Handbook of

North American Indians

1 Introduction

2 Indians in Contemporary Society

3 Environment, Origins, and Population

4 History of Indian-White Relations

5 Arctic

VOLUME 6 **Subarctic, 1981**

7 Northwest Coast

8 California, 1978

9 Southwest, 1979

10 Southwest

11 Great Basin

12 Plateau

13 Plains

14 Southeast

15 Northeast, 1978

16 Technology and Visual Arts

17 Languages

18 Biographical Dictionary

19 Biographical Dictionary

20 Index

Handbook of North American Indians

WILLIAM C. STURTEVANT

General Editor

VOLUME 6

Subarctic

JUNE HELM

Volume Editor

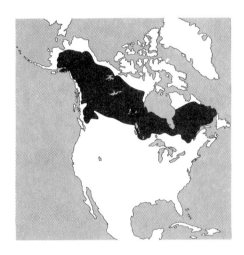

SMITHSONIAN INSTITUTION

WASHINGTON

1981

For sale by the Superintendent of Documents,
U.S. Government Printing Office, Washington, D.C. 20402.
Stock Number: 047–000–00374–1

Library of Congress Cataloging in Publication Data

Handbook of North American Indians.

Bibliography: pp. 741–804
Includes index.
CONTENTS:

v. 6 Subarctic.

1. Indians of North America. 2. Eskimos.
I. Sturtevant, William C.

E77.H25   970'.004'97   77–17162

Subarctic Volume Planning Committee

June Helm, Volume Editor

William C. Sturtevant, General Editor

Catharine McClellan

Edward S. Rogers

James V. Wright

Contents

ix Key to Tribal Territories
x Technical Alphabet
xi English Pronunciations
xii Conventions for Illustrations
xiii Preface

1 Introduction
   June Helm
5 General Environment
   James S. Gardner
15 Major Fauna in the Traditional Economy
   Beryl C. Gillespie
19 History of Ethnological Research in the Subarctic
   Shield and Mackenzie Borderlands
   Edward S. Rogers
30 History of Archeological Research in the Subarctic
   Shield and Mackenzie Valley
   Jacques Cinq-Mars and *Charles A. Martijn*
35 History of Research in the Subarctic Cordillera
   Catharine McClellan
43 History of Research in Subarctic Alaska
   Nancy Yaw Davis
49 Museum and Archival Resources for Subarctic
   Alaska
   James W. VanStone
52 Subarctic Algonquian Languages
   Richard A. Rhodes and *Evelyn M. Todd*
67 Northern Athapaskan Languages
   Michael E. Krauss and *Victor K. Golla*
86 Prehistory of the Canadian Shield
   James V. Wright
97 Prehistory of the Great Slave Lake and Great Bear
   Lake Region
   William C. Noble
107 Prehistory of the Western Subarctic
   Donald W. Clark

Subarctic Shield and Mackenzie Borderlands
130 Environment and Culture in the Shield and
   Mackenzie Borderlands
   Edward S. Rogers and *James G.E. Smith*
146 Intercultural Relations and Cultural Change in the
   Shield and Mackenzie Borderlands
   June Helm, Edward S. Rogers, and *James G.E. Smith*
158 Territorial Groups Before 1821: Cree and Ojibwa
   Charles A. Bishop
161 Territorial Groups Before 1821: Athapaskans of the
   Shield and the Mackenzie Drainage
   Beryl C. Gillespie
169 Montagnais-Naskapi
   Edward S. Rogers and *Eleanor Leacock*

190 Seventeenth-Century Montagnais Social Relations
   and Values
   Eleanor Leacock
196 East Main Cree
   Richard J. Preston
208 Attikamek (Tête de Boule)
   Gérard E. McNulty and *Louis Gilbert*
217 West Main Cree
   John J. Honigmann
231 Northern Ojibwa
   Edward S. Rogers and *J. Garth Taylor*
244 Saulteaux of Lake Winnipeg
   Jack H. Steinbring
256 Western Woods Cree
   James G.E. Smith
271 Chipewyan
   James G.E. Smith
285 Yellowknife
   Beryl C. Gillespie
291 Dogrib
   June Helm
310 Bearlake Indians
   Beryl C. Gillespie
314 Hare
   Joel S. Savishinsky and *Hiroko Sue Hara*
326 Mountain Indians
   Beryl C. Gillespie
338 Slavey
   Michael I. Asch
350 Beaver
   Robin Ridington
361 Subarctic Métis
   Richard Slobodin

Subarctic Cordillera
372 Environment and Culture in the Cordillera
   Catharine McClellan and *Glenda Denniston*
387 Intercultural Relations and Cultural Change in the
   Cordillera
   Catharine McClellan
402 Chilcotin
   Robert B. Lane
413 Carrier
   Margaret L. Tobey
433 Sekani
   Glenda Denniston
442 Kaska
   John J. Honigmann
451 Nahani
   Beryl C. Gillespie
454 Tsetsaut
   Wilson Duff

458 Tahltan
   Bruce B. MacLachlan
469 Inland Tlingit
   Catharine McClellan
481 Tagish
   Catharine McClellan
493 Tutchone
   Catharine McClellan
506 Han
   John R. Crow and *Philip R. Obley*
514 Kutchin
   Richard Slobodin

Alaska Plateau
533 Environment and Culture in the Alaska Plateau
   Edward H. Hosley
546 Intercultural Relations and Cultural Change in the
   Alaska Plateau
   Edward H. Hosley
556 Territorial Groups of West-Central Alaska Before
   1898
   James W. VanStone and *Ives Goddard*
562 Tanana
   Robert A. McKennan
577 Upper Tanana River Potlatch
   Marie-Françoise Guédon
582 Koyukon
   A. McFadyen Clark
602 Ingalik
   Jeanne H. Snow
618 Kolchan
   Edward H. Hosley

South of the Alaska Range
623 Tanaina
   Joan B. Townsend
641 Ahtna
   Frederica de Laguna and *Catharine McClellan*

Native Settlements
664 Native Settlements: Introduction
   June Helm
666 Davis Inlet, Labrador
   Georg Henriksen
673 Great Whale River, Quebec
   W.K. Barger
683 Fort Resolution, Northwest Territories
   David M. Smith
694 Old Crow, Yukon Territory
   Ann Welsh Acheson
704 Minto, Alaska
   Wallace M. Olson

Special Topics
712 Modern Subarctic Indians and Métis
   John J. Honigmann
718 Expressive Aspects of Subarctic Indian Culture
   John J. Honigmann

739 Contributors
741 Bibliography
805 Index

This map is a diagrammatic guide to the coverage of this volume; it is not an authoritative depiction of tribal ranges, for several reasons. Sharp boundaries have been drawn and no territory is unassigned. Tribal units are sometimes arbitrarily defined, subdivisions are not mapped, no joint or disputed occupations are shown, and different kinds of land use are not distinguished. Since the map depicts the situation at the earliest periods for which evidence is available, the ranges mapped for different tribes often refer to different periods, and there may have been intervening movements, extinctions, and changes in range. Not shown are groups that came into separate political existence later than the map period for their areas. In general, the simplified ranges shown are as of the mid-19th century; they are somewhat earlier for the Western Woods Cree, Chipewyan, Yellowknife, and Beaver. For more specific information see the maps and text in the tribal chapters.

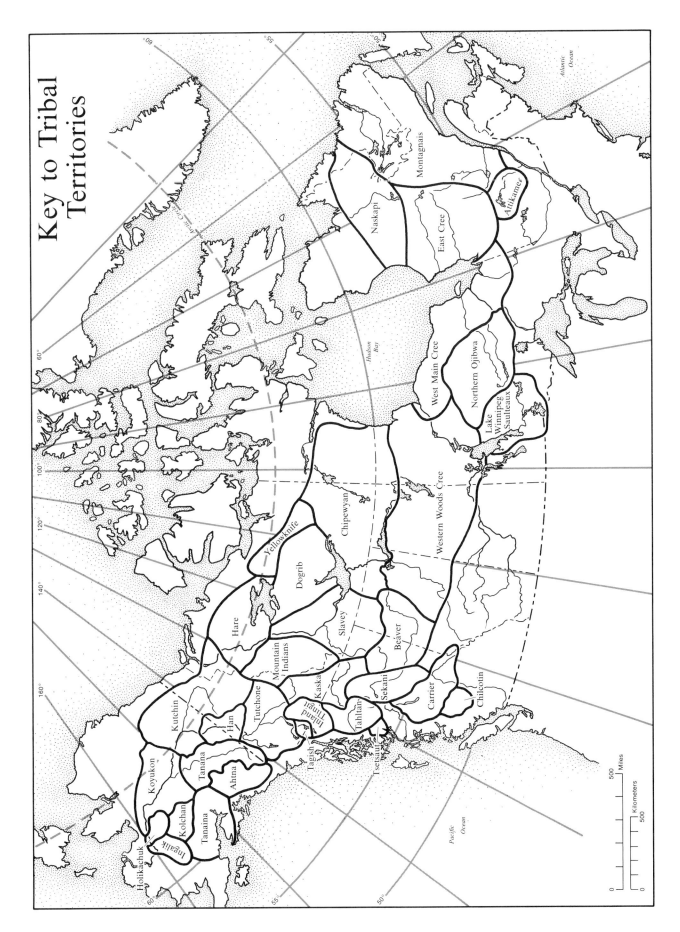

Key to Tribal Territories

Holikachuk
Ingalik
Koyukon
Kolchan
Tanaina
Tanana
Ahtna
Tanana
Han
Kutchin
Tutchone
Mountain Indians
Hare
Kaska
Inland Tlingit
Tagish
Tahltan
Tsetsaut
Sekani
Dogrib
Yellowknife
Slavey
Beaver
Carrier
Chilcotin
Chipewyan
Western Woods Cree
Naskapi
East Cree
Attikamek
Montagnais
West Main Cree
Northern Ojibwa
Lake Winnipeg Saulteaux

Atlantic Ocean
Hudson Bay
Pacific Ocean

Miles
500
Kilometers
500
0
0

60°
55°
50°
60°
80°
100°
120°
140°
160°
60°
55°
50°

Technical Alphabet

Consonants

		bilabial	labiodental	dental	alveolar	alveopalatal	velar	back velar	glottal
stop	vl	p		t	t		k	q	ʔ
	vd	b		d	d		g	ġ	
affricate	vl			θ̂	c	č			
	vd			δ̂	ʒ	ǯ			
fricative	vl	φ	f	θ	s	š	x	x̣	h
	vd	β	v	δ	z	ž	γ	γ̇	
nasal	vl	M		N			N		
	vd	m		n			ŋ	ŋ̇	
lateral	vl				ł				
	vd				l				
semivowel	vl	W				Y			
	vd	w				y			

vl = voiceless; vd = voiced

Other symbols include: λ (voiced lateral affricate), ƛ (voiceless lateral affricate), ʕ (voiced pharyngeal fricative), ḥ (voiceless pharyngeal fricative), r (medial flap, trill, or retroflex approximant). Where in contrast, r is a flap and R is a continuant.

Vowels

	front	central	back
high	i (ü)	ɨ	u (i)
	I		U
mid	e (ö)	ə	o
	ε		ɔ
		Λ	
low	æ	a	a

Unparenthesized vowels are unrounded if front or central, and rounded if back; *ü* and *ö* are rounded; *i* is unrounded. The special symbols for lax vowels *(I, U, ε, ɔ)* are generally used only where it is necessary to differentiate between tense and lax high or mid vowels. *i* and *a* are used for both central and back vowels, as the two values seldom contrast in a given language.

Modifications indicated for consonants are: glottalization (ṭ, ḳ, etc.), fronting (c, ʒ̧, x̧, γ̧, etc.), retroflexion (ṭ), palatalization (tʸ, kʸ, nʸ, lʸ), labialization (kʷ), aspiration (tʰ), length (t·). For vowels: length (a·), three-mora length (a:), nasalization (ą), voicelessness (A). The commonest prosodic markings are, for stress: á (primary) and à (secondary), and for pitch: á (high), à (low), â (falling), and ǎ (rising); however, the details of prosodic systems and the uses of accents differ widely from language to language.

Words in Indian languages cited in italics in this volume are, with one set of exceptions, in phonemic transcription. That is, the letters and symbols are used in specific values defined for them by the structure of the sound system of the particular language. However, as far as possible, these phonemic transcriptions use letters and symbols in generally consistent values, as specified by the standard technical alphabet of the *Handbook*, displayed on this page. Deviations from these standard values as well as specific details of the phonology of each language (or references to where they may be found) are given in an orthographic footnote in each tribal chapter. One deviation from the standard values that is found in the transcriptions of all Athapaskan languages is the use of the voiceless stop and affricate symbols for voiceless aspirates, and of the voiced symbols for the corresponding plain (unaspirated) stops and affricates. For example, in these languages *t* represents phonetic [tʰ] and *d* represents [t]. Exceptionally, italics are used for Chinook Jargon words, which appear in the conventional English-based spellings of the sources. Phonetic transcriptions, even if available, would be variable, and a unified phonemic transcription impossible, since speakers of Chinook Jargon tended to pronounce it using the sounds of their respective languages.

No italicized Indian word is broken at a line end except when a hyphen would be present anyway as part of the word, and words in italicized phonemic transcription are never capitalized. Pronunciations or phonetic values given in the standard technical alphabet without regard to phonemic analysis are put in square brackets rather than in italics. In the chapter "Subarctic Algonquian Languages" a distinction is made between italics, used for general Cree and Ojibwa orthographies suitable for these languages as wholes, and transcriptions between slashes, used for orthographies based on the phonemic analysis of the separate dialects. The glosses, or conventionalized translations, of Indian words are enclosed in single quotation marks.

Indian words recorded by nonspecialists or before the phonemic systems of their languages had been analyzed are often not written accurately enough to allow respelling in phonemic transcription. Where phonemic retranscription has been possible the citation of source has been modified by the label "phonemicized" or "from." A few words that could not be phonemicized have been "normalized"—rewritten by mechanical substitution of the symbols of the standard technical alphabet. Others have been rationalized by eliminating redundant or potentially misleading diacritics and substituting nontechnical symbols. Words that do not use the standard technical alphabet occasionally contain some letters used according to the values of other technical alphabets or traditional orthographies. The most common of these are c for the *Handbook*'s [š]; tc and tᶜc for [č]; ᶜ for [h]; ' for [ʔ]; α for [ʌ]; j for [y] or [ž]; and tr for [c] or [ʒ]. Émile Petitot's transcription uses doubling to indicate glottalization (e.g., tt for [ṭ], tts for [ċ], ttch for [č̣]) and raised apostrophe for aspirated obstruents (t' for *t* [tʰ]; but k' is attested for *g* [k]); other conventions of his include: thl or l' for [ł]; ρ (often transcribed r) for heavy aspiration or [γ]; sh for [θ], th for [θ̂]; dh for [δ]; and œ for [ə]. Early French sources commonly use a digraph here rendered 8 for French ou ([w], [u]).

The transcription from Russian Cyrillic script is not entirely consistent. The Library of Congress transliteration (p. *xi*) has been used in the titles of items in the bibliography and in names and words that were available in Cyrillic, but the names of authors appear in a simplified version. The names of historical personages and place-names are generally in the spellings used in the most available English sources or translations. Group names are transliterated narrowly from the Cyrillic, where available, italics being used for those used as Russian words and roman for cited Indian forms. The older alphabet has been followed when the sources use it.

All nonphonemic transcriptions give only incomplete, and sometimes imprecise, approximations of the correct pronunciation.

Nontechnical Equivalents

Correct pronunciation, as with any foreign language, requires extensive training and practice, but simplified (incorrect) pronunciations may be obtained by ignoring the diacritics and reading the vowels as in Italian or Spanish and the consonants as in English. For a closer approximation to the pronunciation or to rewrite into a nontechnical transcription the substitutions indicated in the following table may be made. The orthographic footnote for most languages contains a practical alphabet that may be used as an alternative by substituting the letters and letter groups for their correspondents in the list of technical symbols in the same footnote.

technical	nontechnical	technical	nontechnical	technical	nontechnical
æ	ae	M	mh	Y	yh
β	bh	N	nh	ž	zh
c	ts	ŋ	ng	ʒ	dz
č	ch	$\mathcal{N}$	ngh	ǯ	j
δ	dh	ɔ	o	ʾ	ʼ
δ̂	ddh	θ	th	ḳ, ṗ, ṭ, etc.	k', p', t', etc.
ε	e	θ̂	tth	aˑ, eˑ, kˑ, sˑ, etc.	aa, ee, kk, ss, etc.
γ	gh	φ	ph	a̧, ȩ, etc.	an, en, etc.
ł	lh	š	sh	kʸ, tʸ, etc.	ky, ty, etc.
λ	dl	W	wh	kʷ	kw
ƛ	tlh	x	kh		

Transliteration of Russian Cyrillic

А	а	a	I	iᵃ	ī	С	с	s	Ъ	ъᵇ	ʺ
Б	б	b	Й	й	ĭ	Т	т	t	Ы	ы	y
В	в	v	К	к	k	У	у	u	Ь	ь	ʹ
Г	г	g	Л	л	l	Ф	ф	f	Ѣ	ѣᵃ	i͡e
Д	д	d	М	м	m	Х	х	kh	Э	э	ė
Е	е	e	Н	н	n	Ц	ц	t͡s	Ю	ю	i͡u
Ё	ё	ë	О	о	o	Ч	ч	ch	Я	я	i͡a
Ж	ж	zh	П	п	p	Ш	ш	sh	Ѳ	ѳᵃ	ḟ
З	з	z	Р	р	r	Щ	щ	shch	V	vᵃ	ẏ
И	и	i									

ᵃ Not in the alphabet adopted in 1918.
ᵇ Disregarded in final position.

English Pronunciations

The English pronunciations of the names of tribes and a few other words are indicated parenthetically in a dictionary-style orthography in which most letters have their usual English pronunciation. Special symbols are listed below, with sample words to be pronounced as in nonregional United States English. Approximate phonetic values are given in parentheses in the standard technical alphabet.

ŋ: thing (ŋ)	ä: father (a)	ə: about, gallop (ə)	ō: boat (ow)
θ: thin (θ)	ā: bait (ey)	ĭ: bit (ɪ)	ŏŏ: book (ʊ)
δ: this (δ)	e: bet (ε)	ī: bite (ay)	ōō: boot (uw)
zh: vision (ž)	ē: beat (iy)	ô: bought (ɔ)	u: but (ʌ)
ă: bat (æ)			

ʹ(primary stress), ˌ(secondary stress): elevator (ˈeləˌvātər) *(éləvèytər)*

Conventions for Illustrations

Map Symbols

- •   Native settlement
- ○   Abandoned settlement
- ▪   Non-native or mixed settlement
- ▫   Abandoned settlement

Mountain range, peak

Marsh, swamp

River or stream

-- -- --   National boundary

-- --- --   Province or state boundary

-- -- -- --   District boundary

Chipewyan   Tribe

Tanacross   Tribal subdivision

Davis Inlet   Settlement, site, reserve

Yukon R.   Geographical feature

Toned areas on tribal maps represent estimated territory.

Credits and Captions

Credit lines give the source of the illustrations or the collections where the artifacts shown are located. The numbers that follow are the catalog or inventory numbers of that repository. When the photographer mentioned in the caption is the source of the print reproduced, no credit line appears. "After" means that the *Handbook* illustrators have redrawn, rearranged, or abstracted the illustration from the one in the cited source. All maps and drawings not otherwise credited are by the *Handbook* illustrators. Measurements in captions are to the nearest millimeter if available; "about" indicates an estimate or a measurement converted from inches to centimeters. The following abbreviations are used in credit lines:

Amer.	American	Histl.	Historical
Anthr.	Anthropology, Anthropological	Ind.	Indian
	ical	Inst.	Institute
Arch.	Archives	Instn.	Institution
Arch(a)eol.	Arch(a)eology, Arch(a)eological	Lib.	Library
		Mus.	Museum
Assoc.	Association	NAA	National Anthropological
Co.	County		Archives
Coll.	Collection(s)	Nat.	Natural
Dept.	Department	Natl.	National
Div.	Division	opp.	opposite
Ethnol.	Ethnology, Ethnological	pl(s).	plate(s)
fol.	folio	Prov.	Provincial
Ft.	Fort	Soc.	Society
Hist.	History	U.	University

Metric Equivalents

10 mm = 1 cm	10 cm = 3.937 in.	1 km = .62 mi.	1 in. = 2.54 cm	25 ft. = 7.62 m
100 cm = 1 m	1 m = 39.37 in.	5 km = 3.1 mi.	1 ft. = 30.48 cm	1 mi. = 1.60 km
1,000 m = 1 km	10 m = 32.81 ft.	10 km = 6.2 mi.	1 yd. = 91.44 cm	5 mi. = 8.02 km

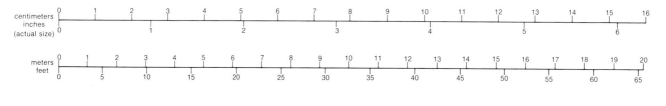

Preface

This is the fourth volume to be published of a 20-volume set planned to give an encyclopedic summary of what is known about the prehistory, history, and cultures of the aboriginal peoples of North America who lived north of the urban civilizations of central Mexico. Volumes 5 and 7–15 treat the other major culture areas of this region.

Some topics relevant to the Subarctic area are excluded from this volume because they are more appropriately discussed on a continent-wide basis. Readers should refer to volume 1, Introduction, for general descriptions of anthropological and historical methods and sources and for summaries for the whole continent of certain topics regarding social and political organization, religion, and the performing arts. Volume 2 contains detailed accounts of the different kinds of Indian and Eskimo communities in the twentieth century, especially during its third quarter, and describes their relations with one another and with the surrounding non-Indian societies and nations. Volume 3 gives the environmental and biological backgrounds within which Native American societies developed, summarizes the early and late human biology or physical anthropology of Indians and Eskimos, and surveys the earliest prehistoric cultures. (Therefore the Paleo-Indian or Early Man period in the Subarctic receives major treatment in volume 3 rather than in this volume.) Volume 4 contains details on the history of Indian-White relations. Volume 16 is a continent-wide survey of technology and the visual arts—of material cultures broadly defined. Volume 17 surveys the native languages of North America, their characteristics and historical relationships. Volumes 18 and 19 are a biographical dictionary; included in the listing are many Subarctic Indians. Volume 20 contains an index to the whole, which will serve to locate materials on Subarctic Indians in other volumes as well as in this one; it also includes a list of errata found in all preceding volumes.

Preliminary discussions on the feasibility of the *Handbook* and alternatives for producing it began in 1965 in what was then the Smithsonian's Office of Anthropology. A history of the early development of the *Handbook* and a listing of the entire editorial staff will be found in volume 1. Detailed planning for the Subarctic volume was undertaken at a meeting of the General Editor and the Volume Editor with a specially selected Planning Committee (listed on page *v*) held in Iowa City, Iowa, October 16–18, 1970. A meeting of the Volume Editor, the Planning Committee, and members of the Athapaskan Conference held in Ottawa on March 17–21, 1971, further developed the tentative table of contents and the proposed assignments of qualified specialists to each topic. More than half the authors who were originally invited contributed to the volume; inevitably, some replacements had to be made as people were unable to accept invitations or later found that they could not meet their commitment to write.

At the time they were invited, contributors were sent a rationale for the plan of this volume that was prepared by the Volume Editor and that gave brief indications of the topics to be covered. This document outlined the volume's theoretical framework, which was informed by consultations with Edward S. Rogers, Catharine McClellan, James V. Wright, and those scholars that attended the Athapaskan Conference. Authors were also sent a "Guide for Contributors" prepared by the General Editor describing the general aims and methods of the *Handbook* and the editorial conventions. One convention has been to avoid the present tense, where possible, in historical and cultural descriptions. Thus a statement in the past tense, with a recent date or approximate date, may also hold true for the time of writing. As they were received, the manuscripts were reviewed by the Volume Editor, the General Editor, and usually one or more referees—frequently including a member of the Planning Committee, and often authors of other chapters. Suggestions for changes and additions often resulted. The published versions frequently reflect more editorial intervention than is customary for academic writings, since the encyclopedic aims and format of this publication made it necessary to attempt to eliminate duplication, avoid gaps in coverage, prevent contradictions, impose some standardization of organization and terminology, and keep within strict constraints on length. Where the evidence seemed so scanty or obscure as to allow different authorities to come to differing conclusions, authors have been permitted to elaborate whichever view they prefer, but the editors have endeavored to draw readers' attention to alternative interpretations in other chapters.

The first manuscript submitted was received in the General Editor's office on April 28, 1972, and the last on August 21, 1980; the first acceptance of an author's manuscript was on January 10, 1973. Edited manuscripts were sent from the Washington office to authors for their final approval between April 6, 1979, and December 10, 1980. These dates are given for each chapter in the list of Contributors. Late dates may reflect late invitations as well as late submissions.

Linguistic Editing

All cited words in Indian languages were referred to consultants with expert knowledge of the respective languages and, as far as possible, rewritten by them in the appropriate technical orthography. The consultants and the spelling systems are identified in an orthographic footnote to each tribal chapter; these footnotes were drafted by the Linguistic Editor, Ives Goddard.

Statements about the genetic relationships of Indian languages have also been checked with linguist consultants, to ensure conformity with recent findings and terminology in comparative linguistics and to avoid conflicting statements within the *Handbook*. In general, only the less remote genetic relationships are mentioned in the individual tribal chapters. The two chapters on the Subarctic Algonquian languages and the Northern Athapaskan languages treat more remote relationships, and further information will be found in volume 17.

The Linguistic Editor served as coordinator and editor of these efforts by linguist consultants. A special debt is owed to these consultants, who provided advice and assistance without compensation and, in many cases, took time from their own research in order to check words with native speakers. The Linguistic Editor is especially grateful to Victor K. Golla, James M. Kari, Michael E. Krauss, Eung-Do Cook, Keren D. Rice, and John T. Ritter.

In the case of words that could not be respelled in a technical orthography, an attempt has been made to rationalize the transcriptions used in earlier anthropological writings in order to eliminate phonetic symbols that are obsolete and diacritics that might convey a false impression of phonetic accuracy.

Synonymies

Toward the end of each "tribal" chapter is a section called Synonymy. This describes the various names that have been applied to the groups and subgroups treated in that chapter (or set of chapters), giving the principal variant spellings used in English, and, frequently, in French and Russian, and often the names applied to the groups in neighboring Indian languages.

Many synonymies have been expanded or reworked by the Linguistic Editor, who has added names and analyses from the literature, from other manuscripts submitted for the *Handbook* (from which they have

then been deleted), and as provided by linguist consultants. Where a synonymy is wholly or substantially the work of the Linguistic Editor, a footnote specifying authorship is given. The synonymies in the chapters on Algonquian-speaking groups are by David H. Pentland.

These sections should assist in the identification of groups mentioned in the earlier historical and anthropological literature. They should also be examined for evidence on changes in the identifications and affiliations of groups, as seen by their own members as well as by neighbors and by outside observers.

Radiocarbon Dates

Authors were instructed to convert radiocarbon dates into dates in the Christian calendar. Such conversions normally have been made from the dates as originally published, without taking account of changes that may be required by developing research on revisions of the half-life of carbon 14, long-term changes in the amount of carbon 14 in the atmosphere, and other factors that may require modifications of absolute dates based on radiocarbon determinations.

Binomials

The scientific names of plant and animal genera and species, printed in italics, have been checked by the General Editor to ensure that they reflect modern usage by biological taxonomists. Scientific plant names have been brought into agreement with those accepted by Gray and Fernald (1950) and Hultén (1968), while zoological nomenclature has been revised in consultation with Smithsonian staff in the appropriate departments.

In most cases the English common names used for animals and plants have also been edited to avoid possible ambiguities. Thus for the various species of salmon the English names recommended by Hart (1973) have been used consistently, except in a few cases (always with the binomial also given) where the Alaskan term king salmon has been used rather than Chinook salmon for *Oncorhynchus tshawytscha*. The snowshoe or varying hare, *Lepus americanus*, is often called rabbit in the Subarctic, but the latter term is preferably restricted to *Sylvilagus* spp., which do not occur in the Subarctic; thus "rabbit" has been replaced by "hare" in this volume. Groundhog refers to *Marmota monax* (also called woodchuck), whereas the (Arctic) ground squirrel is *Spermophilus parryii*. Another confusion in English names that has been avoided here is between crow, properly restricted to *Corvus caurinus* and *Corvus brachyrhynchos*, and raven, properly *Corvus corax*. In the interior of the western Subarctic, where *Corvus caurinus* and *Corvus brachyrhynchos* do not occur, *Corvus corax* is sometimes called crow in English, but it is always raven in this volume; however, moieties named after or identified with the raven are sometimes referred to as Crow, following strong local preference for this usage.

Effort at terminological standardization failed in the case of the burbot, *Lota lota*, an "intriguing fish [that] has received an extraordinary variety of names" (McPhail and Lindsey 1970:299). Besides burbot, this freshwater cod appears in various chapters as loche, ling, and ling cod. (Table 2 of "Major Fauna in the Traditional Economy," this vol., provides synonymies for all economically important fish species.)

Bibliography

All references cited by contributors have been unified in a single list at the end of the volume. Citations within the text, by author, date, and often page, identify the works in this unified list. Wherever possible the *Handbook* Bibliographer, Lorraine H. Jacoby, has resolved conflicts between citations of different editions, corrected inaccuracies and omissions, and checked direct quotations against the originals. The bibliographic information has been verified by examination of the original work or from standard reliable library catalogs (especially the National Union Catalog and the published catalog of the Harvard Peabody Museum Library). The unified bibliography lists all and only the sources cited in the text of the volume, except personal communications. In the text "personal communications" to an author are distinguished from personal "communications to editors." The sections headed Sources at the ends of most chapters provide general guidance to the most important sources of information on the topics covered.

Illustrations

Authors were requested to submit suggestions for illustrations: photographs, maps, drawings, and lists and locations of objects that might be illustrated. To varying degrees most complied with this request. Yet considerations of space, balance, reproducibility, and availability required modifications in what was submitted. In addition much original material was provided by editorial staff members, from research they conducted in museums and other repositories, in the published literature, and from correspondence. Locating suitable photographs and earlier drawings and paintings was the responsibility of the Illustrations Researcher, Joanna Cohan Scherer. Artifacts in museum collections suitable for photographing or drawing were selected by the Artifact Researchers, Cathe Brock (in 1977–1978) and Gayle Barsamian (1979–). All uncredited drawings are by the Scientific Illustrator, Jo Ann Moore.

All maps were drawn by the *Handbook* Cartographer, Judith Crawley Wojcik, who redrew some submitted by authors and compiled many new ones using information from the chapter manuscripts and from other sources. The base maps for all are authoritative standard ones, especially sheet maps produced by the U.S. Geological Survey and the Department of Energy, Mines and Resources, Surveys and Mapping Branch, Canada. When possible, the hydrography has been reconstructed for the date of each map.

Layout and design of the illustrations have been the responsibility of the Scientific Illustrator, Jo Ann Moore. Captions for illustrations were usually composed by Scherer, Barsamian, and Moore, and for maps by Wojcik. However, all illustrations, including maps and drawings, and all captions, have been approved by the General Editor, the Volume Editor, and the authors of the chapters in which they appear, and authors and editors frequently have participated actively in the selection process and in the improvement of captions.

We are indebted to individuals on the staffs of many museums for much time and effort spent in their collections locating photographs and artifacts and providing documentation on them. Many individuals, includings professional photographers, have generously provided photographs free or at cost. Donnelley Cartographic Services (especially Sidney P. Marland, III, general manager) devoted meticulous care to converting the map artwork into final film.

Acknowledgments

Beyond the members of the Planning Committee and those persons whose special contributions are identified in appropriate sections of the text, important aid was also received from Richard V. Bovbjerg, John M. Campbell, Robert W. Cruden, David J. Damas, Gordon M. Day, James E. Fitting, Irving Goldman, Elmer Harp, Irma Honigmann, James M. Kari, Michael Kew, Michael E. Krauss, Virginia Lawson, John Nichols, Wendell H. Oswalt, David H. Pentland, Douglas Sanders, Donat Savoie, Merlin W. Shoesmith, Norman Simmons, James G.E. Smith, and Sam Stanley. Ives Goddard was of particular assistance on matters of historical accuracy as well as on decisions made by the General Editor regarding organization and other editorial procedures.

During the first few years of this project, the *Handbook* editorial staff in Washington worked on materials for all volumes of the series. In 1978, intensive preparation of this volume began. Especially important contributions were provided over the final three years by: the Editorial Assistants, Betty Tatham Arens (until 1979) and Nikki L. Lanza (1979–); the Production Manager and Manuscript Editor, Diane Della-Loggia;

the Bibliographer, Lorraine H. Jacoby; the Scientific Illustrator, Jo Ann Moore; the Cartographer, Judith Crawley Wojcik; the Illustrations Researcher, Joanna Cohan Scherer; and the Artifact Researchers, Cathe Brock and Gayle Barsamian.

The Department of Anthropology, National Museum of Natural History, Smithsonian Institution, released the General Editor and the Linguistic Editor from part of their curatorial and research time.

Preparation and publication of this volume have been supported by federal appropriations made to the Smithsonian Institution in part through its Bicentennial Programs.

For several months Beryl C. Gillespie served as Editorial Assistant to the Volume Editor, checking many points of fact and interpretation. Production at the University of Iowa office of the Volume Editor was greatly facilitated by the energy and organizational skills of Shirley Ahlgren, secretary in the Department of Anthropology, who relieved the Editor of the burden of attending to expense records and who made sure that the flow of photocopying, typing, and mailing ran smoothly and fast.

Many aspects of a research project carried out in 1971–1974 under a grant (GS 3057) from the National Science Foundation augmented the Volume Editor's scholarly resources and comprehensions in the preparation of the volume.

The permission of the Hudson's Bay Company to publish data from the records in its Archives is gratefully acknowledged.

March 1981

William C. Sturtevant
June Helm

Introduction

JUNE HELM

The Subarctic culture area as delimited in this volume encompasses approximately 2,000,000 square miles and extends from the coast of Labrador on the Atlantic Ocean to Cook Inlet and beyond on the Pacific. The sheer expanse of the area has meant that no one anthropologist has traversed all major sectors or had field experience in a representative society within every sector. But from each particular vantage point, Subarctic ethnologists generally recognize that the existence—physical, societal, and cultural—of the hunting peoples of the subarctic expanse has been sharply and immediately keyed to the terrain and its subsistence resources. Furthermore, in late prehistoric and historic times, at least, physiography and resources were paramount in determining the direction and course of intercultural contacts. For these reasons, the culture-areal subdivisions of the subarctic presented in this volume correspond to the major physiographic zones. In adhering preeminently to an environmental-ecological perspective, we depart in a major respect from earlier delineations of cultural subareas of the subarctic (Jenness 1932; Kroeber 1939; Driver and Massey 1957; Murdock and O'Leary 1975, 2), which impose a division at the linguistic boundary between Algonquian speakers and Athapaskan speakers in the lands west of Hudson Bay (fig. 1). Although indicative of ancient cultural relationships, linguistic heritage has but secondary import for the comprehension of cultural adaptations, lifeways, and influences for change among the native peoples of the subarctic.

In his classification of "ethnic environments" or culture areas of native North America, Mason (1896a, 1907) recognized a distinct area he labeled "Athapascan" or "Yukon-Mackenzie," but he included the Subarctic Algonquians with their southern linguistic congeners in his "Algonquin-Iroquois" or "St. Lawrence and Lake" culture area. Wissler (1922:234,363) did not distinguish the Subarctic Algonquian region from his broader "Eastern Woodlands." Jenness's (1932) and Osgood's (1936) geographical subdivisions of the Athapaskan speakers of the western Subarctic, and this volume's departure from them on the basis of closer attention to ecological settings, are discussed in "Environment and Culture in the Cordillera," this volume.

The four major physiographic-ecologic zones under which the tribal chapters in this volume are organized are: the Subarctic portion of the Canadian Shield and the associated Hudson Bay Lowlands and Mackenzie Borderlands, the Cordillera, the Alaska Plateau, and the region south of the Alaska Range. The first division, the Subarctic Shield and borderlands, covers approximately three-fourths of the land mass of the subarctic and places the easternmost Athapaskan groups in the same subarea with all the subarctic Algonquian peoples. In contrast, the region south of the Alaska Range contains but two tribal groups within a relatively small area.

On the whole, the perimeter of the Subarctic culture area corresponds to that of the Hudsonian biotic province (Dice 1943), characterized by the northern coniferous or boreal forest and, as major resource mammals, moose, caribou, and varying hare. The line drawn between the Subarctic and the Northeast culture areas—flanked by Algonquian speakers on either side—conforms to the boundary between the boreal forest and the mixed deciduous-coniferous woodlands of the Great Lakes–Saint Lawrence forest region (Rowe 1972). The cultural-*cum*-environmental break between Eskimo peoples and the Subarctic Indians is almost everywhere sufficiently distinct, as is also that between the Subarctic Indians and the Indians of the Northwest Coast, so that no significant problem arose in assigning groups to one or the other culture area. Except for the Inland Tlingit, linguistic contrasts reaffirm these boundaries. However, on the southwest fringe of the subarctic, linguistic affiliation was used to bring the Athapaskan-speaking Carrier and Chilcotin of British Columbia into this volume, even though in their resource base and certain accompanying cultural attributes these peoples have affinities with the northern Plateau culture area. In contrast, the Athapaskan Sarcee and the Algonquian Plains Cree, who were emigrants from the boreal zone into the northern plains within historic times, became Plains Indians in culture as well as habitat and are treated in the Plains volume.

The identification and demarcation of "tribes" in this volume has been in most cases a matter of judgment. In this vast land there were perhaps—accepting the Mooney-Kroeber (Kroeber 1939:141) estimates—only 60,000 aboriginal inhabitants. Generally, they were de-

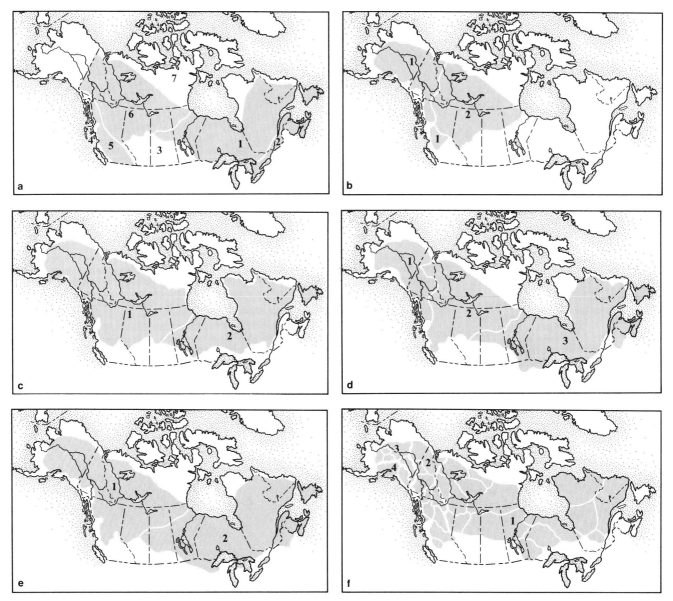

Fig. 1. Anthropologists' interpretations of the Subarctic culture area. a, Jenness 1932 (Canada only): 1, migratory tribes of the eastern woodlands; 2, agricultural tribes of the eastern woodlands; 3, plains tribes; 4, tribes of the Pacific coast; 5, tribes of the Cordillera; 6, tribes of the Mackenzie and Yukon river basins; 7, the Eskimo. b, Osgood 1936: Northern Athapaskan Indians of the 1, Pacific drainage; 2, Arctic drainage. c, Kroeber 1939: 1, Western Subarctic; 2, Eastern Subarctic. d, Driver and Massey 1957: 1, Yukon Subarctic; 2, Mackenzie Subarctic; 3, Eastern Subarctic. e, Murdock and O'Leary 1975: 1, Mackenzie-Yukon; 2, Eastern Canada. f, Subarctic as interpreted in this volume (see Key to Tribal Territories for names): 1, Shield and Mackenzie borderlands; 2, Cordillera; 3, Alaska Plateau; 4, South of the Alaska Range.

ployed over the land in small and often mobile auton-omous groups. Any set of families immediately cores-ident as a local group had wider sociocultural affiliations and identities with like, neighboring groups, but there was no political integration or unity among them, so this often-invoked criterion cannot be used in this re-gion to delimit sets of local and regional groups as "tribes." For some sets there is enough similarity of dialect, social contact and amity, and common historical experience among the units to justify readily enough their inclusion in one "tribe," "people," or "nation."

Such is the case with the Chipewyan, whose range ex-tends 600 miles across central Canada. In other cases, linguistic-cultural gradients between a number of con-tiguous groups may perhaps be of the same order as within the Chipewyan nation, but distinctive features of environmental adaptation and historical circum-stance have led to treatment in two or more chapters. On this basis the Cree of the Hudson Bay Lowlands, here designated West Main Cree, are distinguished from the remainder of the Cree speakers in the boreal forest west of Hudson Bay, who have been unified

2

under the term Western Woods Cree. Similarly the East Main Cree of the east side of the Bay are treated apart from the Cree speakers of the Quebec interior who are presented in this volume under the term Montagnais-Naskapi. Among the Montagnais-Naskapi, the people of the Lake Mistassini area in the previous literature have been variously labeled Cree, Montagnais, and Naskapi. On the Alaskan side of the Subarctic, the Kolchan are here distinguished as a separate cultural-dialectal group although earlier (Osgood 1936) they were tentatively treated as a division of the Ingalik. On the other hand, for the set of groups known as the Carrier we have retained a unitary designation and treatment, although social and linguistic evidence can be brought forward in support of separation into more than one "tribe." These examples by no means exhaust the cases where difficult and somewhat arbitrary decisions on classifying peoples have been made. The various tribal chapters discuss the specifics of each case.

Establishing "boundaries" to tribal territories has been especially arbitrary. A specific disclaimer to this effect accompanies the comprehensive map of the Sub-arctic culture area and its constituent "tribes" (Key to Tribal Territories), but the caveat needs repeating in regard to the tribal maps that accompany the various chapters. It is important to recognize that in response to particular circumstances and in different periods peoples' ranges shifted, sometimes temporarily, and that the historical record is often incomplete or inexact. Furthermore, there was often shared use and occupancy of a region by peoples of the Subarctic or by Subarctic peoples and those of adjacent culture areas; these overlaps have not always been mapped. It is false to historical and ethnographic reality to view the lines around and between peoples drawn on the maps in this volume as constituting a sufficient basis for legal or political definitions on the part of governments, native peoples, or nonnative occupants.

As a label for sociocultural collectivities in the subarctic, the term tribe is even more inappropriate when applied to the Subarctic Métis. These people, whose heritage combines Europeans and Indians (either Algonquian or Athapaskan), live in community association with Indian neighbors and kinsmen throughout the northern reaches of the Prairie Provinces of Canada and north as far as the Mackenzie Delta, but they are perceived and perceive themselves as having a distinctive ethnic heritage and identity.

Three chapters address problems in identifying the ethnic or tribal groups and their territories that are mentioned in the early historical records.

Several chapters of this volume attend to the critical nexus between human survival, culture, and environment in the Subarctic. The chapter on "General Environment" is followed by "Major Fauna in the Tra-ditional Economy," which introduces the main varieties of mammals and fishes by which the aboriginal peoples sustained life in this harsh land. Since major differences in cultural emphases or elaboration across the Subarctic broadly correspond to the four major physiographic-ecologic resource zones, for each of the three largest subareas—the Shield, the Cordillera, and the Alaska Plateau—a general chapter examines the interrelation of culture and environment. Subarctic resources and physiography shaped the course of culture contact between the entering Europeans and the indigenous populations, between the Subarctic peoples and their native neighbors of the Arctic, Northwest Coast, and Northeast culture areas, and among the Subarctic tribes themselves. For this reason, and because most of the knowledge of native lifeways comes from within the historic era after the effects of White-stimulated inter-Indian contacts are discernible, intercultural relations and cultural change in each of the three large subareas warranted chapters.

A distinctive aspect of Indian life in the Subarctic into the late twentieth century is that in many regions the Indian community is the most common kind of settlement to be found in this lightly settled land. The significance of these settlements in shaping Indian life within the historic era deserved explicit attention. An introductory overview of native settlements followed by five community case studies comprises a special section of the volume. These are followed by a chapter on trends in modern native life across the Subarctic.

Certain other topics merited special treatment: the Subarctic Métis as a native people; the social life and values of the seventeenth-century Montagnais, drawn from the masterly accounts in the *Jesuit Relations*; the revivified potlatch complex of the upper Tanana River Indians; the question of what or who were the "Nahani" Indians and the "Attikamègues" of earlier accounts. The final chapter, on expressive culture, offers an integrated perspective on the common and variant styles and themes in the intellectual, religious, aesthetic, and emotional life of the native peoples of the Subarctic.

During the decade that this volume was in preparation, massive projects for the development of hydroelectric, oil, and natural gas energy resources in the subarctic were in planning, underway, or completed. These projects threatened incalculable environmental, political, and cultural consequences for the Natives of the north. They evoked Native concern, protest, and efforts to organize in resistance to the twin juggernauts of big business and big government, in order to seek self-determination of their political and cultural future and affirmation of inalienable rights to their lands. The imposed imperatives of "development" forced the Alaska Native Claims Settlement Act of 1971 and the James Bay and Northern Quebec Agreement of 1975. 3

In defining Native rights and extent of jurisdiction over the land, these "settlements" locked the Native peoples of the affected regions into rigid and bureaucratic relationships with government and among themselves. In appropriate chapters these and other environmental, political, and social transformations emergent in the 1970s are briefly treated. But their portent is beyond our compass. This volume is testimony to the life of the people on the land as it has been.

General Environment

JAMES S. GARDNER

The Subarctic of North America spans the immense country from Alaska to Labrador. Although identified as a coherent region by social, physical, and natural scientists alike, the Subarctic environment displays spatial and temporal variability at a number of scales. There are broad geographical differences in vegetation, climate, geology, and physiography. There are limited and local differences as between barren ridge and wet string bog. Climatic changes occur over millennia and periodic fluctuations occur diurnally and seasonally. Much of the Subarctic bears the imprint of recent glaciations, themselves the result of climatic change. The environment has been responding to the glacial legacy with crustal and sea-level changes, even within historical times (Smith and Barr 1971).

The great expanse of the Subarctic precludes detailed presentation of all its spatial and temporal variability. This environmental description focuses on the geology, physiography, hydrology, climate, and flora. Environmental elements of particular significance to Whites are briefly described for it is they that have stimulated a new dynamism. The impact of Euro-Americans and industrial technology on the environment and people of the Subarctic has been, and will continue to be, profound.

Regional geographic themes are plagued with problems of delimitation and definition. The Subarctic region is no exception. All boundaries are subject to some interpretation and may, in some cases, reflect transitions. Indeed, the term subarctic—like subalpine, subtropical, and subpolar—implies transition between core areas or distinct regions. Many geographers would accept the Subarctic as a regional entity but issue might be taken with boundaries and criteria for determining them (Blüthgen 1970:11–30). Physiographic, climatological, and biogeographic criteria have been used in delimiting a Subarctic region (Wonders 1968, 1972; Bird 1968). In addition, specific limits or boundaries, such as the arctic tree line (Rowe 1972), have been used in defining or discussing the region.

Vegetation is the criterion most frequently used in defining the Subarctic. Blüthgen (1970) includes the wooded zone between discontinuous patch tundra of the Arctic and the economic timber limit of the boreal forest. Wonders (1968), while recognizing that the Subarctic is usually more restrictively delimited, includes both the boreal forest and the transitional forest or forest-tundra ecotone in his discussion.

Interrelationships between vegetation and other environmental factors are evident in most definitions of, and boundaries in, the Subarctic region (fig. 1). For example, the boundary between continuous and discontinuous permafrost approximates the southern limit of tundra vegetation and the southern position of arctic air masses in the summer (Mackay 1972). The northern limit of the Hudsonian biotic province (Dice 1943) corresponds closely to these permafrost and vegetation boundaries. The ethnographic delimitation of the Subarctic used in this volume in turn encompasses the Hudsonian biotic province in its entirety. The southern limit of the Hudsonian province and the ethnographic Subarctic correspond approximately to the southern limit of closed boreal forest. Within the Subarctic, the four ethnographic regions, as defined in this volume, correspond to the four major physiographic provinces. Included are: the Canadian Shield and the associated Hudson Bay and Mackenzie lowlands, the Cordillera, the Yukon-Tanana-Kuskokwim plateaus, and the maritime fringe south of the Alaska Range and the Coast Range.

The following environmental description is by necessity generalized. Data for the Subarctic are scanty and perhaps unreliable for large areas. This qualification is especially pertinent to climatological and hydrological variables, the validities of which are dependent on large numbers of standardized observations made over long periods of time. In addition, large areas exist for which no systematic collection of data has occurred.

Physiography and Geology

The physiography of the Subarctic is so much the expression of the geology that these two environmental elements are treated together. Both are complex west of the Mackenzie River and remarkably uniform to the east. The term physiography is used here to describe the geography of land surface morphology. Geology encompasses factors such as geologic history, geologic structure, bedrock type, and nature of the surface material. Physiography and geology are relatively constant

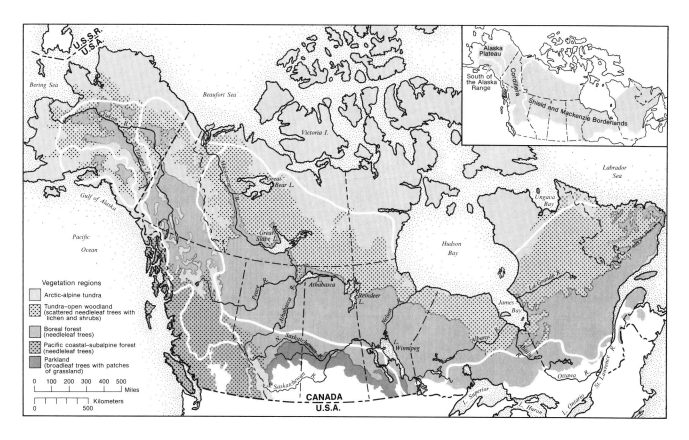

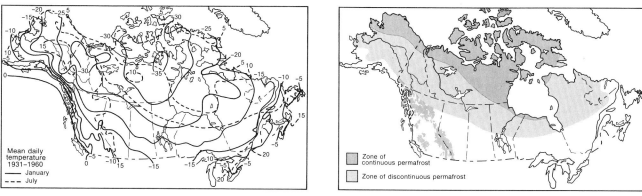

top, after Canada. Surveys and Mapping Branch 1974; U.S. Geological Survey 1970; bottom left, after Bryson and Hare 1974; bottom right, after Canada. Surveys and Mapping Branch 1974; Hunt 1967.

Fig. 1. Vegetation regions and climatic zones. top, Vegetation regions, with the major physiographic zones used in this volume outlined in white; bottom left, atmospheric temperature conditions in degrees celsius; bottom right, permafrost zones.

over short time periods and thus act as a stage on which diurnal and seasonal life processes occur.

The major physiographic regions in the Subarctic of North America are depicted in "Environment and Culture in the Shield and Mackenzie Borderlands," fig. 1, "Environment and Culture in the Cordillera," fig. 1, and "Environment and Culture in the Alaska Plateau," fig. 1, all this volume.

Shield and Associated Lowlands

The Canadian Shield (fig. 2) is one of the major physiographic units of the continent. Bedrock hills and

ridges interspersed with undrained or boggy hollows and valleys are the dominant land forms. Crystalline bedrock of Precambrian age is exposed or near the surface over much of the area ("Dogrib," figs. 6–7, this vol.). Unconsolidated sediments are thin and patchy except in the lowland areas.

The vast and seemingly monotonous Shield surface is not without some significant physiographic and geologic flourishes. The extreme eastern edge of the Shield is uplifted to form the mountainous Labrador coast. The Torngat, Kaumajet, Kiglapait, Benedict, and Mealy mountains rise to nearly 7,000 feet above sea level and have been glaciated to form an impressive alpinelike landscape. Apart from these mountains and some of the interior plateau areas, much of the Shield surface lies at 600 to 1,200 feet in elevation.

Another major geologic variation is found in the Labrador Trough of interior Quebec-Labrador. This feature, made up of parallel ridges trending northwest to southeast, is one of several extensive deposits of Precambrian (Proterozoic) sedimentary, altered sedimentary, and volcanic rocks in the Shield. These, of course, contrast with the predominant intrusive granites, granodiorites, quartz diorites, and granite gneisses.

Two extensive lowland areas, the Hudson Bay and the Mackenzie Lowlands, are physiographically distinct as well. The Hudson Bay Lowlands, situated on the southern and western shores of Hudson and James bays, are flat and poorly drained and maintain a slight slope toward and beneath the waters of the bays. The bedrock is made up of younger Paleozoic rocks, including Silurian and Devonian sandstones, shales, limestones, and dolomites. Surficial deposits, which are relatively thick for the Shield area, are fine sediments of marine origin.

The Mackenzie Lowlands (fig. 3) are a northward continuation of the Great Plains physiographic province. The lowlands consist of a flat surface with a gentle slope toward the Mackenzie River delta. They are interrupted by the Franklin Mountains, which rise to 3,000–4,000 feet in elevation between Great Bear Lake and the Mackenzie River. Substantial thickness of unconsolidated sediments overlie sedimentary rocks of Devonian age with some areas of Cretaceous rocks interspersed. The Mackenzie River delta, a significant physiographic feature in its own right, marks the northern limit of Indian occupation in the lowlands.

Typically, the transition from Precambrian Shield to lowlands is marked by restricted surface exposures of Ordovician age sandstones, quartzites, limestones, and shales.

Cordillera

The Cordillera is the most complex physiographic and geological region in the Subarctic. It is composed of an array of valleys and mountain ranges between the Mackenzie Lowlands and the Yukon River plateau. In a physiographic sense the Cordillera includes all the mountains of western North America. In this chapter the term is applied to the eastern ranges of the Cordillera system.

The Mackenzie and Selwyn mountains (fig. 4) mark the eastern edge of the Cordillera and are northern extensions of the Rocky Mountain system. With the Ogilvie Mountains to the west, the mountains form a drainage divide between the Yukon and Mackenzie watersheds and present a rugged topographic and climatic barrier. The geology of the region is characterized by Paleozoic sedimentary rocks with pockets and, in

Fig. 2. The western edge of the Canadian Shield, east of the Dogrib settlement at Rae Lakes, N.W.T. Spruce forest and Precambrian rock of the Shield are in evidence. Photograph by June Helm, Aug. 1976.

Fig. 3. String bog (lighter areas), and forest of black spruce and jack pine of the Mackenzie lowlands, in Slavey country between Ft. Providence and Ft. Simpson, N.W.T. Photograph by June Helm, June 1951.

some cases, large segments of Precambrian and Mesozoic intrusives. Some of the latter are of economic importance.

The Cordilleran region extends to the north through the Richardson Mountains. It then extends to the west through the Brooks Range in Alaska. The Brooks Range coincides with the transition from the subarctic environment of the Yukon Plateau to the arctic environment of the Alaska coastal plain to the north. Altitudinal differences in the Cordilleran region result in its environment not being uniformly subarctic. There are altitudinal variations among closed forest, transi-

Canadian Dept. of Energy, Mines, and Resources, Surveys and Mapping Branch, Ottawa.

Fig. 4. The Cordillera in the Macmillan Pass area, Selwyn Mountains, near the Yukon and Northwest Territories boundary, in the borderland between Mountain Indian and 19th-century Tutchone country. Typical marked altitudinal zonation, with boreal and montane forest in the major through valleys and alpine or arctic tundra on the uplands and peaks. Photograph by Flight Sgt. Bawden at 13,000 feet, Sept. 1944.

tional forest, alpine tundra, and bare rock, replicating latitudinal variations between subarctic and arctic environments.

Yukon-Kuskokwim-Tanana Plateaus

Interior Alaska and the Yukon Territory are dominated by the Yukon (fig. 5) and Kuskokwim rivers. The river valleys, their floodplains, and surrounding uplands make up the interior plateau region. This physiographic region extends south into British Columbia where it is a complex assemblage of hills, low mountain ranges, valleys, and plateaus. From central Alaska to the interior of British Columbia this region is bounded on the north and east by the Rocky, Mackenzie, Richardson, and Brooks mountains and on the south and west by the Alaska (fig. 6) and Coast ranges.

The bedrock geology of this plateau region is com-

8

plex. Late Proterozoic metamorphic rocks form the largest single unit in the Yukon River area. Mixed with these are pockets of Mesozoic intrusives and sedimentary rocks. The lower reaches of the Yukon and Kuskokwim drainage basins are characterized by younger sedimentary rocks of Tertiary and Quaternary age. Mesozoic and Tertiary sedimentaries with isolated intrusives also characterize the interior plateau region in British Columbia.

In contrast to the Shield and Cordilleran areas, much of the Yukon-Kuskokwim-Tanana plateau region of Alaska was not glaciated during the later stages of the Pleistocene. The legacy is evident in well-developed drainage patterns and soils. The soils are of some economic significance today in Alaska.

Alaska and Coast Ranges and Coastal Fringe

The area south of the inland plateaus in Alaska is dominated by high glaciated mountains. Principal ranges are: the Saint Elias, the Chugach (fig. 7), the Wrangell, the Alaska, the Kenai, and the Aleutian. Altitudes reach 20,000 feet within short distances (50 to 100 miles) of the sea, resulting in a steep Pacific slope. Thus, there is little or no coastal plain with the exception of the area surrounding Cook Inlet. The major mountain ranges are composed of Mesozoic rocks, both intrusive igneous and sedimentary. The coastal fringe, where much of the human occupation of the region is found, contains unconsolidated marine and continental deposits of Tertiary age.

Climate

Climate is a dominant and active element in the Subarctic environment. Weathering, erosion, hydrology,

Fig. 5. Yukon Flats, north-central Alaska, dominated by the meandering Yukon River, one of the most significant rivers of subarctic North America. The territory of the Kutchin extends westward from the adjacent Cordillera into this section of the interior Alaska Plateau. Photograph by June Helm, summer 1971.

Fig. 6. Talkeetna Mountains, south of the Alaska Range that forms the southern boundary of the Alaska Plateau region. Typical upland spruce forest of the Tanaina or Ahtna country borders the deeply eroded upper Matanuska River, which has cut into glacial deposits. Photograph by Edward Hosley, 1967.

Fig. 7. The Tsina, a river carrying glacial debris, in Ahtna territory in southern Alaska with the Chugach Mountains in the background. Photograph by Frederica De Laguna, Aug. 1968.

soil development, and human activities are influenced, and to some degree limited, by climatic factors such as temperature and precipitation.

The climatic characteristics of the Subarctic in North America are remarkably uniform over large areas. Koeppen's climatic classification includes most of the region in the "cold snow forest" category (Dfc and Dfd notations) (Strahler 1969). Warmest and coldest months in this climatic type are characterized by mean temperatures greater than 50°F. and less than 26.6°F. Fewer than four months a year have mean temperatures in excess of 50°F. In this type of climate, a modest degree of precipitation is sufficient to meet the natural demands of evaporation and transpiration in all months of the year. It should be noted that mean annual precipitation over much of the Subarctic is less than 18 inches (46 cms), which would characterize the area as semiarid in many other regions. In fact, low evaporation and transpiration demands result in a surplus of surface moisture in the Subarctic.

9

Major climatic deviations from these general conditions are primarily a function of maritime influences. The influence is evident in figure 1, which portrays mean daily temperatures for January. There is a rapid decline in temperature with increasing distance inland from the Pacific coast. A similar decline in mean annual precipitation occurs on the Pacific coast. Because of the generally eastward flow of air in these latitudes, a similar pattern is not evident on the Atlantic coast. The Coast and Alaska ranges, in combination with the Cordillera, are effective barriers to the inland transport of moisture-laden Pacific air. Much of the Subarctic then, is characterized by a "continental" climate notable for low winter temperatures (fig. 1) and short summers with mean daily temperatures not markedly different from much of the rest of northern and central North America.

The frost-free period is an important distinguishing characteristic of the Subarctic climate. Although maximum temperatures during the summer may be comparable to more southerly locations, the frost-free period is short. The maximum frost-free period in the Canadian part of the Subarctic is 100 to 120 days a year. This is found in the region west of Lake Superior and in small pockets along the Subarctic–Great Plains transition. A frost-free period of 40 to 60 days is more typical of the region. In Alaska, river valley locations have longer frost-free periods (90–120 days) while the coastal fringe in the Tanaina area may have up to 150 days frost-free a year.

A major portion of the precipitation in the Subarctic falls as snow, and the snow cover that develops is an extremely important ecological factor (Pruitt 1970; Seton 1909; Formozov 1964). Animal behavior, flora, human activities, air temperature, lake and river ice, ground ice, and surface waters are all influenced by snow cover. With the exception of the Pacific fringe, most of the Subarctic has a snow cover for at least 140 days each year. Over much of the area, snow cover duration exceeds 200 days a year.

Duration of snow cover is a function not only of general temperature conditions but also of snow depth. A mean annual maximum depth of 20 to 30 inches (50–75 cms) is characteristic of much of the Subarctic. However, in open woods, in hill and valley terrain, and on lakes this average figure has little meaning. Wherever wind is able to redistribute the snow, the snow-cover depth exhibits large variations over short distances. Deep drifts form in the lee of trees and ridges and in valleys of hollows, while ridge tops, lake surfaces, and unwooded bog areas may be swept bare. Snow-cover data from the Cordilleran region and other mountain areas are scanty; however, it is known that large accumulations occur on the windward (west and southwest) slopes of the Coast, the Alaska, and some interior ranges.

Snow cover in the boreal and transitional forests of the Shield is one of the more significant ecological factors in these areas. Accumulations are heavy and the snow cover persists for at least six months. Central Quebec-Labrador is particularly noteworthy for its depth of snow accumulation. Maximum depth ranges between 50 inches (130 cms) and 75 inches (190 cms), among the deepest recorded seasonal snow cover outside mountain areas (Adams et al. 1966; Gardner 1966). The snow cover in Quebec-Labrador is partly a function of a "maritime" influence from Hudson Bay during late fall and early winter when the bay is not yet frozen (Tout 1964) and of severe winter storms that move northeasterly along the Atlantic coast.

Snow density, snow hardness, snow-cover temperatures, and snow-cover structure are additional factors of ecological significance. These factors, as well as snow depth and duration, are influenced by wind speed and direction, air temperature, vegetation structure and distribution, and topography. The light deep snow of the boreal forest, the dense wind-blown sastrugi of the lakes, the deep, dense drifted snow of open woodland, the granular shallow snow at the ground surface, and the "bottomless" water-saturated snow of late spring provide environments and surfaces that encourage or limit activity and movement (Pruitt 1967).

Snow is an effective mediator in the water and energy balances in the Subarctic environment. Large amounts of water are seasonally stored as snow, which affects the behavior of Subarctic rivers. During the long night of Subarctic winters, snow stems the flow (and loss) of terrestrial radiant energy into the cold dry atmosphere. However, the white snow surface reflects (and loses) a large proportion of the incoming solar radiation. Reflection of energy and the expenditure of energy in the melting snow and ice in the spring significantly retard warming of the ground surface and ambient air and thereby the coming of spring.

Hydrology

Rivers and lakes play an important role in transportation and communication in the Subarctic. During freeze-up and breakup they act as an impediment to movement (fig. 8). Otherwise, the drainage patterns and water surfaces are important movement and communication routes and therefore focuses for settlement and other activities during both winter and summer. In addition, rivers and lakes provide habitats for fish of subsistence and commercial significance.

Drainage in the Subarctic is to the Pacific, Arctic, and Atlantic oceans, as well as to Hudson Bay. At a regional or Subarctic scale, the surface drainage appears relatively orderly. However, at the scale of the individual river or drainage basin in the Shield, a dominant characteristic of the surface drainage is the disorderly

Fig. 8. Ice conditions restricting movement. left, Freeze-up on Lac la Martre, N.W.T., with ice forming along the shore while wind and rough water keep the lake open. Dogrib men dismantle a raft and stack the logs for firewood; 3 days later men were on the frozen lake setting fish nets under the ice. right, Breakup near the mouth of a creek discharging into the Mackenzie River, N.W.T., Slavey country, with a stand of aspen on the opposite shore. Photographs by June Helm, left, Oct. 1959; right, May 1952.

and poorly integrated pattern (fig. 9). Watersheds are dotted with myriads of small lakes, bogs, and seemingly aimless interconnected streams. Stream profiles are not steep, and the divides between watersheds are low. These characteristics are, in part, legacies of recent glaciations.

The Yukon and Mackenzie river systems are the largest and best developed in the Subarctic. The Mackenzie has a mean annual discharge of 400,000 cubic feet per second at its mouth while that of the Yukon is 250,000 (Canada. Surveys and Mapping Branch 1974). These discharges are comparable to those at the mouths of the Saint Lawrence and Columbia rivers respectively. An important characteristic of Subarctic rivers is the great seasonal variability in discharge. Snow melt leads to late spring or early summer discharges that are up to 20 times winter discharges (fig. 10). For example, the estimated peak discharge on the La Grande River, which drains part of western Quebec-Labrador, is 208,000 cubic feet per second while the minimum flow is 11,800 (B. Richardson 1972).

Tributaries of the great rivers are significant streams in their own rights. Included are the Tanana, Porcupine, Liard, Slave, Peace, and Athabasca rivers in the western Subarctic. The eastern Subarctic contains a number of smaller but significant watersheds. Those draining radially into Hudson Bay include: the Churchill, the Nelson that is part of the Saskatchewan River system, the Albany, the Moose, the Rupert, La Grande (Fort George), and La Grande Baleine (Great Whale). The last two drain part of interior Quebec-Labrador and form part of a radial drainage pattern on the peninsula

Fig. 9. Bog country about midway between Ft. Rae and Ft. Simpson, N.W.T., 50 or 100 miles west of the western edge of the Shield, in the borderland between Dogrib and Slavey zones. The white lake shores are mineral deposits evaporated from the poorly drained water. Photograph by June Helm, July 1962.

with its center at Caniapiscau Lake. The Caniapiscau and George rivers flow to the north; the Churchill flows to the east; and the Saguenay, Manicouagan, and Moisie rivers flow to the south. Again, drainage divides are low and interdigitated such that human movement from one to the next is relatively simple.

The Shield region is dotted with lakes of all sizes. The largest—Great Bear, Great Slave, and Atha-

Fig. 10. The Copper River in flood, Ahtna territory, Alaska. Photograph by Frederica De Laguna, July 1968.

basca—are at the Shield–Mackenzie Lowlands boundary. Other major lakes on the Shield include: Wollaston, Reindeer, Southern Indian, Mistassini, and Michikamau.

Permanent ground ice is another important facet of Subarctic hydrology. Water is stored as ground ice and the presence of ground ice influences drainage, plant growth, soil formation, and land-forming processes (R.J.E. Brown 1970). The Subarctic, as defined in this volume, encompasses the zone of discontinuous permafrost (fig. 1). Therefore, if permanent ground ice is present, it is located only in favorable situations such as beneath windswept and barren ridge tops exposed to severe winter cold or in bottomlands and bogs where it is buried beneath thick deposits of peat, which serve to insulate the ice from summer warmth (Bird 1964). In the discontinuous zone, thickness of permafrost may be no greater than 200 to 300 feet and is probably less than 100 feet in most instances ("History of Research in Subarctic Alaska," fig. 2, this vol.). Changing technologies and the importation of complex machinery have given permanent ground ice added significance in Subarctic life (Péwé 1966; Ives 1962).

Vegetation

The ethnographic Subarctic encompasses the closed-crown boreal forest and the forest-tundra ecotone or transitional forest (fig. 11). Within these vegetation types are numerous and varied habitats including: dense spruce forest, open bogs, lichen woodlands, tundra-covered ridge tops, alpine tundra, and wet forested depressions or river valleys. Vegetation, a major factor in the definition of habitats, is in turn influenced by climate, moisture conditions, soil conditions, and topography.

Coniferous trees dominate the vegetation of the Subarctic. The particular species present are primarily determined by moisture conditions and secondarily by temperature and wind. The level of species diversity is low relative to temperate and tropical regions. However, the population of individual species may be quite large, as the white spruce in the boreal forest indicates. The white spruce (*Picea glauca*) is the most common conifer and is found in well-drained sites and on southern exposures. Its counterparts in wet sites are the black spruce (*Picea mariana*) and tamarack (*Larix laricina*). In the eastern Subarctic, balsam fir (*Abies balsamea*) and jackpine (*Pinus banksiana*) are important secondary species. The pines tend to occupy better-drained sites. In the west, balsam fir and jackpine are replaced by alpine fir (*Abies lasiocarpa*) and lodgepole pine (*Pinus contorta*). Deciduous species are limited in numbers but of great significance in the region's human ecology. Poplar (*Populus balsamifera*), aspen (*Populus tremuloides*), and white birch (*Betula papyrifera*) are present throughout much of the Subarctic.

The forest-tundra ecotone or transitional forest extends poleward from the boreal forest. In width this zone varies from less than 100 miles to more than 400 miles. Structurally the forest-tundra ecotone is similar to a parkland or savanna with the woody life forms interspersed with areas of open terrain, often lichen-covered. This so-called open lichen woodland is dominated by the same coniferous trees as in the boreal forest and by the "caribou lichens" (*Cladonia alpestris, C. mitis,* and *C. rangiferina*) (E.M. Fraser 1956).

Physiography plays a role in the distribution of the forest-tundra ecotone. The ridges and interfluves in this zone have all the elements of open tundra, whereas the

Natl. Film Board of Canada Photothèque, Ottawa: 62–6776.
Fig. 11. The town of Schefferville, Que., with opencast iron mines in the background. Characteristic Shield granitic glaciated plateau terrain, with the linear ridges typical of the Labrador trough, in Montagnais-Naskapi territory. This shows forest-tundra ecotone, with high exposed ridges carrying tundra association and the valleys boreal forest and transitional forest species. Photograph by Jarrett, Sept. 1962.

12

valleys maintain a cover not unlike the boreal forest. Elsewhere, white spruce, usually of diminishing size, and the caribou lichens predominate. The appearance is one of forest interdigitated with tundra. In the western Subarctic, within the major river valleys with their relatively good fluvially derived soils, vigorous growths of the deciduous species are found within the transitional forest zone.

Tundra vegetation does not cover a large area in the Subarctic. It is restricted to the Arctic margin and to ridge tops and alpine areas. All perennial species are structurally modified to low-growing or recumbent forms. Other species survive the long winter as root stalks, bulbs, and rhizomes, while lichens survive in a desiccated state. A variety of shrubs and dwarf shrubs is found in the tundra and transitional areas. Common examples are: dwarf birch (*Betula glandulosa*), crowberry (*Empetrum nigrum*), cranberry (*Vaccinium vitis-idaea*), alder (*Alnus crispa*), and labrador tea (*Ledum groenlandicum*).

Soils

As an environmental element, soil reflects the combined activity of climate, parent material, topography, and organisms all operating through a period of time. In many regions, soil is of critical importance in economic productivity. In the Subarctic, the factors of soil formation have acted to limit the development of highly productive soils. Most of the Subarctic has been glaciated within the last 20,000 years and is lacking in extensive areas of thick surficial sediments. The climate, being cold, is not conducive to rapid chemical and biochemical breakdown of inorganic and organic material. Mechanical weathering is slow. Neither bedrock nor unconsolidated material is rapidly altered by these processes to form a soil profile. Organic material is slow to decay and accumulates as thick deposits of peat rather than becoming part of a productive soil. In general, Subarctic soils tend to be wet and very high in organic material, and most are frozen for long periods of time.

The podzol is the dominant soil type of the Subarctic. It is characterized by relatively thick leaf mulch, a leached (ash-colored) horizon, and a second horizon with deposits of organic colloids leached from the first horizon. The podzols are generally acidic and not particularly productive. Most of the Subarctic is covered by thin podzol soils interspersed with rock outcrops and peat deposits. On the southern margins, the podzols give way to brown-wooded and gray-wooded soils. If carefully used and properly drained, both of these soils are agriculturally productive. Wooded soils are found in the Hudson Bay Lowlands and its southern margins, in the northward extension of the Great Plains physiographic region, and in some of the interior valleys and

plateaus of British Columbia and Alaska. Alluvial soils, made up of fluvial (river) and lacustrine (lake bottom) parent materials, are found in the Hudson Bay Lowland, in the Lake Athabasca–Great Slave Lake corridor, and in the river valleys of Alaska. Some of these, particularly in the "clay belt" of Ontario (Hearst-Cochrane area) and on the floodplains of Alaskan rivers, are agriculturally productive.

Environmental Resources

Faunal resources are basic to traditional cultures in the Subarctic. At the same time, resources have been the primary stimulus for the movement of Whites into the region. At first, it was the attraction of furs. Some time thereafter, the agricultural potential of areas in northern Ontario, Alberta, British Columbia, and Alaska drew Whites. Fish, lumber, and wood pulp attracted White enterprise as well. However, the mineral resources have consistently provided the greatest attractions of all.

Exploitation of Subarctic mineral resources has occurred for almost 100 years (Tough 1972). Since 1860 it has focused on ores and minerals in the hard rock of the Shield with secondary and short-lived focuses in the gold-bearing alluvial deposits of the Yukon River and its tributaries. The readily discoverable deposits of gold, nickel, and copper were exploited at places such as Sudbury, Yellowknife, Timmins, and Dawson City. Since World War II exploitation has focused on remote, high-grade deposits of gold, radium, uranium, and galena at places like Uranium City and Mayo. In addition, lower-grade deposits such as the lead-zinc ores at Pine Point and iron-ore deposits at Schefferville (fig. 11) have been made economically feasible through technological changes and diminishing supplies of high-grade ores elsewhere. It is very probable that technology will continue to enable further resource recovery, as evidenced by petroleum production and exploration in parts of the Subarctic.

Fossil fuel resources and the hydroelectric energy potential of Subarctic resources are potent factors in changing the Subarctic environment in the late twentieth century. Petroleum and natural gas have been extracted and exported from northern Alberta for a number of years. Potential for future development is high in a zone extending north from northern Alberta and British Columbia through the Mackenzie Lowlands to the Beaufort Sea, as well as the North Slope of Alaska. The rivers of the Shield have attracted hydroelectric power installations of enormous proportions. Churchill Falls in Labrador, the Manicouagan River in Quebec, the Churchill and Nelson rivers in Manitoba, and the La Grande and other rivers draining western Quebec are all in various stages of "development." Others are sure to follow. The myriad lakes and rivers of the Subarctic are also being viewed as potential sources of fresh water for more heavily populated southern regions in North America.

The common feature of resource "development" activities in the Subarctic has been their extractive nature. Gold, silver, nickel, natural gas, petroleum, uranium, electric power, lumber, fish, iron ore, and furs have been extracted and exported. Their exploitation has led to little permanent White settlement within the Subarctic region but to the export of much wealth outside the region.

Conclusion

The Subarctic environment is complex and dynamic. The physiography, climate, hydrology, flora, fauna, and soils, all interacting, provide the stage and context for human life and activity. By the standards of the temperate regions and modern, postindustrial society, it is a harsh and rigorous environment. Yet viable cultures and economies have developed and thrived within it. While it is these that provide the focus for this volume, one cannot ignore the fact that elements of the environment have been, and will continue to be, attractive to outsiders. By this process, the physical environment of the Subarctic and the social, economic, and technological context of life there is being transformed.

Sources

Literature and information on the subarctic environment has increased markedly since 1950. This has resulted especially from the information demands of resource-extraction and transportation industries. As a result, much of the new information is place-specific and problem-specific, and often located in obscure or not easily obtained reports. There remain few comprehensive and general overviews of the physical geography of the subarctic in North America.

For a general overview of the subarctic environment, in particular its special problems, consult Blüthgen (1970). Physiographic features are described generally by Atwood (1940) and Bird (1972, 1972a). *The National Atlas of Canada* (Canada. Surveys and Mapping Branch 1974) and the *National Atlas of the United States of America* (U.S. Geological Survey 1970) present the best maps summarizing the general climatic, hydrological, and biological (plants and animal) characteristics of the subarctic. Permafrost, an important factor in both the arctic and subarctic, is conveniently covered by R.J.E. Brown (1970).

The scholarly journals are the most accessible source for specific information on the subarctic. The physical environment is composed of factors of interest to a variety of disciplines including climatology, meteorology, hydrology, geology, geomorphology, botany, zoology, and pedology, so the information is scattered over a large number of journals. Two journals are particularly devoted to arctic and subarctic issues, *Arctic* and *The Musk-Ox*. Special publications or report series such as *McGill-Subarctic Research Papers* (for example, Adams et al. 1966) are also useful sources for special topics.

Major Fauna in the Traditional Economy

BERYL C. GILLESPIE

"It is a land of feast or famine. The game is afoot with the seasons; the fishes roam over enormous water areas, and they are not easy to find except during the spawning period" (Rostlund 1952:153).

For the entire Subarctic the only significant form of native sustenance has been flesh foods.* Although changes have occurred in the traditional economy throughout the historic period, in the 1970s most native peoples within the Subarctic still relied, at least in part, on hunting, fishing, and trapping.

Subsistence Mammals

Large game animals of primary subsistence importance to the Indians of the Subarctic are the woodland caribou (*Rangifer tarandus caribou*), Barren Ground caribou (*Rangifer tarandus groenlandicus*), and moose (*Alces alces*) (fig. 1). For the Indians living in the Northwestern Transition section of the boreal forest (Rowe 1972:55) of Canada and in the plateau of Alaska the Barren Ground caribou are the subsistence core, with moose an important subsidiary resource. For the rest of the Subarctic the woodland caribou and moose are the essential large game. These animals have also provided the raw materials for much of the material culture of the natives.

In the alpine areas the mountain goat (*Oreamnos americanus*) and Dall sheep (*Ovis dalli*) have been important resources to the Indians, but always in addition to moose and woodland caribou. Elk or wapiti (*Cervus elaphus canadensis*), wood and plains buffalo (*Bison bison athabascae* and *Bison bison bison*), musk-ox (*Ovibos moschatus*), and white-tailed deer (*Odocoileus virginianus*) have very limited distributions and therefore are exploited only in restricted areas. Black bears (*Ursus americanus*) are widely distributed but never have been a major food resource. Grizzly bears (*Ursus horribilis*) have a restricted distribution, are dangerous to hunt, and were not hunted for food.

Of the small mammals, the snowshoe (or varying) hare (*Lepus americanus*) is most widely exploited. While not a preferred source of food for many natives,

---

*The major reference works for fauna classification, distribution, and habitat are by Banfield (1974), Godfrey (1966), McPhail and Lindsey (1970), and Rostlund (1952).

it has been a very important source of midwinter food when large game is difficult to find or kill. Other mammals significant to subsistence in some regions are the beaver (*Castor canadensis*), woodchuck (*Marmota monax*), which is also called groundhog, hoary marmot (*Marmota caligata*), muskrat (*Ondatra zibethicus*), porcupine (*Erethizon dorsatum*), and arctic ground squirrel (*Spermophilus undulatus*).

Sea mammals are of some importance to a few Indian peoples on the eastern and western seacoasts of the Subarctic as well as on the Hudson Bay and the Saint Lawrence River. The harbor seal (*Phoca vitulina*) and the white whale or beluga (*Delphinapterus leucas*) are exploited on the southwest coast of Alaska, the Saint Lawrence River, and, within the historic period, on Hudson Bay. On the Atlantic seacoast the Naskapi Indians traditionally hunted the harp seal (*Phoca groenlandica*) and the ringed or jar seal (*Phoca hispida*), and occasionally the bearded or squareflipper seal (*Erignatus barbatus*).

Animals of the Fur Trade

All Subarctic mammals larger than voles, lemmings, and shrews have been included in the fur-trade economy (table 1). European fur fashions and economy have changed frequently, and fur prices and favored furs changed through time. The preferred furs of the time, their market value, number available, and ease of trapping and hunting have all influenced the activities and income of the native trapper. Besides the many fur-bearing animals that made up the core of the furs traded in all areas of the Subarctic, all large game that has been mentioned as part of Indian subsistence was also incorporated into the fur trade for their hides and for their meat as provisions for workers in the fur trade.

Fish

Along streams of the Pacific drainages that have major salmon runs, Indians have relied heavily on the seasonal catch of several species of salmon. In the other areas of the Subarctic fish were not considered as important as game for subsistence. However, the general availability of fish in most lakes and streams made them sea-

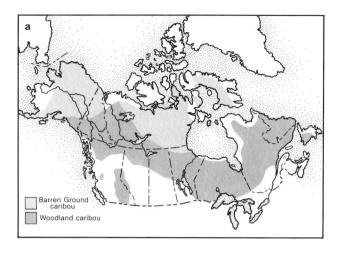
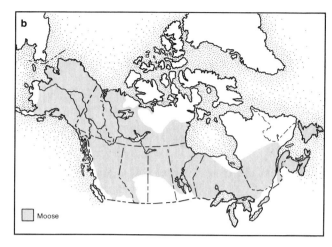
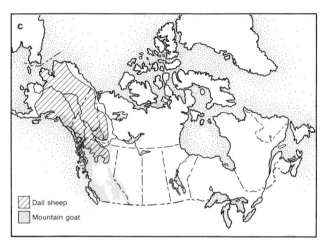
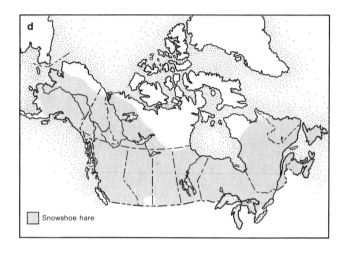

after Banfield 1974; Allen 1979.

Fig. 1. Important subsistence game animals of the Subarctic: a, Barren Ground and woodland caribou; b, moose; c, Dall sheep and mountain goat; d, snowshoe hare.

Table 1. Furbearers

Major economic significance in most of the Subarctic
  Beaver, *Castor canadensis*
  Ermine, *Mustela erminea*
  Lynx, *Lynx lynx*
  Marten, *Martes americana*
  Mink, *Mustela vison*
  Muskrat, *Ondatra zibethicus*
  Red fox, *Vulpes vulpes*
  River otter, *Lontra canadensis*

Minor economic significance or limited distribution
  Arctic fox, *Alopex lagopus*
  Coyote, *Canis latrans*
  Fisher, *Martes pennanti*
  Gray wolf, *Canis lupus*
  Musk-ox, *Ovibos moschatus*
  Red squirrel, *Tamiasciurus hudsonicus*
  Striped skunk, *Mephitis mephitis*
  Wolverine, *Gulo gulo*
  Woodchuck (groundhog), *Marmota monax*

sonally an important resource. During the historic period the importance of fish in the native economy increased. With more effective, European-derived fishing equipment, especially twine for all varieties of nets and metal tools used to break through the ice in winter, there was an increase in the quantity and seasonal availability of fish. After 1850 the introduction of dog traction greatly increased the native need for quantities of fish as a major dog food. Fish also increased in importance in areas, notably in the eastern and central Subarctic, where large game became depleted. Table 2 lists the major fish species exploited by Indians throughout the subarctic.

Fowl

Migratory waterfowl pass through the Subarctic every spring and fall. The snow goose, also called the wavy or blue goose (*Chen caerulescens*), the Canada goose (*Branta canadensis*), and a number of species of duck

Table 2. Fish Species Significant for Indians and their Dogs in the Contact-Traditional Economy

	Shield	Cordillera	Alaska Plateau	South of Alaska Range
Lake sturgeon, *Acipenser fulvescens*	(×)	0	0	0
Longnose sucker, *Catostomus catostomus*	×	×	+	−
White sucker, *Catostomus commersonii*	(+)	0	0	0
Cisco (lake herring), *Coregonus artedii*	(+)	0	0	0
Humpback whitefish, *Coregonus clupeaformis*	×	×	×	+
Broad whitefish, *Coregonus nasus*	(+)	+	+	0
Least cisco, *Coregonus sardinella*	0	+	−	0
Blackfish, *Dallia pectoralis*	0	0	(+)	0
Pacific lamprey, *Entosphenus tridentatus*	0	(−)	0	−
Northern pike (jackfish), *Esox lucius*	+	+	+	+
Goldeye, *Hiodon alosoides*	(+)	0	0	0
Burbot (ling, ling cod, loche, maria, methye), *Lota lota*	+	+	+	0
Pink salmon (humpback salmon), *Oncorhynchus gorbuscha*	0	−	0	×
Chum salmon (dog salmon), *Oncorhynchus keta*	−	(×)	(×)	×
Coho salmon (silver salmon), *Oncorhynchus kisutch*	0	0	(+)	×
Sockeye salmon (red salmon, kokanee), *Oncorhynchus nerka*	0	0	(+)	×
Chinook salmon (king, spring salmon, tyee), *Oncorhynchus tshawytscha*	0	(×)	×	+
American yellow perch, *Perca flavescens*	(×)	0	0	0
Round whitefish, *Prosopium cylindraceum*	+	+	+	+
Rainbow trout (steelhead), *Salmo gairdnerii*	0	+	0	+
Arctic char (Mackenzie salmon), *Salvelinus alpinus*	(+)	0	0	(+)
Brook trout (speckled trout), *Salvelinus fontinalis*	(+)	0	0	0
Dolly Varden (char, salmon trout), *Salvelinus malma*	(+)	0	(+)	+
Lake trout (char), *Salvelinus namaycush*	×	×	−	+
Inconnu (conny, sheefish), *Stenodus leucichthys*	×	×	(+)	+
Yellow walleye (doré, pickerel, walleyed pike), *Stizostedion vitreum vitreum*	×	0	0	0
Arctic grayling (bluefish), *Thymallus arcticus*	(+)	×	+	+
American eel (true eel), *Anguilla rostrata*	(×)	0	0	0
American smelt, *Osmerus mordax*	(+)	0	0	0
Atlantic salmon, *Salmo salar*	(+)	0	0	0

Key: × primary importance, + secondary importance, ( ) limited distribution, − not significant or no mention, 0 absent from the region.

are a source of food for brief periods, especially in the spring. These migratory waterfowl became an important food resource for the Indians of the Hudson Bay Lowland during the historic period. Of greater importance to Indians throughout the Subarctic, but always subsidiary to game and fish, were the various species of grouse. Major grouse species widely distributed are the ruffed grouse (*Bonasa umbellus*), spruce grouse (*Canachites canadensis*), northern sharp-tail grouse (*Pedioecetes phasianellus*), willow ptarmigan (*Lagopus lagopus*), and the rock ptarmigan (*Lagopus mutus*).

Animal Cycles and Fluctuations

Although the quantity and quality of data on Subarctic animals are not uniformly adequate, there is clear evidence of population fluctuations of all animal types sig-

nificant in the native subsistence economy. A complex set of variables results in fairly unpredictable oscillations of the Subarctic populations of large game animals (Waisberg 1975:183). A major factor in the fluctuations in the numbers of large as well as small animals is the various successions of forest stages, each stage supplying adequate food for only certain species. "For any species living in an area undergoing succession, the amount of preferred food that can be taken is gradually reduced. Different animal populations will eventually die or migrate out of their area as their food resource base is transmuted into a different one through vegetational successions" (Waisberg 1975:176).

In addition to the continuous and regular successional stages of forestation is the effect of forest fires (Feit 1973; VanStone 1979b). Whether large or small in size, forest fires alter the vegetational food supply dramatically, thereby radically changing movements and numbers of animals by species. These and other variables,

17

including seasonal weather conditions, contribute to instabilities of animal habitat and populations and to human capacity to procure flesh foods.

Some animals have relatively predictable population cycles. The four-year cycle of certain rodent species sometimes produces the same cycle in their predators, such as fox and marten. The cycle of about 9 to 10 years for the varying hare has been long recognized. It appears that a major decline of the varying hare population in a region is followed within a year by a decline of grouse and ptarmigan since they become the alternate prey for several species of predators. However, these cycles are not regular, either in their temporal or their geographical spans. Clearly, a severe drop in the number of hare, grouse, and ptarmigan—all considered alternate native subsistence foods when large game is not available within a region—can produce dire conditions for the native population (Waisberg 1975).

Ethnographic descriptions suggest that fish species also go through population oscillations seasonally and over years but very little information is available. Perhaps more important for the native subsistence quest are seasonal or transitory climate conditions that render fish unavailable by means of traditional technology.

History of Ethnological Research in the Subarctic Shield and Mackenzie Borderlands

EDWARD S. ROGERS

Ethnological research has been undertaken within the Shield Subarctic, an area extending from Labrador to the Mackenzie borderlands, since the 1880s. Burch (1979a) published a review of northern research that includes the Shield Subarctic. Helm (1976) and Hippler and Wood (1974) provide critical and annotated bibliographies. Several other bibliographies have been published (Feit et al. 1972; Dominique 1976; Helm 1973). The following account first outlines in chronological order the initial entry into the field of those individuals whose primary purpose was to record and analyze the culture of the Indians. At the same time, the increasing coverage of more and more "tribal" groups and bands is indicated. The second part surveys those aspects of Native culture that have been investigated and presents some of the varied interpretations of the data.

Ever since Europeans arrived in the Subarctic, there have been those who took an interest in the Indians' culture and recorded their observations. Some of these accounts have been published, but many more reside in archives such as those of the Hudson's Bay Company and Anglican and Roman Catholic Churches, especially those of the Oblate Order. Traders, explorers, and travelers have provided important materials (for example, Hearne 1958; Isham 1949; McLean 1932; Grant 1889–1890, 2; Cameron 1889–1890, 2; Franklin 1824, 1828; Graham 1969; Boucher 1964; Cartwright 1911; Russell 1898; and J. Rae 1882). Of the missionaries, the early Jesuits' accounts (JR 1896–1901) and those of Petitot (1884–1885, 1891, 1893, 1899) should be noted (fig. 1). Some Indians have contributed (Boulanger 1971; Tetso 1970; Anahareo 1972; Willis 1973; Bouchard 1974–1975; Mestokosho 1977; André 1976, 1979; Williams and Williams 1978a). Indian life has also inspired novels (Lips 1942; Bodsworth 1959, 1967; Thériault 1972, 1972a) and at least two personal accounts of fieldwork (Osgood 1953; Helm 1979).

Survey of Field Research

Ethnographic fieldwork can be divided into three periods: 1882–1920, 1921–1940, and 1941–1980. The transition between each period is marked by a world war when for a number of years fieldwork was rarely undertaken.

1882–1920

The first period, 1882–1920, coincides with the classical period in American anthropology, the first two decades of which saw the establishment of the large North American museums (Mead and Bunzel 1960:276–278) and the last two decades, the dominance of Franz Boas (Mead and Bunzel 1960:400–402). Fieldwork at this time consisted of a few exploratory investigations, in most cases by students of Boas (table 1). A factor inhibiting fieldwork was the difficulty of access. Coastal areas such as the north shore of the Saint Lawrence, the Labrador coast, and Hudson Bay could be reached only by ship. Inland areas were even more difficult to visit. Except on the Mackenzie River, canoes were the only means of transport in summer; in winter, travel was perforce by snowshoe and dog team. Accordingly, few individuals entered the field and then generally in coastal localities.

The first fieldwork that had as one of its specific aims the description of Indian culture was that of Lucien M.

Smithsonian Lib.: Petitot 1891:29.

Fig. 1. Missionaries traveling with dogsleds on Great Slave Lake, N.W.T., in territory of the Dogrib and Yellowknife-Chipewyan. The figure at right probably represents the missionary and linguist-ethnographer Émile Petitot, who signed and dated the 1863 drawing used for this engraving.

19

Turner (fig. 2), who spent 1882–1884 at Fort Chimo on Ungava Bay where some of the northern Naskapi periodically went to trade. Not until 1908 was fieldwork again undertaken in the eastern Subarctic, when Frank G. Speck began work among the Montagnais of Lake Saint John. For the next 30 years he continued to investigate the Montagnais and their neighbors, the southern Naskapi. Although a few others did fieldwork, their contact with the Indians was of short duration.

Fieldwork in this period was scattered geographically, extending from Fort Chimo where Turner worked to the Great Slave Lake area of the Northwest Territories where Frank Russell (fig. 3) and J. Alden Mason (figs. 4–5) made preliminary investigations. Research was supported primarily by museums. The Smithsonian Institution sponsored Turner. The American Museum of Natural History, New York, was responsible for Robert H. Lowie's brief visit to the Chipewyan and presumably those of Alanson B. Skinner among the northern Saulteaux and Cree and of Pliny E. Goddard among the Chipewyan and Beaver. In 1910, Edward Sapir joined the National Museum of Canada, Ottawa, as head of the newly established Anthropology Division, Geological Survey Branch, which supported or at least encouraged investigations by F.W. Waugh, Mason, and some of those by Speck.

Practically all the publications resulting from these field trips were descriptive (see L.M. Turner 1894; Russell 1898; Skinner 1912; J.A. Mason 1946). One, though, went further. Speck (1915a) initiated theoretical studies of the social organization of the Indians, endeavors that continued through the 1970s. Also,

Fig. 3. Frank Russell, wearing his field clothing and holding hunting snowshoes and a Winchester rifle used for collecting mammal specimens. Studio portrait, about 1894–1896, taken after his return from an extended trip in the Subarctic in 1893–1894 to collect for the U. of Iowa museum, where his zoological and ethnological collections survive (including these showshoes, catalogue no. 10,849, and perhaps the Indian moccasins he wears, 10,835).

some attempts at generalizations and historical interpretations of the data collected were being made (Birket-Smith 1918; Hatt 1916; Wissler 1915).

1921–1940

During the second period, 1921–1940, the number of individuals who conducted fieldwork increased slightly (table 1), but the number was minimal considering the vast territory over which the Indians were scattered. Some ethnologists began traveling farther into the interior to study the Native people. Speck continued his work among the Montagnais-Naskapi. John M. Cooper (fig. 6), A. Irving Hallowell (figs. 7–8), and Regina Flannery began their investigations among the Cree, Ojibwa, and Saulteaux, which were to continue for a

Fig. 2. Lucien M. Turner in his winter quarters at Fort Chimo, Que., territory of the Montagnais-Naskapi. Photographed in Feb. 1884.

Fig. 4. J. Alden Mason in a Dogrib canoe with Ft. Rae, N.W.T., in the background, Aug. 1913.

Fig. 5. Tinite, a Slavey resident at Ft. Rae in Dogrib country, one of J. Alden Mason's main informants, recording a song on a wax cylinder. Photograph by Mason, 1913.

number of years, as did Cooper (1926a) and D.S. Davidson (1928d) among the Tête de Boule. Early investigators, such as Strong, ceased work in the Subarctic after their initial venture into the field (fig. 9).

This was a period when new theoretical interests emerged in anthropology, especially concern with social organization and culture and personality, and influenced the work that was undertaken within the Shield Subarctic. Speck (1926:272) outlined some of the areas of concern and noted: "For some time there has been a growing need of a general survey, with an attempt at interpretation, of the cultural properties of the Indians of northeastern America."

The published results during the second period still tended to be descriptive, although specific problems such as trait distributions and origins, band organization, land tenure, cross-cousin marriage, and psychological characteristics began or continued to be investigated. At the same time, field techniques changed somewhat. In the preceding period, direct observations

often were sufficient to secure data since the Indians were still living in a traditional fur-trade economy and many aspects of their culture were considered "aboriginal." But by the second period, the Indians' way of life had begun to change considerably; and the investigators, most of whom were interested in "aboriginal" culture, had to attempt reconstructions frequently based on the memory of their informants (see Speck 1931; Cooper 1934, 1939). Such reconstructions were spurious since there had been some 400 years of contact with Europeans in the east and a century or slightly more in the west. Little attention was paid to historical documents, whether published or unpublished, although museum collections were utilized to some extent (D.S. Davidson 1937). Hallowell (1951), on the other hand, began to use psychological tests to investigate the personality of the Ojibwa and to examine the influence brought to bear upon the personality type by European contact. And Leonard Mason (1967) examined the changes that had taken place through European contact up to the time of his fieldwork (fig. 10).

Museums continued to sponsor research but not to the extent that they had. In 1925, Sapir left the National Museum of Canada; in 1929 Diamond Jenness was appointed chief anthropologist to succeed him. However, the museum was not able to expand its ethnographic endeavors because of the Depression of the 1930s and World War II. With the emergence at this time of departments of anthropology within universities, investigators were usually members of university staffs and sought financial support from their own universities or from organizations other than museums.

1941–1980

Fieldwork was curtailed because of the Second World War. But in the 1950s a new generation of ethnologists emerged and the numbers increased greatly during the 1960s (table 1). Then in the 1970s a research explosion

Fig. 6. John M. Cooper, second from left, with a group of Tête de Boules at Obedijwan, Que. Photographed in 1925.

Table 1. Chronology of Research through 1969: Initial Fieldwork

Investigator	Date	Location	Group
Lucien M. Turner	1882	Fort Chimo	Naskapi
Frank Russell	1893	Fort Rae, Great Slave Lake	Dogrib
Robert H. Lowie	1908	Northern Alberta	Chipewyan
Frank G. Speck	1908	Lake St. John	Montagnais
Alanson B. Skinner	1908	James Bay	Cree
Pliny E. Goddard	1913	Peace and Hay rivers	Beaver
J. Alden Mason	1913	Fort Rae, Great Slave Lake	Slavey, Dogrib, Chipewyan
F.W. Waugh	1921	Davis Inlet	Naskapi
Kaj Birket-Smith	1923	Churchill	Chipewyan
John M. Cooper	1925	Lake St. John	Montagnais
W. Duncan Strong	1927	Davis Inlet	Naskapi
Cornelius Osgood	1928	Great Bear Lake	Bearlake
A. Irving Hallowell	1930	Grand Rapids, Norway House	Ojibwa, Cree
Regina Flannery	1933	James Bay	Cree
Julius E. Lips	1935	Lake St. John, Obedjiwan	Montagnais, Tête de Boule
W.H. Jenkins	1937	Lake Abitibi	Cree
Leonard Mason	1938	Oxford House	Cree
Richard Slobodin	1938	Fort McPherson	Kutchin
John T. McGee	1942	Northwest River	Naskapi
John J. Honigmann	1943	Fort Nelson	Slavey
Eleanor Leacock	1950	Natashquan	Montagnais
June Helm	1951	"Lynx Point"	Slavey
V.F. Valentine	1952	Northern Saskatchewan	Métis
Edward S. Rogers	1953	Lake Mistassini	Cree
Robert W. Dunning	1954	Pikangikum	Saulteaux
Hans Hoffman	1954	Great Whale River	Cree
Asen Balikci	1957	Great Whale River	Cree
Jean Trudeau	1958	Winisk	Cree
Nancy Oestreich Lurie	1959	Lac la Martre	Dogrib
Ronald Cohen	1960	Mackenzie Valley	Athapaskans
James W. VanStone	1960	Snowdrift	Chipewyan
W.D. Johnson	1960	Great Whale River	Cree
Hiroko Sue Hara	1961	Fort Good Hope	Hare
Janice Hurlburt	1961	Fort Good Hope	Hare
D.H.T. Clairmont	1961	Aklavik	Kutchin, Métis
Rolf Knight	1961	Némiscau, Rupert House, Eastmain	Cree
Roger Pothier	1962	Lake Mistassini	Cree
Richard J. Preston	1963	Rupert House	Cree
José Mailhot	1963	Northwest River	Naskapi
A. Michaud	1963	Northwest River	Naskapi
Jack H. Steinbring	1964	Black River, Lake Winnipeg	Ojibwa
Charles A. Bishop	1965	Osnaburgh House	Ojibwa
I.E. La Rusic	1965	Lake Mistassini–Waswanipi	Cree
Robin Ridington	1965	Northeastern British Columbia	Beaver
Georg Hendriksen	1966	Davis Inlet	Naskapi
W.W. Koolage	1966	Churchill	Chipewyan
P.S. Sindell	1966	Lake Mistassini	Cree
Joel S. Savishinsky	1967	Colville Lake	Hare
James G.E. Smith	1967	Brochet	Chipewyan, Cree
Adrien Tanner	1967	Lake Mistassini–Waswanipi	Cree
Mary Black	1968	Weagamow	Ojibwa
Bruce Cox	1968	Hay River	Slavey
Beryl C. Gillespie	1968	Detah	Dogrib
David M. Smith	1968	Fort Resolution	Chipewyan, Métis
Michael I. Asch	1969	Wrigley	Slavey
W. Kenneth Barger	1969	Great Whale River	Cree
S. Richmond	1969	Northern Alberta	Slavey, Beaver
J. Garth Taylor	1969	Lansdowne House	Ojibwa

Maude F. Hallowell, Wayne, Pa.

Fig. 7. A. Irving "Pete" Hallowell with one of his major informants, Chief William ("Willie") Berens of the Saulteaux, Berens River, Man. According to Maude F. Hallowell (communication to editors, 1978) Chief Berens was Hallowell's "mentor, guide, interpreter, informer, friend [and] aside from getting together men and equipment, Willie had relatives and connections in all the settlements up the river. He was also a mine of information about customs and tribal history." Photographed at Berens River, Man., 1934.

occurred, making it impossible to cover here in any detail all the work that was undertaken in that decade, not even the large part that has been published. The topics investigated became extremely varied, reflecting the diversity of interests that were evolving within anthropology. Furthermore, with an increase in the number of investigators a much wider geographical coverage was possible, and most of the major Indian groups were studied to some extent. Yet even among those groups that received the most ethnographic attention, not all aspects of their culture, such as material culture and religion, insofar as it was still possible to secure data on more traditional forms, had been fully documented.

Fieldwork was carried out primarily from universities (Laval in Quebec and McGill in Montreal being most active) with funding coming from either the universities or outside agencies. Among museums, the National Museum of Canada, Ottawa, and the Royal Ontario Museum, Toronto, continued to be involved in research. Important was the Algonquian Project initiated by McFeat (1962) when he was chief ethnologist at the National Museum of Canada.

Starting in the early 1940s, the federal, provincial, and territorial governments became aware of their limited understanding of conditions among the Native peoples and began to provide funds for investigations, including ethnological research, which it was hoped would aid in planning programs in fields such as medical aid, housing, and employment for the "betterment" of the Indians. The first such investigation was the James Bay Survey (Honigmann 1951a), which examined the health of the Cree (Vivian 1948) and their economic and subsistence patterns (Honigmann 1961; Kerr 1950). Similar

projects were sponsored by the Northern Co-ordination and Research Centre (NCRC) of the Department of Northern Affairs and National Resources in the Northwest Territories (e.g., Helm and Lurie 1961; Cohen 1962; Honigmann 1962; VanStone 1963a, 1965) and by the Agricultural Rehabilitation Development Administration (ARDA), which funded the McGill Project (Chance 1969) and the Round Lake Ojibwa Project (Watts 1971). The Research Division, Centre for Community Studies, University of Saskatchewan, funded by the provincial Department of Natural Resources, undertook economic and social investigations in northern Saskatchewan (Worsley, Buckley, and Davis 1961; Kew 1962; Buckley 1962; and Buckley, Kew, and Hawley 1963). Finally, a survey of the contemporary Indians of Canada (Hawthorn 1966–1967), financed by the Department of Indian Affairs, reviewed the economic, political, and educational needs and policies relating to all Canadian Indians including those of the Shield Subarctic.

As the science of anthropology developed, investigators after World War II tended to be more theoretically oriented than those who had undertaken fieldwork during the previous two periods. Reexaminations were made of older interpretations of cultural features such as social organization and land tenure, which frequently resulted in new interpretations of the data. At the same time, approaches to the ethnohistory and cultural ecology of the Shield Subarctic Indians were refined, and new perspectives on their culture began to be gained and a renewed interest in material culture occurred (Gillespie 1970; Bishop 1970a; R. Knight 1965).

Results and Issues

An early concern of ethnologists was the distribution, diffusion, and possible origin of certain aboriginal traits and trait complexes. Hatt (1916) dealt with footwear; D.S. Davidson (1937) examined the distribution of snowshoes; Hallowell (1926) surveyed bear ceremonialism; Speck, birchbark work (1937a) and the double-curve motif in art (1914); Cooper (1938), the distribution of trap systems; G.J. Turner (1955), moose-hair embroidery; and Adney and Chapelle (1964), the distribution and construction of bark canoes.

Most distributional studies were primarily concerned with items of material culture. Yet, in general, little attention was paid to this topic, especially from a historical perspective; and few detailed studies for any particular group exist. Some ethnologists have in their publications given attention to material culture (Birket-Smith 1930; Helm and Lurie 1961; J.A. Mason 1946; L.M. Turner 1894; Skinner 1912; McGee 1961). Few publications are devoted solely to this subject (Hallowell 1938a; Lips 1937, 1947a; Rogers 1967a; Speck

23

HISTORY OF ETHNOLOGICAL RESEARCH IN THE SUBARCTIC SHIELD AND MACKENZIE BORDERLANDS

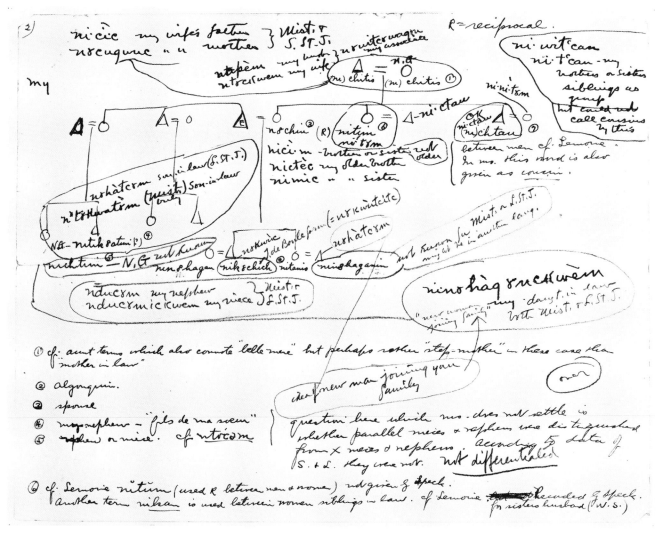

Fig. 8. Part of a manuscript analysis by A. Irving Hallowell of Montagnais-Naskapi and Cree kinship terminology, based on dictionary entries in Lemoine (1901), Lacombe (1874), Silvy (1974), and Fabvre (1970), the last two seen by Hallowell as archival manuscripts, and on other sources including Morgan (1871) (see fig. 12), Speck (1918), and Strong (1929) and personal communications from Strong. This sheet was submitted to Frank G. Speck, who annotated it from his unpublished Pointe Bleue (Lake St. John) and Mistassini data and then returned it to Hallowell, who added a few comments before returning it to Speck. This was part of the research underlying an important paper by Hallowell (1932) on kinship terminology as evidence for cross-cousin marriage among the Montagnais-Naskapi and the Cree.

1930; Steinbring 1966; Taylor 1980; C. Lévesque 1976, 1977; Guy 1970).

Some scholars have essayed broad historical generalizations on the basis of traits and trait complexes. Hatt (1916:248–250) and Birket-Smith (1929:212–219) viewed the Shield Subarctic as part of a world Circumpolar complex exhibiting several evolutionary sequences. Hatt postulated a Coast culture that evolved into an Inland culture. Birket-Smith (1918) renamed Hatt's two stages the Ice-Hunting culture and the Snowshoe culture. Following Hatt's lead Birket-Smith argued that originally Subarctic people lacked snowshoes, moccasins, toboggans, conical lodges, and associated traits and therefore were restricted during the winter to the large lakes where they were forced to live on fish. Later, when the people acquired these specified and associated

traits, they were able to leave the lakeshores during the winter and exploit the boreal forest.

Cooper (1941) utilized the concept of age-area by which he isolated "marginal cultures," those societies most removed from centers of evolutionary change. He placed the Montagnais-Naskapi in this category.

From a basically ecological perspective Wissler (1915, 1922:2–6) included the Subarctic within the "Caribou Food Area." Few investigators followed Wissler's lead but rather distinguished between the Algonquians and Athapaskans on linguistic grounds. Much later Helm and Leacock (1971) defined the Shield Subarctic as a distinctive culture area having many shared features and a similar historical and ecological adaptation. Honigmann (1960a) saw it as continuing to be a distinctive area into the modern era. Speck (1926) argued that the

Smithsonian, NAA: Leonard Mason Coll.

Fig. 10. Leonard Mason in an abandoned York boat near Hudson's Bay Company post at Oxford House, Man., area of the Western Woods Cree. Photographed in July 1938.

NAA, Smithsonian: 80–20134, 80–20133.

Fig. 9. Hunting and fishing as depicted by William Duncan Strong's Naskapi interpreter Joe Rich or Shushebish and "me taking pictures of Mathew" (Strong's label) by a Naskapi boy about 12 years old. Part of a large collection of crayon and pencil Naskapi drawings done in bright but unrealistic colors by children and adults, some of topics suggested by Strong and others evidently not, among the field notes preserved by Strong from his ethnographic research among the Davis Inlet Naskapi in 1928.

Smithsonian, NAA: John J. Honigmann Coll.

Fig. 11. John J. Honigmann with West Main Crees at Attawapiskat, Ont. Photographed in 1947.

cultural features possessed by the Indians of the Labrador Peninsula were so similar that the area constituted a single cultural unit in contrast to the rest of the northeastern North America. Honigmann (1964) with new data reaffirmed Speck's view.

Another area of interest that came under scrutiny was the degree and form of contact between the Indians and Eskimos. Speck (1925, 1935–1936, 1937) investigated this problem within the Labrador Peninsula and concluded that there had been little interaction except of a hostile nature between the two peoples and that what exchanges had taken place were mostly of material items, transferred mainly from the Eskimos to the Indians. Honigmann (1962) and Rogers (1964) came to roughly the same conclusions as Speck. A special symposium dealt with the interaction between the two groups across the whole zone of contact from Labrador to Alaska (J.G.E. Smith 1979).

Perhaps one of the most important topics dealt with from a theoretical (and political) point of view was that of land tenure among the Subarctic Algonquians. Speck (1923, 1927; D.S. Davidson 1928c; Speck and Eiseley 1942) was the first to describe and map the "family hunting territories" of the eastern Subarctic Algonquians and argued for the aboriginality of such a system of land use. Cooper (1939), from a historical perspective, and Hallowell (1949a), from an ecological point of view, supported Speck's thesis. At this time, only Jenness (1932:124) raised a dissenting voice. The po-

25

sition of Speck and his supporters that a concept of private property was to be found in association with a hunting economy went contrary to the view that only communal land ownership was present in such societies, which were seen to represent the initial stage in an evolutionary sequence of social organization. The views of Speck, Cooper, and Hallowell were to influence ethnologists for years to come. Eiseley (1947:681) wrote that it was Speck and Cooper who freed anthropology from the "simplified dogma" of communal ownership of land and Herskovits (1952:335) asserted it was Speck's research that provided "the initial challenge to the doctrine."

Nevertheless, the issue was to be examined again following World War II. The view that "family hunting territories" were aboriginal was judged by a new generation of ethnologists to be erroneous. The fuller use of historical data, more intensive fieldwork, and a new appreciation of Indian culture strongly suggested that these "hunting territories" were in fact "trapping territories" that had developed under the influence of the fur trade (Leacock 1954; Rogers 1963a; R. Knight 1968; Bishop 1970a). The general thesis was that furs, since they were bartered with European traders, were in effect the property of the individual who secured them and not to be shared with the trappers' group. By extension, the animals from which the pelts were obtained came to be looked upon as individual or family property. To make this feasible, "bounded" territories came into use under the control of particular families. Small delimited territories were possible because furbearers in general had limited mobility and therefore remained within a family's territory. The traders may have encouraged this development. Averkieva (1962) concurred but in support of the evolutionary view that initially in human society property was communally owned. Others continued to investigate land tenure among the Algonquians of the Shield Subarctic (Tanner 1973; Morantz 1978).

Sociopolitical organization has been a topic of major concern, starting with Speck (1915a). Primarily, attention has been focused on the maximal and minimal sociopolitical units. The former only occasionally during the course of a year had face to face relations with its members; the latter type of unit maintained intimate relations among its members for all or the greater part of each year. Both units have been designated by several terms. Originally, the larger unit was termed a band and the smaller unit a hunting group. Although the term tribe has appeared in the literature, it has generally referred to a linguistic unit.

Speck (1931) delineated the Montagnais-Naskapi bands of the Labrador Peninsula thought to have existed about 1850. Osgood (1932) mapped the distribution of the Subarctic Athapaskan "groups" or tribes. Speck (1926:277–278) formulated the first definition

of the band among the eastern Subarctic Algonquians:

> a group inhabiting a fairly definite territory with a more or less stable number of families, possessing paternally inherited privileges of hunting within tracts comprised again within the boundaries of the territory, often having an elected chief, speaking with idioms and phonetic forms by which they and outsiders distinguish themselves as composing a unit, often with minor emphasis on this or that social or religious development, often with somewhat distinctive styles of manufacture and art, and finally, travelling together as a horde and coming out to trade at a definite rendezvous on the coast.

Rogers (1969:46) reviewed the topic of band organization among the Subarctic Algonquians and modified Speck's definition to "a loosely structured unit with a patrilineal bias, comprising seventy-five to a hundred and twenty-five people, inhabiting a drainage basin alone or in conjunction with other such groups, uniting during the summer on the shores of a lake within the territory and dispersing for the winter in groups to hunting areas."

Helm (1965, 1968a, 1969) has given considerable attention to the problem of band organizations among the Athapaskans of the Mackenzie drainage; her work is the most meticulous and detailed. She (1965:380) isolated four levels of sociopolitical organization: tribe, regional band, local band (see J.G.E. Smith 1976; Sharp 1977a; Craik 1975), and task group. Her regional band equates with the macrocosmic band of Honigmann (1956:58–59) and the band of Speck and Rogers. Her local band is equivalent to the microcosmic band of Honigmann (1956:59) and the hunting group of Rogers (1963a:54–68; see also J.G.E. Smith 1976; Sharp 1977a; Craik 1975; Morantz 1976 presents a historical reconstruction; Preston 1980, a Cree point of view). Helm (1965:380–381), in part, defines "the Dene socio-territorial groupings" (both regional and local bands) as having "a mode of alliance and recruitment based on the principle of social linkage through bilateral primary bonds of one conjugal pair to another" and the "local group" as "composed of persons whose significant connections may be either affinal or consanguineal." Leacock (1969) attacked the problem of band organization historically, using the Montagnais as an example.

The Subarctic Algonquian band was originally characterized as having patrilocal residence and patrilineal inheritance of land rights. Leacock (1955) suggested that Montagnais residence was formerly matrilocal, giving such units a matrilineal bias, and that under the influence of the fur trade this changed to an emphasis on patrilocal residence and patrilineal inheritance. Eggan (1955:521) on the basis of Strong's (1929) Naskapi data suggested "a bilateral band held together by cross-cousin marriage." Murdock (1965:26), summarizing the available data, characterized Cree bands as "politically autonomous . . . seminomadic . . . agamous," with "ambilocal" residence and "bilateral descent." Helm

(1965, 1968a, 1969) has made a strong case for bilaterality and bilocal residence among the Mackenzie Athapaskans (see Sharp 1977).

Data on the hunters of the Shield Subarctic contributed to Steward's (1955) formulation of band types found throughout the world and Service's (1962) concept of the ubiquitous patrilocal band. Later and more meticulous investigations seem to refute their assertions in regard to the inhabitants of the Shield Subarctic (see M.B. Rogers and E.S. Rogers 1980 for the origin of a "named group").

A growing interest in band societies, generated in part by fieldwork among the Indians of the Shield Subarctic, was evinced when the National Museum of Canada, in 1965, held a conference devoted solely to band organization (Damas 1969). The symposium "Man the Hunter" at the University of Chicago in 1966 also focused attention on band societies (Lee and DeVore 1968).

The documentation and analysis of the kinship systems of Shield Subarctic peoples has had a long history beginning with Lewis H. Morgan (1871) (fig. 12). Later examinations have been made by Helm (MacNeish 1960), Dunning (1959), Rogers (1962), Ridington (1969), D.H. Turner (1977, 1979), and Graburn (1975). A specific problem has been whether or not cross-cousin marriage existed and the structural implications of that pattern. Rivers (1914:49–55), on the basis of Morgan's compiled kinship terms, suggested that cross-cousin marriage did exist among the northern Athapaskans and Cree; but no further interest in the topic was shown for a number of years. Strong (1929) presented evidence for cross-cousin marriage among the Davis Inlet Naskapi. Hallowell (1930, 1932) examined the kinship terminology (fig. 8) (some recorded in dictionaries as early

as the 1600s) and concluded that cross-cousin marriage had been a prominent feature of Subarctic Algonquian social life. Dunning (1959:111–119) provided evidence in support from the Pikangikum Saulteaux. Eggan (1955:520–548, 1966:78–111) reviewed the available evidence and suggested that it was the practice of cross-cousin marriage that held the bilateral bands together (1955:521). Yet Helm (1968a), rejecting her earlier suggestion (MacNeish 1960), presented statistical evidence that cross-cousin marriage had not been practiced among the historic Hare.

Clan organization was lacking except among those Saulteaux in the Lake Winnipeg area and Ojibwa along the upper Albany River of Ontario. Clan organization among the Pikangikum band (Saulteaux), the most northerly occurrence, was examined by Dunning (1959:79–83), who concluded that clans were of minimal importance, a point supporting Eggan (1955:527), who suggested that clans were a late development among the Ojibwa.

Leadership, status, and the role of women in Subarctic society have been other aspects of the Indians' way of life that have been investigated (MacNeish 1956; Rogers 1965; Sharp 1979; Leacock 1958, 1975, 1976). A topic that may have been neglected is the "berdache" status (Broch 1977).

Recreation has been given practically no attention. Some field workers have described toys and games, but only Helm and Lurie (1966) have dealt in detail with this facet of culture, in this case the Dogrib hand game.

Religion has been a topic of limited investigation, frequently without capturing the essence of the religious philosophy nor the integral part it played in the life of the people. Speck (1935) dealt exhaustively with the religion of the eastern Subarctic Algonquians. Unfor-

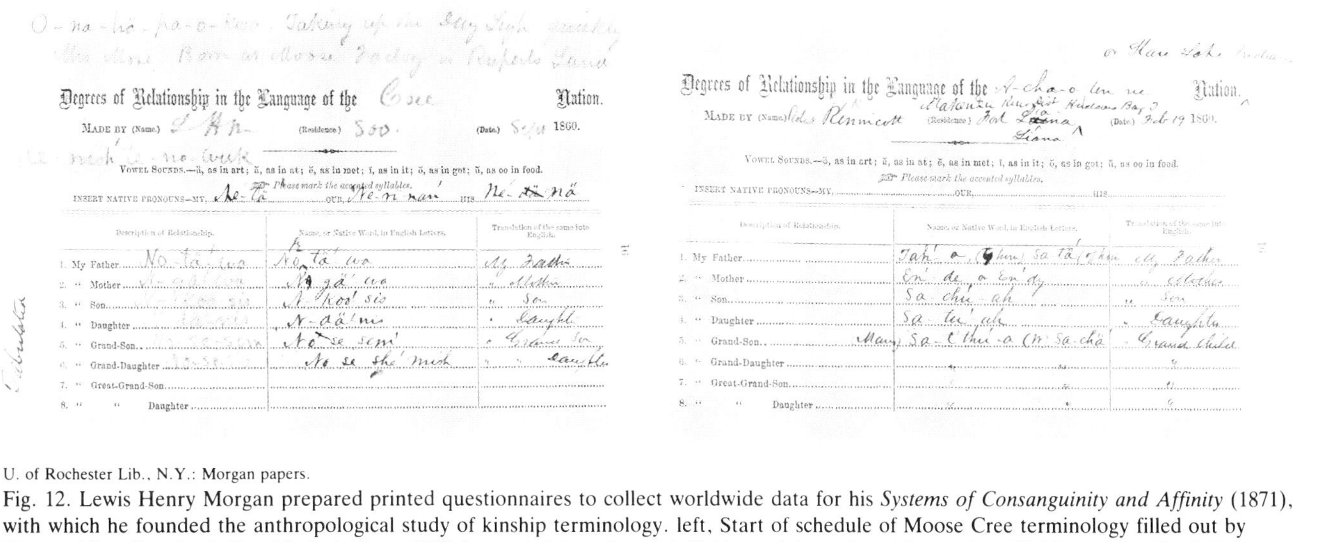

U. of Rochester Lib., N.Y.: Morgan papers.

Fig. 12. Lewis Henry Morgan prepared printed questionnaires to collect worldwide data for his *Systems of Consanguinity and Affinity* (1871), with which he founded the anthropological study of kinship terminology. left, Start of schedule of Moose Cree terminology filled out by Morgan himself at Sault Ste. Marie in Sept. 1860 (or copied later from his fieldnotes) from O-na-hä-ap-o-kwa 'Taking up the Daylight Quickly' (Mrs. More), born at Moose Factory. right, Start of schedule of Slavey terminology filled out by Morgan from data sent him by Robert Kennicott, Feb. 19, 1860, collected at Fort Liard, Mackenzie River District, Hudson's Bay Territory.

tunately, the title of his book, *Naskapi*, is misleading since most of his material is derived from the Montagnais. Tanner (1975, 1979), Preston (1975c), and Flannery (1971) carried on Speck's interest in the religion and belief of the Montagnais-Naskapi, and Meyer (1975) has dealt with ritual concerning geese. Cooper (1934) was concerned with the problem of a supreme being concept among the Indians of James Bay and concluded that aboriginally there had been one. He (1944) also investigated the "shaking tent" ritual, a topic that has been described by other ethnologists (L.M. Turner 1894; Flannery 1939a; Dunning 1959; Rogers 1962) and analyzed by Vincent (1973). From a historical point of view, Hallowell examined the Midewiwin (a shamanistic healing society) of the Lake Winnipeg area (1936a) and the topic of shamanism (1942). Little attention has been given to the religion of the Athapaskans of the Shield Subarctic and Mackenzie drainage (exceptions are Ridington 1968, 1971, 1978; Smith 1973).

Another topic examined in considerable detail over a number of years was the psychological characteristics of the Ojibwa. Hallowell (1936, 1938, 1940, 1941, 1942a, 1946, 1952, 1976) covered these aspects in great detail based in part on his work among the Berens River Saulteaux. Such work led to the debate as to whether or not the Ojibwa were atomistic or cooperative (see Hickerson 1967). Although applied primarily to the Southwestern Chippewa, such characterizations have also been applied to the Shield and Mackenzie peoples (see Honigmann 1946:94, 148 referring to the Slavey, and Honigmann 1975a). Such interpretations led to an impasse because of the polarization of positions. No accepted resolution of the problem has occurred although Cohen and VanStone (1964) have implied that both attributes were operative among the Chipewyan. Savishinsky (1971), Koolage (1975), and Rogers (1969a) have touched upon the topic. This question is vital to undertstanding Shield Algonquians, especially in relation to their forms of social organization.

A topic of some concern has been that of mental health, especially the occurrence of the "Windigo psychosis" (Cooper 1933a). This disorder has been reviewed by Teicher (1960) and Fogelson (1965), and Hay (1971) has formulated a new view. Others who have examined the topic are Bishop (1973), Waisberg (1975), Ridington (1976), J.G.E. Smith (1976c), Preston (1977, 1978a), and D.H. Turner (1977).

Two studies have placed the log cabin all-native settlement in historical perspective (Helm and Damas 1963; Taylor 1972). But most attention has been focused on the contemporary community, be it a "survival" of the more traditional form or a "modern" form (Helm 1961, 1972; MacNeish 1956a; Cohen 1962; VanStone 1965; Liebow and Trudeau 1962; Dunning 1959; Pothier 1965; Honigmann 1961, 1962; McGee 1961; M. Black 1971; Rogers 1962, 1972a; Savishinsky 1974; Savishinsky and Frimmer 1973; Hara 1980; Bone, Shannon, and Raby 1973; J.G.E. Smith 1975; Henriksen 1973). Specific questions relating to changing settlement (Rogers 1963; J.G.E. Smith 1978) and trapping patterns (VanStone 1963; Sharp 1975a), settlement types (Fried 1963), social "disintegration" (Honigmann 1966; Robbins 1973), incentives to work (Honigmann 1949a), and political activity (Preston 1969–1972; Vincent 1978) have been investigated. Practically no concern has been shown for contemporary Indian art and the artists except by M. Black (1970). Little attention has been given to the study of the Métis aside from Valentine (1954), and Slobodin (1966), who has dealt in detail with Métis of the Mackenzie Valley. Brown (1976, 1980) has provided data on the intermarriage of traders and Indian women.

The cultural ecology of Subarctic groups has been treated only to a limited extent. The difficulty of securing adequate quantitative data on the flora and fauna both in time and space has inhibited such work. Speck and Eiseley (1942) utilized ecological concepts when analyzing hunting patterns among the eastern Subarctic Algonquians. They attributed differences in the social organization between the northern and southern Montagnais-Naskapi—communal hunting in the north and family hunting groups in the south—to differences in the environmental conditions within the two areas. Eggan (1966:85) went further to speak of a sociological and ecological gradient from the northeast to the southwest involving the interrelationship of several factors. Hallowell (1949a) reviewed the concept of hunting territories throughout the eastern Subarctic and argued that they were an adjustment to environmental conditions. Further inquiries of an ecological nature have been carried out by Dunning (1959a), R. Knight (1965), Quimby (1960a), Rogers (1969a, 1973), Rogers and Black (1976), J.G.E. Smith (1975, 1976d, 1978), Feit (1973), Sharp (1978), Bishop (1978), VanStone (1974), Weinstein (1977), C. Martin (1980), and Krech (1978b).

A topic that became of greater interest during the 1960s and 1970s was that of ethnohistory (Rogers 1969; Gillespie 1970, 1975, 1975a; Bishop 1970a, 1972, 1974, 1975, 1975a, 1976; Helm et al. 1975; Morantz 1977, 1980; Tanner 1978; Clermont 1974, 1977, 1977a; A.J. Ray 1975, 1975a; Ray and Freeman 1978; Bishop and Smith 1975; C.J. Wheeler 1977; Taylor 1978; Foster 1977; Preston 1975; K.C.A. Dawson 1976a; Morris 1972, 1973; Asch 1975, 1976; H.T. Lewis 1977; Leacock and Goodman 1976; D. Russell 1975; Helm 1980; E.S. Rogers and M.B. Rogers 1980). This field has potentially great theoretical significance for an understanding of the process of culture change under conditions of contact with an alien culture and alteration in the natural environment. Helm and Leacock (1971) have provided a historical overview of the entire Shield Subarctic. A considerable amount of material has been retrieved from the archives by various investigators. Only a limited amount of attention had previously been given to this subject (Lips 1947; Cooper 1946; Hallowell 1946). Occasionally, mention has been made of the historic migrations of Native people, often as background material in studies devoted to another topic (see Cooper 1946:272–278; Hallowell 1955:114–119) and of more recent movements (Piché 1977). Chamberlain (1904) and Nicks (1980) discussed the Iroquois who moved west, some of whom came to reside in the Shield Subarctic.

Despite the great increase in research among the Indians of the Shield Subarctic after 1950, the essence of their culture and way of life, both past and present, is but dimly perceived. Much fine research has been undertaken but the theoretical constructs have frequently been divorced from the people as a living reality. Before the situation can be rectified much more in-depth, truly long-range fieldwork, such as that reported on by Helm (1979), is needed; and the archives must be diligently searched.

History of Archeological Research in the Subarctic Shield and Mackenzie Valley

JACQUES CINQ-MARS AND CHARLES A. MARTIJN

Across the vast expanse of the Subarctic Shield and Mackenzie River valley, the variant features of physiography, geological history, climate, biota, and culture rarely coincide to form discrete divisions. Attempted combinations both through time and across space have yielded a variety of proposed ecological subareas. However, this immense region did possess a historical common denominator in that it remained for a long time relatively inaccessible to most types of anthropological research endeavors because of difficulties in logistics and funding that stemmed from geographical distance and the nature of the terrain itself.

Until the second half of the twentieth century the entire region served as a convenient *terra incognita* to which the eventual solution of all kinds of problems in northern culture history could be relegated. These early speculative efforts tried to deal with broad prehistoric developments on the basis of traditional culture-historical trait distribution studies as well as of fragmentary ethnohistorical data. Some of these conjectures are of specific interest in that they played a prominent role in shaping the initial problem-oriented approaches adopted by archeological researchers, particularly west of Hudson Bay, and in that they still permeate various levels of archeological interpretation.

The Culture-Historical Antecedents

One of the most influential speculations was the proposal of an inland origin for the North American Eskimo, either south of Hudson Bay or somewhere between it and the Mackenzie River in northwestern Canada, as put forward by Rink (1887), Murdoch (1888), Boas (1888), and Steensby (1917). A distributional analysis of arctic footwear led Hatt (1915–1916) to hypothesize two basic culture strata for the whole of the circumpolar area. The oldest of these, the "coast culture," would have been restricted to arctic littoral and riverine regions due to a lack of effective means of travel on deep snow. The subsequent invention of the snowshoe in the Old World and its diffusion in North America would have permitted a later "inland culture" to occupy the entire length and breadth of the northern boreal forest, from Lapland to Labrador.

Elaborating on Hatt's idea, Birket-Smith (1918, 1930a) substituted the Ice-Hunting culture for Coast culture and Snowshoe culture for Inland culture. He suggested that Alaskan and Yukon Athapaskan groups were the first people in the New World to adopt the snowshoe complex and that this exploitative advantage allowed them to spread eastward beyond the Cordilleran system across the boreal forest of the Shield. He further postulated that this resulted in the eventual displacement of lake-oriented "ice-hunting stage" groups such as the Proto-Eskimos who retreated to the arctic coast, and the Proto-Algonquians, who, following adoption of some of the snowshoe complex traits, left their supposed homeland in the Lake Winnipeg region and moved into the interior of the Quebec-Labrador peninsula. Speck (1926) saw this eastern sector of the boreal forest as a refuge area, a marginal zone whose inhabitants retained ancient culture patterns due to their isolated position in a geographical cul-de-sac.

Birket-Smith's views, restated by him in 1929 and 1959, were subsequently supported, enlarged on, or disputed by other colleagues, including Cooper (1946), D.S. Davidson (1937), De Laguna (1947), Gjessing (1944), Mathiassen (1927), and Speck (1931). Debate over an inland origin of the Eskimo was extended to the Eastern Subarctic. The pioneer excavations by Strong (1930) on the Labrador coast led him to define an Old Stone culture, which he regarded as a basic Indian stratum from which later Eskimo and Indian cultures evolved. This issue became crystallized around the topic of the origins of the Dorset Eskimo culture. According to one school of thought the Dorset Eskimo emanated from a northward movement and an adaptive shift to arctic conditions by boreal interior populations. Hoffman (1952), for example, defended the thesis that the antecedents of the Dorset Eskimo culture were to be found in the Great Lakes region, and Meldgaard (1960:75) felt that the Dorset culture "smells of forest" and originally derived from "somewhere in the triangle between the Great Lakes, James Bay and Newfoundland" (1962:94). A similar line of thought was developed by Quimby (1962), who suggested that the use of copper diffused northward from the Great Lakes area over a period of several millennia and was eventually transmitted by Indians to the Copper Eskimos.

Most of these and other early studies reflected in part a long-lasting culture-historical interest in the notion of a circumpolar-circumboreal zone that due to its relative ecological uniformity would have been highly conducive to long-distance cultural movements and diffusion of traits. Archeological variations on this theme, primarily restricted to the northwestern regions but sometimes also extended across the entire length of the North American continent, became frequent in the 1930s and 1940s and were to remain in the forefront of the published literature until the mid-1960s. This was primarily the result of a reassessment of continental prehistoric constructs based on a fast-growing body of archeological evidence obtained from areas located around the entire periphery of the Subarctic region. Major syntheses were put forward by Leroi-Gourhan (1946) and A.C. Spaulding (1946). More trait-specific studies such as those of Osborne, Caldwell, and Crabtree (1956) and Byers (1962) pointed to artifact resemblances between certain Northwest Coast cultures and the Eastern Archaic tradition, which suggested contacts across central Canada. This same route was assumed by McKern (1937) and Griffin (1953) to have served for the diffusion of ceramic traits into the Northeast from Asia, while J.V. Wright (1967) postulated a similar spread of Laurel pottery during Middle Woodland times. This hypothesis has since been discarded (J.V. Wright 1972b).

These views contrasted with Hickerson's (1966:8) belief that "except for an occasional small band of hunters penetrating far inland from the Great Lakes centers on winter hunting excursions, the interior shield region was a wasteland without permanent residents." Because of ethnographical and archeological shortcomings this and other related hypotheses tended to visualize the area as primarily a passageway made use of by human populations moving from the Bering port of entry to more southerly continental claims. Representative of such ideas is the concept of a Mackenzie Valley migration route that at an early date became central to most discussions concerned with the initial peopling of the New World (Johnston 1933; Roberts 1940).

Recourse to the trowel has caused all these hypotheses either to be quietly discarded or else substantially recast. While many aspects of traditional culture-historical approaches continue to influence contemporary thinking, with the passage of time new dimensions have been added to most theoretical discussions. Archeologists in the late twentieth century have come to focus on different kinds of problems and more elaborate levels of analysis.

Early Archeological Forays

The history of archeological fieldwork in the Subarctic Shield and the Mackenzie valley has been dealt with in a succinct fashion by J.V. Wright (1975a). Some passing references to it are also provided by Noble (1973) in his overview of the development of Canadian archeology, and by Dekin (1973) in his treatment of the history of research in those portions of the Arctic that adjoin the boundaries of the Subarctic Shield area. At the regional, territorial, or provincial levels more detailed historical and bibliographical information can be gleaned from the following sources: Cinq-Mars (1973a, 1974, 1976) and D.W. Clark (1975) for the Mackenzie District; T.E.H. Jones (1978) for Saskatchewan; Mayer-Oakes (1967), Hlady (1970), Nash (1975), and Pettipas and Bissett (1976) for Manitoba and Keewatin; Pollock (1975) for northeastern Ontario; and Chevrier (1977), Fitzhugh (1972), Laliberté (1976), Martijn (1972, 1974), Martijn and Cinq-Mars (1970), Martijn and Rogers (1969), McCaffrey (1979), McGhee and Tuck (1975), and W.E. Taylor (1964, 1968) for the Quebec-Labrador Peninsula. "Prehistory of the Western Subarctic" and "Prehistory of the Great Slave Lake and Great Bear Lake Region" (this vol.) provide additional historical perspective on archeological investigations in the Mackenzie River valley and the western edge of the Shield.

Until the 1940s, only scattered archeological investigations had been carried out in the area under discussion. Trait distribution maps for the western sector did not begin to incorporate prehistoric field data until the early 1950s. The interior of the Quebec-Labrador Peninsula was the last large-sized segment of the North American continent to undergo archeological exploration: as late as the 1960s Griffin (1964) published a map marking it as possessing no known prehistoric culture except for the arctic coastal strip along its northern and eastern boundaries.

Prehistoric remains in the Western Subarctic were first noted by geologists such as Robert Bell (1880) and Joseph Tyrrell (1893) while on expeditions into the northern parts of Alberta, Saskatchewan, and Manitoba during the late nineteenth century. In the 50 years that followed, ethnographic collections continued to be commonly used as substitutes for archeological assemblages. With the exception of a single archeological excursion (Bliss 1939, 1939a) that focused on the western edge of the Mackenzie region, partly in search of evidence for early migrations through the "Mackenzie corridor," no professional research was carried out in the Western Canadian boreal forest until well after the end of World War II.

In the Eastern Subarctic, some brief notes regarding archeological findings from southern Labrador were contributed by Lloyd (1875), while Speck (1916) first drew attention to the Tadoussac site on the Gulf of Saint Lawrence upper north shore. Wintemberg (1929) carried out intermittent surveys along this same coastline as far east as the Strait of Belle Isle. He also undertook a more extensive study of the Tadoussac site (Wintemberg 1943), which was continued by Lowther

31

(1965). Additional work was done in the Strait of Belle Isle by Harp (1951), who proposed a preliminary classification (1964) of his prehistoric Indian material into three chronological groupings, which he assigned to the all-inclusive Boreal Archaic tradition that had been defined by Byers (1959).

During the first of a series of epic canoe voyages that commenced in 1947, Rogers and Rogers (1948) surface-collected and sampled sites across a far-flung area of south-central Quebec that included the Lake Mistassini–Lake Albanel region. Their artifacts were analyzed by F. Johnson (1948) who concluded that they could not be classified under any of the broad cultural groupings then in use. After a second field season in that same region, Rogers and Rogers (1950:336–337) stated that:

> a discussion of the distribution of the artifacts in this collection is restricted by the lack of comparative material and by the meagre knowledge regarding human migrations and cultural diffusion in the North during post-glacial and recent times. . . . Until our knowledge of the ecology of the region is more complete we can only assume that the taiga invaded the tundra which covered the region at the close of the Pleistocene. The people who moved into the region are assumed to have been taiga hunters, the theoretical and as yet unproven origin of which has usually been located to the west.

A third field season, this time by Rogers and Bradley (1953), as well as surface collections gathered by Burger (1953) on Lakes Kempt and Manouan, failed to resolve any of the above issues but did establish the existence of a broad transition zone in the eastern Shield containing evidence of southern influences such as Laurentian Archaic traits and later Woodland ceramics. Although Byers (1959) subsequently assigned the Rogers's collections to the northeastern Boreal Archaic tradition, other commentators such as T.E. Lee (1965), Ridley (1966), and J.V. Wright (1968a) laid increasing stress on the unique nature of much of the nonceramic prehistoric assemblages from northern Ontario and central Quebec.

In retrospect, the work of Edward S. Rogers and his companions constituted a watershed insofar as the formulation and problem orientation of later projects in the Subarctic Shield were concerned. It foreshadowed the definition of a Shield Archaic tradition by J.V. Wright (1969, 1972b) and pointed the way to new research approaches that emphasized an understanding of the environmental setting. Interdisciplinary endeavors, beginning with the Glacial Lake Agassiz conference (Mayer-Oakes 1967) and the preliminary synthesis of data on paleoenvironment, prehistory, and ethnohistory in the Lake Mistassini–Lake Albanel district by Martijn and Rogers (1969) were to become standard practice during the late 1960s and the 1970s.

Emergence of Problem-Oriented Approaches

For most of the Subarctic Shield and Mackenzie valley, the threshold of long-term and professional field research was finally reached in the decade of the 1940s when much of the northern boreal interior became slowly integrated, for strategic and various socio-economic reasons, into the southern Canadian communication networks. The change was time-transgressive and was felt well beyond the limits of this area. It led to an initial series of breaches in what A.C. Spaulding (1946:167) had described as "an effective barrier to any final conclusions," that is, "the total lack of information from most of the Canadian forest zone."

Starting in the 1940s, the National Museum of Canada in Ottawa initiated an important program of reconnaissance and limited excavations in the Subarctic Shield, specifically in the Northwest Territories, the northern Prairie Provinces, and northern Ontario. This work was continued at an accelerated pace in the decades that followed. A primary objective was to establish regional cultural sequences and chronology as well as to link existing native populations to late prehistoric assemblages by applying the direct historical approach.

On the basis of a series of surveys in the Upper Mackenzie drainage–Great Slave Lake area (1951) and of the Middle Mackenzie–Great Bear Lake area (1953, 1955), Richard S. MacNeish submitted to the attention of the archeological scientific community an initial series of prehistoric sequences in the western boreal interior. Much of MacNeish's research effort was directed to a search for traces of early migrants through the "Mackenzie corridor." Such evidence eventually began to be sought farther west in the Yukon-Cordilleran regions (R.S. MacNeish 1959a, 1964). Other exploratory activities, this time in the Keewatin District of the Shield, east of the Mackenzie region, were reported on by Harp (1958, 1959, 1961), Forbis (1961), and Giddings (1956, 1967). This work revealed the presence of early Plano Indian hunters and a later interior occupation of the tundra and the transitional taiga by Paleo-Eskimo (the late Arctic Small Tool tradition) that extended south into northern Manitoba. This last-named region was also sampled by J.V. Wright (1965), and northern Ontario was subjected to an array of survey and excavation approaches (T.E. Lee 1954, 1955; R.S. MacNeish 1952; J.V. Wright 1963). In addition, Dewdney and Kidd (1962) launched a study of Canadian Shield rock art, and the Lake Abitibi district in Ontario and Quebec was investigated by Ridley (1956, 1958, 1962, 1964) and T.E. Lee (1965). By the end of the 1950s some of this work had given rise to a series of reassessment papers that were published under the editorship of J.M. Campbell (1962). They attempted to situate and to delimit the prehistory of the boreal in-

32

terior in a broader context of continental culture-history and cultural processes.

The scope of archeological activities gradually increased during the late 1960s, being directed at continuing exploratory work and, sometimes, at a re-evaluation of the working hypotheses and regional sequences that had been proposed in the preceding decades. This situation reflected a growing awareness of research problems specific to the boreal regions on the part of a rapidly expanding company of newly trained prehistorians and informed laymen.

Amateur initiatives predominated in the Lake Saint John–Saguenay River district and along the Saint Lawrence north shore of Quebec (Fortin 1966; Simard 1970; Lévesque 1971), while J.V. Wright (1967, 1967a, 1969), D. Knight (1969), and K.C.A. Dawson (1963–1969, 1976) continued work in Ontario. To the west, Pohorecky and Jones (1967) and Steinbring et al. (1969) pursued the study of rock art. In Manitoba, J.V. Wright (1970, 1971) did further surveys along the shorelines of Southern Indian Lake and God's Lake; Mayer-Oakes (1970) completed the Grand Rapids Reservoir Project; Nash (1969, 1970, 1975) tested a large sample of northern Manitoba tundra-taiga ecotone sites; and Tamplin (1967) undertook more explorations within the limits of Glacial Lake Agassiz. To the north, in Keewatin, Irving (1968a) re-examined portions of the Barren Grounds and reformulated in a more elaborate fashion the sequence initially proposed by Harp (1958, 1959, 1961, 1962). Farther to the west, Noble (1971), following the leads uncovered earlier by R.S. MacNeish (1951), carried out an intensive reconnaissance program in the Great Slave Lake area and vicinity. It brought to light an impressive extension of the geographical range of Paleo-Eskimo remains, permitted a definition of the basic elements of an ancestral Athapaskan cultural entity referred to as the Taltheilei Shale tradition, and culminated in the elaboration of a new regional sequence (Gordon 1976; Noble 1977). The western Great Bear Lake and segments of the middle-lower Mackenzie River areas were revisited by Cinq-Mars (1973a) and, especially, by D.W. Clark (1975), who initiated in the late 1960s a long-term reconnaissance and excavation project. Finally, just beyond the northern limit of the boreal forest, McGhee (1970) excavated a series of Coppermine River sites that yielded among other things evidence of a fairly recent Plano-like lithic technology.

At the theoretical level, J.V. Wright (1969, 1972b) created considerable impact with his proposal that the term Shield Archaic be adopted to designate Archaic Indian remains from a broad belt of the Canadian Shield strung out along both sides of Hudson Bay and including the James Bay region. This concept was provisionally accepted by other researchers since it served as a useful tool in distinguishing cultures adapted to a boreal forest environment from other Archaic manifestations such as the Maritime, Laurentian, and Northern Plains traditions. However, Martijn and Rogers (1969:329) cautioned that it would eventually become necessary to accord recognition to a number of temporal and spatial variations within the Shield Archaic, and perhaps even to view these as having been more in the nature of a co-tradition with different ancestral roots. The applicability of some of Wright's conclusions insofar as the Eastern Subarctic is concerned has been contested by Laliberté (1978).

Economic Imperatives and Research Expansion

The decade of the 1970s witnessed a remarkable expansion of archeological research throughout the entire region under discussion. Several factors contributed to this unprecedented growth. A number of institutions organized programs of a broad interdisciplinary nature that aimed to gain an understanding of the natural environment and concomitant ecological relationships that directly affect human existence in the Subarctic. These integrative trends in archeology stemmed in part from the impetus provided by a rapidly expanding knowledge in other fields such as botany, climatology, and geology. Researchers also profited immensely from a revitalized ethnographic appreciation of boreal hunting and fishing adaptations (Feit 1969, 1978; Tanner 1979; Morantz 1980a; Damas 1969). Some attained some degree of synthetic (ethnographical-archeological) maturity in several conference meetings and publications, such as those devoted to the search for traditional and prehistoric Athapaskan realities (Darnell 1970a; Derry and Hudson 1975; Helmer, Van Dyke, and Kense 1977; Clark 1975a).

Archeological research topics included the economic potential of local natural resources and their seasonal and spatial availability; climatic fluctuations and associated environmental changes as well as disruptions in the boreal forest ecosystem (fires, faunal population dynamics, etc.); and the manner in which such environmental factors affected cultural adaptation, stability, and change among aboriginal hunting and fishing groups. Ethnohistoric data were also used to develop models of environmental exploitation (subsistence-settlement systems) that could be tested not only against prehistoric information but also against a developing body of field archeological data on the historic period (Giroux 1979; Laliberté 1977; Seguin 1979).

Notable programs that put into practice some of these research strategies were those carried out in Hamilton Inlet, Labrador, by the Smithsonian Institution (Fitzhugh 1972); at Mushuaunipi Lake in Nouveau-Québec

33

by the Centre d'Études Nordiques of Laval University (Samson 1977); in the Keewatin Barren Grounds and the eastern Mackenzie District, under the auspices of the Archaeological Survey of Canada and the River-edge Foundation (B.H.C. Gordon 1975); and in the northwestern Great Bear Lake area by the Archaeological Survey of Canada (D.W. Clark 1975). More and more salvage projects have been oriented along similar lines (Denton et al. 1980; Chism 1978; Chevrier 1977; Laliberté 1976; Meyer 1977; Minni 1976).

Of inestimable importance during the early 1970s were decisions or attempts made at both the federal and provincial levels to enact antiquities legislation that ensured the integration of archeology within required environmental impact studies. This, in some cases, obliged governmental and private development agencies to provide monetary and logistical assistance for salvage operations in connection with hydroelectric dam construction, projected oil and gas pipelines, and the building of highways. Examples of this have been the Churchill Falls dam project in Labrador; the La Grande, Kanaaupscow, and Great Whale River drainage basin impact studies in Quebec; various reservoirs connected with the Churchill River Diversion Project in Manitoba and Saskatchewan; and proposed pipelines along the western edge of Hudson Bay and in the Mackenzie River valley. In addition, provincial and territorial agencies were created for the purpose of evaluating and managing archeological and historical resources, thereby significantly increasing financial support (McKay 1977).

A parallel development concerns the efforts made to integrate archeological information or even sites into a series of interpretive centers located in federal and provincial parks. Also, as might be expected, native communities or associations have become increasingly aware of archeological activities and have begun to take a hand in the protection and management of their own cultural heritage (Grand Council of the Crees 1980). By 1980 it was commonly recognized that some of the results of archeological research constitute a valuable educational resource that needs to be more fully exploited and made accessible at the regional and even at the community level. Such thinking has been exemplified by the installation of a territorial museum complex, the Prince of Wales Northern Heritage Centre, which opened in Yellowknife, Northwest Territories, in 1979.

On the other hand, it is all too obvious that the enormous scale and rapidity of the industrial "progress" taking place in the 1980s in the Subarctic represents a crisis for the practitioners of boreal archeology and for the future of boreal prehistory. In attempting to cope with this situation, archeologists working in the Subarctic Shield and the Mackenzie valley will have to revise their priorities, re-evaluate their field methods, and continually question their research objectives in one of the last remaining areas of North America where native groups still intensively exploit the resources of their ancestral lands, and live by hunting, fishing, and trapping.

History of Research in the Subarctic Cordillera

CATHARINE McCLELLAN

Nonprofessional Sources

Traveling in the rugged upper Yukon country of the Cordillera, which he was probably the first White man to see, Robert Campbell (1958:96) of the Hudson's Bay Company wrote in 1851 that "the great attraction was the natives." In 1980 the Cordilleran Indians in some places still outnumbered nonnatives, yet information about them was relatively limited. Throughout the nineteenth century the few accounts of Cordilleran Indians were by explorers, fur traders, missionaries, geologists or other natural scientists; however, many of the best were not published until well into the twentieth century. Others remained in the archives of fur companies, churches, and museums; some are still inaccessible to researchers. Until after World War II few ethnographers worked in the Cordillera. This is equally true of archeologists; the history of archeological investigation in the Cordillera is addressed in "Prehistory of the Western Subarctic," this volume.

Explorers and Fur Traders

The first White man to meet Cordilleran Indians and to publish the information was Alexander Mackenzie (1801, 1970). As an energetic leader of the opposition to the Hudson's Bay Company, he played a key role in the formation and success of the North West Company and of the short-lived XY Company. In 1789, he set off on the first of two epic journeys by canoe to find a route to the Pacific coast. On this trip he descended the Mackenzie River and met briefly near its mouth with a group of eastern Kutchin. In 1792–1793 he traveled through Sekani and Carrier country on his way to the Pacific Ocean, again meeting Cordillerans who had never seen Whites. Mackenzie's interest was not in the Indians themselves but in the potential of their country for the fur trade; nevertheless, he recorded priceless data on Sekani and Carrier Indians. Perhaps his greatest virtue was that he seldom, as he put it, went in for "conjecture" about the Indians.

In the early decades of the nineteenth century during their long winters at remote outposts the men of the North West Company and of the Hudson's Bay Company sometimes wrote about the customs of the local Indians, either as a diversion or because company of-

ficials asked for such reports. Even those most prejudiced against the Indians offer invaluable glimpses of native culture before it had been too greatly changed by White contact. Most of the traders lived in the country long enough to appreciate native skills in surviving in a difficult environment; many married Indians, further enhancing their knowledge of the local customs and language. In addition, they kept records of the goings and comings of the natives, their numbers, the amounts of furs, meat, and fish they brought in to the posts, and the kinds of tools and baubles they bought. The trade records thus give temporal depth, demographic and ecological data, and, in some instances, a surprising amount of ethnographic detail. The records of the Hudson's Bay Company are in Winnipeg, Manitoba.

The journals of early North West Company men such as Simon Fraser (Masson 1889–1890, Series 1:154–221, not Series 2 as in Rich 1967:306; see also Scholefield 1914:240) and Daniel William Harmon (1903, 1957) are richer than those of Mackenzie in data on the Chilcotin, Carrier, and Sekani. Fraser published nothing in his lifetime, but historians and ethnohistorians drew heavily on his letters and journals even in the nineteenth century (Bancroft 1874–1876, 1887), as do anthropologists of the late twentieth century. The gifted explorer and surveyor of the North West Company, David Thompson (1962), also recorded material on the Carrier Indians, though most of his work lay to the south.

John McLean's (1932) memoirs of Hudson's Bay Company service borrowed heavily from Harmon. Unlike Harmon, who married a native and wrote of the Indians with understanding and affection, McLean (1932) was markedly unsympathetic; nevertheless, he too added to knowledge of the Chilcotin and the Carrier in the 1830s. His informal comparisons between the Cordillerans and the Ojibwa, whom he knew far better, are of interest.

The letters and papers of other traders, such as James McDougall, John Stuart, and Peter Skene Ogden, add bits of information on the southern Cordillerans in the first half of the nineteenth century (Scholefield 1914:235–456; Morice 1905) but have not been fully published (Ogden 1961; W.S. Wallace 1934).

An early reporter on the Indians of the more central part of the subarctic Cordillera was Samuel Black

(1955), first of the North West Company and then of the Hudson's Bay Company. In 1824 he explored much of the drainage of the Finlay River, writing in a free-flowing, grandiloquent, and unpunctuated style about almost everything he encountered, including various bands of Sekani. This journal is a vivid, major source on Indians who were just becoming adapted to permanent life in the Cordillera.

John Franklin's (1823, 1828) two overland efforts to find the Northwest Passage, 1818–1823 and 1825–1827, and the subsequent search for Franklin by John Richardson (1851), 1847–1849, resulted in books that had sections describing the native peoples, including the Kutchin of the Cordillera. Both men drew heavily on the knowledge of local fur traders. Richardson especially seems to have talked about the natives with the traders, notably with Murdoch McPherson at Fort Simpson and John Bell at Fort Good Hope. His systematic presentation of all the northwestern natives (Richardson 1851) was a standard source for ethnographers well into the twentieth century. Richardson was familiar with academic publications on native Americans and drew on them. His greatest contribution to Cordilleran research was his decision to include in his book a chapter on the Kutchin and to illustrate it with color plates of Indians, their dances ("Expressive Aspects of Subarctic Indian Culture," fig. 15, this vol.), and their dwellings. These were prepared from original ink sketches by John Murray, who had established Fort Yukon in 1847 for the Hudson's Bay Company, and who had sent both the sketches and a descriptive letter about Kutchin customs to McPherson. Richardson also corresponded with Murray directly. Murray's (1910) journal with the original sketches is one of the most valuable early documents on any of the northern Cordilleran tribes ("Kutchin," figs. 2, 4, 8, this vol.). Additional papers by Murray (1847–1850) remain unpublished in the Hudson's Bay Company archives.

While Murray was at Fort Yukon he was visited by the equally remarkable Hudson's Bay Company trader, Robert Campbell, who came down the Yukon River from Fort Selkirk, which he had built at the mouth of the Pelly River in 1848. Before he explored the Yukon drainage, Campbell had already had considerable experience with Sekani and Kaska Indians who traded at posts in the Liard drainage and had encountered hostile Tahltan and Coastal Tlingit Indians as well. He was the first White to meet some of the Tutchone and the Han Indians. Campbell (1883) published a short account of his Yukon River exploration, but not until the mid-twentieth century did the greater part of his journals appear (Campbell 1958; Wilson 1970). Other of his reports remain unpublished in the Hudson's Bay Company archives. Campbell's materials on the Indians, like those of Murray, are valuable both because they are early and because they are from an intelligent and brave

man who knew the Indians well and discriminated among individuals, some of whom he greatly admired (McClellan 1970; Wilson 1970). Nothing in the published or archival material of other Hudson's Bay Company men in the central and northern Cordillera of the first half of the eighteenth century matches the importance of Murray's and Campbell's data, with the possible exception of unpublished Company records of their close friends, William L. Hardisty (fig. 1) and James Anderson.

Gallatin (1836:2) stated that practically nothing was known of Indian languages west of the Rocky Mountains; by contrast, when Powell's (1891) classification of North American Indian languages appeared, most of the Cordilleran Athapaskan languages had been identified and J.C. Pilling (1892:105–107) listed 15 Kutchin vocabularies, including copies. One reason was that Robert Kennicott (1862), a naturalist, had created a fruitful association between the Smithsonian Institution, which was sponsoring him, and the Hudson's Bay men scattered throughout northwestern North America. In 1861 Kennicott wintered at Fort Yukon in Kutchin country as part of a three-year journey that took him from Fort Simpson on the Mackenzie River over to the Yukon River via the Peel River and back. During this time he taught several of the Company traders how to prepare scientific specimens and reports. Joseph Henry (1860:51), secretary of the Smithsonian, noting a "growing taste for the study of ethnology in this country," had printed up a circular of instructions especially for Company employees. Prepared instructions or questionnaires were characteristic of nineteenth-century scientific inquiry as evidenced in Lewis Henry Morgan's (1871) monumental work ("History of Ethnological Research in the Subarctic Shield and Mackenzie Borderlands," fig. 12, this vol.).

Trader Bernard Ross of Fort Simpson had begun as early as 1854 to send Indian products to the Royal Scottish Museum, Edinburgh, urged by Daniel Wilson, who is considered by some to be the first Canadian anthropologist (Slobodin 1975a:280). Many of the traders received in addition "Instructions for Research Relative to the Ethnology and Philology of America," which western Indian specialist George Gibbs had prepared for the Smithsonian Institution in 1864. As the result of Kennicott's and Gibbs's activities, the Smithsonian Institution Annual Report for 1864 listed 25 names of Hudson's Bay Company employees for special credit. At the 1892 World's Columbian Exposition in Chicago William H. Holmes of the Smithsonian exhibited a model of a Kutchin family group, using dress and items collected in the 1860s by Ross and Chief Factor Roderick MacFarlane (Deignan 1947:3).

Ross, who was probably the most enthusiastic Hudson's Bay Company collector, organized a project among the personnel on the Mackenzie that had no

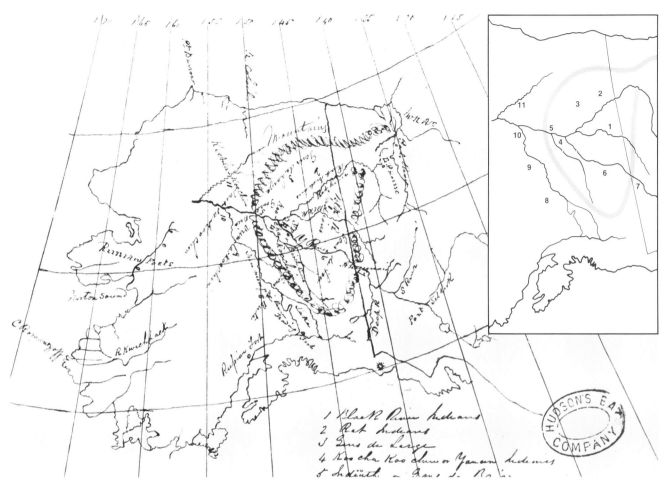

Hudson's Bay Company Arch., Winnipeg, Man.: D 5/38, fo. 77.

Fig. 1. Sketch map, 1853, showing the locations of the Kutchin bands and some neighboring groups in the upper Yukon River drainage, drawn by William L. Hardisty. To a relatively accurate delineation of the Alaskan coast taken from a map published by Richardson (1851) Hardisty has added on a larger scale the area from the lower Mackenzie River and the Pelly River ("Fort Selkirk") on the east to below the mouth of the Tanana River ("Tun nun jie [?] River") on the west. The difference in scale has resulted in a number of distortions, including the depiction of a large lake ("Lake") connected to both the Tanana and Susitna rivers. The names of the Indian groups on the key (with their modern equivalents), redrawn in inset, are: 1, Black River Indians (Black River Kutchin); 2, Rat Indians (Upper Porcupine River Kutchin); 3, Gens de Large (Chandalar Kutchin); 4, Koo cha Koo chin or Yaucen [?] Indians (Yukon Flats Kutchin); 5, Indiūth or Gens de Brie (probably intended to be Gens de l'Abri; Birch Creek Kutchin); 6, Gens de Fou (Han); 7, Ahyunais (Northern Tutchone); 8; Gens de Bute (Tanana); 9, Vunta Koo chin (Crow Flats Kutchin, but misplaced on the Tanana River instead of the Porcupine, called here "Rat River"); 10, Tait sa Koo chin (the Teytseh-Kootchin of Murray 1910:83 and Tătsăh´-Kūtchin´ of Dall 1877:30, an extinct Kutchin band); 11, Keet la Koo chin (unidentified). Enclosed in a letter from Hardisty to George Simpson, Oct. 15, 1853.

exact counterpart in the Cordillera; however, Hardisty (1872), Kirkby (1865), and Jones (1872), who had been in the Yukon drainage, also sent Kutchin specimens to Washington. Their articles, organized along the lines of the Smithsonian Institution's questionnaires, stood along with Richardson's work as standard sources on the Kutchin until well into the twentieth century, and the Kutchin became the best known of the Cordilleran tribes.

In 1867 the Hudson's Bay Company gave up its monopoly in the Pacific northwest, and its power began to wane throughout the Cordillera. Its personnel continued to write privately about the Indians, and to keep records, so archival material remains to be tapped for Cordilleran groups, especially for researchers interested

in locations and movements of the Indians, demography, and cultural change.

Missionaries

Nineteenth-century missionaries who worked in the Cordillera wished to change the natives' mode of living as well as to save their souls, and these concerns are evident in their writings. Nevertheless, several missionaries have left ethnographic materials of value, and, because they wished to communicate effectively with the natives, they were intensely interested in native languages.

As early as 1869 Robert McDonald of the Church Missionary Society of the Church of England developed a writing system for Tukudh Kutchin and printed a Bible in it (1898) ("Northern Athapaskan Languages," fig. 4, this vol.). Thomas Canham (1898) provided a word list of Northern Tutchone. Better known as a linguist was Émile Petitot, an Oblate Father of the Roman Catholic Church ("History of Ethnological Research in the Subarctic Shield and Mackenzie Borderlands," fig. 1, this vol.). Although most of this experience was in the Mackenzie Basin, he studied the Kutchin language (1876). In the southern Cordillera Adrien G. Morice, also an Oblate Father, learned some Chilcotin, invented a syllabary for the Carrier in 1886, between 1891 and 1894 published a newspaper in Carrier, and (1932) issued a Carrier grammar and dictionary.

Both Petitot and Morice gained reputations as ethnographers. Petitot's data on the Kutchin included a substantial body of myths, and he also sketched a Kutchin chief and dwellings (Savoie 1971a:98, 120; Slobodin 1975). Morice, characterized as "missionary, linguist, geographer, journalist, historian, and polemicist" (Carrière 1972:326), was with the Chilcotin from 1882 to 1885 and with the Stuart Lake Carrier from 1885 to 1906. He began publishing ethnography in 1890, but the bulk of his work appeared long after he had left the field, and some professional anthropologists scorned much of it (R.B. Dixon 1921).

Other missionaries active in the Cordillera during the nineteenth and twentieth centuries provided scraps of ethnographic data or popular books (Westbrook 1969; Kirkby 1865; Bompas 1879; Cody 1908; Stuck 1914, 1920; Bobillier 1939, 1976, 1977).

Reports of Government Officials

The various nineteenth-century gold rushes in the Cordillera brought with them public demands for better communications, transportation, and scientific knowledge of the country, especially of its geology. Private enterprise as early as 1864 had tried to link the old and new worlds via a telegraph line that was to run from British Columbia overland to Siberia. The northern end of the telegraph was in the charge of Kennicott, who in 1865 again went north with a staff of six, one of whom was William H. Dall. Like Richardson, Dall (1870) attempted to name and describe all the northern Athapaskan tribes of Alaska and adjacent Yukon Territory and to give their synonymies, drawing heavily on the knowledge of the Hudson's Bay Company men. The only Cordilleran Indians with whom he had firsthand experience were the Kutchin. The Canadian geologist-ethnographer, George M. Dawson, corrected errors in Dall (Dawson 1889:137). As a government paleontologist in British Columbia and the Northwest Territories, he came to know both coastal and interior Indians, especially the Haida of the Northwest Coast and the Cordillerans of northern British Columbia— Carrier, Tahltan, Kaska, and Sekani. In 1876 Dawson

sent Indian foods, artifacts, and photographs of natives to the International Exposition in Philadelphia as a part of the Canadian exhibit. Dawson (1889:appendix II) was intent on reporting all that he could about Cordilleran natives. He (1889) discusses Tahltan and Kaska Indians; however, most of the Tahltan material was by J.C. Callbreath, a trader who had been in the Telegraph Creek area for many years. Callbreath (or Dawson?) made some errors in discussing the rules of exogamy of the Tahltan, but did understand the presence of matriliny among them. Tolmie and Dawson (1884) supplied comparative vocabularies of the Indians of British Columbia. Throughout the late nineteenth and twentieth centuries, other geologists of both the United States and Canada included brief remarks on Cordilleran Indians in their formal reports and in occasional popular accounts of their travels (see Brooks 1953).

Military personnel also reported on Cordilleran Indians. When the United States purchased Alaska in 1867 it sent Lt. Charles Raymond of the U.S. Army to Fort Yukon to determine if it was in U.S. or British territory. Since it proved to be in Alaska the Hudson's Bay Company had to move, but Raymond (1900) added yet another brief glimpse of the Kutchin. The U.S. also sent Lt. Frederick Schwatka on the ludicrous mission of determining whether the Indians of Alaska were a military threat. In his official report Schwatka (1885) wrote the first systematic report on the Tagish, Tutchone, and Han.

Journalists and Photographers

White prospectors have explored the subarctic Cordillera for gold and other minerals since the mid-1880s. Most have had only fleeting experiences with the Indians, whom they did not understand, and for whom they had little sensitivity. Although many popular accounts of the gold rushes in the Cariboo, Cassiar, and Klondike were published, only a few contain source material of anthropological worth. The journalists attracted by the potential news associated with the strikes provided better data.

As early as 1866 Frederick Whymper, a British artist, mountain climber, and pioneer journalist, had traveled to Fort Yukon with William Dall. There he sketched and talked to some of the same Kutchin men known to John Murray, but his information on the Indians, like that of Richardson and Dall, was basically derived from the traders. Whymper (1869) noted that the missionary Robert McDonald had found gold near Fort Yukon, but reporting on the gold find was incidental.

Leslie's Illustrated Newspaper, sparked by reports of numerous gold finds in the upper Yukon drainage, in 1890 sent E.H. Wells, A.B. Shantz, and E.J. Glave across the coastal mountains into the Yukon Cordillera. Most of the party wrote little about Indians, but Glave and two companions traveled in the Alsek drainage, part of the time with a family of Tutchones about whom he wrote at some length. Glave (1892) returned to the Yukon the next summer. He wrote warmly of the Indians and with considerable detail, but as a journalist, not as a systematic ethnographer. He also embellished his articles with many sketches of the Indians, their dwellings and material culture (Glave 1890, 1891). Twentieth-century Tutchones recognized their ancestors in his sketches, some of them evidently made from photographs (McClellan 1975a).

The Klondike gold rush of 1898 drew additional journalists to the northern Cordillera, among them the journalist-artist Edwin Tappan Adney (1900), sponsored by *Harper's* magazine. His article on a winter moose hunt with the Han has charming sketches showing the Indians still wearing many items of aboriginal dress and living in dome-shaped hide shelters.

A few hardy photographers had also entered the Cordillera with the prospectors, so that from the time of the Cariboo rush in Carrier country in 1861, a limited but precious collection of photographs of Cordilleran natives began to accumulate. Supplementing the drawings of the Kutchin by John Murray, Whymper, Dall, and Petitot, and the valuable handful of photographs taken by individuals such as George G. Cantwell, Matthew Watson, and Asahel Curtis, or Eric A. Hegg (M.C. Morgan 1967) were studio portraits, and postcards, soon to be followed by snapshots.

Hunters and Adventurers

The vast Cordilleran wilderness attracted big game hunters, naturalists, and adventurers as well as prospectors. One of the earliest and most famous of the gentlemen sportsmen was Warburton Pike, who in 1892–1893 went up the Stikine to the upper Liard and across to the Pelly River following the steps of both Campbell and Dawson. Describing the remnants of Cassiar mining activity, Pike (1892) observed that the Kaska Indians would soon become extinct unless they received medical attention; he thought the isolated Pelly River Indians to be better off.

Other books by hunters and adventurers included comments on the Indians (M.H. Mason 1924). Some of the photographs and biographical data are useful (Bond 1959; Martindale 1913; R.M. Patterson 1968; Sheldon 1911), but perhaps the chief value of these books is in their documentation of the continuous encroachment of nonnatives into the Cordillera. An example is Walker's (1976) book on the Spasizi area, which the Indians themselves dislike.

Professional Anthropologists

In order to pursue his studies of cultural diffusion, Franz Boas organized the Jesup North Pacific expedition, sponsored by the American Museum of Natural History in New York. Boas's plan was to investigate all the tribes of the north Pacific rim from the Columbia to the Amur rivers, building on the earlier work of the British Association for the Advancement of Science begun by Dawson and others, but most of which he had himself carried out between 1888 and 1897. The bulk of Boas's research had been on the coast, but he had also reported on the Cordilleran Tsetsaut (1895, 1896, 1897)

Boas was interested in the relationship between the coastal tribes and those of the Cordillera. He wanted to know what cultural elements, especially in folklore, had diffused in which directions. Therefore, in 1898, Boas, James Teit (Boas 1922), and Livingston Farrand, a psychologist, followed the Cariboo wagon road into the westernmost Chilcotin villages. Boas reported briefly on the physical anthropology and customs of both the Chilcotin and Carrier (1899a:8–11). Farrand (1899, 1900) and Teit (1907) published on Chilcotin culture and folklore.

Boas believed that one of the most important problems in Canadian anthropology was to learn more about the Northern Athapaskans, including those of the Cordillera. He did not stress the view that has become prevalent among anthropologists since the 1930s, that Athapaskans are highly adaptive (Spencer and Jennings 1965:155; VanStone 1974). Rather, he believed that their cultures represented an old stratum of American Indian culture, lacking intensity (Boas 1910:533).

Teit (1906, 1909, 1914, 1919–1921) continued field investigations in the Cordillera, mostly in folklore. He left unfinished a monograph on the Tahltan (Teit 1956). Teit became involved in the question of registered traplines, which the Canadian government was trying to introduce into northern British Columbia. Perhaps he should be cited as an early applied anthropologist, which is how Boas presented him in his obituary (Boas 1922).

Another protégé of Boas was Lt. George Emmons of the U.S. Navy. While most of his work was with the Coastal Tlingit, Emmons (1911) wrote the only major publication on the Tahltan, the earliest ethnographic monograph on any Cordilleran group.

All this early professional ethnography was descriptive rather than interpretive or theoretical, although Boas drew on that data as he developed his position of historical particularism. The emphasis on folklore also reflected Boas's interests, as did the collections of material culture that reached museums in New York, Philadelphia, and Chicago.

From the late 1920s through the 1930s the major professional figures in Cordilleran ethnography were Diamond Jenness and Cornelius Osgood. Jenness came to the Athapaskans after extensive experience with the Eskimos and also with an interest in giving an ordered and popular account of all of Canada's natives (Jenness 1932). Part of his information was derived from fieldwork with the Sekani in 1924 (1931, 1937) and with the Carrier in 1929 (1929, 1943). Some of his papers (1929, 1933) foreshadow the growing interest in enculturation and in personality and culture that was beginning to emerge in American anthropology, but they lack the developed theoretical framework found in the work on the Kaska by the Honigmanns in the 1950s.

Cornelius Osgood published on the distribution of northern Athapaskans (1936) and an ethnography on the Kutchin (1936a), based on research at Moosehide near Dawson, Yukon Territory, where he had helpful Peel River informants, and at Fort Yukon, Alaska. He collected data from the Han as well (Osgood 1971). In the 1940s Robert A. McKennan (1965) also worked with Kutchin, concentrating on the Chandalar division and on ecological adaptations.

World War II greatly expanded communication and transportation in the north. Many more Whites moved into the northern Cordillera, and, relatively speaking, both the number of ethnographers in the Cordillera and the range of published ethnography increased. Douglas Leechman of the National Museum of Canada visited the Old Crow Kutchin (1948, 1952, 1954). Frederick Hadleigh-West (1963) and E.S. Hall (1969) reported on Kutchin. Richard Slobodin lived with the Peel River Kutchin. He has been concerned with the nature of band organization (1962, 1969a), concepts of reincarnation (1970), and other topics (1960, 1960a, 1969, 1975). Other reports on various Kutchin groups have also become increasingly focused, for example, on hunting techniques (R.K. Nelson 1973); on current conditions as contrasted to the "precontact" culture reconstructed by Osgood (Balikci 1963; Welsh 1970); on nineteenth-century fur trade (Krech 1976) and historical demography (Krech 1978a, 1978b, 1979).

Catharine McClellan and Dorothy Rainier (1950) began fieldwork with the Tutchone, Tagish, and Inland Tlingit in 1948 and 1949, which was continued by McClellan (1948–1975). The early data were used in a descriptive monograph on nineteenth-century culture (McClellan 1975a). Shorter papers discuss early contact conditions and trade, and Indian views of the Whites (McClellan 1964, 1970a, 1970c). Bruce MacLachlan's 1956 work with the Tahltan resulted in a (1957a) paper on folklore.

John J. Honigmann, a student of Osgood, and Irma Honigmann did important research in 1944 and 1945 with the Kaska (fig. 2). Honigmann (1949) emphasized the ethos of the Kaska within the context of a psychoanalytic perspective informed by Rorschach tests, dreams, contemporary events, and patterns of enculturation. His research reflected the interest in the nexus between culture and personality that culminated in the 1940s and 1950s, and a theoretical orientation that was new in literature on Cordillerans. Honigmann (1954) also reconstructed precontact culture.

Fig. 2. John J. Honigmann and Captain Joe, a Kaska Indian of Lower Post, B.C. Photograph probably by Irma Honigmann, 1944.

Irving Goldman and Julian Steward carried out research on the Carrier in the late 1930s and early 1940s. Like Boas, Goldman was interested in contacts between coast and interior Indians, especially as they affected social organization, but he drew his theory from the acculturation studies of the 1940s rather than the earlier ideas about diffusion. Goldman (1940, 1941) adds substantially to Morice's earlier work. Steward too was interested in cultural relations between coast and interior, for he was faced with explaining how the presumed coastal influence on the Carrier could be fitted into his overall theories of cultural ecology and the nature of social units among various kinds of hunting peoples (1955:173–177). Wilson Duff (1951) of the Provincial Museum, Victoria, British Columbia, wrote on Carrier social organization, and Grossman (1965) developed a theory on bilateral descent groups in the Cordillera, using Carrier data.

By 1978 then, the best documented Cordillerans were the Kutchin at the northern end of the Cordillera, the Carrier at the southern end, and the Kaska in the middle, though for the Kaska there was not the historical depth provided by Murray and Richardson for the Kutchin and by Morice for the Carrier.

Interest in culture change and applied anthropology during the 1960s and 1970s is evinced in the research of Cruikshank (1969, 1979) on the roles of Indian women in the Yukon and elsewhere, King (1967) on Yukon native education, Tanner (1966) on Tutchone trappers, R.F. McDonnell (1975) on the Ross River Indian community, Lamers (1976) on culture change in the technology of the Sekani, and Duff (1964) and Fisher (1977) on Indian-White relations in British Columbia.

Some scholars continued Boas's interest in mythology as revelatory of native world view (Cruikshank 1979; McClellan 1970a; Slobodin 1970).

Fig. 3. Richard Slobodin and Rev. Richard Martin, Han, at Moosehide, Yukon Terr. Photographed summer 1961.

Slobodin assessed the general state of northern Athapaskan ethnology, including that of the Cordillera, as "immature," "not, as yet, very interesting theoretically," and "full of lacunae" (1975a:283). Many of the gaps in the ethnographic descriptions of traditional Cordilleran cultures can probably never be filled. However, Cordilleran specialists have challenged some anthropological ideas on the social organization of hunters and gatherers and ecological adaptations, often by drawing on experience with other northern peoples as well.

Natives and Activism

In the late 1960s and 1970s Cordilleran Indians in Alaska and Canada began to make themselves heard in both political and educational contexts. A renewed interest in their traditional languages and cultures accompanied this stirring and resulted in the appearance of Indian-language dictionaries and literature written by Indians or in cooperation with linguists and ethnographers (T. Peter 1973; Peter 1979; Ritter 1976, 1976a; Ritter, McGinty, and Edwards 1977). No Cordilleran has yet published a full autobiography although some have told brief stories of their lives (Cruikshank 1979). This type of publication will probably increase, as projects for taping oral testimony grow. Edith Josie (1966) has for many years written a column in the *Whitehorse Star*, and the Yukon Indians have published a newspaper since 1978.

The push by industry to extract northern oil, gas, and other resources has led to public hearings in which na-

tives gave eloquent statements about their current and past ways of life (Berger 1977; Lysyk, Bohmer, and Phelps 1977). In 1978 the Council for Yukon Indians sponsored an oral history project carried out by Indians and anthropologists together.

The attempts by the Indians to gain or keep control of lands they believe to be their own has resulted too in a proliferation of reports on current conditions by the Indians themselves, by government researchers, and by political activists who sympathize with the Indians (Cumming and Mickenberg 1972; Yukon Native Brotherhood 1973). These add to the material already available in the regular censuses and reports of the U.S. Bureau of Indian Affairs and the Canadian Department of Indian Affairs and Northern Development. The common thread that holds all this literature together is the clear evidence that the Cordilleran Indians have not disappeared, as nineteenth- and early twentieth-century researchers predicted. On the contrary, Cordilleran Indians have declared their intention to direct their own future. Their attention to their past is largely due to their desire to symbolize their roots in Cordilleran country. Because of this they will probably continue to encourage research into traditional cultures both by themselves and by professional ethnographers, who will be held responsible for sharing their research findings directly with the Indians.

Classifications and Bibliographies

Except for the Kutchin, Carrier, and Kaska, the Cordillerans rarely have received much coverage in survey treatments of the American Indians. Data were too scanty and difficult to summarize easily. Hodge's (1907–1910) *Handbook* grouped the Kutchin Indians in the "northwestern" subgroup of the Northern Division of Athapaskans. In the "southwestern" subgroup were the Nahane (which included Kaska and Tahltan), Sekani, divisions of the Carrier (Babine and Takulli), and the Chilcotin. Of the entries for specific Cordillera tribes only two were written by writers who had actually worked in the Cordillera, Emmons (1910, 2:670–671) on the Tahltan, and Farrand (1910:286) on the Chilcotin. Professional ethnographic information on the Cordillera was clearly minimal.

Jenness (1932) grouped together as "Tribes of the Cordillera" the Chilcotin, Carrier, Tsetsaut, Tahltan, and Tagish, together with the Interior Salish and Kutenai. He classified the Sekani, Nahani (Kaska), and Kutchin with other "Tribes of the Mackenzie and Yukon River Basins." Jenness gave short but good ethnographic descriptions of each group.

A.L. Kroeber (1939) still drew largely on Dall's classifications, but he footnoted the section on the Subarctic Indians to alert the readers to Osgood's (1936) paper. *41*

Osgood systemized the nomenclature for all northern Athapaskans. He grouped them into tribes of the Arctic drainage and tribes of the Pacific drainage, characterizing the latter as having a richer culture. This landmark publication also brought up to date major bibliographic references. It remains a valuable and succinct source on Northern Athapaskans. Most of the group names he selected continued in the literature; Osgood rejected the term "tribe," and later scholars recognized its misleading connotations for the northern Athapaskan peoples. In 1974, McClellan proposed a revised grouping of Northern Athapaskans based on more detailed ecological considerations than those used by Osgood. This grouping was adapted by VanStone (1974), who produced the first scholarly book devoted exclusively to Northern Athapaskans.

Bibliographic sources on Cordillerans are generally good. Basic bibliographies that are limited to or include the literature on the Cordilleran Athapaskans have been assembled by Helm (1973), Abler, Sanders, and Weaver (1974), Hippler and Wood (1974), Murdock and O'Leary (1975, 2), Ridge and Cooke (1977), Thomas, Cooke, and Perry (1978), Krech (1980), and the on-going *Arctic Bibliography*. Some are annotated.

Slobodin (1975a), Helm (1976), Burch (1979), and Krech (1980) have written evaluative essays on the literature on northern native peoples, including the Indians of the Cordillera.

History of Research in Subarctic Alaska

NANCY YAW DAVIS

The Tanaina, Ahtna, Ingalik, Kolchan, Koyukon, and Tanana are the Athapaskan-speaking Indians of central and south Alaska, that is, mainland Alaska south of the Brooks Range. This summary history of anthropological research in the region, which is limited to published materials, reviews the often lean accounts of explorers and occasionally rich observations of missionaries; twentieth-century fieldwork in physical anthropology and archeology; the brief period 1929–1937 of early descriptive ethnographies; and the post-1960 period of topical research in cultural anthropology. The chronological organization reveals the intervals when little research took place and highlights the shifts in kinds of data obtained and in research interests.

Explorers' Accounts

The period of recorded exploration begins with the brief account by Capt. James Cook (1785) of Tanaina people in Cook Inlet. On June 1, 1778, Lt. James King went ashore at Point Possession, met 20 natives, planted a bottle containing coins and a map, and claimed the area for the expanding British empire. (The Tanaina Indians of Point Possession continue to tell stories about Captain Cook's bottle, which they still seek.) Other early references to the people of the Inlet are from Portlock (1789), Beresford (1789), and Meares (1791) for the 1780s, Vancouver (1798) who in 1794 spent five weeks battling the tricky tides, and Lisīanskii (1814) who in 1805 reported from Kodiak that Cook Inlet was inhabited by about 3,000 people in 14 settlements. Davydov (1977) described the Cook Inlet and Copper River Athapaskans about 1805.

The interior Athapaskan territory was explored by Andrey Glazunov (VanStone 1959) in 1833–1834. He traveled along the Yukon and Kuskokwim rivers and referred to villages still present in Ingalik territory, such as Anvik and Shageluk. Wrangell (1970) drew on Glazunov's report in preparing the earliest ethnographic summary, published in 1839. The Russian naval lieutenant and scholar L.A. Zagoskin (1967), an unusually astute observer, described the tribes he found living along the Yukon and Kuskokwim rivers during his exploration of 1843–1844.

In 1866 William H. Dall stayed at Nulato in Koyukon territory for seven months. From that experience and

other travels he prepared geographic and ethnographic information on Alaska's "native tribes" (1870, 1877, 1898). Other mid-nineteenth century accounts of the Yukon and Kuskokwim area are given by Whymper (1868, 1869, 1869a), Raymond (1900), and Schwatka (1885, 1900).

In 1884 Abercrombie (1900a) explored the Copper River Valley, and in 1885 Allen (1887, 1889, 1900) led an expedition into the Copper, Tanana, and Koyukuk river areas. The publications of censuses taken in 1880 (Petroff 1884, 1900) and in 1890 (U.S. Census Office. 11th Census 1893) include descriptions of the tribal groups. Population estimates are given; unfortunately, some information was gathered by hearsay instead of by firsthand enumeration.

The end of the nineteenth century was marked by a spate of geological surveys and military explorations. Abercrombie returned to the Copper River area (1899, 1900a) and with Glenn further explored Cook Inlet and the Susitna and Tanana rivers (Abercrombie 1900a; Glenn 1899, 1900, 1900a). Schrader (1900; Schrader and Spencer 1901), Herron (1901), Brooks (1900), Spurr (1900), and Cantwell (1902) also should be consulted by those with specific research interests, though the information on the peoples they encountered is often meager. In sum, accounts of the nineteenth-century explorers are not, for the most part, rich sources of data, but they do contribute toward understanding the setting for the earliest contacts between the Athapaskans and White visitors. In contrast to the Shield area of the Subarctic, no anthropologist went to interior Alaska in the nineteenth century.

Missionaries' Accounts

Three major faiths—Russian Orthodox, Episcopalian, and Roman Catholic—sent resident missionaries into Athapaskan territory during the nineteenth century. Their accounts provide some insight on selected areas.

The earliest record of missionary activity, including a description of Indian response to Christian evangelism, is found in the diary of Hieromonk Juvenal, one of eight Russian Orthodox monks who went to the Russian colonies in 1794. After two years on Kodiak Island, Juvenal ventured into Tanaina Indian territory in the Kenai and Iliamna area of Cook Inlet where he

43

soon lost his life. The authenticity of Juvenal's (1952) diary has been questioned (Townsend 1965). Portions of the journals of three later Russian missionaries—Hieromonk Nikolai, Hieromonk Nikita, and John Bortnovsky—have been translated from archival material. The potential of these data for ethnohistoric reconstruction is well demonstrated by Townsend (1974). Russian Orthodox activity also took place on the Yukon and Kuskokwim rivers. The diary of one priest, Illarion, for the period 1861–1868, has been translated (Oswalt 1960).

The Episcopal church was established in the Ingalik area in 1887. Articles and books on the "Ten'a" Indians were written by the missionary John W. Chapman (1903, 1907, 1912, 1914, 1921, 1948). Later anthropologists, Hrdlička and Osgood, spoke highly of his work and knowledge. Additional writings by Chapman and other Episcopal mission personnel are to be found in various issues of *Spirit of Missions* and *The Alaska Churchman*.

From 1905 to 1913 another Episcopalian, Hudson Stuck, wrote about his travels in the interior, with some references to the Indians he was serving (1914, 1917, 1920). He refers to the knowledge of the Catholic Jesuit priest Jules Jetté (fig. 1), who lived, studied, and served for nearly 30 years at the Koyukon village of Nulato. The thoroughness of Jetté's research (1907, 1906–1907, 1907–1909, 1908–1909, 1911, 1913) has been noted by the anthropologist Frederica De Laguna, who was permitted to incorporate data from Jetté's unpublished ethnographic dictionary in her published work (1947), and by Loyens (1964).

Missionary archival materials often are rich in information about periods and places for which no other ethnographic information is available. Future reconstructive scholarship could profitably include what the missionaries reported. Nothing so thorough as Oswalt's (1963) research and analysis of the Moravian church among the Eskimos on the lower Kuskokwim is available for any of the interior Indians' church experiences. For the location of unpublished church letters, records, and manuscripts, and for information concerning the limited museum collecting in Indian areas, see "Museum and Archival Resources for Subarctic Alaska," this volume.

Anthropological Field Research

Physical Anthropology and Archeology

In 1926 the first anthropologist arrived in Alaskan Athapaskan lands. The physical anthropologist Aleš Hrdlička (fig. 2) spent 16 summer days traveling down the Yukon; he passed through Indian territory from Fairbanks to Paimute, the first Eskimo village on the Yukon at that time. He visited graveyard sites, recovering artifacts as well as skeletal material. His expedition, which extended up the coast to Barrow, was sponsored by the U.S. National Museum and the National Research Council. Unfortunately, very little is learned through him about the living Indians he encountered, though his diary (Hrdlička 1943) is sprinkled with comparisons of Indian and Eskimo physical characteristics based on visual inspection.

Of some ethnographic interest is Hrdlička's (1943:65) note of the marked change in attitudes toward his project, especially the excavation of graves, as soon as he arrived in Eskimo territory. There he did not need to be so secretive, which confirms later studies indicating significant differences in Indian and Eskimo attitudes toward death and the dead.

As questionable as Hrdlička's methods and ethics may be to present-day anthropologists, and undoubtedly to the Indians both then and now, his brief notes, photographs, and anthropometric records are still the only data published on the physical characteristics of the Yukon River Indians. Eskimo remains were far more thoroughly measured and documented by Hrdlička, perhaps by as much as 4 to 1. That ratio is about the same for the relative efforts devoted to Eskimo as against Athapaskan studies in all fields of Alaskan anthropology.

In 1927 Herbert W. Krieger, also from the U.S. National Museum, worked one summer on the lower Yukon River. He contributed additional archeological information and noted the subsistence patterns of the contemporary people in Kachemak Bay on Cook Inlet (1928).

The first extensive archeological excavations in Alaskan Athapaskan territory were accomplished by De Laguna (1934, 1975) in 1931 and 1932 at Cook Inlet after a season of survey and site mapping the previous year. The rich, primarily Eskimo, sites in the Kachemak Bay area received most attention. Only the most recent materials recovered were assessed as Indian, suggesting protohistoric movement of Indians into previously Eskimo-occupied territory. In 1935 De Laguna returned to make an archeological reconnaissance of the middle and lower Yukon River (1936), which resulted in an extended comparative and analytical statement (1947) on the prehistory of northwestern North America.

In 1934 Rainey and others began the excavation of the Campus site located at the University of Alaska in Fairbanks. In reporting a survey of the Tanana Valley and the Copper River in 1936, Rainey (1939, 1940) combined ethnographic information with the locations and descriptions of sites. Most prehistoric sites were found to be along the smaller tributaries of the Tanana River. The move out to the main, muddy rivers took place after the introduction of the fish wheel by miners at the turn of the twentieth century (Rainey 1939).

The period of 1926 to 1936 may be summarized as

Fig. 1. Jules Jetté with his camera, probably one which used dry plate glass negatives; Alick Malimute at right. Jetté's invaluable research on Koyukon linguistics and ethnography is still largely unpublished (Renner 1975) (see "Northern Athapaskan Languages," fig. 3, this vol.). Photographed at Nulato, 1914.

a decade of archeological survey punctuated by significant excavations in two areas—at Kachemak Bay in southern Alaska (although this was predominantly Eskimo in content) and at the Campus site in central Alaska.

For the next several years there was a nearly complete cessation of archeological work. During the 1940s, a site survey was made along the construction route of the Alaska Highway (F. Johnson 1946). Skarland and Giddings (1948) published a summary of sites, or "stations" of finds in central Alaska.

In 1953 Irving (1957) surveyed the Susitna Valley, near the present Tanaina and Ahtna boundary, and excavated some Ahtna sites. VanStone (1955) made the first excavation of a Lower Ahtna site at Taral on the Copper River in the summer of 1954. J.M. Campbell (1961) began research in the Brooks Range in 1956. Skarland and Keim (1958) published another survey, of sites discovered during the building of the Denali

Highway in 1957. On the whole, the 1950s were a continuation, with a slight increase in activity, of the survey-and-test-pit investigations of the previous 25 years.

A third period of research in Athapaskan prehistory began in 1960 and continued with increasing vigor until 1969, when archeological work was further accelerated by the pending construction of the Alyeska Pipeline (J.M. Campbell 1973). For example, in the Iliamna Lake area limited excavations in 1960 (Townsend and Townsend 1961, 1964) were followed by the more extensive excavation in 1966 of the historic site of Kijik (VanStone and Townsend 1970). Elsewhere in the Tanaina area, the northwestern Kenai Peninsula was surveyed in 1960 in preparation for the construction of a gas pipeline (Kent, Matthews, and Hadleigh-West 1964). Dumond surveyed the Knik Arm area of upper Cook Inlet in 1965, and some of those sites were excavated by Mace and Spaulding in 1966 with disappointing results (Dumond and Mace 1968). A few miles

Smithsonian, NAA.

Fig. 2. Aleš Hrdlička, on right, and Harry Lawrence, a local trader, excavating a site in Ingalik territory; the permafrost stopped the digging at this level. Photographed at Bonasila, July 1929, probably by J. Maly.

up the Kenai River in present Tanaina territory, Reger (1977) reported a fish-camp site that appears to be Eskimo. This may confirm earlier speculation that the Tanaina were recent arrivals in the Inlet area.

The 1960s also brought increased activity in other regions. A. McFayden Clark (1970, 1970a, 1970b, 1975) began her work on Koyukon culture. In the Tanana area Hadleigh-West (1967) began a long project at Donnelly Ridge and Tangle Lakes. The excavations at the Donnelly Ridge site beginning in 1963 led to the delineation of the Denali complex, which shares characteristics with the Tuktu complex of north Alaska as well as with the assemblage from the Campus site. Together, they may be part of the Northwest Microblade tradition, a possible Athapaskan tradition (see "Prehistory of the Western Subarctic," this vol.). McKennan and Cook (1970) began excavation in 1967 of a site at Healy Lake that turned out to be rich and old, dating to 9000 B.C., the earliest material yet found in Alaska Athapaskan territory. Another site in Tanana country in the Minto Flats was surveyed by Schlederman and Olson (1969) in 1968, the same year that the first Kolchan excavation was made at the Birches site by Hosley (1968). Discoveries in Eskimo territory at the famous Onion Portage site on the Kobuk River revealed two intrusive bands of artifacts that appear to be Athapaskan (D.D. Anderson 1968, 1970).

The year 1969 marks a point of transition in Alaskan Athapaskan archeology for two reasons. First, Dumond (1969) published a broad reconstruction of the movements over several thousand years of the Na-Dene peoples (Athapaskans and others assumed to be related to them), based on combined linguistic and archeological evidence. His essay indicated the potential of such a combined approach to Athapaskan prehistory (earlier applied to Eskimo prehistory, Dumond 1965) and revealed how incomplete the reconstruction of Athapaskan prehistory was at that time. Second, 1969 was the year of initial surveys along the projected route of the Alyeska Pipeline. Excavations of sites threatened by pipeline construction were continued vigorously through the 1975 season.

Also indicative of a new era in archeological research, in 1975 the Cook Inlet Regional Corporation—formed under the Alaska Native Claims Settlement Act of 1971—supported the Cook Inlet Historic Sites Project, a survey of historical and cemetery sites accomplished by Indian and Eskimo young people working in concert with anthropology students.

Casting back over the history of archeological research, it is a signal fact that the few years between 1969 and 1975 have seen more scholarly effort devoted to Alaskan Athapaskan prehistory than did the entire previous 50 years of professional research. Many questions remain; for example, the boundaries between Athapaskan and Eskimo groups at different times in prehistory have yet to be reconstructed. Yet, answers to many old questions seem soon to be forthcoming, and with them, no doubt, new questions will emerge.

Ethnology

Similar to the history of archeological research, ethnological work among Athapaskans of central and southern Alaska breaks into three periods. There was first a short period of concentrated data gathering, 1929–1937. This was followed by a long hiatus in field research. Then, in 1960, an acceleration of a different kind of fieldwork began.

The first period was one of eight intensive and productive years, 1929–1937, during which three anthropologists, Robert A. McKennan, Cornelius Osgood, and Robert J. Sullivan, worked in Alaska. The data they collected ultimately provided the only substantial reconstructions of central and south Alaskan Athapaskan precontact culture.

McKennan was the first to arrive, in 1929, funded by a fellowship from Harvard. He spent a year with the Upper Tanana Indians recording information on a wide range of subjects such as technology, economy, social organization, and religion (1959). He visited all five bands living in the area at that time, gathering data that allowed for many intracultural comparisons. Since the Upper Tanana had experienced relatively light Euro-American contact, McKennan found much of the traditional Indian life still viable. McKennan augmented his earlier anthropometric material on the Upper Tanana Indians with blood-type data (1964) and dug in 1967 at Healy Lake with Cook. His brief theoretical contribution on central Alaskan bands and territorial boundaries (1969) stands out because such a discussion is so rare.

Osgood began work among the Tanaina Indians of Cook Inlet in 1931. His first field season in Alaska followed discouraging field trips to Canadian Athapaskans. Although the fact that the Tanaina, more than other Alaskan Athapaskans, had experienced a long period of Russian and later American occupation in their area did not augur well for Osgood's interest in reconstruction of precontact culture, he felt his first field season had yielded "encouraging results" (1937:5). He revisited the Tanaina briefly in 1932. Osgood, like McKennan, moved around often during fieldwork, though unlike McKennan his Cook Inlet field periods were limited to summer. This was surely a difficult time to gather data for undoubtedly most of the Indians were at summer fish-camp sites and Osgood visited the winter villages. However, he recorded much data on material culture, technology, and social organization, some knowledge of which was soon lost, particularly regarding the traditional tools and subsistence techniques. Although his most productive work was with informants in Kachemak Bay, Osgood spent between one and two weeks each in Iliamna, Eklutna, Tyonek, Susitna, and Kenai. His studies (1933, 1937) raise the question whether or not the Tanaina were ever one group: the variables affecting the dispersed sectors of Tanaina over a long period of time leave an unanswered question about the degree of sense of unity the Tanaina ever felt.

In 1934 Osgood journeyed to the remote location of Anvik in Ingalik territory, where he met an unusual informant, Billy Williams. Osgood worked primarily with this one knowledgeable and dedicated Indian, an enterprise that ultimately resulted in three complementary volumes (Osgood 1940, 1958, 1959), making the Ingalik the most fully documented Alaskan Athapaskans. Unlike McKennan, who attended a potlatch, Osgood ultimately provided substantial reconstructions of several kinds of ceremonies, though he never attended any. The three Ingalik volumes do not document acculturation or the range of Ingalik variation, but they do provide baseline data for later comparisons and considerations of culture change.

Another valuable outcome of Osgood's commitment to Northern Athapaskan ethnology was his text and map (1936) on the distribution of Northern Athapaskans. With a few modifications in light of later knowledge, his identifications and territorial divisions stand. This is an impressive accomplishment considering the limited state of knowledge at that time.

The third ethnologist, Sullivan, worked in the Koyukon villages of Koyukuk, Nulato, and Kaltag in 1936 and 1937. His emphasis was on subsistence activities (1942) and temporal concepts (1942a). Although her field research was primarily archeological, De Laguna (1936) also recorded ethnographic data in this same decade.

The second period, 1937–1960, is marked by the almost complete absence of any ethnographic field research among the Athapaskans of central and south Alaska. The interruption of World War II may account for part of the hiatus, but the total span remains puzzling, especially when the greater continuity of work in other areas of the Subarctic is considered.

Heinrich (1957) and Heinrich and Anderson (1968) with the Upper Tanana and McClellan (1961) were apparently the only ethnologists in the field in the 1950s. De Laguna (fig. 3) has published an article on Ahtna religious concepts (1969–1970).

In 1960 momentum in field studies picked up, initiating the third period of research. This period is marked by the introduction of information about previously undocumented groups and by a new kind of anthropological inquiry, oriented to specific topics rather than attempted reconstruction of whole cultures.

In 1960 Edward H. Hosley began work among the groups living in the McGrath, Medfra, Nikolai, and Lake Minchumina areas. He found them different enough from the Ingalik to be distinguished as Kolchan (1961, 1968). New data about the Koyukon (McFadyen 1966) began to come in: Clark began her many-faceted research on the prehistory, physical anthropology, and ethnography of the Upper Koyukuk peoples (1970, 1970a, 1975) and Loyens discussed ceremony at Nulato (1964). From her initial work in Tanaina archeology, Townsend's interests expanded into Tanaina ethnohistory and cultural change (1970, 1970a).

The topical interests evinced in publications since 1960 include religion and ceremonialism (Clark 1970; De Laguna 1969–1970, Loyens 1964, Kroul 1974, Guédon 1974), kinship terminology (Clark 1975, Heinrich and Anderson 1968), and territorial groups and organization (McKennan 1969, 1969a). A popularized version of Tanaina folklore became available (Vaudrin 1969). Traditional law ways of Athapaskans were discussed by Hippler and Conn (1972) as they apply to contemporary problems of "bush justice." Hippler's (1973) basically Freudian analysis of Athapaskan child rearing and personality highlights the previous absence of any personality and culture studies and accentuates how little yet is known of Athapaskan family life.

Studies of culture change and adaptation were initiated. Clark (1970b, 1975) noted Koyukon culture change in response to Eskimo contacts. Hosley (1966) looked at Kolchan realignments and factionalism, and Davis (1965) reported the persistence of a kind of modified moiety system in the factionalism of a Tanaina village.

Studies of the languages of subarctic Alaska increased greatly after 1960, most of them being by Michael Krauss and other members of the Alaska Native Language Center. Of general use is a large wall map showing ranges, speaking populations, and linguistic relationships of all native Alaskan languages (Krauss 1975). *47*

Fig. 3. Frederica De Laguna and Frank Charley, one of her Ahtna informants, wearing his dentalium necklaces. Photograph by Catharine McClellan, Aug. 1958.

An exhaustive catalogue of all known materials on Alaskan Athapaskan languages is the annotated bibliography by Krauss and McGary (1980). General surveys are found in Krauss (1973, 1979), and important technical treatments of comparative Athapaskan are by Krauss (1964–1965), Leer (1979), and Kari (1979). Dictionaries, often with ethnographically important information, have been published for Tanaina (Kari 1977; Wassillie and Kari 1979), Ahtna (Kari and Buck 1975), Kolchan (Collins and Petruska 1979), Koyukon (Henry, Hunter, and Jones 1973), and Upper Tanana (Milanowski and John 1979). With this new information on linguistics coupled with new archeological data, a reevaluation and assessment of Athapaskan migrations and prehistory on the order of Dumond's (1965, 1969) earlier effort is in order.

Studies in physical anthropology are still very much neglected. Other than Hrdlička's (1930, 1930a) observations and McKennan's (1964) note on the Upper Tanana, only Corcoran et al. (1959) have published information.

For reference, several bibliographies are available: on Alaska archeology (K. Workman 1972), on central Alaska native populations (Foote and MacBain 1964), and on the Subarctic Athapaskans (Helm 1973; Hippler and Wood 1974; Parr 1974).

Conclusions

48   Viewing the history of ethnological research in central and south Alaska in light of the course of research in the Shield area of the Subarctic (see "Prehistory of the Canadian Shield," this vol.) highlights both distinctive features and deficiencies of the Alaskan research. Developments in the archeology of the two areas are relatively noncontrastive.

By the time professional ethnographic fieldwork began in Alaska, fieldwork in the Shield had been under way for 50 years and had entered its second period (1921–1940). In both areas at that time ethnologists concentrated on the reconstruction of aboriginal cultures, consistent with the major interests of American anthropology in that era. However, not only did Shield research begin much earlier, but also it has been more sustained and has resulted in more frequent and productive theoretical discussions. Contrastively, the Alaskan Athapaskan literature does not offer a series of comparative studies, or discussions of the nature of land tenure, or analyses of the consequences of the shift to a trapping economy. Other than McKennan's (1969a) short article, no general discussion of traditional sociopolitical organization has been put forth, and, excepting De Laguna's (1975) comparative study, there has been remarkably little attention to kinship systems.

The Athapaskan Indians of Alaska were, until the 1920s, on the fringe of the continent and the fringe of anthropological research. However, what was done in descriptive ethnography was accomplished in the classic style of the best monographs of the 1930s; these studies provide a valuable foundation for controlled comparisons and studies of culture change. Alaskan Athapaskan studies can boast a small cadre of devoted anthropologists who have continued to return to the state over long periods of time (McKennan, De Laguna, Townsend, and A. McF. Clark). In addition, several scholars (De Laguna, McKennan, Townsend, Olson, Hosley, A. McF. Clark, VanStone, and Shinkwin) have pursued both archeological and ethnographic investigations, a dual command that provides a sound scholarly base for the reconstruction of long-term culture history.

The Athapaskan peoples of central and south Alaska were in the 1970s located at the scene of profound changes with potentially irreversible consequences. Since 1971 they have experienced, under the Alaska Native Claims Settlement Act, the process of organization into three landholding, profit corporations: Ahtna Inc., Doyon Inc., and Cook Inlet Regional Corporation. A few Athapaskan Indians are enrolled in two other regional corporations, Calista and Bristol Bay, which are predominantly Eskimo. The setting is promising for the development of new kinds of research that will involve the Indians in research into their cultural heritage. Also, as a result of the concern about impending "cultural impact," new levels of awareness of processes and effects of rapid culture change are likely to emerge, for anthropologist and native alike.

Museum and Archival Resources for Subarctic Alaska

JAMES W. VanSTONE

This chapter details major archival source materials and significant collections of Athapaskan material culture from central and south Alaska in American and European museums. Discussion is confined to basic ethnohistorical sources and museum collections of the nineteenth and early twentieth centuries.

Exploration and the Fur Trade

The most important archival source for the study of Russian exploration and the early fur trade in central and south Alaska is the records of the Russian-American Company between 1802 and 1867 in the United States National Archives, Washington. These valuable materials, written in Russian longhand, were transferred to the United States government in accordance with the provisions of the treaty of purchase of Alaska in 1867. The entire collection has been microfilmed and there are copies in a number of major American and Canadian university libraries. Contents of the 77 microfilm reels are as follows: reels 1–25, letters received by the governors general, 1802–1866; reels 26–65, letters sent by the governors general, 1812–1867; reels 66–76, logs of company ships, 1850–1867; reel 77, journals of exploring expeditions, 1842–1864. The Russian-American Company records are particularly important for the study of Russian exploration in western Alaska and the mechanisms of the fur trade on the Yukon River and its major tributaries.

Although some of the most significant archival sources relating to the Russian era in Alaska are in American depositories, there are also important materials relating to central and south Alaska in the Soviet Union. The travel journal of Andrey Glazunov, probably the first Russian to see the Yukon River, is in the Gosudarstvennyĭ arkhiv Permskoĭ oblasti (State Archive of the Perm Region); only excerpts have been published. Journals relating to early explorations of the Copper River are deposited in the Arkhiv Akademii nauk S.S.S.R. Leningradskoe otdelenie (Leningrad branch of the Archive of the Academy of Sciences). These materials and others are discussed in some detail by Fedorova (1973a).

Several members of the Western Union Telegraph Expedition kept journals and diaries that contain useful information on the fur trade and Indians of the Yukon River region. Some of this material is in private hands, but the diaries of Fred M. Smith and George R. Adams are in the University of Washington Library, Seattle; excerpts from the Adams diaries have been published (Taggart 1956).

Another important document relating to the American period is a 91-page manuscript by E.W. Nelson (1880) in the National Anthropological Archives, National Museum of Natural History, Smithsonian Institution. It is an account of a sledge journey made by Nelson from Saint Michael on Norton Sound to the upper Innoko River, a major Yukon tributary, about 1880. This manuscript contains exceptionally detailed information concerning western Athapaskan subsistence activities and resource utilization in the late nineteenth century. An edited and annotated version has been published by VanStone (1978).

Limited information relating to the fur trade in south Alaska during the early American period is found in the Alaska Commercial Company records, 1868–1911, deposited in the Archives and Manuscript Collections, University of Alaska, Fairbanks. An inventory of this material has been prepared by Oswalt (1967a).

Missionary Accounts

Archival sources are of particular importance for the study of missionary impact on the Athapaskans of central and south Alaska. Although there are numerous short published articles by missionaries active in the area as well as a few translations of selected missionary journals from the Russian period (see "History of Research in Subarctic Alaska," this vol.), there is no analytical treatment that evaluates Christian influence in the area.

For the Russian period, the major archival source is the Alaska Russian Church Archives deposited in the Manuscript Division of the Library of Congress. This material is preserved in more than 1,000 box-portfolios, which represent the entire archive of the Ecclesiastical

Consistory of the Russian Church in Alaska. It was placed in the Library of Congress in two installments, the first in 1928 and the second in 1940. Although there is no general index to the collection, Dorosh (1961) describes the archives in some detail. In addition, the first four volumes of a 15-volume typewritten manuscript entitled "Documents Relative to the History of Alaska," compiled as part of the Alaska History Research Project (1936–1938) of the University of Alaska, indexes that part of the archives received by the Library of Congress in 1928 (known as the Alaska Church Collection) and offers selected translations. The original typewritten copy is in the Archives and Manuscript Collections, University of Alaska, Fairbanks, and there is a carbon copy in the Library of Congress. The church archives have not been used extensively by ethnohistorians, but they are essential to an understanding of the impact of Orthodox Christianity on the Indians of the Yukon and Kuskokwim rivers.

Another important archival source for the study of the activities of Russian Orthodox priests in central and south Alaska is the Archive of the Russian Orthodox Church in Alaska, assembled by the Alaska Diocese of the Orthodox Church in America. The collection contains books, pamphlets, and other published information, but the largest part of the documentary materials consists of parish records for the Yukon and Kuskokwim missions covering the period from 1845 until the second decade of the twentieth century. Although some of this material is duplicated in the Alaska Church Collection, there is much new and valuable demographic and ethnographic data relating to the Ingalik and Koyukon Indians. A preliminary survey of the Archive has been published (B.S. Smith 1974). Although the Archive is retained by the Alaska Diocese, the entire document collection has been microfilmed for the Alaska Historical Library in Juneau.

Archival materials relating to activities of the Roman Catholic Church in west-central Alaska are to be found in the Oregon Province Archives of the Society of Jesus at Gonzaga University in Spokane, Washington. Of particular interest are the letters, diaries, and ethnographic and historical writings of Father Jules Jetté; the Alaska Mission Collection, which contains papers, documents, and letters relating to all the Roman Catholic missions in Alaska; and the Holy Cross mission collection, which includes records, diaries, and historical writings concerning the mission and school on the lower Yukon. In addition, the archives contain extensive correspondence and other documents by most of the Jesuit priests and lay brothers who served the church on the Yukon, some of them for many years.

The Episcopal Church, like the Roman Catholic Church, sent missionaries to the Yukon and its tributaries in the late nineteenth century. Valuable unpublished source material concerning their work among the Ingalik, Koyukon, and Tanana Indians is deposited in the Archives and Historical Collections, Episcopal Church, located at the Episcopal Seminary of the Southwest in Austin, Texas. Much relevant material is to be found in the Alaska Papers of the Domestic and Foreign Missionary Society Papers (105 boxes), and the personal papers of John W. and Henry H. Chapman, missionaries at Anvik on the lower Yukon for a total of 60 years. There are also personal papers relating to the activities of Hudson Stuck at Fort Yukon and missionaries at Nenana, Fairbanks, Cordova, and other settlements.

Photograph Collections

Early photographs can be an important ethnohistoric resource and there are a number of important collections relevant to west-central Alaska. John Chapman at Anvik was an avid photographer, and his collection, rich in depictions of subsistence activities and village life, is deposited in the National Anthropological Archives. The Alaska Historical Library, Juneau, also has a collection of photographs relating to central Alaska Athapaskans, particularly the Tanana. Other depositories where relevant material is located are the Pacific Northwest Collection, University of Washington Library, Seattle, and the Archives and Manuscript Collections, University of Alaska, Fairbanks.

Nineteenth- and Early Twentieth-Century Museum Collections

Collections of ethnographic specimens made by L.A. Zagoskin, IU. F. Lisīanskiĭ, I.G. Voznesenskiĭ, and other Russian explorers during the first half of the nineteenth century are in the Muzeĭ Antropologii i Ėtnografii (Museum of Anthropology and Ethnography), Leningrad. Groups represented are the Ingalik, Tanaina, Kolchan, Koyukon, and Ahtna. These collections have been described in varying degrees of detail (Lipshits 1955; Zibert 1967; Troufanoff 1967; Dzeniskevich 1975, 1976). Photographs of materials collected by Zagoskin can also be found in both the 1956 (Russian) and 1967 (English) editions of the account of his explorations. There is also an important early collection of Tanaina specimens in the Suomen kansallismuseo (National Museum of Finland), Helsinki. It was assembled by A.K. Etolin, a Russian naval officer who served as general manager of the Russian-American Company between 1841 and 1845. Some of the specimens are described and illustrated in *The Far North*, a catalogue of an art exhibition at the National Gallery of Art, Washington (Collins et al. 1973).

As is evident from other articles in this volume, relatively few ethnographic collections were made in central and south Alaska by Americans in the late nineteenth century. Members of the Western Union Telegraph Expedition, particularly William H. Dall, obtained some materials, most of which are in the National Museum of Natural History. Capt. J. Adrian Jacobsen (1884), a collector for the Staatliches Museum für Völkerkunde in Berlin, traveled extensively throughout Alaska in 1881–1883. Although he was more interested in obtaining Eskimo and Northwest Coast materials than in assembling a comprehensive collection from the Subarctic, 360 Ingalik and at least 10 Tanaina artifacts collected by him survive in the Berlin museum (Horst Hartmann, communication to editors 1980).

Because of their intensive contact with Russian traders during the first half of the nineteenth century, the Athapaskans of central and south Alaska began to lose their traditional material culture at a relatively early date. As a result, extensive collections of contemporary specimens are virtually nonexistent. In the early twentieth century an excellent assemblage of Ingalik material items, now in the American Museum of Natural History, New York, was made by John W. Chapman. In the 1930s Cornelius Osgood made the collection, so well documented in his monumental study of Ingalik material culture (1940), that is deposited in the Peabody Museum, Yale University. Considering the collections made by Osgood, Chapman, Zagoskin, and Jacobsen, the Ingalik are easily the best represented Subarctic Athapaskans in museum collections throughout the world.

A few additional American, Canadian, and European museums have scattered holdings from the central and south Alaska Athapaskan area. However, it is clear that on the whole these Indians are poorly represented in the collections of major museums, particularly when compared with their immediate western and northern neighbors, the Eskimos.

Subarctic Algonquian Languages

RICHARD A. RHODES AND EVELYN M. TODD*

The indigenous languages of the Subarctic Shield, except for the northwest sector, belong to two of the branches of the Algonquian (ăl'gäŋkēən) language family. The northern branch, here called Cree, comprises the local varieties of speech (dialects) known as Cree, Montagnais, and Naskapi, and the southern branch, here called Ojibwa (ō'jĭbwā), includes the dialects also known locally (and in some historical and technical writings) as Chippewa, Saulteaux ('sō̱,tō̱), Ottawa, and Algonquin (ăl'gäŋkĭn) (figs. 1–2). Each of these branches is conventionally regarded as a single language consisting of a continuum of dialectal varieties, since within each branch every dialect is at least partly intelligible to the speakers of the neighboring dialects. Using stricter criteria of similarity and mutual intelligibility between nonadjacent dialects, the two branches could be said to consist of several languages each. This chapter treats the classification of all varieties of Cree and Ojibwa, including those spoken by groups described in other volumes (see "Southwestern Chippewa," "Southeastern Ojibwa," "Ottawa," "Nipissing," and "Algonquin" in vol. 15; chapters on Plains Cree and Plains Ojibwa in vol. 13); it supersedes the treatment of Ojibwa dialectology in "Central Algonquian Languages" (vol. 15).

Cree and Ojibwa are sometimes referred to as Central Algonquian languages, but this classification is only a convenient geographical one. The Central languages do not form a genetic subgroup of Algonquian, since they do not share unique innovatory features not found in the family as a whole. It is now widely accepted that, while there is a distinct Eastern subfamily of Algonquian languages (as shown by I. Goddard 1967, 1979, 1980), all the other languages, including Cree and Ojibwa, are independently developed from the ancestral language, Proto-Algonquian (PA). The one possible exception is that Ojibwa and Potawatomi may constitute a genetic subgroup that shares some relatively old innovations, though their later developments have diverged ("Eastern Algonquian Languages" and "Central Algonquian Languages," vol. 15).

Several developments serve to distinguish all dia-

lects† of Cree from all dialects of Ojibwa. Two are given here. Phonologically, wherever the protolanguage had *θ, the regularly observed historical development from this (called its reflex) is t in Cree but n in Ojibwa. (Segments and forms in the protolanguage are marked with an asterisk to indicate that they have been reconstructed by inference rather than directly attested.)

	Plains Cree	Eastern Ojibwa	PA
dog	/atim/	/nimoš/	*aθemw-
speaks thus	/itwe·w/	/nwe·/	*eθwe·wa
(that) I lift him	/ohpipitak/	/wmbibnag/	*wempipiθaki

Morphologically, all Cree dialects mark first-person plural in all independent verbs with -na·n (excl.) or -naw or -na·naw (incl.),‡ whereas all Ojibwa dialects mark first-person plural (incl. or excl.) in independent intransitive verbs§ with -min.

	Plains Cree	Southwestern Ojibwa
we (incl.) go home	/kiki·wa·na·naw/	/gigi·we·min/
we (excl.) go home	/niki·wa·na·n/	/ingi·we·min/

Work on Ojibwa dialects (J.D. Nichols 1975; Daviault et al. 1978) has shown that some of the phonological criteria generally used for distinguishing Cree from Ojibwa do not correctly classify some subdialects of Ojibwa. The treatment of PA *nC is a case in point. The reflex of PA *nC is hC in most Cree dialects and nC in most Ojibwa dialects. However, in most of the area covered by the Severn ('sevrən) and Algonquin dialects of Ojibwa, the reflex of PA *nC is C. This is probably not part of the Cree sound shift but a later independent innovation in these dialects, even though in some Severn subdialects some morphemes have hC,

---

*This chapter was first written in 1972 by Todd, then completely revised by Rhodes in 1979 on the basis of the extensive new information on Cree and Ojibwa dialects that became available during the intervening years.

†Because differences in dialects are so important in this chapter, citations are transcribed in such a way as to highlight those differences. Italics (p) indicate citations of General Cree and General Ojibwa (basically the standardized transcriptions of Bloomfield 1946); slashes (/p/) enclose the phonemic forms of individual dialects; and square brackets ([p]) enclose broad phonetic transcriptions.

‡The distinction of inclusive versus exclusive plural in the first person is the distinction between whether the speaker includes his audience or not. Thus first-person plural inclusive means 'we, you and I' or 'we, including you', while first-person plural exclusive means 'we, but not you'.

§The verb systems of Cree and Ojibwa, as of most Algonquian languages, have 2 major subsystems of inflection for person and number, called the independent and conjunct orders.

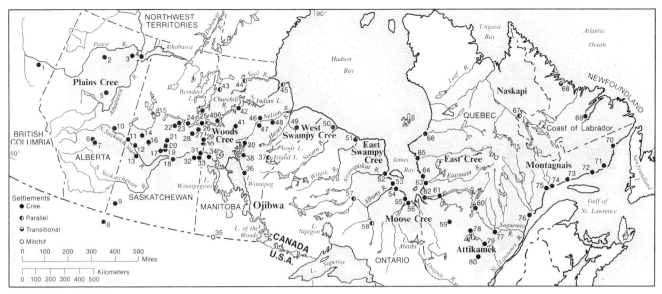

Fig. 1. Cree dialect areas and settlements for which dialect affiliations are known: 1, Saulteau; 2, Fort Vermilion; 3, Cree; 4, Cree; 5, Wabasca; 6, Ermineskin; 7, Samson; 8, Rocky Boy; 9, Maple Creek; 10, Saddle Lake; 11, Onion Lake; 12, Thunderchild; 13, Sweetgrass; 14, Meadow Lake; 15, Île-à-la-Crosse; 16, Pelican Lake; 17, Sturgeon Lake; 18, James Smith; 19, Lac la Ronge; 20–21, Montreal Lake; 22–24, Lac la Ronge; 25–30, Peter Ballantyne; 31, Cumberland House; 32, Red Earth; 33, Shoal Lake; 34, The Pas; 35, Turtle Mountain; 36, Poplar River; 37, Island Lake; 38, Norway House; 39, Cross Lake; 40, Mathias Colomb; 41, Nelson House; 42, South Indian Lake; 43, Barren Lands; 44–45, Churchill; 46, Split Lake; 47, York Factory; 48, Fox Lake; 49, Shamattawa; 50, Fort Severn; 51, Weenusk; 52, Attawapiskat; 53, Fort Albany (Moose Cree dialect); 54, Albany; 55, Attawapiskat (Eastern Swampy Cree dialect); 56, Moose Factory; 57, Martin Falls (Ogoki); 58, Constance Lake; 59, Waswanipi; 60, Mistassini; 61, Némiscau; 62, Rupert House; 63, Eastmain; 64, Paint Hills; 65, Fort George; 66, Great Whale River; 67, Schefferville; 68, Davis Inlet; 69, North West River; 70, Saint Augustin; 71, Romaine; 72, Natashquan; 73, Mingan; 74, Maliotenam; 75, Sept-Îles; 76, Bersimis; 77, Pointe Bleue; 78, Obedjiwan; 79, Weymontachingue; 80, Manouane. Most of the names here and in fig. 2 are official band names rather than settlement names.

which suggests Cree influence. This shows one of the difficulties in trying to formulate simple criteria for determining the linguistic affiliation of any particular group of speakers. For an accurate determination of the linguistic affiliation of a group of speakers, a more comprehensive approach is needed, one which takes into account phonological, morphological, grammatical, and lexical considerations.

Distribution of Cree and Ojibwa

The various dialects of Cree are spoken throughout a wide area of Canada including most of the Quebec-Labrador peninsula, the Hudson Bay coastal region of Ontario, central Manitoba, Saskatchewan, and Alberta. Figure 1 shows the range of Cree and the areas covered by the various dialects. Linguistically, Cree is bounded in the northeast by Eskimo, in the northwest and west by Athapaskan, in the southwest by Blackfoot and Siouan, in the south by Ojibwa, and in the southeast by Eastern Algonquian.

The various dialects of Ojibwa are spoken throughout the area immediately south of the Cree area, from southwestern Quebec through southern Ontario, all of Michigan, the inland regions of northern Ontario, northern Wisconsin and Minnesota, southern Manitoba, and southern Saskatchewan. Figure 2 shows the

range and distribution of Ojibwa dialects. Linguistically Ojibwa is bounded on the north by Cree, in the west by Siouan, in the south by the traditional territories of other Central Algonquian peoples, now mostly displaced, and in the east by Iroquoian.

The discussion and illustration of the range and distribution of the languages and dialects under consideration is complicated by the fact that many of the Algonquian peoples of the Subarctic and northern Plains are seminomadic peoples. They live in the bush in the winter, working extensive trap lines and hunting throughout areas that may cover thousands of square miles, but in the summer they return to permanent settlements. This way of life is typical of the northern and inland bands. On the other hand, the southern bands and those of the Hudson Bay coast are typically permanently settled. This means that the language ranges and dialect areas indicated on the maps may have somewhat different interpretations for different areas. In the northern and inland regions, the areas shown indicate the approximate range of speakers of that dialect (ignoring certain complications such as uninhabitable land). In these regions the dialect boundaries tend to follow the high ground separating river drainages. For the southern and coastal dialects, where the bands or some portion of the bands are more permanently settled, the areas indicated simply encompass

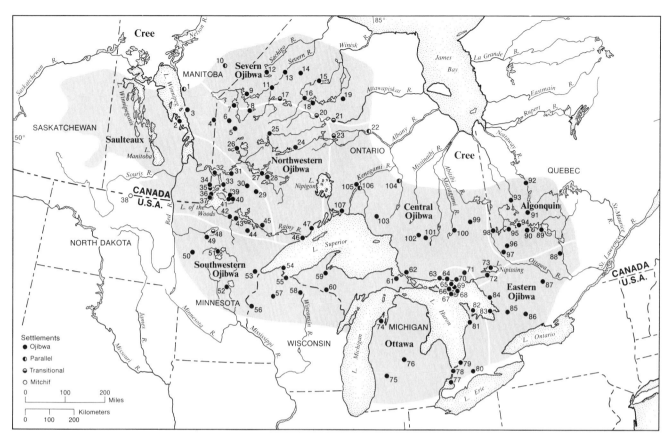

Fig. 2. Ojibwa dialect areas and settlements for which dialect affiliations are known: 1. Poplar River; 2. Jackhead; 3. Berens River; 4. Little Grand Rapids; 5. Pikangikum; 6. Poplar Hill; 7. Deer Lake; 8. North Spirit Lake; 9. Sandy Lake; 10. Island Lake; 11. Muskrat Dam; 12. Sachigo; 13. Bearskin Lake; 14. Big Trout Lake; 15. Kasabonika Lake; 16. Kingfisher; 17. Round Lake (Weagamow); 18. Wunnummin; 19. Webiquie; 20. Summer Beaver; 21. Lansdowne House; 22. Martin Falls (Ogoki); 23. Fort Hope; 24. Osnaburg; 25. Cat Lake; 26. Red Lake; 27. Lac Seul; 28. Sioux Lookout; 29. Wabigoon; 30. Eagle Lake; 31. Grassy Narrows; 32. Islington; 33. Rat Portage; 34. Shoal Lake No. 39; 35. Shoal Lake No. 40; 36. Northwest Angle No. 33; 37. Northwest Angle No. 37; 38. Turtle Mountain; 39. Whitefish Bay; 40. Northwest Angle No. 33; 41. Northwest Angle No. 37; 42. Rainy River; 43. Couchiching; 44. Nett Lake; 45. Lac la Croix; 46. Grand Portage; 47. Fort William; 48. Ponemah; 49. Red Lake; 50. White Earth; 51. Leech Lake; 52. Mille Lacs; 53. Fond du Lac; 54. Red Cliff; 55. Bad River; 56. St. Croix; 57. Lac Court Oreilles; 58. Lac du Flambeau; 59. L'anse; 60. Lac Vieux Desert; 61. Bay Mills; 62. Garden River; 63. Serpent River; 64. Spanish River No. 1 and 2; 65. Sucker Creek; 66. West Bay; 67. South Bay; 68. Manitoulin Island; 69. Sheguiandah; 70. Whitefish River; 71. Whitefish Lake; 72. Dokis; 73. Nipissing; 74. Peshawbestown; 75. Grand Rapids; 76. Mount Pleasant; 77. Walpole Island; 78. Chippewas of Sarnia; 79. Chippewas of Kettle and Stony Point; 80. Chippewas of the Thames; 81. Saugeen; 82. Cape Croker; 83. Christian Island; 84. Parry Island; 85. Chippewas of Rama; 86. Curve Lake; 87. Golden Lake; 88. River Désert (Maniwaki); 89. Barrière Lake (Rapid Lake); 90. Grand Lac Victoria; 91. Lac Simon; 92. Rapide des Cedres; 93. Abitibi (Amos); 94. Rapide Sept; 95. Long Point (Winneway); 96. Hunter's Point; 97. Kipawa; 98. Notre Dame du Nord (Temiskaming); 99. Matachewan; 100. Mattagami; 101. Brunswick House; 102. Chapleau Ojibway; 103. Pic Mobert; 104. Constance Lake; 105. Long Lake No. 58; 106. Long Lake No. 77; 107. Pays Plat. The Saulteaux dialect is also spoken in a number of settlements west of the area covered by this map.

all known settlements and ignore the fact that much of the included region is inhabited by those who speak other languages, mostly English or French. (In Michigan and Wisconsin, shown on the map as Ojibwa-speaking regions, Potawatomi is also spoken, and in Wisconsin, Menominee is spoken as well. There are a number of Ojibwa-Potawatomi bilinguals in these areas, the remnants of an earlier time when the languages were more vital there and when there was considerable multilingualism among the speakers of Algonquian languages.)

Another problem with the interpretation of the maps showing language and dialect range is that settlements through which dialect and language boundaries run are of two types. There is a transitional type, in which the subdialect within the community is fairly uniform but shares features with each of the two dialects on whose common boundary it sits. An example in the Cree area is Davis Inlet, and an example in the Ojibwa area is Weagamow (wē'ägə̩maw) (Round Lake). Older speakers in Weagamow retain their separate dialects, while younger speakers have the transitional dialect (John Nichols, personal communication 1980). On the other hand, there are communities of a mixed type, in which two or more dialects or languages are spoken side by side showing little convergence. Examples of this type of community are Constance Lake, Ontario, where Eastern Swampy Cree and Central Ojibwa coexist and

Schefferville, Quebec, where two Cree dialects, Naskapi and Montagnais, coexist.

Dialects of Cree

The dialects of Cree fall into two groups, Eastern Cree and Western Cree. Given the present state of knowledge, the dialects of Cree are best classified according to phonological criteria. The basic division into Eastern and Western dialects follows the isogloss for the reflex of PA *k before front vowels, a classification first proposed by Michelson (1939). In the east, PA *k appears as č before front vowels. In the west, PA *k remains k.

	Plains Cree	East Cree	PA
he goes home	/kiˑweˑw/	/čiwew/	*kiˑweˑwa
he kicks	/tahkiskaˑkeˑw/	/təhčškačew/	*tankiškaˑkeˑwa

The dialects of Western Cree are Plains Cree, Woods Cree, Western Swampy Cree, Eastern Swampy Cree, Moose Cree, and Attikamek (Tête de Boule) (fig. 1). They can be distinguished from one another by two phonological criteria: whether or not they merge PA *š and *s, and what their reflex of PA *l is. Table 1 gives a summary of the facts. This division of Western Cree dialects is, at least in part, corroborated by data on mutual intelligibility. Wolfart (1973a:11) indicates that Plains Cree is a single mutually intelligible dialect despite the fact that there are two variants, a northern subdialect and a southern subdialect, while David Pentland (personal communication 1980) states that there is a drop in mutual intelligibility between Woods Cree and the adjacent Plains and Swampy dialects. The drop in mutual intelligibility between Eastern and Western Swampy Cree is corroborated by a Summer Institute of Linguistics study (cited in Wolfart 1973a:7) that indicates a drop of mutual intelligibility in the vicinity of the *š > s isogloss. While there are a number of factors, including nonlinguistic ones, that can influence mutual intelligibility, the correlation of the facts of mutual intelligibility with the phonological criteria generally used for distinguishing Cree dialects is a reasonable indication of the validity of these criteria. However, there must be more differences among the various dialects than just the simple ones discussed here, which could not account for the observed diminution of mutual intelligibility. These probably include grammatical and lexical differences as well as phonological differences. Furthermore, the same simple phonological differences occur elsewhere between closely related subdialects; for example the *š > s isogloss subdivides the East Cree dialect into an area on the Hudson Bay coast that preserves the s/š contrast and an area at Great Whale River and inland that does not (MacKenzie 1977). Consid-

Table 1. Phonological Characteristics of Western Cree Dialects

	Plains Cree	Woods Cree	W. Swampy Cree	E. Swampy Cree	Moose Cree	Attika- mek
š and s contrast	no	no	no	yes	yes	yes
the reflex of PA *l	/y/	/δ/	/n/	/n/	/l/	/r/

erable work remains to be done to determine comprehensively what the nature of the differences among the Western Cree dialects is.

One set of differences among the dialects of Cree that is often overlooked because of its subtlety is that which arises from the fact that in the Eastern Cree dialects the General Cree length contrasts in vowels show up as differences in vowel quality, sometimes described as an opposition between normal and short vowels (J.H. Rogers 1958:91; Martin 1980:260). While at first glance it may appear that saying that the Eastern Cree dialects have vowel quality contrast rather than length contrasts is only a matter of how one talks about it rather than a matter of substantive difference, it turns out that viewing the vowel system this way makes more understandable the sizable number of assimilations of vowel quality in these dialects that would otherwise have to be viewed as arbitrary and unmotivated shifts in vowel length. The phonemic transcriptions reflect these differences in the systems of contrast, which are summarized in table 2.

There are three dialects of Eastern Cree: East Cree, Naskapi, and Montagnais, distinguished from one another by a number of features. Three of the most striking are: the correspondence of East Cree-Naskapi /s/ to Montagnais /š/, which has become [h] in most subdialects in many environments; the replacement of East Cree-Naskapi /sč/ by Montagnais /ss/ (or /hc/); and the appearance of Naskapi fricatives in place of General Cree *hkw* and *hp*.[1] Thus, Montagnais has /ntahamət/ 'my snowshoes' and /assi/ 'earth' next to East Cree /ntəsaməč/ and /əsči/, and Schefferville (originally Fort McKenzie) and Davis Inlet Naskapi have [atixw] 'caribou' and [akuφ] 'dress' next to Mistassini East Cree [atihkw] and [akuhp]. There is some controversy over the grouping of the dialects of Eastern Cree, and the issue is somewhat complicated by the fact that many older speakers are polydialectal (MacKenzie 1979), and by the fact that these dialects all have considerable in-

---

[1] This criterion is somewhat tenuous because there is an incipient sound change among the younger speakers of the southeastern coastal subdialect of Montagnais that has a similar effect, but since the question is not whether Montagnais is distinct from Naskapi, but rather whether East Cree and Naskapi are distinct, this criterion may be used.

Table 2. Cree Vowel Correspondences

General Cree	$i\cdot$	$e\cdot$	$a\cdot$	$o\cdot$	i	a	o
Eastern dialects	/i/	/e/[a]	/a/	/o/	/ɪ/	/ə/	/ʊ/
Western dialects	/i·/	/e·/[b]	/a·/	/o·/	/i/	/a/	/o/

[a] Subdialectally in Naskapi and East Cree, General Cree $e\cdot$ and $a\cdot$ merge as East Cree – Naskapi /a/.

[b] Woods Cree and the northern subdialect of Plains Cree merge General Cree $i\cdot$ and $e\cdot$ as /i·/.

ternal complexity, there being three subdialects of East Cree, two of Naskapi, and three of Montagnais (Ford et al. 1978). Here East Cree and Naskapi are considered separate dialects (following Ford et al. 1978), although they form a dialect continuum—the subdialects of each area differing only slightly from those of adjacent areas—and have been considered a single dialect (MacKenzie 1977). In contrast, Montagnais falls into two distinct subdialect regions, with the settlements on the southeastern Atlantic coast from Mingan to Saint-Augustin (the Basse-Côte-Nord 'lower north shore') differing sharply from the rest of the dialect. The Pointe-Bleue (Lake Saint John) subdialect also differs in a number of respects, but this is principally as a result of its retaining archaic features, lost in the rest of Montagnais, that make many words resemble East Cree; for example, Pointe-Bleue is the only Montagnais subdialect that retains the h of General Cree hC-clusters in all positions: Mistassini East Cree and Pointe-Bleue Montagnais /pehtəm/ 'he hears it', Basse-Côte-Nord Montagnais /petəm/. In spite of such archaisms, Pointe-Bleue is shown to be a Montagnais dialect by the many features of lexicon and grammar that it shares with communities to the east, such as Betsiamites (Bersimis) rather than with those to the west, such as Mistassini.

In the Eastern Cree area, several features commonly taken as significant in Cree dialectology are less important than was previously thought. The reflexes of PA *l (/n/, /y/, and /l/) do not distinguish the dialects well, since their distribution does not correlate well with that of other features; however, one study does use the /n/, /y/, and /l/ reflexes as the principal criterion for dividing Eastern Cree into Eastern, Western, and Southern Montagnais, respectively (Pentland 1978). Similarly the merger of $e\cdot$ with $a\cdot$ overlaps the East Cree–Naskapi boundary but does not include all of either dialect.

Another significant fact regarding the dialectology of the Eastern Cree region is that a number of dialect features differ sharply across generations. This was first pointed out by Cowan (1976). For example, in Betsiamites Montagnais, middle-aged and younger speakers substitute [x] for šk and [ɸ] for šp.

	older speakers	middle-aged and younger speakers
my leg	[nɪškat]	[nəxat]
up	[ašpmɪt]	[ɸmət]

The same type of age-graded language variants are found among speakers of Schefferville Naskapi (reported in MacKenzie 1979). Only the oldest generation retains the contrast of $e\cdot$ and $a\cdot$, while only the youngest generation substitutes ss for sč.

	older speakers	middle-aged speakers	younger speakers
fish	[nɪmes]	[nɪmas]	[nɪmas]
kettle	[əsčixw]	[əsčixw]	[əssixw]
he works	[ətʊsčew]	[ətʊsčaw]	[ətʊssaw]

In fact, a number of the most characteristic phonological features of modern Montagnais, such as the change of /š/ to [h], are known to have been rapidly extending their geographical spread in the course of the twentieth century.

There is one further Cree dialect that merits separate attention. Mitchif or French Cree is a dialect based on Plains Cree, but with a heavy borrowing of French nouns.

he built a house	æn	mæzɔ̜	ki·-ošihta·w	
	a	house	past-he build	
French:	une	maison		
we will go to town	dą	la vɪl	niwi·-tohta·na·n	
	to	the town	fut. -we (excl.) go	
French:	dans la	ville		
these are pens	li		plüm	ǫkik
	the-(pl.)		pen	these (anim.)**
French:	les		plumes	
those are my dogs	ni·ya	ne·kik	me	šyæ
	I	those (anim.)	my-(pl.)	dog
French:			mes	chiens

This is not a creole or a pidgin, but a dialect of Cree with all the morphological complexity and extensive lexical resources of other Cree dialects. A grammatical sketch of Mitchif can be found in Rhodes (1977). Mitchif is spoken on the Turtle Mountain Reservation at Belcourt, North Dakota, and in many places in Manitoba, Saskatchewan, and perhaps elsewhere.

Dialects of Ojibwa

Ojibwa falls into eight distinct dialects. They are Saulteaux, Northwestern Ojibwa, Southwestern Ojibwa (which does not include all groups treated in "Southwestern Chippewa," vol. 15), Severn Ojibwa, Central Ojibwa, Ottawa, Eastern Ojibwa, and Algonquin. The areas covered by these dialects are indicated on figure 2. While the best criteria for dialect determination in Cree are phonological, the best criteria for dialect determination in Ojibwa are morphological. The most significant criteria distinguishing Ojibwa dialects are charted in table 3.

**The nouns in Algonquian languages are of two genders, animate and inanimate.

Table 3. Selected Morphological Criteria for Differentiating Ojibwa Dialects

	Saulteaux	Northwestern Ojibwa	Southwestern Ojibwa	Severn Ojibwa	Central Ojibwa	Ottawa	Eastern Ojibwa	Algonquin
2nd-person plural suffix on intransitive verbs	/-m/	/-m/	/-m/	/na·wa·/	/-m/	/-m/	/-m/	/-na·wa·/
1st-person plural suffix on transitive verbs with inanimate object	/-min/	/-min/	/-min/	/-min/	/-min/	/-na·(n)/ᵃ	/-min/ᵇ	/-mɨn/ᶜ
1st-person plural suffix on verbs with 2nd-person subject	/-na·m/	/-na·m/	/-mɨn/	/-na·m/ᵈ	/-mɨn/	/-mɨ(n)/ᵃ	/-mɨn/	/-na·m/
Suffix on verbs meaning 'we do something to you'	/-igo·/	/-igo·/	/-igo·/	/-igo·/	/-igo·/	/-go·/, /-igo·/ᵉ	/-nimin/, /-inmin/	/-inɨm/ᶠ
Separate suffix for obviative plural	yesᵍ	yes	no	no	yes	no	no	no
Suffix on conjunct verbs meaning 'he does something to us (excl.)', contains *m*	no	yes	no	no	no	no	yes	?

ᵃ In Ottawa certain morphemes lose a final *n* when they appear word finally. The two morphemes *-na·n* and *-min* are among these.
ᵇ Some settlements in the Eastern Ojibwa dialect area use both *-min* and *-na·n* in these verbs, for example, Parry Island (J.H. Rogers 1975).
ᶜ Algonquin /ɨ/ corresponds to Common Ojibwa *i* and *a* in most environments.
ᵈ There is an alternate suffix *-nim* on these verbs in the Round Lake (Weagamow) subdialect.
ᵉ Some speakers use the Eastern Ojibwa suffix (Bloomfield 1957).
ᶠ From the combination of /-ini/ + /-nim/ by a regular contraction. The full form *-ininim* is attested as an alternate suffix at Round Lake.
ᵍ Some dialects, especially in the speech of younger speakers, lack this distinction (Paul H. Voorhis, communication to editors 1978; David H. Pentland, communication to editors 1980).

Examples of each of the morphological variants follow. Second-person plural in intransitive verbs may be marked with either *-n* or *-na·wa·*: Central Ojibwa /gdanoki·m/ 'you (pl.) work', next to Severn Ojibwa /gidanoki·na·wa·/. The first-person plural ending on verbs with inanimate objects may be either *-min* or *-na·n*; Eastern Ojibwa /nbi·do·min/ 'we (excl.) bring it, them (inan.)', next to Ottawa /mbi·do·na·/ 'we (excl.) bring it' and /mbi·do·na·nin/ 'we (excl.) bring them (inan.)'. The distinction between singular and plural obviative†† may be marked on animate nouns and on verbs that agree with animate subjects or objects, or it may be left unmarked. If the distinction is marked, the endings are *-an* 'obviative singular' and *-a·* 'obviative plural'; if the distinction is not marked, there is only the one ending, *-an*‡‡ 'obviative': Northwestern Ojibwa /ogozisan/ 'his son', /ogozisa·/ 'his sons'; /owa·bama·n/ 'he sees him', /owa·bama··/ 'he sees them', but Southwestern Ojibwa /ogwisan/ 'his son, his sons', /owa·bama·n/ 'he sees him, them'. The first-person ending on verbs that mean 'you do something to us' may be either *-min* or *-na·m*: Southwestern Ojibwa /giwa·bamimin/ 'you see us', but Algonquin /kɨwa·bmɨna·m/. The ending on verbs meaning 'we do something to you' may be either *-iko·* (which appears as /-igo·/) or *-inimin* from *-ini* + *-min*: Saulteaux /giwa·bamigo·/ 'we see you (sg.)', /gimi·nigo·m/ 'we give it to you (pl.)', but Eastern Ojibwa /gwa·bminmin/ 'we

see you (sg., pl.)', /gmi·nnimin/ 'we give it to you (sg., pl.)'. Finally, the ending on conjunct verbs meaning 'he does something to us (excl.)' may contain an *m* or not. There are several variants of each type: Saulteaux /wa·bamiyangid/ '(if) he sees us (excl.)', Pikangikum Northwestern Ojibwa /wa·bamiyaminj/.

Wolfart (1977) first suggested the value of morphological features for the classification of Ojibwa dialects, but because of a lack of adequate data from several areas his classification is inaccurate. One morphological feature that Wolfart used in his classification requires comment here. There are two endings for marking first-person object on transitive verbs in the conjunct and in those forms meaning 'you do something to me/us'. The two endings are *-i* and *-išši* (/-iži/ in Algonquin): Saulteaux /gino·ndaimin/ 'you hear us', Algonquin /kɨno·daižimin/. However, the distribution of these two endings does not always follow dialect lines. While the data are incomplete, it is known that *-išši* is used in some northern communities of both the Northwestern and Central Ojibwa dialects and throughout Severn Ojibwa, while Algonquin has the variant /-iži/ throughout. Present knowledge indicates that *-i* is used everywhere else.

One of the more obvious phonological differences among Ojibwa dialects is the different treatment of obstruent§§ consonants. While these differences are not usable as diagnostics, they are a particularly prominent

††The obviative is an inflectional category of Algonquian languages that marks one third-person referent as different from some other third-person referent in the immediate context.

‡‡The endings *-an* and *-a·* have the variants *-n* and *-·* after elements ending in vowels.

§§Obstruents are those consonants that involve a major obstruction of the airstream above the glottis (vocal cords). They include both stops like, for example, *p*, *t*, and *k* and fricatives like, for example, *f*, *s*, and *x* and their voiced counterparts, but not *m*, *n*, *l*, *r*, *y*, or *w*, etc.

Table 4. Obstruent Correspondences among Ojibwa Dialects

	p	*t*	*č*	*k*	*s*	*š*
General Ojibwa lenis obstruents not in clusters						
word initial						
Algonquin	/p/	/t/	/č/	/k/	/s/ ‘	/š/
other dialects[a]	/b/	/d/	/ǯ/	/g/	/z/	/ž/
word medial, all dialects	/b/	/d/	/ǯ/	/g/	/z/	/ž/
word final						
Ottawa	/p/	/t/	/č/	/k/	/s/	/š/
other dialects[a]	/b/	/d/	/ǯ/	/g/	/z/	/ž/
General Ojibwa fortis obstruents	*pp*	*tt*	*čč*	*kk*	*ss*	*šš*
Algonquin	/p/	/t/	/č/	/k/	/s/	/š/
Severn Ojibwa, northern Northwestern and Central Ojibwa, and some Saulteaux	/p/ [hp]	/t/ [ht]	/č/ [hč]	/k/ [hk]	/s/ [sˑ]	/š/ [šˑ]
other dialects	/p/ [pˑ]	/t/ [tˑ]	/č/ [čˑ]	/k/ [kˑ]	/s/ [sˑ]	/š/ [šˑ]

[a] Sometimes phonetically voiceless in Severn, in the northern Northwestern and Central dialects, and in Saulteaux.

part of Ojibwa dialectology. Table 4 shows the correspondences among the obstruent consonants of the various Ojibwa dialects and indicates the phonetic realization of those not obvious from the phonemic symbols.

One of the features of Ojibwa dialectology mentioned most often is the fact that there are southern dialects of Ojibwa that have lost short vowels in certain positions. The two dialects most fully affected are Ottawa and Eastern Ojibwa. The deletion arises from a system of alternating stress that still operates in other Ojibwa dialects. A short vowel is stressed when it is to the right of an unstressed vowel, for example, Southwestern Ojibwa [ɪŋgɪtˑɪmíškɪmín] 'we (excl.) are lazy'. Long vowels and the last vowel of the word are always stressed, for example, Southwestern Ojibwa [nɪníbáˑmín] 'we (excl.) are sleeping', [bóˑzɪwág] 'they embark', [níˑmɪškáˀɪgánán] 'bird's crests'. In Ottawa and Eastern Ojibwa all the unstressed vowels are lost, so next to the Southwestern Ojibwa forms [makˑízín] 'shoe', [makˑízɪnán] 'shoes', and [nɪmákˑɪzɪnán] 'my shoes', the Ottawa and Eastern Ojibwa forms are /mkizin/, /mkiznan/, and /nmakzinan/, respectively. However, the overall picture of vowel deletion in Ojibwa as a whole is more complex than this outline might indicate. First, vowel deletion in more restricted environments occurs in other Ojibwa dialects as well; unstressed vowels are lost from word-initial syllables in Central Ojibwa: /kido/ 'he says', /dbikad/ 'it is dark', /gwiškaˑ/ 'it falls over'; compare Southwestern Ojibwa [ɪkˑídó], [dɪbíkˑád], and [gawíškáˑ]. Second, even within the Ottawa and Eastern Ojibwa dialect areas, the loss of short vowels is not uniform. The Maniwaki and Golden Lake subdialects, which are linguistically Eastern Ojibwa (although their speakers call themselves Algonquin), do not show vowel deletion. And even within the region that shows vowel deletion to the fullest extent, the more northerly settlements tend to retain some trace of the deleted vowel in some environments, the most noticeable one being a labialization on velars (*k* and *kk*) and glottal

stop (*ʔ*) before a deleted *o*: Manitoulin Ottawa /aˑkʷzi/ 'he is sick', Curve Lake Eastern Ojibwa /gʷyak/ 'straight, right'. There are also age factors, older speakers retaining more vowels than younger speakers in the same settlement.

Just as in the case of Cree, the individual dialect areas of Ojibwa are not uniform throughout, and the internal complexity of various areas has led to some divergence of opinion on the grouping of subdialects into dialects. For example, Wolfart (1977) groups the subdialects in a somewhat different way. As an example of the kind of internal diversity represented by a single dialect area, the Algonquin dialect will be examined (for the people speaking this dialect, see "Northern Ojibwa," this vol.). Figures 3 and 4 show a set of isoglosses discussed in several articles documenting the subdialects of Algonquin (Daviault et al. 1978; Piggott 1978; Gilstrap 1978; Aubin 1979). This information has been supplemented by Roger Gilstrap (personal communications 1979) to fill in data that are lacking in those articles. It is clear from the maps that there is an "inner" Algonquin area, which includes the bands of Lac Simon and Grand Lac Victoria, and a "transition" area, which includes Amos (Abitibi band), Rapide Sept (Long Point band), Winneway (Long Point band), Hunter's Point, Kipawa, Notre Dame du Nord (Temiskaming band), and Rapid Lake (Barrière Lake band). All these transitional settlements share some, but not all, the distinguishing features of Lac Simon.

Shared Phonological Features in Cree and Ojibwa

In spite of the fact that Cree and Ojibwa have undergone separate development for many hundreds of years, there are a number of phonological phenomena that many dialects and subdialects of these two languages share. Most striking are four chains of phonological change that different dialects and subdialects of Cree

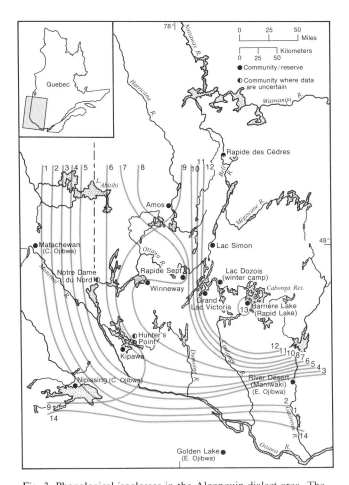

Fig. 3. Phonological isoglosses in the Algonquin-dialect area. The communities on the side of each isogloss on which the number is written have the innovation; those on the other side lack it or have it only optionally (where so indicated). 1, PA *-iwa is reflected by /-iˑ/ in nouns longer than three syllables. 2, Obstruents are devoiced in initial position. 3, Nouns ending in PA consonant plus *y have consonant plus /-iˑ/ in the singular (instead of the consonant alone). 4, Nasalized vowels are denasalized. 5, Obstruents are optionally devoiced in final position. 6, /aˑ/ is pronounced [ɔˑ] after w. 7, Clusters of nasal plus consonant lose the nasal. 8, Obstruents are obligatorily devoiced in final position (optionally for the communities between isoglosses 5 and 8). 9, PA and General Ojibwa *w is lost after a non-velar consonant. 10, General Ojibwa a and i fall together to /ɨ/ between consonants. 11, PA and General Ojibwa *w is lost intervocalically before a back vowel. 12, General Ojibwa p plus a short vowel is obligatorily lost before m. 13, /l/ is found in a few words. 14, Unstressed short vowels are lost. (1 and 3 may be morphologically rather than phonologically motivated; 13 may be a retention, but there are no clear etymologies.)

and Ojibwa participate in to different degrees. The first involves the reduction of the first-person prefix *ni-* before stops. In the first stage of this reduction the combination is reduced to a syllabic nasal plus a stop that in many of the subdialects involved becomes voiced in the process, as in Western Swampy Cree [n̩ditwaˑn] 'I say it' for phonemic /nititwaˑn/ and [m̩baˑɸin] 'I laugh' for phonemic /npaˑhpin/, the latter showing assimilation of the nasal to the point of articulation of the following consonant. In the extreme case the nasal is lost leaving

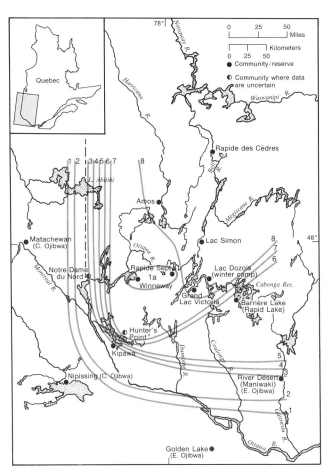

Fig. 4. Morphological isoglosses in the Algonquin-dialect area. The feature described is found in the communities on the side of each isogloss on which the number is written; the feature in parentheses (where given) is found in those on the other side. 1, Third-person conjunct ending is /-ʒ/ (rather than /-d/); 1a, both /-ʒ/ and /-d/ are found. 2, The theme sign for first-person object is /-iʒi/ (not /-i/). 3, In the animate intransitive verb the second-person plural ending is /-naˑwaˑ/ (not /-m/). 4, The locative ending added to nouns is /-ikaˑng/, or /-ikaˑg/(fig. 3, no. 7) (rather than /-ing/). 5, Inanimate nouns are inflected for obviative with the suffix /-ini/. 6, Objectless transitive inanimate verbs (like 'be sad') are inflected like regular transitive inanimate verbs in the first and second persons. 7, /-nan/ is added to the first and second persons singular of animate intransitive verbs. 8, The preverb /oʒi/ is used in the negative past.

only a voiced consonant, as in Sioux Lookout Northwestern Ojibwa [giˑweˑ] for phonemic /ngiˑweˑ/ 'I go home' next to [kiˑweˑ] for phonemic /giˑweˑ/ 'he goes home'. The second chain of phonological changes involves the loss of short vowels between consonants at the same point of articulation, such as Mistassini East Cree /nɪpmᴜhten/ 'I walk'; cf. Plains Cree /nipimohtaˑn/. In the extreme case the first consonant may also be lost, as in Lac Simon Algonquin [waˑmɨk] from /waˑbmig/ 'if I see him' next to [waˑbɨdimaˑn]/waˑbɨdimaˑn/ 'if I see it'; cf. Southwestern Ojibwa /waˑbamag/ and /waˑbandamaˑn/. The third chain of phonological changes involves the assimilation of low vowels a and aˑ to w as in Ottawa [wɒˑbɨdən] for phonemic /waˑbndang/ 'if he sees it' next to [naˑbɨdəŋ] for phonemic /naˑbndang/ 'if he sees it in a vision'. In the extreme case the assimilated vowel may be higher and the *w* may be lost as in Mistassini East Cree [nɪpihtɔn] for /nɪpihtwan/ 'I smoke'. The assimilation of *eˑ* to *w*, though rare, can also be found, as in Mistassini East Cree [miyœyhtəm] for /miyweyhtəm/ 'he likes it'. The final chain of phonological changes found in many Cree and Ojibwa areas involves the loss of semivowels and *h* or glottal stop between vowels. In some areas it is a casual speech phenomenon, for instance, in Manitoulin Ottawa, casual [giˑeˑɪn] for careful /giˑweˑyin/ '(if) you (sg.) go home'. In other areas the semivowels are lacking in all speech styles.

In each language there are dialects or subdialects displaying each stage of each chain of phonological change. Table 5 shows some examples of dialects and subdialects showing the different stages of *ni-* reduction.

Table 5.   *ni-* reduction

	unreduced	syllabic nasal	nasal lost
Cree	East Cree	W. Swampy Cree	Southern Plains Cree
Ojibwa	Algonquin	Saulteaux	southern Northwestern Ojibwa

Prehistory and History

Proto-Algonquian, the common ancestor of Cree, Ojibwa, and the other Algonquian languages, can be reconstructed using the principles developed by Bloomfield (1946). By reconstructing the Proto-Algonquian words for birds, mammals, fish, and trees according to these principles and then mapping the distribution of these species, Siebert (1967:39) concluded that the homeland of the Proto-Algonquians was in southern Ontario, conjecturally about 1200 B.C., with outward migration expanding beyond the lower Great Lakes by about 900 B.C. On the other hand, Snow (1976) postulates a much larger area for the homeland and points out that the conjectural dates are uncertain. Proto-Algonquian, like its descendants, probably had a number of dialects, two of which developed into Cree and Ojibwa. The Cree moved to the north, eventually splitting into two groups that occupied territory on either side of James Bay. The Ojibwa remained closer to the original territory. By the time of contact, the Cree had expanded both east and west. Judging from the apparent complexity of the dialect situation in the east as compared to the west, the eastward expansion is relatively old, while the westward expansion is more recent. Similarly, the Ojibwa dialects in the east reflect a longer occupation, while the westward movement must have been more recent, and the movement of Eastern Ojibwa and Ottawa into southern Ontario and the lower peninsula of Michigan is a matter of recorded history.

The reconstruction of prehistoric population movements from linguistic evidence alone is very difficult. There is reason to suspect that the ancestors of the modern Cree and Ojibwa were nomadic hunter-gatherers and, like their descendants, would range over large areas in hunting. This makes it difficult, even in the historical period, to know what it means to associate a particular group with a particular point on a map. Dialect distinctions like the ones proposed here have been described by authors from the nineteenth century, but changes in the phonology of Cree and, in some instances, the lack of crucial data, have made it impossible to correlate with certainty the reported nineteenth-century dialects with those spoken in the second half of the twentieth century. One attempt to make such a correlation can be found in Pentland (1978). But, even leaving aside the philological problems of deciphering handwritten manuscripts and untangling copyists' errors, there are still significant problems in interpreting linguistic evidence from the early historical period. The most obvious diagnostics, for example, the reflexes of PA *l* and *θ* (Lacombe 1874:xv; Michelson 1939), are not the best diagnostics for modern dialects in many cases and are therefore suspect for the historical cases. Furthermore, the first recorders of Indian languages were not trained phoneticians, and it is not always clear what crucial symbols like "r" and "l" represent phonetically. Judging from some early statements and what is known of the modern languages, it is almost certain that they do not represent simply flap [r] and [l] uniformly throughout all forms of speech recorded in the documents (Jean-Baptiste de La Brosse in Silvy 1974:xxi).

Another approach to unraveling prehistoric population movements is to look at the linguistic relationships among the modern dialects. By evaluating the similarities and differences among the modern dialects, judgments can be made regarding which groups split from which, and what the relative chronology of the splits was. As of 1980, the evidence to make such judgments for Cree and Ojibwa is very limited, but by taking as most significant the degree of mutual intelligibility and shared lexical innovations, a schematic relationship among the Ojibwa dialects can be proposed (fig. 5). In this formulation, shared morphological innovations are taken as less significant in determining the dialect relationships, and shared phonological innovations as least significant.

The most serious problem with the reconstruction of prehistoric population movements from linguistic evidence is the matter of dialect shifting, whereby one group of speakers ends up speaking a dialect different from that of their ancestors. This can render judgments from modern dialects totally useless. For example, at least as early as the first half of the eighteenth century, it is known that the population of the lower peninsula of Michigan included Ottawas, Ojibwas, and Potawatomis (H.H. Tanner 1974). But Baraga, working there in the 1830s, only needed to speak Ottawa. It wasn't until he moved to the upper peninsula of Michigan that he had to learn Ojibwa (Lambert 1967), which can be clearly identified from his writings as Southwestern Ojibwa. The problem of dialect shifting arises, then, with respect to the Ojibwas who had moved into the lower peninsula of Michigan from the north (Kinietz 1940:319). In the 1830s Baraga could speak Ottawa to them, but not to their fellow Ojibwas in the upper peninsula, and in the second half of the twentieth century, their descendants spoke Ottawa as their only Algonquian language.

The probable mechanism of this change of dialect can be worked out from current-day knowledge of Algonquian multilingualism. Even in 1980, multilingualism among the speakers of Algonquian languages is asymmetric. Some languages and dialects rank lower than others, and it is the speakers of the lower-ranking languages who learn the higher-ranking languages and not vice versa. Thus all Ojibwa-Potawatomi bilinguals are natively Potawatomi speakers; Ojibwas do not learn Potawatomi. Assuming a ranking of Ottawa over Ojibwa (presumably Southwestern Ojibwa) over Potawatomi in the lower peninsula of Michigan, it is clear how Ojibwa could have been lost as English made more and more inroads, leaving Ottawa as the only remaining Ojibwa dialect. Throughout the twentieth century Ottawa has been more vital in Michigan than Potawatomi, which, in 1980, was nearly extinct there.

A similar bilingual situation existed involving Mitchif (French Cree) at Turtle Mountain, North Dakota. Stories can still be elicited that reflect a ranking of Mitchif over Plains Cree over Ojibwa (presumably Saulteaux). This explains how the Ojibwas who moved to Turtle Mountain came to speak Mitchif rather than Ojibwa, again under the impact of English, which was the only language of those under the age of 40 there in 1980.

Descriptive Studies

Early accounts of some of the Subarctic Algonquian languages in the Northeast were produced by French missionaries in the seventeenth and eighteenth centuries. The dialects recorded include Montagnais, Algonquin, and Ottawa. Paul Le Jeune's 1634 sketch of Montagnais (JR 7:20–30) described an *r*-dialect, perhaps ancestral to the twentieth-century *l*-dialect, and two published seventeenth-century dictionaries (Fabvre 1970; Silvy 1974) provide extensive documentation of early Montagnais. Unpublished manuscripts on Montagnais, including a 1726 dictionary by Pierre Laure (Hanzeli

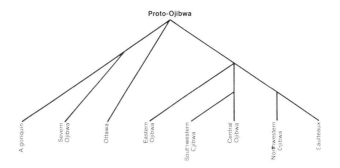

Fig. 5. Family-tree diagram of the Ojibwa dialects.

Ministry of Nat. Resources, Ont. Div. of Mines, Toronto.
Fig. 6. Rev. William Dick, a Cree missionary, in the Anglican church he founded at Trout Lake in Northern Ojibwa territory. The religious texts, including the Ten Commandments on the 2 central panels, are written in syllabics in Plains Cree, which is the liturgical language of the Anglican Northern Ojibwa although not the native language of this community. Photographer not recorded, taken 1883–1917.

1969:127), are an unexploited resource. Although there are significant problems with the transcriptions in these early works, the materials are of high quality and are very useful for historical studies. A guide to the earliest manuscripts can be found in Hanzeli (1969).

In the nineteenth century, there were numerous translations of religious materials, including the Bible and hymns (fig. 6). An exhaustive list of these materials and a description of them can be found in Pilling's (1891) bibliography. For Cree, grammatical studies were published on Moose Cree (Horden 1881), Woods Cree (Howse 1844), Plains Cree (Lacombe 1874), and *l*-dialect Montagnais (Lemoine 1901a), for which there is also a dictionary (Lemoine 1901). For Ojibwa, grammatical studies were published by Baraga (1850, 1878) on the predecessor of the Upper Peninsula subdialect of Southwestern Ojibwa and by Cuoq (1891–1892) on Algonquin (in actuality the predecessor of the modern Maniwaki subdialect of Eastern Ojibwa). Both these authors also produced dictionaries (Baraga 1853, 1878–1880; Cuoq 1886).

In the first half of the twentieth century major new descriptive linguistic studies of the Algonquian languages of the Subarctic were few, but between 1970 and 1980, a number of linguists took to the field and began producing articles, reports, glossaries, dictionaries, and grammatical studies of various dialects of Cree and Ojibwa. The University of Montreal, under the auspices of the Ministère d'Education de Québec, undertook a large project to describe the Cree dialects of Quebec. Ford et al. (1978) is an early product of this effort. The Summer Institute of Linguistics in 1980 had field workers in all the Cree dialects of Quebec and in the Algonquin dialect of Ojibwa. These linguists are a particularly valuable resource because of their continuing close contact with the speakers of the languages they work in.

Language Use

The survival and vigor of the Subarctic Algonquian languages can be attributed to the degree of isolation of the people. A 1960–1962 study of remote communities where the Severn dialect was spoken (Todd 1970) found that Ojibwa was the language of the home, most adults over 50 were monolingual (especially women), and children often did not learn English until they went to school. In contrast, a later survey of Walpole Island, on the Saint Clair River delta (L. White 1978), showed that Ojibwa (Ottawa dialect) was used regularly in only about 25 percent of the homes, and then only among adults. While 50 percent of the population said they they spoke Ojibwa regularly, the youngest fluent speakers in 1980 were in their thirties, and there were only four or five elderly monolinguals.

Bilingual Cree and Ojibwa speakers generally have English as their second language including those in areas in western Quebec in which the Hudson's Bay Company operates, although French is the second language throughout the rest of Quebec. There have been no formal studies of bilingualism involving Cree or Ojibwa and English or French.

Literacy in the native language is found in the older generation among the Cree and among the Ojibwa of northwestern Ontario. Adults read and write (fig. 7) using one of the variants of the syllabic writing system developed by James Evans, called syllabics. The basic system involves a set of characters, the form of which

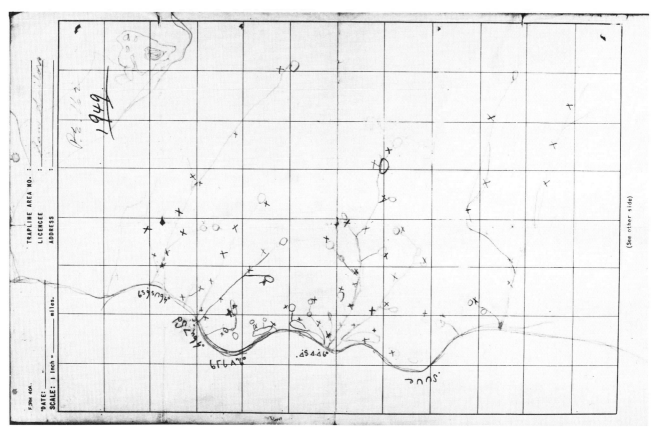

Fig. 7. Map of his trapping territory drawn and labeled by Sam Sailor in 1949 on an application for renewal of his trapping license. North is at bottom, with Kesagami Lake at upper left and the James Bay coast just east of the mouth of the Moose River across the bottom. Circles indicate lakes or beaver ponds, Xs probably beaver houses; coastal points are named in Cree syllabics (here strengthened by retouching), with Netitisiy Point at right. Collected by David H. Pentland at Moose Factory, summer 1973.

62

represents a consonant, and the orientation of which indicates the following vowel (fig. 8). Proponents of this system of writing claim that it is relatively easy to learn and those who know it prefer it to a Roman orthography; however, this may be because the writer is not forced to distinguish between long and short vowels or to write preconsonantal *h*—the very points that are the hardest for beginning writers of Cree and Ojibwa to master. Also, the existence of a special alphabet for the native language clearly has sociological significance. Modifications of the syllabic system have been introduced to accommodate differences among the various dialects of Cree and Ojibwa, and there are two main variants, Eastern and Western, which differ mainly in how *w* and word-final consonants are indicated, and a large number of local and personal modified and mixed varieties.

For the most part the literature that has been available in syllabic printing has been religious literature. Among the Cree especially, this has given syllabics a certain prestige. But syllabics are also used for practical purposes such as grocery lists, advertisements (fig. 9), and correspondence.

During the late 1960s and the early 1970s there was an increased use of syllabics in newspapers and educational materials prepared for native people, and the burst of linguistic interest in Cree and Ojibwa in the late 1970s produced materials, mostly in Roman orthographies, for popular consumption. Because of the expense involved in typing and printing syllabics, various proposals for standard Roman orthographies have been put forward, but the issue of exactly which orthography to use was in 1980 an emotional one. It appeared that in the areas in which the languages had the greatest vitality, syllabics were preferred, while in the areas in which the languages were dying, Roman orthographies were preferred. The impact of teacher training programs, many of which use Roman orthographies, cannot be overlooked for their influence in this matter.

By 1980 no standard Roman orthography for all dialects of either Cree or Ojibwa had emerged. For the dialects of Western Cree, Plains Cree had some prestige, and Ellis's (1970) orthography (based on Bloomfield's work) may possibly become standard, but the presence of French as the dominant language in the Attikamek region made the French-based orthography in use by the Summer Institute of Linguistics workers preferable to the native people there. In the Eastern Cree dialects the situation was less clear. The publication of a substantial Montagnais-French dictionary (Mailhot and Lescop 1977), in a French-based orthography standardized to eliminate subdialectal variation, may well have settled the issue, at least for Montagnais.

Among the Ojibwa, there are numerous different orthographies in use, most of them for teaching purposes, but some appearing in religious literature. A

Consonant	Vowels				Finals	
	e	i/ii	o/oo	a/aa	West	East
none/h/ʔ	▽	△	▷	◁	‖ h	‖ h △ ʔ
w (West)	▽•	△•	▷•	◁•	o	
(East)	•▽	•△	•▷	•◁		o‖ or •△
p	∨	∧	>	<	ı	< ∧
t	∪	∩	⊃	⊂	∕	c ∩
m	˥	Γ	⌐	L	c	L Γ
c	˥	ɼ	J	∪	–	ʃ ˞
k	˥	P	d	ƅ	\	σ ˞
y	⊰	⊱	⊲	⊳	°	ˊ ˎ
s	ヽ	ʼ	ノ	﹨	∩	△ o ˤ
n	⊙	σ	⌓	Ω	⊃	d ˙
š	⌒	ʃ	ↄ	⌣	∪	J ˥
l (West)	{▽	{△	{▷	{◁	{	
(East)	⊃	c	⊅	⊂		⊾
r (West)	⟨▽	⟨△	⟨▷	⟨◁	⟨	
(East)	⟍	⌓	P	ˤ		ˢ
					ˢ	sk ˢ
					×	hk

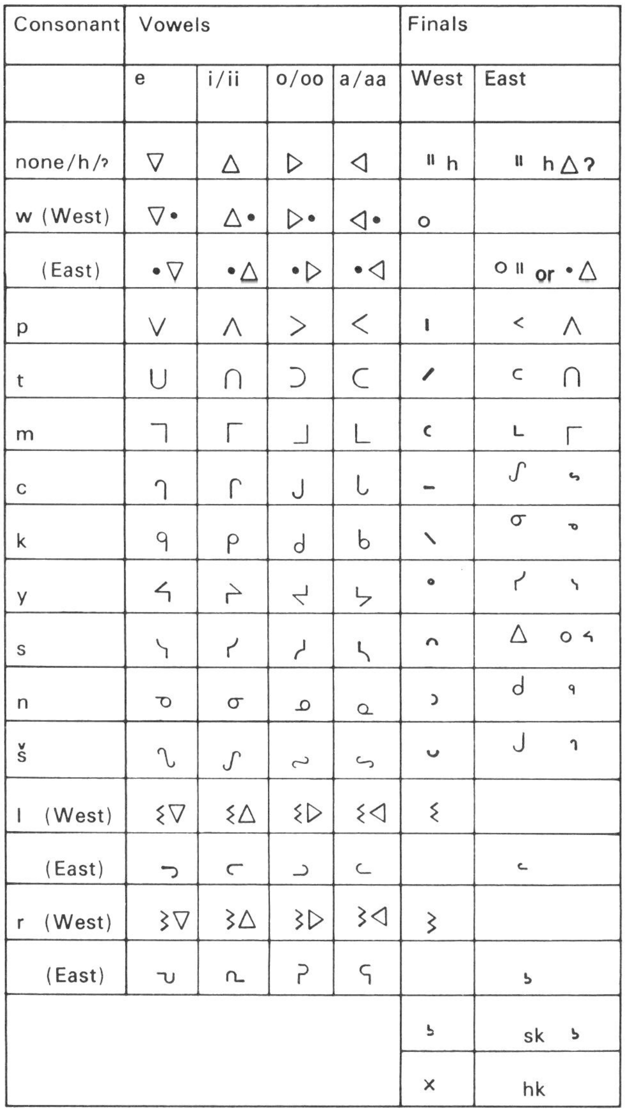

Fig. 8. Cree and Ojibwa syllabics. This way of writing, often called "Cree syllabics," was originally invented for the Ojibwa language by the Rev. James Evans in the 1830s (Burwash 1912; John D. Nichols, communication to editors 1980), but Cree was the first language that syllabics were used to print books in. In the twentieth century syllabics have been used by many speakers of Ojibwa and Cree in Canada and have been adapted for speakers of other native languages including Eskimo and Athapaskan.

chart of the six most prevalent orthographies prepared by John Nichols of the Wisconsin Native American Languages Project is given in table 6. The Fiero (Minnesota) system is gaining in popularity because of its use in the Native Language Teacher Training program in Ontario and in the Ojibwa language courses at Bemidji State University, Minnesota, and at the University of Michigan, and because of its use in the practical glossary of the Southwestern dialect (Nichols and Nyholm 1979) and in the popular *Anishinaabe Giigidowin*, a newsletter for Ojibwa and Potawatomi second-language teachers published quarterly since 1976. For proposals on writing systems, including syllabics, see

Denny and Odjig (1972), Fiero (1967), Jones and Todd (1971), and Todd (1972).

Because both Cree and Ojibwa are dying languages in some areas, there has been an effort on the part of the native people to preserve the languages by developing, or asking to have developed, programs to teach Cree and Ojibwa in the schools (fig. 10). Such programs have arisen throughout the Cree and Ojibwa area at all levels from kindergarten through college. Because of the lack of adequately trained native speakers, programs have been started in the five relevant Canadian provinces to train native-speaking teachers and teachers' aides to prepare materials and teach the native language to English-speaking children. These programs, for example, those of La Macaza in Quebec and the Native Language Teacher Training program in Ontario, have produced a number of speakers of Cree and Ojibwa with a modest amount of linguistic sophistication. In addition, various dialects of Cree and Ojibwa are taught at several colleges and universities as a regular part of the curriculum. These include the University of Alberta, Edmonton; Bemidji State University, Minnesota; Brandon University, Brandon, Manitoba; University of Calgary, Alberta; Cornell University, Ithaca, New York; Lakehead University, Thunder Bay, Ontario; University of Manitoba, Winnipeg; Memorial University of Newfoundland, Saint John's; University of Michigan; University of Minnesota; Northland College, Ashland, Wisconsin; University of Regina, Saskatchewan; University of Saskatchewan, Saskatoon; and Trent University, Peterborough, Ontario.

Synonymy

There is some confusion about the names of different groups of speakers of Cree and Ojibwa. Government documents list groups by officially assigned band names, while linguists and anthropologists tend to list groups by the name of their settlement and their language affiliation or cultural affiliation. On the other hand, the speakers themselves tend to call themselves by their ancestral affiliation or by political affiliations. The differences between band names and other names are too numerous to mention, but the settlement name can generally be identified with a band name by consulting a map. The matter of political names is more difficult. There are two regions in which the linguistic facts run contrary to the names that particular groups use to refer to themselves. In the Severn dialect of Ojibwa, two northwestern bands, the Big Trout Lake band and the Deer Lake band, call themselves Cree. In the Eastern Ojibwa dialect, the River Desert band, settled at Maniwaki, and the Golden Lake band both call themselves Algonquins but align linguistically with Eastern Ojibwa.

In the technical literature there are a number of dif-

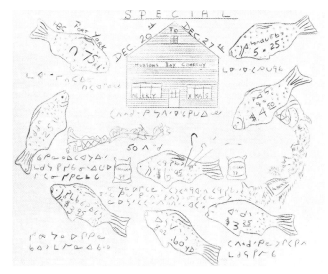

Hudson's Bay Company Lib., Winnipeg, Man.
Fig. 9. A handbill in western Cree syllabics issued at Christmas time in northern Manitoba to advertise Hudson's Bay Company items such as tea, pork, and flour at bargain prices. About 400 of these flyers are said to have been printed and delivered by dog team to nearby Indian camps. Issued in the 1930s by A.W. Scott, a trader at the Island Lake post.

Fig. 10. Two pages from the booklet *Table Talk* (White et al. 1977), an example of language learning materials produced by the Walpole Native Languages Centre; Ottawa dialect written in the local version of the Fiero (Minnesota) orthography. The words given are /ni·bi·ša·bo·na·ga·ns/ (General Ojibwa transcription *ani·pi·šša·po·na·ka·nss*) 'tea-cup'; /dbo·skna·gan/ (*tipo·skina·kan*) 'bowl'; and /zgakna·gne·n/ (*sakakkina·kane·n*) 'Put the dishes away!'. Although the Walpole orthography is designed not to write the vowels deleted in Ottawa, the second and third words show inconsistent writing of some deleted vowels, probably under the influence of materials from other dialects that do not have this deletion.

ferent names for the same groups of both Cree and Ojibwa speakers. Perhaps the most extreme example of alternate (and misleading) names for a single group of speakers involves the Ottawa dialect of Ojibwa. This dialect has been referred to in the linguistic literature

Table 6. Comparative Ojibwa Writing Systems

Fiero (Minnesota)[a]	Baraga[b]	Bloomfield[c]	Fiero (Berens)[d]	Wilson[e]	Traditional[f] (English-Based)
p	p	pp	hp	p	p
b	p-, b-, b	p	p	p-, p, b	b
t	t	tt	ht	t	t
d	t-, d-, d	t	t	t-, d-, t, d	d
ch	tch	cc	hc	ch	ch, tch
j	tch-, dj	c	c	ch-, j, jj	j, dj, g, gg
k	k	kk	hk	k	k
kw	kw	kkw	hkw	qu	qu, qw, kw
g	k-, g-, g	k	k	k-, k, g	g
s	ss	ss	hs	s	s, ss
z	s	s	s	s-, s, z	z, s
sh	sh	šš	hš	sh	sh, sch
zh	j	š	š	sh-, sh, zh	zh, szh, sh, j
m	m	m	m	m	m
n	n	n	n	n	n
w	w	w	w	w	w, u
y	i	y	y	y	y, i
'	not shown	ʾ	ʾ	not shown	h, not shown
h	h	h	h	h	h
a	a	a [e,u]	a	uh, u	a, uh, u, ah, o
aa	a, â	a·	aa	ah, au	a, ah, au, aw, ou, o
e	e, é	e·	e	a	ay, e, a, ey
i	i	i [e,u]	i	e, i	i, e, y, ee
ii	i	i·	ii	ee, e	ee, i, ei
o	o	o [u]	o	o, oo	o, oo, ou
oo	o, ô	o·	oo	o, oo	o, oo, ou, oh

[a] From Fiero (1965). Nasal vowels are marked with a hook (ˎ). This writing system was adopted for use in lesson materials of the Wisconsin Native American Languages Project. A variant of this system with a macron (ˉ) over single vowels to mark the long vowels has been used by Delisle (1970), Snook et al. (1972), and Nichols (1973).

[b] From Baraga (1878–1880). Nasal vowels are not written differently from non-nasal vowels. An early version of this system with some accented vowels (most of them long) marked with ´, the long vowel of the first person conjunct suffix marked with `, and many nasal vowels marked with ^, appeared in Baraga (1850). The Baraga system was used (with some long vowels marked by ˉ) in Verwyst (1901). Much Catholic devotional literature also used this system.

[c] From Bloomfield (1957). In this system, the standard system for linguists, a final nasal vowel is shown by placing a tilde (˜) after it. Other vowels are nasal before combinations of *nʾ* and *ny*. The short vowels *a* and *i* become *e* or *u* and the short vowel *o* becomes *u* in certain positions within the word.

[d] From Quill (1965). Also used in Fiero and Quill (1973). Nasal vowels do not occur except for those in front of nasal-sibilant clusters. Developed for the Pikangikum (Berens River) subdialect of the Northwestern dialect.

[e] From E.F. Wilson (1874). This writing system is somewhat inconsistent and is not recommended for use.

[f] The equivalents given here are drawn from a variety of word lists and phrase books written by both speakers of the language and nonspeakers. These writing systems are not regular or consistent and only some of the possibilities can be indicated here. There are other, somewhat more consistent, traditional systems, but they are no longer in circulation in Wisconsin and Minnesota. A common characteristic of English-based systems is the writing of the diminutive suffix on nouns as *-ance* or *-aynce*.

as: Ojibway (Holmer 1953), Odawa (Kaye, Piggott, and Tokaichi 1971; Piggott and Kaye 1973), Central Ojibwa-Odawa (Rhodes 1976), and Eastern Ojibwa (Bloomfield 1957).

Because of the significance of Bloomfield's work on Ottawa, it is worth mentioning how he came to call it Eastern Ojibwa. Andrew Medler, who was Bloomfield's sole informant, came from a Chippewa family, but the language he spoke was Ottawa. This conclusion has been confirmed by those who knew him and by Volney Jones (personal communication 1979), who arranged for Medler to come to the 1938 Linguistic Institute at which Bloomfield gathered data from him. Moreover, it is demonstrated by the Ottawa features in Medler's speech (Rhodes 1976) and supported by the observation that in the 1970s Ottawa was the socially dominant dialect both on Walpole Island, where Medler lived in the 1930s, and on the lower peninsula of Michigan, where he had been reared. But because his ancestral affiliation was Chippewa, he called the language he spoke Chippewa, though he later confessed uncertainty about the proper name (Carl F. Voegelin, communication to editors 1978). Bloomfield took Ojibwa to be a more technically correct name for Chippewa and arrived at the designation Eastern Ojibwa. It should be pointed out, though, that Medler did have a number of Eastern Ojibwa features in his speech, as is common on Walpole Island, where many speakers are from Chippewa families.

Another dialect that shows some confusion of names in the technical literature is the Cree dialect here called East Cree. Aside from the substantive issue of whether East Cree and Naskapi constitute one or two dialects (MacKenzie 1977, 1979), the names East Cree, James Bay Cree, and even Western Montagnais (Pentland 1978) have been used to designate these groups of speakers.

The final type of confusion of names in the technical literature arises from anthropological usage in contrast to linguistic usage. For example, J.G.E. Smith (1976a, "Western Woods Cree," this vol.) divides the Cree west of James Bay and Hudson Bay into two groups, Woods and Plains, based on the type of land they inhabit. However, his labels divide the speakers of Plains Cree, designating those in the south as Plains Cree, and those in the north as Woods Cree. For him, the term Woods Cree encompasses, in addition to the speakers of northern Plains Cree, the speakers of Woods Cree and of the two dialects of Swampy Cree.

One final comment about the name Ojibwa is in order. There are two variants of this name, Ojibwa and Chippewa. Ojibwa is the Canadian term (generally spelled Ojibway); Chippewa is the American term. Since there are Ojibwa families in Canada who were moved there from the United States in the late nineteenth century but who still call themselves Chippewa, this terminological distinction must have existed since at least that time. In particular, the Ojibwas in the settlements along the Saint Clair River in southern Ontario call themselves Chippewa, if they come from Ojibwa families. Recognition of this historical distinction clarifies a number of naming difficulties that arise in the Ottawa dialect area. Many speakers of this dialect are the descendants of Ojibwas rather than Ottawas. Depending on the settlement history of a particular area, the people will say that they speak a combination of Ottawa and Ojibwa, or Ottawa and Chippewa, or even a combination of Ojibwa and Chippewa. While such comments are often taken lightly by linguists, they are not without linguistic significance.

Northern Athapaskan Languages

MICHAEL E. KRAUSS AND VICTOR K. GOLLA

The 23 languages described in this chapter form a recognized geographical subdivision of the Athapaskan* language family, usually referred to as Northern Athapaskan. They occupy a large, continuous area, mostly in the subarctic interior of Alaska and western Canada, but extending south onto the plains to include the Sarcee of southern Alberta. The Northern Athapaskan group includes the majority of the attested Athapaskan languages.

The other Athapaskan languages are found in smaller clusters in several diverse regions to the south. Various external factors (including the poor attestation of extinct forms of speech) make it difficult to enumerate the languages of these areas according to the same criteria as those used for the Northern group, and the numbers given here are approximate. Pacific Coast Athapaskan is a group of eight languages spoken by riverine tribes in Oregon and California: Upper Umpqua, Tututni–Chasta Costa, Galice-Applegate, and Chetco-Tolowa in southwestern Oregon and the immediately adjacent coast of northern California; Hupa, Mattole, Sinkyone-Wailaki, and Cahto in northwestern California. Kwalhioqua-Tlatskanai was a single language, now extinct, spoken near the mouth of the Columbia River in small enclaves on both the Washington and Oregon sides. The Apachean languages are a group of seven, spoken by tribes in the circum-Pueblo Southwest (Chiricahua, Jicarilla, Mescalero, Navajo, and Western Apache) and on the adjacent Plains (Kiowa-Apache and Lipan).

The Athapaskan family is one branch of a larger genetic grouping, Athapaskan-Eyak, the only other attested branch of which is Eyak, a single language, in 1980 nearly extinct, spoken on the south coast of Alaska near the mouth of Copper River (Krauss 1964–1965, 2, 1973:932–935). Tlingit, a single language spoken across a wide territory along the Alaska panhandle with but moderate dialect differences, bears a close resemblance to Athapaskan-Eyak in phonology and grammatical structure but shows little regular correspondence in vocabulary (Krauss 1969). Sapir (1915) believed he had sufficient evidence to demonstrate a genetic relationship between Tlingit and Athapaskan—no Eyak

*Athabaskan is the spelling preferred by the Alaska Native Language Center, since it reflects more directly the usual American English pronunciation (ˌăθəˈbăskən).

data were known to him at the time—and further claimed that Haida, spoken on the Queen Charlotte Islands to the south of the Tlingit area, was also part of this genetic group, which he named Na-Dene. Later work on Haida (Levine 1977; Lawrence and Leer 1977) has cast serious doubt on Sapir's interpretation of the Haida evidence, and most scholars concerned with the matter now consider Na-Dene to be an untenable hypothesis (Levine 1979; Krauss 1979). However, the nature of the relationship between Athapaskan-Eyak and Tlingit remains an open question (see Pinnow 1976 for a survey of research). While comparative work is hampered by the relative lack of regularly corresponding cognate lexicon, the close similarities between Tlingit and Athapaskan-Eyak verb morphology, in particular, clearly require a historical explanation. Krauss (1973:953–963, 1979) has suggested the possibility of Tlingit being a "hybrid" between Athapaskan-Eyak and an unrelated stock.

Prehistory

Archeologists working with Sapir's partly discredited Na-Dene hypothesis have suggested a correlation between "Na-Dene"–speaking groups and the early spread of the Northwest Microblade tradition in North America (Borden 1975; Dumond 1969, 1974; Carlson 1979). Bearers of the Northwest Microblade tradition were present in Beringia in the terminal Pleistocene and expanded east and south into large areas of Alaska and northwestern Canada by 5000–4000 B.C. If Tlingit is indeed related genetically to Athapaskan-Eyak, the time of their split could perhaps be correlated with the earliest appearance of distinctive Coastal and Interior subtraditions within the Northwest Microblade tradition, not long after 4000 B.C., and the tradition as a whole correlated with the entry of a hypothetical Proto-Athapaskan-Eyak-Tlingit into North America. Incomplete understanding of the relationship between Tlingit and Athapaskan-Eyak makes this highly speculative.

Any reconstruction of the history of Tlingit must take into account the distribution of Tlingit dialects, which are more deeply differentiated in the south than in the north, indicating a northward expansion, perhaps in fairly recent times. Indeed, Tlingit expansion into Eyak

67

territory near Yakutat was still taking place in the historical period. There may not be, then, any long association between Tlingit and coastal archeological traditions in the northern part of modern Tlingit territory. Further, the area of the earliest historical connection between Tlingit and Athapaskan-Eyak, whatever the nature of this connection, must probably be placed in far southern Alaska, or perhaps even British Columbia.

Proto-Athapaskan (PA) and Proto-Eyak, which must have become differentiated from one another by about 1500 B.C. (Krauss 1973:953), were clearly languages of interior-oriented peoples. The distribution of the Athapaskan languages certainly indicates an interior origin; among the Northern Athapaskans only the Tanaina occupied any significant area of coastline. The Eyak, despite their coastal location in the historical period (around Copper River in the twentieth century, somewhat farther to the southeast—from Yakutat to Controller Bay—in the nineteenth century), had a land-based economy and, unlike the Eskimo or Tlingit, never became sea mammal hunters. Wherever it occurred, the linguistic split between Proto-Athapaskan and Proto-Eyak was apparently followed by a total cessation of communication between the groups, for there is no evidence of subsequent linguistic interinfluence. Eyak is, surprisingly, no closer linguistically to its modern Athapaskan neighbor, Ahtna, than it is to Navajo.

The degree of diversity within Athapaskan indicates that Proto-Athapaskan was still an undifferentiated linguistic unit until 500 B.C. or later (Krauss 1973:953). The location of this language was almost certainly somewhere in present-day Northern Athapaskan territory; exactly where is difficult to determine, but some areas seem more probable than others. The areas of greatest (and hence oldest) differentiation in Northern Athapaskan are in the interior of Alaska, the Yukon, and parts of British Columbia. An argument against a central or western Alaskan homeland is the lack of old or intense influence from Eskimo in the languages of that area: Eskimo influence is readily apparent in Athapaskan languages such as Ingalik and Tanaina, which are adjacent to Yupik, but it is virtually absent elsewhere. Since both external connections of Athapaskan, Eyak and Tlingit, are in southeastern Alaska, it seems most likely that the Proto-Athapaskan homeland was in eastern interior Alaska, the upper drainage of the Yukon River, and northern British Columbia, or some part of this area.

The earliest directions of Athapaskan expansion were probably westward farther into Alaska and southward along the interior mountains into central and southern British Columbia. The isolated Pacific Coast Athapaskan languages appear to have been an offshoot from the British Columbia languages, as was Kwalhioqua-Tlatskanai. The degree of differentiation among the more isolated languages indicates that these intermontane and coastal migrations took place for the most part before A.D. 500. At a subsequent period two other Athapaskan expansions occurred. One was eastward into the Mackenzie River drainage and beyond to Hudson Bay; the other was south along the eastern Rockies into the Southwest. These two later movements may have been connected. The Apachean languages of the Southwest appear to have their closest linguistic ties in the North with Sarcee, in Alberta, rather than with Chilcotin or the other languages of British Columbia; however, it is not likely that this is evidence for the Apacheans having moved southward through the High Plains, as some have suggested. The Sarcee in the north, like the Lipan and Kiowa-Apache in the Southwest, are known to have moved onto the Plains in the early historical period from a location much closer to the mountains.

Subgroups, Languages, and Dialects

Attempts to classify the Athapaskan languages into historically meaningful linguistic subgroups have not met with success (see particularly Hoijer 1963 and the criticism in Krauss 1973:943–950). The effort has been hampered to some extent by the lack of good comparative data, but the principal difficulty arises from the fact that Athapaskan linguistic relationships, especially in the subarctic area, cannot be adequately described in terms of discrete family-tree branches. This is because intergroup communication has ordinarily been constant, and no Northern Athapaskan language or dialect was ever completely isolated from the others for long. The most important differences among Athapaskan languages are generally the result of areal diffusion of separate innovations from different points of origin, each language—each community—being a unique conglomerate. Figures 1–2 illustrate the overlapping areal distributions of some representative phonological and morphological innovations in Northern Athapaskan. A geographically isolated group of languages such as Pacific Coast Athapaskan or Apachean can perhaps be treated as a historical unit, but for Northern Athapaskan it is relatively useless to search for the kinds of extensive correlations of phonological, morphological, or lexical features that allow the establishment of a "subgroup" with an assumed common prototype. Between Northern Athapaskan as a whole and the band or community dialects that are its fundamental sociolinguistic units the only useful larger categories are languages, and even these are sometimes arbitrary.

Northern Athapaskan will be treated here as an assemblage of 23 languages. In defining these, several criteria have been applied in a fairly consistent way: strictly linguistic criteria, for the most part differences in the development of the Proto-Athapaskan sound system; sociolinguistic criteria, particularly the ease or difficulty with which speakers from different communities naturally understand—or have learned to understand or profess to understand—each other's speech; and practical and historical criteria, such as the existence of an orthography and teaching materials or some other symbol of a common linguistic tradition, including a name for the language. In striving to attain consistency of definition it has been necessary both to split groups that have previously been considered single languages (for example, Tanacross and Lower Tanana, Babine and Carrier) and to reduce the status of some others from independent languages to dialects of a larger language (Slavey, Bearlake, Mountain, and Hare). In general, previous discussions of Northern Athapaskan languages (Osgood 1936; Hoijer 1963) have relied on a much narrower selection of criteria than that available in 1980.

Whatever the language boundaries, the network of communication in the Northern Athapaskan dialect complex is open-ended. It is probably worth noting that, even in 1980, perhaps most Northern Athapaskans live with only other Athapaskan speakers as neighbors and rarely hear a native language that is not Athapaskan. People from adjacent communities usually expect to be able to understand one another's speech, if not immediately then surely after some practice. Local dialects and languages are important as symbols of social identity, but the native expectation that these differences, even across relatively vast distances, will not be barriers to communication gives the Northern Athapaskan speaker a distinctively open and flexible perception of his social world.

Historical Phonology

Athapaskan words fall into three morphological classes: particles, nouns, and verbs. Particles are usually single morphemes, sometimes compounded. Nouns (speaking only of the morphological class, and excluding the large number of nominalized verbs or verbal phrases that function syntactically as nouns in every Athapaskan language) are also single morphemes for the most part, but unlike particles they can be inflected; nominal inflection consists of a paradigm of possessive prefixes. Verbs, by contrast, are usually quite complex, consisting of a stem morpheme preceded by one or more (often several) prefixes that mark various inflectional and derivational categories. Verb stems, uninflected nouns, and particle morphemes together comprise the phonological class of stems. Stem phonology is the focus of most discussion of the Athapaskan sound system. (For the phonetic values of the symbols used, see p. x and the orthographic footnotes in the respective chapters, this vol.)

The Athapaskan stem normally takes the form CV(C), that is, begins with a single consonant, has a single vowel, and sometimes but not always has a final consonant. Some examples from various Northern Athapaskan languages are: Chipewyan *θe* 'stone', *cez* 'firewood', *-zən* 'black'; Kutchin (Western dialect) *ki·* 'stone', *ca* 'firewood', *-ẓąi̯* 'black'; Ingalik *θa* 'stone', *cəc* 'firewood', *-zəŋ* 'black'.

The Proto-Athapaskan stem-initial consonants[†] are reconstructed as in table 1. The reconstructed obstruents (all the reconstructed consonants except for *w, *$\bar{w}$, *y, *$\bar{y}$, and *n) can be grouped into nine series according to point of articulation and certain other features. In the development of the Proto-Athapaskan sound system in the various languages it is quite common for two or more series to merge as whole units. Much less common is the merger of two or more consonants within a series. A consonant series in Proto-Athapaskan or in a particular language will be referred to simply by citing the aspirated stop or affricate of that series, as is the usual practice in Athapaskanist literature: PA *t (for PA *d, *t, and *t'; Chipewyan *$\hat{\theta}$ (for Chipewyan *$\hat{\delta}$, *$\hat{\theta}$, *$\hat{\theta}$, *θ, and *δ).

Table 2 shows the usual reflexes in the Northern Athapaskan languages of the five obstruent series that have the most diverse developments. These were the series whose development Hoijer (1963) considered diagnostic of the major subgroups within the family.[‡] As can be seen from table 2, different reflexes of these five series often serve to demarcate languages, but the fact that these represent areal interinfluences rather than deep phonological characteristics of a language or group of languages is apparent from a situation such as Tahltan, Kaska, and Tagish, where three dialects of nearly identical grammars and vocabularies nevertheless show three different patterns of series mergers.

The PA vowels are shown in table 3 with their commonest reflexes in Northern Athapaskan. Four full (or long) vowels are reconstructed, and three reduced (or short) vowels. In some languages the PA vowel system is fairly well preserved; in others, particularly where final consonants are reduced or lost, the original pattern is sometimes greatly altered by the introduction of secondary vowels and diphthongs (as in Kutchin). It is hypothesized that PA vowels occurred both with and without a feature identified as glottal constriction (*$\dot{v}$ versus *v). In some languages this feature is lost; in others the constricted/nonconstricted contrast develops into a phonemic tone system, with constricted vowels

† The major differences between the PA reconstructions here and in Krauss 1964 are that the series reconstructed in Krauss 1964–1965,1 as *$\underline{k}^w$ is symbolized here, more accurately, as *$\check{c}^w$ (Krauss 1980), and that voiced fricatives are again posited, with at least allophonic status. Two new sonorants are also included, tentatively reconstructed *$\bar{y}$ and *$\bar{w}$ (but possibly *$ŋ$ and *m, respectively).

‡ Hoijer actually used only 4 PA series, including under PA *$\check{c}$ the reflexes of both *$\check{c}^w$ and *$\check{c}$ as currently reconstructed.

69

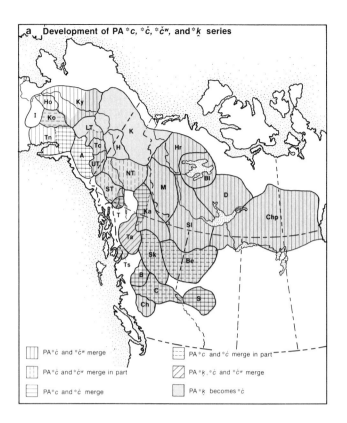

a Development of PA *c̓, *c̄, *c̄ʷ, and *k̲ series

	PA *c̄ and *c̄ʷ merge		PA *c̄ and *c̓ merge in part
	PA *c̄ and *c̄ʷ merge in part		PA *k̲, *c̓ and *c̄ʷ merge
	PA *c̄ and *c̓ merge		PA *k̲ becomes *c̓

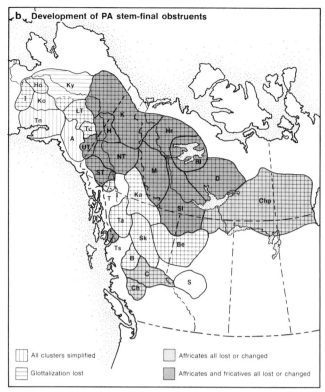

b Development of PA stem-final obstruents

| | All clusters simplified | | Affricates all lost or changed |
| | Glottalization lost | | Affricates and fricatives all lost or changed |

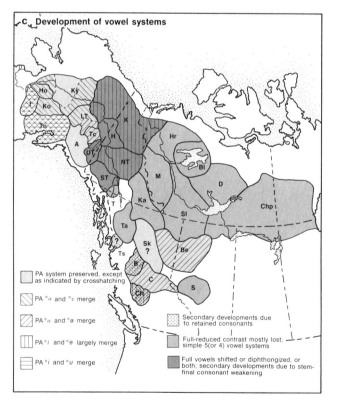

c Development of vowel systems

	PA system preserved, except as indicated by crosshatching
	PA *a and *u merge
	PA *a and *ə merge
	PA *i and *e largely merge
	PA *i and *u merge
	Secondary developments due to retained consonants
	Full-reduced contrast mostly lost; simple 5(or 4) vowel systems
	Full vowels shifted or diphthongized, or both; secondary developments due to stem-final consonant weakening

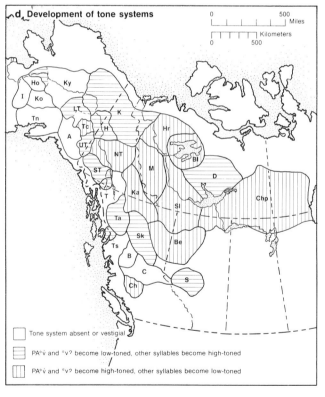

d Development of tone systems

	Tone system absent or vestigial
	PA *v́ and *vʔ become low-toned, other syllables become high-toned
	PA *v́ and *vʔ become high-toned, other syllables become low-toned

Fig. 1. Areal distribution of major phonological developments in the Northern Athapaskan languages. a–c show the overlapping of innovations; d shows the discontinuous distribution of shared innovations. Key to abbreviations: A, Ahtna; B, Babine; Be, Beaver; Bl, Bearlake; C, Carrier; Ch, Chilcotin; Chp, Chipewyan; D, Dogrib; H, Han; Ho, Holikachuk; Hr, Hare; I, Ingalik; K, Kutchin; Ka, Kaska; Ko, Kolchan (Upper Kuskokwim); Ky, Koyukon; LT, Lower Tanana; M, Mountain; NT, Northern Tutchone; S, Sarcee; Sk, Sekani; Sl, Slavey; ST, Southern Tutchone; T, Tagish; Ta, Tahltan; Tc, Tanacross; Tn, Tanaina; Ts, Tsetsaut; UT, Upper Tanana.

70

KRAUSS AND GOLLA

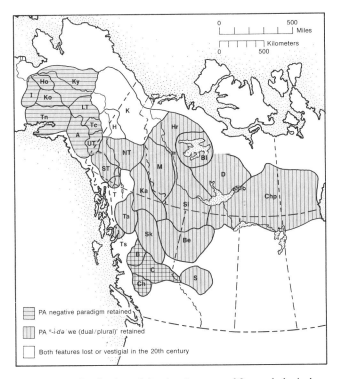

Fig. 2. Areal distribution of the development of 2 morphological categories in the Northern Athapaskan languages. For key to abbreviations see figure 1.

becoming high-toned and nonconstricted vowels low-toned, or vice versa. Tone systems have developed in at least 14 Northern Athapaskan languages. In the remaining 9 tone has either never developed or it has developed and been lost (leaving vestiges in some).

The stem-final consonants reconstructed for PA include most, but not all, of the stem-initial consonants (in stem-final position there is no evidence of contrast between aspirated and unaspirated stops and affricates). The further reduction of phonemic contrasts in stem-final position seems to be a general trend within Athapaskan, with few exceptions. As noted above, the severe reduction of stem-final contrasts (as in Kutchin) is sometimes accompanied by a drastic restructuring of the vowel system.

Northern Athapaskan Languages

Most of the 23 Northern Athapaskan languages are still spoken in 1980 in at least one community. Only Tsetsaut is extinct. Some, such as Dogrib, are actually gaining speakers. Table 4 shows the estimated numbers of speakers of Northern Athapaskan languages in 1979, as well as the viability status of language—the extent to which it is being passed on to the younger generation. A language is called viable when it is spoken by most children in most communities as their first language. A language whose status is precarious is spoken by only some children, usually in remote conservative villages. A moribund language has generally ceased to be learned by children, and without a reversal of this trend it will become extinct in a generation or two.

Ahtna

Essentially the language of the Copper River Indians, Ahtna is spoken at four villages or village clusters along that river in south-central Alaska: Chitina-Tonsina, Copper Center–Tazlina–Glennallen, Gulkana-Gakona, and Chistochina. It is also spoken at Mentasta and

Table 1. Proto-Athapaskan Consonants

	Stops or Affricates			Fricatives	
	Unaspirated	*Aspirated*	*Glottalized*	*Voiceless*	*Voiced*
Obstruent Series					
Dental stop	d	t	t'	—	—
Lateral	λ	$\check{\lambda}$	$\dot{\lambda}$	$\dagger$	l
Dental affricate and fricative	$\mathfrak{z}$	c	$\dot{c}$	s	z
Palatal	$\check{\mathfrak{z}}$	$\check{c}$	$\check{c}'$	$\check{s}$	$\check{z}$
Labialized palatal	$\check{\mathfrak{z}}^w$	$\check{c}^w$	$\check{c}'^w$	$\check{s}^w$	$\check{z}^w$
Front velar	$\hat{g}$	$\underline{k}$	$\underline{k}'$	$\underline{x}$	$\hat{\gamma}$
Back velar	$\dot{g}$	q	$\dot{q}$	x	$\dot{\gamma}$
Labialized back velar	$\dot{g}^w$	q^w	$\dot{q}^w$	x^w	$\dot{\gamma}^w$
Laryngeal	$\mathfrak{z}$	—	—	h	—
Sonorants					
Dental nasal	n				
Semivowels					
Rounded	w				
Nasalized	$\tilde{w}$				
Unrounded	y				
Nasalized	$\tilde{y}$				

Table 2. Development of Unstable Stem-Initial Obstruent Series in Northern Athapaskan

PA	*c	*č	*čʷ	*ḵ	*q
Koyukon[a]	ƛ	c	c	k	q
Holikachuk	θ̂	c	c	k	q
Ingalik	θ̂	c	c̦	č/k	q
Tanaina[b]	c	č	č	k	q
Ahtna[a]	c	c	c	k	q
Kolchan[b]	c̦	c	c̦	č	k
Lower Tanana	θ̂	c	c̦	č	k
Tanacross	θ̂	c	c	č	k
Upper Tanana	θ̂	c	c	č	k
Han	θ̂	c	c̦	č	k
Eastern Kutchin	θ̂/č	c	c̦	č/ć	k
Western Kutchin	θ̂/k	c	c̦	č/c	k
Tutchone[c]	θ̂	c	c	č	k
Tsetsaut	c	c	pf	č	k
Tahltan-Kaska-Tagish					
Tahltan[c]	c	č	č	č	k
Kaska[c]	θ̂	c	c	č	k
Tagish	c	c	c	cᵛ	k
Sekani[b]	θ̂	c	c	č	k
Beaver[b]	θ̂	c	c	č	k
Chipewyan	θ̂	c	c	č	k
Slavey-Hare					
Slavey	θ̂	c	c	č	k
Bearlake	kʷ	c	c	č	k
Mountain	p	c	c	č	k
Hare[d]	f	s	s	š	k
Dogrib	kʷ	c	c	č	k
Babine[a]	c	c	c	k	q
Carrier[b]	c̦	c	c	č	k
Chilcotin[e]	ĉ	c	c	č	k/q
Sarcee	c	c	c	č	k

NOTE: The reflexes shown are for the most conservative dialect of each language. Other, innovating, dialects sometimes show further mergers or phonetic changes.

[a] Some dialects have *ḵ > č.

[b] PA *c and *č series kept distinct only in some dialects or by older speakers.

[c] The continuant *x remains as a front velar, at least in some dialects.

[d] Voiceless affricates merge with fricatives in Hare.

[e] The symbol ĉ indicates c with a "flattening" effect on surrounding vowels. PA *q develops in Chilcotin both into a flattening series q and into a nonflattening series (k).

Table 3. Development of Vowels in Northern Athapaskan

PA	*i	*e	*a	*u	*ə	*α	*υ
Koyukon	i	a[æ]	o[ɔ]	u	ə	ŏ	ŭ
Holikachuk	e	a	ɔ	o	ə	ŭ	ŭ
Ingalik	e	a	o	e	ə	ə	ə
Tanaina	i	a	u	i	ə	ə	ə
Ahtna	i·	e·[æ·]	a·	u·	e	a	o
Kolchan	i	a[æ]	o	u	ə	ŭ	ŭ
Lower Tanana	i	æ	ɔ	u	ə	ŭ	ŭ
Tanacross	i	e[ɪ]	a	u	ǽ	ǽ/ā	ŏ
Upper Tanana	i/ea	e/ea	a/i	u/iu	a/i	a/i	o
Han	i	e	æ	u	ə/ë	a	o
Kutchin	i	i	i/e	io	a	a	o
Northern Tutchone	i	i	e	u	a/o	a/o	a/o
Southern Tutchone	i	e	a	u	a/o	a/o	a/o
Tsetsaut[a]	i	e	a	u	ə	α(?)	o
Tahltan-Kaska-Tagish	i	e	a	u	i/e	a	u
Sekani[a]	i	e	a	u	ə	α(?)	o
Beaver	i	e	a	u	ə	ə	U
Chipewyan	i	e	a	u	ə	a	o
Slavey-Hare:							
Bearlake	i	e	a	u	ɛ	a	o
Hare	i	ie	a	u	e	a	o
Mountain	i	e	a	u	e	a	o
Slavey	i	e	a	u	e	a	o
Dogrib	i	e	a	i	e	a	o
Babine	i	i/e	a/e	o/u	ə	ə	ə
Carrier	i	e	a	o/u	ə	ə	u
Chilcotin	i	i	a	u	e/ɪ	e/ɪ	U
Sarcee	i	α	a	u	α	α	u

NOTE: Diphthongs, secondary contrasts in length and nasality, and some other secondary contrasts develop in many languages. Most of these are not shown here.

[a] The exact correspondences are unclear, due to fragmentary data.

some dialectal variation in exact point of articulation. The full vowels develop into a system of long and short: i·/i, e·/e, a·/a, u·/u; reduced vowels are now e, a, o. Ahtna was little affected by contact with Russian; about 50 Russian loanwords have remained in the noun lexicon.

The language is moribund, the youngest speakers in 1980 being about 30 years of age. In 1974 a practical orthography was developed and the production of teaching materials initiated.

There was no extensive documentation of Ahtna before the ethnographic work of Frederica de Laguna and Catharine McClellan between 1954 and 1968, whose fieldnotes include much cultural vocabulary. Extensive linguistic research was begun in 1973 by James Kari of the Alaska Native Language Center, Fairbanks. A comprehensive noun dictionary (Kari and Buck 1975) and an important technical study of the Ahtna verb (Kari 1979) are available.

Tanaina

The Tanaina language, surrounding Cook Inlet, is a rather well-defined language, not intelligible to any of

at Cantwell. Ahtna is a distinctively defined language, intelligible to neighboring Athapaskans only with considerable practice.

The three PA stem-initial series *c, *č, and *čʷ have all fallen together as [ć] (intermediate between [c] and [č]), a trait shared in Alaska only by the neighboring Upper Inlet dialect of Tanaina. Stem-final glottalized consonants are partly preserved as such except in the Chistochina and Mentasta dialects, but glottal constriction has been lost, with no tonal reflex. The old Mentasta dialect had apparently shifted the PA *ḵ series to č, but Ahtna has otherwise kept the PA velar series *ḵ and *q as such, front and back velars, though with its neighbors, though of these it is most similar to Ahtna. The great diversity of terrain in its area (which includes saltwater coastline, nearly unique for Athapaskan) has given rise to noticeable dialect differences within Tanaina; despite this, Tanaina speakers have a clear feeling for the essential unity of the language. The dialects (see Kari 1975, 1977) are Upper Inlet (Matanuska and Susitna drainage, but with Eklutna the only community); Outer Inlet (straddling Cook Inlet, but now spoken only at Tyonek, the communities on the Kenai Peninsula not having survived); Lake Iliamna (spoken at Pedro Bay and Iliamna); and Inland (at the communities of Nondalton and Lime Village). The extension of Inland Tanaina territory to Lime Village and beyond, as far as Stony River on the Kuskokwim, was not recognized by Osgood (1937).

The main feature distinguishing Tanaina from Ahtna, but which Tanaina shares with Ingalik, is the reduction of the vowel system from seven to four vowels (a system resembling that of Yupik Eskimo, perhaps not by coincidence): PA *i and *u both > i [I], *e > a, *a > u [U], and the three PA reduced vowels *ə, *α, *v all > ə. In all dialects the only major change in the PA stem-initial consonants is the merger of *č and *čʷ as č. However, in Upper Inlet there is a further merger of these with PA *c, while PA *s, *š, *šʷ, and *x all > s, as in Ahtna; further, all the voiced fricatives of these series (*z, *ž, *žʷ, and *γ̂) have shifted to and merged with y. Also as in Ahtna, the velar series *ḳ and *q have remained as such, stem-final glottalized stops have in part retained glottalization, glottal constriction of vowels is lost, and there is no tone.

Except for Lime Village (population about 45), where a very few children spoke Tanaina in 1980, the language is moribund. The Kachemak Bay subdialect is extinct, the Kenai subdialect had two speakers, and only those well over 50 at Tyonek and Eklutna spoke the Outer or Upper Inlet dialects. The Iliamna dialect was spoken only by those over 40. By far the largest group of speakers remaining in 1980 was at Nondalton, where the youngest speakers were about 30.

Relatively intense contact with Russians left over 300 Russian loanwords in Tanaina (by far the largest number in any Athapaskan language). No written literature was attempted by the Russians in Tanaina. Rezanov's (1805) 1,100-word vocabulary of the language was published, together with lesser vocabularies (Radloff 1874). Osgood (1937) contains interesting vocabulary from six locations. A modern orthography was established in 1972, in which a number of teaching materials and texts have been printed. Joan Tenenbaum did fieldwork in Nondalton between 1973 and 1975 and published a series of texts (1976) and a grammar of the verb (1977). James Kari has done extensive Tanaina fieldwork since 1972, publishing several texts and a noun dictionary for all the dialects (Kari 1977). A school dictionary (Wassillie and Kari 1979) has been published. Peter Kali-

fornsky (1977), one of the two remaining speakers of the Kenai subdialect of Outer Inlet, has published some of his own writings in Tanaina in a collection.

Ingalik

Ingalik is the language of Shageluk, Anvik, and the Athapaskan population of Holy Cross (the modern borderline on the Yukon River between Athapaskan and Eskimo areas), as well as of the middle Kuskokwim River, where it was spoken from perhaps as far downstream as Aniak to as far upstream as Vinesale. Although the upper Kuskokwim was also assigned by Osgood (1936, 1940, 1959) to Ingalik, the language of that area is different.

The Yukon dialect of Ingalik has kept distinct all of the stem-initial obstruent series of PA, although with *c, *č, and *čʷ shifted to θ̂, c, and ç, respectively. The Kuskokwim dialect differs from the Yukon dialect mainly in lacking ç, having merged *č and *čʷ as c, and various individual speakers show further mergers. Ingalik has kept PA *q but has split PA *ḳ into č and k (for reasons not fully understood). It also distinguishes PA *qʷ from *q next to a reduced vowel. Ingalik has, as a consequence, a larger number of obstruent series than any other Athapaskan language (except for Kutchin, with its secondary palatalized series): t λ θ̂ c ç č k q qʷ. Glottalization of stem-final consonants is lost, however, as is also glottal constriction of vowels, but there is no tone. Ingalik is also uniquely conservative in the development of sonorants, in that PA *w > v (w in Shageluk), *w̃ > m, and *ỹ > ŋ. The vowel system has developed essentially as in Tanaina. Final suffixal -ə is reduced to "heaviness" (voicing and syllabicity of final consonants), for example, PA *ɫuq̇ə 'fish' > ɫeġ[ɫɛ·ġ]. In a correlated development, all originally final sonorants and fricatives are phonetically voiceless, e.g., ȥaN 'day' (<PA *ȥʷen). This development is found also in Holikachuk and in the Lower dialect of Koyukon.

The Kuskokwim dialect was remembered by fewer than 20 people in 1980, all of them multilingual, living mostly in the vicinity of Stony River; it had been largely replaced by Inland Tanaina, Kolchan, and, above all, Yupik Eskimo (and finally English). The Yukon dialect was itself moribund, spoken only by the oldest generations at Anvik and Holy Cross, and at Shageluk, which had the largest concentration of speakers, the youngest in their thirties.

The Ingalik area was visited and described in 1843 by Zagoskin, who published a small vocabulary under the name "Yug-elnut Inkalit" (Zagoskin 1847, 1967:309–311). The first major documentation of Ingalik was during the initial American missionary period. Perron left some manuscript material, collected between 1894 and 1907, and a prayer book (1904), but best known is the work of Chapman between 1887 and 1930, including a volume of texts (1914). The ethnographic fieldwork of Osgood in 1934 resulted in three monographs (1940, 1958, 1959), which included an important cultural vocabulary. In 1974 a practical orthography was established, and James Kari began extensive linguistic fieldwork. A preliminary noun dictionary (Kari 1978) is available.

Holikachuk

Holikachuk was earlier the language of the upper Innoko River. The lowest and only remaining modern village was Holikachuk; the community moved in the 1960s from there to Grayling on the Yukon. The language is intermediate between Ingalik and Koyukon; it is considered such also by the speakers. Linguistically it is somewhat closer to the Lower dialect of Koyukon, but socially and geographically it is closer to Ingalik. It is partially intelligible to both, but especially to Ingalik because of social contact. It differs phonologically from Koyukon mainly in that PA *c > $\hat{\theta}$, not merging with ł, in that stem-final clusters are not preserved, and in that prefixal *e and *a merge as a.

The language is moribund; the youngest speakers at Grayling were nearly 50 in 1980. Holikachuk has been recognized as a potentially distinct group since Zagoskin (1847), also by Chapman (1914:1), but the language was virtually undocumented until 1961, when Krauss did some preliminary fieldwork. A practical orthography was established in 1974. Kari (1978a) began the first extensive fieldwork on Holikachuk in 1975.

Koyukon

Koyukon is the largest Athapaskan speech community entirely within Alaska. It is spoken in three major dialects, all mutually intelligible: Lower Koyukon, at Kaltag and Nulato; Central Koyukon, at Koyukuk, Huslia, Hughes, Allakaket, Ruby, and Galena; mixed Central and Upper Koyukon at Tanana and Rampart; and Upper Koyukon at Stevens Village. The defining trait of Koyukon (unique in Athapaskan) is the shift of PA *c (probably through intermediate $\hat{\theta}$) to ł, merging with the PA lateral series. This definition excludes Holikachuk, although the latter is partly intelligible to speakers of Koyukon. Upper Koyukon is largely intelligible, also, to Lower Tanana speakers at Minto and Nenana, especially because of social contact. But on the Yukon, between Koyukon and Kutchin, lies perhaps the most abrupt linguistic boundary within Athapaskan.

Another unusual trait of Koyukon is the preservation of some stem-final consonant suffixes in clusters, as in *giłł* 'fishhook' < PA *$\hat{g}$ əs-ł, *čoʔösł* 'we walk along' < PA *$\check{c}^w$ə-γə-ʔ*ə́s-ł, *yiłʔösk* 'he sneezes' < *yə-ł-ʔ*ə́s-x̣. PA *č and *$\check{c}^w$ are merged everywhere as c. PA *ḳ and *q remain as such in the Lower and Central dialects; Upper

Koyukon is distinguished mainly in that PA *ḳ > č (and that in the Minchumina-Bearpaw subdialect suffixal clusters do not appear). Thus, Upper Koyukon has *žiłł* 'fishhook' (Minchumina-Bearpaw *žił*). The PA vowels are practically intact, although PA *α and *υ contrast now only in the Central dialect. Glottalization of stem-final consonants is everywhere lost, but glottal constriction of vowels evidently gave rise to low-marked tone, now lost everywhere except in the Lower dialect, where vestiges of a tonal system remain in verbal prefixes. Distinguishing the Lower dialect also is the loss of suffixal -ə(ʔ) after sonorants and voiced fricatives (as also in Ingalik and Holikachuk). Also in the Lower dialect PA *w > m generally, while in the rest of Koyukon PA *w > b (often m before a vowel followed by n).

It is noteworthy that Koyukon and Kutchin, despite deep phonological differences, share at least one morphological innovation. This is the loss of PA *-d- in the də-classifier in the combinations with the s-perfective marker and with the first-person singular subject marker, PA *š-. Thus Koyukon ʔəsənuN, Kutchin ʔašanąy 'I drink it' < PA *ə-š-də-naỹ.

During the nineteenth century Upper Koyukon dialects spread up the Yukon as far as Stevens Village; up the Tanana as far as Manley Hot Springs and the Zitziana River; and up the Kantishna to Lake Minchumina and Bearpaw, intruding between the Tanana and the Upper Kuskokwim (Kolchan) languages ("Territorial Groups of West-Central Alaska Before 1898," this vol.; Carl Sesuie, personal communication 1962).

During the late Russian period about 85 nouns diffused from Russian into Koyukon, but the language was otherwise unaffected by the Russian presence. The only documentation during the Russian period was a vocabulary by Zagoskin (1847, 1967:309–311), called "Inkilik proper." Missionary literatures in Koyukon began to develop during the initial American missionary period, with Episcopalian literature (mainly by Jules Prevost at Tanana) in the Upper dialect, and Roman Catholic literature in the Lower dialect, by about a dozen Jesuit priests. By far the most important of the Jesuits was Jules Jetté ("History of Research in Subarctic Alaska," fig. 1, this vol.), who published several articles (for example, Jetté 1907–1909) but whose major works are still in manuscript (see Carriker, Carroll, and Larsen 1976), including a highly advanced grammar, and a vast and superb dictionary remarkable for its sensitive ethnographic detail (fig. 3).

In spite of strong initial missionary support, Koyukon is moribund, largely because of suppression of native languages in schools throughout Alaska during the period 1910–1960. In 1980 the youngest speakers were at Allakaket and were in their 20s.

Modern missionary and educational literature was resumed by David Henry of the Summer Institute of Linguistics, who developed a practical orthography in

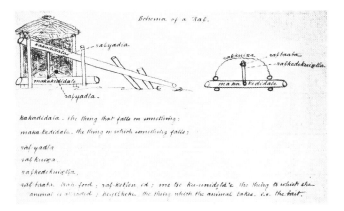

Gonzaga U., Crosby Lib., Spokane, Wash.: Oreg. Prov. Arch.. Jetté Coll.

Fig. 3. The dictionary entry under rał (χał) 'trap'; one of 2,344 manuscript pages in Father Jules Jetté's great work on the Koyukon language, prepared between 1898 and 1927 (Renner 1975).

1961 (subsequently revised). Since 1972 Eliza Jones of Koyukuk has taken a leading role in the documentation of Koyukon, transcribing extensive text materials (see Jones and Henry 1979), editing several dozen school texts (E. Jones 1978), and preparing a comprehensive dictionary of the language, incorporating Jetté's incomparable material. For Koyukon grammar a study of the verbal prefixes by C.L. Thompson (1980) is a major contribution.

Kolchan (Upper Kuskokwim)

The upper Kuskokwim area was tentatively included in Ingalik territory by Osgood (1936, 1940). The language of this area is in fact sharply distinct from Ingalik and from its other immediate neighbors. It is closest to Lower Tanana, with which it is partly intelligible, and was at an earlier period apparently part of the Tanana dialect chain. Kolchan and Lower Tanana have been separated since the nineteenth century by the intrusive Koyukon dialect of Minchumina (now nearly extinct) and have had relatively little social contact. Kolchan is spoken mainly at Nikolai but also at the very small community of Telida and by some of the small native population at McGrath, which includes a few individuals from the Vinesale area, the former border between Kolchan and Ingalik on the Kuskokwim.

The PA *č and *čʷ series are retained distinct in Kolchan as c and c̦, but for all except a few of the oldest generation, who retain PA *c as c̦ (phonetically between θ̂ and c), PA *c has merged with PA *č. PA velars are fronted, PA *k̲ > č, and PA *q > k (even [k̲]). The consonant pattern is thus quite similar to that of Tanana for the older speakers. The vowels also develop as in Lower Tanana; however, unlike Lower Tanana, and like Ahtna and Tanaina, Kolchan has kept some stem-final consonant glottalization, and PA vowel constric-

tion is lost without tone developing (or being preserved).

Zagoskin (1847) penetrated the upper Kuskokwim area to present-day McGrath. Russian influence was mostly indirect, through trading contacts, although the people are Russian Orthodox and the language shows 66 Russian loanwords. Frequent European contact did not come before the twentieth century. The language was still spoken to some extent by the children at Nikolai and perhaps Telida, but according to reports in 1980 the children there too spoke more English than Athapaskan.

The language of the upper Kuskokwim was not clearly documented until 1961 (Krauss 1961), at which time it was finally recognized as distinct. Hosley (1961, 1968) at about the same time recognized the distinctness of the ethnic group. The first sustained documentation of the language was undertaken by Ray Collins of the Summer Institute of Linguistics, who established an orthography in 1966 and began issuing literacy materials. An Athapaskan language program has been in operation in the Nikolai school since 1972, for which by 1980 a few dozen texts had been prepared, including a school dictionary (Collins and Petruska 1979).

Lower Tanana

Lower Tanana (also called Tanana, Krauss 1975) is here defined as the language of the Tanana River from the Tolovana to the Goodpaster. Earlier (Krauss 1973) it was defined as including the dialects upriver through Tanacross ("Transitional Tanana 2").

Lower Tanana is partly intelligibile with Kolchan on the upper Kuskokwim, but social contact between the two groups has been minimal since the late nineteenth century. Social contact between the Lower Tanana of Minto and Nenana and Upper Koyukon speakers at Tanana Village has, on the other hand, been relatively close and the potential for mutual intelligibility has been maximized, although the languages differ more than Lower Tanana and Kolchan. The upriver dialects of Lower Tanana, at Salcha and Goodpaster, were similarly in contact with Tanacross. Definition of the Lower Tanana language as such is probably the most arbitrary and problematical sociolinguistic decision that must be made in delimiting the Alaskan Athapaskan languages.

In the Lower Tanana of Minto-Nenana, the PA *c, *č, and *čʷ series are retained distinct as θ̂, c, and c̦, respectively. The velars, PA *k̲ and *q, are č and k, respectively. Glottalization of stem-final stops is lost; glottal constriction of vowels has given rise to low tone, but the tonal system has become unstable and tone is partly neutralized in noun and verb stems, though still clear in verbal prefixes. Stem-final PA *-k̲ has merged with PA *-q as k, a vanguard trait of the profound stem-final reduction that greatly intensifies as one approaches

Canada. The vowels are as in most Koyukon and in Kolchan, the full vowels preserved with little change, the reduced vowels showing the merger of *α and *ʋ (as ŭ).

The Lower Tanana language is moribund. Almost all of the speakers in 1980 were at Minto and Nenana, the youngest in their 40s. The Chena dialect has probably been extinct since 1976, and there were probably no more than four surviving speakers of the Salcha and Goodpaster dialect in 1980. The consonant system in Chena and Salcha-Goodpaster differs from that of Minto-Nenana mainly in the merger of c and ç as c, and in that a length distinction has developed in the full vowels (in Salcha-Goodpaster).

There was no direct Russian contact in the Lower Tanana area, but about 46 Russian loanwords appear in the language in the Minto-Nenana dialect. The first adequate documentation of Lower Tanana began in 1961 (Krauss 1961a). The practical orthography for the Minto-Nenana dialect was established in 1974, but only a preliminary noun dictionary (Krauss 1974) and one bilingual text (Titus and Titus 1979) have been published.

Tanacross

Tanacross was included as a dialect of Lower Tanana until 1974 (Krauss 1975). It has been separated from Lower Tanana on both social and linguistic grounds. Socially, there is low mutual intelligibility between the Minto-Nenana dialect of Lower Tanana and Tanacross, and a discontinuity has developed with the near-extinction of the intermediate dialects. Linguistically, the following developments differentiate Tanacross from (any dialect of) Lower Tanana: (a) development of vowel constriction into high tone rather than low tone (this development distinguishes Tanacross from all its neighbors); (b) the vowel system, though following the same pattern as Lower Tanana, shows different phonetic reflexes; (c) development of a complete set of length contrasts in the full vowels; (d) stem-initial sonorants *n (and *ỹ) > nd, *y > ž (though PA *-vỹ > -ɣy); (e) stem-initial voiced fricatives are devoiced (though remaining distinctively lenis, in part); (f) first-person singular subject prefix PA *-š- > h, and classifier PA *-ł- > h. Traits c-f are also found in Upper Tanana and were doubtless diffused from that direction. Such similarities, in addition to the close geographical and social relationship between Tanacross and Upper Tanana, make the connection between these two languages stronger than the one between Tanacross and Minto-Nenana Lower Tanana, especially with the loss of the intermediate Lower Tanana–Tanacross dialects.

Tanacross is spoken by the former Healy Lake–Joseph Village and Mansfield Lake (Tanacross)–Ketchumstuk bands, in 1980 both mostly at Tanacross, with some of the former at Dot Lake. There are slight differences between the speech of the two bands; for example, in Healy Lake suffixal -ə tends more to remain, as in Salcha-Goodpaster Lower Tanana, while in Mansfield Lake it tends more to be reduced to voicing ("heaviness") of the preceding consonant, and the devoicing of stem-initial fricatives has not progressed as far in Healy Lake as in Mansfield Lake. Here, as nearly everywhere along the Tanana, the diffusion of traits and the intergradations typical of a dialect chain are evident.

Tanacross was first documented in Wrangell (1839), whose "Copper River Kolchan" vocabulary (obtained at the coast) is clearly of this type. Russian influence was minimal; apparently three Russian loanwords penetrated into and remained in Tanacross. There were some unpublished documentations of the language by De Laguna and McClellan in 1960, and by Krauss in 1961–1962. In 1973 Nancy McRoy designed the first practical orthography and edited some school textbooks. Since then the orthography has been revised and a few more school texts printed as well as a collection of traditional narratives (Paul and Scollon 1980), but there has been no extensive study of the language. In 1980 the youngest speakers were reportedly in their teens.

Upper Tanana

Upper Tanana, at the end of the Tanana dialect chain, is rather sharply distinct from its neighbors on all sides except Tanacross. In 1980 it was spoken in Tetlin and Northway, with slight but systematic differences between the dialects of the two communities. The group was called Nabesna by Osgood (1936), but the "Nabesna" material treated by Hoijer (1963:13–17) was in fact from Tanacross.

The main feature in which Upper Tanana differs from Tanacross (and the Tanana dialects farther downriver) is the treatment of stem-final consonants, which in Upper Tanana have become somewhat reduced. This development links Upper Tanana marginally with Kutchin, Tutchone, and other languages to the east. Many stem-final fricatives and affricates are entirely lost, sometimes with compensatory diphthongization, such as PA *ɬèšʷ 'charcoal' > Lower Tanana ɬæs, Tanacross ɬé's, but Upper Tanana ɬea. The vowel system is fundamentally reshaped, with six vowels i e i a u o (both long and short) and diphthongs ea and iu. In the Northway dialect, in addition, all PA reduced vowels are distinct, with *ə > ë, but in the Tetlin dialect *α and *ə merge as i.

Unlike Tanacross (and Southern Tutchone), but like Lower Tanana, Han, Kutchin, and Northern Tutchone, Upper Tanana appears to have developed a tone system with constricted vowels low-toned, but in 1980 this was either vestigial or—for younger speakers—lost.

Because of the relative isolation of the area, at least until the construction of the Alaska Highway in 1943, children continued to learn the language until the 1960s. In 1980 some young children at Northway still perhaps understood the language, and some at Tetlin may have been able to speak it, but it was rapidly being replaced by English and on the verge of becoming moribund.

The Upper Tanana language was apparently not documented at all until the 1929 fieldwork of McKennan (1959), who included some vocabulary, especially kin terms, in his important ethnographic study of the group. In 1961 Paul Milanowski of the Summer Institute of Linguistics devised an orthography and began publishing literacy and religious materials in the Tetlin dialect. The orthography underwent some modifications in 1975, and more educational material has been published, most notably a school dictionary (Milanowski and John 1979). In 1980 there was no school program for the language.

Han

Han is the language of the village of Eagle, Alaska, with some speakers also on the Canadian side of the border at Dawson. It is sharply distinct from all its neighbors, especially the Tanana dialect chain to the west. Most speakers of Han understand Kutchin fairly well, largely because of practice and the cultural dominance of the Kutchins. Some of the older Han speakers at Eagle make use of Robert McDonald's Kutchin Bible and prayerbook. (Kutchin speakers, on the other hand, do not understand Han easily.) There may also be some small degree of natural mutual intelligibility between Han and Northern Tutchone.

Stem-initial consonants develop basically as in Lower Tanana, but there is a tendency to palatalize in certain series (especially *t*, *ƛ*, and *θ̂*) before high vowels. The loss of stem-final consonants is severe. Only simple stops (*d*, *g*), sonorants (*w*, *y*, *r*, *n*; also *l* in Dawson dialect), and laryngeals (*h*, *ʔ*) are permitted stem-finally, for example, PA *dəł* 'blood' > Han *daw* (Eagle dialect; cf. Dawson *dal*), PA *-čʋč* 'elbow' > Han *-càh*. This reduction is a development shared with Kutchin and Tutchone, and Han is also characteristically "Canadian" in its treatment of stem-initial sonorants: PA *n* > *ⁿd* (or *d*) before nonnasal vowels, PA *y* > *ž*. The vowel system is much reshaped, with some upward shifts in vowel quality as in Kutchin, resulting in seven vowels, long and short. Vowel constriction develops into low tone.

The small group of Han speakers surviving at Dawson in 1980 had a more conservative dialect than the larger community at Eagle. Palatalization of initial consonants

Table 4. Northern Athapaskan Languages, 1979

Language or Dialect	Estimated Speakers	Status
Koyukon	700	moribund
Holikachuk	25	moribund
Ingalik	100	moribund
Tanaina	250	moribund
Ahtna	200	moribund
Kolchan	130	moribund
Lower Tanana	100	moribund
Tanacross	120	moribund
Upper Tanana	250	moribund
Han	30	moribund
Kutchin	1,200	precarious
Tutchone	450	moribund
Tsetsaut	none	extinct
Tahltan-Kaska-Tagish		
Tahltan	100	moribund
Kaska	250?	precarious
Tagish	fewer than 5	nearly extinct
Sekani	100?	moribund
Beaver	900	viable
Chipewyan	5,000?	viable
Slavey-Hare		
Slavey	3,000	viable
Mountain	150–200	viable
Bearlake	450–550	viable
Hare	350–400	viable
Dogrib	2,000	viable
Babine	2,000	viable
Carrier	2,400	viable
Chilcotin	1,725	viable
Sarcee	50?	moribund

and vowel shifts were more strongly developed at Eagle, especially among young speakers.

Before the late 1970s Han was documented only by a short vocabulary attributed to Dall (Anonymous 1865), and some unpublished fieldwork by Gordon Marsh (1956), Michael Krauss (1962, 1967), and Nancy McRoy (1967, 1973). An orthography was established in 1977, and documentation has continued by Krauss and Ruth Ridley (one of the younger speakers from Eagle), and Ritter (1980).

Kutchin

Kutchin is a well-defined language, completely unintelligible to neighbors on all sides except, to some extent, speakers of Han. The Kutchin-Koyukon boundary, in particular, is very sharp and represents the ends of two lines of very divergent phonological development. But, characteristic of Northern Athapaskan, even this extreme discontinuity does not preclude intercommunication and the sharing of at least some linguistic innovations, such as the loss of PA *-d- in the *də*-classifier in certain combinations.

Kutchin is spoken across a wide territory from the Mackenzie River in Canada (where the language is locally and officially known as Loucheux) to the middle Yukon River in central Alaska. A distinction can be made between Eastern (Canadian) and Western (Alaskan) Kutchin dialects. Eastern Kutchin is spoken mainly at Fort McPherson (on Peel River), at Arctic Red River on the Mackenzie Flats, and in the isolated community of Old Crow. Western Kutchin is spoken in the Alaska settlements of Circle, Birch Creek, Beaver, Fort Yukon, Chalkyitsik, Venetie, and Arctic Village.

In Kutchin the PA stem-initial consonants develop basically as in Tanana and Han (PA *č and *čʷ being kept distinct) but, as in Han, with palatalization before certain vowels. The Kutchin palatalizations go much further than those of Han and result in some phonemic mergers; for example, in Eastern Kutchin PA *c > θ (unpalatalized), č (palatalized), and PA *ḳ > č (unpalatalized), ć (palatalized). Eastern and Western dialects differ in the details of palatalization and merger. In most Western Kutchin the palatalization of PA *c is k instead of č, and PA *ḳ is palatalized to c (merging with the reflex of PA *č), so that, for example, PA *ce 'stone' > Eastern Kutchin či·, Western Kutchin ki·; PA *-keʔ 'tail' > Eastern Kutchin -ćiʔ, Western Kutchin -ciʔ. Stem-initial sonorants also develop in a relatively complex way: PA *w > v, PA *y > ž, PA *n, *ȳ > ⁿd (palatalized to ⁿ$\check{\mathrm{z}}$) before nonnasal vowels; for instance, PA *dəne 'person' > Kutchin diⁿži·. The vowels are greatly shifted and the system reshaped, again much as in Han but with further developments, including the merger of PA *i and *e as i (but diphthongized to ia with the loss of certain stem-finals). PA vowel constriction is reflected in Kutchin as low tone, as in Han and Lower Tanana. Stem-final consonants have undergone extensive reduction, but Kutchin (like Tanacross, Upper Tanana, and Han) is conservative in maintaining a distinction between the reflexes of final PA *-ȳ and *-n, at least after PA *a and *e; for example, PA *-tan 'handle stick' (perfective stem) > Kutchin -tin, but PA *-ʔaȳ 'handle small object' (perfective stem) > Kutchin -ʔa̰ḭ.

An extensive religious literature in Eastern Kutchin exists, the work of the Anglican Archdeacon Robert McDonald (b.1829, d.1913), who lived for many years in Peel River. With the help of a woman from Arctic Red River, whose name was Ughaih, McDonald designed a Kutchin orthography and succeeded in translating the entire Bible, the Book of Common Prayer, and a selection of hymns into a conservative form of Eastern Kutchin he called Tukudh. In later life he also published a grammar of Tukudh (R. McDonald 1911). The McDonald Bible (fig. 4), long a source of pride to Kutchin speakers, was still read and studied in both Canadian and Alaskan Kutchin communities in the 1970s, although, since McDonald's orthography was no longer taught, only older people could read it.

This foundation of literacy may have contributed to the relative strength of Kutchin, which in 1980 was still viable, particularly in Alaska. It was spoken by children in several settlements, most notably Venetie and Arctic Village, where it had some chance of survival. A modern orthography was established for Western Kutchin in the 1960s (Mueller 1964), and in this orthography nearly 90 booklets for school use were produced (see Peter 1979). A modern Eastern Kutchin orthography was established by the Yukon Department of Education in the 1970s, and a noun dictionary has been published (Ritter 1976a). There is a large body of older published and unpublished documentation of Kutchin, some dating from as early as the 1840s (Isbester 1850; Murray in Richardson 1851, 2:382–385; Kennicott 1862a). Émile Petitot, Jean Séguin, Isidore Clut, and A. Le Corre gathered extensive data on Eastern Kutchin (Petitot 1876), including an important early collection of traditional texts (Petitot 1887). Particularly important are the field notes of Edward Sapir, who worked with a speaker of Western Kutchin, John Fredson, in 1923, and collected a number of narrative texts (Peter 1974). Extensive later text collections include Peter (1974a, 1979a).

Tutchone

Tutchone is sharply distinct from languages to the south and east (Tahltan-Kaska-Tagish and Slavey-Hare); on the north and west, on the other hand, a number of shared innovations link Tutchone with Upper Tanana, Han, and Kutchin, although it is doubtful that Tutchone speakers understand any of these languages without considerable practice. Within the Tutchone area there

Fig. 4. Two pages from the Tukudh (Eastern Kutchin) New Testament (1886) showing excerpts from Luke 17 translated by Archdeacon Robert McDonald and his Kutchin assistant, Ughaih.

is a major dialect division at Lake Laberge, separating Northern from Southern Tutchone. The Northern Tutchone settlements are at Mayo, Pelly Crossing (formerly at Fort Selkirk), and Carmacks, while Southern Tutchone is spoken at Aishihik, Champagne, Burwash Landing, and Kluane, with a former Lake Laberge group resettled in Whitehorse. Speakers of the two dialects can converse, but with moderate difficulty.

PA stem-initial consonants develop in Tutchone according to the pattern common in languages farther east: PA *c > θ, PA *č and *čʷ merge as c, and PA *ḵ > č. In the Southern Tutchone dialect, affricates and fricatives merge (PA *ʒ, z > δ; *c, s > θ; etc.), similar to a development in recent Hare. The PA full vowels are preserved mostly intact in Southern Tutchone, but in Northern Tutchone PA *i and *e merge as i and there are other changes reminiscent of Han and Kutchin. In both dialects stem-final consonants are drastically reduced, with most obstruents being lost, and a secondary vowel develops (o in Northern, i in Southern), as do nasalized vowels and diphthongs. Reflexes of stem-final PA *-č and *čʷ are distinct in Northern Tutchone: PA *wesᶻʷ 'knife' > mbrà, PA *łèč 'dust' > tyóʔ. Vowel constriction has developed into tone, but the system differs in the two dialects. In Northern Tutchone constricted vowels develop high tone (as in Kaska and Slavey-Hare); in Southern Tutchone, low tone (as in Tagish and Tahltan).

Tutchone, like most Yukon Athapaskan languages, was poorly documented until the 1970s, when fieldwork by John Ritter of the Yukon Department of Education resulted in orthographies and noun dictionaries for Mayo (Ritter 1976) and Selkirk (Ritter, McGinty, and Edwards 1977) as well as much unpublished material on all Tutchone communities. A literacy program, sponsored by the Council for Yukon Indians, has been active since 1973.

Slavey-Hare and Dogrib

The groups known as Slavey, Mountain, Bearlake, and Hare speak closely related dialects of a single language. No convenient name for this language exists, although Slave or Slavey was in 1980 commonly used as a self-designation by most speakers of Mountain, Bearlake, and Hare, as well as of Slavey proper. (The Department of Education in the Northwest Territories considers Hare, Bearlake, and Mountain to be dialects of "Slave.") The language will be referred to here as Slavey-Hare. A very similar language is spoken by the Dogrib. Older Dogribs can understand Slavey-Hare with difficulty; among young speakers the two languages are not mutually intelligible without considerable practice.

It is difficult to assess the degree of continuity between the modern dialects called Slavey, Mountain, Bearlake, and Hare and the speech of the Athapaskan groups assigned these names in the early contact period. Most of the modern settlements in Slavey-Hare territory include descendants of more than one of these groups, and it is certain that some dialect mixture has taken place. The tendency for one dialect in each settlement to become a lingua franca may have preserved many of the old dialect distinctions in a new social setting.

The most widely spoken of the modern Slavey-Hare dialects is Slavey proper. It is the dominant dialect in the communities of Fort Simpson, Jean Marie River, Kakisa Lake, Fort Providence, Hay River, Fort Liard, Trout Lake, and Nahanni Butte, in the Northwest Territories; at Meander River, Chateh Lake (Assumption), and other locations on the upper Hay River in Alberta; and in Fort Nelson, British Columbia. There are also significant numbers of Slavey speakers in Fort Wrigley and Fort Norman. The Slavey of each of these communities is distinguishable by a few phonological and lexical characteristics. The most marked differences occur in the subdialects, quite similar to one another, spoken at Fort Liard and Fort Nelson. Hare is a well-defined dialect with little internal diversity, spoken at Fort Good Hope and Colville Lake. The dialect called Bearlake is the lingua franca of the community at Fort Franklin, and it is also spoken at Fort Norman. Of the Slavey-Hare dialects, Bearlake is the one least likely to reflect the speech of an identifiable precontact group, since the population of both Fort Norman and Fort Franklin, especially the latter, has a very mixed origin, including many Dogribs. Mountain, in precontact times the speech of the inhabitants of the mountains west of the Mackenzie and Liard rivers, is now identified with an important group at Fort Norman and with a few speakers at Fort Wrigley and Fort Liard.

The Dogrib language is primarily spoken at Rae, and also at Rae Lakes, Snare Lake, Lac la Martre, and in the settlement of Detah near Yellowknife. It has become the dominant native language near the Northwest Territories administrative center at Yellowknife.

The Slavey dialect is phonologically the most conservative representative of the Slavey-Hare and Dogrib group. Throughout, the PA stem-initial consonants show the typical "Canadian" developments: PA *c > θ̂, PA *č and *čʷ merge as c, PA *ḵ > č, PA *q > k. In Slavey, θ̂ remains, while in the other Slavey-Hare dialects and in Dogrib this series develops further into a labial or a labiovelar series: gʷ, kʷ, ḵʷ, W, w in Dogrib and Bearlake, gʷ/b, f, ẇ, w, w in Hare, and b, p, ṗ, f, v in Mountain. Hare, the most innovating dialect, is also characterized by a reduction of contrasts within certain consonant series: voiced and voiceless fricatives merge in the ł and f (< PA *c) series (as l and w); aspirated affricates become voiceless fricatives (ł, f, s, š) and merge with the voiceless fricatives of the c and č series. These innovations appear to have occurred in

Hare between the time of Petitot's (1876) documentation and Li's visit in 1929 (Rice 1977a); they may be spreading in the 1970s to other Slavey-Hare dialects. Throughout Slavey-Hare and Dogrib, stem-final consonants are reduced to the bare minimum. In Slavey-Hare a few final consonants occur as underlying segments, preserved before suffixes but neutralized to -*h* or -ʔ in word-final position. In Dogrib, only -*h* occurs as a stem-final consonant in any environment.

As of 1979 all Slavey-Hare and Dogrib dialects were maintaining themselves, even increasing in numbers of speakers. At Fort Liard, Christian and Gardner (1977:50) found that over 75 percent of a representative sample of Indian children were monolingual speakers of Athapaskan. Much the same situation obtains at Rae, Rae Lakes, Lac la Martre, and Snare Lake (Dogrib), and at Fort Franklin (Bearlake).

Petitot (1876) included extensive data from Hare (Peaux-de-Lièvre, obtained at Fort Good Hope) in his comparative dictionary. Hare was studied by Li in 1929 (see Hoijer 1966) and by Rice (1977, 1978), who developed a practical orthography. Dogrib was the focus of Robert Howren's work in the 1960s (Howren 1968), who in addition carried out extensive dialect survey work in Slavey-Hare (Howren 1975). Workers from the Summer Institute of Linguistics have been active in the Slavey area since about 1960 (see P.G. Howard 1963, 1977).

Chipewyan

The language known as Chipewyan was spoken at the time of first contact by the nomadic caribou-hunting Athapaskans who occupied the forest and tundra of northern Alberta, Saskatchewan, and Manitoba, and the Northwest Territories to the east of Great Slave Lake. It was still spoken in 1980 by a relatively large number of people living in various settlements throughout this area, but many if not most of these communities are dominated by other Indian languages, notably Cree (Scollon 1979; Scollon and Scollon 1979). Since a high proportion of Chipewyan speakers are bilingual or multilingual, an estimate of the current number of speakers is difficult and an accurate assessment of surviving dialect differences even more so. The most important Chipewyan settlements are at Cold Lake, Saskatchewan; Fort Chipewyan, Alberta; and Fort Resolution, Northwest Territories. Many other towns or reserves have significant numbers of Chipewyan speakers, including Janvier, Fort McMurray, and Fort McKay, Alberta; Fort Smith and Snowdrift, Northwest Territories; Fond du Lac, Black Lake (Stony Rapids), Hatchet Lake (Lake Wollaston), Peter Pond Lake, and English River, Saskatchewan; and Brochet and Churchill, Manitoba. Carter (1975) noted a dialect division between an eastern group (Hatchet Lake, Brochet,

Churchill) and groups to the west. J.G.E. Smith (1975) believes this reflects an older division corresponding to predation on different major herds of caribou. Earlier records indicate that a distinctive type of Chipewyan was spoken by the Yellowknife Indians, who exploited the Yellowknife and upper Coppermine river drainages in the late eighteenth and early nineteenth centuries. After 1823 they came into continual association with speakers of other varieties of Chipewyan trading into Fort Resolution, and their linguistic distinctness had essentially disappeared by 1913 (J.A. Mason 1946:13). The Yellowknife Chipewyan obtained by Haas (1968) was apparently the speech of a Chipewyan speaker from another area who had taken up residence in Yellowknife.

There is said to be some degree of mutual intelligibility between Chipewyan and Dogrib, but this may reflect the general familiarity these groups have with each other's languages in the area around Great Slave Lake. Mutual intelligibility is usually denied by speakers of Chipewyan and Slavey-Hare.

Stem-initial consonants develop in Chipewyan as in Slavey: PA *c > θ̂, PA *č and *cʷ merge as *c*, PA *ḵ > č, PA *q > *k*. Scollon (1979) found that many speakers in Fort Chipewyan in 1976–1977 merged *c* and *č*, and there is some indication in earlier records that such a merger has long been typical of informal Chipewyan speech (Scollon and Scollon 1979). On the other hand eighteenth-century word lists still show a velar stop as the reflex of *ḵ (Krauss 1980). In the speech of her Chipewyan informant Haas (1968) found PA *t (the phoneme, not the series) > *k*, a recent development that appears to characterize the speech of several northwestern Chipewyan communities (Snowdrift, Fort Resolution) and may be spreading into adjacent Dogrib and Slavey-Hare. Chipewyan shows a moderate reduction of stem-final consonants—affricates and glottalized obstruents are reduced to fricatives—but it is not so far advanced as in Slavey-Hare and Dogrib. The PA full vowel system is preserved, but the reduced vowels are partially merged with the full vowels in a system closely resembling that of Slavey-Hare. PA constriction yields high tone.

Chipewyan is the earliest documented Athapaskan language, with vocabularies dating from 1742 (Thompson, in Dobbs 1744:206–211) and 1743 (Isham 1949:183–191); Alexander Mackenzie (1970:156–159) obtained a vocabulary in 1793. In the second half of the nineteenth century French-Canadian Oblate missionaries devoted considerable attention to Chipewyan (which they called Montagnais). A Chipewyan syllabary (fig. 5) was developed, based on the one in use for Cree, and an extensive religious literature was published. Scholarly descriptions of the language were also published, and of particular note is the copious documentation of Petitot (1876) and Legoff (1889, 1916). The linguist Goddard (1917c, 1917d) worked with Cold Lake Chipewyan in 1911. The most extensive later documentation of Chipewyan comes from Li, who worked at Fort Chipewyan in 1928 and published a stem list (1932), a historical study of the consonant phonology (1933), a grammatical sketch (1946), and texts (Li 1964; Li and Scollon 1976). Carter (1975) carried out an ethnosemantic study at Black Lake, and Scollon and Scollon have studied the speech community at Fort Chipewyan (Scollon 1979; Scollon and Scollon 1979). Linguists affiliated with the Northern Canadian Evangelical Mission have developed a literacy program at Cold Lake and have published a teaching grammar (M. Richardson 1968).

Beaver

Beaver is one of the most poorly demarcated languages in Northern Athapaskan. There is probably some degree of mutual intelligibility between Beaver and all neighboring languages, with the exception of Sarcee; this is apparently highest toward the west, where the dialects of Beaver, Sekani, and Kaska shade into one another without any clear linguistic or social boundaries, but there is also a vagueness about the boundary between Beaver and Slavey in northern Alberta. In 1980 Beaver was spoken in two widely separated areas, between which there was infrequent communication: in British Columbia, in the vicinity of Fort Saint John (with settlements at Doig, Blueberry, Hudson Hope, and Prophet River); and in northern Alberta, at Horse Lakes and Clear Hills on the Eureka River, at Boyer River near Fort Vermillion, and at Rock Lane on the upper Hay River (the Eleske group). The Boyer River and Eleske communities are in close contact with the Slavey speakers at Assumption and Meander River.

Stem-initial consonants develop in Beaver as they do in Chipewyan and Slavey; $\hat{\theta}$ (< PA *c) and c (< PA *č and *čʷ) are kept distinct as such in the eastern communities, where there is considerable Slavey influence, but elsewhere $\hat{\theta}$ has become c̦ or fallen together completely with c. A similar tendency to merge $\hat{\theta}$ and c is found in most languages to the west of Beaver. The vowels are much as in Chipewyan, with PA vowel constriction reflected as high tone. A characteristic of British Columbia Beaver (and found also in neighboring Sekani) is the palatalization of the PA *t series (to č) before reflexes of PA *i, *e, and *u; for instance, PA *tu 'water' > Doig ču. Throughout Beaver, stem-initial PA *n (and *ỹ) loses nasalization before a nonnasal vowel and merges with d (palatalizing in British Columbia to ž); for example, PA *nu 'island' > Boyer River du, Doig žu. Stem-final consonants are more conservatively preserved in Beaver than in Chipewyan, with some final affricates being retained as such.

The only extensive published documentation of Bea-

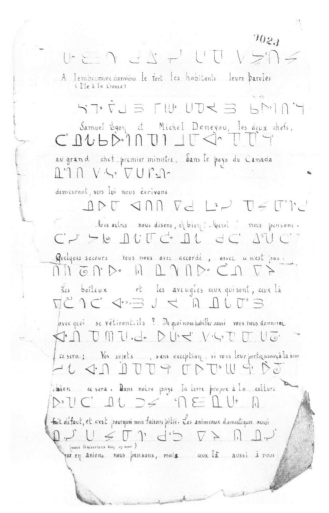

Public Arch. of Canada, Ottawa: R.G. 10, vol. 4006, file 241209–1.

Fig. 5. First page of a 3-page letter, dated July 28, 1883, from Samuel Egon and Michel Deneyou, Chipewyan chiefs at Île-à-la-Crosse, Sask., to John A. MacDonald, superintendent general of Indian affairs, requesting goods for the needs of their people who were not covered by a treaty. The letter is written in Chipewyan (with interlinear French translation added by the bishop of St. Albert) in the syllabic script that was developed by French Catholic missionaries, among them Laurent Legoff, who worked at Île-à-la-Crosse from 1870 to 1881.

ver is Goddard's (1917b) description of the Boyer River (Fort Vermillion) dialect. Robert Young and J.P. Harrington did fieldwork in the same area in 1939, and Patrick Moore began fieldwork with Alberta Beaver in the late 1970s. Linguists affiliated with the Summer Institute of Linguistics have been working with Beaver speakers near Fort Saint John since the early 1960s and have prepared a draft of a phonological study of the Doig dialect (Holdstock and Story 1975). Moore has begun preparing literacy materials for the Boyer River dialect.

Sekani

Sekani is the language of the Indians of the Rocky Mountain Trench area, living at three remote settlements along the Finlay and Parsnip rivers in British Columbia: Ware, Fort Grahame (Ingenika), and Fort McLeod (McLeod Lake). There are also some Sekani speakers living in the town of Mackenzie. It is also possible that the "Bear Lake Nomads" who settled near Telegraph Creek early in the twentieth century and subsequently moved to Kinaskan Lake at the headwaters of the Iskut are speakers of a variety of Sekani.

Accurate information on the Sekani language is scarce. Robert Young and J.P. Harrington obtained some data from a woman from Fort McLeod (Harrington 1939). For a brief time in the 1960s David B. Wilkinson, a linguist from the Summer Institute of Linguistics, worked among the Sekani groups and collected some information on dialect differences (Canonge 1966). From the material available it appears that Sekani rather closely resembles Beaver, with which it is said to be mutually intelligible. PA stem-initial consonants develop as in Beaver, with some speakers maintaining the contrast between $\hat{\theta}$ (or ς) (< PA $*c$) and c (< PA $*\check{c}$, $*\check{c}^w$), others merging these as c. In Fort Grahame and Fort McLeod, but not Ware, PA $*t$ is palatalized before PA $*i$, $*e$, $*u$, as in British Columbia Beaver; however, low tone develops from constricted vowels, whereas in all neighboring languages except Tahltan high tone develops in this environment.

In the 1960s Wilkinson and Wilkinson (1969, 1969a) developed an orthography and prepared a Bible primer, but no further attempts have been made to develop literacy among the Sekani.

Tahltan-Kaska-Tagish

The Tahltan of Telegraph Creek, the various Kaska groups of the Dease and Liard drainage, and the Tagish of the area around Bennett and Tagish Lakes all speak (or spoke) dialects of a single language. In addition, a dialect of this language was apparently formerly spoken by the Athapaskans of the upper Taku River and the area of Atlin and Teslin lakes, who were called Taku by Dawson (1889:193B) and Emmons (1911:5). This language has been referred to as Nahani or Nahane, but the term is no longer used in this sense (see "Nahani," this vol.).

Tahltan is the dialect of the Telegraph Creek Tahltans (as distinguished from other groups who may call themselves by this name, such as the Dease River Kaska). The Anglican missionary Palgrave (1902) compiled a manuscript grammar and dictionary of Tahltan, and some unpublished notes were obtained by Kenneth Hale in 1965.

Kaska is spoken in the region of northern British Columbia and the southern Yukon known as the Cassiar, and at least four subdialects can be distinguished. Frances Lake Kaska was earlier spoken by the inhabitants of the upper Liard River in the area of Frances Lake; most of the remaining speakers of this dialect have moved north to the Pelly River (which may have been within their precontact territory) and in 1980 were living at the settlement of Ross River, where they have been described by the anthropologist McDonnell (1975), who called them Kasini. Upper Liard Kaska was the dialect of the Liard River Indians below Frances Lake, as far downstream as the vicinity of Lower Post. Most speakers of Upper Liard Kaska in 1980 resided in the native settlement of Upper Liard, located just outside the town of Watson Lake. Dease River Kaska was the dialect of the inhabitants of Dease River, especially around McDame Creek. Most speakers of this dialect in 1980 lived at Lower Post, although some were at Dease Lake. This is apparently the dialect documented by E. Cook (1972a) and reported by him as Tahltan. A fourth dialect, Nelson Kaska (or Tselona), was probably spoken originally along the middle Liard River below Lower Post, but the number and location of modern speakers is uncertain and there is no reliable information on this dialect. The Kaska dialects are in general very poorly documented, and the classification here is tentative.

Tagish was spoken in the nineteenth century in the lake area at the headwaters of the Yukon. It and the Athapaskan speech of the Atlin and Teslin lake area was replaced by Tlingit during the nineteenth century and survived into the late twentieth only in the bilingual Tlingit-Athapaskan community at Tagish, Yukon Territory. Fairly reliable data have been collected from the last speakers of Tagish (G. Marsh 1956; Golla 1976).

Tahltan-Kaska-Tagish phonology resembles that of Beaver and Sekani; it is sharply distinct from both Tutchone and Slavey-Hare. There is an interesting diversity in the development of stem-initial consonants. In Kaska, the development is as in Slavey or in conservative Beaver, with PA $*c > \hat{\theta}$, and PA $*\check{c}$ and $*\check{c}^w$ > c. In Tagish, these all fall together as c, and PA $*k$ > c^y, which also seems to have been in the process of merging with c; if this merger had been completed, Tagish would have had the simplest stem-initial consonant system in Northern Athapaskan. Finally, in Tahltan, PA $*c$ is retained as such, and PA $*\check{c}$ and $*\check{c}^w$ merge instead with PA $*k$ as $\check{c}$, a development unique in Northern Athapaskan (although found in some languages of the Pacific Coast group). It is a measure of the superficiality of these seemingly important phonological differences that they hinder the mutual intelligibility of these dialects very little.

The vowel system is conservative, and stem-final consonants are well preserved, although final glottalization is lost. Tone develops from vowel constriction, but, as with the stem-initial consonants, the dialects diverge: constricted vowels develop low tone in Tahltan and Tagish, high tone in Kaska.

Tsetsaut

The language of the Tsetsaut is known exclusively through a vocabulary list collected by Boas from three informants at Kinkolith, on the British Columbia coast, in 1894 (Boas and Goddard 1924). Since the circumstances of the fieldwork were very difficult, and apparently only one of Boas's informants, Levi, was fluent in the language, this material presents many problems. Nevertheless, some startling phonological developments are revealed in the data, and it is clear that Tsetsaut was one of the most divergent of Northern Athapaskan languages. Like the languages of the Mackenzie River area (Slavey-Hare and Dogrib) and the Yukon (Tutchone, Han, Kutchin), but unlike its immediate neighbors (Tahltan-Kaska), Tsetsaut has undergone severe loss of stem-final consonants. Tsetsaut further resembles languages such as Han and Kutchin in preserving the contrast between PA *č and *čʷ, but with the unique shift of *čʷ to a bilabial series (pf) (see Krauss 1964–1965,1, 1973:944–947). Tharp (1972) has argued that Tsetsaut, despite its phonological developments, shows a close relationship to Tahltan, but this interpretation rests on a reanalysis of Tahltan phonology that raises difficulties. The statement of one of Boas's informants that Tsetsaut was mutually intelligible with Tahltan cannot be adequately assessed.

Carrier and Babine

The term Carrier has been used in the twentieth century as the name of a language that includes all the Athapaskan dialects of central British Columbia, from the mouth of Bulkley River in the northwest to the area around Quesnel on the middle Fraser River in the southeast. A sharp linguistic boundary, correlated with cultural and ecological differences, separates the Bulkley River (Moricetown and Hagwilget) and Babine Lake dialects from the rest, and it is probably best to return to earlier usage and consider these northwest dialects a distinct language, Northern Carrier or Babine (Kari 1975a). In the remaining territory, belonging to Carrier proper, a number of local variants can be noted. A distinction is sometimes made between "Central" or "Upper" Carrier—the speech of the groups living to the north of Fort Saint James, around Stuart, Trembleur, and Takla lakes—and "Southern" or "Lower" Carrier, which includes the dialects of Prince George, Cheslatta (Saint Mary's Lake), Stellaquo, Fraser Lake, Stony Creek, Kluskus, Nazko, Quesnel, Ulkatcho, and (in the twentieth century) Anahim Lake. Firm data on Carrier dialectology is sparse, and nearly all the accessible data on the language represent the dialect of Fort Saint James, particularly the somewhat innovative, missionary-sponsored lingua franca that grew up around Stuart Lake in the late nineteenth century. This standardized language is documented in the monumental work of Morice (1932), on the basis of his 50 years' experience with the language.

In stem-initial consonants, Babine and Carrier follow the general pattern of neighboring languages. PA *c, *č, and *čʷ all merge as c, but in Morice's time PA *c was still kept distinct as θ̂ or ç (E. Cook 1976a). Babine is set off from Carrier in its preservation, at least in the Bulkley River dialect, of front-velar ḵ and back-velar q as the reflexes of PA *ḵ and *q. Babine is thus the only Northern Athapaskan language outside of Alaska that has maintained PA *ḵ as a velar stop into the twentieth century (some of the Pacific Coast Athapaskan languages do so as well). Babine is also characterized by several unusual innovations in the vowel system, brought about through consonantal conditioning (Hildebrandt and Story 1974; Kari 1975a). Both Carrier and Babine have lost vowel constriction without developing tone, apparently, although there are some pitch accent phenomena that may be the vestige of a tone system.

The rate of language retention is quite high throughout the Babine and Carrier region and is especially high at Lake Babine, where in 1980 only a scattering of the population was not fully fluent in Babine. Fort Saint James has been the focus of a literacy program sponsored by the Summer Institute of Linguistics that has resulted in a practical orthography, teaching materials (fig. 6), and a dictionary (Antoine et al. 1974).

Chilcotin

Chilcotin is a well-defined language, quite distinct from its only Athapaskan neighbor, Carrier. Chilcotin is spoken in several communities in the vicinity of Williams Lake, British Columbia, including Alexis Creek, Anaham, Nemaiah Valley, Stone, and Toosey, along the Chilco and Chilcotin rivers, as well as Alexandria on the Fraser River. The area around Anahim Lake was once Chilcotin but by the early twentieth century was inhabited by Carrier speakers; the former Anahim Lake Chilcotins moved to Anaham. There is apparently little internal diversity within Chilcotin. It has been suggested (Boas 1924; Harrington 1943) that the Athapaskan language formerly spoken in the Nicola and Similkameen valleys, 150 miles to the southeast of modern Chilcotin territory, was a dialect of Chilcotin. Since only extremely scant attestation exists for Nicola-Similkameen Athapaskan, extinct since about 1910, it is not possible to confirm this. The claim made by Harrington (1943) that the Pacific Coast Athapaskan languages have a closer affinity to Chilcotin than to any other Northern Athapaskan language, though geographically plausible, is not correct.

Fig. 6. A page from *Nak'aẓdli Bughuni*, an instructional workbook in the Carrier language, an outgrowth of the development of linguistic materials by Richard Walker and David Wilkinson, Summer Institute of Linguistics, Inc. Workbook design and development, David B. Wilkinson; Carrier language specialist, Mildred Martin; illustrations, Wilma Reid; composition, Kay Wilkinson.

Sophisticated older speakers of Chilcotin and Carrier are reportedly able to converse, with some difficulty, but to younger speakers the languages are mutually unintelligible. Much of the phonological difference between Carrier and Chilcotin is due to a complex vowel allophony in Chilcotin associated with the "flattening" effect of certain consonants, possibly developed under the influence of Lillooet or another Interior Salish language (Krauss 1975a; E. Cook 1976, 1977).

PA stem-initial consonants develop in Chilcotin generally as they do in Carrier, with PA $*\check{c}$ and $*\check{c}^w$ merging as c, and PA $*c$ kept distinct. The distinctness of the reflexes of the PA $*c$-series, written $\hat{c}$, is most strikingly evident in the "flattening" effect these consonants (but not those from PA $*\check{c}$ and $*\check{c}^w$) have on preceding or following vowels, which are articulated with retracted tongue: Chilcotin $\check{c}i$ [c̀i] 'canoe', but "flattening" $\hat{c}$ in $\hat{c}i$ [cəi] 'stone'. In addition, the reflexes of the PA $*q$ series are split, under various conditions, into flattening (q) and nonflattening (k) variants. These are usually phonetically as well as structurally distinct, although with an asymmetrical distribution and frequency: the common phonemes are nonflattening g and $\mathring{k}$ and flattening q, x, and $\mathring{\gamma}$, with $\mathring{g}$, $\mathring{q}$, k, and x rare; there are also labialized flattening and nonflattening velars.

The Chilcotin vowel system, in addition to the complex allophony of flattening, is also characterized by the merger of PA $*i$ and $*e$ (as i). Significantly, Chilcotin, unlike Carrier, has developed (or preserved) a tone system, with constricted vowels taking on high tone.

Chilcotin was very poorly documented until the 1970s. Fieldwork was undertaken by Krauss (1975a) and E. Cook (1976, 1976a) in conjunction with a literacy program sponsored by the Fish Lake Cultural Centre, and teaching materials were prepared. Chilcotin is surviving vigorously, with most children in 1980 still acquiring it as their first language.

Sarcee

In historical times the Sarcee have been a Plains tribe closely associated with the Blackfoot, although it is likely that their location before the adoption of the horse was near the headwaters of the North Saskatchewan and Athabasca rivers, in territory adjoining the Beaver. The home of the modern Sarcee band is a reserve on the outskirts of the city of Calgary, Alberta.

Sarcee is a sharply defined language, unusual for Northern Athapaskan in that it is spoken by a group with little contact with other Athapaskan speakers, the closest ties of the Sarcee being with other Plains groups: the Assiniboin, the Plains Cree, and especially the Blackfoot. It is noteworthy that none of these non-Athapaskan groups exerted any influence on Sarcee vocabulary. Within Sarcee there are no dialect distinctions that have been noted, although since about 1950, as the use of the language declined, there arose a noticeable difference between the speech of older and younger people.

The segmental phonology of Sarcee is, to some extent, characterized by simplification. Stem-initial consonants show the merger of PA $*c$, $*\check{c}$, and $*\check{c}^w$ (as c), as in the more innovative types of Beaver and Carrier. Sarcee has a simple four-vowel system: PA $*i$ and $*a$ are retained as such; PA $*e$, $*\partial$, and $*\alpha$ merge as α; and PA $*u$ and $*v$ merge as u. On the other hand, Sarcee is decidedly conservative in its retention of stem-final consonants, preserving not only the affricates and glottalization (at least before suffixes) but also some final clusters (the only Northern Athapaskan language other than Koyukon to have done so).

PA constricted vowels become low-toned in Sarcee. The tone system was described by Sapir (1925) and E. Cook (1971) as having three distinctions in level—high, mid, and low. The mid tone apparently results from the lowering of the high tone on unconstricted reduced vowels (Krauss 1980), a feature that may link Sarcee with Navajo and the other Apachean languages, where un-

84

constricted reduced vowels consistently develop low tone instead of the expected high tone.

The most valuable documentation of Sarcee remains Sapir's field notes from 1922, on which are based Sapir (1925), the pioneering study of tone in Athapaskan, Li (1931), a list of verb stems with a discussion of verb morphology, and Hoijer and Joel (1963), a study of noun stems. Beginning in 1969 E. Cook (1971, 1971a, 1971b, 1972) undertook a modern linguistic study of Sarcee.

For most members of the Sarcee band the first language in 1980 was English. No special effort has been made to preserve Sarcee; no more than a dozen older residents of the reserve still carry on conversations in the language, although many of the younger people have a passive knowledge of it.

Prehistory of the Canadian Shield

JAMES V. WRIGHT

The Precambrian Shield covers approximately one-half of Canada extending for some 600 miles both east and west of Hudson Bay and more than 300 miles north and south of it. Over this enormous region physiographic variations do exist but on the whole the area is characterized by a basic sameness except where the dominating boreal forest gradually fades into the northern tundra.

Exclusive of the coastal sections, the area under consideration in this chapter consists of the Precambrian Shield regions of Labrador, northern Quebec, Ontario, Manitoba, and Saskatchewan, extreme northeastern Alberta, and the southern half of Keewatin District and the eastern edge of Mackenzie District of the Northwest Territories (fig. 1). The prehistory of the northernmost part of the Subarctic Shield, which is historically of Athapaskan occupation, is treated in "Prehistory of the Great Slave Lake and Great Bear Lake Region," this volume. To some degree the archeological assemblages of the Subarctic portion of the Shield are also manifested in the southernmost sector of the Shield, which is within the Northeast culture area (vol. 15). The boundary between these two units is that between the boreal and the Great Lakes–Saint Lawrence forest regions.

The relatively close similarities of the archeological assemblages throughout much of the region under consideration is undoubtedly the most striking single characteristic of Shield prehistory. As a somewhat similar degree of cultural homogeneity appears to have existed among the historic Algonquians, who occupied approximately the same area, it would appear that the ethnological and ethnohistorical data are directly pertinent to a greater understanding of the prehistoric situation. Physiographic factors are, of course, an integral part of such an examination. A number of inseparably related physical and cultural phenomena can be proposed to explain the homogeneity of both prehistoric assemblages and historic Algonquians over the enormous tracts of the Shield. First, the river and lake network of the Shield provided not only effective routes of travel and communication, but also throughout most of the area the only feasible means of travel, by birch-bark canoe in summer, and in winter (aided by snowshoes), on the wind-packed snow atop the ice. In addition, food resources were closely associated with the water systems. Second, two major food sources, caribou

and fish, dominate the region. This is not to say that moose, beaver, small game, and local seasonal resources, such as migrating waterfowl, were not at times critical or even temporarily primary, but simply that without the caribou and fish it is very unlikely that humans could have occupied the total area on any permanent basis. Third, the enormous forest fires, which still characterize the region, not only displaced all animals including man but also resulted in a sequence of plant and animal reclamation of the burnt-over area. Fires covering more than 10,000 square miles are not uncommon, and people would have been forced to shift their hunting regions in accordance with the fires and their aftermath. Fourth, the small hunting groups and regional bands of the Algonquians with their flexible residence and marriage patterns and their relative freedom of personal choice favored wide-flung social connections. Women, in particular, appear to have been very mobile under this system. Fifth, the limitations imposed by the boreal environment on the subsistence patterns and attendant social organization inhibited culturally disruptive incursions of peoples and ideas from adjacent regions.

Although other factors had their varying effects it is these five conditions that are regarded as the basic underlying causes of the prehistoric cultural homogeneity seen throughout most of the Shield. In short, a relatively homogeneous physiographic region that could be traversed by interconnecting waterways and that was occupied by small bands of hunters subject to the vagaries of endemic forest fires and big game fluctuations and movements resulted in a degree of cultural uniformity perhaps unequaled in the rest of North America in terms of the square miles involved. In addition to cultural continuity through space the prehistory of the Shield is characterized by cultural continuity through time. From this it is assumed that the indigenous determining forces acting upon the early historic occupants of the region also acted upon their prehistoric predecessors. These generalizations are, of course, oversimplifications, and spatial and temporal variations and discontinuities do occur; however, such variations and discontinuities are minor and frequently explainable and do not seriously detract from the general tenet. Indeed, the Shield region clearly represents a discrete and old culture area. The available evidence strongly suggests that the northern Algonquians at the time of

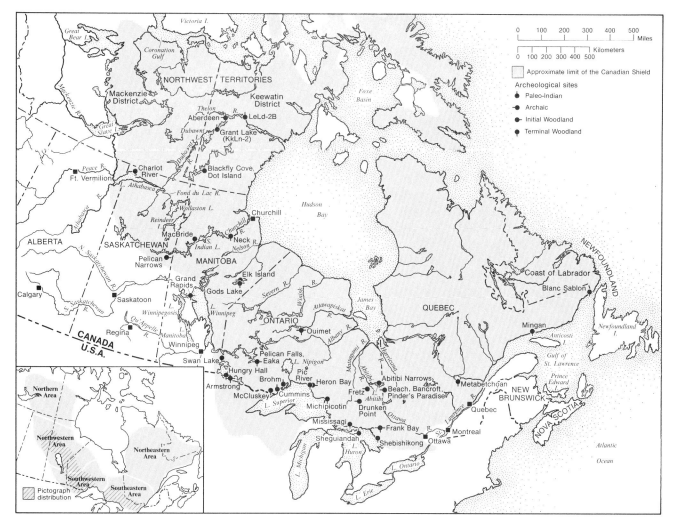

Fig. 1. Archeological sites in the Canadian shield. Inset shows geographic regions discussed for the Terminal Woodland period and the distribution of pictographs (after Dewdney 1970).

initial contact with Europeans followed a way of life that had not changed significantly for more than 7,000 years.

These observations do not apply to the Hudson Bay Lowlands. This region appears to have been virtually unoccupied in prehistoric times and its historic Algonquian population is regarded as a recent phenomenon that is directly related to the establishment of European trading posts around the coast of Hudson Bay.

The prehistory of the Shield will be considered under four periods—Paleo-Indian, Archaic, Initial Woodland, and Terminal Woodland. These groupings are taxonomic conveniences whose major function is to break the time column into more manageable units. They do not represent stages of cultural development.

By Period

Paleo-Indian Period

It is the final portion of the Paleo-Indian period in North America, called Plano, that is pertinent to the Shield

region. A number of regional and temporal varieties of Plano culture have been established on the basis of diagnostic projectile point types. The variety of particular importance to the prehistory of the Shield is called Agate Basin and has been most often dated between 6500 B.C. and 7500 B.C. from sites in northern Ontario, Montana, and Wyoming. Agate Basin projectile points are widely distributed throughout the northern plains, and campsites have been located in the eastern Mackenzie District and the southern half of Keewatin District (fig. 2). The sites in Keewatin District (Harp 1961) are associated with the major caribou crossing places that are also productive of fish. Therefore, it appears that at an early period big game hunters from the northern Plains had moved into the northern and western portions of the Shield and were exploiting the Barren Grounds on a seasonal basis. Farther to the south, in the closed forest, it is an increasingly difficult task to locate Paleo-Indian sites due to the forest cover and the fact that the sites would most likely be associated with the much larger water systems of that period that were produced by the melting of the continental glacier.

Agate Basin projectile points do appear to be the most common Plano point variety found in Manitoba, and similar surface finds extend into the extreme southwestern portion of Northern Ontario. Several quarry sites attributed to Plano culture have been located along the north shore of the Upper Great Lakes (Greenman and Stanley 1943; R.S. MacNeish 1952; T.E. Lee 1957), but no sites have been discovered in the interior of the Shield in Ontario.

As the continental glacier and the associated lakes contracted, early hunters penetrated to the east from out of the northwest, west, and probably also from the south. The Agate Basin point and generalized Plano lanceolate point forms gradually developed into the lanceolate projectile point of the early Shield Archaic, and other changes took place within the stone tool assemblage.

The differentiation of Paleo-Indian from Archaic is an artificial device formulated by the archeologist in order to create manageable units of time. In truth, these are the same people who followed the same way of life but whose stone tool complex was gradually changing through time.

By 4000 B.C. the transition of the late Paleo-Indian culture into the Shield Archaic culture appears to have been completed. The descendants of the Paleo-Indian population, the Shield Archaic, continued to exploit their old territories including the Barren Grounds, but at the same time some continued drifting eastward, along with the caribou, as the eastern portions of the Precambrian Shield were gradually released by the continental glacier and its associated glacial lakes.

Archaic Period

The Shield Archaic represents the first distinctive culture of the Shield as well as the first population to occupy a major portion of the Shield region. The fact that Paleo-Indian materials are largely restricted to the northwest suggests that the major penetration into Ontario and eastward took place after the transition from an Agate Basin culture to a Shield Archaic culture. Most of Quebec and Labrador appear to have been occupied somewhat later than regions to the west and, indeed, the Shield Archaic culture appears to have survived in much of this area until the historic period. Both decreasing game densities and increasing snow accumulations that were probably encountered as these small bands advanced eastward may well have been factors in the late and weaker penetration into the far eastern regions of the Shield. Some of the sparse material from the eastern Quebec and Labrador sites is tentatively placed within the Shield Archaic as many of the specimens involved fit well within a late Shield Archaic context.

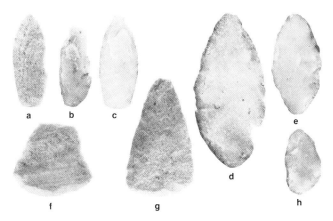

Fig. 2. Paleo-Indian period, Agate Basin artifacts. LeLd–2B site, Schultz Lake, Thelon River, Keewatin District: a-b, burinated Agate Basin projectile points; d, biface blade; e, uniface blade; h, end scraper. KkLn–2 site, Grant Lake, Dubawnt River, Keewatin District: c, Agate Basin projectile point; f-g, end scrapers. Length of a 5 cm, rest same scale.

The radiocarbon time depth of the Shield Archaic ranges from 3000 B.C. into the second millennium A.D. (for specific dates, west to east, see B.H.C. Gordon 1971; J.V. Wright 1970, 1972b; Byers 1959; D. Knight 1971; Harp 1964; Wilmeth 1969; Fitzhugh 1972). It is assumed that research will extend the range both earlier and later.

Eleven archeological sites, located in Keewatin District, Manitoba, Ontario, and Quebec, plus supplementary data, have been used to outline the general characteristics of the Shield Archaic stone tool assemblage (J.V. Wright 1972). Although the information from these sites was not all that could have been hoped for, some patterns have emerged that are generally consistent throughout the region. The most serious limitations of these data are the total absence of bone preservation due to the ubiquitous acid soils, the thinness of the archeological deposits, which made component separation a difficult or impossible task, and the fact that a number of the sites are solely represented by surface collections.

Shield Archaic sites are dominated by three artifact classes—scrapers, biface blades (knives), and projectile points (fig. 3). In terms of approximate averages, scrapers constitute 40 percent, biface blades 25 percent, and projectile points 15 percent of the total stone tool assemblage. Through time the frequencies of both the scrapers and projectile points increase whereas the frequency of the biface blades decreases. The most significant single trend within the projectile point varieties is the decrease through time of the lanceolate points with a corresponding increase of the side-notched points. Some of the scraper varieties also exhibit significant trends through time although the scrapers generally reflect a more regional character than is typical of the projectile points. Most of the other artifact classes are too poorly represented to detect temporal trends although a certain amount of spatial information is suggested by these data. A significant negative trait is the nearly complete absence of stone grinding in tool manufacture. Throughout most of the region the tools decrease in size and in Ontario, in particular, there is a dramatic change that is the result of shifting from the use of massive siliceous deposits such as quartzite to small nodular flints resulting in a concomitant change in the size and variety of tools.

Fluctuations in climate would certainly have had a direct impact upon both the plant and animal occupants of the Shield, including man. There is evidence that several retreats and advances of the tree line have taken place, but the most significant event in terms of the Shield Archaic was the general cooling conditions beginning in 1550 B.C. or 1250 B.C. and lasting until A.D. 1 (Nichols 1971). Shield Archaic populations had occupied the Thelon River drainage in Keewatin District from earliest times, but sometime between 1500 B.C. and 1000 B.C. they abandoned the region. (The late Shield Archaic house structure at the Aberdeen site on the Thelon, for example, has been radiocarbon dated at 1075 B.C. ± 90 [S–506] and this is a minimal date inasmuch as it was obtained from peat within the house.) In the place of the Shield Archaic population a completely different archeological assemblage, the Arctic Small Tool tradition, appears. This assemblage has been equated with Paleo-Eskimo peoples, and their penetration out of the north is relatively well documented (Noble 1971; B.H.C. Gordon 1975). The radiocarbon dates obtained by Gordon for the newcomers are 1210 B.C. ± 95 (I–5978), 940 B.C. ± 125 (S–632), and 890 B.C. ± 95 (I–5975). All these data strongly suggest that the deteriorating climate forced the tree line too far south to permit the Shield Archaic hunters to commute from the forest to their old lands on the Thelon drainage. They were replaced by caribou hunters from the northwest, probably originating from the Coronation Gulf region (Taylor 1972). There is no evidence that a corresponding replacement of Indians by Eskimos took place under similar circumstances in northern Quebec (Martijn and Rogers 1969).

Significant cultural exchange between the Shield Archaic and adjacent and contemporaneous populations appears to be lacking. There is some slight evidence of contacts with the Laurentian Archaic (Ritchie 1965) populations to the southeast of the Shield in the Great Lakes–Saint Lawrence forest country. Such evidence consists of an occasional diagnostic Laurentian Archaic tool occurring in a Shield Archaic site. Evidence of contact with the Plains Archaic to the southwest is equally tenuous, and there is no evidence of contact with the Arctic Small Tool peoples despite their penetration into traditional Shield Archaic country between 1500 and 1000 B.C.

Natl. Mus. of Canada, Ottawa.

Fig. 3. Archaic period, Shield Archaic artifacts. Drunken Point site, Ont.: a, biface blades; f-g, projectile points. Eaka site, Ont.: c, end scraper; e, side scraper; j, copper fishhook. Elk Island site, Man.: b, uniface blade. Aberdeen site, Keewatin District: d, end scraper; h-i, projectile points. Length of a 5.4 cm, rest same scale.

Initial Woodland Period

The Initial Woodland period, formerly referred to as the Middle Woodland period, is introduced by the appearance of pottery. This new period is, once again, an archeological convenience and the only thing that is really new about it is that some of the Shield Archaic people adopt pottery. It has been somewhat of a problem to determine from where this pottery came. It is not similar to any of the ceramic complexes to the south, and there exists a broad zone to the northwest completely lacking in ceramics and thereby precluding a possible Asiatic origin. The only reasonable alternative is that the idea of pottery was adopted from the south via stimulus diffusion and that Archaic populations of the Shield evolved a distinctive ceramic complex after they had acquired the essential techniques of manufacture. Such a possibility is reinforced by the evidence from the Transitional cultures of the northeastern United States where a distinctive ceramic complex was evolved after the introduction of the idea of pottery from the south (Ritchie 1965). It is suggested that the early pottery of the Saugeen and Point Peninsula cultures of Southern Ontario (J.V. Wright 1967) diffused to the Shield Archaic people and was subsequently modified into a complex distinctive to the Shield.

Once again, for the purpose of classification only, it becomes necessary to give a different name to the same culture tradition simply because it has adopted a single new trait—pottery. Thus in some areas the Shield Archaic population of the Archaic period becomes the

89

Laurel population of the Initial Woodland period (fig. 4). Within the Subarctic, Laurel sites have been encountered in east-central Saskatchewan, across most of Manitoba and Ontario, and into extreme western Quebec. Laurel culture also extended to the south as far as northern Minnesota and Michigan. However, the prehistoric populations of the major portion of Quebec and all of Labrador did not adopt pottery and thereby retained a Shield Archaic identification. Although archeological constructs such as distinct periods are artificial and clumsy, they are necessary during the initial stages of investigation into the prehistory of a region. They can be discarded when sufficient information permits the establishment of a single developing tradition or, possibly, several closely related traditions (a co-tradition).

The Laurel people continued a way of life basically indistinguishable from that of their Shield Archaic ancestors. However, along the Shield border region of Ontario and Minnesota south of the Subarctic zone, burial mounds appear for the first time (Wilford 1955). This particular burial trait was only marginally adopted by these southern Laurel people and its origins obviously lay to the south.

Although there is bone preservation in northern Minnesota and Michigan, only one of the major Laurel sites in Canada, the Heron Bay site on the north shore of Lake Superior, produced bone tools and refuse; and even in this instance the preservation was due to the neutralizing effects of the ash from the ancient hearths. At this site beaver incisor tools, awls, toggle harpoon heads, snowshoe netting needles, pendants, beads, pottery markers, and a few other miscellaneous items were recovered. Beaver and moose bones were most common although caribou, muskrat, hare, and bear were present. Fish remains were relatively sparse. Some interesting information bearing upon prehistoric trade networks was also obtained from the Heron Bay site. The items indicative of trade connections were obsidian from Wyoming (1,150 miles away), shell from southern Manitoba (460 miles), and Saugeen culture pottery from Southern Ontario (360 miles).

Within the Laurel development the manufacture of flint tools derived from small nodular cores, which began in late Shield Archaic times, continued, and was expanded. Indeed, the Laurel lithic assemblage could justifiably be referred to as microlithic. Some new traits appeared, such as net sinkers, but on the whole the lithic assemblage is clearly rooted in the previous Shield Archaic assemblage. In the area near the native copper deposits of Lake Superior, sites invariably contain copper implements such as awls, beads, gorges, knives, chisels, and an occasional projectile point, thereby carrying on the metalworking tradition of the earlier Archaic occupants.

Laurel sites have been radiocarbon dated between

Natl. Mus. of Canada, Ottawa.

Fig. 4. Initial Woodland period, Laurel artifacts from the Heron Bay site, Ont.: a, biface blade; b, snowshoe needle fragment; c, copper chisel; d, copper beads; e, rim sherd; f, projectile point; g, worked beaver incisor; h, net sinker; i, toggle head harpoon; j, linear flake; k, copper awl; l, hafted scraper; m-p, range of scraper varieties; q, end scraper; r, lance head. Length of a 6.8 cm, rest same scale.

300 B.C. and A.D. 500 (Wilmeth 1969; Bettarel and Harrison 1962; J.V. Wright 1967; Janzen 1968). If the Saugeen culture and the related Point Peninsula culture of Southern Ontario, the earliest dates for which range between 650 and 400 B.C., provided ceramics to Laurel via stimulus diffusion, then Laurel ceramics should prove to be earlier than these dates suggest. In the face of the evidence, the proposition of stimulus diffusion from more southerly Initial Woodland (Early Woodland) sites resulting in a distinctive ceramic complex that then diffused to the north is not the tenuous proposition it might first appear to be. Certainly it is no more tenuous than attempting to derive the Laurel ceramic complex from unrelated ceramics to the south that are most often dated later in time.

Terminal Woodland Period

The ceramic-producing cultures of much of eastern North America have been temporally segregated into three periods—Early Woodland, Middle Woodland, and Late Woodland. Early Woodland manifestations are very marginal to Canada, and the vast majority of the earliest pottery has been equated with the Middle Woodland period even though the ceramics of eastern Canada and immediately adjacent portions of the

United States bear very little resemblance to the ceramics of most of the northeastern United States. In short, a taxonomic system developed specifically for prehistoric assemblages in the northeastern United States has been applied to distinctly different assemblages in eastern Canada and limited areas of the extreme northern United States and has understandably resulted in a very inadequate taxonomy for that region (R.J. Mason 1970). In order to provide at least a partial resolution of this problem, complexes formerly assigned to the Early and Middle Woodland periods have been placed under a new taxonomic unit called the Initial Woodland period, and the Late Woodland period has been replaced with the Terminal Woodland period (figs. 5–7) (J.V. Wright 1972a).

The separation of the Initial Woodland period from the Terminal Woodland period is unavoidably vague. In simple terms the Initial Woodland period begins with the first appearance of ceramics and only ends as various regional developments differentiate themselves from the Initial Woodland cultural base. The Terminal Woodland period, on the other hand, begins with this cultural differentiation out of a relatively common Initial Woodland base and ends with historically identifiable culture groupings.

When an archeological site contains both aboriginal and European artifacts in association, the ethnic iden-

tification of the original occupants can frequently be established on the basis of the historic documentation. Once the ethnic identification of an historic site is made, the direct historical approach (Steward 1942) can be used to trace the prehistory of the historic group involved back through time. Certain extrapolations based upon the ethnological information for the historic population can also be used to flesh out the archeological skeleton. A somewhat arbitrary figure of A.D. 600 is regarded as the approximate transition of the Initial Woodland period into the Terminal Woodland period. This date is based upon both the evidence for cultural differentiation out of the common Laurel cultural base of the Initial Woodland period and the distance back in time that various historic groupings can be traced by the direct historical approach. Once again, the division of the two Woodland periods is a necessary archeological convenience and is not to be regarded as an indication of any major cultural change or event.

The period under consideration covers approximately the last 1,000 years of prehistory in the Shield. In order to present most effectively the various cultural developments that appear to have taken place during the last prehistoric millennium the Shield has been divided into the following areas: Northern, Northwestern, Southwestern, Southeastern, and Northeastern (fig. 1 inset).

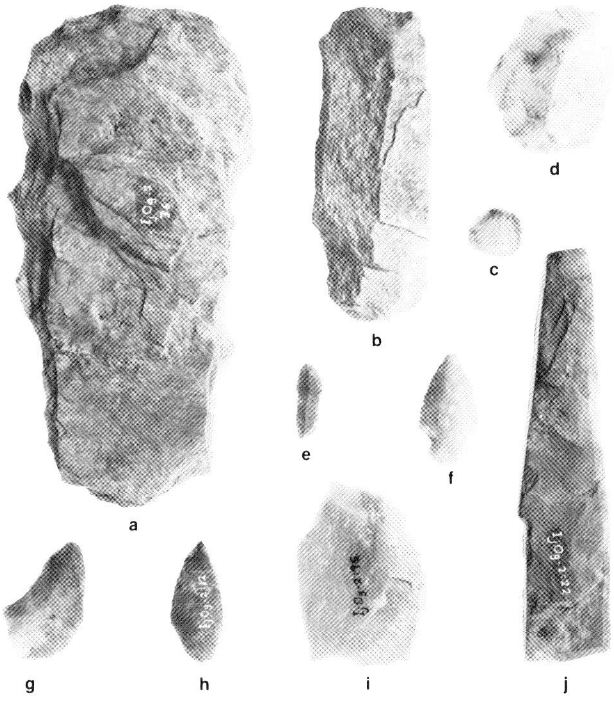

Natl. Mus. of Canada, Ottawa.

Fig. 5. Terminal Woodland period. Northern area material from the Charlot River site, north shore of Lake Athabasca, Sask.: a, chitho; b-d, end scrapers; e, linear flake; f, projectile point; g-i, other scraper varieties; j, rectanguloid abrader. Length of a 13.2 cm, rest same scale.

By Geographic Region

Northern Area

Cultural discontinuities are evident with regard to the prehistoric developments within the Northern area. Indeed, since pottery is absent the area cannot even be placed within the Terminal Woodland period but must be regarded as a contemporaneous but unrelated development. The area will be considered only very briefly and with emphasis on the southeastern portions. For detailed information see "Prehistory of the Great Slave Lake and Great Bear Lake Region," this volume.

After the withdrawal of the late Shield Archaic hunters from the region due to deteriorating climatic conditions, the prehistory of the Northern area of the Shield becomes and remains basically unrelated to prehistoric developments throughout the remainder of the the Shield. It is uncertain how long the Paleo-Eskimo caribou hunters, who occupied much of the area around 1000 B.C., remained, but it appears that they retreated to the coast sometime before 500 B.C. Around A.D. 1 climatic conditions began to improve (Nichols 1971), but before this development a series of archeological assemblages, which have been traced by the direct historical approach to Athapaskan peoples (Noble 1971), began to expand to the east and southeast. Radiocarbon dates pertaining to the newcomers range from 400 B.C.

to A.D. 1450 on the upper Thelon River of the eastern Mackenzie District (B.H.C. Gordon 1974) and from A.D. 660 to 1730 in extreme northern Manitoba (Nash 1970).

Similar remains have been encountered along the northeast shore and eastern end of Lake Athabasca where one date of A.D. 1340 is available. Both archeological and historical information indicates that the (Athapaskan) Chipewyan penetration to the south was a late prehistoric and historic event.

With reference to the Chipewyan the explorer David Thompson stated that "their lands, which they claim as their own country; and to which no other people have a right, are those eastward of the Rein Deer's and Manito [Wollaston] Lakes to Churchill Factory and northward along the interior of the sea coast; all other lands they hunt on belonged to the Nahathaways [Cree], who have returned to the South-westward" (Thompson 1962:126). Thompson also wrote that the Cree "made offerings to" the country around Manitou Falls on the Fond du Lac River between Lake Athabasca and Wollaston Lake at approximately 59° north latitude and 104°28′ west longitude, while they "possessed" it, but "they have retired to milder climates; and the Chepawyans have taken their place" (Thompson 1962:115).

In the 1820s George Simpson (1938:355) wrote of Lake Athabasca that:

> The Chipewyans do not consider this part of the Country to be their legitimate Soil; they came in large Bands from their own barren Lands situated to the North of this Lake, extending to the Eastern extremity of Gt. Slave Lake and embracing a large Track of Country towards Churchill. The Compys. Traders at the latter Establishment, made them acquainted with the use and value of European Commodities and being naturally of a vagrant desposition and those articles becoming necessary to their Comforts, they shook off their indolent habits, became expert Beaver hunters, and now penetrate in search of that valuable animal into the Cree and Beaver Indian hunting Grounds, making a circuit easterly by Carribeau Lake; to the South by Isle a la Crosse; and Westerly to the Banks of Peace River, and so avaricious are they, that the prospect of Gain I have no doubt would lead them much further, did not the more Warlike Tribes to the Southward and Westward intimidate them.

Finally, there is Tyrrell's comment regarding the aboriginal occupations of the Barren Grounds during his visit in 1893 in relation to Samuel Hearne's observations in the same country in 1770: "The conditions which I found were just such as he describes, except that the inhabitants had changed. The Chipewyan Indians, whom he found occupying advantageous positions everywhere as far as the north end of Dubawnt Lake, had disappeared, and in their places the country had been occupied by scattered bands and families of Eskimos, who had almost forgotten the ocean shores of the north, from which they had come" (Hearne 1958:5).

These historical references, which are in essential agreement with the available archeological evidence, indicate a series of population movements for which reasonable explanations exist. The Nahathaways or Cree were in early contact with Europeans and it is suggested that due to a reduction in population resulting from exposure to European diseases and a desire to be closer to the European trading locations the more northerly Cree abandoned their lands and moved south. At approximately the same time the Chipewyans had been drawn into the fur trade, and since their lands were poorly provided with valuable fur animals they expanded into the former Cree territory to obtain the furs necessary to meet their needs for European goods. The areas of the Barren Grounds vacated by the Chipewyans were then occupied by Eskimos in order to exploit the rich game resource.

Northwestern Area

A distinctive complex, called Selkirk, has a core area distribution north to Southern Indian Lake in Manitoba (fig. 6q–z), west to Lac Île-à-la-Crosse in Saskatchewan, south to the Saskatchewan River, and east into the northwestern portions of Northern Ontario (R.S. MacNeish 1958; Hlady 1970a, 1971; J.V. Wright 1971). The Selkirk complex is most readily recognized by its distinctive fabric-impressed pottery, which includes bowls and plates as well as pots. First named by MacNeish for sites in southeastern Manitoba, most of his sites equate more closely with the Blackduck complex of the Southwestern area. The Clearwater Lake and Grass River phases identified by Hlady are included under the more general term of Selkirk.

Radiocarbon dates from Selkirk sites in Manitoba and Ontario range from A.D. 810 to 1620. In addition a number of historic Selkirk sites have been reported from Saskatchewan, Manitoba, and Ontario. In every instance the historic documents indicate that these historic sites are attributable to the Cree. Arrowheads are small side-notched triangular or simple triangular forms that often consist of a simple flake with minor unifacial or marginal retouch. There is a wide range of scraper varieties although the small end scrapers are usually dominant. Bifacially flaked knives are present as well as bifacially flaked celts with grinding largely restricted to the bit edge. Hammerstones, manos, anvils, and abraders also occur, while wedges are very rare. The very few sites where bone preservation exists have produced awls, flaking tools, tubular beads, fleshers, and arrowshaft straighteners.

Archeological evidence strongly suggests that the Cree had a very long period of cultural development in the region under consideration and that they are not easterners who have pushed to the west and northwest in response to the fur trade. From whence they obtained their distinctive ceramic complex is unknown although

Natl. Mus. of Canada, Ottawa.

Fig. 6. Terminal Woodland period. Southwestern Algonquian area Blackduck material from the north shore of Lake Superior, Pic River site: a, typical rim sherd; b-c, atypical rim sherds; d, end scraper; e, scraper; f, copper fishhook; g, linear flake; h, slot abrader; i, biface blade; j-k, projectile points; l, bone bead; m, stone amulet in the form of a beaver; n, stone pipe bowl; o, beaver incisor tool; p, unilaterally barbed harpoon. Northwestern Algonquian area Selkirk material from Southern Indian Lake, Man.: q, typical rim sherd; r, atypical rim sherd; s-t, projectile points; u, side scraper; v, end scraper; w, biface blade; x, flaked and partially ground celt; y, bone awl; z, scraping implement (chitho).

Southeastern Algonquian area material mainly from the northeast coast of Lake Superior, the Michipicoten site: aa, end scraper; bb, linear flake; cc-dd, projectile points; ee-hh, rim sherds representing 3 and possibly 4 different ceramic traditions; ii, chitholike slate implement; jj, copper awl; kk, catlinite stone pipe; ll, Huron-Petun pottery pipe. Length of p 14 cm, rest same scale.

93

some equivocal evidence suggests that a development out of the preceding Laurel ceramics is one possibility. Although changes through time and some spatial variations can be detected in the Selkirk assemblages, the development as a whole is characterized by a basic homogeneity.

There appears to have been an intimate relationship between Selkirk and contemporaneous developments to the south.

Southwestern Area

The core area of the Blackduck archeological assemblage straddles the ethnographic culture area boundary between Subarctic and Northeast culture areas (see "Late Prehistory of the Upper Great Lakes Area," vol. 15). It is distributed from the north end of Lake Winnipeg south into northern Minnesota, west to the Red River in Manitoba, and east to the Michipicoten River in Ontario. This distribution overlaps, to some degree, both the Northwestern and Southeastern areas. R.S. MacNeish's (1958) Manitoba focus is equated with the Blackduck focus, and much of his Selkirk material from southeastern Manitoba is also regarded as Blackduck focus. There is abundant evidence for a long and close interrelationship between the Northwestern area (Selkirk) and the Southwestern area (Blackduck) (fig. 6a–p).

Burial mounds occur in the Southwestern area but are restricted to southeastern Manitoba and the portions of northern Minnesota and southwestern Northern Ontario flanking the international boundary. The occurrence of burial mounds only in the southerly areas of the Blackduck territory, beyond the limits of the ethnographic Subarctic, parallels the case with the preceding Laurel culture. Indeed, there is increasing evidence that Blackduck evolved out of an earlier Laurel culture base (Evans 1961), and it is proposed that the presence of burial mounds in southern Blackduck simply represents the perpetuation of an earlier trait.

Radiocarbon dates from Blackduck sites in Manitoba, Ontario, and Minnesota range from A.D. 620 to 1560. A number of Blackduck sites in Ontario have also produced European trade goods.

A disagreement exists concerning the ethnic identification of the Blackduck complex. A number of archeologists (Wilford 1955; R.S. MacNeish 1958; Hlady 1964) have argued for an Assiniboin authorship. On the other hand, J.V. Wright (1965, 1967a, 1968, 1971) has argued that the Ojibwa are more reasonably equated with Blackduck culture on the grounds of direct archeological and historical evidence and supporting evidence from linguistics, ethnology, and physical anthropology.

The Assiniboin are a Siouan-speaking population who are closely related to the Yanktonai but appear to have split off from them in the mid-seventeenth century (Howard 1966, 1966a). A 1680 French map, for example, locates the Assiniboin in southwestern Manitoba. The prehistoric to early historic Dakota of central Minnesota and westward possessed a Mississippian culture (E. Johnson 1969) whereas Blackduck is purely a Woodland culture. Finally, as can be seen from the inset on figure 1, pictographs of a related style are distributed through the Northwestern (Cree), Southwestern (Ojibwa), and Southeastern (Algonquin) areas. If Blackduck is Siouan then the Assiniboin must have shared in a basic art style related to a common cosmological view with their Cree and Algonquin neighbors.

Further, the Blackduck cultural development has ancient roots throughout the lands occupied historically by various bands of Algonquian speakers referred to collectively as Ojibwa (for example, Thompson 1962:184). The Assiniboin, on the other hand, are the result of a late, probably historic, separation from the Dakota and cannot be equated with the Blackduck development in terms of either time or space.

The attribution of the Selkirk and Blackduck complexes, respectively, to Cree and Ojibwa peoples makes the demonstrable similarities between the two archeological complexes not surprising. The lithic assemblages of the two complexes are very closely related with the exception of the paucity of wedges in the Northwestern area, and a similar observation can be made with reference to the bone tools. In short, the Blackduck and Selkirk complexes are regarded as the products of two related Algonquian-speaking populations. The representation of both ceramic traditions on many sites is probably best explained by female mobility reflecting a situation where Cree men are marrying Ojibwa women and Ojibwa men are marrying Cree women. Generally one of the ceramic traditions dominates, but there are instances where the ratio of the two pottery styles is nearly equal, making the designation of a component as Selkirk or Blackduck a difficult task. Under the circumstances the boundary line between these two areas is somewhat amorphous.

Southeastern Area

Like the Southwestern area, the Southeastern area extends south of the Subarctic, encompassing the portions of the Shield in eastern Ontario and western Quebec. In terms of ceramics the Southeastern area is certainly the most complex area in the Shield. Ceramic complexes from Michigan, Wisconsin, and New York are found in direct association with Selkirk, Blackduck, and Ontario Iroquois pottery. The drawing of women from adjacent regions where they had participated in completely different ceramic traditions is regarded as the major reason for this bizarre heterogeneity of pottery styles. Aside from pottery, the lithic and bone traits and general site features reflect a basically homogeneous culture (fig. 6aa–ll). Certainly the complex interplay of the various ceramic traditions throughout the region is of great value in determining geographic contacts through time, but there exists a danger of permitting the variability in pottery to submerge the basic culture continuity of the nonceramic traits. On the basis of ceramic styles alone eight or more discrete cultural expressions in the Southeastern area would have to be recognized. Further, there are the variable relationships of these different ceramic traditions to one another through both time and space. There also exists a geographic cline in terms of ceramic complexity. As one advances to the north in the Southeastern area both relative quantity of ceramics and the varieties of ceramic traditions decrease (Marois 1974). The temporal and spatial fluctuations of ceramic traditions in the southern portions of this region are clearly expressed at a number of stratified sites (McPherron 1967; B.M. Mitchell 1966; Ridley 1954; J.V. Wright 1965, 1969).

Radiocarbon dates from Terminal Woodland sites in the Southeastern area range from A.D. 710 to 1670. A number of sites containing European trade goods have also been encountered. Following the practice of lumping the various bands of Algonquian speakers under a covering term that possesses some vague degree of discreteness (such as the Cree for the Northwestern area and the Ojibwa for the Southwestern area), the Algonquin are equated with the Southeastern area. Arrowheads are the usual simple triangular and triangular side-notched forms frequently characterized by minimal retouch. Small end and side scrapers are prevalent as are stone wedges. Abraders, manos, hammerstones, and ocher or limonite paintstones are not uncommon; and when close to the natural sources, native copper beads, awls, and knives occur. Due to acid soil conditions limited bone materials have survived on the sites. Unilaterally barbed harpoons, awls, and beaver incisor knives have been recovered as well as dog burials. Some incipient agriculture was practiced along the shores of Lake Huron and the Ottawa River, south of the ethnographic Subarctic.

Northeastern Area

The Northeastern area encompasses Labrador and most of Quebec to the north of the Saint Lawrence River. Most of the Northeastern area is within the Subarctic ethnographic region, but its southern portions and particularly the area along the Saint Lawrence River reveal a close relationship with the Iroquoian populations of southern Quebec and Ontario and northern New York. Pottery is restricted to the southeastern portions of the area (Martijn 1969) and usually consists of Saint Lawrence Iroquoian pottery styles (Pendergast 1966) west

of the Richelieu River, and northern New York pottery styles east of this point as far as the north shore of the Gulf of Saint Lawrence in the Anticosti Island area. Since the Saint Lawrence Iroquois occupied the upper Saint Lawrence valley until sometime in the sixteenth century and the eastern Iroquois of New York State had access to the Saint Lawrence valley via the Richelieu River, the prevalence of their respective ceramics on adjacent and contemporaneous Algonquian sites is not too surprising. However, an examination of the lithic and bone traits permits a ready separation of Iroquoian sites from Algonquian sites sharing an Iroquoian ceramic complex (J.V. Wright 1965).

The Saint Lawrence River has acted as a natural highway for the movement of peoples; however, as one progresses along the north shore into the Gulf of Saint Lawrence, pottery becomes an increasingly rare occurrence on Terminal Woodland sites, and pottery is completely absent from the interior of this area except from Lake Saint John and west. Two reports are available on historic Montagnais sites that also contain prehistoric components; one site is located at Mingan north of Anticosti Island on the north shore (Lévesque 1971) and the other on Lake Saint John (Simard 1970). Both sites contained Iroquois pottery and non-Iroquois lithic assemblages dominated by small end scrapers. Bone was preserved at the Metabetchouan site on Lake Saint John, and the most common bone tools were worked beaver incisors and bone awls. The most common animal species encountered in the faunal remains were moose, beaver, pickerel (walleyed pike), and caribou in descending order of frequency. The much richer site at Mingan, which was occupied from approximately A.D. 1000 to historic times, produced a wide range of corner-notched, side-notched, and simple triangular arrowheads as well as some stemmed points, many of which possess the minimal retouch so typical of Algonquian arrowheads. Some small biface knives, a few polished celts, and abraders were also present.

Assemblages similar to these identified Algonquian sites have been discovered at Brador (fig. 7) (René Lévesque, personal communication 1972) and in Labrador (Harp 1964; Fitzhugh 1972).

The ancestry of the Montagnais and related bands is poorly understood, but there is some evidence to suggest that they evolved from a late Shield Archaic base. With reference to the interior of the Northeastern area the best evidence comes from the Mistassini region, where the Wenopsk complex (circa 4000 B.C. to historic period):

appears to have existed in relative isolation. No abrupt transitions show up in the artifact inventories of any of its major components which could be interpreted as large-scale movements into the area by outside groups. On the contrary, there is a sense of continuity through time. If migrations into the Mistassini Territory did take place during this

Société d'Archéologie de Québec. Institut de Géographie. Université Laval. Ste. Foy. Que.

Fig. 7. Terminal Woodland period. Northeastern area material from a site in the Brador area on the north shore of the Gulf of St. Lawrence, Que. Most of the specimens are manufactured from rama quartzite from Saglek Bay, northern coast of Labrador: a-c, projectile points; d, side scraper; e-f, end scrapers; g, bi-pointed scraper; h-i, large scrapers, j, flake knife. Length of g 11.2 cm, rest same scale.

period they must have come from the Canadian Shield region to the west, rather than from the distant south or north, judging by similarities in artifact types and the scarcity of stone tools made of lithic materials other than quartzite. . . .

The Wenopsk Complex apparently lasted until contact times, and was then transformed into the historical Mistassini Complex by the introduction of European trade goods . . . (Martijn and Rogers 1969:347, 348).

However, some caution is advised since no actual proof yet shows that the Mistassini are directly descended from the prehistoric Wenopsk population (ibid.:334).

Even at this very preliminary stage of knowledge of the Northeastern area it is apparent that there are some significant differences between the late prehistoric complexes of the Saint Lawrence drainage and the Hudson Bay drainage. Only future research can determine whether these differences reflect the cultural development of the Montagnais in the former area and the Cree in the latter area.

Summary

The major portion of the Canadian Shield represents a distinct culture area whose prehistoric antecedents clearly reflect the cultural and linguistic relationships seen to exist among the historic and present Algonquian-speaking populations of the area.

The cultural homogeneity through both time and space are the products of a number of physiographic factors that are collectively unique to the Canadian Shield.

From the earliest human occupation of the Shield to the historic period the way of life has remained basically unchanged and has revolved around a combination of big game hunting and fishing and, inferentially, the use of the bark canoe and the snowshoe.

The prehistory of the Subarctic Shield is essentially the prehistory of the northern Algonquian-speaking peoples.

In order to present this overview of the prehistory of the Shield it has been necessary to make many generalizations supported by very little documentation. Although much of the documentation can be drawn from the references cited, other supporting data have not been published. Due to the nature of the subject matter it has been necessary often to include discussion of areas south of the boreal forest, into the territory of the Northeast culture area, since a substantial portion of the Shield straddles the boreal forest and Great Lakes–Saint Lawrence forest boundary.

Since 1974, a marked increase in the pace of archeological research in the Shield has taken place. This research has further supported the major themes outlined in this article (see "History of Archeological Research in the Subarctic Shield and Mackenzie Borderlands," this vol.).

Prehistory of the Great Slave Lake and Great Bear Lake Region

WILLIAM C. NOBLE

Enveloping the eastern portions of Canada's major northern lakes (Athabasca, Great Slave, Great Bear), the Precambrian Shield frequently outcrops in what is geologically known as the Yellowknife-Churchill province (J.T. Wilson 1952). Here, discontinuous surface tills support a boreal forest (Larsen 1971; Raup 1946; J.S. Rowe 1972) that diminishes and grades into a tundra-taiga ecotone (Larsen 1971a, 1974; Noble 1974) on the continental plateau north and east of those lakes. Beyond this ecotone, which includes the forest border (the outer limit of the area where at least 50 percent of the land is covered by trees; Larsen 1974:343) extends the esker and boulder-strewn tundra of the central-western Barren Grounds.

This presentation of prehistory focuses primarily on the forest and the tundra ecozones of central District of Mackenzie; wider cultural distributions to the east and south are included where appropriate. Throughout, it is clear that most cultural adaptations in this region were made by peoples associated with the forest or the forest-tundra ecotone but who frequented the Barren Grounds in accord with seasonal scheduling associated with caribou hunting. The migratory Barren Ground caribou (*Rangifer tarandus groenlandicus*) summers on the tundra but winters in the adjacent forest. It formed a mainstay in local aboriginal subsistence economics, and, thus, the Barren Ground sequence of human occupation cannot be fully understood without reference to that of the adjacent forest, or vice-versa.

Within this central portion of the District of Mackenzie, initial pioneer archeological reconnaissances were made by R.S. MacNeish (1951) and Harp (1958). Later extensive surveys and excavations by Noble (1966–1969, 1971) have allowed the formulation of a sequence of aboriginal occupation extending back to at least 5000 B.C. Noble (1971:104) recognized and established the presence of three major traditions, each represented by two or more archeological complexes (phases).

As distinct modes of life, the traditions are recognizable through diagnostic elements of material culture in a series of related complexes that occur across space and persist through appreciable time. Earliest is a northern Plano tradition, followed by an Arctic Small Tool variant—Canadian Tundra—and finally there is the Taltheilei Shale tradition, which leads to and terminates with early historic Athapaskans (table 1).

Northern Plano Tradition, 5000 B.C.

The earliest known occupation in the central District of Mackenzie commences with northern Plano Indians circa 5000 B.C. By that time it is apparent that the late Wisconsin Laurentide ice sheet had withdrawn eastward to the Keewatin Ice Divide (Lee 1959; Craig 1960, 1964, 1965; Craig and Fyles 1960), and in all probability Glacial Lake McConnell (Craig 1965), which once joined Lakes Athabasca, Great Slave, and Great Bear, had shrunk to three discrete bodies of water. Significantly, spruce forest made a transgression down the Mackenzie River valley to the Delta Highlands by 6500 B.C. (Ritchie and Hare 1971:338); and at 5000 B.C. the region immediately east of Great Slave–Great Bear lakes was probably covered with spruce parkland grading out to open tundra to the north and east (Noble 1974). A forest fire on Roundrock Lake has been dated to 4960 B.C ±85 (WIS–516) (Sorenson and Knox 1974).

Acasta Lake Complex, 5000 B.C.

Named after the buried homogeneous type site located 80 miles southeast of Port Radium (Forbis 1961; Noble 1969, 1971), the Acasta Lake complex can be traced along a 350-mile distribution from the northern shore of Great Slave Lake northward, east of Great Bear Lake to within 70 miles of the Arctic coast (Coronation Gulf). Twelve sites along this route have yielded more than 1,000 artifacts from locations on sand eskers or blowouts, 850 to 1,400 feet in elevation above mean sea level (fig. 1).

The recovered tool kit (fig. 2a–g) of the Acasta Lake peoples includes items for spearing and fleshing game as well as working bone or wood. Classic Agate Basin lanceolates are most popular in addition to stemmed and incipient-stemmed varieties (Noble 1971:104). Too, the distinctive leaf-shaped, side-notched Acasta points are important as early representatives of the side-notching concept.

Numerous ovate and bipointed quartzite bifaces in various stages of manufacture occur at the Acasta Lake site. Undoubtedly some are preforms for projectiles, while others served as knives and fleshers. Scrapers in many varieties—spall, humped-back, semilunar, stemmed—occur alongside scraper planes and retouched flakes. A single twist drill, multi-gravers, and spokeshaves offer additional tools useful in working wood or bone, although no worked items of these materials are preserved. Transverse burins, rare bipolar pieces (wedges), bladelike flakes, massive cores, and a single whetstone complete the known tool kit of this northern Plano culture.

Situated on the side gully of an esker near a large quartzite quarry erratic, the Acasta Lake type site (LiPk–1) served as a major chipping station and temporary habitation. Seven cases of hearth superimposition clearly indicate recurrent use of the site. In an excavated area of 850 square feet, no less than 105 fire-reddened pit hearths occur in what appear to be five or six distinct ring clusters. Composed of 15 to 25 hearths, each ring measures 8 to 11 feet in diameter, and normal hearth fill includes gray powdery ash liberally mixed with quartzite detritus and artifacts. Such evidence suggests heat treatment of the quartzite prior to percussion chipping.

A large roasting hearth at LiPk–1, number 61, contained charred portions of caribou, black bear, beaver, hare, bald or golden eagle, and fish bone (Savage 1971:11). Taken together, these fauna not only indicate close proximity to a forest border (the black bear, beaver) but also suggest an early fall occupation when such species would be readily available or in prime condition (the caribou). An extensive annual range from the transitional forest into the Barren Grounds appears plausible for the Acasta Lake Plano Indians.

Radiocarbon analyses fix the Acasta Lake complex at about 5000 B.C. While charcoal is extremely sparse in the excavated hearths at LiPk–1, a combined sample from hearths 2 and 3 registers 4900 B.C. ± 150 (GaK–3277) and is complemented by a date of 5020 B.C. ± 360 (I–3957) from hearth 95. Both dates are convincing and help confirm the hypothesis of a general south to north movement of Plano peoples from 8000 to 5000 B.C. Indeed, Acasta Lake appears to represent a final phase of Agate Basin Plano in which there is acculturation with early, contemporaneous stemmed-point Archaic cultures.

Other dated and undated Agate Basin Plano components are present in western and northwestern Canada. The Grant Lake complex in the District of Keewatin (Harp 1959, 1961; Irving 1968a) is well known, and Millar's (1968:316) Agate Basin specimens from Fisherman Lake near Fort Liard have been dated 6770 B.C. ± 190 (GaK–1275). From Alberta, various finds

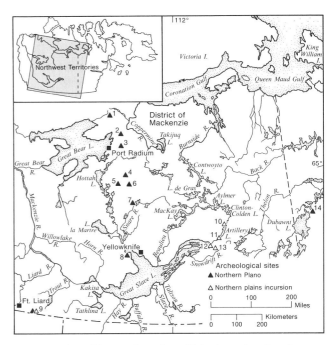

Fig. 1. Northern Plano and northern Plains incursion sites: 1, Dismal Lake 1a; 2, Kamut Lake; 3, Smokey Lake; 4, Acasta Lake; 5, Exmouth Lake; 6, Mesa Lake; 7, Big Quartz; 8, Mosquito Creek; 9, Fisherman Lake; 10, Murphy; 11, Caribou Island; 12, Pike's Portage; 13, Whitefish Lake; 14, Grant Lake.

have been made (Wormington and Forbis 1965), including the 6250 B.C. ± 240 (GX–1435) Waterton Lake site (Reeves 1973). Both Saskatchewan (Minni 1976; Nero 1959) and Manitoba (Nash 1970; Pettipas 1970) also have significant components. Dates between 8000 and 7000 B.C. are reported for even more southerly Plano sites (Wormington 1957; Agogino and Galloway 1965; C.V. Haynes 1967).

The Period 4500–3000 B.C.

Aboriginal occupation in the period 4500–3000 B.C. is poorly represented in the Great Slave–Great Bear lakes region. It almost appears as if there were a cultural hiatus, but this is probably more apparent than real, for there do exist small artifact samples that as yet defy precise classification. One such find is a single ripple-flaked lanceolate of gray silicious shale from Rawalpindi Lake (Noble 1971:106), and there are other amorphous Agate Basin–like lanceolates and expanding stem points that are equally difficult to evaluate precisely. Certainly, there is no manifestation of R.S. MacNeish's (1959, 1964) Northwest Microblade tradition east of Great Bear and Great Slave lakes at this or any later time period.

Of ecological note during this period is the 3120 B.C. ± 140 (I–4376) burning of spruce forest 150 miles north of Yellowknife on Snare Lake (Noble 1971:106, 1974).

Noble 1971:figs. 2–4.

Fig. 2. Northern Plano tradition. Acasta Lake complex artifacts from Acasta Lake (LiPk–1): a, transverse burins; b, Agate Basin point; c,e, Acasta points; d, projectile point; f, stemmed scraper probably for hafting; g, biface. Northern Plains incursion: h, Oxbow complex side-notched quartzite point with convex shoulders and thinned slightly concave base; i, Caribou Island complex distinctively stemmed bifurcate point. Length of b about 7.9 cm, rest same scale.

Northern Plains Incursions

Four very poorly represented complexes from the northern Plains make an appearance in the eastern Great Slave Lake region between 3000 B.C. and A.D. 200. They comprise the Artillery Lake, Oxbow, Caribou Island (Duncan), and Pelican Lake complexes (Noble 1971). None penetrates toward the Barren Grounds farther north than northern Artillery Lake.

Artillery Lake Complex, 3000–2500 B.C.

Originally defined by R.S. MacNeish (1951:38), the sparse and undated Artillery Lake complex is repre-

sented by two sites only. One is the Murphy site (KiNl–3) at the northwest end of Artillery Lake, and the other is the Beaverlodge Portage component (IiOd–1) on northeastern Lake Athabasca (Noble 1971:106). Long, narrow quartzite lanceolates with transverse flaking and mildly concave bases are distinctive (R.S. MacNeish 1951), as are linear bifaces of reddish or white quartzite. Occurring too are small discoidal thumbnail end scrapers, flake scrapers, and choppers. No blades or microblades appear in the Artillery Lake complex.

Probably derived from central Saskatchewan (see Meyer 1970), Artillery Lake points also appear in southeastern District of Keewatin (Irving 1968a:fig. 3, o-p). A date between 3000 and 2500 B.C. is possible for this complex considering the late dates for other Plano-like lanceolates in surrounding regions. For instance, late Plano-like lanceolates occur at Fisherman Lake (Millar 1968) around 2970 B.C. ±110 (I–3190); at Great Bear River between 2854 B.C. ±200 (S–10) and 2694 B.C. ±110 (S–9) (R.S. MacNeish 1955, 1964); and in the Thelon complex dated 2565 B.C. ±140 (I–5976), 3060 B.C. ±225 (S–735), and 3110 B.C. ±310 (S–710) (B.H.C. Gordon 1975).

Oxbow Complex, 2500–1500 B.C.

Well-known from southern Saskatchewan (Dyck 1970; Nero and McCorquodale 1958; Wettlaufer and Mayer-Oakes 1960), Oxbow penetrates to the southeastern end of Great Slave Lake, well within the present forest border. Two surface sites on Pike's Portage (Noble 1971:106) are characterized by side-notched quartzite points with convex shoulders and thinned concave bases (fig. 2h). Small thumbnail end scrapers, knives, and various flakes constitute the remainder of the poorly known tool kit of this weakly represented complex.

Elsewhere in the southern Northwest Territories, an undated Oxbow or Oxbow-like component occurs at Fisherman Lake near Fort Liard (R.S. MacNeish 1954:fig. 68b, 1–2; Millar 1968:328). In southern Saskatchewan, where Oxbow appears earliest, the complex dates 3250–2670 B.C., while in the central portion of the province dates of 2150 B.C. ±90 (S–403) and 1410 B.C. ±120 (S–490) (Dyck 1970) are reported. It has been postulated that the northern components in the southern Territories date between 2500 and 1500 B.C. to account for temporal lag in a south to north diffusion (Noble 1971:107).

Caribou Island (Duncan) Complex, 1500–1000 B.C.

At the mixed surface site (KfNm–5) on Caribou Island, southern Artillery Lake, is yet another weak northern Plains Indian complex. This is distinguished by bifurcated stemmed points (fig. 2i) analogous to Duncan

99

Table 1. Prehistoric Sequences in Central Mackenzie District

Time	Northern Plano	Other Northern Plains Cultures	Canadian Tundra Tradition	Taltheilei Shale Tradition (Chipewyan)	Forest Fires
1500				Reliance Snare River Fairchild Bay	
					A.D. 1385
				Frank Channel	
					A.D. 1210
				Lockhart River	
					A.D. 1160
1000				Narrows	A.D. 1095
					A.D. 720
500				Waldron River Windy Point	
A.D. 1		Pelican Lake		Taltheilei	A.D. 190
				Hennessey	410 B.C.
1000			Timber Point Aurora River Rocknest Lake		
		Caribou Island			
2000					1930 B.C.
		Oxbow Artillery Lake			
3000					3120 B.C.
4000		Ripple-flaked "Plainview"(?)			
5000 B.C.	Acasta Lake				4960 B.C.

points of the Meso-Indian period in Alberta and Wyoming (Wormington and Forbis 1965:29). Other projectiles at this site include a mildly side-notched and an unground lanceolate form that are difficult to assign any precise affinities (Noble 1971:107). Too, linear bifaces of the Aurora River small tool complex complicate clear definition of the Duncan Indian occupation at Caribou Island.

Pelican Lake Complex, A.D. 1–200

Pelican Lake is a weak complex known from two projectiles found at Whitefish Lake (R.S. MacNeish 1951; Noble 1971:107). Other projectiles from this region include a Larter tanged point (R.S. MacNeish 1951:pl. II),and a very late Billings double-spur, basally notched point type, which generally postdates A.D. 1500 in Montana (Mulloy 1958:79).

Dates on Pelican Lake components in the northern Plains range from 280 B.C. (Wettlaufer and Mayer-Oakes 1960) to A.D. 120 (Forbis 1962). It is apparent that the weak Pelican Lake penetration into the eastern Great Slave Lake region temporally overlaps the early phases of the Taltheilei Shale tradition, yet no exchange of ideas (such as side-notching) appears to have taken place.

Canadian Tundra Tradition, 1300–600 B.C.

Initially discovered by W.E. Taylor (1964a, 1967) on Victoria Island, Canadian Tundra is herein broadened and clarified from Noble's (1971:107) first definition. As a regional variant of the late Arctic Small Tool tradition, the Canadian Tundra tradition represents a distinctive caribou-adapted Paleo-Eskimo culture in the tundra-taiga of central-northern Canada. Components are recognizable from Victoria Island (W.E. Taylor 1964a, 1967) southeastward through interior District of Mackenzie to Great Slave Lake (Noble 1971), the Thelon River (B.H.C. Gordon 1975; Harp 1961), the upper Dubawnt (Talzoa) drainage system (Noble 1971:109; James V. Wright, personal communication 1972), North Henik Lake (Irving 1968a), and northeastern Manitoba (Nash 1969) (fig. 3). Indeed, there are indications that it penetrates as far southwest as northeastern Lake Athabasca (J.V. Wright 1975) and Black Lake in northern Saskatchewan (Minni 1976). In short, it has been found on virtually every major river system transecting the forest border in north-central Canada.

Regional variants occur within the Canadian Tundra tradition, and it is clear from distributional, dating (table 2), and artifactual evidence that these people had adapted to the forest border by 1200 B.C. While the

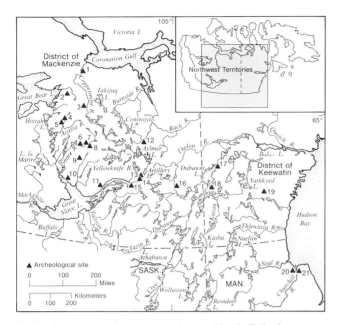

Fig. 3. Canadian Tundra tradition sites: 1, Bloody Falls; 2, Samandré Lake; 3, Rocknest Lake; 4, Esker End; 5, Dry Creek; 6, Deception Point; 7, Canteen; 8, Aurora River; 9, Greenstockings Lake; 10, Frank Channel; 11, MacKinlay River; 12, Sussex Lake; 13, Snowgoose; 14, Timber Point; 15, Pike's Portage; 16, Junction; 17, Migod; 18, Telzoa River; 19, North Henik Lake; 20, Twin Lakes; 21, Sea Horse Gully.

forest border shifted southward between 1500 and 1000 B.C. in District of Keewatin (Sorenson and Knox 1974), available evidence suggests a more stabilized contemporary forest margin in the Great Slave–Great Bear lakes region (Noble 1974). This factor is significant, for the wintering grounds of the Great Slave–Great Bear lakes Barren Ground caribou may not have altered as B.H.C. Gordon (1975) has suggested occurred for the herds of the Thelon-Keewatin region. That Barren Ground caribou were hunted by the Canadian Tundra peoples is attested by excavated calcined bone (Noble 1971:109; B.H.C. Gordon 1975).

The Canadian Tundra tradition has distinctive cultural and technological features. Diagnostic of this tradition are linear and oval bifaces of orange-pink and white quartzites. Thin and well fashioned, such bifaces have no known prototypes in the interior (Noble 1971:108). Highlighting the adaptation to the forest border are woodworking tools including ground adzes and chert drills. Bone tools are not preserved in the inland continental sites, although they are known for the Victoria Island components (W.E. Taylor 1964a, 1967, 1972). Certainly, the small, concave-based triangular and side-notched chert points, lateral insets, asymmetrical knives, burins, burin spalls, microblades, and microcores attest to the close relationship and ultimate derivation of Canadian Tundra with other Arctic Small Tool Paleo-Eskimo manifestations.

In the Great Slave to Great Bear lakes region, components of the Canadian Tundra tradition invariably

are located on sand exposures in protected bays, on sheltered points, on esker fans, or on islands of main waterways. Usually, five to eight hearths demarcated by fire-broken rock (roasting hearths) exist at each component, and sites lie in succession about one-half mile apart from one another. Some sites are up to 150 miles within the present forest border (Noble 1971:107). Osteological remains and burial patterns remain unknown for the Canadian Tundra.

As indicated in table 2, the widespread Canadian Tundra tradition dates about 1300 to 600 B.C., based upon radiocarbon determinations, artifact seriation, and relative beachline correlations. Three complexes are recognized within this time span, and they help demonstrate culture change within the tradition. The complexes include Rocknest Lake, Aurora River, and Timber Point (Noble 1971).

Rocknest Lake Complex, 1300–1100 B.C.

Represented by three components, none of which occurs south of 64° 28′ north latitude, the Rocknest Lake complex takes its name after the type site (LjPh–1) on the middle Coppermine River.

In Rocknest Lake, oval, pink quartzite bifaces and others of black slate and metamorphosed limonite accompany typical Arctic Small Tools, such as small serrated triangular white chert points with concave bases. Asymmetrical knives, semilunar lateral insets, rectangular drill bases, snubnose and flake scrapers complement the tool kit (fig. 4 l–m), as do very rare quartz crystal microblades and chert burins. Clearly distinctive are heavily ground and polished adzes of banded gray-brown chert (Noble 1971:107).

Rocknest Lake bears its closest similarities to the Wellington Bay (NiNg–7), Buchanan (NiNg–1), and Menez (NiNg–10) sites on southern Victoria Island (W.E. Taylor 1964a, 1967). Close ties cannot be drawn with McGhee's (1970:58) 1350 B.C. Bloody Falls site or with the presumably earlier Dismal Lake (MiPr–2) component (Harp 1958:227).

Aurora River Complex, 1100–800 B.C.

The Aurora River complex has a wide distribution in the interior, extending along the Acasta, Snare, Yellowknife, upper Back, and Lockhart rivers down to Great Slave Lake. It also appears to extend eastward to the Thelon River.

Thin pink quartzite bifaces continue from Rocknest Lake and are complemented by the appearance of small, thin ovate bifaces (Noble 1971:108). Small chert tools in the tool kit (fig. 4 a–e,h,n) include drills, concave-base points, various scrapers, small rectangular knives, and rare microblades. Burins are both ground and unground. Of the multicolored cherts distinctive

101

Table 2. The Canadian Tundra Tradition 1300–600 B.C.

Time	Victoria Island (W.E. Taylor 1964a, 1967)	Central Mackenzie District (Noble 1971)	Upper Thelon (B.H.C. Gordon 1975)	Northern Manitoba (Nash 1969)
400 B.C.				
500				
600				
	650 ± 130(GSC–656)?			
700				
		Timber Point 800–600		
800				
			890 ± 95(I–5975)	
900	930 ± 105(I–2058)		940 ± 125(S–632)	
	960 ± 105(I–2053)			Sea Horse Gully
1000	Buchanan-Menez	Aurora River		950 ± 100(S–521)
	1030 ± 150(GSC–713)	1100–800		
	1040 ± 125(I–2054)			
1100				
			1135 ± 70(S–664)	
1200				Twin Lakes
	Wellington Bay	Rocknest Lake	1210 ± 95(I–5978)	
	1230 ± 120(I–2057)	1300–1100		
1300				

in Aurora River components, black chert is particularly conspicuous.

Timber Point Complex, 800–600 B.C.

Typologically late, the Timber Point complex takes its name from the type site (KfNm–13) on southwestern Artillery Lake and appears to be a distinctive local variant of the Canadian Tundra tradition. Burned caribou bone, excavated from a large roasting hearth at the type site and also at the Deception Point site on Snare Lake, indicates one facet of the subsistence pattern.

Innovations are apparent in the Timber Point tool kit (fig. 4f–g, i–k). Not only are a wider range of raw materials being utilized, including welded tuff from the Mackenzie River (Jacques Cinq-Mars, personal communication 1974), but also small convex-based and thin side-notched points appear for the first time (Noble 1971:109). Small quartzite ulus also occur alongside well-fashioned microblades, burins, burin spalls, lateral insets, drills, native copper, and small rectangular knives. Predictably, oval to ovate bifaces (Noble 1971:109) are present.

The fate of the Canadian Tundra tradition peoples is not yet fully documented, but some populations obviously penetrated southeastward through the interior toward northern Manitoba. Others, like Timber Point, apparently remained in local areas.

Taltheilei Shale Tradition, 500 B.C.–A.D. 1840

Named after R.S. MacNeish's (1951:38) pioneer Taltheilei complex, Taltheilei Shale is a major ancestral

Noble 1971:figs. 5–7.

Fig. 4. Arctic Small Tool (Canadian Tundra) tradition. Aurora River complex: a, small concave base white chert point; b, flake scraper; c, snub-nosed scraper; d-e, burins; h, slate whetstone; n, adz. Timber Point complex: f, small convex based, thin side-notched point; g, chert semilunar and biconvex lateral insets; i, distinctive form of "eared" end scraper; j, snub-nosed scraper; k, chert burin with straight base. Rocknest Lake complex: l, asymmetrical knife; m, rectangular based drill bit (tip broken). Length of a about 2.4 cm, rest same scale.

Athapaskan tradition (Noble 1971, 1975). It lies widespread across much of the historic Yellowknife-Chipewyan homeland (fig. 5). From Great Bear Lake to Lake Athabasca, artifact manufacture is characterized by a

102

prolific use of gray silicious shale derived from outcrops on eastern Great Slave Lake, while elsewhere to the east, quartzites provide the most readily available materials.

Taltheilei is most completely known from eastern Great Slave Lake, where 10 successive complexes are found on beaches elevated 5 to 62 feet above mean sea level (Noble 1971). Beginning with Hennessey, the tradition can be traced through Taltheilei, Windy Point, Waldron River, Narrows, Lockhart River, Frank Channel, Fairchild Bay, and Snare River to the early historic and pre-missionary Reliance phase, an aboriginal Athapaskan culture attributable to the Yellowknife-Chipewyan Indians. Outside of this Great Slave Lake core area, distributions and dating for certain of the complexes are being expanded (B.H.C. Gordon 1975; Irving 1968a; Minni 1976; Nash 1970; J.V. Wright 1972, 1975). However, the ultimate origins of Taltheilei Shale remain unknown.

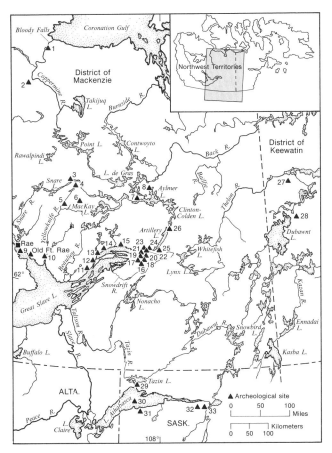

Fig. 5. Taltheilei Shale tradition sites: 1, Sandwillow, Willowherb, Lapointe, and IhOk-1; 2, Kamut Lake; 3, Ft. Enterprise; 4, Windy Point; 5, Snare River; 6, Sandbluff; 7, Drybones; 8, Aylmer Lake; 9, Frank Channel; 10, Giant Mines; 11, Taltheilei; 12, MacKinlay River; 13, Observation; 14, Mining; 15, Waldron River; 16, Pike's Portage, Juncture; 17, Fairchild Bay; 18, Caribou; 19, Ft. Reliance; 20, Narrows (KeNo-2); 21, Back; 22, Hennessey; 23, Many Hearths; 24, Jean; 25, Haig; 26, Lockhart River; 27, Beverly Lake-8; 28, Migod; 29, Charlot River; 30, Beartooth Island; 31, IgOg-4; 32, Black Lake; 33, IhNh-2.

Cultural conservation is a feature throughout the Taltheilei Shale tradition, with changes in artifact styles being few and demonstrably slow over time. For instance, spearing lanceolates continue to be the single most effective weapon in killing caribou right into the historic era (Pike 1892:48, 51). Also, the bow and arrow, as indicated by small corner and side-notched points, appears in the Great Slave Lake region only circa A.D. 1100, whereas such projectiles occur in the eastern Chipewyan territory at least 500 years earlier (Nash 1970:80–85). Persisting throughout the tradition are pointed bifaces, sandstone chithos, barlike whetstones, flake scrapers, bladelike flakes, bipolar hammerstones, and bipolar pieces (Noble 1971).

Hennessey Complex, 500–200 B.C.

Hennessey (fig. 6a–f) marks the beginning of the Taltheilei Shale tradition and, as such, it is remarkably homogeneous over a widespread territory from Great Slave Lake (Noble 1971) to Lake Athabasca (J.V. Wright 1975) and eastward to Keewatin (B.H.C. Gordon 1975; Irving 1968a; Minni 1976). It represents the return of Indians to the transitional forest and tundra east of the Great Slave–Great Bear lakes region after Paleo-Eskimo occupation.

On eastern Great Slave Lake, Hennessey materials appear on beaches elevated 61–68 feet, particularly at MacKinlay River (Noble 1971:111). Dates of 395 B.C. ± 170 (S–737), 405 B.C. ± 80 (S–715), and 490 B.C. ± 120 (S–711) reported for Hennessey from the upper Thelon (B.H.C. Gordon 1975) have allowed a more precise dating estimate for this complex.

Characterized by short, wide-stemmed lanceolates, the Hennessey point type has incipient to well-defined shoulders, and the slightly tapering stems are ground along the lateral margins. Other point forms at this time also include short, unground pentagonal and rare bipointed specimens (Noble 1971:111). Quartzites are particularly abundant as raw materials during this early phase of the tradition, but gray silicious shale, multicolored cherts, basalt, and red slate are also utilized.

Taltheilei Complex, 200 B.C.–A.D. 200

Originally defined by R.S. MacNeish (1951:38) as an early complex, Taltheilei (fig. 6g–j) proves to be an integral phase of the Taltheilei Shale tradition. Occurring on beaches 52 to 57 feet above northeastern Great Slave Lake, this complex has a distribution from Great Slave Lake northward to Kamut Lake, Bloody Falls on the lower Coppermine, Aylmer Lake, and eastward from Artillery Lake to the Thelon. Thus, the known range of the Taltheilei complex extends farther north and south than the preceding Hennessey phase. Caribou bone from the Sandwillow site of this complex dates

103

A.D. 160 ± 70 (S–465) (McGhee 1970:59), but, clearly, more radiocarbon dates are desirable in order to firmly position this complex in time.

In this period, the diagnostic long, ground stemmed Taltheilei point (Noble 1971:111) makes its appearance. It differs from the shorter Hennessey type, but apart from these changes in projectiles, the remainder of the Taltheilei tool kit remains unchanged from Hennessey times.

Windy Point Complex, A.D. 200–400

Distributed from Great Slave Lake to the upper Snare River system, the Windy Point complex sees the replacement of long, ground stemmed lanceolates by short unground stemmed forms, as well as the advent of long unground Agate Basin–like lanceolates. Aside from these differences and the presence of a small native copper awl or punch, the usual bifaces, chithos, scrapers, bladelike flakes, and bipolar pieces continue in unchanging fashion. From excavated bone, dependence upon caribou is evident. Windy Point components invariably lie 42–48 feet above the mean northeastern Great Slave Lake level (Noble 1971:111).

Waldron River Complex, A.D. 400–800

Named after the rich type site (KfNt–1) at the mouth of Waldron River on northeastern Great Slave Lake, this complex (fig. 6k–m) occurs on beach terraces 32–38 feet high. It is distributed from eastern Great Slave Lake through the upper Lockhart River system to the Snare and Emile rivers, to the lower Coppermine River. Dated A.D. 385 ± 90 (I–5821) from the type site, dates of A.D. 500 ± 80 (S–468) and A.D. 570 ± 150 (S–466) are known from the comparable Willowherb and Lapointe sites (McGhee 1970:62–63).

Projectiles in Waldron River include straight to round-based unground lanceolates alongside other unground lanceolates with tapered bases. Sharply defined stemming disappears. Barlike slate whetstones complement the remainder of the tool kit, which duplicates that in Windy Point.

Narrows Complex, A.D. 800–1100

The Narrows complex (fig. 6n–p) is distributed from northern Lake Athabasca (IhOk–1 site—materials in the Saskatchewan Provincial Museum, Regina), along northeastern Great Slave Lake to eastern Artillery Lake. At the type site (KeNo–2) opposite old Fort Reliance, burned caribou bone from a large roasting hearth dates A.D. 940 ± 160 (GaK–1258) and A.D. 1070 ± 130 (I–4973), while another sample from the laterally distributed multicomponent Hennessey site on Artillery Lake returns a date of A.D. 1075 ± 95 (S–587). On

eastern Great Slave Lake, Narrows components lie 27–30 feet in elevation.

Distinctive in the Narrows tool kit are slightly tapered unground lanceolates with straight bases. Apart from this slight developmental change in projectiles, no new developments occur.

Lockhart River Complex, A.D. 1100–1300

Lockhart River represents the best defined of R.S. MacNeish's (1951:33) pioneer complexes, but temporally it falls within the middle period of the Taltheilei Shale tradition. It is during this phase that corner and side-notched points first appear in the tradition in the Great Slave–Great Bear lakes region, and the origin of this concept requires future clarification. Lockhart components are distributed from eastern Great Slave Lake through Artillery Lake to the upper Coppermine drainage. On eastern Great Slave Lake they lie on beaches elevated 25–27 feet above mean lake level.

Frank Channel Complex, A.D. 1300–1500

Named after the type site (KePl–1), seven miles south of Rae, northwestern Great Slave Lake (Noble 1971), the Frank Channel complex (fig. 6q–x) has a distribution from Black Lake, Saskatchewan (Minni 1976), to Lake Athabasca (J.V. Wright 1975), the upper Lockhart River, Artillery Lake (Noble 1971), and eastward to District of Keewatin (J.V. Wright 1972). The type site is elevated 11 feet above northwestern Great Slave Lake, while comparable components lie 20 to 24 feet above the water level of eastern Great Slave Lake.

Dates of A.D. 1280 ± 70 (GaK–1865) and A.D. 1590 ± 180 (GSC–1559) from the type site are complemented at the Haig site on Artillery Lake with a date of A.D. 1410 ± 95 (I–4550) and a date of A.D. 1340 ± 110 (GaK–3799) from the Charlot River component on northern Lake Athabasca (J.V. Wright 1975). Circular tent rings occur at both of these sites.

Frank Channel exhibits delicate side-notched points alongside rare lanceolates and small incipient stemmed projectiles. The usual bifaces, scrapers, chithos, barlike whetstones, and bladelike flakes are complemented by native copper pieces, bone fish gorges, unilaterally barbed bone points, and unstitched birchbark tinder rolls (Noble 1971:114). Faunal resources eaten by the Frank Channel people include: woodland caribou, black bear, beaver, muskrat, snowshoe hare, whistling swans, Canada geese, and fish including inconnu and northern pike. In all, this represents a typical boreal forest subsistence adaptation.

Fairchild Bay Complex, A.D. 1500–1700

Deriving from Frank Channel, Fairchild Bay materials are distributed from eastern Great Slave Lake to Ar-

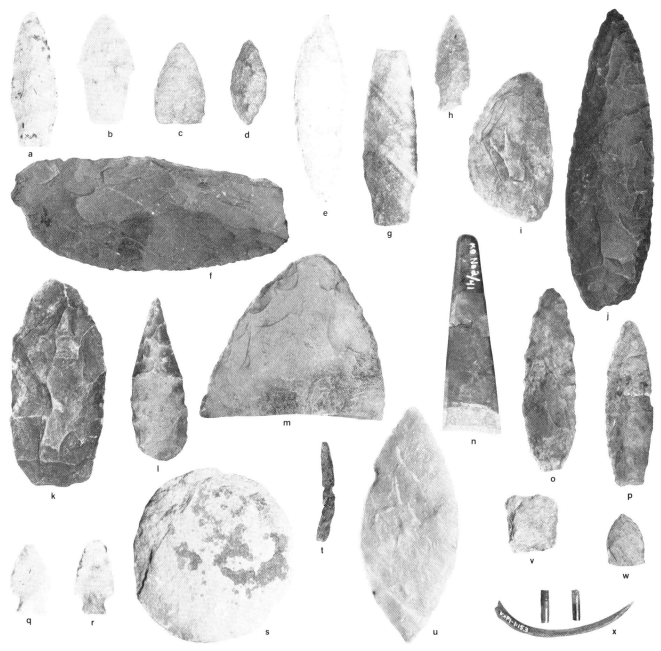

Noble 1971:figs. 9–10, 12–14.

Fig. 6. Taltheilei Shale tradition. Hennessey complex: a-b, Hennessey point; c, pentagonally shaped point with straight thinned base; d, unique bipoint; e, knife; f, linear biface. Taltheilei complex: g, Taltheilei point; h, MacKinlay point; i, semilunar biface; j, red slate knife. Waldron River complex: k, biface; l, knife; m, biface. Narrows complex: n, slate whetstone; o-p, slightly tapered unground lanceolate points with straight bases. Frank Channel complex: q-r, corner removed points; s, circular chitho; t, native copper punch; u, biface; v, "wedge" (*pièce esquillée*); w, stubby triangular point; x, unique incised bone pegs. Length of a about 7.2 cm, rest same scale.

tillery Lake (Noble 1971:114). Few changes in lithics are seen, although overall, workmanship is qualitatively inferior. Side-notched and lanceolate projectiles persist, as do the gray silicious shale bifaces and other standard tools in the tradition.

On eastern Great Slave Lake this complex occurs on beaches elevated 15–19 feet.

Snare River Complex, A.D. 1700–1770

As the final late prehistoric phase of the Taltheilei Shale tradition, Snare River proves useful in linking the prehistoric with the early historic era. The complex occurs on beaches 11–15 feet above eastern Great Slave Lake and is distributed in the triangle bordered by Great

Slave and Artillery lakes northward to Snare and Kamut lakes. Beachlines, typological seriation, radiocarbon and historic dating help bracket the Snare River complex to A.D. 1700–1770.

A date of A.D. 1740 ± 80 (S–474) from the Snare River site augments dates of A.D. 1765 (I–4375) from the Observation site (Noble 1971:115) and A.D. 1740 ± 90 (I–3956) from a four-foot diameter roasting hearth at the Kamut Lake site. None of the above components exhibits historic articles that conceivably could have appeared in 1771–1772 as a result of Samuel Hearne's explorations through the Great Slave Lake–Coppermine River regions.

The late prehistoric Snare River complex sees small side-notched points and slender lithic lanceolates occurring alongside native copper lanceolates. Bifaces, scrapers, barlike whetstones, chithos, bladelike flakes, and birchbark tinder rolls are continuing traits. Excavated calcined caribou bone attests to one facet of the subsistence pattern.

Reliance Complex, A.D. 1770–1840

The early historic, premissionary Reliance complex sees a marked reduction in aboriginal tools in the face of trade with Europeans. Known primarily from items excavated at Franklin's (1823) 1820–1821 Fort Enterprise (Losey 1973) and Back's (1836) 1834–1836 Fort Reliance (Noble 1971), this complex covers northern Great Slave Lake to the lower Coppermine River. Indeed, Reliance represents a last complex of the Taltheilei Shale tradition and can be assigned to the early historic Yellowknife-Chipewyan (Noble 1971, 1975).

In this complex, small side-notched quartzite points continue, as do shale bifaces and scrapers. Indicating the early historic and acculturated nature of the Reliance complex are European blue glass trade beads, kaolin pipe stems, iron and copper bangles, brass and pearl buttons, chinaware, and gunflints (Noble 1971:115). The use of the bow and arrow alongside the gun is a feature of the early historic period, and, indeed, lithic-tipped spears continued to be used until the early 1890s (Pike 1892:48, 51). Burials during this early historic era

are ground interments within spruce-log tombs (Noble and Anderson 1972).

Dogrib Ancestry

In the Great Slave to Great Bear Lake region, the archeological antecedents of the present-day Dogrib remain vague. Only the relatively modern and historic Rae phases of the Dogrib have been defined (Noble 1975). A period of Dogrib-Yellowknife hostilities (about 1780–1823) in the early historic era produced shifts in the territories occupied by the two peoples. By 1823 Back (1836:457) observed that the Yellowknife had withdrawn to the "barren hills bordering on Great Slave Lake." From that time on, the Dogribs held the upper hand and became firmly established on the North Arm of Great Slave Lake, particularly at Old Fort Rae (KdPl-1), after its founding in 1852.

Eskimo in the Interior

As in Keewatin, modern Eskimo penetrations and occupations in central District of MacKenzie are a very recent phenomenon. Two sites demonstrate this. One is the Copper Eskimo site (LiNj–1) observed by Pike (1892) on the middle Back River (Noble 1975:780). It was judged by Pike's Yellowknife Indian guide to have been recently occupied, and the soapstone bowls collected from the site and later forwarded to the National Museum of Canada, Ottawa, are indeed late nineteenth-century styles.

The other known Eskimo site in central District of Mackenzie consists of a find of fresh seal fur picked up by Blanchet (1964:39) at the southwest end of Aylmer Lake in 1924. This find and a large rock cairn recorded by Noble (1975) in 1967 on the same river system most probably are artifacts left by the Kiluhikturmiut band of the Copper Eskimo (David Damas, personal communication 1971). During the mid-1920s these Eskimo people apparently were extending their late summer hunting territory into the former Yellowknife hunting grounds.

Prehistory of the Western Subarctic

DONALD W. CLARK

The regional scope of this chapter is interior northwestern North America—the western Subarctic (fig. 1). With a few exceptions, archeological sites in the western Subarctic are either small and sparse or involve shallow multiple occupations, often over large areas, that are disturbed and mixed through frost action. Organic material seldom is preserved except in late sites.

Within the recent past, the western Subarctic—interior Alaska, the Cordillera, and western Mackenzie District—was occupied exclusively by Athapaskan-speaking groups, but in the remoter past the linguistic and cultural alignments were not necessarily the same. Early historic and late prehistoric archeological material can be linked through the direct historical approach to the ethnographic Indian groups of the region, and, moving further back in time, to probable Athapaskan antecedents of the last two millennia. These cultures postdate a congeries of microblade complexes, certain of which may have an antiquity equal to the latest Paleo-Indian cultures. In fact, some of the sequences suggested here for the early prehistory of the region may ultimately prove to reflect spatial rather than temporal relationships.

History of Research

Almost all understanding of the prehistory of the western Subarctic has been gained since 1940; only in Subarctic Alaska was fieldwork initiated prior to World War II.

The first intradisciplinary anthropological survey of interior Alaska was carried out in 1926 by Hrdlička (1930, 1943), whose work along the Yukon River was followed by archeologically focused surveys and excavations on the lower Yukon by De Laguna (1936a, 1947) and by Rainey (1939, 1940) at various locations in the interior including Dixthada and the Campus site. Work on the Campus site had been started earlier by John B. Dorsh and a brief report published by N.C. Nelson (1937). Before her lower Yukon surveys De Laguna (1934) also had surveyed Tanaina sites on Cook Inlet as part of a program oriented toward prehistoric Indian-Eskimo relationships in interior Alaska.

In 1944 and 1948 the southwest Yukon Territory received its first attention from archeologists (F. Johnson 1946; Johnson and Raup 1964; R.S. MacNeish 1964:201–202 rc Leechman). Later surveys and excavations by

R.S. MacNeish (1960, 1964), including northernmost British Columbia, extended from 1947 through 1960. The first excavations in central British Columbia were made during the period 1950–1952 (Borden 1953). Little additional work was done in central or northern British Columbia until late in the 1960s. Pioneer activity in the western and central Mackenzie District from 1949 through 1952 by R.S. MacNeish (1951, 1953, 1954, 1955) preceded his work on the Arctic coast and in southwest Yukon Territory. Excavations at Pointed Mountain near Fort Liard resulted in the preliminary definition of the Northwest Microblade tradition (R.S. MacNeish 1954). Bliss (1939) had located a single nondiagnostic site on the Yukon-Mackenzie border.

Archeological exploration accelerated greatly throughout the Western Subarctic in the 1960s, with some new areas such as the northern interior Yukon (Morlan 1973; Irving and Cinq-Mars 1974) and the Stikine River drainage (J.W. Smith 1970, 1971) opened to investigation for the first time. During the 1970s surveys and salvage excavations along rights-of-way and communication corridors relating to northern development figured prominently in northern field research (J.P. Cook 1977; Anonymous 1974; Cinq-Mars 1973a, 1974:C1–C20; Janes 1974; Millar and Fedirchuk 1975; Anonymous 1970, 1971).

In 1980 investigations into the prehistory of the northern half of Alberta were only emerging from the pioneer stage. Interpretive analysis of the few excavated sites in that region has consisted largely of their assignment to a few broad cultural units or spheres of influence previously recognized elsewhere in western North America. In Alaska the overall picture is taking form through internally generated and (early) east Siberian models; in the Yukon territory there are reasonably detailed southern and northern sequences; in British Columbia there are numerous data but with many temporal and regional gaps so that there is a diversity of interpretation without universal agreement; while for the western Mackenzie District the many small and poorly dated collections have yet to be acceptably organized.

The Paleo-Indian Horizon

Early man entered the New World from Siberia in the area of the former Bering Sea land bridge and spread

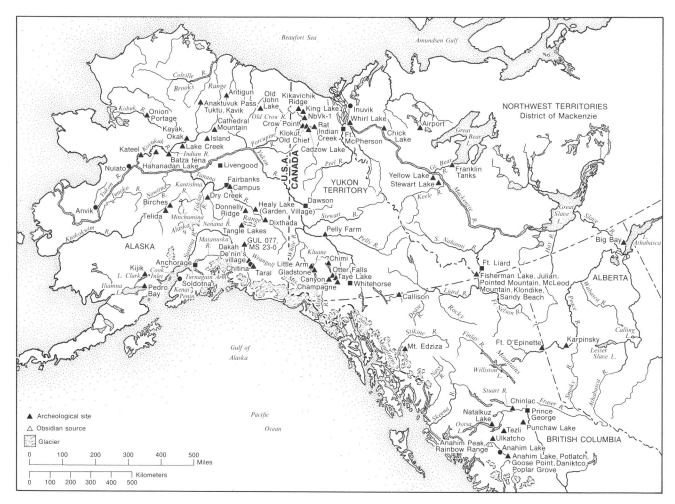

Fig. 1. Primary archeological sites in the western Subarctic area.

eastward through parts of Alaska and the Yukon Territory. When conditions permitted he extended his range southward either through intermountain valleys or along the Mackenzie River drainage.

Of the earliest inhabitants of northwestern North America there are few substantiated finds, but 27,000-year-old bone artifacts from the northern Yukon Territory are offered as evidence of man's presence (fig. 3a) (Irving 1971; Harington, Bonnichsen, and Morlan 1975). Firmer evidence for a later period in the western Subarctic comes in the form of fluted points (fig. 3b–c) that apparently date largely between 9500 and 7500 B.C., although the question of their age and relationships remains unresolved. If, as some archeologists believe, they are a Plains culture element that diffused northward and was adopted by the early indigenous cultures, here identified with microblade production, then there may yet be no known continental Paleo-Indian horizon west of the Mackenzie valley. Early Paleo-Indian material and associated faunal collections, in particular those from the Old Crow River, continued to be amassed, but in situ living sites have yet to be recognized. Somewhat later material (fig. 3d–e) characterized by leaf-shaped projectile points may belong

to a Cordilleran tradition, but this entity is very poorly defined in the region. Much of the central (and eastern) Subarctic had not recovered from the last glaciation until about 8000 to 6000 B.C., at which time the Northwest Territories was colonized by hunters whose non-fluted spear points link them with the later Paleo-Indian culture of the northern Plains. In the Mackenzie valley, however, probable Plano horizon remains (very late Paleo-Indian) continue to be scarce, especially inasmuch as it has been recognized that much of the Franklin Tanks complex at Great Bear Lake, identified by some as Plano (R.S. MacNeish 1955), is stylistically similar to material found elsewhere that is known to be about 2,000 years old. It thus may be related to the Taltheilei Shale tradition. The Paleo-Indian archeological cultures of North America, including those of the Subarctic, are treated in detail in volume 3 of the *Handbook*.

The Middle Millennia (about 8000 B.C.–A.D. 1) and the Microblade Industries

Essentially coterminous with the late Paleo-Indian cultures, a different development, traced ultimately to

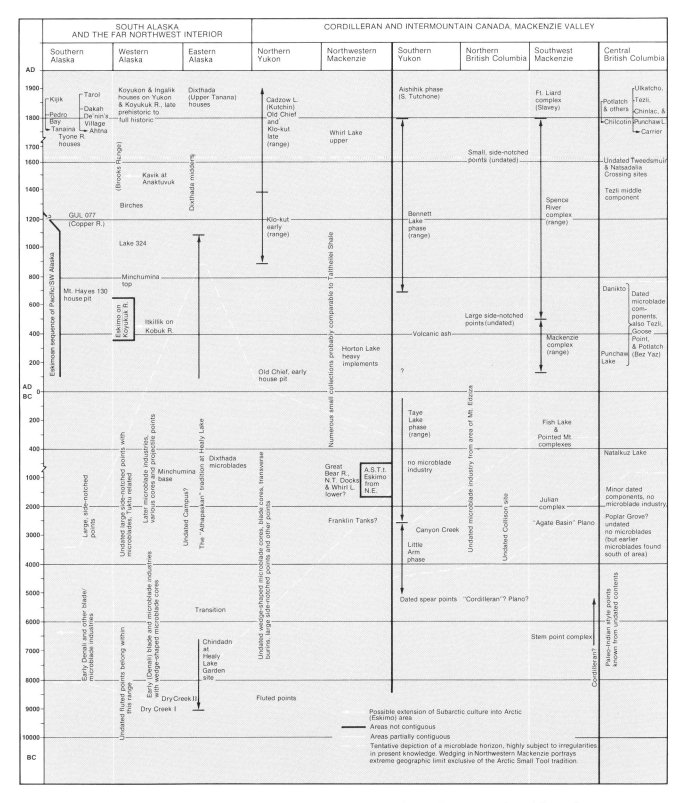

Fig. 2. Chronological subdivisions of western Subarctic prehistory. Millar (1979) redates and renames portions of the southwestern Mackenzie sequence. A.S.T.t. represents the Arctic Small Tool tradition in the northwestern Mackenzie sequence.

Natl. Mus. of Canada, Ottawa: a, M; VI–1 (Loc. 14 N); b, Rk Ig—30:220; c, RI Ig—47:13; d, JcRw—13.113.7; e, JcRw—13.93.18. d-e from U. of Saskatchewan research program.

Fig. 3. Paleo-Indian implements. a, Flesher from Old Crow Flats, Yukon Terr.; b, fluted point, unfinished and broken from Batza téna, Alaska, specimen waxed; c, atypically short obsidian fluted point from Koyukuk River, Alaska, specimen waxed; d, multiple tip graver associated with Cordilleran complex from Julian, Mackenzie District; e, end scraper of Cordilleran complex type from Julian. Length of a 25.5 cm, rest same scale.

northeastern Asia, had become established in Alaska. New populations that traveled across the flooding Bering Sea land bridge had a technology that emphasized long, flat, parallel-sided prismatic stone blades (fig. 4v–x) and more particularly their diminutive counterpart, microblades (fig. 4cc-ii).

Blades and microblades are specialized forms of flakes produced through highly controlled procedures; they can be shaped and hafted for use in a large range of cutting, carving, and scraping implements. Microblade-producing cultures are particular to northern prehistory, of both Indians and Eskimos and their common or separate antecedents, as well as being characteristic of Stone Age cultures of Eurasia. With this technological element they are in contrast to the fluted point, Cordilleran, and Plano Paleo-Indian cultures that have their roots or strongest expression elsewhere, in southern Canada and the contiguous United States.

Widely separated sites of microblade-producing cultures show considerable diversity even at an early time level and form in the north a cultural tradition, or later several related traditions, which underwent development and regional variation over a broad time span (D.D. Anderson 1968, 1970a; J.P. Cook 1971, 1975; Cook and McKennan 1971; D.W. Clark 1977a; Dixon and Johnson 1971; Gordon and Savage 1974; Holmes 1973, 1973a, 1974, 1975; Hadleigh-West 1967; Irving and Cinq-Mars 1974; R.S. MacNeish 1964; Millar 1968; Shinkwin 1975; J.W. Smith 1974; Workman 1974, 1978). Some archeologists have placed the material from the earliest sites of the temporally broad microblade horizon into a "Paleo-Arctic tradition" (Dumond 1977; originally a more restricted American Paleo-Arctic tradition was defined by D.D. Anderson 1970).

Nearly all work in antler, bone, and wood has disappeared from the campsites of the microblade-producing peoples; but in addition to the microblades and cores (less often larger blades) there are in the durable stone implement assemblages various knives and spear points, including in later phases large side-notched points (fig. 4k); large knives (fig. 4a,m), often roughly flaked; rough chopping tools (fig. 4f–i); end and side scrapers (fig. 4d,p–r,t); sometimes notched cobbles or net sinkers (fig. 4rr); and specialized carving, grooving, and scraping implements called burins (fig. 4jj–ll).

Microblade-producing people had reached western Alaska by 9000 B.C. Bearers of this technique had spread into central Alaska by 8500 B.C., to eastern Alaska by 7000 B.C., the southern Yukon Territory before 4000 B.C., and northern interior British Columbia about the same time, while the technique appeared in the western Mackenzie District about 2500 B.C. A largely unrelated early offshoot appears to be responsible for other microblade-producing cultures located along the coast of southern Alaska and British Columbia, which are as much as 9,000 years old. By A.D. 1, or a few centuries later, these industries had passed out of existence throughout much of northwestern North America. Microblade technology was not employed by peoples very far east of the Mackenzie River except when it was brought in relatively late by proto-Eskimos from the north.

Investigations at two sites, Campus in Alaska and Pointed Mountain in Mackenzie District, are of historic importance. N.C. Nelson's (1935, 1937) report indicated the probable early Asian affinities exhibited by the distinctive wedge-shaped microblade cores from the Campus site, an observation that set an interpretive framework that has continued to the present day. Further excavations at the Campus site (Rainey 1939; J.M. Campbell 1968) have revealed the following characteristic implements: leaf-shaped and side-notched projectile points, biface knives and spear heads, rough and very crude bifaces and cleavers, microblade cores and microblades, end scrapers, and burinated flakes of the Donnelly burin variety (Hadleigh-West 1967). It has not been possible to date the Campus site; most artifact types represented there have been found elsewhere in sites that date between 4000 B.C. and A.D. 1, so the original significance of this site has paled.

The Pointed Mountain site, located near Fisherman Lake, Northwest Territories, 800 miles southeast of the

Campus site, has yielded an assemblage also characterized by microblades along with the occasional bifaced blade, burinated flake (Fort Liard burin), and microcore fragment (R.S. MacNeish 1954). The site has a radiocarbon date of 320 B.C. ± 75 (S–194), which is unexpectedly young and is accepted only provisionally pending analysis of later work done at the site. In looking for wider relationships in the Pointed Mountain complex R.S. MacNeish (1954:252) suggested that "in interior northwest North America . . . there is a series of related sites with a distinctive cultural pattern." In defining this pattern MacNeish drew attention to a congeries of crude implements as well as to the microblade and core industry. Included in this pattern were the Campus and Pointed Mountain sites along with others from the intervening area. This pattern became known as the Northwest Microblade tradition, and until the 1970s it was the major synthetic construct for prehistory in the region.

Syntheses of the Middle Millennia and the Microblade Industries

Northwest Microblade Tradition

The first construct to draw widespread attention was the Northwest Microblade tradition, which is not only extremely variable (Irving 1963) but also unverifiable in the estimation of many archeologists.

R.S. MacNeish (1964) redefined the Northwest Microblade tradition on the basis of Yukon prehistory. The Pointed Mountain and Campus sites, upon which the formulation earlier was based, were "more hesitatingly assigned to this tradition because they do not have all the diagnostic traits" (R.S. MacNeish 1964:346). The Tuktu complex of Anaktuvuk Pass was placed in the tradition with the same reservations, while N.T. Docks and others were given an even more peripheral status. This in effect restricted the tradition to a relatively local complex, yet a broader entity seemingly was envisioned.

Denali Complex

In 1967 the Denali complex was proposed as "an early core and blade complex in central Alaska," which included the Donnelly Ridge site, the Campus site, and others (Hadleigh-West 1967). Most Denali traits are present also in the Northwest Microblade tradition although some, such as wedge-shaped microblade cores and Donnelly burins, lack prominence in MacNeish's reports. The Denali complex could, according to some definitions, be regarded as an early segment of a broader tradition. However, if both the early and late age estimates are correct, it must have been very long-lived, through 8,000 years, and thus it would in fact be

a tradition involving continuity of development in technology if not also in peoples.

Hadleigh-West (1972) has limited its application to blade and microblade assemblages lacking stone projectile heads, thus sharpening and narrowing its focus in terms of content and probably early temporal range. However, points may be present (intrusive?) at some Denali sites.

(American) Paleo-Arctic Tradition

Early blade and microblade and core industries found on and north of the Kobuk River in northwestern Alaska belong to the American Paleo-Arctic tradition as adumbrated by D.D. Anderson (1968, 1970a, 1970b). A close relationship is seen between this material, particularly from the Akmak complex, and material dated to 7000–5000 B.C. from the Alaska Peninsula, and both are subsumed within a Paleo-Arctic tradition (Dumond 1977; Henn 1978). Both come from outside the Subarctic boundary as defined for this volume, but they bear directly upon the problem under discussion inasmuch as a close relationship and possible identity is seen with both the Paleo-Arctic tradition and the Denali complex (D.D. Anderson 1970a:7, 1970b:64; Dumond 1977; Hadleigh-West 1972:8).

Northern Archaic Tradition

The Northern Archaic tradition is dated by radiocarbon approximately from 4000 to 2300 B.C. at Onion Portage where it follows the American Paleo-Arctic tradition (D.D. Anderson 1968). Most of the diagnostic elements of the Northwest Microblade tradition are found in the Northern Archaic tradition (D.D. Anderson 1970a:8); the main points of difference are the absence of the microblade industry itself and of burins in the Northern Archaic. Several specialists have extended the term to include a number of early side-notched point complexes usually, but not always, lacking a microblade industry, which are somewhat later than Denali or Paleo-Arctic sites.

Tuktu (Tuktu-Naiyuk) Complex

Although the Tuktu site (J.M. Campbell 1961), like the type sites of the Paleo-Arctic and Northern Archaic traditions, also lies within the historic Eskimo (Arctic) area, it has formed a landmark for the organization of northern interior Alaska archeology. This site, dated early within the Northern Archaic range, contains most of the Northern Archaic diagnostics and, in the Tuktu but not the Naiyuk component, microblades and tabular microblade cores. In the past a distinction between tabular or flat-faced Tuktu cores and narrow wedge-shaped cores has been held to be significant, although inter-

111

41   42   43   44

Natl. Mus. of Canada, Ottawa: a, xi–C:572; b, XI–C:179; c, XI–C:183d; d, XI–C:549; e, XI–C:176; j, KfVd–2; k, RkIn–36:142; l, JiVs–1:34–5a (2774); m, JiVs–1; n, FgSd–1:707; o, XI–C:512b; r, XI–C:170a; s, KkVa–2; t, XI–C:490; y, MgRs–1:16; v, RkIh–28:15; w, JeVc–4; x, LdRq–2:8; dd, JiVs-1:48–46(1054); ee, NcVI–1:12; gg. RkIg–47:65; hh, JiVs:1–34–4a; ii, RkIh–28:27 (lot); jj, JjVg–1:9; kk, MgRs–1:7; ll, JiVs–1:10-5a(2779); mm, RkIh–36:125; nn, JfVg–1:5–4a; oo, JhVf–8; 42. XI–C:522; qq. RkIg–47:90; rr, JfVg–1:7; Natl. Mus. of Canada from U. of Saskatchewan research program: f, JcRx–2.137.6; g, JcRw–10.43.11; h, JcRw–40.15E/14; i, JcRw–13.109.15; p, JcRw–8.123.1; q, JcRx–2.8/10/73; ff, JcRx–2.176.12; U. of Alaska, Fairbanks: x–z; bb; aa, DC–73–4A; U. of Toronto: cc, 70–Sk–2:14.

Fig. 4. Various implements associated with the microblade horizon or otherwise with sites predating A.D. 1. Artifacts from Franklin Tanks, Mackenzie District: a, rough single-edged biface blade; b, small biface blade; c, lanceolate point; d, end scraper on bladelike flake, specimen opaqued; e, lanceolate point of fused tuff, specimen opaqued. Roughly flaked artifacts of Fisherman Lake, Julian technology, Mackenzie District: f, discoidal biface from Pointed Mountain; g, ax or adz from Sandy Beach; h, thick bifacial core tool; i, chisel. Points: j, point from Pelly Farm, southern Yukon Terr.; k, obsidian side-notched point from Batza téna locale, Alaska, specimen opaqued; l, leaf-shaped point from Little Arm, southern Yukon Terr.; m, obsidian oblanceolate point from Little Arm, specimen opaqued; n, fishtail point from Tezli, central B.C.; o, point from Great Bear River, Mackenzie District. Scrapers: p-q, concave beveled flake spokeshaves from McLeod Mountain and Pointed Mountain, Mackenzie District; r, quartzite beveled flake side scraper from Great Bear River; s, uniface from southern Yukon Terr.; t, fused tuff domed end scraper from Great Bear River, specimen opaqued; u, *Limace* shaped uniface from Airport site, Mackenzie District. Blades: v, obsidian core for bladelike flakes from Batza téna, specimen opaqued; w, blade with retouched edges from southern Yukon Terr.; x, fused tuff implement made on blade or bladelike flake, edges and end retouched, from Yellow Lake, western Mackenzie District. Artifacts from Dry Creek, interior Alaska: y, point suggestive of late Paleo-Indian Mohave-type; z, bifacial implement; aa, microblade core; bb, flake exemplifying core technology; cc, tabular microblade core from King Lake no. 2, northern Yukon Terr.; dd, microblade core of a generalized format from Little Arm; ee, wedge-shaped microblade core made on a bifacially prepared blank from Kikavichik Ridge, northern Yukon Terr.; ff, conical microblade core from Pointed Mountain; gg, obsidian platform rejuvenation tablet from microblade core from Batza téna, specimen opaqued; hh-ii, obsidian microblades from Little Arm and Batza téna, all distal ends missing, specimens opaqued. Burins: jj, unusual form, possibly related to notched Donnelly burins, 2 facets, from southern Yukon Terr.; kk, transverse burin from Airport site; ll, obsidian multi-burin of 4 burin facets on a probable biface blank from Little Arm. Other implements: mm, notched pebble chopper from Koyukuk River region; nn, antler hammer head from Canyon, southern Yukon Terr.; oo, larger biface blade from southern Yukon Terr.; pp, fused tuff asymmetrical knife from Great Bear River, specimen opaqued; qq, hammerstone, associated with the production of microblade cores; rr, notched pebble (sinker?) from Canyon. Length of l, 10.0 cm, rest same scale.

mediate forms occur. Tuktu could be classified as early Northern Archaic, as a regional form of the Northwest Microblade tradition, or as a later development out of Denali and the Paleo-Arctic tradition, although the first and the last are incompatible according to some reconstructions of northern prehistory.

The Athapaskan Tradition

For east-central Alaska an "Athapaskan tradition" has been defined as consisting principally of the sequential complexes Tuktu and Denali, along with more recent prehistoric material, Tuktu in this particular case being the oldest (Cook and McKennan 1971). However, Cook (1975) questioned the distinctness as separate complexes, in the local and regional sequences, of Tuktu and Campus or Denali technology.

The Northwest Microblade and the Arctic Small Tool Traditions

The Northwest Microblade and Arctic Small Tool traditions or their equivalents are the two maximum units of synthesis advanced for microblade-producing cultures in the north. Some archeologists have proposed that the two traditions are one and the same thing, or that they are early and late stages of a single tradition. Nevertheless, those most involved with these two traditions early indicated the important differences between them (Giddings 1951; Irving 1962, 1963; R.S. MacNeish 1954). The main characteristics that they have in common are general ones; closer consideration produces critical distinctions. Microblade core types and burin types are quite different and the two traditions present few if any identities, although later in the Arctic Small Tool tradition some Northwest Microblade or seeming interior traits appear in the Choris culture phase. The Denbigh and Pre-Dorset phases of the Arctic Small Tool tradition have many specialized small tools and a distinctive fine flaking style; the Northwest Microblade tradition has many large, rough implements of low characterization and an undistinguished flaking technique.

The two traditions, furthermore, tend to occur in separate geographical and ecological areas. The Arctic Small Tool tradition is essentially a proto- and Paleo- *113*

Eskimo development. The Northwest Microblade tradition, on the other hand, has predominantly a western interior distribution within historic Athapaskan territory.

Early in the history of these tradition concepts it was generally believed that all microblade traditions in the north were related. Ultimately such a relationship probably holds, but it appears to have a time depth of at least 10,000 years, although probably with some later crossties.

The Regional Data

• ALASKA Subsequent to the excavations at the Campus site, early prehistoric material has been excavated at Donnelly Ridge, Healy Lake, Dixthada, and near Livengood northwest of Fairbanks; at Dry Creek, Teklanika River, Lake Minchumina, and numerous sites in the Koyukuk River drainage west of Fairbanks; and in the Tangle Lakes area and near the headwaters of the Susitna River south of the Alaska Range as well as in several other locales but hardly at all in the Copper River basin. In addition, occupations by essentially interior-related cultures have been found in the Brooks Range, on the Kobuk River, and elsewhere within historic Eskimo territory.

One of the more characteristic types of assemblages of northern interior Alaska has been referred to as Tuktu. Among these is the 5,000- to 6,000-year-old Tuktu proper, Bonanza Creek Tuktu (Holmes 1973a), and Batza Téna Tuktu (D.W. Clark 1974). The last two are both from the Koyukuk River drainage and probably are younger than Tuktu proper.

Batza Téna Tuktu is represented primarily by an assemblage from one site located adjacent to the Indian River obsidian source. Obsidian from this source was utilized from Paleo-Indian times onward and was distributed throughout northern interior Alaska and to some coastal locations. A first millennium A.D. radiocarbon date for this site is of dubious validity, but it serves to draw attention to similarly late dates obtained elsewhere for Tuktu- and Denali-like material, thus demonstrating several thousand years of technological continuity for certain traits. Batza téna Tuktu differs from Tuktu at Anaktuvuk Pass (J.M. Campbell 1961) in its relatively low frequency of side-notched and other points (fig. 4k; 4mm is also characteristic of Tuktu), and very low incidence of microblades and microcores. No Tuktu-type (tabular) cores were recovered. A burinlike core found here occurs elsewhere in the northern interior and southward into British Columbia (J.W. Smith 1971: fig. 7–137); technologically it is the Campus-type core described by Hadleigh-West (1967) for the Denali complex.

Farther to the east in interior Alaska at Old John Lake are a number of small sites that appear generally to be related to others of interior Alaska, including particularly those with notched points and microblades that are found in the Koyukuk region to the west (Hall and McKennan 1973).

South of Old John Lake, in the Tanana River drainage, is Healy Lake, one of the more intensively investigated Alaskan localities (Cook and McKennan 1970, 1971; McKennan and Cook 1970). The two principal sites are the Garden and Village sites. The early Chindadn complex at Healy Lake here is considered to be Paleo-Indian, but with traits like microblades in its upper levels that relate it to the Paleo-Arctic tradition. The next several levels have yielded an early to late prehistoric assemblage termed "the Athapaskan tradition." The Athapaskan tradition represents an interior adaptation that developed by 6000 B.C. Radiocarbon assays give late first millennium A.D. dates for Level 1, the first millennium B.C. for Level 2, which is two to four inches below the sod, and the sparse zone (Level 5) between the Athapaskan tradition and the Chindadn complex is estimated to date around 4000 B.C.

Not far from Healy Lake is the Donnelly Ridge site, a principal component of the Denali complex as it first was defined by Hadleigh-West (1967).

The oldest component at the multiple-layered Dry Creek site, located in the Nenana River valley close to the north flank of the Alaska Range, is dated at slightly over 9000 B.C. (Powers 1978). It has not yielded any microblades and appears to be related to the Chindadn complex, which here is classified as Paleo-Indian. One of the earliest radiocarbon dates applicable to a microblade industry in North America—8740 B.C. ± 250 (SI–1561)—applies to the second or principal component (Holmes 1974; Powers 1978; Thorson and Hamilton 1977). This occupation appears to be related to the Denali complex, and in addition to a microblade industry (fig. 4aa) it is characterized by burinated flakes, large biface blades, and smaller bifaces that resemble points but on the basis of wear have been identified as knives (fig. 4y) and other implements (fig. 2z,bb) (Powers 1978). Crossties seen with Siberian Late Paleolithic assemblages suggest not too remote Asian origins although some traits apparently continue into much later times, as, for instance, at the Minchumina site, located west of Dry Creek on Lake Minchumina.

Encountered here is the familiar theme of wedge-shaped microblade cores and burinated flakes. However, there is a great diversity of obsidian, chert, basalt, and sandstone implements, and many varieties of projectile points, apparently reflecting the relatively late date of the site and its proximity to the Eskimo of western Alaska. This site also has a late prehistoric occupation with copper implements and human cremations (Holmes 1973a, 1974:19, 1977). For the end of the early prehistoric period—to A.D. 1 or a few centuries later—this area may have been characterized by a distinctive, albeit extremely eclectic, local culture.

South of the Alaska Range a substantial number of

sites has been investigated in the Tangle Lakes area (Hadleigh-West 1972, 1972a, 1973, 1975; Skarland and Keim 1958). Other sites that have yielded blades or microblades and wedge-shaped cores are located on the Tyone River tributary of the Susitna River (Irving 1957), in the upper Matanuska Valley (Hadleigh-West 1973), on Turnagain Arm near Anchorage (Reger 1977), and elsewhere in lesser sites or outside the area covered by this chapter. In the Tangle Lakes sequence the early Denali complex is followed by sites with notched points and then by a first millennium A.D. house pit occupation. Collections of bifaces also may be very early (Hadleigh-West 1972a), and there are also some blade and core sites that appear to be distinct from the Denali complex. The Denali complex is bracketed at one site by dates of 8200 B.C. ± 280 and 6250 B.C. ± 265 (Hadleigh-West 1975). Notched points have been recovered at sites dated to about 2100 B.C. There is no associated microblade industry (Hadleigh-West 1972), a situation that parallels some "Northern Archaic" sites.

• YUKON TERRITORY AND NORTHERN BRITISH COLUMBIA   Early prehistoric assemblages from the northern Yukon include items such as transverse burins, microblade and core industries, and notched and other projectile points showing crossties with northern interior Alaska (cf. Irving and Cinq-Mars 1974). This section pertains primarily to the southern Yukon Territory.

Originally, in the southern Yukon three stages of the Northwest Microblade tradition—Little Arm, Gladstone, and Taye Lake—were thought to succeed in that order the Champagne complex of Plano culture affiliation and other possible early occupations, and in turn were succeeded by the late prehistoric and historic Athapaskan Aishihik and Bennett Lake phases (R.S. MacNeish 1960, 1963, 1964). However, no sharp break was seen between the late Paleo-Indian Champagne complex and Little Arm. The view that the Northwest Microblade tradition developed out of Champagne through an accumulative process involving the fusion of northern Plano culture elements and elements of Asian origin about 5500 B.C. may be essentially correct for the local area (R.S. MacNeish 1963, 1964), although such origins are indirect.

As redefined, the sequence has only one microblade-producing phase, Little Arm, which includes the former Champagne phase (Plano) material as well as the original Little Arm phase and part of the Gladstone material (Workman 1969, 1974, 1977, 1977a, 1978). Taye Lake is placed in the later Northern Archaic nonmicroblade tradition, which begins before 2000 B.C. and extends into the contact period.

Little Arm is represented by the lowest level of the Little Arm site (R.S. MacNeish 1963, 1964) (fig. 4l,m,dd,hh,ll), the Canyon site lowest levels (Workman 1974) (fig. 4nn,rr), and as a variant by the Otter Falls site (J.P. Cook 1968), all in the Aishihik-Dezadeash-

Kluane area of southwest Yukon. The earliest Little Arm date, from the basal levels of the Canyon site, is 5245 B.C. ± 100 (SI–1117, Workman 1974) or more than 7,000 years old (a convenient reference for all Canadian radiocarbon dates is Wilmeth 1978a). The date is associated with projectile points but not with a microblade industry. However, from various lines of evidence Workman feels that the microblade industry will be found to have an antiquity nearly commensurate with this date. The upper limit of the phase, about 2500 B.C., is set on the basis of the date of 2640 B.C. ± 150 (GSC–942) from related but variant material from Otter Falls and on the basis of slightly overlapping dates from succeeding Taye Lake occupations.

The long-lived Taye Lake phase covers the majority of material from the southwest Yukon Territory including appropriate levels of the Chimi, Gladstone, Little Arm, and Canyon sites. Notched projectile points without any associated microblade industry identify this phase. All Taye Lake components underlie a White River volcanic ash layer formed about A.D. 700 (formerly dated at A.D. 400); the lower limit of the phase is set by the end of the preceding Little Arm phase. A radiocarbon date of 950 B.C. ± 130 (GSC–940) applies to the Chimi site component while dates back to 2780 B.C. ± 320 (W–1125) have been obtained from Taye Lake zones of the Canyon site.

The materials of the Taye Lake phase indicate that between 3000 and 2500 B.C. a new "Northern Archaic" technology characterized by side-notched projectile points, an emphasis on larger bifaces, thick unifaces, and a lack of microblade technology entered the southwest Yukon area. An actual migration of peoples may have been involved inasmuch as this is the only major technological break during the 7,000-year prehistoric record in the area (Workman 1974b:9–10).

In many ways the southwest Yukon sites are like ones from adjacent Alaska, northern British Columbia, and the western Mackenzie District. Thus, Little Arm is suggestive of some Denali complex components. For the next phase, Taye Lake, a Northern Archaic tradition is found as far west as the Kobuk River, in the same time range (Palisades and Portage complexes) (D.D. Anderson 1968) with many of the same implements and again no microblade industry, but in central Alaska similar artifacts are found in association with a microblade industry. Again, just south of the Yukon border in northern British Columbia, the undated Callison site has many Taye Lake characteristics but with a few microblades and a wedge-shaped core. The Fisherman Lake sequence of the southwest Mackenzie District cross-dates with the Taye Lake phase and presents some features in common but here too is accompanied by a microblade industry. These factors suggest that perhaps the microblade industry should not be given primacy as an index trait.

Sites on the Stikine River system in northern British

Columbia have yielded assemblages of the Ice Mountain Microblade phase (J.W. Smith 1970, 1971). The microblade industry is based primarily upon obsidian from Mount Edziza (cf. Souther 1970). Obsidian from this source may occur in archeological sites as far north as Whitehorse, Yukon Territory, and definitely as far south as Skeena River where obsidian from an Anahim area source becomes predominant (Wilmeth 1973).

In the Stikine River area two phases postdate the Ice Mountain Microblade phase. The earlier of the two is distinguished by side-notched points while the later one is considered to lead into the historic Tahltan occupation.

• WESTERN MACKENZIE DISTRICT AND NORTHERN ALBERTA Continued excavations at Fisherman Lake near Fort Liard in the western Mackenzie District have set the Pointed Mountain site into a context illustrating for the local area early and developed phases of the Northwest Microblade tradition, following possible Cordilleran and Plano antecedents, and later phases leading up to the historic Slavey Indian occupation. These are the Julian, Pointed Mountain, and Fish Lake complexes (James F.V. Millar 1968, personal communications 1973; Fedirchuk 1970). In terms of the Northwest Microblade tradition the first complex may be regarded as developmental passing into developed, the second as developed, and the third as a phaseout stage.

Prominent in the first complex is the so-called Julian technology in which many varieties of coarse chopping, scraping, and cutting tools are made from chert cobbles (fig. 4f–i). There are other generalized bifacially flaked tools such as were made also during earlier times. Microblade and core technology appears toward the middle of the complex. Lanceolate points and a corner-notched point are associated. The Julian complex is radiocarbon dated at 1920 B.C. ± 105 (I–3193) and 1660 B.C. ± 110 (I–3195) (Millar 1968).

In the last early prehistoric complex presently considered, Fish Lake, there is a marked decrease in microblade and core technology, and roughly worked lithic material tends to be replaced by more finely knapped implements although the efflorescence in the quality of flaked stone is seen primarily in the following Mackenzie complex. Otherwise, typical artifacts include medium-size notched points and many implement types found in preceding complexes. Conclusions regarding Fish Lake are tentative due to small samples being spread over several localities (James F.V. Millar, personal communication 1973). It is not dated, but dates of 410 B.C. ± 130 (GSC–1033) and 510 B.C. ± 160 (GSC–884) are thought to apply to related material (Millar 1968; Lowdon, Wilmeth, and Blake 1970).

Northward along the Mackenzie valley, near the Keele River approximately halfway between Fort Liard and Inuvik, several small assemblages representing various phases of occupation have been recovered, some of which have a rudimentary blade and core industry (fig. 4x) (Jacques Cinq-Mars, personal communications 1972, 1973). Fused tuff from the Tertiary Hills adjacent to these sites has been traced as a preferred material for stone implements over a wide area, principally in the western Mackenzie District (Cinq-Mars 1973, 1973b).

Near the outlet of Great Bear Lake a sequence of three phases—Franklin Tanks, Great Bear River, and N.T. Docks—has been recovered (R.S. MacNeish 1955). Franklin Tanks (fig. 4a–e) is considered by many to fall within the Paleo-Indian provenance, although this remains a matter of dispute. A Plano affiliation also has been attributed to the Great Bear River complex, but if the radiocarbon dates of 2694 B.C. ± 290 (S–9) and 2854 B.C. ± 200 (S–10) are accepted this complex would have to be an extremely late and derivative Plano (fig. 4o,r,t,pp). A few distinctive Arctic Small Tool tradition implements are recognized in the Great Bear River assemblage. Their presence may indicate that the assemblage dates to about 1000 B.C. or that the collection is from more than one occupation, which is more likely. No blade or microblade industry was recovered, possibly due to the small sample size of about 90 implements. With the exception of Arctic Small Tool tradition sites, cultures producing microblades in the Mackenzie are limited to the western part of the district, and the absence of microblades in the present case could be explained through fluctuation of the eastern limits of the microblade tradition.

A stronger yet somewhat marginal relationship to the Northwest Microblade tradition is found in the N.T. Docks complex, particularly through the presence of microblades. These are not abundant, but the sample is too small for quantitative consideration. Radiocarbon dates for the middle zone of the humic layer in which the N.T. Docks component occurs are 1604 B.C. ± 210 (S–5), and 3050 B.C. ± 200 (S–5 rerun) (R.S. MacNeish 1964; Rutherford, Wittenberg, and McCallum 1975). It is difficult to tell how precisely these dates apply to the archeological site. Related material, including microblades and poorly defined blades, has been found in the undated lower level of the Whirl Lake site located near the Mackenzie delta (Gordon and Savage 1974).

Far to the south, in western Alberta, obsidian microblades have been recovered in surface collections from the middle Peace River area (J.V. Wright 1964). Although it is not possible to say whether these are part of the northern—Northwest Microblade—distribution or part of the Plateau Microblade industry of central and southern British Columbia, in either case they represent an extreme limit. Synthetic constructions used to organize early prehistory in the far northwest probably cannot be applied to northern Alberta, although presently little is known about the early prehistory of that region.

During the middle millennia, Arctic Small Tool tradition people intruded into the area east of the Mackenzie River and north and west of Great Bear Lake. These apparent ancestral Eskimos were in the area sometime between 1200 and 500 B.C. (D.W. Clark 1975; Chambers 1974). By the later date they had been superseded by an unrelated people. This event is better documented and dated elsewhere in the north ("Prehistory of the Great Slave Lake and Great Bear Lake Region," "Prehistory of the Canadian Shield," both this vol.).

• CENTRAL BRITISH COLUMBIA Microblades appear as a persistent element, although often a minor one, at many sites in central British Columbia, including houses of both early and late prehistoric age.

At Tezli a pit house has been dated to 2400 B.C. (Donahue 1975). Later occupations in the house pit complicate the interpretation of this site, and the microblade industry is sparsely represented.

At Natalkuz Lake near Tweedsmuir Park blades, obsidian microblades, and a single blade core have been recovered from a structure that bears evidence of a multiple occupation (Borden 1953). The upper component apparently is a prehistoric Carrier Indian occupation, while the date for the site of 465 B.C. ± 160 (S–4) is considered to apply to the structure and the microblade component.

At Anahim Lake microblades are found in shallow circular house depressions of a number of sites and are associated with stemmed projectile points and other implements (Wilmeth in G.F. MacDonald 1971). No cores have been recovered with the microblades at Anahim Lake, but cores unlike northern varieties have been found elsewhere in central British Columbia. Several radiocarbon dates are available for the microblade phase from the circular houses at the Daniktco, Potlatch (Bez Yaz House), and Goose Point sites. These range from approximately A.D. 80 to 700, the later dates being from Daniktco site (Wilmeth 1971:57, 1977).

Additional probable early prehistoric collections from the Anahim Lake area and Chilcotin Plateau that lack precise dating include the nonmicrolithic Poplar Grove site, for which an age of several millennia B.C. has been proposed (Mitchell 1969, 1970).

Although the dated microblade assemblages are late, they appear to be quite different from the assemblages of the late prehistoric and early contact period Carrier and Chilcotin Athapaskans. Further documentation probably will either provide a transition or show that there was a discontinuity that involved the migration of the Chilcotin and Carrier, and possibly the Navajo, too (Wilmeth 1977; Helmer 1977a). Data from elsewhere in British Columbia lead one to expect the recovery of much earlier prehistoric occupations. Presently there is nothing from the study area to compare with very early assemblages like Dry Creek, and the microblade industry of central British Columbia bears little or no resemblance to either early or late industries of this type found in the north. Relationships are more likely to lie with the southern interior and coastal regions of British Columbia. Although considerable data are available, a diversity of interpretations among specialists prevents ascertaining even the major alignments and connections of prehistory in the region.

One archeologist suggests that the final analyses will show the association between late radiocarbon dates and microblades to be grossly invalid (Donahue 1975). He sees a persistent ongoing Plateau development over the past four millennia in which a microblade industry plays little or no part and that shows strong relationships with the Plains and more southerly Plateau areas.

Others likewise find continuity through time within an area-wide lithic tradition but accept the late dates for microblades and see the strongest relationships to the north instead of to the Plains and Plateau (Helmer 1977a). For the region Helmer proposes three prehistoric periods: the Early Prehistoric period, 2500 B.C. to A.D. 1, characterized by "fish-tailed" points (fig. 4n); the Middle Prehistoric period, to A.D. 1300, characterized by several styles of side- and corner-notched points; and after 1300, small side-notched and triangular points. A more complete representation of early historic artifacts includes also microblades and cores, corner-notched points, leaf-shaped points, and heavy unifaces—but some of these appear also in the middle period.

The Last Two Millennia, about A.D. 1–1900

This horizon extends from A.D. 1, more or less, up to the time of historic contact, then into the contact period when recovered remains still display predominantly the indigenous Athapaskan culture, and finally into the wholly historic period characterized almost exclusively by elements of Euro-American culture. The A.D. 1 beginning date is one of convenience that tends to leave behind the microblade industries discussed in the preceding section, although not always.

In Alaska the interior archeological sequence is interpreted as leading from a microblade tradition into prehistoric Athapaskan culture (Cook and McKennan 1971; McKennan and Cook 1970). In the southwest corner of the Mackenzie District a related microblade tradition also appears to change gradually, with the loss of the microblade industry, into an Athapaskan sequence (Millar 1968). For central British Columbia, events relating to the late microblade industry are variously interpreted, and it is possible that the prehistory of this region involves peoples of several linguistic stocks in addition to the present Athapaskan inhabitants. The apparent earlier demise of the microblade industry in the southern Yukon may be correlated with the fact that a probable Athapaskan tradition—the Taltheilei Shale tradition ("Prehistory of the Great Slave Lake and Great Bear Lake Region," this vol.)—which appeared in the central Mackenzie District by 500 B.C., bears no vestige of a microblade and core industry.

Prehistoric and Contact Periods

Small tapered stem points (Kavik type) (fig. 5i) have been recognized as a diagnostic late northern Athapaskan trait, from British Columbia to northwestern Alaska. For example, an Athapaskan incursion into the area of the Kavik site, located in present Eskimo territory in the Brooks Range of Alaska, proposed on the basis of ethnohistoric accounts (E.S. Hall 1969; Irving 1968), appears to be borne out through recovery of tapered stem points. Small side-notched points (fig. 5e)

Natl. Mus. of Canada, Ottawa: a, JcRw–3.4.B.a (from the U. of Saskatchewan research program); b, LhRk–1:6; c, FgSd–1:1390; d, FgSd–1:609; e, FfSk–1:358; f, FgSd–1:1115; g, FfSk–1:516; h, MjVl–1:266; i, MjVl–1:1256; j. LcRq–2:39; k, LcRq–2:37; l, JfVb–4; m, JfVb–2.

Fig. 5. Flaked stone projectile points and scraper from the last 2 millennia. a, From Klondike (Mackenzie complex), Mackenzie District; b, from Great Bear Lake; c, small triangular biface from Tezli, central B.C.; d, basalt corner notched point from Tezli; e, obsidian side-notched arrow tip (specimen opaqued) from Ulkatcho, B.C.; f, "hooked" concave scraper from Tezli; g, stemmed point from Ulkatcho; h, from Klo-kut, northern Yukon Terr.; i, Kavik point from Klo-kut; j, small "turkey tail" point of fused tuff (specimen opaqued) from Stewart Lake, western Mackenzie District; k, small leaf-shaped point of fused tuff (specimen opaqued) from Stewart Lake; l, obsidian projectile tip from Taye Lake, southwest Yukon Terr.; m, obsidian point from southern Yukon Terr. These objects date between A.D. 1 and contact. Small stemmed or notched points like e, i, and j are relatively recent. Length of b 6.0 cm, rest same scale.

also are generally distributed in the southeastern part of the area under consideration. More or less similar points are found in adjacent areas of North America during late prehistoric time. Some other implement types widely distributed in late prehistoric Athapaskan occupations, but neither universally nor exclusively Athapaskan, are stone slab scrapers (chithos) (fig. 6a), boulder flake implements (mostly also chithos) (fig. 6b), beamers (fig. 6e–f), end of the bone defleshers and skinning implements (fig. 6c–d), heavy grooved (splitting) adzes (fig. 7a–b), slender barbed bone points, and, where preserved, birchbark tray baskets. Rat-tailed points, particularly bone and copper points, and an emphasis on working native copper also may be noted.

For the historic period it is difficult to see very much that is positively and distinctively Athapaskan in any of the sites to be discussed. One explanation for this situation is that native artifacts have been superseded by imported Euro-American items (fig. 8), which as a common denominator over much of the western Arctic and Subarctic have tended to eliminate earlier differences in material culture. Contact and historic period Athapaskan archeology, when divested of its content of imported items, provides very meager fare in the north. Nevertheless, a tenuously consistent pattern emerges in the almost invariable presence of hide scraping stones and frequently of whetstones or abrasive slabs (fig. 7c,e), an occasional stone or bone arrow point, wedge-shaped skinning and defleshing tools, and birchbark basketry. Additional rarely recovered implements have a wide ethnographic distribution, and thus the roster of artifacts, potentially archeological, could be augmented several fold through the inclusion of ethnographically reported types. Nevertheless, the sparse recovery of native artifacts has to be coped with in any analysis (cf. Workman 1974; Dumond 1973). However, in central British Columbia sites of the period are better endowed.

Trade goods may vary according to the absolute date of a site as well as according to its relative age or position in relation to contact and the activities of traders. Thus at some sites there are only a few glass beads and marks on preserved timbers indicative of the use of metal tools; at others there are large quantities of relatively modern trash. Yet there are several consistent elements. These include traits of reuse or remanufacture (fig. 9) found over much of the north, in both Indian and Eskimo sites, particularly cartridge cases used for blunt arrow and toy arrow tips, ulu knife blades and serrated scrapers made from salvaged metal sheet, crooked knives made from files, small pans folded from metal, and various scraper blades of salvaged metal or, more recently, of cut tubing.

In 1970 a symposium held to discuss problems of the definition of prehistoric Athapaskan cultures concluded that there is "no entity identifiable as 'Athabaskan prehistory' " (Morlan 1970a). It would be more appropriate now to say that there is no single entity identifiable as Athapaskan prehistory. Presently, Athapaskan prehistory is a thing of many strands. Almost every area investigated presents a distinctive regional variety of very late prehistoric culture, and it is difficult to see very much less diversity 1,000 to 2,000 years ago. Continuity with the earlier millennia and microblade cultures is not clear; further, there is no reason to expect that all the early prehistoric remains represent a single linguistic stock. Northern Athapaskan prehistory is mainly not an implement trait list but rather the lifeway of a people who had adapted to the largely forested northern interior regions.

The Regional Data

House pits often are singled out for excavation inasmuch as they encompass a systematic body of data, are easier to find than sites without surface features, and localize artifacts and other archeologically significant material in what otherwise would be in most cases a relatively unproductive context.

Semisubterranean house floors have been excavated at several places in Alaska and British Columbia, but

Natl. Mus. of Canada, Ottawa: a, MjVl–7:3; b, MiVo–1:1c; c, KlIg–33:29; d, FcSi–201:198; e, SdIb–2:14; f, MjVl–1:156; g, FcSi–200:21; h, MjVl–1:1521; i, NMM 73–46–11.

Fig. 7. Ground stone and bone implements. a, Grooved pick from Crow Point, northern Yukon Terr.; b, splitting adz from northern Yukon Terr.; c, grinding (honing) slab (incomplete?) from Batza téna locality, Alaska; d, adz blade of greenstone from Potlatch, B.C.; e, abrader (pebble whetstone) from Okak, Koyukuk River region, Alaska; f, pestle from Klo-kut, northern Yukon Terr.; g, bone (?) wedge from Goose Point, B.C.; h, bone awl from Klo-kut; i, red paint palette using natural stone basin from Lake Creek, Koyukuk River region. Implements like a-b were used from about A.D. 1000 to contact, c-i from A.D. 1 or earlier. A few traditional snowshoe makers were still preparing red pigment in basins as recently as 1970. Length of f 17.3 cm, rest same scale.

Natl. Mus. of Canada, Ottawa: a, ScIc–1:23; b, MjVl–1A:213; d, MjVk–7:560; e, MjVl–1:531; c, U. of Alaska, Fairbanks: UA 71–35–182; f, U. of Manitoba, Winnipeg: KS–14.

Fig. 6. Probable skin-working implements. a, Tabular hide-working stone with red pigment stain on one face from Lake Creek, Koyukuk River region, Alaska; b, boulder flake from Klo-kut, northern Yukon Terr.; c, end-of-the-bone flesher (side view) from Dixthada, interior Alaska; d, end-of-the-bone flesher from Old Chief, northern Yukon Terr.; e, decorated beamer fragment from Klo-kut; f, beamer from Kijik, southwest Alaska. These and similar tools were used during the second millennium A.D. and considerably earlier in certain areas. In some communities of the north similar tools were used as recently as the 1950s. Length of f 30.6 cm, rest same scale.

119

only a few are known in the Yukon and the Mackenzie District although leveled or slightly depressed floors are found there. Many of the houses have yielded historic trade material and can be linked to the Athapaskan inhabitants of each area at the time of contact, while others are prehistoric.

• NORTHERN ALASKA: HISTORIC   On the Koyukuk River, Kateel village has been tested (De Laguna 1947) and several houses have been excavated at small one- and two-house settlements farther up the river (D.W. Clark 1969; Clark and Clark 1975; Morlan 1967). Most of the upriver houses appear to date from about the 1880s, the time of direct contact on that part of the river, although there was extraterritorial contact with the Russians at Nulato on the Yukon River as early as the 1840s. Kateel dates closer to this earlier period, but it may have been occupied over several decades (De Laguna 1947:48–51). Two structures tested there yielded a modest collection of native artifacts including potsherds, bone wedges, whetstones, a bone arrowhead, a bone comb, and birchbark baskets, along with other artifacts some of which might be attributed to reported visiting Eskimo traders. Direct evidence of Euro-American contact was limited to glass beads and steel ax-cut timbers.

Consonant with their more recent age, the upriver houses contained a wider array of Euro-American goods (fig. 8a–d,f,h–i) (D.W. Clark 1969). Metal items modified or made into indigenous-style implements include most of those noted above. Among artifacts wholly native are birchbark basket trays, skewer sticks, and a snowshoe netting needle. The only lithics recovered were hide scraping stones in both the boulder flake and chipped slab format (fig. 6a), red paint pigment, a boulder with natural depression used for mixing red paint (fig. 7i), and a natural bar whetstone (fig. 7e). The prime artifacts are the houses, which are reasonably well preserved (Clark and Clark 1975). The houses conform closely to a small semisubterranean four-center-post type with a short tunnel excavated somewhat below floor level (fig. 10). It probably was possible to stand up only near the center line of one of these dwellings.

Elsewhere in the interior north of the Alaska Range historic or contact-period houses have been excavated near Telida on the upper Kuskokwim River (LeFebre 1956:269) and on the lower Yukon River (De Laguna 1947; Dixon 1976). Historic components are known from the surface of other sites, as at Dixthada.

• NORTHERN YUKON TERRITORY: HISTORIC   The Porcupine River drainage of the northern Yukon Territory is another focus of archeological research. Because of physiographic continuity it is discussed in conjunction with the northern interior Alaska distribution, although in terms of spheres of fur traders' activities Alaska-Yukon is split between the Hudson's Bay Company in the Yukon and the Russian-American Company and American traders in Alaska. Historic components have been investigated at Cadzow Lake (Morlan 1972a) and also at Klo-kut, which is primarily a locus of prehistoric occupation (Morlan 1973). An additional historic period camp (NbVk–1), dating within the twentieth century, has an almost exclusively modern assemblage (Morlan 1972). Two Crow Flats Kutchin occupations at the small stratified Cadzow Lake site dating around 1850 and 1880, respectively, show minor Euro-Canadian influence in the form of trade goods. A third camp there is primarily modern. Faunal remains indicate that these camps were occupied chiefly to intercept the northward-bound spring caribou migration.

• SOUTHERN ALASKA: HISTORIC   South of the Alaska Range, contact-period houses have been excavated at Iliamna Lake (Townsend and Townsend 1961; Townsend 1970a, 1970b, 1970d), at the head of Cook Inlet (Dumond and Mace 1968), and on the Kenai Peninsula (Kent, Mattews, and Hadleigh-West 1964) as well as at the later historic Kijik settlement (VanStone and Townsend 1970), all in Tanaina territory. Historic sites and associated refuse piles also have been investigated on the Copper River in Ahtna territory (Rainey 1939; Shinkwin 1979; VanStone 1955; Workman 1971, 1977) and in the region between the Copper and Susitna rivers (Irving 1957). Few of these sites have been rewarding.

The University of Alaska excavated in 1973 parts of a protohistoric Ahtna site, known as Dakah De'nin's village, located near Chitina on the Copper River (Shinkwin 1979). The site is known through oral tradition, and the limited amount of trade goods there coupled with tree-ring dating indicate a prehistoric and protohistoric occupation during the end of the eighteenth and beginning of the nineteenth centuries. The winter village site is a relatively large one with nine rectangular house pits with attached sweat baths and a number of cache pits, but the houses appear not to be all contemporary.

The roster of indigenous-type artifacts includes the following items: boulder-spall hide-working stones, hammerstones, grinding stones and whetstones, picks, and a slate point; copper awls, needles, points (fig. 11c–e), and knife blades (fig. 12g–h); bone points (fig. 11i) and unidentified implements; dentalia, shell beads, and a possible shell labret; and, finally, part of a birchbark object.

Trade objects occurred in the younger contexts of the site and are limited largely to glass beads, small amounts of iron, and a brass bell-like object.

House pits near the Taral site on the lower Copper River are more recent (VanStone 1955:121). At the contact village of Taral proper there were no house pits, but trenching produced a limited late nineteenth-century assemblage, including a clay pipe, which is a type of trade item not common in Alaska.

At the base of the Alaska Peninsula the early contact

Natl. Mus. of Canada, Ottawa: a, SdIb–1:12; b, SdIb–2:27; c, SdIb–1:54; d, SdIb–1:1, 17; e, JbUq–1:12; f, SdIb–2:7; g, FfSk–1:194; h, ScId–1:14; i, ScIc–1:24.
Fig. 8. Trade goods of Euro-American manufacture. a, Powder can top from Kayak, Koyukuk River region, Alaska; b, powder can that contained pitch at time of excavation from Okak, Koyukuk River region; c, powder can screw cap from Kayak; d, musket balls from Kayak; e, gun flint from southern Yukon Terr.; f, 44 caliber rimfire cartridge case from Okak; g, incomplete clay pipe from Ulkatcho, B.C.; h, clay pipe stem fragment stamped "McDougall, Glasgow" from Kayak; i, pocket knife from Lake Creek, Koyukuk River region. These objects are 19th century; those from Alaska had been used 1870–1885. Length of i 9.1 cm, rest same scale.

four-house Pedro Bay site on Lake Iliamna and the late Kijik village on Lake Clark have been excavated (figs. 6f, 9c,e–f,11o) (Townsend and Townsend 1961; Townsend 1970a, 1970b, 1970d; VanStone and Townsend 1970). Pedro Bay is a discontinuously occupied multicomponent site, the houses being of an early contact-period age. Townsend (1970b:37) notes in this ethnic contact area a problem in distinguishing on the basis of artifacts between late prehistoric or early historic Indian sites and Eskimo sites. In discussing the probable Tanaina Pedro Bay site, the later contact Russian Point occupation, and historic Tanaina Kijik village, Townsend draws attention to bone and antler harpoons, ground slate points (fig. 11a–b), slate ulu blades, boulder flake scrapers, and large chipped bifaces. These forms are characteristic also of Eskimos in western Alaska.

The Kijik site is too late to present a very full range of either native artifacts or early contact-period trade goods. Kijik may have been occupied throughout the nineteenth century and into the first decade of the twentieth century, but the bulk of recovered material apparently represents the end of this period (VanStone and Townsend 1970:Appendix 1). VanStone and

Townsend (1970:160) conclude that "it was the influx of trade goods during the early American period and probably after 1875–1880 that practically obliterated almost everything that was distinctively Athapaskan about the material culture of the Indians at Kijik."

• ALASKA: PREHISTORIC To probe behind the historic baseline set above, what is known about earlier Athapaskan archeology? Probable late prehistoric houses on the Copper River, in the Lake Louise–Tyone River area, and on the Kenai Peninsula have yielded disappointingly few artifacts. Likewise, in the original and as yet most extensive survey of Cook Inlet De Laguna (1934:132–156) excavated several recent-appearing although possibly prehistoric house pits, but with poor recovery.

A research problem peculiar to the Cook Inlet region is that of the expansion of the Tanaina Indians toward the outer shores of the Inlet, which formerly were occupied by Eskimos. A find of apparent Eskimo origin

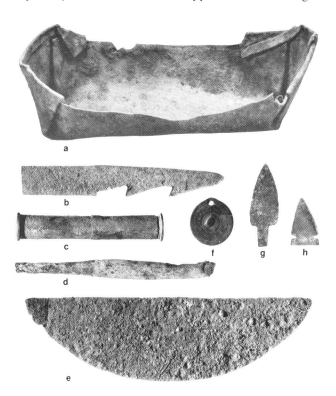

Natl. Mus. of Canada, Ottawa: a, ScIb–1:1; b, FfSk–1:458; v. KS 7; d, SdIb–2:30; e. KT 8; f, KS 14; g, FfSk–1:342; h, FfSk–1:376.
Fig. 9. Artifacts of Euro-American materials or manufacture, modified or remanufactured by Native Americans. a, Metal dish made from a powder can from Lake Creek, Koyukuk River region, Alaska; b, spear or harpoon head made from metal file from Ulkatcho, B.C.; c, brass tube, use unknown, made from 2 joined 45-70 cartridge cases from Kijik, southwest Alaska; d, iron crooked-knife blade from Okak, Koyukuk River region; e, iron ulu (semilunar knife) blade from Kijik; f, pendant made from a copper-alloy button from Kijik; g, stemmed copper point from Ulkatcho; h, side-notched copper point probably manufactured from traded metal sheet from Ulkatcho. These objects date from the second half of the 19th century. Length of b 11.2 cm, rest same scale.

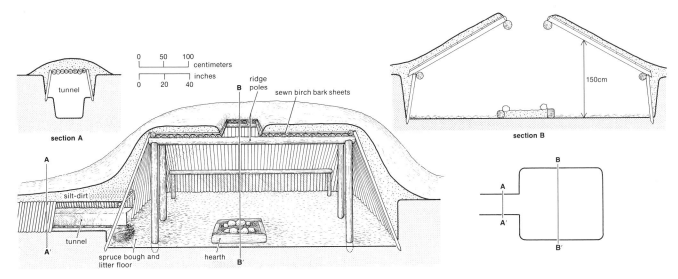

after Clark and Clark 1974:31.

Fig. 10. Reconstruction of a semisubterranean winter house of the Koyukuk division of the Koyukon.

on the Upper Inlet—a large ornate stone lamp with a human figure in the bowl—led Mason in 1928 to propose that the entire Cook Inlet, in addition to the outer part where there still is a remnant Eskimo population, had been Eskimo territory (discussed in De Laguna 1934). Investigations on Cook Inlet (De Laguna 1934; Dumond and Mace 1968) have supported Mason's hypothesis, although for the Upper Inlet no evidence has been found for any substantial prehistoric occupation, either Indian or Eskimo. In 1839 Wrangell (1970:12) proposed that "the Kenay [Tanaina] came to the place they now occupy from across the mountains. These migrant mountain people ultimately became coastal and semisettled.. . . Their favorite occupation remains the hunting of animals in the forests beyond the mountains." When interpreted in terms of ecology and resource utilization the sparse archeological record and Upper Inlet utilization by both Eskimos and Indians may not appear to be unusual.

A 2,000-year-old fishing camp and other sites on the Kenai River near Soldotna show strongest crossties with south Alaskan Eskimo sites and provide more substantial evidence of former Eskimo occupation of the Middle Inlet (Reger 1977, 1977a).

North of the Alaska Range prehistoric sites of the last two millennia have been tested along the Yukon River (De Laguna 1947; Hrdlička 1930; Rainey 1939), near Lake Telida and at Lake Minchumina in the Kuskokwim headwaters region (LeFebre 1956; Hosley 1968a; West 1978), at the Nenana Gorge (Plaskett 1977), and in the Koyukuk drainage (Clark and Clark 1976; D.W. Clark 1974). The Itkillik complex of Onion Portage (D.D. Anderson 1970b) and the Kavik complex from Anaktuvuk Pass and the Antigun site (J.M. Campbell 1968; I.R. Wilson 1978) appear to be Athapaskan intrusions into the present Eskimo area. Ethnohistoric accounts tell also of a Kutchin intrusion into the western Brooks Range (E.S. Hall 1969). For the eastern interior, occupations of the period under consideration are reported from the upper levels of several sites at Healy Lake (Cook and McKennan 1971; McKennan and Cook 1970) and from Dixthada (Shinkwin 1975, 1979). Work done in the 1970s has greatly increased knowledge of prehistory in the Copper River basin, although as yet little is known about early prehistoric times there (Workman 1977).

The Yukon River collections (De Laguna 1947), which come in small increments from a number of sites usually characterized by house pits, appear to belong to the contact period and to the centuries immediately preceding contact although no precise dating is available. They can be attributed to the present inhabitants of the region: the Athapaskan-speaking Ingalik and lower Koyukon. Among the distinctive elements in western Alaska are ceramics—cooking pots and also lamps—most of which, when decorated, would be designated as Yukon line-dot (De Laguna 1947:226ff.; LeFebre 1956:272; Oswalt 1955:37). This type of pottery also is common to the western Eskimo among whom it may not date any earlier than 1600. Ground slate, used for ulus (semilunar knives) and for projectile end blades, is another regional specialty of this and adjacent areas, as is the heavy grooved splitting adz, which is more widespread and includes a related double-edged picklike form that is distinctive of the Yukon drainage extending into the Yukon Territory (fig. 7a). Very few artifacts are flaked in the conventional sense, like arrowheads. Most of the lower Yukon implements have close stylistic counterparts in adjacent Eskimo areas.

Eight house pits, most of them excavated, located farther to the east on Lake Minchumina, have produced

122

an assemblage of a complexion very different from the contact and very late prehistoric sites discussed up to this point. The Birches site, dated to the first and early second millennium A.D., departs from the familiar pattern of recent-appearing houses relatively barren of lithic artifacts (Hosley 1968a; West 1978). The site appears to represent a distinctive regional form of prehistoric culture that apparently is Indian but shows some Eskimoid traits. Other sites in the area extend the sequence to more recent times as well as to earlier periods, and one 2,000-year-old site shows crossties with western Eskimo prehistory (Charles E. Holmes, personal communications 1979, 1980).

For the Koyukuk River drainage there are the assemblages from five semisubterranean houses, located southwest of the Indian River obsidian source, and other sites. The houses are interpreted as the winter dwellings of people either strongly influenced by the Ipiutak Eskimo culture (D.W. Clark 1972a) or in fact as an inland Eskimo occupation (D.W. Clark 1977, 1977a). This complex, Hahanudan, is radiocarbon dated to the middle of the first millennium A.D. Among artifacts related to Ipiutak culture are a ground burin, large and small asymmetrical side inset blades for knives and projectile points, and discoidal biface scrapers. The discoids, a highly distinctive Norton-Ipiutak Eskimo artifact, appear to have been used to the exclusion of conventional end scrapers; and that Athapaskan hallmark, the hide scraping stone (chitho), is absent.

Hahanudan presents a very interesting situation, especially when it is considered in a broader context in conjunction with the Itkillik complex of Onion Portage on the Kobuk River. The Itkillik complex, dated by radiocarbon at A.D. 462 ± 113 (GX–1502; D.D. Anderson 1970), is considered to be an Athapaskan occupation intrusive into an Eskimo one. Thus, at the same time that interior peoples or influence extended westward from the Koyukuk, coastal influence was extending, probably by a slightly more southerly route, into the interior. Coupled with the regional variations and boundary changes discussed here for Cook Inlet, Lake Minchumina, and the lower Yukon River, and found elsewhere in western Alaska and the Brooks Range, in the Kavik complex for instance, these facts point to a very dynamic situation at the Indian-Eskimo interface.

In eastern interior Alaska pertinent information comes from Dixthada located in Upper Tanana territory (Rainey 1939; Shinkwin 1975, 1979 based on McKennan's and Cook's fieldwork). Historic occupation was localized in several house pits, while middens or refuse piles in front of the houses (not excavated) date from historic time back to about A.D. 1000. Underlying the middens is a lower stratum that is the primary locus of a microblade and core industry, which is dated to approximately 500 B.C. Glass beads and iron objects

U. of Manitoba, Winnipeg: a, 40–6, b, 40–137; o, Ks–14; c-e, U. of Alaska, Fairbanks; Natl. Mus. of Canada, Ottawa: f, JiVs–1; g, MjVl–1:66; l, MjVk–6:73; m, MjVl–1:14; n, Xl–c:200.

Fig. 11. Slate, copper, and bone implements. a-b, Ground slate points, base and tip ends missing, from Russian Point, southwest Alaska; c-e, copper points from Dakah De'nin's village, Copper River; f, copper point from Little Arm, southwest Yukon Terr. Bone implements: g, fish effigy (lure ?) from Klo-kut, northern Yukon Terr.; h, unbarbed pointed object (use unknown), from Dixthada, interior Alaska; i, harpoon head from Dakah De'nin's village; j, fragment of barbed point from Dixthada; k, serrated point from Dixthada; l; spear point from Old Crow area, northern Yukon Terr.; m, fishhook shank from Klo-kut; n, blunt point from Ft. McPherson, northern Mackenzie District; o, net sinker, type limited to Indians and Eskimos of western Alaska, from Kijik, southwest Alaska. Length of o 14.9 cm, rest same scale.

were found in the recent refuse layers, while many native copper and bone implements (figs. 6c, 11h,j–k) were found throughout the midden deposits as were lithic artifacts, including some derived from the disturbed lower stratum.

The microblade tradition (part of the "Athapaskan tradition") at Healy Lake persisted into the first millennium A.D. After that there apparently was a hiatus in the occupation of the two principal sites investigated, from about 1200 until the historic period, which can be filled by Dixthada (Shinkwin 1975). However, for much of Alaska such continuity may be little more than a laying of temporal blocks one upon another. Major technological change is the main motive for the division of this chapter into two principal parts, and for the sites discussed Shinkwin (1977:43–44) states: "we are left in the Tanana Valley with archeological components . . . spanning the early part or just preceding the first millennium A.D. characterized by predominantly chipped stone assemblages with wedge-shaped cores and microblades. These . . . are an enigma in terms of their relationships with the later phase [Dixthada is defined as a phase] which cannot be demonstrated. . . . In my opinion, at this point in time in the archaeological record, Athapaskans are invisible in the Tanana River area."

In the Copper River Basin, a region essentially coincident with the historic Ahtna, the paucity of recovered early prehistoric material prevents discussion of a number of the issues raised for other sequences, although the later prehistory is very well represented (summarized by Workman 1977). The two most substantial sites are known simply as GUL 077 and MS 23–0.

MS 23–0 has not produced many artifacts, but it yielded information on settlement features, including two houses. The other site or site area did not contain permanent houses, but there were numerous compound (multi-celled) large cache pits and use of the area must have been substantial judging from the large number of copper and other artifacts recovered. Copper was worked at the site as is documented by the recovery of by-products. Other features include hearths, remains of a sweat bath consisting of fire-altered boulders confined to a small area, and human cremations (probably secondary placements). Both sites are dated to A.D. 1000–1500 and are considered to be seasonally differentiated settlements of a single people, although there also is a later radiocarbon date from GUL 077. In examining this data and that from protohistoric sites Workman (1977) finds a continuity of Ahtna culture from prehistoric times. A number of trends are seen in the details as well, among them the phase-out of flint knapping, which never was especially popular in the area during late prehistoric times.

• NORTHERN YUKON TERRITORY: PREHISTORIC In the Porcupine River drainage of northern Yukon Territory, there are several significant sites, in particular Klo-kut (Morlan 1970, 1973), Rat Indian Creek, and Old Chief Creek (Cinq-Mars 1973a:39–40, 1974:C1–C20).

Occupation of the four- to five-foot-thick Klo-kut site continued more or less intermittently from approximately A.D. 950 into the twentieth century. Contact period occupation occurred during the second half of the nineteenth century and possibly later and is ascribed to the Crow Flats Kutchin. The historic horizon includes a number of indigenous artifact types along with objects of Euro-Canadian origin such as glass beads and a pocket knife.

Prehistoric artifacts include various types of end and side scrapers, rough bifaces, drills, biface knives, probable burins and *pièces esquillées* (stone wedges), Kavik and teardrop-shaped arrow tips (fig. 5h–i), shaped and unshaped boulder flake and stone slab hide scrapers (chithos) (fig. 6b), choppers, pestles (fig. 7f), pecked and ground heavy adzes, barbed bone points, fishhook components (fig. 11n), pointed bone implements including awls (fig. 7h) and unbarbed points, rodent incisor implements, a fish-effigy lure (fig. 11g), and birch-bark tray baskets. Two prehistoric periods are recognized. Radiocarbon dates indicate that the early period extended from about A.D. 950 to 1350, and the late period from then until approximately 1850. The inventory given above is composite. On the basis of apparent continuity the prehistoric occupants of Klo-kut are considered to be the antecedents of the historic Kutchin.

• SOUTHERN YUKON TERRITORY Heavy volcanic ash falls, dated to about A.D. 700, may have dispersed the pre-ash inhabitants of southwest Yukon with far-reaching ripple effects accounting in part for the historic distribution of Athapaskan dialects (Derry 1975; Workman 1977a), but this is largely a matter of hypothesis. The ash does not signal any sharp break in the local archeological record, although it provides a convenient stratigraphic marker.

Two post-ash complexes have been defined for southwest Yukon: Aishihik and Bennett Lake (R.S. MacNeish 1964; Workman 1974, 1977, 1978), which follow in that order the Taye Lake phase. The Bennett Lake phase comprises the contact period within Southern Tutchone territory (MacNeish also included very late prehistoric material). Workman (1974:4) states that "the Bennett Lake Phase is a direct outgrowth of the Aishihik phase, differing significantly only in the addition of European trade goods and an increasing emphasis on the taking of fur bearers." Further, stone and copper tools were phased out by ones of iron and steel, stone boiling was replaced by cooking in metal containers, and log cabins were built and occupied seasonally. As Bennett Lake is the outgrowth of Aishihik, so Aishihik is interpreted, on the basis of artifact continuities, as being based on the antecedent Taye Lake phase. This view presents a single tradition or line of development for approximately 4,500 years succeeding the microblade industry (Little Arm).

Among indigenous-type implements from several

Aishihik and Bennett Lake components are many of native copper (prongs, gorges, tinklers, projectile points—fig. 11f), and others of categories already noted for Klo-kut. Projectile points, in addition to stemmed copper and long multi-barbed bone points, are small side-notched and pointed stem (Kavik) points. These significantly duplicate site inventories in the northern Yukon Territory and Alaska. Native copper implements are particularly widespread during this period in the southern Yukon and interior and south-central Alaska. The copper sources are localities peripheral to the Wrangell Mountains. Copper implements are found also in the Mackenzie District, but there the metal doubtless is derived from a different source.

• MACKENZIE DISTRICT In the southwestern Mackenzie District the Fort Liard complex, dating from 1800 to the present, encompasses essentially the historic horizon (Millar 1968; Fedirchuk 1970a). At Fisherman Lake this complex, identified with Slavey Indian occupants of the region, is characterized by an appreciable range of lithic artifacts as well as by Euro-Canadian goods.

Following the microblade and roughly flaked stone industries of the middle millennia are the Mackenzie and Spence River complexes, represented at several Fisherman Lake sites, which span approximately 2,000 years to the contact period, or Fort Liard complex (Fedirchuk 1970, 1970a; Millar 1968). Preparation of bifacially flaked implements, particularly knives in several forms, has become finer. Also characteristic of both complexes are the large tabular and boulder flake hide scraping implements that are widespread in the north. In the first, Mackenzie, radiocarbon dated to the beginning of the first millennium A.D. (I–3191, A.D. 20 ± 60 years) and estimated to extend to A.D. 500, there is a range of stemmed, round based, lanceolate (fig. 5a), and broadly side-notched or corner-notched points. The second, younger complex, Spence River, is characterized by small points with narrow side notches, a diagnostic type not present earlier.

The most northerly excavated site in the Mackenzie drainage is at Whirl Lake located at the head of the Mackenzie delta. Numerous small assemblages have been recovered, as well, throughout the large intervening area between Fort Liard and the delta (figs. 5j–k, 11n). The upper level, including a dwelling structure and cache pits, is dated at 1740 and 1730 ± 90 (Gak–3266 and I–5840, respectively) and is attributed to the ancestors of the Mackenzie Flats Kutchin (Gordon and Savage 1974). The structure is a five-meter-long semi-subterranean house, but it appears to have been not so well formed as those of western Alaska. Slightly modified bones, a caribou metapodial beamer, and a probable snowshoe netting needle with zoomorphic engraving were recovered as was a fragmented birchbark tray basket. Stone artifacts in the small collection consist of

Natl. Mus. of Canada, Ottawa: a, FgSd–1:1952; b, FcSi–200:187; c, FgSd–1:1116; d, JbUq–1:8; e, FgSd–1:1451; f, Rllg–52:75; g-h, Univ. of Alaska, Fairbanks.
Fig. 12. Flaked stone and beaten copper implements. a, Basalt perforator reshaped from projectile point from Tezli, central B.C.; b, drill bit from Goose Point, Anahim Lake region, B.C.; c, discoidal beveled flake (scraper) from Tezli; d, biface blade from southern Yukon Terr.; e, small biface knife of basalt from Tezli; f, obsidian end scraper (specimen opaqued) from Batza téna locality, Alaska; g-h, copper knife and prong from Dakah De'nin's village, Copper River, Alaska. Implements a-f postdate A.D. l though similar implements may date earlier; copper implements g-h are protohistoric, similar tools in general postdate A.D. 1000. Length of d 10.2 cm, rest same scale.

very roughly fashioned implements neither particularly distinctive nor different in kind from those noted for other northern sites. There are no projectile points.

• CENTRAL BRITISH COLUMBIA Contact-period archeology is represented by several investigations in central British Columbia in the historic Carrier and Chilcotin areas, located primarily south and west of Prince George. Attention also has been directed northward to the Peace River Valley, but primarily for survey and assessment of archeological resources and to excavate Fort D'Epinette (Old Fort Saint John) (Fladmark, Finley, and Spurling 1977). The artifacts recovered from the fort are of interest for understanding the contact period, especially inasmuch as an elaborate industry of native Indian artifacts was recovered. Prehistoric sites discovered in the region have yet to be intensively examined.

Excavations at the protohistoric Carrier village of Chinlac, located at the junction of the Stuart and Nechako rivers, has produced an impressive assemblage of indigenous artifacts and a small number of Euro-Canadian trade goods (Borden 1953). On the basis of the trade goods, the assemblage is considered to date to the second half of the eighteenth century when glass beads and a few iron items could have been traded in from the adjacent West Coast. Dentalia and copper tube beads, also present, may indicate either historic or late prehistoric trade with the coast. Most of the 1,500 or more artifacts from the 40-foot-long multifamily Chinlac house consist of flaked stone implements, and thus the site provides an ideal conjunction of the prehistoric and historic periods. Projectile points include many varieties of small stemmed and side-notched points.

At the abandoned Carrier village of Ulkatcho, located between Anahim Lake and Natalkuz Lake, an area adjacent to the former historically occupied coastal-style longhouse (named Culla culla) was excavated (Donahue 1970, 1973). A broad spectrum of trade and semimodern material was recovered, reflecting the fact that the village, for which there is ethnohistoric documentation, was not completely abandoned until about 1945 (figs. 8g, 9b,g). Evidence is seen in some lithic specimens (fig. 5e,g), for instance in the few microblades, for an early prehistoric occupation of the area also, but most of the flaked implements probably belong to the Carrier component, which is estimated to date back to the protohistoric period (late eighteenth century) when the effects of the fur trade on the coast may have stimulated construction of a potlatch-house trade redistribution center at Gatcho Lake. The stone artifacts show an affiliation with Chinlac as well as with late sites located farther south on the Plateau outside present Carrier territory.

Tezli, located east of Ulkatcho, is a site of intermittent occupation dating from about A.D. 1 to the present (Donahue 1972). Microblades come from a pit house component radiocarbon dated at A.D. 460 ± 100 (Gak-3280), while an additional major occupation is estimated to date around 1400, and a summer camp of three surface dwellings is late prehistoric or protohistoric (figs. 5c–d,f, 12a,c,e).

The multiple occupation Punchaw Lake site, excavated by Simon Fraser University (Fladmark 1973, 1976), is located 35 miles southwest of Prince George and not too far from Tezli, within historic southern Carrier Indian territory. It was occupied from earlier prehistoric times, as attested by microblades, into the contact period. The 43 house-platforms and 53 storage pits make this one of the largest northern Athapaskan sites recorded. House-platforms are not house pits but are "shallow sub-rectangular to oblong benches asymmetrically incised into the sloping stream bank" (Fladmark 1976). Possibly similar platforms are found in the northern Mackenzie District (D.W. Clark 1975), and probably the same type of feature is reported for Healy Lake in Alaska.

Radiocarbon dates associated with these features at Punchaw Lake are largely within the last few centuries and derive from a major Carrier occupation at the site between 1700 and 1800, which is associated with former tree clearing over approximately 14 acres (Fladmark 1976).

Near Anahim Lake several sites have been excavated (Mitchell 1969, 1970; Wilmeth 1970, 1970a, 1971, 1978). For the historic period the Potlatch and Goose Point sites are relevant. Protohistoric and later historic occupation, as well as prehistoric occupation, is recognized in several house pits and associated surface areas (Wilmeth 1970). According to ethnohistorical information a historic Chilcotin occupation preceded the establishment of the Ulkatcho Carrier in the area by gradual movement between 1816 and 1845. The Chilcotin occupation, which is that of the contact and historic period houses, has yet to be recognized in a prehistoric context; this is explained as due either to migration or to an incompletely recovered record.

Potlatch House is a large rectangular house pit believed to have been the home of the Chilcotin chief Anahim, who held potlatches there. It was abandoned about 1869. Recovered artifacts are largely of European or non-indigenous origin (fig. 7d) (Wilmeth 1978).

In contrast to Potlatch House, which architecturally resembles Bella Coola styles and was used to entertain traders from the coast, other historic houses at the site are circular and thus also differ from the rectangular houses of the neighboring Carrier (Wilmeth 1970a:42). They and associated trash mounds produced a much more prolific inventory of native artifacts, such as small stemmed projectile points, as well as Euro-Canadian goods.

Many of the sites discussed above reflect precontact technology, or along with others have late prehistoric components, and seemingly show a gradual technological transition from prehistoric to protohistoric and contact-period occupation. Thus, although few unmixed late prehistoric components have been excavated and dated, a reasonable indication of what is representative of this period is provided by protohistoric and prehistoric sites like Chinlac, Punchaw Lake, Tezli, and others.

Regional specialists see long-established area patterns and trends in those data, while at the same time some propose that the historically known Athapaskan inhabitants of central interior British Columbia are relatively recent migrants from the north. Irrespective of interpretations, there appears to be an area temporal trend. The characteristics of the Early Prehistoric period as adumbrated by Helmer (1977a) were listed above. The succeeding Middle Prehistoric period, from approximately A.D. 1 to 1300, is characterized by several varieties of large corner-notched and side-notched points and by possible continuity of the microblade industry. In the Late Prehistoric period and persisting into the Historic period the many varieties of side- and corner-notched projectile points become very small. Ground and polished adzes are common.

• NORTHERN ALBERTA Data for northern Alberta come primarily from the Peace River and sites in the mixed wood boreal forest. Many of these are located at the southern and eastern limits of the western Subarctic region. It is not surprising then that the affiliation of these sites seems to lie largely with peoples of the Plains or, farther north, that boreal and Plains elements are mixed.

Surveys along the middle Peace River have yielded surface collections of apparent northern Plains affiliation (J.V. Wright 1964, personal communications 1975). Collections reported include a range of cobble tools as well as rough bifaces and various side-notched points. There also are three-quarter grooved splitting adzes suggestive of ones from interior Alaska, the Yukon, and northern British Columbia. R. Thompson (1972) also reports a large number of disturbed surface sites from the Peace River–Saddle Hills area that have yielded all the major point types of the northwest. The first excavated site of the Peace River, the Karpinsky site—barely within the compass of this chapter—consists of a single occupation component characterized by basally thinned lanceolate points (not fluted points), stemmed points, and incipiently side-notched points (Bryan, Conaty, and Steele 1975). The site is dated at A.D. 880 ± 55 (S–517). Recovered implements from Karpinsky show some affinity to central British Columbia (Donahue 1975) and as well to material found far to the north at the outlet of Great Bear Lake in the Franklin Tanks complex, although that complex has been considered to be Plano (Paleo-Indian).

Well east of the Karpinsky site and close to historic Cree Indian territory, at Calling Lake, are a number of excavated sites. One of these (GhPh–103) has yielded a tantalizing collection of side-notched, stemmed, and concave-base oblanceolate points, but the site has been disturbed in recent times and no direct periodization is possible (Gruhn 1966, 1967:fig. B, 1969). Other sites at Calling Lake have yielded radiocarbon dates ranging from A.D. 780 ± 130 to A.D. 1585 ± 55 (respectively GSC–1034 for GhPh–107, and S–518 for GhPh–102, in Lowden, Wilmeth, and Blake 1970:476 and Rutherford, Wittenberg, and McCallum 1973:208, which also cite other dates). However, it has been suggested from typological comparisons with points known to be early in southern Alberta, and also on the basis of stratigraphy, that these dates do not adequately bracket the full range of occupation represented.

An extensive quarry site located farther north in the Athabasca River drainage has produced a large quantity of roughly prepared material, but few finished and diagnostic implements were recovered. Two Besant-like side-notched points put the main utilization of the site around A.D. 400 if cross-dating with the Plains is valid (Syncrude Canada Ltd. 1974:84–87).

The west end of Lake Athabasca is at the very edge of the Shield. Although nominally outside the area of this chapter, the prehistory of this part of Lake Athabasca is significantly different from that of the eastern half (J.V. Wright 1975). Western affiliation with the Besant phase of the northern Plains is seen in the Big Bay site, which is dated at A.D. 690 ± 170 (Gak–3798). Farther to the east at this time affiliations are with the Taltheilei Shale tradition of the north.

The Birch Hills of northern Alberta were a major focal point for exploration during the 1970s. Projectile points recovered from sites there suggest a late northern affiliation—for example, Taltheilei types initially defined for the central Mackenzie District. There is as well material superficially comparable with Plains types (Donahue 1976; Ives 1977). In the nearby Birch Mountains there is the prospect of 5,000 years of radiocarbon dated chronology (Conaty 1977) although present collections are too meager for this to be realized.

Donahue (1976:31) suggests that the co-occurrence of artifacts normally attributed to the Plains and to the northern boreal forest highlights the transitional nature of the region.

Summary and Conclusions

The boundaries of the area dealt with here have been determined by the historic distribution of Athapaskan groups; therefore, especially in the Canadian provinces, the fit with prehistoric patterns has not always been clean and inclusive. The treatment might have been easier—at least it would have been mechanical and simple—if it were merely to attempt to outline the prehistory of each of the score or more of Athapaskan tribes in the area. There are two major blocks to following that procedure: the groups known historically are not necessarily the ones that existed 1,000 years ago, and the data are too incomplete or too unspecific for the prehistory of most groups to be followed. However, considerable attention has been given to detail where particular remains can be linked to a certain people.

Early Cultures

The problem is compounded when one goes back in time, across, for some areas, a seemingly major technological threshold into the microblade and blade cultures. The Athapaskan cultures probably have their roots in the microblade cultures, but this is by no means an established fact. A somewhat different perspective is offered by turning from the direct historic approach ("upstreaming") to one that focuses on the early peopling of the region.

Fortunately, nature in the form of Late Pleistocene glaciation has provided a clean slate, so to speak, throughout much of the area up to 8000–10,000 B.C. and has also created a number of geochronological controls that are mainly of value to Paleo-Indian specialists.

From these factors and the data presented in the preceding pages the following sequence can be developed.

Glaciation did not completely envelop all parts of the north. A great unglaciated zone teeming with wildlife extended from the Yukon Territory through interior Alaska and across the emergent Bering Sea land bridge into Siberia. Man probably was there, but the somewhat disconnected evidence for his early presence does not show relationship to later man in the region. At some time in the past man also had gotten south to the central or subglacial parts of North America and by the end of the Pleistocene had developed a distinctive Paleo-Indian culture there characterized by the use of fluted projectile points.

By 8500 or 9000 B.C. people with an east Siberian blade and microblade culture had entered into the unglaciated interior Alaska-Yukon region. Soon, however, as the global ice caps melted at the end of the Pleistocene, the waters rose to flood Beringia and part North America from Asia. Some people of the Beringian microblade cultures were forced back into Siberia, others into North America. Their numbers were small at first, and they gradually spread eastward, perhaps in some areas occupying lands newly freed from the glaciers, but elsewhere they amalgamated with antecedent peoples or took over areas that had been briefly occupied by Paleo-Indians.

As the continental glaciers receded other Paleo-Indian groups expanded northward from the Plains and Pacific Northwest. They may have become established throughout the available region extending almost to Bering Strait. Shortly before the appearance of the Beringian blade and microblade cultures there were already in Alaska people whose culture was in some ways a distinctive local entity but that also showed cross-ties with the continental Paleo-Indian cultures. In at least one case, in the upper Chindadn levels at Healy Lake, the early local Paleo-Indians may have merged with the Beringian people. However, it is difficult when dealing with the type of evidence available to distinguish between people and technology and all statements on prehistory must be judged against this distinction.

Many millennia passed before the microblade people or technology became established at the eastern limits of their distribution covered in this chapter, and by that time there had been several derivative offshoots whose relationships to the Beringian peoples are so remote as to be of no practical significance—the Arctic Small Tool tradition and the early microblade industries of coastal and southern British Columbia, for instance. Meanwhile, the eastern part of the area was occupied by people whose ancestry probably lies more in derivatives from Paleo-Indians and other Plains and Eastern groups than in groups of Beringian and far northwestern origin.

Until the mid-1970s attempts to periodize or subdivide the Beringian-derived microblade and blade cultures had suffered from insufficiently large assemblages, erroneous dating or usually no dating at all, mixed and thereby invalid assemblages, and from attempts to use as horizon markers traits that have very little temporal significance. The data are still somewhat refractory, but it is possible to see an early stage, represented by the principal component at Dry Creek and some Denali material, in which there are no side- and corner-notched points and in which most points are in fact knives. This is a bifacial industry, although unifaces (implements with a single prepared side) are present. A question of the significance of early exclusively unifacial industries in the prehistory of Alaska has been raised by archeologists, but so far this pertains only to the Arctic littoral, not to the Subarctic interior. Beginning about 4000 B.C. there are side-notched points and points of other forms, and the blade and microblade industry becomes quite variable in its expression and sometimes is absent. Where the appearance of side-notched points signals also the end of the microblade industry it is possible to envision migration of "Northern Archaic" people from regions far to the south and east where such points occur somewhat earlier. But three variables, which combine in permutations, indicate some unresolved questions: in some places side-notched points have short-term existence while in others they persist for several millennia; in some areas such points simply are a trait added to the inventory of a microblade or Beringian-derived culture; and in other places they demark a distinct Northern Archaic culture. It may be noted, too, that this trait is nearly ubiquitous in North America over a long period.

The Last Two Millennia and Athapaskan Prehistory

Factors that have tended to make the microblade cultures refractory also have obscured the transition to nonmicrolithic cultures of essentially modern complexion that are directly or by inference associated with Athapaskan Indians. Enigmatically, the shift in technology occurs about 2500 B.C. in the southern Yukon territory with the appearance of side-notched points. Elsewhere it is later, in some cases after A.D. 1. Whether or not there was an abrupt change or migration may be largely a matter of interpretation; nevertheless, the net change between early prehistoric and late prehistoric technology is very considerable, with the probable exception of central British Columbia.

A large number of late prehistoric sites has been considered in an attempt to represent each region and illustrate the range of variation. For the Subarctic, ethnographic analogy finds a worthwhile application. This is in part because of the detail that has been made available by the very descendants of the later prehistoric inhabitants whose camps are being studied by archeologists, and the operation, probably throughout much of the past after Paleo-Indian times, of an environmentally limited and often patterned set of subsistence alternatives in settings that remain largely in a pristine state in the late twentieth century. Against this backdrop, that of history, and adjacent culture areas (dealt with in other volumes) appears a number of regional variations of prehistoric Athapaskan culture. As constructs of the scholar such variations are almost infinitely mutable depending upon the level of generalization sought, the characteristics emphasized, or the geographic point from which a distribution is viewed.

Among these variations is the Taltheilei Shale tradition of the Mackenzie District, a focus on copper working and de-emphasis of flaked stone found centered in the Copper River Basin, and the slate grinding, pottery making, somewhat Eskimoized Athapaskans of western Alaska. Other variations of more or less local scope are found or may be foreseen on the Chilcotin Plateau of British Columbia and the Kavik phase of northern Alaska and perhaps also the northern Yukon Territory. In some regions there are localized causal factors, such as the Eskimo inhabitants of western Alaska or the occurrence of native copper in the Copper River Basin. Ecological factors vary, but these probably are not expressed in styles and small implement types, and thus except where settlement data are recovered ecological variants often escape detection in the record or, as is usually the case, are inferentially derived. Many local variations may be seen as blends of others. Thus, for instance, copper working is not limited to the Copper River Basin and adjacent reaches of the Tanana River but occurs widely elsewhere, although to a lesser degree, and enters into culture forms that partake also of certain characteristics of other regions. And in the western Mackenzie District and Alberta some projectile points can be related to Taltheilei styles, but this does not mean that the Taltheilei tradition, as originally defined, pervades the whole area. None of these variations can properly be dealt with in terms of the phase concept of conventional archeological taxonomy inasmuch as they are not sharply definable in space and time. But as has already been noted, a number of trends and universals, as well as regional variations, can be seen in the late prehistory of the Northern Athapaskan area. This then is Athapaskan prehistory—a network or chain, depending upon the dictates of geography, of regional variations. It is doubtful if there was significantly less diversity in the deeper past.

Environment and Culture in the Shield and Mackenzie Borderlands

EDWARD S. ROGERS AND JAMES G.E. SMITH

Perhaps one of the most important consequences of the advent of Europeans in the Shield Subarctic, offering a new technology and new economic inducements, was the changes in Indian perception and exploitation of the natural environment. The intent of this chapter is to reconstruct insofar as possible the relationship between native culture and environment before that relationship was altered to any substantial degree by contact with Europeans.

Environment

The term Shield Subarctic is employed in this volume to distinguish an area of basic ethnographic unity—despite the linguistic division within it between Algonquian and Athapaskan speakers—that physiographically is dominated by the Canadian Shield. Included within the Shield Subarctic in its ethnographic definition are some native peoples who in whole or part occupy physiographic regions that flank the Canadian Shield region: the Hudson Bay Lowlands, the Mackenzie Lowlands and the eastern slopes of the Cordillera (fig. 1). Superimposed on the physiographic zones are three major vegetation regions, from north to south: the tundra or barrens; the northern transitional forest or forest-tundra ecotone, of mixed boreal forest cover and barrens; and the full or closed boreal forest. The last two are subdivisions of the boreal forest region per se (Rowe 1972). Although the barrens were seasonally exploited by some of the more northerly Indians, no group occupied them on a year-round basis. The Lake Saint John Montagnais and the Saulteaux of the Lake Winnipeg drainage occupied, in part, subboreal zones (of the Great Lakes–Saint Lawrence forest region); in the west, some Strongwoods Cree occupied the boreal forest–prairie transitional zone.

The overall similarity of the physiographic, climatic, and biotal environment experienced by the inhabitants of the Shield Subarctic guided their cultural adaptations toward a basic uniformity in major aspects of technical and social culture. The regional cultural variations that occurred were, at least in part, due to distinctive combinations of environmental components possible within each region. Variations in environmental features that affected human adjustment included the variations in numbers and combinations of Subarctic floral and faunal species (for example, Rowe 1972 identifies about 26 boreal forest "sections" within the Shield Subarctic); differing behavioral characteristics of each faunal species, such as that between caribou and moose; and the restricted distribution of certain species.

The life cycle of the forest affected its faunal composition and carrying capacity. Periodic forest fires destroyed the climax forest and initiated seral stages, each having its associated fauna. Fires disrupted the forest and game, requiring periodic movements and other adjustments by the human population.

Most of the Shield Subarctic region is characterized by low, rolling relief, interspersed with innumerable lakes, ponds, rivers, streams, and muskeg. The water bodies vary in size, numbers, and spatial distribution, with significant cultural consequences. The Hudson Bay Lowlands, for example, have a limited number of shallow ponds but is nearly devoid of lakes, while the southern and western margins of the Canadian Shield are rimmed by large bodies of water, providing good fishing sites from the Great Lakes to the lower Mackenzie River.

Of great significance to humans was the pronounced summer-winter cycle demarcated by spring breakup and autumn freeze-up ("General Environment," fig. 8, this vol.). Long and severe winters alternated with short and moderately warm summers. It was the winter, especially, that placed its stamp on the inhabitants by limiting their activities and requiring maximal exertions for survival. Powdery snow, deepest in the east, covers the land during the long winter, increasing in depth as the winter progresses. It tends to be deepest within the forest where the winds do not pack it into hard drifts, as occurs in open areas. The variations in snow conditions affect the behavior of the fauna and hence affected native techniques for its exploitation. During the spring thaw or breakup in May-June when ice becomes rotten and the powdery snow becomes granular and water-soaked, human travel was minimal. During summer, travel was on foot, usually following watercourses, or by canoe on open water; but with late autumn (Sep-

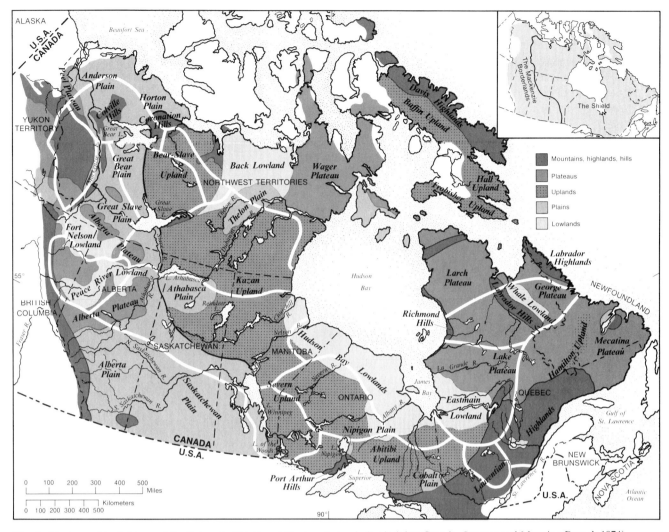

Fig. 1. Physiographic divisions of the Subarctic Shield and Mackenzie borderlands (after Canada. Surveys and Mapping Branch 1974). Approximate tribal boundaries are outlined in white; see Key to Tribal Territories for names.

tember-October) the water again begins to freeze, limiting travel and subsistence activities.

The fauna provided the food and clothing that sustained life. Game animals also provided much of the raw materials, in the form of bone, antler, and hide, for producing articles such as awls, beamers, needles, fleshers, spear and arrow points, fishhooks, bowstrings, lines, bags, and lodge coverings. The forest provided almost all the remaining raw materials for bows, arrows and spear shafts, containers, ladles, dishes, shuttles, net gauges, snowshoe and canoe frames, snow shovels, toboggans, and particularly bark for making dishes, boxes, and coverings for lodges and canoes.

Culture

Subsistence

• TECHNIQUES   The Algonquians and Athapaskans of the Shield Subarctic were big-game hunters. The most

important food animals were the Barren Ground caribou of the northern transitional forest and the adjacent tundra and the moose and woodland caribou throughout the closed boreal forest.

Caribou are concentrated during their migrations between winter and summer foraging ranges (the barren-ground variety more so than the woodland) and, on occasion, within the seasonal foraging ranges. At other times, the animals are scattered in small groups. These behavioral characteristics often dictated the manner in which the animals were taken. During the migratory phases or during periods of concentration within the winter foraging ranges, the chute and pound was widely used. The Chipewyan variety, according to Hearne (1958:49–50), consisted of a circular enclosure up to a mile or more in circumference composed of trees and brush. Within the pound was a "maze" of brush hedges between which snares, made fast to poles or tree stumps, were set. An opening a few feet wide was left in the wall from which two diverging wings

131

composed of brush or poles set 15 to 20 yards apart to represent men extended for a considerable distance, sometimes up to two or three miles. Once a herd had been sighted, the animals were maneuvered into the mouth of the chute and then driven into the pound, to be entangled in the snares and dispatched by spears or, if remaining loose in the pound, shot with arrows.

Frequently in the autumn when the Barren Ground caribou were migrating, they were speared as they crossed rivers and lakes, a favorite technique of the Naskapi (Davies and Johnson 1963:54, 178; Turner 1894) and Chipewyan (Hearne 1958:91). The hunters, two to a canoe, speared the frightened animals by striking them in the area of the kidneys. The spear or lance consisted of a long, light, wooden shaft with a bone or antler point; after European contact the points came to be made of iron. In winter when the animals were often dispersed, the hunters relied upon bows and arrows after first driving the animals into deep snow. Bows were simple without backing (fig. 2), and arrows fletched, and tipped aboriginally with stone or bone heads. Among some Athapaskans, a disguise was sometimes worn by the hunter to enable him to get within arrow range (Anell 1964:3–4). Frequently, snares were erected in caribou trails.

Moose were found primarily within the closed boreal forest, where they were an important source of food and raw materials. Hunting techniques were adapted to the behavioral characteristics of the animal, for moose, in contrast to caribou, do not associate in large numbers. During warm weather, they tend to be solitary; in winter as the snow deepens, they may congregate in favorable forage areas ("yards") where they keep trails open allowing them to reach their food, but rarely are there more than five or so in a yard (Peterson 1955:112). Another characteristic of the animal is its habit when finishing eating of turning back on its trail to the windward to rest. The hunter responded to this trait by a special tracking technique (fig. 3). He followed the trail of the moose to one side and to windward, checking occasionally to see if the moose had turned back to rest. When he discovered that this had occurred, the hunter knew quite accurately where the moose was (Rogers 1962:C42). Moose may have been taken with bow and arrow, especially during the rutting season when they were attracted within range with a birchbark caller. In late winter, the animals were driven into deep snow and speared. It was, of course, at this time of year that they might be forced to restrict their movements and establish yards (Feit 1973:118–120).

Other large ruminants had very restricted distribution: elk or wapiti, mule deer, white-tailed deer, and wood bison in sectors of the southwestern fringe of the Shield Subarctic; musk-ox in the tundra west of Hudson Bay.

132   Although bear were found throughout the forests,

Fig. 2. Athapaskan style of holding a bow and arrow. The horizontal hold of the bow is characteristic of the Athapaskans since at least the 18th century (Thompson 1916:166). The bows are being demonstrated by Harry Bearlake, a Dogrib, and were made by him of willow with twisted caribou babiche bowstrings. The arrows are also of willow, fletched with 3 parallel split duck feathers lashed to the shaft with caribou sinew, which is glued with melted spruce gum. The arrow release shown is the type called secondary; some Dogribs use the primary release. top, Small-game bow with blunt-headed bird arrow. Additional arrows are grasped along the bow to permit rapid shooting. bottom, Big-game hunting bow, showing the wrist guard that prevents the wrist and base of the thumb of the bow hand from being scraped by the released bowstring. Photographs by June Helm, Rae, N.W.T., 1970.

they were not taken frequently enough to bulk large in the diet; however, they were eagerly sought especially for the large quantities of fat they possessed. They were also objects of respect relations for the Algonquian and Athapaskan inhabitants of the Shield Subarctic. Bear were taken in deadfalls and tossing-pole snares and were killed with spears or arrows. They were sought in the fall about berry patches where they came to feast on the ripening fruit; in winter in their dens, often with the aid of small hunting dogs; and in spring, after they emerged from hibernation, at rapids where they came to catch fish.

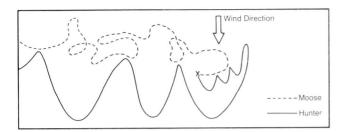

top, after R.K. Nelson 1973:106; bottom, Smithsonian, NAA: 56,963.

Fig. 3. top, Moose tracking technique. A moose normally doubles back after feeding in order to rest at a spot downwind of its previous trail, where it will catch the scent of any following predator. A hunter therefore does not directly follow the trail of a feeding moose, but rather makes semicircular loops downwind from it until the moose's trail doubles back, whereupon he turns back in smaller downwind loops until he encounters the moose (Osgood 1936a:26–27; Rogers 1962:C42–C43; R.K. Nelson 1973:103–106). bottom, Cree man demonstrating the use of a birchbark horn for calling moose. Photograph by Edward S. Curtis, copyright Nov. 1927.

Beaver were an important food mammal to some inhabitants of the Shield Subarctic, especially in the east. Perhaps the easiest time of year to secure them was during the winter, but only when snowfall was light (Davies and Johnson 1963:277), for then their homes could be readily located and at the same time the animals' movements were limited because of ice conditions. To secure the animals, the entrance passages were blocked, the lodge broken into, and the animals killed ("Intercultural Relations and Cultural Change in the Shield and Mackenzie Borderlands," fig. 5, this vol.). Those that escaped would be forced to seek air pockets under the ice, where they could be located and killed. In historic times nets were placed at the entrances to the lodges and retrieved when struck by a beaver. The net acted like a bag, there being a drawstring about the perimeter that the hunter pulled to close the net as he retrieved it. Nets were perhaps most frequently employed during times of open water, set in narrow

streams and hand operated (e.g., by the Mistassini) when beaver were not restricted in their movements by winter conditions. The animals were also taken with a form of harpoon (e.g., by the Montagnais) and with deadfalls. Seals, in the mouth of the Saint Lawrence, were killed with clubs in winter by the Montagnais.

Small animals were caught in a variety of devices (figs. 4–5): snares, including the tossing-pole, spring-pole, and stationary snare; deadfalls of various sizes and trigger mechanisms (Cooper 1938); and bows and arrows. The slow-moving porcupine was often killed with a club. Snares were used to take the widespread varying hare, which in times when big game failed became a critically important food source. Only after European contact were small mammals hunted or trapped primarily for their fur.

The only domesticated animal present aboriginally was the dog, a small variety used for hunting moose, bear, beaver, geese, and perhaps some other animals. Only among the Chipewyan were dogs, in limited numbers, used as pack animals. Not until larger varieties were brought to the Subarctic by Europeans were they used by native peoples to haul toboggans, and this not fully until the twentieth century.

Birds do not seem to have been of great significance to the inhabitants of the Shield Subarctic except for those who may have been living on the Hudson Bay Lowlands where during open water, especially spring and fall, waterfowl were present in vast numbers. Presumably during the time of molt they were captured by hand. However, their importance was only seasonal. In historic times, they became a more significant food resource as a consequence of the introduction of firearms and twine nets. Spruce grouse and ptarmigan were taken in stationary snares and spruce grouse in hand-operated snares; both were shot with blunt-headed arrows (fig. 2).

Fishing may have been a major food source to some groups within the Shield Subarctic, but in general fish provided basic food only at those times of the year when big game was difficult to secure. Rich fishing sites were of social importance, for during the ice-free period they permitted concentrations of population when major social activities took place.

Seasonal climatic conditions, in conjunction with the behavioral characteristics of the fish, indicated the appropriate seasons of exploitation and the techniques to be employed for their taking. Lake trout were taken by hook in open water, or through ice holes in late winter and early spring, or by fish spears. Whitefish spawned during the fall, when they moved into shallows or ascended streams. At this time they were taken by means of dip nets (e.g., by the Rupert House Cree) and weirs (e.g., by Northern Ojibwa). Sturgeon, limited to the central Subarctic, tended to inhabit swift water, especially during the spring spawning, when they were

133

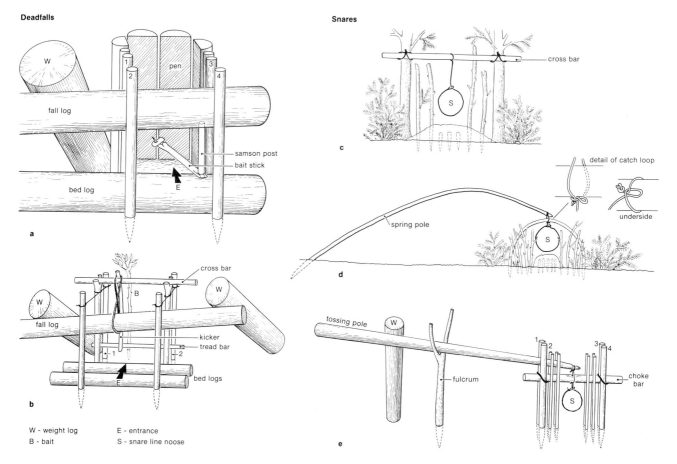

Deadfalls

Snares

W

fall log

pen

samson post
bait stick

bed log

a

cross bar

W

B

W

fall log

kicker
tread bar

bed logs

b

W - weight log   E - entrance
B - bait   S - snare line noose

cross bar

S

c

detail of catch loop

underside

spring pole

S

d

tossing pole   W

fulcrum

choke
bar

S

e

after Cooper 1938:figs. 8, 11, 26, 29, 55.

Fig. 4. Some of the many Subarctic types of deadfalls and snares. *Deadfalls*, set chiefly for marten, fisher, mink, fox, bear, otter, muskrat, beaver, and wolverine. a, Samson-post, an underpropped type. The fall log is positioned over the bed log, held from twisting by the guide stakes (1–4) and balanced between the samson-post and the weight log. The bait stick is positioned under or over the samson-post. The top of the pen is covered with brush to disguise the trap and prevent the animal from entering except through the front. When the animal enters the trap and tugs at the bait (either fish or meat), the bait stick is pulled, upsetting the samson-post and causing the fall log to drop on the back or neck of the animal. b, Kicker, an overhung type. The variety diagrammed is for trapping beaver and is set on a beaver dam. The fall log is suspended by a thong looped over the crossbar to the upper end of the kicker. The lower end of the kicker presses against the tread bar and holds it in place against the back stakes (1–2). Brush is piled up on either side. The beaver in passing through the trap to get to the bait (a poplar sapling), steps down on the tread bar, releasing the kicker, which flips up and releases the fall log. *Snares*, set chiefly for grouse, hare, fox, lynx, bear, caribou, and moose. c, Fox tether snare is stationary with the crossbar lashed between 2 trees. Under the noose 3 stakes covered with moss simulate a windfall; sticks and brush on either side force passage through the snare. The snare line is wire (which the animal cannot bite through) and no bait is used. d, Hare spring-pole snare. The spring-pole is made of peeled sapling or willow bent down and held by a catch loop under a hoop or wicket. The snare noose is held open by branchlets on the flanking uprights, and the animal is led to pass into it by brush placed below and to each side. The catch loop unties when an animal enters the snare noose, releasing the bent spring-pole and lifting the animal off its feet. Spring-pole snares can be used only in warm weather when the sapling is flexible. e, Tossing-pole snare of the choke-toss type, used for bear. A single perforated choke bar is lashed tightly between the uprights (1–4). The snare line passes through the perforation and is tied to the end of the tossing-pole, which is held down by a catch loop. Brush (not shown) is piled under the noose and on both sides of the framework. When an animal enters the noose the catch loop is released and the weight log to the left of the fulcrum causes the tossing-pole to pull up and choke the animal against the bar. Descriptions and terminology based on Cooper 1938. Diagrams are not to the same scale; the size of the deadfall or snare varies with the size of the animal being trapped.

speared. Along the Saint Lawrence River, the Montagnais took eel in weirs during the fall.

Among the Chipewyan, nets were made of babiche; among the Mackenzie River Athapaskans, of willow bast. For the Algonquians in the east, there is no sure evidence that the gill net was present until after European contact, except insofar as some native inhabitants received nets through trade from their southern neighbors (JR 6:309). Gill nets were set under the ice (fig. 6) as well as in open water. Through the thick ice of deep winter, nets could be set or tended only with great difficulty until after the introduced metal ice chisel replaced one of horn.

• FOOD INTAKE Nowhere did vegetal products provide a significant part of the diet, except perhaps berries during late summer and, in the west, the lichen *Gy-*

Fig. 5. Setting traps. left, West Main Cree man constructing a deadfall; photograph by H. Bassett, Moose Factory area, about 1934. right, Marie Bastien, Montagnais-Naskapi from North West River, Newf., setting a hare snare; photograph by Richard Leacock, summer 1951.

rophora, which was made into a nourishing gelatin soup in times of food shortages. In some peripheral zones in the south, wild rice and maple sap were gathered seasonally. Some plants were employed as medicines.

The hunters of the Shield Subarctic required great quantities of food for themselves and their families. Indications are that during the winter approximately 4,500 to 5,000 calories per person per day were needed, and somewhat less in summer (Burton and Edholm 1955:185; Feit 1973:121). An average of at least four pounds of flesh food might be consumed daily by each person (Rogers 1963a:39). Of this a substantial percentage had to be fat in order to secure necessary calories (and also essential fatty acids). It is this situation that gives credence to the common native statement that one can "starve to death on rabbits," since for most of the year they have little body fat.

Although data are meager, it appears that big game yielded the most food with the least labor input (Feit 1973:121; Rogers 1973:table 6, 82). When the yield from big game dropped below 3,500 to 3,600 calories per person per day the hunters turned to small game and fish although at an increase in the labor input (Feit 1973:124). In the eastern part of the Shield Subarctic, when big-game populations dropped below a certain point there were insufficient quantities of small game and fish to adequately augment the food supply. Nineteenth-century records indicate that starvation or depopulation of the particular area resulted. This occurred in the upper part of the Eastmain River drainage basin (Low 1897:101L–102L) and to the southwest of Hudson and James bays ("Territorial Groups Before 1821: Cree and Ojibwa," this vol.).

Figures (table 1) are available for several Cree and Ojibwa bands to indicate the varied reliance placed on big game, small game, birds, and fish. Although these figures are for the mid-twentieth century, they confirm the importance of big game, even at a time when woodland caribou had been drastically reduced in numbers; however, this is not to deny the important role that the other animal species taken for food played in the subsistence economy.

Since the availability of food resources varied seasonally, there were periods when large quantities could be secured and other times when little was available. To equalize the supply over time, some food had to be preserved for the lean periods. During the winter, fish and game were sometimes frozen, but the usual method was to sun-dry or smoke-dry the flesh for later use. If the meat was to be used quite soon, then it was only lightly dried; but if it was to be transported or kept for a considerable period of time, it was thoroughly dried and often pounded and broken up into flakes or powder (fig. 7). Sometimes the end product was mixed with melted fat to form pemmican; berries, when available, were also often added. Meat and fish were dried on a variety of racks. Stone pounders were employed to break up the dried flesh, which was then stored in hide bags or birchbark boxes, which were kept on cache racks to be out of the reach of carnivores. The cache racks were platforms of poles supported by three or four upright poles or trees conveniently placed.

• ANNUAL CYCLE Throughout the Shield Subarctic, there was a basic similarity in the yearly round of activities and movements of the Indian inhabitants. During the summer months, overland travel tended to be restricted. The people then gathered along the shores of lakes and waterways; life was relatively sedentary. Here on the shores the people found protection from the swarms of blackflies and mosquitoes but were somewhat restricted in the game they could secure, although many game animals, such as moose and woodland car-

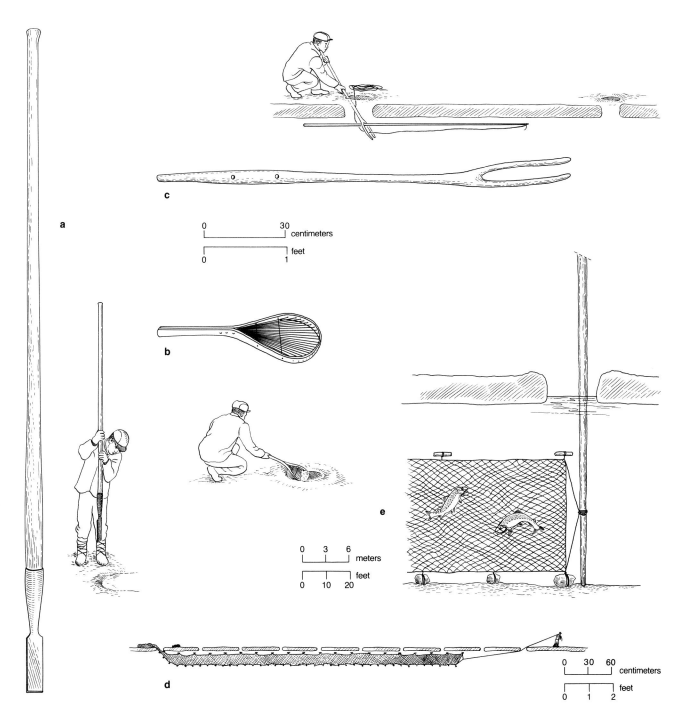

Fig. 6. Setting gill net under the ice. With the substitution of the iron ice chisel, a, for one of horn, and of commercial twine for babiche or willow bast cordage, contemporary Athapaskans set gill nets under ice in much the same manner as that described by Hearne (1958:11–12) in the 1770s: "To set a net under the ice, it is first necessary to ascertain its exact length, by stretching it out upon the ice near the part proposed for setting it. This being done, a number of round holes are cut in the ice, at ten or twelve feet distance from each other, and as many in number as will be sufficient to stretch the net at its full length. A line is then passed under the ice by means of a long light pole, which is first introduced at one of the end holes, and, by means of [one or] two forked sticks [c], this pole is easily conducted, or passed from one hole to another, under the ice, till it arrives at the last. The pole is then taken out, and both ends of the line being properly secured, is always ready for use. The net is made fast to one end of the line by one person, and hauled under the ice [d] by a second [or, as in illustration, the entire operation can be done by one man]; a large stone is tied to each of the lower corners, which serves to keep the net expanded, and prevents it rising from the bottom with every waft of the current [e]. . . . In order to search a net thus set, the two end holes only are opened [and cleared of ice with a scoop, b]; the line is veered away by one person, and the net hauled from under the ice by another; after all the fish are taken out, the net is easily hauled back to its former station, and there secured as before."

Preliminary drawings for this figure were based on 1960s photographs of Dogrib equipment and techniques; these were shown by June Helm to Dogrib informants in 1975 and revised according to their instructions.

ROGERS AND SMITH

Fig. 7. Chipewyan woman pounding dried caribou meat on a stone to powder it before it is mixed with fat to make pemmican.
Photograph by Richard Harrington, near Caribou Post, Man., Feb. 1948.

sought the Barren Ground caribou moved to localities where they intercepted the migrating herds as they moved toward the tree line; those in the boreal forest moved to streams where they secured quantities of whitefish; and those on the north shore of the Saint Lawrence remained on the coast and took eel.

Freeze-up restricted mobility. During this period, canoes could not be used because the thin ice easily cut the birchbark, while at the same time it was not thick enough to walk upon.

Once freeze-up had passed, the people were again mobile. Usually, they established winter camps from which they sought game in the immediate vicinity. If the fall hunt had been successful and game was still plentiful in the area of the winter camp, they might not move again until spring; however, generally their camps had to be shifted periodically to new hunting areas. As winter advanced and snowfall increased, the taking of moose and caribou became easier as the deep snows impeded their freedom and rapid movement (McLean 1932:154; JR 6:277, 8:29; Davies and Johnson 1963:277). January and February were the hardest time of the year because of the intense cold and long hours of darkness. Starvation was sometimes the result, and there were frequently periods of hunger.

With the arrival of spring, those people who relied on water transport began to move to where the previous fall they had stored their canoes or to those localities where birch trees were available for their construction. The period of breakup again prevented the people from moving freely for several weeks; however, it was a time when waterfowl were returning from the south and could be secured along the major flyways. Furthermore, gill nets, for those who possessed them, could be easily set in areas of open water and more fish secured as they began to be more active. Life became easier. With the passing of breakup, the people moved back to their summer campsites.

Travel and Transportation

During the winter months, the accumulation of snow impeded human movements. To overcome this diffi-

ibou, also sought the sanctuary of the shores. Fishing was important for some groups, and at "fisheries" the abundant fish provided subsistence for the larger social aggregates that were important in maintaining social ties.

With the approach of fall, the people left the summer gathering centers to seek food in preparation for the long, cold winter. Hides of big game were then at their best for clothing and the animals had an abundance of fat, an essential nutrient for the winter. Those who

Table 1.   Percentages of Country Game Taken for Food Among Different Bands

	Mistassini 1953–1954	Attawapiskat 1947–1948	Weagamow Lake 1958–1959	Waswanipi 1968–1969	Fort Albany 1964–1965
Big game	65%	18%	53%	64%	82%
Small game	5	12	16	some	1
Birds	4	31	5	some	14
Fish	26	39	26	7	2
Store food	——[a]	——[a]	——[a]	28	——[a]
Sea mammals	0	0	0	0	1

SOURCES: Rogers 1967:75, except Fort Albany (Rogers 1965–1972) and Waswanipi (Feit 1973).
[a] Not included in survey.

culty, the people employed snowshoes that consisted of a frame of larch or birch laced with babiche, for which a bone or wooden needle was employed. A variety of styles of snowshoes (fig. 8) existed: long and narrow in the west, where different right and left foot snowshoes were an Athapaskan feature, tending gradually to become more oval to the east. Within the historic era the long, narrow style diffused eastward into the Labrador Peninsula. Contrary to D.S. Davidson's (1937:138–161) views, solid snowshoes did not come into use until the nineteenth century.

Toboggans, which varied in size but not in style throughout the Shield Subarctic, were used to move supplies in winter. They were constructed of two thin boards of larch or birch secured together by crossbars and turned up in front. Loads were sometimes simply drawn on caribou hides.

In general, winter travel routes were the frozen lakes and rivers that provided a relatively smooth path. Snowshoes and toboggans were well adapted to the light powdery snow that prevailed for most of the winter, but with the arrival of the spring thaw, they were of little use. In that season the canoe-sled ("Davis Inlet, Labrador," fig. 2, this vol.) often replaced the toboggan among the inhabitants of the eastern Subarctic.

Following breakup, conditions of travel altered greatly. To negotiate the open waterways, the native peoples employed birchbark canoes of several distinct regional styles (Adney and Chapelle 1964). Canoes were generally constructed during the spring when the bark of the birch trees could be most easily removed. Cedar, fir, or spruce was used for the frames. Sewing of the birchbark sheathing was done with split black spruce roots, and the seams were pitched with black spruce gum. In restricted areas of the western Shield Subarctic spruce bark was used as a covering ("Slavey," fig. 8, this vol.). As a substitute for canoes, log rafts were sometimes constructed especially to cross streams. Finally, to move goods overland on one's back at all seasons, tumplines were employed among all native peoples of the Shield Subarctic.

Structures

The severe winter temperatures of the Shield Subarctic required some form of shelter, but because the people had to be frequently on the move such shelters had to be readily erected from locally obtained materials or else made of items that could be easily transported. The peoples of the Shield Subarctic had several types of shelter that fulfilled these conditions and at the same time were large enough to house several families (fig. 9).

The conical lodge had a framework of light poles widely spaced; it was covered in the northern part of the Shield Subarctic with hides or boughs ("brush")

and in the south with pieces of bark sewed together to form strips, and/or rush mats. This type of shelter could be used at any time of the year. A second form of shelter was the dome-shaped lodge found among the Algonquians in the eastern part of the Shield Subarctic. Light poles, openly spaced, were thrust into the ground, bent over, and tied together at the tops, then covered with hides, boughs, or bark. This type of structure was not used during the winter when the ground was frozen. Smaller versions were used as sweat lodges. The ridgepole lodge was common among the inhabitants of the eastern Shield Subarctic (fig. 10). It consisted of a frame of light poles supported by a ridgepole resting on an A-frame at either end and covered with bark and hides. Small ones had a door at one end; larger ones housing a number of families had a door at either end. A variation with log walls (fig. 11) occurred among the Slavey of the west (J.A. Mason 1946:20–21).

In the conical and dome-shaped lodges, a fireplace was located at the center; in the ridgepole lodge several fireplaces would be arranged in a line down the center under the ridgepole. Fire was made with a strike-a-light or carried as a smoldering wood from camp to camp. A variety of temporary shelters existed, the most common being the lean-to.

Clothing and Bedding

The severe climatic conditions of the Shield Subarctic dictated that insulating forms of clothing be worn during the winter months, that the people have a high caloric intake, that fire be used, and that when outside one move continuously to maintain body heat.

The making of clothing was the work of the women and occupied a great deal of their time. The resources available from which to prepare clothing were limited; only hides were used. With some exceptions, the hides of moose and caribou were dehaired; softened by soaking, scraping, stretching, and rubbing with brains or grease; and finally, as a rule, smoked to produce a golden brown color on the sueded finish ("Chipewyan," fig. 4, this vol.).

Semitailored shirts and dresses were made of the dressed hides. Coats and parkas with or without a hood were worn throughout the Subarctic during the winter. In the west, they were often of furred caribou or of moose hide. Among the Naskapi, they were also of caribou hide but often dehaired and decorated with elaborately painted designs consisting of the double curved motif. Subarctic Algonquians and some Athapaskans also wore furred beaver robes, and various kinds of furred hats were found everywhere. In addition, a breechclout, leggings, and soft-soled moccasins were worn. The moccasins (fig. 12) were ideal for winter wear—flexible and warm with a grass or hare-skin sock and "working" in perfect combination with the

138

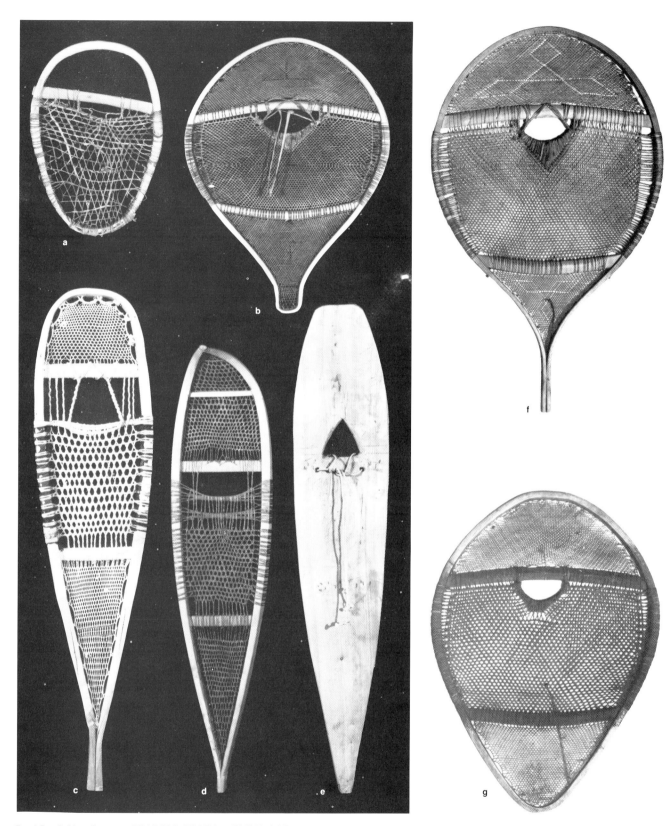

Royal Ontario Mus., Toronto: a, 960.161.34; b, 962.247.3; c, 959.50.80; d, 962.41; e, 959.50.64; f, 956.160.5; g, 930x59.2.

Fig. 8. Snowshoe types, usually distinguished according to the frame shape. The more oval shapes are typical of the east while the narrower shapes are western. a, Bear paw style; crudely constructed snowshoes made for temporary use in an emergency or for young children. b, Beaver tail style. c, Round toe, and d, pointed toe styles. e, Wooden snowshoe. f, Swallowtail style, with geometric designs formed by lacing in toe and heel sections. g, Elbow style, with small area of repaired lacing in heel section. a,b,f,g, Montagnais-Naskapi; c,e, Northern Ojibwa; d, Chipewyan. Length of a, 43 cm, rest same scale.

left, Prov. Arch. of Alta., Edmonton: E. Brown Coll., B3081; right, Natl. Mus. of Canada, Ottawa: 594.

Fig. 9. left, Dogrib and Yellowknife hide lodges at Ft. Resolution. Photograph by Charles W. Mathers, 1895–1901. right, Saulteaux camp at Jack Fish River, Lake Winnipeg area, Man., with birchbark-covered conical and dome shaped lodges. Photograph by T.C. Weston, 1884.

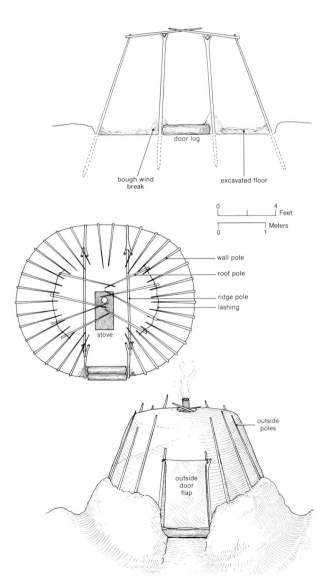

Fig. 10. A variant of the ridgepole lodge used by the Naskapi of Davis Inlet, Lab. The lodge is oval with the 12 by 15 foot floor area slightly excavated and covered with overlapping evergreen boughs. The walls are constructed of both dead and green poles cut in lengths up to 12 feet; about 32 of these are driven into the ground at an angle around the diameter, along with 2 pairs of forked poles to support the ridgepoles. About 8 roof poles are laid across the ridgepoles and their ends firmly lashed to the poles forming the walls. Large pieces of canvas and patched-together deer skins are fitted over the frame with a hole made in the roof for the stove pipe. The covering is held in place by 13 or so poles laid over the outside (additional poles are added in windy weather) and snow is banked up around the bottom. Two logs are laid at the door opening, an inner door flap of canvas is tied to the forked poles, and an outer door flap of skin tied to the outside poles. The construction of a lodge of this kind large enough to house 2 families takes about 5 hours for 2 men and 2 women to complete. After field notes including sketches (Strong 1928, 3:3–6) and photographs (Smithsonian, NAA: Strong 29A–36A) by William Duncan Strong, Feb. 1928.

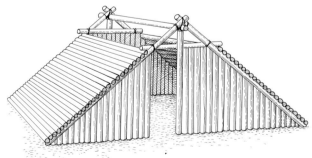

after J.A. Mason 1946:fig. 2.

Fig. 11. Slavey winter house. The ridgepole and its supporting posts each measured about 10 feet, while the long side measured about 20 feet. The large rectangular opening at the top served as a smoke hole. The logs and vertical poles were probably chinked with brush and snow or perhaps mud, earth, or moss (J.A. Mason 1946:20–21). See also "Chilcotin," fig. 3, this vol.

snowshoe—but poor during wet summer weather. Most, if not all, of the Shield Athapaskans had the all-in-one legging with attached moccasin. Moccasin styles varied, but the puckered-toe style may be a late acquisition for some groups, for example, the Northern Ojibwa, Mistassini Cree, and Dogrib. Mittens may also be late. Even at low temperatures, mittens are not essential for protection.

Clothing of hare skins, although undoubtedly an early trait, was not of great importance in much of the eastern Shield Subarctic until after the reduction of caribou and moose within historic times. Originally, hare-skin clothing (figs. 13–14) was worn primarily by the women and children. In the Mackenzie valley, "rabbitskin" robes, coats, vests, and other items of clothing were sometimes worn by men as well, especially by the Hare Indians who derived their name from this use. A netting technique was used in manufacturing items of hare skins that had first been cut into long strips.

Bedding consisted of fabrics made from hare-skin strips or of the furred hides of other animals. Ground sheets consisted of furred bear, moose, and caribou hides.

Technology

Although the equipment possessed by the native peoples of the Shield Subarctic was limited in variety, the people were extremely adaptable to any circumstance that might arise. If a particular tool type was lacking, another could often be substituted.

In dealing with snow and ice, ice chisels, ice scoops, and snow shovels were used. For working wood and bone, there were awls, chisels, wedges, mallets, and perhaps the beaver-tooth knife. The crooked knife with metal blade was a post-European acquisition. For preparing hides, the people employed bone beamers, bone fleshers, and semilunar knives. Two types of stretchers of various sizes were used on which to dry and stretch hides. One, which may have been postcontact, consisted of one or more thin pieces of wood that fitted inside a cased skin. The other was a frame of one or more poles within which the hide was stretched open.

Utensils and containers were prepared from bark, wood, or hide (fig. 15). From birch, spruce, and pine bark were made boxes, dishes, and trays. Birchbark kettles were used for stone-boiling. From wood, primarily that of the white birch, the men made dishes and various styles of ladles and cups. The lower leg skins of caribou were used to prepare the bags typical of the native peoples of the Shield Subarctic, but caribou head skins were also used for this purpose, as was the hide of fetal caribou and moose among Athapaskans. Fish skins and various internal organs of the larger animals were used for containers for liquids such as blood. Coiled spruce-root baskets were made among the Athapaskans of the Mackenzie basin, and occasionally basketry was found in use among a few of the Algonquians of the southern Shield Subarctic. Netted carrying bags of caribou or moose hide thong were made by the Athapaskans.

Population

The Shield Subarctic comprises some 1,500,000 square miles that was exploited aboriginally by a very small population, an estimated 30,000 to 35,000 people (Kroeber 1939:141), giving an overall density of one person for each 50 to 70 square miles. Since population estimates for aboriginal times can be no more than informed guesses the above comments should be taken to mean no more than that the Shield Subarctic supported only a very limited number of individuals.

Social Organization

The development of well-defined territories, whether of bands, smaller groups, or families, was inhibited by the peoples' dependence upon nomadic and migratory big game and by the principle that no one had the right to prohibit others from gaining sustenance from the land. The early literature does not indicate specific hunting or trapping territories. Vague references, assessed in light of the known behavioral characteristics of the game, the techniques of hunting, and the value of sharing held among native peoples of the Shield Subarctic, indicate that regional and local groups occupied and exploited ranges based upon the anticipated movements of big game, the amount of lesser game available in the area, and fisheries resources. Group ranges apparently overlapped somewhat, with indications that neighboring and related groups were on friendly terms and permitted hunting parties to continue their activities undisturbed within their neighbors' accustomed range.

The largest societal group that can be identified in the early European accounts, the "nation," usually consisted of several regional groups, each inhabiting a particular drainage basin or other major cohesive physiographic unit. Collectively such a set of regional groups shared a sense of common identity, language, and culture; exploited contiguous hunting ranges; and was linked by ties of kinship and marriage. Sometimes a single regional group was also referred to by early writers as a "nation." In size, the "nation" ranged from about 50 for the Montagnais "Nation of the Porcupine" to perhaps 4,000 for the Chipewyan. Total populations clearly varied greatly in accordance with the regional situation in aboriginal times, but the varying perceptions of the early European observers as to what constituted the maximal sociopolitical units bring the com-

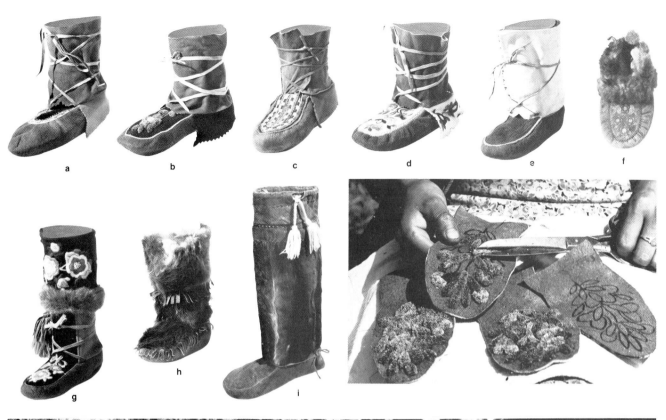

a   b   c   d   e   f

g   h   i

Fig. 12. Moccasin construction and decoration. Footwear is one item of native dress that has been retained and elaborated. bottom, Slavey woman with her sewing equipment, beading a moccasin vamp. Decoration is applied before the moccasin is sewed together. top, Slavey woman trimming dyed moosehair embroidered over a tracing from a paper (before about 1900, birchbark) pattern. Photographs by Richard Harrington, Fort Nelson, B.C., July 1949. a–i, Recent Dogrib moccasins, illustrating the florescence of styles and design. a, Ankle-wrap caribou-hide moccasin with black velveteen vamp bordered with dyed porcupine quillwork band edged with cotton braid, with pinked cuff of red wool. b, Ankle-wrap caribou-hide moccasin with navy-blue vamp and cuff, decorated with dyed moosehair embroidery. c, Ankle-wrap moccasin of moosehide with multi-colored seed bead design on vamp, pinked red wool cuff, caribou-hide ankle wrapping. d, Ankle-wrap caribou-hide moccasin with white wool vamp and cuff with polished cotton floss in satin stitch. e, Ankle-wrap caribou-hide moccasin with black machine-stitched embroidery on vamp, white canvas ankle wrapping and removable sock of white wool edged in black blanket stitch. f, Moosehide moccasin with vamp decoration in cotton thread, floral motifs in chain stitch and edge in herringbone stitch, with pinked red cloth cuff and beaver fur trim. g, Moosehide mukluk with caribou-hide cords, vamp and upper border of blue wool embroidered in multi-colored wool, ankle section faced with red and black wool cloth with beaver fur strip at top; top section has zipper on side (not visible) and tasseled drawstring of braided green and red wool. h, Mukluks with moosehide sole and fringes; vamp and front, back, and top of upper are beaver fur; twisted leather drawstring with tassels (not visible). i, Boots of caribou hide, the leg section tanned with the hair remaining, tasseled drawstring of white wool. Toe to heel length of a 25.5 cm, rest about same scale. a–h collected 1967 by Nancy O. Lurie, i collected 1951 by Helen Elliot.

Fig. 13. Hare-skin blanket construction. Hare skin was cut into continuous strips and twisted into cords such as those hanging from the line in foreground. A selvage cord was attached to a 3-pole frame, which was often propped against a wall (in center of photo). The fur strip was attached to the selvage at upper left of frame and worked in a simple looping technique (detail at right) across the frame from the top to bottom, employing a wooden needle such as that at lower right (length 13.5 cm, collected 1915 at Waswanipi). The finished blanket is furry on both sides, its thickness depending on the width of the hare-skin strips. A blanket for one person (see fig. 14) used about 50 skins. left, Location, photographer, and date not recorded.

parability of the units into question. There is no indication that the "nation" ever assembled, except in the case of the smallest, for communal life or cooperative enterprises.

The regional groups or bands were the largest entities that might, but not invariably, assemble for seasonal hunting and summer fishing, but they were usually dispersed in smaller segments for most of the year, particularly during the winter. The regional band's existence was based in its customary total range, which ordinarily provided all the resources necessary to sustain a population season by season and over generations. Indications are that regional band size generally varied from about 200 to 400 or more. In general, re-

gional bands were not corporate groups but had an amorphous quality based upon constantly shifting allegiances and associations within and between the bands. Thus over a period of years or generations, size and composition were fluid as adaptations were made to changing environmental and social conditions.

As environmental conditions rarely permitted all the members of a regional band to assemble for a long period of time, its members were usually grouped into lesser segments, which may be called hunting groups or local bands. They usually consisted of a few nuclear families related through primary ties of kinship and marriage.

The household unit was usually two or more closely

Fig. 14. Montagnais woman, from Lake St. John, Que., wearing hare-skin robe. Photograph by Frank G. Speck, 1908–1932.

related nuclear families residing together, frequently with aged dependents in a single lodge. The most frequent combinations were those of father and son and their families, brothers and their families, or brothers-in-law and their families. Until the full effects of the later fur trade were felt, reducing resources in some areas and encouraging dispersal for trapping efficiency, the nuclear family rarely operated as an independent residential or economic entity.

The smallest social segment, the extended family lodge or group of lodges, formed the minimal unit of production and consumption. These minimal units were often associated at different times during their life histories with several larger local or regional bands, accounting for the amorphousness of these larger groups.

As a general principle of Shield Subarctic social organization, it appears that the maximum size of the coresidential group was whatever could be supported at those times of the year when the natural resources were concentrated, abundant, and easily procured; the minimum size was that required for efficient exploitation of the resources under the most difficult conditions of scarcity and dispersal of food animals.

The kinship systems were bilateral in type and ego-based, providing a variety of potential consanguineal and affinal relationships for the marital pair on which to base temporary, seasonal, or permanent alliances and for cooperative association, mutual assistance, and hospitality. These features were significant for the survival of small populations, which were susceptible to the skewing of demographic age and sex ratios in the often variable and unpredictable harsh Subarctic environment. The seemingly simple personal bilateral kindred provided the background for a complex system of groupings and patterns of mutual assistance, the flexibility of which has remained evident in the modern context.

Among the early historic Subarctic Algonquians bilateral cross-cousin marriage was preferred and was an effective mechanism for maintaining social linkage between small, isolated, widely dispersed groups (Hallowell 1932, 1937; Strong 1929). Among both Algonquian and Athapaskan peoples, marriages were commonly arranged by the parents. Polygyny, usually but not always sororal, was practiced but generally restricted to leaders and good hunters. The sororate and levirate provided for remarriage of widowed persons under conditions in which the division of labor based on sex was essential. A general pattern of temporary uxorilocal residence after marriage was followed by residence by choice, dependent upon local need but frequently virilocal at least for some years (Helm 1965; Rogers 1963a:55–56).

Leadership was relatively diffuse among the Shield Subarctic peoples and depended upon personal qualities such as male hunting proficiency, generosity, demonstrated wisdom and judgment, and possession of supernatural powers. The dispersed population dictated by the environment and limited technology effectively prevented the development of coercive or complex political institutions. The leader was merely the "first among equals," and important group decisions were based upon consensus. In a climate of egalitarianism, excessive power was feared. Social control was maintained by enculturation, the prevalence of gossip, fear of supernatural sanctions and witchcraft, and the need for cooperative relationships. The value system emphasized generosity, sharing, and hospitality among kinsmen and related groups, of evident value in the context of the uncertainties of life in the Subarctic.

In their subsistence strategies, technology, and social organization, the native people of the Shield Subarctic manifested effective adaptation to severe environmental conditions, an adaptation buttressed and bound together by an ethic of generosity, sharing, and mutual aid.

a, Natl. Mus. of Canada, Ottawa: IV–D–18; b, Lower Ft. Garry Natl. Histl. Park, Selkirk, Man.: HBC 427; Royal Scottish Mus., Edinburgh: c, 848.45; e, 848.19; g, 559.22; d, Smithsonian, Dept. of Anthr.: 395,468; f, Mus. of the Amer. Ind., Heye Foundation, New York: 5/3105.

Fig. 15. Containers. a, Chipewyan woman's meat carrying bag of sinew-sewn strips of caribou leg hide, drawstring at top, collected 1914. b, Bag from skin of 2 swan's feet, lined with black silk, edged with caribou hide decorated with porcupine quillwork, brass and black seed beads, wool tassels; collected 1880s at Ft. Chipewyan. c, Slavey watertight coiled basket for cooking, of spruce roots decorated with brown and red goose quills, collected 1862. d, Chipewyan container of root-stitched birchbark with cloth handle, collected 1931. e, Chipewyan bag made from pelican's pouch, used for quills, moosehair, and other sewing equipment, collected 1862. f, Leather pouch decorated with porcupine quillwork in 2 woven bands and embroidery at top (tribe uncertain, probably 19th century). g, Hare bag of netted babiche, top border of caribou skin with red cotton edging and loops for carrying cord, decorated with red and white goose quills, blue and white beads, and red and yellow wool tassels, the netted area with horizontal bands of red and black pigment, collected 1860. See also "Expressive Aspects of Subarctic Indian Culture," fig. 3, this vol., for beaded bags. Width of g 53.5 cm, rest same scale.

Intercultural Relations and Cultural Change in the Shield and Mackenzie Borderlands

JUNE HELM, EDWARD S. ROGERS, AND JAMES G.E. SMITH

The place of the beaver in Canadian life has been fittingly noted in the coat of arms. We have given to the maple a prominence which was due to the birch. We have not yet realized that the Indian and his culture were fundamental to the growth of Canadian institutions. We are only beginning to realize the central position of the Canadian Shield (Innis 1962:392).

From Labrador to the Rocky Mountains, the essential uniformity of the Subarctic environment overrode the linguistic break between Algonquian and Athapaskan speakers to impel similar adaptations for survival among all the Indian inhabitants. Similarly, the fur trade, the signal feature of Indian-White relations for most of the span of recorded history in the Subarctic Shield and Mackenzie borderlands, evoked a common pattern of native cultural response and change. The climate and physiography of Subarctic Canada precluded the usurpation of land by White agriculturalist-settlers and the retreat or forcible removal of native peoples. As long as fur remained for the European the single great resource of the boreal forest, the Indians freely mobile upon the land served the European purpose. The mutual interest of Indian and European was exchange: furs from the Indian for the products of Western technology.

By 1763, when New France was ceded to Britain, the lure of fur had carried French exploration and trade the length of the southern flank of the Shield and brought Frenchmen in sight of the Canadian Rockies. Over 100 years earlier the English-owned Hudson's Bay Company had established its first post at the "Bottom of the Bay" in an effort to bypass French control of the trade in furs coming out of the Canadian Shield. But in that century span, the company had seen its contacts with tribes in the distant interior from Hudson Bay disrupted by interposed French traders.

The British victory in the imperial contest with France did not eliminate competitors with the Hudson's Bay Company. Entrepreneurial Scottish traders out of Montreal and their French-Canadian worker-allies replaced the earlier French competition and pushed farther west and north. The North West Company, formed by some of these "Montreal peddlers," emerged as the major rival until its coalition with the Hudson's Bay Company in 1821.

From the time of the initial royal charter in 1670, the Hudson's Bay Company had held the legal governance and trading monopoly in a vast domain that had its maximum extent during the second quarter of the nineteenth century, when it embraced all of present-day Canada with the exception of the Great Lakes–Saint Lawrence Basin and the Maritime Provinces. Even when the company's legal monopoly ceased, after purchase of its holdings by the new Dominion of Canada in 1869, the de facto monopoly of the company did not end in many parts of the north. Not until the turn of the twentieth century did "free traders" present a widespread challenge. Whenever intervals of boom fur prices and intense competition receded, Indian-White trading relationships tended to restabilize. The trade itself was the North's greatest resource until its decline during the second quarter of the twentieth century.

Eras of Cultural Impact

The overwhelming import of the fur trade in Indian-White relations divides the contact history of the various Indian peoples into three segments: the period of early, often indirect, exchanges of furs for goods; the period of stabilized and regularized fur-trade activities and relationships between Indians and Whites; and the era when the fur trade shrank to minor importance in the total northern economy and government supervision became the dominating feature in Indian-White relations. Successively, these three periods have been characterized as the early contact era, the contact-traditional era, and the modern era (Helm et al. 1975; Rogers and Trudeau 1969–1972, 3; Helm and Leacock 1971; Helm and Damas 1963 use "contact-traditional" in a more restricted definition).

Early Contact Era, 1500, 1670, 1780–1821

The waterways of the Shield held the key to the penetration of the European and the fur trade into the interior Subarctic. As the European achieved a foothold successively in each of the three great drainages of the Shield, a vast fur land opened to direct trade between

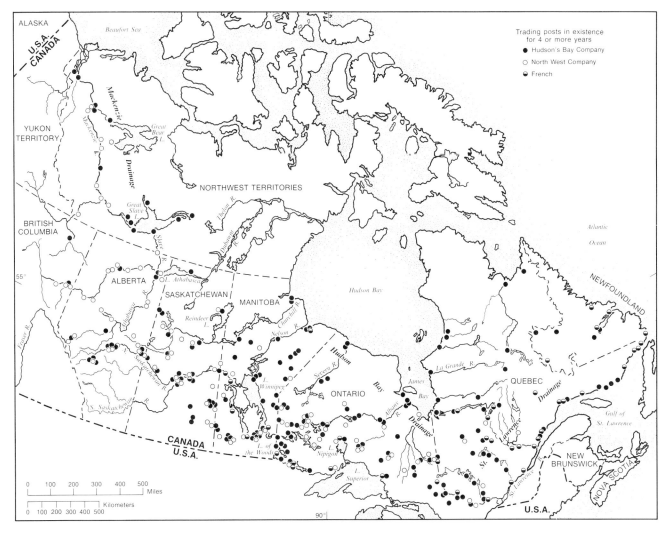

Helm, Rodgers & Smith/Intercultural Relations/SA

Fig. 1. Sectors of early Indian-White contact and fur trading posts (see Canada. Surveys and Mapping Branch 1974).

the European and the Indians within those watersheds. On this basis, the inception of the early contact era for the various native groups divides into three major temporal-spatial sectors: about 1500 in the Saint Lawrence drainage, about 1670 in the Hudson Bay drainage, and about 1780 in the Mackenzie River drainage (see fig. 1).

By the year 1500 Breton fisherman probably had initiated trade with Montagnais along the north shore of the Gulf of Saint Lawrence. Jacques Cartier's voyage in 1535 up the Saint Lawrence as far as the Lachine Rapids pointed the way to the far interior on "that river, large, wide, and broad" (Cartier quoted in Brebner 1955:104). The peoples in this first sector drawn successively into the developing fur trade were the Montagnais groups who occupied the lands draining into the north side of the Saint Lawrence Gulf and River from the Saint-Augustin to the Saint-Maurice River, the Algonquin of the Ottawa Valley, and those Algonquian speakers, probably Ottawa and Ojibwa, who ranged along the northeast-facing shores of Lakes

Huron and Superior. These last came under direct French influence in the mid-seventeenth century. In this period, Northeast tribes (see vol. 15) experienced contact and trade relationships similar to those of Subarctic peoples.

The year of the charter of the Hudson's Bay Company, 1670, serves to mark the inception of the early contact era in the second sector of the Shield. Two years earlier, in fact, Médard Chouart des Groseilliers as an agent of the company had wintered near the site of the present Rupert House at the bottom of James Bay. By 1685 the company had five major forts on Hudson Bay. Each was twice taken by the French between 1685 and 1713, when the entire Bay region was given to the British by the Treaty of Utrecht. However, the first half of the eighteenth century saw the western expansion of French fur trade posts beyond the Saint Lawrence basin as far as the Saskatchewan River section of the Hudson Bay drainage.

The peoples of the Hudson Bay drainage drawn into direct trade relations in this period were, moving clock-

147

wise around Hudson Bay: the Mistassini and other eastern Cree, the Northern Ojibwa, the Lake Winnipeg Saulteaux and the Swampy Cree, the Woods Cree of the Saskatchewan-Churchill river systems, and the Athapaskan-speaking Chipewyan.

In 1778 Peter Pond, proceeding from the Saskatchewan with trade goods, crossed the height of land at Methye Portage (Portage la Loche) to enter the Mackenzie Basin. From Athabasca, where Pond first wintered in 1778–1779, traders in the next few decades ranged north to contact tribes the length of the Mackenzie River and west into the Peace River country. Here, in the third contact sector, are found the rest of Athapaskan-speaking peoples of the Shield and the flanking Mackenzie lowlands: Beaver, Slavey, Dogrib, Hare, Mountain Indians, and eastern Kutchin.

Within all three sectors, and from one to the next, the earliest exchanges of furs for European goods usually preceded direct contact with the European. Middleman tribes, interposed between European points of trade and more distant Indians, passed on "marked-up" trade items. Divisions of Montagnais and Cree were caught up in intermittent conflict with Iroquois and Dakota, respectively, during the seventeenth century, as Indian nations in northeastern North America struggled to make and break Indian-held monopolies. In the Subarctic west of the Bay, the Cree and the eastern Chipewyan enjoyed brief periods of middleman monopoly. Despite traders' efforts to maintain peace among all groups, there were intervals of Cree-Chipewyan and Cree-Beaver conflict, and all three tribes raided Athapaskan neighbors to the north and west.

In the early contact period, European trading stations were often short-lived; therefore, contact with the European trader was for most Indian groups irregular and to some degree unpredictable. Populations at a distance from the waterway-transport routes of the fur trade—the Naskapi within the North Atlantic and Ungava Bay drainages, the eastern Dogrib, and the Mountain Indians, for example—scarcely experienced direct trade contacts until the stabilization of trade throughout the Shield and Mackenzie borderlands after 1821.

Often distant and shifting points of trade, middleman tribes, intertribal hostilities in some areas, and redeployments of populations in response to these conditions are features of the early contact era. So also was the issuance of rum and brandy to Indian trading parties when rival traders vied for furs. Cree and Ojibwa groups notably suffered from the violence and disorder this practice engendered.

One feature of early contact, which was to remain a vicious threat to Indian populations until the modern era, was the introduction of new diseases, both chronic and epidemic—tuberculosis, venereal disease, smallpox, influenza, measles, and scarlet fever. Epidemics often brought starvation as the normally able-bodied

were rendered unable to hunt, fish, and provide the other necessities of life during the course of the disease.

Contact-Traditional Era, 1821–1945

For all sectors of the Shield, the year 1821 serves to mark the beginning of the contact-traditional era, which has been described by Helm and Leacock (1971) as "the stabilized fur and mission stage." In that year began the effective trade monopoly by the new coalition of the Hudson's Bay Company.

The trader had no interest in "civilizing" the Indian in any way that did not promote greater fur production. The impetus to Christianize the native peoples of the Subarctic came from White society far distant from the North. French Catholic missionaries had made contacts in early times with the peoples on the southern edge of the Subarctic in Quebec and along the northern rim of the Great Lakes. The missionary push west and north did not occur until toward the last half of the nineteenth century. Several Protestant denominations became active among the Northern Ojibwa, the Swampy Cree, the Mistassini Cree, and the Naskapi. Anglican missionaries entered the Northwest, but the Roman Catholic Oblate fathers made the greater number of converts in the Shield west of Hudson Bay (see fig. 2). Generally, Indians did not overtly resist proselytization. The aboriginal guardian-spirit complex and shamanistic curing and divination continued to exist throughout the contact-traditional era, if in attenuating form, side by side with Christian church affiliation and practices.

Formal changes in British and Canadian governmental structure and jurisdiction that occurred during the contact-traditional era generally had little immediate effect upon native populations of the Shield region. However, by the end of the era, the Indians of the Prairie Provinces and Ontario had in principle accepted the allotment of Indian reserve lands in partial compensation for land rights relinquished under treaties.

Soon after Confederation, Canada began an active policy of treaty making with Indian populations, for the stated reason of extinguishing aboriginal title to the lands added to the Dominion after 1867. Between 1871 and 1921 the federal government concluded "the numbered treaties," 11 land cession treaties with the Indians of Ontario, Manitoba, Saskatchewan, northeastern British Columbia, and the Northwest Territories ("Chipewyan," fig. 2, this vol.). Most of the "numbered treaties" involve Subarctic Indians entirely or in some part. Various "adhesions" to the treaties were also made. Ojibwa in the area draining into Lake Superior had been included in a pre-Confederation treaty of 1850, the Robinson-Superior Treaty. Several Algonquin, Cree, and southern Montagnais groups of Quebec have been apportioned reserves (Laviolette 1955), but, due to the traditional policy of Quebec, even in the face

Fig. 2. The "Catholic ladder"(detail at left) developed by the Oblate missionary Albert Lacombe among the Blackfoot about 1865–1872, inspired by earlier versions used in the Red River district (Man.) and elsewhere. Many thousands were printed in several editions beginning in 1872; by 1910 these ladders were "in universal use in the [Roman Catholic] missions . . . from Lake Superior to the Pacific" (Morice 1910, 2:290), and they continued through the mid-20th century to be for many Subarctic Indians a highly popular and powerful representation of "salvation history" according to the Roman Catholic faith. Starting with the trinity and creation at the bottom, the ladder summarizes biblical and church history (with each bar representing a century and each circle a year) and ends at the top with alternative routes to heaven, purgatory, and hell (see Hanley 1973). The format—or its early effectiveness—may have been influenced by Indian, especially Plains, pictographic calendar histories. Length 170 cm, width 28 cm; 1872 black and white lithograph.

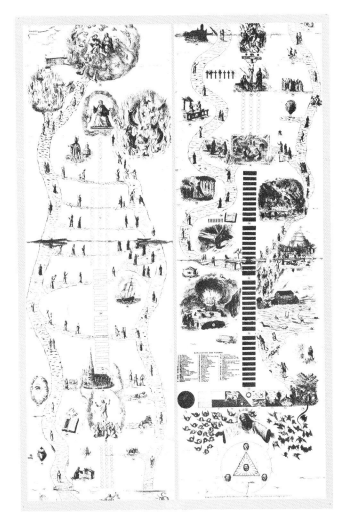

of the contradictory federal policy, the Indians of that province have not signed land cession treaties (see D. Sanders 1974).

Social and technological change throughout the contact-traditional era was generally incremental and untraumatic. Above all else, the stabilized adaptation of the Indian to the fur trade set the tenor of a way of life that endured for more than a century. In the "classic" form of contact-traditional life:

> The only whites in the land are the personnel of the trading post and, in the course of time, the mission. Both are usually at the same site. Indians have no permanent dwellings at the "fort". They live out in the land. Through the decades, a few begin to build cabins at the fort, or at a major fishery or other site occupied for a number of weeks during the year. But they remain seasonally mobile, with ammunition, nets, and a few staples (flour, tea, tobacco) from the trader, often on "credit". They leave the fort before "freezeup" to prepare for winter in the "bush". Hunting, fishing, and snaring is combined with taking of furs during winter. Trading gangs come to the fort at New Year's and debts are paid with furs. With new supplies, they return to "bush" camps or hamlets. In March-April, furs are again traded and supplies obtained. After "breakup" (in June), they come to the fort with furs taken in the "spring hunt". In-

gatherings at the fort are occasions for festivities: feasts, dances, gambling games (Helm et al. 1975:321–322).

In 1970 what living native memory held as the traditional Indian way was not the aboriginal horizon, but the era of the classic fur trade.

Modern Era, 1945–

Beginning in the 1940s, the Canadian government began to assume direct responsibility for native health, education, and welfare needs long neglected. With all other Canadians, Indians received subsidy through the Canadian family allowance and the old-age pension. Physicians and other trained medical personnel were brought into regular contact with the native peoples, resulting in a population take-off. By the end of the 1960s most of the children of primary-school age were in school, and a vigorous federal program in Indian housing ("Dogrib," fig. 2, this vol.) was underway. All these services have tended to induce sedentary town-living.

These changing conditions have coincided with generally declining fur prices, limited subsistence re-

149

Fig. 3. Father Nicolas Laperrière preaching to his Dogrib congregation, Fort Rae, N.W.T. Photographed by Richard Finnie, June 1939.

sources, and greater demand by native persons for the products and services of urban industrial society. The traditional economic base of the Indian societies—subsistence hunting and fishing combined with the taking of furs for the market—has not met the needs of a rapidly growing population with new standards of living. Opportunities for wage work ("Great Whale River, Quebec," fig. 13, this vol.) or other forms of nontraditional employment ("Fort Resolution, Northwest Territories," fig. 11, this vol.) have been at best extremely limited. The modern era has brought heavy dependence upon national welfare and subsidy programs.

During the 1960s, the Indians of the Subarctic Shield joined those of southern Canada in heightened awareness of the threat to treaty rights and aboriginal rights ("Dogrib," fig. 15, this vol.) and to their social and cultural identity in the face of the swamping effect of encroaching Euro-Canadian people and institutions. Proposed government-business ventures in the Shield, such as the James Bay hydroelectric project, the Southern Indian Lake reservoir, and the Mackenzie pipeline, menaced traditional modes of livelihood. In November 1975 the Northern Quebec Inuit Association and the Grand Council of the Cree signed the James Bay and Northern Quebec Agreement with Hydro Quebec, James Bay Energy Corporation, James Bay Development Corporation, and the governments of Canada and Quebec (Quebec (Province) 1976). Five years later, the implementation of the Agreement, essentially a Native land claims settlement, continued to be a source of dissatisfaction and frustration for the native peoples (Anonymous 1980). These and other trends in Subarctic native society within the modern era are discussed more fully in "Modern Subarctic Indians and Métis," this volume.

Whites, Indians, and Métis

Until the modern era, the northern Indians' contact with nonnatives was extremely restricted. Agents of European or Euro-Canadian society were few in kind and number, and face-to-face interaction with them was infrequent. As a result, Indian experience with Western culture and its institutions was channeled selectively and narrowly.

In early times the only Whites in the land were those involved in the fur trade. In the contact-traditional era, the agents of the fur trade were joined by the missionaries. Late in the era, a few law enforcement officers (North West Mounted Police–Royal Canadian Mounted Police) and Indian agents were added, and in some regions "White trappers" during periods of high fur prices.

With the modern era, transient White workers in the extractive industries and in construction began to arrive in certain localities in numbers. However, the major addition to the nonnative population was an increasing number of government employees, most of them in jobs affecting Indian life: game and forest management personnel, welfare workers, health officers, school teachers. The intensity of their instructional and regulatory roles in bringing accommodation and submission of the native people to the Euro-Canadian system far exceeds that of the trader and the missionary of the past.

The centuries of the fur trade brought two main kinds of European ethnics, almost exclusively male, into contact with the Indians—the English and the French. In the lands along the southwest rim of the Shield, the descendants of French-Canadian workers in the fur trade and their Indian wives emerged as a distinctive native ethnic group, the Red River Métis. Roman Catholic, bilingual in French and Cree, Red River Métis moved west and north as workers in the fur trade-and-transport system. In the northern Mackenzie District, Scottish and English recruits to the Hudson's Bay Company posts created by their unions with Athapaskan women the Northern Métis, bilingual in English and an Athapaskan language, Anglican in religion (Slobodin 1966). The Métis have served as cultural intermediaries and interpreters in every sense between the Euro-Canadian and the Indian (see "Modern Subarctic Indians and Métis" and "Fort Resolution, Northwest Territories," this vol.).

Ecological Adaptation

The aboriginal Indian economy of the Shield was based on big-game hunting (moose, caribou), with fishing a secondary or seasonal pursuit. Except for beaver, whose flesh was appreciated and whose skin some groups used for clothing, fur-bearing animals were of little significance in the economy.

left, U.S. Military Academy, The West Point Mus. Coll., N.Y.; Lower Ft. Garry Natl. Histl. Park, Selkirk, Man.: top right, 1318, 1317, 1316, 1314, 1315; bottom right, HBC 59-67.
Fig. 4. left, "Trout Fall Portage, in the Hudsons Bay Country," a depiction based on sketches made in 1821 on the Hayes River, Man.—therefore presumably of West Main Cree—and perhaps also on sketches of Ojibwa in 1821–1826 near present Winnipeg, Man. Trade goods include guns and a copper kettle. Watercolor by Peter Rindisbacher, St. Louis, 1829–1834. right, Common trade items. top right, Covered kettles, ranging from 3 pints to 4 quarts, made from copper sheet, tinned inside. The smaller sizes can be nested inside the larger. Such kettles have been sold by the Hudson's Bay Company from the 18th to the 20th century. Height of 4 quart size (back row left) 19 cm, rest same scale. bottom right, Replica of a tobacco carrot. Prepared by the Imperial Tobacco Company for the Hudson's Bay Company, tobacco was first wrapped in natural-colored cotton and tied at both ends with white string; binder twine was then tightly wound around the entire piece ending in a carrying loop. Weights of up to 15 pounds were prepared in this way. "3 pound net," length 36 cm.

During the first part of early contact times, aboriginal subsistence patterns were largely unaltered. To them were simply added the occasional taking of furs, which were exchanged for a limited variety and quantity of trade goods. Early important trade items (fig. 4) included muskets, knives, axes, files, ice chisels, kettles, and other metal implements, as well as some luxury items.

A major change occurred when the antecedents of the North West Company replaced the French traders operating from Montreal and entered into bitter competition with the Hudson's Bay Company. The competitive period, about 1763 to 1821, brought increased numbers of trading posts, larger numbers of traders, and still larger numbers engaged in the movement of supplies, all largely living from the land. It also brought inexpensive, varied, and abundant trade goods to the Indians of the Saint Lawrence and Hudson Bay drainages and stimulated them to greater exploitation of the fur bearers.

Even before the competitive phase had fully developed, the Crees near the bayside posts of the Hudson's Bay Company had become strongly committed to the fur trade (fig. 6). By the end of this phase, the big-game and fur-bearing animals from the Atlantic to Lake Ath-abasca had been greatly reduced. In some areas moose and woodland caribou were almost exterminated. The briefer and more tenuous penetration of competing traders into the Athapaskan lands north and west of Lake Athabasca forestalled widespread depletions there.

After the amalgamation of the competing companies in 1821, the trade was rationalized by the Hudson's Bay Company and many trading posts were closed. For all but the most marginal peoples, the taking of furbearers had become a regular part of winter activities. In areas that had been depleted of big game, fur trapping* was in uneasy equilibrium with subsistence pursuits and reliance was increasingly placed upon the remaining hare and other small game, fish, and fowl. The trading posts in the eastern and central Shield region were increasingly called upon to provide emergency food rations. In the late nineteenth century the trading posts in some Algonquian areas began to stock food supplies as necessary to the survival of the Indians.

The new subsistence base of these Algonquian groups, in concert with the increased commitment to trapping,

*"Trapping" here refers to the taking of furbearers by whatever means. Actually, in many parts of the Shield the Indian had few commercial metal traps until extensive trading competition was renewed about 1900. Deadfalls were more commonly used.

Fig. 5. Cree beaver trapping and hunting. A diagrammatic sketch done in 1742–1743 by James Isham on the basis of his observations as a Hudson's Bay Company employee at York Factory 1732–1741 and as chief factor since 1741 at Prince of Wales's Fort (Churchill). A small tributary stream (30) runs across the center, bordered by willows (26) and "thick woods" (28), with 2 beaver dams (11). Above it is a cross-section of a beaver lodge (1), with locations of large (3) and small (6) beavers, their exits from the house (4), their food storage area (5), and 4 "vaults" (12) or tunnels into which they escape (8) when disturbed, running about 2 feet underground and 12–14 feet into the banks. An Indian (7) breaks into the house with a chisel attached to a pole, while an escaping beaver is caught in a net (9) set across the stream and removed with a string attached to a stick on the bank. Another Indian (10) sits by a fire watching a net, with a club (29) to kill the beaver caught in the net. Two beavers at left cut down a tree (15) and drag another (13) into the stream, near a row of stakes (14) set to keep the beaver from leaving the stream to enter the river. At upper left (17–23) is a diagram of a beaver showing the internal organs. At center bottom (25) is "a Indian going a hunting," with an Indian "tent" (24) behind him, while in the lower right corner is "a flock of partridges" (27). See Isham 1949:149 for detailed caption by the artist.

emphasized the exploitation of a more limited territory. Under these conditions exploitation was most effectively carried out by very small groups, of two to four nuclear families. Even among the Athapaskans of the Mackenzie drainage, where the traditional food base was unimpaired, effective trapping was best done by these small groups. In parts of the Algonquian area, discrete trapping territories ("Subarctic Algonquian Languages," fig. 7, this vol.) (misnamed in the literature "hunting territories") claimed by small extended family units developed as a means to maintain jurisdiction over the fur resources.

Throughout the Shield, the "trading post band" emerged as an aggregate of groups associated with a specific trading post. Eventually, the government im-

bued these trading post bands with formal membership recorded on "band lists," "chiefs," and a corporate definition pronouncedly at variance with the diffuse, fluid, and pragmatic patterns of traditional leadership and territorial and political organization. After 1900, the constituency of a trading post band could be found variously in tent encampments and in log cabin hamlets oriented to a trading post–mission–village complex. Paradoxically, sedentarization in the form of a "home-base" cabin was encouraged by the introduction of new means of improved mobility and food procurement, such as the dog-team complex (reaching full development in the late nineteenth century), canvas canoes, outboard motors, repeating rifles, and commercial-twine gill nets.

Contact-Traditional Life

Many of the activities and customs that were characteristic of contact-traditional life had their beginnings in early contact times but underwent development, elaboration, or alteration throughout the course of the contact-traditional era. Only a few of the distinctive features of that way of life can be touched on here.

Along with utilitarian objects, certain luxury items entered the Indian material inventory early in the fur trade. From the beginning objects of attire and adornment were attractive goods in the trade. Beads, embroidery silk, and "garterings" were added to aboriginal paint, quill, and hair decorations on clothing and hand and foot wear (fig. 8; "Expressive Aspects of Subarctic Indian Culture," fig. 3, this vol.). Native peoples quickly developed pronounced likes and dislikes for the goods offered, and the trader, anxious to persuade the Indian to procure furs, endeavored to provide the customer with what he wanted. To his superiors in London, the trader James Isham (Davies and Johnson 1965:278–280) wrote in 1739 from York Factory of Indian complaints as to the quality or usefulness of the knives, flints and firesteels (for striking sparks to ignite tinder), gunworms (corkscrewlike devices for cleaning gun barrels), powder, kettles, glove yarn, buttons, rings, blankets, and cloth offered in trade and of their outright rejection of tobacco tongs and "beads large pearl."

Steel needles, awls, knives, and scissors permitted women to make and decorate clothing much more eas-

top left, Amer. Mus. of Nat. Hist., New York: 50.1.7173; top center, Ministère du Tourisme, de la Chasse et de la Pêche, Que.: 58457–53; top right, *Native Press*, Yellowknife, N.W.T.; bottom left and right, Hudson's Bay Company Lib., Winnipeg, Man.

Fig. 6. Beaver skins, their preparation and trade. top center, left to right: Angus Willie Kitchen (child), Mrs. Willie Kitchen, and Widow George Diamond, of the Waswanipi band. Mrs. Kitchen is lashing a beaver skin to its frame, while Mrs. Diamond demonstrates the use of a semilunar scraper. The floor of the house is covered with evergreen boughs, and rolled furs serve as seats. Photographed in Dec. 1952. top left, Montagnais-Naskapi semilunar knife with metal blade and wooden handle. This type of knife is used only for scraping beaver and caribou hides; formerly it may have been made in a single piece cut from a caribou antler. Length of blade about 11.5 cm, collected at Lake St. John by Frank G. Speck, 1913 or before. top right, Trader evaluating a beaver pelt brought in by a Chipewyan or Métis trapper. Photographed at Fort Resolution, N.W.T., 1973. bottom left, Skins, possibly beaver, being pressed at the Hudson's Bay Company Post at Fort Rae, N.W.T., Dogrib territory. Modern presses are turned by a large screw (R. Harrington 1948:29) rather than depressed by a lever. Photographed in 1895. bottom right, Section of a page from a ledger book from York Factory, 1714–1715, giving the value in beaver skins for goods traded: one gun was worth 13 prime pelts, one hatchet worth 1 pelt, 2 mocotaugons worth 1 pelt, etc. The word mocotaugon (from Cree *mo·hkota·kan* 'crooked knife') is an example of the many Cree words used by traders in English (for example, Isham 1949).

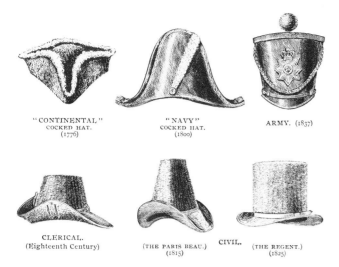

"CONTINENTAL"
COCKED HAT.
(1776)

"NAVY"
COCKED HAT.
(1800)

ARMY. (1837)

CLERICAL.
(Eighteenth Century)

(THE PARIS BEAU.)
(1815)

CIVIL.

(THE REGENT.)
(1825)

after H.T. Martin 1892:125.

Fig. 7. Fur, especially beaver fur, was both an important commodity of exchange and an industrial raw material during the 17th and 18th centuries. Beaver fur was especially important for manufacturing felt for hats, in styles including those shown here (Lawson 1948:34; see chapters on the fur trade, vol. 4). Only toward the mid-19th century did silk begin to replace beaver fur felt as a primary material for such hats.

ily. Woven cloth, first used mainly as blankets and shawls, came more and more to replace dressed hides in making clothing; and European-styled apparel, such as stockings, dresses, trousers, shirts, jackets, and caps, much of it ready-made, eventually became standard contact-traditional garb. European technology provided no effective replacements of hide moccasins and mittens.

The costume of a well-dressed man in the contact-traditional era was an amalgam of Indian, *Canadien* voyageur, and Métis styles tempered by what the trading post had in stock. In 1912, Germain, the chief of the Edge-of-the-Woods Dogribs, wore "a silk handkerchief as a fillet and another around his neck besides a scarlet sash and beaded moccasins, gloves and cartridge bag. Tassels decorated his gun case and dog whip. His leggings were blue stroud [a woolen trade cloth] studded with glass amethysts about as large as silver dollars" (Wheeler 1914:55).

The dog-team complex became a characteristic feature of contact-traditional Indian life. To the hand-drawn toboggan of aboriginal Indian culture, the Europeans and Métis had added a complex of gear and accouterments as well as the dog team itself. The aboriginal Indian dogs were too lightly built to serve as effective draft animals. Traders early adapted dogs for winter transport and developed a stouter breed of animals by importing dogs from England "large and Strong fit to haule the Sledge" (Isbister 1748–1749). For the soft deep snows and narrow trails of the boreal forest the Subarctic dog-team train was composed of a toboggan rather than a runnered sled, with the dogs

in tandem hitch ("Dogrib," fig. 8, this vol.). Besides its moosehide harness, a fully caparisoned team had bells, blankets embroidered and tasseled with wool, and "standing irons" adorned with pompoms (fig. 9). The *Canadien*-Métis driving cry, "Marche!" was incorporated into most Indian languages.

In late contact-traditional times and after, a team was usually composed of four to seven dogs. The support of that many animals required either that large game be taken in quantity for dog food, which in turn required a gun as the only sufficiently effective hunting device, and/or that substantial time and labor be put forth in stockpiling fish in great numbers—possible only with the introduction of the commercial-twine gill net. If fed entirely on fish, a five-dog team, by one rough calculation, consumes in a year about 3,400 pounds of fish by gross weight (Helm and Lurie 1961:63).

Although direct contact was infrequent between the Indian trapper living in the bush and the trader at the fort, their relationship was enduring. The trader kept records of each man's productivity and reliability and determined accordingly the amount of his "credit," issued in the form of ammunition and other supplies for the coming season. Under competitive conditions, the institution of credit was of disadvantage to the trader, as he could not be assured that the trapper would not trade his furs to a rival, instead of repaying his debt. Innis (1962) explains the interlocking complexity of credit, competition, and prices in late contact-traditional times. Purchase of furs with money began only with the period of intense trade competition around the turn of the twentieth century. Before then, no money passed between trader and Indian. The prices of trade goods and of furs of all kinds were reckoned in terms of beaver pelts (Made Beaver, abbreviated MB), the standard unit of value (figs. 6, 10).

From early times, traders had attempted to establish outstanding hunter-leaders as trading chiefs. In an effort to enhance their ability to recruit followers and

Mus. of the Amer. Ind., Heye Foundation, New York: 9/2492.

Fig. 8. Swampy Cree garters, made entirely of trade materials. Black stroud backed with red and black calico, decorated with seed beads and green, blue, and red wool tassels. Seed beads were sold by the strand by the Hudson's Bay Company. Width 10.7 cm, collected at Oxford Lake, Man., about 1919.

top, Hudson's Bay Company Arch., Winnipeg, Man.; bottom, Prov. Arch. of Alta., Edmonton: E. Brown Coll., B 5707.

Fig. 9. Dog transportation. top, "A man and his wife returning with a load of Partridges from their Tent," in the area of Moose Factory on James Bay. The woman, possibly Cree, wears a peaked hood and carries on her back what is probably a cradleboard. The man, possibly a White Hudson's Bay employee, carries a gun, hatchet, and powder horn. The dog in a simple harness pulls a toboggan. Watercolor by William Richards, 1804–1811. bottom, Trader Edward Nagle with cariole dog-sleigh of Western manufacture. Nagle was a principal of the firm Hislop and Nagle that operated a number of trading outlets from Ft. Smith to Ft. McPherson, N.W.T., between about 1895 and 1912 (Usher 1971:159). The photograph was probably taken at Ft. Resolution. The dogs wear blankets decorated with wool embroidery, bells, and wool fringe ("Intercultural Relations and Cultural Change in the Cordillera," fig. 5, this vol.). The "standing irons" above the dog's harness collars appear to be fox tails. Photograph by Charles W. Mathers, 1895–1903.

persuade them to greater fur production, the trading chiefs were accorded uniforms, flags, medals, salutes, and goods for distribution when they came to trade on behalf of their group. The actual authority of such men varied greatly, and the Hudson's Bay Company soon realized it could not require individual trappers to deal through a chief. Still, many trappers saw an advantage in "following" an effective bargainer who "put up feasts" and could be relied on in times of hardship. "Free trader" competition to the Hudson's Bay Company in late contact-traditional times largely eliminated the trading chief.

Hudson's Bay Company Lib., Winnipeg, Man.: 65–66.

Fig. 10. Hudson's Bay Company coins. Brass tokens in one and one-quarter Made Beaver values; others were for one-half and one-eighth. NB was a die-cutter's mistake for MB, usually written joined together; EM stands for East Main, the district for which they were made. These special coins were first issued about 1860–1870, replacing locally stamped bits of metal or wood, counter-stamped coins, and disks of shell or bone, all given in exchange for furs, in Made Beaver denominations, to be used as tokens in purchasing trade goods.

The trading chief was but one of several special roles or occupations created as part of the fur trade. Besides functionaries to serve as organizers or intermediaries between the trader and the Indian trapper, the fur-trade system required provisioning and transport.

As inland posts were established during the early contact era, the trade goods and supplies for the year were brought in and the furs taken out each summer by brigades of birchbark canoes. The crewmen-paddlers were in that era mostly *Canadiens*, along with Iroquois and other Northeastern woodland Indians. Some of the Iroquois eventually merged with the White and Métis populations in the Prairie Provinces.

After consolidation the Hudson's Bay Company replaced canoe with York boats, except in areas where swift waters and numerous portages rendered such boats impracticable, as in the eastern Shield along the Rupert and Nottaway rivers (fig. 12). Adapted from European prototypes, the York boat was a plank craft that on large lakes was fitted with a sail or rowed in the absence of wind (fig. 13). But on the rivers of the fur trade transport system, the York boat had to be "tracked" upstream by the crew hauling on a rope along the shore ("Subarctic Métis," figs. 4–5, this vol.). Crewed by Indians and Métis, a York boat loaded with bales of fur departed from each fort after breakup in the spring. It was joined by other boats of the brigade, fort by fort, on the long journey to the point of transshipment from whence the return trip with the year's supplies for the trading posts would begin.

In the last third of the nineteenth century, paddle-wheel steamboats replaced the York boats on the main

Prov. Arch. of Alta., Edmonton: E. Brown Coll., B-2939.
Fig. 11. Hudson's Bay Company ox train used to transport cargo from one steamboat to another across the 16-mile portage between Ft. Smith and Smith's Landing (later Fitzgerald) on the Slave River, N.W.T. The transfer of cargo might take a week (Stewart 1913:70). Most portaging along the trade routes was accomplished by Métis or native crews without the aid of pack or draft animals. The portage around the rapids in the Slave River was the last impediment to an all-water route of approximately 1,500 miles to the Arctic Ocean, via the Mackenzie River. Photograph by Charles W. Mathers, 1895–1903.

waterways of the western Shield fur-trade routes. Métis usually filled the new, fewer jobs available, both as ordinary crewmen and as pilots, occupations that they continued to follow on the Mackenzie River system after the introduction of diesel power boats and steel barges.

The groups of Crees who attached themselves to the early bayside posts were called "home guards" by the Hudson's Bay Company men. The term also more particularly specified those Indians that came to be employed regularly or seasonally as hunter-provisioners of the forts. In contact-traditional times, the more specialized "home guard" role evolved throughout the central and western Shield into that of the "fort hunter" and his men. The fort hunter, who might be Indian or Métis, was responsible for recruiting and directing a small crew of men to take moose or caribou (or geese at the bayside forts) in quantity for the provisioning of the post personnel. The fort hunter was paid in goods and supplies, much of which he distributed to his men. Fishing crews were also employed in season to stockpile fish for men and dogs. Indian "trippers" carried the mail between various posts.

In the trading establishment itself, a native interpreter-clerk served as the trader's intermediary in dealing with the trading chiefs and individual Indian trappers. The interpreter-clerk was usually a Métis, as few Indians were sufficiently bilingual or attracted to such a sedentary occupation. A similar intermediary status created in late contact-traditional times was the "mountie special" or "special constable," the bilingual Indian or Métis employed as guide, handyman, and interpreter for the RCMP.

The work of the missions was furthered by native catechists and ministers.

With the signing of treaties, the Canadian government required that Indian groups be represented by "chiefs" and subsidiary "headmen" or "councilors." Initially, these men were usually already traditional band leaders or trading chiefs. In areas where the native consensual selection of chiefs and headmen was replaced by a formal elective system, traditional band affiliations and leadership patterns were often cross-cut and distinctions developed between "outside [government] chiefs" and "inside chiefs." The powerlessness of the government chief to influence or alter government policy meant the status per se carried little weight in native society.

Hudson's Bay Company Lib., Winnipeg, Man.
Fig. 12. Némiscau freight canoes in East Main Cree territory, filled with supplies, possibly somewhere along the Rupert River in Que., a major trade route into the interior. Photographed perhaps 1920s–1930s.

HELM, ROGERS, AND SMITH

Fig. 13. York boats, used to transport goods and supplies. right, Under sail on Split Lake, Man., in Cree country; photographed in 1928. left, Dogrib Indians rowing on Great Slave Lake, N.W.T.; photographed by J. Alden Mason, 1913.

Fig. 14. A biweekly plane unloading supplies at Rae Lakes, Dogrib territory. The snowmobile has replaced dog traction in pulling a toboggan loaded with caribou carcasses. Photographed in 1978.

Conclusion

The fur trade brought the Indians of the Subarctic Shield into sustained economic involvement with Western society. This nexus induced accommodations and adjustments in aboriginal patterns of man-to-man and man-to-nature relationships rather than an overthrow of them. Native contact-traditional culture continued to emphasize the ancient skills of bushcraft and the ethic of communal sharing and responsibility. Occupational and leadership roles remained grounded in life lived on the land and sustained by it. The greatest threat to traditional Indian outlook and values has emerged only since World War II, in the form of unparalleled pressures and inducements toward urbanized standards and styles of living.

Territorial Groups Before 1821: Cree and Ojibwa

CHARLES A. BISHOP

In the history of the Subarctic Algonquian-speaking peoples, a critical problem is the identification and placement of territorial groups prior to A.D. 1821.

During the early contact era, the fur trade led to shifts in group boundaries among the Cree and Ojibwa populations in the lands south of Hudson Bay. However, since the evidence is based primarily upon the accounts of a few fur traders and explorers whose concern was primarily with furs, not people, there are often gaps in the data pertaining to specific groups. Sometimes names of groups disappear from the record while new names appear with no explanation. When this occurs it is impossible to determine whether the confusion is due to the name of a group being changed or extended to incorporate several groups, whether a movement of peoples has taken place, or whether a foreign appellation is being used instead of the native term (Bishop 1974).

Except in a few cases, it is not until the nineteenth century that useful dialectal data or specific, recurrent references to a group through time begin to appear in the documents. Furthermore, since the interior region between Lake Superior and Hudson Bay was not permanently occupied by traders until the late eighteenth century, it is impossible to determine the location of inland groups with any degree of certainty before that time, as traders' accounts of groups' locations were generally based on hearsay about lands they had not seen. Often all that can be said is that a named group appears to have shifted its location between two points in time providing that, in fact, it is the same group and not another group or groups called by the same name. An awareness of these major limitations of the historical data justifies caution in making socioterritorial identifications and assessing possible geographical shifts (fig. 1).

Cree, 1640–1670

The earliest accounts of the region west of James Bay and north of Lake Superior compiled by French missionaries and explorers indicate that the inhabitants belonged to the Cree division of Algonquian speakers. In the early literature they were referred to by the term Christinaux or Kilistinon or some variant spelling (see synonymy in "West Main Cree," this vol.; Mooney and Thomas 1907:361–362), which was later abridged to Cree. The Jesuits first mentioned the Kilistinon in 1640, reporting that they "dwell on the rivers of the north sea where Nipissings [an Algonquian-speaking people living near Lake Nipissing] go to trade with them" (JR 18:229). The "north sea" was James Bay.

The *Jesuit Relation* of 1657–1658 listed four "nations" of Kilistinons that Thwaites attempted to locate: "Alimibegouek," or Lake Nipigon Cree; those of "Ataouabouscatouek Bay" probably an early rendering of Attawapiskat, the name later applied to the river flowing into the west side of James Bay and indicating the Cree residing there; "the Kilistinons of the Nipisiriniens," or Nipissings, "because the Nipisirinens discovered their country, whither they resort to trade or barter goods," meaning the Cree between Lake Nipigon and Moose River; and the "Nisibourounik," who resided on the east side of James Bay (JR 44:249). Since the French of the mid-seventeenth century still had no real understanding of the region north of Lake Superior, it is uncertain that these distinctions, derived from Indian informants, reflected actual sociopolitical divisions.

For the seventeenth century, it is not possible to determine the exact geographical demarcation between the Cree groups living nearer Lake Superior and the neighboring non-Cree groups, the Ojibwa and Algonquin proper to the southeast and the Siouan-speaking Assiniboin to the southwest. However, Nicolas Perrot, who was familiar with Indians near the Great Lakes, mentioned (Blair 1911–1912, 1:107–108) that the Kilistinons of the 1660s "often frequent the region along the shores of Lake Superior, and the great rivers, where moose are commonly found."

Bacqueville de la Potherie (1931:265–266), writing of events of the late seventeenth century, stated that in May inland Cree would assemble with other Indian tribesmen in a group of 1,200 to 1,500 persons to construct canoes to travel to the York Factory (Fort Nelson) trading post on Hudson Bay. Other assemblages of over 1,000 Indians of which Cree were a component were met by early explorers at locales west and north

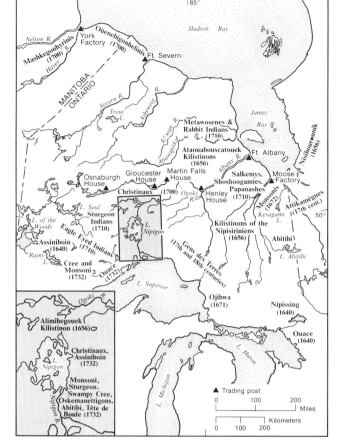

Fig. 1. Approximate locations of Cree and Ojibwa groups before 1821.

of Lake Superior (WHC 11:90–92; Henry 1901:233). Possible regional subdivisions of these Cree are not specified. Furthermore, since by the mid-seventeenth century many inland Cree were involved in warfare with the Dakota and had allied themselves with the Assiniboin, it is impossible to know what proportion of these large gatherings was Assiniboins as against Algonquians. In point of fact, there is no solid evidence either for or against the existence of gatherings of such size in precontact times. In any case, it would seem that these large assemblages were seasonal and temporary.

Although in the mid-twentieth century the Cree of the Hudson Bay Lowlands are often referred to collectively as Swampy Cree (see "West Main Cree" this vol.), the earliest records tend to refer to several specific groups or "nations." Presumably these were socioterritorial units occupying sectors of the major rivers cutting through the Lowlands.

The Jesuits' Indian informants distinguished between the Kilistinons and the Monsonis (Monsounik). An account of 1672 placed the Monsonis on James Bay (JR 56:203), in the southeastern sector of the Lowlands. It has been suggested that they inhabited the Moose River drainage area, which took its name from them (Mooney and Thomas 1907a:932), but Bacqueville de la Potherie

(1931:262–263), who called them People of the Marsh, stated that they were trying to prevent other Indians from trading at York Factory, suggesting that they had shifted farther west by the end of the seventeenth century. However, it is impossible to say whether Bacqueville de la Potherie's Monsonis were the same people as those mentioned 20 years earlier on the Moose River since he only vaguely located them as living inland from Hudson Bay. Nor can anything concrete be said about their numbers, the size of groups, or their dialectal distinctiveness.

There is no strong evidence that the Cree occupied the sea coast until after the Hudson's Bay Company posts were established in the late seventeenth century. At the end of the century Bacqueville de la Potherie (1931:262) did mention the Oüenebigonhelinis or "Sea-Side" Indians living in the area between York Factory and the Severn River in the northern section of the Lowlands. He distinguished them from the Savannahs, "People of the Swamps," a group living inland from York Factory, and the Mashkegonhyrinis, those living near York Factory itself (Bacqueville de la Potherie 1931:258). The term Mashkegonhyrinis and its variants, like Maskegon, became synonyms in later years for Swampy Cree, whose residence near the mouth of the Nelson River seems to have been postcontact.

Groups Trading into Bayside Posts, 1670–1730

Certainly the establishment of trading posts along James Bay and Hudson Bay after 1670 lured Indians to trade from near and far. Although several "nations" are mentioned in the early records, only vague references are made to the regions occupied and usually in terms of the length of time it took them to reach the post. For example, Anthony Beale of Fort Albany in 1707 recorded that a leading Indian named Whatten came "down the River and 16 Canoes along with him" (Beale 1706). Whatten reported that they had been at war and that some French had been killed. From such data, it is only possible to say that these Indians came from somewhere to the south or southwest of the Fort Albany post.

With the construction of several posts on James Bay and Hudson Bay, the fur trade expanded to involve directly all Indian groups between Lake Superior and the coast. The Crees near these posts were designated "home guards" and were particularly important to the traders since it was they who provided the post with geese and other country products. More distant Indians regardless of tribal affiliation (which was specified only occasionally) were called "upland Indians." During the early eighteenth century the bands trading at Fort Albany on James Bay included several unnamed groups plus Salkemys (Kesagami Lake people), Shoshooga-

159

mies, and Papanashes from near Moose River; Metawosenes and Rabbit Indians from the northward; Tibitiby (Lake Abitibi people); Clisteens (Cree from the Shield); the more distant Assiniboin and Eagle Eyed Indians (a division of Assiniboin); and the Sturgeon Indians from west of Lake Nipigon (Beale 1707; Myatt 1716–1719). A few Ottawas also made the journey to the bayside posts (Myatt 1716–1719), and it is possible that such groups included Ojibwa as well as other Algonquians.

Population Shifts, 1720–1770

Since the English posts on the bay were luring many Indians away from the French traders nearer the Great Lakes, the French established a series of forts in the western Great Lakes area during the late seventeenth and early eighteenth centuries. The Iroquois wars of the mid-seventeenth century and the French penetration to the west end of Lake Superior had already produced movements among Indians nearer the Great Lakes. However, the expansion of French traders north and west of Lake Superior during the early eighteenth century marked the beginning of major population shifts westward involving Cree, Ojibwa, and other Algonquians.

Evidence relating to the early 1730s (NYCD 9:1054) indicates a number of groups living northwest of Lake Superior, some of whom appear to have been arrivals from the east. One document estimates the number of "warriors" in each group, referring to the adult males who by this date were involved in open warfare with the Dakota of Minnesota. There were about 100 Cree and Monsoni warriors on Rainy Lake, while along the Nipigon River were 200 Monsoni warriors, 150 Sturgeon warriors, 140 Swampy Cree warriors, and 40 Oskemanettigons (perhaps Ojibwa or Nipissings), along with a few Abitibis and Tête de Boules. On Lake Nipigon itself resided 60 Christinaux and 150 Assiniboin warriors while at the Kaministikwia River were 60 Ouace warriors. If the Monsonis were the descendants of those from the Moose River, a westward movement is indicated. The same interpretation would apply to the Abitibis and Tête de Boules, while the Swampy Cree would appear to have been far to the south of their aboriginal homeland. The Sturgeon Indians (Nameuilini) were probably Cree, although Hodge (1910c) suggests that they were Ojibwa. The Ouace were almost certainly Ojibwa from the north shore of Lake Huron (JR 18:229–233). There is evidence that farther north the Cree of the Shield began shifting westward during the 1720s and 1730s (Barnston 1839).

There is support (Hallowell 1955:114–115; Dunning 1959:3–4; Hickerson 1966:4, 1967a:45) for the argument advanced by Skinner (1912:117) that the Ojibwa began to occupy permanently the central Shield region of the Subarctic during the 1730s, settling in the upper Albany River area west of those Cree in the James Bay Lowlands. According to the Fort Albany trader Joseph Adams in 1733: "the French Cannyda Inds have several of them wintered with the upland Inds. . .about two hundred Miles from this place" (Adams 1733). Prior to this time the "upland Indians" had been either Cree or Assiniboin while the "French Indians" had been Ottawa, Ojibwa, or other Algonquians. This then seems to mark the beginning of Ojibwa expansion into the Subarctic. From the 1720s until the 1770s Crees continued to move westward. In their place came Ojibwas and Algonquins until the 1770s, when their expansion to the north ceased. At that time the Ojibwa had come to occupy the entire Canadian Shield from the mouth of the Ogoki River in the east to Island Lake in the northwest. Some Ojibwa were even on the west side of Lake Winnipeg. Although the exact steps in this expansion are difficult to determine, there can be little doubt that it took place. Reports noting it in progress are made by traders peripheral to the area or at a later time by traders resident in newly occupied zones (Graham 1969:204; Masson 1889–1890, 2:241–242, 346; Barnston 1839).

Conclusion

Although the limited data make ethnographic reconstruction tentative, it is evident that many groups in the central Shield region shifted out of their aboriginal territories within the early contact period. Many of the Cree living north of Lake Superior at the time of contact moved westward during the eighteenth century, while in their place arrived Ojibwas and perhaps other Algonquians. Soon after 1800, the depletion of fur and large game resources resulting from the fur trade competition forced all groups into greater dependence on the trading post, a condition already well advanced among those Crees who had early attached themselves to the bayside forts. In consequence of the territorial shifts, along with a tendency for some groups to coalesce around the trading posts on which they were increasingly forced to rely, new regional identities and affiliations began to take shape. By 1821, when the fur trade stabilized under the monopoly of the Hudson's Bay Company, the major divisions of Cree and Ojibwa of the central Shield region were established in the sections of the lands between Hudson Bay, Lake Superior, and Lake Winnipeg in which they reside in the mid-twentieth century. Their later careers may be followed in the chapters "West Main Cree," "Northern Ojibwa," and "Saulteaux of Lake Winnipeg," in this volume.

Territorial Groups Before 1821: Athapaskans of the Shield and the Mackenzie Drainage

BERYL C. GILLESPIE

The precise locations and groupings of the Athapaskan-speaking Indians of northern Canada in truly aboriginal times will never be known in their entirety. This chapter reviews the documentary evidence that scholars have relied on to infer both aboriginal distributions and possible territorial shifts due to direct and indirect influences and events stemming from the European fur trade (fig. 1). The main concern is with certain early historical references that present problems of interpretation regarding the territorial movements of peoples and the designations of them.

By 1821 most Athapaskans of the Shield and Mackenzie Drainage had been assigned "tribal" names by European traders and their territories designated. In that year the Hudson's Bay Company and North West Company formed a coalition, beginning an era of stable trading relationships throughout this area at permanently located trading posts that were within or near the territories of all major Indian divisions. From the earliest hearsay reports about Athapaskan peoples in the late seventeenth century until 1821 there was a continuous effort on the part of the traders to include more and more of this population in the fur trade. But, except for the Chipewyan whose territorial range was adjacent to Fort Churchill (Prince of Wales' Fort) on Hudson Bay, few other Athapaskans were directly involved in the fur trade until trading posts were established in the interior in the late eighteenth and early nineteenth centuries.

The Athapaskans who exploit the Shield area west of Hudson Bay have been primarily the Chipewyan, including the Yellowknife subgroup. The ranges of the Dogrib and Hare Indians comprise the edge of the Shield and the abutting Mackenzie Valley. Within the rest of the Mackenzie Drainage, except the most western extremities of its tributaries, are the Beaver, Sekani, Kaska, Slavey, Mountain, and Loucheux (eastern Kutchin) peoples. None of these peoples had a "tribal" or "national" unity at the time of European contact. It is likely that, as throughout the historical period, a number of small family-linked groups closely aligned through kin ties, dialect, and shared exploitative zone composed a regional group named after a major resource or topographical feature of their range. All

"tribes" recognized during the historical era are composed of one or more of these regional groups. Since Indians felt no need to label and categorize themselves in any larger sociopolitical units, the names eventually accepted by scholars, and only sometimes by Indians, were names assigned to them by Europeans. The terms eventually settled on by Europeans were usually arbitrary.

The naming of Indian groups by Europeans followed several patterns. Most frequently a general, and often derogatory, term used by a neighboring Indian people that were in direct contact with Europeans provided the first tribal name for people not yet contacted. The Algonquian-speaking Cree trading into Hudson Bay provided the first names for many Athapaskans. The names Chipewyan, Dogrib, Slavey, and perhaps Beaver have their source in Cree designations. The variety of the names applied to one group in different languages was noted by the trader-surveyor of the late eighteenth century, David Thompson (1916:78), in his description of Chipewyan territory: "the country is occupied by a people who call themselves 'Dinnie,' by the Hudson Bay Traders 'Northern Indians' and by their [Cree] southern neighbors 'Cheepawyans'." In addition, information about new groups or areas often resulted in names being applied differently. Although it is not possible to detail all the processes by which names were assigned, juggled, and adopted, some of the confusions surrounding names given Indians by Europeans are treated in order to emphasize the difficulties in the interpretation of early historical documents.

Fur-Trade Influences and Territorial Shifts

In the Mackenzie Valley the advent of the fur trade does not seem to have created major changes in the exploitative ranges of Hare, Loucheux, and Mountain Indians. The present-day Bearlake Indians appear to be an amalgamation mainly of Dogrib and Hare whose ranges overlapped in the Great Bear Lake region, at least by the time of the earliest historical documents. After 1823—the year when the Dogrib took vengeance on the Yellowknife for previous bullying—Dogribs

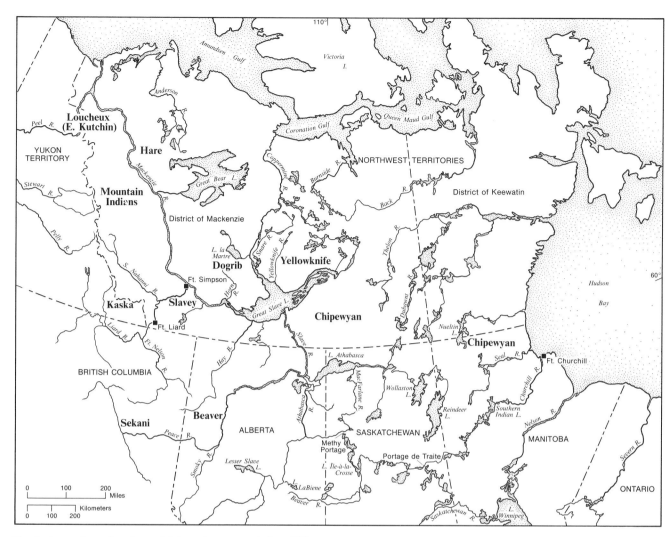

Fig. 1. Approximate locations of Athapaskan groups before 1821.

largely reoccupied areas the Yellowknife had dominated for a limited time. The Yellowknife gradually
retreated from the Yellowknife-Coppermine rivers to
the eastern end of Great Slave Lake. After this realignment between these two peoples there was a peaceful
overlap in the range of the two in the nineteenth century
(Gillespie 1975a:229–232). Some ancestors of the people today known as Slavey possibly were more recent
entrants into the Mackenzie Valley.

The people of the Cassiar region (collectively called
Kaska by twentieth-century scholars) had very little
direct contact with traders until the 1830s. There is little
information in the early records from which to assess
their aboriginal situation. To their south there was contact and intermingling with Sekanis, who had shifted
westward in historic times, but no major realignments
have been recorded between these two populations.
One historical reference mentions a displacement from
the Fort Liard area of a people that may have been a
Kaska group: Keith (1889–1890, 2:68) stated in 1807
that the "*Na ha ne*" left the area because of the intrusion
of a population later classified as Slavey.

The Peace River region has been historically associated with the Beaver Indians; Sekanis, Kaskas, and
Slaveys abutted them to the west, northwest, and north,
respectively. The gradual splitting off of the Sekani
from the Beaver and their western and northern movements in the eighteenth century have been documented
by Jenness (1937:5–16). Historical documents imply
that the Sekani changes in territory were caused by
hostilities with the Cree and Beaver to the east and
Carrier and Shuswap to the south (Jenness 1937:5).

For many Athapaskan peoples of the Shield and the
Mackenzie Drainage no major enduring alterations in
territorial locations with the advent of the fur trade
have been recorded. However, the aboriginal locations
of the Chipewyan, Slavey, and Beaver have been described in the literature as altered in consequence of
the fur trade.

Reconsideration of Historical Interpretations

Scholars have long accepted the idea that the Cree expanded their territory in the eighteenth century, dis-

placing Athapaskan groups, in consequence of their more direct and intensive involvement in the fur trade. This interpretation of the early history of the Subarctic is reflected by Jenness (1932:284) when he states that: "As soon as they [the Cree] obtained firearms from Hudson bay . . . they expanded westward and northward, so that by the middle of the eighteenth century they controlled northern Manitoba and Saskatchewan as far as Churchill river, all northern Alberta, the valley of Slave river, and the southeastern part of Great Slave lake." It seems likely that this thesis of Cree expansion in the Subarctic is an overinterpretation and that the early historical documents now available make this reconstruction incorrect for some regions and doubtful for others. Tracing the sources of this interpretation reveals the ambiguities and limitations inherent in ethnohistorical analysis.

For the Subarctic western interior one of the earliest historical documents (and one of the few available at the beginning of the nineteenth century) was Alexander Mackenzie's account, first published in 1801, of the fur trade and of his journeys to the Arctic Ocean in 1789 and to the Pacific Ocean in 1793. His statements are the basis of almost all later descriptions of territorial shifts due to the advent of the fur trade. Mackenzie (1970:132) describes the extent of Cree territory as including the North Saskatchewan River west into Alberta where it runs north to "the head of the Beaver River to the Elk River [Athabasca River], runs along its banks to its discharge in the Lake of the Hills [Lake Athabasca]; from which it may be carried back East, to the Isle á la Crosse, and so on to Churchill by the Missinipi [Churchill River]." Mackenzie (1970:149) addresses the distribution of Athapaskan peoples and has their southern boundary adjoining that of the Cree along the Churchill River (including Île-à-la-Crosse and Methy Portage) to the Athabasca River and Lake Athabasca, and then "directly West to the Peace River." It is not clear whether these descriptions represent some traditional past extent of lands before fluctuations and specific events occurred (as suggested by other passages in his text) or characterize the territorial ranges at the time of his writing. In any case, Mackenzie does not extend Cree territory as far west or north as later scholars, not claiming that their distribution included the Slave River to the north or northern Alberta to the west. Mackenzie's description of the territorial range of these two language families conforms to their nineteenth-century distributions, and other early documents support his general territorial outlines (Gillespie 1975, 1976).

Mackenzie also mentions on several occasions that the "Knisteneaux" (meaning Cree people in general) were invaders from the east who drove away the natives of the Churchill and North Saskatchewan rivers (Mackenzie 1970:117, 121, 125, 253). These are general comments that are vague as to time of invasion and who the previous inhabitants were. At one point he adds that this westward expansion was still going on up the Saskatchewan, presumably the North Branch (ibid.:117). In one other passage Mackenzie (1970:238) is more specific about changes in territory. This passage has strongly influenced later writers:

> When this country was formerly invaded by the Knisteneaux, they found the Beaver Indians inhabiting the land [the extent of which is not specified] about Portage la Loche [Methy Portage]; and the adjoining tribe were those whom they called slaves. They drove both these tribes before them; when the latter proceeded down the river from the Lake of the Hills [Lake Athabasca], in consequence of which that part of it obtained the name of the Slave River. The former proceeded up the river; and when the Knisteneaux made peace with them, this place [Peace Point] was settled to be the boundary.

It should be noted that this "boundary" concept is European and probably does not reflect an Indian perception of a peace-making event.

Mackenzie's writings were widely read and interpreted by explorers, traders, and scholars. In 1836 Albert Gallatin classified the North American "tribes" and assigned the term "Athapascas" to the Athapaskans of the western Subarctic. Gallatin described the southern boundary of the Athapaskans as from the mouth of the Churchill River to that river's source in the headwaters of the Beaver River near Lesser Slave Lake and westward. He said this was their boundary about "eighty years ago [1750], before encroachments had been made on their territory by the Knistinaux" (Gallatin 1836:17). Gallatin's primary source was Mackenzie but he imposed his own interpretations. However, from Gallatin's article scholars gained the idea that Cree drove Athapaskans, at least the later, historical Beaver and Slavey and perhaps the Chipewyan, from part of their aboriginal territories during the eighteenth century.

Besides the obvious possibility that Mackenzie was sometimes inaccurate, his statements, often ambiguous, demand cautious evaluation. There are several questionable points in the interpretations by Gallatin and later authorities (for example, Morton 1973:12; Jenness 1932:284; Innis 1956:202–203; Curtis 1907–1930, 18:8–10, 57) of Mackenzie's statements. First, Mackenzie's references to a Cree invasion north and west (at an unspecified time in the past) have been interpreted as referring to the Cree war raids of the late eighteenth century. Second, the people driven away by Cree at Portage de Traite and Île-à-la-Crosse on the Churchill River, although not named by Mackenzie, have been identified by scholars as Chipewyan or, more generally, Athapaskans. Third, according to Mackenzie, "Beaver" and "slave" Indians were displaced by Cree (at an unspecified time in the past) from an unspecified extent of country around Methy Portage (Portage la Loche). Scholars have concluded that these two groups were the ancestors of the later Beaver and Slavey Indians and that they were driven away from the Lake Athabasca region and the headwaters of the Churchill River in the second half of the eighteenth century. This last topic is discussed by geographical areas since the terms "Beaver" and "Slave" have been applied to various peoples and sometimes used interchangeably.

Hostilities

In aboriginal times raiding between peoples probably occurred in the Subarctic as elsewhere throughout the world. It seems likely that there was a chronic, sustained enmity between different linguistic-ethnic divisions: between Athapaskans and neighboring Algonquian peoples, and between Athapaskans and Eskimos. This enmity continued between groups of different ethnic and linguistic heritage in historic times. Territorial expansion was not the goal of raiding, nor necessarily was the acquisition of furs or other valuables. Raids by Cree and Chipewyan-Yellowknife, as recorded by several trader-explorers in the late eighteenth century, were usually against peoples at a distance from their customary range and were often referred to as "excursions" rather than invasions (Fidler 1934:498; Mackenzie 1970:233; McDonnell 1889–1890, 1:281; Turnor 1934:365, 399).

A different type of hostility developed as a result of the fur trade when one group had the advantage of direct access to traders.* This form of hostility had an economic base and occurred within as well as between major ethnic and linguistic groupings. Access to traders provided a degree of economic superiority and a probable psychological impact that allowed a group to bully, pirate, and sometimes kill another small group. This type of hostility was often between groups with adjoining ranges of exploitation and apparently in each case lasted for about 60 years or less. Bullying and pirating has been described in the historic literature for Cree groups against various Athapaskans, Chipewyan against their subgroup the Yellowknife and against Dogrib, and Yellowknife against Dogrib (Henry 1901:329; Hearne 1958:115–116; Franklin 1823:246, 287, 289, 291).

In both varieties of hostilities the fear of being attacked sometimes forced people away from an area of easy access or of expected occupation, but this did not mean the aggressor wanted the territory or took it over.

---

*It has been assumed the gun gave great advantage in intertribal warfare. A war raid was characterized by surprise attack, quickly overcoming an unsuspecting encampment, usually at daybreak. The time-consuming process of reloading a muzzle loader and its short range accuracy seem incompatible with this style of "war." Guns may have added terror to some raids because of their noise and foreignness but without providing any technological advantage. In the Chipewyan raid on the Eskimo in 1771 (Hearne 1958:99), the Chipewyan had guns and ammunition but used only spears in their surprise attack.

Chipewyan and Cree

Although Mackenzie (1970:121,125) did not date the Cree "invasion" of the Churchill River and could not identify who the previous inhabitants were, scholars have interpreted his writings to mean that Cree invaded this area after they had firearms and that they drove Athapaskans northward (Curtis 1907–1930, 18:10; Hodge 1907a:276; Jenness 1932:284). All early historical materials associate Cree people with the Churchill River drainage. Chipewyan groups were to the north of the Cree, primarily within the northwest transition section of the boreal forest, extending west and north as far as Great Slave Lake to the Coppermine River. There is almost no information on the area south of Lake Athabasca to the Churchill River from which to ascertain who the aboriginal occupants were, although the Chipewyan have a name for and a story about McFarlane River, which flows into Lake Athabasca (Turnor 1934:429), facts that suggest they were not newcomers to the area. Archeological interpretations conform to the historical evidence that Cree populations prehistorically exploited the Churchill River drainage as well as lands south of the drainage. There is no evidence to support the idea that Cree displaced any Athapaskans from the Churchill River in the eighteenth century.

The gradual and peaceful penetration of Chipewyan groups southward and westward to the Churchill River and the Lake Athabasca region in the last part of the eighteenth century is well documented (see Gillespie 1975:368–385), including a statement to that effect by Mackenzie (1970:125). The Chipewyan expanded into these areas, occupying them along with the Cree, both peoples maintaining their distinct social identities.

"Slave," "Beaver," and the Slavey and Beaver Indians

Crees applied a term translated as "Slave" to several distinct peoples; these included various Athapaskans as well as non-Athapaskan peoples of the Great Plains and Rocky Mountains such as the Blackfoot, Blood, and Peigan (Franklin 1823:108–109; M'Gillivray 1929: lxvii-lxviii; Henry 1897, 2:523). Early historical references to "Slave" Indians can seldom be associated with the Athapaskans later known as the Slavey Indians of the Mackenzie Valley. The Cree term, "Yatchee-thin-yoowuc [and other spellings], which has been translated Slave Indians, but more properly signified Strangers" (Franklin 1823:108), was broadly applied to alien peoples. Mackenzie used the term "Slave" to refer to: a people adjoining the "Beaver" Indians who were once at Methy Portage, the "original inhabitants" of Lesser Slave Lake, and Indians of the western end of Great Slave Lake and of a part of the upper Mackenzie River. It cannot be assumed that these assignments all refer

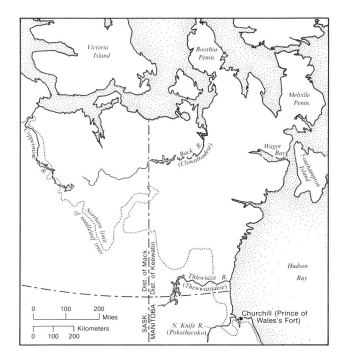

to a single people. Similarly, the very general, descriptive name "Beaver" Indians has been applied to various people over a wide geographical area. Mackenzie used the term to refer to peoples of areas identified above as Methy Portage and Mackenzie Valley as well as to people of the Peace River area. Other authors have considered Lesser Slave Lake as having once been a part of the aboriginal range of the present-day Beaver Indians.

The difficulty of identifying peoples with various areas is further confounded by direct influences of the fur trade. The period of intensive fur-trade competition and expansion, 1790–1821, in the Lesser Slave Lake, Lac la Biche, and Peace River areas brought intrusions of Métis, Assiniboin, Iroquois, and Ojibwa as well as Cree (Thompson 1916:307, 311; A.M. Johnson 1967:196, 216, 242; MacGregor 1966:115–116, 121–122; C. Robertson 1939; Simpson 1938:376–388, 1968:20–21, 30; J.N. Wallace 1929:34, 53; Henry 1897, 2:510). Initially hired into the fur trade or attracted to new sources of furs, these peoples became permanent residents, and

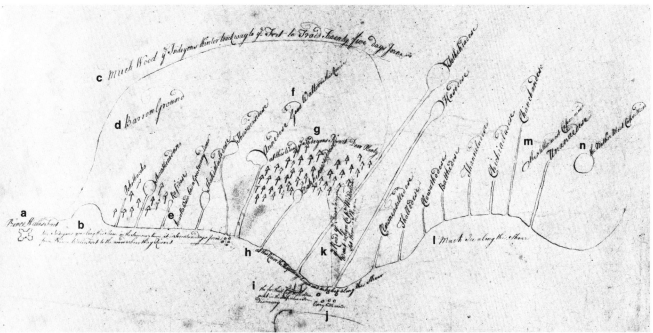

Hudson's Bay Company Arch., Winnipeg, Man.: G. 1/19.

Fig. 2. Manuscript map, about 36 by 44 cm, depicting the rivers flowing into Hudson Bay. The style suggests that the map was drafted by an Indian, the labeling being added by an Englishman; apparently the original pencil has been inked over. Although in 1716 James Knight, the factor at York Factory, received information about 17 rivers from Chipewyan Indians, the map contains as an integral part information on Capt. Christopher Middleton's 1742 sea journey to Wager Inlet that suggests a later date for the whole. The coastline shown horizontally across the map actually runs north-south and then east-west (see key map), between the labeled locations of Churchill and the Coppermine River. The edge of Southampton Island was indicated, but the Melville and Boothia peninsulas and Victoria Island were omitted. The labeling (letters have been added) reads: a, Prince Wales Fort; b, the Indeyons goo along this Shoar in the Summer time it is Seventeen Days Jorne from Prince Wales Fort to the wood whear thay Risort; c, Much Wood the Indeyons Winter track way to the Fort to Traid Twenty five days Jorne; d, Barron Ground; e, hear No Wood bud a Great many Dear; f, Good Watter in this River; g, at this Wood the Indeyons Risort Dear Planty; h, at this River the Usquemays [Eskimos] begen and inhabet along this Shoar; i, the furthist Capt Middleton went in the Ship when aPon Discoverry; j, Very little watter; k, the Road the Two Indeyons went when Capt Middleton Set them a Shoare; l, Much Ice along this Shoar; m, the Sother most Coper mind; n, the Nother Most Coper Mind. The remaining labels are all river names; except for Pokethocoko, which is Cree, the names are Chipewyan as recorded by Knight (transcribed in Warkentin and Ruggles 1970:opp. 86).

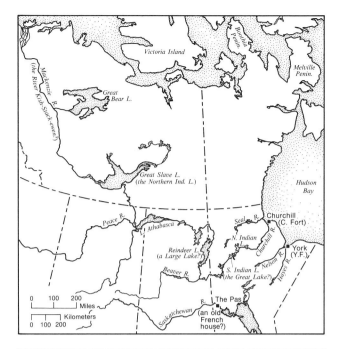

after Hudson's Bay Company Arch., Winnipeg, Man.: G. 2/8.

Fig. 3. A map in pencil on parchment, about 81 by 61 cm, titled "Moses Norton's Dr[aught]t of The Northern Parts of Hudson Bay Laid Down on Ind'n Inform'n & Brot Home by Him. Anno 1760." The map appears to have been drawn by Indians and labeled by Norton during interviews with them at Fort Churchill; Warkentin and Ruggles (1970:88) identify the Indians as Chipewyans, but the extent of the information about the more southerly French trading posts indicates that they must have been Crees. It depicts Indian geographical knowledge of much country at that time unexplored by the Hudson's Bay Company. Redrawn and labels transcribed from photographs and from Warkentin and Ruggles 1970:opp. 88. For the identifications on the key map, see also Ruggles 1971:238–239.

Methy Portage

Gallatin and later scholars have interpreted the extent of land Mackenzie (1970:238) was describing when he mentioned the flight of "slaves" and "Beaver Indians" from Methy Portage to encompass the northern half of the Athabasca region and the headwaters of the Churchill River, including Beaver River, and sometimes Slave River and Lesser Slave Lake. Unfortunately the slight archeological evidence from this area cannot be safely associated with any historical distribution of peoples or used to support or reflect ethnohistorical interpretations of population movements.

In the 1760s two groups of Cree trading into Fort Churchill from the interior were referred to as Athapescow (or some variant spelling) and as Beaver River Indians (Gillespie 1975:373). A 1760 map (fig. 3) drawn by Cree Indians (or from their account by Moses Norton, factor at Fort Churchill) identifiably outlines Lake Athabasca, Slave River, and Great Slave Lake, labeling the first "the Athapeeska Indians Country" and the last "the Northern Indian Lake" (Warkentin and Ruggles 1970:89). The first reports based on travels in the western interior, including Mackenzie's, identified Cree groups with, respectively, the Athabasca River and Lake and the Beaver River (Gillespie 1975:375–380).† Early historical sources do not suggest that Cree groups were recent arrivals to this area, displacing Athapaskans. Mackenzie's (1970:238) statement remains ambiguous.

Mackenzie (1970:149) considered lands north of Lake Athabasca a part of Athapaskan territory and made no mention of Cree invading this area. But his statement

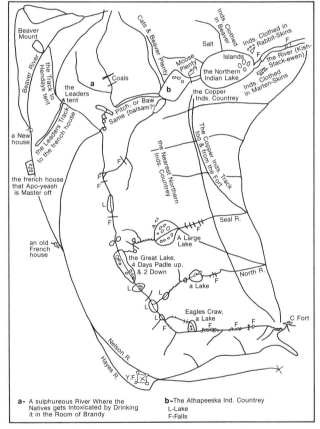

a- A sulphureous River Where the Natives gets Intoxicated by Drinking it in the Room of Brandy

b-The Athapeeska Ind. Country
L-Lake
F-Falls

no doubt some of their descendants are members of groups recorded as Cree by the Canadian government (Canada. Department of Indian Affairs and Northern Development. Indian Affairs Branch 1970:26–27) in these locales in the twentieth century.

---

†In 1772 Hearne identified Great Slave Lake as "Arathapescow Lake," a baffling error that makes interpretations of his map (Warkentin and Ruggles 1970:93) difficult. He places the "Arathapescow Indians" south and west of Great Slave Lake and the "Northern Indians" (Chipewyan) extending east and south of the lake. In the southwest corner of his map he has demarcated the "Tuskey Moginicks or Beaver Indians." He probably learned about these peoples from Indians accompanying him on his journey. Whether Hearne placed these "Beaver Indians" in relationship to Great Slave Lake or Lake Athabasca, in either case most likely they were Athapaskans since they are located outside the range of the Beaver River Cree of the Churchill drainage.

that "slaves" fled from Methy Portage by way of Slave River has led scholars to consider Slave River, as well as Lake Athabasca, a part of the aboriginal territory of the later-designated Slavey Indians and to believe that the region came to be "controlled" by Cree about the middle of the eighteenth century (Jenness 1932:389; Hodge 1907b:439). In 1772, a few years before Mackenzie's travels, Hearne (1958:173–174) and his Chipewyan companions anticipated meeting Cree along the Slave River and observed previous seasons' campsites. Small Cree groups returning from war raids against the Athapaskans were still met by Mackenzie (1970:233) in 1789 and by Fidler (1934:498) in 1791 on the Slave River. How long Cree had traveled in this area and whether they were using it only as a raiding road is not clear; Jenness (1932:424) estimated the Cree had "controlled" the area for 10 to 20 years before Hearne's travels. It does appear that the Cree had been in the area for only a limited time. For instance, they were unfamiliar with the fish inconnu (*Stenodus leucichthys*) (Turnor 1934:416), which is found in the Hay, Slave, and rivers southeast of Great Slave Lake (Fuller 1955:769–770), a fact that shows that this area was not part of the Cree exploitative range. Crees referred to Great Slave Lake and the Slave River with a term translated as 'slave' (Turnor 1934:399–400), which suggests that these were within the traditional lands of an alien group that they considered inferior. By the last two decades of the eighteenth century Slave River had become part of the Chipewyan range. It remains unknown what people exploited this area in the early eighteenth century, but they were most likely Athapaskans with a full boreal forest orientation in their exploitative pattern.

Lesser Slave Lake

In the 1970s the Indian population around Lesser Slave Lake is identified as Cree. Mackenzie (1970:249) reported that the "original inhabitants" of Lesser Slave Lake were called "Slaves" by the Cree. He also mentioned that the Cree were familiar with the area because they "formerly" traveled through it from the banks of the Saskatchewan River on the way to their "war-road" between Lesser Slave Lake and the Peace River. Jenness (1932:382–383) has interpreted this passage of Mackenzie's to mean that before 1760 armed Cree "drove out or destroyed the 'Slave' Indians" and that these "Slaves" were probably a band of Beaver Indians. Goddard (1917:209ff.) retells a Beaver Indian account of a Beaver group that at one time lived at Lesser Slave Lake, but, so the account goes, they died out and after that Crees moved into the area because of the good supply of fish. Goddard recorded many stories from Beaver Indians about Cree war raids on their people. The Cree were a feared enemy, but none of the stories

suggests the Beaver Indians were forced to flee from a part of their aboriginal lands. There are stories in which both peoples were able to kill most or all of an enemy camp. Goddard (1917:216) mentions that in times when game failed, Beavers went to fish lakes that were south and east of Peace River (Lesser Slave Lake included); according to their stories, these lakes were also visited by Crees. This suggests that some of the hostilities between these two peoples occurred when a lack of game and a need for an alternative food resource directed groups of both peoples into the same area.

Slavey Indians of the Mackenzie Valley

Mackenzie (1970:172, 182, 229, 435) makes reference to "Slave" Indians on the western half of Great Slave Lake and along part of the Mackenzie River, locations consistent with the historical range of Slavey Indians. But Mackenzie also refers to "Beaver" Indians in the same area and specifies their lands as the Horn Mountains (ibid.:172, 177, 229, 445). He provides no explanation for a distinction between "Slave" and "Beaver" in this area, adding to the confused application of both terms.‡

Two traders writing in 1807 mention the possibility that the Indians of Fort Liard and Fort Simpson regions (later designated the Slavey) were once Beaver Indians. Both traders relate native accounts that tell about how they were Beaver Indians of Peace River until they were driven north by enemies. Wentzel (1889–1890,1:85) retells the story and identifies the enemy as Cree but Keith (1889–1890, 2:68) does not identify the enemy and describes the account as happening "some ages ago." Both men treat these native accounts with some doubt, especially pointing out the distinctiveness of the Slavey language from that of the Beaver Indians. If this people's separation and move away from the Beaver Indians occurred, it may well have happened before the last half of the eighteenth century when Cree were making their farthest northern and western excursions with firearms in hand.

Beaver Indians of Peace River

An Athapaskan people have been associated with the Peace River region and called Beaver Indians since the earliest historical documents relating to this area. There have been no major difficulties of group designations with the Peace River region, but there has been con-

‡Mackenzie's (1970:facing 67) map confuses his tribal designations further. He places "Beaver Indians" in the Horn Mountains and leaves the Peace River area blank. On his map he does not use "Slave Indians," as he does in his text, for people of the Mackenzie Valley but uses the term "Strong Bow Indians" for those adjacent to the "Beaver Indians" of the Horn Mountains and in an area associated with later-designated Slavey Indians.

fusion between the Athapaskan-speaking Beaver Indians of the Peace River region and the Beaver River Cree. (Peace River is called by the Chipewyan "the Chaw hot-e-na Dessa or Beaver Indian river"—Turnor 1934:401). The Indians of Heart Lake, headwaters of the Beaver River, are misidentified by the Canadian government as Athapaskan Beaver Indians (Canada. Department of Indian Affairs and Northern Development. Indian Affairs Branch 1970:26–27); they are Cree.

Conclusion

The ambiguities of tribal names and unknown effects that the fur trade had in the western interior before any direct contact make it impossible to state with any definiteness whether Athapaskan people were permanently displaced from any areas by the Cree. In the early historic era, except for the expansion of the Chipewyan southward and westward, only minor changes in exploitative range—between Athapaskan and Algonquian speakers as well as among the Athapaskans—have been documented for the peoples within the Shield and the Mackenzie Drainage.

Synonymy§

In this synonymy are discussed the name Athapaskan and its synonyms.

The name Athapaskan (ˌăθəˈbăskən) was introduced in the form Athapascas by Gallatin (1836:16–20) as an "arbitrary denomination" of the linguistically related Indian groups in the interior of northwestern North America beyond the Churchill River. This was an extension of his usage in a manuscript sent to Alexander von Humboldt, in which he had called Sarcee a dialect of Athapescow, his name for Chipewyan (Balbi 1826,1:307). As Gallatin defined it in 1836, Athapascas included all the Athapaskan-speaking Canadian groups, except for the Kutchin and some western groups that were then unknown to ethnologists; later investigators added the rest of the Canadian groups, and those of Alaska, the Pacific Coast, and the Southwest to the family (Powell 1891:51–52; Harrington 1940:508). Gallatin based the name on that of Lake Athabasca, which he took to be also the name of the central part of the country inhabited by the Indians so designated; the choice probably reflects in part reliance on Hearne,

§This synonymy was written by Ives Goddard.

who applied the name Athapuscow to Great Slave Lake and the Indians of the Slave River, although the Athapuscow Indians were clearly Crees. The form Athabascan was used by Latham (1848:161), other spellings being Athabaskan (Latham 1850:302), Athapascan (W.W. Turner 1856:84), and German athapaskisch (Buschmann 1856). The spelling Athapaskan has been in fairly general use among anthropologists since Sapir and Osgood "settled on" it about 1930, in part to give maximum differentiation from Athabasca (Osgood 1975a:13). Athabaskan is preferred by some because it better fits the usual pronunciation (for example, Krauss 1975; cf. Krauss 1973:904).

The name of Lake Athabasca is from Woods Cree aδapaska·w '(where) there are plants one after the other', a reference to the Peace-Athabasca delta region just west of the lake (Harrington 1940:506; Turnor 1934:400; Lacombe 1874:323–324, 705). For variants of the name of the Athabasca subgroup of the Cree, see the synonymy in "Western Woods Cree," this volume.

A number of writers have used names for the Athapaskan family based on words for 'man' or 'person' in various Athapaskan languages that reflect Proto-Athapaskan *dənæ; these include Ingalik and Koyukon dəna, Kutchin diⁿʒi·, and Chipewyan dene. The various renderings of these names have been used for single groups and, most commonly, for various combinations of Subarctic Athapaskans. Examples are Dinnie, 1790s (Thompson 1916:78); Dinneh (Franklin 1824, 1:241); 'Tinnè or 'Dtinnè (Richardson 1852:244); and Tinneh, 1866 (Ross 1872:303; Dall 1877:24); Zagoskin (1956:248, 1967:242–243, 300–301) used ttynaïfsy, a Russianized form of ttynai or ttynaï, which was his rendering of the Koyukon word influenced by an assumed connection with Kenai (see the synonymy in "Tanaina," this vol.). Petitot (1876:xiii) coined the name Dènè-Dindjié for the Northern Athapascans by combining the Chipewyan word and the Kutchin word, and Morice (1890:109, 1893:110–111, 1895:8–10) argued for the adoption of Déné as the name for the whole family: "after the native name of the most central . . . and one of the most populous branches." Since 1960 (MacNeish 1960), Dene has come into use by anthropologists for individual groups and for Athapaskans in general, especially in reference to Canadian Athapaskans; the general and particular uses sometimes appear without distinction in the same source (for example, Christian and Gardner 1977:2, 30, 31, 38). In Canada Indians have expressed a preference for Dene, as in the name adopted by the Dene Nation of the Northwest Territories in the 1970s.

Montagnais-Naskapi

EDWARD S. ROGERS AND ELEANOR LEACOCK

Since the earliest historic period, at least, those Indians designated by Speck (1926:275, 1931) as Montagnais-Naskapi (ˌmôntən'yā nəs'käpē) have inhabited the greater portion of the Labrador Peninsula, the land mass east of Hudson and James bays that is divided politically between the Canadian provinces of Newfoundland and Quebec. Within the overall designation Montagnais-Naskapi, a three-fold division into the Montagnais in the south, the Naskapi in the north, and the East Cree in the west accords roughly with the drainage patterns—the Saint Lawrence River and Gulf, the North Atlantic and Ungava Bay, and James and Hudson bays, respectively (fig. 1)—and dialect divisions ("Subarctic Algonquian Languages," this vol.). The Montagnais-Naskapi speak dialects of the Cree language of the Algonquian family, forming a subgroup of Cree that has been called Eastern Cree, Montagnais-Naskapi, or simply Montagnais (Michelson 1939; Pentland 1978).* The Montagnais-Naskapi who occupy lands within the James Bay drainage have sometimes been designated Cree, as in James Bay Cree, East Main Cree, or Mistassini Cree; in this chapter this subdivision is designated the East Cree.

Much has been written about the Montagnais-Naskapi of the twentieth century, but many gaps remain in knowledge about earlier changes in their way of life. This chapter utilizes data drawn primarily from the East Cree of Lake Mistassini (see Rogers 1963a, 1964, 1972a,

1973) and to a lesser extent from the Montagnais and Naskapi occupying the eastern part of the peninsula and recorded during the first part of the twentieth century. For additional information see "Seventeenth-Century Montagnais Social Relations and Values," "Davis Inlet, Labrador" (for a discussion of a Naskapi group of the mid-twentieth century), and coverage of the "Coasters" of James Bay and their relationship to their immediate inland congeners in "East Main Cree," all in this volume.

Regional Variations

The Montagnais-Naskapi lived in the past by hunting, trapping with deadfall and snare, fishing, a little gathering, and, after the advent of Europeans, by trading furs. Since the Montagnais-Naskapi lived almost entirely on the animal resources of the country, specific features of technology and patterns of seasonal movement were attuned to the distributions, specific combinations, and behavioral characteristics of the fauna in the three major drainage divisions of the peninsula. These divisions roughly correspond to the three subdivisions of the Montagnais-Naskapi—East Cree, Naskapi, and Montagnais.

The principal animal resources depended upon by the seventeenth-century Montagnais of the Saint Lawrence region were fresh eels in September and October; smoked eels, porcupine, and beaver in early winter; moose and some caribou with the coming of the deep snows; and bear, beaver, and fowl in the spring and summer (JR 6:277). Waterfowl were especially important in the swampy lands to the west, bordering on James Bay. The East Cree of the boreal interior exploited big game and, during the summer, the fish of the large lakes. In more northeasterly areas, the Naskapi moved in late summer and early fall out onto the tundra to encounter migrating herds of caribou. These Naskapi commonly used hides for lodge coverings, rather than the birchbark characteristic of other areas.

In addition to variations in subsistence patterns and material culture in the tripartite division into western, northern or northeastern, and southern groupings, there were also some differences in cultural features such as religious and mythological traditions and kin-

---

*The Montagnais-Naskapi words appearing in italics are written in a standardized phonemic orthography using the following symbols: *p, t, č, k; s, š, h; m, n, l; w, y; i, a, u; iˑ, eˑ aˑ, uˑ*. The orthography basically follows the standardized Montagnais orthography of Mailhot and Lescop (1977), with the substitution of the standard technical symbols of the *Handbook*; however, *h* and *l* are written (instead of nothing and *n*, respectively) in forms from dialects having these phonemes, and some consonant clusters are written differently according to dialect. *s* and *š* are distinct phonemes only in some subdialects of East Cree (East Main Cree); elsewhere *s* is a predictable allophone of *š* in consonant clusters. The extensive degree of phonetic variation among the numerous subdialects of Montagnais-Naskapi is obscured by the standardized transcriptions used. The italicized Montagnais-Naskapi words cited in the text are from Mailhot and Lescop (1977: 392–394) and Michelson (1939:81); those in the synonymy are phonemicizations by David H. Pentland of transcriptions in the sources cited. In Pentland's phonemicizations *r* is used for the segment corresponding to modern *l*, and *kʸ* for the segment that becomes modern *č* nonfinally and phonetic [č], [c], or [t] (standardized as *t*) in word-final position.

ship terminology, in dialect (Michelson 1939; "Subarctic Algonquian Languages," this vol.), and in physical traits like blood types (Blumberg et al. 1964). The three subdivisions also reflect differing historical influences. The Montagnais of the Saint Lawrence River visited and traded for cornmeal and tobacco with Iroquois, Algonquin, and Abenaki neighbors. In post-Columbian times, the East Cree became involved with Europeans of English background, by contrast with the Montagnais of the north shore of the Saint Lawrence River who came into contact with the French. The Indians of the northern interior have maintained greater independence from Euro-Canadian influences than other Montagnais-Naskapi groups, although since the beginning of the twentieth century they have attached themselves to Indian groups wintering on the north shore of the Saint Lawrence River or have moved down to the Atlantic coast where the settlers from Europe were British.

Territory and History

No precise boundaries can be drawn at any period between northern, southern, and western groupings, for the pattern of seasonal movements led to frequent interchange of people among neighboring bands. During the short summer, everyone came out of the mosquito-infested woods to gather on the shores of large interior lakes, or at the mouths of rivers that emptied into the Saint Lawrence River or Gulf, Hudson or James bays, or Davis or Hamilton inlets. The summer season was one for festive gatherings and, judging from the assemblages that came together in later times at summer mission stations, also a time for courtship.

When the time came to break up into smaller groups and move back upriver, new alliances would often be formed, altering the composition of the loosely related groupings. Furthermore, the fact that a well-defined height of land crosses the peninsula from west to east, narrowly separating the headwaters of the rivers that run into the Saint Lawrence River from those that flow into other coastal waters, meant that groups that had summered at widely spaced shore locales might meet in the winter near the headwaters of the different rivers they had ascended. Since the late nineteenth century it has been commonplace for people to descend to the coast by a river other than the one they had taken inland and to attach themselves to a group at a summer camp far from their previous one. There is no reason to think that this was not always the case.

With regard to the boundary of the Montagnais-Naskapi as a whole, archeological evidence shows a long history of hunting peoples in the Labrador Peninsula but does not indicate when the ancestors of the present Montagnais-Naskapi arrived. In the west, to draw a

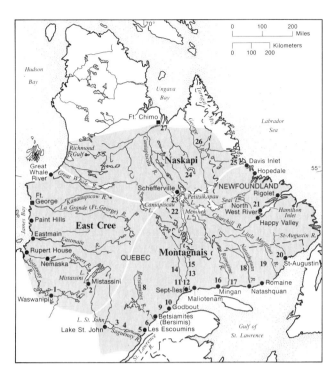

Fig. 1. Territory and approximate locations of bands and subgroups, 1600–1980: 1, Waswanipi; 2, Mistassini; 3, Lake Saint John–Saguenay River; 4, Chicoutimi; 5, Tadoussac; 6, Escoumains; 7, Bersimis; 8, Papinachois; 9, Oumamiouek; 10, Godbout; 11, Ouchestigouek; 12, Sept-Îles; 13, Shelter Bay; 14, Sainte-Marguerite; 15, Moisie; 16, Mingan; 17, Esquimaux; 18, Natashquan; 19, Romaine; 20, Saint-Augustin; 21, North West River; 22, Menihek Lakes; 23, Petitsikapau; 24, Michikamau; 25, Davis Inlet; 26, Barren Ground; 27, Chimo.

boundary for early times between the East Cree and other Cree serves ethnographic convenience but scarcely reflects the reality that obtained. In the Atlantic coastal region to the east, the evidence shows a pattern of shifting boundaries between more land-oriented and more marine-oriented cultures, a pattern that continued into historical times with the southward advance and later retreat of the Eskimo (Fitzhugh 1972:187–197). Territorial demarcations between the hunters of the Labrador Peninsula and the agricultural peoples to the south were also changeable. Agricultural peoples were well established in the upper Saint Lawrence River region at the time of Jacques Cartier. They are presumed to have been Iroquoian speakers, although this is not absolutely certain (see "Saint Lawrence Iroquoians," vol. 15). In any case, they had given way to hunting peoples by the time of Samuel de Champlain, possibly as a result of the fur trade; and in the early seventeenth century the Montagnais were in the habit of crossing the Saint Lawrence to hunt inland from the south shore.

From the earliest times, then, the ebb and flow of changing cultural adaptations was continuous; however, the pace was slow. By contrast, when the first trading vessels from Europe brought wondrously laborsaving iron tools and copper kettles, the fur trade—a new focus for both seasonal and long-term movements—was introduced, and it markedly increased the tempo of change among the peoples of the Labrador Peninsula.

During the sixteenth and seventeenth centuries, the effect of trade brought by the European ships was to draw Montagnais-Naskapi groups toward the Saint Lawrence; later the trade encouraged movement back into the northern and eastern hinterlands. It is as yet unclear how far toward the Strait of Belle Isle the Montagnais-Naskapi journeyed for hunting at the time of the first European incursions. Since the late nineteenth century at least they have lived and hunted in the wooded areas from Hamilton Inlet down the Little Mecatina and Saint-Augustin river drainages but have found little use for the rocky coast at the southeastern tip of the peninsula. Sporadic trading by Europeans with inhabitants of the lower Saint Lawrence had occurred previous to the voyage of Cartier, who wrote of the people he met either at Natashquan or farther west as coming "as freely on board our vessels as if they had been Frenchmen" (Cartier 1924:76). They were not Eskimo, although within a century the Eskimo were apparently moving south, and some were occasionally reported to be at the large summer gatherings that met the trading vessels (Taylor 1974:6–10; Zimmerly 1975:39–40). Cartier's visitors could have been Iroquoian speakers, traveling or living beyond their later range; however, in all likelihood, the Indians Cartier encountered somewhere along the lower Saint Lawrence were Montagnais-Naskapi.

By the 1600s there are many references to Montagnais living east of the Lake Saint John area. In 1640 the Chisedeck (Shelter Bay band) and Bersiamites (Bersimis band) Indians were mentioned as living upriver from "Esquimaux," who occupied country near the Strait of Belle Isle (JR 18:227). Rather than being Eskimo speakers, these people may have been Algonquians (Taylor 1978). In 1694 Louis Jolliet met Montagnais in the vicinity of the Saint-Augustin River, although they may have come from farther west (Delanglez 1944a:179). By 1700, the Montagnais-Naskapi were clearly recorded as familiar with the north shore of the Saint Lawrence as far east as the Strait of Belle Isle, although they may not have ordinarily hunted that far east. However, during the 1700s some Montagnais-Naskapi were definitely living permanently in the southeast corner of the peninsula, as mentioned by Cartwright (1911:159–160, 207–209).

During the eighteenth and nineteenth centuries, White settlements grew along the Saint Lawrence, and some of the settlers turned to trapping. This, plus the establishment of trading posts in the central interior and in the eastern parts of the Labrador Peninsula, encouraged the movement of Native people away from coastal areas. During these centuries, the fur trade grew to a position of central importance in the economy of most Montagnais-Naskapi groups, and what may be called "trading-post bands" emerged as a characteristic form of organization.

By 1800, if not before, the Montagnais-Naskapi clearly occupied most of the Labrador Peninsula south of the forest-tundra ecotone. With regard to their northern boundary, early mentions of Indians inland from Hopedale on the Atlantic coast of Labrador may indicate a northern movement during the 1700s, to search for furs and to investigate the new mission stations (J.B. Holmes 1827:85; Packard 1885; J. Garth Taylor, personal communication 1971). The Davis Inlet and Barren Ground bands have been in the habit of traveling to the coast only in the twentieth century and at first only briefly to trade (Hubbard 1908:158; Strong 1929:278). By mid-century they were spending more and more time on the coast.

On the other side of the Labrador Peninsula, Montagnais-Naskapi were mentioned by the mid-eighteenth century as living quite far north, perhaps as far as Richmond Gulf (Davies and Johnson 1963:xvii). In 1755, several Indians visited Richmond Post (Davies and Johnson 1963:xxiii). However, the interior of the Ungava Peninsula and the Torngat Mountains remained, as they probably always had been, uninhabited by Indians. In fact, as late as the second half of the eighteenth century, the forest-tundra ecotone was probably exploited seasonally, rather than occupied the year round. Erlandson said the North West River Indians seldom went beyond Seal Lake except during the summer for caribou (Davies and Johnson 1963:257).

Fort Chimo was established in Ungava Bay around 1830 and a few Indians were reported to be living in the area (Davies and Johnson 1963:97, 103); however, their occupancy was tenuous. McLean (1932:204, 215, 218), who worked at Fort Chimo from 1837 to 1841, reported that the Indians had left the district for North West River and had to be persuaded to return. The fort was closed from 1853 to 1866 (Low 1897:16L–17L). Even as late as 1892, Indians who had traded into Ungava Bay for some years returned to Great Whale River to make it their permanent post (Batty 1893:213).

The pattern of extensive movement by the Montagnais-Naskapi, both in terms of seasonal cycles and in relation to changing band membership, was a constant concern of missionaries who wished the Indians to "settle down." Early intrepid missionaries traveled from the Saint Lawrence into the interior as guests of the Indians to contact far-flung groups, baptize them, and enjoin them to come regularly to the missions. A few did indeed turn to farming near the mission stations that were set up on the Saint Lawrence, and some joined the colony near the convent and school founded in 1637 at Sillery. However, eventually the missionaries all but gave up their efforts to make farmers of the Indians, at odds as they were not only with the needs of Indian economy but also with the interests of the fur traders. On different grounds, the cosmopolitan attitudes of the Indians were also of concern to the traders, who wished the Indians to become permanently attached to one or another specific post as these became established. Not only did the wide-ranging movements of the Montagnais-Naskapi interfere with efficient fur trapping, the paramount interest of the traders, but also it made difficult the collection of debts incurred when Indians were staked by a trader to winter supplies.

Throughout the nineteenth and into the twentieth century the Indians continued to travel widely in response both to social interests and the needs of the hunt, apparently indifferent to the traders' listings of "their" Indian families. Complaints about Indians having left one or another post, for a season or permanently, keep recurring in the Hudson's Bay Company records. Nonetheless, the trade of furs for metal goods and dried foods was becoming sufficiently important in Montagnais-Naskapi economy for seasonal movements to revolve more consistently around trips to a post. Toward the middle of the nineteenth century, the Hudson's Bay Company had obtained a near monopoly of the fur trade and had established a series of posts strategically located both along the coast and in the interior so as not to compete with one another (table 1). As groups of Indians became more firmly attached to one or another post, a new form of organization emerged: the "composite band" or "trading-post band," along with the so-called family hunting territory, actually a trap-line arrangement.

By comparison with coastal posts, those of the interior were difficult to supply. Moreover, trade in the Labrador Peninsula as a whole sank to minor importance by the second half of the nineteenth century by comparison with parts of western Canada. Therefore, once the Indians become committed to the equipment and staple foods that could be had in return for furs, the interior posts began to be closed in favor of those at the coasts. What had been a series of small trading-post bands began to coalesce into larger groupings that summered together near the coastal posts or mission stations. In 1931, 27 local bands were identified that either were or had been associated with trading posts both on coastal river mouths and on lake shores in the interior (Speck 1931: map 2, 565; Cooper 1928, 1933a; D.S. Davidson 1928b:pl. 1). By 1950 Leacock (1954:19) found that the Petitsikapau, Kaniapiskau, and Michikamau bands of the interior Lake Plateau identified by Speck had merged with the Sainte-Marguerite, Moisie, and Shelter Bay bands around the large post and growing settlement at Sept-Îles, although some of their former separation could still be traced.

By the middle decades of the twentieth century, the trading-post bands were in most cases replaced by relatively large centers of permanent Indian settlement,

Lib. of Congress: Champlain 1613.
Fig. 2. A Montagnais man and woman shown on Champlain's engraved map of New France. The woman holds a decorated canoe paddle; behind her is a container, possibly bark, with loop handle. The man carries a wooden shield, bow (perhaps conventionalized), oversize quiver with arrows, and probably a ball-headed club. Many details are dubious, but the depictions seem ultimately based on 1608–1612 firsthand observations. Engraving by David Pelletier.

notably by Betsiamites on the Saint Lawrence; Mistassini in the interior; Fort George on James Bay; Schefferville near the interior iron mine; Sept-Îles, a railhead on the Saint Lawrence River; and Happy Valley near the Goose Bay air base on Hamilton Inlet. An example of the few remaining "bands" that are still to be found is the Davis Inlet group, north of Hamilton Inlet (see "Davis Inlet, Labrador" this vol.). While most Indians who live in towns work as wage laborers at the enterprises near their homes, work is often seasonal, and some still derive a part of their income from winter trapping.

Population

Since the advent of Europeans, there has been a continuous decrease in Montagnais-Naskapi population that has only reversed itself since about 1945. The Mistassini are an example of these trends (Pothier 1965:129). European diseases, especially smallpox (Heagerty 1928, 1:17–65) and tuberculosis, to which the indigenous inhabitants had little resistance, were a major factor contributing to the decrease. With modern health services, childhood diseases have been brought under control, and the population has been rapidly increasing.

Guns, steel traps, and the encouragement to overhunt and trap caused a reduction in the faunal resources

Table 1. Population Estimates, 1857

Tadoussac	100	"Kibokok"	100
Chicoutimi	100	Great Whale River	250
Lake St. John	250	Little Whale River	250
Île-Jérémie	250	Fort George	200
Godbout	100	Rupert House	250
Sept-Îles	300	Mistassini	200
Mingan	500	"Temiskaming"	75
Musquaro	100	Waswanipi	150
Natashquan	100	"Pike Lake"	80
North West River	100	Nitchequon	80
"Fort Nascopie"	200	Caniapiscau	75
Rigolet	100	Total	3,910

SOURCE: Hind (1863, 2:117), also Speck (1931:597–598), with names modernized; the modern equivalents of names in quotation marks are not known.

of the peninsula, and death by starvation often resulted. However, localized famines had probably always occurred. During the winter of 1645–1646, starvation and reports of cannibalism were recorded (JR 8:29, 31). In 1820 the Indians were starving at Mistassini (Davies and Johnson 1963:15), a recurrent pattern (Lips 1947:454–481). The region to the north of Lake Mistassini had a long history of starvation and for a time the area was abandoned. Not until about 1906 had the furbearers increased and the Indians returned, but starvation followed due to a lack of large game. To compensate for the low game densities, store food was imported, and by the early 1900s some families coming from Lake Saint John took with them as much as one-third of the food they would consume in one winter (Cabot 1922:202).

Alcohol also contributed to the decimation of the population. Its effects began in the early part of the seventeenth century, or perhaps earlier, in the southern portion of the Labrador Peninsula (Bailey 1969:66–74; JR 6:251, 253). In addition destructive forest fires at various times and in various areas ravished the land, destroying resources on which the people depended, and causing depopulation and movement (Hind 1863, 1:203–208; Low 1897:36L–37L; Cabot 1922:191–192, 215).

In the early years of contact, warfare altered population densities and movements to a limited extent. Montagnais-Naskapi were among the Algonquians who urged Champlain to lead a raid to the south against Iroquoian peoples. Later, during the middle of the seventeenth century, the Iroquois retaliated and terrorized the Montagnais-Naskapi in the southwestern part of the peninsula. This may have become possible only after the Montagnais-Naskapi had been reduced in numbers. The Montagnais-Naskapi carried on a desultory warfare with the Eskimo, both in the eastern part of the Gulf of Saint Lawrence and along the east coast of Hudson Bay.

Good population estimates for the Montagnais-Naskapi are virtually impossible to make for the early years of European contact, especially since the exact territorial extent of the Indians at that time is not known. The fact that over 1,000 Indians gathered at trading posts during the seventeenth century before being decimated by smallpox (Leacock 1969:11) suggests that population densities were greater than has been commonly assumed. It may be that the number of Indians exceeded 4,000 in an area of about 300,000 square miles.

There were at least that many Montagnais-Naskapi inhabiting perhaps 400,000 square miles around the middle of the nineteenth century (table 1). However, at the end of the century Low (1897:41L) estimated that there were no more than 3,000 to 3,500 Montagnais-Naskapi. In the intervening half-century, many Indians had died from starvation. At Fort Chimo in 1892, for example, a famine reduced the population from 350 Indians to less than 200 (Low 1897:41L).

Beginning in the second quarter of the twentieth century, the population of Native Americans began to increase rapidly due to medical aid and traded food. In 1967 the number of Montagnais-Naskapi was given at 10,353, but this excluded the North West River and Davis Inlet Indians (Canada. Department of Indian Affairs and Northern Development. Indian Affairs Branch 1967:9–10). In 1977 North West River was estimated at 550 and Davis Inlet at 300 (Lazore and Gardner 1977). Figures for 1971 (table 2) include individuals who did not reside within the Labrador Peninsula. A number of younger Montagnais-Naskapi had gone away to school or for employment. No accurate figures exist, but perhaps as many as 1,000 or more had left.

Table 2. Population, 1971

Waswanipi	650
Natashquan	351
Romaine (Saint-Augustin)	544
Betsiamites	1,631
Escoumains	114
Mistassini	1,511
Great Whale River	326
Fort George	1,309
Paint Hills	557
Rupert House	874
Schefferville	414
Eastmain	268
Sept-Îles (Maliotenam)	1,192
Mingan	253
Nemaska (Némiscau)	135
Pointe-Bleue, Lake St. John	1,568
Davis Inlet	?
North West River	?
Total	11,697 +

SOURCE: Orenstein 1973, 1:105–106.

Traditional Culture

Subsistence

The Montagnais of the Saint Lawrence region, in contrast to other Montagnais-Naskapi, inhabited an environment that offered them a wide variety of food resources, before they were pushed north by European settlement. According to a seventeenth-century account, the Montagnais of the upper Saint Lawrence River ate moose, caribou, bear, beaver, porcupine, fox, hare, marten, woodchuck, "badger" (wolverine?), and squirrel, as well as a variety of fowl: Canada geese, snow geese, brants, ducks, teals, loons, grouse, woodcocks, snipes, and passenger pigeons. Eel were important, and other fish taken were salmon, pike, walleye, sucker, sturgeon, whitefish, catfish, lamprey, and smelt. Seals were hunted, and turtles caught and eaten. Raspberries, blueberries, strawberries, cherries, wild grapes, hazelnuts, and wild apples were gathered, as well as "red martagon" bulbs, a plant with licoricelike roots, and what was probably the Indian potato (*Apios tuberosa*). Maple trees were tapped for their sap (JR 6:271–273).

During September and October, large numbers of eels were caught and dried to be taken into the interior. Chains of stones were laid in the sand at the river edge, to guide eels, when waves lashed the shore, into weirs large enough to hold 500–600. Eels were also attracted to canoes at night with torches and speared with iron-pointed leisters (JR 6:309, 311). Eels, along with porcupine and beaver, were an important source of food until the deep snows of late winter made it possible to track moose and kill them with spears. When the snow was still light, only a very lucky hunter could get close enough to a moose to kill it with a bow and arrow (JR 6:277, 307). Moose meat was smoke-dried by cutting the two sides away from the bones, tramping and pounding the sides to get the juices out, slashing the meat if thick to let the smoke penetrate, and stretching it on poles over a fire. The dried meat was folded up for storage (JR 6:297).

Deadfalls and snares were set for bears in the spring; bears might be found hibernating during the winter (JR 6:307). Hares were either caught in nets or snares or shot with arrows. Porcupines were usually snared, and all manner of small animals were caught and eaten when other food was unavailable. The variety of ingenious devices that continued to be employed in the Labrador Peninsula into the twentieth century has been described by Lips (1936) ("Environment and Culture in the Subarctic Shield and Mackenzie Borderlands," fig. 4, this vol.).

In the winter, beaver were sometimes caught in nets that were set through slits cut in the ice near their houses. Or beaver houses were broken into with hatchets and picks, after escape routes to neighboring streams or ponds had been blocked off by stakes planted close together through holes chopped in the ice. The hunters would sound the ice for hollow places into which the beavers had escaped to breathe and would cut through the ice to spear them (JR 6:299–303). Even with traded iron tools, the method was arduous, and it was not until the breakup of the ice in the spring that beavers were taken in large numbers.

In the lake areas of the western Labrador interior, the Mistassini of the early eighteenth century were said to "live on fish, with which the lakes are well stocked. There are but few beaver among them, but herds of caribou compensate for that" (JR 68:47). By the late nineteenth century, caribou had become scarce in Mistassini territory, but large numbers of fish were taken in the fall and smoked for winter use. All the larger species were eaten, but whitefish and lake trout were considered the most desirable. Of the 28 species of mammals indigenous to the area, more than half were taken for food. Practically every species of bird was regarded as edible, but in general only the larger ones

bottom, after Turner 1894:321; top, Smithsonian, NAA: 80–20260.

Fig. 3. Wooden swimming paddles. bottom, One of a pair collected by Lucien M. Turner in 1882–1884 from the Naskapi of Little Whale River (Petite rivière de la Baleine) in western Que. top, Drawing in pencil and orange and blue crayon by Nok', a 6-year-old Naskapi boy of Davis Inlet, Labr., of "Boys using swimming paddles" (labeled by William Duncan Strong, for whom the drawing was done in 1928). Speck (1937b) reported such paddles among the Montagnais of Lake St. John; here as among the Naskapi (Turner 1894:20) their use was evidently not recreational but rather was required for safety since most men were poor swimmers.

were utilized. Gathering was of minimal importance (Rogers 1963a:32–36).

The Mistassini originally used only the simple bow and arrow (see "Davis Inlet, Labrador," fig. 4, this vol.); probably after contact with Europeans, they adopted the cross-bow for ptarmigan and spruce grouse. Perhaps the chute and pound in which stationary snares were set was used for the capture of caribou as it was among the Naskapi who lived to the northeast. Spears may also have been used for caribou. Moose, which entered the Mistassini area only after 1900, were attracted toward the hunter with a "call."

Nets were set for beaver and otter. Small hunting dogs were trained to locate beavers and hibernating bears (Rogers 1967a:79, 1973:45). To lure geese, black ducks, and American mergansers within range, locally made decoys were sometimes used, the idea derived perhaps from trade contacts with Rupert House. Blinds might be placed on the bows of canoes or on shore when hunting waterfowl.

In the western part of Mistassini territory, sturgeon were taken either in nets or with metal-tipped leisters. Trout were taken on set lines or by jigging. Gill nets for catching fish were made by Mistassini women with net shuttles and traded twine. Among the Davis Inlet Naskapi gill nets used to be made of babiche and were said by the Indians to be old.

Technology

The basic woodworking tool all over the Labrador Peninsula since at least the 1820s has been the crooked knife (fig. 4). Made from a bent and hafted file, and used like a draw knife held in one hand, it was employed for planing snowshoe frames, canoe ribs and planks, wooden shovels, and other wooden items. Ice chisels, used to set fish nets or secure drinking water in winter, were an important early trade item. Although adopting a variety of European tools, the Montagnais-Naskapi long continued to make tools and equipment from bone, antler (especially caribou), bark and wood of the white birch, wood from larch and white spruce, hides, ligaments and organ tissues, and fish skins. Stone, extensively used prehistorically, continued to be used only for netsinkers, pounders, and hones.

Women employed a number of special tools in the preparation of hides: a beamer made from the cannon bone of caribou or moose; a flesher, mounted on a larger wooden weight; and a semilunar knife of caribou antler, in later times of iron, to scrape beaver pelts. Large wooden needles were used to weave hareskin blankets (Rogers 1967a:39–48).

In early times, the Montagnais-Naskapi cooked their meat by either roasting or stone-boiling, but the copper or iron pot rapidly became an ubiquitous item. Eating vessels and utensils were made of birchbark or wood,

with local stylistic variations. Large feast trays were made by joining several pieces of birchbark and securing the ends with strips of wood. Fish spoons, grease ladles, and drinking cups, the last often with incised designs, were made of wood. All these have been replaced by metal dishes and containers. Storage containers were made from the leg skins of caribou, other animal skins, or from birchbark (Turner 1894:300–302; Lips 1947a:31–32; Speck 1930:436–437; Rogers 1967a:34–39). In early times, when the people of the Saint Lawrence River traded moose skins to the Hurons for maize and tobacco, they made a tobacco pouch from the whole skin of a muskrat with a little opening at the head (JR 6:131, 273).

Structures

The most common dwelling in early times in the Labrador Peninsula was the conical lodge that housed 15–20 people, several nuclear families. As Le Jeune described the building of such a lodge, the women went into the forest with axes to cut poles, while the men drew a circle in the snow and cleared it away with snowshoes or wooden shovels to a depth of two to four feet. Some 20 to 30 poles were set in the snow, converging at the top. They were covered with large rolls of birchbark that had been stitched together, with an opening left at the center over an open fire. The snow was cleared back from where the doorway was to be, and a skin to cover the opening was fastened to the two side poles. The ground and snow walls were covered with small branch ends of fir. In 1616, Biard wrote that over the fir floor "are often thrown some mats, or sealskins as soft as velvet; upon this they stretch themselves around the fire with their heads resting upon their baggage. And, what no one would believe, they are very warm in there around that little fire, even in the greatest rigors of the winter" (JR 3:77).

Sometimes elliptical or rectangular lodges were built, with a ridgepole down the center. Le Jeune visited a summer home that was long and narrow, with "three fires in the middle, distant from each other five or six feet" (JR 5:27). This ridgepole lodge (Rogers 1967a:11–13) was probably more commonly employed than the literature indicates ("Environment and Culture in the Subarctic Shield and Mackenzie Borderlands," fig. 10, this vol.). Dome-shaped lodges were also built in western areas, and small dome-shaped structures served as sweat lodges all over the Labrador Peninsula. In the western part of the Peninsula, another shelter type was the moss-covered conical lodge, probably first used in the late nineteenth century. Poles, often split in half, were set side by side to make a large cone-shaped dwelling that was covered with moss and turf to within several feet of the apex. Such lodges were not built during the

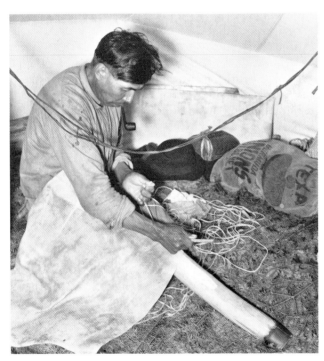

bottom left. Natl. Geographic Soc.. Washington: 115817.

Fig. 4. Montagnais snowshoe construction. top left, Philip Michel, North West River, shaving a snowshoe frame with a crooked knife. top right, Michel bending a frame into shape. bottom left, Man of Lake St. John band slicing moosehide into babiche. His tent floor is covered with balsam fir boughs. bottom right, Marie Mestokosho, Natashquan band, lacing an elbow-style snowshoe with babiche. She is wearing an old-style hat (tuque), made on a manual sewing machine. top left and right, Photographs by Richard Leacock, summer 1951; bottom left, by Harrison Howell Walker, summer 1938; bottom right, by Eleanor Leacock, summer 1950.

winter, when it would have been difficult to secure the moss and turf covering (Rogers 1963b).

Temporary lean-tos were erected by men when stopping overnight on the trail. When Strong (1929) was living with the Davis Inlet Naskapi, a temporary overnight shelter was made by piling up snow and scooping out a hollow big enough for several men to curl up in. Cache racks, consisting of platforms of poles about five feet off the ground or snow, were other structures ("Davis Inlet, Labrador," fig. 3, this vol.). A special rack on which the bones of game animals were placed was an essential feature of all Mistassini hunting camps (fig. 5). Small temporary lodges were also built according to prescribed specifications for holding the important religious event, the shaking-tent rite.

Clothing

In the past, hide, especially that of caribou, was the major material used for clothing. Generally, the hair was removed, the hide dressed and smoked, and the clothing cut and sewed with sinew thread and a bone needle. Le Jeune (JR 4:205, 7:13–15, 25) described the clothing of the Montagnais in the seventeenth century as consisting of leggings, moccasins, and robes with detachable sleeves. The leather leggings extended high up in front where they were fastened to a belt, and they had a loop under the instep at the bottom. The stitched edge of the leggings was cut into a fringe, to which bead or shell ornaments were attached. Robes were usually made of bear or moose hide in the Saint Lawrence area, or from five or six beaver skins. The sleeves, added as the weather demanded, were broad at the top, almost uniting when tied on. Both robes and sleeves were painted with long stripes, giving them a lacy effect (fig. 6). When the weather was warm, the robes were worn casually over an arm, or with leather strings tied across the front. When it was cold, they were pulled tighter and belted, sometimes with a cord or dried intestine. A flap was often looped up over the belt by both sexes, to serve as a capacious pocket in front. Often clothes were casually laid aside in the warmth of the lodge.

Fig. 5. A special rack at an abandoned Mistassini campsite, with caribou antlers decorated with colored ribbons and the skulls of small mammals, so placed to show respect for the game animals and to ensure good luck in future hunting. Photograph by Adrian Tanner, 1969–1970.

To the north, clothing approached the style of the Eskimo, and caribou-hide parkas, with the hair left attached, were common. In this area, hide clothing continued to be worn long after European clothing had come into use in the rest of the peninsula (Turner 1894:281–292). Moccasins, both of caribou and moose hide and of the more water-resistant sealskin, were the item of clothing that continued in use the longest. During the winter, several pairs were worn over one another.

Formerly, hare skins were dried, cut into strips, and made into parkas and blankets ("Environment and Culture in the Subarctic Shield and Mackenzie Borderlands," figs. 13–14, this vol.). Bear skins were used as floor coverings. Infants, diapered with sphagnum moss, were wrapped with soft materials, such as the skin of a caribou embryo, or placed in a decorated moss-filled leather bag. In western areas within historic times mattresses were occasionally made from canvas filled with moose or caribou hair, and small pillows filled with duck feathers were used.

Transportation

Mobility was of vital importance to the Montagnais-Naskapi, and the characteristic means used were, in the summer, the canoe, and in the winter, snowshoes and toboggans. Light and maneuverable birchbark canoes of several styles (fig. 8) (Adney and Chapelle 1964:99–106) were ideal for summer travel through the networks of lakes and ponds connected by rivers and streams, often obstructed by rapids, that cover the Labrador Peninsula. Women usually sat at the stern of the canoes, steering, while the men sat toward the front. Materials for making canoes varied somewhat according to the resources of an area. For example, cedar, used for canoe ribs by the Mistassini, extends only as far north as the southern tip of Lake Mistassini, so bands living to the north either traded for it or used some substitute. Birchbark, the most desirable covering, had to be traded into some northern areas. Eventually canvas replaced birchbark as sheathing for canoes.

Log rafts were sometimes constructed to cross streams or small lakes. The Montagnais early used the French open boats or shallops on the Saint Lawrence. Canoes and shallops were cached in the fall to be recovered in the spring when the ice melted. During the spring, when the snow became waterlogged, the Montagnais-Naskapi used a canoe-sled, consisting of two runners with a raised platform for carrying supplies, or two cross-bars for supporting a canoe (Rogers 1963c:74–76; Mason 1896:572–573). After 1900, to the hand-drawn toboggan the Mistassini as well as the Northern Naskapi added sled-dogs and komatik-type sleds of Eskimo origin (see "Davis Inlet, Labrador," fig. 2, this vol.). However, in Mistassini country both sleds and Eskimo

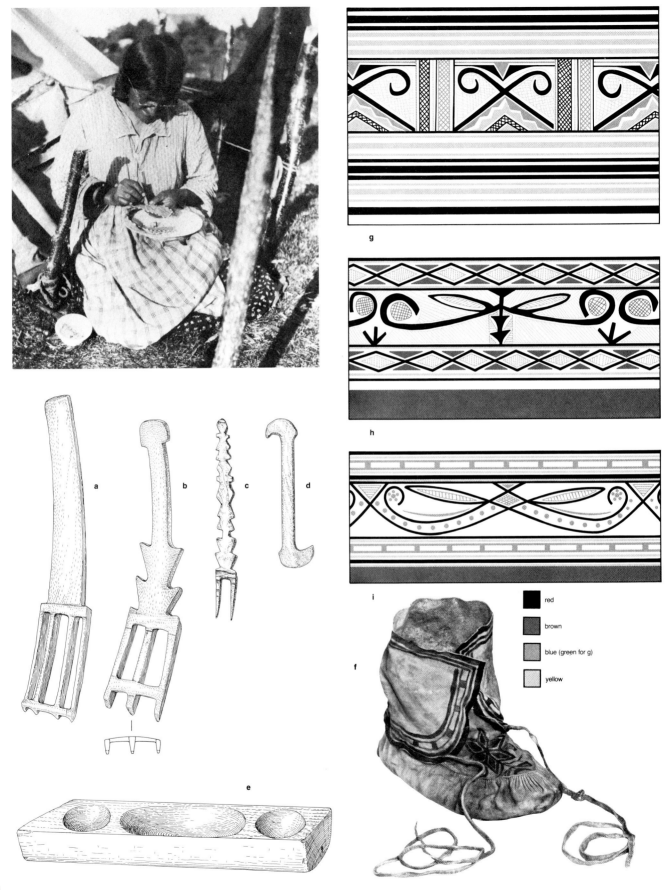

top left, Mus. of the Amer. Ind., Heye Foundation, New York: 12117; Smithsonian, Dept. of Anthr.: a, 90264; b, 89967; c, 90171; d, 90174; e, 89993; h, 74458 (border detail); f, U. of Pa., U. Mus., Philadelphia: 30-3-16; g, Natl. Mus. of Canada, Ottawa: Speyer Coll., III-B-590 (border detail); i, after F.H. Douglas 1939:42.

Fig. 6. Naskapi hide painting. top left, Old Margaret, from the Ungava band, demonstrates painting on smoked hide. Photograph by Frank G. Speck, Sept-Îles, Que., 1924. Men's, women's and children's hide garments with painted decoration were made into the early 1900s when they were replaced by cloth clothing. Women sewed the hide garments and then decorated them with often intricate designs in paint applied freehand with painting tools of bone, a–d, or wood. Parallel lines were achieved with a multiple-pronged tool, a–c, which varied in size and number of tines. Fine single lines were applied with a paint stick, d, rather than the fingers. Paint was derived from red and yellow ocher; indigo (usually in the form of washing blue) and vermillion obtained in trade; and fish roe. Pigments were also combined to produce additional hues. Water, oil or tallow, and fish roe for binder were added to pigments to obtain desired consistency. Single wooden bowls or wooden paint trays with multiple hollows, e, were used to hold the mixed colors. Length of a, 13.7 cm, b–d to same scale, e, 26.8 cm; a–e collected by Lucien M. Turner, Ungava Bay, Que., 1882-1884. f, Moccasins with painting on vamp and ankle wrap. Length 24.7 cm, collected by Frank G. Speck, from the Barren Ground band, 1930. Coats were more frequently and more elaborately painted than other items of clothing. The double-curve motif was common; the variations shown here are all from the lower borders of men's coats. g, Collected about 1740; h, collected 1884; i, collected about 1926. It is unclear whether any elements had symbolic importance, but there was some association of painted coats with luck in hunting (Speck 1914, 1935). Also see "Expressive Aspects of Subarctic Indian Culture," fig. 2, this vol.

dogs were soon replaced by imports from the south, probably from Lake Saint John (Speck 1925a). In the 1970s both were replaced by snowmobiles ("Davis Inlet, Labrador," figs. 5–6, this vol.).

Snowshoes were made in a variety of styles ("Environment and Culture in the Subarctic Shield and Mackenzie Borderlands," fig. 8, this vol.) (Turner 1894:309–311; Rogers 1967a:91–94; Speck 1930:457; Lips 1947a:69–77). For example, among the Mistassini the beavertail snowshoe was used by men when traveling through the bush during the height of winter, when the snow was deepest and most powdery. The swallowtail, another common style, was used by women, and by men when on a trail, or during early winter and spring. The pointed snowshoe was adopted by the western Montagnais-Naskapi sometime after 1900 (Rogers 1967a:93). Other styles were the "bear paw" and "elbow." Wooden snowshoes were also occasionally used, perhaps necessitated on occasion by a lack of hide from which to make babiche for lacing.

Long toboggans, narrow enough to be pulled along forest trails, were dragged by a cord across the chest. They were ideal when everything was covered with deep snow, for their relatively extensive bearing surface prevented them from sinking too deeply into the powdery snow. In early times, children too dragged loaded toboggans, made small enough for them to handle (JR 7:111). The old and the sick were carried along on toboggans as long as it was possible. However, they were sometimes hard to maneuver. Le Jeune described with some dismay a man letting his aged mother roll down a hill too steep for the toboggan she was riding, then fetching her at the bottom. Later he described himself as learning the accepted technique of rolling down steep slopes in the snow, or sliding down icy banks with no discomfort (JR 5:141, 149).

Social Organization

• ECOLOGICAL ADAPTATION AND THE BAND In the early twentieth century, the Montagnais-Naskapi band was characterized as:

a group inhabiting a fairly definite territory with a more or less stable number of families, possessing paternally inherited privileges of hunting within tracts comprised again within the boundaries of the territory, often having an elected chief, speaking with idioms and phonetic forms by which they and outsiders distinguish themselves as composing a unit, often with minor emphasis on this or that social or religious development, often with somewhat distinctive styles of manufacture and art, and finally, travelling together as a horde and coming out to trade at a definite rendezvous on the coast. Intermarriage, in the majority of cases, is also within the families of the band (Speck 1926:277–278).

It was later recognized that this description fits, not the aboriginal Montagnais-Naskapi band, but the population that traded into a particular trading post in historic times. In place of these relatively large collectivities of nuclear-family units, the *Jesuit Relations* suggest that the social organization of the Montagnais of the seventeenth century was based on lodge-groups of three or four families, of some 15 to 20 people, as the basic socioeconomic units. Several such lodge-groups stayed together or near one another through the winter season in groups averaging about 50 people, and two or more of these aggregates, in turn, comprised the named regional groupings of some 150 to 300 people who gathered on their way to the Saint Lawrence shore from the interior (Leacock 1969:9–11). There were no formal chiefs; the principle of elected chiefs was introduced by the Jesuits with indifferent success (Leacock 1958). Effective orators were put forth, presumably by some kind of consensus, to present the Montagnais viewpoint to the French on formal occasions, but these spokesmen had no authority to make decisions.

Since the time of first interchanges with European traders and missionaries, the Montagnais-Naskapi have been altering their sociopolitical organization in accord with new conditions. Through the sixteenth and seventeenth centuries, the fur trade increased in importance and more posts were established, some becoming permanently located. As the Indians became more dependent on the tools, utensils, clothes, and food that they exchanged for pelts, they were faced with the con-

Fig. 7. Women's hairstyle and hats. left, Women wearing traditional hats and hairstyle. The hair is wound on a small rectangular piece of wood (bottom right) with concave ends and then bound with cloth or beads. Hair tied on a form beside each ear in this manner is known as *še·čipitwa·kan*. The hand-sewn cloth hat (tuque), upper right, is made of 6 alternating sections of red and navy blue wool. The seams are covered with red cloth tape, and the lower edge is bound in blue cotton and decorated with seed beads in red, greens, and blue; the inside is lined with undyed fabric. The hat rests atop the head with the upper portion folded over on itself rather than standing up straight. left, photograph by Frank G. Speck, Sept-Îles, Que., 1924. upper right, Height 26.5 cm, collected near North West River, Que., 1891. bottom right not to same scale.

stant choice to remain part of larger groups with more chance to socialize and with greater security in case of poor hunting, accident, or illness; or to spend more time apart in small groups and trap for furs. Individuals and groups made different decisions at different times, but over the years there was an increasing tendency for the lodge-groups to fragment into smaller units for more efficient trapping and to stay at some distance from one another within specific areas that have been called "hunting territories."

During the first part of the twentieth century, a variety of economic arrangements existed among the Indians of the Labrador Peninsula. Some small cooperative bands were still to be found, much like the old winter clusters of lodge-groups. Such were the Davis Inlet people with whom Strong (1929) wintered in 1928, who spent most of their time fishing and hunting but who went after valuable fox furs when they could. More common were the trading-post "bands," with sets of the constituent families living together during the winter in small hamlets or hunting groups, something like the old lodge-groups, and dividing their time between hunting and trapping. Trappers laid short lines, usually of no more then several dozen traps.

In time, more stabilized "bands" or communities began to replace the above arrangements, as individual family heads became part-time wage workers and part-time hunters and trappers and as some became virtually full-time professional trappers. The trappers left their families at the trading post or coastal settlement during the winter season and tended full time to their permanent lines of several hundred traps, usually along with a male kinsman or in-law (Leacock 1954). All these arrangements were flexible and graded into each other, shifting in accord with the availability of wage work or the price of furs on the world market.

• THE TRADING-POST BAND: THE MISTASSINI EXAMPLE The Mistassini were first mentioned by that name in early seventeenth-century accounts. Between about 1650 and 1800, Europeans occasionally traveled through Mistassini country, and the Mistassini visited trading posts at Lake Saint John or James Bay. However, Mistassini culture was not greatly altered until after 1800, when the fur trade reached its height. In the early 1800s, traders were still attempting to engage the Mistassini and other East Cree more actively in trapping, but by the end of the century, they had become heavily dependent upon the capture of fur-bearing animals for a

bottom, Natl. Mus. of Canada, Ottawa: 54533.

Fig. 8. Canoe construction. top, Joe Rich or Shushebish, a Naskapi chief from Davis Inlet, Labr., building the frame of a modern canoe that will be covered with canvas and sealed with several coats of paint. Photograph by Fred Bruemmer, July 1968. bottom, Canvas-covered crooked canoe being constructed among the Natashquan band. The Montagnais crooked canoe was particularly well adapted to rivers with rapids (Adney and Chapelle 1964:106; Taylor 1980). Photograph by F.W. Waugh, 1921–1922.

living. Following 1925, increasing land pressure and the depletion of game, prospecting, mining, and the building of roads all brought new and often disruptive influences to the Mistassini; and changes have been steadily increasing in tempo (Martijn and Rogers 1969:69–139; Pothier 1965; Feit 1973a; Chance 1967).

During the nineteenth century, trading-post bands were rather small, numbering no more than 250 individuals, frequently fewer. However, with the closing of several trading posts in the interior, and a slowly increasing population after about 1945, the remaining bands increased in size and their membership became more stable. The introduction of dog traction around 1900 no doubt facilitated the increase in size, since longer distances could be covered more easily than before.

Although trading-post bands were amorphous units, their members were linked together by affinal and con-sanguineal bonds. Yet little formal political, religious or economic cooperation took place. The lands of al. the hunting groups comprising a trading-post band formed an unbroken block of territory, the outer limits of which delimited the band boundary; however, these territorial limits were elastic. A family on the border might join a neighboring trading-post band while remaining on their ancestral grounds, thereby decreasing the extent of their former band's territory. This was possible since no band was an isolated unit but rather the member families were linked with neighboring bands through kinship ties and common cultural traditions. There is no evidence that the bands ever acted as political units to arbitrate disputes regarding their boundaries or those of their component hunting groups; instead the hunting groups that were involved apparently arranged a settlement among themselves (Rogers 1963a:24–27, 1969:32–35).

Never has the band been a landowning unit. Nor, before 1850 (and perhaps earlier, Morantz 1978), did "family hunting territories" as constituted around 1900 exist; instead all resources were "free goods" (Leacock 1954; R. Knight 1965). However, hunting groups commonly utilized particular districts or "hunting areas," and as furbearers, especially beaver, became important trade items, regularized access to such areas took on new significance. With the emergence of a full-fledged trapping economy, usufructuary rights to trap in specific territories became established (D.S. Davidson 1928c:42–59; Speck 1923) and along with them the distinction between resources used for group needs and those that were sold or traded to Europeans. The former remained available to anyone, while the latter became the property of the hunting group or individual on whose territory they occurred. Trespass with the intent of securing furs or other products for trade was resented and threatened with punishment through shamanistic performances (Rogers 1963a:71–73, 82–86).

Each trapping territory involved several lakes and rivers that formed a unified physiographic region. It was encircled by a boundary known only within a limit of several miles. Territory sizes varied widely: in 1953–1954 the largest trapping territory among the Mistassini band was 2,000 square miles; the smallest, 300 square miles. The average area for each trapper was about 260 square miles. This was a considerable reduction in the size of territory previously exploited by an individual trapper, which in 1828–1829 is estimated to have been about 1,000 square miles (Rogers 1963a:69–70).

The hunting groups that made up the trading-post band were the fundamental sociopolitical units in Mistassini society. Composed of from three to five nuclear families, each hunting group was the maximal unit of exploitation and generally the largest religious congregation for nine months of the year, traveling and working together from the middle of August until late May or early June exploiting its "family hunting territory." Only in summer at the trading-post settlement did the hunting groups dissolve as functional units.

In late August the hunting groups left the summer camp, and until mid-September the time was spent in moving to their trapping territories, transporting as much essential winter supplies and equipment as they could afford. On arrival at their territories, the men hunted big game and fished, and the women dried the flesh for later use. Starting about the middle of October, several weeks were spent in erecting a winter camp. November and December were devoted to intensive trapping of furbearers, using the traps that had been cached in the previous year in different locations within the territory. Around New Year's, a feast was held. Following this event, the group might dismantle its camp and move to another section of its territory to hunt big game and, when time allowed, furbearers. Additional movements to new areas might continue until the middle of April, at which time the group returned to the vicinity of the fall camp where the canoes had been left. Here the major activities were hunting ducks and loons and trapping muskrats and otter. In gratitude for having survived the winter, a thanksgiving feast would be held. About the middle of May, the group repaired its canoes and motors and made any equipment that was needed for the return trip to the summer settlement. Once the ice had broken up, the group started back to the trading post, and by the first of June, most groups had usually reassembled there (Kerr 1950:135–155; Rogers and Rogers 1959; Rogers 1963a:45–53).

From late August until early June, members of a hunting group cooperated in the quest for food and furs and in the distribution of items essential for survival. Generally, two or more men operated as a team when hunting moose, bear, or caribou. Frequently for companionship, two men set traps together, or several women went together to collect boughs or berries. All members of the group participated in occasional games and feasts (Rogers 1963a:54). Early in a child's life, a concept of generosity was instilled, since the ideal person was one who gave both his time and food to other members of the group or to anyone in dire need, especially a friend. The successful hunter gave to member families moose and caribou meat and hides, lake trout, and on occasion, beaver, hare, grouse, and waterfowl. Food was also distributed at feasts. Furs, on the other hand, were infrequently shared (Rogers 1963a:59–61).

The winter camps of the hunting groups were separated from one another by distances of 10–50 miles. Hunting groups varied in size from 10 to 20 individuals. Some groups were larger; rarely were they smaller. As a rule, each nuclear family occupied its own lodge; however, occasionally they all inhabited a communal dwelling (fig. 9). The core of the group consisted of the leader

and his family, and the same families usually were together year after year. Nevertheless, changes in group affiliation could occur quite easily (Rogers 1963a:54–58).

Because of the informality of leadership, relations among the men were usually amicable. Leaders were most often men 40 years or older with the greatest religious and practical knowledge, whereby they derived their influence. They were sensitive to the wishes of others and quickly lost prestige if they tried to force their will upon the group. Furthermore, if any member of the group felt that the leader's decisions were unacceptable, he could move to another group or start his own. A conscientious leader worked in the best interests of the group, although policies were discussed jointly. The leader's initiative was usually followed with regard to travel, hunting, and trapping. He decided when the group would leave in the morning and where and when to make camp at the end of the day. While leaders were normally in charge of subsistence activities, there were occasions when a leader relinquished his position. Dreams afforded clues about good hunting, and the leader might defer to a man who had received a dream indicating where game was to be found. Furthermore, any individual who killed big game decided when and how it was to be brought to camp and supervised the allocation of the meat (Rogers 1963a:62–63).

Women made decisions on behalf of their families and the group with regard to their activities and spheres of influence. They organized the ongoing operations of the camp, the distribution of supplies, the collection of necessities such as firewood and boughs for flooring, and various tasks such as processing skins for different uses. They might also, on occasion, influence the decisions of the men.

• THE TRANSITIONAL BAND: THE SOUTHEASTERN MONTAGNAIS EXAMPLE   In the southeastern part of the Labrador Peninsula, the fur trade, and with it the trading-post band, did not become so firmly established as they did to the west. In 1950 the Montagnais bands that summered along the lower Saint Lawrence River, at the mouths of the Natashquan, Mecatina, and Saint-Augustin rivers, did not have defined hunting territories; and, although some hunting partnerships involved strong ties of kinship and friendship and persisted for years as the cores of hunting groups, many other partnerships were more casual, and there was frequent change in hunting group composition. Similarly, although some areas had become habitually used by groups that formed around such core partnerships, there was still a great deal of leeway for deciding how all hunting groups would distribute themselves during any given winter. Final decisions might not be made until the time for leaving the trading-post settlement and journeying upriver into the interior arrived.

Leadership among the southeastern Montagnais was

182

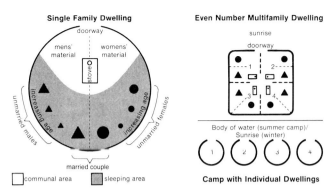

Single Family Dwelling

doorway

mens' material | womens' material

stove

increasing age

unmarried males

increasing age

unmarried females

married couple

□ communal area ▨ sleeping area

Even Number Multifamily Dwelling

sunrise

doorway

1   2
3   4

Body of water (summer camp)/ Sunrise (winter)

1 2 3 4

Camp with Individual Dwellings

after Tanner 1979:figs. 3.6, 8–9.

Fig. 9. The organization of social space for the Mistassini. Despite the pattern of frequent residential changes during the annual cycle, the internal arrangement of the dwelling is standardized; in a sense the place of residence never changes. The family unit, which lives and eats together, never contains more than one married couple. During the winter hunting and trapping season, family units usually live in their own separate dwelling, while often between freeze-up and mid or late winter the units occupy a communal lodge. Within the single-family dwelling each person has his own private space near the outside wall, while the area near the stove is used by the whole family. Because of the limited space inside the dwelling, members of the family generally do not walk around inside except to enter or leave. At night the family sleeps with heads oriented to the outside wall and feet toward the stove. All goods and materials within the dwelling are divided into male and female areas so that, for example, the food supply is kept on the women's side while the hunting and trapping supplies are kept on the men's side. The oldest unmarried female takes charge of the cooking, while the married female is in charge of preparing animal skins. The fire, the only thing not categorized as male or female, is tended by both sexes. In the single-family dwelling the family inside orients itself toward the door; the door in a summer camp usually faces the water, while in a winter camp it faces the sunrise.

In a communal dwelling the family units orient themselves toward the stoves in the center. The doorway always opens to the rising sun. Family units are set up internally following the same principles as for an individual dwelling with 2 additional points of consideration: the females of the 2 families on either side of the door must be closest to the door, and adjacent families must not have members of the opposite sex next to each other. In communal dwellings with an odd number of families either an alcove or recess is constructed between the opposite sexes of 2 families or the unmarried men are separated out at the rear of the lodge. See Tanner 1979:73–87.

even more informal and flexible than among the East Cree, such as the Mistassini. Although men of wisdom and experience often became leaders of hunting groups, their leadership, like the group composition itself, was temporary and seasonal. In 1950, the people at Natashquan had begun the practice of descending to the coast for the bitter and windy months of January and February, rather than staying inland as previously. During March and April, parties of men either with or without their families would return to the interior to trap, but not necessarily in the same groups, or to the same areas, or with the same leaders as in the fall.

At various times, different individuals from southeastern bands or bands hunting on the interior Lake Plateau had experimented with setting up permanent lines of several hundred traps, with cabins located a day's journey from each other along the line, after the fashion of full-time White trappers. However, the institution has not been maintained (Leacock 1954:31–32).

By the 1970s the summer camp of southeastern bands had been replaced by year-round villages of frame houses, and hunting and trapping trips into the interior had diminished considerably in frequency and duration. However, groups of kin and friends continued to perform many of the cooperative functions that characterized the hunting groups of the past (Dominique and Pelletier 1975).

• MARRIAGE AND KINSHIP Among the Mistassini band, and no doubt elsewhere, until at least the middle of the twentieth century, practically all men married, generally when they were in their early twenties and women when in their late teens. The choice of a mate depended upon the demonstrated capabilities of the prospective spouses and kinship. Most commonly, marriage alliances were between families whose territories were in close proximity to each other. After marriage, the ideal was for a man to reside with his parents, although one winter within the first three years of marriage had to be spent with his wife's parents. Traditionally, bilateral cross-cousin marriage was practiced, the sororate was perhaps the norm, and the levirate permissible. Polygyny was practiced, although few men had as many as three wives. Neither band exogamy nor endogamy prevailed (Rogers 1963a:27–31).

Genealogies were not of particular interest, and people were often unable to trace their specific relationships with distant relatives for whom they used kin designations. Among the northern bands a cross-cousin was still preferred as a spouse in the 1920s, a practice reflected in the erotic association and joking relationship connected with the term *ni·timuš* 'my cross-cousin or sibling-in-law of the opposite sex' (Strong 1929). The joking relationship obtained not only between marriageable cross-cousins themselves but also between cross-cousins of the same sex (*niwi·če·wa·kan* for a woman, *ni·sta·w* for a man). The ribaldry and sexual license allowed between cross-cousins of the same sex involved asking for the other's brother or sister, leading to temporary unions that often evolved into permanent marriages characterized by brother-sister exchanges (Strong 1929). In the past among the northern bands, the same term was used for son-in-law and cross-nephew, and another for both daughter-in-law and cross-niece, but these terms have apparently changed as the importance of cross-cousin marriage has faded (Hallowell 1932). In the eastern part of the peninsula, Roman Catholic law is apparently one factor that has discouraged cross-cousin marriages since at least 1900, but the former existence of this practice appears to be reflected by the use of *ni·timuš* as a general term for 'my sweetheart' in this area (Hallowell 1932; Leacock 1950–1951).

Religion

The Montagnais-Naskapi ritualized their relations to supernatural powers primarily around three basic concerns: good health, good hunting, and successful birth (Speck 1935; Tanner 1979). Religious practices involved: the shaking-tent rite, in which a shaman conversed with the spirits in a lodge specially constructed for the purpose; the respectful disposal of the bones left after butchering and eating large game and beaver (fig. 5); the holding of special "eat all" and other kinds of feasts; ceremonial drumming (Rogers 1963a:64–67, 1973:10–15); and scapulimancy (fig. 10), the scorching of a caribou or hare shoulder blade or grouse sternum, to determine the whereabouts of game or people. No line can be drawn, of course, between the "social" and the "religious" aspects of these functions.

Religion was a highly personal affair among the Montagnais-Naskapi, and individuals who "lived the right life" acquired increasing powers of communion with the spirit world as they grew older. Individuals who obtained considerable power through conscious effort became shamans, capable of performing the shaking-tent rite (Vincent 1973). In early times, women as well as men acquired shamanistic powers, but this has not been the case for some time. Shamans were important for their aid in healing and their assistance in ascertaining where game was to be found, and there was usually at least one shaman in each band or hunting group. Among the Mistassini, this was often the oldest man and hunting group leader.

The important ritual act of drumming was not a group endeavor among the Montagnais-Naskapi, and only one man drummed at a time. Among the Mistassini, the leader of the group drummed first, and when finished handed his drum to the next senior member. As a man drummed, he sang the hunting songs given him by the spirits ("Expressive Aspects of Subarctic Indian Culture," fig. 16, this vol.) (Rogers 1963a:67). Drumming always followed a feast, but it occurred many other times as well. Since it was used in the Mistassini band as a way of obtaining knowledge of events that might occur during the winter, it was frequent during the fall months. A performance might take one or two hours or might last all night.

Since the arrival of the Jesuits in the early 1600s, the Montagnais-Naskapi have been visited by missionaries of various persuasions. The Anglicans became influential among the East Cree, where they have worked since the mid-1800s, while at an earlier date, the Indians of the Saint Lawrence and the eastern part of the Labrador Peninsula became Roman Catholics. Adherence

bottom, U. of Pa., U. Mus. Philadelphia: 31–7–171, 31–7–172.

Fig. 10. Scapulimancy. top, A Mistassini hunter using a burnt shoulder blade of a hare to predict some phenomenon. bottom, Hare shoulder blades used for divination. These bones are "subjected to heat, and the burnings, in the form of blackened spots, cracks and breaks, are then interpreted by the cunning and ingeniousness of the practitioner. Imagination suggests the likeness of the marks produced by the heat, to rivers, lakes, mountains, trails, camps and various animals—the latter either single or in groups. The direction of the burnt marks and their respective locations are also significant. Persons are also believed to be represented by the spots or outlines. Abstract ideas may be represented: life, death, success, failure, plenty, famine, sickness . . . . and general good or bad luck are likewise indicated by the cabalistic figures" (Speck 1935:139). Individual interpretation rather than formalized rules are the basis for reading bones; interpretation depends in part on which bone is used from what kind of animal (Tanner 1979:117–124). top, Photograph by Adrian Tanner, 1969–1970. bottom, Length 5.5 cm, collected by Frank G. Speck, Lake St. John, Que., 1931.

to Catholic observances, which these people had to practice most of the time without benefit of a priest, coexisted with older practices. Biblical stories were told as well as older myths about *čahka·pe·š* (Djokabish, Chikapis, etc.), the trickster-transformer figure who with his sister can be seen on the face of the moon, and other important figures, such as the man who married a caribou-woman and played a leading role in cementing relations between people and the animal on whom they so largely depended. The most feared malevolent beings were Windigos or cannibal monsters.

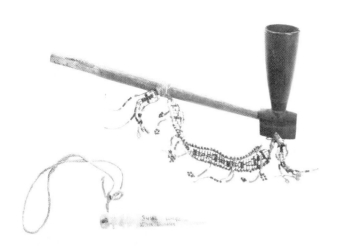

Smithsonian. Dept. of Anthr.: 90306, 90024.
Fig. 11. Black slate pipe with incised lines at top and bottom of characteristic deep bowl. The attached loom-woven beaded ornament indicates the pipe was used in feasts honoring dead game. Smoking items such as the pipe and accompanying carved horn pipe cleaner were part of a man's spiritual hunting equipment and were used to aid luck in hunting (Speck 1935:219). Length of pipe 21 cm, collected by Lucien M. Turner, Ungava Bay, Que., 1882–1884.

Sociocultural Situation in the 1970s

By the 1970s, the old ways of the Montagnais-Naskapi had been radically altered in all external aspects and to a large extent also in those aspects of culture not so visible. The Indians dressed in Western clothing, lived in permanent prefabricated houses provided by the government; traveled by snowmobiles, motor vehicles, and aircraft; sent their children to White-run schools; attended Christian churches; and published accounts of their experiences (André 1976, 1979; Willis 1973; Bouchard 1977). No longer were they self-sufficient and able to gain a livelihood from the land. Government support programs maintained the modern standard of living since the renewable natural resources were insufficient and wage employment was limited. By 1980 they had become settled villagers, a life imposed upon them through the activities of the Euro-Canadians who have come to own the land. Yet they refused to remain confined to one place (Piché 1977).

Synonymy†

The Indians north of the Saint Lawrence River have been called Montagnais 'mountaineers' by the French since the early seventeenth century, "because of the high mountains" in their territory (JR 23:302). Most variants of the French name originated with Champlain

† This synonymy was written by David H. Pentland.

(1922–1936): Montagnes, 1603 (1:103; same as Montagnés [sg.; JR 9:821]); Montaignes, 1603 (1:109); Montagnez, 1603 (1:124); Montaignez, 1603 (1:124); Mōtaignars = Montaignars, 1605 (1:342); Mōtaignets = Montaignets, 1609 (2:57); Montagnets, 1609 (2:64); Montagnars, 1609 (2:97); Montaignairs, 1615 (3:40); Montagnairs, 1632 (map). The modern spelling Montagnais first appeared on Lescarbot's 1609 map (Winsor 1884–1889, 4:117). Other spellings are: Montagnards, 1632 (JR 5:54); Montagnaits, 1633 (JR 5:92); Montaignets, 1643 (JR 23:302); Montagners, 1808 (McKenzie in Masson 1889–1890, 2:412). Mountaineer is occasionally used as an English equivalent (Long 1791:155; Pierronet 1800); Chappell's (1817:152) Mountain Indians are probably the same. The English name Montagnais has usually been applied to the Indians of the southeastern quadrant of the Labrador Peninsula (Hind 1863, 2:9–10), but also more narrowly to just those west of Sept-Îles (Jenness 1932:266–270) and more broadly to those of the whole peninsula (Cooper 1933—as a linguistic term; Flannery 1936; Murdock and O'Leary 1975, 2:166–167). The compound Montagnais-Naskapi was introduced by Speck (1926:274, 1931:576) and Hallowell (1929:337) to include all the Algonquians of the Labrador Peninsula, but it and expressions like Montagnais and Naskapi are sometimes intended to exclude the East Cree (Jenness 1932:266, 270). The names Montagnais and Montagnard have also been used for the unrelated Chipewyan (see the synonymy in "Chipewyan," this vol.) and other peoples living in hilly regions. There are no equivalents in Montagnais or neighboring Algonquian languages for the term, though Hind (1863, 2:10) gives Tshe-tsi-uetin-euerno 'people of the north-north-east' as the self-designation used by the Indians he called Montagnais.

Naskapi is said to be a derogatory term meaning 'uncivilized people' or 'those who have no religion' (Speck 1931:559), but no satisfactory etymology has yet been put forward. The name is generally applied to the northern and especially northeastern bands (Hind 1863, 2:97) but has also been extended to those of the Basse-Côte-Nord east of Sept-Îles (Jenness 1932:266, 270). It first appears in 1643 as Ounachkapiouek (JR 24:154), probably representing Montagnais *unaska·hpi·wak^y* (pl.). The proposed phonemicization takes into account some of the later recordings, especially Skoffie (Pierronet 1800) and Scoffis (Latham 1850:328), which reflect the Labrador dialects' pronunciation of *hp* as [f]. Other spellings of the name (from Hodge 1907–1910, 2:32, unless otherwise marked) are: Cuneskapi, an error for Ouneskapi, 1731 (Pierre Laure in Hind 1863, 1:34, and Speck 1931:559); Naskapis, Naskupis, 1733; Ounescapi, 1755; Nasquapicks, 1774; Unescapis, 1779; Nascapees, 1808 (McKenzie in Masson 1889–1890, 2:412); Nascopies (Latham 1850:328); Nascobi, 1861 (De Boilieu 1969:88); Nasquapee (Hind 1863), Ounascapis, 1863;

Nascopi, Nascupi, and Ounadcapis, 1884; Naskopis, Neskaupe, 1885; Naskopie, 1894; Nascaupee (Low 1929:146). Hodge's (1907–1910, 2:30–32) entry uses Nascapee.

In the seventeenth century the Montagnais around Tadoussac called themselves *ne·hirawiriniw* 'Montagnais-speaking person', from *ne·hirawe·w* 'he speaks our language, he speaks Montagnais' (Silvy 1974:89; Fabvre 1970:188); the prenoun form is attested as nehiro-iriniui (La Brosse 1767). This name seems to have gone out of use among the Montagnais, although Hind (1863, 2:10) recorded it as Ne-e-no-il-no and it is still the self-designation of the Attikamek and Western Woods Cree. Like many other Algonquian-speaking groups, the Montagnais use the word for 'human being' (Southern Montagnais *ilnu*, Eastern Montagnais *innu*) to refer to themselves and related tribes as opposed to Eskimos and Whites, but this should not be uncritically taken to mean that they perceive the other groups as non-human.

Local Groups

Numbers in parentheses below correspond to locations shown on figure 1.

Waswanipi (1). The Southern Montagnais call the people of Waswanipi *wa·šwa·nipi·wilnu* 'jack-lighting person' (after Speck 1931:579).

The Mistassini band (2), named after the great rock (*mistasiniy*) in the lake of the same name, call themselves *mistasini·wiyiyu* 'great rock person' (Speck 1931:592); the same name (with the change of *y* to *n*) is used by the Eastern Montagnais in referring to them (Mailhot and Lescop 1977:129). The version *mistasini·w* was recorded in 1643 as Mistasiniouek (pl., JR 24:154). The name was borrowed into French in a variety of shapes: Mistasiriniens, 1665 (JR 50:36); Mistassinirinins, 1672 (JR 56:156); Mistasirinis, 1672 (JR 56:168); Mistassins, 1674 (JR 59:28). Raudot in 1709 subdivided them into the Grands and Petits Mistassins (Kinietz 1940:365). In English the name appears as Mistissinnys, 1801 (Mackenzie 1970:map), and Mistassins (Chappell 1817:166).

Lake Saint John–Saguenay River (3). The Lake Saint John band people call themselves Piɔkwágami·wilnúts· 'flat lake people' (Speck 1931:580), the Piekouagamies of Mackenzie's (1970) map of 1801. They are named after the lake, which was called Piék8agami (Laure 1889:28; miswritten Piouagamik in JR 31:250), but their neighbors seem to have misunderstood the name: the Eastern Montagnais call them *pi·kwa·kami·winnut* 'turbid lake people' (Mailhot and Lescop 1977:230), the Attikamek *pe·kwa·kamiriniwak* (not translatable; Béland 1978:542), and French Piek8agamiens is also attested (Laure 1889:40).

The tribe named *ka·kuš* '(little) porcupine'—so called

because of the numerous porcupines around Lake Saint John (JR 56:154)—earlier lived in the same vicinity. The name was usually recorded in the plural: Kaк8azakhi, 1641 (JR 21:118); Kaкouchakhi, 1643 (JR 24:154); Kakovchaqvi, 1660 (Creuxius [Du Creux] in JR 46:map); Kaкouchac, 1672 (JR 56:154); kak8chak, about 1679 (Silvy 1974:44); Kak8echak, before 1696 (Fabvre 1970:90). In French they were called nation des Porcs-épics in 1638 and nation du Porc-épic in 1640 (JR 14:224, 18:226).

The missionaries sometimes spoke vaguely of les peuples du Sagné 'peoples of the Saguenay River' (as in JR 9:218) but more often mentioned specific groups. The most prominent from their point of view were the people of Tadoussac (5) or Sadiseg8 (misprinted as Sadilege, JR 29:122) '(some kind of) river mouth'. Around 1685 Radisson called them the Sagseggons (1961:160), reflecting *usa·čise·ku·w* 'Sadiseg8 person' (from Silvy 1974:112 and Fabvre 1970:247); the locative was Shatshegutsh (La Brosse 1767). Speck (1931:581) gives the variant Wɔca·t'cékwilnuts· (c = š), which he translates 'gulf people' or 'steep river-mouth people'. Those from Chicoutimi (4) are called *še·kutimi·wilnuč* 'head of the tide people' (from Speck 1931:581), in French sometimes Chek8timiens (Laure 1889:40) or Chicoutimiens (as in Kinietz 1940:365). Below the mouth of the Saguenay are the (6) *e·šiši·pi·wilnuč* 'clam river people' or *e·šiši·pi·wiši·puwilnuč* 'river of clam-brooks people' (phonemicized from Speck 1931:581). The modern band name is Escoumains and the place-name Les Escoumins, earlier attested as the locative Iskuamiskutsh (La Brosse 1767).

Betsiamites (7). To the self-designation petsiámiwilnúts· (Speck 1931:559) corresponds Eastern Montagnais *pe·ssia·mi·winnut* (pl.; Mailhot and Lescop 1977:227); these forms and the 1643 recording Oubestamiouek (JR 24:154) mean 'people of *pe·sčia·mi·č·*'. The translation of the place-name is not certain, but Speck's (1931:559) rendering 'they come out by way of the river' is probably close. The French more often referred to the band by the place-name: Sauvages Bersiamiste, 1632 (Champlain 1922–1936, map); Bersiamites, 1635 (JR 8:40); Bersiamitæ, 1660 (Creuxius in JR 46:map); Bertiamistes, 1665 (NYCD 3:122). The modern French form is Betsiamites, in English Bersimis. Le Jeune in 1635 was not sure whether the ouperigoue ouaouakhi were the same as the people of Bersimis (JR 8:40). Other spellings are Oueperigoueiaouek in 1643 (JR 24:154) and 8iperig8e8a8ak, around 1695 (Fabvre 1970:235).

At the mouth of the Manicouagan and neighboring rivers in the seventeenth century were the *uma·mi·wak^y* 'downstream people' (9). The Montagnais form was variously spelled: 8mami8eкhi, 1641 (JR 21:116); 8mami8ek, 1650 (JR 35:274); Oumamiouek, 1651 (JR 36:224); 8mami8ec, 1666 (JR 50:192); 8mami8etch,

1673 (JR 59:56). It also appears as a French word, Oumamiois, in 1664 (JR 49:68). This tribe was said to be allied with the "Esquimaux" in 1652 (JR 37:232); in 1673 they were simply described as a tribe of Esquimaux (JR 59:56). Garth Taylor (1978), following the lead of Burgesse (1949), has shown that until the end of the seventeenth century the name Esquimaux was applied to a Montagnais-speaking band on the north shore of the Saint Lawrence (17), and cites the following spellings: Esquimawes, 1584; Excomminquois, Excomminqui, 1612; Esquimau, 1648; eskimeaux, 1673; Aesquimaux, 1676. In 1691 the Algonquian group was called the petits Eskimaux to distinguish them from the grands Eskimaux or Inuit (Taylor 1978:100). The identification is complicated by Silvy's (1974:11, 35) translation of Montagnais *ayaščime·w* as 'gaspésiens' in about 1679, followed a few years later by Fabvre (1970:16, 69) with 'gaspésiens, mikmaks'.

Inland from the Oumamiouek lived the Papinachois (8), a name Speck (1931:558) would derive from *pabi·nácuwe* (c = *š*) 'one who wanders from place to place'. Laure (1889:63) described them as living from the Bersimis River to Labrador and related their name to *ni-papinach* 'I laugh a little'. The earlier recordings suggest the Montagnais form *upapinašiw* (vowel lengths uncertain): 8papinachi8eκhi, 1641 (JR 21:116); Oupapinachiouek, 1643 (JR 24:154); 8papinachi8ek, 1650 (JR 35:274); Ovpapinachoveti, 1660 (Creuxius in JR 46:map). These are all plurals, as is the Latin 8papinachi8j, created in 1673 from the Montagnais singular (JR 59:62). Other versions are given with Montagnais plural endings but without the initial *u-*: Papinachi8ekhi, 1642 (JR 22:218); Papinachioueκhi and Papinachioueki, 1662 (JR 47:220, 230); Papinachioec, 1667 (JR 50:210). French borrowed the singular, spelling it Papinachiois, Papinachois (JR 47:60, 48:278) and Papinacheois (Laure 1889:40); the French plural is the same.

The seventeenth-century inhabitants of the Sept-Îles area (11) called themselves *učiše·stiku·wak^y* 'people of the great river'. Early spellings are: Chichedec, 1612; Chicedec, 1613; Chisdec, 1632 (all from maps in Champlain 1922–1936); Chisedech, 1640 (JR 18:226); Chisedeck, 1685 (Radisson 1961:160); and Latinized Chichesedecum, 1660 (Creuxius in JR 46:map). The Jesuit recordings were more accurate: Oukesestigouek, 1643 (JR 24:154); Ouchestiguetch, Ouchestigouetch, Ouchestigouets, and Ouchestigueti, 1664 (JR 49:60–64); Ouchestigoüek, 1665 (JR 50:28). The Latinized form 8tchisestig8 natione, 1673 (JR 59:60) lacks the plural suffix. A different formation with similar meaning, *mista-ši·pi·winnu* 'big river person', is the modern name of the Moisie band (15) (Mailhot and Lescop 1977:129; Speck 1931:584).

Montagnais from North West River (21) are known as *(či)še·ša·či·winnu* 'great lake-outlet person', a name

also used by the Indians at Davis Inlet in the 1920s (Speck 1931:588); what is conceivably a variant of this name was spelled Sheshatapooshshoish in 1800 (Pierronet 1800), later shortened to Sheshatapoosh (Latham 1850:328).

Other modern subgroup names (from Speck 1931 and Mailhot and Lescop 1977) are: (10) Godbout, *wa·wiya·pe·ku·wilnu* 'whirlpool person'; (13) Shelter Bay, Wəsakwopətá·nwilnut‘ (pl.) 'mossy portage people'; (14) Sainte-Marguerite, *če·ma·nipistikwinnu* 'steep-edged river (?) person'; (16) Mingan, *(a)kwa·niči·winnu* 'jetsam person' or *manitu·w-ši·pi·winnu* 'spirit river person'; (12) Sept-Îles, *wa·ša·winnu* 'bay person'; (18) Natashquan, *nu·taskwa·ni·winnu* 'bear hunting person'; (19) Romaine, *unaman-ši·pi·winnu* 'vermilion river person', or Musquaro, probably *maskwa·nuwinnu* 'bear tail person'; (20) Saint-Augustin, *pakut-ši·pi·winnu* (Speck translates 'bastard, or fatherless boy, river people'); (24) Michikamau, *mišikama·winnu* 'great lake person'; (23) Petitsikapau, Petəs·əkupáuwi·nút‘ (pl.) 'lake that is narrow in the middle people' (?); (22) Menihek Lakes, *minaikwinnu* 'white spruce person'; (25) Davis Inlet, *učima·ssi·winnu*, possibly 'Hudson's Bay Company land person' (compare *učima·wat* 'the bosses, the Hudson's Bay Company'); (26) Barren Ground, *mu·šawa·winnu* 'tundra person' used in the form mushuau innu as the French name for the modern Davis Inlet dialect (Ford 1978); (27) Chimo or Ungava, *(pwa·t-)čišaimu-innu* '(Fort) Chimo person' (borrowed from English; ultimately from Eskimo).

Sources

Although ethnographic data are relatively rich for a few Montagnais-Naskapi groups, information is scattered through many publications, covers a time span of 400 years, and has been recorded by missionaries, traders, geologists, biologists, and ethnographers. An exhaustive bibliography for the Labrador Peninsula that includes a most comprehensive coverage of the Montagnais-Naskapi is by Cooke and Caron (1968). Feit et al. (1972) published one for the western part of the area and Dominique (1976), for all Montagnais-Naskapi except the Coasters of James Bay. A general survey of the history and culture of the Indians of the Labrador Peninsula can be found in Fried (1955) and Malaurie and Rousseau (1964).

Some of the earliest information pertaining to the Montagnais-Naskapi is found in the writings of the Jesuit missionaries, especially the mid-seventeenth-century *Jesuit Relations*, which often give quite detailed descriptions of the Indians' way of life. Other early writers present only minimal information (for example, Cartier 1924; Champlain 1922–1936; Jolliet in Delanglez 1944, 1944a; Dobbs 1744; Oldmixon 1741; Boucher 1964). Bailey (1969) has drawn upon these materials to examine from a historian's point of view the impact of the Europeans upon the Montagnais. Hoffmann (1961) has critically examined the early sources, especially the maps.

Following the mid-seventeenth century and for the next two centuries only limited observations were recorded. Cartwright (1911) and McLean (1932) are exceptions, McLean in the 1840s giving the first rather detailed account of the northern Naskapi. Other information is to be found in Chappell (1817) and the journals of Hudson's Bay Company traders (Davies and Johnson 1963). Hind (1863) left an account of the Indians living inland along the Moisie River with valuable illustrations made during the trip by his brother. W.H.A. Davies (1854) published observations on the Naskapi of Fort Chimo, and Horden (Batty 1893) left some notes on the Indians on the west side of the peninsula. Barnston (1861) presented the first quantitative data on the utilization of waterfowl by the Indians of James Bay.

Beginning in the late nineteenth century, an increased interest in the inhabitants of the Labrador Peninsula began, and more information was recorded. The geologist Low (1897) traversed the peninsula in many directions and recorded a few sparse remarks on many Montagnais-Naskapi groups. Others were to follow (Newnham in Shearwood 1943; Cabot in Grenfell 1909; V. Tanner 1944; D. Wallace 1907; Hubbard 1908; C.W. Townsend 1910, 1913; Bryant 1913; J.W. Anderson 1961; Leith and Leith 1912; Curran and Calkins 1917; E.T.D. Chambers 1896; Comeau 1909). Elton (1942), using the Hudson's Bay Company archives, presented data on animal population cycles and the Naskapis' dependence on caribou. The botanist Rousseau (1945, 1946, 1946a, 1947; Rousseau and Rousseau 1948, 1948a, 1952) and the trader Burgesse (1943, 1944, 1944a, 1945) added their observations.

Ethnographic investigations started remarkably early in the Labrador Peninsula. Turner (1894) was the first, working from 1882 to 1884 among the Naskapi who traded at Fort Chimo. His research initiated the scientific study of the Indians of the Shield Subarctic. In 1908 Speck began investigations among the Montagnais of Lake Saint John, later expanding his work to other groups; he initiated the study of Montagnais-Naskapi social organization (1915a), mapped and proclaimed the aboriginality of "family hunting territories" (1923, 1927, 1928; Speck and Eiseley 1939, 1942), and published the most comprehensive analysis of Montagnais-Naskapi religion (1935). Vincent (1973) and Tanner (1975, 1979) added further insights. Lips undertook fieldwork a little later than Speck and investigated the legal systems (1947, 1947a), economic organization (1939), and hunting technology (1936) of the southern Montagnais-Naskapi. He was the first ethnographer to utilize the Hudson's Bay Company archives to examine

in historical perspective the sociopolitical organization of these people, an approach continued by Morantz (1976, 1977, 1978, 1980).

Waugh (1925) and Strong (1929) worked among the eastern Montagnais-Naskapi. Leacock (1954), working among the southeastern Montagnais, questioned the idea that the "family hunting territory" was a precontact feature of Indian life, as others had proposed (Speck 1923, 1927, 1928; Cooper 1939; Hallowell 1949a). Leacock (1955) further argued for an aboriginal matrilocal social system replaced by a patrilocal system under the impact of the fur trade. She also investigated the role of women (1975, 1976; Leacock and Goodman 1976). McGee (1961) and Mailhot and Michaud (1965) worked in the community of Northwest River. Henriksen (1971, 1973) analyzed sociopolitical organization among the Indians of Davis Inlet. Dorian (1967) has dealt with place-names of the Montagnais-Naskapi of the Mingan Reserve.

Skinner (1912) undertook the first fieldwork among the Indians of the east coast of James Bay. He was followed by Cooper (1930, 1935, 1939, 1946), Flannery (1938, 1939a, 1946, 1962), D.S. Davidson (1928b), R. Knight (1965, 1968), and Preston (1964, 1968–1972, 1971b, 1975b, 1980). Hallowell (1929, 1932, 1946) also contributed to knowledge of the Montagnais-Naskapi. In the 1940s the James Bay Survey was undertaken (Honigmann 1951a). As part of this program, Kerr (1950) investigated the economic system of the Rupert House Cree. Later Honigmann (1952, 1962) and Barger and Earl (1971) studied the interrelationship between the Indians and Eskimos of Great Whale River. Honigmann also reviewed the culture of the northern Montagnais-Naskapi (1964). Rogers (1963a, 1967a, 1973) pursued further Speck's (1923, 1930) interest in the Mistassini. The McGill-Cree project (Chance 1968) furthered research among the Indians of the Mistassini area (Pothier 1965, 1968; La Rusic 1971; Tanner 1968, 1971, 1973; Sindell 1968; Holden 1968, 1969; Feit 1971, 1971a, 1973). An excellent source on modern Mistassini winter hunting is Richardson and Lanzelo (1974), a documentary film on a 16-person camp. As part of the Algonkian Project McFeat (1962) encouraged investigations among the Montagnais-Naskapi. The National Museum of Man, Ottawa, sponsored these investigations (C. Lévesque 1976; Taylor 1980). At about this time, the Centre d'Études Nordiques, Université Laval, Quebec, was formed and began a monograph series, some titles of which relate to the ethnography of the Labrador Peninsula. This activity stimulated an increased interest in the Montagnais-Naskapi (Désy 1963, 1968; Lachance 1968; Lebuis 1971). The journal *Recherches amérindiennes au Québec*, which was initiated in 1971, provides considerable information about the Montagnais-Naskapi, including some analyses of Montagnais mythology (Savard 1969, 1971, 1972, 1973).

Finally, the James Bay Hydroelectric project, which resulted in a settlement in November 1975, brought about interest in the Indians of this area (B. Richardson 1975; Quebec (Province) 1976). As a consequence, further studies have been undertaken of their way of life (Salisbury et al. 1972; Spence 1972), and the Indians of the Quebec Association commissioned a comprehensive study on their own history (Orenstein 1973).

Seventeenth-Century Montagnais Social Relations and Values

ELEANOR LEACOCK

Among the many seventeenth-century accounts of New France that were written by explorers, traders, and missionaries, the fullest record of everyday Montagnais life was given by Paul Le Jeune, a Jesuit missionary, who wrote detailed letters to his superiors in Paris on the progress of his mission near Quebec. Of greatest importance is his report on the winter he spent in 1633–1634 with a group of Montagnais who traveled inland from the south shore of the Saint Lawrence River. The following précis of social life and attitudes among the Montagnais is drawn primarily from Le Jeune's accounts as published in the *Jesuit Relations* (see also Le Jeune 1973).

Ecological Adaptation

The principal animal resources depended upon by the Montagnais with whom the Jesuit missionary Paul Le Jeune worked, were fresh eels in September and October; smoked eels, porcupine, and beaver in early winter; moose and some caribou with the coming of the heavy snow; and bears, beaver, and fowl in the spring and summer (JR 6:277, 7:107). In order to tap these resources, the Indians not only went into the interior in the fall and back down to the Saint Lawrence in the spring but also made continual smaller moves, both along the river in the summer and through the forests in the winter. Between November 12, 1633, and April 1634 the group with which Le Jeune lived broke camp 23 times in a period of as many weeks. This may have been more often than usual, since it was a difficult winter, with the snow that made it possible to track moose and caribou coming late. Some people died of starvation. A Montagnais commented to Le Jeune that the Indians were like the caribou that "go in troops," and "hardly stop in one place, continually travelling," while the French were sedentary like "elks [moose]" (JR 29:221).

The groups that stayed together varied seasonally in size. Nineteen people shared the lodge in which Le Jeune spent the winter, and this group traveled inland with two other lodge-groups of 10 and 16. During the most difficult season, the 45 people had to divide, and one lodge-group left the others in order to spread out over a wider area in search of game. In the spring some members of Le Jeune's lodge-group stayed inland to hunt moose, while the others kept to the stream beds to hunt beaver. Le Jeune traveled with the second group, who smoked the best meat "for the feasts they were to give . . . at the place where they had appointed a rendezvous" (JR 7:185; Leacock 1954:14–15).

Scattered references in the *Jesuit Relations* illustrate further the coming together and separating of multifamily lodge-groups. An aggregate of several such groups apparently made up a "winter band" of some 35 to 75 people. In turn, two or three of these aggregates probably constituted the named band of 150 or upward of 300 that shared a general area. Finally, there were large summer gatherings at the Saint Lawrence River shore of members from several named bands, as well as groups of other peoples—Abenaki, Algonquin, Huron, even Eskimo. Such gatherings became as large as 1,500 and more. Although the actual size of these was probably increased by the fur trade and the staple foods that were available, the pattern of summer gatherings for trade and socializing was probably old (Leacock 1969:9–12).

Survival during the difficult winter season depended upon the dual principles of spreading out for maximum access to game while keeping in touch so that others could be turned to for help. People came together when they could but separated "for fear that, by keeping together in too great numbers, they may suffer from hunger" (JR 62:223). When people were in trouble, food was unstintingly shared. Le Jeune was chagrined when he saw his group's meager resources being readily given to others who came for help during the worst of the winter.

People moved about in traditionally used lands, on the whole, and apparently checked with others when moving into lands they were occupying. However, there is no indication of anything like the individual trapping territories that were to develop later. Le Jeune referred to others "coming to hunt upon our very grounds [*jusque nos marches*], taking away our game and our lives at the same time" (JR 7:171) and to a starving family that was fed and "not asked why they came upon our boundaries [*sur nos limites*]" (JR 7:177), but Le

Jeune's actual experiences, in conjunction with the entire body of seventeenth-century materials, indicate that such phrases have no more reference to land ownership than do phrases such as "our school" and "our neighborhood." Indeed, the Jesuits repeatedly bemoaned the extent to which the Montagnais with whom they made contact moved about and changed their affiliations (for example, JR 6:147). It was Le Jeune's expressed wish that "it will be so arranged that, in the course of time, each family of our Montagnais [will] . . . become located" so that "it will take its own territory for hunting without following in the tracks of its neighbors" (JR 8:57, 59).

Leadership and Decision-making

Individual autonomy, a fundamental principle of Montagnais social relations, was based upon and defined by the direct dependence of each member on the group. "Obedience" was owed not to any individual, but to the practical and moral order of the group. It was defined by constant teasing and banter and ultimately enforced by necessity.

Deploring Montagnais pride and hauteur, Le Jeune wrote:

> They imagine that they ought by right of birth, to enjoy the liberty of Wild ass colts, rendering no homage to any one whomsoever, except when they like. They have reproached me a hundred times because we fear our Captains, while they laugh at and make sport of theirs. All the authority of their chief is in his tongue's end; for he is powerful in so far as he is eloquent; and, even if he kills himself talking and haranguing, he will not be obeyed unless he pleases the Savages (JR 6:243).

The "captains," "sagamores," or "chiefs" referred to in the *Relations* and other accounts were apparently men of personal influence and rhetorical ability. Everyone was impressed with the skill of the speaker who put forth the Montagnais view of French-Indian relations when he greeted Samuel de Champlain in 1632 (JR 5:205–211). Such men were spokesmen, who acted as intermediaries with the French or with other Indian groups, but they held no formal power, a situation that the Jesuits wanted to change by introducing organized elections (JR 18:99–105). "Alas!" Le Jeune complained, "if someone could stop the wanderings of the Savages, and give authority to one of them to rule the others, we would see them converted and civilized in a short time" (JR 12:169). However, he commended the lack of avarice and ambition in Montagnais social practice, for since there were no "offices nor dignities nor any authority" among them, "they never kill each other to acquire these honors. Also, as they are contented with a mere living, not one of them gives himself to the Devil to acquire wealth" (JR 6:231).

Important matters were resolved through considered discussion. Le Jeune was impressed by the patience with which people listened as each spoke, rather than all talking at once (JR 5:25). At that time, as in more recent times (Leacock 1958), leadership in specific situations apparently fell to the individual who was knowledgeable, for instance, the one who best knew the route to a certain place (JR 7:109). Shamans were influential as individuals but held no formal power. In Le Jeune's time, women as well as men learned the shamanistic arts of communicating with spiritual beings (JR 8:261, 9:113, 14:183).

The principle of autonomy extended through the social fabric to relations between women and men. There was little distinction between formal and informal or public and private spheres of life. "Formal" decisions about group movements and activities were in effect also "household" decisions, for there was no institutionalized decision-making structure superimposed on the groups of several nuclear families that constituted the households. Decisions were made by those responsible for carrying them out. Le Jeune commented on the way this arrangement smoothed the process of daily life: "It is true that the Savages are very patient, but the order which they maintain in their occupations aids them in preserving peace in their households. The women know what they are to do, and the men also; and one never meddles with the work of the other" (JR 5:133, 6:233).

Some observers saw women purely as drudges and "slaves" (JR 2:77, 4:205), but those who came to know the Montagnais more intimately saw women as holding "great power" (JR 5:181) and as having, "in nearly every instance . . . the choice of plans, or undertakings, of journeys, of wintering" (JR 68:93). Indeed, the independence of women was considered a problem to the Jesuits, who lectured the men about "allowing" their wives sexual and other freedoms (JR 5:181, 6:255). As in the case of chiefs, the Jesuits sought to introduce European principles of obedience. Montagnais converts to Christianity took up the Jesuits' exhortations, and lectured women to obey their husbands, children to obey their parents, and people to obey their new formally elected captains (JR 18:107, 22:81, 85, 115–121, 125).

Social Institutions and Social Ethics

Le Jeune wrote that the Montagnais preferred "to take the children of their sisters as heirs, rather than their own, or than those of their brothers" (JR 6:255), and residence was referred to in the *Relations* as matrilocal (JR 31:169, 44:307). However, the matter was apparently casual, for there was little to inherit and there were no formal kinship groups or clans. Postnuptial residence seems to have been flexible. While there are *191*

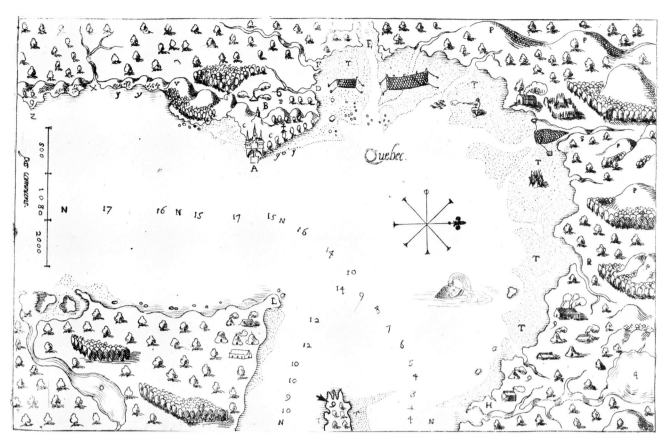

Fig. 1. Samuel de Champlain's map of the region around Quebec (at "A") in 1608–1612. At least 2 types of Montagnais houses are shown—gabled or barrel-vaulted and conical or domed—as well as an Indian eel trap at the mouth of the Moulin River (top right; cf. Champlain 1922–1936, 2:44), and 2 fish nets set on tidal flats (top center). The figure 9 (arrow) shows 4 "places where the Indians often encamp." The scale at left indicates 2,000 *pas communs* (about 1,500 m); for modern identifications of places see Champlain 1922–1936, 2:pl. 3.

frequent references to households with father-in-law and son-in-law living together, or with sisters in coresidence, at least one of whom is married, there are also mentions of other arrangements. Le Jeune lived with three brothers, who, temporarily at least, were wintering together. Since it was easy to change affiliations, presumably there was then, as later (Leacock 1955), a certain expediency in working out living arrangements that assured a compatible nucleus of adults and a balance of sexes and ages.

Marriage could be polygynous, and divorce was easy and at the desire of either partner. Both were conditions the Jesuits wished to change, although for the most part with indifferent success in the early days (JR 12:261, 16:41, 22:81–85, 229). "Since I have been preaching among them that a man should have only one wife," wrote Le Jeune, "I have not been well received by the women; for, since they are more numerous than the men, if a man can only marry one of them, the others will have to suffer" (JR 12:165). Women and men were both expected to contribute to the household according to the sexual division of labor. A man who was a poor hunter might have difficulty keeping a wife (JR 7:173). Although there were no taboos against doing the work

of the other sex according to expediency, a man might be teased for doing a woman's tasks for it showed he could not hold a wife (JR 5:133).

There was considerable formality about eating, which was conducted in near silence; talking and maybe singing and drumming came later. Care was taken in the disposal of certain animal bones, and children were sent away from a lodge where a bear was being eaten. Eating to the full was important, and it was good manners to comment that one had. Feasting was ritually as well as socially meaningful, and, while everyone in a lodge ordinarily ate together, certain ritual feasts for bringing good weather and successful hunting were attended by men only. In turn, when meat was plentiful, women held feasts for themselves only. Except for special "eat-all" feasts, food was kept for those not present (JR 6:217–219, 279–291).

All children were cherished, and orphans were well cared for (JR 6:239). While care for infants fell mainly to women, responsibility for young children was apparently shared among older children and adults, and men were not incompetent in this area. Le Jeune described a father holding a sick baby, soothing it with, in his view, "the love of a mother," as well as "the

192

firmness of a father'' (JR 11:105). Children shared in work early and were disciplined by the social pressures and material realities of their lives, apparently, for they were not punished. Le Jeune wrote that "all the Savage tribes of these quarters. . .cannot chastise a child, nor see one chastised" nor "even scolded, not being able to refuse anything to a crying child" (JR 5:221, 6:153). He related an incident where a French drummer boy had hurt an Indian with his drum stick, and the Indian had asked for a gift in recompense. The French said instead they would whip the boy. At this, the Indians argued that the boy was only a child, who "had no mind," and "did not know what he was doing." When the French persisted and brought a whip, an Indian took off his robe and threw it over the boy, saying to hit him, not the child (JR 5:219–221). Le Jeune's view was that the Montagnais refusal to punish a child would make the mission's educational task a very difficult one and that it would be best to take children away from their home localities for schooling (JR 5:221, 6:153).

Within the group, the social ethic called for generosity, cooperation, and patience, and Le Jeune commented on the good humor, lack of jealousy, and willingness to help that characterized daily life. Those who did not contribute their share were not respected (JR 5:105), and it was a real insult to call a person stingy (JR 6:237). Le Jeune wrote that they "cannot endure in the least those who seem desirous of assuming superiority over the others; they place all virtue in a certain gentleness or apathy" (JR 16:165). However, this did not mean that the people's style of interaction was muted or restrained. On the contrary, Le Jeune was unnerved by the loud, jocular, lewd discourse of both women and men, laced with constant banter and ridicule (JR 6:253). There was "neither gentleness nor courtesy in their utterances," he wrote, marveling that their voices could be so sharp without their becoming angry (JR 6:235). "Their life is passed in eating, laughing, and making sport of each other, and of all the people they know," he stated (JR 6:243). The ridicule was apparently taken in good spirit, and people were not upset at hearing they had been made sport of in their absence. "They are harmonious among themselves, and their slander and raillery do not disturb their peace and friendly intercourse" (JR 6:247). Yet they were sensitive to any implication that real criticism was being conveyed; Le Jeune referred to "fear of being blamed" as a compelling motivation (JR 6:241).

It was important to keep in good spirits, and laughter was a common reaction to misfortune (JR 7:83, 6:237). "Take courage," Le Jeune was told when food was short during the winter, "let thy soul be strong to endure suffering and hardship; keep thyself from being sad, otherwise thou wilt be sick; see how we do not cease to laugh, although we have little to eat" (JR 6:233). When Le Jeune became sick, he was told: "Do not be sad; if thou art sad, thou wilt become still worse; if thy sickness increases, thou wilt die. See what a beautiful country this is; love it; if thou lovest it, thou wilt take pleasure in it, and if thou takest pleasure in it thou wilt become cheerful, and if thou art cheerful thou wilt recover" (JR 7:191). The sick were given what they asked for but otherwise not urged to eat. "To coax . . . with love and gentleness, is a language which they do not understand," Le Jeune stated. As long as sick people were able to eat, they were carried on sleds with the group, but people who no longer wished to eat were given up for dead and might be killed to relieve their suffering when there was a journey to make. They "do this through compassion," wrote Le Jeune (JR 5:143). When he expressed concern for an old woman whose son was dragging her on a sled, he was told: "She is going to die. . .; take her and kill her, since thou hast pity for her; thou wilt do her a service, because she will not suffer so much; perhaps her son will leave her in the midst of the woods, as he is unable either to cure her or to drag her after him, if he does not find something to eat" (JR 5:141–143). When game was scarce, and constant moving imperative, the sick had to be abandoned (JR 5:103). The Montagnais soon took advantage of the alternative of leaving them at the missions, where the Jesuit fathers were eager to baptize the dying or convert those who lived. The Jesuit fathers report many instances when the ill were abandoned to their care (for example, JR 6:135, 139). The mission narratives also suggest the fear and confusion engendered among the Montagnais by the new deadly illnesses that were appearing among them.

The importance of not feeling angry was explained to Le Jeune, for "anger brings on sadness, and sadness brings sickness" (JR 7:83). Le Jeune wrote that the Montagnais recognized "scarcely any sin more enormous than anger" (JR 16:165). However, the conscious effort at restraint did not seem to entail guilt-linked repression in the psychoanalytic sense of not recognizing the feeling of anger as valid, as has been suggested for northeastern Algonquians (Hallowell 1946). Le Jeune discussed anger as follows:

> They make a pretence of never getting angry, not because of the beauty of this virtue, for which they have not even a name, but for their own contentment and happiness, I mean, to avoid the bitterness caused by anger. . . . I have only heard one Savage pronounce this word, *Ninichcatihin,* "I am angry," and he only said it once. But I noticed that they kept their eyes on him, for when these Barbarians are angry, they are dangerous and unrestrained (JR 6:231).

As an example of such dangerous anger, a man who suspected his wife was going to leave him, was reported to have nearly killed their infant in an outburst of fury before she grabbed it and ran away (JR 6:127). Usually bitter enmities were kept hidden, although it was sometimes feared they could lead to attempted murder by witchcraft (JR 12:11, 13). Anger was openly expressed in the merciless and protracted torture of Iroquois prisoners, in which women and even children took part, the women often with greater fury than the men. The Iroquois "do still worse; that is why we treat them as cruelly as we can," Le Jeune was told (JR 5:53). One old woman asked permission of the French to "caress" some Iroquois prisoners, for they had killed, roasted, and eaten her father, husband, and children (JR 27:237). Le Jeune wrote: "So enraged are they against every one who does them an injury, that they eat the lice and other vermin that they find upon themselves,—not because they like them, but only, they say, to avenge themselves and to eat those that eat them" (JR 5:31).

Le Jeune's account followed some hundred years of disruptive events for the Montagnais, including terrorization by the Iroquois who made deep forays into their lands; new and deadly epidemic diseases; confrontation with numerous, powerful, and proselytizing strangers; and the availability of alcohol with its ambiguous properties of both relieving and creating anxieties (cf. Bailey 1937). The evidence in the *Jesuit Relations* indicates a contrast between the smoothness of interpersonal relations Le Jeune experienced during his winter inland and the recurrence of friction and conflict around the mission settlement that seems more than just a matter of greater numbers. Fighting and destruction of property often occurred when people were drunk, although the liquor, or the French who had supplied it, were said to be responsible rather than the individual (JR 6:231, 7:73, 75). Increasing numbers of individuals were attaching themselves to the missions and the French settlements and enjoining their relatives and friends to follow suit. "We have burned all our songs," one convert said, "all our dances, all our superstitions and everything that the Devil has taught our forefathers" (JR 22:237). Excessive expressions of guilt and punitiveness among some new converts expressed what must have been widespread feelings of doubt and anxiety (Bailey 1937).

Traditionally in Montagnais society, hospitality was accorded freely to all who came in friendship. The Montagnais were always ready to take in outsiders; a Montagnais woman was mentioned as having an Iroquois husband who came with her to the mission at Tadoussac (Anonymous 1854). Le Jeune reported lying, ingratitude, and generally disagreeable behavior as common in Indian relations with the French (JR 6:239, 247), but he was astute and honest enough to note that such behavior followed French rejection of Indian hospitality, and the fact that the French stayed aloof, "despising" Indian laws and customs (JR 6:259).

Le Jeune himself was subjected to all manner of practical jokes and ridicule during the winter he spent in the interior (JR 6:245, 7:63), and it is hard to assess to what extent this was the usual teasing or to what extent it was in rebuff for his open disapproval of what he saw as gluttony, immodesty, and lack of concern for cleanliness of clothes and food on the part of his hosts (JR 6:239, 253, 259). He lectured them constantly about their beliefs and actions and wrote about his running battles with the shaman whose home he shared. Whatever his hosts' attitudes may have been, and despite what he saw as a lack of sympathy for him, their consideration was revealed in a passage wherein he described his suffering from the bitter cold, while waiting after a day's march for a new lodge to be built. Upon feeling his hands, one of the men expressed surprise that he really was so cold, and thereafter men would give him their warm mittens and take his cold ones (JR 7:113). Another passage describes consideration, Montagnais style. Le Jeune noted the lack of formal greetings, and the seeming indifference accorded a man coming from a journey, who was given food in silence, with no one bursting out talking as would be the case among the French.

> But they told me rightly that one ought not to weary a man who has more need of rest than of words. If anyone comes from some other quarter, having entered the cabin he makes himself comfortable. . . . Knowing that he brings news, people come to see him and sit down near him; yet no one says a word to him, for, as he came for the purpose of talking, it is for him to begin. After resting a while, he speaks without being questioned, or interrupted in any way. After he has related his news, the old men question him, and engage in conversation with him (JR 11:211, 213).

The generally good spirits that prevailed in the Montagnais camp would at times give way to fear of starvation and death (JR 6:233, 7:171, 173). In a final fight to survive, each would then have to "play, so to speak" at saving himself (JR 7:49).

Attitudes toward the Supernatural

Gods and other supernatural beings were not held in awe. Le Jeune was critical that the Montagnais lacked any "fear of God" but were concerned, in his view, only with "their own pleasure and satisfaction" (JR 6:241, 7:85). They showed their gods not "the slightest honor," at most throwing some grease, their most valued food, into the fire for them (JR 6:173). The children's form of prayer was to come out of the lodges in the morning and shout, "Come Porcupines; come Beavers; come Elk," or they would call out wishes for better weather or cure of illness (JR 6:203, 205).

People showed respect for dead animals with a series of practices, such as keeping certain bones from dogs (JR 6:211, 5:165) or not spilling beaver blood around (JR 5:179), perhaps some of them practical matters of housekeeping that had become ritualized (McGee 1961:138). Scapulimancy (JR 6:215) and the interpretation of dreams (JR 5:161) were then, as still, ritualized ways of organizing discussion as to plans. People were casually persistent about such practices in the face of Le Jeune's arguments. At times they laughed at inconsistencies he pointed out in their beliefs; nonetheless, he complained, they did not "cease to act upon their own ideas" (JR 5:131, 151). At other times, his hosts chided him for his presumption in claiming knowledge of things he could not know (JR 6:181, 183), while Le Jeune criticized their vaguely defined feelings about shadowy souls and an afterlife (JR 6:175–181). Upon being pressed for their beliefs about creation,

> They answered that they did not know who was the first Author of the world,—that it was perhaps Atahocham, but that was not certain; that they only spoke of Atahocam as one speaks of a thing so far distant that nothing sure can be known about it; and, in fact, the word "Nitatahokan" in their language means, "I relate a fable, I am telling an old story invented for amusement" (JR 6:157; cf. JR 12:149).

Along with this philosophical stance, there was also a deep respect for and attachment to their mythology. The same account of Djokabish, the trickster-transformer who can be seen with his sister on the face of the moon, that was told to Le Jeune (JR 12:31–37) in the 1630s was still being told in 1950 on the north shore of the Saint Lawrence at Natashquan.

The Montagnais listened to Le Jeune and other missionaries with interest and respect, although debating with them and testing their sincerity. Eventually they integrated old and new beliefs and practices in their Roman Catholicism (Rousseau and Rousseau 1952), although they departed from Europeans in following their adopted social codes with a direct piety and lack of hypocrisy that constantly amazed the Jesuit fathers. And, catholic in the original sense, they lectured Le Jeune on tolerance: "They said that when I prayed God they greatly approved of it, as well as of what I told them; and hence, that I must also approve of their customs, and I must believe in their ways of doing things; that one of their number was going to pray in their way, soon, and that I should listen patiently" (JR 9:239).

Sources

On April 18, 1632, the Jesuit Paul Le Jeune left his convent at Dieppe, France, to assume the position of Father Superior of the Residence of Quebec, a post he held for about 25 years. After spending a year attempting to build up his mission and to master the Algonquin and Montagnais languages, Le Jeune accepted an invitation to share a lodge with three Montagnais families, a group of 19 who wintered on the south shore of the Saint Lawrence River, leaving Quebec in late October 1633 and returning in late April 1634. The account of his winter that Le Jeune sent back to his superiors in Paris stands unparalleled among seventeenth-century records of the Canadian north in the wealth of its detail and the honesty of its attempt to understand Indian life and attitudes (JR 5–7); there is a usefully annotated edition of this (Le Jeune 1973). Further information on the seventeenth-century Montagnais is scattered through mission reports of the following years.

East Main Cree

RICHARD J. PRESTON

Territory

The East Main Cree ('krē) are that part of the East Cree and Naskapi who occupy the land in Quebec on the east side of James Bay and the south part of the east side of Hudson Bay (in contrast with the west side of these bays, the West Main). The term was probably coined in the 1600s (Oldmixon 1741) and was used by the Hudson's Bay Company to refer to a department or district for their fur-trade enterprise. It included those Indians living between Richmond Gulf in the north and the Nottaway River drainage in the south, extending inland from the coast to the height of land, deep in the interior of the Ungava Peninsula (fig. 1). In 1974 the Indians of this area (including Mistassini and Waswanipi Crees) formally set up the Grand Council of the Crees (of Quebec).

Language

The East Main Cree speak the East Cree dialect of the Cree-Montagnais-Naskapi language (see "Subarctic Algonquian Languages," this vol.).* East Cree is closely related to Cree proper (Western Cree), but while the East Main people can often understand Moose or Attikamek Cree to a considerable extent, speakers of dialects of Cree proper usually cannot follow a conversation in the East Main language at all (Michelson 1939; Pentland 1970–1979). The subdialect of Fort George and Great Whale River is somewhat different from that of Rupert House and Mistassini, but not enough to cause any difficulty in communication. In the 1970s most individuals under 30 were bilingual in English or French.

*East Cree words appearing in italics are in a phonemic orthography that uses the following symbols: *p, t, č, k; s, š, h; m, n; w, y; i, a, u; i·, e·, a·, u·*. The transcriptions of East Cree words in the text were provided by Marguerite MacKenzie (personal communication 1979), except for *pi·simuta·wiyiyu·č*, which is based on transcriptions by Preston and by Faries (1938:178, 417). The italicized East Cree words in the Synonymy are phonemicizations by David H. Pentland of transcriptions in the sources cited; for the special symbols used, see the orthographic footnote in "Montagnais-Naskapi," this vol.

Coasters and Inlanders

There are several identifiable groups on the East Main. The *wi·nipe·ku·wiyiyu·č* 'salt-water (i.e., James Bay) people' or Coasters stay and get their living along the coast. Subdivisions are the *atima·pi·simwiyiyu·č* 'northern people', Coasters living to the north of the Fort George (LaGrande or Big) River, and *pi·simuta·wiyiyu·č* 'southern people', Coasters living to the south of the river. There are many smaller divisions or groups, according to the settlements, legal "bands," particular spring goose-camp locations, and other criteria. Contrasting with the Coasters is the category of Inlanders (*nu·hčimi·wiyiyu·č* 'bush people'), whose living has traditionally been got inland but who traded at the coastal trading posts. In the journals and records of the Hudson's Bay Company and others, these people were usually referred to as Uplanders or as Inlanders ("Montagnais-Naskapi," this vol.). Another category that is often found in historical documents is the Home or

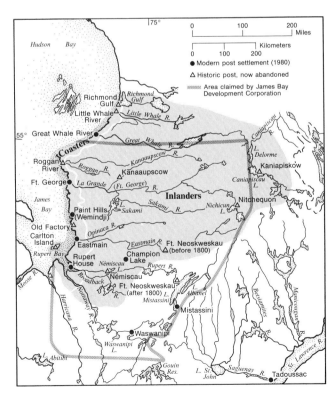

Fig. 1. East Main Cree territory.

Home Guard Indians, Indians who were in the steady employ of the Hudson's Bay Company or other White organizations. The Inlanders, Coasters, and Home Guard were quite similar in history, language, and culture (Cooper 1946); the most significant differences are those relating to subsistence adaptations and to related distinctions in attitudes, thoughts, actions, and social organizations.

The Coaster-Inlander distinction becomes more pronounced as one goes geographically northward from the bottom of James Bay, along the coastal lowland belt that narrows and then disappears as one proceeds northward along the east coast of Hudson Bay proper to the area round Richmond Gulf. The Coasters historically got their living by hunting, fishing, fowling, and gathering, with maritime efforts, especially seal hunting, similarly increasing in importance toward the more northerly area. Parallel with this directional gradient is the extent of interaction with, and sometimes displacement of, Inuit (Eskimo) and the degree to which the Hudson's Bay Company whale-oil enterprise in the second half of the 1700s engaged those Indians most accessible for employment; both of these contacts were directed north. A particularly strong Coaster distinction is noticeable at Fort George, where the Kanaaupscow band, whose members ranged over a large area, far inland, emigrated for summer residence, supplies, and services to this essentially Coaster community in 1965, when the Hudson's Bay Company closed the Kanaaupscow post. Probably due to their separate arrival, Inlanders and Coasters lived in distinct sections of the settlement. Similarly, when Némiscau (Nemiska) was closed in 1970, these Inlanders took separate residence at Rupert House and at Mistassini, where there was

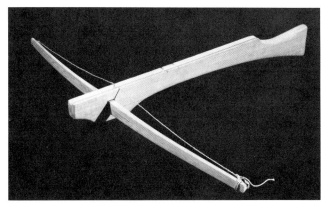

Natl. Mus. of Canada, Ottawa: III-D-419.
Fig. 2. Crossbow of cedar, with bowstave inserted through a gunstock-shaped stock. The arrow or bolt is placed in the groove on the top edge of the stock, and the bowstring is set in one of the 2 notches. This example does not have the trigger mechanism sometimes used to release the string. Crossbows were widely used by Indians of the eastern Subarctic and the Northeast, usually by boys for hunting or as toys. However, the introduction of the artifact type may be due to European influence (Burgesse 1943a). Length of stock 72.5 cm, collected at Eastmain, Que., 1973.

space for them to remain together as a group. While subsistence, especially maritime hunting differences, varies on a north-south axis, the Coaster distinction is recognized all along this axis.

The Inlanders who associated with the Coasters and with the coastal trading posts and settlements have always ranged inland for hundreds of miles. Those hunting in the more northerly areas around Lakes Kanaaupscow, Caniapiscau, and Nichicun sometimes intermarried with the Naskapi Barren-Ground hunters trading into Fort Chimo or into the posts on the Atlantic coast. While Nitchequon outpost was open, people were able to replenish their supplies of twine, gunpowder, shot, traps, and other basic tools of trapping and hunting. But for their summer trading, they traveled downriver (usually via the Eastmain River) to the coastal posts, or to Mistassini post. But the posts were not their homes; their hunting-trapping territory or ecological range was home, so that they were normally very widely scattered, and only gradually became more committed to the coastal or inland posts, which have become the eight East Cree towns (Preston 1975). Other lakes of importance to the Inlanders include Neoskweskau and Némiscau, and groups of Inlanders might identify themselves according to these hunting ranges. Indians from the areas of Lakes Mistassini and Waswanipi also traded into James Bay at times and sometimes worked on the canoe brigades, freighting the trade goods to inland posts.

Environment

The Coasters have lived for an unknown length of time in the narrow lowland (swampy or muskeg) area bordering the east side of James Bay and the adjacent southerly portion of Hudson Bay, including islands offshore, and rivers on and near the coast. The subsistence areas or "territories" involved range in depth from about 10 to 40 miles inland from the coast. Briefly, if one proceeds from offshore toward the inland area, a shallow salt sea with many coastal islands gives way to tidal flats of up to a mile; then beaches variously of sand, rock, or clay; a belt of muskeg ranging in width up to 40 miles in the south; and finally to drier, firmer ground (Robinson 1968:222–225). Species especially important to human life include caribou, seal and beluga, polar and black bear, moose, beaver, otter, lynx and hare, geese, ducks, ptarmigan, cisco, whitefish, trout, sturgeon, and pike.

Within this environment, the occupancy of territory by Coastal Cree varied with time, circumstance, and the particular individuals involved. A definition of Coaster given by John Blackned (Rupert House Cree) specifies those people who, when going out from the post to their territory, did not use a canoe. Trips inland were short and by snowshoe; people remained along the coast and river mouths during the summer months to avoid the soft and soggy muskeg and the biting insects that bred there. The Inlanders, by contrast, did use canoes (Taylor 1980) for their longer, pre–freeze-up trips to their territories and the postbreakup return to the trading posts (listed in table 1). Coasters' territories, by this definition, would probably extend inland about 40 miles.

Blackned's conception is in marked contrast to one described by Geordie Georgekish (Paint Hills Cree) as imposed by a Hudson's Bay Company manager at Old Factory, who mapped out a strip 10 miles wide along the coast, in sections about 10 miles square. Such an orderly imposition seems anomalous; it is likely that White influence on Coaster territories was usually more subtle, and boundaries much more variably defined (Cooper 1939). A major influence was to redefine "territory" into an individual, bounded piece of real estate, where the Cree had maintained a traditional notion of an ecological range of rivers and trails that were commonly recognized as the hunting locus of a group that was usually led by a particularly competent, knowledgeable man (Preston 1963–1979, 1975).

External Relations

Twentieth-century Cree regard Coasters and Inlanders as "the same" people who get their living under different circumstances. Inlanders regard the Coasters as having a less demanding life but also a poorer standard of living and quality of life (Preston 1963–1979). Smaller territories and easier access to the post also involved the Coasters in summer periods of working for the Hudson's Bay Company.

Even into the early decades of the twentieth century, the Inlanders sometimes did not bring their families down to the coast, only bringing their furs down, staying scarcely a month, and returning with their trade goods. They had no time to work for the company. "Post groups" were most often recruited from among the Coasters. They were Indians who spent substantial portions of summer and winter in working and procuring food for the company, living most of the year in the vicinity of the post, and tending to be the most closely dependent on the post's economic resources and social values.

The Coasters' relationships with Inlanders were normally peaceful and, on occasions such as feasts, cooperative and sometimes competitive. Cooperation was manifested also in occasional marriages between Coasters and Inlanders, and in cases of an individual Coaster man who decided, for practical and congenial reasons, to change his hunting and trapping area by going with a group of Inlanders, or vice versa.

Feasts and rivalries characterize seasonal occasions in Coastal-Inlander relations. The typical feast pattern

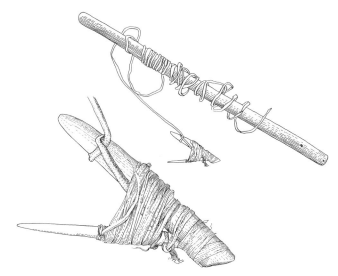

Natl. Mus. of Canada, Ottawa: III-D-312.
Fig. 3. Hook and rod for catching lake trout. Bone barb lashed with sinew to wood shaft notched at opposite end to hold leather line running to rod. Length of hook shaft about 10 cm, rod 51.3 cm, collected at Fort George, Que., 1967.

was narrated by Geordie Georgekish (Inlander) and translated by Gertie Murdoch:

> The Coasters are called wi·nipe·ku·wiyiyu·č because they stay along the coast, and the Inlanders are referred to as being "bush."
>
> The Coasters mainly get geese, and the Inlanders mainly get beaver and any wild meat. The Inlanders came back to the coast about the 24th of June. The Coasters usually go for just a short time inland, and then they come back to the coast for geese. And then in the spring, they only go for a short period in the bush.
>
> And the Inlanders, they kill caribou, and dry up the meat and save all the grease. And the Coasters kill the geese, and dry them, and also save the grease from the geese.
>
> And then they take the meat and the grease to the Coasters, usually the oldest man in the group. And then the Coasters go to the oldest Inland man, and give him the dried goose meat, and also the grease. And then they build a big wigwam. And when they are finished all the people join in the feast, with all that they got from the Inlanders, and vice versa. The old people start dancing and using their drum. And the Inlanders start singing about shooting down the rapids, and the Coasters start singing about the geese. They used to build a long tent for all of them, and then they don't use it after the feast, they take all the bark off and tear it up. When it's cold there are three fires going. The Inlanders and the Coasters shared their food at this time. And they usually do it in the spring, when all the people from inland come in for supplies (Preston 1963–1979).

The degree to which feasts were rivalries (for quantity and quality of food, dancing and songs) is not clear; one can more appropriately emphasize the cooperative side rather than the competitive aspects. Events encouraged by the Company, with games including canoe races and tug-of-war, typically set one group or individual against another, often on the Inlander-Coaster basis. These contests reflect a more general and constant sense of differences between the two, but it would distort reality to portray Inlanders and Coasters as separate cultures (Morantz 1976). Where rivalries were manifested, they were often drawn on the Inlander-Coaster basis. Yet similar rivalries were drawn on other bases. At Old Factory in the 1940s and 1950s, for instance, the people located on two islands, with the Hudson's Bay Company on one and the Oblates of Mary Immaculate mission on the other, and rivalries in games were also a way for the boys of one team to visit the girls on the other island. Again, the men of different posts might compete as canoe brigademen for speed and amount of cargo carried.

Shifting to stay with another group might occur with a marriage between an Inlander and a Coaster, or without intermarriage, simply for practical and congenial reasons. Individual Inlanders, for instance, spent some seasons on the coast, always by going with a Coaster group (for safety, guidance, good company, and no problem of trespass), then returned to their Inland territory in subsequent winters. A Coaster, similarly, would always join an Inlander group, thereby making himself a member of a food-sharing alliance and benefiting from the leader's competence in directing the hunt. Old stories also relate how individual Whites would winter under the guidance of the leader, giving their meat and furs to the group leader (Morantz 1977).

The Coasters' relationship with post Indians is both more complex and probably closer. The complexity is partly due to the different ways that the relationship was viewed. Post Indians were a part of a small but well-defined social hierarchy, with the post manager at the top and servants and post Indians at the bottom. When Coasters were given (or obliged to take) jobs laboring for the company or tasks arranged through the company, the particular Coasters involved would be temporarily at the very bottom of the hierarchy, at least from the point of view of others in the hierarchy. It is possible that these particular Coasters were, until recently, viewed by the Inlanders as virtual slaves, since the value placed on individual autonomy and responsibility for one's decisions and actions was strongly believed to be very high.

The Coasters' view of themselves, at least in the nineteenth century, probably tended to be rather less hierarchical, although some may have found prestige and security in their dependent status. Most individuals have probably always viewed their work and other ties to the Company in a practical, event-specific way. That is, they may have seen themselves as outside of the company's "society" and as independent agents (like the Inlanders) who would temporarily accede to work for the Company when the press of recruiting or the need for trade goods, or both, was great enough.

The situation is also complicated by the historic

Public. Arch. of Canada, Ottawa: C 16429.
Fig. 4. Repairing a birchbark canoe near a log cabin and 2 conical wigwams. Photograph by Bernard Rogan Ross at Rupert House, Que., 1867.

changes in the locations of trading posts. Prior to 1668, an unknown degree of contact with Indian middlemen and White traders at Tadoussac and elsewhere on the Saint Lawrence probably had little effect on the Indians exploiting the drainages of James Bay other than stimulating them to meet a demand for furs and to seek more trade goods. After 1668 the coastal posts and inland outposts opened and closed often (see table 1), and populations responded by shifting the direction of summer travel to and from the posts, thereby altering their contacts with other local Indian groups and sometimes moving more permanently to closer access to a post.

It is not clear how closely the people of the East Main were related to the people of the West Main, but it appears that intergroup ties and cultural uniformities were stronger from East Main Coasters toward Inlanders than they were to Coasters on the west side of the Bay (see "Subarctic Algonquian Languages," this vol. for dialect differences). Archival sources imply a contrast between the two coasts. With a reference to "habitual raids of the James Bay Indians on the Eskimos of the East Main," in the summer of 1736 about 50 men from the Moose and Albany area are reported to have killed 20 adults and captured 10 children (Davies and Johnson 1965:273), with no mention of the Indians of the East Main. Only two years later, in 1738, there was poor trade due to war with the "Christian Indians" (Cree to the west), and "due to the poor starving condition of the natives of the East Main" (Davies and Johnson 1965:274). From these sources, one senses an implicit separation between the East Main Indians and the Moose-Albany Indians at the south and west side of James Bay.

Relations with the Eskimo are remembered in Cree narratives (Preston 1963–1979), which trace a period (the 1700s?) of occasional but violent conflict leading to a peace parley and to continuing amicable relationships. On the basis of material culture, Rogers (1964)

Table 1. Chronology of Trading Posts and Outposts

Precontact—1670s—Early fur trade—1763—Fur company rivalry—1821—Classic fur trade—1930—Commercialism

Coaster Posts

Richmond Gulf	1749–1756				1923–	
Little Whale River		1756–1759	1793–1794	1820?–	1851–1890	
Great Whale River		1756–1780		1813–1822	1857–	
Roggan River					dates uncertain; closed about 1940	
Fort George				1803–1813, 1816–1824, 1837–		
Paint Hills						1959–
Old Factory						1938–1959
Eastmain[a]	sloop 1698–1740[b]		post 1722–1837		since 1870 as outpost or post	
Charlton Island		1680–1686, 1713?–early 1800s? later dates uncertain, closed about 1930				
Rupert House	"Charles Fort" 1668 "Fort Charles" 1670–1693		Rupert's House 1776–			

Inlander Posts

Kaniapiskow				1836–1844		
Nitchequon	1725?–			1816–1822, 1834—1910?		
Neoskweskau				1793–1822	1925?–	
Némiscau	1695–1713?		1794–1799		1923?–1970	1977–
Kanaaupscow			1802–1809		1921–1965	

SOURCES: Davies 1963; Voorhis 1930; Preston 1963–1979.

[a] East Main (Slude) River was Albany's first permanent subordinate post (Davies 1963:xli). In the 1670s a small post building was constructed.

[b] The Albany sloop wintered at Eastmain (or Old Factory) for safety from the ice of the Albany River during spring breakup.

finds little cultural exchange between the two, and close contacts seem to have amounted to individual friendships and rather rare intermarriage.

Finally, relations with the *na·tawe·wiyiyu·č*, presumed to be Iroquois raiding parties (in the 1600s and 1700s), were fearful, bloody, and remembered in many vivid narrative accounts (Preston 1963–1979). Perhaps related are Cree narratives regarding the *pwa·t* or Bod (probably variant representations of the same word) Indians, where threat is common and violence is occasional; the term refers to dangerous and strange (but probably Subarctic) Indians. Like other northern Algonquians, the East Main Cree regarded the mythic Windigo cannibals as the most fearsome and damaging of all peoples (Preston 1980a).

History of the Coasters

Indian adaptations to the influences of the Hudson's Bay Company included, according to the writings of the 1700s and 1800s, Home or Home Guard individuals who spent some substantial part of their time hunting for or otherwise serving the needs of the company personnel. Also mentioned, apparently in contrast to the Home Indians, are the Uplanders. Later common parlance refers to a different contrast, of Inlanders and Coasters. The referent of Inlanders is probably quite close to the older Uplanders. Much more problematic is the relationship between the Coasters and the Home Indians of the earlier records.

There are two alternatives to explain the existence of Coasters. One is that the Coasters are an artifact of the fur trade, drawn into the coastal areas by dependency on the trading posts or by being squeezed out of inland trapping territories by competition or accident. The other alternative is that the ancestors of the Coast-

Public Arch. of Canada, Ottawa: Geological Survey of Canada Coll., PA 38008.
Fig. 5. Group at Fort George, Que., in front of their hide-covered conical wigwam with a birchbark crooked canoe. Photograph by A.P. Low, 1888.

ers aboriginally were regularly exploiting the coastal zone, at least seasonally. Unfortunately there is not sufficient evidence for or against either hypothesis.

It is with the accounts of the few explorers and traders of the seventeenth century that the first direct evidence of Indians on the coast appears. In 1611, toward the end of Henry Hudson's wintering at the southeast corner (Rupert Bay) of James Bay, a lone Indian appeared to barter a few skins for trinkets (Asher 1860:114–115). When Médard Chouart des Groseilliers and Capt. Zachariah Gillam brought the next ship to winter in the same area in 1668, at the present site of Rupert House, Indians came out to meet them. Gorst's (1943) journal for the period 1670–1675 refers also to an expedition south and west, contacting other (Coaster?) Indians at the Moose River. Therefore, Indians were definitely in the coastal area at the bottom of the bay at this time. Except for the Gorst extract, Hudson's Bay records from 1668 to 1700 are apparently not found (Davies and Johnson 1963:x). The 1700s and 1800s are better documented, and frequent mention of the Home, or Home Guard, Indians seems to refer to those who stayed in the lowlands area at or near the coast, acting as hunters, canoe brigademen, or casual laborers for the English and French traders. It is likely that these were mostly drawn from the Coasters, and that those who became particularly dependent upon the Whites became what are now called "post Indians."

The reconstructed traditional (1500?–1821) yearly cycle of activities for Coasters consisted of hunting, trapping, fishing, and fowling along the lowlands of James Bay, with periods of labor for the fur company during the summer. Killing food was done, prior to the gradual adoption of trade goods, with snares, deadfalls, bow and arrow (and perhaps the crossbow), spear, bird bola, and fishnets of roots or babiche. While the technology was simple in design, it was sophisticated in application. For instance, a rabbit might gnaw through a babiche snare, but when the babiche was rubbed with lynx dung, the rabbit would not attempt to gnaw it.

Snaring was used even for caribou, using braided strips of caribou hide. Geese were killed with bow and arrow, and perhaps with a bola or crossbow, which were all replaced with muskets as these were obtained in trade. Geese were dried, and some were bought by the Hudson's Bay Company to be salted in barrels. Other kinds of meat and fish were preserved by drying; the extent of drying depended on how long the meat was to be kept. Dried fish was pounded into a kind of flour and sometimes mixed with cooked berries. Bear grease, a particular delicacy, was kept in a caribou stomach or a special birchbark container; it did not congeal even in cold weather.

The size and activity of groups varied during the seasons as different food animals were sought and as the food availability waxed and waned. Periods of severe starvation were not uncommon and put pressure on groups to split up, even though the ideal was to remain together, since the chances were that at least one of the several men would manage to kill food, and then everyone would have a chance to eat something. Going on one's own was a risk sometimes taken on the possibility that one's particular direction of travel would be more fortunate than that taken by the others. Respect for the food animals was shown in the care taken to place the bones of animals in the trees, in songs sung to the animals (either in anticipation of the hunt or in thanks for a past success), and in the care to keep men's hunting from contact with the contamination of menstruation.

Epidemic illnesses allowed little means for their alleviation; perhaps this is why they are little mentioned in the Cree oral tradition, although large proportions of the population died from these diseases.

Although posts were often built at sites Crees had used for their own gatherings, periods spent in the vicinity of the Hudson's Bay Company posts were brief, and Skinner (1912) reports only a two-week summer residence in 1908. Labor periods varied with the amount of work required. The Inland Indians did not stay out of the bush long enough to work at the posts or on the

left, Public Arch. of Canada, Ottawa: PA 44225; right, Royal Ontario Mus., Toronto: 79 ETH 92.
Fig. 6. Dome-shaped lodges. left, Willow framework at Rupert House, Que., photographed in 1929; right, occupied lodge with canvas covering and stove pipe at Némiscau, Que., photograph by Edward S. Rogers, summer 1964.

canoe brigades that supplied the inland outposts, and so the Coasters worked on the brigades until well into the 1930s. Besides the canoe brigades, hay gathering for cattle (ranging widely for wild-growing grasses) and log cutting for firewood and for whipsawing into boards were major jobs in the 1800s.

Missionaries were little in evidence until the Anglican Rev. E.A. Watkins was stationed at Fort George in 1852. The Manitou concept (Cooper 1934), intended by missionaries to refer to the Christian God, was taken by the East Main Cree as an additional spirit person (in the existing world of spirit persons), whose power, while somewhat greater than that of other spirits, was personal and finite and served as protection against sorcery, perhaps as a master of spirits in a way similar to the notions of masters of species. Native catechists were sometimes also conjurors, although some other catechists were strongly opposed to aboriginal belief in spirits. Perhaps they were more opposed to the conjuror's personal spirit ally *mista·pe·w* 'great man' (sometimes *ačahkw* 'soul') than to songs and beliefs relating to food animals (Preston 1975b). Probably the most profound missionary effects were exercised by Rev. W.G. Walton, stationed at Fort George from 1892 to 1924; memories of him and of his admonitions were strong at least through the 1960s.

The Oblate missions began at Fort George, where during the early 1920s they developed a substantial medical, educational, and maintenance facility as well as the mission church. In the 1940s missions were built in the other towns on the East Main, but they have had very few converts and rather limited religious importance. Evangelical missions began in the late 1950s on a more modest scale with similarly limited effects. Pentecostalism in the early 1970s regularly drew over 100 to services at Rupert House, although it was unsuccessful elsewhere on the coast (Preston 1975a).

Traditional ideology for the Coasters varied from that of the Inlanders mostly in the emphasis put on particular food animals. Geese, for instance, were shown respect by hanging their bones in a tree in order to assist in future hunting attempts, and a special *ni·ma·pa·n* (ceremonial cord) was worn by the man most capable at shooting geese (fig. 7). The wearing of the cord required the man to catch in his hands each goose that he shot (at close range with bow and arrow) before it hit the ground. If a goose should hit the ground, the person could no longer wear the ceremonial cord (Preston 1978). The master of fish, *misina·kw*, was also of special though not exclusive importance to the Coasters and was often called into the conjuring tent to be asked for future success in fishing. The persistence of beliefs and ritual practices into the 1960s and early 1970s was quite strong, probably an expression of the continuing importance of "bush" life for the East Main Cree (Preston 1975b).

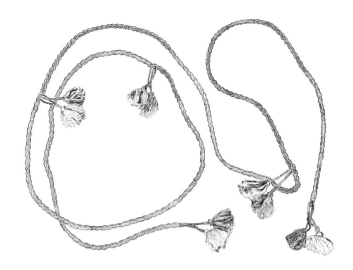

Natl. Mus. of Canada, Ottawa: III-D-245.

Fig. 7. Ceremonial carrying strap, *ni·ma·pa·n*, of plaited caribou hide dyed red with wool tassels hung from strands of seed beads. The decorations show respect for the game killed and may be symbolic. This example was used for geese, but similar cords were also used by hunters to drag bear, beaver, and other animals back to camp (Speck and Heye 1921; Speck 1935:210–220; Tanner 1979:142–143). Length about 260 cm, collected by R.J. Preston, Rupert House, Que., 1963–1965.

Sociocultural Situation in the 1960s and 1970s

The historic image of the Hudson Bay settlement, a trading post and mission located at a river mouth for accessibility to shipping from Europe and canoes from and to the inland areas, was transformed by the 1960s into that of a small multiethnic town that is primarily defined by the Indian band that is based there. Besides Great Whale River, the towns were Fort George, Wemindji (Paint Hills) (Canadian Broadcasting Corporation 1976), Eastmain, Némiscau, and Rupert House (table 2), the populations of which were about 90 percent Indian people. About 10 percent were Euro-Canadians whose purpose for residence was commercial, religious, medical, educative, or administrative, usually as responsible local officials in a bureaucratic chain. Band government gradually shifted from the informal leadership, based on example and respected suggestion of the older persons, to the elected chief and councilors (one councilor per 100 band members) and the appointed band manager. While these formal roles partly displaced the older Indian leadership, they also partly displaced the Euro-Canadian (most notably the Indian agent's) influence (Preston 1969–1972, 1974).

Occupations also shifted towards more formally differentiated, wage-oriented alternatives to full-time hunting and trapping. Besides the paid band manager, individuals might be more or less permanently employed by outside commercial interests (airline, oil distributor, Hudson's Bay Company) or within the more

Table 2. Band Population by Post, 1949–1970

Post	1949	1954	1970
Eastmain	180	175	257
Fort George	684	784	1,233
Kanaaupscow (inland)	probably included	included	closed
Great Whale River	181	182	306
Old Factory/Paint Hills	266	319	527
Rupert House	416	535	829
Némiscau (inland)	113	118	173
Totals	1,840	2,113	3,325

SOURCES: Leechman 1953: Laviolette 1955; Canada. Department of Indian Affairs and Northern Development. Indian Affairs Branch 1970.

NOTE: Coasters and Inlanders trading into these posts are combined.

community-based educational or service occupations. Temporary occupations included construction work on community projects, work with the James Bay hydroelectric project in the 1970s, and a variety of casual labor jobs in or near the towns. There was relatively little work migration, either seasonal or more permanent. The relative importance—economic as well as psychological—of getting a living in the bush remained strong in the 1970s.

Religious participation ranged from a stable and vigorous blend of traditional Cree and Anglican (at Wemindji) to a more complex and variable differentiation of Cree-Anglican, Pentecostal, Evangelical, and Roman Catholic (at Rupert House). Relative to Canada as a whole, a large proportion of the Indians were deeply religious. Significantly, it is in the matter of religion and ethics that Inlanders were most expressive of a difference between themselves and Coasters. Inlanders believed that traditionally held respect for animals and the symbolic disposition of their remains were less felt and less manifested by Coasters. Similarly, the qualities of family bonds, gentleness, self-esteem, and self-control (Preston 1976, 1979) were thought to be more pronounced in Inlander families, and their children did well when they went out to school. Because they had a poorer and harder life, the Coasters were characterized by one informant as lacking the closeness of kin bonds and inner strength, relying more on physical abilities than spiritual or social strength. As a result, arguing, trespassing, and even fistfights would occur over territories, children might start slingshot wars, and some other rivalries might stem from this contrast. Also, the network of relationships that was extended by marriage made Coaster-Inlander unions less desirable and less common, particularly at Fort George. These distinctions were held with quite variable degrees of conviction and were less manifest at Eastmain and Rupert House than at Fort George and Wemindji. Perhaps most important, these distinctions seemed to be

diminishing, and the integration of Coasters and Inlanders increasing.

Formal education was a rapidly developing factor. During the 1960s a considerable amount of money and planning was put into shifting the locus of schooling from residential schools to day schools in the home community. The schools' curriculum and administration became increasingly integrated into the community (Preston 1979a) and came under band influence, and in 1975 the Rupert House school committee was for the first time elected by the band. The Coaster-Inlander distinction did not appear to be relevant there at all.

In summary, the 1960s and 1970s showed a trend toward greater responsibility for leadership on the part of band councils, until the whole process of self-government was made critically important by the advent and rapid development of the James Bay hydroelectric project during the 1970s. The hydroelectric project began in 1971, centered on the northerly drainage and diversion into the Fort George (La Grande) River; the southern stage began in 1979, combining the drainages of the Nottaway, Broadback, and Rupert rivers. It involved the relocation of the town sites of Fort George, Waswanipi, Némiscau, and perhaps Rupert House. The Cree response was a resistance effort made through legal and political negotiation, leading to the formation of the Grand Council of the Crees (of Quebec) and of a new political unity among the eight bands (six bands of East Main plus Mistassini and Waswanipi). Negotiations resulted in the James Bay and Northern Quebec Agreement among the Grand Council of the Crees, the Northern Quebec Inuit Association, the province of Quebec, and the government of Canada, which was ratified in 1975 and subsequently incorporated into a series of provincial and federal acts of legislation (Quebec (Province) 1976). However, the native people have experienced difficulties vis-à-vis the Quebec government in implementing their rights (Anonymous 1980).

The consequences included the Cree Villages Act, the formation of the Cree Regional Authority, the Cree School Board, and similar arrangements for health, housing, communications, economic development, and other aspects of self-government. While the agreement was criticized as a sell-out of land rights, or as just another treaty, these criticisms miss the importance to the Crees' future of a large capital fund and continuing major obligations of provincial and federal governments, plus a carefully planned local and regional self-government. These factors have brought about radical and remarkably conflict-free changes in the political, economic, and social organization of the Cree region. Mindful of the problems and discontent that plagued the "from-the-top, down" government of the Department of Indian Affairs (and many other Native and non-Native organizations), the Cree bureaucracy has deliberately emphasized a "ground level, up" orga- 203

Natl. Film Board of Canada, Ottawa: top left, 68–12421; top right, 68–12374; center left, 68–12453; bottom left, 68–12398; bottom right, 68–12394.

Fig. 8. Activities at Rupert House, Que. in the late 1960s. top left, Filling empty oil cans with water from Rupert River; top right, water from the river, heated at open fire, used in washing machine; center left, hanging wash to dry with modern houses in background; bottom left, cutting firewood while girl swings; bottom right, men playing a form of checkers using black and white pebbles on painted gaming board. Photographs by Terry Pearce, June 1968.

nization to maintain effective representation for the whole constituency. This was shown in their assistance to the Nemaska band, who had lived for seven years in enclaves at Rupert House and at Mistassini. In 1977 the Cree Grand Council made possible the gathering of the people of the Nemaska band, with resource persons, at the Champion Lake site, and the week of planning resulted in the decision of the band to remain there and build their town where the hydroelectric project flooding would not reach them.

Synonymy†

The term East Main has been used by the Hudson's Bay Company since the seventeenth century to distinguish the east coast of James and Hudson bays from the other coast (the West Main) and inland parts of their possessions. By 1716 the inhabitants of the area were being referred to as East Main Indians (Davies and Johnson 1965:55). In the eighteenth and early nineteenth centuries those north of the Eastmain River were usually called Northward Indians (Davies and Johnson 1965:72, 1963:265, 333), or occasionally Northern Indians (Coats 1852:61, 64, 88); those to the south were sometimes distinguished as Southward Indians (Davies and Johnson 1965:124, 303). Skinner (1912) coined the term Eastern Cree to refer to the bands on both sides of the bays, but it is sometimes limited to the Montagnais-speaking group discussed in this chapter (Preston 1975d; MacKenzie 1979). James Bay Cree (as in Feit et al. 1972) and East Main Cree are other terms employed in the twentieth century to designate, without differentiation, all Algonquian Indians in the northwestern quarter of Quebec.

In the seventeenth and eighteenth centuries three partially similar names were used for groups living in what is now East Main Cree territory. One of the four Cree bands listed in 1658 was the Kilistinons Nisibourounik (JR 44:248); Creuxius gave the garbled version Kilistones Nisibouʀ8nici in 1660 (JR 46:map). Gorst (in Tyrrell 1931:390) in 1670-1671 mentioned a tribe "near akin to the Eskeimoes" called Pishhapocanoes. This later appeared in the forms Oupeshepow, 1775 (Graham in Isham 1949:315); Oupeeshepow and Oupeshepou, 1791 (Graham 1969:204, 207); and Upe-shipow (Richardson 1852:265). The link between these two terms is provided by a third from 1660, Pitchib8renik (JR 45:228), also spelled Pitchiboutounibueʀ, 1672 (JR 56:202), Pitchibourouni, 1703 (J.K. Fraser 1968:244), Pitchiboueouni, 1779 (Hodge 1907–1910, 2:264), Pitchiboucouni, 1784 (ibid.). The last three are given as the name of a river, possibly the Eastmain but more likely the Roggan River farther north, which in 1828 was called Pishop Roggan (Hendry in Davies and John-

†This synonymy was written by David H. Pentland.

son 1963:78). The river name is from Attikamek Cree pi·hčipora·kan or Old Montagnais pi·hčipura·kan 'fish weir' (from Faries 1938:413 and Fabvre 1970:311); related forms meaning 'one who uses a weir' may underlie the group names.

Coaster is a well-established local term (Shearwood 1943:200) corresponding to the self-designation wi·nipe·ku·wiyiyu 'salt-water person' (Marguerite MacKenzie, personal communication 1979). Cognate forms are used to refer to the East Main Cree by other Montagnais-speaking groups: Eastern Montagnais (n-dialect) wi·nipe·ku·winnu (Mailhot and Lescop 1977:385) and Southern Montagnais (l-dialect) wi·nipe·kwilnu (after Speck 1931:580). A Cree form wi·nipe·ko·wak (pl.) is probably reflected in the spellings Wine pesk ko wuck, 1775 (Graham in Isham 1949:317), Uinnipiskowuck, 1791 (Graham 1969:207), and Winne-peskowuk (Richardson 1852:265), but the medial s is an unexplained problem. Albanel's reference in 1662 to the gens de la mer (JR 56:202) is a French translation of the Montagnais name.

The name Inlander is also established in local usage (Shearwood 1943:201). It is equivalent to the East Cree self-designation nu·hčimi·wiyiyu 'inland person' (Marguerite MacKenzie, personal communication 1979). The variant nu·hčimi·w 'inlander' (Speck 1931:594, respelled) was given as a self-designation of the old Ungava band, with nu·hčimi·wilnu as the Southern Montagnais equivalent; in Eastern Montagnais nu·čimi·winnu refers to any inland Indian (Mailhot and Lescop 1977:198).

At the end of the nineteenth century Newnham distinguished a part of the Inlanders with the name Voyageurs, those who annually went from Nitchequon and Waswanipi to the coast (Shearwood 1943:201). Low (1929:46) called the people of Nitchequon the Western Nascaupee.

Bands

Fort George, Great Whale River. The self-designation čiše·-si·pi·wiyiyu 'great river person' was given by Speck (1931:593, respelled) as the name of both the Fort George and Great Whale River bands. Eastern Montagnais has čiše·-ši·pi·winnu for Fort George (Rivière La Grande) and wa·pame·kustiku·winnu 'beluga river person' for Great Whale River (Mailhot and Lescop 1977:342, 360); according to Speck (1931:593) the last name referred to the White Whale River band, who hunted north of the Little Whale River.

Kaniapiscow. Speck (1931:590) gives Kani·ápəckau wi·′nut‘, presumably ka·-ne·ya·piska·winnut (pl.) 'rocky point people', an Eastern dialect form. The name of the lake on which they lived is spelled Caniapiscau.

Nichikun. Their own name is ničikwani·wiyiyu 'otter hunting person?' (from Speck 1931:591), the same as

Fig. 9. Sod house used in winter, built about 1973 at Opinaca Lake, Que., probably by Charlie Mayapoo of Eastmain. top, View from the southwest with firewood stacked under porch, ladder laid against left side of house so repairs can be made without stepping on sod covering. bottom left, Front door seen from the covered porch, which is not attached to the house. bottom right, Interior, with poles for drying rack set at head height, ax-split wall siding, flooring of evergreen boughs. The house, with floor diameters 25 and 20 feet, was heated by 2 stoves. Photographs by G. Heberton Evans III, 1975.

Eastern Montagnais *ničikuni·winnu* (Mailhot and Lescop 1977:192). Canadian maps give Nitchequon outpost on Nichicun Lake.

Rupert House. For the Rupert House band Speck (1931:592, respelled) has *wi·nipe·ku·wiyiyu* 'Coaster' and *wi·nipe·ku-wa·skahikanis iyiyu* 'salt-water house person'.

Sources

Of the historical sources on the East Main Cree, the most useful are the early report of Gorst (1943) of which only an extract from the journal has yet been found, the early history of the area by Oldmixon (1741), and a volume drawn from materials in the Hudson's Bay

Company archives for the period of the early 1800s (Davies and Johnson 1963).

Anthropological sources include Skinner's (1912) detailed monograph that uses data from Rupert House and Eastmain. Cooper's work includes significant debate on religion (1934), land tenure (1939), and culture history (1946). Flannery, a student of Cooper's, did work on women's roles (1935), cross-cousin marriage (1938), infancy and childhood (1962), and religion (1939a, 1971). Preston (1963–1979) has concentrated especially on the topics of world view (1975b, 1980a) and education (1974, 1975a, 1979a).

Rupert House as a community was studied in the late 1940s by A.J. Kerr (1950) and in the 1960s by R. Knight (1968) and Preston (1969–1972). Work has been done at Fort George (Désy 1968) and Great Whale River ("Great Whale River, Quebec," this vol.). Bibliographies have been published (Feit et al. 1972; Feit 1976).

Attikamek (Tête de Boule)

GÉRARD E. MCNULTY AND LOUIS GILBERT

The group of Cree-speaking* Indians who inhabit the Upper Saint-Maurice River region in the province of Quebec have generally been referred to in the ethnographic literature as Tête de Boule (Mooney 1910; Cooper 1926; Michelson 1933). In the 1970s these people preferred the name *atihkame·k^w* or Attikamek. The term *atihkame·k^w* recalls the bands of nomadic Indians designated Attikamègues in the *Jesuit Relations* and other documents of the era, who roamed the Upper Saint-Maurice River area during the seventeenth century. According to one historical viewpoint, these Attikamègues mysteriously disappeared between the years 1670 and 1680 (Mooney 1907; Clermont 1977). Another view holds that the present-day Tête de Boule–Attikamek of Manouane, Weymontachingue, and Obedjiwan—give or take some intermingling with surrounding bands (JR 56:154–156)—are the direct descendants of the seventeenth-century Attikamègues (Sulte 1911; Joyal 1915; and missionary tradition in general).

During the entire period of documented history, and no doubt earlier, the Attikamègue–Tête de Boule have occupied a country rich in beavers (fig. 1), which provided a primary resource both for use and for trade. In the early period, beaver pelts were exchanged with the Huron and then the French. The techniques for locating beaver show remarkable continuity from the earliest period to the present, although the killing methods have shifted with the introduction of new weapons, traps, and tools (Clermont 1974).

Attikamègues in the Contact Period

Europeans began to record information about the upper watershed of the Saint-Maurice River in the 1630s. At that time, the term Attikamègue was borrowed by the French from their Algonquin neighbors to designate the 550 or so Indians occupying the region, who were recognized as linguistically and culturally similar to, but distinct from, the adjacent Crees, Montagnais, and Algonquins.

The Attikamègue seem to have been united by ties of marriage and visiting, and in reaction to Iroquois raids from the south, but they were not politically unified. There were, apparently, three constituent bands, wintering at locations about 25 leagues apart, each with its own territorial range and with distinct trading relations with the French and, soon, differential acculturative influences from them. Each band was composed of several family groups, some polygynous, and had several leaders, one of whom in each band evidently had more authority than the rest.

The aboriginal economy was based on hunting and fishing. The large game of the region were beaver, caribou, moose, and bear. The fish depended on were probably those now most important in the region: northern pike, walleyed pike, gray trout, speckled trout, and whitefish. Summer was largely a fishing season, while the population divided into smaller groups for winter hunting; in bad winters starvation was common. At least by early historic times maize, maize flour, dried fish, and probably tobacco were obtained by trade from the Huron, in exchange for furs (Sulte 1911:123). A traditional intertribal trading center—a "fair"—was reported to be located at Necouba Lake. Intense fur trading with the French began in the late 1630s, with Attikamègue expeditions once or twice a year to Trois-Rivières, or sometimes to Tadoussac or Sillery (JR 16:72, 18:112, 24:66, 26:100, 27:276, 31:208, 36:228, 44:200). Algonquin and French traders also went to the Attikamègue country (JR 38:48–50, 43:50).

The Attikamègue were reputed to be essentially peaceful. Only with the Iroquois, beginning at least by 1636, were hostilities constant. Iroquois raids in 1651 and 1652 even appear to have disrupted the fur trade until 1657 (JR 36:147, 37:69, 73, 38:48–50). The Iroquois attacks coupled with smallpox epidemics were responsible for a marked decline of the Attikamègue population. An epidemic in 1669–1670 was especially severe, and by the 1670s they were on the brink of extinction.

Late Seventeenth Century

The dwindling remnants of the Attikamègue were scattered from Mistassini and beyond to Tadoussac (JR 56:156, 37:203), thereby leaving empty the Upper Saint-Maurice region, which they had exploited as far back

---

* The Attikamek (Tête de Boule) dialect of Cree has the following phonemes: *p, t, č, k, k^w; s, š, h; m, n, r; w, y; i, a, o; i·, e·, a·, o·.* Transcriptions of Attikamek words are from Béland (1978).

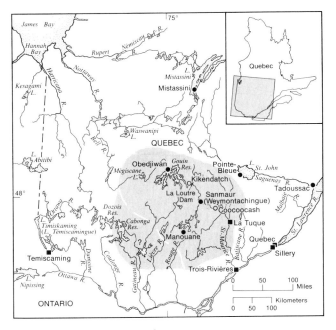

Fig. 1. Eighteenth-century territory.

as historical records go. The last reference to this tribe as such appears in the parish registers of Trois-Rivières in 1698 (Clermont 1977:18).

The decimation and dispersal of these Attikamègues left their vast fur-rich zone open to neighboring bands who might wish to expand their own hunting grounds or exchange their native territories for more promising ones. Following R.G. Thwaites's comment on a 1684 letter of Daniel Greysolon Dulhut (WHC 16:114), supported by other historical references, Clermont (1977:19–20) concluded that a group of Indians living between Lake Superior and Hudson Bay called the Gens des Terres migrated eastward to fill the territory left vacant by the disappearance of the Attikamègue. These Gens des Terres came to be known as Tête de Boule. The Trois-Rivières parish registers mention both the Tête de Boule and the Attikamègue in the last decade of the seventeenth century, thereby indicating that they were perhaps looked upon as being two distinct peoples (Clermont 1977:18), and other sources make the same distinction (Raudot 1904:98, translated in Kinietz 1940:366).

On the other hand, the records of the ranges of the Attikamègue and the Gens des Terres in the seventeenth century tend to imply the lack of a sharp distinction between them. "The Iroquois penetrated into the country of the Attikamegues, as far as the lake called Kisakami," located "about twenty days across the snow" from Trois-Rivières (JR 37:69). This 1651 statement by the missionary Father Jacques Buteux indicates that the Attikamègue range was not limited to the Upper Saint-Maurice River watershed area but was an immense territory that extended northwestward in the James Bay drainage at least as far as Lake Kesagami

just south of present-day Hannah Bay.† In other records of this era, the Attikamègue are said to have come from the "fond des terres," meaning far inland (JR 29:108, 20:270–272, 21:116).

The *Jesuit Relation* of 1670 (JR 55:98) describes the Gens des Terres or Gens de la Mer du Nord as the Indian groups in the general area north of Lake Superior.‡ In 1684 the Gens des Terres (referred to as Opemens d'Acheliny) were one of a number of named groups west of James Bay that were said to be shifting their trade from the English on Hudson Bay to the French at the Nipigon River (WHC 16:114; Margry 1876–1886, 6:51). Barbezieux (in Dunn 1975:129) comments that before the advent of the French, "les Têtes de Boules et les sauvages du Nord" met the Hurons for trade at the mouths of the Dumoine, Gatineau, and Lièvre rivers, which debouch into the Ottawa. However, a record dating to 1736 (Maray de La Chauvignerie 1928:541; NYCD 9:1052) indicates that the term Tête de Boule had a broad rather than particular connotation: "The Têtes de Boule or Tribes of the Interior (*gens des terres*). These are wandering Savages who have no knowledge either of the order or form of villages. . .; they inhabit the mountains and lakes in the interior, from Three Rivers to Lake Superior." In 1753 Franquet (1889:23–24) summed up the hinterland situation: "Apart from the Algonquin Indians there are also Tête de Boule and Montagnais. The former are so named because of their round heads. They have no villages, are quite numerous, and generally inhabit the area between the north shore of the [St. Lawrence] river and Labrador. . . . The latter, called Montagnais, are likewise nomadic having no fixed abode and occupy the area between the [St. Lawrence] river and Hudson's Bay. These Indians and the Tête de Boule as well are usually referred to as Gens de Terre." Franquet's geographical placement of the Tête de Boule vis-à-vis the Montagnais is disconcerting, for it reverses their relative locations, which are well documented in the literature. But the importance of Franquet's statement for the present problem is that it indicates that the term Gens de(s) Terre(s) was a popular all-embracing expression that referred to all those wandering Algonquian bands,

† A band of *r*-dialect Cree Indians still inhabited Lake Kesagami in the late 1880s. The survivors of this small group moved to Moose Factory where Cooper (1945) interviewed them in 1927 and gathered some scanty linguistic and ethnographic material. Between these westernmost *r*-dialect speakers and the main body of the 18th- and 19th-century Tête de Boule–Attikamègues in Upper Maurice was the Indian group at Megiskan, a summer meeting place and trading post situated between present-day Senneterre and the Indian settlement of Obedjiwan. The Megiskan group joined the Obedjiwan band after the withdrawal of the Hudson's Bay Company post from Megiskan around 1890.

‡ These roving bands have left their mark on the modern map of Quebec—the Gens de Terre River, which empties into the Baskatong Reservoir just north of Mont-Laurier, Que., the headwaters of the Gatineau River (Dunn 1975:111).

209

Mus. of the Amer. Ind., Heye Foundation, New York: a, 14/2068; b, 14/7845; Smithsonian, Dept. of Anthr.: c, 395.375; d, 395.376.

Fig. 2. Rectangular birchbark containers with lids. a, A common type was undecorated except for dyed spruce-root lid design and rim lashing. To decorate containers patterns (later saved and reused) were cut from birchbark and traced onto the outer surface, which was then moistened so that a sharp tool could be used to remove the dark outer layer from around the designs. b, The lid and each side of the container were treated as separate design areas with different patterns on each. The inside of the container shows the rough outer surface of the birchbark. c, Ducks were a favorite design element but d, geometric designs were also used (see D.S. Davidson 1928e). Height of a 28 cm, rest same scale. a and b collected by D.S. Davidson, Weymontachingue band, 1925–1926; c and d collected by John M. Cooper, Obedjiwan band, 1925.

including groups known as Tête de Boule, who exploited the territories adjacent to the headwaters of the Gatineau, Lièvre, Dumoine, and Saint-Maurice rivers, and areas beyond.

The foregoing accounts lead to the following interpretation. Peoples known in the seventeenth century as the Tête de Boule and the Attikamègue exploited the area between James Bay and the Saint Lawrence River, including the Lake Kesagami region. Those known to Europeans as Tête de Boule descended the rivers south to trade at Sault Sainte Marie and at the mouths of the Dumoine, Gatineau, and Lièvre rivers, whereas the Attikamègue's contacts were farther to the east and southeast at Lake Saint John and Trois-Ri-

vières. But they were essentially the same linguistic and cultural group known and reported under different names according to their points of trade. The term Gens des Terres encompassed these two groups and many others and seems to have had much more a broad geographical significance for the writers of that period than a specific tribal or linguistic reference.

It is significant that coincident with the closing of most French forts and trading posts in the Upper Great Lakes region at the end of the seventeenth century the Tête de Boule as such appeared at Trois-Rivières. With the closing of their long-established bartering and fur-trading outlets, the Tête de Boule simply moved across a region that was traditionally theirs to follow the east-

Fig. 3. Gill net construction and tools. Marie Louise Tshatsha making a net of commercial twine; inset, her tools. Twine is held on the wooden netting needle as knotting progresses and the wooden mesh gauge is used to keep mesh size consistent. Length of needle 23.5 cm. Collected and photographed by John M. Cooper, Obedjiwan, Que., June 1925.

erly trade routes of their linguistic brothers, who until then had been known in those parts as Attikamègue but who had recently suffered great losses at the hands of the Iroquois and from the scourge of smallpox. D.S. Davidson (1928d:18, normalized) affirms that in the 1920s the Tête de Boule called themselves Chekamek-iriniwak, so recalling the historical Attikamègue. He also notes that Frank G. Speck, while questioning the Lake Saint John Montagnais, discovered that they referred to the Tête de Boule of the early twentieth century as Sagami Indians. Another name for this same group furnished Speck by a Tête de Boule resident at Pointe Bleue was Ogishakamiiu 'person from Lake Kesagami'. The last two designations refer to Lake Kesagami, which was said to be within Attikamègue territory in the 1650s.

Tête de Boule Period

1680–1820

An account from 1692 refers to "Algonquins à têtes-de-Boule" arriving at Montreal to trade their furs (NYCD 9:535). Henry (1901:62, 208) referred to the Gens des Terres of the 1760s, "also called *Tetes de Boule*," as O'pimittish Ininiwac 'men of the woods', using an Ojibwa name for them and making clear the equivalence of Gens des Terres and Tête de Boule at least in some usages. In fact, some accounts imply a broad application of the name as though Tête de Boule were an inclusive term embracing many bands of roving Algonquian-speaking Indians canoeing the inland waterways from Trois-Rivières to Lake Superior. Franquet's (1889) broad usage and (apparently confused) placement has already been noted. Maray de La Chauvignerie (NYCD 9:1052–1053) reported in 1736 that the Tête de Boule were situated between Trois-Rivières and Lake Superior and numbered some 600 warriors; they traded at Trois-Rivières, Lake Timiskaming (Témiscamingue), and the Nipigon River. Raudot (1904:99) mentioned them in 1709, giving Machatantibis as a synonym, without locating them geographically. In 1757–1758 the "Têtes-de-Boule, ou Gens de Terre" were trading at Fort Timiscamingue (Bougainville 1964:212).

Historical documentation on the Tête de Boule over this 140-year period is so scanty that one can hardly say anything certain about them except that they hunted, trapped, traded, and moved about between the Upper Great Lakes and Trois-Rivières. Their family and larger social organization, religion, and linguistic traits are undocumented for this period.

Modern Tête de Boule–Attikameks descend from the seventeenth-century Attikamègue, from the seventeenth- and eighteenth-century Tête de Boule, and probably from Ojibwa groups located farther west in the eighteenth century (Clermont 1977:17–24). In addition, modern genealogies show links with the eastern Montagnais, the northern Waswanipi Cree, the Algonquins of Rapid Lake, and the Mistassini Cree.

1821–1913

The nineteenth-century culture and history of the Weymontachingue band is relatively well documented (Clermont 1977), and the following materials refer particularly to them. The other two bands may have differed in some respects. The Manouane band differentiated from the Weymontachingue band beginning in the 1860s, while the Obedjiwan band, always considered somewhat distinct from the Weymontachingue band, has undergone a series of displacements since the end of the eighteenth century (Norman Clermont, communication to editors 1979).

When the North West Company took over most of the fur trade in the formerly French-controlled Indian territories in 1774, it set up a network of trading posts. One of these nerve centers was built on the Upper Saint-Maurice River in the same year, thus drawing the Indians away from urban Trois-Rivières on the Saint Lawrence and insuring a monopoly that, in 1821, was passed along to the Hudson's Bay Company when it merged with its rival.

Clermont (1977:31) estimates that roughly 150 Indians or from 22 to 25 families traded at the Weymontachingue post between 1820 and 1830. This sparse population explains why the Hudson's Bay Company profits were so low in the years 1824 and 1826. These Indians roamed the Upper Saint-Maurice region hunting, fishing, and trapping. Economic restraints did not permit the Tête de Boule to stay idle around the post as a group for more than five weeks at a time; otherwise food reserves would run out (Bourassa 1845:248).

At that time the Tête de Boule were divided into hunting-trapping groups each composed of a few families who constituted a dwelling cluster as well. A chief hunter and his wife formed the nucleus of the unit with the married sons and daughters revolving around them.

The hunting-trapping season (October to June), a period of intense collaboration, gave way to the summer season, a time of social gathering among hunting groups. These dwelling clusters showed a high degree of regularity in their seasonal activities, which undoubtedly upheld and prolonged their traditions and ancestral way of life.

It was not until 1837 that the Roman Catholic missionaries established sustained contact with the Tête de Boule by traveling into the Upper Saint-Maurice area to evangelize them. During the seventeenth and early eighteenth centuries contact with missionaries, French or English, had been so sporadic that two missionaries in 1837 noted the survival of many aboriginal ritual and religious observances (Dumoulin 1839; Bourassa 1845). The priests soon set about expunging the cultural and religious practices that were anchoring the Tête de Boule in paganism. By the middle of the nineteenth century the annual Roman Catholic retreat was as much a part of Indian life as was their seasonal rhythm in exploiting the territory they roamed. Their involvement in the world economy lay in their systematic harvest of commercial faunal resources and in their economic dependence on "credit" from the fur trader. J. Adams (1831:28) summed up the situation: "These people, once a formidable race, are now reduced by smallpox, and more especially by the baneful effects of rum . . . [and] are generally . . . much in debt for clothing, arms, ammunition, and provision."

During the entire period the traditional way of life was cumulatively altered through contact with Europeans and their culture. The Indians slowly assimilated many foreign cultural elements and yet maintained their language and sense of group identity.

From the beginning of the nineteenth century the province of Quebec became increasingly interested in the natural resources of the Upper Saint-Maurice region. Logging companies, woodcutters, and surveyors gradually moved northward into this rich woodland area to harvest white pine. Parallel to the creation in 1852 of forestry concessions for the benefit of exploiting companies, the reserve of Weymontachingue was established for the Indians in 1851. The entire Lower Saint-Maurice River was harnessed to render easier the floating of logs to mills downstream; makeshift roads were opened up thereby fostering the thrust of southern civilization northward toward the Upper Saint-Maurice watershed. In 1910 the completion of the railway line linking La Tuque with Abitibi split the traditional Tête de Boule territory in half, and Weymontachingue, the ancestral gathering place of this tribe, became the hub for many of these new enterprises. The Manouane and Kikendatch subgroups were still relatively insulated from rampant acculturation.

1914–1972

During the years 1914 through 1950 the Tête de Boule underwent the ravages of accelerated acculturation. Between 1914 and 1917 the construction of the La Loutre Dam on the Upper Saint-Maurice River some 60 miles north of present-day Sanmaur brought an influx of heavy machinery and White manpower into the Weymontachingue region. Upon completion of the dam in 1917 the Brown Corporation set up operations for exploiting forestry resources, thereby adding over 1,000 lumberjacks to the ever-increasing White presence in that region. The International Paper Company followed suit 13 years later.

Two other factors that abetted the acculturation process of the Tête de Boule were the setting up of summer schools (June to September) at Weymontachingue and Obedjiwan in the mid-1920s simultaneously accompanied by the building of many wooden houses around the Hudson's Bay Company stores and Catholic missions. The former nomads were rapidly acquiring sedentary habits, reversing their nineteenth and early twentieth century pattern of 9 to 10 months on the traplines and two to three months at the post or mission until by 1950 just the opposite pattern was true.

Still other elements were at work helping to hasten the Indians' abandonment of their traditional lifeways. The forest was being leveled, accompanied by the din of lumberjack and construction camps. The construction of the La Loutre and other, secondary, dams flooded two Tête de Boule villages, Kikendatch and Coocoocash, plus hundreds of square miles of rich hunting territory and brought a scarcity of fur-bearing animals. Forest fires also took their toll. However, the greatest problem was the ever-growing presence of White poacher-trappers, tourists, and private hunting clubs. During the 1930s the Hudson's Bay Company bought more beaver pelts from Whites than from the Indians (Guinard 1945:134). There was simply less game for the Tête de Boule.

With the outbreak of World War II most of the lumberjacks enlisted; this opened logging jobs to the surrounding Indian population. By 1950 several male adults at Weymontachingue had relatively stable employment in the forest industry while their tribesmen at Obedjiwan and Manouane were eking out a paltry living through hunting, trapping, and fishing and from meager government handouts or sporadic seasonal work.

From 1950 to 1972 the trend toward sedentary life and outlook became an irreversible reality. More and more wooden houses were built in Manouane and Obedjiwan. Children were sent to boarding schools at La Tuque or Pointe Bleue for a nine-month school year. Some of these youngsters were repatriated in the late 1960s and early 1970s when grade schools were constructed in Manouane and Obedjiwan and a new village was built at Weymontachingue. The new schools brought ever-increasing numbers of White teachers and government agents. As time passed the Indians became more dependent upon the Hudson's Bay Company and its wares, the missionary, woodcutting jobs or other seasonal work, the White educational systems, and, above all, government aid.

Attikamek Period, 1972–

Nobody seems to know exactly when and how the old name Attikamek came to be revived or who instigated its reincarnation; however, most Attikameks agree that the revival took place sometime in or around 1972. The principal reason behind the resuscitation by these people of their former appellation appears to lie in their developing educational and political awareness. This has been manifested in their sustained interest in the Amerindianization Programme for Quebec Indian schools, coupled with their blossoming political union with the Montagnais in order to strengthen their bargaining power at the negotiating table on land and cultural rights.

In the late 1970s, most of the Attikamek people were to be found in the settlements of Manouane, Weymontachingue, and Obedjiwan. In December 1978 their respective populations were 984, 595, and 1,069 (Canada. Department of Indian Affairs and Northern Development 1980:16–17). They were organized politically in the Conseil Attikamek-Montagnais.

The language, an *r*-dialect of Cree, was in 1979 well spoken at all age levels of Attikamek society. Children entering kindergarten were 100 percent monolingual Attikamek speakers.

Synonymy§

The name Attikamek (Montagnais *atihkame·k^w* 'whitefish, *Coregonus clupeaformis*') was recorded in the seventeenth century with several spellings: Attikamegouekhi, 1635 (pl., JR 9:114); Attikamegouek, 1643 (pl., JR 24:154); Attikameg, 1645 (JR 27:158); Attikameg8ek, 1647 (JR 31:208). The 1647 form was spe-

§ This synonymy was written by David H. Pentland.

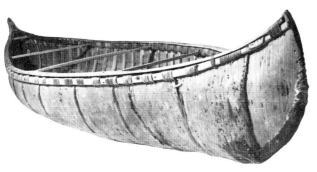

cifically stated to be their own name, the French equivalent being Attikamegues, also written Atikamegues and Atticameges, 1643 (JR 23:298, 24:36) and Aticamegues, 1709 (Raudot in Kinietz 1940:366). In the modern period the spellings Attikamègues (Lacombe 1874:705) and Atikamègues (Cuoq 1886:68) have been used, and more recently also Attikamek (feminine Attikamèque) (Le Conseil Attikamek Montagnais 1979:172). The Ojibwa form of the name is *atikkame·k(ok)* (from Cuoq 1886:68). The modern Attikamek call themselves *atihkame·kʷ(ak)* (Béland

1978:401), but like many other groups prefer to be known as Cree (Béland 1978:3; see the synonymy in "West Main Cree," this vol.). The name Attikamek was translated into French as Poisson-blanc (pl. Poissons-blancs, JR 16:72).

The Tête(s)-de-Boule (French for 'round-heads') are first mentioned in 1692 (NYCD 9:535) and first appear in the parish registers of Trois-Rivières in 1697 (Clermont 1977:18); the only variations in the name are the frequent omission of the circumflex and hyphens required by modern French spelling rules. An Ojibwa equivalent is Machantiby, 1697 (Aubert de la Chesnaye in Margry 1879–1888, 6:6), Machandibi or Machadibi, 1709 (La Hontan in Winsor 1884–1889, 4:208), Machatantibis ou Têtes de Boules, 1709 (Raudot 1904:99; miscopied in Kinietz 1940:366); except for the medial *-a·ntip-* 'head' the word is unanalyzable. The 1697 form Testes de boeuf (Aubert de la Chesnaye in Margry 1879–1888, 6:6) is probably an error for Têtes de boule.

The name Tête-de-Boule is sometimes equated with Gens des Terres (Maray de La Chauvignerie 1928:541; Henry 1901:62, 208), raising questions about the ref-

Natl. Mus. of Canada. Ottawa: top left. 78–5451; top center. 78–5449; top right. J–19551–19; center left. J–19551–9; center right. J–19551–17; bottom. III–L–228.

Fig. 4. Construction of a birchbark one-man hunting canoe by Albert Birote. commissioned for the National Museums of Canada's collections (Guy 1970). top left. Centering the building frame on the bark, which has been laid out on a slightly convex bed prepared in the sandy ground. After the frame is weighted with stones to hold it in position and keep it flat, the bark is slit and shaped upward around the frame and stones (top center). The frame and bark are outlined with stakes, laths inserted lengthwise to align the sides, and opposing pairs of stakes are lashed together. Shorter stakes inside are tied to the outer ones to hold the bark firmly in position, overlapping at each slit. The joints in the bark are lashed together, the stones and internal stakes removed, and the building frame raised to gunwale height (top right). The bark is then trimmed flush with the gunwales. Holes are made in the bark with an awl, and women stitch the gunwale to the bark with thongs made from split jack pine roots that have been boiled in water for many hours to make them pliable. The outer stakes are removed when the lashing is finished leaving the rough shape of the canoe. The ribs are shaped with a crooked knife, soaked with boiling water and prebent over the knee, and then bent in the canoe for drying in the desired shape. After drying, they are removed and reinserted later. The tips of the canoe are strengthened and finished off, and the gunwale caps and final thwarts are installed. Next the interior is caulked with a gum made from pine and spruce resin mixed with store-bought pitch and commercial vegetable fat. This mixture is applied with a cloth-covered spatula over joints, a cloth strip adhered to it and a second coat added (center left). center right, The final insertion of the cedar sheathing and ribs, which are tapped into place with a birch mallet. Last, the exterior is caulked to complete the construction. bottom, Finished canoe. Length 3.9 m. Photographs by Camil Guy at Dam C, near Weymontachingue, Que., July 1966.

erence of both terms. According to Raudot in 1709, the wandering bands of Algonquian Indians north of the Great Lakes were all called Gens des Terres, because they lived *dans les terres* 'inland' (Raudot 1904:98, translated in Kinietz 1940:366). Alexander Henry the Elder (1901:62, 208) added that the Gens de Terres ("also called Tetes de Boule") ranged from the Gulf of Saint Lawrence to Lake Athabasca, making it most unlikely that all of them were ancestors of the modern Attikamek. Although he met Gens des Terres in 1762 and 1767, Henry (1901:246) mentions that until 1775 he had never seen a Cree; the identity of the Gens des Terres as a whole is thus made even more of a mystery. They first appear as Gens des Terres and Gens de la Mer du Nord ('people of the northern sea [Hudson Bay]') in 1671 (JR 55:98); other terms are: Nations du nord, 1674 (Jolliet in Winsor 1884–1889, 4:208); Gens du Nord, 1709 (Raudot in Kinietz 1940:365); and Wood-Indians, 1809 (Henry 1901:62). The Ojibwa name is *no·ppimink taše· inini* (sg., phonemicized from Cuoq 1886:288) 'person (who lives) in the woods' or *no·hpimink tašininiwak* 'people of the bush' (William Jones in Hodge 1907–1910, 2:82, who gives additional forms), recorded about 1678 as Noupiming-dach-iri-niouek, representing Old Algonquin *no·ppimink*

taširiniwak (Nicolas 1930, following 79). This resembles the name recorded as Opemens d'Acheliny, 1684 (Greysolon Dulhut, in Margry 1876–1886, 6:51) and O'pimittish Ininiwac 'Men of the Woods', 1809 (Henry 1901:62). Montagnais *nu·čimi·winnu* 'inland person' may have formerly referred to the Gens de Terres but is no longer the name of a specific group (Mailhot and Lescop 1977:198).

The employees of the Hudson's Bay Company referred to the Gens des Terres (and perhaps other groups south of them, including northern bands of Ojibwa) as the Upland Indians from as early as 1670–1671 at Rupert House (Gorst in Tyrrell 1931:388); the variant form Uplanders was used at Moose Factory in 1706 (Williams 1975:53). References in the York Factory records to Upland Indians in 1717 (Davies and Johnson 1965:72) and Uplanders in 1716 (Knight 1932:58) indicate Algonquian groups far to the west of the peoples treated in this chapter.

Early names of subgroups are known only in the northern part of Attikamek territory. The Cuscudidah band, which spent the winter of 1670–1671 at Rupert House (Gorst in Tyrrell 1931:390), is assigned to the Attikamek dialect group on the basis of a short vocabulary (Pentland 1978:104–105). The people who lived around Kesagami Lake (Cree *(ki)sa·kamiy*, probably 'hot lake', Pentland 1970–1979) are known to have spoken a similar dialect (Cooper 1945). Speck (1931:579; D.S. Davidson 1928d:18) recorded as names of the Attikamek (of the Saint-Maurice River) Lake Saint John Montagnais Sagamì, Montagnais Otcàkamiilnuts, and Attikamek Ogicà'kαmiiu (the last two said to mean 'people of the other watershed'); and in 1652 the Iroquois penetrated the Attikamek territory as far as a lake called Kesagami (JR 37:68): it is possible that these names refer to the same lake, but there is no proof. The Kesagami Lake people were called the Salkemy or Salcomy Indians in 1706 (Williams 1975:50, 63) and the Sockemy Indians in 1727 (Davies and Johnson 1965:124); perhaps the same were the Shaggamies (Shiagamies, Shiogamys, Williams 1975:56–58), but there are linguistic objections to equating the two names.

Speck (1931:579; D.S. Davidson 1928d:18) recorded Mótacéwilnuts' and Mαtacèwilnuts, probably *mu·taše·wilnuč*, conjecturally translated 'lookout people', as the Montagnais name of the Weymontachingue band. The other modern bands are known in Attikamek as *manawa·n* 'where one picks up gull's eggs' (Manouane), *opi·čiwan* 'where the stream goes back' (Obedjiwan), *ki·ke·nita·č* (translation unknown) (Kikendatch), and *ko·hko·ka·šš* (translation unknown) (Coocoocash) (all from Béland 1978). Other spellings in use, especially in English, for some of these bands include: Weymontachie, Manowan, and Kikendash. In the 1950s some Attikameks were said to call themselves Barrières (Rue 1961:27), but the people described were members of the Barrière Lake band of Northern Algonquin.

Sources

The largest corpus of cultural information concerning the Attikamek–Tête de Boule is conserved in the field notes of Cooper (1926–1937), reflected in part in Cooper (1926a, 1938, 1939). Other modern sources include Skinner (1912), D.S. Davidson (1928d, 1928e), M. Raymond (1945), Burger (1953), Pepin (1957), Guy (1966, 1967, 1970), and Gilbert (1967). J. Adams (1831) reports an earlier situation. The Hudson's Bay Company Archives, in the Provincial Archives of Manitoba, Winnipeg, contain valuable information concerning economic transactions at the different posts.

Clermont has combined ethnographic and documentary sources for studies of aspects of Attikamek-Tête de Boule culture and history: on identities (1974a), on beaver hunting (1974), on parish registers and Hudson's Bay Company account books as sources (1975), on economic history (1977a), on general cultural history (1977), and on Windigo beliefs (1978).

West Main Cree

JOHN J. HONIGMANN

Territory, Language, and Environment

The Indians occupying the low-lying west coast of James and Hudson bays from the Moose River in northeastern Ontario to the Churchill River in northern Manitoba have generally been known as Cree ('krē) or Swampy Cree. In this chapter they are designated West Main Cree, to parallel the name for the Cree of the east coast, the East Main, of Hudson and James bays ("East Main Cree," this vol.). Inland the territory of the coastal Indians is hard to delimit, but for purposes of this chapter it includes the area exploited by Cree-speaking people trading with the settlements listed in table 1 (see fig. 1). In 1947 a few Attawapiskat families trapped as far as 160 miles inland, but most wintered considerably closer to the coast or on Akimiski Island. The inland groups of Swampy Cree in Manitoba and Saskatchewan are treated in "Western Woods Cree," this volume.

Language is one trait that enables the West Main Cree to distinguish themselves from the Ojibwa Indians on the upper reaches of the Albany and Attawapiskat rivers, and it is also a basis on which they consider themselves different from Indians on the east coast of James Bay. The west coast people speak an *n*-dialect of the Cree language, except at Moose Factory where an *l*-dialect is used ("Subarctic Algonquian Languages," this vol.). Literacy in the Cree language, using the syllabary developed by James Evans in the nineteenth century (Logan 1951), was widespread. As late as 1955 the syllabary was still being taught to children in the Roman Catholic boarding school at Lac Sainte Anne, located a short distance upriver from Fort Albany (Trudeau 1966:54).*

* The Cree dialects spoken in the areas covered by this chapter may be written with the following phonemic symbols: *p, t, č, k; s, š, h; m, n, l; w, y; i, a, o; i·, e·, a·, o·* (Ellis 1962). The Moose Cree dialect (spoken at Moose Factory and by some people on the Kasechuan Reserve near Ft. Albany) has this full set of phonemes; the Eastern Swampy dialect (spoken at Ft. Albany, Attawapiskat, Winisk, and by some residents of Moosonee) lacks *l*, substituting *n* instead; and the Western Swampy dialect (spoken from Ft. Severn to Churchill) lacks both *l* (substituting *n*) and *š* (substituting *s*) and pronounces *č* as [c]. The Cree words given in italics in this chapter are in the Eastern Swampy dialect; the phonemic transcriptions were provided by C. Douglas Ellis (communication to editors 1973), except for *pape·we·win* (phonemicized from Lacombe 1874:535 and Faries 1938:115, 439), and the words in the synonymy.

Several large and numerous small rivers drain the low-lying muskeg territory of the West Main Cree. The rivers, starting at the southern end, include the Moose, Albany, Kapiskau, Attawapiskat, Ekwan, Lakitusaki (Lake River), and—coming to streams entering Hudson Bay—the Sutton, Winisk, Severn, Hayes, Nelson, and Churchill rivers. The drainages of the Kapiskau and other northerly streams as far as the Winisk tend to converge on a common catchment basin, making it easy to travel by portaging from the headwaters of one to those of another.

Spruce, tamarack, and willow are the trees most common to the region. A narrow coastal strip of tundra begins below Cape Henrietta Maria, the northwestern extreme of James Bay, and extends west and north. Here caribou were taken (Bishop 1972:64; Rogers 1967:90), and in small numbers they formerly ventured south of the Albany River. By the early decades of the twentieth century, or possibly earlier, moose had started to frequent the country between the Moose and Winisk rivers. In addition to large numbers of geese, one of whose main flyways lies over the coastal marshes of James Bay (East 1951), and ducks, the country has provided hunters and trappers with bear, beaver, hare, porcupine, fox, otter, marten, mink, muskrat, weasel, groundhog, and squirrel. These forest animals, however, have not come coastward in great numbers. Polar bears drift to the shore on the ice around Cape Henrietta Maria from farther north. The rivers contain trout, pike, sturgeon, and other species of fish, and their estuaries attract occasional seal or belugas. While West Main Cree did not relish these sea mammals for food, they caught them for oil and later fed the meat to dogs.

History of Indian-White Relations

The Fur Trade

Little is known about west coast culture history from 1697, when Bacqueville de la Potherie (1931:222–238, 261–267) observed a few customs of the Indians who visited York Factory (Fort Nelson, Fort Bourbon) to trade, until 1908, when Skinner (1912) took note of the extent to which Indian life reflected Euro-American cultural influences. The events bringing those influences

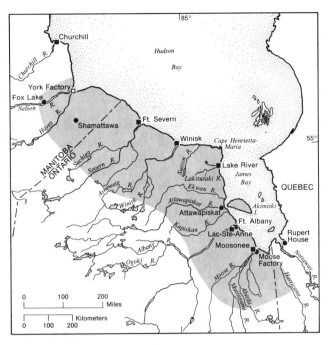

Fig. 1. Nineteenth-century territory.

about go back to 1668, when the first trading post was built at Rupert House, and 1671, when Moose Factory was founded in the southwest corner of James Bay. Soon Fort Albany was in operation (Kenyon 1965); and the establishment of York Factory (Fort Nelson), Fort Severn (Macfie 1967, 1970), and Fort Churchill (originally Fort Prince of Wales) followed.

The extent of Indian occupation and exploitation of the coastal area prior to the establishment of the trading posts is problematic. In any case Bishop (1972:63) points out the almost immediate effect Fort Albany had in encouraging Indians to become dependent on the traders. In 1717 the Cree looked to the Hudson's Bay Company not only for an annual supply of European goods, including special guns for the Indian trade (Gooding 1951), cloth, blankets, and food, but also even for wild goose meat, which the Company preserved in quantity for the winter to feed its own men and hungry Indians.

By the middle of the nineteenth century, Indians from Attawapiskat and Winisk were visiting Fort Albany to trade (D. Anderson 1873:98). After 1882 the Hudson's Bay Company built an outpost at Winisk and, following 1893, smaller posts on James Bay between Fort Albany and Winisk. Revillon Frères and other trading companies also entered the area, initiating a period of very competitive fur buying from which the Indians benefited materially.

Missionaries

From 1686 to 1693 Jesuit missionaries lived in what became Fort Albany. Not until 1823, when a Church of England prelate was stationed at York Factory (Marsh 1957:4), were Christian missionaries again active among the West Main Cree. Northern coastal Indians, however, probably witnessed laymen performing Christian rituals (Macfie 1970:45, 49). A Wesleyan missionary at Moose Factory converted many Indians before Roman Catholic Oblates began missionizing there in 1847 (Nadeau 1954:105ff.; Paul-Émile 1952:81ff.; Saindon 1928:13). Gradually the Oblates extended their efforts northward to Albany, where they met with little success, and to Attawapiskat and Winisk, where practically the entire populations became Catholic. The attraction and encouragement of the Catholic missions at Attawapiskat and Winisk caused Indian families to establish themselves closer to the coast (Chipman 1903).

Alternatives to Trapping

During World War I, military authorities sent a small number of native men from west coast James Bay communities to Great Britain where they worked in sawmills but learned very little English. The postwar years were especially hard for the inhabitants of the lowlands, never an easy area in which to secure a dependable food supply. (As early as 1671, Oldmixon 1931:392 reported starvation on the Ekwan; see also Isham 1949:80; Bishop 1972.) Overtrapping had depleted fur resources, and the small settlements contained no income-producing alternatives to trapping. However, the region was becoming more closely integrated with the rest of Canada as two railway lines pushed northward, one terminating at Churchill and the other across the river from Moose Factory at Moosonee. Ten years after World War II, Moosonee became a port supplying military installations at Great Whale River and Winisk, while Churchill grew into a busy town and military base. Increasingly, Indians drifted into those places in search of jobs and moved south along the railways, which offered major sources of employment for unskilled workers. The Canadian government also began to take more active interest in all northern people; on the west coast it invested social capital in the form of a large modern hospital at Moose Factory, local nursing stations, schools, and a beaver preserve, as well as providing more social assistance for the aged and indigent.

Population

It is impossible to say how many of Mooney's estimated 17,000 Eastern Subarctic Cree (Kroeber 1939:141) correspond to the 4,722 "Indians" belonging to West Coast bands located between Moose Factory and Churchill in 1970. Table 1 gives figures for different periods, but it should be kept in mind that official figures exclude Métis and Indians who have asked to be removed from

218

Table 1. West Main Cree Population

	1793[a]	1829[a]	1858[a]	1947[b]	1954	1962	1964[c]	1966	1967	1970[d]	1978[e]
Moose Factory[f]					567		598			1,099 (783)	1,380
Moosonee[g]							700		1,200[h]		
Fort Albany (Albany band)	190	259	387		762		800			1,399 (921)	1,774
Lac Ste. Anne[g]				197							
Attawapiskat band				645	743	375[i]	200			1,077 (486)	1,375
Weenusk band (Winisk)							100			218	240
Severn band							115			240	272
York Factory band										335 (109)	419
Churchill band								223[i]		354	
Fox Lake band											316
Shamattawa band											569
Total						2,513				4,722	6,345

[a] From Bishop 1972:64, 68, based on Hudson's Bay Company Archives.

[b] Starting in 1947, Moose Factory, Fort Albany, Attawapiskat, Winisk, Severn, and York Factory figures are from government band lists unless otherwise credited. Totals do not accurately represent settlement population, most importantly because not all band members remain in the settlement from which the band is named. Also, "enfranchised" Indians are not included in a band list.

[c] Figures are from Rogers and Trudeau 1968–1972, 3, who credit "most" of the Ontario figures to the Ontario Department of Lands and Forests. The authors claim that these are band enrollment figures, but compared to 1947 and 1970 government numbers they make more sense interpreted as resident populations.

[d] Canadian Department of Indian Affairs and Northern Development figures; numbers in parentheses are reserve residents only.

[e] From Canada. Department of Indian Affairs and Northern Development 1980:18–28. Total enrollment.

[f] Excluding patients in the hospital and children in the residential school belonging to East Main Cree bands.

[g] Indians in Moosonee and Lac Ste. Anne belong mainly to the Attawapiskat and Weenusk bands.

[h] An average of several written estimates provided by local persons.

[i] Trudeau's 1963:89 estimate of resident population.

[j] Excluding Chipewyan.

band lists. With the exception of Lac Sainte Anne, Moosonee, and Churchill, west-coast communities have lost population since the late 1940s. York Factory Indians have migrated, some to Churchill; families from Winisk and Attawapiskat moved to Lac Sainte Anne or, along with Moose Factory and Fort Albany families, to Moosonee and farther south. Persons moving to another settlement are not usually removed from band lists unless the move is by a woman who marries a man belonging to another band.

Traditional Culture

Technology

Informants in Attawapiskat in 1947 scarcely knew that Indians of the region formerly made ground stone knives and axes, the axes grooved according to Skinner (1912:51, 52), who also reports stone adzes. Most of the primary tools expected in a Subarctic Indian culture occurred in the lowland area: bone awls, sewing needles (with tubular needle cases of hollow bird bone), bone fleshers, skin scrapers, and beaver tooth chisels.

Preparing caribou skin, the basic clothing material, was a long process. Women fleshed the hide as it lay pegged on the ground and shaved the hairs while holding the skin against a log. Skinner (1912:33) illustrates a hafted semilunar metal knife used for fleshing after contact. (Possibly a semilunar slate knife was used prior to contact.) Once the hide had been soaked in a brain mixture, rinsed, dried, stretched, and smoked, it was ready for tailoring. Tanning seal and white whale (beluga) skin required similar hard work, compared to which cleaning the skins of hares and cutting them into strips to make garments and blankets were relatively simple.

The West Main Indians employed the full complement of northern lines and cords, made from rawhide, dressed hide, sinew for garment sewing, willow bark, and spruce root.

Because the strike-a-light method of fire making was difficult, fire was carried in the form of a glowing pole or glowing tinder stored in a birchbark container.

Subsistence

Fish may have formed the dietary mainstay of former times. The Indians had a variety of techniques and implements to catch them, including: angling with barbless bone or spruce hooks, leisters, weirs, and gill nets of willow-bast cord. An ice scoop served to clear the hole made for nets in the frozen river. Harpoons for seal and beluga were introduced within the contact era.

The bow, arrow, and lance furnished the principal hunting weapons. Simple bows, in height sometimes reaching to a standing man's forehead but usually smaller, were strung with bark or babiche. Arrows were fitted with antler, bone, or stone points suited for particular types of game. Deadfalls ("Environment and Culture in the Shield and Mackenzie Borderlands," fig. 5, this vol.) caught black bears and many smaller fur-bearing animals. Traps fitted with falling trapdoors were built in water to catch beaver, an animal also taken by nets and sometimes simply by a man's crashing into its dwelling ("Intercultural Relations and Cultural Change in the Shield and Mackenzie Borderlands," fig. 5, this vol.). Snares were used to take geese, ducks, hare, and larger land animals. In caribou hunting, groups of several families cooperated in constructing surrounds or driving the animals through a narrow valley. Individual hunters also hunted them by semicircular tracking (Honigmann 1956:35) and by running them down in soft snow, techniques that later came to be used in moose hunting.

Heat-drying enabled meat and fish to be preserved; sometimes the dry meat was pounded, larded with grease, and enriched with berries ("Environment and Culture in the Shield and Mackenzie Borderlands," fig. 7, this vol.). Grease rendered from seal blubber was added to dried fish; fish or meat without fat was little relished, whether fresh or dried.

For boiling, the usual method of preparing meat and fish, people used clay-covered woven spruceroot kettles and caribou stomachs (Honigmann 1956:40). Skinner (1912:30) also mentions carved soapstone cooking vessels. The sexes followed no special order in eating, a task in which wood or bone knives served to cut the meat and horn or wood spoons to transport food to the mouth. Among the few magically conceived food taboos that encumbered eating were those requiring women to avoid certain parts of game animals in order that hunters might take game again. An Attawapiskat informant mentioned the ritual eating of dog, claiming it was done for the purpose of enhancing a shaman's ability to ascertain the location of a caribou herd.

Structures

Attawapiskat informants described the basic dwelling as frequently consisting of a conical lodge (fig. 2) with a three-pole foundation on which a series of poles was laid to support a further cover that varied with the time of the year. It might consist of bark, skins, brush, or, for winter use, earth (that is, pieces of turf), for which the underlying poles must have been set close together indeed. Indians reported that the floor of a winter earth lodge was excavated a foot or so below the ground surface. South-coast informants also recalled dome-shaped dwellings walled with bark sewed to a willow framework. The sudatory was constructed according to such a plan, but with dimensions smaller than a dwelling. A low conical lodge sheltered a girl undergoing isolation at menarche.

Other nonresidential structures included a four-pole platform cache, pole-lined subterranean cache for storing dried fish and meat, and a ceremonial enclosure fenced with willow or spruce brush used for special dances (Honigmann 1956:57).

Clothing and Adornment

Men always wore a breechcloth held in place by a belt. Then, depending to some extent on the season, they completed their attire by choosing items from an assemblage that included a short coat of dressed hide or of fabric made from hareskin strips; an outer belt to pull the coat tight; leggings with garters; moccasins; a warmer coat, perhaps a fur robe, for cold weather; mittens; and cap. (For drawings reconstructing former dress see Scott and Leechman 1952.) Women omitted a breechcloth, except possibly at menstruation, according to an Attawapiskat informant, or, according to Isham (1949:110), in winter. They wore a long dress or smock to which they added the five last-mentioned items of the man's clothing assemblage. Hare skins or other fur duffel protected the hands and feet in cold weather. Skinner (1912:17, 19) reports hooded cloaks (parkas), but Attawapiskat informants maintained that those garments appeared only after the White man's woolen capote had been introduced.

Attawapiskat informants gave the impression that dress remained quite plain until late fur-trade times

Public Arch. of Canada, Ottawa: C 75915.

Fig. 2. Conical bark-covered wigwam with built-out entryway. The women wear peaked caps of a type sometimes elaborately decorated. Photographed about 1900; place not recorded.

220

when elaborate beadwork came into use. In an earlier period Isham (1949:110) and Graham (1969:146) noted quill and bead decoration extending even to the breechcloth. Men plucked facial hair and women their eyebrows; accounts are inconsistent regarding depilation of other body hair (cf. Graham 1969:144). Without question one or both sexes painted the face, tattooed at least the hands and part of the face with sinew thread rubbed in charcoal, pierced the ears for ear plugs, braided the hair, and on the north coast bored a hole in the nasal septum where in postcontact times they wore a bead (Isham 1949:110).

Travel and Transportation

Means of transportation obviously altered with the sharp swing of the seasons. During time of open water, Indians hunted in small canoes and moved family and possessions in larger traveling craft ("Intercultural Relations and Cultural Change in the Shield and Mackenzie Borderlands," fig. 4, this vol.). Both were covered with birch or spruce bark. The vessels also ventured into the salt water. Wintertime, goods were loaded on toboggans made of tamarack and pulled by human power, for the small dogs used in hunting lacked strength to haul those vehicles; however, by the middle of the eighteenth century at least the northern coastal people used dogs for traction ("Intercultural Relations and Cultural Change in the Shield and Mackenzie Borderlands," fig. 9, this vol.) and also packed them (Isham 1949:164). Elongated snowshoes, some seven or eight feet long, likewise made of tamarack and filled with a lacing of babiche, greatly facilitated travel and hunting in soft snow.

Games and Music

Games were played by adults and children. Some, like cup and pin, ball-in-the-air, football, lacrosse (Skinner 1912:38), pull tug-of-war, and string figures, required simple equipment; but there were also sports that relied solely on physical skill. Children played hide and seek, scaled stones, played hunting games (fig. 3), and amused themselves with buzz toys, bull-roarers, toy bows, carved wooden dolls, and pea shooters.

Evenings, people told stories, sometimes about the culture heroes, čahka·pe·š (Djokabish) and wi·sake·ča·hk (Wisakedjak). Although singing and dancing were sometimes recreational, they might also be devoted to serious purposes, for example, when men sang or danced to obtain success in hunting.

Social Organization

The household frequently consisted of two nuclear families, each headed by brothers or by men who had mar-

Fig. 3. Children from Moose Factory playing the wavey (snow goose) game, a simulated hunt engaged in only by children. Photograph by Regina Flannery-Herzfeld, Aug.-Sept. 1935.

ried sisters. A household might also be a temporarily extended family created through bride service, after which residence was bilocal or neolocal.

Kinship terminology in use in 1947 suggests that the levirate, cross-cousin marriage, sororal polygyny, and the sororate were practiced at one time, but Attawapiskat informants recalled only the last three customs. They possessed Iroquois cousin terminology that merged siblings and parallel cousins according to sex and age relative to ego. Cross-cousins of opposite sex were called ni·tim, a term also used for spouse's siblings of opposite sex. Separate terms distinguished parents and parents' siblings. A single term for father's sister and wife's mother and another for mother's brother and husband's father were consistent with cross-cousin marriage.

Mother-in-law avoidance did not occur, but wife exchange and sexual hospitality did, along with easily secured divorce.

Skinner (1912:56) states that the Albany Cree recalled former patrilineal "clans" symbolized by animals; the clans might have been derived from the Northern Ojibwa. Nowhere else are unilineal descent groups reported, and Skinner's own data become suspect when he adds that young men occasionally dreamed the clan that they were to join.

Political Organization

In the closing years of the seventeenth century, Bacqueville de la Potherie (1931:266–267, 357) noted that Indians who came to Fort Nelson (York Factory) to trade chose several chiefs to take charge of the trading for their people (cf. Isham 1949:82ff.). A chief spoke

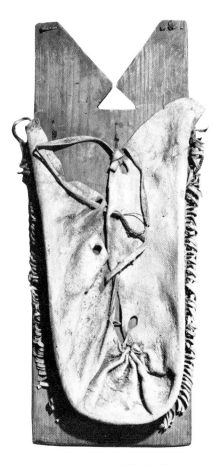

Fig. 4. left, Model cradleboard with white leather cover attached with vegetable fiber cord over a U-shaped wooden hoop on the front of a wooden board. The edge of the cover is painted red, and the cut fringe is wrapped alternately with red and white porcupine quills. A leather strap decorated with colored beads and hair is tied to a wooden strip on the back. This cradleboard, almost identical in design to one about 3 feet long illustrated by Isham (1949:105), was collected about 1740 by John Potts, a surgeon under Isham at York Factory. right, Pair of fetal caribou legs that were tied to a baby's cradle to bring luck hunting caribou in later life. Collected by John M. Cooper at Moose Factory, Ont., 1934. Length of left 37 cm, rest same scale.

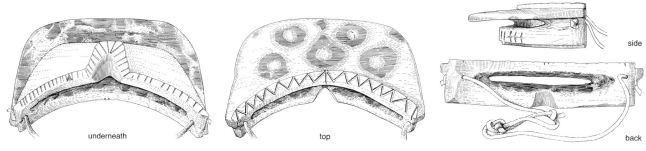

underneath · top · side · back

Fig. 5. Snow goggles carved from a single piece of wood. The wide visor extending horizontally above the eye-slit (top right) is fire-darkened on the underside (left) to help cut glare from snow and ice. The top (center) is decorated with fire-blackened circles and incised lines. Leather ties hold the goggles in place. Width 18 cm, collected by John M. Cooper at Moose Factory, Ont., 1934.

for his hunters, requesting the trader's kind consideration and prices at least no higher than those charged to other Indians. These men may have been band leaders. According to Attawapiskat informants, bands of from 2 to 10 families recognized the authority of leaders who, on the basis of expert knowledge, advised their followers where to hunt and fish and helped them make other advantageous decisions. Leaders possessing the "right to tell the people what to do" were explicitly denied for olden times.

222

Informants distinguished between two kinds of divination. Scapulimancy belonged to the first type (collectively called *pape·we·win* 'good luck'), which was matter of fact in nature ("Montagnais-Naskapi," fig. 10, this vol.). Receiving information about the future and other matters from nonhuman helpers in dreams or in the shaking tent ("Saulteaux of Lake Winnipeg," fig. 9, this vol.) belonged to the second type (*mite·wiwin*), which was the province of the shaman (*mite·w*).

Both men and women attempted to become shamans by securing nonhuman helpers through dreaming, but apparently men made the more earnest efforts. Some men acquired extraordinary power through dreaming and became renowned for their success in divination, curing, and possibly even sorcery.

Early accounts that report Indian belief in good and evil deities (cf. Graham 1969:159) should be viewed cautiously, for, as Thompson (1962:74–75) observed, Indians answering questions about religion "give the answer best adapted to . . . please the enquirer." Some of the sources Cooper (1933) cites to prove that aboriginally the Cree believed in a personal supreme being, called *manito·w* or *kihči-manito·w*, may have been affected by that tendency. At any rate Skinner's (1912:59) and Honigmann's (1956:66–67) data contradict Cooper and support the conclusion that *manito·w* refers to an abstract, impersonal power. The coastal Indians also conceived of several personalized entities that influenced human affairs, including underwater creatures, dwarfs, animal "bosses," and cannibalistic beings like the Windigo (Cree *wi·htiko·w*) whose tracks travelers unexpectedly encountered in the forest.

The most ceremonial activities were those following the killing of a bear and involved carefully depositing the animal's skull (sometimes painted) into a tree ("Expressive Aspects of Subarctic Indian Culture," fig. 5, this vol.). Other animal bones were also reverentially disposed of in order to retain favor with the species and thus to continue to kill game. Other rituals included seclusion of menstruants (at menarche only) and widows.

Not all curing depended on the agency of a shaman. People also resorted to a considerable variety of herbal medicines, each suited to a specific ailment. Additional curing procedures, sometimes employed in shamanistic contexts, included sucking, confession, sweatbathing, and administration of enemas.

When a person died, relatives washed the body and provided a birch- or spruce-bark shroud in which either to bury the extended corpse or, if it was winter, to cache it on the ground surface. Eating utensils, bones of game animals, clothing, and weapons were placed on the grave or hung from a crossed stick (Isham 1949:94).

The New Culture of the Fur-Trade Period

Starting in the late seventeenth century and accelerating during the next 200 years, the coastal Cree Indians substantially redesigned both the adaptive and expressive components of their way of life in response to the opportunities and pressures of the fur trade and of missionization. To obtain trade goods, Indians took up the specialized pursuit of fur trapping, which in turn worked changes in resource utilization and societal arrangements. Missionary teaching planted new ideas that also called for a host of adjustments in many cultural domains.

Implements formerly made by the Indian were sooner or later replaced in whole or in part by ready-made equipment bought at the store. Metal cutting tools were quickly substituted for those of bone, antler, and stone. Fishnets and snowshoe lacing were eventually made with cotton twine instead of native cordage. The steel trap became the mainstay of trapping, replacing native deadfalls. Canvas replaced bark as the sheathing for canoes and the canvas tent became the common dwelling.

Firearms altered and eased subsistence hunting; especially, they allowed the Indians to rely on waterfowl (figs. 7–9) as a seasonal staple food. Besides fish and other native food resources, flour, tea, sugar, oatmeal, and other imported food items from the traders as-

Fig. 6. A man from Moosonee bringing in his beaver catch. He wears snowshoes, moccasins with decorated vamp, and gloves with embroidered floral cuffs. He carries a hatchet and rifle in cloth or skin case. Photograph by John Macfie, 1959.

Anonymous 1978.

Fig. 7. Goose hunt camp. Canvas tent has interior stove with smoke stack visible. Drawn by Clayton Cheechov, Cree pupil, for Sept. 'blue or snow goose month', for 1978 school calendar.

sumed a major place in the diet. Tobacco and alcohol were much desired, especially tobacco, which was easier to obtain.

Manufactured garments (like the parka) and cloth changed traditional Indian apparel in practically every respect except the moccasin. For working in the coastal marshes, traders introduced imported Eskimo-made sealskin boots and later rubber boots. In winter, hands and feet were protected by woolen duffel. New forms of personal adornment appeared, especially colorful beadwork.

Euro-Canadian cultural influence affected recreation through the diffusion of board games (checkers, fox and geese), card games, and new kinds of music, instruments, and dancing.

In the realm of social life, polygyny, the sororate, and wife exchange disappeared, and only ambivalently did the churches tolerate occasional cross-cousin marriages. Decimation of large game led large winter bands to split up into smaller units of one, two, or three families (Bishop 1972:65) to whom the sovereign Hudson's Bay Company assigned trapping territories.

In no sphere of life was substitution more extensive than in the realm of religious belief. With the help of denominational boarding schools, Anglican and Catholic missionaries succeeded in implanting an entire new belief system and eradicating practically all adherence to the old one. In this respect the West Main Cree contrast with those on the East Main, where, despite conversion, a considerable part of the old belief system

persisted beyond the middle of the twentieth century (Speck 1935; Preston 1971a). Literacy in the Cree syllabary enabled every adult to read Christian prayer-books, hymnals, and other religious literature. As Indians became committed to the new faiths, the churches joined the trading posts as focal points in the social structure of their settlements.

Mid-Twentieth Century Readaptation

By 1947, when Attawapiskat, midway on the west coast of James Bay, was studied, it was apparent that the Indians' specialized adaptation to fur trapping no longer served their needs. Not only had the population of fur-bearers declined, but also, even more important, fur prices were low compared to the prices of the many things on which the people had come to depend. About half the Attawapiskat Indians' total income came from unearned sources, chiefly the Canadian family allowance and social assistance. Even with considerable reliance on fish, geese, and other country food, the people felt themselves deprived.

The Hudson's Bay Company was attempting to maintain trapping by stocking and carefully harvesting a vast

Public Arch. of Canada, Ottawa: C 1917.

Fig. 8. Hunter from York Factory returning with his catch. He wears a blue, yellow, and red peaked hat decorated with feathers, blue chief's coat with yellow, blue, and red Assomption sash, red, black, and yellow flat pouch hanging from neckband, powder horn, blue leggings, undecorated moccasins. The woman is wearing a red bead necklace, blue leggings, and no upper garments except a Hudson's Bay Company blanket and is carrying a child in a cradleboard on a chest tumpline. Watercolor by Peter Rindisbacher, 1821.

224

Fig. 9. Goose decoys. left, Decoy of oak driftwood. The body has a flat bottom and rounded front; the neck and head are carved from a separate piece of wood and nailed to the body. Length 76 cm, collected at Moose Factory, Ont., 1973. Decoys were also made from other materials. right, These set up near York Factory, are of twigs, earth, and real goose heads and necks. Photograph by Vernon Smith, 1945–1949.

beaver preserve (Denmark 1948), but a number of Indian families had already quit trapping and sought to readapt economically by leaving the community for wage labor in Moosonee or Lac Sainte Anne. By 1952, 262 members of the Attawapiskat band had been drawn off from that settlement: 157 of them were living at Moosonee; 55 at Fort Albany (probably Lac Sainte Anne); and 50 elsewhere, probably on the railroad line south of Moosonee. By 1964, 48 percent of the Attawapiskat band had left the settlement (Hawthorn 1966–1967, 1:113). Other small west-coast communities were also losing people to larger centers, but the migrations are not well documented.

Attawapiskat Community Organization, 1947

The trading store and Catholic church were both focal points in community organization in Attawapiskat in 1947, but the dominant role belonged to the Church. In the 35 years since a permanent mission had been established in the settlement, the Church had preempted guidance of the Indians' intellectual and moral life. It even exercised a minor economic role through selling food and offering summer jobs. The Hudson's Bay Company was undoubtedly of much greater economic importance. The resident manager advanced credit to capitalize a family's winter trapping, bought the bulk of furs, supplied most wares and imported foodstuffs, acted as the government's representative in issuing family allowances and relief, and provided summer jobs. But whereas the manager dealt with the Indians through

an interpreter (for part of the year, a Moose Factory Indian), the Oblate missionaries spoke Cree fluently.

The priests celebrated Mass and other rituals to which the almost exclusively Catholic Indian community responded intensely, adults and young people vigorously singing the Mass as they had learned to do while attending boarding school. The Oblates also exercised an educational role through preaching, running a day school, and offering informal advice on personal problems. They sought to provide medical assistance, issuing pharmaceuticals deposited with them by the Indian agent. If a case seemed serious, a priest used the church radio to send a message to the Indian agent at Moose Factory, who was also a physician. Some aspects of the relationship between the Indians and priests showed strain, but generally the fathers were respected, which enabled them to maintain a dominant moral role and to be a strong force for social control in the community.

Acculturation in Winisk: 1955 to 1961

The Catholic Church and Oblate priests also won the Indians' respect in Winisk, where a permanent mission was founded in 1924. But construction of a radar base, begun in 1955, promoted a revolutionary change in values that severely curtailed the priests' influence. Employment in military construction brought a temporary halt to trapping and stimulated a brief economic boom in which the average cash income for an Indian family climbed from $1,000 to about $5,000. When the boom ended in 1960, Indian men who were not hired for the

Fig. 10. Bannock, a staple of Subarctic Indian cuisine. A kneaded dough of flour, baking powder, salt, lard, and hot water fills the bottom of a greased frying pan, which is propped in front of embers (left, by Alfred Mitchell) so that the bannock cooks from the top down. It is turned several times, basting with lard, until a thick crust forms (Macfie 1956). Bits are dipped in melted lard (right, by Duncan Gray) before eating. Photographs by John Macfie at Ft. Severn, Ont., 1955.

few maintenance jobs left at the radar base drifted back to their trap lines, but without taking wives and children along as they had formerly done. First employment on the base and then the change in trapping from a family enterprise to primarily a masculine occupation severely altered customary patterns of social relations among Indians. Both married and unmarried men reduced their interaction with wives and parents. Disparate experiences between young and old of both sexes attenuated intergenerational relationships and eroded parental authority. Behavior problems increased, partly due to the large number of nonnative (largely White) men working on the base who illegally sold beer and other alcoholic beverages to the Indians and sought women for sexual relations. When parents tried to control young people's behavior, most discovered that they lacked the power to do so. Native gossip and verbal remonstration, hitherto a highly effective means of social control in this small community, had declined to a point of ineffectuality. Parents who appealed to the elected chief and the more influential priest for assistance learned that those two men also lacked power to impose forceful sanctions and that the priest had lost much of his former prestige and authority.

Attawapiskat, 1961

The social upheaval that radically transformed the Indian community in Winisk was not apparent to Nonas (1963) visiting Attawapiskat in 1961. Summer for trappers back from the bush was still vacation time, as it had been in 1947, and there were no signs of greater economic prosperity. The mission and Hudson's Bay Company provided a little wage labor, and Indians quickly took the few jobs available. About three years later, a survey revealed a real per capita cash income in Attawapiskat of $247, $194 of which derived from "transfer payments," including $45 in the form of social assistance. Over one-third of the Indian households received some welfare money (Hawthorn 1966–1967, 1:49, 51, 116).

The Church permeated community life. The priest in charge and three brothers even furnished entertainment. They provided an athletic field, and each Sunday evening they played amplified recorded music from the church steeple: opera arias, musical comedy numbers, fiddled jigs, Gregorian chants, and organ hymns. The Indians respected the churchmen in their religious role; but as men running a profit-making store, cannery, and sawmill, the people sometimes criticized their conduct. Toward the federal government, the Indians voiced strong indignation at its unfulfilled promises regarding welfare and other matters.

Though the Cree could objectively sort out some elements of their culture as "White" or "Indian," they valued the one no more consistently than the other. They did not feel themselves becoming Whites or Canadians. They felt, rather, "that they [were] living in

226

a world to which things are somehow added; a growing world to which they were able to adapt as their fathers did to theirs" (Nonas 1963).

Synonymy†

The usual self-designation of all West Main Crees is *omaške·ko·w* 'muskeg person, swamp person' (Honigmann 1956:24–25). Other groups call them by variants of the same name: Plains Cree *maske·ko·wiyiniw* (from Lacombe 1874:443 and Faries 1938:192), Woods Cree *maski·ko·w* (Pentland 1970–1979), and Ojibwa *omaški·ko·* (from Cuoq 1886:193). Mooney (1907b:813) suggested that the 1671 form Masquikoukioeks (Margry 1879–1888, 1:97) may be the same name, but the identification is questionable. The same is true of the Miscosinks, whom Coats described as a group trading at Moose Factory in 1727–1751 (Coats 1852:41). More reliably ascribed to the West Main Cree are the following forms (those in *-u(c)k* are Cree plurals, those in *-s* French or English borrowings): Mashkegonhyrinis and Maskegonehirinis, 1753; Musce ko uck, 1775 (Graham in Isham 1949:316); Maskego, 1786; Muskekowuck, 1791 (Graham 1969:206); Masquigon, 1804 (Cameron 1889–1890, 2:241); Maskegons, 1809 (Henry 1901:26); Muscagoes and Muskagoes, 1820 (Harmon 1957:52, 97); Muskeggouck, 1820 (J. West 1967:16); Muskegoe, Muskegoag, 1830; Muskigos, 1841; Omashkekok, 1850; Omush-ke-goag, Omushke-goes, 1852; Maskègowuk (Richardson 1852:264); Mas-ke-gau, 1859 (Kane 1971:76); Muskeegoo, 1861; Machkégous, 1884; Machkégons (Cuoq 1886:193) (unattributed forms from Mooney 1907b:813–814). The modern French form, borrowed from Cree *(o)maške·ko·w*, is Maskégon (as in Lacombe 1874:ix). In English the translations Swampy Cree or just Swampy (Indian) are used, replacing older Swamp Indian (as in J. West 1967:16).

The more general term *ininiw* (Moose Cree *ililiw*) 'person, Indian' is also often used as a self-designation. In the seventeenth century the speakers of the δ-dialect (the Woods Cree dialect of the twentieth century) used *ne·hiδaw* (see the synonymy in "Western Woods Cree," this vol.), but this term seems to have gone out of use in the West Main by the early nineteenth century, when there were no longer speakers of this dialect in this area (Pentland 1979:61).

Crees use the name Cree to refer to themselves only when speaking English or French. It derives from the name of an obscure band of Indians who roamed the region south of James Bay in the first half of the seventeenth century. In 1640 they were listed as the Kiristinon among the tribes north of the Nipissing (JR 18:228), but no information was given that would permit identification of either the language or the territory of

the group. The name itself is Ojibwa, in the Old Algonkin dialect form *kirištino·*, but the presence of the foreign (Cree) consonant cluster *št* shows that it was borrowed by the Ojibwa, presumably from the group to which it referred. Graham (1969:206) was surely wrong to list them as an Ojibwa-speaking group as of 1770–1791, but nowhere is a Cree form of the name recorded.

The name *kirištino·* was immediately adopted by the French (with plural *-s* rather than *-k*) and by 1658 was used as a generic term to refer to all Cree-speaking groups (JR 44:248). Some of the spellings of the name are: Kyristin8ns, 1641 (JR 21:124); Kiristinous, 1653 (Du Val in Warkentin and Ruggles 1970:33); Christinos, 1671 (Margry 1879–1888, 1:97); Kristinos, 1679 (Greysolon Dulhut in Margry 1879–1888, 6:31); Christinaux, 1685 (Jaillot in Warkentin and Ruggles 1970:53); Cristinaux, 1697 (Hennepin in Winsor 1884–1889, 4:252); Cristinos, 1697 (Aubert de la Chesnaye in Margry 1879–1888, 6:7); Kiristinnons, 1713 (Marest in Tyrrell 1931:139); Cristineaux, 1790 (Umfreville 1954:101); Cristinau (Cuoq 1886:168).

The French name was quickly shortened, probably by the coureurs de bois, to its modern form Cris (usually both singular and plural, but a singular Cri occasionally appears). Variants are: Kris, 1685 (Silvy in Tyrrell 1931:95); Kriqs, 1713 (Marest in Tyrrell 1931:139); Crists, Crics, 1717 (Greysolon Dulhut in Margry 1879–1888, 6:496, 505); Cris, 1729 (La Vérendrye in Warkentin and Ruggles 1970:73); Criqs, 1809 (Henry 1901:208).

The English, too, had heard of the Kiristinon band, although they seldom visited the Hudson's Bay Company's posts. The following spellings appear in fur trade documents: Cristeens, 1706 (Williams 1975:57); Gristeen, 1743 (Isham 1949:112); Christeens, 1717 (Davies and Johnson 1965:71). The name was soon confused with the word Christian, which the semiliterate traders wrote: Christean, 1732 (Davies and Johnson 1965:167); Christian, 1738 (Davies and Johnson 1965:274); Cristians, 1751 (Coats 1852:40); Christianux, 1770 (Graham in Richardson 1852:265); Christianaux, 1775 (Graham in Isham 1949:317). The last two spellings are due to Graham's acquaintance with the French form Christinaux. By 1780 English traders had adopted the shortened form Cree as a generic term (Umfreville 1954:101; Fidler 1934:498), probably under French influence: Umfreville thought Cree was the French form, and Thompson (1962:73) gave Krees as the name used by the French traders.

During the seventeenth century the Old Algonquin dialect of Ojibwa began to use *l* (like Ottawa) instead of *r*. The form *kilištino·* was recorded in 1667 as Kilistinouc (pl.; JR 51:56) and in 1790 as Ka-lis-te-no (Umfreville 1954:chart opp. p. 104). Other spellings reflect its use as a French loanword: Kilistinons, 1658

† This synonymy was written by David H. Pentland.

(JR 44:240–248); Kilistones, 1660 (Creuxius in JR 46:map); Guilistinous, 1670 (JR 54:154); Kilistinaux, 1670 (JR 54:192); Kilistinos, 1684 (Du Val in Margry 1879–1888, 6:51); Killistinoes (Carver 1778:76); Klisteno, Kilistheno (Latham 1850:328).

Another dialect of Ojibwa (probably the ancestor of modern Saulteaux) had *n* where Algonquin used *l* or *r* (see "Central Algonquian Languages," vol. 15); by the end of the eighteenth century all Ojibwa dialects used *n*. The form *kiništino·*, which is the modern Ojibwa for the Cree, was earlier taken over as a French name, written Kinistinons in 1672 (JR 56:202). A few traders who spoke Ojibwa gave forms with *n*, but always as alternatives to their own choice, Cree: Knisteneaux, 1801 (Mackenzie 1970:179); Kinistinaux, 1809 (Henry [the elder] 1901:208); Kinishtineau, 1811 (Henry [the younger] 1897, 2:537); Knisteneux, 1816 (Harmon 1957:199).

In their post journals, Hudson's Bay Company factors seldom referred to Cree bands by name. More often they were too specific—giving an individual's name—or too vague—stating only that their customers came from the north, or down the river, or from their unnamed hunting grounds. A common distinction was between Northern and Southern Indians. At York Factory and Churchill (Fort Prince of Wales) the name Northern or Northward Indian meant Chipewyan, as shown by Isham's (1949:37) "Northward Indian" vocabulary, but the Northward Indians who were reported to have married "this country Indians" at Fort Albany in 1716 (Davies and Johnson 1965:50) were more likely Crees from farther up the west coast of the bay. During his voyages to Hudson Bay in 1727–1751 Coats applied the name Northern Indians both to Chipewyans seen at York Factory and to East Main Crees on the Great Whale River (Coats 1852:31, 64, 88).

The term Southern or Southward Indian almost always refers to the West Main Cree. At York Factory in 1743 Isham (1949:34–36) distinguished between the Common Indian (Cree) and the Southward Indian (Mohawk) languages, but this usage is unique. More typical was Hearne's (1958:161) contrast between the Southern Indians—the Cree of the Hudson Bay Lowlands—and the Athapuscow (Western Woods Cree) and Neheaway (Plains Cree) to the west. In 1705 the Albany journal recorded the arrival of "a southward Indian from the northward" (Williams 1975:34), showing that it was not meant literally even in the earliest days.

The most important group of West Main Cree to the traders was the Home Indians, a term used at York Factory by 1690 (Kelsey 1929:2) and at Albany by 1706 (Williams 1975:51). The variant form Home-guard Indians was defined by Hearne (1958:51) in 1795 as "certain of the natives who are immediately employed under the protection of the Company's servants, reside on the plantation, and are employed in hunting for the Factory." At most posts the Home-guards were Cree, but at Churchill some were Chipewyan (Graham in Isham 1949:312).

Regional Groups

In the seventeenth century the ancestors of the West Main Cree probably occupied almost all of northern Ontario, with extensions into Manitoba and Quebec, but since then they have come to occupy a smaller area (Pentland 1979:61). Some of the major regional groups of the earlier West Main Cree territory noted in the early records are listed below; of these the Abitibi, Nipigon, and Piscotagami probably lived in areas occupied by Ojibwa speakers in later times.

Abitibi. The people living around Lake Abitibi in the seventeenth century were probably Cree, although in the twentieth century they speak an Ojibwa dialect (Speck 1915:3). Cuoq (1886:8) derives the name from Ojibwa Abitiping '(at) the half lake', so called because it is at the height of land where half the water flows north, the other half south. As the expected Ojibwa form with this meaning would be **a·pitta·pi·nk*, not *a·pittipi·nk*, his etymology must be considered doubtful. Speck (1915:3) recorded Abít·ibi· anicǝnàbi 'blue-water people' (probably *apittipi· aniššina·pe·*, sg.) as the Temiskaming Ojibwa name of the band; if his translation is correct Ojibwa has borrowed a Cree form *(ot)apihtipi·w*, which is unattested but a properly formed Cree name for a person from a dark-colored lake. Earlier spellings of the name, most of which omit the initial *o-* or *ot-*, are: Outabitibek, 1660 (misprinted Outabitikek in JR 45:232); 8tabitibecus, 1660 (Creuxius in JR 46:map); Tabittee, 1671 (Gorst in Tyrrell 1931:390); Outabitibecs, 1674 (JR 59:28); 8tabitibeux, 1677 (JR 60:244); Tabitibis, 1684 (Greysolon Dulhut in Margry 1879–1888, 6:51); Abitibis, 1709 (Raudot in Kinietz 1940:366); Tibithebe, 1722 (Davies and Johnson 1965:82); Abbitibbes, 1801 (Mackenzie 1970:map). The forms with final *-s* in addition to or in place of *-k* are French or English plurals. Coats in 1727–1751 knew of both Great and Little Tabitabies (Coats 1852:41), a distinction of unknown significance.

Albany. The Cree name of the Albany River, *ke·šičiwan* 'swift current' (Ellis 1962), is also applied to the settlement at the mouth of the river, called in English Kasichuan Reserve. It first appears in Radisson's 1685 list of tribes (Radisson 1961:193) in the form Kechechewan. Later spellings are: Kitchichiouan, 1688 (Franquelin in Warkentin and Ruggles 1970:49); Ka stich e wan, 1775 (Graham in Isham 1949:316); Kastechewan and Kesichewan (Sepee), 1791 (Graham 1969:206, 251); Kà-stichewanuk (locative; Richardson 1852:264). The Roman Catholic settlement at Lac

Sainte Anne is called *pi·hta·pe·kohk* 'at the old river channel'.

Attawapiskat. The Cree form is unknown, but in 1658 the Ataouabouscatouek (pl.) were listed as one of the four Cree divisions (JR 44:248). Creuxius (in JR 46:map) used the Latinized form Ata8ab8skat8ci in 1660. The Bouscouttons, mentioned in 1671 (Margry 1879–1888, 1:97), are probably the same people.

Monsoni. In 1672 Albanel encountered the Monsou-nik (Ojibwa *mo·nsoni·k*, pl.) on the shore of James Bay (JR 56:202). Borrowed into French the name appears in the following shapes: Monsonis, 1679 (Greysolon Dulhut in Margry 1879–1888, 6:31); Monsony, 1688 (Franquelin in Warkentin and Ruggles 1970:49); Mon-saunis, 1697 (Bacqueville de la Potherie 1931:263); Monzoni, 1709 (Lahontan in Winsor 1884–1889, 4:258–259); Monsonnis, 1729 (La Vérendrye in Warkentin and Ruggles 1970:73); Monsoni or Mosonique (Dobbs 1744:33). Horden created the form Moosonee in 1872 for the name of an Anglican diocese (J.K. Fraser 1968:243), but there is no evidence that it is an acceptable Cree word, although the locative *mo·soni·hk* '(at) Moose Factory' exists (Pentland 1970–1979). A Cree group-name *omo·soni·w* 'moose person' (the translation is inaccurate insofar as it leaves the segment *-ni(·)-* unexplained) probably underlies the place-name and the French form Aumoussonnites, a tribe mentioned in 1671 (Margry 1879–1888, 1:97); the Ojibwa name is either cognate with or borrowed from Cree.

Cheyenne traditions mention the Móĭseo (Mooney 1907a:368–369, 427), a group that accompanied the Cheyenne onto the Plains but later returned to the Woodlands. Mooney claimed that the Móĭseo were the Monsoni, apparently basing his argument on the similarity between the two names, but there is no connection: if the Cheyenne had already known the name of the Monsoni before their westward migration, they would now pronounce it **méhene* (pl.).

In English sources the Moose Cree are called the Moose River Indians (as by Gorst [1670–1671] in Tyrrell 1931:390), sometimes misspelled Mouse River (Williams 1975:42). The name is a translation of Cree *mo·so-si·piy*, which Graham wrote Moose waw sepe (in Isham 1949:317) and Moosu-Sepee (Graham 1969:207). Richardson's (1852:265) Muswà-sipi is an ungrammatical combination of Cree *mo·swa* 'moose' and *si·piy* 'river'; this and other group names were re-elicited by Richardson from a list that Thomas Hutchins copied from Graham.

Since Albanel said that the Mousousipiou (Moose River) was also called Kichesipiou (Old Cree *kiše·-si·piw*, modern *kiše·-si·piy* 'great river'), the Kichesi-piiriniouek mentioned in 1658 (JR 44:250) and Radisson's misspelled Kischeripirini (Radisson 1961:160) may refer to the same band. The Moose Cree are also the most likely candidates for the Kilistinons des Nip-

isiriniens (JR 44:248), so called because the Nipissings had "discovered" them.

Nipigon. An Old Ojibwa form *alimipi·k*, perhaps meaning '(where) the water begins' (referring to the height of land north of Lake Superior), is attested from 1658 as the name of Lake Nipigon (Alimibeg) and the band of Kilistinons Alimibegouek who lived near it (JR 44:242, 248). In 1685 Jaillot published a map on which the name was misspelled Alemenipigon (Warkentin and Ruggles 1970:53); confusion was heightened by vague knowledge of a Lake Ouinipigon (Winnipeg) in the same direction from Sault Sainte Marie. Carver (1778:415) mentions the Nipegons, but by his day the area was probably Ojibwa (Bishop 1974).

Piscotagami (perhaps Cree *piskwata·kamiy* 'mound lake'?). In the second quarter of the eighteenth century the Piscotagemies were among the groups trading at Moose Factory (Coats 1852:41). In 1709 Raudot (1904:99; Kinietz 1940:366) gave the name as Pisouotagamis, perhaps an error for Piscoutagamis, but the only clue to their location and identity is that they are listed between the Monsonis and Abitibis, which is about where Jaillot showed a Lake Piscoutagamy on his 1685 map (Warkentin and Ruggles 1970:53).

Severn. The Cree place-name *wa·šaha·w si·piy*, *wa·saha·wi-si·piy* 'bay river, Severn River' (Pentland 1970–1979; Faries 1938:502) was borrowed by the Hudson's Bay Company traders with or without *si·piy* 'river': Washahoe or New Severn Indian, 1671 (Gorst in Tyrrell 1931:392); Quashe·o, 1743 (error for Ouashe·o; Isham 1949:113); Owashoes, 1727–1751 (Coats 1852:41); Washe ho Sepe, 1775 (Graham in Isham 1949:316); Washeo-Sepee, 1791 (Graham 1969:206); Washè-u-sipi (Richardson 1852:264).

Winisk (Cree *wi·nask* 'groundhog'). The Winisk River flows north from what is now Northern Ojibwa territory to the Cree settlement at its mouth. Graham listed a Winisk River band of Ojibwa (see the synonymy in "Northern Ojibwa," this vol.), but Honigmann (1956:24) gives a Swampy Cree form Wii´-niskiiwiisakahiikaniiwi´niiwak (equivalent to *wi·nasko-sa·kahikan-ininiwak* 'groundhog lake people') as the name of the Winisk Cree. The modern band name is also spelled Weenusk.

Winnipeg. There were perhaps two groups who called themselves *wi·nipe·ko·wak*, besides the Coasters on the east side of James Bay. The Cree word *wi·nipe·k* 'foul water, salt water' refers primarily to Hudson Bay but was also the name of Lake Winnipeg; the West Main Cree apparently used *wi·nipe·ko·w* for a person from either area. The Oüenebigonhelinis or Oüenebigonchelinis, whom Bacqueville de la Potherie (1931:337, 341, 355, 1753, 1:122, 131) saw in 1697 at York Factory, were confused with the Winnebago by Hodge (1907–1910, 2:961; corrected by Michelson 1934), and the Ovenigibonc, one of the bands who came

229

to Sault Sainte Marie from the north in 1670, were misidentified as the Winnebago by Thwaites (JR 54:133–134, 73:210, 214); both references are probably to Hudson Bay Cree. Coats (1852:41) mentions both Great and Little Winipeggons, perhaps 'coast Indians' and 'Lake Winnipeg Indians'; Graham (1969:192, 206) gave Winepeg and Winnepeg as the inland Indians' name for the Home-guard, those who lived with the traders on the shore of the bay.

During the early nineteenth century groups came to be called after the post they frequented, and these names became fixed with the signing of the treaties. In the 1970s most West Main Cree belonged to the Moose Factory, New Post, Albany, Attawapiskat, Weenusk (Winisk), Fort Severn, and York Factory bands, but not all the names were still appropriate: most of the New Post band lived in Moosonee, and no one had lived at York Factory since its closing in 1957.

Sources

For reconstructing the culture as it probably was prior to heavy European influence, there are the firsthand observations made at York Factory and Churchill between 1697 and 1791 by Bacqueville de la Potherie (1931:222–238, 261–267), Isham (1949:61–177, 316–317), and Graham (1969:141–212). Graham's data are sometimes hard to identify as pertaining specifically to coastal Cree. For a history of the fur trade in the seventeenth and eighteenth centuries, see Williams (1970:9–15); for nineteenth-century painted scenes of southern James Bay trading posts see A.M. Johnson (1967a).

In 1909 at Fort Albany Skinner (1912:8–116) gave considerable attention to eliciting customs of former times. He also described contemporary behavior patterns and beliefs that a knowledge of areal ethnography indicates to be of autochthonous origin. In 1947–1948, with additional checking in 1955, Honigmann (1956) at Attawapiskat probed for recollections of culture patterns uninfluenced by factors of contact.

Honigmann's studies of the contemporary culture of Attawapiskat in 1947–1948, 1955, and 1956 resulted in a report emphasizing ecology and foodways (Honigmann 1961) and several papers (1949a, 1953, 1957, 1958) dealing with special topics. Trudeau studied acculturation in Winisk 1958–1960 (Trudeau 1966; Chance and Trudeau 1963; Liebow and Trudeau 1962). Nonas (1963) did fieldwork in Attawapiskat. Koolage (1971) gives some attention to the Cree and Cree Métis adaptations to the town of Churchill (see also Egloff, Koolage, and Vranas 1968). Papers by Rogers (1966, 1967), Rogers and Trudeau (1968–1972, 3), and Bishop (1972) discussing demography and ecology for the coastal Cree and other areas are based on a variety of primary sources, including, in Bishop's case, Hudson's Bay Company Archives. Detailed accounts of the Roman Catholic church in James Bay have been written by Paul-Émile (1952) and Nadeau (1954). For a James Bay bibliography see Feit et al. (1972). Hoffmann (1961) has analyzed culture and personality adaptation among Attawapiskat Indians.

Northern Ojibwa

EDWARD S. ROGERS AND J. GARTH TAYLOR

Language, Territory, and Environment

The name Northern Ojibwa (ō'jībwā) here refers to the Ojibwa Indians that live along the upper courses of the rivers that flow generally northeast into Hudson and James bays, from Island Lake, Manitoba, to Ogoki, Ontario (fig. 1). It thus refers to only the northernmost of the groups called Northern Ojibwa by Dunning (1959:5) and includes only Island Lake, Sandy Lake, and Deer Lake of the groups east of Lake Winnipeg to which the name was applied by Hallowell (1955:112–113). The territory occupied by the Northern Ojibwa corresponds essentially to the Patricia portion of the Precambrian Uplands of northern Ontario with a slight extension west into Manitoba and a possible extension southeast. The total area comprises approximately 100,000 square miles. The people within this region appear to have had a somewhat distinctive cultural history in relation to other Ojibwa due in part to the nature of the country they inhabit and in part to influences exerted by the Cree to the north and east. It has also been argued that the distinctive features exhibited by the Northern Ojibwa are attributable to their recent arrival in the north (see "Territorial Groups Before 1821: Cree and Ojibwa," this vol.).

Data are not sufficiently complete to draw a rigid boundary for the territory of the Northern Ojibwa at any period in their history. Population movements and intermarriage with surrounding groups, as well as the infusion of other Indian and European culture traits, have contributed to a blurring of boundaries. Nevertheless, the Northern Ojibwa do form, at least in part, a distinct dialect unit, being coextensive with the Severn dialect (Todd 1970; J.D. Nichols 1975) except for including also a few groups of somewhat different speech immediately to the south.* To the northwest (Wolfart 1973), north, and east are Cree; to the southwest, the Northwestern dialect of Ojibwa (J.D. Nichols 1975). In addition to their partial dialectal distinctness, the

*The orthography used to spell words in all varieties of Ojibwa in the *Handbook* follows the analysis of Bloomfield (1946, 1957), using the following phonemic symbols: *p, t, č, k, ʾ; s, š; m, n; w, y; i, a, o; iˑ, eˑ, aˑ, oˑ*. This is the transcription referred to as General Ojibwa in "Subarctic Algonquian Languages" (this vol.), where details on pronunciation in the different dialects are given. In the Severn dialect preaspirated stops (such as *hk*) appear instead of the geminate stops of the other dialects (*kk*), and *h* appears for *ʾ*.

Northern Ojibwa lacked, except along their southern margin, certain cultural traits found among their Ojibwa neighbors to the west and south. Notably lacking are social and religious elaborations such as patriclans and the Midewiwin and (excepting Sandy Lake) *manitoˑhkeˑwak* ceremonies (Rogers 1958–1959; cf. "Saulteaux of Lake Winnipeg," this vol.). In regard to environment, for example, most Northern Ojibwa were outside the range of wild rice and the sugar maple, a fact that limited the subsistence potential of their area compared to that of their southern neighbors.

History and Culture

Lack of information makes it difficult to distinguish precise time periods enabling one to describe the cultural changes that have taken place since contact with Europeans. Tentatively, four periods are proposed: the early fur-trade period, 1670–1821; the early contact-traditional period, 1821–1900; the late contact-traditional period, 1900–1950; and the modern period, since 1950.

Early Fur Trade Period, 1670–1821

No doubt some of the ancestors of the Northern Ojibwa had had direct contact with Europeans prior to 1670, the year in which the Hudson's Bay Company was incorporated. Yet not until the 1740s can the Northern Ojibwa be dimly perceived as a distinct group, included under the name Nakawawuck (Isham 1949:314–315; cf. Graham 1969:204; Richardson 1852:265).

During the period 1670–1821, the Northern Ojibwa gradually became dependent upon European trade goods, which they secured in return for furs. For approximately a century following contact, the Northern Ojibwa secured goods, although not food to any extent, from trading posts located on James and Hudson bays—Fort Albany, Fort Severn, and York Factory—and from French posts in the vicinity of Lake Nipigon and along the middle course of the Albany River (Bishop 1969:317–318, 320). For more than half the period, the trading posts were located outside the territory of the Northern Ojibwa. Only after about 1740 did traders establish posts within Northern Ojibwa country (fig. 1). Prior to

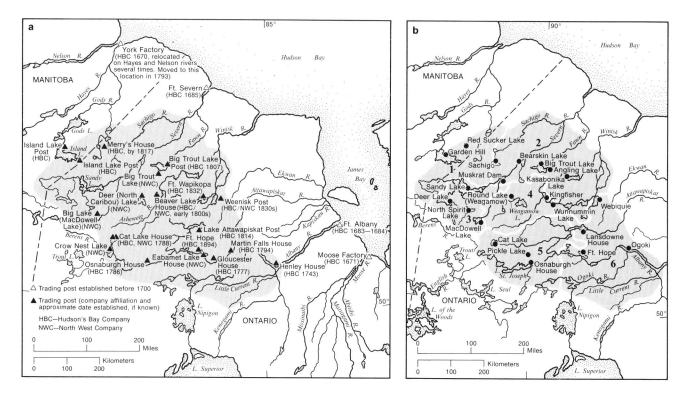

Fig. 1. Nineteenth-century territory with a, historic trading posts, and b, 1970s settlements and bands designated by the government at the time of treaty: 1, Island Lake; 2, Trout Lake; 3, Deer Lake; 4, Caribou Lake; 5, Osnaburgh House; 6, Fort Hope.

this time, the Northern Ojibwa secured goods either through Indian middlemen or from relatively long trips each summer to the southern or coastal posts. Such long trips may initially have posed a food problem since the northern Subarctic Algonquians apparently did not have gill nets (Skinner 1912:128) with which to exploit the available fishing sites along the routes of travel. In the late 1600s, the Hudson's Bay Company had authorized net makers to be sent to the bay to provide the Indians with gill nets so that they might more easily make the trip to the coast (Rich 1945:297); however, even as late as about 1800, remarks of Cameron (1889–1890, 2:255) suggest that Indians still did not make extensive use of gill nets.

During the late eighteenth and early nineteenth centuries, basic changes began to take place in trade relations between the Northern Ojibwa and Europeans. From 1784 to 1821, the North West Company and the Hudson's Bay Company engaged in an energetic trade war. To obtain the Indians' furs, the rival traders supplied the Northern Ojibwa with an abundance of trade goods (Cameron 1889–1890, 2:296). As long as rival traders were present in the country, the Ojibwa remained independent and could play one trader against another for trade concessions.

The abundance of trade goods brought about certain changes in the material culture of the Northern Ojibwa. It is estimated that by the late eighteenth century every adult male owned a gun. At an even earlier date, metal tools had begun to replace those of bone; and stone

and metal containers, those of hide and bark (table 1). Furthermore, although caribou, moose, beaver, marten, lynx, and otter skins provided material for clothing—moccasins, leggings, robes, and jackets—garments of European manufacture and cloth were offered by the traders and many Northern Ojibwa made use of these materials (Bishop 1969:324–352).

Prior to the late eighteenth and early nineteenth centuries, data are too limited to allow the definition of a regular yearly cycle for the Northern Ojibwa. Apparently, they might visit the nearest trading post at any time of the year. As early as about 1780, according to Long, people near the Albany River may have been selling sturgeon to the traders (Thwaites 1904:155). By about 1800, bands generally assembled at the trading posts in the early part of the summer to await the arrival of the brigades that brought new "outfits" (the year's supplies for the posts) for the coming season. Occasionally, such concentrations of Indians exhausted the supply of food in the immediate vicinity of the posts and starvation occurred.

Once the Indians had secured trade goods, they moved to a fishery. As fall approached, the people picked berries and killed whatever animals they could find: beaver, otter, and big game (Bishop 1969:268–269). Shortly thereafter the deep winter snows would arrive; as they increased in depth, moose and caribou could be more easily killed. Yet it was a time of year when the people had to be frequently on the move in search of food (Cameron 1889–1890, 2:258). With the coming of spring, the Northern Ojibwa took beaver and big game, and during May they hunted waterfowl that had returned from the south. At the same time, some groups fished for sturgeon (Bishop 1969:269). Soon it was time to seek a congenial trading establishment where they might profitably secure a new supply of trade goods for the furs taken during the winter.

The sociopolitical organization of the Northern Ojibwa during the late 1700s and early 1800s is not clearly discernible. The people appear to have been organized in bands, the core of which consisted of an elder and his married sons with male affines often included. This extended family may have numbered between 20 and 40 people. With the addition of other nuclear families, most likely relatives, the total aggregate may have been anywhere from 50 to possibly 75 individuals (Bishop 1969:275–281).

Some bands may have been named after the leader of the core family. Although no complete census of Northern Ojibwa bands exists, several have been mentioned for the late eighteenth century: the Cranes, of Weagamow Lake; the Suckers, part of Sandy Lake (Rogers and Rogers 1980; Bishop 1969:277–278; Skinner 1912:164; D. Anderson 1873:239; Godsell 1938:41); and some of the Nakawewuck bands living north of Lake Superior and east of Lake Winnipeg that traded with the Hudson's Bay Company—Nameu-Sepee, Wapus, Uinescaw-Sepee 'Winisk River', Mistehay Sakahegan 'big lake'; Lake Winnipeg', Shumataway 'Shamattawa(?)' (Graham 1969: 204, 206; Richardson 1852:265).

Each band was led by a senior male of the core family. Frequently, if not always, these individuals acted as the "trade-chiefs" (Bishop 1969; Cameron 1889–1890, 2:278). The position of leader appears to have been based on his ability to secure for his followers abundant trade goods, to excel as a hunter, and to command superior religious knowledge. Nevertheless, such individuals were charismatic, not autocratic leaders. Their followers could sever their allegiance at will (Bishop 1969:278–282).

Each band tended to habitually exploit a particular territory, a "hunting range" or "hunting area" (Rogers 1962:C22). Such territories were not rigidly bounded and trespass was not resented. Indications are that when big game was abundant, the band remained together as a unit throughout the year.

The religion of the Northern Ojibwa revolved around the concept of "power" (manito·hke·win). An individual received "power" from the spirits through a vision quest and dreams (Cameron 1889–1890, 2:260–261). The "power" obtained could be used for both good and evil. It could be used to manipulate the supernatural, the natural environment, and people. An example was combatting the Windigo (wi·ntiko·), a cannibal being who in winter often preyed on humans. Those who received the most "power" became shamans (Cameron 1889–1890, 2:249–250), and the type of instructions received when "power" was acquired determined the type of shaman the person would be. At least five different types of shamans existed, the most important being the shaking-tent performer (Cameron 1889–1890, 2:264), the mite·-na·pe· ("spirit-man"), and the herbalist (Rogers 1962:D10).

Early Contact-Traditional Period, 1821–1900

Starting in 1821, when the Hudson's Bay Company and North West Company joined forces, the way of life of the Northern Ojibwa began to alter rapidly. Since the reorganized Hudson's Bay Company had no rivals and furbearers had then become scarce, the Company closed many trading posts and restricted the import of trade goods. Because of these changes, the trappers could no longer "dictate" to the traders (Bishop 1969:308). Furthermore, by 1825 furbearers and caribou had been greatly reduced in numbers and moose had been annihilated (Bishop 1969:292; Cameron 1889–1890, 2:296). During the second half of the nineteenth century, moose began to reappear (Peterson 1955:45–49), and caribou may have increased somewhat in numbers.

Because of the alterations that had occurred in the faunal resources by 1825 the Northern Ojibwa instituted a new adaptive strategy to gain sustenance from the land. They began to take fish and hare intensively, soon being forced to depend upon these species as their mainstay. Since the country had been largely depleted of furbearers, the Northern Ojibwa had to intensify their trapping endeavors. In times of dire need Northern Ojibwa relied upon food supplied by the traders, such as fish, potatoes, and flour (Bishop 1969:272, 287–288, 292; Cameron 1889–1890, 2:296; Rogers and Black 1976).

With the quantity and variety of trade goods restricted and faunal resources altered, the Northern Ojibwa had also to make alterations in certain items of their material culture. No longer could they clothe themselves exclusively with moose and caribou hides or European cloth. Instead, they had to rely upon hare skins for clothing—parkas, hoods, mittens, breechclouts, leggings, and occasionally moccasins (Skinner 1912:122)—a material that had been worn primarily as the garb of women and children (Bishop 1969:291). Moccasins were sometimes also made of sturgeon skin (Skinner 1912:123–124).

Since the Northern Ojibwa during the first half of the period often lacked sufficient hides of moose and caribou from which to make babiche for lacing snowshoes, they devised as a substitute snowshoes of solid wood (Skinner 1912:146; Bishop 1969:289, 290). The laced snowshoes in use were of two styles: a long, narrow,

Table 1. Selective Inventory of Northern Ojibwa Material Culture

Trait	Early Contact 1670–1821	Contact-Traditional 1821–1900	1900–1950	Modern 1950–1970
Subsistence				
bow and arrow complex				
simple bow	x	x	x	o
arrow, 3–4 feathers		x	x	o
blunt head simple	x	x	x	o
crossbow	o	1870	x	o
firearms				
muzzle-loaders	1780	r	r	o
shotguns	o			x
rifles	o			x
snares				
large game	?	x	x	o
beaver	o	o	1930?	x
small game	x		1920-, wire	x
deadfalls	x	x	x	o
nets for birds		x	x	o
commercial traps	o	r	r	x
decoys for geese	?	x	x	
fishing devices				
gill net		r	r	x
iron ice chisel		x	x	x
metal fishhook		?	x	x
spear (sturgeon)	?	x	x	
weir	?	x	x	r
Travel and Transportation				
birchbark canoe				
small, 15 feet	x	x	x	r
large		x	x	r
canvas-covered canoe	o	o	r	x
outboard motors	o	o	r	x
tumpline		x	x	r
snowshoe				
round toe	x	x	x	x
pointed	o	1850	x	x
wooden	o	1820	x	o
toboggan				
native	x	x	x	x
commercial	o	o	o	r
dog-team	o	1880	x	x
canoe-sled	o	1880	x	x
sled	o	1880	x	x
snowmobile	o	o	o	x
cradleboards	x	x	x	x
Structures and Heat				
dwellings				
conical spruce bough		x	x	r
conical birchbark		x	x	
conical hide		x	x	o
conical earth-covered		1880	x	o
ridge-pole lodge		x	x	o
dome-shaped lodge		x	x	o
log cabin	o	1880	x	x
government houses	o	o	o	1960
canvas tent	o	1880	x	r

234

Table 1. Selective Inventory of Northern Ojibwa Material Culture (*Continued*)

Trait	Early Contact 1670–1821	Contact-Traditional 1821–1900	Contact-Traditional 1900–1950	Modern 1950–1970
open fire	x	x	x	o
clay chimney	o	1880	x	o
metal wood stove	o	?	x	x
Clothing				
beaver skin	x	r?	r?	o
hare skin	r	x	x	r
parkas		x	x	r
hoods		x	x	r
mittens		x	x	o
breechclout		x	x	o
pants		x	x	o
leggings		x	x	o
socks		x	x	o
blankets		x	x	r
moose or caribou hide	x	r	r	r
moccasins	x	x	x	x
slipper	?	x	x	r
pointed	?	x	x	r
puckered	o	o	1930	x
mittens	?	?	x	x
mukluk	o	o	1930	x

NOTE: Approximate date of inception of trait is given when known.
x = trait present, o = trait absent, r = trait rare.

and pointed type and a shorter one with rounded toe (Skinner 1912:145–146). The former was quite likely adopted during the 1800s from native peoples to the west. Other items of winter transport equipment were toboggans for moving supplies and canoe-sleds used in the spring (Skinner 1912:145). Toward the end of the period or soon thereafter, large dogs were acquired and used to haul the toboggans and sleds.

Presumably, the birchbark canoe (fig. 2) for summer travel remained unaltered from the previous period. The frame was made by the men and the covering secured to the frame by the women (Cameron 1889–1890, 2:257; Skinner 1912:131–132). Another transportation device was the cradleboard (fig. 3) in which infants were secured (Cameron 1889–1890, 2:256). Skinner (1912:144) claims that the type without a hoop was the oldest.

Limited information is available regarding subsistence technology. The trap for whitefish (Skinner 1912:137; McInnis 1912:134; Camsell 1912:93) may have been introduced at this time. Furthermore, since fewer trade guns were now available, it can be surmised that indigenous deadfalls and snares were used more commonly than had been the case in former years.

No doubt, the Northern Ojibwa made other adjustments to the changes in the resource base such as the more extensive use of brush and birchbark as a substitute for hides in lodge coverings. Yet the basic dwelling styles presumably remained the same, consisting of the ridgepole and conical lodges (Cameron 1889–1890, 2:255–256; Skinner 1912:119–120). According to Skinner (1912:153), the dome-shaped lodge was common. Toward the end of the period, the moss-covered lodge came into use (Rogers 1963). Lodge floors were covered with boughs or, in the south, mats made from the inner bark of cedar or bulrushes (Skinner 1912:127). Open fireplaces provided heat and light; fire was made with a bow drill (Skinner 1912:138).

Many of the indigenous tools, containers, and utensils continued in use throughout the period: bone fleshers and beamers (Skinner 1912:125–127), bone and wooden snowshoe needles (Skinner 1912:128), sewing needles of bone or thorn (Skinner 1912:132), and birchbark boxes (fig. 4) were common. The southern bands also utilized splint baskets, woven bags of cedar bark, wicker baskets, and netted bags (Skinner 1912:128–129).

Following 1825, the yearly cycle began to alter in response to the new economic and subsistence conditions. During the summer, the bands assembled at profitable fishing sites. From there the men made trips to the nearest trading post. With the coming of fall, each band broke up into hunting groups, each moving to a favorable rapid to continue fishing. There the men built traps for whitefish, a species that at this time of the year ascended and, several weeks later, descended the streams. With luck, sufficient fish could be secured and preserved for the weeks ahead.

Fig. 2. Boy in a birchbark canoe built by his grandmother, Maria Mikenak, at a time when most of the Northern Ojibwa had been using canvas canoes for several decades. The dark caulking is spruce gum mixed with lard and charcoal. Photograph by John Macfie, near Osnaburgh House on the Albany River, Ont., 1956.

Fig. 3. A woman from Lansdowne House, Ont., carrying a baby in a wooden cradleboard. The baby, wrapped in blankets, is laced into a bag decorated with appliqué work and tied with lacing cut from tanned hide. Traditionally, sphagnum moss, to serve as a disposable diaper, was packed around the infant's front and buttocks. Photograph by John Macfie, 1954.

As winter intensified, the hunting groups had to leave the site of their traps, which were frozen in; furthermore, few if any fish were still available at such spots. If possible, camps were situated near a lake where fishing through the ice might be profitable. Presumably set lines and jigging were the methods employed in under-ice fishing, the hook being a composite type with wooden shank and bone barb (Skinner 1912:137).

With the arrival of spring, the people often moved to sites near the outlets or inlets of lakes where open water would first occur and where fishing was easier and waterfowl would soon be arriving from the south. Shortly thereafter the hunting groups returned to the summer gathering spots (Rogers 1962:A22–A25).

As the annual cycle altered, modifications took place in the sociopolitical organization of the Northern Ojibwa. The band now assembled as a unit with face-to-face relationships only during the summer at a fishing station or trading post. As in earlier times, the band was under the direction of one of the elder males known for his hunting abilities and superior religious powers.

At other times of the year, the band was fragmented into three or four hunting groups. The hunting group was a social unit that apparently evolved during this period. Hunting groups ranged in size from approximately 15 to 25 individuals; each was in effect a bilateral extended family (Rogers 1969:24–32). At the same time, as the Northern Ojibwa came to depend more on the limited fur resources of the area, they evolved a concept of vaguely demarcated "hunting territories." These were in reality trapping territories and served to facilitate an equitable allocation of fur resources. At first, only beaver lodges were marked to denote "ownership" of the beaver therein, but in time territorial boundaries were established for each hunting-trapping group. Within each territory the group had exclusive rights to the fur resources but not to other resources or to the land itself (Bishop 1970a; Rogers 1962:C22–C24).

The kinship terminology during the nineteenth century was bifurcate collateral with Iroquois cousin terminology. Cross-cousin and polygynous marriages were permitted (Skinner 1912:151; Cameron 1889–1890, 2:242–252; Rogers 1962:B10–B13, B48). The levirate and sororate were also practiced (Cameron 1889–1890, 2:252). In addition, clans were said to exist among the more southerly groups (Skinner 1912:149–150) but have not been reported among the bands to the north. Skinner (1912:149) reported that the clans were matrilineal, but Bishop (1969:185) doubts that this was the case.

Late Contact-Traditional Period, 1900–1950

The period from 1900 to 1950 was characterized by a significant decline in the mobility that marked the ear-

Fig. 4. William Moore making a birchbark container. left, Splitting white spruce root to make lacing; center, soaking the split spruce root in hot water to make it more pliable; right, applying reddish stain to completed container by rubbing it with boiled alder bark. Photographs by John Macfie at Mattagami Reserve, Ont., 1957.

lier period. Accompanying this decline was a transition from native house types to log cabins and the emergence of what has been referred to as all-native settlements (Helm and Damas 1963).

Government involvement in the lives of the Indians had started in the earlier era with the signing of treaties and establishment of "treaty bands." Those bands along the north shore of Lake Superior made treaty in 1850. They were followed by Lac Seul in 1873, by Osnaburg, Fort Hope, and Martin Falls in 1906 (D.C. Scott 1906), and by Island Lake in 1909 and Deer Lake in 1910. In 1929 and 1930 the last treaties were signed with the people of Trout Lake and Caribou Lake (J.L. Morris 1943). In addition to making annual treaty payments, the government issued emergency rations and supported schools in a few of the larger trading post centers; however, contact with government agencies remained minimal for the vast majority of people in the area.

Contact with the outside world was increased dramatically by major developments dating from the close of the prior period. The first significant event was the construction of the Canadian Pacific Railway along the north shore of Lake Superior. This line, completed in the 1880s, was followed by the more northerly Canadian National Railway just prior to World War I. With these developments, most trading centers in the area began to obtain their supplies from new railway towns, rather than from the old posts on the shores of Hudson and James bays.

Another major development in transportation was the advent of "bush flying" in the years that followed World War I. By the 1930s airplanes were flying supplies into the most remote regions from bases on or near the railway. The use of airplanes increased the amount and variety of supplies that could be supplied

to northern settlements. Air transportation eventually spelled the doom of the canoe brigades that had formerly been an important source of summer employment for the Indians.

After the advent of the railways, canvas-covered canoes became common and by the 1920s had almost completely replaced locally made birchbark canoes. Although the number of imported goods continued to increase and included items such as violins, guitars, and even a few gramophones, many utilitarian items (fig. 6) of local manufacture persisted throughout the period. Prominent among such items were mittens, moccasins, snowshoes (fig. 7), and birchbark boxes (Skinner 1912:119–149; Rogers 1962:C62–C64).

Throughout this period, there was a steady increase in the variety of foods obtained. This resulted partly from the return of caribou and moose to many of the regions and partly from the greater availability of imported staples such as flour, sugar, lard, and suet. In many areas gardening was undertaken, the main crop being potatoes. Although sporadic gardening efforts had begun in some regions during the late nineteenth century, local gardens did not become common until the 1930s and 1940s.

Concomitant with the increase in material goods and food supplies was the development of semisedentary all-native settlements. A detailed reconstruction, based on 1949 census material, reveals that in the Lansdowne House area the average size of six all-native settlements was 62 persons (Taylor 1972:22). Within each of the six settlements the majority of married couples were connected by means of primary kin ties with other members of the community. Most couples that did not have primary ties in 1949 appear to have lost their kin connections through deaths occurring just prior to that date (Taylor 1972:25). The six settlements in the sample *237* was that the former encouraged and trained local men to be catechists. By the end of the period most of the Anglican settlements had native catechists who gave services in their own homes or in the small local churches that began to appear in the early 1930s. Some of the catechists were powerful local leaders, exerting their influence in secular as well as in religious matters.

The Modern Period, 1950–

After 1950 most all-native settlements were abandoned, as more and more people moved into larger communities. In the new centralized communities, many of which grew up around former trading posts, several new services were available. Most, such as health and education services, were provided by Euro-Canadians from outside the area.

Health services were increased considerably with the construction of the Indian Hospital in Sioux Lookout in 1949. At about the same time, nursing stations were built in some of the larger communities such as Trout Lake, Osnaburgh House, and Lansdowne House. One of the most dramatic results of the increase in health facilities was the sharp decline in infant mortality. This resulted in a rapid growth of population.

Government programs in the field of education also

Ministry of Nat. Resources, Ont. Div. of Mines, Toronto.

Fig. 5. Robert Fidler, chief of the Sandy Lake Ojibwa, Deer Lake band. The suit was probably issued to him by the federal government, along with his chief's medal (not here worn). Photographed in July 1937.

showed a relatively well-developed tendency to local endogamy. The percentage of endogamous marriages ranged from 33 percent to 89 percent, with an overall average of 65 percent. In the 23 marriages that were not endogamous, the immigrant spouse was the wife in 17 cases and the husband in only six. This suggests a tendency to virilocal residence at the settlement level.

Many of the more overt features of the native religion, such as the shaking-tent rite, gave way under the increasing influence of Christianity. The first baptisms were made by Anglican and Roman Catholic missionaries who had entered the area prior to the turn of the century. Two of the earliest Anglican missionaries were the Rev. William Dick ("Subarctic Algonquian Languages," fig. 6, this vol.), who built a church at Trout Lake around 1883, and the Rev. R. Faries, who built a church at Fort Hope in 1895. Both men were Cree Indians who had been ordained at the older missions on the coast of Hudson and James bays. The Roman Catholic missionaries were usually nonnatives.

One of the main differences in the proselytizing methods of the Anglican and Roman Catholic missionaries

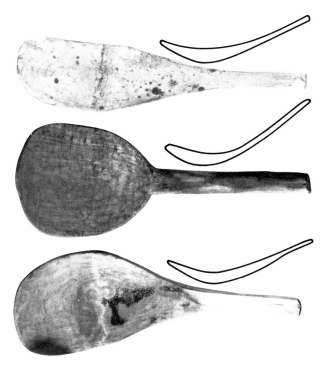

Amer. Mus. of Nat. Hist., New York: 50.7450, 50.8070, 50.8069.

Fig. 6. Wooden spoons in a variety of shapes were used for preparing and eating food. They were usually carved from the wood at the juncture of the trunk and roots of birch trees (Skinner 1912:134). Length of top spoon about 28 cm. All collected by Alanson Skinner, top at Martin Falls, Ont., rest at Fort Hope, Ont., 1909.

ROGERS AND TAYLOR

Fig. 7. Willie Coaster, from Ogoki, Ont., shaping the frames for a pair of pointed-toe snowshoes. Once the frames dry thoroughly in this shape, holes are drilled to take the lacing ("Montagnais-Naskapi," fig. 4, this vol.). Photograph by John Macfie at Ogoki, Ont., 1959.

Royal Ont. Mus., Toronto: 959.50.117a.
Fig. 8. Hare-skin sock, used as duffel inside moccasins. Length about 28 cm, collected by Edward S. Rogers at Weagamow Lake, Ont., 1958–1959.

expanded rapidly. At the end of World War II the only formal education available to most children in the area was that provided by residential schools located in Sioux Lookout, Kenora, and McIntosh. By 1970 day schools had been constructed in almost all the communities. With the construction of day schools, many women who had formerly accompanied their husbands on the trapline now remained in the village to care for school-age children.

Trading posts in the modern communities have taken on the character of ordinary retail stores with the increased importance of cash in the economy. Although the Hudson's Bay Company remained the largest trade

and retail organization in the area, there were smaller independent stores in most communities, some of which were run by native people.

The modern period witnessed a further decline in the number of material possessions of native manufacture, and a corresponding increase in the number and variety of factory-made consumer goods, the most obvious of which were outboard motors, chain saws, and snowmobiles. Automobiles began to make their appearance in those communities, such as Osnaburgh House, that were reached by roads.

One of the most significant changes in the economy was a decline in the relative importance of trapping as a source of earned income. An analysis of fur harvests in the Weagamow Lake area during the 1949–1967 period revealed a decline both in total value of the fur harvest and in average income per trapper (J. Watts 1971:74–77). This was attributed largely to a decrease in fur prices. There was no evidence of any overall decline in the harvest per trapper or in the number of active trappers (J. Watts 1971:75). However, the fact that the number of trappers remained constant in spite of a rapidly increasing population indicates a decrease in the percentage of men engaged in trapping.

The decline in trapping income was offset by the growth of other seasonal or part-time employment opportunities, such as short-term construction jobs, logging and sawmill operations, tourist guiding, and commercial fishing. In addition, many men from northern settlements held temporary jobs outside their home communities as fire fighters and tree planters (Taylor 1969). Although some men in the southern part of the area found permanent employment in mining and on the railroad (Baldwin 1957), full-time jobs remained rare throughout most of the area. In the north they were restricted mainly to service occupations in local stores, schools, and hospitals.

In addition to an increase in the amount of income from new types of employment, there was a sharp increase in the amount of government assistance. In 1969 government subsidy payments represented approximately 33 percent of the total income at Lansdowne House (Taylor 1969) and approximately 47 percent of the total income at Weagamow Lake (M. Black 1971:188). With the increase in cash income there was a decrease in the use of wild foods for domestic consumption and also in the cultivation of local gardens.

The modern trading-post villages (table 2) were usually composed of members from several of the earlier all-native settlements. In many of the villages, such as Weagamow Lake (Rogers 1962:B89) and Lansdowne House (Taylor 1969), the members of the former settlements remained in close residential proximity, thus forming relatively distinct "neighborhoods." In others, such as Osnaburgh House (Bishop 1969:71), the old settlement groups became somewhat mixed due to gov- *239* ernment housing and road-building projects. However, the preference for residing in close proximity to near kin has remained (Taylor 1972). The modern villages have become increasingly endogamous as their populations have expanded, while the populations of the officially recognized bands (table 3) are often scattered in more than one settlement. Differences between the lists in table 2 and table 3 are due to the fact that some bands are found in more than one often mixed settlement or at a settlement with a different name. For example, the Martin Falls band is at Ogoki, the Caribou Lake band is at Round Lake, the Deer Lake band is at Deer Lake and Sandy Lake, and members of the Fort Hope band are also at Lansdowne House and Webiquie. Many of these bands are officially listed as linguistically Cree (Canada. Department of Indian and Northern Affairs 1980) or as Cree and Ojibwa (Canada. Department of Energy, Mines and Resources 1980); for the identification of their speech as Ojibwa see "Subarctic Algonquian Languages," this volume.

The nature of the household unit shows considerable variation throughout the region. In Round Lake multifamily households seem to be extremely rare, with no cases reported in 1958 (Rodgers 1962:B68) and only one case reported in 1968 (M. Black 1971:237). In Lansdowne House and Webiquie single-family households were also in the majority, but it was by no means unusual for two or even three nuclear families to share a single dwelling (Taylor 1969, 1970). Most of such households contained a father and his married sons. In Osnaburgh House there was not a single case of a father and son sharing a household, although some households were shared with wife's parents (Bishop 1969:74).

Traditionally patterns of leadership and authority appear to have declined sharply in many modern villages, such as Osnaburgh House (Bishop 1969:78) and Lansdowne House (Taylor 1969). In Weagamow Lake, this decline was partly counter-balanced after 1958 by an increase in the political influence of the elected chief and councilors (Rogers 1962:B89–B92; M. Black 1971:279). In some of the more isolated Anglican communities, such as Webiquie, Kingfisher, and Kasabonika, the church catechists continued to hold important leadership positions (Taylor 1970).

In villages that had members from different Christian churches, religion often acted as an impediment to social integration. In Lansdowne House, the "split" was even evident in the settlement pattern, with the Anglicans living on the mainland and the Roman Catholics on a nearby island (Taylor 1969). Even more potential for social and spatial division was created by the arrival of new sects. For example, at Weagamow Lake a Northern Evangelical church was established in 1952, and a Pentecostal church in 1968 (M. Black 1971:283). The Pentecostals have been followed by the Mennonites.

Synonymy†

The Northern Ojibwa have never been recognized by themselves and seldom by others as a distinct group of people: the names that have been recorded refer either to small subdivisions or to groups of which the Northern Ojibwa are only a part.

The name *očipwe·* was originally the self-designation of a band north of Sault Sainte Marie, which Graham (in Isham 1949:317) listed as a band of Nakawewuck around 1775 (see the synonymy in "Southeastern Ojibwa," vol. 15). The name has been borrowed by the Cree as *ocipwe·w*, the West Main Cree term for all people living upstream from themselves (Honigmann 1956:25). Variants of Ojibwa/Chippewa and its near synonym Saulteaux have often been used to refer to the Northern Ojibwa as well as their relatives in other areas. Early historical sources use variants of the term *no·ppimink* and its French equivalent Gens des Terres

Table 2.   **Population Estimates by Settlement, 1972**

Settlements	Population
Angling Lake	60
Bearskin Lake	270
Cat Lake	160
Deer Lake	250
Fort Hope	450
Garden Hill (1970)	1,265
Kasabonika	230
Kingfisher	125
Lansdowne House	350
MacDowell Lake	30
Muskrat Dam	80
Ogoki	150
Osnaburgh House	300
Pickle Lake	75
Round Lake	335
Red Sucker Lake (1970)	235
Sachigo	140
Sandy Lake	700
St. Theresa Point (1970)	913
Trout Lake	500
Wasagamack (1970)	381
Wunnummin Lake	225
Webiquie	330
Total	7,554

SOURCES: Wolfart 1973; Canada. Department of Indian Affairs and Northern Development. Indian Affairs Branch 1970; Rogers 1965–1972.

†This synonymy was written by David H. Pentland, incorporating some materials furnished by Edward S. Rogers and J. Garth Taylor. Included are discussions of the names of some Ojibwa groups that are not certainly classed as Northern Ojibwa but appear in early sources with the Northern Ojibwa and are not discussed elsewhere in the *Handbook*, namely the Gens de la Sapinière, Outoulibis, Ouassi, Sturgeons, Moose, and Wapus.

Table 3. Official Band Populations, 1978

Ontario

Angling Lake	170
Bearskin Lake	345
Big Trout Lake	672
Caribou Lake	483
Cat Lake	278
Deer Lake	1,978
Fort Hope	1,904
Kasabonika Lake	397
Kingfisher	231
Martin Falls	252
Muskrat Dam Lake	178
Osnaburgh	862
Sachigo Lake	326
Wunnumin	284

Manitoba

Garden Hill	1,623
Red Sucker Lake	330
St. Theresa Point	1,275
Wasagamack	590
Total	10,555

SOURCE: Canada. Department of Indian Affairs and Northern Development 1980:18–28.

for the 'Indians of the interior', sometimes perhaps including the Northern Ojibwa or their ancestors (see the synonymy in "Attikamek (Tête de Boule)," this vol.).

Hallowell (1955:112–124) first used the term Northern Ojibwa but restricted it to the Lake Winnipeg area. Dunning (1959:5–6) used Northern Ojibwa for all those groups living in the northern and western part of Ojibwa territory. In this chapter the Northern Ojibwa are more narrowly delimited on the basis of new linguistic and cultural evidence. Skinner's (1912:10, 117–118) term Northern Saulteaux is nearly equivalent to Northern Ojibwa as here employed.

The northern bands of Northern Ojibwa prefer to be called Cree, a usage that has confused students and government officials: the Trout Lake, Deer Lake, and Caribou Lake bands of Northern Ojibwa are not distinguished from their Cree-speaking neighbors to the north in Canadian government publications (for example, Canada. Department of Indian Affairs and Northern Development. Indian Affairs Branch 1970:12–17). A factor contributing to the confusion is the fact that Cree is the liturgical language for many Northern Ojibwa, and they use Cree translations of the Bible and other Christian religious literature (J.D. Nichols 1975).

The most common Ojibwa self-designation is *aniššina·pe·* 'ordinary man', used by other Ojibwa groups besides the Northern Ojibwa. Some of the latter use the variant *aniššinini* 'ordinary person'. The term *ni·ʔina* 'one of us', a derivative of *ni·ʔinawe·* 'he speaks our language, he speaks Ojibwa' (Cuoq 1886:271; Baraga 1878–1880, 2:288) is also sometimes given by

Ojibwa of all areas as their own name. The form Nena Wewhck, an error for Nenawewhok or Nenawewack on Arrowsmith's 1795 map of North America (Warkentin and Ruggles 1970:133), is probably *ni·ʔinawe·wak* (pl.), although it might represent the unattested Swampy Cree cognate **ne·hinawe·wak*.

The Cree of Manitoba and farther west call the Northern Ojibwa and the closely related Saulteaux *nahkawiyiniw* (Faries 1938:372; Pentland 1970–1979), a name for which no translation is recorded. A form *nahkawe·wak* (pl.), which has been recorded in the twentieth century only as a verb meaning 'they speak Ojibwa', appears in English documents with the following spellings: Nakawawuck, 1743 (Isham 1949:112); Nackowewuck, 1772 (Graham 1969:292); Naka we wuck, 1775 (Graham in Isham 1949:317); Na,kow,wa,vouck, 1778 (Rich and Johnson 1951:210); Naka-we-wuk (Richardson 1852:264). The longer form *nahkawe·wiyiniw* 'Ojibwa-speaking person' appears in the dictionaries (Lacombe 1874:475; Faries 1938:160); the Woods Cree cognate *nahkawe·wiδiniwak* (or perhaps the modern form *nahkawi·wiδiniwak*; both are plural) was given by Alexander Henry the Younger (1897, 2:537) as Nahcowweeethinnuuck. The Northern Ojibwa have borrowed this Cree element and use the name *nahkawe·-aniššinini* as a relative term for bands to the south; at Weagamow (Round Lake) this name is applied to the people at Cat Lake, Lansdowne House, and Osnaburgh, but at Trout Lake, to the north, it includes those at Round Lake as well (Rogers 1962:A23).

In 1839 George Barnston reported that the Ojibwa at Martin's Falls (Ogoki), who were mostly Suckers, were called Bungees at York Factory and Fort Severn, a name he correctly derives from their frequent use of the word *panki·* 'a little' (Bishop 1975:203). Simms (1906:330) refers to the "Bungees, or Swampy Indians" as living between Norway House and York Factory as well as around Lake Winnipeg (cf. Michelson 1939:89). Bungee or Bungi was also frequently applied to the Plains Ojibwa, especially in Manitoba.

Seventeenth-century documents mentioned "the people of the spruce grove" in contexts that place them in the southern part of Northern Ojibwa territory. The name is rendered as Gens de la Sapinière, 1684 (Greysolon Dulhut in Margry 1879–1888, 6:51); peuples de La Sapinère, 1697 (Aubert de la Chesnaye in Margry 1879–1888, 6:7); gens de la Sapinerie, 1709 (Raudot 1904:99). In Canadian French *sapin* means 'fir', not 'spruce', which is *épinette*, as in the Epinette Nation mentioned by Dobbs (1744:32) as a tribe of Sauteurs (Ojibwa) north of Lake Superior.

Another seventeenth-century group who may have been part of the Northern Ojibwa were known by the Ojibwa name *oto·ripi·* (Old Algonquin dialect) or *oto·lipi·* (Old Ottawa dialect) 'tullibee, *Coregonus artedii*'. They were called les Outurbi in 1640 (JR 18:228),

241

misspelled Orturbi by Radisson (1961:160); the *l*-dialect form was used as a French word (with plural -*s*), written Outouloubys by Greysolon Dulhut in 1684 (Margry 1879–1888, 6:51) and Outoulibis by Jaillot on his 1685 map (Warkentin and Ruggles 1970:53).

In 1804 Duncan Cameron (1889–1890, 2:246) listed the following "tribes" among the Ojibwa north of Lake Superior: moose, reindeer, bear, pelican, loon, kingfisher, eagle, sturgeon, pike, rattlesnake, sucker, and "barbue." Most of these Ojibwa titulary names appear in other writers' lists from the seventeenth century on, but not all are represented in the Northern Ojibwa.

Barbue is a French name for the brown bullhead, a species of catfish (*Ictalurus nebulosus*), in Ojibwa called *waˑssįˑ*. Radisson referred to the Ovasovarin (Radisson 1961:160), probably equivalent to Ojibwa *waˑssįˑ irini* 'bullhead person'; the name also appears as Ouassi (Dobbs 1744:32) and Wasses (Long 1791:45). The Owashoes (Coats 1852:41; cf. Oldmixon 1741:555) or Washeo-Sepee (Graham 1969:206) are more likely the Severn or other bands of West Main Cree.

The Cranes, who can be identified as the Weagamow Lake Ojibwa or a part thereof (M. Black 1968–1973; Rogers and Rogers 1980) and a segment of the Sandy Lake Ojibwa, hunted between Osnaburgh House and Big Trout Lake (Bishop 1975:201) and were frequently mentioned in the early part of the twentieth century (Miller 1912:87–92; Lofthouse 1907:14; Skinner 1912:164–165). The Suckers (*nameˑpin*) or Red Suckers (*miskomeˑpin*), who may have been somewhat more widespread (Bishop 1975), make up a part of the Island Lake and Sandy Lake populations (Boyle 1908:101; Wolfart 1973; Stevens 1919).

The Sturgeons (Ojibwa *nameˑ* 'lake sturgeon, *Acipenser fulvescens*') were recorded as the Sturgeon Indians (Dobbs 1744:34) and Sturgoon Indians (Coats 1852:40). It is not clear whether the Nameu-Sepee (Cree *nameˑw siˑpiy* 'sturgeon river') in Graham's (1969:206) list of the Cree names of Nakawewuck bands are the same, especially since he earlier called them Nama kou sepe (Cree *nameˑ koˑsiˑpiy* 'trout river'; Graham in Isham 1949:317). In 1814 the Sturgeons were reported to hunt southwest of Osnaburgh House, together with the Moose (Bishop 1975:201); these Ojibwa Moose should not be confused with the Moose Cree (see the synonymy in "West Main Cree," this vol.).

In 1743 Isham (1949:112) mentioned the Wappuss (Cree *waˑpos* 'hare'), no doubt the same as Graham's Waupus (Isham 1949:317) or Wapus (Graham 1969:206) band, which he classed as Ojibwa. Richardson (1851, 2:37, 1852:264) who re-elicited a 1770 copy of Graham's list, gives the form Wà-pusi-sipi, an ungrammatical version of Cree *waˑposo-siˑpiy* 'hare river', but the name probably was not originally a geographic one.

Graham's list of Nakawewuck subdivisions includes the Win nes cau sepe (Isham 1949:317) or Uinescaw-

Sepee (Graham 1969:206), those living on the *wiˑnasko-siˑpiy* 'groundhog river' (Winisk River), and the Shu mattaway (Isham 1949:317) or Shumataway (Graham 1969:206), probably *kišeˑ-maˑtaˑwaˑw* 'great river junction'. Since he states that the latter band traded at York Factory they are probably from the place in northern Manitoba still called Shamattawa; however, this is not certain, as Shamattawa is in a traditionally Cree area, and Richardson (1852:264) identifies the Ojibwa group with Henley House on the lower Albany River.

Sources

For the early contact and early contact-traditional periods, 1650–1900, little has been published. Isham (1949:191) was the first to mention the Northern Ojibwa or the Nakawawuck, as he referred to them, in 1743 when he presented a short list of words and phrases. Graham in Isham (1949:314–315) in 1775 wrote a very short general description of the Nakawawuck, naming some, perhaps all, of the constituent groups (Graham 1969:204, 206). In the early years of the nineteenth century, Peter Grant and Duncan Cameron, traders for the North West Company, wrote more extended accounts of the Ojibwa, including but not distinguishing the Northern Ojibwa (Masson 1889–1890, 2). Only Bishop (1969, 1970a, 1972) and Rogers and Rogers (1980, 1980a) have examined archival material pertaining to the Northern Ojibwa.

For the late contact-traditional period, 1900–1950, published information on the Northern Ojibwa is rather scarce and consists for the most part of scattered references in the accounts of geologists (Camsell 1912; McInnis 1912), traders (Godsell 1939), missionaries (Lofthouse 1907, 1922; Stevens 1919), travelers (North 1929), and government officials (D.C. Scott 1906). The first anthropologist in the area was Skinner, who based a monograph (1912) on a trip he made down the Albany River in 1909. Skinner's time in the field was extremely limited, and he concentrated mainly on describing material culture. Hallowell (1938a) published on the material culture recorded at Island Lake. Taylor (1972) has published a reconstruction of the size and composition of several of the all-native settlements that were typical of this period. Rogers and Black (1976) dealt with subsistence strategy.

For the modern period, since 1950, there are published descriptions of several Northern Ojibwa communities, mostly written by anthropologists. The village of Round Lake, now Weagamow, was described in a standard ethnographic account by Rogers (1962) and has been the object of a detailed restudy by M. Black (1971). Greenwood has undertaken a socioeconomic study of Big Trout Lake (Sametz 1964), and Baldwin (1957) has written an article on social problems in the

Fort Hope and Collins area. Bishop (1969) gives some attention to the contemporary situation in his ethnohistoric study of the Osnaburgh House area. M. Black (1970) has reported on modern art at Weagamow. Taylor has done ethnographic research in Lansdowne House (1969), Webiquie (1970), and Wunnummin Lake (1971). Wolfart (1973) has described the Cree influence in the dialect of Island Lake.

OTHER SUBARCTIC OJIBWA AND ALGONQUIN GROUPS

The classification of the Ojibwa-speaking groups has given rise to inconsistencies and disagreements among specialists and government agencies, some of which are reflected in the treatment of these groups in the *Handbook*.‡ For example, in *Northeast* (vol. 15:745) the Pikangikum, Fort Hope, and Martin Falls bands are classed as Southwestern Chippewa, but in this volume the Pikangikum band is treated in "Saulteaux of Lake Winnipeg" and the other two in "Northern Ojibwa." The Constance Lake band, which contains both Ojibwa speakers and Cree speakers but is officially classified as Cree (Canada. Department of Indian Affairs and Northern Development 1980:19), has not been treated in any Ojibwa chapter and is only nominally covered in "West Main Cree."

The speakers of subdialects of Algonquin (as defined in "Subarctic Algonquian Languages," this vol.) have not been treated as a unit. The official category Algonquin excludes the northernmost Algonquin-speaking bands, Abitibi Dominion and Abitibi Ontario, and includes the linguistically and historically distinct Golden Lake and River Desert (Maniwaki) bands of Ojibwa speakers. In the official 1970 Canadian listing of linguistic affiliations the Cree-speaking Attikamek were also included as Algonquin (with one band inconsistently given as Algonquin and Cree, in different places), but they were correctly reclassified on the official 1980

‡ This paragraph and the next two are by Ives Goddard.

map; however, the 1980 listing still gives the language of the Obedjiwan band of Attikamek as Algonquin (Canada. Department of Indian Affairs and Northern Development. Indian Affairs Branch 1970:9–10; Canada. Department of Indian Affairs and Northern Development 1980:16–17; Canada. Department of Energy, Mines and Resources 1980). The chapter "Algonquin" (vol. 15) treats the bands officially called Algonquin in 1970 except for the Attikamek. The Abitibi Dominion and Abitibi Ontario bands are officially classified as linguistically "Ojibway" and Cree; this probably explains why they were not treated in the chapter "Algonquin," but by oversight they are not treated in this volume either. The Algonquin-speaking bands, their location if not indicated by their name (all in Quebec), and their population in 1978 are as follows: Abitibi Ontario (57) and Abitibi Dominion (412), at Amos and Rapide-de-Cèdres (Matagami Lake); Lac Simon (466); Grand Lac Victoria (231), also with a winter camp on the Réservoir Dozois; Barrière Lake (289), at Rapid Lake; Kipawa (197), formerly Kippewa; Wolf Lake (40), formerly Wolfe Lake, at Hunter's Point and Lac des Loups; Long Point (311), at Winneway and Rapide VII (Rapide Sept); and Timiskaming (427), formerly Temiskaming, at Notre Dame du Nord. The Brennan Lake and Argonaut bands formerly recognized as Algonquin no longer exist (Canada. Department of Indian Affairs and Northern Development 1980; Canada. Department of Indian Affairs and Northern Development. Indian Affairs Branch 1968, 1970; Canada. Department of Indian and Northern Affairs. Indian and Inuit Affairs Program 1978:map 2B).

The Abitibi bands formerly lived and hunted around and north of Lake Abitibi, astride the Ontario-Quebec border; the official recognition of two bands merely reflects their former location in two provinces, though all now reside in Quebec. Their subsistence activities have been described by Jenkins (1939), and a manuscript by MacPherson (1930) provides a general ethnography. Some sources for the other Algonquin-speaking bands are given in "Algonquin" (vol. 15:797).

Saulteaux of Lake Winnipeg

JACK H. STEINBRING

The Saulteaux ('sō,tō) bands that now occupy the shores and in-flowing rivers of Lake Winnipeg have moved, since the mid-eighteenth century, from more easterly lake-forest locations (Bishop 1974:331–335). In doing so, many have adapted to Canada's third largest lake, the thirteenth largest in the world.

The Indians treated in this chapter as the Lake Winnipeg Saulteaux are essentially the same as those called the Northern Ojibwa by Hallowell (1955:112) but differ from those called Northern Ojibwa in the *Handbook* ("Northern Ojibwa," this vol.) in having several traits the others lack, including the Midewiwin or Grand Medicine Society (W.J. Hoffman 1891; Landes 1968), totemic affiliation inherited in the male line, the use of sucking tubes in curing, and the exploitation of wild rice (*Zizania aquatica*). These traits, which suggest some cultural distance between the Lake Winnipeg Saulteaux and the Northern Ojibwa, may at the same time be seen to relate the Lake Winnipeg Saulteaux more closely to the southern Ojibwa or Chippewa (Hickerson 1962). The Island Lake band, though included by Hallowell in what he called Northern Ojibwa or Saulteaux, is covered in the chapter "Northern Ojibwa."

The term Saulteaux is used for self-identification and is the customary regional term used by everyone. Older persons readily confirm that they are Ojibwa (or Ojibway), a more general term, and they occasionally use the term *aniššina·pe·* 'person'.

Language and Territory

Linguistically, the Lake Winnipeg Saulteaux are distinct from the northernmost Northern Ojibwa, who use the Severn dialect (Todd 1970:7; Wolfart 1973:1318).* Those from the Bloodvein River and Lac Seul north speak the Northwestern dialect of Ojibwa, also used by the Ojibwa and Northern Ojibwa to the east, while those to the south speak the Saulteaux dialect also used to the immediate south and west ("Subarctic Algonquian Languages," this vol.).

The boundaries of the Lake Winnipeg Saulteaux are difficult to set because of discontinuities in ethnographic

fieldwork and because of a general failure to detail linguistic boundaries (Wolfart 1973:1306). Basically, they occupy lands in Ontario and Manitoba that drain into Lake Winnipeg from the east and south (fig. 1). Provisionally, the northern boundary of the Lake Winnipeg Saulteaux is represented by bands occupying the Poplar River. It skirts the Severn drainage in the southeast as far as Lac Seul in Ontario, which may be taken as the ultimate eastern limit. The bands along the Berens River in Manitoba at Little Grand Rapids, Pauingassi, Poplar Hill, and, in Ontario, Pikangikum form the northeastern elements on a line southeast from Poplar River to Lac Seul. The southern limits include the Lake of the Woods and lie essentially along the international boundary, which in many sections demarcates the Southern Ojibwa, or Chippewa, even though this boundary remains arbitrary and cuts across several population sources in western river drainages. On the west, the Red River constitutes the boundary from Lake Winnipeg south past the junction with the Assiniboine River, and to the north this boundary is fixed by bands living along rivers flowing directly into Lake Winnipeg from the west. This western boundary is in part coincidental with the eastern boundary of the Plains Ojibwa or Bungee (Howard 1965:11). Most of the communities that form the basis of the descriptions in this chapter are in the Canadian province of Manitoba.

History of Indian-White Contact

The Lake Winnipeg Saulteaux appear to be derived from Ojibwa populations that originally occupied the lake and river country of the Precambrian Shield to the east.

It is generally assumed that an enormous territorial expansion of the Ojibwa that began in the late seventeenth century had its origins in a relatively restricted area around the eastern shores of Lake Superior. To the south, these movements had partially displaced the Fox and the Sioux by 1750. To the west and northwest, they displaced the Cree—especially in the Lake Winnipeg drainage ("Territorial Groups Before 1821: Cree and Ojibwa," this vol.). It seems likely that, prior to this Ojibwa expansion, all of the nearer Lake Winnipeg drainage had been occupied by the Cree, with possibly

*For the transcriptional system used to write italicized Saulteaux words, see the orthographic footnote in "Northern Ojibwa," this vol.

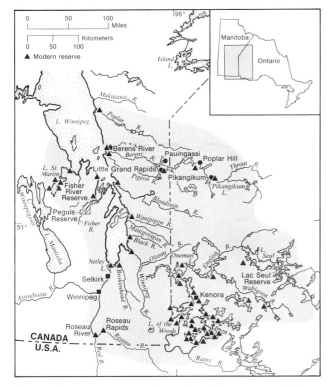

Fig. 1. Nineteenth-century territory with settlements in the 1970s.

some few elements of the Assiniboin remaining scattered around the southern and eastern shores. In 1775 Alexander Henry the Elder encountered a Cree village at the mouth of the Winnipeg River (Henry 1897,1:35), but by the beginning of the nineteenth century, the Cree no longer occupied the areas east, south, and west of Lake Winnipeg (Hallowell 1955:115). In 1794 the Ojibwa are reported at The Pas and well up the Saskatchewan River (Hallowell 1936a:35), apparently attesting to aggressive northwesterly movement around the northern end of Lake Winnipeg; however, the area through which these elements passed remained Cree.

The Ojibwa who came to occupy the Lake Winnipeg area moved west from many scattered and isolated locations deep within the complex topography of northwestern Ontario. The main arteries of this general movement included the Poplar, Berens, Bloodvein, Wanipigow, Manigotagan, Black, Winnipeg, Brokenhead, and Roseau rivers. The last two of these do not originate in the Shield but did carry people classed as Lake Winnipeg Saulteaux from sources very close to the Lake of the Woods–Winnipeg River route, probably the most extensively utilized one.

During the nineteenth century, Cree from bands such as Oxford House and Norway House took employment on the York boats transporting trade goods between York Factory on Hudson Bay and the Lake Winnipeg lakehead. Cree families moved down from the north via the York boat routes and settled with Saulteaux groups prior to the treaties of the 1870s. Cree men also

married Saulteaux women and in some cases started whole family lines within a Saulteaux group. To some extent, intermarriage between Cree and Saulteaux has been sustained. At times the degree of intermixture makes it difficult to classify a band as either Cree or Saulteaux, the people themselves not being completely sure which English label is appropriate. Island Lake in the Severn drainage has often been cited as an example of this, but this situation is complicated by the fact that Hallowell's (1938a:131–132) hypothesis of an ancient blend there of Cree-Ojibwa language characteristics has been succeeded by a picture of a basically Ojibwa form of speech with some Cree admixture (Wolfart 1973:1317–1318). On the other hand, autonomy for both Cree and Ojibwa is expressed on the Fisher River Reserve area in the Manitoba Interlake. Here Cree relocated from Norway House in 1875 still do not commonly intermarry with the immediately adjacent Peguis Saulteaux, who were moved to the same area in 1909.

Since the final settling of the Lake Winnipeg bands and the signing of treaties (the last one in 1875), new groups have been formed, small groups have been attached to larger ones, and there have been many relocations.

Band Relocations

The Pauingassi group, situated 15 miles up the Berens River from the Little Grand Rapids band, was formed as a splinter of traditionalists from the Little Grand Rapids band during the 1940s. These people were reacting to what they felt to be an excessive rate of westernization.

The Hole River (Wanipigow, Hollow Water) band now includes, through an addition to the reserve, a group formerly located at the mouth of the Rice River a few miles to the north. The river gets its name from the wild rice in Shallow Lake, which it drains. Some members of the Hole River band still exploit this rice annually, but many also travel to Lone Island Lake 175 miles to the southeast by road. Here they collect rice annually with many other bands of road-connected Lake Winnipeg Saulteaux. While this practice has fallen off since the 1960s, it follows the traditional summer aggregates and has benefits in the renewing of friendships and family ties throughout the region.

The Hole River–Rice River area yields clues to suggest that the eighteenth-century Ojibwa movements, at least to the northwest within the boreal forest–Precambrian Shield habitat, may be seen as a return to some former environmental breadth. Numerous prehistoric rock paintings, lost to the memory of living informants, are readily compared with Ojibwa birchbark pictography of the Grand Medicine Society (Lipsett 1970). However, only one case of an actual Saulteaux rock painting is recorded, and it was created at Hole River in 1904. In form the painting compared directly with paintings found in the Shield country in the deep interior of Ontario. It depicted a turtle flanked by two snakes, common elements of Ojibwa mythology and ritual. The painting was executed on a sedimentary rock face that has since weathered away (Steinbring 1978:13).

Oral traditions of the Little Black River band identify its eastern origin as "One Man" Lake in northwestern Ontario. Actually "One Man" is an English corruption of the word *wanamin* 'red ocher'. This lake is located near the southern part of the boundary between Ontario and Manitoba; it should not be confused with the Wunnummin Lake settlement recorded by Rogers and Taylor ("Northern Ojibwa," this vol.). Contacts between the established Little Black River Reserve on Lake Winnipeg and the One Man Lake group were directly maintained by canoe until the early 1900s when a dam project forced the One Man Lake group to relocate to the road-connected White Dog Reserve northwest of Kenora, Ontario. With the introduction of the road system to Little Black River in 1963, contact was immediately resumed. An important reason for this renewal of active relationship has been medical treatment, there being highly respected traditional practitioners at White Dog.

A controversial relocation of a Lake Winnipeg Saulteaux band occurred in 1909. It stemmed from the "surrender" by the Saint Peter's band of its reserve on Netley Creek along the Red River just north of the present city of Selkirk, Manitoba. The details of this are fully described by Chief Albert E. Thompson (1973), whose great-great-grandfather, Chief Peguis (d. 1864), was easily the most celebrated of historic Lake Winnipeg Saulteaux leaders (fig. 2).

Peguis and his followers entered Lake Winnipeg by one of the main rivers, probably the Winnipeg, and traveled to what was then called the Nee-poo-win River (Netley Creek). The initial occupation there was around 1790 and immediately followed the extermination by smallpox of a Cree community. Through Canada Treaty No. 1, August 3, 1871, the descendants of the original Peguis group under Henry Prince, his grandson, became the Saint Peter's band with a defined reserve. In 1909, the Saint Peter's band was relocated on the Fisher River in the Manitoba Interlake adjacent to the Fisher River Reserve, which is Cree. The Saint Peter's band became renamed the Peguis band, and the Reserve is also thus identified.

The controversy surrounding the surrender of the Saint Peter's Reserve centered upon political manipulations, collusion, bribery, inadequate publicity, and lack of Native representation. The Saint Peter's band was awarded a total of $5,000 for approximately 48,000 acres of land, which now includes part of the thriving city of Selkirk, Manitoba. A.E. Thompson (1973:35–52) conveys the essential information on these negoti-

Fig. 2. Chief Peguis wearing a triangular neck ornament (probably a mirror) edged with tinklers and suspended from a decorated neckband, blue belted fur (?) breechclout, fringed leggings, red and white garters with tinklers, and red decorated moccasins. He is armed with a bow attached to a quiver of arrows, a gun and powder horn, a red gunstock club with metal blade, and, evidently, a knife at his left hip. Watercolor by Peter Rindisbacher at the mouth of the Red River, 1821.

ations. The Lake Winnipeg Saulteaux commonly refer to the incident as a "sell-out" and express the opinion that the small number of Natives participating were given much liquor and then offered the settlement in cash. Documentation, in the form of contemporary letters provided by Chief Thompson, tends to confirm their beliefs. The new Peguis Reserve on the Fisher River contained 75,000 acres of land, and the precise location was largely determined by the band on the basis of the great abundance of whitefish in the area and upon the potentials for farming. Since its settlement on the Fisher River the Peguis band has become the most successful Native farming community in the province of Manitoba.

Other Lake Winnipeg Saulteaux have also experienced major movements, although mostly upon the basis of individual and family choices (Anonymous 1974a:7, 8). Table 1 shows population estimates for the bands in the mid-twentieth century.

Table 1. Lake Winnipeg Saulteaux Band Population

	1949	1970	1978
Manitoba			
Little Black River (O'Hanly)[a]	96	194	283
Bloodvein	124	339	454
Hole River[a] (Hollow Water, Wanipigow)	170	358	464
Brokenhead (Scanterbury)[a]	227	434	552
Roseau River[a]	328	725	953
Berens River	368	719	914
Fort Alexander[a]	962	2,023	2,620
Peguis[a]	1,266	2,060	2,534
Little Grand Rapids (includes Pauingassi)	413	733	878
Jackhead	122	256	360
Fairford	321	720	921
Lake Saint Martin	284	581	818
Poplar River	178	392	511
Ontario			
Pikangikum	342	764	1,086
Islington	227	622	815
Grassy Narrows	242	485	590
Shoal Lake No. 39	134	187	236
Shoal Lake No. 40	170	220	243
Northwest Angle No. 33	70	158	192
Northwest Angle No. 37	59	85	124
Dalles	82	89	85
Rat Portage	164	310	247
Whitefish Bay	175	363	516
Eagle Lake	85	146	163
Wabigoon	140	129	133
Wabauskang	68	67	68
Lac Seul	548	1,153	1,297
Big Island	113	163	207
Big Grassy	—	212	280
Sabaskong	—	229	325
Totals	7,478	14,916	18,869

SOURCES: Leechman 1953; Canada. Department of Indian Affairs and Northern Development. Indian Affairs Branch 1970:12–20: Canada. Department of Indian Affairs and Northern Development 1980:18–27.

NOTE: Cree and other Status Indian peoples are not distinguishable from Saulteaux in these figures.

[a] Year-round road connection.

Culture

Despite the effects of migration, change in habitat, Cree admixture, and accelerating Euro-Canadian influences, distinctive aspects of traditional Saulteaux culture can be identified.

Subsistence

The basic adaptation to lake and river country of the forested Shield is manifest in a hunting and fishing economy abundantly supplemented by seasonal col-

Prov. Arch. of Man., Winnipeg.

Fig. 3. Living area of a temporary ricing camp at Big Whiteshell Lake where many bands congregate to harvest wild rice in early September, each band camping in its traditional place. The modern tent is of canvas, and the woman heating an iron is dressed in recent-style, with trousers. Photographed at Whiteshell Provincial Park, Man., about 1958.

lecting of many forms. Innovations such as pulp cutting, mining, and guiding relate directly to indigenous patterns, especially in their seasonal and male-oriented characteristics. While wild rice is limited to the eastern and southern section of the Lake Winnipeg region, its importance is seen in the fact that almost all the Saulteaux groups who migrated beyond its limits still return each year to the rice lakes of the Whiteshell Forest Reserve (fig. 3). By 1970 this activity was becoming purely economic, but in past generations it constituted as much a social institution as an economic one.

Fish undoubtedly constituted a very basic and continuous dietary source in the original Ojibwa adaptation. The Lake Winnipeg setting served to accentuate this element. Added to it were the new techniques of open-water net fishing and the construction of large, plank boats of spruce on a European model. Original fishing techniques involved a more individual focus than they do in the twentieth century. Spears of various kinds were used both in summer and winter, and pole snares were commonly employed in the spring. The only indigenous fishing practice of a collective character was the use of the stone weir, which consisted of huge boulder lines, usually in the form of parallel chevrons, across the rivers with points directed upstream. Whole families participated in spearing, gaffing, or snaring the fish during spring runs. Preparation by drying, pounding, and flaking, and the smoking of several shapes of fillets, was accomplished on the spot. The last major weir used

247

by the Lake Winnipeg Saulteaux was abandoned in the early 1900s. It is still visible on the Roseau River Reserve (Waddell 1970:70).

The high proportion of members of the Sturgeon totem around Lake Winnipeg probably reflects the importance of this fish in the original economy. Hallowell (1936a:49) notes also that the central figures in the Grand Medicine Society of the Lake Winnipeg region "were members of the sturgeon sib." Their great size and high nutritional values (Quimby 1960:4) made sturgeon an important object of economic venture until depletion required the imposition of controls in the 1930s. It is probably accurate to say that sturgeon of over 20 pounds were caught in extensive numbers for home consumption until the 1920s.

Technology

Birchbark canoes (fig. 4) were last made in the early 1940s. Outboard motors had been adopted in the 1930s, and a few of the early models were still operating in the 1960s. None was ever discarded, and people traveled many miles to trade for a needed part. Gaskets of moosehide and even bark served in emergencies as people adopted this artifact, learned its nature, and applied their practical skills to its maintenance. As roads penetrated and spread through the area of the Lake Winnipeg Saulteaux, cars entered the culture in nearly the same way as did outboard motors. None is ever totally abandoned. Parts are commonly traded between bands and families, and it is not uncommon for a man to retain several old cars for salvage.

The Lake Winnipeg Saulteaux have traditionally produced snowshoes with pointed toes. Made in June of white ash, they feature a high arch at the toe where two laterally bent staves are joined. This preference in snowshoe style follows that depicted in George Catlin's famous painting of Ojibwas, *Snowshoe Dance at First Snowfall,* executed at Fort Snelling in 1835 (McCracken 1959:167). A few snowshoes are still made for commercial markets. Birchbark containers are only rarely made; the traditional form seems to have been the squared base, tapering type common to many Algonquians (Webber 1973). Spruce root was used to stitch them, and the ulna of a deer was squared in cross section and pointed for use as a perforator. The bone has been replaced by Phillips screwdrivers, modified harness-making tools, filed-down kitchen fork handles, and the like.

Two forms of rush mats were being made by some eastern Lake Winnipeg bands up until the 1960s. In shape, size, and technology these do not vary from those described for the Minnesota Chippewa (Petersen 1963:pl. 54). The distribution of these mats is limited to the east side of Lake Winnipeg.

248   One relatively complex material trait of significance

Dept. of Energy, Mines, and Resources, Geological Survey of Canada, Ottawa: 960.
Fig. 4. Wekemouskunk and son with birchbark canoe and conical lodges covered with birchbark sheets. Photographed at Lake St. Martin, Man., 1888, probably by J.B. Tyrrell.

in linking Saulteaux bands in the eastern Lake Winnipeg watershed is a highly distinctive pipe, always made from black stone. From Fort Alexander to Berens River, this type was shared among shoreline bands, and it was found as far inland on the Berens as Poplar Hill. The type consists of a modified monitor form (fig. 5). These pipes are distinct from the Micmac type attributed to the Cree (G.A. West 1934:228–229) and from the red catlinite pipes of Siouan origin.

Craftswomen, especially along the Berens River, make profusely beaded mittens with a gauntlet sleeve that reaches nearly to the elbow. These "mitts" commonly have beaver fur trim. Essentially floral, the beadwork motifs form an unbridled exaggeration of the restrained, miniature bead designs of an earlier period.

U. of Winnipeg, Dept. of Anthr., Man.: E5–48, E5–235.
Fig. 5. Pipes of blackened steatite with incised decoration. Length of top about 8 cm; collected by Jack Steinbring and Norman Williamson from the Pauingassi band on the Berens River, 1970.

The boldness and complexity of these designs mark them as a real art form (fig. 6). There has been some degree of social symbolism in these as well, since they are worn proudly by adult males in public. The skills of the women are thus openly exhibited. A girl may make her brother a pair of mitts or fancy moccasins. Young unmarried males, then, can judge the skills of a potential bride. Mitts can be readily identified as to band, and often as to a particular woman.

While the manufacture of fish-skin containers has been reported for the Southern Ojibwa (Hilger 1951:132), the Lake Winnipeg Saulteaux appear to be unique in making one from the skin of a sturgeon (Steinbring 1965:3). A bottle-shaped container was made by Lake Winnipeg bands north from Fort Alexander, which was adopted also by some neighboring Cree groups such as the Cross Lake band. The containers, called *name·waya·n*, were used up to about 1930 to store the extracted oil of the sturgeon, which was widely used for cooking and flavoring. It was also used in the treatment of a psychotic urge to eat human flesh known to anthropologists as "Windigo psychosis" (Rohrl 1970:97).

Curing

Bloodletting, now rarely practiced, was a traditional form of medical treatment among the Lake Winnipeg Saulteaux. It must be regarded as a strictly practical form of medicine; it was not associated with drumming, incantations, or other ritual activities. It involved specialists not necessarily associated with the Grand Medicine Society and there is evidence at Little Black River that the art was transmitted from father to son. A substantial knowledge of the circulatory system was re-

Prov. Arch. of Man., Winnipeg.
Fig. 7. Charlie Assiniboin (left) and his brother, sons of Assiniboin, who was a Saulteaux chief of the Portage band in southern Man. around 1900. They wear vests, pouches on sashes, leggings, and one pair of garters, all elaborately beaded. The Portage band had migrated north from Red Lake, Minn. and were officially recognized in the Selkirk Treaty of July 17, 1817. Studio photograph by J.F. Rowe, Portage-la-Prairie, Man., 1890s.

quired, and over 200 physiological terms were collected in 1965 (Steinbring 1965a).

Social Organization

The Lake Winnipeg Saulteaux moved into their present locations possessing the nonresidential totemic clans† characteristic of the Ojibwa nearly everywhere. Affiliation with the clan, or totem as it may be called, is inherited in the male line and is retained by both sexes for life. The totemic groups are exogamous and follow the rule of band exogamy. Thus, even if other totems are present in a young man's band, he must marry some-

†Hallowell (1955) preferred the term sib to denote the characteristics associated with the totemic groupings of Lake Winnipeg Saulteaux. This was to accord with a distinction made between sib and clan, the latter requiring veneration and food proscriptions for totem animals, residentiality, and changing affiliation upon marriage. None of these attributes is present among the totemic groupings of Lake Winnipeg Saulteaux. The controversy over Ojibwa clans has been reviewed by Bishop (1974:341).

U. of Winnipeg, Dept. of Anthr., Man.: E5–346, E5–347.
Fig. 6. Mitten gauntlets of moosehide with beaver fur trim and multi-colored seed bead decoration. Length 41 cm; collected by Jack Steinbring and Norman Williamson from the Little Grand Rapids band on the Berens River, 1970.

one from another totem who is also from another band. The totemic animal does not figure in a clan's mythical ancestry, and there are no food restrictions on it. Sturgeon, caribou, bear, mallard, lynx, snake, and bullfish are prominent totems among the Lake Winnipeg bands. Some of the original Cree families established among the Saulteaux in the nineteenth century can now be identified because the Cree did not have totems; yet people without them are considered (and consider themselves) to be Saulteaux. The lack of a totem for some persons is expressed as a positive fact, as though not having one is a kind of variation of the many possible ones. The significance of totemic affiliation is rapidly becoming defunct, as many young people do not know theirs.

There is no evidence that a residential condition was associated with any of the Saulteaux clans upon migration into the region. Only the demographic and social significance of the Sturgeon (*name·*) totem would suggest such a trend, and this would appear to be within postsettlement history. Clan and band exogamy were widely practiced until the 1960s.

Residence after marriage among Lake Winnipeg Saulteaux is basically patrilocal (in the bridegroom's band), but with a period of matrilocal residence during which time the young man serves his father-in-law, usually in trapping, fishing, or pulp cutting. This period of service, of course, takes place in the bride's band. The temporary matrilocal residence has normally been of two or three years duration but in recent years has lessened. In many cases through the early 1970s, there was no temporary matrilocal residence, and there was also a strong tendency toward initial neolocal residence—in some cases urban.

Hallowell (1937) has conveyed the data on cross-cousin marriage preference and on its historical decline in the region. The only surviving indication of this is in the kin terminology (illustrated for male ego), which classes father's brother's daughter and mother's sister's daughter as *nintawe·ma·* 'sister' and mother's brother's daughter and father's sister's daughter as *ni·nimošše·n ʔ*, also used for 'sweetheart'. There are joking relationships between a young man and his sister-in-law, and close bonds are expressed between him and his brother-in-law, called *ni·tta·*, the term that also designates a male ego's male cross-cousin and (at least in current usage) his male parallel cousin. Mother-in-law avoidance was commonly practiced in the bands for which there are data, but it no longer appears significant.

Traditionally, marriage was hardly ever by choice. Parents arranged marriages. Not infrequently the young woman's expressed preference was taken into account, perhaps in keeping with customary romantic aggressiveness of adolescent girls (Dunning 1959:101). Data collected along the east shore of Lake Winnipeg suggest that jilted young women were sometimes the cause of

Fig. 8. Saulteaux family on the Red River, drawn from life in 1821. A domed lodge is at right and 2 conical ones at left, all bark-covered. Men's clothing and ornament includes a blue breechclout, red leggings with decorated flaps, moccasins with red vamps, black and white neck bands, bear-claw necklace, nasal septum ornament, and red face paint. One smokes a long-stemmed pipe. Women wear red leggings, moccasins with red vamp, blue dress with red and white straps, green and yellow bead necklaces, green bead ear ornament; one woman carries a baby on her back, the other has a trade blanket over her lap. A trade pot is near the fire. Watercolor by Peter Rindisbacher.

profoundly complex and vigorous exchanges of sorcery between families.

Religion

Aboriginally, the Lake Winnipeg Saulteaux experienced shamanistic contests in which two rival shamans competing for power and authority would incite each other to the highest pitch of evil-dealing sorcery. Hallowell (1955:277) has described a number of these contests, and their occurrence was general throughout the Lake Winnipeg region.

A most interesting aspect of continuity of concern with the power inherent in shamanism and sorcery features the fiddle. The love of fiddling came through contacts with the White settlers on Red River and their descendants. From them, the Lake Winnipeg Saulteaux learned the Scottish jigs and reels and made modifications of their own. Certain persons were accorded special respect for fiddling, and men, perhaps unconsciously, came to wish for this. In all probability, sorcery was diminishing because of missionary influence, and fiddling posed an acceptable vehicle for achieving prestige.

An incident reflects this fusion. In one small band there were several fiddlers, but two stood out as about equal. They played alternately at the square dances, as did the other fiddlers. Both expressed themselves as being the best fiddler or at least made remarks that could be so interpreted. Just as in the traditional shamanistic competitions, the weight of this began to affect these men. They performed their very best. Finally, one night as one of them was fiddling at a dance, and the other was watching closely, the fingers of the fiddling man turned, in the eyes of his opponent, into snake heads (the observer's nickname was Snake-eye). The viewer took this as an omen of profound power and immediately stopped playing his fiddle. He did not take it up again until the other man was defeated as a candidate for chief, in the band elections two years later.

• THE VISION QUEST AND GUARDIAN SPIRIT Isolation, fasting, and meditation were universal components in the efforts of Lake Winnipeg Saulteaux boys to achieve a vision. The behaviors and expectations of this activity follow closely those of the general North American Indian model. Adolescent boys in the Lake Winnipeg region would travel to a remote location in the bush. Here they would fast for four days, concentrating on the appearance of a supernatural figure. The vision would usually come in the form of a bird or animal that would then be identified as the communicant's guardian spirit or "helper." This protective spirit would be available to the recipient for his lifetime and could be summoned in cases of need by renewed fasting and concentration, offerings of tobacco or food, and through dreams. Shamans were in alliance with the more powerful of these spirits, and normally had access to several. Among the mythologically prominent ones used by the Lake Winnipeg Saulteaux were Turtle, Frog, and the Thunderer.

The vision quest, as such, does not seem to have been practiced by girls; however, there is substantial evidence for the unpremeditated reception of visions by girls. These commonly led to semishamanistic roles for women, especially as applied to the treatment of the sick. Some women also became sorcerers through the experience of a vision.

The psychological dimension of guardian-spirit phenomena among the Lake Winnipeg Saulteaux is probably very deep-seated. Motivations in initial television program selection (S. Davidson 1973:85; Steinbring 1980:221) may be related to this, and the use of alcohol as a guardian-spirit substitute in the process of acculturation (Hamer 1969:239) appears to be a legitimate hypothesis in some cases.

Fiddling became fused with the vision quest. The best available examples of it would appear to have occurred around the turn of the century. This fusion comes about in the requirement that during a four-day fast, the male initiate must learn to play the fiddle. An old man completely departed from the norm of Ojibwa stoicism when he wept in relating his failure to accomplish this feat. He had taken his fiddle to a deep, interior location on Black Island, a sacred place. For four days, he tried his best. At the end of the period his fingers were torn

and bleeding, and he could not play tunes. It was his greatest personal disaster. He later became a strong advocate of Christianity.

• THE SHAKING TENT The shaking tent rite, a widespread Algonquian phenomenon, involves the shamanistic use of a special cylindrical lodge (fig. 9). The practice was present throughout all bands of the Lake Winnipeg Saulteaux, although at times any given band might not have a person capable of performing it. The shaman with this capability (said to be derived from a vision) erected his round, open-topped rawhide tent at dusk. After dark he entered it and started singing and drumming to summon his spirit helpers. Their arrival was marked by the swaying of the tent, strange lights, and the appropriate animal cries. The shaman then used his spirit helpers in locating lost objects (and people), in curing, and in anti-sorcery. The shaman was engaged for a negotiated fee by a client. The practice does not appear to have survived the 1950s among the Lake Winnipeg Saulteaux, but an authentic performance was secretly conducted at the Cree community of Norway House in 1974.

• THE MIDEWIWIN For the Lake Winnipeg Saulteaux, as for the Southern Ojibwa, the Midewiwin was the major religious institution in traditional culture. This was a society that centered on training in the medical arts. The instructional ceremonies were carried out by the members of the Midewiwin or Grand Medicine Society under the leadership of the Mide priests, who also instructed initiates in the rituals of the society and in the songs and secrets of the "degree" that each was taking (fig. 10). The degrees or grades were ranked. There were normally four, but in the Kenora area several have been added. Attainment of each degree in-

Prov. Arch. of Man.. Winnipeg.

Fig. 9. A shaking tent (conjuring lodge) at Little Grand Rapids, Man., with canvas and birchbark covering on a pole framework about 4 feet in diameter at the base (Hallowell 1942:36–37). The traditional covering was untanned hides of moose, caribou, or deer. Photograph by A.I. Hallowell, 1934.

Fig. 10. left, Mide lodges with a complete superstructure were typical of the Berens River Saulteaux; this one was photographed before 1926 at Pikangikum Lake on the Upper Berens River, Ont., while a nearly identical one was photographed a few years later at Pauingassi. right, Morning Star (*wa·panank*) (d. 1932), of the Hole River band, who served about 1919–1925 as one of the last Mide leaders in the Lake Winnipeg region (Hallowell 1936a:45); photograph by A.I. Hallowell, 1930–1932. The Midewiwin flourished at shifting centers near Lake Winnipeg. The society trained young men and women in practical and ritualistic medicine. A tutor was engaged for a fee, and training culminated in secret and public ceremonies in a Mide lodge that lasted nearly a week and featured a death and rebirth ritual. The neophyte was magically shot and killed with small shells and brought back to life by a shaman who sucked the shells out of the neophyte's body. The young person was then "licensed to practice"; much of this practice involved preparing and administering plant remedies. The lore of the Midewiwin was kept on pictographic birchbark scrolls (fig. 11), invested with great inherent power by the mere act of producing them. Some were made for hunting medicine; one such scroll was sold to a trapper in the early 1960s for $1,000.

volved payment to the priests in charge, in exchange for the secret formulas for curing associated with that degree. Birchbark scrolls bearing symbols and representations of the medicine lodges (in order of their rank) served as mnemonic aids to the priests. These often elaborate scrolls might also represent, in idiosyncratic symbolism, the elements of a magical song.

Curing seems to have always dominated the Grand Medicine Society in the Lake Winnipeg region. While numerous nonmedical activities were peripherally associated with annual gatherings, an earlier "spiritual" emphasis, as postulated for the Southern Ojibwa (Ritzenthaler and Ritzenthaler 1970:9–91), cannot be confirmed in this region.

Hallowell's (1936a, 1942) accounts provide descriptions of the last northern manifestations of the Grand Medicine Society, and indicate the shifting centers of influence: these include Roseau River, Fort Alexander, Hole River, Dog Head, Jackhead, Bloodvein, and Berens River. The last regional celebrations of the Midewiwin among the Lake Winnipeg Saulteaux occurred in the summer of 1926 on Black Island north of Hole River.

Some previously unrecorded information pertaining to the Jackhead Midewiwin was provided by Keewatin (Mrs. Scott), who lived at the Hole River Reserve. She is the maternal granddaughter of George Traverse, the last highly celebrated Jackhead Mide priest. Keewatin

was interviewed in June 1970 in the hope of identifying and interpreting Midewiwin scrolls found by pulp company employees in the remote bush. She identified two scrolls (fig. 11) as belonging to her grandfather and reported that there had originally been four scrolls, her grandfather's "Master Scroll" and three others that he had used in training leaders from the other participating bands—Brokenhead (Scanterbury), Bloodvein, and Hole River. He did not train a follower at Jackhead.

At Jackhead, there were three ranked earth degrees and the one sky. This sky category was an unranked lodge into which families could sponsor a deceased member as a posthumous honor. The names are not known, but the third earth degree was symbolized by a bear, just as the fourth is so symbolized among the Southern Ojibwa.

According to his granddaughter and others, George Traverse (d. 1914) committed suicide by hanging while in prison, after refusing to become a Christian through baptism. Peter Traverse (d. 1955), a son, is reported to have put George's Mide paraphernalia in a "quiet place."

The Jackhead ceremonial lodge was a large, open affair like that of the Southern Ojibwa (W.J. Hoffman 1891:256). In the center was placed a very large *mi·kiss* (marine shell), which was abraded during ceremonies to produce a powder for the curing rites. Sick people were initiated into the Jackhead Midewiwin (and ap-

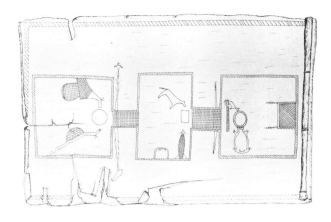

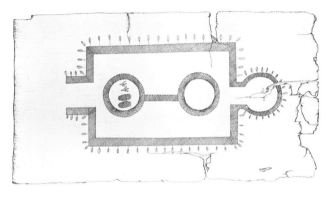

U. of Winnipeg. Dept. of Anthr., Man.
Fig. 11. Drawings of birchbark scrolls attributed to the Mide priest George Traverse. The scrolls were secreted in the forest near the Jackhead Reserve at the time of his death about 1914, along with his other Mide paraphernalia. He had used these materials to train Mide leaders from Hole River, Scanterbury, and Bloodvein. The last Midewiwin celebration at Jackhead is reported to have occurred in 1942. For possible interpretations of these scrolls see Dewdney (1975:150–153). Tracings by Edward Sawatzky of incised designs on original birchbark scrolls. Width of top 44.3 cm.

parently other Lake Winnipeg groups) as a condition of their treatment. The Jackhead lodge differed in design from that at Pauingassi on the Berens River, which had a superstructure, with only the sides completely covered.

Mythology

The Windigo (*wi·ntiko·*), a cannibalistic monster who haunts the winter forests of the Ojibwa everywhere, is a prominent figure in Lake Winnipeg Saulteaux mythology. Most describe the Windigo as a giant, human male who appears dramatically and devours the people he happens upon. Windigo is, however, quite separate from "becoming (or being) Windigo." This latter denotes an identifiable psychological disorder that involves a craving for human flesh. One may contract the ailment by confrontation with Windigo, or one may be sorcerized by a shaman into "becoming Windigo." In the event of the latter, copious doses of hot grease (including bear fat, melted deer tallow, and sturgeon oil) are said to bring about a quick cure. Those who have the Windigo psychosis can be identified in the bush at night by bright, sparkling lights that surround and follow them. In the 1970s a very acculturated young man was asked if he believed in Windigo. He answered, "No, but I saw his tracks."

Manitou (*manito·*), an immanent, pervasive power, is regionally acknowledged as a paramount spiritual concept of long standing. This power is neither negatively nor positively valued; however, its use may be conditioned by human motivations. Kitchi-Manitou (*kičči-manito·*), on the other hand, is a supreme beneficent force, frequently with anthropomorphic endowments. Missionaries utilized this apparently indigenous concept in explaining the God of Christianity.

A quasi-religious figure of regional importance is Nanibush (Nanabozho). In keeping with his very widespread appearance in Ojibwa mythology, he is a form of comic hero about whom there are endless stories. A standard form of these stories among the Lake Winnipeg Saulteaux involves his violations of taboo and the inevitable punishments he gets for these violations. In one story, for example, Nanibush is tied to a tree, then encircled by a group of old ladies who all proceed to urinate on him.

Sociocultural Situation in the 1960s

In the 1960s there were probably very few who overtly practiced elements of indigenous religion. The large denominational Christian churches have vigorously competed for dominance in many of the Lake Winnipeg Saulteaux communities, which struggle often created highly destructive factionalism. Since the 1950s fundamentalist groups have come to achieve a large following and appear on the threshold of producing a powerful reformative upsurge of basically Native identification. The Pentecostal movement appears favored among the Lake Winnipeg Saulteaux; the Fairford Reserve hosted in 1973 a large gathering from places as distant as the Pikangikum band.

With the introduction of roads, sources of Euro-Canadian material goods became greatly expanded. For most bands located on Lake Winnipeg, road connection did not commence until the 1950s. Prior to that time, travel to stores in the southern segment was by boat. Larger markets became generally accessible at about the same time as the relatively inexpensive transistor radio was first being widely distributed. This constituted in the early 1960s the first major impact by mass media.

With roads came active urban connection. At first this was strictly experimental. People would drive to the north outskirts of Winnipeg, park their car, and take a bus into the city center. In the initial phases of urban exploration, only middle-aged and older persons could afford to make the trips, and few of these spoke English effectively enough to handle themselves adequately in the city. They walked untold miles, got on wrong buses, went hungry because they hired a taxi that took all their money.

As urban experience broadened and driving cars became more common, urban communication by road became greatly accelerated. Related to this was a strong movement in the mid-1960s by social planners and some politicians to encourage Indians to move to the city where they could get jobs, better medical attention, and good housing. For a time public policy reflected this, and Winnipeg, as the regional center, experienced very heavy pressures from reserve migrants. The Native population in Winnipeg for 1975 was estimated at more than 30,000.

Any population estimate on Native peoples in Winnipeg, however, must be viewed against the factor of transiency. Most Native families in the city do not make it their permanent home. They move back and forth from city to reserve, usually winter in the city, summer on the reserve. Those moving in the early 1960s had made a studied decision to change. Only a few actually succeeded, but they formed a basic group to which persons coming later could apply for advice, a few nights lodging, or a meal. For a very brief span of time, the old clan system entered urban movements, since a pattern of obligations existed within a totem. A man belonging to any given totem might, when he was in a strange place, find his totem-mate. This person, then, was obligated to provide him food and lodging during his stay. The social conventions of city life and the poverty of city migrants, who often had whole families with them, did not sustain this practice very long.

The medical needs of all Treaty Indians in Canada are met by the government, but the advantages of better medical assistance in the city are an added attraction for some. Families often have at least one elderly person receiving an old age pension from the government. With the standard Canadian family allowance for the youngsters in the family and one or two old age pension checks, supplemented by welfare payments and occasional employment, a family can survive in the city. The old age pension checks constitute a major proportion of the money income. These elderly people must have continuous access to the best medical facilities. It is not uncommon to find grandfather and grandmother coming to the city with their children and enjoying lavish attention.

Alcoholics Anonymous had an extremely active spurt during the 1960s along the east shore of Lake Winnipeg (Steinbring 1980a). It followed the spread of the road system. Many joined. In doing so they formed chapters in their own communities and used their own language. While the groups sought to eliminate alcohol consump-

tion, some members had never really been alcoholics, and at least a few had not even been drinkers. Since alcohol at the time had evolved into a symbol of past misfortunes and failures, Alcoholics Anonymous could be seen in the early 1960s as kind of reformative movement. As a Native institution, however, it did not survive. More and more it came to reflect its urban origins, ceasing to operate as a collection of reserve-centered, exclusive groups. Many withdrew but the overall effect on drinking behavior was substantial. It reduced the most destructive effects of alcohol at a very critical time.

The history of the Lake Winnipeg Saulteaux tends to reflect a persisting identity, threats to which have always prompted defense or specialized accommodation. This resilient people probably will resist for some time still those influences that they see as inconsistent with Saulteaux life.

Synonymy‡

Saulteaux and its variants are French terms for 'people of the rapids' (that is, Sault Sainte Marie). The Algonquian equivalent appears first in 1640 as Baouichtigouian (JR 18:230), a form that has been interpreted as Cree (Pentland 1978:104) and as Ojibwa (synonymy in "Southeastern Ojibwa," vol. 15). Subsequently recorded forms are based on Ojibwa paˑwittik 'rapids' or paˑwittink '(at) Sault Ste. Marie': Paüoitigoüeieuhaκ, 1642 (JR 23:222); Paoutig8ejenhac, 1653 (Du Val in Warkentin and Ruggles 1970:33); Pagouitik, 1658 (JR 44:250); Pa8itig8ecii, 1660 (Creuxius in JR 46:map); Paouitikoungraentaouak, 1670 (Gallinée in Margry 1879–1888, 1:163); Pahoüiting dach Irini, 1670 (JR 54:132); Paouestigonce, Pouoestingonce, 1685 (Radisson 1961:93, 113).

French translations of the Algonquian name are: Nation des Gens du Sault, 1640 (JR 18:230); Habitans du Sault, 1642 (JR 23:222); Peuples du Grand Sault, 1658 (JR 44:250); Nation du Saut, 1663 (JR 48:172). Radisson in 1685 translated it into English as Nation of the Sault and the Sault [Indians] (1961:93, 113). The shorter French form Sauteur soon became the standard name, although there has never been complete agreement on the spelling. Some of the variants are: Sauteurs, 1663 (JR 48:74); Saulteurs, 1670 (JR 54:132); Saulteux, 1670 (Gallinée in Margry 1879–1888, 1:163); Sauteux, 1789 (McKenzie in Masson 1889–1890, 1:32); Sautaux, 1820 (Hood 1974:87); Seauteaux (Ryerson 1855:143); Saulteaux, 1859 (Kane 1971:65). The last spelling is the one used by the Canadian government (Canada. Department of Indian Affairs and Northern Development. Indian Affairs Branch 1970).

English adaptations of the French name are Sautors (Carver 1778:96), Sotees (Chappell 1817:199), Sotoos

‡ This synonymy was written by David H. Pentland.

(Richardson 1852:264), and Sotto, 1859 (Kane 1971:153). Modern Plains Cree *so·to·wiyiniwak* (pl.) is also based on the French term. The English form Leapers, 1698 (Hennepin 1903:116) is a mistranslation of French Sauteurs.

Saulteaux has been used since the seventeenth century as an exact synonym of Ojibwa/Chippewa (JR 51:60; Margry 1879–1888, 1:163, 6:6). Similarly, the Ojibwa names *nakkawe·* and *očipwe·* and their cognates in other Algonquian languages (see the synonymies in "Northern Ojibwa," this vol., and "Southeastern Ojibwa," vol. 15) are used at least as often to refer to the Saulteaux as to other Ojibwa-speaking groups: Faries (1938:382) notes that Cree *ocipwe·w* is "often applied to the Saulteaux by those who do not live near enough to become acquainted with the tribal differences," and Wolfart (1973:1322) reports that "Cree speakers use the [English] term *Saulteaux* for dialects other than their own in a way highly reminiscent of the Greek term *barbaros.*"

Sources

One of the foremost contributions of the Lake Winnipeg Saulteaux to world anthropology has been through Hallowell's (1955) analyses of Saulteaux personality and world view. The work dealing with this was accomplished over nearly a decade of field studies along the Berens River, which has been followed up by others elsewhere (Barnouw 1950). A great many other psychologically oriented contributions by Hallowell were published in journals of psychology, social work, medicine, and sociology (Dunning 1959:210–211; Barnouw 1950:146). Hallowell's (1942) monograph on conjuring is based largely upon Berens River data and constitutes the primary regional source on this subject. This monograph and his (1936a) article on the passing of the Midewiwin provide the only professionally established basis for comparisons with the major nineteenth-century descriptions of the Southern Ojibwa (W.J. Hoffman 1891).

Except for the work of Hallowell, only short-term, specialized studies are available for the development of an ethnography of the Lake Winnipeg Saulteaux (Steinbring 1964, 1965, 1966, 1967, 1969–1972, 3, 1978, 1980a; Steinbring and Elias 1968; Elias and Steinbring 1967; Elias 1967, 1967a). Most of this work has been done in only a few of the Lake Winnipeg shoreline communities.

The only major residential study on a directly related group is that done by Dunning (1959) at Pikangikum, at the easternmost extension of the Lake Winnipeg drainage. With an emphasis on social and economic change, this work also contains a wealth of ethnographic data, especially on social structure. Except for A.E. Thompson (1973), historical descriptions of the Saulteaux in the Lake Winnipeg drainage are virtually nonexistent. This is probably owing to the facts that the Saulteaux were migrating during the two centuries of initial contact and that they normally occupied remote localities, off the main arteries of commercial and exploratory travel. They may also have been commonly mistaken for Cree. Henry (1897) constitutes the most widely used historical source on Saulteaux in the immediate vicinity of Lake Winnipeg.

255

Western Woods Cree

JAMES G.E. SMITH

The term Western Woods Cree ('krē) encompasses three major divisions, the Rocky Cree, the western Swampy Cree, and Strongwoods or Bois Fort Cree. In this chapter, the recent data refer to the western Swampy Cree and the Rocky Cree; information is lacking on the Strongwoods Cree, and the Swampy Cree of the Hudson Bay Lowlands and coast are considered in detail in "West Main Cree," this volume. The former existence of a fourth group, the Athabasca Cree, may be inferred from the presence of a distinct *r*-dialect south of Lake Athabasca in the eighteenth and nineteenth centuries (Pond 1930; Lacombe 1874:xv; Pentland 1978:106–107).

Language

Linguistically the Western Woods Cree include all speakers of the Woods Cree (δ) dialect, most or all of the Northern Plains Cree (*y*) dialect, and the speakers of the western Swampy Cree (*n*) dialects; a fourth dialect, Misinipi Cree (*r*), extinct since the nineteenth century, was also spoken in the Western Woods Cree area* (Pentland 1978). The dialect boundaries correspond only approximately to the ethnographic divisions, and have shifted a considerable distance westward during historical times.

The Northern Plains dialect of the Strongwoods Cree is almost identical to the Southern Plains dialect of the Plains Cree proper (described in the grammatical sketch of the Cree language in vol. 17). Woods (or Rocky) Cree is somewhat different, but not enough to cause any problems in communication: Woods Cree speakers use the Plains Cree translation of the Bible, and there is a small minority of Plains Cree speakers living among them in Saskatchewan. The Swampy Cree dialects form a chain running from the mouth of the Albany River in Ontario to the Cumberland House area of Saskatchewan. Eastern Swampy speakers have no difficulty communicating with the Moose Cree, while the westernmost Swampy Crees easily understand the neighboring Woods and Plains dialects. The major break in the Swampy dialect continuum, separating Western Swampy from Eastern Swampy ("Subarctic Algonquian Languages," this vol.), falls between Fort Severn and Winisk and hence does not correspond to the eastern boundary of the area covered in this chapter.

Territory and Environment

The Western Woods Cree occupy the full boreal forest west of Hudson and James bays, including the northern portions of Ontario, Manitoba, Saskatchewan, and Alberta. Some groups of the three divisions are beyond the perimeters of the full forest: the eastern Swampy or West Main Cree occupy the Hudson Bay lowland, and some of the Rocky and Strongwoods Cree are in the forest areas transitional to the prairies and to the Rocky Mountains (fig. 1). The Swampy Cree reside in the region from James Bay, westward to Cumberland House, Saskatchewan; the Rocky Cree are in and west of the Nelson River drainage in northwestern Manitoba and Saskatchewan; and the Strongwoods Cree are north of the Saskatchewan River in Saskatchewan and Alberta (Canada. Department of Indian Affairs and Northern Development. Indian Affairs Branch 1970; J.G.E. Smith 1967–1970, 1975a; Wolfart 1973a:7–11; Smith 1976a). The dividing lines among these groups may have varied in the past, as some major shifts occurred as a result of the introduction of the fur trade (Hlady 1964; Mandelbaum 1940).

The full boreal forest is characterized by a heavy forest cover, predominantly of white and black spruce but including other conifers such as tamarack, balsam fir, and jack pine; broad-leaved trees include white birch, trembling aspen, and balsam poplar. In the Hudson Bay Lowlands and in northern Manitoba and Saskatchewan, the boreal forest changes gradually to a zone of transition to the tundra: the forest cover be-

---

* The Cree dialects spoken in the areas covered by this chapter may be written with the following phonemic symbols: *p, t, c, k; s, h; m, n, δ; w, y; i, a, o; i·, e·, a·, o·*. The phonology of these dialects is very close to that of Southern Plains Cree (Wolfart 1973a; see chapter on Cree in vol. 17), except that Woods Cree has a phoneme δ that is lacking in Swampy (which substitutes *n*) and in Plains (which substitutes *y*), and that Woods and Northern Plains Cree have replaced *e·* with *i·* since about the late nineteenth century. Also, older speakers of Saskatchewan Woods Cree have a cluster δk ([θk]), replaced by *sk* in the speech of younger speakers, by *hk* in Plains, Manitoba Woods Cree, and most Swampy Cree, and apparently by *htk* in Saskatchewan Western Swampy (Pentland 1978:109, 113).

Italicized Cree words in the text of this chapter have been phonemicized by the editors, in part on the basis of communications from David H. Pentland (1980) and C. Douglas Ellis (1973).

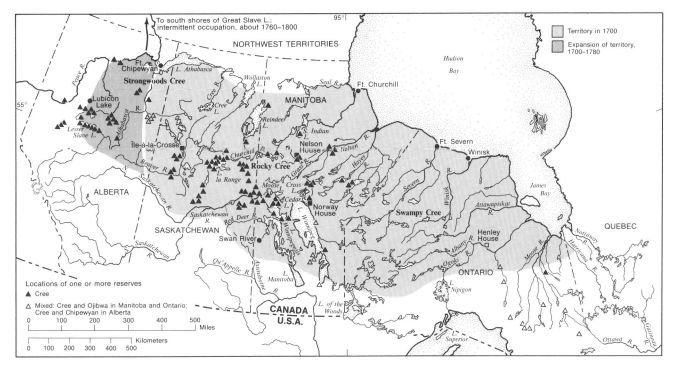

Fig. 1. Territory in the 18th century with locations of modern reserves.

comes predominantly black spruce and tamarack, the subarctic open lichen-woodland interspersed with patches of tundra. On the southwest margin there is a transition to the prairies, with a transitional aspen grove forest (cf. Rowe 1972:20–55). Physiographically, the area occupied by the Western Woods Cree is primarily the Precambrian Shield, and, on the west, the forested interior plain. The region is characterized by a low, rolling relief, with a few major hills, and a vast number of lakes, rivers, and streams.

Major animal species of importance for food and useful by-products include the woodland caribou, moose, elk or wapiti, wood bison, and white-tailed deer. Of these, moose and woodland caribou were most important for subsistence, the others having limited distribution. Black bear were important for ritual purposes. Small mammals utilized for food include the varying hare, beaver, woodchuck, muskrat, porcupine, and squirrel; of these, the most important as a source of subsistence was the varying hare. North of the Churchill River in Manitoba, and around Lake Athabasca in Saskatchewan, Barren-Ground caribou were sometimes present when the herds were at maximum size and penetrated more deeply to the south. Fur-bearing animals of major importance include the beaver, mink, marten, otter, lynx, fox, and muskrat; those of lesser significance were the squirrel, woodchuck, gray wolf, wolverine, and fisher (Peterson 1966). The most important fish species were whitefish, lake trout, pickerel, and pike (McPhail and Lindsey 1970). Waterfowl were seasonally utilized in the areas of their flyways (Godfrey 1966). Vegetal products were limited seasonally and restricted to a number of varieties of berries.

History

The Swampy Cree in the seventeenth century occupied the region between Hudson and James bays and were known to the French as Christinaux (JR 18:229, 44:249; Blair 1911–1912, 1:107–108, 224; "Territorial Groups Before 1821: Cree and Ojibwa" and synonymy in "West Main Cree," this vol.).

The history of the Western Woods Cree has not yet been adequately pursued by scholars, but accumulating evidence indicates that earlier interpretations of territorial movements are incorrect. It has generally been considered that the western Cree represent a late eighteenth and early nineteenth-century westward migration resulting from the depletion of game and fur-bearing animals in the region east of Lake Winnipeg (Jenness 1932:284; Hlady 1964; A.D. Fisher 1969; Pentland 1978:109–110). However, there is evidence that although the Swampy Cree were migrating during this period, the Rocky and Strongwoods Cree had been long present in the west: it was apparently merely the name Cree that was at this time extended westward to apply to these divisions, previously known by generic terms such as Southern or Upland Indians (J.G.E. Smith 1976a).

Archeological survey and excavation at Southern Indian Lake indicate cultural continuity and Cree occupation from about A.D. 900 to the present (J.V. Wright 1971:3). The band located there now is Rocky Cree, associated with the Nelson House band. Selkirk pottery, the type identified with Cree at Southern Indian Lake, is also found around Reindeer Lake (Downes 1938), and James V. Wright (personal communication 1970) has identified similar pottery from Lac la Ronge. Archeologically, the Churchill River drainage as far west as Lac la Biche, Alberta (Meyer 1978), must be considered as Cree in late prehistoric times, rather than Chipewyan. Indeed, Gillespie (1975) and J.G.E. Smith (1975) have identified the aboriginal territory of the Chipewyan as to the north of the Seal River, in the forest-tundra ecotone to the west of Hudson Bay, and Gillespie has documented the southern movement of the Chipewyan, from regions north of Lake Athabasca south to the Churchill River region in the late eighteenth and the nineteenth centuries.

Historical data confirm the archeological record. Jérémie (1926:20–21), French officer and commandant at Fort Bourbon, as York Factory was known during the French occupation of 1694–1714, gave the southern boundary of the Chipewyan as the Seal River. Bacqueville de la Potherie (1931:265, 356), writing in the same period, observed that the Chipewyan dared not traverse the territory of the Maskegonehirinis (Swampy Cree) to reach York Factory. When the British began to explore seriously in the last third of the eighteenth century, they encountered Cree as far west as Alberta, and only late in the century were Chipewyan beginning to occupy part of the area. Thompson (1962:91), writing in the 1790s, asserted that the old people had told him that their ancestors had always hunted in this western territory. It was presumably Cree with whom the earlier French posts were trading. The "history" recorded by Petitot (1883) was the apparent basis for the theory of westward movement. Up to 1670, the territory of the Cree then known to the French extended approximately from Hudson Bay to the north shore of Lake Superior; western boundaries were not given. The Indians are reported to have lived by hunting, fishing, and collecting wild rice (JR 51:57) but were possibly hunting fur-bearers more than in the past, and their material culture was beginning to be modified by the introduction of trade goods. If Cree to the west of Lake Winnipeg and the Nelson River were not trading directly with Europeans, there would appear to be little question that some trade goods were beginning to reach them through intermediaries.

By the early eighteenth century, the French had extended their forts and other establishments west of Lake Superior, and in the north the English were established on the shores of Hudson Bay. By 1751 the French had established forts as far west as the foothills of the Rocky Mountains, although the Hudson's Bay Company had by then only one inland post, Henley House (Innis

1956:84–113), and interior exploration had been limited to the journey of Kelsey (1929). After the conquest of New France and the Treaty of Paris in 1763, the west was opened to the "Montreal peddlers," whose partnerships were the antecedents of the North West Company; the Hudson's Bay Company established inland posts to meet the competition (Innis 1970:149–282; Masson 1889–1890). Prior to the period of competition, the Indians had to travel great distances to trade, but in this phase trading posts were located conveniently, the variety of trade goods expanded, and prices were low.

The period of competition that lasted from the 1760s until the coalition of the two companies in 1821 provided the incentives for the Cree to increase their take of fur-bearing animals, eventually leading to severe depletion of this important resource, although they were increasingly dependent upon trade goods for essential technology. The period also led to a decrease in moose and caribou, as large amounts of game were needed to supply the needs of the trading post staffs, the Indians employed by the companies, and the large "fur brigades" that brought supplies in and took furs out. In some areas game depletion was drastic and responsible for depopulation and migration (Cameron 1889–1890, 2:241–242; Thompson 1962:103–104, passim; A.J. Ray 1971).

It was during this time, the late eighteenth and early nineteenth centuries, that the western movement of the Swampy Cree occurred. The human population was also depleted as hitherto unknown epidemic diseases were introduced. In 1781 a smallpox epidemic was introduced from the Sioux and Ojibwa that, according to the Cree, killed half the population, although the recorder (Thompson 1962:92) estimated three-fifths had perished. Subsequent outbreaks occurred until 1838 (Heagerty 1928, 2:17–65), and other diseases, such as tuberculosis, began to have effect. Following the smallpox epidemic of 1781, there appears to have been a southerly move and consolidation of the western Cree toward the Saskatchewan River drainage, with Chipewyan moving into the abandoned regions (Gillespie 1975). However, by the end of the century there was a gradual return to northern areas.

With the coalition of the Hudson's Bay and North West companies, the company rationalized its posts, eliminating competing establishments and closing those that were not profitable. Hitherto the Cree had maintained a traditional seminomadic life, with the major changes occurring in technology and increased hunting of small, nonmigratory, fur-bearing animals. Subsequent to the establishment of a trading monopoly in 1821, there was an increased tendency for the bands to be localized and oriented to a specific post, a first stage in the process of sedentarization. There is no evidence in the early literature to support the existence of individual or family hunting or trapping territories, although the family trapping territory had emerged well before the end of the nineteenth century (Rossignol 1939). The period from 1821 to the end of World War II was that of the classic fur trade or contact-traditional era (see "Intercultural Relations and Cultural Change in the Subarctic Shield and Mackenzie Borderlands," this vol.). In the latter part of the era, in the twentieth century, all-native log-cabin communities came into existence in favorable locations, oriented to a trading post–mission complex, which became the summer social center as well. Summer transportation was still based on the canoe, but the introduction of dog traction increased both mobility and the amount of goods that could be transported. The material culture was, by the end of the period, almost entirely Euro-Canadian.

Missionary activity began in earnest in the mid-nineteenth century, and in the twentieth the population was largely Christian, at least nominally (primarily Roman Catholic or Anglican). However, traditional beliefs, practices, and world view continued to coexist with Christianity, particularly in more isolated regions. Government involvement with the Indians began with the establishment of treaties, intended to extinguish the bands' territorial claims, in the decades following the cession of the Hudson's Bay Company Territories to the Dominion of Canada in 1870. Although reserves were created under the treaties made between 1876 and 1906 (Laviolette 1956:109–110), the Cree were able to continue the use of traditional territories. It was not until the modern period that the encroachment of industry began to affect traditional territorial exploitation as mining and lumbering operations commenced and further sedentarization was encouraged by the introduction of commercial fishing operations.

The trading post–mission complex was the Euro-Canadian center, but it also was the home of the Cree employed by the Hudson's Bay Company (the Home Guard or Home Indians) to hunt, to transport supplies, to carry on the "camp trade," and to perform other tasks. After World War II the extension of government services and other facilities resulted in the complex's becoming the basis for the modern village with a sedentary population, with only men leaving for the traplines and hunting territories in the winter.

Traditional Culture and Culture Change: The Eighteenth Century

The following account is based primarily upon late seventeenth, eighteenth, and early nineteenth-century documents that, taken together, permit a reconstruction of many aspects of Cree life in the eighteenth century. There are serious gaps, as there are for the contemporary situation, for lack of adequate ethnographic research. The documentation on the Woods Cree rarely

differentiates among the major divisions, but there do not appear to have been significant differences other than those associated with specific subsistence areas.

Social Organization

Information on socioterritorial organization is fragmentary for the entire history of the Western Woods Cree, which may be a function of both the flexible nature of organization and the lack of interest or perception by early travelers and writers. However, the earliest fragments seem to be consistent with the information from the late contact-traditional period.

The smallest unit was the nuclear family of husband, wife, and children. Sometimes the family was an extended polygynous family, the second wife commonly the sister of the first. A chief might have as many as seven wives. The household consisted of a lodge occupied by 10 to 14 relatives, but added extensions (probably temporary) could more than double the size.

Local bands, which usually consisted of several related families, constituted the hunting group of the autumn, winter, and spring. It was led by a leader (okima·w) whose authority was based on his experience, ability as a hunter and organizer, and possession of spiritual powers. A decline in his powers led to his replacement or to the dispersal of his band as the constituent families joined other bands.

Local or hunting bands came together for several months during the summer, to the shore of lakes where, escaping the mosquitoes and black flies, they could subsist by fishing and hunting. These summer groupings drew together the regional band, the largest cooperative unit, which was led by a chief (okima·w). In the nineteenth century, bands were known by the leaders' names, and it is probable that this reflects the custom of an earlier period.

Membership in the local and regional bands was flexible, varying according to the leaders' abilities, supply of game and other environmental conditions, and family realignments. There is no indication that the regional or local bands had definite territorial boundaries, and families were free to leave one and join another, permanently or temporarily, in which they had kinsmen. The flexibility of band size and composition was directly related to the environmental exploitation and seasonal adaptations. The early sources give little information as to band size, but local bands seem to have consisted of from two to four or five men and their families, or about 10 to 30 individuals (perhaps sometimes more), and regional bands may have been from one to several hundred.

The kinship system reflected the Subarctic demands for adaptability. It was bilateral in type, allowing for a maximum of possible affiliations. Bilateral cross-cousin marriage, that is, marriage to a mother's brother's or father's sister's child, was preferred, although marriage to any unrelated person was permitted. Cross-cousins were not considered kinsmen, while parallel cousins, that is, the children of parents of the same sex, were considered as siblings and marriage was prohibited. This structuring of marriage maintained kin relations between neighboring families and bands and assured cooperation and hospitality when needed.

Political Organization

There were no formal political institutions. The chief lacked coercive power; leaders could influence, but not control, individual behavior. Murder was avenged by kinsmen.

Warfare, or intermittent raiding, took place on the margins of Cree territory. On the northeast, near Hudson Bay, the Eskimo were the enemy and were hunted. On the north, the Chipewyan were the enemy until the Hudson's Bay Company made peace in the eighteenth century. In the area adjacent to the Plains, the Cree were allied with the Assiniboin against the Sioux. Shortly before the time of contact, the Assiniboin had separated from the larger body of Sioux and fled to Cree lands where they were well received and entered into this alliance.

Annual Cycle

During the summer, for two or three months, the regional band congregated on the shores of lakes where abundant fish, supplemented by game and berries, permitted population concentration. This was the time of major socializing, reinforcement of social ties, realignment of families, and planning for the winter dispersal.

In late summer or early autumn the local bands began departing by canoe for the wintering territory before freeze-up. During freeze-up travel and other activities were limited. Hunting was the major activity of early winter: moose and elk were hunted by bow and arrow, while the migrating herds of woodland caribou were snared or speared in pounds. Fur-bearing animals were also hunted or trapped, but the main concentration of trapping activity was during November and December, when the furs were of the highest quality. In January and February, when the weather was most severe, activities were limited. Intervals of enforced leisure encouraged the recounting of legends and other traditional oral literature. It was also a time when hides and pelts were processed, clothing made or repaired, and other routine activities performed. As winter moderated, hunting and trapping resumed.

During the period of breakup travel was again restricted. Woodland caribou were again the object of collective hunting at the time of their spring migration. With open water, the families and local bands returned to their prearranged summer location. Some men, acting for themselves and others, traveled to the distant trading posts on Hudson and James bays. By the end of the eighteenth century, inland trading posts had been established, and long-distance travel became less necessary.

Life Cycle

The birth of a child was attended with little ceremony. If it occurred while traveling under adverse conditions, only the briefest halt was made. In general, the birth was attended by two or three older women acting as midwives. Confined to a cradleboard, the baby was kept dry and clean with dried moss. If twins were born, one was immediately killed; the boy was allowed to live if one twin was a girl. There are statements that female infanticide occurred; infanticide was sometimes a necessity under the harsh conditions of Subarctic life, for a woman could not care adequately for two nursing children.

The child was given a name within a few months after its birth. The name was chosen by an older person, usually male, and was commonly related to environmental features, such as animals, plants, or seasons. There was no ceremony associated with the naming, although if the father had a successful hunt a feast was held. Other names were often adopted because of special events or dreams.

Children were treated with great affection and little apparent discipline; corporal punishment was not employed. Children were usually not weaned for at least one year, and sometimes not until age three. As they grew older, they began to assist the parents and to learn the skills necessary for adult life. At adolescence the individual underwent periods of isolation and fasting, to obtain through dreams spiritual powers from the manitous or spirits that would appear. For the growing boys, a ceremonial feast was held on the occasion of the first kill of big game.

When the girl reached puberty she was isolated in a small lodge some distance from the camp, and food was brought to her by her mother or other adult female

Mus. of the Amer. Ind., Heye Foundation. New York: 17/6836.

Fig. 2. Bull-roarer of wood with serrated edge attached with string to stick. Length 31 cm, collected by A.I. Hallowell at Cross Lake, Man., 1930.

Franklin 1823:facing 169.

Fig. 3. Interior of a skin-covered lodge near Cumberland House with family around the fire. Woman on right with baby in cradleboard wears a beaded pink, yellow, and white bib or collar, while the man on left smokes a long-stemmed black pipe. Bow and 2 arrows with gun at left. Colored lithograph based on lost 1820 watercolor by Robert Hood.

relative. After the isolation of the first menses she returned to her family tent. For a month or two after, she wore her hair disheveled, head hung low, and a cap with fringe to cover her face; she drank only from a vessel hung from the belt.

Marriage was arranged or at least influenced by the parents. Frequently friends would betroth children even before birth to solidify an alliance. It was not uncommon for a girl to move to the lodge of her husband at age 8 to 10, where she was treated with great affection; the marriage was not consummated until later. In other cases, a young man would obtain the consent of the girl's father or brother and then visit her with a present of beads or cloth. Her acceptance of the gift indicated consent. Marriage was not associated with any ceremony. Immediate postnuptial residence was matrilocal (uxorilocal) during which time the groom hunted and provided service for his wife's family, until a child was born, after which the couple usually moved to the camp of the husband. A successful hunter or leader might thereafter take an additional wife, often the sister of the first; co-wives referred to each other as sisters.

Wives were sometimes exchanged by men who thus cemented a long-term partnership or alliance. The lending or exchange of wives for specified periods (as much as a year) was permitted or valued, but adultery by the wife was severely punished or cause for divorce. In the event of divorce small children accompanied the mother. For the unmarried, there were few restrictions on sexual activities.

The division of labor was based on sex. Men were responsible for hunting, trapping, and fishing, and associated activities, including the manufacture of equipment. Women were frequently responsible for bringing the game to the camp. In general, women's activities were associated with the camp, pitching the tent, cutting firewood, dressing game, preparing hides and pelts, making clothing, cooking, and caring for the children. In addition, women snared hare and fished.

Sickness

Sickness and injury were considered the result of malevolent forces, and shamans were called upon for treatment. Herbal remedies and setting of limbs were supplemented by the shaman's use of spiritual forces,   *261* including those summoned in the rituals of the shaking tent. The sweat lodge was used both for curing and for cleanliness.

Fatal illness was met with resignation and serenity. The dying person was dressed in his finest clothing, his face painted, and his pipe always prepared. The man would then issue final instructions to his family—disposing of his equipment, making any last request, and giving the mandate to his survivors to avenge his death, for death was regarded as the result of witchcraft perpetrated by an enemy. Immediately after death a rifle was fired within the tent, to deter the spirit of the dead from returning. Burial was in a circular or oval grave, in a rectangular mound of earth with wooden stakes to provide the wall, or on a scaffold. In each case, the corpse was covered by wood; and personal possessions, such as smoking equipment, snowshoes, gun and ammunition, were included in the interment. The dead person's drum and birchbark vessel were attached to the grave or a nearby tree. Following the burial and loud lamentations, the remainder of the day and through the night a silent vigil was kept against the return of the deceased's soul. After that night the name of the deceased could not be mentioned again. The eldest son succeeded the deceased as head of the household.

In some cases, death was by request when an aged and helpless man or woman decided that he or she was an encumbrance on the family. In such cases, the individual sat in a prepared grave and was garroted with a bow string by a member of the family.

Structures

Shelter was provided by the conical lodge or the larger oblong variation. The former was constructed of 30–40 poles, 16–20 feet long, tied together at the top with leather thongs, covered by elk, caribou, or moose hides. A gap at the top permitted light to enter and smoke to leave; and a flap served as a door, facing south. The hearth was in the center, raised slightly on a mound of earth or stones. The lodge served as shelter for two or more families. In winter, lodges were placed in the forest to avoid the wind; in the summer on lake or riverbanks to take advantage of the breezes that repelled the biting insects. A semilunar lean-to or barricade was often constructed, especially when traveling.

Clothing

For most of the eighteenth century, dress was largely traditional, although toward the end of the century European cloth was introduced and styles modified. Traditionally clothing was made from the tanned hides of moose, caribou, and elk, and sometimes decorated with geometric designs of porcupine quills, later sup-

plemented by beads and thread that permitted floral designs. The men wore a tunic that reached almost to the knee over which, in winter, another of caribou or beaver with the hair on was worn. Over the outer tunic a cloak or blanket of beaver, caribou, or otter was worn; it doubled as a blanket at night. A hide belt around the waist supported a long breechcloth, ornamented with quills or beads. Hide leggings reached from the upper thighs to ankles, tied below the knees with decorated garters. Moccasins were made from one or two pieces of moose or caribou, and sometimes decorated. In winter, an extension reached to the knee, and socks of caribou or hare, with the fur inside, were worn. In winter a cap of cloth or animal pelt was worn; in summer men went bareheaded or wore caps fashioned from skins of caribou, otter, eagles, and other birds and animals. Mittens for summer were made of unlined moose or caribou skin; those for winter were of beaver, lined with cloth or hide.

Women wore dresses of moosehide, the sleeves attached only by thongs decorated with quills, beads, or brass, as was the bottom of the dress itself. A belt of hide was worn, often elaborately decorated. Other garments were like those of the men, although with more decoration, including painted designs. The clothing of children was similar to that of parents.

Technology

The simple bow of aboriginal times was largely replaced by the musket by the late eighteenth century. Snares were used for game, and deadfalls for furbearers, later largely replaced by metal traps. Fishing was not of major importance, except in times of scarcity, for it was considered a demeaning activity for a hunter. Fish were speared and caught by angling; winter fishing was limited until the introduction of the iron ice chisel.

The most important items of traveling equipment were snowshoes, toboggans, and canoes. Snowshoe frames were made of birch, the lacing of babiche, and were of two varieties, elongated oval and pointed. The toboggan was made of planks of juniper, curved at the front end, usually 12 feet long, 16 inches wide, and one-quarter inch thick. A leather thong attached to the curved end was passed over one shoulder and under one arm for pulling. Women normally pulled the toboggan, but occasionally a dog was used; it was not until the twentieth century that dog teams were commonly employed. Canoes were ribbed with birch, sheathed with birchbark, and caulked with turpentine boiled to the consistency of pitch. They were generally about 18 inches deep and weighed about 80 pounds. A canoe held two adults, children, and equipment.

Bear pelts were used for bedding and seating, and blankets were made from moose, caribou, or elk hides. Birchbark containers were used for storage; and others

262

Fig. 4. Camp at Oxford House, Man., with conical wigwams and birchbark canoes on the shore. Photograph by Robert Bell, 1880.

were used for cooking, hot stones being placed in the water or broth for boiling. From an early period copper kettles began to replace the birchbark containers. The aboriginal equipment was rapidly replaced by metal implements, although some items persisted. Bone scrapers, fish spears, and fishhooks, for example, were preferred to those of iron; but metal axes, awls, knives, crooked knives, ice chisels, and needles were standard equipment.

Religion

Cree religious beliefs are only poorly understood, for the people have from early contact (Thompson 1962:75) to the present (J.G.E. Smith 1967–1970) been reticent to speak on the subject. They believed in the existence of the benevolent Great-Great Spirit or Kitchi-Kitchi-Manitou (*kihci-kihci-manito·w*), to whom on very rare occasions sacrifice of a dog was made. Although the provenience of the Great Spirit (*misi-manito*) is not definite, Cooper's (1933) argument that the concept was aboriginal is supported by eighteenth-century references (Isham 1949:65; Graham 1969:160–161). The *maci-manito·w*, or Evil Spirit, was feared and propitiated by sacrifices. The Windigo (*wi·htiko·w*), a cannibal with heart of ice (often a giant) who also possessed humans and caused them to become cannibals, was

greatly feared. Individuals thought to be Windigos were killed; these were frequently people of suspect behavior (Fogelson 1965; Hay 1971). Manitous or spirits could inhabit all living things, as well as objects or forces (such as wind and thunder); and many of these were considered animate. Manitous appeared in dreams and gave special power or protection to the individual. Some men obtained great powers from the manitous; in curing they called upon manitous for help. Each man had his medicine bundle, containing objects of great spiritual power.

Creative Expression

The traditional oral literature has not been systematically gathered or analyzed. Trickster (Swampy *wi·sake·ca·hk*, Plains *wi·sahke·ča·hk*) or Wisakedjak tales were, and in some places are still, told during the winter, when the animal spirits are asleep. Singing and dancing occurred on the occasion of successful hunts and the feasting that followed. Various games were played, particularly games of chance and skill, including the hand game. Artwork was limited by the nomadic life, but clothing was decorated with bead and quill work, and the face and body were tattooed and painted with complex designs.

Contact-Traditional Culture: The Nineteenth and Twentieth Centuries

Little information is available for the early contact-traditional culture of the nineteenth century. The prior period had seen an intensification of hunting of furbearers as well as severe depletion of the big game supply as meat was needed to support both the Native peoples and the European residents and fur brigades. This was a factor in the movement of many Swampy and other Cree to the Plains in the late eighteenth and early nineteenth centuries (Hlady 1964; Mandelbaum 1940). For example, at Norway House in 1815, the chief factor reported only 26 (Swampy) Cree families in his district, most having come from the York Factory district because of the poor game and fur supply. The former inhabitants of the Norway House district had left for the west to seek better hunting and trapping grounds (Sutherland 1815). At the same time, the factor at Swan River (west of Lake Winnipeg) reported that of the newly arrived Cree, some were hunting on the Plains with Saulteaux and Assiniboin, while others were hunting and trapping in the forest (Hudson's Bay Company 1815).

The presence of essentially the same *y*-dialect among both the Strongwoods Cree and the Plains Cree suggests that many of the Strongwoods Cree of northern Saskatchewan and Alberta moved onto the Plains. According to A.J. Ray (1974), the Cree occupying the transitional forest-parkland-prairie ecotone were preadapted to a Plains adjustment by virtue of seasonal adaptations to the Plains fauna. Other sources (Hlady 1964; Mandelbaum 1940) indicate that Swampy Cree (speaking an *n*-dialect) were another major component of the Plains Cree population.

During the nineteenth century, some important modifications were made in Cree culture. There is no evidence for individually or family-owned hunting or trapping territories in the early period, but trapping territories had emerged by the end of the nineteenth century, and combined hunting and trapping territories could exist where subsistence was based on nonmigratory small game, furbearers, and fish. The size of the trapping territories was a function of the interplay of ecological factors (Hallowell 1949a; Leacock 1954; Bishop 1970a, 1974). With the decrease in big game and the introduction of the metal ice chisel and twine gill net (fig. 5), fish became a more important part of the diet and later became of still greater significance when dog teams

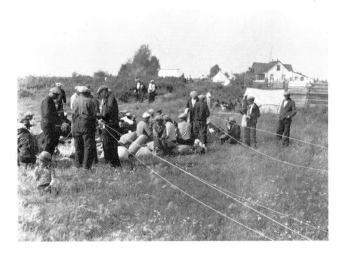

Fig. 5. Dividing commercial cord received as part of treaty payment. Such cord was used in making fish nets, which were "sixteen meshes wide and forty or fifty yards long" (L. Mason 1967:33). Photograph by Leonard Mason, Oxford House, Man., July 1940.

became the basic form of winter travel. The technology was largely of European origin, and the interdependence of trader and trapper, with the attendant credit economy, led to increasing stability of band membership oriented to a specific trading post (L. Mason 1967:19–35). Communal hunting of big game gave way to individual hunting and trapping, or to the cooperative group of two or three men and their families, closely related by kinship or marriage. The common association was that of father and son(s) or son-in-law, or of brothers or brothers-in-law. By the early twentieth century, all-native log-cabin communities served as base camps, oriented on the one hand to the traplines and on the other to the trading post–mission complex.

The Hudson's Bay Company factor at the post was the economic authority through his control of the credit system, but he was also the representative of the company in its role as government of Rupert's Land; he gradually became known as *okima·w* 'chief, leader, person of authority or influence', while the Cree chiefs became *okima·hka·n* 'elected or appointed chief', literally 'surrogate or substitute chief' (Ellis 1960; Faries 1938:383) as traditional leadership roles decreased in scope and importance. After several treaties were made between 1871 and 1890, the government recognized chiefs and councilors, but their powers were limited and they acted largely as intermediaries with the Euro-Canadian authorities. In many areas the consensual form

top, Glenbow-Alberta Inst., Calgary, Alta.: AP1838; bottom left, Mus. of the Amer. Ind., Heye Foundation, New York: 7/2410; lower right, Man. Mus. of Man and Nature, Winnipeg: H4.12–99.

Fig. 6. Leather garments with satin-stitch floral embroidery. top, Jacket with silk embroidery work, mink trim, leather fringe, and buttons (not visible) bearing the Hudson's Bay Company insignia; collected at Norway House, Man., 1960. bottom left, Leggings with light-colored leather panel (detail) with silk embroidery edged with red and green silk ribbon appliqué; collected 1917. bottom right, Gloves decorated with embroidery of mercerized cotton and leather fringe; collected at Norway House, Man., about 1900. Moccasin vamps are also decorated in this manner. Length of jacket 86 cm; except detail, rest to same scale.

WESTERN WOODS CREE

of chief selection was eventually changed to elective. The leaders of trapping groups, those designated captains and lieutenants, disappeared when trading and credit were handled on an individual basis. Traditional methods of social control were complemented or replaced by Euro-Canadian personnel, especially the Royal Canadian Mounted Police.

Effective missionary activity was made possible by the increased sedentarization characteristic of this era. Father Silvy (1931) complained in 1684 that conversion of the Western Woods Cree was impossible because of their ceaseless wandering, but after missionary effort was initiated in the 1840s, conversion to Christianity became common. The effects of conversion were numerous. Polygyny and the levirate were banned. Cross-cousin marriage was frowned upon, but it persisted nevertheless; it began to disappear only in the twentieth century (Hallowell 1937; L. Mason 1967:49–51; Rossignol 1938) and in more isolated areas was to be found even in the 1960s (J.G.E. Smith 1975a). Missionaries also attempted to overcome traditional behavior and beliefs pertaining to the supernatural, for example, the curing methods of the shaking-tent ritual, and to substitute Christian morals and beliefs (L. Mason 1967:57–67). Their efforts were not completely successful, and many practices and values persisted, particularly in the more isolated areas of the north (Rossignol 1938a; J.G.E. Smith 1967–1970).

The trading post–mission complex increasingly became the focal point of band life and was visited at the end of the main trapping season at Christmas, at Easter, and in the summer for the rituals of treaty payment. The increased sedentarization and orientation to the center was paralleled by a decline in extensive interband relations. It was the trading post–mission complex that in the modern era became the village site.

Until after World War II, most Crees lived a traditional way of life that had evolved as a result of the changes brought about by the fur trade. Relatively few were bilingual, and still fewer had received any formal education, although some were literate in the Cree syllabary. Traditional medical practices were to some degree supplemented by the government medicine chest provided to missionaries or Hudson's Bay Company officials for use of the Indian population; access to medical facilities was limited. Hunting, fishing, and trapping provided the basis for subsistence (fig. 7). Besides trapping (fig. 8), cash income was received from the treaty annuities, five dollars a person each year for most persons, and some men were permanently or seasonally employed by the Hudson's Bay Company in carrying supplies to the posts and furs to the larger centers. For most Cree, the annual seasonal cycle remained much as it had been, although commercial fishing was beginning to develop in a few areas.

Sociocultural Situation in the 1960s

Following the Second World War, the Canadian government began to extend social services to the Native peoples of the boreal forest, aided by technological

Hudson's Bay Co. Lib., Winnipeg, Man.

Fig. 7. Women skinning muskrats. The skins on stretchers are hung to dry while the meat is dried or smoked on a rack (right foreground) for later consumption. Photograph by Donald Denmark at Cumberland House, Sask., before March 1941.

Hudson's Bay Co. Lib., Winnipeg. Man: 77–29.
Fig. 8. Isaiah Clark of Norway House, Man., setting a steel trap with a fish head to catch mink. He wears a fur trimmed, fringed skin jacket with beaded decorations and beaded gloves.
Photograph by J. Ferdie Dalman, 1940–1943.

developments that made access and communication relatively easy and rapid. Young people were encouraged to attend residential schools in the south, and later elementary schools were established on many reserves; some schools, both elementary and secondary, were operated by provincial governments and provided services for both status and non-status Cree. Nursing stations, sometimes very modern, provided basic medical care, and radio communication and aircraft were used to remove serious cases to central hospitals. The family allowance system was introduced at the beginning of this period, the amount being disproportionately important to Native peoples because of its certainty. It was often used to provide necessities, such as ammunition and milk, while most subsistence still came from the land. Emergency welfare became generally available, supplementing the trapping and commercial fishing income. Government housing programs began to provide lumber and plywood houses to replace the log cabins typical of the earlier part of the twentieth century. In many areas all-weather roads were built, and most reserves were served with fair regularity by scheduled air service.

A process of sedentarization was well underway: the mission–trading post complex became the center of a developing micro-urban community, with all the institutions of Euro-Canadian society present or indirectly affecting the population. As the young people returned from residential schools, they were often no longer fit-

ted for, nor interested in, life in the "bush," and economic opportunities were very limited. Some, including the few with advanced or university education, had begun in the late 1960s to speak aggressively on behalf of the rights of the Native peoples. The provincial Indian Brotherhoods were beginning to unite the various bands to consult with the Canadian Department of Indian Affairs and Northern Development in the formulation of a new Indian policy.

Although there had been much in the way of social and cultural change, economically the position of the Western Woods Cree was depressed. Increased education was not paralleled by increased economic opportunity, although some were being employed on band business and as guides at fishing resorts. The establishment of the Canadian Freshwater Fisheries Board was a promising innovation in the development of commercial fishing. On the whole, however, the potential economic resources of the boreal forest have been limited, and, probably, will be inadequate to the increasing population.

Population

The aboriginal population of Western Woods Cree cannot be more than approximated. Mooney (1928:4) estimated that there were 20,000 Cree and Maskegon at the time of contact and 19,000 in 1906. Jenness (1932:286) gave a figure of 20,000 for all Cree in 1924 but noted they had suffered enormously from tuberculosis and other epidemic diseases. These figures were prepared under the assumption that the Cree of northwestern Manitoba and northern Saskatchewan and Alberta were recent immigrants from the east; they are likely to be underestimates. The population for the western Cree is not even hinted at by any of the early observers, and no projection can be made from the number of Cree who came to the coastal forts by canoe, since only a small number came to trade in any one year. A figure of about 20,000 for the aboriginal population would not seem excessive for the combined Swampy, Rocky, and Strongwoods Cree. Present-day Canadian government figures are ethnographically imprecise. The population registered to 61 official bands in table 1 does not include Cree who are classed as Métis, although many are linguistically, culturally, and genealogically identical to Treaty Cree or status Indians.

Synonymy†

The Western Woods Cree usually refer to themselves as *ne·hiyawak* (singular *ne·hiyaw*, which becomes *ni·hiyaw, ni·hiδaw* in the modern local dialects) 'those who speak the same language' (Hayden 1863:235), a

† This synonymy was written by David H. Pentland.

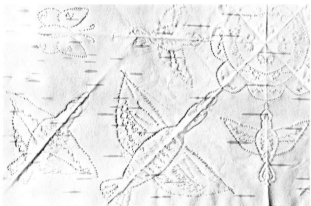

Fig. 9. Angelique Merasty of Beaver Lake, Sask. (b. 1927), demonstrating birchbark biting. The designs are made using both the side and front teeth, biting sharply and rapidly into a piece of folded thin birchbark to form intricate and delicate patterns (Moody 1957:9–11). Such birchbark designs were sold in 1980 for about $25 for a 5-inch square. Photographs by Frank Fieber, 1978.

derivative of *ne·hiyawe·w* 'he speaks our language, he speaks Cree'. The name is often taken to be a derivative of *nah-* 'proper, correct', whence the translations 'exact people' (Howse 1844:2) and 'precise speakers' (Logan 1958:12), but the Ojibwa cognate *ni·ʔinawe·* 'he speaks our language, he speaks Ojibwa' shows that this interpretation is incorrect. The Woods Cree form *ne·hiδaw(e·w)* appears as Nayhaythaways, 1690 (with English plural -s; Kelsey 1929:9); Nahetheway, 1775 (miscopied with Nak-, Graham in Isham 1949:311); Nahathaway, 1785 (Thompson 1962:12); Ne-heth-aw-a, 1790 (Umfreville 1954:92); Ne-he-tha-way, Ne-heatha-way, 1791 (Turnor 1934:338, 458); Něhethówuck (pl.; Howse 1844:2); Nehethè-wuk, Nithè-wuk (both pl.; Richardson 1852:264). Plains Cree *ne·hiyaw(e·w)* is recorded as Neheaway, 1772 (Hearne 1958:130); Nahhahwuk, 1830 (pl.; Tanner 1956:316); Né-a-ya-óg (pl.; Hayden 1863:235); Nehiyawok (pl.; Lacombe 1874:x). Faries (1938:350) also gives the variants *one·hiyaw* and *ne·hiyawiyiniw* in his Plains Cree dictionary; the Woods Cree cognate of the latter, *ne·hiδawiδiniw*, was written Nathèwy-withinyu by Richardson (1852:264). In 1743 James Isham (1949:113) mentioned a group called Unnahathewunnutitto; the first part of the name is Woods Cree *one·hiδaw,* but the remainder is unidentified.

The eighteenth-century Woods Cree also referred to themselves as Atheneuwuck (*iδiniwak* 'people') (Graham 1969:143, 207).

The Western Woods Cree distinguished themselves from other Cree-speaking groups by the name *saka·wiyiniwak* (Plains dialect), *saka·wiδiniwak* (Woods dialect) 'bush people', recorded as Sackaweé-thinyoowuc (Richardson in Franklin 1823:108) and Sakawiyiniwok (Lacombe 1874:x). The name Cree and its variants (see the synonymy in "West Main Cree," this vol.) are seldom used without modifiers to refer specifically to the Western Woods Cree; however, compounds with translations of *saka·wiyiniw* are common: French Cristinaux du Bois fort, 1749 (La Vérendrye in Margry 1879–1888, 6:616) and Cris des Bois (Lacombe 1874:xv); English Strong Wood Crees, 1792 (McDonald in Masson 1889–1890, 2:17) and Thick Wood Crees (Richardson in Franklin 1823:108). The Plains Cree proper also call the Western Woods Cree *saka·wiyiniwak*; another Plains Cree name is *natikamiwiyiniwak*, perhaps meaning 'northern people' (Pentland 1970–1979).

To the Chipewyan, the Cree are known as *ʔená* 'enemy' (J.G.E. Smith 1967–1973, 1975a; Ronald Scollon and Eung-Do Cook, communications to editors 1979). The Hare use the cognate *ʔeda*, with the same reference and connotation (Keren Rice, communication to editors

Table 1. Population of Western Woods Cree by Government Bands, 1978

Ontario		Saskatchewan	
Brunswick House[a,b]	219	Canoe Lake	449
Chapleau Cree[a]	36	Cumberland House	276
Constance Lake[b]	600	Lac la Ronge	2,713
Flying Post[a,b]	32	Montreal Lake	1,236
Matachewan[a,b]	141	Peter Ballantyne	2,170
Missanabie Cree[a]	64	Red Earth	477
New Post	48	Shoal Lake	252
Timagami[a,b]	189	Sturgeon Lake	950
		Waterhen Lake	649
Manitoba			
Bloodvein	454	**Alberta**	
Chemahawin	449	Cree	876
Cross Lake	2,091	Driftpile	647
Fisher River[b]	1,302	Duncan's	52
God's Lake	1,073	Fort McMurray[c]	119
Grand Rapids	359	Grouard	65
Mathias Colomb	1,192	Little Red River	1,283
Moose Lake	336	Lubicon Lake	136
Nelson House	1,942	Sawridge	44
Norway House	2,333	Sturgeon Lake	734
Oxford House	1,076	Sucker Creek	572
Peguis[b]	2,534	Swan River	196
Poplar River[b]	511	Wabasca (Bigstone)	1,608
Split Lake	1,194	Whitefish Lake	531
The Pas	1,340		
		Total	35,550

SOURCE: Canada. Department of Indian Affairs and Northern Development 1980.

NOTE: Band names are the official designations of the Canadian Department of Indian Affairs and Northern Development; many are commonly known by other names. Some of the largest bands are located on several different reserves and exploit different territories; for example, the officially designated Nelson House band also has a "band" at Southern Indian Lake. Incidents of transferring band membership, especially on the margins of Western Woods Cree territory, also confuse the population rolls; for example, the Barren Lands band of Chipewyan included approximately 200 Rocky Cree in 1970 that are not included here.

[a] Officially designated Cree but cultural and linguistic affiliations undetermined.

[b] Includes Ojibwa.

[c] Includes Chipewyan.

1979). Other Athapaskan names for the Cree recorded by Petitot (1896:105) are: Beaver déchiné, Slavey enda, and Eastern Kutchin tattinœ.

Bands

During the eighteenth and nineteenth centuries, subgroups were usually called by the name of the lake or river from which they came; the following bands (and, no doubt, many others) probably lived within the area covered by this chapter.

Athabasca (*ahδapaska·w* 'there are reeds here and there'). Athapeeska Indians, 1760 (Norton in Warkentin and Ruggles 1970:89); Athapuscow, 1771 (Hearne

1958:161); Thopiskow, 1775 (Rich and Johnson 1951:16); Athup pe scau, 1775 (Graham in Isham 1949:316); A'Thopuskow, A,thup'pes'cau, Atha,pus,kow, A,tho,pus,cow, 1776–1777 (Rich and Johnson 1951:60, 87, 185, 236); Athupescow, 1791 (Graham 1969:206); Atha-pis-co, 1791 (Turnor 1934:335); Arabuthcow, Athapuscow, Athabasca, 1809 (Henry 1901:326); Athăpèskow (Richardson 1852:264); Rabaskaw, Athabaskaw, Ayabaskawiyiniwok (Lacombe 1874:x, xv). The form Arathapescow Indians, 1772 (Hearne in Warkentin and Ruggles 1970:93), appears to be a garbling of two dialect variants.

Beaver River (*amisko-si·piy* 'beaver river'). Omisk a sepe, 1775 (Graham in Isham 1949:316); Amiska-Se-pee, 1791 (Graham 1969:206); Omiska-sipi (Richardson 1852:264).

Churchill River (*misi-nipiy* 'great water'). Meshinnepee, Mishenepe, 1717 (Knight 1932:163); Missinnepee, 1743 (Isham 1949:112); Mis se ne pe, 1775 (Graham in Isham 1949:316); Missinepee, 1791 (Graham 1969:206); Misi-nipi (Richardson 1852:264); translated as Great Water Indians, 1717 (Knight 1932:165). Another band lived on the part of the Churchill called *manite·w si·piy* 'strangers' river', written Mantua-Sepee in 1791 (Graham 1969:206).

Cross Lake (*pimicikama·w* 'cross lake'). Peme chic emeou, 1775 (Graham in Isham 1949:316); Pimmechikemow, 1791 (Graham 1969:206); Pemmichi-ke-mè-u (Richardson 1852:264).

Firesteel River (*ahpiht si·piy* 'firesteel river'; now considered part of the Hayes River). Apet-Sepee, 1791 (Graham 1969:206).

Grass River (*maskosi·ska·w si·piy* 'lots-of-grass river'). Mus cus is cau, 1775 (Graham in Isham 1949:316); Muscasiscow, 1791 (Graham 1969:206); Muska-siskow (Richardson 1852:264). The traders usually called this band the Grass River Indians (Rich and Johnson 1951). Perhaps the same were the Muchiskewuck Athinuwick, 1768 (Graham 1969:192).

Hayes River (*pinasiwe·ciwan si·piy* 'flows-down-the-bank river'). Pennesewagewan, 1743 (Isham 1949:112–113); Pena say witchewan, 1775 (Graham in Isham 1949:316); Penesewichewan, Penesiwichewan Sepee, 1791 (Graham 1969:206, 250); Penesay-wichewan sipi (Richardson 1852:264).

Hill River (*cahkatina·w si·piy* 'pointed-hill river'; now considered part of the Hayes River). Chuckitanau, 1775 (Graham in Isham 1949:316); Chucketanaw, 1791 (Graham 1969:206); Chuki-tanu sipi (Richardson 1852:264).

Île-à-la-Crosse (*sa·kihtawa·w* 'river mouth'). Sakittawawiyiniwok (Lacombe 1874:x); Sakitowawuk, Sakitawaweyinewuk (Faries 1938:445).

Moose Lake (*pi·ka·kama·w* 'muddy lake'). Pegog eme ou, 1775 (Graham in Isham 1949:316); Pegogamow, 1791 (Graham 1969:206); Pegogĕ-mè-u nipi (Richardson 1852:264). Another band with the same name—spelled Pigogomew, etc. (Rich and Johnson 1951)—lived somewhere on the plains near the South Saskatchewan River during the same period.

Nelson River (Cree form unknown). Poethinicau, 1775 (Graham in Isham 1949:316); Poethinicaw, 1791 (Graham 1969:206); Po-i-thinnè-kaw-sipi (Richardson 1852:264). Usually this band was called the North River Indians by the Hudson's Bay Company traders (Rich and Johnson 1951). Perhaps the same is Pechepoethinue, 1743 (Isham 1949:316).

Red Deer River (*wa·ske·siw si·piy* 'elk river'). Waske su sepe, 1775 (Graham in Isham 1949:316); Wuskesew-Sepee, 1791 (miscopied Musk-; Graham 1969:206); Wuskèsew-sipi (Richardson 1852:264).

The Pas (*opa·skwe·ya·w* 'wooded narrows'). Basquio Indians, 1776 (Rich and Johnson 1951:34); U'Basquio, Bas,qui,a, 1777 (Rich and Johnson 1951:129, 183); U'Bas,qui,a, Bas,que,ah, U'Bas,que,a, 1778 (Rich and Johnson 1951:209, 240, 241).

Part of the modern Woods Cree call themselves *asini·ska·wiδiniwak* (phonemicization uncertain) 'people of the rocky area', that is, the Precambrian Shield (J.G.E. Smith 1967–1970); others say there is no name to distinguish themselves from other *saka·wiδiniwak* (Pentland 1970–1979). Names for the Swampy Cree are listed in the synonymy in "West Main Cree," this volume.

Sources

Source material on the Western Woods Cree is unsatisfactory in many respects for all periods of their history. They were first—by 1640—and marginally known to the Jesuits Albanel and Allouez (JR 18:229). With the establishment of forts on Hudson Bay, they became known to the traders and other officials. With the exception of Kelsey (1929), inland exploration of the interior by the Hudson's Bay Company did not begin until the mid-eighteenth century. Early reports from Hudson Bay were made during the French occupation of York Fort by Marest (1931), Silvy (1931), Bacqueville de la Potherie (1931), and Jérémie (1926). By mid-century, La Vérendrye (1927) had explored the interior, and major accounts became available on the Cree trading there (Dobbs 1744; Graham 1969; Isham 1949). After Hendry's (1907) inland exploration of 1753, accounts were left by the traders of the rival companies (Cameron 1889–1890, 2; Cocking 1908; Fidler 1934; Harmon 1903; Hearne 1934, 1958; Henry 1901; Mackenzie 1927; Thompson 1962; Turnor 1934). Some collections of early documents have been published by Blair (1911–1912), Kellogg (1917), Masson (1889–1890), and Tyrrell (1931), and the Hudson's Bay Record Society continues its publications from the archives. Other officials or explorers (Chappell 1817; Franklin 1823; Richardson 1852) left some record of the Western Cree that they encountered.

Ethnographic research has been extremely limited; the major sources are A.D. Fisher (1969), Hallowell (1932, 1937), L. Mason (1967), J.G.E. Smith (1967–1970, 1975), and the brief papers of the Oblate missionary Rossignol (1938, 1938a, 1939).

Chipewyan

JAMES G.E. SMITH

Language, Territory, and Environment

The Chipewyan (ˌchĭpəwī'ăn or -'än, or ˌchīpə'wīən) belong to the Northeastern Athapaskan dialect group of the Mackenzie–Hudson Bay drainages. Dialect variations among the Chipewyan are minor and correspond to regional zones of occupation.* The Chipewyan consider the neighboring Athapaskan Dogrib and Slavey as similar but ethnically distinct. The Eskimo to the north are known as *hotél'ená* 'enemies of the flat area' (that is, the Barren Grounds); the Cree to the south are simply *'ená* 'enemy'.

Several major Chipewyan divisions were recognized during the nineteenth century if not earlier. As distinguished by Petitot (1876:xx), supported by comparisons with other sources (Petitot 1844–1885, 1:51, 1891:363; Legoff 1889; Penard 1938; Curtis 1907–1930, 18:3–4; J.G.E. Smith 1967–1976, 1970, 1975), these were as follows:

(1) T'atsan ottiné (*tacán-hotine, talʒá̧-hotine*), translated by Petitot 'copper people', the Yellowknife. In the historical sources these are usually presented as a distinct tribe (see "Yellowknife," this vol.).

(2) Kkpest'aylékkè ottiné (*k̓estait-hotine*) 'dwellers among the quaking aspen', the Athabasca division; this includes the people along the Slave River elsewhere distinguished by Petitot (1891:363) as the Des-nèdhè-

kkè-nadé (*desneδe-k̓e-náde*) 'they (who) dwell on the wide river'.

(3) Thi-lan-ottiné (*θílą-hotine*) 'dwellers at the top of the head' (of the ice giant; Petitot 1891:363), the people of the upper Churchill River drainage. Petitot (1876:xx, 1884–1885, 1:48) termed these the Chipewyan proper, believing that the center of dispersion was the Peace River region and that northern and eastern groups were relatively recent migrants. This erroneous interpretation, based on local legend unsupported by historical or archeological data (J.G.E. Smith 1975, 1976a), has been commonly repeated in later literature.

(4) Ethen-eldèli (*'eθə́n heldéti*) 'caribou eaters', the bands along the forest edge west of Hudson Bay. They have also been called by variants of Sa-i-sa-ˈdtinnè (*sayise dene* 'east (rising-sun) people', now the name of the Churchill band) and Thè-yé-Ottinè (*θeye-hotine* 'dwellers at Stone Fort', the name of Fort Prince of Wales and later of Churchill) (Richardson 1852:246; Petitot 1891:363; Hodge 1907h:440–441; Ronald Scollon, communication to editors 1979).

The Chipewyan are the most numerous and most widely distributed of the Northern Athapaskans (fig. 1). Aboriginally, they occupied the forest-tundra ecotone (the "edge of the forest") from near Hudson Bay, north of the Seal River, in a wide northwesterly arc to north of the Arctic Circle, near the mouth of the Coppermine River (see "Yellowknife," fig. 1, this vol.). In historic times, they extended westward into the region between Great Slave Lake and Lake Athabasca and beyond, and south of Lake Athabasca to the lakes of the Churchill River drainage (Gillespie 1975). On the north they had occupied the south and central Barren Grounds but in the nineteenth century abandoned much of it, limiting themselves in the twentieth century to the margins, the vacuum being substantially filled by the emerging Caribou Eskimo (Smith and Burch 1979).

The territory occupied by the Chipewyan in protohistoric and earliest contact times was the northern transitional zone of the boreal forest and the Barren Grounds beyond. Winters there are long and severe, with freeze-up occurring by mid-October, and breakup not complete until June or July. Summers are cool or moderate, seldom excessively warm. The forest has a dominant cover of black spruce, with limited white

---

*The italicized Chipewyan words cited in the *Handbook* are transcribed according to the standard technical alphabet, except that, as with all the Athapaskan languages, the usual Athapaskanist practice is followed of using the voiced stop and affricate symbols for the corresponding voiceless consonants. The Chipewyan phonemes are: (voiceless lenis stops and affricates) *b, d, λ, δ̂, ʒ, ǯ, g, gʷ, ʔ*; (aspirated stops and affricates) *t, λ̓, θ̂, c, č, k, kʷ*; (glottalized) *t̓, λ̓, θ̂̓, č̓, c̓, k̓, k̓ʷ*; (voiceless fricatives) *t, θ, s, š, x, xʷ, h*; (voiced fricatives) *l, δ, z, y, γ, γʷ*; (nasals) *m, n*; (trill) *r*; (plain vowels) *i, e, a, o, u, ə*; (long vowels) *iˑ, eˑ, aˑ, uˑ*; (nasalized vowels) *i̧, ȩ, a̧, u̧*; (long nasalized vowels) *i̧ˑ, ȩˑ, a̧ˑ, u̧ˑ*; (tones) high (v́), low (unmarked), rising (v̌), falling (v̂). The distinction between *e* ([ɛ], [e]) and *ə* is problematical; Li (1946) distinguished ɛ ([ɛ]) from *e* ([e], [ə]). There is considerable variation among regional and age dialects.

Phonemic transcriptions of words and information on Chipewyan phonology were provided by Ronald Scollon and Eung-Do Cook (communications to editors 1979), supplementing the account of Li (1946); the editors are responsible for making selections from these materials. Phonemicizations of kegwi and Nunarna'dene were not available.

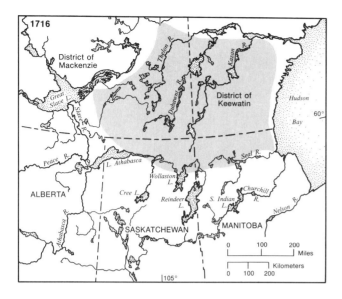

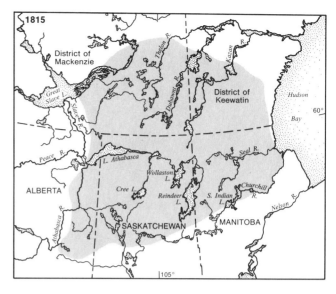

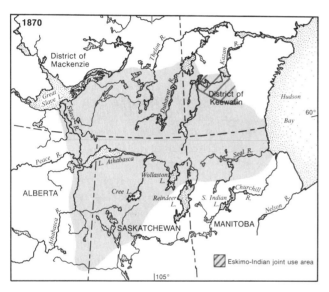

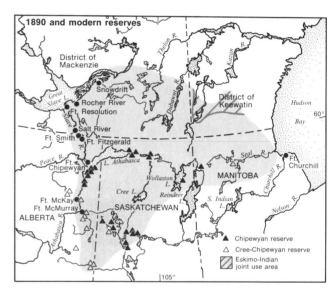

Fig. 1. Chipewyan territory in historic times.

spruce, birch, and aspen, and is interspersed with patches of tundra (Rowe 1972:55). It is locally known as "the land of the little sticks," because of the severe climatic limitations imposed upon growth. Beyond the treeline, in favorable but limited protected areas, some stunted trees and shrubs occur (Rowe 1972:62). In both forest and tundra, the ground vegetation is mainly mosses and lichens, upon which the caribou feed, and some berries grow. After about 1775 some Chipewyans moved into the full boreal forest.

The major game animal was the Barren Ground caribou or reindeer (*Rangifer tarandus groenlandicus*), which wintered in the northern fringes of the forest and migrated into the tundra to calve and forage in the summer (Banfield 1961; Kelsall 1968; Parker 1972). The musk-oxen in the tundra were only occasionally utilized by the Chipewyan for food, and the Arctic and varying hare were normally of minor significance. The

major fur-bearing animals in the tundra included the wolf and Arctic fox.

Within the boreal forest, furbearers included, in addition to the wolf, black bear, colored fox, beaver, ermine, fisher, lynx, marten, mink, muskrat, otter, and wolverine. All species were more plentiful in the full boreal forest than in the transitional zone. In the full forest moose and woodland caribou (*Rangifer tarandus caribou*) were the important game animals (Peterson 1966). Fish of importance to man included whitefish, pickerel, pike, lake trout, and char (McPhail and Lindsey 1970).

Above all, the Barren Ground caribou was of overwhelming importance to the Chipewyan, structuring their seasonal cycle, seasonal distribution, socioterritorial organization, and technology; it was the focus of religious beliefs and oral literature. It is readily apparent why those Chipewyan who clung to their traditional

272

lands, with whom this chapter is primarily concerned, were still known in the 1970s as the Caribou Eaters.

History of Indian-White Contact

Of the Northern Athapaskans, the Chipewyan have been longest in continuous contact with the Europeans, and their history is potentially the most documentable. At York Factory, established by the Hudson's Bay Company in 1682, the English and French first learned of the Chipewyan from Chipewyan women and children who were occasionally taken captive by the Cree. After the company regained York Factory from the French after the War of the Spanish Succession, Capt. James Knight sent William Stewart in 1715, guided by Thanadelther, the famous Chipewyan known as the Slave Woman, and accompanied by 150 Southern (Cree) Indians, to find the Northern (Chipewyan) Indians and invite them to trade and to make peace with the Cree. Stewart accomplished this mission in the winter of 1715–1716 (Knight 1715–1717). Churchill (known sometimes as Prince of Wales's Fort) was established in 1717 for the Chipewyan trade (Knight 1932; A.M. Johnson 1952; Van Kirk 1974).

The Chipewyan were marginal to the fur trade for, as Samuel Hearne (1958:135–136) pointed out, in their lands furbearers were scarce and the Chipewyan required little in the way of trade goods, as the caribou provided almost all their needs. In 1769–1772 Hearne (1958) was the second European to visit the Chipewyan in their own territory. Guided by the Eastern Chipewyan leader Matonabbee, he traveled overland from Churchill, on the bay, to the lower Coppermine River near the Arctic coast. There, the Chipewyan, joined by Yellowknife, annihilated an Eskimo band at Bloody Falls (Hearne 1958:96–104).

During this early period, the Chipewyan were intermediaries in the fur trade between the Hudson's Bay Company and the Yellowknife and Dogrib (Hearne 1958:78). The Chipewyan monopoly of the Athapaskan trade was broken in the late eighteenth century, when the Scots traders from Montreal (eventually amalgamated as the North West Company) entered the northwest, establishing numerous posts. Their entry was countered by the Hudson's Bay Company, which established competitive forts inland, and a period of intense economic rivalry began. Competition ended in 1821 when the companies joined together under the title and royal charter of the Hudson's Bay Company.

The demand for furs in the competitive period and the low prices for trade goods were significant in the shift of some Chipewyans from the forest-tundra ecotone into the full boreal forest. The traders of both companies always encouraged the Chipewyan to trap in the closed forest where furbearers were more numerous and the distractions of the Barren Ground caribou were not present. In the late eighteenth and early nineteenth centuries, many Chipewyans responded to the traders' urging and became the nucleus of the upper Churchill River and Athabasca divisions, while the Caribou Eaters remained in their traditional territories (Gillespie 1975; J.G.E. Smith 1975). In this period, too, the Yellowknife were at war with the Dogrib, ultimately losing their linguistic and cultural identity (Gillespie 1970, 1975). The move into the interior forest had been facilitated by the peacemaking efforts of the Hudson's Bay Company and by the loss of half or more of the Cree population by the smallpox epidemic of 1781–1782 (Thompson 1916:109, 321–325). Although Hearne (1958:115) estimated that 90 percent of the Chipewyan bands known to him were also killed by the disease, this estimate must refer only to the eastern bands near Churchill.

The period of competition, about 1763–1821, was one in which early but sketchy observations on the Chipewyan from the posts on Hudson Bay (Jérémie 1926; Knight 1932; Isham 1949; Dobbs 1744; Graham 1969) were supplemented by the firsthand reports, sometimes equally sketchy, of traders and explorers (Back 1836; Fidler 1934; R. King 1836; Pond in Innis 1930; Mackenzie 1927; Simpson 1938; Thompson 1916; Turnor 1934a; Wentzel 1889–1890, 1) who traveled or dwelt with them. The first North West Company post established for trade with the Chipewyan, in 1789, was appropriately named Fort Chipewyan, and others were soon added, with the Hudson's Bay Company countering with rival establishments (Innis 1956:149–282; Voorhis 1930). Few of the posts were in the heartland of the Chipewyan because of logistic problems in the transport of trade goods and furs.

After the coalition of the companies, the administration of Sir George Simpson rationalized the trade by eliminating competing and unprofitable posts. Meanwhile, the marginal position of the Caribou Eaters kept them peripheral to the stabilized fur trade.

In the 1840s the task of conversion of the Chipewyan was entrusted to the missionary order of the Oblates of Mary Immaculate. From their center at Île-à-la-Crosse, they immediately began the conversion of the Chipewyan, a task that was at least nominally completed by 1905.

The cession of the Hudson's Bay Company Territories to the newly created Dominion of Canada in 1870 had few immediate effects on the Chipewyan. Under Treaty No. 8 of 1899, and Treaty No. 10 of 1907, the federal government moved to extinguish Chipewyan claim to their lands in return for providing five dollars per capita annuities, annual supplies of ammunition, twine, and other articles, and a medicine chest.

The Chipewyan, as other Subarctic peoples, were seriously affected by European-introduced diseases. In

273

left, Prov. Arch. of Man., Winnipeg: A.V. Thomas Coll., 126; top right, Natl. Mus. of Canada, Ottawa: Geological Survey of Canada Coll.: 18770; botom right, Public Arch. of Canada, Ottawa: Natl. Medal Coll., 1642.

Fig. 2. Ft. Churchill at Treaty time. left, Newly elected chief French John and councilors Sam Chinashagun and Thomas Crazy. The men are draped in a flag and wear medals showing Edward VII profile. Photograph probably by Alfred V. Thomas, Aug. 1, 1910. lower right, Edward VII medal, of bronze, was issued in 1907 in connection with the signing of Treaty No. 10. The reverse side shows the Canadian treaty commissioner shaking hands with an Indian chief; a tomahawk lies on the ground between their feet. Unlike previous medals the Edward VII does not carry a date or treaty number on the reverse (Jamieson 1936). Diameter about 7.5 cm. top right, Gathering at Hudson's Bay Company Post at time of signing adhesions toTreaty No. 5. Photograph by James Macoun July 26–Aug. 1, 1910.

addition to smallpox, tuberculosis was widespread, and there were outbreaks of influenza in the 1920s. As late as 1948 a measles epidemic among the isolated Barren Lands band killed about 80 adults of a total of about 300 individuals, resulting in substantial social realignments.

After 1945, an increasing number of children were sent to residential schools to receive a Euro-Canadian education. Nursing stations were also established; and family allowances, old-age pensions, welfare payments, and other social services were made available. Commercial fishing was introduced, and, later, provincial fishing cooperatives were founded. By the 1960s elementary schools had been built in most band centers, with the percentage of children enrolled increasing.

Population

The early records of the Hudson's Bay Company generally do not provide population estimates for the Chipewyan. Isham (1949:177) estimated 1,000 families in the period 1743–1749. The size of bands was sometimes noted by Hearne and other traders, but no overall figures were suggested. Since Chipewyan in the early years of the trade did not visit Churchill annually, or even regularly, and only sporadically trapped, the Churchill records stand as equally vague. Mooney (1928:4), probably projecting from Hearne's journal, estimated that at time of contact there were about 4,000 Chipewyan (430 Yellowknife, 2,250 "Chipewyan," and 1,250 Caribou Eaters). For 1906 his estimate was 2,670

(250 Yellowknife, 1,520 "Chipewyan," and 900 Caribou Eaters). On the basis of the carrying capacity of the caribou herds, H.P. Thompson (1966) estimated a figure between 4,760 and 10,652, but his calculations underestimate the number of hides needed and the enormous waste that often occurred. Thompson's lower figure corresponds roughly to that of Mooney, and it appears reasonable to suggest a figure of 4,000–5,000. It may be noted that this figure is not significantly different from the 1970 census (table 1) of somewhat more than 5,000 (when the Cree enrolled in the Cold Lake, Lac La Hache, and Barren Lands bands are excluded). Until the population explosion of the 1960s and 1970s, the population tended to remain relatively constant, apparently rapidly recovering from epidemic disease. In any case, Chipewyan population density has always been very low, less than one person per 100 square miles.

Culture: Early Contact, 1715–1821

An unusually high amount of information is available for the period in which the Chipewyan had limited contact with the English at Churchill, and when sociocultural change was minimal. Hearne (1958), the first European to live among them, left an informative and perceptive journal, subsequent travelers left additional commentary, and the Hudson's Bay Company Archives add supplementary data. In general, the temporal span of this period may be set between 1715 (the date of first direct contact between the Chipewyan and fur traders in their own territory) and 1821; however, because of the marginal position of the Caribou Eaters most cultural attributes of the early contact period persisted among them until the beginning of the twentieth century. For many aspects of culture, ethnographic data recorded after the 1820s may be regarded as representing practices in the early contact period; some of these have been incorporated in this account of that period.

Socioterritorial Organization

The Chipewyan occupied the forest-tundra ecotone, in which the most important element in the environment was the Barren Ground caribou, of which three great herds (Kaminuriak, Beverly, and Bathurst) provided their basic subsistence. The herds migrated in great columns from the tundra at the onset of severe winter (usually November) to the winter foraging ranges within the forest, within which they were nomadic in small bands. In late winter (April or May) the return migration was made to the area of the lakes in the tundra that were the calving centers of the herds, and from which they derive their names (Kelsall 1968; Parker 1972). Chipewyan territorial organization corresponded to that of the caribou. The Chipewyan concentrated in larger groups when the caribou were concentrated and dispersed into smaller units within the foraging ranges as the herds dispersed (J.G.E. Smith 1975, 1976, 1976a, 1976b).

The Hudson's Bay Company officials early recognized two divisions of the Chipewyan, the "Northern Indians" and the Yellowknife, the latter differentiated on the basis of their possession of copper used in the making of tools. Linguistically, the dialects were very close, Hearne (1958:80) commenting that they were of the order of English county variations. A dialect distinction has also been noted (J.G.E. Smith 1975) that differentiates the bands east of Black Lake, Saskatchewan, from those to the northwest. Thus three dialects existed, corresponding to the divisions based upon predation on each of the major caribou herds: the Yellowknife were associated with the Bathurst herd; the bands historically known as the Black Lake, Fond du Lac, and other "Athabaskans" (Petitot 1884–1885) with the Beverly herd; and the Hatchet Lake, Barren Lands, and Duck Lake bands with the Kaminuriak herd.

Band movements were based on the herds. The largest aggregations, the regional bands, gathered in preparation for the caribou migrations, when the animals

Table 1. Chipewyan Population by Bands, 1970

	Population
Manitoba	
Northland(1976)	334
Churchill	346 (63)
Saskatchewan	
English River	374
Fond Du Lac	552
Lac La Hache	232 (75)
Peter Pond	448
Portage La Loche	249
Stony Rapids	447
Alberta	
Cold Lake	841 (500)
Fort Chipewyan	242
Fort McKay	173
Fort McMurray	91
Janvier	178
Northwest Territories	
Fitz-Smith	295
Resolution	309
Snowdrift	251
Total	5,362
Chipewyan	4,724

SOURCES: Canada. Department of Indian Affairs and Northern Development. Indian Affairs Branch 1970 except Barren Lands, Lac La Hache, and Cold Lake from J.G.E. Smith 1967–1976, and Churchill from Koolage 1968:63 and Egloff 1968:132.   .
NOTE: Numbers in parentheses are estimates of Crees enrolled in the band.

were taken by the method of the chute and pound ("Environment and Culture in the Cordillera," fig. 4, this vol.), in which they were snared, speared, or shot with arrows. During the dispersal of the herds in winter and summer, the regional band separated into a number of smaller local bands, although larger aggregations could gather even at these times. In the winter of 1715–1716, for example, Stewart encountered a band of 400, but Thanadelther told Captain Knight there had been 100 tents, or 800 to 1,000 persons, in the area (Knight 1715–1717:fo. 28d). In July 1770 Hearne (1958:25) was with about 70 tents, or at least 600 persons, and he rarely traveled with less than 200 companions.

The regional band historically has consisted of about 200 to 400 or more individuals, occupying a vaguely delimited territory, and adjacent to other such groups to which they were tied by links of kinship and affinity. Band membership was fluid, as bilateral kinship and marriage provided the avenues for new affiliations to meet the requirements of the severe environment, the fluctuating size of foraging ranges of the herds, and other environmental features, as well as social needs. The degree of interrelationship is, perhaps, indicated by Hearne's journey, for his guide, Matonabbee, and companions invariably had "friends" (relatives?) in almost every band that they encountered (J.G.E. Smith 1975).

Local bands were similar in composition and flexibility but smaller in size than the regional bands (J.G.E. Smith 1976, 1976b). The local bands varied in size from perhaps 25 to over 100 persons, with 50 or 60 perhaps more common. Their size permitted them to utilize the chute and pound effectively. For example, in March 1771 Hearne (1958:54) encountered a group of five tents (perhaps 40–50 people) who had spent the "great part of the winter" snaring caribou at a site that had been repeatedly utilized. In the summer, groups of this size speared caribou from canoes at lake or river crossing points (Hearne 1958:23).

By the mid-eighteenth century, the trading band under a trading leader or "captain" had emerged, to undertake the long overland trek to Churchill (J.G.E. Smith 1976, 1976b). Most men remained in their lands, with the women and children, while some went to trade. Only the trading chiefs were allowed inside the fort, where they bargained on behalf of their followers and those left behind. The fur trade was of limited importance to the Chipewyan; they required only axes, knives, ice chisels, muskets, and files. These could be procured for a limited number of furs, much to the displeasure of the company traders who sought to involve them more fully in the fur trade.

Furs were sparse in the Chipewyan territory and were largely obtained from the Yellowknife and Dogribs, who in turn received trade goods from the Chipewyan at suitably increased prices. While most Chipewyan

men had visited Churchill at least once, travel to the post was not common.

To the English, the bands were known by the names of their leaders, such as Keelshies and the distinguished Matonabbee, although the Chipewyan and other Athapaskans used regional designations (Curtis 1907–1930, 18:3–6; J.G.E. Smith 1975). Chiefs appear to have been of two types: those recognized by the Hudson's Bay Company as excellent hunters and rewarded with titles, like Captain and Lieutenant, and other honors; and traditional leaders who led by virtue of their abilities and powers, including supernatural power, for example, Chawchinahaw (Hearne 1958:xvi), although both kinds of attributes were sometimes combined in one person.

Ethnographic fieldwork in the 1960s and 1970s documented two features of Chipewyan social organization, the hunting group and the personal kindred, that in all likelihood represented continuations of aboriginal modes of affiliation. The local band consisted of several hunting groups. The hunting group was established around a founding male with sufficient authority and ability to hold or recruit sons' and daughters' conjugal families. The hunting groups (which subsequently became the basis for trapping or fishing groups) were distributed in a line of some depth across the area of expected seasonal caribou migration or shifts in their foraging zones, forming a communication network. There is little question that the hunting group and its distribution (Sharp 1977, 1977a; J.G.E. Smith 1978, 1978a) represent basic adaptations to the exploitation of the caribou and as such are of great antiquity. Of the bilateral or personal kindred, two degrees were recognized and have distinct names. ʔełehotine refers to all kinsmen, including affines, but may also designate only those who habitually live and cooperate together. ʔełenakʷi (literally 'brothers') defines bilateral consanguineal kinsmen only. The widely dispersed bilateral kindred provided the basis for cooperation, sharing, and hospitality (J.G.E. Smith 1970, 1975).

Annual Round

Because the seasonal cycle was based upon the caribou herds, winters were spent within the forest, from November to April or May, with the Chipewyan moving as necessary to follow the herds. The concentrations of caribou were sometimes so great that an encampment might not have to move its tents more than once or twice (Hearne 1958:50–51). When the herds moved to the tundra in spring, the Chipewyan placed themselves on the migration routes for the great kill; at the time of the great migration of November, the same occurred. As late as the twentieth century, it is reported that at the southwest edge of Nueltin Lake enough caribou could be killed in November to provide food for the

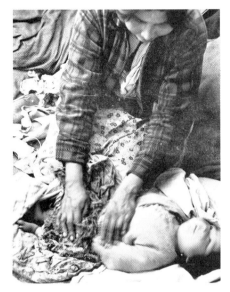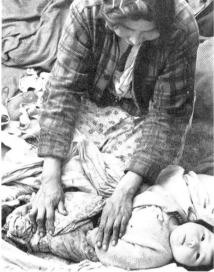

Fig. 3. The making of a moss bag. The baby is packed with absorbent moss and swaddled in layers of cotton cloth with an outer covering of wool laced with thong. Photographs by Richard Harrington near Duck Lake Post on Nejanilini Lake, Man., 1947.

winter, and enough in spring to last for the summer. During the summer, the Indian bands were in the Barren Grounds, gathered or dispersed with the caribou.

Hunting of fur-bearing animals was marginal to subsistence. The journey to Churchill on Hudson Bay was usually made in late winter, on foot. Later, when trading posts were established in the inner forest, the Chipewyan tended to bring their furs in on foot, build birchbark canoes (birch was not abundant at the edge of the forest), and return by water.

Life Cycle

The Chipewyan life cycle was marked by a minimum of ceremony. If birth occurred while traveling, the woman might be on the march within a matter of hours. The parturient was usually attended by other mature women of the local group, usually close relatives. According to Hearne (1958:201), the child was carried on the mother's back, under her clothing against the naked skin, with moss used to keep the infant dry; mossbags (fig. 3) therefore seem to be a later development. There is some indication that female infanticide was sometimes practiced (Thompson 1916:130); children were usually spaced about three years apart, and the number of children was small, usually two or three. As the children grew older, they began to learn appropriate behavior from the parents, but the responsibilities fell heaviest on the girls.

In adolescence, the boy was learning the skills of a hunter, but there were no ceremonies to recognize puberty or social adulthood. At the menarche, the girl stayed apart from the camp, but thereafter she was required only to observe certain taboos, occupying a "small hovel" apart from the other tents, staying away from the men's equipment, not stepping across the trail of game animals, and refraining from eating certain parts of the caribou and other animals (Hearne 1958:201–205).

First marriage was arranged by the parents, and a girl was often betrothed as a child. The husband was often much older than the bride, for a demonstrated good hunter was desired for a son-in-law. Curtis (1907–1930, 18:41, 148–151) states that the Chipewyan practiced preferential patrilateral cross-cousin marriage. There are scattered references in early accounts of exploration that cousins could marry, and kinship terminologies (when complete) are congruent with the practice (Petitot 1876a; Legoff 1889; Penard 1938; Sharp 1973). The early marriage records (to the early 1900s) of Mission Saint Pierre de Lac Caribou, at Brochet, Manitoba, contain some remarriage of the same partners with dispensation given for the close degree of relationship, the exact nature of which cannot be reconstructed. Analyses indicate that among the eastern bands, from Wollaston Lake to Churchill, marriage was generally proscribed between persons genealogically closely connected, but pseudo–patrilateral cross-cousin marriage was permitted or encouraged. Pseudo–cross-cousin categories arise from marriage, adoption, or a step-parental relationship (J.G.E. Smith 1967–1976). Among the bands from Black Lake, Saskatchewan, to the west the kinship terminology is of a generational type and marriage of genealogically close kin is prohibited, as are the institutions of the sororate and the levirate (Sharp 1973, 1975). Marriage tends to develop close alliances between hunting groups for several generations but in the long term emphasizes an extensive network of potentially cooperative relationships over a wide range.

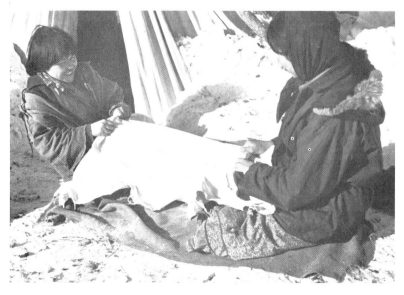

278

No ceremony marked the marriage, but the husband lived with his bride and her family and hunted on their behalf. After the birth of a child, sometimes only after several years because of the girl's youth, the couple were free to affiliate with his family. Polygyny was permitted, often with sisters, and was most common among leaders or good hunters. Large numbers of wives, such as those of Matonabbee, were probably restricted to trading leaders who needed them to transport furs and trade goods. Wives, especially young and childless, were the prizes in wrestling matches (Hearne 1958; Jenness 1956).

In the division of labor by sex, the women were concerned with matters pertaining to the camp. They erected the lodge and broke camp, pulled the toboggan on the trail or carried loads on their backs, prepared fires and cooked, prepared hides (fig. 4) and made clothing, carried the game to the camp or the camp to the game, made caribou dry meat ("Environment and Culture in the Shield and Mackenzie Borderlands," fig. 7, this vol.), and cared for the children. They also snared small game, especially hare, and in late summer picked berries. The men were thus free to pursue game as opportunity arose. The men also angled for fish in winter or caught them in gill nets in summer.

Old age was an unfortunate time, as the old and feeble were of little value and, indeed, a detriment under the conditions of nomadic life. Sometimes the aged were eventually abandoned to the elements when they could no longer keep up with their group. The bodies of the dead were left on the ground surface; there was no effort made to bury them. After a death, the camp was abandoned, and the deceased's and his family's personal effects destroyed or left behind (Hearne 1958:218–219).

Mythology and Beliefs

Oral traditions included the legend of the Copper Woman and the origin of the Coppermine River (J.G.E. Smith 1967–1976) and of the origin of the Chipewyan from the union of primeval woman with a dog that was transformed into a man at night (Hearne 1958:219–220; Franklin 1824, 1:13–14; J.G.E. Smith 1967–1976), a legend that probably gave rise to the early designation of the Chipewyan and other Northern Athapaskans as the "dog-ribbed" or "dog-sided" Indians.

The story of the historical Slave Woman, Thanadelther, who guided the English to the Chipewyan (Davies and Johnson 1965:410–413; A.M. Johnson 1952; Van Kirk 1974; Knight 1715–1717), became an enduring and oft-told tale (J.G.E. Smith 1967–1976). Other historical traditions include those of being taught how to prepare pelts for the Hudson's Bay Company, how to hold a musket, the fall of Prince of Wales's Fort to the French (in 1782), and of fights with the Cree.

An important set of traditions dealt with the relationship of man to nature. In these the Chipewyan are identified with the wolf, whose pattern of predation and reliance on the caribou is remarkably similar to the traditional Chipewyan pattern. Reincarnation as man or wolf may occur, often with extraordinary or miraculous powers, including those of curing (Sharp 1973, 1976; J.G.E. Smith 1967–1976).

Traditional magico-religious beliefs were based on the concept of *ʔiɬ̨aze* or power given in dreams by spirit-animal beings. The power thus obtained was used in curing and in controlling game and other natural phenomena; it could also be used for evil purposes (Smith 1973). Possession of power was at least sometimes a factor in leadership.

Games and Music

Games of chance were commonly played. Hearne (1958:215) recorded the hand game played by two persons; if not aboriginal, the two-team hand game (*huʒi*) was later present (J.G.E. Smith 1967–1976) and perhaps identical to that described by Helm and Lurie (1966) for the Dogrib. Other games included competitive shooting at sticks and the ring and pin game (kegwi) (Curtis 1907–1930, 18:37–39; J.G.E. Smith 1967–1976).

Dancing and singing occurred, but descriptions are inadequate; drums were the sole musical instruments.

Hudson's Bay Company Lib., Winnipeg, Man.

Fig. 4. Tanning caribou hide. The animal is killed, skinned, and butchered by men, then the laborious tanning process is conducted by women. The hide is stretched over a log (top left) and the inner side defleshed with defleshing tool with a serrated edge, made from a section of moose femur. After the hide is soaked in water most of the hair is removed with a steel knife (top right); the remaining hair is scraped away with a caribou-bone beamer. The brains from a caribou skull are removed (center left) and kneaded into a paste, to which water is added to form a thick soup. This is thoroughly worked into the hide (center middle) by soaking and rubbing—the crucial chemical step in tanning that prevents the hide from deteriorating. The hide is stretched to dry (center right), often (as here) aided by freezing. The holes are from an infestation of the live animal by warble or bot fly larvae. The tanning solution is then removed by soaking the hide in water, sometimes with commercial soap added. The hide is made pliable by repeatedly stretching it over a wire (formerly over a stick) and by pulling it with the hands (bottom left) as the hide dries. If brown leather is desired, as for moccasins, the hide is then smoked (bottom right) on a tripod over a smudge from burning hardwood smothered with moss. There are variations in this complex process, both in the sequence of the stages (especially defleshing, dehairing, and beaming) and in repetitions of some stages (especially working in the brain solution, stretching, and smoking). Photographs by Richard Harrington, near Caribou Post, Man., Feb. 1947.

Aboriginal Chipewyan material culture was based on a complex of equipment made from antler, bone, hide, stone, and wood. The caribou was central to this complex, as the object of the chase that provided both subsistence and a set of basic raw materials. Hides provided clothing (fig. 5), bedding, and lodge coverings, and also the babiche (rawhide thong) used for bow strings, snowshoe lacing ("Environment and Culture in the Shield and Mackenzie Borderlands," fig. 8, this vol.), gill nets, tumplines, drum-heads, and other objects. Antlers and bones provided hafts and points, fishhooks, fleshers, and scrapers. Wood, particularly birch, supplied arrow and spear shafts, planks for toboggans, the frame work for canoes, and other items. Birch was not common, and trips into the inner forest were necessary to obtain the bark to sheathe canoes. Canoes were used primarily to cross rivers or hunt caribou, for the travel routes tended to run across, rather than with, the drainage systems.

Immediately following the establishment of trade relations with the English the technology was modified by the adoption of metal axes, knives, ice chisels, files, and muskets that soon replaced the aboriginal equivalents. Among the Caribou Eaters, however, much of early contact period material culture persisted in a very conservative fashion (cf. Birket-Smith 1930).

Culture: Contact-Traditional, 1821–1960

Because of their marginal position to the transportation and trade routes, dependence upon the caribou, and relative indifference to most European trade goods, sociocultural change was slow and limited among the Caribou Eaters who remained in their ancestral lands; they did not undergo a substantial impact of the "modern" era until the 1960s. Among those Chipewyan who had moved into the full boreal forest, in proximity to the trading posts, change was somewhat more rapid. There, where subsistence was based on moose and woodland caribou, they necessarily made adaptations in hunting strategies and in some areas developed the family-owned trapping territory (Penard 1938; Jarvenpa 1976). Through time, traditional band affiliations tended to alter and weaken as some families became more strongly associated with the trading posts, as at Snowdrift (VanStone 1965) and Fort Resolution (Smith 1973b).

For sharper focus, discussion in this section concentrates on the Caribou Eater Chipewyan.

Socioterritorial Organization

From about the mid-nineteenth century into the modern period, the Caribou Eaters were divided into five

Nationalmuseet, Copenhagen: H1:24.
Fig. 5. Woman's dress of caribou hide, fur side out, with wrists edged in dark striped cloth. Length 139 cm, collected by K. Birket-Smith, 1923.

regional bands, deriving their names from some geographic characteristic: the *sayisedene* 'east people', officially known as the Duck Lake or Churchill band; the *hotél-náde dene*, 'flat-area-dwelling people', known officially as the Barren Lands band; the Nunarna'dene, 'people of the south' or *θęł-tue dene* 'hatchet-lake people', the Hatchet Lake band; the *yoday dene* 'upland or western people' or *delzən-tue dene*, the Black Lake or Stony Rapids band; and the *gane-kų́ę́ dene* 'pine-house people', the Fond du Lac band. There is some evidence that these band territories have been occupied consistently since the time of early European contact (J.G.E. Smith 1976, 1976b).

Band territories were located primarily within the forest; however, until the 1950s the margins of the tundra were still exploited, in early fall primarily for caribou hides and in winter for Arctic fox. The Caribou Eaters were torn between an orientation to the edge of the forest because of the caribou subsistence base and to the interior forest where furbearers were more numerous and where the trading post–mission complexes were located. The tension of the twin pulls persisted in 1973 (J.G.E. Smith 1967–1976). The establishment of posts, combined with the Hudson's Bay Company monopoly and credit system of "grub stakes" repaid with furs, tended to attach each band to a specific post.

Each regional band was associated with a major wintering foraging range of the caribou, and with major migration routes, thus almost insuring a continuing food supply. Communal hunting by the method of chute and

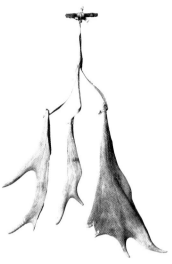

left, Natl. Mus. of Canada, Ottawa: Geological Survey of Canada Coll., 74880; right, Nationalmuseet, Copenhagen: H1:44.

Fig. 6. Caribou hunting. left, Camp with traditional conical tepees probably of caribou skin. Man on right in foreground wears a full-length fur coat with cuffs probably of cloth. Photograph by Robert Bell, near Ft. Churchill, 1880. right, Decoy of antler pieces tied with leather thongs to a toggle worn under the hunter's belt. The sound made by the pieces rattling together imitates bulls fighting thus attracting other bulls in rutting season. Total length 51 cm, collected by K. Birket-Smith, 1923.

pound was discontinued in the early twentieth century, as more efficient rifles became available. The metal ice chisel made fishing with the gill net in deep winter possible, commercial twine provided more and better nets, and fish for dog food became of greater importance in the twentieth century when the dog team became the chief means of transportation. As the tundra was gradually abandoned, summer subsistence was increasingly based upon fish, for the principal caribou summer ranges were too distant to be readily exploited. The process of sedentarization was further increased by these factors.

Regional bands usually ranged in size from about 200 to 300 persons. The shift of families, or perhaps of local bands, from one regional band to another, has given the regional bands an amorphous character. Such shifts doubtless reflected connections of families within the widespread bilateral kindreds, the ʔełehoṯine and ʔełenakʷi (J.G.E. Smith 1970, 1976, 1976b, 1978).

Local bands varied from about 30 persons to well over 100 after the people began to live in log cabin

Fig. 7. Ridge-pole lodges (nịbále) at hunting camp near Ft. Smith. Photograph by René Fumoleau, March 1970.

settlements, about 1920 and later. Research in the archival sources indicates such figures to be consistent with those of the eighteenth and nineteenth centuries (J.G.E. Smith 1973, 1975, 1976, 1967–1976). These bands consisted of families related to one another through primary ties of descent and affinity, and they have had a relatively high continuity from generation to generation, although families shifted occasionally from one band to another, permanently or temporarily.

The Barren Lands band is typical of the regional bands of the Caribou Eater Chipewyan. Their main encampment had been near the treeline, on the southwest of Nueltin Lake, near a major caribou migration path and near a lake known for its excellent and abundant fish. Here the regional band gathered for the great hunts of early winter and spring, then dispersed to the local band camps at Misty Lake, Lac Brochet, Maria Lake, Fort Hall Lake, and on the Lueaza and Cochrane rivers. These locales were central to the usual winter foraging ranges of the caribou, well situated for fishing, and centrally located with respect to traplines. While the tent camps gradually became log cabin settlements, they remained essentially base camps and rendezvous points for the local bands. The greater mobility provided by dog traction made possible the exploitation of a considerable area around the settlements.

Trapping territories, more properly the right to utilize trapline areas, developed but without a concept of ownership. A family had the right to use the trapline as long as it was utilized; if abandoned, it could be taken by another. As the land was sparsely occupied, shifts to establish new traplines were not infrequent. When the Manitoba government established registered traplines in 1958, the Barren Lands band Chipewyan

281

chose to have one registered "trapline" for the entire group, while the Rocky Cree to the south chose to register family territories. The land chosen by the Chipewyan was caribou country, where furbearers were relatively rarer than to the south. While trappers' territory was limited by convention the people placed no restrictions on the areas for the hunting of the caribou or the relatively few moose.

Sociocultural Situation in the 1960s

The 1960s were traumatic for the Caribou Eater Chipewyan as the contact-traditional way of life suddenly ended. In 1958 the federal government relocated the Duck Lake (Churchill) band to the outskirts of the ethnically heterogeneous rail head and port town of Churchill on Hudson Bay. The relocation of traditional Chipewyan to this Subarctic town, described by one government committee as Canada's worst slum, was without preparation and was followed by disorientation and demoralization (Koolage 1968). In 1971 about 70 to 80 members of this band returned to the bush, first reestablishing themselves at Duck Lake, then in 1973, at Tadoule Lake (J.G.E. Smith 1967–1976).

In 1967, as a result of the extension of federal social services to the North, the Barren Lands band settled in the village of Brochet, Manitoba (J.G.E. Smith 1970, 1967–1976, 1978). The near-final stage in the process of sedentarization was brought about by a variety of specific factors and pressures. These included new government housing to supplement or replace the few existing log cabins, the monthly payment of family allowances and old age pensions, the availability of emergency rations, the establishment of a nursing station and a visiting nurse, a radio that permitted rapid contact to bring aircraft to remove the seriously ill, the establishment of a provincial elementary school (originally established for the non-Treaty Cree), a greater variety of goods at the Hudson's Bay Company, the presence of the mission, some periodic wage labor opportunities, and the threat of withdrawal of the family allowance if school-aged children were not enrolled. The last threat was of considerable importance, for the value was disproportionate to the amount; the regular cash income provided not only milk for children but also ammunition for hunting. Commercial fishing, originally limited to Crees and a few Chipewyans, was also beginning to be a significant economic factor.

While the Chipewyan from the north were the new settlers at Brochet, the Cree were also present in roughly equal numbers. These had originally come as "Home Guard Indians" of the Hudson's Bay Company, hunting, fishing, and transporting supplies for the post. They were joined by others moving north to the sparsely inhabited and better hunting and trapping territories. Thus in 1967, the trading post–mission complex became a multi-ethnic village of some 300 Chipewyans, 300 Crees (Treaty and non-Treaty), and a score of Euro-Canadians.

Chipewyan reaction to village life was mixed. The advantages were offset by the necessity of men leaving their families behind while they hunted or spent lonely weeks or months on the traplines, without the efficiency of the traditional division of labor. Moreover, Brochet was geographically marginal to the normal range of the caribou, particularly with the decreased range resulting from the greatly reduced size of the herds (Kelsall 1968; Parker 1972). The distance made difficult the killing of large numbers and the transportation of the meat and hides to the village by the dog team and toboggan of limited carrying capacity. In addition, the traditional hostility of Cree and Chipewyan was still present, although restrained, and interethnic tensions occurred. Even within the Chipewyan community problems occurred as a large group, composed of the several local bands, was concentrated for long periods of time. Traditional patterns of reciprocity and sharing began to break down under the influence of a cash economy and increased emphasis on the individual and nuclear family (J.G.E. Smith 1970, 1978).

The tensions eventually resulted in some families returning to the bush. In 1969–1970, several families returned to their traditional settlement at Misty Lake, and in 1972–1973 the local band had reconstituted itself at that point. In the summer of 1973, the Misty Lake band was relocating a few miles to the south, at Lac Brochet, where they were constructing log-cabin homes, a one-room school, and a nursing station. The Indian Affairs Branch of the government had agreed to provide, if possible, a teacher; a nurse was to visit regularly, and a radio was available for emergencies. The local band subsistence economy was again substantially based on the caribou, and its cash economy on fur and commercial fishing, for which a local band cooperative was successfully established. In the summer of 1973 the larger part of the Barren Lands band was dispersed in local bands along the northerly parts of Reindeer Lake, where they were engaged in commercial fishing in a very successful cooperative that had been greatly supported by the local Indian Affairs officials and the Oblate missionary. The village of Brochet was, at least for the summer, being avoided. By 1976 almost all Chipewyans had left Brochet and were at Lac Brochet (J.G.E. Smith 1978).

The Black Lake (Saskatchewan) band was also considering a return to its traditional area on the edge of the forest in the Northwest Territories, closer to the caribou, and provisional upon the availability of certain modern amenities—a store with basic supplies, a nursing station, and a radio for emergencies.

While the adjustment of many Chipewyans to the forces of the modern period has been similar to that of other Subarctic peoples, that of the Caribou Eaters in their marginal position in the caribou lands has continued to demonstrate their traditional relationship to the caribou as a "moral commitment" (Sharp 1977). In the late 1700s Hearne (1958:51–52) observed that "the real wants of these people are few, and easily supplied; a hatchet, an ice chissell, a file, and a knife, are all that is required to enable them, with a little industry to procure a comfortable livelihood. . . ." In 1967, almost two centuries after Hearne's journey, a Hudson's Bay Company manager noted, as did Hearne, that the Caribou Eater Chipewyan were less committed to the fur trade than the adjacent Cree (J.G.E. Smith 1967–1976). In the late 1960s and early 1970s, while some Caribou Eater Chipewyan were involved in the Indian Brotherhoods and the evolution of a federal Indian policy, others were still constrained to a traditional relationship to the caribou and their lands.

Synonymy†

The name Chipewyan was borrowed into English from Cree by the North West Company men and other "free traders" in the late eighteenth century, appearing as Chepewyans, 1776 (Henry 1969:333); Otchipiweons, Orchipoins, Ochipawayons, 1785, 1787 (Peter Pond in Davidson 1918:maps facing 23, 36, 42); Chi-pa-why-ans, U-che-pi-wy-an, Chepawyans, 1790 (Turnor and Ross in Hearne 1934:338, 341, 359); Chepewyan, 1801 (Mackenzie 1970). Later renderings included Chippewyans and Chip-pe-wi-yan, 1830 (J. Tanner 1956:391); Chippeweyans, 1849 (McLean 1932:134); Cheepawyans (Thompson 1916:78, 1962:72); and in other spellings listed by Hodge (1907a:276). Its Cree source was apparently *či·pwaya·n* (Faries 1938:176, emended and phonemicized), appearing dialectally as Northern Plains Cree *oči·pwaya·ni·w* (David H. Pentland, communication to editors 1979; cf. Curtis 1907–1930, 18:158), both meaning '(those who have) pointed skins or hides'. This is commonly regarded as an allusion to their manner of cutting their hunting shirts or preparing beaver pelts, which the Cree ridiculed (Petitot 1876:xix; Mackenzie 1970:120–121), but the Chipewyan believe that the Cree told the English at York Factory that they had tails and were not true humans (J.G.E. Smith 1967–1976). Early recordings by a Hudson's Bay Company trader are Wee-chip-y-an-i-wuck and Wechippiane-wuck distinguished from Weechepowack, Wechepa-wuck, and Wechepowuck, given as a general term for Athapaskans (Graham in Isham 1949:311, 316; Graham 1969:201, 205). In local English in the twentieth century the name is usually abbreviated colloquially to Chip.

†This synonymy was written by Ives Goddard and James G.E. Smith.

CHIPEWYAN

The Chipewyan call themselves *dene* 'the people' (see synonymy in "Territorial Groups Before 1821: Athapaskans of the Shield and the Mackenzie Drainage," this vol.). The Hare call them *ǩáselehtine* (Keren Rice, communication to editors 1979), given by Petitot (1876:247) as Kkpay-tsele-'ttiné 'dwellers among the small willows'; their Dogrib name is *teh3ǫt̨į* (Robert Howren, communication to editors 1979).

In the late seventeenth and eighteenth centuries the Hudson's Bay Company men at the bayside posts usually called the Chipewyan the Northern Indians, less commonly Northward Indians: 1689 (Kelsey 1929:25), 1743 (Isham 1949:3, 177), 1770–1772 (Hearne 1958:9), 1790 (Turnor 1934:338), in contradistinction to the Southern Indians or Cree. The earliest references to Chipewyan may be the Louzy Indians, 1689 (Rich 1957:58, 66) or Nation des Poux, 1699 (Warkentin and Ruggles 1970:51), presumably to be identified with the Ikovirinioucks (which would be Woods Cree *ihko-iriniwak* 'louse people'), 1694 (Marest 1931:142). The frequent nineteenth- and twentieth-century French name Montagnais (Petitot 1876:xx; Penard 1938), used at least as late as 1950 (J.G.E. Smith 1978a:73–74), appears sometimes in English as Mountainees, 1821 (Simpson 1938:370) or Mountaineers, 1830 (J. Tanner 1956:391); these are not to be confused with the Algonquian-speaking Montagnais of Quebec and Labrador.

Renderings of Cree *atimospikay* 'dog rib' and variants of the French translation Plats-Côtés de Chien are sometimes used by eighteenth-century writers to refer to the Chipewyan (Jérémie 1715–1724, 5; Bacqueville de la Potherie 1931:285, 265). This may reflect the use of the Cree term for Athapaskan groups generally, though an early listing (Graham in Isham 1949:316; Graham 1969:205) gives Ateem Uspeki (Atim-uspiki) and Wee-chip-y-an-i-wuck (Wechippianewuck) as distinct groups. See the synonymy in "Dogrib," this volume.

Sources

The first contact of the English with the Chipewyan in their own lands in 1715–1716 by William Stewart is recorded in Captain Knight's (1715–1717) journals at York Factory. If Stewart kept a journal, it has long been lost. The archives of the Hudson's Bay Company provide the basic source of data for early and later periods; many of the early journals of exploration, which have been published by the Champlain Society and the Hudson's Bay Record Society, are cited in the section on history. Anthropologists have begun utilizing the Hudson's Bay Company Archives (Gillespie 1975a, 1975; J.G.E. Smith 1976, 1976b, 1978).

Birket-Smith (1930) spent a month at Churchill, as

part of the Fifth Thule Expedition, and Curtis (1907–1930, 18:3–52) briefly visited the Cold Lake Chipewyan. VanStone (1965) did a major study of the Snowdrift band. The late 1960s and early 1970s witnessed a surge of field research: Koolage (1968) studied the Chipewyan relocated at Churchill; J.G.E. Smith (1970, 1973, 1967–1976, 1975, 1976, 1976a, 1976b, 1978, 1978a) worked with the conservative Barren Lands band, Sharp (1973, 1975, 1975a, 1976, 1977, 1978) with the Black Lake band; Bone, Shannon, and Raby (1973) with those of the Stony Rapids region; Smith (1973, 1973b), those of Fort Resolution; Jarvenpa (1976), those of Upper Churchill; and Müller-Wille (1974) with the Fond du Lac group.

Yellowknife

BERYL C. GILLESPIE

The Yellowknife ('yĕlō͵nīf) Indians, Athapaskan speakers, were a Chipewyan regional group mentioned in the historical literature of the eighteenth and nineteenth centuries. They were no longer an identifiable dialectal or ethnic entity in the twentieth century.* This chapter deals only with the specific history of the Yellowknife; their culture is described in "Chipewyan," this volume.

Territory and Ethnic Affiliation

The Yellowknife exploitative range was in the Transitional Boreal Forest and adjacent Barren Grounds of western Canada. At the beginning of the nineteenth century their range included the north shore of the eastern half of Great Slave Lake, the Yellowknife and Coppermine rivers, and eastward from these rivers into the Barren Grounds (fig. 1). Some alterations in their

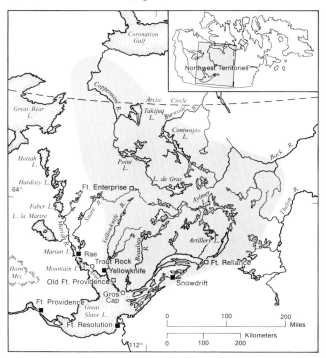

Fig. 1. Territory in the 18th and early 19th centuries.

*Haas (1968) has published a word list of the dialect spoken by a Chipewyan from the town of Yellowknife, N.W.T. This, however, does not represent the dialect of the historic Yellowknife; no linguistic record or analysis of that dialect is known to exist.

range occurred within the nineteenth century in response to locations of trading posts and their relationships with neighboring peoples.

Their subsistence quest was centered around the movements of the Barren Ground caribou, and the Yellowknife range, to some degree, corresponds to the range of the Bathurst caribou herd. J.G.E. Smith (1975:416–419) suggests that the Chipewyan regional groupings and their ranges coincide with three great caribou herds that overlap spatially but can be defined by their separate zones of concentration.

Throughout the historical literature the Yellowknife have been repeatedly described as very much like the Chipewyan (summarized in Gillespie 1975a:203–204). On first meeting two Yellowknife Indians in 1721, the chief factor at Fort Churchill commented that "as far as I can find they are some that boarders upon the Northern Indians [Chipewyan]; for theire Language nor aperill is nothing Diferant from the Rest" (Hudson's Bay Company 1718–1721:fo. 132).

Historic Period

Table 1 documents the significant events and conditions in Yellowknife history.

Early Contact

From the beginning of the eighteenth century traders on the west coast of Hudson Bay showed interest in reports of copper deposits in the interior and the associated "Copper Indians." Although Yellowknife Indians did visit Fort Churchill with other Chipewyans a few years after its establishment on Hudson Bay in 1717, they were infrequent visitors throughout the eighteenth century. The distance from their exploitative range to Hudson Bay and the harrassment by other Chipewyans discouraged any steady contact with European fur traders.

Hostilities and Fame

Soon after the establishment of trading posts in the Great Slave Lake–Great Bear Lake region late in the eighteenth century, the Yellowknife achieved a warlike reputation among both Europeans and their Indian

285

Smithsonian Lib.: Franklin 1823:facing title page.

Fig. 2. Keskarrah, a Copper Indian guide for the Franklin expedition, and his daughter Green Stockings who is mending a snowshoe. The daughter, then about 16 years old, was said by Franklin to be "considered by her tribe to be a great beauty"; she bore a daughter to Lt. Robert Hood, a member of the expedition (Hood 1974:xxxi–xxxii). Colored lithograph based on lost watercolor by Hood done at Ft. Enterprise in winter 1820–1821.

neighbors. The Yellowknife began to plunder, bully, and occasionally kill Slavey, Hare, and especially Dogrib Indians. This Yellowknife ascendency forced the Dogrib, and perhaps others, to avoid certain sectors of their traditional exploitative ranges. By 1820 Akaitcho (fig. 3) was their prime leader. Strong and aggressive, his predations were vividly remembered by Dogribs in the 1960s (Gillespie 1970:63). Akaitcho became known in Canadian history through his involvement, along with other Yellowknifes, in exploration expeditions, especially Sir John Franklin's first expedition of 1819–1822. After that expedition, in 1823, Dogribs made a revenge attack for past aggressions on a camp of Yellowknifes. Long Legs, a Yellowknife leader mentioned by Franklin (1823:306, 310, 334) was killed (E. Smith 1823–1827:fo. 9) along with his entire encampment of 34 (Hudson's Bay Company 1826–1827:fo. 1). This constituted a loss of one-fifth of the Yellowknife population and precipitated the gradual decline of the group.

Decline and Amalgamation

After 1823—as a consequence of consolidation of the North West Company with the Hudson's Bay Company—the Yellowknife no longer had trading establishments within their exploitative range. They then directed all their trade to Fort Resolution on the south side of Great Slave Lake. Some hostilities and tensions existed between them and other Chipewyan of that region for about a decade, followed by amicable and more frequent contact between these two groups. By the sec-

ond half of the nineteenth century the process of Yellowknife amalgamation with other Chipewyans of the Fort Resolution area was underway.

After the Yellowknife "defeat" by the Dogribs, the former avoided areas they had frequented during the period of their famed prowess. The Yellowknife immediately retreated from the eastern end of Great Bear Lake and gradually restricted themselves to the east arm of Great Slave Lake and north to the Barrens. By the end of the nineteenth century the Dogrib had expanded their range into areas formerly associated with the Yellowknife. Dogribs were also sharing the east arm of Great Slave Lake with Yellowknifes before 1900. The amicable sharing of their ranges began the same process of intermarriage and amalgamation that had started earlier with the Chipewyan. Within the twentieth century the Dogrib or Chipewyan populations of the Yellowknife Bay, Snowdrift, and Fort Res-

Smithsonian Lib.: Franklin 1823:facing p. 203.

Fig. 3. Akaitcho and his son. Akaitcho wears a native caribou hide robe and leather shirt, moccasins, and mittens, and also items of European origin: red breechclout trimmed in white and green, 2 white-edged blue chest sashes, red and white yarn belt supporting a powderhorn, red cuffs and trim on mittens. The boy has a red and white neckband, leather shirt with red lower border and green sleeves, red-trimmed mittens on a red cord across his neck, and red garters. Colored lithograph based on lost 1821 watercolor by Robert Hood.

Table 1. Events and Conditions in Yellowknife History

EARLY CONTACT

Limited Contact with Traders Outside the Yellowknife Exploitative Range

1714 First apparent record of Yellowknife, Indians dwelling in lands containing copper (Davies and Johnson 1965:62).

1721 Two "Copper Indians" visit Fort Churchill with a group of Chipewyan (Hudson's Bay Company 1718–1721:fo. 132).

1771 Hearne meets "Copper Indians" within their exploitative range and locates the "copper mines" (Hearne 1958:76–77, 85, 91, 94).

1778 Pond establishes the first trading post in the Athabasca River region (Simpson 1938:413).

late 1770s? Hearne records from hearsay that "Dog-ribbed Indians" had killed many "Copper Indians" (Hearne 1958:116).

1784 Pond is visited by 40 Yellowknifes at his post on Athabasca River (Davidson 1918:260).

1786 North West Company post established on Great Slave Lake near site of Fort Resolution (Simpson 1938:416).

1788 North West Company post established on Lake Athabasca near site of Fort Chipewyan (Simpson 1938:414).

Frequent Contact with Traders near the Yellowknife Exploitative Range

1789 Mackenzie (1970:172) meets Yellowknifes in Yellowknife territory on the North Arm of Great Slave Lake.

1792 Fidler (1934:540, 551) meets Yellowknife Indians on the south side of Great Slave Lake, trapping and traveling to Lake Athabasca with Chipewyans.

1796–1823 North West Company post near Yellowknife River on Great Slave Lake, Fort Providence (Simpson 1938:423).

1799–1815 North West Company post on Great Bear Lake at site of Fort Franklin (Stager 1962:38).

18??–1820 North West Company outpost on Mountain Island, Great Slave Lake, at site of "Old Fort Rae," intermittently used (Simpson 1938:420).

1800–1801 Yellowknife trading throughout the year into North West Company post at location of later Fort Resolution (Porter 1800–1801:80).

 Report of a band of Yellowknife, "say about 30 men," on the Mackenzie River. Yellowknifes winter with Mackenzie River Indians but no mention of any hostilities (Porter 1800–1801:5, 69).

1805–1806 One group of Yellowknife trading into Great Bear Lake post throughout the year, have a camp on Bear Island (off Leith Peninsula) (A. McKenzie 1805).

 "25 men with their families" trade into Great Bear Lake post; estimate that 100 men trade at Great Slave Lake (A. McKenzie 1805:20).

Suggestion that "Slave" (or Dogrib) near the entrance of Mackenzie River fear Yellowknife (A. McKenzie 1805:31).

Some Yellowknifes reside "near" Lac la Martre (A. McKenzie 1805:70).

HOSTILITIES AND FAME

1812 Yellowknifes trading into Great Bear Lake post are "about 15 married men" (Keith 1889–1890, 2:106).

 Yellowknifes plundering Mackenzie River and Lac la Martre Indians and making them avoid part of their lands (Keith 1889–1890, 2:112).

1815 Yellowknife reported to have killed "Hare" Indians of Great Bear Lake (Hudson's Bay Company 1822–1823:fo. 52).

1820–1822 Yellowknife with their leader Akaitcho are guides and provisioners for the Franklin expedition. Franklin (1823:211, 275, 291, 314) reports Yellowknife past aggressions toward Dogribs and Dogribs' continued anxieties.

1823 In June Lac la Martre Dogribs flee in the direction of Fort Simpson away from the Yellowknife "who had murdered 4 of their men this year" (Hudson's Bay Company 1822–1823a:fo. 45).

 In the spring near Fort Providence Yellowknifes kill 4 "Dog Rib" women, another escapes (E. Smith 1823–1827:fo. 8).

 In October Dogribs retaliate on a Yellowknife camp, probably near the Hottah Lake area; Long Legs and his group are killed (E. Smith 1823–1827:fo. 9).

 Dogribs killed 34 Yellowknifes in the October attack—4 men, 13 women and 17 children (Hudson's Bay Company 1826–1827: fo. 1).

1824–1825 Numerous mentions of Yellowknife at Lac la Martre, Marian Lake, and Mountain Island (Hudson's Bay Company 1824–1825).

1824–1826 Dogribs staying away from Lac la Martre, which is considered part of their exploitative range, because of fear of Yellowknife (Hudson's Bay Company 1825–1827).

 Dogribs near Mackenzie River (Hudson's Bay Company 1823–1824:fo. 5).

1825 Yellowknife will not join Franklin's 2nd expedition to Great Bear Lake to avoid area where relatives were killed in 1823 (Franklin 1828:10; (Hudson's Bay Company 1826–1827:fo. 1).

prior to 1826 Great Bear Lake "Outer Indians," probably Hare of Colville Lake, "frequently meet with the Copper Indians who take the same advantage of them that they take of the Hare Indians and pillage" (Hudson's Bay Company 1826).

1825–1835 Reports of aggressive tensions between Yellowknife and Chipewyan trading into Great Slave Lake (Hudson's Bay Company 1824–1825, 1826–1827, 1825–1827; Back 1836:212, 458).

Table 1. Events and Conditions in Yellowknife History (Continued)

1831	Yellowknife killed a Lac la Martre Indian, probably Dogrib. Hudson's Bay Company concerned to keep peace between Yellowknife and Dogrib Indians (E. Smith 1831).
1833–1835	Akaitcho and other Yellowknifes guide and provision expedition at Fort Reliance at east arm of Great Slave Lake (Back 1836).
	Akaitcho an old man, sick and not the chief he used to be (Back 1836:311, 456–457).
	Fears still exist between Dogrib ["slave"] and Yellowknife Indians (Back 1836:121).
1838	Akaitcho dies in the spring (Hudson's Bay Company 1838–1839).

DECLINE AND AMALGAMATION

1848	Yellowknife have retreated from Great Bear Lake and stay more toward the east end of Great Slave Lake (Richardson 1851, 2:4).
1850	Dogribs hired to supply the expedition at the east end of Great Bear Lake and the Coppermine River (J. Rae 1953:lv, 147).
1855	Temporary post at end of east arm of Great Slave Lake where Yellowknifes are the provisioners and frequent visitors (Hudson's Bay Company 1855).
1858	Dogribs and a few Yellowknifes trading into Old Fort Rae (on Mountain Island, 1852–1906) and Chipewyan, Yellowknife and a few Dogribs and Slaveys trading into Fort Resolution (Anderson 1858).
1890	Yellowknifes in the east arm of Great Slave Lake and are visited by Dogribs from Old Fort Rae (Pike 1892:153).
1892	Band of Indians at the mouth of the Yellowknife River identified as both Dogrib and Yellowknife (Russell 1898:74, 165)
1895	Both Dogribs and Yellowknifes are provisioners of caribou for Fort Resolution (Whitney 1896:160).
1900	Treaty No. 8 signed at Resolution by Dogribs from Trout Rock to Gros Cap and by Yellowknife from the east arm of Great Slave Lake.
1907	Seton (1911:185) meets Dogribs and Chipewyans in east arm of Great Slave Lake.
1908	"Dog Ribs and Yellowknives are the only natives that inhabit these parts," Artillery Lake and the east arm of Great Slave Lake to the Barrens (Canada. Royal Canadian Mounted Police 1910:148).
1914	Yellowknife losing their tribal identity, "preferring to be known as Chipewyan." Two bands of "Yellowknife-Dogrib" trade into Fort Resolution and "live along the Yellowknife River" (J. A. Mason 1946:12–14).
1926	Snowdrift established (Usher 1971:50).
1928	Influenza epidemic: native populations of Yellowknife River and eastward into the east arm of Great Slave Lake suffer many deaths.

Smithsonian Lib.: Petitot 1891:93.

Fig. 4. Three Yellowknife men. European trade goods include the coat of the man leaning on the tree, pipes (at least the one on the right), and the smoking tobacco. The man in the center wears around his neck a knife in a sheath with geometric designs. Engraving from an unknown sketch by Émile Petitot, 1863.

olution areas continued to incorporate descendants of the historic Yellowknife, especially in the wake of the devastating influenza epidemic of 1928. The Canadian government applied the erroneous designations of "Yellowknife 'A' Band" to Chipewyans in the Snowdrift area until the 1960s (Canada 1959) and "Yellowknife 'B' Band" to Dogribs residing in and near the town of Yellowknife, Northwest Territories, until the 1970s (Canada. Department of Indian Affairs and Northern Development. Indian Affairs Branch 1970:37).

Population

Europeans described the Yellowknife as demoralized, suffering periods of starvation and disease, and losing population after their losses in the 1823 "war" (for example, Hudson's Bay Company 1825–1827:fo. 14; Back 1836:209, 456–457; McLean 1932:347–348). However, the majority of European estimates of their population, from 1819 to 1900, range around the figure of 200 (summarized in Gillespie 1975a:233).

Synonymy†

The recorded names for the Yellowknife in Athapaskan, Algonquian, and European languages all appear to refer ultimately to the copper found in their territory from which they made cutting tools for trade to other Indians (Morice 1906–1910, 1:265–266). Their Woods Cree name appears as Mithcocoman (presumably *miθkohkoma·n* 'red metal, red knife') in a list of the three Athapaskan groups known at Fort Churchill in the 1770s (Graham 1969:205). The same word was given with the gloss 'copper metal' in a 1714 report from York Factory that includes the first reference to

†This synonymy was written by Beryl C. Gillespie and Ives Goddard.

Natl. Mus. of Canada, Ottawa: 26098.

Fig. 5. Canvas-covered lodges of Indians trading into Ft. Resolution, possibly Yellowknife. At the time of the photograph canvas was replacing caribou hides as lodge coverings (J.A. Mason 1946:20). Photograph by J. Alden Mason, 1913.

Yellowknife (Davies and Johnson 1965:62), and subsequent reports use the expression "Copper Indians" (table 1). Peter Fidler in 1791 used the terms Coppermine Indians and Coppermine river Indians (1934:546–547, 551). Another term was Red-knife Indians (Mackenzie 1801:17) or Red Knives, 1789 (McKenzie 1889–1890, 1:30), in French Couteaux rouge, 1784 (Peter Pond in Davidson 1918:260), a literal translation of the Cree name. George Simpson (1938:252, 371) in 1821 was apparently the first to use Yellow Knife (attributive) and Yellow Knives, equivalent to French Couteaux Jaunes (Petitot 1876:xx); Simpson explained the name as derived from that of the Yellowknife River.

The Chipewyan name was given by François Mandeville in 1928 as *talʒáhotinɛ* 'Yellowknives' (Fang-Kuei Li cited by Ronald Scollon, communication to editors 1979). According to Petitot (1876:xx, 108, 1891:95, 158) this name means 'copper people' (Gens du Cuivre). It is formed with an archaic word for 'copper' (literally 'pond scum', alluding to the green color of oxidized copper) that was not recorded by later investigators, and it has not been analyzable by twentieth-century Chipewyan speakers (Smith 1973a; Ronald Scollon, communication to editors 1979). The same word appears in the name of the Taltson River, recorded by Fidler (1934:520–21, 524) in 1791 as Tall chu dezza 'Red Knife [river]' and called on King's (1836, 2:288) map "Copper Indian River." In the 1960s the Chipewyan of Fort Resolution used tatsọtine, perhaps a phonetically evolved equivalent, for those Chipewyan who may be, in part, decendants of the Yellowknife branch and who have maintained their Indian heritage to a greater degree than those they identify as Métis (Smith 1976:13, 15). Other recordings of this name are in table 2 and in Hodge (1910a:699); the early interpretation

'birchbark Indians' has no known linguistic support. The term t'etsọt'ine, which J.A. Mason (1946:12) recorded in 1913 for the Yellowknife remnants (who preferred to be known as Chipewyan), can be compared to *tehʒọt̜į*, the generic Dogrib name for the Chipewyan.

Sources

Almost no information on the Yellowknife Indians is available for the eighteenth century. Hearne (1958) provides some description as he met them in 1770 within their exploitative range.

In the first part of the nineteenth century the major descriptions and accounts of the Yellowknife come from the explorers Franklin (1823), Back (1836), and King (1836). A brief sketch of them was also written by fur trader Keith (1889–1890, 2) in 1812. The Hudson's Bay Company archival materials for this period provide especially rich material on the Yellowknife relationship to the fur trade.

For the second half of the nineteenth century only scanty references to the Yellowknife are made; the most valuable are by traveler-adventurers Pike (1892) and Russell (1898). The Hudson's Bay Company, Winnipeg, Manitoba, archives and Oblate missionary records (Fort Smith, Northwest Territories) for the second half of the nineteenth century have not been reviewed by scholars; they would undoubtedly add historical perspective.

Table 2. Variants of the Chipewyan Name for Yellowknife

Chipewyan name	Translation	Source
Tantsawhot-dinneh	Birch-rind Indians	Franklin 1823:287
Tantsa-ut-'dtinnè	Birch-rind people	Richardson 1851, 2:4, 1852:245
T'atsan ottiné[a]	gens du cuivre	Petitot 1876:xx
Tpatsan-Ottinè, Tpaltsan Ottinè	Gens du Cuivre	Petitot 1891:95, 158
Tpa-'ltsan-Ottinè	gens de la crasse de l'eau ('pond-scum [i.e. copper] people')	Petitot 1891:363
Thatsan-o'tinne	none	Morice 1906–1910, 1:265
Tandzán-hot!ínnĕ	none	Curtis 1907–1930, 18:4
t'etsọt'ine[b]	none	J.A. Mason 1946:12
tatsọt'ine[b]	none	Smith 1975:114

[a] The spelling Tatsanottine was adopted as standard by Hodge (1910a).

[b] Perhaps not the same word.

In 1913 ethnologist J.A. Mason (1946) made brief mention of the Yellowknifes he met at Fort Resolution (fig. 5). The "disappearance" of the Yellowknife in the twentieth century precludes any research other than with historical materials. Ethnohistorical articles by Gillespie (1970, 1975a) are based on published sources and on fieldwork among the Dogrib of Yellowknife Bay, Northwest Territories.

Dogrib

JUNE HELM

Language, Territory, and Environment

The Dogrib ('dôg‚rīb) Indians speak a language of the Northeastern Athapaskan language group.*

The Dogrib range is between 62° and 65° north latitude and between 110° and 124° west longitude in the Northwest Territories, Canada (fig. 1). South to north, Dogrib land lies between Great Slave Lake and Great Bear Lake and extends, west to east, from the lowlands on the east side of the Mackenzie River to Contwoyto, Aylmer, and Artillery lakes. The Mackenzie River Lowlands are heavily forested, supporting large specimens of spruce, poplar, and birch. But the greater portion of the Dogrib range is in the low hills and rock outcrop of the Canadian Shield, where the forest cover becomes progressively more sparse and stunted toward the east. Dogribs enter the tundra beyond the treeline only seasonally, for caribou, and in former days, for musk-ox and white fox.

In the northwestern sector of their range, Dogribs meet Bearlake Indians; in the western and southwestern sector, Slaveys; along the eastern edges, Chipewyans; and in the Contwoyto Lake region at the northeastern apex, they have occasionally encountered Eskimos.

*The phonemes of Dogrib are: (unaspirated stops and affricates) b, d, λ, ʒ, ǯ, g, gʷ, ʔ; (aspirated stops and affricates) t, ƛ, c, č, k, kʷ; (glottalized) t̓, ƛ̓, c̓, č̓, k̓, k̓ʷ; (voiceless continuants) ł, s, š, x, W, h; (voiced continuants) l, z, ž, γ, w; (prenasalized stops) ᵐb, ⁿd (nasals) m, n; (resonants) r (retroflex resonant or apico-alveolar tap), y; (plain vowels) i, e, a, o; (nasalized vowels) į, ę, ą, ǫ; (long vowels) e·, a·, ǫ·; (tones) high (unmarked) and low (v̀). There is considerable variation among individuals in the pronunciation of Dogrib in the twentieth century; for example, ą tends to be pronounced like ǫ and ž like y, and hotį̀ 'people of' may also be gotį̀ or otį̀. Furthermore, the phonemicizations of Petitot's band names given in this chapter reflect the language as spoken in the nineteenth century, before the loss of some suffixes and other changes.

In the practical orthography used by the Department of Education of the Northwest Territories the Dogrib phonemes are written as follows: b, d, dl, dz, j, g, gw, ʼ; t, tł, ts, ch, k, kw; t', tł', ts', ch', k', kw'; ł, s, sh, x, wh, h; l, z, zh, gh, w; mb, nd; m, n; r, y; i, e, a, o; į, ę, ą, ǫ; ee, aa, ǫǫ; low tone (v̀).

Information on Dogrib phonology and the practical orthography was furnished by Keren Rice, who also checked the transcription of the forms cited (except for the spirit names žekʷį and cįčo). Howren's (1979) technical discussion of some aspects of Dogrib phonology uses essentially the same phonemic system.

Dogrib in the 1960s

The Dogrib are one of the largest "tribal" Indian populations in the Northwest Territories. They comprised about 1,700 persons in 1970. Of that number, the 1,200 Dogribs living at or trading into the settlement of Rae made up the bulk of the Dogrib population. Most of the Indian persons living in the urbanized town of Yellowknife or its vicinity, including those at nearby Detah (fig. 2) or "Indian Village," consider themselves Dogribs (see "Yellowknife," this vol.). Persons of full or partial Dogrib descent who live or trade at Fort Franklin make up, by one estimate (Denis 1972), perhaps 80 percent of the native population at that fort. Some of the Indians at Snowdrift, on the east arm of Great Slave Lake, are said to have Dogrib ancestry, but their language now is Chipewyan (Helm 1959–1971).

In the early 1940s, most Dogribs lived a life comparable to that of their ancestors 50 or more years earlier: they were largely monolingual, with no formal schooling, receiving little or no modern medical services, and with no source of income for the purchase of Western products except that gained by the trapping of furs. Trapping was conjoined with hunting and fishing for subsistence throughout the year, as parties moved about the land from one station to another according to season.

After the Second World War, a series of responsibilities successively assumed by the Canadian government toward northern native populations greatly affected Dogrib life. The Canadian family allowance and expanded welfare services provided subsidies that augmented trapping income. Greatly expanded health and medical services laid the base for the growth of the native population (table 1). During the 1960s the government moved emphatically into other domains of native life. Through the government housing program for Indians, lumber and plywood houses largely replaced log dwellings. The majority of children of school age were, for the first time, in primary schools. The completion of the Mackenzie Highway link to Yellowknife brought greatly increased communication between the Dogribs of Rae and Yellowknife and opened direct contact and interaction with other Indian groups as far distant as southern Alberta.

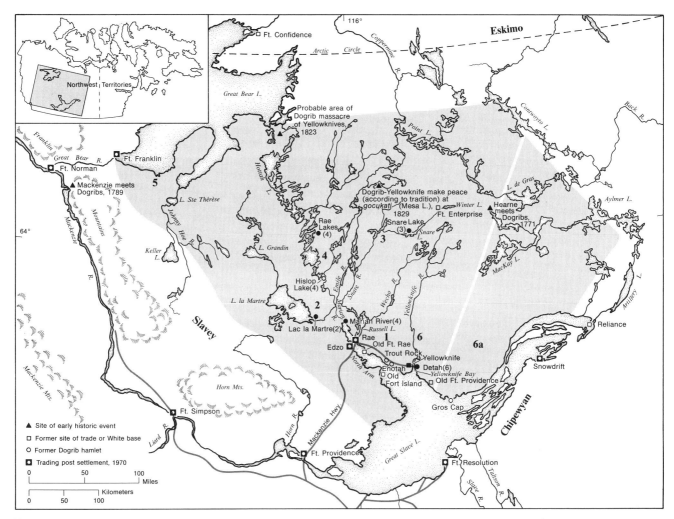

Fig. 1. Tribal territory, 1850–1970, with approximate centers of exploitation or travel of regional bands: 1, *ta ga hoṭ* 'Follow the Shore People'; 2, *cǫ́tì hoṭ* 'Filth Lake People'; 3, *dečįla hoṭ* 'Edge of the Woods People'; 4, *ʔeʔaṭ* (*ʔeʔa hoṭ*) 'People Next to Another People'; 5, *sati hoṭ* 'Bear Lake Dogrib'; 6, *Wulede hoṭ* 'Connie River People'; 6a, no native term (former camp and hamlet area of Dogribs who perished in 1928 influenza epidemic). Band affiliation of Dogrib hamlets is given in parentheses.

Fig. 2. Settlement at Detah. Houses were built in the 1960s under a federal housing program. Poles at right are covered with canvas when used for smoking hides or making dry fish or dry meat. Photograph by René Fumoleau, April 1971.

In the last half of the 1960s youths began to return from government and Roman Catholic boarding schools with full fluency in English and with knowledge of and commitment to Euro-Canadian living standards. This generation began to provide leadership in pan-Indian and Indian rights movements.

One of the most significant by-products of the various government aids and interventions has been the increasing sedentarization of the Dogrib in the towns of Rae and Yellowknife, and, since 1970, Edzo.

Despite political and cultural changes, the earned income of most male household heads was in the 1960s perforce based on the precarious trapping economy. Other than trapping, casual and occasional labor was all that most were able to find. Such work included employment as fishing guides at tourist lodges on Great Bear Lake and as laborers in the construction of roads and government housing for Indians. A few Dogribs, bilinguals, had full-time jobs, such as janitors for government installations and as clerks in local stores.

Table 1. Population

Date	Rae	Elsewhere	Total	Source
		Population		
1825	—	Norman, Simpson	760[c]	E. Smith 1825
1858	657[a]	133 Norman	790	Anderson 1858:282–283
1858	620	23 Resolution 150 Simpson 133 Norman	926	Hodge 1910b:744
1859	1,200	—	1,200[c] (too high)	Petitot 1891:189
1864	788			Petitot 1884–1885:53
1869		47 Norman, Franklin		Petitot 1884–1885:53
1881	615	—	615	Russell 1898:160
1882	633	—	633	OMI 1882
ca. 1893	711	—	711	Russell 1898:160
ca. 1900	all "divisions"		1,150[c] (too high)	Morice 1906–1910, 1:265
1913	700	—	700[c]	J.A. Mason 1946:13
1921	800	—	800[c]	Canada 1966:4
1924	all groups Bear Lake to Gros Cap		997	Canada 1924:54
ca. 1930	—	—	750[c]	Jenness 1932:393
1941	686	232 Yellowknife area	918	Robinson and Robinson 1947:153
1949	718[b]	279[b] Yellowknife area	997[b]	Leechman 1953
1959	906[b]	332[b] Yellowknife area	1,238[b]	Anonymous 1959
1964	968[b]	433[b] Yellowknife area	1,401[b]	Canada. Department of Citizenship and Immigration. Indian Affairs Branch 1964
ca. 1970	1,202[b]	504[b] Yellowknife area	1,706[b]	Canada. Department of Indian Affairs and Northern Development. Indian Affairs Branch 1970

[a] Including "A few Slave and Yellowknives." Dogribs at Fts. Simpson and Resolution are mentioned but not distinguished within the counts for these forts.

[b] These figures represent "Treaty Indians" registered at Rae and Yellowknife. Descendants of Métis who "took Treaty" are included.

[c] Estimate.

History of Indian-White Contact

1680–1850

In the historical literature, the Dogrib identity—as a total societal-territorial body and in its regional subdivisions—remains elusive until after 1850. In the French and English writings from about 1680 to 1770 there are several references to people who are designated as "Dogribs" or by some variant term. But within this interval almost no contact with peoples identified by this term was made by the Europeans of the northern fur trade. "Dogrib" was often a generic term applied to Athapaskan-speaking peoples northwest of the Cree, apparently often including the Chipewyan. Furthermore, most observers between 1770 and 1850 (for example, Hearne, Fidler, Wentzel, Franklin, Richardson) did not distinguish Dogrib from Slavey populations in the sense that has become standard since 1860.

On a journey along the edge of the woods from Fort Prince of Wales to the Coppermine River, Samuel Hearne and his Chipewyan companions encountered some "Copper Indians" (Yellowknife) and a few "Dogrib Indians" on October 23, 1771, while in the region tentatively identified as between Point Lake and MacKay Lake (Hearne 1958:63). This is the first recorded contact with Dogribs in their own territory.

In the next decade far-off events altered conditions of Dogrib life. In 1782 the capture of Fort Prince of Wales (later Fort Churchill) by the French closed for a few years the source of trade goods to those Chipewyans who had been operating as middlemen between the Dogrib and Yellowknife and the English point-of-trade (Hearne 1958:114–116).

Mackenzie (1966:50) in 1789 was the next explorer to record meeting "Dogrib Indians" encamped with Slaveys on the Mackenzie River near the mouth of Great Bear River. Although Mackenzie was also on the North Arm of Great Slave Lake, he identified no groups met there as Dogribs. Petitot (1888:578–584), however, records a native account of the meeting of Dogribs (L'intchanɋe 'Flancs-de-Chien') with a White trader on Great Slave Lake, probably on Old Fort Island, apparently a few years before Mackenzie's journey.

Old Fort Providence† was founded on the North Arm

†Not to be confused with later Fort Providence on the Mackenzie River.

Fig. 3. Inside a lodge. The woman standing on the left and the man seated behind the fire are wearing decorated knife sheaths. The knives are probably trade goods, as are the Hudson's Bay Company blankets on the two figures at the right and the copper pot at bottom right. All the clothes show ornamentation including both fringes and geometric designs, and the women's chins are tattooed. Engraving from a sketch by Émile Petitot, probably 1860s.

of Great Slave Lake by the North West Company in the 1790s as a meat-provisioning post and for "the convenience of Copper [Yellowknife] and Dogrib Indians" (Franklin 1824, 1:325). In 1812, at a trading station on Great Bear Lake that later became Fort Franklin, Keith (1889–1890, 2:112) recorded that Marten Lake Indians (Dogribs) attempting to frequent the post were often restrained by the bullying of the Yellowknife. Sir John Franklin's account of his 1819–1822 expedition confirms that the Dogrib were in this period in fear of the Yellowknife, most of whom were led by the chief Akaitcho ("Yellowknife," fig. 3, this vol.). Following information gained from the fur trader W.F. Wentzel, Franklin described the "Thlingcha-dinne" (Dogribs) of this period and stated that they were called "Slaves" by the Cree. He located them west of the Yellowknife Indians as far as the Mackenzie River, confounding the later distinction between Dogrib and Slavey territory. He identified the "chief tribe of the Dog-rib nation" as "Horn Mountain Indians," extending that group's zone beyond the Horn Mountains to include all the country between Great Bear Lake and the west end of Great Slave Lake. He noted that small detachments of Dogribs frequented Marten Lake and hunted around Fort Enterprise in the summer and that "indeed this [latter] part of the country was formerly exclusively theirs," lakes and hills bearing Dogrib names. "As the Copper [Yellowknife] Indians generally pillage them of their women and furs when they meet, they endeavour to avoid them, and visit their ancient quarters on the barren grounds only by stealth" (Franklin 1824, 2:80–83).

Between Franklin's departure from the Canadian Northwest in 1822 and his return in 1825 peace had been secured between Dogrib and Yellowknife Indians. According to contemporary documents, the destruction of a "considerable party"—"about one-fifth" (McVicar 1825–1826:fo. 14) or 34 (McVicar 1826–1827) Yellowknifes by Dogribs broke the former's aggressive spirit (T. Simpson 1843:318), and peace between the two groups was mediated by representatives of the Hudson's Bay Company (Franklin 1828:9); however, Dogrib oral history attributes the establishment of amity between Dogrib and Yellowknife solely to the Dogrib Edze or, as he is now more generally known, Edzo, who by his oratory shamed and terrified Akaitcho and his Yellowknife into enduring peace (Helm 1959–1971; Gillespie 1970; see also "Yellowknife," this vol.). Excepting one equivocal entry, Edzo remains undocumented in the historical literature.

Old Fort Providence was closed in 1823. Not until the establishment of Fort Rae in 1852, farther down the North Arm of Great Slave Lake, did Dogribs again have a point of trade well within the area they inhabited. Before 1852, most of the Dogribs had "resorted to Fort Simpson, hauling their provisions and furs from 15 to 30 days distance; the consequence was they hunted little either of furs or provisions [for the trading fort]. Many of them had never even seen a white man" (Anderson 1858:104). Forts Norman, Franklin, Confidence, and Resolution also drew Dogrib trade.

1850–1900

The founding of Fort Rae in 1852 and the entry of the first Roman Catholic missionary into the Dogrib region in 1859 marked the inception of a way of life that was to endure for 100 years. Now the bulk of the Dogrib nation had a single point of trade that became the focus of tribal rendezvous at Christmas–New Year's, at Easter time, and in June after the spring beaver hunt.

For decades the Indians of the lands on the east side of Great Slave Lake had been more important to the fur trade as provisioners of caribou meat than as fur procurers (Franklin 1824, 1:325; Simpson 1938:371). With the founding of Fort Rae, "for many years the best provision post in the Mackenzie district" (Russell 1898:70), the Dogrib entered a golden era in their trading economy.

Caribou began to decline in the 1880s as a commercial resource for the Dogrib. By then, Fort Rae was a major station in the trade in musk-ox robes (Russell 1898). In the Mackenzie District, musk-ox robe production began to accelerate in 1876 and did not pronouncedly decline until 1902 (Tener 1965:113–115).

In 1859 the first Dogribs, 139 children, were baptized in the Roman Catholic faith. Within five years, over 600 Rae Dogribs had been baptized; the missionization of the Dogrib was essentially completed within a decade (Petitot 1891; Duchaussois 1928).

Economic and cultural changes in Dogrib life from 1900 to 1945 were generally incremental and untraumatic. After 1900 fur trapping became much more important in the Dogrib economy. In that first decade, "free traders" in competition with the Hudson's Bay Company were providing the Dogrib with a greater variety of European goods and brought the removal of Fort Rae to another site farther down the North Arm of the lake. In 1921 representatives of the Rae Dogribs "signed" Treaty No. 11 with "His Majesty's Commissioner," along with the other Indian peoples north of Great Slave Lake; those Dogribs who traded in Fort Resolution had already "signed" Treaty No. 8 there in 1900 (table 2). The gold discovery on Yellowknife Bay in the mid-1930s created the boom town of Yellowknife, but the bulk of the Dogrib population was not immediately much affected.

Socioterritorial Groups

Regional Bands

The maximal socioterritorial division of the Dogrib, the regional band, is identified by one or more terms that refer to a locus of occupation or area of exploitation in which a substantial number of the group can be found during a significant part of the year (fig. 1).

The first record of distinct Dogrib regional bands (French *gens*) comes from Petitot. His named groups and their regions do not fully correspond to those distinguished by Dogribs in the 1960s. For the period about 1860–1870, Petitot (1891:363) distinguished four major Dogrib groups. Making no mention of Dogribs south of the Old Fort Rae region, Petitot identified (1) Klin-tchanpè (ʎįčɑγe), the group in the vicinity of Fort Rae, which he calls the "Dogribs proper"; (2) Tsan-tpié-pottinè (cǫtiè goṭine), the Marten Lake group; (3) Ttsè-pottinè (či goṭine), the "Canoe People," hunting along the southern shores of Great Bear Lake; and (4) Tpa-kfwèlè-pottinè (takᵂele goṭine), *gens de l'Anus-de-l'Eau*, a group to whom he assigns a vast range that in later times is split between two regional bands (dečįla hoṭį and ʔeṭaṭį)—the territory between the North Arm of Great Slave Lake and Great Bear Lake and the lands east to the source of the Coppermine River. Later regional band identifications (Osgood 1932:33; Duchaussois 1928:438) approximate the four regional groups trading into Rae identified by Helm (1968a). Note that a publisher's error in table 2 of Helm (1968a) places Marian River hamlet in the wrong regional band area; its correct affiliation is with the ʔeṭaṭį.

Regional band affiliations were still recognized in the 1960s, although occupation and exploitation of the region had become attentuated for many Dogribs. These bands, as recognized by Dogribs since at least 1900, are as follows:

(1) *ta ga hoṭį* 'Follow the Shore People', so identified because of the camps and log-cabin hamlets they occupied along the east shore of the North Arm of Great Slave Lake.

Fig. 4. Dogrib Indians on Great Slave Lake, probably arriving at Ft. Resolution for trade from their camps and villages across the lake between Gros Cap and Yellowknife River. The birchbark canoes in the background are of indigenous manufacture, while the plank boats in the foreground are Euro-Canadian; "Ste. Marie" is painted on the bow of the one on the right, suggesting that it is on loan from the Roman Catholic mission. Many oars are painted with geometric designs. Photograph by Charles W. Mathers, 1900.

Table 2. Historical Events and Conditions 1766–1975

1975 DEVELOPING CONFRONTATIONS BETWEEN INDIAN SPOKESMEN AND GOVERNMENT; INCREASING SOCIAL AND POLITICAL COMMUNICATION BETWEEN NWT INDIANS AND THOSE TO THE SOUTH

1971 Edzo town-site and day school opens.

1970 Rae-Edzo becomes incorporated hamlet with governing council.

GOVERNMENT SERVICES AND SUBSIDIES INCREASE: EDUCATION, HOUSING, MEDICAL CARE, WELFARE

1969 Indian Brotherhood of NWT formed.

1967 Yellowknife becomes capital of NWT.

mid 1960s Yellowknife-Rae-Edmonton highway completed; commercial bus service.

1959 Alcohol consumption legalized for NWT Indians.

1950s Physician attached to Rae Mission hospital. Rae day school begins.

POPULATION GROWTH BEGINS.

OLD AGE PENSION, TUBERCULOSIS ALLOWANCE, OTHER GOVERNMENT WELFARE MEASURES BEGIN.

INCREASING SEDENTARY LIVING IN TOWN.

1950

1940s Tuberculosis hospital for Northern natives established in Edmonton. Rae Catholic Mission hospital opens.

1934 Goldstrike: Yellowknife begins as gold camp.

1928 Influenza epidemic (Godsell 1934:304). Many deaths (about 110); Gros Cap population wiped out (Helm 1959–1971).

1924 RCMP post established at Rae (Robinson and Robinson 1946, 2:46).

RAE DOGRIBS COME UNDER TREATY

1921 Treaty No. 11 signed; Monphwi becomes "government chief" of Rae Dogribs; traditional band leaders become councilors (Helm 1959–1971).

PERIOD OF GENERALLY HIGH FUR PRICES (Gimmer 1966:25; Innis 1956:357; Helm 1959–1971)

1914 Bear Lake Chief and his brigade cease to trade at Rae, affiliate with Norman-Franklin (Osgood 1932:33).

1906 New Fort Rae: Hudson's Bay Co. and mission follow "free trader" firm of Hislop and Nagle to new site (Duchaussois 1928:292; Helm 1959–1971).

END OF HUDSON'S BAY MONOPOLY AT RAE AND POINTS NORTH. FUR TRAPPING BECOMES MORE IMPORTANT IN DOGRIB ECONOMY (Russel 1898:70)

1900 Treaty No. 8 signed at Resolution by Drygeese, representing Dogribs from Trout Rock to Gros Cap.

1900

1890s "Free traders" arrive at Fort Resolution (McGregor 1970:13).

1890

MUSK-OX ROBE TRADE (Tener 1965:113–115)

1880

1859 First Roman Catholic missionary to Rae, first baptisms (Duchaussois 1928:293).

"Mal du Ft. Rae": first recorded severe epidemic (Petitot 1891:189).

ERA OF DRY MEAT TRADE (Helm 1959–1971; Innis 1956:300)

MAIN GROUPS OF DOGRIBS SHIFT TRADE TO FT. RAE (Russell 1898:70)

1852 Old Fort Rae established by Hudson's Bay Co. (Robinson and Robinson 1946:46).

NO CENTRAL POINT OF TRADE FOR DOGRIBS: BANDS VARIOUSLY TRADE AT SIMPSON, NORMAN-FRANKLIN, CONFIDENCE, RESOLUTION

1829 Edzo and Akaitcho make peace, Dogrib version (Gillespie 1970; Helm 1959–1971; E. Smith 1829–1830); 1824: Dease and McVicar negotiate peace, White version (Franklin 1828:10).

1825

1823 Dogribs destroy group of Yellowknife (T. Simpson 1843:318). Old Ft. Providence abandoned (Rich 1938:423).

HUDSON'S BAY CO. MONOPOLY BEGINS

1821 Hudson's Bay Co. absorbs North West Co.

DOGRIB-YELLOWKNIFE HOSTILITIES (Hearne 1958:116; Franklin 1824, 1:235).

1804–1799 North West Co. posts established near sites of future Forts Simpson, Norman, Franklin (Stager 1962:38).

1796 or 1790 Old Fort Providence established (Rich 1938:423; Robinson and Robinson 1946:253).

1790

1789 Alexander Mackenzie meets a few Dogribs near Great Bear River; Laurent Leroux trades at Lac la Martre (Mackenzie 1966:50, 109).

1786 Trader-Dogrib contact on Great Slave Lake (Petitot 1888:584).

Trading post established on Great Slave Lake near site of future Fort Resolution (Innis 1956:199).

1785

CREES AGGRESS AGAINST "DOGRIBS" (Fidler 1934:498; Hearne 1958:171).

1775

1771 Hearne of Hudson's Bay Co. meets a few Dogribs between (probably) Point Lake and Mackay Lake (Hearne 1958:63).

1770

CHIPEWYAN AS MIDDLEMEN BETWEEN DOGRIBS AND HUDSON'S BAY CO. (Hearne 1958:115; Rich 1967:146).

1766 A few "Dog Ribb Indians" visit Churchill (Hudson's Bay Company 1765–1766).

(2) *còti hotį* 'Filth Lake People', Marten Lake People, whose main hunting and trapping area was along the streams and lakes draining into Lac la Martre. A major hamlet of *còti hotį* has been long established near the lake outlet.

(3) *dečįla hotį* 'Edge of the Woods People', one of their designations. Members of this regional troup traveled and hunted along the waterways (notably the Snare and Wecho rivers) draining into Russell Lake, which discharges into the end of the North Arm of Great Slave Lake at Rae. For the spring caribou hunt Snare Lake was a focal point for the whole band and drew Dogribs of other regional bands as well. For all caribou hunting, Dogrib range extended to Point Lake and, in some years, into the barrens as far as Contwoyto Lake.

(4) *ʔeįatį* (*ʔeįa hotį*) 'People Next to Another People'. These Dogribs ranged along the chain of lakes draining into Marian River (which discharges into the northernmost extension of Great Slave Lake) and crossed the height of land to continue along the northward chain of lakes that drains into Great Bear Lake. The Emile River, also draining into Marian River, was a major route of access to the fall caribou-hunting grounds.

(5) *sati hotį*‡ 'Bear Lake Dogrib'. These people apparently were formerly not regionally distinguishable from the *ʔeįatį* band. As a total set of people, members of the *ʔeįatį* and *sati hotį* groups ranged between Rae up the chain of lakes to Great Bear Lake and along its southside to the Fort Franklin area. After 1914 (Osgood 1932:33; Helm 1959–1971), the *sati hotį* ceased to trade into Rae and traded only into Forts Norman and Franklin. Their descendants form a substantial part of the Fort Franklin population (see "Bearlake Indians," this vol.). They continue to exploit the southwest side of Great Bear Lake and the area of the Johnny Hoe River.

Except for the disassociation of the *sati hotį* from Fort Rae after 1914, these five regional groups ingathered into Rae for trade after its establishment in 1852. Groups 1–4 represented by Monphwi (Morphy) as head chief, "signed" Treaty at Rae in 1921. They are "the Dogribs" of most prior ethnographic maps and summaries.

(6) *Wulede hotį* 'Connie River People'. These people have been commonly misidentified as Yellowknife Indians. Their more permanent camps and cabin sites were around Yellowknife Bay and on the adjoining shores of the North Arm of Great Slave Lake, to the north as far as the Enotah–Trout Rock area where they overlapped with the *ta ga hotį*. For fall caribou hunting, their route to the barrens often followed the waterways along the Yellowknife River to Snare Lake and beyond. In 1900 these people and those of region 6a, represented by Drygeese as head chief for both groups, "signed" Treaty at Fort Resolution, where they were

accustomed to trade. Their trading orientation to Fort Resolution, combined with some admixture by marriage with Chipewyans, gave them a degree of distinctiveness.

(6a) No encompassing native term is known for these people, who, prior to 1928, were closely commingled with the *Wulede hotį*. They occupied a series of camps with local leaders along the east shore of the North Arm of Great Slave Lake down to Gros Cap and across the lake at the mouth of the Taltson River (Camsell 1916:22). They hunted along both sides of the east arm of Great Slave Lake and to the north of it. The few survivors of the influenza epidemic of 1928 joined the people of region 6. The merging of some of these people with the Snowdrift Chipewyans had probably occurred earlier. No permanent hamlets or stabilized camps were to be found in the 6a area after that time.

Nature of Dogrib Groups

The regional band was not necessarily "banded together" as a compacted residence group. Sets of families coalesced or fragmented into larger or smaller units according to the exigencies of the food and fur quest. These relatively short-term groupings have been described as "task groups" (Helm 1968a, 1972).

Sometimes within a regional band a small group of related nuclear families came to form a "local band" or group, by remaining together for a "few or many years as a community body resident in one settlement or, formerly, in a series of relatively compacted camp areas" (Helm 1972:76). The hamlets presented on figure 1 are such modern local groups.

Any socioterritorial group or grouping, as recognized by the Dogrib, can be identified by the name of the region or current locale of the group (for example, *còti hotį* 'Marten Lake People', *kʷeka telį hotį* 'the group [currently] at the water-over-rocks-place') or, especially when traveling together or engaged in a particular "task," by the name of its leader (for example, *žimičeke* 'Jimmy's bunch'). An individual thus might at any one time "have social identity as a member of a regional band and of a local band, and, by the simple fact of his presence, also be a member of a task group" (Helm 1968a:118).

No group had sharply defined or exclusively claimed territory. Correspondingly, personnel was not fixed: residential movement from one group to another followed ties by blood or marriage (Helm 1965).

Leadership

Dogrib leadership has been closely tied with economic pursuits and contact relations. Designations as well as roles of leaders have changed in pragmatic recognition of altered conditions. Yet, through historic time and

---

‡Dogribs use the same term to refer to Bearlake Indians in general.

circumstance, the status of the leader has rested on consensual recognition that he is a superior producer-provider, generous and committed to the welfare of the group.

Before traders came, Dogrib oral history goes, a band formed around a great hunter to whom supernatural control over game was attributed, *weʒihta*. Such a great provider-leader could also be termed *weꝁahočehde* 'we follow him'.

The period of effective Hudson's Bay Company monopoly (until 1905) created the 'people's trader' *done ꝁawi*. (The title of *ʔeꝁawi* is applied equally to the Hudson's Bay manager and the trading chief.) The status of the trading chief derived from his role as spokesman and middleman between his followers and the company. In one Dogrib's account (somewhat edited; cf. Helm 1965a:40–41):

> The Hudson's Bay Company used to give all kinds of supplies, clothing and ammunition to the *done ꝁawi*. If his bunch ran short of supplies, the *done ꝁawi* could send two of his men to Resolution or wherever. Those two men would say, "*ʔeꝁawi* sent us for grub," and the trader had to send what he was asked for back to the *ʔeꝁawi*. In the springtime or Christmas the *ʔeꝁawi* paid back the trader with fur.
>
> The *done ꝁawi* had five or six helpers, hunters and fishermen. . . . *done ꝁawi* and his helpers had to feed the whole band, so pretty nearly all of the Indians had to follow him to whatever place was a good hunting place, a good trapping place. Maybe there would be a hundred people following him (as a band) and everybody got the same amount.

The coming of free traders "cut out *done ꝁawi*." Now, Indian entrepreneurs (*naeⁿdi dǫ* 'buy-and-sell men') received goods from one or another competing trader that they exchanged for furs. They were figures around which a group tended to gather.

The native-recognized leader of a regional band or a major subgroup was called *done ɣa ꝁawo* 'boss for (a) people'. (A few were also of the stature of *ʔeꝁawi*.) With the taking of Treaty, the several *done ɣa ꝁawo* became in official White reckoning the "councilors" of the two government-designated "bands," the "Rae band" and the "Yellowknife band." Up to 1970 councilors continued to be chosen by consensus of their respective regional groups. As "councilors" they are called *gʷati* (or its diminutive) 'he talks straight'. The official head chief is also *gʷati* (or *gʷatiⁿde* 'big chief'), as is the government police officer. Up to the 1970s, the "head chief" line of the Rae Dogribs descended ideologically (and to some extent genealogically) from the great trading chief Ekawi Jimi (Jimmy). In Dogrib oral tradition (Helm 1959–1971), the chiefly line leading to Ekawi Jimi begins with Edzagwo, a legendary figure, one of whose many children was Edzo (Edze), the leader in the 1820s who confronted and broke the spirit of the Yellowknife leader Akaitcho. Edzo probably appears in the historical record (Richardson 1851,

298

2:133) as Tecon-ne-betah ('Tecon's father') who died after 1850. As Dǫnęꝁǫ or Dek'on, Tecon (d. by 1864) is identifiable in Dogrib oral history and mission records as the father of Ekawi Jimi (Timoleon Nate'a, b. 1835) who was trading chief from about 1865 to his death in 1897. Ekawi Jimi designated Monphwi (Murphy, Morphy, b. 1866) as his successor as prime chief of the Rae Dogribs. Monphwi became the first *gʷatiⁿde*, official head chief, when he "signed" Treaty No. 11 in 1921. On Monphwi's death in 1936, Jimmy Bruneau (Bruno, b. 1882, d. 1975), son of Ekawi Jimi, became head chief. He retired as chief in 1969, upon consensual agreement that his son Joseph (Susie) Bruneau would succeed him. In 1971, Joseph Bruneau was replaced as Rae head chief in the first formal election held for that office. Within the decade of the 1970s, three men were successively elected head chief.

Finally, the general term *ꝁawo* 'boss' applies to any person acting in any leadership capacity. Specifically it refers to the temporary 'boss' selected by consensus of a traveling or hunting group, and to a temporary or 'permanent' executive officer appointed by a chief or headman to organize and direct group events. The term *ꝁawo* may also refer to the chief or regional band leader in his total capacity (Helm 1972:77).

Culture

Annual Cycle

Prior to about 1950, almost all Dogribs spent most of the year in "bush" living, apart from a point of trade or other Euro-Canadian installation. The annual cycle followed in those days was still carried out by some Dogribs in the 1960s. The major seasonal activities of this traditional pattern are summarized below (stressing the Rae Dogribs) and in figure 5.

In late June or early July the men come to the fort to trade beaver and muskrat furs taken in the "spring hunt." Some bring their families with them (fig. 6); others leave the women and children in bush camps or hamlets. Feasting, dances, and hand games are held at the fort.

In late July and early August men and their families return to the bush. During August the women prepare dry fish at fish camps while hunters travel by canoe and portage to the edge of the woods or beyond to meet the caribou moving toward the forest. The caribou at this time are moving in small bands. From a successful hunt each man returns with a bale of caribou dry meat and a bale of skins, which at this time of the year are in prime condition for apparel—moccasins ("Environment and Culture in the Shield and Mackenzie Borderlands," fig. 12, this vol.), mitts, parkas.

Gill-net fishing continues through September as families stockpile a reserve for early winter and the coming

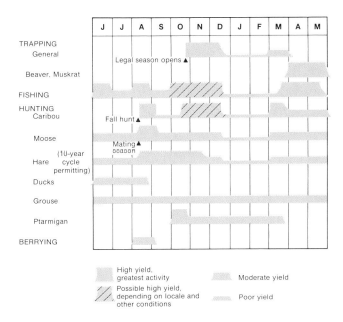

	J	J	A	S	O	N	D	J	F	M	A	M
TRAPPING												
General			Legal season opens ▲									
Beaver, Muskrat												
FISHING												
HUNTING												
Caribou			Fall hunt ▲									
Moose			Mating ▲									
Hare (10-year cycle permitting)												
Ducks												
Grouse												
Ptarmigan												
BERRYING												

High yield, greatest activity

Moderate yield

Possible high yield, depending on locale and other conditions

Poor yield

Fig. 5. Annual cycle.

trapping season. The fish are strung on poles through their gills or tails and hung on a rack-stage. The cool weather obviates the need to convert fish to dry fish.

Freeze-up occurs during the first weeks of October. The gill nets are taken out of the water just before the ice forms and are set under the ice again as soon as it is thick enough to support human weight. The ptarmigan migrate from the barrens into the woods.

November and December are the best period for trapping fine furs. The caribou are moving through the woods in large herds. When word comes of a herd, the best hunters with their dog teams head for the area. They are followed by other men and youths with dog teams to help bring back the kill. During December, men begin to bring furs to the fort to trade and to participate in the festivities of Christmas and New Year's.

January and February are the hardest time of the year; fish, hares, and fur animals are in poor supply. Because the intense cold carries sound at great distances, caribou and moose are hard to approach.

As the days lengthen and the cold lessens in March, fishing, snaring, hunting, and trapping improve. Caribou hunting is especially good at Snare Lake as the herds move along the narrow lake toward the barrens for their summer pasturage and calving.

During April and May the men gather at the fort for Easter time, to sell their furs and attend services at the mission; feasts, dances, and hand games occur. As the snow begins to melt at the end of April, men leave the fort, the bush camps, and hamlets by dog team (fig. 8) for the spring beaver and muskrat hunt. As breakup occurs in the smaller streams, the hunters abandon their toboggans and make canoes.

The larger waterways open during June. The beaver

hunters return to their families at the base camps or hamlets. The Dogribs gather into the fort in the late days of June. After 1921 Treaty payment about the end of June became an additional attraction at Rae.

Life Cycle

As Roman Catholics, Dogrib observe the major rites of passage of the church. Of aboriginal belief and practice regarding major stages of the life cycle, only bride service and restrictions around the female menstrual cycle were in the 1960s still observed, and only by more tradition-minded families. Except where indicated, the following account represents normative belief and practice as held in the memory culture of mature Dogribs (Helm 1959–1971).

top, Natl. Mus. of Canada, Ottawa: Geological Survey of Canada Coll., 26058.
Fig. 6. Indian encampments at Ft. Rae. top, Tepee with caribou hide cover. Photograph by J. Alden Mason, summer of 1913. bottom, A canvas tent set up at Treaty time. When returning to Ft. Rae from hunting and trapping some families had houses to move into (background), but others used tents with adjacent small wood-burning stoves. The woman in the center is carrying a baby in a shawl, supported by a carrying strap. Granite outcropping of the Precambrian Shield, common in this area, is evident. Photograph by Richard Finnie, Ft. Rae, 1939.

bottom, Hudson's Bay Company Lib., Winnipeg, Man.:73–185.

Fig. 7. Treaty activities. top left, Treaty payment, 1939. District Indian agent checks the Indian's name in his ledger book and gives out 5 one-dollar bills, while the constable guards the cash. Identification cards (right foreground) showing the number of family members were examined before payment was made. Except for the chief (who received $25) and the councilors (who received $15), every man, woman, and child was eligible for a $5 payment. Photograph by Richard Finnie. top right, Treaty feast at Rae, 1962. Tents have been joined together to accommodate from 200 to 400 adults. Men and women sit separately. Each person brings his or her own utensils and container, which are placed on strips of oilcloth on the ground. Twenty or so men serving as waiters pass up and down the rows putting the food in each person's container. Photograph by June Helm. bottom, Feast at Ft. Rae following treaty payment, 1936. Traditionally the Hudson's Bay Company, other traders in town, and the Indian agent contributed "store" food. The man standing on the left is one of the Indian waiters who will serve the entire assemblage. Bare area is granite outcropping. Photographer not known.

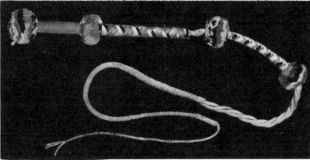

bottom, Natl. Mus. of Canada, Ottawa: VI–E–48.
Fig. 8. Dog team and equipment. top, Isadore and Rose Sangris of Detah traveling by toboggan-type dog sled on Great Slave Lake; photograph by René Fumoleau, April 1970. bottom, Dog whip made of wool woven over a wooden handle, decorated with 4 woolen pompoms, and ending in a caribou babiche cord; length 220 cm, collected about 1940.

Women removed to a special shelter for childbirth. They were attended by other mature women, often close relatives. The mother knelt to give birth, over a pad of moss prepared to receive the baby. Female infanticide was once practiced (Anderson 1858:107).

The child's name was appropriately bestowed by a grandparent. It might reflect a wish for future abilities, such as Good Paddler.

No formal recognition was accorded the boy's approach to puberty. But to assure that he would not be weak or of poor account, his easy childhood association with girls now ceased.

With the menarche, the girl was placed apart from the group camp in a small shelter. Her mother visited her once a day to bring her food. During this period she was kept busy at women's tasks, in order that she learn to be a hard worker. For the rest of her reproductive life, each menstrual or postpartum period re-quired that she stay apart from men's gear, that she walk aside from the trail, and that, generally, she remain apart from the family so that her condition would not adversely affect her husband's hunting or her children's health.

Prior to the introduction of the Christian wedding services, no ceremony marked the advent of marriage. Courtship became de facto marriage, which apparently stabilized after the birth of a child. At least until the birth of the child, a young man served his prospective parents-in-law, hunting and bringing water and firewood. Young persons should not marry without parental approval, which was largely contingent upon the parents' mutual regard for the working standards of each young person and that person's family. In the pre-Christian past some some superior providers had more than one wife. As among other Mackenzie drainage Athapaskans, young wives not yet with children might be won by another man through wrestling contests or gambling. The "giving" of children by one family with many to a related couple with none continued to be common through the 1960s. In that decade the Canadian government began to legalize these transfers of children as adoptions.

It is said that stage burial was once practiced. Since missionization, disposal of the dead has been by burial in a blessed ground, with a picket fence erected about the grave. Some personal possessions of the deceased may be burned nearby, or smashed and broken, a trait widely documented for aboriginal Mackenzie drainage Athapaskans.

Kinship

A Dogrib's relatives are embraced by the term *sehoṭi* 'my people', which can also refer to one's band or hamlet group. Dogrib social organization lacks clans or any other form of descent group. Kinship reckoning radiates bilaterally from each ego. As it conveys the Dogrib sense of kinship—those whom one is "related to"—*sehoṭi* includes relatives by marriage as well as consanguines. Figure 9 presents the terminology system as applied by the speaker to closer relatives.

Traditional Dogrib norms required reserved behavior between a man and his sister. A man should not look directly into his sister's face or joke with her. A milder reserve relationship was maintained between a man and his brother-in-law. They should not joke directly or allude to sexual matters, but cooperation in hunting and trapping with the brother-in-law is a common feature of Dogrib work relationships. A man also practiced a mild reserve toward his father-in-law, who had the same right to command the energies of a young man that his father and older brother had.

Although young persons were expected to be obe-

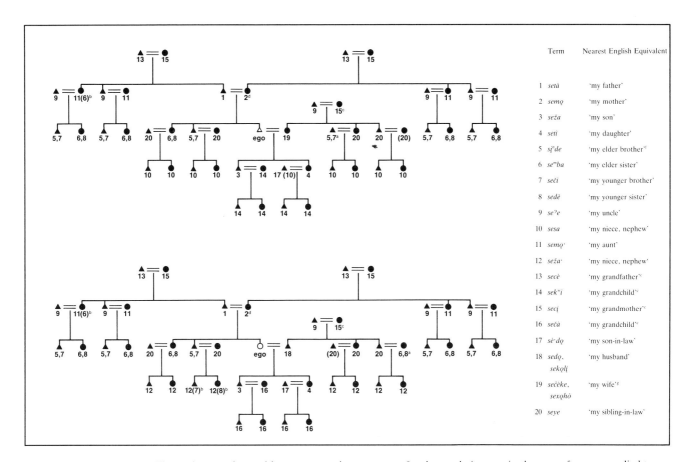

	Term	Nearest English Equivalent
1	setà	'my father'
2	semǫ	'my mother'
3	seža	'my son'
4	seti	'my daughter'
5	sįⁿde	'my elder brother'ᶠ
6	seᵐba	'my elder sister'
7	seči	'my younger brother'
8	sedè	'my younger sister'
9	se²e	'my uncle'
10	sesa	'my niece, nephew'
11	semǫ·	'my aunt'
12	seža·	'my niece, nephew'
13	secè	'my grandfather'ᵉ
14	sekʷi	'my grandchild'ᵉ
15	secį	'my grandmother'ᵉ
16	secä	'my grandchild'ᵉ
17	sé·dǫ	'my son-in-law'
18	sedǫ, sekǫlį	'my husband'
19	secèke, sexǫhò	'my wife'ᵍ
20	seye	'my sibling-in-law'

Fig. 9. Kinship terminology. Figures in parentheses either represent alternate terms for those relatives or, in the case of *seye* as applied to man's wife's brother's wife and woman's husband's sister's husband, indicate that those kin types are beyond the limit of kin-term assignments by some speakers. The distinction between male ego (top) and female ego (bottom) is that of sex of ego as the point of reference rather than of speaker's sex per se. Thus, a man uses the woman's term when speaking of a woman's grandchild or to a woman about her grandchild or other relative that requires the sex of ego distinction. Each term as given includes the first-person possessive prefix *se-*; the corresponding vocatives (address forms) have the indefinite prefix *²e-* or *²eh-*: e.g., *²età* 'father', *²eᵐba* 'elder sister', *²ehcè* 'grandfather', *²ehcį* 'grandmother'.

Notes to charts: a, Men married to sisters and women married to brothers address one another by brother and by sister terms, respectively. The criterion determining the use of *sįⁿde* versus *seči* and of *seᵐba* versus *sedè* is that of the relative ages of the linking spouses, not the relative ages of ego and alter. Thus, a man aged 50 addresses his wife's sister's husband aged 70 as *seči* ('my younger brother') if that sister of his wife is younger than his own wife. b, Some Dogrib women apply *seči* and *sedè* to brother's son and brother's daughter but not to sister's son or sister's daughter. Reciprocally, father's sister is then addressed as *²eᵐba*. c, Some Dogribs recall that *²ehᵐbe* is "an old-time word" applied to a mother-in-law (see MacNeish 1960:280 on Slavey kin-term usages). d, Some speakers use *²enę*, the irregular vocative of 'mother', for both address and reference to their own mother; others consider this form archaic in all uses. e, Grandparent and grandchild terms are commonly employed in address between any 2 persons of the appropriate generational distance, whether related or not. f, The polite form for one's older brother is *kįⁿde*. g, The term *sexǫhò*, as a secondary alternate to *secèke*, has been provided by Keren Rice (communication to editors 1979).

dient and helpful toward older persons, with parents and especially grandparents and aunts and uncles, the relationship was ideally one of easy affection. Men were not "shy" with sisters-in-law or with cousins of either sex.

Mythology and Beliefs

The legends around Edzo, notably his leadership in making peace with the Yellowknife chief Akaitcho, form a body of lore distinctive to the Dogribs. With neighboring tribes—Slavey, Chipewyan, Yellowknife— they share a number of myths and traditions. These include the saga of the Two Brothers (Petitot 1888; Williamson 1955–1956; MacNeish 1955; Helm 1959–1971), the Copper Woman (Petitot 1888; Helm 1959–1971), the Slave Woman (Petitot 1888; Helm 1959–1971; Davies and Johnson 1965:410–413), and the tribal creation by the mating of a woman with a dog (Mackenzie 1970:149; Petitot 1888, 1891; Helm 1959–1971).

Traditionally, magico-religious beliefs and practices centered on the concept of *²įk̇ǫ* 'power' or 'medicine'. Power was given to men or women by animal-spiritual beings, who directed them in curing, divination, or controlling game and weather. A possesser of curing abilities had to be persuaded or shamed into performing; part of the cure might require the sufferer's confession of misdeeds in the presence of the assembled group.

Ceremonies and Spiritual Life

Two kinds of traditional mimetic "ceremonies" apparently have not been enacted since the 1950s. In one of these an actor imbued with the spirit of ʒekʷi̜ wore a birchbark mask and dressed as a hunchback. He clownishly handed out spruce boughs as "meat," then mistook the male spectators for caribou, and eventually caught one of them whom he sat on while he struck about with an ax as though he were butchering a caribou. In the other "play," several men who had the spirit of ci̜čo dressed and painted one of themselves, who took up a pole with which he detected metal objects in the ground. He chased spectators, and when he caught one of them he could predict how long a lifetime remained to that person (Helm and Lurie 1966:85). Both these enactments occurred only in the springtime, for apparently they revolved around life, sustenance, and increase.

Mass and other Catholic services provide ritual and social occasions in Dogrib life. While in camp in the bush or at isolated hamlets, Dogribs carry out their own Sunday services.

In the winter of 1966–1967, upon the opening of the Mackenzie Highway, a Slavey prophet from northern Alberta visited Fort Rae. One Rae Dogrib became a major prophet, recruiting followers. The sermons, songs, dances, and rituals—largely borrowed from or influenced by the southern prophet—blend Roman Catholic and aboriginal concepts and practices (Helm 1969a).

Another notable Dogrib prophet of the 1960s was Naidzo, "the Bear Lake Prophet" (b. 1887, d. 1973). Naidzo did not carry out ritual or ceremonial activities. Greatly esteemed, he confined his role as prophet to exhortation to moral behavior and adherence to Catholic practices, and to eloquent narrations of Dogrib legends (see "Bearlake Indians," fig. 6, this vol.).

Christmas–New Year's, Easter, and "Treaty time" serve as focal times for Dogrib ingathering to Rae and for native celebrations of feasting, dancing, and playing of the hand game. Multiple weddings are commonly performed in the church at this time.

As among other Athapaskan tribes of the Mackenzie drainage, traditional dance is accompanied by the communal singing of men. In the so-called Tea Dance, men and women move clockwise, facing inward, in a dance circle (see "Expressive Aspects of Subarctic Indian Culture," fig. 17, this vol.). In the Drum Dance a set of drummer-singers provides song and tempo while dancers form a line front to back. Some dance songs are attributed to individual innovators (Helm and Thomas 1966:53–54). Individual shaman songs and love songs might also be created (Helm 1959–1971).

Games

The hand game (figs. 10–11) is a hidden-object guessing game between two teams, played to the accompaniment of vigorous drum beats and chanting. It is a marked feature of tribal ingatherings. Opposing teams are made up from regional bands or, when the occasion allows, of a set of Dogribs against members of a neighboring tribe (see Helm and Lurie 1966).

Other traditional games included a version of the ring and pin game (fig. 12), competitive play with bow and arrow, stick throwing, and other contests of skill (Helm and Lurie 1966:78–89; Helm 1959–1971). Betting on the outcome of play is a feature of most traditional games, as it is with poker, rummy, pedro, and Chinese checkers, borrowed games much enjoyed by Dogribs.

Technology

Aboriginal Dogrib technical culture had essentially the inventory of tools and techniques common to other Athapaskans of the Mackenzie drainage. Basic items included the snowshoe, toboggan, birchbark canoe (fig. 13), gill net (fig. 14) with winter under-ice fishing, the simple bow ("Environment and Culture in the Shield and Mackenzie Borderlands," fig. 2, this vol.), and snares.

Dogribs were probably indirectly receiving pieces of European iron and a few other items before 1750. Some had commenced direct trading relations by 1800. Yet many aspects of technology remained aboriginal either fully or in modified form into the twentieth century.

Table 3 gives some indication of time and rate of technological introductions, modifications, and replacements within the contact era for four main classes of artifacts. Objects are placed in eras. Aboriginal times are from precontact into the early contact period, ending about 1820. Even if adopted before 1820, traits obviously borrowed from the European are placed in the following era. Contact-traditional, about 1820–1945, embraces the period of fur-trade dominance. Modern times indicates since 1945. A trait's presence is shown by x; absence, by o; rarity, by r.

Synonymy

The difficulty of equating "Dogribs" of early accounts with those people so identified after 1850 is indicated in the chronological list of designations given below. The conclusions best drawn from these data follow. From the Cree, interposed between the Whites on Hudson Bay and the northeastern Athapaskans, Europeans first learned of the people they called *atimospikay* 'dog

Fig. 10. The hand game at Rae. top, With their hands hidden under jackets or between thighs the men are each shuffling a small object (rock, tinfoil, etc.) from one hand to another and swaying to the double beat of the chanters' drums. bottom left, Each with a hidden object, idzi, in one of his hands, the players are moving in rhythm to the drums while posed so that the guesser selected by the opposing team can make his assessment of the location of each idzi. bottom right, Holding hands forward the players are at the second stage of presenting their idzi. Chief Jimmy Bruneau is in center wearing hat and checkered jacket. opposite page left, Alexis Arrowmaker (later chief) as guesser for his team indicates by hand signal which hand of each player of the opposing team holds idzi. By a single or compound hand signal the guesser can designate which hand of every opponent has the hidden idzi. The sticks keep count of the score. opposite page right, Chief Jimmy Bruneau serving as guesser for his team is signaling his guess that all opponents to the left of the V formed by his thumb and forefinger hold their idzi in the right hand and all those to the right of the V hold their idzi in their left hand. Photographs by June Helm, July 1962.

Fig. 11. Young boys playing at the hand game. The boy at right rear is the guesser against his two opponents. He is employing a variant of the same signal used by Chief Jimmy Bruneau (see fig. 10). His team companion is simply watching the play; as in the adult game, only one guesser is active at one time. Photographed at Rae Lakes, 1978.

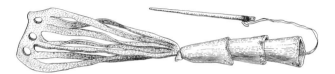

after Culin 1907:fig. 716.

Fig. 12. Ring and pin game. Bone needle and cones attached with sinew to caribou hide strip. The player holds the needle near the sinew while swinging the rest upward and outward. The object of the game is to put the needle through the center of the cones or a slit in the leather. Total length about 37 cm, collected at Ft. Rae by F. Russell, 1892–1894.

side'. Possibly the epithet stemmed from Cree knowledge of the widely shared Athapaskan legend of tribal creation by the mating of a woman with a dog. The term may have been a reference to Athapaskans in general; at the least, it seems not to have been specifically applied to the people that became known as Dogribs after 1850.

Before 1700 the English on Hudson Bay were distinguishing Chipewyans from the "dogside Nation," but the French were calling both Plats-Côtés de Chien 'dog sides', using an expression for 'side' that refers to the ribs of a half carcass. By 1800 the English came to apply

Natl. Mus. of Canada, Ottawa: Geological Survey of Canada Coll., 26142.

Fig. 13. Birchbark portage canoes. Photograph by J. Alden Mason at Ft. Rae, 1913.

Fig. 14. Elise Abel of Detah repairing a gill net. Photographed in 1974.

Fig. 15. Chief Charles Charlo (holding document) and councilors of the Rae Dogribs with proposed amendment to Treaty No. 11, "To read as follows: 'The Dogrib People *do not* cede, release, surrender and yield up to the Government of the Dominion of Canada, their rights, titles and privileges to the lands . . .'." Photographed in 1977.

their term to Athapaskan groups between Great Slave and Great Bear lakes and along the Mackenzie River, but not until after 1850 did they consistently distinguish the Dogrib from the Slavey.

Prior to the contact era λįčǫ 'Dogrib' was almost certainly not a term of self-reference for the ancestors of those who so identify themselves in the 1970s. In the 1860s Petitot (1891) limited the term to the Indian group immediately around Fort Rae. Since that time, the term has been extended to the total "tribal" group as an accepted self-designation, employed when contrasting themselves with neighboring Athapaskan peoples such as the *tehʒǫt̨į* 'Chipewyan'. When contrasting themselves and other Athapaskans with persons of Eu-

306

ropean descent, Dogribs use the term *done* ('people', 'men') to emphasize their Indianness.

An attempt has been made to include here all sources written before 1800. From these, repetitions of synonymous terms meaning Dogrib are presented with comments, for the purpose of documenting for that era the degree of ambiguity of the referent tribe or tribes. Dating of the sources has been based, when possible, on known date of contact, actual writing (or, failing that, the earliest edition), rather than the date of the publication available for citation. After 1800 only synonymies from primary sources have been selected—those whose authors had direct contact with peoples identified as Dogribs—except for the reference works by Morice (1906–1910, 1), Hodge (1907–1910), and Swanton (1952).

1678: Alim8spigoiak (Franquelin 1970:39), placed schematically at headwaters of Mississippi River but in the latitude of Hudson Bay. (8 stands for ou.)

1689: dogside Nation (Kelsey 1929:25), distinguished from Chipewyan ("no[r]thern Indians"); Doggside Indians (Rich 1957:58, 66).

1694–1714: Plascôtez de Chiens (Jérémie 1715–1724, 5; see also Jérémie 1926:20, 21, 31), shown by internal evidence to be Chipewyan-Yellowknife Indians.

1694: Alimouspigut, Alimouspigui (Marest 1931:128, 142), translated by Marest's editor, J.B. Tyrrell, as "Dog Ribs"; Marest's description—"c'est une Nation nombreuse: elle a des Villages, & s'étend jusques derriere les *Assiniboëls* [Assiniboin], avec qui elle est presque toûjours en guerre"—is not a correct description of the Dogrib but may have been based on Franquelin's vague map.

1700: Atticmospiscayes, Attimospiquaies (Bacqueville de la Potherie 1931:258, 265), indicated by context to be Chipewyans.

1721: Plats côtez de Chiens (Charlevoix 1744, 3:181), indicated by geographical context to be eastern Chipewyan.

1744: Plascotez de Chiens or Tete Plat Nation; Plats cotes de Chiens; Attimospiquay, which signifies the Coast of Dogs; Attimospiquais, Tete Plat, or Platscotez de Chiens, a Nation living Northward on the Western Ocean of America (Dobbs 1744:map, 19, 25, 44); by his own statements Dobbs follows Jérémie and Bacqueville de la Potherie and an account by a French-Indian, Joseph la France.

1761: Plats cotee de Chiens, Lowland dogs (Jefferys 1761, 1:44), description and placement taken directly from Charlevoix.

1766: DogRibb Indians (Hudson's Bay Company 1765–1766), distinguished from Chipewyan.

1771: Dog-rib Indians (Hearne 1958), distinguished from Yellowknife and Chipewyan.

1772: Western Dog-ribbed Indians (Hearne 1958:168–

Table 3. Selective Inventory of Dogrib Material Culture

	Aboriginal	Contact-Traditional	Modern
Weapons, Food Procurement Equipment			
bow and arrow complex	x	x	o
simple bow, without guard	x	x	sport, child's
with guard	x	x	
arrow, 3 feathers	x	x̄	
blunt head, simple and compound (birds)	bone, horn, copper?	iron	
detachable unbarbed point (large game)	bone, horn, copper?	iron	
fixed unbarbed point (small game)	bone, horn, copper?	iron	
bow held horizontal, waist high	x	x	
primary release	x	x	
Mediterranean release	?	r?	
secondary release	?	r?	
caribou-hide quiver, draw string	x	x	
firearms	o	x	x
muzzle-loaders	o	-1930	o
shotguns	o	1890-	x
rifles	o	1920-	x
caribou spear, unbarbed point	bone,[a] horn	iron	o
snares			
large game, babiche line	x	x	r?
with brush fence (caribou)	x	-1870?	o
small game (especially hares), sinew	x	x	o
twine	o	x	x
deadfalls	x	x	x[b]
commercial traps	o	1905-	x
fishing devices			
gill net, willow bast	x	-1900	o
commercial twine	o	1900-	x
ice chisel, horn	x	o	o
iron	o	early-	x
fishhooks			
bone, claw, or tooth point lashed to willow shank	x	x	o
commercial metal	o	x	x
fish spear			
single point	horn	iron	o
2 or 3 prongs	horn	iron	o
fish weir	r?	r?	o
Travel and Transportation			
water transport			
birchbark canoe			
small: "portage canoe," 12–18 feet, stern and bow "decked"	x	-1920	o
large: "freighter" or "family" canoe 20–22 feet	o	-1920	o
spruce-bark canoe	?	r	o
canvas-covered canoes, small and large	o	1920-	x
plank scows	o	1920-	x
outboard motors	o	late-	x
land transport			
tumpline and chest strap	x	x	x

Table 3. Selective Inventory of Dogrib Material Culture (*Continued*)

	Aboriginal	Contact-Traditional	Modern
snowshoe, narrow, pointed, upturned toes:			
for "trail" (3 feet) and hunting (5 feet)	x	x	x
woman's rounded-toe snowshoe	o[c]	r	r
toboggan			
native, birch	x	x	o
commercial	o	1920-	x
dog-team complex (tandem hitch)	o	1850?-	x
snowmobile	o	o	1967-
Shelter and Heat			
dwellings			
facing half-conical shelters of poles, branches, and bark, fire between	x	?	o
conical spruce-bough lodge	x	x	o
caribou-skin tepee	x	x	o
split-log dwelling, open at 2 ends	x	x	o
"open camp" against snowbank, lined with spruce boughs	x	x	x
log cabin	o	x	r
canvas tent	o	1920-	x
lumber-plywood houses (government)	o	o	1960-
fires and stoves			
open fire in lodges, tepees	x	x	o
clay chimney-fireplace in cabins	o	x	o
metal fire-drum or stove (in tents, cabins, houses)	o	1920-	x
oil space-heater (in houses)	o	o	1960-
Clothing			
outer garments, men and women			
caribou-hide shirts or capotes, furred and unfurred	x	x	r
netted hareskin robes	x	x	o
hide mitts on neckcord	x	x	x
hide gauntlets, men's	o	r	r
skin garments generally	x	-1875	r
European-style cloth garments generally	o	1875-	x
men's clothing			
fringed hide pubic tassel	x	?	o
caribou-hide breechclout	?	x	o
caribou-hide trousers	o	x	o
over-the-knee hide or stroud leggings	?	x	o
women's clothing			
cured hide breechclout	x	x	o
slit, toggled hide underpants	?	x	o
tailored hide dress	o	x	o
knee-high stroud leggings	o	x	o
footgear			
all-in-one soft-soled "shoe" plus leggings	x	-early	o
ankle-wrap moccasin, seamed, pointed toe, T-seam heel	?	x	r
puckered-toe, T-seam heel	o	1930-	x
mukluk moccasin-boot, mid-calf	o	1930-	x
slipper moccasin	o	by 1913-	x
moccasin pac: furred hare, muskrat, caribou skin	x	x	o
blanket cloth (duffel)	o	x	x
moccasin rubbers	o	late?-	x

Sources: Helm 1959–1971; Helm and Lurie 1961; Lurie 1962; Mackenzie 1966; J.A. Mason 1946.

[a] Mackenzie (1966:54) reports a spear with a point of "barbed Bone 10 Inches long, with this they Spear the Rein Deer in the Water," but as a barbed point would hold in the animal and threaten the canoe with capsizing, the accuracy of this statement must be questioned.

[b] Instructions in deadfall construction are now available from Game Management authorities, Wildlife Service, Department of Northern Affairs and Natural Resources.

[c] Probably not aboriginal, as rounded-toe is designed to prevent its catching in long skirts.

172); geographical context indicates Slavey Indians may be the referents.

1775: Ateem Uspeki (Graham 1949:316), Atim-us-peki (Graham 1969:205), distinguished from Chipewyan.

1789: Dog Rib Indian (Mackenzie 1966), distinguished from Slavey, Chipewyan, and Yellowknife. Lac la Martre ("Lac la Merde") Indians identified as "Slave" Indians, not Dogrib.

1791: Thlee-chaug-a or Dog Rib (Turnor 1934:399). "[Great] Slave Lake called by the Southern [Cree] Indians . . . the Arch-a-thin-nu ['stranger'] or Wau-con ['slave'] Sack-a-ha-gan or Slave Lake and by the Chepawyans Thlee-chaug-a Too-a or Dog Rib Lake."

1791: Dog ribbed tribe (Fidler 1934:498); geographical context suggests Slavey Indians may be the referents.

1805: DogRibb Indians; Slaves (or DogRib) (McKenzie 1805); source does not distinguish Slavey from Dogrib.

1812: Filthy Lake Indians (Keith 1889–1890, 2:106, 111ff.). These are the Indians of Lac la Martre. Keith distinguishes them from Yellowknife Indians, stating that they consider themselves a distinct tribe from the "Grand River Indians" (Slaveys), although he considers them essentially the same; he does not identify "Dogribs" in his writings.

1821: Dog Ribs (Wentzel 1821), in the text; Horn Mountain Indians are the "principal branch of the Dogrib Indians," and there is no mention of Slavey. On the accompanying map, "Dogribs" are placed in the Lac la Martre area and distinguished from "Horn Mountain Indians."

1821: Dog Rib Tribe (Simpson 1938:395), distinguished from Slavey.

1824: Thlingcha-dinneh; Dogribs; called Slaves by the Cree (Franklin 1824, 2:80); given as synonyms.

1851: Thling-è-ha-'dtinnè; Dog-ribs; "slave" (from Richardson 1851, 2:3, 5, the Cree designation); given as synonyms.

1865: Lin-tchanpe, Flancs-de-Chien, Plat-coté-de-Chien (Petitot 1868:489).

1891: Dounè, Côtes-de-Chien (Petitot 1891:363), in addition to the terms above.

1906: Lintchanre, Duné (Morice 1906–1910, 1:264); Morice's data on the Dogribs are derivative and contain misstatements.

1910 and 1952: Thlingchadinne (Hodge 1910b:744; Swanton 1952:604), apparently taken from Franklin (1824), with a shift in orthography. Other secondary sources appear to have borrowed or embroidered the terms Thlingcha-dinneh (Franklin 1824) or Thling-è-ha-'dtinnè (Richardson 1851; see Hodge 1910b:745)

Sources

Only scraps of information can be gleaned from the published writings of the traders and explorers who contacted Dogribs between 1770 and 1850. Most of these references are cited above. Unpublished Hudson's Bay Company archival documents hold promise of fuller comprehension of the history of the Dogrib in relation to the fur trade.

In the last half of the nineteenth century, the prolific Petitot was the single committed scholar of the Mackenzie drainage Athapaskans. The travel accounts of Petitot (1891) and Russell (1898), unfortunately rare volumes, are the two major sources on Dogrib life in that period. Russell collected specimens of Dogrib material culture, described in his book, which are in the museum collections of the University of Iowa. Wheeler (1914) presents piecemeal but lively firsthand observations.

J.A. Mason (1946) was the first ethnologist to do fieldwork among the Dogrib, in the summer of 1913. The next ethnological report based on fieldwork is that of Helm and Lurie (1961) on the subsistence economy of the Lac la Martre Dogribs. Helm and Lurie (1966) deal with the Dogrib hand game; Helm and Thomas (1966), with Dogrib legends; and Helm (1965, 1965a, 1968a), with aspects of social organization. Schmidt (1971) emphasizes subsistence activities and the changing economy of the Rae Dogrib. For a general summary description of Dogrib culture, see Helm (1972).

Linguistic fieldwork was begun in 1965 by Howren (1968, 1970, 1971, 1975, 1979) and Ackroyd (1979).

Unless otherwise specified, data presented in the text are from Helm's (1959–1971) field notes.

Bearlake Indians

BERYL C. GILLESPIE

The Bearlake ('bārlāk) Indians speak a language of the Northeastern Athapaskan language group closely related to Mountain, Hare, and Dogrib (Howren 1975:583).*

The population of Bearlake Indians is made up of the descendants of mainly Dogrib, Hare, and Slavey Indian groups who came into frequent contact with one another after the establishment of fur-trading posts at or near Great Bear Lake. Chapters (in this vol.) on the Dogrib, Hare, and Slavey adequately describe the various aspects of native life and culture that also characterize the Bearlake Indians. The emphasis of this chapter is the historic factors that gave rise to the Bearlake population as a distinctive people.

Territory and Environment

The Bearlake Indians exploit the shores of Great Bear Lake (the largest lake fully within Canada's boundaries) and the adjacent areas (fig. 1). Great Bear Lake lies between 65° north latitude and the Arctic Circle in the Northwest Territories. The region has a subarctic climate and vegetation. It is within the northwest transition section of the boreal forest. Stands of stunted black and white spruce, birch, poplar, and willow are intermixed with muskeg, outcroppings of rock, and many small lakes (J.S. Rowe 1972:55).

*The phonemes of Bearlake are: (unaspirated stops and affricates) b, d, λ, ʒ, ǯ, g, gʷ, ˀ; (aspirated stops and affricates) t, ƛ, c, č, k, kʷ; (glottalized) t̓, ƛ̓, c̓, č̓, k̓, k̓ʷ; (voiceless continuants) ł, s, š, x, W, h; (voiced continuants) l, z, ž, γ, w; (nasals) m, n; (resonants) r, y; (plain vowels) i, e, ε, a, o, u; (nasalized vowels) į, ę, ą, ǫ, ų; (long vowels) e·, a·, o·, ǫ·; (tones) high (v́), low (unmarked). There is considerable diversity among Bearlake speakers, reflecting both age-dialect differences and contacts with Hare, Mountain, and Dogrib. ž is in free variation with y, ą and ų generally merge with ǫ, and there are a number of types of variation affecting certain sounds in certain words. The speakers who use ẇ for kʷ in certain forms have one additional phoneme.

In the practical orthography used by the Department of Education of the Northwest Territories the Bearlake phonemes are written as follows: b, d, dl, dz, j, g, gw, ˀ; t, tł, ts, ch, k, kw; t', tł', ts', ch', k', kw'; ł, s, sh, x, wh, h; l, z, zh, gh, w; m, n; r, y; i, i̱e, e, a, o, u; į, ę, ą, ǫ, ų; ee, aa, oo, ǫǫ; high tone (v́). The writing of e as i̱e and ε as e (to conform to Hare orthography) was tentative in 1979.

Information on Bearlake phonology and the practical orthography was furnished by Keren Rice (communication to editors 1979), who also checked the transcription of the cited form.

History and Identity

There is a general agreement throughout the historical literature that Hare Indians exploited the region from Great Bear Lake northward to the tree line and that Dogrib ranged between Great Bear Lake and Great Slave Lake. A part of the Slavey Indian exploitative range was southwest and west of Great Bear Lake. From 1799 to 1815 (Stager 1962:38), during the existence of the North West Company's trading post on Great Bear Lake at the later location of Fort Franklin, a good fishery site, traders reported that groups from these three populations visited the post, as did the Yellowknife who were coming by way of the east end of the lake (McKenzie 1805; Keith 1889–1890, 2). Whether the Yellowknife aboriginal range included the eastern end of Great Bear Lake is not known since the attraction of a trading post might have encouraged them to travel and exploit new areas. With their "defeat" in a Dogrib revenge attack in 1823 the Yellowknife permanently retreated from the Great Bear Lake region.

With the establishment of the Hudson's Bay Company monopoly in 1821, Fort Norman on the Mackenzie

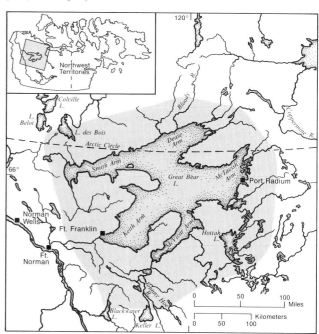

after Rushforth 1976:map 1.8.
Fig. 1. Twentieth-century territory.

Natl. Mus. of Canada, Ottawa: VI–G–55.

Fig. 2. Bearlake wooden leister, moose-bone point, lashed with sinew and babiche. Used for small fish, especially herring (Gillespie 1972). Shaft shortened, present length 110 cm, collected by C. B. Osgood in 1929.

River became the main point of trade for Indians in the Great Bear Lake region for the next 130 years. In the nineteenth century there were several expedition posts on Great Bear Lake, and Fort Norman was moved to that lake from 1863 to 1869 (Petitot 1893:65, 51), but these were only temporary installations.

With the establishment of Fort Rae on the North Arm of Great Slave Lake in 1851, some Dogribs changed trading posts, as seen from the statement in the Hudson's Bay Company Fort Rae account book for 1854 that: "Those Indians entered as 'Fort Norman Indians' [12 men] are from the vicinity of Great Bear Lake, and may now be considered as belonging to Fort Rae" (Hudson's Bay Company 1854). Although some Dogribs changed their point of trade, they continued to exploit the south side of Great Bear Lake. One group mentioned both in the literature (Russell 1898:70, 165; Wheeler 1914:60; J.A. Mason 1946:14) and in 1911 Fort Rae mission records (Helm 1962) stopped trading into Fort Rae in 1914 and changed their allegiance to Fort Norman (Osgood 1932:33). An elderly member of the original migrant group recalled in 1971 that when they moved to Great Bear Lake the people there were good to them, encouraging them to stay permanently (Naedzo 1971). In 1972 the priest at Fort Franklin estimated that 80 percent of the people of that hamlet "are Rae people to a certain extent" (Denis 1972).

From scattered and limited historical materials it can be gleaned that there were a couple of groups of both Dogrib and Hare that were associated with the Great Bear Lake region. At least one group of each people, as well as some Slavey and Mountain Indians, were continuously trading at Fort Norman and gradually merging with the others through intermarriage. Osgood (1932) in 1928 was the first ethnographer to see the Bearlake Indians as a distinct entity, following their self-designation. Rushforth (1976:38) has identified the regional exploitative areas within the Great Bear Lake region as perceived by the Bearlake Indians in the mid-1970s. These areas closely conform to those described by Osgood (1936:7) from his 1928 fieldwork, indicating continuity in land use and occupancy patterns over a half-century.

There were a number of small trading operations around Great Bear Lake during the first half of the nineteenth century (Usher 1971:71–72), but they had little effect on the focus of trade at Fort Norman. With the discovery of pitchblende and silver at Port Radium in the 1930s there was greater activity in the area but modest impact on the native way of life.

Fort Norman continued to be the point of trade for Bearlake Indians as well as for some Slavey and Mountain Indians. The mission records of Fort Norman in the 1930s still distinguished Slavey and Mountain Indians as well as the Bearlake Indians (Gens du Lac d'Ours), who consisted of two sectors, Dogrib and Hare (Gillespie 1971). With the re-establishment of the Hudson's Bay Company store at Fort Franklin in 1950 a majority of the Indians shifted their trade to that post. Since the 1950s the settlement of Fort Franklin has had government administration (fig. 3) and service installations as well as a Roman Catholic church (fig. 4). Especially the school, nursing station, and federally supported housing program have settled the population at Fort Franklin.

Population

At least one and sometimes two groups of Dogribs associated with the Great Bear region traded into Fort Rae in the second half of the nineteenth century and the first part of the twentieth century. Similarly a group of Hare Indians trading into Fort Good Hope exploited

Native Press, Yellowknife, N.W.T.

Fig. 3. Federal Indian Affairs representative (right) shaking hands to open the annual treaty payments to Indians registered under Treaty No. 11 signed in 1921. Photographed at Ft. Franklin, June 1975.

Fig. 4. An aerial view of Ft. Franklin with the Roman Catholic church in the center. Photograph by René Fumoleau, Jan. 1968.

Fig. 5. Family at their fish camp near Ft. Norman. Photographed about 1971.

Fig. 6. Naidzo (b.1887, d.1973) a Dogrib Indian known as The Bearlake Prophet. He was a great moral leader, and he excelled in relating traditional legends. Photograph by René Fumoleau, Ft. Franklin, July 1968.

the Great Bear Lake region. But Fort Norman was the primary center of trade and represented the main body of Indians exploiting the Great Bear Lake region. In 1851 the Hudson's Bay Company trader James Anderson (1858) estimated for Fort Norman 103 Hare, 133 Dogrib, 84 Slave, and 43 "Nahanies" (Mountain Indians), giving a total of 363. In 1892 Ducot (1892) estimated the Fort Norman Indian population to be 352.

Population figures for the first half of the twentieth century are meager but do indicate an almost negligible increase for the total population. With adequate medical services introduced in the 1950s, the population figures for the 1960s and 1970s show a substantial increase in total population as shown in table 1. Table 1 also shows the great proportion of the population formerly counted at Fort Norman that became registered at Fort Franklin after it was re-established.

Synonymy†

The people of Great Bear Lake refer to themselves as *sahtú gotine* 'bear-lake people' (Osgood 1932:35; Keren Rice, communication to editors 1979), or in English as Bearlake Indians. Osgood introduced as an English

†This synonymy was written by Beryl G. Gillespie and edited by Ives Goddard, incorporating suggestions from Keren Rice (communication to editors 1979).

designation the arbitrarily shortened form Satudene, but although this has been used in the secondary literature (for example, Murdock and O'Leary 1975), Osgood (1936:7) himself later referred to these people only as the Bear Lake Indians.

The main difficulty with the term Bearlake Indians, as used historically, is the imprecision that results from the fact that the Hare and the Dogrib have employed

Table 1. Population

Year	Fort Norman	Fort Franklin	Total	Source
1914	366		366	Ducot 1914
1924	370		370	Canada, Dominion of 1924:57
1941	374		374	Robinson and Robinson 1947:153
1952	129	238	367	Gillespie 1971
1964	136	289	425	Canada. Department of Citizenship and Immigration. Indian Affairs Branch 1964:45
1969	164	360	524	Canada. Department of Indian Affairs and Northern Development. Indian Affairs Branch 1970:37
1973	189	408	597	Canada. Department of Indian Affairs and Northern Development. Indian Affairs Branch 1973
1978	214	466	680	Canada. Department of Indian Affairs and Northern Development 1980:47

in their own languages terms cognate with *sahtú gotine* to refer to any people exploiting the Great Bear Lake region, including members of their own groups. Petitot's (1876a:xx) reference to one group of Hare as the Sa-tchô t'u gottiné 'people of Great Bear Lake' (the Athapaskan is 'people of big-bear lake') may reflect this usage at a time when the Bearlake Indians had perhaps not yet emerged as a separate group, though it is noteworthy that in his dictionary Petitot (1876a:xlvi) indicates some words as belonging to the distinct dialect of the Hare of Great Bear Lake (Peaux de Lièvre du grand lac des Ours). On the other hand, in the genealogical record that he began in the 1860s Petitot (1867–1920:2) included both Hare and Dogrib Indians of the Great Bear Lake region under the category of Gens du Lac d'Ours 'Bear Lake People'.

Sources

Osgood's (1932) monograph on the Bearlake Indians is the only ethnography on these people. In the historical literature only brief references are made to Dogrib and Hare Indians in the Great Bear Lake region. The first descriptions of these populations are from two North West Company traders, McKenzie (1805) and Keith (1889–1890, 2). Sir John Franklin's (1828) account of his second arctic expedition, which first gave the name Fort Franklin to the present site, provides some descriptions of native life. On later expeditions in the nineteenth century T. Simpson (1843) and Richardson (1851) made brief comments on the Indians exploiting the region. Petitot (1893), an Oblate priest who lived with the Indians of the Great Bear Lake region in the 1860s, provides some ethnographic and historical information.

From his field notes of 1928 Osgood (1975) has compiled the native terms and descriptions of topographical features of the Great Bear Lake area. Morris (1973) has reviewed the historical literature on the region with an emphasis on demographic and ecological data. Rushforth (1976, 1977) made a thorough report on the Bearlake Indians' hunting and trapping economy as it continued with vigor in the 1970s.

Hare

JOEL S. SAVISHINSKY AND HIROKO SUE HARA

Language and Territory

The Hare ('hār) Indians are a group of Athapaskan-speaking people who have lived, since at least the late eighteenth century, in the forested areas of northwestern Canada that border the lower Mackenzie River valley.* In their nomadic pursuit of a hunting, fishing, and trapping way of life, the Hare have utilized a territorial range extending eastward from the Yukon side of the continental divide, across the Mackenzie River, into the regions to the west and northwest of Great Bear Lake. In their traditional pursuits, members of the various bands in this area, who have been collectively designated as Hare by Whites and neighboring indigenous peoples, have also traveled as far north as the Mackenzie delta and periodically crossed the tree line along the Horton and Anderson rivers to hunt caribou on the Barren Grounds (fig. 1).

Identity

Traditionally, the Hare were not organized into a unified tribal entity and did not recognize any central authority or corporate group structure among their numbers. The tribal designation of Hare is as much a reflection of administrative and ethnographic convenience as it is of cultural identity (cf. Osgood 1936:3; MacNeish 1956:132–133). Both before and until well

*The phonemes of Hare (as spoken at both Fort Good Hope and Colville Lake) are: (unaspirated stops and affricates) *b, d, λ, ʒ, ǯ, g, gʷ, ʔ*; (aspirated stops) *t, k*; (glottalized stops, affricates, and continuant) *ƚ, x̣, c̓, č̓, k̓, w̓*; (voiceless continuants) *f* [f~ɸ], *ł, s, š, x, h*; (voiced continuants) *l, z, ž, γ, w*; (nasals) *m, n*; (resonants) *r, y*; (plain vowels and diphthong) *i, ie̯, e* [ɛ], *a, o, u*; (nasalized vowels) *į, ę, ą, ǫ, ų*; (tones) high (v́), low (unmarked). There is some variation among individuals in the pronunciation of certain sounds and words. *ų* is pronounced like *ǫ* and *ž* like *y* by all but the most conservative speakers; the pronunciation of *ǫ* as *ǫ* is also common. There is variation between *gʷ* and *b, x* may be replaced by *k* or *f* in some words, and for some speakers *t* and *ƚ* vary with *k* and *k̓* before front vowels.

In the practical orthography used by the Department of Education of the Northwest Territories the Hare phonemes are written as follows: b, d, dl, dz, j, g, gw, '; t, k; t', tł', ts', ch', k', w'; f, ł, s, sh, x, h; l, z, zh, gh, w; m, n; r, y; i, ie̯, e, a, o, u; į, ę, ą, ǫ, ų; high tone (v́).

Information on Hare phonology and the practical orthography was furnished by Keren Rice (communication to editors 1979), who also checked the transcription of the forms cited.

after the establishment of fur-trading posts in the nineteenth century, the native people of the lower Mackenzie area composed a series of semiautonomous, nomadic bands whose membership, size, and location fluctuated considerably over time. These bands shared many cultural similarities with the neighboring eastern Kutchin, Dogrib, Mountain, and Slavey Indians; but in some regards, including geographical, technological, behavioral, and possibly linguistic features, the Hare were distinctive enough as a people to warrant being given an ethnic designation by their Athapaskan-speaking neighbors.

In 1789 Alexander Mackenzie made the first journey by a European into this region. His Indian guides and the members of other native groups whom he met along his route identified the Hare to him as a separate people. In his report, Mackenzie (1801:44) noted the people's distinctively heavy reliance upon hare skins for clothing, but he also emphasized that the Hare otherwise closely resembled the different native bands he

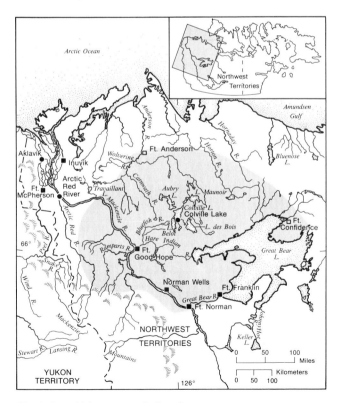

Fig. 1. Late 19th-century tribal territory.

had already encountered. Later explorers (for example, Richardson 1851, 2:3–4) also stressed that the Hare's dependence upon the varying or snowshoe hare for food and apparel was one of their few distinguishing characteristics as a people. The members of constituent bands gathered together several times a year for ceremonial purposes and for joint hunting and fishing pursuits during caribou migrations and spawning seasons. The communal feasting, dancing, and gambling that accompanied these activities undoubtedly contributed to a sense of group identity among them (Hurlbert 1962:72). In addition to these ecological and ceremonial dimensions, the Hare also had a wide reputation for timidity, as indicated by their reported fear of the Kutchin, the Eskimo, and strangers in general, and this was similarly emphasized by early writers as another distinctive trait that set them apart from neighboring ethnic groups (Mackenzie 1801:44, 50; Richardson 1851, 1:211–212, 352–353; Jenness 1932:392–395).

The Hare were probably also characterized by some dialectal differences from the surrounding Athapaskan peoples, for although there are no adequate linguistic data for the periods of early contact, studies in phonology and morphology indicate a pattern of dialectal divergence in the area dating back to at least the mid-nineteenth century (Hoijer 1966; Howren 1970, 1975). However, for older people in the mid-twentieth century the Hare dialect was mutually intelligible with Bearlake, Mountain, and Slavey, spoken at Fort Norman and Fort Franklin, and this mutual intelligibility must have obtained in earlier times as well; the mutual intelligibility with Dogrib is, and probably was, much less (Keren Rice, communication to editors 1979). These five forms of speech make up the distinct linguistic subgroup called Northeastern Athapaskan by Howren (1975; see "Northern Athapaskan Languages," this vol.).

Corresponding to this linguistic continuity between the Hare and their neighbors was a geographic overlap among many of these groups. The seasonal pursuit of caribou to the north, east, and northeast brought some of the Hare bands into contact with the Eskimo, the Dogrib, and perhaps the Chipewyan, while hunting and fishing activities to the north, south, and west by bands along the Mackenzie involved contact with the eastern Kutchin, Slavey, Mountain Indians, and Mackenzie Eskimo. Twentieth-century folklore among the Hare emphasizes the hostile nature of certain of these experiences, especially the encounters with the Eskimo. If evidence from the nineteenth century is indicative of other aspects of these earlier relationships, then trade and intermarriage with other Indian groups were undoubtedly present as interethnic features during the precontact situation as well. One nineteenth-century band on the northwestern periphery of the Hare area was called in Hare *ne la gotine* 'end of the earth people'

and in French *Bâtards Loucheux*, signifying this group's biological and cultural overlap with one such neighboring people, the Loucheux or eastern Kutchin (Petitot 1876:xx). Therefore, in regard to aboriginal conditions, the available evidence indicates that the Hare comprised a number of bands that shared linguistic, cultural, kinship, and territorial bonds that only partially distinguished them from other such loose groupings in the Mackenzie area.

One long-range consequence of Euro-Canadian influence in the North since the early nineteenth century has been the development of a much more clearly defined sense of identity among the Hare. Traditionally, since large regional groupings were seasonal and transient in nature, Indian people in the area were identified primarily in terms of their affiliation with local geographic bands; however, band identity was also highly variable over time because of the mutability of these groups. Migration, intermarriage, ecological fluctuation, and population decimation through starvation and epidemic diseases are factors that have led to the continual redefinition, reconstitution, and relocation of Hare bands throughout the nineteenth and twentieth centuries. This is borne out by the inconsistencies contained in the several band lists that have been published since the mid-nineteenth century (Petitot 1875, 1876, 1889, 1891, 1893; Osgood 1932; Hurlbert 1962; Sue 1964).

In contrast to the fluctuating nature of band organization among the Hare, the establishment of trading posts (or "forts") in the nineteenth century encouraged regional concentrations of Indian populations. Ethnic groups have been simultaneously redefined and made more sedentary through their mutual identification with, and congregation at, a home town or "point of trade" (Helm and Damas 1963:10). Since trading forts were strategically placed to maximize trade and supply possibilities, they often attracted native people from several ethnic or dialectal groups. Later developments, especially the governmental organization of fort populations into official "bands" for the signing of treaties and for administrative purposes and the subsequent creation of mutually exclusive "game areas" for some of these "bands," have further intensified the people's sense of geographic and ethnic separateness from other officially defined "bands" (Sue 1964:1–5).

Since the mid-eighteenth century, different Hare groups have been drawn into the populations of Forts Good Hope and Norman on the Mackenzie and Fort Franklin on Great Bear Lake. In terms of aboriginal groupings, the ethnic composition of the last two forts is complex, and native identities have consequently been altered: the Hare descendants at Franklin identify themselves as Bearlake Indians, and many of the natives at Fort Norman, although officially designated Hare by the government, consider themselves to be

Fig. 2. Indians (left) and 3 Métis interpreters (right) for the Hudson's Bay Company at Ft. Good Hope. Several men wear caps of the "smoking hat" type, popular at the time, which were sometimes highly decorated with floral and geometric designs. Photograph by Elizabeth Taylor, 1892.

Slavey or Bearlake Indians (see "Slavey" and "Bearlake Indians," this vol.). Although it is also ethnically mixed, the situation in the Fort Good Hope area is less ambiguous, for its Indian population is primarily of Hare origin. The people at Good Hope, and those of the satellite community of Colville Lake—which developed from the fort's population in the early 1960s and whose members are primarily descended from a nineteenth-century Hare band, *Gens du Large*, that was centered around old Fort Anderson in the Colville area—thus constitute the greatest concentration of Hare within that people's traditional territory.

The native peoples distinguished by the Hare are the Eskimos and several kinds of Indians: (1) themselves; (2) the Mountain Indians, who are considered to be most closely related by the Hare through kinship ties and linguistic proximity; (3) Bearlake Indians, with whom the Hare feel friendly because of intermarriage; (4) the eastern Kutchin, with whom the Hare also intermarry, but with whom they feel a bit uneasy; (5) the Dogrib Indians, with whom contemporary Hare have relatively little direct contact, except in the Great Bear Lake region; and (6) more southerly groups such as the Slavey and Chipewyan, with whom the Hare recognize a distant linguistic and historical connection, and the Cree, whose postcontact encounters with the Hare are often characterized as hostile in the people's contemporary folklore. Among themselves, the Hare also distinguish a number of localized bands that are formed on a seasonal basis for subsistence and trapping activities; as in earlier centuries, individuals and families are thought of in terms of their affiliation with one of these

groupings. The bands are usually identified by descriptive terms consisting of a locational expression followed by *gotine* 'people'. Examples of such groups are the *die̥ho gá gotine* 'along-the-river people' along the Mackenzie and the *duta gotine* 'among-the-islands people' at the north end of Colville Lake.

The Hare have a consciousness of themselves as a distinct people and an even sharper sense of their membership in more localized groups. They apply the concept and term *segotine* 'my people' not only to their close relatives but also to all the people with whom they have a sense of group affinity. For the Hare at Fort Good Hope and Colville Lake this includes not only the native people in these two neighboring communities but also many persons at Forts Norman and Franklin and selected individuals who have migrated to other regional settlements.

Culture

The aboriginal culture of the Hare Indians is difficult to reconstruct because of a paucity of descriptive material immediately after contact. For several decades after Mackenzie's initial contact with them, accounts of the Hare by traders and explorers were fragmentary, and it is probable that the Hare were already being indirectly influenced by the fur trade prior to Mackenzie's journey. More substantial material on the Hare is included in the writings of missionaries and travelers during the second half of the nineteenth century, especially in the works of Émile Petitot, John

316

Richardson, and Bernard R. Ross, and these sources provide valuable discussions of Indian culture during an era when many aboriginal elements were still a viable part of the people's lifeway. Detailed ethnographic studies of the Hare in the twentieth century yield a picture of their culture that includes both aboriginal features and their modified persistence under more recent conditions (Osgood 1932; MacNeish 1960; Hurlbert 1962; Sue 1964, 1965; Helm 1965, 1968, 1969; Savishinsky 1970, 1970a, 1971, 1972, 1974, 1975; Savishinsky and Frimmer 1973). Given these limits on knowledge of earlier times, then, and the fact that the Hare's sense of their own past is actually a mélange of aboriginal and contact-era elements, it is both necessary and appropriate to consider the people's traditional culture in these historical terms, rather than as a strictly aboriginal phenomenon.

Subsistence

The precariousness of Hare existence was one of the most striking and persistent features of their early condition. The dependence of many bands upon the snowshoe hare for subsistence led to periodic starvation whenever the cyclically fluctuating hare population reached a low point every 7 to 10 years (cf. Rand 1945:74). Caribou, moose, and fish were often not sufficient or reliable enough as food sources to compensate for this cyclical phenomenon, and death from starvation occurred regularly throughout the nineteenth century and as recently as 1920 (Wentzel 1889–1890, 1:106–107; Keith 1889–1890, 2:118–119; Hooper 1853:305; Petitot 1889:39–44; Sue 1964:53, 55, 231). Even a Western technology of iron, netting (fig. 3), and guns, which was gradually made accessible to the Hare beginning in the early nineteenth century, was no guarantee of survival during much of the contact era.

Hare Indian population was small and low in density, with perhaps 700 to 800 people occupying an area of about 45,000 square miles at the time of European contact (Mooney 1928:26; Osgood 1936). The size and membership of Hare bands fluctuated as a consequence of the mobility imposed by the food quest and the periodic depopulation to which the people were subjected.

The territory utilized by the Hare was ecologically diversified, including mountain, taiga, tundra, and transitional zones, and particular bands may have focused their subsistence activities on different regions within this range. Groups to the southwest, along the Mackenzie, were within a birch, poplar, and willow zone; hence, their major large game animal was moose. Barren Ground caribou rarely migrated into this zone, but groups to the northeast were in the heart of the caribou's winter range, and by following the herds across the tree line and onto the barrens during the late sum-

Fig. 3. Charlie Codzi tying a rock sinker onto his nylon gill net; wooden floats in foreground await attachment. Photograph by Joel Savishinsky at Lugetenetue Lake, north of Colville Lake, N.W.T., May 1968.

mer as well, these northeast bands had a much more plentiful, though much more migratory, source of food and clothing (J.S. Rowe 1972; Kelsall 1968:53).

Freshwater lakes in the northeast region were well stocked with trout, whitefish, and other species, and the Mackenzie River was an important source of fish, especially during the summer. Large game were taken with bows, arrows, spears, snares, pounds, and deadfalls. Smaller game such as hare and ptarmigan were snared, and fish were caught with hooks, willow-bark nets, and by the use of weirs and dams along narrow streams (Sue 1964:163–212).

Plant substances were of minor significance in the people's diet: rose hips and several types of berries were eaten in the summer and fall, certain mosses and lichens were boiled to make beverages and medicines, and the vegetable matter in the stomachs of caribou, moose, and other herbivores was also consumed. Spruce sap was chewed as a gum and utilized as a poultice and covering for wounds. Cooking methods included roasting and stone-boiling, with some of the people's favorite delicacies being caribou tongue, caribou fetus, muskrat, and beaver tail. Meat and fish were sometimes pounded up with grease and berries to make pemmican. Excess foodstuffs were preserved by freezing and cacheing during the winter and by drying (fig. 4) and smoking techniques during the summer (Sue 1964:163–225).

Clothing and Adornment

Moose, caribou, and fur-bearing animals supplemented hare skins for clothing and blankets. During the winter caribou and moose hides were used with the hair left on for pants, leggings, hoods, jackets, skirts, and capes; tanned hides with the hair removed were made into mittens and footwear. Hare skins were cut spirally into long, continuous strips and woven to form capes, shirts, blankets, and other items of apparel ("Environment and Culture in the Shield and Mackenzie Borderlands," fig. 13, this vol.). Porcupine quills and possibly moose hair were used for decorative motifs on clothing. The Hare also practiced facial tattooing and painting for body ornamentation (Keith 1889–1890, 2:121–122; Richardson 1851, 1:357, 380, 392–393, 2:3, 7–11, 25–26; Sue 1964:184, 191, 237–263).

Transport

Spruce, birchbark, and occasionally moose-hide canoes were utilized for summer transport on lakes and rivers. Winter travel was mainly accomplished on foot and on snowshoe since the Hare possessed few dogs for traction purposes until the early twentieth century (Sue 1964:279–299). In the nineteenth century, a small breed of dog is reported to have been used for moose hunting on the spring crust (Richardson 1851, 2:25–26; Wentzel 1889–1890, 1). Toboggans made of wood or caribou leg hides, loaded with the minimal possessions of families, were usually dragged by women during the migratory phases of the annual cycle.

Technology

Knives, blades, bows, arrows, spears, scrapers, chisels, needles, and containers were variously manufactured from stone, bone, antler, wood, bark, and beaver teeth. Caribou intestines also served as containers for fat and grease. For snares, snowshoe lacing, sewing, and cordage, caribou sinew and babiche were essential materials

Fig. 4. A summer camp near Ft. Good Hope with inconnu fish drying on rack and Martha Rabesca tanning a hide. Photograph by René Fumoleau, Aug. 1969.

Native Press, Yellowknife. N.W.T.

Fig. 5. Chief Kotchile and family at their camp. A tanned moosehide hangs over a line behind the tent, and snowshoes, ax, and bow saw are wedged in the snow. Sled dogs are staked (left) as they always are now when not in harness or working. Photograph possibly by David Kelly, March 1971.

("Environment and Culture in the Shield and Mackenzie Borderlands," fig. 15, this vol.) (Sue 1964:113).

Tepee and lean-to structures of poles were covered with hides, moss, and brush to provide shelter.

Social Organization

Kinship was traced bilaterally, and the terminology was of the bifurcate merging type, with the Iroquoian system of cousin classification (MacNeish 1960). Marriage forms alluded to by early observers included sister-exchange, sororate, and levirate unions, with polygyny being a possibility for those few men who could maintain large families. Polyandry is also reported, which may have been a consequence of an imbalance in the sex ratio among the Hare (cf. Sue 1964:422 ff.). These traditional marriage patterns, evidence for which often consists primarily of casual comments by informants and early observers, are difficult to substantiate or quantify (see Helm 1968 for a statistical refutation of cross-cousin marriage as an actual practice among the Hare). Although bands were without institutionalized or formal leadership, good hunters and powerful shamans of reputation could attract a following of kinsmen and affines, thus providing an organizing principle for such groupings. Clusters of male siblings and their bilaterally related kin also served as the focus for the creation of seasonal or long-term bands.

People usually entered into marriage relations by their early teen years (Keith 1889–1890, 2:114; Ross 1872:305; Petitot 1876a:32). Children were often betrothed by their parents at a young age, although unions were easily dissolved if the partners were incompatible. Although the Hare had no formal marriage ceremony, a man was expected to fulfill a period of bride service for his wife's family, and postmarital residence was therefore initially uxorilocal. Couples, families, and individuals could shift residence between different bands on the basis of bilateral and affinal ties, and a far-flung and diffuse kinship system of this type was a key feature of the fluidity that characterized Hare social organization (Savishinsky 1970). This structural flexibility was adaptive both for redistributing the population among scarce and variable ecological resources and for allowing the people to re-form bands following the decimations caused by raids, diseases, and episodes of widespread starvation. Individuals were also wary of prolonged, solitary separation from people because of its dehumanizing consequences: a belief in forest-dwelling "bush men" (*rare²į*, literally 'he hides'), persons who had become cannibalistic because of their isolation from people, reinforced the necessarily social nature of existence (Sue 1964:225–227).

Shamanism and Curing

Supernatural powers and practices were also relied upon by the Hare to contend with the problems and challenges of existence. Although visions were usually not sought in a purposeful quest, they were frequently achieved in dreams, and the people placed great faith in the predictive efficacy of dreams to guide them in their actions and decisions. Medicine men (*²ećene gotine*), who had established special relationships with guardian spirits through dreams and visions, demonstrated their power by sleight-of-hand, and they were looked to by the people for assistance in the face of hardship and danger. By singing and invoking the aid of their spirits, they could call game and caribou in times of starvation and overcome enemies in cases of raids and warfare. In cases of diseases and bodily ailments, the medicine men sought cures by utilizing their supernatural powers in conjunction with trance states, singing, the use of native medicines, and sucking and removing from the afflicted part of the body a small object (cf. Keith 1889–1890, 2:118; Sue 1964:336–376). According to Jenness (1932:395), Hare medicine men "permitted themselves to be suspended in the air to facilitate communion with their guardian spirits." In the nineteenth century, Franklin (1824, 2:83) and McLean (1932:324) both wrote that the medicine men of the Hare were greatly respected by the Indian people of the area, although Richardson (1851, 2:22) notes their declining influence by the mid-nineteenth century as a result of White contact. Yet over 100 years later, the people of Colville Lake and Fort Good Hope still turned to those individuals who had "strong medicine" to cure them of ailments when Western techniques were unavailable, insufficient, or ineffective (Sue 1964:366–375; Savishinsky 1970a:96–100).

Life Cycle

Hare culture also involved various kinds of ceremonial and proscriptive procedures that marked events and crises in the lives of individuals or groups. At menarche, young girls were isolated in a special shelter and required to observe a series of food and touching taboos. There were a large number of such proscriptions that females were expected to observe following this recognition of their maturity. Menstruating women were forbidden to step over fish nets and hunting implements and prohibited from skinning or eating the parts of certain animals in order to insure the success of the men in subsistence activities and to safeguard the well-being of their families and children. All adults followed a series of comparable restrictions on the killing, cooking, and handling of game animals, taboos that were held to be prophylactic measures against hunger, disease, death, and bad weather (cf. Sue 1964:119ff.). The people as a whole refrained from eating wolves, wolverines, and dogs, a proscription explained by their belief that dogs were "dirty" animals and that wolves and wolverines ate them. These taboos may also be related to a widespread mythological concept among the northern Athapaskans concerning their aboriginal descent from a dog or wolflike ancestor (Birket-Smith and De Laguna 1938:57, 427–429, 492; "Dogrib," this vol.; McKennan 1959: 162–163; Savishinsky 1975).

There was no ritual elaboration of birth or of male puberty among the Hare, although a feast would often be given to mark the first kill of a large game animal by a young adult male. Petitot notes a form of bear ceremonialism (1893:13) and also a ritual feast marking the advent of spring (1876a:95). In some accounts the spring rite is reported to be held only in conjunction with a lunar eclipse (Osgood 1932:86; Hurlbert 1962:65). In regard to other temporal concepts, the Hare divided the year into a series of lunar months, most of which were named for major ecological events, and they considered the spring equinox to mark the beginning of a new yearly cycle (Petitot 1876:xxii).

Scaffold burials were used to dispose of the dead, and a pennant was erected near the site in order to amuse and keep the deceased's ghost (ʔewį) near the grave, thus preventing it from haunting the living (Hurlbert 1962:66). Ghosts were greatly feared, and a number of propitiatory acts were performed to placate them: travelers passing near a grave offered food to the deceased, and morsels of food were thrown into a fire when it hissed in answer to what was interpreted to be a call from the dead. Nonkinsmen recruited to conduct a burial for a family henceforth occupied the special status of seċeʔǫ to these people, and they were required to follow an avoidance relationship with the deceased's kin. Traditionally, all the property of the deceased, and the possessions of all his immediate kinsmen, were destroyed at death, but by the mid-twentieth century, the destruction of kin's belongings had been modified to the point where houses, dogs, radios, and other valuable material possessions were instead preserved and redistributed. The Hare continue to maintain a firm belief in reincarnation, and a newborn infant or child who physically or behaviorally resembles a recently deceased person, or who dreams about such an individual, is often named after that person in accord with the concept that he or she is that individual's avatar (Sue 1964:344–361).

Values

The Hare placed a strong emphasis upon sharing, a value that is still manifested by them in many ways. Children were easily adopted between different families, thus assisting both childless couples and parentless children and redistributing young people among those who most needed and could best care for them. Traditionally, surplus food was also shared within the band, and a successful hunter usually gave away large game, such as moose and caribou, to another person, who then distributed the kill among the people (Savishinsky 1970; Sue 1964:299–304, 433–436). There was no ownership or inheritance of territory or resources among the Hare, and groups and individuals enjoyed control only over those areas that they were currently using. Local bands might periodically alternate among a series of seasonal camping sites, but such patterns were subject to the stability and availability of resources, features that did not have a high degree of predictability. Seasonal and long-term mobility was thus maintained at a high level, vitiating the need for, or the possibility of, family or band-owned hunting or trapping territories. The periodic aggregation of several small bands for ceremonial and subsistence activities allowed for the renewal of ties on a regional basis. The sociability of these reunions, involving upward of perhaps 200 people, was invested with drum dancing, the recitation of folklore, the arrangement of marriages, and forms of communal gambling such as ʔuʒi, a type of Athapaskan hand game. These seasonal assemblages counterpointed the extreme and prolonged dispersals that characterized the bulk of the Hare's annual cycle under these traditional conditions (Hurlbert 1962:72; Savishinsky 1970a:86–91).

History of Indian-White Contact

With the advent of direct White contact in the late eighteenth century, the Hare Indians became increasingly involved with the fur trade and with the array of Western goods, services, and institutions that accompanied it. During the preceding century, as European fur companies expanded westward from lower Hudson Bay, some trade goods had probably already reached the Hare, since, according to Mackenzie (1801:83), the neighboring Dogribs were in possession of iron and other materials by the time of his journey in 1789. It is also possible that the Hare may have been forced into a more northerly territory during this period because of the pressures created by the raids of the Cree and Chipewyan on the peoples of the Mackenzie valley.

Following two attempts to establish posts near the present site of Fort Franklin at the turn of the nineteenth century, Fort Good Hope was the first post north of the Great Bear River to be built in the region of the Hare. At its establishment by the North West Company in 1806, it was the most northerly fort of its time (Petitot 1887; Robinson and Robinson 1947:133–134). Erected at the mouth of the Bluefish River near the Mackenzie (67°27′ north latitude), the commercial interests at the post were later taken over by the Hudson's Bay Company, which absorbed the North West Company in 1821. In the next several years, the fort's location was changed several times. In 1823 it was moved two days' travel downriver to the intersection of the Mackenzie

and Travaillant rivers in order to facilitate trade with the eastern Kutchin and Eskimo; then, in 1827, to allow for more satisfactory provisioning and access to the Hare, its location was shifted southward to Manitou Island, across from the site of the present fort (fig. 6). Finally in 1836, after the island site had been damaged for several years by severe ice conditions during the annual breakup, the fort was moved to the east bank of the river (Hurlbert 1962:10; Sue 1964:46–49).

Trapping was encouraged through the provision of trade goods to the Hare, thus creating an irreversible and ever-increasing commitment on their part to Western technology. As at other posts in the Northwest, the people's involvement was enhanced by the institution of a debt system, and it was routinized by the traders' creation of native "trading chiefs" or "leaders" who exercised authority over the people during their trips to the fort. The trading possibilities at Good Hope attracted Mountain Indians, Kutchin, and other peoples as well as the Hare, with the result that, during the first half of the nineteenth century, members of several ethnic groups were drawn into the fort's population (Franklin 1824, 2:83–87; Richardson 1851, 2:7; Sue

Fig. 6. Aerial view of Ft. Good Hope, N.W.T. Mackenzie River is at left, Jackson Creek at right. Photograph by René Fumoleau, May 1969.

1964:3). While trade with the Eskimo fell off at Good Hope because of traditional Indian-Eskimo hostility, the eastern Kutchin continued to use the fort during the 1820s and 1830s, since it was the most accessible trading post for them prior to the establishment of Peel River Post in 1840. The propinquity of the Hare and the Kutchin at Good Hope during this era is indicated by the Hudson's Bay Company's population statistics for 1829–1830, which are given in table 1.

In 1859 Father Grollier of the Roman Catholic Oblates of Mary Immaculate order arrived in Good Hope, and a mission was built there. A church was completed at the fort in 1866, and by the early twentieth century almost all the Hare were nominally Catholic through baptism and confirmation, and the people were mostly monogamous. Father Émile Petitot, who served the Good Hope congregation in the late nineteenth century, traveled widely throughout the Northwest and published extensively on Athapaskan culture and language.

The various Hare groups in the forested regions around the fort traveled to Good Hope periodically to trade, socialize, arrange marriages, seek medical assistance, and participate in religious holidays and observances. The Catholic priests inaugurated an annual religious cycle in which three major holidays were emphasized—Christmas, Easter, and the Feast of the Assumption in mid-August—and these events, along with the arrival of the trading company supply barges each summer, have since structured the timing of community ingatherings. Despite the presence of European facilities and materials, starvation was still occurring among the Hare at cyclical intervals throughout this period, and cannibalism and infanticide were reported in conjunction with famines (McLean 1932:343; Hooper 1853:303–304; Lefroy 1938:88; Hodge 1907j:667; Duchaussois 1923:279; Sue 1964:53–56, 444–445). Epidemic European diseases also decimated the population on several occasions during the nineteenth century (Sue 1964:21; Hurlbert 1962:73).

Between 1858 and 1866, the Hudson's Bay Company tried to establish a trading relationship with the Eskimo by constructing a fort on the Anderson River (68°30′ north latitude, 128° west longitude). Increasing tensions between the Kutchin and the Eskimo at this post and the outbreak of virulent scarlet fever and measles there in 1865–1866 led to the closing of Fort Anderson (Sue 1964:54–55). With the exception of this failure, the fur trade flourished in the Hare region during the last decades of the nineteenth century: the Northern Trading Company opened a store at Good Hope in the 1890s to rival the Hudson's Bay Company, while the latter expanded its own facilities at the fort. Some White employees at the post married Hare women, or had children by them, and in the first two decades of the twentieth century, some children from the fort were

Fig. 7. Roger Boniface holding beaver skins being prepared for sale. The fresh pelts are stretched on willow-hoop frames, scraped, and dried. Photograph by René Fumoleau near Ft. Good Hope, May 1969.

sent to the Fort Providence Mission Boarding School run by the Roman Catholic Church. Many gained a considerable fluency in French as a result of this experience. By 1912 some of the better Indian hunters employed by the Catholic mission and the trading companies at Good Hope had built log cabins for their homes at the fort.

Between 1860 and 1921, the Hare comprised three major geographic groups for hunting and trapping activities: the síhta goṭine, the Mountain People to the west of the Mackenzie, who are not to be confused with the Mountain Indians; the sinta goṭine, the River People along the Mackenzie; and the dela goṭine, the Lodge People, in the forested lake district to the east and north of Good Hope. It was also during this time that some of the people extended their activities westward to Lansing Creek and Mayo Lake of the Yukon drainage, in some cases as a result of the gold rush in the Dawson area, which began in 1898 (Sue 1964:53–61).

The Canadian government concluded treaties with the Mackenzie area Indians in 1921, and the Hare in the Good Hope vicinity were administratively grouped together as Band Number 5. In exchange for treaty payments and the promise of government medical and educational services, the people gave up title to their traditional lands but retained the right to utilize the natural resources for subsistence and trapping purposes.

In 1923 a Royal Canadian Mounted Police post was opened at Good Hope, and in 1926 Hare children began attending a new Catholic residential school at Aklavik, where English replaced French as the official language. Tuberculosis had become endemic by the 1930s, and by the early 1960s, when the disease had finally been brought under control, more than half the adult Hare had undergone hospitalization for it. Numerous other

Table 1. Indian Population of the Fort Good Hope Area, 1829–1830

Leaders, Chiefs	Men Hunters	Boys	Girls	Children	Women	Total	Identity
1	51	32	28		39	151	Mackenzie River Indians or Rapid Indians
2	57	51	33		44	187	Mackenzie River Indians or Outer Hare Indians
1	43	43	14		30	131	Mackenzie River Indians, Lower or Bastard Loucheux (Kutchin)
1	33	10	18		16	78	Mackenzie River Indians, Upper Loucheux (Kutchin)
1	30			37	25	93	Mackenzie River Indians, or Lower Rat Hunters, Loucheux (Kutchin)

SOURCE: Sue 1964:50, based on figures from Hudson's Bay Company records at Fort Good Hope.

European diseases continued to afflict the people on a periodically epidemic scale. In 1928, following an especially severe outbreak of influenza and cholera that killed many (table 2), ground burials were instituted to replace the more traditional scaffold interments (Sue 1964:21, 64).

The fur trade continued to flourish in the 1920s and 1930s, and people began to make much more extensive use of steel traps as compared to deadfalls. With trapping incomes at a high level, some local people opened up commercial stores of their own, although most of these collapsed with the decline of fur prices, which began in the mid-1940s; however, while the fur boom persisted, many more people built homes at Fort Good Hope, and a number of winter trapping cabins were constructed at Colville Lake as well. The 1920s and 1930s also witnessed the increasing use of Western materials such as outboard motors, firearms, kerosene lamps, and sewing machines. There was also a greater involvement in the consumption of home brew (kǫ́túé? 'fire water'), a fermented drink that the people had learned to manufacture from early traders.

The period of the Second World War introduced a number of sweeping and radical changes in the lifeways and orientations of the Hare. Larger amounts of wage labor became available, and both men and women found employment at the Norman Wells oil refinery as well as with the construction crews laying the Canol pipeline to the Yukon. As more people acquired new skills and greater levels of education, increasing numbers of them started to spend more time at the fort in pursuit of wage labor positions. With most of the people still active in hunting and trapping, a new immediacy was given to the Hare's distinction between kǫ́ę́? 'the settlement' and destta 'the bush', because of these emerging differences in native lifeways.

The collapse of fur prices after the war and the high rate of tuberculosis accelerated the concentration of people at the fort. Trapping became less economically viable as a lifeway, while at the same time more construction jobs were being created as a result of the

Canadian government's northern development policy. The opening of a school and nursing station at Good Hope in the late 1940s and the provision of government-sponsored housing and community services, including welfare, rations, and family allowances, decreased the people's involvement in bush life and cooperative living. Yet wage employment remained basically seasonal in nature, with only a handful of native people qualifying for the few full-time jobs available at the fort (Cohen 1962; Balikci and Cohen 1963; Hurlbert 1962; Sue 1964).

The experience of schooling and the economic insecurity of a more urbanized existence lengthened the process of social maturation to the point where people postponed marriages until their late teens and twenties. The decline of bush life diminished the amount of skill and competence that younger adults had for subsistence pursuits, so that although the Hare still proudly thought of the bush as a uniquely Indian world where Whites, by contrast, were ill at ease and incompetent, the cooperation, sharing, self-reliance, and involvement that once characterized native existence in the bush were becoming less and less a part of Hare reality. The older and more knowledgeable people in these traditional areas led a more secure life because of government old-age pensions. In a parallel process, the native mythology, folklore, and gambling games that they had preserved were suffering a comparable decline as radios, magazines, movies, card games, and drinking superseded them as leisure activities. The availability of Western health services also cut into the influence and role of traditional medicine men as curers, just as the presence of the RCMP and White administrators undermined the power of the medicine men, good hunters, dreamers, "treaty" chiefs, and community public opinion as the people's main sources of leadership and social control.

In the face of these trends toward increasing sedentariness and population concentration and the related decline in economic self-sufficiency, one major revitalizing move occurred among the Hare in the late

Table 2. Population of the Fort Good Hope Area, 1827–1970

Date	Men	Women	Total	Sources
1827	197	124	301(?)	Hurlbert 1962:16
1858			364	Ross in Hodge ed. 1907j:667
1867			422	Petitot 1883:653
1871	244	276	520	Hurlbert 1962:16
1921	103	105	208[a]	Hurlbert 1962:16
1922	162	162	324[a]	Hurlbert 1962:16
1923	176	183	359[a]	Hurlbert 1962:16
1928	179	171	350[a]	Hurlbert 1962:16
1929	162	146	308[a]	Hurlbert 1962:16
1934	170	156	328[a](?)	Hurlbert 1962:16
1944			337	G. Taylor 1947:72
		Whites	14	
1951			257	Hurlbert 1962:16
		Whites	28	
1955	157	134	291	Hurlbert 1962:16
1957	156	145	301	Hurlbert 1962:16
1958	170	157	327	Hurlbert 1962:16
1970	184	181	365	Canada. Department of Indian Affairs and Northern Development. Indian Affairs Branch 1970
1978	—	—	430	Canada. Department of Indian Affairs and Northern Development 1980:47

[a] Based on the Treaty Records, these figures include only those Indians who are Treaty Indians; that is, they exclude those who have become enfranchised or are the children of an enfranchised father. Members of Hare Indian Band 5 are registered whether they lived in the community that year or not. In 1921, the year of the initial treaty signing, it is probable that not all Indians had been registered in the Treaty Book.

1950s. This was largely the result of a decision taken by regional administrators to encourage greater use by the Hare of the territory's natural resources and to decrease their reliance upon welfare and wage labor. In 1959 a winter road was cut to the fur, caribou, and game-rich area of Colville Lake, and by 1962, with the help of local officials, a small community had been built up around a store and mission that had recently been established there. Fourteen families from several different bands of the Hare migrated to or resettled in this community, and these people were able to pursue a hunting, fishing, and trapping way of life with only a minimum of government assistance, and without the welfare, drinking, and unemployment problems that characterized the larger fort towns of the Mackenzie. With this partial decentralization, the majority of the Hare were thus redistributed into two permanent settlements, and since Colville Lake and Fort Good Hope are less than 100 miles apart, the members of these two communities continue to visit, communicate, and intermarry with one another, thereby maintaining their sense of a common identity.

Synonymy†

The Hare have been called the Hare Indians at least since the late eighteenth century (Mackenzie 1801:44);

†This synonymy was written by Joel S. Savishinsky and Ives Goddard, incorporating information from Hiroko Sue Hara and (where indicated) from Keren Rice.

the name refers to their heavy dependence on the varying hare for clothing and food. The French name is Peaux de Lièvre 'hare-skins' (Petitot 1876:xx); variants are Peau de Lièvre (Petitot 1875:chart) and Peaux-de-Lièvres (Petitot 1891:362). The name Hare is not used by the people of Good Hope and Colville Lake as a self-designation, though there is some acceptance of Rabbitskins, a translation from French, which is often employed by local Roman Catholic missionaries (also in McLean 1932:339).

Nineteenth-century sources give what appear to be variants of an Athapaskan name for the Hare that the sources consistently translate as 'Hare Indians' or the like: Kawchodinneh (Franklin 1824, 2:261); Kā-cho-'dtinne (Richardson 1851, 2:3, 1852:245); Kah-cho tinneh 'Arctic Hare people' (Ross in Gibbs 1865); K'a-tchô-gottinè 'people among the large hares (= arctic hares)' and K'a-t'a-gottinè 'people among the hares (= varying hares)'—two bands of Hare (Petitot 1876:xx, 231), also given as Kha-tchô-Gottinè 'people among the hares' and Kha-tpa-gottinè 'people among the rabbits' (Petitot 1891:362). If such terms existed in Hare they would have contained the Hare elements *gah* 'hare', *čo* 'big' (modern Hare *šo*), *ta* 'among', and *gotine* 'people (of)' (rather than *dene* 'man, person, Indian'), but no such name based on *gah* has been found in use in the twentieth century. The name used by the Hare to refer to themselves is rather *ǩá šo gotine* (Keren Rice, communication to editors 1979), earlier recorded as *ǩá čo gotine* (Osgood 1932:33, phonemicized). Though the meaning of this name is not clear to some

Hare speakers (Sue 1964:6), those who do give it an English meaning consistently translate it as 'big willow people', based on a variant *ká* of *káy* 'willow' often appearing in compounds (Osgood 1932:33; Keren Rice, communication to editors 1979). A less common self-designation used in the 1970s is *gahwi̦é goṭine* 'rabbit-skin people', but this appears to be merely a recent coinage translated from English (Keren Rice, communication to editors 1979).

Other names recorded for the Hare are Kancho (Gallatin 1836:19), Tä-nä´-tin-ne (Morgan 1871:289), Eskimo Nouga 'spittle' (Hind 1863, 2:258), and Chipewyan Kkɒayttchare Ottiné 'dwellers under willows' (Petitot 1865, 1869a). In several sources the Hare are treated collectively with other northern Athapaskan peoples under the general names Dene, 'Tinne, Chipewyans, Slave, and Slavey; see, for example, Richardson (1851), Anonymous (1859), Ross (1861, 1862, 1872), Petitot (1875), and Morice (1906–1910). Sue (1964:30a–30d) provides a regional-band synonymy for the Hare covering reports from the nineteenth and twentieth centuries.

Sources

Mackenzie (1801) is the only firsthand, significant source on the Hare for the late eighteenth century. Explorers and traders provide valuable information about the people during the early decades of trade and contact in the nineteenth century (Wentzel 1889–1890; Keith 1889–1890; Franklin 1824; T. Simpson 1843; Lefroy 1938; Richardson 1851; Hooper 1853; McLean 1932; Anonymous 1859; Ross 1861, 1862, 1872). Petitot (1875, 1876, 1876a, 1883, 1887, 1889, 1891, 1893) is the most important source for ethnographic and linguistic material during the late nineteenth century. Hodge (1907j:667) made an early attempt to summarize the literature. Morice (1906–1910) treats the Hare in an extended series of essays covering the northern and southern Athapaskans. The most extensive research on the Hare in the twentieth century can be found in the writings of Osgood (1932, 1936), Hoijer (1966, based on linguistic data collected by F.-K. Li in 1929), MacNeish (1956, 1960), Cohen (1962), Balikci and Cohen (1963), Hurlbert (1962), Sue (1964, 1965), Helm (1965, 1968, 1969), Helm and Damas (1963), Villiers (1967), Howren (1970, 1975), and Savishinsky (1970, 1970a, 1971, 1972, 1974, 1975; Savishinsky and Frimmer 1973; Hara 1980). Unpublished material and manuscripts that deal with the Hare in the nineteenth century can be found in the National Anthropological Archives, the Smithsonian Institution; in the records of the North West and Hudson's Bay Companies, Winnipeg; and in the diaries and parish records of the Oblates of Mary Immaculate, Ottawa, who have served at various Hare communities since the 1860s. Unless otherwise noted, statements in the text are based on Savishinsky (1967–1971, 1970a) and Sue (1961–1963, 1964).

Mountain Indians

BERYL C. GILLESPIE

Language, Environment, and Territory

The Mountain Indians are among a number of groups that have been associated with the Mackenzie Mountains, the heights of which define the boundary between the Yukon and Northwest Territories and the western limits of the Mackenzie River drainage. Various bands called Mountain Indians have been associated with the eastern slopes of the Mackenzie Mountains between Forts Liard and Good Hope during the nineteenth century. Since the last half of the nineteenth century this wide dispersal has been gradually reduced, and Fort Norman on the Mackenzie River has become the only place associated with the Mountain Indians. Therefore, the Mountain Indians here described, except within the environmental and historical sections, represent those bands that have traded into Fort Norman continuously since 1823 as well as additional individuals and small groups of other so-called Mountain Indians that have merged with this population.

In linguistic usage the name Mountain is used more broadly to refer to the language spoken in the 1970s at Fort Norman and Fort Wrigley and reportedly also by a few people at Fort Liard (Keren Rice and Victor Golla, communications to editors 1979). Mountain is a language of the Northeastern Athapaskan group* (Howren 1975) most closely related to Hare and Bearlake.

---

*The phonemes of the Fort Norman dialect of Mountain are: (unaspirated stops and affricates) b, d, λ, ʒ, ǯ, g, ʔ; (aspirated stops and affricates) p, t, ƛ, c, č, k; (glottalized) p̓, t̓, ƛ̓, c̓, č̓, k̓; (voiceless continuants) f, ł, s, š, x, h; (voiced continuants) v, l, z, ž, γ; (prenasalized stops) ᵐb, ⁿd; (nasals) m, n; (resonants) r, y; (plain vowels) i, e, a, o, u; (nasalized vowels) į, ę, ą, ǫ, ų; (tones) high (v́), low (unmarkd). The inventory of the Fort Wrigley dialect differs in having i and į for Fort Norman u and ų. Fort Norman ų is generally pronounced ǫ, and the ą of both dialects is generally ǫ also. ž is used in conservative speech, generally being replaced by y. There is free variation among b, m, and ᵐb in prefixes and also between d and ⁿd and between b and ᵐb in stems.

In the practical orthography used by the Department of Education of the Northwest Territories the Mountain phonemes are written as follows: b, d, dl, dz, j, g, '; p, t, tł, ts, ch, k; p', t', tł', ts', ch', k'; f, ł, s, sh, x, h; v, l, z, zh, gh; mb, nd; m, n; r, y; i, e, a, o, u; į, ę, ą, ǫ, ų; high tone (v́).

Information on Mountain phonology and the practical orthography was furnished by Keren Rice (communication to editors 1979), who also checked the transcription of the forms cited.

Historically, and presumably aboriginally, the various "Mountain" Indian groups exploited the eastern slopes of the Mackenzie Mountains between 61° and 66° north latitude (fig. 1). This area encompasses more than 44,300 square miles from the area west of the Mackenzie River lowlands to the alpine peaks of the Mackenzie Mountains. Between the high peaks, often above the timberline, are alpine tundra and river valleys covered mainly with white and black spruce; and birch, tamarack, and willow are found in certain areas (Porsild 1945). Throughout the mountain area there are lakes, but they are usually very small with a short ice-free season. The rivers of the eastern slopes are fast running and follow narrow, rugged valleys. The major rivers, which flow into the Liard and Mackenzie rivers, are the South Nahanni, North Nahanni, Root, Redstone, Keele (Gravel), Carcajou, Mountain, Arctic Red, and Peel. The rivers are open for four to five months of the year but are dangerous even for lightweight craft because of their swiftness and shallowness. For most of the year the frozen rivers served the Indians as forest-free paths through a rugged, mountainous terrain to various hunting locations.

The major big game hunted by the Indians of the eastern slopes of the Mackenzie Mountains are moose, woodland caribou, and Dall sheep. Mountain goats "are very thinly distributed in the south half of the range, mostly south of the 63rd parallel and west of 126° west" longitude (Simmons 1968:37). If recent biological studies reflect faunal conditions 200 years ago, the eastern slopes have had a plentiful amount of large game animals, especially caribou and sheep. The area is not rich in animals valued in the fur trade (Rand 1945a:28–44). Fish are in all the streams and lakes of the eastern slopes. The snowshoe hare, an important food and clothing resource for the people of the Mackenzie basin, is scarce in the mountains. The ground squirrel is found throughout the mountains and was frequently used for clothing and occasionally as food.

Within the Mackenzie mountain range the Mountain Indians associated with Fort Norman exploited the territory between the Redstone and Mountain rivers. The Keele River was the river used most frequently for travel in the historical period and apparently was an important part of the zone exploited aboriginally. "The Mountain Indians have hunted on the Gravel [Keele]

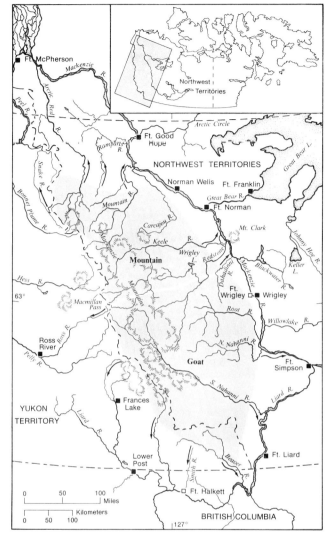

Fig. 1. Historic territory and routes to points of trade.

river for a long time; there are meat-drying racks everywhere along the stream banks. Some of their signs are very old, showing evidence of stone implements having been used" (Keele 1910:12). Some lakes were locations of seasonal camps; Drum (Wrigley) Lake in the North Redstone River area has been the most frequently mentioned lake where people camped. When Keele traveled across the Mackenzie Mountains in 1908 he estimated that "about 100 Indians hunt and trap on the Gravel river and its branches, trading fur and dried meat at . . . Fort Norman" (Keele 1910:11). This description probably represents the people of one regional group who for most of the year were dispersed into smaller groups exploiting various locations within this general territory.

Nineteenth Century

Because these Indians in the mountains had contact with Whites only beyond their own territory at trading

posts on the Mackenzie River and later in the Yukon, their history is little known (table 1). Mackenzie in 1789 learned from Mackenzie River Indians that the Mackenzie Mountains were inhabited (1966:56, 88). Mackenzie placed these Mountain Indians, whom he never met, on his map directly west of the future site of Fort Norman. By 1807 Wentzel, at the North West Company post near present-day Fort Simpson, still knew of these Indians in the mountains only through Indian reports as "namely *Nahanies, Dahoteena* and *Nombahoteenais*, besides many others" (1889–1890, 1:78). The only addition to his information by 1821 was that their territorial range was "the Rocky Mountains from Liard River to Fort Good Hope" (Wentzel 1821). Within this area he states that on the west side of the Mackenzie River, north of Fort Simpson in an area "occasionally visited by the dog ribs & Hare Indians, are the Dahodinne's, natives & inhabitants of the Rocky Mountains, they are seen sometimes on Mackenzies river." Some of these Mountain Indians were trading to Forts Norman and Good Hope in 1822–1823 (Hudson's Bay Company 1822–1823b).

In the summer of 1823 Fort Norman was moved 30 miles up the Mackenzie River from Great Bear River (until 1851) "to be in the most Centrical place for the accomodations of the Dahautinnes and part of the Dog Rib Indians" (Hudson's Bay Company 1823–1824a). Two "families" of "Dahautinne" visited Fort Simpson in 1825 (Hudson's Bay Company 1824–1825a), and in 1827 10 of them along with six "Nahanny" came to trade for guns (Hudson's Bay Company 1826–1827a). At this time the chief factor at Fort Simpson, E. Smith, distinguished between the Upper and Lower Dahotinnes as those who traded at Fort Simpson and Fort Norman respectively. In 1828 Smith got the first description from the Upper Dahotinne Indians of themselves and their neighbors. They said the South Nahanni River was the dividing line between themselves and the Nahani Indians and that "those of the Umbahotinne who reside in this vicinity [Fort Simpson] are the same Indians as the Dahotinnes resorting to Fort Norman—speak the same language and are the same people—and the difference in name is only to distinguish those living in the Goat country from those Lower down—on whoes Lands we may inferr this Animal is scarce or not to be found" (Hudson's Bay Company 1826–1828).

Tribal nomenclature has continued to become more confused since these early accounts; the early accounts in fact provide the better comprehension of peoples' territorial dispositions at the beginning of the fur trade. These first reports suggest that there were three regional groups exploiting the eastern slopes of the Mackenzie Mountains in the early 1800s. The "Nahanny" group mentioned was most likely Kaska speaking and correlates in territorial location with Honigmann's

Table 1. Chart of Historical Events

Date	Events
1969	Airplane landing strip built at Fort Norman
1950s–1960s	Canadian government programs for Indians
1950	Fort Franklin reestablished
1948	Canadian Game Service established at Fort Norman. Nursing station built at Fort Norman (Bull and Bull 1972)
1945	U.S. army wives begin day school at Fort Norman (Bull and Bull 1972)
1942–1943	Canol Road and pipeline built from Norman Wells across Mackenzie Mts. by U.S. army
1941–1947	Hospital built at Fort Norman by Anglican mission; taken over 1943 by Canadian government, burned 1947 (Bull and Bull 1972)
1939	First permanent Indian Affairs agent at Fort Norman (Bull and Bull 1972)
1931	Northern Transportation Company established at Fort Norman (Bull and Bull 1972)
1928	Influenza epidemic, 26 recorded flu deaths at Fort Norman and 23 other deaths that summer, 9 from tuberculosis (OMI 1927–1965)
1921	RCMP establish permanent detachment at Fort Norman (Bull and Bull 1972)
1920	Discovery of oil at Norman Wells
1908	Keele surveys Mackenzie Mts.; first exploration of Keele River (Keele 1910)
1902	Measles epidemic at all posts on the Mackenzie R. (Camsell 1954:152)
1900	Trading post established at mouth of Ross River, Yukon (Keele 1910:11)
1898	Klondike gold rush, greater contact between Mountain Indians and Indians of Yukon
1892	Mountain Indian chief of Fort Good Hope and most of family die of starvation in mountains (Gillespie 1968–1971; Petitot 1867–1920)
1892	15 individuals from the Yukon on Fort Norman records (Ducot 1892)
1886	Last war in the Mackenzie Mts.; survivors of Pelly River Indians join Mountain Indians of Fort Norman (Field 1957:48)
1886	First steamboat on Mackenzie R.—*Grahame* (Camsell 1954:19)
1885	Roman Catholic mission permanently established at Fort Norman
1872	Permanent site of Fort Norman at mouth of Great Bear R. (Robinson and Robinson 1946, 1:253)
1868–1943	Anglican missionaries sporadically at Fort Norman (Robinson and Robinson 1946, 2:46)
1867	Mountain Indians of Fort Liard and Yukon Indians included with Mountain Indians of Fort Norman (Petitot 1867–1920)
1865	Measles epidemic (Petitot 1893:87)
1864–1872	Fort Norman moved to Great Bear L., near site of Fort Franklin (Robinson and Robinson 1946, 1:253)
1860s	Oblate priests visit Fort Norman annually
1855	Some Mountain Indians of Good Hope trade to Peel's River Post (Hudson's Bay Company 1855–1856)
1851–1864	Fort Norman at two sites: 1851–1860 at Great Bear R. on Mackenzie; 1860–1864 a short distance north of this site (Robinson and Robinson 1946, 1:253)
1851–1852	Many Mountain Indians die of starvation (Anderson 1849–1859)
1850	Mountain Indians of Forts Norman and Good Hope killing "Gens du Roche" (Peers 1847–1853)
1844	Mountain Indians to Fort Norman with a "Gens des Fou" boy (Hudson's Bay Company 1844–1845)
1844	Influenza reported at Norman and other forts, "fatal to some" (Hudson's Bay Company 1843–1844)
1843	"Ahbahaetais" and Mountain Indians of Fort Norman reported killing Frances Lake Indians (Hudson's Bay Company 1834–1864)
1843	Over 50 die at Fort Good Hope of starvation and 25 at Fort Norman in 1842 (Hudson's Bay Company 1843–1844)
1837	"A great number of the Mountain Indians have died of starvation last winter" (Hudson's Bay Company 1837–1838)
1837	Starvation among Mountain Indians, 32 or more died in winter of 1836–1837 (Hudson's Bay Company 1837–1838a)
1837	No "Nahanny" or "Dauhaudinnes" trading at Fort Simpson (Hudson's Bay Company 1836–1837)
1837	First mention of Mountain Indians using canoes down the Keele R. (Hudson's Bay Company 1837–1838a)
1835–1836	Mountain Indians report war with other Indians in the mountains in 1834 (Hudson's Bay Company 1835–1836)
1835	Mountain Indians at Fort Norman report wars in mountains in past two years (Hudson's Bay Company 1835–1836)
1834	Fort Simpson "Mountain" Indians trading at Fort Liard (Public Archives of Canada, Series MG19, D8:4–12)
1831	Starvation for Indians trading on Mackenzie R. (Hudson's Bay Company 1831–1832)
1830	Mountain Indians at Good Hope report war in mountains (Hudson's Bay Company 1829–1830)
1829	Hudson's Bay Co. encourages peace between "Goat Indians" and "Touetchoetinne" (Kaska speakers near Frances L.) (Hudson's Bay Company 1829–1830a)
1828	"Nahanny" and "Goat" Indians trading to Fort Simpson; "Dahotine" trading to Fort Norman (Hudson's Bay Company 1826–1828)

Table 1. Chart of Historical Events (*Continued*)

Date	Events
1823	40 Mountain Indians at Fort Norman (Hudson's Bay Company 1823–1824a), 24 at Good Hope (lower post) (Hudson's Bay Company 1822–1823c)
1822	Hudson's Bay Co. contact with "Dahotinnais" at Forts Simpson and Good Hope (Hudson's Bay Company 1822–1824)
1822–1851	Fort Norman established by Hudson's Bay Co. for "Dahautinnes and part of the Dog Rib" (Hudson's Bay Company 1823–1824a)
1821	"Daudinnes" said to be in mountains, Liard R. to Fort Good Hope (Wentzel 1821)
1804–1821	North West Co. intermittent posts between Keele and Great Bear Rs. on Mackenzie R. No information on which Indians traded there (Stager 1962:38)
1807	The yet unseen Indians of the mountains are named "Nahanies, Dahoteena, and Nombahoteenais" (Wentzel 1889–1890, 1:78)
1789	Mackenzie (1966:37, 186) is told of Indians inhabiting the Mackenzie Mts.; places "Mountain Indians" west of Great Bear R.

(1949, 1954) Kaska division called the Nelson Indians. The other two regional groups mentioned, the "Umbahotinne" and "Dahotinnes," very likely constituted the Goat and Mountain Indians of the nineteenth century.

The "Umbahotinne," adjoining the so-called Nahani to the north, have also been referred to as the Espatodena or Goat Indians. Honigmann (1954:20) placed the Goat Indians in the area "north of the Liard, including the drainages of the Beaver, South Nahanni, and perhaps Upper Nahanni rivers. With contact some came to trade at Fort Halkett and Lower Post [near Watson Lake] while others congregated at Fort Liard." Almost all historical sources have also located the Goat Indians within this general area (table 2). The Hudson's Bay Company records at Fort Simpson recorded these Goat Indians as coming first to Fort Simpson to trade but many shifting to Fort Liard in the 1830s.

The distinction between the "Umbahotinne" (Goat Indians) and "Dahotinne" (Mountain Indians) made in the 1828 native account, based on territory and the limits of the mountain goat, is in agreement with the memory culture of several Mountain Indians (Gillespie 1968–1971). The Mountain Indians whose ancestors traded to Forts Norman and Good Hope say that the people to the south of them in the mountains were friends, just like them, but hunted the mountain goat and traded to Forts Simpson, Liard, and Wrigley. They refer to these neighbors as the *ehba goṭine* 'mountain goat people'. The distinction between two regional bands based on who hunted the mountain goat also agrees with the twentieth-century faunal distribution.

Simmons's (1968) data indicate that the mountain goat is at the northern fringe of its habitat at about 63°30′ north latitude, slightly south of the Redstone River. This places the goat just south of the territory exploited by the Mountain Indians and within Goat Indian territory, corresponding exactly with the 1828 Hudson's Bay Company account.

External Relations

From the earliest reports by Mackenzie (1966:56, 88) and Wentzel (1821) it is clear that Dogrib, Slavey, and Hare peoples were familiar with Mountain and Goat Indians aboriginally. They occasionally visited them in the mountains and encountered them when they came to the Mackenzie River to fish. Since all historical sources but one (T. Simpson 1843:95) as well as the Mountain Indians deny any hostilities with these neighbors, it is safe to state that they all have been on friendly terms for a long time.

Some internal feuds have been remembered by the Mountain Indians, but most hostilities were with Yukon peoples. Aboriginal contact by Mountain and Goat Indians with Yukon Indians is implied in Mackenzie's (1966:86, 88) journal. Historical sources and Mountain Indian tradition refer to numerous wars with Yukon groups in the nineteenth century (table 1). At least some of these conflicts were instigated by the Mountain Indians who went to the Yukon for furs (Gillespie 1968–1971).

If Field's fieldwork in 1913 provides an accurate account, warfare continued in the Mackenzie Mountains until late in the nineteenth century. According to the last survivor of the original Pelly River Indians, that group was extinct because of internal feuds, other Indian peoples' raiding them, and an attack on them near Macmillan Pass by "Mackenzie" Indians in 1886 (Field 1957:48). After this attack a few survivors went to live with "the Indians called the Mountain Indians and then trading at Fort Norman" (Field 1957:49). This corresponds with statements of Mountain Indians in 1971 who recalled hearing about "the last war" that resulted in a few families from Ross and Pelly rivers following them back to Fort Norman (Gillespie 1968–1971).

The Mountain Indians considered the Yukon to be foreign and hostile territory until the twentieth century. With the Klondike gold rush in 1898 and the following years of greater traffic over the mountains, as well as the establishment of trading posts on Pelly and Ross rivers, more Mountain Indians traveled to the Yukon as guides or as traders. The traditional fear of Yukon Indians had disappeared by 1900 (Keele 1910:11).

Dispersal

Both the Goat Indians and the Mountain Indians proper seemed to experience population decreases through the

Table 2. Terminology for 2 Mountain Indian Groups

Date	Name	Area	Name	Area	Source
1807	Dahoteena	Rocky Mts.	Nombahoteenais	Rocky Mts.	Wentzel 1889–1890, 1:79
1821	Dahodinnes	Rocky Mts. between Liard R. and Fort Good Hope			Wentzel 1821
1822	Dahotinnais	Trading to Forts Simpson, Norman, and Good Hope			Hudson'sBay Company, 1822–1824
1828	Lower Dahotinne	Trade to Fort Norman, live north of Goat Indians	Upper Dahotinne or Umbahotine	Trade to Fort Simpson, hunt goats	Hudson's Bay Company 1826–1828
1837	Dauhaudinnes	Trading to Simpson, some trading to Liard			Hudson's Bay Company 1834
1821			Ambawtawhoot-din-neh, Sheep Indians	Trade to Good Hope, live at source of "Dahoot-dinneh" R.	Franklin 1824, 1:292
1843			Ahbahaetais	Probably on west side of mts., trade to Frances Lake	Hudson's Bay Company 1834–1864
1851	Daha-'dtinne	Trade to Fort Norman, descend Keele R.	Amba-ta-ut-'tinne, Sheep People	Trade to Good Hope, live near 65° north latitude	Richardson 1851, 2:7
			Ah-bah-to-din-ne	Trade to Forts Liard and Simpson	Hardisty 1872:311
1860s	Eta-gottiné	Live in mts. between Kutchin and Esba-t'a-ottiné	Esba-t'a-ottiné	'dwellers among the mountain goats (French *Argali*)'	Petitot 1876:xx
	Ehta-Gottinè	In Rocky Mts. south of 66° north latitude; associated with groups at Fort Norman	Espa-tρa-Ottinè	'people of the goats', 'people of the big-horns'; Rocky Mts. along Liard R.	Petitot 1891:301, 362
1915			Espatoten, Goat tribe	North and South Nahanni, Beaver Rs.	Teit 1956:46
1932			Esbataottine, Goat Indians	Beaver and South Nahanni Rs.	Jenness 1932:396
1936	Ehta-Gottine	Live in Keele R. drainage	Esbataottine, Sheep Indians	Beaver and South Nahanni Rs.	Osgood 1936:13, 15
1946			Espato-tena, Goat Indians	Beaver and South Nahanni Rs., trade to Liard and Simpson	Honigmann 1946:35
1971	Edaot'ine	Trade to Norman and Good Hope, live in Keele R. drainage	Ehba got'ine, Goat People	Southern neighbors to Edaot'ine, trade to Simpson and Liard	Gillespie 1968–1971

nineteenth century (table 3). In part this apparent loss of population was caused by dispersal to several trading posts. In Anderson's (1849–1859) Mackenzie River District Report of 1858 the "Mountain" Indians (whom he interchangeably calls Nahanny) are scattered from Fort Liard to Peel's River Fort as well as at Fort Halkett in northern British Columbia.

One explanation for the fanning out of the Mountain and Goat Indians in every direction to various posts is to be seen in the drainage pattern of the Mackenzie Mountains (fig. 1). Groups in the headwaters of the eastern slopes could be in close proximity to one another but travel to posts 1,000 miles apart. Although information is meager for the last half of the nineteenth century, it appears that the Mountain and Goat Indians were so dispersed among various posts that some amalgamated with more populous native groups along the Liard and Mackenzie rivers and in the Yukon. Probably a major reason the Goat Indians disappeared as a territorial entity by the twentieth century was this dispersion to widely separated points of trade.

Population

What kept the population small aboriginally is not fully understood, but Mountain and Goat Indians seem to have suffered from starvation to a greater extent than other Indians in the Mackenzie River drainage. Starvation was also a main cause of infanticide and reported cannibalism (Petitot 1869:286–287). The worst famine reported was for the winter of 1851–1852: "With the exception of one band saved by the exertions of Taylor [Hudson's Bay Company manager] at Fort Norman, it is feared that all the Mountain tribes attached to Forts Norman and Good Hope have perished" (Anderson 1849–1859:15). In 1854 the number of Indian trappers at Fort Norman was greatly reduced, from 150 to 60: "Some have gone to Martin [Marten Lake], some to Simpson, most of the Mountain Indians dead" (Anderson 1849–1859, 5:1a). Among the various native groups at Fort Norman in 1971, only Mountain Indians could recall stories of past starvation. One story correlates in time with the winter of 1851–1852 and another reports the death of a chief and many of his relatives in 1892 (Gillespie 1968–1971). By the twentieth century starvation cases disappeared, but European diseases continued to keep the population from increasing until modern medical attention became available in the 1950s (see table 1).

In addition to trading dispersal, starvation, and disease, intertribal hostilities influenced the shifts of peoples in the Mackenzie Mountains. As a part of this process some people merged with the Mountain Indians trading into Forts Norman and Good Hope. Intermarriage of these latter with the Hare, Slavey, and Dogrib was also occurring by at least the second half of the nineteenth century.

Genealogical records started in 1867 by Petitot (1867–1920) separated the Mountain Indian group from other local native populations of the Fort Norman area. Within this group are listed families previously registered at Forts Liard and Good Hope. From 1879 on there are also included a number of families from west of the mountains, supporting statements made by Mountain Indians in 1971 and by Field in 1913.

Genealogical records made at Fort Norman in 1892 (Ducot 1892) distinguished the Mountain Indians from other natives of the fort and also listed 15 recent immigrants from the Yukon. A later genealogical list for Fort Norman (Ducot 1914) listed separately Mountain Indian families whose ancestors were associated with Fort Norman, Fort Good Hope, and the Yukon. What is then recognized as the Mountain Indians of Fort Norman in the twentieth century is the result of merging of groups and individuals from a wide geographical range within the Mackenzie Mountains and Yukon.

Mid-Twentieth Century

The Mountain Indians had remained a social entity distinct from those Indians of the Mackenzie River and eastward primarily by their different exploitative territory. By the late 1960s they had reduced their exclusive use of the Mackenzie Mountains and thereby any territorial separation from the Fort Norman native population. By this time they hunted, trapped, and fished within the proximity of the fort as well as the Mackenzie Mountains along with other Indians of the locale.

Table 3. Population Estimates of Mountain Indians 1827–1971

Year	Location	Men	Women	Boys	Girls	Total	Source
1827	Fort Simpson	30	25	50		105	Hudson's Bay Company 1826–1828
1829	Fort Simpson	60	40	101		201	Hudson's Bay Company 1829–1930a
	Fort Norman	30	24	27	19	100	
1858	Fort Simpson	13	14	47	13	87	Anderson 1849–1859
	Fort Norman	8	9	18	8	43	
	Fort Good Hope	1	1	3	3	8	
	Fort Liard "Mountain" and Kaska	9	9	13	7	38	
	Fort Halkett "Mountain" and Kaska	63	63	76	57	259	
1880	Fort Norman (at Great Bear Lake)					43	Petitot 1884–1885:53
1908	Keele River area					100	Keele 1910:11
1914	Fort Norman					48	Ducot 1914
	Portage (?)					17	
	Fort Good Hope					37	
1958	Fort Norman					43[a]	Michéa 1963:51–52
1971	Fort Norman					87[b]	William Bull, personal communication 1972

[a] This figure is too low; it omits several Mountain Indian families that have been trading to Fort Norman for a long time.

[b] This figure does not include spouses and adoptions of Mountain Indian families that are not Mountain Indian. Since all other population estimates are based on family counts, a population total consistent with others would be about 100.

By the mid-twentieth century, their lifeway, featuring increased involvement in the Euro-Canadian economy and sociopolitical system, corresponds to that of the other Indian peoples of the Northwest Territories ("Intercultural Relations and Cultural Change in the Shield and Mackenzie Borderlands," this vol.). Major events in the Fort Norman area introduced by the Whites were the discovery of oil at Norman Wells (50 miles north) in 1920, the discovery of pitchblende at Port Radium (Great Bear Lake) in 1931, and the United States Army's construction of the Canol Road and pipeline across the Mackenzie Mountains to the Yukon in 1942–1943. All these events brought an influx of Whites for short periods and tended to make Fort Norman an important establishment on the Mackenzie River from 1920 to 1945. With the reestablishment of Fort Franklin on Great Bear Lake as a native settlement and point of trade in 1950 and the increased development of Norman Wells, Fort Norman lost much of its importance. By 1971 Fort Norman had become a relatively isolated, small settlement with a native population of 272, of which about one-third were Mountain Indians. The population of Fort Norman in 1978 was 214 (Canada. Department of Indian Affairs and Northern Development 1980:47).

Culture

Subsistence

Little is recorded of the Mountain Indians' annual subsistence patterns since no Whites traveled into the Mackenzie Mountains to document any aspects of Indian life until 1957. In the late 1950s Michéa (1963) observed a very late contact-traditional annual cycle that included long periods of residence at Fort Norman. At that time those Mountain Indians who still exploited the mountains left the fort in July or August, walking directly westward with their pack dogs into the mountains. By October small groups of families came together at the headwaters of the Keele River where they built large mooseskin boats to descend the river to the Mackenzie River and then downstream to Fort Norman. They loaded these boats with dry meat, which they traded at Fort Norman for supplies. After a week or two they moved across the Mackenzie River to several lowland lakes, often accompanied by some Hare Indians, to fish and trap until Christmas, when they returned to the fort. In January they returned to the mountains, making their longest expedition into their heights where they remained until spring. When the streams were again open for navigation, usually in late May, they returned by mooseskin boats to Fort Norman. There they spent most of the summer, relying on local fish and moose supplies as well as groceries (Michéa 1963:54).

332   The departure of the Mountain Indians from the fort

to the mountains in late summer and their return after breakup in the spring correlate with important caribou-hunting seasons. Simmons (1968) reports that the woodland caribou begin to group and move toward their winter range after the first snowfall sometime in mid-September, following the river shores down into the wooded valleys and plateaus. It is at this season the caribou are to be found in larger herds and their skins are at their prime for making clothing. About mid-March the caribou move upstream on the ice toward their calving grounds and are channeled by the terrain through certain predictable areas that allow for relatively easy killing. It is after this spring caribou hunt that another trip to Fort Norman used to be made. It was meat more than furs that the traders expected from the Mountain Indians in the contact-traditional period.

The most complete account of aboriginal subsistence was given in 1971 by Tatsi Wright, a 99-year-old Mountain woman at Fort Norman (Gillespie 1968–1971). She stated that before the fur trade and even a long time afterward the Mountain Indians stayed in the mountains almost all the time, seldom traveling to the lowlands and Mackenzie River. Dall sheep and caribou are remembered to have been the major food resources of the aboriginal economy and the preference then was always for meat over fish, as has been the case in the historical period. Sheep and caribou were most easily caught in the summer months. Indian groups moved from one valley to another and along streams to favorite feeding grounds where these two species were snared in brush fences. The animals were butchered on the spot and the meat hauled to a nearby camp. What was not eaten was dried and cached for winter. Most of the sheep were killed in the summer and, in general, most of the large game. Moose were snared or chased down but were more difficult to kill than caribou and sheep. Norman M. Simmons (personal communication 1972) supports this native account: he has seen "quite a few of the old drift fences and snare locations used in the 'old times' . . . to capture and kill caribou and mountain sheep. I saw one set-up that probably was used to snare moose or at least guide them close to hunters, but this was not a common situation."

During the summer and fall hunting, each major kill was at least in part sun-dried and cached for future use. Then the group would move on to the next predictably good hunting area. This pattern continued until November. During the winter they would stay in a place as long as cached meat and freshly taken game supported them. Then they would move on to the next closest cache from the summer hunt. Wright said it was very hard to kill enough animals throughout the year. Winter starvation apparently resulted not from a scarcity of large game but from the difficulty of killing it in winter. With the scarcity of the snowshoe hare and the lack of large lakes where ice fishing was feasible in the coldest months, the Mountain Indians had few resources other than large game for the lean mid-winter. With guns the Mountain Indians found it much easier to kill everything, but most especially the moose. Even so, the muzzle-loading guns of the nineteenth century did not prevent cases of winter starvation.

Technology

The material culture of the Mountain Indians has never been recorded in any detail but seems to conform to that of their Subarctic Athapaskan neighbors in general. Only those somewhat distinctive variations in material culture that were adaptations to the Mackenzie Mountain environment will be emphasized here.

Birch was not available to any degree in the mountains; therefore, canoes were always made from spruce bark instead of birchbark. Containers, mainly used for stone-boiling cooking, were made of coiled spruce roots tightly sewed together.

Transportation

Methods of transport reflect Mountain Indian adaptation to a rugged, mountainous terrain. The use of dogs to pack (fig. 2) and to haul toboggans was a development of the last half of the nineteenth century. Mountain Indians in 1971 (Gillespie 1968–1971) were definite that dogs were not used for transport until that time. It is said that families in the late 1800s had only two or three dogs for packing, but by the 1920s they had up to five or seven. In earlier times, a small dog was used for hunting only, mainly to chase sheep up the mountainside and to run down moose in the snow. Families had one dog at most.

Mountain Indians in 1971 also said that they never used toboggans until the second half of the nineteenth century. The aboriginal way of hauling supplies, mainly meat, was with a skin blanket pulled by a strap around the shoulders. These blankets were made of 30 to 40 animal leg skins or several caribou or moose hides.

The other item of transport distinctive to the Mountain Indians has been the large mooseskin boat (figs. 3–4). The first good description of this boat comes from the 1890s:

> At the end of the summer the Indians descended the river in boats made of raw moosehide. Eight or ten skins sewn together, with the seams sealed with hard grease, were stretched over a framework of green pliable poles to make a serviceable boat twenty or twenty-five feet in length with perhaps a five-foot beam. It was the most suitable craft possible for Gravel [Keele] River, a roaring mountain stream, because if it hit a rock it slid over easily . . . (Camsell 1954:49).

Although the mooseskin boat has become one of the distinctive traits of the Mountain Indians, it was not invented until the late 1800s. A local Fort Norman In-

Fig. 2. Transporting goods by dog pack and back pack across a branch of the Little Bear River. Photograph by Jean Michéa, 1957–1958.

dian on a trip with the Mountain Indians to the Keele River constructed the first mooseskin boat (Gillespie 1968–1971). Few mountain rivers were deep enough for this type of craft, and it was used almost exclusively on the Keele River.

Mountain Indians state that only the spruce-bark canoe was used before they made the mooseskin boats. The spruce-bark canoe was small and broke easily once it dried out, making it of limited used in gaining a livelihood in the mountains. Mountain Indians claimed that they traveled less extensive distances at any one time until they had dogs and larger boats in the late nineteenth century (Gillespie 1968–1971).

Structures

The simple brush lean-to or open fire was probably the most common campsite traditionally. The conical brushwood or split-log shelter was used only for semipermanent winter camps. Within the historical period Mountain Indians made caribou-hide lodges that housed two to four families. The hide lodge followed the earlier wood lodge in floor layout, having two entrances with the families occupying the area along the walls between the entries. The lodge, either of wood or hide, was supported by three or four poles. The wood lodge had additional poles to support the horizontally stacked brush or logs (Gillespie 1968–1971).

Clothing

Aboriginal Mountain Indian clothing probably did not differ greatly from other Mackenzie drainage Athapaskan peoples'. Both men and women wore the caribou hide all-in-one moccasin and legging that came up

333

Fig. 3. The construction of a moosehide boat on Gravel (Keele) River in the Mackenzie Mountains. Photograph by Norman Simmons, May 1968.

over the thighs and was held in place by strings wrapped around the waist. Sometime in the nineteenth century this foot-legging was abandoned. Leggings were cut off at the ankle, and the ankle-wrapped moccasin was used.

Men wore hide shirts that slipped over the head and fell to about the thigh in length. The woman's shirt was the same style, but its length was almost to the ankles. Caribou hide was used most frequently for leggings and shirts, but sheep and moose hides were also used, at least in the nineteenth century. Over this basic outfit the people wore robes, or blankets, made of three or four caribou or sheep hides. Netted ground-squirrel skins were also used to make these robes as well as children's clothing.

Wright emphasized the great difficulties in tanning and sewing hides, especially moose, before the introduction of metal knives, scissors, awls, and needles. Before metal blades, Indians had to cut hides with beaver teeth or birds' beaks attached to wooden handles. She said that before White trade items were available they tanned young or unborn-calf skins whenever possible because they were softer and easier to work with. Also, netted ground-squirrel clothing was used for adult

clothing more often since these skins required no tanning (Gillespie 1968–1971).

Social Organization

During the nineteenth century the people living on the eastern slopes of the Mackenzie Mountains were reduced to one regional band (Helm 1968a). This band was a unit of social identity based on common dialect, interlocking kin ties, and mutual exploitation of a general region. The regional band survived through generations as a social group even though the membership was always changing to some degree, especially during the nineteenth century. As segments of this general social unit, smaller groups traveled, camped, and pursued the various exploitative tasks together. The minimal social-economic unit of the Mountain Indians was two to four nuclear families who shared the same shelter or fire. This small unit was closely connected through blood and marriage ties and shared in most of the economic activities of the annual cycle. In the winter when people had to disperse into small groups, it was this linked-family unit of 10 to 20 individuals that was the

334

Fig. 4. Moosehide boats. left, Mooseskin boat beached in front of a shore camp. The sweep rudder in the water is used for steering. right, A close-up of the prow of a moosehide boat. A caribou stomach filled with grease is hanging over the side. To prevent water leakage grease was applied to the seams before and during the use of the boat. left, Photograph by D.B. Dowling at Ft. Norman, 1921. right, Photograph by Jean Michéa, 1957–1958.

Fig. 5. A tent encampment at the tree line in the Mackenzie Mountains. One end of the dry meat rack is secured to the tent while some of the tent poles are used for household gear. The tent is canvas, a trade item introduced in the first part of the 20th century that gradually replaced hide and brushwood coverings. Photograph by Jean Michéa, 1957–1958.

minimal unit. Mountain Indians estimated that during the summer when hunting permitted it, there were usually "10 fires, 10 different family groups traveling and hunting together, about two families to a fire" (Gillespie 1968–1971). A group of 40 to 80 individuals was probably the maximal number in close proximity at any one time.

Leadership

A man who was a good hunter, could make decisions on when and where to hunt, and had general respect attracted followers. Each linked-family unit had a recognized leader, a man in his mature years who had some of these leadership qualities but who had no authority except through consensual recognition by the group. In any one generation there were one or two

men who were generally considered great leaders. They excelled in the natural leadership qualities, which included a high amount of generosity, and each was considered to have in addition special powers from his own "medicine."

With the signing of Treaty No. 11 in 1921 a chief and councilors were selected to represent the natives of Fort Norman, as elsewhere. In the following 50 years these native "councilors," as defined by the Canadian government, only sometimes included Mountain Indians.

Life Cycle

Childbirth occurred without ceremony. A woman gave birth away from the camp or in a shelter with only women about her. Infanticide was practiced into the nineteenth century but was done only because of general hardships. Wright emphasized the difficulty of supplying clothing for children as a major reason infanticide was sometimes considered necessary. Baby girls were usually those allowed to die because they were considered less important than boys, who would eventually be hunters (Gillespie 1968–1971).

There was no formal recognition for boys' reaching puberty. They were encouraged to camp away from the main camp occasionally in order that they might dream of and gain their "medicine." Some believed their dreams had provided them with special supernatural powers and these used their "medicine" as shamans in their mature years.

The most ritualized event was a girl's menarche. A shelter was built away from the camp where she remained for weeks to over a month. The girl was visited only by her mother or a couple of close female relatives during this period of isolation. The girl was under a series of special rules of behavior and had to wear a special hat that hid her face from view. She was ex-

Natl. Mus. of Canada. Ottawa: VI-K–5.
Fig. 6. Man's hat, velvet with beadwork, made for special occasions and for well-to-do men whose wives are good sewers. The style was in fashion in the late 19th and early 20th centuries (see "Hare," fig. 2, this vol.). Width 25.5 cm, made by Harriette Gladu, collected by Beryl Gillespie, Ft. Norman, N.W.T., 1973.

pected to devote most of her time to work—chopping wood and sewing—to insure that she became a hard-working woman. Traditionally some girls were married before their menarche. The husband recognized the onset of his "child-bride's" menarche by wearing hide strips around his neck and ankles. He brought cut wood to each family in the camp to announce his wife's condition while she remained in isolation from the group.

Menstrual blood was always treated as dangerous to men's ability to kill animals. Women during menstruation were expected to walk off the path used by men, either not to use the main entrances to the family shelter or to use a separate shelter, and not to touch or walk over any hunting weapons.

Marriage took place without ceremony until Christianity came in the second half of the nineteenth century. It is said that women were scarce in the "old days" and marriage contracts were often made between a man and a girl's parents when she was still a small child. A man would usually live with and help the girl's family until they had their own child. A couple could choose residence among any group of close relatives from either side. There was brother-sister reserve after puberty, but this did not prevent married brothers and sisters from being a part of the same family camp. There was some quarreling over women, and men did occasionally steal wives.

Beliefs

Almost nothing is known of aboriginal Mountain Indian expressive and ideational culture, but it can be assumed that it was very similar to that of the other native groups of the Mackenzie River and eastward. In the twentieth century the Indians of Fort Norman have considered the Mountain people the leaders of traditional song-making and dances.

The Mountain Indians have also been viewed as having greater "medicine" powers, both good and bad, than the people of the Mackenzie River area. By 1971 the few men who were considered to have native "medicine" were no longer practicing their skills. Some of the older Mountain Indians still followed food taboos and special behavior toward some animals (fig. 7).

Synonymy†

The name of the Mountain Indians is either an independent descriptive phrase or a translation of their name for themselves, *sĭh gotine* 'mountain people' or *šĭhta gotine* 'among-the-mountains people'. Similar names are used in the other Northeastern Athapaskan languages. Recordings include Cheta-ut-tdinnè (Richardson 1851, 2:7, 1852:247), šitagottine (Osgood 1936:15, normalized), Chi-tra-gottinékhé (Petitot 1867–1920), Chitra-gottinéké (Michéa 1963:49), and the arbitrarily shortened Shi-ta-dene (Osgood 1932:48). This term has been used mainly for the Mountain Indians that have traded into Fort Norman, but the Hare have also used it for a band of their own group that exploits lands west of the Mackenzie River.

Many other names have been used in the literature to designate the same people of the eastern slopes of the Mackenzie Mountains. The term Nahani has been used since the early 1800s and was still used by the Canadian government in the 1960s as a tribal-linguistic designation. It has been the primary tribal name under which "Mountain" Indians have been categorized by anthropologists.

Osgood (1936:13, 15) eliminated the "Nahani" tribal category, the "Nahane" of Swanton (1910:10), and divided the Athapaskans of the eastern slopes of the Mackenzie Mountains into two major groups: Kaska and Mountain. He put the people called the Esbataottinè in his Kaska division, and following Petitot (1891:362) he put together three small groups associated with Fort Norman as his Mountain division; however, only one of these groups is here analyzed as part of the Mountain Indians: the Ehta-Gottinè.

The Ehta-Gottinè and Esbataottinè were the main regional groups of "Mountain" Indians in the nineteenth century. Table 2 presents the most frequently used native terms (in their variant spellings) for these two groups that are recorded in the literature. Although there are contradictions as to location and inclusiveness of these terms, the Ehta-Gottinè are the group most frequently associated with the Keele River and Forts

†This synonymy was written by Beryl C. Gillespie and Ives Goddard.

336

Fig. 7. As an offering to the spirit of the moose, pieces of the viscera are suspended in a tree at the time of butchering. Photograph by Jean Michéa, 1957–1958.

Norman and Good Hope, and the Esbataottinè are the group most frequently associated with the Beaver and North and South Nahanni rivers and Forts Simpson and Liard.

According to information obtained by Richardson (1852:112, 247), Dahadinnè(s) or Dahā-'dtinnè was the Dogrib name for Indians on the Keele River that called themselves Cheta-ut-tdinnè. Petitot (1876:xx, 1891:301, 362) used the name Eta-gottinè, Éta-Gottinè, or Ehta-Gottinè, which he glossed as 'people in the air' (gens en l'air) and 'mountain people' (gens de la montagne, gens des montagnes), the latter presumably an explanation or identification rather than a literal translation. This name is probably ʔehda goṭine, but the analysis is uncertain (Keren Rice, communication to editors 1979).

The names of the Esbataottinè reflect ʔesbata goṭine 'among-the-mountain-goats people' or ʔehba goṭine 'mountain-goat people'. Modern Mountain has ʔehba for 'mountain goat', but other dialects and languages, including nineteenth-century Slavey and Mountain, have ʔesba (Petitot 1876:250; Keren Rice, communication to editors 1979). The forms like Umbahotine apparently contain another dialect variant. The early sources, including some writings of Petitot (1876:250, 1891:362), give the mountain sheep (Dall sheep) as the referent of the name, but later information, including other writings of Petitot (1876:xx, 1891:301) and data

from Keren Rice (communication to editors 1979), specifies the mountain goat; this disagreement was briefly noted by Osgood (1936:13) but is not completely resolved.

The Mountain Indians were not treated clearly by Hodge (1907o:1, 1907p:432, 1907l; Swanton 1910:10). They appear there in the entries for the Abbatotine, Esbataottine, and Etagottine, which are grouped together as part of the "Nahane." One reference to the "mountain Indians" from Hardisty (1872:311) mistakenly appears in the Tutchone ("Tutchonekutchin") synonymy (Hodge 1910i:855). Swanton (1952:583–585, 608) continued these confusions.

The name Montagnards was applied to the Mountain Indians by Petitot (1867–1920) and Ducot (1892, 1914), though Petitot (1876:xx) also used it in a broader sense to include several groups in the mountains west of the Mackenzie River (also Hodge 1907l:934). The designation Gens des Montagnes was used in English by McLean (1932:339), apparently for the Mountain Indians. Petitot (1891:362) reported that the Mountain Indians (of his classification) were commonly called Montagnais in French, but he himself regularly used Montagnais to mean 'Chipewyan' (Petitot 1876). Entirely distinct are the Algonquian-speaking Montagnais of Quebec and Labrador (so-called in both English and French), and the Rocky Mountain Indians of historical sources (Mackenzie 1801:163).

Sources

Throughout the nineteenth century Mountain Indians are merely mentioned or very briefly discussed. Petitot (1869, 1878, 1888, 1891, 1893) mentioned them most frequently but seldom described them distinctively from other native groups; most of Petitot's materials are very rare in North American libraries. In the twentieth century very little has been added to information on the Mountain Indians. Keele (1910) on his explorations of the Keele River in 1908 and Camsell (1954) provide brief statements about the Mountain Indians. The only published anthropological source is Michéa (1963), whose fieldwork was in 1957–1958 at Fort Norman and in the Mackenzie Mountains. His essay deals primarily with the annual cycle and the modes of transportation used by the Mountain Indians while in the Mackenzie Mountains and their adaptations to Canadian society at Fort Norman.

Primary sources for this article are Gillespie (1968–1971) and other unpublished sources, especially the Hudson's Bay Company archival records.

Slavey

MICHAEL I. ASCH

Territory

The terms Slave ('slāv) and Slavey ('slāvē) have traditionally been used to describe one grouping of Athapaskan-speaking people living in the boreal forest region of northwestern Canada. Osgood (1936:17), following Petitot (1891:363), places this group at the time of first European contact in "the region of the Slave River and the drainage of the western end of Great Slave Lake continuing some distance down the Mackenzie River." According to Osgood's (1936:4) map the northern boundary of Slavey territory extends to a point near the settlement of Wrigley, while Jenness (1932:389) would place it somewhat farther north near the settlement of Fort Norman (fig. 1).

Although popularly described as a "tribe," there is no evidence to support the notion that the Athapaskans of the Slavey region constituted a single entity in any political, cultural, or linguistic sense either in late aboriginal times or in the period since European contact. Rather, data both from early historical sources and from ethnographic fieldwork indicate that the Athapaskans of the region have always identified themselves as members of smaller groups and used geographic location, peculiarities of behavior, differences in local dialect, or variation in some cultural feature to differentiate among these groups (Honigmann 1946:23). Indeed, there is no equivalent in any Athapaskan language for a single group living in the region defined as Slavey and the only general collective means of designating the people in this area in native terms is by use of the label *dene* 'people', which implies the inclusion of all Athapaskan-speaking peoples. However, in the twentieth century, some Athapaskans, while using community residence to identify themselves in the Slavey language, have adopted the label Slavey to differentiate between themselves and Whites, Crees, and other Athapaskan groups such as Hare, Dogrib, and Chipewyan, for whom English language labels are known, when communicating in English.

Thus, as it seems clear that the "Slavey" Indians never formed a single tribal unit, the term Slavey is defined here as applying to those Athapaskans who, in the twentieth century, accept this label, at least when speaking English. Geographically, their region encompasses the lands along the west end of Great Slave Lake, an area south and west of the lake bounded by the Hay River to the east and the Liard drainage to the west, and the Mackenzie River valley north to Great Bear River. It includes people living in or near the settlements of Fort Norman, Wrigley, Fort Simpson, Fort Providence, Hay River, and Fort Liard in the Northwest Territories; Fort Nelson in British Columbia; and the Hay Lakes region of the upper Hay River (near Fort Vermilion) in Alberta. In 1974 the Prophet River band was administratively divided from the Fort Nelson band; these Indians, variously described as Sekanis or Beavers, are treated in "Beaver" in this volume.

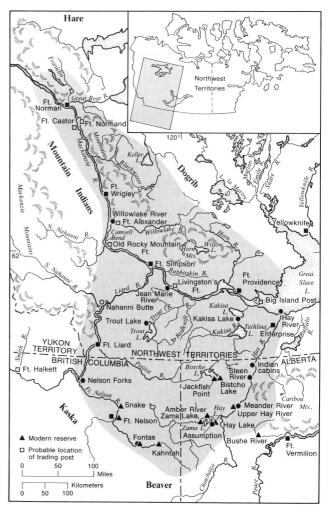

Fig. 1. Tribal territory about 1850.

Environment

The Slavey territory is a region characterized by small lakes, rivers, and waterways cutting through low-lying plains. The predominant forest cover is white spruce, birch, and jack pine typical of the Mackenzie lowlands region of the boreal forest (Halliday 1937:13). The climate is continental, with long, cold winters and short, but surprisingly mild, summers, separated by brief transition periods known as breakup and freeze-up (G. Taylor 1947:43).

The lakes and waterways that dominate the region are rich in fish, the most common of which are trout, loche, whitefish, northern pike, and inconnu. Major furbearers are beaver, marten, muskrat, lynx, and mink. Varying hare and, in season, migratory waterfowl are major small game. Of the big game animals, only the moose and woodland caribou are found extensively throughout the region; however, black bear are present especially in the west and north, and wood bison were known aboriginally in the south and east (Honigmann 1946:22). Barren-land caribou are rare, though until the 1960s herds would usually appear at least one year in six in the Mackenzie valley region (Asch 1969–1970). Summer provides an intense growing season for a wide variety of plants including edible berries such as saskatoons, rosehips, strawberries, and raspberries.

Language

Slavey has been grouped with Dogrib, Chipewyan, Hare, Mountain, and Bearlake as a language of the Northeastern Athapaskan subgroup (Howren 1975); however, it is not likely that the Slavey Indians ever spoke one unique variety of Athapaskan but rather spoke a number of mutually intelligible dialects, at least some of which were more comprehensible to Athapaskans of adjoining regions than they were to each other.* In the twentieth century, the Athapaskans began to adopt English as a lingua franca. Thus, by the 1960s, while the older people of Wrigley, a northern Slavey settlement, could understand Hare, Mountain, Dogrib, Bearlake, and most Slavey dialects, the younger people

were able to understand only the Slavey spoken in their own and neighboring communities and used English to communicate with others.

Culture

The reconstruction of aboriginal Athapaskan culture for the Slavey region is hampered by the lack of an adequate archeological record, the inadequacy of early travelers' reports, and the possible inaccuracies in descriptions from native informants, who are several generations removed from precontact times. Therefore, any interpretation of the aboriginal culture here is bound to contain errors and must be considered tentative at best. Nonetheless, Honigmann (1946) has provided an extensive and reasonable reconstruction of aboriginal Athapaskan culture in the Fort Nelson area based on informant descriptions. The account presented here will rely heavily on the Fort Nelson data but will also make use of descriptions provided by informants at Wrigley (Asch 1969–1970) and information taken from some early travelers' reports.

Subsistence

The aboriginal population of the region in late precontact times has been estimated at approximately 1,250 people (Kroeber 1939:141). The primary economic and social unit was the local group of perhaps 10 to 20 individuals. As the region is relatively poor and not ecologically diverse, it is most likely that local groups lived in semi-isolation from each other for most of the year, staying within a small geographic zone centered near a fish lake. In this way, each group could minimize the threat of starvation by exploiting a dependable supply of fish and small game animals while searching for moose and the other big game essential for both food and raw materials. However, some time during the summer when subsistence conditions permitted, local groups came together at a central campground such as at Great Slave Lake where they formed a temporary assemblage of perhaps 200 to 250 people; this assemblage lasted until conditions again necessitated dispersal.

---

*The phonemes of Slavey are: (unaspirated stops and affricates) *b, d, ƛ, δ̂, ʒ, ǯ, g,* ʔ; (aspirated stops and affricates) *t, ƛ, θ̂, c, č, k*; (glottalized) *t́, ƛ́, θ́, ć, č̓, ḱ*; (voiceless continuants) *ł, θ, s, š, x, h*; (voiced continuants) *l, δ, z, ž, γ*; (prenasalized stops) ᵐ*b,* ⁿ*d*; (nasals) *m, n*; (resonants) *r, y*; (plain vowels) *i, e, a, o, u*; (nasalized vowels) *i̧, ȩ, a̧, o̧, u̧*; (long vowels) *i·, e·, a·, o·, u·*; (long nasalized vowels) *i̧·, ȩ·, a̧·, o̧·, u̧·*; (tones) high (v́), low (unmarked). There is phonological and lexical variation among and within the several Slavey-speaking communities. For example, there is a general fluctuation between *ž* and *y*, but with a preference for *ž* in Fort Simpson and Fort Providence and for *y* in Fort Liard and elsewhere. Before nonnasal vowels there is generally free variation between the nasals and the corresponding

prenasalized stops, except that in Fort Simpson, Fort Providence, and Hay River the prenasalized stops are obligatory in this position in stems. In all dialects, *ǫ* and *ǫ·* often merge with *o* and *o·*.

In the practical orthography used by the Department of Education of the Northwest Territories the Slavey phonemes are written as follows: b, d, dl, ddh, dz, j, g, '; t, tl, tth, ts, ch, k; t', tl', tth', ts', ch', k'; ł, th, s, sh, x, h; l, dh, z, zh, gh; mb, nd; m, n; r, y; i, e, a, o, u; i̧, ȩ, a̧, ǫ, u̧; ii, ee, aa, oo, uu; i̧i̧, ȩȩ, a̧a̧, ǫǫ, u̧u̧; high tone (v́).

Information on Slavey phonology and the practical orthography was furnished by Keren Rice (communication to editors 1979), who also checked the transcriptions of the forms cited. The phonemicization of nola in the term for Tea Dance was not available.

Snaring with babiche and sinew snares was the main hunting technique for taking both large and small game. Moose and other big game were also hunted with bow and arrow, club, or spear when crossing water or open country. Beaver were dispatched by clubbing after they had been aroused from their lodge. Fishnets made of woven willow bast or caribou babiche were used in both lakes and rivers. Weirs were used in running water. Edible berries and roots were gathered in bark baskets. Men were responsible for taking large game and fish, women and children for small game, berries, and roots.

Food preparation was the women's task. Most commonly, food was cooked by stone-boiling in a vessel made of bark or "plaited" (coiled?) spruce root sometimes lined with clay ("Environment and Culture in the Shield and Mackenzie Borderlands," fig. 15, this vol.). Meat was also broiled on a skewer, fish on red-hot rocks or by hanging over a fire. Occasionally fish was baked under hot ashes. Fat was rendered from beaver, muskrat, and porcupine as well as big game animals. In summer, surplus food was preserved by smoking and drying (fig. 2) over a smudge fire; in winter it was frozen

and cached. Berries were eaten raw or pounded with meat, fish, and fat to make pemmican. Food was served in birchbark dishes and eaten with the fingers or wooden spoons.

Clothing and Adornment

Clothes were generally made from moose hide (figs. 3–4) though on occasion women's and children's wear was made of hare skins. Clothing was the same for men and women, consisting of a cloak, a shirt, leggings attached to moccasins, and in winter a pair of mittens attached by a cord hung from the neck. All winter garments except headwear and footwear were made with the hair still on the hide and sewed together with moose sinew. Fringes and moose-hair or porcupine-quill ornamentation (figs. 5–7) served as decorative motifs.

Bracelets, wrist and arm bands, and necklaces made of wood, horn, or bone were worn, as were belts and garters made of dressed hide. Men usually had their facial hair plucked out by the roots and were tatooed

Native Press, Yellowknife, N.W.T.

Fig. 2. Indian students learning to make dry meat at Drum Lake Lodge on the shore of Lake Wrigley. The lodge was run by Paul and Mary Rose Wright, formerly of Ft. Norman, as a Wilderness Education Center, to teach Athapaskan youths the traditions and culture of their ancestors. Photographed in 1975.

ASCH

Fig. 3. Celine Gargan dehairing a moose hide using a curved-end scraper made from a piece of metal from a trap or an iron file. Photograph by June Helm, near Ft. Simpson, N.W.T., April or May 1952.

with a double line of black or blue on each cheek from ear to nose. A hole was pierced in the septum of the nose through which a quill or stick was passed. Hair style for both sexes was either long or long in the back but cropped from the crown to the ears (Mackenzie 1970:184).

Structures

The Slaveys used two types of dwellings. One, a conical structure that resembled a tepee, was made by leaning three or four poles at right angles to one another and covering them with bark or moose hide. According to Mackenzie, they were pitched so that two families could share a communal fire (Mackenzie 1970:185). When abandoned, the skin covering was packed and carried, but the frame was left standing for the use of other parties. The other shelter resembled a low oblong cabin with walls made of logs chinked with moss or cemented, a pitched roof covered with spruce boughs, and two doorways (J.A. Mason 1946:20, 21). The fire was placed in the center of the dwelling, and smoke escaped through a firehole in the roof.

In the Fort Nelson area, the conical structure is re-

ported to have been more commonly used than the pitched-roof one (Honigmann 1946:50); however, in the eastern region, the conical structures were mainly found at large camping grounds such as Great Slave Lake (J.A. Mason 1946:20) and along main river routes (Mackenzie 1970:185), thus suggesting a summer usage. The pitched-roof dwelling, on the other hand, may have been associated primarily with small fish-lake encampments and was perhaps a winter structure (Jenness 1932:390; J.A. Mason 1946:20).

When traveling, temporary shelters were made by bending small trees and covering them with moose hide. Several types of caches were constructed. The most common was a smooth pole 10 to 15 feet high with the bark removed. In winter, ground caches were also used (Honigmann 1946:51).

Travel and Transport

Summer travel was primarily by water in shallow-draft, one- or two-man canoes sheathed with spruce bark (fig. 8) or birchbark. Rafts, although known, were rarely used. In summer overland travel was by foot with essential goods carried on the back by means of straps secured over the crown of the head. The women carried babies strapped to their backs in moose-hide bags called mossbags. Women were also responsible for carrying the fire in both summer and winter.

All travel in winter depended upon foot power. At least two types of snowshoes were used: a narrow type for breaking and following trails and a wider and longer variety used in tracking big game animals. These were made of babiche lacing stretched on a spruce-wood frame. Toboggans pulled by the women carried essential goods. During the transition periods of breakup and freeze-up the water systems were impassible, making travel at any distance impossible.

The designation of geographical directions seems not to have been uniform throughout the total region. In the Fort Nelson area, north was defined as 'downstream', south as 'upstream', east as 'where the sun rises', and west as 'where the sun sets' (Honigmann 1946:49). Among the groups along the Mackenzie River, direction was apparently indicated by wind direction (Asch 1969–1970).

Social Organization

• KINSHIP RECKONING While it is known that aboriginal social organization was structured by kinship relations, Slavey kinship terminological features for the precontact period remain unclear. Ethnographic and historical accounts appear to agree that in the grandparental generation only sex and age were used to differentiate kinship relations, while for the second descending generation distinctions were based exclusively

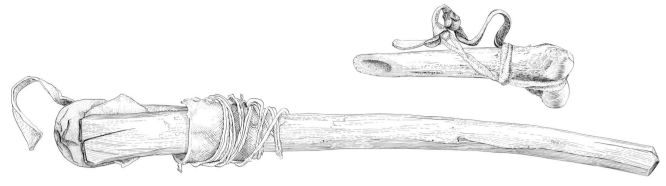

Fig. 4. Hide-working tools. top, Flesher with moosehide handstrip; bottom, hide softener of flaked stone wrapped with moosehide and hafted with string and canvas. Length of bottom 75 cm, other same scale. Collected by J.J. Honigmann at Ft. Nelson, B.C., 1943.

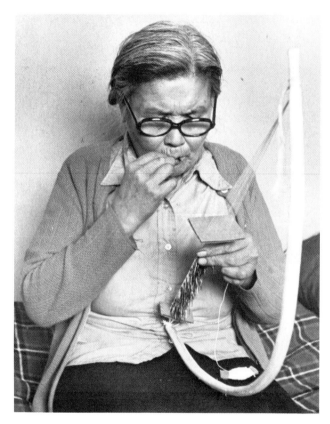

Fig. 5. Margarite Sabourin weaving porcupine quills on a traditional wooden bow loom with cardboard warp spacers. She is softening and flattening the quills between her teeth. Photographed at Ft. Providence, 1978.

on generation with terminological differentiation made on the basis of the sex of the speaker. Concerning the first ascending generation, some reports (MacNeish 1960:280ff.; Asch 1972:47) indicate use of a bifurcate merging system at least in the historical period, while others (Honigmann 1946:68) give a more complicated picture. For ego's generation, Honigmann (1946:68) reports a Hawaiian system, Asch (1972:48) an Iroquoian, while MacNeish (1960:280ff.) records use of

both types. In the first descending generation, Honigmann (1946:68) suggests a Hawaiian pattern, while MacNeish (1960:280, 281) and Asch (1972:48) indicate the use of an Iroquoian parallel-cross designation. According to informants at Wrigley, in the first descending generation, ego designated as his own children the children of his same sex siblings, same sex parallel cousins, and opposite sex cross-cousins. The children of his opposite sex parallel cousins and same sex cross-cousins were given a "cross" designation (Asch 1969–1970). A similar kind of differentiation is found in MacNeish (1960:280).

The Slavey did not have clans or other forms of unilineal descent groups. Relations between individuals were most likely traced laterally through the use of sibling and marriage links between living persons rather than lineally by means of descent principles and a precise genealogical record. Nonetheless, the Slavey classificatory kinship network was quite extensive in scope.

• THE LOCAL GROUP   The primary economic and social unit was the local group. According to informants at Wrigley (Asch 1969–1970), local groups were commonly structured around a core of parallel relatives of a single sex, although a powerful and important individual could establish such a group regardless of kinship considerations. Most likely, membership in a local group could be established merely by operationalizing real or classificatory parallel ties to a person of the same sex already belonging to the group. This allowed for great flexibility in the nature of the local group's composition and so enabled smooth transitions during times of economic, social, or even individual crisis. Without a strong descent principle, groups were probably dissolved on the death of a core member.

Members of the local group were expected to share food and material things. Leadership in economic matters was provided by a successful male hunter who often also served as the medicine man. There was no institutionalized political structure within the local groups, and so disputes were settled informally with banishment

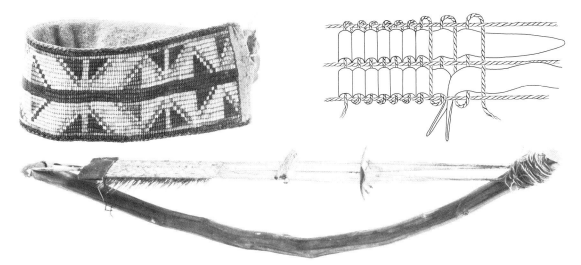

Fig. 6. Loomed quillwork. bottom, Bow loom with red, white, and blue porcupine quillwork in progress. Warp strands of sinew are stretched through 2 birchbark spacers and tied to the ends of the bow. The sinew weft on a wooden shuttle is passed over and under the warp with the flattened quills being alternately bent up or down over the weft thread with each pass. After each pass of the weft the quills are pushed tightly together to conceal the weft. New quills are added as shown in the diagram; the ends that protrude at the back of the work are cut off close to the weave after the piece is finished. Length 59.5 cm, collected 1862. top left, Bracelet of white, red, and blue woven porcupine quills, backed with leather. Width 3.5 cm, collected by B.R. Ross at Ft. Simpson in 1860–1861.

Fig. 7. Quilled band, probably used as sling to support small child on mother's back (see "Old Crow, Yukon Territory," fig. 6, this vol.). Purple, red, black, and white quills are laid flat (see detail, front side has tone) rather than woven, and backed with canvas. Wool and bead tassels, leather ties. Length of band 110 cm (plus ties), collected at Hay River, 1924.

Fig. 8. Spruce-bark canoe made of a single sheet of bark, sewed with spruce root fore and aft, with holes plugged with moss and spruce gum. The ribs and gunwales are of spruce. The canoe was constructed by Louis Norwegian, who is pictured, and his trapping partner for their return from the spring beaver hunt after breakup. Mackenzie River and ice floes in background. Photograph by June Helm, near Ft. Simpson, May 1952.

being the most severe form of punishment commonly administered.

• INTERGROUP RELATIONS   Relations among local groups were characterized by friendship and warmth. Meetings, whether chance winter encounters between two local groups or large gatherings at a summer camp, were generally pleasant occurrences that provided an opportunity for gossip, exchanges of information, and, for the young people, courtship. They were occasions that called for feasting and dancing. There were two kinds of dances: the Drum Dance (ʔeɣele čę́ dagoδe) in which the dancers stood behind one another and the Tea Dance or Round Dance (nola dagoδe) in which they danced side by side in a circle. The Drum Dance was performed to the accompaniment of a tambourine drum (ʔeɣele) made of caribou hide stretched over a birchwood frame.

Disputes between local groups were usually resolved peacefully by means of a hand-game competition or a ritual contest of medicine men. In extreme cases, physical reprisal was permitted, though premeditated murder was probably not sanctioned.

• MARRIAGE RULES   While no prescriptive regulations have been reported in the region, Wrigley informants

(Asch 1969–1970) suggest that the preferred type of marriage was between individuals belonging to different local groups for whom parallel kinship ties could not be established. Unions of parallel cousins not living in the same local group were considered permissible but were not encouraged. Only marriages between members of the same local group were said to be strictly taboo. Unions between the sons of one local group and the daughters of another were highly approved of and encouraged. Sister exchange, the levirate, and the sororate were practiced. Honigmann (1946:85) also reports polygyny.

Life Cycle

The choice of a marriage partner was usually left to the individual, though the girl's parents generally played a key role in the decision. During courtship, the boy had to prove his worth to the girl's parents by giving gifts and performing services. Marriage was formalized only after a period of bride service usually lasting until the birth of the couple's first child, after which the couple was free to establish residence where it pleased. Permanent matrilocal residence was common in the Fort Nelson region (Honigmann 1946:83). According to informants, divorce in aboriginal times was virtually non-existent (Asch 1969–1970).

Births were attended only by the women. Delivery was accomplished in a kneeling position on a blanket of moss. When giving birth, the woman was cautioned to remain silent as outbursts were considered to have a detrimental effect on the unborn baby. Upon delivery, the afterbirth and the moss blanket were burned or buried. The mother then remained away from the camp until she had fully recovered so as to minimize the spiritual danger to the men.

For about two years after birth the mother nursed and carried the infant in a moosehide moss-lined bag (fig. 9). Diapers were made from moose hide, moose-calf skin, or hare pelts. Diaper lining consisted of dried moss. Lullabies were often sung. Naming generally occurred during the early years after the child revealed his character through some act. The parents usually adopted a teknonym based on the name of their first-born. Children were highly valued among the Slavey, and, at least in the eastern area, adoption was easy.

For girls, menarche marked the beginning of adulthood. At the outset of her first menstrual flow, the girl was removed from the camp to a small shelter where she remained for 10 days (Honigmann 1946:85). From then on, she was expected to reside away from the camp during menstruation. For boys, adulthood was achieved upon the first kill of a large game animal, after which a ceremony was held. Often, a young man would acquire spiritual power for curing and hunting from an animal spirit who appeared in a dream and gave the

boy a special song by which the spirit could be summoned when needed.

The attribution of cause for most illnesses in aboriginal times is not known; however, serious illnesses and deaths in certain cases are known to have been attributed to witchcraft. Common ailments were cured by herbal remedies and perhaps sweat baths. Serious sickness required the service of a strong medicine man who summoned his spiritual animal to fight the invading supernatural force ("Expressive Aspects of Subarctic Indian Culture," fig. 1, this vol.).

At the moment of death, the individual was considered to possess great spiritual power and his dying words were carefully remembered. After death, the corpse was either interred or placed in a tree scaffold. Some personal possessions were placed with him. Other property was burned or discarded. Death feasts were sometimes held, but there were no mourning songs.

The Supernatural World

The supernatural world was inhabited by spirits that could dispense power to or create danger for mortals. Spirits presented themselves to humans usually in animal forms such as the beaver, otter, wolf, and raven. Some individuals possessed personal animal-spirits who could warn them of danger in a dream or could be called upon to aid in a crisis. Shamans possessing such a spirit would avoid killing or eating the animal that represented it. Two of these animal-spirits, the raven and the wolf, played a central role in the creation of the world (Asch 1969–1970). Honigmann (1946:90) mentions the raven in this context but not the wolf. Other supernatural creatures for the Slavey included monsters who lived at the mouth of the Mackenzie

Anglican Church of Canada, General Synod Arch., Toronto, Ont.:P7517–328.

Fig. 9. Indians and/or Métis at Hay River. The woman is holding a baby in a moss bag covered with elaborate floral designs probably of beads. Photograph by Henry W. Jones, about 1910.

River (Mackenzie 1970:182ff.) and bushmen (*náhgane*) who were represented as unsocialized giants who stole careless young children.

History of Indian-White Contact

A few European trade items such as iron were introduced into the region by Cree or Chipewyan middlemen probably by the mid-eighteenth century. In the late part of the eighteenth century, the European trade rivalries stimulated the Cree to raid into Slavey territory, disrupting normal travel and settlement patterns as far north as Camsell Bend (Mackenzie 1970:179, 181).

Initial European contact in the region occurred with Alexander Mackenzie's expedition in 1789. About 1796, the North West Company established Livingston's Fort, the first post in Slavey territory, on the Mackenzie River at a point about 80 miles downstream from Great Slave Lake (Voorhis 1930:104). About five additional posts, some short-lived, were established along the Mackenzie and Liard rivers between 1800 and 1810. After the fur-trading companies' consolidation of 1821, the Hudson's Bay Company maintained several permanent posts in the region. Throughout the nineteenth century expansion by the company was slow and cautious. In 1879, Wrigley, the last post to be established in the region, was opened. This brought the total number of trading forts frequented predominantly by Slavey to seven: Fort Norman, Wrigley, Fort Simpson, Fort Providence, Hay River, Fort Nelson, and Fort Liard. All were still functioning in the 1960s (see table 1).

Christian missionaries from both the Anglican and Roman Catholic churches arrived in the North in 1858. Through the rest of the nineteenth century, the two denominations competed for converts. As a result, in several communities some Slaveys became nominal Roman Catholics and others nominal Anglicans. According to Duchaussois (1923:242), virtually all the Slaveys had been contacted by Christian missionaries by the end of the nineteenth century, the final converts being the people at Trout Lake in 1902.

The government of Canada, although it had been ceded Rupert's Land by the Hudson's Bay Company in 1869 and had appointed a lieutenant governor in 1875, did not begin to assert its presence in much of the company's former domain until the start of the twentieth century. The government's first land-cession treaty with segments of Slaveys was made at Fort Res-

Table 1. Major Trading Posts in the Slavey Region

			Missionary Contact		
Post and Founding Company	Founded-Abandoned	Other Names	Catholic	Anglican	Treaty Signing
North West Company					
Livingston's Fort	ca. 1796[a]–1799[j]	Trout River Post			
Old Rocky Mountain Fort	ca. 1800[d]–ca. 1805[d]				
Fort Simpson	1804[a]–	Fort of the Forks[d] 1802–1821	1858[f]	1858[b]	1921, No. 11
Fort Liard	1804[j]–	Fort Riviere-du-Liard[d]	1860[f]	1858[f]	1922, No. 11
Fort Nelson, B.C.	1804[h]–1812[j]		1868	—	1911, No. 8
Reestablished by Hudson's Bay Company	1865[d]–				
Forts Castor and Norman	ca. 1810[d]–1822[a]		—	—	
Hudson's Bay Company					
Fort Norman	1822[a]–		1859[f]	1871[b]	1921, No. 11
Fort Halkett	1829[k]–1875[d]		—	—	
Big Island Post	1849[l]–1868[l]		1858[f]	—	
Hay River, N.W.T.	ca. 1868[c]–		1869[f]	1893[a]	1900, No. 8
Fort Providence	1868[l]–		1861[f]	—	1921, No. 11
Wrigley	1877[j]–	Little Rapid[d]	1881[f]	1885[j]	1921, No. 11

NOTE: Because the Slaveys of the Upper Hay River–Hay Lakes region (Alberta) had only short-lived trading posts in their area, they generally traded into Fort Vermilion in Beaver Indian territory; thus, they are not represented here.
[a] Robinson and Robinson 1946.
[b] Tucker 1908.
[c] Canada. Department of Citizenship and Immigration. Indian Affairs Branch 1957.
[d] Voorhis 1930.
[e] Usher 1971.
[f] Duchaussois 1923.
[g] Canada. Department of Northern Affairs and Natural Resources. Indian Affairs Branch 1966.
[h] Honigmann 1946.
[i] Asch 1969–1970.
[j] Innis 1956.
[k] Fleming 1940.
[l] Rae 1963.

olution and Fort Vermilion in 1900 as part of Treaty No. 8. This was followed in 1911 by the addition of the Fort Nelson Slavey to the same treaty. The aboriginal lands of these groups became, respectively, part of the Northwest Territories and of the provinces of Alberta and British Columbia, thus dividing the Slavey region into three political jurisdictions (see table 2). A treaty with the rest of the Slavey living in the Northwest Territories was not made until 1921 (1922 in Fort Liard). The provisions of the treaties called for cession of aboriginal title by the Slavey in return for treaty payments, future reserve lands, and certain governmental services. These terms were still disputed by the Indians in the 1960s.

In the Northwest Territories, where the majority of the Slavey reside, assertion of governmental authority in the period prior to the Second World War was limited to the larger settlements by poor lines of communication. This problem was alleviated when the Canadian and United States governments constructed airstrips and provided radio communications in formerly remote settlements such as Hay River, Fort Simpson, Fort Providence, and Wrigley during the Second World War. Since the war, the government of Canada has established a permanent telecommunications line (including telephone) along the east bank of the Mackenzie River and has inaugurated scheduled airline service to many of the smaller communities, which allowed for more intensive political and juridical control over the region. In 1967 a number of governmental responsibilities and aspects of administration were transferred from the federal government to a new, quasiprovincial government of the Northwest Territories located at Yellowknife.

By the end of the 1930s, exploitation of mineral resources had displaced the fur trade as the dominant industry in the Northwest Territories (Robinson and Robinson 1947:139); however, it was not until after the Second World War that finds of oil and natural gas were made in Slavey territory near Fort Simpson. As a result of these and other finds throughout the North (especially along the Alaskan north slope) the resource industry proposed about 1970 the construction of a gas pipeline along the Mackenzie through the heartland of the Slaveys. This project was approved by the government of Canada, which proposed an energy corridor with pipelines and a road along the east bank of the Mackenzie River. Road construction for this project was started in the summer of 1972. Following the recommendations of the Mackenzie Valley Pipeline Inquiry (Berger 1977), plans for the pipeline were halted in the late 1970s.

Effects of Contact

During the period between initial contact and the First World War, change was, for the most part, related to

the adoption of certain trade goods. Of these, the most significant were: metal implements; firearms; new foods such as tea, flour, rice; and tobacco. The trading post began to replace the lake shore as the summer camping ground; and, after the introduction of a calendrical cycle of feasts by the missionaries, the trading post and mission settlements became the gathering places for the surrounding local groups at midwinter (Christmas–New Year's) and early spring (Easter).

Despite such innovations, major aspects of Slavey culture remained fundamentally unaltered or changed only slowly during this period. Many items of material culture, such as clothing, were still of native manufacture in the late 1800s, and some stone tools were still being made (Bompas 1888:40, 92). Subsistence still depended upon bush resources taken by hunting, gathering, and fishing; and, even after the introduction of firearms, hunting was still primarily a snaring activity, with firearms used only in situations that had previously called for the bow and arrow or the spear. The local group was still the primary economic and social unit, and leadership, despite the traders' attempts to introduce trading chiefs, was still in the hands of the able hunters. In short, survival still required the traditional qualities of self-reliance and mobility set within a stable but flexible social order.

Two factors appear to have been most important in maintaining Slavey independence from European influence during this period. The first was the high cost of trade goods relative to the price paid for raw fur, which kept purchases to a minimum. As a result most European goods never became indispensable to the Slavey and trapping for trade remained a subsidiary activity. The second factor was the precariousness of the European presence in the region. Survival by the Whites in times of need depended directly upon Slavey good will, and starvation occurred when the Indians could not provide relief. Thus it was the Slavey strategy for survival and not the European one that was considered the more successful.

Relations between the Indians and Whites during this period were peaceful. There was only one incident of violence directed at the Whites. This occurred at Fort Nelson early in the nineteenth century and resulted in the deaths of a factor and his family along with the destruction of the post (Honigmann 1946:30).

The period of Slavey autonomy from European influence lasted until the start of the First World War, when a rapid rise in fur prices persuaded most Indians to begin serious trapping for furs (Asch 1969–1970). Although prices fell again after the war, most Slaveys continued to trap for income, and since that time the availability of sufficient money to purchase trade goods has been a primary economic concern.

Euro-Canadian influence has greatly increased in the period since the Second World War. This is due mainly to the introduction of programs by the government of

Table 2. Indian Population of Settlements Occupied or Frequented by Slaveys

Settlement	1858[a]	1881[b]	1883[b]	1921[c]	1924[d]	1931[e]	1941[f]	1970[g]	1978[j]
Northwest Territories									
Hay River	—[h]	—[h]	—[h]	127	104	129	147	239	276
Fort Providence	—[h]	456	436	256	301	251	376	473	585
Fort Liard	281	216	219	207	227	225	202	321	442
Fort Simpson	658[i]	500[i]	234	356	376	343	378	623	704
Wrigley			164	80	83	91	77	169	199
Fort Norman	84[i]	254[i]	324[i]	204[i]	370[i]	346[i]	200[i]	164[i]	214
British Columbia									
Fort Nelson		209[i]	224[i]		120	74	75	334[i]	287
Alberta									
Hay Lakes Region	—[h]	—[h]	—[h]	—[h]	440	—[h]	—[h]	1,011[i]	1,262
Totals	1,023	1,635	1,601	1,230	2,021	1,459	1,455	3,334	3,969

[a] Anderson 1858:282.
[b] Russell 1898:160.
[c] Canada. Department of Interior. Northwest Territories and Yukon Branch 1923:18.
[d] Canada. Department of Indian Affairs 1924:56.
[e] Bethune 1937:48.
[f] Wherrett 1947:230.
[g] Canada. Department of Indian Affairs and Northern Development. Indian Affairs Branch 1970:26, 29, 37.
[h] Not available.
[i] Known or reasonably suspected to include non-Slavey Indians by 15% or more.
[j] Canada. Department of Indian Affairs and Northern Development 1980:34, 38, 47–48. Non-Slavey percentage not determined.

Canada to improve the economic and social conditions of northern Indian life. Government policies such as monetary assistance (especially welfare), compulsory education, and improved medical services have sharply decreased dependence on bush resources, mobility, and self-reliance and have resulted in a weakening of traditional leadership and the ability to enculturate the young to traditional Slavey values.

By the 1960s in the large communities such as Hay River, Fort Providence, and Fort Simpson, where the government policies had already become effective, many Indians had opted for a sedentary existence based on monetary income and the purchase of store goods. On the other hand, in the smaller communities such as Wrigley and "Lynx Point" (Helm 1961) the population—while it had become dependent on many Western material items such as store-bought clothing, scow and motor for transportation on water, the snowmobile, and the radio—still relied in large measure on bush resources for subsistence and maintained many aspects of traditional social organization. However, by the late 1960s, with the extension of local community schools, governmental services, and medical assistance to these settlements, these Slaveys too have come under increasing pressure to reject their traditional pattern of life and conform to the model adopted in the larger communities.

In response to increasing pressures from Euro-Canadian society, Slaveys have become hostile to the presence of the Whites in the region. In the late 1960s Slaveys, especially in the larger communities, began to take political action, such as seeking elective office and joining pan-native political organizations, as a means to check White influence in the region and thus regain the initiative in controlling their affairs.

Synonymy†

The name Slavey continues that used by Hudson's Bay Company traders in the nineteenth century (Kennicott 1862a); it was apparently originally a language name, the designation "broken Slavé" being attested for the Athapaskan-based jargon formerly used in the northwestern parts of British America (Dall 1870:106). Presumably the name Slavé was formed by adding the ending of French group and language names like *français* and *anglais* to the English word slave. Another spelling is Slavi (Reeve in Pilling 1892:88).

English Slave and its French equivalent *Esclave* are applied to a number of Athapaskan groups in the early sources. Often the names Slave and Dogrib are interchanged or the Slave are equated with the "Rocky Mountain Indians" or some other group. The epithet Slave was also applied on occasion to the tribes of the Blackfoot confederacy (for example, Rowand 1842). However, by the mid-nineteenth century the term Slave was commonly used by Whites specifically for the Athapaskans of what is defined here as the Slavey region. In the twentieth century these Indians generally refer to themselves and their language as Slavey, except for those in Alberta and British Columbia, who use the name Slave (Keren Rice and Patrick Moore, communications to editors 1979; Honigmann 1946:22).

†This synonymy was written by Michael I. Asch and Ives Goddard. *347*

The name Slave is a translation of Cree *awahka·n* 'captive, slave' (pl. *awahka·nak*) (Petitot 1888a:293; Faries 1938:403, phonemicized), though some sources refer it to a Cree word meaning literally 'stranger': Northern Plains Cree *ayahciyiniw* 'Slavey' (David H. Pentland, communication to editors 1979), but Southern Plains Cree *aya·hciyiniw* 'member of the Blackfoot confederacy' (Faries 1938:243, phonemicized). According to Mackenzie (1970:238) the Cree applied the pejorative label 'slave' to groups of Athapaskans that they had driven out of the Lake Athabasca region in late precontact times, and Petitot (1876:xx) stated that it was a reference to "their timidity." Peter Pond in 1790 reported what appear to be Swampy Cree names for Great Slave Lake and the Slave River that contain Iotchinine and Iotchyniny, and he gave the explanation "Iotchininy signifies Slaves, or a savage and uncultivated people" (Davidson 1918:opp. 42–43). The two Cree terms were equated by Turnor (1934:399) in 1791 when he wrote that the (Woods) Cree called Great Slave Lake "the Arch-a-thin-nu or Wau-con Sack-a-ha-gan or Slave Lake."

Petitot (1891:363) differentiated four regional bands within Slavey territory: (1) Des-nèdhè-yaρè-l'Ottinè 'people of the great river below' (modern Slavey *deh neδe gotine*) or Tρi-kka-Gottinè 'people on the water' (both names apparently equivalent to 'Mackenzie River people'; Petitot 1891:75); (2) Él'é-idlin-Gottinè 'people of the forks' (now *łí·λį kǫ́ę́ gotine* 'Fort Simpson people'); (3) Ettchéri-dié-Gottinè 'people of the swift current' (*ʔečide deh gotine*) along the Liard River; (4) Etcha-Ottinè 'sheltered people' (now *ʔeča gotine* 'Fort Liard people'). An earlier listing (Petitot 1876:xx) differs somewhat and gives the Etchaρè-ottiné of the Liard River as a group separate from the rest of the Slavey. These are apparently the people referred to as the Echel-la-o-tuna or Gens des Bois Forts, 1807 (Wentzel 1889–1890, 1:85), Tsillawdawhoot-dinneh (Franklin 1824, 2:87), Tsilla-ta-ut-'tinnè 'brushwood people' (Richardson 1852:247), and Bastard Beaver Indians (Ross in Gibbs 1872:308); they called themselves Beaver Indians but were distinct from the Beaver of the Peace River (Keith 1889–1890, 2:68). In this connection it is noteworthy that the three early contact-period groups indicated on Mackenzie's (1970:opp. 164–165) map in the region defined here as Slavey are the Strong Bow Indians (perhaps a translation of Gens des Bois Forts), the Inland Indians, and the Beaver Indians.

The Slavey have no name to refer to themselves in their own language except the very general *dene* 'people'. Chipewyan names recorded for them are Tesscho-tinneh 'great river (Mackenzie) people' (Gibbs 1872:303), and *desneθéhotįne, desnáhotįne,* and *desnátįne* (Li and Scollon 1976:275, 299; Ronald Scollon, communication to editors 1979); these names seem to refer especially (or perhaps only) to the Mackenzie River Slavey. The name Grand River Indians (Keith 1889–1890, 2:106, 111) translates an expression of this type. Other names identified with the Slavey are in Hodge (1907b:440). Kutchin *ʔa·čin* 'Slavey people' (Ritter 1976a:46) may refer to the Mackenzie Athapaskans generally.

In the late 1970s the name Dené Thá was adopted to replace the band name Slaves of the Upper Hay River (Canada. Department of Indian Affairs and Northern Development 1980:34); this represents Slavey *deneδa* 'real people'.

Petitot (1876:xx) used Esclave as a name for the Mackenzie valley Athapaskans generally, including the Liard River Slavey, the Slavey proper, the Dogrib, the Hare, and the Mountain Indians; this usage is noted, with some confusion, in the entry "Slaves" in Hodge (1910d:600). In modern local usage in the Northwest Territories, the name Slavey is applied also to the Hare, Bearlake, and Mountain Indians of Forts Good Hope, Franklin, and Norman (but not to the Dogrib) and is used by these Indians in English as a self-designation and linguistic label (Keren Rice, communication to editors 1979).

Sources

Honigmann provides an extensive account of aboriginal culture as reconstructed by twentieth-century informants. Other reconstructions appear in J.A. Mason (1946) and Jenness (1932). A brief summary of aboriginal Slavey life based primarily on Honigmann appears in Spencer and Jennings (1965).

The primary firsthand account of the time of first direct contact appears in Mackenzie's journals of his explorations in 1789 and 1793. Several versions of these journals are available, but Mackenzie (1970) and Mackenzie (1966) provide commentary concerning specific geographic locations found in Mackenzie's entries. Wentzel (1889–1890, 1) and Keith (1889–1890, 2) provide excellent information on the early contact period, 1807–1824, while for the last half of the nineteenth century, Bompas (1888) and Petitot (1891) give the most complete information. In addition, Russell (1898) provides some useful data on the Slavey, including population statistics. Duchaussois (1923) gives a history of the Roman Catholic missions in the district, while Bompas (1888) and Tucker (1908) provide this data for the Anglicans. Voorhis (1930) contains the most complete historical record of trading posts in the region but is not always accurate. Primary unpublished sources for the nineteenth and twentieth centuries can be found in the archives of the Hudson's Bay Company (microfilm series, Public Archives of Canada, Ottawa), the Anglican missions (Records of the Anglican Dioceses of the Mackenzie River and of Athabasca, Provincial Archives of Alberta, Edmonton), and the records of the

Roman Catholic order of the Oblates of Mary Immaculate, Archives Deschâtelets, Ottawa.

The primary sources of ethnographic information on Slaveys in the twentieth century are Honigmann (1946), Helm (1961), and Asch (1972). In addition, information on Slavey folk tales can be found in MacNeish (1955) and Williamson (1955–1956). Slavey folk beliefs are discussed by MacNeish (1954) and Slavey music by Asch (1972).

A short description of the history and customs of the people of the Slavey region appears under the heading "Etchareottine" in Hodge (1907b).

Beaver

ROBIN RIDINGTON

Language and Territory

The Beaver (ˌbēvər) Indians are the Athapaskan-speaking people of the Peace River of British Columbia and Alberta.* To the west of the Beaver are the closely related Sekani. To the north are Athapaskan Slavey Indians and to the east the Chipewyans of Lake Athabasca. Beginning in the late eighteenth century, Algonquian-speaking Crees moved into the Lower and Middle Peace River areas of the traditional Beaver lands.

The Beaver Indians will be portrayed as they were before the twentieth century, a people who moved from place to place because of their dependence on hunting, gathering, and fishing for subsistence, a pattern that persisted even after the fur trade altered the rhythm of their movement.

The Beaver Indians call themselves *dəneẕa* 'real people'. Before the White world altered the fabric of their society the term *dəneẕa* meant the people with whom one could establish a kinship connection, with whom one could discover a reciprocal term of relationship.

Among those who recognized one another as being *dəneẕa* there were groups with names containing the

element *wədəneˀ* 'people of' or *ne* 'people'; these were collections of people sharing common territory, kinsmen, and dialect. They had names like *yaˀ kwǫ wədəneˀ* 'lousy camp people'; *ƛeže ne* 'grizzly bear [hunting] people'; *çe k̓e wədəneˀ* 'rocky mountain people'; *caˀ čuge wədəneˀ* 'beaver lake people'. These *wədəneˀ* groups were not fixed permanent political or territorial units. They changed composition frequently in adaptation to changes in the availability and distribution of resources.

The name a person used to identify his own *wədəneˀ* group was often different from the name more distant people used to classify him. An old person might think of himself as belonging to the *wədəneˀ* group in which he had spent his childhood, while a young person would see more clearly the old person's membership in his own group. Thus, the name used to refer to a person's *wədəneˀ* group was relative to the social space between him and the observer. To a Beaver Indian, one's *wədəneˀ* group and one's own place in a constellation of kinsmen constantly changing form over time and space was as natural as the movements and changes among the animals upon whom their lives depended.

If an objective model of Beaver social classification is needed perhaps it would be useful to see their social groups as having been like a series of partially overlapping circles within an area bounded by geography, common history, language, and culture. For every person there was a circle of people who were seen regularly and clearly known and recognized as kinsmen. Those on the circumference of an individual's circle of recognition would themselves recognize ties with people outside his usual range of contact, but because of their mediating ties and a common system of classification they could be aware of one another as Beaver. The *wədəneˀ*-group designations can be used either to mean the people who are living together at a particular time, or to mean a group or related groups sharing a common history and genealogy, or to mean all the people of an area some distance away.

In the early twentieth century, Goddard (1917:208) identified three geographical groups of Beavers from the "eastern base of the Rocky Mountains in British Columbia along the Peace River to the falls about forty miles below Vermilion [in north-central Alberta]." Their westernmost extension, a movement in historic

---

*The phonemes of the Beaver of Doig River, B.C., are: (unaspirated stops and affricates) *b, d, λ, ǯ* (dental), *ʒ* (alveolar), *ǯ, g, ˀ*; (aspirated stops and affricates) *t, ƛ, c̣, c, č, k*; (glottalized) *t̓, ƛ̓, c̣̓, č̓, č̓, k̓*; (voiceless continuants) *ł, ṣ, s, š, x, h*; (voiced continuants) *l, ẕ, z, ž, γ*; (nasals) *m, n*; (resonants) *w, y*; (plain vowels) *i, e, æ, a, o, u*; (short vowels) *ɪ, ʊ, ə*; (nasalized vowels) *ę, æ̨, ą, ǫ, ą̇*; (tones) high (v́), low (unmarked). There is extensive but poorly known diversity among the dialects of Beaver; for example, the dialect of Boyer River, Alberta, has an interdental series of affricates and continuants instead of the alveolar series and is in many ways closer to the Slavey of nearby Assumption than it is to Doig Beaver (Patrick Moore, communication to editors 1979).

In the practical orthography used by the Summer Institute of Linguistics the phonemes of Doig Beaver are written as follows: b, d, dl, dz, dz, j, g, `; t, tl, ts, ts, ch, k; t', tl', ts', ts', ch', k'; ł, s, s, sh, h, h; l, z, z, zh, gh; m, n; w, y; ii, e, eaa, aa, o, uu; i, u, a; ę, ęąą, ąą, ǫ, ą; high tone (v́) marked on verbs.

Information on Doig Beaver phonology and the practical orthography was furnished by Gillian L. Story, and the transcriptions of Beaver words were supplied by Marshall and Jean Holdstock (Gillian L. Story, communication to editors 1979). The phonemic analysis of Beaver vowels given here follows the phonetic realizations and the practical orthography; a more abstract analysis positing vowel clusters for certain syllable nuclei and *w*-plus-vowel sequences is preferred by Story.

times, has been into the mountains along the Halfway River, tributary of the Peace, and across the height of land into the headwaters of the Liard drainage along the Sikanni Chief, Prophet, and Muskwa rivers (fig. 1). The Prophet River band is sometimes designated Sekani (Godsell 1934:319; Honigmann 1946:23), for, as Jenness (1937:8) pointed out, "it is impossible to draw a sharp line between Sekani and Beaver Indians, and the Indians of Hudson Hope, who are usually classed as [western] Beaver, might be included with almost equal justice among the Sekani."

Population

According to government records (Canada. Department of Indian Affairs and Northern Development. Indian Affairs Branch 1970, 1980), in 1978 there were 468 Beavers of Treaty-Indian status in Alberta and 444 in British Columbia, totaling 912; the figures in 1970 were 371 and 348, totaling 719. Treaty records of 1929 show 590 Beavers between Fort Vermilion and Hudson's Hope. Faraud (1866:364) estimated 800 in 1859 and believed the population to have been depleted by disease by that time. Assuming an aboriginal population of about 1,000, the population density of the 75,000 square mile area would have been one in 75 square miles or .013 persons per square mile.

Culture

Subsistence

The Beaver depended almost entirely upon animals for food. There are not many lakes in Beaver Indian territory, and fish seem to have been important only as emergency rations when hunting failed. Hares were abundant at the peak of their population cycle but were not preferred food. Beaver were plentiful and were an important food source in addition to their value in the fur trade.

Large game was more important to the Beaver Indians. Bison were in sections of their territory and were a source of food until their extinction in the nineteenth

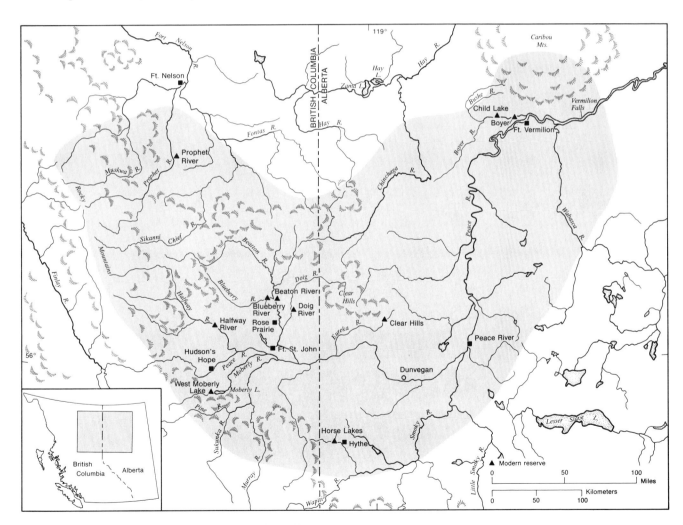

Fig. 1. Territory in 1800. Reserves were established after 1900.

century. Woodland caribou also were limited to certain areas but were important where available. The most significant source of food was the moose, dispersed throughout the area. Besides meat, moose and caribou provided skins for clothing and, in the nineteenth century at least, covers for tepees (Goddard 1917:210), although winter lodges of logs covered with moss and sod were also made.

The Beaver had to organize their lives so that a minimum of about two pounds of meat per capita a day was regularly available. A group of 10 people needed 140 pounds of meat a week or at least one moose every three weeks. A group of 100 people needed 1,400 pounds of meat a week or almost four moose a week. Because of these requirements groups tended to form around an optimum size of 30 individuals. If a group was too large a short period of bad luck, illness, cold weather, or a temporary shortage of game would bring the whole group quickly to starvation, but if a group was too small it risked overdependence on the health and well-being of only one or two hunters. In a group of 30 about one moose a week was required.

Groups changed size easily in response to the availability of resources. In summer and fall when hunting was good many people might come together to sing and dance and renew contacts with one another, but in the lean season of late winter and early spring people usually split up into smaller groups that were less vulnerable to sudden starvation. Both the larger summertime groups and the smallest winter band may be *wədəne⁹* groups. Hunting and trapping territories were not individually owned but the *wədəne⁹* group had definite territorial rights.

Kinship

The basic social and territorial unit may be called a bilaterally extended family band. Because their life was hard, bringing death from many directions, those who lived to an old age and had living children and grandchildren counted themselves fortunate and sought to keep both daughters and sons within their group. To do this meant that wives for the sons and husbands for the daughters were recruited from among relatives whose families had been split apart by death. A successful extended family band included several brothers and their wives but sometimes also sisters and their husbands; a younger generation of active adults, the sons and daughters of the older generation; their spouses; and a generation of children.

The system of terminological classification of relatives accommodated this kind of extended family band

Natl. Mus. of Canada, Ottawa: 60719.

Fig. 2. Structures at Hudson Hope. Typically Athapaskan are the lean-to (right) with brush walling and canvas cover, and the pole drying rack (left) with horizontal member on 2 conical supports. The tepee (center) with canvas cover pinned together shows Plains influence, although the poles are stacked in the Beaver manner rather than the Plains style that yields a more tightly closed cover. Photograph by Diamond Jenness, 1924.

well. Basically, relatives in one's own and adjacent generations fell into two categories, those called 'brothers' and 'sisters', 'mothers' and 'fathers', or 'sons' and 'daughters'; and those called by a term for a potential spouse or spouse of someone in the first category. Thus, every group contained people in each category. Once a successful band had become established, marriage within the band was encouraged as long as it did not grow beyond the size that was ecologically advantageous. It was common for a person's first marriage to be with someone of an older generation. Older men took young girls, often as second or third wives, and young men moved into the ongoing households of widows in need of a new husband.

When a successful family band continued to thrive for several generations it usually split into several linked groups that reunited when seasonal conditions were favorable. The large *wədəne*ʔ group that came together in the summer was actually an evolved form of the *wədəne*ʔ group that was an extended family band. A group of married siblings and their children living together was the basic social unit from which larger associations could grow.

From a small group of actual siblings, relationship could be traced in an expanding circle outward to parallel cousins (children of parents' same-sex siblings) who were also called 'brothers' and 'sisters', and cross-cousins (children of parents' opposite-sex siblings) who were called 'husbands' and 'wives' of oneself or one's brothers and sisters. Ultimately everyone who was a Beaver Indian could be placed in his proper form of relationship to oneself. Half the people in one's own generation were 'brothers' and 'sisters'; the other half, their 'husbands' and 'wives.' Similarly half the people in one's parents' generation were like mothers and fathers (the parents of those called 'brother' and 'sister'), and the other half were the parents of those called 'husbands' and 'wives' (Ridington 1969).

The Beaver explain their kinship system with a story about a brother and sister who were the sole survivors of an attack by a giant animal. The boy and girl knew that a group containing only brothers and sisters is incomplete and barren. If the *wədəne*ʔ group were to continue there would have to be husbands and wives, so they set out walking around a mountain in opposite directions from one another. If they met on the other side it was to be a sign of completion and transformation. When they did meet on the opposite side of the mountain from where they had lived as brother and sister, they became husband and wife. Their children grew and married one another and with the third generation there were again both brothers and sisters, husbands and wives among the Beaver and life has continued in the same way since that time. Every group was able to move self-sufficiently and was a complete social unit from which larger associations might grow.

From the bilaterally extended family band, relationship could be established with any other of the Beaver.

World View

• ANIMALS When a hunter killed an animal he gave meat to everyone in his camp. The people received life from one another just as the hunter received life from the animals. The man who gave away meat one time received it another. The man who received the gift of an animal's life had given away his own life to an animal during a childhood vision quest. Before the people were settled on reserves it was unthinkable for some people in camp to eat while others went hungry. The moose was usually divided at the kill site, each family sending someone to pack in the meat. In camp the meat was then distributed so that everyone was fed.

Persons slept with their heads pointing to the place where the sun rises. A medicine bundle hung behind where the hunter slept. In the bundle were tokens of the animals to whom he had given his life when he went into the bush alone as a child. His dreams came from the place where the sun rises. In them he traveled with his mind ahead of his tracks. When he dreamed he entered the time when he made contact with his medicine animal as a child. He entered the time that is told of in traditional stories about the time of beginning and transformation when giant animals who ate men became the real animals that are eaten by men. In dreaming to the sunrise the Beaver left the sequential time in which tracks are laid down, one after another, and entered an essential time where what was and what shall be might be experienced simultaneously. When the hunter left camp he sought a point of intersection between his own tracks and those of an animal that he had already experienced in his dreaming. When he made contact with an animal and took its life he then revealed his dreaming to the people.

Each species of animal had its song that it gave to the person who sought it out. The word for spiritual power or medicine is *məyɪne*ʔ 'his song'. The same term was used to refer to a person's medicine bundle. Every child was sent into the bush to make contact with an animal. He or she spent several days away from the people. When the child returned, the camp seemed strange and unfamiliar to him. He reacted to it as an animal would react. Usually an old person had been dreaming about him and when the child was seen at the edge of the camp it was he who brought the child back into the circle of the people. The old person placed the skin of his own medicine animal around the body of the child who slept, perhaps for several days. When the child returned from sleep he was a person once more but the memory of his vision remained with him. The old person knew many stories and passed them on to the young. The stories were about the time of beginning, but they were at the same time an account of what every person would experience during the course of his life.

• CREATION The world took on its form when *ya k̓e ṣədę̌*, 'heaven sitter', the creator, drew a cross on the water and sent down various animals to find land. When muskrat came up with a speck of dirt underneath his nails *ya k̓e ṣədę̌* placed the earth at the center of a cross on the water and told it to grow. The structure (fig. 3) laid out in this creation story is the structure within which both the visionary experience and everyday reality took place. In it are laid out the cardinal directions and their point of intersection from which up and down, heaven and the underworld, future and past spring into being. The people slept with their heads pointing to where the sun rises and watched the sun's movement across the sky in reflection of the moment of creation told about in the story. When they traveled through otherwise featureless country they directed their path with reference to the sun's position. Story and reality intersected in their experience. Creation was constantly taking place.

Many stories were about the giant animals that used to live on the world and hunt humans. They talked and lived like people and their game was the animal called *dəneẓa*. The stories of these monsters were set in the distant past and yet when the child went into the bush alone he became one of the *dəneẓa* of long ago who

after Ridington and Ridington 1970:52; Ridington 1978: cover, 50.
Fig. 3. The Beaver cosmos as painted by Kayan, about 1915, on one head of a double-headed drum later owned by his pupil, the dreamer Charlie Yahey. The diagram represents the dreamer's magic flight to the world beyond the sky. Creation began at the center of the cross; the lines slanting outward from it lead to the hatched path to heaven, discovered by the culture hero on his vision quest for Swan medicine.

was eaten by a giant animal. The reality of the stories lay in their relevance to the experience that a person had during his life.

Although in the mid-twentieth century both the stories and the experience of receiving power from the animals have weakened, the old people still tell them to those who will listen. The central figure in many stories is Saya or Usakindji, the culture hero. The events of his life reflect symbolically the experiences of a person growing up among the nomadic hunting Beaver. Here is a short version of the story of Saya. It takes the hero from his birth in the east to the south, west, and finally back to the east. The cardinal directions thus suggest stages in the growth of a person's understanding. The text of this and other stories may be found in Ridington (1978).

• A BOY NAMED SWAN Once there was a boy named Swan. He lived with his mother and father. His mother was a good woman but she died when Swan was young. Before she died she told her husband, "When I die and you take another woman I want you to find one who will be good to my son. Do not take a woman from where the sun goes down. Do not take a woman from where the sun comes up. Take a woman from the South where the sun is at dinner time. That kind of woman will be good to my boy."

Swan's father looked for a woman where the sun was highest but he could not find one. Then he went to look for a woman from where the sun sets. He came to the ocean and stopped there. In that country he found a nice looking woman and brought her back for his son. He made a bow and arrow for Swan and taught him to hunt rabbits.

Swan's father went out to hunt and left his son and his wife in camp. The woman said to her stepson, "Swan, go out to hunt rabbits. I'll go with you."

They went out. She told him, "Every time you see a rabbit shoot it in the head. You can shoot anything you want." When he shot a rabbit in the head that woman would take it and put it under her dress between her legs. As it died it kicked and scratched her legs. When you shoot an animal in the head it always kicks like that.

"Step-mother, why do you do that? We have to eat that meat."

"Well," she said, "I hold him that way so he will die quickly." Every time Swan shot a rabbit through the head that woman did the same thing.

When they got back to camp the father went to sleep with his wife and saw that her legs were all scratched up and covered with dried blood.

"What happened," he asked. "You weren't like that the last time I saw you."

Then that woman lied to her husband. She told him, "Well, your boy did that. He threw me down and did that. He's a big boy now and he is stronger than I am."

Swan's father believed what she said and got mad at his own boy. He told Swan, "Let's go hunting out where the sun goes down in the ocean." He planned to leave Swan on an island in the ocean.

They made a canoe and paddled to an island almost out of sight of land. "Swan, you go around one side. I'll go around the other. We'll find out how big this ground is."

As soon as Swan was out of sight the Old Man turned around and went back to his canoe. He waited for his son some distance offshore. When Swan got back to the place they had left the canoe he saw his father, who said, "I am leaving you here. We both shared the same hole. We can't both go in the same place."

Swan tried to tell his father that the woman had tricked him, but the father did not listen. He went back to their country.

Swan lay down next to the water and cried. He cried himself to sleep. Then he heard someone talking to him but no one was there. It must have been *ya ke șadę* who was helping him. The voice said, "Why do you cry? Don't cry. You are going to live. Do you see all those geese and ducks flying over going to a different place? You get a lot of pitch and put it on the rocks of this island wherever the sun strikes. The ducks and geese will get stuck there. You can live like that."

Swan put pitch on the flat rocks and began to make a house by digging a hole in the ground. The next morning he found ducks and geese stuck in the pitch. He took their feathers and put them in the hole he had dug. He cut up the birds and made dry meat. All fall he prepared for the winter in this way. Swan lived in his house and the cold winter did not bother him. When spring came he had very little left to eat, and it was not warm enough to melt pitch and catch the ducks and geese on their return to the North. When his food was almost gone he thought, "Maybe my father will come back."

One day he heard somebody singing out on the water and hitting a canoe like a drum. It was his father. "Swan, you're smart enough. You fooled around with my woman and now I want to see how your headbone sets. Is it in the water or the bush."

The Old Man went around one side of the island. Swan had been careful not to leave any tracks there. When he was out of sight Swan jumped into the canoe and paddled away. "Now you are going to live the way I did," he called to his father. When he returned to the island in ten days he found his father dead with feathers in his mouth. Then Swan became angry at the bad woman who did that.

He went back to his country and met that woman. He took an arrow and shot it in the ground by her feet. The arrow caught fire when it hit the ground. The woman ran away and Swan fired into the earth after her until she ran into the water. When his flaming ar-

rows hit the water it boiled, and when the woman emerged from the other side she was just bones. That is how Swan killed that bad woman.

After that time Swan stayed with one of the giant animals who eat people. When the giant animal came to a camp of people and killed them Swan became angry. He shot the giant animal in the breast. After that he took the name Saya, and he began to travel around the world killing the giant animals and changing them into the ones that the people see today.

The story of Swan is followed by a heroic cycle of stories about how Saya overcame the giant animals and transformed them into the ones now on the earth. Every person underwent experiences similar to those of Swan. Children were sent out into the bush alone after the mother who nursed them for the first several years of life turned her attentions to a younger child. The father or grandfather sent a child of about six years out into the bush alone to meet for himself the animals that had been calling for him. The stories were as much a part of the reality as the experience itself. Story gave form to experience, and experience gave vitality to tradition.

The stories provide an insight into nearly every aspect of life before the coming of Whites. The qualities that stand out in them are an intimacy with and dependency on nature. The Beaver lived in a vast wilderness and were obliged to move often to maintain a steady supply of meat on which life depended. Many of the stories told of times when they were brought to the point of starvation by bad luck or illness or severe weather. Saya was the one who taught the people many of their essential arts. It was he who first learned to make arrows and it was he who first lay down to receive assistance through a dream. It is the child Swan who overcame the fear of darkness and isolation to become Saya the man. Besides providing entertainment the stories were the medium through which a philosophy combining self-reliance and interdependence was taught.

The transformation of Swan into Saya was paralleled in the life of a man growing up to be a hunter. Saya was self-reliant but his powers came to him through dreaming. The hunter too was self-reliant, but the animal he took was always one that first came to him in a dream. Men and women were equal in their mastery of the arts that were given to them and were equally necessary to the successful completion of a way of life.

• DREAMING Dreaming was central to the experience of the Beaver (Ridington 1971). Every person dreamed. Even the dreams of children were given significance, but until a person dreamed back to the time of his vision quest and had been given instructions for making a medicine bundle, his dreaming was seldom focused to a particular purpose. The medicine bundle hanging behind where a person slept, head to the east, was a sign of his maturity and an instrument of his dreaming. It was usually only when a person was married and responsible for a family that he or she dreamed of a medicine bundle and song. A person's dreams could then aid him in providing for and protecting his family. Both men and women used dreams in this way. Each story about the transformations that Saya effected upon the giant animals was also a story of the vision quest for that animal and the dream that told a person how to construct the medicine bundle for that animal. The stories were actually descriptions in words of the experiences a person might come to have in his dreaming. The story of how Saya emerged from the child Swan tells how a person first abandoned himself to dreaming during his vision quest. Thus, tradition and experience constantly reinforced each other.

Every person who dreamed of 'his song' also learned that he must not eat certain foods or have contact with certain kinds of activity. These were foods and activities that pertained to the giant animal in the story. Even

Fig. 5. Áma or Emma Skookum (b. about 1873, d. about 1967), a woman dreamer, who sang songs sent to her in dreams but was not a ceremonial leader. She was said to have become a dreamer when her sight was restored after some years of blindness. Photograph by Robin Ridington, Halfway River Reserve, 1966.

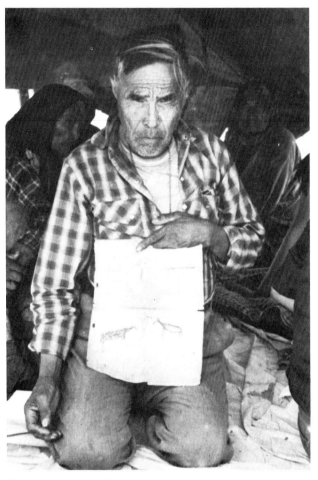

Fig. 4. Augustine Jumbie, a respected medicine man although not a dreamer, holding drawings done by the dreamer Decutla about 1900 and kept as ceremonial objects. The lower page shows game keepers—individual animals who control the entry of ordinary animals of their species into this world and into hunters' dreams—flanking a human figure that probably represents a dreamer. The buildings on the upper page depict the heaven of the historic prophet tradition. The woman to Jumbie's left is Bella Yahey; to his right may be Áma. Photograph by Robin Ridington, Halfway River Reserve, 1966.

the smallest child knew what foods an older person could not eat and what activities should not be performed in his presence. For instance, in one story, Giant Spider kills men by attracting them with the sound of a sharp stick swung around his head from a string. In the story Saya turns the giant's weapon against him and changes him into the spiders of present times. Around a person who knew Spider one was not supposed to make any noise with a string or stretched hide thong. To do so would risk making the person "too strong," that is, changing him back into the giant animal of the story.

• MEDICINE POWERS   Someone whose personal medicine taboos were violated by another was said to become transformed into the giant man-eating animal of mythical times. Such a person was called *wehčuge* (Ridington 1976). *wehčuge* was a cannibal who sang the song of the giant animal in the story, then began to eat his own lips and finally completed the transformation by hunting down and eating his own people like the giant animals before Saya changed them into their present form. The flesh thus eaten turned to ice within him, and he could only be killed by burning for seven days. *wehčuge* was like the Algonquian Windigo in eating his own lips and becoming filled with ice, but unlike the Windigo *wehčuge* did not kill from hunger and fear of starvation so much as from a violation of his medicine powers. The giant animals that eat people emerged from within the people who experienced the story of them in their dreaming. Within every person who knew the nature of his medicines the giant animal *wehčuge* was lurking. Because of this the Beaver showed great care and respect of one another's personal spaces. To violate another person's space intentionally was to risk bringing on the cannibal *wehčuge*. When a person had begun to undergo the transformation from man into *wehčuge* it was still possible to bring him back. To do this another person used his medicines to overcome the strength of the monster. He faced *wehčuge* and sang his own songs. He might even wrestle with him and then cover him with his own medicine robe. Once the transformation to *wehčuge* had been completed by eating his own lips the only way people could save themselves was to burn the monster for seven days, until all the ice had melted.

Dreaming was also used to defend oneself from the possible aggressive use by another person of his medicine powers. A medicine fight resulted when a person believed that another was using his powers harmfully against him. No one admitted to using his powers to harm others, but everyone believed that there were those who misused their powers and that it might be necessary to defend oneself from attack. Medicine fights were brought on by secret attacks (Ridington 1968).

• THE DREAMER Everyone dreamed and used dreams to make contact with events that existed within the realm of possibility, but the Beaver recognized people with special powers who followed their own trail ahead of them past the point of their own death. These people were called *načę*, dreamer or prophet, because of their ability to relate what happens in the present to past and future experience through dreaming of future possibilities. The present tradition of prophets began about 1870 when a dreamer took the name *məkænunətəne* 'road over the top(?)' and has taken on Christian influences and symbolism. There have been perhaps 20 of these dreamers who have symbolically died, gone to heaven, and returned with songs. There was at least one dreamer alive in the late 1960s. The songs called *načę ne yɪneʔ* 'dreamers' songs' are distinguished from *məyɪneʔ*, medicine songs. The dreamers' songs were sung publicly and for the benefit of all, while individual medicine songs were sung privately for the protection of individuals in specific situations.

• SINGING AND DANCING From time to time the people came together to sing and dance. The dance was always done around a fire following the path of the sun. It might be either outside or within a large temporary dance tepee. Men, women, and children danced together, but they were seated around the fire according to age and sex. Men sat in the northern half and women in the southern half. The singers, men who were hunters, sat to the eastern side of the men's half. Thus their songs came from the east just as the animals they

brought into camp came from their dreaming to the east. The old men sat to the western side and the old women often sat by them on the western edge of the women's half. Young women and children sat by the south near the entrance to the dance lodge. The dreamer sat to the west because he had experienced the place beyond the setting sun.

The songs of the dance were dreamers' songs brought back from the people in heaven by particular dreamers whose names and lives were remembered, but they were also the prayers that animals sing in hard times. Dancing was symbolically walking to heaven, and the dreamer told people that when they died they would follow a trail of song to where the old people are singing for them. In mid-summer several hundred people came together to sing and dance, each group setting up a dance lodge and fire. Together they reaffirmed the kinship ties that linked them to one another in the past and laid the foundation for new ties that would emerge in the future. The ritual was not complicated or esoteric, yet the experience of coming together in a circle around a common fire and dancing to the songs that the old people in heaven sent down to them was a powerful form of communion (Ridington 1971, 1978a).

History of Indian-White Contact

The Beaver felt the effects of Western culture even before they came into direct contact with Whites. Before 1760, according to Mackenzie (1970:238), gun-bearing Crees drove Beaver Indians out of the Athabasca River region. Peace between the two groups was made at a point on the Peace River, thereby giving that river its name, and "this place was settled to be the boundary." The Beaver have an extensive oral tradition dealing with their experiences during this period and the later period of direct contact (Ridington 1979).

Beaver Indians moved farther west into the eastern slopes of the Rocky Mountains of British Columbia in the late eighteenth century. They displaced Sekani groups farther up the Peace and Smoky rivers and mixed with Sekani at Hudson's Hope (Jenness 1937:7). By the nineteenth century movements of the various peoples stabilized with the establishment of trading posts throughout this part of the northern interior.

In the first quarter of the nineteenth century the bison of the Peace River prairies were nearly exterminated by Indians hunting for the North West Company (MacGregor 1952). Throughout the nineteenth century the Beaver became increasingly involved in the fur trade, but this trade did not alter their basic dependence on hunting for subsistence. Firearms increased the efficiency of their food gathering, but according to stories of these times, supplies of powder and shot were unreliable and shortages often led to great hardship.

The first Roman Catholic missionary reached the Beaver in 1845 (Duchaussois 1928:936). Although their first reaction was to resist baptism (Faraud 1866), they later accepted Catholic ideas and symbols. The prophets held their own services and made drawings of the road to heaven that showed the influence of the Catholic Ladder, a pictorial catechism used by the missionaries (see "Intercultural Relations and Cultural Change in the Shield and Mackenzie Borderlands," fig. 2, this vol.). By the turn of the century nearly all Beavers were nominally Roman Catholics, but in fact they had assimilated Catholic ideas in enrichment of their own traditions rather than giving them up in favor of the religion of the missionaries.

The last quarter of the nineteenth century brought independent traders to the Peace River country and with them for the first time Euro-Canadian foods like flour, sugar, and potatoes. The Beaver tell colorful stories about Twelve Foot Davis and the new goods he introduced. By this time horses had become common, first among the eastern Beaver and later among those of the northwest. The horses were allowed to range free during the winter, but were used for transportation and hunting in summer. In the 1960s, old people recalled the tremendous difference that horses made in their lives when they first became common.

The twentieth century brought contact between Beavers and Whites other than traders (fig. 6) and missionaries. By 1930 most of their territory along the Peace River had been settled by farmers; Beavers con-

Fig. 6. Trading furs in a Hudson's Bay Company store at Ft. Vermilion, managed by Francis D. Wilson. The Indian wears an Assomption sash, and other sashes hang from the rafters among other items of clothing. Photograph by Ernest Brown about 1904–1909.

tinued hunting and trapping along the Blueberry, Half-way, and Prophet rivers in British Columbia and north of the Peace toward Hay Lake and the Caribou Mountains in Alberta. The building of the Alaska Highway in 1942 opened up the last territory in which bands of Beaver were living a more or less nomadic life.

The Beaver Indians of Dunvegan and Fort Vermilion signed Treaty No. 8 in 1899, and those of Fort Saint John in 1900. Those of the Prophet River area signed Treaty at Fort Nelson in 1910. In consequence of the treaty, several small reserves were eventually established. Beaver reserve communities in British Columbia are Prophet River, at Mile 234, Alaska Highway; Halfway River, northwest of Fort Saint John; Doig River, near the village of Rose Prairie; Blueberry River, north of Fort Saint John, which is part Cree, part Beaver; and the groups at the west end of Moberly Lake. In Alberta, the reserves established were Clear Hills on the Eureka River, Horse Lakes near Hythe, and Child Lake and Boyer on Boyer River near Fort Vermilion.†

Sociocultural Situation in the 1960s

Since the building of the Alaska and Mackenzie Highways, the Beaver of Alberta and British Columbia have lost contact with one another. Hunting and trapping have decreased in importance while guiding for big-game hunters and clearing "bush" for roads, pipelines, and powerlines have taken their place, for a source of cash income. On two of the reserves in British Columbia, Halfway River and Doig River, the Canadian government has successfully begun raising grain and beef cattle. Although in Alberta farming and stock raising had begun earlier on the Boyer reserve, these activities declined in the 1960s.

Most of the people who grew up after the construction of the Alaska Highway have been to school and are literate in English. Beaver was still the first language, but because of increasing contact with English-speaking people the generation that spoke Beaver in the 1970s will probably be the last. The forces of history are undermining the purposes that brought the people together in the past. Like many other Indian groups, they are in danger of becoming merely a disadvantaged minority, but the changes have been so rapid that the full richness of skills and powers still remains within the experience of many of the people.

---

†The Department of Indian Affairs publications and maps formerly identified the small Indian group of Heart Lake, east-central Alberta (Reserve No. 167), as Athapaskan-speaking Beaver Indians, apparently because of the nearby Beaver River. The Heart Lake group is Cree and Chipewyan.

Fig. 7. Mary Wolf, at left, with scarf and beaded bracelet sometimes worn at first menstruation, when the girl is taught traditional crafts by women and must not look directly at men, particularly her father. Traditionally the girl was also secluded in a special shelter, but this is no longer practiced. Photograph by Robin Ridington, Halfway River Reserve, 1966.

Synonymy‡

The name Beaver Indians has been used from the beginning of historical records, when Pond (Davidson 1918:32–33) used the term on his map to refer to at least part of the people labeled Beaver Indians in later times. Other names have been used; according to Jenness (1937:7) the section of Mackenzie's "Rocky Mountain Indians" that lived between the junction of the Peace and Smoky rivers and the Rocky Mountain Canyon was a group of Beaver Indians. In 1791 Turnor (1934:401, map) located the Beaver Indians along both sides of the Peace River, which he said was called by the Chipewyan "the Chaw hot-e-na Dez-za or Beaver Indian river." In contrast Petitot (1888a:292) gave the Chipewyan name for Peace River as Tsa dès 'beaver river', suggesting that the people were named after the river. In French the Beaver are called Gens de Castor or simply Castors. Tsa-ttiné 'habitants parmi les Castors (dwellers among the beavers)' (Petitot 1876a:26), adopted by Hodge (1910j:822) without the accent, was the name used by the Chipewyan of Lake Athabasca (Petitot 1876:75). The northern Plains Cree name is *amiskiwiyiniw* 'beaver person' (David H. Pentland, communication to editors 1979).

Sources

Little has been written about the Beaver. Goddard's (1917, 1917a, 1917b) work is important for linguistics

---

‡This synonymy was written by Beryl C. Gillespie and Ives Goddard.

and for the stories he has recorded. Ridington (1968, 1968a, 1969, 1969a, 1971, 1972, 1976, 1978, 1978a, 1979; Ridington and Ridington 1970) has written on Beaver social and religious life. Ridington (1965–1972) has collected a large number of stories as well as tapes of Beaver music and oratory. General histories of the Peace River area by MacGregor (1952) and Bowes (1963) include some information on the Beaver Indians. The best history by far is that provided by the people themselves; their stories give a rich, detailed, and accurate picture of their experience from prehistoric times to the present.

Subarctic Métis

RICHARD SLOBODIN

In one sense the Métis ('mā͟,tē, mə'tīs) comprise a sector of the North American population whose status is defined by their perceived mixed descent from both aboriginal American and non-American ancestry. At some periods and in some places they have constituted a more structured grouping than is implied in the foregoing statement. This occurred most notably in the Red and Saskatchewan river valleys and adjacent plains during the middle and late nineteenth century, where the "Métis Nation" emerged.

The Métis form a regional example of a social and demographic phenomenon that has marked the frontiers of European colonial expansion in the post-Renaissance era: the "mixed" population.

Identity

In law, the Métis have no collective identity, except the negative one that they in part include individuals or families who have renounced Indian treaty rights. However, this is not a sufficient criterion of Métis status, as there are many Métis families that have had nothing to do with Indian treaties and many "non-Treaty Indians" who are culturally and socially members of Indian bands.

Métis do not have a specific homeland or habitat as do Indian tribes, communities, or dialect groupings. A majority of Subarctic Métis reside in the northern parts of the prairie provinces of Canada and in the Mackenzie District of the Northwest Territories, Canada; there are also some in the Yukon Territory of Canada and in Alaska. Dispersed throughout a vast region, they live in many communities, in most of which they form a decided minority.

Certain traditions, sociocultural characteristics, and external conditions, such as discriminatory pressures, combine to give this scattered population greater and more enduring significance than that of a mere social category and to imbue in its members a sense of identity as Métis.

Ethnicity and Descent

Like other "hybrid" populations of the world, the Métis are defined in terms of "mixed" ancestry and syncretized culture; however, the status of Métis is a socio-logical condition rather than a genetic fact. Although a large majority of Métis are in fact of combined aboriginal American and non-American, usually European, ancestry, there are many individuals of Indian status and some of Eskimo status who have more non-American ancestors than do many Métis. It is also possible, and it has frequently happened, that a person with no known non-Indian ancestry is sociologically and culturally Métis. Furthermore, a person whose known ancestry is exclusively White may be Métis. This situation has been rare in recent generations but was not uncommon among *coureurs de bois* during the fur-trade era in Canada.

Nevertheless, it is true that a large majority of Métis have an ancestry that is "mixed" in the commonly understood sense. However, there are considerable differences among Métis populations in terms of the ingredients and the histories of the mixtures or miscegenations involved.

Regional Distinctions

As canoemen and packers, Métis moved into the Subarctic with the fur trade in the late eighteenth and early nineteenth centuries. They were offspring or descendants of French or French-Canadian *coureurs de bois* and Ojibwa or Cree women; their first language was almost surely that of their maternal ancestors. They were joined by Iroquois bateaumen, for the most part Mohawk, whose way of life had become largely Métis. In the service of the North West Company and Hudson's Bay Company, these men traveled the major waterways into the western Arctic. There are Kutchin traditions of Cree-speaking and Mohawk-speaking canoemen in the Mackenzie Delta and on the middle reaches of the Yukon. However, those of the early Métis rivermen who remained in the far northwest settled at trading posts in the southern Subarctic, marrying Cree and, in a few cases, Chipewyan women. After the final defeat of the "Métis Nation" at the close of the second Northwest Insurrection in 1885, these rivermen were joined by refugee families from the Saskatchewan River region.

The older population of Métis in the Subarctic and the refugees from the Plains shared several important cultural attributes: predominantly French and Algonquian-speaking backgrounds, with minorities of Scottish and Iroquoian descent; adherence to the Roman Catholic Church; the use of a distinctive dialect of French (called in English Country French) beside Broken Slavey and other, regional, trade jargons; and a major association with the transportation industry. A distinction existed in the Plains Métis' former heavy involvement in large-scale buffalo hunting, whereas the secondary (in some situations, primary) occupation of the Subarctic Métis was a combination of riverine and lake fishing, caribou and moose hunting, and fur trapping.

The Plains Métis soon adapted to Subarctic subsistence and economic necessities; however, they brought with them many cultural features and traditions with which they had long been identified, and as they outnumbered the earlier Subarctic Métis, these traditions became characteristic of the Métis in the southern Subarctic. The Plains Métis and their way of life had continued to be called Red River Métis, even after the center of Métis settlement had shifted westward from the Red River valley to that of the Saskatchewan. For this reason, and because Red River Métis is a phrase carrying much historical significance in Canadian and United States history, the "mixed" population of the southern Subarctic are called Red River Métis.

From Fort Simpson, Northwest Territories, downstream or northward on the Mackenzie River to the Arctic coast and over the Cordillera into the northern Yukon Territory and eastern Alaska, few families identified as of "mixed" ancestry share the culture and traditions of the Red River Métis. In the 1960s the term Métis was little known in this subregion. The original native-European unions rarely dated as far back as a century. Although nonaboriginal ancestry is much more varied there than among the southern Subarctic Métis, the White ancestry most heavily represented in northern Mackenzie genealogies is Scottish (Slobodin 1966:13).

The absence until the 1960s of the term Métis in everyday discourse reflects the brevity of tradition in the more northerly "mixed" population. Whereas the original mixed unions in Red River families occurred in eastern Canada between the seventeenth and nineteenth centuries, most of the lower Mackenzie Métis are descendants of "mixed" unions that took place in the subregion since 1850. This population is here termed the Northern Métis. Besides their descent from relatively recent miscegenation, the Northern Métis are distinguished from their Red River congeners by their predominantly Athapaskan maternal ancestry and northern European paternal background (Scottish, Scandinavian, English, Irish, German); preponderantly Protestant church affiliation, although there is a large Roman Catholic minority; and the possession of traditions not autonomously Métis, but deriving from their mothers' tribal affiliations or from their fathers' work

in the local fur trade. Further distinctions between Red River and Northern Métis are summarized by Slobodin (1966:158).

Social Organization

The distinctive features of Subarctic Métis social organization are the more inclusive ones. Household composition and family structure are only marginally different from those of the peoples among whom Métis reside; in some instances, they are not different at all. The surname-groups, which are more extensive, are also more distinctive, while participation in the Métis communications network not only binds Métis together but also goes far toward distinguishing them from members of other ethnicities.

Family and Household

Among Subarctic Métis the nuclear family is the basic social grouping as it is in the Euro-American (and Euro-Canadian) society and, with some qualifications, the aboriginal American societies that produced the Métis' ancestors.

Although the Métis fertility rate is higher than the national average, Deprez and Bisson (1975:88) found that at Fort Resolution the Indian rate is consistently higher than the Métis.

The modal household type for Subarctic Métis, both Red River and Northern, comprises a married couple with minor offspring; in a 1963 survey of Mackenzie District Métis, 36 out of a sample of 77 households were of this type. The size of households studied was comparable to the general Canadian average. Various co-resident arrangements found among Indians of the Mackenzie District, such as the paired family and the couple with one or more aged parents, were absent from the sample and have been rare among Métis during the twentieth century (Slobodin 1966:37).

The kinship system of Subarctic Métis is essentially Euro-American. What is not at all obvious, but may be discerned upon prolonged acquaintance, is that Northern Métis also operate in terms of Eskimo and Indian kinship patterns when interacting with their kinsmen of those communities.

Marriage

Older Métis throughout the region remember marriages as having been arranged, in contrast to the prevalence of marriage by choice in the 1970s. However, the Métis appear in the mid-twentieth century to choose marriage partners with the same kinds of social characteristics as did their seniors at the turn of the century.

Beyond prohibition of marriage within the incest group, which includes first cousins for members of certain Christian denominations, there is no stated prescription in marriage choice. However, in fact, no cases of marriage within the wide limits of the surname-groups were found in the 1963 survey (Slobodin 1966:74).

Characteristics of Subarctic Métis life are physical mobility and far-ranging social ties. These are reflected in the high proportion of Métis who marry outside their communities and the considerable proportion of couples who reside away from the home community of either spouse.

Love Affairs

Linton (1936:175) has observed that "all societies recognize that there are occasional violent emotional attachments between persons of opposite sex." This is true for Northern and Red River Métis, but what is distinctive for Red River Métis is an ideology of sexual passion, a sense that each person's life is likely to include an irresistible, stormy love affair. "Among Red River Metis . . . a strong passionate attachment is one of the common values as well as one of the common hazards of life. Such attachments . . . always seem to bring troubles in their train. Indeed, one gains the impression they would not be considered the real thing if they did not involve disturbance, outrage, and violence. . . . When Red River Metis reminisced . . . retrospective resentment and anxiety were expressed, but also, in every case, some pride and satisfaction. . . . The feeling conveyed was that 'Tis better to have loved and lost . . .' In no case was a marked sense of guilt to be noted, although the narrator may have deserted spouse and children" (Slobodin 1966:40–41). However, of 22 Red River Métis—6 women and 16 men—who provided narratives of significant love affairs, all but one were living with spouse and children when interviewed, in some cases having returned after an extended absence. Several observers have noted that the Red River Métis love affair, like the courtly love of the late Middle Ages in Europe, is not regarded as a basis for marriage.

Surname-Groups of the Mackenzie District

The bearers of a dozen or so family names constitute a majority of Métis in the Mackenzie District, with another dozen surnames slightly less common. Almost all of these are names well known and frequently encountered in the history of the northwest and of the fur trade: Beaulieu, Mercredi, Mandeville, Lafferty, Cardinal, Bouvier, Fabien, Isbister, Jones, Flett, Hardisty, Fraser, Camsell, Hodgson, Firth, Stewart, McKay,

Linkletter, Berens, and Houle (see "Fort Resolution, Northwest Territories," figs. 4, 10).

Among Red River Métis, the more common surnames have been established since the mid-nineteenth century. A bearer of one cannot trace genealogical connections with most others of the same name. Nevertheless, "there is a sense of being 'a Beaulieu' or 'a Mandeville' as something distinct within the Red River Metis universe. This in-group sentiment is reinforced by a consciousness of boundaries. There are many Indians in the southern [Mackenzie] District and in the neighbouring provincial areas, bearing the Old Metis surnames. No doubt in most cases these people share common ancestry with the Metis, but [there appears to be no] sense of unity among Indians and Metis similarly named" (Slobodin 1966:71).

There are traditions and legends associated with some, at least, of the Red River Métis surnames. The most elaborate are those told about the Beaulieu connection in the lower Slave River–Great Slave Lake region. The family appears to have been established by François Beaulieu (b. ca. 1775, d. ca. 1875) (Burger and Clovis 1976:101; cf. Petitot 1888a:314, 1888:584). His antecedents and career are archetypal of the earliest Subarctic Métis. His father, either a Frenchman or a

Hudson's Bay Company Lib., Winnipeg, Man.

Fig. 1. Charlotte Jones cutting birch tree for sap. The collection of such sap was introduced into the Ft. Resolution area by the Métis or Whites probably during the last half of the 19th century. The sap was boiled down into syrup and often mixed with dry pounded fish meal for eating (David M. Smith, communication to editors 1978). Photograph by Henry W. Jones, Ft. Resolution, about 1912.

Fig. 2. Catherine Lafferty with her children James and Edward. The baby, outfitted in a lace bonnet and lace fringed cotton blanket, is in a beaded moss bag. Photograph by Henry W. Jones, at Ft. Resolution, N.W.T., about 1912.

Métis, was a *coureur de bois* in the service of the Sioux Company, and his mother was Chipewyan. François

> saw the arrival in 1780 of Peter Pond, the first explorer of Great Slave Lake; then, in 1789, Sir Alexander Mackenzie. His uncle, Jacques Beaulieu, served as interpreter [for Peter Pond]. In 1825 [François] was an interpreter for Sir John Franklin.
>
> Chosen by the Yellowknives as their chief, Beaulieu became the terror of the Dogrib, Slavey, and Sekani. . . . This Metis sultan . . . had three wives, Cree, Dene [probably Chipewyan], and Metis. He left offspring in every tribe where he had traveled, not counting 10 married children, fathers and mothers of families or already grandparents, who lived with him (Petitot 1888a:313; translation by Richard Slobodin).

Polygynous until converted to Christianity in middle life (some Métis traditions credit him with 10 wives) François Beaulieu served as a strong-arm man for the North West Company and later for the Hudson's Bay Company. Like many other nineteenth-century Métis, he also operated in semi-independent fashion, engaging in some trading at his farm on the Salt River, where early missionaries reported a large and busy establishment (cf. Usher 1971:47–48).

Joseph Beaulieu (b. ca. 1836, d. 1916) was the first family member to receive the sobriquet "King" (Slobodin 1966:71–73). In the eastern Great Slave Lake region he established Beaulieu Fort (later, Snowdrift, Northwest Territories) and also the short-lived King

Post. There have been a succession of Beaulieu men christened Joseph, nicknamed Sousi or Suzie, and also called King, for example, Joseph King Beaulieu (b. 1859, d. 1929) and his namesake and nephew (b. 1900, d. 1974). The King family also claims descent from "Old Man" Beaulieu and the first "King" Beaulieu.

Other particularly strong and widespread Red River Métis surname-groups are the Mercredis and the Mandevilles.

Surname-groups among the Northern Métis are shallower than those of the Red River people. In some cases the eponymous ancestor was known to persons alive in the mid-twentieth century, for example, widely known traders such as Julian S. Camsell (originally Onions), John Firth, and Charles Philip Gaudet. In keeping with the relatively brief histories of Northern Métis surname-groups, affiliation is determined genealogically. Stories and traditions exist in connection with these descent groups, as with the Red River Métis surname-groups, but the Northern Métis traditions are much less autonomous and more likely to chronicle service with the Hudson's Bay Company or other Euro-Canadian agencies.

The Communications Network

News and messages travel fast and far in the North and did so long before the advent of electronic media. Members of all ethnic groups participate in one or another communications network, from the "bush telegraph" or "moccasin telegraph" of the native peoples to various professional and occupational channels among salaried and wage employees.

Métis have long had the reputation of being the most active news and rumor distributors. Long-distance sociability is so characteristic of Subarctic Métis that it may be regarded as a criterion of Métis ethnicity. Traditionally associated with travel and transport, Mackenzie Métis have probably always been more mobile than most Indians and Eskimos. They enjoy more numerous, varied, and intimate social ties throughout the Mackenzie District than do most Whites. "The result is that from each Metis extend threads of awareness and sentiment reaching throughout the Northland and, in many cases, into the south" (Slobodin 1966:66).

The half-dozen "circuits," as they have been called, of the Subarctic Métis "bush telegraph system" carry messages through visits, letter writing, message-sending by travelers and radio broadcast message services, and gift-exchange, as well as by other expressions of interest such as gossip and story-telling. Some of these are remarkably long, such that a Métis at Fort Smith, near the Alberta border, or even in the northern portions of the prairie provinces, may maintain regular communication with congeners on the Yukon.

Métis communications linkages are distinguishable from those of Indians and Eskimos, on the whole, by their greater extension, and from those of Whites by their greater inclusiveness; the Whites' networks tend to be associated with occupational status.

Occupations

As Métis existence is by definition postcontact, there has been no independent Métis economy in the sense that may be discerned for Indian and Eskimo social groupings. Leaving aside the "Métis Nation" of the Plains as being outside of the Subarctic, the nearest approach to independence must have been the semi-nomadic (but also semilegendary) "tribes" of Beaulieu and Mandeville. Even these, if their way of life was anything like its description in folklore, trapped for the Euro-Canadian fur trade and provided labor for fur-trade transport.

From their historical beginnings, Subarctic Métis have been engaged in a wide variety of employment, a variety noticeably greater than that of most Indian, Eskimo, and White workers. This variety of occupation is seen in the work careers of individual Métis as well as of the ethnic group as a whole. It is usual for a Métis to have turned his hand to many kinds of job. It is also characteristic that throughout Subarctic Métis history, most Métis men have been wage-earners rather than self-employed.

Trapping and Subsistence Hunting and Fishing

The "bush" or "land" occupations of trapping and subsistence hunting and fishing form a partial exception to the generalization that Métis have usually been wage-earners. Until the 1960s every able-bodied Subarctic Métis male, and many females, engaged in these occupations periodically or sporadically. A great many continued to do so in the 1970s (fig. 3). However, full-time trappers for the fur trade have always been in a minority among Subarctic Métis, excepting insofar as the traditions of the nineteenth-century surname-groups are to be credited. No doubt since their earliest emergence, Métis have had recourse to hunting and fishing for home consumption. However, hunting and fishing as an economic way of life has been no more characteristic of Métis domestic economy than it has been for that of the Whites on the fur-trade frontier.

Hunting and fishing as wage-earners or for the market is another matter. The highly organized large-scale hunts that were the most spectacular feature of Plains Métis culture did not extend into the Subarctic, but many Métis have been "post hunters" for trading establishments.

Because few Métis have been full-time trappers, there has been a tendency in the past for full-time In-

Native Press, Yellowknife, N.W.T.
Fig. 3. Isadore and Elizabeth Beaulieu from Ft. Resolution, N.W.T., camping in the bush. Photographed in 1974.

dian trappers to disdain Métis as trappers who were afraid to venture far from the trading posts. However, examination of trapping returns at a number of settlements in the Mackenzie District and the Yukon Territory suggests that Métis have been among the most successful and venturesome of trappers in the Subarctic.

Transportation

If the Métis "might be called the offspring of the Canadian fur trade" (Morton 1972, 7:53–56), their principal and characteristic function in that far-flung enterprise has been as movers of men and materials. Indians were primarily harvesters of the renewable resources and Whites were primarily merchants, but there were Métis engaged in these activities while also dominating, in terms of manpower, the transportation function that was the lifeline of Euro-Canadian penetration into the North as well as the West. Métis served as canoemen, York boat men, mail-drivers, "fore-runners," steamboat deckhands, stevedores, and river pilots (figs. 4–5) (Slobodin 1966:80).

The voyageur heritage was evidenced, during many decades, in the esprit de corps of the bateaumen and in certain rituals and symbols. Among these were work songs, drinking songs, and love songs of habitant origin or genre and also decorative gear and its use ("Expressive Aspects of Subarctic Indian Culture," fig. 3g, this vol.). In the full fur-trade or contact-traditional era, when a "brigade" of freighting canoes or bateaux approached a settlement, the men donned festive attire. Universal in the Subarctic as decoration for boatmen was the Assomption or arrowpoint sash (figs. 6–7), which had its origin in Lower Canada (Barbeau 1939). Other items of finery, not so widely used as the sash, were fancy ribbon leggings and the "feather hat" adorned and partly constructed of Canada goose quills

Prov. Arch. of Alta., Edmonton: E. Brown Coll., 2873, 2974, 2981.
Fig. 4. Tracking on the Athabasca River and portaging on the Slave River. Photographs by Charles W. Mathers, 1901.

Public Arch. of Canada, Ottawa: PA 18789.
Fig. 5. Tracking scows. Photograph by Carl Engler, chief of surveying expedition in Alta., 1910.

and feathers. Some of these hats were associated with medicine power.

During the first half of the twentieth century a number of riverboat pilots were Métis, both Northern and Red River; pride in their work and their skills has remained high in the dwindling ranks of these men.

Trading

In the fur trade of the western Subarctic, Whites formed a majority of post factors (later termed managers), clerks, and others engaged in the actual commercial operations of the trade. This kind of occupation cannot be regarded as characteristic of Subarctic Métis. Nevertheless, a significant minority of fur traders were Métis. In this region as elsewhere Métis were at first employed at trading posts as interpreters, but some became assistant post managers or managers of outposts and a few rose to be post manager, a responsible position, especially in the employ of the Hudson's Bay Company and some of the larger and more stable "independent" trading concerns.

Data are not available, but it seems likely that Red River Métis who rose to responsible positions did so almost exclusively in the service of "independent" firms. Some became traders on their own, as François Beaulieu is said to have done. Northern Métis were

employed for the most part with the Hudson's Bay Company. This variance seems to reflect a continuation of the relatively independent position assumed by Red River Métis at the period of conflict between major trading interests. The Northern Métis, "White men's sons," were likely to have been trained and brought along in the fur trade by their fathers, Hudson's Bay Company functionaries.

It would appear that the employment of Subarctic Métis as traders reached a peak, for both Red River and Northern Métis, in the early decades of the twentieth century. With expansion and improvement of travel facilities in the 1930s, more Whites moved into the Subarctic, and employment of Métis in commerce began to diminish. Numerous economic and social changes since World War II have furthered this tendency. The general decline in the fur trade and the spread of literacy among Indians have reduced the demand for Métis' special knowledge of local conditions, fur values, and aboriginal languages. Sophisticated techniques of merchandising in what has become a general retail trade have placed at a disadvantage those Métis who have not received modern commercial training.

Métis are employed in retail trade, but a smaller proportion of Métis than formerly are self-employed entrepreneurs or employees in positions of responsibility and trust with southern-based firms.

Fig. 6. The Half-Breed Scrip Commission's boat leaving Ft. McMurray to ascend the Athabasca River. In 1899 a double commission was appointed to negotiate a treaty with the Cree, Beaver, and Chipewyan Indians as well as to issue scrip certificates to the Métis who were not included in the treaty. Scrip was readily convertible into cash (Mair 1908:68–69). The members of the commission were Major Walker, J.A. Coté, J.F. Prudhomme, and Charles Mair (with white moustache seated at back). Pierre Cyr or Sawyer, a Métis wearing an Assomption sash, is the bowsman. Photographed in Aug. 1899.

Fig. 7. Finger-woven sash of red, blues, greens, buff, and yellow. Probably made in Assomption, Quebec; the style was popular throughout the Subarctic. Once owned by J.B. Lagimodiere, a prominent Red River Métis. Length 185.4 cm, width 22.9 cm, collected 1870s.

Commercial Fishing

Métis were hired as post fishermen in the nineteenth and early twentieth centuries, providing food for humans and sled dogs at trading posts, missions and mission schools, and to a lesser extent at police posts. At the end of World War II, the Northwest Territories Council opened the Mackenzie District to large-scale commerical fishing, which "encouraged a number of fishing companies to be established at Hay River where they built docking and warehousing facilities and arranged to ship fresh fish to markets in Chicago, Detroit, and New York" (Jenness 1963:1).

Great Slave Lake remains the site of the largest commerical fishing enterprise in the Mackenzie District, and the only one heavily involving Métis. Many of these are Red River Métis from the northern prairies, where they had been commercial fishermen. Métis from almost every province and Whites from a score of nationalities are represented among those holding commercial fishing licenses at Hay River. Commercial fishing is a major occupation of Red River Métis not only at Great Slave Lake but also at the older-established fisheries in Saskatchewan and Alberta, at Lesser Slave, Athabasca, Wollaston, and Reindeer lakes.

Summer or openwater fishing is a form of seining. A boat, motor, and nets are rented to an experienced fisherman regarded as a good risk. He in turn hires four to six men on a wage basis. The families of the operator and his men buy supplies from local stores on credit,

Brown U., Haffenreffer Mus. of Anthr., Bristol, R.I.: E.S. Colcleugh Coll., 57–542.

Fig. 8. Métis mittens, made extra large to allow wearing of duffel mittens underneath, decorated with silk embroidery and appliquéd ribbonwork. Length 26 cm, collected at Ft. McMurray 1880s–1890s.

in the same manner as do the town-dwelling families of trappers.

Winter fishing, from December through March, is carried out from small movable cabins on skids, known as cabooses. Fishing is done with gill nets set under the ice. Some cabooses and the motorized winter vehicles used for hauling them and the fishing catch are owned by fishing firms, but many are owned or rented by local entrepreneurs, including Métis, who employ hands as in summer fishing.

Many more Métis are engaged in summer fishing than in the winter pursuit. Ice fishermen tend to be the more bush-oriented men. Some of these, when conditions allow, have their cabooses set near isolated stretches of shoreline so that they may combine fishing with trapping.

Backwoods Labor

Métis have been self-employed in the special sense of this term that applies to trappers. As small scale "independent" fur traders and as commercial fishing contractors, some Métis have been entrepreneurial while most have worked for wages; however, until the 1960s few have clocked in to work at repetitive tasks. Especially far removed from clocked employment has been work on the winter trail or the waterways, but trading-post jobs have also been quite different from rationalized labor; "though most of them are only laborers, no other laborers are so free, and none spice life with so much of adventure" (Ralph 1892:215).

This is less true of any regular employment in the North than was formerly the case; but still many kinds of wage employment open to Métis in the North, such as fire suppression crewmen, boatmen, game patrolmen and police special constables, even construction laborers, road maintenance men, and drivers do not involve repetitive work in a shop or plant. There is, however, an increasing number of Subarctic Métis in technical and clerical employment under "southern" conditions in the major administrative and industrial centers of the Mackenzie District.

Social Problems

Conditioning Métis existence is the fact that they have been perceived, at least during the twentieth century, in terms of social problems. This perception has been strengthened by the struggle of Métis organizations in the provinces and territories for what they have regarded as Métis rights (fig. 9) and against social abuses. The perception is also a reflex of the socially and culturally marginal position of Métis and of the very considerable bigotry of which Métis have been the object.

Prejudice against Métis has many sources; a key condition has been the position of Métis as pioneers and groundbreakers, among northern North Americans, in urbanization and acculturation. It must be understood that both of these processes have been relatively restricted in the Subarctic. Urbanization has occurred in communities that would be very small in southern terms; for example, in the Northwest Territories in 1976, the population of Inuvik was 3,116; Yellowknife, 8,256; Hay River, 3,268; Fort Simpson, 1,136; and Aklavik, 781. Yet each of these is an urban center in the North, with its hinterland and its administrative, commercial, and social functions (Canada. Statistics Canada 1976).

Throughout the contact-traditional era, acculturation took place along a very narrow front (Slobodin 1964:52). Nevertheless, for many generations Subarctic Métis have been pioneers and agents in culture change, for instance, in language and in kinship usage. At the same time, since Métis are neither Indian nor White socioculturally, they have been perceived by both Indians and Whites as inherently deviant from, hence inadequate to, accepted standards. An example of such a prejudicial view and of its unrealistic nature is the folk belief on the part of both Indians and Whites that Métis have been tied to settlements through lack of skill, courage, and enterprise, a notion expressed in former generations by the stereotype phrase "[trading] post 'breed." In point of fact, taken as a group Subarctic Métis have been the most widely traveled of all northern peoples.

The Métis are unique among Subarctic peoples in their lack of political power. Indians and Whites cannot disregard each other, vastly unequal as their power relationship may be, because each controls resources. Those of the Whites are manifold and obvious. The Indians deal in several kinds of political power, but principally in rights to land, rights that in the modern world the Whites, through the national state, cannot

Fig. 9. Métis Association meeting at Hay River, N.W.T. Photographed Jan. 1973.

ignore. The Métis have had no political or economic leverage and insufficient social cohesiveness to act as a political force, although an emerging leadership is seeking through organization to change this aspect of the situation.

Population

Insurmountable difficulties lie in the way of arriving at a realistic estimate of Subarctic Métis population. No two researchers, even making head counts within one small community, can agree, mainly because of the difficulties in the definition of Métis, and also because of Métis physical mobility. For example, in the 1960s at Fort Resolution Gendron (1963) counted 138 Indians and 332 Métis; Slobodin (1966) estimated 200 Indians and 250 Métis; and Deprez and Bisson (1975:38) found 233 Indians and 214 Métis. Figures for total native population agree rather closely—470, 450, and 447 respectively—but there is disagreement on how this population is categorized.

Efforts in the 1970s to arrive at a population count of Métis in the Northwest Territories exemplify the problem at a regional level. Certainly too high is one estimate of 10,000 in the Northwest Territories (Hoople and Newberry 1974:map, 20–21). An official of the Metis Association of the Northwest Territories provided an estimate of 7,700 (Gemini North 1974, 2:71). Helm (1977:30) estimated "possibly 3,500–4,500 Metis and Non-Status Natives." The Commissioner of the Mackenzie Valley Pipeline Inquiry concluded that there was a maximum of 4,500 nonstatus Indians and Métis combined and that "the population that regards itself as distinctively Metis would lie currently between 1,000 and 1,500 people" (Berger 1977, 1:147).

Estimates of Métis populations in the prairie provinces and the Yukon Territory would no doubt evince comparable ranges. Equally, any guess as to the size of the Métis population in former times would be quite misleading.

Sociocultural Situation in the 1970s

The Subarctic Métis constitute a regional proletariat. Their region has never been agricultural and is just beginning to undergo industrialization. Hence the Métis have been at the same time workingmen and backwoodsmen. They have had no opportunity to develop the life-styles, work habits, or attitudes of farmers or factory workers. The type of life-style and attitude most analogous to those of the Subarctic Métis are those developed by highly skilled, itinerant workers such as nonferrous miners, oil riggers, and heavy construction operators. These, and other less skilled workers for whom they serve as models, have come into the North in some numbers and have married Métis women. The result is a cultural and social situation rather unusual for North America, a type that is found in some industrializing, developing nations. A regional style of life appears to be emerging that partakes of Western working-class traditions and also Métis traditions. It is a life-style that is problem-laden, rough and crude by middle-class standards, and not, as yet, very well adapted to the environment, but it is highly dynamic. In order for this way of life to be adaptive, bigotry against Métis, and more generally, mutual distrust and contempt among ethnic groups in the region must be overcome, and the exploitative attitude of the Whites toward the land and its resources must be transcended. If this is not accomplished, the future of the Subarctic Métis is likely to be one of social dependency. If it is done, the Subarctic Métis will play a key role in the future of the northern lands, along with those Indian, Eskimo, and White working people who have joined and to some degree assimilated to the Métis in a regional populace (see D.G. Smith 1975:40–74).

Synonymy*

The name Métis is taken over from standard French *métis* (pronounced [metis]; feminine *métisse*) 'half-breed, half-caste'. Only in the second half of the twentieth century has it come into wide use in English, though it was already used as an English word the century before. Of the common pronunciations, 'mā͵tē (also ͵mā'tē and 'mātē) is an (incorrect) approximation of the French, ͵mā'tēs and mə'tīs are probably oral imitations of French, or Canadian French [metɪs] (also [metˢɪs]), and 'mētīs is a complete anglicization. Canadian French also has an old variant *métif* [metˢɪf]

---

*This synonymy was written by Ives Goddard, incorporating some material from Richard Slobodin.

(feminine *métive*), which has been reported in the form Mitchif as the self-designation used by some Métis (La Société du Parler Français au Canada 1968:452; Rhodes 1977); Metif also appears in nineteenth-century English accounts.

Names earlier in use but now considered pejorative include half-breed, breed, mixed-blood, and French *bois-brûlé* (literally 'burnt-wood', an allusion to skin color); these do not always have the specific meaning of Métis. Indian language terms include Cree *a·pihtawikosisa·n*, literally 'half son' (Faries 1938:92, phonemicized), Ojibwa *aya·pittawisit* 'one who is half', and *wi·ssa·kkote·winini* 'Métis man' and *wi·ssa·kkote·wikkwe·* 'Métis woman' based on *wi·ssa·kkote·* '(partly) burnt forest'. "They call the half-breeds so, because they are half-dark, half-white, like a half-burnt piece of wood, burnt black on one end, and left white on the other" (Baraga 1878–1880, 2:4, 421, phonemicized). The Athapaskan languages of the Mackenzie use expressions meaning 'half White person' (Hare *tadi móla*; Bearlake *tani móla*), 'yellow (or burning) hair' (Ft. Simpson Slavey *neɣá dékǫ́*) (Keren Rice, communication to editors 1979), or 'Whiteman's child' (Peel River Kutchin *čí· žak gʷičin gí·* or *o·ⁿžít gí·*). Petitot (1876:242) records also Chipewyan *bèρa rédhkkρaṇ* 'bois brûlé', Hare *éwié-étti* 'he who pulls death behind him', and Kutchin tattîn.

Sources

There is an extensive literature on Red River Métis political and economic history insofar as these have affected the general course of Canadian history (see the chapter on Red River Métis in vol. 13). The history of the Northern Métis is bound up with that of the fur trade in the far northwest.

Essential to an understanding of the development of Subarctic Métis and of their life in the early contact and contact-traditional eras are frontier and fur-trade histories (A. Ross 1855, 1856; Begg 1894–1895; Morton 1973; Innis 1956). Also informative are histories of the Métis Nation on the Plains (Cameron 1926; De Trémaudan 1935), of which Giraud (1945) and Howard (1952) are the best.

Sportmen's and travelers' chronicles of the late nineteenth and early twentieth centuries contain many observations, for the most part couched in terms contemptuous of the "half-breeds." The best and least biased of these is by Seton (1911). The American journalist Ralph (1892) and the veteran missionaries Breynat (1945–1948, 1) and Stuck (1914, 1917) present much interesting detail, related realistically and sympathetically. Ralph's book is also valuable for the pen-and-ink illustrations of Métis life by the distinguished artist of the vanishing frontier, Frederic Remington.

Outstanding monographs are those by Lagassé et al. (1959) on the economic condition of Métis and non-reserve Indians in Manitoba; Buckley (1962) on the economics of trapping and fishing among Saskatchewan Métis; Card, Hirabayashi, and French (1963) on the epidemiology of tuberculosis in northern Alberta and the factors relating to a high disease rate among Métis there; and Deprez and Bisson (1975) on demographic distinctions between the Indian and Métis populations of Fort Resolution.

D.G. Smith's (1975) close and thorough analysis of social interaction among natives and outsiders in the Mackenzie River delta contains many searching observations on the total social setting of Métis residing on the northern border of the Subarctic.

A valuable collection of historical photographs with useful commentary has been produced by the Metis Association of the Northwest Territories (Burger and Clovis 1976).

The one general survey of Mackenzie District Métis (Slobodin 1966) draws upon observations made over many years but principally during fieldwork in 1963. This chapter is based largely upon this work.

"Fort Resolution, Northwest Territories," this volume, provides additional information on the Métis people of that settlement.

Environment and Culture in the Cordillera

CATHARINE MCCLELLAN AND GLENDA DENNISTON

The Subarctic Cordillera is a magnificent high plateau country. In it are large and small rivers and lakes, floodplains and muskeg swamps, patches of meadow, and vast stretches of boreal forest, but there are also alpine tundra, bare slopes of scree, craggy mountain peaks, small glaciers, and huge icefields.

As defined here, the area includes the northern half of interior British Columbia, the western edge of northern Alberta and of the District of Mackenzie of the Northwest Territories, all of Yukon Territory, and much of northeastern interior Alaska (fig. 1).

Population

Estimates of aboriginal population density are based on very poor data, but they suggest a difficult habitat for human beings. There was probably less than one person per 100 square kilometers, and the total number of Indians in the entire Subarctic Cordillera may not have exceeded 25,000 (Dobyns 1976:10–21; Kroeber 1939:141–142; Krech 1978a; cf. VanStone 1974:11).

Native Groups

The native groups of the Subarctic Cordillera are distinguished in this volume under the names Chilcotin, Carrier, Sekani, Kaska, Tsetsaut, Tahltan, Tagish, Inland Tlingit, Tutchone, Han, and Kutchin. Throughout the nineteenth century all these peoples spoke Athapaskan languages, many of them closely related, except that the Inland Tlingit and Tagish adopted Tlingit as their chief language in the nineteenth century. All groups also shared much in common in their cultures, which partly reflected the rugged environment to which they had adapted over the centuries.

Plausible arguments can be made to include as Subarctic Cordillerans bordering groups such as the Mountain Indians and the upper Tanana River and Upper Koyukon Indians who had quite similar habitats and cultures, or to exclude some such as the Sekani who are probably recent in the area, or the Chilcotin who were heavily influenced by their Salish neighbors and who are at the southern extreme of the environmental area.

The set of peoples here designated as Subarctic Cor-

dilleran Indians differs from that of Jenness (1932), who listed together as "Tribes of the Cordillera": the

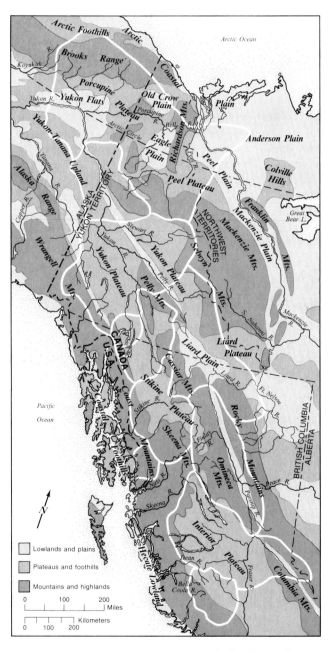

Fig. 1. Physiographic divisions of the Subarctic Cordillera (after Wahrhaftig 1965; Canada. Surveys and Mapping Branch 1974) with approximate tribal distribution. See Key to Tribal Territories for tribal names.

372

Salish of the Fraser River, Kutenai, Chilcotin, Carrier, Tsetsaut, Tahltan, and Tagish. Jenness separated this group from another comprised of northern Athapaskan speakers whom he designated as "Tribes of the Mackenzie and Yukon River Basins"—Sekani, Beaver, Chipewyan, Yellowknife, Dogrib, Slavey, Hare, "the little known Nahani" and "rather confused Kutchin" tribes—even though the Cordilleran and the Mackenzie-Yukon divisions did not correspond very well to either the physiographic Cordillera or Interior Plains shown on his maps (Jenness 1932:10–14).

The present grouping of the Subarctic Cordillerans does not coincide exactly either with the distinction made by Osgood (1936) between Northern Athapaskan speakers of the Pacific drainage and those of the Arctic drainage. He classed the former as salmon fishermen having a richer culture than that of the latter people who had no access to salmon. Osgood's dividing line, which runs along the height of land between the two drainage systems, ignored the reality of the Cordilleran physiography and the varied econiches it contains. He underrated the importance of caribou and of other land animals and freshwater fish in the lives of the Cordilleran peoples. Thus, while most of the tribes counted as Subarctic Cordillerans in this volume lived exclusively in the Pacific drainage at the time of contact (Carrier, Tsetsaut, Tahltan, Inland Tlingit, Tagish, Tutchone, and Han), others, such as the Kaska, lived wholly in the Arctic Ocean drainage. The Chilcotin, Sekani, and Kutchin occupied parts of both systems, sometimes moving back and forth across the height of land that separated the two (McClellan 1970c; VanStone 1974).

What justifies the Subarctic Cordilleran grouping adopted here is the unity of the physiographic bloc in which the people have lived and their distinctive subsistence and deployment patterns, which combine big and small game hunting with fishing and some gathering into an annual round of high mobility. Unless otherwise noted, this chapter describes major environmental and cultural conditions of the early nineteenth century.

Environment in Relation to Native Locations

Physiography

The physiography of the Cordillera is characterized by an eastern Continental facade and a western Pacific mountain system, between which stretches a complex plateau that can itself be further subdivided (see Bostock 1948; Clibbon and Hamelin 1968:57–62, fig. 3–1; Johnson and Hartman 1971:14–15, 25, pls. 6, 11). The Continental facade includes the Rocky, Columbia, Yukon-Mackenzie, and Franklin mountains in Canada, then swings west between 60° north latitude and the Arctic Circle into the Brooks Range of northern

Alaska. South of the Peace River, the Rocky Mountains may rise more than 10,000 feet in height; they are somewhat lower to the north, but because of the high latitudes, timberline is often reached by 2,500 feet. Much of the Brooks Range is covered by alpine tundra. Throughout the facade, but especially in southern British Columbia, ice fields are common at high altitudes.

Beyond the facade are intermontane belts of mountains, deeply dissected tablelands, trenches (such as the Great Rocky Mountain trench that runs north to the Liard River), and glacial plains that rise slowly in elevation toward the higher latitudes. This vast highland country is where the Cordillerans found most of their livelihood (Barker 1977).

The Pacific Mountain system includes a spectacular high massif composed of a southern and a northern arc. The significance of the southern Pacific arc for the Subarctic Cordillerans is that it effectively cuts off the wet, warm coast from the dry, cold interior Cordillera and also restricts contact between coastal and interior peoples. Some native Cordillerans hunted in the coast mountains, but in most places, their cold, glacier-studded heights loomed as uninhabited buffer zones between them and the Indians of the coastal strands. The marked contrast between the interior and coastal environments meant great differences in raw resources, which led to a well-developed aboriginal trade between the two areas. The few rivers and passes that led through the mountain barriers channeled both internative relationships and later contacts between Indians and Whites (fig. 2).

The northern arc of the Pacific mountain system includes the mountains of the Canadian-Alaskan border that extend into the great Alaska Range. The eastern part of that range is relatively low, so that the Tutchone and Han could meet rather easily with upper Tanana River Indians. The central Nuzotin and Mentasta Mountains rise more than 9,000 feet and are glaciated, but the copper deposits in the difficult Scolai Pass area attracted Tutchone, Ahtna, Upper Tanana, and perhaps Han Indians to the vicinity because they could make superior tools and weapons from the raw metal.

For detailed maps of the Cordilleran ecosystems see Joint Federal-State Land Use Planning Commission for Alaska (1973), Oswald and Senyk (1976), Chapman and Turner (1956), and Canada. Surveys and Mapping Branch (1974).

Climate

Subarctic lands are characterized by great extremes in annual and diurnal temperatures. Thus, at the abandoned village of Snag on the border of Tutchone and Upper Tanana country, summer days may range into the high eighties, while the mean low for January is −14° F., and a winter low of −81° has been recorded. *373*

For five months the mean daily maximum does not rise to 32°, and the mean daily minimum remains below zero. The higher latitudes, of course, have the greatest cold for the longest periods of time, but altitude, lay of the land, and relationship to maritime influences all affect local conditions (Kendrew and Kerr 1955; Johnson and Hartman 1971:51–57).

As striking as the variation in temperature is the variation in amount of daylight throughout the year. In Chilcotin and Carrier country day and night are more equal in length throughout the year than farther north, but deep mountain shadows make winter days seem much darker than those on the prairies at the same latitude. Those Kutchin who live north of the Arctic Circle have continuous sunlight on the longest day of the year in June, but on the shortest day, the sun does not rise at all. Although curtailment of light affects outdoor activity, except in periods of extreme cold it is possible, if not desirable, to move about in the twilightlike conditions of deep winter. Moonlight nights are surprisingly bright when there is snow on the ground. The most difficult times to travel are when the lakes and streams begin to freeze in the fall, and even more so during the spring breakup when people may be immobilized by mud and melt waters.

Precipitation in the Subarctic Cordillera is light and much of it falls as snow. The amount of snow cover varies greatly with the terrain. For example, average snow depths in the upper Yukon country are 50 to 70 inches in the valleys, but in the Saint Elias Mountains range from 100 to 400 inches (Selkregg 1974:4–7, fig. 5). Snow rarely melts in winter but thanks to the forest usually blows only in the mountain heights.

Vegetation

The forest cover is part of the boreal coniferous forest, which has several subtypes within it (Shelford 1972:120–180, figs. 5:1, 5:15). From the spruce-pine cover of Chilcotin and most of the Carrier terrain, one moves north to a forest of black and white spruce mixed with lodge-pole pine. This starts at about 58° north latitude in the Stikine River drainage occupied by the Tahltan and characterizes the country of the Inland Tlingit, Tagish, Tutchone, and Han in the upper Yukon basin (Oswald and Senyk 1976).

At about 61° north latitude on the northern edge of Han country begins a spruce-birch mix characteristic of the higher latitudes where the Kutchin live, and north of 68° pure stands of birch sometimes make up the entire forest. All the trees here are small. The Kutchin of Old Crow have trouble finding trees with butt diameters of more than two inches (M. H. Mason 1924:7).

Throughout the Cordillera, the forest is interspersed by meadows as well as swampy muskeg.

Fig. 2. Alpine tundra in southern Tutchone territory, near the summit of Chilkat Pass in the Coast Range. Photograph by Frederica de Laguna on the Haines Highway, Yukon Terr., 1954.

North of 55° the intermittent patches of alpine tundra increase in frequency and extent. The Cassiar region of British Columbia, home of the Tahltan, Kaska, and Sekani, has a great deal of alpine cover as compared to adjacent sections of the interior plateau, and the Chandalar Kutchin of north Alaska used to spend long periods hunting above the timberline, since only their river valleys were wooded (McKennan 1965:17; F.B. Watts 1968:88, fig. 4).

The distribution of various kinds of berries and other types of subarctic plants used by Indians as seasonal food has only been partially mapped for both boreal forest and the alpine tundra. The more southern Indians used a wider variety of berries and roots than those in the far north (Shelford 1972:206–210).

Fish

Several species of salmon spawn in the river systems that drain into the Pacific Ocean, although not all species run in all streams. From south to north the first major salmon stream is the Fraser, the upper reaches of which were inhabited by Chilcotin and some Carrier. Other Carrier lived on the upper Bella Coola and Skeena rivers. The Cassiar section of the interior plateau, occupied mostly by Tahltan, is also drained by the upper Skeena, and by the Nass, Stikine, and Taku rivers. The upper reaches of the Stikine are blocked so that salmon cannot go much above Telegraph Creek, nor are they in the eastern headwaters of the Taku River.

The Inland Tlingit used to take a good supply of salmon from the Nakina tributary of the Taku River, but during the nineteenth century most of the Indians moved to the upper Yukon River basin across the coastal divide. While salmon also ascend the Yukon drainage system, they become progressively poorer as they reach the extreme headwaters where the Inland Tlingit, Tagish, and many Tutchone live. The Han and some Yukon drainage Kutchin caught better-quality salmon. The few Tutchone at the head of the Alsek River got salmon of excellent quality, since unlike the Yukon salmon, these fish come but a short distance from the ocean.

The Chandalar Kutchin and those who lived in the Mackenzie rather than the Yukon drainage lacked salmon but caught quantities of whitefish and char as did most of the Sekani and the Kaska, who were also Mackenzie drainage peoples. All groups, including those with good salmon supplies, took various kinds of freshwater fish for food during some parts of the year. This was especially true of those in the more northern latitudes.

Mammals and Birds

Within the forest and on the open uplands are typical subarctic animals. Chief large game to be found almost everywhere are moose, caribou, and, of lesser significance as food, black bear. Caribou, both tundra and woodland subspecies, are most numerous in the northern areas. Grizzly bears live largely above the tree line, and the mountain heights also support Dall sheep (from northern British Columbia northward), marmots, and, in the coastal ranges, mountain goats. Wood bison used to range in parts of Carrier, Sekani, Kaska, Tahltan, and Inland Tlingit country but were rare or extinct by the nineteenth century as were the musk-oxen of the Chandalar Kutchin (Banfield 1974:383–390, 395–401; McKennan 1965:28). Chilcotin Indians had some wapiti in the past, and they, the Sekani, and some Carrier could perhaps get mule deer (Banfield 1974:383–390, 395–401). Important furbearers such as lynx, wolf, wolverine, fox, marten, mink, otter, and beaver are ubiquitous but variable in concentration, as are the small game animals such as snowshoe hare, porcupines, muskrats, ground squirrels, marmots, and so on. Ptarmigan (in the north), grouse, and in season, migratory waterfowl have always been part of the native diet.

Characteristic of boreal fauna are the cyclical fluctuations in numbers of many of the species. The intricate interrelationships between these fluctuations and the forest fires, snow depths, and other climatic factors are just beginning to be understood, as are the variations in salmon runs, but the practical consequences have long been a reality to those who aboriginally depended on caribou, moose, hare, or salmon as important parts of their food supply, or who later tried to incorporate successful fur harvests into their econo-

mies. When mice, voles, and hare drop in numbers, so do fox, lynx, and other furbearing predators.

Culture

Subsistence—The Annual Round

Although the exact aboriginal subsistence patterns of the Subarctic Cordillerans cannot be known before the indirect, if not the direct, effects of the Euro-American fur trade were being felt, it is known that well into the nineteenth century seasonal movements appear to have been dictated more by the availability of food and traditional social interests of the Indians than by the goal of trapping furs. Since all Cordillerans exploited a succession of animal and supplementary plant foods, nowhere could the Indians live year round in one place.

In summer, those who had access to salmon were busy catching and drying them for winter use ("Carrier," figs. 9–10, this vol.). The Chilcotin and some Carrier had both early and late runs, so that they could hunt in the mountains for an intervening period in July. Other groups usually had only one fishing season. But neither the Chilcotin nor Stuart Lake Carrier could count on regular runs in the upper Fraser, so they sometimes had to trade with neighboring Shuswap or Bella Coola for winter supplies of salmon. The Carrier, who fished the headwaters of the Nass and Skeena rivers along with one group of Sekani, the Tsetsaut, and Gitskan of the Northwest Coast, had ample supplies in most years. Some Tahltan benefited from large runs up the Stikine River to a short distance above Telegraph Creek, an area that also attracted the Tlingit of the rainy lower Stikine because of the ease of drying fish in the sunny interior. Other Tahltan and those Inland Tlingit who had not yet crossed the divide to the Yukon drainage got Taku River salmon. These people often met with coastal Taku Tlingit who likewise preferred to dry their fish in the hinterland. In the same way the Chilkat and Yakutat Tlingit had summer fish camps far up the Alsek River near the southernmost Tutchone. These summer fish camps facilitated trading between coast and interior peoples. Shells, seal skins, eulachon oil, dried sea weed, and other maritime delicacies passed inland, while tanned moose and caribou hides, ground squirrel skins, and other products moved to the coast. The trading intensified after the late eighteenth-century arrival of Russian, British, and American trade vessels on the coast and the subsequent establishment of coastal trading posts. Native trade fairs became important summer events and were supplemented by both summer and winter trading expeditions into the interior by coastal Indians who for most of the nineteenth century controlled the trade because they had easiest access to the cheapest Euro-American goods ("Intercultural

Relations and Cultural Change in the Cordillera," this vol.).

As noted, the Tagish and those Inland Tlingit who had moved into the Yukon headwaters could only get salmon of poor quality in contrast to those taken by many Tutchone, Han, and Kutchin, while Mackenzie drainage Kutchin, Sekani, and Kaska had to depend on char and whitefish.

Throughout the Cordillera the men prepared the fishing gear, put in the weirs and traps, and did most of the fishing. They removed the fish from the traps or dip-netted them, while the women cut hundreds of fish daily and attended to the drying (fig. 3). The split fish were air-dried on racks and had to be turned several times in the course of several days or weeks as dictated by local weather conditions. Small smudge fires were kept going to discourage the flies.

When the dried fish had been stored in caches, people moved into the high mountains for the late summer meat hunts critical for the survival of all groups. As households moved upland, they got ground squirrels, marmots, and also berries. Later they hunted moose, caribou, sheep, and goat, depending on what was to be found in the area. The aim was to get prime meat and skins. Where great caribou herds could be expected, as high in Tutchone, Han, and Kutchin country, many families gathered together to drive the animals into long straight fences or circular corrals (fig. 4) where the animals were snared or shot with arrows. Some of the Kutchin also intercepted the caribou at river crossings. As with the fish, much of the meat was dried and stored. Most potlatching was done in the fall because fresh meat supplies were at their maximum.

Toward the coldest part of the year all groups, from the Chilcotin to the Kutchin, gathered in settlements, usually of two or more households, to live on stored food and supplementary fresh fish and small game. So long as the food supplies held, men did not try to hunt much for big game, though when they traveled to distant caches to bring in new stores of dried meat or fish they sometimes killed moose or caribou. Families made their winter quarters where there were ample supplies of firewood, where they would be sheltered from the winds, and where the snow was not too deep. The summer salmon fishing sites often did not meet these requirements. For some groups, winter ice-fishing at good fish lakes was essential (fig. 6).

People tried to stay together at least through the coldest and darkest times. The winter solstice was marked by story telling, riddling, ceremonial gift exchange, and other indoor recreational activities such as dancing and singing. It was at this time in particular that the old people passed on much of their cosmological knowledge to the young and taught them rules of social behavior.

Fig. 3. Kutchin woman preparing whitefish for drying. Photographed at Arctic Red River, N.W.T., 1977.

By late winter, even before the fur trade had made trapping profitable, large winter camps usually broke into small units of one or two households that traveled independently in order to find big game, better fish lakes, and more abundant small game. As the fur trade grew the lengths of time that people dispersed in winter probably increased, since wide scattering of the population led to the best trapping.

This period of high mobility was halted by the difficult conditions of the spring thaw. Just before and during the thaw was when starvation most often threatened. People usually stayed where whitefish might be expected to run or beaver and muskrat were available. By this season the hare and grouse that earlier in the winter often supplemented big game and fish had become too thin and poor to provide much nourishment. Hare, in particular, are subject to great fluctuations in numbers. In years when both hare and salmon failed, hardship was inevitable. People listened eagerly for the first whistles of ground squirrels and the cries of migratory fowl, for they were welcome sources of food before the salmon arrived again. This too was the season when black bear were sought on the sunny side hills.

Since little is known of the actual amounts or the nutritional value of the meat, fish, and seasonal vegetable foods utilized by any of the nineteenth-century Cordillerans, no statements can be made as to which groups may have been better supplied than others. Unstudied data in the Hudson's Bay Company Archives could probably provide some useful insights. Starvation has been reported for all Subarctic Cordilleran groups, including the Chilcotin farthest to the south. In order to survive the winter Carrier families sometimes lived with the Bella Coola or the Gitksan, and early White traders sometimes starved. The starvation of natives for which historical records exist undoubtedly resulted in part from debility due to new diseases introduced by the Whites and from the alterations of subsistence patterns to accommodate to the fur trade, but some of the Indian stories about starvation seem to refer to precontact times. Only rarely did starvation lead to cannibalism, although Kaska, Tahltan, Han, and Kutchin warriors ritually ate parts of their slain enemies (McClellan 1975b:205–206; Krech 1978b).

Technology

Cordilleran technology was admirably adapted to mobility. People carried little with them, since many things could be made rather quickly with materials close at hand. Although production was often aligned by sex, and some persons were much more skilled than others, highly specialized techniques of manufacture were not critical for survival. Some Han and Kutchin had beautifully constructed birch canoes; others had less elegant watercraft that were still fully adequate for fishing and travel purposes. A snare, depending on its strength, could be used to catch an animal of any size from a bear to a ptarmigan. What was absolutely critical was

the knowledge of how to use the equipment effectively in varying situations, where best to set the snare or deadfall or to build a caribou surround, where to go on one's snowshoes to locate a moose, how to bait (fig. 8) a wolverine deadfall or to disguise the human odor on a beaver net. The successful hunter had to know the landscape, the habits of his prey, and the probable course of the weather. Equally essential to his mind was the knowledge of how to behave in a personalized universe in which many animal spirits were thought to be more powerful than humans.

The major raw materials of the artisans were bone, antler, horn, skin, sinew, wood, bark, and roots, with a lesser dependence on stone, teeth, earth ochers, and on raw copper in the few places that it was available. Manufacturing techniques were cutting, adzing, pounding, steaming, soaking in hot water, netting, lashing, tying, scraping, and smoking. Men made the bulk of the tools, hunting and fishing equipment, and weapons; women made containers, nets, and clothing. The two sexes worked together to produce skin toboggans, skin-covered boats, snowshoes, shelters, and a few other objects.

• HUNTING AND TRAPPING GEAR The importance of the snare can scarcely be overstressed. Portable and effective, snares could be used high in the mountains for sheep, caribou, ground squirrels, or ptarmigan; in the forest for bear, moose, caribou, wapiti, hare, grouse, and several kinds of furbearers; in the tall grass for waterfowl; and under water for beaver and some fish. Snares for small animals were of a few strands of sinew, babiche (semisoftened hide that had been slightly scraped after dehairing, defleshing, and wash-

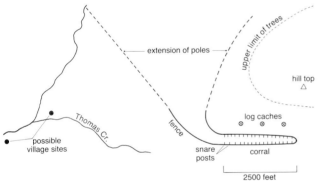

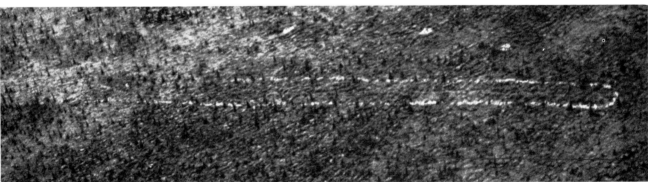

top, after 1968 sketch by W.N. Irving.

Fig. 4. Kutchin caribou surround, last used in 1894 (Richard E. Morlan, communication to editors 1978), at the head of Thomas Creek in northwestern Old Crow Flats, Yukon Terr. The corral, shown in aerial photograph, was about one-half mile long and consisted of 2 parallel fences about 20–30 yards apart and closed at one end, constructed of upright poles about 8 feet tall set 4–5 feet apart, once probably interlaced with brush with narrow openings in which, as well as inside the corral, hundreds of caribou-babiche snares were set. The diverging arms of the corral were made of smaller, more widely spaced poles. The whole impressive construction may have included 10,000 poles. In Sept.–Oct. caribou herds crossing the area were driven toward the surround by small groups of people running behind the animals and imitating wolf cries, while hunters with bows and arrows and spears were stationed at the entrance and along the corral—although most caribou were caught in the snares. The corral itself was concealed from the approaching animals by the dense timber and by a low ridge across the extended arms (Morlan 1973:71–73). Photograph by Richard E. Morlan, July 1967.

Fig. 5. Andrew Koe, Peel River Kutchin, at his hunting camp from which he was mainly trapping for furs. Photograph by Richard Slobodin on the Rat River portage near the divide between the Yukon and Mackenzie drainages, Jan. 1947.

ing), or the rib of a feather, while those for large animals might be 8-, 14-, or even 20-ply ropes of rawhide. Large snares usually had toggles or dragpoles. Spring and toss-pole snares such as those preferred for ground squirrels (fig. 9) and hare were more complicated to set than the simple choke loops.

Deadfalls are also highly adaptable. In the uplands they could be made of stones to catch marmots, or they could be elaborately balanced affairs of heavy poles set in the forest to take bears and furbearers such as fox and wolverine. Lighter constructions were set in trees to catch marten. Again the materials were all readily at hand, but one had to know how to use them—where to set up the sansom posts and triggers, how to choose an effective bait, how to erase human smells.

All tribes used bows and arrows, and everywhere the ideal bow was of birch. The southern tribes such as the Chilcotin, Carrier, Tsetsaut, and Sekani had sinew-backed as well as simple bows, as did the Kutchin adjacent to Eskimo, but other groups apparently did not. Although not specifically reported for Chilcotin, Carrier, or Sekani, most groups lashed a distinctive wooden wrist guard to the inner shaft of the bow. Bow strings were of twisted babiche, rawhide, or sinew. Arrows were of straight-grained spruce or birch and were carefully feathered with three or four feathers from eagles

or hawks. Bunting arrows for small animals had fixed bone or antler heads carved into conical or pyramidal shapes, sometimes beautifully incised. Big-game arrow heads were of antler or bone, often barbed on one side. These were often detachable so the shafts dropped at impact and the points worked into the animals' flesh to cause internal bleeding. Some groups had pressure-flaked stone arrow points that were fixed, as were the raw copper arrowheads of the Tutchone. Hunters carried skin quivers ("Han," fig. 2, this vol.) suspended from their left sides so they could quickly grasp the arrows with their right hands. Bows were usually held almost horizontally.

Bows and arrows could be used to kill bear, but the appropriate weapon for bears and men was the spear with a lanceolate head of bone, antler, or copper fixed onto a stout pole about six feet long. Some Cordillerans, such as the Tagish, Tutchone, Han, and Kutchin, speared caribou from hunting canoes. Beaver were either netted or speared.

Bone, stone, or native copper knives were made in a variety of shapes depending on the intended use. The Carrier, Tahltan, Inland Tlingit, and Tagish acquired through trade coastal-style fighting knives with wooden or bone handles carved to represent clan crest animals (fig. 10). The Tutchone, Han, and Kutchin had copper,

Fig. 6. Chief Isaac, Han (b. about 1847), fishing through a hole in the ice. Photograph by George G. Cantwell at Moosehide, Yukon Terr., 1898.

and later, iron knives with fluted double-edged blades and voluted handles ("Kutchin," fig. 4, this vol.). These too were for human combat and may have been Russian imports or copies.

• FISHING GEAR Fishing gear was just as ingeniously adapted to the differing kinds of fish and habitats as was the land hunting gear. It probably reached its greatest complexity among the southern Cordilleran groups. Tied brush and sapling weirs of various sorts and cylindrical funnel traps (fig. 11) were known to all tribes; however, box and tongue traps were restricted to the groups who had closest contact with coastal salmon fishers. The Chilcotin, Carrier, Tahltan, Han, and Kutchin took many of their fish in dip nets, sometimes in conjunction with a platform and weir, sometimes by means of a canoe (Osgood 1971:66–69; McKennan 1959:62–64).

Willow bast, nettle fiber, and sinew gill nets for fish were widely used in the nineteenth century. Some scholars think all gill nets were postcontact or else that Whites taught the Indians how to set them under the ice in winter ("Inland Tlingit," fig. 5, this vol.). Data are inconclusive (Rostlund 1952:84).

All Cordilleran natives speared large fish using leisters with barbed center spikes and springy side prongs. The Tutchone, Tagish, Inland Tlingit, and perhaps others tied a cross-piece to the handle just above the side prongs. This sighting device enabled a man more easily to spear the fish crossways. When men speared the fish through holes cut into the ice, they covered themselves with brush or skins to cut down the light and attracted the fish by dangling lures covered with fish skin. Barbed spears were used by all groups who caught salmon, and the heads were usually detachable. Fishhooks were little used in the past and may be postcontact. They are reported only for Sekani, Kaska, Inland Tlingit, Tagish, Tutchone, and Han. The use of

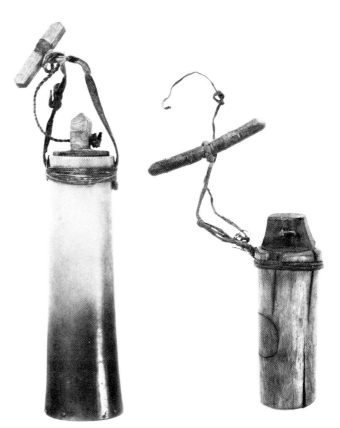

Smithsonian. Dept. of Anthr.: 248370, 248371.

Fig. 8. Tahltan containers for castoreum. Cylindrical boxes of bone with wooden base (left) and of wood (right), fitted with wooden stoppers, used to hold castoreum (a substance from beaver glands), which was smeared over and around traps and snares to attract game. They were carried toggled to the hunter's belt. Length of left about 20 cm, collected by G.T. Emmons, 1904–1906.

gaffs ("Carrier," fig. 9, this vol.) and gorges was more widespread.

Structures

Substantial houses did not fit well with the seasonal round of Cordilleran life. Perhaps some of the Chilcotin came closest to permanent residency, since they could often spend an entire winter in their semisubterranean dwellings similar to those of their Salish neighbors or the more characteristic ridge pole winter houses ("Chilcotin," fig. 3, this vol.). However, even they did not return to the same house every year, and like the other Cordillerans they also had various kinds of simple frame shelters: rectangular single or double frame lean-tos and gabled or conical pole structures that were roofed with moss, bark, and sometimes with skins. The Carrier, Tahltan, Inland Tlingit, Tagish, Tutchone, Han, and Kutchin made rectangular bark-covered structures at summer fish camps both for drying fish and as living quarters ("Tahltan," fig. 7, this vol.). Those of the southern groups closest to the coast were often quite large structures of poles and spruce slabs. Where

Fig. 7. Rack for equipment in the Tutchone settlement at Aishihik, Yukon Terr., with fish nets, moosehide hung out in preparation for further processing, dog harnesses, and toboggan. Photograph by Catharine McClellan, late winter, 1963.

379

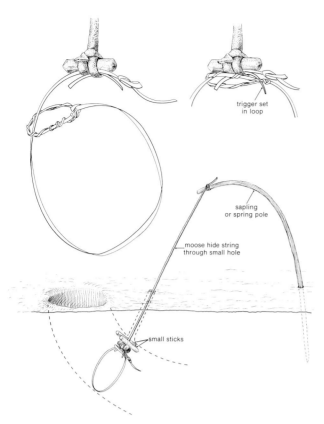

Natl. Mus. of Canada, Ottawa: VI-Q-102.

Fig. 9. Gopher (arctic ground squirrel) snaring. Southern Tutchone snare made by forming a loop at one end of a strip of an eagle feather quill and passing the other end through it to create a sliding noose. The remaining end of the quill is knotted and a wooden toggle and a trigger of quill is attached near it with a length of tanned hide. This strip is sometimes rubbed with red ocher to prevent stretching in the rain. A number of snares would be stored together in a bag containing an aromatic plant used to counteract the human scent. To set the snare, a woman uses a stick with a terminal hook to perforate the roof of the burrow a few inches from its opening, and to draw out through this hole the string from the snare placed inside the burrow. A green spring-pole placed several feet away or a nearby sapling is bent over and the string is tied to the end. Two small sticks are placed inside the burrow, one on each side of the string, and the trigger is set in the loop. As the gopher exits the burrow pulling on the noose the sticks are upset and trip the trigger. The noose is tightened by the tension of the spring pole and the gopher is caught in it (McClellan 1975a:158–159; Johnson and Raup 1964:194). Diameter of noose about 6.5 cm, collected by Catharine McClellan, 1963.

coastal ideas of social stratification became embedded, a high-ranking man sometimes built a substantial structure of timber to be used as a lineage house for part of the winter or for a specially important potlatch. The more northern Cordillerans—Tutchone, Han, and Kutchin—had portable dome-shaped winter houses of tied frameworks covered with tanned or semitanned mooseskins. The Sekani made only conical brush- or skin-covered tepees. Every camp or village had, in addition to dwellings, various kinds of drying racks and ground or raised caches ("Tutchone," fig. 2, this vol.). Small domed sweathouses were widespread, but their

full distribution is uncertain. Brush shelters for menstruants or parturients were constructed some distance from the main settlements and were used by every group (McKennan 1959:73–77).

Transportation

Most Subarctic Cordillerans moved about on foot. Only the Han and some of the Kutchin were to any extent water travelers. Like their neighbors farther down the Yukon, they made hunting and traveling canoes of birchbark on spruce frames that were better constructed, and in the case of the traveling canoe, larger than the canoes of any other Cordilleran group (McKennan 1959:92–93). Elsewhere in the Cordillera, the Indians lacked birchbark, or the swift rivers and windy lakes did not favor canoe transportation (Osgood 1971:80–81). The Sekani, Kaska, Tahltan, Inland Tlingit, and Tagish had only heavy spruce-bark canoes. The Carrier, Tahltan, Inland Tlingit, Tagish, Tutchone, and Sekani had small dugouts ("Sekani," fig. 2, this vol.) of various sorts, and all groups used rafts and temporary frame boats covered with rawhide. These could carry six or seven people as well as heavy loads of meat.

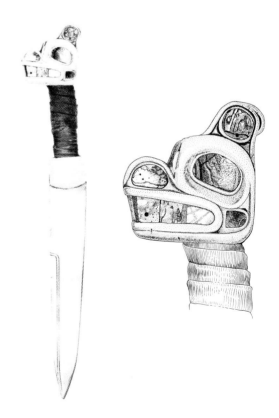

Mus. of the Amer. Ind., Heye Foundation, New York: 1/921.

Fig. 10. Tahltan knife showing coastal influence. Carved bone handle with abalone shell inlay hafted to a Euro-American metal blade. The quality and style of the carving indicate it is probably of Tlingit manufacture (Emmons 1911:116). Length about 43 cm, collected by G.T. Emmons, 1904–1906.

Fig. 11. Carrier salmon trap and dugout canoe at the outlet of Stuart Lake near Ft. St. James, B.C., with a brush fire in the distance. Photograph by James McDougall, Aug. 1891.

Cordilleran Indians of the northwest made excellent snowshoes, but the Chilcotin and Carrier say that only in the nineteenth century did they learn of snowshoes from Indians and traders farther east. This may also be true of the Tsetsaut, Tahltan, and Inland Tlingit. Carrier shoes of the twentieth century are either bear paw in type or else have small squared-off tips on the toes and rather long tails. The Sekani, Tahltan, Inland Tlingit, Tagish, and some of the Tutchone preferred upturned pointed toes on both the large hunting shoe and the smaller trail shoe, but northern Tutchone, Han, and Kutchin shoes were almost always round-toed (fig. 12). Toes and heels were usually filled with babiche and the foot section with strong rawhide. The Kutchin also did a fine lacing of sinew, even in their hunting shoes, which sometimes reached eight feet in length. Snowshoes are essential for moving about in the fine powdery snow of the boreal forest, which rarely crusts until late spring.

The Chilcotin and Carrier denied the aboriginal use of toboggans and sleds, but the Carrier and all the Cordillerans to the north or east used drags made of the leg skins of moose or caribou sewed together. Usually the women pulled them to transport household goods or meat, while the men went ahead hunting. Possibly the Kaska had steamed-wood toboggans in precontact times, but more probably they came in with the fur trade.

Whether because they were near the Eskimos or because of Siberian influence spreading up the Yukon River, the Kutchin apparently had wooden sleds with rather high runners in precontact times. They too were drawn by humans (Osgood 1936a:59, 64). Dog traction for toboggans ("Intercultural Relations and Cultural Change in the Cordillera," fig. 4, this vol.) and sleds and possibly dog-packing ("Kaska," fig. 3, this vol.) came in only with the Whites. The chief aboriginal use of dogs was for hunting wapiti, moose, or bear in the spring.

Cooking and Containers

Some raw foods such as fish heads and eggs, or skinned ground squirrels were fermented in bags or holes in the ground. Dried meat, dried fish, and berries were usually eaten raw. Other food was cooked by stone-boiling, roasting on an open fire, or in earth ovens. People made fires with strike-a-lights, drills, or plows, but in winter they liked to carry fire brands with them.

Carrying and storage containers (fig. 13) were light and flexible. They were of bark, tanned skin or rawhide, netted sinew or babiche, woven spruce root and the stomachs, bladders, guts, feet, or heads of animals. Each man had a netted (fig. 14) or hide hunting bag and a tool bag with fire-making equipment and other essentials such as an awl and crooked knife ("Tahltan,"

381

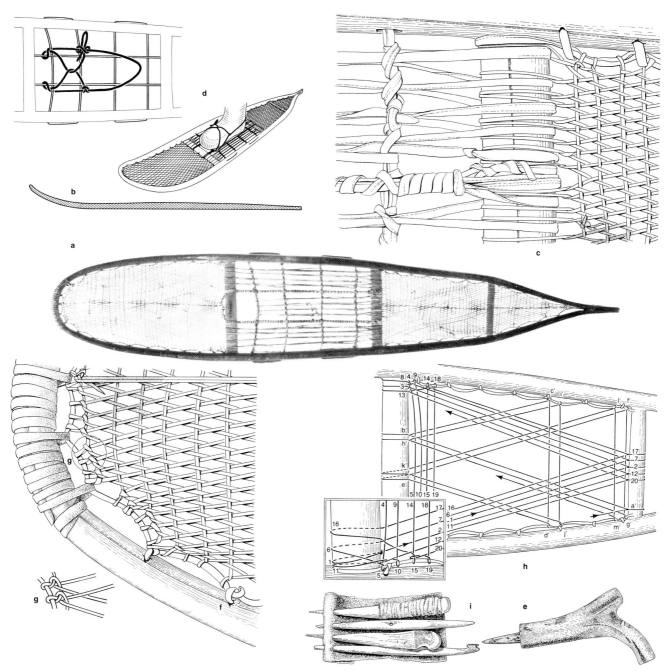

a, Smithsonian, Dept. of Anthr.: 234027; Natl. Mus. of Canada, Ottawa: e, VI–H–30; i, VI–Q–129.

Fig. 12. Round-toed snowshoe and lacing details. a, Kutchin snowshoe with rounded slightly turned-up (b) toes. The center portion (c, partial detail) of the snowshoe supports the foot, bearing the user's weight. For this reason the lacing is simpler and the babiche stronger than the finer mesh of the toe and heel sections, which serves to keep the snowshoe on the snow surface. Toe and heel section lacing is most often done by women and the foot section by men. The harness for attaching the snowshoe to the foot is usually heavy babiche or moosehide attached to the snowshoe at 2 points and crossed over the forefoot (d) (Osgood 1936:77–82). It is possible to insert the foot into the harness without undoing it, although adjustments when necessary can be made at the single loop bow knot that lies on the outside of the forefoot (and thus also serves as an indicator of right or left foot). Snowshoe lacing tools include a Kaska awl (e) with antler handle and short, sharply pointed metal blade used to make the V-shaped holes on the inside of the snowshoe frame (f). The holes are usually evenly spaced, with intervals measured by finger widths; the finer the lacing, the closer the spacing. Selvage loops (g) are knotted through these holes and the filler is attached along these loops. The hexagonal filler of the toe and heel (h) sections is created with fine babiche dampened for pliability and laced in a complicated triangular pattern. Lacing is begun at 1 in the lower left and proceeds in order through 20 and in the same manner beyond until the midbrace is filled at a´; a new pattern is then begun (a´–m´) and is continued in the same manner until the hexagonal pattern fills the whole area (see Osborne, Appleby, and Kershner 1977). The Southern Tutchone bone tool kit (i), kept in a leather holder, is used in working the lacing. It includes, top to bottom, an awl wrapped in babiche, a netting needle pointed at both ends with a hole in the center, another awl, and a hooking tool square at one end and with a short notched hook at the other. Individual preference dictates tool use. In addition to the pattern created by the lacing, decoration of red ocher on the lacing (such as the barely visible dots down the center of the Kutchin snowshoe here) might be added. Wool tassels are sometimes tied on the outer edge of the frames and serve to muffle the sound of breaking through the crust. a, Length 107 cm, collected by Edward A. Preble, Mackenzie District, N.W.T., before 1905; e, length 15 cm, collected by J.A. Teit, Cassiar, B.C., 1915; i, length of hooking tool about 14 cm, collected by Catharine McClellan, Aishihik, Yukon Terr., 1963.

top, Natl. Mus. of Canada, Ottawa: J–2190; bottom, Smithsonian, Dept. of Anthr.: 381.2621.
Fig. 13. Berrying baskets. top, Inland Tlingit child holding a coastal-style berrying basket of twined spruce root, which is rolled for storage then dampened to open when in use. It was probably made in the upper Taku River region, where the Inland Tlingit formerly lived. Photograph by Dorothy Rainier Libby at Teslin, Yukon Terr., 1948. bottom, More typical in the Cordillera region were containers of birchbark such as this Carrier fiber-stitched woman's berry basket with leather carrying strap. The upper edge is reinforced with a wood strip and bound with red and green dyed fiber. Height 14 cm, collected by Julian H. Steward at Ft. St. James, B.C., 1940.

fig. 6, this vol.). Each woman had a sewing kit with awl and sinew (fig. 15).

Clothing

Cordilleran women were skilled in dressing and tailoring animal hides. Skin dressing was a complex process

of cleaning the skins, then rendering them soft by soaking them in a solution of water and fermented animal brains or other substances and breaking down the fibers through the physical means of scraping and smoking ("Carrier," fig. 3, this vol.).

All but the Chilcotin, who wore kilts in summer, dressed in well-cut shirts and leggings or one-piece combinations of trousers and moccasins. The men's shirts were shorter than those of the women and in the north often ended in points at both front and back ("Kutchin," fig. 4, this vol.). Fringes, seeds, quills, bird or beaver claws, bits of bird down, and red ocher paint embellished the finest clothing. Robes, hoods, and hats of fur or netted hareskin kept people warm in winter, as did mitts with neck strings and high-topped moccasins that could be stuffed with hareskin or grass duffle as a warm lining. Soft moccasin soles were essential for easy snowshoeing.

Mothers carried their babies laced into special carriers. These usually had semirigid bark backs but were padded with soft moss and covered with tanned skin. Broad baby-carrying straps might also be used ("Old Crow, Yukon Territory," fig. 6, this vol.), whether or not the infant was in a moss bag.

Social Organization

The aboriginal social organization of the Subarctic Cordillerans is even harder to reconstruct than their material culture. Crucial factors to be considered include the degree to which population movements and sizes were directly or indirectly affected by the Euro-American fur trade, which introduced disease and altered band compositions, and which certainly made increased social stratification possible among those Indians closest to the source of trade goods. Some of them made

Lower Ft. Garry Natl. Histl. Park, Selkirk, Man.: HBC 61–165.
Fig. 14. Kutchin game bag of moosehide with netting of caribou hide, yellow, green, and purple wool tassels, and design in silk embroidery along the top. Width 53.3 cm, collected on the Mackenzie River, N.W.T., about 1910.

U. of Alaska Arch., Fairbanks: Charles Bunnell Coll., 58–1026–1549.
Fig. 15. Woman, probably Han, sewing tanned hide. A sewing kit is by her knees. Photograph by George G. Cantwell, at Moosehide, Yukon Terr., probably about 1900.

great profits acting as middlemen between the Whites and Indians farther away, and they began to accumulate guns, knives, and other surplus goods themselves. Several scholars have argued that much of the social organization of the Cordillerans at the time of contact had been recently borrowed from their coastal neighbors and that the process was still going on. Thus, some of the Southern Carrier adopted Bella Coola–like ranked lineages and reckoned descent bilaterally, while others, along with one Sekani group, had a system of Tsimshian-named matrilineages grouped into phratries. Nineteenth-century Tahltan, Inland Tlingit, Tagish, and some Tutchone had Tlingit-named matrilineal clans organized into moieties that paralleled those of the Northwest Coast. Even the Kaska had Tlingit-type moieties. Some of these incorporations of coastal social organization were certainly recent; nevertheless, it is possible to argue that matriliny, clans, and moiety organization are basically very old in the Cordillera. The matter is of special interest to those who think that hunting peoples are usually bilaterally or patrilineally organized. For most nineteenth-century Subarctic Cordillerans matriliny was certainly the rule—that is, an individual belonged to the descent group of his or her mother (McClellan 1964). The only exceptions were the Sekani, who probably entered the Cordillera in the eighteenth century, the Carrier with closest ties to the Bella Coola, and the Chilcotin who were so heavily influenced by the Shuswap. Clan and moiety organization of the Cordillerans and their neighbors has been summarized by De Laguna (1975), who argues that clan alignments shifted rather easily from group to group in response to demographic and cultural factors.

Most authorities (but cf. McDonnell 1975) assume the fundamental importance of the nuclear family in the past, but it is clear that the minimal domestic or co-residential units everywhere were extended families of some sort. The family links were often between two adult siblings of same or opposite sex, or between parents and their married children; however, sometimes the linkage was between hunting partners who were only distant classificatory kin. What was important was that in the course of its existence, any nuclear family or any other segment of a domestic group might leave to join another household unit. The system was extremely flexible, and arrangements of many kinds were worked out in terms of general expedience and personal preference. In the northern area, at least, husbands were responsible for the welfare of their wives' parents until they died, so they often met this obligation by living with them.

Because of the constant fission and fusion, the sizes of local groups at any particular time varied greatly. A local group might consist of a single extended family. More often two or three families camped and traveled together. Many more might gather for the fall caribou hunt or summer fishing or for the midwinter cold season. Such groups of people or local bands were in certain contexts designated by the areas that they habitually exploited, for they were held together by their territorial as well as their kinship ties. All the households usually saw each other face to face during some part of the year, even though they did not always stay together. Others who joined the group and undertook to hunt, fish, or trade in its area had to validate their presence either through primary kin ties or by setting up a formal partnership with someone in the band (McClellan 1975a:13–16).

Large social units predicated on formal territorial claims did not exist. It has been argued that the Kutchin had a sense of "nationhood," derived from their distinctive language and culture ("Kutchin," this vol.; McKennan 1965:14–15), and this may also have been true of the Han (Osgood 1971:20–28). To a lesser extent, other groups also recognized a commonality of linked dialects, shared customs, and contiguous territory, but it was the Whites who gave them the overall "tribal" names used in this volume. The stealing of women or territorial trespass sometimes led to feuding or raids between local groups or segments of them, but there was no full-scale warfare between large regional groups.

Neither the fluidity of band composition nor the presence of coastal-type clans, phratries, or moieties, where found, were conducive to the development of formal offices of political leadership until after the fur traders created "trading chiefs." Aboriginal leadership depended on hunting or shamanistic skills, wisdom, a strong personality, and oratorical persuasiveness. When a headman's personal powers declined, so did his authority, and his followers left to find better providers elsewhere. Even where Northwest Coast influence was strongest and a ranked position as "chief" was fixed, it had to be maintained through potlatching and other acts befitting the high rank. Furthermore, a chief was recognized only within his own lineage, clan, or phratry. The aboriginal Cordillerans were basically egalitarian.

Life Cycle

In keeping with their egalitarian ethos, the Cordillerans stressed the development of individual self-reliance well suited for subarctic survival. Human life was thought to be part of a continuous cycle of life and death. During life a person's immortal spirit was incarnated in an earthly body that was usually, although not always, human. The rebirth of some, but not all, specific individuals was recognized and sometimes deliberately induced through ritual. A physical sensation, such as a chill, signaled the arrival of the baby's spiritual essence in the mother.

All groups ritualized birth, puberty, loss of a spouse, and death, primarily through food taboos and restrictions on ordinary social contacts and sexual activity. A prolonged training period at puberty marked the end of a basically permissive childhood. Every effort was made to ensure a successful transition to adult status, for in the small populations every adult counted heavily. Girls were isolated from the main camp or village for a month to as long as two years. They wore enveloping puberty hoods, used scratching sticks, were forbidden fresh foods, and observed a host of symbolic acts designed to ensure their own future well-being and that of their children. Except for sewing, emphasis was less on their practicing domestic skills, many of which they had already acquired, than on their thorough learning that as mature women they had the inherent power through menstrual and birth effluvia to offend the spirits of the game animals and other natural phenomena. They therefore had to learn how to manage this power through proper social restraints and ritual behavior, since people's livelihood depended on their behavior. Many of the puberty observances were repeated at parturition and widowhood. Boys too had to learn how to please the powerful spirits of the universe, and when they were quite young they began to acquire personal spirit helpers. The more southern groups stressed formal vision quests. Adult men taught the boys hunting skills and put their charges through rigorous physical exercises. A boy's first major kill was formally recognized by all in camp. In the northern area young men often lived together in loose age sets while they were being trained.

Marriage was arranged by the couple's parents, and it involved exchange of gifts between families. Where present, lineages, clans, phratries, or moieties structured the choice of spouses and also of reciprocal social actions at public ceremonials, especially at death and at the final memorial feast for the deceased. Corpses were usually cremated.

Although varying somewhat in form, the memorial rite was a prime ceremonial event for most of the Cordilleran tribes. Usually described as a "potlatch," it brought together maximum numbers of people for oratory, singing, dancing, display of ceremonial garb and symbolic crests, feasting, and distribution of wealth to members of the moiety or phratry opposite that of the deceased ("Tagish," fig. 5, this vol.). It marked the finish of an individual's current earthly life and his kin group's discharge of all outstanding debts for reciprocal services to him during that life. Then society was in a position to start a new round of social interactions. Where the profits from the fur trade had made stratified rank a possibility, potlatching also became a means to enhance or maintain rank and to assume or reaffirm lineage prerogatives.

Beliefs and Religion

Because they were widely scattered, few in number, and nonliterate, the Cordillerans had no dogmatized belief systems. However, every group had oral traditions about the nature of the universe and the beings in it. Each told of a trickster-transformer or culture hero who changed the world and its inhabitants to the state in which the recent Indians knew it. He often put the heavenly bodies in position, altered geography, killed off or reduced in size giant man-eating animals, and saw to it that people would be able to eat, talk, and give birth in human fashion. People believed that animals and a great many other natural phenomena were inhabited or controlled by powerful spirits and also that dwarfs, giants, and other superhuman creatures lived in the world.

The public religious practitioners were shamans, who undertook to control the spirit powers so as to locate game, change the weather, cure sickness, or perform other marvelous acts. Each shaman had his individualized way of "knowing" aspects of the universe and had a series of spirit helpers whose aid he might enlist in dreams or who might possess him while he and his audience sang the spirit songs at night-time services.

Every person also acted privately to come to terms with the world of personified power. A successful hunter had at least one spirit helper and often more. Each adult had, too, a store of practical knowledge suitable for his or her sex. This included weather lore, a roster of home remedies for minor illness, and so on. Elders had to have, in addition, accurate knowledge of genealogical data, lineage or clan traditions, and past historical events such as feuds, wars, and so on. Much of this information was learned by listening to stories from childhood. A good raconteur was much appreciated, and creative variation was condoned. The repertoire of stories was constantly expanded by additions from coastal and White traders, or the Algonquian and Iroquois hunters attached to them. Many tales involved marriages between humans and animals or other superhumans during which the humans learned the proper relationships between themselves and these beings, including the way animals liked to have their bodies cared for after they have been killed. Others illustrated what was desirable or undesirable in human interrelationships. Some tales had a high comic quality, but all oral traditions were believed to be basically true, whether set in the mythological past or more recent times.

Music, Dance, and Art

Individual skills in singing and dancing were likewise valued. Both sexes composed lyric expressions of their emotional state—grief, happiness, loneliness. The best songs soon became public; however, the specific ownership of lineage or clan songs was formally recognized. Dancing was lively and was often imitative. Men and women did various round and line dances as well as solos. Musical instruments were drums ("Inland Tlingit," figs. 8–9, this vol.), beating sticks, clappers, and whistles. As with stories, every group tried to acquire songs and dances of neighboring or more distant peoples.

The aboriginal and later trade networks facilitated the movement of all these forms of expression much more than of the graphic and plastic arts. In spite of their proximity to the great art style of the Northwest Coast peoples, even the Cordillerans closest to the coast could not easily copy the coastal peoples' monumental cedar carving or painted house screens. They lacked the straight-grained coastal timber, and their mobile way of life militated against the creation of large or fixed heirloom objects. Their own artistic expression was in spare geometric black or red painted designs or incisions on wooden or antler plates, spoons (fig. 16; "Tutchone," fig. 7, this vol.), or gambling sticks (fig. 17) and in the tasteful decoration of clothing. Psychologically, they apparently preferred not to fix in realistic representative form the frequently metamorphosing beings of a universe that they conceptualized as fluid

and open. Almost every aspect of Cordilleran behavior emphasized individual adaptability and self-reliance in an uncertain world.

Natl. Mus. of Canada, Ottawa: VI–F–3.

Fig. 16. Han spoon. Mountain-sheep horn decorated with incised lines stained red. Length 54 cm, collected at Dawson, Yukon Terr., 1901–1906.

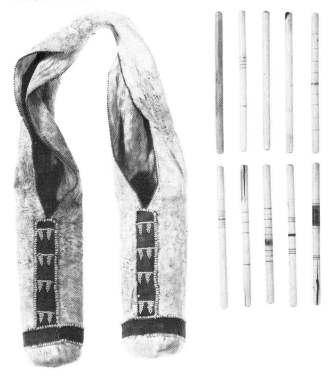

Smithsonian, Dept. of Anthr.: 230.019.

Fig. 17. Tahltan gambling sticks and carrying case. Sticks are of rounded and smoothed wood; most have black and red designs, which determine value and name. A set of 18 to over 30 sticks is kept in a tanned caribou hide band with a pocket at each end decorated with red flannel and green, pink, and clear beads, which is carried over the shoulder or grasped in the hand. Emmons (1911:88–98) explains the game. Length of band 67 cm, sticks about 12.5 cm. Collected by G.T. Emmons about 1904.

Intercultural Relations and Cultural Change in the Cordillera

CATHARINE McCLELLAN

The Subarctic Cordillera stretches north in Canada from central British Columbia through the southwest corner of Northwest Territories and all of Yukon Territory except the arctic coast. From the Yukon Territory it bends west into north-central Alaska in the United States. This vast mountain-plateau area thus straddles two nations with distinctive political histories.

Until 1858 the Hudson's Bay Company, under a charter from the British Crown, had nominal control of the Canadian part of the Cordillera. British Columbia then became a Crown Colony until 1871 when it entered the confederation of Canada and became a province. In 1869 the Hudson's Bay Company also turned over to Canada what became the Northwest Territories; the small part of the Cordillera within it subsequently became part of the Mackenzie District. Yukon Territory was separated from the Northwest Territories in 1898. Russia claimed sovereignty over Alaska from 1741 until 1867, when it was sold to the United States. Alaska became a territory in 1912 and a state in 1958. Each political change carried immediate or eventual repercussions for the Indian peoples of the Cordillera.

Native Cordillerans have always been few, but twentieth-century authorities usually distinguish 10 groups. South to north these are: Chilcotin, Carrier, Sekani, Kaska, Tahltan, Inland Tlingit, Tagish, Tutchone, Han, and Kutchin. The Tsetsaut disappeared early in the twentieth century, as may have happened also to other groups in the upper Taku and Yukon river drainages.

These peoples shared aboriginal cultures that were quite similar, and most of them spoke related Athapaskan languages. Furthermore, the pattern of culture change after Whites arrived was much the same for all, regardless of the exact time of contact or of national dominance. This chapter stresses the types of change that all Cordilleran natives have experienced.

The Subarctic Cordillera was one of the last regions of North America to be occupied by Whites. Broadly, three historic periods of culture change may be distinguished. The early period (mid-eighteenth to mid-nineteenth century) was marked by the initial meetings between Indians and White traders who introduced new technology and new diseases to the natives. They also generated considerable hostility among various Indian groups, each of whom tried to monopolize the sources of Euro-American trade items. The second period (mid-nineteenth to mid-twentieth century) was characterized by a more stabilized fur trade, early missionary work, and several political changes that affected the Indians. A series of nineteenth-century gold strikes periodically stimulated rapid, though often transient, growths in the White population and in transportation facilities and government controls. The modern period (mid-twentieth century on) brought greatly increased contacts with urban Canada and the United States, the decline of the fur trade, the development of extensive government programs for natives, and native activism. Within the Cordillera, the sequence of these broad "periods" of successive change has generally been later in the northwest than in the south or northeast.

An important factor to Cordillerans throughout their history has been their proximity to the environmentally rich Pacific coast, which in the eighteenth and nineteenth centuries supported a dense Indian population with sophisticated cultures.

Mid-Eighteenth to Mid-Nineteenth Century

In the period just before White contact, almost all the small groups of Indians living in the Subarctic Cordillera were Athapaskan speakers. Bands using different dialects evidently met unexpectedly from time to time where large caribou herds could be anticipated or at good fishing spots. Whether the strangers fled, fought, or became friends varied from situation to situation. The safest way for aliens to make or maintain contact was through trading relationships, which often led to the linking of groups by marriage as well.

Cordillerans bartered both among themselves and with their neighbors, particularly those of the Pacific coast. Far up the major salmon streams in the sunny interior the Cordillerans and Northwest Coast Indians met, both to catch and dry salmon and to exchange the dressed elk, caribou, and moose hides, babiche and sinew, ground squirrel, marmot, and mountain goat skins, fine land animal furs, quillwork, lichen dyes, and raw copper of the interior for marine products such as abalone and dentalium shells, dried seaweed, clams, and eulachon grease, as well as for steamed-wood boxes, spruce-root basketry, iron daggers, and, occasionally, for slaves from the southern coast.

In this exchange the coast Indians dominated their near Cordilleran neighbors, who did the same to the Cordillerans farther inland to whom they passed on some of the coastal products. The entire trade network, which was usually structured as a kind of reciprocity system between real or fictive kin, was facilitated by the existence of matrilineal clans (often grouped into moieties or phratries) among the northern coast Indians and most of the adjacent Cordillerans. Farther south, the Bella Coola and most of the Kwakiutl of the coast, as well as the Cordilleran Chilcotin with whom they traded, were bilaterally organized; however, each group had named ambilineal descent groups that could be linked through kinship or marriage (De Laguna 1975; McClellan 1950, 1964).

Less is known about precontact trade between the northern Cordillerans and their eastern neighbors in the Rocky Mountain foothills and Mackenzie Lowlands, or between the Chilcotin and Carrier and the adjacent Shuswap to their east and south, or between the Tutchone, Han, and Kutchin with the Upper Tanana and Koyukuk to their west and north. The natural resources and ways of life of all these peoples were quite similar.

On the Arctic plains and Arctic slope of the Brooks Range north of the Kutchin were Eskimos. They sometimes bartered lines of walrus hide, sealskins, whalebone, and ivory for the wolverine pelts and dressed moosehide of the Kutchin, but trade was sporadic because of environmental, linguistic, and cultural factors (Burch 1979; Krech 1979a).

At the time of White contact the only Cordilleran Indians who had not lived in the area for many centuries were probably the Sekani. Their ancestors, fearful of the Cree and Beaver, began to stay permanently in the mountains only in the late eighteenth and early nineteenth century. The introduction of Euro-American goods into the aboriginal trade networks led to movements by Indians already in the Cordillera. For example, in the nineteenth century some Inland Tlingit crossed from the Taku River into the Yukon River drainage, and the Chilcotin began to expand south. There were undoubtedly other population shifts too, because, just as had happened earlier in the central-eastern Subarctic, each native group in the Cordillera or on its borders tried to monopolize the distribution of the new items. In the Cordillera the situation was complicated by the simultaneous appearance in the east of North West Company traders and, in the west, of American and British trade ships competing with the Russians.

By 1800 the sea otter, on the pelts of which the Whites had built a thriving trade with China, had been almost exterminated. The traders then had to turn to fine land furs, but until they established posts in the interior mainland they had to rely on coast Indian middlemen to supply the beaver, marten, fox, and lynx furs that replaced the sea otter pelts. At the same time, competition began to increase from land-based American fur traders to the south.

The Cordilleran natives took what advantage they could of the situation, realigning their positions with native middlemen of the coast or Rocky Mountain foothills as the sources of goods changed, and traveling about looking for White traders with whom they could themselves trade directly. Indians who in early times would never have met encountered one another at expanded native trade fairs on the great salmon streams and, later, at trading posts newly established within their homelands. The coastal Indians almost always prevented the Cordillerans from going down to trade with White sea captains.

The first direct contact between Whites and Cordilleran Indians probably took place in 1789 when Alexander Mackenzie of the North West Company met some eastern Kutchin along the lower part of the river that now bears his name. Four years later, after wintering near present-day Fort Vermilion, Mackenzie followed the Peace River into the Rocky Mountains and ascended the Parsnip River in what was becoming Sekani territory. He then crossed the divide to the Fraser River in Carrier country and finally cut overland to reach the Pacific Ocean in the land of the Bella Coola just seven weeks after Capt. George Vancouver had reached the same spot by sea (Cooke and Holland 1978:113; Rich 1967:184–185). Although the Carrier had never before met Whites, Mackenzie found some of them already supplied by the Shuswap, Bella Coola, and Tsimshian with iron tools of European manufacture. The Carrier feared the Shuswap because of their guns and metal knives and feuded with each other and with the Chilcotin over access to new trade goods. The Sekani had fled westward into the mountains, fearful of the Cree and Beaver who were also armed with guns (Black 1955:10–58, 108–123; Mackenzie 1801:297–314; Morice 1905:160).

Farther north, the Kaska and Tsetsaut were raiding the Tahltan nearest the coast, and all were trading with well-armed and arrogant Tlingit and Gitksan who were in direct contact with Euro-American ship captains. By mid-century, when the Tutchone first met Whites, they were describing as dangerous enemies the Han who lived below them on the Yukon River and who were being supplied with metal goods procured by Kutchin traders from posts on the lower Mackenzie drainage, from Tanana Indian middlemen, from Russians on the middle Yukon, or else from Ahtna and Tanaina middlemen who visited Russian forts at the mouth of the Copper River, in Prince William Sound, or in Cook Inlet. But even more than the Han, the Tutchone feared the coastal Tlingit who were making annual trading trips far inland. The Tutchone themselves alternately raided or traded with Upper Tanana River Indians (Boas 1895; McClellan 1975a:501–518; Black 1955:l–lii, lxxiv–lxxvi).

The various Kutchin bands either traded or quarreled among themselves and became increasingly hostile to the Eskimos of the Mackenzie delta, who were trying to break the strategic trade position of the eastern Kutchin (Burch 1979; Krech 1979a; Pullen 1979:141–145). In short, as elsewhere in the Subarctic, the introduction of White goods strongly affected intergroup relationships among the natives decades before the Whites themselves appeared in the Cordillera.

The North West Company established the first posts within the Cordillera itself, in Sekani and Carrier country, beginning with Fort McLeod in 1805 (fig. 1). In 1821 the intense competition between the Hudson's Bay Company and the North West Company ended in a merger. The revived Hudson's Bay Company then began to consolidate its position all along the Pacific coast and to put new posts farther north in Cordilleran country among the northern Sekani, Kaska, Tutchone, and Kutchin. Some of them (Fort Halkett, Dease Lake, Pelly Banks, Fort Frances, Fort Selkirk) were short-lived, for the bitter fact was that the post managers often found themselves less well stocked than the coastal Indian traders who also often charged 50 percent less than the company. Whites often found it difficult, if not impossible, to live in the harsh Cordilleran environment, and Tlingit hostility aggravated their problems in the middle Cordillera region (Black 1955:125–175; Wilson 1970:11–40, 53–110).

Extending its posts still farther northwest, in 1847 the Hudson's Bay Company founded Fort Yukon (fig. 2) among the western Kutchin in what was technically Russian territory. The Russians were by this time advancing up the Yukon from its mouth, as well as up the Copper River toward the low pass separating it from the Yukon drainage. As a result of all this activity of White traders, the various Kutchin bands were having a glorious and profitable time as middlemen par excellence (Murray 1847–1850, 1910; McClellan 1950:177–185; Osgood 1936a:17–18).

Altered Economy and New Technology

Throughout this early period, much of the interaction between Indians and Whites was of a reciprocal nature. The incoming White traders wanted the Indians to continue as hunters, but they also offered rewards for increased catches of furbearers. Traditionally, most Cordillerans tried to acquire enough food so they could

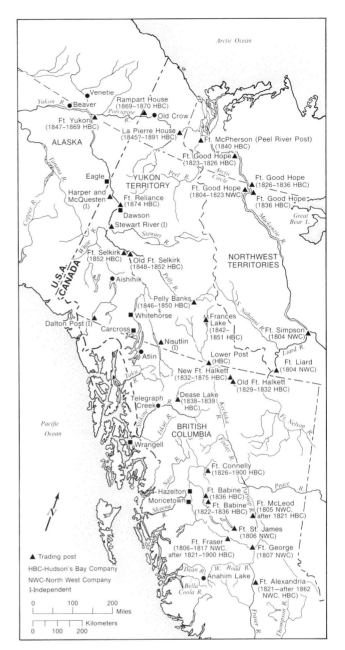

Fig. 1. Trading posts in the Cordillera and adjoining Mackenzie borderlands, with approximate dates when they were established and abandoned, when known.

stay together as long as possible in winter camps or villages. After the traders arrived, the local natives began to congregate for short periods of time near the trading posts after the fall hunt and perhaps again at Christmas, but they spent the rest of the winter widely scattered in their hunting and trapping areas. In the late spring and summer they returned to the trading posts, which were usually at good fishing spots.

As a consequence of the focus on trapping, the Indians soon acquired a new or improved technology of metal traps, files, knives, axes, and so on, which also became increasingly incorporated into all their subsistence activities. Guns received in exchange for furs pro-

Smithsonian Arch.: 80–1394, 80–1395.

Fig. 2. Fort Yukon in June 1867, a principal trading post operated until 1869 by the Hudson's Bay Company in western Kutchin country. "All the houses were strongly built, roofed with sheets of spruce bark pinned and fastened down by long poles. The sides were plastered with a white mortar made from shell-marl, obtainable in the vicinity. Most of the windows were of parchment, but those of commander's house were of glass" (Dall 1870:103). A narrow fur press is also shown here (see 'Intercultural Relations and Cultural Change in the Subarctic Shield and Mackenzie Borderlands,' fig. 6, this vol.). Although the Indians themselves sometimes used spruce bark roofing, the Kutchin and other northern Cordillerans were impressed by the construction of the trading post buildings because unlike some of the southern Cordilleran groups nearer the coast they, themselves, had no permanent structures. Sketches by William H. Dall.

vided new ways to kill game, but aboriginal hunting techniques using snares, caribou and moose fences, deadfalls, spears, and bows and arrows continued in many places even after guns became common.

Careful study of ethnohistoric sources is needed before it can be determined whether there was greater plenty or greater hardship in any given place after the introduction of the Whites' technology. Short-term climatic shifts, the cyclical nature of subarctic faunal populations and the effects upon them of forest fires, which probably increased as Whites traveled through the area, all affected subsistence production. Other factors to be weighed are the amount of time that the Indians spent seeking fur and fur traders rather than game, the impact of introduced diseases, and the interpretation of what the Indians really meant when they reported "starvation."

Changes in modes of travel and transportation may ultimately have been almost as significant in altering subsistence patterns as the introduction of guns. The aboriginal Cordillerans in the north always made fine snowshoes for winter travel, but some of the Tahltan and Carrier evidently learned of them only from the White traders, and the Whites certainly introduced dog traction with wooden sleds or toboggans to all the Cordillerans (fig. 4). It is a moot point whether they also brought in dog packing. These new modes of transportation enabled the Indians to move faster and with more weight than was possible with the traditional skin drags. On the other hand, as they began to keep dogs, the Indians had to get more meat and fish to feed them, even though guns sometimes made it easier to take

Hudson's Bay Company Lib., Winnipeg, Man.

Fig. 3. Rampart House, one of 3 posts by that name successively established by the Hudson's Bay Company on the Porcupine River in Kutchin country. This depiction is probably of the first Rampart House, which was at Howling Dog. The domed structures may be either sweathouses or Indian dwellings. The tents were probably all occupied by Indians. Watercolor, signed and dated 1870 by the missionary Émile Petitot.

game. The Whites had introduced fishhooks, fish net twine, and gill netting in winter.

A few Indians learned how to make lumber boats such as were used by some of the traders, but only slowly did they begin to abandon their traditional bark and skin canoes, dugouts, and rafts. Among the Cordillerans only the Han and Kutchin were really skilled rivermen.

A few Cordilleran posts specialized in manufacturing articles needed by the Hudson's Bay Company. The Yukon posts in the Northern District, for example, sent leather east of the mountains, and many of the skins were supplied by the Kutchin or Han. Fort Babine and

Fig. 4. Watson Smarch, an Inland Tlingit, leading a loaded toboggan on a trapping trail. Photograph by Catharine McClellan, March 1951.

Fort Connelly in Carrier country were famous for salmon. Local Indians were encouraged to bring in fish and meat even if they were not actually employed by the company (Innis 1956; Scholefield 1914, 1:289–291; Morice 1905:176).

In favored places traders planted gardens and kept a few cattle. As early as 1849 Fort Yukon had a cow, calf, and bull. The southern Cordilleran posts gradually got horses, but during this period no Cordilleran Indians planted or ate vegetables or kept livestock. Nor did they, for the most part, receive processed foods in return for their furs. Their basic diets were little changed.

New Luxuries and Social Patterns

The Cordillerans had evidently chewed tobacco before the Whites arrived, acquiring it in the early eighteenth century through native trade from Siberia and later from Indian middlemen on the Pacific coast and to the east. The North West Company tried half-heartedly to keep liquor out of its Rocky Mountain posts, and after 1831 the Hudson's Bay Company too forbade its sale. It remained available to the natives nonetheless. Partly in response to the pattern set by the Whites (Morice 1905:116–118) the natives very soon began to see rum,

whiskey, or other intoxicants as splendid additions to their traditional ceremonial feasting and gift giving. These occasions had already been enhanced by other luxury items—metal kettles that facilitated cooking and serving of food, woolen cloth, stroud, blankets, needles, pearl buttons, feather cockades, vermilion paint, and, above all, glass beads, which opened new possibilities both in creating ceremonial regalia and in reciprocal gift exchange.

Just as Indians from distant parts of the Cordillera and the coast encountered one another at native trade fairs, at the White trading posts they met, in addition to English, Scottish, French, or Canadian Whites with alien cultural backgrounds, Indians and Métis who had come from far east of the Cordillera. Some Iroquois entered the south and central Cordillera as trappers or fort hunters. Cree and other Algonquians were often employed at the more northern posts, and the Cordilleran Athapaskans themselves traveled widely. In 1829–1830 Cree, Slavey, Chipewyan, and Beaver Indians were all smoking and dancing with the Sekani at Fort Halkett. Dease Lake Tahltan were at Frances Lake in 1843, and Han and Tutchone visited Fort Yukon in the 1850s (Innis 1956:300; Murray 1910:59–60).

The wives or associated females of many of the North West or Hudson's Bay Company employees were either local natives or Indians or Métis from east of the Rockies, and a great deal of acculturation took place in the domestic units associated with the trading posts (Harmon 1903:230–231). The basic socialization of the children must have been in the hands of the Indian and Métis women. The fates of the mixed-blood children

Fig. 5. Kutchin dog blanket. Black velvet, backed with canvas and edged with red, black, white, and blue wool fringe. Eight large sleigh bells, on a leather strap, divide the piece. One half is decorated with seed beads, the other with appliquéd commercial cotton braid. Placed with the strap around the dog's middle, such a blanket was part of the embellishment added just before a sled team entered a settlement (McClellan 1975a:274). Length of strap 42 cm, collected on the Yukon River before 1928.

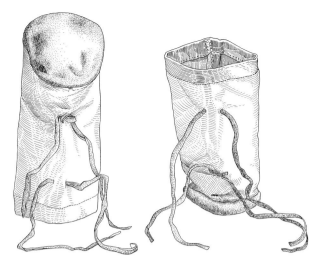

Natl. Mus. of Canada, Ottawa: VI–Q–54.

Fig. 6. Southern Tutchone dog moccasins (2 of set of 4 shown), used in spring to protect the dog's feet from sharp ice. Round tanned moosehide sole with a canvas upper that is secured around the dog's leg with 2 leather ties. Diameter of sole about 7.5 cm, collected by Catharine McClellan at Aishihik, Yukon Terr., 1963.

of fur trade employees were variable. Some were sent to England, eastern Canada, or the Red River to be educated. Some rose in the ranks of the Hudson's Bay Company. Others remained "common Indians," but those who stayed in the country and especially those who returned to it were probably powerful agents of change (Brown 1980:4).

Language interpreters, usually mixed-bloods, not only conducted business but also no doubt informally transmitted aspects of differing ideologies between Whites and Indians. At least one trade language is known to have been used in the Cordillera. This was Broken Slavey, used on the Peel and Yukon rivers, apparently basically pidginized Athapaskan with words from French, English, Chipewyan, Slavey, and Cree. Also some White traders learned Indian languages (Savoie 1971; Black 1955:14; Whymper 1869:226).

Along with the ethnic and linguistic diversity came fresh patterns of social organization and behavior. The hierarchical organization of trading-post personnel could not escape the notice of the Cordillerans. Perhaps they knew too of the stratified organization of the coastal trading ships. In any case, whatever the particular model, the formal organization of the Whites was enough like the status-structured organization of the prestigious Northwest Coast Indians to reinforce the interest of the Cordillerans in achieving such structures themselves.

To some extent the traders' attempts to incorporate the Indians into the Euro-American economic system also strengthened the native systems of prestige based on wealth, by introducing additional bases for them. The traders preferred to deal with "chiefs" rather than all the Indians in a band. They therefore created "trad-

ing chiefs" who usually were already the true native headmen in the group (McClellan 1950:125–121, 1975a:489–494). However, no Indian headmen had the coercive and economic controls locally associated with high-status Whites. The positions of native headmen depended on hunting skill, kinship, and frequent redistribution of wealth rather than continuous accumulation of capital.

The incoming traders accommodated to some extent to the preliminary gift giving, oratory, singing, dancing, and other rituals characteristic of the traditional native trading (Murray 1847–1850). They sent gifts of tobacco and clothes to native leaders when they heard they were approaching the post and fed the Indians when they first arrived. In the course of their visits to trading posts the Indians learned stories and styles of music and dance that they adapted in varying degrees to their own expressive cultures. They developed new fashions in clothing, made possible by the imported fabrics and decorations that the Hudson's Bay Company encouraged them to buy. Women began to decorate clothing (fig. 7), moccasins, hunting bags, and other items with elaborate floral designs of glass seed beads or silken embroidery (Kate Duncan, personal communication 1979; "Expressive Aspects of Subarctic Indian Culture," fig. 3, this vol.).

The traders and mixed-bloods passed on some knowledge of the western world in an informal fashion and

Natl. Mus. of Canada, Ottawa: VI–I–3.

Fig. 7. Kutchin woman's leggings. The panels of heavy floral beadwork on these cloth leggings are characteristic of Athapaskan decoration after the mid-19th century; earlier clothing had geometric designs in quillwork. Length 66 cm, collected on Mackenzie River, 1911.

392

mostly from a male point of view, but few natives had any grasp of the great "outside" during the early contact period. However, the Cordilleran natives did associate the outside world with increased illness. The record of diseases introduced to the Cordillera is spotty but sufficient to show that the population was hit early and often by diseases to which they had no immunity—smallpox, measles, and others (Helm et al. 1975:table opp. p. 350). Since, however, the demographic data for the early period are so poor, the effect of the diseases cannot be accurately gauged, either the numbers of those who died from them directly or indirectly from aftereffects such as starvation because there were not sufficient able-bodied adults to maintain the food supply.

In any event, the Indian population far outnumbered that of the Whites. During this period White traders and Indians came to know outstanding people of the other race as individuals and assessed each other's characters quite realistically. Both groups were interested in economic profit, but since the traders had no wish to acquire Indian lands, political sovereignty never became an issue.

Mid-Nineteenth to Mid-Twentieth Century

From the mid-nineteenth century on, events and people less directly connected with the fur trade progressively affected both the Indians and the traders themselves. The relative proportions of natives to Whites began to alter, slowly in some places, by great spurts in others. To the extent that they could, the Indians continued to take from the Whites only what seemed relevant to their own cultures, but in the end, their traditional ways of life (especially their subsistence patterns) were not able to withstand the onslaughts of gold prospectors, missionaries, roads, railroads, steamboats, changing government policies, and continued disease and depopulation. Throughout much of the area an impoverished Indian population continued to live mostly from the land but also came to rely on flour, rice, sugar, and tea, which the traders began to stock in the 1860s. The Indians had become almost wholly dependent on west-

left, Smithsonian, Dept. of Anthr.: 248514; right, Natl. Mus. of Canada, Ottawa: VI–B–319.

Fig. 8. left, Tahltan elbow-shaped wooden pipe, fitted with brass and separate wooden stem. Length 27.5 cm, collected by G.T. Emmons on Stikine River, 1904–1906. right, Carrier gunpowder pouch of tanned caribou hide lashed with babiche to an incised bone tube. Length 19.5 cm, collected at Moricetown, B.C., before 1925.

ern technological items such as guns, ammunition, traps, axes, and kettles, and ultimately they gave up much of their former nomadism to cluster around trading posts, churches (fig. 10), and schools. In central British Columbia some groups were assigned reserves.

Changes in the Fur Trade

As the Indians came to rely upon White trade goods, they entered into an unending cycle of debt and re-

Yale U., Peabody Mus.: 30891.

Fig. 9. Tahltan gun case of tanned caribou hide decorated with beadwork on black stroud bands bordered with red, pink, and yellow tape and hide fringe. Length 128 cm, collected on Stikine River, B.C., 1910.

393

payment. Most could not trap seriously unless the trader outfitted them for the winter on credit, to be repaid with the season's fur catch. The Hudson's Bay Company tried to manage the fur catch so as to prevent overtrapping of desirable species and, in spite of fluctuations in the world market, found it best to maintain a steady price system for the Indians. Only when company prices seemed too steep did Indians then turn temporarily to independent traders if they were present. The Hudson's Bay Company lost its monopoly in 1858. By about 1900 the importance of the trader had greatly declined in many parts of the Cordillera. The values of furs dropped drastically during World War I. Although they rose again sharply during the 1920s, they became almost worthless during the 1930s and 1940s. By World War II the trader's position had become marginal. Missionaries and government officials had usurped much of his social prestige and moral leadership, and in British Columbia the Hudson's Bay Company had more often ignored than profited from the gold rushes.

Prospectors and Gold Strikes

In the last half of the nineteenth century four major gold strikes profoundly affected portions of the Cordillera, and each resulted in further opening up the area to Whites, in larger numbers than the natives had ever before encountered. First came the rush along the Thompson and Fraser rivers that peaked in about 1855 on the southern edge of Chilcotin country; next came the Cariboo gold rush, which climaxed in 1862. Both affected the Chilcotin and Carrier Indians. Third were the closely linked Omineca and Cassiar gold rushes of 1871 and 1873, which involved Carrier, Sekani, Kaska, and Tahltan. Finally, the 1898 Klondike gold rush of Yukon Territory and adjacent Alaska radically changed the lives of many Kaska, Tahltan, Inland Tlingit, Tagish, Tutchone, and Kutchin and virtually destroyed the Han who had lived in the Dawson area.

Each event was prefaced by a trickle of prospectors, followed by a sudden mass of would-be millionaires, many of them ill equipped to deal with the conditions of the rough Cordilleran environment. Although short-lived, each rush resulted in easier access to that section of the country where it occurred, a greater number of permanent White settlers, and changed relations between Indians and Whites (Akrigg and Akrigg 1977:48–54, 88–340; Fisher 1977:95–118; Henning, Loken, and Olds 1979:39–42, 53–65; McClellan 1975a; Wright 1976).

Some of the Indians themselves became prospectors; others became engaged in wage labor as packers or deckhands on steamboats, or they sold meat and fish, or cut cord wood for the steamboats on the rivers and lakes. Indians for the first time became aware of road

Fig. 10. The Carrier Indian village at Ft. Babine with Roman Catholic church on right. Photograph by Frank Cyril Swannell, 1927.

houses, saloons, and dance halls, and saw more White women than had ever before come to their country, even though females were a small minority compared to the White males. Indians had easier access to liquor, but at the same time they began to come under the surveillance of the Northwest Mounted Police.

The Cariboo gold rush of the early 1860s brought the building of the Great Cariboo Wagon Road into the gold fields. Finished in 1865, it was linked to the head of navigation on the Fraser River and provided a route to Chilcotin country far easier than the steep trails from Bella Coola. By then, the Bella Coola, Chilcotin, and Lower Carrier had been hard hit by a smallpox epidemic. The number of Indians who died may have been overestimated (Fisher 1977:115–116), but it is not surprising that one cause of the Chilcotin uprising of 1864 was said to be the threat by a White man that he would send sickness to destroy the whole tribe. However, the igniting incident revolved around building the Cariboo road through Chilcotin country and the molestation of Chilcotin women. The Chilcotin killed a number of Whites, but the affair ended with the defeat of the Indians and the hanging of five Chilcotins (Akrigg and Akrigg 1977:297–305). This was the only instance when Cordilleran natives made a concentrated attack on Whites, and it occurred where pressures from Whites were greatest.

The Chilcotin uprising and several bloody episodes on the coast ended all Indian resistance in British Columbia. Whites increasingly began to settle in the southern and interior part of the territory. Most had very negative images of the Indians about whom they knew much less than did the fur traders. The settlers usually stereotyped the Indians as "savages," and they thought they would soon die out. However, they esteemed the hunters of the Cordillera more than the coastal natives (Fisher 1977:89–94).

MCCLELLAN

Northern British Columbia remained almost totally isolated until the Cassiar strike. Then in 1873–1874 the population of Whites suddenly ballooned to 2,000 or more from a handful of prospectors who had drifted from Omineca Mountain in Sekani country to Dease Lake in Kaska-Tahltan country. The boom settlements soon became ghost towns, but new roads had been made to the area of the upper Skeena and Stikine rivers, and they were further developed as the routes to the Klondike gold fields in 1898 (Morice 1905:322–323; Zaslow 1971:43–45).

The Klondike gold rush probably had the greatest impact on the native peoples of any of the Cordilleran strikes. It crushed the trade blockade of the coastal Tlingit, and for the first time some of the Tagish, Tutchone, and Inland Tlingit saw Whites come through their own country—more than 40,000 of them. At first the Indians packed much of the goods (figs. 11–13), but by the early twentieth century there was a railroad across the White Pass through Tagish country, well-developed steamboat travel on the Yukon River through Tutchone, Han, and western Kutchin lands, and several small towns. Some Indian families began to cut wood for the river boats. Cordilleran Indian crews regularly traveled from Whitehorse in Yukon Territory to Saint Michael on the Bering Sea, meeting other Athapaskan Indians and also Eskimos, whom they feared. Everybody wanted to go to Dawson City. The numbers of marriages that the Indians made with natives outside their own groups far surpassed those of the early contact period.

The Indians around the temporary boom centers entered into inflated cash economies quite different from the old trading-post credit system. Indians who were prospectors or packers, or who sold meat and fish, became temporarily well off. But when the prospectors left, the Indians who had been caught up in the strikes often found themselves worse off than they had been before.

Missionaries

Concerted missionary efforts within the Cordillera began only in the mid-nineteenth century. Roman Catholic Jesuits and, later, Oblates were strongest in the southern Cordillera, while the Church Missionary Society of the Church of England and Oblate Catholics dominated the northern Canadian section and Alaska. American Episcopalians replaced the Anglicans among the Kutchin after the Hudson's Bay Company withdrew from Fort Yukon in 1869. Methodists and Presbyterians also became active in the late nineteenth century. In most places the missionaries supplanted the Hudson's Bay Company managers or other traders as the White dictators of acceptable social and religious morality for both the Indians and post personnel. Each new gold strike also quickened missionary activity, for the White miners were viewed as a godless lot as much in need of salvation as the heathen natives (Duchaussois 1923; Veillette and Gray 1977).

True conversions by natives to the new faiths were slow. The individualistic Cordillerans did not take ea-

Natl. Mus. of Canada, Ottawa: J–2162.
Fig. 11. Annie Stevens, Tutchone from Aishihik, demonstrating the old method of packing with a tumpline over the head. Photograph by Dorothy Rainier Libby at a camp on Kluane Lake, Yukon Terr., 1948.

Prov. Arch. of B.C., Victoria: A–7417.
Fig. 12. Tagish or Coastal Tlingit packers at rest on the Dyea Trail. Oxen were useful pack animals in the warm months since they could be sold for meat after they crossed into the interior (Cruikshank 1975:25). Photograph by La Roche, 1897–1898.

INTERCULTURAL RELATIONS AND CULTURAL CHANGE IN THE CORDILLERA

Fig. 13. Tagish or Coastal Tlingit packers and the photographer Lloyd Winter hauling gear over the Taiya (Dyea) River to the Chilkat Pass. Photograph by Winter and Pond, 1897.

Fig. 14. Four-door Chevrolet sedan purchased by George Johnston, an Inland Tlingit, and shipped to Whitehorse on the White Pass Railway and then to Teslin on this barge. It was the first car in Teslin (Cruikshank 1975:64), and there being no road there at that time, Johnston's sororal nephews cleared one for his use (McClellan 1975a:431), which was later followed by builders of the Alaska Highway. Johnston painted the car white and used it on frozen lakes to hunt wolves. It still ran in the 1950s. Photograph by George Johnston, 1928.

gerly to dogmas that appeared to ignore their own fundamental religious concern, which was the proper relationship between human beings and nonhuman spirits, such as the powerful spirit owners of game and fish. The natives' beliefs about illness and reincarnation were totally alien to the Christian message. Furthermore, some missionaries vigorously attacked long-standing native social customs and ritual that were integral to the core of native culture—polygamy, girls' puberty seclusions, hand games and gambling, native dancing and singing, especially that associated with the potlatch cremation, and, above all, shamanistic performances. In some places, native religious practitioners independently borrowed bits of Christian ritual and belief to develop their own "churches" or prophet movements (fig. 15). A number of these movements surged through the Cordillera during the nineteenth and early twentieth century, evoking a fervor and excitement in their participants that Christian churchmen rarely could (Duff 1964, 1:88–89; Fisher 1977:123–124; Honigmann 1949:47–48; McClellan 1956, 1975a:547–549).

The Catholics were usually fairly tolerant of those parts of native culture that were not in direct conflict with their theology, but they did not train Indians themselves to become part of the clergy. By contrast, the Protestants, especially the Anglicans, systematically tried to incorporate the Indians into the church hierarchy.

Bitter rivalry developed between the Catholic and Protestant missionaries, both on the coast and in the Cordillera. Church records are laced with intemperate statements from clergy on both sides. The Indians themselves were sometimes caught in the conflict, which continued into the mid-twentieth century in parts of British Columbia and Yukon Territory (Carrington 1963; Morice 1905, 1910).

Perhaps the most radical innovation brought by the missionaries was schooling. The Anglican Robert McDonald settled into Fort Yukon in 1862, published a Bible in the local Kutchin dialect, and taught both adult and young Kutchins to read and write. After 1867, the Episcopalian churchmen took over the Anglican activities. William C. Bompas founded an Anglican boarding school in Carcross for Yukon Indians (fig. 16), which continued as a church-run school until after 1950. The Anglicans also had local schools intermittently from the 1890s at some of the other Cordillera settlements. During the late 1940s an evangelical sect of Baptists ran a combined boarding and day school in Whitehorse in Yukon Territory. In 1951 the Oblates opened a large boarding school at Lower Post in Kaska country for more than 100 young Indians from northern British Columbia and Yukon Territory (Bullen 1968:169–179).

The boarding schools especially had a strong acculturative effect on the native children who attended them. This was never the majority of Indian children. In Yukon Territory, for example, in 1931 there were only 26 students at the Carcross school and some stayed only for a year or so. In 1954 enrollment reached 160 but declined to 80 by 1966, probably because after 1948 Indian students were allowed to attend federally run public schools in their own communities. The regimented routine, kinds of skills acquired, and strict emphasis on learning English all contrasted greatly with permissive patterns of traditional Cordilleran socialization and learning. Many of the children were very unhappy (Bullen 1968:138–180; King 1967) at the schools, but when they returned to their families they

Fig. 15. Albert Edward Tritt (b. about 1880), a Chandalar Kutchin of the Arctic Village band. At one time a powerful shaman, he became the leader of a revitalization movement about 1910, preaching the Christian gospel in a small log chapel, advocating a nativistic revival (McKennan 1965:86–88), and teaching reading and writing using Robert McDonald's Kutchin alphabet. Photograph by Robert McKennan, July 1933.

often felt alienated from traditionally oriented older people. At the boarding schools children from a number of different Indian groups came to know each other, and the school experiences meant an expanded social network among the native pupils. Sometimes they formed ties that led to marriage.

Communications, Transportation, and White Contacts

In 1864–1865, telegraph survey parties briefly entered the country of the Carrier and of the Kutchin, but the successful laying of the transatlantic cable ended all work in 1866 in both British Columbia and Alaska. The Carrier used the abandoned wire to build suspension bridges across Hagwilget Canyon ("Carrier," fig. 2, this vol.) and elsewhere. During the Klondike gold rush a telegraph line was constructed from Dawson to Whitehorse in Han and Tutchone country and then linked to a line extending south through Atlin in Inland Tlingit country, Telegraph Creek in Tahltan country, and on south through Hazelton to Quesnel in Carrier country (Akrigg and Akrigg 1977:324–330; Dawson 1889:185–186; Lawrence 1965:36–38, map facing 86).

Between 1871 and 1879 there were five separate investigations of the upper Peace River district by surveyors, geologists, and botanists seeking a northern

route for the Canadian Pacific Railway as an alternative to the rival southern approach to Vancouver. Because of the Cassiar gold rush, regular steamboat service had been instituted in 1874 from Wrangell to Telegraph Creek, and the next year the government bought and improved the horse trail from Telegraph Creek to Dease Lake. In 1890 steamboats began to run up the Skeena to Hazelton. The Tahltan and Carrier Cordillerans had thus become accessible from the coast and now they were to be linked to the east by rail (Zaslow 1971:48–49); however, in the end the railroad was routed far to the south. There was little further penetration of the subarctic Cordillera by Whites from any direction until the Klondike gold rush in 1898, which resulted in the building of the White Pass and Yukon Railway from the Alaskan coast to Yukon Territory. Not until 1914 did a Canadian National Railway branch through Hazelton finally link Upper Carrier Indians to the head of the Skeena by land (Zaslow 1971:20–29, 203).

Each railroad opened up travel opportunities for both Whites and Indians and also incorporated a few more Indians into a wage economy. Some became permanent railway employees maintaining the tracks. Others were hired on a temporary basis.

As the riverboats and railways built up a tourist trade in the twentieth century, the local Indians became suppliers of the fresh fish and moose meat that were served in the dining rooms on stern-wheelers, such as those on Lakes Tagish and Atlin or on the Yukon River, or at dining stops such as Bennett on the White Pass Railway. By this time Indians were supplying meat and fish to mission schools and to retailers in various White settlements as well. Indian women increased their sales of handicrafts to tourists.

Anglican Church of Canada, General Synod Arch., Toronto, Ont.: P7517–83.

Fig. 16. Bishop Isaac O. Stringer (back row right) with the staff and students in front of the Carcross Indian School (Choutla School), Yukon Terr. Photographed in June 1921.

Some Indians who served as packers, suppliers, and guides for the surveyors and scientists exploring the Cordillera began to handle the pack trains (fig. 17) and boats for the big game hunters who were attracted to the northern wilderness. A few Indians themselves became big-game hunting outfitters, for the northern Cordillera offers choice specimens of coveted game animals.

Some of the prospectors and White trappers who came into the Cordillera married native women and, like the missionaries and later the settlers who came with their families, became long-term residents in Indian country. As communications and transportation systems became established, a handful of small towns of mostly White residents grew up at the sites of old trading posts and mining centers. As late as 1911, none had more than 1,000 people. Not until 1931 did Prince George in Carrier country reach a population of between 1,000 and 5,000 (Farley 1979:3–23). By 1911 in Yukon Territory the high population figures of the Klondike days, about 10,000 in Dawson City alone, had dropped precipitously, so that all of Yukon Territory contained only 8,512 people, and by 1921, 4,157, less than half of which were Indians. So, as elsewhere in the Cordillera, the relative proportion of Whites to Indians continued to grow, and more Whites began to covet Indian lands (Morrison 1968:5; Leechman 1947:28).

Government Policies

Government policies toward the Indians evolved somewhat differently in British Columbia, the Northwest Territories and Yukon Territory, and in Alaska.

Fig. 17. The Hudson's Bay Company store at Telegraph Creek, B.C., during the outfitting of a big-game hunting party. The Indian youth holding the horse is probably Tahltan. Photograph by Richard Harrington, 1953.

Soon after he became governor of Vancouver Island in 1851 and, in 1858, of British Columbia, James Douglas instituted a policy of purchasing land from Indians and of laying out reserves where pressure from White settlers was greatest. Douglas retired in 1864, and succeeding governors, supported by prospectors and would-be settlers, rejected the idea that Indians had any claims to the land, a position that ran counter to that of the Imperial (British) government and the Canadian government established by confederation in 1867. The British Columbia Indians remained caught in a continuing struggle between White lawmakers who favored the restrictive British Columbia land policy toward Indians and those who pressed for the slightly more liberal federal policy (Cumming and Mickenberg 1972:171–193; Duff 1964, 1:60–63; Fisher 1977:146–211).

The British North America Act of 1867 had given the federal government overall responsibility for the Indians, and the 1876 Indian Act finally set up an administrative framework. The federal policy was at that time to grant to Indians reserves of equal and rather large size (for example, 160 acres per family of five), as carried out in the "numbered treaties" in the prairie provinces. However, the British Columbia commissioners preferred to negotiate treaties following the earlier pattern of eastern Canada. Declaring that the hunters and fishers did not need as much land as did potential farmers, they usually allotted areas far smaller than the standard federal reserves of the prairies (Fisher 1977:64–72). More generally, White settlers, missionaries, and educators continuously debated whether it was possible to civilize and Christianize the Indians or whether they were irredeemable or would in any case all soon die. If one assumed the Indian could be civilized, then there were the questions of how long it would take, whether the Indians should be protected from corrupt Whites or exposed to the edifying influence of Christian Whites, kept on their lands as hunters and fishers, or changed into farmers and laborers in permanent settlements. There was little or no government response to what the Indians themselves might wish nor did all the Cordilleran Indians have the same views (Fisher 1977:146–211; Patterson 1972:100–144).

The controversy between the federal and provincial government over Indian land rights continued until 1927, when a special committee of the House of Commons rejected the validity of Indians' land claims in British Columbia. The question was reopened in a 1964 court case. In the long course of these events, the Northwest Coast Indians of British Columbia learned to cooperate with one another in order to present their cases in Ottawa (Cumming and Mickenberg 1972:189–191). By contrast, even in the late 1960s, many of the Cordilleran Indians of British Columbia were still unaware of the political controversy over whether the Indian peoples of that province had or ever had aboriginal title to their lands. No Subarctic Cordillerans in British Columbia signed treaties, even though a 1959 map showed Treaty No. 8 lands taking in Kaska and Sekani territory.

The eastern Kutchin of the Northwest Territories became Treaty Indians in 1921, thereby presumably extinguishing their original land title (Fumoleau 1973:165–168, 183–190), but the position of the Kutchin in Yukon Territory and Alaska was different. None of the Yukon Indians (Inland Tlingit, Tagish, Tutchone, Han, Kutchin) had signed treaties.

Eventually, whatever the provincial, territorial, or federal policies in Canada might be, or whatever the legal status of the Indian lands, agencies of the federal Department of Indian Affairs were established at certain communication centers within the various Indian people's countries (Duff 1964, 1:63). The presence of an Indian agent meant only modest beginnings in social welfare for the Indians. The programs were limited and many northern Indians still remained isolated in the bush for much of the year, so that the agents' effects on Indian lives were usually negligible.

Perhaps the greatest acculturative impact of the agencies was in their efforts to see that Indian children attended school, usually by contracts with church-run boarding or local schools.

In Alaska the few Han living near Eagle and the western Kutchin were affected by United States government policy only late in the nineteenth century. The Russians had certainly never had any political control over their lives.

By 1871, four years after the Alaska Purchase, Congress forbade further treaty-making with Indians in U.S. lands. The result was that the Alaskan natives including those of the Cordillera never had a chance to settle either their land claims or legal positions. The Organic Act of 1884, which made Alaska a Land District rather than a Customs District, meant that the U.S. mining laws applied, but it also said that Indians and others should not be disturbed on lands that they claimed or where they lived, and that Congress would settle at a later date just how legal title to the lands should be acquired.

Alaskan legal policy in relation to Indians then became even more complex. Congress ignored the Alaskan Indians with respect to the 1887 Dawes Severalty Act applicable to Indians in the rest of the United States, and when an equivalent law was passed in 1905 for Alaska, it was so unsuitable that by as late as 1959 only 80 allotments had been issued—mostly to Northwest Coast Indians. When Alaska became a territory in 1912, the legislature enfranchised the Indians, but not until 1924 did an act of Congress make all Indians of the United States citizens. In 1943 Secretary of the Interior Harold Ickes created several reservations in Alaska at the request of the Indians. One of these was the Venetie Reservation asked for by the Chandalar Kutchin. The rest of the Alaska Kutchin and the Han had no clear land ownership status, a fact that became of major importance following World War II (Rhodes et al. 1976).

Mid-Twentieth Century to the 1970s

The construction in 1942 of the Alaska Highway across northern British Columbia, Yukon Territory, and central Alaska ushered in the modern period. Built in less than a year as a military supply road for World War II, the Alaska Highway brought a massive influx of mostly White males into the heart of what had remained until then a vast area of Indian hunting and trapping grounds, the lands of the Sekani, Kaska, Inland Tlingit, and Tutchone. For a short while there was a boom economy reminiscent of the Klondike gold rush, but, as before, most of the Whites left after the initial construction. Only a few natives were hired to work on the highway; however, their lives were deeply affected by it and subsequent expansions of transportation and communication in the Cordillera (Cruikshank and McClellan 1976).

Transportation, Communications, and Economy

The highway and the roads and airfields that were developed during the war and in following years increasingly made many areas of the Cordillera attractive and accessible to nonnatives. Settlers arrived in sufficient numbers so that by 1976 Yukon Territory had a total population of about 20,000, of which roughly 3,000–4,000 were "Indian." By contrast, after an initial population spurt northernmost British Columbia began to lose White population in Inland Tlingit and Kaska country.

By the 1950s stern-wheelers had disappeared from the rivers, and with them went the need for the cordwood that had supplied cash to Yukon Indian families throughout the first half of the century. With the extension of the road system, by the mid-1970s of all the Subarctic Cordillerans only a few Sekani and Kaska and the Kutchin around Old Crow in Yukon Territory and Fort Yukon and Venetie in Alaska needed to depend on small boats or airplanes for rapid transportation. After World War II Cordilleran Indians everywhere who became ill or who had to do business with the government were able to radio for planes without much difficulty. They became accustomed to flying out for medical treatment in Edmonton, Vancouver, Anchorage, or Seattle. They went by air or road to visit relatives who had already established themselves in towns and cities. Another acculturative force of great magnitude was the advent of transistor radios in the 1950s, followed in the late 1960s by television in the major towns. Knowledge of a world beyond the Cordillera was enormously expanded for Indians of all ages.

For most natives, the social trend was to nuclear families and the economic trend has been to almost total dependence on cash wages or welfare payments. Although there was an upswing in fur prices in the late 1960s and early 1970s, by then only a limited number of Indian families spent entire winters in the bush. In the 1970s trappers were going out for only a week or so at a time, or else they visited their traps on day trips made from their permanent home settlements. Increasingly, trappers began to replace dog teams with snowmobiles (fig. 18). Only older men and their wives attempted to live primarily on game and fish. Younger Indians had come to feed their families almost exclusively from supplies purchased in stores. They still tried to supplement their diets whenever possible with fish and meat, but this became difficult to do since so many of them had moved to towns looking for jobs.

Unfortunately, in the 1960s and 1970s the range of steady jobs, especially for young males, remained limited in most northern settlements. A few worked on railway and highway maintenance or in construction. In Canada some were taught trades, either in local vocational schools or in Edmonton or Vancouver where they were sponsored by various government programs. But whether they stayed in the north or returned, they usually were among the last hired or they did not find jobs at all. Some Indian women were trained as nurses's aides, secretaries, beauticians, and in food service. A few went "outside" for advanced vocational training; there, they might not finish their courses but marry White men and remain in one of the large cities in the south. In the late 1960s federally funded local band offices and other programs for Indians began to hire Indians, especially those with some education, as secretaries, aides, and administrators. Few natives had finished college, and even fewer had become lawyers, teachers, doctors, or nurses. Few Indians became engaged in mining activities, although large new company towns sprang up close to their settlements (B. Sharp 1977).

Statistics are scant, and the specific situation has varied from locality to locality, but many Indians have spent a disproportionate amount of their income on alcohol, especially since changes in Canadian laws after World War II made it legal for them to drink in public places and to buy packaged liquor. Because so many Indians had moved into towns, if they became drunk they were much more visible to the Whites than was earlier the case. This often provoked increased White prejudice against natives. Increased financial and other aid to Indians from government services added to the resentment of natives felt by some northern Whites. The natives, in turn, became more open in expressing their dislike of both the paternalism shown to them by

River Times, Fairbanks, Alaska.
Fig. 18. Robert Cruikshank, a Kutchin from Beaver, Alaska, playing a guitar in his family's snowmobile. Photograph by Mary Beth Smetzer, 1973.

some of the older White settlers and the ignorance of Indian behavior and values exhibited by later White immigrants.

As a result of the building of the trans-Alaska oil pipeline in the 1970s, the Han and Kutchin of Alaska experienced many of the kinds of changes associated with the building of the Alaska Highway. The construction of the pipeline depended on the prior settlement of the Alaska native land claims.

Government Programs in Canada and Alaska

In Canada, only since World War II has there been aggressive government programming for Indians in health, education, and welfare. The benefits of these various programs have been mostly restricted to status Indians. The former dependence on contracts with church-run boarding schools changed in favor of local grade schools in Indian settlements or funding the housing of Indian students in government or church-run hostels in the larger northern towns where Indians could attend high schools or vocational schools along with Whites. The effort was toward integration, but racial prejudice often ran high in the mixed schools (King 1967). Major Indian settlements have nursing stations, and X-ray teams and other traveling clinics visit the settlements regularly. Native women have been incorporated into programs for midwifery and other kinds of health care. Native health has improved and the birth rate has begun to rise rapidly. A third area of government aid has been expanded welfare payments, in addition to the family allowance and old-age pension that all qualified Canadians receive. In the 1970s the government encouraged local crafts and industries—skin sewing, canoe building, snowshoe manufacturing, and sawmills.

In Alaska, too, government services to the Indians increased after World War II. Some of the Han and Kutchin benefited from the educational programs and from improved health services that followed the transfer in 1956 of native health care from the Bureau of Indian Affairs to the Public Health Service. Indeed, after Alaska became a state in 1959, there was a period of confusion when federal and state agencies vied with each other to see who could offer the most services and welfare checks. Sometimes they duplicated their programs; at other times needy Indians were ignored. With government help, larger numbers of young Indians began to attend high schools and college. During the 1950s students had to leave their villages in order to get advanced education, but by the 1970s the policy of having local high schooling was paramount.

Native Activism

The Canadian minister of northern affairs and the United States secretary of the interior have both been in the paradoxical position of being charged to keep the government trust with the natives and at the same time to promote development of extractive industries and other enterprises that Indians see as detrimental to their interests. In the northern Cordillera matters came to a head in the late 1960s and early 1970s over the projected building of oil and gas pipelines.

Cordilleran natives of both Canada and Alaska became more politically aware from the experiences of returned war veterans and increased communications. They became caught up in the native political movements of the 1960s and 1970s. In the northern part of the Cordillera the White population was still relatively small, and the Indians came to realize that they had considerable political power if they exercised their vote. They also had growing contact with Northwest Coast Indians, some of whom had been activists since the first part of the century, when they had organized the British

Columbia and the Alaska Native Brotherhoods in an effort to compete fairly with White fishermen.

The Tsimshian Niska succeeded in presenting the first land claims case to the government of Canada in 1913 (Cumming and Mickenberg 1972:189). Although the case was lost, native agitation for land control continued. In Canada it climaxed in the 1970s among the Indians of the Northwest Territories (eastern Kutchin, Mountain, Hare, Bearlake, Slavey, Dogrib, and western Chipewyan) and the Cordilleran Indians of the Yukon Territory. The Mackenzie Valley Pipeline inquiry in the Northwest Territories and the Lysyk Commission in the Yukon Territory gave these Indians a chance to be heard when the building of a gas pipeline from the Alaska North Slope became a major political issue, since it would run through lands claimed by Eskimos and northern Indians, including some of the northern Cordilleran groups. As the energy crisis deepened through the 1970s, negotiations over land claims and rights of way for pipelines became very complex. The Indians of the Yukon Territory refused to agree to a pipeline until the land claims issue was settled. Status and nonstatus Indians united to push their views (Yukon Native Brotherhood 1977).

The Canadian Indians had as a precedent for their position the events surrounding the settlement of the land claims of Alaska natives, which was concluded in 1971 as a condition for the building of the oil pipeline from Prudhoe Bay, part of which runs through Kutchin country. Under the terms of the settlement, most Alaska natives were organized into 12 corporations. Of the Cordilleran groups, the Venetie Kutchin preferred to keep reservation status, but the rest of the Kutchin and Han became members of the Doyon Corporation (Arnold 1976; Burch 1979).

The vigorous efforts of the Alaska Indians to cope with their current and future problems has been termed rational nativism (Lantis 1973).They have not tried to preserve their past or to control their destiny by appealing to supernatural means as has sometimes been done by native peoples elsewhere. Instead they have rationally tried to maintain and create their own kind of native culture for the present and future. In doing this they have drawn heavily on deep-rooted traditional values, but they have also been ready to adapt them when necessary to the contemporary world. This approach is shared by most northern Cordillerans.

Chilcotin

ROBERT B. LANE

Language and Territory

The Chilcotin (chīl'kōtən) speak a distinct Northern Athapaskan language* that shares some areal features with that of the adjacent Carrier Indians. The Chilcotin have been influenced strongly by Plateau culture and some authorities classify them in the Plateau rather than the Subarctic culture area (cf. Ray 1939:147).

In the early twentieth century the Chilcotin occupied the drainage system of the Chilcotin River and the upper reaches of the Homalco, Klinaklini, and Dean rivers, which lie between the Chilcotin watershed and the Coast Range. In pre-European times their territory did not extend so far eastward (fig. 1). Chilcotin territory encompasses Cariboo Parklands, Subalpine Forest, and Northern Alplands biotic areas (Cowan and Guiguet 1973).

The Chilcotin probably moved from a more northerly region onto the Chilcotin plateau in the not too distant past. Their own recollections carry no hint of such a move. They have no traditions of migration or of the origin of themselves as a people.

Many older Chilcotins believed that other peoples once lived in parts of what is now Chilcotin territory and that the Chilcotin at that time occupied the drainage system of the Chilcotin River above where it joins

*The phonemes of Chilcotin are: (unaspirated stops and affricates) b, d, λ, ẑ, ʒ, ž, g, gʷ, g̣, g̣ʷ, ʔ; (aspirated stops and affricates) p, t, ƛ, ĉ, c, č, k, kʷ, q, qʷ; (glottalized) ṭ, ƛ̓, ĉ̓, c̓, č̓, k̓, k̓ʷ, q̓, q̓ʷ; (voiceless continuants) ł, ŝ, s, š, xʷ, x, x̣ʷ, h; (voiced continuants) l, ẑ, z, y, w, γ̇, γ̇ʷ; (nasals) m, n; (lax vowels) ɪ, e ([ɛ]), ʋ; (tense vowels) i, a ([æ]), u; (tones) high (v́), low (unmarked). Phonetic nasalized vowels are interpreted as vowel plus n. The pharyngealized alveolar (ĉ, etc.), back velar (q, etc.), and labialized back velar (qʷ, etc.) series cause "flattening" (backing or lowering) of the adjacent vowels. Next to such a consonant a is [a], u is [o], and e is [ə] or [ʌ]; i is [e] before an affecting consonant but [əi] after one; the lax vowels ɪ and ʋ are affected in ways parallelling the effects on the respective corresponding tense vowels. A few older speakers have also a voiceless nasal N.

In the practical orthography used by the Education Centre of Williams Lake, B.C., the phonemes of Chilcotin are written as follows: b, d, dl, dẑ, dz, j, g, gw, gg, ggw, ʔ; p, t, tl, tŝ, ts, ch, k, kw, q, qw; t', tl', tŝ', ts', ch', k', kw', q', qw'; lh, ŝ, s, sh, wh, x, xw, h; l, ẑ, z, y, w, gh, ŵ; m, n; i̠, e, o; i, a, u; tone as in the technical alphabet.

Information on Chilcotin phonology and practical orthography and the transcriptions of the Chilcotin words cited were provided by Eung-Do Cook (communications to editors 1979, 1980). This supersedes the analysis in A. King (1979).

the Chilko River and perhaps the upper Nazko River. They believed that the Bella Coola once controlled most of the habitable lands along the east front of the Coast Range south of Anahim Lake. Salish people lived around the headwaters of the Homalco river. The main valley of the Chilcotin River was the home of a semi-mythical people, the ʔenayčel 'little Salishan(s)' who lived in pit houses and subsisted on salmon. The Chilcotin entered the valley, scared the ʔenayčel away, and took over the salmon fishery.

Culture

This description of traditional culture is as older Chilcotin believe it to have been prior to European settlement in their territory.

Technology

Chilcotin material culture was not elaborate. A family's basic equipment would include: for fishing—dip net,

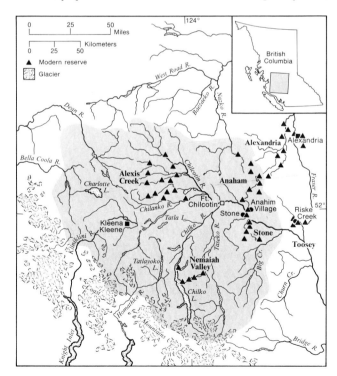

Fig. 1. Aboriginal territory with bands and modern reserves recognized as Chilcotin by the Canadian government in 1971.

gill net, gorges, gaffs, bone and horn trident fish spears and harpoon points; for hunting—bow, arrows, quiver, stone-pointed spear, bone trigger pieces for marmot traps; for gathering—digging stick, bark stripper, sap scraper (fig. 2); for food preparation—bone knife, bark and woven baskets and trays, horn spoons, grinding slab, wooden pestle; for fire making—fire drill, hearth, tinder, and carrying case; tools—horn chisel, straight adz, stone scraper, drill point, stone knife, bone awls and needles; weapons—stone-headed club; transportation—pack straps, skin sacks, snowshoes; for personal use—bone tweezers and simple carved wooden combs; household furnishings—grass and reed mats, woven wool and fur blankets, snow shovel; miscellaneous—single-headed skin drum, flute, lahal (bone game) bones and beaver-tooth dice, black and red paint, buckskin-covered frame cradle.

Clothing and Adornment

Men and women wore moccasins, short buckskin aprons, and fur robes. Robes were commonly of marmot, beaver, or woven hare skin. In the winter leggings and round fur caps were added. Women also used knee-length buckskin kilts.

Men generally wore their hair shoulder length or shorter. Some let it grow longer and wore it gathered by a thong in back or braided into one or two braids. Women wore their hair long and often gathered into two braids. Bone or shell ear and nose ornaments and necklaces of shells and animal teeth and claws were worn. Dentalia and bear claws were especially prized.

Both sexes tattooed or painted their faces. Except for red and black face paint worn by fighters and black eye shadow used in winter, facial painting was decorative in purpose. In cold windy weather the body, face, and hair were heavily greased.

For cleanliness, people bathed or took sweat baths in dome-shaped brush-covered sweathouses. There were no strong spiritual or ritual connotations to sweat bathing.

Structures

Houses were rectangular and gable roofed. The simplest consisted of a ridge pole connecting two end posts. Poles were laid against the ridge pole. Winter houses (fig. 3) had one or two ridge poles against which several rafters were laid. Roof poles were laid horizontally. Space was left open at the top to allow smoke to escape. Sometimes low walls of poles were built up inside the gabled roof but the outward appearance was unaltered. Roofs were covered with grass, bark, brush, and earth.

Pit houses were less common. They were probably copied in the recent past from those of the Shuswap and they went out of fashion in the mid-nineteenth century.

In warm weather and when traveling, people built casual shelters of mats, boughs, or bark.

Travel and Transportation

Most travel was by foot. Snowshoes were used. Sleds and toboggans were unknown. Skin or basketry packs were used with tumplines. Dogs carried packs. Casually built spruce-bark and dugout canoes were used mainly for fishing and for crossing rivers. Terrain was such that there was little travel by watercraft. Pole bridges were maintained at major crossing points along the Chilcotin River.

Division of Labor

Women did camp work, prepared skins and clothing, wove baskets, and gathered plant foods and materials. Men hunted, fished, fought, and manufactured tools

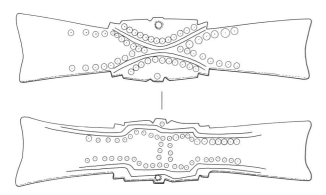

after Teit 1909b:780.
Fig. 2. Double-ended sap scraper of incised caribou antler used to collect the cambium layer of black pines, which was eaten. Length 15 cm, collected 1897.

Fig. 3. Remains of a traditional winter house near Puntzi Lake, built before 1930. The large vertical post supporting the ridge pole is about 12 feet long. Photograph by Robert B. Lane, 1951.

and equipment. Men and women often shared tasks and some individuals by preference engaged in tasks traditionally performed by the opposite sex. This was not considered deviant or noteworthy.

Wealth

Sharing was the ideal. If someone had something to spare it would be given on request and a return would be made later. Beyond one's group, exchanges became a form of trade. For example, a man might take furs to the Bella Coola. He would "give" his produce to a trading partner. When he left to return home, the partner would provide an ample exchange. There was no bargaining.

Although there was little individual control over resources or possibility for amassing wealth such as foods, hides, and furs, some men through their knowledge, skills, and energy accumulated more than others. Most of the accumulation was channeled into gifts and feasts. A wealthy man was one who produced for distribution.

Life Cycle

Birth occurred out of doors and away from camp. The woman kneeled with arms supported by two horizontal poles. A midwife or the husband aided in delivery. There were dietary and behavior restrictions on the husband and wife before and after delivery. Nursing usually continued until another child was born. Weaning was gradual.

Twins were considered lucky, but one might be given away if the mother were unable to care for both. The parents of twins observed no special proscriptions.

Children had much freedom, but they were given tasks and encouraged to become self-sufficient as early as possible. They collected fire wood, watched for fish in traps, and cleaned debris from weirs. As soon as they were able, they helped their parents in adult activities.

At puberty children underwent training and trials related to the development of physical and mental character. Boys commenced with a year on a restricted diet

Natl. Mus. of Canada, Ottawa: top left, 50156; top right, VI–B–342; bottom left, after Teit 1909b:787.

Fig. 4. Cradle construction and use. top left, Jennie West making a cradle frame; photograph by Harlan I. Smith, 1920. top right, Completed framework, length about 54 cm. bottom left, The framework covered with leather or cloth on the outside, length 63 cm, collected 1900; bottom right, Julia Stum carrying her baby in a covered cradle with strap over one shoulder and across her back. Photograph by Robert B. Lane, Anahim Reserve, 1950.

of dried foods and soups. They exercised by running and working hard. They arose early to swim in cold water. Following the training, a boy would go off for several days in the mountains, carrying only dried fish and a bark drinking container. He would run until tired and dive in streams and lakes. He napped without fire or shelter. On awakening he would be off again. The emphasis was on endurance, agility, and mobility. When he returned home, the boy's family gave a feast and the boy was considered an adult.

For girls, the aim was similar, a testing of character with stress on patience and diligence. At the first menses a girl was confined to an isolated temporary shelter. She ate dried foods and drank water through a drinking tube. She made baskets and performed tedious tasks. When she went out, she ran about, constantly on the move. She could touch herself only with a scratching stick.

Boys and girls might acquire spirit power during this period.

Marriage occurred soon after puberty. Promiscuity was disapproved, but premarital sex with a prospective spouse was tolerated.

Parents arranged marriages for their children but boys and girls had some say in choosing partners. They could run away to avoid an undesired union. Often such flight involved elopement with a more desired partner. Such a couple usually stayed away until a child was born.

In arranged marriages, gifts were exchanged between the parents-in-law and a marriage feast was held. Usually the newlyweds lived with the man's parents for a while and then alternated between the residences of the two sets of parents. After the first child, the new couple usually set up housekeeping for themselves.

Many marriages were brittle, but some couples remained together throughout life. Polygyny occurred but was not common.

Old people were respected. Efforts were made to care for them although this was sometimes difficult or impossible. An old person who was weak or injured was sometimes moved from camp to camp slung under a pole carried on the shoulders of two men.

At death the body was hung in a tree until it could be cremated. The remains were deposited under a rock cairn. In an earlier period earth burial was practiced. The house or camp in which a death occurred was abandoned. Cremation ceased in the late nineteenth century, replaced by interment with small houses built over the graves (fig. 5).

Subsistence

• HUNTING The large animals hunted were elk, deer, caribou, mountain goats, and sheep. Black bears were occasionally taken. In the twentieth century moose re-

Fig. 5. Graveyard at Redstone Flats with grave houses, carved fences, and crosses, typical of the postcontact period and showing some Northwest Coast influence. Photograph by Robert B. Lane, 1951.

placed elk in the country. Marmots, hares, beaver, muskrats, and porcupine were important, as were ducks, geese, ptarmigan, and grouse. Few animals were not eaten. Only wolves, owls, frogs, and snakes were strongly tabooed.

Game was stalked or ambushed, sometimes from concealed pits, along trails. In deep or crusted snow, game would be run down by men on snowshoes aided by dogs. Also in the winter, bears were driven from their dens into barricades of poles held over the entrances and clubbed to death.

Deadfalls and snares were used, often in conjunction with game fences built across game migration routes. Snares were of tossing-pole, tether, clog, and less commonly, spring-pole types. Pit falls, sometimes with stakes in the bottom, were used for deer.

When men hunted together, the person who first struck an animal distributed the parts. The meat was divided into piles. One man pointed to each pile while the successful hunter, his back to the piles, named the man to whom the share was to go. This practice made the division impartial.

• FISHING The important fish were trout, whitefish, suckers, and salmon (*Oncorhynchus nerka*, both land-locked or kokanee and sea-run or sockeye). All of these were taken during spawning in basketry traps set in weirs. The weirs were in shallows in lakes or in streams up which the fish moved to spawn.

Gill nets were set through holes in lake ice in winter. They were also used with canoes and rafts in the fall. Some older Chilcotin doubted the antiquity of the gill net. They also claimed that dip nets for salmon were acquired late from the Shuswap.

Gorges were used with bait and artificial lures through holes in lake ice in winter. Compound fishhooks may have been used.

• GATHERING Plant foods were important diet supplements. Some served as "starvation" foods, particularly in early spring. A few roots and berries were gathered in sufficient quantities to be stored for winter use.

In the growing season people moved about the country to take different kinds of game and fish. Almost every move was calculated to coincide with the availability of particular plant foods.

• STORAGE   Dried fish was stored in pits concealed near the fishing sites or near winter campsites. Pole and tree storage were temporary camp expedients. Open platform caches were probably recent.

• ANNUAL ROUND   In November people moved into winter camps. These were near lakes well stocked with fish. Houses were built close to, but often out of sight of, one another. While winter quarters were being prepared, people hunted and fished. A few hunters might travel to or remain in the mountains to hunt sheep and mountain goats.

Early in December most hunting (except for hares) stopped, and ice fishing was the main occupation.

In late December and through January when really cold stormy weather arrived almost all hunting stopped. Thick ice and poor returns reduced fishing. People stayed inside as much as possible living on stored food. If the weather was mild or food supplies low, some hunters might go into the river valleys to hunt big game.

Late February and March could be difficult when stored food was low or exhausted. In March, when periods of sunshine, cold winds, and crusted snow could be expected, hunters on snowshoes could run down game. People would leave their winter camps to travel in search of game. At this season game was easy to kill, but it was scarce and in poor condition. This could be a critical period, for if the change in weather did not come or if snowfalls became heavy and wet, people could be immobilized and reduced to starvation.

Toward the end of March the thaw started. Travel was restricted to early morning and camp was made as soon as the snow softened. Soft wet snow would clog snowshoes and slacken their webbing. People moved back to the lakes for more ice fishing or toward lower ground where roots and new plants provided food.

April and May brought the spring runoff. Weirs and traps were prepared and fishing began in the streams in which lake fish spawned. Some of these fish were dried and stored for future use. Muskrats were trapped and plant foods were gathered. Because of the wetness, there was little travel for hunting; but if game trails were nearby, traps were set for game moving from the valleys toward the mountains.

In May and June as the land dried, hunting intensified. Men would hunt cooperatively along game trails while the women continued fishing.

In late June as fish runs declined, people would move gradually toward the mountains, hunting and berrying. By July most people were in the mountains in the south. The women dug roots for food and for baskets and

lines. The men trapped marmots. The marmots were at their prime in August and September, but most people preferred to take them early in order not to miss the salmon runs of the later months. These trips to the mountains were made in large groups for there was danger from strangers in the mountains on similar business.

Some groups went in other directions, to the Aitcha Mountains in the west for caribou or to Anahim Peak for obsidian. Some men might leave their groups to raid neighboring people at their salmon fishing sites where the runs were earlier.

The time in the mountains was enjoyed. It was an escape from mosquitoes, food was plentiful, people from different bands and camps intermingled, and there was dancing and gambling.

After mid-July, or when it was known that the Chilcotin sockeye salmon run was coming, people moved back into the Chilcotin valley, berrying along the way.

When the salmon arrived, almost everyone gathered at fishing sites along the Chilcotin and Chilko rivers. The fishing and preparation of the fish for storage was hard work, but there was visiting to camps up and down the rivers and gambling and dancing. Men made snowshoes and other equipment for winter while women wove baskets from the roots collected earlier.

In September after the salmon runs, family groups dispersed in different directions. Some went back to the southern mountains for more marmot trapping. Others went northwest for caribou and some went back to the lakes to fish for kokanee. Those who went to the lakes often prepared game fences and traps for the coming migration of game out of the mountains. When the game began to move in late September and October, the people in the mountains followed it down and joined people from the lakes at the ambush sites along the game trails. By November most people were back at the lakes preparing for another winter.

Band location, individual need and interest, weather, interpersonal relations, and a variety of other things could alter these patterns. In a mild winter, some people might never settle down in a winter camp. Some men lingered in preferred activities. An inveterate gambler might remain long at fishing sites, while another man might prefer the solitude to be found hunting in the mountains.

Sometimes families would join the Shuswap for early salmon fishing. Some might winter in Shuswap villages. Others might travel westward to hunt on the upper Klinaklini. They might then take skins and furs north to trade to the Bella Coola and winter there.

Sociopolitical Organization

The Chilcotin shared a common language, culture, and territory. They had a sense of common identity and expectations of aid and cooperation from fellow Chilcotin unless personal friction precluded it. Non-Chilcotin could expect cooperation only from Chilcotin with whom they had established personal relationships.

Among Chilcotin information was shared about intruders into their territory. There was likelihood of group action against such intruders if they were hostile. Chilcotin could call upon other Chilcotin for help in time of trouble.

This unity was not highly structured. It was a matter of ideals and good behavior. There were no rules enjoining it and there was no group leadership to enforce it. The entire Chilcotin never assembled or acted together. Feuding occurred between Chilcotin but attacks were against specific individuals rather than entire communities; however, given kinship ties, an attack against an individual inevitably drew in others.

• KINSHIP Kinship terms for consanguines are given in table 1. Among mid-twentieth century Chilcotin there was confusion about some terms and usages, and the list is not definitive.

There is no ethnographic evidence that suggests descent groups, such as clans and moieties, among the Chilcotin. Within the loose framework of Chilcotin sociopolitical groupings, kinship connections were important determinants of individual affiliation and action. Parents and their married children often camped and traveled together. Brothers often hunted and fought as teams. Feuds and some raids were usually conducted by groups of close kin. Skills and abilities tended to be linked to kinship. The son or nephew of a good hunter tended to be a good hunter. The son or niece or nephew of a shaman was more likely to be a shaman than were others. Close consanguineal connection tended to outweigh connection through marriage. In conflicts loyalty to parents outweighed loyalty to spouses.

• TYPES OF GROUPS The minimal social unit, the nuclear family, could operate independently. However, the more common coresident group was the camp, a small collection of families, often those of brothers, and associated kin camping within sight or sound of each other. Such groups cooperated closely in daily activities but they were informal and of indefinite duration.

A number of these camps would associate on the basis of kinship, friendship, geographical proximity, and mutual interest in cooperative or concurrent exploitation of particular resources. Such camp clusters would often cooperate in building fish weirs or game fences. Both the camp and the camp cluster varied in family composition from season to season and from year to year.

A number of interrelated camp clusters formed a band. A band was all the people customarily wintering in an area. Most band members were related but coresidence rather than kinship was the basis of band identity. Bands were social communities of people living near one another and voluntarily accepting common

Table 1. Kinship Terms Applied to Consanguines

1. Father *setá*; *ʔábá* (vocative)
2. Mother *seban*; *ʔinkwél* (vocative)
3. Son (man speaking) *seyi*
4. Son (woman speaking) *seyaz*
5. Daughter (man speaking) *seĉi*
6. Daughter (woman speaking) *seyaĉí*
7. Father's brother, mother's brother *seẑʔi*
8. Father's sister, mother's sister *sebiz*
9. Nephew, niece *sazi*; also *seĉoy* (*seẑʔi?*) for 'nephew'
10. Elder brother and male cousin *sunaγ*
11. Younger brother and male cousin *seĉel*
12. Elder sister and female cousin *sadi*
13. Younger sister and female cousin *sedíz*
14. Grandfather *secí*; *ʔincí* (vocative)
15. Grandmother *secu*; *ʔincu* (vocative)
16. Grandchild (man speaking) *seĉuy*
17. Grandchild (woman speaking) *seĉáy*

NOTE: *se-* (or *s-*) is the first-person singular possessive prefix.
SOURCE: Lane (1948–1951), phonemicized by Eung-Do Cook (communication to editors 1979) except for nos. 14 and 15, which are phonemicized on the basis of the vocatives. Cook is the source of the distinction between the 2 grandchild terms and reports an alternate term *seĺes* 'my cousin'.

interests. They were not organized political units. All members of a band were informed about and directly interested in the affairs of comembers, but they rarely assembled or acted together. Movement was on a camp or family basis.

The number of bands, their names, and their territories varied over time. Since the late nineteenth century there have been six bands: Toosey (Riske Creek), Stone, Anaham, Alexis Creek (Redstone), Alexandria, and Nemaiah Valley. Each of these bands has a major settlement (fig. 1) and a number of satellite reserves.†
In the northwest there are a few scattered families who have not closely affiliated with any of these bands. Modern bands have geographic names with the exception of Anaham, which is a personal name. Earlier, bands were named for the lake where the members wintered.

Bands occupied but did not exclusively control territory. However, members did resent intrusions of persons not connected to and associated with them or the territory in question. Beyond the winter quarters area, the definition of band territory was vague since areas used depended upon seasonal activities. Families from one band might travel to different areas and families from different bands might utilize resources in a single area.

Because different bands had more or less different geographical orientations, their relations with non-Chilcotin people tended to differ in kind and intensity.

†In 1875–1876 and again in 1916, governmental commissions gave official recognition as "reserves" to various lands already occupied by Chilcotin groups.

This in turn led to minor cultural and dialect differences.

• LEADERSHIP There were no chiefs or formal leaders until Whites came. Leadership depended on skill in particular activities combined with the ability to direct and advise people in those activities. A leader in any activity was one whom others accepted as a mentor and supervisor in that realm. Since skills were in a very loose sense inherited, there was a potential for the inheritance of leadership. A person who was a leader in hunting, fishing, fighting, or shamanism, who was long established in the particular geographic area, and who was central and senior in the kinship network of the area was likely to be the political leader of a group. Leaders existed only by virtue of a voluntary following. Loss of confidence in a political leader resulted in individuals joining other bands, or in the band splitting with some following the old leader and others a new leader, or replacement of the old leader by a new one.

• SOCIAL CONTROLS Formal social controls were minimal. Individuals had a high degree of autonomy. In theory, beyond the confines of the family, no one could force anyone else to do anything. People were guided to internalized morality and recognition of the need to maintain good relations with others in anticipation of the need for future aid and support. Where these did not suffice, gossip and ostracism were effective. The offender was not exiled; rather others moved away from and avoided him. A dangerous deviant was liable to be killed either by direct physical assault or by shamanistic attack. The executioner usually acted on his own initiative but with an awareness of community feelings about the victim. A common situation, in which such an extreme solution was resorted to, was in the case of a fighter who became so aggressive that his activities brought unbearable retaliation from enemies or who fought and killed fellow Chilcotin without real provocation.

Warfare

Despite an ideal of peaceful existence, fighting occurred. There were striking occasions when large numbers of Chilcotin joined to make determined attacks upon non-Chilcotin communities.

Aggressive activities were murder, feuding, and raiding. These occurred to avenge threats and insults or to acquire loot. Aggression initiated through fear that someone was planning or engaged in physical or magical attack, or fear that someone was threatening one's family relations, or fear that a stranger in the wilderness was up to no good were recurrent themes in Chilcotin accounts and discussions of fighting.

Disputes of every kind and most particularly those leading to murder (real or assumed) generated feuds. There were customary mechanisms, including payment, for settling disputes; however, settlements rarely satisfied injured parties or their kin. People bided their time patiently waiting opportunities for revenge.

Murders and feuds occurred among the Chilcotin but raids were usually against non-Chilcotin. In time of extreme hardship (severe winters or periods of starvation), small groups of Chilcotin might attack small isolated foreign communities, kill the occupants, and remain until captured food supplies had been consumed.

The weapons for fighting were bows and arrows, spears, daggers, and clubs. Hide and slat armor were sometimes used but shields were not. Fighting men used red and black facial paint in combat. Success in raiding depended on surprise, favorable omens, and, sometimes, aid from an accompanying shaman.

Attacks began at dawn and were pressed with determination. The aim was to fight until the enemy was destroyed or scattered. If raiders were successful, they celebrated on the spot, feasting on the enemy's supplies, dancing and singing of their exploits. If a raid were for vengeance, scalps might be taken and the bodies of the enemy dead mutilated. On the way home, the scalps were left under rocks in streams and body parts might be hung in trees along the trail. Such trophies were not carried home. On the return home, there was a dance and feast at which the raiders sang their songs and acted out events of the raid. Later, the raiders drank water and induced vomiting to purify themselves. Anyone who had killed an enemy lived apart from the group for a period of time, accompanied by his wife.

Some of the Chilcotin reputation as a dangerous people may stem from their defensive tactics. They gained security from being dispersed in small groups that were physically apart but close enough to communicate readily. This made it difficult for an enemy to surprise a whole community. Once an enemy was detected, the rest of the community could quickly rally to defense or could slip away into hiding as required. In either case, raiders gained little from such an attack, and once they were on the way home they could expect ambushes and harassment.

The people surrounding the Chilcotin, except for some of the Carrier, lived in sedentary or semisedentary communities that were known to the Chilcotin and vulnerable to attack. The Chilcotin were capable of devastating attacks against more "powerful" but less mobile enemies.

Religion and Curing

There was no belief in a supreme being or in major deities. Supernatural monsters were believed to exist but they had no direct interest in human affairs and were only dangerous when directly confronted.

Every human being had a soul that could leave the

408

body for short periods. Permanent soul loss caused death. When this happened, the soul became a ghost. People were uncertain as to what ultimately happened to ghosts. At least some of the time they wandered near the place of death. Ordinarily they did not bother the living, but if surprised or provoked they might seize a soul. Ideas about a final resting place for ghosts or about a land of the dead were vague and conflicting. Some people deny that such existed before Christian concepts were introduced. Others claim an aboriginal belief in a land of the dead across water.

Anyone could seek a guardian spirit although not everyone did and not all those who sought were successful. Guardian spirits were most commonly acquired between puberty and middle age. In later life, their acquisition was more often due to chance encounter than to seeking.

The basic pattern of the spirit quest was similar to training at puberty. A person was sent out by an older relative. He remained in the wilderness one to three days, bathing, fasting, and exercising. Spirits might be animals, birds, mythological figures, ghosts, or natural phenomena such as thunder, lightning, rainbows, or winds; but they appeared to the seeker in human form in a dream. They gave the seeker a song and dance, power, and advice. The power given usually focused on activities such as hunting, fishing, gambling, or fighting.

At the conclusion of the successful quest, the recipient of the spirit power returned home but did not reveal the outcome for a year or more, except indirectly to his mentor. During this time, the novice perfected his spirit relationship and experimented with the newly acquired powers. People suspected the fact and nature of the spirit encounter but did not inquire about it. Finally, at a dance, the recipient sang and danced in ways that enabled people to learn what had happened. Girls and women engaged in spirit quests, but they more commonly acquired spirit aid in chance encounters. Not so many women as men had spirit power.

There was no limit to the number of spirits that a person might get. A person who acquired several might become a shaman. Most powerful shamans had as one of their spirits the ghost of a dead shaman. It also added to the shaman's reputation if he had been initiated by a group of practicing shamans. The initiation consisted of a power contest in which the novice vied with and demonstrated his power to the satisfaction of the attending shamans. All shamans had certain general abilities: curing, killing or injuring, and clairvoyance. Specialized skills were associated with specific spirit helpers. Trout spirits were good for removing constrictions in the throat, wolves for finding lost persons, and hummingbirds for killing.

The major types of illness treated by shamans were soul loss, intrusive spirit, and intrusive object. The de-

tails of treatment varied from one shaman to another. The general pattern was for the shaman to sit beside the patient and call in spirits to aid in diagnosis. In the case of soul loss, spirits might also be sent after the soul. After the trouble was diagnosed, the shaman would manipulate the patient's body either to draw out the cause of illness or to return the lost soul. An audience was desirable but not necessary. The audience provided a chorus while the shaman sang.

There was no standard fee for a shamanistic treatment. It was considered right that if there were no cure, there should be no payment. Illness such as colds, and aches and pains, and injuries such as cuts and broken bones could be treated by a shaman but were usually treated by anyone with knowledge of appropriate plant medicines.

Shamans could use their powers to injure or kill as well as to cure. The major technique involved projection of power from the hand or mouth into the victim. The most powerful shamans could do this from a distance. Some shamans could also send their spirits to steal souls or to cause injury. Shamanistic attacks were not considered inherently evil. They only became so in the hands of vicious or unscrupulous persons. Usually, shamans served as guardians of order and morality. Wrongdoers could expect to come under shamanistic attack and this expectation often enough inhibited wrongdoers. The shaman did not act in a public capacity. Wrongdoing was seen as acts against individuals and it demanded revenge from the injured persons and their kin. The shaman acted as an instrument of revenge for a group of kin, but, since the kin tended to be co-extensive with the community, the effect was as if he were acting in a public capacity.

Many of the powers and activities of the shaman could be described as magical. People without shamanistic power could also practice magic of various types—divination, love magic, or magical attack. Magical attack included devices such as placing bits of material closely associated with the intended victim in a human skull or hollow bone. Such practices were essentially mechanical and anyone with the knowledge could perform them.

Bear ceremonialism involved special songs while skinning, placing the bear skull streaked with charcoal in a tree, ritual feasting, and other ritual acts. It related primarily to black bears. Grizzly bears were normally avoided. A clash with a grizzly entailed the ritual associated with that of fighting humans.

The wolf was also a special animal feared by most people. If one were accidentally killed, apologies were given by the hunter. It was believed that physical contact with a wolf would cause nervous illness and, ultimately, death.

Mysterious strangers, *dešini*, were often reported in the vicinity of camping places, although they were seldom actually seen. They were supposed to steal women. Suspicions of their presence alarmed people. They were frightening because they were elusive.

Art and Music

Plastic and graphic arts were little developed. Occasionally human heads were carved on tree stumps, but apart from this there was practically no decorative carving. Geometric designs and stick figures were painted on equipment and implements. A noteworthy craft of the Chilcotin was the geometric representations of men and animals imbricated on baskets (fig. 6).

Singers and dancers used round single-headed skin drums (fig. 7). Hollow-log drums and plank drums were also used. Young people made bark whistles and flutes of bird bones or grass stalks. Rattles may have been used by shamans.

Dancing was graceful and without jerky or violent movement. Most dances were performed solo. Dancers imitated animals or acted out events. Most often the dancer sang alone; occasionally others provided a chorus.

Mythology

Stories were told by old people to children in the evening and in winter time. They were well known, but a good teller could always delight and interest an audience. Skill in mimicry of characters was much appreciated.

Myths and tales seldom contained explicit moralizing, but they were told for moral effects. For example, through them young people learned not to be greedy like Raven or they would suffer misfortune. They were told to be industrious and to be kind to those with misfortunes, for then, like myth characters, they would reap supernatural aid and wealth.

The stories themselves were a mixture of Northern Athapaskan and Plateau tales with an overlay of Northwest Coast materials such as Raven as a trickster-transformer. Cosmic myths were unimportant and the Dog Husband and Salmon Boy were the only cyclical tales. The Dog Husband and his sons were the only culture heroes. Generalized animal characters were relatively unimportant. Where animals appear in stories of neighboring peoples, human beings often are substituted by the Chilcotin. Transformation of people into animals and of animals into people was a common theme.

Recreation

Feasts and parties were an important feature of life. They were held whenever people came together. On such occasions games (snowsnake, ring and arrow, ball) and athletic contests (swimming, foot racing, wrestling) were held, invariably accompanied by gambling.

History Since Contact

In the late eighteenth century, a European-stimulated trade in furs began between the interior and the coast. Locally, much of this trade followed old routes from the upper Fraser River westward through Carrier territory to the Bella Coola valley.

Shortly thereafter, explorers and fur traders from the east entered central British Columbia. None of the early European travelers entered Chilcotin territory.

The first recorded European contact was about 1815 with Ross Cox, a trader. In 1821 a fur-trading post, Fort Alexandria, was established in Carrier territory on the Fraser River; and Fort Chilcotin, a small subsidiary, was built on the middle Chilcotin River.

It seems probable that the Carrier early established themselves as the middlemen in the fur trade between

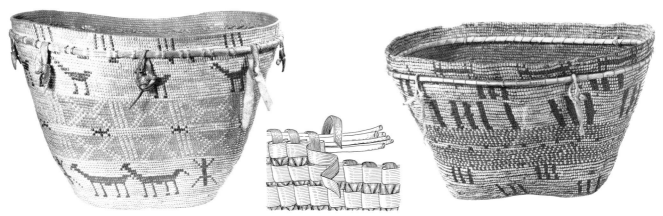

left, U. of B.C., Mus. of Anthr., Vancouver: A2.658; right, Smithsonian, Dept. of Anthr.:247, 691.
Fig. 6. Coiled baskets with imbricated designs. Willow hoops beneath the rim are for added strength. The greater height of the rim at the ends is typical and resembles the shape of some birchbark containers. left, Animal and line figures worked in bullrush and cherry bark on cedar root. Height about 33 cm, collected 1885–1911; right same scale, collected by G.T. Emmons before 1907.

Fig. 7. Old Sulin beating a single-headed drum made from a wooden box with hide covering. He is singing the song "Hudson's Bay Rum" in his native language. Photograph by Robert B. Lane, near Nimpo Lake, B.C., 1951.

the coast and the interior. Fragments of evidence suggest that the Chilcotin were unhappy with this. This dissatisfaction may have been the root of a number of extraordinary attacks that they made on Carrier groups in this period, the most spectacular of which were on Chinlac village on the Nechako River trade route and on the Carrier at Fort Alexandria.

During the Fort Alexandria attack in 1826, Europeans at the trading post gave arms and ammunition to the Carrier. This caused the Chilcotin to retreat, angry with the Europeans: "On their departure they denounced vengeance against us, and threatened to cut off all white men that might thereafter fall in their way" (Cox 1831:371). In this period, the Chilcotin may have pressed to the northwest to develop direct fur-trading contacts with the Bella Coola.

The Cariboo gold rush started in 1857, and by 1858 prospectors were in Chilcotin territory; but they found little gold and there is no record of friction. However, there were indirect repercussions of the gold rush. In the early 1860s, pack trains began to carry supplies from the Bella Coola valley to Alexandria and the gold fields beyond. They opened a new route through the grasslands of the Chilcotin plateau. Also, parties began to enter the country in the search for railway routes to the sea.

The packers and work parties often treated the Chilcotin harshly and arrogantly. Some of them may have deliberately introduced the smallpox that had devastating results on the population, which aboriginally was probably 1,000 to 1,500 (see table 2). In 1864 some Chilcotin lost patience and killed a trader, some packers, and most of a party of workers in three separate but related incidents. A large military force was sent into the area. After a ludicrous "campaign," seven Chilcotin, who had been visiting the camp of the militia, were identified as the culprits, seized, and taken away. Five were hanged and two were released. This was the "Chilcotin War."

The 1870s and 1880s were periods of radical change. Missionaries had visited the Chilcotin in the 1840s but it was not until the 1870s that serious missionary work began. By the 1880s, most of the Chilcotin were nominal Christians. The Roman Catholic priests who worked among the Chilcotin were largely responsible for the development of villages, which became the centers for reserves. The missionaries were also influential in the development of the idea of chiefs and in the

Table 2. Population

Bands	1823[a]	1837[b]	1864[c]	1905[d]	1970[e]	1978[f]
Alexandria					52	64
Alexis Creek (Redstone)					311	383
Anaham					606	731
Nemaiah Valley					193	222
Stone					146	195
Toosey (Riske Creek)					93	105
Total	252	600	1,500	550	1,401	1,700

[a] Men only? Cox (1831, 2:393).
[b] Estimate (Douglas 1839).
[c] Prior to 1864 smallpox epidemic (Morice 1897:39).
[d] Estimate (Teit 1909:760).
[e] Canada. Department of Indian Affairs and Northern Development. Indian Affairs Branch (1970:28–32).
[f] Canada. Department of Indian Affairs and Northern Development (1980:36–45).

formation of a semitheocratic local government structure.

Around 1880 ranches were being established in the Chilcotin valley. This development had a great impact upon Chilcotin life. Men and boys took rapidly to the cowboy role, and they remained enthralled by it in the mid-twentieth century. Many lived in close association with pioneer ranchers. To the extent that White culture was evidenced in this frontier life, Chilcotin came to know it intimately. As the ranches developed, haying became important. Chilcotin families were able to take over this chore and they remained indispensable until the 1950s, when haying was mechanized.

Trapping was never important for the Chilcotin. They took fur-bearing animals as the opportunity arose, but only a few individuals had trap lines.

From the beginning of the twentieth century to World War II, the Chilcotin, with their reserves as bases, roamed the country in wagons, living in tents and hunting and fishing much as before. The men found excitement in working as cowboys and most families, at one time or another, built up small cattle herds for themselves. The sale of a few cattle, a few furs, and the haying contracts provided what cash was needed.

Old ways died out but new ways were only slowly introduced. The first mission schools were started in 1914, but in the early 1950s many Chilcotin children were still not attending school and the Alexis Creek and Nemaiah bands had no schools at all. Only a few Chilcotin had entered high school by the 1960s, and none had gone on to higher education.

In the 1950s the horse and the horse and wagon were still the main means of transportation. Life in the area in the mid-twentieth century was much like that in other parts of the west in the early twentieth century. Whatever the hardships and disadvantages of this life few Chilcotin seemed anxious to escape it. Even in the mid-twentieth century, when people from neighboring groups were traveling widely in northwestern North America, few Chilcotin had traveled beyond areas known to their ancestors.

By the 1960s this equilibrium was shattered. The Chilcotin area became popular with people seeking escape from the modern world. Hunters and fishermen, home seekers, and would-be ranchers came in increasing numbers. Inevitably and usually unknowingly, these people usurped resources upon which the Chilcotin have depended. The Chilcotin reserves are mainly living sites. Subsistence and economic activities—hunting, fishing, grazing, and haying—are largely carried out on public lands that the Chilcotin assumed were available to them by right. Due to the pressure of non-Chilcotin interests, these resources are no longer readily available or abundant. Almost every development in the 1950s and 1960s has led to a decrease in resources upon which the Chilcotin have depended or to a decline in economic opportunities available to them.

Synonymy‡

The name Chilcotin first appears in English as Chilkhodins, 1808 (Fraser 1889–1890, 1:165) and with the spelling Chilcotin as early as in Cox (1832:326). Hale (1846:202) referred to them as Tsilkótin or Chilcotin, and Tsilkotin is the spelling adopted by Farrand (1910:826), who gives other nineteenth-century variants. The English name is a borrowing of their name for themselves, *ĉinɬqutin* (phonetically [tsǝ̂ɬqotin]) 'people of the Chilcotin River' (Eung-Do Cook, communication to editors 1979). The Carrier call them *ciɬkotin* (Morice 1895:22, phonemicized).

Sources

Sources on the Chilcotin are few. The best published account of their culture is that of Teit (1909b). Farrand (1899, 1910) has also written on them and provides (1900) a summation in English of their mythology. Ray (1942) adds further data on their culture in his Plateau culture element distribution study, but he notes that his data for the Chilcotin are the least adequate of all that he collected for his study. Beyond these sources, the major collection of ethnographic data for the Chilcotin is Lane's field notes (1948–1951) and dissertation (1953).

‡This synonymy was written by Ives Goddard.

Carrier

MARGARET L. TOBEY

Language and Territory

The Carrier ('kărēər) Indians speak a Northern Athapaskan language.* They live in the mountainous north-
central interior of British Columbia between the Rocky
Mountains and the Coastal Range. Their settlements
have for centuries been located along the numerous
lake and river tributaries of the upper Skeena and
Fraser rivers. The line of 56° north latitude marks the
approximate northern boundary of the territory. The
southern boundary until the nineteenth century angled
northward from Alexandria in the east to a point midway between Ulkatcho and Anahim Lake in the west
(fig. 1).

*The phonemes of the Fort St. James dialect of Central Carrier
are as follows: (unaspirated stops and affricates) *b*, *d*, λ, ȝ̂, ȝ, ẓ̌, *g*,
*g*ʷ, ʔ; (aspirated stops and affricates) *t*, ƛ, ç, *c*, *č*, *k*, *k*ʷ; (glottalized)
t̓, ƛ̓, ç̓, *c̓*, *č̓*, *k̓*, *k̓*ʷ; (voiceless continuants) ł, ṣ, *s*, *š*, *x*, *h*ʷ, *h*; (voiced
continuants) *l*, ẓ, *z*, *y*, γ, *w*; (nasals) *m*, *n*, ŋ; (vowels) *i*, *e*, *a*, *o*, *u*,
ə; (tones) high (v́), low (unmarked). The fronted alveolar series (ȝ̂,
ç̣, etc.) is distinct from the alveolar series (ȝ, *c*, etc.) in the speech
of only a few of the oldest speakers. Also, some local dialects of
Central Carrier lack ŋ as an independent phoneme.
    Southern Carrier appears to have the same phonemic inventory as
Central Carrier, except for lacking the fronted alveolar series and ŋ.
It has phonetic nasalized vowels, but these may be analyzed as sequences of vowel plus *n*.
    The Bulkley River dialect of Northern Carrier (or Babine) has the
following phonemes: (voiceless unaspirated stops and affricates) *b*,
d, λ, ȝ, *g*, ġ, ġʷ, ʔ; (aspirated stops and affricates) *t*, ƛ, *c*, *k*, *q*, *q*ʷ;
(glottalized) *t̓*, ƛ̓, *c̓*, *k̓*, *q̓*, *q̓*ʷ; (voiceless continuants) *h*ʷ, ł, *s*, *x*, *x̣*, *x̣*ʷ,
h; (voiced continuants) *l*, *z*, *y*, γ, *w*; (nasals) *m*, *n*; (full vowels) *i*, *e*,
a, *o*, *u*; (short vowel) ə (with a range of environmentally determined
central-vowel allophones); there are no phonemic tones. The velar
series is fronted ([ġ], [ḳ], [ḳ̓], [x̣]), and in the Babine Lake dialect
of Northern Carrier the stops of this series are replaced by affricates
(ž, *č*, *č̓*).
    In the practical orthography used by the Carrier Linguistic Com-
mittee and the Summer Institute of Linguistics the phonemes of Central Carrier are written as follows: b, d, dl, d̲z̲, dz, j, g, gw, ' (written
word-initially); t, tl, t̲s̲, ts, ch, k, kw; t', tl', t̲s̲', ts', ch', k', kw'; lh,
ṣ, s, sh, kh, wh, h; l, ẓ, z, y, gh, w; m, n, ng; i, e, a, o, oo, u; tone
as in the technical alphabet.
    Information on Carrier phonology, dialectology, and practical or-
thography was obtained from Antoine et al. (1974), Walker (1979),
Kari (1975a), Cook (1975), Hildebrandt (1974), and Hildebrandt and
Story (1974). The editors are responsible for the synthesis of information from these sources in this footnote. Information on the local
distribution of Carrier dialects and transcriptions of Central Carrier
words was provided by Richard Walker (communication to editors
1979).

Anahim Lake was a population center of the Chilcotin through the 1850s, when the tribe began moving
east. During the years that followed, Carrier families
from Ulkatcho migrated sporadically to the Anahim
Lake settlement. In 1916 land was set aside near the
lake for a few Ulkatcho families, and by 1945 the move
from Ulkatcho was complete. In 1949 the Carrier reserve at Anahim Lake was officially established (Davis
1970). Another expansion of Carrier territory occurred
in the late nineteenth century when Carriers moved
into Sekani hunting territory on and north of Takla
Lake and set up a village next to Fort Connelly, a
Hudson's Bay Company post, on Bear Lake (Morice
1895:26–27); these Carriers, with some Sekanis, apparently constitute the subsequently recognized Takla
Lake band (Duff 1964, 1:34–35). With the exception
of Ulkatcho and Takla Lake, Carrier bands occupy reserves within the boundaries of their aboriginal subtribe
territories. Morice (1893, 1895) recorded the names
and locations of more than 20 nineteenth-century
villages.

Component Groups

The Carrier tribe was and is composed of a number of
divisions most commonly referred to as subtribes (Jenness 1943; Duff 1951). Tribe as used here simply refers
to a linguistic grouping, the speakers of Carrier, who
may be distinguished on the basis of language from
neighboring Athapaskans, the Chilcotin and Sekani,
and from the Gitksan, Haisla, Bella Coola, and Shuswap whose territories adjoin the Carrier range.
    Carrier subtribes are named and localized socioter-
ritorial units. By drawing on a variety of sources, including the journals of explorers and fur traders and
the writings of missionaries and anthropologists, 14
distinct subtribes may be identified (fig. 1). In general
these sources agree quite well, but fusion and fission
of these units have occurred in the past. The Stony
Creek subtribe, for example, is an amalgamation of two
formerly distinct units (Jenness 1943:586). The Carrier
bands recognized by the Canadian government for administrative purposes correspond fairly closely to the
aboriginal subtribal divisions, except that some subtribes include more than one official band. In addition,

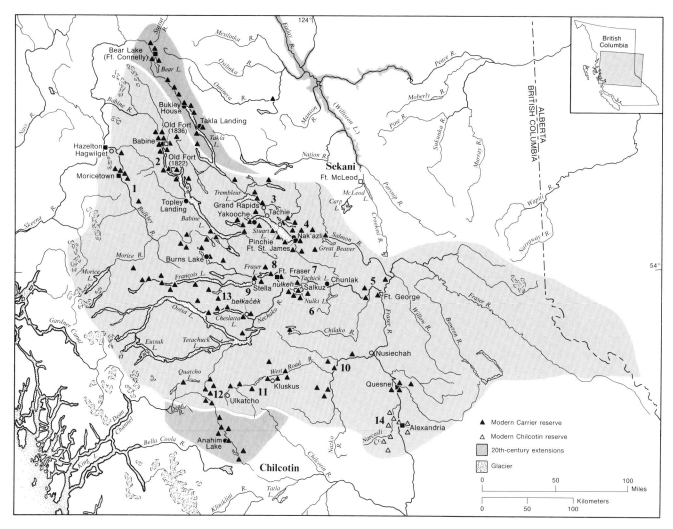

Fig. 1. Late 19th-century tribal territory with regional subtribes: 1, Bulkley River; 2, Babine Lake; 3, Stuart-Trembleur Lake; 4, Stuart Lake; 5, Fort George; 6, Nulki; 7, Tachick; 8, Fraser Lake; 9, Stellaquo; 10, Nazko; 11, Kluskus; 12, Ulkatcho; 13, Cheslatta; 14, Alexandria. For a discussion of subtribe names see the Synonymy; the locations and affiliations of modern reserves are given in Canada. Department of Indian and Northern Affairs (1978), which also gives their names.

the government publication (Canada. Department of Indian Affairs and Northern Development. Indian Affairs Branch 1970) listing the linguistic and cultural affiliations of Canadian Indian bands wrongly identifies the Hagwilget band as all Gitksan. The Alexandria band, formerly Carrier, has been a Chilcotin group since the early 1900s (Kew 1974, personal communication 1977; cf. Morice 1895:23, 24).

The nature of Carrier subtribes as socioterritorial units prior to their correspondence with government-recognized bands has been confused by the variety of labels attached to them in the literature. Hale (1846:202) called the subtribes "clans, or minor tribes," and Morice (1895) referred to them as "tribal subdivisions" or "septs"; others (for example, Hudson 1972:107) prefer to call them "bands." However, it is clear that the subtribes were neither corporate kinship groups nor unified political divisions. Rather, each subtribe was identified by its association with a particular territory

and had a name consisting of a place-name or a description of a place followed by *hʷəʔen*, or contracted *-ʔen* (pl. *-ne*), 'people of'. The subtribes correspond closely to the regional bands of the Mackenzie drainage Athapaskans (Helm 1965, 1968a; Kobrinsky 1977).

The social identity of the Carrier subtribe (as in the regional band of the Mackenzie drainage) was found in the persons exploiting the various resources within a recognized range or territory (Helm 1968a:119). The resources of the territory were sufficient to permit the subtribe to endure as an identifiable unit for generations. Characteristically, the constituent units of a regional band or subtribe were not physically together or co-resident. In the case of the Carrier, the constituent units of the subtribe were distinct villages that correspond in the structural hierarchy to the local bands of the Mackenzie drainage Athapaskans (Helm 1965, 1968a). The villages that comprised a subtribe may have occasionally united and operated as a task group in the

414

exploitation of seasonally abundant resources such as the annual salmon runs.

Subtribal unity was enhanced by a uniform dialect that differed slightly from other subtribe dialects (Morice 1895:3). The ties that bound the individual to the subtribe were less important than the cohesiveness of the constituent villages and families. It was only the frequent association, the links of marriage and kinship, the uniform dialect, and the pressure to share resources within a territory that counteracted the strong centrifugal tendencies of the smaller-scale residence and kinship units, knitting these units into a definite, though clearly acephalous, subtribe (Jenness 1943:482).

Relations among subtribes were generally friendly but varied in intensity. The Bulkley River, Babine Lake, and Takla Lake subtribes visited and traded with one another frequently. Interactions with subtribes farther south were less frequent, although their occurrence in the early historic period is confirmed by Harmon's (1957:140–141) record of an 1811 visit to Stuart Lake by Babine Lake Indians.

Morice (1895:24–30), in his detailed classification of Carrier subtribes and villages, relied on dialectal similarities and geographical distribution in formulating a tripartite division of the tribe into Babines (Bulkley River, Babine Lake), Upper Carriers (Stuart Lake, Stuart-Trembleur Lake), and Lower Carriers (the remaining groups to the south). In contrast, Goldman (1941:397, 411), using sociopolitical organization as his main criterion, extended the label Upper Carrier over all of Morice's Babines and Upper Carriers and some of his Lower Carriers to cover all subtribes that share an apparently Gitksan-influenced sociopolitical system not found among the subtribes Goldman called Lower Carrier (Ulkatcho, Kluskus, and Nazko), who interacted more frequently with the Bella Coola. Duff (1964, 1:33–34) restored a tripartite division into Babines (Morice's Babines), Upper Carrier (the rest of Goldman's Upper Carrier), and Lower Carrier (Goldman's Lower Carrier plus the extinct Alexandria subtribe).

In the earliest nineteenth-century reports the Chilcotin are described as "a tribe of Carriers" (Fraser 1889–1890, 1:165; cf. Hale 1846:202; MacDonald 1862:126) or as speaking a Carrier dialect (Cox 1832:326). This error was eventually corrected by the linguistic research of Tolmie and Dawson (1884) and Morice (1890:110).

Linguistic research on Carrier dialects in the 1960s and 1970s has confirmed in a general way Morice's tripartite division, in particular the distinctness of Northern Carrier (Babine) as virtually a separate language (Morice 1895:27, 1932, 2:506; Krauss 1973:916, 1979:864–865; Walker 1979:96), but the major dialect groupings recognized by linguists (Richard Walker, communication to editors 1979) do not correspond exactly to those of the other classifications. The Northern Carrier dialect is spoken by the Takla Lake Carrier in addition to Morice's Babines, and the Southern Carrier dialect is that of Duff's Lower Carriers plus the Cheslatta Lake subtribe; the rest speak Central Carrier. Within these major groupings each subtribe has a distinct local dialect showing clear but minor differences from the others. In distinction from the linguistic usage, the terms Northern Carrier and Southern Carrier in this chapter refer to the sociopolitically defined groupings called, respectively, Upper and Lower Carrier by Goldman. This follows later anthropological usage, for example, DeLaguna (1975).

Prehistory

Jenness (1929:22) and other scholars have assumed that the Carrier originally lived east of the Rocky Mountains but moved many centuries ago into their present homeland in northern British Columbia. Between 1950 and 1974, seven Carrier villages were investigated by archeologists, but the studies have produced two somewhat contradictory interpretations of Carrier prehistory: on one hand, Athapaskan-speaking groups are recent migrants to the central interior of British Columbia whose southward movements may have pushed Salish-speaking groups farther south (Borden 1953; Wilmeth 1975); on the other hand, cultural continuity and stability as evidenced by materials from the Tezli village site do not necessarily negate the possibility of population replacement but suggest instead that the Athapaskan migration southward may have begun early enough and occurred slowly enough "for cultural assimilation to the then extant systems to take place" (Donahue 1975:55; "Prehistory of the Western Subarctic," this vol.). A definitive interpretation must await further research.

The precontact population estimate of 8,500 for all Carrier (Mooney in Kroeber 1939:141) represents the

Natl. Mus. of Canada, Ottawa: 60313.

Fig. 2. Indian bridge made of timber and telegraph wire over Bulkley River, in Hagwilget Canyon, 4 miles east of Hazelton. Photographer and date unknown.

highest population density of any Subarctic Athapaskan group (see table 1).

Despite the barriers posed by mountains and rapids, the Carrier were linked in well-established precontact trade networks with two Northwest Coast tribes. The Northern Carrier traded almost exclusively with the Gitksan of the Skeena River. The Gitksan acted as middlemen for the Coast Tsimshian in the exchange of shell objects, copper, wool and bark blankets, and eulachon oil for the prepared hides and furs of the interior. The same products were exchanged by the Southern Carrier and the Bella Coola along a mixed overland-riverine trade route that followed the Bella Coola River northward to the Dean (Salmon), Blackwater, and up-per Fraser rivers. Trade with the Northwest Coast is indicated archeologically by the presence at Chinlac of dentalium shells, copper, and a Chinese coin dated about 1125 (Borden 1953:33–34).

History of Indian-White Contact

The established trading relationships were intensified and expanded in the last two decades of the eighteenth century by the maritime fur trade along the coast of British Columbia. Although the sea otter was the favored fur in the early period of trade, the furs of the interior (beaver, marten, lynx, and fox) became in-

Table 1. Population

Bands	Precontact	Estimates by Trading Posts				Censuses					
		1806–1831[b]	1839[c]	ca. 1845–1883[d]	ca. 1890[e]	1929[f]	1939[g]	1944[h]	1963[i]	1970[j]	1978[m]
Northern Carrier		2,000	181								
Lake Babine (2)				300	310	400	400	398	739	879	988
Bulkley River (1)				300	300						
Moricetown						180	280	278	464	584	697
Hagwilget						130	125	117	170	187[k]	261[k]
Omineca						79	84	89	133	158	202
Burns Lake						17	17	13	25	28	28
Central Carrier		1,000									
Stuart-Trembleur Lake (3)			288	346	90	293	248	283	500	617	797
Takla Lake						29	125	135	221	264	338
Necoslie (Stuart Lake) (4)					180	235	257	288	418	534	691
Fort George (5)			187	343	130	53	60	51	67	78	81
Stony Creek (6,7)				no data	153	166	187	211	328	387	451
Fraser Lake (8)			285	285	135	102	87	82	143	169	190
Stellaquo (9)						84	81	88	146	158	182
Southern Carrier	600		747	150							
Quesnel (10)					90	55	41	34	17	28	45
Nazko (10)						67	96	100	123	141	163
Kluskus (11)						38	50	56	65	108	124
Ulkatcho (12)					135	120	134	127	240	293	381
Cheslatta (13)						97	87	93	98	123	146
Alexandria (14)					15	—[l]	—[l]	—[l]	—[l]	—[l]	—[l]
Totals	8,500[a]	3,600	1,688	1,724	1,538	2,145	2,359	2,443	3,897	4,736	5,765

NOTE: Numbers after band names correspond to the subtribe listing in the Synonymy.
[a] Mooney in Kroeber 1939:141.
[b] Harmon 1957; Morice 1905.
[c] A.C. Anderson's census in Morice 1905:195.
[d] Morice's (1905:196) revisions of Anderson's census.
[e] Morice's (1895:24–29, 221) estimates.
[f] Canada. Department of Indian Affairs 1930:46, 47, 50, 51.
[g] Canada. Department of Mines and Resources 1940:4, 5, 10, 11.
[h] Canada. Department of Mines and Resources 1945:4, 5, 10, 11.
[i] Duff (1964, 1:33–34, table 2).
[j] Canada. Department of Indian Affairs and Northern Development. Indian Affairs Branch 1970:28–32.
[k] Officially listed as Gitksan; estimated in 1980 to be only 25% Babine speakers (Henry Hildebrandt cited by Randy Bouchard, communication to editors 1980).
[l] Now composed of Chilcotin Indians.
[m] Canada. Department of Indian Affairs and Northern Development 1980:37–46.

416

creasingly valuable cargo (Goldman 1940:340), and the wealth of the Carrier in terms of iron tools and other manufactured goods increased accordingly. The Bella Coola and Tsimshian continued to act as middlemen in the expanded trade network—interior to coast to ship—and presented a formidable challenge to the North West Company traders who penetrated British Columbia from the east via interior routes in the late eighteenth and early nineteenth centuries.

A significant consequence of the new-found wealth of the Carrier was the stimulus it gave to intermarriage with high-ranked Gitksan and Bella Coola families. Such intermarriage was probably infrequent prior to the establishment of the commercial fur trade on the Pacific coast because the rank-conscious Bella Coola and Gitksan would have disdained the Carrier as marriage partners. The commercial value of pelts from the interior reversed the attitudes of the Gitksan and Bella Coola, among whom wealth was a decisive factor in building rank (Goldman 1941:414–416). The potential for monopolizing a steady source of furs through affinal ties and purchasing valuable new prerogatives with the wealth thus gained diminished the Bella Coola–Gitksan resistance to marriage with the Carrier. A concomitant of intermarriage was the rapid adoption by the Carrier of Northwest Coast systems of social organization and stratification, the "potlatch-rank complex" as defined by Goldman (1940, 1941). The transformation in Carrier sociopolitical organization began, then, in the last decades of the eighteenth century among the western subtribes who had direct and frequent contact with the Gitksan and Bella Coola. The westernmost Carrier, in turn, acted as middlemen in the movement of both manufactured goods and the potlatch-rank complex to Carrier living farther east and to the neighboring Sekani and Chilcotin (Goldman 1941:408–410; see also Morice 1893).

The first reference to the Carrier Indians appears in Alexander Mackenzie's account of his 1792–1793 journey from Lake Athabasca to the Pacific Ocean. On June 9, 1793, Mackenzie and his party encountered a small group of Sekani Indians, well armed with iron-tipped weapons, camping south of the Anzac River on the Parsnip (Mackenzie 1970:286). Mackenzie learned from these Sekani that:

> Their iron-work they obtained from the people [i.e., the Carrier Indians] who inhabit the bank of that [Fraser] river, and an adjacent lake, in exchange for beaver skins, and dressed moose skins. They represented the latter as travelling, during a moon, to get to the country of other tribes, who live in houses, with whom they traffic for the same commodities; and that these also extend their journies in the same manner to the sea coast, or, to use their expression, the Stinking Lake, where they trade with people like us, that come there in vessels as big as islands (Mackenzie 1970:287).

The trade in iron, originating on the Pacific coast and reaching the Sekani via the Carrier, may have begun

prior to direct contact with overseas traders when the Northwest Coast Indians discovered the valuable metal in the woodwork of Japanese and Russian ships carried westward by the Japan current and wrecked off the Alaskan coast (Hackler 1958:22–23).

By June 18, 1793, Mackenzie had reached the Fraser River and was traveling downstream within traditional Carrier territory. The following day he sighted Indians but was unable to make contact. Continuing down the Fraser, Mackenzie and his party passed several large spruce plank houses, undoubtedly erected by the Carrier but temporarily abandoned. On June 21, at the junction of Narcosli Creek and the Fraser River, a confrontration between Mackenzie's party and several Carrier men in canoes at last resulted in conversation and the exchange of gifts for information concerning the course of the river.

1806–1821

Mackenzie represented the interests of the North West Company in his journey to the Pacific Ocean in 1793. His reports revealed the potential value of interior British Columbia to the commercial fur trade. Simon Fraser established Fort McLeod, the first post west of the Rockies, in 1805. Posts followed at Stuart Lake and Fraser Lake in 1806 and at the confluence of the Nechako and Fraser rivers in 1808 (Fort George). The last three were located near Carrier population concentrations, and the Stuart Lake post (Fort Saint James) served as headquarters for the entire fur trading district known as New Caledonia (Morice 1905; Harris and Ingram 1972).

The establishment of posts resulted immediately in an influx of European goods such as guns and metal implements, but the more far-reaching consequences of the fur trade included changes in hunting techniques, living habits, settlement patterns, and resource allocation (Harris and Ingram 1972:186). The Carrier derived perhaps 50 percent of their subsistence from annual salmon runs in their major rivers. Large game animals such as caribou and moose were not abundant, but the territory was rich in small fur-bearing animals (Steward 1960:733). The Indians were expected to process enough salmon during the late summer runs to provide for themselves all winter and to provision, in exchange for goods, the personnel stationed at the trading posts. The traders hoped a stored surplus would free the Carrier men for winter trapping, but the salmon runs occasionally failed and the late winter months had always been a lean period when people dispersed to take advantage of scattered food sources.

1821–1860

Following the merger of the North West Company with the Hudson's Bay Company in 1821, fort-building activities in New Caledonia were renewed. A depot at Alexandria on the Fraser was established in 1821 to facilitate the transport of goods from the Columbia River to Stuart Lake (Morice 1905:122). In 1822 the Company built Fort Kilmars (more commonly known as Old Fort) at the base of the two arms projecting from the north end of Babine Lake. Fort Connelly was built in 1826–1827 at Bear Lake, a meeting place and trading center of Gitksan, Carrier, and Sekani.

The major goal in establishing new Hudson's Bay Company posts was to counteract the native trade network, which was siphoning off interior furs to the coast. The Bulkley River and Babine Lake Carrier in particular continued to trade most of their furs to the Gitksan at Hazelton. Around 1850 the Coast Tsimshian attempted to eliminate the Gitksan as middlemen in the trade by annually ascending the Skeena River to its junction with the Bulkley River. On an open flat between the two rivers, the Indians held a large market where the Tsimshian traded goods obtained from Hudson's Bay Company traders stationed on the coast for the Carrier furs (Morice 1905:209; Jenness 1943:478). An additional stimulus to extending Company control over the northern part of the district was the richness of the salmon runs at Babine Lake. The Company resolved, therefore, to move Fort Kilmars in 1836 to the northern tip of the northwest arm of Babine Lake in a further attempt to monopolize Northern Carrier furs and salmon. Nevertheless, the trade settled into a fixed pattern in these decades interrupted only briefly by tragic breakdowns in Indian-trader relationships that resulted in loss of life on both sides, and by the measles epidemic that swept through the region in 1848–1849 (Harris and Ingram 1972:182; Morice 1905).

1860–1970s

After 1860 settlement and mining on the upper Fraser River brought improved lines of communication and broke down the wilderness buffer that had kept New Caledonia in relative isolation. In the 1860s and 1870s prospectors passed through Fort Saint James on their way to the Omineca and Cassiar gold fields to the north (Harris and Ingram 1972:182). Their arrival hastened the spread of a smallpox epidemic that nearly destroyed the Chilcotin population in 1862 but that had less disastrous effects among the Carrier (Morice 1905:307–308; Jenness 1943:485–486). "Free traders" established themselves at Quesnel, the commercial center of the Cariboo mining district, and offered an alternative to the Hudson's Bay Company. The gold miners and free traders were the first serious intrusions on the Hudson's Bay Company domination over the interior of British Columbia (Harris and Ingram 1972:182–183).

Competition and declining returns forced drastic cut-

backs in personnel and in the number of posts at the turn of the century. Fort George and Fort Fraser were closed, and Fort Saint James, after 1918, emphasized retail sales over fur trading. The building of the Grand Trunk Pacific Railway and the Pacific Great Eastern Railroad opened the district to extensive commercial mining and lumbering. Indian trappers began registering individual lines with the provincial government in 1926 and relied heavily on their yield until the late 1940s when the market dropped considerably. Individuals continued to trap through the 1970s, but wage work overshadowed trapping as a source of income.

Culture

Social Organization

In the eighteenth century the Carrier were hunters and fishers who apparently lacked social stratification and potlatching, but there is nothing in the ethnographic record that clearly indicates the nature of early Carrier social organization (Steward 1960:732–733). Goldman (1940) and Steward (1960) believe that certain elements of Southern Carrier social organization are retentions indicative of general Carrier social structure prior to the period of Northwest Coast influence.

Goldman (1940:334–335) suggests that the relatively cohesive Carrier social unit in the pre–Northwest Coast period was the extended family consisting of a group of male siblings, their wives, children, and married sons' wives and children. The members of this exogamous group, which he refers to as the sadeku, recognized the limited authority of a headman, the first-born male of the sibling group, which he calls the detsa. The status of these words as technical terms in Carrier is uncertain; they correspond to Central Carrier *snadneke* 'my close relatives', *snadneku* 'my distant relatives', and *tnadneke* 'relatives' (the inclusive collective form of *nenadən* 'our relative, generally belonging to the same household'); and *ʔədeco-ən* 'first one, eldest' (Antoine et al. 1974:19, 389; Morice 1932, 1:97–98, 156). The detsa regulated the joint hunting and fishing activities of the group. Each sadeku was associated with a hunting territory that was not further subdivided among the constituent nuclear families. The concept of individual ownership of land was not developed, and the sadeku monopolized hunting territories and fishing sites only during their period of seasonal use. Inheritance of property (fig. 5) and use rights was bilateral, but because residence was predominantly patrilocal after a period of bride service, economic privileges tended to pass in the patriline (see also Jenness 1929:22).

• THE POTLATCH-RANK COMPLEX   According to Goldman (1940, 1941) and Steward (1955, 1960), adoption of the potlatch-rank complex entailed, among the Northern Carrier, a shift in the descent system from bilateral to matrilineal. The Gitksan were divided into clans and phratries based on the principle of matrilineal descent, and it was this system (with important variations) that the Northern Carrier subtribes adopted; however, the Bella Coola recognized the principle of bilateral descent, and their ambilineal corporate kinship groups, "ancestral families," were composed of individuals who had chosen to activate membership in an ancestral family either through the maternal or paternal line (McIlwraith 1948). Thus, according to Goldman (1940:338), the Bella Coola were instrumental in maintaining an emphasis on bilaterality among the Southern Carrier (primarily Ulkatcho) with whom they traded and intermarried.

A fundamentally different view of the changes in Carrier sociopolitical organization is offered by Dyen and Aberle (1974:410–418). Based on their lexical reconstruction of the Proto-Athapaskan kinship system, they suggest that the Carrier (and most Athapaskans) were originally matrilineal, that only the potlatch-rank complex and not the matrilineal descent rule was adopted by the Northern Carrier, and that the Southern Carrier lost the rule of matrilineal descent under Bella

Natl. Mus. of Canada, Ottawa: 56902.
Fig. 3. Woman scraping a moosehide with a stone-bladed scraper. Photograph by Harlan I. Smith, 1922.

Coola influence. De Laguna (1975) also believes that matrilineality may be very ancient among Athapaskans. Her excellent comparison of matrilineal kinship institutions, particularly clan, moiety, and phratry names, in northwestern North America neither proves nor negates such a possibility but offers synthesized data for further study. This interpretation certainly deserves investigation, but the more widely held view of the changes in Carrier social organization is the basis for analysis in this chapter. Another suggestion that should be considered is that the lack of uniformity in resources among Carrier subareas may underlie the lack of uniformity in social organization among the Carrier subtribes (Michael Kew, personal communication 1977).

• NORTHERN CARRIER POTLATCH-RANK COMPLEX The concepts of rank and matrilineal descent diffused eastward from the Bulkley River and Babine Carrier, who were directly influenced by the Gitksan. The transmission to the eastern subtribes was by no means uniform. The most important modifications occurred in the clan-phratry system, which underwent reduction and simplification. When Jenness (1943:482, 485, 584–586) did fieldwork in 1924–1925 he found that six of the seven Northern Carrier subtribes he visited had five phratries then or in the recent past; the Stony Creek subtribe had two. Morice (1895:203–205) reported four phratries in the groups known to him, and later investigators have found five, four, three, and two in the subtribes Jenness studied (Hackler 1958:55–56; Steward 1960:739; Duff 1951:29–30; Hudson 1972:110–118; Shirley Walker in Antoine et al. 1974:385). The data are complex and in part conflicting, and the phratry names vary in the different groups and sources. The standardized names used by Jenness (1943), the major variants used by him and Duff (1951), and the transcriptions of Morice (1895:203, phonemicized) are as follows: (1) Gitamtanyu, Tamtanyu, *təmtényu*; (2) Gilserhyu, Jilserhyu; (3) Laksilyu, Yiselyu, *yəsilyu*; (4) Laksamshu, Llsamashu, Lsamasyu, *lĉəmásyu*; (5) Tsayu, *cayu*. Alternate names recorded include Kwanpahotenne (*kʷən ba hʷəténne* 'people of the fire-side') for phratry (1), (2), or (3); Grand Trunk (the name of a railroad) for (1) and (3); Tso'yezhotenne and Tsuyaztotin for (2) and (3); and others. The five Bulkley River Carrier phratries were equated with the four Gitksan phratries for purposes of potlatching and regulating marriage, as follows: Carrier phratry (1) with Gitksan *lax gibuˑ* 'Wolf

Smithsonian, Dept. of Anthr.: 381282.
Fig. 4. Hide scraper. The stone blade is lashed with leather and cord to wooden shaft. Length 76.5 cm, collected by Julian H. Steward near Fort St. James, B.C., in 1940.

Smithsonian Lib.: Morice 1895:174, 176.

Fig. 5. Ceremonial wigs worn only by persons of high rank; each was considered part of the associated hereditary title (Kahul for the one at left). Both are based on netted sinew caps, with rows of dentalia beneath and long trains of twisted human hair (one with smaller dentalia strung on) with terminal tassels of human hair, while bundles of artificially curled human hair hang below the dentalia; the top is decorated with 2 bundles of sea-lion whiskers (left) or strips of ermine skin (right).

phratry'; phratries (2) and (3) with *lax se·l* 'Frog or Raven phratry'; (4) with *gisqaha·st* 'Fireweed or Killer-Whale phratry'; and phratry (5) with *lax čimilix* 'Beaver clan' of *lax xsgi·k* 'Eagle phratry' (Jenness 1943:483; Hindle and Rigsby 1973).

Four of the Bulkley River phratries were subdivided into three clans each while the fifth phratry contained only one clan (Jenness 1943:484). According to Steward (1960:732–740), only the Bulkley River phratries were subdivided into clans; thus "phratry" is a misnomer for the corporate descent groups of the other subtribes. Hackler (1958:48) believes that the Babine Lake phratries were at one time divided into clans that had never equaled the phratries in social importance. The practice of phratric exogamy varied as well from subtribe to subtribe. The Bulkley River Carrier apparently adhered to the rule while the other subtribes viewed exogamy as a matter of choice or denied the existence of such a rule (Jenness 1943:483; Duff 1951:29–31; Steward 1960:732–740).

These reported variations in subtribal social structure result from the combined factors of physical proximity to the Gitksan, the relative richness of each subtribe's salmon runs as the quantitative basis of potlatching (Steward 1960:732–740), and the ethnographic time frame of the anthropological reports. Only the Babine and Bulkley River Carrier were in frequent and direct contact with the Gitksan, and only those women wore the Gitksan-style labret that signified high rank. Furthermore, the salmon runs in the Bulkley and Babine

rivers were the richest in Carrier territory. Finally, Jenness, more than Steward or Duff, relied on memory culture in his study of the Bulkley River Carrier in an effort to reconstruct their social life during the florescence of the potlatch-rank complex. For these reasons, this description of the Northern Carrier potlatch-rank complex is based on Jenness's (1943) monograph on the Bulkley River people.

Each Bulkley River clan owned a number of titles that were inherited through the matriline and that bestowed high rank on their individual holders. The usual successor to a man's title was his sister's son or daughter. Full accession to a title depended upon the ability to give a potlatch. If proper heirs were lacking and a more distant kinsman in the same clan had the means to potlatch, the title might go to him even if he had previously held low rank. Similarly, high-ranking families who had become impoverished were often unable to bestow titles on their heirs, who then descended in rank. Boundary lines between high and low rank were therefore rather fluid.

Titles apparently never passed from one phratry to another although they could be transferred, temporarily or permanently, to other clans within the phratry. Most of the Bulkley River titles were in the Tsimshian language, many also being used by the Gitksan in the nineteenth and early twentieth centuries.

The Bulkley River Carrier symbolized their division into clans by the display of crests (fig. 6). Each clan possessed at least one, or, more often, several crests that were carved or painted on the chief's house, grave box, ceremonial hats, and blankets. Clan members bore a tattooed version of the crest. The crests were associated with origin legends that could be related by any subtribe member except at potlatches, where only the highest ranking clan member had the privilege of recounting the tale. The crests themselves were considered clan property and were jealously guarded. Crests that were deeply rooted in local history occasionally ranked higher than the other crests and were protected from abuse by the entire phratry.

Clan crests depicted a variety of natural phenomena, mythical beings, and manufactured objects such as raven, beaver, weasel, swan, fungus, stars, monsters, and logs carved as men. Although animal crests predominated, they carried no totemic significance, and their living counterparts were killed and eaten without restriction.

Personal crests were owned by all clan chiefs and most of the titleholders in each clan. When a man's personal crest coincided with his clan title, it was considered the inalienable property of the clan; otherwise, personal crests could be purchased and traded. In addition, these crests were inherited matrilineally.

The sponsor of a potlatch used the feast as an opportunity to dramatize his or her personal crest and thus gain public recognition and endorsement of own-

420

Fig. 6. Cloak of clan chief, broadcloth with clan crests appliquéd in cotton and decorated with buttons. Length 119 cm, collected by Diamond Jenness at Ft. Fraser, 1924.

ership. The right to dramatize the crest's theme then became the exclusive property of the holder. A Bulkley River man purchased the "man who pinches others" crest from a Babine Lake Carrier in 1923. He dramatized his crest at potlatches by pinching with long sticks the arms of leading title-holders ("Expressive Aspects of Subarctic Indian Culture," fig. 11 left, this vol.).

The clan chieftainship was inherited through the matriline, and the usual successor to a chief was his sister's son. The successor was often chosen some years before the chief's death to avoid disputes. Actual succession to the position was achieved after six potlatches had been sponsored by the candidate and his kinsmen. The dead chief's funeral potlatch constituted the first in the series, the others following at rather long intervals. The sixth potlatch was occasionally marked by erecting a totem pole (fig. 7), an event that attracted visitors from other subtribes and tribes.

A clan chief was expected to build a house much larger than those of the clan members to serve as a shelter for his family and visitors and as the center for his clan's potlatching activities. He was responsible for settling disputes between clan members, relieving the wants of the poor, and representing the interests of his clan in its relations with the other clans and phratries. Chiefs were not exempt from subsistence activities, although they were generally relieved of portage duties.

Despite the expense and limited authority associated with the clan chieftainship, the position was highly coveted.

The chief of the highest ranking clan generally held the position of phratry chief. The duties of the phratry chief paralleled on a higher organizational level those of the clan chiefs. In disputes between phratries, the phratry chiefs consulted with their clan chiefs and then with each other to arrive at an appropriate settlement. In theory, the phratry chiefs shared equal rank, although the one who represented the largest membership might possess more influence and authority. The ranking of clans within the phratries apparently fluctuated.

The territory of the subtribe was partitioned among the phratries, and trespass on the territory of another phratry often led to quarrels and bloodshed. The chief of each phratry controlled the division of the phratry hunting and fishing territories among the clans. Each clan chief administered the territories assigned to his clan, but if a dispute over territorial rights arose be-

Fig. 7. The 4 totem poles at Hagwilget. left to right: Totem pole of the Owl House, Laksamshu phratry (originally belonged to the Tsayu phratry, which was decimated by the 1862 smallpox epidemic); totem pole of the Grizzly House, Gitamtanyu phratry; totem pole of the House in the Middle of Many, Gitamtanyu phratry; totem pole of the House of Many Eyes, Laksilyu phratry. Identification of the poles derived from Jenness 1943:486–487, fig. 63. Photograph by Harlan I. Smith, 1915.

tween members of different clans in the phratry, the phratry chief was generally responsible for resolving the conflict. Each clan had exclusive fishing rights over the lakes and rivers within its territory; however, fishing stations and portions of hunting territories were often exchanged or given away in payment for certain services. If the members of one phratry contributed generously to the potlatch of another phratry, the receiving phratry might publicly deed over certain territorial rights. Such transactions were not usually permanent, and original ownership might be restored within two or three generations.

• SOUTHERN CARRIER POTLATCH-RANK COMPLEX Bella Coola influence resulted in the formation among the Ulkatcho Carrier of crest groups that were incorporated into the existing social structure based on the sadeku. Crest groups did not develop among the Nazko and Kluskus Carrier where the sadeku remained the largest kinship group (Kew 1974:33). Ulkatcho informants described the crest group as a local group whose members lived together in the same village, shared common fishing sites and hunting territories, and potlatched together. In the vicinity of Ulkatcho, three crest groups were dominant in the nineteenth century—the Beavers, the Grizzly Bears, and the Ravens. Other less significant crest groups in the area of Ulkatcho were associated with the Black Bear and Owl crests. The Timber Wolf crest group was localized in the Ootsa Lake region (Goldman 1941:399–400).

Membership in the crest groups was inherited bilaterally. Children were assigned to the crest group of either the paternal or maternal lines or to both. Thus it was possible for an individual to inherit membership rights in all three major groups by acquiring, for example, rights in two of the groups from one parent and rights in the third from the other parent (Goldman 1941:399); however, only those individuals who, with the aid of their kinsmen, could distribute property at a series of potlatches were entitled to display the group's crest and exercise associated ceremonial prerogatives. These prerogatives included songs, dances, house styles, and a variety of special privileges. Furthermore, additional personal crests, titles, and honorific prerogatives could be purchased from both the Northern Carrier and the Bella Coola. Poor members were permitted to use the common hunting and fishing sites but could exercise none of the crest group's ceremonial prerogatives and were not considered active members in the group.

The patrilocal sadeku continued to be an important social unit after the development of the crest groups, a fact that poses fundamental analytical problems. Goldman's informants claimed that both groups served to determine residence and allocate resources. It is clear that the membership of the sadeku did not necessarily coincide with the membership of a crest group because

Natl. Mus. of Canada, Ottawa: 70386.

Fig. 8. Round Lake Tommy, a Hagwilget Indian of the gəlulém society (Jenness 1943:577–580), in special ceremonial clothes including cedar-bark headband and neck-ring, a ribbon-appliquéd cloth dance apron with thimble and deer-hoof tinklers, cloth leggings with tinklers, and a hide jacket with pearl buttons and floral embroidery on cuffs. Photograph by Harlan I. Smith, 1927.

brothers had the privilege of validating membership in different crest groups. This privilege so exercised could seriously disrupt the essential unity of the sibling group as a residence and resource-sharing unit. More significantly, marriage between members of the same sadeku was prohibited while the crest groups were not exogamous. Therefore, the crest group was not simply a sadeku that acquired new ceremonial functions under Bella Coola influence.

The Southern Carrier crest groups may have originally been modeled in part after the phratry organization of the Northern Carrier and were at first superimposed on the sadeku organization but "as emphasis upon the honorific aspects of crest prerogatives made for greater fluidity in crest group membership, the crest group slipped out of gear with the sadeku exogamic pattern and was transformed into an honorific society" (Goldman 1941:406). Thus in Goldman's view the functions of the two social units gradually became dichotomized: the sadeku retained its position as the primary cooperative economic unit while the crest group became in practice a ceremonial and honorific society.

Grossman (1965) interpreted the crest group as a stem lineage as defined by Sahlins: "a stem lineage has a core of patrilineal relatives supplying the lineage head — . . . evidently through primogeniture. To this patrilineal stem are attached cognates of various description, affiliated with full and equal rights save that of succession. The lineage holds land corporately, but administration is vested in and monopolized by the core line" (Sahlins quoted in Grossman 1965:254). In this scheme, the administrative core of the Southern Carrier stem lineage (the crest group) is the sadeku whose headman did indeed inherit his position through primogeniture. However, if the possibility existed, as Goldman claims it did, that brothers could validate membership in different crest groups, the core of the stem lineage would be fragmented and administratively ineffectual. Goldman's view that the functions of the sadeku and the crest group gradually dichotomized does not present this problem and is therefore preferred.

Unfortunately, resolution of these questions may be impossible because the potlatch-rank complex had begun to erode by 1860 under the impact of missionaries, fur traders, and gold seekers. Thus the changes integrating the potlatch-rank complex into the pre-existing social structure occupied so short a time span (three or four generations) that native accounts may necessarily be confused (Goldman 1941:400).

Potlatching dominated the ceremonial functions of the crest groups. Each crest group potlatched as a unit under the direction of its chief. Intravillage potlatches were generally hosted by one crest group and attended by the members of the village's other crest groups. Occasionally, the crest groups of a village united to sponsor an intervillage potlatch that attracted Bella Coola and Chilcotin guests as well as residents of other Carrier villages.

An intravillage potlatch was modest by Bella Coola standards, lasting two days and involving perhaps 10 blankets and food for all participants. Property was symbolically "thrown into the fire" but was never actually destroyed (Goldman 1940:347). Each crest group had its own songs and dances, the performance of which required a distribution of gifts to the gathering.

Potlatches were held for a variety of reasons—to celebrate the naming of an infant, to mark the individual's assumption of the family crest or crests at an age of economic maturity, to secure and strengthen the potlach sponsor's personal rank, and to commemorate the death of high-ranking individuals. Newly rich families acquired crests, titles, and honorific prerogatives by sponsoring the funeral potlatch of a deceased person of high rank or by direct purchase from another family line (Goldman 1941:404). Crests and titles could also be purchased from the Northern Carrier and the Bella Coola. Frequent property distributions were required of all crest-holders, regardless of mode of acquisition, to validate and maintain their high rank. Intracrest group potlatches also gave members opportunities to elevate their social standing within the group (Goldman 1941:402).

• TWENTIETH CENTURY The impact of fur traders, missionaries, gold seekers, and the provincial government had begun to erode the potlatch-rank complex by the late nineteenth century. Interest in the retention of manufactured goods acquired through the fur trade gradually overshadowed the importance of status achieved through ceremonially giving away such goods. This trend was bolstered by an increasing dependence upon Euro-Canadian foodstuffs, hardware, and clothing, which compelled each individual to trade his furs to the company in order to support his family rather than accumulating a surplus for potlatching. Private trap lines registered under provincial law undermined clan and phratry control of resources and furthered the process of individualization (Steward 1960:740–741).

The Roman Catholic church, more than any other agency, has worked hard to transform Carrier culture and, particularly, to eliminate the potlatch. By the 1930s, social rank distinctions and the rivalrous elements of potlatching had been eliminated, but potlatches were still held to commemorate the dead (Goldman 1940:378–379). While the Canadian government enforced its sanctions against the potlatch, Carrier Indians living in certain isolated areas held their potlatches in secret (Steward 1960:741).

By the mid-twentieth century, the basic social group was the individual nuclear family, each economically and politically independent. However, the phratry organization of the Northern Carrier had not been entirely abandoned. When Duff (1951:29–33) conducted his fieldwork in 1951, these phratries still functioned at social events such as funerals. Membership continued to be traced through the matriline, but the rule of exogamy was no longer maintained.

Kinship Terminology

Duff (1951) compared the kinship terminology he recorded for the Fort Fraser Carrier with the terminologies recorded in the 1920s and 1930s by Jenness (1943) and Goldman (1941) for the Bulkley River and Ulkatcho Carrier, respectively. Duff believed that differences in the terminologies reflect the degree to which each group had shifted toward a phratry organization. Both Duff (1951:33) and Goldman (1941) have suggested that the Ulkatcho terminology is the original Carrier type from which the others developed.

At Ulkatcho, cousins are not distinguished from siblings in the terminology, and first or second cousins are not permitted to marry. Among the Fort Fraser Carrier, separate terms are used for siblings and cousins, but cross- and parallel cousins are not terminologically distinguished. However, cross-cousins are permitted to marry at Fort Fraser, thus suggesting that the cross-parallel distinction is behaviorally if not terminologically important. At Bulkley River, cross- and parallel cousins and siblings are all distinguished terminologically. According to Jenness (1943:526), the Bulkley River Carrier preferred cross-cousin marriage.

All three subtribes distinguish lineal from collateral relatives in the first ascending and first descending generations. The Ulkatcho Carrier do not distinguish between maternal and paternal uncles and aunts, and all nieces and nephews are called by a single term, regardless of sex. Among the Fort Fraser and Bulkley River Carrier, maternal uncles and aunts are called by the Ulkatcho terms while separate terms are used for paternal uncles and aunts (Duff 1951:33). Furthermore, a cognate of the Ulkatcho niece-nephew term is applied to sisters' children (who are in ego's phratry) while the terms used for brothers' children (who are not in ego's phratry) are cognate with the Ulkatcho terms for younger male and younger female sibling/cousin.

Most of the Carrier subtribes have a simple grandmother-grandfather distinction, but the Bulkley River and Babine Lake Carrier distinguish mother's mother from father's mother, thus producing a three-term system that suggests a greater emphasis on maternal kin (Duff 1951:33; Hudson 1972:147).

Technology

Table 2 summarizes the basic items of Carrier material culture at the time of their first White contact in 1793. However, the Carrier were receiving iron tools and weapons some years earlier via their Gitksan and Bella Coola trading partners, who obtained the metal products from the skippers of ocean vessels.

By the 1940s the Carrier purchased locally all clothing except moccasins, food other than meat and fish, lumber, motor vehicles, household tools, metal traps, and firearms. Carrier moccasins were the standard footgear in the country for both Indians and Whites. Traditional snares were still in use for taking some food animals (Goldman 1940:373).

424

Table 2. Precontact Material Culture

Subsistence and Trapping Equipment
fishing
    fish weirs of woven branches
    conical fish traps of split fir in open trellis work, 15–18 feet long, 12–15 feet in circumference
    fishing scaffolds erected over turbulent water
    wood fish rakes
    3-pronged wood spears
    nets of willow and alder bark, nettle fibers
    wooden net floats
    stone net sinkers
    horn and bone 3-pronged harpoons
    bone fish lures and hooks
hunting and trapping
    sinew-backed bows, sinew strings
    arrow and spear points of wood, bone, horn, flint, quartz, and obsidian
    wooden spear and arrow shafts
    hunting surrounds of sticks laced with cedar roots
    various snares and deadfalls
    babiche beaver nets
food and hide processing
    cooking, serving, and storage vessels made of birch and spruce bark, wood, and woven cedar roots
    spruce-bark berry boilers
    wood and horn spoons and ladles
    bone and antler sap and bark scrapers
    stone pestles
    bone hide scrapers and fleshers
    bone awls and needles
    serrated stone salmon knives
    T-shaped digging sticks
general use
    skin fire bags
    fire drill
    cedar root ropes
    knives of stone and beaver tooth
    moose molar pressure flakers
    polished and chipped stone axes and adzes
    stone clubs

Clothing and Adornment—Women
short skin tunic (moose or caribou), skin leggings, skin apron
fur pectoral blanket
wooden labrets (Bulkley River and Babine Lake subtribes)
dentalium braid ornaments
haliotis ear pendants

Clothing and Adornment—Men
skin breechcloth, skin leggings, long skin tunic
dentalium, bone, and beaver-claw helix ornaments
moose hide armor

Clothing and Adornment—Both Sexes
fur robes (beaver, lynx, marmot, muskrat; woven strips of hare fur)
marmot fur cap
moose or caribou skin moccasins
fur mittens
skin bags

Table 2. Precontact Material Culture (Cont'd)

fringed skin hair ornaments
bracelets of wood, sinew, bone, horn, and copper traded from
  the Northwest Coast
dentalium septum ornaments and necklaces
horn or copper tweezers
bone tattooing needles

Transportation[a]
spruce bark and birchbark canoes
dugout canoes, especially of cottonwood
babiche and cedar-bark tumplines
wood and birchbark cradleboards with skin wrappings

Structures
rectangular A-shaped houses
gabled plank houses, style adopted from Northwest Coast
circular semisubterranean earth-covered lodges (Southern
  Carrier)
brush and branch shelters
raised fish and meat caches
sweat lodges
fishing lodges
smoke houses
decoy huts for waterfowl hunting
menstrual huts

Ritual and Curing Equipment
shaman's gear
    bear- or wolf-skin cloaks
    skin, wood, and bone images of guardian spirits
    wood rattles
    hide-covered drums
    carved wooden masks
    necklaces of grizzly bear claws and beaver teeth
    coronets of grizzly bear claws
life cycle ritual gear
    adolescent girl's fringed skin bonnet, bone drinking tube,
      wooden head scratcher
    carved wooden funeral posts
    wooden boxes for the deposition of cremated remains

SOURCES: Morice 1890, 1895, 1906–1910; Goldman 1940; Jenness
1943.
   [a] Morice (1890:131, 1895:151) makes the assertion and Jenness
(1937:42, 1943:532) repeats it that the Carrier lacked snowshoes in
precontact times. However, Michael Kew (personal communication
1977) seriously doubts that this widely shared Athapaskan trait was
absent among the Carrier.

Subsistence and Economic Trends

• ANNUAL ROUND IN THE PROTOHISTORIC PERIOD   The
Indians gathered at their major weirs in the late summer
to intercept migrating salmon in large conical basketry
traps. Scaffolds were also erected where the fish could
be harpooned, gaffed (fig. 9), or netted. Most of each
local run generally occurred during a two-week period,
but the Bulkley and Babine Carrier had access to a
more abundant supply of salmon for a greater period

of time. Purely freshwater species were taken as well.
Women dried (fig. 10) and stored the fish for use in the
fall and early winter. The salmon trapping season was
generally one of abundance when the diet was supplemented with fresh berries, wild turnip roots, bulbs, and
greens. Several types of berries were boiled to the consistency of a paste, shaped into cakes, and dried for
future use. Mountain goats were hunted during short
trips to the mountains. Late summer was the season for
potlatching, visiting, and trading. The Carrier subtribes
contributed to one another's potlatches and the potlatches of the Gitksan and Bella Coola.

Before snow accumulated on the ground, the villages
broke up and individual families dispersed to their hunting territories and trap lines where they lived in relative
isolation. Beaver, bear, marmots, goats, and caribou
were caught in snares, deadfalls, and surrounds. Hunting was done with spears and bows and arrows. Meat
was preserved by drying, and surplus caribou fat was
melted and stored to provide food for the winter and
for long journeys. As the commercial fur trade expanded on the Pacific coast and in the interior, fur-
bearing animals were trapped in greater quantities.

Very little game was secured during the severe winter
months. Families tended to congregate in or near their
permanent settlements where stored foods were available. The Bulkley River Carrier frequently wintered
with the Gitksan at Hazleton, while some Ulkatcho
Carrier spent the lean months at Bella Coola.

When the snow began to melt in the spring, hunting
became even more difficult, and families gathered on
the frozen lakes and rivers for a brief season of ice
fishing. The food supply was at its lowest point in the
cycle. All the preserved foods had been consumed, and
the spawning season was months away. People dispersed widely to take advantage of small but concentrated runs of trout and suckers. Many families sustained themselves on the inner bark of the hemlock
until the salmon arrived.

• NINETEENTH AND TWENTIETH CENTURIES   As long as
New Caledonia remained in relative isolation, the annual round continued to be followed despite the increased trapping of fur animals. But the 1858 gold rush
upset this pattern, with most serious consequences
among the Southern Carrier whose easternmost lands
contained the Cariboo gold fields. Thousands of Whites
poured into their country—farmers and ranchers on the
heels of miners—while the Indian population steadily
declined (Kew 1974:6–7). Most of Carrier territory
held no promise of gold and attracted few permanent
settlers until transportation routes were improved and
expanded in the late nineteenth and early twentieth
centuries. As the interior opened to economic development, the need to set aside land for the Indians became urgent.

The joint federal-provincial Indian Reserve Com-

B.C. Prov. Mus., Victoria: left, PN 3272; right, after PN3267 and 3268.

Fig. 9. Salmon gaffing. Fishing from a scaffold or standing by rapids as shown here, the fisherman jerks upward to hook the fish; the metal hook and wooden foreshaft are pulled off (remaining attached with a leather lanyard) so that the fish does not come free or break the shaft. Photograph by Wilson Duff, Moricetown, 1952.

mission established most of the reserves in British Columbia between 1876 and 1908, but these were soon recognized as inadequate. Between 1913 and 1916, the McKenna-McBride Commission evaluated the allotment of lands and established a number of additional small reserves among the Carrier. In the 1970s the 17 Carrier bands recognized by the Canadian government held approximately 63,000 acres in more than 200 separate reserves varying greatly in size and nature. A few contained villages; others were set aside as fishing stations, hay meadows, and cemeteries (Michael Kew, personal communication 1977).

The growth of British Columbia's forest industries since the 1940s has had a tremendous impact on the lives, land, and resources of the Indians. Occasional employment was available in the sawmills and logging camps, but the damage to the environment was of greater concern to many Indians than the potential income. Most were still hunters, fishermen, and berry pickers during certain seasons, and they depended on local natural resources to supplement purchased foodstuffs. The Nazko and Kluskus bands joined in 1973 to establish their right to choose a plan of development for their resources. The Indians held that sponsors of government projects in the timber industry have failed to consider the adverse impact of logging and logging roads on fish and other wildlife, still the major source of protein in the native diet. A detailed chronology of the Nazko-Kluskus efforts to compel the government to respond to their complaints and suggestions may be found in *Coyoti Prints* (Caribou Tribal Council 1976); see also Kew (1974).

In general, the small amount of wage employment available was of short duration and seasonal. Some Bulkley River and Babine Carrier found seasonal employment in the coastal fisheries and canneries. In the south, men occasionally worked as ranch hands, and during a two-month period in the fall both men and women were employed as guides by Whites who hold outfitters' licenses and permits for registered guiding areas. A few young men aspired to become outfitters themselves (Kew 1974:27–29). Funds from the Department of Indian Affairs and Northern Development paid the salaries of a number of public sector employees, including each band's administrator, welfare administrators, teachers, and teachers' aides.

Most Indian families derived a modest cash income from various kinds of self-employment such as trapping, stock raising in the south, and handicrafts, particularly beadwork and buckskin, but the greatest proportion of

426

TOBEY

Fig. 10. Salmon preparation. left, Drying salmon along the Babine River. Plank smokehouse on right, drying racks in center with gill nets hung in front, dugout canoe on the shore. right, Smoking salmon heads at Fort St. James Dominion Day celebration. left, Photograph by John M. Cooper, Aug. 1925. right, Photograph probably by Frank Cyril Swannell, at Stuart Lake, Aug. 20, 1909.

regular cash income came from unearned family allowances, old-age assistance, and welfare payments (Kew 1974:27–30).

Life Cycle

• BIRTH, NAMING, AND CHILDHOOD This account describes practices in the protohistoric period.

The pregnant Carrier woman was subject to numerous food and behavioral taboos. As childbirth approached, the husband built his wife a special hut that he but no other male could enter. The husband or a female relative assisted in the delivery, and cut the umbilical cord, placed the baby in its cradleboard, and wrapped the placenta in bark or fur. The mother later concealed the placenta in a tree.

Naming might be delayed for several weeks or months. According to Morice (1890), among the Stuart Lake Carrier children who were not heirs to high rank were given names that had been communicated in dreams to their parents or some other person. The name given to a child of high rank recalled a maternal ancestor and was bestowed at a potlatch sponsored by the maternal relatives.

The Bulkley River child initially received a name suggestive of one of the crests in his or her father's clan or phratry. People who held no titles rarely changed this name in later life, and individuals of high rank often retained it for everyday use. The child of elevated social status received during adolescence a second name, which linked him or her to the mother's clan and established the young person's rank among the title-holders of the clan (Jenness 1943:520).

When children began to walk, they started their systematic training along two lines, which Jenness (1929:25) referred to by the Northern Carrier words geretne and gidete. Geretne, or secular training, was instruction in the various manual tasks required of adults. Girls learned to carry wood and water; cure and cook fish, meat, and berries; tan skins; sew clothing; and make baskets and sinew thread. Boys were instructed in housebuilding, the manufacture of tools and weapons, and the methods of hunting and fishing. Parents and grandparents were primarily responsible for the training of young children. Among the Northern Carrier, this responsibility was gradually transferred to the mother's brothers and sisters as the child grew older. Gidete, or religious training, involved instruction in etiquette, morals, and the supernatural significance of natural phenomena through the medium of the folk tale. In addition to their instructive purpose, the tales were used to draw a confession from an errant child who recognized his breach of conduct in the tale chosen for narration (Jenness 1929:25).

• PUBERTY The training of boys and girls was intensified during adolescence. Boys prepared for successful hunting by running uphill and by observing numerous food taboos. Heart, head, tripe, and marrow were all forbidden to the young hunter because these foods were thought to impair his hunting and running abilities.

The menarche marked the beginning of a one- or two-year period of seclusion and restricted activity for the adolescent girl. She lived alone in a small isolated hut and consumed dried fish, dried berries, roots, and bark. Fresh red meat was considered especially dangerous to the young woman. Liquids were taken

427

through a drinking tube of goose or swan bone, and the head was scratched with a comb or scratcher. The adolescent girl's face was hidden by long fringes attached to a skin bonnet. Food and drink were provided by the girl's mother, grandmother, or sister. Female relatives used the period of seclusion to further instruct the young woman in the domestic arts. When she accompanied her family on hunting or food-gathering expeditions, the girl avoided the trails followed by hunters and crossed streams on logs laid across for that purpose. When the young woman emerged from her seclusion, she was eligible for marriage. A much briefer seclusion accompanied all subsequent menstrual periods (Jenness 1943:522–525).

• MARRIAGE   The choice of a husband rested with both the girl and her parents unless a chief asked for her in marriage or she was given in atonement for a murder or other crime (Jenness 1943:527). The Bulkley River Carrier apparently preferred marriages between cross-cousins because family titles and privileges were thus retained within a small circle of kin. The sororate and levirate were practiced. Polygyny was generally the prerogative of wealthy chiefs.

When a young man had been accepted as a suitor, he presented the girl's mother with a large quantity of furs, moccasins, arrows, and other valued goods. The girl's father asked the suitor to join his household and assist him in hunting and other subsistence activities. The couple did not marry immediately even though they now lived in the same household. The young man and woman used this intermediate period to become better acquainted and to confirm their intention to marry. Finally, when all circumstances seemed favorable, the young man crept under the sleeping robe of his bride and remained there through the night. The couple was recognized as formally married the following morning (Jenness 1943:527).They resided with the wife's parents for a year or more longer while the husband contributed his labor to the household of his father-in-law. A widowed chief who remarried was exempt from any period of bride service.

• DEATH   The Carrier practiced cremation of the dead until the 1830s when White pressure to bury led to its abandonment (McLean 1932; Morice 1905). Funeral customs associated with cremation are described by Harmon (1957), McLean (1932), and Cox (1957). A woman whose husband had died was expected to embrace his burning body until she could no longer stand the smoke and flames. If her husband's kinsmen were displeased with her performance as a wife, they had the right to push her repeatedly into the fire. Both widows and widowers were required to serve the kinsmen of their deceased spouses for at least one year, after which they were free to remarry.

Among the Northern Carrier, the father's phratry was responsible for all funeral arrangements and for gathering the burned bones on the day following cremation. The bones were placed in a box and given to the mother's phratry (of which the deceased had been a member), who repaid the gift with a potlatch. After the typical mourning period of one year, the father's phratry built a grave house over the cremation site, and the mother's phratry placed the bones on top of a post carved with the crest of the deceased's clan or phratry (Jenness 1943:534). The easternmost Carrier apparently required widows to carry on their backs the bones of their deceased husbands during the mourning period, hence the tribal name Carrier. The Bulkley River Carrier have no recollection of such a practice (Jenness 1943:535).

Religion

• ABORIGINAL BELIEFS   Aboriginal beliefs centered on the concept of a world populated by a number of spirits, mostly animal, to whom the individual appealed for guidance and protection. The animal spirit, like man, was believed to possess a mind and a soul and differed from man only in its corporeal form; however, the corporeal form was not immutable, for animal spirits were able to assume at will the shapes of human beings (Goldman 1940:364; Jenness 1943:539–540). The numerous regulations and taboos associated with hunting and fishing reflected the Carrier hunter's respect for the animal spirits and his dependence upon their good will toward him.

Communications with animal spirits took place during dreams when the souls of men wandered and as-

Natl. Mus. of Canada, Ottawa: 60592.
Fig. 11. Upper part of tombstone of the Hagwilget "Chief Caspit, died Mar. 11, 1917, aged 74 years," with his crest. Photograph by Diamond Jenness, 1923–1924.

428

sociated with the souls of animals. The Carrier distinguished the soul, which occasionally left the body during dreams, from the ghost, which emerged only at death. Every young man attempted to acquire his own animal protector or guardian spirit by sleeping in isolated and dangerous places that were conducive to vivid soul-wandering dreams (Jenness 1943:542). The Stuart Lake Carrier believed that every youth obtained a guardian spirit, but only a few favored individuals acquired, through dreams of a special character, the medicine power that ranked them as shamans. The Fraser Lake and Stony Creek subtribes believed that most youths failed in their quests for guardian spirits and that the few young men who succeeded became shamans.

Among the Bulkley River Carrier, the doctrine of the guardian spirit quest was modified due to increased Gitksan influence after 1800 (Jenness 1943:543); they developed the doctrine that guardian spirits and medicine power could not be sought but were instead thrust upon the individual even if he were unwilling. This unsought spirit possession caused a wasting sickness in the afflicted man that only a shaman could diagnose and cure. The cure was accomplished by removing the spirit from the patient's body entirely or by training the patient to perceive and control the spirit, thereby acquiring medicine power, and following a validating potlatch, the status of shaman himself. A similar medicine sickness was caused by the imprisonment of a man's soul in the homeland of an animal spirit. A shaman was called upon to restore the captured soul.

• THE PROPHET MOVEMENT   The Prophet Dance that swept through the Salish tribes of the interior Northwest Coast area around 1800 reached the Carrier in the mid-1830s (Spier 1935:7). Spier distinguishes two waves of the Prophet Dance: an early form that apparently subsided during the 1820s and a later Christianized form that spread rapidly during the 1830s among the tribes of Oregon, Idaho, Washington, Montana, and British Columbia. It is the later Christianized form that is documented among the Carrier. A Hudson's Bay Company employee stationed at Stuart Lake wrote in the winter of 1834–1835 or 1835–1836:

> Two young men, natives of Oregon, who had received a little education at Red River, had, on their return to their own country, introduced a sort of religion, whose groundwork seemed to be Christianity, accompanied with some of the heathen ceremonies of the natives. This religion spread with amazing rapidity all over the country. It reached Fort Alexandria, the lower post of the district, in the autumn; and was now embraced by all the Nekaslayans [Stuart Lake Carrier]. The ceremonial consisted chiefly in singing and dancing (McLean 1932:159).

The names of the major Carrier prophets and a summary of their religious activities from the mid-1830s to the 1870s are given by Jenness (1943:547–559). The Carrier prophets most commonly received their messages while in a death state and returned to life to preach. Since they often perceived the Whites as sources of abundant food and horses, their prophetic messages lack the elements of earth renewal and destruction of Whites that are so prominent in the proselytizing of the 1890s Ghost Dance prophets.

• CONVERSION TO CHRISTIANITY   Prior to the arrival of the Roman Catholic priests, Carrier contact with Christianity was through the men stationed at the fur-trading posts and through Indians of other tribes who had been exposed to Christianity in diverse ways. Missionaries did not visit the Carrier until 1842 when Father Modeste Demers preached and baptized sporadically in the summer months. Father John Nobili, a Jesuit, worked in Carrier territory from 1845 until 1847. This activity was followed by a 21-year hiatus in missionizing.

Rapid missionization began in 1869. The Babine Lake Carrier apparently resisted and resented the efforts of the missionaries to a greater degree than did other Carrier subtribes (Hackler 1958:110). Bishop L.J. D'Herbomez and Fathers Jean LeJac and A.G. Morice were the principal missionaries to Carrier territory during the last half of the nineteenth century. The priests endeavored to instill the acceptance and performance of Catholic rituals and to eliminate those native customs, rituals, and beliefs that they believed to be immoral—particularly potlatching, polygyny, and faith in the efficacy of the shaman's healing powers.

As late as 1958, there were indications that the Church had yet to gain the unanimous support of the

Catholic U., Dept. of Anthr., Washington.

Fig. 12. Chief Daniel of Babine village wearing a fringed leather jacket decorated with floral embroidery. Photograph by John M. Cooper, Aug. 1925.

Babine Lake Carrier (Hackler 1958:118). At Ulkatcho, too, relations with the Church were highly tenuous (Goldman 1940:373). The surface rituals of Catholicism were accepted easily and without friction, but the depth of belief in the basic tenets is difficult to evaluate, and, as in any community of Christians, Carrier individuals differ in their devotion to religion.

Synonymy†

The name Carrier has been used in English since the first recorded contact by Mackenzie (1970:322, 338) in 1793: Carrier-Indians and Carriers. It is a translation of French Porteur, itself a rendering of the meaning of Sekani ʔaɣeɬne (Morice 1893:111, 1932, 1:xi and Harrington 1939, phonemicized), an apparent allusion to the custom of widows carrying on their backs the cremated remains of their husbands (Harmon 1957:149; Hale 1846:203–204; Morice 1893, 1932). In early usage, attested by Harmon's (1957) journal from the period 1810–1819, the name Carrier was applied only to the eastern groups and not to the Babines. The Carriers call themselves dakeɬne (sg. dakeɬ), also used for 'Indian(s)' in general (Antoine et al. 1974:74). Renderings of earlier forms of this word include Nagailas and Nagailer, 1793 (Mackenzie 1970:322, 338), Tâcullies and Tâ-cullies, 1820 (Harmon 1957:134, 135, 242), Tahkali (Hale 1846:201), Takellies and Tekallies, sg. Takelly, 1849 (McLean 1932:160–161), and Takulli (Tolmie and Dawson 1884:map), used as the standard name by Hodge (1910l:675–676), who lists other spellings. The meaning of this name is 'people who go upon water' (Harmon 1957:242), 'people who go by boat on the surface' (Morice 1932, 1:xi), though Mackenzie's recordings with apparent na- 'about' for da- 'on top' point to an earlier meaning 'people who go about by boat'. The last meaning would fit even better with Morice's explanation that the name is "from their habit of moving about on the lakes and rivers which dot and drain their country."

The Northern Plains Cree name is onayahciki·w 'packer, i.e. carrier' (David H. Pentland, communication to editors 1980).

The Bella Coola call the Carrier ʔax̣smx 'interior person' (Philip W. Davis, communication to editors 1980), rendered Atlāshimih by Tolmie and Dawson (1884:122B), and the Gitksan call them Akwilgét, a name applied specifically to the Bulkley River Carriers and their village Tsitsk (Hagwilget) (Morice 1895:27). The Gitksan name was used in local English and appears as Hoquel-got in early government reports as the name of the Carrier (or Northern Carrier) in general (Loring 1891:97).

†This synonymy was written by Ives Goddard incorporating references furnished by Margaret L. Tobey.

Subtribes

The Carriers usually refer to themselves by the names of the subtribes. Lists of these, showing extensive agreement, are given by Hale (1846:202); Dawson (1881:20B, 30B), for Northern Carrier only; Morice (1895:24–30, 221), here phonemicized; and Jenness (1943:476, 584–586), the Bulkley River Carrier names collected in 1924–1925. The following list correlates the names in these sources (referred to by date) and a few others with the subtribes supposed to have existed in 1850 (Duff 1964, 1:33–34), given first, and the official band names of 1916 (Duff 1964) and 1964 (Canada. Department of Citizenship and Immigration. Indian Affairs Branch 1964:33, 34, 41, 43, 44).

(1) Witsiwoten, 1964: not mentioned in 1846; mentioned but not named in 1881; hʷocoɩenne 'people of the Bulkley River', Northern Carrier dialect Hwotsu'tinni, 1895; Hwitsowitenne 'clever people' or Bulkley Carrier, 1943; Bulkley River (Duff 1951:31); the Moricetown and Tsitsk (Hagwilget) bands, with offshoots having become the François Lake "tribe," 1916, and the Omineca and Burns Lake bands, 1964.

(2) Nataotin, 1964: Nâte-ote-tains and misprinted Nâle-ale-tain, 1820 (Harmon 1957:140, 174); Babine Indians, 1846; Na-taw-tīn 'people of Babine Lake', 1881; nadoɩenne or Babines, Northern Carrier dialect Nitu'tinni or Nétu'tinni, 1895; U'anwitenne or Babine Lake, 1943; Lake Babine, 1964. Subtribes (1) and (2) together were referred to as the Hagwilget "tribe" in 1916. The name Babine, from French babine 'labret', was originally applied by traders only to the Babine Lake Carrier. Morice (1895:27) extended it to include both them and the Bulkley River Carriers "since in language they are practically one, and the custom of wearing labrets which gave its distinctive name to one of them was common to both." The wearing of labrets specifically by Babine Lake women was described in 1820 by Harmon (1957:257; cf. Dawson 1881:25B).

(3) Tachiwoten, 1964: Tatshiáutin, 1846; Kus-chē-o-tin, 1881; x̣azɩenne 'people of the end of the lake', 1895; Tatchetenne, 1943; Tatche "tribe," 1916; Stuart-Trembleur Lake, 1964. The names used in 1846, 1916, and 1943 are based on that of the village Tachie (tače), and that used in 1881 on that of Grand Rapids (k̓əzče) (Morice 1895; Antoine et al. 1974:124).

(4) Necosliwoten, 1964: Nikozliáutin, 1846; Nekasly, Nekaslay, Nekaslayans, 1849 (MacLean 1932:163, 158, 159); Na-kas-le-tīn 'people of Stuart Lake', 1881; nak̓azλitenne, 1895; k̓otene, 1943; Stuart Lake "tribe," 1916; Necoslie (Fort St. James), 1964. The term k̓udəne is applied by the Babines to subtribes (3) and (4) according to Morice (1895) and is used in Central Carrier for the villages of the Stuart Lake area (Richard Walker, communication to editors 1979). There are slight disagreements on membership: Pinchie village

(*binče*) is put in (4) in 1895 but in (3) in 1916; the Takla Lake band, called North Takla Lake in 1916 (North Tacla Lake is also attested), is part of (3) in 1895 (agreeing with Duff 1964) but in (4) on Jenness's map.

(5) Tanoten, 1964: Thetliótin, 1846; not mentioned in 1881; *tanoíenne* 'people a little to the north', 1895; Tannatenne, 1943; Laydliwotin (Duff 1951:28) or *łeiλi hʷəíenne* 'river-confluence people' (Richard Walker, communication to editors 1979); Fort George, 1916 and 1964; also referred to by the name of the modern town as the Prince George subtribe (Duff 1951:28).

(6) Nulkiwoten, 1964: Nulaáutin (perhaps miscopied), 1846; Nool-kē-otīn, 1881; means 'people of *nułkeh* village' or 'of Nulki Lake' (cf. Morice 1893:109, 1932, 1:xiv); also Laketown or *nułke*, 1895.

(7) Tachickwoten, 1964; Tsatsnótin (perhaps miscopied), 1846; Ta-tshik-o-tīn, 1881; means 'people of Tachick Lake'; also Stony Creek or *saiḱəz*, 1895. Subtribes (6) and (7) amalgamated into a single subtribe, and Morice (1895:221) refers to them as two villages of one "subdivision": *hʷozahne*, 1895; Yutawotenne and Yuta'wotenne, 1943; Saykuswotin or *ẕaiḱəz hʷəíenne* 'people on the sand or gravel' (Duff 1951:28; Antoine et al. 1974:208); called by others *ʔazehne hʷəíen* (Richard Walker, communication to editors 1979); Stony Creek band, 1916 and 1964.

(8) Natliwoten, 1964: Natliáutin, perhaps including subtribe (9), 1846; Nau-tle-a-tīn, 1881; *naλoíenne* 'people of *naλeh* village', includes subtribe (9), 1895; Nattlewitenne or Fraser Lake Subtribe, 1943; Fraser Lake, 1916 and 1964. (9) Stellawoten, 1964: Stel-a-tīn, 1881; Stella village (*stela* 'cape, peninsula'), included in subtribe (8), 1895; Nu'tseni or Endako River subtribe, 1943; Stellawotin or *stela hʷəíenne* 'people of the peninsula or cape' (Duff 1951:28; Richard Walker, communication to editors 1979); Stellaquo band, 1916 and 1964.

(10) Nazkoten, 1964: Nascud Denee, 1793 (Mackenzie 1970:338); Nasquitins, 1808 (Fraser 1889–1890, 1:158); Nus-koo-tain, 1815 (Harmon 1957:173); Naskotins (Cox 1832:344); Naskótin, 1846; *nazkuíenne* 'people of the Nazko River', 1895; Naskotenne, 1943; the Nazko and Euchinico bands of the Kluskus "tribe," the Blackwater "tribe," and the Quesnel "tribe," 1916; Nazko and Quesnel bands, 1964. They refer to themselves as *čəntezniʔai*, but other Carriers call them *nazko hʷəíen* (Richard Walker, communication to editors 1979).

(11) Kluskoten and (12) Algatcho, 1964: Ntshaáutin, 1846; *nučaíenne* 'people down against (?) the island', 1895; Nētcā'ut'in (Boas 1899:665); Nitchaotenne, 1943: Nətca'-hwoten (Goldman 1953:2); *nečauten* (Davis 1970:59, normalized). Morice includes in one subtribe Kluskus (*łusḱəz*), Ulkatcho (*łḱačo*), and villages at Cheslatta (subtribe 13) and Trout lakes, and Hale's term probably had a comparable inclusiveness; Hodge

(1910o:766) describes Tluskez (Kluskus) as a Ntshaautin village. The other names were collected for the Ulkatcho of Anahim Lake; other renderings of their name are Alkatcho and Lkátcoten (Goldman 1940, 1941, 1953:2), and *ʔəłḱačo* (Morice 1932, 1:xiv; Richard Walker, communication to editors 1979). Garbled renderings of *łusḱəz hʷəíenne* and *nučaíenne*, probably miscopied, are Sloua-cuss-Dinais 'Red-fish Men' and Neguia Dinais, 1793 (Mackenzie 1970:347–348, 354); for the first Cox (1832:327, 344) gives an again miscopied "Slowercuss, Dinais" beside Those Kuz Lake ("tribe"). These groups perhaps belonged to a single subtribe, but they are now recognized as two bands: Kluskus and Ulkatcho, 1916 and 1964.

(13) Cheslatta, 1964: apparently subsumed in subtribes (11) and (12) in the nineteenth century, the village on Cheslatta Lake being referred to as Pel'catzék (Morice 1893:109) and *bełḱaček*, 1895; Tatchatotenne or Cheslatta Lake Indians, 1943; *tačik hʷəíen* (Richard Walker, communication to editors 1979); Cheslatta "tribe," 1916, and band, 1964.

(14) Tauten (Talkotin), 1964: Tahowtin, 1808 (Fraser 1889–1890, 1:159); Talkotins (Cox 1832:344); Taūtin or Talkótin, 1846; *łtauíenne* 'people of Fraser River', 1895; Ltautenne, 1943; Alexandria band, 1916. According to Morice (1895) fewer than 15 remained in their village *stela* 'cape' near Fort Alexandria; these disappeared as a separate subtribe, and the Alexandria band subsequently consisted entirely of Chilcotin Indians and was so listed officially in 1964 (Canada. Department of Citizenship and Immigration. Indian Affairs Branch 1964).

Sources

The journals of Alexander Mackenzie (1970), Simon Fraser (1889–1890, 1), Daniel Harmon (1957), and John McLean (1932) date from the period in Carrier history of early White contact and the build-up of the fur trade, 1793–1837. Mackenzie and Fraser provide the earliest but briefest observations of the Carrier. Harmon was stationed in New Caledonia from 1810 to 1819, serving at both the Stuart Lake and Fraser Lake posts. He was the first White man to visit the Babine Lake Carrier, and his culture sketch of the Carrier is invaluable despite obvious misconceptions. McLean's journal (1833–1837) repeats much of Harmon's information.

The most prolific recorder of Carrier history, language, and culture was Father Adrien Gabriel Morice, who was resident priest at Stuart Lake in the late nineteenth century. Morice published from about 1880 to 1930 and presented comparative data on the Sekani, Chilcotin, and Athapaskans generally as well as specific descriptions of Carrier culture. Morice had a tendency both to moralize and to generalize from Stuart Lake

Carrier data, but his treatments (1890, 1895, 1906–1910) of material culture and subsistence are the most detailed available. His history of New Caledonia (1905) deals with Indian-White relations and is thus more balanced than many such histories of the fur trade era. A comprehensive bibliography of Morice's work has been compiled by Carrière (1972).

The monograph of Jenness (1943), who worked with the Bulkley River Carrier in 1924–1925, is indispensable. The Ulkatcho Carrier have been well documented by Goldman (1940, 1941, 1953) who conducted fieldwork in the winter of 1935–1936. Both Jenness and Goldman focused in their published works on social organization and the potlatch-rank complex, but Goldman's (1953) manuscript is an excellent comprehensive ethnography.

Steward (1941) worked briefly among the Stuart Lake Carrier. His Carrier data contributed significantly to the development of his theory of culture change (Steward 1955, 1960; Murphy and Steward 1956). Duff (1951), who studied the Fort Fraser Carrier, emphasized variations in the forms of the clan and phratry system adopted by the Northern Carrier subtribes.

Hackler (1958) conducted fieldwork at Babine Lake in 1956, and his thesis concentrates on the forces of social and economic change. Hudson's (1972) thesis is a detailed analysis of the historical determinants of Northern Carrier matrilineality.

Kew's (1974) paper, prepared at the request of band officials and members of the Nazko-Kluskus Study Committee, focused on life in the 1970s and the problems created by continued extension of logging into the Nazko-Kluskus area.

Rejecting ancient matrilineality among the Carrier, Kobrinsky (1977) has argued that the Northern Carrier system of matri-phratry territories was adopted within historic times in order to delimit and regulate access to valuable fur-trapping areas.

Sekani

GLENDA DENNISTON

The language of the Sekani ('sekə͵nē or sə'känē) belongs to the Beaver-Sarcee-Sekani branch of Athapaskan.* This fact plus clear cultural similarities with the Beaver Indians suggest that before the Cree influenced the Beaver, Beaver and Sekani could have been classed as one people, as Daniel Harmon (1957:130, 256) conjectured in 1810.

Territory and Environment

The probable limits of the territories of the Athapaskan bands that can be classed as Sekani are shown in figure 1. As cultural markers these boundaries are quite arbitrary, especially on the east and north; eastern Sekani could almost as easily be called western Beaver, and northern Sekani could be called Kaska. Cultural and linguistic disparities are more abrupt to the west and south where Sekani territory meets that of Carrier and Shuswap groups. By convention, the term Sekani has, at least after the first quarter of the nineteenth century, been reserved for the Athapaskan inhabitants of the mountainous areas of British Columbia drained by the Finlay and Parsnip branches of the Peace River. In the late 1700s many of the bands ancestral to modern Sekani probably spent the late fall to early spring season on the east side of the mountains.

The country of the Sekani includes rolling foothills, mountains, and high plateau areas, dotted with lakes and cut by numerous rivers and streams. Most of Sekani country is part of the Mackenzie (Arctic) drainage system and lacking in salmon. Sekani lands are quite dry, and most of the precipitation is in the form of winter snow. Winters are severe; temperatures often are well below zero and in some areas there is deep snow as well.

*The phonemes of Sekani are: (unaspirated stops and affricates) b, d, ƛ, ʒ, ǯ, g, gʷ, ʔ; (aspirated stops and affricates) t, ƛ, c, č, k, kʷ; (glottalized) t̓, ƛ̓, c̓, č̓, k̓, k̓ʷ; (voiceless continuants) ł, s, š, x, hʷ, h; (voiced continuants) l, z, γ, γʷ; (nasals) m, n; (resonants) w, y; (vowels) i, ı, e, ɛ, a, o, u, ə; (nasalized vowels) i̧, etc.; (tones) high (unmarked), low (v̀). Field notes collected by Harrington (1939) at Ft. McLeod suggest that some dialects of Sekani may also have had a fronted alveolar or interdental series (c̓, etc., or θ̇, etc.).

Information on Sekani phonology is from David B. Wilkinson (in Canonge 1966).

Phonemic transcriptions of the Sekani words cited in the *Handbook* were not available; the orthography of the quoted sources is followed.

Especially in the lower altitudes, there is a dense forest cover of the Engelmann spruce–Alpine fir type, or, especially in extensive fire-marred areas, a subclimax cover where poplars predominate. There are many high areas with subalpine vegetation and virtually bare mountain tops. In the northwestern plateau, drained by the upper Finlay, Stikine, and Liard rivers, there is an extensive grassy area rich in game animals. East of the mountains, along the Peace River, stands of boreal forest are also interspersed with broad prairies.

Socioterritorial Groups

It is extremely difficult to determine the kinds of socioterritorial groups that can be ascribed to the Sekani at the time of earliest contact. Early references to these people include only minimal demographic information. Some guesses can be made from the few indications in accounts of early traders of the number of Sekanis who came to a particular fort at one time or were said to be together up a certain river. Samuel Black's (1955) account has by far the best information, at least for the northernmost regional band in 1824.

The information obtained from these spotty sources as well as that elicited from Jenness's (1937) informants 100 years later is not incompatible with the levels of socioterritorial groupings defined by Helm (1968a:118–120) for the Dogrib and other Mackenzie drainage Athapaskans: regional bands identified with a general territorial range, with constituent subsistence-camping units in the form of local bands and task groups. For the Sekani, as with other Mackenzie drainage peoples, the territorial groupings appear to have had a focus of identity and membership based on bilateral kinship ties. The loose bilateral organization of the Sekani allowed maximum individual choice in the exploitation of a difficult environment. A boy learned to hunt in the territory of his parents. When he married, he lived and hunted with his wife's family until the birth of the first child, or longer, thus becoming familiar with another territory if this was outside his own.

Jenness (1937:11) recorded the names and ranges of four regional bands of the early nineteenth century as recalled in 1924 by the Sekani of Forts Grahame and McLeod. First, the Tsekani inhabited the region from McLeod Lake south to the height of land and east to

433

the edge of the prairies. The "Big Men" of the McLeod Lake area, as designated by Fraser (1960:165 passim) in 1806, could have been this group, the Yutuwichan, or both. Second, the Yutuwichan exploited the region from the north end of McLeod Lake down the Parsnip River to Rocky Mountain canyon on the east and westward to the upper Salmon of the Fraser drainage, and to Carp Lake and the headwaters of the Manson and Nation tributaries of the Parsnip. Third, the Sasuchan were in the basin of the Finlay River from the mouth of the Omineca north and west; Bear and Thutade lakes were in their range. Fourth, the Tseloni occupied the plateau country between the headwaters of the Finlay and the Liard rivers; the upper Fox and Kechika rivers flowed through the center of their country. Most of the Tseloni and Sasuchan amalgamated when Fort Grahame was established in the 1890s; so also with the Yutuwichan and Tsekani, who came to occupy a single village at McLeod Lake.

Besides these four regional bands recalled by the Sekani as being in existence in the early 1800s, two groups occupying other ranges have been recorded for that period. The Meadow Indians of 1806, as identified and located by Fraser (1960:164–165, 175–176), inhabited the upper reaches of the Halfway River. However, Jenness (1937:7, 19) placed Meadow Indians as recalled by the Sekani in the 1920s in a more southerly range that included the Pine and upper Smoky rivers. The Baucanne or Says-thau-dennehs were so designated by Fraser (1960:220) in 1806 from an Indian's report that this group was on the upper Fraser River (or at the headwaters of the Smoky, according to Jenness 1937:7). They may have been the survivors of the Sekani band who, according to Shuswap tradition, were attacked and expelled from the lands of the North Thompson Shuswap (Teit 1909a:524–525, 546–548).

Two new socioterritorially discrete bands emerged around the turn of the twentieth century. The T'lotona or "Long Grass Indians" were a group formed of Sasuchan Sekani intermarried with Gitksan; they occupied the Groundhog country, the grassy plateau region of the upper Stikine and Skeena, at the end of the nineteenth century (Jenness 1937:12–15, 18). This was former Tahltan country; in 1826 its Tahltan inhabitants, the Thloadenni, were contacted by Samuel Black through friendly Sekani intermediaries. "Davie's band," designated Otzane, formed in the early 1900s around the son of a French Canadian trapper and a Sasuchan mother; their range was the Fox and Kechika River area. Through marriage with a Tseloni woman, Davie gained hunting rights in the old Tseloni territory, his group taking "the name [Otzane] and territory of a kindred band that had recently dissolved" (Jenness 1937:14–15).

In sum, within the historic era, Sekani socioterritorial alignments have been marked variously by movement,

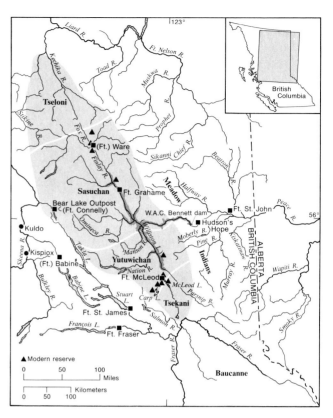

Fig. 1. Tribal territory with regional bands in the early 19th century.

splitting, amalgamation, and regroupings as well as by intermarriage with other tribes.

The size of regional bands apparently varied depending on the resources of their areas. When Fraser (1960:178) brought together all the "Meadow Indians" or "Les Gens du large" in the vicinity of Rocky Mountain Portage (near modern Hudson Hope) in 1806, he counted 44 men, 30 women, and 79 children. These were said to have belonged to one band. According to Fraser (1960:175), their territory was somewhere around the upper reaches of Halfway River, that is, the eastern foothills of the Rocky Mountains north of Peace River. At the time of his account they were being forced westward into the mountains by the Beaver Indians. Another regional band present at the same post would, Fraser (1960:178) estimated, bring the total population of the two groups to "about 60 men, 40 women, and upwards of 100 boys, girls, and children." The second band, said to be relations and allies of the Meadow Indians, gave information concerning the Finlay River and its headwaters and even Bear Lake (Fraser 1960:170). It is possible that they were members of the northernmost regional band of Sekani, the people described in some detail by Black (1955) in 1824.

In 1793 Mackenzie (1970:287) came upon three families (three men, three women, and seven or eight children) near Table River along the upper Parsnip River. These people told him that their group (most likely the regional band called Big Men by Fraser and Tsekani by Jenness) numbered no more than 10 families (perhaps 50 individuals).

According to Black (1955:51, 101–114, 189), in 1824 the sole inhabitants of the upper Finlay beyond the Big Bend, exploiting the headwater tributaries of the Liard River and the plateau country of the Finlay-Stikine-Liard divide, were members of a regional band led by one old man. This band consisted of seven married men, "about as many young men," and an unspecified number of women and children, perhaps about 40 in all (Black 1955:51). These people were in the country of the Tseloni, as identified in later times. When Black was with this northernmost band he learned of two families of Sekani who were possibly then at Bear Lake. In 1828 Simpson (1947:23) noted that Bear Lake (where Fort Connelly was established about 1826) was frequented by about 30 Sekani men who hunted in the mountain territory of the Finlay headwaters. This figure (which by extension must imply at least 100 or so men, women, and children) probably included at least two regional bands, perhaps the Sasuchan as well as the Tseloni, as identified by Jenness's (1937:11) informants. Members of other groups might also have been included.

Permanent or even semipermanent settlements were unknown in early contact times, with the exception of villages of Sekani groups who had moved into salmon-producing areas. In 1810 Harmon (1957:135) recorded the population of a Sekani village in Carrier territory on Fraser Lake at about 90 individuals, about twice the size of any of the mountain bands so far noted. Clearly, the salmon of the Pacific drainage lake enabled the concentration of larger and more stable populations than was possible in Sekani territory proper. Two years later, Harmon (1957:148) identified another village of "mostly Sicannies" in the Pacific drainage near Tachy in the Stuart Lake area but gave no population estimate. The total population of the Sekani in the areas drained by the Finlay and Parsnip rivers was probably no more than 200 in the early nineteenth century. The inclusion of groups located in the eastern foothills of the Rocky Mountains and the inhabitants of villages in Pacific drainage areas probably would double or triple this estimate.

External Relations

In the early nineteenth century, relations with peoples east of the Rocky Mountains were predominantly hostile. The most feared enemies were the Beaver and the Cree. Both of these peoples had access to firearms, putting the Sekani, armed only with traditional weapons, at a great disadvantage. Sekani who in earlier times had wintered east of the mountains were forced to relinquish large portions of their former range and to

remain year round in the mountains where resources were limited. In this same period Iroquois hunters and trappers came in limited numbers into the upper Fraser River and Finlay River country, further depleting the area.

To the south were the Shuswap. Again, relations were mostly hostile. Teit (1909a:547) recorded evidence among the North Thompson Shuswap of the virtual annihilation of a large group of Sekani who had moved into their territory on the upper Fraser and even the upper Thompson River. In 1793 Mackenzie (1970:318) encountered a Sekani woman enslaved by the Shuswap who gave him a similar account. The period of active encroachment and warfare was thought to be about 1780 to 1790.

Most contact to the west, across the Arctic-Pacific divide, was with various Carrier groups. Sekani of the Parsnip and Finlay basins, probably of the Sasuchan band, often visited the Bulkley Carrier at the north end of Babine Lake in the nineteenth century and probably earlier (Jenness 1943:481). The Yutuwichan band visited, traded, and intermarried with the Carrier of Stuart and Fraser lakes and were much influenced by them (Harmon 1957:257). The Tsekani band probably had dealings primarily with the Carrier of the upper Fraser.

Although relations between Carrier and Sekani were, on the whole, friendly, the two peoples looked down on each other; sometimes there were bloody quarrels between them. Certain Sekani bands had predominantly hostile relations with certain Carrier groups, for example, the "Baucannes" of Fraser (1960:220) with the Stuart Lake Carrier (also Jenness 1937:19).

The European items traded by the Carrier for furs and other products of Sekani hunts were for the most part obtained from the Pacific coast. One major route of these trade goods was from the Tsimshian up the Skeena River to the Gitksan to the Carrier of the Bulkley River area to the Sasuchan Sekani. About 1850, the Tsimshian tried to eliminate the middlemen by ascending the Skeena nearly to its junction with the Bulkley. After Fort Connelly or Bear Lake Post was established for the Sekani about 1826, the Sasuchan Sekani met there not only the Carrier but also the Gitksan villagers of Kispiox, Kiskargas, and Kuldo. Although there was some intermarriage, relations between Sekani and Gitksan were mostly hostile. After about 1840 relations improved and the T'lotona band of mixed Sasuchan Sekani and Gitksan was formed (Jenness 1937:12–15, 18).

To the north and northwest the Sekani met only members of groups of poor and scattered hunters who, like most of themselves, had no access to salmon and only indirect contact with the coast. In 1824 the northernmost band of Sekani met in friendship with the "Thloadennis" (evidently the southeasternmost Tahltan band) in the headwater country of the upper Stikine

435

(Black 1955:51, 107–115). The Sekani said that the previous year they had traded part of their hunt to the Thloadennis in exchange for powder and small balls. These trade goods came ultimately from the Russian-American Company at Sitka. The Thloadennis had gotten them from the "Trading Nahannies" who came up the river from the "Taodennis Doadennis" (Tlingits) who got them from the Whites.

Relations in early times between the northern Sekani and the Kaska farther to the north and northwest are unclear, due to uncertainty as to the boundary between the groups and the problem of distinguishing Kaska from other peoples designated Nahani. The "Meadow Indians" told Fraser (1960:176) of frequent contact with "Nakanés," probably Kaska, of the Liard drainage in the country beyond the upper reaches of Halfway River. Jenness (1937:19) reported that his Sekani informants "remember no conflicts with the Tahltan or Kaska Indians."

Culture

Subsistence

At the time of earliest White contact the Sekani were primarily hunters; fishing also was important. Major food mammals were moose and caribou, mountain sheep and mountain goats (in certain areas), bears, beaver, whistlers or marmots, hares, and porcupines. At least in the late eighteenth and early nineteenth centuries, bison, wapiti, and moose were hunted in the foothills and prairies east of the Rockies by at least some Sekani. Significantly, the Sekani word for the lunar month of midsummer meant "the buffalo ruts" (Morice 1895:106). With the coming of White traders, fur animals increased in value; far more time was spent in winter and early spring obtaining furs than previously had been the case. Beavers soon were threatened with extinction (Morice 1890:131).

Most streams in Sekani lands were Arctic drainage streams, devoid of salmon; the fish available to the Sekani were largely whitefish, trout, and suckers. Even in Jenness's time (1932:379) the Sekani retained "the scorn of true hunters for fishermen," but it must be noted that at every opportunity, it seems, groups of Sekani moved into salmon country and exploited this relatively rich resource. This was the case at Bear Lake, the northern end of Takla Lake, and near the Carrier on Stuart Lake. Conflict with the Shuswap in the late eighteenth century was occasioned by Sekani encroachment on Shuswap fishing grounds (Teit 1909a:524, 542, 546–548).

In Jenness's (1937:2) characterization: "The Sekani generally spent the period from about November until mid-summer on the plateaux and mountain slopes running down the caribou and moose on the snow, and when the snow had melted driving them into snares and trapping groundhogs. About mid-summer they resorted to the lakes to fish, or visited the various tribes beyond their borders." According to Black in 1824, the Sekani of Rocky Mountain Portage usually wintered in the plains on either side of the fort along the foot of the mountains. In March, on the snow crust, they began their wanderings in the mountains and in fall returned again to the plains. On the other hand, the northernmost Sekani band often chose to winter in the mountains. In the winter the Sekani who remained in the mountains, whether by choice or necessity, often scarcely survived, moving constantly in search of game (Black 1955:188).

Technology

Deadfalls and snares were of primary importance. Many of these devices were ingenious and were specifically designed for particular species. Deadfalls were used for marmots, small furbearers, lynx, and bears. Forty or 50 snares were often set in a line in passes and caribou driven into them, and many grouse were snared simultaneously by using snares set in brush fences. Snares were also used to take mountain sheep and goats, bears, lynx, marmots, hares, and even waterfowl (Morice 1895:95–104). Beavers were taken in spring and summer with the aid of castoreum lure and in winter were caught in babiche nets set in holes cut into the ice near a lodge (Morice 1895:66–67).

Other hunting methods used by the Sekani involved stalking and killing animals with bows and various types of arrows, some designed for specific kinds of mammals or birds. The longbow described by Mackenzie (1970:290) for Parsnip River Sekani was six feet long with a short iron spike at one end. Morice (1895:58–59) described a sinew-reinforced bow, the sinew fastened with "sturgeon glue." Spears of different sorts were used as well, a stone-headed lance for bears and a barbed bone toggled spear for beaver. For fishing there were three-pronged leisters, hooks, and gaff hooks, as well as gill nets and weirs.

In warfare, bows and arrows and spears, moose jaw clubs, and "skull crackers" or "temple lancets" were used; so, too, was the bayonet on the end of the long-bow (Morice 1895:60–62). There was a tradition among the McLeod Lake Sekani of an oblong wooden shield coated on the outside with pitch and pebbles (Jenness 1937:37).

Dried meat prepared in summer for winter use was stored on platforms atop posts or erected against trees and covered over with spruce bark or hides. Cooking was done by dropping red hot stones into watertight kettles of woven spruce roots. Also, bark vessels were used over direct heat out of reach of the flames. Meat and fish were also roasted on spits or smoke-dried.

Dishes and vessels were made of bark and wood, bags of leather and leather netting, and spoons of horn and wood. Some scrapers were made of bone and of split cobbles, one end chipped, hafted in a cleft stick. Beaver-tooth knives were used, as were other knives and adzes of chipped stone until they were replaced by iron tools.

Transportation

Travel was primarily by foot; possessions were carried on backs. Traditionally, dogs were not used as pack animals, and toboggans came into use only in modern times. Unlike their neighbors to the west, the Sekani made use of snowshoes; these were indispensable for winter and early spring hunting. Spruce bark canoes were used in the summer along major rivers and in other spots for crossing streams. Crude cottonwood dugouts (fig. 2) were made in postcontact times, on the model of Carrier and Gitksan craft.

Structures

In early times, the winter shelters of the Sekani were conical lodges covered with spruce bark. Later, moose skins often were substituted, sometimes lined around the perimeter with horizontal bundles of spruce branches (Morice 1895:192–193). The conical tent sometimes was used in summer, but more usual shelters were lean-tos or crude conical windbreaks covered with spruce-bark, hides, or boughs. On the windbreaks the sheath-ing extended no more than four or five feet up the sides; the top was left open. By 1924 most of the Sekani occupied cloth tents in summer, and several log or frame houses were in use at the trading posts (Jenness 1937:32–34).

Clothing

Aboriginally, basic items of dress for both sexes consisted of moccasins and leggings of dressed moose or caribou skin, topped by a sleeveless shirt, also commonly of moose or caribou hide although furred pelts, sewn together, of small animals might be used. In cold weather a rectangular robe of marmot or hare skins, fastened on one shoulder and cinched with a belt, was added, as were furred caps.

Life Cycle

In the old days, according to Jenness's (1937:54–55) informants in 1924, a woman in labor camped away from her husband so that he would not have bad luck in hunting. She knelt, sometimes with the help of a female relative, supporting herself with a stick. The umbilical cord was cut with a sharp stone and the placenta hidden in a tree. There was no abortion or infanticide reported. A baby received a name soon after birth from the father or from a man known to have many dream guardians. Babies were carried everywhere on their mothers' backs and nursed for about three years.

left, B.C. Prov. Mus., Victoria: PN 3376; right, Natl. Mus. of Canada, Ottawa: 60664.

Fig. 2. Cottonwood dugout canoes. Sekani, but of a type made by the Carrier and Gitksan (Jenness 1937:42). left, Members of the McLeod Lake band in a canoe on the Crooked River about 1912; photographer unknown. right, Beached canoe on McLeod Lake; photograph by Diamond Jenness, May 1924.

Fig. 3. A rectangular shelter with pole framework; roof and lower walls covered with spruce bark; a log cabin is at right (Jenness 1937:33–34). Photograph by Diamond Jenness at McLeod Lake, June 1924.

When a boy approached puberty he was sent into the woods to seek a vision and spiritual help, which would give him good hunting medicine (Jenness 1937:55–56, 61). Food taboos were observed and special items of adornment worn in order to assure his development into a proper hunter.

During menstruation, girls and women had to camp apart in small brush huts, drinking from special cups and eating dried meat or dried fish. These and other taboos served the same purpose: to prevent any contact, physical or spiritual, between menstruating women and men or the animals they hunted; such contact would ruin the hunt.

Marriage was prohibited between close relatives on either side. Polygyny was not uncommon and frequently took the form of marriage with two sisters. If a wife died, her husband could marry her sister if he so chose; the sister could not refuse. When a man wanted to marry a woman he simply asked her, usually after consulting with his father. If her parents approved the woman set up a brush tent near the residence of her parents, and the man moved in with her. For a year or longer he was obligated to hunt for her father. He was free from this obligation with the birth of the first child. Divorce was a simple matter of separation, at the will of either partner, but it seldom took place if there were children.

In the early nineteenth century the Sekani around Fort McLeod cremated their dead, while those living east of the Rocky Mountains buried them. Harmon (1957:148) described cremation at a village near Stuart Lake. Later, the practice of burning the dead was discontinued; older customs were revived or continued. The dead were covered with the brush shelters in which they had lived their last days, and the localities were deserted for a time. Influential persons were placed in coffins of hollowed logs and raised on platforms or in trees; some were enclosed in the natural hollows of standing trees. In the late nineteenth century Christian burials in the ground became the rule (Jenness 1937:59).

In imitation of the Carrier, McLeod Lake Sekani women sometimes carried the crushed remains of their husbands' cremated bodies in bags suspended from their necks. The eldest son or a near relative gave a feast for the entire band six months to a year after his father's death. This practice might have been borrowed from the Carrier. Both widows and widowers could remarry at will; there was no prescribed period of mourning. The T'lotona band's feast in memory of the dead was tied to the phratry system, which was borrowed from the Gitksan and Tahltan. For all Sekani groups, mourning was expressed by loud piercing wails. This was true even in 1924, when Jenness observed it. The wailing took place generally at dawn or dusk, and the daily mourning sometimes continued for months or even years after the death of a loved one (Jenness 1937:59–60, 62).

Social Organization

Sekani social organization was originally bilateral. When Sekani began to intermarry and have other close contact with the Gitksan and Carrier to their west, however, they tried to organize themselves into exogamous matrilineal phratries; they even began to hold potlatches, though on a scale much reduced from the extravagant feasts of their neighbors. The two McLeod Lake bands, Tsekani and Yutuwichan, imitated the Carrier of Stuart Lake; the Sasuchan band of Bear Lake and the Finlay River basin copied the Carrier and the

Fig. 4. Women and children at Ft. Grahame, B.C.; 4 wear moccasins, and the 2 women at right wear Assomption sashes. Photograph by Diamond Jenness, June 1924.

Gitksan who also frequented Fort Connelly; and the T'lotona band derived their phratry system from the Tahltan and Gitksan.

In the course of recorded history, the phratry system as it was established among different groups of Sekani broke down several times and later was tried again. When Jenness visited the Sekani in 1924, phratries recently had been revived among the Finlay River Sekani due to renewed contacts with the Carrier and Gitksan around Babine Lake and River. Crests and potlatches were a part of this system. Phratries were exogamous, and members of one phratry were buried by those of one of the others. For the most part, the system functioned primarily during the summer months, and even then mostly to facilitate dealings with groups in which phratries were more important (Jenness 1937:46–50).

Beliefs

There was a pervasive belief among the Sekani that man and the animal world were linked by a mystic bond, and that animals possessed special powers that they could grant a seeker. The powers resided not in individual animals but in the species as a whole and were transmitted to individuals through dreams and visions. "Hunting medicine" was sought in quests, especially at puberty, which involved fasting and dreaming in solitude in the wilderness. Hunting medicine was very specific; it was useful only for particular animals or in special situations. It often was associated with songs and amulets, taught or specified by the spirit helper (Jenness 1937:67–71).

Sickness was believed to be caused by the wandering away of a soul, a shaman's machinations, or the breaking of a taboo associated with medicine power (Jenness 1937:72–79). Shamans were called upon and paid for their help in treating illness. A shaman sometimes entered a sweathouse where the cause of the sickness was revealed to him. He then treated the patient by catching and restoring his soul, or magically extracting a bone or other object from him (implanted by an unfriendly shaman). The treatment characteristically entailed singing, rubbing the patient with an amulet, breathing on him, massaging him, or sucking out objects. A shaman's medicine powers were obtained through dreams and given by animal spirit helpers. They were thought to be inherited mystically from some ancestor. It was possible for a great shaman to transfer some of his powers to a son. Women could not become professional healers, but they could become dreamers; they might, for example, gain the power to foretell the future. A violent form of hysteria, sometimes resulting in complete dementia, occurred among the Sekani. This hysteria was thought to be caused by the land-otter, who was able to take on human form. It sometimes could be cured by shamans.

The concept of monotheism was first introduced by White traders in the early nineteenth century; Iroquois and other Indians in the service of the traders helped to spread Christianity. A messianic cult, a distortion of missionary teachings in Oregon, arose and spread up the Fraser River through the Shuswap to the Carrier and Gitksan and from there to the Sekani about 1830. The cult involved trance and "death," a stay with God, and the return to the living with Christian influenced teachings and songs. Revivals of similar cults were reported about 1870 to 1880 and in the early twentieth century. The messianic cults appear to have been modifications of the older belief in spirit helpers, the helpers being replaced by the God of Christianity (Jenness 1937:64–67). About 1870 the Roman Catholic Oblate order began intensive missionary work in the area. Jenness reported that Sekani were, in 1924, faithful Roman Catholics.

History of Sekani-White Contact

In 1793 Mackenzie (1970) traveled through the territory of the southern Sekani on the Parsnip River and met people who had never seen Whites before. A few years later, in 1805, after preliminary explorations by John Finlay and James McDougall, Simon Fraser (1960:16–23) established two posts for the North West Company: Rocky Mountain Portage near Hudson Hope and Trout Lake (later Fort McLeod). In 1806 he established two more in Carrier lands: Nakazleh or Fort Saint James on Stuart Lake and Natleh or Fort Fraser on Fraser Lake. In 1807 Fort George was built at the mouth of the Nechako. In 1824 Samuel Black (1955) explored the Finlay River to the lakes at its source and the country to the northwest. In 1826 or 1827 Fort Connelly was established on Bear Lake for the northern Sekani as well as some Carriers and Gitksans, and in 1829 the old Fort Halkett was founded in Liard headwaters flowing into Fort Nelson River; its exact location is uncertain. In 1833 it was moved to the confluence of the Smith and Liard, outside Sekani territory (Hudson's Bay Company 1829–1830b). Some of the trading posts used by Sekani at various times were: Dunvegan, Fort Saint

Natl. Mus. of Canada, Ottawa: VI–M–1.
Fig. 5. Beaded belt. Red, blue, white, yellow, pink, purple, and green beads couched on cotton print backed with moosehide; the metal clasp bears the Hudson's Bay Company insignia. Length 1 m, collected at Ft. Grahame, B.C., before 1925.

John or Saint John's House, Fort d'Epinette, Rocky Mountain House, Rocky Mountain Portage, Trout Lake or Fort McLeod, the Carrier posts of Fort Saint James, Fort Fraser, Fort George, and Fort Kilmars, Bear Lake or Fort Connelly, Old and New Fort Halkett, Fort Grahame or Bear Lake Post, Fort Ware, and Finlay Forks or McDougall's posts in Kaska and Tahltan territories in later times.

In 1846 at Jasper House, a traveling artist, Paul Kane, painted what may be the first depiction of a Sekani (fig. 6).

The Omineca gold rush in the western Sekani range began in 1861 (Patterson 1968:68). Ten years later, at least 1,200 Whites were reported in the area, cutting trails, trapping Sekani lands, and building towns. By 1916 most of the Whites had left, but the damage was done: the total population of Sekani was reported as 70 in 1916 (Lamers 1976:13–18). It is likely that many Sekani had moved out of their own territory during the height of the gold rush. About 1917, Davie's band or Otzane, as they were called, moved into the Fox and Kechika area from Lower Post, in Kaska territory (Jenness 1937:14; Lamers 1976:18). This group, of mixed background and complicated history, became the Fort Ware band. In the 1960s the W.A.C. Bennett Dam created an enormous artificial lake, Williston Lake, separating some Sekani groups from others with whom they previously had contact.

Population

The size of the Sekani population is difficult to estimate, even in 1980, because of the way census figures are recorded. Canadian Indian groups are named according to the post or settlement with which they are affiliated. Department of Indian Affairs records only list "status" Indians, that is, those who are considered Indian under the terms of the Indian Act and are registered members of a band (Elizabeth Snider, personal communication 1975). Thus, Sekani in the minority at any particular post would not be distinguished, nor would non-Sekani at predominantly Sekani posts. Métis or nonstatus Indians are not counted.

Earlier, precensus figures probably are highly inaccurate, especially in the first part of the nineteenth century. Morice (1890:112) estimated no more than 250 Sekani in British Columbia at the time of his stay there. A census made by the Department of Indian Affairs in 1923 gave the total Sekani population as 160, 61 around Fort McLeod and 99 around Fort Grahame (Jenness 1937:13). In 1924, when Jenness (1937:13) visited the Sekani, there were 36 adults, of whom 25 were of pure Sekani origin, near Fort McLeod and 25 (or 21—Jenness's counts do not match) adults, of whom 16 were pure Sekani, at Fort Grahame. In 1934, the Canadian government reported 76 Sekanis at Fort Con-

nelly, 133 at Fort Grahame, and 81 at McLeod Lake, for a total of 290 (Canada. Department of Indian Affairs 1934:34–35). Although not exact, government census figures indicate an increasing population, from 336 to 523, between the years 1949 and 1973; the figure for 1978 was 586 (Canada. Department of Indian Affairs and Northern Development 1980:38–41).

Synonymy†

The name Sekani was established in this form by Hodge (1910n:498–499) and used by Jenness (1931, 1937) and Osgood (1936:16). It is based on their name for themselves, recorded as tθhéek'ehneh, and variants (Harrington 1939), and Tsé-'kéh-ne (Morice 1895:28); the meaning is 'people on the rocks', that is, 'people on the mountains'. Jenness (1937:5) suggested that the earliest form of this name in English might be Cigne, frequently mentioned in the Journal of the Rocky Mountain Fort in the winter of 1799–1800 (O'Neil 1928:260), but this may be just a French nickname (*cygne* 'swan') for a local Indian leader. In any case the references by Mackenzie (1970:316, 318, 319) to "Rocky-Mountain Indians" near Rocky Mountain Portage and along the Parsnip River in 1793 could reflect a translation of the name Sekani, probably from the Beaver equivalent.

Fraser (1960) referred to various groups as "Big Men," "Meadow Indians," "relations of the Meadow Indians but of a different tribe," and "Baucannes" or "Says-thau Dennehs" but did not unify them under a single tribal designation. Jenness (1937:5) believed that Harmon (1957:130, 131, 160, 199) was the first to use the term Sicannies (sg. Sicanny) and Sicaunies for the entire people in 1810. He thought that Harmon had used the name of the band nearest the first post at McLeod Lake as a name for all Sekani. At any rate, the name came into general use in the first quarter of the nineteenth century. By 1824, Black (1955) was using Thecannies as a general term that included even the northernmost band, as were these band members themselves, at least when speaking to Black.

Additional variants of the name include: Secunnie (Hale 1846:202); Tsitka-ni (Richardson 1852:260), Siccany and Siccanies (Pope 1866:28); Thikanies (Hardisty 1872:311); Chicanee (McDonald 1872); Seccanies (Simpson 1947); Tsekanies (McLean 1932:141); French Sékanais and Athapaskan Thè-kka-nè 'those who dwell on the mountain' (Petitot 1876:xx); Sikani and Siccanie (Dawson 1881:30B, 45B, 1889:192B, 200B); "Tsekenné more commonly called Sékanais" (Morice 1890:112); Siccannies (Canada. Department of Indian Affairs 1930:47). Minor variants are listed in Hodge (1910n:499).

† This synonymy was written by Glenda Denniston and Ives Goddard.

The Carriers call the Sekani ƚtaiˀən (Antoine et al. 1974:145), said to mean 'people of the beaver dams' (Morice 1895:29). This was rendered Al-taˊ-tin by Dawson (1889:192B, 200B).

Sources

The main sources of information concerning the period of early Sekani-White contact are the records and journals of traders and explorers of the North West Company and the Hudson's Bay Company. Notable among these are Alexander Mackenzie's journal of 1792–1793 (1970), Simon Fraser's of 1806–1808 (1960), Daniel Harmon's of 1800–1816 (1957), and Samuel Black's of 1824 (1955). By their very nature, trading records have only spotty ethnographic information. Most early information is in the form of reports of brief sightings of new Indians, attempts to monitor families' contributions of furs, and hearsay information concerning groups farther from trading posts. Black's account is somewhat more informative, as he traveled for a number of weeks with members of one band.

In the late 1800s Roman Catholic missionaries began to remain for extended periods among Indians of interior British Columbia. Morice (1895), missionary to the Carrier, recorded much valuable information about them and their Sekani neighbors as well. The main

work on the Sekani after Morice was done by Jenness (1931, 1937) in 1924. Unless otherwise indicated, data in this chapter are usually derived from Jenness.

Fig. 6. *A-Chis-a-lay, The Call of the Wind*, identified by the artist in his portrait log kept on an 1846–1848 journey as a member of "The As-ick-an-a tribe from Peace River" (Kane 1971:315), which would make the subject a Sekani. However, the portrait was made at Jasper House on the Upper Athabasca River, southeast of the usual Sekani range, and Kane confused his "As-ick-an-a tribe" with Alexander Mackenzie's "Carriers," so there is some doubt on the subject's tribal identification. Watercolor by Paul Kane, possibly Nov. 5, 1846.

Kaska

JOHN J. HONIGMANN

Language and Territory

The Kaska ('kăsku) Indians of northern British Columbia and the southern Yukon are affiliated culturally with the northern Athapaskans of the Mackenzie drainage subarea (Osgood 1936a). However, with moieties named Wolf and Crow, potlatching, animal masks, and a few other traits, they share some cultural attributes with the Athapaskans of the Pacific drainage and with the Northwest Coast culture area. The Kaska are closely related linguistically to the Tahltan and the Tagish, and in fact the three or four Kaska dialects,* Tahltan, and Tagish may all be considered varieties of a single language ("Northern Athapaskan Languages," this vol.).

The accounts on which this chapter is based (Honigmann 1947a, 1949, 1954; Honigmann and Honigmann 1945) largely pertain to two Kaska divisions, the Upper Liard Indians living northwest of Lower Post and, in less detail, the Dease River people who are adjacent to the Tahltan Indians (fig. 1). Little ethnographic information is available concerning the Frances Lake Indians on the upper reaches of the Frances River and around Frances Lake and the Nelson Indians (Tselona), east of Lower Post on the Liard and Kechika rivers, who sometimes crossed the Rocky Mountains to trade at Fort Nelson, where they are known as "Grand Lakers" (Honigmann 1946:72, 1954:19).

Kroeber (1939:141) overstated the aboriginal Kaska population at 500. According to the December 31, 1970, list of "Registered Indians" belonging to Band 24 of Agency 991 Yukon, the Kaska group comprised 281 males and 258 females or a total of 539 persons, not all of whom resided locally. The first Indian Affairs Branch enumeration of 1914 counted 238 persons in

the agency; the figure rose to 323 in 1934, but 10 years later inexplicably dropped to 175.

History of Indian-White Contact

Continuous contact for the Kaska Indians began in the 1820s at the Hudson's Bay Company post of Fort Halkett on the Liard River (Honigmann 1949). In 1838 a trading post opened on Dease Lake but survived only three years. Another post started operating on Frances Lake in 1843 but closed in 1851 to be briefly reinstituted in 1880. In 1873 gold seekers in large numbers penetrated the Cassiar, as the territory of the Kaska Indians is called, and they came again in 1897–1898 when the country became a route to the Klondike goldfields. White trappers and several trading companies have been in the area since the end of the nineteenth century. Intensive contact with White miners and trappers no doubt accounts for the fact that in 1944–1945 ethnographic fieldwork could be conducted in English, a lan-

Fig. 1. Nineteenth-century territory with regional bands: 1, Frances Lake; 2, Upper Liard; 3, Dease River; 4, Nelson Indians (Tselona).

---

*The phonemes of the Dease Lake and Lower Post dialects of Kaska are: (unaspirated stops and affricates) b, d, λ, δ̂, ʒ, ž̦, g, ʔ; (aspirated stops and affricates) t, λ, θ̂, c, č, k; (glottalized) ț, λ̦, θ̦̂, č̦, č̦, k̦; (voiceless continuants) ł, θ, s, š, x, h; (voiced continuants) l, δ, z, ž, γ; (nasals) m, n; (resonant) y; (short vowels) i, e, a, u; (long vowels) i·, e·, a·, u·; (tones) high (v́), low (unmarked).

Information on Kaska phonology was furnished by Victor Golla (communication to editors 1979), on the basis of unpublished field notes collected by George W. Tharp and Eung-Do Cook in 1971.

None of the Kaska words cited in the *Handbook* was available in phonemic transcription, and they therefore appear here in the phonetically imprecise spellings of the sources.

442

guage spoken in a characteristic style by almost all Kaska (Darnell 1970).

Protestant and Roman Catholic missionaries visited the Kaska Indians prior to 1926, the year when the Catholic Oblate Father E. Allard established a mission at McDame Creek on Dease River. From a secular point of view, more momentous events took place with the building of the Alaska Highway in 1942. The road passed within a few hundred yards of the riverbank settlement of Lower Post, opening that settlement to frequent visits by construction workers, military men, and police. New buildings went up along the road, and many activities shifted toward the highway, along which flowed the merchandise that had formerly arrived by river from Dease Lake and Wrangell, Alaska. Upper Liard and Nelson Indians, too, began to use the highway for travel to and from their winter trapping grounds. Casual sexual contacts and illegal drinking appear to have increased during the war years as a direct result of increased contact with non-Indian strangers whom the highway brought to Lower Post.

Culture

Technology

Pecked and polished, close-grained stone; flaked siliceous rock; bone, antler, and horn were the materials used for tools in precontact times. The lithic implements included axes, knives, hafted scrapers, and crude pestles that were used to crack marrow bones. Multipurpose knives varied in size depending on their intended use, and they were usually hafted with a mountain goat's horn. Bone provided material for knives, scrapers, awls, eating utensils, needles, and arrow points. Other implements were made from the horn of Dall sheep, mountain goats, and woodland caribou.

Objects of wood and bark also played important roles in daily living; but with only bone and stone tools at hand, cutting down trees and making planks was an arduous task. Easily available, spruce wood was the variety most frequently used. Bark, too, was used for a wide variety of objects ranging from canoes to drinking and storage vessels.

Using animal pelts the Indians sewed and plaited garments, sleeping robes, lines, and storage bags. Processing the pelts varied in accordance with the purpose for which the skin was intended. Fur-covered pelts required basically only fleshing, after which they were dried and perhaps stretched. Tanning moose and caribou hide constituted a more complex process involving scraping, treating with a mixture of water and brain, washing, drying, and smoking. Sinew, spruce roots, and willow bark were among other materials used to make cordage.

During postcontact times the White men's hardware, purchased in exchange for furs, became the primary technical basis of almost everything that a family made and did. In 1944, even the moderately well-equipped household shifting between Lower Post and its winter bush camp transported axes, snare wire, metal pots, kettles, a washtub, needles, scissors, knives, a carpenter's drill, nails, and other items. One complex technical routine that in the 1940s perpetuated aboriginal habits was skin tanning, the finished hide being largely used in making moccasins and mittens. Baking soda was sometimes added to the brain mixture in which moose and caribou skins were soaked for tanning. From semitanned skin women made babiche, used in netting snowshoes, and they also preserved sinew for sewing moccasins.

Subsistence and the Annual Round

In precontact times the Kaska secured food through gathering, trapping, hunting, and fishing. Women did the principal collecting, chiefly berries, including the soapberry, high- and lowbush cranberry, salmonberry, raspberry, strawberry, currant, and blueberry. Other vegetables products sought were fern roots (in spring), lily bulbs, birch sap, mushrooms, muskeg apples, wild onions, rose petals, and wild rhubarb.

Wild game was secured with the least expenditure of energy by setting traps in the form of snares, deadfalls, nets, and perhaps pitfalls. In hunting, men employed bows and arrows, spears, gaff hooks, slings, and clubs. The atlatl is thought to have been used by the Dease River Kaska. Hunting techniques sometimes required hunters to wait in ambush for the game, while at other times they drove, tracked, or pursued the animals. In hunting caribou, herds were stampeded into corrals where hunters waited to fire arrows. Decoys brought birds within range to kill. The Upper Liard Kaska regarded game as the most attractive food, but fish constituted the dietary mainstay. Clubbing, angling, spearing, shooting with bows and arrows, netting, and trapping were employed to catch fish. Although strongly repulsed by the thought of eating human flesh, the Kaska, according to their oral history, practiced cannibalism in times of famine and ceremonially consumed the "belly fat" of a slain enemy.

Boiling provided the primary method of cooking, a hardened moose stomach often serving as a vessel supported over an open fire. In another boiling method, a covered vessel was placed in a pit lined with hot stones. Only on rare occasions did people consume raw meat or fat. For preservation they cut meat into strips and sun-dried them. A light pounding later softened the dried meat and readied it for storing in a skin bag. The simplest food cache found in the mountainous areas consisted of a spruce-lined hole in the ground covered with stones. Small quantities of meat were also cached on a pole that was then lashed to a tree.

Variations in the seasonal cycle brought about notable changes in the habits and conditions of the game animals. The Indians responded by altering their routines and moving their homes to take advantage of what the country offered. For example, in late summer, when game fattened, hunters and their families moved into the mountains to hunt goats, sheep, woodland caribou, and "gophers" and "groundhogs" (marmots). Women busied themselves drying meat and caching it for winter use, while men readied snowshoes, toboggans (fig. 2), and walking staves. As the cold season progressed, families gathered at a "fish lake" where they subsisted on fresh fish or dried meat fetched from autumn caches.

With the advent of fur trapping, the annual cycle came to involve two major shifts of residence. The following description is of activities in the decade of the 1940s. In spring, families left the trap lines, taking along furs that had accumulated since the men last visited the store prior to the breakup of the rivers and lakes. Traveling by water, the family came to the trading post settlement, sold the last of its furs, and proceeded to live on fish locally netted plus canned goods, potatoes, bacon, and other food purchased from the store with the winter's earnings. Smoked salmon occasionally brought down the Dease River from Tahltan country were a special summer treat. Young men might occasionally venture into the bush to hunt moose, but not often; the mosquitoes, which were not too obnoxious in the cleared space of the settlement, were much thicker in the enclosed forest and no one suffered them gladly. With autumn, the family started the slow trip back to the trap line, the boats heavily loaded with food supplies, soap, candles, gasoline, kerosene, ammunition, new traps, and household equipment. The group might stop for a week or so at a good fishing site. After the return to the winter settlement more fishing, moose hunting, and berry picking took place. People counted on fall hunting to provide meat for part of the winter. If little was brought in, the family would quickly exhaust its store food. Sometimes hunting was prolonged until it cut into the trapping season that legally began on November 1.

Compared to some other northern Canadian Indians, the Kaska of the 1940s ate a varied, modern diet, probably as another outcome of their intensive contact with Whites, but more immediately as a result of the profitability of trapping. Flour figured prominently in many meals and was often consumed in the form of bannock prepared with lard and baking powder.

Travel and Transportation

Food gathering in early times depended completely upon mobility, with modes of travel necessarily varying with the seasons. When snow lay on the ground and the waterways froze, toboggans and snowshoes aided movement, while during the summer months, travelers could use mooseskin boats, dugouts, bark canoes, or rafts. Toboggans were made from the exterior layers of a green tamarack or birch tree. Snowshoes had a wood frame. For trail breaking, a snowshoe about three and one-half feet long would suffice, while snowshoes as tall as the wearer were needed for hunting to support him on the surface of powdery snow.

By the 1940s, the gasoline engine mounted on a scow about 18 feet long had become an indispensable adjunct for travel to and from the winter settlements. Snowshoes and handmade toboggans or sleds drawn by from three to six tandem-hitched dogs were relied on to get around on the trap line and to make the several-days' journey to the trading post. Meat from spring and autumn hunts was packed out of the bush by people or in canvas packs (fig. 3) on the same dogs that were harnessed in winter. Once the Alaska Highway was finished, trucks rented from local White men came into use to transport winter outfits part way to winter settlements located on the upper Liard or toward Fort Nelson.

Structures

Traditional shelters varied in complexity from a sprucebush windbreak to a large dwelling capable of accommodating two or more families. The most common houses were the conical lodge (made from closely placed poles covered with sod or moss) and the A-shaped house, a composite structure made by placing two lean-tos together. Both types served as semipermanent winter dwellings. Simpler lean-tos provided temporary shelter, as did occasional snow houses. The Kaska built no ceremonial structures, and the only nonresidential building they made was the sudatory. To generate fire, a prerequisite for many technological operations, people used the strike-a-light method, tinder consisting of soft, dry grass or birchbark. In winter travelers carried fire in the form of glowing embers.

In the annual cycle that developed as an adaptation to fur trapping, the Kaska family alternated between occupying a log cabin located in the winter settlement and a wall tent, tent-frame, log cabin, or (just beginning in 1944) a frame house at the trading post settlement. Enroute, tents were pitched. Unfloored tents and other dwellings were carpeted with spruce boughs that were renewed approximately fortnightly. The simple furnishings of winter homes were homemade except for the stove. Winter settlements contained one or more caches, either of a simple platform or a walled type; located on posts about 10 feet high, they were reached via a ladder. No latrines were built, the bush near a dwelling serving as a toilet and dump.

444

Fig. 2. Shaping green planks of birch for a tobbogan on a bending frame made of the lower trunk and root of a spruce tree. After bending, the planks are held in position by lashing until they dry (Honigmann 1949:58, 72–74). Photographs by John J. Honigmann at Lower Post, B.C., 1944–1945.

Clothing and Adornment

Women formerly made all the clothing, tanned caribou skin being the principal material. Sewing was done with sinew line and bone needles. During the summer months, each sex wore a tanned skin breechcloth supported from an inner belt, a tailored coat with a girdle of tanned skin or woven porcupine quills, and trousers. In winter this basic wardrobe was retained with certain additions, such as a fur parka of caribou or sheep skins. Decoration of clothing consisted of porcupine quill embroidery, of the "hard pellets" obtained from the tripe of moose sewed on women's dresses, or of skin fringes sewed along the shoulders and bottom of men's parkas.

Body adornment included tattooing (done with a porcupine quill coated with charcoal that was drawn under the skin), nasal rings, ear plugs, labrets, and, for potlatch dancers and on ceremonial occasions, face painting. Normally people did not cut their hair or put it up in any other way than by braiding.

By the mid-1940s, men's clothing was of a casual, frontier type, suited to outdoor living: woolen shirts (with arm garters in some cases), woolen trousers, and purchased parkas or windbreakers. Young women had come to prefer slacks and even older women donned men's trousers for winter travel. Both sexes wore moccasins over which rubber overshoes were put when the ground was damp. Moccasins and mittens, made of moose or caribou hide, were the main apparel that women still made, and their embroidered decoration took more time than the cutting and sewing.

Recreation

The Indians prior to contact times enjoyed contests of strength and skill, including throwing, arrow shooting, wrestling, and racing. Games included blindman's buff, hide and seek, and in postcontact times, rope jumping and tug of war. The hand game took place in the summer, when a number of family bands gathered and the weather permitted players to assemble outdoors. Feasts marked several points in the life cycle, such as the birth of a child, the first game killed by a youth, and marriage. Potlatches commemorated a person's death.

Recreational patterns that in 1944–1945 aroused the strongest interest and widest participation were (in descending order of interest): home-brew drinking parties, summer dances enlivened with the music of fiddle and guitar ("Wabash Cannonball" was a popular tune), and the summer hand game. Dancing was by couples, though Tahltan visitors occasionally put on a square dance. The summer of 1945 saw two potlatches (reportedly the first since 1930). The first, described as a feast ("party") sponsored by the Wolf moiety, was actually organized by a man belonging to the Crow division aided by his Wolf daughters. It was to honor the man's married daughter who had died a few months before. Members of both moieties were served food.

445

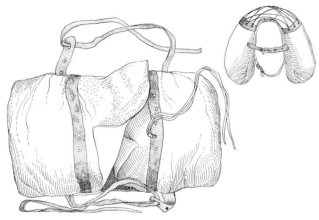

Fig. 3. Dog pack construction and use. This pack is made from a single piece of canvas folded at each end and sewed along the edges to form pockets. The central section between the pockets goes over the dog's back while the top flaps overlap to protect the pack contents. The moosehide strips, sewed along one edge at the top of each pocket, are perforated to take lashing across the dog's back (detail, bottom right). Leather lines attached lower down on the pockets run through the opposing perforated tabs, one under the dog's neck and the other under its body. Length of bottom left, 50 cm, collected by J.A. Teit at Cassiar, B.C., 1915. top, Women packing dogs. The dogs usually carry no more than 35 pounds for a walk of 20 miles (Honigmann 1949:45). Photograph by John J. Honigmann, Lower Post, B.C., 1944–1945.

A few weeks later a few members of the Crow moiety made a "return" potlatch. No gifts or tokens were exchanged in those affairs.

Family and Kin

Among the aboriginal Kaska, the nuclear or conjugal family was coresident with a larger, extended family. Typically, an extended family included a man, his wife, perhaps her sisters and their husbands, married daughters and their husbands, unmarried sons and daughters, and the unmarried children of the married daughters. The extended family often constituted the local band, though not all bands conformed to the matrilocal extended family type.

Kin terms collected from Upper Liard, Dease River, Tselona, and Frances Lake Kaska in 1944–1945 revealed several relatively common features linking the kin-term systems. Crow-type cousin terminology was a feature, except in the east, where Crow terms gave way to Iroquois terms. Bifurcate-merging terminology was manifested in the same term for mother and mother's sister. Such merging failed to appear among the Tselona. Bifurcate merging also appeared in common terms for son and brother's son and for daughter and brother's daughter; however, children of a sister were frequently distinguished from own and brother's children. Bifurcate merging also resulted in the same term for grandparents and parents-in-law, and in the frequency with which son's wife and granddaughter were classed together. Daughter's husband was consistently designated by a distinctive term. Mother's brother and sister's son frequently used a reciprocal kin term.

Rules of behavior formerly and to a large extent still observed in the 1940s between kinsmen included a tendency to warm, friendly symmetry between grandparents and grandchildren, warmth between a woman and her sister's children, circumspect behavior between siblings of opposite sex, strong reserve between a man and his mother-in-law, and a warm camaraderie between brothers-in-law. A man was freely allowed to tease his brother's wife, often by sexual allusions.

Households, the most important economic group in postcontact Kaska society, consisted in the 1940s primarily of the nuclear family, but occasionally contained an aged relative or related orphan children. Authority was ideally vested in the husband. In winter camps and during summer visits to the trading post, matrilateral extensions of the nuclear family might occur, but the extended family group was not a highly cohesive unit.

Social Organization

The local band—an extended family group including unrelated hangers-on and adopted children—was a segment of an unorganized and highly amorphous regional band designated by some feature of its territory. Only the local band recognized a headman, generally a family head. Local bands did not enjoy exclusive ownership rights to any territory. People felt free to hunt or fish anywhere within their own country, but generally they avoided regions known to be currently exploited by another family. The only areas owned exclusively by a family were beaver creeks. (It is not known if this was a development of the fur trade period.)

In the aboriginal culture, inheritance pertained to names as well as material goods. Following a man's death, half of his possessions went to his brother, while his children divided up the other half. The widow might be allocated a share of the goods that her brother-in-law received, but he retained permanent rights of possession. At the death of a wife, her goods went to her husband, who customarily gave all or most of it to his brother's wife.

The aboriginal community found itself compelled to deal with offenses like lying, assault, manslaughter, infanticide, murder, sorcery, incest, unwed motherhood, and adultery. In general, the major sanctions consisted in unfavorable public opinion, but for some serious offenses exile, indemnities, and blood revenge were also employed. No one individual or group held explicit authority to impose judgment or punishment on behalf of the total community.

War was motivated by group retaliation for offenses committed by strangers upon members of the community or by a desire to steal women. Since military revenge in turn promoted the desire for fresh vengeance by the opposite side, antagonism tended to be chronic. But large-scale aggression did not occur frequently, and the Kaska did not value fighting for its own sake. The office of war leader was distinct from that of band headman since several groups provided recruits for a military expedition. The expedition itself contained two divisions: one comprised young men about 19 or 20 years old who packed goods, and the other contained fully adult men who did the actual fighting.†

The majority of the Kaska belonged to one of two exogamous matri-moieties named Wolf and Crow. These groups prepared for burial bodies of persons belonging to the opposite group. Whatever the bonds of moiety membership may have been in the past, in 1944–1945 kinship sentiments were not extended to include members of one's moiety with whom meaningful genealogical links could not be traced. Nor did people acknowledge any kind of direct or mystical relationship to the eponymous crow and wolf. Nelson Indians were unaffiliated with unilinear descent groups but, upon marrying someone belonging to one, received a conventional moiety identification. Very slightly did individuals feel emotionally linked to their regional divisions, like the Upper Liard Indians or Dease River Indians, though they found those rubrics useful to identify themselves or their winter ranges. More significant was the sense of social identity that separated the Kaska from the Tahltan, despite some intermarriage with that tribe. The total Kaska "tribe" or community had a government-appointed chief, appointed probably in the 1930s, who exercised almost no manifest political role. Informal gossip and criticism were the most used means

† This description of well-organized warfare was obtained chiefly from one Upper Liard informant. It appears to be out of keeping with the looser organization of other behavior and does not conform to warfare among other Mackenzie drainage Athapaskan tribes. The pattern might be based on the informant's hearsay knowledge of fighting among the Tlingit.

of adult social control, though they were not often openly directed to the offending person.

Life Cycle

The pregnant woman formerly ate a diet of soft meat and intestines and was advised not to lift heavy weights. The only dietary restriction imposed on the father was with respect to kidneys. Due to the sense of pollution associated with birth, delivery took place in a windbreak located 10 or 15 feet from the dwelling, with assistance provided by the parturient's mother and sisters. A shaman intervened only if the birth became difficult. The afterbirth, wrapped in birchbark, was cached in a tree away from camp.

Parents did not neglect punishing a child to keep him from socially disapproved behavior. Discipline was ideally administered by the like-sexed parent, but in fact a mother always exerted more authority because of her constant interaction with her child. Physical punishment was never more severe than a light whipping inflicted with a willow switch.

Coinciding with the vision quest, which marked the completion of childhood, a boy began to train himself for hardihood and endurance by plunging into icy water and being whipped with willow switches. A competitive element accompanied these exercises; the youth who could stand the most gained a reputation of toughness. For girls, menstruation and the beginning of reproductive life brought accompanying taboos, including menstrual sequestration in an open camp away from the village. The menstruating woman also avoided stepping across snowshoes or bows and arrows for fear of causing bad hunting.

In earlier times, boys married around the age of 18, or when they were old enough to bear the responsibility of earning a living by hunting. Girls married at 16 or shortly thereafter, after menarche had occurred. Too great disparity in age between marital partners was regarded unfavorably. Blood relatives as close as parallel cousins of the second or third degree came under the incest taboo and so did anyone belonging to the same matrilineal moiety. Cross-cousins, on the other hand, were preferred as spouses among the Dease River people and Tselona, and marriage by exchange of sisters also occurred. A period of bride service, involving matrilocal residence and sometimes lasting two years, initiated a marriage. Later, after two or three children had been born, a husband might ask his father-in-law for permission to camp by himself. Though ideally marriages were permanent, and a person who wanted to leave a spouse would be urged by others to reconsider, actually divorce was common. Sororal polygyny occurred more rarely than monogamy, and fraternal polyandry was still scarcer, being limited to old men. Both the sororate and levirate were practiced.

Several beliefs stated by informants in 1944–1945 as of contemporary vintage are undoubtedly old, such as the theory that conception results from an amalgamation of blood in the uterus following coitus and the opinion that more than one act of sexual intercourse is required to complete conception. In 1944–1945 babies were mostly born at home. Not fed for the first day of life, they thereafter received breast milk supplemented with a bottle. Nursing continued for about two years. Sphincter control, mildly instituted, came between one and two years but no serious notice of lapses was taken before the child was three.

The Kaska Indians were always ready to show affection and attention to infants and most mothers were reluctant to leave a small baby alone or even in someone else's care. In a short time, however, the warmth that these normally unexpressive people demonstrated to an infant declined, and the mother unconsciously became much less openly affectionate toward the child and responded sharply to its crying.

Scolding, corporal punishment, and threats were the main techniques of parental discipline. Few children attended school in 1944–1945, and at home education for daily living continued to be unformalized, starting earlier for girls than boys. Puberty brought few major changes in a girl's life, for her economic role began early, and menarche no longer received ceremonial observance. For boys, adolescence marked the beginning of serious participation in the tasks of trapping and hunting. Marriage signaled full entry into adult status. Preferential marriage still occurred between father's sister's daughter and mother's brother's son.

Though men recognized no intrinsic difference between the sexes, they claimed superiority over women, and, in fact, women were economically dependent on their husbands. Men, however, were far from content to live alone, and a widower showed great readiness to remarry.

The Kaska Indians were nominally all Roman Catholic in 1945. Though they were not devout, they favored church marriage on the ground that, being legally binding, it increased marital stability.

• DEATH In the past the Kaska recognized several interrelated causes of death: overexertion, accidents, natural causes, and sorcery. They believed in several afterworlds. Up in the sky lay the realm reserved for the souls of good persons, while the place reserved for the wicked, inhabited by various snakes, monsters, and fire, resembled the Christian hell. One part of the dead person remained around the vicinity of the grave until it was reincarnated. A corpse was disposed of by the opposite moiety through cremation, inhumation, abandonment, or caching in a tree. Following disposal, the close relatives of the deceased cut their hair above their ears, but other forms of mutilation were rare.

In aboriginal belief (still held in the 1940s), death, resulting from old age, illness, or an accident and indicated by cessation of the heart's movement, severed the connection between body and soul (the soul called tajuš 'wind'). While death represented the final dissolution of body and soul, the two might also be temporarily estranged, as happened during dreaming when the soul "walked around," perhaps to discover what would happen to the dreamer in the future. For a few days after death the soul lingered near the body, and at that time it was dangerous, especially to children, whom it stole for company. It also menaced relatives who had offended the deceased during life, and on whom it might take vengeance. During this time, the soul might try to communicate with the living through the crackling of burning wood, whereupon a piece of food was cast into the stove as an offering. After a few days, the soul went to the afterworld (in the 1940s the Christian heaven or hell) whence it might return as a ghost.

Relatives of the same sex as the deceased, but (in the 1940s) not necessarily of the opposite moiety, washed the corpse and invested it with clothing that was as fresh and attractive as possible. Then the extended corpse, hands folded across the abdomen, was wrapped in a cotton shroud and placed in a coffin. Burial came as soon after death as possible in order to alleviate the distress of the surviving kinsmen. Cloths worn by the deceased at the time of death might be burned. Other possessions were either distributed among relatives as mementos or burned. The Kaskas showed little inclination to follow a cult of the dead. A memorial was erected at a burial place, but no later attention was given to the grave.

Shamanism

The power to perform as a shaman came from "dreaming of animals in a lonely place." Generally the aspirant ate and drank sparsely during his one or two days of isolation. Every night as he lay down to sleep he wished that a source of power would be revealed to him. Communications from animals or other beings were the mark of a successful "vision quest" and promised that a portion of a being's "wind" had passed into the dreamer to enhance his natural powers. The successful quester could now rely on the aid of the helper. A man did not avoid eating the animal source of his power.

Every young man formerly had the opportunity to acquire extra power that would enhance his personal capacities. Hence every man was a potential shaman. By working hard and successfully at shamanism, some persons acquired a widespread reputation as curers, diviners, and conjurers. Ordinarily no special dress distinguished a shaman; however, when called to practice, he might represent his power source by donning the skin of an animal helper.

Curing and divination or clairvoyance were probably the commonest tasks of a shaman. Many, but not all, sicknesses were treated by shamans. Sometimes the practitioner "blew" water from his mouth on the sore part of a patient's anatomy, or he might transfer the intensive illness into a foreign object, such as a rock. Confession helped to alleviate sickness resulting from broken taboos. With or without the aid of external oracles, a shaman "dreamed" of the location of game or perhaps foresaw somebody's imminent death. Some shamans enhanced their prestige by public conjuring, sometimes in competition to test who was more powerful (cf. Ridington 1968).

In 1925 five Kaska Indians were convicted of murdering a youth accused of witchcraft (Honigmann 1947a). Some years previously, two other children, one 5 and the other between 10 and 14 years old, were reported to have been executed for the same reason. Witchcraft does not appear to have been a trait of aboriginal Kaska culture as it was in Tlingit culture, whence the pattern probably diffused to the Kaska as well as to the Tahltan (Emmons 1911:113–114) and Pelly River Tutchone (Field 1957:50) during late post-contact times. The murders referred to were apparently the last sign of witch fear among the Kaska.

Beliefs

Judging from informants' statements, cosmological speculation remained unelaborated in aboriginal Kaska culture. People believed that the world had several times altered. In an earlier period the animals alone inhabited the earth. Then came a time when both humans and animals lived, which ended in a great flood after which Crow restored the world. Several culture heroes have existed, including Kliatata, who bestowed the bow and snowshoe and taught the Indians to make fish nets from willow bark, and Tsuguya, who had many adventures and narrow escapes. Spiritual beings of the old culture included: counterparts of at least some of the empirically sensed animals; Gusłina, an evil being or "devil;" the North Wind Man who brought suffering through the cold he controlled; cannibalistic giants; a giant who befriended man; dwarfs helpful to human beings; but apparently no supreme being.

Some contemporary beliefs undoubtedly possess considerable antiquity, including, for example, ideas regarding conception, knowledge of animal habits, and evaluations of certain animals as smart, such as hare and beaver, and others as foolish, like the bear because he attacks enemies, namely men, who can defeat him. Kaska informants of the 1940s explained that the world, man, and other creatures were created by Jesus.

Teleologically speaking, many animals were made so that man would have them to eat. Such conceptions obviously indicate assimilation of Christian (Catholic) teachings. The Indians also conceived of the clouds, water, earth, and animals as having "bosses," executory forces, who were not always conceived of anthropomorphically. A supreme being, alternatively called God and Jesus, is "head man" and rules over the nature bosses. The devil instigates evil both in men and in animals like the grizzly bear.

Social Personality

Kaska social personality and emotional style, as observed in 1944–1945, manifested six interrelated themes. (1) The Kaska take a practical and resourceful attitude toward problems of living and are prone to concrete rather than abstract thinking. (2) Persons subordinate external necessity and duty to personal inclination, with the result that habits are not rigid, and behavior sometimes becomes indecisive and procrastinative. (3) They value deference in human relationships and reject aggression as a permissible form of coping with others. (4) The Kaska are emotional suppressors and their behavior is therefore marked by little emotional display or involvement. (5) They place a high valuation on personal independence, meaning that persons are self-oriented rather than group-oriented. And, finally (6), despite the value placed on independence, a contrary tendency also exists to become dependent under certain conditions. In general, Kaska personality wavers between the idea that experience is manageable and the idea that life is difficult and uncertain. People value self-reliance, but they also abandon striving and revert to passivity when things become complex or difficult. None of these traits is incapacitating. The Kaska have survived many difficult experiences associated with acculturation, and they give every indication of continuing to adapt to their changing circumstances.

Synonymy‡

The name Kaska has been used by anthropologists since the early reports of Dawson (1889:199B) and Morice (1903:519). It is a local English borrowing of the Kaska name for McDame Creek, which Morice writes KasHa ("the H representing a peculiar gutturalo-sibilant aspiration"), also borrowed as Cassiar, the name applied to the mining region between the Coast Range and the Rocky Mountains. Other recordings are kaša and (Tahltan) kɔswa (Honigmann 1954:20–21). The spelling Casca is much less frequent (Canada. Department of Indian Affairs 1930:50).

‡ This synonymy was written by Ives Goddard.

Earlier the Kaska were referred to by variants of the name Nahani, such as Nakane, 1806 (Simon Fraser in Jenness 1937:6), but this name has been applied to other groups as well. Morice (1905) used Nah·ane and Teit (1956:44–46) Nahani for an Athapaskan subgroup comprising the Kaska, Tahltan, and others, and Nahani has continued in official use as the linguistic denomination of the Kaska (Liard River and Ross River bands) and some Southern Tutchone (Whitehorse band) (Canada. Department of Citizenship and Immigration. Indian Affairs Branch 1964:44–45). For a full discussion of the name Nahani, see "Nahani," this volume.

The synonymy of the various band and local group names of the Kaska has not been completely worked out. The Upper Liard Kaska are also referred to as Tichotina, recorded as Ti-tsho-tī-na (Dawson 1889:200B) and Titcoténa (Teit 1956:45), but Honigmann (1954:20) applies this name to the Frances Lake Kaska. The Dease River Kaska have been called Sa-zē-oo-ti-na (Dawson 1889) or Sêzoténa (Teit 1956), though Honigmann (1954:23) believed this name to be proper to the Bear Lake Sekani. The Tselona, referred to locally as Nelson Indians, Grand Lakers, and Fort Grahame Nomads (Honigmann 1954:19–20), also have a name resembling that of a reported Sekani band, the Tseloni (Jenness 1937:11).

Sources

At the foot of Dease Lake between 1912 and 1915 Teit (1917, 1956) collected Kaska tales and made a few other observations. In 1929 the Rev. E. Allard, O.M.I., published some notes on the Kaska made after 1926, the year he was posted to a mission in the area. John J. Honigmann spent the summer of 1944 in Lower Post doing mainly ethnographic reconstruction with Dease River and Upper Liard informants but also observing contemporary life (Honigmann 1954; Honigmann and Honigmann 1945). The results of further ethnographical research in 1945 at Lower Post and in a Liard River winter settlement are in Honigmann (1949, 1970). No later information is available; therefore, the account in this chapter of Kaska society and culture is carried only to 1945.

The assistance of Alan McGinigle and of the Community Affairs Branch of the Department of Indian Affairs and Northern Development (Canada) in the preparation of this account is gratefully acknowledged.

Nahani

BERYL C. GILLESPIE

The term "Nahani," with variants, appears in historical, ethnological, and Canadian government publications as the name of a cultural and linguistic division of the Athapaskan populations of northern British Columbia, the Yukon territory, and the Northwest Territories. It has been variously used to refer to or include the Kaska, Mountain, Taku (the Athapaskan-speaking ancestors of the eastern Inland Tlingit), Slavey, Tsetsaut, Tagish, Tahltan, and Tutchone; Swanton (1910) grouped in this "division" 13 "tribes" that supposedly shared an Athapaskan language. However, the term Nahani is not generally considered by anthropologists to be an acceptable label for any tribal, cultural, or linguistic group. Accordingly, this chapter outlines the history of the application of the term, in view of its widespread and continued use in the literature.

The Sources of the Name

The term Nahani is derived from a word used by several Athapaskan groups to refer to certain Athapaskan speakers other than themselves, but as with some other "tribal" designations in the Subarctic it came to be used by Europeans for Indians who would never have applied it to their own group. In the attestations of the name as used by Indians it sometimes refers to a specific neighboring group and sometimes has a vague or mythological reference; its use as a self-designation in a few instances seems to derive from its application by White traders and other outsiders.

Variants of Nahani with specific reference include: Kutchin Naheiy, for the people living along the Gravel (Keele) River in 1848, presumably Mountain Indians (Murray 1910:61); Northern Tutchone Na-ai´, for the Pelly River Indians (Dawson 1889:201B); Kaska na.ani (also naha.ne and other spellings) for the Tahltan and the Pelly River Kaska (Teit 1956:45, 48; Honigmann 1954:21); Sekani nahʔáˑneh, for the Indians at Caribou Hide, British Columbia, who summered at Bear Lake (presumably the Bear Lake Sekani), and Carrier náhʔáneˑ with the same reference (Harrington 1939, normalized)—but the Sekani name referred to the Tahltan and the Upper Liard Kaska and the Carrier to the Tahltan, according to Jenness (1932:427) and Morice (1903:517). However, Honigmann (1956a:36) concluded from discussions of the term Nahani with Fort Nelson Slaveys and Lower Post Kaskas that it was used by various Athapaskan peoples for "relatively remote or distrusted Indian groups" that were considered "evil, untrustworthy, or hostile," and that in contemporary usage it was applied to evil Indians, sometimes portrayed as giants, that had lived in the mythical past. Names used in this way in the twentieth century include Slavey nahʔani or nahʔǫa (Keren Rice, communication to editors 1980) and Peel River Kutchin nahʔáíˑ (John T. Ritter, communication to editors 1980).

The analysis of the Athapaskan forms is uncertain, and none of the translations that have been proposed (Petitot 1891:363; Morice 1903:517; Jenness 1932:427; Teit 1956:48; Honigmann 1956a:36) is supported by linguistic analysis (Victor Golla, John T. Ritter, and Keren Rice, communications to editors 1980).

The groups specifically referred to as Nahani in native usage are in two general areas, the Upper Stikine (Tahltan and Bear Lake Sekani) and the Pelly–Upper Liard–Keele area (northern Kaska and perhaps others), and in fact the Tahltan at Telegraph Creek (Teit 1956:48) and the Pelly River Kaska at Ross River (Tharp 1971) are the only groups known to accept this as a name for themselves. However, as Teit points out, the "Tahltan recognize themselves as Nahani because [they are] so called by Indians living east of them" (the Kaska), and the use of the term has been spread by White traders. Hence there is no guarantee that any of these usages are of precontact date. Nevertheless, the name Nahani was still used in the 1970s by the Canadian government, inappropriately, to designate the language of the Yukon Territory Indians at Whitehorse, Ross River, and Liard River (Watson Lake) (Canada. Department of Indian Affairs and Northern Development. Indian Affairs Branch 1970:37), who in fact speak Southern Tutchone and Kaska.

Nahani in Early Reports

On the map of his 1789 journey Mackenzie (1966:20) placed the "Nathana" Indians between the Mackenzie River and Great Bear Lake but did not mention them in his journal. This location does not coincide with any later references to Nahani. In 1807 trader George Keith (1889–1890, 2:68) at Fort Liard reported that the Slavey Indians had driven away the previous inhabitants of the area, the "Na ha né." Trader W.F. Wentzel (1821), describing the various Indian groups of the Mackenzie River drainage, mentioned the native account of a tribe in the mountains west of the (lower) Liard River called "Nahannies." Wentzel named the river associated with these yet unseen Indians the Nahanny River (now the South Nahanni). These so-called Nahani Indians began to trade at Forts Liard and Simpson by the late 1820s and were probably Kaska (Hudson's Bay Company 1826–1828). By the 1830s Nahani was used by traders and explorers more generally for Indians from the mountains west of the Mackenzie and Liard rivers. Well into the twentieth century Mountain Indians as well as Kaska were often called Nahani.

During the nineteenth century the Hudson's Bay Company extended the fur trade into the Cordillera with only limited success. The mountains hindered traders from developing efficient trading routes into the Cordillera from the south and east, while on the west the Tlingit Indians blocked the European traders in order to keep their trade monopoly with the interior natives. Northern British Columbia and the Yukon remained poorly known throughout the nineteenth century, and most Indian groups within this area were referred to as Nahani at various times.

Robert Campbell established the Dease Lake Post for the Hudson's Bay Company in 1838. The Indians that Campbell encountered at the post and to the westward he called Nahannies (Wilson 1970:27, 37). They were presumably Tahltan Indians. Anderson reported a few so-called Nahani at every post on the Mackenzie River and at Peel's River, Liard, and Halkett posts. He described the Fort Halkett population as Sekani and "Nahanies of different tribes" (1858:121). By the 1850s the term was used so generally that it often referred to any Indians of the Cordillera other than Kutchin, as well as to the Mountain Indians.

Other attempts to name and group natives of the Cordillera came from writers far removed from the area. The Oblate priest Émile Petitot, who missionized the Indians along the Mackenzie River in the 1860s and 1870s, attempted to classify all Northern Athapaskans. For Petitot the Nahani (which he spelled differently in various publications) were just one tribe within his Rocky Mountain, or " Montagnard," division of Athapaskan speakers. He vaguely locates them on the western slopes of the Rocky Mountains with a small section on the eastern slopes, south of the Mountain Indians, an area that corresponds with that of the Kaska (1868:489, 1876:xx, 1891:362).

Dall (1877:32–34), in his classification of the natives of Alaska and the adjacent interior, was the first to use the term "Nehaunees" to label a cultural grouping, though this was merely a residual category of poorly known groups in the Cordillera that he listed on the basis of information from others. He gave six "bands," which correspond to the Kaska, Taku, Tagish, and Pelly River Northern Tutchones (perhaps including some Mountain Indians).

The only nineteenth-century report on northern British Columbia and the southern half of the Yukon based on scientific exploration was by George M. Dawson in 1887. His efforts to name and locate Indian groups have remained acceptable in most respects. He was aware that names given by Indians for various neighbors might not be accurate. He hesitated to combine them into larger cultural classifications. Omitting the Nahani category from his list of Indian groups, Dawson (1889:201B) explained: "The Kaska form a portion of the group of tribes often referred to by the Hudson Bay Company's people as the Nahanie or Nahaunie, and so classed collectively by Dall in the absence of more definite information." In spite of Dawson's attempt to eliminate the Nahani category, it continued to appear in the literature as an extensive cultural-linguistic classification.

Nahani as a Cultural-Linguistic Division

The Oblate priest A.G. Morice began his missionary work in northern British Columbia during the 1880s. He soon worked out ethnic and linguistic divisions for the Northern Athapaskans based on information from various sources. Morice (1903:517–522) described the Nahani as a dialect grouping of peoples known at present as Tahltan, Kaska, Taku, Mountain, and perhaps the Tsetsaut. His classification of the Tahltan and Kaska was based on first-hand linguistic investigation, and the inclusion of the Taku followed Dawson's (1889:193B) statement that they spoke the same dialect as the Tahltan. The Mountain Indians were included because Petitot (1876:xx, 1875:262) had used the name Na″anné for this group or parts of it, and the Tsetsaut on the basis of Boas's informant's claim that their language was mutually intelligible with Tahltan, though Morice expressed serious doubts about the inclusion of the Tsetsaut. Morice's classification was the basis of Swanton's (1910) "Nahane" list, though for unclear reasons Swanton added to Morice's list other "tribal" names given by Petitot (including some groups of Slavey) and claimed of the entire set of Indian groups under "Nahane" that "[t]hey correspond with Petitot's Montagnard group, except that he included also the Sekani" (1910:10). Actually Petitot's (1876:xx) Montagnard "group" included the Beaver, Sarcee, and Sekani, and also a sector of Mountain Indians (Goat Indians) and a sector of Kaska, as known today; within this group he applied the name Na″annè (Nahani) specifically to a small band located vaguely on "the east slope of the mountains," probably another sector of Kaska.

Other twentieth-century classifications treat the Nahani as a basic division of Athapaskan Indians, but with different listings of the component groups. Teit's (1956:45–46) list of Nahani "tribes," based on information obtained from the Tahltan in 1912 and the Kaska in 1915, includes the Tahltan, three groups of Kaska, and apparently two groups each of Northern Tutchone and Mountain Indians. After working with the Tahltan in the early 1900s Emmons (1911:5–6), considered them one of the four populations of the Nahani linguistic division. Jenness (1932:370, 376, 396, 427–429), using mainly the earlier published material, retained the Nahani category to group within it Mountain Indians and the Kaska, including those on the upper Pelly River, but he made the Tahltan and Tagish distinct. Swanton (1952:583–584), alluding to these inconsistencies, listed Kaska, Mountain, Tagish, Taku, and possibly Tahltan as included in the "Nahane" division. Osgood (1936:13) was the first anthropologist authoritatively to eliminate Nahani as a basic division of Northern Athapaskan Indians on the grounds that the term "has been used most indiscriminately as a label for Indians about whom little is known."

Tsetsaut

WILSON DUFF

Language and Territory

The Tsetsaut (tsə'tsäwt, 'tsets‚äwt) spoke an Athapaskan language. The fragmentary linguistic materials collected from the last handful of speakers in 1894 (Boas 1895; Boas and Goddard 1924)* attest a set of unique phonological developments that make it "the most strikingly aberrant . . . of all Athapaskan languages" (Krauss 1973:917), and its genetic relationships within the family have not yet been completely worked out (Hoijer 1963; Tharp 1972; Krauss 1973:946–947).

From the interior Cordillera of British Columbia, the Tsetsaut had penetrated across the southern headwaters of the Stikine River and the northern headwaters of the Nass as far as the Pacific coast (fig. 1) but failed to achieve a viable long-term adaptation to the natural and cultural environments of these major river systems or the sea coast. From the traditions of the adjacent Gitksan and Coastal Tlingit it is evident that many families of the Tsetsaut were assimilated into these tribes and thereby lost their separate identity. Some others were likewise assimilated into the mixed Sekani-Gitksan people of the vicinity of Bear Lake, at the headwaters of the Skeena. Those who remained Tsetsaut continued to be vulnerable to attack and exploitation by their more powerful neighbors, until they were brought to the verge of extermination. In 1885, a forlorn remnant consisting of 12 men and their families moved from the upper reaches of Portland Canal to the Anglican mission village of Kincolith, there to be finally assimilated by the Niska. Their fate in its broad outlines may have repeated that of other Athapaskans who reached the Northwest Coast in earlier times.

The evidence suggests that the Tsetsaut were most closely related to the Kaska. Emmons (1911:22) wrote of the Tsetsaut that "the Tahltan of today claim relationship to them [the Tsetsaut] only through the Kaska, from whom they say they [the Tsetsaut] are descended."

*There is no phonemic orthography for Tsetsaut, which became extinct early in the twentieth century. The Tsetsaut words cited in the *Handbook* are given as found in the sources, with a phonetic transcription into the *Handbook* technical alphabet added in brackets for those words available in Boas and Goddard (1924). The editors have been unable to check the spelling of the words cited from Thorman's (1915) manuscript.

An ecological factor that supports the suggestion of Kaska-Tsetsaut connection is the absence of salmon from the greater part of the Stikine drainage basin. Rich spawning areas a short distance above Telegraph Creek were exploited by all the bands of Tahltan, but blockages in the major tributaries turned the upper parts of the river system into what was in effect a salmonless corridor extending from Kaska territory almost to the sea coast.

Identity

A persistent suggestion that the Tsetsaut were nothing more than a displaced offshoot of the Tahltan (McKay in Boas 1895:559; Morice 1906–1910:276; Emmons 1911:22; Drucker 1965:52, 105) does not fit the evidence and has been convincingly disproved (Boas 1895; Tharp 1972). A particular cause of confusion has been the application of the name Tsetsaut to the southernmost band of Tahltan, the Nassgotin, who were in fact the Tsetsaut's most relentless enemies (see "Tahltan," this vol.). At an early time, perhaps about the beginning of the nineteenth century, this Tahltan band displaced the Tsetsaut on the upper Nass and established a fishing

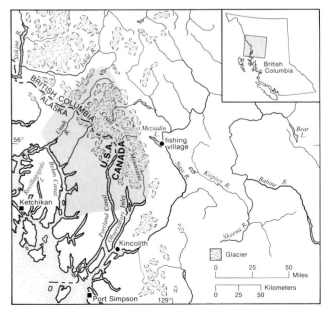

Fig. 1. Maximum extent of Tsetsaut territory, mid-19th century.

village on Meziadin Lake, which they held until about 1865, when they themselves were so reduced in wars with the Kitwancool (Gitksan) and Niska that they withdrew to the Stikine, leaving most of the upper Nass in the possession of the Kitwancool (fig. 1). This Tahltan band was also known to Tsimshian speakers as Lakwiyip (Lackweip, Laq'uyî´p [laxʔuyíp]) or Gitlakwiyip '(people of) on large flat ground' although that too was an undiscriminating term applied to the groundhog (marmot) country of the Nass and Stikine headwaters and its occupants. As applied here, the name Tsetsaut is not used for any of those who were also Tahltan or Sekani, but only for those who, not having any other identity, might with irony be called "Tsetsaut proper."

Tribal Subdivisions

Three named bands of Tsetsaut, or fragments of earlier bands, have been distinguished. Thorman (1915) was told by the Tahltan of three groups that were disrupted by the southward advance of the Nassgotin. Two of these were displaced to the west of the Nass, the third to the east. He recorded their names as follows: Suss to'deen 'people of the black bear raiment', of the Unuk River area; Tse etseta 'people of the adult marmot headgear', farther south; and Thlakwair khit 'they of the double house', who were driven east. Thorman's notes described in some detail the invasion by the Nassgotin and their establishment of a summer village at a place that they called Thluwe'thlun'dahl and that, judging from Kitwancool traditions, was by the falls at the foot of Meziadin Lake.

> Driving the *Suss to'deen* mercilessly before them to the Ningunsaw River [a southern tributary of the Iskut] and beyond, they slaughtered the adult males and aged females, making slaves of the younger women and children, many of whom were taken to Tahltan. They penetrated the *Suss to'deen* country to the Ocean Water at the Unuk River, from which inhospitable country they quickly returned. Farther south they harassed the *Tse etseta* into retreat among the crags and forests of the coastal range, also taking slaves (Thorman 1915).

On the other flank of their advance "they harassed a small group, the *Thlakwair khit* (they of the double house, double in the sense that they were reinforced in strength to withstand the very heavy snowfall of that area)" (Thorman 1915).

Boas also recorded the names of the two western bands in the winter of 1894 when he eagerly sought out the remnants of the Tsetsaut at Kincolith and recorded the great bulk of the known ethnographic and linguistic information on them (Boas 1895, 1896, 1897, 1969:155–170; Boas and Goddard 1924). His main informant Levi (Dandjalee) told him that "before our times the country was inhabited first by the *ts'ak'ê´*, who wore marmotskins; later on, by the *futvūd'iê´*, who wore bear-skins.

Both were said to have spoken the Ts'ɛts'ā´ut language" (Boas 1897:48). The latter name, given the sound correspondences between Tsetsaut and Tahltan, is cognate with Thorman's Suss to'deen; the former, while etymologically different from Thorman's Tse etseta, clearly refers to the same group, the marmot-skin people.

Levi distinguished these Tsetsaut from another group that was clearly the Nassgotin band of Tahltan. He called that band, in Niska, Laq'uyî´p, and in Tsetsaut, Naqkyina [naxkyina] ('on the other side'); its village was called Gunaqä´ [gunaxʸɛ·ʔ] (Boas 1895:555). Boas commented that the dialect of this village differed somewhat from the Tsetsaut, the latter being considered slaves of the Gunaqä´ (Boas and Goddard 1924:16).

That Thorman's third band, the double-house people, were also Tsetsaut seems likely in view of the information obtained by Teit (1915) from Tahltan and Niska informants. Teit's description of Tsetsaut territory differs from that of Boas in that it extends eastward as far as Bear Lake and Sustut River. Teit failed to distinguish clearly enough between the Tsetsaut proper and the Nassgotin and between the Niska and the Kitwancool. Despite that, the following seems to refer to an eastern remnant of Tsetsaut: "Some Indians claim that Tsetsaut were the same as the old Bear Lake tribe. . . . Part of the tribe still live around Bear Lake and Sustut Lake . . . After the Nishga [Niska] took the central part of their country away the Tsetsaut were divided, one band in the west and the other around Sustut River. The latter became mixed with Sekani proper, Carrier, Babine, Tahltan, Gitksan, and later most of them moved to among Tahltan and elsewhere" (Teit 1915). This corresponds with Thorman's description of the fate of the double-house people. In any event, they lost their identity as Tsetsaut.

The western Tsetsaut occupied an area that included the Unuk River and reached saltwater along the eastern side of Behm Canal and the upper reaches of Portland Canal and Observatory Inlet (fig. 1). According to Levi, they formerly spent most of their time on the Behm Canal side in intermittent friendly relations with the Sanyakwan Tlingit, but on the death of the chief of that group they began to frequent Portland Canal more and came under the domination of the Niska.

Niska traditions tell how Eagle clan chiefs of the Gitxadin or downriver Niska, while scouting for new territories, discovered the Tsetsaut at Tombstone Bay on Portland Canal (Barbeau 1950, 1:27–29). Portland Canal, and the Salmon and Bear rivers at its head, were claimed by Chief Gitkun. When his family declined in numbers he permitted another Eagle chief named Sagawan or Chief Mountain to use the area, and the Tsetsaut came to be known as the Tsetsaut slaves of Chief Mountain. Sagawan lived for a time at the site of Kincolith, to be close to the trading ships and the Hudson's

Bay Company post at Port Simpson, and he held a monopoly of trade with the Tsetsaut. When William Duncan established the new Christian village of Metlakatla in 1862 and entered the competition for furs, this monopoly was broken. In anger, Sagawan moved back to Gitiks on the Nass. Robert Tomlinson, who established the mission at Kincolith in 1867, was in frequent contact with the Tsetsaut, and in 1885 his successor, W.H. Collison, invited the last 12 men and their families to take up residence in Kincolith. When Boas visited them in 1894, he found their total number to be 12, reduced from an estimated population of 500 just 60 years earlier (1895:555). Emmons (1911), in 1907, found only seven: four men, two old women, and a girl. Later writers do not identify any persons as Tsetsaut.

Traditional Culture†

Boas (1895), the source for this section, makes it clear that the Tsetsaut economy was based on inland game hunting. Only in the summer when they descended the rivers to Portland Inlet did they take salmon, drying their excess catch for winter use. Their principal food was the marmot, though they also relied on mountain goat, bear, and porcupine. With the beaver (and excepting the porcupine?) these animals also provided the skins for their clothing. For both sexes traditional clothing consisted of pants of cured skins and thigh-high marmot skin "boots" (probably the Athapaskan all-in-one moccasin legging). Mittens, jackets, short coats, robes, and belts, all of skins, completed the costume.

The Tsetsaut had no fixed villages but moved camp as the subsistence quest dictated. Their shelters were temporary, single or double lean-tos (fig. 2) covered with bark. For winter travel they used snowshoes with lacing of beaver skin. Canoes, made of the bark of the yellow cedar, were seldom used. Each man hunted alone, "confining his operations to one valley at a time" (Boas 1895:565). For taking marmots, deadfalls were commonly used. In hunting other animals, besides lances and clubs they employed the sinew-backed bow. The bow also served as a fire drill, and fires were kindled by means of strike-a-lights as well.

In Boas's (1896:257) judgment the tales and myths of the Tsetsaut resembled "in character" those of the Athapaskan peoples of the Mackenzie drainage, but had "evidently . . . been greatly influenced by Tlingit tales." With all surrounding groups they shared reliance

on shamans for curing and the emphasis on girls' puberty seclusion and ritual observances.

Boas's information from Levi led to the conclusion that the Tsetsaut had been divided into two matrilineal exogamous "clans," Eagle and Wolf, named in Levi's time in the Niska-Gitksan language. By the time of Boas's field research in 1894 the Eagle clan was extinct, and the few remaining members of the Wolf clan maintained exogamy by marrying members of foreign tribes. Boas (1916:480) rejected the validity of Emmons's (1911:22) statement that the Tsetsaut survivors he met in 1907 claimed to have recognized three divisions, Raven and Eagle, both extinct by 1907, and Wolf, represented by seven surviving individuals. De Laguna's (1975:59) statement that Tsetsaut "social organization seems to have been very similar to that of the Tlingit" reflects a preference for Boas's conclusion regarding a dual division in Tsetsaut social organization.

Synonymy

Much confusion over the identity and history of the Tsetsaut has been caused by the name itself and the ways in which it has been used. This name was not used by any group for itself but was said by Boas (1895:555) to be a Tsimshian word, meaning 'those of the interior', applied by the Gitksan and Niska indiscriminately to the Athapaskans to the north and northeast of themselves. It thus included bands of Tahltan and Sekani as well as the Tsetsaut, but since the "native name of the [latter] is forgotten, . . . we must . . . continue to designate them as Ts'ɛts'ā́ut," i.e. [čəčá·ut] (Boas 1895:555). Boas also used the spelling Ts'ets'aut (Boas and Goddard 1924), and Emmons (1911:22) rendered the Niska name as Tsits Zaons. Emmons (1911:21–23) referred to the people in question as "the Portland Canal People" and said that they called themselves Wetalth, presumably [wətał]; Tharp (1972:16) considered this form to be "a phonological impossibility in the language" but does not justify this judgment. The Tahltan called them Tseco to tinneh (Emmons 1911:22).

Sources

Boas's 1894 fieldwork among the Tsetsaut living at Kincolith is a classic example of the salvage ethnography he so vigorously promoted. Of the three men interviewed by Boas, only his elderly informant Levi spoke the Tsetsaut language fluently. The two younger men used the Niska-Gitksan language almost exclusively. Boas (1895:555) freely acknowledged that "all the ethnological and historical data were given by Levi." Boas's (1895) brief report remains the primary source on the Tsetsaut; it includes notes on social or-

---

†Before his death in 1976, Wilson Duff had completed his informed analysis of the scanty yet complex data bearing on the tribal identity and tribal subdivisions, the movements, and the history of the Tsetsaut, and the source of the name. The sections of this chapter on those topics are by Wilson Duff (with a few editorial emendations). Margaret Tobey checked references and wrote the section on Sources. She and June Helm prepared the section on Traditional Culture.

Boas 1895: figs. 1–2, pp. 561–562.

Fig. 2. Frameworks for houses, for a single family (left) and for 2 families (right). In use, the pole framework was covered with bark except for door openings next to the tree (left) or on each vertical side (right). Between uses, the poles (the longest about 14 feet) were dismantled and stored tied to a tree.

ganization, material culture, subsistence patterns, and history. Myths and oral histories of the Tsetsaut recorded during the 1894 visit were also published (1896, 1897). Boas and Goddard (1924) collaborated on a rel-atively extensive treatment of the Tsetsaut language, principally as spoken by Levi. Tharp (1972) has evaluated the position of the Tsetsaut among Northern Athapaskan languages.

Tahltan

BRUCE B. MACLACHLAN

Language

The Tahltan ('täl,tän) are a group of Athapaskan speakers centered on the upper basin of the Stikine River in northern British Columbia. The remnants of five or six bands of Tahltan plus a band of Sekani that migrated into the region in the late nineteenth century comprise the officially delimited Tahltan Band associated with the settlement of Telegraph Creek. In 1972 this band was administratively divided into the Tahltan and Iskut bands, the Iskut comprising the component of Sekani origin living in Eddontenajon village at Kinaskan Lake.

The Tahltan speak a dialect of the Tahltan-Kaska branch of the Athapaskan language family.* Besides the Kaska, the ancestors of some of the twentieth-century Inland Tlingit also probably spoke a variety of Tahltan-Kaska (Dawson 1889:193B; Emmons 1911:22; Boas 1895). The Bear Lake Sekani accretion to the Tahltan speak an Athapaskan dialect of the Sekani-Beaver grouping.

Territory and Environment

What is probably the farthest extent of Tahltan occupation or use in the nineteenth century is shown in figure 1. The southern portion, assigned to the Nassgotin band, overlaps the range ascribed in other sources to the Tsetsaut (assimilated into the Niska about 1885). The Bear Lake Sekani replaced the Thlegtotin, who vacated the eastern sector before 1870. The upper Dease River, in the Arctic drainage, was considered Kaska country until late in the nineteenth century. The Stikine Tlingit controlled the Stikine River to Glenora, and there was overlapping use of the river and its shores

*The phonemes of Tahltan as spoken in Telegraph Creek are: (unaspirated stops and affricates) b, d, λ, ꝫ, ǯ, g, ˀ; (aspirated stops and affricates) t, ƛ, c, č, k; (glottalized) ṭ, ƛ̓, c̓, č̓, k̓; (voiceless continuants) ł, s, š, x, h; (voiced continuants) l, z, ž, γ; (nasals) m, n; (resonant) y; (short vowels) i, e, a, u; (long vowels) i·, e·, a·, u·; (tones) high (v́), low (unmarked). Information on Tahltan phonology was furnished by Victor Golla on the basis of unpublished field notes collected by Kenneth L. Hale in 1965 and by George W. Tharp in 1971. The phonemicizations should be considered tentative.

The group names and place-names not available in phonemic transcription are given in the spelling of the sources, except that the obsolete phonetic symbols c and tc have been replaced by sh and ch, respectively; these spellings are not phonetically accurate.

from Glenora to the Tahltan River mouth. The headwaters of the Sheslay and Nahlin rivers were contested by the Inland Tlingit of the upper Taku River and perhaps by the Taku Tlingit of the coast.

The part of the Tahltan sphere within the Coast Range is cold, damp, and relatively unproductive of game and utilized plants. It was subject to hunting expeditions, but it was never settled.

The rugged plateau country of the Stikine drainage above Glenora is dry (annual precipitation, 38–64 centimeters), sunny, and usually relatively moderate in both summer and winter temperatures, although the range between extremes is high. Natural forest fires encourage berry thickets and berry-eating animals. Parkland and coniferous and deciduous forest support plentiful moose and mountain caribou, although the absolute numbers and relative frequency of the two animals have fluctuated greatly in the period for which there is some record. Five varieties of salmon run and spawn in the major rivers. Conditions are unusually favorable for simultaneously catching salmon, picking berries, and preserving both foods. It was to exploit these conditions that the Stikine Tlingit established use rights so far up the river.

Mountain sheep and goats are found at the higher elevations. Muskrat, mink, marten, beaver, and other furbearers are present in numbers significant to the fur trade.

External Relations

The frontiers or degree of control over territory fluctuated with the relationships with neighboring groups. Relationships with the Stikine Tlingit on one side and with the Kaska and Bear Lake Sekani on the other side were peaceful and commercial. Marriages and movement between groups were exploited and elaborated. With the Inland Tlingit, the Coastal Tlingit of the Taku River, and the Tsimshian, competition and conflict were endemic. There was little possibility for reciprocal support of complementary interests (although there was some intermarriage at least with the Inland Tlingit); instead, there was merely contest for fishing sites, hunting ranges, trap lines, and rights as middlemen in trade along the coast-to-interior axis.

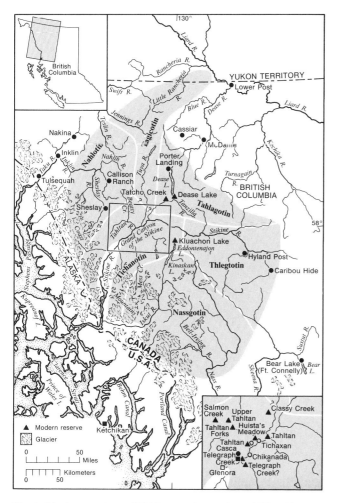

Fig. 1. Maximum extent of Tahltan territory, about 1830, with regional subdivisions.

History of Intercultural Contact

Central to Tahltan history is a continuous process of adapting a culture probably very similar to that of early historic Arctic-drainage Athapaskans to the special, more generous conditions of the Pacific drainage and of response to contact with the richer, more complex culture of the coast. Major external events changed the direction and intensity of Tahltan development, and these events are reference points along the time continuum; however, particular trends worked at different rates and at different times among the several Tahltan groups, so that the reference points do not mark off qualitatively different basic processes. The reference points are: Athapaskan (Tahltan) infiltration into the Stikine basin, contact with the Tlingit, arrival of Whites at the Stikine mouth in 1799 and the beginning of Tlingit-controlled participation in the White fur trade, and effective penetration of the upper Stikine by Whites around 1874.

The Stikine Basin

Although human occupation of the region may have begun as early as 30,000 years ago (J.W. Smith 1971:200), the gradual infiltration of small groups of Athapaskans was into an unpopulated region less than 300 years ago (J.W. Smith 1969:8). The new land had large, reliable annual runs of nourishing salmon, which can be preserved for long periods; a limited number of good fishing sites; and more concentrated sources of game. More or less directly these ecological conditions permitted or encouraged: increase of gross population size and density; increase in the size and duration of concentrations of people; shift of the annual settlement cycle from a more nearly nomadic movement among alternative customary campsites of approximately equal centrality to a more nearly transhumant pattern of annual concentration upon a fixed headquarters, with dispersal of subgroups to customary hunting ranges, and emergence of clearer membership boundaries among groups; elaboration of the technology of fishing, preservation, and storage; appearance of more permanent and substantial structures; increase in the number and variety of less portable or more valuable objects; increasing differentiation in wealth and control of resources, both between groups and within groups on the basis of rights in limited numbers of preferred fishing sites; increasing differentiation of political leadership consistent with economic differentiation and increasing size and concentration of population; and increase in the significance of institutions governing the transmission of rights between generations, that is, greater emphasis upon line of descent.

Tlingit-Tahltan Contact

The precise form of the last six developments was decisively influenced by contact with coastal people. Wood smokehouses, wooden boxes, and ornate pipes of coastal pattern became part of the material inventory. Other coastal imports—dentalium shell, eulachon grease, possibly slaves—also appear. The nascent social forms—social classes, chieftainship, matrilineal descent groups—and their expression—titles, crests, ceremonial gift exchanges—were less elaborate versions of Northwest Coast culture.

The barrier of the Coast Range is pierced by the Taku, Stikine, and Nass rivers. Small groups of Athapaskans reached the coast, and some became assimilated into the coastal clan system. Coastal Indians established contacts in the interior, and the coastal tribes established control up the major river valleys and over the major passes. The Taku and the Nass rivers became established as "grease trails" along which passed eulachon oil from the coast in exchange for hides, fur, copper, and other interior products. The relatively later deep penetration by the Tlingit of the Stikine valley seems to have been primarily to secure the favorable fish-drying sites, although trade presumably was a part of contact and became increasingly significant.

Intensified Tlingit-Tahltan Relations

Relations between the Tahltan and the Stikine River Tlingit were greatly intensified after White contact on the coast. European trading vessels had appeared in the mouth of the Stikine by 1799 (Emmons 1911:11). Although European trading rights passed from Russian to English hands in 1840, the coastal Indians' middleman control over the trade was unchanged. During this period, the gradient of power, prestige, and wealth from coast to interior became much steeper. Epidemics of European origin were spread into the interior by coastal Indians, reducing the number of Tahltans by as much as three-fourths during the nineteenth century (table 1) (Duff 1972; Emmons 1911:12, 34). External pressures on territory increased as coastal Indians, Tsimshian as well as Tlingit, pushed more aggressively into the interior.

A number of consequences of these conditions may be inferred. To the Tahltan the Tlingit fur trade increased the importance of trade and production of exports. Participation in the coastal system of clans became far more important as an entrée into the fur trade, since certain coastal families maintained monopolies on coast-interior trade, barring interior Indians from the coast and Whites from the interior. Limited opportunities for trade, like limited fishing sites, became objects of rights exercised to the exclusion of others. The amount and variety of wealth increased; its distribution became more uneven. Inheritance of exclusive rights and the kinship institutions governing inheritance became more prominent, and the number of hereditary rights was roughly fixed. At the same time a large part of the population was disappearing, including some of the holders and heirs of rights. Opportunities for great social mobility encouraged competition. The result was accelerated assimilation to the Tlingit way of life.

White Penetration of the Upper Stikine River

Although Tlingit control of the Stikine River had been weakened before 1874, it was broken by the Cassiar gold rush of 1874–1876. That boom and the Klondike gold rush of 1898–1899 brought thousands of Whites and hundreds of Chinese and Northwest Coast Indians through and into the region. Traders, missionaries, policemen, Indian agents, tourists, and sportsmen were not far behind the prospectors.

The White invasion brought Tlingitization of the Tahltan to its furthest. About 1875 the remnants of several Tahltan bands (including some individuals who

Table 1. Population

Date	Population	Source
1800	1,000	Estimate based on Kroeber's (1939:141) ratios and Teit's (1915) boundaries
1837	500	Wilson 1970:28; "Nahany" probably refers to Tahltan.
1850	300–325	Duff 1972
1907	220	Canada. Department of Indian Affairs 1907–1915
1915	217	Canada. Department of Indian Affairs 1907–1915
1934	240	Canada. Department of Mines and Resources. Indian Affairs Branch 1935
1949	357	Canada. Department of Citizenship and Immigration. Indian Affairs Branch 1952
1954	397	Canada. Department of Citizenship and Immigration. Indian Affairs Branch 1955
1959	503	Canada. Department of Citizenship and Immigration. Indian Affairs Branch 1961
1963	637	Duff 1964:36
1970	709	Donat Savoie, personal communication 1972
1978	793	Canada. Department of Indian Affairs and Northern Development 1980:39, 45

had prospered packing and freighting for prospectors), decimated by repeated epidemics, coalesced into a single unit, or tribe, with a paramount chief. They built a village, Tahltan Village, with European-style log houses. The subdivisions of the Tahltan, having lost much of their territorial rights, became groups defined almost entirely by descent.

Hunting, trapping, and fishing remained basic to Tahltan subsistence from 1874 through the middle of the twentieth century. In addition, the Tahltan were drawn into the wider market, wage, and welfare economy. Guiding, packing, and wrangling for White prospectors and sportsmen, and government jobs, became wage sources (Muir 1917:95–96). Following World War I Tahltan Village was gradually abandoned in favor of Telegraph Creek, where a school for Indians was established in 1906 and a regular school district in about 1915. During World War II supplies for the construction of the Alaska Highway were shipped to Telegraph Creek for trucking to the highway. Many Tahltans were involved in the construction and freightage, and some went farther afield. Discovery of asbestos in 1950 led to the establishment of the Cassiar asbestos works, the first major, modern private industry in the region.

By 1874 a segment of Bear Lake Sekani (T'lotona 'Long Grass Indians', Tahltan name: T'lukotene, T'lokotan) had replaced the Thlegtotin Tahltan in the upper Stikine. The T'lotona were a mixed Sasuchan Sekani and Gitksan band that arose around Fort Connelly (established 1826). These people ranged the "Groundhog country" at the sources of the Stikine, Nass, and Skeena rivers. When the Hudson's Bay Company withdrew from Fort Connelly about 1890, a segment of the Groundhog people remained. Gradually the focus of the group shifted to Telegraph Creek. By 1923 they were trading regularly there, and in 1954 they settled across the river from the town (Jenness 1937:v, 8–19; MacLachlan 1956:11, 31). In 1964 the group, accompanied by a missionary, withdrew to Kinaskan Lake, reportedly to minimize unnecessary contact with Euro-American civilization (Anonymous 1964).

Tribal Subdivisions

During the protohistoric and early historic periods a system of matrilineal descent groups was emerging out of a looser system of amorphous local and regional groups, a process that culminated in the 1870s. Until then the "subdivisions" of the Tahltan probably were the effective groups, and a Tahltan "tribe" or nationality was relatively nebulous.

There were in Tahltan Village four named matrilineal clans. Some of the clans apparently immigrated as such. For at least one of these there is a tradition that it immigrated from the coast as a clan segment. Other clans appear to have formed by stages out of local groups on the immigrant model, in such a way as to articulate with it or them. The final stage of this process and the foundation of Tahltan Village are closely related.

Of the subdivisions extant in the nineteenth century, Taxtlowedi, Naneai, and Tahlagotin have been reported as descent groups of the Wolf moiety, while Kachadi and Nahlotin were mentioned as descent groups of the Raven moiety. Catharine McClellan (personal communication 1972) points out that Taxtlowedi, Naneai, and Kachadi are "Tlingit terms for clans known on the coast;" in Tlingit their names are *daqɬawe·dí* (Inland dialect *dax̣ƛawe·dí*), *na·nya·ʔa·yí*, and *qa·č̓ádi* (Jeff Leer, communication to editors 1979). Tahlagotin and Nahlotin were also reported along with Tichanotin, Nassgotin, and Thlegtotin as names of either a local group or a group occupying and exploiting a large region (Emmons 1911:14–19; Teit 1906:349, 1915, 1919–1921:212, 1956:41; Duff 1964:36; De Laguna 1975:75–79).

The following are names of lesser groups or traditional groups, and synonyms for those listed above: Klabbahnotin, a local division of the Kachadi on a flat beyond the Tahltan River (Emmons 1911:18); Karkarkwan, a synonym, probably Tlingit, for Tahlagotin (Emmons 1911:19); Tikaihoten (Teit 1915), apparently

the same as Tichanotin and the "Tahltan" subdivision shown on McClellan's (1950), map I, which is based on Teit's, while Teit (1956:47, normalized) gives Tičaxhanoté·n as the Tahltan name for the whole tribe; Tlepanoten (Teit 1915), a synonym for Thlegtotin (MacLachlan 1956; Duff 1964); Thloadenni (Black 1955), apparently a Sekani name for the Thlegtotin; Tagishoten, McClellan's (1950:map I) substitute for Teit's Taxtlowedi, which is a coastal clan name, Shutin, an offshoot of the Tichanotin on Tahltan Lake and later on the Chutine River (Thorman, quoted in Duff 1972 and in MacLachlan 1956:14–15); Lakuyip (Teit 1956:44), also Laqʼuyî´p (Boas 1895) and Lakweip (Hodge 1907k:754; Scott 1870:563), apparently the Tsimshian name for the Nassgotin, equivalent to Tsetsaut Naqkyina (Boas 1895).

The Nassgotin and Nahlotin regional groupings persisted after 1874, but they disappeared in the twentieth century.

Division into nonlocal, exogamous, matrilineal moieties was probably developed soon after contact with the Tlingit and was well established before 1800. It was still sporadically observed in the mid-1950s.

Settlements

Telegraph Creek (fig. 2) has been the headquarters of the Tahltan Band since early in the twentieth century (MacLachlan 1957), while Kinaskan Lake has been the headquarters of the Bear Lakers since 1964. Tahltan, on a high terrace 1.5 miles down the Stikine from the Tahltan River mouth, flourished from about 1875 to about 1920 (Emmons 1911:31, 34). Chikanada, at the foot of Grand Canyon, eight miles below Tahltan, was a major fishing station and rendezvous for Nassgotin and Thlegtotin that was abandoned in the 1830s (Emmons 1911:86; Duff 1972; MacLachlan 1956:14). Gunakhe (Gunaqä´), on a westerly branch of the Nass River, constituted the chief village of the Nassgotin (Hodge 1907k:754; Boas 1895:555; Scott 1870:563). Tsala, at the confluence of the Nahlin and Sheslay rivers, was the principal fishing station of the Nahlotin (Teit 1915; Duff 1972; Honigmann 1954:22).

A number of other traditional names for locations have been reported, and some of these have been associated with specific sites. Additional unnamed sites have been located (Emmons 1911:16, 32–33; Swanton 1952:601–602; MacLachlan 1956:14–16; Honigmann 1954:22).

Culture

Subsistence

Like other Athapaskans, the Tahltan had a keen sense of the value of innovations, pragmatically adopting or

Fig. 2. Town of Telegraph Creek, on west bank of Stikine River. Missionaries, government officials, traders, enfranchised Indians, and Métis lived here, while the enrolled Indians (except the Bear Lakers) lived on a small reserve on a high terrace above Telegraph Creek, to left of gabled building at upper left. The Bear Lakers' settlement is marked by the narrow bare strip on the lowest terrace on the opposite (east) bank. Photograph by Bruce B. MacLachlan, 1956.

retaining the useful and manageable and ignoring or dropping the less useful. Most of the objects and techniques described and illustrated by Emmons (1911) and Teit (1906, 1956) had at the time of their fieldwork been replaced by Euro-American elements and incorporated into the fundamental pattern of alternating dispersed hunting and trapping in the winter with summer assembly at fishing sites.

Before 1874 people dispersed about the beginning of October to their hunting grounds, usually in groups of two families. The summer season (June-September) at the fishing stations was marked by feasts, visiting, and trading. The climax of the season was the great trading rendezvous with the Tlingit in September, with a lesser peak of trading activity in June. After 1874 White shopkeepers displaced the Tlingit traders, and it became customary to break the winter hunting by a return to Tahltan for the Christmas season.

The Tahltan were by origin and preference exploiters of land resources and eaters of big game—mountain caribou, moose, wood buffalo, black bear, grizzly bear, mountain sheep, mountain goat—plus smaller animals, such as beaver, muskrat, marmot. At times fish may have been the principal nutritional source.

The snare and deadfall, seconded by spear and bow and arrow, were the most productive hunting tools. The most effective techniques with the important caribou involved channeling the herds with brush surrounds or stake-and-brush fences at suitable locations. Natural impediments, including deep, soft snow, were also extensively exploited. Groups of men could then slaughter several animals with spears or bows and arrows. Such hunting probably entailed the cooperation of the full manpower of the two-family hunting groups, but not more.

Prehistoric fishing employed traps, gill nets, barbed spears, toggle spears, and gaff hooks, with large traps and weirs built and tended by men at the major salmon fisheries. Cutting and preservation of fish was women's work, as is tending of the modern gill nets suspended from floating booms. Running the modern fish camps is often done by the women while the men hunt or work for wages.

Travel and Transportation

In contrast to their mastery of the land, the Tahltan did not elaborate water transportation. Bark canoes and rafts were rare, poorly constructed, and short-lived. With Tlingit immigration, canoes with sails were adopted by a few Tahltan, but the lucrative freight canoeing between Glenora and Telegraph Creek during the gold booms was done by Tlingit.

Snowshoes and moccasins were well made and existed in a number of forms. Tumplines (fig. 3) and backpack harnesses were well developed, widely used, and often ornate and personalized. Dog packing came in about 1850, and prospectors introduced dog sledges.

Clothing

Clothing prior to 1870 was tanned hide or fur. Basic dress consisted of a shirt (fig. 4), trousers or leggings with or without attached feet, breechclout, moccasins, belt, and garters. A woman's dress was cut like a man's shirt, only longer, and in winter it was supplemented by a skin blanket.

Many men and women carried a small tool bag (fig. 6) containing several well-assorted, simple, effective tools.

Trade

Tahltan-cured hides, leather goods, and babiche were valued on the coast and were export items, as were robes, furs, and quillwork. Eulachon oil, slaves, woodwork, salmon oil and eggs, dentalia and haliotis, copper plates, ceremonial clothes and blankets were imported from the coast. Metal traps, knives ("Environment and Culture in the Cordillera," fig. 10, this vol.), firearms, glass beads, buttons, tobacco, and liquor were added after 1800.

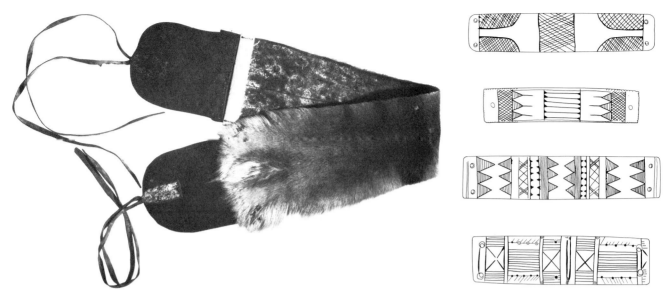

Fig. 3. Tumpline of caribou leg fur, with heavy moosehide end pieces and caribou hide tie strings. Back packs were always supported by a plaited strap across the chest; for heavier loads or on long journeys, a tumpline of this type also passed across the forehead, with the tie strings attached to loops on the pack bag. The strap was kept flat by a bone spreader (right) at each end, usually decorated with ocher-filled incising (Emmons 1911:52). left, Length of strap 88 cm (excluding tie strings), right, length of top about 12 cm, rest same scale; collected by G.T. Emmons, 1904–1906.

Structures

Tahltans often camped overnight without shelter. The basic shelter was a low, inverted V formed by a lean-to framework and covered with brush or bark (later, canvas) (Emmons 1911:36–37, pl. VId).

An old form of structure is the rectangular combined fish smokehouse and dwelling with vertical walls and gabled roof (fig. 7). The sides are of vertical, stripped saplings spaced to permit circulation of air. The houses built at Tahltan Village were of the current Euro-American horizontal log construction, with wood floor and glass windows.

The Tahltan continue pragmatically and flexibly to use any means or material known to them from traditional, coastal, or Euro-American culture, depending upon circumstances and resources.

Social Organization

The Tahltan sense of personal status was highly developed. Individuals and groups were ranked in society; and realty, movables, and intangibles were objects of alertly defended, exclusive rights. Social position was indicated by a set of titles for which eligibility was inherited; however, assumption of the titles had to be validated by appropriate behavior, including acquisition, distribution, and consumption of symbolic and utilitarian goods. The most important and valued rights were exercised by the leaders of families and clans. Holders of important hereditary rights were thought of as an aristocratic class as contrasted with ordinary individuals. Slaves, aliens acquired through capture or exchange, formed a third category. In practice class boundaries were indistinct. Mobility was achieved through aggressiveness, skill, acquisition of wealth, marriage, and trade; these possibilities were greatly intensified in the nineteenth century.

The most dramatic expression of social arrangements and of attempts to maneuver within the arrangements was the ceremonial distribution or destruction of property at a feast given for members of the opposite moiety. Beyond this the leader or aspirant must have become a focus for the continual redistribution of goods, a coordinator of activities, and an executor of rights in important resources.

Each family and matriclan had its leader. The leaders of the clans constituted an informal council for the combined clans. When the clans amalgamated under a single leader, about 1875, the leaders of the clans involved agreed that the leader of the most powerful clan should be the chief. This was the leader of the Kachadi clan, with the hereditary title Nan-nok.

Intraclan disputes were mediated by the clan leader. Disputes involving individuals of different clans were regarded as corporate responsibilities of the clans, represented in their negotiations by their respective leaders.

All succession to titles and all inheritance of significant rights were matrilineal. Access to resources and trading channels was along lines established between descent groups by marriages, especially "noble" mar-

Natl. Mus. of Canada, Ottawa: left, 33103, right, 33099; center, Smithsonian, Dept. of Anthr.: 248442.

Fig. 4. Skin shirts and knife sheath. left, Teltah or Mrs. Martin (age 42) wearing old-style fringed dress of caribou, fur hat, and bead necklace with what appears to be a charm made of stone wrapped in leather hanging from the end (Teit 1956:75). right, Dandy Jim (age 50), a member of the Nahlotin clan of the Raven phratry and Teit's (1956:40–41) main informant, wearing old-style fringed shirt, fur hat with feather, and knife sheath. center, Knife sheath of caribou skin covered with blue cloth trimmed with red and decorated with beadwork, worn as part of costume for dances and ceremonies; length 72 cm, collected by G.T. Emmons, 1904–1906. Photographs (left and right) by James A. Teit, 1915.

riages. Moiety exogamy was strict. Polygyny was rare but permissible. Proper marriage was negotiated between responsible clanswomen of the parties, and the participation of clansmen of the groom was required in the form of tangible values; hence, marriage was a matter between families, and a disapproving family could block almost any union.

A man assuming a deceased 'mother's brother's' title was expected to marry his predecessor's widow; it would be quite proper for him to marry a second woman closer to him in age. A widower was expected to marry his deceased wife's 'sister', if he remarried. In both cases, the governing consideration seems to be continuation of the attachment of the male to his wife's matrilineal group. Cross-cousin marriage must have been permissible, and matrilateral cross-cousin marriage may have been preferred.

A boy might live with his mother's brother instead of his parents. Where a man lived and worked was determined with reference to the location of his matrilineal territorial rights and the matrilineal territorial rights of his wife's family; it was not determined directly with reference to the location of the residence of either spouse's parents or of his own boyhood residence.

Initially, and for an indefinite period, the groom was expected to "work for" and live with his wife's parents. Later he would establish an independent household, if possible. However, he would be limited by the loci of hereditary or maritally acquired privileges.

Divorce was rare. Women appear to have been relatively secure, well-off, and influential, even exercising leadership (Wilson 1970:28, 32–33; Parnell 1942; cf. Emmons 1911:27).

Art and Expression

Many utilitarian objects were ornamented apparently for aesthetic effect. Geometric designs predominated.

MacLACHLAN

Fig. 5. A Tahltan family visiting Lower Post. B.C. (in Kaska territory). The young girl wears a coat decorated with coins, and the man and woman wear moccasins. Photograph by John J. Honigmann, 1944–1945.

Ceremonial pipes, grave houses, and grave posts sometimes bore clan animal crests.

A special shelter and special dress, utensils, and accouterments were used during the seclusion and education of a pubescent girl, who was also subject to food and behavioral regulations ("Expressive Aspects of Subarctic Indian Culture," fig. 9, this vol.).

Concentrations of people were exploited for dances and feasts, which were instrumental and expressive as well as recreational and convivial ("Environment and Culture in the Cordillera," fig. 17, this vol.). Feasts or potlatches were held on occasions such as assumption of a title, completion of a girl's puberty seclusion, marriage, or the anniversary of death. Formal dances with appropriate songs were integral to the death feast and the peace feast.

Oral literature was usually recited in a recreational context, but it was overtly didactic and moralistic, and it was used for making topical points. The competitiveness of the Tahltan was sometimes manifested in storytelling contests to see which side knew the most stories. Much of the corpus is in the Northwest Coast tradition, for example, the Raven cycle, but the inland milieu and interior origins of the Tahltan are also reflected (Teit 1909, 1919–1921; MacLachlan 1957a).

Beliefs

Although most of the original man-animals were destroyed in a great flood, there were animal spirits that could appear in human form. Game Mother controlled the animals, and would recall the game if hunters lacked respect.

Otter, mink, marten, wolverine, wolf, and dog were considered to have supcranimal qualities, and they were eaten only in emergencies. Otter especially was a potent form of spirit entering women and causing both good fortune and illness. Possession by spirits and sorcery were recognized causes of illness, and shamans performed public ceremonies extracting alien objects.

Ghosts, particularly of the uncremated, wandered the earth, and sometimes the dead, particularly young children, were reborn to their former parents. The dead needed the help of the living to reach and maintain themselves in the afterworld. Funeral services were performed by members of the moiety opposite to the deceased. For this they were honored and feasted by the deceased's moiety. Special grave houses, enclosures, and posts were constructed and maintained.

Young men actively sought patron spirits and personal songs in the wilderness.

One variety of humanoids in the forests was said to kidnap people; another variety, to eat them.

Synonymy†

The name Tahltan was used in this form by Palgrave (1902); other spellings are Tahl-tan (Dawson 1889:192B), Tātltan (Boas 1895), and Toltan (Muir 1917:95). It is taken from Tlingit *ta·ɬta·n*, the name of a low flat at the mouth of the Tahltan River that was an important trading ground (Teit 1956:47–48). The Tahltan appear to have borrowed this name, unaltered, into their own language; although Tahltan folk-etymological interpretations have been offered, Emmons (1911:13) reported that the "older people generally agree that it is from some foreign tongue," and Teit (1956:47–48) was told that it was Tlingit. Tlingit also has *ta·ɬtanqʷá·n* 'Tahltan people'. The name of the village of Tahltan is also reported as Talyan (Smith in Colyer 1870:567).

Other names used by the Tahltan for themselves are tičaxhanoté·n 'people of tičaxhan' (Teit 1956:47, normalized), recorded in 1912 and 1915 (tičaxhan being a former village site at the mouth of the Tahltan River opposite *ta·ɬta·n*, the name of which is also given by Emmons [1911:13] as Tutcher anne or Tchaane), and

†This synonymy was written by Ives Goddard incorporating some materials from Bruce B. MacLachlan. The Tlingit words cited in italics are in phonemic transcriptions provided by Jeff Leer (communication to editors 1979); see the orthographic footnote in "Inland Tlingit," this vol.

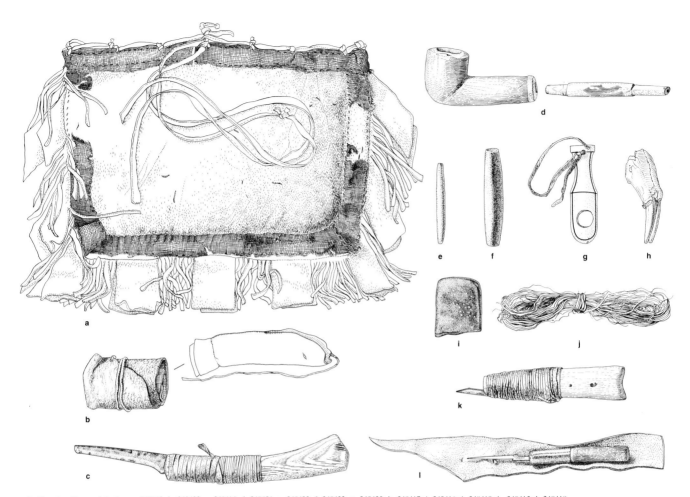

Fig. 6. Man's work bag and contents. a, Caribou bag trimmed with red cloth and fringed around edge; b, caribou skin paint bag; c, knife with iron blade; d, wooden pipe bowl, with brass ferrule, and stem; e-f, gambling bones used in the guessing game; g, bone slide for drawstrings on beaver net; h, beaver teeth in jawbone used to put edge on metal tools; i, whetstone for sharpening metal tools; j, caribou sinew for sewing and lashing; k, awl for piercing snowshoe frame for lacing; l, awl for sewing with sinew, steel point with mountain goat horn handle. Width of a, about 29 cm, rest same scale; collected by G.T. Emmons, 1904–1906.

ke·yeho·ti·ne 'people of Tahltan Village (key·e)', recorded in 1965 (Kenneth L. Hale, communication to editors 1979). It may be that the name recorded by Teit was originally that of a band centered at the Tahltan River mouth but came to apply to all Tahltan after they had coalesced in this area about 1870.

The Kaska call the Tahltan tačotena or tučotena (Honigmann 1954:21, normalized), not to be confused with the Titshotina band of Kaska. The Tsimshian name for the Tahltan is reported to be estikhe.n, derived from Tlingit štaxhí·n 'Stikine River' (Teit 1956:48). In local English the Tahltan are sometimes called Stikine or Stikine Indians (the same as the designation of the Stikine Tlingit in some sources), and their language is called Telegraph Creek language (Victor Golla, communication to editors 1979).

The Tahltan have also been referred to by terms applied generally to interior Northern Athapaskans. The Tlingit use ǧunana· 'strangers' in this sense, early spellings of which include Connenagh (Pope 1865:32, 1866:27–28), Kunana (Veniaminof, in Krause 1956:218), Kŭn-ŭn-ah´ and Khŭn-ŭn-āh´ (Dall 1886:376, 379), and Konē´.na (Teit 1956:48). Of similar scope was the term Stick Indians or Sticks (Smith, in Colyer 1870:567; Dall 1886:376, 379), a loan translation of Chinook Jargon stick siwash 'forest Indian' (Pope 1866:27). The name Nahani, and variants, has been widely used by Northern Athapaskans to refer to some group other than one's own (Honigmann 1956a), and it was used specifically for the Tahltan (and for "the Pelly River Indians") by the Kaska, being recorded by Teit (1956:48) as na.ani, naha.ne, nêhrane, nExa.ne, and nexōni. In earlier ethnic and linguistic classifications the Tahltan were included in a Nahani, or Nahane, grouping (Swanton 1910:10) that is no longer recognized (see "Nahani," this vol.). More specifically the Tahltan have been called the Western Nah·ane (Morice 1890), perhaps including other groups. Pope has been cited as distin-

466

Fig. 8. Koshon 'old wolf' and his wife Thlogosqin from the Stikine River region, in ceremonial costume. She is wearing a cloak made of the fur of small mammals with a border of bead-embroidered hide, tied near the neck and around the waist (Emmons 1911:43). He is wearing a shirt with appliquéd and probably partly beaded designs and a tight-fitting fur cap. Photograph by G.T. Emmons, 1904–1906.

Fig. 7. Structures serving simultaneously as shelters and smokehouses, in a fishing village on the Tahltan River at its junction with the Stikine River. This vicinity is the mythical home of the Tahltan and the location of their first known settlement. The rectangular structures, framed with heavy poles, have walls of saplings twined together at the top with a rope of willow bark and twigs, and a roof of lengthwise poles lashed on with willow bark rope and overlaid with spruce bark and brush, held down by small logs (Emmons 1911:37–38). bottom, Interior of Louise Dick's fish house at this site. top, Photograph by James A. Teit, 1912. bottom, Photograph by Bruce MacLachlan, 1956.

guishing the Tahltan as the Nahanies of the Upper Stikine (Emmons 1910:671, citing Pope 1865:32), but this phrase is to be taken to mean 'the Nahanies, who are on the Upper Stikine', since elsewhere Pope (1866:27–28) clearly uses "Nahany or Connenagh tribe" specifically for the Tahltan.

Sources

Observations of the ethnographers Morice (1890), Emmons (1911), and MacLachlan (1957) at Telegraph Creek have been published. Emmons's monograph (1911) remains the basic source, but Teit's (1906, 1909, 1914, 1919–1921, 1956) articles are necessary supplements to Emmons. Unpublished field notes by Teit (1915) repose in the National Museum of Canada, Ottawa, with artifacts and song recordings he collected. Anthropometric measurements of 36 Tahltans are reported by Boas (1901). Barbeau (1933) recorded phonographically at least one Tahltan song.

Heavy reliance has been given to information supplied by several long-term White residents of the area, J.C. Callbreath (Dawson 1889), Frederick Ingles (Emmons 1911), George Adsit (Teit 1956), C.F. Palgrave, and William P. Thorman (MacLachlan 1956; Duff 1972).

Artifacts collected by Emmons were placed in the University Museum, University of Pennsylvania, Philadelphia, and the Washington State Museum, University of Washington, Seattle.

Black's (1955) 1824 journal gives eyewitness observations of what are probably Tahltan near Caribou Hide. Journals and records of early White explorers and settlers in the upper Stikine drainage are found in the archives of the Hudson's Bay Company, Winnipeg, Manitoba; the Charles S. Hubbell collection of Alaskan manuscripts, Manuscript Department, University of Washington Library, Seattle; and the Bancroft Library, University of California, Berkeley. A partial copy of the Palgrave grammar (1902) and some other documents collected by R.J. Meek are located in the Provincial Archives of British Columbia, Victoria.

Inland Tlingit

CATHARINE McCLELLAN

Territory and Language

The Inland Tlingit ('klĭŋkĭt, 'klĭŋgĭt, 'tlĭŋkĭt, 'tlĭŋgĭt) of the twentieth century have mostly lived in Teslin village (fig. 1), which grew up around a trading post established in 1903 on Teslin Lake in southeastern Yukon Territory, and in the mining town of Atlin founded in 1898 on Atlin Lake in extreme northern British Columbia. Some are also in Whitehorse and other settlements of Yukon Territory, or in Juneau, Alaska. In 1974 the Canadian government formally recognized the Teslin and Atlin bands, members of which usually refer to themselves as Tlingit, although the Department of Indian Affairs and Northern Development designates the Atlin band as Tahltan. The Inland Tlingit have never formed a cohesive tribe nor made a treaty with the government of Canada, either as a total group or severally (Cumming and Mickenberg 1972:194–199).

Although their ancestors formerly lived along the upper Taku River, during the nineteenth and twentieth centuries most of the Inland Tlingit moved permanently across the divide to the headwaters of the Yukon River, perhaps splitting the ancestors of the Athapaskan-speaking Tagish from those of the Athapaskan Tahltan. Some or all of the Inland Tlingit may themselves be descended from Athapaskan-speaking Indians that adopted Tlingit as their chief language owing to extensive trade and intermarriage with coastal Tlingits during the nineteenth century. Specifically, they may be the descendants of the Athapaskans that Dawson (1889:193B) and Emmons (1911:5) called Taku and described as speaking Tahltan or a closely related dialect and in fact the Tlingit they speak* diverges somewhat from that of the Coastal Tlingit, who class them

as *ġunana·* 'strangers'. By 1970, most Inland Tlingit children spoke only English.

Although both Tlingit and Athapaskan speakers may share common roots in interior northwestern America, Barbeau (1947:277) was probably wrong in describing the Inland Tlingit as remnants of a classic Tlingit society that was once widespread in Yukon Territory and British Columbia. Rather, they represent a late expansion of Coastal Tlingit, or of their influence, triggered by the growth of the Euro-American fur trade. The main impetus for the Inland Tlingit move to the Yukon headwaters was the availability of fine land furs for which the demand swelled following the near destruction of the sea otter in the late eighteenth century (McClellan 1950:163–173, 1975a:7–8, 515–518). The Klondike and Atlin gold rushes of 1898 led to the final concentration of the Inland Tlingit in the Yukon drainage.

Because the Inland Tlingit shifted their areas of exploitation, the size of their territory at any given time is difficult to estimate, but the whole of the Taku and the Teslin-Nisutlin plateaus, which they intermittently occupied, comprises about 4,000 square miles (fig. 2).

External Relations

Throughout the nineteenth century, the Inland Tlingit married Tahltans to the south, but they also feuded with them continuously over the right to exploit both the upper Taku and the upper Yukon River basins. By 1900 the Inland Tlingit controlled the portion of the Yukon drainage where they now live, and most of the upper Taku drainage above the Tulsequah River; Coastal Taku Tlingit dominated the Taku below that

---

*The phonemes of Inland Tlingit are: (unaspirated stops and affricates) *d, ƛ, ʒ, ǯ, g, ġ, gʷ, ġʷ, ʔ;* (aspirated stops and affricates) *t, ƛ, c, č, k, q, kʷ, qʷ;* (glottalized) *t̓, ƛ̓, c̓, č̓, k̓, q̓, k̓ʷ, q̓ʷ;* (voiceless spirants) *ł, s, š, x, x̣, xʷ, x̣ʷ, h;* (glottalized spirants) *ł̓, s̓, x̓, x̣̓, x̓ʷ, x̣̓ʷ;* (nasals) *m, n;* (resonants) *w, l, y;* (short vowels) *a, e, i, u;* (long vowels) *a·, e·, i·, u·;* (tones) high (v́), low (unmarked). Sequences of velar (or back velar) plus *w* are distinct from unitary labialized phonemes, and sequences of obstruent plus *ʔ* are distinct from glottalized obstruents. The phoneme inventory of Inland Tlingit differs from that of Coastal Tlingit only in having the additional rare consonants *m* and *l*, but there are also differences in lexicon and in the phonemic shapes of some words. The basic sources for Tlingit pho-

nology are Boas (1917:9–13) and Leer in Williams and Williams (1978:6–17); specific information on Inland Tlingit and the phonemic transcription of Tlingit words was provided by Jeff Leer (communication to editors 1979), based on collaboration with John Marks.

In the practical orthography now in use (Story and Naish 1973; H. Davis 1976) the Tlingit phonemes are written as follows: d, dl, dz, j, g, g̲, gw, g̲w, .; t, tl, ts, ch, k, k̲, kw, k̲w; t', tl', ts', ch', k', k̲', k'w, k̲'w; ł, s, sh, x, x̲, xw, x̲w, h; ł', s', x', x̲', x'w, x̲'w; m, n; w, l̲, y; a, e, i, u; aa, ei, ee, oo; high tone (v́), low tone unmarked. Word-initial glottal stop is not written but is predictably present before all orthographically word-initial vowels. This orthography differs slightly from that of Naish and Story (1963), which it replaces.

Fig. 1. A street in Teslin village, with houses lined up in the style of the Coastal Tlingit and 3 flag poles. Lumber for some of the houses was sawed at the head of Teslin Lake during the height of the Klondike gold rush of 1898 and was later floated down to the village, which grew up around a trading post established at a native fishing site (McClellan 1975a:233–234, 237–240). Photograph by Douglas Leechman, 1948.

point (Emmons 1911:11–21; Goldschmidt and Haas 1946:57–70a; McClellan 1975a:49–64).

East and northeast of the Inland Tlingit are Kaska, with whom the nineteenth-century Inland Tlingit also traded, feuded, and sometimes intermarried. However, contacts have been greatest since the building of the Alaska Highway in 1942 (Honigmann 1954:15–23).

The Inland Tlingit traded and sometimes intermarried too with Pelly River Athapaskans to the north and with the Tagish to the west, who were originally Athapaskan speaking but who adopted the Tlingit language in the nineteenth century partly because of Inland Tlingit ties.

Population

Demographic data are unsatisfactory. The Taku plateau has been unpopulated since the first quarter of the twentieth century, except for one or two Atlin families who worked at Tulsequah mine until it closed in 1956, and who since then have sporadically trapped along the Nakina River. However, archeology and ethnography attest to at least a dozen former settlements in the area, although even the largest probably never exceeded 50 persons at any one time (French 1974; McClellan 1975a:48–64). In the Yukon drainage, the Inland Tlingit probably never numbered more than 400 (table 1). Official band lists omit women married to non-Indians who have hence lost Indian status for themselves and their children, or those of either sex who have for other reasons lost their legal Indian status.

Environment

The natural environment of the Taku plateau contrasts somewhat with that of the upper Yukon drainage (Bos-

tock 1948:50, map; Kerr 1948:4). Cutting through the rugged coastal range that rises above 8,000 feet in some places, the Taku River flows southeast along the edge of the great Juneau ice fields into the Pacific Ocean. Its lower reaches fall into the Sitkan biotic zone where rainfall is heavy. Where the Inland Tlingit lived, the climate is drier, and the flora and fauna become increasingly boreal, but steep relief and tangled brush along the river edges make overland travel difficult. Water travel, where possible, is often hazardous because of the fluctuating levels of the glacier-fed streams. Winter ice too is often treacherous.

The chief food resource is salmon. Large runs of chinook (king) (*Oncorhynchus tshawytscha*), coho (silver) (*O. kisutch*), and sockeye salmon (*O. nerka*) spawn in the Taku headwaters; pink salmon (*O. gorbuscha*) are blocked by a rockfall part way up the Nakina River. The major game animals since the mid-eighteenth century have been moose, caribou, sheep, goats, and bear, but moose were scarce until early in the twentieth century, and sheep too have been rare.

Two major trails lead from the Taku plateau across relatively low passes into the Yukon drainage. One goes up the Sloko River and into Atlin; another up the Nakina River to the head of Teslin Lake where, from 1897 until 1901(?), the Hudson's Bay Company had a post that also marked the end of a trail from Telegraph Creek in Tahltan country.

The Teslin-Nisutlin plateau is about 2,000 feet high, with surrounding mountains of over 6,000 feet (Bostock 1948:64–65). Climate, flora, and fauna are distinctly subarctic; however, while midwinter temperatures can drop below −60° F. at Teslin, neither Teslin nor Atlin has the extremes of climate characteristic of areas a little farther inland (Kendrew and Kerr 1955:147–156).

With lengths of 75 and 85 miles respectively, Teslin and Atlin are sizable lakes; other large and small lakes

Table 1. Population

Year	Teslin	Atlin	Source
1900	30[a]		Hudson's Bay Company 1899; L.W. Hall 1899
1944	150	?	Office of the Indian Agent, Whitehorse, Yukon Terr.
1950	150	?	Office of the Indian Agent, Whitehorse, Yukon Terr.
1951	?	55	Hawthorne, Belshaw, and Jamieson 1958:28
1961	135	?	Bullen 1968:46
1974	256	164	Canada. Department of Indian Affairs and Northern Development, Whitehorse, Yukon Terr.
1978	250	161	Canada. Department of Indian Affairs and Northern Development 1980:48

[a] "Most of which belong to the Takio (sic) Tribe," at "Old Post" at head of Teslin Lake.

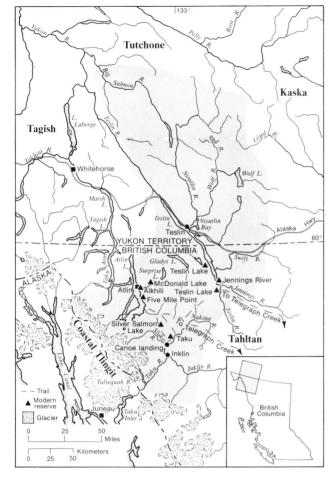

Fig. 2. Late 19th–early 20th century territory with modern reserves.

dot the country as well. Most contain freshwater white-fish, trout, pike, and ling cod. Some rivers are clear; others are full of glacial silt. Chinook salmon and chum salmon (*Oncorhynchus keta*) arrive in the Teslin River in late summer, and they reach the Nisutlin River in sufficient numbers so that on it during the nineteenth century Teslin Indians had an important fish camp. However, because they have swum more than 2,000 miles, many salmon are fit only for dog food. Atlin Indians must cross back to the Taku drainage for salmon fishing.

As on the Taku plateau, caribou and moose popu-lations have fluctuated through time. In the nineteenth century people most often hunted caribou, and in ear-lier times they also got wood bison, which are now extinct in the area (Cowan and Guiguet 1973:388; McClellan 1975a:108–120). The numbers of small game, furbearers, and game birds constantly increase and drop off in complex interrelated cycles.

Traditional Culture

This section is an account of reconstructed nineteenth-century Inland Tlingit culture. Historical sources are both few and meager, so that knowlege of nineteenth-century ways has depended almost wholly on the mem-ories of twentieth-century Indians. The picture that emerges tends to be idealized and timeless, but signif-icant changes known to have occurred in either century are indicated.

Subsistence

The Inland Tlingit knew that gaining a successful live-lihood from their natural environment was an uncertain matter. They met the challenge by combining an inti-mate knowledge of the varied terrain and weather, learned physical skills, ingenious technology, and a strong faith in the possibility of gaining the favor of the superhuman spirits whom they believed to control the universe. Ritual observances to please these spirits were an essential part of the food quest.

In the Taku basin, the Inland Tlingit relied heavily on the summer salmon catch, part of which they stored. Some lower Taku River Tlingit also came upstream in

Natl. Mus. of Canada, Ottawa: J-729.

Fig. 3. Man putting a mink skin on a wooden stretcher. Mink were not trapped until the 20th century; they were formerly associated with bad luck, especially for women (McClellan 1975a:142–145). Photograph by Catharine McClellan, Flat Creek, Yukon Terr., April 1951.

summer where they could dry salmon more easily than on the rainy coast and could also trade with the Inland Tlingit for valuable land furs. By September they returned home, and the Inland Tlingit, after several weeks of berrying ("Environment and Culture in the Cordillera," fig. 13, this vol.), and upland hunts for ground squirrels, groundhogs, and big game, began to gather in settlements near their supplies of stored salmon. But no group could remain sedentary for the entire winter. The food stored in pits on the gravel ridges rarely lasted past January, and in order to get either large or small game, or to trap furs, households had to disperse widely—a pattern that the fur trade surely intensified. Units of two or three nuclear families increasingly crossed to the Yukon to hunt and trap, not to return to the Taku until after the spring beaver hunt. Some families then continued downstream to trade on the coast, while others remained to prepare again for summer fishing and the upriver trade. Throughout the year feuding with the Tahltan and Coastal Tlingit clans was endemic. By the late nineteenth century many of the Inland Tlingit had begun to live permanently in the Yukon headwaters. There the salmon supplies were never so great as on the Taku River, and although hunters cached meat from the fall hunt at various spots in the mountains, by midwinter small family groups

were constantly moving from one fresh moose or caribou kill to another, or from one fish lake to another. Spring was the leanest season of all until spawning whitefish enabled the families to reunite at favorite spots such as Nisutlin Bay near present Teslin. In all seasons of the year much of the diet consisted of freshwater fish and small game instead of the preferred salmon and big game. Berries, either fresh or preserved, Hedysarum roots, and inner spruce bark were the chief vegetal foods. To the extent that it is known, the Inland Tlingit subsistence cycle was quite marginal compared with that of the more sedentary and numerous Coastal Tlingit.

Technology

In both the Taku and the Yukon drainages, Inland Tlingit technology was typical of neighboring Cordilleran peoples. The essential materials—stone, wood, hide, sinew, bone, antler, horn, bark, and roots—were readily available and easily worked.

Men and women trapped, speared, hooked, gaffed, and gill-netted fish. During the 1950s some Teslin Indians drifted gill nets by torchlight for salmon, a technique said to have been learned from Whites. Gill-netting under the ice (fig. 5) was probably also introduced

Yukon Arch., Whitehorse: Jim Robb Coll.

Fig. 4. Beaver skins stretched in the oval shape preferred by traders until the 20th century when the round shape replaced it (see "Hare," fig. 7, this vol.). The man in the center is looking through binoculars. Photograph by George Johnston, Teslin, 1934.

Fig. 5. Daisy Sheldon pulling a gill net through a hole in the ice. Photograph by Catharine McClellan, Teslin, 1951.

shot with bunting arrows or snared. Brave men fought bears as they did their human enemies by spearing them at close quarters. Less adventurous hunters caught them in heavy deadfalls or toss-pole snares.

The arrowheads for large game were of bone or antler. They were detachable and unilaterally barbed to cause internal bleeding. Bows were simple or recurved slightly and had wooden wrist guards. Metal arrowheads and a wide variety of introduced firearms gradually replaced these traditional weapons by the end of the nineteenth century.

Beaver were netted under the ice or speared. Hunters left enough adults in each colony for "seed." Because steel traps do not allow for this selectivity, they never became popular for beaver.

Other furbearers such as fox, wolverine, and marten were best caught in wooden deadfalls, but lynx were most often snared. Although a few mid-twentieth century trappers still preferred such methods, most had come to rely on steel traps.

Mink, otter, and wolves were seldom killed, because all were thought to be so very dangerous spiritually. Hunters who caught such animals took especially stringent ritual precautions, as they did with grizzly bears. They carefully disposed of all animal corpses, paying greatest attention to the heads so that dogs did not chew them. (For further details on Inland Tlingit subsistence, technology, and ritual see McClellan 1975a:95–231, 253–257, 261–297.)

Structures

The nineteenth-century Inland Tlingit built several rectangular houses along the Taku River in imitation of coastal-style structures, and at least one lineage head constructed a special "potlatch house" in which to display goods accumulated for a memorial feast, but this was never finished as a permanent dwelling. Most houses were impermanent double lean-tos of brush, sheltering two to four nuclear families. Sometimes a second and third house shared side walls with a central dwelling. The walls had hidden pockets where children could hide in case of an enemy attack. Other brush shelters were conical.

By the end of the century, people began to cluster near trading posts, churches, schools, and mining centers and to build log cabins or lumber houses holding only a single nuclear family with an additional relative or two. Since World War II, the variety of single or multiroomed houses has increased in the villages. Tents or log cabins have continued to serve on the traplines.

Necessary adjuncts to traditional camps were storage caches and menstrual and birth huts, which were always a good distance from the center of activities (McClellan 1975a:237–251).

by them. It increased in importance as the numbers and sizes of dog teams grew after their introduction in the late nineteenth century. The advent of snowmobiles in the 1960s reduced the need for dogs and therefore of fishing activity.

Animals of all sizes were taken in snares and deadfalls, probably more often than with arrows, spears, or clubs. Hunters shot bison with arrows, but it is not known if they also used other methods to get them or how important they once were in the basic economy. Nor is it certain whether the Inland Tlingit constructed circular caribou corrals with V-shaped dromoi such as were used by the neighboring Kaska (Honigmann 1954:37). They certainly made long brush fences into which they set drag-pole snares at intervals to catch both caribou and moose. Drag-pole snares were also set singly along game trails, or hunters shot moose with arrows. Goats and sheep were shot with arrows or snared. Groundhogs (*Marmota monax*, woodchuck) and ground squirrels (*Spermophilus parryii*) were snared, or caught in deadfalls. Other small game and birds were

Clothing

Aboriginally, both men and women wore trousers with moccasins attached and tailored skin shirts cut and decorated in typical Cordilleran style. In very cold weather they donned goat wool trousers and overshirts of caribou or netted hare skin, with separate collared hoods. Each adult had a fur robe that served both for extra clothing and bedding. Skillful trappers boasted robes of pieced-together fox or lynx paw skins (McClellan 1975a:299–324).

By the end of the nineteenth century most Inland Tlingit had adopted Western-style clothing and begun to wear shoes or boots, but some late twentieth-century adults still preferred moccasins with ankle wrappings that keep out the snow in winter and the insects in summer.

Late summer skins of caribou or moose were best for traditional clothing and footwear. Commercially tanned skins were introduced in the 1960s for making items for the tourist trade. They were not very satisfactory but were welcomed by younger women unwilling to undertake the arduous soaking, wringing, smoking, and scraping by which the heavy raw skins used to be transformed to fine suede (McClellan 1975a:256–257, 264–267).

Whether Inland Tlingit women ever wove Chilkat blankets of bark and goat wool is doubtful. Some people certainly owned them, as well as dance blankets and shirts of imported navy blue and red wool. The shirts, derived in style from Western military dress, were embellished with floral designs and clan crests (figs. 6–7) worked in seed beads, pearl buttons, and appliqué. Headdresses, dance bibs, and special face paintings also symbolized clan affiliations. Since about 1960, nativistic movements have revived interest in heirloom ceremonial garb and resulted in a proliferation of modern replicas and new creations (McClellan 1975a:299–324, 1948–1975).

Transportation

During the nineteenth century a few lineage heads bought large dugout canoes on the coast, so they could easily bring goods up the Taku River. One such canoe was even carried across the divide to Atlin Lake. Ordinarily, Canoe Landing at the junction of the Sloko and Nakina rivers marked the head of navigation. The trip from there downstream to Juneau required only a few days; however, the return journey—made in the high water or summer when the wind blew steadily upstream—took at least a week. Boatmen tried to sail wing on wing, using moosehide (and later canvas) sails, but crews often had to thread along steep banks and treacherous sandbars pulling the heavily laden boats

Anglican Church of Canada, General Synod Arch., Toronto, Ont.:P7517–326.
Fig. 6. Joe Sqwam, headman of the *de·ši·ta·n* or *tuqwe·dí* clan at Teslin, with his 2 wives. He wears a beaver-fur hat with ribbons and a mirror and a shirt with a beaded design showing his beaver crest animal. The shirt of his wife Annie, to his right, shows her *yanye·dí* eagle crest. Her sister Mary, to his left, wears a coast-style button blanket. Photograph by Heber Wilkinson, summer, 1923–1925.

with ropes. At Canoe Landing they cached the craft and walked farther inland.

In the interior people had rafts, small cottonwood dugouts, or light frame boats that could be temporarily covered with raw moosehides, but they preferred walking when possible. Summer trails followed major watercourses, usually staying high above the streams and cutting across smaller drainages. In winter people also traveled on frozen lakes and rivers.

Snowshoes, with either round or pointed toes, were essential in winter, and they remain so for those on foot. Hunting shoes ran six feet or more in length; trail shoes were shorter. Since the 1960s several Teslin families have made snowshoes for commercial sale (White 1972:44–56).

Traditional drags were made from the foreleg skins of moose or caribou, the skins being pieced together so that their hair ran in the same direction and the drags moved easily over the snow. Women used them to pull household goods from camp to camp, while the men went ahead hunting. They were also used to bring in meat. Steamed-plank toboggans and dog traction were both introduced in the nineteenth century from the Mackenzie River area, as were all forms of sleds. While useful on the ice or well-broken trails, sleds often fail in the powdery snow of the bush. Whether dog packing is aboriginal is uncertain, but it has long been common in both summer and winter.

As they traveled, people bent branches or set up sticks with charcoal marks indicating the directions they were going, the location of game, or other information. They signaled their whereabouts with smoke.

Natl. Mus. of Canada, Ottawa: J–733–5; drawings after McClellan 1975a:107, 481, 299.

Fig. 7. Mary Jackson, Jake Jackson (headman of the *deˑšiˑtaˑn* clan), and Annie Geddes recording ceremonial songs. They are wearing red dance shirts decorated with animal crests, beads, and button work, representing beaver, double-limbed beaver—both of the *deˑšiˑtaˑn* clan of the Crow moiety—and killer whale of the Old *yanyeˑdí* clan of the Wolf moiety. Jake Jackson wears the same hat worn by Joe Sqwam in fig. 6. Photograph by Catharine McClellan, Teslin, 1951. Drawings left to right: single double-limbed beaver (from back of shirt), double-limbed beavers, and killer whales.

Following the gold rush of 1898 an influx of horses, stern-wheelers, and, later, motor boats revolutionized travel. The building of the Alaska Highway in 1942 brought cars, trucks, buses, and airplanes and linked the Inland Tlingit indissolubly with the "outside" industrial world. By the late 1960s radio and television likewise were powerful forces in cultural change (McClellan 1975a:267–279, 1948–1975).

Social Organization

The Inland Tlingit tell their history as a set of specific traditions associated with five or six Tlingit named clans (exogamous matrilineal descent groups), local segments of which also existed among the Coastal Tlingit. The clans themselves were dually grouped so that the entire population was divided into the Crow moiety (Tlingit *yéˑɬ*, translated on the coast as 'Raven') and the Wolf moiety (Tlingit *ġuˑč*), sometimes designated instead as Eagle (Tlingit *čáˑḵ*).

In any given locality a clan achieved its relative rank through one or more resident lineages, that is, through a group or groups of individuals who easily traced their kinship to each other through their mothers. Theoretically, all lineages within a clan were related to each other, no matter where they were located.

Rules of clan and moiety exogamy meant that a husband always belonged to a lineage and clan of one moiety, while his wife and children belonged to a lineage and clan of the opposite moiety. The matrilineally related males who most often acted together were brothers, and maternal uncles and nephews, but a man's paternal grandfather and his son's sons might also be included. This was because ideally two lineages should exchange spouses from generation to generation so that persons bearing the same names, with their associated ranks and prerogatives, produced offspring whose names also remained constant but whose ranks might rise if they successfully met the requirements of their ascribed statuses. High-ranked families—those composed of senior lineal and collateral members of the lineages—made every effort to sustain the ideal through manipulation of the kinship system and strategic distribution of wealth on public occasions. Although descent was matrilineal, reciprocity was constant between one's own matrilineage and that of one's

475

father. "Father's people," whether reckoned closely or in the extended sense allowed by the kinship terminologies, were as important in determining individual social position as were "mother's people" (De Laguna 1952:8–12, 1972, 1:476–498; McClellan 1954, 1975a:439–478).

The kinship system was of a Crow type like that of the Coastal Tlingit. One set of terms could be extended to designate all within one's own lineage, clan, and moiety in the first ascending and descending generations. Another set encompassed individuals in one's father's lineage, and by extension those of all lineages and clans of the opposite moiety. Grandparent and grandchild terms were also widely extended, but the terms themselves did not distinguish lineage affiliations. There were affinal terms too, although ideally one's affines were also often one's consanguines (De Laguna 1954; 1972, 1:475–496; Durlach 1928:17–67; McClellan 1975a:418–438; Swanton 1908:423–425).

Every lineage constantly tried to increase its prestige. However, various quarrels and other misfortunes have led to fissions and fusions of lineage and clan that have resulted in complex and contradictory claims to crests and other prerogatives. For example, three distinct lineages of the Inland Tlingit have asserted that they represent the *yanye·dí* clan (usually translated 'hemlock people') of the Wolf moiety. In the twentieth century two lineages have been centered in Teslin and one in Atlin. Each has attempted to operate as a separate clan claiming a special *yanye·dí* Wolf crest, conceptually distinct from the Wolf associated with all clans of the Wolf (or Eagle) moiety. However, the first *yanye·dí* lineage to arrive in the Teslin area in the nineteenth century asserts it has the greatest right to the *yanye·dí* Wolf and names.

Important nineteenth- and twentieth-century clans of the Crow moiety at Teslin have been the *de·ší·ta·n* 'end-of-the-trail people', also sometimes called *tuqwe·dí* (translation uncertain), and the *qú·kʷhítta·n* 'cellarhouse people' and *ʔiški·ta·n* 'salmon-hole people', both of which are also represented in Atlin. Some *qú·kʷhítta·n* equated themselves with *ʔatdú·guhítta·n* 'skin-house people', and both groups claim to be closely related to the coastal *ġa·naxʔádi* 'people of Ganax', and sometimes identify themselves as such. (For further discussion of Inland Tlingit clans see McClellan 1950:77–98, 112–115, 1975a:418–438.)

The exact composition of various residential units during the nineteenth century remains uncertain, but fluid membership was characteristic. A man and his son-in-law and family, two or more like-sex siblings, their spouses, children, and perhaps their parents, or a brother and sister who had married another cross-sex sibling pair and their offspring and parents might join to hunt and trap together, but other combinations were possible. In twentieth-century settlements groups of

Catharine McClellan, Madison, Wis.

Fig. 8. Participants in a costumed dance at the July 1, 1949, Teslin village Sports Day celebrating Queen Victoria's birthday. top, left to right, Old Fox (headman of the Old *yanye·dí* clan) with feather dance fans and wearing a beaded dance shirt showing the clan crest of an eagle and its young, the drummer William Johnston (New *yanye·dí*, elected chief of Teslin), and Jake Jackson (headman of the *de·ší·ta·n* clan) wearing his clan's beaver dance shirt. bottom, Dance in progress. Photograph by Dorothy Rainier Libby.

siblings tended to build single-family houses side by side. Brothers-in-law were expected to cooperate with each other and act as intermediaries in many reciprocal obligations between lineages of opposite moieties.

No chief had coercive power over all, although ranking lineage heads or good hunters with powerful personalities often attracted followers and acted as de facto leaders of localized exploitative groups. Ideally, each local clan segment formed a distinct corporate group within which all crime or unrest had to be settled as

476

best as possible through the skill and persuasion of the head man and his advisors. Disputes between clans of the same or opposite moiety often led to feuding if high-ranking lineage heads could not settle matters through appeals to the respect owed to 'father's people' or to other real or putative kin (McClellan 1975a:418–438).

Following World War II, the Department of Indian Affairs instituted elected band chiefs and councils. Since the early 1970s each band has also had a paid band manager and a secretary.

Life Cycle

The Inland Tlingit throughout the nineteenth and most of the twentieth centuries have viewed life as a continuous round from birth to death and a subsequent rebirth of one's soul into a new body. How much variation from the psychological and social behavior of a previous incarnation was allowed or expected is uncertain. Souls could be reborn to individuals of different sex and with different names (De Laguna 1954, 1972, 2:757–790; McClellan 1975a:376–399).

• BIRTH AND CHILDHOOD Every couple hoped for children. Ideally a woman of the parturient's father's lineage delivered the baby, but in practice the best midwife in a small local group would serve.

Children spent their first few months in hooded skin carrying bags, graduating to cases with tailored legs and feet, and finally, to ones with openings through which they could thrust their legs. Adults, especially grandparents, indulged the very young who led unrestricted lives until they "came to their senses" and could begin to understand the nature of the universe and accept their responsibilities within it. By the age of five or six children started to internalize the intricacies of the kinship systems and its related behavior. Equally important, they learned the constant necessity to please the superhuman spirits of animals and other phenomena of their environment. At play, children often imitated their elders, taking on their respective sex roles.

• PUBERTY Mothers prepared their daughters for puberty, warning them that at the first flow of blood they should wait until they were discovered and could be properly isolated by their female relatives. Ideally a girl then remained in a special puberty shelter for two full years. Throughout her isolation, she wore a large "bonnet" of dressed hide propped out in front of her on a willow framework. The period was marked by many restrictions on the girl's behavior, and numerous ritual acts, but her only practical training was in sewing. The ultimate purpose of all the symbolic observances was to insure a successful life for her and all her clan members. Some of the ritual was repeated at the births of each of her children and the death of her husband.

Some of it was also followed by young fathers and by widowers.

Throughout their reproductive lives women were regarded as potentially dangerous to, or in danger from, the many spirits of the natural environment, and a host of ritual precautions effectively cut females off from sources of power available to adult males. Women thought their lives to be much harder than men's, but this view of sex roles slowly shifted as traditional beliefs died out and women became leaders in the nativistic organizations of the 1970s (McClellan 1975a:385–395; Cruikshank 1969).

Boys too underwent rigorous training at puberty. The young males of a camp lived together in a loose age group. Although cross-sex siblings who had reached puberty (as well as uterine brothers) had to avoid direct speech or glances, the boys' sisters usually prepared their food. Their maternal uncles and other knowledgable males of their clans were their stern mentors. Fathers helped in the training, but it was thought they might be overindulgent since they belonged to the opposite moiety.

In 1907 the Roman Catholics opened a religious school for Indians near Atlin, and in 1910 the Anglicans established the first of a series of local schools for both Indians and Whites at Teslin. Since 1900 Inland Tlingit have also attended boarding schools run by Roman Catholics, Anglicans, or Baptists or have gone to high school or vocational school in Whitehorse under programs set up by the Department of Indian Affairs in the 1960s (Bilsland and Ireland 1971:51; Bullen 1968:137–200; King 1967).

• MARRIAGE AND OLD AGE First marriage was often to someone much older, since lineage status dictated the proper alliance, which was arranged by the elders. Both polyandry and polygyny were practiced. A considerable bride price was required for a high-ranking girl, and all marriages entailed initial bride service, which continued in the sense that a son-in-law had to provide for his wife's parents until their deaths. If there were few daughters in a family, a man might travel with his parents-in-law for many years. Often his father-in-law was his paternal grandfather, mother's brother, or his brother, since ideally he married his maternal uncle's widow (who was ideally also his father's sister), his maternal uncle's daughter, or his brother's daughter, and frequently these were uterine, not merely classificatory kin. A man acted formally to or avoided these males as he did his mother-in-law, even though prior to his marriage she was usually a joking relative. A girl respected but did not avoid her parents-in-law (McClellan 1961:110–114, 1975a:418–438). Most twentieth-century marriages have been solemnized in Christian churches.

The entire social system stressed relative seniority, and the old commanded respect. As people aged they were thought to become more closely allied with the superhuman world. Some developed abilities to foretell events though body portents or dreams. A few used their spiritual powers to achieve ends they could no longer obtain through physical means. Children were taught to be kind to the old, both because they would some day need help and because offended elders might bewitch them.

• DEATH A death always triggered intensive reciprocal social behavior. The closest relatives in the moiety opposite that of the deceased prepared the corpse for cremation, or, in the twentieth century, burial. They gathered at once to eulogize the dead person and to smoke, eat, and sing with his clan members. Smoking, the fire into which some of the food was put, and songs were all channels of communication between the living and the dead.

Potlatching

The final deposition of a person's ashes took place about a year after cremation, by which time his lineage had collected enough food and wealth either to host or to participate in a memorial potlatch. Local and sometimes geographically distant clan members of the moiety opposite that of the deceased were formally invited as guests.

Only a high-ranking person would inaugurate a potlatch to which people from afar were invited, but whenever such ceremonies were held, the lesser-ranked members within the clan or moiety of the chief host would contribute to the costs and like him would distribute gifts to any guests to whom they were indebted for earlier services, whether for a death or other reason. Wealth from the fur trade enabled the nineteenth-century Inland Tlingit to hold potlatches lasting a week or more.

Most potlatches occurred after the fall hunt, since several days of feasting, singing, and dancing preceded the major ritual. At the beginning of the main ceremony the personal possessions of the dead person were claimed by close lineage relatives, and the guests deposited the ashes in a grave house that they themselves built. This was followed by a solemn meal for the dead, a collection of wealth by the hosts from among themselves, and its subsequent distribution to the guests. By these acts appropriate living members of the host moiety socially validated their assumption of the names and statuses of the dead, with all associated prerogatives and obligations. Both hosts and guests sang honored clan songs, danced, displayed their crests, and engaged in notable oratory. Those who had performed specific duties for the deceased were specially paid, but all guests received gifts commensurate with their ranks and relationship to the dead person or persons being honored.

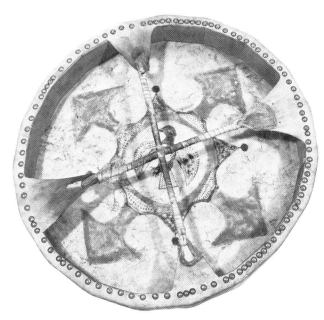

Natl. Mus. of Canada, Ottawa: VI–J–80.

Fig. 9. Single-headed drum, skin stretched over a wooden frame and secured with brass tacks; the underside of the head is painted with eagle and arrow designs. Diameter 18 cm, collected at Teslin Lake, 1911.

Many features of memorial potlatches also characterized other potlatches held to wipe off a person's shame or to signalize some other event requiring public validation. Traditional-style potlatching continued in the 1970s.

Trade and Warfare

Until the twentieth century the Coastal Tlingit prevented direct trading with the Whites, even when the Inland Tlingit visited the coast. The lower Taku River Tlingit annually went well into the Yukon drainage to collect furs. In this trade they took advantage of the Inland Tlingit who, in turn, exploited the Athapaskans farther inland. Although trading partners structured their relationships in a framework of real or fictive kinship (McClellan 1950:50–150, 160–204, 1964:7–8, 1975a:515–518), much of the feuding between the Tahltan and Inland Tlingit or between upper and lower Taku River Tlingit flared over efforts to monopolize sources of fine fur or of trade goods. Marriage alliances cemented for trading purposes were highly vulnerable to dispute, and sudden raids for revenge were common, but local clan heads rarely united to conduct group warfare. Specific war leaders were chosen for each raid; raiders also relied heavily on shamanistic aid (McClellan 1975a:519–527, 1975b:188–198).

Peacemaking was highly ritualized. Reciprocal hostages called "deer" were symbolically clothed, fed, and waited upon, until the headmen of each faction worked out ways to settle the dispute, whether by death or payment, which would equalize damages inflicted by each side. Several important peace ceremonies between the Inland Tlingit and Tahltan during the nineteenth century were commemorated by pictographs along the Taku River (McClellan 1975a:519–527).

World View and Religion

The world view included a belief in the creator trickster, Crow (*yé·ł*, the Raven of the Coastal Tlingit), and stories about him and other mythical beings help explain the nature of the universe and of acceptable behavior in it. To coastal clan traditions the Inland Tlingit added their own specialized lineage histories, and they also told many stories widespread among neighboring Athapaskans: for example, Star Husband, Bear Husband, The Adventures of Two Brothers, and others. With the Tagish and Tahltan, they shared the myth of Animal Mother who gave birth to all the game animals (McClellan 1970a:89–91).

Religious observances related primarily to powerful spirit owners of the mountains and the water as well as to those of various creatures and other phenomena within their domains and elsewhere. Since these spirits could work either good or evil and were usually more powerful than humans, the essential philosophical problem was how to maintain proper relationships with them. A man who conducted himself wisely could gain personal power from such spirits, and almost every adult male had one or more spirit helpers who enabled him to influence the weather, to kill game easily, or to have good luck of other kinds. Imitative rituals could also accomplish some of these ends and could be practiced by all.

Professional shamans deliberately sought out the most powerful spirit helpers, even though contact with such power might backfire and kill them. Some shamans inherited the helpers of their maternal uncles or fathers, but all had to endure long periods of ritual withdrawal before they were ready to practice publicly.

A shaman ideally acted for everybody's benefit, controlling the weather, locating game, healing sickness, or dueling with threatening shamans from elsewhere. Successful shamans gained prestige and wealth but also risked accusations of witchcraft. Most shamans were men, since reproductively active women were believed to offend animal spirits (McClellan 1956, 1975a:529–565).

Since the late nineteenth century the Russian Orthodox, Anglican, Presbyterian, Roman Catholic, and a few fundamentalist churches have converted all Inland Tlingit to a syncretistic Christianity. By 1950 many had accepted White ideas of moral behavior and scientific knowledge (McClellan 1956; Bilsland and Ireland 1971: 49–52; Bullen 1968:98–180, 235–249). In the 1960s, however, the Inland Tlingit began to participate actively in native organizations that aim both to revive traditional value systems and to gain important civil rights (Yukon Native Brotherhood 1973).

Synonymy†

The name Inland Tlingit was introduced by McClellan (1950:102–124) because these people, though in an interior location, have Tlingit as their native language, at least in the twentieth century, and usually designated themselves as Tlingit.

Early references to the Indians at the headwaters of the Taku and Yukon rivers applied to them the name Taku (Dawson 1889:193B; Teit 1906:337, 1909:314, 1914:484; Emmons 1911:5), a rendering of Tlingit *ta·qú* 'Taku River'. However, this name has more often been used for the better-known Coastal Tlingit Indians of the lower Taku River and Taku Inlet (Swanton 1908:396–412, 1910b).

Dall (1877:33) gave Tāh'ko-tin'neh as a name used by "some of the traders" for a small, poorly known group of Indians inhabiting "the basin of the Lewis River"; this name is presumably 'Taku people', although it is not known from what Athapaskan language, if any, it was taken. As Dall was never in the upper Yukon area the location he gave was vague; at the time he wrote the entire course of the Yukon River above its confluence with the Pelly was called the Lewes River, but the Athapaskan-speaking ancestors of the Inland Tlingit probably never lived west of the Teslin River, in the southeastern part of the area he indicates. Dawson (1889:193B) distinguished between Tahltan-speaking Taku in the interior, whom he equated with Dall's Lewes River group, and Tlingit-speaking Taku on the coast; nevertheless, he used the same name for both.

Hodge (1910k) apparently coined Takutine on the basis of Taku and Dall's name, but he included under this term also the Ta-koos-oo-ti-na of Dawson (1889:200B–201B) and the "Nehaunees of the Chilkaht River" of Dall (1877:33); accordingly he describes the Takutine as living on Teslin River and Lake and the upper Taku River, with hunting grounds that included the Big Salmon River and extended to the Pelly and upper Liard rivers. However, both of Hodge's inclusions are incorrect. Ta-koos-oo-ti-na was recorded by Dawson as a Kaska name for the Pelly River Indians, who were probably Tutchone; they are entirely distinct in his account from the Athapaskan group he called Taku. The "Nehaunees of the Chilkaht River" were described by Dall as an Athapaskan group of the Upper Yukon drainage that traded goods from the Chilkat Tlingit to the "Crows" (Tutchone) and "Nehaunees"

†This synonymy was written by Ives Goddard incorporating materials and references from Catharine McClellan.

(other interior Athapaskans); to judge from their location they may have been the Tagish.

Osgood (1936:17–18) lists the Taku and Tahltan as the two divisions of his Tahltan group; in this he followed Emmons, who had classed the Taku, Tahltan, and Kaska together as "Nahane," but with the exclusion of the Kaska, whom Osgood recognized as a separate major group. These varying usages and many ambiguities have led to the dropping of the name Taku in favor of Inland Tlingit for the interior Tlingit-speaking group.

The Canadian Department of Indian Affairs and Northern Development. Indian Affairs Branch (1968) listed the Teslin and Atlin bands as Tagish, although in 1974 they designated the Atlin band as Tahltan. In 1968 both bands were classified as linguistically Tlingit.

Sources

Documentation on the Inland Tlingit is meager and often confusing because of the variable use of Taku as a "tribal" name.

Simpson (1847, 1:214–217) briefly mentioned trade between the lower Taku River Tlingit and the Indians (Inland Tlingit) farther upstream. Dall (1877:33) published two lines on the Tāh´ko-tin´neh, succinctly describing them as "scarcely known to the Whites." Both authors wrote from hearsay.

Dawson, who traveled near Inland Tlingit country in 1887, devoted a few paragraphs to the Inland Tlingit under the name Taku (Dawson 1889:193B,200B). Dall and Dawson are the only sources cited by Hodge (1910k:676).

Unpublished Hudson's Bay Company Records from the end of the nineteenth century tell something of the trading and hunting of the Inland Tlingit at the head of Teslin Lake, and there are some unpublished notes by the Canadian geologist, William Ogilvie, who met Inland Tlingit on the upper Taku River in 1895 and saw their grave houses at the confluence of the Sloko and Nakina rivers (McClellan 1975a:48–64; Ogilvie 1894–1895).

Following the discovery of gold in the Klondike in 1896 and at Atlin in 1898, Indians who were certainly Inland Tlingit begin to be mentioned briefly in travel books, newspapers, and various geological and missionary reports, but important data remain in manuscripts written by prospectors or missionaries (for example, Bobillier 1939).

Emmons (1911) and Teit (1906, 1909, 1914, 1956), who did ethnographic work with the Tahltan at Telegraph Creek, include a small amount of data on the Inland Tlingit as does Honigmann (1954:22–23), but only McClellan and Rainier have done ethnography directly with them. This was carried out intermittently between 1948 and 1974, mostly in Teslin, and focused on traditional culture (McClellan and Rainier 1950; McClellan 1950, 1953, 1954, 1956, 1961, 1970, 1970a, 1975, 1975a, 1975b). In 1968 French (1974) began archeological and ethnographic work in Atlin and the Taku drainage, following up a brief archeological survey by McClellan and Osborne in 1956 (McClellan 1975a:59–64). Bilsland and Ireland's (1971) history of Atlin includes virtually nothing on the Indians. Bullen's (1968) study of the Indian education system describes Teslin in the 1960s, and White (1972) published a popular account of modern Teslin Indian crafts. The Teslin Women's Institute's (1972) history of Teslin contains material on native life written by Indians. Tommy Peter, a Teslin Indian, with the help of Nora Florendo, published the Bear Husband story in Tlingit (T. Peter 1973). Twentieth-century pictures of Inland Tlingit may be found in Cruikshank (1975:33, 39, 42–45, 48–51, 52, 58, 64, 67, 71–72, 75–76, 85–90, 96–104, 117, 119, 132–135, 143–144).

Tagish

CATHARINE MCCLELLAN

Territory, Environment, and Language

The Tagish ('tăgĭsh) live on the Yukon River head-waters in southern Yukon Territory and northern British Columbia (fig. 1). Little was known about them ethnographically until the 1940s.

Prior to 1898 the Tagish exploited about 4,000 square miles of the Yukon plateau (Bostock 1948:64–67). The northern limits ran from Marsh Lake northeast to Teslin River drainage; the southern limits, from the vicinity of White Pass through the northern portion of Atlin Lake. Westward, the Tagish hunted high in the headwaters of the Watson River but probably did not cross to the Takhini drainage. The rugged coastal range, with some peaks of more than 7,000 feet, has two passes that cut through to Tagish country from Lynn Canal, a deep ocean fjord along which lived the Chilkoot Tlingit. The Chilkoot Pass begins at Dyea, Alaska. The White Pass, which starts at Skagway, Alaska, was the route chosen for the building of the White Pass and Yukon Railway in 1900, which first linked the Tagish easily with the outside world.

Most of the Tagish country consists of the broad Lewes and Teslin plateaus, which are between 3,500 and 4,000 feet high (Bostock 1948:65–66). Several large lakes run in a generally north-south direction feeding the silt-laden upper Yukon (or Lewes) River. Precipitation is slight, and the climate is subarctic. Temperatures drop to −60° F. in winter and sometimes rise above 90° F. in summer. Valleys are timbered with boreal forest, but there are also extensive meadowlands, and, on the mountain heights, an alpine tundra (McClellan 1975a:34–36).

The Tagish seasonally exploited all types of terrain from the river bottoms to above the timberline. The subarctic fauna provided both food and fine-quality pelts, but its cyclical fluctuations required the Tagish to employ the same kind of flexible technology and exploitative strategies for which other northern Cordilleran Indians have been noted.

Since 1900 the caribou population has declined markedly, so that only a few small herds live in the high coastal range. None has been seen at Carcross since the 1920s, although the town's name is a shortened form of Caribou Crossing, which referred to the large herds that used to swim the river annually. However,

moose have increased greatly, perhaps because of an increase in forest fires following the Klondike stampede (McClellan 1975a:108; Feit 1969:67–93, 106–109).

The Athapaskan language* spoken by the Tagish is closely related to the Tahltan-Kaska branch (Krauss 1973:913–914); in 1974 it was remembered by only two or three people. The older Tagish spoke Tlingit, and the young spoke English. The shift to Tlingit clearly resulted from the close contact in the nineteenth century with the coastal Chilkoot, although Tagish Tlingit differs in some details from Coastal Tlingit. Already in 1887 Dawson (1889:192B, 204B) considered the Tagish to be Tlingit-speaking Indians with an Athapaskan culture.

External Relations

Although the Tlingit to the south traded and intermarried with the Tagish, the coast range that separated the two groups is a formidable physical barrier, made the more effective during most of the nineteenth century by a Tlingit blockade of the passes. The Tlingit prevented White traders from entering the interior and the Tagish from going down to the coast. Instead, they themselves carried trade goods to the Tagish, who began to adopt the Tlingit social organization and language. After the Klondike gold rush of 1898 broke the Tlingit trade monopoly, the Tagish could more freely visit the coast, especially if they had established kin ties there; but as internative trade declined, contacts between the Tagish and the Tlingit lessened.

---

*The phonemes of Tagish are: (unaspirated stops and affricates) *d*, λ, ʒ, ʒᵛ, *g*, ʔ; (aspirated stops and affricates) *t*, ƛ, *c*, *cᵛ*, *k*; (glottalized) ƭ, ƛ̇, ċ, ċᵛ, ƙ; (voiceless continuants) ɫ, *s*, *sᵛ*, *x*, *h*; (voiced continuants) *l*, *z*, *zᵛ*, γ; (prenasalized stops) ᵐ*b*, ⁿ*d*; (nasals) *m*, *n*; (resonant) *y*; (short vowels) *i*, *e*, *a*, *u*; (long vowels) *i·*, *e·*, *a·*, *u·*; (tones) high (unmarked), low (v̀). The palatalized alveolar series (ʒᵛ, etc.) is not consistently distinguished from the alveolar series (ʒ, etc.) and may not be distinct at all for some speakers. Information on Tagish phonology and the transcription of Tagish words was provided by Victor Golla on the basis of his own fieldwork in 1976 and field notes collected in 1953 by Gordon Marsh.

The phonemic transcription of the Tlingit clan names was furnished by Jeff Leer (communication to editors 1979); see the orthographic footnote in "Inland Tlingit," this vol. The Coastal Tlingit place-name Dáqxuq has been left in the orthography used by Garfield (1947).

481

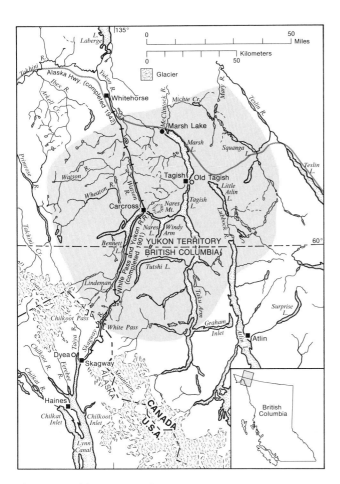

Fig. 1. Late 19th-century territory.

To the east lived the Inland Tlingit, some of whose ancestors had crossed to the Yukon drainage during the nineteenth century. This movement may have split off the Tagish from a previous Tagish-Tahltan-Kaska dialect continuum. Since consolidating their position in the Yukon drainage, the Inland Tlingit have frequently married Tagish Indians.

West, north, and northeast of the Tagish are Athapaskan Tutchone with whom the Tagish also formerly traded and intermarried, and with some of whom they feuded. In the 1970s Tagish, Inland Tlingit, and Tutchone individuals were constantly meeting in Whitehorse, at schools, and elsewhere. They continued to intermarry and to attend one another's potlatches.

History of Indian-White Contact

The slaughter of the Pacific sea otters that resulted from White demand for their furs had led to the animals' near extinction in the late eighteenth century. As a consequence the value of land animal pelts increased greatly, and this was why the Coastal Tlingit jealously guarded their middleman position between the White traders and the Tagish, who could provide such furs.

The first Whites to meet the Tagish were a few prospectors whom the Chilkoot Tlingit allowed to cross the coastal passes in the last quarter of the nineteenth century and Lt. F. Schwatka and his party who passed through the country on a United States army military reconnaissance in 1883. By this time some Tagish had begun to be attracted to trading posts in Han territory, down the Yukon River, where prospectors were becoming more numerous, and by the late 1890s a few Tagish dared to visit the Tlingit-dominated coast.

Gradually the native way of life was altered as western trade goods became available and new contacts were made with Whites, but it was the Klondike gold rush of 1898 that brought major changes in almost every aspect of traditional Tagish life. Three Tagish—Skookum Jim, his sister Kate, and his sororal nephew, Dawson Charlie (fig. 2)—were with the White prospector, George Carmack, who set the rush in motion in 1896, and Skookum Jim probably picked up the first nuggets in Bonanza Creek downstream from Tagish country. By 1900 more than 40,000 Whites had passed through Tagish territory, and Skookum Jim and his relatives (fig. 3) had become famous and relatively wealthy (McClellan 1950:65–101, 138–149, 1963, 1975a:37–44; Carmack 1933; Mathews 1968:148–156; Ogilvie 1913:125–136).

The chief nineteenth-century gathering place of the Tagish was at present-day Tagish, at the confluence of Tagish and Marsh lakes. There, late in the century, the Tagish had built two substantial lineage houses imitating Coastal Tlingit structures. During the gold rush the North West Mounted Police established a Canadian customs post at Tagish, and a trading post was also started (Hamilton 1964:119). However, most Tagish had moved to Carcross in 1900, attracted by the completion of the railroad and the establishment of an Anglican school ("Intercultural Relations and Cultural Change in the Cordillera," fig. 16, this vol.) and church (McClellan 1975a:40–41; King 1967; Bullen 1968:149–167).

The majority of the Tagish still lived in the 1970s on the south side of the Nares River. They formed the nucleus of the Carcross Indian band, which in 1974 had an elected chief and council as well as a band manager and secretary. The Tagish have never made a formal treaty with the Canadian government. At the end of the 1970s the political status and land claims of the Indians of the Yukon Territory, including the Tagish, were still under review. In 1967 Skookum Jim Hall was built in Whitehorse with a legacy from Skookum Jim as a friendship center for all Indians, but Tagish Indians especially have been involved in its activities. Both status and nonstatus Tagish were leaders in native movements of the 1970s that aimed to better the economic position of Yukon natives while at the same time preserving important aspects of their cultural heritage.

Yukon Arch., Whitehorse: McBride Mus. Coll., 3870.
Fig. 2. Dawson Charlie, one of the discoverers of Klondike gold. Photographed in photographer's studio in 1898.

Population

Although reliable demographic data for the Tagish are lacking, they have probably always been a very small group. Schwatka (1885:83) thought they did "not certainly exceed fifty altogether," and in 1887 Dawson (1889:204B) estimated 70 to 80 individuals. In 1950 McClellan (1950) estimated a total of about 112 status and nonstatus Tagish. The Indian Affairs Branch numbered the Carcross band at 96 in 1974 and 111 in 1978, but the figures exclude nonstatus Tagish, of which there are several large families in Carcross and Whitehorse.

Culture

Subsistence

The Tagish remember their subsistence cycle only as it existed in the late nineteenth and early twentieth centuries when the emphasis on fur trapping and the arrival of the Whites had altered the earlier patterns. In the decades just before the gold rush, the households gathered together in early summer where fish were abundant and they could also get small game and waterfowl. Salmon came only to the McClintock River at Marsh Lake, but other lakes and streams had whitefish,

trout, ling cod, and other freshwater species. While at fish camps, the Tagish were visited by Coastal Tlingit eager to exchange Euro-American goods for the winter fur catch.

By late summer, families began to move upland in groups of two or three households to hunt groundhogs (woodchucks, *Marmota monax*), caribou, moose, and sheep. They cached the dried meat in convenient spots to which the younger men could return for supplies in winter or to which the families themselves could move.

In early December most people returned to Tagish, where they lived in the two large lineage houses or smaller shelters nearby, but by late January they again scattered in order to get enough food and to trap. Able-bodied adults sometimes left the elderly and mothers with young children by good fishing lakes while they hunted meat elsewhere. One or two families usually made a winter trek to Pelly River to buy furs, which they could in turn sell to Tlingit entrepreneurs (Mc-

Fig. 3. Patsy Henderson, a nephew of Skookum Jim, wearing a beaded jacket that he frequently wore while lecturing to tourists about the gold rush days. He accompanied Skookum Jim and Dawson Charlie to Klondike country but was not with the others when they discovered gold—because, he said, when he was a young boy he cried when he heard Wealth Woman's baby (McClellan 1975a:572–573). Photograph by Catharine McClellan, Carcross, 1950.

Clellan 1950:138–149, 1975a:510–515; Moore 1968:92).

The move to Carcross at the turn of the century did not at first affect the annual cycle very much, but as children began to attend school and the men took jobs on the railway, families became increasingly sedentary. Table 1 summarizes a yearly round of the 1920s as remembered by a woman in 1950. By the 1930s the fur market had collapsed, and since then few Tagish have spent the entire winter on the trapline. The improved fur prices of the 1970s increased trapping, but snowmobiles made it possible for those with steady jobs or children in school to use Carcross as a base of operations.

Technology

Traditional Tagish technology of the nineteenth century was similar to that of other Cordilleran Athapaskans ("Environment and Culture in the Cordillera," this vol.), and throughout the period stone and bone tools were steadily replaced by metal counterparts, usually brought by the Tlingit.

The Tagish did some hunting with bows and arrows, but much game and fur were procured with deadfalls and snares. Men, women, and children drove caribou into snares set in long brush fences, and sometimes they drove varying hares into similar, but lower fences. Moose too were snared in fences, although they cannot be driven. Mountain goats and sheep, smaller game, and furbearers were snared or trapped in deadfalls;

beaver were netted under water and clubbed, or else speared. Stout fixed-head spears were employed for killing both grizzly bears and humans. By 1900, guns had become the chief means of killing game, and steel traps had supplanted the earlier snares and deadfalls.

Although the Tagish like to think of themselves as big-game hunters, a good part of their daily diet in the nineteenth century consisted of small game and fish. Bark or sinew gill nets were perhaps aboriginal, but setting them under the ice was introduced by Whites. The chief aboriginal technique for winter fishing was spearing through holes in the ice; however, where the streams still ran open in December, adults drove whitefish into funnel traps by beating the water with long poles. In summer, the salmon at McClintock River were caught in box and tongue traps and dried in rectangular frame shelters where people also slept.

The chief vegetable foods were berries and Hedysarum roots. All hunting, fishing, and gathering activities included stringent rituals designed to ensure a harmonious relationship between the Tagish and the powerful spirits whom they believed to control most natural phenomena (see McClellan 1975a:95–103, 107–182, 189–194, for details of subsistence cycle, technology, and hunting ritual).

Structures

Except for the two timber houses at Tagish, nineteenth-century dwellings were impermanent double lean-tos

Table 1. Tagish Annual Cycle in the 1920s

October	November	December	January	February	March	April	May	June-July	August	September
Complete drying and caching meat from fall hunt.	Move slowly to main trapping cabin toward Squanga Lake. Set up food caches, tents, and brush camps in 10-mile radius. Men trap wolf, coyote, lynx. Women snare hares. Set mink and weasel traps. Women cut wood. Moose and caribou hunted throughout the winter.				Women set out muskrat traps. Move to second trapping cabin. Young adult male may take furs by dog team to trading post for Easter and return with new supplies. Late March move slowly along string of lakes for beaver and muskrat. Fish for dog food. Cross lake in previously cached boat and then travel overland to Tagish by foot. Trade furs. Net whitefish, trout, and sucker; dry them for dogs.			Summer at Tagish and Carcross. Some lake fishing. Women pick berries, and families dry ground squirrels and groundhogs (woodchucks) in the mountains around Lake Bennett. Some men on big game hunts as guides. Leave Carcross by boat for Tagish and cache boat. Go overland to Little Atlin Lake. Use moosehide boat to cross lake. Get fish for dogs. Start summer meat hunt in the mountains and cache dried meat by the lake.		

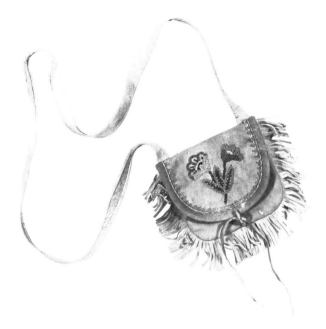

Fig. 4. Ammunition bag of tanned caribou with moosehide trim and fringe, a reconstruction of an older form but decorated with modern beadwork. Width 16 cm, excluding fringe. Made by Angela Sidney, 1949.

of brush, conical brush shelters, or hemispherical moose-skin tents (McClellan 1975a:233–234, 236–237, 240–251).

Clothing

Precontact clothing was of tanned caribou or moose hide and, for cold weather, of sheep or mountain goat skin with the fur worn against the body. Both sexes wore one-piece moccasin-trousers with tailored overshirts, decorated with fringes and quillwork. Glass beads were available by the mid-nineteenth century. Older women still made beaded skin jackets and moccasins for the tourist trade of the 1970s.

Late nineteenth-century ceremonial dress copied Tlingit styles on which clan crests were portrayed. Skookum Jim ordered a Chilkat shirt of goat wool and cedar specially woven for a potlatch he helped to host at Carcross in 1912. It shows his clan crest, the Wolf (figs. 5–6) (see McClellan 1975a:260–264, 299–323 for details of clothing).

Transport and Travel

Land travel was traditionally by foot. People carried their belongings on their backs in netted bags or in large packs supported by broad chest straps and tumplines. In winter men snowshoed ahead hunting, while women snowshoed behind, pulling skin drags. Dog traction and plank toboggans (fig. 7) were introduced only late in the nineteenth century by those who had been in con-

tact with White traders downriver. Previously each family kept only one or two dogs to help hunt or to carry supplies into the mountains in small saddle bags.

During the gold rush, Tagish men, women, and children all "packed" goods across the mountains for Whites, and they became noted for their ability to carry huge loads.

For water transportation the Tagish used rafts, cottonwood dugouts, spruce-bark canoes, or temporary frame boats covered with raw moosehide. They justifiably feared sudden wind storms on large lakes, which they avoided crossing when possible.

Smokes, blazes, and charcoal-marked sticks were traditional signals and guides. After guns became numerous, people signaled each other with shots. Great fusillades marked the arrival of trading parties or of guests for potlatches. By the early twentieth century, horses the railway, and stern-wheelers had markedly altered mobility and social patterns. One Tagish family became big game outfitters; others began to fish commercially as outboards became available. World War II brought even greater change, when the building of the Alaska Highway in 1942 linked Tagish and Carcross to Whitehorse by a good road, and the Indians began to drive cars and trucks. Air travel too became commonplace (McClellan 1975a:267–279, 294).

Social Organization

Far back in their history the Tagish may have had matrilineal descent and exogamous clans and moieties with Athapaskan names; however, by the late nineteenth century they had adopted Tlingit names for both clan and moiety and had incorporated as well Tlingit ideas of rank, proper names, and related aspects of social behavior.

The late nineteenth and twentieth-century Tagish have had only two matri-clans, one in each moiety, and each represented by a single lineage—that is, by a group of matrilineally related individuals who can trace their relationships with some accuracy. One clan identifies itself as a segment of the Coastal Tlingit *daqławe·dí* ('people of Dáqxuq' Garfield 1947:447) clan of the Wolf moiety, and the other as part of the *tuqwe·dí* (meaning unknown) of the Crow moiety (that is, the Raven moiety of the Coastal Tlingit). The *tuqwe·dí* also equate themselves with the *de·ši·ta·n* ('end of the trail people') of the Inland Tlingit and the Coastal Tlingit, tracing their ancestry to Angoon (De Laguna 1960:132–137; Garfield 1947; McClellan 1950:77–129, 1975a:439–440, 468–479; R.L. Olson 1967:7, 28–30, 32–33). A few individuals of other Tlingit clans have married Tagish but have not established local lineages.

Each clan has honored traditions accounting for its presence. The ancestors of the *daqławe·dí* were once traveling near Telegraph Creek in Tahltan country, but

Fig. 5. Potlatch participants of both the host moiety (Wolf) and the guest moiety (Crow) on the occasion of raising a tombstone to Dawson Charlie (see fig. 6). The principal host of this potlatch was Skookum Jim, whose house is in the background. back row, left to right: 1, Johnny Frazer (Tutchone), holding a long dance pole; 2, Johnny Dawson or Dawson Johnny (possibly Tutchone or Han), holding feather fans in his hands; 3, Big Salmon Jim (Tutchone), wearing a shirt with floral decoration on the cuffs, bib, and skirt and holding a rattle; 4, Johnny Brown (possibly Tutchone); 5, Charlie Burns (Tagish), holding a rifle in the air; 6, Whitehorse Billy (Tutchone or Tagish); 7, Billy Johnson (Tagish), with a large plume or cockade in his headband; 8, Sam Smith (Tagish), wearing a shirt with a crest design; 9, Patsy Henderson (Tagish); 10, Tagish Jim (Tagish), wearing a jacket with a long rectangular design; 11, Slim Jim or "Captain Slim" (possibly Tutchone); 12, Joe Kane (Tutchone); 13, Big Salmon Harry (Tutchone), wearing a feather headdress and holding a feather fan above his head; 14, Skookum Jim (Tagish), holding a small totem pole and wearing two octopus bags and a bib with crest designs. 15, Billy Bone (Inland Tlingit), wearing a crest headdress and holding a killer whale dance pole with the whales' blow holes depicted (dark areas) and a British flag attached to one end. He is wearing the Chilkat shirt with Wolf crest that Skookum Jim ordered for this potlatch. 16, Paddy Smith (Tutchone), wearing a fur robe and beating a drum. 17, Big Lake Charlie (Tutchone), wrapped in white cloth; 18, Jo Jackie (Tutchone); 19, unidentified; 20, Frankie Jim (Tutchone); 21, David Hammond (Tagish), with white band around his head; 22, Johnny Johns (Tagish), with a Tlingit mask over his face; 23, Shakoon (Tagish); 24, Johnny Joe (Tutchone). Photograph by Matthew Watson at Carcross, autumn, 1912.

after a young man caused an explosion by kicking a Thunderbird feather, the group split up and one branch moved north to Tagish.

The *tuqwe·dí* tell of three, sometimes four, high-ranking sisters whose families long ago moved from Angoon to Chilkat on the coast. From there the girls migrated up the Taku River where one married a Tahltan, another a Tagish, while the third found a Tutchone husband (McClellan 1950:78–79, 1975a:445–479, 1975).

Subsequently each clan built a lineage house at Tagish and decorated it with its respective crests. The *daqɬawe·dí* claim Wolf because one of their clansmen once watched Animal Mother order the physical attributes of various species of animals born to her. She gave each a name while it danced and sang on a "swing" hung between four mountain peaks near Carcross. The man learned the song of each animal, and that of the Wolf—the last animal to dance—remains the honored clan song. Another *daqɬawe·dí* crest is the Killer Whale, about which the clan tells a story widely known on the coast (McClellan 1975a:445–468).

The *tuqwe·dí* claim to Beaver rests on a tradition similar to that recorded on the coast at Angoon and elsewhere about how a pet beaver once flooded a town in which their ancestors lived (McClellan 1954:78–84, 1975a:468–474, 1975).

Because of rules of clan and moiety exogamy, every traditional Tagish family includes a spouse from each moiety, the children belonging to the lineage of the mother. Tlingit kinship terminology fits well with this system (see vol. 7), and by the late nineteenth century most Tagish used Tlingit rather than Tagish terms, especially for public occasions, although some families still retained the Tagish term for 'mother'. The few

Fig. 6. Dawson Charlie's tombstone with his crest figure, a wolf, on top. The inscription reads "Dawson Charlie Died Dec. 26, 1908 Aged 42 Yrs." Stone was erected at a potlatch in 1912 (see fig. 5). Photograph by Catharine McClellan, at Carcross, Sept. 1977.

Fig. 7. Albert James with sled-dog puppy sitting on sled loaded with firewood. Photograph by Catharine McClellan, Carcross, 1950.

Tagish speakers of the 1950s and later could remember only fragmentary bits of their Athapaskan terminology, which was apparently close to that of the Tahltan. In both Tagish and Tlingit systems consanguine and affinal kin terms can be extended to an individual's entire lineage, clan, and moiety, so that persons reckon relationships to each other in several different ways. Knowledgable Tagish of the 1970s still delighted in selecting the most appropriate terms by which to address or refer to each other on a given social occasion. At formal potlatches persons preferred to address individuals by the Tlingit proper names that they had inherited.

Nineteenth-century individuals tried to make the exact same marriages as did their predecessors who bore the same personal names, so that members of the two clans would forever be linked together in identical manner. This was thought to be possible because ideally the pool of clan names and accompanying statuses remained constant. What changed externally were the persons who temporarily held these names and their prerogatives while alive, and those who once held the same names, but who had died. Because the Tagish believed in reincarnation, all these persons really represented the same social individual in a system that thus incorporated the living and the dead indissoluably. Actually, of course, demographic variability and other exigencies meant that the ideal system was constantly manipulated to meet the realities of life (De Laguna 1952, 1972, 1:476–496; McClellan 1975a:412–413, 416–438).

Life Cycle

Nineteenth-century Tagish believed in the reincarnation not only of humans but also of animals. A dying person could actively ensure rebirth to a particular woman, or a bereaved mother entice back her own dead child or someone else who had died (De Laguna 1954:181–187; McClellan 1975a:349–350). Whether or not it was a matter of planned reincarnation, a woman knew she had conceived when a sudden chill marked the arrival of the spirit of the child to be born to her. A pregnant woman kept physically active and carried out magical ritual directed toward her own welfare and that of the coming child.

Birth was in a hut some distance from the main dwellings, for birth fluids were especially dangerous to the spirit helpers of shamans and the male hunters in camp. Before the mother returned to the camp, she repeated much of the ritual she had undergone during her puberty seclusion, although the restrictions lessened with each birth. The new father was expected to be very industrious and to perform services for the whole camp.

An infant spent much of its first year in a bark-backed skin carrying case of tanned moose or caribou hide, which could be carried on its mother's back or placed in a net hammock safe from the dogs. Young children led relatively free lives, but by the age of five or six they were expected to begin to act responsibly toward other humans as well as toward the nonhuman spirits of the natural world.

There were few competitive games. Children mostly imitated adults, the girls acting as mothers and housewives, the boys as fathers and hunters. Even before puberty the sexes kept more and more to themselves, and puberty brought formal avoidance between both uterine and clan siblings of opposite sex (McClellan 1961:114–116).

Her first menstruation brought a girl's abrupt withdrawal to an isolated brush shelter and the imposition of strict taboos relating to her diet and most other activities. The isolation was a kind of extreme avoidance behavior with respect to the rest of the group, perhaps symbolizing fetal life and rebirth. The girl wore a large hood stretched over a willow frame so that she could neither see out nor be seen. Ideally she stayed under it for two years, although few girls managed to complete the full period, for they often had to emerge earlier to help with the demanding business of gaining a living. Nevertheless puberty observances were extremely important, for the Tagish believed that the girl's future and the welfare of her entire group depended upon it. Indeed, throughout her fertile years a woman isolated herself monthly and was also daily constrained by a host of rules designed to prevent her direct confrontation with the spirits who controlled the world and who found offensive the power inherent in female biological functioning.

Puberty seclusion entailed much advice on proper moral and social behavior given by the girl's mother and women of her father's clan. The chief technical training was in sewing, and women of the 1950s declared that after they had been through it, they could never bear to be idle and were always "hungry for sewing." The seclusion effectively insured that all women in this small society could carry out their roles as spiritually responsible and practically effective adults.

Male puberty was equally important, but observance was not so dramatic. Grandfathers, fathers, and uncles all gave the boys rigorous physical training and taught them the technical and ritual aspects of subsistence activities, their moral obligations, and the traditions and prerogatives of their matrilineages.

A girl married soon after she came out from her puberty isolation. The groom's parents arranged the match with her parents, who expected a period of bride service. Some marriages were arranged at birth, for women were scarce. Growing Tlingit influence meant that considerations of social rank increasingly structured marriage alliances so that spouses were often of quite different ages. The son-in-law remained responsible for the welfare of his wife's parents until their deaths. Traveling with his father-in-law, he often acquired knowledge of a terrain different from that of his boyhood, thus enhancing survival chances in a marginal environment (McClellan 1964:9–10).

Polygyny and polyandry were allowed but were rare. Few marriages were dissolved, because this required the return of goods exchanged between lineages at the time of marriage as well as lineage obligations to provide substitute spouses.

Until the introduction of welfare programs in the 1950s no widow or widower remained single after the proper commemorative potlatch had been held for a spouse who had died. The lineage of the deceased then offered a new spouse, usually a uterine sibling, or a maternal niece or nephew of the dead person. Sometimes a man married his step-daughter. After the gold rush the frequent marriage of Tagish girls to Whites made it difficult to maintain the traditional marriage system. Since World War II Tagish men too have been marrying Whites; as a consequence, the clan system has been disappearing.

Before twentieth-century schooling changed their way of life, the Tagish valued the aged for their experience and because it was thought that they became increasingly in touch with the spiritual power of the superhuman world. Some old people employed their powers to work evil on any who slighted or mistreated them.

At death all members of the clan opposite that of the deceased came to prepare the body for cremation, to sing mourning songs, and to comfort the survivors through oratory. All smoked and ate so that the spirits of the dead ancestors as well as of the newly dead person would have food and tobacco in the other world. Christianity, introduced at the turn of the century, altered some of these patterns, and burial became the rule; but in the 1970s most life crises, particularly death, still activated reciprocal services between those of opposite moieties (see McClellan 1975a:349–376 for details of the Tagish life cycle).

Potlatches

During the late nineteenth century, after a person died the closest matrilineal kin began to save food and other wealth so that about a year after the death their ranking member could host a memorial feast or potlatch. Those of the opposite clan were publicly paid for their help at the death and for finally depositing the ashes of the deceased in his lineage "dead house" at the time of the potlatch itself. At the potlatch the names, rank, and prerogatives of the deceased passed to the heir, and these rights were reaffirmed through clan songs, dances, and ceremonial dress (figs. 5, 8) and through distribution of gifts to the guests, who always belonged to the moiety opposite that of the dead person or persons being honored. If the deceased were high ranking, Tutchone, Inland Tlingit, and even Coastal Tlingit might be invited. Memorial potlatches were essential, but potlatches could also be held to raise the status of an individual, or, on occasion, to wipe out a social blunder. Potlatching continued into the 1970s with relatively minor changes although the dead were buried rather than burned (McClellan 1954, 1975a:373–375).

Fig. 8. George and Angela Sidney wearing ceremonial clothing. She is Tagish of the Crow moiety. He is Inland Tlingit, and his dance shirt and grizzly bear ear headdress were inherited through the Old *yanye·dí* clan of the Wolf moiety (see "Inland Tlingit," fig. 8, this vol. for a previous holder wearing the same costume). Photograph by Catharine McClellan, Carcross, 1963.

Political Organization

The size of nineteenth-century co-residential groups varied according to seasonal and other circumstances. Sometimes the entire population gathered at Tagish. When the people again scattered, the minimal exploitative units usually had at least two adult males and two adult females. Often a pair of siblings and their spouses and children traveled together. Households were flexible and were built on whatever primary kin ties seemed most congenial and economically advantageous at a given moment.

The Tagish lacked formal political structure. With the help of other high-ranking males and females, the senior males of each lineage organized certain hunting and trading activities, directed potlatches, and arbitrated disputes within the clan. If members of opposite clans quarreled, the headmen tried to settle matters through negotiation and payments; otherwise feuding usually resulted. In theory no one person ever controlled an entire local group, let alone the entire Tagish band, since members of two clans were always present. In practice, an excellent hunter, wise in human relationships, often dominated everybody in his own household and others allied with it regardless of clan affiliations. As the fur trade grew, a man could build up an economic surplus to consolidate power and prestige

beyond the limits that his lineage status would have enabled him to do in earlier days. How often a leader acquired power through shamanistic activity is uncertain.

Most of the land was held in clan trust, the *daqɫawe·dí* claiming the area around Tagish Lake, and the *tuqwe·dí*, that around Lake Bennett. However, any group could, in fact, use whatever land was not being actively exploited by others. Male household heads could claim the right either because they were members of the "owning" clan, or because they could call on ties to "father's people" or "brothers-in-law" that required reciprocal generosity. Only since the introduction of individually owned trap lines after World War II has conflict arisen over land use (McClellan 1975a:481–487, 492–493).

Trade and Warfare

Nineteenth-century Tagish trading developed on relations extending far back in time, for the environmental contrasts of Northwestern North America mean varied natural resources. Aboriginally, the Coastal Tlingit brought wooden boxes, dried clams, sea weed, eulachon oil, and other marine products to the Tagish, exchanging them for ground-squirrel robes, lichen dyes and goat wool for Chilkat blankets, and tanned moose and caribou hides (McClellan 1950:138–149, 1964:7–8, 1975a:510–515).

When the demand for land furs accelerated Tlingit trade with the Tagish, a coastal family might spend an entire winter trapping with a Tagish family, although the Tlingit knew so little about the rugged interior existence that the Tagish report having to look after these guests "like babies." Sometimes coastal men then chose Tagish wives or gave their own women to Tagish husbands, so that they could later call on affinal kin ties to secure the best possible bargains in fur. All trade was structured by the fictive, if not actual, kinship that the matching clan and moiety systems made possible. Each Tagish had a Tlingit trading partner with whom he traded annually or semiannually. Gift exchange, feasting, and story telling marked the opening of trade, which was conducted through barter. Through all these means the Tagish became effectively Tlingitized. However, ill feeling, and even fighting, sometimes arose when the Tlingit took advantage of the Tagish, seizing Tagish women temporarily or cheating their partners too blatantly.

The Tagish in turn operated as middlemen, taking some of the White man's goods they had acquired from the Tlingit farther inland to Indians on the upper Pelly River, from whom they demanded far more for each item than they had themselves given. A highlight of this trading was the gambling games that accompanied the exchange of goods. Some Tagish also used to guide Coastal Tlingit traders to Han country below Fort Selkirk (De Laguna 1972, 1:248, 350; McClellan 1950:138–149, 160–208, 1975a:501–502, 510–515).

World View

Children of the nineteenth century learned major aspects of the Tagish world view by listening to stories during the long winter evenings, by attending shamanistic seances, and through observing the ritual of their elders.

The Tagish believed the universe to be full of power manifested in various kinds of spirits. Most spirits had more power at night than in the day, and much in the spirit world was a reverse of the human world. Since animal spirits were believed to be far more powerful than human beings, humans tried to obtain them as allies. One hoped at the very least to prevent the spirits from becoming vindictive so that they produced bad weather, caused illness, or refused to be caught in the animal bodies that the Indians had to kill to stay alive.

Almost every adult male had one or two spirit helpers who aided him in his hunting and other affairs. Certain persons, who had enough power to perform in public, became shamans. They were mostly men, but women past menopause could also be shamans. All shared common beliefs about the nature of the universe, but their specific dogmas and the amulets and rituals they prescribed for their clients were quite individualistic. Each had a set of powerful spirit helpers acquired either through inheritance from a maternal uncle or father or by quest. The novice had a long period of hardship and abstinences while he gained control of these spirits, whose symbolic attributes he kept in a medicine or "dream" bag. At a public performance an aide beat the drum, joining both the shaman and the audience in singing to summon the shaman's spirit helpers so that he could send them out on special missions. Each spirit helper had a different song. At other times, when a shaman was dreaming in private, his own spirit might leave his body to locate the cause of an evil or to retrieve a lost soul. The shaman undertook to control weather, locate game, and cure the ill. He was well paid for his services (from $5 to $200 in the 1950s and 1960s, and probably the equivalent in native goods in earlier times), but he was often feared because of his potential for working evil as well as good (McClellan 1956, 1975a:529–565).

By the beginning of the twentieth century most Tagish had become devout Anglicans or had joined other Christian denominations (McClellan 1956). Since the 1960s a number have been very active in the Baha'i faith.

Tagish oral literature is rich. One series of stories tells of humans who spent time in the animal spirit world as a consequence of breaking taboos. On their return to the human world they brought knowledge of how to treat both the living animal species and their corpses so as to please the spirit owners of the animals. Thus, Bear Husband explains the ritual expected of hunters who kill a grizzly bear and also dramatizes the complex relations between animals and humans and among humans themselves (McClellan 1970a). The Tagish tell Star Husband in classic northern form, which further extends its known distribution (Thompson 1953:93–163; Lévi-Strauss 1968:164–165, 185–250, 1971:23–24, 502–558), and they know many other widespread Athapaskan and Tlingit stories, including the Crow (Raven) cycle. Specific clan stories such as the *daqławe·dí* Animal Mother myth constitute another important genre. Animal Mother is also told by the Inland Tlingit and Tahltan, but uniquely Tagish is the account of how Skookum Jim's aid from a Frog spirit helper and his encounter with Wealth Woman led to the gold rush of 1898. All categories of stories are regarded as equally true (Cruikshank 1979; McClellan 1963, 1970a:66–67, 1970:115–118). Tagish sing and dance in both Athapaskan and Coastal Tlingit styles (Mark 1955).

Synonymy†

The name Tagish is in origin a place-name, now applied to a lake and a town. It is from Inland Tlingit *ta·gíš* and *ta·giš qʷá·n* 'Tagish people' (Jeff Leer, communication to editors 1979), ultimately from Tagish *ta·gizi*, a place name meaning 'it (spring ice) is breaking up', and *ta·gizi dene* 'Tagish Indian' (McClellan 1948–1974; Gordon Marsh cited by Victor Golla, communication to editors 1979). The English name Tagish appears as early as Dawson (1889:192B) and was used by Swanton (1910a:669) and Jenness (1932:376). Other spellings are Tahk-heesh and Tahkeesh (Schwatka 1885:21, 1885a, 1893; G. Davidson 1901:76–79) and Tahgish (G. Marsh 1958). The Krause brothers gave a German rendering as tagisch (A. Krause 1882:308–325; Krause 1885:194).

Schwatka (1885a:80) also gives the name Si-him-E-na, of uncertain analysis.

Like a number of interior Athapaskan groups the Tagish have been referred to under the general terms Stick Indians (Dawson 1889, Schwatka 1885, 1885a, 1893) and Tlingit *ǧunana·* 'stranger', variously spelled (see the synonymy in "Tahltan," this vol.). Under a rendering of this Tlingit word, Dall (1886:379) put two Indian groups he had earlier called the Tāh´ko-tin´neh, said to be on the Lewes River (i.e., the Yukon above the confluence with the Pelly), and the "Nehaunees of the Chilkaht River" (Dall 1877:33); the Tagish and

†This synonymy was written by Ives Goddard incorporating references supplied by Catharine McClellan.

490

Natl. Mus. of Canada. Ottawa: VI–P–3.
Fig. 9. Octopus bag of red flannelette with beadwork decoration, said to be from the Crow moiety. Length 45 cm, collected at Tagish Lake, 1911.

some of their neighbors are presumably the people included in some confused way in these categories.

Sources

Historical sources for the Tagish are limited. In 1882 a German geographer (A. Krause 1882:308–325; Krause 1956) accompanied some Coastal Tlingit across the Chilkoot Pass to Lake Lindeman. He met some White prospectors but no interior Indians, although he and his brother knew of Tlingit trade at Tagish (Krause 1956:136). For his 1883 trip Lieutenant Schwatka had employed two Tagish packers and an interpreter whose mother was Tagish and whose father was Tlingit. Schwatka's brief official description of the Tagish (1885:2180) was repeated in a popular book (1885a:59–63, 82–83) and reissued with a changed title and minor emendations (1893:59–63, 82–83).

Dawson, a geologist who met Tagish Indians while traveling through their country to the coast in 1887, recorded a "Tagish" vocabulary that is about 90 percent Tlingit (1889:192B, 203B–205B, 208B–213B). Recognizing this, he considered the Tagish themselves to be basically Tlingit. Dawson (1889:164B–169B, 177B–181B) added material on the Tagish and judiciously reviewed the history of White penetration of Tagish country. Ogilvie, who explored the White Pass guided by Skookum Jim, and who knew of George Carmack and his Tagish wife (although he did not mention them by name in early reports), stressed the Chilkoot dominance over the Tagish (Ogilvie 1898a:22–24, 35, 1898:407, 1913:125–136, where he changed the spelling of Cormac to Carmac; Moore 1968:19, 90–91). G. Davidson (1901:76–79) published a map drawn by a Chilkat chief showing Tlingit trade routes through Tagish country. See McClellan (1950:14–19, 65–70, 1975a:3–8) for other brief nineteenth-century references.

The early prospectors who preceded Krause, Schwatka, and Dawson did not leave written accounts of the Indians, but the more than 50 published accounts of the Klondike stampeders usually mention the Tagish or Sticks, giving widely varying accounts of their involvement in the discovery of gold. Few add ethnographic data of value, and some are distinctly derogatory. Moore (1968:19, 62, 92, 156–159, 186), who with his father founded Skagway, has interesting data on Skookum Jim and other Tagish in the late 1890s. For samples of gold rush literature with mentions of the Tagish see McClellan (1950:80–81), Lotz (1964:67–83), and Hemstock and Cooke (1973:204–221).

Swanton (1910a:669) wrote a short piece on the Tagish and Jenness (1932:376) gave a brief account of them. Drawing chiefly on Dawson, both scholars described the Tagish as Athapaskans who had adopted Tlingit as a second language. This position was sustained by ethnographic fieldwork by McClellan and D. Rainier Libby in Carcross in 1948 and 1949, and by McClellan in 1950–1951, and 1974. Fullest published sources on the Tagish are by McClellan (1961, 1963, 1970, 1970a, 1975a). G. Marsh's (1958) linguistic study is unpublished as is a manuscript map drawn by Teit (1912–1915), who worked with the Tahltan in the early twentieth century. The map shows the Tagish-oten as a northernmost Tahltan division in the vicinity of Teslin Lake. Later he located a "Tagish" group near Atlin Lake. Both lakes are in Inland Tlingit country to the east of the Tagish (McClellan 1975a:40).

For a period before World War II, Patsy Henderson, Skookum Jim's sororal nephew, had a museum of Tagish materials at Carcross, but it burned down. During the 1950s and 1960s he lectured to tourists on the Klondike discovery and on traditional Tagish culture. He sold the lecture in pamphlet form, from which it was also reprinted (Henderson 1950; Martinson 1960). In 1973 the Tagish began an oral history project under the sponsorship of Skookum Jim Hall; they have emphasized collecting accounts of Skookum Jim from those who knew him personally. Some of these interviews have been published in the *Yukon News*. Others are available on tape in the Yukon Archives in Whitehorse, Yukon Territory, which also has a collection of photographs, manuscripts, and documents relating to the

Tagish (see also McClellan 1963, 1975 for stories about Skookum Jim from Indian informants). Cruikshank (1979) includes autobiographical material of a Tagish woman and some myths.

Studio photographs and snapshots of Tagish, including several of Skookum Jim, are in Cruikshank (1975:16–21, 37–38, 46–47, 49, 66, 86–88, 113, 116, 120, 121, 123).

Tutchone

CATHARINE MCCLELLAN

Language

The Tutchone (tōō'chōnē) Indians of southern Yukon Territory are a small population whose ancestors were held together in the past by their contiguous territories, intermarriage, and closely related Athapaskan dialects.

Linguistically, the Tutchone seem to divide into a Northern and Southern group, but further research may modify this classification.* The exact position of Tutchone in relation to neighboring clusters of Athapaskan dialects remains ill defined. Probably it is to be distinguished from Tagish, Kaska, Mountain, Han, and Upper Tanana but is closer to the last two (Denniston 1966; Krauss 1973:913–914, 1975; McClellan 1975a:13–14, 1948–1975; Ritter 1976b; Ritter, McGinty, and Edwards 1977).

Environment

The Tutchone homeland is the Yukon Plateau between the towering Saint Elias Mountains on the west (which merge into the coastal range on the south) and the Pelly and Selwyn mountains on the east (fig. 1).

*The phonemes of the Mayo and Selkirk dialects of Northern Tutchone are: (unaspirated stops and affricates) d, λ, $\hat{\delta}$, ʒ, ž, g, gʷ, ?; (aspirated stops and affricates) t, ƛ, $\hat{\theta}$, c, č, k, kʷ; (glottalized) $\dot{t}$, $\dot{ƛ}$, $\dot{\theta}$, $\dot{c}$, $\dot{č}$, $\dot{k}$, $\dot{k}ʷ$; (voiceless continuants) ł, θ, s, š, x, xʷ, h; (voiced continuants) l, δ, z, ž, γ, γʷ; (prenasalized stops) ᵐb, ⁿd, ⁿʒ; (nasals) m, n; (resonants) r (retroflex), y, w; (vowels) i, e, a, o, u, ɔ; (nasalized vowels) į, etc.; (tones) high (v́), mid (v̄), low (unmarked). The Carmacks dialect of Northern Tutchone and Southern Tutchone have additional front velar continuants x̱ and ɣ̱. Southern Tutchone lacks the nonglottalized affricates of Northern Tutchone (except for the lateral affricates), replacing them with the corresponding continuants, and it has an additional high back unrounded vowel ɨ. The Carmacks dialect has a complex 5-tone system, and Southern Tutchone has on most syllables the reverse of the Northern Tutchone tones. There are many differences among the dialects in the shapes of individual words.

The practical orthography used for the Mayo and Selkirk dialects of Northern Tutchone by the Yukon Native Languages Project spells the above phonemes as follows: d, dl, ddh, dz, j, g, gw, '; t, tl, tth, ts, ch, k, kw; t', tl', tth', ts', ch', k', kw'; ł, th, s, sh, kh, khw, h; l, dh, z, zh, gh, ghw; mb, nd, nj; m, n; r, y, w; i, e, a, o, u, ä; nasalized vowels and tones as in the technical alphabet.

Information on Tutchone phonology, dialectology, and practical orthography was derived from Ritter (1976, 1976b), Ritter, McGinty, and Edwards (1977), and John T. Ritter (communications to editors 1980).

Dotted with numerous small and some very large lakes, the Plateau is also dissected by many rivers. The chief drainages are the upper Yukon River system, which runs northwest toward the Bering Sea, and the Alsek River, which cuts south through the coastal range to the Pacific Ocean.

The climate is one of extremes, with hot summers and very cold winters, especially in the lower-lying "frost holes." Precipitation is slight, so that snow depths rarely exceed two feet except high in the mountains and near the coastal range (Kendrew and Kerr 1955:147–208; McQuesten 1952:14). The meadowlands, boreal forest, and alpine tundra support typical subarctic flora and fauna, with moose, caribou, mountain sheep, and mountain goat being the chief large game. Marmots, ground squirrels, and varying hare are important small game animals. Foxes, wolverines, marten, beaver, and mink provide pelts of fine quality. Grizzly and black bear are common but are of limited economic importance. Migratory waterfowl and various kinds of grouse and ptarmigan are common, as are both freshwater fish and salmon. King (*Oncorhynchus tshawytscha*) and chum salmon (*O. keta*) run up the Yukon and many of its tributaries but, having come such a distance, are of poorer quality than those of the Alsek drainage, which has runs of sockeyes (*O. nerka*) and cohos (*O. kisutch*), as well as kings and chums (Johnson and Raup 1964:22–34; McClellan 1975a:16–20, 1971 in 1948–1971; Oswald and Senyk 1976).

Territory

The Tutchone have always been highly mobile. Aboriginally, they moved about in small groups, annually exploiting hundreds of square miles of their varied habitat. Periodically too they adjusted their movements either to gross changes in their traditional subsistence resources—such as shifts in the ranges of caribou, moose, or salmon—or to take advantage of new resources stemming from the growth of the western fur trade on the peripheries of their homeland. Since their first direct contact with Whites in the mid-nineteenth century, the Tutchone have repeatedly moved their "headquarters," realigning their bands in response to the activities of the newcomers (fig. 1, table 1).

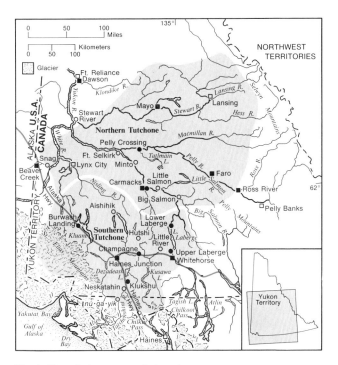

Fig. 1. Twentieth-century tribal territory.

The Canadian Department of Indian Affairs did not use the term Tutchone in any context in 1976; however, it listed six bands whose members were wholly or partly Tutchone speaking: Ross River, Selkirk, Carmacks, Whitehorse, Champagne, and Kluane. Two of the band names (Selkirk and Champagne) better reflect earlier twentieth-century gathering places of the Tutchone than the situation in 1976. Of the 12 communities recognized for representative purposes by the Council for Yukon Indians in 1976, Whitehorse, Carmacks, Champagne–Aishihik–Haines Junction, Kluane, Pelly Crossing, Mayo, and Ross River had partly or completely Tutchone populations. In the 1970s most of the Indians at Ross River were speakers of the Frances Lake dialect of Kaska, but they are treated in this chapter because of their political and cultural associations with the Northern Tutchone.

In the nineteenth century, and perhaps earlier, some Northern Tutchone ranged as far east as the height of land dividing the Yukon from the Mackenzie drainages, intermittently trading, marrying, and fighting with Peel River Kutchin, Mountain Indians, Upper Pelly River "Knife"Indians (who may themselves have been a Tutchone group), and Frances Lake Kaska. From about 1900 members of all these groups have at different times congregated with Tutchone at various trading posts and mining centers on the upper Stewart River (chiefly in the vicinity of Lansing and Mayo) and along the Pelly River and some of its branches, especially at Pelly Banks and Ross River. Local group boundaries never became firmly fixed (Cruikshank 1974:v, 50–59; Denniston 1966; Dominique Legros, personal communi-

cation 1974; McClellan 1975a:15–16, 22; R.F. McDonnell 1975:36–47, 380–387; Tanner 1966:9–10).

External Relations

During part of the nineteenth century, the Northern Tutchone along the Yukon River were blocked by the Han farther downstream from easy access to the goods stocked at the Hudson's Bay Company post established at Fort Yukon in 1847. However, the Klondike gold rush of 1898, which drew thousands of Whites as well as Indians from a wide area into Dawson City, virtually destroyed the Han (Jarvenpa and Williams 1970; McClellan 1967, 1970b:107–114, 1975b:214–218; Osgood 1971:62–65, 77–78).

Nineteenth-century relationships also shifted constantly between the Northern and Southern Tutchone, the Han, the Upper Tanana, and a few Ahtnas at the headwaters of the White River, especially in the Scolai–Chisana Pass Region. Various headmen from each of these groups tried to monopolize local sources of native copper as well as to gain advantage with respect to the changing sources of White men's trade goods. Throughout the early part of the century, the Upper Tanana got tobacco, guns, and other Western trade items chiefly from the Southern and Northern Tutchone traders, who, in turn, had to buy them from Coastal Tlingits. This intergroup trade sometimes led to feuding. Indeed, the arrogance of several Southern Tutchone headmen toward their Upper Tanana trading partners (combined with trouble over stolen women) finally led the Upper Tanana to massacre most of the Southern Tutchone from Neskatahin (Old Dalton Post) while they were at their spring fishing camp near an outlet of Dezadeash Lake. This probably happened in mid-century. By 1875 the Copper Chief (whose first language was apparently an Upper Tanana dialect) evidently controlled the White River copper sources. He married a Northern Tutchone from Fort Selkirk, and four of his sons subsequently became headmen of the Tutchones gathered respectively at Fort Selkirk, Carmacks, Snag, and Burwash Landing, while yet another son lived first at Hutshi and then at Aishihik. By this time the Upper Tanana and Han, as well as the Tutchone, had begun to trade at Fort Reliance, Dawson, Fort Selkirk, and Carmacks. During the early twentieth century, many of these same Indians also converged in the upper White River drainage in short-lived settlements of White prospectors such as Lynx City, Copper City, and Snag. Feuding ceased and intermarriage increased.

The development of transportation throughout Yukon Territory and adjacent Alaska after World War II further increased social interaction among all the Tutchone and their Athapaskan neighbors. Attendance at potlatches in distant villages became common, and in-

Table 1. Population

Place	Year	Number	Source
Fort Selkirk locale	1843	"a large band"	Campbell 1958:68
Kah-Tung (N. Tutchone village near Fort Selkirk)	1883	175–200	Schwatka 1885:185b
Kitl-ah-gon (N. Tutchone village near Minto)		"log house" and brush shelter	
Neskatahin	1891, estimate	100	Glave 1892:682
Hutshi village	1897	3 houses and graveyard	McArthur in Ogilvie 1898a:22
Lower Laberge	1898	ca. 20	Steele in Cruikshank 1974:v-27
Hutshi village	1902, estimate	200	Jim Boss cited in Cruikshank 1974:v-28
Klucho (Kloo Lake?) (S. Tutchone)		25	
Iseaq (Aishihik)		250	
Klukshu		80	
Gaysutchu (Big Salmon)		50	
Tatsuchu (Carmacks?)		15	
Kloosulchuk (Minto?)		35	
Haseena (Ross River)		90 (not all Tutchone)	
Klukshu-Champagne band	1944, census	64	Office of Indian Agent, Whitehorse, Yukon Terr., cited by McClellan 1975a:20
Kloo Lake band		20	
Hutshi band		"One family"	
Burwash Landing band		49	
Champagne	1967, census	130	Canada. Department of Indian Affairs and Northern Development. Indian Affairs Branch 1967:23–24
Aishihik		65	
Kluane (Burwash Landing, Beaver Creek)		100	
Ross River		126	
Selkirk (Pelly Crossing)		256	
Carmacks (Little Salmon, Minto)		247	
Ross River (includes non-Tutchone)	1974, census	138	Office of Indian Agent, Whitehorse, Yukon Terr.; McClellan 1974 in 1948–1975
Selkirk (Pelly Crossing)		306	
Carmacks (includes Little Salmon, Minto, and other N. Tutchone)		245	
Whitehorse (all Indian residents)		595	
Champagne-Aishihik band (includes Haines Junction, Kloo Lake, and Canyon)		199	
Kluane (Beaver Creek, Snag, White River, Burwash Landing; includes Upper Tanana)		97	

tergroup marriages even more frequent (Cruikshank 1974:v17–v21; McClellan 1948–1975, 1975a:24–25, 30–31, 509–510).

Before the fixing of the boundary between British Columbia and the Yukon Territory in 1899–1908, some Southern Tutchone had occupied parts of the Alsek River basin in northern British Columbia, and centuries ago their ancestors may even have lived at the river mouth on the Alaskan coast in the Dry Bay country later claimed by Coastal Tlingit (De Laguna 1972, 1:81–90; McClellan 1975a:23–29, 1948–1975). However,

even though a few Alsek drainage Tutchone were related to Dry Bay or Yakutat Tlingit, during the nineteenth century it was the Chilkat Tlingit who most regularly supplied them with White trade goods and native coastal products. Chilkat domination over the Southern Tutchone was greater than that of the Tutchone over the Upper Tanana. The Chilkat forbade the Tutchone to cross the passes to the coast, but they themselves made long trading trips throughout much of Tutchone country, sometimes three a year. At the height of the trading activity in the first half of the nineteenth century, Chilkat members of the *ǧa·naxte·dí* (called *ǧa·nax̣ʔádi* farther south) and *šanguke·dí* clans of Klukwan maintained the special trading and fishing village called in Tlingit *nú·ǧa·yík* (Nuqwa'ik' in McClellan 1975:32) far up the Alsek River, about 30 miles below Neskatahin. However, they found the interior habitat very difficult, and after a smallpox epidemic swept up the river in midcentury most of the survivors returned to the coast. A few joined the Southern Tutchone at Neskatahin (De Laguna 1972:1, 81–89; McClellan 1948–1975, 1964, 1975a:21–29, 502–508).

Tutchone dependence on the Tlingit lessened as White prospectors and traders slowly penetrated the upper Yukon drainage, finally precipitating the Klondike gold rush of 1898, which completely destroyed the Coastal Tlingit blockade. But interaction between coastal and interior natives again intensified with the building of the Haines Road across the Chilkat Pass during World War II and in response to the growing pan-Indian movement associated with Tlingit land claims in both Alaska and Yukon Territory.

With the Tagish east or south of them the Southern and Northern Tutchone were usually on good terms, and they often intermarried (McClellan 1975a:25).

Culture in the Nineteenth Century

Unless another period is specified, this culture section describes Tutchone life of the nineteenth century. However, much of the technology and many of the customs date from earlier times, and some of them continued in conservative families in 1975.

Subsistence—Annual Cycle

Traditional Tutchone often characterized themselves as either salmon eaters or big game eaters, even though their daily diet frequently was small game or freshwater fish. All Tutchone followed the same basic exploitative cycle. Early in "summer," which the Tutchone reckoned as running from May to October, 5 to 10 small domestic units gathered together to catch either salmon or freshwater fish that they dried and stored for early winter. By August several family groups moved upland together to kill whatever game was most plentiful in the area and to dry and store the meat in scattered caches. Some units might then go off independently to trap, but in December and January during the coldest part of "winter" (which ran from November to April) they usually gathered together again with other families to live mainly off stored foods. Young men brought meat or fish from the distant caches into sheltered camps, which were often at good fishing lakes. By late winter, people had to disperse once more in order to find enough game to stay alive.

March and April were the leanest months of the year, drawing the hungry people together at places where the whitefish spawned, although some families might continue to trap muskrat and beaver late into the season. All looked forward to the fresh, fat meat of ground squirrels and migrant waterfowl of late May, to the more abundant fish and small game of summer, and to the arrival of Coastal Tlingit traders at well-established trading centers.

Of course, special local resources meant slightly differing emphases in the exploitative patterns. Thus, the Southern Tutchone of Neskatahin and Klukshu who had access to the rich salmon of the Alsek River identified themselves as "Fish People" in contrast to the "Meat People" of Hutshi, Aishihik, and Kluane Lake who relied more heavily on mountain sheep and caribou than on the salmon they caught in the Nisling River or the whitefish from the lakes. The "Flat Place People" of Lake Laberge lived mainly on whitefish and mountain caribou. Most Northern Tutchone dried quantities of Yukon-drainage salmon in summer, but the people depended equally on dried meat. The Stewart and Pelly River people had specially good sheep hunting, and they also got mountain caribou. All groups came to depend heavily on moose hunting as these animals increased at the end of the century, and the numbers of caribou dwindled (McClellan 1975a:108–119; McCandless 1976:36–38).

The chief vegetable foods were berries, Hedysarum roots, and the inner bark of several kinds of trees, but these were never the main part of the diet.

Hunting and Fishing Technology

Traditional hunting and fishing equipment was like that of other Cordilleran Athapaskans—light, easily made, and well suited for taking a range of fauna in a variety of ecological niches. Those Tutchone who had access to raw copper for making weapons and other tools felt themselves specially favored.

Many large and small animals as well as birds were snared ("Environment and Culture in the Cordillera," fig. 9, this vol.). Moose and caribou snares were set singly along trails or else in openings in roughly constructed brush fences. Some caribou fences ran in a straight line for several miles, but the more northerly Tutchone also made round corrals with V-shaped entrances into which they drove the animals that they snared, shot with bows and arrows, or speared. Mountain sheep and goats as well as hares were also occasionally surrounded and snared or shot with bows and arrows.

Arrow heads were of antler, bone, or native copper. Those for large game were barbed and detachable. Smaller animals and birds were stunned by bunting arrows of several kinds.

Men killed both bears and human beings with stout spears that had fixed lanceolate heads of native copper or bone. Spears for beaver and salmon had detachable barbed harpoon points. Furbearers such as wolverines, foxes, or marten, as well as bears, were killed in deadfalls; and pitfalls were also occasionally used for bears.

Salmon, trout, pike, and large whitefish were caught with fish leisters or in several kinds of funnel and box traps into which they were directed by weirs (fig. 2). According to tradition, the Coastal Tlingit taught the Tutchone how to make the box traps. Fish were also taken in sinew dip nets, gill nets, and by hooks, gaffs, spears, and lines.

After the mid-nineteenth century, guns, steel traps, wire snares, and twine fish nets began to supplant the aboriginal technology, but in 1975 older men still knew how to make and use bows and arrows and still snared some furbearers and small game or caught them in deadfalls (McClellan 1975a:107–189).

Settlement Pattern

People returned to good fishing spots year after year, and these were also often native trading centers. Usually they were on lakes or on tributaries of the major rivers. No villages were inhabited year round. Winter

bottom left, Natl. Mus. of Canada, Ottawa: J-2144.

Fig. 2. The fish camp at Klukshu. top, Part of the camp with log cabin houses, tents, brush shelters, and raised caches; bottom left, bridge and fish trap across stream; bottom right, close-up of salmon in trap. bottom left, Photograph by Douglas Leechman, 1948. top and bottom right, Photographs by Frederica de Laguna, 1954.

camps were sheltered from the wind, but summer camps were in open grassy places where the breezes would keep down the mosquitoes.

By the twentieth century every Tutchone family had a main log cabin at "headquarters"—near trading post, school, and church—although people seldom stayed in such settlements year round until after World War II. Most families had auxiliary cabins and tent frames at fish camps and in trapping areas.

Structures

Only at the end of the century did some Southern Tutchone begin to build coastal-style rectangular houses of logs or split planks (fig. 3). Traditional shelters were conical brush affairs or rectangular single or double lean-tos with tied pole frameworks, brush walls, and roofs of moss, bark, or skin. Some Northern Tutchone had domed winter tents of six or seven raw caribou or moose hides stretched over frameworks of saplings (McClellan 1975a:240–249; Osgood 1936a:48–57).

Several families lived in each house, sharing a central fireplace, or, in the case of the double lean-tos, one that ran the length of the dwelling; however, each family cooked for itself unless a special feast were given. If an adult died in the house, it was abandoned at once.

Near the main dwellings were storage caches of various sorts, meat and fish drying racks, racks for boat frames and toboggans, sweathouses, and skin-tanning and smoking frames. Small huts for menstruants and parturients were in the bush nearby.

In 1975 the Tutchone lived in a variety of western-style frame houses that they built themselves or that were provided by the Department of Indian Affairs.

Travel

In summer the Tutchone preferred to walk overland. They feared the sudden winds on the large lakes and the treacherous river rapids. However, they occasionally used log rafts, cottonwood dugouts, frame boats covered with raw moosehide, or small canoes of spruce bark or birchbark. Only the Northern Tutchone near Fort Selkirk had really good birch canoes like those of the Han and other downstream neighbors (McClellan 1956, 1960 in 1948–1975; Osgood 1971:79–80).

Winter travel was by snowshoe. Most Tutchone made round-toe shoes laced with partially tanned caribou or moosehide string, but some also had pointed-toe shoes more characteristic of the Mackenzie drainage Indians. These may have been introduced late in the century by the White traders, as was dog traction with wooden toboggans or sleds. Before contact the women usually used "drags" made of caribou leg skins when moving camp while the men went ahead hunting. In the nineteenth century each domestic group usually had one or

Yukon Arch., Whitehorse: MacBride Mus. Coll., 3869.
Fig. 3. Group in front of John Kha Sha's house at Neskatahin village. The heavy beam framing, carved designs on roof edge, beams, door, and wind screen on the roof suggest Northwest Coast influence. Photographed near Old Dalton Post, April 1898.

two pack dogs, but whether dog packing was aboriginal is uncertain (McClellan 1975a:267–279; McDonnell 1975:44, 48–49).

The Tutchone readily took to horses and to skiffs with outboard motors when they became available. After 1950 some trappers hired planes to fly them into their winter trapping grounds. By 1975 almost every family owned a car or truck, and a few persons had snowmobiles and trail bikes.

Clothing and Adornment

Clothing was expertly tailored of well-dressed hides or of fur. Both sexes wore trousers (or possibly leggings) with set-in moccasins and pullover shirts decorated with fringe wrapped with dyed quills or strung with bird down, beaver claws, beads of dried berries or seeds, and, later, of glass. Heavy smoking of the skins may have been introduced during the nineteenth century from down the Yukon River. In earlier times grease and red ocher were rubbed into the skins as waterproofing. Cold-weather clothing included overshirts of caribou or netted hare skins, hoods of dressed hide or fur, trousers of mountain sheep or mountain goat fur, and mitts. Everyone also had a fur robe for extra warmth out of doors and for sleeping. Women showed much skill and taste in making the clothing. The same kind of spiritual relationship was thought to exist between an individual and his clothes as between an animal's carcass and his pelt or "clothes."

Both sexes wore long hair, and, if they were wealthy, copper nose rings or pins, bracelets, and sometimes neck rings. Dentalium shells procured in trade were made into necklaces and hair, nose, and ear ornaments. Adults painted their faces with red designs for ritual

Natl. Mus. of Canada, Ottawa: J – 2161 and J – 2160.
Fig. 4. Sophie Watt of Burwash Landing wearing a ground squirrel robe and carrying a baby in a strap. Photograph by Dorothy Rainier Libby at the Big Arm of Kluane Lake, 1948.

occasions, and with soot to prevent sunburn. Some women had lines tattooed from their lower lips to the outer edges of their chins (McClellan 1975a:301–311).

Social Organization

The Tutchone reckoned descent matrilineally. Most Tutchone were organized into two exogamous groups, called in English Crow (Northern Tutchone *čeḱi* 'raven', locally called "crow," or *haⁿdyát*) and Wolf (*ʔegay* 'wolf' or *haguⁿde*).† While these matri-moieties paralleled in some respects the Coastal Tlingit division into Raven and Wolf, dual organization is probably old in the interior. At the height of the Tlingit-Tutchone trading, the Southern Tutchone centered at Little River and Neskatahin became so heavily intermarried with the Chilkat Tlingit that they also adopted the Coastal Tlingit clan system, with Tlingit-named lineage houses and ranked lineage statuses.

The few marriages between Coastal Tlingit and Tutchone in the more northerly bands did not result in the adoption of Tlingit-named clans, but the dual organi-

†In the Carmacks dialect the moiety names are *haⁿẓ́ɔt* and *ʔegumⁿde* (John T. Ritter, communication to editors 1980).

zation into localized 'Crows' and 'Wolves' could easily be interpreted as equivalent to matrilineal clan segments (De Laguna 1972:449–461, 1975:79–88; McClellan 1975a:439–445).

Pelly River Tutchone who incorporated bilaterally reckoning Indians from the Mackenzie into their local groups usually assigned them to the Wolf moiety. Other Tutchone successfully aligned their moiety system with the multi-clan systems of the Upper Tanana and Han. The social structure was flexible enough to accommodate various expedient adjustments of clan or moiety organization (De Laguna 1975:75–113, 136–139; Denniston 1966:19; McClellan 1948–1975; R.F. McDonnell 1975:339–368; McKennan 1959:123–127; Osgood 1971:39–41).

The moiety organization everywhere structured modes of social reciprocity. It dictated moiety exogamy and governed social obligations at life crises and on public occasions such as potlatches. Many Tutchone still adhered to matrilineal reckoning and to moiety exogamy and other rules of reciprocity in 1975, stating that "Crow and Wolf—it's the law," thus differentiating themselves from Indians farther down the Yukon River.

499

Fig. 5. Elsie Smith carrying her youngest son in a strap decorated with floral beadwork; at right, her son Frankie. Photograph by Catharine McClellan at Haines Junction, July 1966.

Tutchone kinship terminology was congruent with matrilineal reckoning and was extended to include all members of each moiety. Parallel cousins were grouped with siblings and differentiated from cross-cousins. Some of the Northern Tutchone kinship systems more closely resembled those of the Han or the Kaska than of the more southern bands of Tutchone (Dyen and Aberle 1974:236–428; McClellan 1975a:402–416, 1966, 1970 in 1948–1975; R.F. McDonnell 1975:199–338; Ritter 1976:38–39).

A minimal domestic group ideally had at least two able-bodied individuals of each sex. The chief consideration was to link together enough adults to meet subsistence needs. Often the unit was structured around adult siblings of same or opposite sex or an older couple and their daughter and son-in-law. Such a unit might travel about alone during part of the year and then join with others who were linked to them by kinship ties of some sort. Local band membership was very fluid.

The Tutchone lacked formal political organization. A man of forceful character who was a good hunter or trader attracted other domestic groups to his own, and all helped him in activities such as fishing, driving caribou, trading, or potlatching.

Such a headman or "chief" harangued his group in the morning, with the aim of directing the day's activities, preventing overhunting, and endeavoring to set a proper moral tone. The growth of the Western fur trade enabled some headmen to gain considerable prestige and social control because of the wealth they derived from astute trading rather than hunting ability,

and some of them married many wives. Succession of local group leadership was never strictly matrilineal, for a son often succeeded his father, as in the case of the sons of the Copper Chief of the White River, but where Tlingit-style lineage structure was stressed, a brother or sororal nephew usually took over the position of a deceased headman (McClellan 1975a:489–492).

Life Cycle

The Tutchone ritually emphasized birth, puberty, and death. The goal was to promote the welfare of both the individual and the group, and it prescribed varying degrees of withdrawal from daily activities, sexual abstinence, bathing, the use of bone drinking tubes and bone body scratchers, restrictions on the use of sharp-edged tools (which might symbolically cut a person's life line), and a host of other imitative magical acts pertaining to bodily health and successful living. The most stringent observances were associated with attainment of puberty, for at this critical juncture the boys and girls had to become fully capable and responsible adults in a small society where every individual counted. At menarche a girl ideally was secluded for several months or longer in a small shelter some distance from the main household. She wore a large hood (see "Expressive Aspects of Subarctic Indian Culture," fig. 8, this vol.) held out in front of her on a willow framework. In her seclusion she perfected the practical art of sewing by stitching clothing for the entire local group, but what was most strongly impressed upon her was that her female physiology had now become a powerful force in relation to the pervasive spiritual aspects of the world about her. Her conduct could affect either favorably or unfavorably the state of the weather, mountains, rivers, and the animals and plants on which the welfare of the group depended. It could also affect the course of her own life—the ease with which she would bear children, her health, her social character.

Although males were not so completely isolated at puberty as females, they often lived together in separate camps, where they received rigorous training from both maternal and paternal kin in the technology and the ritual aspects of hunting and trapping. They tried to strengthen their personal powers both through vigorous physical exercise and by acquiring spirit helpers.

Only a knowledgeable hunter could hope to gain a well-trained wife. Young men often traveled for several years in order to gain experience in learning how to exploit different parts of the country and to find good wives. During the nineteenth century marriageable females were scarce due to occasional female infanticide and perhaps to other factors (McClellan 1975b:206–221). The ideal of marrying a father's close female kins woman such as his sister's daughter was not easily achieved, although the dual organization and extended kin terminology meant that one could always find a cross-cousin.

When a man married, he usually stayed with his wife's family for several years helping his parents-in-law with hunting and fishing. The son-in-law was responsible for the welfare of his wife's parents until they died. Depending on circumstances, such as the number of daughters in his wife's family, the ages of her parents, and whether or not her father was his maternal uncle, he might travel with the domestic unit for years. Alternatively he might take his wife to live with a different domestic unit and visit his parents-in-law only periodically to give them gifts and to see how they fared. A man avoided his mother-in-law in looks and speech and behaved formally to his father-in-law, from whom he often learned the specifics of a new hunting territory and important social and cosmological lore.

The oldest brother and sister of a family were responsible for the welfare of their young siblings and sometimes advised them verbally, although strict cross-sex avoidance was enjoined between siblings who had reached puberty. Siblings of the same sex, especially brothers, also showed considerable reserve toward each other. The stringency of avoidance lessened among distant classificatory siblings, but respectful behavior to one's elders was the rule.

Some Southern Tutchones had Tlingit-named lineages and crests as well as Tlingit personal names, which were an integral part of a ranked system based on primogeniture. This system was absent among Tutchone farther from the coast. All Tutchone felt that death required moiety-structured reciprocity of services and payments. Those of the opposite moiety of the deceased cremated the body, prepared the grave fence or grave house (fig. 6) erected a year afterward, and carried out other duties for which they were publicly feasted and paid by the matrilineal kin of the deceased at feasts known as potlatches. Some said the custom was first instituted by the leader at Minto, Yukon Territory, called by the Tlingit name *lingít ẋe·n* 'big person' after the death of his mother by famine just prior to 1848. They may have meant to imply a coastal-style memorial feast; however, some form of public memorial ritual was undoubtedly old in the interior.

New parents, widows, and widowers repeated many of the ritual observances that marked their puberty, and to a lesser degree so did those who either handled the dead or who gave potlatches. All such individuals were thought to be so highly vulnerable with respect to their spiritual powers that they could jeopardize through inappropriate actions the welfare of the entire social group.

Although the fleshly body died, the essential soul spirit of a person was reborn as a new individual. Certain people remembered their previous incarnations with exactitude, while for others the situation was much vaguer (McClellan 1970c:xii, 1975a:343–349).

The "Potlatch" and Other Ceremonies

The feast and accompanying payments that marked both the funeral and the later completion of a person's grave house became known to the late nineteenth-century Tutchone by the borrowed term potlatch. The term was often used too when individuals publicly gave gifts to persons of the opposite moiety, for example, at a feast held to celebrate recovery from a serious illness, to mark some other good fortune, or to restore social standing after a public humiliation of some sort. Traditional gifts were furs and food, but later guns, beads, calico, and other Western trade goods became suitable. Not until about 1920 did cash distributions become common. For a death or memorial potlatch, all local matrilineal kin of the deceased were expected to contribute, the closest kin giving the greatest amount of wealth. By the mid-twentieth century at memorial feasts when deaths were "finished" by the construction of grave houses, several thousands of dollars might be collected and distributed.

top, Natl. Mus. of Canada: Ottawa: 98077.

Fig. 6. Grave houses. top, At Aishihik, older style, of planks with surrounding wooden fence. bottom, At Champagne, made of corrugated metal. A grave is covered with canvas (foreground) until the memorial potlatch is held, when the grave house is constructed by the moiety opposite that of the deceased. top, Photograph by Douglas Leechman, 1945. bottom, Photograph by Frederica de Laguna, May-June 1968.

501

The development in transportation has meant the growth of the potlatch network, and tape recorders have enabled people more easily to practice mourning and dance songs and to exchange them over long distances.

Also referred to as "potlatches" by some, or as "Indian Christmas" by others, were midwinter festivals during which people circulated about the camp singing and dropping strings with hooks down the smoke holes of their trade and hunting partners' houses while they whistled the names of the gifts they wished. When those inside guessed what was desired, they put the articles on the hooks.

World View

Each Tutchone had somehow to relate to a world full of superhuman power made manifest in spiritualized aspects of mountains, rivers, plants, and—most particularly—of animals and certain other nonhuman beings. It was a world marked too by fluidity of the forms and functions of spirits and of uncertainty as to the consequences of human behavior. What was good at one moment, might, on another occasion, or if pushed too far, suddenly become bad. Every human tried through personal ritual to enlist the help rather than to incur the ill will of the spirits, especially those of the animals whose bodies he had to kill for a livelihood. Bear, wolf, wolverine, lynx, and beaver had specially powerful spirits. Almost every adult man and many women acquired one or more spirit helpers, either through dreams or through unique encounters when the person was alone in the bush. Each spirit gave its protegé a symbol of its power, such as a song, a food taboo or prescription, or a special body feeling. The spirits also told individuals what to keep in their personal dream bags, for example, an eagle feather or claw, a bit of a special kind of shrub, or a Hudson's Bay post ledger. Persons who had several strong spirit helpers and who were willing to use their powers publicly became professional shamans or "dream doctors." They showed their status by wearing their hair long and uncombed. While asleep or in a trance they sent their spirit helpers out to locate game and to call it to a place where hunters could easily kill it. They also cured the sick by retrieving souls that had been frightened out of their bodies or stolen, dueled with the spirit helpers of rival dream doctors from other groups, foretold future events, or carried out other missions. Location or control of game seems to have been fully as important as curing, if not more so. Some dream doctors held seances simply to show off their great abilities to bend guns, handle magic bullets, or produce special effects likened to motion picture shows. In times of famine or for difficult cases of any sort, two or three dream doctors might cooperate, singing for several days and nights as they huddled under a large blanket and sending their own spirits out to accompany their spirit helpers. The rest of the people kept vigil, preventing the dogs from barking, and increasing the doctors' power by singing the spirit helpers' songs to the accompaniment of drumming. All shamanistic paraphernalia had to be kept ritually clean, away from dogs and menstruating women. Dogs were categorized separately from other animals, and after Christian teaching was introduced in the second half of the nineteenth century, they were usually linked with the devil (McClellan 1975a:161–167, 529–563).

Some Tutchones who had contact with the Upper Tanana or Ahtna bought from them secret "words" that enabled them to cure wounds, clear the trail, prevent attacks by bears, or to accomplish other desirable ends (McClellan 1975a:568–569; McKennan 1959:165–166). Tutchones close to the coast sometimes patterned their search for power as did Tlingit shamans. This involved finding and slitting the tongue of a representative of each kind of animal whose spirit help one acquired. It was a very dangerous act that might result in death due to a kind of backfiring of the power. The Tutchones in touch with the Kaska and the Coastal Tlingit seem to have developed certain ideas about witchcraft more fully than the other Tutchones (Honigmann 1947a, 1954:104–116; McClellan 1975a:563–565, 1970 in 1948–1975).

Mythology

The major myth cycle of the Tutchone accounts for the present nature of the human world. It is about Beaver Man, or Beaver Doctor, who traveled about reducing giant man-eating animals of myth time to their current size, dictating to them their present-day diets. But the Tutchone also knew a cycle of stories about Crow (the Raven of the coast), and they delighted in a wealth of other stories that they told in individualized, novelistic fashion, skillfully developing the psychological possibilities of the plots. A striking characteristic of their tales about their encounters with the first Whites or other strangers is that they often stress their numbskull reactions to the events.

Music and Art

The ability to dance or sing well was prized, and both sexes composed lyric songs about romantic love, loneliness, the beauty of their country, the pleasures of drinking with their affinal relatives, and poignant mourning songs for those who had died (McClellan 1970, 1970a).

Graphic art was relatively meager, abstract, and highly symbolic, confined mostly to paintings in red ocher or black on wooden gaming sticks or dishes, engravings of sheep-horn spoons (fig. 7) and, among the

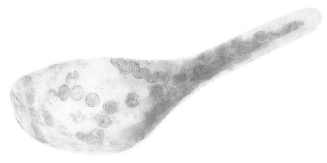

Natl. Mus. of Canada, Ottawa: VI–Q–17.

Fig. 7. Sheep-horn spoon with incised circle and dot designs on bowl and handle. Large decorated spoons were used for ceremonial grease drinking; holding the bowl in the left hand and the handle in the right, a person drank from the side of the spoon (McClellan 1975a: 281–282). Length 23 cm, collected at Hutshi, 1912.

Tlingit-influenced bands, to a few Tlingit-style carvings and paintings in houses. Perhaps the fluidity inherent in the Tutchone world view did not encourage fixed representations of beings and other features of their world. Their greatest artistic skills were often exhibited in their personal dress and adornment.

History of Indian-White Contact

Robert Campbell of the Hudson's Bay Company was probably the first White to see Tutchones in their home country, when, in 1842, he met people whom he called "Wood Indians" at the confluence of the Pelly and Yukon rivers. These people were probably Northern Tutchone. They warned Campbell against the Han downstream but were themselves far more friendly than the Upper Pelly River "Knife" Indians whose identity is uncertain. In 1848 Campbell set up Fork Selkirk at the mouth of the Pelly River. This post attracted natives from the surrounding area who may have been the ancestors of the Selkirk and Tatlmain Lake Tutchone bands of the first half of the twentieth century. In 1852 jealous Chilkat Tlingit traders (perhaps with the help of some Han from downstream and some Northern Tutchone from near Minto) routed Campbell and his men permanently from Fort Selkirk.

Not until 1874 did White traders again penetrate the upper Yukon drainage when Arthur Harper and Leroy (Jack) McQuesten established Fort Reliance in Han country on the Yukon River, in order to serve gold prospectors trickling into the area from downstream. Although reliable records of their movements are lacking, some prospectors were undoubtedly exploring Tutchone country at this time. By 1886 Harper, McQuesten, and Alfred Mayo had set up another post at the mouth of the Stewart River well inside Northern Tutchone country, and in 1893, just three years before the discovery of the Klondike gold, Harper reopened

Fort Selkirk (Brooks 1973:212–320; Campbell 1958:79–138; G. Davidson 1901; Denniston 1966:10–19; McClellan 1967, 1970:107–114; Osgood 1971:3–28; Wright 1976:103–133).

The Coastal Tlingit blockade prevented White entry from the south until the end of the nineteenth century, although a few prospectors may have crossed the Chilkat Pass as early as 1875. Arthur Krause, a German geographer, reached its summit in 1882, but the first White to reach Tutchone country from the coast and to publish a brief account of the Indians was Lt. Frederick Schwatka, who, in 1883, rafted down the Yukon River with six men on a reconnaissance for the U.S. Army (McClellan 1975a:32–34, 38; Osgood 1971:16, 31; Schwatka 1885:32, 38, 80, figs. 14, 15, 16, 1894:200, 224–234; Wright 1976:132–140).

George Dawson and William Ogilvie, Canadian geologists who explored the Pelly and Upper Yukon rivers in the late 1880s, and four men of the 1890 *Frank Leslie's Illustrated Newspaper* Alaska expedition who went down the Yukon River after crossing the Chilkat Pass, saw or met briefly only a few natives who may have been Tutchone. However, two additional members of the Leslie's Expedition, E.J. Glave and Jack Dalton, and their Tlingit interpreter encountered a Southern Tutchone family near Lake Kusawa (Arkell) and traveled with them to Neskatahin. Dalton subsequently set up trading posts at Neskatahin in 1896 (?) and at Champagne in 1902. During the gold rush he also developed the "Dalton trail," following the old Tlingit route to Fort Selkirk via the Tutchone trade centers of Neskatahin, Hutshi, and Aishihik (Dawson 1889; Glave 1890:7, 1891:414, 1892; Ogilvie 1913:84–136; Roppel 1975; Schanz 1890; Schanz and Wells 1974; Tero 1973; Wells 1890, 1891, 1974).

Of the thousands of White prospectors who swarmed through Tutchone country during the gold rush of 1898, most soon left. However, since 1900 several subsequent mineral finds have sporadically drawn Whites to traditional Tutchone areas—to the White River for copper and gold, to the Ruby Range and Scotty Creek for gold, and to Mayo for silver and lead.

Mining continues to dominate the twentieth-century economy of Yukon Territory. Few natives have been directly involved in it, but the building of the company mining town of Faro in 1970 opened up the northeastern Tutchone region, which had been relatively inaccessible even after World War II. Since then White and native populations of Pelly Crossing and of Ross River have greatly expanded, and the characters of these two settlements have changed rapidly (Denniston 1966; Sharp 1976).

The construction of the Alaska Highway in 1942 for military purposes and of subsequent branch roads made these newer mining developments possible. The building of the Alaska Highway also brought a second great influx of Whites into the southern Yukon, involving at least 34,000 military and civilian personnel, almost all males. As happened after the the Klondike rush, most of the men soon left; nevertheless, by 1975 the population of Yukon Territory had climbed from a 1921 low of 4,000 natives and Whites combined to over 18,000. Most of these were living in Whitehorse, which became the territorial capitol in 1950, or in other smaller settlements in traditional Tutchone country (Cruikshank and McClellan 1976).

The building of the roads meant the end of the large river boats for which Indians had begun to cut wood shortly after the gold rush. After the collapse of the fur market in the 1930s, wood cutting had become a main source of cash income for many Tutchone families, but when the boats disappeared, the Indians abandoned their riverbank settlements, such as Big Salmon, Little Salmon, and Stewart River, and moved to Whitehorse or along the highways where they hoped to find steady employment but rarely did.

Until World War II whatever formal education the Yukon natives received was largely in the hands of the missionaries—first the Anglicans and Church of Canada and later the Roman Catholics and Baptists as well. In 1950 the federal and territorial governments began to take over most of the educational, welfare, and developmental services for natives and to expand them. The Tutchone, being close to the administrative centers, were early involved in such governmental programs. They also began to participate in various pan-Canadian native movements. From 1965 through the 1970s several Southern Tutchones were leaders in negotiating land settlement claims with both the federal and territorial governments and in acting to retain certain aspects of their traditional ways of life (Yukon Native Brotherhood 1973).

In less than two centuries the Tutchone have had to adjust to the impact of the western fur trade, to two short-lived boom economies (the Klondike gold rush and the building of the Alaska Highway), to a steadily growing permanent population of Whites, to new schooling and religious sytems and, especially since 1950, to a rapidly increasing transportation network and expanding ties with industrial Canada and the United States (Cruikshank 1974; Cruikshank and McClellan 1976; Cumming and Mickenberg 1972:194–199; Hamilton 1964; Lotz 1971; McClellan 1970:107–114, 1975a:16–33; Mathews 1968:32–122; Tanner 1966; Yukon Native Brotherhood 1973).

Population

The precontact Tutchone population was small, although for no period are there reliable overall figures. Census figures do not identify the Tutchone as a named Indian group, nor do they include any nonstatus Indians (notably women who have married nonnatives or the children from such unions). Important, but incomplete, archival data of the Church of Canada, Roman Catholic and other churches, and of the Department of Indian Affairs remain to be analyzed. Figures available in 1975 are summarized in table 1, which also reflects something of the changing locales where Tutchone have congregated in the past.

Synonymy‡

The name Tutchone was introduced by Osgood (1936:19) as a shortening of Tutchonekutchin (Hodge 1910i:855), a name that originated as Tŭt-chone´-kŭtchin´ in the influential classification of Dall (1877:32). Earlier Dall wrote Tutchon Kutchin (Dall 1870a:271) and Tutchóne Kutchín (Dall 1870:109, 429), and he reverted to a clearly disyllabic first element in Tŭt-chohn´-kŭt-chin (Dall 1886:379). The fact that Dall learned this name at Fort Yukon points to this being a Kutchin name, and the more accurate renderings Tŭtchŭn tā´h kūtchĭn, applied to the Indians above Fort Selkirk (Kennicott 1862), and Touchon-ta-Kutchin 'wooded-country Indians' (Kirkby 1865:418) can be compared directly to Peel River Kutchin dačan tat gʷičin 'dwellers in the woods', used for the Mayo Indians, the northernmost group of Northern Tutchone (Ritter 1976a:45); western Kutchin would have te· for tat. This corresponds exactly in form and meaning to dečan to hoṭyan, which the Mayo people recognize as "the original name for the people who lived in the Stewart Valley" (Ritter, McGinty, and Edwards 1977:13). It is an open question whether this was always a name for this one group of Tutchones or was a translation of the general name Stick Indians (from Chinook Jargon stick siwash 'forest Indians') applied by coastal Indians and traders to the interior Athapaskans of the Cordillera (see Synonymy in "Tahltan," this vol.). The French equivalent Gens de Bois (Campbell 1958:81; Whymper 1869:255; Hardisty 1872:311) or Gens des Bois (Dawson 1889:202B) was used by traders; Dall (1870:109, 1870a:271, 1877:31–32) confused this with Gens de(s) Foux, the name of the Han, and Raymond (1900:38) copied this error. In English the trader's name was Wood Indians, 1842 (Campbell 1958:68, 108, 136; cf. Dawson 1889:202B), also used by Anglican missionaries among the Northern Tutchone (Canham 1898).

Whymper's (1869:254) Tatanchok Kutchins probably reflects a misperception of the Kutchin name, and Raymond's (1870:593) Tatanchaks and Gens-de-wiz are further garblings of this and Gens de Bois. Dall's (1870:109, 1877:32–34) idea that Tutchóne Kutchin meant 'crow people', whence his name Crows, is probably based on a presumed connection with Kutchin de·činʔ 'raven' (in local English "crow").

‡This synonymy was written by Catharine McClellan and Ives Goddard.

Variants of Tlingit *ǵunana·* 'stranger, Interior Athapaskan' have been applied to the Tutchone: Gunana (Krause 1956:218), Gunena and Goonennar (Glave 1890:352, 1892:678, 876), Kŭn-ŭn-ah´ and Khŭn-ŭn-āh´ (Dall 1886:376, 379); see Synonymy in "Tahltan" (this vol.). The Tutchone were in part included in Dall's (1877:32–34) Nehaunees, a widely applied term (see "Nahani," this vol.), and they have also been called by variants of a third general name, appearing as A-yan or Ai-yan Indians (Schwatka 1885:82), I-yan (Schwatka 1885a:227, 1894:227), and Pelly River Kaska eiyô·na (Denniston 1966:11–12). Variants of this general name are also applied to the Han.

Dall (1870:428–430) classified the Tutchone as one of the "Kutchín tribes" (see Synonymy in "Han," this vol.), and they have been called Kutchin in some popular and government publications (Leechman 1947:29, 1950a:253–254; Canada. Department of Citizenship and Immigration. Indian Affairs Branch 1964:44).

Bands and Local Groups

The synonymy of Tutchone band and local group names has not been completely worked out; some problems in identification have been discussed by McClellan (1975:20–34, 1975a:3–7, 13–21), R.F. McDonnell (1975:380–387), and especially Osgood (1971:20–28). It is essential to know the specific contexts in which a name was elicited as well as the time period.

Two bands of Northern Tutchone can probably be identified with the ancestors of the Stewart River Indians and those of the lower Pelly River. The first group is referred to as: Frawtsee-Kootchin (F- probably miscopied for T-) 'people of the forks', classified as the uppermost of the four bands of the Gens du Fou, 1848 (Murray 1910:82), and given as Trātzè-kutchi by Richardson (1852:234); Tr´ōtsĭk kū´tchĭn '[people] of the forks' or Upper Gens de Fou (Kennicott 1862); Totshik-o-tin, on the lower Stewart (Dawson 1889:202B); and Netch-on´-dees or Na-chon´-des, on the Stewart River and the Yukon nearby (Schwatka 1894:227–228). The second appears as: Fathzei-Kootchin (F- probably for T-) 'people of the ramparts' (perhaps Kutchin *ŝahčai· gʷ ičin* 'people of the mountain side'—John T. Ritter, communication to editors 1980), below the Pelly-Yukon confluence and above the Han, 1848 (Murray 1910:82), given as Tathzey-kutchi by Richardson (1852:234), who confuses this group with the Han as a result of skipping several lines in Murray's manuscript; Tī·ⁿzĭt kutchin or Rampart Indians, on the Yukon up to Fort Selkirk (Kennicott 1862). Other names that appear to refer to Tutchone groups are: Caribou Indians (Dall 1877:32); perhaps the Knife Indians, on the Pelly River (Campbell 1958:101, 107, 110, 124, 140; Dawson 1889:202B); Klo-a-tsul-tshik´, from Rink Rapid

(below Carmacks) to the upper Nisling and on the Yukon down to the confluence with the Pelly (Dawson 1889:202B); and Little Salmon River Indians (Field 1913:1–2, 1957:50; Denniston 1966:12).

In the late nineteenth century some of the people on the Upper Pelly, Macmillan, and Stewart rivers were referred to as Abbāto-tenā´ (Bernard R. Ross in Dall 1877:32–33), Es-pā-to-tī-na (Kaska), Spo-to-ti-na, and perhaps Ta-koos-oo-ti-na, and (Northern Tutchone) Na-ai´ (Dawson 1889:200B–202B). These people were not Tutchones but Mountain or Goat Indians connected with those on the South Nahanni and Beaver rivers called Ah-bah-to-din-ne ("mountain Indians") (Hardisty 1872:311) and Esba-t'a-ottiné (Petitot 1876:xx); see "Mountain Indians" (this vol.). The name Kasini was applied by R.F. McDonnell (1975:380–387) to the Kaska speakers at Ross River on the Pelly in the twentieth century; this is the name used by them for the Ross River, apparently of Tlingit origin (McClellan 1975a:476, 586).

Modern Tutchone names for some local populations are listed by Ritter, McGinty, and Edwards (1977:81–82) and McClellan (1975a:13–34). The Ross River people are called *ḱálat hoṭyán³*. The Tutchone at Pelly Crossing generally refer to themselves as Selkirk people, after their former location near Fort Selkirk (Ritter, McGinty, and Edwards 1977:7–8).

Sources

The journalist E.J. Glave (1892) provided valuable accounts and drawings of the Southern Tutchone of the Alsek drainage in the late nineteenth century, but the articles are short. Other nineteenth-century sources are scattered and even more limited in nature, although Campbell's journals (published in 1958) give priceless glimpses of the Tutchone near Fort Selkirk in midcentury. Schwatka (1885:82–84) located camp and village sites in 1883.

Twentieth-century ethnographic data remain scant. Cruikshank (1974, 1975), Johnson and Raup (1964), McClellan (1950, 1964, 1970a, 1970b, 1975a, 1975b), and Tanner (1966) are the fullest sources. McClellan's (1948–1975) field research data during the 1960s centered at Aishihik and Haines Junction. R.F. McDonnell's (1975) manuscript on Ross River deals mostly with the population derived from the Liard River drainage, while Denniston's (1966) stresses Tutchone elements. Arcand (1966) has done fieldwork with Northern Tutchones around Carmacks. Important linguistic studies of the Mayo and Fort Selkirk dialects of Northern Tutchone have been carried out by Ritter (1976) and Tutchone associates (Ritter, McGinty, and Edwards 1977).

Han

JOHN R. CROW AND PHILIP R. OBLEY

Language, Territory, and Environment

The Han ('hän) speak an Athapaskan language that is quite distinct from those of their neighbors, though in the usual Northern Athapaskan pattern it shares certain features with each of them.* Han is most similar to Kutchin but only at best partially mutually intelligible with it, though some older Han speakers can read the Kutchin orthography of Robert McDonald and use his Anglican bible and prayer book; Han shows fewer affinities to Northern Tutchone and Upper Tanana. At the time of the gold rush in the late nineteenth century Peel River Kutchins, Tutchones, Tagishes, and Upper Tananas were drawn into Han territory, especially to the Moosehide settlement near the later site of Dawson, and Han became the local Athapaskan lingua franca for about a generation, until displaced in this function by English. This circumstance probably accounts for both the extent of the passive knowledge of Kutchin among the Han and the relatively small number of fluent speakers remaining, estimated to number only about 35 in 1979 (Michael Krauss, in Osgood 1971:147–149; Ritter 1979; Robert Jarvenpa, communication to editors 1978).

The area inhabited by the Han in protocontact times fell approximately between 64° and 65°30′ north latitude along the Yukon River on both sides of the United States–Canada boundary (fig. 1). The part of the Yukon River occupied by the Han is a heavily forested region just upstream from the area known as the Flats. The numerous rivers and lakes contain many varieties of fish, most significantly salmon, whitefish, pike, grayling, and loche. Important mammals included Barren Ground caribou, moose, bear, beaver, and porcupine. Monthly mean temperatures in the region range from −17° to 60° F., with recorded maximum and minimum of 95° and −73° F.

Traditional Culture

Technology

Aboriginally the material items of the Han were much like those of other Subarctic Athapaskans, especially those within the Pacific drainage. Commonly used hunting implements were the bow (with guard) (fig. 2) and several types of arrows, including a blunt-tip variety for bird hunting. Spears for bear and caribou hunting as well as babiche and sinew snares for both large and small animals were used. Fish were taken in weirs and traps, by gill nets and dip nets, and with spears and harpoons.

For travel the Han depended upon birchbark canoes, mooseskin boats, hunting and trail snowshoes, and sleds. In protocontact times they did not have toboggans. Cooking was often done in woven spruce-root baskets by the stone-boiling method. Skin bags were used for food storage.

Clothing

Clothing, sewn primarily of caribou skins, consisted of a shirt or coat that reached nearly to the knees. For extra warmth the shirt was sometimes made of plaited hare skin. The leggings and moccasins were often in one piece, usually made of caribou hide, though some-

---

*The phonemes of the Eagle dialect of Han are: (unaspirated stops and affricates) *b, d, λ, δ̂, ȝ, ʒ̇, ǯ, g, ʔ*; (aspirated stops and affricates) *t, ƛ, θ̂, c, c̣, č, k*; (glottalized) * t̓, ƛ̓, θ̂, c̓, c̣̓, č̓, k̓*; (voiceless continuants) *ł, θ, s, ṣ, š, x, h*; (voiced continuants) *l, δ, z, ẓ, ž, γ*; (nasals) *m, n, ŋ*; (resonants) *w, r* (retroflex), *y*; (plain vowels) *i, e, æ, a, o, u, ë* (mid back unrounded), *ɔ*; (long vowels) *i·*, etc.; (nasalized vowels) *i̧*, etc.; (long nasalized vowels) *i̧·*; (tones) high (unmarked), low (v̀), falling (v̂), rising (v̌). In syllable-final position, partly devoiced resonants and nasals (analyzed as *n, w, r, y*) contrast with their fully voiced counterparts (analyzed as *n·, w·, r·, y·*). In the Dawson dialect many words differ from their cognates in Eagle according to systematic sound correspondences, and there are the following additional phonemes: (prenasalized stops) *ᵐb, ⁿd*. The dental stops are palatalized in some environments to [tʸ], and in the speech of the younger speakers at Eagle to [č], thus falling together with the palatal affricate series.

In the practical orthography used by the Yukon Native Languages Project and the Alaska Native Language Center the phonemes of Han are written as follows: b, d, dl, ddh, dz, dr, j, g, ' (not written word-initially); t, tl, tth, ts, tr, ch, k; t', tl', tth', ts', tr', ch', k'; ł, th, s, sr, sh, kh, h; l, dh, z, zr, zh, gh; m, n, ng; w, r, y; i, e, a, ä, o, u, ö, ë; ii, etc.; i̧, etc.; i̧i̧, etc.; tones as in the technical orthography. Syllable-finally the voiceless resonants are written n, w, r, y, and their voiced counterparts nn, ww, rr, yy. The Dawson prenasalized stops are spelled mb and nd.

Information on Han phonology, dialectology, and practical orthography was furnished by John T. Ritter, who also provided the phonemic transcriptions of the Han forms cited (communications to editors 1980), and by Michael Krauss (communication to editors 1980).

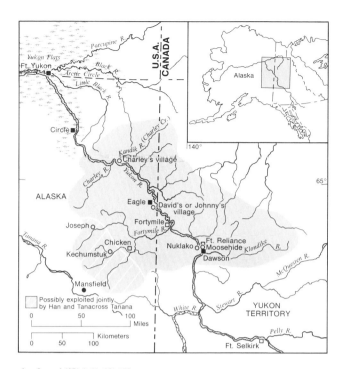

after Osgood 1971:4, 11, 151–153.
Fig. 1. Territory in 1850.

times separate moosehide moccasins were worn. Fur caps and hare or mountain-sheep robes were also worn in the winter.

Structures

Two main types of shelters were built. The first, called a moss house by Osgood (1971:84), was a semisubterranean square structure made of split wooden poles and insulated with moss; the second was a domed skin house for temporary use while traveling.

Subsistence—Annual Cycle

The Han were, according to Osgood (1971:115), more dependent on fish than on meat as the basis of their food supply; and salmon was certainly the most important of the several species taken. Beginning in June with the king salmon and in August with the chum salmon, the fish appeared in large numbers in the Yukon River and its tributaries. In anticipation the Han settled on the river banks in early spring to begin preparing the necessary canoes, nets, and other imple-

Fig. 2. Chief Isaac (d. 1933), leader of the Klondike band of the Han (Osgood 1971:153). He holds a bow with a projecting wooden string guard and wears a hide quiver with painted borders and beaded fringe. Photograph by Asahel Curtis, 1898.

ments for harvesting the fish. The moss houses were repaired or new ones built while the Indians awaited the beginning of the salmon run. During this interval hunters sought moose, caribou, and small game, as well as other types of fish. The salmon run began in July and continued until September. Large quantities were taken, and much of it was dried and stored for winter use.

When the run ceased, the river camps were abandoned and small bands moved into the woods to seek game. While the men hunted moose and other game, the women fished the lakes and streams and worked to ready the caribou impounds for the coming winter migrations. Any surplus meat was cached for later use.

In about the middle of October the bands returned to the river camps, where they remained for about the next two months. Items for the winter months, such as snowshoes and additional clothing, were manufactured at this time. Members of the group not involved in these preparations hunted and fished.

The riverbank camps were occupied for most of the winter, except for a brief trip to hunt caribou and another to bring back cached meat. The latter journey took only a week or two in mid-January, while the caribou hunt lasted from mid-February to mid-March. Upon finishing the hunting trip the Han returned to the rivers and began preparing once again for the summer salmon runs.

Social Organization

Little is known of aboriginal forms of Han social organization. According to Osgood (1971:40) there were

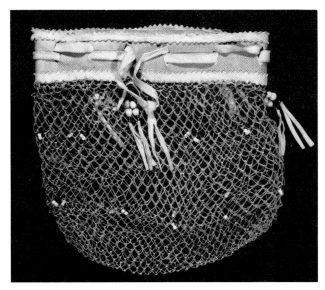

Yale U., Peabody Mus.: 53033.

Fig. 3. Bag of babiche in simple looping topped by band of smoked moosehide, edged with notched white caribou skin and decorated with pairs of black and white trade beads and tassels with seeds between black trade beads. Depth 30.5 cm, collected by Cornelius Osgood at Eagle, 1932.

apparently three exogamous, matrilineal clans, two of which belonged to one moiety. The remaining clan constituted the other moiety. There is no evidence concerning the existence of distinct classes of people, though there was at least some concept of clan stratification based, at least in part, on wealth. Accumulation of goods was the chief means of becoming rich, but it is unclear what the goods consisted of, or how they were accumulated. It is known that the potlatch served to distribute the property of the wealthy deceased.

Wealth also was an important factor in the selection of clan leaders, though intelligence and ability were considered. At least one of Osgood's (1971:42) informants indicated that chiefs were formerly elected by a council of clan members.

Within the clan the most important social unit was ideally a conjugal pair and its dependents, operating in close contact with another such group, usually tied by a link of two close relatives, such as brothers. These two groups then operated within a sphere of several other such groups, getting together at various times of the year according to the needs at hand.

Kinship terminology was probably bifurcate collateral, and relative age was recognized in sibling terminology. Cousin terminology has not been determined. Cross-cousin marriages were preferred, with uxorilocality the preferred residence pattern for at least the first few years of marriage.

Life Cycle

Birth took place with the mother isolated from her husband and aided by two women. The mother squatted to give birth, supported by a horizontal pole padded with moosehide. The newborn child was washed in warm water by the midwives, then dressed in hare skins. The placenta was wrapped in skin and either placed in the top of a tree or buried to protect the child's health. In some cases the umbilical cord was put in a sack and saved as a source of "medicine."

Following the birth of the child the father gave a banquet for the entire village. Generally this event took place at least two weeks after the birth to be sure that the child would live. The name could be assigned by anyone, but most often it was done by a shaman.

Only minimal ceremony followed a young man's achievement of puberty, but girls were subject to elaborate ritual behavior at menarche. To celebrate the event, a girl's father held a banquet for the entire community. Then the girl was isolated from her home in the care of a relative of her betrothed. She was not permitted to eat any fresh meat for a year, subsisting on dried meat, fish, and berries. Restrictions during succeeding menstrual periods were not so severe.

Marriages were generally arranged by parents during their children's infancy, although consideration was

508

given later for the wishes of those involved. Usually marriage took place between the ages of 16 and 20, though occasionally as late as 25. Wealthy men sometimes practiced polygyny, and cases of polyandry were known.

The dead were usually cremated and the remains collected in a wooden box. Chiefs were sometimes interred in a hollow log that was placed on a platform. Cremation was usually attended to by men of the opposite moiety of the deceased. These men ate no fresh meat for a year after the cremation, for fear of death. Mourning was demonstrated by performance of a dance before cremation. The surviving spouse was not permitted to remarry for several years.

Religion

Information is sparse with regard to aboriginal Han religious beliefs. They did share with other Athapaskans the belief in Nakani, the Bad Indian. There is also mention of Fireman, a dream figure. The mythological narratives extant deal largely with the origins of man and the world and with the relations of men to other creatures.

Shamans in Han society shared most of the functions of those in other Athapaskan groups: curing disease and providing aid to insure success in hunting and warfare. Either men or women could fill this role, and they could be either good or bad according to how they used their power. This power was derived from a variety of sources, though commonly it was from an animal being seen in a dream. One who wished to learn shamanistic skills slept under the same blanket with an accomplished shaman. As the new shaman drew power from the old one the latter tended to lose power.

Art and Music

Aboriginally, plastic and graphic arts were limited to the decoration of a few items ("Environment and Culture in the Cordillera," fig. 16, this vol.). Han women used dyed porcupine quills and hair to decorate clothing and accessories and worked small geometric designs into woven baskets. Schmitter (1910:10) reports that red ocher was mixed with grease as a paint for faces or with mud for painting unspecified wooden articles.

Songs were of four types: love, war, potlatch, and shamanistic. The only instrument used to accompany singing was the tambourine drum. There is no specific mention of oration as a highly developed art.

Games

The Han shared many games with surrounding groups. These included wrestling, tug of war, foot races, shinny, hoop-and-pole, and the hand game. Some apparently unique games included throwing-the-stick, the object of which was to knock down stakes placed in two rows by tossing a club. They also had a game similar to volleyball. It was a team sport in which the object was to keep a ball from touching the ground within one's own area.

History and Culture Change

The Han were among the last of the Northern Athapaskans to encounter Europeans. Initial meetings occurred shortly after the establishment of Fort Yukon to the northwest of Han territory in 1847. The Han had already obtained some European goods (for example, guns and iron tools) through contact with other Indians, and they traveled to the fort to seek additional items. Not until 1851 did Whites actually penetrate Han territory. Robert Campbell, a Hudson's Bay Company factor, left the newly established Fort Selkirk and followed the Yukon River down into Han country. In 1852 he repeated the trip and this time passed through to Fort Yukon before returning to Fort Selkirk (Osgood 1971:3, 4).

The next 15 years saw no Europeans entering Han lands, though the Han continued to make the trip to Fort Yukon. Whites next entered the area in 1867, but still no European settlements were established among the Han.

With the purchase of Alaska by the United States, in 1869 the Hudson's Bay Company closed Fort Yukon. Moses Mercier, an ex-trader from that fort, returned to Alaska in 1873 and founded a post on Belle Isle, just offshore from the present town of Eagle (Osgood 1971:8). A year later Fort Reliance was established as the second post in Han territory. Further trade developed as the Alaska Commercial Company franchised the operations of a team of three men as the sole traders on the Yukon River in the area of the Han. From that time on, White men with their goods regularly plied the waters of the Han region.

During this first period of White contact the Indians began to shift from the traditional hunting and fishing economy toward one based on trapping. The Han were relying more and more on store goods. Guns, European clothing, and certain food items were becoming necessities. Skin tents were being replaced with canvas and log structures, clustered near the White communities. Caribou became less important as their skins were no longer in such demand. Thus the hunting trips for migrating caribou declined in frequency.

The systems of clans and moieties, as well as patterns of preferred marriage and residence, were gradually breaking down. Christianity was being rapidly accepted by the Indians, though the influence of shamans continued into the twentieth century.

Although detailed documentation is lacking, Murray (1910) and Schwatka (1885a) indicate that epidemics occurred during this period.

The Gold Rush

Gold was known in the Yukon River area as early as the 1850s, but news of its presence apparently did not spread until 1875 when the first gold was actually taken out of Alaska. Prospectors began to arrive, and small strikes were made in a number of places. The first major strike was not until 1885, southeast of Han territory. In 1886 a big find was made at the mouth of the Fortymile River, and 30 to 40 men wintered there the following year. Other strikes in Han country were made in 1888, 1894, and 1895.

The peak of the rush followed the discovery of gold on the Klondike River in 1897. The town of Dawson, at the mouth of the river, swelled to 5,000 people in 1897 and to an estimated 20,000 to 30,000 the next year. Other towns were subject to similar expansion, though on a smaller scale. Eagle, for example, had a population of about 1,000 by 1898. As the gold rush ended, the towns were abandoned, and only Dawson and Eagle remained by the early twentieth century.

Missionaries had first contacted the Han at Fort Yukon in the 1860s. Robert McDonald of the Church of England was instrumental in Christianizing the Han,

bottom, U. of Alaska Arch., Fairbanks: Selid-Bassoc Coll. 64–92–402; top, U. of Wash. Lib., Seattle.
Fig. 4. Dancing in the Alaska Commercial Company's yard at Dawson. Photographs by Goetzman, May 24, 1901.

through contact with them at Fort Yukon (Osgood 1971:13). The first mission actually within Han territory was established in 1887 at Fortymile. It was headed by Bishop William C. Bompas until 1901. As the gold rush peaked and declined, so did mission activities.

With the sudden arrival of thousands of Whites and the goods associated with them, the Han entered a period of extremely rapid change. The shift to a cash economy became nearly complete as the Indians relied less on salmon and devoted more time to supplying meat and furs to the Whites. Some Han men worked on the steamers that plied the river and thus saw much that was outside the experience of usual Han life. Some women married White men, hastening the disintegration of aboriginal marriage patterns.

The increase in mission activity associated with the gold rush effectively ended most of the traditional Han religious beliefs.

Epidemics, especially of diphtheria, were still common during this period. Some attempts were made to vaccinate against smallpox.

After 1900

As the number of gold strikes dwindled, so did the White population. Most of the mining camps were abandoned and the once-thriving Dawson had only a few hundred people. The Han, greatly affected by White contact and disease, were once again becoming isolated. For many years the Han were in contact only with government agents and a few die-hard miners. This continued until the opening of the first roads into their territory in the 1950s. Despite their isolation, they suffered epidemics of influenza, mumps, and measles, especially in the years between 1919 and 1925 (Jarvenpa 1978).

Most of the remaining elements of Han aboriginal material culture disappeared early in the twentieth century. Salmon fishing continued, but with the use of introduced devices such as the salmon wheel. The Han who survived the period of intense White contact did, however, retain some aspects of traditional culture. Even in the 1960s, Slobodin (in Osgood 1971:145) reported that women were still isolated at the time of their first menstruation.

By the 1960s most Han lived around Dawson, Yukon Territory, with a smaller community near Eagle, Alaska. Like many White-dominant Northern communities, the town of Eagle proper was populated by Whites, while the Han lived just outside of town in a separate village. The Indian village at Eagle had a population of around 40 individuals. Most of the men in the village were seasonally employed, and a few had full-time jobs. A majority of the positions were with the government, such as road construction workers or fire fighters. Women too held seasonal jobs, often through the school system. In addition they produced beadwork for sale in the town.

Trapping provided many families with extra income, and hunting was still an important activity in the village. Moose and caribou were hunted for meat, which was packed to the village and preserved. The hides were no longer tanned. Fish remained as a Han staple, but few families were actively engaged in fishing. Most families preferred to buy their fish from the Indians and Whites who still set nets.

Few traditional Han religious beliefs were discernible in Eagle in the 1960s. The Han of Eagle were active and devout Episcopalians; however, some Han believed that a dead person's spirit comes back to check on those he left behind. There are some who continued to believe that a child born shortly after someone's death will take on some of the characteristics of the deceased.

Traditional material culture was nearly gone. One woman could still make thin babiche, and another, birchbark baskets. Older men still made snowshoes, but these skills were ebbing (Judith Maxwell, personal communication 1973).

Population

At the time of contact there were three Han bands, with a total population according to Osgood (1971:33) of perhaps 1,000. By the end of the gold rush nearly all the Han lived in Johnny's Village, Fortymile, or Nuklako, those at Nuklako later moving across the river to Moosehide. Information reported by Schmitter (1910:11, 14) about a memorial potlatch held in 1909 indicates that the Han then viewed themselves as consisting of four bands, living at Charley Creek, Eagle, Moosehide, and Kechumstuk, though other sources claim that Kechumstuk was a caribou-hunting camp jointly used with Tanacross speakers from Mansfield Village ("Tanana," this vol.). When Osgood visited the Han in 1932 only the villages of Eagle and Moosehide remained. In the 1960s Richard Slobodin (personal communication 1973) found that nearly all Han lived in or near Dawson, with the rest living outside of Eagle. There were no longer any Han living at Moosehide, but approximately 215 to 250 Hans lived nearby in the Dawson area. In addition there were about 50 Hans in and around Eagle (Judith Maxwell, personal communication 1973), for a total Han population of 265 to 300.

Synonymy†

The name Han was introduced by Osgood (1936:11) as a shortening of Hankutchin (Hodge 1907m:531), which

---

†This synonymy was written by Ives Goddard.

Fig. 5. Mary McLeod and her granddaughter, who is wearing a dentalium and bead necklace. Photograph by Catharine McClellan, Dawson, 1966.

first appeared as Han-Kootchin (People of the Water), 1848 (Murray 1910:82). This is the Kutchin name for the Han, *han-g^wičin* 'people of the river' (John Ritter, communication to editors 1980). Other early spellings are Hun-koo-chin (Hardisty 1872:311), Hong-Kutchin (Strachan Jones 1872:321), An Kutchins (Whymper 1869:254), Han Kutchin and Han-Kutchín (Dall 1870:107, 430), and Hăn-Kŭtchin´ (Dall 1877:31); apparently influenced by published forms are Au Kotchins (Raymond 1870:593, misprint) and Hun-Kutchin (Raymond 1900:38). Hungwitchin is the spelling in McPhee (1977:378).

The Han have no name in their language for themselves as a separate group but traditionally used only the names of the local bands. The self-designation Takon, reported somewhat diffidently by Schwatka (1885a:86), has not been confirmed by any other source; Schwatka (1893:242) later wrote this name Tahk-ong. Some Hans have borrowed the Kutchin name, either in its Kutchin shape or more or less adapted to Han phonetics (for example as *hǫ hwəčin*), and Han Gwich'in (the spelling in the Kutchin practical orthography) has been used in English in literacy publications of the Council for Yukon Indians (Richard Slobodin, personal communication 1973; Robert Jarvenpa, communication to editors 1978; John Ritter, communication to editors 1980).

Dall (1870:428–430) classed the Kutchin bands, the Han, the Tutchone, and the Tanana together as the "Kutchin tribes," apparently because they all "form their tribal name by the addition of the word Kutchin." But since the names Dall had for these groups were the Kutchin names, obtained at Fort Yukon, they naturally all contained Kutchin *g^wičin* 'people of', and this fact indicates nothing about the relationship of these groups. Nevertheless, the classification of the Han as Kutchin became established (Hodge 1907m:531) and has been used in official publications for the Han and Tutchone, even when the Kutchin have been separately classed as Loucheux (Canada. Department of Citizenship and Immigration. Indian Affairs Branch 1964).

The French name for the Han used by Hudson's Bay Company traders was Gens du fou (Murray 1910:82), Gens de Fou (Hardisty 1872:311), or Gens de Foux (Whymper 1869:245), meaning 'fool people', appearing in garbled form as Gens-de-fine (Raymond 1870:593). The traders applied this name to the Han and some Northern Tutchone ("Upper Gens de fou") because of their "remarkably *energetic* . . . manner of dancing" (Kennicott 1862). Dall (1870:109, 429, 430, 1870a:271) gives Gens de Bois (Gens des Bois) as the traders' name for the Han and Gens de Foux (Gens des Foux) as their name for the Tutchone, an incorrect reversal that is perpetuated elsewhere (Dall 1877:31–32; Raymond 1900:38).

According to Dawson (1889:200B, 202B) the Ti-tsho-tī-na (Frances Lake Kaska) called the people next beyond the Pelly River people Ai-ya´-na, and the Fort Selkirk Indians (Northern Tutchone) called the people next below the lowest Han band Ai-yan´, but other evidence suggests the Han may have been included under this name. Although related forms are used in several Athapaskan languages for relatively distant groups, Robert Campbell reported that the "Ayonais" were below the "Wood Indians" (Northern Tutchone) (Dawson 1889:202B), and the modern Northern Tutchone equivalent *ʔeža·n* (with *ž* regularly for *y*) is applied specifically to the Han ('Dawson people') (Ritter, McGinty, and Edwards 1977:81; Ritter 1976:40). A version of this name induced Dall (1886:379) in his final classification to give the name of the Han as Hai-ăn´-kŭt-chin´; since he specifies that the territory of this group extended to Fort Selkirk (at the confluence of the Pelly and the Yukon), he appears to include under this new name the Northern Tutchone, called by Schwatka (1885a:82) the A-yan or Ai-yan Indians.

Schwatka (1885a:86) gives the "Ingalik" (Koyukon) name of the Han as Tchi-cargut-kotan.

Band names

Designations are attested for three Han local bands within what is now recognized as Han territory (Ritter 1979).

The northernmost Han band was found at the mouth

of Kandik River (Charley Creek) in Charley's village (also Charlies Village), named after their "head chief" (Petroff 1884:map; Schwatka 1885a:88–90, map part 2 sheet no. 8); Schmitter (1910:14) refers to them as the Charlie Creek Indians. The Han name of their village site was k̀àyⁿdik 'willow creek' (Ritter 1979), whence Kandik. They were called Charley's Indians and, according to a local trader in 1883, the Tadoosh, a name he is also said to have used for both them and the next band south (Schwatka 1885a:90, 1893:262); Tadoosh appears in Hodge (1910m:668) as Tadush. Dawson (1889:202B) gives their name as Ka-tshik-o-tin. Osgood (1971:26) followed Baker (1906:170) in using the name Charley Village, but Baker gives Charley's Village as the local usage.

The middle Han band was at Johnny's village (also John's Village), named for their "head chief" (Schwatka 1885a:87, map part 2 sheet no. 7), just above Eagle Bluff; this is the present site of Eagle, called θeˑ t̀àwλin 'where it flows by the rock (bluff)'. Several diverse renderings of this name appear as designations of the middle band or their village: Fetoutlin (Petroff 1884:map, 1900:68); "Fetutlin (now called Eagle City)" (Wickersham 1938:313; cf. Hodge 1907f:458); Klat-ol-klin Indians and Klat-ol-klin´ village (Schwatka 1885a:86, 1893:255), obtained from a half-Russian interpreter and hence apparently with Koyukon λa- 'bluff' replacing its Han cognate θeˑ; Tsit-o-klin-otin (with -otin 'people of'), obtained from Indians near Fort Selkirk (Dawson 1889:202B); Θetahʊklį and Θtahuliⁿ, used at Eagle (Osgood 1934:176, 1971:27). Dawson and perhaps Petroff locate this group at the mouth of Fortymile River, where they seemed to have sometimes had their village (Schmitter 1910:17), but the identity of all these names with that proper to the Eagle area shows that only a single band is involved, not two as Osgood (1971:26–27) thought. Petroff in 1884 (1900:68) also referred to them as David's people, and in the following census "David's camp" and "the native village of Klot-ol-tin" were enumerated as one unit (U.S. Census Office. 11th Census 1893:162, 165). Osgood (1971:26) adopted the spelling Johnny Village to conform to his use of Charley Village.

Indians from Eagle have given anthropologists a name ežan kučin, said to be ezzin kučin in Kutchin (probably Peel River) and ežana in (Northern) Tutchone, as that of the Eagle people (Slobodin in Osgood 1971:27, normalized; Robert Jarvenpa, communication to editors 1978), which has led Osgood to compare Dawson's name Ai-ya´-na. However, ežan kučin is a modern coinage given as a literal translation of 'Eagle people'; here ežan and its variants are words for 'golden eagle': Han čəžæn'ʔ, ʔəžæn'ʔ, Peel River Kutchin ʔežìn; Fort Yukon Kutchin čìžìnʔ (Ritter 1976a:26;

Peter 1979:3; John Ritter, communication to editors 1980). Schmitter (1910:1, 15), who reported that the Eagle people called themselves kkwi dyik and were called vun tte kwi chin 'people of the Willow Creek (Charlie Creek)' in the "Porcupine" language, adopted the name Vuntakutchin for them; he thus confuses completely Han k̀àyⁿdik (modern pronuciation also [k̀àydʸik]), the designation of the lower Han band discussed above, and Kutchin van tcˑ gʷičin 'people among the lakes; Old Crow people, Vunta Kutchin' (formerly of the middle Porcupine River).

The southernmost (uppermost) Han band was on the Klondike River and near its mouth in the village of Nu-kla-ko (also Noo-klak-ó, Nuclaco, and miswritten Nuctaco) (Schwatka 1885:86, map part 2 sheet 7, 1894:246) opposite Fort Reliance, whose name was used for the band by Petroff (1900:68), and later at Moosehide and Dawson. Schmitter (1910:14) called them the Moosehide Indians. The Han name for the Klondike is čoⁿdik 'stone-for-driving-in-fish-trap-poles river' and the Klondike band is called čoⁿdik hwət̀in (Dawson dialect) or čožuˑ wəčin (modern Eagle dialect) (John Ritter, communication to editors 1980); these names have been rendered Tro-chu-tin (Adney in Osgood 1971:27), tɣatcɪk and tɣačik (Osgood 1934:176, 1971:27), and tronžiuk or troⁿčik (Slobodin in Osgood 1971:27). Schwatka (1885:84) used the name Takon Indians for this band, but he indicated uncertainty about it and said it was also used by the Indians of the middle band. In addition to these three bands Murray (1910:61, 75–76, 82) in 1848 reported Frawtsee-Kootchin 'people of the forks' (with F- probably miscopied for T-) as the uppermost of four Han bands, a name rendered by Richardson (1852:234) as Trātzè-kutchi 'people of the fork of the river', but judging from the apparent location of this group it was probably a Northern Tutchone band.

Sources

Osgood (1971) is the best reference on the Han. This monograph is based on Osgood's own field data from a visit in 1932 as well as information from Slobodin's fieldwork in 1961 and 1962. Early sources of some value include Murray (1910), Schwatka (1885a), Schmitter (1910), Campbell (1958), Dall (1870a), and Adney (1900).

Unless otherwise noted, the data presented in this chapter are taken from Osgood (1971). Personal communications from Slobodin (1973) and Judith Maxwell (1973) provided information on the Han of the 1960s. McPhee (1977:183–438) is a sensitive journalistic account of the Han and other inhabitants of the region around Eagle in the mid-1970s.

Kutchin

RICHARD SLOBODIN

Language, Territory, and Environment

The Kutchin (kōō'chĭn) comprise several communities in each of which is spoken a dialect of the Kutchin language, a member of the Athapaskan family.* The Kutchin as a whole are rather sharply bounded, both by the relative distinctiveness of their language in the Athapaskan family and by a strong consciousness of kind among Kutchin speakers. Moreover, Kutchins tend to feel that they differ from their neighbors in psychological makeup.

It is probable that the territory of the Kutchin shifted eastward in late prehistoric and early historic times.

*The phonemes of the Peel River (Fort McPherson) dialect of Eastern Kutchin are: (unaspirated stops and affricates) b, d, λ, δ̂, ʒ, ȝ́, ǯ, ǯ, g, gʷ, ʔ; (aspirated stops and affricates) t, ƛ, θ̂, c, ć, ç, č, k, kʷ; (glottalized) ṭ, ƛ̓, θ̇, ċ, ḉ, ç̣, č̣, ḳ; (voiceless continuants) ł, θ, s, ś, ṣ, š, x, h; (voiced continuants) v ([β] ~ [v]), l, δ, z, ź, ẓ, ž, γ, γʷ; (prenasalized stops) ⁿd, ⁿȝ; (nasals) m, n; (voiceless nasal) N; (resonants) r, y; (voiceless resonant) R; (short plain vowels) i, e, a ([ə]), o, u; (long plain vowels) iˑ, eˑ, aˑ, oˑ, uˑ; (nasalized vowel) ą; (diphthongs) ai, aiˑ, eiˑ, ao; (tones) high (unmarked), low (v̀). In the production of the alveopalatal series (ȝ́, ć, etc.) the articulation starts at the lamino-alveolar position and moves to the apico-alveolar (or palatal) position. The continuants of this series are found in the speech of only a few older speakers, and younger speakers have merged the entire series with the palatals (ǯ, č, etc.). Of the other Eastern Kutchin dialects, Crow River (Old Crow) is similar to Peel River, and Mackenzie Flats (Arctic Red River) differs most notably in having the full set of vowels and diphthongs also nasalized (į, įˑ, ąįˑ, etc.). The Western Kutchin dialects also have a full complement of nasalized vowel nuclei, but they have consonants of the alveolar series (ʒ, c, etc.) corresponding to those of both the alveolar and alveopalatal series of (conservative) Eastern Kutchin. The shapes of many words differ among the various dialects; Kutchin words cited in the *Handbook* are given in both Western and Eastern forms, where available, except when these are identical.

In the practical orthography used by the Alaska Native Language Center, the Summer Institute of Linguistics, and the Departments of Education of the Yukon and Northwest Territories the phonemes of Kutchin are written as follows: b, d, dl, ddh, dz, dzh, dr, j, g, gw, ' (not written word-initially); t, tl, tth, ts, tsh, tr, ch, k, kw; t', tl', tth', ts', tsh', tr', ch', k'; ł, th, s, ssh (or sh), sr (or shr), sh, kh, h; v, l, dh, z, zzh (or zh), zr (or zhr), zh, gh, ghw; nd, nj; m, n; nh; r, y; rh; i. e, a, o, u; ii, ee, aa, oo, uu; nasalization and tones as in the technical alphabet, when written.

Information on Kutchin phonology, dialectology, and practical orthography was obtained from Ritter (1976b), Peter (1979), and from John T. Ritter and Richard Mueller (communications to editors 1979, 1980), who also provided phonemic transcriptions for the Kutchin forms cited. The editors are responsible for selecting from and interpreting the available materials.

There are strong suggestions that a Kutchin group, first identified in 1935 (McKennan 1935), occupied most if not all the southern slopes of the Brooks Range in Alaska, whence it was evicted by Eskimo pressure in the early nineteenth century (Gubser 1965:45–49; E.S. Hall 1969). On the other hand, since the middle of the nineteenth century Kutchin have increasingly utilized and in a measure occupied territory east of the lower Mackenzie River.

The climate of Kutchin territory is "interior Subarctic" (Nordenskjöld and Mecking 1928:197), characterized by long, cold winters and short, warm summers. The land is for the most part covered by boreal forest. This cover is absent from periodically flooded islands and lowlands of the Yukon Flats and the Mackenzie Delta, and from elevated areas; the tree line at this latitude lies at 1,200 feet above sea level. Overall, the terrain is varied, including rugged, geologically new mountains—the Brooks Range and sections of the Cordillera—and also the broad river valleys and floodplains of the middle Yukon and lower Mackenzie. The fact that both these great rivers pass through Kutchin territory has been a major factor in the ecology and the culture history of this people.

Societal Groupings: Regional Bands

At the time of contact, the Kutchin speakers were grouped into nine (or perhaps 10) regional bands. The habitat of each centered in the drainage of a major river (fig. 1). A century later, dialect differences were observable among all the surviving communities; it is probable that such dialects were at least as distinct in the early nineteenth century.

1. Arctic Red River Kutchin (Osgood 1934, 1936a:13). Their range was the Arctic Red River, the Mackenzie River at the head of the Mackenzie Delta, and the land east of the Mackenzie from the Delta up to Travaillant River, eastward to the proximity of the upper Anderson River. Krech (1979) argued that the people on the lower Mackenzie and those east of that area were two distinct bands.

2. Peel River Indians. Their territory was almost the entire drainage of the Peel River. In late precontact times and well into the third quarter of the nine-

teenth century, the lower Peel River itself does not seem to have been regularly occupied by this band.

3. Upper Porcupine River Kutchin (Osgood 1934).
4. Crow Flats Kutchin (Osgood 1934). They lived along the middle reaches of the Porcupine River; its northern tributaries, the Crow River, including the Crow Flats; and the Coleen River (see also "Old Crow, Yukon Territory," this vol.).
5. Black River Kutchin (Osgood 1934), Cache River People (Cadzow 1925), the Chalkyitsik (chäl'kētsĭk) people, the Salmon Indians.
6. Yukon Flats Kutchin (Osgood 1934), Fort Yukon Indians. They ranged along the middle Yukon River between the mouths of Sam Creek and the Chandalar River. In historic times this band has had a strongly riverine orientation.
7. Birch Creek Kutchin. They were located along Birch Creek, west of the upper Yukon Flats, and in the mountains to the southwest of Birch Creek.
8. Chandalar Kutchin. "The early traders called them the 'Gens du Large,' which, corrupted to Chandelar [now standardized as Chandalar], became the name of the river flowing through their territory" (Osgood 1934:172). McKennan (1965:16) states that their territory "centred about the drainage of the East Fork of the Chandalar River. It also included the headwaters, at least, of the Sheenjek River to the east, together with the intervening valley of the smaller Christian River."
9. Dihai Kutchin. Their range was north of the Yukon River and west of the Chandalar East Fork, but its extent is uncertain. E.S. Hall (1969) suggests that Kutchin speakers may have ranged as far west as the headwaters of the Noatak and Kobuk rivers at the beginning of the nineteenth century.

The westernmost Kutchin band, the Dihai, appears to have been dispersed during the first half of the nineteenth century, probably under pressure from Kobuk and Nunamiut Eskimo (E.S. Hall 1969). Survivors moved eastward and appear to have joined the Chandalar and Yukon Flats bands.

The Upper Porcupine band dwindled during the second half of the nineteenth century and by the early twentieth had ceased to exist. The reasons are not clear; an important factor may have been the band's remoteness from trading centers. Most members joined the neighboring Crow Flats and Peel River bands, but some families continued to dwell in the Upper Porcupine habitat, dealing with independent traders, until the 1930s. Robert McDonald used the Kutchin name of the Upper Porcupine band, which he wrote Tukudh (and Takudh), to designate the language of his translations of Anglican scripture and prayers after 1873, and this has led some to conclude that these materials are in their dialect (which, if it was a separate dialect, is now extinct). However, although the form of the language

used by McDonald contains some archaisms not found in any modern Kutchin dialect, it has some features especially indicative of the Arctic Red River dialect and some recognizable elements from the Peel River and Crow Flats dialects (John T. Ritter, communication to editors 1980). It seems, then, that McDonald's dialect may represent an artificial compromise, an attempt at a standard Kutchin literary language. In contrast, Roman Catholic religious translations rely predominantly upon the dialect of Arctic Red River, the only Kutchin community that is Roman Catholic.

In 1977 there were six bands and several subcommunities, using the term band in an ethnological rather than a legal-administrative sense. The bands were: Arctic Red River, Peel River, Crow Flats, Black River, Yukon Flats, and Chandalar.

The subcommunities were the Mackenzie Delta Loucheux and Birch Creek. The Loucheux of the Mackenzie Delta are centered in the towns of Aklavik and Inuvik. Some families from there have trapped on the lower and middle Anderson River. The Delta Loucheux are mainly of Peel River and Arctic Red River background. At Birch Creek a very small number of families have maintained year-round residence, trading into Fort Yukon, Yukon Territory, or Circle, Alaska.

There have been other subcommunities, more or less ephemeral, in the historic period; one such was called the Rat Indians, trading into the now abandoned post of La Pierre House on the Porcupine River. Probably the largest such community was that formed at Moosehide, near Dawson, Yukon Territory, during the Klondike gold rush. It was largely a satellite settlement of Peel River people (Slobodin 1963).

Culture

Subsistence

Almost every type of edible fauna, from the wide variety of these available, and many types of flora, were utilized by the Kutchin; however, in their own eyes the Kutchin were "people of the deer" almost as fully as were natives of the Subarctic Shield. Several subspecies of caribou are found in Kutchin territory, and mammalogists (Preble 1908; Kelsall 1968; Banfield 1961, 1974) provide no unequivocal guidance on the major type or types hunted by the Kutchin. The most widespread, if not most numerous, in Kutchin territory is *Rangifer tarandus granti*, a race of the Barren Ground caribou. *R.t. caribou*, a woodland type, is also found, along with occasional members of other subspecies. A factor in the modern situation is the genetic contribution of strays from the Siberian-Alaskan reindeer herd driven through Kutchin country in the early 1930s for the establishment of the government reindeer station in the Mackenzie delta.

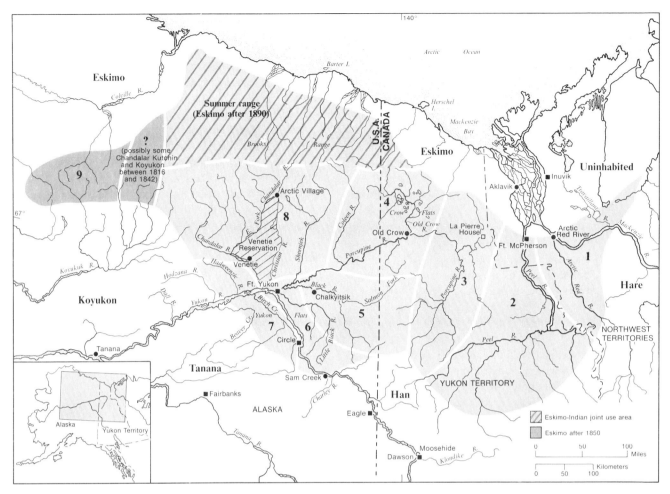

Fig. 1. Nineteenth-century territory with regional bands: 1, Arctic Red River; 2, Peel River; 3, Upper Porcupine River; 4, Crow Flats; 5, Black River; 6, Yukon Flats; 7, Birch Creek; 8, Chandalar; 9, Dihai (displaced by Eskimos about 1850). The northern extension of Chandalar Kutchin territory (not discussed in the text) follows Burch (1980:261 and communication to editors 1980).

For day-to-day subsistence throughout the year, reliance was placed on the harvesting of fish and of small mammals such as hares, beaver, muskrats, tree squirrels, ground squirrels, and porcupine. These were usually taken by deadfalls or babiche snares.

Anadromous fish—such as several species of salmon in the Yukon drainage, Arctic char in the Mackenzie drainage, and herring—as well as whitefish were taken in post-and-withe weirs into which basket fish traps were set. There were many variations in these suited to variant types of current, bottom, season, and type of fish. Dip nets with netting of spruce root or babiche were employed by Yukon-drainage Kutchin to take fish trapped at the weir, but these appear to have been little used by Mackenzie-drainage Kutchin.

Freshwater fish, including whitefish, lake trout, pike, and loche (or burbot) were taken by means of bone hooks, unbaited except in fishing for trout. Gill nets captured almost all varieties of fish, including inconnu and grayling. Leisters were also used for the larger species. While weir fishing was exclusively an open-water or warm-weather activity, the other devices were used both in open water and through holes in the ice.

With the coming of warm weather, migratory birds, especially geese, ducks, and swans, were hunted in considerable number, although nowhere in Kutchin territory were they as plentiful as at points farther south where flyways converged. The principal hunting method was shooting at the sitting or swimming bird with blunt arrows. Ptarmigan and grouse were also taken, sometimes by means of snares.

Larger animals taken for food were the caribou, moose, Dall sheep, and black bear.

Prior to establishment of the European fur trade, the fur of the beaver, muskrat, hare, ermine weasel, wolf, wolverine, lynx, and several other mammals was used in clothing and for intertribal trading.

Although Kutchin could not have survived without exploitation of the smaller mammals, birds, and fish, there is no doubt that the hunting of the large mammals, preeminently the caribou, was of central importance ideologically. It is also true that from the larger animals, again especially the caribou, came a high proportion of food and the raw materials for clothing and a mul-

516

titude of tools, weapons, ornaments, and ritual objects. The sociocultural importance of the larger mammals is evidenced in elaboration of hunting ritual, in many refinements and variations in stalking and taking the game, in the customs for sharing out the kill—practices that were relatively rigid for a culture marked by pragmatic flexibility—and in the prestige attached to successful hunting of these animals.

Depending upon the terrain and the season, and the grouping of caribou, these animals might be pursued by men stalking individually or in small groups. They might be shot with arrows or speared while swimming, or they might be driven over steep banks. However, the main method for large-scale caribou hunting was the surround or corral ("Environment and Culture in the Cordillera," fig. 4, this vol.). Under favorable conditions, a surround would produce the largest harvest of food experienced by the Kutchin, surpassing the results of marine fish-runs in Kutchin territory.

Moose were hunted by individuals or, preferably, by a pair of men who in many cases were brothers, brothers-in-law, or partners. The chase of moose was never an easy matter. Under the best conditions, in spring when there was a crust on the snow, men on hunting snowshoes could run on the surface while the animals plunged through the crust, laboring in deep snow. Even this "easy" hunt required speed and stamina. At other seasons, for example in the summer, moose tracking was, and to large extent remains, a complex technique (Osgood 1936a:26–27; R.K. Nelson 1973:84–114).

Technology

Tools included a wide range of implements for working wood, bone, and animals' skin, including axes, adzes, chisels, mauls, knives, awls, scrapers, and fleshers. Tool blades were of stone and bone, although a few copper knives and arrow points were obtained in trade from the Pacific Coast, especially by the western Kutchin. Copper blades were prestige items, symbols of wealth.

The Kutchin employed a simple longbow, generally of birch, strung with twisted caribou sinew. In shooting, the bow was held by the left hand at angles variously reported from 45 degrees to "slightly off the horizontal" (McKennan 1965:36). The Mediterranean arrow release (Morse 1885) was used. The manufacture of well-balanced bow stave and arrow shafts was regarded as among the essential skills of a man.

Fire was ignited by means of pyrites or with a fire plough. Some Kutchin report the use of the bow drill, probably due to Eskimo influence.

Snowshoes were a necessity in this region of fairly deep and, in timbered areas, loosely packed snow. Those of the Kutchin were well made; the "Loucheux snowshoe" came to be regarded as the type for the western Subarctic ("Environment and Culture in the Cordillera," fig. 12, this vol.). In most cases, the frame was of birch or willow, the lacing of babiche. The trail snowshoe averaged four and one-half feet long for an adult male; the hunting snowshoe, five to six feet long.

Clothing and Adornment

Clothing prior to 1870 was of finely tanned white caribou skin or of fur. Both sexes wore pullover shirt and trousers with or without attached feet of tanned mooseskin (table 1). Soft-soled moccasins were worn with the footless trousers. Lower hems of the men's shirt reached the hips and slanted down to points, at knee level, fore and aft. Women's shirt hems, pointed in back, tended to be horizontal in front (fig. 2). All skin garments, including caps, belts, mitts, garters, knifesheaths, and the fringes of these, were decorated with vegetable-dyed porcupine quillwork (fig. 3) and with beads worked from dentalium shells or from the silverberry (*Elaeagnus commutata*) or soapberry (*Shepherdia canadensis*) (Richardson 1851, 2:380; J. Thompson 1972:161). Garments were also painted, preferably with red ocher. In cold weather coats of various furs, tied in front, were worn.

Decoration with paint and shell-strings was applied on special occasions to the face and hair (fig. 4), as well as to snowshoes. Red facial paint and shell strings through the nasal septum were marks of beauty and to some extent of wealth and high status. A degree of supernatural power was attributed to the preferred red mineral, *caih*, which was probably hematite. Certain locations where the pigment was extracted were regarded as sacred, and offerings were left when *caih* was obtained.

Well-groomed head hair was a particular mark of beauty and status; much folklore describes the recognition of an important personage by the fine condition of his or her hair.

Tattooing was applied to the chins of women as a mark of beauty, and to the upper arms and occasionally the cheeks of men as a war honor.

Social Organization

Kutchin society featured certain kinds of status relationships that either resulted in particular groupings or cross-cut groups and linked members of different groups. All aspects of Kutchin social life exemplified two further and overriding principles, namely, flexibility and opportunism, and a tendency to act out and mark status relationship in terms of physical relationship (see Slobodin 1960). For example, the placement of dwellings within a large encampment reflects many of these relationships (fig. 7).

Flexibility is seen in the kinship system. This was, in

Table 1. Change in Some Kutchin Culture Traits

	to 1840	1840 to 1950	1950-
Large game hunting			
hunting with dogs	x	r	
caribou surrounds	x	-1910	
semicircular moose tracking; moose called with antlers	x		
scapulimancy	x	r?	
dreaming about game; giving away kill	x		
Clothing			
woven hare skin clothing	x	x (infants)	
parka	x		
shirt	x	r	
one-piece trousers and footgear	x	o	
moccasins with anklewrap; slipper-moccasins		x	
cradleboard	x	d	
strap baby carrier	x		
clothing decoration:			
skin fringe	x	o	x
feather	r	o?	
fur	x		
paint	x	o	
porcupine quill, geometric designs	x	r	i
oleaster fruit (*Elaeagnus*) seeds	x	o	
bead, geometric design	x	r	r
steel and glass bead, flower design		x	
Structures			
surface rectangular log house	r(e), x(w)	x	
semisubterranean log house	x	r	
semispherical shelter	x	o	
canvas tent		x	
frame house		1925-	x
menstrual lodge	x	o	
sweathouse; special ceremonial ground	x	?	
Travel and Transportation			
birchbark canoes, various types	x	o	
decked canoes	x	plank scows	
mooseskin boats	r	x	o(e), x(w)
Loucheux-type snowshoe, trail and hunting types	x		
sleds	x	o	
toboggans	x	x	r
dog traction	o	x	r
Technology			
tanning	x		
woven basketry	x	o	
matting	x	o	
skin weaving	x	r	
babiche, rawhide, and sinew lines	x		
willow bark; spruce root	x	r	
gill net	x		
basket trap fish weir	x	o	
leister fish spear	x		r
barbed bone fishhook	x		
snares for small mammals	x		
deadfalls and figure-4 traps	x	-1920	o
pitfalls	x	r	
bows and arrows	x		children only
bone, stone, and copper knives	x	o?	
ulu	x	r	
bone scraper	x		
stone scraper	x	r	

Table 1. Change in Some Kutchin Culture Traits (*Continued*)

	to 1840	1840 to 1950	1950-
steel scraper		x	
breech-loading rifles		x	
Social Organization			
matrilineal clans	x	d(e)	
slaves (war captives)	x(w), r(e)	o	
chieftainship	x		elective
partnership	x		
joking relationship	x		
Life Cycle			
naming			
teknonymy	x		
name chosen by shaman	x	d	o
exchanging names with partner	x		
father's or mother's baptismal name as surname		x	
standardization of patrilineal surnames			x
disposal of the dead			
cache, on ground or elevated	x	o	
cremation	x	o	
grave gifts	x		r
Religion			
belief in:			
forest spirits; lake monsters	x	d	
giants	x	?	
bushmen	x		
moon and star beings	x	o	
afterworld; reincarnation	x		
offerings at special places	x		r
Knowledge			
Big Dipper as time indicator	x	r	
herbal remedies	x	r	r
sweat and hot spring bathing	x	?	
surgical practices	x	d	o
importance of red pigment; weather omens; drawing on snow	x		
Circle Dance; War Dance	x	d	
European folk dances		x	
games			
wrestling	x		d
dog-team races		x	
shinny; footraces	x		
ball games	x	football 1900–	
swings	x		
stick and hand games	x		d
story telling	x		

SOURCES: Osgood 1936a:174–188; Petitot 1876, 1876a; Slobodin 1938–1968; McKennan 1965; R.K. Nelson 1973.

NOTE: x = present; o = absent or lapsed; r = rare; i = more frequent occurrence or increase in importance; d = decreased occurrence or diminished importance; e = occurring solely or predominantly among eastern bands; w = occurring solely or predominantly among western bands; ? = relative date of culture change uncertain. The last symbol to the right indicates the 1980 status of the trait or set of traits.

formal terms, bifurcate collateral with a Hawaiian cousin terminology. However, "except for close kin, people are addressed according to simple categories based primarily upon age" (Osgood 1936a:117); secondarily, but in large measure, upon relative status; and in the third place, upon mutual esteem or disesteem. Thus two or more Kutchin of the same sex and the same geneal-ogical distance from a third party might address and refer to him or her by quite different terms.

Important aspects of kin behavior were the close bonds among siblings, a category that in Kutchin terms includes first cousins in the European sense, and joking relationships among siblings-in-law of both sexes and between members of alternate generations. A major

519

Fig. 2. Women's costume. left, Woman carrying a baby in a bark carrier ("Tanana," fig. 12, this vol.) and wearing a dress of caribou hide with the hem pointed in back but straight in the front. The child wears a caribou-hide parka. The woman, child, and baby are all shown with nose ornaments. According to Osgood (1936a:42), few women wore nose ornaments and they were never worn while performing ordinary work, but only on festive occasions. Photo copy, with some retouching, from Murray 1910:82 of sketch by Alexander Hunter Murray, 1847–1848 (known only from a photostat now in the B.C. Prov. Arch., Victoria). right, Caribou-hide dress decorated with trade beads and red ocher lines, probably worn in the summer, since winter garments usually had fur on the inside. Length about 129 cm, collected on the Peel River by Robert Kennicott, 1859–1862.

quasi-kin relationship was that of partners (*šiȝyà·ʾ* 'my partner'), persons of the same sex who in early years formed a lifelong alliance, signalized by an exchange of names.

• INFRABAND GROUPS The nuclear family was fundamental. In addition, every Kutchin in the course of his life was at times a member of other groupings, kin-based and non–kin-based. These included the paired family and several larger special-purpose groups.

With a married couple and their dependent children, one or more aged and dependent parents of the child-rearing couple were often present, sleeping by preference in a separate shelter near the family dwelling, but eating and spending much time with the nuclear family.

A paired family household involved two nuclear families, customarily the families of brothers or sisters. The component families dwelt and worked together during a period ranging from a season of subsistence activities to several years. Since in this society the kinship terms and to a large extent the behavior appropriate between uterine siblings obtained between cousins, and since in addition, partners might also pair their families, the choice of linkages was fairly wide. During its working career, a family might pair with several other families.

A local group was one that, unlike all other groupings except the fish camp, occupied a particular locale and exploited the territory around it during a number of years. The modal duration of local groups among the Peel River Kutchin in the nineteenth and early twentieth centuries was three generations. The group comprised a senior family or the families of two siblings, some or all of their married offspring of both sexes, and their grandchildren, married and unmarried.

Such a grouping developed on occasion because the economic competence of certain family heads enabled them to exploit the resources of a particularly favorable locality. Their sons and sons-in-law were then willing to stay in the area and submit in some respects to the authority of the senior men, and, in lesser degree, to that of senior women. Other band members, claiming close kinship, might be accepted into the group, which would then be able to hold the area against pressure from other families. It does not appear that more than 15 percent of any band belonged to local groups at any one period.

The local group consisted as a rule of six to eight households, composed of nuclear or paired families, who resided within a few miles of each other and interacted more frequently among themselves than with other families of the regional band. In the nineteenth century, and indeed, well into the twentieth century in some bands, hereditary chiefs and other leading people

Fig. 3. Caribou-hide suit decorated with quillwork and seeds. a, Shirt; b, detail of shirt showing quilled band, quill-wrapped fringe, and *Elaeagnus* seeds; c, trousers with attached moccasins, quillwork strip in red, blue, and white; d, mittens; e, hood, with fringe decorated in the same manner as shirt fringe. All pieces are unsmoked finely tanned hide, sinew sewn. Originally the costume may also have included a decorated knife sheath or quiver. Length of shirt 129.5 cm, rest same scale (except detail), collected by James McDougall, 1864–1869.

Fig. 4. Men's costume. left, Hunters, wearing "a capot or shirt of dressed deer skin [early writers consistently use "deer" for caribou]; pointed in front and behind . . . a broad band of beads is generally worn across the breast and shoulders, and behind a fringe of fancy beads, and small leathern tassels wound round with porcupine quills and strung with the stones of a white berry common in the country" (Murray 1910:84). Also worn is "a pair of deer skin pantaloons, secured by a narrow band around the lower part of the body; a strip of beads about two inches broad is worn on each side of the trousers from the hip to the ankle, bands of beads are fastened around the legs and ankles. The shoes and pantaloons are the same piece, the stripes of beads on the legs are in alternate squares of red and white, but frequently only single fringes are worn and those who are poor use only porcupine quills" (Murray 1910:84). A dressed hide gun case and quiver, bow, volute-handled knife, dentalium hair band, nose and ear ornaments, hair feathers, and small skin bags are also shown. The plain bag suspended from the neck by a string carried fire stones and luck charms (Osgood 1936a:39). Murray (1910:85) stated that the facial designs were a matter of individual fancy, "most commonly the upper part of the checks and around the eyes are black, a black strip along the top of the nose, the forehead is covered with narrow red stripes, and the chin with strips of red and black." right, Man wearing beaded shirt, volute-handled knife through waistband, necklaces, hair ornaments, nose pin, ear ornaments, and facial design. Photo copies, with some retouching, from Murray (1910: 94, 90) of sketches by Alexander Hunter Murray, 1847–1848 (known only from photostats now in the B.C. Prov. Arch., Victoria).

all belonged to local groups. Caribou surrounds were as a rule constructed by local groups, although used by others on invitation or permission from the local group seniors.

The larger groupings within the band, ranging in size from 10 to 50 families, were not based upon kinship. They were temporary assemblages organized for a specific purpose, economic or ritual. The hunting camp, fish camp, and trading party were economic, although ritual was involved in their functions; the band assembly was primarily for public ceremony. Leadership in these groupings was more likely to be administrative than it was in the smaller groups; that is, the leader or leaders

directed rather than participated in all major tasks.

To some extent this was true even of the most specialized of larger groupings, the war party. For tactical reasons, and also because warfare and homicide involved many magico-religious precautions, warfare was hedged about with very many restrictions (Slobodin 1960a, 1975).

Intertribal commerce also necessitated use of supernatural power against the dangers inherent in close contact with strangers. As in the war party, leadership of the trading party was in large measure executive, and was, for Kutchin society, unusually authoritarian. Indeed, trading and raiding were closely connected in

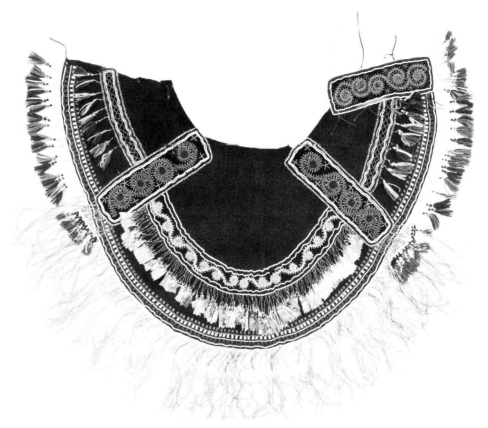

Fig. 5. Man wearing clothing of a style later than that in fig. 3, with elaborate beadwork. Photograph by Edward W. Nelson at Ft. Yukon, 1877–1881.

Fig. 6. Cape or yoke of blue stroud worn over the shoulders and tied in front. Beaded velvet stripes are applied at the shoulders and front. The center section has a fringe of tin tags and caribou skin bordered by bands of curvilinear and geometric beadwork, while the lower edge at the back bears a moosehide strip with a fringe of quill-wrapped leather. The side sections, bordered by geometric beadwork, have fringes of caribou skin and wool tassels. Radius 30.5 cm, collected by F.H. Mayhew along Mackenzie River about 1910.

Kutchin thought; one kind of activity might easily be replaced by the other. However, at any given period trading in some directions was relatively stable and pacific, signalized by trading partnerships among leading men in both (or all) the participant communities. Hence a trading party might comprise adults of all ages and children, whereas only active men went on a war party.

The precontact trading pattern persisted for at least a generation after the establishment of fur-trade posts, in that high-status, wealthy men largely monopolized interaction with Euro-Canadians and Euro-Americans.

The systems of status relationship that cross-cut groupings were: matrilineal clans, wealth-ranking, and age-grading.

• CLANS The three matrilineal clans each had reputed characteristic traits. Naatsaii (Fort Yukon dialect *nancąį·*, Arctic Village *ną·cąį·*, Peel River *nà·cai·*) was associated with the raven; some speakers of the Crow Flats and Peel River dialects associate the name with *caih* 'hematite, red paint'. The alleged traits of members were large stature, dark complexion, and passionate

temperament. The meaning of the name of the clan Ch'itshyaa' (Crow Flats *čićyà·ʔ*, Peel River *ʔićyà·*) is not clear. The associated animals are wolf, herring gull, and "fish" (Hardisty 1872), and the alleged traits of its members are stature below medium, light complexion, and equable temperament. Teenjiraatsyaa (*te·ⁿžirà·cya·*, intepreted as 'friends on each side; linked with each side') is associated with the glaucous gull and the arctic tern; the traits attributed to its members are intermediate between those of Naatsaii and Ch'itshyaa'.

The matrilineal clan system had certain social characteristics. It was to some extent intertribal or extratribal, as it existed not only among all Kutchin bands but also among the neighboring Han and Koyukon. Other Alaskan Athapaskan peoples had unilineal descent groups in varying numbers and phratry groupings. In the course of trading activity, joint ceremonial, or other peaceable interaction between tribes or communities with differing languages, equation would be made between each Kutchin clan and one or more of the foreign descent groups. McKennan (1965:61) provides some of these equations.

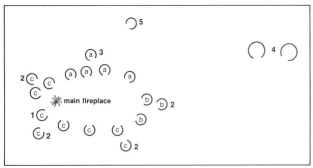

after Slobodin 1962:62.

Fig. 7. Schematic plan of a large-group camp: a, household headed by member of "upper" clan; b, household headed by member of "middle" clan; c, household headed by member of "lower" clan; 1, camp leader; 2, aged dependents of nearest household; 3, girl in puberty isolation; 4, unmarried youths; 5, aged person or persons with no near kin in the group. In this example the camp leader is designated a member of the "lower" clan to emphasize that leadership and high status were not related to clan membership or to the ideological ranking of clans. It is stated that a chief of the Crow Flats Kutchin might not be chosen from the "middle" clan (Balikci 1963:22, 26); however, this is not true for several other bands.

The Eskimo and the Athapaskan speakers eastward of the Kutchin lack clan systems. The Kutchin are at the northeastern extremity of the northwestern American clan distribution. Among Kutchin, clans are less important as one moves eastward.

There was a vague but persistent sentiment that the clans were ranked, with the Naatsaii as the highest, Teenjiraatsyaa intermediate, and Ch'itshyaa' lowest. The Kutchin, at least in modern times, are perfectly aware of the inconsistencies involved in ranking exogamous sectors of society.

There is also a feeling that the Naatsaii and the Ch'ityshyaa' are the principal clans, and that the third clan is something of an anomaly. It is sometimes stated that the Teenjiraatsyaa is small in membership. This has led some Kutchin and others to maintain that Kutchin have essentially a moiety system and that the middle clan is merely a category for "classifying the descendants of endogamous marriages" (Balikci 1963:23). However, genealogical study of eastern Kutchin indicates that, while some Teenjiraatsyaa are indeed offspring of endogamous marriages, many are children of Teenjiraatsyaa women married to men of other clans. Moreover, in the twentieth century the middle clan has been the largest in one band and the second largest in another.

Aside from marriage regulation, clans functioned principally in ceremonial. In the relatively attenuated Kutchin potlatch, in feasts, games, and on other public occasions, clans were ranged against each other and served each other.

• WEALTH-RANKING The range of variation in material possessions among Kutchin households was not great, measured on a world scale. Nevertheless, in precontact and in historic times, some households have lived in considerable comfort, while others have been at the bare subsistence level. Sharp distinction is made between those regarded as wealthy and those classed as poor. Prestige usually accompanied wealth; among the synonyms for 'wealthy' in Kutchin are terms meaning 'shrewd' and 'industrious'. However, the converse is not true; the poor are designated by terms indicating degrees of deprivation, rather than personal qualities. There is a Kutchin saying: "A rich man has many relatives; a poor man has few." The wealthy were claimed as kin by many, while few people would assert their relationship to the poor and low-ranked.

A wealthy person in the Kutchin view was endowed with traits such as unusual energy, resourcefulness, and industry, and also with a proper balance between, on the one hand, shrewdness and an eye to the main chance, and, on the other, generosity and concern for the common weal. A person with these qualities, or a pair of siblings endowed with them, might form the core of a local grouping.

• AGE-GRADING The third cross-cutting type of status relationship was age-grading. A Kutchin who survived into advanced years, which in the early postcontact period was the age of 50 or more, passed through childhood, youth, maturity, and old age or seniority.

Of these stages, the periods of youth and of seniority are those most clearly distinguished by social and physical segregation from the band; this is especially true of youth. The period of youth began shortly before puberty and terminated at marriage.

In late boyhood, a year or two before puberty, a boy was, as the Kutchin say, "thrown out" of the parental lodge and sent to live with other youths in a special lodge, larger than those of most individual households. Under the close supervision of various mature men chosen by the chief and elders, he resided in this group until his marriage. As a first marriage might occur at any time from the young man's late teens until his mid-twenties, a bachelor remained in the group for a period ranging from 6 to 12 years. During this time, he remained on a strict regimen, arising very early in the morning, hunting or scouting for enemies all day on many days, eating and drinking sparingly, enjoined from partaking of many foods (including all delicacies) and from a number of other activities. He improved his knowledge and skill in the subsistence activities, the making of snowshoe frames and other woodwork, the techniques of war, bushcraft, and tracking.

At menarche a girl was sequestered, either in a small lodge or in a screened-off sector of the parental home. She was subject to a number of taboos, the most important of which prevented her dangerous condition from harming others. She was attended by a mature woman, preferably past the menopause. Because her gaze was baleful, to men especially, she wore when out of the tent a headgear with a deerskin cowl hanging

524

down so that she could see only her feet. It was fringed with dried caribou hoof rattles to warn others of her presence. When an encampment was on the move, the cowled girl was led along devious paths away from the main trail. Reports differ on the duration of girls' puberty isolation, ranging from three months to a year.

People defined as old, that is, those past the years of child-rearing and of major subsistence activities, were segregated to some extent. An aged couple or widowed parent of a household head might dwell in a small tent close behind that of the main household. In other cases, the dependent seniors lived in the household lodge (fig. 8), being assigned a warm place to sleep, farthest away from the entrance. The luckless aged who had no active mature children in the group lived a hand-to-mouth existence on the fringe of the camp.

• MARRIAGE Several forms of marriage existed. At any given time, most marriages were monogamous, but a minority were polygamous. According to Kutchin ideas of propriety, monogamous marriages were arranged by the parents, with the mothers taking the initiative.

When the marriage linked families of approximately equal social standing, postmarital residence was uxorilocal until at least the birth of the first child. During this time much of the young couple's labor was contributed to the household of the bride's parents.

A high-ranking family preferred that their sons marry girls from lower-ranking but reputable families. It was said that a poor girl would be grateful and industrious. Postmarital residence in these cases was virilocal. There was little or no bride service by the husband; the wife's parents would benefit in less direct ways.

Insofar as the ideal of masculine hypogamy was attained, the marital arrangements of wealthy girls and poor bachelors are of interest. Exceptionally desirable and high ranking females might become prime objects for kidnapping by neighboring peoples, including Eskimo; there was a special term for such women, translatable as 'she who is stolen back and forth' (Petitot 1886, 1887; Slobodin 1975). However, only a very few women attained this status. Other high-ranking girls did in fact marry chiefs: still others married men of their own or slightly lower rank, whereupon the couple resided, at least for several years, with the wife's parents. Where both the young women and the young men of a family stayed with their parents after marriage, a local group was formed.

Other young women of fairly high rank entered temporary polyandrous unions. This occurred when a pair of young men, or very occasionally three, not having accumulated sufficient working capital to make individual marriages, banded together and arranged to share a wife. Usually, it appears, she was of higher rank than the co-husbands. In all known cases, the co-husbands were brothers, in Kutchin terms, or partners. In time, other women joined the household, which even-

Fig. 8. Winter lodge with sled in foreground and round-toed snowshoes protruding from the snow. According to Alexander Murray, this lodge was made of caribou skin with hair attached to maintain warmth. It is "put up on willow poles which they generally carry with them on their sledges. Snow is then packed half way up, the inside is lined with small pine brush, and the small hole used for a door closed with a double deer [caribou] skin" (Murray 1910:85–86). This semispherical skin-covered lodge (*niˑvyàˑžeh*) was used in camp sites in late winter and spring. In summer a similar lodge was used, but the skins were more frequently hairless (Osgood 1936a: 49–50). Photo copy, with some retouching, from Murray (1910:85) of sketch by Alexander Hunter Murray, 1847–1848 (known only from a photostat now in the B.C. Prov. Arch., Victoria).

Fig. 9. A dome-shaped structure used for smoking moose hide. Photograph by Douglas Leechman, Old Crow, Yukon Terr., summer 1946.

tually broke up into monogamous couples. The Kutchin pattern of close collaboration and frequent coresidence of siblings and siblings-in-law formed the background for these transitional marriage forms.

On the other hand, chiefs and other high-ranking men might be polygynous. A large number of co-wives is reported for several well-known Yukon chiefs. Only a few eastern Kutchin chiefs were polygynous, and none had more than two wives.

Another western Kutchin chiefly practice was cicisbeism (see MacCulloch 1908; Rivers 1915:428; Piddington 1950–1957, 1:114–115). A polygynous chief would attach young men to his household who would have sexual access to the chief's young wives. This practice bore some resemblance to the polyandry of low-ranking men and also to bride service, with the marked differences that offspring of the chief's wives were all offspring of the chief, and during the chief's lifetime such arrangements did not develop into monogamous unions between the younger men and the chief's wives.

There is no clear evidence of marriage preference in terms of kinship.

For 10 days at menstruation, sexual intercourse was to be avoided. The wife kept count of the days by means of small sticks. Sexual intercourse after child-bearing was also disapproved. This injunction was not a strict taboo, but it was regarded as praiseworthy for a man to refrain from intercourse with his wife while an infant was nursing. In general, it appears that restraint in sexual intercourse was a feature of the Kutchin ideal of manhood and womanhood.

Supernaturalism

The religious and cosmological ideas of the Kutchin were not organized and systematized, as there were no full-time religious practitioners. The ideas or sentiments in this sphere that seem to have been fundamental and to have had the widest currency were those concerning time, or in philosophical terms, being and becoming, and the relationship of man, that is, the Kutchin, and nature.

• TIME In mythic time, man was hardly differentiated from other natural phenomena. Humans and other animals communicated at will and exchanged forms. Humanity as such emerged in a lengthy process, involving, in its most dramatic aspects, the activities of the culture-hero. The culture hero himself, Ataachookaii, became differentiated from his fellows as the result of long isolation enforced by an accidental fratricide. The theme of change in state consequent upon physical and social isolation is an enduring one in Kutchin ideology (Slobodin 1960). Within the body of Kutchin mythology, it is in the culture-hero adventures that sequences of events are most clear. Time begins to move, in a spiral; patterns of events and relationships repeat themselves, but with a difference. In historic tales time moves lineally; however, one sequence of events has no relation temporally or causally to another. The supernatural plays some part in historic tales, but much less than in myth, and not much more than in stories told of postcontact events. Some legends involve no magic at all. In postcontact oral literature, time and causation become increasingly similar to those in Euro-Canadian culture. Kutchin speak of the precontact events as occurring "before we knew how to tell the time." Nevertheless, "spiral" time continues to exist alongside sequential clock time, evidenced by such persistent concepts as those of reincarnation, of "family curses"—physical blemishes or behavioral peculiarities held to be inherited matrilineally—and of bushmen and other creatures originally human or animal, who live a vague semisupernatural existence outside of clock time.

• MAN AND NATURE Kutchin have a particular affinity with caribou. In mythic time, the Kutchin and the caribou lived in peaceful intimacy, although the people were even then hunters of other animals. When the people became differentiated, it was agreed that they would now hunt caribou. However, a vestige of the old relationship was to remain. Every caribou has a bit of the human heart (ʔeʒiˑʔ, literally 'heart') in him, and every human has a bit of caribou heart. Hence humans will always have partial knowledge of what caribou are thinking and feeling, but equally, caribou will have the same knowledge of humans. This is why caribou hunting is at times very easy, at other times very difficult. All hunted creatures are to be respected, but none, except the bear, more so than the caribou.

There are other man-animal ties. By virtue of clan membership, every Kutchin inherits matrilineally a special relationship with one or more animals associated with the clan. As with other clan functions, these are

526

much more important among the Yukon-drainage Kutchin than in the eastern bands. Among the western bands particularly, one is enjoined from killing one's clan animal, and to kill that of another clan is an insult to members of that clan. Some persons, but by no means everyone, can "talk to" their clan animals. It is not believed that clan members are descended from the clan animals.

A special, individual relationship obtains between some Kutchin, male or female, and certain animals, a relationship similar to that in the guardian-spirit concept of many North American tribes. The relationship begins in persistent dreaming of the animal. It may also be said that one "talks to" a particular kind of mammal, bird, or fish. It is assumed that at times he may assume the form of this creature, usually in dreaming.

In postcontact times only a small minority of Kutchin have enjoyed this special relationship. It is said, as it is of all types of supernatural power or privilege, that in earlier times this was more common. One possessing such power wore an emblem of it, a feather if it were a bird, or, commonly, a roughly carved representation if it were fish or mammal, for a person must not, except in dire emergency, harm members of the species with which he talks. An animal-dreamer may learn a great deal from his nonhuman friends; hence, this power is cherished and admired.

• SUPERNATURAL BEINGS The Kutchin were encompassed by myriad supernatural beings, friendly, hostile, and unpredictable. Besides the supernatural manifestations of familiar animals, there were monsters in large lakes and some other locations, which added to the hazards of travel; the underwater creatures were thought of as large hairy worms. There were several zooanthropomorphic types of creature, usually malevolent. Kutchin "bushmen" (Eastern *nana·ʔih*) were beings who had been human and who became differentiated due to long isolation following some catastrophe or untoward event; the characteristic attitude toward the bushmen was, and remains, ambivalent: they were feared but also pitied (Slobodin 1960). There were also moon- and star-personages.

• AFTERLIFE Concepts of life after death, like concepts of the soul, became so markedly influenced by Christian doctrine that the aboriginal formulations are extremely difficult to discern. It would seem that after death, the spirit traveled westward, down the Yukon toward the sunset. In one respect, Christian indoctrination has not produced much effect; even among the most devout churchgoers, there is little or no eschatology of reward and punishment after death.

One of the most durable of pre-Christian religious ideas is that of reincarnation. A small fraction of the population at any given time consists of the reborn (Slobodin 1970).

• SHAMANS For the most part, a Kutchin dealt with life problems, including relationship with the unseen, by means of whatever physical and supernatural power he happened to possess, or with the aid of kinsmen. There is reason to believe that the power of shamans, and the extent to which they dominated Kutchin life, have been somewhat overstated. Certainly, some shamans were respected and influential; some were feared. However, most Kutchin got along most of the time without the benefit or the hazard of shamanistic activity. The status of shaman, like that of chief, was more important among western Kutchin than in the eastern bands.

Ceremonies

Some shamanistic performances were public; however, the principal ceremonials involving large-scale public participation were the spring and lunar eclipse dances, the memorial potlatch, and feasts marking life crises.

The spring dance took place the night of a new moon near the vernal equinox, and on the next night. Participants danced in line, winding among the tents and singing mournfully (Petitot 1876a:95–98, 1887:61–62). A similar dance was held on a night of lunar eclipse.

Detailed descriptions of potlatches are given by Hardisty (1872) and Jones (1872). McKennan's (1965:64) summary account for the western bands holds also for the eastern Kutchin:

> Its function was to help the giver assuage his sorrow following the death of a member of his family and at the same time to reward the members of the opposite clan for their assistance at the funeral. . . . Gifts . . . were hung from . . . [a] fence, and dances, games, and feasts took place. . . . At one stage of the ceremony a caribou skin was tossed into the midst of the guests, who struggled good-naturedly to cut off small strips from it. At another stage a caribou bladder or paunch filled with marrow fat was tossed into the crowd and everyone tried to get a little of the fat to eat.

Members of the potlatch giver's own clan did not receive gifts. Among western bands, recipients were expected eventually to return half the value of the gifts, but among the eastern Kutchin, whose potlatches were relatively modest, there appears to have been no such expectation.

Feasts marked a birth, the conclusion of a girl's puberty isolation, a boy's first kill, and among Yukon-drainage bands, the appearance of the first salmon. These are probably more deeply rooted in the culture than the potlatch and have, in fact, survived ("Old Crow, Yukon Territory," fig. 5, this vol.).

Mythology

Besides individual myths there are three myth cycles, each centering around a major supernatural being: The culture hero Ataachookaii, the Raven, and the trickster

Vasaagijik. These terms are not fully descriptive, since Raven (Western *de·cyà̠ʔ*, Eastern *de·çinʔ*) is a trickster, and both Raven and Vasaagijik perform feats appropriate to a culture hero. The culture hero par excellence is the anthropomorphic figure Ataachookaii, known to the Peel River Kutchin as *ʔata·čò·kai·* 'he paddled the wrong way'; the cognate Western Kutchin name *čatayù·kąį̠·* or *čite·hà·kʷai·* has been rendered for the Chandalar dialect as Jateaquoint (McKennan 1965:98–122). Raven is a shape-changer, but Vasaagijik (Eastern *vasa·gìžik*, Western *vasa·gihʒak*) is so changeable that his basic form is not clear, although some identify him with the Canada jay (*Perisoreus canadensis*), whose Kutchin name is (Western) *čidin-gʷaían* or (Peel River) *ʔedin-gʷaían* 'greasy-mouth'.

The name of Vasaagijik suggests a derivation from Wisakedjak, the Cree culture hero–trickster (Skinner and Satterlee 1915; Skinner 1916; Teit 1921; D.S. Davidson 1928, 1928a). The name may have been brought down the Mackenzie by French Canadian, Métis, or even Cree *voyageurs*.

Legends include tales of important persons or events, told as Kutchin history, as well as domestic stories ranging in tone from the grim and grisly, such as "The Two Men Who Married One Wife" (McKennan 1965:153–154) to the grotesque and farcical. Historical tales center around important figures, usually war leaders (M.H. Mason 1924:294–299; Petitot 1886:43–55; Osgood 1936a:166–167; Slobodin 1975). The domestic tales include a modicum of the supernatural; the historic tales, little or none.

Music, Dance, and Games

Music and dancing were important to the Kutchin and appear to have been closely associated with sport. According to both Kutchin tradition and unofficial Hudson's Bay Company reports (Pendleton 1840–1915), the first Euro-Canadians to ascend the Peel River, in 1840, found the indigenous band at a spring meeting place, engaged in sports and dancing. Sports included footraces, tug-of-war, wrestling, and a kind of football with a skin spheroid stuffed with dry grass.

Yukon Flats dances are recorded in the lively sketches and description of Murray (1910) ("Expressive Aspects of Subarctic Indian Culture," fig. 15, this vol.). The principal musical instruments were tambourine drums, wooden gongs, and willow whistles. Singing was highly regarded; supernatural power was manifested in song, which was judged for tone, voice production, and style, as well as text. A song belonged to its composer and ordinarily might not be sung by others. Verbal skills may be regarded as entertainment, since the Kutchin keenly appreciated style and wit in oratory and in repartee.

Among other favored recreations were two stick

games. In one, a man held a short stick and challenged others, one at a time, to pull it from his grasp. This was played "among the tents," or between families. The other was a gambling game preferably between representatives of different clans. This was of the widespread American hand game type, closely resembling the Dogrib hand game ("Dogrib," figs. 10–11, this vol.) described by Helm and Lurie (1966).

Knowledge

Kutchin ethnoscience, that is, the accumulated and roughly systematized knowledge of the environment, and its application, as in folk medicine, has been little recorded. Most of this has become irrecoverable, with the passing of older people who retained this knowledge. Information about the fauna and flora of their habitat was very extensive. Of 103 bird species identified at Old Crow, Yukon Territory, in 1957, an ornithologist has found that the Crow Flats Kutchin had names for 99 species (L. Irving 1958, 1960). An admittedly incomplete list of 400 names of local plants and animals identified by Peel River and Arctic Red River Kutchin has been collected (Slobodin 1938–1968). For the animals of greatest interest to the Kutchin a large number of discriminatory terms exist; Mueller (1964) lists 17 terms for caribou, distinguishing by sex, size, age, markings, and physical condition. On the basis of a brief study, Leechman (1954) lists 22 genera of plants employed for medicinal purposes by the Crow Flats Kutchin. Star and weather lore were also extensive.

History of Indian-White Contact

In the late precontact period there was probably increased intertribal trade, with Kutchin as middlemen, between tribes to the southwest on the one hand and on the other, the Mackenzie Eskimo and Athapaskans east of the Mackenzie River. At the same time it is likely that conflict with neighboring peoples intensified.

Early Contact Period, to 1840

The earliest recorded encounter between Kutchin and Europeans occurred on July 9, 1789, when Alexander Mackenzie's exploring party encountered several "Quarreller" families fishing on what was to be called the Mackenzie River, just above its delta (Mackenzie 1801:51; for an estimate of the precise location, see Lamb in Mackenzie 1970:195). About 1806 the North West Company established Fort Good Hope "for the convenience of the tribe of Indians whom Mackenzie calls the Quarrellers, but whom the traders . . . name the Loucheux" (Franklin 1828:23). Trade at this post was troubled by "hostilities between the Esquimaux

528

and Loucheux," as reported in 1831 by Sir George Simpson, governor of Rupert's Land (quoted in Fleming 1940:lxiii). To bypass this obstacle and to exploit the basin of the Peel River, discovered in 1826, a trading post was built in 1840 on the Peel some 30 miles from its confluence with the main river. This post came to be known as Fort McPherson.

Contact-Traditional Period, 1840–1950

In 1847, a Hudson's Bay Company party crossed the mountains from the Peel River to the Yukon and established Fort Yukon ("Intercultural Relations and Cultural Change in the Cordillera," fig. 2, this vol.) in what was actually Russian territory. In ensuing decades, other outposts from Fort McPherson (fig. 10) were set up in Kutchin territory, as well as on the western Canadian Arctic coast.

In addition to European influences through the fur trade, Kutchin experienced White contact in other ways. In the 1860s both the Roman Catholic Church and the Church of England sent missionaries to them. Major epidemics struck the Kutchin in the 1860s and 1870s. The whaling boom in the western Arctic, 1889–1904, drew the Kutchin to Herschel Island and the nearby Arctic Coast. The effects of the Klondike gold rush and its aftermath involved especially the Peel River and Yukon Flats bands from about 1898 to 1915. A scarlet fever epidemic took its toll in 1897.

In 1903 the Northwest Mounted Police (later Royal Canadian Mounted Police) first arrived among the Canadian Kutchin. From about 1905 to the 1940s Roman Catholic and Anglican residential schools were established in Canada while in Alaska the government developed day schools for the primary grades as well as residential schools. Many Kutchin children experienced at least a few years of schooling.

In 1904 there was a measles epidemic and an Eskimo-Kutchin battle at Fort McPherson was narrowly averted. In 1921–1922 and again in 1928 influenza was epidemic.

The Kutchin continued to be affected by the fluctuations of the fur trade. In 1916 they benefited from a great rise in the price of muskrat fur, but in the 1930s the end of the monopoly fur trade with Canadian Kutchin brought a decline in fur prices. In the 1940s fine-fur trapping was revived with the price rise, but the 1950s saw another decline in fur prices.

Two linguistic developments in the contact-trad{}tional period were the use of Broken Slavey and literacy in Tukudh. "Broken Slavey" was a trade jargon associated with the fur trade along the Athabasca, the Mackenzie, and the middle reaches of the Yukon rivers. It was learned by many Kutchin and Kutchin Métis who traveled for the fur trade in the nineteenth and early twentieth centuries. It has been obsolete among Kutchin since the 1930s.

Hudson's Bay Company Lib., Winnipeg, Man.

Fig. 10. Part of Hudson's Bay Company establishment at Ft. McPherson. left to right, Storehouse, company store, fur press, unidentified log structure, and hide tepee. Photograph by Henry W. Jones, 1904.

Tukudh (Takudh) was the name given by the pioneer Anglican missionary, the Rev. Robert McDonald, to the Kutchin language and the system of orthography that he devised in the 1870s for translation of religious texts. Many Kutchin men and some women became literate in it and used it not only in church services but also as a medium for letter writing and other secular communications. Some even claimed that the use of McDonald's materials had induced changes in their own speech (McKennan 1965:15). In the 1970s people of the middle and older generations could read Scriptures and prayers in "Tukudh" or its Roman Catholic equivalent. However, its use in writing was confined to a few older persons.

Modern Period, 1950–

In 1953 the formation of the Department of Northern Affairs and National Resources in the government of Canada facilitated the construction of government schools and hostels. Inuvik, the administrative center in the Mackenzie Delta, was built 1955–1961. The Alaska Native Cooperative movement developed in the 1950s.

In the 1970s most Kutchin were fairly fluent in English. The Kutchin language has taken in a very large number of words and phrases, and some locutions, from English, and in early postcontact times, from French. Conversely, and expectably, the English of Kutchin speakers reflects Kutchin phonology and grammar.

A dwindling number of the aged are monolingual in Kutchin. Increased opportunity for and participation in government schooling, plus wage employment and dealings with agencies requiring the use of English, *529*

Natl. Mus. of Canada, Ottawa: 100601.

Fig. 11. Chief Peter Moses and his wife Myra. He wears a visored cap with a badge lettered "Chief"; the medal on his coat is also a sign of his office. She wears a pin in the shape of the Canterbury Cross, which signifies her life membership in the Women's Auxiliary of the Anglican Church. Photograph by Douglas Leechman, Old Crow, Yukon Terr., summer 1946.

have hastened the change; however, in 1973 an organized effort was underway among the Peel River Kutchin to sustain the use of the aboriginal language.

Population

Mooney (1928; reiterated by Kroeber 1939:141) estimated the aboriginal (presumably eighteenth-century) population of seven "Kutchin tribes" at 4,600 but included in this some non-Kutchin Indian groups (Krech 1978a:90). VanStone (1974:11) offered a total Kutchin figure of 1,200 for 1860 (here following Osgood 1936:15; cf. Krech 1978a:90). On the basis of extensive archival research, Krech (1978a) estimates a total of 5,400 for Kutchin population in the mid-eighteenth century, followed by a sharp decline due to introduced disease both before and after actual contact with Europeans. He estimates that in the 1860s the total population declined below 1,000, its lowest point in the known history of the Kutchin.

The principal features of Kutchin demography in the Modern period are: a marked decrease in death rate, especially in infant mortality rate, with consequent population increase; and movement away from the land and into towns. Although many Kutchin engage in hunting trips for meat and skins, and probably a majority take part in the spring hunt for muskrats, which involves several weeks' camping, most are residents of fixed communities dominated by Euro-American or Euro-Canadian institutions and agents (table 2). A majority of Kutchin, other than younger Mackenzie Delta residents, retain a sense of belonging to one or another of the six extant bands.

Natl. Mus. of Canada, Ottawa: 100562.

Fig. 12. Robert Steamboat of Old Crow, Yukon Terr., taking a salmon from a net. Nets are always put in the same place in the stream by their owners, and this right is generally recognized (Leechman 1954:11). His canoe, small and not decked, is covered with canvas instead of the traditional birchbark. He wears netting over his head for protection from the insects, especially mosquitoes, which have been known to kill dogs by the loss of blood and constant irritation (Leechman 1954:3). Photograph by Douglas Leechman, summer 1946.

There are a few Kutchin families resident at Eagle, Alaska; Dawson, Yukon Territory; Fort Good Hope, Northwest Territories; and elsewhere.

Synonymy†

The name Kutchin first appeared in print in the account of Richardson (1851, 1:214, 1852:223), based in part on notes and letters from Murray (1910:84), who had written in 1848 "they call themselves, as do all other tribes, the *People* 'Kootchin'." The use of this name, presumably current among Hudson's Bay Company traders in the 1840s, derives from a misunderstanding of the Kutchin band names, which consist of a place-name or description of an area followed by the word $g^w i\check{c}in$ 'people of, dwellers at' (Murray's Kootchin). This usage was continued by the standard classifications of Dall (1877:25) and Osgood (1936:14–15) and by Hodge (1907–1910, 1:739–740), though Dall by the same error extended his name Kŭtchin over other groups as well (see synonymies in "Han" and "Tutchone," this vol.). Nevertheless, the name Kutchin has never come to be used as a self-designation, though in the 1970s Gwich'in (the practical-orthography spelling of $g^w i\check{c}in$) was gaining some currency in educational materials produced in Alaska as the English name for

†This synonymy was written by Ives Goddard and Richard Slobodin. In the forms cited from Kennicott (1862) th is written for his th with superposed 4 (indicating [θ]), dh for th with superposed 5 ([δ]), and ⁿ for n with superposed 3 (indicating a nasalized vowel).

Table 2. Population, 1968

	Kutchin	*Other*
Alaska		
Arctic Village	150	10
Venetie	80	5
Fort Yukon	320	80
Circle	125	40
Chalkyitsik	80	0
Canada		
Old Crow, Yukon Terr.	180	25
Fort McPherson, N.W.T.	550	80
Arctic Red River, N.W.T.	80	5
Aklavik, N.W.T.	250	400
Inuvik, N.W.T.	275	2,100
Total	2,150	

SOURCES: Slobodin 1938–1968, except Arctic Village Kutchin figure, which is based on R. Mueller, personal communication 1968, and non-Kutchins in Canada, for which Canada Census 1971 was also used.

the Kutchin language (Peter 1979). This usage was a novelty in Canada (Ritter 1976a:3).

The Chipewyan name for the Kutchin is *degeδe* 'squint-eyed' (Petitot 1876:233). The Canadian French translation of this, Loucheux 'squinters' (sg. Loucheu), was borrowed into English in the fur-trade period (Murray 1910:30,84; Dall 1877:30–31), and Loucheux (with the pronunciation ˈlōōšōō) has come to be the usual English name for the Eastern Kutchin in Canada, both locally and officially (Canada. Department of Citizenship and Immigration. Indian Affairs Branch 1964:45; Ritter 1976a:1). Different explanations have been given of the significance of this name: Diguthe Dinees (printed text: Deguthee Dinees) or Quarrellers, 1789 (Mackenzie 1970:195); "the literal meaning of their Indian name is the Sharp Eyes," 1825 (Franklin 1971:27); "They were very shy and quick sighted, which made the *Voyageurs* say they could see on both sides at once" (Masson 1889–1890, 1:110).

The Kutchin call themselves *di^nǯi· žuh* or *di^nǯi· žu·*, sometimes translated 'Indian' (Peter 1979:title, 70; Ritter 1976a:4, 6, 45). Petitot (1876:233) gives dindjié 'person', reflecting the Arctic Red River pronunciation [dinǯ^ye·].

The Hare name for the Kutchin is *degewi goṯine* (Keren Rice, communication to editors 1979). The neighboring Eskimo call them and all Indians itkpéléïṯ or ipkpélit (Petitot 1876a:xi, 43) said to mean 'nits' (perhaps 'those who have many nits', an uncomplimentary allusion to Northern Athapaskan hair-style).

Subdivisions

The most important sources for the names of the Kutchin regional bands are Murray (1910), Hardisty (1872:311), Dall (1877:30–31), Petitot (1876:xx,

1893:361), and Hodge (1907–1910). The following list gives the names from these sources (with Hodge and Murray cited by date and page, the others by date alone), a few from other writers, and the modern Kutchin transcriptions in a Western dialect (Fort Yukon, from Richard Mueller, communication to editors 1979) and an Eastern dialect (Peel River, from John T. Ritter, communication to editors 1980).

(1) Arctic Red River Kutchin. Also called Mackenzie Flats Kutchin. Their usual name is (Eastern) *g^wičyàh g^wičin* 'people of the flat-land'; they are also called *ci·gèh^nǯik g^wičin* 'people of the Arctic Red River'. Earlier sources give the first name as that of a band living northeast of the lower Mackenzie between it and the Anderson River: Kwitcha-Kuttchin 'dwellers on the steppes' (1876) or 'tundra' (Savoie 1971:110); Kwitcha-Kouttchin or Kodhell-vén-Kouttchin 'people of the edge of the Eskimo barren lands' (1893) or 'caribou grazing grounds' (Savoie 1971:110); Kwitchakutchin (1907–1910, 1:748). These sources give a different name for the band along the lower Mackenzie: Nakotchpô-ondjig Kuttchin 'people of the Mackenzie River' (1876); Na-kotchpô-ondjig-Kouttchin 'people of the river with huge banks' (1893); Nakotchokutchin (1907–1910, 2:14); this is (Eastern) *na·g^wačo·^nǯik g^wičin*. However, Kennicott (1862) gives Kū´tchä Kū´tchĭn and Nä´kūtchū´ūnjūk kū´tchĭ´n as synonyms. A discussion of the evidence for a distinction between these bands, with additional spelling variants, is in Krech (1979).

(2) Peel River Kutchin. Peels River Indians (1910:40); Tã-tlit-Kutchin, Peel's River Indians (Kirkby 1865:417–418); T'etllet-Kutchin (1876); Tpè-tliet-Kouttchin 'people of the end of the water' (1893); Tatlitkutchin (1907–1910, 2:698); (Eastern) *te·k̇it g^wičin* 'people of the head of the waters' (Ritter 1976a:4–6, 45); also called Fort McPherson people.

(3) Upper Porcupine River Kutchin. Tã-küth-Kutchin, Lapiene's (for La Pierre's) House Indians (Kirkby 1865:418); Tãkū´rdh 'twisted' or Njidh 'between others' (Kennicott 1862); Tuk-kuth or Rat Indians (1872); Tŭkkŭth´-kŭtchin´ (1877); Dakkadhè 'squint-eyed', assuming a connection with the Chipewyan name, and other names (1876); Dakkadhœ and others (1893); Tukkuthkutchin (1907–1910, 2:834); Arctic Red River dialect *dagaδ g^wičin*, other dialects *dago· g^wičin*; Han *dəgë·* (John T. Ritter, communication to editors 1980). The name of this band, in the spellings Tukudh and Takudh, was used by Robert McDonald as the name of the language of his Eastern Kutchin religious translations (Pilling 1892:57–60), which displays grammatical features from several dialects (John T. Ritter, communication to editors 1980). According to Kennicott (1862) the name Louchioux (Loucheux) was "properly applicable—if at all—only to" this band.

(4) Crow Flats Kutchin. Vanta Kootchin 'men of the lake(s), people of the lakes', or distant Rat Indians

(1910:35, 56, 83); Van-tah-koo-chin (1872); Vuntá Kutchin or Rat Indians (Dall 1870:109); Vŭntá´-kŭtchin´ and Gens des Rats (1877); Vœn or Zjen Kuttchin 'people of the lakes or of the [musk] rats' (1876); Vànœ-ta-Kouttchin or Zjén-ta-Kouttchin (1893); Vuntakutchin (1907–1910, 2:882–884); (Western) *van te· g*ʷ*ičin*, (Eastern) *van tat g*ʷ*ičin* 'people among the lakes'. Also called Old Crow Indians, Crow River Kutchin, and in the ethnographic literature usually Vunta Kutchin. Murray (1910:26–27, 32, 56, 83) seems to distinguish between the Rat Indians or Youcon Indians (apparently the Indians of Rat River, later Bell River, a tributary of the Porcupine), whose chief was Grand Blanc, and the "distant Rat Indians" (the name used at Peel River Post for the "Vanta-Kootchin"), whose chief was Letter Carrier. This agrees with Hardisty's (1872) equation of the Rat Indians with the Upper Porcupine band, but later sources equate them with the Crow Flats band.

(5) Black River Kutchin. Tran-jik-koo-chin (1872); T'trānjĭ´k kutchin 'Big Black River [people]' (Kennicott 1862); (Western) *ȝàh*ⁿ*ȝik g*ʷ*ičin* 'people of Black River', (Eastern) *ȝà·*ⁿ*ȝik g*ʷ*ičin*. Hodge (1907–1910, 2:685, 820) confused this group with the Teenjiraatsyaa clan and with Kennicott's (1862) Tr´ōtsĭk kū´tchĭn, who were apparently a band of Northern Tutchone.

(6) Yukon Flats Kutchin. Kootcha-Kootchin or people of the low lands (1910:59, 82, 83); Kutch-a-Kutchin or Youcan Indians (Kirkby 1865:418); Koo-cha-koo-chin (1872); Kotch-á-kutchins (Whymper 1869:254); Kutchá Kutchin or Fort Yukon Indians (Dall 1870:107); Kŭtchā´ Kŭtchĭn´ 'lowlanders' (1877); Kutchiá-Kuttchin´ 'giant people' on the Upper Yukon (1876); Kouschâ-Kouttchin (1893); Kutchakutchin (1907–1910, 1:739); (Western) *g*ʷ*ičya· g*ʷ*ičin* 'Fort Yukon dwellers, dwellers on the flats', (Eastern) *g*ʷ*ičà· g*ʷ*ičin* and *g*ʷ*ičyà· g*ʷ*ičin*. Although the names of this band and the first are similar in form and meaning, they are distinct words in Kutchin. Kennicott (1862) gives their English name as Fort Indians.

(7) Birch Creek Kutchin. (Western) *de·*ⁿ*dyu· g*ʷ*ičin* 'people on the other side' or (Fort Yukon dialect) *ixe·*ⁿ*ȝik g*ʷ*ičin*, (Arctic Village dialect) *iše·*ⁿ*ȝik g*ʷ*ičin* 'people of Birch Creek'; they call themselves tsətet'aič'in 'dwellers on the converging streams' (Slobodin 1938–1968). Perhaps these were the Tēⁿuth or Middle Indians of Kennicott (1862) and the Tennŭth´-kŭt-chin´ or Birch Indians of Dall (1877:30).

(8) Chandalar Kutchin. Ney-et-se-Kootchin or Gens du large 'people of the wide country' (1910:35–36, 62, 83); Na-tsik-koo-chin (1872); Natché Kutchin or Gens de Large (Dall 1870:109); Nâtsit´-kŭt-chin´ 'strong people' (1877), the gloss being wrong; Nā´-tsĭ't kū´tchin 'outer-country people' (Kennicott 1862);

Tρè-ttchié-dhidié-Kouttchin or gens du Large 'people who live away from the water' (1893); Natsitkutchin (1907–1910, 2:39); (Western and Eastern) *ne·čit g*ʷ*ičin*, (Eastern) *ne·čąį· g*ʷ*ičin*, applied to the people of Arctic Village and Venetie.

(9) Dihai Kutchin (McKennan 1935). Tēähī´ⁿ kūtchĭn '[people of] the country below the others' or Gens de Siffleur (Kennicott 1862). (Western) *diˀhąį· g*ʷ*ičin* 'downriver people'.

Other bands are mentioned by Murray (1910:82), Dall (1877), and Petitot (1876, 1893) that cannot now be identified.

Sources

The relevant remarks of the early explorers, Mackenzie (1801), Franklin (1828), and Richardson (1851, 2:377–402) are important as historical evidence. Later travelers' tales, from the nineteenth and early twentieth centuries, are a mixed group, presenting reports and observations ranging from the fairly acute to the absurd. Of these, the most insightful and dispassionate is M.H. Mason's (1924) narrative. A. Graham (1935) is very good on native medical practices at the turn of the century.

Of what might be termed proto-ethnography, Murray's (1910) 1847–1848 journal is invaluable, within the limits of his observation, for its account of western Kutchin before almost any acculturation. Other Hudson's Bay Company post managers (Hardisty 1872; Jones 1872) and an Anglican missionary (Kirkby 1865), replying to or stimulated by a questionnaire from L.H. Morgan, have provided source material on kinship and social organization. The extensive ethnographic observations, folklore collection, and dictionary of Petitot (1876, 1876a, 1886, 1887) are extremely valuable, if one overlooks his theoretical flights.

The first modern ethnographical work on the Kutchin, by Osgood (1936a), remains the basic and most important monograph on this people. Osgood (1934) discusses territory and synonymy. McKennan's (1965) study of the Chandalar Kutchin is indispensable. Slobodin examined social organization (1960a, 1962, 1969, 1969a), belief (1970), and folklore (1975). Balikci (1963) has studied Crow Flats Kutchin social change. R.K. Nelson (1973) has provided a circumstantial account of subsistence techniques and other survival strategies of the Black River Kutchin.

Krech's (1974) fieldwork among the eastern Kutchin has been followed by ethnohistorical research on Kutchin fur trade (1976), demography (1978a, 1979), and interethnic relations (1979a).

Environment and Culture in the Alaska Plateau

EDWARD H. HOSLEY

The Alaska Plateau region forms a crescent that extends from the mountain uplands of the upper Tanana River and the northern and western slopes of the Alaska Range toward the tundras and deltas of western coastal Alaska (fig. 1). The Athapaskan groups of the Alaska Plateau utilized the same basic set of techniques for extracting a livelihood from a generally harsh environment; differences among the groups were simply those of emphasis upon one resource as against another in response to the specific features of each group's ecological niche. As Van Stone (1974:121) has pointed out, the Athapaskan adaptive strategy was a highly flexible one with a close fit to the environment and with a strong tendency to exploit the total environment.

The Environment

The overall physiography of the Alaska Plateau is determined by two major geosynclines (the Kuskokwim and Yukon basins) and an intervening geanticline (the Kuskokwim Mountains and the Yukon-Tanana uplands) ("General Environment," this vol.). The general southwesterly course of the major rivers is controlled by these structural features. The main rivers have cut channels into the dissected plateau, which stands generally 1,000 to 2,000 feet higher than the valley lowlands. These plateau uplands slope upward away from the rivers and join the major mountain ranges at elevations of 3,000 to 4,000 feet. The treeline varies but tends to be around 3,500 feet in elevation (Hunt 1967:405–419).

The Alaska Plateau region generally has a subarctic continental climate of short, warm summers and long, cold winters. There is precipitation throughout the year, ranging from 10 to 20 inches annually, with much of the region in the 10-inch range. The area lies north of the 30° isotherm, indicating that the average annual temperature is below 30° F. (Hunt 1967:421). Though this area was not glaciated during the Pleistocene epoch except for the higher mountain ranges, great amounts of glacial outwash and loess filled large structural basins, creating vast flats across which the major rivers now meander (Hunt 1967:417).

Although it will drift to greater depths in open areas, the maximum snow depth in winter is from 20 to 30 inches. More significantly, snow covers the ground for five or six months of the year. In addition, lakes and streams are frozen from late October or early November through mid-May of each year. These factors create an environment that requires a different set of adaptive techniques from that needed for the other half of the year when the plateau region is a vast network of lakes, rivers, small streams, sloughs, ponds, and muskeg. In response the Athapaskans developed a complex of tech-

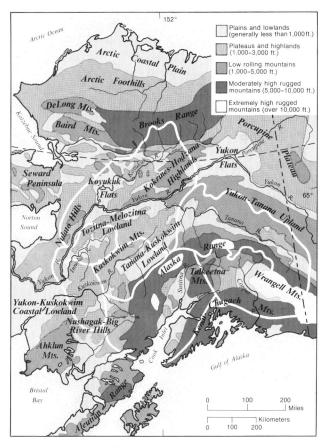

Fig. 1. Physiographic divisions of Alaska (after Wahrhaftig 1965) with approximate distribution of Alaska Plateau tribes and those south of the Alaska Range in about 1880. See Key to Tribal Territories for tribal names.

niques designed to exploit the opportunities and minimize the disadvantages of each season. Separating the two halves of the year, at freeze-up and breakup, are two- to three-week periods when travel is nearly impossible.

The Alaska Plateau, except for the higher elevations where tundra prevails, is covered by an interior forest dominated by white spruce and birch. In areas characterized by discontinuous permafrost, shallow-rooted species such as black spruce prevail. Other trees common to the region include tamarack, poplars, and aspen, the last two especially common in burned-over areas and along stream courses. Stands of willow are frequent near streams.

Most of the varied animal life of interior Alaska was utilized by the native populations in one way or another. The Barren-Ground caribou were widely available in aboriginal times. They moved up the mountain slopes to the open tundra in the spring around May, and returned to the upland forests in the fall, September through November. The interior tribes responded to the seasonal movements of the caribou with specialized hunting techniques. The Indians stressed the fall hunt when the caribou were fat and the skins prime for making clothing.

Mountain sheep were of seasonal importance, being hunted in the ranges in late summer prior to the fall caribou hunts. They were highly prized, for both their meat and their skins. Moose were widespread in the region, generally found at lower elevations and in valley lowlands where the young vegetation on which they lived was plentiful. Solitary animals, they did not lend themselves to the cooperative hunting techniques utilized for the caribou. Black bear were fairly common, especially in the valley lowlands, while the grizzly bear was found at higher elevations. Other animals of value to the Athapaskans included the varying hare, as well as beaver, muskrats, and various other furbearers.

Of great significance were the fish that were to be found in this well-watered region, both anadromous and freshwater varieties. Where they were found, salmon provided a predictable and relatively reliable food source for up to four months of the year. Runs were heaviest in the downstream portions of the Yukon and Kuskokwim rivers and tended to decrease upstream as the fish diverged into tributaries.

In the areas outside the salmon runs, varieties of whitefish assumed major importance. These fish, together with the grayling, make spawning runs from the lakes and rivers to the smaller streams from mid-summer through early winter. Other fish of importance to subsistence, many of which were taken through the ice in winter, included inconnu or sheefish, blackfish, suckers, loche or ling, and pike (Graburn and Strong 1973:65).

Territories and Intergroup Relations

It is difficult to assign precise tribal or group boundaries to the Alaskan Athapaskans (cf. Osgood 1936:3; McKennan 1969:98; VanStone 1974:8; "Territorial Groups Before 1821: Athapaskans of the Shield and the Mackenzie Drainage," this vol.). By convention, anthropologists have generally followed the territorial designations set forth by Osgood (1936). While some adjustments in these boundaries will be evident in the maps that accompany these chapters, the general terms have been retained, with some exceptions (Hosley 1966; McKennan 1969). However, it should be emphasized that in many respects these groups form a cultural continuum, and most differences between any two adjacent groups are slight. The sharpest boundaries are those between languages, but adjacent languages are similar and adjacent dialects of different languages may share features having a distribution that cuts across language boundaries.

The Alaska Plateau was occupied by four major groups: the Tanana of the middle and upper Tanana River; the Koyukon of the Yukon, Koyukuk, and lower Tanana rivers; the Ingalik of the lower Yukon and lower Kuskokwim rivers; and the Kolchan of the upper Kuskokwim River drainage. These groups speak seven distinct languages ranging from Holikachuk, spoken in a single village in the Ingalik area, to Koyukon, spoken in several dialects over a wide area.

Estimates of the aboriginal or early historic population of these groups vary widely and are based on limited data. For the Tanana, one estimate is 550; for the Koyukon, 940; for the Ingalik, 2,000; and for the Kolchan, perhaps 250–300 (Hosley 1960–1964; McKennan 1969:105; VanStone 1974:11). It seems clear that populations were always sparse with the exception of the Ingalik, who had a richer resource base. In general, the populations ranged from 1 to 1.4 persons per 100 square miles for most of the Alaska Plateau region (cf. McKennan 1969:105–106).

Culture

Subsistence

The Indians of the Alaska Plateau region were primarily hunters, and only secondarily fishermen, although the degree to which fish were sought varied widely. The single most important source of food was caribou, which were taken during the fall and spring migrations. Local Indian bands and groups of bands constructed pole fences across the caribou migration routes. Snares were placed in gaps in the fences to trap the caribou; alternatively, two converging lines of fences would lead to a large surround or corral (fig. 2) where the driven animals would be snared and killed. These fences often led to the taking of several hundred caribou by a band of 20 or 30 hunters; this was sufficient to provide food and clothing for an extended period.

Snares were used to take a wide variety of other game, from hares to grizzly bears and Dall sheep. In its several variations—spring pole, tossing pole, and tether snares—the snare was one of the most sophisticated and widely applied hunting devices of the Alaskan Athapaskans. Deadfalls and the bow (figs. 3–4) were also used to take a variety of animals, and the lance or spear (fig. 5) was widely used to kill denned bears and to stab moose and caribou from a canoe (fig. 6) as they crossed lakes or streams.

The other major cooperative venture of the Athapaskans was the fish weir ("Kolchan," fig. 2, this vol.)—a fence built across a stream or the mouth of a lake. Either adjacent to the weir or in openings along its length, cylindrical basket traps were placed to collect the fish ("Koyukon," fig. 3, "Ingalik," fig. 6, this vol.). Dip nets (fig. 7) and leisters were also used throughout the area.

Food was prepared (fig. 9) by roasting over fires, stone-boiling in birchbark baskets, and, among the Yukon River groups and the Kolchan at least, through the use of crude pottery vessels (McKennan 1959:45; Hosley 1960–1964). Fire was made by the strike-a-light and, perhaps more widely, with both the cord drill (fig. 10) and the bow drill.

Travel and Transportation

Spring breakup results in great quantities of standing water held in place by the underlying permafrost. This condition prevents easy cross-country land travel except in the drier upland regions. As a consequence, several

Fig. 4. Nabesna John (Upper Tanana) wearing cloth shirt with button decoration and fur fringe, demonstrating birch bow and big-game arrow. The typical wooden guard attached to take the impact of the bowstring projects above his left hand; the bow is held in the near-horizontal position widely used in the Alaska plateau region, while the arrow release is a variant of the secondary type common among Northern Athapaskans (McKennan 1959:55–57). Photograph by Robert A. McKennan at Upper Nabesna, 1929.

Fig. 2. Koyukon shooting caribou driven into a corral. Engraving after Frederick Whymper sketch of 1866–1867.

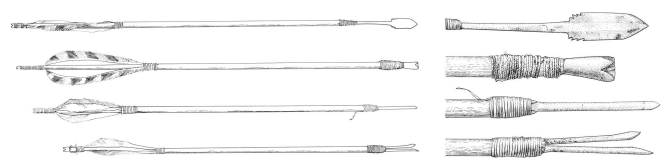

Fig. 3. Upper Tanana arrows of spruce with 3 split feathers radially attached with sinew lashing. top to bottom, Big-game arrow with steel point (formerly copper, sometimes horn) designed to separate from the shaft on impact; small-game arrows, with conical bunt (for birds and rabbits), with spiked head made from iron nail, and with 2-pronged head. top about 74 cm, rest same scale; collected by Robert A. McKennan in 1929.

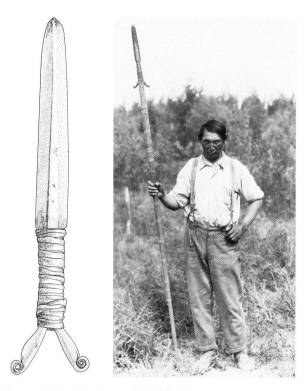

Fig. 5. left, Upper Tanana steel knife with flaring, voluted handle, copying form of older copper knives. Length 39 cm; collected by Robert A. McKennan in 1929. right, Titus Alexander, of Tanana and Russian descent, with copper hunting knife lashed to long shaft for use as a bear spear. Photograph by Frederica De Laguna at Baker on the Tanana River, 1935.

Fig. 6. A Koyukon or Tanana River Indian hunting moose with a knife in the Yukon River above the mouth of the Dall (Whymper 1869:240, 246; Dall 1870:95–96, 100). Engraving after Frederick Whymper sketch of June 1867.

Fig. 7. Joe John, an Upper Tanana Indian, fishing with a dip net from a platform that overlooks the fishing dam behind him. Photograph by Frederica De Laguna, at Tetlin, July 1968.

Fig. 8. Ingalik man holding an ice chisel in his left hand and an ice scoop in his right, used in winter fishing for cutting hole in the ice and clearing the hole of chipped ice. Photograph by John Wight Chapman near Anvik, about 1925.

Fig. 9. Ingalik girl cutting chum salmon on a piece of bark. In the several containers to her left she places the fish eggs, entrails, and heads. The filleted fish are skewered flat and hung on racks to dry (Osgood 1940:192–193). Photograph by John Wight Chapman at Anvik, about 1903.

kinds of watercraft were developed. The most widespread of these was the small, wood-framed canoe covered with birchbark (fig. 11). Such boats were constructed in the spring, when the bark was most readily removed from the trees, sewed with spruce roots (fig. 12), and sealed with spruce pitch. These canoes were partly decked at the forward end or, less frequently, both fore and aft (McKennan 1959:93). The canoes were propelled with single-bladed paddles (fig. 13) and poled upstream. Larger, skin-covered craft (fig. 14) were built for carrying heavy loads. Rafts were also utilized on occasion. Because canoes were small and light, weighing as little as 40–50 pounds, they were easily portaged. On the occasions where loads were carried overland for any distance, both the forehead tumpline and the chest strap were used. The Tanana used dogs for packing ("Tanana," fig. 2, this vol.), as did the Kolchan and the Ingalik (McKennan 1959:92; Hosley 1960–1964).

Winter in the Alaska Plateau presented quite a different set of conditions. Following the period of no travel at freeze-up in early November, straight-line cross-country movement was possible, but numerous technological devices were required to make such travel efficient. In the boreal forest the snowfall accumulation usually does not pack but remains soft for extensive periods, thus requiring a means of supporting a person's weight on the surface. The universal answer to this problem was the snowshoe. Two types were manufactured. In widespread use, although probably a more evolved and later form, was a long-tailed snowshoe with a rounded, slightly raised front (fig. 15). The large sur-

face area of these so called Loucheux-type shoes was well-adapted to hunting and traveling over unbroken or fresh snow. A second type was smaller, with a pointed front formed by the joining of the two side pieces, and with a rather more sharply upturned toe. The smaller surface area, while more easily handled, sank more deeply into the snow. Such shoes were better adapted to old snow and previously broken trails (McKennan 1959:90–91; VanStone 1974:26).

For carrying heavy loads in the winter, two means of conveyance were utilized. In the eastern part of the Alaska Plateau region the toboggan with an upturned prow was used. This device appears to have had its origin farther east. The Kolchan, Koyukon, and Ingalik used a relatively short, double-ended sled. In addition, the Ingalik and probably the Koyukon had the built-up, single-ended sled (fig. 16) that undoubtedly was borrowed from the Eskimo. Dog traction was not developed by the Alaskan Athapaskans until after historic contact.

It is important to note that by taking advantage of the two most characteristic features of the Alaska Plateau, extensive watercourses in the summer and vast expanses of snow in the winter, the Athapaskans were able to cover great distances with little difficulty. The nomadism forced on them throughout the year by an

Fig. 10. Chisana Joe (Upper Tanana) making fire by means of a cord drill and fungus hearth, a technique probably diffused from the Eskimos (McKennan 1959:68–69). Photograph by Robert A. McKennan, Upper Nabesna, 1929.

environment of widely scattered subsistence resources was thus facilitated by the very nature of that environment.

Structures

As would be expected of peoples who were seasonally on the move under varied conditions, the Athapaskans of the Alaska Plateau had a variety of shelter types. The most widespread form for summer use was the rectangular bark house. Sheets of bark were placed between vertical poles with a flat or gabled roof. Such dwellings were easily constructed and provided excellent protection from summer rains. For more temporary use, the single or double-facing lean-to was also

left, *Tundra Times*, Anchorage, Alaska; right, Smithsonian, NAA: 10,455–2.

Fig. 11. left, Making a birchbark canoe within upright, outside supports driven into the ground; the flat floor rack is in place. Photographed possibly in the 1960s. right, Manufacture of an Ingalik birchbark hunting canoe. The floor rack lies next to the canoe. The bark cover is fastened to the stem and stern posts with special pegs, which are removed when the cover is sewed. The man at right is splitting softened spruce roots for sewing the seams. Photograph by John Wight Chapman near Anvik, 1899.

River Times, Fairbanks, Alaska.

Fig. 12. Mabel Charlie of Minto (Lower Tanana) collecting birchbark (left) probably for baskets and spruce roots (right) used for sewing birchbark baskets and also canoes. Photographed in the 1970s.

538

Fig. 13. Koyukon boy paddling fore-decked birchbark canoe. Photograph by Frank DuFresne, July 1927.

Fig. 14. Upper Tanana caribou-skin boat, similar to the Eskimo umiak (McKennan 1959:93), used to carry heavy loads or many people. Photograph by Robert A. McKennan at Upper Nabesna, 1929.

used. An alternative portable shelter, used particularly in the eastern areas while hunting on the barren uplands, was the skin-covered conical tepee. Lean-tos and tepees also served as temporary trail shelters during the winter.

Several forms of winter shelter were used. A less permanent shelter was the dome-shaped, circular winter house of poles covered with skins (fig. 17). These were sometimes slightly semisubterranean. The more permanent form of winter dwelling consisted of layers of moss or dirt placed over a framework of poles and excavated one to a few feet into the ground, often with a protected entryway facing away from the prevailing winds. The Ingalik, Yukon Koyukon, and Koyukuk

Koyukon constructed particularly substantial forms of these semisubterranean houses. Still another type of dwelling had a scattered distribution. It was a log or pole house that resembled a log cabin, except that the ends of the horizontal poles were held by vertical timbers placed in the ground rather than by notching (VanStone 1974:33–34).

Also worthy of mention are two other shelters: the crude brush menstrual hut and, for some but not all groups, the bath house used for steam bathing. Steam bathing was accomplished by heating stones in a fire within a small, skin-covered, roughly dome-shaped enclosure. After the stones were heated, water was thrown on them to produce steam. While it was primarily a pleasurable and relaxing social activity, the year-round use of the steam bath provided temporary surcease from the mosquitoes and black flies of the summer and relief from the extremely low humidity of the cold winter periods.

Clothing and Bedding

The tailored skin clothing of the Athapaskans provided protection in the extreme climate while permitting unrestricted movement. Both summer and winter costumes were essentially the same, the difference being that winter clothing was made of skins with the fur left on, while summer dress was made of dehaired skins. Skins of caribou, moose, sheep, and occasionally other animals were used (figs. 18–19). The skins were tanned using a paste of caribou or moose brains to break down the fibers, and usually they were smoked as well. The basic style for both sexes consisted of a sleeved shirt, often belted, with the edges of the shirts being pointed front and rear for men, more frequently straight for women. The edges of the shirts were often fringed, and a second band of decorative fringing ran over the shoulders and across the breast. The shirts for women were often longer than those for men. In winter, trousers with moccasins attached were worn beneath the shirts; these were often of sheepskin for those groups with access to this animal. In the summer, these were replaced by knee-high legging moccasins. Also in winter, socks, mittens, and caps or an attached parka hood were worn for added warmth. A set of clothing had an average life-span of one or two seasons, and hence a continuing supply of skins was needed to manufacture replacements.

Clothing was often decorated with dyed porcupine quills in horizontal and vertical bands. Dentalium shells traded from the Northwest Coast were highly prized as a sign of wealth and were widely used in decorating clothing (fig. 21).

Bedding consisted of the skins of moose, caribou, hare, or sheep, with the fur left on.

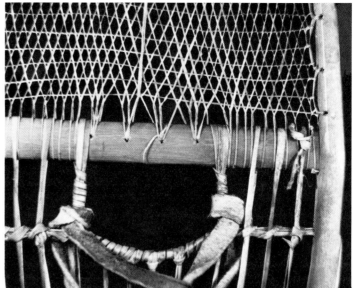

center and right, Dartmouth College Mus., Hanover, N.H.: 30–2–4600.

Fig. 15. left, Scottie Creek Titus, an Upper Tanana River shaman of the Upper Nabesna band, holding snowshoe frames with lever-frames inserted to shape the upturned toes (McKennan 1959:90, 226). Photograph by Robert A. McKennan at Upper Nabesna, 1929. center and right, Upper Tanana showshoes. Detail shows lacing and mode of attachment to frame. Length 90 cm; collected by Robert A. McKennan, 1929.

Whitehorse Star, Yukon Terr.

Fig. 16. Steven Frost, a Kutchin from Old Crow, winning the dog race at Whitehorse during the Sourdough Rendezvous. The runnered sled is pulled by dogs in a center-trace hitch, the standard modern Alaskan type. As the snowmobile displaced dog traction for hauling and normal transportation, dog teams became important in recreation. Photograph by Bob Erlam, Feb. 1965.

Social Organization

For all Athapaskans of the Alaska Plateau region, and especially those in the upper reaches of the major rivers who were least sedentary, the social organization was flexible. Long-lived socio-territorial units were unusual except for the salmon-dependent groups on the lower rivers.

The nature of the seasonal round was such that many of the economic tasks required the cooperative efforts of from a few to many individuals. Accompanying this was commensalism, a basic economic pattern that had obvious survival value. It is not surprising, then, to find that for all the Alaskan Athapaskans the basic household unit was that of two families, customarily sharing the widespread double lean-to. The household functioned as a single economic unit throughout the annual cycle.

A more or less durable association of from two to five households (perhaps 15–75 persons) constituted the next level of social organization. In their most sedentary phase, these households constituted the "winter village." In this group the focus was usually upon one dominant extended family. The tendency was to remain together throughout the year, sharing dwelling sites, resources, and a territory. This group, perhaps best referred to as a local band, exploited both summer fishing grounds and winter hunting grounds, areas that may have been 50 or more miles apart. A band's territory consisted of perhaps as much as 5,000 square miles. Only at very lean times of the year would the local band scatter into individual foraging households. The local band tended to be exogamous, marrying into adjacent local bands.

Several local bands within the same river drainage or foothill region would be linked by ties of marriage and tradition, share a regional dialect, and possess some idiosyncracies of culture. Such a group is best termed a regional band (cf. Helm 1965:375; McKennan 1969:104–105). A regional band was largely endogamous, with the local bands of which it was composed sharing one another's territorial resources on occasion

540

Fig. 17. Tananas (Tanacross) of the Healy River band standing in front of their skin-covered, domed winter lodge on Middle Fork of the Fortymile River. Photograph by C.S. Farnsworth, on the preliminary survey of the Eagle-Valdez Military Telegraph line, March 1901.

and sometimes coming together as a unit for major cooperative endeavors. The regional band was also a closed unit in warfare, feuding frequently taking place with other regional bands.

For most of the peoples, cross-cutting the local and regional band structure was a system of named exogamous matrilineal descent groups or clans. There tended to be three of these, of which one was less clearly defined and seen as somehow intermediate between the other two. Although the clan names varied somewhat, the same clans were geographically widespread and served to counteract the isolated nature of the local and regional band structure. An individual could expect hospitality from clan mates in a distant community even though he had no other ties with the group.

The tripartite matri-clan structure also served minimal corporate functions in regulating marriage and in the feasts for the dead. There was a preference for marrying cross-cousins, with a tendency for a man to marry toward the matrilateral side. Upon death, a man's funeral was handled by the members of another clan. This duty was later repaid by the kinsmen of the deceased in a commemorative feast that has come to be known as the potlatch.

Fig. 18. An Upper Tanana River girl dehairing a caribou skin. Photograph by Robert A. McKennan at Tetlin, 1930.

Fig. 19. An Upper Tanana River woman softening a tanned skin. Photograph by Robert A. McKennan at Tetlin, 1930.

541

ENVIRONMENT AND CULTURE IN THE ALASKA PLATEAU

Fig. 20. A Koyukon family in winter parkas. The adults wear caribou-skin parkas with fur trim, the hoods edged in wolverine, and the woman's parka has bands of sewed appliqué designs. The parka worn by the child on the right appears to be made of hare fur. Photographed about 1900–1910.

The kinship system for all except the Eskimoized Ingalik and the lower Yukon River Koyukon had bifurcate collateral terms for the parent's generation and Iroquois cousin terms. Since attribution of kinship terms tends to mirror social definitions, it is noteworthy that not only are cross-cousins outside a person's own clan, but also, being set apart from the siblings–parallel cousins category, they terminologically fall within a marriageable class. Such a kinship system, when combined with local exogamy, functions well in giving a kin group multiple ties with adjacent groups.

The Koyukon were divided by a line just above the village of Nulato. Above this line, the tripartite matrilineal clan structure was found. South of this line, it was absent (Jetté 1906–1907, 1:402; Loyens 1964:133); however, the Lower Yukon Koyukon maintained an Iroquois system of kinship nomenclature, which is consistently associated with matrilineal clans in the Alaska Plateau region and suggests their former presence. Among the Ingalik of the lower Yukon the cousin terminology was of Eskimo type, reflecting a thorough bilaterality and absence of a unilineal emphasis.

Marriages were frequently arranged, with the women marrying soon after the menarche, men somewhat later. The most common residence pattern was for a man to move into his wife's local band after marriage, entering into a form of bride service to her parents that sometimes lasted a year or two. Following this, families

were free to establish their own residence, but often they remained with the wife's local band. For the husband this residence pattern resulted in his becoming familiar with at least two band territories. This would have obvious advantages in that a familiarity with a wider habitat would enhance the chances of survival during times of scarcity.

In addition to clan and local band exogamy, a third pattern uniting family groups was also widespread. This was the so-called partner system. Every adult male had at least one male partner, an especially close and usually life-long friend, with whom he shared special bonds of mutual aid, hospitality, and respect. A man's partner normally belonged to another clan, frequently was a member of another local band, and sometimes was both his cross-cousin and wife's brother. Partners were on occasion members of the same two-family household group.

Annual Round

The relative abundance of big game and fish is highly variable in the Alaska Plateau region. The downstream portions of the major rivers tended to have the heaviest salmon runs, and the Athapaskans located in those re-

Fig. 21. Tanana Chief Thomas and daughter, wearing fine clothing decorated with beads and dentalia. Birchbark containers are on the ground. Photograph by Cann, 1930s.

542

gions usually emphasized fishing in their subsistence patterns, were the least mobile, and had the greatest population densities. In addition to more extensive caribou hunting, groups farther upstream, on the Koyukuk, middle Tanana, and upper Kuskokwim rivers, generally supplemented salmon fishing with exploitation of other fish, especially whitefish. Finally, those in the headwaters had little or no salmon, and they stressed caribou hunting and seasonal trapping of whitefish (fig. 22). As would be expected, these latter groups were the most mobile and had the smallest population densities.

Descriptions that have emphasized the salmon dependence of the Alaskan Athapaskans may have drawn too heavily for their content upon the study of Athapaskans in salmon-rich areas whose cultures were heavily influenced by adjacent groups of riverine and maritime Eskimo. The Athapaskans of the Alaska Plateau can best be understood as upland big-game hunters who adapted the seasonal round to include an emphasis upon fishing in those environments where the fish were abundant (VanStone 1974:7).

While there was sufficient snow remaining on the ground for travel, those groups dependent upon caribou hunting left their winter camps or "villages" as early as mid-March or early April. Usually several villages of a regional band moved to the caribou fences in the uplands. These were run on a cooperative basis under

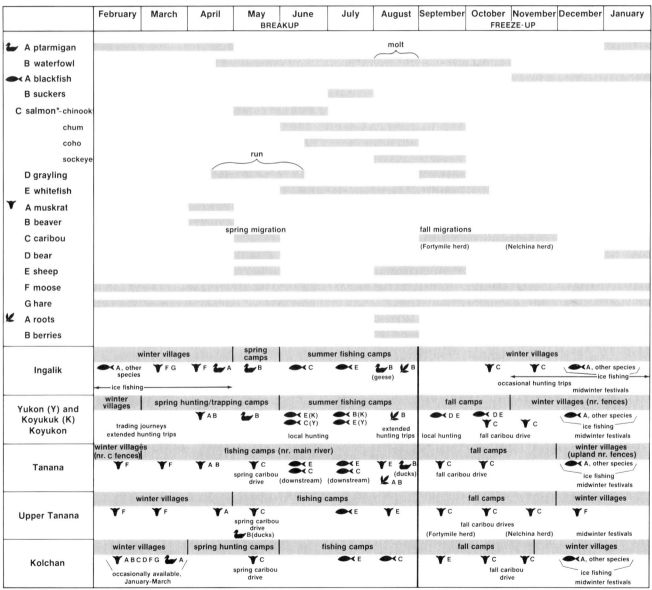

*All varieties of salmon were not available to all groups (especially the Kolchan of the upper Kuskokwim, the Koyukon and Ingalik of the upper Innoko, the Koyukon of the Koyukuk, and the Tanana).

Fig. 22. Seasonal food and fur resources and traditional subsistence and trapping rounds of the Alaska Plateau. The chart shows optimum periods of availability, when animals were sought intensively; nonmigratory species of animals were available and taken year round as need and opportunity arose. This is a generalized depiction, which may not be accurate in detail for a particular band or subgroup for every year.

543

the leadership of certain men, often those who had supervised the original construction of the fences. Following the spring caribou migration, those groups least dependent upon fishing continued to hunt sheep, bear, and caribou in the uplands until early or mid-summer. In June or July whitefish and grayling began their summer spawning migrations, and the Athapaskans established summer fishing camps near the outlets of lakes. Several village groups or local bands might come together to build and repair their fish dams. Fishing for salmon, in those areas where they were abundant, was conducted in a similar manner with the use of larger weirs. The location was often nearer to the main streams than the whitefish camps. The fish were cut, dried, and stored for winter use in underground caches lined with birchbark. Added to this were summer acquisitions of game and berries.

In late summer and early fall, families moved once again to fall camps at the outlets of lakes where they trapped grayling and whitefish. Geese and other waterfowl were taken during the August molt, often by netting. Following this, those Athapaskans adjacent to the high foothills of the Brooks and Alaska ranges sent hunting parties into the mountains in search of Dall sheep.

From mid-October through November, the fall caribou migration took place, and groups moved once again to their fences. Following the fall caribou hunt, the local bands returned to their individual winter villages, which were often situated near a lake close to the caribou fences. The winter activity consisted of local hunting of big game. In addition, ice-fishing was pursued with gill nets and cylindrical, keyhole, and other forms of traps set beneath the ice.

At the height of winter when the days were the coldest and shortest, people subsisted primarily on stored food. It was at this time that villages visited one another, and funeral potlatches and other mid-winter ceremonials or festivals were conducted (fig. 23). Sometimes individuals or families departed on long-distance trading journeys.

By late winter food stocks were low and game scarce. These were frequently lean times, with occasional starvation. Hare and ptarmigan were snared, and moose run down on the soft snow. The months of March and April were generally the most difficult of the annual cycle. The welcome arrival of migratory birds and the first salmon in May marked the resumption of the active phase of the seasonal round.

Trade and Economic Change

Before the intervention of Europeans in Alaska, all-native trading networks extended from northeast Asia into interior Alaska. Furs, hides, ivory, iron, shells, and copper were widely traded. Annual trade fairs were

Gonzaga U., Crosby Lib., Spokane, Wash.; Oreg. Prov. Arch., Jetté Coll.
Fig. 23. Koyukon potlatch participants and dancers. The women are wearing antlerlike headdresses such as those worn at the feast for the dead (see "Koyukon," fig. 7, this vol.). Photographs probably by N.B. Clemons, at Kokrines, Dec. 1911.

held, most notably in Kotzebue Sound, Norton Sound, and the Yukon delta region, to which large numbers of Athapaskans and Eskimos came. These trade fairs usually took place in summer.

In the late eighteenth and early nineteenth centuries the Russians established trading posts and redoubts on Cook Inlet, on the lower Kuskokwim and Yukon rivers, and on the Bering Sea coast. Their purpose was to implement the fur trade with the Athapaskans of the interior. Initially, the furs traded were those of animals such as beaver, which were trapped primarily for food. However, as the Athapaskans became more dependent upon trade goods, especially after the United States purchased Alaska in 1867, the winter-to-early-spring seasonal round was modified to permit more intensive and varied fur trapping, which fostered individual rather than cooperative group effort.

Individual traplines were established. The use of dog sleds, along with a larger breed of dog, was adopted from the Eskimo by the Athapaskans of the interior in the late nineteenth century. More dogs meant that more food had to be provided for them, and the best and easiest source of such food was dried fish. As a consequence, fishing came to be ever more emphasized in the annual cycle.

In the late nineteenth and early twentieth centuries missions and trading posts increasingly became the focus of at least temporary settlement, and diseases and White gold rushes disrupted native society. In this period, also, the introduction of the fish wheel (fig. 24) made feasible the exploitation of the main rivers (excepting the Koyukon) for salmon and other migratory fish. This, combined with dog-food needs and a general reduction in the availability of caribou, led to a shift away from an upland-hunting and clear-water-tributary fishing pattern. The interior Indians spent more time on the main rivers, the fishing aspect of the economic cycle was stressed at the expense of the older patterns, and the interior Athapaskans came increasingly to resemble the more sedentary riverine and coastal Eskimos and Athapaskans. Their former mobile, nomadic, hunting-fishing-collecting way of life was replaced by a dual pattern of winter villages and summer fish camps. The nucleation of population increased to the point where, in some cases, an entire regional band came to occupy a single winter village, although small groups continued to exploit traditional family fishing grounds

Fig. 24. Kolchan fish wheel in operation on North Fork of the Kuskokwim River. Fish wheels were introduced in the early 1900s and greatly increased the number of fish caught. Photograph by Edward Hosley, Aug. 1960.

in the summer. By the second quarter of the twentieth century the fall and spring caribou hunts and the construction of fish dams and caribou fences existed only in the memory culture of the people.

545

Intercultural Relations and Cultural Change in the Alaska Plateau

EDWARD H. HOSLEY

It is not uncommon for the European to believe that his influence upon other societies does not begin until he is in direct contact with them. For Alaska, as elsewhere, this is incorrect. Not only items of European material culture in indirect trade but also knowledge of Whites preceded White people, as a tale from the Tanana Indians illustrates: "For generation after generation, maybe for 300 years (sic), the Indians have heard that a strange, new people were coming to kill the Indians and take away their hunting grounds. These new people would have yellow hair and pale skin. My father told me this story; his father told him; and his father told him" (McKennan 1959:174).

As McClellan (1964:5) has noted, "nowhere in the north can we hope to peer back into a pristine aboriginal past." With the arrival of European goods and, somewhat later, the Europeans themselves, the ancient processes of social and material cultural change accelerated. The history of intercultural relations and cultural change in western and southwestern Alaska is predominantly the history of the fur trade, the Christian missionary effort, the gold rush, and White-introduced diseases—each with different but significant and often inseparable consequences.

The region being considered here is that of the Alaska Plateau, including the Yukon, Koyukuk, Tanana, and Kuskokwim river drainages ("Environment and Culture in the Alaska Plateau," fig. 1, this vol.). Included are the Athapaskan groups termed the Ingalik, Koyukon, Kolchan, and Tanana (including the Upper Tanana).

With the partial exception of those groups in closest contact with the Eskimo, such as the Ingalik and some Koyukon, the aboriginal cultural patterns and annual round were based on highly nomadic, family-based bands. Originally adapted to hunting in an upland coniferous environment, the Athapaskans had added a moderate fishing emphasis to their basic caribou-hunting economy. Carrying out spring and fall caribou hunts, combined with fishing and some gathering, the bands were thinly scattered over relatively large territories centered on the clear-water tributaries of the major rivers of the area. Due to the relatively low carrying capacity of the land, the subsistence economy was based on extensive utilization of all available resources, and population densities were low—perhaps no more than 4,000–6,000 natives for the Alaska Plateau region at the time of contact. Band membership and structure were fluid and temporary, a particular band enduring perhaps for a maximum of three generations.

Protohistoric Period, to 1800

A well-established network of trade relationships existed in protohistoric times and appears to have had ancient roots. This trade not only connected the groups in this area but also linked them, often indirectly, to Athapaskan and Eskimo groups far to the east and west, including linkages with the so-called Chukchi trade between Siberia and western Alaska. This trade accelerated with the addition of items of European material culture during the late seventeenth and early eighteenth centuries.

Trade from Asia to Alaska is apparently ancient. There is evidence of iron of nonmeteoritic origin in Eskimo archeological contexts in eastern Siberia and western Alaska about A.D. 1 (Bandi 1969:76, 105). Ease of travel along the broad valleys and extensive river systems of western Alaska gave rise to annual trade fairs. Such fairs were held, usually in summer, in Hotham Inlet in Kotzebue Sound, in Norton Sound, and on the Yukon Delta, among other places. Goods from Siberia included iron tools and weapons, tobacco, metal utensils, and reindeer skins. Moving in the opposite direction were furs and manufactured objects of wood. Also, inland tribes exchanged jadeite, red ocher, and skin clothing for sealskin (for snare thongs) and seal oil. Traded goods changed hands again at inland trade fairs. Similarly, there were trade contacts from the Plateau to the east via the Tutchone and Chilkat Tlingit for the products of the Northwest Coast Indians. These trade networks promoted widespread cultural uniformity, and new cultural traits diffused fairly rapidly.

For reasons that probably relate to greater efficiency in the use of environmental resources, the Eskimo gradually expanded up the major rivers at and prior to White contact. This was especially notable on the lower

Kuskokwim and Yukon rivers, where the Ingalik were strongly Eskimoized by the time the Russians arrived in the area (Oswalt 1962:2–4, 1967:241; Zagoskin 1967:244). This is to be seen not so much as Eskimo displacement of Athapaskans as it is the Athapaskans adapting themselves to the fishing-oriented economy of the Eskimo and being absorbed by them.

Russian Contacts Before 1800

The Russians were in Siberia by the mid-seventeenth century. Following the discovery of Alaska in 1741, the Russians confined their activities initially to the Aleutians and occasional coastal trading contacts; however, in order to expand their trade, they began to establish trading posts or "redoubts" (fortified posts) in southern Alaska (fig. 1). Following a fight with the Koniag Eskimo, the Russians, under the direction of the Shelikhov-Golikov Company, established their first post at Three Saints Bay on Kodiak Island in 1784. The rival Lebedev-Lastochkin Company established a second post at Saint George (Kasilof) on the Kenai Peninsula two years later. The Lebedev-Lastochkin Company established another post, Nikolaevskiy Redoubt (Saint Nicholas Redoubt), at the mouth of the Kenai River in 1791. For a time, the two Russian trading companies engaged in amicable competition. This later developed into hostility and mutual raiding. The Shelikhov-Golikov Company reorganized as the Russian-American

Company and under an imperial charter was granted exclusive rights to the trade and occupation of the Russian possessions in North America in 1799. This privilege extended until Alaska was purchased by the United States in 1867 (Brooks 1906:113–114). The Lebedev-Lastochkin Company ran into financial difficulties and by 1800 had abandoned its last foothold on Cook Inlet to the Russian-American Company (Bancroft 1886:343; Tompkins 1952:117; Zagoskin 1967:79).

As a result of the presence of these and other trading posts in the Cook Inlet area, the Tanaina quickly took on the role of middlemen in the developing fur trade with the Russians.

In 1794, a number of Russian Orthodox priests arrived in Kodiak to begin missionary efforts in the region. By 1796, a trading base had been established at Iliamna Lake, from which the Russians sent trading expeditions into the Kuskokwim region.

The access to items of Western material culture in this early period did little to disrupt aboriginal cultural and economic patterns, as furs had long been an item in the intertribal and coastal trade. In addition, European goods such as iron, copper kettles, knives, and similar items simply were more efficient substitutes for native implements, disrupting the economy probably very little at first. It is likely that some individuals, leaders and self-selected traders, gained prestige as a consequence of access to European goods and their use in the potlatch. The protohistoric period is best understood as a time when old patterns were built upon and added to, but there was as yet no extensive social or economic change.

Russian Fur-Trade and Mission Period, 1800–1867

The early part of the nineteenth century saw the Russians spread rapidly west from Cook Inlet into southern and western coastal Alaska and up the major rivers until they were in contact with the interior Athapaskans from three sides—east, south, and west. (The English, meanwhile, were moving northwest from central Canada; by 1800 they were in contact with the Eastern Kutchin of the northern Mackenzie drainage.)

In 1818, Aleksandrovskiy Redoubt (Nushagak) was established at the head of Nushagak Bay, so as to serve more conveniently the southern coast of Alaska. In 1832, Pëtr Vasil'evich Malakhov established a trading post at the mouth of the Holitna River on the lower Kuskokwim under the Creole Semën Lukin. After several moves the post was designated Kolmakovskiy Redoubt (Kolmakof) and conducted the trade for the Kuskokwim River. The Russians then established posts at Mikhailovskiy Redoubt (Saint Michael) in Norton Sound in 1833, and Ikogmiut (Russian Mission) on the lower Yukon in 1836. In 1839, in an effort to cut off the Koyukon trade in furs to the coastal Eskimos, Ma-

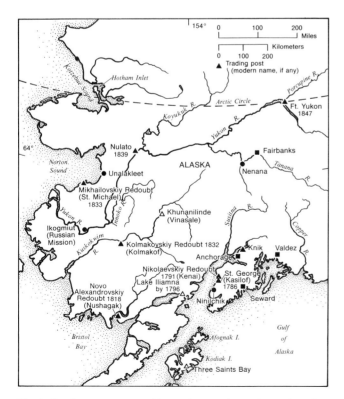

Fig. 1. Trading post communities and approximate dates when they were established (if known).

lakhov founded the post of Nulato (fig. 2) just south of the junction of the Koyukuk and Yukon rivers. In 1847, the English established Fort Yukon at the juncture of the Porcupine River with the Yukon in Western Kutchin territory, and the English and Russians shared the fur trade of the Yukon River. By the late 1830s traders from Kolmakovskiy Redoubt were making regular journeys to the upper Kuskokwim for furs, establishing regular trade at Khunanilinde (Vinasale) by the early 1840s. In addition, Tanainas from Cook Inlet were crossing the Alaska Range as early as 1844, trading with the upper Kuskokwim Kolchan as middlemen from Nikolaevskiy Redoubt (Oswalt 1962:2; Zagoskin 1967:269–272). Notwithstanding exploratory journeys by Andrei Glazunov in 1834, L.A. Zagoskin in 1843–1844, and Ivan Semënovich Lukin (son of Semën Lukin) in 1863, the Russians never expanded farther into the interior (VanStone 1959; Sherwood 1965:21–22; Zagoskin 1967).

Although the missionary effort and the fur trade had different, if not conflicting, goals, the two often worked together. Because the number of Orthodox priests in Alaska was so small, the missionary effort frequently took the form of mass baptisms carried out during visits made primarily for the purpose of trading (Oswalt 1960). While the Athapaskans of the interior appeared not to resist Christianity, it is doubtful whether they had any depth of understanding of Orthodox belief. The argument can be made that the natives viewed the acceptance of Christianity as one of the costs of the fur trade. Perhaps the most visible addition to the aboriginal culture imparted by the Orthodox Church was substituting inhumation of the dead for the earlier practices of cremation or exposure.

Hudson's Bay Company Lib., Winnipeg, Man.
Fig. 2. Nulato trading post, near the Koyukon village of Nulato below the confluence of the Koyukuk and Yukon rivers. This post was founded in 1839 by Pëtr Vasil'evich Malakhov and added to and rebuilt in following years, the fort shown here having been constructed in 1859 (Dall 1870:349). Watercolor by Frederick Whymper, 1867 (evidently after his field sketches of Nov. and Dec. 1866; cf. Whymper 1869:frontisp., 196).

With direct access to the redoubts and trading posts, change came more rapidly for the Athapaskans of the interior. In addition to the introduction of metal tools, skin clothing was rapidly replaced by clothing made of cloth. In part this was due to pressure from traders against utilizing valuable furs for clothing, and in part to the trading posts making cloth available at relatively low prices. Although the bow and lance continued to be used into the early part of the twentieth century, firearms were being traded into the Yukon Plateau region as early as the 1840s.

As a result of increased dependence upon the traders for material goods, there came a gradual shift in the annual round. More time was devoted to fur trapping, and less to other economic pursuits. This led to an increasing dependence upon certain food items obtainable by trade, such as flour and sugar. Increasingly, the Indians became affiliated with the trading posts.

By the middle of the nineteenth century, European impact upon the Indians of the Alaska Plateau was extensive, with the fur trade as the primary means of access to European goods, which were gradually becoming necessities.

On June 20, 1867, the United States signed the Alaska Purchase, and Russian control in the area came to an end. The Russians, having already abandoned Kolmakovskiy Redoubt and closed Vinasale station in 1866, closed the remainder of their trading stations the following year, and control of the territory and the fur trade passed to the Americans. The Russian Orthodox Church continued its presence in Alaska despite the end of Russian political control, and the Orthodox religion remained strong on the Kuskokwim River and portions of the lower Yukon River.

American Fur-Trade and Mission Period, 1867–1900

Beginning in the 1860s, and continuing through the 1870s and 1880s, gradually increasing numbers of Whites arrived in the Alaska Territory. They were, aside from service and governmental personnel, traders, trappers, missionaries, prospectors, and even a few homesteaders. Until the gold rushes at the close of the century, they remained relatively few in number and their influence upon the native Athapaskans was primarily that of mediators of Euro-American material and religious culture.

Following the Alaska Purchase the Alaska Commercial Company took over, and expanded, the fur trade of the Russian-American Company. Some of the old trading stations were reopened, and new ones established. Firearms became increasingly available, and Indian dependence on Western trade goods continued to increase. The first steamer ascended the Yukon in 1869, opening a period of expanded and increasingly efficient transportation. This improved transport, in combination with a rising world market for furs, and the later gold rushes, resulted in increases in the prices paid to the Indians for their furs. As a consequence, the Indians were able to acquire still larger quantities of goods (Graburn and Strong 1973:101).

The rifle, by enabling the hunter to kill game with accuracy at long range, had several consequences. Large numbers of caribou could be taken with relative ease, and this contributed to their declining numbers. The caribou along the lower rivers and coastal regions all but disappeared in the late nineteenth century. Moreover, the rifle reduced the need for the older communal hunting techniques. This led to an increased emphasis upon individualistic hunting patterns and was in keeping with the already significant individualism brought on by the fur trade. The moose, normally a solitary animal not easily taken by traditional communal techniques, became a much more important food resource with the general advent of the rifle.

As families increasingly stressed fur trapping in their seasonal round, they became more dependent upon the trading posts for tools, weapons, and nonnative food supplies. The traders, in an effort to tie the Indians even more closely to them, instituted the practice of extending "debt" or credit to the Indians. By advancing sufficient supplies to a family to enable it to trap for a winter, the trader hoped to ensure that he would receive the family's furs in trade the following spring.

In the late Russian and early American periods, the use of dogs for pulling sleds spread from the coastal Eskimo regions to the Athapaskans of the interior. This rapid means of conveyance enabled the Indians to make their trapping efforts more efficient. Another effect of this was an increased emphasis upon fishing to supply dog food for the greater numbers of dogs. This resulted in a period of increased sedentariness during the summer and a consequent increase in the importance of fish in the economy and diet of the people.

As late as the 1860s, the few White traders of the interior had only begun to attract the Indian groups away from their trapping and fishing grounds on the clear-water tributaries in the uplands of the Alaska Plateau region. Although the natives occasionally established seasonal settlements on the main waterways, the bulk of the year was still spent away from the muddy main streams such as the Tanana, Yukon, and Kuskokwim.

Although gold was known to be present in Alaska earlier, the first major strike came in 1885. This was followed by others, culminating with the major discoveries on the Klondike in 1897. Thousands of Whites entered Alaska and adjacent areas of Canada, profoundly affecting native life in the regions. For the first time, the presence of Whites in significant numbers offered opportunities for employment, but the Whites also brought disease, drunkenness, and disruption of native social and sexual mores.

With the close of the nineteenth century, American control and exploration of interior Alaska was completed. The American fur-trade and mission period saw substantial changes in the way of life of the Athapaskans of the Alaska Plateau. Not only was extensive replacement of traditional material culture by White goods underway, but also subsistence patterns shifted, and fishing came to be emphasized at the expense of hunting, especially caribou hunting. The Indians became somewhat more sedentary, frequently settling for periods of time near missions and trading posts. As people came increasingly to frequent the same areas, the log cabin gradually replaced aboriginal forms of dwellings. To this was added, in the late nineteenth century, the elevated log cache (fig. 3). The decrease in nomadism coincided with the decline in the importance of cooperative activities, and the increase in the economic importance of the nuclear family and family-owned traplines.

American Period of Stabilization, 1900–1940

By 1910 the gold strikes began to dwindle, and with them went most of the White population. There remained behind a die-hard cadre of White miners and trappers who settled in the Yukon, Kuskokwim, and Innoko river drainages. They gradually developed a seasonal cycle of mining in the summer supplemented by winter fur trapping. Communication with the outside world became easier after river steamers (fig. 4) began regular runs up the Yukon and Tanana rivers from Saint Michael (Mikhailovskiy Redoubt) following the establishment of Fairbanks in 1902. To provide communication and the movement of supplies and mail during the winter, a widespread network of winter trails was established in the 1910s and 1920s, largely following earlier Indian trails. Roadhouses were built at intervals along these trails and served as rest stops and trading posts (fig. 5). During the 1920s and early 1930s, when fur prices were high, the roadhouses were frequently the site of fur farms. While some Indians obtained seasonal employment carrying mail and supplies on the winter trails, larger numbers obtained work at the roadhouses as cooks and in supplying fish and game. Thus they came into more frequent contact with the White population of the region.

Beginning in 1905, the Alaska Road Commission extended the Richardson Trail from Valdez to Fairbanks. The following year, construction began at Seward on the Alaska Railroad. In 1912, the Richardson Trail was widened to accept horse-drawn vehicles, and by 1927 it was capable of handling automobiles. By 1923, the Alaska Railroad was completed to Nenana with a branch line to Fairbanks, thus opening up the interior in a major way.

549

Fig. 3. left, The Koyukon village of Nulato showing the mission (1), Indian-owned store (2), and White-owned store (3). Photograph probably by Jules Jetté, 1899. right, Nulato, with elevated log caches behind the houses. Photograph by Frederica De Laguna, 1935.

Fig. 4. The steamboat *Nenana* going north. Photograph by Frederica De Laguna, below Kalland, July 1935.

Fig. 5. The Sourdough Roadhouse on the Valdez-Fairbanks Road, an area adjacent to the Alaska Plateau on a main travel route into the region. Photograph by Guy F. Cameron, about 1920.

Because of the rapidly improved means of transportation and access to the outside world, both White populations and the impact of European technology grew rapidly. Formerly isolated Indian groups came to be more frequently and intensively involved with religious and governmental institutions and their representatives. The Indians became gradually more aware that factors such as the prices of trade goods and furs were largely determined by events far distant from Alaska.

Finally, the beginning of regular airplane flights (fig. 6) into the interior across the Alaska Range in the middle and late 1930s put an end to the long river voyages and the period of winter isolation. Soon afterward, the winter trail and roadhouse system was abandoned.

In the first decade of the twentieth century, the European fish wheel ("Environment and Culture in the Alaska Plateau," fig. 24, this vol.) was introduced on the Yukon River by Whites. It had spread to the lower Kuskokwim River by 1914 and was in use on the upper Kuskokwim by 1918. This technological innovation allowed fish to be taken on the deep, muddy main rivers, where nets and weirs were ineffective. The taking of large quantities of fish allowed the Indians to keep larger dog teams, thus extending their traplines. As late as the 1920s and early 1930s, fur prices were good, and although there was a decline in the game herds, there were still enough game, fish, and waterfowl available so that a modified subsistence economy could continue for some of the more remote bands.

By the mid-1930s the use of repeating rifles and the indiscriminate burning over of large areas reduced the caribou herds drastically. The caribou fences and the cooperative hunting techniques were no longer utilized, and the older leadership patterns thus underwent a change. Decades of intensive fur trapping had also re-

550

Tundra Times. Anchorage. Alaska.

Fig. 6. Plane delivering mattresses and goods to the Tanana town of Old Minto during the summer floods of Aug. 1967. Photograph by Ellwood M. Slee, of the American Red Cross.

U. of Alaska Arch., Fairbanks: Richard Frank Coll., 73–71–9.

Fig. 7. Arthur Grant, Sr., and his wife and children with fox furs (including one silver fox pelt) brought for sale to Andrew Vachon (background), manager of the Tanana Commercial Company 1907–1912. Traders paid about $100 for each silver fox skin the trapper brought in (Cameron 1910:127, 260). Photographed at Tanana, about 1910.

River Times, Fairbanks, Alaska.

Fig. 8. Snowmobile attached to a single-ended or built-up sled at Nulato, a Koyukon village. Before 1962 there were no snowmobiles on the upper Kuskokwim River above McGrath; since then snowmobiles have almost completely replaced dog teams for sled traction. Photographed in 1970s.

sulted in a decline in the fur-bearing animals, and this, along with a general drop in fur prices in the mid-1930s, led to fur trapping no longer providing the income it once had (fig. 7).

Indian populations continued to nucleate into fewer, and larger, settlements on the main rivers, with the decreased nomadism yielding to a summer-winter dualism. Families tended, by the mid to late 1930s, to occupy fish camps during the summer and to operate traplines out of fixed villages during the winter.

Although a few Indians had operated power boats in earlier years, outboard motors began to be employed in appreciable numbers around 1935. This device had an effect upon mobility and settlement patterns that was not to be repeated until adoption of the snowmobile (fig. 8) in the 1960s. Water travel was made more efficient, and winter and summer villages could be more widely separated, thus making settlement in or near White communities more feasible. The relatively high cost of purchasing and maintaining outboard motors also encouraged the Indians to become increasingly dependent upon a wage economy.

With the changes in the economic and demographic spheres came changes in political structure as well. Band leaders came increasingly to be the intermediaries between the band and the world of Whites. By 1906, the concept of elected chiefs (fig. 9) had been introduced by American government agents, with the village or band council being the most widespread organizational pattern. The Indian Reorganization Act of 1934 was extended to Alaska in 1936, and it added to the strength of the formal governing structures being developed by the native groups of the Alaska Plateau region.

By the early 1900s virtually all Athapaskans were at least nominally Christians (figs. 10–11), and shamanism had begun to decline in importance. In the native mind, shamanism never really directly came into conflict with

Fig. 9. Council of Tanana and Koyukon leaders and Whites who met with James Wickersham, Alaska's delegate to Congress, in Fairbanks, July 5–6, 1915. The meeting had been sought by the Indians and their friends to convey their concern for protection of Indian land (Patty 1971:2–18). left to right, top row: Julius Pilot, Nenana; Alexander Titus, Manley Hot Springs; G.F. Cramer; Thomas Riggs, Jr.; C.W. Ritchie; Chief Alexander William, Tanana village. middle row: Jacob Star, Tanana village; Chief William, Tanana village; Chief Alexander, Tolovana; Chief Thomas, Nenana; James Wickersham; Chief Ivan, Cosna; Chief Charlie, Minto. front row: Chief Joe, Salchaket; Chief John, Chena; John Folger, Tanana village; Rev. Guy H. Madara; Paul Williams, Tanana village (interpreter). Photograph by Albert J. Johnson, Fairbanks, July 1915.

Fig. 10. Uniformed Indian boys parading in front of the priest's residence at Holy Cross, a Roman Catholic mission on the Yukon River in Ingalik territory. Photograph possibly by Jules Jetté, about 1912–1914.

Fig. 11. Russian Orthodox church at Nikolai village, a Kolchan community on the South Fork of the Kuskokwim River. Photograph by Edward Hosley, 1962.

Christianity, for it was seen by the natives as dealing with a domain distinct from the teachings of the Church. Missionaries, however, viewed it as a threat and preached strongly against it (cf. Oswalt 1960:113). By the mid- to late 1930s, few Indians would admit to being shamans, and most restricted their practice to herbal remedies and simple divination. With the general economic decline of the Depression years, the old midwinter festivals came to be fused with the Christian celebration of Christmas, and the potlatch became once again primarily a funeral feast.

The Modern Era, Since 1940

With the early 1940s and World War II, Whites, modernization, and change came to Alaska and its native population to an extent much greater than before. Large numbers of troops were stationed in Alaska, and many airstrips were built at isolated communities. In addition the construction in 1942 and 1943 of the Alaska Highway from the continental United States through Canada opened up Alaska to the rest of North America.

By this time, the great majority of Indians of the Alaska Plateau region were living permanently in villages that had formerly served only as winter headquarters. During the 1940s and early 1950s the establishment of village schools served to nucleate populations at a single location for most of the year. Although the education provided did little initially to improve the economic situation of the Indians, it did expose them increasingly to a knowledge of the outside world. The major contribution of the schools was in imparting a knowledge of English. The establishment of schools also had an impact on the annual round. The fact that they operated during the active fall hunting and winter-to-spring trapping seasons reduced family mobility and set up conflicts that often led young males to drop out of school early in order to participate in hunting and trapping expeditions.

By the mid-1950s tuberculosis was endemic in Alaska, and the U.S. Public Health Service launched an extensive control program involving chemotherapy and modern hospital care. This, along with ancillary services such as periodic dental examinations of school children and innoculation programs, led to a sharply reduced death rate among children and a subsequent population growth in the late 1950s and early 1960s. Lack of knowledge of effective birth-control techniques led to the increasing incidence of large families, thus exacerbating the economic strain on an already marginal subsistence pattern.

The decline of the fur market after World War II, combined with the end of the employment opportunities afforded by military installations during the war years, contributed to a general economic decline in the region. While many continued to pursue winter fur trapping out of economic necessity, it was an economically unrewarding activity except to the most skilled and dedicated men. With the decline in the fur economy, dog teams were reduced in numbers, and this in turn led to a decrease in the amount of fishing done during the summer months.

During the summers, occasional wage labor at various extractive industries such as fish canneries and mines provided an income for those men willing to leave their families behind in the fish camps. Since the 1960s, firefighting in the interior forests for the Bureau of Land Management, Department of the Interior, has become a major source of cash income for many during the summer.

More important on a year-round basis has been the increased governmental support. The unearned income provided by aid to dependent children and old age programs, Social Security benefits, food stamps, and other supportive services constitute in many cases a major part of the cash income of an Indian community. More important, it has made older people less dependent upon relatives for support and has permitted them to maintain separate households well into old age.

Both the Bureau of Indian Affairs and the Alaska State Housing Authority have instituted extensive programs of subsidized housing construction, including the installation of safe water supplies and electric power plants in many isolated communities.

The period since the late 1940s has seen an appreciable increase in the dependence upon modern technology. In the post-World War II era outboard motors became first common, then necessary as an aid to transportation. A second device that has become nearly indispensable is the gasoline-powered chain saw, used for securing firewood, the preparation of logs for house construction, and cutting holes in the ice in winter for setting beaver snares or fish nets.

The device that has had perhaps the greatest influence has been the gasoline-powered snowmobile. Although in isolated use in the early 1960s, its impact did not reach maximum proportions until the middle of that decade. The introduction of safe, dependable, motorized winter transportation with good speed and range at a reasonable price eliminated the use of dog teams for trapline travel and other winter transportation needs. While it led to a further decline in summer fishing for dog food, it enabled individual hunters and trappers to range much farther afield with increased efficiency. While dogs continue to be raised in some Athapaskan communities for the competitive dog-racing market, they are no longer a significant element in the annual round.

Industry in Alaska in the postwar years has continued to be predominantly extractive, and this is as true of

553

the Alaska Plateau region as it is elsewhere. Mining, fishing, lumbering, and the oil industry have been the major employers in this field. While some jobs for natives have become available in these industries, it has been the pattern for the companies involved to import the majority of their labor because of the high skill levels required. Thus the work available to the natives has generally been at lower-paying levels.

Through the late 1960s and early 1970s, the trend among the Indian populations of the Alaska Plateau has been to an almost total reliance upon manufactured goods, mechanical devices, and processed, store-bought food supplies. Concomitantly, there has been a complete involvement in and dependence upon the wage-labor economy and welfare income payments to pay for these needs. Aside from occasional trapping, fishing, and seasonal moose and caribou hunting, traditional subsistence activities are no longer followed.

Some 30 years or more of exposure to formal schooling has resulted in the younger adult population in the mid-1970s being largely literate and aware of the outside world. Many have traveled to high schools in southeastern Alaska and elsewhere in the United States. An increasing number have attended college. In this experience, the teacher has been an important agent of change, as well as a role model and source of information about the outside world. Radio and television increasingly fill this role. As would be anticipated, the decline of native language usage has been rapid and universal in all but the most conservative and traditional communities.

Since the 1960s, fundamentalist Christian religious sects have increased their missionary efforts in interior Alaska. In some cases, conversions in communities that were previously uniformly of one faith has led to friction and factionalism over religious issues.

The Alaska Statehood Act of 1958 set the stage for perhaps the most momentous change in the history of European contact with the natives of Alaska. In accordance with the Statehood Act, the government of Alaska began state selections from federal landholdings for eventual transfer to state ownership. In response, the 1960s saw the rapid growth of political awareness and organization (fig. 13) among the interior Athapaskans, as well as other Alaska native groups. By 1967, 12 regional associations had united into a single statewide group, the Alaska Federation of Natives. The native groups pressed their claims to federal lands, and the federal government placed a freeze on the state land selections until the matter of the native claims could be resolved. The result was the Alaska Native Claims Settlement Act of 1971. Under the terms of the act, the natives of Alaska relinquished their claims on

Tundra Times, Anchorage, Alaska.
Fig. 13. left to right: Eben Hopson of Barrow, state senator for 3 terms between 1959 and 1966; Emil Notti, an Athapaskan from Ruby (a Koyukon village) and president of the Cook Inlet Native Association, who later became the first president of the Alaska Federation of Natives; and Charlie Edwardson, Jr., of Barrow, one of the founders of the Arctic Slope Native Association. All were interested in establishing an organization to promote native land claims. This meeting in 1965 foreshadowed the Oct. 1966 meeting that organized the Alaska Federation of Natives. Photographed in 1965.

River Times, Fairbanks, Alaska.
Fig. 12. Kaarina Abel, Koyukon from Huslia, making beadwork band on a commercial bead loom (for the earlier bow loom see "Slavey," fig. 5, this vol.). She is basing her pattern on Dakota designs from Hunt and Burshear (1951) open to her right. Photographed about 1975.

554

HOSLEY

the basis of aboriginal use to most of the territory of Alaska. In return, they gained the right to select 40 million acres of land and to receive cash payments ultimately totaling $962 million.

Doyon Limited, one of the 12 regional corporations, encompasses the Athapaskan-speaking groups of the interior, including the Indians of the Alaska Plateau. Covering over one-third of the area of Alaska, Doyon Limited will receive in excess of 12 million acres of land, and 34 village corporations in Doyon's region will receive an additional 3.6 million acres. Satellite sensing has been used to assist in the land selection process (Haynes 1975:201–207).

Most of the land will not be allocated to individuals but will remain under corporate ownership. The potential for long-range development by the regional and village corporations is excellent but depends in part upon timber and mineral resources available on the selected lands and the skill with which development is carried out. In the 1970s, the political unity provided by Doyon Limited, supported by a valuable land and resource base, appears to be able to go far toward providing a secure economic future for the natives of the Alaska Plateau region.

Territorial Groups of West-Central Alaska Before 1898

JAMES W. VANSTONE AND IVES GODDARD

The Athapaskan-speaking inhabitants of west-central Alaska were contacted relatively late by Europeans. In fact, there are few areas in all of North America where European penetration was delayed as long as it was in the valley of the Yukon River and its tributaries. Nevertheless, there were some population movements and territorial shifts in this area between the time of the earliest European contact and the turn of the twentieth century. This chapter surveys the evidence of the nineteenth-century territorial distributions of the Ingalik, Holikachuk, Kolchan, Koyukon, and Tanana.

Russian explorers may have reached the middle Kuskokwim and lower Yukon rivers overland from Iliamna Lake as early as the 1790s, but it was not until 1833 when the Russian-American Company established Mikhailovskiy Redoubt north of the mouth of the Yukon that they were able to penetrate the interior of Alaska by way of its major river (fig. 1). Successful explorations of west-central Alaska prior to the purchase of the territory by the United States in 1867 were those of Vasiliy Ivanov apparently to the Kuskokwim and perhaps to the Yukon about 1790 (Davydov 1977:200–202; Chernenko in Zagoskin 1967:9–10, 29–30; Fedorova 1973b:121), Pëtr Korsakovskiy and Eremey Rodionov to the Kuskokwim via the Mulchatna and the Holitna or Hoholitna in 1818 (Fedorova 1973b:64–68, 308–310), Ivan Ya. Vasil'ev to the Kuskokwim via the Nushagak and Holitna in 1830 (Fedorova 1973b:256; Wrangell 1970:13–14), Fëdor Kolmakov to the Kuskokwim by the same route in 1832 (VanStone 1967:10–11), Andrey Glazunov on the Anvik, Yukon, and Kuskokwim rivers in 1834 (VanStone 1959), Pëtr Malakhov on the middle Yukon in 1838 (Chernenko in Zagoskin 1967:10; Fedorova 1973b:140) resulting in the establishment of a trading post at Nulato, Pëtr Kolmakov on the upper Innoko River in 1839 (Zagoskin 1967:81, 236–237; VanStone 1978:4), and Lt. Lavrentiy Zagoskin on the Yukon, Koyukuk, Kuskokwim, and Innoko rivers in 1843–1844 (Zagoskin 1967). Zagoskin's report, first published in 1847–1848 and in an English translation in 1967, is the primary source for information on the history, geography, and ethnography of west-central Alaska during the Russian period. All these explorations were sponsored

by the Russian-American Company (after Ivanov's, sponsored by the Lebedev-Lastochkin Company), and they resulted in the opening of large areas of west-central Alaska to direct contact with European traders (VanStone 1979:43–62).

At the time of the transfer of Alaska from Russia to the United States, American explorers were already in the newly acquired territory. Members of the Western Union Telegraph Company expeditions surveyed the Yukon and some of its tributaries between 1865 and 1868 (Whymper 1869; Dall 1870; Sherwood 1965:22–30), as did Capt. Charles W. Raymond, U.S. Corps of Engineers, in 1869 (Raymond 1871, 1873). Other explorers who made useful contributions to knowledge of the geography and inhabitants of west-central Alaska during the early American period were Edward William Nelson on the Innoko River in 1880 (VanStone 1978), and Yukon explorers Capt. J. Adrian Jacobsen in 1882 (J.A. Jacobsen 1977), Lt. Frederick Schwatka in 1883 (Schwatka 1893), and William C. Greenfield in 1890 (U.S. Census Office. 11th Census 1893:117–128). Lt. Henry T. Allen explored the Tanana and Koyukuk rivers in 1885 (Allen 1887). Except for the work of Allen there were no truly comprehensive explorations of the Yukon River country after those of Zagoskin. Nevertheless, since useful information was contributed by travelers during the early American period, the date 1898, the year of the Klondike gold rush, has been selected as an appropriate cut-off date for this survey of territorial boundaries in west-central Alaska. The gold rush marks the beginning of rapid culture change throughout the region and, in some areas at least, had important effects on settlement patterns.

Ingalik

The earliest historical references to the inhabitants of west-central Alaska concern the Ingalik. Information obtained by Vasil'ev in 1830, including a vocabulary (Wrangell 1970:13–14), indicates that Ingaliks occupied the Holitna River, a Kuskokwim tributary, thus documenting the southernmost extent of their territory at the time of first contact. At that time the Tanaina of Cook Inlet used the name Tutna for these Athapas-

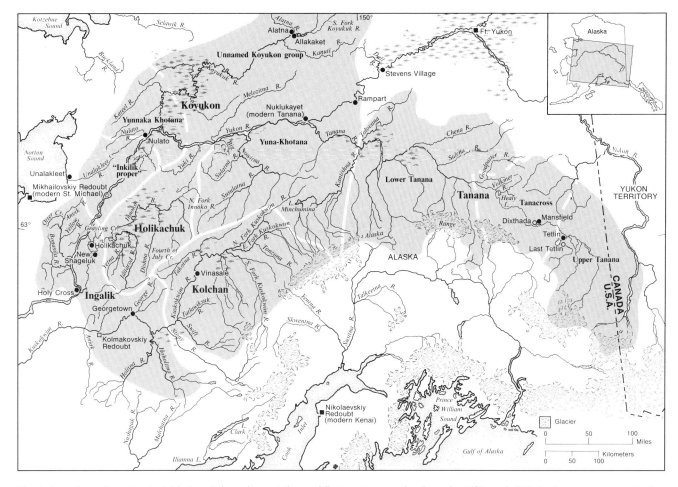

Fig. 1. Locations of west-central Alaskan Athapaskans at times of first contact, ranging from the 1830s and 1840s in the western areas to the 1880s on the Tanana and the upper Koyukuk rivers.

kans on the Holitna as well as for the Eskimos on the Nushagak River and Bristol Bay, although in the twentieth century Tanaina *dutna* refers only to Yupik-speaking Eskimos (Kari 1977:94); variants of the name Tutna are associated with the Kuskokwim and its peoples in the accounts of the Ivanov and Rodionov expeditions also.

Glazunov visited the Ingalik in 1834 by way of the Anvik River (VanStone 1959) and noted that their southern boundary on the Yukon was at the Ingalik settlement of Anilukhtakpak. He also reported these Indians as living on the Kuskokwim and lower Innoko. Zagoskin (1967:190–193, 243) in 1843 documented the Ingalik villages on the Yukon as extending from Va-zhichagat at the entrance of Shageluk Slough down to Anilukhtakpak at the Eskimo boundary, but Ingalik subsistence territory seems to have extended as far up as Blackburn Creek to judge from his statement that this creek was the boundary between two Athapaskan tribes with different languages (cf. DeLaguna 1947:29). The next year he visited the Innoko, where there were Ingalik settlements as far upriver as Khuligichagat at the confluence with Holikachuk Slough, and the Kusko-

kwim, where Ingaliks who were strongly influenced by the neighboring Eskimos inhabited a short stretch from the Kolmakov River to the Holitna (Zagoskin 1967:231–268). It would appear from his account that those Ingaliks reported as living on the Holitna in 1830 had already moved to the Kuskokwim, though men with summer camps in the George River area still hunted on the Holitna, or its tributary the Hoholitna (Zagoskin 1967:266).

Late Nineteenth Century

Ethnographic fieldwork among the Ingalik in the 1930s provided evidence for three subgroups of the Ingalik (Osgood 1940:31), and later ethnohistorical and settlement-pattern research (VanStone 1979, 1979a) has provided information on their late nineteenth-century boundaries.

The Anvik-Shageluk group of Ingalik inhabited the village of Anvik, at the confluence of the Yukon and Anvik rivers, and settlements on the Innoko River below Holikachuk village, the largest of which was Shageluk. The Anvik River as far as the mouth of Otter

557

Creek was utilized for summer fishing and winter trapping camps and the Ingalik boundary in this area would appear to have been the height of land separating the Yukon drainage from those rivers flowing into Norton Sound. Similarly, the high country to the east of the Innoko including the Shageluk Mountains and the headwaters of the Yetna River was utilized by trappers and caribou hunting parties in the early spring. To the north, the Ingalik boundary can be put a couple of miles below the mouth of Grayling Creek; Ingalik fish camps extended up the Yukon to this point, above them being the summer fish camps of upper Innoko River people (VanStone 1979a:45–53).

A second group of Ingalik lived in the now abandoned village of Bonasila on the Yukon approximately 22 miles above its confluence with the Innoko (Osgood 1940). This settlement was occupied at the time of Glazunov's exploration (VanStone 1959:44) and is said to have been abandoned in 1898 following an epidemic of measles (De Laguna 1947:71). Shortly thereafter, another settlement, called New Bonasila, was established two miles downriver, which continued to be occupied until the late 1950s (VanStone 1979a:55–59). Hunters and trappers from both Bonasila and Anvik utilized the upper Bonasila River and its tributaries.

A third group of Ingalik inhabited the villages of Holy Cross on the Yukon and Georgetown on the Kuskokwim (Osgood 1940). Holy Cross was established in 1888 as a Roman Catholic mission station at or near the former settlement of Anilukhtakpak. A village rapidly grew up in the vicinity of the mission and attracted people who previously lived at Koserefsky, a large settlement across the river, and from several lower Innoko River settlements.

A fourth Ingalik subdivision, the McGrath group occupying the drainage of the upper Kuskokwim, was tentatively suggested by Osgood (1940:31, 480). It is now known that the people on the upper Kuskokwim are a separate, non-Ingalik group (see "Kolchan," this vol.), but Osgood based his suggestion on information about a few families of Kuskokwim Ingalik who by late in the nineteenth century had moved as far up the river as Vinasale and the mouth of the Takotna and had a village at the mouth of Fourth of July Creek (Chapman 1914:1, 1948:103; James M. Kari, personal communication 1979).

The evidence is, then, that at the end of the nineteenth century the territory of the Ingalik included the banks of the Yukon River from just below Grayling Creek to Anilukhtakpak-Koserefsky, the Anvik River as far up as the mouth of Otter Creek, the Innoko River from its mouth up to but not including the settlement of Holikachuk, and small portions of the Kuskokwim drainage. In addition, extensive areas inland from these rivers were utilized at various times during the yearly subsistence cycle. Earlier in the century their northern boundary had been farther north, on both the Yukon and the Innoko, and a larger area of the Kuskokwim drainage had been exploited.

Holikachuk (Upper Innoko)

The existence of the Holikachuk as a separate group was suggested by Glazunov (VanStone 1959:44), who noted that two languages were spoken on the Innoko River. In the 1830s and 1840s Pëtr Kolmakov and Zagoskin noted five villages on the Innoko from near the mouth of the North Branch to just below that of the Iditarod (Zagoskin 1967:81, 300; VanStone, 1978:4; Russian-American Company 1841). In 1844 Zagoskin stopped at the Ingalik village of Khuligichagat, which was on the left bank of the Innoko just below the mouth of Holikachuk Slough. This was apparently nearly opposite the site of the settlement of people from the upper Innoko known as Holikachuk, which seems not to have been established until after the explorer's visit (VanStone 1979a:22–24, 30). Hieromonk Illarion, the Russian Orthodox priest at Ikogmiut on the lower Yukon River, visited the Holikachuk in 1860 (Oswalt 1960:109, 116–117) as did Edward William Nelson in 1880 (VanStone 1978:12), but there is little information on the exact location of their settlements (VanStone 1979a:27–30).

The upper Innoko people, who had few salmon in their own river, had fish camps on the Yukon. In the summer of 1843, for example, Zagoskin encountered a group of upper Innoko Indians who were fishing on the Yukon not far below the mouth of the Nowitna River. They had also brought with them furs to trade (whether at Nulato, at Nuklukayet, or to passing Koyukon middlemen is not specified), and they indicated that they also took their furs down the Innoko (perhaps to Anilukhtakpak) and down the Kuskokwim (Zagoskin 1967:167–169). At least by 1860 they had fish camps on the lower Yukon (Oswalt 1960:117), presumably about the entrance to Shageluk Slough in the area in which their descendants later lived. For their later history, see the section on the Holikachuk in "Ingalik," this volume.

Kolchan

The name Kolchan and its many variations was applied by early explorers to people living on the upper Kuskokwim River and is so used here (see "Kolchan," this vol.). However, it is apparent that this term was simply the transliteration of a designation in several Athapaskan languages serving to identify populations who lived inland from the speakers. Zagoskin (1967:300) understood this and noted that the name was what the Tanaina called the Athapaskans of the interior.

The Kolchan (Upper Kuskokwim people) may be alluded to in Vasil'ev's information reported by Wrangell (1970:14), who noted that a people called Galtsan inhabited the upper "Kviklok" River, possibly a reference to the upper Kuskokwim. In 1834 Glazunov learned that the Kolchan traded with the Stony River Tanainas and the upper Innoko people and raided the Kuskokwim Ingalik (VanStone 1959:46–47). Zagoskin (1967:267–272) visited the upper Kuskokwim in 1844 and applied the term Goltsan to the local inhabitants. He believed that Pëtr Kolmakov, whose map he had examined, was in error in extending the use of this term to include those Indians living along the upper Innoko River (Zagoskin 1967:243, 300). At this time Cook Inlet Tanainas traded directly with the Kolchan at a trade fair on an upper tributary of the Kuskokwim. The Kuskokwim Ingaliks who accompanied Zagoskin up the river considered the Swift and Tatlawiksuk rivers to be in Kolchan territory, which extended indefinitely far up the Kuskokwim.

In 1860 these Indians were trading with the manager of Kolmakovskiy Redoubt at the mouth of the Holitna River (Oswalt 1960:107), but they may not have utilized this area of the river for subsistence. Later they withdrew from the southern part of their territory, and by late in the nineteenth century some Kuskokwim Ingaliks had moved upriver as far as the mouth of the Takotna. In the 1970s the Stony River Tanainas claimed the Swift River as part of their subsistence territory (James M. Kari, personal communication 1978).

Koyukon

Zagoskin (1967:190, 243, 306–307) traveled in the territory of the Koyukon in 1843 and described three subdivisions of these people. The Yunnaka-khotana included the inhabitants of the lower Koyukuk River below the mouth of the Kateel and those on the Yukon from Nulato up to about Fish Island, the Yuna-khotana lived on tributaries of the Yukon from above Fish Island (Big Creek and the Nowitna are specifically mentioned), while the third group (his "Inkilik proper") occupied the banks of the Yukon from just below Nulato down to Blackburn Creek. Included in the "Inkilik proper" were the Ulukagmyut on the Unalakleet River and the Takayaksa of the Kaiyuh Slough area. He also learned of a group far up the Koyukuk who differed in speech and customs from those at the mouth of the Kateel. The "Inkilik proper" and the Ingalik were described as having adopted many cultural practices from the Eskimo, including clothing and personal adornment, some food preferences, some dances and ceremonies, and the use of the kazhim, the large Eskimo-type sweathouse and ceremonial center. These Eskimo cultural features were sparsely represented among the Yunnaka-khotana and absent among the Yuna-khotana

and the upper Innoko people (Zagoskin 1967:243–246).

It is possible that the Ulukagmyut had moved from the Yukon to the Unalakleet River sometime before 1838 (Zagoskin 1967:146) in response to the trade with the Norton Sound Eskimos in European goods and native products that had by then been going on for more than 50 years; in the 1960s Unalakleet Eskimos claimed that this river—the main route from Norton Sound to the middle Yukon—had always been Eskimo territory (Ray 1975:171). In any event by Zagoskin's time population shifts and changes associated with the arrival of Russian fur traders on the Yukon had already begun. Below Nulato the ravages of the 1838–1839 smallpox epidemic caused the abandonment of some settlements (Zagoskin 1967:188, 248).

The Nulato post had been established in 1839, in an area apparently near the boundary between the territories of the Yunnaka-khotana and the "Inkilik proper," and it had drawn inhabitants downriver from the former group into an area the "Inkilik proper" used for fishing (Zagoskin 1967:147, 177, 243, 307). Friction between the two Koyukon groups erupted about 1846 in the massacre of the people of Kełroteyit on the lower Koyukuk by a party of Ulukagmyut and allied Eskimo, in retaliation for which Indians from the lower Koyukuk attacked the Nulato post in February 1851, killing a number of Ulukagmyuts and Whites in what came to be known as the Nulato Massacre (Jetté 1910a:frames 639, 641; Dall 1870:48–52). The Ulukagmyut remained on the Unalakleet into the early twentieth century; they had two settlements there in 1843 and in 1866, but only a single settlement in 1885 and when reported about 1910 (Zagoskin 1967:135; Dall 1870:32; Whymper 1869:175; Allen 1887:111–112; Jetté 1910a:frame 641; Correll 1972:177).

There is ample evidence for extensive trade between Eskimos of the upper Kobuk and Selawik rivers and the Koyukuk River Koyukon in the late nineteenth and early twentieth centuries. However, there were apparently no movements of Indians into Eskimo territory in this area (Clark and Clark 1976; Anderson 1974–1975), though some intermarriage with the Eskimos on the Selawik is suggested by a statement that the Kateel River Koyukons had "kinsmen" there in 1843 (Zagoskin 1967:126). On the other hand some Kobuk River Eskimos did use the Koyukuk for subsistence purposes; movements and intermarriages between these two areas increased toward the end of the nineteenth century and many Eskimos eventually settled on the Koyukuk, at Alatna and elsewhere (Allen 1887:102, 104; Jetté 1910a:frames 642, 644–645; Burch 1979).

On the middle Yukon the Yunnaka-khotana already in 1843 dominated trade up to the Nuklukayet trading ground at the mouth of the Tanana (Zagoskin 1967:165–175), and they increased their presence and influence in this area in the following decades. Jetté (1910a:frames 655–657) documented the movement of a large number of Koyukons from the Koyukuk to the Yukon and eastward along the Yukon between 1860 and 1910 (cf. U.S. Census Office. 11th Census 1893:119); this movement incidentally seems to account for why the name Koyukon, originally meaning a person from the Koyukuk, came to be used for the people on the Yukon as well. During the same period there was also migration from the lower Koyukuk to the upper Koyukuk, from the upper Koyukuk to the Yukon, and from the Yukon up the Kantishna (Jetté 1910a; Michael Krauss, personal communication 1978).

It is necessary to take account of these nineteenth-century population shifts when correlating the twentieth-century Koyukon subgroups and dialects with those delimited by Zagoskin. Zagoskin's "Inkilik proper" are continued by the Lower Yukon subgroup, speaking the Lower Koyukon dialect, and the descendants of his Yunnaka-khotana are the Central Koyukon speakers on the Koyukuk up to Allakaket and on the Yukon up to Rampart. The Yuna-khotana, whose speech Zagoskin's interpreters from downriver had difficulty understanding, and the people he heard of far up the Koyukuk presumably spoke Upper Koyukon; speakers of this dialect were in the mid-twentieth century at Allakaket on the Koyukuk (having come from the South Fork), on the Yukon at Stevens Village and (interspersed with Central Yukon speakers) at Rampart and Tanana village, and on (or recently from) the Kantishna and the lower Tanana (Zagoskin 1967:170, 175; Henry, Hunter, and Jones 1973; Krauss 1973:908; Michael Krauss, personal communication 1978). However, although it is clear that the people on Big Creek and the Nowitna River in 1843 were displaced by Central Koyukon speakers in the second half of the nineteenth century (Jetté 1910:49, 1910a), their movements and those of the Koyukon groups farther upriver are not known with certainty. It is possible that some of the Nowitna River people encountered by Zagoskin were among the Koyukons that later moved up the Kantishna.

There is little information to be found in nineteenth-century sources concerning the Koyukon-Kutchin boundary on the Yukon, but it appears to have been downriver from its present location, perhaps in the area of the "ramparts." In 1867 a former Kutchin settlement just above the mouth of the Dall River was found abandoned as the result of an epidemic of scarlet fever five years earlier (Dall 1870:100); this would have been near the later location of Stevens Village, founded by Koyukons at the end of the nineteenth century. Similarly, the Koyukons living on the lower Tanana are seldom mentioned, though Allen (1887:138) recognized their resemblance to the Yukon River people, and Schwatka (1900:346–347) noted an alliance between

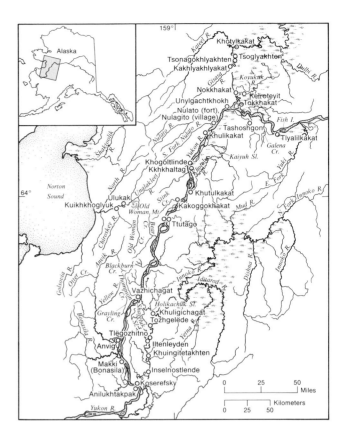

Fig. 2. Ingalik and Koyukon settlements in the middle Yukon area as recorded by Zagoskin in 1843–1844 (spelled as in Zagoskin 1967), with the addition of the contemporaneous settlements of Koserefsky (VanStone 1979a) and Keḷroteyit (Jetté 1910a). The absolute locations of most are approximate, and some are shown here on the opposite bank from their locations on Zagoskin's map. For the settlements on the upper Innoko and the Kuskokwim in this period see "Ingalik," figs. 1 and 16, this vol.

the Koyukon of the lower Tanana and the Indians of the Kantishna and the Kuskokwim. Direct information on Koyukuk River Koyukon east of the lower Kateel River was not available until Allen explored the Koyukuk from its upper reaches to its mouth. He reported scattered settlements as far upriver as the lower South Fork (Allen 1887:140) but gave no clear indication of subdivisions.

Tanana

Allen, the pioneer explorer of the Tanana River, recognized the linguistic and cultural distinctiveness of the Indians on the upper river, whom he met at three villages named after their chief—Nandell's (Last Tetlin), Tetling's (Tetlin), and Kheeltat's or Khiltat's (Dixthada site near Mansfield). The Indians in this area in the twentieth century are those speaking the Tanacross (at Mansfield) and Upper Tanana languages. The settlements and fish camps of the lower-river Indians were observed from the mouth of the Goodpaster River down (Allen 1887:83–84, map 3). If the fish camp seen at the mouth of the Volkmar River was a salmon fish camp (as Allen implies), it also probably belonged to the lower Indians rather than to those later at Healy Lake. Allen noted the similarities between the lower Tanana River people and those on the Yukon, but did not differentiate any subgroups. In the twentieth century speakers of the Lower Tanana language were found only as far down as the Tolovana, the lowermost stretch of the Tanana being inhabited by Koyukons. There is no evidence of significant population movements along the Tanana River in the historic period.

Prehistoric Territorial Boundaries

Though only population shifts in the historic period can be documented with certainty, it is probable that even before the Russians entered the Yukon valley significant shifts in boundaries and settlement locations in west-central Alaska took place as a result of adjustments made necessary by participation in the Siberia-Alaska trade. This expanded trade network, which began in the late eighteenth century and involved the Chukchi of Siberia, the Eskimos of the Bering Strait area, and the Indians of the lower and middle Yukon River and its tributaries, necessitated changes in subsistence emphasis long before initial direct contact with Russian traders. In fact, given the known extent of this trade early in the nineteenth century (Ray 1975:97–102; VanStone 1979a:63–75), it is likely that for most of the Indians of west-central Alaska, the truly "aboriginal" period came to an end not long after 1750.

Although clear proof is lacking, it may not be an exaggeration to suggest that early-contact settlement patterns in west-central Alaska reflected almost entirely the requirements of the coast-interior trade. This would mean that many of the major settlements in the area may not predate the beginning of the nineteenth century. If this is indeed the case, then there is no great historical depth to the group boundaries that were observed at the end of the nineteenth century and are described here.

Lieutenant Zagoskin recognized the significance of the Siberia-Alaska trade and, indeed, had been sent into the interior to determine how it might be diverted to the posts of the Russian-American Company (Zagoskin 1967:81–82). Unfortunately, his careful delineations of native territorial groupings were obscured by the later work of William Healy Dall, a member of the Western Union Telegraph Company expedition and a noted American authority on Alaska, who unfairly denigrated Zagoskin and had little understanding of the extent of his explorations or the care with which he compiled ethnographic data (Dall 1870:432, 1877:26, 1886:365). Such was the influence of Dall on later observers of the inhabitants of the Yukon valley that it was only in the 1960s that anthropologists' understanding of the territorial and linguistic groups in this area reached the level attained by Zagoskin in 1844.

561

Tanana

ROBERT A. McKENNAN

The Indians treated in this chapter under the name Tanana ('tănə‚nô) inhabited the watershed of the Tanana River from its uppermost tributaries, Scottie Creek and the Chisana River, downstream as far as the Tolovana River, including the Tolovana and Toklat drainages. Like other Northern Athapaskan peoples, the Tanana Indians had no self-defined "tribal" identity. Rather they thought of themselves in terms of small local bands that constituted both social and geographical units. Frequently several contiguous bands would be sufficiently interlocked through marriage, geography, and common interests for them to consider themselves a larger unit, or regional band, of which the Upper Tanana division is a good example (McKennan 1969a:99).

Osgood (1936), whose pioneering study brought order out of the chaos that had characterized Northern Athapaskan nomenclature, established the term Tanana. At the time nothing was known regarding the linguistic affiliations of these people, and Osgood relied largely on geographic considerations in delineating their territory. It has since been pointed out that the Indians at the extreme lower end of the valley, as well as those on the upper Kantishna River, spoke dialects of Koyukon (McKennan 1969:341; Krauss 1973:908); consequently they are treated in "Koyukon," this volume. However, the spread of these Koyukon speakers eastward up the Yukon and southward between the Kolchan and the Tanana groups seems to have occurred only shortly before the period of White contact in the area.

The name Tanana has taken on a much broader meaning in the name of the Tanana Chiefs Conference, territorially the largest of 12 Native associations resulting from the Alaska Native Claims Settlement Act of 1971, which includes all the Alaskan Athapaskans of the Yukon, Koyukuk, Chandalar, and Porcupine rivers as well as those of the Tanana drainage. On the other hand, the Alaska Native Language Center uses the term Tanana in a much narrower sense, restricting it to only the lowermost of the three languages spoken by the Indians called Tanana in this chapter (Krauss 1975).

Languages

According to Krauss (1975, 1978, communication to editors 1978) the three languages spoken by the Tanana

Indians are Upper Tanana,* Tanacross,† and Tanana, but his Tanana will be called Lower Tanana‡ in this

---

*The phonemes of the Tetlin dialect of Upper Tanana are: (voiceless unaspirated stops and affricates) b ([b, mᵇ]), d, λ, δ̂, ʒ, ʒ̣, ǵ, ʔ; (aspirated stops and affricates) t, ƛ, θ̂, c, č, q; (glottalized) t̂, ƛ̂, θ̂, ĉ, č̂, q̂; (voiced continuants) m, n ([n, nᵈ]), l, δ, z, šʼ, y; (voiceless continuants) N ([nN]), ł, θ, s, š, x, h; (short vowels) i, e, i (high back unrounded), a, u, o; (long vowels) iˑ, eˑ, iˑ, aˑ, uˑ, oˑ; (nasalized vowels) i̧, i̧ˑ, a̧, a̧ˑ, o̧, o̧ˑ; (diphthongs) ea, iu. Tone is vestigially present but has not been analyzed. The Northway dialect has in addition the mid back unrounded vowel ë.

In the practical orthography used by the Summer Institute of Linguistics the Upper Tanana phonemes are written: b, d, dl, dh, dz, j, g, ' (not written word-initially); t, tl, th, ts, ch, k; tʼ, tlʼ, thʼ, tsʼ, chʼ, kʼ; m, n, l, dh, z, shy, y; nh, ł, th, s, sh, x, h; i, e, u, a, u, o. Long vowels are indicated by doubling and nasal vowels by the nasal hook (γ). Northway ë is written a̧.

Information on Upper Tanana was furnished by Paul G. Milanowski (Tetlin dialect; communication to editors 1979) and Michael E. Krauss and Jeff Leer (Northway dialect; communications to editors 1978, 1979).

†The phonemes of Tanacross are: (unaspirated stops and affricates) d, λ, δ̂, ʒ, ʒ̣, g, ʔ; (aspirated stops and affricates) t, ƛ, θ̂, c, č, k; (glottalized) t̂, ƛ̂, θ̂, ĉ, č̂, k̂; (voiced continuants) ł, θ, s, š, x, h; (voiced continuants) m, n, l, δ, z, šʼ, γ, y; (short full vowels) i, e, a, u; (long full vowels) iˑ, eˑ, aˑ, uˑ; (reduced vowels) æ, ö; (nasalized vowels) i̧, i̧ˑ, ȩ, ȩˑ, a̧, a̧ˑ, u̧, u̧ˑ; (tones) v́ (high) and unmarked (low). The word-final sonorant system has the following distinctions: y ([x]), yˑ, yʔ, yˑʔ; n ([N]), nˑ, nʔ, nˑʔ. Non-nasal stem-initial voiced continuants are voiced only in their release.

In the practical orthography used by the Alaska Native Language Center the Tanacross phonemes are written: d, dl, dh, dz, j, g, ' (not written word-initially); t, tl, th, ts, ch, k; tʼ, thʼ, tsʼ, chʼ, kʼ; ł, th, s, sh, x, h; m, n, l, dh, z, shy, gh, y; i, e, a (in stems) and ä (in prefixes); u; ii, ee, aa, uu; a, o. The word-final sonorant system is rendered: ih, iy, iʼ, iyʼ; nh, nn, nʼ, nnʼ. High tone is shown as v́ and nasalization as γ. Since a does not contrast with æ in stems (a appears before h, ʔ, x, and γ, and æ appears elsewhere), the same symbol (a) can be used for both.

Information on Tanacross was furnished by Ronald Scollon and Michael E. Krauss (communications to editors 1978).

‡The phonemes of the Minto-Nenana dialect of Lower Tanana are: (unaspirated stops and affricates) b, d, λ, δ̂, ʒ, ʒ̣, ʒ̣, g, ʔ; (aspirated stops and affricates) t, ƛ, θ̂, c, ç, č, k; (glottalized) t̂, ƛ̂, θ̂, ĉ, č̂, k̂; (voiceless continuants) ł, θ, s, ş, š, x, xʷ, h; (voiced continuants) n, l, δ, z, ẓ, y, γ; (full vowels) i, æ, u, ɔ; (reduced vowels) ə (with several central and front allophones) and ŭ; (tones) v́ (high), v̀ (low), v̇ (nasal high). There is devoicing in final position of n to [N] and y to [x̣]; b is optionally [m] if the next consonant in the word is n. In the Chena and Salcha-Goodpaster dialects the retroflex consonants (ʒ̣, ç, and so forth) each merge with the corresponding member of the alveolar series (ʒ, c, and so forth).

Information on the Lower Tanana language was provided by Michael E. Krauss (communication to editors 1978).

562

chapter to avoid confusion with the other uses of the term Tanana. Upper Tanana has two dialects, one spoken by the Tetlin–Last Tetlin band and the other by the bands farther upriver (Lower Nabesna, now known as Northway, Scottie Creek, and perhaps Upper Nabesna–Upper Chisana). Within the Tanacross language there are slight dialectal differences between the speech of the Mansfield-Kechumstuk ('kechəm,stäk) band and that of the Healy River–Joseph band. In contrast there are somewhat greater differences among the three dialects of Lower Tanana, that of the Salcha-Goodpaster band or bands (3 speakers in 1978), that of the Chena band (dialect extinct in 1978), and that of the lowermost bands (Wood River, Nenana-Toklat, and Minto). Krauss's linguistic classification closely matches the delimitation of ethnographic and dialectal differences among the Tanana bands revealed by McKennan's 1962 demographic survey of the entire region from Snag to Tanana village. The five regional bands that McKennan recognizes (fig. 1) correspond exactly to the three dialects of Lower Tanana and the Tanacross and Upper Tanana languages. One of the most important ethnographic breaks on the river separates the bands on the Goodpaster River and below, who fished for salmon, from the bands in the valley above the Goodpaster, an area with no salmon (McKennan 1969:338); this break coincides with the line between the Lower Tanana and Tanacross languages, a significant linguistic boundary that demarcates, for example, the different tonal systems of the languages above and below it (Michael E. Krauss, communication to editors 1978).

It should be emphasized that the grouping of Indian bands treated here under the name Tanana is to a certain extent an arbitrary one. The Athapaskans on the Tanana and Yukon rivers, from the Tutchone to the Ingalik, do not fall easily into a number of discrete cultural or linguistic blocks; rather, they constitute a continuum of local bands whose respective microcultures and dialects differ only slightly from those of their immediate neighbors. Over a span of several bands the linguistic differences are compounded, with mutual intelligibility diminishing in rough proportion to the intervening distance. Within this continuum the Tanana show more linguistic diversity than any of the other named groups given separate-chapter treatment in this volume, though the three languages of the Tanana are probably more similar than any other three comparable linguistic units. Also, it is hard to say whether the linguistic jumps from the Minto dialect (of Lower Tanana) to Upper Koyukon and from Upper Tanana to Southern Tutchone are greater than the jump from Minto to Upper Tanana (Michael E. Krauss, communication to editors 1978). Indeed, both Tanacross and Upper Tanana speakers told McKennan that they are able to converse with Lower Tanana speakers less easily than with speakers of Han, Ahtna, and Southern Tutchone, although it is not clear whether or not this is because they have acquired some degree of competence in these languages through extensive and often intimate contact. Nevertheless, some form of classification is necessary in describing the bands of the Tanana-Yukon continuum, and the Tanana group as here delimited is a reasonable and convenient unit. However, the use of a single name for the Indians of the Tanana valley should not be taken to imply any sense of communality, for this did not exist among them until the mounting pressure for a settlement of native land claims produced an embryonic pan-Athapaskan movement in the 1960s.

Environment

The Tanana River, a major tributary of the Yukon, is formed by the confluence of the Nabesna and Chisana rivers and flows northwest some 440 miles to its junction with the Yukon a few miles above the village of Tanana. The Nabesna and Chisana rivers in turn have their origins in glaciers in the rugged Wrangell Mountains near the international border. North of the Nutzotin Mountains the rivers join in the Northway-Tetlin lowlands, a lake-dotted plain through which the rivers flow slowly. Below Tanacross (formerly Tanana Crossing) the valley becomes quite narrow and the Tanana contains several rapids that make upstream navigation difficult for small boats. Below the Goodpaster the valley begins to broaden again, and the river breaks into a maze of swift-flowing channels, the Bates Rapids. These rapids extend almost to Fairbanks, below which the valley continues to broaden and the river resumes a more leisurely course. Nearly all the major tributaries entering the Tanana from the south are typical glacial streams, many-channeled and heavily silted. Thus, they did not lend themselves to aboriginal fishing methods. However, some of the shorter and smaller streams are nonglacial and clear. The tributaries entering the Tanana from the north are consistently clear. The Tanana itself is heavily silted.

The terrain to the south beyond the river floodplain consists first of a series of rolling hills, and behind them comes the rugged Alaska Range, with peaks ranging from 10,000 to over 20,000 feet. Extending east from the Alaska Range are the Wrangell Mountains, equally rugged although less high.

Due to the aggrading action of its glacial tributaries the Tanana River hugs the northern edge of the valley floor. Here begin the Yukon-Tanana uplands, a series of rounded ridges rising 500 to 1,500 feet from the valley level and culminating in rugged mountains ranging from 4,000 to 6,000 feet in height. At the lower end of the valley these uplands are broken by the Minto Flats, a low-lying, lake-dotted plain on the lower Chatanika, ecologically similar to the Tetlin-Tanacross lowlands. At the upper end, in the region of Tetlin Junction, the

563

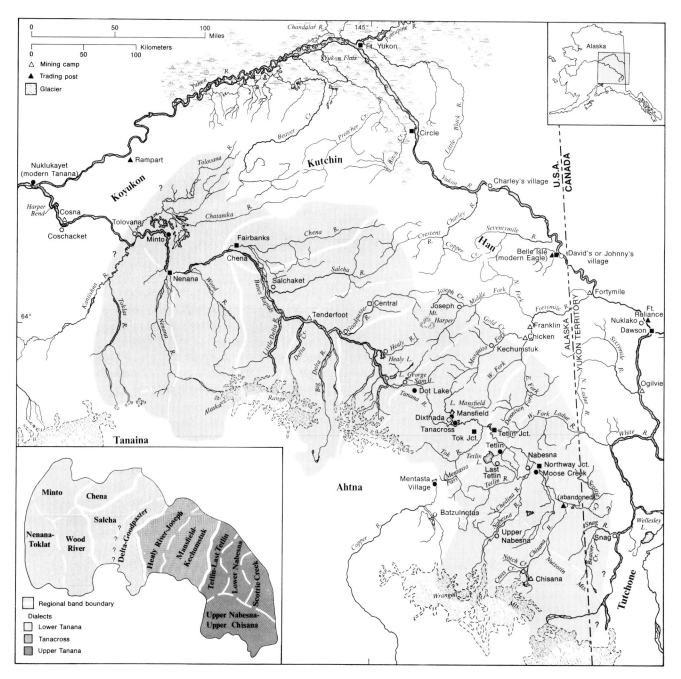

Fig. 1. Tribal territory, about 1880. Inset shows approximate band areas.

headwaters of both the Dennison fork of the Fortymile and of the Ladue River are within a few easy miles of the Tanana (less than five in some places); and this adjacent area, like the upper White River, was exploited by the Upper Tanana natives.

Because it is separated from the ameliorating influence of the Pacific Ocean by high mountain ranges, the area has the continental climate typical of the Alaskan interior. In spite of the watery appearance given it by the many shallow thaw lakes that dot the land's surface, precipitation is actually slight, about 12 inches a year on the average. Winter temperatures are severe, −70° F.

and even below on occasion, while summer temperatures can climb into the 90s.

Spruce constitutes the major timber cover. Over much of the area these trees are small, scraggly, and shallowly rooted since the underlying soil is permanently frozen. However, between the Tok and Big Delta rivers stands of merchantable timber occur. Tree line is at about 3,500 feet, varying somewhat with local conditions, so that much of the terrain away from the main river valleys consists of either tundra or high, rocky slopes. Deciduous trees include poplar and aspen, particularly abundant on burned-over areas, as

564

well as birch, alder, and willow. Berries, which did not play a large role in the native diet, include the blueberry, highbush cranberry, mountain cranberry, crowberry, bearberry, and wild-rose hips. Other vegetable foods used by the Indians included hedysarum roots and mushrooms.

Caribou, formerly the most important single food source of the natives, are found throughout the area. Moose are more restricted to the valleys and lower altitudes where browse is plentiful. Mountain sheep are found in the higher mountains. Both black and grizzly bear are found throughout the area, although the latter are more common at higher elevations. Small game of importance to the natives includes the varying hare, marmot, and ground squirrel, the latter two being found only at higher altitudes. The principal furbearers are the red fox (including its cross and black phases), lynx, coyote (a twentieth-century migrant), wolverine, marten (at the higher altitudes), beaver, mink, otter, and muskrat, the last named being particularly abundant in the Minto Flats and the Northway-Tetlin lowlands. Resident birds utilized by the natives include ptarmigan, ruffed grouse, and sharp-tailed grouse. In the spring large numbers of migrant waterfowl (ducks, geese, and swans) pass through the area on their way to their breeding grounds farther north. However, many ducks nest on the myriads of small lakes and ponds that dot the valley, and the Minto Flats and Healy Lake are famous for the abundance of their duck populations.

Of the fish resources exploited by the Indians the whitefish (at least two species) is the most widely distributed and possibly the most important. Other freshwater fish used are the grayling, northern pike, sucker, and ling. Three varieties of salmon (Chinook, chum, and coho) ascend the Tanana and its principal, clearwater tributaries, as far upstream as the Goodpaster River, and are, of course, an important food fish in the areas where found. The Salcha River apparently enjoys a larger run than some of the other rivers, but good data are lacking.

Territory

At the time of White contact, about 1880, the speakers of Lower Tanana did not extend completely to the mouth of the river but rather began with the drainages of the Tolovana and Toklat rivers (fig. 1). The country below these tributaries was utilized by Koyukon speakers. It is quite possible that at an earlier time this may also have been Tanana territory, since the Koyukon seem to have been gradually pushing their way up the Yukon. The Alaska Range and Wrangell Mountains formed a natural barrier on the south, thus limiting intercourse with the Tanaina and the Ahtna to the few accessible passes. The headwaters of the White River

were used by the Tanana Indians as were portions, perhaps all, of the Snag drainage. Sometime before White contact, relations between the Upper Tanana and their Southern Tutchone neighbors to the east were interrupted by a "war," which was still a vivid part of native legendary history in 1929. This may account for the uncertain nature of this eastern boundary.

Like that to the south, the northern boundary is a natural one, consisting of the rugged mountains of the Yukon-Tanana uplands from the head of the Tolovana east along this range as far as Mount Harper at the head of the Healy River. Beyond this point the Tanana territory also included the upper tributaries of the Fortymile River, specifically the Middle Fork downstream to below Joseph (a caribou hunting camp of the Healy River band), the Mosquito Fork downstream to the mouth of Gold Creek some miles below Kechumstuk, and the Dennison Fork as well as the headwaters of the Ladue River. Influenced by a statement of Stuck's (1914:261–262) that his dog-driver and interpreter could not understand the language of a band of Kechumstuk Indians whom they met on the trail, Osgood (1971:150–153) assigned this upper Fortymile area, including Kechumstuk, to the Han. However, Tanacross informants, several of whom were born at Kechumstuk, and one of whom, indeed, had been a member of the very group that Stuck met on the trail, reaffirmed in 1972 that Kechumstuk was the caribou hunting camp of the same Tanana band that had its summer fishing camp at Mansfield Village. They also said that because of the abundance of caribou in the upper Fortymile area, Han people sometimes joined them in communal hunts, a situation also true of the Healy River band on the Middle Fork.

It is evident that except for natural boundaries such as high mountain ranges, it is extremely hard to draw precise territorial limits for these nomadic people. Adjacent local bands often came together for purposes of communal hunting, trade, or potlatch ceremonies except for those periods when local "wars" (more often vendettas) temporarily separated them. Intermarriages between bands often took place, as the native genealogies attest. Indeed the small size of the local bands, some 20 to 75 people (McKennan 1969a:102–103), combined with the clan exogamy that prevailed would make some out-marriages inevitable.

Subsistence

Good data on the territorial ranges of local bands are available only for the area above the Goodpaster River. Such territories reflected the basic subsistence quest that was much the same throughout the Tanana valley.

Of primary importance was the fall caribou hunt, which began in late August at caribou fences constructed near the edge of timber, either in the form of a long fence, set with snares, or two long fences, converging to form a corral. The trapped caribou were then killed with lances or arrows. One such fence, often mentioned by early White travelers, extended from a few miles beyond Lake Mansfield on down the Mosquito Fork nearly to Kechumstuk, but many other such fences once dotted the Yukon-Tanana uplands. The southward-migrating caribou were taken in such quantity that the band was able to subsist largely on the dried meat throughout the winter; thus the winter camps or "villages" were located in the uplands. Kechumstuk and Joseph (both abandoned well before 1967) constituted such winter villages.

In the spring, before the disappearance of the snow made toboggan travel difficult, the Indians repaired to the vicinity of their fishing spots nearer the main river. Here they hunted and snared moose, intercepted caribou on their northward migration through the timber, and killed muskrat and beaver.

By June the whitefish started running up the clearwater streams to spawn. These fish were taken in both cylindrical fishtraps and large dip nets at weirs built across the streams, generally near the outlets of lakes. Like the caribou fences, the fish weirs required considerable collective effort in their construction and use, and so they also served as nucleating centers. However, where the streams were small, the band would divide into smaller units during the fishing season. Most of the fish were dried and stored in underground caches for later consumption and, after the coming of Whites, for dog food. In 1885 Allen (1887:75–80) found such fishing communities at Nandell's (Last Tetlin), Tetlin, and Kheeltat's (Dixthada). Farther down the valley in large clearwater rivers such as the Goodpaster, Salcha, Chena, and Tolovana, salmon were taken in much the same fashion except that the weirs were, perforce, much larger, with a number of interstices, each opening operated by a single family. Because of the several runs of salmon the fishing season also lasted somewhat longer. Salmon were also taken on the main river in small dip nets used from canoes.

Following the fishing season the native larder was supplemented by berries, roots, and ducks, the ducks easily killed by blunt arrows during their molt. In late summer came a sheep-hunting trip to the mountains both for meat and for skins used for winter moccasin-trousers. While the men hunted sheep the women snared marmots and ground squirrels, both for food and for their skins, which were sewed into robes. Following the sheep hunt the band would move to its caribou fence and the yearly cycle would begin anew.

The band territories outlined on figure 1 are to be regarded as only an approximation of the situation as it existed in the late nineteenth century. Between the 1920s and the 1960s the situation of the Upper Tanana changed markedly. By 1962 no Indians inhabited the intermontane basins of the Chisana, Nabesna, and White rivers; and the few survivors of the Upper Nabesna–Upper Chisana band were at Tetlin, as were the survivors of Last Tetlin. The Scottie Creek group no longer existed as a band although two native families still resided in the area. The Lower Nabesna band was leading a largely sedentary existence at its old fishing camp on Moose Creek near modern Northway. Kechumstuk was deserted, Mansfield largely so, and the members of that band together with a few natives from the upper Copper River were living at Tanacross. A small native settlement had sprung up at Dot Lake, peopled by families from Tanacross, Healy River, and Mentasta. The former villages at Joseph and Healy Lake were deserted although two native families were still living at the lake in 1972. In 1962 there were no Indian settlements along the Tanana valley from Healy Lake to Nenana, although at the time of White contact the Salcha certainly had at least two local bands. The Chena band was evidently always a small one; its two survivors were living in Fairbanks, as were, of course, Indians and Eskimos from many parts of Alaska. The descendants of the Wood River and Nenana-Toklat bands had moved to the native section of Nenana together with Athapaskan migrants from the lower Tanana and middle Yukon. The native village of Minto, while containing some descendants of the old Tolovana and Minto bands, also contained migrants from a variety of groups.

Obviously band organization is a thing of the past as is the old, nomadic way of life. It should be noted that even in aboriginal times specific local bands were probably transitory in nature. The bands were of such small size that periodic famines, warfare, and later, diseases introduced by Whites could easily reduce them to a point where they were no longer viable. The survivors would be forced to join another and larger band or starve. On the other hand, under optimum conditions some bands no doubt increased to a size where they were forced to split into smaller units and seek new territory.

History of Indian-White Contact

Although the first published description of the Tanana Valley is Lt. Henry T. Allen's account of his pioneer exploration in 1885 (Allen 1887), the early trader-prospectors, A.C. Harper and Bates, had traversed it 10 years earlier after coming overland from Belle Isle. Harper later made several other trips up the lower Tanana River and at various times he maintained a trading post above its mouth at Harper Bend. Previously the Indians from the lower Tanana, and occasionally from as far upstream as Mansfield, were in the habit of making annual visits to Nuklukayet at the mouth of the river, where they traded with the Russians from Nulato and Hudson's Bay Company men from Fort Yukon. Even earlier some trade goods made their way to the Tanana from the Russian posts on the coast. Although the bulk of this trade was conducted through intermediaries, some of it was direct (McKennan 1969a:95). This early trade probably did little to change the native subsistence pattern, but it could well have reinforced distinctions based on wealth and thus enhanced the status of the traditional band leaders.

By the 1880s the pioneer traders—Harper, Al Mayo, Jack (L.N.) McQuesten, and Joe Ladue—were operating trading posts along the Yukon at Rampart, Belle Isle (Fetoutlin, David's Camp, Eagle), Fort Reliance (below Dawson), and Ogilvie (mouth of Sixtymile), and it was at these posts that the Tanana Indians largely traded until the gold discoveries at the end of the nineteenth century brought a sudden influx of White miners to the area. This dramatically changed the nature of native life along the upper Yukon and the lower Tanana. In the early twentieth century, beginning with W.H. Newton (personal communication 1931) at Healy River in 1907, a series of posts was established by various traders along the upper Tanana. These operated until World War II when the building of the Alaska Highway with its adjacent airfields at Tanacross and Northway put an end to the relative isolation of this region and the importance of fur trapping. The trading post was then replaced by the native-owned cooperative store. Following statehood in 1958 the enforcement of fish and game laws, equally applicable to both Indians and Whites, sounded the death knell to the old pattern of living off the land.

The development of the fur trade not only brought obvious changes in Tanana material culture but also affected profoundly the subsistence pattern, round of seasonal activities, social organization, and demography. Semipermanent villages (Healy Lake, Tanana Crossing, Nabesna, Cross Creek, and Snag) grew up in the neighborhood of the trading posts. The introduction of the dog team and its growing use on the trapline increased both the need and the market for dried fish, an easily transportable dog food. Where salmon were available, the introduction of the Whites' fish wheel in the early 1900s further promoted the importance of fishing as well as transferring this activity from clearwater tributaries to the muddy waters of the lower Tanana. Native economic life centered more and more around the activities of the nuclear family at the expense of the earlier, collective activities of the band with its network of kinship responsibilities and perquisites. Also it increased the magnitude, if not the importance, of the potlatch ceremony.

Christian missions also exercised a centripetal force on the Tanana Indians. The first missionary to visit the Tanana was Rev. V.C. Sim, an Anglican, who in 1884 briefly accompanied a group of Tanana Indians from Nuklukayet upriver to a point apparently near present Fairbanks (Wesbrook 1969:39). The natives also had some occasional contacts in the 1880s and 1890s with Anglican missionaries at the settlements of Fortymile and Eagle. With the influx of White miners, Protestant Episcopal missions and mission schools were established at Tanana, 1887; Nenana, 1907; Chena, 1908; Salchaket, 1909, an old Salcha fish camp; Tanana Crossing, 1912; and Minto, 1929 (P.T. Rowe 1920:80ff.). These drew Indians from various bands to settlements along the river, further confusing traditional clan, kinship, and residence patterns. In addition to its obvious effect on native religious beliefs, the mission work increased the use of the English language by the natives and introduced new standards of personal cleanliness and sanitation. While the early missions were Episcopalian, other sects, particularly the evangelical ones, have made some Indian converts in the period since World War II.

Beginning with the 1930s the Indian Bureau (later to become the Bureau of Indian Affairs) took over the responsibility for native education. Since Alaska's assumption of statehood, this function has gradually been assumed by the local communities, a shift that reflects the migration from native villages to the predominantly White settlements of Fairbanks, Nenana, and Tok.

The development of mining likewise materially changed the nature of Indian life. Placer gold was first discovered in nearby Han country on the Fortymile at Franklin Creek in 1886 and at Chicken Creek shortly thereafter. As a result most of the prospectors then along the Yukon quickly congregated on the Fortymile, and short-lived mining camps sprang up that were visited frequently by the neighboring Tanana bands for both trade and diversion. Although the famous Klondike stampede of 1897–1898 did not have the traumatic effect upon the Tanana Indians that it did upon the Han, numbers of gold seekers did make their way through the upper Tanana country, having come up the Copper River to Mentasta Pass, thence down to the Tanana River and across to Dawson by way of two old Indian trails—one through Mansfield and Kechumstuk and on down the Fortymile and another across country from the Tetlin area, essentially the route followed by the Taylor Highway.

The discovery of gold in the Fairbanks area in 1901 transferred some of this feverish gold-seeking activity to the Tanana. In 1902–1903 hundreds of miners, many of them from the Klondike, flocked to the newly established town, and by 1909 there were some 12,000 Whites living in the area (Hulley 1970:282) with consequent disruptive effects on the small Chena band that originally inhabited this region. For a few years they maintained a village at Chena Mission, some miles away on the Tanana proper, but the group eventually disintegrated and the village was abandoned. Later placer finds on the Kantishna, 1904; at Tenderfoot, in Salcha territory, 1905; Chisana, 1913; and the upper Tolovana in 1914 drew the local Indians to these vicinities. Satellite native settlements sometimes sprang up, but like the mining camps they were of short duration. While very few Indians worked in the placer mines, the miners provided a ready market for fresh meat and fish and many Indians made a business of market-hunting. The mining era not only disrupted former demographic patterns but also brought considerable social demoralization in the form of drunkenness, debauching of women, and venereal disease. Roads were built to connect Fairbanks with the coast (Richardson Highway) and with the Yukon (Steese Highway). The Alaska Railroad reached Nenana in 1917 and transformed that former mission village into a bustling, commercial town where freight destined for both Fairbanks and the Yukon was transferred to river steamboats.

A military telegraph line connecting Fort Egbert (Eagle) and Valdez with a branch line traversing the Yukon-Tanana uplands to Fort Gibbon (Tanana) was constructed in 1902. Maintenance stations were established every 40 or 50 miles along its route and two or three soldiers were assigned to each. These isolated posts, located at places such as Kechumstuk, Joseph, Tanana Crossing, Central, Minto, and Tolovana, tended, like the mining camps, to draw the local natives to the vicinity; and semipermanent native villages often resulted (fig. 2). The Eagle-Valdez line was abandoned in 1910, but some Indian villages such as Tanana Crossing and Minto persisted. In 1915 Minto was founded a few miles downstream from the site of the telegraph station of that name. The major changes in experience and circumstance that the Tanana Indians in general have undergone in the twentieth century are encapsulated in the chapter "Minto, Alaska" in this volume.

Population

The little available data indicate that the native population was always sparse. Petroff (1900:66), who never visited the region, gives a total population of 700 for the "Tanana Villages" in 1880. Allen (1887:137), who traversed the area in 1885, estimated the native population at between 550 and 600, although he actually saw less than half that number. Brooks (1900:493), who came down the Tanana in 1898, estimated the population to be less than 400. The census of 1910 (U.S. Bureau of the Census 1915:16), which made a careful attempt to enumerate natives by language and "tribe," gives a population of 415 for the "Tenankutchin." All such figures undoubtedly include some of the Koyukon-speaking groups at the lower end of the river. Census

U. of Alaska Arch., Fairbanks: Archie Lewis Coll., 896–64.

Fig. 2. Fish camp at mouth of Tolovana River. Canoes decked fore and aft are on the beach. In 1903 a telegraph station was established here, and it was also the location of a trading post. Photographed about 1919.

figures since 1910 are of little use for comparative purposes, since they include so many Indians who have migrated to the Tanana from other areas following the occupation of the valley by Whites.

Legends of epidemic diseases are a part of the folk history. A smallpox epidemic ravished the native population of the lower Yukon in 1838–1839. A scarlet fever epidemic was introduced to the Southern Tutchone by the Chilkat in 1851; and the same disease, brought to Fort Yukon in 1865, took a heavy toll among the natives along that section of the Yukon in the years following. One or more of these diseases may have spread to the Tanana. More direct contact with Whites in the late nineteenth and early twentieth centuries brought epidemics of measles, and the influenza epidemic of the 1920s devastated many villages. Tuberculosis also became endemic with the Indians until it was finally brought under control when the U.S. Health Service took over the responsibility for native health in the mid-twentieth century and built modern hospitals at Anchorage and Tanana to which the Tanana natives are sent for treatment.

Culture

Numerous aspects of Tanana life have already been mentioned in connection with the aboriginal subsistence pattern. An attempt will be made here to give only a general summary of the culture as it existed at the time of direct White contact, about 1880. Much of this information was originally obtained from Upper Tanana informants, some of whom could recall their first meetings with Whites in the persons of Joe Ladue, Jack McQuesten, or Lieutenant Allen. Later discussions with informants at Tanacross, Dot Lake, and Healy Lake confirmed the fact that the culture of their group was almost identical with that of the Upper Tanana although their language differed. The testimony of informants from all the remaining groups indicates that the same general culture pattern prevailed along the entire length of the river with only minor differences, chiefly reflecting the presence and use of salmon. Thus the Salcha group, although largely dependent on caribou and moose, spent more time in their summer fishing camps than did their upriver neighbors and consequently made more use of semipermanent dwellings—the bark house and semisubterranean log house covered with moss. These camps were located on the Goodpaster and the Salcha rivers rather than on the main Tanana. What little data there are for the Chena Indians indicate that their caribou hunting was largely confined to the drainage of the Chena River, a clearwater stream that does not have a large salmon run. On occasion they also hunted on the upper Chatanika; therefore, they may be grouped culturally with the Salcha, who are apparently also their closest linguistic kin.

The lowermost Tanana bands seem to have done more fishing along the main river, although they also fished in the clearwater streams and, of course, depended greatly on the caribou resources in the hill country on each side of the valley. On ecological grounds then it is possible to subdivide the Tanana Indians into three general groups: those inhabiting the territory above the Goodpaster River, those inhabiting the valley from the Goodpaster to below the mouth of the Chena, and those inhabiting the lower part of the valley to the Tolovana. Such subdivisions are probably more meaningful to ethnographers than they were to the Indians; however, it is interesting to note that the early travelers Peters and Brooks (1899:74), who traversed the valley in 1898, suggested essentially this same division.

Technology

The caribou hunt by means of the fence or corral was basic to the economic life of all the groups. Moose and mountain sheep were also taken in snares as well as hunted with bows and arrows. The bows were made of birch with a projecting attachment to take the impact of the string and serve as a wrist guard ("Environment and Culture in the Alaska Plateau," fig. 4, this vol.). The arrow points showed a variety of forms depending on the purpose ("Environment and Culture in the Alaska Plateau," fig. 3, this vol.). Arrow points for big game were made of antler, bone, or copper and were serrated. Various snares and deadfalls were used for smaller game. Fish were taken in cylindrical traps and by large dip nets in openings in the fish weirs. Large salmon were also taken in dip nets from canoes. Netting was of twisted bast cordage. Fish were also speared using a three-pronged leister with serrated tines of bone or antler.

Fire was made with a simple cord drill ("Environment and Culture in the Alaska Plateau," fig. 10, this vol.) with a piece of birch fungus as punk. Food was roasted over the fire or boiled in birchbark vessels by means of hot stones. Grease was rendered from the marrow of the long bones and, in cold weather, soup was also made by boiling broken bones. Cooking was generally done by the men.

Snowshoes, vital to winter travel, were of the two-piece, bowed type ("Environment and Culture in the Alaska Plateau," fig. 15, this vol.). Baggage was hauled on toboggans and double-ended sleds. Women supplied most of the traction, since dogs were neither harnessed nor used for pack animals until after White contact (fig. 3). Water travel was by means of small, birchbark canoes, partially decked and propelled by a single paddle. In upstream travel these were propelled by a short pole held in each hand. Larger, skin-covered boats were used for carrying heavy loads, usually meat, downstream ("Environment and Culture in the Alaska Plateau," fig. 14, this vol.).

Smithsonian, NAA.

Fig. 3. A woman, possibly from the Salcha band, with pack dogs along Richardson Highway. Dog packing was a woman's responsibility. Photograph by Ordway, late 1920s.

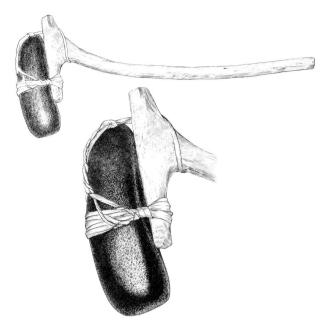

Dartmouth College Mus., Hanover, N.H.: DCM 30–2–4613.

Fig. 4. Upper Tanana stone maul consisting of a cylindrical stone grooved for tying with babiche to an elbowed stick. Mauls were used in the construction of houses and fish weirs, and for other purposes. Length 49.5 cm, collected before 1930.

Stone adzes were used rather than axes. A pointed version of this adz, often double-ended, was used in hand-to-hand fighting, as was a club fashioned from caribou antler and then made heavy by being saturated with grease. A distinctive form of dagger with hilt ending in spiraling antennae was made of native copper ("Environment and Culture in the Alaska Plateau," fig. 5, this vol.). Warfare featured stealth, trickery, and hand-to-hand fighting. Other tools included stone mauls (fig. 4), pestles, crooked knives fashioned from bones, and drills utilizing fox and beaver teeth set in wooden handles. Women used fleshers and beamers made from caribou and moose tibia and semilunate scrapers (chithos, Upper Tanana čỉ·θo·) made from schistlike rock ("Environment and Culture in the Alaska Plateau," figs. 18–19, this vol.). Sewing was done with a bone awl and sinew. Spruce roots and babiche were used for bindings, and the babiche was also twisted and braided into a variety of cords.

Clothing and Adornment

Clothes were made of tanned skins, generally of caribou. Trousers and moccasins were of one piece. Winter moccasin-trousers were of sheepskin (fig. 5). Hoods were often attached to the shirts, which for men had pointed tails. Dyed porcupine quills were used to decorate clothing, while wood and bone items were often incised with simple designs of lines, circles, and chevrons (figs. 6–7). Dentalium shells, secured by trade

Fig. 5. Boy wearing sheepskin moccasin-trousers with hair inside and caribou skin parka with attached hood, with beaded decorations on parka and mitten. Photograph by Robert A. McKennan at Tetlin, Feb. 1930.

570

from the coast, were a sign of wealth and were much prized for personal adornment (figs. 8–9). The men wore their hair in a single, heavy braid that was often stiffened with grease. The nose and ears of both men and women were pierced for the wearing of ornaments (fig. 10), but facial tattooing was confined to the women.

Structures

A variety of house styles was used, the form depending on the season and the duration of stay. A skin-covered, domed lodge was used in the winter camps (fig. 11). The double lean-to, housing two families, was used for more transitory camps. Bark-covered huts were also constructed, particularly at the fish camps. Domical sweathouses were separate and were much used.

Music

Singing and dancing were common, accompanied by a tambourine-type drum. Both songs and dances were highly individualistic and hence varied somewhat from group to group and from time to time. In general they were associated with ceremonial occasions.

Life Cycle

A man was permitted several wives, who quite often were sisters. Although there was no formal bride purchase, the prospective husband customarily secured his spouse as a result of gifts and services to her parents. For the first few years after marriage the young couple normally lived with the girl's parents or with their band.

Fig. 6. Moses Charlie, wearing dentalium necklace and beaded moccasins, carving a spoon with a crooked knife. Photograph by Wallace M. Olson at Old Minto, 1967.

Dartmouth College Mus., Hanover, N.H.: 30–2–4624, 30–2–4626–7.
Fig. 7. Upper Tanana decorated spoons. top, Sheep horn, length 44 cm; bottom, wooden, length 38 cm. Collected by Robert A. McKennan, 1929.

U. of Alaska Arch., Fairbanks: Kristeatter Coll., 67–121–1.
Fig. 8. Chief Healy of Healy River band wearing a beaded leather shirt and a dentalium necklace; the heavy mustache was common (McKennan 1959:85). Photographed about 1920s.

Childbirth took place in a hut specially constructed for the purpose, and a neighboring woman served as midwife. The mother and father were subject to a host of taboos and restrictions, particularly as to their food

571

Fig. 9. White River Johnny (Little John) and family, of the Scottie Creek band. Two wear dentalium necklaces. The small child is carried in a blanket supported by a chest strap. Photograph by Frederica De Laguna at Tanacross, July 1960.

Smithsonian Lib.: Whymper 1869: facing 239.

Fig. 10. Man with nose ornament, dentalium ear pendant, and typical knife or dagger in decorated scabbard hung from neck. Men wore feathers in the hair on festive occasions, the small ones held in red clay applied to the back of the head (Whymper 1869:239). Engraving after Frederick Whymper sketch, June 1868.

and drink, both before and after the child's birth. Babies were carried in a distinctive type of birchbark sitting-cradle (fig. 12). While the birth rate appears to have been high, high infant mortality together with the hardships of Subarctic existence resulted in relatively small families. Boys underwent austere training emphasizing endurance and dexterity, the qualities needed for the role of hunter and warrior.

Menstruation was regarded as a critical period for a woman, particularly the first menses, and at this time she was compelled to live in a special menstrual hut, avoid gazing upon men or upon the sun, refrain from eating fresh meat, take her drinking water only through a bone tube, and observe other taboos of a similar nature.

In the old days the Tanana Indians usually cremated their dead together with the deceased's personal property. With the first White influence burial replaced cremation, and a small house was built over the grave.

Social Organization

Tanana social organization featured exogamous matrilineal descent groups. The basic number of maximal descent groups apparently was three, and this tripartite system was particularly marked among the peoples on the lower river. At least two of the maximal units were composed of a number of clans. The third, or middle, descent group might be a single clan. It seems to have enjoyed an intermediate and somewhat amorphous position, "almost a cousin to us all" as informants sometimes put it. (See "Upper Tanana River Potlatch," this vol., for further discussion of Tanana descent groups.) Although the descent groups were not totemic, they were often associated with animals, such as the caribou and the bear, and had various migration legends. Quite evidently they constitute an old element in Tanana social organization.

The matrilineal descent groups were regarded as large consanguineous families that cut across group boundaries, and when in need an Indian could look to his fellow moiety members or clansmen for help or hospitality. In addition to his clansmen an Indian could turn for aid to his formalized "partner," who was often both his cross-cousin and his brother-in-law due to the practice of preferential cross-cousin marriage. Rights and duties were reciprocal between partners and included the specified division of any game taken by either.

The kinship terminology of the Tanacross and Upper Tanana bands is bifurcate collateral for the parental generation. For ego's own generation siblings and parallel cousins were called by the same term, while cross-cousins were terminologically differentiated from siblings and parallel cousins, but not from each other—

U. of Alaska Arch., Fairbanks: C.S. Farnsworth Coll., 75–175–267.

Fig. 11. Old Sam and family of the Healy River band in their winter hunting camp on the Middle Fork of the Fortymile River, near the later village of Joseph. Domed skin-covered lodge at right; a platform at left holds caribou meat and skins. Photograph by C.S. Farnsworth, during the preliminary survey for the Eagle-Valdez Military Telegraph line, March 1901.

left, Natl. Mus. of Canada, Ottawa: VI–X–1 b; right, Alaska Histl. Lib., Juneau.

Fig. 12. left, Birchbark baby carrier stitched with spruce root. After padding of an absorbent material such as moss is added, the infant's legs hang over the sides, separated by the vertical tonguelike structure. Length 32.5 cm, collected 1886. right, Baby in birchbark carrying cradle. Spruce boughs serve as tent flooring. Photograph by Albert J. Johnson of Fairbanks, about 1915.

the so-called Iroquois system. The Lower Tanana kinship terminology system is essentially the same (Michael E. Krauss, communication to editors 1978).

The Tanana set great store by the "potlatch," or ceremonial giving-away feast, usually honoring a dead relative. The potlatch was an important part of the native ceremonial life, and it served to bring the members of different bands together. It also enabled a chief to validate his position as a successful hunter and a wealthy man (see "Upper Tanana River Potlatch," this vol.).

Political Organization

Each band had its headman or "chief" (fig. 13), who was assisted by a "second chief." The caribou fences on which the bands' welfare depended were considered the property of the chiefs. Chiefs were characterized as having been rich, wise, and able orators. Often they had shamanistic powers as well, which further strengthened their position. Chieftainship tended to follow certain family lines but under no rigorous rule of inheritance; it might pass from a father to either a son or a maternal nephew, or even to a son-in-law.

Religion

The native religious beliefs and practices centered around shamanism. The shaman was believed to pos-

sess special spiritual power, which he secured by means of dreams. This power was most commonly used to cure sickness. Since sickness was believed to be the result of some evil spirit that had gotten into one's body, treatment consisted of removing this sprit and was accomplished by means such as sucking on the afflicted part, blowing, or exorcising, the exact method varying with the individual medicine man. Shamans were also believed to possess the power to bring misfortune, illness, or even death, and hence were much feared. They likewise were credited with powers of divination, although this ability was possessed by other individuals as well.

In addition to shamanism the native religious life featured a host of taboos, many of which clustered around critical occasions such as childbirth, menstruation, giving a potlatch, hunting, and fishing. Certain beliefs appear to have been general: the fear of a bogeyman or "Brush Indian" who hovered about camps; the belief in a race of manlike monsters with tails who formerly inhabited the area; a reverence for both the dog and the otter with the result that the Indians were reluctant to kill these animals. In addition to a variety of legends and folk tales the native mythology contained two distinct myth cycles that were told the length of the river. One cycle, narrated only in the winter, dealt with the exploits of a mythical culture-hero and

Episcopal Church Arch., Austin, Tex.

Fig. 13. Some of the participants who attended the chiefs' conference at Fairbanks in the summer of 1915 (see "Intercultural Relations and Cultural Change in the Alaska Plateau," fig. 9, this vol.) (Patty 1971:2–18). Photographed on a less formal occasion and wearing less traditional garb. standing, Chief John, Chena; Chief Charlie, Minto; Alexander Titus, Manley Hot Springs; Jacob Starr, Tanana village; Chief William, Tanana village; Chief Thomas, Nenana; Rev. Guy H. Madara of the Episcopal Church; Chief Ivan, Cosna; Julius Pilot, Nenana. seated, Paul Williams, Tanana village (interpreter); Chief Alexander, Tolovana; Chief Alexander William, Tanana village; and Chief Joe, Salchaket. Photograph probably by Albert J. Johnson, Fairbanks, 1916.

the other centered on the exploits of an anthropomorphized Raven, who was something of a trickster.

Prehistory

Only two sites pertinent to Tanana prehistory will be mentioned here. The Village site at Healy Lake (McKennan and Cook 1970; Cook and McKennan 1970) is located where an Indian settlement was thriving in 1930 but was deserted by 1962. Systematic excavations in 1966, 1967, 1969, and 1970 underneath the debris from the historic village have revealed a more or less continuous occupation beginning at about 9000 B.C. and lasting until about A.D. 1400 based on a series of 22 radiocarbon dates. Because the upper levels show no cultural disconformity, with the stone projectile points and knives manifesting a continuity in their development, Cook and McKennan (1970a) have suggested that Athapaskans or proto-Athapaskans occupied this site as early as 2000 B.C., although it is obvious that continuity in lithic tradition does not necessarily imply continuity in language. Microblades (small prismatic flakes, presumably made to fit into grooves cut into bone and antler projectile points) are found at all levels, and this trait, at least, can be considered part of prehistoric Athapaskan culture.

Dixthada, some 50 air miles to the southeast, is clearly an Athapaskan site, since it is Kheeltat's village visited by Allen in 1885. Excavations there by Rainey (1939:365–366) in 1936–1937 and by McKennan and Cook (1972) in 1971 produced a variety of tools and ornaments of native copper, stone tools, microblades, and serrated leister points of bone with incised decorations, plus trade goods of the historic period. The 1971 excavation demonstrated that there had been an earlier occupation of this site featuring a core and microblade industry with a date of about 500 B.C. and a later occupation beginning at about A.D. 1200, thus completing the seriation begun at Healy Lake. Although it is possible that the microblades of the later occupation resulted from the excavations by natives for their semisubterranean houses, the evidence from Healy Lake indicates that microblades were used by protohistoric Athapaskans. The copper ornaments and incised decorations also add an aesthetic element to early Athapaskan culture.

Synonymy§

The Tanana Indians are named from the Tanana River; they have been called Tananas (Whymper 1869:240) or Tanana Indians, 1883 (Schwatka 1900:345) since the period of first contact with Americans, these terms usually including the Koyukon bands on the lower part of the river. Other early references use the Kutchin name *tanan g^wəčín* (or *gučín*) 'Tanana River people' (Katherine Peter, communication to editors 1979), learned by Hudson's Bay Company men at Fort Yukon; this appears as Tannin-Kootchin, 1848 (Murray 1910:83), Tanna-Kutchi (Richardson 1851, 1:398), Tā-non Kutchin (B.R. Ross in Gibbs 1865), Tenán-Kutchín (Dall 1870:108, 431), Tenăn´–Kŭt-chin´ (Dall 1877:29, with the incorrect statement that this is "their own tribal name"), and Tpanata Kuttchin, Tanan Kuttchin, Tpananæ-Kouttchin (Petitot 1865, 1876:xx, 1891:361). Neither the translations of the type 'people of the bluffs', 'gens des buttes', 'mountain men' (Murray, Richardson, Petitot, Dall, Whymper; Hodge 1910:727) nor those of the type 'large river people' (Ross) are supported by linguistic analysis (Michael E. Krauss, communication to editors 1978). Equivalent is Koyukon *tənən hŏtanə*.

In 1885 Allen (1887:136–137) coined the names Tananatána (for all the Tanana River Indians), Nabesnatána (for the Indians on the upper Tanana), and Nukluktána (for the "two or three small tribes" on the lower part of the river). These were formed by adding -tána, Allen's rendering of Ahtna *Wie·ne* 'people of', to the name of the Tanana River (from Koyukon or Kutchin), to Ahtna *nabe·sna?* (Kari and Buck 1975:85), which Allen took to be the name of the Tanana, and to Nuklukayet (Koyukon *nukələɣoyət*, Henry, Hunter, and Jones 1973:34), the name of the traditional intertribal trading ground at the confluence of the Tanana and the Yukon. The information that the river was called Tananá by the Indians of the lower river and Nabesná by the upriver Indians (Allen 1887:68, 84, 136) most likely reflects familiarity with different foreign names, since these are not the names for the river in any of the three Tanana languages. Osgood (1936:15–16, 19) shortened Allen's names to Tanana and Nabesna and applied them differently. Allen had used Nabesnatána (and Upper Tananatánas, Allen 1887:25, appearing as Upper Tananas in Allen 1900:415) for the Tanacross speakers at Mansfield (Kheeltat's village) as well as for the Upper Tanana speakers, but Osgood's Nabesna covers only the latter. Allen's Tananatána were the people of the whole river, while Osgood's Tanana included Allen's Nukluktána, the Tanacross-speaking part of Allen's Nabesnatána, and several Koyukon bands on the Kantishna and the Yukon. The term Upper Tanana, reintroduced by McKennan (1959:17), follows local English usage.

Tanana self-designations are Upper Tanana *dineh šu·* and Tanacross *dandé·y ín*, both meaning 'the people'.

§This synonymy was written by Ives Goddard, incorporating material supplied by Robert A. McKennan. The Upper Tanana names were furnished by Paul G. Milanowski (communication to editors 1979), the Tanacross by Ronald Scollon (communication to editors 1979), the Lower Tanana by Michael E. Krauss (communication to editors 1978), and the Koyukon by Eliza Jones (communication to editors 1978). The Ahtna names (Mentasta dialect if with *Wie·n* 'people of') are from Kari and Buck (1975:58).

Northern Tutchone has ӡan to hoṫyán? as a general name for 'Tanana people' (Ritter, McGinty, and Edwards 1977:82).

A list of "tribes along the Tanana" was recorded by Allen (1887:137) from a Yukon River Indian but has not been confirmed from other sources; in order from the upper river down are: Nutzotin, Mantotin, Tolwatin, Clatchotin, and Huntlatin. Also of uncertain identity are the San-to-tin´ and Sa-tshi-o-tin´ groups reported to be in the same area (Dawson 1889:203B). The village names Allen (1887:74–79, map 3) gives are simply the names of their chiefs: Nandell's (Last Tetlin), Tetling's (Tetlin), and Kheeltat's or Khiltat's (Dixthada site near Mansfield), incorrectly located by Hodge (1907c:679) on the Nabesna. Local group designations recorded in the 1970s are: (Upper Tanana) čo· godn ni·gn ṫi·n 'Scottie Creek people', (Upper Tanana) θe· cą· ӄa· ṫi·n, (Ahtna) ӡełtnaWṫe·n 'upper Nabesna–upper Chisana people', (Upper Tanana) na·biah ṫi·n, (Ahtna) ǫesci·ge Wṫe·n 'Northway people' (cf. Upper Tanana ƙeh θi·gn 'Northway fish camp'), (Ahtna) natǫeӡi Wṫe·n 'Tetlin people', (Ahtna) WdisaWṫe·n 'Tanacross people' (cf. Upper Tanana dihθa·dn 'Mansfield'), (Ahtna) salca Wṫe·ne 'Salcha people', (Ahtna) taγṫi·l Wṫe·ne 'Nenana people', (Lower Tanana) bəntəxʷṫǽnæ, (Koyukon) bəNtə hŏṫanə, (Ahtna) bentaWṫe·ne 'Minto people'. Other recorded Upper Tanana place-names are te·łąiy 'Tetlin', nahƙadn 'Last Tetlin', and še·ki·h če·gn 'Ketchumstuk'.

Sources

The starting point for knowledge of the Tanana is Allen's (1887) account of his journey down the river from Tetlin to the Yukon in 1885. The geologists Peters and Brooks (1899) who traveled the length of the Tanana River in 1898 likewise have left an excellent account of their boat journey although their emphasis is more on the geography than on the native inhabitants. Brooks (1953), who spent the next 30 years in Alaska with the U.S. Geological Survey, is rich with information on many aspects of the interior during the early mining years. Wickersham (1938), an active participant in Alaskan affairs during this same period, provides much helpful information, historical and otherwise, including an account of his trip up the Kantishna River in 1903.

The only published accounts of an anthropological nature that deal with the natives are those of McKennan on the Upper Tanana (1959) based on nine months' residence with these people in 1929–1930, on Athapaskan social organization (1969a) based on a demographic field study along the entire length of the Tanana River in the summer of 1962, on ethnohistory (1969), and on physical anthropology (1964). McKennan's military service, 1942–1943, in the area and several summers between 1966 and 1972 devoted to archeological fieldwork in Tanana country permitted incidental ethnographic work with the natives. Admittedly much of the cultural information contained in this chapter was obtained from the Indians of the upper valley. This is partly because good ethnographic information for the lower Tanana is much harder to acquire and partly because the Indians of that area had somewhat earlier contacts with Whites and also suffered more drastically from the disruptions and dislocations that accompanied the early mining era.

Upper Tanana River Potlatch

MARIE-FRANÇOISE GUÉDON

The potlatch was in 1970 the only traditional public ceremonial occasion of the upper Tanana River Indians. The midwinter ceremony had been replaced by Christmas festivities and survived only in a few riddles, a strong feeling against telling myths in spring or summer time, and the native names of the month corresponding to December: 'hook game month' or 'big month'. Other ceremonies, such as the ritual procession protecting the village during a lunar eclipse and the meal for men only following the killing of a bear, are but a memory.

Between July 1969 and September 1970, nine potlatches took place in the area west of the Yukon-Alaskan border, involving speakers of the Upper Tanana, Tanacross, and Ahtna languages. The participants came from the villages of Tetlin, Northway, and Tanacross (see "Tanana," fig. 1, this vol.)—the last two including the people formerly at Mansfield, Kechumstuk, Last Tetlin, and Healy Lake—and also from Mentasta, an Ahtna village (see "Ahtna," fig. 1, this vol.). The following description is based on data and recordings gathered during the preparation of and participation in seven of these feasts, supplemented by comments about the potlatch, past and present, from Tetlin and Tanacross people (Guédon 1969–1972).

In 1969 the inhabitants of the three upper Tanana River villages of Northway, Tetlin, and Tanacross were divided into exogamous matrilineal descent groups, or clans, cross-cutting villages and bands. The clans were grouped into two moieties, or "sides." Of the 17 clan names mentioned by the people living at that time, seven (including ʔał ċą ʔ dine· and nį·si·, both related to Marten) were of the nalci·n 'Raven' (or "Crow") side and 10 were of the čą· 'Sea Gull' side, also known as the Wolf Side.* The Crow population was much larger than the Sea Gull population—99 as opposed to 15 adults. The members of the čika·k yu· clan, although it belongs to the Crow side, were allowed to marry with both Sea Gull people and members of the other Crow clans. This created three exogamous groups of clans. However, the dual pattern was emphasized by cross-cousin marriage and by the recognition of the father's clan as opposed to the mother's clan: one's father's clan, which was often one's husband's or one's wife's clan, was described as the "opposite" clan or the "people on the other side." In the more extended social world, the "opposite side" included members of all the clans that were related to one's father's clan, namely all Crow clans if one was a Sea Gull, all Sea Gull clans if one was a Crow. čika·k yu· people might then merely remark that they are "in the middle." The term cross-relatives is used here to designate all relatives who do not belong to one's " mother's side"; they are grouped in a single category by the Upper Tanana people.

The Circumstances for Potlatch

The native term ti·ł is usually translated as 'potlatch'. One does not "hold a potlatch;" one "gives a potlatch" as a host to mark or commemorate an event in the life of another person. ti·ł designates the formal and public distribution of gifts to cross-relatives of that person and to members of his or her opposite matriclans. This giving away is preceded by one or several sessions of dancing, eating, and feasting and occurs on various occasions—a child's first kill, indemnity for an offense, remarriage, any special celebration, and death.

When a child, especially a boy, kills various meat animals for the first time, the particular animal cannot be kept or eaten by the boy or his family. It has to be given away to the child's cross-relatives. If it is small game, it can be given together with two or three blankets without other ceremony. If the parents are rich enough or if it is a large meat animal (moose, caribou), a potlatch has to be given. A favorite daughter may also have a potlatch given for gathering her first berries.

A potlatch can also be given as a payment for an offense—murder, a fatal accident, or an injury—to a member of an opposite clan. Given by the offender, or sometimes by a relative in the name of the offender, to the offended party, this ceremony is a very serious matter.

A person who wants to remarry after the death of a spouse is supposed to give a potlatch to the members of the former spouse's clan. There are some indications that in former days the clan could claim almost all of this person's wealth (McKennan 1959:134).

*The Indian words appearing in italics in this chapter are in the Upper Tanana language, written in the phonemic system described in the Upper Tanana orthographic footnote in "Tanana," this vol. They were furnished by Paul G. Milanowski.

A potlatch may be given to honor someone after a special deed or to celebrate the return, recovery, or rescue of someone. The guests are the cross-relatives of the person for whom the potlatch is given, and most especially those relatives who have expressed sympathy or provided help during the preceding hardship. Older people of Tetlin found quite normal, and praiseworthy, the potlatch given in 1969 by an Ahtna man to children at Chistochina for a dog which had recovered from a broken leg.

Death is the most imperative circumstance for a potlatch. After the death of any person, a potlatch has to be given for the deceased by one or several close relatives (father, mother, brother, sister, child; father's or mother's sibling; sometimes a parallel or cross-cousin; more rarely a grandparent or grandchild). Several years may pass between the funeral and the potlatch; the potlatch can also be given prior to the death of the person. In such cases, a small potlatch is given to conclude the funeral, thank the visitors, and pay the deceased's cross-relatives who took care of the funeral and all other matters pertaining to the disposal of the corpse. These persons are the guests of honor, but every person who has expressed his or her participation in the sorrow of the hosts is usually repaid by some gift.

While a small potlatch is given for a deceased child, an adult requires as important a potlatch as possible. A small potlatch may also be given for a favorite dog, to pay the owner's cross-relatives who take care of the dog's body. Although the exact date of the event has been forgotten, a bear that once killed two Tetlin men was subsequently captured and forced to attend their funeral and feast as guest of honor and prisoner. The bear was then choked on the fumes of the pyre, which were intended to make him cry.

Several persons may give a potlatch at the same time. Usually there is a main host who meets most of the expenses, but less wealthy people often take advantage of the occasion to give away a few blankets. Each giver has his own pile of blankets or his own heap of gifts, and speeches specify exactly who gives what. The givers do not have to belong to the same clan. However, all the persons for whom a potlatch is given should preferably belong to the same "side," that is, to clans grouped together in the same moiety.

Whatever the circumstances, a potlatch is basically a transfer of goods from the host to the cross-relatives of the person for whom the potlatch is given.

A person who gives a potlatch for a relative belonging to his or her own clan has little difficulty in amassing goods from this clan. On the other hand, a person who gives a potlatch for somebody of a clan different from his or her own clan has to provide most of the wealth, for he or she will not receive much help from others. For example, if a man gives a potlatch for his wife or for his child, that is, a person belonging to his wife's clan, he may expect some help from his wife's clan but practically none from his own family except from a few relatives, maybe his brother or his parents, who are going to act as cohosts with him. It would thus seem that the potlatch is based on an opposition between a clan acting as a host and a clan or group of clans acting as guests. The opposition is still more evident when, as is supposed to be the case, the host-clan is represented by a whole localized clan and many or most of the guests come from other bands or villages, although the localized clan may sometimes be joined by the other members of the local band so that the whole village acts as a unit during most of the potlatch; this could be done, for example, at the death of an important chief. Yet, during the last evening, the characteristic opposition between host clan and guest clans reappears in the transfer of gifts.

Fundamentally, the potlatch is a payment, whether this payment is for concrete services or for settling a disagreement. In broadest terms, this "payment"—going to the cross-relatives of the person for whom the potlatch is given—seems to express a concept of basic indebtedness to the father's clan. As one man from Tanacross summarized it, "you are born because of your father's people, that is why you pay back." The potlatch has additional social and psychological functions. The death potlatch, for example, allows the living to mourn their dead relative in an orgy of grief before being told in the next speeches to forget him in the following merrymaking. As "payment" to the people who cry for the dead person, it settles the deceased's debt and thereby frees him from his ties with the living; being contented, he understands he has to go away. Finally, no matter what the occasion for a potlatch, the hosts almost invariably gain prestige and subsequent power. According to one participant, a potlatch is a social occasion on which one gives away everything one owns, leaving oneself with nothing but the resulting good reputation and "big name," becoming thereby a "rich woman." Thus anyone who gives a potlatch is in fact rich, but without potlatching no amount of personal wealth gives high status.

The Potlatch Sequence

Preparation

A person who wants to give a potlatch does not talk much about it. For several months or years, the host-to-be piles up blankets, food, and other goods in his cache. These are not supposed to be touched for any other purpose, are treated with respect, and are protected from bad influence that might "spoil the luck." Little by little, the whole village becomes aware of the host's intentions and involved in the preparations. Each household makes room for three or four guests, for the adult population is likely to double in size during the several days of the ceremony.

Formerly, potlatches were held inside a special enclosure out of doors, where the gifts were exhibited to everyone's sight. By 1969–1970 each Tanana, upper Tanana, and Copper River village had a community hall—a large log cabin usually furnished with benches along the wall, some tables, and a cooking stove—where potlatches were given.

Invitation

The invitations are supposed to be formally delivered. A certain formality is still observed as far as the old people of the upper Tanana River and high-ranking Ahtna Indians are concerned; they prefer to wait until the invitations are delivered in the proper way, by one or two well-esteemed messengers. The messengers are supposed to adopt a pleading attitude when inviting and the guests must look reluctant to accept.

A serious potlatch in the upper Tanana area includes guests from at least all upper Tanana groups and most of the northern Copper River villages of the Ahtna Indians. Upper Tanana Indians are often invited to potlatches given by the Ahtna Indians.

A potlatch in any one of the upper Tanana villages is likely to attract people from the whole upper Tanana area, invitation or no invitation. Some come to help the hosts; some come as guests, even if they have to invite themselves. The kinship connections are so tight that practically every upper Tanana native has a right to sit at a potlatch given for somebody living or having lived in Tetlin, Northway, or Tanacross. So, it may be sufficient to invite by "passing the word around."

Reception of Guests

Only the formal visit to the host recalls the elaborate reception that used to be organized to greet the guests. In the 1920s groups of guests announced their coming by lighting smoke on the trail. Each group mustered around its chief some distance from the host village, waiting for the others. When properly dressed, all the guests entered the village as a unit. The welcome ceremonial included volleys of rifle shots, beating of drums or rattles, offering of small gifts, and welcoming songs and dances. Endicott (1928:120) recorded a spectacular reception of this kind when Chief Healy gave a potlatch at Healy Lake in July 1927.

The arrival of the guests in the mid-twentieth century has been more casual. In the 1960s, as before, the main meal held in the afternoon brought together the local people and the guests. Meanwhile the guests visited around the village.

Feasting

In the feast house, the chiefs and the most important guests ideally are seated along the wall facing the door.

In the past, guests were probably grouped according to clans, regardless of the locale from which they came. In the mid-twentieth century the guests tend to gather according to village membership, apparently not daring to sit near a relatively unfamiliar person. The hosts do not eat with their guests but may sit occasionally with them.

The distribution of food is organized so that some persons stand out as guests of honor. Those persons are given basins and baskets of food, and it is their privilege to "give it away" or share it with the people seated near them.

In former days, a host of a death potlatch could bring some of his guests to share a part of his sorrow by giving them very strong tea or "something to make them sick"—cups of fish grease or an infusion of tobacco leaves. The guests so treated were chosen people who would receive many gifts later as compensation. Such "tricks" were also used to silence a man who was speaking too much.

During the meal, songs and speeches burst out to thank the hosts or to express satisfaction and wishes. Empty pans are thrown rolling on the floor while the men utter special calls. The general atmosphere is always joyful.

Dancing and feasting go on for several days, as long as there is enough food. On the last day, all the remaining food is to be distributed to the guests.

Songs, Dances, and Oratory

People may start singing and dancing at any time during the afternoons. The main performances are held after the meal. All new songs are carefully rehearsed. Upper Tanana Indians proudly recall that during all the twentieth century they have never really stopped dancing and singing. The vitality of the local traditions is recognized by the neighboring Indian groups who appreciate the new songs being composed. A few composers, including a group of women in Tetlin, and some of the best drummers in the area have become famous from Copper Center to Minto.

Since 1969 the tape recorder has been an essential element of the rehearsals. Recordings help the singers to remember the songs, especially the first measures, which are difficult to catch. Besides, a new song is subject to changes and may be forgotten rapidly if it is not recorded in some way. With a tape recorder one can fix a song even while it is being composed. Tape recorders are also used more and more frequently during the ceremony, and people have begun collecting tapes of the songs and speeches.

The Indians divide the songs performed during a potlatch into three categories: "potlatch songs" or "lucky songs," "sorry songs" or "worry songs," and "dance songs." The "potlatch song" is sung once in the evening and marks the beginning of the serious celebration. It is slow and ceremonious, its purpose being to "bring back money and meat, bring good luck." It has to be sung, without any mistake, by the hosts and the singers of the host village who have participated in the preparation of the ceremony, at the host's request. They simply enter in a procession and stand in a semicircle. The atmosphere must be very quiet. During or before the potlatch song, the air may be "cleaned" by burning fragrant plants or other smoky material. A fire that catches quickly and burns strongly with enough smoke means good luck.

The potlatch song is followed by "sorry songs." Composed at the death of one's relative or dear friend, they are repetitions of short sentences expressing one's grief, and their slow rhythm is very close to sobbing. They are accompanied by a gesture of the hands held in front of the body and moving up and down, "as if they were catching the tears." The dancers hold feathers or scarves in their hands. The original circle of singers moves slowly, usually clockwise. Little by little men and women who are serving as assistants are progressively invited to join the circle, and others enter by themselves, close relatives first, then neighbors, followed by distant acquaintances. Songs composed for previous funerals or potlatches are soon introduced. Since the guests are then reminded of their own dead relatives, the whole hall is soon involved in a general crying and mourning. Everybody is brought into the singing and dancing. The songs are led by a few renowned local drummers; the composers of the songs may take the lead, helped by a drummer friend.

When the song leaders judge that the mourning has lasted long enough, they introduce "dance" songs of a more lively nature. Yet mourning can start again at any time, so that crying and laughing alternate for a while, until dancing predominates. (While mourning may last several hours for a potlatch following a funeral, it may be reduced to a few songs on other occasions.) The "dance songs" are diversified in rhythm, tune, and meaning. They are accompanied by energetic dances that often act out, in a very stylized manner, the words of the song. Many songs are said to have been introduced from other Indian groups. The "gunho dances" are supposed to have been brought by the Dawson City Indians of the Yukon. They are named for the long dance paddles (*ganho·k*) decorated with beads and ribbons that are used by the best male dancers to direct the dances of the other men or simply to accentuate the dancing. The so-called Eskimo dances are characterized by a double beat and accompanied by a jumping back and forth, feet together, "just like a puppet." Other dance songs are said to have come from the Tlingit Indians via the Ahtna of the Copper River. Sorry songs are sometimes treated as dance songs and sung to a slightly faster tempo. Love songs may also be performed during a potlatch, often jokingly, but not war songs or shaman songs. The dances are led sometimes by the local singers, sometimes by groups of guests. In 1969 and 1970 Tetlin and Northway singers were known to offer a number of new songs and steps, while the Copper River people usually brought traditional ones.

During the dances performed by the men, competition is discernible between individuals as well as between villages. It is also a characteristic of some of the oratory during the recesses. These oratorical contests are often likened by the Indians to fights. They oppose speakers of different clans, one after another responding to a challenge. Speeches of this kind are delivered in an archaic language and are based on tradition and native history, including wars and former potlatches, all elements being referred to in obscure allusions. Boasting is allowed, as are comments about one's ability to sing, drum, and dance. Later, just before the gifts are distributed, speeches of a different kind will announce the amount and kind of the contributions, but although these may contain old-style references, there is no competition involved. From time to time, between the mourning songs and the dance songs, a small group grotesquely dressed comes in to entertain the assistants and make them laugh with their antics.

Gifts

On the last afternoon or evening of the series of feasts and activities, the main and most serious part of the ceremony takes place. The hall has to be carefully swept. Blankets or sheets are laid on the floor "so everything is clean, nothing dirty or dusty." The gifts are brought in through a window rather than the door, for "with potlatch things you have to be careful" and should a menstruant walk through the door the "good luck" would be spoiled.

The host piles on the floor the blankets, furs, clothes, guns, tools, and scarves that comprise his gifts. When there are several hosts, each one stands near his or her pile. In effect, while the feasting is a communal affair, the distribution of gifts is organized so as to identify carefully each participating host, so that there are several smaller potlatches going on in addition to the main one. A "chief" or famous old man makes a speech on behalf of each giver to identify the gifts, their provenance, and the total amount of money expended by the host and those who helped him accumulate the items; he also specifies the nature of the kin ties between the host and the person so honored. In addition to the main reason for a potlatch, the host may announce an honor bestowed on someone, such as a name given to a child. The gifts are then distributed and carried to the recipients by the host and by helpers he chooses among his close relatives. A host is guided in his choices by the persons who contributed to his pile of gifts. The distribution often lasts several hours. At the end, the important guests may stand up to thank the hosts, yet there is no formal ending to the potlatch and the participants simply drift away, carrying sleeping children, piles of blankets, and boxes of food back home.

Aftermath

Ideally a host is supposed to strip himself of all his possessions. If his distribution has been large, his newly established prestige will enable him to receive many gifts at later potlatches. A man from Tanacross explained: "Potlatching is just like a bank. When you give away, those people have to give you back next time. What I put down, they have to remember." His enhanced prestige will encourage aid from his relatives and clanmates in future potlatches. On the other hand, a host must remember who helped him and the amount of each contribution: "You have to give them back the same, later. If you give me two blankets, maybe next time I will help you the same way. That's the way they're supposed to do."

After a potlatch, the hosts have to be careful. The events may leave them vulnerable to bad luck. Furthermore, the excesses of grief, the excesses in food and dance, and the boasting, whether in speeches or dancing demonstrations that took place during the feast, may draw the attention of the nonhuman powers to the participants, especially to the donors who, by giving away so much wealth, seem to claim they are rich.

To avoid repercussions, for two 30-day periods the host should practice the same ritual taboos as a girl reaching her puberty: staying quietly at home, or, better, in an isolated place, without talking, laughing, touching his face, or stretching his legs; eating sparingly and only bits of dried fish or meat; drinking very little and only lukewarm water, ideally with a straw so as not to open his mouth and not to let the water touch his lips; keeping clean and taking frequent steambaths; and keeping away from the sky, the woods, the fire, game animals, and women.

Some people are said to know magic songs or tricks to help them regain their money faster. These include keeping a little bag of duffel taken from a potlatch blanket or a pinch of the dust from an ant nest, for ants are thought to give potlatches: one can see them carrying food all the time, the ant eggs resemble blankets, and *ya· mạ·gn te·šaiy* the mythical 'he who travels around the earth' is said to have heard the faint sound of tiny drumming coming from an ant nest.

Koyukon

A. McFADYEN CLARK

The Koyukon (ˌkäyōō'kän) are the northwestern-most Athapaskans of Alaska. They inhabit regions adjacent to the lower and middle Yukon River, the Kantishna River (a tributary of the Tanana) as far up as Lake Minchumina (Hosley 1968:9; Henry, Hunter, and Jones 1973; Loyens 1966:277; McKennan 1969), and the Koyukuk River as far north as the south slope of the Brooks Range (fig. 1). They are fragmented into a number of bands or territorial village groups and recognize no tribal unity.

The Koyukon have generally been divided into two or three major divisions, though the criteria used and the details of the classification have varied (Zagoskin 1967:243; Osgood 1936:14; De Laguna 1947:27–31; Dall 1877:25–28; Loyens 1964; Clark 1974). Here three geographically and culturally defined divisions are recognized: (1) the Upper Yukon division, which includes the Koyukon living along the Yukon River from Stevens Village down to Koyukuk just below the mouth of the Koyukuk River; (2) the Lower Yukon division, which includes the Koyukon along the Yukon from Nulato to the Blackburn Creek and those in the Kaiyuh Slough–Khotol River region; and (3) the Koyukuk River division, which includes the Koyukon living along the Koyukuk River and its tributaries.

This tripartite division appears to correspond to the Indians' own perception of the major distinct groups of Koyukon, and it delimits the subunits of the Kuyokon that differ from one another culturally. For example, the Lower Yukon division differs significantly from the other two in social structure, belief system, and many aspects of ceremonial life. The Koyukon of the Lower Yukon and Koyukuk divisions have long interacted with their Eskimo neighbors, and their culture bears unmistakable marks of Eskimo influence not present in the Upper Yukon division. The three divisions also differed in their relations with other groups and with one another. The Lower Yukon people traded with the Yupik and Inupiat Eskimos of Norton Sound, while those of the Koyukuk division traded with the Inupiat Eskimos of Kotzebue Sound, the Kobuk and Selawik rivers, and the Anaktuvuk Pass area and occasionally intermarried with the Kobuk and Selwik people. Members of the Upper Yukon division traded with the Tanana and had amicable relations with the Koyukuk division, but the two were frequently on hostile terms

with the Lower Yukon division, with which they traded as well. In the 1840s Zagoskin (1967:137, 178, 190–191) reported both trade and warfare between the Lower Yukon Koyukons (of different subdivisions) and the Ingalik.

A number of subdivisions of the Koyukon may be recognized, though lack of complete information makes it impossible to be certain of their exact distribution throughout the entire Koyukon area, especially since it appears to have changed somewhat in the course of the nineteenth and twentieth centuries. De Laguna (1947:27–31) distinguished six Koyukon subdivisions on the basis of dialectal differences and Indian opinion in 1935, and three more can be added by making further sociopolitical distinctions (Clark 1974:1–6; Zagoskin 1967:243). The subdivisions thus recognized are as follows: in the Upper Yukon division, Stevens Village–Tanana, Tanana-Nowitna, and Nowitna-Koyukuk; in the Lower Yukon division, Ulukagmyut and Takayaksa (or Kaiyuhkhotana proper); and in the Koyukuk division, Yukon-Kateel, Huslia-Dalbi(Dulbi)-Hogatza, Todatonten-Kanuti, and South Fork. In addition, the poorly known Koyukons of the lower Tanana River and the Kantishna River appear on the basis of linguistic evidence to have comprised two groups, Minchumina–Bearpaw and Cosna-Manley (Krauss 1979; "Northern Athapaskan Languages," this vol.). The delineation of the Upper Yukon subdivisions is particularly uncertain, as there have been extensive population movements in this area in the historical period and the modern settlements are of mixed origin.

Language

The Koyukon speak a language of considerable internal diversity that has three major dialects and several distinct subdialects* (Clark 1961–1972; Henry, Hunter, and Jones 1973; Krauss 1979; "Northern Athapaskan

---

*The phonemes of Central Koyukon are: (voiceless unaspirated stops and affricates) b, d, λ, ʒ, g, g̣, ʼ; (aspirated stops and affricates) t, ƛ, c, k, q; (glottalized) t̓, ƛ̓, c̓, k̓, q̓; (voiceless continuants) N, ł, s, Y, x, h; (voiced continuants) m, n, l, z, y, γ̇; (full vowels) i, a ([æ·, a·]), o ([ɔ·]), u; (reduced vowels) ə (with several central and front allophones), ȯ, ü. Prevocalic x is optionally pronounced [h]. In Lower Koyukon m replaces b. Within Central Koyukon the Upper Koyukuk subdialect (spoken at Hughes and Allakaket) differs in having the

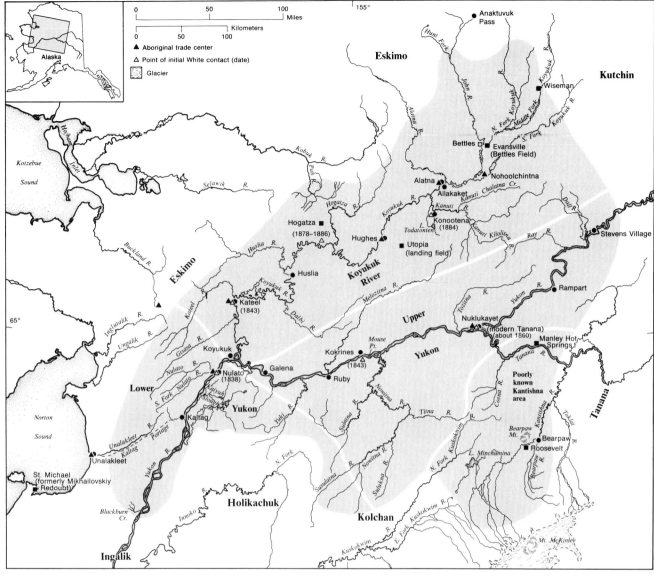

Fig. 1. Tribal territory in the 19th century with major cultural divisions.

Languages," this vol.). The three dialects are Lower Koyukon, Central Koyukon, and Upper Koyukon; in an earlier classification (Krauss 1973:907–908) the Lower and Central dialects were grouped together as Outer Koyukon and the Upper dialect was called Inner Koyukon. Lower Koyukon is spoken by the Lower Yukon division, but the other two dialects cut across the other two divisions. Central Koyukon is spoken by members of the three lowermost subdivisions of the Koyukuk division and by the two lowermost Upper Yukon subdivisions, while Upper Koyukon is the dialect of the South Fork Koyukuk subdivision and of the Stevens Village–Tanana subdivision of Upper Yukon, as well as of the lower Tanana–Kantishna Koyukons. Within Central Koyukon the so-called Upper Koyukuk subdialect, spoken originally by the Todatonten-Kanuti subdivision, differs in certain words and other features (Clark 1961–1972; Henry, Hunter, and Jones 1973). In

pronunciation [ɣ] for *y*. Upper Koyukuk and the Upper Koyukon dialect have *ŭ* for the *ŏ* and *ŭ* of the other dialects. Upper Koyukon also differs from all of Central and Lower Koyukon in shifting the velar series (*g, k, k̇, Y*) to *ž, č, č̇, š*, respectively. Other differences among the dialects involve especially the presence or absence of word-final segments.

In the practical orthography in use since 1977 the phonemes of Koyukon are written as follows: b, d, dl, dz, g, gg, ' (the last not written word-initially); t, tł, ts, k, kk; t', tł', ts', k', kk'; nh, ł, s, yh, h, h; m, n, l, z, y, gh; ee, aa, o, oo; i and a (depending on allophone),

ʉ (or u), u. The shifted Upper Koyukon consonants are: j, ch, ch', sh. A hyphen is used to separate clusters of affricates and glottal stop; hence *c*ʔ is written ts-' to distinguish it from unit *č*. This orthography differs from that of Henry, Hunter, and Jones (1973), especially in eliminating all underlined letters.

Information on Koyukon phonology, dialectology, and the correct transcription of Koyukon words was provided by Eliza Jones and Michael Krauss (communications to editors 1978). Cited Koyukon words are in the Central Koyukon dialect, except where otherwise specified.

the twentieth century people originally from different bands came together in settlements along the major rivers, and as a result both Central and Upper Koyukon were spoken in the villages of Allakaket, Tanana Village, and Rampart. By the 1970s, although there were several hundred speakers of Koyukon, no children were learning the language and the lower Tanana–Kantishna subdialects were nearly extinct.

Territory and Environment

The Koyukon territory is a vast region that cross-cuts several ecozones (see "Environment and Culture in the Alaska Plateau," fig. 1, this vol.). All regions share a strong continental climate with short hot summers, when temperatures sometimes reach 95° F., and long cold winters, when in the northern part of the Koyukuk River division the temperature may drop to −84° F. It is also a region of little precipitation and light snowfall. Parts of all three regions are underlain by permafrost. The two Yukon divisions share the lowland flats with their myriad bogs, sloughs, and small lakes, as well as the adjacent forested rolling and mountainous upland areas. The terrain along the lower Koyukuk River is quite similar to that along the Yukon River, but as one goes farther north it becomes more arid with numerous uplands and mountains, and a proportionately greater extent of open taiga. The regions of all three divisions share many types of flora and fauna although in different proportions.

Among the flora are: black and white spruce, juniper, poplars (including aspen and cottonwood), birch, alder, and willows, with a ground cover of *Cladonia*, sphagnum, various grasses, sedges, heather, fireweed, and the myriad tundra flowers. Edible products of the land include blueberries, lowbush cranberries (lingonberries), highbush cranberries, cloudberries (salmonberry but different from the salmonberry of southern Alaska), raspberries, edible rose hips, wild rhubarb (*Polygonum alaskanum*), wild onion (chives), licorice root (*Hedysarum alpinum*), and wild parsnip (*Pastinaca*).

A variety of ducks, geese, swans, swallows, ptarmigan, and spruce hens (grouse) are important to Indian subsistence, while the loon, eagle, raven, owl, and hawk are important in myth and ritual or are used for other nonculinary purposes. Fish of greatest economic importance are king salmon, primarily on the Yukon with only a few on the Koyukuk River, coho and chum salmon, several varieties of whitefish, blackfish, shee (inconnu), grayling, lingcod, and pike. The most important mammals, used either for subsistence or materials for manufactures, are moose, caribou, Dall sheep, brown, grizzly, and black bear, porcupine, beaver, hare, lynx, wolf, fox, wolverine, mink, marten, otter, weasel, marmot, and ground squirrel.

The two Yukon divisions of the Koyukon have a far greater abundance of salmon than does the Koyukuk. In the 1970s moose were plentiful in the regions of all three, but in the past quantities have varied in different areas from none to only a few, and they were especially scarce about 1900. The people of the Koyukuk have had more caribou, which were nearly absent from the Yukon divisions from the early 1900s and have only returned there in any numbers since 1970; and they alone among the Koyukon have access to Dall sheep in the Brooks Range.

History of Contact

Direct contact by Europeans with the Koyukon on their own soil came late, in 1838, when Pëtr Vasil'evich Malakhov of the Russian-American Company first reached the Yukon River from Mikhailovskiy Redoubt on Norton Sound. He established a trading post at Nulato to cut off Koyukon trade with the Eskimos of Norton and Kotzebue sounds. Less than 50 years later all major riverways in Koyukon territory had been explored. Sustained contact was uneven among the three divisions, and as a result differential culture change was still evident in the 1970s, with the Koyukuk River division villages of Allakaket and Hughes continuing to be the most traditional.

Initial Russian contact was with members of the Lower Yukon division, who then numbered about 425 (see table 1). Prior to exploration by the Western Union Telegraph Company in 1866–1867, Russians had explored the lower Koyukuk River to Kateel in 1843 and about 1860 the Upper Yukon division territory as far as the native trading ground of Nuklukayet near the mouth of the Tanana River. In 1866 and 1867 Ivan Semënovich Lukin, William H. Dall, and Frederick Whymper of the Western Union Telegraph expeditions ascended the Yukon by boat to the Hudson's Bay Company post in Kutchin territory at Fort Yukon. The next 20 years saw development of river transportation and trading posts concomitant with the coming of prospectors, military exploration, and missionaries. Military parties on the Kobuk River (Stoney 1899) and the Yukon River (Allen 1887) entered the virtually unexplored Koyukuk River region in 1885. Except for the Yukon-Kateel group, initial home territory contact with the Koyukuk had been only the year before, at Konootena, by traders from the Yukon.

During the 1890s gold prospectors entered the Yukon Territory of Canada and eastern Alaska by the thousands. By 1898 the gold rush was in full swing, creating considerable traffic and settlement along the Yukon River. There also were local gold rushes in other parts of Koyukon country. On the Koyukuk River this was followed by missionization at Allakaket, but on the Yukon several missions preceded the gold rushes. After

584

Table 1. Population Estimates

Division	1843[a]	1880[c]	1885	1903	1973[f]	
Lower Yukon	264	447		346[e]	(503)	647
Upper Yukon		485			(902)	1,228
Koyukuk River	289[b]	150	276[d]		(491)	645
Total	about 1,100?	1,082			(1,896)	2,520

[a] From Zagoskin (1967:307); after the smallpox epidemic of 1839.
[b] Lower Koyukuk and associated Yukon River settlements only.
[c] Calculated from census figures given by Petroff (1884:12).
[d] From Allen (1887:141).
[e] From Loyens (1966:142).
[f] Based on Department of Interior Draft Environmental Statement DES 73–97:table IV on the Proposed Koyukuk National Wildlife Refuge, Alaska. Figures in parentheses represent native residents of Koyukon villages, while main figures are the enrollment of natives irrespective of location. Eskimos are here excluded, but some non-Koyukon Athapaskans are included.

the gold rushes until the beginning of World War II, itinerant miners and traders as well as missionaries worked in Koyukon territory, but during this period many Indians continued to follow their earlier subsistence and settlement patterns. Table 2 gives an outline of contact history, a periodization of events and the types of impact these made on Koyukon culture.

Culture: Contact-Traditional Lifeways, about 1843–1906

Exploitative Groups and Territoriality

Each major Koyukon geographic division was subdivided into smaller areas, which were at the same time both residential and exploitative in nature. The concomitant social group was the band with its semipermanent village, its households and nuclear families. In the Upper Yukon and Koyukuk divisions band populations were small. Some had not many more than 50 persons at the time of contact, although each band covered a rather large well-defined territory frequently 50–75 miles across.

Bands of the upper two divisions were based on a core of several matrilineal extended families, to which a few other unrelated people frequently attached themselves. Among the Lower Yukon people where clans were absent, band territory was exploited by members of primarily endogamous semisedentary village groups. In all divisions, two families usually shared a dwelling and together formed a household, except in cases where a hunter had a large polygynous family and had an entire dwelling of his own. Several household units were located close to one another and formed a small village. Members from these smaller aggregates—family, household, and village—variously worked together as cooperatives at different times of the year within the band territory. But at certain times, especially during caribou migrations in the fall and spring, members from several villages and sometimes from different bands gathered to exploit resource areas together.

Parts of each band region were shared communally, while others were considered to be private, family-held property. Among the Koyukuk beaver houses and ponds, muskrat swamps, fishing locations, bear hibernation holes, certain big game territories where fences were built, berrying grounds adjacent to fish camps, and some bird hunting areas were privately held. After 1900 mink and marten traplines and after 1940 wood lots were added to the list. Most large game hunting, fowling, and berrying grounds were considered open land and were jointly exploited.

There was no tribal unity, but persons from the several bands within each division recognized affiliation with others with whom they married and with those who spoke closely similar dialects. Even though there was no political centralization, members from the bands within a division considered themselves to be one people, as opposed to all others whom they designated as outsiders. Amicable interdivision interaction obtained only between the Koyukuk and Upper Yukon division people who occasionally intermarried and formed alliances for trade and war. These two considered the Lower Yukon Koyukon to be members of a different and frequently hostile "tribe" (Clark 1974, 1975; Loyens 1966; Dall 1870; Zagoskin 1967).

Just as no tribal unity was recognized, there were no divisional or tribal chiefs. Village chiefs have only been elected since 1906 (cf. Loyens 1966:179) when the concept was introduced by United States territorial officials. Exceptions to this include several outstanding individuals, such as "Chief" Moses (fig. 2), who acted as a major spokesman for the upper Koyukuk people just prior to the gold rush in 1898. However, at the band as well as at the semipermanent village level, there were local "rich men," "big traders," or caribou fence and fish-trap "bosses" as well as important warriors and medicine people to whom others turned for guidance. Among the Lower Yukon Koyukon, a council of elders sometimes was called upon to make decisions in time of crisis.

585

Table 2. Koyukon Historic Events

Period	Date	Characteristic or Special Events	Source
Indirect contact (1649–1827)	1649	Russian trading post on Anadyr River in Siberia provides extra stimulus for native trade.	Bogoras 1904–1909, 1:53–54
	1789	Anyui Trade Fair established on Kolyma River (Siberia) to trade in tobacco; intercontinental native trade.	D.J. Ray 1964
Protohistoric (1829–1837)	1829	Russian reconnaissance of Norton Sound for site for post to control Yukon-Siberia native trade.	Zagoskin 1967
	1832	Post established on Kuskokwim River (among Ingalik). Named Kolmakovskiy Redoubt in 1841.	Zagoskin 1967: 251–252 Bancroft 1886:553
Direct contact on the lower Yukon and lower Koyukuk rivers (1837–1844), and contact-traditional period there (1838–1900) begins	1837	Glazunov makes initial contact with Koyukon in their own territory.	Zagoskin 1967:135, 189
	1838	Malakhov reaches Nulato on the Yukon and in 1839 builds cabin, the first trading post among the Koyukon (permanently manned after being rebuilt in 1841).	Zagoskin 1967:146–147, 183
	1839	Koyukon ravaged by smallpox.	Zagoskin 1967:147
	1843	Koyukuk and Yukon rivers explored by Zagoskin to Kateel and confluence of the Nowitna River respectively.	Zagoskin 1967
	1844	Russian Orthodox missionaries present at Mikhailovskiy Redoubt on the coast.	Loyens 1966:115
	1847	Hudson's Bay Co. post established by Murray at Ft. Yukon above Koyukon territory; trade among natives is stimulated.	Murray 1910
	1847–1851	Koyukon obtain muzzle loaders from Kotzebue Sound and Ft. Yukon through intertribal trade.	Starbuck 1878:450–451; Raymond 1900; Murray 1910
	1851	Nulato massacre: one of many Koyukuk River division raids against Lower Yukon Koyukon.	Clark 1961–1972; Bancroft 1886
Opening of the interior, exploration (1865–1885)	1865–1867	Fear of reprisals from 1851 Nulato raid causes movement of some members of Koyukuk River division up the Koyukuk River.	Clark 1961–1972; Dall 1870
	1865–1867	Western Union Telegraph parties explore Koyukon region of Yukon River.	Dall 1870; Whymper 1869
	1867	United States purchases Alaska; administration, trading, and treatment of Indians change.	
	1869	Nulato trading post reestablished by Americans but not continuously maintained.	Raymond 1900:22, 24
	1870–1873	Fr. Petitot and other Roman Catholic missionaries reconnoiter Yukon and baptize Indians at Nulato.	Loyens 1966:116; Thomas 1967:42
	1883	Yukon River explored.	Schwatka 1885
	1883	Epidemic kills many people on Koyukuk River.	Allen 1900
Direct contact with Middle and Upper Koyukuk River division Koyukon in their own territory and beginning of Koyukuk River division contact-traditional period (to 1906)	1884	The trader, Mayo, and an engineer go overland from the Yukon River to trade with Koyukuk at Konootena.	Allen 1900
	1885–1886	Members from Stoney's Kobuk River exploration party explore trade route from upper Kobuk River to Nulato and St. Michael.	Stoney 1899
	1885	Allen contacts Koyukuk at Konootena.	Allen 1887
	1884–1885	Mineral wealth becomes an economic-historic factor. Gold prospecting begins at Hughes on Koyukuk and becomes intense along the middle Yukon River in Upper Yukon division territory.	Orth 1967:436
Missionization, schooling, gold rushes, and initial sedentarization (1887–1906)	1887	Intensive missionization and education begins. Roman Catholic Mission established at Nulato, with contract school.	Thomas 1967; U.S. Bureau of Education 1893

Table 2. **Koyukon Historic Events** *(Continued)*

Period	Date	Characteristic or Special Events	Source
	1887	St. James Mission and school established at Tanana by Canham, Missionary Society of London. Classes taught in Athapaskan. In 1891–1892 this mission is transferred to Episcopal Church.	Canham 1887–1891; Thomas 1967; U.S. Bureau of Education 1893: 1250; Prevost 1892
	1895	Medical missionary at St. James Mission, Tanana, with hospital built by 1900.	U.S. Bureau of Education 1896: 1429; P.T. Rowe 1910–1940
	1897	U.S. Post Office opened at Nulato.	Couch 1957
	1897	First steamboat ascends Koyukuk River.	
	1897–1906	Gold rushes: several thousand prospectors enter Koyukon territory. Extensive two-way traffic on the Yukon, by steamboat and overland, which peaks around 1900 with 46 steamers in operation.	Schrader 1900:458; Grinnell 1901:32; Maddren 1913:76; Mendenhall 1902
	1899	U.S. Army post, Ft. Gibbon, established near Tanana.	Cantwell 1902
	1900	Measles epidemic and food shortage kill 58–67 Koyukon at Nulato.	Cantwell 1902
	1901–1939	Telegraph links Nulato, St. Michael, and other stations along the Yukon River.	Loyens 1966:114
	1901–1902, 1905	Reindeer herds established near Nulato and Bettles; impact of reindeer on Koyukon is nil.	U.S. Bureau of Education 1906
	1903	River boats being converted to oil causes a decrease in wood-cutting jobs for Koyukon.	Kitchener 1954:112
	1905	At Bettles Athapaskan woman opens first school on the Koyukuk River.	Stuck 1906, 1906a, 1914
Early village period (1906–1945)	1906	Episcopal Mission St. John's-in-the-Wilderness established at Allakaket with a day school and medical missionary. Indians and Eskimos settle semipermanently near the mission.	Burke 1961
	after 1906	Most prospectors and miners from initial gold rushes leave Koyukon territory. Local strikes in 1911, 1915, 1917. Mining has continued in the Wiseman district through early 1970s.	R. Marshall 1933; Clark 1961–1972
	ca. 1910	Fish wheels introduced and become popular on the Yukon; tried but not used on the Koyukuk.	Loyens 1966:151–152
	1919	Lead prospectors arrive near Galena.	Orth 1967:358
	1920s	Gasoline boat engines increase mobility from semisedentary villages.	Clark 1974, 1961–1972
	1923	Alaska Railroad reaches Nenana near the Yukon River (in Tanana territory).	Couch 1957:58
	1940s–1950s	U.S. Air Force builds at Galena, Bettles Field, Utopia (Indian Mountain), and Tanana.	
	1942–1945	Koyukon men join U.S. military forces; later others go to Korea and Vietnam.	Clark 1961–1972
Semisedentary lifeways shift to sedentary village focus— all Koyukon divisions 1945	1956	Territorial or federal schools in nearly every Koyukon village, replacing mission schools.	Ray 1959
	1958–1959	Alaska granted statehood; Koyukon schools come under state administration.	
	1970s	Renewed oil exploration of Alaska's North Slope stimulates wage labor and increases nonnative traffic through Koyukon territory.	
	1971–	Native land claims settlement enacted; correlated with increased strength in Tanana chiefs' native organization; Doyon Corporation organized to manage land claims.	cf. G.W. Rogers 1971; Arnold 1976

Episcopal Church Arch., Austin, Tex.
Fig. 2. Chief Moses (b.ca. 1845, d.1935) wearing winter fur parka with wolverine ruff on hood, marten skin hat, high mukluks, and decorated mittens. He was the first recognized chief of the Koyukuk Division of the Koyukon and was known for his strong leadership ability. He traded from the interior directly to Kotzebue instead of trading through intermediaries, which increased his wealth and reputation. He died near Allakaket. Photographed in 1912.

Subsistence

Annual activities (cf. Sullivan 1942 for Lower Yukon division) were distinctly structured in terms of time, place, type of activities, and type of interacting units. These units at various appropriate times consisted of families and households, fishing encampments, and hunting-foraging groups that comprised major portions of a band, entire bands, joint hunting groups from two bands, and, for trading and festivals, various aggregates of Koyukon as well as other Athapaskan and sometimes Eskimo groups.

Soon after breakup, at the end of May or early in June, spring hunting and trapping camps were vacated and people gathered at the mouths of major tributaries to hold communal feasts of ducks, geese, and muskrat, which had been killed during spring hunting.

When the salmon run began, families moved from their rendezvous points to their fishing sites where they gathered around "bosses" who directed the construction or repair and installation of salmon traps and weirs. Women also set gill nets in sloughs or quiet eddies or near the mouths of major tributaries along the Koyukuk River; only infrequently were nets set in the Yukon. In years when the salmon run was small, some families left the rivers and installed traps in tributaries to catch whitefish and suckers. Later, with the introduction of commercial twine, nets almost completely supplanted the use of traps on the Koyukuk; and with the introduction of the fish wheel about 1910 (U.S. Bureau of Education 1911:1362; Loyens 1966:151) the Yukon people began to use it almost exclusively. On the Koyukuk the net fishery resulted in a proliferation of smaller fish camps, while the introduction of the fish wheel created large camps on the Yukon. Concomitant with fishing, hunting continued but it usually was limited to the vicinity of the fish camp. As soon as berries began to ripen women, children, and old people picked them to store for winter use. Late in the summer men from several local groups joined one another to hunt in the hinterlands. Hunters made frequent moves and cached their meat at strategic points to be picked up on their return. During the hunters' absence women, children, and old people continued to fish and gather berries that would later be cached in birchbark-lined pits or taken with them to their next encampment.

The men returned from their hunting forays as the days began to get cooler and darker and together with their families went to fall camps on outlet streams adjacent to larger lakes. Men set grayling and whitefish traps in the streams and continued to hunt locally, while women and children dried fish and snared small game. About this time of the year people moved into their winter villages, which consisted of several semisubterranean houses. Winter villages were usually a short distance from their fall camps and frequently near a caribou fence.

Around the middle of October southward-migrating caribou usually began to arrive in northern Koyukon territory, especially along the Koyukuk where people from the Upper Yukon division, accompanied by their families, sometimes joined those from the Koyukuk to kill caribou as they came through the passes onto the adjacent uplands. After the major migration, families withdrew to their long caribou fences ("Environment and Culture in the Alaska Plateau," fig. 2, this vol.) and, under the direction of the fence boss, set snares and worked the fence as a cooperative enterprise. Between breaks in hunting, keyhole (fig. 3) or basket traps, and in later times nets, were set under the ice in rivers to catch ling, shee, whitefish, and pike; inverted traps were set in lakes to catch blackfish, a fish that frequently sustained these small populations in periods of otherwise poor fishing and hunting. As the fur trade became increasingly important, in November when pelts were becoming prime, men began to work their traplines while those not so engaged continued to fish through the ice. Along the lower Yukon hunting was intensified as caribou began to spread out in small herds throughout the willow country.

When the shortest days of winter arrived, there was little hunting and trapping and practically no fishing because the ice usually was too thick. During this period the Indians visited nearby groups for their high season festivals.

When the darkest days of winter had passed, Koyukuk traders, some accompanied by their families, went on trips to the Brooks Range or to the Kobuk and Selawik rivers to trade with the Eskimos, or to villages of the Upper Yukon division and, after Russian contact, to Nulato. Some Lower Yukon division people went to Norton Sound, or their Eskimo trading counterparts visited Koyukon territory. Others went out from their winter houses on extended hunting-foraging-trapping trips, while the oldest people remained behind to fend for themselves. In years when game was scarce, this was an especially difficult period and people would then be nearly constantly on the move in search of food. Since 1900 men trapped marten on late winter treks and some had trapping camps at their turnaround points. In some places the caribou fences were again manned during spring.

In April people began to move to muskrat camps located near ponds and lakes. Snow was still on the ground, but soon the lakes thawed sufficiently around the edges for canoeing. Men hunted muskrat, beaver, and waterfowl, while the women set nets for pike, small whitefish, and suckers. Women too trapped muskrats, sometimes at camps separate from the men. Spring break-up comes during middle to late May. When the rivers were clear, people went back to their summer locations along the rivers, or, en route, tarried awhile on one of the tributaries near their spring camp to take advantage of runs of fish coming from the lakes and to continue hunting ducks and geese.

Social Organization

Members of Upper Yukon and Koyukuk River divisions of Koyukon had a matri-Iroquois system of kin-

Poldine Carlo, Fairbanks, Alaska: Carlo 1978:77.

Fig. 3. Joseph Stickman (Otzosia) (left), a medicine man who died in 1933, his wife Anna Stickman (K'Oghotaaineek) (center), and their son-in-law Andrew Johnson (right), checking winter fish traps. Joseph Stickman was from the upper Innoko. Photograph by Bernard Hubbard, Nulato, 1930.

River Times, Fairbanks, Alaska.

Fig. 4. Marylene Esmailka ice fishing on the Yukon, with snowmobile attached to sled in foreground. Photograph possibly by C. Perdue at Kaltag, in the 1970s.

ship nomenclature. Among the people of the Koyukuk in 1885, at the time of direct contact, descent was reckoned lineally through one of three exogamous matriclans. These were: *toniʒəʔ ɣəlcilə* '(one) continually made in the middle of the river', *bəʒəY tə χŏtanə* 'caribou people' and *nolcinə* (variously explained as referring to iron, copper, or bear) (Clark 1975). De Laguna (1975) and Jetté (1906–1907) list quite similar names for the clans of the Upper Yukon division. The system was classificatory, and certain terms, for example, those for older or younger brother and sister, mother's brother, mother's sister and her children, as well as terms for grandparents and grandchildren, were extended to one's clan mates within the division as well as to those from similarly named clans elsewhere (cf. De Laguna 1975). Clan as well as band exogamy was the rule among the Koyukuk, and initial matrilocal residence was preferred. A similar system appears to have existed among the Upper Yukon division people (De Laguna 1975; Jetté 1906–1907), although it is not so well documented for them as for the Koyukuk. After 1900 the structure of the Koyukuk system began to change, and by 1970 nearly all knowledge of the three-clan system had been lost. Most people, except the most traditional ones, thought and operated in terms of a bilateral structure, which was rapidly losing all nuances of the earlier system (Clark 1975).

The Lower Yukon Koyukon differed in that they, like some Ingalik, did not, so far as is known, have clans (De Laguna 1975; Jetté 1911:714, 1906–1907:402), though their kin nomenclature is classificatory and of the Iroquois type (Loyens 1966:79), which may represent a retention of terminology from an earlier clan system. Unlike the other two divisions, the Lower Yukon of earlier times practiced both village and band endogamy.

Among all three divisions marriage was preferentially division endogamous, although by 1885 there had been a few marriages between the Koyukuk and Upper Yukon bands and some with Eskimo from the Kobuk. By 1915 on the Koyukuk, clan and band exogamy had also begun to break down. The Lower Yukon division people seldom married outside their own, but when they did it was with Ingalik and infrequently with Norton Sound Eskimo. Only on very rare occasions did they marry members of the other two Koyukon divisions.

Marriage to anyone with whom close kin relationship was recognized was forbidden in all three divisions, except to cross-cousins and certain affinals such as one's deceased brother's wife or sister's husband. Initial marriage with matrilateral cross-cousins was preferred, while patrilateral ones were second choice. Because parallel cousins were equated with sisters and brothers, marriage to them was forbidden; and since missionization and a general shift to bilaterality among the Koyukuk and Upper Yukon divisions, cross-cousin marriage has not been permitted either.

Polygyny was practiced and was not restricted to the marriage of sisters. In most polygynous marriages the man had only two wives, but some wealthy ones had as many as seven or more. Polyandry also existed, but it usually was not of the fraternal type and appears to have occurred primarily out of exigency in times of decimation of population by warfare or disease.

Life Cycle

Some aboriginal belief and practice on marking life passages continued in the 1970s although in attenuated form, while others fell into disuse only in the 1960s. By 1970 the major observances still practiced by the more

traditional families were certain menstrual cycle restrictions, strong parental influence in selection of mates by their offspring, when practicable temporary bride service with initial matrilocal residence, and funeral feasts for the dead that are locally called "potlatches" (fig. 5). Unless otherwise specified, the following patterns are described as they were remembered rather than practiced (Clark 1961–1972) and were particularly typical of the Koyukuk River division.

• BIRTH Women continued to work during pregnancy, practicing a few food restrictions, such as taking only cold food and drink and avoiding freshly killed game. As the fetus enlarged the expectant mother sometimes wore a soft, tanned strap of caribou or moose skin below her abdomen to support the additional weight. Birth almost always occurred outside the family dwelling.

An older woman, or infrequently the woman's husband, acted as midwife. During delivery the mother assumed a squatting or kneeling position, while the attendant pushed down on her abdomen and back to assist delivery. As an alternative a horizontal pole was suspended above her head over which she placed her arms to help her force the child from the uterus. After birth, the umbilical cord was tied with sinew, severed from the placenta with a stone knife, then rubbed with black soot. Part of the cord was saved and sewed into a small bag that was worn by the child to ward off danger, and the afterbirth was wrapped in skin and hung in a tree far from the trail. Infants were not fed for a day or two and usually were not named until they were about a year old, or when there was some assurance they would live. Following the birth, both the

Fig. 5. Participants in a potlatch at Tanana, with women wearing feather headdresses. Photograph by Coagen and Allen, Jan. 1917.

mother and father ate only cold food and drink and avoided freshly killed game. The father also refrained from working with sharp tools, and he was restricted from hunting for at least a month. Infanticide was practiced occasionally but was not limited to females.

• PUBERTY Female puberty rites were very strict, whereas almost none other than first-game ceremonies were imposed on the males. At the onset of menses the girl was secluded in a small hut, sometimes as far as a half-mile from her people, where she remained for nearly a year. By 1900 seclusion had been shortened to less than six months, by 1960 the longest was for two months, and by 1970 a girl was no longer secluded away from the family, although her bed was separated from others by a blanket or partition. While in seclusion, a girl's mother, mother's sister, or other older woman attended her from time to time, brought food, and instructed her in domestic arts. She ate only cold foods that were not freshly killed, kept her head elevated even while she slept, wore a menstrual hood and mittens, and used a drinking tube and a special cup and bowl. The cup and bowl she continued to use during succeeding menses after her seclusion ended. On leaving her hut for her daily ablutions, a girl was required to keep her head down and was prohibited from walking on game or hunter's trails. After initial seclusion, women continued to cover their heads (in the 1970s only kerchiefs were used) and take separate trails during each menstrual period until they reached the menopause.

• MARRIAGE Marriage partners were selected by one's parents; selections were based on the skills of the respective partners and the standing of their families. Rich men and shamans selected whomever they wished as spouses. Additional wives were sometimes obtained through barter, for example, after contact for copper pots or metal knives. Yet in other instances, female children were betrothed to older men several years prior to the onset of menstruation. There was no marriage ceremony until the mission period, which began with visits of Russian priests as early as the 1840s on the lower Yukon but not until 1906 on the upper Koyukuk. Usually the prospective groom lived with the bride's family while she was in puberty seclusion and worked and hunted with her father and unmarried brothers. When additional wives were taken, often the first wife retained the position of control and authority, while the younger ones worked under her supervision. Especially pretty young wives enjoyed privileges, and it was they who accompanied their husbands on trips to other territories.

Divorce was easy, but sometimes acrimonious. The woman and children usually returned to her family.

• DEATH Elaborate mortuary ceremonialism followed death, a time the Koyukon considered to be very dangerous because the newly released spirit of the deceased

could bring harm to his fellowmen or take them with him to the land of the dead. Careful attention to prescribed ritual could allay his wrath and assist him on his way to the land of the dead where he would remain until reincarnated.

The following is a description of Koyukuk people's practice in the past, but many of the customs are still followed. In all three regions rites attendant to death, in addition to those of the Christian faith, continue, but by 1910 inhumation in graveyards was the rule, periods between initial and final feasts had been shortened, ornamental grave houses (fig. 6; "Expressive Aspects of Subarctic Indian Culture," fig. 10, this vol.) had been added, the number of days spent in feasting had been shortened, and the gifts distributed included contemporary items.

On the Koyukuk as death approached, the person was taken from his dwelling to a small shelter or covered with skins outdoors. People from a clan other than the dead person's moved the body to a safe place and washed and dressed it in entirely new garments, then placed it on a scaffold away from the dwelling. Female relatives in the encampment began to wail intermittently and continued to do so for several days. A fire was set in front of the dead person's dwelling, and most people remained inside to prevent the spirit of the deceased from taking someone with him to the land of the dead. The next morning, men assembled and attempted to run the spirit upriver, away from the settlement.

As soon as practicable, the body was wrapped in caribou skins, taken preferably to an area of large trees, and placed on a scaffold between two of them; if the locality was devoid of large trees, the body was placed in a dry spot at the base of a small one and covered either with logs or during later periods by a conical cache. Some useful possessions, such as a sled, bow and arrows, a knife, or a cup, were placed either with the body or on the grave.

Disposal of the body set in motion a series of feasts or "potlatches" of varying size and participation ("Environment and Culture in the Alaska Plateau," fig. 23, this vol.). The first was at graveside when those involved with the burial ate a bit of food and burned some for the deceased. The second was given that night when the same individuals and members of the bereaved family again ate together, sharing bits of their food with the deceased by burning some in the fire.

These were but preludes to the major feast for the dead (fig. 7), which preferably was held during the winter solstice a year after death. Each day during the week-long festival, which was held inside a log enclosure, now inside the community hall, was characterized by special events in addition to communal feasting. During the mortuary festival special foodstuffs were distributed to guests to take home with them. Days

Frederica De Laguna, Bryn Mawr, Pa.

Fig. 6. Overall view (top) and close-ups of graves in cemetery at Koyukuk. left, Grave houses built about 1918 with poles, one at left with carved bird on top and cagelike structure that appears to be blackfish trap belonging to the woman buried there. right, Older graves with pyramidal roofs probably related to those on old semisubterranean houses. Photographs by A.J. Eardley, 1935.

592

CLARK

were also devoted to games, riddling, feats of strength, and dancing. These culminated with the final feast, presentation of eulogies, and with especially composed commemorative songs frequently accompanied by dancing. There were other dances where participants carried wolf and wolverine skins, and in later times unrolled bolts of cloth, and then the final distribution of gifts was made to those who had assisted at the time of death. All the possessions of the deceased were distributed to invited guests. In the 1970s many items were retained by the immediate family, including all major household accoutrements, dogs, and dwellings. It was thought that those who took part in distributing the goods were acting solely as intermediaries for the dead person and that the recipients received some of the power of the deceased along with the gifts.

Until after the gifts had been distributed circumlocutions were used when referring to the deceased. Once these prescribed functions had been performed, his spirit usually was satisfied and content to go to the land of the dead and remain there until time for rebirth. Some spirits, particularly those of shamans, continued to stay nearby either to help friends and relatives or to cause evil to enemies.

Religion

The Koyukon view of their supernatural universe was based on a concept of all-pervading spirits who controlled the world and constantly posed obstacles to the maintenance of health and welfare of the people. They developed a workable system for dealing with the spirits in their universe that stemmed from their transition world myths (*q̇ədon čədni*), which date from the time when people could change into animals and animals could change into people (Clark 1970a; Jetté 1907, 1908–1909). This system involved an intricate network of taboos and concomitant practices and abstinences that permeated the fabric of their culture and permitted them to meet effectively the challenges advanced by their unseen adversaries. Beside their belief in a hierarchy of primarily malevolent spirits was a belief that all humans and animals as well as many inanimate objects also had spirits, which could be turned to good or evil practice at the whim of their owners.

Bear, wolf, lynx, wolverine, most of the furbearers, and some birds, like man, were believed to have two spirits: a major life spirit that left the body only at death and a second spirit that could "come out easy" and temporarily leave the body during illness or shamanistic performances. The animals named above were considered to be "rich" or prominent "people" in Koyukon mythological time. Some also were denoted by human kinship terms, for example, bear was called "grandfather" and wolf "brother," while all were considered to be ones who at will could change back and forth from man to animal or vice versa (Clark 1970a; Jetté 1907; Loyens 1966; Sullivan 1942). The killing of a bear, lynx, wolverine, and in earlier times a wolf, was followed by a special ritual and a feast. Names of these ceremonial animals were not mentioned, and when they were being hunted circumlocutions were used.

Other animals, for whom a feast was not given, were treated with respect when they were killed, and almost all furbearers were fed after they had been shot or trapped. The bones, skins, hair, and inedible parts of game animals, birds, and fish were disposed of in a specified manner in the animal's habitat to ensure they would return to life, procreate, and thus be a continuing source of food. Strict observance of nearly all these practices began to diminish by 1960, but some were continued into the 1970s, especially by the more traditional people on the upper Koyukuk River.

In addition to feasts given for ritual animals, ceremonial feasts, which continued into the 1970s, were held during the winter solstice, now coincident with Christmas, when members from the local group, and frequently guests from other groups as well, gathered to celebrate the time when the "long and short days meet" in expectation of the longer brighter days to follow. Memorial potlatches or feasts for the dead frequently were held in conjunction with the winter festival. Activities, exclusive of the memorial feasts, included: exchange of gifts and elaborate distribution of food; communal banquets; speeches by elder clan members; games; dog, snowshoe, and snowmobile races; feats of strength; dancing; and presentation of newly composed songs. Earlier there were riddling contests, which would not be given until after the shortest days had arrived. These heralded the end of the recitation of the *q̇ədon čədni* myths told in fall. Smaller celebrations with somewhat similar motifs were held in earlier times when the first salmon arrived, especially among the Lower Yukon Koyukon (Sullivan 1942:20–21), and during trading festivals. Practice in the mid-twentieth century was also to have a "potlatch" and dancing on the occasion of the construction of new houses, marriages, major wedding anniversaries, carnival and dog races in the spring, and the Fourth of July, as well as on some other legal and Christian holidays (cf. Kroul 1974 for discussion of "potlatch" at Koyukuk on the Yukon).

• SHAMANISM Shamanism earlier played a leading role in control and guidance of many beliefs and practices of the Koyukon (Jetté 1907). It was extant in the 1970s but in a much attenuated form, and most people living in the 1970s who have felt the call to shamanism have refused it and have been successfully aided by others to avoid becoming active. Power has diminished markedly since the 1960s although some persons continue to practice in minor capacities. Each person is thought to have some supernatural ability, but only the

River Times, Fairbanks, Alaska (upper left); Tanana Chiefs Conference, Inc., Fairbanks, Alaska (upper right and all lower).

Fig. 7. The Stick Dance (*xiyo*) (upper left) is one of the major events of the Feast for the Dead or memorial potlatch organized by family and friends to commemorate the memory of the deceased and to thank publicly those who helped at the time of the death. The ceremony includes eulogies to the deceased, feasting, dancing, singing, and gift giving. The name refers to the special spruce stick or pole that is carried around the village (upper right) and then lashed to a crossbeam in the skylight of the community hall (lower left) where dancers move clockwise around it, men closer to it and women on the periphery. The pole is decorated with colored ribbons (lower center) that are torn off for luck and with wolf or (as here) wolverine skins that are later cut into strips and distributed to guests to be used as ruffs on parkas (Carlo 1978:61–70; Loyens 1964:134–136). Women dance in special potlatch dresses with feather headdresses, such as worn by Jessie Sipary here (lower right). Photographs by Doug Tobuk at Nulato, 1974 (upper left); by Barry McWayne at Nulato, 1975 (upper right and all lower).

594

shaman, who may be either male or female, had strong pervasive power and among them only a few achieved the highest rank of the five possible attributed to shamans by the Koyukuk. Shamanistic power was usually inherited and could come through either the father's or mother's lineage. It lasted for four generations, then usually disappeared, only to return to the line at a later time. Spirits of powerful deceased shamans could also become reincarnated in the body of a newborn or young person. Recognition of power was obtained through dreaming. Frequently, once power was obtained, other practitioners guided one in attaining greater power. Among the shamans' repertoires were: curing the sick; warding off evil produced either by spirits or other shamans; finding lost objects; giving or conversely taking away one's luck in hunting, war, or love; waging war through telepathic communication; and predicting future events. Koyukon shamans frequently but not always performed under a large animal-skin blanket; traveled great distances either through the sky or under the rivers, usually in the guise of their familiars; used dried animal skins that represented their spirit helpers—for example, frog, mink, marten—through whom they projected their voices while in a trance; used special amulets and other paraphernalia; and almost always charged for their services.

Mythology

The Koyukon had a highly developed and sophisticated repertory of myth and legend, related variously to different periods of their five-period universal time-reckoning scale: the hazy time before light and land were found; the time when people could change into animals and animals into people; the time that started when their culture hero *k̓ətətalqani* 'he who went off visiting by canoe', went around the world and changed all things into their present form; legend time or long, long time ago; and the period they and their immediate ancestors knew, or memory culture time that extends to the present. This rich oral tradition, which was used to teach the young the ways of the culture as well as to entertain, had central themes that included the Raven myths, the *k̓ətətalqani* cycle, orphan boy makes good, cannibals and giants, sky-earth motifs, bushman, feats of shamans, riddling-game stories, funny occurrences, and "historic" events.

Music

Many Koyukon songs and dances were related to myth and legend, but there were other songs and dances that were composed locally. Most music and dance of the 1970s was of Western or international origin and have been learned from radio, records, or contacts away from the villages. In the 1970s traditional native dancing was done only at festivals and potlatches. The older people also still enjoyed the Western two-step, square dance, and Virginia reel.

Trade

The Koyukon had long played an important role in aboriginal intertribal commerce, trading interior goods to their Eskimo partners on the coast, where, in turn, the Alaskan Eskimo bartered North American goods to their Siberian counterparts for both native and European items. From Siberia the Alaskans obtained reindeer skins, tobacco, metal pots, knives, lances, and strike-a-light steels, which at the time of Russian contact in North America were being exchanged for wooden utensils and furs (Zagoskin 1967:100–101). In addition to furs and other wares designated for intercontinental trade, inland goods such as red paint stone, fringed garments, and other manufactured items were traded from the interior to the coast for seal oil, sealskin, and bearded seal hide for mukluk soles (Bogoras 1904–1909, 1:53, 7:681–682, 686–687; Kitchener 1954:156; Whymper 1869:162–165; Dall 1870:161–162; Stoney 1899:808–810; Allen 1887:102; Clark 1974:205–247; Rainey 1947:267). In fact it was for the specific purpose of intercepting the native inland-coastal-Siberian trade that the Russian traders first explored the Yukon and established their deepest interior post at Nulato ("Intercultural Relations and Cultural Change in the Alaska Plateau," figs. 2–3, this vol.). Competition in trade also appears to have been one of the prime movers in development of hostile relationships between peoples of the Lower Yukon division and those of the Upper Yukon and Koyukuk River divisions inasmuch as both the Koyukuk and people from the Lower Yukon division had direct links to the coast. Further, these two vied for control of trade with the Upper Yukon division.

Inter- and intradivisional trade was transacted both at intermediate points and at large trade fairs. Intermediate points were at the mouth of the Nulato River on the Yukon, sometimes at the mouth of the Koyukuk, on the Koyukuk near the Kateel River, and at points adjacent to the contemporary villages of Huslia, Hughes, and Allakaket, at the mouth of the South Fork, and also at Hunt's Fork on the John River, where trade was conducted primarily between the Upper Yukon division, Koyukuk River Koyukon, and Eskimo. The Lower Yukon division people attempted to trade at the mouth of the Koyukuk and sometimes near the mouth of the Tanana with the Upper division Koyukon (Zagoskin 1967:177–178), but primarily they traded at Nulato and Kaltag Portage, and at Unalakleet on Norton Sound.

Larger trade fairs were held periodically at Nuklukayet on the Yukon near the mouth of the Tanana and at Norton Sound where the Russians later established Mikhailovskiy Redoubt (Saint Michael); a few Koyukuks went to the Eskimo fair at Hotham Inlet on Kotzebue Sound. At Nuklukayet Yukon and Koyukuk River people met traders from the Tanana and probably the upper Innoko rivers (Zagoskin 1967:167–168; Dall 1870:93; Whymper 1869:210). At the coast, the Lower Yukon division people met Ingalik as well as local Norton Sound and visiting Eskimo (Zagoskin 1967:137 for Ingalik on the coast; Van Stone 1979:66, 70 for Ingalik and Koyukon on the coast).

Trade was almost always transacted through well-established partnerships. These have continued, especially between the Koyukuk River Koyukon and their Eskimo counterparts, through the 1970s. From the 1920s until the mid-1960s little native trade was carried on, but since that time with increased ease of transportation there has been a modest reaffirmation of old trade relationships and a concomitant resurgence of trade between Koyukuk Indians and the Nunamiut, Kotzebue Sound, and Kobuk Eskimos (Clark 1974:205–247; Clark and Clark 1976).

Hostilities

From precontact times until about 1870 the Koyukon carried out raids on other Koyukon villages, on the Eskimo, and on neighboring Athapaskans. Those from the Koyukuk and Upper Yukon frequently joined together in raids against people of the Lower Yukon division. These raids may have been an important factor in dividing the Koyukon into the present three sections, if indeed they ever were a single discrete group. One of the better known altercations was the Nulato Massacre of 1851, although according to informants it was only one of a continual series of raids between the Koyukuk and the Lower Yukon division people.

Exclusive of intra-Koyukon relationships, the lines of least hostility, especially for the upper Koyukuk River people, were with the Kobuk and Nunamiut Eskimo, whereas greatest hostility obtained for both the Koyukuk and Upper Yukon Koyukon with their Kutchin-speaking neighbors to the east. Koyukuk River Indians have listed competition for hunting territory, revenge for wrongs, capture of women, evil shamanistic acts, and competition in the fur trade as being the primary reasons for waging "war."

Technology

The Koyukon share many material traits with other Athapaskans whom they border and with neighboring Eskimo who inhabit similar environments (Clark 1974). Most of their manufactured items were fashioned from bone, stone, wood, birchbark, caribou hides, moose hides, and caribou fawn skins, as well as fish skins and squirrel skins, the last two used almost exclusively by the Lower Yukon Koyukon (Clark 1974; Whymper 1869; Zagoskin 1967). Sinew was used for sewing clothing and tentage; spruce root was used for stitching bark on house roofs and canoes and for containers. Willow bast was used for nets on the Koyukuk, but the Yukon people also used fine babiche or sinew. The Koyukon, like the Ingalik and neighboring Eskimo, made pottery, a feature that distinguishes them from most other interior Athapaskans. They produced Yukon line-dot ware as well as the more widely distributed plain pottery.

Clothing

Clothing featured double-V tailed caribou-skin tunics and single-piece trouser-moccasin suits, depilated for summer and with the hair left on and turned inside for winter. This type of clothing, with matching mittens and cap, was frequently exquisitely decorated with dyed porcupine quillwork, plant seeds, red paint along the seams, dentalia, and fine fringe—a costume that was worn especially when a person attended feasts, visited other encampments, or went trading. A less ornate caribou-skin pullover jacket, usually with hood attached, had straight hems and was cut longer for women than for men ("Environment and Culture in the Alaska Plateau," fig. 20, this vol.). Trouser-moccasins were also worn with these. Ornate clothing similar to that worn by the Eskimo about Kotzebue Sound was also used as were caribou-skin mukluks with moose-hide soles (fig. 8).

Structures

Many types of shelter were made by the Koyukon that were in most ways similar to other northwestern Athapaskans. They also built semisubterranean winter houses, which on the Koyukuk were somewhat like those of the Kobuk Eskimo (Clark and Clark 1974; Clark 1974), while Lower Yukon houses were structurally related to Ingalik and probably Norton Sound dwellings (Zagoskin 1967; De Laguna 1947). These houses had tunnel entrances with cold traps and a central hearth. Some also had sleeping bunks.

Transportation

In addition to birchbark and improvised skin boats and the ubiquitous snowshoes, dog traction, used in conjunction with the Innoko sled (Osgood 1940:358), was used to a limited degree at the time of contact. The teams were very small and usually consisted of one to three dogs, a half-grown child or two, and sometimes a wife—a picture that again parallels the Eskimo. During gold rush times and later, teams increased in size to 10–16 dogs or more. Dogs were still popular in the

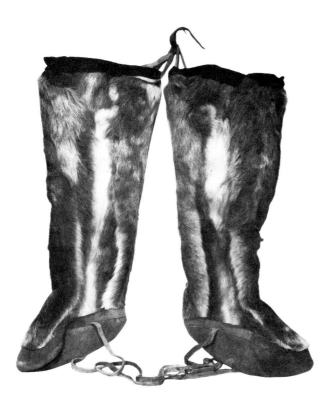

Natl. Mus. of Canada, Ottawa: VI–V–1ab.
Fig. 8. Woman's winter boots of caribou skin with the fur turned outside and moosehide soles. This pair was sewn with dental floss. Length 28 cm, collected in 1970.

1970s, and raising racing dogs for sale and competition was a major enterprise, especially for those on the Koyukuk and upper Yukon rivers.

Sociocultural Situation, 1950s–1970s

In 1973 the Koyukon from all three regions had a total estimated population of about 2,000, including those working out of the villages or away at school (table 1). They had been undergoing slow change from the time of White exploration of 1838–1885, through the ensuing gold rush of 1898–1906 and, at the same time or a few years earlier, the period of missionization. But it has been especially since the late 1940s and early 1950s when the men who had served in the military returned to their homes with new perspectives and technical training that the people entered the period of most rapid change. Completion of the shift to a more sedentary village life, modern transportation and communication, better and more efficient health services, education, increased wage employment both within and outside the villages, and attendant demands for goods and services appear to have been the prime movers.

Sedentary Village Life

In the 1940s and earlier in some local regions, the Koyukon modified their mobile settlement pattern, which had followed their annual subsistence round, and settled permanently into the villages they had used earlier as their winter headquarters, in some places adjacent to missions or old mining towns. Their villages are along the major waterways at Kaltag, Nulato, Koyukuk, Galena, Kokrines, Ruby, Tanana, Rampart, and Stevens Village on the Yukon and at Huslia (earlier Cutoff), Hughes, Alatna-Allakaket, and Bettles Field–Evansville on the Koyukuk. Some people continue to spend part of each summer at fish camps (fig. 9); and during hunting and trapping season some men and women leave their villages to hunt big game—moose, caribou and bear—and trap furbearers, which materially add to both the larder and the bank account. Nearly all villages have electricity; a few have wells, but they still depend primarily on the rivers for their water supply. In most villages, houses are log cabins but they are well insulated, and many have thermopane windows and corrugated aluminum or steel roofs.

Education

When people settled permanently into villages, parochial, Bureau of Indian Affairs, territorial, and later state of Alaska schools providing general education through the eighth grade were opened in nearly all Koyukon villages. Earlier most of the educational function had been carried out by the mission schools on an intermittent basis or by the individual families as they moved from place to place. During the 1960s a far greater number of students who had completed eighth grade went on to boarding high schools in Alaska, Oregon, or elsewhere, or enrolled in the home boarding program to attend city high schools in Fairbanks and Anchorage. In the 1970s many adult Koyukons spoke their own language (Krauss 1973:908) in addition to English, and some spoke Inupiat Eskimo as well.

Health

Health facilities have greatly improved since the mid-1950s. Infant mortality and tuberculosis have dropped to within the national average. Family planning has become popular, and many are now spacing their children in order that they can better provide for them. Much of the improvement at the village level has been due directly to the U.S. Department of Health, Education, and Welfare's Public Health Service program for training local village women as nurses' aides to take care of the day-to-day health needs of members of their own villages. All severe cases of illness and injury are dealt with through air evacuation to modern hospitals at Tanana and elsewhere where the services of specialists are available.

Employment

From the time of the gold rush until after World War

Fig. 9. Alexei's summer fish camp below Kaltag, which was destroyed by ice in 1930. The large plank structure is a salmon drying shed. Photograph by Aleš Hrdlička, 1929.

II, there was little opportunity for supplementing income other than by trapping because wage labor in Alaska was scarce. But from the late 1940s until the early 1970s a gold-dredging operation on the Hogatza River employed up to 100 men from the area during the summer. Additional work became available at military establishments at Bettles Field, Utopia, Galena, and Tanana and at airfields both in the area and outside Koyukon territory in the larger centers, especially in Fairbanks, for those with skills. During the 1960s and 1970s Indian men and women took jobs such as postmasters, workers in native-owned cooperatives, airfreight agents, school maintenance personnel, teaching aides, or nurses' aides in their villages. Most work other than village service positions is seasonal, and thus many must rely upon unemployment checks to carry them through the winter. Retired people and the maimed receive old-age, social security, or disability pensions while many, young and old alike, are eligible for sup-plementary food stamps. One of the most esteemed industries among the Koyukon during the 1960s and early 1970s was the raising and racing of dogs. Racing prizes were large; for example, in the revived Idatarod races winners may receive as much as $15,000 in a single race. The sale of a well-trained lead or seasoned racing dog brought in excess of $1,500. During the winter fur trapping continued, but it made only a small contribution to the income of most Koyukon.

Political Organization

With larger aggregates of people living in villages, political awareness has heightened. There is greater power in the hands of the elected village chiefs and councils and in the extra-village Tanana Chiefs' Conference and Doyon Ltd., instrumental in land claims issues in the 1970s and with which all Koyukon are affiliated, as well as participation at the state and national level. Koyukon

598

CLARK

women are deeply involved in political action; a number sit on local councils and are elected mayors or chiefs in some villages.

Religion

Since the 1880s both Roman Catholic and Episcopalian missionaries have ministered to the Koyukon on the Yukon, and since 1905–1906 the Episcopal church has had missionaries on the Koyukuk River. In addition to their spiritual concerns the missionaries served the sick and acted as welfare agents and educators until state and federal instititutions took over these functions, in some places as late as the 1950s. By the 1960s the native people began to take more active roles in religious activities. Some have become priests or deacons and others are lay readers or members of their bishops' committees. In some villages the Indians have taken over ministry of the faith to their own people.

Synonymy†

The name Koyukon was introduced with approximately its present reference by Osgood (1936:14), who explicitly adapted it from the Co-Youkon (also Co-yukon) of Whymper (1869a:173, 1869:204), respelling it to suggest the names of the Koyukuk and Yukon rivers. Whymper had used this name for the Indians of the Koyukuk and of the Yukon "virtually from below" the confluence of the Koyukuk to that of the Tanana; to these Osgood added the Lower Yukon division, which previous classifications had grouped with the Ingalik. Osgood included as Koyukon the upper Innoko people, now recognized as a separate Holikachuk group ("Ingalik," this vol.), and did not include the speakers of the Upper Koyukon dialect on the Yukon, lower Tanana, and Kantishna, whom, following earlier writers, he grouped with the Tanana River Indians as Tanana. The name Koyukon was not given its present eastern and southeastern extent in these areas until the field surveys of McKennan (1969:339–341) and Krauss (1973:907–908, 1975) in the early 1960s (cf. De Laguna 1947:27–28). The Koyukon language has no term referring to Koyukon speakers as a group.

Nineteenth-century observers other than Whymper used the name Koyukon only for the inhabitants of the Koyukuk River, including an area on the Yukon at the confluence of the two rivers; variants in this meaning are Koyúkun (Dall 1870:77) and Kóyukuns (Allen 1887:94), beside Kuyukuks, 1869 (Raymond 1900:35) and Kóyukuks (Allen 1887:92). Whymper's usage is explained by Raymond's (1900:36) remark that the Yukon Koyukons from the Koyukuk to the Tanana

river were "usually called by the Russians Kuyukunski" although the name Kuyukuk belonged "properly" to the Koyukuk River people. The prominence of Koyukuk River Koyukons, who frequently appeared on the middle Yukon to trade and fish, presumably accounts for the Russians' use of their name for the Yukon River people as well. Russian *kuñukantsy* (pl. noun) and *kuñukanskiĭ* (adjective), implied by the forms cited by Dall (1877:27), Raymond (1870, 1900), and Oswalt (1960:112), are derivatives from *Kuñukak*, the name Malakhov gave to the Koyukuk River in 1838 on the basis of an Eskimo word (Zagoskin 1956:136, 1967:146); cf. Inupiat *kuiyuk* 'river that always flows' (Emily Brown, communication to editors 1978). To have a distinctive name for the Koyukuk people, Dall (1870a:270) coined Koyúkokhotáná by combining Koyukuk with khotana, Zagoskin's rendering of Koyukon *xŏtanə* 'people of'; variants are Koyúkukho-tána (Dall 1870:431; cf. Dall 1877:27) and Koyukukhotana (Hodge 1907g:729–730; Osgood 1936:14). Koyukon uses both *yunəġə xŏtanə* 'back-from-the-river people' and *q̇ŏyəx̣očənə xŏtanə* 'head of willow river people' for the Koyukuk division (Eliza Jones, communication to editors 1978). The first was rendered in Russian as Yunnaka-khotana (Zagoskin 1956:300, 1967:307); the second was obtained by De Laguna (1947:29) in 1935 as the self-designation of the Koyukuk people exclusive of the South Fork subdivision. Variants of Zagoskin's and Dall's terms in the secondary literature are in Hodge (1907g:730).

The Upper Yukon division Koyukons, at least those between the mouth of the Koyukuk and that of the Tanana, have sometimes been referred to by renderings of the Koyukon terms *yuqənə xŏtanə* 'Yukon River people' and *yuna⁷ xŏtanə* 'far upriver people': Yuna-khotana (Zagoskin 1967:243, 306); Yukonikhotana and Unakhotána (Dall 1870a:270; Hodge 1910e:867, 1910f:1009). These Koyukon terms have a general reference and do not indicate precisely bounded divisions; there is no basis in the primary sources for differentiating them as Hodge (1910e, 1910f) does.

The Lower Yukon division is called in Koyukon *yudo⁷ xŏtanə* 'downriver people' (Eliza Jones, communication to editors 1978). They were distinguished by Zagoskin (1956:249, 1967:243) as *sobstvenno inkiliki* 'Inkilik proper', and when Dall (1870) and Whymper (1869) use Ingalik and Ingelete without qualification they are referring to Koyukons of this division. However these authors also use the name Ingalik (and its variants) in a broader sense to include the modern Ingalik and different combinations of other neighboring groups (see the synonymy in "Ingalik," this vol.). This name, from Yupik *iŋqiliq* 'Indian', is now unknown to Athapaskans, but Zagoskin (1956:123, 1967:136) indicates that it was formerly used by at least some Koyukons (perhaps only those bilingual in Yupik) as a

---

†This synonymy was written by Ives Goddard, incorporating some information and references from A. McFadyen Clark.

self-designation in dealing with outsiders. Dall (1870a:270) also introduced as equivalent to his Ingalik (Lower Yukon Koyukon, Ingalik, Holikachuk, and Kolchan) the name Kaiyuh-khotaná, although he elsewhere states correctly that this is the name specifically of the subdivision of Lower Yukon Koyukon that lived in the Kaiyuh Slough–Khotol River area (Dall 1870:53). Variants are Kaíyuh-khatána, Káiyuhkatána, Káiyuh-kho-tána, and Kainhkhotana (Dall 1870:28, 53, 431; Petroff 1884), standardized as Kaiyuhkhotana by Hodge (1907e:643); Osgood (1936:14) used this name for the Lower Yukon Koyukon specifically. Similarly the name Ten'a, from Ingalik and Koyukon *dəna* 'man, person', was introduced by Jetté (1906–1907) for all the Koyukon and Ingalik from the confluence of the Tanana to that of the Innoko; De Laguna (1947:27) adopted Tena in this sense, with the explicit inclusion also of the Lower Tanana, the Koyukon on the Yukon from Rampart to the mouth of the Tanana River and on the Koyukuk, and the Upper Innoko people (not then recognized as surviving at Holikachuk).

The Athapaskan and Eskimo neighbors of the Koyukon generally have no names for them as a unit but use geographical expressions for local or areally defined subgroups. Yukon Ingalik *'eneʒ həʔan* and Holikachuk *yonaʔ həʔan*, both literally 'upriver people', are virtually equivalent to 'Koyukon', but in Kuskokwim Ingalik *'eneʒ həʔan* refers to the Kolchan (James M. Kari, communication to editors 1978). Petitot (1865, 1876:xx, 1891) recorded the Kutchin names of several Koyukon groups, but it is not clear which divisions or subdivisions they are: Hattchénœ, Intsi-Dindjitch, T'éttchié-Dhidié, Ounhann-Koutànœ. Inupiat Eskimo *taɣɣaviɣmiut* 'people of the place where boats are pulled upstream with a line' (Ingstad 1954; Edna Maclean, communication to editors 1979; cf. Gubser 1965) refers to the two uppermost Koyukuk division bands.

It should be noted that terms such as Upper Koyukuk, Lower Koyukuk, and Upper Koyukon have been used by different anthropologists and linguists with quite different applications and have no consistent and firmly established reference (cf. Clark 1974:3–4, 1975:151–154; De Laguna 1947:27–29; Loyens 1966; Henry, Hunter, and Jones 1973).

Subdivisions

For some of the subdivisions specific names have been recorded; these generally have a geographical reference.

Within the Upper Yukon division a major subdivision was the *noɣi xŏtanə* 'Nowitna River people', also called Noggoykhotana, a rendering influenced by a folk-etymological connection with *noɣoyə* 'frog' (Zagoskin 1967:172, 175), and (after the summer camp at the Nowitna mouth) Newicargut (Whymper 1869:22a),

Nowikákat (Dall 1870:85), and Noyokakat and Noyakakat (Petroff 1900:68, 258). According to Jetté (1910) the Indians who hunted on the Nowitna River settled on the Yukon at Kokrines and Mouse Point below the mouth of the Nowitna and were called the Kokrines Indians, but De Laguna (1947:28) put the people Zagoskin found coming from the Nowitna in 1843 in her Tanana-Nowitna subdivision; population shifts may account for the discrepancy.

Within the Lower Yukon division two subdivisions are named in the sources. The Ulukagmyut (Zagoskin 1967:103, 135–136, 243) were known by their Eskimo name, based on that of their village Ulukak on the Unalakleet River; this name apparently represents Yupik *uluaɣkaq* 'ulu (woman's knife) material' (or Inupiat *ulukaq*), to judge by Zagoskin's (1967:294) explanation and by the Lower Koyukon name for this subdivision, which is *ƛamas xŏtanə* 'ulu people' (Steven Jacobson, communication to editors 1979; Eliza Jones, communication to editors 1978). The name of the Takayaksa was said by Zagoskin (1967:103, 149, 180) to mean 'swamp', a reference to the area of lakes and lowlands east of the Yukon below Nulato. The Russianized noun *takaīaksantsy* (pl.) and adjective *takaīaksanskiĭ* (Zagoskin 1956:138, 149) appear in several imprecise renderings in translations and secondary sources (De Laguna 1947:29). The usual Koyukon name is *qayəx xŏtanə* 'people of the Kaiyuh Slough area' (Eliza Jones, communication to editors 1978), rendered Káiyuhkatná 'lowland people' by Dall (1870:53); variants of this name were used by Dall and his successors in various much wider applications (see above). The distinction implied by Hodge (1907e:644, 1910g:673) between the Kaiyuhkhotana "division" and the Takaiak is without foundation.

Within the Koyukuk division several subdivision names are attested. The Yukon-Kateel subdivision is in Koyukon *kodilqaɉə xŏtanə* 'people of the area of the mouth of the Kateel River' (Eliza Jones, communication to editors 1978). The Todatonten-Kanuti subdivision is named after Todatonten Lake and the Kanuti River, site of the former village called Konootená by Allen (1887:97); these names in Koyukon are *todaƛtoNdəN* and *q̇unutnə* 'Kanuti River', after which the village was named (Eliza Jones, communication to editors 1979). These people call themselves *q̇unutnə xŏtanə* 'Kanuti people' and are referred to by the South Fork people as *yudo yung̈ot* 'down at a place back away from the river' (Clark 1961–1972, phonemicized; Eliza Jones, communication to editors 1978). The South Fork people are called by other Koyukuk Koyukons *tuloɣə xŏtanə* 'people who live at the head of the river' (De Laguna 1947:29; Clark 1961–1972; Eliza Jones, communication to editors 1978), and they call themselves nikhto hot'ana (D.W. Clark 1968).

Sources

Zagoskin's (1967) journal of his explorations along the Yukon in 1843 is the earliest and most valuable of the contact-period documents for the Koyukon.

From the second half of the nineteenth century the diary of Kennicott (James 1942) and works by Dall (1870, 1877) and Whymper (1869), members of the Western Union Telegraph exploration party, provide further insight into the conditions and habits of the people of the middle Yukon. Whymper and Dall both give lively accounts of incidents such as the Nulato Massacre, which undoubtedly adversely affected opinions of later explorers who were to enter Koyukon territory, as well as good descriptions of material culture, ecology, and belief. The artist, Whymper, also left some fine sketches of the people and their environment.

From later in the nineteenth century, when prospectors, traders, and missionaries began to infiltrate the region, bits of information are available in letters and obscure journals and in reports from trading companies such as the Alaska Commercial Company and the Northern Commercial Company (Kitchener 1954) as well as in early exploration and military reports (Stoney 1899; Allen 1887; Cantwell 1902; Schwatka 1885; Raymond 1873, 1900; Schmitter 1910).

Initial ethnographic work was done at the turn of the twentieth century by Father Jules Jetté, the single most important early scholar of the Yukon River Koyukon. Regrettably, he did not visit people living on the middle and upper Koyukuk. His published works (1906–1907, 1907, 1908–1909, 1911, 1913) as well as his manuscripts on deposit at the Oregon Provincial Archives, Gonzaga University, Spokane, Washington, are invaluable guides. Archdeacon Hudson Stuck (1914, 1917, 1920) collected some ethnographic information on the Koyukuk River people; his surviving papers are deposited in the Church Historical Society Archives, Episcopal Church of the United States, Austin, Texas, which also has information from other Episcopal missionaries who worked among the Koyukon.

In 1935 De Laguna (1947) made an archeological reconnaissance of the Koyukon region and also collected invaluable ethnographic information from people along the Yukon and lower Koyukuk. Sullivan (1942) made an ethnographic study of the people between Koyukuk and Nulato; Robert McKennan collected information from the Upper Yukon Koyukon during the 1940s and earlier while doing ethnographic work among the Chandalar Kutchin. In the early 1960s Loyens (1964, 1966) continued ethnographic work among the Lower Yukon division people. Henry and Henry (1965, 1969, 1969a) and Henry, Hunter, and Jones (1973) treat the language of the Koyukon, especially concentrating on Upper Yukon and Koyukuk division dialects. The major ethnographic and archeological work for the Koyukuk River division was done between 1961 and 1972 (McFadyen 1964, 1966; Clark 1970, 1970a, 1974, 1975; D.W. Clark 1972, 1974; Clark and Clark 1974, 1976). Unless otherwise stated data presented in the text for the Koyukuk division are from Clark (1961–1972), and D.W. Clark (1968).

Collections of Koyukon artifacts are very limited. Items collected by Zagoskin in 1843 are in the Museum of Ethnography and Anthropology, Leningrad; some of these catalogued as Ingalik are in fact Lower Yukon division Koyukon. Late nineteenth- and early twentieth-century specimens may be found in the Museum of Natural History, Smithsonian Institution, Washington, and the Venneti Collection, University of Alaska Museum, Fairbanks. For twentieth-century specimens, the best collections are at the National Museum of Man, Ottawa, and the University of Alaska Museum.

Ingalik

JEANNE H. SNOW

At the time of contact with the Russians in the 1830s the Ingalik (ĭŋ'gälĭk) occupied parts of two river systems. One sector lived along the lower Yukon River and its tributary the Innoko from Blackburn Creek and Holikachuk Slough to Holy Cross. The other was on the middle Kuskokwim from the Holitna River to the Kolmakof River (fig. 1), an area in part shared with Kuskowagamiut Eskimos, with whom they had a joint village on the Kolmakof called Kvygympaynagmyut (Yupik *kuiɣəm paiŋamiut* 'people of the mouth of the river') (Zagoskin 1967:190, 193, 210, 243, 252, 268; De Laguna 1947:29; Wrangell 1970:13; Oswalt 1962:2–3; Michael E. Krauss, communication to editors 1978). The Ingalik speak a distinct Athapaskan language with slight internal dialectal differences.* However, as a consequence of intermarriage with the more numerous Kuskowagamiut, the Kuskokwim Ingalik spoke Eskimo more than Ingalik by the beginning of the twentieth century (Chapman 1907:15), and by 1978 the Kuskokwim dialect of Ingalik was spoken by fewer than 20 scattered individuals (James M. Kari, communication to editors 1978).

In the nineteenth century the middle and upper Innoko River area was inhabited by speakers of a distinct Athapaskan language known as Holikachuk, the name of the village their descendants lived in until moving to Grayling on the Yukon in 1963 (Kari 1978a:1; VanStone 1979:16–17). These people, poorly known to anthropologists, have previously been grouped for convenience with the Koyukon (Osgood 1936:14, 1940:480), though they were recognized as a distinct people as early as 1844 (Zagoskin 1967:235, 307; De Laguna 1947:29). They are treated here with the Ingalik because in the historic period their closest ties have been

with that group.

The major work on the Ingalik (Osgood 1940, 1958, 1959) deals only with the traditional culture as described by informants for the Anvik-Shageluk populations, and there are very few additional sources on Ingalik and Holikachuk† culture. Therefore, unless the Kuskokwim Ingalik or Holikachuk are specifically referred to, information presented in this chapter refers to the Ingalik who lived along the Yukon and lower Innoko rivers. The Indians Osgood (1936:13) tentatively labeled McGrath Ingalik are not Ingalik; they are treated in the chapter "Kolchan," this volume.

Territory and Environment

The Yukon and Kuskokwim river basins are two extensive lowland areas formed by the valleys of the two great rivers. Not far above the point where the Yukon loops around a high ridge and escapes to the sea, the long river is joined by two tributaries, the Anvik and the Innoko. The larger waterways alternate between high banks and low areas filled with willows and scrub poplars (VanStone 1974:18). These waterways played a dominant role in Yukon Ingalik life not only by providing the major food resource but also by serving as a network of communication among villages (Osgood 1940:33). Kuskokwim resources were far poorer than those of the Yukon in terms of number, variety, and size of fish. Zagoskin (1967:220) reports that for this reason the natives on the central Kuskokwim near Kolmakovskiy Redoubt relied more heavily on hunting than on fishing.

There are highland areas of tundra and barren country covered with small shrubs, lichens, sedges, grasses,

---

*The phonemes of Ingalik are: (unaspirated stops and affricates) d, λ, δ̂, ȝ, ȝ̇, ž, g, ġ, ʔ; (aspirated stops and affricates) t, ƛ, θ̂, c, ȼ, č, k, q; (glottalized) t́, ƛ́, θ̂́, ć, ȼ́, č́, ƙ, q́; (voiceless continuants) N, N̦, ł, θ, s, ṣ, š, Y, x, h; (voiced continuants) m, n, ŋ, v, l, δ, z, ẓ, y, γ̇; (full vowels) e, a, o; (reduced vowels) ə (with several central and front allophones), ŭ. The unaspirated stops and affricates are voiceless prevocalically and voiced word-finally. The v is pronounced [v] at Anvik and [w] at Shageluk.

In the practical orthography used by the Alaska Native Language Center the Ingalik phonemes are written: d, dl, ddh, dz, dr, j, g, gg, ' (not written word-initially); t, tl, tth, ts, tr, ch, k, q; t', tl', tth', ts', tr', ch', k', q'; nh, ngh, ł, th, s, sr, sh, yh, x, h; m, n, ng, v, l, dh, z, zr, y, gh; e, a, o; i, u.

Information on the phonology of Ingalik and the transcription of Ingalik words was provided by James M. Kari (communication to

editors 1978; Kari 1978).

†The phonemes of Holikachuk are: (unaspirated stops and affricates) d, λ, δ̂, ȝ, g, ġ, ʔ; (aspirated stops and affricates) t, ƛ, θ̂, c, k, q; (glottalized) t́, ƛ́, θ̂́, ć, ƙ, q́; (voiceless continuants) N, ł, θ, s, Y, x; (voiced continuants) m, n, ŋ, l, δ, z, y, γ̇; (full vowels) e, a, ɔ, o; (reduced vowels) ə (with several central and front allophones), ŭ. The unaspirated stops and affricates are voiceless prevocalically and voiced word-finally.

In the practical orthography used by the Alaska Native Language Center the Holikachuk phonemes are written: d, dl, ddh, dz, g, gg, ' (not written word-initially); t, tl, tth, ts, k, q; t', tl', tth', ts', k', q'; nh, ł, th, s, yh, x; m, n, ng, l, dh, z, y, gh; e, a, o, oo; i, u.

Information on the phonology of Holikachuk and the transcription of Holikachuk words was provided by James M. Kari (communication to editors 1978; Kari 1978a).

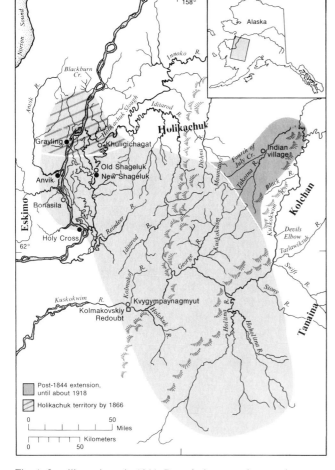

Fig. 1. Ingalik territory in 1844. Boundaries away from major rivers are uncertain.

In the map legend:

Post-1844 extension, until about 1918

Holikachuk territory by 1866

0 50 Miles

0 50 Kilometers

weeds, and mosses. Dense stands of spruce and birch are typical of the areas adjacent to the main rivers. One also finds poplar, aspen, and cottonwood. Willows grow along the banks of the streams and in the boggy areas. Tamaracks, alders, and mountain ash are surrounded in summer by diverse species of berries and wild flowers (Osgood 1940:33–34).

The animal life of the region is typical of that reported for much of interior Alaska. Of importance to the Ingalik for food or hides were bear, moose, caribou, and mountain sheep as well as mink, marten, red fox, porcupine, muskrat, otter, hare, wolf, wolverine, ermine, and several species of squirrels. Several species of salmon spawn along the tributaries of the Yukon and the Kuskokwim. Freshwater fish include whitefish, pike, blackfish, grayling, and burbot (VanStone 1974:18; Osgood 1958:280). Most of the birds that were used for food are migratory—ducks, geese, swans, and loons for example—but grouse and ptarmigan remain through the winter as do birds considered inedible, such as the raven, pine grosbeak, and Canada (or Alaskan) jay. One other form of life is eloquently described by Osgood (1940:34): "One may not remember the soft springy touch of the muskeg under the feet, the smell

of the virgin spruce, or even the sight of a golden sky dripping the reflection of the midnight sun, but none can forget the sound of the swarming insects which creep from their bark houses to descend cloud-like on all living things, making for a few months [in summer] of an Ingalik paradise something nearer hell. There are mosquitoes and gnats, big flies and little flies, wasps and bees, besides a score of silent comrades to creep in and out of everything."

External Relations

At the time of historic contact, the Ingalik were described as living in an environment rich in resources (Zagoskin 1967:162). They were not dedicated traders, as the Koyukon were, and when they did trade, it was mostly with the Eskimo. The Yukon Ingalik traded with the Norton Sound Eskimo, exchanging wooden bowls and wolverine skins for seal oil and sea mammal skins and furs for tobacco, caribou skins, sealskin thongs, and seal hides. They also occasionally visited Nulato Post, and some Koyukon traders visited the Ingalik villages, though trade with the Koyukon was recalled in the 1930s as not having been very extensive (Zagoskin 1967:191–192, 235, 244; Osgood 1958:62–63). The Kuskokwim Ingalik traded beaver, marten, and wolverine skins, spruce gum, caribou sinew, and birch-bark canoes to the Kuskowagamiut Eskimo downstream in exchange for seal skins, seal oil, frozen and dried fish, squirrel skins, and dentalia (Zagoskin 1967:197; Osgood 1958:63; Oswalt 1962:11). They also were visited by Stony River Tanaina traders in the nineteenth century (Zagoskin 1967:268).

Compared to the Athapaskans living farther up the Yukon, the Ingalik were a peaceful people, according to Osgood's informants. Osgood (1959:77) notes that historical evidence seems to verify their view of the past. Raids and other hostile actions did of course take place. The traditional enemies of the Yukon Ingalik were the Koyukon. At contact hostilities were reported between Koyukon and the Yukon Ingalik, between the Kuskokwim Ingalik and the Kuskowagamiut Eskimo, and between the Kuskokwim Ingalik and the Kolchan (Zagoskin 1967:191; Petroff 1900:60; Osgood 1958:63, 1959:77). However, Oswalt (1962:11) concludes that there was no conflict of any significance between the Kuskowagamiut and the Kuskokwim Ingalik. The relationships between the Ingalik and the Eskimo seem to have been far less hostile than those with neighboring Athapaskans.

The Yukon and Kuskokwim Ingalik intermarried with the Eskimo and borrowed heavily from them. Eskimo influence was strong in ceremonial matters, clothing, subsistence techniques, food preferences, and house styles (Zagoskin 1967:244–247; Chapman 1907:16; Whymper 1869:175–177; Stuck 1917:177; De Laguna

1936:569; Loyens 1964:145; Oswalt 1973:131–132). The Yukon Ingalik only partially followed the interior Athapaskan subsistence pattern; they did hunt, but fishing dominated their economy. Thus they occupied an intermediate position between neighboring riverine Eskimo and inland Athapaskan patterns of subsistence (McKennan 1969a:98).

Culture

Settlement Pattern

Osgood's informants described traditional Yukon Ingalik life as divided among three kinds of settlements, depending upon the season of the year: the home-base winter village (qay), the canoe (spring) camp (ċeqay), and the summer camp (saN qay). All three were relatively close together, within approximately a six-mile radius.

A typical winter village consisted of a kashim (ċał θet) and a row of wooden houses. The kashim, a large, rectangular, semisubterranean building, was the ceremonial center, the men's social center, and the workshop. The typical residence in a winter village held two nuclear families, perhaps 12 individuals. A village included 10 or 12 of these dwellings, with sloping pole entryways and dome-shaped, dirt-covered roofs on which grass grew (figs. 2–3). Behind the houses were caches, mounted on high posts, in which food was stored, and between and in front of the houses were racks for sleds and canoes, which were also on poles.

Subsistence

Subsistence activities are detailed in figures 4 and 5. Men tended to cooperate in economic activities when winter villages were occupied. It was then that they built guides and surrounds for taking caribou, fished for lamprey, and occasionally hunted bear.

At the winter villages, gill net fishing was an important activity from September through early December. Nets for whitefish were set from the banks in eddies of main streams. Winter traps were set for burbot (ling) (fig. 6). They remained under the ice all winter and also provided pike, whitefish, and a few suckers. These traps were frequently set in pairs facing each other to catch fish swimming up or down stream. The fish were guided into the traps by weirs and removed from the trap with a special rake, six to eight feet long. (A detailed discussion of the construction of these traps and all other aspects of Yukon Ingalik technology is given by Osgood 1940.)

The fish trap most often set in the small lakes was for blackfish. It was set beneath the ice at the end of a weir extending a short distance from the shore or in a pothole where the blackfish came up "to breathe."

The traps were visited nearly every day and were moved frequently (unless placed at potholes) to maximize the catch. The villagers caught pike by line fishing with a piece of caribou bone used as a hook on a sinew line tied to a short pole.

Hare were an important winter food source. Women used tossing pole snares to catch them, although the men sometimes hunted them with bows and arrows. The women also set tether snares for ptarmigan.

Caribou were hunted, for their skins and meat, in winter, when they were plentiful. Hunters tracked them alone or cooperated in groups to take them in surrounds. At times two men might decide to spend a winter in the woods to hunt and trap; if they took their families with them, they set up a semipermanent winter camp (xəY qay) apart from the village (Osgood 1958:167). Moose were also hunted during the winter, although there were easier times of the year to do it. Using tether snares, bows and arrows, and three varieties of deadfalls, the Yukon Ingalik took beaver, lynx, ground and red squirrel, mountain sheep, river otter, marten, fox, mink, ermine, wolf, and wolverine.

In the spring up to 10 families might decide to sled their canoes ("Environment and Culture in the Alaska Plateau," fig. 11, this vol.) into sites located on small lakes in search of fresh fish. They returned in their canoes on the spring flood. These camps, or "canoe villages," were only six or seven miles from the winter villages. People built inverted V-shaped shelters, made of spruce poles and boughs, for their stay. During May, side-stream traps were set under the ice to catch grayling, salmon trout, and burbot. In April and May dip nets with babiche mesh were used, from a canoe, to catch two kinds of whitefish, and the pike-run traps were set at sites shared by a group of men. By May the blackfish trap was set in a small channel at the outlet of a lake; it might be filled overnight. Other activities at this time of year included snaring ground squirrels and ducks, hunting muskrat, and occasionally shooting ducks with bow and arrow.

The summer camps were nearer the winter villages than were the canoe camps, but they were smaller, as people dispersed to take advantage of the best fishing sites on the rivers. The camp had fish-drying racks near the river, smoke houses, and dwellings that were less solidly built than those in the winter village. One or two might have spruce plank walls, but most were faced with spruce bark, split cottonwood logs, or strips of birchbark.

At a summer camp the most important activity was fishing. Occasionally a caribou or moose was taken but people were primarily concerned with fish. Because salmon did not ascend the Innoko River in appreciable numbers, Shageluk and other Innoko River people maintained summer fish camps on the Yukon (James W. VanStone, personal communication 1975). In June

Smithsonian, NAA: 10,455–D–1.
Fig. 2. A section of Anvik. left to right, Log cabin, caches, and a small semisubterranean winter house. Photograph by John Wight Chapman, about 1923.

a summer or whitefish trap was set at a man's principal site on the main stream. The trap was set in a pole frame, covered with latticelike fencing, which began at the swiftest run of water in the Yukon and ran to the shore. A man expected to catch three different species of whitefish and perhaps some salmon (*Oncorhynchus*). Chinook salmon were taken with a seine. This large net of willow bast line, with floats and sinkers, measured 50 by 8 feet. It drifted downstream from a canoe. By the end of June a chum salmon trap, which was 18 feet long, was set in the same place and in the same manner as the summer or whitefish trap. In it, chum, Chinook, coho, sockeye, and pink salmon were taken. In July and August the women of the Shageluk area set gill nets for whitefish. What Osgood (1958:280) refers to as salmon trout are probably landlocked Arctic char (*Salvelinus alpinus*) (McPhail and Lindsey 1970:142–144). "Salmon trout" and grayling traps were set on small side streams. The men speared fish with long, toggle-headed harpoons, principally on the Anvik River and the Innoko River, where screens and weirs were placed to block the passage of the fish. Spear fishing was of minor importance in the overall economy of the Yukon Ingalik.

Although not a major item in the diet, berries were a favorite Ingalik food. Gathering took place from mid to late summer on into the fall. The mossberry, mouse berry, bunchberry, high-bush and low-bush cranberry, blueberry, red raspberry, salmonberry, and winter-berry were enjoyed. Indian potato (*Hedysarum alpinum*) was gathered near the Anvik River in September, and wild rhubarb was gathered in May, June, and July. The "cotton" from the pods of cottonwood trees

was combined with oil, snow, and berries to make "ice cream" (*vaNgəq*) (Osgood 1940:193–194). A cabbage-like plant was gathered in July, mixed with salmon eggs, cooked, and stored for later consumption. A green plant resembling parsley was eaten raw. Bird eggs were also collected, duck and sea gull eggs being the most popular.

The only information on subsistence and the annual cycle among the Kuskokwim Ingalik comes from Zagoskin's (1967:252) early account. He reported that the Kuskokwim natives were more interested in hunting caribou and fur-bearing animals like beaver and river otter than in fishing.

A major change occurred in faunal resources of the tundra country and interior highlands of Alaska after the 1870s. The caribou virtually disappeared (Townsend 1973:410). Since there is little information on the subsistence practices of the Ingalik prior to that period, it is difficult to ascertain the impact of such a change. In his record of travels in Yukon Ingalik country be-

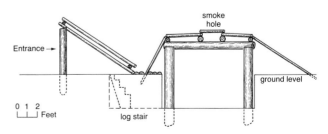

after Osgood 1940:303.
Fig. 3. Cross-section showing construction of a small semisubterranean winter house. The interior dirt walls are hung with grass mats.

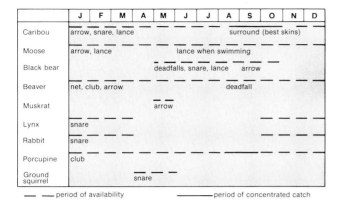

	J	F	M	A	M	J	J	A	S	O	N	D
Caribou	arrow, snare, lance								surround (best skins)			
Moose	arrow, lance				lance when swimming							
Black bear				deadfalls, snare, lance				arrow				
Beaver	net, club, arrow								deadfall			
Muskrat				arrow								
Lynx	snare											
Rabbit	snare											
Porcupine	club											
Ground squirrel				snare								

— — period of availability   ———— period of concentrated catch

after Osgood 1958:281.

Fig. 4. Seasonal cycle of mammal hunting in traditional Yukon Ingalik culture.

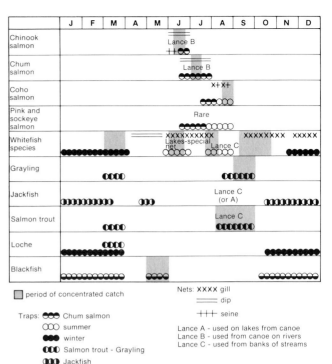

after Osgood 1958:280.

Fig. 5. Seasonal cycle of fishing in traditional Yukon Ingalik culture.

tween 1904 and 1916, Stuck (1917:178) reported that caribou, moose, and mountain sheep were extremely rare and that the diet among these Ingalik was varied by little else than spring and autumn waterfowl supplemented to a limited extent by hare, squirrel, "small deer" (caribou), and vegetables from small garden plots. The scarcity of large game plus the introduction of the fish wheel probably increased the Ingalik reliance on fishing. Chapman (1913:50) records the introduction of the fish wheel into the Yukon Ingalik area. He refers to fish wheels having been towed across the river to take advantage of a good run of coho salmon. Stuck (1917:174, 182) noted that fish wheels were "creak[ing] and groan[ing]" resulting in "acres and acres" of racks covered with red flesh of fish early in the salmon season. The fish wheels did not replace traps immediately. Residents at Anvik in the 1970s recalled that wicker traps were in use during the summers into the early 1920s (James W. VanStone, personal communication 1975). By 1936 the fish wheel was reported as universal on the lower Yukon (Sullivan 1942:2).

Among the Kuskokwim Ingalik, the fish wheel was in use at Georgetown in 1914 (Oswalt 1963:44). Oswalt (1962) suggests that the final ascendency of the Kuskowagamiut over the Kuskokwim Ingalik came about because the Ingalik lifeway had to be drastically redirected after the disappearance of the caribou. Survival lay in more intensive salmon fishing, which in turn fostered more intimate Kuskowagamiut Eskimo contact, because the Kuskowagamiut had already established themselves as the salmon fishers of the region.

Social Control

When a person was known to be a thief, all the men, but only the old women, held a meeting in the kashim. During the discussion one man (not necessarily the same one on each occasion) usually acted as leader. It was he who told the offender that he would be banished

Smithsonian, NAA: 10455–L–1.

Fig. 6. Man removing fish from a winter fish trap raised through a hole cut in the ice of the Yukon River. Behind him is an ice chisel and a scoop (see "Environment and Culture in the Alaska Plateau," fig. 8, this vol.); he holds a shorter ice scoop in his left hand. Traps of this type were used mainly for ling. The form of the sled at left is not typical for the Ingalik, showing White influence. Photograph by John Wight Chapman, 1898.

or killed if he did not stop, these apparently being the only two choices open. Murder activated blood revenge. There was no organized response such as there was for thievery unless one man murdered several people.

Considerable pressure to marry was brought by the villagers on a young man who was old enough to have made his first kill and who had begun to trap. The attitude seemed to be that a young man of 16 years would probably marry within the village, which was desirable. Young girls were not encouraged to have foreign suitors (Parsons 1921–1922:63).

Shamanism

A shaman (dəyanəN) was believed to have a more powerful soul than an ordinary human being. No one could inherit the role of shaman. It was something for which one had to have a "peculiar aptitude" (Chapman 1907:13). Osgood's (1959:130) informants said that the shaman's power was derived through the "dreaming of animals." Shamans could be either men or women (Parsons 1921–1922:68).

One of the most important elements in the Ingalik belief system was the concept of "songs" or magical spells (Osgood 1959:118). Although almost everyone acquired "songs," they were the specialty of the shaman. He used his powers to aid the sick, exorcise evil spirits, and even to kill people. An especially powerful shaman might be able to influence a fish run; in at least one masked dance, shamans invoked game (De Laguna 1936:585).

At Anvik, four- and five-year-old children were consigned to the care of the shaman in a special ceremony, even though the welfare of the children rested with the villagers as a unit (Parsons 1921–1922:56). Parsons's (1921–1922:65) informant reported that a highly respected shaman was entitled to other men's wives.

Supernaturalism

The relationship between the Ingalik and the world of nature was very close. The principal support of human beings was thought to be the various "animal people," on the flesh of which people lived (Osgood 1959:115). All these animals required respectful treatment or they would no longer be available for food. The function of "songs," or magical spells, was to bring into equilibrium the conflicts that existed among the worlds of the spirit, nature, and society. The songs created good relations between the Ingalik and the spirits of the fish and food-giving mammals. A younger man could "buy" a song from an older man; they were classified as ordinary, very powerful, or unique (Osgood 1959:121). People wore amulets (gaqen), almost always associated with "songs," which were usually acquired by inheritance or purchase, although they could be made by an individual (Osgood 1959:126). The songs and amulets were magical instruments used to obtain a desired end. As Osgood (1959:167) explains:

> The Ingalik universe is distinguished by its animation and by the modesty with which the Indians regard man's place in the natural order. To get along successfully is to have good relationships with other forms of life. The key to

these mutual adjustments is communication, but unfortunately every living thing does not necessarily understand the Ingalik language. Therefore one is forced to utilize magical incantations or "songs" to make up for this deficiency. Through this medium one can exert the necessary influence for support when it is needed.

Ceremonies

The Yukon Ingalik observed seven major ceremonies in traditional times. Four of the seven ceremonies involved invitations to neighboring villages for feasting, ceremonial exchange, gift giving, and symbolic and imitative dances against a background of songs: these were the Partner's Potlatch (nixoʔoʔ), the Mask Dance (gəyema) ("Expressive Aspects of Subarctic Indian Culture," figs. 12–13, this vol.), the Death Potlatch (gətolyat), and the Hot Dance. The villages that exchanged these invitations in the 1930s were Anvik, Shageluk, and Holikachuk (De Laguna 1936). The Feast of the Animals' Souls (doθton) resembled a pageant to which, with its accompanying feasts, the neighboring villagers came without special invitation. The other two ceremonies involved only the residents of a single village, who assembled to propitiate the animals in the Bladder ceremony (gələhəθ) and to discover what omens for the coming year the Doll's ceremony would provide. Several of the ceremonies showed heavy Eskimo influence (De Laguna 1936:569).

Only the Partner's Potlatch and the Death Potlatch lacked the themes of ensuring the occurrence and increasing the quantity of economically important animals. These ceremonies brought prestige to the host of a ceremonial exchange of goods and honored the dead. The Partner's Potlatch was an occasion for fun and took place at any time of the year, whereas the Death Potlatch was considered the most solemn occasion of the year and was held in midwinter. In both ceremonies exchange relationships worked on two levels. There was a host-guest relationship between two villages and exchanges between individuals. The Partner's Potlatch (Osgood 1958:73–81) involved an invitation from one village to another, usually the nearest of equivalent size. Acceptance of the invitation by the guest village conveyed the obligation to provide the host village with "an untanned bear skin for the kashim door and a new bear gut cover for the smoke hole" (Osgood 1958:75). Individuals in the host village had "parka partners" of either sex in the guest village. Being a "parka partner" meant having an exchange relationship established either by mutual agreement or by taking the partner of a deceased parent at the parent's death. During the potlatch, the dead were honored by the display of a gift by a relative who wished to "remember" the deceased in front of his friends and neighbors. When the guests arrived, each one also had a "feeding partner" who provided food during the ceremonies.

Smithsonian, Dept. of Anthr.: top 339811, bottom 339812.

Fig. 7. Ceremonial batons used by male leaders of two groups of a host village during Partner's Potlatch. One baton was decorated to symbolize the caribou, and the other, the wolf (Osgood 1958:73–74). Top length 41 cm; collected 1928.

For the Death Potlatch (Osgood 1958:138–143) invitations were extended to particular individuals. A man and his wife might decide they had acquired enough goods to hold a potlatch, normally to honor the man's father. Once they had selected the men that they would potlatch, the man went to the kashim to announce the names of the individuals they had chosen. The invitations were sent by this man in honor of the deceased person to other men from his own and neighboring villages. It was possible for a man to extend an invitation to a woman, but if he did so, the return invitation came through her father, husband, or son (Osgood 1958:138). Honored guests were selected on the basis of their ability to reciprocate, because of past obligations, or in order to help a friend. Even though invitations were to individuals, it was understood that all the men and women of the guests' villages were invited to participate. The prestige that the host acquired came not only through hosting the event but also from the quality of the gifts. If the host were wealthy enough, he gave the traditional mittens, boots, and parka as presents not only to his honored guests but also to all the men who had helped with the duties surrounding the death. Food was provided for everyone. An adjunct to the Death Potlatch was the Hot Dance—a night of singing, dancing, sexual license, and gift giving (Osgood 1958:143–146).

The Feast of the Animals' Souls was very different from the "potlatches." The ceremonies, dances, costumes, and masks created an occasion for artistic expression, amusement, and communion with the world of nature. This 14-to-21-day ceremony, which preceded or followed the Death Potlatch, was the highlight of the ceremonial year. The ceremony was directed by the song leader, who learned the order of the songs and dances and saw to it that they did not vary from year to year. The major performers were the "red male mask" and the "red female mask" (fig. 8). These parts in the pageant were inherited roles, passed down from father to son. They performed solemn dances symbolizing the hunt and imitating fish and animals. The "black mask" by contrast was a clown who provided comic relief. He bellowed when he came on "stage" because he could not speak. He fished and caught people, stole food during the ceremonies, and performed in skits in which he seduced little old ladies by mistake. Other stock characters in the pageant were the "funny face mask," "grandma" and "granddaughter" masks. There were other masks, called variable masks, which people who attended the ceremony wore.

The fourteenth night of the Feast of the Animals' Souls was the most important, and everyone wore new clothes for the occasion. Bowls of "ice cream" were decorated with small models of snares or deadfalls, and gifts were presented to the song leader. The long evening was a combination of dances, either solemn, as was the "song of the fishes" that the red masks performed, or dramatic, as in an enactment of the legend called "murder of the woman." Or the dances could be funny, as was the skit where the "funny face mask" chased the "black mask" all around the kashim trying to murder him with a cudgel. The entertainment ended with an exchange called the "skin thimble." Women chose men to whom they gave gifts and "ice cream" and the men responded in kind. Following evenings were devoted to tugs of war, wrestling, races, and food exchanges.

In addition to the seven major ceremonies, the Ingalik held ceremonies that centered principally around "putting down," for prestige or privilege. "Putting down" involved bringing food into the kashim to be shared by everyone present. These ceremonies included public recognition of a boy's first kill, a girl's first menstruation, a marriage, and obtaining the privilege of dancing at a Partner's Potlatch. Other feasts took place at the first salmon run, when a man killed a wolf or a wolverine, and when an eclipse occurred (Osgood 1958:65–73).

Ranking

The Yukon Ingalik recognized three status groups: rich men (*qŭsqa*), common people, and ingilaninh (*əŋəlanəN* 'people who do nothing') (Osgood 1959:61). A rich man had a surplus of food and goods that he was expected to share with those less fortunate. Indeed, his prestige depended upon it. The ideal of Ingalik society was not "to have and to hold" but "to have and to

608

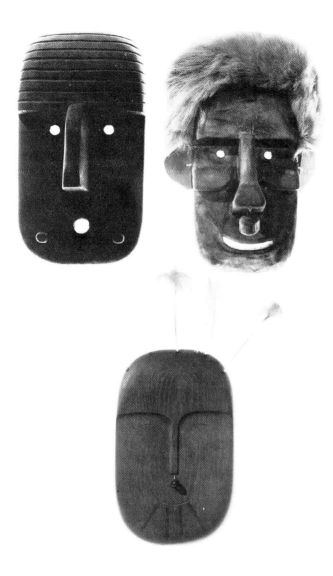

Yale U., Peabody Mus.: top left, 29453; top right, 29457; bottom, 29456.
Fig. 8. Animal ceremony masks. top left, Big brother mask, painted black; the little brother mask (not shown) is similar but lacks the 2 pegs representing labrets. top right, 'Comes in to throw' mask, black with red eyes, ears, cheek knobs, and nose tip, trimmed with caribou hair. bottom, Red female mask, painted red with 5 feathers (2 missing) at top; the red male mask (not shown) is similar but has a pair of labrets below the corners of the mouth, while the female is distinguished by the red glass bead suspended from the nose and black lines representing chin tattoos; the use of these masks is an inherited privilege (see Osgood 1958:16, 98–101). Height of top right about 28 cm, others same scale. All collected in 1935 from Billy Williams of Anvik and Shageluk.

give" (Osgood 1959:72). One of the rewards for giving was taking the lead in ceremonial activities.

The ingilaninh were the irresponsible and could be of either sex. They were those who by "indolence and disregard of customs, live off the community at large by doing as little work as possible" (Osgood 1959:61). One of the distinguishing features of the ingilaninh was that no one would consider such a person as a marriage partner. They could not be counted on to undertake

the necessary share of labor in a household (Osgood 1959:65).

These ranks were fluid. People could, and did, shift from one to another by their own effort or lack of it (Osgood 1959:61).

Wealth was composed first and foremost of fish. One of Osgood's (1959:71) informants expressed it this way: "fish oil looks like gold dust to the people." A man was regarded as a person of means when he had accumulated substantial quantities of fish, meat, fur, logs, and bark. Certain furs were highly valued by the rich. A man went to a good deal of trouble to obtain a wolverine skin. Other attributes of wealth were the possession of an elaborate dwelling, the ownership of a fine canoe, wooden bowls of superior quality, ceremonial drums, stone adzes, or any item distinguished by fine carving and skilled workmanship. Other kinds of objects embodying wealth were red ocher and dentalia. Dentalia were especially valuable because they could be acquired only through trade (Osgood 1959:71).

Life Cycle

• MARRIAGE Marriage was endogamous within the village, with prohibitions against marrying within the range of first cousin (Parsons 1921–1922:63; Osgood 1958:190). Parsons's (1921–1922:60) informant reported that a young man interested in a girl worked for the parents for a time, but "if the old man does not like him, thinking he has not done enough, the young man cannot get the girl." On the other hand, informants reported that the mother determined the marriage partner of a daughter or son, always ensuring that the elder daughter married before the younger (Osgood 1958:190). A few Yukon Ingalik, generally the rich, acquired a second wife. The husband first obtained the permission of the first wife and they all lived in the same household. The levirate was "relatively common"; the sororate was less so (Osgood 1958:200, 198). A divorced wife returned to her mother. Upon the death of her husband, a widow returned to her mother's house to live. A widowed person's mother-in-law controlled any remarriage, and a widower might be expected to reside in his mother-in-law's household after his wife's death (Osgood 1958:203, 200, 198).

Postnuptial residence is not clearly defined in the source material. Parsons's (1921–1922:61) informant reported that for the first two or three years after marriage a woman lived with her husband in her parents' home. At the end of that time a man built his own house, perhaps near the woman's parents' home. Osgood's (1958:159) informants reported that a boy brought his bride to his parents' home for a period of time during which they prepared to build a house of their own. Where that house was eventually built was apparently not important.

• BIRTH Upon becoming pregnant, a woman did not change her daily routine. At delivery she was assisted by a midwife, who sang a "caribou song." The afterbirth was placed in a birchbark basket and tied to the fork of a tree. After the delivery a number of taboos surrounded the behavior of the mother and father. For about 12 days, the mother remained seated on the bench where she had given birth, bound about the stomach and legs with soft skin bands and old garments. The period of restriction ended on the twentieth day after birth (Osgood 1958:173). The father did not work for those 20 days nor did he eat fresh fish or meat. There were many taboos about the things he could touch. He was to avoid in particular White men's goods, things of steel and iron. Other taboos extended for many months past the birth of the child. For example, if the baby was born in the spring, the father would not go lamprey fishing the next fall (Parsons 1921–1922:52).

At the end of the initial 20-day restriction, the father had a "sun song" chanted for him by a friend. He then went off into the woods for a brief period of purification. He was expected to bring back edible meat. When he returned, he went to the kashim to reward the man who sang the "sun song" for him with caribou skins.

The baby was treated gently by his parents. When he cried, he was fed. He was played with, weaned when he began to walk, and early in life carefully taught the many taboos that had to do with the welfare of the family (Parsons 1921–1922:53; Osgood 1958:176–179).

• PUBERTY Unlike some Athapaskan groups, there was no isolation for boys at puberty. The most significant thing that happened to mark the occasion was "putting down" for a name, which took place at the Partner's Potlatch (Osgood 1958:188).

At her menarche, a girl was segregated from the community for a year ("Expressive Aspects of Subarctic Indian Culture," fig. 7, this vol.). She occupied a corner of her father's house, around which a little enclosure of grass mats had been constructed by her mother (Osgood 1958:183–184). She wore a beaded forehead band to which bear claws were attached. As the year went by, she mastered all the skills of a "worthy woman." She learned to sew, to cook, and to make beadwork, baskets, and fish nets (Parsons 1921–1922:57–58). She, and indeed any menstruating woman, was believed to be dangerous to men if she looked them in the eye. A man could lose his hunting, fishing, and "community" (public speaking) powers (Parsons 1921–1922:57). When a girl "went into the corner," her father observed taboos very much like those he carried out following the birth of his child. This period of restriction also lasted 20 days. During the year he took it upon himself to guide young men courteously to the kashim instead of inside his front door when they came to visit. At the end of this year of seclusion for his daughter, a wealthy man "put down" a gift of food in the kashim in her honor (Osgood 1958:189). His daughter could then be courted by young men.

During courtship in traditional times, a young man called on a girl many times until she finally consented to share a dish of food with him. Once this occurred, they slept together and were considered to be husband and wife (Osgood 1958:189–195). A somewhat different view was presented by Parsons's (1921–1922:61) informant who reported that premarital sex was permitted among the Yukon Ingalik, with marriage following if pregnancy occurred.

• DEATH Two ceremonies marked the death of an individual. First, there was the "funeral" itself, which took place in the kashim. Men for whom great respect was felt were accorded a full four nights of ceremony. During that time the deceased person was symbolically fed by close relatives. The food was then distributed among the elderly. New and old songs of mourning were sung by members of the community. Two or three men might show respect by acting as song leader (Osgood 1958:151–153). After the funeral, burial in the village graveyard (fig. 9) took place. If a man was considered important he was buried in a casket (fig. 10); if not, he was buried without one. Property was burned, inhumed, or given away. After burial, close relatives observed a number of taboos for a variable period of time. His status and the attitude toward the individual who died determined the period of mourning (Osgood 1958:155).

The second ceremony was the Death Potlatch. After a member of the community gave the Death Potlatch for the first time, taboos governed his behavior for a period of 20 days. At the end of that time, the villagers in the kashim were feted by the host on fish and "ice cream" (Osgood 1958:138).

Kinship

Kinship terminology among the Yukon Ingalik was Eskimoan in that lineal relatives consistently were distinguished from collateral relatives. Typical Athapaskan construction was evidenced in the terminological distinction between elder and younger brother and between elder and younger sister, plus man-speaking and woman-speaking terms for son and for daughter (Osgood 1959:162).

According to Osgood's (1958:231) informants, in traditional times certain forms of avoidance were practiced among Yukon Ingalik "close relations." A man did not eat "ice cream" made by his mother, his sister, his brother's wife, or his grandmother until he grew old. Joking relationships occurred between male and female first cousins.

The literature does not indicate any form of descent group existing among the Yukon Ingalik.

Smithsonian, NAA: 6912.

Fig. 9. Holikachuk graveyard at the confluence of Holikachuk Slough and the Innoko River. There were about 30 graves here, with a pole in front of each, on most of which a rifle was fastened horizontally some 10 feet from the ground (VanStone 1978:31). Photograph by E.W. Nelson, Dec. 1880.

Division of Labor

After marriage, as the Ingalik said, a man "runs the chase"—that is, he provides the major portion of the food (Parsons 1921–1922:58). He depended upon his wife to care for the children, prepare all the clothing and food (fig. 12; "Environment and Culture in the Alaska Plateau," fig. 9, this vol.), get the wood and water, and acquire what food she could from the area close to the village. She snared hare, duck, and grouse, tended the gill net, and gathered plant products (Parsons 1921–1922:58; Osgood 1958:235, 239, 248). She also made pottery, a rather uncommon trait among northern Athapaskans.

Table 1 lists the tools of subsistence and type of clothing used by the Yukon Ingalik.

Contact History and Culture Change

The Russians established a trading station along the Kuskokwim River at the mouth of the Holitna River in the winter of 1832–1833. This was on the eastern fringe of Kuskokwim Ingalik territory. In 1834 Andrei Glazunov explored the Yukon River, stopping at Anvik and then proceeding down the Yukon River to the site of Holy Cross and up the Kuskokwim, where he ascended the lower Stony River (VanStone 1959:42–47). As a result of the Russian contact, the first of the great epidemics occurred in 1838–1839. An estimated 50 percent of the neighboring Kuskowagamiut Eskimo perished in that epidemic (L.D. Mason 1975:68). The number of Ingalik who died is unknown, but according to Zagoskin (1967:193) the disease had a less severe effect on the Ingalik communities than on the Lower Koyukon.

The Russians introduced the Russian Orthodox faith. They established trade with the natives at Aleksan-

Smithsonian, NAA: top, 10455–0–4; bottom, 76–6602.

Fig. 10. Coffins, probably outer coffins or coffin houses, with figures painted in red or black (see Osgood 1940:409–414, 1958:149–154; De Laguna 1947:80–82). top, Grave near Anvik of a man said to have died before 1884, with depiction of the notable killing of a beluga. Photograph by John Wight Chapman, after 1895. bottom, Grave of a caribou hunter, on the lower Innoko River. Photograph by Aleš Hrdlička, 1929.

Fig. 11. Ralph stitching the rim of a birchbark basket with spruce root. This was a woman's activity, but Ralph was a berdache (although here dressed as a man). Photograph by Frederica De Laguna at Anvik Point, 1935.

drovskiy Redoubt, Kolmakovskiy Redoubt, Mikhailovskiy Redoubt, Ikogmiut, and Nulato ("Intercultural Relations and Culture Change in the Alaska Plateau," fig. 1, this vol.) (Osgood 1940:35). After the United States took possession of Alaska on June 20, 1867, the steamboat era on the Yukon began. The fur trade was 611

Yale U., Peabody Mus.: a, 200222; b, 25431; Amer. Mus. of Nat. Hist., New York: c. 60.5013; d, 60.4981.

Fig. 12. a-b, Spruce wood pestles for preparing foods by mashing in wooden dish. a, Size used for pounding fish eggs and rotten fish heads, collected 1956; b, for crushing berries and wild rhubarb, collected 1934. c-d, Pottery vessels, made with ptarmigan feather temper, shaped with paddle, and fire-dried. c, Lamp used for lighting with moss wick and whitefish or seal oil; d, small cooking vessel. c-d, Collected at Anvik between 1903 and 1935. Height of d about 15 cm, rest same scale.

expanded by the Alaska Commercial Company and continued on the Kuskokwim (Osgood 1940:43).

In 1887 the Episcopalians founded a mission at Anvik; and in 1888 the Roman Catholic Mission at Holy Cross was established (fig. 14). These churches maintained boarding schools (fig. 15) and "the effect on the Ingalik was considerable;" by 1940 nearly all the Indians were members of a Christian church (Osgood 1940:44).

Unfortunately, studies that deal with culture change or contemporary life of the Yukon Ingalik are lacking.

Population

Population estimates for the Ingalik since contact are given in table 2. The factor of mixed descent (European and Indian) should also be considered. Between 1900 and 1930 about 16 percent of births in the Anvik District were mixed-blood, and by 1940 the figure was 20 percent (Osgood 1940:481). Oswalt (1962:11) indicates that some time after 1900 the Kuskokwim Ingalik met their "cultural demise" as a result of the increasing frequency of intermarriage with the Kuskowagamiut Eskimo.

Table 1. Selective Inventory of Yukon Ingalik Traditional Material Culture

Subsistence and fur procurement equipment

bow and arrow complex
    plain bow, sinew back bow (rare); blunt bird arrows; detachable point arrows; multi-tipped arrows; bone foreshafts; arrow, 2 or 3 rows of feathers; Mediterranean arrow release; underarm quiver
knives
    notched stone ulu; stone skinning knife; stone wood trimming knife; caribou horn knife; wood snow knife
club; lance; bear spear
snares
    free tossing pole snare (hare)
      nettle line
    clog snare (caribou)
      babiche line
    tether snare
      sinew or babiche (ptarmigan, grouse, lynx)
      babiche and willow back line (black bear)
      twisted nettle line (tree squirrel)
    caribou surround and guide fence
deadfalls
    toppling trigger deadfall (bear, fox, wolf, and wolverine)
    friction trigger deadfall (marten, otter, mink, squirrel, ermine, and porcupine)
    beaver deadfall
beaver nets
spear thrower and darts (ducks)
fishing devices
    gill, seine, and dip net; simple and basket-trap fish weir; simple and toggle headed detachable fish spears; lances; netlike fish drags; ice chisel, ice scoop, ice needle; lamprey sticks; line fishing hooks (rare)

Implements and utensils

materials
    bone and stone
types
    side and end scrapers; cut bone awl; stone adz; wooden wedges; wooden maul

Containers

wooden dishes, one-piece or sewed
wooden spoons
bags of intestine or skin
clay pots
clay lamps
snow shovel
netting needle
bark remover
baskets
    sewn birchbark
    twined, of twisted grass or willowbark line

Travel and transportation

birchbark canoe
    hunting (ordinarily used by one man)
    transport (requires more than one person to handle; ordinarily used by 2 or 3 women)
mooseskin boat (rare)

SNOW

Table 1. Selective Inventory of Yukon Ingalik Traditional Material Culture (*Continued*)

Travel and transportation (Continued)

square raft
sled

Structures

winter village
    kashim: semisubterranean log ceremonial and men's house
        with tunnel entrance
    semisubterranean log house without tunnel entrance
summer village
    spruce (or cottonwood) plank gabled house
    hemispherical shelter
    spruce-bark gabled house
    rectangular birchbark house
    rectangular grass mat house
spring village
    inverted V-shaped house (spruce poles and boughs)
simple tepee
dugout snow house

Clothing

materials
    tanned animal skins, gut, fish and bird skin
types
    parka (marten, summer calf caribou or mountain sheep,
    mink, hare, muskrat in order of preference); shirt; one-
    piece trousers and footwear; trousers
    caribou boots
    robe/blanket
    mittens
    belts
    skin hats
    strap baby carrier

SOURCE: adapted from Osgood 1940.

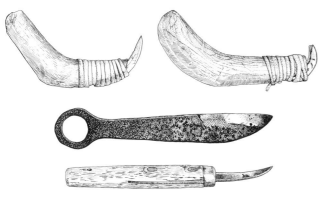

Yale U., Peabody Mus.: 50112, 50111, 200228, 200227.

Fig. 13. Woodworking tools. top, Old forms of chisels, made from beaver incisors attached with spruce gum and babiche to spruce wood hafts, left has two upper incisors used for rougher preliminary shaping, right has single lower incisor used for subsequent shaping (and for first gash in removing birchbark from tree). center and bottom, Newer forms are crooked knives made from cut down, curved, and resharpened Euro-American knives. Center, 20 cm long, rest same scale; chisels collected in 1937, knives in 1956.

In the 1970s population figures for the Ingalik come only from the Holy Cross, Anvik, and Shageluk area of the Yukon River. In 1975 Anvik had a population of 129, and Shageluk had a population of 185. Although the territory of the Yukon Ingalik falls within the Doyon Corporation, which is Athapaskan, in 1914 Holy Cross was the dividing line between Ingalik and Kuskowagamiut Eskimo (Sniffen and Carrington 1914:20). At that time, one-half the residents of Holy Cross were Eskimo. Holy Cross had a population of 429 in 1975 (Alaska Native Foundation 1975). It is not possible to establish what the Indian-Eskimo ratio actually is in Holy Cross. If it were still 50 percent Eskimo (discounting the complication of mixed descent), one could estimate that there were 215 Ingalik in Holy Cross and therefore 530 Yukon Ingalik in all. (It is important to note that under the terms of the Alaska Native Claims Settlement Act, not all people who claim a place as residence actually live there.)

Synonymy‡

The name Ingalik first appears as Russian Inkality (and German Inkaliten) in Glazunov's 1834 journal and derived sources (Wrangell 1839:69, 1839a:120, 151, 152, 155, 1970; VanStone 1959), referring to the Yukon and Kuskokwim Ingaliks. Subsequently, Zagoskin (1956:81, 123, 249, 1967:103–104, 136, 243) in 1843–1844 used Inkiliki (also Inkality, Inkaliki) as a general term for the Koyukon and Ingalik, of whom he considered the Lower Koyukon (below Nulato) to be *sobstvenno inkiliki* 'Inkilik proper', perhaps because he had encountered members of this group first. This name was borrowed by American explorers from Alaskan Russian and standardized in English as Ingalik (then pronounced 'ĭŋgə̩līk), applied to the Lower Koyukon and the Ingalik together (Dall 1870a:270, 1870:53; Allen 1887:143); Whymper (1869:175, 264) used Ingelete. The name Ingalik passed out of use in Alaska and is unknown to the Ingalik themselves, but it was revived by Osgood (1936:12–13) to refer to the Ingalik as distinct from the Lower Koyukon. Because of a lack of information he included the Holikachuk and Kolchan (Upper Kuskokwim) under the name as well, and only after the recognition in the 1960s of the distinctness of these two groups has the name Ingalik been explicitly restricted to the people so designated here (Krauss 1973:908, 1975). Russian originally borrowed the name from Yupik Eskimo *iŋqiliq* 'Indian' (pl. *iŋqilit*), literally 'having many nits', a reference to the Athapaskans' uncut hair style (James M. Kari, communication to editors 1978; Zagoskin 1967:105).

Dall (1870a:270, 1870:28, 53, 431, 1877:25, map) introduced Kaiyuhkhotana (also variously hyphenated

‡This synonymy was written by Ives Goddard.

Fig. 14. Holy Cross Mission on the Yukon River. left, Mission in June 1912 or 1914; left to right, storehouse, boys' residence, fathers' residence, post office, church, and sisters' residence. Photograph by Loman Brothers. right, Photograph by Frederica De Laguna, 1935.

Fig. 15. Indian students in sewing class at Holy Cross Mission, with the sister in the background. The large sewing machine was for repairing shoes and boots. Photograph possibly by Jules Jetté, about 1900–1915.

and accented) as a synonym of his Ingalik (Lower Yukon Koyukon, Ingalik, Holikachuk, and Kolchan), and this term had some use in secondary sources. Hodge (1907:609, 1907e:643) in two brief entries uses Ingalik and Kaiyuhkhotana synonymously in this broad sense. (Further discussion of these terms is in the synonymy in "Koyukon," this vol.) Equivalent is Ten'a, or Tena, introduced by Jetté (1907) and generally used in the anthropological literature (for example Chapman 1914; De Laguna 1947:27) until Ingalik and Koyukon became established; it is based on Ingalik and Koyukon *dəna* 'man, person' (see the synonymy in "Territorial Groups Before 1821: Athapaskans of the Shield and the Mackenzie Drainage," this vol.).

Zagoskin (1956:239, 300) used Russian *inkiliki–ūg-el'nut* and *inkality ūg-el'nut* to differentiate the Ingalik in exactly the current sense, including the Yukon, lower Innoko, and Kuskokwim groups but excluding the Holikachuk and the Kolchan. These incorporate a Yupik

term he gives as *ūg-el'nuk, ūg-el'nut* 'foreigners, mutes' (Zagoskin 1956:80), apparently *yuɣŋalŋut* 'those resembling Eskimos' (Michael E. Krauss, communication to editors 1978). Sometimes the Yukon Ingalik are differentiated from the Koyukon by expressions such as Ingaliks of the Lower Yukon or Lower Ingaliks (Dall 1870:214, 219). The Yukon-Innoko Ingalik and the modern Holikachuk are De Laguna's (1947:27) Tena of group 8.

The Ingalik call themselves *deg həian* 'people from here', and Deg Hit'an, the practical-orthography spelling, is used as the English name for the Ingalik by the Alaska Native Language Center (James M. Kari, com-

Table 2. Population

Date	Population	Area
contact	1,500	Anvik, Makki, Holy Cross, and Kolmakovskiy Redoubt
1834	1,500	all Ingalik
1842–1844	405	Anvik, Makki, Holy Cross, and Kolmakovskiy Redoubt
1844	900	all Ingalik
1880	451	Anvik, Makki, Holy Cross, and Kolmakovskiy Redoubt
1890	382	Anvik, Makki, Holy Cross, and Kolmakovskiy Redoubt
1900	565	Anvik District (Anvik, Anvik River, Bonasila, Shageluk Slough, Shageluk, and neighboring villages)
1900	600	all Ingalik
1914	452	Anvik District
1930	440	Anvik District
1934	500	all Ingalik
1974	530	Yukon River Ingalik (Anvik, Shageluk, and Ingalik of Holy Cross)

SOURCE: Osgood 1940:481, except for 1974, Alaska Native Foundation 1975.

SNOW

munication to editors 1978). The Koyukon call all downriver peoples (Holikachuk, Ingalik, and Yupik) *doċǝ xŏtanǝ* (Eliza Jones, communication to editors 1978).

HOLIKACHUK§

Territory and History

The people on the Innoko River above Holikachuk Slough had five known villages when first visited by Pëtr Kolmakov in 1839 (fig. 16). As named by the Russians (with modern locations and Holikachuk names in parentheses) these were, in order going downstream: Tlëgon (Davenport?; *toɣŭN*), Tlegokokhkakat (*toq̇akŭxnɔʔ*), Tleket, Kkholikakat (Hammer Creek; *q̇alekaɡ̇*), and Ttality (Dementi; *yałdǝkacaɡ̇*). Ttality had three winter houses and a population of 45 in 1844 and the middle three villages were described as "small" (Zagoskin 1967:236–238, 307; VanStone 1979a:27; James M. Kari, communication to editors 1979). It seems unlikely that the total population was greater than a few hundred, though in 1834 Glazunov was told of 40 "villages" on the Innoko (including the lower Innoko Ingalik), and in 1880, after smallpox and other diseases had reduced their numbers to 125, they were said to have once been "a numerous tribe having several hundred men" (VanStone 1959:44; Nelson 1978:45).

In 1844 Khuligichagat, on the east bank of the Innoko just below the outlet of Holikachuk Slough, was an Ingalik village, but by 1866 "Holiaktzagmute" in the same general area was the southernmost village of the upper Innoko people (Zagoskin 1967:235; Oswalt 1960:117). In 1880 there was also still a village at Dementi and one far upstream, perhaps at Dishkakat (*dǝYkaɡ̇*), as well as perhaps a few others. In the 1890 census 114 people in 28 houses were reported for Holikachuk village; other upper Innoko villages are not identifiable, but a total population of 300 was estimated for them and the Kolchan (U.S. Census Office. 11th Census 1893:156, 165). Most of these people eventually ended up in the modern village of Holikachuk on the west bank of the Innoko, which was abandoned in 1963. The remaining population then joined others who had moved to Grayling on the Yukon. Here there were "native houses" in 1869 and a year-round Indian village of about 40 people in 1900, though it appears to have been abandoned for a time from the 1920s on (Nelson 1978:18, 46; De Laguna 1947:65–67, 74–76; Kari 1978a:1; VanStone 1979a:50–51; Orth 1967:388). Grayling is below the site of Vazhichagat, which was the uppermost Ingalik village on the Yukon in 1843 and later (Zagoskin 1967:192). As a consequence of their shift southward, the original upper Innoko people have

§This section was written by Ives Goddard.

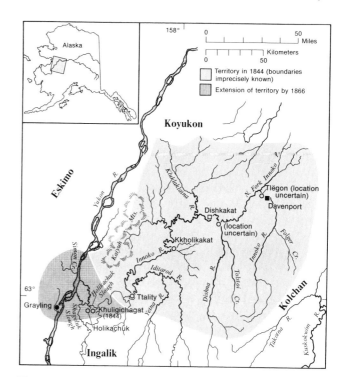

Fig. 16. Holikachuk territory.

ended up in what was earlier Ingalik territory (cf. Osgood 1940:480), except that a few who went to Nulato have descendants among the Koyukon (Carlo 1978:21–24).

Culture

At the time of contact the upper Innoko people traveled long distances out of their territory for trade and salmon fishing, salmon not being found in the Innoko. After trapping furbearers in the winter and completing the spring caribou hunt, they took their furs to the lower Innoko, the middle Yukon, or the Kuskokwim, where they traded for beads, dentalia, iron, tobacco, and (from the Kuskokwim) Eskimo-style clothing. On the middle Yukon, at least, they stayed to hunt beaver and to catch and dry fish until the first snow, when they returned to the Innoko country and scattered to their winter camps. In 1866 the Indians from the lower Innoko were said to fish for salmon on the Yukon, and the implication is that people from Holikachuk and perhaps farther up were among them. This was definitely the case in later years when Grayling was settled; fish camps of Holikachuk people were on the Yukon above and below Grayling by the 1890s, and one was at the mouth of Simon Creek in 1935 (Zagoskin 1967:167–170; Oswalt 1960:109, 117; VanStone 1979a:49–53; De Laguna 1947:64).

The culture of the upper Innoko people resembled that of the Ingalik, but with fewer Eskimo borrowings. Clothing was of painted moose and caribou skins, until replaced (by 1880) by clothing of cloth and sea-mammal   *615* skins obtained from White and Eskimo traders. Winter villages had a small number of semisubterranean houses, and summer villages, often built nearby, had brush- and bark-covered huts. Kashims were built originally only for the use of visiting traders, but "three or four years" before 1880 they were constructed in "several of their villages" for ceremonies and to serve as men's houses, though they lacked sleeping platforms. Cemeteries had plank grave boxes, roofed and supported above ground, typically with black-painted figures of caribou for a man and of "hunting shirts" for a woman. Grave goods were placed under shelters or on a tall pole set next to each grave, and new clothing was provided after one year; the graves of shamans, who could be men or women, received special additional treatment, including offerings of food and tobacco. In December each village held a potlatch for the dead that differed in some respects from the corresponding Ingalik ceremony (Zagoskin 1967:170, 236; Nelson 1978:18–21, 31–33, 44–46).

Synonymy

The people of the upper Innoko were distinguished by Zagoskin (1967:243, 307) as the Innoka-khotana or Tlëgon-khotana, the latter being specifically the name used by those on the Tlëgon River (the Innoko above where the North Fork comes in). These names correspond to Holikachuk *yonəq həian* 'middle Innoko River people' and *toγŭn^ʔ həian* 'uppermost Innoko River people' (Ingalik *ʔenŭq həian* and *teγetno^ʔ həian;* Koyukon *λuγotno^ʔ xŏtanə* from Eliza Jones, communication to editors 1978), with the element for 'people of' normalized by Zagoskin to a rendering of Koyukon *xŏtanə.*

The upper Innoko and upper Kuskokwim people were both called Inkalikhlyuat by the Yupik, apparently *iŋqiliⱥłuat* 'strange, different Indians' (Steven Jacobson, communication to editors 1979), and they were both called Kolchan (Kuilchana, etc.) in local Russian and English usage (Glazunov in Wrangell 1839a:149, 155; Zagoskin 1967:105, 243; Illarion in Oswalt 1960:109, 117; Nelson 1978:18; U.S. Census Office. 11th Census 1893:156; synonymy in "Kolchan," this vol.). Inkalichmüten (Wrangell 1839a:148) is an error for Inkalichlüaten, a German rendering of Glazunov's Russian *inkalikhlūaty.* Ethnographers after Zagoskin generally lost track of the upper Innoko people as a distinct group and lumped them with the Koyukon or the Ingalik under various labels.

After the rediscovery by Michael Krauss in 1962 that a distinct language was spoken at Holikachuk and Grayling (Kari 1978a:1; cf. Glazunov in VanStone 1959:44; Chapman 1914:1), the name Holikachuk came into use by linguists for this language and the people speaking it. The name Holikachuk was transferred from an earlier village, or succession of villages, in the area; it has also been rendered Khuligichagat, for the Ingalik village in 1844 (Zagoskin 1967:235); Holiaktzagmute (Oswalt 1960:117), apparently for Holikatzag with Eskimo *-miut* 'people of'; Holikitsak (U.S. Census Office. 11th Census 1893:7, 165); Rolukekakat (Jetté 1910); and Hologochaket (De Laguna 1947:74). The Holikachuk name for Holikachuk village is *həyeγeləNdə* (Kari 1978a:1).

The Holikachuk people call themselves *doγ həian* 'people from here' (James Kari, communication to editors 1978).

SOURCES

The earliest information on the Ingalik is in Glazunov's short description of the people of Anvik in 1834 (VanStone 1959) and the brief comments of Wrangell (1839, 1839a, 1970). Zagoskin's (1967) detailed account of his exploration of the Yukon and Kuskokwim river drainages over a period of a year and one-half, 1843–1844, provides substantial ethnographic data on the Ingalik and the Holikachuk. A major contributor to information on the Yukon Ingalik was Chapman (1903, 1907, 1913, 1914, 1921), whose work reflects his interest in folklore and religion during more than 40 years at Anvik. Other articles by Chapman in *The Spirit of Missions* and *The Alaskan Churchman* deal with various aspects of cultural change (James W. VanStone, personal communication 1975). Stuck's brief comments on Ingalik subsistence (1917) and the effects of epidemics (1914) are the only references available for that time period. Parsons (1921–1922) published a narrative from a native of the Yukon Ingalik territory that contains valuable ethnographic data.

Archival sources include the Archives of the Episcopal Church, Episcopal Seminary of the Southwest at Austin, Texas. These archives contain all the letters and papers of Chapman as well as much material from later priests and church workers at Anvik. The Oregon Province Archives of the Society of Jesus at Gonzaga University in Spokane, Washington, contain the unpublished writings of J. Jetté as well as much correspondence with a large number of Yukon River churchmen and women and the diaries of the Holy Cross Mission. There is considerable Ingalik material in the Alaska Church Collection, Library of Congress, and the Russian-American Company Records, National Archives. B.S. Smith's (1974) survey of archives contains important material relating to the lower Yukon; of particular importance are the diaries of Netsvetov, the first priest at Ikogmiut.

Other contributions include De Laguna on Holikachuk ceremonialism (1936) and on Yukon River prehistory (1947), Oswalt (1962) on historical populations on the Kuskokwim River, Nelson's (1978) notes on Ingalik and Holikachuk ceremonies and beliefs, and

VanStone's (1979, 1979a) ethnohistorical research on the Ingalik and Holikachuk area. Preliminary noun dictionaries of Ingalik (Kari 1978) and Holikachuk (Kari 1978a) have appeared.

The major source on the Yukon Ingalik is Osgood (1940, 1958, 1959), whose substantial artifact collection is at the Peabody Museum of Natural History at Yale University.

Kolchan

EDWARD H. HOSLEY

Language, Territory, and Environment

The Kolchan (ˌkol'chăn) are the Athapaskan Indians of the upper Kuskokwim River. They speak a distinct Athapaskan language more closely related to Tanana than to Ingalik, spoken on the middle Kuskokwim.* The Kolchan were originally not so much a "tribe" as a collection of autonomous contiguous bands having cultural and linguistic similarities.

The area occupied by the Kolchan in protohistoric times extended from the western foothills of the Alaska Range to the eastern slope of the Kuskokwim Mountains, and from the Swift River on the southwest to the divide between the Kuskokwim and Kantishna river drainages in the north (fig. 1). The Kolchan extended their territory northeastward in late prehistoric times into a region that was previously occupied by Athapaskans from the lower Tanana River. The ethnographic baseline of this chapter describes the period between first contact, about 1835, and the beginning of depopulation around 1900. There were six fairly well-defined bands, somewhat intermarried and on peaceful terms.

The Kolchan utilized a region of the upper Kuskokwim basin totaling more than 22,000 square miles. The principal unifying feature of this area is the main Kuskokwim River and its northward extension, the North Fork, which runs northeast to southwest along the base of the Kuskokwim Mountains. The river is generally silt-laden and meandering, as are the lower reaches of its main tributaries, which trend northwest from the western slopes of the Alaska Range. Approaching the range, the tributaries become clear and rocky. It was

in this area that the Kolchan spent the bulk of their time, rarely coming to the main river except to trade.

The biota is subarctic, with the climax forest composed of mixed spruce, birch, and willow and frequented by the usual variety of associated animal life. Whitefish are abundant in the lakes and streams, and most of the tributaries receive runs of several varieties of salmon.

External Relations

The Kolchan were surrounded by other Athapaskan groups. Their friendliest relations, including intermarriage, mutual potlatching, and close cultural similarities, existed with the Tanana to the north. Attitudes toward the Koyukon to the west were hostile, with cultural differences stressed, and mutual raiding taking place. Relations with the Ingalik to the southwest, who were seen by the Kolchan as Eskimo-like in their culture, were marred by disputes over the caribou grounds between their respective territories (Osgood 1959:77). Contacts with Eskimos from the lower Kuskokwim River were restricted to occasional hunting expeditions by Eskimo into Kolchan territory. The aggressive Tanaina flanked the Kolchan on the south at Stony River and also east of the Alaska Range. They made frequent trading journeys into the upper Kuskokwim region, and in the mid-nineteenth century they established a village in the upper Big River drainage. This led to hostilities, and the Kolchan eventually forced them to abandon the area (Hosley 1960–1964).

Culture

The Kolchan seasonal round focused upon hunting, with fishing of secondary importance. Winter camps were villages of semisubterranean dwellings. Winter subsistence depended largely upon small game, caribou, and hibernating bears, supplemented by ice fishing. The winter camps were located on lakes or clearwater tributaries of major streams toward the Alaska Range.

In late March, preparations were made for the spring caribou hunt. The lightweight birchbark canoes and personal belongings were loaded on hand-drawn toboggans, and small packs were carried by dogs. Bands

---

*The phonemes of Kolchan are: (unaspirated stops and affricates) d, λ, ȝ, ʒ̇, ǯ, g, ʔ; (aspirated stops and affricates) t, ƛ, c, ç, č, k; (glottalized) t̓, ƛ̓, c̓, ç̓, č̓, k̓; (voiceless continuants) N, ł, s, ṣ, š, x; (voiced continuants) m, n, l, z, ẓ, y, γ; (full vowels) i, a [æ], o [ɔ], u; (reduced vowels) ə (with a range of central and front allophones), ŭ. Some older speakers have a contrast between the c-series and a series with fronted ([ç]) or almost interdental ([θ̂]) pronunciation.

In the practical orthography introduced by Collins and Collins (1966) the Kolchan phonemes are written: d, dl, dz, dr, j, g, ʼ (not written word-initially); t, tł, ts, tr, ch, k; t', tł', ts', tr', ch', k'; n̦, ł, s, sr, sh, h; m, n, l, z, zr, y, gh; e, a, o, u; i, w.

Information on the phonology of Kolchan and the transcription of Kolchan words was provided by Raymond L. Collins (communication to editors 1973).

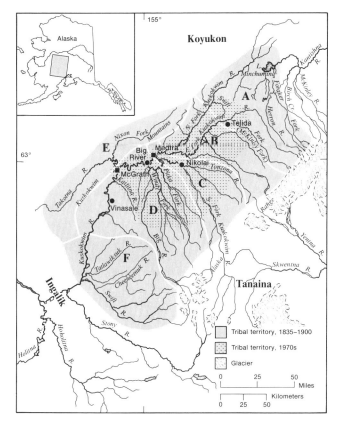

Fig. 1. Tribal territory, 1835–1960s, with approximate areas of 6 main bands: A, Telida-Minchumina; B, East Fork; C, Nikolai; D, Vinasale; E, Takotna; F, Tatlawiksuk.

traveled to the upland caribou grounds before the river ice broke. Caribou were hunted in both spring and fall, the fall season being the more important. Hunting techniques frequently involved more than one band, for example, use of the caribou surround. Caribou were also stalked by individuals in skins, and during mating season they were attracted by rubbing caribou scapulae together.

The summer was spent in the ranges hunting caribou, sheep, and bears. The meat was dried and prepared for packing back to the winter camps. Summer dwellings were tepeelike structures covered with skins. In the early fall, some families moved downstream or to the lakes to fish camps for the whitefish and salmon runs. Both set nets and weirs (fig. 2) were employed.

In late October, following the fall caribou hunt, the return trip to the winter camps was made by canoe and skin bullboats. In preparation for the winter, clothing was made from tanned caribou hides and various furs. The tanning process included breaking down the fibers by a paste of caribou brains and smoking over fires. The shirts were straight-bottomed, with a fringe at the lower edge and across the chest. Moccasins and high leggings decorated with porcupine quills were also worn, and separate parka hoods or fur caps completed the normal attire. Fur mittens and sheepskin socks were added in cold weather, and capes of salmon skin were

used for rain. Bedding consisted of sewed rabbit or sheep skins.

Though the Kolchan made crude pottery, most cooking was done by stone-boiling in birchbark containers. Fire was produced by both the bow drill and hand drill. Firearms were in use as early as the 1840s (Zagoskin 1967:269), but as late as 1898 the Kolchan were still hunting largely with spears (fig. 3) and the bow (Spurr 1900:72). In aspects not discussed here, the Kolchan had the general material technology of the Western (Yukon drainage) Athapaskans.

The Kolchan social organization was based upon three exogamous matrilineal descent groups or clans: *dəčalayuɣ* 'fish people', *toniʒɣəlčiłna* 'people in the middle', and *məʒəštəhŭtana* 'caribou people'. A fourth clan, *nolcina* or *nalcina*, was present as a result of intermarriage with the Tanana. A man belonged to the clan of his mother, and the mother's brother was often an authority figure. Marriages were arranged, cross-cousin marriage was preferred, and there was a tendency to seek a maternal uncle's daughter for a bride. Brothers frequently married into a single band, often to sisters, and brother-sister exchange in marriage was common.

Upon her menarche, a girl went into seclusion, remaining under a number of taboos for several weeks. She was then considered eligible for marriage, and courtship usually followed immediately. After the initial arrangements between the two families, the youth made gifts of food and skins to the girl's mother and performed various services for her family. The marriage was announced to the band members, and the husband joined the wife's group without ceremony. They con-

Fig. 2. Nikolai Alaxia of Nikolai village spearing salmon in an impoundment between 2 weirs (in background and behind the camera) on the Hidzulhgashno or Ch'idzulhgashno' (*čəʒułgašno*ʔ, interpreted as 'salmon spearing creek'), a clearwater tributary of the Tonzona River 20–25 miles upstream from Nikolai.
Photograph by Edward Hosley in 1962; at that time the weirs were still used only by the Alaxia family.

Fig. 3. Chief Devian Wassilia (b.1883, d.1963) standing in front of his cabin in Nikolai village holding a knife with flaring, voluted handle formerly attached to a long lance—shaft wrapped with rawhide thongs in a series of half hitches to improve the grip—which he had used as a young man to kill bears. Photograph by Edward Hosley, 1962.

tinued to live with the wife's band for a year or more. Following this period of bride service, though free to establish their own household, the couple usually remained with the wife's group. Polygyny was occasionally practiced, there were isolated instances of fraternal polyandry, and both the sororate and levirate were present.

The Kolchan kin terminology employed Iroquois cousin terms and bifurcate collateral terms for parents' siblings and siblings' children. Band leadership shifted with the task at hand, usually resting with the eldest males and the shaman of the group.

The ideological life of the Kolchan focused upon explanations of events and upon divination, particularly in connection with the hunt and death. Interpretations of signs, omens, dreams, and the cries and movements of animals played an important part. It was believed by the Kolchan that in ancient times the animals spoke with and helped men. Some still were able to speak a few words in the Indian language and used this ability to help men. Animals also communicated among them-

selves, and hunters needed their cooperation in order to kill them. Thus apologies were made to bears and wolves at the time of a kill, and they were treated with great respect so as not to offend them. For the same reason, fur-bearing animals were taken into a warm dwelling before skinning.

In the supernatural realm, the Kolchan believed in the Nahani or Bush Indian, an elusive creature who served as a scapegoat for unexplained events. There were also the Hill People of the caribou ranges who were propitiated with food thrown into the fire. The mythology revolved about two major figures. One was čəcʼətazkani 'one who is paddling around', a culture hero. The other was doçonʔ or doçocəla 'Raven', a trickster figure about whom many tales, frequently humorous, were told.

Both sexes served as shamans, the specialty passing down family lines. Power was acquired by dreams, and the shaman was assisted by animal familiars. The shaman treated illness, interpreted dreams and other omens, assisted in warfare, and entertained at social gatherings. Bands without resident shamans were considered to be weak, and a shaman could occasionally rise to a position of strong leadership.

The Kolchan had little concept of an afterlife, although they believed the spirits of dead persons lived after them and were often harmful to the living. Cremation followed by tree exposure of the remains was the customary means of disposal, and it was believed that newborn children were the reincarnated spirits of the deceased.

History of Contact

Because the Kolchan were remote from the earliest Russian settlements, initial trading was through other groups, such as the Tanaina. Later, by 1834, a permanent trading station was established by Fëdor Kolmakov at Kvygympaynagmyut on the lower Kuskokwim (Zagoskin 1967:252). By 1844 officials from that station, called Kolmakovskiy Redoubt, were traveling up the Kuskokwim to trade. From the 1840s well into the early part of the twentieth century, Vinasale, a Kolchan fishing camp, was an intermittent trading post (Oswalt 1963:107–109; Spurr 1900:94–95). Conversion to Russian Orthodox Christianity was rapid, with some Kolchans baptized as early as 1838 (Zagoskin 1967:249). As trade increased, the new wealth led to a change in the Kolchan "funeral potlatch" from a simple commemorative feast to a four-day event in which large amounts of food and goods were given away.

As the Kolchan involvement in the fur trade increased, their seasonal round changed. They became more sedentary and permanent villages were established. As the land gained an economic value, band ownership of trapping areas weakened in favor of family rights. By the turn of the twentieth century, Kolchan contact with Whites greatly increased. The region was visited by a geological party in 1898 (Spurr 1900), by a U.S. Army survey expedition in 1899 (Herron 1901), and by trappers, prospectors, and Orthodox priests. From 1900 to 1910 the Kantishna and Innoko gold fields were opened, prospectors in the upper Kuskokwim River area became numerous, and additional trading posts were established.

The last major potlatch was held in 1915, following which the institution merged with the Russian Orthodox Christmas. The first churches were built at Nikolai and Telida villages in 1914–1915, and these two communities became the focal points for the remaining Kolchan.

By 1915, decreased mobility and the introduction of the fish wheel had caused an increased emphasis upon fishing ("Environment and Culture in the Alaska Plateau," fig. 24, this vol.). In addition, by the late 1920s, the use of repeating rifles had so destroyed the caribou herds that the seasonal movement to the caribou hunting grounds was largely abandoned, and the moose became the main game animal. Work in the mines was available between 1910 and the late 1930s. Many Indian families worked at the roadhouses established by Whites along the winter trails; however, the introduction of the airplane in the 1930s caused the abandonment of the winter-trail network. As a result of the Depression, trapping, fur farming, and mining decreased in importance.

By 1935 the population was concentrated at Vinasale, Big River, Nikolai, and Telida. The government of Nikolai and Telida villages was organized on the village council pattern. With the abandonment of Vinasale in 1940, Nikolai village (fig. 4) became the center of Kolchan settlement. A school was established at Nikolai in 1950, contributing to the coalescence of the Kolchan in this community. Because of this nucleation of the population at Nikolai, the region exploited was reduced to less than half the original Kolchan territory, with the areas about Lake Minchumina and south of McGrath no longer utilized (fig. 1).

Population

The Indian population of the upper Kuskokwim area probably did not exceed 250 to 300 in aboriginal times (Spurr 1900:71; Gordon 1917; Hosley 1960–1964). Warfare, the emphasis on large game over fish, and recurrent periods of starvation probably served to keep population densities low. Following European contact, the introduction of diseases, primarily diphtheria and influenza, led to population decline. By 1910 the population of the 10 winter village groups of the Kolchan totaled only 68. By 1935 the low point of about 50 persons had been passed, and a population of 69 had amalgamated into four winter village groups. By 1968 the population had risen to an estimated 135, largely due to better medical care.

Sociocultural Situation in the 1960s

By the mid-1960s, 135 Kolchan were living in Nikolai village. Winter trapping was still important, although population pressure had caused a decline in the income from this source. In the spring, families left the village and moved to summer fish camps elsewhere in the upper Kuskokwim region, frequently near the trading-post communities of Medfra and McGrath where occasional summer employment was available. Fire fighting, airfield and road maintenance, and work in the few operating mines were the most common jobs. In the fall, the emphasis was on the salmon and whitefish runs, as well as on moose hunting.

By the late 1960s, the dog team was rapidly being replaced by the snowmobile (fig. 6), and outboard motors had become the norm for river travel. Employment opportunities in the area were still limited, although lumbering had some potential. Other than trapping and seasonal employment, the major sources of income for the Kolchan were various state and federal assistance programs. Better health care had led to an expanded population, with increased outward migration to larger population centers in Alaska. With the Alaska Native

Fig. 4. Nikolai village on the South Fork of the Kuskokwim River. Tall poles support radio antennas. Photographed facing east by Edward Hosley, 1960 or 1962, copyright 1966.

Fig. 5. Single- and double-ended sleds used by the Kolchan of Nikolai village. Photograph by Edward Hosley, 1960.

Tundra Times, Anchorage, Alaska.
Fig. 6. Phillip and Dora Esai on snowmobile. Photographed late 1960s or early 1970s.

Claims Settlement Act of 1971, the remaining Kolchan may in time obtain the necessary economic base to survive as a viable and distinct ethnic unit.

Synonymy†

The name Kolchan was introduced by Hosley (1968:6–7) in order to have a distinctive name for the native inhabitants of the upper Kuskokwim River, who had not been consistently distinguished in the earlier literature. This usage follows Zagoskin (1967:243, 268–269, 300), who in 1844 had applied the name Goltsan to the same people. Goltsan is a rendering of Tanaina *ɣəlcana*, a general name for all interior Athapaskans used in the Upper Inlet dialect specifically for the upper Kuskokwim people (Kari 1977:93). The first distinctive use in English may be by Elliott (1875:29), who refers to "the *Kolchans*, or people of the Upper Koskoquim River," though his population estimate of 6,000 to 7,000 may indicate that the interior groups generally are meant. Variants of this name used in broader or different meanings are Kyltschanes (German Kyltschanen), Galtzanes (Galzanen), Koltschanes (Koltschanen) (Glazunov in Wrangell 1839a,1:148; VanStone 1959:43–44); *Kol'chane* and *Gal'tsane* (Wrangell 1839:54); kalchan (P. Kolmakov in Zagoskin 1967:300); Kolchanes (Illarion in Oswalt 1960:104, 117); and Kol-

†This synonymy was written by Ives Goddard, incorporating materials supplied by Edward H. Hosley.

chan (Nelson 1978:18); see also the entry "Kulchana" in Hodge (1907d:733–734). The Athapaskan languages use this word to refer generally to alien Athapaskans, especially those for whom there is no specific name: Inland Tanaina *ɣəlcuna* (Kari 1977:93); Ahtna *ɣalca·ne* (Kari and Buck 1975:58); Koyukon *ɣəlχonə* (Eliza Jones, communication to editors 1978). Nineteenth-century Russian sources give the translations 'strangers', 'visitors', or 'nomads' (VanStone in Nelson 1978:12–13), but a likely analysis suggests 'those who are recognized' (Eliza Jones, communication to editors 1979).

In the influential classification of Osgood (1936:13, 1940:31) the Kolchan were called the McGrath group of Ingalik, though with the qualification that they might "after further study, prove a distinctive group," independent of the Ingalik. Hosley's (1968) delineation of the ethnographic distinctness of these people rendered Osgood's tentative label inappropriate. Also in the 1960s the linguistic distinctiveness of this group was identified by Collins and Collins (1966) and Krauss (1973:908, 1974), who employ the designation Upper Kuskokwim Athapaskan.

The Kolchan refer to themselves as *dəna'ina* 'people, Athapaskans', a name identical to the self-designation used by the Tanaina. They are called *yun'əhtan* in Lime Village and Nondalton Tanaina (Kari 1977:93) and *'eneʒ hətan* in Kuskokwim Ingalik (James Kari, communication to editors 1978), both meaning 'upriver people'. Koyukon uses *dəkənaniqə hŏtanə* for all Kuskokwim Athapaskans (Eliza Jones, communication to editors 1978). Zagoskin (1967:105, 243) records Yupik Inkalikhlyuat for both the upper Innoko and the upper Kuskokwim people and sometimes uses the compound name Goltsan-Inkalikhlyuat; see the synonymy for Holikachuk in "Ingalik," this volume.

Sources

The available literature on the Kolchan is limited, since they were not studied ethnographically until Hosley's (1960–1964) fieldwork. In the 1960s and 1970s, there was some linguistic work done by Raymond L. Collins (Collins and Collins 1966; Collins and Petruska 1979) and Michael Krauss. The primary source of data on the Kolchan in 1972 remained Hosley (1966). Additional information may be obtained from the journals of early explorers and their references to the region. Most readily available are Michael's translation of Zagoskin's (1967) journals, and the journals of Gordon (1917), Herron (1901), and Spurr (1900).

Tanaina

JOAN B. TOWNSEND

Tanaina (təˈnīˌnu) is the name used by twentieth-century anthropologists to designate the Athapaskan Indian population of southwestern Alaska in the vicinity of Cook Inlet and the region immediately north and west (fig. 1). The Tanaina speak closely related dialects of a distinct Athapaskan language* and recognize their shared ethnic identity, at least in the twentieth century, but they have never formed a separate socio-political unit and they exhibit a broad range of aboriginal ecological adaptations.

External Relations

Like other peoples of Alaska, the Tanaina were never isolated socially from other populations. Trade networks crisscrossed Alaska, and intergroup contacts and exchanges of ideas were common long before the Russians arrived. Warfare occurred between the Tanaina and neighboring Eskimos, slaves being taken by both sides, and there were also hostilities among Tanaina villages and with other Athapaskans. However, Tanaina war stories seem to recount conflicts mainly with Eskimos (Osgood 1937:109, 183; Tenenbaum 1976, 4; Kalifornsky 1977:77; Townsend 1960–1973, 1979). While societal endogamy was the norm, marriages occasionally did occur between the Tanaina and other

*The italicized Tanaina words cited in the *Handbook* are in the phonemic system of Kari (1977) transcribed as follows: (voiceless unaspirated stops and affricates) b, d, ƛ, ʒ, ǯ, g, ġ, ʔ; (aspirated stops and affricates) t, ƛ̓, c, č, k, q; (glottalized) t̓, ƛ̓, c̓, č̓, k̓, q̓; (voiceless continuants) ł, s, š, x̣, x, h; (voiced continuants) v, l, z, ž, ɣ̣, ɣ; (nasals) m, n; (semivowels) w, y; (vowels) a, i, u, ə. In the practical orthography used by the Alaska Native Language Center these are written: b, d, dl, dz, j, g, gg, ' (not written word-initially); t, tl, ts, ch, k, q; t', tl', ts', ch', k', q'; ł, s, sh, x, h, hh; v, l, z, zh, y̱, gh; m, n; w, y; a, i, u, e.

The Upper Inlet dialect has 8 fewer consonants, as follows: ǯ, č, and č̓ merge with ʒ, c, and c̓, respectively, which here have an intermediate pronunciation; š and x̣ merge with s; z, ž, and ɣ̣ merge with y. b, v, and w were originally dialect variants of a single phoneme, which in most environments was [b] in Upper Inlet and Outer Inlet (except Kachemak Bay), [v] in Iliamna and Inland, and [w] in Kachemak Bay; but the introduction of b and v in loanwords has made the contrast distinctive.

Village and group names are given in the local dialect; otherwise, unspecified forms are in the Outer Inlet dialect. James M. Kari (communications to editors 1978, 1979) has provided information on the meanings and transcriptions of Tanaina words.

Indian and Eskimo groups. The Tanaina share many cultural elements with neighboring Athapaskans, Eyak, and Tlingit. Their culture is somewhat less complex than that of the Coastal Tlingit but more complex than the interior Athapaskans such as the Ingalik, Koyukon, Kutchin, and Tanana, particularly in their having a greater number of clans and a greater emphasis on rank.

Language

Tanaina, one of the most internally diverse Alaskan Athapaskan languages (Kari 1977a:274), falls into two major linguistic divisions, Upper Inlet and Lower Inlet. Upper Inlet is a single dialect, but there are three Lower Inlet dialects, Outer Inlet, Iliamna, and Inland. The Upper Inlet dialect is or was spoken at the head of Cook Inlet, along Knik Arm, the lower Knik, Matanuska, Susitna, and Yentna rivers, and along the northwestern shore of Cook Inlet as far south as Nikolai Creek on Trading Bay. A small Upper Inlet–speaking village, Nikita, was founded at Point Possession on the northwest corner of Kenai Peninsula in the nineteenth century but was abandoned in the 1930s (De Laguna 1934:136; Kari 1977a:277). The Outer Inlet dialect is or was spoken on the Kenai Peninsula as far south as Kachemak Bay, where there was a major subdialect. At least by the late nineteenth century, Outer Inlet speakers also occupied the western shore of Cook Inlet in the West Foreland–Tuxedni Bay area, particularly at Polly Creek, a commercial clam digging station, and Kustatan. The Iliamna dialect is spoken at the eastern end of Iliamna Lake and perhaps formerly at Chinitna Bay. The Inland dialect is spoken on Lake Clark, along the Stony River, and formerly along the Mulchatna River (Kari 1975, 1977, 1977a).

Upper Inlet Tanaina is very sharply distinct from the Lower Inlet dialects in having eight fewer consonants, a reduction that largely parallels that in neighboring Ahtna (Kari 1977a:281–282). The Lower Inlet dialects differ mostly in details of grammar and lexicon; however, the distribution of some linguistic features cuts across the dialect boundaries, and some modern settlements, such as New Tyonek, have dialectally mixed populations drawn from different areas.

Societies

The people speaking the Tanaina language comprised at least three societies (Levy 1966:20–21; Aberle et al. 1950) in the past (fig. 1). These correspond roughly but not completely with the dialect divisions identified by Kari for Tanaina of the twentieth century. Societal divisions reflect differences in marriage patterns, sociocultural elements, degree of interaction, and proximity. Variations in adaptation to the diversity of ecological environments found in the region were basic, with resultant variations in emphasis on specific subsistence activities, and different degrees of sociocultural elaboration. These societies existed generally in the nineteenth century, but they ceased to exist as societal entities in the twentieth century.

The hazards of water travel in Cook Inlet with its enormous tides inhibited but did not completely preclude contact across the inlet. For example, people from both sides of Cook Inlet exploited Kalgin Island for hair seals, birds, and clams (U.S. Census Office. 11th Census 1893:71; De Laguna 1934:13), and, at least after 1900, some Kustatan people hunted moose on the Kenai Peninsula (Kalifornsky 1977:23). However, the most intense and constant relations occurred along the shores of the inlet rather than across it, effectively creating two societies, Kenai Peninsula (Outer Inlet dialect) and Susitna (Upper Inlet dialect). The third society, Interior, was to the west. Most marriages recorded by the Nushagak and Kenai Russian missionaries in the last half of the nineteenth century were within the societal boundaries, although some intermarriage occurred between societies (Alaska Russian Church Archives 1842–1931, 1845–1933).

All societies maintained winter villages. In spite of movements to and from these semipermanent villages and fish camps and hunting and trapping locales, there was a continuity of social and political interaction among village members, which contributed to the evolution of ranking and other complex forms of village life. The degree of this elaboration varied among the societies.

The most complex elaboration was in the Kenai society, which in part reflected its more stable and lush land and marine subsistence resources. The Kachemak Bay area was the most intensely marine oriented and was almost completely sedentary. Iliamna region people of the Interior society not only had access to the lake resources, which included salmon runs and a resident population of seals, but also exploited adjacent lands for game and portaged to Cook Inlet to obtain marine and littoral resources. Further inland, people of the Interior society concentrated more heavily on hunting and fishing in interior waterways. Although resources were more abundant for Iliamna people and their social structure was somewhat more elaborate than those farther north, the high degree of interaction throughout the area maintained a single society. For the same reasons, Susitna remained a single society despite internal variations in subsistence and cultural complexity.

Although societal and dialect boundaries were maintained during the eighteenth and nineteenth centuries, intermarriage among the Tanaina societies and also between Tanaina and other linguistic groups did occur. For example, during the nineteenth century some Western Ahtna moved into the Talkeetna River drainage from the Upper Susitna and consolidated with Tanaina there to become the group known as the Mountain People (Kari 1977a:276–278). Also, some Koniag and Creole employees of the Russians who were posted at Iliamna in the 1850s married local Tanaina women (Alaska Russian Church Archives 1845–1933, 1842–1931; Townsend 1960–1973).

In 1881, Hieromonk Nikita noted that the language of the people "beginning from" Kustatan village and along the northwest shore of Cook Inlet was different from that of the Kenai people, indicating the presence of two dialects on the western shore. Subsequently there was increased contact across the inlet, including marriages arranged by the priest at Kenai (Townsend 1974:11, 17–18), and people from several areas including Iliamna and Kenai Peninsula came to the Polly Creek–Kustatan area to participate in the commercial clamming enterprises (Kalifornsky 1977:5). Whatever the extent of the nineteenth-century population movements might have been, Kustatan people interviewed in the 1930s and later were found to speak the Outer Inlet dialect (Kari 1975:50, 1977a:274).

A number of factors including disruption of interior resources and population declines brought about consolidation of Interior people during the last few decades of the nineteenth century. In the 1970s the Interior Tanaina were mainly at Lime Village, Nondalton, and Pedro Bay.

In the last few decades of the nineteenth and the early twentieth centuries, population decimation from epidemic diseases, changes in resource availability, acceleration of fur trading activities from competing companies following the sale of Alaska to the United States, introduction of commercial fishing and canning enterprises, and improved transportation disrupted older cultural patterns and encouraged greater movement of people across societal lines, further weakening the old societal distinctions. These ceased to exist by the beginning of the twentieth century, when the Tanaina became an enclaved ethnic unit within the Euro-American society.

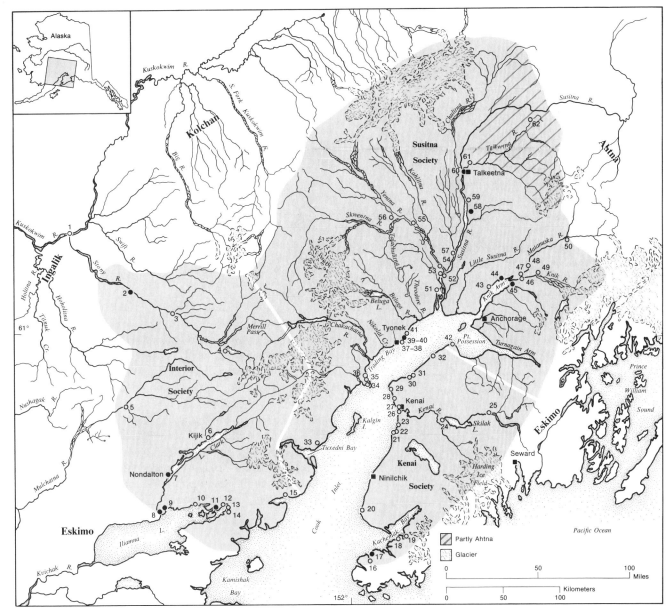

Fig. 1. Tanaina local groups, with settlements of various periods in the 18th through 20th centuries. (Townsend 1960–1973; James M. Kari, communication to editors 1980). INTERIOR SOCIETY   Inland dialect. Stony River Tanainas: 1, Stony River village (partly Ingalik and Yupik); 2, Lime Village; 3, Canyon Village. Telaquana Lake Tanainas: 4, Trail Creek village. Mulchatna Tanainas: 5, *čałčikaq̇* 'Chilchitna River mouth'. Lake Clark Tanainas: 6, Kijik; 7, Nondalton.   Iliamna dialect. Iliamna Lake Tanainas: 8, Newhalen; 9, New Iliamna villages (mostly Yupik); 10, Chekok; 11, Pedro Bay; 12, Lonesome Bay; 13, Pile Bay; 14, Old Iliamna village; 15, Chinitna Bay (dialect uncertain).

KENAI SOCIETY   Outer Inlet dialect. Kenai Peninsula Tanainas, including East Foreland Tanainas, Kenai River Tanainas, Kenai Mountain Tanainas, and Seldovia Tanainas: 16, Old Seldovia village; 17, Seldovia; 18, China Poot Bay village; 19, Soonroodna; 20, Kasnatchin; 21, Cape Kasilof village; 22, Coffee Point village; 23, Kalifornsky village; 24, Stepanka's village; 25, Skilak; 26, Chinila; 27, Skittok; 28, Salamatof; 29, Nikishka I; 30, Nikishka III; 31, *tiduqilčэtt* 'abandoned place'; 32, Libby Creek settlement.

SUSITNA SOCIETY   Outer Inlet dialect. Kustatan Tanainas: 33, Polly Creek; 34, Old Kustatan; 35, Packer's Creek village; 36, New Kustatan.   Upper Inlet dialect. Tyonek Tanainas: 37, Robert's Creek site; 38, Old Tyonek; 39, New Tyonek; 40, *qaǵэýślat*; 41, Chuit River village. Knik Arm Tanainas: 42, Point Possession village; 43, Fish Creek village; 44, Cottonwood Creek village; 45, Eklutna; 46, Matanuska village; 47, Old Kinik; 48, *nił'aca'iłut* 'rocks together'; 49, *xutnayuťi* 'glittering'; 50, Chikaloon village. Lower Susitna River Tanainas: 51, Alexander Creek village; 52, Susitna or Susitna Station; 53, Old Susitna; 54, Yentna River village; 55, Fish Lake village; 56, Hewitt Lake village. Kroto Creek Tanainas: 57, Kroto village; 58, Montana Creek village; 59, Sunshine Creek villlage; 60, Talkeetna. Talkeetna River Ahtna-Tanainas: 61, Chunilna Creek camp; 62, Stephan Lake village.

Culture

Subsistence

All five species of salmon, chinook (*Oncorhynchus tshawytscha*), coho (*O. kisutch*), sockeye (*O. nerka*), pink (*O. gorbuscha*), and chum (*O. keta*), are available during the summer months in Cook Inlet; sockeye is abundant in the Interior, particularly at Iliamna and Clark lakes. It is salmon that provides the basis of Tanaina subsistence. Aboriginally, and until the early twentieth century, salmon were taken in weirs and basket traps set in streams; dip nets were used as a secondary method. Antler fish spears, usually single-barbed with detachable heads, were occasionally used. Men usually fished; women split (fig. 2) and dried the catch. Since the beginning of the twentieth century, gill nets have replaced all other techniques of salmon fishing. Seining and set and drift netting are employed (fig. 3).

Pike, trout, grayling, and other freshwater fish were caught in earlier times with bone fishhooks and more recently with metal hooks. Nets are also set in ponds for pike and are often placed under the ice.

The Pacific harbor seal (*Phoca vitulina richardii*) is common in Cook Inlet; in addition, Iliamna Lake is one of the few freshwater lakes in the world with a resident seal population. These mammals, while secondary in importance to fish and usually to land mammals, were taken in summer with both bows and arrows and toggle harpoons at Cook Inlet and Iliamna Lake until the twentieth century. Iliamna informants state that seals were also hunted at their breathing holes in the lake ice during winter (Townsend 1960–1973). Beluga whales were hunted by people of Cook Inlet and Iliamna people who portaged to Cook Inlet, particularly Kamishak Bay, for that purpose.

Fig. 3. Seining with gill net at Pedro Bay, Iliamna Lake. With one end of the net attached to the shore, the other end is rowed out to enclose a school of salmon and force them near the beach. Photograph by Joan Townsend, 1969.

Land animals were hunted throughout the year, but during the fall men made special trips for caribou (*Rangifer tarandus granti*) (Skoog 1968:1–12). Moose (generally more common than caribou), bear, mountain goats, and Dall sheep were hunted annually in the areas adjacent to the winter villages. For large game, sinew-backed bows and arrows with antler, native copper, or chipped or ground stone points were the main weapons. Spears, from four to eight feet in length with large stone points, were also used. After contact, iron was used for many arrow and spear points. Spear throwers increased the efficiency of the spears. Caribou were hunted by driving the herds into lakes where they were speared by hunters in canoes. Dogs were also used to surround the caribou and drive the herd toward men waiting with bows and arrows. Alternatively, long fences with hidden snares and surrounds were used for caribou. A range of other hunting techniques and equipment was used depending on the kind of animal hunted and the local conditions. These included sling shots, snares, deadfalls, and pitfalls.

Birds, particularly ptarmigan, grouse, and ducks, were hunted in the summer and autumn with bolas and bows and arrows. In the late nineteenth century, spent rifle cartridges were jammed onto wood shafts to be used as blunt arrowheads for birds.

Guns began to be available to the Tanaina by the 1840s (Zagoskin 1967:247, 268–270) and possibly earlier. By the turn of the twentieth century, Tanaina had muzzle-loading guns, percussion rifles, and small gauge double-barreled shotguns (Abercrombie 1900a:402; VanStone and Townsend 1970:107–111).

Data on subsistence are provided by Osgood (1937), Townsend (1965, 1960–1973), VanStone and Townsend (1970), and Wrangell (1970).

• ANNUAL ROUND From aboriginal times through the early part of the twentieth century, and at some places

Fig. 2. Filleting salmon with a semilunar knife, or ulu (Tanaina *vašlu*), formerly of stone, now of reworked piece of saw blade. Photograph by Joan Townsend, 1969.

through 1970, when the salmon runs began in summer Tanainas left their winter villages to live at camps at particularly good fishing locales. In some areas fish camps were consolidated; others, for example, Nondalton in the 1960s, were strung out along the river or lakeshore for several miles. In either case, all residences in the community were within short distances of each other so that village unity was maintained.

After the salmon run ended in late summer Tanainas of most groups traveled into the mountains to hunt caribou and mountain sheep. Among the Kenai and Inland Tanaina these trips were usually short and by men only, but among the Susitna Tanaina and other local groups that had to make longer trips families traveled together. During the hunting trips into the interior, trading occurred with other groups encountered. Although caribou were hunted prior to the twentieth century on the Kenai Peninsula, there is no evidence that the animals were ever very numerous, and by the turn of the century caribou numbers were so reduced as to be no longer of economic significance (Lutz 1956:82–86). On the Peninsula, moose and fish were probably always more important food resources (Skoog 1968:176–177; Petroff 1884:38). Inland Tanainas were still hunting caribou in the 1970s, but the Susitna people ceased their hunts in the Alaska Range and the Talkeetna valley after the disruptions of the 1918 influenza epidemic (James M. Kari, communication to editors 1978). In most areas women and children went to snare ground squirrels in the mountains while the men went hunting. By the beginning of winter, all had returned to the villages. When on hunting expeditions, temporary tent-like structures of birchbark or skins were used for shelter. Along frequently traveled trails, small relatively permanent huts were built for shelter of travelers.

After the European fur trade became an important aspect of Tanaina economy, trapping was introduced as part of the seasonal round. This activity, in the fall and early spring, was combined with subsistence hunting trips of several weeks' or, occasionally, months' duration. It did not seem to alter extensively the seasonal round of the people.

• TRADE   Aboriginally the Tanaina were involved in intertribal trade with all the surrounding tribes, as well as intratribal trade between Tanaina villages in different ecological zones. Rich men (*qəšqa*) with trade partners were especially active. Fairs were held for the express purpose of trade. Items exchanged included native copper for projectile points, caribou and other animal skins and furs, porcupine quills, sea mammal products, dentalium shells, and slaves. This trade continued until the beginning of the twentieth century.

At the beginning of the nineteenth century when the fur trade was initiated by the Russian mercantile monopoly, the Indians incorporated fur for that market into their already existing trade system. Some Tanainas, particularly Susitna men, acted as middlemen for the Russians in trade for the valuable furs of the more interior regions of Alaska. In addition to trade, they trapped for commercial purposes themselves.

Although most Indians participated in trapping, those who had been leaders in aboriginal trade more readily adapted to fur marketing and utilized their trading expertise with interior peoples. In the early years, the Russians provided extensive credit to successful Indian fur trappers and traders in order to keep them indebted to the Russian-American Company and actively obtaining furs. Items traded to the Indians by the Russians, such as beads and particularly dentalium shells, were highly valued as prestige symbols. Thus, rich men continued to participate in the fur-trade activities in order to obtain more prestige within their own society.

During the period of rising economic prosperity and easy credit of the late nineteenth century the rich men grew in importance and were able to entice a large entourage of relatives to work for them, assisting them in advancing their prestige even more. When the local fur market crashed after 1897, the rich men were no longer able to maintain their economic levels and many of their supporters left their households.

• THE TWENTIETH CENTURY   Commercial salmon fishing had replaced trapping as the major source of cash income by the mid-twentieth century, and most Tanainas in the Lake Clark, Iliamna Lake, and Cook Inlet areas participated in it extensively. A man may work for a cannery and have his gear provided or he may own a skiff or fishing boat and contract his labors. Other means of gainful employment for Indians not living in urban areas include some minor trapping, government construction, commercial flying, and acting as hunting and fishing guides for sportsmen.

In the mid-twentieth century oil activity in the Cook Inlet area increased and Tyonek received a large sum from oil leases for exploration purposes on land it owned. The funds were used not only to modernize and improve facilities within the village but also to invest in real estate in Anchorage to provide a steady revenue for the Tyonek people. This farsighted strategy has become a model for the Alaska Federation of Natives.

Structures

Aboriginally a Tanaina village consisted of as few as one or as many as 10 or more multi-family dwellings (*ničił*, sg.). These house units, in historic times and possibly earlier, were semisubterranean, excavated as much as three or four feet into the ground with an entry tunnel in front, a central fireplace, and one or more smaller rooms attached to the rear and sides. The main room, often up to 20 feet square, was used for daily activities of the extended house group. Around the walls were sleeping compartments for couples, their younger children, and adolescent girls. Adolescent boys slept on benches above the compartments. The smaller attached rooms, about 12 feet square, were used as additional sleeping quarters, sweatbaths, and isolation rooms for menstruating women and young girls undergoing puberty confinement (Osgood 1937:55–62; Townsend and Townsend 1961:31–36).

Until the mid-nineteenth century, permanent winter villages often were hidden because of threat of attacks. In the last half of the nineteenth century and throughout the twentieth, Tanaina villages have been located either as clustered units or in a linear plan along the shore of a lake or river.

Following Russian contact during the nineteenth century, houses began to be built totally above ground, although the log side walls were still banked with dirt (VanStone and Townsend 1970:29–45). During the early part of the twentieth century, winter houses became smaller, accommodating usually one nuclear family. This, in part, probably reflects the economic slump and the rich men's loss of ability to support large numbers of people. The nuclear family dwelling continued to be the predominant style in the mid-twentieth cen-

tury. In the late nineteenth century some steambaths, originally attached to the house, were built separately from the winter residence, and in the mid-twentieth century all were built separately. Other structures around a 1960s village included one or more caches built on posts for storage of dry foods and equipment and outdoor latrines, since the villages do not have sewage disposal.

While the winter houses (fig. 4) prior to the early twentieth century were normally lineage dwellings, summer fish-camp residences often contained only nuclear or extended families. Earlier, the fish-camp house was a small surface log and sod structure, but in the first half of the twentieth century white canvas side-wall tents became common for fish-camp housing. Fish-drying racks and smoke houses are additional separate constructions. By the mid-twentieth century, in some places the winter residence was used throughout the year.

Clothing and Adornment

Until the second half of the nineteenth century the Tanaina retained their aboriginal dress. During the

628   Fig. 4. Natives from Seldovia. The roofs are thatched with grass held down by poles. Photograph by Case and Draper, 1898–1907.

summer both sexes wore a tailored one-piece undergarment of dehaired caribou skin, resembling somewhat a suit of underwear, which extended from the neck to halfway between the knees and ankles. A similar winter garment had footwear attached to the legs and might have the hair left on but turned inside. Over the basic garment a dehaired shirt of caribou, which was pulled over the head, was worn in summer. Dehaired skins were often dyed brown or red and decorated with porcupine quill embroidery (fig. 5), ermine tails, and dentalium shells. After contact, glass beads were added to the garment decoration (fig. 6). Furred shirts, coats, and cloaks were worn in winter. Knee boots were made of caribou or sheep skin and might be dehaired. Soles were of brown bear or beluga hide. Waterproof boots were fashioned from salmon skins and a waterproof parka was made of whale membrane (Beresford 1789:239; Richardson 1851, 2:405; Osgood 1937:46–50; Townsend 1965:141–147).

Bone labrets were worn in the lower lip. Men's and women's ears and nasal septums were pierced in order to insert shell decorations (Beresford 1789:240; Richardson 1851:404; Petroff 1884:25; Townsend 1965:149).

Women of wealthy families had tattoo lines of charcoal drawn from their mouths to their chins and on their hands (Osgood 1937:53–54; Townsend 1965:150–151). Red and black face paints were apparently used as clan designations (Beresford 1789:237; Richardson 1851, 2:403; Osgood 1937:53; Townsend 1965:150).

Men often wore their hair in a long single braid, which was covered with grease, bird down, and feathers. Otherwise they tied their hair behind in knots or let it hang loose. Women used two braids or let the hair fall naturally (Richardson 1851, 2:403; Petroff 1884:25; DRHA 2:60, 63; Osgood 1937:52–53).

After contact with Western civilization, the first elements of adornment to disappear, about 1860, were the labrets, the practice of piercing the nasal septum, and tattooing (Townsend 1965:149). Russian priests attempted to induce Tanaina men to cut their hair according to European fashion, but the Indians did not do so until about 1880 (DRHA 2:60; Townsend 1974:11). Apparently not until the entry of the American traders after 1867 was a quantity of fabrics and ready-made clothing and shoes easily available (DRHA 2:60; Schanz in U.S. Census Office. 11th Census 1893:94).

Suomen Kansallismuseo, Helsinki: left, 174; right, 167.
Fig. 5. left, Caribou(?) skin tunic, decorated with fringes; white, black, and brown porcupine quills; and thread. right, Woman's dress of caribou(?) skin decorated with porcupine quills, seeds, fox fur, eagle down, and thread, with pointed bottom both in front and back. Length of right 134 cm, other same scale, collected before 1847 (cf. Collins et al. 1973:142, 145; Zibert 1967:pls. 4, 8).

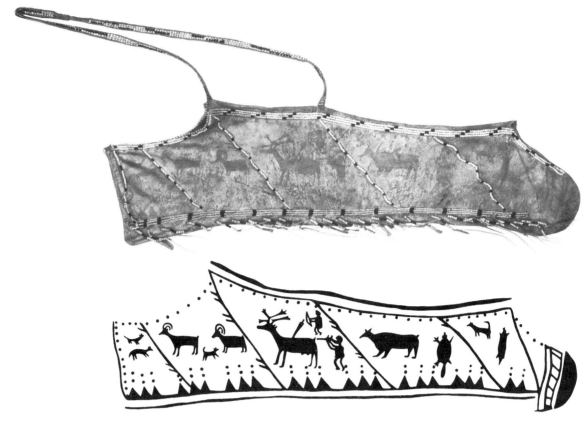

Muzeĭ Antropologii i Etnografii, Akademiĭa Nauk SSR, Leningrad: 2667–30.

Fig. 6. Skin quiver decorated with lines of white and black trade beads, bead fringe ending in porcupine quills, and red-painted figures (detail shows partial reconstruction) of caribou, mountain sheep, other animals, and 2 hunters. Length 77 cm, collected 1840–1842 (Zibert 1967:62, 73).

Transportation

The Tanaina have always traveled widely throughout southwestern Alaska, using an extensive network of trails. Winter transportation, until about the 1850s, was by foot. Snowshoes were manufactured of birch wood with webbing of bear or moose rawhide (babiche). Dogs were used for packing as well as for hunting throughout the year, but apparently dog traction was not used until the mid-nineteenth century. Tanainas then began to use a sled with dogs harnessed in pairs to a center trace, a technique presumably introduced from Siberia by the Russians (Zagoskin 1967:127). Persons who did not own dogs used smaller sleds and propelled themselves on them with poles. By the mid-1960s snowmobiles had become an additional means of winter transportation, although many families retained their dog teams (Townsend 1960–1973, 1965:129–141).

Travel in summer was primarily by water along the rivers, lakes, and sea coast. Birchbark canoes and mooseskin boats were common conveyances. At some time, perhaps protohistoric, the Tanaina also adopted the Eskimo sealskin boats, both the decked-over kayak and the open umiak. After the Russians became active in southwestern Alaska two and three-holed bidarkas (fig. 7) (a variation on the Eskimo kayak) became universal (Wrangell 1970:12; Osgood 1937:67–70; Townsend 1965:124–126). In the early part of the twentieth century wooden skiffs, at least 18 feet long, replaced the birchbark and skin boats. Sails were used on skiffs for propulsion until outboard motors became readily available in the mid-twentieth century. In the 1960s each family in the Iliamna region had at least one skiff and motor. In addition to the skiffs, some of the more affluent families in the Iliamna region and Cook Inlet owned commercial fishing boats.

Because of poor surface transportation networks, including the lack of roads, the airplane became a significant mode of transportation in southwestern Alaska after the 1940s. By the 1960s some young Tanainas had acquired their own small planes and a few were flying charter flights.

Social Organization

Tanaina social organization has changed considerably during the nineteenth and twentieth centuries, and some of these shifts seem to have occurred in response to the elaboration and then collapse of the trading system and its concomitant distribution of wealth.

Alaska Histl. Lib., Juneau: Case and Draper Coll., 269.
Fig. 7. Men from Seldovia using single-bladed paddles to propel themselves in a 3-hole bidarka made of dehaired sealskin over a wooden frame. Single-hole kayaks and perhaps 2-hole bidarkas, both probably adopted from the Eskimo, were extensively used by the Tanaina in Cook Inlet and at Iliamna in pre-European times. The 3-hole bidarka, designed to carry a Russian passenger paddled by 2 Aleuts or other native servants, is a postcontact borrowing by the Tanaina. Photograph by Case and Draper, 1898–1907.

• KINSHIP Tanaina kinship terminology, as collected in the twentieth century, shows divergences among the various local groups and some inconsistencies in the data recorded by different scholars (Osgood 1937:144–147; Townsend 1965:232–233, 416, 1960–1973; Kari 1977:82–86, 1977a:280; Tenenbaum 1975:32–35, 1977:12); it is likely that these differences reflect the separate nature of the original societies as well as changes resulting from 200 years of contact with European types of social organization. Cousin terminology is Iroquois in the Upper Inlet and Iliamna dialects, Crow in the Inland dialect, and Hawaiian in recent Outer Inlet. The terminology in the first ascending generation is bifurcate merging in Inland and recent Iliamna, bifurcate collateral in Upper Inlet and earlier Iliamna (Osgood 1937), and mixed (with lineal aunt terms and merged or collateral uncle terms) in Outer Inlet.

• CLANS Tanaina were divided into matrilineal clans, segregated into moieties that were the focal point of social organization. In traditional times there were between 11 and 18 active clans. The clan system remained well known in the 1970s although in Lime Village it was no longer active. In Iliamna and Nondalton clans continued to function at death and to some extent in the selection of a spouse. Clan affiliation cross-cut societal and linguistic divisions, so that a member of the

Raven clan might have "relatives" among the Ravens of the Eyak, Ahtna, and "Galtsan" (probably the Upper Tanana and other interior Athapaskan groups) (Wrangell 1970:9; De Laguna 1975).

• RANK Tanaina society can be considered a ranked society with a redistributive economic system (M.H. Fried 1967). A village was composed of one or more rich men who were the most prestigeful individuals of their respective local lineage groups of their clans. In the ideal situation the rich man was aided by a group of relatives, presumably males of his clan, who seem to have resided avunculocally (a couple resides with the husband's mother's brother or another man standing in this classificatory relationship), either with him within the large communal dwelling or in individual houses nearby.

The rich man functioned as a headman and acted as the center of the redistributive system. Goods flowed from the rich man's group to him and he redistributed these according to need. He was responsible for the care of orphans, widows, and the infirm; made certain that his kin group was well cared for; and tried to see that traditional values were instilled in the people. In exchange for this service, leadership, and protection, people worked for him assisting in subsistence pursuits, fur trapping, and manufacture of trade goods. Persons were not forced to give allegiance to a particular rich man, nor were they required to support any rich man. Further, if a rich man became selfish or domineering, the people were free to leave him and live by themselves or join forces with another rich man.

After the Russians entered the Alaska fur trade, they appointed influential men, usually already established "rich men," as chiefs (duyun, duyuq sg.). The nonaboriginal nature of the office of chief (tyone, doyon, and other spellings) is reflected by the fact that duyun is a borrowing of Russian toïon (toën, toïën; Zagoskin 1956:416), a word of Yakut origin (Böhtlingk 1964:97) used in the Russian colonies for appointed native spokesmen. These men acted as liaison between the Russians and their people and were the main contacts within the fur-trade system.

Major trading trips were made by a rich man and some of his assistants to Eskimo or other Indian villages where the man had established a trading partnership with an individual. Trading partners seemed to have served a dual purpose; in addition to trade, a man's trading partner might arrange peace negotiations and the exchange of prisoners during hostilities.

Important criteria for becoming a rich man were a man's generosity, his willingness to assist others, his hunting ability, and his bravery and ability in warfare. An individual who manifested these qualities and aspired to become a rich man accumulated quantities of movable goods, including animal skins and items manufactured from them. He rose within the system by trading these items with other native groups, and after contact also with Europeans, and converting some of the proceeds to prestige symbols such as dentalium and glass-bead belts. While inheritance of prestige symbols from a matrilineal uncle might aid an individual in his aspirations, he also needed leadership qualities and generosity in order to marshall the assistance of his kin group in acquiring goods needed in his trading ventures. Without their support, a man could never acquire sufficient wealth to become a rich man. A shaman was also usually a rich man.

Potlatches were given by the rich man with the co-operation of his kin group at deaths of clansmen. Marriages and other occasions, such as an attempt to aid a poor man or welcome back a returning relative, provided additional opportunities for a rich man to potlatch. It was through the mechanism of the potlatch with its massive amount of gift giving to the guests that a rich man validated his position and attempted to increase his prestige within the society. Prestige symbols were ostentatiously displayed on the clothing of the rich man and his family not only in the kinds of fur worn but also in the valuable glass-bead and dentalium-shell belts.

Rich men had more wives than other men, as they were able to afford the necessary bride price and potlatches. Women were of particular value to a rich man. Not only were they active in preparing the winter food necessary for the people the rich man assisted, but also they trapped ground squirrels, whose fur was used for parkas, and manufactured garments that were rich in porcupine-quill embroidery and other decoration, which made these items valuable in intertribal and European trade. Women had considerable status and prestige in Tanaina society and could, by skillful negotiations, accrue wealth in their own right.

Slaves, often Eskimos, were obtained in trade or during battles and kept by Tanaina rich men.† Slaves were well treated and often permitted to return home after a number of years of service. A rich man's prestige was enhanced considerably if a slave, given his freedom, elected to stay with his master. Slaves were important commodities in intersocietal trade and an individual might be transferred a number of times from one tribe to another.

After the drop in the value of furs in 1897, the rich man was no longer able to maintain his position of wealth and prestige vis-à-vis other people of his kin group. Thus, during the early years of the twentieth century the position of rich man became decreasingly important and the clans, as corporate units, seem to have been reduced in function. Perhaps the last who could be considered rich men of anything like the traditional type were Simeon Chickalusion of Tyonek, who died about 1963, and Mike Alex of Eklutna, who died in 1977 (James M. Kari, communication to editors 1978).

• SOCIAL CONTROL Gossip has perhaps always been one of the more effective means of social control in Tanaina society (Townsend 1960–1973). However, among aboriginal Tanaina, an additional mechanism for social control was vested in the clan and moiety structure: the revenge killing or beating. If the disruption occurred within a moiety, revenge normally was carried out by the injured party or a close relative. On the other hand, if the aggrieved person was of the opposite moiety, the member clans of the moiety normally acted as a unit for revenge. Occasionally this erupted into civil war in which prisoners were not kept as slaves but ransomed back to their respective kin groups. An alternative to revenge was provided by paying wergild (compensation) to the offended moiety (Wrangell 1970:11; Osgood 1937:139).

By the mid-twentieth century clan and moiety mechanisms for social control had ceased to be effective, although gossip continued to play its role. On rare occasions when a major social disruption developed involving violence, an Alaska State Trooper, summoned from Anchorage or Dillingham, removed the offending individual. Village councils have been in operation since the mid-twentieth century with an elected mayor or president. The council acts primarily as liaison between the village and the Euro-American society outside, particularly the various government departments that have dealings with the villages.

• PROPERTY OWNERSHIP Much ownership of property seems to have been vested ultimately in the clan with the rich man in nominal control. Hunting and fishing areas were also frequently controlled by clan. Personal property was often destroyed at the death of an individual but that which remained was passed matrilineally from mother's brother to sister's son. By the early twentieth century when the rich man and the clans were losing their position and Euro-Americans were becoming more influential, much property began to be passed down through the nuclear family from parent to child.

Life Cycle

• BIRTH AND CHILDHOOD Traditionally, at childbirth the mother was confined in a special shelter of bark and was assisted by women acting as midwives. Mother and child remained in seclusion for about 40 days. In the early twentieth century the use of a separate birth

---

†It has been claimed that the Tanaina word ʔułčəna 'Pacific Eskimo' is derived from ʔułčaq̇a 'slave' (Wrangell 1970:11, 1839a:110) or itself means 'slave' (Radloff 1874:24), but ʔułčəna means only 'Pacific Eskimo' and ʔułčaq̇a is 'drudge, poor person assigned to work for a chief'. Linguistic analysis does not support any relationship between the words (James M. Kari, communications to editors 1978, 1979; Osgood 1937:134, 214), but some Tanainas draw an analogy between them.

Yale U., Peabody Mus.: 15864.
Fig. 8. Large food dish from Iliamna, carved from white spruce, with black painted design in interior, rim and bottom design painted red, blue-filled groove around outside, crack repaired with 2 babiche stitches. Length 33 cm, collected 1931.

house was abandoned and women had their infants at home. After 1960, many were going to hospitals in cities for childbirth.

Until the early twentieth century the child was placed in a birchbark cradle with dry moss in the bottom for a diaper. A child was often named after one of its parents' siblings or, after the coming of the Russian Orthodox religion, for a saint. Teknonymous names were used in addressing a parent among Outer Inlet Tanainas (Osgood 1937:161), but Upper Inlet speakers followed the Ahtna conventions, with teknonymous names ending in -tu or -tukda 'father' used in address and reference for men, and women having nonteknonymous names in a suffix -na (Kari 1977a:280–281).

Adoption has been common, and seemingly the adopting family did not have to be of the same clan as the child. The child retained his clan membership. A rich man often cared for orphans as part of his duties in the community.

Traditionally, when a boy was old enough to learn to hunt he was placed under the tutelage of his mother's brother. The boy was taught to swim, work, and endure hardships, including cold and little food.

• PUBERTY Until the early part of the twentieth century puberty in both boys and girls was recognized by special ceremonies. According to Osgood (1937:162–163), boys at 15 years of age in the Susitna society were sent to the woods for a five-day fast. In the Interior society (Townsend 1960–1973), a boy was kept alone

in a room for about a week and permitted little food. Each morning he was to run a distance but return to his room before the rest of the household had risen. Spruce root ropes were tied at his arm and leg joints. At Tyonek Osgood (1937:163) noted a similar practice. In addition, when a boy killed his first game of any kind, the village people were invited to partake of the meat (Townsend 1965:222).

A girl's puberty recognition was more arduous. At the onset of menstruation, a girl was confined to a small room attached to the main house, where she remained for most of the following year. There she learned sewing, other skills, and behavior proper for a woman. She was prohibited from touching herself. When she ventured outside, she was to pull her parka hood over her face and look only at the ground for her look was dangerous. After the year, the girl was considered ready for marriage, but she returned to confinement each month during her menstrual period (Townsend 1965:223–224).

• MARRIAGE Before the early twentieth century, clan and moiety exogamy rules applied to the selection of marriage partners but there was no rule regarding village endogamy. Marriages were to some extent arranged by the couple's parents, although apparently the young man did have some say in the matter. Cross-cousin marriage, particularly of a boy to his father's sister's daughter, was preferred (Townsend 1965:238–241; DRHA 2:330).

Upon marriage, the young husband resided in the home of his wife's parents for at least a year for bride service. Occasionally a wealthy man would simply pay bride price and agree to assist the girl's parents for the privilege of taking the girl immediately. At the end of the bride service, the couple was free to establish residence where they wished and occasionally they remained with the girl's family. More commonly the couple returned to the boy's "home," which seems usually to have been avunculocal. Under avunculocality male clan members formed an efficient work force to enhance the economic position of their clan and their rich man. A couple was free to establish a household completely independent of either set of relatives and independent of any village if they so desired, but this situation was rare.

When the couple left the wife's parents' home after the year of bride service, the husband received gifts from her parents. These were repaid if the marriage was dissolved (Wrangell 1970:10). In the mid-nineteenth century, and perhaps before, the husband needed to give a potlatch in order to validate his marriage (Townsend 1965:245; Osgood 1937:165). This correlates with the period when the European fur trade was expanding the wealth concepts in Tanaina society.

Polygyny, most commonly sororal, was permitted but it was practiced primarily by the rich men who could afford it. At the death of a wife the sororate was also practiced.

By the mid-twentieth century young people seemed comparatively free to select their own spouses. Although clans were not very active, clan endogamy was extremely rare, at least in the Iliamna region. Cross-cousin marriages were no longer very common in the 1960s. Bride price, bride service, polygyny, and avunculocal residence were no longer practiced. Residence remained often within the village of one of the couple's parents, and some villages seem to have been composed basically of several lineages representing different clans. Marriages often were contracted between people in neighboring Tanaina villages, although a few spouses came from farther away.

• DEATH Until the later nineteenth century, practices surrounding death remained essentially aboriginal. When a person was dying, loud noises were made to frighten away evil spirits (DRHA 2:62; Petroff 1884:163). At death, members of the deceased's moiety assembled in the house to grieve. A prominent man, probably the rich man of the local segment of the deceased's clan, eulogized the dead. The deceased's clothing was distributed to the people of his moiety, although, according to Osgood (1937:166), some possessions were destroyed with the body. Members of the opposite moiety attended and gave presents to the grieving moiety to console them. It was the obligation of the opposite moiety to make funeral preparations and conduct the body disposal. The body was removed from the house through a window, not through a door (DRHA 2:62), and was cremated (Wrangell 1970:10; Osgood 1937:166–167; Townsend 1965:224–225). Afterward, the bones were gathered, placed in a box, and either buried or placed under a shed set on posts (Wrangell 1970:10; Davydov 1810–1812:147; Lisiansky 1814:188).

As the Tanaina converted to Christianity in the mid-nineteenth century, cremation was replaced by burial. Small houses were constructed over the graves or else fences surrounded them (fig. 9). Grave offerings were left on the grave much to the disconcertion of the priests (DRHA 2:60; Petroff 1884:163). By the mid-twentieth century this practice had ceased, although fences were still placed around each grave. People who were not members of the deceased's clan continued to make all funeral arrangements in the Iliamna region.

Until after the beginning of the twentieth century in most areas and until 1969 at Nondalton, a potlatch was held for the deceased approximately a year following the death. The dead man's moiety amassed food, animal skins, and other valuable gifts, inviting the opposite moiety to a feast to honor the deceased and in appreciation of their assistance during the bereavement. After feasting, the gifts were distributed to the opposite moiety, and it was during these distributions that a rich man demonstrated his prestige.

Natl. Arch.: 126–AR–7A–3.
Fig. 9. Indian grave houses and fences at Old Kinik. Photographed Oct. 1918.

Religion

Shamanism was the focal point of Tanaina aboriginal religion, continuing throughout the nineteenth century. A person became a shaman, often unwillingly, through dreams. The shaman acted as magician, priest, and medical practitioner. The shaman could be of either sex and either "good" or "bad."

In curing, the shaman, wearing a carved wooden mask, performed rituals with a small doll that he sent magically into the sick person to locate and exorcise the illness. He might also use a shaman's stick, about four feet long, to drive out evil forces. Although all people were believed to have familiars, the shaman made use of his in searching for lost souls and in curing (Osgood 1937:177–182; Vaudrin 1963:27–34; Townsend 1965:302–310).

The Russian Orthodox priests became active in Tanaina territory after 1845, and the people were nominally converted to Christianity within the next quarter-century. However, the shaman remained active in a syncretic role merging Christian belief with the traditional, and shamanism probably continued through the first half of the twentieth century. Shamans often proved to be the most "devout" Christians. By the 1960s the overall religious system was a blend consisting of both Christian and traditional Tanaina elements.

Fundamentalist missionaries entered the Iliamna area after 1900 and converted some Tanainas from Orthodoxy to their particular doctrines. Inter- and intrafamily conflicts developed occasionally over the different interpretations of beliefs, but these were to a great extent related to the fervor of the particular missionaries active in a village at that time.

Beliefs

Within the Tanaina belief system there are a number of spirit and quasi-spirit beings. These can be classified into four broad categories of phenomena.

The first is purely mythological. The Tanaina trickster, Raven (ǵuǵuyni; Upper Inlet dəlǵa; Inland and Iliamna čulyin) is the best known. Raven stole the sun and the moon so people could see but is an amoral creature who continually plays pranks and breaks the norms of Tanaina society. The exploits of Raven as well as a number of other creatures are documented in legend cycles called sukdu, which were used in the past for the instruction of children (Kari and Kalifornsky 1974; Osgood 1937:183–184; Tenenbaum 1976, 2; Townsend 1965:310–312, 1969:xxxv; Vaudrin 1969).

A second category involves supernatural beings. Some of these are evil, such as qaxdascidi who is heard as a mysterious noise and is related to other spirits around the villages that attempt to harm people (Osgood 1937:170). There are also People of the Woods who take fish from smokehouses and kidnap people (Townsend 1965:316). A Tyonek man believed they were souls of people who had been lost in the woods (Krenov 1951:180–181). Osgood (1937:171–172) equated them with the Nakani believed in by many Northern Athapaskans. There were also giants who came from the north creating Iliamna Lake and other natural geological formations in the area and killing people (Petroff 1884:163–164; Townsend 1965:316). Other supernatural beings are harmless such as the one heard in the crackling of the fire. The sus lik̓a 'mountain-pass dog' (ʔəlnən xlik̓a 'dog from the earth' in Upper Inlet and Iliamna) lives under the hills and is heard barking but never seen. Tree people (čvala dnayi) come out of the trees at night waving their arms (Osgood 1937:170–171). There are also spirits called "whistlers," because they often make whistling sounds, which live in the mountains and look like rats that have been cut in half (Townsend 1965:317). Iliamna Lake Tanaina recognize a spirit that, although powerful and held in awe, usually seems benign toward people; it may take animal form and is capable of appearing and disappearing (Townsend 1960–1973).

The close relationship between people and various animals and animal spirits comprises a third category. The loon is the shaman's bird and assists him. The Tanaina feel a close comradeship with the bear and respect it highly. Wolves are considered brothers. If a man is hungry and lost in the woods, he need only ask his brother, the wolf, for help and help will be given (Townsend 1965:314).

A fourth category includes a class of strange, powerful creatures that lack truly supernatural powers: the Hairy Man and the Big Fish. They are considered by the Tanaina as objectively real and distinct from the spirit and supernatural creatures just discussed. The Hairy Man, similar to the Sasquatch described from the western United States and British Columbia, is harmless or helpful to humans unless injured. It is a large, hair-covered, grayish biped with pupilless eyes, who likely lives in villages in the mountains (Townsend 1960–1973; Michael Dorris, personal communication 1977). These creatures have occasionally been confused with the "People of the Woods."

The Big Fish has been reported from a number of lakes (see, for example, DRHA 2:56; Townsend 1974:9). However, the Big Fish of Iliamna is probably the most famous. These are described as huge and strong with the ability to bite the bottoms out of boats. They dislike red and will attack things of that color. The Hairy Man and the Big Fish have been reported throughout the twentieth century by a number of people in the Iliamna region including Eskimos, Indians, and Whites (Townsend 1965:319–321, 1960–1973). Ichthyologists have speculated that the Big Fish might be large sturgeon.

Various means to obtain good luck are known. To insure a successful hunt, offerings were made to k̓əluyəš, the chief of the mountain people and controller of the animal spirits, and other taboos and special practices were observed, including substitution of "mountain language" words for many words of ordinary Tanaina, which he did not like to have used in his domain (Doroshin in Radloff 1874:vii). Until the mid-twentieth century good luck offerings were made near the grave of a shaman at Iliamna Lake and at various places along the portage from Iliamna to Cook Inlet (Townsend 1965:315).

History of Contact

Early Contact Period, Until 1784

In 1741, Vitus Bering discovered Alaska and within a short time Russian fur hunters began to exploit the rich sea otter grounds along the Aleutian chain. Capt. James Cook arrived in southern Alaska in 1778 where, at Cook Inlet, Tanainas came to his ship trading furs and fish for iron. A few European goods were already in the Indians' possession (Cook 1784:552). Although southern Alaska Indians and Eskimos were eager to extend their trading enterprises to include Europeans visiting in ships, they were adamant in opposing any attempted settlement. With the exception of the Aleuts, they remained virtually free of European influence.

Conflict Period, 1784–1799

In 1784, the Shelikhov-Golikov Company established at Kodiak a post that was destined to become one of the main headquarters of the later Russian-American Company and from which Tanaina contact was implemented.

Taking hostages to insure peaceful and advantageous relations with native groups was a general Russian practice. In 1785 a Russian party from Kodiak explored Cook Inlet and took 20 hostages. The following year, the Lebedev-Lastochkin Company, a rival, established the first mainland post, Saint George, on Kenai Peninsula well within Tanaina territory (Bancroft 1886:314). In 1791 they built another post on the Kenai River. During the last decade of the eighteenth century, violent conflicts between the rival companies and with Indians beset the area. Although the Shelikhov-Golikov Company was finally able to take over the Cook Inlet posts and restore relative peace, Tanainas in the interior prevented any attempt to settle there until about 1818.

Although eight Russian Orthodox clergymen arrived at Kodiak in 1794 to begin missionization (Bancroft 1886:352, 360; DRHA 1:172), it was more than 30 years before much real evangelical activity began.

Trade and Missions, 1799–1867

In 1799 the Russian-American Company mercantile monopoly was established, and in 1804 Novo-Arkhangel'sk was founded on Sitka Island. In 1808 it became the headquarters of the Chief Manager and the center of the Russian possessions (Fedorova 1973:134). With the move of the headquarters from Kodiak and the decline of the sea otter herds, Russian activity increased in the east and lessened in the Kodiak–Cook Inlet region; however, the posts there continued to be maintained and hunting persisted.

During the first half of the nineteenth century, Tanainas were drawn more actively into the fur trade, and Indians near Russian posts, particularly on Kenai Peninsula, became increasingly dependent on the Russians. Occasionally marriages between Russians and native women occurred; although some marriages were with Tanainas, far more common were those with Aleuts and Koniags. From these, a Creole population emerged who were frequently used as traders in more remote areas. Because it was Creoles who often had the direct contacts with the interior people, the impact of Western civilization on native populations was somewhat lessened.

Russians also used native peoples as middlemen in fur activities. Cook Inlet Tanainas were acting in this capacity to interior groups by the first decade of the nineteenth century (Davydov 1810–1812:145). At the time of Zagoskin's (1967:81, 268) visit in 1844, the Stony River Tanainas were engaged in the fur trade between Cook Inlet and the Kuskokwim, and Glazunov (in VanStone 1959:46) reported the existence of this trade as early as 1834.

With the fur trade, epidemic diseases plagued native populations. The most disastrous was the smallpox epidemic of 1836–1840, which took the lives of at least 4,000 natives, including many Tanainas (Bancroft 1886:560–562; Tikhmenev 1861–1863:366–368). The real number, including people in remote villages, will never be known. In addition, syphilis, tuberculosis, and other contagious diseases took a heavy toll.

Intensive missionization did not begin until after the disastrous smallpox epidemic. In 1845 Hieromonk Nikolai became the first priest at Nikolaevskiy Redoubt (Saint Nicholas Redoubt) serving Cook Inlet, Prince William Sound, and the interior (DRHA 1:354–355; Townsend 1965:291, 1974). In 1853 interior Tanainas came under jurisdiction of the Nushagak mission (Townsend 1965:58, 1974). Missionization was a slow process because of the few priests and the great distances to cover. Villages were usually visited less than once a year. Although Tanainas near the Cook Inlet mission began to participate more actively in the Russian Orthodox Church in the 1840s, the remote interior Tanaina villages of Mulchatna and Kijik were little affected until after 1870.

The American Period, 1867–

In 1867 Russia sold Alaska to the United States; the Russian-American Company assets were assumed by the Alaska Commercial Company. With the monopoly ended, the Alaska Commercial Company had to contend with competition from other fur traders. As a consequence, prices of furs rose while prices of some trade goods were lowered. At the high point of competition, prices paid to the Indians for furs were equal to those paid in San Francisco (Abercrombie 1900a:400). In 1897 the prices of fur at all stores dropped and continued a downward spiral for several years. Prices never again reached the peaks of the early 1890s (Alaska Commercial Company Records 1872–1899, 1875–1903; DRHA 2:73, 83, 186–187), and a long period of hardship began. The Alaska Commercial Company sold its southwestern interests to private traders in 1911.

Salmon canneries, established in the 1880s, monopolized the best fishing streams in Cook Inlet, preventing the Indians access to the most productive places for subsistence. The canneries also purchased quantities of the Indian catch destined for winter use so that, to compensate for sold fish, Indians had to depend on cash to purchase winter food from traders, whose stocks usually ran out before spring (Alaska Commercial Company Records 1875–1903). In Bristol Bay until 1907, canneries often blocked the mouths of the Nushagak and Kvichak rivers so that few salmon escaped to the lakes and major food shortages occurred. The game and fur-bearing animals also were rapidly being depleted.

Miners were active in the Tanaina territory between 1903 and 1906 (Martin and Katz 1912:21). Contacts with Indians were minimal, although a few miners did marry Indian women and remain.

By the late 1800s, Russian priests were well accepted in Indian communities in Cook Inlet and were actively attempting to eradicate shamanism and other Indian traditions.

Until the end of the first quarter of the twentieth century, epidemics, including diphtheria, measles, whooping cough, pneumonia, and influenza, plagued the Tanaina, and tuberculosis was pandemic (cf. DRHA 2:330). The effects of epidemics and new illnesses on Tanaina social organization and economy throughout this period were extensive. Only since the mid-twentieth century have health conditions improved appreciably.

Tanainas began to participate in work at salmon canneries about 1915. Since 1940 they have become intensively involved in actual commercial fishing, and by the 1960s a major portion of cash income was derived from that enterprise.

In 1892 reindeer were imported from Siberia to Alaska to bolster the native economy. A herd was established at Iliamna in 1905, and some Tanainas acted as herders. Although reindeer were a secondary economic activity, they did not prove profitable, and by the 1940s the activity had virtually ceased.

Trapping continued through 1970, but its economic importance had decreased and few engaged in the activity.

Tanainas remain, on the whole, devout Russian Orthodox Christians (fig. 10), and lay readers conduct services if a priest is not available. Fundamentalist Protestant missionaries entered the Iliamna area after 1900, and occasionally conflicts have arisen regarding membership and specific doctrines.

Until the mid-twentieth century opportunities for formal education were limited. During Russian times, only Tanainas near missions received a little education (cf. Zagoskin 1967:286). In the early 1900s schooling was provided at a few villages on a rather haphazard basis. Between 1926 and 1952, no school was readily available to many interior Tanaina, but by the 1960s schools through the eighth grade were located in many Tanaina villages. After grade school, students may leave to attend boarding schools for secondary education.

During the early twentieth century, there were major population shifts among the Tanaina. People migrated from Kijik and Stony River to Nondalton and Old Iliamna. In the 1930s Old Iliamna was abandoned in favor of Nondalton and later the new village of Pedro Bay. Some moved to Anchorage (Townsend 1960–1973). The Tyonek population has been augmented by people from the Susitna River area (Michael Dorris, personal communication 1970). By executive order in

Fig. 10. St. Nicholas Russian Orthodox church at Tyonek, with starving moose in foreground eating tree limbs due to poor winter forage. Photograph by Michael Dorris, April 1971.

1915, 26,918 acres were set aside as the Moquawkie Reserve for the Tyonek people (Federal Field Committee for Development Planning in Alaska 1968:445). Many Kenai Peninsula Tanaina remain there although some have moved to Anchorage. The Eklutna population, near Anchorage, is composed of people from that vicinity as well as a few from the Iliamna region (Davis 1965:12–13; Townsend 1960–1973). Some Tanainas spend at least some years outside Alaska, particularly in the West Coast states.

Throughout Tanaina history, contact with Western civilization has been more intensive in the more accessible Cook Inlet region than in the more remote Iliamna, Susitna, and Interior areas. Contact with all Tanainas is increasing through village schools and city experience, and change has become more rapid since about 1960. Even so, the Tanaina retain their cultural identity and seem to be welding this with elements from Euro-American civilization into a viable and coherent culture (Townsend 1979).

Population

The Tanaina population before European contact and during the nineteenth century is difficult to calculate, and some figures (for example, Tikhmenev 1861–1863; Petroff 1884) are almost certainly grossly inaccurate. Calculations based on data from explorers and the Russian church archival vital statistics (Townsend 1965:85–99) indicate that the aboriginal Tanaina population must have been at least 4,000–5,000, while the numbers between 1860 and 1875, after several severe epidemics had decimated the populations, were a minimum of 1,500. The 1970 United States census does not provide separate figures for Indian groups so that only an estimate can be made of the total Tanaina population at that time. Persons in completely ethnically Tanaina villages (Nondalton, Pedro Bay, Tyonek, Lime Village, and Eklutna) numbered 531 in 1970 (U.S. Bureau of the Census 1973:11–12, table 6). Tanainas also continue to live on the Kenai Peninsula, as well as in cities in Alaska and other parts of the United States.

Synonymy‡

The name Tanaina has been standard in English since Osgood (1933). It is a rendering of the Tanaina self-designation *dəna'ina* 'the people', recorded as Tnaína (in Russian, Wrangell 1839:56, 1970:9), tēnaina (Radloff 1874:29), and Thnaina (Holmberg 1856:287). The Alaska Native Language Center uses the Tanaina practical orthography spelling Dena'ina as the English name. Dall (1870:430, 1877:35) used Tehanin-Kutchin, from Ross, said to be the name used by "the Yukon Indians."

The Pacific Eskimo call the Tanaina *kənaiyut* (sg. *kənaiyuq*) (Leer 1978:106), recorded as kina-īut (in Russian, Wrangell 1839:56, 1970:9) and kinajut (in German, Wrangell 1839a:103). From this was derived the Russian noun *Kenaïtsy* (sg. *Kenaeťs*) and adjective *Kenaïskĭĭ* (Wrangell 1839:56–57) and the German *Kenayer* and *Kenaier* (Wrangell 1839a:103, 259 table) and *Kinai* (Radloff 1874:29). There are numerous slight variants of these names (Hodge 1907i:716–717), including the local English terms Kenaitze (Petroff 1884:25, 1900:85; Ackerman 1975) and Kenai Indians, sometimes restricted to the Tanaina of the Kenai Peninsula but also used at Iliamna. Dall (1870a:270) introduced the erroneous Kenai-tená, later replaced by K'naí-ā-kho-tana (Dall 1877:35, 1886:379), which was used by Hodge (1907i:715) as Knaiakhotana; this name, which Dall obtained from Ahtnas, appears to be an overnormalization of Ahtna *nkoxtna' Wie·ne* 'Kenai people' (Kari and Buck 1975:58). Another rendering may be the "Kankünă or Kankünats Kŏqtana" of Staffeief and Petroff (1885–1886). Zagoskin (1956:249, 1967:243) used the name *Ttynaïtsy* in Russian (or *sobstvenno Ttynaïtsy* 'Ttynai proper'), in the belief that *Kenaïtsy* contained a corruption of Tanaina *dəna'ina*; this appears as Tinnats-khotana (and variants) in Petroff (1884:162, 164, 1900:260, 263), incorrectly said to be "their own name."

The Ahtna name for the Tanaina is *dastne·y* (James M. Kari, communication to editors 1978).

Local Groups and Settlements

Tanaina settlements and named local groups known to have existed at some time in the nineteenth and twentieth centuries are listed here, arranged by dialect; numbers refer to figure 1, which also gives the societal af-

filiations. These settlements were not all villages of equal importance and were not all occupied at the same period. The listing follows James M. Kari (communications to editors 1979, 1980) and Townsend (1960–1973), with additional information from De Laguna (1934), Kari (1977:92–93, 127–130), Kalifornsky (1977:125–135), Kari and Buck (1975), and Kari (1977a).

Inland dialect. Stony River Tanainas (*ḱqizaɣətnu xtan* 'distant river people' or *dɣili 'učen xtan* 'outside-the-mountains people'): Lime Village, 2 (*xəḱdičən xdakaq̇* 'abundance mouth'), erroneously called Hungry Village in the 1939 census (Orth 1967:576); Canyon Village, 3 (*qəɣnilən* 'flows through'); Stony River village, 1 (*ḱqizaɣətnu xdakaq̇*), partly Ingalik and Yupik.

Telaquana Lake Tanainas (*caynən xtan;* Iliamna *xcaxtana*), of the Telaquana–upper Stony–upper Mulchatna area (*caynən*): Trail Creek village, 4 (*čqulčištnu* 'willow-sprout creek'), also called Old Village (Orth 1967).

Mulchatna Tanainas (*vałcatnaxtan*), of the Mulchatna River (*vałcatnaq̇*), also called Molchatna (Petroff 1884:17): several villages including *čałčikaq̇*, 'Chilchitna River mouth', 5.

Lake Clark Tanainas (*qiž̌ʒəx xtan*): Kijik, 6 (*qiž̌ʒəx*), also Kichik (Petroff 1884:17) and numerous spellings in Orth (1967), referred to as Nikhkak in 1891 (U.S. Census Office. 11th Census 1893:94; VanStone and Townsend 1970:17–19); Nondalton, 7 (*nundaltin* or *nuvəndaltin* 'lakes extend').

Iliamna dialect. Iliamna Lake Tanainas (*nilavəna xtana* or *nilamna xtana*): Chekok, 10 (*čixkaq̇* 'red ocher mouth'), also Chikak (Petroff 1884:17); Pedro Bay, 11, and Lonesome Bay, 12 (perhaps no Tanaina names); Pile Bay, 13 (*cayanq̇tnu* 'on-the-cliff river'); Old Iliamna village, 14 (*čaḱdalitnu* 'flows-out river'), also Ilyamna (Petroff 1884:17); Newhalen, 8 (*nuɣilən* 'flows down'; Noghelingamiut in U.S. Census Office. 11th Census [1893:95]), and New Iliamna villages, 9, which are mostly Yupik; perhaps the Chinitna Bay settlement, 15 (*canitnu* 'cliff island river').

Outer Inlet dialect. Kustatan Tanainas (*qəzdəɣtna;* Upper Inlet *qəydəɣtna*): Polly Creek, 33 (*taľin čiltant* 'where we found a whale'); Old Kustatan, 34 (*qəzdəɣnən* 'point of land; West Foreland'), Kustatan in Petroff (1884:29); New Kustatan, 36 (*x̌əɣ ditčikt* 'yellow grass place'), Kustatan in Orth (1967); Packer's Creek village, 35 (*ḱətnuka'a* 'big creek'; k'núka in De Laguna [1934:139]).

Kenai Peninsula Tanainas (Upper Inlet *yaxtana*), including East Foreland Tanainas (*qəɣnənxtana*), Kenai River Tanainas (*kaxtnuxtana*), Kenai Mountain Tanainas (*caxtana*), and Seldovia Tanainas (*'angidaxnuxtana*): Libby Creek settlement, 32 (*quqəɣniḱtələxt*, the name of the creek, also called Seven Egg Creek); Nikishka No. 3 (Orth 1967), Nikishka III

‡This synonymy was written by Ives Goddard.

(De Laguna 1934:134, switched with Nikishka I on map, pl. 1), apparently the Kultuk of Petroff (1884:29) and the *dẏažalaxt* 'where sticklebacks run; Bishop Creek', 30, of Kalifornsky (1977:127); *tiduqilčətt* 'abandoned place', 31, placed by De Laguna (1934:134) at Nikishka II (the Nikishka of USGS maps) but not locatable there, placed by Petroff (1884:29, map) south of East Foreland as Titukilsk (probably switched with his Nikishka), but placed by Kalifornsky (1977:127) between Swanson River and Bishop Creek; Nikishka I, 29 (*tuqəyankda* 'clearing'), the Nikishka of Petroff (1884:29, map) if this has been switched with Titukilsk, now Nikiski Wharf (Orth 1967); Salamatof, 28 (*kən dəčəxt* 'brushy flat'), perhaps the Kandazlit mentioned as a village by Doroshin (Radloff 1874:vi) if this is not the beach called *qandazλənt* by Kalifornsky (1977:128); Skittok, 27 (*škituẋt* 'where we slid down'), also Chkituk (Petroff 1884:29); Chinila, 26 (*čanilnat* 'camping-out place'), also Chernila (Petroff 1884:29) and Chinilof (De Laguna 1934:133); Stepanka's village, 24 (*q̇əsdudilənt* 'where it flows into an outlet'); Skilak, 25 (*sqilant* 'ridge place'), also Skilakh (Petroff 1884:29); Kalifornsky village, 23 (*ʔunx̣ẏənəsditnu* 'last creek over'), misspelled Kalifonsky on USGS maps (Kalifornsky 1977:iii, 9–10); Coffee Point village, 22 (*nintuduṧt*); Cape Kasilof village, 21 (*kəčan datkizt* 'where grass lies'), also Kassilof (Petroff 1884:29); Kasnatchin, 20 (*q̇əs nalčint* 'where the outlet is made'), also Laïda (Petroff 1884:29) (from Siberian Russian *laïda* 'beach below high-water mark'), modern Anchor Point; Soonroodna, 19 (Jacobsen 1884:369), apparently the Halibut Cove site (De Laguna 1934:23), perhaps *čunẏutnu*; China Poot Bay village, 18 (*cayəx̣q̇at* 'cave beneath the cliff'); Old Seldovia village, 16 (*čəslaxtnu* 'rock spawn river'), also Chesloknu (Dall and Becker 1895); Seldovia, 17 (*ʔangidaxtnu*), reported as an Eskimo village in 1880 (Petroff 1884:27, 29) but probably then as later partly Tanaina; the Russian and Creole settlements of Kenai (St. Nicholas, Nikolaevskiy Redoubt, *kaxtnu*), Kasilof (*ġasilaxtnu*), and Ninilchik (*niqnalchint* 'where a lodge is built') had Tanaina residents in later historical times.

Upper Inlet dialect. Tyonek Tanainas (*təbuẏna*; Inland and Outer Inlet *tuvuẏna;* Ahtna *tuba·ẏne*): Robert's Creek site, 37 (*čələxtnu* 'spawning creek'); Old Tyonek, 38 (*tubuẏnən(q̇)* 'land on the beach'), also Toyonok (Petroff 1884:29) and Tujun (Doroshin in Radloff 1874:iii), New Tyonek, 39, referred to in Tanaina by the name of Old Tyonek or as *qaġəyšlat*, 40, the name of a creek and an old village site (De Laguna 1934:139) nearby; Chuit River village, 41 (*ču ʔitnu, čubətnu*), also Chubutnu (Townsend 1974:19), at the site of modern Ladd.

Lower Susitna River Tanainas (*susitnu x̣iana*, Ahtna *sasutnaʔ Wie·ne*): Alexander Creek village, 51 (*tuqənkaq̇* 'warm water mouth'), the daqoléstaqta of De Laguna (1934:139), a chief's name, *diqələš tukda*; Old Susitna,

53 (*taniʔi* 'fish weir'); Susitna or Susitna Station, 52 (*catukəẏ* 'below the big rock'); Yentna River village, 54 (*suḱ qayəx̣* 'old village'); Fish Lake village, 55 (*bəntalit* 'where the lake flows'); Hewitt Lake village, 56 (*tiq̇ax̣əna*).

Kroto Creek Tanainas (*dasq̇əx̣iana*): Kroto village, 57 (*dasq̇ə*, whence the superseded name Deshka River), the Croton of De Laguna (1934:139); Montana Creek village, 58 (*qiduġat* 'where it overflows and freezes'); Sunshine Creek village, 59 (*suḱ qayəx̣* 'old village'); Talkeetna, 60 (*ḱdalkitnu* 'river where food is stored, Talkeetna River'), a White town with some Tanaina residents.

Talkeetna River Ahtna-Tanainas (*dẏəlaytəx̣iana*, Ahtna *dẏela·y taWie·ne* 'mountain people'): Chunilna Creek camp, 61 (*čaniltnu*); Stephan Lake village (*titiḱiniłtunt;* Ahtna *titiyʔniłta·ndə* 'game trail goes out').

Knik Arm Tanainas (*ḱənax̣tana*): Fish Creek village, 43 (*ḱənakatnu,* apparently including the nearby Knik Lake site for which De Laguna 1934:141 obtained the name šúnta), the Knakatnuk of Petroff (1884:29); Cottonwood Creek village, 44 (*łaʒəẏt* 'by the mud place'); Old Kinik (De Laguna 1934:140), the Kinik of Petroff (1884:29) and Knik Village of Abercrombie (1900:map); perhaps *tux̣nayiłkict* 'where fabric is' near Matanuska, 47, *niłʔacaʔiłut* 'rocks together' in Palmer, 48, or *x̣utnayuti* 'glittering' at Bodenburg Butte, 49; Matanuska village, 46 (*nitəx̣* 'among islands'), the Nitakh of Petroff (1884:29); Chickaloon village, 50 (*nuḱdinʔitnu* 'log bridge goes across'); Eklutna, 45 (*ʔəyλuẏət* 'where things are'; cf. *ʔəyλuytnu* 'Eklutna River'), the Zdluiat of Petroff (1884:29), from the Outer Inlet form *ʔəzλuẏət;* Point Possession village, 42 (*čaẏəłnikt* 'protection on one side'), also Nikita.

Sources

Osgood (1937) intended to describe aboriginal Tanaina culture largely on the basis of work with Cook Inlet Tanainas in 1931 and 1932, but much of his material reflects the culture of the mid-nineteenth century, after extensive contact with both Russians and Americans. Townsend (1965) presents a diachronic study of the culture from precontact times through the 1960s.

Studies of specific topics include VanStone and Townsend's (1970) archeological description of a late nineteenth century site on Lake Clark, Townsend's (1970b) survey of Iliamna Lake archeology, and Townsend and Townsend's (1961) Pedro Bay archeological study. Davis (1965) is an ethnographic study of Eklutna. Ethnohistoric and culture change studies were made by Townsend (1970, 1970a, 1970c, 1973, 1974, 1975, 1975a). Townsend (1980) also studied social organization in the broader context of southern Alaskan ranked societies and (1979) the intersocietal relationships between Tanainas, Eskimos, and other Indians. Vaudrin (1963, 1969) and Krenov (1951) wrote English versions of Tanaina stories. Later Tenenbaum (1976, 1–4) edited and translated texts from Nondalton, and Kari and Kalifornsky (1974), from Kenai. Peter Kalifornsky (1977), a Kenai Tanaina, published a set of stories and reminiscences. P.R. Kari (1977) provides an ethnobotany in a popular fieldbook format. Kari (1975, 1977a) discusses Tanaina dialect differences and wrote (1977) a Tanaina noun dictionary, which contains much information on Tanaina culture.

From the nineteenth century valuable historic and ethnographic materials are in Wrangell (1839, 1839a:103–116, 1970), Radloff (1874), Petroff (1884:17, 25–29, 162–164, 1900:84–89, 260–263), U.S. Census Office. 11th Census (1893:69–71, 156, 163), Bancroft (1886), Tikhmenev (1861–1863, 1978), and the translations from Russian sources in Documents Relative to the History of Alaska (DRHA).

Ahtna

FREDERICA DE LAGUNA AND CATHARINE McCLELLAN

Language, Territory, and Environment

The Ahtna ('ätnu, 'ătnu) speak an Athapaskan language that is sharply distinct from those of their neighbors; however, the Ahtna language* shows some similarities to Tanaina, especially to the Upper Inlet dialect, which has been strongly influenced by Ahtna phonology and lexicon (Kari 1977). The Mentasta dialect of Ahtna shares some features with Upper Tanana.

Ahtna territory in the nineteenth century included the 23,000 square miles of the Copper River valley, minus the delta, for south of the Chugach Mountains lived the Eyak of the delta and adjacent coasts and, farther west, the Chugach Eskimo of Prince William Sound. The Alaska Range, from the Mentasta Mountains on the east to the gateway of present McKinley Park on the northwest, formed the Ahtna northern boundary. The volcanic Wrangell Mountains marked the eastern edge of Ahtna territory, which also extended up the valley of the Chitina River, a major tributary of the Copper River that rises in the eastern icefields where the Wrangell and Saint Elias ranges merge. On the west, the Ahtna spread over the lake-studded plateau into the drainage basins of the Matanuska, Talkeetna, and Susitna rivers. The extreme northwestern part of this area was hunting territory shared by the Ahtna, Tanaina, and Lower Tanana Indians and lacked clear boundaries. There may have been no permanent Ahtna villages northwest of Tyone

Lake in aboriginal times, and the Ahtna frontier marked on figure 1 may include disputed territory.

The climate of the Copper River valley is transitional from maritime to continental. The upper valley and plateaus near the Alaska Range are more continental than the lower valley near the Chugach Mountains and therefore experience greater variations in temperature, but less cloudiness and humidity and less precipitation. Snow cover in the inhabited areas generally lasts from mid-November to mid-April.

The Russians recognized two groups along the Copper River, Lower Ahtna and Upper Ahtna. Although they were not distinguished by the Russians, it was known by the end of the nineteenth century that there were also the Middle and Western Ahtna, ranging through the Tazlina-Mendeltna, Gakona, and Gulkana drainages, into the upper Susitna country as far as the Talkeetna Mountains (and beyond?) and the Alaska Range.

The Lower Ahtna and the Middle and Western Ahtna (including Cantwell) all spoke the lower dialect. The Upper Ahtna, from Sanford River and Chistochina to Slana, Suslota, and Batzulnetas, spoke a slightly different dialect; the speech of Mentasta was still more divergent.

Figures 1 and 2 show former and present communities, settlements, and camps. Of these, only Chitina, Copper Center, Tazlina, Gulkana, Chistochina, Mentasta, and Cantwell existed in 1975. A few individuals lived at Lower Tonsina, Mendeltna, Gakona, Slana, and Twin Lakes (near site of Batzulnetas). Residents from abandoned settlements have moved chiefly to Copper Center, Glennallen, Anchorage, and Fairbanks.

Formerly each local group was autonomous. The Ahtna have never formed a tribal political unit, nor have they ever held a council of all Ahtna chiefs, even when threatened by enemies. After the adoption of Alaska statehood in 1968, the Copper River Native Association (Ahtna Tannah Ninnan Association) was formed, and after 1971 Ahtna, Inc., the corresponding Native regional corporation.

External Relations

The Ahtna regarded the Tanaina as friends and relatives, the Western Ahtna being most closely linked to

---

*Ahtna words cited in italics in the *Handbook* are in a transcription that recognizes the following phonemes: (unaspirated stops and affricates) b, d, λ, ʒ, g (mid velar [k] to [kʸ]), ġ (back velar), ʔ; (aspirated stops and affricates) t, ƛ, c, k, q; (glottalized) i̇, ẋ, ċ, k̇, q̇; (voiceless continuants) W, ł, s, Y, x, h; (voiced continuants) m, n, ŋ, w, l, z, y, γ; (short vowels) i, e[ɛ], a[ʌ], o[ŏ], u[ū]; (long vowels) i·, e·[æ·], a·[ɔ·], o·, u·. Word-initial vowels contrast with vowels preceded by ʔ. Only the Mentasta dialect has phonemic Y.

In the practical orthography used by the Alaska Native Language Center (Kari and Buck 1975) the above phonemes are spelled as follows: b, d, dl, dz, g, gg, ʼ; t, tl, ts, c, k; tʼ, tlʼ, tsʼ, cʼ, kʼ; hw, ł, s, yh, x, h; m, n, ng, w, l, z, y, gh; i, e, a, o, u; ii, ae, aa, oo, uu.

The spelling of Ahtna words has been checked by James M. Kari (communications to editors 1975, 1978). Kinship terms and terms of clan relationship are given with the first-person singular possessive prefix s-. Forms cited with an initial hyphen cannot be used as independent words but must be preceded by some element.

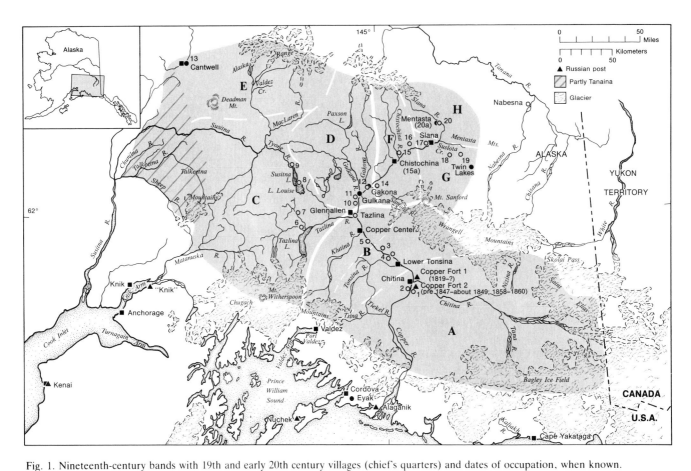

Fig. 1. Nineteenth-century bands with 19th and early 20th century villages (chief's quarters) and dates of occupation, when known.
LOWER AHTNA   A, Chitina-Taral band: 1, Taral (1847 or earlier–1911); 2, Dakah (1816–1838, completely abandoned by 1885).
B, Tonsina-Klutina band: 3, 'Copper Place' (before 1885); 4, Liverstake or Leibigstag's (chief's village of Lower Tonsina band after Tonsina-Klutina band divided; inhabited 1885, beginning and end dates unknown); 5, Conaquanta's or Stickwan's (chief's village of Klutina-Copper Center band after Tonsina-Klutina band divided; inhabited before 1885–1907).
MIDDLE AND WESTERN AHTNA   C, Tyone-Mendeltna band: 6, Mendeltna, at mouth of Mendeltna River (before 1848–?); 7, "Matanuska Village" (after Abercrombie 1900: map; inhabited 1898, beginning and end dates unknown); 8, Lake Louise (prehistoric and historic; 9, Tyone Lake (prehistoric and historic).   D, Gulkana-Gakona band: 10, Dry Creek (?–1939); 11, Gulkana River (occupation dates unknown); 12, Gakona (may have been an Upper Ahtna village; ?–1935).   E, Cantwell-Denali band (may not have existed in the 19th century): 13, Cantwell (1916–1970s).
UPPER AHTNA   F, Sanford River-Chistochina band: 14, Sanford River (after 1885?–1900?); 15, old Chistochina (after 1885–?); 15a, modern Chistochina (date first inhabited by Ahtnas unknown); 16, Indian River (?–1939).   G, Slana-Batzulnetas band: 17, Slana (before 1819–1909); 18, Batzulnetas (before 1847–1940); 19, Suslota (before 1885–1948).   H, Mentasta band: 20, Old Mentasta (?–1899); 20a, Modern Mentasta (1951–1970s). The Russian post "Knik" is located according to Abercrombie (1900:map); the exact location and identification is uncertain.

the Indians of Knik Arm and Susitna River. The Upper Ahtna and the Upper Tanana were usually friendly, but there was once a "war" between some Western Ahtna hunting near the Alaska Range and Tanana raiders from Nenana. After four years of fighting back and forth, into which the Mentasta Ahtna and Upper Tanana were drawn, the men of the Nenana party were all killed near Valdez Creek on the Upper Susitna.

On the whole, the Eyak were regarded as good people, but inferior to the Tlingit who were much admired for their wealth and sophistication, especially in ceremonial regalia and dance songs; however, until the twentieth century, the Ahtna had little direct contact with the Tlingit.

The inveterate enemies of the Ahtna were the Chugach Eskimo (sometimes called Aleuts locally). Many stories tell how the Chugach went up the Copper River to Batzulnetas, timing their visits so they could rob and destroy the fish caches while the Ahtna were hunting in the mountains, and pillaged Ahtna settlements all the way down the river. The Eskimo wanted copper bracelets, dentalia, good snowshoes, wooden dishes, and women. Once they killed the Klutina chief (Lower Ahtna) but were themselves defeated by a one-armed hero and an ingenious woman. After several such raids, the Ahtna claim to have slaughtered the Chugach on Mummy Island in Prince William Sound, thus ending the Eskimo attacks and justifying the composition of

DE LAGUNA AND McCLELLAN

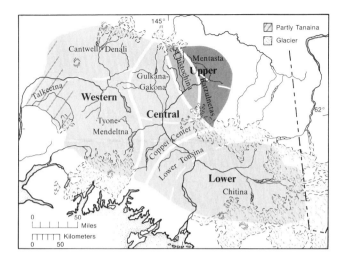

Fig. 2. Twentieth-century speech communities (James M. Kari, communication to editors 1978).

several victory songs. Although these raids occurred some time in the nineteenth century, the two peoples remained unfriendly in the mid-twentieth.

History of Indian-White Contact

Ahtna history falls into five periods: early Russian, 1783–1806; late Russian, 1807–1867; early American, 1876–1900; twentieth century to World War II, 1900–1941; and recent, 1941–1975.

Expanding first from headquarters in the Aleutians, later from Kodiak (founded in 1784), and from posts in Prince William Sound (Nuchek) and Cook Inlet (Kenai, Knik), the Russians discovered the Copper River and the Ahtna. Although the Lower Ahtna were at first friendly but secretive, Russian attempts to enter their country were unsuccessful. News of the destruction by Tlingit of the Russian post at Yakutat in 1805 inspired threats by Ahtna, Tanaina, and Chugach Eskimo.

In 1819 Andrei Il'ich Klimovskiy successfully penetrated Lower Ahtna territory and established Copper Fort near Taral, but the hostile Upper Ahtna blocked expeditions led by Pëtr Vasil'evich Malakhov and by Gregoriev in 1843 and by Ruff Serebrennikov in 1847–1848. The massacre of Serebrennikov's party led to closing of the Taral post, and when it was briefly reopened, trade with the Ahtna was of little value. Smallpox killed many Ahtna in 1837–1839; only a few were baptized.

After the purchase of Alaska by the United States, the post at Taral was not reopened, so the Ahtna traded directly with the Alaska Commercial Company at Nuchek and indirectly with posts on the Yukon. Abercrombie (1900a) failed in 1884 to ascend the Copper River but discovered the route from Valdez Arm into the interior. In 1885 Allen (1887) ascended the Copper

River to Batzulnetas, crossed to the Tanana, and descended the Koyukuk and the Yukon. The gold rush of 1898–1899 brought thousands of prospectors into Ahtna territory, hundreds wintering at Copper Center. In 1899 military exploring and rescue expeditions were led by Glenn (1900) and Abercrombie (1900). These resulted in Ahtnas' first intensive contacts with Whites. Luxuries were introduced, and tuberculosis became endemic.

At the beginning of the twentieth century the pack trail from Valdez to the Yukon River was brushed out for the Army Telegraph Line; by 1905 it became the Richardson Highway to Fairbanks, passable at first by horse-drawn vehicles and by 1927 by automobiles. The roadhouses for travelers also served as trading posts for the natives. Hunting for the roadhouses and for mining camps depleted the game; overfishing in World War I nearly destroyed the salmon runs; yet subsistence hunting and fishing continued until World War II. The ax, repeating rifle, fish wheel, tent, and stove eliminated the caribou fence, dipping platform, and large native house, and with them the native chiefs. The building of the railroad from Cordova to the Kennecott mines in 1911 shifted the Taral population to Chitina, but when the mines closed in 1938, Chitina was gradually abandoned. Closing of the Valdez Creek mines in 1935 drove Ahtna workers to Cantwell. Influenza in 1918 and other epidemics greatly reduced the native population (table 1). By the 1930s all Ahtnas had been baptized in the Russian Orthodox faith. Bureau of Indian Affairs schools were established by 1941.

After World War II the shift to a cash economy was completed, although there were few jobs for natives, except for the brief period of building the oil pipeline. Increase in population was checked by epidemics, especially in 1942 and 1946. The Alaska Native Brotherhood was introduced in 1954. The Alaska Central Missions have been active since 1950, with Faith Hospital at Glennallen and an annual Bible Conference at Copper Center, and they are credited by the Ahtna with saving them from drink and teaching them literacy. The Ahtna have been unprotected against the flood of settlers, wealthy sportsmen, and industrial entrepreneurs, who are attracted by the highway, electrification of the valley, and the construction of the pipeline, which runs through the heart of Ahtna country. Although a few natives have found local jobs since its completion, especially in the tourist lodge established by Ahtna, Inc., at Glennallen, many young people have left home to seek work in Anchorage.

The Ahtna are learning to write and read their own language; five were fully literate by 1979 (James M. Kari, communication to editors 1979). Nevertheless, they fear the loss of their separate identity. "We lost the track—like we go out with snowshoes, and the wind

Table 1. Population

	Group	Number			Sources
		Men	Women	Total	
1818	Lower Ahtna	294	273	567	Petroff 1884:33; Tikhmenev 1861–1863, 1:253
1839	Lower Ahtna			300	Petroff 1884:36
1860	Lower Ahtna	17	1	18	
	Upper Ahtna	97	93	190	Tikhmenev 1861–1863, 1:246
1863	Lower Ahtna			500	Petroff 1884:40
1880	Lower(?) Ahtna			250	Petroff 1884:29
1882–1884	Lower Copper River Indians			350–400	Abercrombie 1900a:404
1885	Lower Ahtna: Copper River			209	
	Chitina River			30	
	Tazlina River and Lake			20	
	Upper Ahtna			117	Allen 1887:128
1890	Lower(?) Ahtna	89	53	142	U.S. Census Office. 11th Census 1893:158
1898–1899	Lower Ahtna			75?	
	Upper and Western Ahtna			75	
	Western Ahtna			150	Abercrombie: 1900:578–579
1910	All Ahtna	161	136	297	U.S. Census Office. 13th Census 1913, 3:1137
1967	All Copper River natives			500	Federal Field Committee for Development Planning in Alaska 1968:504

blows the tracks away. . . . That's the way it's going to be."

Culture in the Nineteenth Century

Historical documents and memories of elderly informants of the mid-twentieth century give some idea of Ahtna culture in the nineteenth century, but it is uncertain how far back in time this picture can be projected. Some of the earlier customs and beliefs have persisted, but much has changed, particularly in technology, subsistence, settlement patterns, and the politico-legal system.

Settlements

Ahtna settlements (*qayax̱*) were either winter "villages" or hunting and fishing camps, the camps purely temporary or regularly occupied in season. Settlements were more numerous than modern Ahtna villages, and also smaller, a winter village consisting of a maximum of nine multifamily houses, or of only one such house and perhaps a few huts. These dwellings were not always closely grouped but, as in modern Copper Center, might be scattered along a stretch of several miles, with several local designations for the parts of such a single residential site.

Each winter establishment was under a "chief," either an important rich man who was the leading chief of the region, or the head of an extended household, subordinate to a leading chief. As the fortunes of regional chiefs rose and fell, the alignments of their followers in the various "bands" and the identities of their principal villages changed through time.

Each village or cluster of settlements within a 20-mile area appears to have had its own distinctive dialect (local manner of speech), which was retained even by members who married into other communities. Each village claimed a nearby hill for its symbol: the "chief's face" or "grandfather's face" of its people, invoked in potlatch oratory and song. The community also cherished traditions of great victories or splendid potlatches, displayed heirlooms, and was proud of the wealth, eloquence, and power of its chief.

Every major community or group of settlements had its own areas for hunting, fishing, and berry picking. Fish weirs and caribou fences in the most advantageous spots tended to attract visitors who could claim blood relationship to a local resident. This was usually easy to do, but foreigners could not enter the territory of any group without permission from its local chief. A stranger speaking an alien tongue and lacking a proper introduction risked being killed on sight. The major territorial lines were between Lower, Middle and Western, and Upper Ahtna.

Although some modern Ahtna speak of certain villages or localities as "belonging" to particular matrilineal clans, it is doubtful that such territory was actually claimed and controlled by a clan, as among the Tlingit; rather the clan was well represented in the area and the leading chief, at the time in question, was a member of that clan. Succession might easily go to a leader in another clan. In every community there were likely to be semipermanent visitors, married-in persons from distant Ahtna villages, or even foreigners in search of wives or in trouble at home, who were permitted to establish residence and serve the chief in return for his protection.

Technology

Aboriginal Ahtna technology was well suited to a seminomadic life. Most items were light, rather easily made, and fairly expendable. A man and a woman might work together in constructing a house, a moosehide boat, or a pair of snowshoes; and group cooperation was necessary for building the larger winter houses, caribou or moose fences, fish weirs and dip-net platforms. Otherwise, any normal adult could produce at almost any season the critical tools appropriate to his or her sex.

Stone, bone, horn, antler, wood, skin, sinew, roots, willow withes, bark, feathers, quills, ochers, and vegetable dyes were widely available, and they were used to make the items characteristic of northwestern Athapaskans. Only raw copper, which one Ahtna described as "the greatest story ever told," was limited in distribution, demanded religious precautions to secure the nuggets, and specialized knowledge to shape it into knives, daggers, spear heads, harpoon heads, and arrowheads. The Lower Ahtna, especially under Chief Nicolai of Taral (d. 1899), held a monopoly on the sources of most native copper, which further enhanced their position as middlemen between the Eyak and Tlingit of the coast and the Upper Ahtna, the Upper Tanana, and the Indians of the White River.

Structures

The largest Ahtna constructions were the big winter houses occupied by chiefs and their close dependents, including as many as six nuclear families. The main part of the house was rectangular, with excavated floor, walls of vertical poles or planks, and gable or hip roofs, thickly insulated with moss and heavy spruce bark. An untanned bearskin hung as a door at the small porch entry in front. Just inside were storage places, partitioned off by bark, for food, water, and wooden dishes. Slaves and persons of lowest rank lived and worked in this area. Along each side wall ran a platform about four feet high, the space below which was divided by bark walls to form private cubicles where the women and children slept and the men visited their wives. Married men were supposed to sleep on top of the

bench or in the sweatbath. During the day they often sat on the platforms, while the women worked below in front of their cubicles.

Cooking was done at the central fireplace, from which embers or hot rocks were taken to warm the cubicles, and hot rocks were passed through a circular door in the back wall into the low rectangular sweathouse. This had a flat roof with a skylight of bear gut that could be removed. Water poured on the hot rocks produced clouds of steam. Here men and older women bathed; unmarried youths, sometimes men, or even little girls might sleep there in winter.

At winter settlements, or nearby, there were apt to be also smaller "moss houses," of horizontally laid split logs, chinked with moss, and shed-type roofs of turf and moss (fig. 4). Families that scattered for winter trapping and hunting built such shelters deep in the woods where there was little wind.

More temporary dwellings included the double lean-to (fig. 5) with brush walls, bark roof and sides, held firm by heavy poles. When families moved, they carried with them sheets of sewn bark to make such huts. Hunters and trappers made even simpler kinds of brush shelters, but some wealthy men covered domed frames with five or six tanned moosehides, decorated with feathers and beads.

Every living site had a sweathouse, pit caches, a variety of tree or platform caches, as well as small enclosures for menstruants and parturients set at a distance.

Good fellowship and cooperation prevailed in the large houses, where tasks were assigned by the head man and his first wife. The sweatbath was enjoyed at the end of the day, not only because it brought physical well-being, but because it was a social time of story

James VanStone, Chicago: Abercrombie 1900b: pl. 158.

Fig. 3. Lower Ahtna man, woman, and child outside a dwelling made of bark sheets held down by poles. Fish drying rack to the right. Photographed a mile above Taral, before 1900.

Fig. 4. Permanent house of Doctor Billum (Lower Ahtna) at Lower Tonsina, where he ran a horse ferry across the Copper River. Log cabin with turf and moss roof, canvas tents, and elevated food cache. Photograph possibly by Guy F. Cameron, 1910–1920.

Fig. 5. Double lean-to of brush and canvas possibly at Taral. Small animal skins hang from the overhead poles. Photograph by Miles Bros., probably 1902.

telling, instruction, and fun. While some Ahtna believe that sweatbathing was aboriginal, the Russians undoubtedly reinforced the custom, if they did not introduce it. They were probably responsible for attaching the bathhouse as an annex to the large winter house, and the word for the alder switch used in bathing (*beni·k*) is a borrowing of Russian *venik*. Many Ahtna in the 1970s still sweatbathe almost every evening.

(For archeological details of Ahtna houses, see Rainey 1939; VanStone 1955; Irving 1957; Workman 1971; Shinkwin 1974.)

Subsistence

Each local group, in addition to fishing a part of the Copper River or a major tributary, exploited a section back from the river that included smaller streams, lakes of differing sizes, marshes, forests, open uplands, and mountain heights. The extent of each type of terrain and the ease of access to it varied, creating minor divergences in the annual subsistence cycles. Thus, the Lower Ahtna could hunt mountain goats in the Chugach Range, unavailable to groups farther upstream, while the Middle and Upper Ahtna got more muskrat and caribou than did the Indians of the lower river. All could find Dall sheep on the slopes of the Wrangell Mountains or the Alaska Range.

The Ahtna divided the solar year into two parts or "years"; "summertime," which began in late April or May with the melting of snow and breakup of river ice, and "wintertime," which began in November (although October was known as "half-summer, half-winter," and September was the "first month"). There were 12-odd lunar months of 30 days each (not 15 months as stated by Wrangell 1970:8). Month names were either ordinal numbers or descriptions of important seasonal events, but they varied to reflect local conditions.

In spring and summer people lived first in the salmon camps, after which they moved upland to meat camps, hunting small game on the way. In fall they descended once more to the rivers, trapping and hunting, until the several families gathered in the winter houses. These were usually near summer fish camps where the salmon were stored. By late January or February, families again were scattering to secure what game or freshwater fish they could. In precontact times this movement probably depended upon the condition of the food caches; as fur trapping became more profitable, the Middle and Upper Ahtna bands probably dispersed more widely in winter. The Lower Ahtna, who controlled much of the fur trade, did little trapping but bought furs from the upriver Ahtna to take to the coast on winter and spring trips.

• FISHING Probably the most important food resources of the Ahtna were the sockeye salmon (*Oncorhynchus nerka*) and Chinook salmon (*O. tshawytscha*), the first of which were taken early in June by the Lower Ahtna. With the introduction of fish wheels, about 1910, the late season coho salmon (*O. kisutch*) and steelhead trout (*Salmo gairdnerii*) became important.

Varying summer weather may rapidly alter the level of the glacier-fed Copper River; as the salmon are very sensitive to the water level, it is impossible to predict accurately the arrival of the runs. Sockeye and king (Chinook) salmon usually reach the lower river by late May or early June, and the upper drainage about two weeks later, but they may become soft and begin to spoil by the time they have reached the middle river, especially if battered by high water. High water may also make it difficult or impossible to catch the fish in wheels, although traditional fishing techniques may not have been so much affected by water level.

Of the 36 places for taking salmon remembered by modern Ahtna or mentioned in early sources, 13 were along the lower river and 8 each on the middle and the upper river. Spearing or harpooning of salmon and other fish was feasible only in clearwater streams and lakes. In the silty waters of the Copper, Chitina, and other glacial streams, people used dip nets of willow withes (fig. 6). At a few places, there were rocky points from which one could easily dip into the current, but usually the men had to make short fences to deflect the salmon to the ends of dipping platforms. These platforms, poles lashed together and supported on staging that could be moved to suit changing water conditions, were "owned" by the head men of large houses who kept all the fish caught by their households. When they had enough fish, others could use the platform. Both sexes dipped fish.

Large funnel traps of spruce saplings were apparently common in clearwater streams, like the Gulkana River. Middle and Western Ahtna used them in February for ling cod. Funnel traps were used for several kinds of freshwater fish, such as whitefish, ling cod, suckers, and trout. These were also taken with hook and line, and in winter were speared through holes chopped in the ice. Such ice fishing was sometimes critical for the survival of the Ahtna in the late winter.

In spite of their well-developed technology, the Ahtna sometimes failed to secure enough salmon even for early winter. If the first salmon runs were late, the people starved. In an attempt to secure bountiful catches and to avoid the epidemics believed to accompany the fish from salt water, the Ahtna followed a series of rituals and taboos, which included a feast given by each family for the first salmon caught, and rules for the treatment of fish and the disposal of their remains. These regulations, according to the myth, were learned by a young boy who lived with the Salmon People for a year.

• HUNTING AND TRAPPING   Until late in the nineteenth century, the Ahtna secured game and furbearers with bows and arrows, spears, snares, deadfalls, and pitfalls. But skill was only one part of hunting success. The series of ritual observances accorded to the spiritual aspects of the animals were thought to be equally essential for good luck.

Hunters learned the landscape intimately and kept continuously alert to the direction of the wind and the state of the weather. They did not practice scapulimancy but sometimes divined the location of game by means of beaver hip bones. Shamans or medicine men could locate animals in their dreams and send the hunters to them. The hunters prayed to animal spirits and before setting out sang special magic songs (especially those of the Wolf, Canada Jay, Fox, or Wolverine), but they never announced what they hoped to kill. They usually referred to all animals by circumlocutions, not by their "true" names. This was especially necessary in the case of valuable furbearers or dangerous animals like the grizzly. Before and after the hunt, a man was supposed to be sexually continent. While he was out, neither he nor the women associated with him could

Fig. 6. Lower Ahtna fishing. left, Tenas Charley's dip net, made of willow twined with spruce root; rim diameter about 45 cm. Photograph by Frederica De Laguna at Copper Center, Aug. 1954. right, Woman fishing for salmon with dip net, from platform near Lower Tonsina. Photographed about 1910.

wash their persons or belongings, lest they wash away his luck. No menstruant was allowed any contact with a hunter, his food, clothing, or weapons.

The Ahtna divided animals into three groups: "game" or meat animals, furbearers (some of which were eaten, too), and a third less easily characterized group. The meat animals (caribou, sheep, goats, moose) required fewer ritual observances than did furbearers, although their bones were burned (never given to dogs), and they were sometimes designated by special names when hunted. For three days after death, their flesh and hides were still associated with their spirits (kuniˑs), contact with which made babies sick. Meat and hides were never brought into the house through the door, but through the smoke hole (later, the window).

The pelts of valuable furbearers (lynx, wolverine, marten, fox, beaver, otter) had to be kept apart until dried. Some were too dangerous to children ever to bring into the house. Bones and carcasses not eaten by humans were burned, but beaver bones, like fish bones, were consigned to the water. The hunter had to offer excuses for killing certain species, place gifts beside the dead animal, or pray to it for luck.

Caribou and moose were caught either in drag-pole snares or in snares set 200–300 feet apart in long brush fences. Caribou fences were mostly above the timberline, but moose fences might run for seven or eight miles through the forest. During both spring and fall migrations, the natives drove the caribou into brush corrals with V-shaped entrances, where they were speared, shot with arrows, or entangled in snares. Several men, under the local chief, built and maintained such fences and corrals. At a few places, such as Paxson Lake, men and women stampeded the caribou into water where the hunters waited in small canoes to spear the swimming animals.

While there were caribou in the Klutina area (Remington 1939:79) and probably elsewhere in Lower Ahtna country where they are no longer, the Middle and Upper Ahtna were able to exploit part of the great Yukon-Tanana herd, which occasionally came as far south as Copper Center (Murie 1935:70–73). Mentasta Ahtna often joined Upper Tanana relatives to work the profitable caribou fence at Kechumstuk in the upper Tanana drainage.

After guns were obtained, moose were most successfully hunted in April, when the thawed snow froze at night to a crust that hampered the animals, but not the man on snowshoes.

Sheep and goats were caught in drag-pole snares set in stone fences or were shot with arrows.

Only a brave man deliberately hunted the grizzly or the black bear. Bears were most prized in fall for their fat, though some persons refused to eat grizzlies. Bears were snared, killed by spiked deadfalls, or stabbed with stout copper-bladed spears. All bears were believed to possess great physical and spiritual powers; they were especially taboo (ʔengiˑ) to babies and were surrounded by ritual precautions.

Wolves were seldom hunted, for it was believed that whoever killed one would starve to death. Only an old man, with suitable magical care, could remove the pelt.

Furbearers, such as wolverines, fox, and lynx, and small game like mountain squirrels and rabbits, were usually taken in snares and deadfalls. Rabbits and porcupines often became the main food during late winter and early spring.

Dogs that had been specially trained in practical and magical ways were occasionally used to hunt bear and to track other animals. To kill any dog or a pup meant death to the slayer or his child.

People pole-snared ducks and geese along their trails in the tall grass; spruce hens could also be taken in this way. Ptarmigan were caught in simple loop snares, set in the willows where they fed.

Before the end of the nineteenth century, guns of various sorts became the chief means of hunting most kinds of game, while steel traps supplanted the earlier snares and traps. Repeating rifles were not introduced until the twentieth century.

• GATHERING The Ahtna ate "Indian potatoes" (*Hedysarum* sp.), "wild rhubarb" (*Rumex* sp.), a few other kinds of greens, the inner bark of the poplar tree, and at least 10 kinds of berries. Some berries were eaten fresh; others were stored in pit caches, together with *Hedysarum* roots, for winter use. The roots were pried up in the fall with digging sticks, or women took them from the nests of mice, leaving small gifts so that the aggrieved mice would not retaliate by robbing human caches.

• FOOD PROCESSING The Ahtna traditionally ate moose, caribou, goat, sheep, black and grizzly bear, lynx, beaver, porcupine, rabbit, ground squirrels, muskrats, game birds, fish, and some vegetable foods. But even when starving they refused to eat wolf, mink, or dog and only in extremity ate tree squirrels and marten. Wrangell (1970:7) stated that Ahtna existence depended upon the spring and fall caribou hunts, citing widespread starvation when the hunts were poor. Allen (1887:129) thought that fish was the most important food, with rabbit next. Probably both often made up the bulk of the daily fare, though the Ahtna like to picture themselves as big-game hunters.

Men usually cooked the large game and other choice food. The principal ways of cooking were by stone-boiling in spruce-bark baskets or in moose or caribou stomachs and by roasting on a spit. Grease was rendered from caribou and moose as well as from fish. Caribou meat, mixed with berries and grease, was stored in bark buckets.

Food was also stored so that the long dark hours of midwinter could be devoted to local community festivities, with singing, dancing, gift giving, story telling and riddling, through which the elders instructed the young on the nature of the universe and men's moral obligations to the beings in it.

Women did most of the work of preparing salmon and other fish for storage. Using sharp semilunar copper knives, the women sliced the salmon and spread the flesh thin enough to dry quickly in the air on an open drying rack. Despite a smudge, wasps became too dangerous in late summer to permit this activity. When dried, the fish were folded together and pressed into bales of 40 for winter storage or trade. Women also rendered grease from water-soaked fish heads to store in fish-skin bags. Many fish taken in the 1970s are lost to blowflies or rot in the rain; the same was true in the past, when Allen (1887) in 1885 found many fish caches moldy or maggotty.

Men ate first at meals, even young boys taking precedence over the women. Each person had his or her own oval wooden dish and wooden or horn ladle from which to drink soup.

Clothing and Adornment

Nineteenth-century writers describe the Ahtna as a fine-looking tall people, with rather smooth olive complexions and well-kept hair. Their dress was much like that of neighboring Athapaskan tribes. Women made the clothing, which was mostly of tanned caribou or moosehide. Processing the skins was arduous and time consuming.

Both men and women wore one-piece trouser and moccasin combinations and fringed shirts (fig. 7), although the style differed by sex (Allen 1887:131–132, pls. opp. 48, 52, 130; Dall 1877:34; A.M. Powell 1909:218, 299, 300). Quill and feather spine embroidery and, later, beadwork, pearl buttons (fig. 8), and dentalia outlined the yokes of the shirts and made decorative stripes down the outer sides of the trousers. People might also wear loose shirts of mountain-squirrel skins and robes of netted rabbit-fur cord. Men had fur hats, and women, collared hoods (later kerchiefs). Mittens or gloves were worn in winter or for certain ritual tasks.

Both sexes wore ear and nose ornaments (fig. 9) of metal or dentalia, and they painted their faces for special occasions. Men wore beaded sheaths, day and night, to hold their large copper daggers with double-spiraled handles. Wealthy men had beaded ammunition pouches, and necklaces (fig. 10) and bandoliers decorated with dentalia and glass beads.

Transportation

Travel was largely on foot; women, children, and dogs carried packs (fig. 11), leaving the men free for hunting

Smithsonian Lib.: Petroff 1884:pl. 6.

Fig. 7. A Copper River man wearing caribou-skin leggings and fringed shirt decorated with porcupine quills. The bag around his neck was perhaps for carrying firemaking equipment. Part of a lithograph after a depiction done in 1881.

or defense. In winter they used fine round-toed snowshoes, often traded by the Upper Ahtna to the Lower, and loads were hand drawn on toboggans and sleds. Dog traction was not adopted until about 1899. Traditional toboggans were of moose leg skins, sewn with the hair pointing backward; bent plank toboggans were probably introduced through European influence. The aboriginal sled was of "Kutchin type," about six feet long, with runners turned up high at both ends, and three struts on each side to support the bed for the load. In summer large dogs carried packs of 25 to 40 pounds (Allen 1887:133).

A mother carried her baby on her back, the child tied into a chairlike birchbark cradle (fig. 12), which allowed the legs to dangle on each side of a central flap that was fastened to the chest by cross ties. (The cradle

Fig. 8. left to right: Aysenatah (Charlie Sanford); Nel-cotly, his wife; Etetnot-otna (Susie); Frank; Setin-setna (Ina); Exch-na (Katie, the smallest); Kotenich-etl (Lena, the eldest). All are Upper Ahtna. Photograph by A.M. Bailey at Batzulnetas, Dec. 1919.

Fig. 9. left to right: Tenanichna (daughter of Suslota John), wearing one-piece trouser-moccasins and earrings of dentalia; her 6-year-old daughter; her husband, Estaloda (i.e., *u'eł dila· ta'* 'Rattles-Dishes' father'; the name refers to noise at potlatch time); and Tsacotina or Mary Ann (later married to Douglas Billum) wearing a nose ring. Estaloda and his wife were of Upper Ahtna origin, although living in Lower Ahtna territory. Photograph by Miles Bros., near Lower Tonsina, 1902.

650

Fig. 10. Mary Ann and Douglas Billum (Lower Ahtna). He is wearing a dentalium shell necklace and a red cloth coat decorated with beads, appliqué, and a fur border. Photograph by Frederica De Laguna at Copper Center, Aug. 1954.

is often incorrectly illustrated upside down, as if the flap protected the head, as in Mason 1896:fig. 99.) The whole was carried in a fold of the woman's robe or blanket, held by a wide beaded band around the shoulders.

River travel was limited by dangerous currents, and rivers, especially the Copper River, were treated with religious precautions. Game killed upstream was sometimes simply allowed to float down, or hunters packed the meat into boats made of their hides on a light frame. Large boats of moose, sheep, goat, or caribou skins were also made for river travel and for trading trips to the coast. These boats were up to 30 feet long and held from 10 to 30 paddlers, one old man often acting as pilot but doing no paddling (Abercrombie 1900a:405). Rafts were used for short trips on rivers or lakes. One-man hunting canoes of birch or spruce, propelled by double-bladed paddles, were used on quiet water, especially for hunting swimming caribou.

Trade

The Ahtna belonged to an ancient and widespread trade network involving the Eskimo, other Athapaskans, the coastal Eyak and Tlingit, and probably the Chukchi of Siberia. In the late eighteenth century, the Lower Ahtna, probably more than the Eyak, served as middlemen between the interior tribes (Upper Ahtna,

Smithsonian. NAA: 75–5648.

Fig. 11. Chief Stickwan's girls (Lower Ahtna) carrying camp equipment with tumplines. The girl on the right is wearing trouser-moccasins. Photograph by Miles Bros., probably near Lower Tonsina or Taral, 1902.

Upper Tanana, Tutchone) and the Russians on the coast, although the Chugach Eskimo at first tried to prevent contact between the Ahtna and the Russians (Bancroft 1886:187, 190, 191; Tikhmenev 1861–1863, 2:suppl. 6:61); however, by the end of the century, the Ahtna were trading directly with the Russians at Nuchek in Prince William Sound. Shortly afterward the Eyak, who moved westward to the Copper River mouth, began to serve also as middlemen.

Wrangell's information, in part based on Klimovskiy's explorations of 1819, indicates that the Lower Ahtna obtained moose, lynx, and beaver pelts from the Upper Ahtna to trade with the Russians, who, since 1819, had a small post on the Copper River near Taral, which the Upper Ahtna also sometimes visited. Moreover, the Upper Ahtna (of Slana and Batzulnetas) used to meet the Tanaina from Knik Arm and Susitna River at "Lake Khtuben," somewhere at or near the source of the Susitna in the Alaska Range. Here they traded, hunted caribou, or even went on together to "Titlogat," a lower Tanana village at the confluence of the Toklat-Kantishna River with the Tanana. From the Upper Ahtna of Slana ("Nutatlgat"), the Tanaina sometimes obtained English guns, copper money, and beads that were not of Russian make, goods said to have come from a third tribe who obtained them from people living in a fort. Since there were no Hudson's Bay Company posts on the Yukon for a decade after Wrangell's re-

port, it is quite possible that these English goods came from posts on the Lower Mackenzie and Liard rivers (Wrangell 1839a, with map).

Other trade routes led via the Matanuska River, or via Tazlina River and Lake (Allen 1887:61, fig. 18), to Knik Arm, and to Russian posts in Tanaina country. To reach Nuchek, the Ahtna went via Klutina River and Lake, thence over the glaciers of the Chugach Range to Port Valdez in Prince William Sound; but those who used this route had to pay the Chugach Eskimo not only for the use of their boats but also for the privilege of passing through their country. This arrangement was abandoned about 1850 or 1860, after an Indian party was slaughtered by the Chugach, who in turn were destroyed by an epidemic believed sent by Ahtna shamans (Abercrombie 1900a:391). All subsequent trade with Nuchek was via the Copper River valley. In the 1880s mixed parties of Upper and Lower Ahtna often made three trips a year: in March when the river was frozen, in May when the ice was out, and in September when the water was low.

In precontact times the Ahtna had also carried copper via an overland route from the Tana River across the Bagley Icefield, to the Eyak and Tlingitized Eyak on the Gulf Coast near Kaliakh River and Cape Yakataga. The Ahtna emigrants who became the Tlingit Raven moiety's *ga·naxte·dí* clan of Cordova and *kʷá·šk qʷá·n* clan of Yakutat were supposed to have traveled this way. The coastal natives themselves sometimes took this route into the interior, and it was used by a few prospectors in gold rush days, in preference to the

Smithsonian. NAA: 75–5343.

Fig. 12. Lower Ahtna infants in bark baby carriers; moss for diaper shows on left. Photograph by Miles Bros., probably at Taral, 1902.

Copper River valley (Rohn 1900:781; A.M. Powell 1909:3–4; De Laguna 1972, 1:100–101, map 16).

Another important route led up the Nizina and over Skolai Pass (via summer and winter routes), to Russell Glacier and the headwaters of the White River; or a descent of the Chisana or Nabesna rivers could be made to Upper Tanana country. Native copper was obtained from at least four localities on or near this route (Hayes 1892:120–125; Rohn 1900a:793–798). This copper was passed on by Tutchone groups in Yukon Territory to the Kutchin on the Yukon and to the Chilkat Tlingit.

In 1884 Bremner (in Seton-Karr 1887:212; cf. Schwatka 1885:92–93) reported that guns and ammunition were reaching the Lower Ahtna via the Upper Ahtna and Upper Tanana, who obtained them along with beads and dentalia from the Hudson's Bay Company at Fort Selkirk, 1848–1851, and Fort Yukon, 1847–1867, and later from independent posts. Even in 1899, the Upper Tanana Indians on the Nabesna had bullets and knives obtained from such sources and arrow points of native copper from the Ahtna (Rohn 1900a:793). Chief Nicolai of Taral in 1885 was accustomed also to leave Russian beads and ammunition in his house on the Nizina River, where the "Colcharnies" (Upper Tanana and Tutchone) from across Skolai Pass would leave furs in exchange.

Warfare

Disputes between Lower and Upper Ahtna were sometimes called wars but, like quarrels between bands of the same division, were more apt to be settled by discussions and payments than by fighting.

An Ahtna war party was led by a special war chief, not by the regular chief (*qasqe·*). He could demand assistance of his own clan or moiety but had to pay members of the opposite moiety to accompany him.

Warriors wore armor of wooden rods or else of rabbit or beaver fur pitched and coated with sand and gravel. They were armed with spears, weighted horn clubs (fig. 13), bows and arrows with three-cornered bone heads designed to remain in the wound, and daggers of copper (later of iron).

Warriors practiced dodging before setting out, gulped raw meat, and painted their faces red. If anyone tripped, he was dismissed, for this was a death omen.

A warrior who had killed (*dene· zeł'ye·nen*) was traditionally a little crazy. He wanted to be alone, yet dared not sleep at night, fearing vengeance. He was supposed to sing his victory song once, then throw it away lest someone else die. He was subject to 100 days of isolation, hair hanging unkempt, with strings around his hands, wrists, knees, and ankles, sitting under a blanket in the corner of the house, eating from his own dishes, unable to hunt or fish lest he poison everything. In short, he observed all the stringent life-crisis taboos. He could avoid this period of taboo and also his terror if he cut open his victim and ate a little fat from near the heart. This resembles the tasting of game killed by a hunter, and perhaps both rites were to subdue the spirit of the slain.

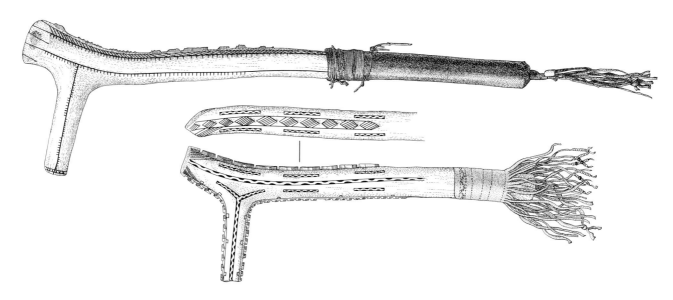

Muzeĭ Antropologii i Étnografii Akademiia Nauk SSR, Leningrad: 571–32b (top), 2667–14 (bottom).

Fig. 13. War clubs of caribou antler collected along the Copper River in 1839–1845. The distal ends are sharpened, and the incised decorations are filled with brown coloring, probably red ocher. One at top has hole in end of tine for (missing) stone or metal blade, and irregular sharp bits of iron inserted along back; one at bottom has raised rhomboids carved along back and carrying cord through hole drilled near proximal end. Proximal ends covered with tanned hide, with tassels strung with European beads; one at bottom has wavy embroidered line of red and black moosehair(?) near top of wrapping. Top 68 cm long (plus tassel), bottom same scale. See Troufanoff 1970.

• CLANS AND MOIETIES The Ahtna were in the 1970s and in the past composed of some 8 to 10 matrilineal clans (*ẏatci·tne*), with traditionally about 5 in each exogamous moiety, the number fluctuating as some clans became extinct or were so reduced in numbers that they merged with another or new clans were introduced (table 2). The moieties were identified as those who called the Raven (*saẏani*, locally translated 'crow') and Sea Gull (*nalbe·y*) their respective "grandfathers," though there was no belief in descent from these birds. In mythology, Raven is the creator-trickster-transformer, but Sea Gull appears only as a minor character. According to one story, all clans were descended from a set of sisters who ascended the Copper River from the coast, some of the sisters going to the Upper Tanana River, others to Cook Inlet.

Moieties ranged individuals as "opposites" who intermarried, helped each other at life crises, and gave each other potlatches. Since dualism between kin groups was stressed through cross-cousin marriage, clans were more significant than moieties. Neither ever gathered as a whole on any occasion.

In any small community, the accidents of birth and death might produce a numerical imbalance between moieties, leading to marriage between members of two clans on the same side. Such an intramoiety union, though not condemned as an incestuous intraclan marriage would be, did create kinship problems, since the spouses and siblings-in-law could not be "opposites" at potlatches, and their children were confused by having some parallel cousins (or "siblings") in the opposite moiety, and some cross-cousins ("sweethearts," or "joking relatives," or gift-exchanging and hunting "partners") in their own. But a sufficient number of such marriages would eventually result in a reclassification of the two clans as "opposites," one of which thereby shifted its moiety affiliation. A similar shift could occur when a clan was introduced into a foreign community. For a time, as a "middle clan," it might contract marriages with both sides, since both were strangers, but it would eventually become associated with one. Population movements also split single clans into branches that became distant enough to intermarry. Dual division was probably fundamental to the alignment of clans among the Ahtna and their neighbors—Tanaina, Koyukon, Tanana, and Kutchin (De Laguna 1975; Pitts 1972:79–96).

While succession to chieftainship was not determined by matrilineal descent, there was some feeling that certain villages, or their chiefs, should "belong" to particular clans; some regions were designated as the home or 'land' (*nen*ʔ) of certain clans. This suggests that Ahtna clans were semilocalized groups, the origins of which were probably, and traditionally, traceable to particular areas.

Most clan names refer to some object "found" by an ancestor (usually an ornament for the face or head); other clans claimed some animal from which they were derived or with which an ancestor was associated; however, these objects or associated animals did not develop into representational clan crests like those of the Northwest Coast Indians. Comparison of Ahtna clans or clan names, or of units recognized as their equivalents, suggests widespread migrations and intermarriages among the Western Athapaskans and even the Eyak, the closest affiliations of the Ahtna being with the Tanaina and the Upper Tanana.

Sib and moiety organization has remained important in structuring social relationships and ceremonials.

• KINSHIP Ahtna kinship terms reflect the matrilineal clan-moiety system and the importance of cross-cousin marriage. Since both husband and wife should belong to each other's father's maternal line, paternal and affinal kin are ideally the same, and the two matrilineal lines are continually linked in marriage so that there is no distinction between matrilateral and patrilateral cross-cousins (table 3).

Grandparents and grandchildren are free and affectionate in their relations; the terms of address reflect the sex of the grandparent.

Terms used by the parental generation for their children and for nephews and nieces vary according to the sex of the speaker. For relatives in the parental generation, male and female speakers employ the same terms. Father's sister and mother's brother's wife take the same term, as do mother's brother and father's sister's husband, reflecting the intermarriage of the two lines. A "mother's brother" is treated with greatest respect by his maternal nephew; the uncle reciprocates with polite reserve but has authority over both his nephew and niece. The maternal uncle and his niece are "shamed together" (avoid each other, do not address each other face-to-face), and the same avoidance obtains between a fraternal nephew and his "father's sister," while the "father's sister" exercises authority over her respectful niece.

The terms for father's brother and his sister are usually not extended to the father's more distant parallel cousins, because the father's clanmates (*sta*ʔ *belda·n*ʔ*ne*), other than his siblings and immediate cousins, are one's joking relatives and potential spouses. These include, of course, one's cross-cousins, who are possible sweethearts or partners (*slaci·n*), depending on their sex, or possible siblings-in-law. There is only one term of address used between male and between male and female cross-cousins, but a special term is used between females. After the marriage of a cross-cousin to one's close consanguineal relative, the appropriate affinal

Table 2. Clans and Moieties

Name of Clan	Reported Origin and Emblem	Present Ahtna Distribution
Sea Gull Moiety		
1. Red Paint People *cisyu*	Poor people on lower Copper River. Found red face paint. "Have the Bear and the Pigeon Hawk."	Among all Ahtna divisions. Reported as originally chiefs, displaced by They Came Down from the Sky. Now intermarried widely with Caribou People.
2. Striped Painted People (?) *necisyu*	(Western or Northern variant of Red Paint People?) "Have the Bear."	Only 3 persons among Middle and Upper Ahtna.
3. Caribou People *uʒisyu*	Ancestor found among caribou herd, near Tangle Lakes or Tazlina Lake. Or used caribou skin bedding.	All major Ahtna divisions. Many married to Red Paint People.
4. Fish [Salmon] Tail People *kelaʔyu, k̇ek̇elaʔyu*	Probably from Upper Tanana or Yukon. Put on fish tail as hat. Considered equivalent of Red Paint People.	None.
5. Canyonberry People *dengigeʔ taWie·ne, dembaʔ Wie·ne, or ceŋohie·ne;* Canyonberry Place People *nigeʔ qule·n Wie·ne*	Found among berries, ate them, or wore them as beads. Seem to have been local groups, with local names for *Elaeagnus argentea*, which were amalgamated or equated.	Among Cantwell Ahtna; formerly among Lower (?) and especially Middle and Western groups.
6. Snow Bunting People *ġe·xyu, Wġe·xyu*	Wore snow bunting feather in nose. Possibly same as Canyonberry clan.	None, although mentioned by all informants.

According to one story, all were descended from sisters that came up Copper River from the coast, some going to Upper Tanana, others to Cook Inlet. Caribou People are usually ascribed to the northwestern caribou hunting grounds.

Name of Clan	Reported Origin and Emblem	Present Ahtna Distribution
Raven Moiety		
1. They Came Out of [Wood] Canyon *diči ʔilci·ne*	From Tlingit. Attacked Red Paint People, enslaved by them, freed by They Came Down From the Sky.	Among Lower Ahtna; formerly also among Middle Ahtna.
2. They Came Down from the Sky *nalci·ne* Name used as moiety designation.	Descended from younger sister of ancestor of They Came Out of Canyon, via Star Husband. Succeeded Red Paint People as Lower Ahtna chiefs; reputed shamans.	Throughout Ahtna territory.
3. Cotton People (from fireweed or cottonwood down) *diq̇a·giyu*	From the coast. Put cotton on heads instead of feather down.	Among Lower Ahtna; once reported on headwaters of the Gulkana.
4. Single-Minded or Fierce People a. "real" *ʔałčeʔ tne·y*	From Midway Lake; derived from water plant.	Middle and Upper Ahtna. Descendants of groups a and b among Upper Ahtna. Group c not among Ahtna. The 3 groups may intermarry.
b. "middle" *ʔałčeʔ tne·y*	From Middle or Lower Tanana; associated with the Marten.	
c. "Northway group," *nenʔ Wza·* [a]	From Canada, use the Fox Tail.	
5. They Came Out of the Water *talci·ne* a. main body b. Mountain People *dẏela·y taWie·ne* Mountain Squirrel People *celes ẏantenaʔ* [b] Ice People *ten Wie·ne*	From Cook Inlet. Derived from Sea Otter, or more probably from Land Otter.	Group a moved east to Middle Copper River; among Middle and Western Ahtna; a few among Upper Ahtna. Group b went up Susitna River; at Cantwell, a few among Middle Ahtna. The 2 groups may intermarry.

SOURCES: DeLaguna 1975; Wrangell 1970 and Osgood 1937 for the Tanaina.

[a] Literally 'open country', that is, nonmountain people, a general name for Athapaskans on the other side of Northway (James M. Kari, communication to editors 1978); apparently equivalent to the Upper Tanana clan name *nị·sí·*.

[b] Literally 'arctic ground-squirrel trail creek', a place-name occurring in several parts of Ahtna territory (James M. Kari, communication to editors 1978).

654

Table 3. Kin Terms

Ahtna Term	Speaker's Sex	Primary Meaning	Application and Extensions
sciye	m, f	Grandfather	Includes grandparents on both sides, their sib-
scukde	m, f	Grandmother	lings, parallel cousins, and spouses; sometimes their clanmates; one's spouse's grandparents.
scu·ye	m	Grandchild	Reciprocal of grandfather. Extended.
ska·y	f	Grandchild	Reciprocal of grandmother. Extended.
sta²	m, f	Father	
sta·y	m, f	Father's Brother "little father"	Includes father's close male parallel cousin; step-father; husband of mother's sister or of her female parallel cousin.
sna·n	m, f	Mother	
saǫeye	m, f	Mother's Sister	Includes mother's female parallel cousin; step-mother, wife of father's brother or of his male parallel cousin.
sez²e·	m, f	Mother's Brother	Includes mother's male parallel cousin, even one's older clan-brother; husband of one's father's sister or of his female parallel cousin.
sbeče²	m, f	Father's Sister	Includes his close female parallel cousin; the wife of one's mother's brother or of one's mother's female parallel cousin.
si·²e·	m	Son, stepson	Includes son of wife's sister.
si·²e·	m, f	Brother's son	Includes son of male parallel cousin; son of clan-brother.
sce²e	m	Daughter	Includes wife's sister's daughter.
sce²e	m, f	Brother's Daughter	Includes daughter of male parallel cousin, of clan-brother.
sya·ze	f	Son	Includes son of sister and of female parallel cou-sin, and of husband's brother; may be extended to all boys in own clan.
syače·	f	Daughter	Extended similarly to the above.
saze·	m	Nephew/Niece	Child of his sister or female parallel cousin.
sunɣe·	m, f	Older Brother	Includes half-siblings, stepsiblings, parallel cous-
skele	m, f	Younger Brother	ins (even if in different clans), and clanmates.
sade·	m, f	Older Sister	
sde·ʒe²	m, f	Younger Sister	
ski·le²	m, f	Brother	
stełče²	m, f	Sister	
sude·	m	Cross-cousin (m or f)	Extended to the clanmates of cross-cousins on occasion.
sude·	f	Cross-cousin (m)	
sezde·	f	Cross-cousin (f)	
sχen	m	Brother-in-law	Wife's brother and wife's maternal uncle; hus-band of sister and of sister's daughter.
sẏe·	m	Sister-in-law	Wife's sister; Brother's wife; extended to the fe-male parallel cousins or clanswomen of the sister-in-law.
sẏe·	f	Sibling-in-law (m or f)	Similarly extended.
s²eł zda·nen	m, f	Spouse	
s²a·t	m	Wife	
sqan²	f	Husband	

Note: First-person possessed forms, used for reference. The same terms are used for direct address (in the Lower dialect often without the s-), except that avoidance rules exclude sez²e·, sbeče², si·²e·, saze·, and the sibling terms from being addressed to individuals of the opposite sex. The terms stełče² and ski·le² are from James M. Kari (communication to editors 1978).

term is substituted for the cross-cousin term: "brother-in-law," used between men, who concomitantly treat each other with mutual generosity and respectful reserve, and "sibling-in-law," used between women and between men and women. Siblings-in-law of opposite sex continue or adopt the joking, flirting relationships of cross-cousins.

The same terms are used by both sexes for older brother, older sister, younger brother, and younger sister. These terms are extended to half-siblings, parallel cousins, and clanmates. But there is avoidance ("shyness," "shaming") not only between brother and sister (including parallel cousins of opposite sex) but also between older and younger sibling and between parallel cousins of the same sex, varying in degree according to difference in age, upon which authority also rests (McClellan 1961).

The various degrees of reserve, respect, and avoidance toward certain kinsmen are first exhibited about the time of puberty, to be slowly relaxed in old age. Except at Mentasta, the second-person plural pronoun *xanyu·* is used in an honorific function to call an avoidance or respect relative when absolutely necessary; but the relatives may not look at each other. A senior may use an honorific third person plural when addressing a junior, but the junior is not supposed to answer back. Circumlocutions are substituted for kin terms in referring to a dead father, mother, or oldest sibling.

The levirate and sororate replaced a deceased spouse with his or her sibling or parallel cousin. Failing an appropriate mate in his own generation, a man might marry his maternal uncle's widow (his cross-cousin's mother), provided she were not closely related to his own father. Or, he might marry the daughter of a female cross-cousin.

Affinal relations always took precedence over the consanguineal in determining kin terms and behavior. Since generation lines could be disregarded in marriage, a man's female cross-cousin who married, for example, one of his "mother's brothers" became a "father's sister." In such cases, the union transformed the joking cross-cousin into a respect or avoidance relative. Not only was a daughter equated with mother and mother's sister but also the uncle and nephew were equated with each other. Because of this, a man used the term "brother-in-law" for his wife's maternal uncle and his sister's daughter's husband.

There are only descriptive terms for father-in-law, mother-in-law, son-in-law, and daughter-in-law (such as 'she whose daughter I married' for mother-in-law), for they were never addressed. A man is respectfully reserved or "shy" with his father-in-law and son-in-law (including the husband of his brother's daughter or of his wife's sister's daughter), but he is "shamed" and avoids his mother-in-law and the sisters of her parents, as well as his daughter-in-law (including the wife of his sister's son or his brother's son). This reserve and avoidance behavior is mutual, the strongest prohibitions separating father- and daughter-in-law, and mother- and son-in-law, who must not even look at each other.

Political Organization

Every major settlement had a chief (fig. 14), *qasqe·* 'spokesman' or *dene·* 'chief' or 'rich man'. He was usually referred to by suffixing the forms *-denen* 'chief of' or *-ɣaxen* 'prominent resident of' to the name of the locality. Although he was often a shaman (since the 1840s, a "Christian sleep doctor" adopting bits of Russian Orthodox ritual), his power was primarily economic. When he lost his vigor to hunt and trade, a younger male relative would take his place and attract his followers. While he held his position, he could command the labor of his dependents to hunt and fish; to build or repair houses, caribou and moose fences, fish weirs, and fishing platforms; and to construct and fill food caches. He usually led trading parties and firmly controlled all transactions (Allen 1887:53, 61). Minor headmen were under the major chiefs of their district or "band," but one might become the leader by deposing the old chief.

Chiefs, their wives, children, and other close relatives formed an aristocracy distinguished by fine clothing, the best food, and seats of honor in the big house on formal occasions, when "lines of caste [were] rigidly drawn" (Allen 1887:59). Poor dependents, drudges, or

Smithsonian, NAA: 75–5663.

Fig. 14. Chief Stickwan (or Stephen), wearing a dentalium necklace; he was leader of the Klutina–Copper Center band of Lower Ahtna after Conaquanta's death, and in 1898 was living at "Stephen's Village" (Abercrombie 1900: map). Photograph by Miles Bros., probably 1902.

656

slaves performed the menial labor for the aristocracy, although the chief's maternal nephews, as prospective sons-in-law, also fetched firewood and water, and did similar chores.

A chief or rich man might single out a first or beloved child to become an aristocratic "favorite child" (ʒuʹǵi); if he were wealthy enough, all his children, or even a pet dog, would be so treated. Such young favorites were adorned with beads and dentalia, well fed, and honored at potlatches given by their fathers; but after marriage a "favorite child" usually had to work, except for a chief's daughter married to a wealthy chief. It is said that one so indulged in childhood would suffer in later life, perhaps starve to death, while those who had been deprived would become rich.

In addition to the ordinary retainers or free men, the chief had drudges or servants (ʔelnaʹ) who worked for bare subsistence. In hard times poor people might sell their own children to a chief (girls being worth more than boys), but most drudges were widows or orphans, whose treatment depended upon the good will of the deceased husband's or father's relatives. There were also captives taken in war, or slave children purchased from the "Kolchane" (Upper Ahtna?) (Wrangell 1970:8). No stigma attached to an Ahtna who had been a slave but became free through escape or ransom by his chief. Slaves were not killed at ceremonies.

An important chief was always accompanied by 10 to 20 clansmen who acted as his helpers and bodyguard (ukiʹleʔ; also 'his brothers'). In feuds or war he usually relied on a subordinate as war chief. It would appear that the chief was more the leader of a community than of a descent group, or rather, that a shift in status from localized clan head to political leader was taking place in historic times but was still incomplete.

The chief was responsible for feeding his people, for delivering moral lectures, for enforcing the traditional "law" within his own settlement, and for defending his people in legitimate grievances involving other groups. Deliberate murder and theft of food were punishable by death, and a chief might order the execution of a troublemaker unless he escaped to relatives in a distant place. When disputes arose between communities, their respective chiefs met to decide the rights of the case, hearing witnesses. In this way, payments made by the culprit's clansmen in cases of accidental death might avert a feud, or a determined show of force by one side could decide the issue. A chief could rely on his own clansmen, his sons, and his brothers-in-law to back him up. To acquire such relatives, a powerful chief took wives from all clans, including his own.

Life Cycle

• BIRTH   In the past and sometimes in the 1970s, magical precautions were observed by both parents for the welfare of the unborn and the newborn child (especially to prevent dangerous contact with freshly killed animals). Most of the rituals of childbirth and couvade, like those of puberty, were to confine and remove contamination and to bring health and wealth to the parents.

Birth (until the 1950s) took place in a special shelter, where mother and child were isolated for 30 days. For the first 10, both parents had to remain quiet, not to injure the new fragile soul, then had to work hard, as in other ritual situations. The parents repeated many of the observations of adolescence (see below), the major difference being that no hood was necessary, and the woman's old clothes would be kept for her next confinement. Otherwise there was the same isolation, the same count on two sets of strings, and the same food taboos, to be followed separately by man and wife. Couples lessened the 70-day ritual after each successive birth.

• CHILDHOOD   The education of children was to produce skilled and lucky hunters and industrious and accomplished housewives. Laziness, improvidence, stinginess, lying, stealing, and spreading malicious gossip were countered by admonitions, spankings (by parent, older sibling, or mother's brother), by rigorous physical training (early rising, running, hard work, cold baths), and especially by the magical exercises of puberty. Amulets (worn only a day or two, for any excess was dangerous) imparted desired traits.

Unruly children were threatened by the Owl, by huge monsters (ǵuʹx) underground or in deep lakes, by Bush Indians who kidnap those who stray, or by xayuǵeʹ, an abductor of naughty children, impersonated especially at the winter solstice festivals by a man with painted face, huge pack, and knife. Adults might tease noisy children at other times with the song that heralded his approach.

A child's first kill of any food animal, however small, was the occasion for a ceremony in which the food, together with gifts, was given to the child's cross-cousin, while the child and his or her immediate family fasted for three days. Ideally, the taboo against eating one's own kill and the obligation to distribute it to one's opposites applied to the first of every species; but after the very first the ceremony was usually neglected until the first big meat animal was killed.

• PUBERTY   Puberty was the most critical time in the life of boy or girl, when he or she observed, in complete and elaborate detail, the system of prescriptions and proscriptions to be repeated, in shortened and modified form, by the parents of a new baby, by the potlatch-giver and his wife, by the killer, by the menstruant, and by those who handled a corpse. Their purpose was to insure health and long life, free from afflictions of old age; to bring luck in hunting and wealth in trade and potlatch; to remove pollution that could drive away fish and game, ruin the berry crop, raise storms, or cause death to others. It is difficult to reconstruct the details of aboriginal puberty rituals, since they were already being abandoned before 1900, and no one living in 1970 had observed them all, although most elderly persons in 1955–1960 had endured some and were inclined to blame bad weather, scarcity of fish or berries, and poor teeth of the young upon their failure to "take care of themselves" at adolescence.

The adolescent was under severe restrictions for 70 days (in 3 stages: 30 plus 30 plus 10) and followed less stringent rules for a whole year. The first days were counted by tying knots in a string fastened to the neck, but the last 10 ("for luck") by slipping a cord ring from finger to finger.

The girl at first menstruation (*tiniya·nen*) and the adolescent boy might be called 'the one in training' or 'the hood-wearer'. The huge hood (later a black calico kerchief for a girl and a fur cap for a boy) was of moose skin, had fringes falling over the face to shield living things and the sky from the wearer's baleful glance, and was hung with rattling hoofs to warn others. The hood was worn for a full year and after use was saved for a younger sibling.

The adolescent was isolated in a brush hut or tent. For the first three days, neither the boy nor girl might speak, eat, or drink, but sat with bowed head and bent knees, a position to be maintained for 10 days, and resumed as much as possible for 60. To insure limber joints and small bones, strings of caribou hide were tied around wrists, elbows, knees, and ankles and laced around the fingers of both hands. The girl also wore a string around her waist.

At the end of the first 10 days the adolescent might bathe (but a sweatbath was forbidden for a year), and a series of observances and exercises began to insure the qualities desired in adult life (industry, smooth skin, lack of body odor).

At the end of the first 30 days, the adolescent bathed, donned cleaned clothes incensed with "perfume" (*Pyrola* sp.?), and moved to a new brush hut closer to the family dwelling, beginning a second string count to attract riches. The first counting string (which removed contamination), the strings from the body, and the old clothes were hung in trees where the wind could blow away body odor.

Food taboos and restrictions on handling food lasted for a year. These required a drinking tube of swan bone and of special dishes. Hot food, flesh less than three days old, and handling a knife or cooking were all tabooed. Someone else had to care for the youngsters.

Young girls married shortly after puberty, but a man was apt to be 30 years old, since he should have given (or participated in) three potlatches before marriage.

• MENSTRUATION At each menstruation, a woman isolated herself in her own hut, where special utensils, bedding, and old clothes were kept for her use. When the period ended, she bathed, put on fresh clothes, and returned home. In the 1970s some still observed these precautions; others remained at home, let their husbands cook, but used their own dishes. At menopause, a woman became "just like a man—no more taboo."

• MARRIAGE Polygyny and polyandry were practiced into the beginning of the twentieth century, wealthy men taking two or more wives, of whom the senior had authority over the junior. Sororal polygyny was felt to promote domestic harmony, but important chiefs took wives from as many clans as possible, even their own, for political reasons.

A girl's parents, and especially her mother's brother, might arrange her marriage, although love affairs between cross-cousins often became permanent unions. Divorce was supposed to be easy, but unhappy wives, far from home, might commit suicide. Unless the suitor were already established, he had to live for some time (formerly a year or more) in the house of his prospective parents-in-law, working for them. Such bride service often resulted in permanent matrilocal or avunculocal residence, especially if this offered advantages to either couple. The last daughter to be married often lived with her parents, so that her husband could support them, or the parents moved to their daughter's settlement. Assistance, when practical, was extended to uncles and aunts, and especially to maternal grandparents.

There has always been great fluidity of residence: a husband from a distant Ahtna community or even non-Ahtna group might live with his wife's people, or take her back to his own home. It was also common to seek a bride in the community from which one's maternal grandmother had come, for there a young man had suitable cross-cousins.

• DEATH Old age came early in former days. In good times, old people might be able to stay all year at the winter village, but in periods of starvation, when people had to travel and were too feeble to carry them, the aged were abandoned. Sometimes the house was simply pulled down as they lay on their beds; or they were smothered ("a soft death").

Death brought not only sorrow, often violently manifested and most keenly felt at the loss of a spouse, but also danger through contamination by the corpse and the gathering of ghosts. Death was not explained to children, who were sent to stay with relatives, and it was strictly taboo to mention the real name of the deceased (not applicable to American, Russian, or teknonymous nicknames).

For fear of contamination, the dying person was removed to a small shelter, if possible. Friends and relatives washed and dressed the corpse with new moccasins and gloves and watched over it for three days while the spirit still lingered. They informed the deceased that he was now dead and should go away without taking with him the soul of another. Customarily members of the opposite moiety, preferably cross-cousins or siblings-in-law, disposed of the dead. A corpse was taken out of the house through the smoke hole or window, not the door. The structure in which an adult died was abandoned and burned with all its contents.

The corpse and his personal possessions were cremated. The ashes might be left at the spot but were usually buried in a birchbark box. Those of a rich man might be kept by his children. In one case, his adolescent daughter, accompanied by her brothers, carried the box for a year, revisiting the places where her father had lived.

By mid-nineteenth century, Russian influence introduced burial in a plank-lined grave, marked by a cross and surrounded by a fence. In a little house above were placed the belongings of the deceased, especially his bedding, clothes, and the nail parings and hair combings he had saved. In the 1970s ordinary coffins were used and wealthy families provided marble tombstones, but the fence was retained.

The corpse-handlers were contaminated and for 10 days had to stay quietly at home, eating alone and abjuring fresh flesh. Then they took a sweatbath and donned new clothes provided by the relatives of the deceased.

For 30 days (under Russian influence, 40), the ghost was summoned by the appropriate kin term at each meal, when the spouse or daughter put food in the fire to feed it. The ghosts of the dead were believed to haunt the graveyard or to live in Mount Wrangell, the sulphurous fumes of which were their cooking fires; some might be reincarnated.

A widow or widower had to mourn for a year. The widow also worked during that time for her dead husband's brother (or near kinsman), before remarrying. If she showed insufficient grief, she might be beaten; the hard work was supposed to ease her sorrow and make her industrious. Widows were often abused as drudges, as were fatherless children, but widowers seem to have had an easier lot.

After a year or two, the bereaved might remarry, supposedly a clanmate of the deceased. If the widow chose a man of a different clan, he had to pay the relatives of her former husband. Some men never remarried.

Potlatches

The Ahtna potlatch remains in the 1970s the center of native ceremonial life. Although conceived in terms of relationships between individuals in opposite moieties, it is actually an occasion on which a village may host guests from other communities, often irrespective of their moiety affiliations. Even the smallest potlatch, perhaps a one-day affair, requires guests from another settlement. A major potlatch given by a wealthy chief is an intervillage, interband, and intertribal political and economic institution, linking the most important Ahtna and Upper Tanana communities. It may last a week or two and cost several thousand dollars. The number of guests, the length of their stay, the value of the food and presents given to them—all redound to the credit of their hosts, especially to the chief who organized the affair. Through frequent and lavish potlatching a wealthy man becomes recognized as a chief, both by his own people who give him economic support and by the guests who come from afar.

Occasions for potlatching may include rejoicing at the recovery from illness of a close relative or the accomplishment of a favorite child. One Ahtna leader in 1970 gave a potlatch for his favorite dog, giving toys to the children. At a potlatch for the living, the person honored distributes the gifts at the direction of the giver, and the occasion is purely joyful.

Most potlatches are to mourn and honor a dead relative by repaying those who helped at or attended the funeral and showed sympathy. Only in this way can grief be extinguished. A poor person may be able to afford only the small feast that always follows a funeral, with inexpensive payments to those who "worked on the body," or he may be able to save enough over time to "go in on someone else's potlatch" and so repay his debts.

Every adult, except the poorest, gives several potlatches in his or her lifetime, and any one potlatch may involve several hosts, each of whom has his or her pile of gifts to distribute, while acknowledging assistance in their accumulation, and each has his or her own mourning song, composed for the occasion. The several hosts need not be from the same clan or moiety, but all are related to the person being honored. If several dead are to be mourned, they are always of the same clan.

The invited guests are the affinal relatives of the person (or persons) being honored, their married cross-cousins or siblings-in-law. Such relatives include the spouses of half-siblings, of parallel cousins, or even of clanmates. Thus, if a man honors his mother, maternal uncle or aunt, sibling or parallel cousin, or his sister's child—all members of his own moiety, usually of his own clan—the guests will belong to the opposite moiety, and he will expect economic assistance from his own clanmates. But if he honors his father, wife, his own or a brother's child, he must give to members of his own clan and moiety, the "opposites of the person honored," and may therefore expect no help from his own clansmen, since they come as guests, although any close relative of the person being honored may also be a host at the same potlatch. The only affinals or relatives who receive nothing at a death potlatch are the spouse of the deceased, the orphaned child, and bereaved parent. (Persons whose irregular intramoiety marriages have made them affinals of the honored person may be present as slightly embarrassed guests.)

A potlatch may involve a year or more of planning and saving, composing special songs and dances, rehearsing older ones, making fancy costumes and paraphernalia (drums, song leader's wand, dancers' feather pompoms, fig. 15), sending messengers to invite the guests, gathering and preparing native foods, incensing the potlatch house for luck, receiving the guests (formerly by friendly exchanges of gunfire), speeches by the principal hosts and guests (chiefs or noted elders), singing the hosts' special potlatch song to mourn the dead and to insure the return of the wealth to be disbursed, singing of other mourning songs, feasting the guests (who formerly ate alone; since the 1970s both sides eat together), the guests calling for more food and drink or banging their dishes on the floor when sated. Then follows the introduction of happy dance songs by the guests (old mourning songs in a lively tempo, or foreign dance songs), perhaps a tug-of-war with a length of calico or competitive dancing between rival guest villages, oratorical contests between guests and the hosts who have now shed their grief, or perhaps the settlement of some old dispute. Chiefs and wise men are expected to know the traditions of their hosts' village so they can respond properly to oratorical riddles or to the display of village heirlooms and can make flattering reference to the village hill or "grandfather." They know these things because their own grandfather or grandmother came from the village.

On the last day of the festivities the gifts (blankets, clothing, firearms) are passed in bags into the house through the window (not the profane door) and are arranged in piles in front of each host, who distributes them to those guests to whom an obligation is owed.

After speeches of thanks for coming and thanks for hospitality, the guests depart, and the potlatch hosts and their spouses begin a ritual period of taboos and magical exercises, patterned on those of puberty and childbirth-couvade, in order to regain their wealth. Thus, while the potlatch marks the end of a life and of mourning the deceased, it is also a life-crisis for the giver.

The potlatch giver and spouse observe the same taboos as at the birth of a child. For a first potlatch, the ritual period is 100 days (30 plus 30 plus 30 plus 10), but the number is reduced for succeeding potlatches, so that by the eighth there need be no more, though some people may continue. A very old man, unable to accumulate more wealth, observes only the last 10-day finger count "for luck."

At the time of the famous potlatch at Healy Lake in 1927, attended by some Ahtna (Endicott 1928:93–118), the Copper River people had almost forgotten how to dance because potlatching was nearly obsolete among

Fig. 15. Bill and Maggie Joe (Upper Ahtna) in potlatch dance costumes. They hold feather wands for gesturing during the dance. These cotton garments are patterned after the aboriginal ones of tanned caribou skin. Since 1964 the colors of the cloth may indicate the clan or the moiety of the wearer. Here, Maggie Joe, a member of the *uʒisyu* clan, is wearing red to symbolize the Seagull moiety, and her husband, Bill Joe, of the *nalci·ne* clan, is wearing black for the Raven moiety. Other dance costumes may be in bright colors without clan or moiety symbolism. Photograph by Frederica De Laguna, at Chistochina, Aug. 1968.

them. Since 1954, learning of Tlingit songs from the Tlingit who introduced the Alaska Native Brotherhood to the Ahtna, interest in tape recordings of their own and foreign songs, dancing at commercially sponsored festivals, and attendance at potlatches of the Upper Tanana have all revived potlatches and song composition on the Copper River.

Shamanism

During the nineteenth century, every older person was likely to be something of a shaman, especially after experiencing a personal misfortune, such as the death of a relative or crippling injury, but certain men and women became noted as great "dream doctors," sometimes even while young. Women shamans were believed to be more powerful than men, though most stories are about men.

The shaman (*dyenen;* Lower dialect *genen*) was called a "different" or transformed person, a 'singer' (*k̯edeλi·nen*), or 'dreamer, clairvoyant' (*tete·sen*), because it was through dreaming and singing that he acquired and exercised the powers that transformed him. He might have up to eight powers or spirits and their songs, and while there is disagreement as to the ultimate sources of power, all agree that the novice had to dream of a dead shaman performing—"then gets his job"—for he thus obtained his predecessor's spirits (sometimes his name) and also rights to his songs and paraphernalia. Shamanistic powers and techniques were therefore inherited by close relatives (children, younger siblings, nephews or nieces), and, while most shamans were jealous of each other, in one case two brothers exercised the same powers simultaneously and assisted each other.

A dead shaman was never cremated, and unless he had bequeathed his paraphernalia to someone, these magic objects were left on his grave, perhaps to be duplicated by his successor as the result of a dream. Some shamans were said to be able to return to life again after even eight years, provided surviving relatives observed strict rules during that period and no dog barked at the critical moment of resurrection. Women avoided the graves as well as the sleeping places of doctors.

When shamanistic dreams began, they might last a year or more and should not be revealed. The novice secluded himself for at least 30 days, avoiding places where women walked. He dared not refuse the call, although another shaman might remove the new power if the novice were "mean" and likely to become a "bad doctor."

A shaman could not cut his hair or change his clothing but wore some of the magic things (*k̯eze?*) he had dreamed. These magic aids might be a flag, an embroidered "map of the world," a beribboned cane, a little stuffed weasel that could be sent to find lost persons, a doll that could dance, an image that warned of danger, or an object that could shoot disease into a victim.

Each shaman specialized: some cured certain types of illness, such as soul loss or object intrusion, or performed operations that left no scars; others healed wounds because they had dreamed of an ax or gun that made such wounds; others could hold burning coals in the mouth, or call game, or control the weather, or rescue children from the Bush Indians.

Although accounts of shamanistic powers vary, all power was based on knowledge acquired only by dreaming. Some say that every species or natural object, like bears, the Copper River, the moon, or the sun, is subject to six Owners, and that the shaman dreamed of each in the set of six until he gained knowledge and power over the species or object. Others think that he dreamed of mythological characters and so could imitate their accomplishments (restore sight like the Loon); others dreamed of the Thunderbird, or of Bush Indians (who transform their victims by surgery and restore them to life). The power-giving spirit would not come to the shaman in a seance or possess him but rather imparted power to him by teaching him a song and a skill while he dreamed. The varied character of the dreams thus explains the differences between the specialties of the different shamanistic lines.

The practicing shaman became "crazy." He sang one or more of his songs but often was "timid" and needed the encouragement of an audience that sang with him. He was paid for his services, small fees for each of his helpers, "to keep them happy," but these were returned if he failed in his mission.

Shamans cured the sick or injured in a variety of ways, but a shaman could not help anyone in his own household because he was too close to the patient. To accomplish anything, he had to sleep in another dwelling. If bad luck or prolonged illness were thought to be caused by a bad shaman, the unfortunate victim would usually have to bribe the one who was injuring him.

Each shaman had one or more "roads," or ways of traveling. Sometimes he might send his spirit to fight that of another shaman in a different place (usually among the Upper Tanana). If defeated, the spirit would return to inform his master, who then knew that he would die. More often the shaman himself wandered in sleep. Such journeys might make him very hungry, and when he found what he thought was meat, he ate it, but it would really be the "soul" of someone in another village. Therefore, a death in one's own community was often blamed on an alien shaman, avenging a killing in his own. Too often, the shaman had not meant to kill anyone but was overpowered by hunger. On awakening, he could remember only where he had been and would worry about whom he might have eaten. In a similar manner, the shaman in his dreams might kill the "soul" of a moose, thereby delivering the animal to the hunter whom he would instruct where to find it.

It is no wonder that shamans were ambivalent figures, and they remain so in the 1970s, especially for their sons or nephews who are often leaders in missionary activities.

Synonymy†

The name Ahtna is from Russian *Atna,* originally the name of the Copper River (Wrangell 1839:52, 1970:5; Sokolov 1852; Radloff 1858; Tikhmenev 1861–1863),

---

†This synonymy was written by Ives Goddard, incorporating material supplied by Frederica De Laguna.

itself from Ahtna *ʔatnaʔ* 'lower Copper River' (a placename of unknown etymology). It appears in German as Atnaer and Athnaer (Wrangell 1839a:97; Holmberg 1856:7) and in English as Atnah, Ahtnah, and Atna (Scouler 1841:218, 1848:232; Latham 1857:68; Bancroft 1874–1876, 1:137; Petroff 1884:146; U.S. Census Office. 11th Census 1893:156; De Laguna 1972). The spelling Ahtna is that used by the people themselves, as in the name of Ahtna Incorporated, the regional native corporation. The spelling Ahtena (Huntington 1907) was introduced as Áh-tená by Dall (1870:429), who was in error in taking this as "their own name for themselves" (1877:34) and in assuming that it contained the widespread Athapaskan word for 'man' or 'people' (Koyukon *dəna*, Ahtna *tneˑy*, and cognates). The supposed meaning 'ice people' (Dall 1877:34; Huntington 1907) is a mistranslation of a misinterpreted passage in Wrangell (1839a:98) that discusses the Ahtna name for the Russians.

Chugach Eskimo has *wiˑɬit* 'Ahtnas', applied particularly to those at Chitina (Birket-Smith and De Laguna 1938; Birket-Smith 1953:99; Jeff Leer, communication to editors 1978); this was rendered as Yullit by Nagaev in 1783 (Tikhmenev 1861–1863, 2: suppl. 7, 8). Tlingit has *ʔiqkaˑ qʷaˑn* or *ʔiqkahaˑ qʷaˑn* 'copper diggers' (Boas 1917:155; Jeff Leer, communication to editors 1978).

Ahtna *ʔatnaʔ Wiˑne* 'lower Copper River people' (also *ʔatnaWiˑne* and Lower dialect *ʔatnahiˑne*) (Kari and Buck 1975:57; James Kari, communication to editors 1978) has been rendered as Atnakhtîane (Wrangell 1839:52, 1970:5) and Atnatána (Allen 1887:128). Equivalent expressions are Tanaina *ʔutnuxiana* (Kari 1977:93), Eyak *ʔaˑdnaʔyaʔdəlahgəyuˑ* (Krauss 1970:490), Chugach Eskimo aˑtnaɣmiut (Birket-Smith and De Laguna 1938), and Upper Tanana atnaˑtʼene (Guédon 1974:21) or *taχoˑ tiˑn* (Paul G. Milanowski, communication to editors 1979). These Lower Ahtnas are the ones the Russians called *Mĭednovskĭe* or *Mĭednovťsy*, after the Russian name for the Copper River (*Rĭeka Mĭednaya*, from *mĭedʼ* 'copper', modern *medʼ*; compare their Tlingit name) (Wrangell 1839, 1970; Fedorova 1973:361), whence the Midnoósky and Midnóvsti of Allen (1887:128) and other variants listed by Huntington (1907). They include the Chettyna and Klutena of Abercrombie (1900:579), who are the Ahtna of the Chitina and Klutina rivers (*cedinaʔ* 'copper river' and *ḵatinaʔ*). In the Mentasta dialect they are called *ɋetnaWiˑn* (Kari and Buck 1975:57).

The upper Copper River Ahtnas have distinct names: Ahtna *taχaWiˑna* 'headwater people' (Kari and Buck 1975:57), whence Tatlatán (Allen 1887:128); Tanaina *tuχuxiana* (Kari 1977:93); Eyak *xədəgdəlahgəyuˑ* 'upland people' (Krauss 1970:490); Upper Tanana *taˑχaˑ tiˑn* (Paul G. Milanowski, communication to editors

1979). The Russians called them *Mĭednovskĭe Galʼťsane* (or *Kolchane*) 'Copper (River) Kolchanes' (German Kupfer-Galzanen) or nearer Kolchanes (Wrangell 1839:65, 1970:8–9), though the former name is also used for a Tanacross vocabulary (1839a:101–102, table opp. 258; Krauss 1964:410). The term Kolchane and its variants (Ahtna *ɣalcaˑne*) is generally applied to Athapaskans of other tribes, especially unnamed ones (see synonymy in "Kolchan," this vol.) but was formerly used by the Lower Ahtna for the Ahtnas on the upper Copper River, at or above Chistochina. The Chugach Eskimo distinguished between the *wiˑɬit* and the Shukturalit, the Ahtnas at Copper Center, whom they believed to be cannibals (Birket-Smith 1953:99).

The Western Ahtnas, including those at Cantwell since 1916, are Ahtna *caˑy Wiˑne* or *Wcaˑy Wiˑne* 'jack-spruce people' and Upper Inlet Tanaina *caxiana* or *xcayexiana* (Kari and Buck 1975:57; Kari 1977:93, 1977a:283, communication to editors 1978). The Taxlena (Tazlina) and Matanuskas of Abercrombie (1900:579) are the Central and Western bands, and his "Gakona Indians" were the remnants of the Upper Ahtna. Eyak names were *təχeˑldəlahgəyuˑ* 'Taral (Chitina) people, lower Copper River Ahtnas' and *yaˑnahgəyuˑ* 'Ahtnas, especially from middle Copper River' (Krauss 1970:490).

The elaborate list of reputed Ahtna subdivisions (with Eskimo names) recorded by Hoffman (Osgood 1936:7; Swanton 1952:530; Federal Field Committee for Development Planning in Alaska 1968:261) is completely fanciful.

Sources

The best early source on the Ahtna is Wrangell (1970). The German version (1839a) includes information and a map not found in the English translation. A later excellent account is by Allen (1887). Additional information from the last half of the century can be found in Abercrombie (1900, 1900a), Seton-Karr (1887), A.M. Powell (1909), Remington (1939), and sections in Petroff (1884) and U.S. Census Office. 11th Census (1893).

Historical and other background data are in Bancroft (1886), Sherwood (1965), Brooks (1973), Colby (1939), and Federal Field Committee for Development Planning in Alaska (1968). Sokolov (1852) remains in Russian, but Tikhmenev (1861–1863) is available in English (Tikhmenev 1978), minus the appendices and maps. The general ethnographic position of the Ahtna in relation to other tribes is discussed by Osgood (1936), Birket-Smith and De Laguna (1938), McClellan (1964), McKennan (1969), and De Laguna (1972, 1975).

Reports dealing directly with the Ahtna are by McClellan (1961), De Laguna (1969–1970), Troufanoff

(1970), B.S. Strong (1972), and John and John (1973). Field notes of De Laguna and McClellan (1954–1960) and De Laguna and Guédon (1968) remain largely unpublished.

Archeological reports are available (Rainey 1939; VanStone 1955; Irving 1957; Workman 1971; Shinkwin 1974). The noun dictionary of Kari and Buck (1975) covers many areas of traditional culture.

Native Settlements: Introduction

JUNE HELM

The Indians of the Subarctic stand apart from those whose heritage lies in southern Canada and the United States in that, in general, they have not suffered displacement from their traditional lands nor severe restriction of use and movement within them. Within the historic era, they have reoriented their interests and activities in response to the redefined resources of their natural surroundings and to the offerings and demands of the intruding, European-derived society. But, by and large, they have not been pushed or driven from their old locales within their lands. Rather, increasingly they have been drawn to new ones that offer easier access to the goods, services, and occupations of Euro-American society.

The historic process of White penetration into the Indian world has had its effect upon the nature of the native community. Local and regional identities have come to focus upon *settlements,* visible as clustered dwellings, often with one or several White institutional facilities present.

Upon the land where aboriginally camps of temporary or movable shelters were to be found, the European superimposed the fur-trade post or "fort." The trading post at first simply provided a focus for annual ingathering for trade. As Euro-American installations expanded from the trading post to include the mission, and then the school, nursing station, and other buildings housing Whites and their institutions, some native families began to erect their own permanent dwellings, usually in the form of log cabins, at these points of trade and services. Others established satellite all-native hamlets. Those who remained more mobile camped in temporary shelters at these loci in season. Expanded government services, especially, finally led almost all Indians to adopt an at least seasonally sedentarized existence in town or hamlet.

Many of the once all-native hamlets had by 1970 attracted White installations, such as schools, stores, and game warden cabins. Some Indian villages in the Canadian north are in fact recently reconstituted hamlets—a response to government efforts to disperse the congregated Indians at the trading settlements into the hinterland and into smaller settlement units.

Many of the settlements in the Subarctic, in some areas the bulk of them, were created either by natives or by Whites in response to the native role as fur procurer. Only after 1900 in the western Subarctic (notably Fairbanks, Anchorage, and Whitehorse) and only after World War II in the Shield Subarctic (e.g., Yellowknife, Schefferville) did a few urban centers emerge, towns and cities that had not been created in response to or sustained by the presence of a native population. Directly or indirectly, mining provided the initial impetus in the development of these centers. Most of the Whites resident in the Subarctic are concentrated in such centers. In those smaller settlements in which native peoples predominate, most of the resident Whites are transient employees, not settlers (cf. Fried 1963, 1968). Their jobs are for the most part to deal in some respect with Indians or Indian activities—as missionaries, merchandisers, administrators, teachers, public health personnel, welfare agents, game wardens, and so on.

Of the major political divisions within the Subarctic, native peoples—Indian, Métis, and Inuit (Eskimo)—are in the majority in the Northwest Territories and Nouveau Québec (Arctic Quebec). In 1971 the combined population of the Yukon Territory and the Northwest Territories, approximately 53,000 persons, divided, in terms of ethnic heritage, roughly into Indian, 20 percent; Métis and "nonstatus" Indians, 28 percent;* Inuit, 21 percent; nonnative (predominantly White), 32 percent (Canada Year Book 1972; Hoople and Newbery 1974). Of the total residents in the two territories, about one-fourth—most of them Whites—lived in Yellowknife or Whitehorse. In Alaska, in contrast, in 1970 only one-seventh of the population of 300,000 was native Indian, Aleut, and Inuit. Of these about 8,500 (16%) were Subarctic Athapaskans (McNickle 1973:179). The two urban complexes of Fairbanks and Anchorage accounted for over half the total population of the state. Yet, in 1967 over 70 percent of the natives in Alaska dwelt in predominantly native settlements having populations of 25 to 2,450 (Federal Field Committee for Development Planning in Alaska 1968).

*Nonstatus Indians are those who have relinquished or lost legal definition as Indians. Like Métis, nonstatus Indians "differ from registered Indians in their access to services, since the Federal Government claims no official responsibility for their well being" (Hoople and Newbery 1974:5).

The chapters that follow do not cover all the Subarctic settlement types that in mid-twentieth century contained Indian and Métis peoples (fig. 1). Native populations enclaved or dispersed within an urban complex such as Fairbanks, Yellowknife, or Inuvik are not directly represented (cf. Ervin 1969; Honigmann and Honigmann 1970). The all-native satellite hamlet is missing (cf. Helm 1961; Helm and Damas 1963; Taylor 1972), although two communities of the sample, Minto and Old Crow, began as such settlements. However, the settlements described are of a kind common throughout the Subarctic. They are small, predominantly native settlements containing one or more White installations and are especially significant on two counts. First, they have come to serve as a focal point of societal identification and interaction, not only for those natives in residence but also for those who have immigrated to urban centers as well as for those who reside in the settlement's hinterland. Second, historically they have been the locus where most of the direct contact and experience of the Subarctic Indians with agents of White society have taken place.

It is impossible to give an accurate count of native-based versus White-based settlements throughout the area defined as the ethnographic Subarctic. To do so one would have to know the history of every settlement as well as the native versus nonnative proportion of population in each. Sometimes, by combining data from disparate sources developed for other purposes, quantified approximations of native-based versus nonnative-based settlements may be gained for certain areas. The following approximations refer to the 1960s.

About half of Ontario lies north of the east-west railroad line and 50° north latitude. In this area about 40 small settlements are mapped (treating the mining cluster of Pickle Lake–Central Patricia–Pickle Crow as one). Of these, 14, about one-third, have been identified as Indian-based (Rogers 1962:A3–A4).

In the province of Manitoba north of 55° north latitude, an area of roughly 115,000 square miles, 26 settlements are mapped. Of these 18 are White settlements, all on the two railroad lines of the region. There are eight predominantly Indian settlements, none on transportation facilities although a number of Indians reside in Churchill, the grain port at the end of the railroad line on Hudson Bay (Manitoba. Department of Agriculture and Conservation. Social and Economic Research Office 1959:32.–34). In other words, about one-third of the settlements in northern Manitoba are Indian-based settlements.

In the District of Mackenzie, Northwest Territories, there are 18 major settlements in the area defined as Subarctic for this volume (thereby excluding Aklavik and Inuvik). Of these, three have developed into White-dominant administrative and transportation centers, although two were founded for the fur trade. Two others are small extractive-industry sites. The rest are native-based trading post communities. In addition there are about 10 to 15 outlying native satellite hamlets.

Within Subarctic Alaska (Athapaskan Indian lands), there are about 59 predominantly native settlements, most of them with a population between 25 and 200 (Federal Field Committee for Development Planning in Alaska 1968:map).

Several considerations led to the selection of the five settlements presented in the chapters that follow: recent, intensive fieldwork in the communities; geographical distribution; representation of the two linguistic families of the Subarctic, Athapaskan and Algonquian; and variety and contrast in the history of settlement creation and growth and in the ethnic components of the population.

The settlements of Davis Inlet, Old Crow, and Minto manifest a single, profound line of ethnic cleavage between the Indian residents, who share to a full or substantial degree a similar linguistic-cultural heritage, and the Whites. In Fort Resolution the Métis sector, distinguishable from yet bound into the Indian community, adds another dimension to the two-part picture. At Great Whale River the sociocultural distance separating resident Crees, Eskimos, and Whites (discounting the Whites' internal ethnic differentiation) creates a tripartite division.

Of these settlements, Minto and Old Crow began as all-native hamlets, apart from a point-of-trade (although traders soon came to them). First and foremost, Fort Resolution, Davis Inlet, and Great Whale River came into being as settlements around the trading post. All have accreted additional White installations and personnel. All are increasingly subject to "the ethnic, economic, social and political complexities" imposed by the workings of the modern national state (J.G.E. Smith 1970:63). These trends are detailed in "Modern Subarctic Indians and Métis," this volume.

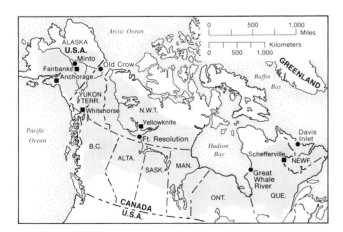

Fig. 1. Native settlements.

Davis Inlet, Labrador

GEORG HENRIKSEN

History of the Settlement

This chapter focuses on the life of the Davis Inlet Naskapi in the decade of the 1960s (Henriksen 1966–1968, 1971, 1973), here treated in the present tense.

For more than half of the year these Naskapis live in the interior of Labrador hunting the caribou. There, a social life unfolds that is only superficially affected by Whites and that is radically different in quality from that at the coastal settlement at Davis Inlet.

The Naskapi are conscious of this contrast. When at the coast they continuously express a longing for the interior, the Barren Grounds, and express their contempt for the life in Davis Inlet, saying that "the salt water is no good."

Traditionally, the "home" area of the Algonquian-speaking people now known as the Davis Inlet Naskapi was around Indian House Lake on the George River (see "Montagnais-Naskapi," fig. 1, this vol.). Being hunters who relied on the caribou as their principal source of food, they were forced to move to the trading post at Davis Inlet about the year 1916, when the annual migration of caribou herds failed to come through their area. After this event, the Naskapi became increasingly attached to the store for reasons of security.

At that time the Naskapi of the area consisted of two groups: the Barren Ground band and the Davis Inlet band. Arriving at the coast, the former kept itself in Voisey's Bay, while the latter lived some 30 miles farther south at Davis Inlet. However, both before and after the move to the coast, the two bands often resided together and intermarried. The nucleus of the Davis Inlet band was originally from North West River (Strong 1929:278).

In the summer of 1924, a Roman Catholic missionary arrived at Davis Inlet. He proclaimed an English-speaking Naskapi as "chief" and promised to come back every summer if the "chief" could gather all the people for the event. From 1927 the missionary made annual summer visits, and gradually the two bands merged into one and came to spend the summers around Davis Inlet. Since 1952 there has been a missionary in the settlement all year round.

Traditionally the Naskapi never undertook regular seasonal migrations to exploit the resources of the coast. Even after they moved to the coast around 1916,

they kept their orientation toward the interior, staying at the head of the bays where they scarcely utilized the resources of the sea. Caribou and other land animals were still their most important food, and their social and ritual life revolved around the hunting of big game.

As early as 1831, the Hudson's Bay Company had established a trading post at Davis Inlet (fig. 1). However, both reports from the post managers trading with the various Indian bands of the northern Labrador Peninsula (Williams 1963) and accounts from Henriksen's (1966–1968) informants make it clear that all the northern Indians did very little trapping for furs. Finding small profit in its trade with the Naskapi, the Hudson's Bay Company gave up its business in northern Labrador in 1942, when the Newfoundland government took over the trade and the responsibility for the welfare of the population. Recognizing the inability of the local population to participate successfully in the market economy on the basis of the local resources, Newfoundland transferred the administration of northern Labrador from the Department of Natural Resources to the Department of Public Welfare in 1951, and created a special organization, which became the Northern Labrador Service Division (N.L.S.D.). This organization has carried out essentially a welfare policy, issuing relief and statutory income to the Naskapi and other residents of northern Labrador through its government stores. It also operates fisheries, trying to motivate the Naskapi to engage themselves more actively in money-earning activities.

In this the missionary resident in the 1960s has played an active role. Through various strategies, this missionary induced some of the Naskapi to embark upon individual economic careers within the money economy. By rendering a variety of services he tied the Naskapi closer to the mission, so that they spent most of the summer season at Davis Inlet itself.

Population

The present settlement of Davis Inlet, where the Naskapi have lived since 1967 in houses built by the government, is located on the coast of Labrador at 59° 55' west longitude and 55° 53' north latitude (see "Native Settlements: Introduction," fig. 1, this vol.). This chapter describes the old settlement, which was situated

Fig. 1. Hudson's Bay Company post at Davis Inlet, in summer and winter. Photographed about 1883.

three miles south of the present site. There, the Naskapi lived in tents, except the Naskapi "chief" and one of his sons and their families who shared a house built for them with the help of the missionary. The only other wooden houses in this settlement were the school building and the missionary's residence.

The other Euro-Canadian residents in the community—the storekeeper and his family, an old store clerk with his family, and a young, unmarried store clerk—all employed by the Northern Labrador Service Division, lived in two houses on an island across the Davis Inlet, facing the Naskapi settlement. The missionary and the storekeeper were the only Euro-Canadians who played a prominent role in the social life of the Naskapi community.

Strong (1929:278) reports that in 1927 the two bands that later merged around the trading post at Davis Inlet totaled 92 individuals. In 1968 the population had increased to 145. It is a young population: in 1965, 46 percent of the population was under 16 years of age. In 1968 there were 33 households in the band, of which two no longer traveled into the interior since the heads of these households were no longer active hunters. There were 31 active hunters among the Naskapi in 1968. In addition there were two young men in their late teens who had not yet established their own households and therefore did relatively little hunting.

Relations with the Outside

The settlement is relatively isolated. The nearest communities are Hopedale and Nain, some 50 to 60 miles south and north of Davis Inlet respectively. These communities consist of Eskimos and White settlers. Each of these communities has a Royal Canadian Mounted Police station, one of which serves Davis Inlet.

The nearest Indian settlement is North West River, which lies some 150 miles south of Davis Inlet by air. The Davis Inlet Naskapi have many kinship ties into this community. However, they usually visit North West River in connection with illness, as the nearest hospital is located there. The Davis Inlet Naskapi also have relatives among the Indians at Knob Lake, but they do not visit one another.

The Naskapis' knowledge of, and contact with, the Euro-Canadian society is extremely limited. Only a few Naskapis have briefly visited modern Euro-Canadian towns. Until 1968 only one child had reached grade five. Generally, the Naskapis' command of English is very limited.

The Natural Environment

The hunting grounds of the Naskapi, which are not an Indian reserve, lie roughly within a semiellipse, stretching 150 miles west and 50 miles north and south of Davis Inlet. The interior, western part of this area consists mainly of barren mountains and rolling mountain plains. In this exposed landscape the Naskapi find lee for their camps in scattered patches of conifers in the river beds and on a few sheltered hillsides. This barren land provides the setting for the crucial caribou hunt of the Naskapi. The coast in this area consists of numerous islands and bays that cut 10 to 20 miles inland. The outer islands lie naked and exposed to the Atlantic Ocean, but some of the inner islands are quite heavily forested.

The climate in the Barren Grounds may be characterized as arctic; the air is very dry and the winter temperature often sinks to −50° C. The coastal climate is wetter and a little milder than the interior in the winter, but may be cooler with fog and rain in the summer due to the cold and damp air from the Labrador Current. During the winter the sea ice freezes a long way out from the coast.

This is a harsh environment, but by hunting and fishing the Naskapi continued in the 1960s to wrest a living from a country that is not rich in terms of renewable resources.

The Economic Bases of the Community

The caribou are by far the most important food resource for the Naskapi; they play a prominent role in their social and ritual life. Caribou are hunted all the year round, although only sporadically in the summer time. From October/November to March/April the people live with their families in the Barren Grounds, where they hunt and live off the caribou. If there is enough caribou, other types of food are sought only for variety in the diet. Porcupine, which are sometimes caught in the woods as the Naskapi travel to and from the Barrens, are eaten with relish, as are foxes and wolves. A small amount of red char is fished through the ice. Ptarmigan are often abundant and easily hunted. However, very little time is spent in hunting and catching animals other than the caribou. The Naskapi bring food from the store with them to the Barrens: on an average 100 to 150 pounds of flour, 50 to 75 pounds of sugar, 20 to 40 pounds of lard and margarine, salt pork, tea, and tobacco for each household. These goods, since they are irreplaceable, become very precious as soon as one is away from the coast.

Sometime during March or April the Naskapis travel back to the coast and Davis Inlet. Immediately they start hunting seal and continue to do so throughout their stay in the settlement. The harp seal and the jar seal are the most common, while the squareflipper is the most sought after since its skin provides the watertight soles for the sealskin moccasins used by the Naskapi during spring, summer, and fall. Seal hunting is not very significant as a source of cash income.

Later in the spring the Naskapi hunt for the Canada geese and various species of ducks. They fish for brook and lake trout through the ice, and hunt the black bear when it comes out of hibernation.

In July the cod fish reach the Labrador coast. They formerly provided the main source of cash income for the Naskapi; however, their numbers have rapidly declined due to overexploitation by the offshore trawlers. In place of cod, the Naskapis, as well as the White settlers and Eskimos, have turned to catching salmon and arctic char for sale.

In September/October the Naskapi load their dogs, sleds, and other equipment into their trap boats and punts to travel into the bays, where they spend a month hunting seals and at the same time fishing for arctic char in nets set under the ice on the lakes. When the big rivers finally are frozen, they start their travel inland in search of caribou. In this period and later throughout the winter some Naskapi may sporadically put out a few traps to catch mink, otter, and foxes.

These, then, are the most important renewable resources that the Naskapi exploit and that provide by far the largest part of their diet; however, they do receive some additional food through the store, mainly those items mentioned above. As "relief" issue, the Naskapi may receive store food and other goods, such as axes and cotton duck for their tents.

The various forms of income that the Naskapi received through the government store in the period April 1966 to April 1967 were: total cash income from work, $20,035; statutory income (family allowance, old age pension, and fishermen's unemployment insurance), $20,000; relief (or social assistance), $10,921. All totaled $50,956. Of the cash income, $8,550 came from the cod fisheries, $101 from the sale of furs, $749 from the sale of snowshoes and moccasins. The rest of the amount was earned through wage labor for N.L.S.D., mostly in connection with the clearing of the site for the new village.

In the Barren Grounds

Hunting Camps

When the Naskapi travel inland (fig. 2) toward the Barrens in the fall, they face a situation of extreme uncertainty as they have no way of knowing exactly when and where they will first encounter caribou. Thus, a common strategy is for some men to travel without their families into the Barren Grounds early in the fall to shoot a supply of caribou that they leave on scaffolds. They then return to the coast to fetch their families. As the Naskapi keep practically no secrets about their hunts, all the Naskapi at Davis Inlet at once know about the success or failure of the hunt, as well as the exact location of the stored meat. Hence, most families make this stored caribou their first destination when they leave Davis Inlet.

The cache of stored caribou becomes a kind of base camp. Having thus provided for themselves and their families, the men at once start to hunt farther into the Barren Grounds. This strategy is possible for the Naskapi, first, because they all have equal rights in the hunting grounds and its various resources. Thus, everybody is free to go where and when he likes, as no person or family can claim any exclusive rights to portions of territory or any particular resources of a delimited area. Second, people cannot be excluded from a hunting camp. Any Naskapi family may join any hunting camp whenever they wish. Third, the Naskapi practice a form

Fig. 2. Family with their loaded komatik pulled by dogs, traveling to their next camp, left to right, Shushebish (or Joe Rich), Napiou (baby in sled), Akat, and Penashaway. Penashaway is wearing a caribou skin fur coat. The hood is made from the whole skin of the caribou head and the protrusions are the ears of the caribou. When traveling Napiou was diapered with moss, wrapped in a piece of old tent, covered with a skin jacket, and then wrapped in a blanket (Strong 1928). Photograph by William Duncan Strong, Jan.-March 1928.

Fig. 3. Canvas tents of winter hunting camp, with protruding stove pipes. A storage rack is in center; snowshoes are impaled on sticks in front of tents to keep dogs from eating the rawhide lacing. Photograph by William Duncan Strong, Jan.-March 1928.

of sharing where everybody is entitled to a share of the game that the hunters bring down.

This system allows for an extreme mobility in physical and social space. Among the Naskapi there are no permanent groups and no permanent leaders with any predetermined following. It is therefore impossible to predict the exact composition of a hunting camp. Three main factors enter into the decisions the Naskapi make with regard to where, when, and with whom they shall travel: environment and game conditions, prestige and influence, and kinship and sentiments.

As to the first factor, a Naskapi family prefers not to travel alone, but to have the company of one or more families as insurance in case of sickness or accident. With an abundance of game the Naskapi may merge into large camps with 10 to 20 families, while in periods of scarcity they may split into smaller units (fig. 3) that scatter more widely over their large hunting grounds.

Second, Naskapi men compete among themselves for prestige and leadership. This competitiveness is an important factor in the formation of hunting camps and their splitting and merging, as any man may seek to establish a following for himself by traveling to an unoccupied territory.

As practically all the Naskapi are in some way related to each other, it is impossible to predict on the basis of kinship who will participate in hunting camps. Temporary feelings of friendliness and antagonism are more important. The women also influence the choice of which hunting camp a family will join. Naturally they want to join camps where the relations between the women may be congenial, and they do influence the decisions of where to travel.

The Ethic of Sharing

The Naskapi practice a form of sharing that makes it possible for families to join any hunting camp they wish and still be guaranteed their share of the meat that is procured in the camp. A hunter and his family may even travel into the Barrens without a rifle and still get their share. This means that as long as the Naskapi live away from the settlement of Davis Inlet, they adhere to a set of rules that obligates any individual who is the holder of meat to share the good equally with any other individual, regardless of his relationship to the receiver, while the act of receiving does not carry with it any obligation to reciprocate. These strict rules of sharing are crucial in the cultural and social life of the Naskapi; they allow the individual households a high degree of mobility. They also allow the Naskapi to attain an exceptionally high degree of individual autonomy, as the possibilities for a Naskapi to manipulate and control other people and their labor are severely limited.

Leadership

By being a good hunter and through sharing the spoils of the hunt according to societal rules, a man can attain prestige and a following. This is so because every Naskapi recognizes the risks of traveling into the Barren Grounds and therefore prefers to follow a man who has proved his skills in hunting and staying alive in the Barrens under adverse conditions.

The Naskapi have no system of institutionalized leadership. One becomes a leader, or first man (*učima·w*), simply by taking the initiative in joint actions such as hunting trips or the moving of a camp. As soon as the task is finished, the leader is no longer *učima·w*. Since any Naskapi hunter may become a *učima·w*, hunters are constantly competing among themselves for prestige and leadership.

Rituals

Various animals are objects of ritual commensality among the Naskapi. The most significant of these rituals is the *makuša·n,* where all the hunters in a camp led by the *učima·w* sit for a whole day scraping the meat off the long bones of all the caribou that have been shot since the last *makuša·n.* The ends of each long bone are crushed and boiled, and the fat extracted. Finally, the bones are cracked open and all the men eat the raw marrow. Later they call in the women and the older children to let them have their share of the sacred food (cf. Henriksen 1973; Speck 1935; Strong 1929; Turner 1888; Williams 1963).

The *makuša·n,* as well as the other communal meals, expresses the unity and mutual dependence of all Naskapi, and their relationship to the natural environment, its animals, and their spirits. More directly the rituals may be viewed as confirmations of the relationships between the Naskapi and the various animal spirits. The Naskapi are under the obligation not to kill more animals than they need or to waste any of the usable parts of the animals, and they must share with one another the products of the hunts according to the rules of sharing. Otherwise the animal spirits hold the animals back from the Naskapi.

Social values derive largely from the adaptation of the Naskapi to their environment. Manliness is reckoned in such terms as traveling speed, number of animals hunted and killed under difficult conditions, blizzards survived, the ability to run faster than an otter and finally kill it with an ax, and so on. Their social life is continually filled with contexts where the hunters may act out these values and receive immediate recognition and social rewards. Mythology, ritual life, hunting, the rules of sharing, leadership, and prestige are intimately interconnected in such a way as to give a consistent frame of reference for one's choice of actions. Although the Naskapi value keeping for themselves what they procure of material wealth, in the Barren Grounds the situation is such that risk reduction and saving can only be achieved by distributing the products of the hunt according to the rules of sharing. Thus, when in the interior, a Naskapi faces relatively few dilemmas with regard to the allocation of his time and energy, his meat and skins.

At the Davis Inlet Settlement

As soon as the Naskapi reach the settlement of Davis Inlet, the value of sharing versus the value of having creates an acute dilemma. This is mainly due to an extreme change in opportunities.

670

Field Mus., Chicago: 61512.

Fig. 4. Shushebish demonstrating the method of using bow and arrow. The bow and arrows were made of dried juniper; the Mediterranean arrow release was used. Blunt-headed arrows similar to these were used in hunting hare and ptarmigan (Turner 1894:312–313); these were made for use in a competitive game (Strong 1928). Photograph by William Duncan Strong, March 1928.

Relatively speaking, it is safer to live on the coast than in the Barren Grounds, as enough fish to feed one's family may nearly always be caught if one should fail to procure other game. Also, if need be one can always depend upon the store for supplies. Thus, the main reason for being a follower in the Barrens is absent on the coast. In addition, on the coast the Naskapi pursue most of their economic activities either alone or in small groups, returning to the settlement in the evening. This pattern gives limited opportunities for a would-be leader to demonstrate his abilities as a hunter to an audience. Thus, since a would-be leader fails to gather a following, a major incentive for sharing one's produce is lacking at the coast.

While the opportunity situation in the interior favors the sharing of one's produce and there are strong ritual and social sanctions against keeping for oneself, at the coast it is both possible and desirable to undertake untraditional transformations of economic goods. The storekeeper is there to buy the fish, fur, and skin products that one produces, at the same time that goods are available from the store and mail order catalogs. The Naskapi have developed a desire for expensive capital equipment such as motor-powered boats and snowmobiles (fig. 5), as well as luxury items such as radios and phonographs. They have private accounts in the store and deal individually with the storekeeper. Some of the Naskapi have embarked upon individual economic careers, where they sell and save to invest in industrial goods.

Since the choices made on the basis of the new opportunities in a money economy are contradictory to the traditional ideas, the individual Naskapi is caught in a dilemma: shall he give away without asking for anything in return, or shall he ask to be paid in kind or in cash? Shall he share, or shall he keep for his own consumption or for later sale to the store or other White men? Since the Naskapi cannot agree upon how goods should circulate in this new context, incessant conflicts and quarrels arise. Even persons within the nuclear family may be in serious conflict, blaming one another for selling goods instead of sharing them according to the traditional rules that are still observed in the interior.

With their extremely limited knowledge of the English language and of the Euro-Canadian culture and society in general, the Naskapi are totally dependent upon the White middlemen in Davis Inlet in their economic endeavors within the money economy and in their dealings with the outside world. This is the basis for the influence enjoyed by the storekeeper and, especially, the missionary.

The missionary at Davis Inlet in the 1960s lived in the middle of the settlement and spoke Naskapi fluently. His stated aim was to bring to an end the

Fig. 6. The rewards of a caribou hunt. Two snowmobiles at right. Photograph by Winston White, in the Kukicapike Mountains, 80 miles north of Nain, April 1979.

drinking among the Naskapi and to help them to an effective adaptation to the money economy during their stay at the coast in the summer. To accomplish these goals he employed various strategies whereby he accumulated and wielded considerable influence in Davis Inlet. He rendered services such as lending money to people who wished to buy an outboard engine or a motor boat (on the condition that the borrowers promise to stop drinking). He was the only mechanic in the community able to repair and maintain the various machine equipment in Davis Inlet. He provided medical help through his large stock of medicines and gave out vitamins and powdered milk to mothers with young children.

As their priest the missionary gained information through confession. More important, however, is the fact that the Naskapi came to him with their internecine quarrels and complaints as they had no "court of appeal" among themselves.

The clergyman's role as middleman between the Naskapi and the outside world was also of great importance. He operated a radio on which he could call in the hospital plane in cases of emergency. With his knowledge of the Naskapi language, he served as a necessary link between the Naskapi and the storekeeper, the storekeeper's superiors, government officials, and other representatives from the Euro-Canadian society. Thus he came to control all strategic information flowing between Davis Inlet and the outside world.

These assets were all the more important since the Naskapi had created no middleman-leader of their own, nor had they organized to take joint actions concerning the White men and their society. The mission-appointed "chief" served merely as the ostensible spokesman of the Naskapi, used by the missionary in his strategies toward the outside world (Henriksen 1971:31).

Fig. 5. William Katchinak, Jr. (right), John Poker (background left), and others examining a disabled snowmobile. Photograph by Winston White at Davis Inlet, April 1975.

Barren Ground and Coast

On the Barren Grounds, the Naskapi are united through hunting (fig. 6) and commensality. There is no activity at the coast that unites the Naskapi in a similar manner. In consequence, social life in the settlement of Davis Inlet is full of conflicts, quarrels, and gossip. More than half the adult population indulges in heavy drinking of home-brewed spruce beer, which heightens discord. The opportunity situation confronting the Naskapi on the coast leads to choices that muddle the unambiguous codifications of their traditional culture. In the economy of sharing in the interior everybody contributes to the material well-being of the group, the rewards of the hunter being social recognition and prestige. There, the activities themselves are of central value. In the money economy on the coast, material goods and comforts are made the central objects of value, while the productive activities themselves have very little social significance. By enforcing individual careers measured in terms of individual economic profits, involvement in the market economy has led to the destruction of traditional community values and relations.

672

Great Whale River, Quebec

W.K. BARGER

Great Whale River, or Poste-de-la-Baleine, Quebec, located on the east coast of Hudson Bay (see "Native Settlements: Introduction," fig. 1, this vol.), is one of the many trading-post settlements of the contact-traditional era in northern Canada that have been transformed since World War II into modern towns. By 1970 some 300 East Main Cree Indians, 550 Inuit (Eskimos), and 150 Anglophone and Francophone Canadians had settled there, one of the few places in the North where all four groups are represented. The town borders the inland taiga and riverine environment, traditionally exploited by the Cree, and the coastal and tundra environment, traditionally exploited by the Eskimos. This chapter deals primarily with those Eskimos, Crees, and Whites in Great Whale during the period 1969–1971, and descriptions of life in the town are largely representative of younger and middle-aged males who have spent a significant portion of their adult lives in the town (Barger 1977; Barger and Earl 1971).

History of the Settlement

The first European point of contact on the east coast of Hudson Bay was established in 1732, when a trading post was built at Richmond Gulf. Several posts were subsequently opened and closed by the Hudson's Bay Company along the coast over the next century. A permanent post was built at Great Whale River in 1857, and in 1891 this post became the main site for trade activities in the region (figs. 1–2). In 1876 the Rev. Edmund J. Peck of the Church of England introduced Christianity to the area. Around the turn of the century, Rev. W.G. Walton, continuing this mission activity, urged the Eskimos and Crees to a strong commitment to Christianity. Using a system of syllabic writing developed for missionary purposes in the North, he and his wife translated religious literature into both languages and taught both peoples to be literate in their own tongues.

Subsistence during this contact-traditional, fur-trade period was enhanced by new weapons, tools, materials, and foods, though new diseases and starvation often threatened death. The long winters were spent in scattered multifamily camps, the Crees in the inland areas and the Eskimos along the coast. Summers were spent at the post, where furs were traded for goods or used

to pay credit advanced the previous fall and where the people participated in social and religious activities.

Smithsonian, NAA.

Fig. 1. The Hudson's Bay Company trading post complex at Great Whale River, summer 1949, looking west. The river is on the left and Hudson Bay, filled with ice floes, is in the background. The Hudson's Bay Company has operated a store here continuously since 1857. Photograph by John J. Honigmann.

Smithsonian, NAA.

Fig. 2. Hudson's Bay Company supply ship at Great Whale River in summer 1949, one of the few links this community then had with the outside world. Photograph, looking south, by John J. Honigmann.

In 1955 a radar control base was constructed at Great Whale, and this formed the nucleus for a new modern town. When military operations were phased out in 1967, Great Whale became a regional administrative center for the federal and provincial governments. Significant Euro-Canadian influences were introduced to the Eskimos and Crees with the new town, including wage employment, greater access to material goods, housing, education, and medical care, and more intense exposure to Western society through travel and movies. Furthermore, a distinct White community emerged in Great Whale, providing for the first time a model of modern Euro-Canadian life. It is this period of the new town setting and adaptation to town life experienced by the Crees and Eskimos that is considered here.

The People of Great Whale

Euro-Canadians (Whites)

Most of the Euro-Canadians in Great Whale live in a segregated neighborhood in the former base site, known as "the Hill" (see figs. 3–4). There were 138 Whites in Great Whale at the end of 1970 (table 1). About half the adult males were married and had families with them. Euro-Canadians have tended to be highly transitory, and most have gone North for only a year or so.

The terms Euro-Canadian, White, and Western are used here to identify all Whites in Great Whale as a unitary ethnic group; however, distinctly English and French backgrounds are evident among them. The English Canadians have traditionally been the source of Western influence in the area through the Hudson's Bay Company, the Anglican mission, and federal government agencies, while the French Canadians have been associated primarily with Quebec government agencies. Many of the English Canadians come from rural settings and through their jobs tend to interact regularly with the native peoples, as in teaching school. Many of the French Canadians come from urban settings, and, except for provincial teachers, have had more limited contact with the Eskimos and Crees.

The Euro-Canadians of Great Whale resemble in part a middle-class community in southern Canada. Most hold white-collar, administrative, or professional jobs (table 2). Some are skilled technicians and supervise natives in service and construction work. Most Whites receive wages and bonuses significantly above

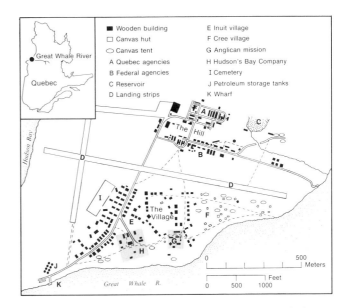

Fig. 3. Town plan of Great Whale River (Poste-de-la-Baleine). After a sketch map by Barger, July 1969.

Fig. 4. Great Whale River in 1969 as seen from the south. The poles are for electricity and telephones. In the foreground is "the Hill," the former military base where almost all the Euro-Canadians live, with the regional administrative complexes of the Quebec provincial government in foreground and at right and the Canadian federal government at left background. In the far background across the airstrip and along the river are the Indian (Cree) village (far left) and the Inuit village (center). Fuel storage tanks are right center, and on the far right the river flows into Hudson Bay. Photograph by W.K. Barger, summer 1969.

those for similar employment in southern Canada, the stated purpose being to draw qualified personnel to work in the North.

The standard of living provided to most White families is comfortable, including electricity, hot running water, upholstered furniture, and special food rations. All Euro-Canadians are eligible to belong to a social club located in the former base headquarters, which has a bar and sponsors regular movies and seasonal parties. Whites also participate in organized activities such as a snowmobile club and various sports groups, some of which are open to native peoples. Personal relations with other Whites tend to be based on social class and English or French background. Certain tensions are evident in the Euro-Canadian community. Some frictions are related to differences in class, religion, English-French and rural-urban backgrounds, and association with federal or provincial agencies; however, tensions generally emerge only around specific issues such as the creation of a school board for Nouveau Québec (the northern division of Quebec), the only appointed, or nonelected, one in the province.

The Euro-Canadian sector in Great Whale, as in other towns in the North, reflects a variation of contemporary Western society. Unique characteristics include: the high proportion of single adult males, the low proportion of children and elderly, the highly transitory nature of community members, and the high proportion of white-collar occupations. The absence of an industrial or other economically viable base and the administrative nature of most agencies in the town are the factors that underlie the unusual sociological pattern. Yet the life-style, standard of living, activities, values, and beliefs of the Euro-Canadians in Great Whale reflect the middle-class Western heritage from which most come.

Inuit (Eskimos)

The Inuit community of Great Whale forms a distinct neighborhood of "the Village" (see fig. 3). There were 543 Inuit, in 115 families, making their home in Great Whale at the end of 1970 (table 1), compared to 193 in 1949 (Honigmann 1962:4). About half the Inuit have immigrated from other regions since the modern town was formed. Of the 93 Inuit male family heads at the end of 1970, 49 percent were associated with the Great Whale post during contact-traditional times, and 12 percent came from the Belcher Islands, also associated with the Great Whale post in the past. Eleven percent came from the James Bay area, and 28 percent came from Port Harrison or other places in Northern Quebec.

The Inuit of Great Whale have altered much in their way of life in response to the new town. A significant proportion of the adults hold regular jobs in the town

(see table 2). About half of these are nonskilled workers, such as janitors and boiler operators. The others are skilled workers, such as mechanics and carpenters, or hold administrative positions such as interpreters, clerks, and teaching assistants. Only a few families gain their subsistence through traditional means, such as hunting and producing crafts and works of art; however, almost every household has its subsistence supplemented by local hunting (figs. 5–6), production of arts and crafts, and various forms of government assistance. The standard of living among the Inuit, while much lower than among the Euro-Canadians, is significantly higher than in contact-traditional times. Every Inuit lives in a frame house, though most are shared by related nuclear families. Inuit homes all have oil heating, and many also have electricity, though none has running water or plumbing. Many Inuit own major items such as agitator washers and snowmobiles, and almost all have smaller items such as cameras and radios. Many Inuit raised in traditional times express appreciation for the economic security and relative comforts associated with town life.

Social interaction among the Great Whale Inuit is shaped by kinship and place of origin. Close kinsmen regularly participate together in activities such as hunting, and they visit each other frequently; however, social bonds have been widening as schools, jobs, and other recent circumstances place individuals in close association and provide common experiences. Though some strains exist, the Inuit have maintained a notable level of social cohesion in the congregated town setting. They actively participate in community recreational events such as movies and dances, as well as in seasonal festivals. The Inuit tend to predominate in these events, though Crees and those occasional Whites who wish to come also participate.

The Inuit have actively participated in political affairs. Most of those elected to the Community Council have been individuals who have demonstrated an ability to integrate into town life. They effectively represent their people in dealing with government and other agencies and also manage many aspects of internal community affairs. Inuit leaders are also actively involved in regional and national political issues affecting native peoples, particularly in their opposition to the transfer of administration of native affairs from the federal to the provincial government. Almost all adult Inuit belong to the Quebec Indian Association, and local leaders were involved in a movement to form an autonomous native regional government. Though they do not always comprehend Western political and bureaucratic processes, most Inuit are knowledgeable about key political issues affecting their lives.

Most Great Whale Inuit are dedicated Anglicans. They regularly attend religious services and generally adhere to the teachings of the church as interpreted by

675

Table 1. Population Distribution in Great Whale River, 1970

Age	Inuit		Cree		Euro-Canadian		Total	
	Male	Female	Male	Female	Male	Female	Male	Female
0– 9	90	76	50	58	15	17	155	151
10–19	74	55	30	31	3	6	107	92
20–29	43	40	21	25	27	20	91	85
30–39	33	33	13	14	19	10	65	57
40–49	22	20	14	18	6	2	42	40
50–59	17	19	12	3	11	1	40	23
60–69	6	6	3	8	1	0	10	14
70–79	3	1	5	3	0	0	8	4
80–89	1	1	0	1	0	0	1	2
Unknown	1	2	1	5	0	0	2	7
Subtotals	290	253	149	166	82	56	521	475
Totals	543		315		138		996	

SOURCE: Barger 1974.

the missionaries. In many cases, values (such as disapproval of males and females associating in public other than at group events), beliefs (that sewing on Sunday offends Jesus), and knowledge of the world (for example, geography), have clearly been influenced by the church and Western education. However, other values and beliefs, such as respect for individual autonomy and a belief in "the people who live in the rocks," reflect more traditional thought.

Some social problems are evident, of course (see L.W. Hall 1973); however, on the whole the Inuit appear to have adequately adjusted to new stresses, and a low occurrence of mental health problems was indicated by a survey. As a group, it is evident that the Inuit of Great Whale have achieved significant integration into the new town setting (Barger 1977; Barger and Earl 1971), as have Eskimos in other areas of the North (Chance 1960, 1966; Chance and Trudeau 1963; Graburn 1969; Honigmann 1975; Honigmann and Honigmann 1965, 1970).

Cree Indians

The Cree community in Great Whale also forms a distinct neighborhood of "the Village" (see fig. 3). At the end of 1970, 315 Crees in 72 families were making Great Whale their home (table 1), compared to 171 in 1949 (Honigmann 1962:4). There has been little immigration of Crees from other regions since the formation of the town, though some have spouses from Fort George.

The Great Whale Crees have made some alterations in their way of life in face of the new modern town context. Many Crees hold regular jobs in the town (table 2). Most of these are nonskilled workers, though a few are skilled workers and some hold administrative positions. The number of families subsisting primarily by hunting and trapping declined from 24, or 40 per-

Natl. Mus. of Canada, Ottawa: J–14212.

Fig. 5. Butchering a bear. Most of the participants appear to be Inuit. Photograph by Asen Balikci, 1957.

Smithsonian, NAA.

Fig. 6. An Inuit woman skinning seals on the linoleum floor in her house. Photograph probably by William M. Schneider, 1965.

676

cent, in 1968–1969, to 5, or 8 percent, in 1970–1971. This shift in subsistence is primarily related to the increased availability of construction and other jobs. Local hunting supplements the subsistence of most Cree families (fig. 7), as does craft production and various forms of governmental assistance. By Euro-Canadian measures, the standard of living among the Crees is the lowest among the three ethnic groups in Great Whale. In 1969 only 16 houses were available to Crees, and some 43 percent of the Cree families lived in tents or in canvas huts (fig. 8) while an additional 23 percent shared the homes of relatives; however, a new housing program has been providing more homes for Cree families. Though the people voice a desire for comfortable living conditions, they are generally not materialistic in their value orientations.

Social relations among the Crees are stongly dominated by kinship. Many traditional activities, such as hunting and gathering firewood, have important personal and social significance among the Crees, and close kinsmen participate in these together; however, participation in community events such as movies and dances tends to be passive. Some social factionalism is evident in the congregated town setting. This is seen by some Whites as evidence of disintegration of Cree society; however, the basic Cree social units are the nuclear and extended families, and these provide the individual with a viable source of identity and support in the town setting. Though there is evidence of change and adjustment, these do not necessarily reflect disintegration. In many ways, more social factionalism exists in the Euro-Canadian community than among the Crees.

Decisions on matters affecting the Cree community are generally reached by consensus, a process in which the opinions of lineage elders are influential. The band council is the primary body for dealing with government

Smithsonian. NAA.

Fig. 8. Cree temporary summer tent of canvas near the Great Whale post, with woman carrying firewood. Photograph by John J. Honigmann, summer 1949.

and other agencies external to the Cree community, and the younger men who are the council leaders at times aggressively represent their people. Almost all adults belong to the Quebec Indian Association. While many Crees are not personally involved in major political issues, most support the council in such affairs as opposition to the transfer of administration to the Quebec government.

Most Great Whale Crees are devout Anglicans. They regularly participate in religious activities and follow the teachings of the church. The missionaries have had considerable influence in the Cree community, in private and social matters as well as in religious ones. Values, such as an emphasis on equality and social tranquillity, are strongly based in traditional systems, though these have at times been influenced by Western thought. Though some social problems have been evident among the Crees, stresses appear to be adequately handled, and there was low occurrence of mental health problems in 1971 (Barger 1977).

Although some significant changes have occurred in the life ways of the Great Whale Crees since the development of the town, traditional orientations, though expanded and modified, remain the basic framework

Fig. 7. Cree duck hunters. Although the Cree do not normally hunt seal, the man on the right shot one for its fur value when it was surprised on an ice floe. Hunting, expeditions to cut firewood in the bush, and other traditional activities are highly valued by the Crees. Photograph by W.K. Barger, June 1969.

Public Arch. of Canada, Ottawa: PA 27645.
Fig. 9. Cree men playing a checkerlike board game with pebble markers; beached canoes in background. Photograph by S.J. Bailey, 1948.

for experiencing life; and the new circumstances have been reinterpreted in these terms (Barger 1977; Barger and Earl 1971). This pattern is consistent with responses to Western settings made by other Cree peoples in the North (Chance and Trudeau 1963; Tanner 1968).

Interethnic Relations

Personal relations among all three ethnic groups in Great Whale occur almost exclusively within their own ethnic communities (Barger 1979, 1980). Interaction between ethnic groups generally takes place in specific and relatively defined contexts, such as on the job, in meetings (fig. 10), and in exchange of goods and services. Though some tensions do exist, the general lack of intensity in interethnic relations contributes to a relatively relaxed atmosphere.

The overall social structure in Great Whale in many ways defines the interaction among the ethnic groups there (Barger 1979, 1980). The Euro-Canadians are in the dominant position in terms of economic and political power and of social prestige. This circumstance existed in contact-traditional times (Honigmann 1952) but has become more intensified and prominent with the establishment of government agencies and the emergence of a distinct Euro-Canadian community. The Whites comprise an upper social stratum, and the Eskimos and Crees jointly comprise a lower "native" stratum, in which the Eskimos possess greater social and economic advantages than the Crees.

The View From the Hill

Many Whites in Great Whale are dedicated and sincere in their sense of service toward the native peoples there;

however, few are adequately prepared for optimal interaction with the Crees and Inuit, as Murdoch (1972) has vividly described. Almost all have had no experience with native peoples and have received little training or indoctrination regarding native ways of life. The background of most Euro-Canadians has instilled in them the view that modern technological society is the "highest" form and at the same time "primitive" peoples are relatively free of stress in their "simple" life. Most of their knowledge of the Inuit and Crees has been acquired from other Whites, particularly those who have lived in the North for a number of years. Though observation has also provided some information on native ways, relatively little such knowledge has come from interaction with native people. Much of the knowledge among Whites about the personal lives of Inuit and Crees tends to emphasize unfavorable aspects, such as drunkenness. Generally, then, most Whites interpret the behavior of the Crees and Inuit in terms of their own Western background, and it appears that in the minds of most Euro-Canadians the responsibility for interethnic adjustment is on the native peoples.

The social structure of the town serves to limit personal relationships between Whites and natives. Most interaction involves formal roles based in Western culture where the Euro-Canadian is in the superior position, such as administrator to client, boss to worker, and teacher to pupil. An unofficial policy of segregating the White community from the native peoples has discouraged personal relations between the Hill and the Village. Most personal and informal interaction that does occur between Whites and natives generally takes place outside the Euro-Canadian community, as when a White goes hunting with an Inuit or Cree. Euro-Canadians, then, live in a social atmosphere that insulates them from friend relationships with native individuals.

Fig. 10. The Inuit and Cree councils meeting at Great Whale River with Jean Chrétien, Canadian minister of Indian affairs and northern development. Photograph by W.K. Barger, summer 1969.

One important influence affecting relations between ethnic groups in Great Whale is the Whites' preference for the Inuit over the Crees. Both the federal and provincial administrative agencies have provided more opportunities for the Inuit than for the Crees, as in employment and education. Historically, the original federal agency in the town, the Department of Northern Affairs, was responsible for administration of Eskimos but not of Indians. Developmental programs, such as job training and housing, have been readily accessible to the Eskimos. The Crees had to rely alternately on the Department of Indian Affairs agency in Fort George and the local agency, which was less familiar with programs for Indians. This discrepancy has been resolved with the consolidation in 1973 in the Canadian federal government of the Department of Northern Affairs and the Department of Indian Affairs into the Department of Indian Affairs and Northern Development. However, many problems remain, both in the carryover of prior orientations of administrative personnel and in bureaucratic organization.

The provincial Département Général du Nouveau Québec has also been more oriented toward the Inuit than the Crees. This is due in part to the larger proportion of Inuit under its jurisdiction, the overseeing of a vast territory traditionally occupied mostly by Inuit, and an effort to salve the stringent opposition of the Inuit to the transfer of administration from the federal to the provincial government.

The Euro-Canadians have also generally shown a personal preference for the Inuit as a group over the Crees, though there are some individual exceptions. Considerable difficulty is experienced in approaching at the same time two peoples with distinct ethnic backgrounds. The orientation of government agencies has somewhat influenced the personal orientations of their employees. Euro-Canadians have also experienced greater personal validation with the Inuit than with the Crees. White administrators, for instance, have seen relative success in the educational program for the Inuit and can personally share in a sense of accomplishment regarding it. However, the Whites also tend to polarize the two native groups and positively evaluate the Inuit in comparison to the Crees in terms of key Western values. Much of Inuit behavior tends to please and impress the Euro-Canadians. They see the quick smiles of Inuit as "friendly" and "happy" and interpret other traits in such ways as "honest" and "industrious." At the same time, many Whites have generally experienced something on the order of a "personality clash" with Crees. Whites tend to interpret Cree reticence, for example, as dislike, suspicion, and personal rejection and are thus offended. Other Cree traits are seen in terms such as "lazy," "greedy," and "manipulative." Thus, many Euro-Canadians admire Inuit ways but are annoyed or alienated by Cree behavior.

Relatively little overt tension is seen between Whites and the native peoples. Some frictions do exist, of course, but these are related more to specific occasions and issues. Though there are at times clashes of values and personalities, Euro-Canadians are generally cordial, relaxed, and somewhat patronizing toward Eskimos and Crees.

Some White men, particularly single individuals, have sought sexual relations with several Inuit women, and there are a number of cases where Euro-Canadian men have married Inuit women and two cases where Euro-Canadian women have married Inuit men. Liaisons between Whites and Crees have occurred only rarely. By 1971 there was one case where a White man had married a Cree woman.

In contrast to the general pattern of insulation from native peoples, several Whites have made a conscious effort to understand and respect the Inuit and Indians, and a few have learned to speak a native language. Those personal relations between Euro-Canadians and native peoples that do exist have involved these few Whites. These individuals have on occasion served as a catalyst in interethnic relations by presenting in Western terms native wishes and points of view to other Whites.

Several factors, then, have influenced the way Whites of Great Whale approach and interact with Crees and Inuit. Interaction with native peoples tends to be with the Whites in the socially dominant position and based on the initiative of the Whites concerned. The distance in relations in many ways serves to maintain interaction at a relatively comfortable level for all concerned.

The View From the Village

There are many similarities in the manner in which the Crees and Inuit of Great Whale approach the Euro-Canadians. These similarities reflect, among other fac-

Table 2. Occupational Patterns in Great Whale River, 1970–1971

Type of Occupation	Euro-Canadi-ans	Inuit	Crees	Total
Traditional (hunting, trapping, crafts, etc.)	0	9	7	16
Pension	0	16	5	21
Irregular	0	28	24	52
Nonskilled	0	38	23	61
Skilled	17[a]	18	2	37
Administrative	78[b]	18	7	92
Totals	95	127	68	290

SOURCE: Barger 1974.

[a] 6 worked for federal agencies, 9 for provincial agencies, and 2 for other agencies.

[b] 25 worked for federal agencies, 42 for provincial agencies, and 11 for other agencies.

tors, their common lower status in face of the Whites and the shared challenge of adapting to a Western town setting from a hunting and trapping way of life.

Well over half the adult Cree and Inuit men, and some women as well, speak some English, though there are varying degrees of proficiency. With the founding of the federal school in Great Whale, most young people and children speak some English also. English serves as the standard language for interethnic communication in Great Whale, though the Anglican and Roman Catholic missionaries and a few other Whites speak Eskimo, Cree, or both. Only a couple of Crees and Inuit speak any French.

Both Inuit and Crees reveal a sense of awe at some complex aspects of Western culture. Both peoples esteem certain useful material and technical items that enhance their standard of living and life-style, such as snowmobiles and cameras. They recognize at times that they lack clear understanding of important facets of the larger Canadian society such as political systems and bureaucracy. Both peoples also readily recognize the social and economic power that Whites possess and generally exhibit deference and accommodation in interaction with them.

In many ways, the Euro-Canadian community serves as a model for town life and as a source of ideas for adaptation. Inuit and Crees have both adopted certain attitudes and values that are standard among Whites in town, such as a desire for adequate housing and an acceptance of formal education. Many concepts and courses of action have originated from Whites, such as a brief movement to form a regional native government. The Crees and Inuit have also found elements of the Euro-Canadian society useful in facing new problems in the congregated town setting. The White policeman, for instance, may be called on to remove a drunk and troublesome member of their community.

One major phenomenon related to the formation of a town is a heightened sense of ethnic identity among the Inuit and Crees. The emergence of a distinct, technically adept White community, more intense exposure to Western society through travel and movies, and contact with native organizations such as the Quebec Indian Association have enhanced Indians' and Inuits' awareness of their own ethnic heritages. Such identity is expressed in many ways, such as beaded patches depicting Indians worn by Crees and the desire expressed by Eskimos at a regional meeting to be termed "Inuit." The development of a conscious ethnic identity also stems in part from reactions to political issues such as the transfer of native administration from the federal to provincial government, which both the Inuit and Crees have opposed. Both peoples assert that they were "here first" and that the area is "our land." They voice resentment at various government policies and actions that seem to lack regard for their native rights, such as

provincial laws that prohibit their holding title to the land they live on and a proposal to make Richmond Gulf a provincial park where native hunting and fishing would be restricted, as happened at Mistassini Lake. They also assert they should be "boss in our own land" and express resentment at the formulation of administrative policies without their participation or prior consultation. Much in these attitudes contrasts with traditional orientations and so reflects concepts that have been modified in response to new circumstances. Some of the information and interpretations in these views has originated with particular Whites. The Great Whale Inuit and Crees are in the process of defining themselves in relation to the larger Canadian setting as they increasingly participate in the national society.

Though many attitudes and responses toward the Whites are shared, the Great Whale Inuit and Crees also display important differences in interaction with Euro-Canadians. In many cases these reflect patterns of social behavior within their separate communities.

Great Whale Inuit are generally accepting of White behavior. They display a great deal of tolerance toward Whites, as they do among themselves. In those instances where they might feel uncomfortable, as when White inquisitiveness is perceived as prying, Inuit generally react with accommodation or, if too much pressure is felt, withdrawal. These tactics reduce tensions felt by the Inuit and also generally do not offend Euro-Canadians, who may be left confused at times. Flexibility is also evident in interaction with Whites. If a White boss appears to be arbitrary in stating how he wants a job done, for instance, an Inuit worker willingly tries it out.

Frictions do exist, of course. Inuit interpret some behavior of Whites as "unfriendly," as when a Euro-Canadian fails to exchange greetings in passing or when Whites talk among themselves in French and thus exclude an Inuit who is present. Inuit also strongly resent the White policeman's shooting their loose dogs without prior notice. Tensions felt by Inuit tend to be related to specific individuals, incidents, and issues, rather than being categorical attitudes.

The Crees, for their part, tend to see much of White behavior in negative terms. The Euro-Canadian manner of asking direct questions, for instance, is sometimes perceived as intrusive. And some Euro-Canadian norms, such as competitiveness, strongly violate Cree values. Crees also at times see White behavior in such terms as overly demonstrative, obsessed with cleanliness, naive, and selfish. There are also instances when Crees clearly resent some White behavior, as when a Cree outhouse in the way of new construction was bulldozed down without the owner's knowledge or consent. Yet the Crees do not normally show offense or resentment. This is in keeping with their lower social status in face of Whites, with their reticence, and with their tendency to wait and see how each individual and each circumstance will turn out.

Not all relations between Great Whale Crees and Whites are abrasive, of course. Several Crees and Whites have developed friendships and participate in various activities together, like hunting. These cases are more related to the individual Cree and White involved than to group relations.

The View Across the Village

Relations between Inuit and Crees in Great Whale have been significantly altered in the town setting (Barger 1979). The formal greetings, visiting, joint participation in games, trade, and other forms of interaction between the two groups reported in 1950 (Honigmann 1952) were not prevalent in 1970, although some exchange of services still occurs. Inuit women, for example, have prepared deceased Crees for burial, and Cree hunters give the meat of a seal to various Inuit women in exchange for processing its fur for sale. However, each group has a distinct concept of its own neighborhood, and Crees and Inuit do not normally enter each other's neighborhood except in passing. Though a few casual relations are evident (fig. 11), most interaction between the two groups is limited to specific purposes, as when a Cree woman obtains a pair of sealskin boots from an Inuit woman. There is only one known case of intermarriage, when in the first quarter of the century a Cree man married an Eskimo woman and "went Eskimo." Sexual relations between the two groups have also been rare, and when they have occurred mostly young Inuit males and Cree females have been involved.

Despite the lack of frequent interaction, both Inuit and Crees are knowledgeable of events and affairs that take place in the other community, as both are of those in the White community. Well over one-third of the adult Inuit men, and some women as well, speak some Cree. Only a couple of Crees, however, speak any Eskimo. Younger Crees and Inuit, when the occasion calls for it, communicate with each other in English.

In events where both groups are present, the Inuit tend to dominate the activities and the Crees tend to observe or participate more passively. At movies, for instance, the Crees generally sit in the rear behind the Inuit, and at dances most of the participants are Inuit while the Crees generally observe from the sidelines.

Few tensions are evident between the Crees and Inuit, even though each tends to regard the other in terms of its own ethnic standards. In addition, the Crees somewhat resent the greater opportunities of the Inuit in the town setting. Inuit and Crees have been in regular association with each other for over a century, are aware of the other's way of life, and personally know a number of individuals in the other community. These and other factors, then, serve to maintain a general attitude of tolerance between the Inuit and Crees in Great Whale.

Adaptation to Town Life: Summary

Great Whale River has in recent times evolved from a trading post to a town. It is an administrative town, with little internal economic base. It is marked by the joint, and sometimes conflicting, presence of both federal and provincial authorities, and it is one of the few places in the North where Eskimos and Indians come together. Euro-Canadians are locally in the minority but are socially, economically, and politically dominant due to their ties with the larger society. The native peoples have shifted much of their subsistence and life

Fig. 11. Cree tents. An Inuit woman (left) is visiting a Cree woman (right) in front of tent with entranceway. Communication on such casual visits was largely nonverbal (Honigmann 1962:19–20). Photograph by John J. Honigmann, summer 1949.

orientations from a dispersed hunting and trapping life on the land to a settled and congregated life in a contemporary town setting.

The Great Whale Inuit have experienced relatively easy integration into town life. They have received significant opportunities and encouragements for participation in town life. A continual government program for Inuit housing and a preference by White employers for Inuit in the higher-status and higher-paying skilled jobs (fig. 12), for example, have made it possible for many Inuit to settle in town with relative economic and social security. Furthermore, many elements in their ethnic heritage have also contributed to Inuit integration into the town. A behavioral value comparable to Euro-Canadian "industriousness," for instance, has proved compatible with expectations for job performance on the part of White foremen.

The Great Whale Crees have demonstrated potential for selective participation in town life. Traits such as strong self-reliance and persistence, for example, have undoubtedly contributed to the stable employment records of those who hold regular jobs (fig. 13); however, this potential has been limited by both their reception in the town and the ways they brought with them to the town. The lack of opportunities to participate more fully in town life has discouraged the Crees from seeking greater integration. For instance, lack of adequate housing in comparison to Whites and Inuit, unofficial job discrimination in favor of the Inuit, and negative

reactions by Whites toward various Cree ways have restricted participation in town life. It is also evident that some traditional behavioral norms have also inhibited integration. Cree reticence, for instance, has tended to make Whites feel uncomfortable, and has also contributed to Cree discomfort with White demonstrativeness.

Two main influences, then, have contributed to the distinct adaptations of the Inuit and Crees to the emergence of a town at Great Whale. One is the different circumstances each has encountered in the town setting. The other is the different cultural heritage each has brought to the town situation.

Sources

For descriptions of life among the Inuit and Cree peoples of Great Whale during the contact-traditional period, see Honigmann and Honigmann (1953, 1959), Honigmann (1951, 1952, 1960, 1962), and Walker (1953). Other reports referring to Great Whale include Balikci (1964), Honigmann (1964), Marsh (1964), and Rogers (1964). W.E. Taylor (1964) deals with the prehistory of the region.

For information on the town period in Great Whale, see Balikci (1959, 1961), Barger (1977, 1979, 1980), Barger and Earl (1971), L.W. Hall (1973), Honigmann (1975), Johnson (1962), P.A. Rogers (1965), and Wills (1965).

Smithsonian, NAA.
Fig. 12. Inuit carpenters building cargo canoes in the shop operated by the Department of Indian Affairs and Northern Development, typical of the skilled jobs held by many regularly employed Inuit. Photograph probably by William M. Schneider, 1965.

Fig. 13. Cree construction workers. Most jobs open to Crees involve nonskilled, seasonal work. Photograph by W.K. Barger, summer 1970.

Fort Resolution, Northwest Territories

DAVID M. SMITH

The settlement of Fort Resolution is on the south shore of Great Slave Lake a few miles south of the Slave River delta. It is at the end of what passes for an all-weather road (completed in the late 1960s), linking it with the lead-mining community of Pine Point, and from thence with the Mackenzie Highway.

In January 1972 the native population of Fort Resolution numbered 541. Of this total 210 persons were listed on the Fort Resolution band roll, that is, as having the legal status of Indian; 331 persons were not. Most of the second group are of mixed Indian-European ancestry and are known locally to themselves and others as "half-breeds." In this chapter these people will be referred to by the French-derived term, Métis, which is commonly used in southern Canada. The dominant Indian culture component of Fort Resolution is Chipewyan, although other heritages, such as Slavey, Dogrib, and Cree, have minor representation.

In the 1960s Fort Resolution had about 65 White residents. All but a few of these were there as employees of a number of governmental agencies.

Fort Resolution is descendent from the first trading post on Great Slave Lake, scene of earliest fur trade activity in what is today the Northwest Territories. At one time Resolution was the foremost center of commercial and social activity on the lake. It became a major center of Métis settlement and the first site of missionary activity in the Great Slave Lake area. Since World War II, however, with the shift in the northern economy away from the fur trade, and with the concomitant shift of the major routes of commerce from the waterways to the skyways and roads, Fort Resolution's importance has vastly diminished. Even so, Fort Resolution has become the locus of settlement for many of the native peoples who had traditionally traded there.

The Founding

In the summer of 1786 Cuthbert Grant of the North West Company and Laurent Leroux of Gregory, McLeod, and Company went to the south shore of Great Slave Lake to establish trading posts. By 1794 only the North West Company remained. Its main trading house was by this time on Moose Deer Island (now Mission Island), close to the present onshore site of Fort Resolution.

In 1803 the Hudson's Bay Company established Chiswick House in the Slave River Delta. Chiswick House was abandoned after the 1805–1806 season, and it was not until 1815 that the company returned, this time to stay.

After 1815 the Hudson's Bay Company was also located on Moose Deer Island and its post was named Fort Resolution in October 1819. In July 1822 the company moved its post to Point Brules, the present site of Fort Resolution, and from that time until the 1890s it enjoyed a virtual monopoly of the fur trade in the area.

Indians Trading into Fort Resolution

In his District Report for 1825–1826, Chief Factor Robert McVicar (1825–1826) set forth the range of the native groups then trading into Fort Resolution: west to east, from the outlet of the Mackenzie River to the upper reaches of the "Thulloodessy" (probably the Thelon River); north to south, from the Lac La Martre drainage to the Caribou Mountains. Through the next 100 years, the territory whose residents traded into Fort Resolution became progressively smaller as additional trading posts were established in the Great Slave Lake area (fig. 1).

In his report on the Athabasca District for 1820–1821, Simpson (1938:371) stated that Fort Resolution was meant to serve "three classes" of Indians. These he termed "Mountainees, Carribeau Eaters and Yellow Knives." He regarded all these as Chipewyan because of their similarities in language and custom. He maintained that the "Mountainees" (no doubt equivalent to Montagnais as the early French term for the Chipewyan, but not to be confused with the Algonquian Montagnais of Quebec and Labrador) were "home guards," meaning that they were more involved in the fur trade than the other "classes."

The Chipewyans had entered full boreal forest areas as a consequence of their involvement with the fur trade, as traders encouraged their hunting furs in those areas. The lands along the Slave River and westward were therefore new regions for the Chipewyans drawn to trade at Fort Resolution. The lands east of the Slave River, however, are winter range for the migratory caribou, the traditional source of food, shelter, and clothing for the Chipewyans, and McVicar (1825–1826)

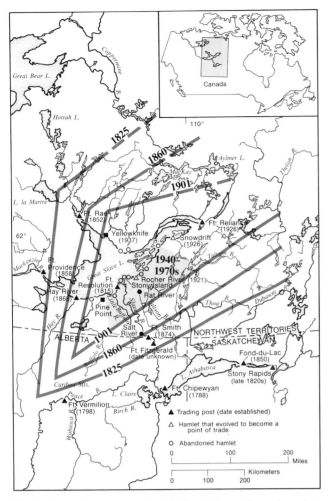

Fig. 1. Approximate areas using Ft. Resolution as the major point of trade, 1825–1940. Dates given for the establishment of trading posts are the earliest dates known; locations of some trading posts and forts may have changed slightly over time.

the east arm of the lake as well as interior regions northeastward to the barren lands. The Yellowknife gradually lost their distinctive identity and in the early twentieth century had "disappeared" by virtue of intermarriage and assimilation with Dogribs and Chipewyans.

The "Carribeau Eaters" mentioned by Simpson were the Chipewyan bands who remained most closely associated with their precontact range in the forest-tundra transition zone to the southeast of Great Slave Lake. A few westerly Caribou Eaters have occasionally traded into Resolution since the early 1800s.

Some Dogribs were trading at Fort Resolution by the 1850s (Anderson 1858). Dogrib trade into Resolution did not completely cease until about 1930. In the second half of the nineteenth century and the early years of the twentieth century, a few Slavey Indians living along the lower Hay River also traded at Fort Resolution.

The Chipewyan people trading into Fort Resolution during the nineteenth century lived in nomadic hunting, fishing, and trapping bands. The size of these bands and the amount of time they spent at any given camp varied with the season and with their immediate economic situation. Especially during the late nineteenth century, large bands gathered at major fisheries during the fall and spring when various species of fish made their spawning runs. Also, in the fall and late spring throughout the nineteenth and early twentieth centuries, large bands of 200 or more people assembled at the edge of woods at caribou hunting camps.

Freedom to live in any band in any region of the country was valued, yet a man's decision to join a particular band usually meant having one or more relatives by blood or marriage as members of it.

There seem to have been four non–mutually exclusive categories of leaders in traditional Chipewyan society in the Great Slave Lake area. One kind of leader, who is said to have been aboriginal, was called *beká bá̧θdeli*.* Another kind of leader, which existed until about 1950, was the *dene-gą k̓álδər*. There were also "trading chiefs" during the nineteenth century, deliberately created by the early traders, whose role was to facilitate trade with the people. Finally, there were men, and a few women, who were magically and medically adept. There was no special term applied to them.

Native people translate the word *beká bá̧θdeli* as 'the one who is at the center while others talk around him'. In part, his role was like the *dene-gą k̓álδər*, in that he directed the exploitative quest of his band. The *beká bá̧θdeli* is said to differ in that he had considerably more authority, assumed leadership in war ("if it came to that" as one elderly man put it), and had exceptional

*The Chipewyan terms in this chapter have been phonemicized by Ronald Scollon (communication to editors 1979) and written in the orthography described in the orthographic footnote in "Chipewyan," this vol.

noted that their proximity presented a "serious and lasting obstacle" to fur production in the Great Slave Lake area. This prediction proved to be true through most of the nineteenth century; the natives ranging north and east of Fort Resolution preferred trading caribou meat and hides for the few trade goods they required, rather than taking furs. Until the 1890s, the involvement in the fur trade for all peoples trading at Fort Resolution was light.

Throughout the nineteenth century most of the people who traded into Fort Resolution were known either as Chipewyan (or Montagnais) or Yellowknife. The Chipewyans primarily occupied regions south of Great Slave Lake and it was mainly bands of these people who exploited the lands west of the Slave River. They were more adept at hunting moose than the Yellowknife (cf. Weekes 1949:7; Anderson 1858) and appear to have been more reliant on trade goods.

The Yellowknife primarily occupied those lands from Yellowknife Bay eastward along the northern shore of supernatural adeptness. He was able to punish people supernaturally who did not comply with his wishes. *bɛǩá báθdeli* are said to have disappeared with the coming of the White traders.

The term *dene-gą ǩálδər* is usually translated 'boss of the people'. These men were band headmen who had limited authority, although this varied with their charisma. They were leading hunters, trappers, and "travelers," selected by casual processes of consensus to direct the exploitative activities of the band.

"Trading chiefs" were given clothing and medals to enhance their authority and were responsible for trading the furs and distributing the trade goods for their "trading gangs" (cf. MacNeish 1956:146). Only one or two trading chiefs, such as the famous Akaitcho of the Yellowknife (see "Yellowknife," fig. 3, this vol.), are recalled today. The degree of authority they had among their followers while in the "bush" is not known. A few, such as Akaitcho and perhaps Le Grand Jeune Homme and Whitefish, may have had considerable influence among the people (Simpson 1938:370; Back 1836:83).

The final category of leader among the people trading into Fort Resolution was the adept magico-medical practitioner. Most leaders had some supernatural skills in the early days since it was supernatural skill that enabled a man to excel as a hunter. There were also men and women who had no formal leadership role who were called upon to cure the sick, to predict the future, and to enable the band to be successful in the exploitative quest. The importance of such persons declined after the coming of the missionaries and after the introduction of Euro-American medicine. In the 1960s some old people pointed out that year-round "bush" living was no longer possible as there are no adept persons of any consequence left (Smith 1973).

The Métis

Most of the early Métis people went north in the service of the early traders. They were originally from the Red and Saskatchewan river valleys, where, during the eighteenth century, a distinctive Métis culture had evolved (Slobodin 1966:12–14). For the most part, the Métis of the southern Mackenzie District were Red River Métis of French-Cree heritage.

At least two of the earliest Métis names still associated with Fort Resolution—Beaulieu and Mandeville—go back to the very beginning of the fur trade on Great Slave Lake. The Beaulieus, who first settled at Salt River (about 15 miles downstream from present-day Fort Smith) were acquainted with Great Slave Lake before the first representatives of a trading company arrived (Petitot 1884–1885:47).

The early Métis manned the birchbark canoes and York boats of the Mackenzie fur brigade. They were

interpreters, fort hunters, and fishermen. Most worked for the traders during the transportation season and hunted and trapped during the winter months, either from the fort itself or with bands of Indians. A few Métis rose to serve in very important capacities, such as post manager, for the trading companies.

There also were Métis known as "freemen." They were men who had once worked for the traders or who worked for the traders only occasionally (Innis 1956:288–289). Some of these freemen lived with Indian people and became virtually indistinguishable from Indians in their cultural identity. While many Fort Resolution Métis have spoken French and to a lesser extent English, nearly all have spoken Chipewyan (and other Indian languages) and have considered Chipewyan their first language.

Many early Fort Resolution Métis took Chipewyan wives. Through the years, the Métis and Indian populations have become linked by complexities of kinship. The children of Métis-Indian marriages were often raised in the "bush" as Indians. Some early Métis assumed positions of leadership in the society of Chipewyans who traded at Fort Resolution. The Métis François Beaulieu II, "le Patriarche," was a major Indian leader about whom the legends are legion in the southern part of the Mackenzie District.

The Missionaries

In 1852 Father Faraud, O.M.I. (*Oblats de Marie Immaculée*) arrived at Fort Resolution. In 1856 a mission house was constructed on Moose Deer Island (fig. 2) and in 1858 the bishop of Saint Boniface stationed two fathers and a lay brother there permanently.

The conversion of the peoples trading into Fort Resolution seems to have been accomplished with ease (Duchaussois 1923:196). Both the oral history of Fort Resolution peoples and the historical literature suggest

Fig. 2. St. Joseph Mission and Indian tepee on Moose Deer Island. Ft. Resolution is in the background. Engraving after original drawing by Emile Petitot, probably 1863.

that the presence of Christian Whites and Métis had prepared the way for the priests (McVicar 1825–1827; Casterman 1965).

In 1890 the Roman Catholic mission establishment was moved to the mainland site of Fort Resolution, and in that same year the Anglican Church sought a foothold there (Robinson and Robinson 1946:46). The

Fig. 3. Indian tepee, possibly Dogrib, in front of Hudson's Bay Company trading post at Ft. Resolution. Photograph by Charles W. Mathers, 1900.

Anglicans soon abandoned their efforts in Fort Resolution, and other attempts by Protestant missionaries in succeeding years met with a similar lack of success.

The Nineteenth Century

Fort Resolution was not outstanding as a "fur post" during most of the nineteenth century. From earliest years until the decline of the fur-trade economy in the north, Fort Resolution's importance rested primarily on its location for the fur trade transport. All northern commerce, from the Mackenzie River, the north arm of Great Slave Lake, and later the east arm of the lake, passed through Fort Resolution (Rae 1963:128–129).

Fort Resolution was also a "fish post" in the nineteenth century, providing quantities of fish for the fur brigades. Fort Resolution also produced dry meat, pounded meat, grease, and hides for the "general service," mostly brought to the fort by Indians whose hunting grounds were along the east arm of the lake. However, after Fort Rae was established in 1852, it was the

Fig. 4. Hudson's Bay Company manager J.F. Cunningham and clerk Louis Roy grading a fox skin with Joseph Houle, a Métis interpreter, looking on. Photograph by Henry W. Jones, 1916–1917.

Fort Rae Dogribs who provided the majority of the dry meat required for general service (Innis 1956:300).

In years of the nineteenth century when the fur and provision trade failed, disease and starvation of the area Indians were often cited as causative factors. Starvation was a threat in the nineteenth century when game was scarce or when the quest for furs led people into lands where food resources were limited. Very few foodstuffs

Prov. Arch. of Alta., Edmonton: E. Brown Coll. B–2935.
Fig. 5. Scows filled with supplies being pulled into Ft. Resolution by the Hislop and Nagle steamboat. Photograph by Charles W. Mathers on Great Slave Lake, 1895–1903.

were available from the traders until the end of the century. Periods of illness and extremely bad weather sometimes combined with food shortages to produce a large number of deaths.

The Expansion of the Fur Trade

It was not until 1893 that the Hudson's Bay Company (figs. 3–4) experienced serious competition on Great Slave Lake with the coming of the firm of Hislop and Nagle (figs. 5–6), which was headquartered at Fort Resolution (Russell 1898). The coming of "free traders" was made possible by improvements in transportation, such as the completion of the railroad to Edmonton, Alberta, in 1890 and the operation of steamboats both north and south of the Fort Smith rapids by the mid-1880s (Innis 1956:344–345). By the turn of the century, Resolution was the foremost fur-trade post on Great Slave Lake, and in 1902 there were no less than six different trading companies located there (Usher 1971:41). The growing importance of Fort Resolution in the early part of the twentieth century is indicated

Prov. Arch. of Alta., Edmonton: E. Brown Coll. B–2875.
Fig. 6. The Hislop and Nagle trading post. Photograph by Charles W. Mathers, 1895–1903.

by the construction of a mission school (fig. 7), orphanage, and convent in 1903 and the permanent stationing of a Royal Northwest Mounted Police detachment there in 1913.

Improvements in transportation and the competition between traders provided an increased quantity and variety of trade goods. Native peoples responded by becoming more committed to trapping furs for trade.

Native Hamlets

The growing commitment of native peoples to trapping is reflected in the establishment, between 1895 and 1915, of native log-cabin hamlets. These hamlets indicate a definite break with the more fully nomadic mode of life characteristic of earlier times (Helm and Damas 1963). They were located at sites that had been major fisheries for years, and most were at the mouths of the major streams that fall into the Lake. They consisted of from two or three families up to 50 people (Canada. Dominion Bureau of the Census 1941). In addition to the proximity of fisheries, the selection of sites for these hamlets was influenced by the quality and accessibility of hunting and trapping in the vicinity and the ease of travel by canoe (fig. 8) and dog toboggan to the fort.

In the early part of the twentieth century, people stayed in their hamlets for perhaps three weeks or a month in the fall and spring for fishing, and briefly at other times if their food supplies permitted. As fur prices became higher, and as more and more supplemental food stocks were available from the traders, people were able to spend longer periods of time at their hamlets. In some cases by the 1930s men had built additional cabins out on their trap lines to which they took their families during the trapping season.

The hamlets closest to Fort Resolution were the first established, and all of these were founded or cofounded by Métis.

Treaty No. 8

Another decisive event in the lives of native peoples at the turn of the century was the "signing" of Treaty No. 8 in Fort Resolution on July 25, 1900. In addition to the Chipewyan and Yellowknife, some Slavey and Dogrib people who then traded at Fort Resolution also "took Treaty" at this time. The dominion government created the institution of "chiefs" (fig. 9) and "headmen" (or "councilors") in order to deal with the people. An annuity of five dollars per person was promised (but $25 for chiefs and $15 for headmen) along with small amounts of "rations" in the form of axes, hand saws, ammunition, netting twine, flour, slab bacon, and tea (MacRae 1900). In return the Indians ceded their territory and became subject to dominion law.

Hudson's Bay Company Lib., Winnipeg, Man.
Fig. 7. Indian, White, and Métis children with Sister McQuillan at the Roman Catholic mission school at Ft. Resolution. Photograph by Henry W. Jones, 1913.

Until the 1930s, all the chiefs and councilors of the Chipewyans were respected traditional leaders in native culture; they were dene-gą k̓ál̃ɔr. But as elderly leaders died, and as times changed, few eminent leaders continued to emerge. Since World War II, with much more individualized relations between native peoples and White governmental personnel, chiefs and headmen have not been seen as very important. By the early 1970s it was difficult to hold elections for such leaders as few people would come to a meeting for that purpose. It was felt that the White man had the power and chiefs could do very little to gain for the people what they wished.

On the occasion of the first signing of the treaty, Chipewyans trading into Fort Resolution had had but minimal contact with Whites; few if any "bush" people understood English. It is thus understandable that these people first put forth Pierre Beaulieu (fig. 10), a respected Fort Resolution–dwelling Métis, for their chief. This choice was not permitted by the government treaty commissioner, as anyone in some way recognized as being Métis was not permitted to "take Treaty."

Instead of a treaty, Fort Resolution Métis were given a "scrip payment." This payment acknowledged their Indian ancestry and was meant to settle their legal claims with the government "once and forever." The Métis were excluded from the treaty because it was felt they lived as Whites (Cumming and Mickenburg 1972:202). After 1900 "Indian" describes those natives with treaty status, and "Métis" is synonymous with nontreaty status. However, this categorization of population (table 1) does not coincide with cultural boundaries. In the early 1930s, some Métis were permitted to "take Treaty" if they desired. This apparently was the result of the urging of the Indian agent stationed at Fort Resolution at this time, Dr. Clermont Bourget

Fig. 8. Dogrib Indians arriving at Ft. Resolution. Bales of fur, blankets, bark strips, personal gear, and tepee poles and coverings are already unloaded. Birchbark freighter canoes are in the Chipewyan style. Photograph by Charles W. Mathers on Great Slave Lake, 1901.

(1929), who argued that there were many Métis leading lives essentially like the Indians who were therefore deserving of the "protection" of a treaty. Some Métis "took Treaty" at this time and became legally Indian in the eyes of the government. Most did not, being proud of their non-"ward" status, and being fearful that the government would someday establish a reservation (a provision of Treaty No. 8 never acted upon) to which treatied people would be confined.

Although Métis people were initially excluded from the treaty, Fort Resolution treaty Indians have always included Métis leaders in their discussions of Indian-government matters. Métis leaders were continuously consulted, for it was recognized that their language ability and occupational involvement in the White world had given them a better understanding of White motivations and actions.

The Boom Period of the Fur Trade, 1916–1929

Between the years 1916 and 1929 the fur trade underwent a boom in the Fort Resolution area. There were several major trading concerns, and most seasons found several itinerant free traders coming to Fort Resolution with scow loads of goods. This expansion was again made possible by improved means of transportation, such as the completion of the Alberta and Great Waterways Railroad to Waterways, Alberta, in 1925 (Phillips 1967:147) and the use of trucks and tractors on the portage at Fort Smith.

Competition among the traders at Fort Resolution was so strenuous that sometimes the native trappers received prices for their furs in excess of the actual outside market value. Despite the tremendous increase in the abundance and variety of goods, trading was so vigorous that the stores were sometimes out of goods prior to the beginning of the next shipping season. As a consequence, native peoples, by now much more dependent upon the stores, sometimes underwent periods of considerable hardship.

In Fort Resolution, the number of Métis people increased as they went there to work for the traders and at other White installations (table 1). The steady increase in the Métis population correlates well with the expansion of the fur trade as more Métis people came to Fort Resolution. It also reflects greater numbers of

689

Fig. 9. Chief Vital Lamoëlle, Chipewyan from Buffalo River Village, and Bishop Gabriel Breynat, bishop of Mackenzie River District. Chief Lamoëlle was one of the cosigners of Treaty No. 8 in 1900. Photograph by Henry W. Jones at Ft. Resolution, 1912.

Fig. 10. Pierre Beaulieu (b.1833, d.1910), adopted son of François Beaulieu. Photographed about 1900.

Métis-Indian and Métis-White marriages and the better access Fort-dwelling Métis have had to medical care. The increase and decrease in the number of Whites in Fort Resolution also correspond well with the expansion and decline of the fur trade.

Although there was an increased flow of Whites into the north, pushing Métis people out of more prestigious and higher-paying occupations, Fort Resolution is said to have been one of the better settlements in the north in which to find summer work, and trapping was relatively good. Fort Resolution became the base for several schooners manned by Métis, which served the posts and outposts around the lake. The mission establishment provided work in the form of haying for its livestock, fishing, and working at the mission sawmill. There were also other jobs, such as hauling the mail by dog sleigh, and working for the RCMP as "special constables" (for example, as forerunners, interpreters, and general workmen).

High prices for furs brought an increase in the number of White trappers in the Fort Resolution area. Many of these, approaching trapping as a business, came into the country just before the trapping season—with rather complete "grub stakes" and up to 500 steel traps—and left at the end of the trapping season. The fur animal populations in the Fort Resolution area were seriously affected by their activities, and the federal government, in order to protect native trappers (who set about 20 traps in addition to living off the land) established a native trapping preserve in the region (see Rea 1968:75–76).

Some White trappers, however, came north in an evident search for a new life. Settling in satellite communities such as Rocher River and Rat River, they intermarried and became fairly well integrated members of these communities.

Métis-Indian Relations Until 1940

Until the late 1930s, Indian people from all around the lake came into Fort Resolution to receive payment of treaty annuities, to trade, and to participate in Roman Catholic religious observances. These in-gatherings were important festive occasions, with feasts, dances, and gambling.

For people traveling to Fort Resolution, the hamlets of Stony Island and Jean River were important stopover points. Especially at Jean River, Indian-government matters were discussed, for this community had been founded and was headed by the Métis patriarch, Jean-Marie Beaulieu. He was widely known for his wisdom and generosity, and since his village was fairly close to the Fort, he was in a good position to obtain any information that the Indian agent or others had received from Ottawa. While nontreaty in status, he was always politically active and concerned about the welfare of all native peoples.

An influenza epidemic in 1928 had a devastating effect upon Fort Resolution peoples, for many old native leaders died. In the 1930s, when native peoples thought of electing a new chief "not afraid to talk for the people," they thought of Jean-Marie as he was one of the few surviving native leaders. The Indian agent was asked to prevail upon Jean-Marie to "take Treaty" and become chief, which he did. (Many of his relatives at Jean River "took Treaty" because he had.) While he was an effective chief, he was already an old man in his seventies, and he died in 1935. His son, Alexis Jean-Marie Beaulieu, succeeded him as chief, and although he was a respected man and for a time was an effective chief, the great economic and social transformations that occurred during and after the Second World War thwarted his efforts to continue successfully.

In Fort Resolution itself, the foremost Métis leaders, who were elder members of the major patronymic groups living there, were often consulted during ingathering. One man in particular was consulted from the 1930s on, after many treaty Indian leaders had died. His son has described his role: "People would come to see him: 'Se?e [sɛ?ɛ 'my uncle'], this chief we got now is just for his bunch and he talks just for nothing. We got to have a chief for all of the people.' So maybe he would call a meeting of the wise old men . . . and they would fix it up good" (Smith 1968–1972).

The Life of Native Peoples Since 1940

In the 1930s world economic depression and a declining market for furs saw the Hudson's Bay Company close many of its outposts in the north, and many of their competitors soon closed as well. In 1938 Northern Traders Limited sold its assets to the Hudson's Bay Company (Usher 1971:28) and only "the Bay" and one major "free trader" (Pinsky and Necrasoff) were still operating in Fort Resolution.

In the 1940s a major transformation of the northern economy—from an emphasis on the fur trade to an emphasis on the extractive industries—was clearly evident (Rea 1968:122–124). In 1948 the Mackenzie Highway was completed to Hay River; Fort Resolution was bypassed by the road.

In addition to a decisive shift in the economy, the 1940s saw the beginning of active large-scale government concern for native peoples as the federal family allowance and old age pension programs were initiated. Throughout the 1950s, several major steps were taken by the federal government in the realms of welfare, health care, and education. After 1958 a federal day school was operating in Fort Resolution, and the government took over full responsibility for native health care with the establishment of a nursing station, which replaced the mission hospital first opened in 1939.

After the Second World War, fewer and fewer native people found that they were able to continue the older trapping, hunting, and fishing way of life lived in the "bush," and they began to settle at Fort Resolution on a more or less permanent basis. Most native hamlets were abandoned by the early 1950s, although a few families have continued (but decreasingly through the years) to return to a few of them for trapping and fishing at different times.

There were several reasons people came to live in Fort Resolution permanently. With fur prices relatively low, were it not for government aid in the form of welfare, family allowances, old age pensions and the like, people would have been compelled to lead a poverty-stricken existence in the "bush." Native peoples well knew times were changing and came to live at Resolution so that their children might have schooling to enable them to find wage employment. Since the federal school was a day school, at least one parent had to be home to look after the children when school was

Table 1. Population of Fort Resolution, 1823–1971

Year	Natives Trading or Residing at the Fort — Indians		Métis	Total Natives	Whites	Total Population	Source
1823	564	(372 Chipewyan 192 Yellowknife)	ca. 10	563	ca. 5	568	McVicar 1825–1827
1863	577	(245 Chipewyan 332 Yellowknife)	25	602	15	617	Petitot 1884–1885
1910	580		82	662	44	706	St. Joseph's Mission 1852–1972
1920	624		111	735	ca. 65	800	St. Joseph's Mission 1852–1972
1930	439		219	658	ca. 85	743	St. Joseph's Mission 1852–1972
1940	305		277	582	83	665	St. Joseph's Mission 1852–1972
1950	338		254	592	67	659	St. Joseph's Mission 1852–1972
1971	210		331	541	ca. 65	606	St. Joseph's Mission 1852–1972

out. The older pattern of families living together in the bush was therefore no longer feasible, and trappers were understandably reluctant to stay away from their families in the "bush" for the seven or eight months required for successful trapping. The necessity to pick up periodic family allowance, old age pension, and other checks also held people to the community, and town came to provide the setting for the things that present-day native peoples much desire (for example, warm houses, parties, movies).

The most important reason for people deciding to reside in Fort Resolution, however, seems to have been the presence of health-care facilities there. From the 1920s through the 1940s Fort Resolution people saw the deaths of many respected elders from influenza, tuberculosis, and other diseases and watched in anguish as their children died in the "bush." Thus, when it became economically possible, people were often willing to move into the town to stay. When people are asked why the residents from this or that hamlet decided to move into the town, the following reply is rather typical: "You see, there weren't that many people left, and it was breaking their hearts. They wanted to go away from that place. So they gave up and came over here" (Smith 1968–1972).

Thus, the pressures to abandon the older life were great; however, for the native people who have settled in Fort Resolution, there has been little wage work. Most men have continued to do some trapping, but the average annual trapping income has been low. For the years 1957–1965, for instance, the trapping income averaged just under $350 (see Makale, Holloway, and Associates 1966:48). Most families have had to rely upon welfare assistance to help them meet basic needs, and men have worked at casual and occasional jobs when available (for example, fighting forest fires, constructing roads and government low-cost housing, staking claims, working at the sporadically operating local sawmill—fig. 11).

Since the Second World War the life situation of most Métis and most Indians who joined them in Fort Resolution has become much the same; however, the legal distinction between treaty and nontreaty status, which has roughly distinguished the Indian from the Métis population, has become more important. In general, treaty people receive more assistance from the federal government. This form of governmental discrimination has exacerbated bitter feelings on the part of some members of both groups toward the other group. Inequities in the treatment of Indian compared to Métis were especially obvious in the realm of government low-cost housing. Construction began in the 1960s, but

692

Native Press, Yellowknife, N.W.T.
Fig. 11. The Ft. Resolution planer mill with native male and female employees. This mill burned down in Oct. 1976 but was back in operation within 2 years. Photographed in 1975.

until 1969 when the territorial government took over the housing program, it was available to treaty Indians only, despite the fact that the need of many nontreaty families was just as great.

At least in part because of a lack of opportunity for employment, an emigration of young native people from Fort Resolution occurred during the 1950s and 1960s. This emigration has offset the population increase that would otherwise have occurred because of marked improvements in health care. Young native women have been especially successful in leaving the community, marrying out of the settlement to men with jobs (often White men). In 1971 there were 56 people 20 years of age and older, either living in Fort Resolution or living there frequently, who were considered eligible for marriage. Of this total, 52 were male and only 4 were female. This surplus of single men (tables 2–3) has added to the problems of the people.

In summary, the post-World War II years have seen a sharp decline in Fort Resolution's commercial and social importance, and the sedentarization of the native people in the settlement itself, a combination that has created new and complex social and economic problems for the native people.

Sources

Valuable knowledge of native life during the initial period of the establishment of trading posts on Great Slave Lake may be gleaned from Fidler's (1934) account of his journey between Lake Athabasca and Great Slave Lake during the winter of 1791–1792. The un-

Table 2. Native Population of Fort Resolution, by Age and Sex, 1971

Age Category	Male	Female	Total
0– 4	33	34	67
5– 9	49	40	89
10–14	47	30	77
15–19	32	35	67
20–24	31	13	44
25–29	15	10	25
30–34	7	9	16
35–39	19	10	29
40–44	18	14	32
45–49	14	10	24
50–54	7	6	13
55–59	8	7	15
60–64	8	10	18
65–69	6	2	8
70–74	5	3	8
75–79	1	3	4
80 and over	4	1	5
Totals	304	237	541

SOURCE: Louis Menez, personal communication 1972.

Table 3. Single Native People Emigrating from Fort Resolution, 1956–1971

	Married to:		Living in:			
Males	N	O	N	O	Single	Total
1956–1966	8	2	20	2	12	22
1967–1969	0	1	2	0	1	2
1970–1971	2	0	10	0	8	10
Females						
1956–1966	10	24	20	23	9	43
1967–1969	1	8	12	8	11	20
1970–1971	1	4	8	2	5	10
Total Single People Emigrated = 107						

N = Northerner, North; O = Outside of the Northwest Territories. Outsiders are, by and large, Whites.
SOURCE: Louis Menez, personal communication 1972.

published documents of the Hudson's Bay Archives, Winnipeg, include important bits of information on the native peoples of Fort Resolution for the entire nineteenth century. Simpson's (1938) journal gives some indication of the nature of these materials.

Between 1820 and 1855, the explorers Franklin (1823, 1828), Back (1836), and Richardson (1851), passed through Fort Resolution and often used this post as their supply base. Limited but useful data on native people trading into Fort Resolution are given, especially data on the Yellowknife. The single most important observer during the nineteenth century was Father Émile Petitot, who contributed several excellent works on the native peoples of the north that include information on Indians and Métis of the Great Slave Lake area (Petitot 1891). Other nineteenth-century materials include the writings of other Catholic priests (Duchaussois 1919, 1923), the memoirs of a trader (Weekes 1949), and traveler accounts (Russell 1898). General accounts of the development of the fur trade with materials on Fort Resolution include Innis (1956), Usher (1971), and Rae (1963).

Firsthand accounts of times during the fur-trade boom in the twentieth century include Godsell (1934) and Bourget (1938). Phillips (1967) and Rea (1968) provide extensive data on the economic transformation in the north during World War II that profoundly altered the lives of Fort Resolution peoples.

The only professional ethnologists who have been in Fort Resolution for any length of time are Slobodin (1966) and Smith (1968–1972, 1973). Slobodin was in Fort Resolution briefly during 1963 and provides some excellent information on Métis community organization. Smith has benefited greatly from the meticulous scholarship of Father Louis Menez of Saint Joseph's Parish, Fort Resolution, who freely shared data he had personally gathered. Finally, the best source of information on Fort Resolution history has been the accounts of the resident native peoples themselves, who freely welcomed Smith in their homes and shared their knowledge.

Old Crow, Yukon Territory

ANN WELSH ACHESON

By the 1960s, the Kutchin Indian village of Old Crow, northern Yukon Territory, was one of the best-known—or at any rate best publicized—Northern Athapaskan villages in Canada. It was the subject of a *Life* magazine article (Hamblin 1965) and a Canadian television broadcast. One local Indian resident, Edith Josie (fig. 1), was writing a regular town news column for the *Whitehorse Star;* a collection of these columns was published in a book, *Here Are the News* (Josie 1966). In addition to such popular treatments, Old Crow has attracted the attention of scientists over a period of many years, including archeologists (Morlan 1969, 1970, 1971, 1973; Irving 1967), physical anthropologists (Hildes, Wilt, and Parker 1965; Lewis et al. 1961; Marshall 1970), and cultural anthropologists (Acheson 1977, 1977a, 1980; Balikci 1963, 1963a, 1968; Leechman 1948, 1950, 1952, 1954; Welsh 1970, 1970a), and a geographer (Stager 1974).

With this interest and attention, there has been a tendency for Old Crow to be idealized, both by White outsiders and even by natives of other towns. "Old Crow is sure a nice place," is a phrase one hears often when traveling in the North, and the village's inhabitants strive to maintain this image; they are concerned that outsiders should hear or read "good news for Old Crow," as they put it. In the eyes of many outsiders, Old Crow is a harmonious Indian community, where people still live as trappers and hunters, for the most part untouched by the "evils of civilization."

The popular image of Old Crow as an indigenous Indian social form is misleading on two counts. First, the village itself is recent, formed in the early twentieth century. Permanent, sedentary town living did not commence for most of the population until the early 1960s, with the decline in importance of trapping and the establishment of increased government services at Old Crow. Second, the village developed largely through the presence and stimulation of outside, White institutions.

History

The establishment and growth of Old Crow village must be understood within the general framework of changes taking place in the surrounding region. Before White contact, the vicinity of the present village, which is located about a mile below the confluence of the Old Crow and Porcupine rivers at 67°35′ north latitude, 139°50′ west longitude (see "Native Settlements: Introduction," fig. 1, this vol.), was known as a good fishing area by the Crow Flats Kutchin band. The spring Barren-Ground caribou crossing site of Klokut (Irving 1967; Morlan 1969, 1970, 1971) is nearby, and the Crow Mountains just north of the Porcupine River are a good area for fall caribou hunting. After the Crow Flats Kutchin became involved in the fur trade, their seasonal round underwent major changes, including a shift in orientation from Crow Flats and the hilly uplands north of the Flats toward a greater riverine emphasis. During this period, the vicinity of Old Crow contained several

Whitehorse Star, Yukon Terr.: Bob Erlam Coll.

Fig. 1. Edith Josie, a well known reporter of local news who published regularly in the *Whitehorse Star* and the Edmonton (Alta.) *Journal*. Photographed at Old Crow, December 1967.

summer fishing sites. It was also a gathering spot for Kutchin families arriving from Crow Flats via Old Crow River and for families from bands farther up the Porcupine who were going to trade downstream, first at Fort Yukon and later at Rampart House. The first permanent log cabin dwelling at Old Crow is reported to have been built around the turn of the century by John Tizya, whose fishing camp was nearby, and who served as catechist for the band when the Anglican missionary was not present. The name of the village is said to have come from a former chief who had a fishing camp near the mouth of the Old Crow River in the mid-nineteenth century.

Epidemic disease was a significant factor in the development of Old Crow in the early twentieth century. The Crow Flats and Upper Porcupine bands had both been depopulated. Many Upper Porcupine Kutchin intermarried with the Crow Flats people and began to shift into their area. Other Upper Porcupine people drifted eastward and joined with the Peel River Kutchin band. Today, the upper Porcupine River area is uninhabited, though people from Old Crow occasionally travel there for hunting and trapping. In 1911–1912, there was a disastrous smallpox epidemic at Rampart House, which had been the point of trade for most of the Crow Flats Kutchin and several other bands as well, and most of the native houses at that site were burned down. In 1912, two traders opened a store at Old Crow, and the population began shifting there from the Rampart House area and from the upper Porcupine. Trading posts have been in operation at Old Crow more or less continuously ever since, the most recent one being run by a local Indian trader. In 1970 this trader sold out, and a cooperative store (fig. 2) was formed. Old Crow is perhaps unique in the area in that trade has never been conducted there by the Hudson's Bay Company.

By the early twentieth century, the people of the region were fully involved in the fur trade. Steel traps, guns, twine fish nets, tents, log cabins, tin and iron stoves, and a variety of hardware, clothing, and foodstuffs were standard throughout the region. The seasonal round involved the typical pattern of dispersal to small trapping, muskratting, and fishing camps during most of the year, with in-gathering at Old Crow during the summer and Christmas and Easter holidays. In addition to the trading post, an Anglican church was built by the Indians in 1926, and in 1928 the Royal Canadian Mounted Police post was moved to Old Crow from Rampart House. The presence of trading post, church, and police reinforced the importance of the village for people of the surrounding area, who increasingly began to have Old Crow as their town of orientation. In this period, there were also several small, all-native settlements farther up the Porcupine. Trading was carried on sporadically by a local Indian trader at two of these, Whitestone and Johnson Creek villages, which were

Whitehorse Star, Yukon Terr.

Fig. 2. The new coop store at Old Crow being built next to an old-style log and sod house. Photograph by Bob Erlam, 1969.

abandoned by the early 1950s. Those who trapped in the upper Porcupine region did not visit Old Crow as frequently as those dwelling in the mid-Porcupine and Crow Flats areas, going instead to Eagle (Alaska), La Pierre House, or Fort McPherson.

During the height of the fur trade period Old Crow physically consisted of a few log cabins, many tents during in-gathering periods, a log church, R.C.M.P. establishment, and trading post, all huddled close together in several rows facing the Porcupine River. A few natives had permanent cabins in town, usually those who spent relatively more time in the area, for example, elderly people who no longer went trapping; persons who were employed by the police, trading post, or mission; and those whose summer fishing sites were nearby. There were also a number of White trappers and retired prospectors resident in Old Crow at times, in addition to the missionary, police, and storekeepers. A number of the White trappers were married to native women. Indian dwellings, both cabins and tents, were generally located "uptown" (upriver), while the Whites and mixed bloods had their homes "downtown," a pattern persisting in the 1970s.

The designation Métis (mixed blood) is not used locally, and the Métis in Old Crow have never formed a large, distinct, or self-identified group. The local Indians usually refer to them as "half-breeds" or as being "on the White side," referring to the legal status of those with White or White-status fathers.

Some effort was made at providing education and health services when people were in town, primarily by a succession of Anglican missionaries and their wives. A few children were shipped out to church-run boarding schools (some never to return).

Since the early 1950s, Old Crow has presented a different picture, both physically and socially, than it did during the fur-trade period. The Canadian government is the dominant local institution, and it has come to play an increasingly active role in the Indians' lives. Economically, it provides direct welfare payments, old-age pensions, and family allowances, as well as indirect subsidies in the form of payment for labor and services. Those requiring medical care, particularly for tuberculosis, began to be sent "outside" for care on an extensive basis with the building of Camsell Hospital in Edmonton, Alberta, in 1947. In 1961 a permanently staffed nursing station with complete modern facilities was opened at Old Crow, and a new installation was erected by the R.C.M.P. during the mid-1960s.

In 1958 government teachers replaced Anglican missionaries as educators. By 1969 the large school built in 1961 had classes through grade 9. This building, with three classrooms and attached teachers' apartments, burned in 1969 and was succeeded by another one in 1970. For high school, young people were being sent to Whitehorse where most were placed in vocational programs.

The building of these institutional structures, and also the advent of government housing programs (primarily for old people or those on welfare) provided increased wage labor opportunities at Old Crow at a time when fur prices had been on the decline, and stimulated increased periods of in-town residence.

The building of the school was probably the single greatest factor in causing most people to settle more or less year-round in the village. In addition to the construction projects, the government institutions also offered a few permanent positions to those willing to stay in town all year, and they provided a ready market for firewood. In addition to economic considerations, education had come to be highly valued, and people felt compelled to send their children to school. By the late 1960s, trapping for fine furs had all but ceased, and almost no one lived out in the bush for trapping; however, quite a few families (at least half in 1968) continued to go to their muskratting areas (fig. 3) in the spring

when school was out, perhaps as much for sentimental as economic reasons. Oil exploration activities in the area brought in yet another source of wages during the late 1960s. When these jobs are available, even the highly valued "ratting" (spring muskrat hunt) is given up, at least temporarily.

Mass media (especially the radio, but increasingly also written materials) and modern transportation facilities have broken Old Crow's previous isolation. Regular service by Great Northern Airways was instituted in the 1960s, allowing a tremendous volume of freight and mail to be brought in by air. A permanent airstrip, built largely at the encouragement of oil interests, was completed in 1970–1971. In addition, oil companies built a winter road into the area from the south in the early 1970s, bringing the beginnings of automotive and truck traffic to Old Crow.

Knowledge of English was widespread by the 1960s, and exposure to the White world had increased greatly. As of 1969, most of those under age 50 were bilingual, and many children no longer spoke the native language, though most could understand it.

The Modern Village

Population and Social Organization

The modern population of Old Crow includes three categories of people: transient Whites and their families, primarily church and government personnel (not more than 20 individuals usually); permanently resident White-status persons (almost entirely Métis); and persons of Indian status, or Old Crow band members. Table 1 gives available population data. Figures prior to the 1960s reflect numbers trading into Old Crow, rather than those permanently resident. Since the government band list of persons of Indian status is not an accurate estimate of actual village residence, where possible the figures shown are those of actual village censuses, excluding transient Whites.

Social organization of modern Old Crow native society is marked by the abandonment of many aboriginal forms, combined with the persistence of certain aboriginal traits—particularly certain features of the kinship system. New kinds of forces have influenced social organization, most notably the formation of the permanent village rather than the band as the basic large-scale unit, the introduction of various governmental services, and the exposure of the Indians to the White man's way of life and White values.

Traditional kinship principles continue to operate in many spheres of life, but in modified and diminished form.

Aboriginally, there was a division into two or possibly three nonlocalized matrilineal descent groups or clans: *nà·cai·* and *čičyà·ʔ* being the predominant ones, with

Fig. 3. Families with their possessions, including sled dogs, returning from the spring muskrat hunt in canvas-covered boats. Photograph by Ann Acheson at Old Crow, June 1968.

Table 1. Old Crow Population: Permanent Residents

	Indian Status	White Status (mainly Métis)	Other	Total
1931[a]	168	not given	6 Eskimo	174?
1941	167	15		182
1951	126	27		153
1956				173[c]
1959	152	not given		152?
1961	151	58		209[d]
1964[b]	172	not given		172?
1968	148	40		188

SOURCES: Northern Coordination and Research Center, Dept. of Northern Affairs and Resources, mimeo, compiled from Dominion Bureau of Statistics Records, 1961, except for 1968, from Acheson 1977:149.

[a] Includes general Old Crow area, with 75 listed for Old Crow proper and the remainder in smaller trapping settlements.

[b] Band list, not actual residents.

[c] Breakdown not given by legal status. Probably represents band list.

[d] Balikci (1963a:65–67) reports a total of 198, with "about 140" Indians and "about 50" Métis.

the *te·nǯirà·cya·* possibly consisting of individuals born of clan endogamous marriages.* Among other clan functions, each clan's members had the responsibility of disposing of the other's dead, in return for which they were often given a feast (fig. 4). For further discussion of Kutchin clan organization and potlatching see Balikci (1963:22–24), Leechman (1954:27–28), McKennan (1965:60–61), and Osgood (1936a:107, 122–123).

Clan exogamy is no longer practiced, and by the 1970s many younger people were barely aware of their clan affiliations, but "moose feasts" were still being given ostensibly along clan lines (fig. 5). Visiting and interaction generally are more intensive among close kin than between those more distantly related or unrelated. Sharing and redistribution of bush food are still practiced to a large extent, but survival is no longer dependent on sharing, and community pressure is not strong enough to enforce the old norms on the unwilling.

Kinship principles still affect placement of houses and residence choices of individuals. Of 35 village household dwellings in 1968, 23 were located next to one or more sets of close kinsmen. There were seven such "kin clusters," ranging in size from two to five households, including one cluster of Métis. In the past, initial uxorilocal residence was the norm, the young couple usually residing in the same structure as the older one. The modern tendency is toward virilocality, the most common residential cluster at Old Crow consisting of an elderly couple (or remaining widow) and their sons

*The phonemic transcriptions of the Crow Flats Kutchin words in this chapter were provided by John Ritter. See the orthographic footnote in "Kutchin," this vol.

and families; however, separate households are maintained.

The village in 1968–1969 (Acheson 1968–1969) contained 35 Indian and Métis households, each occupying a separate log-cabin dwelling. In the summer, boys and unmarried men sometimes had tents near their parents' houses but did not maintain separate households.

Household Size, December 1968

Number of Persons	1	2	3	4	5	6	7	8	9	12	16
Number of Households	3	5	6	2	4	2	3	6	2	1	1

Average household size was 5.2 individuals, with 14 (40%) of the households consisting of three people or less.

There is a greater range in household size than in aboriginal times, according to modern informants. The larger households result primarily from the increase in numbers of surviving children due to better medical care. Smaller households consisting primarily of old people living alone or with an adult, unmarried child are also more common than in the past, when older people would normally have dwelled with married children or other close kin in larger units.

Economic changes and sharp changes in marriage patterns have greatly affected modern household composition. The following factors are of particular significance:

(1) the disappearance of family-arranged marriages and the introduction of White standards of "free choice," a situation strongly urged by the Anglican Church but also influenced by education and mass media;

(2) increase in government assistance and wage-labor opportunities, combined with year-round village residence, leading to a decrease in the importance of the nuclear or extended family as a survival unit;

(3) temporary and permanent out-migration by many younger people to larger towns, with a greater proportion of those leaving permanently being women;

(4) sharp decline in the frequency of marriage and remarriage, probably due largely to economic factors, especially the inability of many men to make a living locally, and the increasing self-sufficiency of women made possible by government assistance in various forms. Furthermore, since the Anglican Church disapproves of divorce, women may remain separated from their husbands for many years and are not free to remarry.

A high proportion of adults remain unmarried or do not dwell with their spouses. Because of this, the number of households organized on a nuclear family basis was only 51 percent of the total in 1968. Households headed by women alone, a relatively new phenomenon in Kutchin life, are coming to be quite common (37% of the households in 1968).

Fig. 4. Men and older women sitting at a funeral feast. The younger women and children eat after the men are finished. Chief Peter Moses sits at the head of table (Leechman 1954:32). Photograph by Douglas Leechman at Old Crow, July-Aug. 1946.

Fig. 5. Preparations for a moose feast being made by members of the čičyà·ʔ clan and other kinsmen of the feast-giver. Note storage cache (left background) and platform tent (right) now used occasionally in the summer, but during the fur-trade period a much commoner year-round dwelling than the log cabin. Photograph by Ann Acheson at Old Crow, July 1968.

Social units above the level of family or household are not of very great significance, except perhaps for the village itself, and have been largely imposed from the outside or are connected to White institutions. These include church-related groups such as the women's auxiliary, men's group, and confirmation classes, all supervised by the Anglican church, and various groups connected with the school such as sporadic sports teams, a group of adolescent cross-country skiers, and a "school board" (consisting of about three parents appointed by the principal as "advisors," or, more accurately, intermediaries between the school authorities and the Indian community).

Friendship and partnership appear to be persisting social institutions beyond the family and kinship level. The term šižyà·ʔ 'my partner' referred to an aboriginal relationship between two men, established for life, who owed each other mutual obligations of material assistance and revenge for each other's death, combined with privileges of wife-exchange (see Osgood 1936a:113–114, 124, 132). Although the formalized šižyà·ʔ partnership form has pretty much vanished, the term continues to be used to refer to any kind of friendship or temporary partnership. Partnerships seem to have strong economic functions, usually being formed in connection with specific tasks, normally bush tasks. They are formed between people of the same sex, and usually about the same age, who may or may not be kinsmen. Occasionally, an older man with some sort of economic asset such as a motor boat or chainsaw will form a temporary alliance with a young man who helps provide labor. Some partnerships are short-lived, perhaps lasting for only a season, while others persist over years and more closely approximate the aboriginal pattern. There is a strong element of sociability in the operation of partnerships, over and above their economic functions. In Old Crow, the line between simple friend and partner is a hazy one, which in fact may shift back and forth over time for any given pair.

698

ACHESON

Fig. 6. Mrs. Joe Netro carrying her 8-month-old baby Linda in a blanket supported by a florai beaded strap with wool tassels. Photograph by Richard Harrington at Old Crow, 1960.

R.C.M.P.). Table 2 summarizes major subsistence activities observed in 1968.

Commercial trapping, both for fine furs and for muskrat, has been on the decline since the 1950s, both in terms of the number of people actively involved and the total time they spend in such activities (table 3).

The gross cash income of Old Crow in the 1960s derived more from wage labor, various forms of government assistance, and woodcutting than from trapping. More people were involved in cutting wood for sale (primarily for the school and for occasional building projects) than were engaged in either trapping or wage activities. However, on an individual or household basis, woodcutting does not bring so high an income as regular, full-time wage labor does, and the local market for wood is a limited one.

The people of Old Crow engage in three kinds of wage labor: temporary jobs in larger towns, usually lasting from several months to several years; permanent jobs in Old Crow, some part time and some full time, but all limited in number and connected with local White institutions; and sporadic, temporary jobs around town, usually in the summer, involving activities such as construction, guiding, and assisting in various research projects (table 4). After 1968 the tempo of oil exploration and pipeline survey greatly increased, and many more men were employed, particularly in the warmer months.

Economy

The people of Old Crow since the 1950s have been shifting quite rapidly from bush orientation to town orientation. Trips out of town for subsistence activities are sporadic and short-term. Still, in 1968 approximately half the food consumed by people and dogs consisted of bush products, predominantly caribou and fish (although in the 1960s snowmobiles began to replace dogs in some households, 25 households still maintained teams in 1968–1969, and there were a total of 146 dogs in the village excluding those owned by the

Spatial Organization

In general layout, Old Crow is similar to many other Northern towns that grew up primarily in connection with the fur trade. Its buildings stretch for about three-fourths of a mile in a narrow row facing the Porcupine River, with the Indian cabins "uptown" and the White and Métis structures "downtown." Spacing of buildings in the two sections of town is quite different, the Indian structures being placed much closer together than those of the Whites or Métis (fig. 7). Indian homes, furthermore, do not have any "yards" or private territories

Table 2. Subsistence Activities at Old Crow, April 1968–Jan. 1969

Activity	People	Households	Locale	Season	Average Time Spent
Fishing					
Camp set up	13	10	Old Crow, Porcupine R.	May–Oct.	1–2 months
Nets tended from village	9	9	Porcupine R.	June–Oct.	8–10 hours/week
Caribou hunting[a]	14	10	Crow Mt., Porcupine R.	Aug.–Sept.	2–3 days
Moose hunting	10	9	upper Porcupine R.	Aug.–Sept.	3–7 days
Rabbit snaring	15	12	near town	all seasons	4–6 hours/week

SOURCE: Acheson 1977:155.

[a] Unusually low number of man-hours spent in fall hunt because of temporary shift in caribou migration routes.

699

Table 3. Trapping Activities, Old Crow Area, April 1968–Jan. 1969

Activity	People	House-holds	Average Time Spent
Trapping camp residence	3	3	2–3 months
Sporadic trapping	6	5	2–3 weeks
Staking muskrat houses	6	6	2–3 weeks
Muskrat camp residence	21	16	2–3 months
Muskratting by boat after breakup	5	4	2–3 weeks

SOURCE: Acheson 1977a:159.
Note: Minor children are excluded.

Table 4. Employment at Old Crow, June 1968–Jan. 1969

	Num-bers	Amount of time	Time of year
Permanent Jobs			
School janitor	4–5[a]	full	
Nursing station janitor	1[b]	half	
Nursing station, domestic	1	half	
Mission, domestic	1	half	
R.C.M.P. special constable	1	full	
Store owner	1	full	
Store clerk	1	full	
Postmaster	1	sporadic	
Newspaper correspondent	1	sporadic	
Airline agent	2[b]	sporadic	
Power plant operator	1[a]	sporadic	
Temporary Jobs			
Guide (paleontology)	1	full	6/15–8/15
Archeological excavation	2	full	6/15–8/31
Construction	2	full	6/15–7/15
River piloting	2	full	6/1–7/31
Assist physiological research	2	sporadic	2 weeks, Aug.
Assist physiological research	2	sporadic	1 week, Oct.
Guide (oil exploration)	1	sporadic	Aug.–Sept.
Unloading freight	5–6	sporadic	All months
Assist electrician	2	full	1 week, Dec.

SOURCE: Acheson 1977:167.
[a] 4 employed in summer, 5 in winter; one janitor also ran power plant.
[b] One man held 2 jobs, as airline agent and janitor.

surrounding them, while the recently built White establishments (school, nursing station, R.C.M.P. buildings) have low, symbolic fences surrounding their grounds. To a lesser extent, the Métis homes and older institutional structures have private outside territories, marked by patches of grass or paths on their perimeters.

A significant feature of modern village spatial organization is the ever-increasing structural and functional differentiation of buildings. Aboriginally, all aspects of living took place in and around the one type of structure, which served as living quarters, meeting place, and for every other function. In the modern village various activities tend to be confined to buildings or areas specialized for particular purposes—school, church, community hall, R.C.M.P. barracks, post office, store, freezer, baseball field. This specialization and differentiation in the way village space is utilized is being paralleled by increasing social differentiation and fragmentation. Winston Churchill's remark, "We shape our buildings, and they shape us," is very appropriate to Old Crow in the modern era.

Physical differentiation and specialization in space use can also be observed in the ways in which people divide up their houses. The use of interior space in houses gives a useful measure of relative acculturation. There is a continuum ranging from traditional, one-room, multiple-use cabins, with little furniture except stoves, storage boxes, mattresses on the floor, and perhaps a table, through multiple-roomed dwellings with kitchen, living room, wash room, and bedrooms, furnished with sofas, tables, chairs, bedsteads, and various large and small electrical appliances. In between, there are some families who hang curtains around sleeping or toilet areas, achieving some visual, though not auditory privacy, or who have a separate room where all the family sleeps, beds pushed side by side.

Government-built housing often causes social disruption and psychological discomfort, when a traditionally oriented older person or family is moved into a White-style cabin where functional areas are divided physically by walls and doors. Such discrepancies between housing style and life style markedly affect interaction patterns within the household, visiting behavior, and communication in general.

Political and Legal Affairs

The aboriginal political and legal system has almost entirely disappeared. The Indian population is enrolled in the official government Old Crow band, which elects a chief and three councilors. When the system was first instituted about 1930, the elected chiefs were the same kinds of individuals who would have been chiefs under aboriginal circumstances. They were generally respected, their advice was sought, and their opinions and suggestions were usually heeded. In the 1970s with increasing White intervention and the breakdown in Old Crow's isolation from the outside world, the elected chiefs and councilors have very little power and are apt to lack the respect of the majority of the people, except insofar as they exhibit skill in serving as cultural brokers between the Indian and the White worlds. Besides the government-imposed band organization, there is no political body representing the village as a whole. This means essentially that the White-status villagers

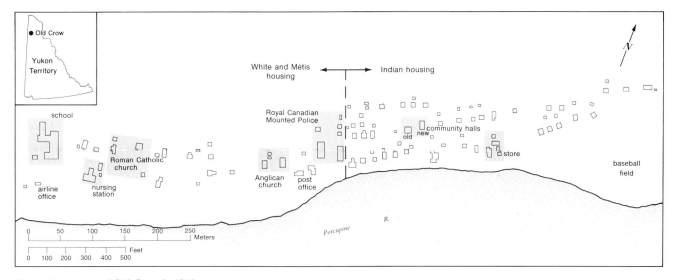

Fig. 7. Town plan of Old Crow in 1968.

have no formal local voice. All villagers do, however, have the right to vote in national and territorial elections.

Some traditional forms of social control are still in evidence, particularly general community pressure exerted through gossip, innuendo at public gatherings, joking, and admonitions by older kinsmen. The more extreme forms of social deviance are kept in check by the R.C.M.P. There has been one murder in recent years, a Métis man killing his cousin, and two cases of attempted suicide, one of them successful (both men were also Métis). Most common crimes stem in one way or another from drinking, the two most usual offenses being assault and "being drunk off the reservation." The latter charge is a contrived one, since Old Crow is not a reservation. Most physical conflicts that occur during drinking involve husbands and wives or young men, who often get into disputes over women. Stealing within the native community has been rare but by the 1970s appeared to be on the increase. People go to the R.C.M.P. quite readily in cases of assault or fighting but appear loathe to report stealing, even though they may get quite angry and talk to everyone about it, reasoning that the culprit (who is usually known) is probably poor and in need. Meat, fish, wood, and occasionally gasoline are the most usual items appropriated.

Religion

The Kutchin in the Yukon Territory were converted to Christianity primarily by the Anglican Archdeacon Robert McDonald during the late 1800s, although the first Anglican missionary to reach them was W.W. Kirkby, who visited Fort Yukon in 1862. The people of Old Crow are all Anglicans. Until recently, church activities were a major social focus, and for most older

people, they still are. Since the people of Old Crow built their first log church in 1926 there has been a minister, White or Indian, in residence almost continuously (fig. 8). Two Roman Catholic Oblate priests built a church in the early 1950s but never won any converts, focusing instead on working with the Indians in other ways. The one priest who remained developed a very successful ski-training program and club, which at one time brought a good deal of fame and notice to the town through national and international competition.

Most people in Old Crow are quite devout, attending church regularly; many pray and sing at home and speak sincerely of God and Jesus in their conversations. Although there are no longer any shamans (or "medicine men," as they are called in English locally), many elements of aboriginal belief and practice still exist, seemingly without much conflict with Christian beliefs. These include the use of various substances or "medicines" (for gambling luck, producing good dogs, attracting women), several taboos (such as those associated with menstruation), and a number of beliefs, fears, and practices surrounding death, ghosts, and evil creatures (particularly "bushmen") who continue to reside out in the bush.

Is Old Crow a Community?

From the point of view of settlement pattern and institutional services, Old Crow in the 1970s is a community. It has many of the kinds of structures and services found in any small Canadian or American town. The permanent residents of the town live in a world dominated by White institutions, though the number of Whites they have come in contact with is relatively small. The early relationship of Indians and Whites was

Fig. 8. Bishop Tom Greenwood, Rev. George Hamilton, and Indian deacons greeting parishioners at the Anglican Church at Old Crow. Photograph by Richard Harrington, 1960.

generally nondirective and nonintensive. Interaction was confined to the brief periods of town residence by Indians during summers and holidays. Furthermore, during the early phases of contact, most Whites lived much as the Indians did, hunting and cutting wood. Many married native women or became permanent residents. Since the 1950s there has been a growing trend for more specific and impersonalized relations between Indians and Whites. As each new White institution is introduced in the village, there is a new building, each larger and more modern. Each time, the building and its staff are further removed from the native people's way of life and standard of living.

If one approaches the question, "Is Old Crow a community?" with the concept of reference group in mind, then the answer must be no. Old Crow is not one community, but two—the White and the Indian—with the Métis occupying a hazy middle ground between. The Whites, stationed for one to three years in their comfortable buildings in "stranger town" (as the villagers sometimes refer to the "downtown" area) do not identify themselves as members of an Old Crow community, and the permanent residents do not consider them as such either.

The relationship among Indians, Métis, and Whites can be poignantly observed in one of the few surviving aboriginal observances—the institution of feasting. Aboriginally, the Crow Flats Kutchin practiced a form of the potlatch, whereby relatives of an important de-

ceased person assembled food and goods and invited members of another clan, preferably from distant bands, to partake. Other kinds of aboriginal feasting also existed, all of them apparently involving the elements of host group–guest group and competitive reciprocity between the two.

In Old Crow in the 1970s the most important feast takes place when a man kills a moose. If moose have been scarce (as they usually are) he gives the animal to a respected older person in the other clan to give a feast with. Ostensibly, the feast is for the "guest" clan, but in actual practice everyone in the village partakes. Speeches are made, and there is dancing (White square dances and jigs), sometimes lasting all night. White-status (Métis) villagers are never given moose to make feasts with, nor do they formally give any themselves (though they do share meat along less formal kinship lines).

The moose feast and similar gatherings and dances (such as Christmas, New Year's, Easter, and Dominion Day celebrations) are the modern equivalents of the potlatch, but the Whites, rather than the other clan, have become the "opposing group" for whom the feast is prepared, and to whom speeches are made. White people are placed at a head table in the community hall, using special plates and serving dishes set out especially for them. The Indians and Métis sit on benches around the sides and on the floor, using dishes brought from home and being served out of large, communal pots.

Whites new to the village, or simply passing through, are subtly coerced into the guest-recipient role, to the extent that someone (usually the school principal or head R.C.M.P. officer) usually feels obliged to offer a thank-you speech in response to the feast giver's traditional oratory, much as a leader from the receiving clan did aboriginally. For the Indians, and to a lesser extent the Métis (who are never put in the guest role), feasts and dances appear to be used as a way of reciprocating, actually of "getting back at," the donors whose largesse and services are at the same time desired and humiliating. Always on the receiving end, the Indians seize on these occasions as one of the few ways they have of giving, and, as in the past, the giving serves both as a reinforcer of in-group solidarity and as a means of expressing veiled hostility toward members of an opposing group.

Old Crow in the 1970s

The 1970s saw a great rise in political awareness and activism at Old Crow, beyond the symbolic level. A new generation of more educated and widely traveled younger people began to assume a larger role in local affairs. Legally, the Indians of Old Crow do not have a reservation and never signed a treaty ceding their

702

lands to Canada. Nonetheless, the government considers the area to be Crown lands, with the natives being permitted to hunt, fish, and trap; even those rights could be suspended. As the villagers have begun to realize their insecure legal and economic position, they have begun to initiate inquiries and actions to clarify their situation and to protect the land and their future. Prospects of a gas pipeline through the area served to accelerate this "politicization" (Stager 1974).

Unfortunately, like many Northern towns, Old Crow has a very inadequate economic base. With a decline in fur prices, trapping would hardly be a viable way of life, and if fur prices rose and stayed at attractive levels it is doubtful whether large numbers of people from Old Crow would return to the kind of trapping way of life they followed earlier in the twentieth century. The town exists largely through government support. If oil or gas resources are developed in the region, Old Crow could become a service town—perhaps a small boom town. This has elsewhere usually proved to be highly disruptive to native communities. Even if economic circumstances do not change appreciably, trends suggest that the town's inhabitants will tend to become increasingly reliant on outside resources, both material and social, and will continue to become further removed from the bush way of life.

Sources

Major ethnographic and archeological sources on the Kutchin provide important background information for an understanding of Old Crow village, as well as summaries of overall historical data and documents (Acheson 1977; McKennan 1965; Morlan 1973; Osgood 1936a; Slobodin 1962). The 1960s and 1970s saw a rise in studies centered on residents of particular Kutchin settlements. This trend is in line with the increasing sedentarization of the Kutchin and other Subarctic peoples. Most noteworthy of these are R.K. Nelson's (1973) study of Chalkyitsik, Alaska, and Krech's work at Fort McPherson, Northwest Territories (Krech 1974, 1978, 1978a) in addition to works on Old Crow.

While Old Crow is mentioned in a number of earlier works, the first anthropologist to publish specifically on the basis of fieldwork in the village was Leechman (1948, 1950, 1952, 1954). Balikci (1963, 1963a, 1968) spent the summer of 1961 in the village. Acheson's nine months of research in Old Crow in 1968–1969 resulted in a dissertation (1977) and several articles and papers (Welsh 1970, 1970a; Acheson 1977a, 1980). A geographer did a contracted study of Old Crow in 1973 as part of the Canadian government's effort to assess possible impacts of a gas pipeline in the area; his report (Stager 1974) includes summaries of demographic, economic, and attitudinal data drawn primarily from survey instruments and documents. Several short-term studies of the health and physical characteristics of Old Crow native residents have been carried out (Hildes, Wilt, and Parker 1965; Lewis et al. 1961; Marshall 1970). In the area of folklore, besides tales included in works cited above, there is a collection of Kutchin stories (Keim 1964) narrated by an Old Crow woman.

Old Crow has drawn a good deal of notice from the popular press; daily newspapers and news magazines have carried articles on the village with some regularity. Josie's (1966) *Whitehorse Star* town news columns were published, and she and the town were the subject of an article in *Life* magazine (Hamblin 1965). L. Harrington's (1961) photo-essay is a further example of this kind of popular interest.

Minto, Alaska

WALLACE M. OLSON

Most of the residents of the village of Minto are descendants of the Lower Tanana Athapaskans who lived along the many clearwater streams that flow into the Tanana River. The original native settlement of Minto (now Old Minto) was located on the Tanana River approximately 30 miles downstream from Nenana. In 1971 it was relocated as New Minto to a site on the Tolovana River on the western side of the Minto flats (fig. 1). Other Lower Tanana Indians live either in Nenana or in the city of Fairbanks.

Aboriginally, the Lower Tanana people followed the general subsistence pattern of other Subarctic Athapaskans. They hunted caribou and moose in the hills during the winter months and fished and hunted waterfowl in the summer. Historically, small bands, averaging perhaps 100 persons or less, exploited the drainages of the Salcha, Chena, Wood, Nenana, Tolovana, Chatanika, and Toklat rivers, and, at some periods, the Kantishna. At times each band would subdivide into smaller groups depending on the availability of food supplies so that there were many variations in the actual size and composition of groups through the seasons.

Prior to contact, the ancestors of the present-day residents of Minto intermarried with other Indians along the length of the Tanana River. There does not seem to have been any set pattern for residence after marriage. Accounts of early times indicate that postmarital residence (after perhaps initial uxorilocality) might be either uxorilocal or virilocal. The Tanana Indians had exogamous matrilineal descent groups, and this system appears to have influenced the selection of marriage partners and cooperation in feuds and warfare. Beyond the kinship bond, many men had trading partners in other bands whom they considered "as close as blood brothers." These partnerships allowed them to interact with other bands in extended bonds of alliances.

Within the contact era, intermarriage with other bands continued, and, as small settlements died out, the people moved into Nenana, Minto, or Fairbanks. Hence, the residents of Minto are actually a composite of peoples from throughout the area. For many years, families have moved into Minto temporarily and then moved elsewhere. This accounts for the fact that many names that appear in the early census reports are no longer found in the village. Also, some individuals who were born and raised for a few years in Minto still consider it their home although neither they nor their families have lived there for many years.

Until fairly recent times, there were only a few marriages between Minto people and Whites. There were some common-law marriages or extra-legal unions, usually between White men and Indian women. The children of such unions were considered Minto people. Since 1950 there has been an increase in the number of marriages between Minto women and White men. Marriages between Minto men and White women have been very rare.

History

Early Contact, 1850–1900

The Tanana Indians were one of the last groups of the Subarctic to have contact with Whites in their own land. The Russian-American Company established a redoubt on the Yukon River near the present village of Nulato in 1835. Upstream, in the Yukon flats, the Hudson's Bay Company founded Fort Yukon in 1847. The Minto people could either portage over the hills to the north to reach Fort Yukon or go down the Tanana and Yukon rivers to Nulato. Trade was also carried on at the confluence of the two rivers near the site of the present

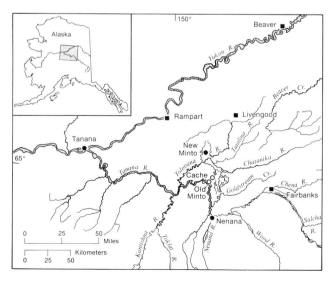

Fig. 1. Minto and surrounding area.

704

village of Tanana. But as late as 1868, Dall (1898:107) reported that no Whites had yet been into Lower Tanana territory.

During this early stage of contact, in exchange for furs the Tanana people acquired some trade goods, such as firearms, traps, and other metal tools. Apparently, the Tanana Indians traveled to the trading posts to obtain goods and then returned to the relative isolation of their own territory. Several early reports refer to them as "warlike," and Whites were warned to stay out of their territory.

Lt. Henry T. Allen descended the Tanana River in 1885 and saw only a few Indians along the entire route. The natives were evidently still following the old subsistence pattern and were not on the large Tanana River, but rather fishing the small, clearwater streams. A few early prospectors ventured into the area prior to 1900, but it was not until the discovery of gold (and the consequent founding of Fairbanks) in 1902 that any large number of Whites began to settle along the lower Tanana.

1900–1915

The years between 1900 and 1915 were a period of intensive contact in which many major changes took place in the lives of the Lower Tanana Indians.

With the discovery of gold, riverboats began to make regular trips from Saint Michael at the mouth of the Yukon to the new town of Fairbanks. Trading posts and small settlements grew up along the major rivers. Small mining camps sprang up along the eastern and northern boundaries of the Minto region. In 1902 a telegraph line was constructed from Fairbanks along the length of the Tanana River to Tanana (sometimes known as Fort Gibbons). The station along the way that was called Minto was actually several miles upstream from where the village of Minto came to be located. The telegraph line was kept in operation until 1918.

• ECONOMY About the turn of the century the fish wheel was introduced into the interior of Alaska. It brought great changes in the native way of life. Prior to its introduction, the people fished principally on the smaller streams with weirs and nets. The new invention allowed them to fish the Tanana and other large rivers successfully and provided a surplus of fish both for human consumption and to feed large dog teams. With large teams, they increased their winter trapping.

The growth of the trapping industry accounted for an increase in the traditional potlatch. Before contact, the people had midwinter celebrations that could best be termed "gatherings" and a form of mortuary potlatch. But with the increased availability of trade goods and high fur prices, thousands of dollars worth of goods were distributed at the potlatch. One of the largest

celebrations ever held was in the winter of 1915 when natives from as far away as Tanana and Fairbanks came to join the festivities in Nenana.

• MINTO BAND During the first decades of the twentieth century, the bands headquartered on the Wood, Toklat, and Kantishna rivers relocated in Nenana or Fairbanks. Some of their members married into the Minto band.

The local territory of the Minto band—generally the flats and lake area—remained relatively untouched through the gold rush days. A few prospectors searched the hills for gold, but with little success; however, eventually gold mining operations near Fairbanks did affect the fishing and trapping in the flats. The washout from mining operations on the Chatanika and the Little Goldstream was carried out into the flats where it polluted the water and reduced the fishing.

During this period the main settlement of the Minto people appears to have been in the center of the flats at Cache. A few elevated caches still mark this site, with a small cemetery upstream on the Little Goldstream. Here the people lived in canvas tents. They utilized the site both for summer fishing and winter trapping and hunted the surrounding hills to the north, east, and west. In 1915 a few families constructed log cabins on the banks of the Tanana at the site today known as Old Minto.

• NENANA In 1915 the federal government began the construction of the Alaska Railroad, and a settlement grew up at the present site of the town of Nenana. The completion of the railroad came in 1923 when the bridge spanning the Tanana River at Nenana was completed, joining Fairbanks with the coastal port of Seward. Nenana had a post office, a general store, a bank, and even a newspaper.

Brooks (1903:467) reported that in 1902 there was just a small settlement of log cabins at Nenana. In 1903 Jimmy Duke opened a trading post there. Saint Mark's Episcopal Mission began operations a couple of years later. The church and a "native section" were about one-half mile upstream from the main part of town. To sell their furs and obtain trade goods, the Minto people began to travel to Nenana, and eventually some established homes there. Both Chief Thomas from the Wood River and Chief Charlie from Minto had residences in Nenana at one time. The city attracted Indians from all over the interior as it became the center for all river freighting in Alaska. Some of the Minto men worked on the riverboats and traveled the Tanana and Yukon rivers. The modern town of Nenana contains natives whose forefathers came from Fort Yukon, Beaver, Tanana, and Cantwell. Even some Eskimos settled in the town after finding employment with either the riverboats or the railroad. With the growth of Nenana as a trade center came many of the problems associated with sudden, intensive contact. Excessive drinking became a serious problem. In fact, the mission officials considered moving the mission to some other place to protect the Indians from what the officials considered harmful contact situations.

One of the most influential contact agents of the 1900–1915 period was the Episcopal mission at Nenana (fig. 2). A few of the Minto children, mainly boys, attended school there. Most of them completed only a few grades and then returned to their band to hunt, fish, and trap. In spite of the fact that they only spent a year or so at the school, for many it was a period of intensive contact with Whites. They learned the basic skills of reading and writing, but they also learned about life in a frontier town. There were some unfortunate consequences. The discipline at the school was strict in comparison to Indian patterns. Oftentimes the young boys had to hunt for food or collect firewood to help provide the basic necessities for the mission. Looking back in later years, they felt that they had been "used" or exploited.

• THE QUESTION OF RESERVATIONS In 1915 a meeting was called in Fairbanks to discuss the possibility of establishing reservations for the Indians. Chiefs from the lower portions of the Tanana River met with government officials ("Intercultural Relations and Culture Change in the Alaska Plateau," fig. 9, this vol.). When the conditions of reservation life were explained and descriptions of reservations in other parts of the country were given, the chiefs decided against such a life for their people. It was not that they were not interested in the land, but they felt that there would be plenty of room for everyone. At this time the interior of Alaska was in a "boom" period. Gold mining was profitable, trapping and hunting were still very productive, and there were only a few White men living outside the major settlements or gold fields.

U. of Alaska Arch., Fairbanks: Charles Bunnell Coll., 58-1026-2296.

Fig. 2. St. Mark's Mission under construction at Nenana. Minto children went to school here. Photographed about 1906–1908.

1915–1935

The years from 1915 until the 1930s brought few major events or dramatic changes to the Minto people. During the 1920s and early 1930s, the price of fur was very good, and there were still enough moose and caribou, along with fish and waterfowl, to provide the people with an adequate supply of country game for basic subsistence.

One brief but serious threat was the widespread influenza epidemic that struck Nenana in 1920. Many people, both Indian and White, died in the epidemic. Elderly Minto people recall being advised to leave the town of Nenana to avoid the illness. Many did move back to the old sites, and only a few of the Minto people died from the disease. It was soon after this that many of the influential leaders passed away.

The 1920s witnessed the decline of Nenana as the hub of the interior. The Alaska Railroad moved its headquarters out of Nenana, and river freighting remained the only local industry.

As the city of Nenana decreased in importance, the village of Minto grew. Within a few years of its founding in 1915, every family of the Minto band had a cabin in the new village. There were also a few other smaller settlements, usually one or two houses, at other points along the river, and a trading post was located at the mouth of the Tolovana River (fig. 3). Johnny Campbell, a White prospector, purchased a small roadhouse just below Minto and operated a trading post there for many years.

In 1929 Rev. Arthur Wright went to Nenana as a deacon for the Episcopal Church. For a period of time he lived in Minto and attempted to conduct an elementary school there, but only a few students attended. His mother was an Indian, his father a White miner; Wright married a White woman from the mission. After a few years, he moved upriver. Not until 1954 did the village again have a full-time missionary. Occasionally a missionary would visit the village, but there was very little formal training in Christianity.

1935–1955

The 20 years bracketing World War II brought the Minto people into new and more intensive involvements with American Whites and their institutions.

In the mid-1930s the caribou herds began to diminish, and trapping declined as a source of income. Although hunting and trapping continued as important economic activities into the 1940s, the Minto people began to consume more store-bought food, and many maintained gardens. They also began to depend more and more on Euro-American tools and equipment. Though some individuals had owned power boats before, it was during these later years that the outboard motor became common.

Fig. 3. Tolovana fishing camp and site of trading post, post office, and telegraph station established in 1903. Photographed July 1919.

In 1938 a few of the old people in Minto began to receive old-age assistance and the number of recipients increased over the years. The early payments ranged from $12 to $15 a month, less than $200 a year.

The village began to operate under a village council system in 1937. It received its charter from the Department of the Interior in 1939. In 1937 a federal school was opened in Minto. Only from this point onward is there an accurate census for the region. The school report of January 1, 1938 (Anonymous 1937–1940, 1:"p") recorded a total of 15 Whites and 168 Natives for Minto and the immediate vicinity.

The school teachers kept a record of annual events. Some indications of introduced change can be seen in the mention of large celebrations held on Lincoln's birthday, Halloween, Thanksgiving, and Christmas. It was apparently during this period that the use of the native Athapaskan language began to decline. Hardly any children born after 1940 became fluent speakers of the language.

In 1953, a White woman lived in the village working on behalf of the Episcopal Church, and one year later a full-time missionary was sent to replace her. The Assembly of God also sent a full-time missionary to Minto in the same year. Between the school and the missions, the villagers were brought into daily, face-to-face contact with agents of change within their own territory and settlement.

During World War II four of the Minto men went into service. American soldiers were stationed at Nenana and at Tanana. Although the war did not affect the Minto people directly, except for rationing, the influx of the military into the region gave them even broader exposure to Euro-Americans. Increased contact with Fairbanks, via Nenana, followed when Fairbanks grew to be a major Alaskan city in World War II. After World War II a large airstrip was constructed at Minto and regular air service provided.

Following World War II, the young people began to continue their education through the secondary level. To do so, they had to leave the village and spend the school months at Mount Edgecumbe near Sitka, Alaska, or go to Chemawa in Oregon. Some went as far away as Chilocco, Oklahoma.

Indian-Government Relations, 1950–1971

In the 1950s and 1960s the village came into more frequent contact with government agencies such as the Public Health Service, Bureau of Indian Affairs, Alaska Rural Development, and the Office of Economic Opportunity. The form of communication between the agencies and the people became the source of many problems over the years for all involved. As in many other places in the Subarctic, the agency representatives arrived in the village, spent a few hours or a day at the most, and then left. Often a meeting was called, matters briefly discussed, and the people asked to make a decision. After the choice was made and the agency people left, there were often questions and second thoughts, but no means of clarifying the issues. Correspondence was often equally confusing.

There are indications that from the earliest contacts the Minto people resented the intrusion of outsiders into their traditional hunting and fishing areas. The reaction to White intrusion became more overt in the 1930s and increased as more and more Euro-Americans from Fairbanks and other places began to build hunting camps on the Minto flats. The Minto people had no power to restrain the Whites until the land became a legal issue.

With statehood achieved in 1958, Alaska began to select federal lands to be transferred to state ownership. In response, the Minto as well as other native groups challenged this action of the state of Alaska and began to push for recognition of their aboriginal territorial lands. By the 1960s native political organizations had formed in order to obtain settlement of native land claims for which they could show "use and occupancy" since time immemorial. The Minto people were convinced that they had to present a united front if they were to succeed in the claims contest. The villagers engaged an attorney to represent them and began to press for legal action. The land claims issue solidified the village in opposition to the White government, and the people of Minto became leaders in the interior in the fight for a land settlement. Settlement came in December 1971 with the Alaska Native Claims Settlement Act, which included a cash award of nearly one billion dollars for all legally defined natives of Alaska and the right to select 40 million acres of land. Each village, and each of the 12 regional corporations throughout the state, began the process of selecting the lands they wished to retain. Minto joined with other interior Athapaskan settlements to form their own regional corporation.

It is almost impossible to understand the role of the Minto people in these events without considering the character of Chief Peter John (fig. 4). In response to the land claims issue in the 1960s, Chief John developed sophisticated skills and techniques for dealing with government agencies. As both the officially elected chief and the charismatic leader, he captured the leadership and the confidence of the Minto people as far as dealing with government agencies was concerned. He was recognized by the villagers as one of the most knowledgeable persons regarding the old culture and local history. He used this background to great advantage in dealing with various officials. When the question of "use and

708

Tundra Times, Anchorage, Alaska.
Fig. 4. Chief Peter John testifying before a congressional committee on land claims in Anchorage, Feb. 1968.

occupancy" of the land arose, Chief John was able to provide the Athapaskan name for every hill, creek, burial place, and old settlement site, to the consternation of those questioning the Minto claim. Although there have been intravillage disputes, Peter John's leadership of the group in regard to the government was unchallenged.

New Minto

Another matter, peculiar to the village itself, that united the people was the need to relocate the village. Since its founding in 1915, the Tanana River had eroded away a major portion of the original village, and several times the inhabitants had been forced to move their houses farther back from the original river frontage. Over a period of 50 years, the river had eroded nearly 150 feet of the riverfront. By the mid-1960s, the village was inundated almost every summer. By 1967, it was evident to the people that they had to move to an entirely new location. After long discussions with government officials, it was decided to construct a new village at an old occupation site at the north fork of the Tolovana River.

Work began on the new village in 1969 and was nearly completed by the end of 1971 with some work remaining on the road and airstrip. Final costs for this relocation have been estimated at nearly one million dollars (Wally Craig, personal communication 1974).

The new village sits on a high ridge overlooking a clearwater stream at the northern end of the Minto flats. The remains of a few cabins built nearby in the 1920s can still be seen. The new site is about 25 air miles north of Old Minto, and 60 miles north and west of Fairbanks. It is also accessible by road via the Elliott Highway, but by road it is approximately 120 miles to Fairbanks. The road is not paved nor is it maintained in the winter months. However, hunters from Fairbanks can drive to New Minto, leave their cars at the village, and take boats out into the flats for hunting and fishing. Hence, there has been an increase of White utilization of the flats. Several Minto residents have purchased automobiles and drive to Fairbanks in the summer months.

In the winter months, foodstuffs are flown into the village from Fairbanks. In the summer months many families obtain rides to and from Fairbanks and do their shopping in the city. One individual has attempted to open a general store in the village.

The new village is composed of 41 homes, all frame houses approximately 24 by 20 feet in size. They are mounted on pilings above the ground; a few of the residents have enclosed the lower portion for added insulation. About half the people heat their houses with local firewood while others heat with stove oil. All the homes have running water and sewer systems, but the occupants must install their own water heaters if they want hot water. A majority of the houses are partitioned into a living room–dining room–cooking area with one bedroom and a bath. Others have reduced the living room area and made two bedrooms. Half the houses were built through the Alaska State Housing Authority, which is both a loan and grant agency. Residents of these houses must pay back part of the loan in monthly installments. The remainder of the houses were built by the Bureau of Indian Affairs under a simple grant system, and the occupants of these do not make any return payments. There is a combination well-house and power plant, and electricity is metered to each home. Nearly all the residents have electric appliances including freezers, television sets, irons, and toasters.

Even prior to relocation, the villagers had moved increasingly to a wage or money economy and away from old subsistence patterns. For example, with introduction of the snowmobile, the number of dog teams was drastically reduced. Fishing for salmon for dog feed decreased accordingly. At the new location, fish wheels are no longer used since they are rather ineffective on clearwater streams. A few older couples spend part of the summer fishing on the Yukon, but in general fishing has decreased.

Relocation has altered patterns of social interaction. The village is composed of two parallel lines of houses facing each other and is nearly one-eighth mile in length. Those living at one end of the village tend to associate with their immediate neighbors rather than those at a distance. Prior to relocation and a dependable source of electric power, game killed during the summer months had to be consumed, dried, or shared with others; and there was a great deal of sharing (fig. 5). In the 1970s most of the residents have freezers and keep their summer catch for their own winter use.

The Christmas season, however, still evokes a period of traditional sharing and community interaction. Minto people, even if they are living in Fairbanks or Anchorage, make an attempt to return to the village for the Christmas season, which harkens back to the traditional midwinter gathering in aboriginal times. Even young people away at school try to find a means to be home for a few days over this period. It appears to be a time in which village identity as "Minto people" is strengthened.

Another occasion when village identity is renewed is after the death of a member of the village. Approximately a year after a person dies, there is a potlatch with a large dinner and gift giving (fig. 6). Sometimes these activities continue throughout several days and people as far away as Tanacross may be invited to attend. The members of the immediate families of the deceased—irrespective of descent group affiliation—will often join together to host the ceremony. Gifts are given to all guests and all adults from the village.

The importance of the clan system has decreased to the point where it no longer even influences marriage patterns. Matrilineal clan identity has been replaced by village identity vis-à-vis any outside group. This is manifested during the Eskimo-Indian Olympics in Fairbanks. Beginning in the early 1960s the Minto partic-

Fig. 5. The sharing of first salmon. Photograph by Wallace M. Olson at Old Minto, 1967.

Tundra Times, Anchorage, Alaska.
Fig. 6. Matthew and Dorothy Titus at a potlatch feast. Necklaces and headband are of dentalia. Photograph by Jennifer Ortiz, 1970s.

River Times, Fairbanks, Alaska.
Fig. 7. Minto dancer Neal Charlie, son of Moses and Bessie Charlie, in modern dance dress. His use of gloves while dancing may be a personal innovation. Photographed possibly at Eskimo-Indian Olympics, 1970.

ipants—especially the dancers—have come with traditional matching costumes and take pride that they have won many awards as the "Minto Dancers" (fig. 7).

On a broader cultural level, there has been an effort in Minto to revive the Athapaskan language among the young people. Some are studying the language under the guidance of an older man in the village. The adults are encouraging this effort since they know that if the language dies, no one will know or understand the songs and dances that have become their hallmark. Arts and crafts, such as basketmaking and skin sewing, have continued on a limited basis.

The village experienced a Christian religious revival beginning in the late 1960s. A former Episcopal missionary through his studies became interested in the phenomenon of "speaking in tongues" and soon several village people were discovered to possess that gift. Others have advocated a return to a fundamentalist form of Christianity as a solution to excessive drinking and other social problems. Many of the young people have become active in church activities.

Relationship to the Urban Center

The ties to Nenana have weakened in proportion as the people have come to rely on goods and services from Fairbanks. There is almost daily commerce between New Minto and Fairbanks throughout the year. On some days as many as three or four flights are made between the two points. On the average, nearly one person from every family at Minto is in Fairbanks at least once a month. They go in to shop, to see the doctor, to procure food stamps. Almost every family has at least one close relative residing in Fairbanks.

When people from the village travel to Fairbanks, they usually find a relative in town who has an apartment and stay there temporarily.

In the city Minto families live on a very low economic scale. Many of the houses or apartments they rent are substandard. Most Minto people have no special skills and are employed in manual labor. Sometimes the men will lose or quit their jobs; on these occasions, they often return to Minto until a new job comes along.

The Minto children in the 1970s all go on to high school, usually in Fairbanks or Anchorage. A handful of young people attend the University of Alaska at Fairbanks. Some of the young men have served in the military and like to go to Fairbanks for the excitement and social life. In 1974 about half of those between 20 and 30 years of age lived in the village; the others lived in Fairbanks or other Alaskan towns. Only a couple of the young men actively trapped in the early 1970s.

Since first contact, the Lower Tanana people have gone to trade centers, but historically they have been able to a substantial degree to withdraw from intensive

Fig. 8. "Johnny" David, age 13, son of Jonathan David of Minto, dancing in a contest. He wears a smock decorated with feathers and beads. Photographed in 1969.

contact. In spite of the presence of missionaries, school teachers, and others, the village remained comparatively isolated. The issue of land claims and increased intrusion into their traditional area amplified their sense of village identity in the face of outsiders (Olson 1968). In spite of the relocation, there is still a strong sense of community. However, the highway provides direct access between Fairbanks and New Minto, and more and more outsiders are coming into the village in the summer months. The opportunities to earn a cash income at the new site are limited, and many young people are beginning to live and work in Fairbanks and return to Minto only to visit. The former self deter mined isolation of the Minto people appears to be weakening under the pressure of intrusions and lures from beyond the village.

Sources

The sources available on the Lower Tanana Indians (including Minto) are principally early historical articles and observations in newspapers, church publications, and a few scholarly journals. There are a few unpublished descriptions such as Drane's (1928) manuscripts compiled during the years 1915 to 1924 when he was an Episcopalian missionary to the area. Works by McKennan (1959, 1965), Loyens (1966), and Osgood (1936a, 1971) concerning Alaskan Athapaskans provide useful comparisons and insights. Hosley (1966a) did a study of acculturation and factionalism in a neighboring Alaskan community, which is useful for an understanding of modernization in interior Alaska. Olson (1968) studied historical influences on group identity.

In 1973, there were still a number of elderly Indians in the Tanana Valley who could recall much of the history of contact. They are perhaps the most valuable resource for research.

Modern Subarctic Indians and Métis

JOHN J. HONIGMANN

Without having adopted an overall White style of life, the Indians and Métis of the Subarctic have come to use a number of modern appliances and energy resources of Euro-American technology. The numbers and proportion of native people engaged in wage employment have steadily increased, and their social roles have become more differentiated. Family form, recreation, and patterns of associational and recreational life correspond, at least superficially, to analogous forms in Euro-American mainstream society, both Canadian and United States variants. However, in many respects Subarctic Indian culture of the 1970s is Euro-Americanized only to a very partial extent, especially so in the realm of knowledge and ideas, and the distribution of such traits among the native people is very uneven.

A major share of this chapter will be devoted to Canada, for which more information on Indians and Métis was available to the author than for Alaska.

Ethnically plural and culturally heterogenous communities were created the moment when the first local agents of the fur companies, churches, and governments settled in Alaska and northern Canada (see "Intercultural Relations and Cultural Change in the Alaska Plateau," "Intercultural Relations and Cultural Change in the Shield and Mackenzie Borderlands," "Intercultural Relations and Cultural Change in the Cordillera"). In central and northwestern Canada, European workers in the fur trade who married Indian wives furthered pluralism by producing a new ethnic group, the Métis. Although native people predominated numerically over nonnatives in those communities, the Euro-American population in colonial fashion controlled economic, ideological, and legal power.

The Subarctic remained a frontier area compared to other parts of Canada and the United States. When the fur-trade period drew to a close with the end of World War II, few jobs existed apart from trapping to provide cash incomes. Few communities possessed local schools. Most native people had poor access to doctors and hospitals, though unscheduled air transportation helped in emergency cases. And most native people had very limited communication with the mainstream society (see Honigmann 1960a, 1971).

Beginning in World War II, the isolation of the North began to recede. Winter tractor trails and all-weather roads crept northward (Hewetson 1947). Scheduled air service reduced passenger and freight rates. Enormous amounts of equipment and thousands of persons moved north as military installations went up and as oil and minerals became the raw materials primarily sought in the region by metropolitan society. The Hudson's Bay Company and Canadian provincial governments attempted to increase the productivity of trapping by replenishing muskrat, mink, and beaver resources. However, fur-enhancement programs achieved less than was expected, for they coincided with a postwar drop in fur prices that ushered in the slow decline of trapping as an industry.

More far-reaching for many people were the changes in native life that resulted from government decisions of the 1940s and 1950s to establish local day schools and community health stations, to inaugurate housing programs, and, in Canada, to introduce the family allowances. Northern settlements became sites of prodigious capital investment as hospitals, schools, radar sites and other defense installations, and administrative headquarters were located in or near them (Fried 1964; J.G.E. Smith 1978). New towns, like Schefferville, Quebec, and Inuvik, Northwest Territories, mushroomed in a few years' time.

The spurt of postwar military and other construction begun in the 1950s partly alleviated the problem brought on by the economic collapse of trapping by offering at least temporary wage employment to some Indians and Métis. Quitting the "bush" settlements, many Indian families moved, or were moved, into Schefferville, Great Whale River, Churchill, Inuvik, Whitehorse, and other expanding towns where steady employment beckoned or where persons with chronic ailments could be near hospitals. Thus, low-key urbanization began to characterize areas of the Subarctic (Liebow and Trudeau 1962; Fried 1964; Rogers and Trudeau 1969–1972, 3; La Rusic 1970). Women and children increasingly abandoned the annual pattern of mobility to and from the trapline. Shedding a number of their economic roles, they remained in the settlements while husbands and older sons went off to visit the traps (Honigmann 1951; Rogers 1963; Pearson 1971:258–259).

Income

Since World War II, wage labor and government subsidies (also called transfer payments, see Usher 1971, 2:101–102), including old-age security and assistance, disabled persons' allowances, social assistance or "welfare," and in Canada family allowances, have increasingly replaced trapping as the main sources of personal and family income. Wage labor and social subsidies have created a greater socioeconomic integration into metropolitan society.

Wage Labor

The amount and type of wage labor available in a Subarctic locality depend on the industries that are present, the amount of capital invested by government or private enterprise in those industries, and the qualifications set for employment. Nonnatives control the basic factors governing native employment and make the basic decisions in far-off capital cities. They decide where to locate industries or build government installations and when to terminate such facilities.

The great majority of jobs for native men and women lie in service industries covering tasks such as maintaining streets, roads, and buildings; driving taxis and other vehicles; cleaning public buildings; doing housework in private homes; serving as nurses' and teachers' aides; and performing clerical and administrative roles. On a part-time basis there are jobs fighting forest fires; guiding tourists, fishermen, and hunters; and babysitting (Hawthorn 1966–1967, 1:148–159). Forestry, mining, and commercial fishing are the chief industries employing Indians in parts of Alaska, at Great Slave Lake, and in northern Ontario (Hippler 1972b:54–60; Radojicic 1969:93ff.; Rogers 1972). A very few Indians or Métis work in manufacturing industries, such as sawmills, power plants, smelting, pulp making (in northern Quebec and Ontario), and government-sponsored workshops for fur garments in Aklavik (see Lotz 1962; Bissett 1967:483). Others work at home supplying hand-crafted items like mittens, moccasins, and models of canoes and cradleboards to local resale outlets.

Trapping

Trapping by the 1970s varied considerably in economic importance from one place to another. In a large town like Inuvik, only four Indian family heads (21% of all Indian family heads) devoted themselves to trapping in 1967; among Métis, eight male and one female family heads were committed to that occupation (24% of all Métis family heads) (Honigmann and Honigmann 1970:244).* However, in the Fort Liard Indian band,

*Inuvik's Métis (called "Other Natives" by Honigmann and Honigmann 1970:11–12, 259) numbered 318 persons; in addition to persons of Indian-White extraction they included 8 married persons of Indian-Eskimo ancestry and 29 school-age children of part-Eskimo descent.

living in an area where fur resources were underexploited, 44 out of 55 households trapped in 1967–1968. Yet, 35 of those households also managed to participate in wage labor (Higgins 1969:133ff.). The Tanaina of Lake Iliamna, Alaska, have similarly succeeded in combining winter trapping with summer jobs and commercial fishing (Hippler 1972b:54–60).

Social Legislation and Social Assistance

Studies completed in Canada in 1947 (Honigmann 1961) showed that by that decade an Indian band had come to derive an important proportion of its income from government sources. Family allowances (in Canada) and other subsidies became increasingly vital as the cost of living rose and the economic value of furs declined (see Usher 1971, 2:103). Even when some food was obtained through hunting and fishing, family allowances provided a substantial part of many Canadian Indian families' living expenses (table 1; for comparable information see Bock 1966:45–47; Helm 1961:36–37; Honigmann 1961:101–114, 128; Honigmann and Honigmann 1970:75–76; Rogers 1962:C76).

Unlike family allowances, which are paid to all eligible persons regardless of other income, social assistance is provided only in circumstances of need. Some older native people have come to regard social assistance as a right, though they recognize that securing it from local government agents requires considerable effort and perseverance. Other Indians and Métis share the views, held frequently by middle-class Whites, that social assistance is shameful and that providing it too readily makes people less willing to work.

Material Culture

Native people are able to incorporate modern appurtenances in their lives partly through the money they

Table 1. Comparative Sources of Income: Fort Liard Indians and Osnaburgh House Indians

Income Source	Fort Liard, N.W.T. 1967–1968	Osnaburgh House, Ont. 1965–1966
Wage labor	32.2%	12.4%
Trapping	28.0	15.2
Commercial fishing		23.0
Sale of handicrafts	1.4	
Social legislation (e.g., family allowances, old-age security)	28.0	18.6
Social assistance	6.6	29.2
Annuity payments		1.4
	96.2%	99.8%

SOURCES: Higgins 1969:181, 182; Charles Bishop, personal communication 1970.

receive in wages or subsidies and partly through the readiness of governments and private corporations to provide materials for new housing, to build electrical generators and telephone exchanges, and to provide other installations requiring heavy capital. Alaskan native people have formed cooperatives to secure electric power (Cruikshank 1972).

Some items of industrial technology are ubiquitous. Every person wears some modern clothing; every Northern home contains items like a clock, table, chairs, usually a radio; every family serves commercially packaged foods. Other items of technological modernity—refrigerators, freezers, televisions, automobiles, snowmobiles, telephones, and electricity—were more spottily distributed in the 1970s, but their ownership was growing. To be sure, the cultural configuration in which these items are used remains distinctive and not identical with North American middle-class culture. Indians and Métis live amidst the material apparatus of the larger society, but they have their own norms governing buying and their own ways of using the products of modern technology (Chance 1969:22). Furniture and houses show signs of hard wear; men's suits and women's dresses may be worn with moccasins; and meals, as often as possible, include locally caught game and fish. There are Indians and Métis whose values lead them to fully endorse mainstream cultural norms, but they are often constrained in emulating the middle-class culture pattern by low incomes or by the social and economic expectations of their relatives and neighbors who hold different values.

Social Structure

Starting with the first trading posts and missions but increasing greatly with the coming of wage labor and the development of towns has been the agglomeration of Indians belonging to different bands and linguistic groups. The result, best seen in towns, is that people live, work, and attend school with companions of diverse ethnic extraction and backgrounds. Linguistic and other boundary-maintaining mechanisms limit interpersonal access, especially between adults, and are particularly effective where Indians or Métis and Eskimo have been brought together. Widely divergent cultural traditions and experience also create strong barriers to interaction between Indians or Métis and nonnatives (mostly Whites), though marriage does occur between those ethnic groups (Fried 1964:58).

A paramount problem facing Indians and Métis in pluralized communities is how to cope effectively with nonnatives, who hold controlling power with respect to housing, welfare, and jobs as well as in school and in the law. Métis as a group possess more favorable chances of employment and success in school than Indians, probably because their early home life has better equipped them for meeting the normative expectations of Euro-American society (Honigmann and Honigmann 1970; Wolforth 1971:114–115). Competition between Indians, Métis, and other ethnic groups over housing and jobs exists to some degree, but it remains largely covert and expressed mainly as individual resentment.

Social Differentiation

The pattern of social roles has partially shifted from multifaceted roles, executed principally in kin groups, to specialized roles carried out in nonkin social settings. Such a role change constitutes a familiar adjunct of modern life; in the North it has emerged as involvement with Euro-American institutions has increased. Formerly each household manufactured its own capital equipment, secured a major part of its food, provided housing and transportation, and created a substantial part of its recreation. With the fur trade, the family became an income-producing group, but members did not at once shed their many-faceted functions. The responsibilities of spouses to one another and of parents to children shrank only when key activities formerly carried out in the household came to be done in shops, schools, hospitals, restaurants, taverns, or on playing fields and wherever people congregate, directed by nonnative schoolteachers, nurses, and other specialists who were induced to go North because of their skills. Consequently, natives have become significantly involved with nonnatives whom they meet primarily in highly segmental relations (Slobodin 1966:142). Natives and nonnatives tend to know only fractional parts of each other, whereas Indians and Métis in a community know each other much more totally.

Indian-Métis populations in Subarctic communities of the 1960s revealed no clear-cut evidence of being stratified in socially ranked classes that pursued diverse economic interests, maintained social distance from one another, and followed different styles of life. Naturally, these native people ranked one another according to various criteria, and observers noted economic differences between families, but whether social classes will appear on the basis of such differences is not predictable.

Political Organization

Historically, Subarctic Indians have been slow to undertake assertive political action on an organized basis. Until the 1960s, the various interest groups in which Indians and Métis participated—band meetings, trappers councils, community councils—were essentially creations of Canadian and American government divisions and often dominated by them. Elected chiefs and councilors were allocated extremely restricted responsibility and decision-making powers (Honigmann

1966; Kupferer 1966; Preston 1969-1972, 3; Robbins 1967).

The 1960s saw the development or expansion of native-created political interest groups such as the Native Brotherhoods of Alaska and Canada, COPE (Committee for Original Peoples' Entitlement) of the Northwest Territories, and the Métis Associations of the Canadian provinces and territories (Patterson 1972:172). Often guided by young bicultural natives, these groups have carried out emphatic and concerted action to seek redress in matters relating to land use and occupancy. Claims to the continuing viability of aboriginal title to land have been advanced in the courts or over the negotiation table in Alaska, British Columbia, Yukon Territory, and Northwest Territories—political divisions in which the resident Indians had not signed treaties, or in which the validity and good faith of the treaties have been effectively called into question. Two results have been the Alaska Native Claims Settlement Act of 1971 and the imposition in 1973 of a caveat on land use and development by Whites in the Canadian Northwest Territories. Other grievances relating to land usurpation and destruction, such as that of the affected Indian population of Quebec against the James Bay hydroelectric power development project, were taken to the courts.

Education and Awareness

Traders, mission boarding schools, travel and hospitalization outside of the North, and contact with visitors have given Subarctic Indians and Métis a modicum of awareness of the greater world. However, older people's knowledge is frequently based on limited information that has undergone considerable reinterpretation (Wills 1965). Traders and missionaries for a long time also constituted the main sources of secular knowledge pertaining to subjects like Western hygiene, economy, political authority, and current history. When local radio stations began to broadcast in Alaska and Canada, they did so mostly in English and naturally could not promote awareness among people who did not know the language. Native-language broadcasts, movies, and, in Northern towns, taped television programs have partly overcome the language barrier, but their influence remains to be studied.

School is undoubtedly the most effective agency disseminating modern knowledge, basic skills, and specialized vocational training. Northern schools generally follow a curriculum differing little from the one used elsewhere in Canada and the United States, which is geared to Euro-American goals and heritage (Grantham 1951; Phillips 1967:233–241; Robertson 1967). Most teaching is done in English, although for lower grades native speakers are employed as teachers' aids in some places (Rosenstiel 1971).

In the 1970s, only small settlements were without a school. Children who happen to live in a place without one, as well as young people seeking education beyond locally available grades, including those who want high school and vocational training, travel by plane at government expense to residential schools located in larger centers.

Anthropologists who have investigated formal education in the North have often called attention to the cultural bias in educational content and school organization and to difficulties that schooling has generated. They have noted education's disruptive effects on economic cooperation carried out in the family (Bishop 1970) and the break that residential schools impose on the continuity of a child's experience, thereby creating wrenching problems of choice and identity (King 1967; Wintrob and Sindell 1969). Several investigations have demonstrated that native children often lag behind White children in academic tasks (Slobodin 1966:118–126; Honigmann and Honigmann 1970:185–206), but evidence also indicates that school to an appreciable extent achieves its mission. Such evidence is seen in the sophistication and English language competency of the native people of the Mackenzie drainage area who have spent time in the residential school, and in results of research conducted in Inuvik in 1966–1967. Approximately half the school children from Indian or Métis households earned average or advanced ratings on New Basic Reading Tests developed and standardized with United States schoolchildren. In Metropolitan Achievement Test scores for reading and arithmetic, native children in the town of Inuvik performed better than pupils in the wider Inuvik region as a whole, which includes many settlements (Aklavik, Fort McPherson, Arctic Red River, Fort Good Hope, Fort Franklin, Reindeer Station, Tuktoyaktuk, Sachs Harbour, and Paulatuk). It is impossible to say whether school is better taught in Inuvik, whether town children are apt to possess greater aptitude for those subjects, or whether other factors exist that favor the town-dwelling group (Honigmann and Honigmann 1970:185–206).

Recreation

Northern recreation, especially in the bigger settlements, often depends on resources supplied by the larger society. Commercial movie theaters and local recreational associations show United States feature movies; theatrical or musical groups travel north to provide currently popular entertainment, and most radio fare and television programs originate in the south. As in present-day society generally, recreation in the North has become largely passive; adults especially are given to watching and listening rather than doing. A number of recreational events, such as bingo games in church or association halls and midwinter festivals, are organized by nonnatives with the intention of raising money for local community purposes. Modern sports, including baseball, basketball, hockey, and soccer, have considerable appeal for young people as do modern dancing and rock music, the latter played live by local combos or on records. In place of home brew, the common alcoholic beverage of fur-trade times, commercially made beer and liquor have become popular. Studies in Inuvik and Churchill in 1966–1968 indicated that 60–76 percent of the adult Indian and Métis populations in those towns used alcoholic beverages purchased from government-controlled stores. Considering only men, the proportion is higher. In addition, natives in these towns also drank in taverns.

Natives in Modern Society

Since their "discovery" by Europeans, people of Indian background have increasingly come into relationship with more people, and the intensity of those social relationships has steadily deepened (Wilson and Wilson 1945). The range and intensity of Indians' and Métis' social involvement in the larger society may be examined from several standpoints, including the limits that involvement reached in the early 1970s.

Many factors govern an individual's adaptation to modern life, including his or her interests, aptitudes, opportunities, financial means, and previous experience. As a result of differences in such factors, acceptance of features of the larger society is unevenly distributed in the Subarctic from one individual to another. Differential responses to modern society by individuals or households can be described in terms of the relative frequency with which traits such as wage employment, use of clinics, modern possessions, adaptation to school, and others are manifested. Thus, Indian mothers in Inuvik in 1967 varied in their willingness to take advantage of the free well-baby clinic for immunization of their children. Half of the 18 children three months to two years of age with Indian mothers had received from half to all immunization treatments appropriate for a given age; three had received some but less than half; and six had received none (Honigmann and Honigmann 1970:121–122, 252). In Great Whale River in 1969, 76 percent of 38 Indian households owned a table radio, only 47 percent possessed a table and chairs, and only 18 percent a sofa or washing machine (Barger 1969; Barger and Earl 1971).

Variation also occurs by social catetory. Age and education are important factors (Holden 1969:A–8), the aged not unexpectedly tending to be underrepresented in jobs, which of course limits their access to modern homes and possessions. Young men face difficulty in securing jobs, partly because men with family responsibilities have priority, but also because some young men are unwilling to work steadily.

In terms of native ethnic divisions Métis have historically been more culturally and economically integrated into the greater society than have Indians. Comparative research in three northern Canadian towns where both Indians and Eskimos reside reveals that on a variety of measures Indians are proportionately more often in the poorest position with respect to employment and rank lower in possession of Euro-American traits (Honigmann and Honigmann 1970:109, 249; Koolage 1971). The objective differences in the way Canadian society, especially northern federal administration, has impinged on Eskimos and Indians is one possible reason for the disparity.

From the time fur trapping began to the present day when native people are occupying jobs in shops, offices, commercial fishing, and other enterprises, Indians have increased the extent to which they have been producing and exchanging goods jointly with the larger society. Simultaneously, Canadian and United States taxpayers have expanded their economic contribution to the Subarctic, thereby providing jobs, capital for fur-enhancement programs, health and other social services, and subsidies for the native as well as the White population of the North.

As literacy has increased among natives, the volume of communication between northern native people and world society has grown. (However, the literacy level of the natives of Northern Canada and Alaska remains far below national averages.) Radio, motion pictures, and television have also promoted communication, but, as with the written word, almost entirely in a one-way flow. That is, Euro-American society has been sending religious, administrative, and entertainment messages to the Indians and Métis far more than natives have originated communication to it. When Indians have, it has usually been in face to face relations with representatives of the larger society who were present in northern communities.

The Indians' felt identification with the national society has been largely channeled through sentiments of citizenship, military service, and membership in world religions. Evidence suggests that the power of religious symbols is declining as young people lose the devoutness marking their parents and grandparents. But as that channel of identification weakens, others broaden. Particularly, schools make pupils aware of their national identities and of the mutual responsibility linking them and their government.

Finally, the integration of northern communities has been accomplished by coercive pressure exerted on natives by police, courts, and other agencies of the wider society. Laws pertaining to income tax, school attendance, crime, and alcohol are binding. In addition,

716

local regulations govern sanitation, zoning, dogs, and curfews, for example. In school, church, and associations another form of social pressure—convention—is imposed on Indians and Métis to regulate their forms of speech, work, dress, sexual behavior, and personal habits. A third form of pressure, logic, also comes into play when the teacher, minister, nurse, foreman, or judge alerts the native that his behavior or reasoning deviates from the premises generally accepted in Euro-American society.

The one-sidedness of social pressure is apparent; not only do nonnatives under ordinary circumstances remain relatively impervious to pressure that Indians and Métis might seek to exert on them, but also the laws, norms, and logical premises sanctioning conduct have practically without exception been introduced by the mainstream society through its representatives. In these ways their subordinate position in modern society is impressed forcefully upon Indians and Métis. Only as native people gradually adopt the larger society's legal or other norms and logical premises and themselves apply them to one another and nonnatives does their position in society approach a condition of full participation, but on the terms of a historically alien culture.

In the past Subarctic Indians and Métis have rarely sought deliberately to resist integration into Euro-American society on an organized basis, nor have they expressed strong hostility to Whites or sought to promote a separate unity of their own. Nevertheless, subtle contraintegrative and contraassimilative tendencies can be discerned in native behavior and sentiments. By adhering to certain preferred attitudes and activities that conflict with or limit closer integration—whether through choice or economic necessity does not matter—Indians and Métis to some degree reduce their involvement in modern society (Honigmann and Honigmann 1970:228–229; Spaulding 1966, 1). Adherence to such cultural forms may symbolically help forge a sense of separate native cultural identity, especially in conjunction with participation in the pan-tribal political action groups of the 1970s.

Sources

Contemporary Alaskan sources either deal with Eskimo or merge Eskimo and Indians in an undifferentiated category of "native people." For much information on recent Subarctic Canadian culture, anthropologists are indebted to the Northern Coordination and Research Centre, now Northern Science Research Group, under its perceptive chiefs, Victor F. Valentine and A. J. Kerr. Also useful are the area economic surveys done by the Industrial Division of the Northern Administration Branch. Another Domesday-like record is the four-volume *Settlements of the Northwest Territories*, assembled for the Advisory Commission on the Development of Government in the Northwest Territories and published in mimeographed form in 1966. Helm (1976:28–32) provides annotated citations of 30 publications treating contemporary conditions of Subarctic Indians and Métis.

Expressive Aspects of Subarctic Indian Culture

JOHN J. HONIGMANN

Expressive culture has to do with symbols and meaning. This chapter explores two kinds of meaning. The first arises from the explicit and implicit beliefs, sentiments, conceptions, and values of a society as they bestow significance on what members do, think, or feel; the ceremonies and symbols people create; individuals with whom a person interacts; or situations and events people encounter. This kind of meaning, the relationship between events and the understandings and interpretations people bring to them, is called cognitive meaning.

The second kind of meaning, which need not be independent of cognitive meaning, arises from the total context in which people experience an event, whether with pleasure, sorrow, or whatever emotion. The event's significance derives from the context of experience, and people recall, look forward to, or dread the event's repetition by remembering the emotions and associated experiences that made it significant. This kind of meaning, a relationship between an event and its ambiance, will be called contextual meaning (Lewis 1969:17–24; see also Barthes 1967:43).

To see a cognitive state or emotion expressed in behavior one must choose a perspective. A phenomenological vantage point enables an observer to grasp the meaning of events as the actors perceive it. An Ojibwa patient, for example, guided by the Ojibwa world view, saw his illness as due to a moral transgression he committed (Hallowell 1961). An Athapaskan Indian construed a child's recognition of a place where the child had never before been as evidence that the youngster incorporated the soul of a recently deceased person (Slobodin 1970). Each event is in its own way expressive to someone who knows the native conceptual "code" that unlocks its meaning for the Indians.

Another way of understanding significance adheres less exclusively to the actors' own perspective, though the main clues may come from there. Using this perspective, the meaning of an event is interpreted theoretically according to concepts held by an observer. Often he assumes that a similar extended meaning could not have escaped the actors, though they were not explicitly aware of it. Indians played games relying heavily on physical skill in an ambiance of fun and competition. According to a theory of games (Roberts and Sutton-Smith 1966), the prominence of games of physical skill in Subarctic culture expresses the high value the Indians placed on physical competence and achievement.

The topics covered in this chapter meet the specification that they reveal meaning or emotion without necessarily being adaptive or contributing to survival. Hence not much will be said about the role of empirical beliefs or knowledge and their expression in the practical survival activities of everyday life. Due to limits of space not all expressive aspects of Subarctic culture are represented. Furthermore, the emphasis is on aboriginal culture, insofar as it can reasonably be reconstructed. If more prominence is given to precontact Athapaskan culture than Algonquian, that is partly due to more of that culture having survived, at least in native memory, until it could be recorded by ethnographers. Also, more elaborated expressive forms in the precontact culture of the Pacific drainage region enrich the Athapaskan ethnographic data.

Power, Shamanism, and Sorcery

From the Indian's point of view, many things a man successfully accomplished revealed that he held power granted by nonhuman helpers who attended him. In the old days, there were no gods, only medicine, the Slavey Indians told J.A. Mason (1946:37), thereby indicating their conception of the nonpersonalized, immanent power in the universe that could be tapped by people to gain food, long life, and other vital goals. The eastern Cree, however, tended to personalize power and called it the Mistapew (*mista·pe·w* 'Great Man') (Speck 1935:41–52; Preston 1966, 1971a:26–166). Whether conceived of in personal or impersonal terms, Indians regarded power as an adjunct of the individual personality, as a quality that a man gained through his own efforts and could lose. Unhappy events in human life, a man's misfortune or a family tragedy, might be interpreted as desertion by the power that he had once possessed, or as evidence that another's power had outdone him (Speck 1935:18, 41–44, 47–49; Osgood 1936a:158–159, 1937:180–181, 1958:56–61, 1959:130–135, 1971:37–39; Hallowell 1938, 1939, 1961; J.A. Mason 1946:37–40; Honigmann 1954:104–107, 1956:71–75; McKennan 1959:149–151, 1965:78–83; Rogers 1962:D5–D36; Preston 1966).

Though human life expressed the workings of power, no person was every moment conscious of particular events hinging on his power. Judging from the ethnographic sources, knowledge that one had the blessings of the nonhuman grandfathers—as the Berens River Ojibwa put it around 1930 (Hallowell 1961)—normally remained in the background of consciousness. Such knowledge moved into the forefront of awareness only when something out of the ordinary happened that called for explanation.

Even when power was conceived impersonally, it appeared to the recipient, usually in dreams, in the guise of specific, anthropomorphic manifestations. Something—typically an animal—let the dreamer know that from henceforth he could count on its help. Everywhere, except among the eastern Cree, Naskapi, and Atlantic Slope Algonquians, a boy at about puberty hoped to find supernatural helpers while in solitude in the forest, through a dream that conformed to the right type. On returning to camp he must not tell others what he had dreamed, though he made known that his quest had been successful. The strong desirability of dreaming for power is apparent in the zeal with which men pursued it and from the way a generally dissatisfied, bewildered, 26-year-old Kaska Indian in 1945 admitted his misfortune of never having dreamed successfully. "Nothing saw me . . . nothing wanted me," he complained (Honigmann 1949:352). An Attawapiskat Cree Indian in 1946 compared the dream quest to attending church (Honigmann 1956:71). There can be no doubt that for Cree and Ojibwa the dream quest and associated activities connoted the holy or pertained to the numinous (Otto 1959; Honigmann 1956:72–73; Rogers 1962:3; Landes 1968:4).

Although nearly all men, and in some groups, women, acquired power, individuals obviously differed in their abilities and talents. A few men displayed outstanding skill in hunting or luck in gambling. Some won reputations for powerful sorcery. Power to cure was especially prized. Reasoning from the prevailing belief system, Indians saw extraordinary accomplishments in these areas as evidence that the adept and his spiritual helpers incorporated stronger than average power. Such a person, especially one who manipulates or controls a class of events, such as illness and death, that affects the social body, may be termed a shaman.

In many tribes, shamans possessed special paraphernalia that symbolized their role or the power they relied on. One such object, a medicine bag that held a Slavey shaman's amulets and other repositories of his power that were probably used for curing, was collected in Fort Nelson in 1943. The pouch (fig. 1), made of moosehide and decorated with beaded patches of black velvet, contained several packets wrapped in printed or dyed cloth, tinfoil, and silk handkerchiefs. Within the wrappings were red ocher, seeds, pieces of root, and to-

Yale U., Peabody Mus.: a, 57343a; b, 57343k; c, 57343v; d, 57343e; e, 57343l; f, 57343h.
Fig. 1. Medicine bag of Old Matoit, a Slavey shaman, with some of the contents. a, Bag with shoulder strap; b, black velvet bag decorated with braid bands, containing tinfoil-wrapped packet of bark or roots; c, "Old Chum" tobacco sack dated 1915, containing bark or reeds; d, cloth wrapping with baking powder tin containing red ocher; e, used Winchester No. 10 cartridge shell stuffed with cloth-wrapped packet; f, "Turlington's Balsam" medicine bottle containing brown fluid. Width of a about 25 cm, rest same scale, collected in 1943, last used some years earlier.

bacco. Other contents of the bag included a spent cartridge shell, empty pill boxes, and a rectangular wooden box about five inches long with sliding cover, somewhat resembling a Tlingit medicine box. (The bag is described in Honigmann 1946:78; cf. Swanton 1908:468 for the Tlingit box. For Ingalik amulets and other shamanistic paraphernalia see Osgood 1940:417–421, 1959:126–130.)

Viewed as performance, shamanism provided a dramatic way of demonstrating power, and some shamans became quite legendary in their society for the feats they performed. Wonderworking and, among the Cree and Ojibwa, the shaking tent furnished impressive means of validating shamanistic status in public (Hallowell 1942; Rogers 1962; Preston 1966, 1971a:29ff.). Sorcery, using power to cause illness or other misfortune, offered a similar opportunity in a less visible but, from the community's standpoint, no less credible and convincing manner. By no means did a sorcerer need to do acts of sorcery in order to acquire his reputation. If someone accused a person of sorcery, and the accused tacitly accepted the charge instead of denying it, the way was free for the community to declare the person a sorcerer (Ridington 1971, 1968). Sorcery was legitimate if people regarded it as being in retaliation for an offense; if they believed it to be used wantonly for the sake of misfortune, it was illegitimate, and a person so accused projected an aura of fear.

Sentiments regarding sorcery were not solely confined within the community. They were also imposed to characterize neighboring Indian groups. The Fort Nelson Slavey as late as 1943 dreaded the "Grand Lakers" (Kaska) across the Rocky Mountains because of their reputation for dangerous, wanton sorcery (Honigmann 1946:79, 130; cf. Rogers 1962:D29).

From a non-Indian point of view, power, shamanism, and sorcery seem quite congruent with an ecology, social structure, and means of social control that left much to the resources of the individual and placed a premium on traits of independence, achievement, and self-reliance.

Ethnographic fieldwork since about 1940 has revealed a variety of attitudes toward what survives of the power complex. It has shown that the eastern Cree (at least older men) retained warm, positive feelings toward the Mistapew concept (Preston 1971a). Across James Bay, however, in 1947–1948, Attawapiskat Indians regarded the Midewiwin as having been supported by the Devil. They relegated shamanism to a past with which they were done (Honigmann 1961:18, 68). Other Indian groups came to equate the power concept with sorcery or interpret it as standing in opposition to Christianity, as if it were a rival religion. Still others accepted the syncretism by shamans of Christian and aboriginal concepts and practices (McClellan 1956; Rogers 1962:D20–D21, D40; Ridington and Ridington 1967 in the tale titled "Makenunatane").

Values

Illness among the Subarctic Indians, when more serious than a cold or ache, did not always signify sorcery. Physical illness and behavioral disorders might also mean automatic retribution for sin committed, perhaps through carelessness or deliberately to gain an illicit reward. Retribution could fall on the sinner himself, on his spouse, or on his child. Indians suspected of having caused sickness through a moral transgression stood forth in their own eyes and in public opinion as symbols of guilt. With good fortune, confessing the offense brought cure, but sometimes sin led to death (Hallowell 1936, 1961; Honigmann 1946:82, 1954:112; Dunning 1959:180).

Among cases cited by Hallowell (1936:1299–1302, 1306–1307) from the Berens River Ojibwa is that of a shaman who in the 1930s suffered from an incapacitating phobia that did not allow him to go into the bush by himself. He interpreted his malady as the consequence of having once deceived the people by moving the shaking tent himself, leaving others to think it was done by his nonhuman helpers.

A number of actions, whether or not they threatened to cause illness and other misfortunes, held moral significance. Among Algonquians, a greedy hunter who wantonly destroyed game was dangerous because the animals on which life depended would henceforth withhold themselves (Hallowell 1950:736). Certain acts were in themselves bad, like niggardliness, laziness, and causing embarrassment. A longer list of undesirable behavior recognized by the Ingalik (Osgood 1959:99–102) includes gossiping, feuding, masturbation, excessive sexual intercourse, and aggression. Even the weapons used to kill someone acquired an indelible evil character that caused the Ingalik to burn them or throw them away.

A Kaska Indian, verbally sketching some of the psychological types (all male) of former times, revealed how values were used to appraise behavior (Honigmann 1954:24–25; cf. Osgood 1959:65). There were all-around handymen, capable of doing almost any task, skillful enough to provide all the implements needed to make a living, confident, and perhaps a shade too eager to see that others became aware of so much talent and acumen. Men of that type contrasted with inept individuals whose practical skills and knowledge were minimal, who could not get themselves to move, who wasted time when they could have been doing something worthwhile, and who were consequently poor (Slobodin 1969:69). Even giving an inept man what he lacked did not help, for "pretty soon his wife came back and said that they're starving." Another character, whom everyone liked, exuded warmth and friendliness. People also enjoyed the "crazy man," who couldn't resist playing jokes and teasing the girls.

Indians did not judge behavior in moral terms only; they also made aesthetic judgments. They acknowledged with approval evidence of skill, good craftsmanship, competence, and wit. Kutchin Indians recognized two styles of leadership. There was the "hard," incisive task leader who planned and directed a trapping party, and his fun-loving, "soft" lieutenants. The Indians primarily appreciated the hard leader for his ability to accomplish a task and the soft leader for his sympathetic understanding of people and the desirable emotional effect he had on a group (Slobodin 1969:66, 81–82).

Aesthetic judgments were extended beyond behavior. The richness and sophistication of women's aesthetic values are manifested in the decorative art they created variously in quillwork ("Slavey," figs. 5–7, this vol.), painted garments (fig. 2; "Montagnais-Naskapi," this vol.), moosehair work, silk embroidery, and beadwork (fig. 3). An Ingalik informant assured Osgood (1959:97–99) that people in precontact times enjoyed beauty for beauty's sake. They found different juxtaposed colors attractive. The smoother spruce wood planks could be made, the "prettier" they were considered. Skin fringes and fur decoration were used on clothing primarily to enhance its appearance. Bags were made of bear gut just because the material looked beau-

left, Natl. Mus. of Canada, Ottawa: Speyer Coll., III–B–588; right, Dept. of Anthr., Smithsonian: 90241.
Fig. 2. left, Naskapi painted caribou skin of yellow, red, and blue-green, red border once decorated with diagonal lines of red porcupine quill embroidery, cut fringe edges originally wrapped with red quills, and the fringes on corner tabs quill-wrapped and strung with brass cones and red hair tassels. Width 105 cm, collected about 1740. right, Naskapi man's summer coat of white-tanned caribou skin, sewn with sinew, with painted designs in light red, brownish red, blue, and yellow. Length 118 cm, collected 1882–1883.

tiful. A man who was tall and muscularly well-built had intrinsic appeal; and men found a woman attractive if she was short and stout, had large breasts, and possessed a flat nose rather than one with a high bridge. For many of these judgments Osgood offers reasons obtained from the Indians, but the reasons seem more like secondary rationalizations provided to satisfy an inquirer rather than postulates from which evaluations are made.

New experiences in the course of the contact era, including the introduction of a cash economy and the teachings of Christianity, stimulated new assessments of values throughout the northern forest. Given a choice between food obtained by hunting or fishing and food purchased from the store, Indians nearly invariably ranked game before rice, flour, and other purchased staples on which, however, they had become heavily dependent. The eastern Kutchin went even further. For them reliance on store food boded decadence. The physical and spiritual decline they perceived in themselves and in neighboring Indians they attributed to too great dependence on imported edibles (Slobodin 1969:85; Savishinsky 1970:48–49). Food that had to be paid for, whose availability did not depend primarily on a family's effort and resourcefulness, came to be very reluctantly shared, although former sentiments extolling generosity continued to prevail (Honigmann 1949:141–142, 216, 1961:191; cf. Osgood 1959:69–71; Hallowell 1960:47).

Indians having learned lessons taught by more puritanical missionaries in some communities brought sex under a cloud of moral disapproval. They imposed severe sanctions against sex play, premarital sexuality, and illegitimacy (Honigmann 1961:63). Nowhere in the Subarctic during pre-Christian times had heterosexual intercourse and unwed motherhood been so stringently condemned.

Ceremonial

Ceremonies, ranging from rituals of interpersonal etiquette completed in a few moments to dramatic performances lasting days or weeks, provide a community with its preeminent means for expressing sentiments and marking the significance of important occasions. Made up of expressive words, gestures, and objects capable of arousing emotion, ceremonies dramatize that which is culturally significant. But, as is well known, symbols that allow for emotional expression in one culture may possess little meaning for people of an alien way of life. The problem is compounded when, in reconstructing a bygone culture, the ethnographer is unable to learn the significance attached to ritual symbols.

Avoidances

The most elementary rites in any society, requiring neither special apparatus nor time for prior preparation, occur when people take note of an important goal, role, or occasion by refraining from doing something that otherwise they could quite properly do. Of the many ritual avoidances (taboos) reported for the northern Indians, a few will illustrate the kinds of meaning they express.

Rules in many Athapaskan groups enjoined young men from taking too much water, grease, or marrow;

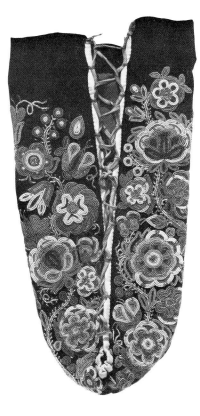

a   b   c

Natl. Mus. of Canada, Ottawa: a, III–C–512; c, VI–I–5; d, VI–J–4; e, VI–M–2; Lower Ft. Garry Natl. Hist. Park, Selkirk, Man.: b, HBC 2260; B. C. Prov. Mus., Victoria: f, 14828, U. of Iowa, Mus. of Nat. Hist., Iowa City: g, 9634; U. of Calif., Lowie Mus., Berkeley: h, 2–2636; U. of Pa., U. Mus., Philadelphia: i, NA 5840a.

Fig. 3. Subarctic beadwork. Bead embroidery, a major Subarctic art form still produced, reached an apex in the decades around 1900. The sewing technique is nearly always couching (also called overlaid or spot stitch), where beads strung on a sinew or thread are attached to the hide or fabric surface by tiny stitches of a second thread between every 1 to 3 beads (Orchard 1929:fig. 127). Beads are Venetian and Czechoslovakian glass seed beads (about 1/16 to 3/32 inch in diameter) in a variety of colors and tiny faceted gold and silver colored metal beads. a, Hood from the Attikamek at La Tuque. The colors (white, blue, green, pink, and crystal) and the design of multiple delicate bands of serpentine leaf-edged stems and distinctive bell and bud forms characterize a small group of exquisite hoods that appear to have been produced at about the mid-19th century by the James Bay Cree. Height 51 cm, collected about 1890. b, Pouch said to have been given to Sir George Simpson by Cree Indians in 1854. Black broadcloth edged with red silk ribbon, beaded primarily in blues, pink, green, white, and crystal. This pouch is stylistically related to hoods such as a. Bags of this shape, often called octopus bags (because of the 8 tabs) or finger bags, were popular 19th-century costume elements in parts of the Subarctic, the Plains, and the Northwest Coast. Width about 41 cm. c, Moss bag for baby, collected among the Eastern Kutchin. The design is characteristic of the Mackenzie River–Great Slave Lake area, densely beaded on black velvet with precise, elaborated rosette, bell, bud, and leaf forms. Contour shaded pinks and greens dominate, accentuated with gold and silver metal beads at leaf and petal points, and rosette and petal-edge centers. Length 55 cm, collected 1911. d, Moccasins from the Inland Tlingit. These are representative of many produced around 1900 by the Tlingit and Inland Tlingit, often for sale to tourists. Outlined semifloral and cartouche forms, largely in primary colors, are typical. The eagle was a popular Alaskan motif. Length 25 cm, collected in 1912 at Teslin Lake. e, Firebag. The earred, ruffed fabric firebag, a type produced by the Sekani early in the 20th century, is heavily and exuberantly beaded on front and back in a wide range of colors. Loose stylized floral forms merge with abstract background elaboration. Length 2.6 cm plus tassels, collected at Fort Graham, made about 1900. f, Pouch from the Tahltan at Telegraph Creek. The typical Tahltan pouch, of leather and fabric beaded on one side, is organized into multiple horizontal design registers. A geometric band of sinew-woven beadwork is often countered with one or more fabric bands of couched symmetrical curvilinear-abstract motifs. White, plus black, blue, or red beads on red fabric are common. Width 15.7 cm, probably early 20th century. g, Shot pouch made by a Métis woman from Norway House. The Métis produced much elaborate floral embroidery. Enlarged detail shows skilled control of form and technique; the couching stitches are visible, as are occasional remnants of white, probably flour paste used to draw the design on the fabric before beading. Sash about 6.5 cm wide, collected in 1892–1893. h, Sled bag from the Upper Yukon. The form is typical of this region, as is the design lightly beaded in muted colors, of simple small semifloral motifs, outlined or filled, attached to a dominant, central focused network of white stems. Width 49.5 cm, collected 1894–1901. i, Pouch from the Ingalik at Anvik. Western Athapaskans bordering on the Eskimo produced little beadwork. Some Ingalik women made pouches for sale to steamboat passengers, framing a skin insert (here of birdskin) with a netted bead edge and light bead patterning. Length 28 cm, collected in 1917. Kate Corbin Duncan selected and described the items in this figure.

722

HONIGMANN

d

e

f

g

h

i

723

EXPRESSIVE ASPECTS OF SUBARCTIC INDIAN CULTURE

eating the leg tendons and hind quarters of large animals; and eating too much in general. Magically, the object was to preserve the tyros' health, stamina, and endurance. The taboos may be interpreted as symbolizing the values of physical achievement and prowess, indispensable qualities for young men preparing to play the role of hunter.

Though simple to execute, avoidances might severely curtail a person's customary activities, in certain cases for long periods of time. An Ingalik father counted 20 days of enforced idleness following the birth of a baby. During that time he ate no fresh meat or fish and left off good clothes in favor of old (Osgood 1958:172–173). Symbolically, the observance links him to the mother, for she simultaneously underwent a series of restrictions. So, husband and wife expressed their common concern, as mourners also do when they unite around a death that affects them all.

Roman Catholicism brought new avoidances that Indians adopted, including the custom of commemorating Christ's death by not eating meat on Fridays. By special dispensation the bishop exempted James Bay Cree Indians from Friday observance, in exchange for which he enjoined them from social dancing. Though Attawapiskat Indians mostly observed the ban, nothing indicates that it carried much meaning for them (Honigmann 1947–1948). Even the priests explained it quite practically as a stratagem to prevent premarital sexual relations from occurring after dances ended at night.

Respect for Animals

Subarctic Indians behaved as if a close bond existed between human beings and the animals on which they depended for survival. The eastern Cree Indians, viewing their relationship to caribou from the animals' perspective, pictured it in metaphorical terms as founded on sexual attraction or love. The caribou, they said, are willing to be taken in hunting because they love men (Preston 1970, 1971:207, 1971a). Animals used for food as well as other kinds were ceremoniously treated with avoidances and other rites that signified fear and respect and, as Father Chrétien Le Clercq learned in 1691, insured that the animals would continue to allow themselves to be caught (cited in Speck 1935:76).

Old Lady Matoit, a Slavey Indian at Fort Nelson, echoed the same idea in 1943. She recalled warning young people that they would not be able to kill moose if they threw the bones all over instead of piling them in one place. Time, she remarked, had proved her right (Honigmann 1946:76).

Generally, simple observances executed for the bear, moose, beaver, caribou, and other game included no wanton killing, prescribed careful butchering (fig. 4) so as not to break the vertebrae or other bones, and above

Fig. 4. An Attikamek woman preparing to skin and butcher a bear. The bear has a pipe in his mouth, symbolic of giving the animal its last smoke; however, at this period this was done more in jest than as ritual (Cooper 1925). Photograph by John M. Cooper at Obedjiwan Lake, June 1925.

all enjoined careful disposal of the skull (fig. 5) and other bones so that dogs could not debase them (Skinner 1912:68, 73; Speck 1935:113–116, 122–124; Honigmann 1946:76–79, 1956:69–70; Rousseau 1952; Hallowell 1960:47; Preston 1964; Helm 1961:119).

The Montagnais-Naskapi and adjacent Cree reserved a much more elaborate animal-deference ceremony for bears. Varying in details from place to place, it generally called for adorning the carcass with trinkets (fig. 5), honoring the dead animal in a pipe-smoking rite, and butchering in formal fashion. Then the men ate some portion of the carcass, usually the head, in a prescribed manner, being careful to finish the meat at a single sitting (Skinner 1912:69–71, 75, 162–164; Hallowell 1926; Speck 1935:103–110; Honigmann 1949:221, 1956:69).

Along with rituals symbolizing respect for game animals, Athapaskans carried out special magical precautions upon killing certain creatures that were not used for food, such as the wolf, otter, mink, and lynx. On the Upper Liard River, for example, Indians burned a mink that had been inadvertently caught in a deadfall and covered the charred remains with feathers to put the mink in a "good mind" (Honigmann 1946:76, 1954:108–109; Helm 1961:119).

724

HONIGMANN

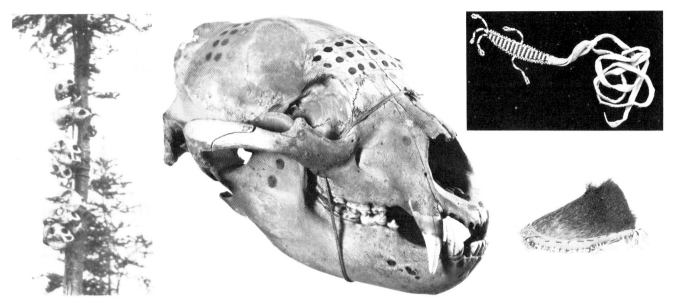

left, Natl. Geographic Soc., Washington; center, Royal Ontario Mus., Toronto: 964.140.28; Natl. Mus. of Canada, Ottawa: top right, III-B-318; bottom right, III-D-61.

Fig. 5. Eastern Cree and Naskapi representations signifying respect for bears. left, Bear skulls hung on a tree out of respect to the animal, near Rupert House. Photograph by E.S. Covell, Nov. 1931. center, Ceremonial bear skull decorated with painted dots, from Rupert House, collected 1964. top right, Naskapi hunting charm with part of a bear tongue inside a beaded decoration, hung on a gun for good luck, from Shango Bay, Davis Inlet, collected 1960. bottom right, Charm made from lower lip of black bear, decorated with beads, from Rupert House, collected 1934. Length of center 35 cm, rest about same scale.

Distribution of Game

Sharing game, although often obligatory, was usually done so informally that it scarcely resembled what Euro-Americans are apt to regard as ceremonial. Nevertheless, it gave public expression to the value of generosity, to the high regard in which Indians held meat, and to the claims that people had on one another.

Writing about a band of 65 Hare Indians at Colville Lake, Northwest Territories, in 1967–1968, Savishinsky (1970:47–49) describes three patterns of sharing different kinds of game. A moose the hunter usually gave to someone else, his father or a close friend, for example (who, one suspects, was publicly honored by being chosen). Then all the men of the settlement and some young women traveled to the site of the kill where the person who had received the animal supervised the butchering and distributed the meat among the people (Rogers 1962:B80, C69, C72; Helm 1965a:37–38; see also Honigmann 1946:133).

Unlike moose, caribou were usually plentiful around Colville Lake in the winter and spring, and all 14 Indian households had a good chance of acquiring some. Correspondingly, no binding obligation compelled people to distribute caribou meat as was the rule for moose. However, families differed in the success with which their members killed caribou, and a successful hunter was expected to give meat to families having little or none, especially if he made a very large kill at one time.

No one felt obliged to share the daily catch of fish taken from nets set through much of the year. Only a particularly "meaty" fish, such as a large trout, or an especially favored one, like the loche, was shared with close relatives: parents, a married son or daughter, or a married sibling. Fish were distributed in larger quantities only if a close or distant relative or friend ran out of a supply to feed his family or his dogs.

The style with which food is distributed by Subarctic Indians, including the emotional quality of the attendant behavior, appears to have largely escaped ethnographers' attention. A party of Fort Nelson Slaveys going to fetch a moose in the summer of 1943 revealed little formality that an embryonic ethnographer could observe (certainly much less than was witnessed among Eskimo) and little patterned emotional expression be-

Royal Ont. Mus., Toronto: 964.140.24.

Fig. 6. Stuffed goose head from Rupert House used for ceremonial purposes, decorated with strings of beads with woolen tassels at the end of the severed neck and through the ear openings, and a wool cord through the nostrils. Length 26.7 cm, collected 1964.

yond elation (Honigmann 1946:106). However, something may have been missed due to being unfamiliar with the Indians' controlled style of emotional expression. Possibly for this reason, the same observer failed to catch any more emotional expression or formality in a similar event among the Kaska Indians a year or so later (Honigmann 1949:65). In the Cree settlement of Attawapiskat in 1946–1947, a woman or child bringing some fresh meat or fish as a gift to the ethnographer's house came with a smile; the food was always covered; but nothing special was said. It seems safe to conclude that the Subarctic Indians have not elaborated fine points of interpersonal etiquette to a high level. An Ingalik man offering dinner prepared by his wife to friends in the kashim (men's house), simply said: "If you fellows would like to eat, go ahead" (Osgood 1958:37). According to Indian norms, his invitation quite conformed to what good breeding demanded.

Biological Symbolism

Menstruation and childbirth, points in a woman's reproductive cycle when her femaleness is most clearly revealed, were ritually marked in a number of Subarctic cultures. Menstruation was especially emphasized among the Athapaskan Indians, the most elaborate observances occurring at the menarche (Morice 1906–1907, 1906–1910:971–978; Jetté 1911:699–704; Skinner 1912:152; Osgood 1937:160, 162, 1958:183–188; Honigmann 1954:122–126, 1956:70; Wallis and Wallis 1955:244, 245, 251; Dunning 1959:100).

Women exuded danger to themselves and others each time they entered the critical status of menstruant or parturient. By sequestration of menstruating girls (fig. 7) and of women in childbirth the threat was contained or kept at a distance. A menstruant wearing a hood (fig. 8) to restrict where her glance might fall, being pegged to the ground so she could not stray away from the menstrual camp, using a drinking tube (fig. 9) so that her lips did not touch water, employing a scratching stick to prevent her fingers from touching her hair, keeping out of a hunter's track, and observing food taboos—all these customs and associated beliefs also say symbolically that menstruation was dangerous and threatened men's hunting ability. A man, too, took precautions in his contacts with female sexuality, especially at times when his masculinity was most clearly evident—evident, that is, in cultural guise; for after all, he did not menstruate or give birth, and comparable biological signs of his sex were lacking—thus, in conjunction with hunting and war he avoided coitus (Honigmann 1954:96, 110), he cached his cut hair in a safe place, and he disposed of wood shavings where a menstruant could not walk over them. Thus, to a degree he paralleled women's precautions.

726

Smithsonian, NAA: 10,455–G–2.

Fig. 7. Ingalik, the older 2 girls wearing kerchiefs and hoods because they are in seclusion having recently reached puberty. Photograph probably by John Wight Chapman at Anvik, 1918.

Yet, anthropologists, for some groups, may have exaggerated the sense of danger with which those biological events were surrounded. A Tahltan Indian woman describing the restrictions of menarche that she had experienced about eight or nine years previously did not give the impression that she and another girl had been seriously intimidated. Nor did boys dread them as perils of pollution.

> I stayed in the house one month. . . . Not allowed to laugh. . . . When a man come into the house I must not look at him. . . . My grandma always watch.
> I wanted to go to dance. I sneak out when grandma went. . . . I tell grandma I want to go, but she say no. Gee, I get mad.
> All the boys go in May's tent. . . when grandma sleep. In morning they all go. Grandma never know. . . . That's why we lose our auntie. They say that's May's fault (Honigmann 1954:125).

Clearly grave danger threatened if the rules were broken. The informant's attempt to evade the rules by going to a dance and the young people who ignored

Natl. Mus. of Canada, Ottawa: VI-Q-6.
Fig. 8. Tutchone girl's skin hood worn during puberty seclusion. The hood has a skin thong to close the sides and conceal the face. Length 50 cm, collected before 1913.

them may have been products of postcontact cultural change, through which the forms survived without conviction. But it is also possible that, as with ritual expression in general, danger connected with menstruation had long been something people were supposed to feel, but not everyone did.

Some Athapaskan cultures tended to symmetrize the ceremonial attention paid to boys' and girls' puberty. The Chandalar Kutchin and Tanaina even provided boys with ceremonial appliances found in the girl's puberty complex: a drinking tube and a similar special hat. Other Indians compared celebration of a youth's first game kill to the rites of menarche. However, in the Subarctic generally, boys' puberty rites were more attenuated than girls' or were absent. The lack of ritualization cannot be wholly explained by saying that masculine biology does not offer material on which Indians' imagination could have seized for the purpose of ceremonial elaboration, for other cultures have managed to heighten boys' puberty far beyond the slim biological material it naturally provides (Osgood 1936a:147, 1937:162–163, 1971:48; Honigmann 1954:125; McKennan 1965:59).

Death

Rituals revealed a number of loosely connected meanings of death and—as in most, if not all, cultures— confirmed death as one of the most significant events befalling a family or small community.

Death in the Subarctic frequently meant that inimical forces—evil spirits, ghosts, or the effect of sorcery— had intruded in human affairs; however, that folk explanation throws no light on the symbolism brought into play at death (Goddard 1917:228–230; Osgood 1936a:145–146, 148–149, 1937:165–168, 1958:156–157, 1959:73, 1971:52; Honigmann 1949:207, 1954:139–142; Field 1957:56; McGee 1961:52–53; Rogers 1962:B63; McKennan 1965:59; see also Honigmann 1945).

Like people everywhere, the northern Indians expressed grief for the deceased. Death produced a sense of loss to which the survivors gave expression by wailing, fasting, destroying their possessions, and abstaining from work. A widow went about unkempt and remained celibate for a long time; her stylized cry of mourning rang through the camp for months. Thus the living dramatized that life without the deceased had lost its zest and become painful. The rituals of mourning created a context of bleakness and liminal living, thereby confirming that death had changed the normal course of life and brought pain and depression.

The survivors also revealed respect for the deceased by dressing a corpse in new clothes, furnishing it with what the soul might need in the afterlife, and accompanying it to the grave. In Pacific drainage tribes, signs of respect varied in proportion to the prestige of the dead person. Western Athapaskans also memorialized the dead in the death potlatch (see "Koyukon," fig. 7, this vol.), where stand-ins represented specific dead persons. There as well as elsewhere people enshrined the memory of a dead mother or other individual through mementos, consisting of things that once belonged to the person, and perpetuated it in grave markers (figs. 10–11) (Isham 1949:93–94; McKennan 1959:147). (Through the influence of missionaries grave markers were elaborated in postcontact times and, in fact, introduced where they had not been before.) Also, by feeding the fire with bits of food, Athapaskans from time to time nourished the souls of the departed.

Most northern Athapaskans appear to have entertained more fear of the ghosts of the recently dead than did Algonquians, but not to the degree held by the southern Athapaskans, the Navajo. Actually, the northern Indians did not do much to neutralize the dangerous power of ghosts. The Kaska thought it unwise for a child to look at a dead body, because doing so allowed the ghost to see and take a fancy to the child. Circuitous removal of a corpse from a dwelling was intended to prevent the ghost from finding its way back. And, on the theory that the ghost clung to the body it once inhabited, fleeing the scene of death put survivors beyond the zone of danger. But mostly ghost fear simply lingered, contributing to an ambiance of disturbed feelings.

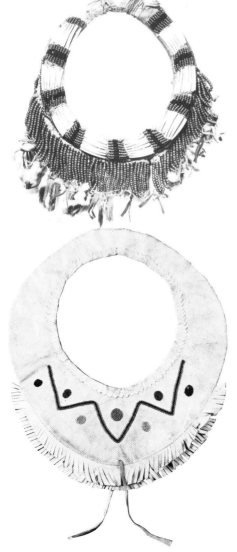

Natl. Mus. of Canada, Ottawa: top left, VI–0–57ab; top right, VI–0–60; bottom, VI–0–56; center, Mus. of the Amer. Ind., Heye Foundation New York: 1/865.

Fig. 9. Tahltan female puberty accessories. top left, Bone drinking tube and small packet attached to caribou skin tube carrier decorated with purple, blue, green, black, and brown beads and red paint, with down-covered cord. Used during girl's puberty seclusion when she was required to use only the tube for drinking and to smear her lips daily with grease from the packet so she would need little food. Other items used by young women after puberty seclusion until marriage are: top right, Hair ornament, one of a pair worn at the sides of the head covering the ears, made of caribou skin with dentalium, red and blue beads, and tassels of yellow, black, and red wool. center, Wooden neck ring with dentalia and bead-strung leather fringe; bottom, caribou skin collar with red, blue, green, and black beads. Length of top right 40.5 cm, rest same scale; center collected 1904, rest collected 1915.

Ingalik Ceremonies

Nowhere in the Subarctic prior to contact did Indians enact any ceremonies so spectacular as the "great ceremonies" held by the sedentary Ingalik Indians of Alaska in the village kashim during the winter and other leisureful nonsummer months. The "great ceremonies" were complex, many-faceted performances continuing for as long as 17 nights (most were shorter); and their meaning was correspondingly rich and composite (Osgood 1958:73–146). Meaning lay partly in content: what masks represented (figs. 12–13), other objects denoted, and dancers, mimics, or clowns enacted. Meaning also lay in the myth that gave the reason for the affair or in the purpose for which it was performed. Thus the death potlatch honored both the recently deceased and living individuals who were potlatched to; the Bladder ceremony sought to increase the supply of desirable animals; the Hot Dance too served to increase the food animals and was very much anticipated for the sexual license it permitted when the kashim lights were put out. Wealthy and ambitious men had special interest in the ceremonies, which they promoted. They saw the affairs as opportunities to enhance their reputations

Fig. 10. Koyukon images of guardian spirits on a grave house at Koyukuk village. left to right: White rabbit; yellow fox; gray bear; red moose with a tin beard, ears, and horns; and red tin fish (De Laguna 1947:304). Photograph by Frederica De Laguna, 1935.

HONIGMANN

Natl. Mus. of Canada, Ottawa: 70418, 70419.
Fig. 11. Views at the ceremony for erection of a tombstone to Big Seymour (d. 1924), a Carrier Indian of Hagwilget. left, Young relative with tongs seizing a man probably in an enactment of a crest right (see "Carrier," this vol.); right, man wearing a ceremonial blanket with appliqué designs of 2 whales and a human form. The whale design is partly outlined with pearl buttons. Photographs by Harlan I. Smith, 1927.

by meeting standards of generosity and hospitality. Other persons benefited in esteem from displaying their skills in dancing, miming, and other arts or from the honor paid them as valuable gifts were publicly bestowed in their names.

Finally, the meaning of the elaborate performances lay in the ambiance they created. These affairs were holidays when most normal work was suspended (at least by men). Objects decorating the kashim gave the building a distinctive appearance, appropriate to the ceremony that was being performed. Preparing the decorations, masks, or other appurtenances and, for some ceremonies, sending messengers to invite guests from other villages built up a pleasant tension of anticipation. Good things happened in the ceremonies that affected their atmosphere. People received gifts of value; they wore new clothes (unless old clothes were required to symbolize death); stories, singing, and music entertained them; they received good food lavishly served.

The fun-giving character of the ceremonies should not be overstated. The four-day death potlatch that

Smithsonian, NAA:10,455-N-1.
Fig. 12. Ingalik masks used during the Mask Dance, an important ceremonial for the purpose of increasing the quantity of economically important animals. (For the mask types see Osgood 1958:80–95.) Photographed by John Wight Chapman, 1890s–1920s.

Fig. 13. Ingalik painted wooden masks. a, Painted flat white, red lips, blue beads for labrets, representing man; b, forehead and nose painted dark gray, black around eye, chin red, representing "Half Man," used in Mask Dance; c, forehead painted gray (with white spots, now faded), black around eyes, white over eyes, red around mouth, formerly had large bead suspended from nose, representing a mythical "siren," used in Mask Dance; d, forehead and line above mouth painted gray, ears and edges gray, representing an Innoko man, probably from Mask Dance; e, painted gray (with white stripes and spots, now faded) except for cheeks, top movable, separate plug in mouth, fishskin straps in back, once had 3 feathers inserted in top, representing ruffed grouse, used in Mask Dance. Length of e about 45.5 cm, rest same scale; collected at Anvik in 1905. See Chapman 1907.

took place during the shortest days of the year had an austere significance and was devoid of social amusement. Symbols of death were conspicuous, including a guest from the land of the dead, people identifying themselves as specific persons who had died, and coffin handlers who received presents for services they had rendered. At the end of the ceremony everyone in the kashim jumped on the wooden floor to be answered by everyone in the houses jumping. The action paralleled the stamping done at the moment of a funeral when a dead person was removed from the kashim.

Feasts

Less lavish than the Alaskans' ceremonies were the feasts that individual Indians gave as rites of passage to mark the birth of a first child, a boy's first killing of game, marriage of a daughter, or a hunter's success in killing game. As with ceremonies in general, meaning jointly resided in people's understanding of what the events celebrated and in the emotions that the celebration aroused (Turner 1894:322–323; Speck 1935:201–202; Osgood 1936a:121, 125, 141, 147, 1958:66, 71; Flannery 1946:267; Honigmann 1956:61–62; McKennan 1965:64).

Other feasts expressed pleasure or gratitude at the seasonal arrival of highly desirable food, like the first salmon in spring (see "Minto, Alaska," fig. 5, this vol.). Algonquians had eat-all and spring thanksgiving feasts. For the spring feast, the best parts of game animals were saved up during the winter. A bit of dancing accompanied both (Osgood 1936a:52; Honigmann 1946:89, 1956:44–45; Oldmixon 1931:388 may be describing a spring thanksgiving feast observed by him in May 1671 at Rupert House).

Postcontact Ceremony

Christian church services in which sacred symbols predominate, as well as calendrical holidays possessing mostly secular significance, have become ceremonial occasions in postcontact times.

Only a few ethnographers have said much about how the sacred symbols and theological ideas of Christianity were understood by Indians (Honigmann 1958; McGee 1961:125–137, 142; Rogers 1962:D9). That many aspects were reinterpreted and recast in native idiom is evidenced in the prophet movements among the Subarctic Indians of the nineteenth and twentieth centuries. Fort Nelson Slavey prophets of 1925 patterned their behavior and attire after those of Catholic priests. At feasts, to which hunters contributed meat, the prophets preached broad moral values while enjoining church-like silence and forbidding people to walk around during the service (Honigmann 1946:132–134).

Ridington and Ridington (1967: "Charlie Yahey") quote a Beaver prophet's version of the soul's ascent to heaven (see also "Beaver," fig. 3, this vol.):

> If some person is really good, something just like a car comes to meet him. You just sit on that thing that flies like a plane. You just sit on top of that thing; you go up really fast. Just like a saucer. It just goes to heaven like a car. When you get on the road to heaven, there's a cleft in the middle of the road. If you are good, some angel will take you across. When you get there, you're never cold, never worried. That kind of person is really safe in heaven. Its very hard but some people pass that. Some people get stuck; some people are not very good.

Persons educated in mission boarding schools learned to conform much more closely to orthodox Christian belief and practice. (Spier 1935 summarizes the early period; for the Fort Nelson area in the 1920s see Honigmann 1946:132–134; Ridington and Ridington 1967 probably refer to the same period in an immediately adjacent area in narratives titled "Charlie Yahey" and "Prophet Teachings." For accounts of other Athapaskan prophet movements see McClellan 1956:134–136; McKennan 1965:86–87; "Dogrib," this vol. A new religion among the Lake Superior Ojibwa in 1830 is fully cited in Mooney 1896:677; Cooper 1933:83 describes an equally early James Bay religion.)

In some places the missionaries allowed Christian rituals to develop local meanings, for example, the Micmac "national holiday" in honor of the patron, Sainte Anne (Wallis and Wallis 1955:283ff.), and Rat Sunday in the lower Mackenzie valley, a day of thanksgiving that came after the spring muskrat hunt. When the collection plate was passed at that service, Indians

contributed a part of the winter fur catch to support the Anglican church in their community (Honigmann and Honigmann 1970:37, pl. 30).

New Year's provided a secular occasion for celebrating, especially in Canada where Scottish Hudson's Bay personnel popularized the holiday (Helm 1961:97–108; Honigmann and Honigmann 1970:48). In Fort McPherson on New Year's morning the Kutchin Indian chief and councilors, wearing uniforms supplied by the government, went round the settlement shaking hands with the occupants of every house and wishing them "Happy New Year!" Members of each house joined the procession, which moved back to the chief's home where he made a speech and served tea with bannock or pilot biscuits. That evening there was a community feast and dance.

Canadian Indians also recognized treaty payment as a festive time and observed it by feasting and dancing. Accompanied by a Royal Canadian Mounted policeman in his ceremonial red tunic, the Indian agent visited each trading post in early summer, just after the Indians had returned from their winter trap lines, and using crisp paper currency made the mandatory payments (see "Dogrib," fig. 7, this vol.). Then came a feast at which the chief uttered appropriate sentiments (fig. 14) and the people prayed (Helm and Lurie 1966:7–12). As in the rest of Canada, White Canadians in the north promote the celebration of Dominion Day on July 1. In 1967 Indians in Aklavik and Inuvik celebrated the national holiday by competitive sports, carnival-type games, and an evening dance. The money raised went,

Ont. Arch., Toronto: 2475 S–7600.

Fig. 14. Missabay, a blind Northern Ojibwa traditional leader, making a speech at the celebration of the signing of Treaty No. 9, the James Bay Treaty, at Osnaburgh House in July 1905, when he was elected chief. Photograph by Duncan Campbell Scott, one of 3 commissioners who negotiated the treaty.

like profits from the late winter celebration held in Inuvik, to a community purpose (Honigmann and Honigmann 1970:95, pl. 30).

Church services and a number of calendrical holidays shared a feature characteristic of modern recreation in the North: arranged and dominated by non-Indians, they were events in which most Indians participated largely passively or as paying customers. In the case of the holidays, the meaning for the native people lay less in the myth or in the significance of the event they commemorated than in the pleasure they furnished. It was different with the community feast or family reception that celebrated a marriage following a church service. There people both understood the meaning and enjoyed the occasion. So it was, too, with the Kaska Wolf moiety's party (potlatch) in 1945, designed to honor a woman of the Crow moiety who had recently died, and the reciprocal Crow party tendered a week later by the other moiety (Honigmann 1949:169–172).

Recreation

Games

On adult play in precontact times, there are data on the Ingalik (Osgood 1958:46–53) and the eastern Cree (Honigmann 1956:54–55). The large repertory of play reveals a light side of Subarctic existence that at first glance contrasts with the harsh environment and the occasional famines. However, by applying the theory of games developed by Roberts and Sutton-Smith (1966), the character of the games is seen to be congruent with the everyday concerns of a food-gathering society in which survival depended on the initiative and resourcefulness of individuals.

Most of the games fell into two types: either based primarily on physical skill or loaded heavily with the factor of chance. In the former, the outcome depended much on the physical agility, strength, or weight of the individual contestants or of teams pitted against each other, as in wrestling or push-pole tug of war. They reflect the Indians' concern with physical competence and achievement, traits important in a hunting society. The latter type, games in which the result was produced by the throw of a die, hidden objects (see "Dogrib," figs. 10–11, this vol.), or by some other random factor were appropriate to a people whose technology and habitat often exposed them to the contingencies of chance.

Music and Dancing

In traditional culture, musical performances were often not recreational amusements but rather served serious purposes (fig. 15), as in courtship, mourning, and summoning by song and drum nonhuman helpers for successful hunting (fig. 16) or curing. However, among the Athapaskan tribes of the Mackenzie drainage, male communal singing provided melody and rhythm in purely recreational group dancing whenever people gathered. These "tea dances" and "drum dances" continued to be enthusiastically performed through the mid-twentieth century (fig. 17). (For a technically competent treatment of traditional Mackenzie Athapaskan dancing and musical styles see Kurath 1966.)

New musical styles, dances, and instruments were adopted during the cultural florescence promoted by diffusion and growing prosperity in late fur-trade times (Helm and Lurie 1966:98; Honigmann 1968a). To the jigs and reels introduced in that era have been added a one-step dance by couples to "cowboy music" and in mid-twentieth century the loudly amplified music of rock with its vigorously animated dance forms. As new styles appeared, old ones did not immediately disappear; sometimes they remained as alternatives or as preferences of the older generation or of particular ethnic groups (Honigmann 1962:65–66; L.W. Hall 1971). It is not known whether any style of dancing was ever exclusively the property of any generation until the 1960s when rock became the prerogative of young people, virtually a symbol of youth culture (Honigmann 1949:173–174; L. Mason 1967:55; Honigmann and Honigmann 1970:97, 182, 215; Alexander 1972:55–56).

Alcohol

During the fur-trade era, Indians learned how to set malt beer or to prepare a fermented brew from yeast, water, dried fruits, and sugar. Brew parties became the most popular social gatherings in many small settlements. These convivial gatherings, comprised of friends and kin, provided one of the most emotionally unrestrained settings of Indian social relations. As the brew increased intoxication, the drinkers grew more and more elated. They talked and joked, affirmed good fellowship, engaged in sexual badinage and overtures, and sometimes broke into quarrels and violence that a spouse or good friend sought to restrain lest serious injury ensue (Honigmann and Honigmann 1945, 1970:46–47; Helm 1961:102–107; Bock 1966:81; Hippler 1972b; Dailey 1968 reviews the early role of alcohol among American Indian tribes as reported in the *Jesuit Relations*).

Especially as distilled liquor became available in the larger settlements, many Indians adopted the heavy use of alcohol and public drunkenness that was part of the White frontier style of life with which native people tended to identify (see, for example, Honigmann and Honigmann 1970:14–15, 111, 224, 229).

The drinking party, in the isolated camp or in the public bar, meant "having a good time." It provided a change of social and emotional pace from the every-

732

Smithsonian, NAA: 44.314–D.

Fig. 15. Dance of the Kutchin, which was accompanied by leaping, wrestling, and feats showing strength and agility. Such dancing often occurred when friendly bands met. The fringed skin clothes were decorated with beads and porcupine quills (Murray 1910:84, 87). Colored lithograph (Richardson 1851:397) from unlocated original drawing by Alexander Hunter Murray, 1847–1848, which is known only from a photostat in the B.C. Prov. Arch., Victoria (Murray 1910:87; Wilson 1947:41).

day life that offered little variety or means of entertainment. Another aspect of the complex meaning of alcohol was based on the recognition of the social-psychological use that the individual could make of its intoxicating properties. For example, in the iron-mining town of Schefferville, intoxication enabled Naskapi Indian men, drinking at home or in hotel bars, to bolster their self-image by making unrestrained claims for deference in ways they would never employ when sober (Robbins 1973).

For many Subarctic Indians, however, alcohol and drunkenness came to acquire a negative meaning as they learned the traumatized attitude with which alcohol has been regarded in North American culture and witnessed the violence, loss of jobs, and other distress caused by drunkenness. Rupert House Cree deemed drinking inappropriate in the ceremony of the shaking tent (Preston 1971:66). The preachments of the Rae Dogrib prophet stressed the social evils of drink (Helm 1972:80). Former drinkers among the Kutchin of Inuvik and the Saulteaux of the Lake Winnipeg area joined fundamentalist churches that forbade the use of alcohol, or they affiliated with Alcoholics Anonymous

to secure help in giving up drinking (Bock 1966:81; Steinbring 1969–1972, 3; Hippler 1972a).

Speech Use

Narrative served the Cree as a device that enabled an Indian to communicate the precise and often complex or obscure meaning of a particular fact (Preston 1971a:13ff.). The context of the story—a mythical tale or a factual one—communicated the correct way to understand the topic. Preston reports that Indians dealing with him chose narrative to answer his direct questions in preference to offering generalizing, definitional responses such as he had expected. More than one ethnographer has been disconcerted by the northern Indian's tactic of apparently ignoring certain questions (cf. Rogers 1962:4). Preston believes that when a Cree informant answers numerous questions with "I don't know," he means, "I don't know how to reply to your question in a way that will be satisfactory to us both," and when something in the interpersonal situation inhibits him from resorting to narrative to bring out the

Field Mus., Chicago: 61540.

Fig. 16. Shinabest, Naskapi of the Davis Inlet band, singing a hunting song. The drum head, held between two ring frames, is a tanned whole young caribou skin, and the lashings are babiche; bird quill snares are attached to a cord across the head. Photograph by William Duncan Strong, March 1928.

complex meaning of what is being discussed. Preston supports his theory of narrative largely by his own experience as an ethnographer among the eastern Cree, but he is inclined to believe that under certain circumstances Indians followed the same mode of speech among themselves.

Narratives as means of expressing complex meanings are, in the broadest sense, metaphors, devices whose use Preston (1971) describes among the Cree. Metaphors served to convey the essential or inward aspect of phenomena whose complete nature could not be fully communicated by attending merely to outward appearance.

Though Algonquian and Athapaskan Indians held verbal skill in high regard, their patterned use of speech 734 also included silence under certain circumstances,

avoidance of certain topics or emotions in conversation, and other kinds of verbal restraint.

Remaining silent when dangerous or socially ambiguous subjects came up in conversation was a good way of avoiding offense (Darnell 1970). The Ingalik considered it extremely painful for the speaker to express an unfavorable opinion directly to a person's face (Osgood 1958:218). Nevertheless, they knew terms of opprobrium and uttered them in moments of extreme provocation. The worst thing one person could say to another was "Die!" Another terrible expletive was "Dirty!" but the English word fails to convey the full force of the native expression. Songs of ridicule, an expressive form that the Ingalik borrowed from the Eskimo and sang during ceremonies, were less likely to provoke fighting than direct expressions of displeasure or anger. The person made fun of, perhaps by being likened in an uncomplimentary manner to a bird or an animal, simply retaliated in kind.

Kaska manifested verbal restraint by omitting strong warm feelings from speech as well as hostile feelings, except that warmth was fully conveyed to a young child. They trained their children not to shout and to suppress other forms of verbal exuberance. Yet, a limit existed to restraint, for an excessively taciturn person disturbed people.

Humor and Sarcasm

Humor occurs when someone or something, deliberately or inadvertently, expresses the ridiculous. Laughter is evidence of the humor in absurd situations and in the incongruous actions of people, animals, and mythological beings. It was humorous when a person, making no attempt to deceive, said something directly contrary to what all eyes could see, as when an old man was called young, or when someone, without intending offense, acted contrary to the norm for a situation. That happened, for example, when guest Ingaliks warned their potlatch host that he would not be repaid for the gifts he gave, or a speaker used the third-person singular to refer to the victim of a joke while looking at someone else (Honigmann 1947–1948; Osgood 1958:78, 219; Dunning 1959:127; see also Preston 1969:10).

A relaxed, convivial group allowed for prolonged, elaborate, humorous play built up of word and gesture (Slobodin 1969:76–77). What was humorous to one person might not amuse another. When Indians laughed at actions that struck them as absurd but were not so intended—a man stumbling, for example—the target of their laughter might react in good grace and join in. Or he might interpret the laughter as scorn and become angry. Hence laughter was somewhat ambiguous and could be dangerous, as children learned from being warned not to show disrespect for animals by laughing at them (Flannery 1946:264).

Certain occasions were especially rich in humor. The great ceremonies of the Ingalik frequently rang with

Native Press, Yellowknife, N.W.T.
Fig. 17. left, Dogrib drummer-chanters for Drum Dance at Detah Village. left to right, Angus Charlo, Narcisse Charlo, Harry Martin, Alfred Baillargeon, Chief Joe Charlo, Noel Croockedhand, Isadore T'setta, and Gabriel Doctor. right, Dogrib Indians dancing the Tea Dance to their own choral accompaniment at Fort Rae. left, Photographed in 1976. right, Photographed by Tapwe Chrétien, July 1976.

laughter and were favorite times for clowning and other kinds of contrived absurdity. Somewhat surprisingly, shaking-tent performances among the Cree and Ojibwa were recognized occasions for joking. The *mista·pe·w* spirits visiting the shaman in his lodge threw out humorous remarks, much to the onlookers' delight (Dunning 1959:179; McGee 1961:84; Preston 1966, 1971a:26–166).

Humor shades into sarcasm, a scornful comment about an event that may be too pungent to draw a laugh. An Attawapiskat Indian man referring to an allegedly promiscuous woman remarked that at night she was as active as a rabbit (Honigmann 1947–1948). An Ingalik reprimanded a man fighting a brother by saying scornfully: "Why don't you kill your brother and eat him? You treat him just like an animal!" (Osgood 1958:219). Apparently Indians found metaphor useful to sharpen a stinging comment.

Cross-cousins

All social interaction contains an expressive element; therefore, all kinship relationships do. Relatives symbolize through appropriate words, gestures, gifts, or visits sentiments they hold, or are supposed to hold, toward one another. Many times the actors themselves are unaware of the symbolism informally expressed in kinship behavior, though they know that the correct outward forms must be observed. In such cases, ethnographers must interpret the expressive component in the manifest behavior occurring in a kinship dyad. Accounts of how cross-cousins of opposite sex interacted among the Northern Ojibwa need such interpretation (Dunning 1959:129–130; Rogers 1962:B12–B34; Hallowell 1949:110–111).

The ethnographers report that an adolescent boy freely engaged in roughhouse teasing with his female cross-cousin and directed salacious, joking remarks to her. Considering that the Ojibwa language lacked polite terms for sexual topics, some of his allusions were plain indeed. The girl, stimulated by his attention, took no offense but maintained as becoming an air of modesty as her confusion allowed. With age, however, the female cross-cousin's confusion under such circumstances disappeared and her behavior changed dramatically. An old woman unashamedly met her cousin's wit with ribald barbs of her own. Good-naturedly, she warded off his mock sexual intrusions, while her husband laughed, as the spirit of the affair called for him to do.

The attractiveness and excitement of sex was the dominant theme expressed by Ojibwa in the patterned interaction of these cross-cousins. The vehicles of expression—verbal joking and horseplay—reflected the ambiguity and ambivalence surrounding the appeal of sex. For sex in its permitted forms of expression was no more free and untrammelled in Ojibwa culture than anywhere else. Outside of the legitimizing context of marriage or between cross-cousins of the opposite sex one or both of whom might be married to another, sexually toned behavior remained ambiguous. Joking defined the ambiguous and disabled the threatening. When initiated by boys to youthful female cross-cousins, joking and horseplay closely resembled the teasing with which boys in many Subarctic communities made premarital sexual advances to unrelated girls; in both contexts it symptomatized their ambivalence (Honigmann 1947, 1949:160–161; Wallis and Wallis 1955:285; Dunning 1959:102; Rogers 1962:B43–B45).

Social Personality

Social personalities describe populations, not individuals. A description of social personality sums up a group's intellectual approach to problems of living, the values by which its members prefer to rule their lives, the level or degree of control people exert over drives and feelings, and the circumstances when they relax control and freely vent emotion. Such features can, of course, be known only from what individuals belonging to a society say and do.

A social personality is an ideal type in the sense of an archetypal construct, not in the sense of "perfect" or "desirable." The observer constructs it from dozens of clues gathered in studying a sample of the population, testing and observing people in a variety of public situations. By definition, no individual possesses the ideal type of personality in its entirety. Personality research in the Subarctic has produced ideal types constructed by studying Indians belonging to identifiable communities, but in samples that are not statistically representative, so that this is not the "modal personality" (the constellation of personality attributes that occurs most often in a population, cf. Wallace 1952; Gue 1971). Limited though ideal types may be for prediction, they are useful to compare different cultural groups. This discussion will be exclusively concerned with feelings and values in Subarctic social personality, not with its intellectual aspects.

Inner Control

Anthropological research on Subarctic Indian social personality, beginning with Hallowell, has discovered several correspondences in behavioral style between a number of Indian communities belonging to both the Athapaskan and Algonquian language divisions (cf. Spindler and Spindler 1957). Some of the same anthropologists working among Eskimo find that they do not belong to this psychological type. One Athapaskan-Algonquian similarity, variously described by different observers, is a tendency to maintain strong inner control over behavior. (What follows concerning inner control is supported by evidence in Hallowell 1946:204–207, 210–214, 216–220, 224, 1949:123; Honigmann 1949:253, 264–267, 288–291, 299–302; Helm, DeVos, and Carterette 1963:127; Helm 1961:89–90, 92; Preston 1971a:26, 107, 181, 184–185, 255, 1976; Savishinsky 1971:612.) Hippler's (1972, 1972b) analysis of social personality in interior Alaska diverges greatly from the others'. Relying more than they on indirect evidence such as folktales, he finds evidence for very poor internal control and hence a necessity for strong external sanctions, which were manifested in the legal system and chieftainship of former times.

Several kinds of evidence illustrate the restraint that Indians exerted over themselves. Shyness marked by comparative facial immobility on occasions when Indians felt uneasy with one another or when they were in the presence of strangers is one illustration. In an unfamiliar situation, the Indian did nothing to help overcome feelings of strain, much to the discomfort of White people who are inclined to become garrulous in such circumstances. Indians also revealed self-restraint when they were provoked, irritated, or frustrated. Evidence indicates that control even extended to the level of feeling. Indians sought to suppress or blunt the intense conscious impact of negative feelings accompanying disappointment, personal tragedy, fear, and other unpleasant emotions. They not only controlled negative emotions but also restrained signs of exuberance, joy, and elation, so that those feelings acquired a relatively measured expression that gave someone unfamiliar with Indians an initial impression of emotional flatness in their behavior (cf. Savishinsky 1970:44). Longer acquaintance, of course, revealed peaks and troughs in their style of emotional expression and made clear that Indians were not total emotional suppressors.

Above all, Indians normally controlled the release of hostility. Direct aggressive behavior, verbal or physical, toward other people was rigorously checked. Eschewing aggression was quite likely not the outcome of a saintly value placed on nonviolence. It may have been consciously motivated by fear of retaliation that could take the form of sorcery or by the realization that showing anger would lead to prolonged and highly unpleasant strain in relations with someone seen regularly. Whatever the consequences the individual was to avoid, he was guided by the social norm of repression of aggressive behavior.

Inner control implies that the Indian responded to situations after they had been cognitively assimilated. His action stemmed from internal rather than primarily external stimuli. The same idea is contained in descriptions of the Indian social personality as strongly introverted, a conclusion consistently supported by Rorschach test results. The Ingalik Indian, Osgood (1959:165) observes, is "constantly intervolving the things that he sees, that he hears, that he smells, into a meaningful pattern—and in his real world, this is the truth of it. Seeing particulars is very much less reliable." Preston (1969a:9) in like terms describes the eastern Cree as placing a high evaluation on mental events. They "define certain truth value on the basis of what a man can see with his own eyes, complemented by what he may perceive with his 'mind's eye' " (Preston 1971a:144, 180).

Restraint was a matter of degree. First, it varied in strength among individuals and groups. This is illustrated in a comparison of Slavey and Dogrib Indian personality by Helm and DeVos (1963). Compared to the Slavey, the Dogrib gave evidence of quicker emotional responsiveness, meaning less inner control.

Nevertheless, the Dogrib in test data showed up as relatively placid individuals who avoided hostile feelings and were little moved by strong positive emotion. Control likewise altered with situation. Drunkenness has long been noted as an occasion when emotional restraint and controlled behavior almost disappeared among Indians (Hallowell 1946:214–215; Honigmann 1949:237–239). Apparently flamboyant emotionality, ready expression of anger, and loss of other inhibitions after heavy drinking occurred not, as used to be thought, because alcohol acted on cortical centers—almost literally dissolving inhibitions—but because Indians had learned to structure drunkenness in cultural terms (MacAndrew and Edgerton 1969). Drunkenness became an occasion when people might release control, vent emotion freely and feel it intensely, and know that, within limits, drunkenness made such behavior expectable and socially excusable.

Personal Autonomy

"They hold it as a maxim that each one is free: that one can do whatever he wishes: and that it is not sensible to put constraint upon men," the missionary Le Clercq observed about seventeenth-century Micmac (quoted in Hallowell 1946:207). The Indians' maxim points to another pronounced quality in Subarctic social personality: high regard for personal autonomy or independence. It is an attribute of motivation and behavior and not the quality of northern social organization that has been termed "atomistic" (see Hickerson 1967; Honigmann 1968). Personal autonomy refers to a claim that individuals manifested when they resisted bossiness or other interference in their personal lives. The suppression of hostility and aggression in interpersonal relations was consistent with a high degree of personal autonomy, since in avoiding domination of others through aggression a person showed that he respected and recognized others' freedom of action. (For documentation see Hallowell 1946:207–208; Honigmann 1949:250–258; Helm and DeVos 1963; Helm, DeVos, and Carterette 1963:127; Slobodin 1960; Helm 1961; Balikci 1963; Savishinsky 1971:611).

Some anthropologists, including Hallowell (1938), have offered a different interpretation: they have traced nonaggression in interpersonal relations to psychological sources such as pervasive anxiety, social distrust between people, and hostility unconsciously projected by one person upon others (cf. Slobodin 1960). According to them, nonaggression expressed fear, not respect for another's autonomy. People were afraid of what might happen should they infringe on the rights of somebody else. Up to a point the two interpretations can be reconciled: looked at from the standpoint of motivation, fear of engendering a hostile emotional re-

action moved people to use tact in giving directions or making suggestions and to avoid criticism; while from an outside vantage point, Indians showed regard for one another's feelings. However, that does not explain parental behavior, for it is unlikely that anxiety or social distrust induced Indian adults to respect children's independence. Rather, sensitivity to the youngsters' feelings guided the parents' treatment, which in turn, along with other supportive experiences children encountered, fostered development of independent personalities.

Subarctic culture contained symbolic warnings that the desire for independence could be carried too far. The inhuman isolate of the northern Algonquians, the Windigo (Cree *wi·htiko·w,* East Main Cree *atoš*), symbolized the danger that befalls persons who become so asocial that they treat people like animals by feeding on human flesh. Although many theories (see Parker 1960; Fogelson 1965; Rohrl 1970 who was criticized by Brown 1971; and Bishop 1971) consider Windigo disorder as a culture-specific or folk illness, there are no well-authenticated cases of the supposed ailment. The primary sources consist of descriptions written at second- or thirdhand, and the etiological theorists have never studied a patient suffering from the syndrome. By empirical standards, it is much more defensible to regard Windigo disorder as an Indian belief (as Bishop 1971 tends to do and as analyzed by Sadler 1976).

Slobodin (1960) collected Kutchin myths of persons who were feared and mistrusted because they had grown too isolated from communal life. He points out that stories of "bush men," isolated prowlers of the forest, also symbolized dangers associated with extreme aloneness and, from a functional point of view, reinforced centripetal tendencies in a structurally simple society.

Nevertheless, much of Subarctic culture during pre-contact and fur-trade times expressed and supported the value Indians placed on personal autonomy. Most technical tasks and many social forms left individuals with considerable scope to determine for themselves when and how to act. People were hardly ever subordinated in hierarchical chains of command. Modes of cultural adaptation left the individual relatively free by placing a premium on personal initiative, self-reliance, and individual responsibility. These were essential traits for maintaining life in the small residential bands (cf. Barry, Child, and Bacon 1959). But the atomistic quality of social life must not be exaggerated to the nonsense point. Leadership did exist in the small bands; and some tasks, like hunting with caribou surrounds, required cooperation with members outside the family. Like human beings everywhere, Indians depended on one another, sharing of food being one form of their mutual dependence. Consequently, people strongly deplored the individualistic trends of later fur-trade

737

times that curtailed sharing (Honigmann 1949:280–287; Helm, DeVos, and Carterette 1963:128; Savishinsky 1971:611).

Plainly, the value placed on personal autonomy did not imply total social atomism; it was not so great that it prevented all cooperation and exercise and acceptance of authority. Nevertheless, it is likely, judging from what anthropologists observed in the late fur-trade period, that the claim for personal autonomy introduced a dynamic tension into interpersonal relations to which leadership and other structural forms perforce adapted. The individual, in his turn, despite a positive evaluation of independence, also had to adjust, however reluctantly at times, to his dependence on others, to their claims on him, and to the manifest advantages of leadership in certain circumstances.

Contributors

This list gives the academic affiliations of authors at the time this volume went to press. The dates following the entries indicate when each manuscript was (1) first received in the General Editor's office; (2) accepted by the editors; (3) sent to the author (or, if deceased, a substitute) for final approval after revisions and editorial work.

ACHESON, ANN WELSH, Bangor, Maine. Old Crow, Yukon Territory: 7/11/72; 6/18/73; 5/9/79.

ASCH, MICHAEL I., Department of Anthropology, University of Alberta, Edmonton. Slavey: 8/2/72; 4/30/73; 1/15/80.

BARGER, W.K., Department of Anthropology, Indiana University, Indianapolis. Great Whale River, Quebec: 11/15/72; 6/8/73; 4/20/79.

BISHOP, CHARLES A., Department of Sociology/Anthropology, State University of New York at Oswego. Territorial Groups Before 1821: Cree and Ojibwa: 5/22/74; 7/10/74; 11/24/80.

CINQ-MARS, JACQUES, Archaeological Survey of Canada, National Museums of Canada, Ottawa, Ontario. History of Archeological Research in the Subarctic Shield and Mackenzie Valley: 4/30/79; 12/2/80; 12/3/80.

CLARK, A. McFADYEN, Canadian Ethnology Service, National Museums of Canada, Ottawa, Ontario. Koyukon: 9/15/75; 8/22/77; 5/31/79.

CLARK, DONALD W., Archaeological Survey of Canada, National Museums of Canada, Ottawa, Ontario. Prehistory of the Western Subarctic: 6/5/73; 7/26/78; 5/27/80.

CROW, JOHN R., Jaffrey, New Hampshire. Han: 7/16/73; 8/6/73; 3/25/80.

DAVIS, NANCY YAW, Cultural Dynamics, Ltd., Fort Washington, Maryland. History of Research in Subarctic Alaska: 9/8/77; 9/8/77; 7/30/80.

DE LAGUNA, FREDERICA, Department of Anthropology (emeritus), Bryn Mawr College, Pennsylvania. Ahtna: 7/15/75; 9/30/75; 4/16/79.

DENNISTON, GLENDA, Madison, Wisconsin. Environment and Culture in the Cordillera: 9/18/78; 7/3/79; 7/14/80. Sekani: 2/26/80; 4/16/80; 5/8/80.

DUFF, WILSON (deceased), Department of Anthropology and Sociology, University of British Columbia, Vancouver. Tsetsaut: 5/24/73; 8/2/79; 12/20/79.

GARDNER, JAMES S., Department of Geography, University of Waterloo, Ontario. General Environment: 6/9/72; 1/13/76; 8/21/80.

GILBERT, LOUIS, Outremont, Quebec. Attikamek (Tête de Boule): 4/11/78; 11/8/79; 10/24/80.

GILLESPIE, BERYL C., Iowa City, Iowa. Bearlake Indians: 1/19/78; 10/17/78; 10/11/79. Major Fauna in the Traditional Economy: 1/27/78; 10/17/78; 6/18/80. Mountain Indians: 8/21/72; 10/23/72; 12/20/79. Nahani: 7/23/73; 7/23/73; 3/26/80. Territorial Groups Before 1821: Athapaskans of the Shield and the Mackenzie Drainage: 7/29/77; 8/3/77; 12/10/80. Yellowknife: 9/19/77; 10/17/78; 9/17/79.

GODDARD, IVES, Department of Anthropology, Smithsonian Institution, Washington, D.C. Territorial Groups of West-Central Alaska Before 1898: 2/27/79; 7/16/79; 9/28/79.

GOLLA, VICTOR K., Department of Anthropology, George Washington University, Washington, D.C. Northern Athapaskan Languages: 12/28/76; 6/2/80; 8/21/80.

GUÉDON, MARIE-FRANÇOISE, Department of Anthropology and Sociology, University of British Columbia, Vancouver. Upper Tanana River Potlatch: 9/7/77; 9/7/77; 4/6/79.

HARA, HIROKO SUE, Women's Studies Program, Ochanomizu University, Tokyo, Japan. Hare: 5/18/72; 10/11/73; 11/9/79.

HELM, JUNE, Department of Anthropology, University of Iowa, Iowa City. Dogrib: 7/28/72; 9/24/73; 1/15/80. Intercultural Relations and Cultural Change in the Shield and Mackenzie Borderlands: 3/21/74; 3/21/74; 8/8/80. Introduction: 1/16/76; 10/4/80; 10/30/80. Native Settlements: Introduction: 8/20/73; 1/12/76; 4/20/79.

HENRIKSEN, GEORG, Department of Social Anthropology, University of Bergen, Norway. Davis Inlet, Labrador: 6/6/72; 3/27/79; 4/20/79.

HONIGMANN, JOHN J. (deceased), Department of Anthropology, University of North Carolina, Chapel Hill. Expressive Aspects of Subarctic Indian Culture: 9/21/72; 7/16/73; 7/5/79. Kaska: 4/28/72; 2/2/73; 4/7/80. Modern Subarctic Indians and Métis: 9/1/72; 12/11/73; 5/7/79. West Main Cree: 7/31/72; 3/29/73; 11/25/80.

HOSLEY, EDWARD H., Department of Anthropology, State University of New York, Potsdam. Environment and Culture in the Alaska Plateau: 5/14/76; 11/24/78; 4/24/79. Intercultural Relations and Cultural Change in the Alaska Plateau: 7/2/76; 12/20/78; 5/4/79. Kolchan: 6/13/72; 2/13/73; 4/11/79.

KRAUSS, MICHAEL E., Alaska Native Language Center, University of Alaska, Fairbanks. Northern Athapaskan Languages: 4/19/74; 6/2/80; 8/21/80.

LANE, ROBERT B., Victoria, British Columbia. Chilcotin: 6/15/72; 10/11/73; 4/3/80.

LEACOCK, ELEANOR, Department of Anthropology, City College, City University of New York, New York. Montagnais-Naskapi: 10/26/76; 11/1/76; 11/17/80. Seventeenth-Century Montagnais Social Relations and Values: 12/19/75; 12/28/76; 12/3/80.

MACLACHLAN, BRUCE B., Department of Anthropology, Southern Illinois University, Carbondale. Tahltan: 5/3/72; 2/13/80; 4/28/80.

McCLELLAN, CATHARINE, Department of Anthropology, University of Wisconsin, Madison. Ahtna: 7/15/75; 9/30/75; 4/16/79. Environment and Culture in the Cordillera: 9/18/78; 7/3/79; 7/14/80. History of Research in the Subarctic Cordillera: 8/21/80; 12/1/80; 12/14/80. Inland Tlingit: 9/22/76; 7/31/79; 3/17/80. Intercultural Relations and Cultural Change in the Cordillera: 2/29/80; 3/20/80; 6/26/80. Tagish: 9/13/76; 10/21/77; 3/17/80. Tutchone: 1/2/80;1/24/80; 5/1/80.

McKENNAN, ROBERT A., Department of Anthropology (emeritus), Dartmouth College, Hanover, New Hampshire. Tanana: 8/27/73; 5/21/74; 4/6/79.

McNULTY, GÉRARD E., Département d'Anthropologie, Université Laval, Ste-Foy, Quebec. Attikamek (Tête de Boule): 4/11/78; 11/8/79; 11/3/80.

MARTIJN, CHARLES A., Service du Patrimoine Autochtone, Ministère des Affaires Culturelles, Quebec, Quebec. History of Archeological Research in the Subarctic Shield and Mackenzie Valley: 4/30/79; 12/2/80; 12/3/80.

NOBLE, WILLIAM C., Department of Anthropology, McMaster University, Hamilton, Ontario. Prehistory of the Great Slave Lake and Great Bear Lake Region: 5/12/72; 10/27/75; 6/19/80.

OBLEY, PHILIP R., Havertown, Pennsylvania. Han: 7/16/73; 8/6/73; 3/25/80.

OLSON, WALLACE M., Division of Humanities and Social Sciences, University of Alaska, Juneau. Minto, Alaska: 4/24/72; 6/21/74; 4/10/79.

PRESTON, RICHARD J., Department of Anthropology, McMaster University, Hamilton, Ontario. East Main Cree: 6/6/75; 7/31/75; 11/14/80.

RHODES, RICHARD A., Department of Linguistics, University of Michigan, Ann Arbor. Subarctic Algonquian Languages: 12/18/78; 6/20/80; 10/31/80.

RIDINGTON, ROBIN, Department of Anthropology and Soci-

ology, University of British Columbia, Vancouver. Beaver: 6/12/72; 7/10/74; 11/16/79.

ROGERS, EDWARD S., Department of Ethnology, Royal Ontario Museum, Toronto. Environment and Culture in the Shield and Mackenzie Borderlands: 5/1/72; 3/31/75; 10/7/80. History of Ethnological Research in the Subarctic Shield and Mackenzie Borderlands: 5/27/75; 7/8/80; 8/28/80. Intercultural Relations and Cultural Change in the Shield and Mackenzie Borderlands: 3/21/74; 6/13/74; 8/8/80. Montagnais-Naskapi: 10/26/76; 11/1/76; 11/17/80. Northern Ojibwa: 5/1/72; 7/24/74; 10/17/80.

SAVISHINSKY, JOEL S., Department of Anthropology, Ithaca College, New York. Hare: 5/18/72; 10/11/73; 11/9/79.

SLOBODIN, RICHARD, Department of Anthropology, McMaster University, Hamilton, Ontario. Kutchin: 10/23/73; 9/7/77; 6/4/80. Subarctic Métis: 8/29/77; 9/7/77; 1/15/80.

SMITH, DAVID M., Department of Sociology/Anthropology, University of Minnesota, Duluth. Fort Resolution, Northwest Territories: 8/25/72; 9/6/72; 8/29/79.

SMITH, JAMES G.E., Museum of the American Indian, Heye Foundation, New York, New York. Chipewyan: 2/20/75; 2/24/75; 1/14/80. Environment and Culture in the Shield and Mackenzie Borderlands: 5/1/72; 3/31/75; 10/7/80. Intercultural Relations and Cultural Change in the Shield and Mackenzie Borderlands: 3/21/74; 6/13/74; 8/8/80. Western Woods Cree: 3/24/75; 4/8/75; 11/25/80.

SNOW, JEANNE H., Iowa City, Iowa. Ingalik: 7/19/76; 7/20/76; 5/3/79.

STEINBRING, JACK H., Department of Anthropology, University of Winnipeg, Manitoba. Saulteaux of Lake Winnipeg: 5/31/74; 4/9/75; 10/20/80.

TAYLOR, J. GARTH, Canadian Ethnology Service, National Museums of Canada, Ottawa, Ontario. Northern Ojibwa: 5/1/72; 7/24/74; 10/17/80.

TOBEY, MARGARET L., Washington, D.C. Carrier: 4/77; 7/31/79; 4/4/80.

TODD, EVELYN M., Department of Anthropology, Trent University, Peterborough, Ontario. Subarctic Algonquian Languages: 11/30/72; 6/20/80; 10/31/80.

TOWNSEND, JOAN B., Department of Anthropology, University of Manitoba, Winnipeg. Tanaina: 7/12/72; 8/12/77; 4/16/79.

VANSTONE, JAMES W., Department of Anthropology, Field Museum of Natural History, Chicago. Museum and Archival Resources for Subarctic Alaska: 9/10/76; 10/3/77; 7/10/80. Territorial Groups of West-Central Alaska Before 1898: 2/27/79; 7/16/79; 9/28/79.

WRIGHT, JAMES V., Archaeological Survey of Canada, National Museums of Canada, Ottawa, Ontario. Prehistory of the Canadian Shield: 5/15/72; 7/7/75; 6/30/80.

Bibliography

This list includes all references cited in the volume, arranged in alphabetical order according to the names of the authors as they appear in the citations in the text. Multiple works by the same author are arranged chronologically; second and subsequent titles by the same author in the same year are differentiated by letters added to the dates. Where more than one author with the same surname is cited, one has been arbitrarily selected for text citation by surname alone throughout the volume, while the others are always cited with added initials; the combination of surname with date in text citations should avoid confusion. Where a publication date is different from the series date (as in some annual reports and the like), the former is used. Dates, authors, and titles that do not appear on the original works are enclosed by square brackets. For manuscripts, dates refer to time of composition. For publications reprinted or first published many years after original composition, a bracketed date after the title refers to the time of composition or the date of original publication.

Abercrombie, William R.
1899   Reports of Explorations in the Territory of Alaska (Cooks Inlet, Sushitna, Copper and Tanana Rivers), 1898. Made Under the Direction of the Secretary of War, by Capt. Edwin F. Glenn and Capt. W.R. Abercrombie. Washington: U.S. Government Printing Office.

————
1900   A Military Reconnoissance of the Copper River Valley. Pp. 561-628 in Compilation of Narratives of Explorations in Alaska. Washington: U.S. Government Printing Office.

————
1900a   Report of a Supplementary Expedition into the Copper River Valley, Alaska, 1884. Pp. 381–408 in Compilation of Narratives of Explorations in Alaska. Washington: U.S. Government Printing Office.

————
1900b   Alaska 1899: Copper River Exploring Expedition. Washington: U.S. Government Printing Office.

Aberle, David R., A.K. Cohen, A.K. Davis, Marion J. Levy, Jr., and F.X. Sutton
1950   The Functional Prerequisites of a Society. *Ethics* 60(2):100-111.

Abler, Thomas A., Douglas Sanders, and Sally M. Weaver
1974   A Canadian Bibliography, 1960-1970. Toronto: University of Toronto Press.

Acheson, Ann Welsh
[1968-1969] [Ethnographic Fieldnotes from Approximately Eight Months' Fieldwork Among the Kutchin at Old Crow, Yukon Territory.] (Manuscripts in Acheson's possession.)

————
1977   Nomads in Town: The Kutchin of Old Crow, Yukon Territory. (Unpublished Ph.D. Dissertation in Anthropology, Cornell University, Ithaca, N.Y.)

————
1977a   Kutchin Feasting: Continuity and Transformation. (Paper presented at the 17th Annual Meeting of the Northeastern Anthropological Association, Providence, R.I., March 24-26.)

————
[1980]   The Kutchin Family: Past and Present. In The Canadian Family: Ethnic Variations. K. Ishwaran, ed. Toronto: McGraw Hill-Ryerson. In Press.

Ackerman, Robert E.
1975   The Kenaitze People. Phoenix: Indian Tribal Series.

Ackroyd, Lynda
[1979]   Dogrib Verb Structure. (Unpublished manuscript in Ackroyd's possession.)

Adams, J.
1831   Sketches of the Tête de Boule Indians. *Quebec Literary and Historical Society Transactions* 2:25-39. Quebec.

Adams, Joseph
1733   [London Inward Correspondence, July 31, 1733.] (Manuscript A.11/2 in Hudson's Bay Company Archives, Provincial Archives of Manitoba, Winnipeg, Canada.)

Adams, W.P., W.R. Cowan, B.F. Findlay, J.S. Gardner, and R.J. Rogerson
1966   Snowfall and Snowcover at Knob Lake, Central Labrador-Ungava. Pp. 114-140 in Hydrological Studies in Labrador Ungava. *McGill University, Subarctic Research Laboratory Paper* 22. Montreal.

Adney, Edwin T.
1900   Moose Hunting with the Tro-chu-tin. *Harper's New Monthly Magazine* 100(598):494-507.

Adney, Edwin T., and Howard I. Chapelle
1964   The Bark Canoes and Skin Boats of North America. *United States National Museum Bulletin* 230. Washington.

Agogino, George A., and Eugene Galloway
1965   The Sister's Hill Site: A Hell Gap Site in North-central Wyoming. *Plains Anthropologist* 10(29):190-193.

Akrigg, G.P.V., and Helen B. Akrigg
1977   British Columbia Chronicle, 1847-1871: Gold and Colonists. Vancouver: Discovery Press.

Alaska Commercial Company Records
[1872-1899] [Iliamna Trading Post.] (Manuscripts in Library, University of Alaska, College.)

————
[1875-1903] [Tyonek Trading Post.] (Manuscripts in Library, University of Alaska, College.)

Alaska Native Foundation
1975   Village Corporations Eligible for Land and Money Benefits. In Village Corporations Established Pursuant to the Alaska Native Claims Settlement Act. Washington: U.S. Government Printing Office.

Alaska Russian Church Archives
[1842-1931] [Vital Statistics, Nushagak Mission.] (Manuscripts in Russian in Library of Congress, Washington.)

————
[1845-1933] [Vital Statistics, Kenai Mission.] (Manuscripts in Library of Congress, Washington.)

Alexander, Frank S.
[1972]   Contemporary Fort Yukon Culture. (Unpublished fieldnotes in possession of John J. Honigmann.)

Allard, Edward
1929   Notes on the Kaska and Upper Liard Indians. *Primitive Man* 2(1-2):24-26.

Allen, Henry T.
1887   Report of an Expedition to the Copper, Tananá, and Koyukuk Rivers, in the Territory of Alaska, in the Year 1885. Washington: U.S. Government Printing Office.

————
1889   Atnatanas: Natives of Copper River, Alaska. Pp. 258-266 in Pt. 1 of *Annual Report of the Smithsonian Institution for 1886*. 2 Pts. Washington.

————
1900   A Military Reconnoissance of the Copper River Valley, 1885. Pp. 411-488 in Compilation of Narratives of Explorations in Alaska. Washington: U.S. Government Printing Office.

Allen, Thomas, ed.
1979   Wild Animals of North America. Washington: National Geographic Society.

Anahareo
1972   Devil in Deerskins: My Life with Grey Owl. Toronto: New Press.

Anderson, David
1873   The Net in the Bay; or, The Journal of a Visit to Moose and Albany. 2d ed. London: Hatchards. (Reprinted: Johnson Reprint, New York, 1967.)

Anderson, Douglas D.
1968   A Stone Age Campsite at the Gateway to America. *Scientific American* 218(6):24-33.

1970   Athapaskans in the Kobuk Arctic Woodlands, Alaska. *Bulletin of the Canadian Archaeological Association* 2:3-12. Ottawa.

1970a   Microblade Traditions in Northwestern Alaska. *Arctic Anthropology* 7(2):2-16.

1970b   Akmak: An Early Archeological Assemblage from Onion Portage, Northwest Alaska. *Acta Arctica* 16. Copenhagen.

1974-1975   Trade Networks Among the Selawik Eskimos in Northwestern Alaska During the Late 19th and Early 20th Centuries. *Folk* (16-17):63-72. Copenhagen.

Anderson, James
1849-1859   [Correspondence and Reports to Sir George Simpson [and Others] on the Affairs of the Mackenzie River District, 1849-1859.] (Manuscript Series MG19/A 29, copied in 1907 from original documents, in Public Archives of Canada, Ottawa.)

1858   [McKenzie River District Report.] (Copyist's Manuscript [1907] of a report dated Fort Simpson 19 May, 1858. Pp. 104-139 in Manuscript Series MG 19/A 29, in Public Archives of Canada, Ottawa.)

Anderson, James W.
1961   Fur Trader's Story. Toronto: Ryerson Press.

André, Anne
1976   Eukuan nin matshimanitu innu-iskueu; Je suis une maudite sauvagesse. José Mailhot, trans. Montreal: Editions Leméac.

1979   Tante nana etutamin nitassi; Qu'as-tu fait de mon pays? Antane Kapesh and José Mailhot, trans. [Montreal]: Les Editions Impossibles.

Anell, Bengt
1964   Animal Hunting Disguises Among the North American Indians. *Studia Ethnographica Upsaliensia* 21:1-34. Upsala. Sweden.

Anonymous
1854   Relation de ce qui s'est passé de plus remarquable aux missions des pères de la Compagnie de Jesus, en la Nouvelle France ès années 1676 et 1677. Albany: Weed, Parsons.

1859   On the Indian Tribes of McKenzie River District and the Arctic Coast. *Canadian Naturalist and Geologist* 4(3):190-197. Montreal.

[1865]   [Wordlist in Hong Kutchin; Also a Copy with Appended Notes by F.L.O. Roehrig Attributing the Vocabulary to William H. Dall.] (Unpublished manuscripts Nos. 148 and 165 in National Anthropological Archives, Smithsonian Institution, Washington.)

[1937-1940] [Unofficial Records Found at B.I.A. School, Minto, Alaska.] (Records in possession of Wallace M. Olson, Juneau, Alaska.)

1959   [Alphabetical List, Yellowknife Indian Agency No. 139.] (Mimeograph, dated May 21st 1959 of "All Treaty Indians" of the Yellowknife Agency of Indian Affairs Branch, Canada; copy in June Helm's possession.)

1964   Drink Drives Indians Back to Northland. *New York Times* February 2:65. (Brief Canadian press dispatch from Vancouver in non-final edition of this issue.)

1970   Report of Archeological Survey and Excavations Along the Alyeska Pipeline Service Company Haulroad and Pipeline Alignments. College: University of Alaska, Department of Anthropology.

1971   Final Report of the Archeological Survey and Excavations Along the Alyeska Pipeline Service Company; Pipeline Route to Fulfill Requirements of Task Order 9. College: University of Alaska, Department of Anthropology.

1974   Report on 1973 Program Archaeological Impact Study Mackenzie Highway System; Composite Volume—Fort Simpson to M.P. 939. [Fort Simpson]: Department of Public Works.

1974a   The Saulteaux, 1700's. Pp. 4-8 in The Interlake Flyer. Winnipeg: Fund for Rural Economic Development.

1978   [Cree Calendar, Compiled by Students of Main School, Moose Factory, Ontario.] (Copy in June Helm's possession.)

1980   James Bay Disagreement. *National Indian* 3(2): 8. Ottawa.

Antoine, Francesca, Catherine Bird, Agnes Isaac, Nellie Prince, Sally Sam, Richard Walker, and David B. Wilkinson
1974   Central Carrier Bilingual Dictionary. Fort Saint James, B.C.: Carrier Linguistic Committee.

Arcand, Bernard
1966   Ethnographie des Tutchone: Organisation socioéconomique et processus acculturatif. (Unpublished M.A. Thesis in Anthropology, University of Montreal, Montreal.)

Arnold, Robert D., ed.
1976   Alaska Native Land Claims. Anchorage: Alaska Native Foundation.

Asch, Michael I.
[1969-1970] [Ethnographic Notes, from Approximately 12 Months' Fieldwork Among the Slavey Indians, Wrigley, Northwest Territories, Canada.] (Manuscripts in Asch's possession.)

1972   A Social Behavioral Approach to Music Analysis: The Case of the Slavey Drum Dance. (Unpublished Ph.D. Dissertation in Anthropology, Columbia University, New York City.)

1975   The Impact of Changing Fur Trade Practices on the Economy of the Slavey Indians. Pp. 646-657 in Vol. 2 of Proceedings of the Second Congress of the Canadian Ethnology Society. Jim Freedman and Jerome H. Barkow, eds. 2 vols. *Canada. National Museum of Man, Mercury Series, Ethnology Service Paper* 28. Ottawa.

1976   Some Effects of the Late Nineteenth Century Modernization of the Fur Trade on the Economy of the Slavey Indians. *Western Canadian Journal of Anthropology* 6(4):7-15.

Asher, G.M., coll.
1860   Henry Hudson the Navigator: The Original Documents in Which His Career Is Recorded. (Works Issued by the Hakluyt Society 27) London: Printed for the Hakluyt Society.

Atwood, Wallace W.
1940   The Physiographic Provinces of North America. Boston: Ginn.

Aubin, George
1979   Golden Lake Algonquin: A Preliminary Report. Pp. 121-125 in *Papers of the Tenth Algonquian Conference*. William Cowan, ed. Ottawa: Carleton University.

Averkieva, Julia
1962   The Problem of Property in Contemporary American Ethnography. (Translated from *Sovetskaya Etnografiya* 4, 1961). *Soviet Anthropology and Archeology* 1(1):50-63.

Back, Sir George
1836   Narrative of the Arctic Land Expedition to the Mouth of the Great Fish River, and Along the Shores of the Arctic Ocean, in the Years 1833, 1834, and 1835. London: John Murray.

Bacqueville de la Potherie, Claude C. Le Roy
1931   Letters of La Potherie [1700]. Pp. 143-370 in Documents Relating to the Early History of Hudson Bay. J.B. Tyrrell, ed. (Publications of the Champlain Society 18) Toronto: The Champlain Society.

Bailey, Alfred G.
1969   The Conflict of European and Eastern Algonkian Cultures, 1504-1700: A Study in Canadian Civilization [1937]. 2d ed. Toronto: University of Toronto Press.

Baird, P.D.
1949   Expeditions to the Arctic. The Beaver 280 (June):41-47.

Baker, Marcus
1906   Geographic Dictionary of Alaska. Rev. ed. U.S. Geological Survey Bulletin 299, ser. F: Geography 52. Washington.

Balbi, A.
1826   Atlas ethnographique du globe en classification des peuples anciens et modernes d'après leur langues. Paris: Rey et Gravelier.

Baldwin, William W.
1957   Social Problems of the Ojibwa Indians in the Collins Area in Northwestern Ontario. Anthropologica 5:51-124. Ottawa.

Balikci, Asen
1959   Two Attempts at Community Organization Among the Eastern Hudson Bay Eskimos. Anthropologica n.s. 1(1-2):122-135. Ottawa.

1961   Relations inter-ethniques à la Grande Rivière de la Baleine, Baie d'Hudson, 1957. Anthropological Series 50, National Museum of Canada Bulletin 173:64-107. Ottawa.

1963   Vunta Kutchin Social Change: A Study of the People of Old Crow, Yukon Territory. (NCRC 63-3) Ottawa: Department of Northern Affairs and National Resources, Northern Co-ordination and Research Centre.

1963a   Family Organization of the Vunta Kutchin. Arctic Anthropology 1(2):62-69.

1964   The Eskimos of the Quebec-Labrador Peninsula: Ethnographic Contributions. Pp. 375-394 in Le Nouveau-Québec: Contribution à l'étude de l'occupation humaine. Jean Malaurie and Jacques Rousseau, eds. Paris: Mouton.

1968   Bad Friends. Human Organization 27(3):191-199.

Balikci, Asen, and Ronald Cohen
1963   Community Patterning in Two Northern Trading Posts. Anthropologica n.s. 5(1):33-45. Ottawa.

Bancroft, Hubert H.
1874-1876   The Native Races of the Pacific States. 5 vols. San Francisco: The History Company.

1886   The History of Alaska, 1730-1885. (The Works of Hubert H. Bancroft 33) San Francisco: A.L. Bancroft.

1887   The History of British Columbia, 1792-1887. San Francisco: The History Company.

Bandi, Hans Georg
1969   Eskimo Prehistory. Ann E. Keep, trans. College: University of Alaska Press.

Banfield, Alexander W.F.
1961   A Revision of the Reindeer and Caribou, genus Rangifer. Biological Series 66, National Museum of Canada Bulletin 177. Ottawa.

1974   The Mammals of Canada. Toronto: University of Toronto Press.

Baraga, Friedrich
1850   A Theoretical and Practical Grammar of the Otchipwe Language, the Language Spoken by the Chipewa Indians; Which Is Also Spoken by the Algonquin, Ottawa, and Potawatomi Indians, for the Use of Missionaries and Other Persons Living Among the Indians of the Above Named Tribes. Detroit: Jabez Fox.

1853   A Dictionary of the Otchipwe Language, Explained in English... Cincinnati: Printed for J.A. Hermann.

1878   A Theoretical and Practical Grammar of the Otchipwe Language for the Use of Missionaries and Other Persons Living Among the Indians. Montreal: Beauchemin et Valois.

1878-1880   A Dictionary of the Otchipwe Language, Explained in English. 2 vols. Montreal: Beauchemin et Valois. (Reprinted: Ross and Haines, Minneapolis, 1966.)

Barbeau, Charles M.
1933   Songs of the Northwest. Musical Quarterly 19:101-111.

[1939]   Assomption Sash. Anthropological Series 24, National Museum of Canada Bulletin 93. Ottawa.

1947   Alaska Beckons. Caldwell, Ida.: Caxton Printers; Toronto: Macmillan Company of Canada.

[1950]   Totem Poles. 2 vols. Anthropological Series 30, National Museum of Canada Bulletin 119. Ottawa.

Barger, W. Kenneth
1969   Adaptation to Town in Great Whale River. (Unpublished M.A. Thesis in Anthropology, University of North Carolina, Chapel Hill.)

1974   Great Whale River: Adaptation to Modern Life in the Canadian North. (Unpublished Ph.D. Dissertation in Anthropology, University of North Carolina, Chapel Hill.)

1977   Culture Change and Psychosocial Adjustment. American Ethnologist 4(3):471-495.

1979   Inuit-Cree Relations in the Eastern Hudson Bay Region. Arctic Anthropology 16(2):59-75.

[1980]   Inuit and Cree Adaptation to Northern Colonialism. In Contemporary Political Organization of Native North Americans. Ernest L. Schusky, ed. San Francisco: American Indian Historical Press. In Press.

Barger, W. Kenneth, and Daphne Earl
1971   Differential Adaptation to Northern Town Life by the Eskimos and Indians of Great Whale River. Human Organization 30(1):25-30.

Barker, Mary L.
1977   Natural Resources of British Columbia and the Yukon. Vancouver: David and Charles Douglas.

Barnouw, Victor
1950   Acculturation and Personality Among the Wisconsin Chippewa. Memoirs of the American Anthropological Association 72(4):5-148. Menasha, Wis.

Barnston, George
1839   [Martin Falls Report on the District for 1839.] (Manuscript B.123/e/14 in Hudson's Bay Company Archives, Provincial Archives of Manitoba, Winnipeg, Canada.)

1861   Recollections of the Swans and Geese of Hudson's Bay. Canadian Naturalist and Geologist 6(5):337-344.

Barry, Herbert, III, Irvin L. Childs, and Margaret K. Bacon
1959   Relation of Child Training to Subsistence Economy. American Anthropologist 61(1):51-63.

Barthes, Roland
1967   Elements of Semiology. Annette Lavers and Colin Smith, trans. London: Jonathan Cape.

Batty, Beatrice
1893   Forty-two Years Amongst the Indians and Eskimo: Pictures from the Life of the Right Reverend John Horden, First Bishop of Moosonee. London: The Religious Tract Society.

Beale, Anthony
1706   [Fort Albany Post Journal, May-June 1706.] (Manuscript B.3/a/2 in Hudson's Bay Company Archives, Provincial Archives of Manitoba, Winnipeg, Canada.)

1707   [Fort Albany Post Journal, May 2, 1707.] (Manuscript B.3/a/2 in Hudson's Bay Company Archives, Provincial Archives of Manitoba, Winnipeg, Canada.)

Begg, Alexander
1894-1895   History of the North-west. 3 vols. Toronto: Hunter, Rose.

Béland, Jean P.
1978   Atikamekw Morphology and Lexicon. (Unpublished Ph.D. Dissertation in Linguistics, University of California, Berkeley.)

Bell, Robert
1880   Report on Explorations of the Churchill and Nelson Rivers and Around God's and Island Lakes, 1879. *Geological Survey of Canada, Report on Progress for 1878-79.* Pt. C. Ottawa.

Beresford, William
1789   A Voyage Round the World; But More Particularly to the North-west Coast of America Performed in 1785, 1786, 1787, and 1788, in the King George and Queen Charlotte. George Dixon, ed. London: George Goulding.

Berger, Thomas R.
1977   Northern Frontier, Northern Homeland: The Report of the Mackenzie Valley Pipeline Inquiry. 2 vols. Toronto: James Lorimer in Association with Publishing Centre, Supply and Services Canada.

Bethune, William C., assembler
1937   Canada's Western Northland: Its History, Resources, Population, and Administration. Ottawa: King's Printer.

Bettarel, Robert, and Sidney Harrison
1962   An Early Ossuary in Michigan. *Michigan Archaeologist* 8(4):37-42.

Bilsland, W.W., and W.W. Ireland
1971   Atlin, 1898-1910: The Story of a Gold Boom. Atlin, B.C.: Atlin Centennial Committee. (Reprinted from *British Columbia Historical Quarterly* 16(3-4):121-179.)

Bird, John B., ed.
1964   Permafrost Studies in Central Labrador-Ungava. *McGill University, Subarctic Research Laboratory Paper* 16. Montreal.

1968   The Arctic. Pp. 508-528 in Canada: A Geographical Interpretation. J. Warkinton, ed. Toronto: Methuen.

1972   The Natural Landscapes of Canada. Toronto: Wiley.

1972a   The Physical Characteristics of Northern Canada. Pp. 1-24 in The North. Le Nord. William C. Wonders, ed. Toronto: University of Toronto Press.

Birket-Smith, Kaj
1918   A Geographic Study of the Early History of the Algonquian Indians. *Internationales Archiv für Ethnographie* 24:174-222.

1929   The Caribou Eskimos: Material and Social Life and Their Cultural Position. W.E. Calvert, trans. *Report of the Fifth Thule Expedition 1921-24,* Vol. 5, Pt. 1. Copenhagen.

1930   Contributions to Chipewyan Ethnology. W.E. Calvert, trans. *Report of the Fifth Thule Expedition 1921-24,* Vol. 6, Pt. 3. Copenhagen.

1930a   Folk Wanderings and Culture Drifts in Northern North America. *Journal de la Société des Américanistes de Paris* 22:1-32.

1953   The Chugach Eskimo. *Nationalmuseets Skrifter Etnografisk Raekke* 6. Copenhagen.

Birket-Smith, Kaj, and Frederica De Laguna
1938   The Eyak Indians of the Copper River Delta, Alaska. Copenhagen: Levin and Munksgaard.

Bishop, Charles A.
1969   The Northern Chippewa: An Ethnohistorical Study. (Unpublished Ph.D. Dissertation in Anthropology, State University of New York, Buffalo.)

1970   The Effects of Formal Education on Two Northern Ojibwa Communities. (Paper presented at the Algonquian and Iroquoian Conference, Peterborough, Ont.)

1970a   The Emergence of Hunting Territories Among the Northern Ojibwa. *Ethnology* 9(1):1-15.

1971   The Historical and Ecological Basis of Windigo Behavior. (Unpublished paper presented at the Algonquian Conference, Big Moose, N.Y.)

1972   Demography, Ecology and Trade Among the Northern Ojibwa and Swampy Cree. (Special Issue: The Fur Trade in Canada) *Western Canadian Journal of Anthropology* 3(1):58-71.

1973   Windigo: Canni[b]al Devil of the North. *Bulletin of the Field Museum of Natural History* 44(8):12-16. Chicago.

1974   The Northern Ojibwa and the Fur Trade: An Historical and Ecological Study. Toronto: Holt, Rinehart and Winston.

1975   The Origin of the Speakers of the Severn Dialect. Pp. 196-208 in Papers of the Sixth Algonquian Conference, 1974. William Cowan, ed. *Canada. National Museum of Man, Mercury Series, Ethnology Service Paper* 23. Ottawa.

1975a   Ojibwa, Cree and the Hudson's Bay Company in Northern Ontario: Culture and Conflict in the Eighteenth Century. Pp. 150-162 in Western Canada Past and Present. A.W. Rasporich, ed. Calgary: McClelland and Stewart West.

1976   The Emergence of the Northern Ojibwa: Social and Economic Consequences. *American Ethnologist* 3(1):39-54.

1978   Cultural and Biological Adaptations to Deprivation: The Northern Ojibwa Case. Pp. 208-230 in Extinction and Survival in Human Populations. Charles D. Laughlin, Jr. and Ivan A. Brady, eds. New York: Columbia University Press.

Bishop, Charles A., and M. Estellie Smith
1975   Early Historic Populations in Northwestern Ontario: Archaeological and Ethnohistorical Interpretations. *American Antiquity* 40(1):54-63.

Bissett, Don
1967   The Lower Mackenzie Region: An Area Economic Survey. *Canada. Department of Indian Affairs and Northern Development, Industrial Division Report* 66/1. Ottawa.

Black, Mary
1968-1973   [Ethnographic Fieldnotes from Weagamow Lake. Weagamow, Ontario.] (Manuscript in Black's possession.)

1970   Legends and Accounts of Weagamow Lake. *Rotunda: Bulletin of the Royal Ontario Museum* 3(3):4-13. Toronto.

1971   The Round Lake Ojibwa, 1968-1970. Pt. 3 in The Round Lake Ojibwa, the People, the Land, the Resources, 1968-1970. J. Watts, ed. (Indian Development Study in Northwestern Ontario, A.R.D.A. Project 25075) Toronto: Ontario Department of Lands and Forests.

Black, Samuel
1955   A Journal of a Voyage from Rocky Mountain Portage in Peace River to the Sources of Finlays Branch and Nort West Ward in Summer 1824. E.E. Rich, ed. (Publications of the Hudson's Bay Record Society 18) London: The Hudson's Bay Record Society.

744

Blair, Emma H., ed.
1911-1912 The Indian Tribes of the Upper Mississippi Valley and the Region of the Great Lakes as Described by Nicolas Perrot, French Commandant in the Northwest; Bacqueville de la Potherie, French Royal Commissioner to Canada; Morrell Marston, American Army Officer, and Thomas Forsyth, United States Agent at Fort Armstrong. 2 vols. Cleveland: Arthur H. Clark.

Blanchet, Guy
1964 Exploring with Sousi and Black Basile. *The Beaver* 295 (Autumn):34-41.

Bliss, Wesley L.
1939 Early Man in Western and Northwestern Canada. *Science* 89(2312):365-366.

1939a An Archaeological and Geological Reconnaissance of Alberta, Mackenzie Valley, and Upper Yukon. Pp. 136-139 in *Yearbook of the American Philosophical Society for 1938.* Philadelphia.

Bloch, Bernard, and George L. Trager
1942 Outline of Linguistic Analysis. Baltimore: Published by Linguistic Society of America at the Waverly Press.

Bloomfield, Leonard
1946 Algonquian. Pp. 85-129 in Linguistic Structures of Native America. Harry Hoijer, ed. *Viking Fund Publications in Anthropology* 6. New York.

1957 Eastern Ojibwa: Grammatical Sketch, Texts and Word List. Ann Arbor: University of Michigan Press.

Blüthgen, Joachim
1970 Problems of Definition and Geographical Differentiation of the Subarctic with Special Regard to Northern Europe. Pp. 11-33 in Ecology of the Subarctic Regions: Proceedings of the Helsinki Symposium, 1966. Paris: UNESCO.

Blumberg, Baruch S., John R. Martin, Fred H. Allen, Jr., Judith L. Weiner, Elaine M. Vitagliano, and Alan Cooke
1964 Blood Groups of the Naskapi and Montagnais Indians of Schefferville, Quebec. *Human Biology* 36(3):263-272.

Boas, Franz
1888 The Central Eskimo. Pp. 399-669 in *6th Annual Report of the Bureau of American Ethnology for the Years 1884-1885.* Washington.

1895 The Indians of British Columbia: Physical Characteristics of the Tribes of the North Pacific Coast, the Tinneh Tribe of Nicola Valley, the Ts'ets'ā'ut, the Nisk'a'. Linguistics of Nisk'a' and Ts'ets'āut, and Vocabulary of the Tinneh Tribes of Canada. *British Association for the Advancement of Science, Annual Meeting Report* 65:523-592. London.

1896 Traditions of the Ts'ets'ā'ut, I. *Journal of American Folk-Lore* 9(35):257-268.

1897 Traditions of the Ts'ets'ā'ut, II. *Journal of American Folk-Lore* 10(36):35-48.

1899 Linguistics. Pp. 654-666 in The North-Western Tribes of Canada: Twelfth and Final Report. *Report of the 68th Meeting of the British Association for the Advancement of Science for 1898.* London.

1899a Summary of the Work of the Committee in British Columbia. Pp. 667-683 in The North-Western Tribes of Canada: Twelfth and Final Report of the Committee. *Report of the 68th Meeting of the British Association for the Advancement of Science, 1898.* London.

1901 A.J. Stone's Measurements of Natives of the Northwest Territories. *Bulletin of the American Museum of Natural History* 14:53-68. New York.

1910 Ethnological Problems in Canada. *Journal of the Royal Anthropological Institute of Great Britain and Ireland* 40:529-539. London. (Reprinted: Pp. 331-343 in Race, Language and Culture, by Franz Boas, New York, Macmillan, 1940.)

1916 Tsimshian Mythology, Based on Texts Recorded by Henry W. Tate. Pp. 29-881 in *31st Annual Report of the Bureau of American Ethnology for the Years 1909-1910.* Washington.

1917 Grammatical Notes on the Language of the Tlingit Indians. *University of Pennsylvania Museum, Anthropological Publication* 8(1). Philadelphia.

1922 James A. Teit. *American Anthropologist* 24(4):490-492.

1924 Vocabulary of an Athapascan Tribe of Nicola Valley, British Columbia. *International Journal of American Linguistics* 3(1):36-38.

1969 The Ethnography of Franz Boas. Ronald P. Rohner, ed. Hedy Parker, trans. Chicago and London: University of Chicago Press.

Boas, Franz, and Pliny E. Goddard
1924 Ts'ets'aut, an Athapascan Language from Portland Canal, British Columbia. *International Journal of American Linguistics* 3(1):1-35.

Bobillier, Marcel
[1939] [Journal d'un missionnaire au Yukon.] (Manuscript, original in Dawson City Museum, Dawson, Yukon Terr.; Copy in Archives of the University of British Columbia, Vancouver.)

1976 Souvenirs du Yukon, I: Un voyage en traîne à chiens. *North* 23(6):18-23.

1977 Souvenirs du Yukon: Nöel sous la tente au lac Wolf. *North* 24(6):20-25.

Bock, Philip K.
1966 The Micmac Indians of Restigouche: History and Contemporary Description. *Anthropological Series 77, National Museum of Canada Bulletin* 213. Ottawa.

Bodsworth, Fred
1959 The Strange One. New York: Dodd, Mead.

1967 The Sparrow's Fall. Garden City, N.Y.: Doubleday.

Böhtlingk, Otto N. von
1964 Über die Sprache der Jakuten [1851]. The Hague: Mouton. (Facsimile reprint of the 1851 edition, St. Petersburg.)

Bogoras, Waldemar
1904-1909 The Chukchee. Vol. 7 of Publications of the Jesup North Pacific Expedition. Franz Boas, ed. 12 vols. New York: G.E. Stechert; Leiden, The Netherlands: E.J. Brill. (Also issued as Memoirs of the American Museum of Natural History 11, New York; reprinted AMS Press, New York, 1975.)

Bompas, William C.
[1879] Portions of the Book of Common Prayer, Hymns, etc. in the Chipewyan Language, by Archdeacon Kirkby. Adapted for the Use of Slavi Indians by the Right Rev. W.C. Bompas. London: Society for Promoting Christian Knowledge.

1888 Diocese of Mackenzie River. London: Society for Promoting Christian Knowledge.

Bond, J.H.
1959 Moose-skin Boat. *The Beaver* 290 (Winter): 44-45.

Bone, Robert M., Earl N. Shannon, and Stewart Raby
1973 The Chipewyan of the Stony Rapids Region: A Study of Their Changing World with Special Attention Focused upon Caribou. *University of Saskatchewan, Institute of Northern Studies, Moadsley Memoir* 1. Saskatoon.

Borden, Charles E.
1953 Results of Archaeological Investigations in Central British Columbia, 1952. *Anthropology in British Columbia Memoir* 3:31-43. Victoria.

1975   Origins and Development of Early Northwest Coast Culture to About 3000 B.C. *Canada. National Museum of Man, Mercury Series, Archaeological Survey Paper* 45. Ottawa.

Bostock, Hugh S.
1948   Physiography of the Canadian Cordillera with Special Reference to the Area North of the Fifty-fifth Parallel. *Canada. Department of Mines and Resources, Geological Survey Memoir* 247. Ottawa. (Reprinted in 1965.)

Bouchard, Serge, ed.
1974-1975   Les Récits de Mathieu MestoKosho: Chronique de chasse d'un Montagnais de Mingan. *Recherches Amérindiennes au Quebec* 4(2):17-25; 5(2):19-23.

———, ed.
1977   Chroniques de chasse d'un Montagnais de Mingan. [Quebec]: Ministère des Affaires Culturelles.

Boucher, Pierre
1964   Histoire véritable et naturelle des moeurs et productions du pays de la Nouvelle-France vulgairement dite le Canada [1664]. Boucherville: Société Historique de Boucherville.

Bougainville, Louis A. de
1964   Adventures in the Wilderness: The American Journals, 1756-1760. Edward P. Hamilton, ed. and trans. Norman: University of Oklahoma Press.

Boulanger, Tom
1971   An Indian Remembers: My Life as a Trapper in Northern Manitoba. Winnipeg: Peguis.

Bourassa, A.M.
1845   Lettre au Révérend Père Honorat, Trois-Rivières, le 25 juillet, 1844. *Annales de la Propagation de la Foi* 17:243-252. Lyon.

Bourget, Clermont
1929   [Letter of February 18, to the Assistant Deputy and Secretary, Department of Indian Affairs, Ottawa.] (Manuscript at St. Joseph's Parish, Fort Resolution, N.W.T. Canada.)

1938   Douze ans chez sauvages au Grand-Lac Esclaves comme médecin et agent des Indiens (1923-1935). Ste. Anne-de-Beaupré, Que.: Printed for the Author.

Bowes, Gordon E., ed.
1963   Peace River Chronicles: Eighty-one Eye-witness Accounts from the First Exploration of 1793 of the Peace River Region of British Columbia, Including the Finlay and the Parsnip River Basins. Vancouver: Prescott Publishing Company.

Boyle, David
1908   The Killing of Wa-Sak-Apee-Quay by Pe-Se Quan and Others. Pp. 91-120 in *Annual Archaeological Report for 1907, Being Part of Appendix to the Report of the Minister of Education, Ontario*. Toronto.

Brebner, John B.
1955   The Explorers of North America, 1492-1806. Garden City, N.Y.: Doubleday.

Breynat, Gabriel J.E.
1945-1948   Cinquante ans au pays des neiges. 3 vols. Montreal: Fides.

Broch, Harold B.
1977   A Note on Berdache Among the Hare Indians of Northwestern Canada. *Western Canadian Journal of Anthropology* 7(3):95-101.

Brooks, Alfred H.
1900   A Reconnaissance in the Tanana and White River Basins, Alaska, in 1898. Pp. 425-494 in *20th Annual Report of the U.S. Geological Survey for the Years 1899-1900*. Washington.

1903   An Exploration to Mt. McKinley, America's Highest Mountain. *Journal of Geography* 2(9):441-469.

1906   The Geography and Geology of Alaska: A Summary of Existing Knowledge. *U.S. Geological Survey Professional Paper* 45. Washington.

1953   Blazing Alaska's Trails. Burton L. Fryxell, ed. College: University of Alaska and Arctic Institute of North America. (Reprinted in 1973.)

Brown, R.J.E.
1970   Permafrost in Canada. Toronto: University of Toronto Press.

Brown, Jennifer S.H.
1971   The Cure and Feeding of Windigos: A Critique. *American Anthropologist* 73(1):20-22.

1976   A Demographic Transition in the Fur Trade Country: Family Sizes and Fertility of Company Officers and Country Wives, ca. 1759-1850. *Western Canadian Journal of Anthropology* 6(1):61-71.

1980   Stranger in Blood: Fur Trade Company Families in Indian Country. Vancouver: University of British Columbia Press.

Bryan, Alan L., Gerald Conaty, and D. Gentry Steele
1975   A Prehistoric Athapaskan Campsite in Northwestern Alberta, with Appendix: Analysis of a Human Tooth. *Western Canadian Journal of Anthropology* 5(3-4):64-91.

Bryant, Henry G.
1913   An Exploration in Southeastern Labrador. *Bulletin of the Geographical Society of Philadelphia* 11(1):1-15. Philadelphia.

Bryson, Reid A., and F. Kenneth Hare, eds.
1974   Climates of North America. (World Survey of Climatology 11) Amsterdam, London, New York: Elsevier Scientific Publishing Company.

Buckley, Helen
1962   Trapping and Fishing in the Economy of Northern Saskatchewan. *University of Saskatchewan, Research Division, Center for Community Studies, Economic and Social Survey of Northern Saskatchewan Report* 3. Saskatoon.

Buckley, Helen, J.E.M. Kew, and John B. Hawley
1963   The Indians and Métis of Northern Saskatchewan: A Report of Economic and Social Development. Saskatoon: Centre for Community Studies.

Bull, William, and S. Bull
1972   [Tape Recorded Letter to Beryl C. Gillespie, April 1972.] (Manuscript in Gillespie's possession.)

Bullen, Edward L.
1968   An Historical Study of the Education of the Indians of Teslin, Yukon Territory. (Unpublished M.A. Thesis in Education, University of Alberta, Edmonton.)

Burch, Ernest S., Jr.
1979   Indians and Eskimos in North Alaska, 1816-1977: A Study in Changing Ethnic Relations. *Arctic Anthropology* 16(2):123-151.

1979a   The Ethnography of Northern North America: A Guide to Recent Research. *Arctic Anthropology* 16(1):62-146.

1980   Traditional Eskimo Societies in Northwest Alaska. *National Museum of Ethnology, Senri Ethnological Studies* 4. Osaka, Japan.

Burger, Joanne Overvold, and Allan Clovis, eds.
1976   A Portrayal of Our Métis Heritage. Yellowknife, N.W.T.: The Métis Association of the Northwest Territories.

Burger, Valerie
1953   Indian Camp Sites on Kempt and Manowan Lakes in the Province of Quebec. *Pennsylvania Archaeologist* 23(1):32-45.

Burgesse, J. Allan
1943   Montagnais-Naskapi Nomenclature. *Primitive Man* 16(1-2):44-48.

1943a   Montagnais Cross-bows. *The Beaver* 274 (Winter): 37-39.

1944   The Woman and the Child Among the Lac-St.-Jean Montagnais. *Primitive Man* 17(1-2):1-18.

1944a   The Spirit Wigwam as Described by Tommie Moar, Pointe Bleue. *Primitive Man* 17(3-4):50-53.

1945   Property Concepts of the Lac-St.-Jean Montagnais. *Primitive Man* 18(1-2):1-25.

1949   Esquimaux in the Saguenay. *Primitive Man* 22(1-2):23-32.

Burke, Clara Heintz
1961   Doctor Hap. As Told to Adele Comandini. New York: Coward-McCann.

Burton, Alan C., and Otto G. Edholm
1955   Man in a Cold Environment; Physiological and Pathological Effects of Exposure to Low Temperatures. (Monographs of the Physiological Society 2) London: Arnold.

Burwash, Nathaniel
1912   The Gift to a Nation of Written Language. *Proceedings and Transactions of the Royal Society of Canada*, 3d ser., sect. 2, Vol. 5: 3-21. Ottawa.

Bushmann, Johann K.E.
1856   Der athapaskische Sprachstamm. *Abhandlungen der Königlichen Akademie der Wissenschaften für 1855*. Berlin.

Byers, Douglas S.
1959   The Eastern Archaic: Some Problems and Hypotheses. *American Antiquity* 24(3):233-256.

1962   New England and the Arctic. Pp. 143-153 in Prehistoric Cultural Relations Between the Arctic and Temperate Zones of North America. John Campbell, ed. *Arctic Institute of North America Technical Paper* 11. Montreal.

Cabot, William B.
1922   The Indians. Pp. 184-225 in Labrador: The Country and the People. Wilfred T. Grenfell, ed. New ed. New York: MacMillan.

Cadzow, Donald A.
1925   Habitat of Loucheux Bands. *Museum of the American Indian, Heye Foundation, Indian Notes* 2(3):172-177. New York.

Cameron, Agnes Deans
1910   The New North: Being Some Account of a Woman's Journey Through Canada to the Arctic. New York and London: D. Appleton.

Cameron, Duncan
1889-1890   A Sketch of the Customs, Manners and Way of Living of the Natives in the Barren Country About Nipigon. Pp. 229-300 in Vol. 2 of Les Bourgeois de la Compagnie du Nord-Ouest. L.R. Masson, ed. 2 vols. Quebec: A. Coté.

Cameron, William B.
1926   The War Trail of Big Bear: Being the Story of the Connection of Big Bear and Other Cree Indian Chiefs and Their Followers with the Canadian North-west Rebellion of 1885, the Frog Lake Massacre and Events Leading Up to and Following It, and of Two Months' Imprisonment in the Camp of the Hostiles. London: Duckworth.

Campbell, John M.
1961   The Tuktu Complex of Anaktuvuk Pass. *Anthropological Papers of the University of Alaska* 9(2):61-80. College.

————, ed.
1962   Prehistoric Cultural Relations Between the Arctic and Temperate Zones of North America. *Arctic Institute of North America Technical Paper* 11. Montreal.

1968   Arctic. *American Antiquity* 33(2):272-278.

1968a   The Kavik Site of Anaktuvuk Pass, Central Brooks Range, Alaska. *Anthropological Papers of the University of Alaska* 14(1):33-42. College.

1973   Archaeological Studies Along the Proposed Trans-Alaska Oil Pipeline Route. *Arctic Institute of North America Technical Paper* 26. Montreal.

Campbell, Robert
1883   The Discovery and Exploration of the Pelly (Yukon) River. Pp. 435-443 in The Royal Readers: Fifth Book of Reading Lessons. Toronto: T. Nelson and J. Campbell.

1958   Two Journals of Robert Campbell, Chief Factor, Hudson's Bay Company, 1808 to 1853; Early Journal, 1808 to 1851, Later Journal, Sept. 1850 to Feb. 1853. Seattle: Shorey Book Store.

Camsell, Charles
1912   Country Around the Headwaters of Severn River. Pp. 87-93 in Reports on the District of Patricia. Willet G. Miller, ed. *Reports of the Ontario Bureau of Mines* 21(1). Toronto.

1916   An Exploration of the Tazin and Taltson Rivers, Northwest Territories. *Canada. Department of Mines Geological Series 69, Geological Survey Memoir* 84. Ottawa.

1954   Son of the North. Toronto: Ryerson Press.

Canada. Département des Affaires Indiennes
1925   Recensement compilé par inspectorats départementaux, par agences et par districts, 1924. P. 57 in *Annual Report of the Department of Indian Affairs for the Year Ended March 31, 1924*. Ottawa: King's Printer.

Canada. Department of Citizenship and Immigration. Indian Affairs Branch
1952   Census of Indians in Canada, 1949. Ottawa: King's Printer.

1955   Census of Indians in Canada, 1954. Ottawa: Queen's Printer.

1957   Copy of Treaty No. 11 (June 27, 1921) and Adhesions (July 17, 1922) with Reports, etc. Ottawa: Queen's Printer.

1961   Census of Indians in Canada, 1959. Ottawa: Queen's Printer.

1964   Traditional Linguistic and Cultural Affiliations of Canadian Indian Bands. Ottawa: Queen's Printer.

Canada. Department of Energy, Mines and Resources
1980   Canada: Indian and Inuit Communities and Languages. Ottawa: Surveys and Mapping Branch.

Canada. Department of Indian Affairs
1907-1915   Annual Reports for the Years Ending March 31 (*Sessional Paper* 27). Ottawa: King's Printer.

1924   Annual Report for the Year Ended March 1924. Ottawa: King's Printer.

1930   Census of Indians in Canada, 1929. Ottawa: King's Printer.

1934   Annual Report of the Department of Indian Affairs for the Year Ended March 31, 1934. Ottawa: King's Printer.

Canada. Department of Indian Affairs and Northern Development
1980   Linguistic and Cultural Affiliations of Canadian Indian Bands. Ottawa: Queen's Printer.

Canada. Department of Indian Affairs and Northern Development. Indian Affairs Branch
1967   Linguistic and Cultural Affiliations of Canadian Indian Bands. Ottawa: Queen's Printer.

1968   Indian Bands with Linguistic Affiliations. Map. Ottawa: Department of Energy, Mines and Resources, Surveys and Mapping Branch.

1970   Linguistic and Cultural Affiliations of Canadian Indian Bands. Ottawa: Queen's Printer.

1973   [Registered Indians as of June 30, 1973: Band 06, Fort Franklin, N.W.T.] Mimeo.

Canada. Department of Indian and Northern Affairs
1978   Atlas of Indian Reserves and Settlements, Canada, 1971. Ottawa: Indian and Inuit Affairs Program, Reserves and Trust Group.

Canada. Department of Mines and Resources
1945   Census of Indians in Canada, 1944. Ottawa: King's Printer.

Canada. Department of Mines and Resources. Indian Affairs Branch
1935   Census of Indians in Canada, 1934. Ottawa: King's Printer.

————
1940   Census of Indians in Canada, 1939. Ottawa: King's Printer.

Canada. Department of Northern Affairs and National Resources. Indian Affairs Branch
1966   Copy of Treaty No. 8, Concluded June 21, 1899 and Adhesions, Reports, etc. *Department of Indian Affairs and Northern Development Publication* QS-0576-000-EE-A-16. Ottawa.

Canada. Department of the Interior. Northwest Territories and Yukon Branch
1923   Local Conditions in the Mackenzie District, 1922. J.F. Moran, comp. Ottawa: King's Printer.

Canada. Dominion Bureau of the Census
1941   Native Indian and Eskimo Population Area of Health District W 10 [as of 1966]. Ottawa: The King's Printer.

Canada, Dominion of
1924   Annual Report of the Department of Indian Affairs for the Year Ended March 31, 1924. (*Sessional Paper* 14) Ottawa: King's Printer.

Canada, Government of
1959   Alphabetical List: Yellowknife Indian Agency, No. 139. Mimeo.

————
1966   Treaty No. 8 Made June 21, 1899 and Adhesions, Reports, etc. [1899]. Ottawa: Queen's Printer.

Canada. Mackenzie Valley Pipeline Inquiry *see* Berger, Thomas

Canada. Northwest Mounted Police *see* Canada. Royal Canadian Mounted Police

Canada. Royal Canadian Mounted Police
1910   Report of Inspector Pelletier of the Royal Northwest Mounted Police in 1908. P. 148 in *Sessional Paper* 28. Ottawa: King's Printer.

Canada. Statistics Canada
1976   Census of Canada. Vol. 1, Population: Geographic Distributions. Ottawa: Queen's Printer.

Canada. Surveys and Mapping Branch
1974   The National Atlas of Canada. 4th rev. ed. Ottawa: Department of Energy, Mines and Resources.

Canada Year Book
1972   Statistical Annual of the Resources, Demography, Institutions, and Social and Economic Conditions of Canada. Ottawa: Statistics Canada.

Canadian Broadcasting Corporation
1976   The Crees of Paint Hills. 16mm Color Film, Sound, 57 Minutes. From the Series, The Nature of Things. Distributed by The National Film Board of Canada.

Canham, A.S.
[1887-1891] [Papers.] (Domestic and Foreign Missionary Society Papers, in Alaska Papers, 1884-1939, Box 48. The Church Historical Society, Austin, Tex.)

Canham, Thomas H.
1898   Vocabulary, English–Wood Indian. London: Society for Promoting Christian Knowledge.

Canonge, Elliott
[1966]   The Swadesh 100-Word List in 27 Athapaskan Languages. Mimeo.

Cantwell, J.C.
1902   Report of the Operations of the U.S. Revenue Steamer Nunivak on the Yukon River Station, Alaska, 1899-1901. Washington: U.S. Government Printing Office.

Card, Brigham Y., G.K. Hirabayashi, and C.L. French
1963   The Métis in Alberta Society: With Special Reference to Social, Economic, and Cultural Factors Associated with Per-

sistently High Tuberculosis Incidence. Edmonton: University of Alberta.

Caribou Tribal Council
1976   Nazko-Kluskus: The Future is Now. *Coyoti Prints* 3(9):Sept. 20, 1976. Fish Lake Cultural Education Centre, Box 6000, Williams Lake, B.C.

Carlo, Poldine
1978   Nulato: An Indian Life on the Yukon. Drawings by Glenn Carlo. Fairbanks, Alaska: no publisher.

Carlson, Roy L.
1979   The Early Period on the Central Coast of British Columbia. *Canadian Journal of Archaeology* 3:211-228.

Carmack, George W.
1933   My Experiences in the Yukon. [Seattle]: Privately Printed.

Carrière, Gaston
1972   Adrien-Gabriel Morice, O.M.I. (1859-1938): Essai de bibliographie. *Revue de l'Université d'Ottawa* 42:325-341. Ottawa.

Carriker, Robert C., Clifford A. Carroll, and W.L. Larsen
1976   Guide to the Microfilm Edition of the Oregon Province Archives of the Society of Jesus Indian Language Collection: The Alaska Native Languages. Spokane: Gonzaga University.

Carrington, Philip
1963   The Anglican Church in Canada: A History. Toronto: Collins.

Carter, Robin W.
1975   Chipewyan Semantics: Form and Meaning in the Language and Culture of an Athapaskan-speaking People of Canada. (Unpublished Ph.D. Dissertation in Anthropology, Duke University, Durham, N.C.)

Cartier, Jacques
1924   The Voyages of Jacques Cartier. Henry P. Biggar, ed. *Publications of the Public Archives of Canada* 11. Ottawa.

Cartwright, George
1911   Captain Cartwright and His Labrador Journal. Charles W. Townsend, ed. Boston: Dana Estes.

Carver, Jonathan
1778   Travels Through the Interior Parts of North-America, in the Years 1766, 1767, and 1768. London: Printed for the Author. (Reprinted: Ross and Haines, Minneapolis, 1956; Coles Publishing Company, Toronto, 1974.)

Casterman, O.
[1965]   [Notes.] (Manuscript, in the Provincial House Archives, Fort Smith, N.W.T., Canada.)

Chamberlain, Alexander F.
1904   Iroquois in Northwestern Canada. *American Anthropologist* n.s. 6(4):459-463.

Chambers, Edward T.D.
1896   The Ouananiche and Its Canadian Environment. New York: Harper and Brothers.

Chambers, R.W.
1974   [Chick Lake Archaeological Project.] (Manuscript in University of Saskatchewan, Department of Anthropology and Archaeology, Saskatoon.)

Champlain, Samuel de
1613   Les Voyages de sievr de Champlain, Xaintongeois, capitaine ordinaire pour le Roy, en la marine... Paris: Jean Berjou.

————
1922-1936   The Works of Samuel de Champlain [1626]. Henry P. Biggar, ed. 6 vols. Toronto: The Champlain Society. (Reprinted: University of Toronto Press, Toronto, 1971.)

Chance, Norman A.
1960   Culture Change and Integration: An Eskimo Example. *American Anthropologist* 62(6):1028-1044.

————
1966   The Eskimo of North Alaska. New York: Holt, Rinehart and Winston.

748

1967   The Changing World of the Cree. *Natural History* 76(5):16-23.

————, ed.
1968   Conflict in Culture: Problems of Developmental Change Among the Cree; Working Papers of the Cree Developmental Change Project. Ottawa: Saint-Paul University, Canadian Research Centre for Anthropology.

————, ed.
1969   Developmental Change Among the Cree Indians of Quebec. Rev. ed. (McGill University, Cree Developmental Change Project, Summary Report) Ottawa: Department of Forestry and Rural Development, Rural Development Branch.

Chance, Norman A., and John Trudeau
1963   Social Organization, Acculturation and Integration Among the Eskimo and the Cree: A Comparative Study. *Anthropologica* n.s. 5(1):47-56. Ottawa.

Chapman, John D., and D.B. Turner, eds.
1956   British Columbia Atlas of Resources. Vancouver: British Columbia Natural Resources Conference.

Chapman, John W.
1903   Athapascan Traditions from the Lower Yukon. *Journal of American Folk-Lore* 16(62):180-185.

1907   Notes on the Tinneh Tribe of Anvik, Alaska. Pp. 7-38 in Vol. 2 of *Proceedings of the 15th International Congress of Americanists*. 2 vols. Quebec, 1906.

1912   The Happy Hunting-ground of the Ten'a. *Journal of American Folk-Lore* 25(95):66-71.

1913   A Message from Anvik. *The Alaskan Churchman* 7(2):50.

1914   Ten'a Texts and Tales from Anvik, Alaska. With Vocabulary by Pliny Earle Goddard. (Publications of the American Ethnological Society 6) Leyden, The Netherlands: E.J. Brill.

1921   Tinneh Animism. *American Anthropologist* 23(3):298-310.

1948   A Camp on the Yukon. Cornwall-on-Hudson, N.Y.: Idlewild Press.

Chappell, Edward
1817   Narrative of a Voyage to Hudson's Bay in His Majesty's Ship Rosamond, Containing Some Account of the Northeastern Coast of America and of the Tribes Inhabiting That Remote Region. London: Printed for J. Mawman. (Facsimile Reprint: Coles, Toronto, 1970.)

Charlevoix, Pierre F.X. de
1744   Histoire et description générale de la Nouvelle France, avec le journal historique d'un voyage fait par ordre du Roi dans l'Amérique septentrionnale. 3 vols. Paris: Rolins fils.

Chevrier, Daniel
1977   Préhistoire de la région de la Moisie. *Ministère des Affaires Culturelles, Direction Générale du Patrimoine, Cahiers du Patrimoine* 5. Quebec.

Chipman, C.C.
1903   [Fur Trade Reports, Feb. 7, 1902, and February 3, 1903.] (Manuscripts in Hudson's Bay Company Archives, Provincial Archives of Manitoba, Winnipeg, Canada.)

Chism, James V.
1978   Archaeology at Washadimi: The 1978 Field Summary. 3 vols. (Unpublished manuscript in Ministère des Affaires Culturelles, Service du Patrimoine Autochtone, Direction Générale du Patrimoine, Quebec.)

Christian, Jane, and Peter M. Gardner
1977   The Individual in Northern Dene Thought and Communication: A Study in Sharing and Diversity. *Canada. National Museum of Man, Mercury Series, Ethnology Service Paper* 35. Ottawa.

Cinq-Mars, Jacques
1973   A Propos de la signification archéologique d'un matériau découvert dans la région de la rivière Keele (T.N.O.). *Bulletin of the Canadian Archaeological Association* 5:1-25. Ottawa.

1973a   Preliminary Archaeological Study, Mackenzie Corridor. (IAND Publication QS-1506-000-EE-XA1) *Northern Pipelines Task Force on Northern Oil Development, Environmental-Social Committee Report* 73-10. Ottawa.

1973b   An Archaeologically Important Raw Material from the Tertiary Hills, Western District of Mackenzie, Northwest Territories: A Preliminary Statement. Appendix E in Preliminary Archaeological Study, Mackenzie Corridor. Jacques Cinq-Mars, ed. *Northern Pipelines Task Force on Northern Oil Development, Environmental-Social Committee Report* 73-10. Ottawa.

1974   Preliminary Archaeological Study Mackenzie Corridor (Second Report). Jacques Cinq-Mars et al., eds. *Northern Pipelines Task Force on Northern Oil Development, Environmental-Social Committee Report* 74-11. Ottawa

1976   Preliminary Archaeological Study: Mackenzie Corridor (Final Report 1975). (ALUR 1974-75) Ottawa: Minister of Indian and Northern Affairs.

Clark, Annette McFadyen
[1961-1972]   [Fieldnotes and Records, 1961, 1968, 1969, 1970, 1971, 1972.] (Manuscripts in Archives of the Canadian Ethnology Service, National Museum of Man, Ottawa.)

1970   The Athabaskan-Eskimo Interface. *Bulletin of the Canadian Archaeological Association* 2:13-23. Ottawa.

1970a   Koyukon Athabascan Ceremonialism. Pp. 80-88 in Athabascan Studies. Regna Darnell, ed. *Western Canadian Journal of Anthropology* 2(1).

1970b   Archaeology of the Batza Tena Obsidian Locality of West Central Alaska. (Paper presented at the 21st Alaska Science Conference, August 16-19, 1970, University of Alaska, College.)

1974   Koyukuk River Culture. *Canada. National Museum of Man, Mercury Series, Ethnology Service Paper* 18. Ottawa.

1975   Upper Koyukuk River Koyukon Athapaskan Social Culture: An Overview. Pp. 147-180 in Vol. 1 of Proceedings: Northern Athapaskan Conference, 1971. A. McFadyen Clark, ed. 2 vols. *Canada. National Museum of Man, Mercury Series, Ethnology Service Paper* 27. Ottawa.

————, ed.
1975a   Proceedings: Northern Athapaskan Conference, 1971. 2 vols. *Canada. National Museum of Man, Mercury Series, Ethnology Service Paper* 27. Ottawa.

Clark, Annette McFadyen, and Donald W. Clark
1974   Koyukon Athapaskan Houses as Seen Through Oral Tradition and Through Archaeology. *Arctic Anthropology* 11(suppl.):29-38.

1976   Koyukuk Indian-Kobuk Eskimo Interaction. Pp. 193-220 in Contributions to Anthropology: The Interior Peoples of Northern Alaska. Edwin S. Hall, Jr., ed. *Canada. National Museum of Man, Mercury Series, Archaeological Survey Paper* 49. Ottawa.

Clark, Annette McFadyen *see also* McFadyen, Annette

Clark, Donald W.
[1968]   [Fieldnotes.] (Manuscript in Archives, Archaeological Survey of Canada, National Museum of Man, Ottawa.)

1969   Archaeological Survey on the Koyukuk River, Alaska. (Manuscript in Archaeological Survey of Canada, National Museum of Man, Ottawa.)

1972   Archaeology of the Batza Tena Obsidian Source, West-central Alaska: A Preliminary Report of Initial Reconnaissance Surveys. *Anthropological Papers of the University of Alaska* 15(2):1-22. College.

1972a   An Interior Alaskan Settlement of Ipiutak Affiliation. (Unpublished manuscript in Archaeological Survey of Canada, National Museum of Man, Ottawa.)

1974   Filaments of Prehistory on the Koyukuk River, Northwestern Interior Alaska. Pp. 33-46 in International Conference on the Prehistory and Paleoecology of Western North American Arctic and Subarctic, Calgary, 1972. Scott Raymond and Peter Schledermann, eds. Calgary: University of Calgary, Archaeology Association.

1975   Archaeological Reconnaissance in Northern Interior District of Mackenzie: 1969, 1970, and 1972. *Canada. National Museum of Man, Mercury Series, Archaeological Survey Paper* 27. Ottawa.

1977   Hahanudan Lake: An Ipiutak-related Occupation of Western Interior Alaska. *Canada. National Museum of Man, Mercury Series, Archaeological Survey Paper* 71. Ottawa.

1977a   Arctic and Subarctic America: Current Early Man Research. *Early Man News* 2:24-33. Tübingen, Germany.

Clark, Donald W., and A. McFadyen Clark
1975   Fluted Points from the Batza Tena Obsidian Source of the Koyukuk River Region, Alaska. *Anthropological Papers of the University of Alaska* 17(2):31-38. Fairbanks.

Clermont, Norman
1974   Qui étaient les Attikamègues? *Anthropologica* n.s. 16(1):59-74. Ottawa.

1974a   Le Castor et les indiens préhistoriques de la Haute-Mauricie: Un problème d'identification. *Recherches Amérindiennes au Québec* 4(1):4-8. Montreal.

1975   L'Archéologie historiques et les registres. *Recherches Amérindiennes au Québec* 5(1):47-49. Montreal.

1977   Ma Femme, ma hache et mon couteau croche: Deux siècles d'histoire à Weymontachie. (Collection Civilisation du Québec, Série Cultures Amérindiennes 18) Quebec: Ministère des Affaires Culturelles.

1977a   La Transformation historique des systèmes économiques algonquiens. Pp. 182-187 in *Papers of the Eighth Algonquian Conference.* William Cowan, ed. Ottawa: Carleton University.

1978   Les Kokotchés à Weymontachie. *Recherches Amérindiennes au Québec* 8(2):139-146. Montreal.

Clibbon, Peter B., and Louis-Edmond Hamelin
1968   Landforms. Pp. 57-77 in Canada: A Geographical Interpretation. John Warkentin, ed. Toronto, London: Methuen.

Coats, William
1852   The Geography of Hudson's Bay: Being the Remarks of Captain W. Coats, in Many Voyages to That Locality, Between the Years 1727 and 1751. (Works Issued by the Hakluyt Society 11) London: Printed for the Hakluyt Society.

Cocking, Matthew
1908   An Adventurer from Hudson Bay: Journal of Matthew Cocking, from York Factory to the Blackfeet Country, 1772-73. L.J. Burpee, ed. *Proceedings and Transactions of the Royal Society of Canada,* 3d ser., Vol. 2:89-121. Ottawa.

Cody, Hiram
1908   An Apostle of the North: Memoirs of the Right Reverend W.C. Bompass. New York: E.P. Dutton.

Cohen, Ronald
1962   An Anthropological Survey of Communities in the Mackenzie-Slave Lake Region of Canada. (NCRC 62-3) Ottawa: Department of Northern Affairs and National Resources, Northern Co-ordination and Research Centre.

Cohen, Ronald, and James W. VanStone
1964   Dependency and Self-sufficiency in Chipewyan Stories. *Anthropological Series 62, National Museum of Canada Bulletin* 194:29-55. Ottawa.

Colby, Merle E.
1939   A Guide to Alaska, Last American Frontier. New York: Macmillan.

Collins, Henry B., Frederica De Laguna, Edmund Carpenter, and Peter Stone
1973   The Far North: 2000 Years of American Eskimo and Indian Art; Catalog of an Exhibition Held at the National Gallery of Art, March 7-May 15, 1973. Washington: National Gallery of Art.

Collins, Raymond L., and Sally Jo Collins
1966   Dinak'i: Upper Kuskokwim Athapaskan Dictionary. Anchorage: University of Alaska, Summer Institute of Linguistics.

Collins, Raymond L., and Betty Petruska, comps.
1979   Dinak'i, (Our Words): Upper Kuskokwim Athabaskan Junior Dictionary. Anchorage: University of Alaska, National Bilingual Materials Development Center.

Colyer, Vincent
1870   Report of the Hon. Vincent Colyer, United States Special Indian Commissioner, on the Indian Tribes and Their Surroundings in Alaska Territory from Personal Observation and Inspection in 1869. Pp. 533-616 in *Annual Report of the Commissioner of Indian Affairs for the Year 1869.* Washington.

Comeau, Napoléon A.
1909   Life and Sport on the North Shore of the Lower St. Lawrence and Gulf, Containing Chapters on Salmon Fishing, Trapping, the Folk-lore of the Montagnais Indians and Tales of Adventure on the Fringe of the Labrador Peninsula. Quebec: Daily Telegraph Printing House.

Conaty, Gerry
1977   Excavations at Wentzel Lake. Pp. 31-36 in Archaeology in Alberta, 1976. J.M. Quigg, ed. *Archaeological Survey of Alberta Occasional Paper* 4. Edmonton.

Le Conseil Attikamek Montagnais
1979   Nishastanan Nitasinan: Notre terre, nous l'aimons et nous y tenons; revendications territoriales des bandes attikamèques et montagnais. *Recherches Amérindiennes au Québec* 9(3):171-182. Montreal.

Cook, Eung-Do
1971   Vowels and Tones in Sarcee. *Language* 47(1):164-179.

1971a   Morphophonemics of Two Sarcee Classifiers. *International Journal of American Linguistics* 37(3):152-155.

1971b   Phonological Constraint and Syntactic Rule. *Linguistic Inquiry* 2:465-478.

1972   Sarcee Verb Paradigms. *Canada. National Museum of Man, Mercury Series, Ethnology Service Paper* 2. Ottawa.

1972a   Stress and Related Rules in Tahltan. *International Journal of American Linguistics* 38(4):231-233.

1975   A Phonological Study of Chilcotin and Carrier. (Unpublished report to the National Museum of Man, Ottawa.)

1976   Flattening and Rounding in Chilcotin Velars. (Unpublished paper read at the Victoria Conference on Northwestern Languages, Victoria, B.C., November 1976.)

1976a   A Phonological Study of Chilcotin and Carrier. Pt. 1: Chilcotin Phonology; Pt. 2: Central Carrier Phonology. (Unpublished report to the National Museum of Man, Ottawa.)

1977   Syllable Weight in Three Northern Athapaskan Languages. *International Journal of American Linguistics* 43(4):259-268.

Cook, James
1784   A New, Authentic and Complete Collection of Voyages Round the World Undertaken and Performed by Royal Authority... Successfully Performed in the Years 1768, 1769, 1770, 1771-1772, 1773, 1774, 1775-1776, 1777, 1778, 1779, and 1780. George W. Anderson, ed. London: Alex Hogg.

1785   A Voyage to the Pacific Ocean, Undertaken by the Command of His Majesty, for Making Discoveries in the Northern Hemisphere. 3 vols. 2d ed. London: G. Nicol and T. Cadell. (New ed.: The Journals of Captain James Cook on His Voyage of Discovery. John C. Beaglehole, ed., Vol. 3, Hakluyt Society, Extra ser. 36, Cambridge, United Kingdom.)

Cook, John P.
1968   Some Microblade Cores from the Western Boreal Forest. *Arctic Anthropology* 5(1):121-127.

1971   Summary. Pp. 457-465 in Final Report of the Archeological Survey and Excavations Along the Alyeska Pipeline Service Company Pipeline Route. College: University of Alaska, Department of Anthropology.

1975   Archaeology of Interior Alaska. *Western Canadian Journal of Anthropology* 5(3-4):125-133.

————, ed.
1977   Pipeline Archeology. Fairbanks: University of Alaska, Institute of Arctic Biology.

Cook, John P., and Robert A. McKennan
1970   The Village Site at Healy Lake, Alaska: An Interim Report. (Paper presented at the 35th Annual Meeting of the Society for American Archaeology, Mexico City, April 30-May 2, 1970. Mimeo.)

1970a   The Athapaskan Tradition: A View from Healy Lake in the Yukon-Tanana Upland. (Paper presented at the 10th Annual Meeting of the Northeastern Anthropological Association, Ottawa, May 1970.)

1971   The Athapascan Tradition: A View from Healy Lake. (Paper presented to Athapascan Conference, Museum of Man, Ottawa, March 1971.)

Cooke, Alan, and Fabien Caron, comps.
1968   Bibliography of the Quebec-Labrador Peninsula. 2 vols. Boston: G.K. Hall.

Cooke, Alan, and Clive Holland
1978   The Exploration of Northern Canada, 500 to 1920: A Chronology. Toronto: Arctic History Press.

Cooper, John M.
[1925]   [Fieldnotes on Obedjiwan Lake.] (Manuscript in Department of Anthropology, Catholic University of America, Washington.)

1926   The Têtes de Boule of the Upper St.-Maurice. Abstract. *Journal of the Washington Academy of Sciences* 16(5):138. Washington.

1926a   The Obidjiwan Band of the Têtes de Boule. *Anthropos* 21(3-4):616-617.

1926-1937   [Notes on Ethnographic Fieldwork Among the Attikamek–Tête de Boule, Mostly at Obedjiwan.] (Manuscript in Department of Anthropology, Catholic University of America, Washington.)

1928   Some Notes on the Waswanipi. Pp. 459-461 in Vol. 2 of *Proceedings of the 22d International Congress of Americanists*. 2 vols. Rome, 1926.

1930   Field Notes on Northern Algonkian Magic. Pp. 513-518 in *Proceedings of the 23d International Congress of Americanists*. New York, 1928.

1933   The Northern Algonquian Supreme Being. *Primitive Man* 6(3-4):41-111.

1933a   The Cree Witiko Psychosis. *Primitive Man* 6(1):20-24.

1934   The Northern Algonquian Supreme Being. *Catholic University of America Anthropological Series* 2. Washington.

1935   Supreme Being Concept of the Montagnais-speaking Peoples. *Anthropos* 30:228.

1938   Snares, Deadfalls, and Other Traps of the Northern Algonquians and Northern Athapaskans. *Catholic University of America Anthropological Series* 5. Washington.

1939   Is the Algonquian Family Hunting Ground System Pre-Columbian? *American Anthropologist* 41(1):66-90.

1941   Temporal Sequence and the Marginal Cultures. *Catholic University of America Anthropological Series* 10. Washington.

1944   The Shaking Tent Rite Among Plains and Forest Algonquians. *Primitive Man* 17(3-4):60-84.

1945   Tête-de-Boule Cree. *International Journal of American Linguistics* 11(1):36-44.

1946   The Culture of the Northeastern Indian Hunters: A Reconstructive Interpretation. Pp. 272-305 in Man in Northeastern North America. Frederick Johnson, ed. *Papers of the Robert S. Peabody Foundation for Archaeology* 3. Andover, Mass.

Corcoran, Patricia A., F.H. Allen, Jr., A.C. Allison, and B.S. Blumberg
1959   Blood Groups of Alaskan Eskimos and Indians. *American Journal of Physical Anthropology* n.s. 17(3):187-193.

Correll, Thomas C.
1972   Ungalaqlingmiut: A Study in Language and Society. (Unpublished Ph.D. Dissertation in Anthropology, University of Minnesota, Minneapolis.)

Couch, James
1957   Philately Below Zero. State College, Pa.: American Philatelic Society.

Cowan, Ian McT., and Charles J. Guiguet
1973   The Mammals of British Columbia. 5th ed. *British Columbia Provincial Museum Handbook* 11. Victoria.

Cowan, William
1976   The Generation Gap in Montagnais Dialectology. Pp. 323-338 in *Papers of the Seventh Algonquian Conference, 1975*. William Cowan, ed. Ottawa: Carleton University.

Cox, Ross
1831   Adventures on the Columbia River, Including the Narrative of a Residence of Six Years on the Western Side of the Rockey Mountains, Among Various Tribes of Indians Hitherto Unknown, Together with a Journey Across the American Continent. 2 vols. London: H. Colburn and R. Bentley.

1832   The Columbia River; or, Scenes and Adventures During a Residence of Six Years on the Western Side of the Rocky Mountains, Among Various Tribes of Indians Hitherto Unknown. 2 vols. in one. 3d ed. London: Henry Colburn.

1957   The Columbia River. Edgar I. Stewart and Jane R. Stewart, eds. Norman: University of Oklahoma Press.

Craig, Bruce G.
1960 Surficial Geology of North-central District of MacKenzie, Northwest Territories. *Geological Survey of Canada Paper* 60-18. Ottawa.

————
1964 Surficial Geology of East-central District of MacKenzie. *Geological Survey of Canada Bulletin* 99. Ottawa.

————
1965 Glacial Lake McConnell, and the Surficial Geology of Parts of Slave River and Redstone River Map-areas, District of MacKenzie. *Geological Survey of Canada Bulletin* 122. Ottawa.

Craig, Bruce G., and J.G. Fyles
1960 Pleistocene Geology of Arctic Canada. *Geological Survey of Canada Paper* 60-10. Ottawa.

Craik, Brian
1975 The Formation of a Goose Hunting Strategy and the Politics of the Hunting Group. Pp. 450-465 in Vol. 2 of Proceedings of the Second Congress of the Canadian Ethnology Society. Jim Freedman and Jerome H. Barkow, eds. 2 vols. *Canada. National Museum of Man, Mercury Series, Ethnology Service Paper* 28. Ottawa.

Cruikshank, Julie
1969 The Role of Northern Canadian Indian Women in Social Change. (Unpublished M.A. Thesis in Anthropology, University of British Columbia, Vancouver.)

————
1972 Cultural Responses to the Alaska Village Electric Cooperative Program in Alaska Native Villages. *Arctic Anthropology* 9(1):35-42.

————
1974 Through the Eyes of Strangers: A Preliminary Survey of Land Use History in the Yukon During the Late Nineteenth Century; Report to the Yukon Territorial Government and the Yukon Archives. Whitehorse: no publisher.

————
1975 Their Own Yukon: A Photographic History by Yukon Indian People. Photos Collected by Jim Robb. Whitehorse: Yukon Native Brotherhood.

————
1979 Athapaskan Women: Lives and Legends. *Canada. National Museum of Man, Mercury Series, Ethnology Service Paper* 57. Ottawa.

Cruikshank, Julie, and Catharine McClellan
1976 Preliminary Investigation of the Social Impact of the Alaskan Highway on Yukon Indians: Probable Parallels to the Impact of the Pipeline Construction; Testimony for the Mackenzie Valley Pipeline Inquiry. (Manuscript in possession of its authors.)

Culin, Stewart
1907 Games of the North American Indians. Pp. 3-809 in *24th Annual Report of the Bureau of American Ethnology for the Years 1902-1903*. Washington.

Cumming, Peter A., and Neil H. Mickenberg, eds.
1972 Native Rights in Canada. 2d ed. Toronto: Indian-Eskimo Association of Canada in Association with General Publishing Company.

Cuoq, Jean André
1886 Lexique de la langue algonquine. Montreal: J. Chapleau et fils.

————
1891-1892 Grammaire de la langue algonquine. *Proceedings and Transactions of the Royal Society of Canada*, sec. 1, Vol. 9: 85-114; 10:41-119. Montreal.

Curran, William T., and Harold A. Calkins
1917 In Canada's Wonderful Northland: A Story of Eight Months of Travel by Canoe, Motorboat, and Dog-team on the Northern Rivers and Along the New Quebec Coast of Hudson Bay. New York: G.P. Putnam's Sons.

Curtis, Edward S.
1907-1930 The North American Indian: Being a Series of Volumes Picturing and Describing the Indians of the United States, and Alaska. Frederick W. Hodge, ed. 20 vols. Norwood, Mass.: Plimpton Press. (Reprinted: Johnson Reprint, New York, 1970.)

DRHA = Documents Relative to the History of Alaska
[1741-1900] Alaska History Research Project, 1936-1938. (Manuscripts in Library of Congress, Washington, and University of Alaska Library, College.)

Dailey, Robert C.
1968 The Role of Alcohol Among North American Indian Tribes as Reported in the Jesuit Relations. *Anthropologica* n.s. 10(1):45-57. Ottawa.

Dall, William H.
1870 Alaska and Its Resources. Boston: Lee and Shepard.

————
1870a On the Distribution of the Native Tribes of Alaska and Adjacent Territory. Pp. 263-273 in *Proceedings of the American Association for the Advancement of Science for 1869*. Salem, Mass.

————
1877 Tribes of the Extreme Northwest. Pp. 1-106 in Vol. 1 of *Contributions to North American Ethnology*. J.W. Powell, ed. 9 vols. Washington: U.S. Geographical and Geological Survey of the Rocky Mountain Region.

————
1886 The Native Tribes of Alaska: Address. Pp. 363-379 in *Proceedings of the American Association for the Advancement of Science for 1885*. Ann Arbor, Mich.

————
1898 Travels on the Yukon and in the Yukon Territory in 1866-1868. Pp. 1-242 in The Yukon Territory, by William H. Dall et al. London: Downey.

————, et al.
1898a The Yukon Territory, the Narrative of W.H. Dall, Leader of the Expedition to Alaska in 1866-1868; the Narrative of an Exploration Made in 1887 in the Yukon District by George M. Dawson... Extracts from the Report of an Exploration Made in 1896-1897 by Wm. Ogilvie. London: Downey.

Dall, William H., and George F. Becker
1896 Sketch of Part of the Alexander Archipelago Showing Route of Mess'rs Becker, and Dall and Localities Examined by Them, 1895. Map. Pl. 48 opp. p. 772 in *17th Annual Report of the U.S. Geological Survey for the Years 1895-1896*. Washington.

Damas, David, ed.
1969 Contributions to Anthropology: Band Societies. Proceedings of the Conference on Band Organization, Ottawa, August 30 to September 2, 1965. *Anthropological Series 84, National Museum of Canada Bulletin* 228. Ottawa.

Darnell, Regna
1970 The Kaska Aesthetic of Speech Use. Pp. 130-139 in Athabascan Studies. Regna Darnell, ed. *Western Canadian Journal of Anthropology* 2(1).

————, ed.
1970a Athabascan Studies. (Special Issue) *Western Canadian Journal of Anthropology* 2(1).

Daviault, D., M. Dufresne, S. Girouard, J.D. Kaye, and P. Legault
1978 L'Algonquin du nord. Pp. 55-60 in *Papers of the Ninth Algonquian Conference*. William Cowan, ed. Ottawa: Carleton University.

Davidson, Daniel S.
1928 Folk Tales from Grand Lake, Victoria, Quebec. *Journal of American Folk-Lore* 41(160):275-282.

————
1928a Some Tête de Boule Tales. *Journal of American Folk-Lore* 41(160):262-274.

————
1928b The Family Hunting Territories of the Grand Lake Victoria Indians. Pp. 69-95 in Vol. 2 of *Proceedings of the 22d International Congress of Americanists*. 2 vols. Rome, 1926.

752

1928c   Family Hunting Territories of the Waswanipi Indians of Quebec. *Museum of the American Indian, Heye Foundation, Indian Notes* 5:42-59. New York.

1928d   Notes on Tête de Boule Ethnology. *American Anthropologist* 30(1):18-46.

1928e   Decorative Art of the Têtes de Boule of Quebec. *Museum of the American Indian, Heye Foundation, Indian Notes and Monographs* 10(9):115-143. New York.

1937   Snowshoes. *Memoirs of the American Philosophical Society* 6. Philadelphia.

Davidson, George
1901   Explanation of an Indian Map of the Rivers, Lakes, Trails and Mountains from the Chilkaht to the Yukon Drawn by the Chilkaht Chief, Kohklux, in 1869. *Mazama* 2(2):75-82.

Davidson, Gordon C.
1918   The North West Company. *University of California Publications in History* 7. Berkeley.

Davidson, Sally
1973   Saulteaux Ethnomusicology and the Background Music of T.V. Soap Operas: A Cognitive Study of T.V. Adoption in a Manitoba Reserve. Pp. 70-87 in Preliminary Report on the Adoption of Television by Native Communities in the Canadian North, by J. Homer et al. Ottawa: Department of Communications.

Davies, Kenneth G., and A.M. Johnson, eds.
1963   Northern Quebec and Labrador Journal and Correspondence, 1819-35. (Publications of the Hudson's Bay Record Society 24) London: The Hudson's Bay Record Society.

1965   Letters from Hudson Bay, 1703-40. (Publications of the Hudson's Bay Record Society 25) London: The Hudson's Bay Record Society.

Davies, W.H.A.
1854   Notes on Ungava Bay and Its Vicinity. *Transactions of the Literary and Historical Society of Quebec* 4:119-137.

Davis, Clark A.
1970   The Identity of Nētcä'ut'in. *International Journal of American Linguistics* 36(1):59-60.

Davis, Henry, comp.
1976   English-Tlingit Dictionary: Nouns. Rev. ed. Sitka, Alaska: Sheldon Jackson College.

Davis, Nancy Yaw
1965   Eklutna, Alaska: A Tanaina Indian Village. (Unpublished M.A. Thesis in Anthropology, University of Chicago, Chicago.)

Davydov, Gavriil Ivanovich
1810-1812   Two Voyages to America. 2 vols. St. Petersburg: Naval Printing Office.

1977   Two Voyages to Russian America, 1802-1807. Richard A. Pierce, ed. Colin Bearne, trans. *Materials for the Study of Alaska History* 10. Kingston, Ont.

Dawson, George M.
1881   Report on an Exploration from Port Simpson on the Pacific Coast to Edmonton on the Saskatchewan Embracing a Portion of the Northern Part of British Columbia and the Peace River Country, 1879. Pp. 1B-177B in *Report of Progress of the Geological and Natural History Survey of Canada for 1879-1880.* Montreal.

1889   Report on an Exploration in the Yukon District, N.W.T., and Adjacent Northern Portion of British Columbia, 1887. Pp. 7-277 in Pt. 1 of *Annual Report of the Geological Survey of Canada for the Years 1887-1888* n.s. 3(B). Montreal.

Dawson, Kenneth C.A.
1963-1969   [Fieldnotes: Northwestern Ontario Archaeological Surveys.]

(Unpublished manuscript in Archaeological Survey of Canada, National Museum of Man, Ottawa.)

1976   Algonkians of Lake Nipigon: An Archaeological Survey. *Canada. National Museum of Man, Mercury Series, Archaeological Survey Paper* 48. Ottawa.

1976a   Historic Populations of Northwestern Ontario. Pp. 157-174 in *Papers of the Seventh Algonquian Conference, 1975.* William Cowan, ed. Ottawa: Carleton University.

De Boilieu, Lambert
1969   Recollections of Labrador Life [1861]. Thomas F. Bredin, ed. Toronto: Ryerson Press.

Deignan, H.G.
1947   HBC and the Smithsonian. *The Beaver* 1(287):3-7.

Dekin, Albert E.
1973   The Arctic. Pp. 15-48 in The Development of North American Archaeology. James E. Fitting, ed. Garden City, N.Y.: Anchor Press/Doubleday.

De Laguna, Frederica
1934   The Archaeology of Cook Inlet, Alaska. Philadelphia: Published for the University Museum by the University of Pennsylvania Press.

1936   Indian Masks from the Lower Yukon. *American Anthropologist* 38(4):569-585.

1936a   An Archaeological Reconnaissance of the Middle and Lower Yukon Valley, Alaska. *American Antiquity* 2(1):6-12.

1947   The Prehistory of Northern North America as Seen from the Yukon. *Memoirs of the Society for American Archaeology* 3. Menasha, Wis.

1952   Some Dynamic Forces in Tlingit Society. *Southwestern Journal of Anthropology* 8(1):1-12.

1954   Tlingit Ideas About the Individual. *Southwestern Journal of Anthropology* 10(2):172-191.

1960   The Story of a Tlingit Community: A Problem in the Relationship Between Archeological, Ethnological and Historical Methods. *Bureau of American Ethnology Bulletin* 172. Washington.

1969-1970   The Atna of the Copper River, Alaska: The World of Men and Animals. *Folk* 11-12:17-26. Copenhagen.

1972   Under Mount Saint Elias: The History and Culture of the Yakutat Tlingit. 3 Pts. *Smithsonian Contributions to Anthropology* 7. Washington.

1975   Matrilineal Kin Groups in Northwestern North America. Pp. 17-145 in Vol. 1 of Proceedings: Northern Athapaskan Conference, 1971. A. McFadyen Clark, ed. 2 vols. *Canada. National Museum of Man, Mercury Series, Ethnology Service Paper* 27. Ottawa.

De Laguna, Frederica, and Marie-Françoise Guédon
1968   [Ahtna Fieldnotes.] (Manuscripts in authors' possession; Microfilm copy at American Philosophical Society, Philadelphia.)

De Laguna, Frederica, and Catharine McClellan
[1954-1960]   [Ahtna Fieldnotes.] (Manuscripts in authors' possession; Microfilm copy at American Philosophical Society, Philadelphia.)

Delanglez, Jean
1944   Document: The Voyage of Louis Jolliet to Hudson Bay in 1679. *Mid-America* 26 [n.s. 15](3):221-250.

1944a   Journal de Louis Jolliet allant à la découverte de Labrador, 1694. Pp. 147-206 in *Rapport de l'Archiviste de la Province de Québec pour 1943-44.* Quebec.

753

Delisle, Gilles
1970   Southwestern Chippewa: A Teaching Grammar. Minneapolis: University of Minnesota, Department of American Indian Studies.

Denis, J.
1972   [Typed Page of Information on Dogrib Families at Fort Franklin, Northwest Territories, Dated 25 April 1972.] (Manuscript in Beryl C. Gillespie's possession.)

Denmark, D.C.
1948   James Bay Beaver Conservation. *The Beaver* 279 (September):38-43.

Denniston, Glenda
1966   The Place of the Upper Pelly River Indians in the Network of Athabaskan Groups. (Unpublished manuscript in author's possession; Copy in National Museum of Man, Ottawa.)

Denny, J. Peter, and Lorraine Odjig
1972   Guide to Possible Writing Systems for Ojibway. (Paper distributed by the Native Resource Center, University of Western Ontario, London, Ont.)

Denton, David, Marie Ferdais, Jean-Yves Pintal, Claude Rocheleu, Michel Bouchard, Pierre Richard, and Pierre Grégoire
1980   Investigations archéologiques dans la région du futur réservoir Caniapiscau, 1979: Un rapport préliminaire. 2 vols. (Unpublished manuscript in Ministère des Affaires Culturelles, Service du Patrimoine Autochtone, Direction Générale du Patrimoine, Quebec.)

Deprez, Paul, and A. Bisson
1975   Demographic Differences Between Indians and Métis in Fort Resolution. Winnipeg: University of Manitoba, Centre for Settlement Studies.

Derry, David E.
1975   Later Athapaskan Prehistory: A Migration Hypothesis. *Western Canadian Journal of Anthropology* 5(3-4):134-147.

Derry, David E., and Douglas R. Hudson, eds.
1975   Athapaskan Archaeology. (Special Issue) *Western Canadian Journal of Anthropology* 5(3-4).

Désy, Pierrette
1963   Acculturation et socio-économie chez les Montagnais et les Naskapi du Lac John près de Schefferville. (Unpublished M.A. Thesis in Geography, Université Laval, Quebec.)

_____
1968   Fort George ou Tsesa-sippi: Contribution à une étude sur la désintégration culturelle d'une communauté indienne de la Baie James. (Unpublished Ph.D. Dissertation in Anthropology, Université de Paris, Paris.)

De Trémaudan, August-Henri
1935   Histoire de la nation métisse dans l'ouest canadien... Montreal: Albert Lévesque.

Dewdney, Selwyn H.
1970   Dating Rock Art in the Canadian Shield Region. *Royal Ontario Museum, Art and Archaeology Division Occasional Paper* 24. Toronto.

_____
1975   The Sacred Scrolls of the Southern Ojibway. Toronto: University of Toronto Press.

Dewdney, Selwyn H., and Kenneth E. Kidd
1962   Indian Rock Paintings of the Great Lakes. *Quetico Foundation Series* 4. Toronto.

Dice, Lee R.
1943   The Biotic Provinces of North America. Ann Arbor: University of Michigan Press.

Dixon, E. James
[1976] The Pleistocene History of Arctic North America. Pp. 168-198 in Habitats humains antérieurs à l'Holocene en Amérique. *Union Internationale des Sciences Préhistoriques et Protohistoriques, IXe Congrès, Colloque XVII*. Paris.

Dixon, George *see* Beresford, William

Dixon, Greg, and William Johnson
1971   A Core and Blade Site on the Alaska Peninsula. Anchorage: Alaska Methodist University.

Dixon, Roland B.
1921   [Review of] Essai sur l'origine des Dénés de l'Amérique du Nord. *American Anthropologist* 23(2):218-220.

Dobbs, Arthur
1744   An Account of the Countries Adjoining to Hudson's Bay, in the North-west Part of America. London: J. Robinson. (Facsimile reprint: Johnson Reprint Corporation, New York, 1967.)

Dobyns, Henry F.
1976   Native American Historical Demography: A Critical Bibliography. (The Newberry Library Center for the History of the American Indian, Bibliographical Series) Bloomington and London: Indiana University Press.

Dominique, Richard
1976   Bibliographie thématique sur les Montagnais-Naskapi. (Service d'Archéologie et d'Ethnologie Dossier 21) Quebec: Ministère des Affaires Culturelles.

Dominique, Richard, and Celine Pelletier
1975   Une Etude de la technologie de la trappe chez les Montagnais-Naskapi de la Moyenne-côte-nord. Quebec. (Unpublished manuscript in the possession of the authors.)

Donahue, Paul F.
1970   Excavations at Algatcho and Tezli on the Central Interior Plateau of British Columbia. (Report to the National Museum of Man, Wenner-Gren Foundation for Anthropological Research, and Archaeological Sites Advisory Board. Mimeo.)

_____
1972   Preliminary Report of Excavations at Tezli (FgSd-1), British Columbia. (Report to the National Museum of Man, Explorers Club, and Archaeological Sites Advisory Board. Mimeo.)

_____
1973   Ulkatcho: An Archaeological Outline. *Syesis* 6:153-178.

_____
1975   Concerning Athapaskan Prehistory in British Columbia. *Western Canadian Journal of Anthropology* 5(3-4):21–63.

_____
1976   Research in Alberta, 1975. *Archaeological Survey of Alberta Occasional Paper* 2. Edmonton.

Dorian, Henri
1967   Les Noms des lieux Montagnais des environs de Mingan: Contribution à la connaissance de la choronymie aborigène de la côte-nord. (Groupe d'Etude de Choronymie et de Terminologie Géographique 2) Quebec: Presses de l'Université Laval.

Dorosh, John T.
1961   The Alaska Russian Church Archives. *Quarterly Journal of the Library of Congress* 18(4):193-203.

Douglas, Frederic
1939   A Naskapi Painted Skin Shirt. *Denver Art Museum Material Culture Notes, Reports from the Ethnographic Laboratory* 10:38-40. Denver.

Douglas, James
1839   New Caledonia Census, Spring 1839. (Unpublished manuscript in Private Papers of Sir James Douglas, microfilm A-92, frame 9 in University of Washington Library, Seattle.)

Downes, P.G.
1938   Reindeer Lake Pottery. *American Antiquity* 4(1):48

Drane, Frederick B.
1928   The Indian As I Knew Him. (Manuscript in possession of Rev. Drane, Edenton, N.C.)

Driver, Harold E.
1961   Indians of North America. Chicago: University of Chicago Press.

Driver, Harold E., and William C. Massey
1957   Comparative Studies of North American Indians. *Transac-*

tions of the American Philosophical Society n.s. 47(2). Philadelphia.

Drucker, Philip
1965   Cultures of the North Pacific Coast. San Francisco: Chandler.

Duchaussois, Pierre
1919   The Grey Nuns in the Far North, 1867-1917. Toronto: McClelland and Stewart.

_____
1923   Mid Snow and Ice: The Apostles of the Northwest. Thomas Dawson, trans. London: Burns, Oates and Washbourne.

_____
1928   Aux Glaces polaires: Indiens et Esquimaux. New ed. Paris: Editions SPES.

Ducot, X.F.
1892   [Statistique des indiens de la Mission Ste. Thérèse au Fort Norman, June 1892.] (Manuscript, copy, No. KIS IC3 in Archives Historiques Oblates, Ottawa.)

_____
1914   [Statistique de la Mission Ste. Thérèse: Fort Norman.] (Manuscript at Ste. Thérèse Mission, Fort Norman, N.W.T., Canada.)

Duff, Wilson
1951   Notes on Carrier Social Organization. *Anthropology in British Columbia* 2:28-34. Victoria.

_____
1964   The Indian History of British Columbia. Vol. 1: The Impact of the White Man. *Anthropology in British Columbia Memoir* 5. Victoria.

_____
[1972]   [Notes for the Indian History of British Columbia.] (Manuscript in Duff's possession.)

Dumond, Don E.
1965   On Eskaleutian Linguistics, Archaeology, and Prehistory. *American Anthropologist* 67(5):1231-1257.

_____
1969   Toward a Prehistory of the Na-Dene, with a General Comment on Population Movements Among Nomadic Hunters. *American Anthropologist* 71(5):857-863.

_____
1973   Reviews of Kijik: An Historic Tanaina Indian Settlement, by James W. VanStone and Joan B. Townsend, and Akulivikchuk: A Nineteenth Century Eskimo Village on the Nushagak River, Alaska, by James W. VanStone. *American Antiquity* 38(2):247-248.

_____
1974   Remarks on the Prehistory of the North Pacific: To Lump or not to Lump? Pp. 47-55 in International Conference on the Prehistory and Paleoecology of Western North American Arctic and Subarctic. Scott Raymond and Peter Schledermann, eds. Calgary: University of Calgary, Archaeological Association, Department of Archaeology.

_____
1977   The Eskimos and Aleuts. (Ancient Peoples and Places 87b.) London: Thames and Hudson.

Dumond, Don E., and Robert L.A. Mace
1968   An Archaeological Survey Along Knik Arm. *Anthropological Papers of the University of Alaska* 14(1):1-21. College.

Dumoulin, S.N.
1839   Lettre datée du 17 juillet 1838. *Notices sur les Missions du Diocèse de Québec* 1:24-31.

Dunn, Guillaume
1975   Les Forts de l'Outaouais. Montreal: Editions du Jour.

Dunning, Robert W.
1959   Social and Economic Change Among the Northern Ojibwa. Toronto: University of Toronto Press.

_____
1959a   Rules of Residence and Ecology Among the Northern Ojibwa. *American Anthropologist* 61(5):806-816.

Durlach, Theresa Mayer
1928   The Relationship Systems of the Tlingit, Haida and Tsimshian. *Publications of the American Ethnological Society* 11. New York.

Dyck, Ian G.
1970   Two Oxbow Settlement Types in Central Saskatchewan. *Na'pao* 2(2):1-29. Saskatoon.

Dyen, Isidore, and David F. Aberle
1974   Lexical Reconstruction: The Case of the Proto-Athapaskan Kinship System. London and New York: Cambridge University Press.

Dzeniskevich, G.I.
1975   Okhotnichii i rybolovnyĭ promysly u Tanaĭna (Alĭaska) v XIX v (Hunting and Fishing Trade of the Tanaina (Alaska) in the 19th Century). *Sbornik Muzeĭ Antropologii i Etnografii* 31:52-68. Leningrad.

_____
1976   O kultovykh elementakh v ornamente iz igl dikobraza u Atapaskov Alĭaski. Pp. 166-175 in: Pervovytnoe Iskusstvo. R.S. Vasilevskiy, ed. Novosibirsk: Akademia Nauk SSR.

East, Ben
1951   Waveys Over the Bay: The Migrating of the Geese Across the Marshes of James Bay Forms: One of the Most Thrilling Wildlife Spectacles on This Continent. *The Beaver* 282(September):10-13.

Eggan, Fred, ed.
1955   Social Anthropology of North American Tribes. 2d ed. Chicago: University of Chicago Press.

_____
1966   The American Indian: Perspectives for the Study of Social Change. Chicago: Aldine.

Egloff, Margaret Stephens
1968   Cree-Métis and Other People on the Flats. Pp. 129-143 in Ethnographic Survey of Churchill. John J. Honigmann, ed. *University of North Carolina, Institute for Research in Social Sciences Working Paper* 3. Chapel Hill.

Egloff, Margaret S., William W. Koolage, and George Vranas
1968   Ethnographic Survey of Churchill: Urbanization in the Arctic and Subarctic. John J. Honigmann, ed. *University of North Carolina, Institute for Research in Social Science Working Paper* 3. Chapel Hill.

Eiseley, Loren C.
1947   Land Tenure in the Northeast: A Note on the History of a Concept. *American Anthropologist* 49(4):680-681.

Elias, Douglas
1967   The Effects of Water Level Fluctuations Upon the Peoples Dwelling on Lake Winnipeg and Inflowing Rivers. (Unpublished manuscript in University of Winnipeg, Department of Anthropology, Winnipeg.)

_____
1967a   Gossip. (Unpublished manuscript in University of Winnipeg, Department of Anthropology, Winnipeg.)

Elias, Douglas, and Jack Steinbring
1967   Animal Designs in Rock Paintings. *Zoolog: Quarterly Journal of the Zoological Society of Manitoba* 8(4):10-11. Winnipeg.

Elliott, Henry W.
1875   A Report Upon the Condition of Affairs in the Territory of Alaska. Washington: U.S. Government Printing Office.

Ellis, C. Douglas
1960   A Note on Okima·hka·n. *Anthropological Linguistics* 2(3):1.

_____
1962   Spoken Cree, West Coast of James Bay. Pt. 1. Toronto: Anglican Church of Canada, Department of Missions.

_____
1970   A Proposed Standard Roman Orthography for Cree: A Report Submitted to the Canadian Department of Indian Affairs and Northern Development, Ottawa. Mimeo.

Elton, Charles S.
1942   Voles, Mice and Lemmings: Problems in Population Dynamics. Oxford, England: Clarendon Press.

Emmons, George T.
1910   Tahltan. Pp. 670-671 in Vol. 2 of Handbook of American
        Indians North of Mexico. Frederick W. Hodge, ed. 2 vols.
        Bureau of American Ethnology Bulletin 30. Washington.

1911   The Tahltan Indians. *University of Pennsylvania Museum,
        Anthropological Publication* 4(1). Philadelphia.

Endicott, Henry W.
1928   Adventures in Alaska and Along the Trail. New York: F.A.
        Stokes.

Episcopal Seminary of the Southwest
1957   [Alaska Papers of the Domestic and Foreign Missionary So-
        ciety, 1884-1952.] (Manuscripts in St. John's in the Wilder-
        ness Mission, Allakaket, Alaska.)

Ervin, Alexander M.
1969   Conflicting Styles of Life in a Northern Canadian Town.
        Arctic 22(2):90:105.

Evans, G. Edward
1961   Ceramic Analysis of the Blackduck Ware and Its General
        Cultural Relationships. *Proceedings of the Minnesota Acad-
        emy of Science* 29:33-54. St. Paul.

Fabvre, Bonaventure
1970   Racines montagnaises, compilées à Tadoussac avant 1695.
        Lorenzo Angers and Gérard E. McNulty, eds. *Université
        Laval, Centre d'Etudes Nordiques, Travaux Divers* 29. Que-
        bec.

Faraud, Henri
1866   Dix-huit ans chez les sauvages: Voyages et missions de Mgr.
        Henry Faraud. Paris: R. Ruffet. (Reprinted: Johnson Re-
        prints, New York, 1966.)

Faries, Richard, ed.
1938   A Dictionary of the Cree Language, as Spoken by the Indians
        in the Provinces of Quebec, Ontario, Manitoba, Saskatche-
        wan and Alberta. Toronto: The General Synod of the Church
        of England in Canada.

Farley, Albert L.
1979   Atlas of British Columbia: People, Environment and Re-
        source Use. Vancouver: University of British Columbia
        Press.

Farrand, Livingstone
1899   The Chilcotin. Pp. 645-647 in *Report of the 68th Meeting of
        the British Association for the Advancement of Science, 1898*.
        London.

1900   Traditions of the Chilcotin Indians. *Memoirs of the American
        Museum of Natural History* 4(1): 11-54. New York.

1910   Tsilkotin. P. 826 in Vol. 2 of Handbook of American Indians
        North of Mexico. Frederick W. Hodge, ed. 2 vols. *Bureau
        of American Ethnology Bulletin* 30. Washington.

Federal Field Committee for Development Planning in Alaska
1968   Alaska Natives and the Land. Washington: U.S. Government
        Printing Office.

Fedirchuk, Gloria
1970   Recent Archaeological Investigations at Fisherman Lake:
        The Julian Site. Pp. 105-112 in Early Man and Environments
        in Northwest North America. R.A. Smith and J.W. Smith,
        eds. (Proceedings of the 2d Annual Paleo-environmental
        Workshop of the University of Calgary Archaeological As-
        sociation) Calgary, Alta.: The Students' Press.

1970a   Archaeological Investigations at Fisherman Lake 1970. Al-
        buquerque: University of New Mexico, Department of An-
        thropology. Typescript.

Fedorova, S.G.
1973   The Russian Population in Alaska and California: Late 18th
        Century, 1867. R.A. Pierce and A.S. Donnelly, eds. and
        trans. *Materials for the Study of Alaska History* 4. Kingston,
        Ont.

1973a   New Data on Russian Geographic and Ethnographic Inves-
        tigations in Alaska [First Half of the 19th Century]. (Paper
        presented at the 9th International Congress of Anthropo-
        logical and Ethnological Sciences, Chicago.)

Feit, Harvey A.
1969   Mistassini Hunters of the Boreal Forest: Ecosystem Dynam-
        ics and Multiple Subsistence Patterns. (Unpublished M.A.
        Thesis in Anthropology, McGill University, Montreal.)

1971   L'Ethno-écologie des Cris Waswanipis, ou comment des
        chasseurs peuvent aménager leurs ressources. *Recherches
        Amérindiennes au Québec, Bulletin d'Information* 1(4-5):84-
        93. Montreal.

1971a   Exploitation des ressources naturelles en expansion dans la
        région de la Baie James. *Recherches Amérindiennes au
        Québec, Bulletin d'Information* 1(4-5):22-26. Montreal.

1973   The Ethno-ecology of the Waswanipi Cree: Or, How Hunters
        Can Manage Their Resources. Pp. 115-125 in Cultural Ecol-
        ogy: Readings on the Canadian Indians and Eskimos. Bruce
        A. Cox, ed. Toronto: McClelland and Stewart.

1973a   Twilight of the Cree Hunting Nation. *Natural History* 82(7):48-
        57, 72.

1976   Bibliographie concernant la Baie James. *Recherches
        Amérindiennes au Québec* 6(1):61-64. Montreal.

1979   Waswanipi Realities and Adaptations: Resource Manage-
        ment and Cognitive Structure. (Unpublished Ph.D. Disser-
        tation in Anthropology, McGill University, Montreal.)

Feit, Harvey A., M.E. MacKenzie, José Mailhot, and Charles A.
Martijn
1972   Bibliography: Native Peoples, James Bay Region. *Re-
        cherches Amérindiennes au Québec, Bulletin d'Information*
        2(1 spécial). Montreal.

Fidler, Peter
1934   Journal of a Journey with the Chipewayans or Northern In-
        dians to the Slave Lake and to the East and West of the Slave
        River, in 1791 and 1792. Pp. 493-556 in Journals of Samuel
        Hearne and Phillip Turnor Between the Years 1774 and 1792.
        J.B. Tyrrell, ed. Toronto: The Champlain Society.

Field, Poole
1913   [Communications on the Ethnology of the Athabascan-
        speaking Peoples Between the Yukon and Mackenzie Riv-
        ers.] (Manuscript 35, Pts. 1-4 in National Museum of Man,
        Ottawa.)

1957   The Poole Field Letters [1913]. June Helm MacNeish, ed.
        Anthropologica 4:47-60. Ottawa.

Fiero, Charles E.
1965   Ojibwa Language Course, Pt. 1. Red Lake, Ont.: no pub-
        lisher.

1967   Ojibwa Assimilation. Freeport, Pa.: Fountain Press.

Fiero, Charles E., and Norman Quill
1973   Ojibwa Assimilation. Red Lake, Ont.: Northern Light Gos-
        pel Missions.

Fisher, Anthony D.
1969   The Cree of Canada: Some Ecological and Evolutionary
        Considerations. *Western Canadian Journal of Anthropology*
        1(1):7-19.

Fisher, Robin
1977   Contact and Conflict: Indian-European Relations in British
        Columbia, 1774-1890. Vancouver: University of British Co-
        lumbia Press.

Fitzhugh, William W.
1972   Environmental Archeology and Cultural Systems in Hamil-
        ton Inlet, Labrador: A Survey of the Central Labrador Coast

from 3000 B.C. to the Present. *Smithsonian Contributions to Anthropology* 16. Washington.

Fladmark, Knut R.
1973 Archaeological Investigations at Punchaw Lake, North-central British Columbia. *Midden* 5(4):1-2, 11. Vancouver.

————
1976 Punchaw Village: A Preliminary Report; Archaeology of a Prehistoric Settlement. (Current Research Reports) *Simon Fraser University, Department of Archaeology Publication* 3. Burnaby, B.C.

Fladmark, Knut R., Finola Finlay, and Bruce Spurling
1977 Archaeological Investigations in the Peace River Basin of British Columbia: Summer 1975. Pp. 276-320 in *Annual Report for the Year 1975 of the Archaeological Sites Advisory Board of British Columbia.* Victoria: Ministry of Recreation and Conservation.

Flannery, Regina
1935 The Position of Woman Among the Eastern Cree. *Primitive Man* 8(4):81-86.

————
1936 Some Aspects of James Bay Recreative Culture. *Primitive Man* 9(4):49-56.

————
1938 Cross-cousin Marriage Among the Cree and Montagnais of James Bay. *Primitive Man* 11(1-2): 29-33.

————
1939 An Analysis of Coastal Algonquian Culture. *Catholic University of America Anthropological Series* 7. Washington.

————
1939a The Shaking-tent Rite Among the Montagnais of James Bay. *Primitive Man* 12(1):11-16.

————
1946 The Culture of the Northeastern Indian Hunters: A Descriptive Survey. Pp. 263-271 in Man in Northeastern North America. Frederick Johnson, ed. *Papers of the Robert S. Peabody Foundation for Archaeology* 3. Andover, Mass.

————
1962 Infancy and Childhood Among the Indians of the East Coast of James Bay. *Anthropos* 57(3-6):475-482.

————
1971 Some Magico-religious Concepts of the Algonquians on the East Coast of James Bay, Canada. Pp. 31-39 in Themes in Culture: Essays in Honor of Morris Opler. Mario D. Zamora, J. Michael Mahar, and Henry Orenstein, eds. Quezon City, Philippines: Kayumanggi Publishers.

Fleming, R. Harvey, ed.
1940 Minutes of Council, Northern Department of Rupert Land, 1821-31. (Publications of the Champlain Society 3) Toronto: The Champlain Society.

Fogelson, Raymond D.
1965 Psychological Theories of Windigo "Psychosis" and a Preliminary Application of a Models Approach. Pp. 74-99 in Context and Meaning in Cultural Anthropology: In Honor of A. Irving Hallowell. Melford E. Spiro, ed. New York: Free Press; London: Collier-Macmillan.

Foote, Don C., and Sheila K. MacBain
1964 A Selected Regional Bibliography for Human Geographical Studies of the Native Populations of Central Alaska. *McGill University, Geography Department Publication* 12. Montreal.

Forbis, Richard G.
1961 Early Point Types from Acasta Lake, Northwest Territories, Canada. *American Antiquity* 27(1):112-113.

————
1962 The Old Women's Buffalo Jump, Alberta. *Anthropological Series* 57, *National Museum of Canada Bulletin* 180:56-123. Ottawa.

Ford, Alan
1978 L'Alternance n/yod en mushuau innu. Pp. 237-245 in *Papers of the Ninth Algonquian Conference.* William Cowan, ed. Ottawa: Carleton University.

Ford, Alan et al.
[1978] Rapport préliminaire sur la dialectologie des parlers cri-montagnais de Québec. Première partie: Phonologie et morphologie des flexions. (Manuscript in Richard Rhodes's possession.)

Formorzov, A.N.
1964 The Snow Cover as an Integral Factor of the Environment and Its Importance to the Ecology of Mammals and Birds. William Prychodko and William Pruitt, trans. *University of Alberta, Boreal Institute Occasional Publication* 1. Edmonton.

Fontin, J.-Henri
1966 Archéologie au Saguenay: Un site de Royaume du Saguenay, rapport préliminaire, site O (section 4). Lac St.-Jean, P.Q. Saint-Jérôme, Que.: Société d'Archéologie du Saguenay.

Foster, John E.
1977 The Home Guard Cree and the Hudson's Bay Company: The First Hundred Years; Approaches to Native History in Canada. *Canada. National Museum of Man, Mercury Series, History Division Paper* 25. Ottawa.

Franklin, Sir John
1823 Narrative of a Journey to the Shores of the Polar Sea in the Years 1819, 20, 21, and 22. London: John Murray. (Reprinted: M.G. Hurtig, Edmonton, Alta., 1969.)

————
1824 Narrative of a Journey to the Shores of the Polar Sea, in the Years 1819-20-21-22. 2d ed. 2 vols. London: John Murray.

————
1828 Narrative of a Second Expedition to the Shores of the Polar Sea, in the Years 1825, 1826, and 1827 Including an Account of the Progress of a Detachment to the Eastward. London: John Murray. (Reprinted: M.G. Hurtig, Edmonton, Alta., 1971.)

Franquelin, Jean-Baptiste
1970 Section of Map, "Carte Gnlle de la France Septentrionalle" [1678]. Reproduced: Pp. 38-39 in Manitoba Historical Atlas. John Warkentin and Richard I. Ruggles, eds. Winnipeg: Historical and Scientific Society of Manitoba.

Franquet, Louis
1889 Voyages et mémoires sur le Canada. Pp. 23-40 in *Annuaire de l'Institut Canadien de Québec.* Quebec.

Fraser, E. Morton
1956 The Lichen Woodlands of the Knob Lake Area of Quebec-Labrador. *McGill University, Subarctic Research Laboratory Paper* 1. Montreal.

Fraser, J. Keith
1968 Place Names. Pp. 236-262 in Vol. 1 of Science, History and Hudson Bay. C.S. Beals, ed. 2 vols. Ottawa: Department of Energy, Mines and Resources.

Fraser, Simon
1889-1890 Journal of a Voyage from the Rocky Mountains to the Pacific Coast, 1808. Pp. 155-221 in Vol. 1 of Les Bourgeois de la Compagnie du Nord-Ouest. L.R. Masson, ed. 2 vols. Quebec: A. Coté.

————
1960 The Letters and Journals, 1806-1808. W. Kaye Lamb, ed. Toronto: Macmillan of Canada.

French, Diana E.
1974 Taku Recovery Project: A Preliminary Report for the Atlin Band. Archaeological Sites Advisory Board Permit No. 29-73. Mimeo.

Fried, Jacob, ed.
1955 A Survey of the Aboriginal Populations of Quebec and Labrador. (Eastern Canadian Anthropological Series 1) Montreal: McGill University.

————
1963 White-dominant Settlements in the Canadian Northwest Territories. *Anthropologica* n.s. 5(1):57-67. Ottawa.

————
1964 Urbanization and Ecology in the Canadian Northwest Territories. *Arctic Anthropology* 2(2):56-60.

757

1968   Peoples of European Origin. Pp. 172-200 in Vol. 1 of Science, History, and Hudson Bay. C.S. Beals, ed. 2 vols. Ottawa: Queen's Printer.

Fried, Morton H.
1967   The Evolution of Political Society: An Essay in Political Anthropology. New York: Random House.

Fuller, W.A.
1955   The Inconnu (Stenodus leucichthys mackenziei) in Great Slave Lake and Adjoining Waters. *Journal of the Fisheries Research Board of Canada* 12(5):768-780.

Fumoleau, René
[1973]   As Long as This Land Shall Last: A History of Treaty 8 and Treaty 11, 1870/1939. Toronto: McClelland and Stewart.

Gagnon, François-Marc
1979   L'Expérience ethnographique de Louis Nicolas. *Recherches Amérindiennes au Québec* 8(4):281-295. Montreal.

Gallatin, Albert
1836   A Synopsis of the Indian Tribes Within the United States East of the Rocky Mountains, and the British and Russian Possessions in America. Pp. 1-422 in *Archaeologia Americana: Transactions and Collections of the American Antiquarian Society* 2. Cambridge, Mass.

Gardner, James S.
1966   Snow Studies at Schefferville, 1954-1964. *McGill University, Subarctic Research Laboratory Paper* 20:14-20. Montreal.

Garfield, Viola E.
1947   Historical Aspects of Tlingit Clans in Angoon, Alaska. *American Anthropologist* 49(3):438-452.

Gemini North
1974   Social and Economic Impact of Proposed Arctic Gas Pipeline in Northern Canada. 7 vols. Calgary, Alta.: Canadian Arctic Gas Pipeline.

Gendron, Peter
1963   [Notes on Fort Resolution.] (Unpublished manuscript in Department of Northern Affairs and National Resources, Northern Administration Branch, Welfare Division.)

Gibbs, George
[1865]   [Notes on the Tinné or Chipewyan Indians of British Columbia.] (Manuscript No. 126 in National Anthropological Archives, Smithsonian Institution, Washington.)

1867   Instructions for Research Relative to the Ethnology and Philology of America. *Smithsonian Miscellaneous Collections* 7(11). Washington.

1872   Notes on the Tinneh or Chepewyan Indians of British and Russian America. Pp. 303-327 in *Annual Report of the Smithsonian Institution for 1866*. Washington.

Giddings, J. Louis, Jr.
1951   The Denbigh Flint Complex. *American Antiquity* 16(3):193-203.

1956   A Flint Site in Northernmost Manitoba. *American Antiquity* 21(3):255-268.

1967   Ancient Men of the Arctic. New York: Alfred A. Knopf.

Gilbert, L.
1967   Organisation économique et relocalisation à Weymontachie. (Unpublished manuscript at Université Laval, Quebec.)

Gillespie, Beryl C.
[1968-1971] [Ethnographic Notes from Fieldwork Among Dogrib, Bear Lake Indians and Mountain Indians, Northwest Territories, Canada.] (Manuscripts in Gillespie's possession.)

1970   Yellowknives: Quo Iverunt? Pp. 61-70 in Migration and Anthropology: Proceedings of the 1970 Annual Spring Meeting of the American Ethnological Society. Seattle: University of Washington Press.

1971   [Ethnographic Notes of Fieldwork at Fort Norman and Fort Franklin, N.W.T.; Population Lists in Record Books of the Roman Catholic Church at Fort Franklin and Hudson's Bay Company at Fort Norman.] (Manuscript in Gillespie's possession.)

1975   Territorial Expansion of the Chipewyan in the Eighteenth Century. Pp. 350-388 in Vol. 2 of Proceedings: Northern Athapaskan Conference, 1971. A. McFadyen Clark, ed. 2 vols. *Canada. National Museum of Man, Mercury Series, Ethnology Service Paper* 27. Ottawa.

1975a   An Ethnohistory of the Yellowknives: A Northern Athapaskan Tribe. Pp. 191-245 in Contributions to Canadian Ethnology, 1975. David B. Carlisle, ed. *Canada. National Museum of Man, Mercury Series, Ethnology Service Paper* 31. Ottawa.

1976   Changes in Territory and Technology of the Chipewyan. *Arctic Anthropology* 13(1):6-11.

Gilstrap, Roger
1978   Algonquian Dialect Relationships in Northwestern Quebec. *Canada. National Museum of Man, Mercury Series, Ethnology Service Paper* 44. Ottawa.

Gimmer, David H.
1966   Milady's Fur... The Trapper. Pp. 25-28 in People of Light and Dark. Maja van Steesel, ed. Ottawa: Department of Indian Affairs and Northern Development.

Giraud, Marcel
1945   Le Métis canadien: Son rôle dans l'histoire des provinces de l'ouest. *Travaux et Mémoires de l'Institut d'Ethnologie* 44. Paris.

Giroux, Claude
1979   L'Utilisation contemporaine du territoire: Réservoir de LG-3, Complexe La Grande Baie James. 2 vols. (Unpublished manuscript in Ministère des Affaires Culturelles, Service du Patrimoine Autochtone, Direction Générale du Patrimoine, Quebec.)

Gjessing, Gutorm
1944   Circumpolar Stone Age. *Acta Arctica* 2. Copenhagen.

Glave, Edward J.
1890   The Alaska Expedition. *Frank Leslie's Illustrated Newspaper* 70:84, 86, 87, 266, 286-287, 310, 328, 332, 352, 374-376, 485, 572.

1891   The Alaska Expedition. *Frank Leslie's Illustrated Newspaper* 71:414, 438.

1892   Pioneer Packhorses in Alaska. 2 Pts. *Century Illustrated Monthly Magazine* 44(5):671-682, (6):869-881.

Gleason, Henry A.
1961   An Introduction to Descriptive Linguistics. Rev. ed. New York: Holt, Rinehart and Winston.

Glenn, Edward F.
1899   Reports of Exploration in the Territory of Alaska (Cooks Inlet, Sushitna, Copper and Tanana Rivers), 1898. Washington: U.S. Government Printing Office.

1900   Explorations in and about Cook Inlet, 1899. Pp. 713-724 in Compilations of Narratives of Explorations in Alaska. Washington: U.S. Government Printing Office.

1900a   A Trip into the Tanana Region, 1898. Pp. 629-647 in Compilation of Narratives of Explorations in Alaska. Washington: U.S. Government Printing Office.

Goddard, Ives
1967   Notes on the Genetic Classification of the Algonquian Languages. Pp. 7-12 in Contributions to Anthropology: Linguistics I (Algonquian). *Anthropological Series 78, National Museum of Canada Bulletin* 214. Ottawa.

758

1979   The Evidence for Eastern Algonquian as a Genetic Subgroup. *Algonquian Linguistics* 5(2):19-22.

1980   Eastern Algonquian as a Genetic Subgrouping. Pp. 143-158 in *Papers of the Eleventh Algonquian Conference.* William Cowan, ed. Ottawa: Carleton University.

Goddard, Pliny E.
1917   The Beaver Indians. *Anthropological Papers of the American Museum of Natural History* 10(4):201-293. New York.

1917a   Beaver Texts. *Anthropological Papers of the American Museum of Natural History* 10(5):295-397. New York.

1917b   Beaver Dialect. *Anthropological Papers of the American Museum of Natural History* 10(6):399-546. New York.

1917c   Chipewyan Texts. *Anthropological Papers of the American Museum of Natural History* 10(1):1-65. New York.

1917d   Analysis of Cold Lake Dialect, Chipewyan. *Anthropological Papers of the American Museum of Natural History* 10(2):67–170. New York.

Godfrey, W. Earl
1966   The Birds of Canada. *Biological Series 73, National Museum of Canada Bulletin* 203. Ottawa.

Godsell, Philip H.
1934   Arctic Trader: The Account of Twenty Years with the Hudson's Bay Company. New York: G.P. Putnam's Sons.

1938   Red Hunters of the Snows: An Account of Thirty Years' Experience with the Primitive Indian and Eskimo Tribes of the Canadian North-west and Arctic Coast, with a Brief History of the Early Contact Between White Fur Traders and the Aborigines. Toronto: Ryerson Press.

1939   The Vanishing Frontier: A Saga of Traders, Mounties and Men of the last North West. London: Robert Hale.

Goldman, Irving
1940   The Alkatcho Carrier of British Columbia. Pp. 333-386 in Acculturation in Seven American Indian Tribes. Ralph Linton, ed. New York: D. Appleton-Century.

1941   The Alkatcho Carrier: Historical Background of Crest Prerogatives. *American Anthropologist* 43(3):396-418.

1953   The Alkatcho Carrier of British Columbia. (Manuscript in the British Columbia Provincial Museum, Victoria.)

Goldschmidt, Walter R., and Theodore H. Haas
1946   Possessory Rights of the Natives of Southeastern Alaska: A Detailed Analysis of the Early and Present Territory Used and Occupied by the Natives of Southeastern Alaska, Except the Natives of the Village of Kake (Partially Treated), Hydaberg and Klawock: A Report to the Commission of Indian Affairs. Mimeo.

Golla, Victor K.
1976   [Fieldnotes on Tagish, Collected from Mrs. Angela Sidney, Tagish, Yukon Terr., Summer 1976.] (Manuscript in Golla's possession.)

Gooding, S.J.
1951   H.B.C. Trade Guns. *The Beaver* 282(December):30-31.

Gordon, Bryan H.C.
1971   Interim Report: Upper Thelon River Archaeological-Botanical Project. (Mimeograph copy in Archives of the Archaeological Survey of Canada, Ottawa.)

1974   Of Men and Herds in Barrenland Prehistory. (Unpublished Ph.D. Dissertation in Archaeology, University of Calgary, Calgary, Alta.)

1975   Of Men and Herds in Barrenland Prehistory. *Canada. National Museum of Man, Mercury Series, Archaeological Survey Paper* 28. Ottawa.

1976   Migod—8,000 Years of Barrenland Prehistory. *Canada. National Museum of Man, Mercury Series, Archaeological Survey Paper* 56. Ottawa.

Gordon, Bryan H.C., and Howard Savage
1974   Whirl Lake: A Stratified Indian Site Near the Mackenzie Delta. *Arctic* 27(3):175-188.

Gordon, George B.
1917   In the Alaskan Wilderness. Philadelphia: John C. Winston.

Gorst, Thomas
1943   Extract of Mr. Thomas Gorst's Journal in the Voyage to Hudsons Bay Begun the 31 Day of May 1670. Appendix 2. Pp. 286-292 in Caesars of the Wilderness: Médard Chouart, Sieur des Groseilliers and Pierre Esprit Radisson, 1618-1710, by Grace Lee Nute. New York: D. Appleton-Century.

Graburn, Nelson H.H.
1969   Eskimos without Igloos: Social and Economic Development in Sugluk. Boston: Little, Brown.

1975   Naskapi Family and Kinship. *Western Canadian Journal of Antropology* 5(2):56-84.

Graburn, Nelson H.H., and B. Stephen Strong
1973   Circumpolar Peoples: An Anthropological Perspective. Pacific Palisades, Calif.: Goodyear Publishing Company.

Graham, Andrew
1949   Extract from "Observations on Hudson's Bay" [1775]. Pp. 309-317 in James Isham's Observations on Hudson's Bay, 1743. E.E. Rich, ed. App. B. Toronto: The Champlain Society.

1969   Andrew Graham's Observations on Hudson's Bay, 1767-1791. Glyndwr Williams, ed. (Publications of the Hudson's Bay Record Society 27) London: The Hudson's Bay Record Society.

Graham, Angus, assembler
1935   The Golden Grindstone: The Adventures of George M. Mitchell. Philadelphia: J.B. Lippincott.

Grand Council of the Crees
1980   Position of the Grand Council of the Crees (of Quebec) and the Crees of James Bay Respecting the Future of Archeological Research in Northern Quebec. Pp. 81-84 in *Actes du Colloque sur l'Archéologie Québécoise,* 5-7 avril 1979. Quebec: Ministère des Affaires Culturelles, Centre de Documentation, Direction Générale du Patrimoine.

Grant, Peter
1889-1890   "The Sauteux Indians," vers 1804. Pp. 306-366 in Vol. 2 of Les Bourgeois de la Compagnie du Nord-ouest: Récits de voyages, lettres et rapports inédits relatifs au nord-ouest canadien. L.R. Masson, ed. 2 vols. Quebec: A. Coté.

Grantham, E.N.
1951   Education Goes North. *Canadian Geographical Journal* 42(1):45-49.

Granville, Charles Bécard de *see* Nicolas, Louis

Gray, Asa, and Merritt Fernald
1950   Gray's Manual of Botany: A Handbook of the Flowering Plants and Ferns of the Central and Northeastern United States and Adjacent Canada. 8th ed. New York, Cincinnati, Boston, Atlanta, Dallas, San Francisco: American Book Company.

Greenman, Emerson F., and George M. Stanley
1943   The Archaeology and Geology of Two Early Sites Near Killarney, Ontario. *Papers of the Michigan Academy of Science, Arts and Letters* 28:505-530. Ann Arbor.

Grenfell, Wilfred T.
1909   Labrador: The Country and the People. New York: Macmillan.

Griffin, James B.
1953   A Preliminary Statement on the Pottery from Cape Denbigh, Alaska. Pp. 40-42 in Asia and North America: Transpacific

Contacts. Marian W. Smith, ed. *Memoirs of the Society for American Archaeology* 9. Salt Lake City.

1964   The Northeast Woodlands Area. Pp. 223-258 in Prehistoric Man in the New World. Jesse D. Jennings and Edward Norbeck, eds. Chicago: University of Chicago Press.

Grinnell, Joseph
1901   Gold Hunting in Alaska. Elizabeth Grinnell, ed. Chicago: David C. Cook.

Grossman, Daniel
1965   The Nature of Descent Groups of Some Tribes in the Interior of Northwestern North America. *Anthropologica* n.s. 7(2):249-262. Ottawa.

Gruhn, Ruth
1966   Summary of Field Work at Calling Lake, Northern Alberta. Pp. 2-4 in *Archaeological Society of Alberta Newsletter* 16 Edmonton.

1967   Summary Report of 1967 Fieldwork at Calling Lake, Northern Alberta. (Unpublished manuscript No. 87 in National Museum of Man, Archaeological Survey of Canada, Ottawa.)

1969   Summary of Field Work at Calling Lake, Northern Alberta, Summer 1968. Pp. 8-14 in *Archaeological Society of Alberta Newsletter* 19. Edmonton.

Gubser, Nicholas J.
1965   The Nunamiut Eskimos: Hunters of Caribou. New Haven, Conn.: Yale University Press.

Gue, Leslie R.
1971   Value Orientations in an Indian Community. *Alberta Journal of Educational Research* 17(1):19-31.

Guédon, Marie-Françoise
[1969-1972]   [Fieldnotes for Upper Tanana Indians.] (Manuscripts in National Museum of Man, Ethnology Division Archives, Ottawa.)

1974   People of Tetlin, Why Are You Singing? *Canada. National Museum of Man, Ethnology Division, Mercury Series Paper* 9. Ottawa.

Guinard, J.E.
1945   Mémoires: Journal des missions. (Manuscripts in Séminaire de Trois-Rivières, Quebec.)

Guy, Camil
1966   L'Organisation socio-territoriale des Indiens de Weymontaching. (Unpublished manuscript in National Museum of Man, Ottawa.)

1967   Les Indiens du Québec: Désagrégation culturelle et prolétarisation. *Parti-Pris* 4:165-181.

1970   Le Canot d'écorce à Weymontaching. *Canada. National Museum of Man, Anthropological Paper* 20. Ottawa. (English translation published in 1974.)

Haas, Mary R.
1968   Notes on a Chipewyan Dialect. *International Journal of American Linguistics* 34(3):165-175.

Hackler, James C.
1958   The Carrier Indians of Babine Lake: The Effects of the Fur Trade and the Catholic Church on Their Social Organization. (Unpublished M.A. Thesis in Anthropology, San Jose State College, San Jose, Calif.)

Hadleigh-West, Frederick
1963   The Netsi Kutchin: An Essay in Human Ecology. (Unpublished Ph.D. Dissertation in Anthropology, Louisiana State University, Baton Rouge.)

1967   The Donnelly Ridge Site and the Definition of an Early Core and Blade Complex in Central Alaska. *American Antiquity* 32(3):360-382.

1972   Archeological and Palaeoecological Research in the Tangle Lakes, Central Alaska, 1966-1972: A Report of Progress. (Unpublished manuscript in Alaska Methodist University, Anchorage.)

1972a   The Significance of Typologically Early Site Collections in the Tangle Lakes, Central Alaska: A Preliminary Consideration. (Paper presented at the Conference on Prehistory and Palaeoecology of the Western Arctic and Sub-Arctic, Calgary, Alta., November 1972.)

1973   Old World Affinities of Archaeological Complexes from Tangle Lakes, Central Alaska. (Paper prepared for All-Union Conference on the Bering Land Bridge, Khabarovsk, USSR. May 10-15, 1973.)

1975   Dating the Denali Complex. *Arctic Anthropology* 12(1):76-81.

Hale, Horatio E.
1846   Ethnography and Philology. United States Exploring Expedition During the Years 1838, 1839, 1840, 1841, 1842 Under the Command of Charles Wilkes, U.S.N. Vol. 6. Philadelphia: Lea and Blanchard.

Hall, Edwin S., Jr.
1969   Speculations on the Late Prehistory of the Kutchin Athapaskans. *Ethnohistory* 16(4):317-333.

Hall, Edwin S., Jr., and Robert A. McKennan
1973   An Archaeological Survey of the Old John Lake Area, Northern Alaska. *Polar Notes* 13:1-31.

Hall, L.W.
1899   [Report of Teslin Post.] (Manuscript B.356/e/1 in Hudson's Bay Company Archives, Provincial Archives of Manitoba, Winnipeg, Canada.)

Hall, Lawrence W., Jr.
1971   Great Whale River Eskimo Youth: Enculturation into the Northern Town Life. (Unpublished M.A. Thesis in Anthropology, University of North Carolina, Chapel Hill.)

1973   Great Whale River Eskimo Youth: Socialization into the Northern Town Life. *Anthropologica* n.s. 15(1):3–19. Ottawa.

Hall, Raymond E., and Keith R. Kelson
1959   Mammals of North America. 2 vols. New York: Ronald Press Company.

Halliday, William E.D.
1937   A Forest Classification for Canada. *Canada. Forest Service Bulletin* 89. Ottawa.

Hallowell, A. Irving
1926   Bear Ceremonialism in the Northern Hemisphere. *American Anthropologist* 28(1):1-175.

1929   The Physical Characteristics of the Indians of Labrador. *Journal de la Société des Américanists de Paris* n.s. 21:337-371.

1930   Was Cross-cousin Marriage Practiced by the North-central Algonkian? Pp. 519-544 in *Proceedings of the 23d International Congress of Americanists*. New York, 1928.

1932   Kinship Terms and Cross-cousin Marriage of the Montagnais-Naskapi and the Cree. *American Anthropologist* 34(2):171-199.

1936   Psychic Stresses and Culture Patterns. *American Journal of Psychiatry* 92(May):1291-1310. (Reprinted: Pp. 21-39 in Culture and Mental Health, by M.K. Opler, Macmillan, New York, 1959.)

1936a   The Passing of the Midewiwin in the Lake Winnipeg Region. *American Anthropologist* 38(1):32-51.

1937   Cross-cousin Marriage in the Lake Winnipeg Area. Pp. 95-110 in Twenty-fifth Anniversary Studies. D.S. Davidson, ed.

Publications of the Philadelphia Anthropological Society 1. Philadelphia. (Reprinted: Pp. 317–332 in Contributions to Anthropology: Selected Papers of A. Irving Hallowell, Raymond D. Fogelson et al., eds., University of Chicago Press, Chicago, 1976.)

1938   Fear and Anxiety as Cultural and Individual Variables in a Primitive Society. *Journal of Social Psychology* 9:25-47. (Reprinted: Pp. 41-62 in Culture and Mental Health, by M.K. Opler, Macmillan, New York, 1959.)

1938a   Notes on the Material Culture of the Island Lake Saulteaux. *Journal de la Société des Américanistes* n.s. 30:129-140. Paris.

1939   Sin, Sex and Sickness in Saulteaux Belief. *British Journal of Medical Psychology* 18(2):191-197.

1940   Aggression in Saulteaux Society. *Psychiatry* 3(3):395-407. (Reprinted: Pp. 277–290 in Culture and Experience, by A. Irving Hallowell, University of Pennsylvania Press, Philadelphia, 1955.)

1941   The Social Function of Anxiety in a Primitive Society. *American Sociological Review* 6:869-881. (Reprinted: Pp. 266–276 in Culture and Experience, by A. Irving Hallowell, University of Pennsylvania Press, Philadelphia, 1955.)

1942   The Role of Conjuring in Saulteaux Society. *Publications of the Philadelphia Anthropological Society* 2. Philadelphia. (Reprinted in 1971.)

1942a   Some Psychological Aspects of Measurement Among the Saulteaux. *American Anthropologist* 44(1):62-77. (Reprinted: Pp. 203–215 in Culture and Experience, by A. Irving Hallowell, University of Pennsylvania Press, Philadelphia, 1955.)

1946   Some Psychological Characteristics of the Northeastern Indians. Pp. 195-225 in Man in Northeastern North America. Frederick Johnson, ed. *Papers of the Robert S. Peabody Foundation for Archaeology* 3. Andover, Mass. (Reprinted: Pp. 125–150 in Culture and Experience, by A. Irving Hallowell, University of Pennsylvania Press, Philadelphia, 1955.)

1949   Psychosexual Adjustment, Personality and the Good Life in a Non-literate Culture. Pp. 102-123 in Psychosexual Development in Health and Disease. Paul H. Hoch and Joseph Zubin, eds. New York: Grune and Stratton.

1949a   The Size of Algonkian Hunting Territories: A Function of Ecological Adjustment. *American Anthropologist* 51(1):35-45.

1950   Values, Acculturation and Mental Health. *American Journal of Orthopsychiatry* 20:732-743. (Reprinted: Pp. 358–366 in Culture and Experience, by A. Irving Hallowell, University of Pennsylvania Press, Philadelphia, 1955.)

1951   The Use of Projective Techniques in the Study of the Sociopsychological Aspects of Acculturation. *Journal of Projective Techniques* 15:27-44.

1952   Ojibwa Personality and Acculturation. Pp. 105-112 in Vol. 2 of *Proceedings of the 29th International Congress of Americanists*. 3 vols. New York, 1949.

1955   Culture and Experience. Philadelphia: University of Pennsylvania Press.

1960   Ojibwa Ontology, Behavior, and World View. Pp. 19-52 in Culture in History: Essays in Honor of Paul Radin. Stanley Diamond, ed. New York: Columbia University Press.

1961   Ojibwa World View and Disease. (Paper prepared for a Conference on Medicine and Anthropology, Sponsored by the New York Academy of Medicine, Committee on Special Studies, and The Wenner-Gren Foundation for Anthropological Research, Harriman, N.Y.)

1976   Contributions to Anthropology: Selected Papers of A. Irving Hallowell. Chicago: University of Chicago Press.

Hamblin, Dora J.
1965   "Everybody Sure Glad." *Life* 58(20):69-70, 74, 76.

Hamer, John H.
1969   Guardian Spirits, Alcohol, and Cultural Defense Mechanisms. *Anthropologica* n.s. 11(2):215-241. Ottawa.

Hamilton, Walter R.
1964   The Yukon Story: A Sourdough's Record of Goldrush Days and Yukon Progress from the Earliest Times to the Present Day. Vancouver, B.C.: Mitchell Press.

Hanley, Philip M.
1973   Father Lacombe's Ladder. *Etudes Oblates* (April-June):82-99. Ottawa.

Hanzeli, Victor E.
1969   Missionary Linguistics in New France: A Study of Seventeenth- and Eighteenth-Century Descriptions of American Indian Languages. (*Janua Linguarum Series Maior* 29) The Hague: Mouton.

Hara, Hiroko Sue
1980   The Hare Indians and Their World. *Canada. National Museum of Man, Mercury Series, Ethnology Service Paper* 63. Ottawa.

Hara, Hiroko Sue *see also* Sue, Hiroko

Hardisty, William L.
1872   The Loucheux Indians. Pp. 311-320 in Notes on the Tinneh or Chepewyan Indians of British and Russian America. *Annual Report of the Smithsonian Institution for the Year 1866*. Washington.

Harington, C.R., Robson Bonnichsen, and Richard E. Morlan
1975   Bones Say Man Lived in Yukon 27,000 Years Ago. *Canadian Geographical Journal* 91(1-2):42-48.

Harmon, Daniel W.
1903   A Journal of Voyages and Travels in the Interior of North America. New York: A.S. Barnes.

1957   Sixteen Years in the Indian Country: The Journal of Daniel Williams Harmon, 1800-1816. W. Kaye Lamb, ed. Toronto: Macmillan of Canada.

Harp, Elmer, Jr.
1951   An Archaeological Survey in the Strait of Belle Isle Area. *American Antiquity* 16(3):203-220.

1958   Prehistory in the Dismal Lake Area, N.W.T., Canada. *Arctic* 11(4):219-249.

1959   The Moffatt Archaeological Collection from the Dubawnt Country, Canada. *American Antiquity* 24(4):412-422.

1961   The Archaeology of the Lower and Middle Thelon, Northwest Territories. *Arctic Institute of North America Technical Paper* 8. Montreal.

1962   The Culture History of the Central Barren Grounds. Pp. 69-75 in Prehistoric Cultural Relations Between the Arctic and Temperate Zones of North America. J.M. Campbell, ed. *Arctic Institute of North America Technical Paper* 11. Montreal.

1964   Evidence of Boreal Archaic Culture in Southern Labrador and Newfoundland; Contributions to Anthropology 1961-62, Pt. 1. *Anthropological Series 61, National Museum of Canada Bulletin* 193:184-261. Ottawa.

Harrington, John P.
[1939]   [Carrier and Sekani Vocabulary Recorded at Fort St. James, British Columbia, December 1-7, 1939.] (Manuscript in

Northern Athapaskan Fieldnotes, Boxes 28-32, J.P. Harrington Papers, National Anthropological Archives, Smithsonian Institution, Washington.)

1940   Southern Peripheral Athapaskawan Origins, Divisions, and Migrations. *Smithsonian Miscellaneous Collections* 100:503-532. Washington.

1943   Pacific Coast Athapascan Discovered to Be Chilcotin. *Journal of the Washington Academy of Sciences* 33(7):203-213. Washington.

Harrington, Lyn
1961   Old Crow: Yukon's Arctic Village. *The Beaver* 292(Winter):4-10.

Harrington, Richard
1948   Trapline to Trading Post: A Fur Trade Picture Story. *The Beaver* 279 (December):16-29.

Harris, Donald A., and George C. Ingram
1972   New Caledonia and the Fur Trade: A Status Report. Pp. 179-194 in The Fur Trade in Canada. *Western Canadian Journal of Anthropology* 3(1).

Hart, J.L.
1973   Pacific Fishes of Canada. *Fisheries Research Board of Canada Bulletin* 180. Ottawa.

Hatt, Gudmund
1915-1916   Kyst- og Inlandskultur i det Arkiske. *Geografisk Tidskrift* 23(8):284-290. Copenhagen.

1916   Moccasins and Their Relation to Arctic Footwear. *Memoirs of the American Anthropological Association* 3:151-250. Menasha, Wis.

Hawthorn, Harry B., ed.
1966-1967   A Survey of the Contemporary Indians of Canada: A Report on Economic, Political, Educational Needs and Policies. 2 vols. Ottawa: Department of Indian Affairs and Northern Development, Indian Affairs Branch.

Hawthorn, Harry B., C.S. Belshaw, and S.M. Jamieson
1958   The Indians of British Columbia: A Study of Contemporary Social Adjustment. Berkeley: University of California Press and University of British Columbia.

Hay, Thomas H.
1971   The Windigo Psychosis: Psychodynamic, Cultural, and Social Factors in Aberrant Behavior. *American Anthropologist* 73(1):1-19.

Hayden, Francis V.
1863   Contributions to the Ethnography and Philology of the Indian Tribes of the Missouri Valley. *Transactions of the American Philosophical Society* n.s. 12:231-461. Philadelphia.

Hayes, Charles W.
1892   An Expedition Through the Yukon District. *National Geographic Magazine* 4:117-162.

Haynes, C. Vance
1967   Carbon-14 Dates and Early Man in the New World. Pp. 267-286 in Pleistocene Extinctions: The Search for a Cause. Paul S. Martin and Herbert E. Wright, Jr., eds. New Haven, Conn: Yale University Press.

Haynes, James B.
1975   Land Selection and Development Under the Alaska Native Claims Settlement Act. *Arctic* 28(3):201-208.

Heagerty, John J.
1928   Four Centuries of Medical History in Canada and a Sketch of the Medical History of Newfoundland. 2 vols. Toronto: Macmillan of Canada.

Hearne, Samuel
1934   Journals of Samuel Hearne and Philip Turnor Between the Years 1774 and 1792. J.B. Tyrrell, ed. (Publications of the Champlain Society 21) Toronto: The Champlain Society.

1958   A Journey from Prince of Wales's Fort in Hudson's Bay to the Northern Ocean in the Years 1769, 1770, 1771, and 1772 [1795]. R. Glover, ed. New ed. Toronto: Macmillan.

Heinrich, Albert C.
1957   Sib and Social Structure on the Upper Tanana. Pp. 10-22 in Science in Alaska: Proceedings of the 8th Alaskan Science Conference. Anchorage: American Association for the Advancement of Science, Alaska Division.

Heinrich, Albert C., and Russell Anderson
1968   Co-affinal Siblingship as a Structural Feature Among Some Northern North American Peoples. *Ethnology* 7(3):290-295.

Helm, June
1959-1971   [Ethnographic Notes, from Fieldwork Among the Dogrib at Lac La Martre and Rae in the Years 1959, 1960, 1962, 1967, 1968, 1969, and 1970, 1971, Totaling Approximately 22 Months.] (The Notes of 1959, 1967 and part of 1962 are jointly authored with Nancy O. Lurie, collaborator in the field. Manuscripts in Helm's possession.)

1961   The Lynx Point People: The Dynamics of a Northern Athapaskan Band. *Anthropological Series 53, National Museum of Canada Bulletin* 176. Ottawa.

1962   [Fort Rae Roman Catholic Mission Record of 1911.] (Manuscript in Helm's possession.)

1965   Bilaterality in the Socio-territorial Organization of the Arctic Drainage Dene. *Ethnology* 4(4):361-385.

1965a   Patterns of Allocation Among the Arctic Drainage Dene. Pp. 33-45 in Essays in Economic Anthropology. June Helm, ed. (Proceedings of the Annual Spring Meeting of the American Ethnological Society) Seattle: University of Washington Press.

1968   The Statistics of Kin Marriage: A Non-Australian Example. Pp. 216-217 in Man the Hunter. Richard B. Lee and Irven DeVore, eds. Chicago: Aldine.

1968a   The Nature of Dogrib Socio-territorial Groups. Pp. 118-125 in Man the Hunter. Richard B. Lee and Irven DeVore, eds. Chicago: Aldine.

1969   A Method of Statistical Analysis of Primary Relative Bonds in Community Composition. Pp. 218-230 in Contributions to Anthropology: Band Societies. David Damas, ed. *Anthropological Series 84, National Museum of Canada Bulletin* 228. Ottawa.

1969a   An Annotated Description of a Dogrib Prophet Cult Ceremony; Part of 1968 Final Report to National Museum of Canada. (Manuscript, copy at National Museum of Man, Ottawa.)

1972   The Dogrib Indians. Pp. 51-89 in Hunters and Gatherers Today: A Socioeconomic Study of Eleven Such Cultures in the Twentieth Century. M.G. Bicchieri, ed. New York: Holt, Rinehart and Winston.

1973   Subarctic Athapaskan Bibliography: 1973. Iowa City: University of Iowa, Department of Anthropology.

1976   The Indians of the Subarctic: A Critical Bibliography. (Bibliographical Series, The Newberry Library Center for the History of the American Indian) Bloomington and London: Indiana University Press.

1977   Indian Dependency and Indian Self-determination: Problems and Paradoxes in Canada's Northwest Territories. (Revised manuscript of a paper read at the 1976 Annual Meeting of the American Anthropological Association; copy in R. Slobodin's possession.)

1979   Long-term Research Among the Dogrib and Other Dene. Pp. 145-163 in Long-term Field Research in Social Anthropology. G.M. Foster, T. Scudder, E. Colson, and R.V. Kemper, eds. New York: Academic Press.

1980   Female Infanticide, European Disease, and Population Levels Among the Mackenzie Dene. *American Ethnologist* 7(2):259-285.

Helm, June, and David Damas
1963   The Contact-traditional All-Native Community of the Canadian North: The Upper Mackenzie "Bush" Athapaskans and the Igluligmiut. *Anthropologica* n.s. 5(1):9-21. Ottawa.

Helm, June, and George DeVos
[1963]   [Dogrib Indian Personality: Rorschach, Thematic Apperception Test, and Observational Data Collected in 1959 and 1960, N.W.T., Canada.] (Unpublished manuscript in Helm's possession.)

Helm, June, and Eleanor B. Leacock
1971   The Hunting Tribes of Subarctic Canada. Pp. 343-374 in North American Indians in Historical Perspective. Eleanor B. Leacock and Nancy O. Lurie, eds. New York: Random House.

Helm, June, and Nancy O. Lurie
1961   The Subsistence Economy of the Dogrib Indians of Lac La Martre in the Mackenzie District of the Northwest Territories. Ottawa: Department of Northern Affairs and National Resources, Northern Co-ordination and Research Centre.

1966   The Dogrib Hand Game. *Anthropological Series 71, National Museum of Canada Bulletin* 205. Ottawa.

Helm, June, and Vital Thomas
1966   Tales from the Dogribs. *The Beaver* 297 (Autumn):16-20, (Winter):52-54.

Helm, June, George A. DeVos, and Teresa Carterette
1963   Variations in Personality and Ego Identification within a Slave Indian Kin-community. Pp. 94-138 in Pt. 2 of Contributions to Anthropology, 1960. 2 Pts. *Anthropological Series 60, National Museum of Canada Bulletin* 190. Ottawa.

Helm, June, Terry Alliband, Terry Birk, Virginia Lawson, Suzanne Reisner, Craig Sturtevant, and Stanley Witkowski
1975   The Contact History of the Subarctic Athapaskans: An Overview. Pp. 302-349 in Vol. 1 of Proceedings: Northern Athapaskan Conference, 1971. A. McFadyen Clark, ed. 2 vols. *Canada. National Museum of Man, Mercury Series, Canadian Ethnology Service Paper* 27. Ottawa.

Helm, June see also MacNeish, June Helm

Helmer, James W.
1977   Points, People and Prehistory: A Preliminary Synthesis of Culture History in North Central British Columbia. Pp. 90-97 in Problems in Prehistory of the North American Subarctic: The Athapaskan Question. J.W. Helmer, S. VanDyke, and F.J. Kense, eds. Calgary: University of Calgary, Archaeological Association.

Helmer, James W., S. VanDyke, and F.J. Kense, eds.
1977   Problems in the Prehistory of the North American Subarctic: The Athapaskan Question. Calgary: University of Calgary, Archaeological Association.

Hemstock, C. Anne, and Geraldine A. Cooke, comps. and eds.
1973   Yukon Bibliography Update 1963-1970. *University of Alberta, Boreal Institute for Northern Studies Occasional Publication* 8(1). Edmonton.

Henderson, Patsy
1950   Early Days at Caribou Crossing and the Discovery of Gold in the Klondike. J.M. Moyer, ed. Bremerton, Wash.: Privately Printed.

Hendry, Anthony
1907   York Factory to the Blackfeet Country: The Journal of Anthony Hendry, 1754-55. Lawrence J. Burpee, ed. *Proceedings and Transactions of the Royal Society of Canada,* ser. 3, Vol. 1:307-354. Ottawa.

Henn, Winfield
1978   Archaeology on the Alaska Peninsula: The Ugashik Drainage, 1973-1975. *University of Oregon Anthropological Paper* 14. Eugene.

Hennepin, Louis
1903   A New Discovery of a Vast Country in America. [1698]. Reuben G. Thwaites, ed. 2 vols. Chicago: A.C. McClurg.

Henning, Robert A., Marty Loken, and Barbara Olds, eds.
1979   The Stikine River. *Alaska Geographic* 6(4). Anchorage.

Henriksen, Georg
1966-1968   [Ethnographic Fieldnotes on Davis Inlet, Labrador, June 1966-June 1967, December 1967-June 1968.] (Manuscript in Henriksen's possession.)

1971   The Transactional Basis of Influence: White Men Among Naskapi Indians. Pp. 22-33 in Patrons and Brokers in the East Arctic. Robert Paine, ed. (*Newfoundland Social and Economic Papers 2*) St. Johns: Memorial University of Newfoundland, Institute of Social and Economic Research.

1973   Hunters in the Barrens: The Naskapi on the Edge of the White Man's World. (*Newfoundland Economic Studies 12*) St. Johns: Memorial University of Newfoundland, Institute of Social and Economic Research.

Henry, Alexander
1897   New Light on the Early History of the Greater Northwest: The Manuscript Journals of Alexander Henry... and of David Thompson... 1799-1814, Exploration and Adventure Among the Indians on the Red, Saskatchewan, Missouri, and Columbia Rivers. Elliott Coues, ed. 3 vols. New York: F.P. Harper. (Reprinted: Ross and Haines. Minneapolis, 1965.)

Henry, Alexander (the Elder)
1901   Travels and Adventures in Canada and the Indian Territories Between the Years 1760 and 1776 [1809]. James Bain, ed. Boston: Little, Brown.

1921   Alexander Henry's Travels and Adventures in the Years 1760-1776. Milo M. Quaife, ed. Chicago: R.R. Donnelley and Sons.

Henry, David, and Kay Henry
1965   Koyukon Classificatory Verbs. *Anthropological Linguistics* 7(4):110-116.

1969   Dinaak'a Our Language: Koyukon, Athapaskan Indian. Fairbanks: Summer Institute of Linguistics.

1969a   Koyukon Locationals. *Anthropological Linguistics* 11(4):136-142.

Henry, David, Marie D. Hunter, and Eliza Jones
1973   Dinaak'a Our Language: Koyukon Athapaskan. 2d ed. Fairbanks: Summer Institute of Linguistics.

Henry, Joseph
1860   A Circular to Officers of the Hudson's Bay Company. Washington: Smithsonian Institution.

Herron, Joseph S.
1901   Explorations in Alaska, 1899, for an All-American Overland Route from Cook Inlet, Pacific Ocean, to the Yukon. Washington: U.S. Government Printing Office.

Herskovits, Melville J.
1952   Economic Anthropology: A Study in Comparative Economics. 2d ed. New York: Alfred A. Knopf.

Hewetson, H.W.
1947   Transportation in the North-west. Pp. 185-225 in The New North-west. Carl A. Dawson, ed. Toronto: University of Toronto Press.

Hickerson, Harold
1962   The Southwestern Chippewa: An Ethnohistorical Study.

Memoirs of the American Anthropological Association 92. Menasha, Wis.

1966   The Genesis of Bilaterality Among Two Divisions of Chippewa. *American Anthropologist* 68(1):1-26.

1967   Some Implications of the Theory of the Particularity, or "Atomism," of Northern Algonkians. *Current Anthropology* 8(4):313-343.

1967a   Land Tenure of the Rainy Lake Chippewa at the Beginning of the 19th Century. *Smithsonian Contributions to Anthropology* 2(4):41-63. Washington.

Higgins, G.M.
1969   The Lower Liard Region: An Area Economic Survey. *Canada. Department of Indian Affairs and Northern Development, Industrial Division, Area Economic Surveys Report* 68/3. Ottawa.

Hildebrandt, Henry F.
1974   [Babine Phonetic Statement.] (Manuscript in Hildebrandt's possession.)

Hildebrandt, Henry F., and Gillian L. Story
1974   A Historically Oriented Study of Babine (Northern Carrier) Phonology. (Unpublished manuscript in possession of the authors.)

Hildes, J.A., J.C. Wilt, and W.L. Parker
1965   Surveys of Respiratory Virus Antibodies in an Arctic Indian Population. *Canadian Medical Association Journal* 93(19):1015-1018.

Hilger, M. Inez
1951   Chippewa Child Life and Its Cultural Background. *Bureau of American Ethnology Bulletin* 146. Washington.

Hind, Henry Y.
1863   Explorations in the Interior of the Labrador Peninsula, the Country of the Montagnais and Nasquapee Indians. 2 vols. London: Longman, Green, Longman, Roberts and Green.

Hindle, Lonnie, and Bruce Rigsby
1973   A Short Practical Dictionary of the Gitksan Language. *Northwest Anthropological Research Notes* 7(1):1-60. Moscow, Ida.

Hippler, Arthur E.
1972   The Athabascans of Interior Alaska: A Culture and Personality Perspective. (Unpublished manuscript in Hippler's possession.)

1972a   Fundamentalist Christianity: An Alaska Athabascan Technique for Overcoming Alcohol Abuse. (Unpublished manuscript in Hippler's possession.)

[1972b]   The Tanaina of Lake Iliamna. (Unpublished manuscript in Hippler's possession.)

1973   The Athabascans of Interior Alaska: A Culture and Personality Perspective. *American Anthropologist* 75(5):1529-1541.

Hippler, Arthur E., and Stephen Conn
1972   Traditional Athabascan Law Ways and Their Relationship to Contemporary Problems of "Bush Justice": Some Preliminary Observations on Structure and Function. *University of Alaska, Institute of Social, Economic and Government Research Occasional Paper* 7. Fairbanks.

Hippler, Arthur E., and John R. Wood
1974   The Subarctic Athabascans: A Selected Annotated Bibliography. Fairbanks: University of Alaska, Institute of Social, Economic and Government Research.

Hlady, Walter M.
1964   Indian Migrations in Manitoba and the West. Pp. 24-53 in 10,000 Years of History in Manitoba. Walter M. Hlady, ed. *Papers of the Manitoba Historical and Scientific Society*, 3d ser., Vol. 17. Winnipeg.

————, ed.
1970   Ten Thousand Years: Archaeology in Manitoba, Commemorating Manitoba's Centennial, 1870-1970. Altona: Manitoba Archaeological Society.

1970a   Manitoba: The Northern Woodlands. Pp. 93-121 in Ten Thousand Years: Archaeology in Manitoba. Walter M. Hlady, ed. Altona: Manitoba Archaeological Society.

1971   An Introduction to the Archaeology of the Woodland Area of Northern Manitoba. *Manitoba Archaeological Newsletter* 8(2-3). Winnipeg.

Hodge, Frederick W.
1907   Ingalik. P. 609 in Vol. 1 of Handbook of American Indians North of Mexico. Frederick W. Hodge, ed. 2 vols. *Bureau of American Ethnology Bulletin* 30. Washington.

1907a   Chipewyan. Pp. 275-276 in Vol. 1 of Handbook of American Indians North of Mexcio. Frederick W. Hodge, ed. 2 vols. *Bureau of American Ethnology Bulletin* 30. Washington.

1907b   Etchareottine. Pp. 439-440 in Vol. 1 of Handbook of American Indians North of Mexico. Frederick W. Hodge, ed. 2 vols. *Bureau of American Ethnology Bulletin* 30. Washington.

1907c   Khiltats. P. 679 in Vol. 1 of Handbook of American Indians North of Mexico. Frederick W. Hodge, ed. 2 vols. *Bureau of American Ethnology Bulletin* 30. Washington.

1907d   Kulchana. Pp. 733-734 in Vol. 1 of Handbook of American Indians North of Mexico. Frederick W. Hodge, ed. 2 vols. *Bureau of American Ethnology Bulletin* 30. Washington.

1907e   Kaiyukhotana. Pp. 643-644 in Vol. 1 of Handbook of American Indians North of Mexico. Frederick W. Hodge, ed. 2 vols. *Bureau of American Ethnology Bulletin* 30. Washington.

1907f   Fetutlin. P. 458 in Vol. 1 of Handbook of American Indians North of Mexico. Frederick W. Hodge, ed. 2 vols. *Bureau of American Ethnology Bulletin* 30. Washington.

1907g   Koyukukhotana. Pp. 729-730 in Vol. 1 of Handbook of American Indians North of Mexico. Frederick W. Hodge, ed. 2 vols. *Bureau of American Ethnology Bulletin* 30. Washington.

1907h   Etheneldeli. Pp. 440-441 in Vol. 1 of Handbook of American Indians North of Mexico. Frederick W. Hodge, ed. 2 vols. *Bureau of American Ethnology Bulletin* 30. Washington.

1907i   Knaiakhotana. Pp. 715-717 in Vol. 1 of Handbook of American Indians North of Mexico. Frederick W. Hodge, ed. 2 vols. *Bureau of American Ethnology Bulletin* 30. Washington.

1907j   Kawchodinne. P. 667 in Vol. 1 of Handbook of American Indians North of Mexico. Frederick W. Hodge, ed. 2 vols. *Bureau of American Ethnology Bulletin* 30. Washington.

1907k   Lakweip. P. 754 in Vol. 1 of Handbook of American Indians North of Mexico. Frederick W. Hodge, ed. 2 vols. *Bureau of American Ethnology Bulletin* 30. Washington.

1907l   Montagnard. P. 934 in Vol. 1 of Handbook of American Indians North of Mexico. Frederick W. Hodge, ed. 2 vols. *Bureau of American Ethnology Bulletin* 30. Washington.

1907m   HanKutchin. P. 531 in Vol. 1 of Handbook of American Indians North of Mexico. Frederick W. Hodge, ed. 2 vols. *Bureau of American Ethnology Bulletin* 30. Washington.

1907n   Kutchin. Pp. 739-740 in Vol. 1 of Handbook of American Indians North of Mexico. Frederick W. Hodge, ed. 2 vols. *Bureau of American Ethnology Bulletin* 30. Washington.

1907o   Abbatotine. P. 1 in Vol. 1 of Handbook of American Indians North of Mexico. Frederick W. Hodge, ed. 2 vols. *Bureau of American Ethnology Bulletin* 30. Washington.

1907p	Esbatottine. P. 432 in Vol. 1 of Handbook of American Indians North of Mexico. Frederick W. Hodge, ed. 2 vols. *Bureau of American Ethnology Bulletin* 30. Washington.
1907q	Etagottine. P. 439 in Vol. 1 of Handbook of American Indians North of Mexico. Frederick W. Hodge, ed. 2 vols. *Bureau of American Ethnology Bulletin* 30. Washington.
———, ed.	
1907-1910	Handbook of American Indians North of Mexico. 2 vols. *Bureau of American Ethnology Bulletin* 30. Washington.
1910	Tenankutchin. Pp. 727-728 in Vol. 2 of Handbook of American Indians North of Mexico. Frederick W. Hodge, ed. 2 vols. *Bureau of American Ethnology Bulletin* 30. Washington.
1910a	Tatsanottine. Pp. 698-699 in Vol. 2 of Handbook of American Indians North of Mexico. Frederick W. Hodge, ed. 2 vols. *Bureau of American Ethnology Bulletin* 30. Washington.
1910b	Thlingchadinne. Pp. 744-745 in Vol. 2 of Handbook of American Indians North of Mexico. Frederick W. Hodge, ed. 2 vols. *Bureau of American Ethnology Bulletin* 30. Washington.
1910c	Nameuilini. P. 18 in Vol. 2 of Handbook of American Indians North of Mexico. Frederick W. Hodge, ed. 2 vols. *Bureau of American Ethnology Bulletin* 30. Washington.
1910d	Slaves. P. 600 in Vol. 2 of Handbook of American Indians North of Mexico. Frederick W. Hodge, ed. 2 vols. *Bureau of American Ethnology Bulletin* 30. Washington.
1910e	Unakhotana. P. 867 in Vol. 2 of Handbook of American Indians North of Mexico. Frederick W. Hodge, ed. 2 vols. *Bureau of American Ethnology Bulletin* 30. Washington.
1910f	Yukonikhotana. Pp. 1009-1010 in Vol. 2 of Handbook of American Indians North of Mexico. Frederick W. Hodge, ed. 2 vols. *Bureau of American Ethnology Bulletin* 30. Washington.
1910g	Takaiak. P. 673 in Vol. 2 of Handbook of American Indians North of Mexico. Frederick W. Hodge, ed. 2 vols. *Bureau of American Ethnology Bulletin* 30. Washington.
1910h	Nascapee. Pp. 30-32 in Vol. 2 of Handbook of American Indians North of Mexico. Frederick W. Hodge, ed. 2 vols. *Bureau of American Ethnology Bulletin* 30. Washington.
1910i	Tutchonekutchin. P. 855 in Vol. 2 of Handbook of American Indians North of Mexico. Frederick W. Hodge, ed. 2 vols. *Bureau of American Ethnology Bulletin* 30. Washington.
1910j	Tsattine. Pp. 822 in Vol. 2 of Handbook of American Indians North of Mexico. Frederick W. Hodge, ed. 2 vols. *Bureau of American Ethnology Bulletin* 30. Washington.
1910k	Takutine. P. 676 in Vol. 2 of Handbook of American Indians North of Mexico. Frederick W. Hodge, ed. 2 vols. *Bureau of American Ethnology Bulletin* 30. Washington.
1910l	Takulli. Pp. 675-676 in Vol. 2 of Handbook of American Indians North of Mexico. Frederick W. Hodge, ed. 2 vols. *Bureau of American Ethnology Bulletin* 30. Washington.
1910m	Tadush. P. 668 in Vol. 2 of Handbook of American Indians North of Mexico. Frederick W. Hodge, ed. 2 vols. *Bureau of American Ethnology Bulletin* 30. Washington.
1910n	Sekani. Pp. 498-499 in Vol. 2 of Handbook of American Indians North of Mexico. Frederick W. Hodge, ed. 2 vols. *Bureau of American Ethnology Bulletin* 30. Washington.
1910o	Tlukez. P. 766 in Vol. 2 of Handbook of American Indians

North of Mexico. Frederick W. Hodge, ed. 2 vols. *Bureau of American Ethnology Bulletin* 30. Washington.

Hoffman, Bernard G.
1952   Implications of Radiocarbon Datings for the Origin of the Dorset Culture. *American Antiquity* 18(1):15-17.

Hoffman, Walter J.
1891   The Midewiwin, or "Grand Medicine Society" of the Ojibwa. Pp. 149-300 in *7th Annual Report of the Bureau of American Ethnology for the Years 1885-1886*. Washington.

Hoffmann, Hans
1961   Culture Changes and Personality Modification Among the James Bay Cree. *Anthropological Papers of the University of Alaska* 9(2):81-91. College.

Hoijer, Harry
1963   The Athapaskan Languages. Pp. 1-29 in Studies in the Athapaskan Languages. Harry Hoijer, ed. *University of California Publications in Linguistics* 29. Berkeley.

1966   Hare Phonology: An Historical Study. *Language* 42(2):499-507.

Hoijer, Harry, and Janet Joël
1963   Sarsi Nouns. Pp. 62-75 in Studies in the Athapaskan Languages. Harry Hoijer, ed. *University of California Publications in Linguistics* 29. Berkeley.

Holden, David E.W.
1968   Friendship Choice and Leader Constituency Among the Mistassini-Waswanipi Cree. Pp. 69-81 in Conflict in Culture: Problems of Developmental Change Among the Cree; Working Papers of the Cree Developmental Change Project. Norman A. Chance, ed. Ottawa: Saint Paul University, Canadian Research Centre for Anthropology.

1969   Modernization Among Town and Bush Cree in Quebec. *Canadian Review of Sociology and Anthropology* 6(4):237-248.

Holdstock, Marshall, and Gillian Story
1975   A Synchronic and Diachronic Study of Beaver (Doig, Ft. St. John) Phonemes. (Unpublished manuscript in the possession of its authors.)

Holmberg, Heinrich J.
1856   Ethnographische Skizzen über die Völker des russischen Amerika. *Acta Societatis Scientiarum Fennicae* 4:281-421. Helsinki.

Holmer, Nils M.
1953   The Ojibway on Walpole Island, Ontario. (A Linguistic Study). *Upsala Canadian Studies* 4. Lund, Sweden.

Holmes, Charles E.
1973   Preliminary Testing of a Microblade Site at Lake Minchumina, Alaska. (Paper presented at the International Conference on the Prehistory and Paleoecology of the Western North American Arctic and Subarctic. Calgary, Alta.. November 23-26, 1972.)

1973a   The Archaeology of Bonanza Creek Valley, Northcentral Alaska. (Unpublished M.A. Thesis in Anthropology, University of Alaska, College.)

1974   New Evidence for a Late Pleistocene Culture in Central Alaska: Preliminary Investigations at Dry Creek. (Paper presented at the 7th Annual Meeting of the Canadian Archaeological Association, Whitehorse, Yukon Territory, March 1974.)

1975   A Northern Athapaskan Environment System in Diachronic Perspective. *Western Canadian Journal of Anthropology* 5(3-4):92-124.

1977   3000 Years of Prehistory at Minchumina: The Question of Cultural Boundaries. Pp. 11-15 in Prehistory of the North American Subarctic: The Athapaskan Question. J.W. Helmer, S. VanDyke, and F.J. Kense, eds. Calgary: University of Calgary, Archaeological Association.

Holmes, John B.
1827   Historical Sketches of the Missions of the United Brethren for Propagating the Gospel Among the Heathen, from Their Commencement to the Year 1817. 2d ed. London: Printed for the Author.

Honigmann, Irma, and John J. Honigmann
1953   Child Rearing Patterns Among the Great Whale River Eskimo. *Anthropological Papers of the University of Alaska* 2(1):31-50. College.

Honigmann, John J.
1945   Northern and Southern Athapaskan Eschatology. *American Anthropologist* 47(3):467-469.

1946   Ethnography and Acculturation of the Fort Nelson Slave. *Yale University Publications in Anthropology* 33. New Haven, Conn.

1947   The Cultural Dynamics of Sex: A Study in Culture and Personality. *Psychiatry* 10:37-47.

1947a   Witch-fear in Post-contact Kaska Society. *American Anthropologist* 49(2):222-243.

1947-1948 [Ethnographic Notes from Approximately 10 Months' Fieldwork Among the Cree Indians of Attawapiskat, Ontario.] (Manuscript in Honigmann's possession.)

1949   Culture and Ethos of Kaska Society. *Yale University Publications in Anthropology* 40. New Haven, Conn.

1949a   Incentives to Work in a Canadian Indian Community. *Human Organization* 8(4):23-28.

1951   An Episode in the Administration of the Great Whale River Eskimo. *Human Organization* 10(2):5-14.

1951a   The Logic of the James Bay Survey. *Dalhousie Review* 30:377-386.

1952   Intercultural Relations at Great Whale River. *American Anthropologist* 54(4):510-522.

1953   Social Organization of the Attawapiskat Cree Indians. *Anthropos* 48(5-6):809-816.

1954   The Kaska Indians: An Ethnographic Reconstruction. *Yale University Publications in Anthropology* 51. New Haven, Conn.

1956   The Attawapiskat Swampy Cree: An Ethnographic Reconstruction. *Anthropological Papers of the University of Alaska* 5(1):23-82. College.

1956a   Are There Nahani Indians? *Anthropologica* 3:35-38. Ottawa.

1957   Interpersonal Relations and Ideology in a Northern Canadian Community. *Social Forces* 35(4):365-370.

1958   Attawapiskat—Blend of Tradition. *Anthropologica* 6:57-67. Ottawa.

1960   The Great Whale River Eskimo: A Focussed Social System. *Anthropological Papers of the University of Alaska* 9(1):11-16. College.

1960a   Circumpolar Forest North America as a Modern Culture Area. Pp. 447-451 in Men and Cultures: Selected Papers of the Fifth International Congress of Anthropological and Ethnological Sciences, Philadelphia, 1956. Anthony F.C. Wallace, ed. Philadelphia: University of Pennsylvania Press.

1961   Foodways in a Muskeg Community. *Canada. Department of Northern Affairs and National Resources, Northern Co-ordination and Research Centre Publication* 62(1). Ottawa.

1962   Social Networks in Great Whale River: Notes on an Eskimo, Montagnais-Naskapi, and Euro-Canadian Community. *Anthropological Series 54, National Museum of Canada Bulletin* 178. Ottawa.

1964   Indians of Nouveau-Québec. Pp. 315-373 in Le Nouveau-Québec: Contribution à l'étude de occupation humaine. Jean Malaurie and Jacques Rousseau, eds. (*Bibliothèque Arctique et Antarctique 2*) Paris: Mouton.

1966   Social Disintegration in Five Northern Canadian Communities. *Canadian Review of Sociology and Anthropology* 2(4):199-214.

1968   Interpersonal Relations in Atomistic Communities. *Human Organization* 27(3):220-229.

1968a   The Fur-trade Period as a Developmental Stage in Northern Algonkian Culture History. (Unpublished paper prepared for the First Algonquian Conference, St. Pierre de Wakefield, P.Q.)

1970   Field Work in Two Northern Canadian Communities. Pp. 39-72 in Marginal Natives: Anthropologists at Work. Morris Freilich, ed. New York: Harper and Row.

1971   Formation of Mackenzie Delta Frontier Culture. Pp. 185-192 in Pilot Not Commander: Essays in Memory of Diamond Jenness. Pat Lotz and Jim Lotz, eds. *Anthropologica* n.s. 13(1-2). Ottawa.

1975   Five Northern Towns. *Anthropological Papers of the University of Alaska* 17(1). College.

1975a   Psychological Traits in Northern Athapaskan Culture. Pp. 545-576 in Vol. 1 of Proceedings: Northern Athapaskan Conference, 1971. A. McFadyen Clark, ed. 2 vols. *Canada. National Museum of Man, Mercury Series, Ethnology Service Paper* 27. Ottawa.

Honigmann, John J., and Irma Honigmann
1945   Drinking in an Indian-White Community. *Quarterly Journal of Studies on Alcohol* 5(4):575-619.

1959   Notes on Great Whale River Ethos. *Anthropologica* n.s. 1(1-2):106-121. Ottawa.

1965   Eskimo Townsmen. Ottawa: St. Paul University, Canadian Research Centre for Anthropology.

1970   Arctic Townsmen: Ethnic Backgrounds and Modernization. Ottawa: Saint Paul University, Canadian Research Centre for Anthropology.

Hood, Robert
1974   To the Arctic by Canoe, 1819-1821: The Journal and Paintings of Robert Hood, Midshipman with Franklin. C. Stuart Houston, ed. Montreal and London: Arctic Institute of North America, McGill-Queen's University Press.

Hooper, William H.
1853   Ten Months Among the Tents of the Tuski: With Incidents of an Arctic Boat Expedition in Search of Sir John Franklin, as Far as the Mackenzie River, and Cape Bathurst. London: John Murray.

Hoople, Joanne, and J.W.E. Newbery
[1974] And What About Canada's Native Peoples? Ottawa: Canadian Council for International Cooperation.

Horden, John
1881   A Grammar of the Cree Language, As Spoken by the Cree Indians of North America. London: Society for Promoting Christian Knowledge.

Hosley, Edward H.

[1960-1964] [Ethnographic, Archeological, and Linguistic Fieldnotes, from Approximately 12 Months' Fieldwork Among the Kolchan, Upper Kuskokwim River, Alaska.] (Manuscript in Hosley's possession.)

1961   The McGrath Ingalik. *Anthropological Papers of the University of Alaska* 9(2):93-113. College.

1966   Factionalism and Acculturation in an Alaskan Athapaskan Community. (Unpublished Ph.D. Dissertation in Anthropology, University of California, Los Angeles.)

1966a   The Kolchan: Athapaskans of the Upper Kuskokwim. (Unpublished manuscript at University of Alaska, College.)

1968   The Kolchan: Delineation of a New Northern Athapaskan Indian Group. *Arctic* 21(1):6-11.

1968a   Grant · No. 4083—The McGrath Ingalik Indians, Central Alaska. Pp. 544-547 in *American Philosophical Society Year Book for 1967*. Philadelphia.

Howard, James H.

1965   The Plains-Ojibwa or Bungi: Hunters and Warriors of the Northern Prairies, with Special Reference to the Turtle Mountain Band. *University of South Dakota Museum Anthropology Paper* 1. Vermillion.

1966   The Wičíyela or Middle Dakota. *University of South Dakota Museum News* 27(7-8). Vermillion.

1966a   The Dakota or Sioux Indians. *University of South Dakota Museum News* 27(5-10). Vermillion.

Howard, Joseph K.

1952   Strange Empire: A Narrative of the Northwest. New York: Morrow.

Howard, Philip G.

1963   A Preliminary Presentation of Slave Phonemes. Pp. 42-47 in Studies in the Athapaskan Languages. Harry Hoijer, ed. *University of California Publications in Linguistics* 29. Berkeley.

1977   A Dictionary of the Verbs of the Slave Language. Ottawa: Department of Indian and Northern Affairs, Northern Social Research Division.

Howren, Robert

1968   Stem Phonology and Affix Phonology in Dogrib (Northern Athapaskan). Pp. 120-129 in Papers from the Fourth Regional Meeting of the Chicago Linguistic Society. B.J. Darden et al., eds. Chicago: University of Chicago, Department of Linguistics.

1970   A Century of Phonological Change in a Northern Athapaskan Dialect Group. (Paper presented at the 9th Conference on American Indian Languages, San Diego, Calif.)

1971   A Formalization of the Athabaskan 'D-Effect.' *International Journal of American Linguistics* 37(2):96-113.

1975   Some Isoglosses in Mackenzie-drainage Athapaskan: First Steps Toward a Subgrouping. Pp. 577-618 in Vol. 2 of Proceedings: Northern Athapaskan Conference, 1971. A. McFadyen Clark, ed. 2 vols. *Canada. National Museum of Man, Mercury Series, Ethnology Service Paper* 27. Ottawa.

[1979]   The Phonology of Rae Dogrib. *National Museum of Canada Bulletin*. Ottawa. In Press.

Howse, Joseph

1844   A Grammar of the Cree Language; With Which Is Combined an Analysis of the Chippeway Dialect. London: J.G.F. and J. Rivington.

Hrdlička, Aleš

1930   Anthropological Survey in Alaska. Pp. 19-374 in *46th Annual Report of the Bureau of American Ethnology for the Years 1928-1929*. Washington.

1930a   The Ancient and Modern Inhabitants of the Yukon. Pp. 137-146 in *Explorations and Field-work of the Smithsonian Institution in 1929*. Washington.

1943   Alaska Diary, 1926-1931. Lancaster, Pa.: Jacques Cattell Press.

Hubbard, Mina Benson

1908   A Woman's Day Through Unknown Labrador: An Account of the Exploration of the Nascaupee and George Rivers. London: John Murray.

Hudson, Douglas R.

1972   The Historical Determinants of Carrier Social Organization: A Study of Northwest Athabascan Matriliny. (Unpublished M.A. Thesis in Anthropology, McMaster University, Hamilton, Ont.)

Hudson's Bay Company

1718-1721   [Fort Churchill Post Journal.] (Manuscript B.42/a/1 in Hudson's Bay Company Archives, Provincial Archives of Manitoba, Winnipeg, Canada.)

1765-1766   [Fort Churchill Post Journal, 1765-66.] (Manuscript B.42/a/64 in Hudson's Bay Company Archives, Provincial Archives of Manitoba, Winnipeg, Canada.)

1815   [Swan River Post District Report.] (Manuscript B.213/e/1 in Hudson's Bay Company Archives, Provincial Archives of Manitoba, Winnipeg, Canada.)

1822-1823   [Fort Resolution Post Journal.] (Manuscript B.181/a/4 in Hudson's Bay Company Archives, Provincial Archives of Manitoba, Winnipeg, Canada.)

1822-1823a [Fort Simpson Post Journal.] (Manuscript B.200/a/1 in Hudson's Bay Company Archives, Provincial Archives of Manitoba, Winnipeg, Canada.)

1822-1823b [Mackenzie River District Report.] (Manuscript B.200/e/1 in Hudson's Bay Company Archives, Provincial Archives of Manitoba, Winnipeg, Canada.)

1822-1823c [Fort Good Hope Post Journal.] (Manuscript B.80/a/1 in Hudson's Bay Company Archives, Provincial Archives of Manitoba, Winnipeg, Canada.)

1822-1824   [Mackenzie River District Report.] (Manuscript B.200/e/2 in Hudson's Bay Company Archives, Provincial Archives of Manitoba, Winnipeg, Canada.)

1823-1824   [Mackenzie River District Report.] (Manuscript B.200/e/4 in Hudson's Bay Company Archives, Provincial Archives of Manitoba, Winnipeg, Canada.)

1823-1824a [Mackenzie River District Report.] (Manuscript B.200/e/3 in Hudson's Bay Company Archives, Provincial Archives of Manitoba, Winnipeg, Canada.)

1824-1825   [Fort Resolution Post Journal.] (Manuscripts B.181/a/5 and B.181/a/6 in Hudson's Bay Company Archives, Provincial Archives of Manitoba, Winnipeg, Canada.)

1824-1825a [Mackenzie River District Report.] (Manuscript B.200/e/5 in Hudson's Bay Company Archives, Provincial Archives of Manitoba, Winnipeg, Canada.)

1825-1827   [Fort Resolution District Report.] (Manuscript B.181/e/1, in Hudson's Bay Company Archives, Provincial Archives of Manitoba, Winnipeg, Canada.)

1826   [Fort Good Hope District Report.] (Manuscript B.80/e/1 in Hudson's Bay Company Archives, Provincial Archives of Manitoba, Winnipeg, Canada.)

1826-1827   [Fort Resolution Post Journal.] (Manuscript B.181/a/7, in Hudson's Bay Company Archives, Provincial Archives of Manitoba, Winnipeg, Canada.)

1826-1827a   [Mackenzie River District Report.] (Manuscript B.200/e/7 in Hudson's Bay Company Archives, Provincial Archives of Manitoba, Winnipeg, Canada.)

1826-1828   [Mackenzie River District Report.] (Manuscript B.200/e/8 in Hudson's Bay Company Archives, Provincial Archives of Manitoba, Winnipeg, Canada.)

1829-1830   [Fort Good Hope Journal.] (Manuscript B.80/a/8 in Hudson's Bay Company Archives, Provincial Archives of Manitoba, Winnipeg, Canada.)

1829-1830a   [Mackenzie River District Report.] (Manuscript B.200/e/9 in Hudson's Bay Company Archives, Provincial Archives of Manitoba, Winnipeg, Canada.)

1829-1830b   [Fort Halkett Journal, July 23, 1829-May 31, 1830.] (Manuscript B.85/a/1 in Hudson's Bay Company Archives, Provincial Archives of Manitoba, Winnipeg, Canada.)

1831-1832   [Fort Simpson Correspondence Book.] (Manuscript B.200/b/7 in Hudson's Bay Company Archives, Provincial Archives of Manitoba, Winnipeg, Canada.)

1834   [Mackenzie River District Report.] (Manuscript B.200/e/11 in Hudson's Bay Company Archives, Provincial Archives of Manitoba, Winnipeg, Canada.)

1834-1864   [Fort Simpson Correspondence Inward.] (Manuscript B.200/c/1 in Hudson's Bay Company Archives, Provincial Archives of Manitoba, Winnipeg, Canada.)

1835-1836   [Fort Norman Post Journal.] (Manuscript B.152/a/14 in Hudson's Bay Company Archives, Provincial Archives of Manitoba, Winnipeg, Canada.)

1836-1837   [Fort Simpson Correspondence Book, 1831-1832.] (Manuscript B.200/b/9 in Hudson's Bay Company Archives, Provincial Archives of Manitoba, Winnipeg, Canada.)

1837-1838   [Fort Good Hope Post Journal.] (Manuscript B.80/a/14 in Hudson's Bay Company Archives, Provincial Archives of Manitoba, Winnipeg, Canada.)

1837-1838a   [Fort Norman Post Journal.] (Manuscript B.152/a/16 in Hudson's Bay Company Archives, Provincial Archives of Manitoba, Winnipeg, Canada.)

1838-1839   [Fort Resolution Post Journal.] (Manuscript B.181/a/14 in Hudson's Bay Company Archives, Provincial Archives of Manitoba, Winnipeg, Canada.)

1843-1844   [Fort Simpson Correspondence.] (Manuscript B.200/b/17 in Hudson's Bay Company Archives, Provincial Archives of Manitoba, Winnipeg, Canada.)

1844-1845   [Fort Norman Post Journal] (Manuscript B.152/a/26 in Hudson's Bay Company Archives, Provincial Archives of Manitoba, Winnipeg, Canada.)

1854   [Fort Rae Account Book.] (Manuscript B.172/d/1 in Hudson's Bay Company Archives, Provincial Archives of Manitoba, Winnipeg, Canada.)

1855   [Fort Reliance Post Journal.] (Manuscript B.180/a/1 in Hudson's Bay Company Archives, Provincial Archives of Manitoba, Winnipeg, Canada.)

1855-1856   [Fort Good Hope Account Book.] (Manuscript B.80/d/3 in Hudson's Bay Company Archives, Provincial Archives of Manitoba, Winnipeg, Canada.)

1899   [Report of 1899 Relating to Teslin, Yukon Territory, Canada.] (Manuscript B.356/c/1 in Hudson's Bay Company Archives, Provincial Archives of Manitoba, Winnipeg, Canada.)

Hulley, Clarence C.
1970   Alaska: Past and Present. 3d ed. Portland, Oreg.: Binfords and Mort.

Hultén, Eric
1968   Flora of Alaska and Neighboring Territories: A Manual of the Vascular Plants. Stanford, Calif.: Stanford University Press.

Hunt, Charles B.
1967   Physiography of the United States. San Francisco: W.H. Freeman.

Hunt, William B., and J.F. Burshear
1951   American Indian Beadwork. Milwaukee: Bruce Publishing. (Reprinted: Macmillan-Collier, New York, 1971.)

Huntington, Frank
1907   Ahtena. Pp. 30-31 in Vol. 1 of Handbook of American Indians North of Mexico. Frederick W. Hodge, ed. 2 vols. *Bureau of American Ethnology Bulletin* 30. Washington.

Hurlbert, Janice
1962   Age as a Factor in the Social Organization of the Hare Indian of Fort Good Hope, N.W.T. (NCRC 62-5) Ottawa: Department of Northern Affairs and National Resources, Northern Co-ordination and Research Centre.

Ingstad, Helge M.
1954   Nunamiut: Among Alaska's Inland Eskimos. F.H. Lyon, trans. New York: W.W. Norton; London: George Allen and Unwin.

Innis, Harold A.
1930   Peter Pond, Fur Trader and Adventurer. Toronto: Irwin and Gordon.

1956   The Fur Trade in Canada: An Introduction to Canadian Economic History [1930]. 2d ed. Toronto: University of Toronto Press.

1962   The Fur Trade in Canada: An Introduction to Canadian Economic History. Rev. ed. New Haven, Conn.: Yale University Press.

Irving, Laurence
1958   Naming of Birds as Part of the Intellectual Culture of Indians at Old Crow, Yukon Territory. *Arctic* 11(2):117-122.

1960   Birds of Anaktuvuk Pass, Kobuk, and Old Crow: A Study in Arctic Adaptation. *United States National Museum Bulletin* 217. Washington.

Irving, William N.
1957   An Archaeological Survey of the Susitna Valley. *Anthropological Papers of the University of Alaska* 6(1):37-52. College.

1962   A Provisional Comparison of Some Alaskan and Asian Stone Industries. Pp. 55-68 in Prehistoric Cultural Relations Between the Arctic and Temperate Zones of North America. John M. Campbell, ed. *Arctic Institute of North America Technical Paper* 11. Montreal.

1963   Northwest North America and Central United States: A Review. *Anthropological Papers of the University of Alaska* 10(2):63-71. College.

1967   Klo-kut: A Late Prehistoric Kutchin Site in Northern Yukon Territory. (Paper presented at the 32d Annual Meeting of the Society for American Archaeology, Ann Arbor, Mich.)

1968   Legend and Prehistory in the Brooks Range. (Paper presented at the 2d Annual Meeting of the Canadian Archaeological Association, Toronto; Abstract in *Bulletin of the Canadian Archaeological Association* 1:35, 1969.)

1968a   The Barren Grounds. Pp. 26-54 in Vol. 1 of Science, History and Hudson Bay. C.S. Beals, ed. 2 vols. Ottawa: Department of Energy, Mines and Resources.

1971   Recent Early Man Research in the North. *Arctic Anthropology* 8(2):68-82.

Irving, William N., and Jacques Cinq-Mars
1974   A Tentative Archaeological Sequence for Old Crow Flats, Yukon Territory. *Arctic Anthropology* 11(suppl.):65-81.

Isbester, J.A.
1850   On a Short Vocabulary of the Loucheux Language. *Proceedings of the Philological Society* 4:184-185.

Isbister, Joseph
1748-1749   [Fort Churchill Post Journal.] (Manuscript B.42/a/32 in Hudson's Bay Company Archives, Provincial Archives of Manitoba, Winnipeg, Canada.)

Isham, James
1949   Observations on Hudson's Bay, 1743, and Notes and Observations on a Book Entitled A Voyage to Hudsons Bay in the Dobbs Galley, 1749. E.E. Rich, ed. Toronto: Published by the Champlain Society for The Hudson's Bay Record Society.

Ives, John D.
1962   Iron Mining in Permafrost, Central Laborador-Ungava: A Geographical Review. *Geographical Bulletin* 17(May):66-77.

Ives, John W.
1977   The Excavation of HkPA-4 Birch Mountains, Alberta. Pp. 37-44 in Archaeology in Alberta, 1976. J. Michael Quigg, ed. *Archaeological Survey of Alberta Occasional Paper* 4. Edmonton.

JR = Thwaites, Reuben G., ed.
1896-1901   The Jesuit Relations and Allied Documents: Travel and Explorations of the Jesuit Missionaries in New France, 1610-1791; the Original French, Latin and Italian Texts, with English Translations and Notes. 73 vols. Cleveland: Burrows Brothers. (Reprinted: Pageant, New York, 1959.)

Jacobsen, Johan A.
1884   Captain Jacobsen's Reise an der Nordwestküste Amerikas, 1881-1883 zum Zwecke ethnologischer Sammlungen und Erkundigungen nebst Beschreibung persönlicher Erlebnisse. A. Woldt, ed. Leipzig, Germany: Max Spohr.

1977   Alaskan Voyage, 1881-1883: An Expedition to the Northwest Coast of America [1884]. Erna Gunther, trans. Chicago: University of Chicago Press.

James, James A.
1942   The First Scientific Exploration of Russian America and the Purchase of Alaska. *Northwestern University Studies in the Social Sciences* 4. Evanston and Chicago.

Jamieson, Melville A.
1936   Medals Awarded to North American Indian Chiefs, 1714-1922 and to Loyal African and Other Chiefs in Various Territories within the British Empire. London: Spink and Son.

Janes, Robert R.
1974   The Archaeology of Fort Alexander, N.W.T. *Northern Pipelines Task Force on Northern Oil Development, Environmental-Social Committee Report* 74-34. Ottawa.

Janzen, Donald E.
1968   The Naomikong Point Site and the Dimensions of Laurel in the Lake Superior Region. *University of Michigan, Museum of Anthropology Anthropological Papers* 36. Ann Arbor.

Jarvenpa, Robert
1976   Spatial and Ecological Factors in the Annual Economic Cycle of the English River Band of Chipewyan. *Arctic Anthropology* 13(1):43-69.

1978   [Letter to June Helm, Dated October 23, 1978.] (Copy in June Helm's possession.)

Jarvenpa, Robert, and Susanne Williams
1970   [Fieldnotes from Dawson, Yukon Terr.] (Manuscript in National Museum of Man, Ottawa.)

Jefferys, Thomas
1761   The Natural and Civil History of the French Dominions in North and South America. 2 vols. in 1. London: Printed for T. Jefferys.

Jenkins, William J.
1939   Notes on the Hunting Economy of the Abitibi Indians. *Catholic University of America Anthropological Series* 9. Washington.

Jenness, Diamond
1929   The Ancient Education of a Carrier Indian. *Annual Report for 1928, National Museum of Canada Bulletin* 62:22-27. Ottawa.

1931   The Sekani Indians of British Columbia. Pp. 21-34 in *Proceedings and Transactions of the Royal Society of Canada*, 3d ser., sec. 2, Vol. 25. Ottawa.

1932   The Indians of Canada. *Anthropological Series 15, National Museum of Canada Bulletin* 65. Ottawa. (Reprinted in 1934.)

1933   An Indian Method of Treating Hysteria. *Primitive Man* 6(1):13-20.

1937   The Sekani Indians of British Columbia. *Anthropological Series 20, National Museum of Canada Bulletin* 84. Ottawa.

1943   The Carrier Indians of the Bulkley River: Their Social and Religious Life. *Anthropological Papers 25, Bureau of American Ethnology Bulletin* 133. Washington.

1956   The Chipewyan Indians: An Account by an Early Explorer. *Anthropologica* 3:15-33. Ottawa.

Jenness, Robert A.
1963   Great Slave Lake Fishing Industry. (NCRC Report 63-10) Ottawa: Department of Northern Affairs and National Resources, Northern Co-ordination and Research Centre.

Jérémie, Nicolas
1715-1724   Relation du detroit et de la baye d'Hudson. Pp. 396-432 in Vol. 5 of Recueil de Voiages au Nord. Jean F. Bernard, ed. 9 vols. Amsterdam: J.F. Bernard.

1926   Twenty Years of York Factory, 1694-1714: Jérémie's Account of Hudson Strait and Bay. Robert Douglas and J.N. Wallace, trans. Ottawa: Thorburn and Abbott.

Jetté, Jules
1906-1907   L'Organisation sociale des Ten'as. Pp. 395-409 in Vol. 1 of *Proceedings of the 15th International Congress of Americanists*. 2 vols. Quebec, 1906.

1907   On the Medicine-men of the Ten'a. *Journal of the Royal Anthropological Institute of Great Britain and Ireland* 37:157-188. London.

1907-1909   On the Language of the Ten'a. *Man* 7:51-56; 8:72-74; 9:21-25. London.

1908-1909   On Ten'a Folk-lore. *Journal of the Royal Anthropological Institute of Great Britain and Ireland* n.s. 38(11):298-367; 39(12):460-505. London.

[1910]   On the Geographical Names of the Ten'a. (Manuscript in the Oregon Province Archives of the Society of Jesus, Indian Language Collection: The Alaska Native Languages, Gonzaga University, Spokane, Wash.)

[1910a] Migrations of the Ten'a. (Manuscript, microfilm reel 22, frames 627-658 in the Archives of Gonzaga University, Spokane, Wash.)

1911 On the Superstitions of the Ten'a Indians (Middle Part of the Yukon Valley, Alaska). *Anthropos* 6:95-108, 241-259, 602-615, 699-723.

1913 Riddles of the Ten'a Indians. *Anthropos* 8: 181-201, 630-651.

John, Fred, and Katie John
1973 The Killing of the Russians at Batzulnetas Village. *Alaska Journal* 3(3):147-148.

Johnson, Alice M.
1952 Ambassadress of Peace. *The Beaver* 283 (December):42-45.

———, ed.
1967 Saskatchwan Journals and Correspondence: Edmonton House, 1795-1800; Chesterfield House, 1800-1802. (Publications of the Hudson's Bay Record Society 26) London: The Hudson's Bay Record Society.

———
1967a James Bay Artist, William Richards. *The Beaver* 298(Summer):4-10.

Johnson, Elden
1969 The Prehistoric Peoples of Minnesota. St. Paul: Minnesota Historical Society.

Johnson, Frederick
1946 An Archaeological Survey Along the Alaska Highway, 1944. *American Antiquity* 11(3):183-186.

———
1948 The Rogers' Collection from Lakes Mistassini and Albanel, Province of Quebec. *American Antiquity* 14(2):91-98.

Johnson, Frederick, and Hugh M. Raup
1964 Investigations in Southwest Yukon: Geobotanical and Archaeological Reconnaissance. *Papers of the Robert S. Peabody Foundation for Archaeology* 6(1). Andover, Mass.

Johnson, Philip R., and Charles W. Hartman
1971 Environmental Atlas of Alaska. 2d ed. College: University of Alaska, Institute of Arctic Environmental Engineering.

Johnson, William D.
1962 An Exploratory Study of Ethnic Relations at Great Whale River. Ottawa: Department of Northern Affairs and National Resources, Northern Co-ordination and Research Centre.

Johnston, W.A.
1933 Quaternary Geology of North America in Relation to the Migration of Man. Pp. 11-45 in American Aborigines, Their Origin and Antiquity; A Collection of Papers... Published for Presentation at the Fifth Pacific Science Congress, Canada, 1933. Toronto: University of Toronto Press.

Joint Federal-State Land Use Planning Commission for Alaska
1973 Major Ecosystems of Alaska. Map. Fairbanks: U.S. Geological Survey.

Jones, David, and Evelyn M. Todd
1971 A Revised Spelling System for Ojibwa. Peterborough, Ont.: Trent University, Department of Anthropology.

Jones, Eliza
1978 Dinaakkanaaga Ts'inh Huyoza: Junior Dictionary for Central Koyukon Athabaskan. Anchorage: University of Alaska, National Bilingual Materials Development Center.

Jones, Eliza, and Chief Henry
1979 Chief Henry Yugh Noholnigee; The Stories Chief Henry Told. Eliza Jones, ed. and trans. Fairbanks: University of Alaska, Native Language Center.

Jones, Strachan
1872 The Kutchin Tribes. Pp. 320-327 in Notes on the Tinneh or Chepewyan Indians of British and Russian America. *Annual Report of the Smithsonian Institution for the Year 1866*. Washington.

Jones, Tim E.H.
1978 Archaeological Resource Management in Saskatchewan: An Overview. (Pastlog 1) Regina: Government of Saskatchewan, Department of Culture and Youth.

Josie, Edith
1966 Here Are the News. Toronto: Clark, Irwin.

Joyal, Arthur
1915 Excursion sacerdotale chez les Têtes-de-Boule. Quebec: Imprimerie Commerciale.

Juvenal, Iëromonakh
1952 A Diary Journal Kept by the Rev. Father Juvenal. One of the Earliest Missionaries to Alaska. *Kroeber Anthropological Society Papers* 6:26-59. Berkeley, Calif.

Kalifornsky, Peter
1977 Kahtnuht'ana Qenaga: The Kenai People's Language. Jim M. Kari, ed. Fairbanks: University of Alaska, Native Language Center.

Kane, Paul
1971 Paul Kane's Frontier, Including Wanderings of an Artist Among the Indians of North America [1859]. J. Russell Harper, ed. Toronto: University of Toronto Press.

Kari, James M.
1975 A Classification of Tanaina Dialects. *Anthropological Papers of the University of Alaska* 17(2):49-53. College.

———
1975a Babine, a New Athabaskan Linguistic Grouping. (Unpublished report to the National Museum of Man, Ottawa.)

———
1977 Dena'ina Noun Dictionary. Fairbanks: University of Alaska, Native Language Center.

———
1977a Linguistic Diffusion Between Tanaina and Ahtna. *International Journal of American Linguistics* 43(4):274-288.

———
1978 Deg Xinag: Ingalik Noun Dictionary. (Preliminary Printing) Fairbanks: University of Alaska, Native Language Center.

———, comp.
1978a Holikachuk Noun Dictionary (Preliminary Printing) Fairbanks: University of Alaska, Native Language Center.

———
1979 Athabaskan Verb Stem Categories: Ahtna. *Alaska Native Language Center Research Paper* 2. Fairbanks.

Kari, James M., and Mildred Buck, comps.
1975 Ahtna Noun Dictionary. Fairbanks: University of Alaska, Native Language Center for Northern Educational Research.

Kari, James M., and Peter Kalifornsky
1974 K'ela: The Mouse Story. Told by Peter Kalifornsky. James Kari, trans. College: University of Alaska, Native Language Center.

Kari, Priscilla Russell, comp.
1977 Dena'ina K'et'una: Tanaina Plantlore. Kathleen Lynch, illus. Anchorage: University of Alaska, Adult Literacy Laboratory.

Kaye, Jonathan, Glyne L. Piggott, and K. Tokaichi
1971 Odawa Language Project: First Report. Toronto: University of Toronto, Department of Anthropology.

Keele, Joseph
1910 A Reconnaissance Across the Mackenzie Mountains on the Pelly, Ross and Gravel Rivers, Yukon and North West Territories. Ottawa: Government Printing Bureau.

Keim, Charles J., ed.
1964 Kutchin Legends from Old Crow, Yukon Territory. *Anthropological Papers of the University of Alaska* 11(2):97-108. College.

Keith, George
1889-1890 Letters to Mr. Roderic McKenzie, 1807-1817. Pp. 61-132 in Vol. 2 of Les Bourgeois de la Compagnie du Nord-Ouest: Récits de voyages, lettres et rapports inédits relatifs au Nord-

Ouest Canadien. L.R. Masson, ed. 2 vols. Quebec: A. Coté. (Facsimile Reprint: Antiquarian Press, New York, 1960.)

Kellogg, Louise P., ed.
1917   Early Narratives of the Northwest, 1634-1699. New York: Charles Scribner's Sons.

Kelsall, John P.
1968   The Migratory Barren-ground Caribou of Canada. Ottawa: Department of Indian Affairs and Northern Development, Canadian Wildlife Service.

Kelsey, Henry
1929   The Kelsey Papers. Arthur C. Doughty and Chester Martin, eds. Ottawa: King's Printer.

Kendrew, Wilfred G., and Donald Kerr
1955   The Climate of British Columbia and Yukon Territory. Ottawa: Queen's Printer.

Kennicott, Robert
[1860]   [Words from the Language of the Kutch-á kutch-iń—the Indians of the Youkon River at the Mouth of the Porcupine River in Russian America.] (Manuscript No. 160 in National Anthropological Archives, Smithsonian Institution, Washington.)

————
1862   Tribes of Kutchin Indians of Lower Mackenzie and Youkon Region. (Manuscript No. 203-b in National Anthropological Archives, Smithsonian Institution, Washington. This Manuscript and Kennicott 1862a were formerly catalogued as part of NAA No. 203-c and referred to in Hodge (1907-1910) as "Ross, Ms. Notes on Tinne, BAE.")

————
1862a   [Memoranda in Reference to Kennicott's Indian Vocabularies of Arctic America.] (Manuscript No. 203-a in National Anthropological Archives, Smithsonian Institution, Washington.)

Kent, Frederick J., John V. Matthews, and Frederick Hadleigh-West
1964   An Archaeological Survey of the Portions of the Northwestern Kenai Peninsula. Anthropological Papers of the University of Alaska 12(2):101-134. College.

Kenyon, Walter A.
1965   The 'Old House' at Albany. The Beaver 296 (Autumn):48-52.

Kerr, A.J.
1950   Subsistence and Social Organization in a Fur Trade Community: Anthropological Report on the Rupert's House Indians for the National Committee for Community Health Studies, Department of Indian Affairs and Northern Development, Ottawa. (Manuscript in Kerr's possession.)

Kerr, F.A.
1948   Taku River Map-area, British Columbia. H.C. Cooke, comp. Canada. Department of Mines and Resources, Geological Survey Memoir 248. Ottawa.

Kew, J.E.M.
1962   Cumberland House in 1960. University of Saskatchewan, Research Division, Center for Community Studies, Economic and Social Survey of Northern Saskatchewan Report 2. Saskatoon.

Kew, Michael
1974   Nazko and Kluskus: Social Conditions and Prospects for the Future. (Paper prepared for the Nazko-Kluskus Study Committee.)

King, A. Richard
1967   The School at Mopass: A Problem of Identity. New York: Holt, Rinehart and Winston.

King, Quindel
1979   Chilcotin Phonology and Vocabulary. Pp. 41-66 in Contributions to Canadian Linguistics. Canada. National Museum of Man, Mercury Series, Ethnology Service Paper 50. Ottawa.

King, Richard
1836   Narrative of a Journey to the Shores of the Arctic Ocean, in 1833, 1834, and 1835, Under the Command of Capt. Black, R.N. 2 vols. London: R. Bentley.

Kinietz, W. Vernon
1940   The Indians of the Western Great Lakes, 1615-1760. University of Michigan, Museum of Anthropology Occasional Contribution 10. Ann Arbor.

Kirby, William see Kirkby, William W.

[Kirkby, William W.] "Kirby, William"
1865   A Journey to the Youcan, Russian America. Pp. 416-420 in Annual Report of the Smithsonian Institution for the Year 1864. Washington.

Kitchener, Lois D.
1954   Flag Over the North: The Story of the Northern Commercial Company. Seattle: Superior Publishing Company.

Knight, Dean
1969   Archaic of North-central Ontario: Montreal River (GgGu-1). Pp. 8-15 in Palaeocology and Ontario Prehistory. William M. Hurley and Conrad E. Heidenreich, eds. University of Toronto, Department of Anthropology Research Report 1. Toronto.

————
1971   Archaeology of the Lake Temiskaming Region—Progress Report. (Manuscript in Archives of the Archaeological Survey of Canada, Ottawa.)

Knight, James
1715-1717   [York Fort Post Journal by Captain James Knight, Governor-in-chief in the Bay.] (Manuscript B.239/a/1-3 in Hudson's Bay Company Archives, Provincial Archives of Manitoba, Winnipeg, Canada.)

————
1932   The Founding of Churchill: Being the Journal of Captain James Knight, Governor-in-Chief in Hudson Bay, from the 14th of July to the 13th of September, 1717. James F. Kenney, ed. Toronto: J.M. Dent and Sons.

Knight, Rolf
1965   A Re-examination of Hunting, Trapping, and Territoriality Among the Northeastern Algonkian Indians. Pp. 27-42 in Man, Culture and Animals: The Role of Animals in Human Ecological Adjustments. Anthony Leeds and Andrew P. Vayda, eds. (Publication 78) Washington: American Association for the Advancement of Science.

————
1968   Ecological Factors in Changing Economy and Social Organization Among the Rupert House Cree. National Museum of Canada Anthropology Paper 15. Ottawa.

Kobrinsky, Vernon
1977   The Tsimshianization of the Carrier Indians. Pp. 201-210 in Problems in the Prehistory of the North American Subarctic: The Athapaskan Question. J.W. Helmer, S. VanDyke, and F.J. Kense, eds. Calgary: University of Calgary Archaeological Association.

Koolage, William W., Jr.
1968   Chipewyan Indians of Camp-10. Pp. 61-127 in Ethnographic Study of Churchill. John J. Honigmann, ed. Chapel Hill: University of North Carolina, Institute for Research in Social Science. Mimeo.

————
1971   Adaptation of Chipewyan Indians and Other Persons of Native Background in Churchill, Manitoba. (Unpublished Ph.D. Dissertation in Anthropology, University of North Carolina, Chapel Hill.)

————
1975   Conceptual Negativism in Chipewyan Ethnology. Anthropologica n.s., 17(1):45-60. Ottawa.

Krause, Arthur
1882   Die Expedition der Bremer geographischen Gesellschaft nach der Tschuktschen-Halbinsel und Alaska, 1881-1882. (Reisebriefe des Dr. Arthur Krause.) Deutsche Geographische Blätter 5:308-326. Bremen, Germany.

Krause, Aurel
1885   Die Tlingit Indianer. Jena, Germany: H. Costenoble.

_____
1956   The Tlingit Indians: Results of a Trip to the Northwest Coast
            of America and the Bering Straits [1885]. Erna Gunther,
            trans. (American Ethnological Society Monograph 26) Se-
            attle: Published for the American Ethnological Society by
            the University of Washington Press.

Krauss, Michael E.
1961   [Lexical and Phonological Notes on Upper Kuskokwim from
            Mr. and Mrs. Carl Sesuie, Telida, Alaska.] (Manuscripts in
            Krauss's possession.)

_____
1961a   [Lexical Fieldnotes and Texts in Lower Tanana, from Teddy
            Charlie and Moses Charlie.] (Manuscripts in Krauss's pos-
            session.)

_____
1962   [Han Notes, 1962.] (Manuscript in Krauss's possession.)

_____
1962-1964   [Letters (April 20, 1962, Feb. 8, 1964, and Feb. 22, 1964) to
            Robert A. McKennan on Tanana Dialects.] (Letters in
            McKennan's possession.)

_____
1964   Review of Studies in the Athapaskan Languages, by Harry
            Hoijer et al. International Journal of American Linguistics
            30(4):409-415.

_____
1964-1965   Proto-Athapaskan-Eyak and the Problem of Na-Dene. 2 Pts.
            International Journal of American Linguistics 30(2):118-131;
            31(1):18-28.

_____
1967   [Han Notes, 1967.] (Manuscript in Krauss's possession.)

_____
1969   On the Classification in the Athapaskan, Eyak, and Tlingit
            Verb. Indiana University Publications in Anthropology and
            Linguistics, Memoir 24. Bloomington.

_____
1970   Eyak Dictionary. College: University of Alaska.

_____
1973   Na-Dene. Pp. 903-978 in Linguistics in North America. Cur-
            rent Trends in Linguistics. Thomas A. Sebeok, ed. Vol. 10.
            The Hague, Paris: Mouton. (Reprinted: Plenum Press, New
            York, 1976.)

_____
1974   Minto-Nenana Athabaskan Noun Dictionary, Preliminary
            Version. Fairbanks: University of Alaska, Native Language
            Center.

_____
1975   Native Peoples and Languages of Alaska. Map. Fairbanks:
            University of Alaska, Native Language Center.

_____
1975a   Chilcotin Phonology, a Descriptive and Historical Report,
            with Recommendations for a Chilcotin Orthography. (Un-
            published manuscript in Krauss's possession.)

_____
1979   Na-Dene and Eskimo. Pp. 803-901 in The Languages of Na-
            tive North America: An Historical and Comparative As-
            sessment. Lyle Campbell and Marianne Mithun, eds. Austin:
            University of Texas Press.

_____
1980   Proto-Athabaskan*k in 18th-Century Chipewyan: Philolog-
            ical Evidence. (Unpublished typescript in Krauss's posses-
            sion.)

Krauss, Michael E., and Mary Jane McGary
1980   Alaska Native Languages: A Bibliographical Catalogue. Pt.
            1: Indian Languages. Alaska Native Language Center Re-
            search Paper 3. Fairbanks.

Krech, Shepard, III
1974   Changing Trapping Patterns in Fort McPherson, Northwest
            Territories. (Unpublished Ph.D. Dissertation in Anthropol-
            ogy, Harvard University, Cambridge, Mass.)

_____
1976   The Eastern Kutchin and the Fur Trade, 1800-1860. Eth-
            nohistory 23(3):213-235.

_____
1978   Nutritional Evaluation of a Mission Residential School Diet:
            The Accuracy of Informant Recall. Human Organization
            37(2):186-190.

_____
1978a   On the Aboriginal Population of the Kutchin. Arctic An-
            thropology 15(1):89-104.

_____
1978b   Disease, Starvation and Northern Athapaskan Social Orga-
            nization. American Ethnologist 5(4):710-732.

_____
1979   The Nakotcho Kutchin: A Tenth Aboriginal Kutchin Band?
            Journal of Anthropological Research 35(1):109-121.

_____
1979a   Interethnic Relations in the Lower Mackenzie River Region.
            Arctic Anthropology 16(2):102-122.

_____
1980   Northern Athapaskan Ethnology in the 1970's. Annual Re-
            view of Anthropology 9:83-100.

Krenov, Julia
1951   Legends from Alaska. Journal de la Société des Américanistes
            n.s. 40:173-195. Paris.

Krieger, Herbert W.
1928   Tinne Indians of the Lower Yukon River Valley. Pp. 125-
            132 in Explorations and Field-work of the Smithsonian Insti-
            tution in 1927. Washington.

Kroeber, Alfred L.
1939   Cultural and Natural Areas of Native North America. Uni-
            versity of California Publications in American Archaeology
            and Ethnology 38. Berkeley. (Reprinted in 1953.)

Kroul, Mary V.
1974   Definitional Domains of the Koyukon Athapaskan Potlatch.
            Arctic Anthropology 11(suppl.):39-47.

Kupferer, Harriet J.
1966   Impotency and Power: A Cross-cultural Comparison of the
            Effects of Alien Rule. Pp. 61-71 in Political Anthropology.
            Marc J. Swartz, Victor W. Turner, and Arthur Tuden, eds.
            Chicago: Aldine.

Kurath, Gertrude
1966   Dogrib Choreography and Music. Pp. 13-28 in The Dogrib
            Hand Game, by June Helm and Nancy O. Lurie. Anthro-
            pological Series 71, National Museum of Canada Bulletin 205.
            Ottawa.

La Brosse, Jean Baptiste
1767   Nehiro-Iriniui Aiamihe Massinahigan [Prayer Book in the
            Montagnais Language]. Uabistiguiatsh [Quebec]: Massina-
            hitsetuau, Broun gaie Girmor.

Lachance, Denis
1968   L'Acculturation des Indiens de Sept-Îles et Maliotenam.
            (Unpublished M.A. Thesis in Anthropology, Université
            Laval, Quebec.)

Lacombe, Albert
1874   Dictionnaire de la langue des Cris. Montreal: C.O. Beau-
            chemin et Valois.

_____
1874a   Grammaire de la langue des Cris. Montreal: C.O. Beau-
            chemin et Valois.

Lagassé, Jean H., Jean K. Boek, Walter E. Boek, Walter M. Hlady,
and Ralph B. Poston
1959   The People of Indian Ancestry in Manitoba. Winnipeg:
            Queen's Printer.

Laliberté, Marcel
1976   Bilan du programme de recherche archéologique à la Baie
            James, 1972-1976. Ministère des Affairs Culturelles, Direction
            Générale du Patrimoine, Dossier 22. Quebec.

_____
1977   Les Schèmes d'établissement des Cris de la Baie James.
            (Unpublished manuscript in Ministère des Affaires Cultu-
            relles, Service du Patrimoine Autochtone, Direction Générale
            du Patrimoine, Quebec.)

1978   La Forêt boréale. Pp. 87-97 in Images de la préhistoire du Québec. Claude Chapdelaine, ed. *Recherches Amérindiennes au Québec* 7(1-2). Montreal.

Lambert, Bernard
1967   Shepherd of the Wilderness: A Biography of Bishop Frederic Baraga. L'Anse, Mich.: no publisher.

Lamers, Frans
1976   Sekani Adaptation: An Analysis of Technological Strategies and Processes. (Paper read at Northwest Coast Studies Conference, May 12-16, 1976; manuscript in Catharine McClellan's Possession.)

Landes, Ruth
1968   Ojibwa Religion and the Midéwiwin. Madison: University of Wisconsin Press.

Lane, Robert B.
[1948-1951]   [Chilcotin Ethnographic Fieldnotes.] (Manuscripts in Lane's possession.)

1953   Cultural Relations of the Chilcotin Indians of West Central British Columbia. (Unpublished Ph.D. Dissertation in Anthropology, University of Washington, Seattle.)

Lantis, Margaret
1973   The Current Nativistic Movement in Alaska. Pp. 99-118 in Circumpolar Problems: Habitat, Economy, and Social Relations in the Arctic; a Symposium for Anthropological Research on the North, September 1969, Lulea, Sweden and Tromsø, Norway. Gösta Berg, ed. (Wenner-Gren Center International Symposium Series 21) Oxford, New York: Pergamon Press.

Larsen, James A.
1971   Vegetation of Fort Reliance, Northwest Territories. *Canadian Field-Naturalist* 85(2):147-178.

1971a   Vegetational Relationships with Air Mass Frequencies: Boreal Forest and Tundra. *Arctic* 24(3):177-194.

1974   Ecology of the Northern Continental Forest Border. Pp. 341-369 in Arctic and Alpine Environments. Jack D. Ives and Roger G. Barry, eds. London: Methuen.

La Rusic, Ignatius
1970   From Hunter to Proletarian. Annex B in Developmental Change Among the Cree Indians of Quebec. Norman A. Chance, ed. Ottawa: Department of Regional Economic Expansion. Mimeo.

1971   La Réaction des Waswanipis à l'annonce du projet de la Baie James. *Recherches Amérindiennes au Québec, Bulletin d'Information* 1(4-5):15-21. Montreal.

Latham, Robert G.
1848   On the Languages of the Oregon Territory. *Journal of the Ethnological Society of London* 1:154-166.

1850   The Natural History of the Varieties of Man. London: J. Van Voorst.

1857   On the Languages of Northern, Western and Central America. Pp. 57-115 in *Transactions of the Philological Society for 1856*. London.

Laure, Pierre
1889   Mission du Saguenay: Relation inédite, 1720 à 1730. Notes biographiques et chronologiques, by Arthur E. Jones. Montreal: Archives du Collège Ste. Marie.

La Vérendrye, Pierre Gaultier de Varrennes de
1927   Journals and Letters of Pierre Gaultier de Varennes de la Vérendrye and His Sons... Lawrence J. Burpee, ed. (Publications of the Champlain Society 16) Toronto: The Champlain Society.

Laviolette, Gontran
1955   Notes on the Aborigines of the Province of Quebec. *Anthropologica* 1:198-211. Ottawa.

1956   Notes on the Aborigines of the Prairie Provinces. *Anthropologica* 2:107-130. Ottawa.

Lawrence, Erma, and Jeff Leer, comps.
1977   Haida Dictionary. Fairbanks: University of Alaska, Native Language Center, and The Society for the Preservation of Haida Language and Literature.

Lawrence, Guy
1965   40 Years on the Yukon Telegraph. Vancouver: Mitchell Press.

Lawson, Murray G.
1948   Fur Traders vs. Feltmakers. *The Beaver* (September):34-37.

Lazore, Melissa, and Eddie Gardner
1977   An Interview with Bart Paul Jack, Land Claims Director, Naskapi Montagnais INNU Association of Labrador. *The Native Perspective* 2(7):15-16. Ottawa.

Leacock, Eleanor
1950-1951   [Ethnographic Notes from Six Months' Fieldwork Among the Montagnais-Naskapi of Natashquan, Quebec, and Northwest River, Newfoundland-Labrador.] (Manuscript in Leacock's possession.)

1954   The Montagnais "Hunting Territory" and the Fur Trade. *Memoirs of the American Anthropological Association* 78. Menasha, Wis.

1955   Matrilocality in a Simple Hunting Economy (Montagnais-Naskapi). *Southwestern Journal of Anthropology* 11(1):31-47.

1958   Status Among the Montagnais-Naskapi of Labrador. *Ethnohistory* 5(3):200-209.

1969   The Montagnais-Naskapi Band. Pp. 1-17 in Contributions to Anthropology: Band Societies. David Damas, ed. *Anthropological Series 84, National Museum of Canada Bulletin* 228. Ottawa.

1975   Class, Commodity and the Status of Women. Pp. 601-616 in Women Cross-culturally: Change and Challenge. Ruby Rohrlich-Leavitt, ed. (9th International Congress of Anthropological and Ethnological Sciences, Chicago, 1973) The Hague: Mouton.

1976   Women in Egalitarian Society. Pp. 11-35 in Women in European History. Renate Bridenthal and Claudia Kooz, eds. Boston: Houghton, Mifflin.

Leacock, Eleanor, and Jacqueline Goodman
1976   Montagnais Marriage and the Jesuits in the Seventeenth Century: Incidents from the Relations of Paul LeJeune. *Western Canadian Journal of Anthropology* 6(3):77-91.

Lebuis, François
1971   Le Complexe culturel de la pêche de subsistance à Namiska, au Nouveau-Québec. (Unpublished M.A. Thesis in Anthropology, Université de Montréal, Montreal.)

Lee, Hulbert A.
1959   Surficial Geology of Southern District of Keewatin and the Keewatin Ice Divide, Northwest Territories. *Geological Survey of Canada Bulletin* 51. Ottawa.

Lee, Richard B., and Irven DeVore, eds.
1968   Man the Hunter. (Symposium on Man the Hunter, University of Chicago, 1966) Chicago: Aldine.

Lee, Thomas E.
1954   The First Sheguiandah Expedition, Manitoulin Island, Ontario. *American Antiquity* 20(2):101-111.

1955   The Second Sheguiandah Expedition, Manitoulin Island, Ontario. *American Antiquity* 21(1):63-71.

1957   The Antiquity of the Sheguiandah Site. *Canadian Field-Naturalist* 71(3):117-137.

———
1965 Archaeological Investigations at Lake Abitibi, 1964. *Université Laval, Centre d'Etudes Nordiques, Travaux Divers* 10. Quebec.

Leechman, Douglas
1947 Aborigines in Yukon Territory: A Brief Description of Its History, Administration, Resources and Development. *Canada. Northern Administrations, Department of Resources and Development Report* 28-32. Ottawa.

———
1948 Old Crow's Village. *Canadian Geographical Journal* 37(1):2-16.

———
1950 Loucheux Tales. *Journal of American Folklore* 63(248):158-162.

———
1950a Yukon Territory. *Canadian Geographical Journal* 40(6):240-267.

———
1952 Folk-lore of the Vanta-Kutchin. *National Museum of Canada Bulletin* 126:76-93. Ottawa.

———
1953 Population Statistics of the Canadian Aborigine Arranged by Linguistic Stocks, 1949. (Mimeo. Copy in June Helm's possession.)

———
1954 The Vanta Kutchin. *Anthropological Series 33, National Museum of Canada Bulletin* 130. Ottawa.

Leechman, Douglas, and Richard Harrington
1948 Caribou for Chipewyans. Text by Douglas Leechman; Photos by Richard Harrington. *The Beaver* 278(March):12-18.

Leer, Jeff, comp.
1978 A Conversational Dictionary of Kodiak Alutiiq. Fairbanks: University of Alaska, Native Language Center.

———
1979 Proto-Athabaskan Verb Stem Variation. *Alaska Native Language Center Research Paper* 1. Fairbanks.

LeFebre, Charlene Craft
1956 A Contribution to the Archaeology of the Upper Kuskokwim. *American Antiquity* 21(3):268-274.

Lefroy, John H.
1938 Sir Henry Lefroy's Journey to the North-West in 1843-4. W.S. Wallace, ed. Pp. 67-96 in *Transactions of the Royal Society of Canada*, 3d ser., sect. 2, Vol. 32. Ottawa.

Legoff, Laurent
1889 Grammaire de la langue montagnaise. Montreal: no publisher.

———
1916 Dictionnaire français-montagnais. Lyon: Société Saint-Augustin, Desclée, de Brouwer.

Leith, Charles K., and Arthur T. Leith
1912 A Summer and Winter on Hudson Bay. Madison, Wis.: Cartwell.

Le Jeune, Paul
1973 Le Missionnaire, l'apostat, le sorcier: Relation de 1634 de Paul Le Jeune. Edition critique par Guy Laflèche. Montreal: Les Presses de l'Université de Montréal.

Lemoine, Georges
1901 Dictionnaire français-montagnais avec un vocabulaire montagnais-anglais, une courte liste de noms géographiques et une grammaire montagnaise. Boston: W.B. Cabot and P. Cabot.

———
1901a Une Grammaire montagnaise. Boston: W.B. Cabot and P. Cabot.

Leroi-Gourhan, André
1946 Archéologie du Pacific-nord, matériaux pour l'étude des relations entre les peuples riverains d'Asie et d'Amérique. *Université de Paris, Institut d'Ethnologie, Travaux et Mémoires* 47. Paris.

Lévesque, Carole
1976 La Culture materielle des Indiens du Québec: Une étude de raquettes, mocassins et toboggans. *Canada. National Museum of Man, Mercury Series, Ethnology Service Paper* 33. Ottawa.

———
1977 Production et artisanat dans la communauté indienne de Fort-George. Pp. 32-35 in *Papers of the Eighth Algonquian Conference*. William Cowan, ed. Ottawa: Carleton University.

Lévesque, René
1971 La Seigneurie des Iles et des Ilets de Mingan. (Archéologie du Québec) Montreal: Leméac.

Levine, Robert D.
1977 The Skidegate Dialect of Haida. (Unpublished Ph.D. Dissertation in Linguistics, Columbia University, New York City.)

———
1979 Haida and Na-Dene: A New Look at the Evidence. *International Journal of American Linguistics* 45(2):157-170.

Lévi-Strauss, Claude
[1968] L'Origine des manières de table. (His Mythologiques 3) Paris: Plon.

———
[1971] L'Homme nu. (His Mythologiques 4) Paris: Plon.

Levy, Marion J.
1966 Modernization and Structure of Societies: A Setting for International Affairs. 2 vols. Princeton, N.J.: Princeton University Press.

Lewis, Henry T.
1977 Maskuta: The Ecology of Indian Fires in Northern Alberta. *Western Canadian Journal of Anthropology* 7(1):15-52.

Lewis, Marion, J.H. Hildes, H. Kaita, and B. Chown
1961 The Blood Groups of the Kutchin Indians at Old Crow, Yukon Territory. *American Journal of Physical Anthropology* 19(4):383-389.

Lewis, Phillip H.
1969 The Social Context of Art in Northern New Ireland. *Fieldiana: Anthropology* 58. Chicago.

Li, Fang-Kuei
1931 A Study of Sarcee Verb-stems. *International Journal of American Linguistics* 6(1):3-27.

———
1932 A List of Chipewyan Stems. *International Journal of American Linguistics* 7(3-4):122-151.

———
1933 Chipewyan Consonants. Pp. 429-467 in *Bulletin of the Institute of History and Philology of Academia Sinica, Suppl., Vol. 1: Ts'ai Yuan P'ei Anniversary Volume*. Taipei.

———
1946 Chipewyan. Pp. 398-423 in Harry Hoijer et al., Linguistic Structures of Native America. *Viking Fund Publications in Anthropology* 6. New York.

———
1964 A Chipewyan Ethnological Text. *International Journal of American Linguistics* 30(2):132-136.

Li, Fang-Kuei, and Ronald Scollon
1976 Chipewyan Texts. *Academia Sinica, Institute of History and Philology, Special Publication* 71. Taipei.

Liebow, Elliot, and John Trudeau
1962 A Preliminary Study of Acculturation Among the Cree Indians of Winisk, Ontario. *Arctic* 15(3):191-204.

Linton, Ralph
1936 The Study of Man: An Introduction. New York, London: D. Appleton-Century.

Lips, Julius E.
1936 Trap Systems Among the Montagnais-Naskapi Indians of Labrador Peninsula. *Statens Ethnografiska Museum, Smärre Meddelanden* 13. Stockholm.

774

1937   Notes on Some Ojibway-traps (Metagama Band). *Ethnos* 2(6):354-360.

1939   Naskapi Trade: A Study in Legal Acculturation. *Journal de la Société des Américanistes* n.s. 31:129-195. Paris.

1942   Tents in the Wilderness: The Story of a Labrador Indian Boy. Philadelphia and New York: Frederick A. Stokes.

1947   Naskapi Law (Lake St. John and Lake Mistassini Bands): Law and Order in a Hunting Society. *Transactions of the American Philosophical Society* n.s. 37(4):379-492. Philadelphia.

1947a   Notes on Montagnais-Naskapi Economy (Lake St. John and Lake Mistassini Bands). *Ethnos* 12(1-2):1-78.

Lipsett, Brenda McGee
1970   A Comparative Study to Determine the Origin of Some Canadian Shield Rock Paintings. Pp. 181-189 in Ten Thousand Years: Archaeology in Manitoba. Walter M. Hlady, ed. Winnipeg: Manitoba Archaeological Society.

Lipshits, B.A.
1955   O kollekt͡siakh Muze͡ia antropologii i ͡etnografii, sobrannykh russkimi puteshestvennikami i issledovatel͡iami na Al͡iaske i v Kalifornii (The Collections of the Museum of Anthropology and Ethnology Gathered by Russian Travelers and Explorers in Alaska and California). *Sbornik Muze͡i Antropologii i Etnografii* 16:358-369. Leningrad.

Lis͡ianskii, Iur͡ii Fedorovich
1814   A Voyage Round the World in the Years 1803, 1804, 1805, and 1806. Performed by Order of His Imperial Majesty Alexander the First, Emperor of Russia, in the Ship Neva. London: Printed for John Booth and Longman, Hurst, Rees, Orme, and Brown.

Lloyd, T.G.B.
1875   Notes on Indian Remains Found on the Coast of Labrador. *Journal of the Anthropological Institute of Great Britain and Ireland* 4:39-44. London.

Lofthouse, Joseph
1907   Letter from Bishop Lofthouse, Diocese of Keewatin. *Moosonee and Keewatin Mailbag* 5(1):13-14. London.

1922   A Thousand Miles from a Post Office; or, Twenty Years' Life and Travel in the Hudson's Bay Regions. London: Society for Promoting Christian Knowledge; New York: Macmillan.

Logan, Robert A.
1951   The Precise Speakers: The Cree Language with Its Variety and Exactness Makes a Highly Interesting Study. *The Beaver* 282(June):40-43.

1958   Cree Language Notes. Lake Charlotte, N.S.: Loganda.

Long, John
1791   Voyages and Travels of an Indian Interpreter and Trader. Describing the Manners and Customs of the North American Indians; with an Account of the Posts Situated on the River Saint Laurence, Lake Ontario, etc. To Which Is Added a Vocabulary of the Chippeway Language... a List of Words in the Iroquois, Mohegan, Shawanee, and Esquimeaux Tongues, and a Table Shewing the Analogy Between the Algonkin and Chippeway Languages. London: Printed for the Author. (Reprinted: Coles, Toronto, 1971.)

Loring, R.C.
1891   The Hoquel-gots. P. 97 in *Canada. Annual Report of the Department of Indian Affairs for the Year 1890.* Ottawa.

Losey, T.D., ed.
1973   An Interdisciplinary Investigation of Fort Enterprise, Northwest Territories, 1970. *University of Alberta, Boreal Institute for Northern Studies Occasional Publication* 9. Edmonton.

Lotz, James R.
1962   Pelts to Parkas. *The Beaver* 293 (Autumn): 16-19.

1964   Yukon Bibliography. (*Yukon Research Project Series 1*) Ottawa: Department of Northern Affairs and National Resources, Northern Co-ordination and Research Centre.

1971   Northern Realities: Canada-U.S. Exploitation of the Canadian North. Chicago: Follett.

Low, Albert P.
1897   Report on Explorations in the Labrador Peninsula. Along the East Main, Koksoak, Hamilton, Manicuagan, and Portions of Other Rivers, in 1892-93-94-95. *Annual Report of the Geological Survey of Canada* n.s. 8(L). Ottawa.

1929   Extracts from Reports on the District of Ungava or New Quebec. 3d ed. Quebec: Department of Highways and Mines, Bureau of Mines.

Lowdon, J.A., R. Wilmeth, and W. Blake, Jr.
1970   Geological Survey of Canada Radiocarbon Dates. X. *Radiocarbon* 12(2):472-485.

Lowther, G.R.
1965   Archaeology of the Tadoussac Area. Province of Quebec. *Anthropologica* n.s. 7(1):27-37. Ottawa.

Loyens, William J.
1964   The Koyukon Feast for the Dead. *Arctic Anthropology* 2(2):133-148.

1966   The Changing Culture of the Nulato Koyukon Indians. (Unpublished Ph.D. Dissertation in Anthropology. University of Wisconsin, Madison.)

Lurie, Nancy O.
1962   [Ethnographic Notes, from Fieldwork Among the Dogrib at Lac La Martre, Northwest Territories.] (Manuscript in Lurie's possession.)

Lutz, Harold J.
1956   Ecological Effects of Forest Fires in the Interior of Alaska. *U.S. Department of Agriculture Technical Bulletin* 1133. Washington.

Lysyk, Kenneth M., Edith Bohmer, and Willard L. Phelps
1977   Letter Addressed to the Honorable Warren Allmand, Minister of Indian Affairs and Northern Development. House of Commons, Ottawa. Pp. v-vxi in Alaska Highway Pipeline Inquiry. Ottawa: Minister of Indian Affairs and Northern Development.

MacAndrew, Craig, and Robert B. Edgerton
1969   Drunken Comportment: A Social Explanation. Chicago: Aldine.

McCaffrey, Moira
1979   Annotated Bibliography of Central and Northern Quebec and Labrador Prehistory. (Unpublished manuscript at McGill University, Department of Anthropology, Montreal.)

McCandless, Robert G.
1976   Trophies or Meat: Yukon Game Management, 1896 to 1976. (Unpublished manuscript No. 550.025 in the Yukon Archives, Whitehorse, Yukon Terr.)

McClellan, Catharine
1948-1974   [Notes on about 6 Months' Fieldwork with the Tagish at Carcross, Yukon Territory.] (Manuscript in the Archives of the National Museum of Man, Ottawa.)

1948-1975   [Ethnographic Fieldnotes from Yukon Territory.] (Manuscripts in the Archives of the National Museum of Man, Ottawa.)

1950   Culture Change and Native Trade in Southern Yukon Territory. (Unpublished Ph.D. Dissertation in Anthropology, University of California, Berkeley.)

1953   The Inland Tlingit. Pp. 47-51 in Asia and North America: Transpacific Contacts. Marian W. Smith, ass. *Memoirs of the Society for American Archaeology* 9. Salt Lake City.

775

1954   The Interrelations of Social Structure with Northern Tlingit Ceremonialism. *Southwestern Journal of Anthropology* 10(1):75-96.

1956   Shamanistic Syncretism in Southern Yukon Territory. *Transactions of the New York Academy of Sciences*, 2d ser., Vol. 19(2):130-137. New York.

1961   Avoidance Between Siblings of the Same Sex in North America. *Southwestern Journal of Anthropology* 17(2):103-123.

1963   Wealth Woman and Frogs Among the Tagish Indians. *Anthropos* 58(1-2):121-128.

1964   Culture Contacts in the Early Historic Period in Northwestern North America. *Arctic Anthropology* 2(2):3-15.

1967   Through Native Eyes: Indian Accounts of Events in the History of the American Northwest. (Unpublished manuscript in Archives of the National Museum of Man, Ottawa; copy in McClellan's possession.)

1970   Indian Stories About the First Whites in Northwestern America. Pp. 103-133 in Ethnohistory in Southwestern Alaska and the Southern Yukon: Method and Content. Margaret Lantis, ed. (Studies in Anthropology 7) Lexington: University Press of Kentucky.

1970a   The Girl Who Married the Bear: A Masterpiece of Indian Oral Tradition. *Canada. National Museum of Man, Publications in Ethnology* 2. Ottawa.

1970b   [Fieldnotes, Yukon Territory.] (Manuscript in Archives of the National Museum of Man, Ottawa; copy in McClellan's possession.)

1970c   Introduction to Special Issue: Athabascan Studies. *Western Canadian Journal of Anthropology* 2(1):vi-xix.

1975   My Old People's Stories: Oral Literature of the Indians of Southern Yukon Territory. (Manuscript in McClellan's possession; copy in National Museum of Man, Ottawa.)

1975a   My Old People Say: An Ethnographic Survey of Southern Yukon Territory. 2 Pts. *Canada. National Museum of Man, Publications in Ethnology* 6. Ottawa.

1975b   Feuding and Warfare Among Northwestern Athapaskans. Pp. 181-258 in Vol. 1 of Proceedings: Northern Athapaskan Conference, 1971. A McFadyen Clark, ed. 2 vols. *Canada. National Museum of Man, Mercury Series, Ethnology Service Paper* 27. Ottawa.

McClellan, Catharine, and Dorothy Rainier
1950   Ethnological Survey of Southern Yukon Territory, 1948. (Preliminary Report). *National Museum of Canada Bulletin* 118:50-53. Ottawa.

McCracken, Harold
1959   George Catlin and the Old Frontier. New York: Dial Press.

MacCulloch, John A.
1908   Adultery (Primitive and Savage Peoples). Pp. 122-126 in Vol. 1 of Encyclopedia of Religion and Ethics. James Hastings, ed. 13 vols. Edinburgh: T. and T. Clark. (Reprinted: Charles Scribner's Sons, New York, 1928)

McDonald, Archibald
1872   Peace River: A Canoe Voyage from Hudson's Bay to the Pacific, by the Late Sir George Simpson (Governor, Hon. Hudson's Bay Company) in 1828. Journal of the Late Chief Factor, Archibald McDonald (Hon. Hudson's Bay Company) Who Accompanied Him. Malcolm McLeod, ed. Ottawa: J. Durie and Son.

MacDonald, Duncan G.F.
1862   British Columbia and Vancouver's Island: Comprising a Description of These Dependencies... Also an Account of the Manners and Customs of the Native Indians. London: Longman, Green, Longman, Roberts, and Green.

MacDonald, George F.
1971   The Archaeological Survey of Canada. *Archaeological Survey of Canada Research Report* 1:1-3. Ottawa.

McDonald, Robert, trans.
1886   The New Testament of Our Lord and Saviour Jesus Christ. Translation into Takudh. London: Printed for the British and Foreign Bible Society.

1898   Ettunettle Rsotitinyoo Sheg Ako Ketchid Kwitzugwatsui (Holy Bible). London: British and Foreign Bible Society.

1911   A Grammar of the Tukudh Language. London: Society for Promoting Christian Knowledge. (Reprinted: Canarctic Publishing Ltd., for Curriculum Division, Department of Education, Government of the Northwest Territories, Yellowknife, 1975.)

McDonnell, John
1889-1890   Some Account of the Red River (About 1797) with Extracts from His Journal, 1793-1795. Pp. 265-295 in Vol. 1 of Les Bourgeois de la Compagnie du Nord-ouest. L.R. Masson, ed. 2 vols. Quebec: A. Coté.

McDonnell, Roger F.
1975   Kasini Society: Some Aspects of the Social Organization of an Athapaskan Culture Between 1900-1950. (Unpublished Ph.D. Dissertation in Anthropology, University of British Columbia, Vancouver.)

McFadyen, Annette M.
[1964]   [South Fork Koyukuk Social Organization.] (Unpublished manuscript in McFadyen's possession.)

1966   Koyukuk River Culture of the Arctic Woodlands: A Preliminary Survey of Material Culture, with an Analysis of Hostility and Trade as Agents of Cultural Transmission. (Unpublished M.A. Thesis in Anthropology, George Washington University, Washington.)

McFadyen, Annette M. *see also* Clark, Annette McFadyen

McFeat, Tom F.S.
1962   Museum Ethnology and the Algonkian Project. *National Museum of Canada Anthropology Paper* 2. Ottawa.

Macfie, John
1956   Bannock. *The Beaver* 287(Autumn):22-23.

1967   The Coast Crees. *The Beaver* 298(Winter):13-21.

1970   Centenary at Severn House 1770. *The Beaver* 300(Spring):42-49.

McGee, John T.
1961   Cultural Stability and Change Among the Montagnais Indians of the Lake Melville Region of Labrador. *Catholic University of America Anthropological Series* 19. Washington.

McGhee, Robert
1970   Excavations at Bloody Falls, N.W.T., Canada. *Arctic Anthropology* 6(2):53-72.

McGhee, Robert, and James A. Tuck
1975   An Archaic Sequence from the Strait of Belle Isle, Labrador. *Canada. National Museum of Man, Mercury Series, Archaeological Survey Paper* 34. Ottawa.

M'Gillivray, Duncan
1929   The Journal of Duncan M'Gillivray of the North West Company at Fort George on the Saskatchewan, 1794-95. Arthur S. Morton, ed. Toronto: Macmillan.

MacGregor, James G.
1952   The Land of Twelve Foot Davis: A History of the Peace River Country. Edmonton: Applied Art Products.

1966   Peter Fidler: Canada's Forgotten Surveyor, 1769-1822. Toronto: McClelland and Stewart.

1970   The Klondike Rush Through Edmonton, 1897-1898. Toronto: McClelland and Stewart.

McIlwraith, Thomas F.
1948   The Bella Coola Indians. 2 vols. Toronto: University of Toronto Press.

McInnis, William
1912   Report on a Part of the Northwest Territories of Canada Drained by the Winisk and Attawapiskat Rivers. Pp. 108-138 in Reports on the District of Patricia. Willet G. Miller, ed. *Reports of the Ontario Bureau of Mines* 21(2). Toronto.

McKay, Alexander G., ed.
1977   New Perspectives in Canadian Archaeology. *Proceedings of the 15th Symposium of the Royal Society of Canada.* Toronto.

Mackay, J. Ross
1972   The World of Underground Ice. *Annals of the Association of American Geographers* 62(1):1-22. Washington.

McKennan, Robert A.
1935   Anent the Kutchin Tribes. *American Anthropologist* 37(2):369.

1959   The Upper Tanana Indians. *Yale University Publications in Anthropology* 55. New Haven, Conn.

1964   The Physical Anthropology of Two Alaskan Athapaskan Groups. *American Journal of Physical Anthropology* n.s. 22(1):43-52.

1965   The Chandalar Kutchin. *Arctic Institute of North America Technical Paper* 17. Montreal.

1969   Athapaskan Groups of Central Alaska at the Time of White Contact. *Ethnohistory* 16(4):335–343.

1969a   Athapaskan Groupings and Social Organization in Central Alaska. *Anthropological Series 84, National Museum of Canada Bulletin* 228:93-115. Ottawa.

McKennan, Robert A., and John P. Cook
1970   Prehistory of Healy Lake, Alaska. Pp. 182-184 in Vol. 3 of *Proceedings of the 8th International Congress of Anthropological and Ethnological Sciences.* 3 vols. Tokyo and Kyoto, 1968.

1972   The Dixthada Site, Central Alaska. (Paper presented at 37th Annual Meeting of the Society for American Anthropology, Bal Harbour, Fla., May 1972.)

Mackenzie, Sir Alexander
1801   Voyages from Montreal on the River St. Laurence, Through the Continent of North America, to the Frozen and Pacific Oceans; In the Years 1789 and 1793, with a Preliminary Account of the Rise, Progress, and Present State of the Fur Trade of that Country. London: T. Cadell and W. Davies. (Reprinted: University Microfilms, Ann Arbor, Mich., 1966.)

1927   Voyages from Montreal, on the River St. Laurence, Through the Continent of North America, to the Frozen and Pacific Oceans; in the Years 1789 and 1793, with a Preliminary Account of the Rise, Progress, and Present State of the Fur Trade in That Country. Toronto: The Radisson Society of Canada.

1966   Exploring the Northwest Territory: Sir Alexander Mackenzie's Journal of a Voyage by Bark Canoe from Lake Athabasca to the Pacific Ocean in the Summer of 1789. T.H. McDonald, ed. Norman: University of Oklahoma Press.

1970   The Journals and Letters of Sir Alexander Mackenzie [1789-1819]. W. Kaye Lamb, ed. Cambridge, England: Published for the Hakluyt Society at the University Press.

McKenzie, Alexander
1805   [Journal of Great Bear Lake.] (Manuscript AB40/M193 C.2 in Provincial Archives of British Columbia, Victoria; copy in Beryl C. Gillespie's possession.)

MacKenzie, Marguerite
1977   Montagnais Dialectology. Mimeo.

1979   Fort Chimo Cree: A Case of Dialect Syncretism. Pp. 227-236 in *Papers of the Tenth Algonquian Conference.* William Cowan, ed. Ottawa: Carleton University.

McKenzie, Roderick
1889-1890   Réminiscences, mémoires, extraits de lettres de Sir Alexander Mackenzie, etc. Pp. 1-66 in Vol. 1 of Les Bourgeois de la Compagnie du Nord-Ouest. L.R. Masson, ed. 2 vols. Quebec: A Coté.

McKern, William C.
1937   An Hypothesis for the Asiatic Origin of the Woodland Pattern. *American Antiquity* 3(2):138-143.

MacLachlan, Bruce B.
1956   [Ethnographic Notes from Approximately Eight Weeks' Fieldwork, at Telegraph Creek, British Columbia.] (Manuscripts in MacLachlan's possession.)

1957   An Anthropological Reconnaissance to Telegraph Creek, B.C. (Unpublished manuscript in MacLachlan's possession.)

1957a   Notes on Some Tahltan Oral Literature. *Anthropologica* 4:1-9. Ottawa.

McLean, John
1932   John McLean's Notes of a Twenty-five Years' Service in the Hudson's Bay Territory [1849]. W.S. Wallace, ed. Toronto: The Champlain Society.

MacNeish, June Helm
1954   Contemporary Folk Beliefs of a Slave Indian Band. *Journal of American Folklore* 67(264):185-198.

1955   Folktales of the Slave Indians. *Anthropologica* 1:37-44. Ottawa.

1956   Leadership Among the Northeastern Athabascans. *Anthropologica* 2:131-163. Ottawa.

1956a   Problems of Acculturation and Livelihood in a Northern Indian Band. *Contributions à l'Etude des Sciences de l'Homme* 3:169-181.

1960   Kin Terms of Arctic Drainage Déné: Hare, Slavey, Chipewyan. *American Anthropologist* 62(2):279-295.

MacNeish, June Helm *see also* Helm, June

MacNeish, Richard S.
1951   An Archaeological Reconnaissance in the Northwest Territories. *Annual Report for 1949-50, National Museum of Canada Bulletin* 123:24-41. Ottawa.

1952   A Possible Early Site in the Thunder Bay District, Ontario. *Annual Report for 1950-51, National Museum of Canada Bulletin* 126:23-47. Ottawa.

1953   Archaeological Reconnaissance in the Mackenzie River Drainage. *National Museum of Canada Bulletin* 128:23-39. Ottawa.

1954   The Pointed Mountain Site Near Fort Liard, Northwest Territories, Canada. *American Antiquity* 19(3):234-253.

1955   Two Archaeological Sites on Great Bear Lake, Northwest Territories, Canada. *Annual Report for 1953-54, National Museum of Canada Bulletin* 136:54-84. Ottawa.

1958   An Introduction to the Archaeology of Southwest Manitoba. *Anthropological Series 44, National Museum of Canada Bulletin* 157. Ottawa.

1959 Men Out of Asia; as Seen from the Northwest Yukon. *Anthropological Papers of the University of Alaska* 7(2):41-70. College.

1959a A Speculative Framework of Northern North America Prehistory as of April 1959. *Anthropologica* 1(1-2):7-23. Ottawa.

1960 The Callison Site in the Light of Archaeological Survey of Southwest Yukon. *National Museum of Canada Bulletin* 162:1-51. Ottawa.

1963 The Early Peopling of the New World—As Seen from the Southwestern Yukon. *Anthropological Papers of the University of Alaska* 10(2):93-106. College.

1964 Investigations in Southwest Yukon: Archaeological Excavations, Comparisons, and Speculations. *Papers of the Robert S. Peabody Foundation for Archaeology* 6(2):201-488. Andover, Mass.

McNickle, D'Arcy
1973 Native American Tribalism: Indian Survivals and Renewals. London, New York: Oxford University Press.

McPhail, J.D., and C.C. Lindsey
1970 Freshwater Fishes of Northwestern Canada and Alaska. *Bulletin of the Fisheries Research Board of Canada* 173. Ottawa.

McPhee, John
1977 Coming into the Country. New York: Farrar, Strauss, and Giroux.

McPherron, Alan
1967 The Juntunen Site and the Late Woodland Prehistory of the Upper Great Lakes Area. *University of Michigan Museum of Anthropology, Anthropological Papers* 30. Ann Arbor.

MacPherson, John T.
1930 An Ethnographical Study of the Abitibi Indians. (Unpublished manuscript in National Museum of Man, Ottawa.)

McQuesten, Leroy N.
1952 Recollections of Leroy N. McQuesten of Life in the Yukon, 1871-1885. Dawson City, Yukon Terr.: no publisher.

MacRae, J.A.
1900 Treaty No. 8 and Adhesions, Reports, etc. Ottawa: Queen's Printer.

McRoy, Nancy
1967 [Han Fieldnotes.] (Manuscript in McRoy's possession.)

1973 [Han Wordlists.] (Manuscript in McRoy's possession.)

McVicar, Robert
1825-1826 [Report on Fort Resolution District, 1825-1827; Great Slave Lake Outfits.] (Manuscript B.181/e/1 in Hudson's Bay Company Archives, Provincial Archives of Manitoba, Winnipeg, Canada.)

1826-1827 [Fort Resolution Post Journal.] (Manuscript B.181/a/7 in Hudson's Bay Company Archives, Provincial Archives of Manitoba, Winnipeg, Canada.)

Maddren, A.G.
1913 The Koyukuk-Chandalar Region, Alaska. *U.S. Geological Survey Bulletin* 532. Washington.

Mailhot, José, and Kateri Lescop
1977 Lexique montagnais-français du dialecte de Schefferville, Sept-Iles et Maliotenam. *Ministère des Affaires Culturelles, Direction Générale du Patrimoine, Dossier* 29. Quebec.

Mailhot, José, and Andrée Michaud
1965 North West River: Etude ethnographique. *Université Laval, Centre d'Etudes Nordiques, Travaux Divers* 7. Quebec.

Mair, Charles
1908 Through the Mackenzie Basin: A Narrative of the Athabasca and Peace River Treaty Expedition of 1899. Toronto: William Briggs.

Makale, Holloway and Associates
1966 Fort Resolution: NWT Planning Report and Development Plan. Edmonton: no publisher.

Malaurie, Jean, and Jacques Rousseau, eds.
1964 Le Nouveau-Québec: Contribution à l'étude de l'occupation humaine. (Bibliothèque Arctique et Antarctique 2) Paris: Mouton.

Mandelbaum, David G.
1940 The Plains Cree. *Anthropological Papers of the American Museum of Natural History* 37(2):155-316. New York. (New edition: University of Regina, Canadian Plains Research Center, Regina, Sask., 1979.)

Manitoba. Department of Agriculture and Conservation. Social and Economic Research Office
1959 A Study of the Population of Indian Ancestry Living in Manitoba. 3 vols. Winnipeg: Department of Agriculture and Immigration.

[Maray de la Chauvignerie, Michel]
1928 Dénombrement des nations sauvages qui ont rapport au gouvernement de Canada; des guerriers de chaque nation avec les armoiries, 1736 [1726]. *Bulletin des Recherches Historiques* 34:541-551. Ottawa and Quebec.

Marest, Gabriel
1931 Letter from Father Marest, Missionary of the Company of Jesus, to Father de Lamberville of the Company of Jesus, Overseer of the Missions of Canada. Pp. 103-142 in Documents Relating to the Early History of Hudson Bay. J.B. Tyrrell, ed. (Publications of the Champlain Society 18) Toronto: The Champlain Society.

Margry, Pierre, ed.
1876-1886 Découvertes et établissements des Français dans l'ouest et dans le sud de l'Amérique septentrionale, 1614-1754. 6 vols. Paris: D. Jouaust.

_____, ed.
1879-1888 Découvertes et établissements des Français dans l'ouest et dans le sud de l'Amérique septentrionale, 1614-1754. 6 vols. Paris: Maisonneuve.

Mark, Lindi Li
1955 Structure of Tlingit Melodies. (Unpublished M.A. Thesis in Anthropology, Northwestern University, Evanston, Ill.)

Marois, Roger J.M.
1974 Les Schèmes d'établissement à la fin de la préhistoire et au début de la période historique: Le sud du Québec. *Canada. National Museum of Man, Mercury Series, Archaeological Survey Paper* 17. Ottawa.

Marsh, Donald B.
1964 History of the Anglican Church in Northern Quebec and Ungava. Pp. 427-437 in Le Nouveau-Québec: Contribution à l'étude de l'occupation humaine. Jean Malaurie and Jacques Rousseau, eds. Paris: Mouton.

[1967] A History of the Work of the Anglican Church in the Area Now Known as the Diocese of the Arctic. Toronto: no publisher.

Marsh, Gordon
[1956] [Fieldnotes on Tagish, Summer 1956.] (Manuscript in Marsh's possession.)

1958 Tentative Placing of the Tahgish Language within the Athapaskan Stock. (Paper presented at the Annual Meeting of the Canadian Linguistic Association, 1958.)

Marshall, H.
1970 Problems of a Contemporary Arctic Village. *Arctic* 23(4):286-287.

Marshall, Robert
1933 Arctic Village. New York: H. Smith and Robert Haas.

Martijn, Charles A.
1969 Ile-aux-Basques and the Prehistoric Iroquois Occupation of

Southern Quebec. *Cahiers d'Archéologie Québecoise* 3:53-113. Trois Rivières.

——— 1972 James Bay Region (Quebec): Prehistory Bibliography. Pp. 50-62 in Bibliography: Native Peoples, James Bay Region, by Harvey Feit, M.E. Mackenzie, José Mailhot, and Charles A. Martijn. *Recherches Amérindiennes au Québec, Bulletin d'Information* 2(1). Montreal.

——— 1974 Etat de la recherche en préhistoire du Québec. *Revue de Géographie de Montréal* 28(4):429-441.

Martijn, Charles A., and Jacques Cinq-Mars
1970 Aperçu sur la recherche préhistorique au Québec. *Revue de Géographie de Montréal* 24(2):175-188.

Martijn, Charles A., and Edward S. Rogers
1969 Mistassini-Albanel: Contributions to the Prehistory of Quebec. *Université Laval, Centre d'Etudes Nordiques, Travaux Divers* 25. Quebec.

Martin, Calvin
1980 Subarctic Indians and Wildlife. Pp. 73-81 in Old Trails and New Directions: Papers of the Third North American Fur Trade Conference. Carol M. Judd and Arthur J. Ray, eds. Toronto: University of Toronto Press.

Martin, G.C., and F.J. Katz
1912 A Geologic Reconnaissance of the Iliamna Region, Alaska. *U.S. Geological Survey Bulletin* 485. Washington.

Martin, Horace T.
1892 Castorologia, or the History and Traditions of the Canadian Beaver. Montreal: Wm. Drysdale; London: Edward Stanford.

Martin, Pierre
1980 Les Semi-voyelles en Cris-Montagnais de Fort George. Pp. 247-262 in *Papers of the Eleventh Algonquian Conference.* William Cowan, ed. Ottawa: Carleton University.

Martindale, Thomas
1913 Hunting in the Upper Yukon. Philadelphia: G.W. Jacobs.

Martinson, Ella Lung
1960 Patsy Henderson's Klondike Story. Pp. 75-76 in The Alaska Book: Story of Our Northern Treasureland. Chicago: J.G. Ferguson.

Mason, J. Alden
1946 Notes on the Indians of the Great Slave Lake Area. *Yale University Publications in Anthropology* 34. New Haven, Conn.

Mason, Leonard
1967 The Swampy Cree: A Study in Acculturation. *National Museum of Canada Anthropology Paper* 13. Ottawa.

Mason, Lynn D.
1975 Hard Times Along the Kuskokwim. *Natural History* 84(7):66-73.

Mason, Michael H.
1924 The Arctic Forests. London: Hodder and Stoughton.

Mason, Otis T.
1896 Primitive Travel and Transportation. Pp. 239-593 in *Report of the United States National Museum for 1894.* Washington.

——— 1896a Influence of Environment Upon Human Industries or Arts. Pp. 639-665 in *Annual Report of the Smithsonian Institution for 1895.* Washington.

——— 1907 Environment. Pp. 427-430 in Vol. 1 of Handbook of American Indians North of Mexico. Frederick W. Hodge, ed. 2 vols. *Bureau of American Ethnology Bulletin* 30. Washington.

Mason, Ronald J.
1970 Hopewell, Middle Woodland, and the Laurel Culture: A Problem in Archaeological Classification. *American Anthropologist* 72(4):802-815.

Masson, Louis F.R., ed.
1889-1890 Les Bourgeois de la Compagnie du Nord-ouest: Récits de voyages, lettres et rapports inédits relatifs au Nord-ouest canadien. 2 vols. Quebec: A. Coté. (Reprinted: Antiquarian Press, New York, 1960.)

Mathews, Richard
1968 The Yukon. Carl Carmer, ed. (Rivers of America) New York: Holt, Rinehart and Winston.

Mathiassen, Therkel
1927 Archaeology of the Central Eskimos. 2 Pts. *Report of the Fifth Thule Expedition, 1921 1924,* Vol. 4. Copenhagen.

Mayer-Oakes, William J., ed.
1967 Life, Land and Water: Proceedings of the 1966 Conference on Environmental Studies of the Glacial Lake Agassiz Region. *University of Manitoba, Department of Anthropology Occasional Paper* 1. Winnipeg.

——— 1970 Archeological Investigations in the Grand Rapids, Manitoba, Reservoir, 1961-1962. *University of Manitoba, Department of Anthropology Occasional Paper* 3. Winnipeg.

Mead, Margaret, and Ruth L. Bunzel, eds.
1960 The Golden Age of American Anthropology. New York: George Braziller.

Meares, John
1791 Voyages Made in the Years 1788 and 1789, from China to the N.W. Coast of America... in the Ship Nootka. 2 vols. London: no publisher.

Meldgaard, Jørgen
1960 Origin and Evolution of Eskimo Cultures in the Eastern Arctic. *Canadian Geographical Journal* 60(2):64-75.

——— 1962 On the Formative Period of the Dorset Culture. Pp. 92-95 in Prehistoric Cultural Relations Between the Arctic and Temperate Zones of North America. John Campbell, ed. *Arctic Institute of North America Technical Paper* 11. Montreal.

Mendenhall, Walter C.
1902 Reconnaissance from Fort Hamlin to Kotzebue Sound, Alaska, by Way of Dall, Kanuti, Allen, and Kowak Rivers. *U.S. Geological Survey Professional Paper* 10. Washington.

Mestokosho, Mathieu
1977 Chroniques de chasse d'un Montagnais de Mingan. Georges Mestokosho, trans. Serge Bouchard, ed. (*Série Cultures Amérindiennes, Civilisation du Québec 20*) Quebec: Ministère des Affaires Culturelles.

Meyer, David A.
1970 Plano Points in the Carrot River Valley. *Saskatchewan Archaeology Newsletter* 29:8-21. Regina.

——— 1975 Waterfowl in Cree Ritual—The Goose Dance. Pp. 433-449 in Vol. 2 of Proceedings of the Second Congress of the Canadian Ethnology Society. Jim Freedman and Jerome H. Barkow, eds Canada. *National Museum of Man, Mercury Series, Ethnology Service Paper* 28. Ottawa.

——— 1977 Pre-Dorset Settlements at the Seahorse Gully Site. *Canada. National Museum of Man, Mercury Series, Archaeological Survey Paper* 57. Ottawa.

——— 1978 Prehistoric Pottery from Northern Saskatchewan. *Na'Po: A Saskatchewan Anthropological Journal* 8(1-2):5-29. Regina.

Michéa, Jean
1963 Les Chitra-gottinéké: Essai de monographie d'un groupe Athapascan des Montagnes Rocheuses. Pp. 49-93 in Contributions to Anthropology, 1960. Pt. 2 *Anthropological Series 60, National Museum of Canada Bulletin* 190. Ottawa.

Michelson, Truman
1933 The Linguistic Classification of Tête de Boule. *American Anthropologist* 35(2):396.

1934   Oüenebigonchelinis Confounded with Winnebago. *American Anthropologist* 36(3):486.

1939   Linguistic Classification of Cree and Montagnais-Naskapi Dialects. *Anthropological Papers 8, Bureau of American Ethnology Bulletin* 123:67-95. Washington.

Milanowski, Paul G., and Alfred John, comps.
1979   Nee'aaneegn': Upper Tanana (Tetlin) Junior Dictionary. Anchorage: University of Alaska, National Bilingual Materials Development Center.

Millar, James F.V.
1968   Archaeology of Fisherman Lake, Western District of Mackenzie, N.W.T. (Unpublished Ph.D. Dissertation in Anthropology, University of Calgary, Calgary, Alta.)

1979   Interaction Between the Mackenzie and Yukon Basins During the Early Holocene. (Paper read at the 12th Annual Conference of the University of Calgary Archaeological Association, Calgary, Alta.)

Millar, James F.V., and Gloria Ferdichuk
1975   Mackenzie River Archaeological Survey. *Northern Pipelines Task Force on Northern Oil Development, Environmental-Social Committee Report* 74-47. Ottawa.

Miller, Willet G., ed.
1912   Reports on the District of Patricia. *Reports of the Ontario Bureau of Mines* 21(3). Toronto.

Minni, Sheila J.
1976   The Prehistoric Occupations of Black Lake, Northern Saskatchewan. *Canada. National Museum of Man, Mercury Series, Archaeological Survey Paper* 53. Ottawa.

Mitchell, Barry M.
1966   Preliminary Report on a Woodland Site Near Deep River, Ontario. *National Museum of Canada Anthropology Paper* 11. Ottawa.

Mitchell, Donald H.
1969   Excavations at Three Sites on the Chilcotin Plateau. (Unpublished report to the Archaeological Sites Advisory Board of British Columbia, Victoria, and to the National Museum of Man, Ottawa.)

1970   Archaeological Investigations on the Chilcotin Plateau, 1968. *Syesis* 3(1-2):45-65.

Moltke, Gertrude von *see* Anahareo

Moody, Harry
1957   Birch Bark Biting. *The Beaver* 287(Spring):9-11.

Mooney, James
1896   The Ghost-dance Religion and the Sioux Outbreak of 1890. Pp. 641-1136 in Pt. 1 of *14th Annual Report of the Bureau of American Ethnology for the Years 1892-1893.* 2 Pts. Washington.

1907   Attikamegue. P. 116 in Vol. 1 of Handbook of American Indians North of Mexico. Frederick W. Hodge, ed. 2 vols. *Bureau of American Ethnology Bulletin* 30. Washington.

1907a   The Cheyenne Indians. *Memoirs of the American Anthropological Association* 1(6):357-442. Lancaster, Pa.

1907b   Maskegon. Pp. 813-814 in Vol. 1 of Handbook of American Indians North of Mexico. Frederick W. Hodge, ed. 2 vols. *Bureau of American Ethnology Bulletin* 30. Washington.

1910   Têtes de Boule. Pp. 735-736 in Vol. 2 of Handbook of American Indians North of Mexico. Frederick W. Hodge, ed. 2 vols. *Bureau of American Ethnology Bulletin* 30. Washington.

1928   The Aboriginal Population of America North of Mexico. *Smithsonian Miscellaneous Collections* 80(7). Washington.

Mooney, James, and Cyrus Thomas
1907   Cree. Pp. 359-362 in Vol. 1 of Handbook of American Indians North of Mexico. Frederick W. Hodge, ed. 2 vols. *Bureau of American Ethnology Bulletin* 30. Washington.

1907a   Monsoni. P. 932 in Vol. 1 of Handbook of American Indians North of Mexico. Frederick W. Hodge, ed. 2 vols. *Bureau of American Ethnology Bulletin* 30. Washington.

Moore, J. Bernard
1968   Skagway in Days Primeval. New York: Vantage Press.

Morantz, Toby
1976   L'Organisation sociale des Cris de Rupert House, 1820-1840: Quelques exemples de l'utilité des études ethnohistoriques. Daniel Chevrier and Claude Chapdelaine, trans. *Recherches Amérindiennes au Québec* 6(2):56-64. Montreal.

1977   James Bay Trading Captains of the Eighteenth Century: New Perspectives on Algonquian Social Organization. Pp. 77-89 in *Papers of the Eighth Algonquian Conference, 1976.* William Cowan, ed. Ottawa: Carleton University.

1978   The Probability of Family Hunting Territories in Eighteenth Century James Bay: Old Evidence Newly Presented. Pp. 224-236 in *Papers of the Ninth Algonquian Conference.* William Cowan, ed. Ottawa: Carleton University.

1980   The Fur Trade and the Cree of James Bay. Pp. 39-58 in Old Trails and New Directions: Papers of the Third North American Fur Trade Conference. Carol M. Judd and Arthur J. Ray, eds. Toronto: University of Toronto Press.

1980a   The Impact of the Fur Trade on Eighteenth and Nineteenth Century Algonquian Social Organization: An Ethnographic-ethnohistoric Study of the Eastern James Bay Cree from 1700-1850. (Unpublished Ph.D. Dissertation in Anthropology, University of Toronto, Toronto.)

Morgan, Lewis H.
1871   Systems of Consanguinity and Affinity of the Human Family. *Smithsonian Contributions to Knowledge* 17. Washington.

Morgan, Murray C.
1967   One Man's Gold Rush: A Klondike Album. Seattle: University of Washington Press.

Morice, Adrien G.
1890   The Western Dénés: Their Manners and Customs. Pp. 109-174 in Proceedings of the Canadian Institute for 1888-1889, ser. 3, 7. Toronto.

1893   Are the Carrier Sociology and Mythology Indigenous or Exotic? Pp. 109-126 in *Proceedings and Transactions of the Royal Society of Canada for the Year 1892,* ser. 1, sect. 2, Vol. 10. Ottawa.

1895   Notes Archaeological, Industrial, and Sociological on the Western Dénés with an Ethnographical Sketch of the Same. *Transactions of the Canadian Institute* 4:1-222. Toronto.

1903   The Nah-ane and Their Language. *Transactions of the Canadian Institute* 7:517-534. Toronto.

1905   The History of the Northern Interior of British Columbia (Formerly New Caledonia), 1660-1880. 3d ed. Toronto: William Briggs.

1906-1907   La Femme chez les Dénés. Pp. 362-394 in Vol. 1 of *Proceedings of the 15th International Congress of Americanists.* 2 vols. Quebec, 1906.

1906-1910   The Great Déné Race. *Anthropos* 1:229-277, 483-508, 695-730; 2:1-34, 181-196; 4:582-606; 5:113-142, 419-443, 643-653, 969-990.

1910   History of the Catholic Church in Western Canada, from

Lake Superior to the Pacific (1659-1895). 2 vols. Toronto: The Musson Book Company.

1932   The Carrier Language (Déné Family): A Grammar and Dictionary Combined. 2 vols. St. Gabriel-Mödling, Austria: Verlag der Internationalen Zeitschrift "Anthropos."

Morlan, Richard E.
1967   Siruk House 1, Alatna River, Alaska: The Mammalian Fauna. (Unpublished manuscript at the University of Wisconsin, Madison.)

1969   Recent Excavations at the Klo-kut Site, Northern Yukon Territory. (Paper presented at the 34th Annual Meeting of the Society for American Archaeology, Milwaukee.)

1970   Toward the Definition of a Prehistoric Athabaskan Culture. *Bulletin of the Canadian Archaeological Association* 2:24-33. Ottawa.

1970a   Symposium on Northern Athabaskan Prehistory: Introductory Remarks. *Bulletin of the Canadian Archaeological Association* 2:1-2. Ottawa.

1971   The Later Prehistory of the Middle Porcupine Drainage, Northern Yukon Territory. (Unpublished Ph.D. Dissertation in Anthropology, University of Wisconsin, Madison.)

1972   NbVk-1: An Historic Fishing Camp in Old Crow Flats, Northern Yukon. *Canada. National Museum of Man, Mercury Series, Archaeological Survey Paper* 5. Ottawa.

1972a   The Cadzow Lake Site (MjVi-1): A Multicomponent Historic Kutchin Camp. *Canada. National Museum of Man, Mercury Series, Archaeological Survey Paper* 3. Ottawa.

1973   The Later Prehistory of the Middle Porcupine Drainage, Northern Yukon Territory. *Canada. National Museum of Man, Mercury Series, Archaeological Survey Paper* 11. Ottawa.

Morris, J.L.
1943   Indians of Ontario. Toronto: Department of Lands and Forests. (Reprinted in 1964.)

Morris, Margaret W.
1972   Great Bear Lake Indians: A Historical Demography and Human Ecology, Pt. 1: The Situation Prior to European Contact. *The Musk-Ox* 11:3-27. Saskatoon, Sask.

1973   Great Bear Lake Indians: A Historical Demography and Human Ecology, Pt. 2: The Situation after European Contact. *The Musk-Ox* 12:58-80. Saskatoon, Sask.

Morrison, David R.
1968   The Politics of the Yukon Territory: 1898-1909. Toronto: University of Toronto Press.

Morse, Edward S.
1885   Ancient and Modern Methods of Arrow-release. *Bulletin of the Essex Institute* 17(10-12):145-198. Salem, Mass.

Morton, Arthur S.
1973   A History of the Canadian West to 1870-71: Being a History of Rupert's Land (the Hudson Bay Company's Territory) and of the North-West Territory (Including the Pacific Slope). Lewis G. Thomas, ed. 2d ed. Toronto: University of Toronto Press.

Morton, W.L.
1972   Métis. Pp. 53-56 in Vol. 7 of Encyclopedia Canadiana. 10 vols. Toronto, Ottawa, Montreal: Grolier of Canada.

Mueller, Richard J.
1964   A Short Illustrated Topical Dictionary of Western Kutchin. Fairbanks: Summer Institute of Linguistics.

Müller-Wille, Ludger
1974   Caribou Never Die! Modern Caribou Hunting Economy of the Dene (Chipewyan) of Fond du Lac, Saskatchewan and N.W.T. *The Musk-Ox* 14:7-19. Saskatoon, Sask.

Muir, John
1917   Travels in Alaska. Boston: Houghton, Mifflin.

Mulloy, William
1958   A Preliminary Historical Outline for the Northwestern Plains. *University of Wyoming Publications* 22(1). Laramie.

Murdoch, John
1888   Dr. Rink's "Eskimo Tribes." *American Anthropologist* 1(2):125-133.

Murdoch, John S.
1972   A New Direction. (Paper presented at the Annual Meeting of the Society for Applied Anthropology, Montreal.)

Murdock, George P.
1949   Social Structure. New York: Macmillan.

1965   Culture and Society: Twenty-four Essays. Pittsburgh: University of Pittsburgh Press.

Murdock, George P., and Timothy J. O'Leary
1975   Ethnographic Bibliography of North America. 4th ed. 5 vols. New Haven, Conn.: Human Relations Area Files Press.

Murie, Olaus Johan
1935   Alaska-Yukon Caribou. (*U.S. Bureau of Biological Survey, North American Fauna 54*) Washington: U.S. Government Printing Office.

Murphy, Robert F., and Julian H. Steward
1956   Tappers and Trappers: Parallel Process in Acculturation. *Economic Development and Cultural Change* 4(4):335-355.

Murray, Alexander H.
1847-1850   [Fort Yukon Journal.] (Manuscripts B.240/a/1, B.240/a/2, and B.240/a/3 in Hudson's Bay Company Archives, Provincial Archives of Manitoba, Winnipeg, Canada.)

1910   Journal of the Yukon, 1847-48. J.J. Burpee, ed. *Publications of the Public Archives of Canada* 4. Ottawa.

Myatt, Joseph
1716-1719   [Fort Albany Post Journal, May-June, 1716, 1717, 1718, and 1719.] (Manuscript B.3/a/9 in Hudson's Bay Company Archives, Provincial Archives of Manitoba, Winnipeg, Canada.)

NYCD = O'Callaghan, Edmund B., ed.
1853-1887   Documents Relative to the Colonial History of the State of New York; Procured in Holland, England and France, by John R. Brodhead. 15 vols. Albany: Weed, Parsons.

Nadeau, Eugène
1954   Sapier, prêtre de misère: Le père François-Xavier Fafard, O.M.I. (1856-1946). Montreal: Editions Oblates.

Naedzo, J.
1971   [Taped Account. V. Thomas, trans.] (Manuscript in June Helm's ethnographic fieldnotes on Rae, N.W.T.)

Naish, Constance M., and Gillian L. Story
1963   English-Tlingit Dictionary: Nouns. Fairbanks: Summer Institute of Linguistics.

Nash, Ronald J.
1969   The Arctic Small Tool Tradition in Manitoba. *University of Manitoba, Department of Anthropology Occasional Paper* 2. Winnipeg.

1970   The Prehistory of Northern Manitoba. Pp. 77-92 in Ten Thousand Years: Archaeology in Manitoba. Walter M. Hlady, ed. Altona: Manitoba Archaeological Society.

1975   Archaeological Investigations in the Transitional Forest Zone: Northern Manitoba, Southern Keewatin, N.W.T. Winnipeg: Manitoba Museum of Man and Nature.

Nelson, Edward W.
1880   [Tinné Tribes of Alaska; Information Mainly from Anvik Indians, with Some Information from Yukon Indians and

Kolchan Indians of Innoko River.] (Manuscript No. 2109 in National Anthropological Archives, Smithsonian Institution, Washington.)

1978　　E.W. Nelson's Notes on the Indians of the Yukon and Innoko Rivers, Alaska. James W. VanStone, ed. *Fieldiana: Anthropology* 70. Chicago.

Nelson, Nels C.
1935　　Early Migration of Man to America. *Natural History* 35(4):356.

1937　　Notes on Cultural Relations Between Asia and America. *American Antiquity* 2(4):267-272.

Nelson, Richard K.
1973　　Hunters of the Northern Forest: Designs for Survival Among the Alaskan Kutchin. Chicago: University of Chicago Press.

Nero, Robert W.
1959　　An Agate Basin Point Site in Saskatchewan. *The Blue Jay* 17(1):32-41. Regina, Sask.

Nero, Robert W., and Bruce A. McCorquodale
1958　　Report of an Excavation at the Oxbow Dam Site. *The Blue Jay* 16(2):82-90. Regina, Sask.

Nichols, H.
1971　　Summary of the Palynological Evidence for Late Quaternary Vegetational and Climatic Change in the Central and Eastern Canadian Arctic. (Paper presented at a Symposium on Climatic Change in Arctic Areas Over the Past 10,000 Years, Oulu, Finland.)

Nichols, John D., ed.
1973　　Ojibwe-ikidowinan/Ojibwe Words: A Brief Ojibwe-English Word List. (*Papers in Indian Studies 1*) Bemidji, Minn.: Bemidji State College, Area of Indian Studies.

1975　　Northwestern Ontario Dialect Survey Research Report. (Paper read at 7th Algonkian Conference, Niagara-on-the-Lake, Ont.)

Nichols, John D., and Earl Nyholm, eds.
1979　　Ojibewewi ikidowinan: An Ojibwe Word Resource Book. St. Paul: Minnesota Archaeological Society.

Nicks, Trudy
1980　　The Iroquois and the Fur Trade in Western Canada. Pp. 85-101 in Old Trails and New Directions. Carol M. Judd and Arthur J. Ray, eds. Toronto: University of Toronto Press.

[Nicolas, Louis]
1930　　Les Raretés des Indes, "Codex Canadiensis" [1678] . . . Paris: Librairie Maurice Chamonal. (Facsimile of a Manuscript, now Granville 1701 in Thomas Gilcrease Institute of American History and Art, Tulsa. Formerly Attributed to Charles Bécard de Granville. For the attribution to Nicolas see Sioui 1979 and Gagnon 1979.)

Noble, William C.
[1966-1969] Archaeological Sites in the Central Northwest Territories, 1966-69. (Manuscript in Noble's possession and in Archaeological Division, National Museum of Man, Ottawa.)

1969　　The Acasta Lake Site, N.W.T., Canada. P. 35 in Abstracts of Papers of the 34th Annual Meeting of the Society for American Archaeology. Milwaukee.

1971　　Archaeological Surveys and Sequences in Central District of MacKenzie, N.W.T. *Arctic Anthropology* 8(1):102-135.

1973　　Canada. Pp. 49-83 in The Development of North American Archeology. James Fitting, ed. Garden City, N.Y.: Anchor Press/Doubleday.

1974　　The Tundra-Taiga Ecotone: Contributions from the Great Slave-Great Bear Lake Region. Pp. 153-171 in 5th International Conference on the Prehistory and Palaeoecology of Western North American Arctic and Subarctic. Scott Raymond and Peter Schledermann, eds. Calgary, Alta., 1972.

1975　　Applications of the Direct Historic Approach in Central District of Mackenzie, N.W.T. Pp. 759-797 in Vol. 2 of Proceedings: Northern Athapaskan Conference, 1971. A. McFadyen Clark, ed. 2 vols. *Canada. National Museum of Man, Mercury Series, Ethnology Service Paper* 27. Ottawa.

1977　　The Taltheilei Shale Tradition: An Update. Pp. 65-71 in Problems in the Prehistory of the North American Subarctic: The Athapaskan Question. J.W. Helmer, S. VanDyke, and F.J. Kense, eds. Calgary: University of Calgary, Archaeological Association.

Noble, William C., and James E. Anderson
1972　　Contributions to Central Northern Athapaskan Osteology and Burial Patterns. (Manuscript in possession of its authors.)

Nonas, Richard
1963　　The Ever-winking Eye: An Account of the Cree Indians of Attawapiskat, James Bay, and the Limitations of Ethnographic Method. (Manuscript, microfilm, Wilson Library, University of North Carolina, Chapel Hill.)

Nordenskjöld, Otto, and Ludwig Mecking
1928　　The Geography of the Polar Regions. 2 Pts. (*American Geographical Society Special Publication 8*) New York: American Geographical Society.

North, Robert C.
1929　　Bob North with Dog Team and Indians. New York: G.P. Putnam's Sons.

OMI = Oblats de Marie Immaculée
1882　　Schedule for Taking Census of Indians at Fort Raë. (Manuscript at St. Michael's Mission, Rae, N.W.T.)

1927-1965　[Registre de Sépultures, Fort Norman.] (Manuscript of various authorship by Oblate priests, at St. Thérèse Mission, Fort Norman, N.W.T.)

Ogden, Peter S.
1961　　Snake Country Journal, 1826-27. K.G. Davies and A.M. Johnson, eds. (Publications of the Hudson's Bay Record Society 23) London: The Hudson's Bay Record Society.

Ogilvie, William
1894-1895　Diary of 1894-95. (Manuscript No. 36 in the Public Archives of Canada, Ottawa.)

1898　　Extracts from the Report of an Exploration Made in 1896-1897. Pp. 385-423 in The Yukon Territory. F. Mortimer Trimmer, ed. London: Downey.

1898a　　The Klondike Official Guide; Canada's Great Gold Field, the Yukon District, with Regulations Governing Placer Mining. Toronto: Hunter, Rose.

1913　　Early Days on the Yukon and the Story of Its Gold Finds. London and New York: John Lane.

Oldmixon, John
1741　　The British Empire in America, Containing the History of the Discovery, Settlement, Progress, and State of the British Colonies on the Continent and Islands of America... 2d ed. 2 vols. London: Printed for J. Brotherton, J. Clarke (etc.).

1931　　The History of Hudson's-Bay Containing an Account of Its Discovery and Settlement, the Progress of It, and the Present State of the Indians, Trade, and Everything Else Relating to It: Being the Last Chapter of Vol. 1 of The British Empire in America (London, 1708). Pp. 371-410 in Documents Relating to the Early History of Hudson Bay. J.B. Tyrrell, ed. Toronto: The Champlain Society.

Olson, Ronald L.
1967　　Social Structure and Social Life of the Tlingit in Alaska. *University of California Anthropological Records* 26. Berkeley.

Olson, Wallace M.
1968　　Minto, Alaska: Cultural and Historical Influences on Group

Identity. (Unpublished M.A. Thesis in Anthropology, University of Alaska, College.)

O'Neil, Marion
1928   The Peace River Journal, 1799-1800. *Washington Historical Quarterly* 19(4):250-270. Seattle.

Orchard, William G.
1929   Beads and Beadwork of the North American Indians. *Contributions from the Museum of the American Indian, Heye Foundation* 11. New York.

Orenstein, Toby E.
1973   The First Peoples in Quebec: A Reference Work on the History, Environment, Economic and Legal Position of the Indians and Inuit of Quebec. G. William Craig, ed. 3 vols. Montreal: Thunderbird Press.

Orth, Donald J.
1967   Dictionary of Alaska Place Names. *U.S. Geological Survey Professional Paper* 567. Washington.

Osborne, Carolyn M., Kristyn Appleby, and Pat Kershner
1977   A Technical Analysis of Three Forms of Sub-Arctic Snowshoes. *Arctic Anthropology* 14(2):41-78.

Osborne, Douglas, Warren W. Caldwell, and Robert H. Crabtree
1956   The Problem of Northwest Coastal-interior Relationships as Seen from Seattle. *American Antiquity* 22(2):117-128.

Osgood, Cornelius
1932   The Ethnography of the Great Bear Lake Indians. Pp. 31-97 in *Annual Report for 1931, National Museum of Canada Bulletin* 70. Ottawa.

_____
1933   Tanaina Culture. *American Anthropologist* 35(4):695-717.

_____
1934   Kutchin Tribal Distribution and Synonymy. *American Anthropologist* 36(2):168-179.

_____
1936   The Distribution of the Northern Athapaskan Indians. *Yale University Publications in Anthropology* 7:3-23. New Haven, Conn.

_____
1936a   Contributions to the Ethnography of the Kutchin. *Yale University Publications in Anthropology* 14. New Haven, Conn.

_____
1937   The Ethnography of the Tanaina. *Yale University Publications in Anthropology* 16. New Haven, Conn.

_____
1940   Ingalik Material Culture. *Yale University Publications in Anthropology* 22. New Haven, Conn. (Reprinted: Human Relations Area Files Press, New Haven, Conn., 1970.)

_____
1953   Winter. New York: W.W. Norton.

_____
1958   Ingalik Social Culture. *Yale University Publications in Anthropology* 53. New Haven, Conn.

_____
1959   Ingalik Mental Culture. *Yale University Publications in Anthropology* 56. New Haven, Conn.

_____
1971   The Han Indians: A Compilation of Ethnographic and Historical Data on the Alaska-Yukon Boundary Area. *Yale University Publications in Anthropology* 74. New Haven, Conn.

_____
1975   An Ethnographical Map of Great Bear Lake. Pp. 516-544 in Vol. 2 of Proceedings: Northern Athapaskan Conference, 1971. A. McFadyen Clark, ed. 2 vols. *Canada. National Museum of Man, Mercury Series, Ethnology Service Paper* 27. Ottawa.

_____
1975a   Athapaskan? Pp. 12-16 in Vol. 1 of Proceedings: Northern Athapaskan Conference, 1971. A. McFadyen Clark, ed. 2 vols. *Canada. National Museum of Man, Mercury Series, Ethnology Service Paper* 27. Ottawa.

Oswald, Edward, and J.P. Senyk
1976   Ecoregions of Yukon Territory. Map. Victoria, B.C.: Pacific Forest Research Centre, Department of Environment.

Oswalt, Wendell
1955   Alaskan Pottery: A Classification and Historical Reconstruction. *American Antiquity* 21(1):32-43.

_____, ed.
1960   Eskimos and Indians of Western Alaska, 1861-1868: Extracts from the Diary of Father Illarion. *Anthropological Papers of the University of Alaska* 8(2):101-118. College.

_____
1962   Historical Populations in Western Alaska and Migration Theory. *Anthropological Papers of the University of Alaska* 11(1):1-14. College.

_____
1963   Mission of Change in Alaska: Eskimos and Moravians on the Kuskokwim. San Marino, Calif.: Huntington Library.

_____
1967   Alaskan Eskimos. San Francisco: Chandler Publishing Company.

_____
1967a   Alaska Commercial Company Records, 1868-1911. College: University of Alaska Library.

_____
1973   This Land Was Theirs: A Study of the North American Indian. 2d ed. New York: John Wiley.

Otto, Rudolf
1959   The Idea of the Holy: An Inquiry into the Non-rational Factor in the Idea of the Divine and Its Relation to the Rational [1917]. John W. Harvey, trans. Harmondsworth, England: Penguin Books.

Packard, Alpheus S.
1885   Notes on the Labrador Eskimo and Their Former Range Southward. *American Naturalist* 19(May):471-481; (June):553-560.

Palgrave, Francis M.T.
1902   A Grammar and Dictionary of the Language Spoken by the Tahl Tans on the Stikine River, British Columbia, a Tribe Belonging to the Tinne Branch of North American Indians. (Manuscript in possession of William P. Thorman, Telegraph Creek, B.C.; partial copy in British Columbia Provincial Archives, Victoria.)

Parker, Gerald R.
1972   Total Numbers, Mortality, Recruitment, and Seasonal Distribution. Pt. 1 of Biology of the Kaminuriak Population of Barren-ground Caribou. *Canadian Wildlife Service Report Series* 20. Ottawa.

Parker, Seymour
1960   The Wiitiko Psychosis in the Context of Ojibwa Personality and Culture. *American Anthropologist* 62(4):603-623.

Parnell, C.
1942   Campbell of the Yukon, Pt. 1. *The Beaver* 273(June):4-6.

Parr, Richard T.
1974   A Bibliography of the Athapaskan Languages. *Canada. National Museum of Man, Mercury Series, Ethnology Service Paper* 14. Ottawa.

Parsons, Elsie Clews
1921-1922   A Narrative of the Ten'a of Anvik, Alaska. *Anthropos* 16-17:51-71.

Patterson, E. Palmer, II
1972   The Canadian Indian: A History Since 1500. Don Mills, Ont.: Collier-Macmillan of Canada.

Patterson, Raymond M.
1968   Finlay's River. New York: William Morrow.

Patty, Stanton H.
1971   A Conference with the Tanana Chiefs: A Memorable Gathering at Fairbanks in the Summer of 1915. *Alaska Journal* 1(2):2-18.

Paul, Gaither, and Ronald Scollon
1980   Stories for My Grandchildren. Told by Gaither Paul; Ron Scollon, ed. Fairbanks: University of Alaska, Native Language Center.

Paul-Emile
1952   Amiskwaski, la terre du castor. (La Baie James, trois cents ans d'histoire militaire, économique, missionnaire.) Ottawa: Editions de l'Université d'Ottawa.

Pearson, Roger
1971   Settlement Patterns and Subarctic Development: The South Mackenzie, N.W.T. Pp. 255-270 in Pilot Not Commander: Essays in Memory of Diamond Jenness. Pat Lotz and Jim Lotz, eds. Anthropologica n.s. 13(1-2). Ottawa.

Peers, Augustus R.
1847-1853   Journals of Augustus R. Peers, 1847-1853. (Manuscript MG19/D12 in Public Archives of Canada, Ottawa.)

Penard, Jean Marie
1938   Grammaire montagnaise. Le Pas, Man.: no publisher.

Pendergast, James F.
1966   Three Prehistoric Iroquois Components in Eastern Ontario: The Salem, Grays Creek, and Beckstead Sites. Anthropological Series 73, National Museum of Canada Bulletin 208. Ottawa.

Pendleton, George
[1840-1915]   [Notes on MacKenzie River District Posts.] (Unpublished manuscript in File "Posts, Miscellaneous No. 2," Fur Trade Department, Hudson's Bay Company Archives, Provincial Archives of Manitoba, Winnipeg, Canada.)

Pentland, David H.
1970-1979   [Fieldnotes on Cree Dialects of Ontario, Manitoba, Saskatchewan, Alberta, and North Dakota.] (Manuscript in Pentland's possession.)

————   1978   A Historical Overview of Cree Dialects. Pp. 104-126 in Papers of the Ninth Algonquian Conference. William Cowan, ed. Ottawa: Carleton University.

————   1979   Algonquian Historical Phonology. (Unpublished Ph.D. Dissertation in Anthropology, University of Toronto, Toronto.)

Pepin, Pierre-Ives
1957   Les Trois réserves indiennes du Haut Saint-Maurice: Ouémontachingue, Obidjiouane, Manouane. Revue Canadienne de Géographie 11(1):61-71. Montreal.

Perron, Joseph
1904   Canotlé Rannaga Kelekak: Délochét Roka. Winnipeg: Free Press.

Peter, Katherine, ed.
1974   Sapir John Haa Googwandak. [Sapir-Fredson Stories] 3 vols. College: University of Alaska, Native Language Center.

————   1974a   Dinjie Zhuu Gwandak: Gwich'in Stories. Anchorage: Alaska State Operated Schools. (Reprinted: Dissemination and Assessment Center for Bilingual Education, Austin, 1976.)

————, comp.   1979   Gwich'in, Junior Dictionary [Dinjii' Zhuh Ginjik Nagwan Tr'i ł tsąįį]. Anchorage: University of Alaska, National Bilingual Materials Development Center.

————   1979a   Elders Speak. Anchorage: University of Alaska, National Bilingual Materials Development Center.

Peter, Tom
1973   The Bear Husband. Nora Florendo, ed. and trans. Fairbanks: University of Alaska, Tlingit Readers and the Alaska Native Language Center.

Peters, William J., and Alfred H. Brooks
1899   Report of the White River-Tanana Expedition. Pp. 64-75 in Maps and Descriptions of Routes of Exploration in Alaska in 1898. 55th Congress, 3d sess., Senate Executive Doc. No. 172. (Serial No. 3737) Washington: U.S. Government Printing Office.

Petersen, Karen Daniels
1963   Chippewa Mat-weaving Techniques. Anthropological Papers 67, Bureau of American Ethnology Bulletin 186:211-285. Washington.

Peterson, Randolph L.
1955   North American Moose. Toronto: University of Toronto Press.

————   1966   The Mammals of Eastern Canada. Toronto: Oxford University Press.

Petitot, Emile
1865   Chippewyan Vocabulary, and Notes: An Account of the Montagnais or Chippewyan Tribe, Their Habitat, and Division into Nations and Tribes. (Manuscript No. 172 in National Anthropological Archives, Smithsonian Institution, Washington.)

————   [1867-1920]   Noms des Indiens du Grand Lac d'Ours, de Fort Norman, T'u-Ce-itta, et d'autres localités, appartenant aux deux missions Ste. Thérèse. (Started by Petitot and added to by later priests. Manuscript, copy in Archives Historiques Oblates, Ottawa.)

————   1868   Etude sur la nation montagnaise. Mission des Missionnaires Oblats de Marie Immaculée 7:484-499. Paris. (Reprinted: Pp. 41-47 in Annales de la Propagation de la Foi pour les Provinces de Québec et Montréal, Montreal, 1871.)

————   1869   Journal du R.P. Petitot, Grand Lac d'Ours, 30 juin 1867. Missions des Missionnaires Oblats de Marie Immaculée 8:286-316. Paris

————   1869a   [Comparative Vocabulary of Chipewyan, Hare, Kutchin and Eskimo. Fort Norman-Franklin-Great Bear Lake, Jan. 11, 1869.] (Manuscript No. 221 in National Anthropological Archives, Smithsonian Institution, Washington.)

————   1875   Géographie de l'Athabaskaw-Mackenzie et des grands lacs du bassin arctique. Bulletin de la Société de Géographie ser. 6, Vol. 10:5-42, 126-183, 242-290. Paris.

————   1876   Dictionnaire de la langue Dènè-Dindjié, dialectes Montagnais ou Chippewyan, Peaux de Lièvre et Loucheux, etc. Paris: E. Leroux; San Francisco: A.L. Bancroft.

————   1876a   Monographie des Dènè-Dindjié. Paris: E. Leroux.

————   1878   Monograph of the Dènè-Dindjié Indians. Douglas Brymner, trans. (Manuscript, copy in the Public Archives of Canada, Ottawa.)

————   1883   On the Athabasca District of the Canadian North-West Territory. Proceedings of the Royal Geographical Society 5(11):633-655. London.

————   1884-1885   On the Athabasca District of the Canadian North-west Territory. Canadian Record of Science 1:27-53. Montreal. (Reprinted from Proceedings of the Royal Geographical Society, November 1883)

————   1886   Traditions indiennes du Canada nord-ouest. (Les Littératures populaires de toutes les nations 23) Paris: Maisonneuve frères et C. Leclerc.

————   1887   Traditions indiennes du Canada nord-ouest. Société Philologique Actes 16-17:169-614. Alençon, France.

————   1888   Traditions indiennes du Canada Nord-ouest (Textes originaux et traduction littérale). Alençon, France: E. Renaut de Broise.

1888a   En Route pour la mer glaciale. 2d. ed. Paris: Letouzey et Ané.

1889   Quinze ans sous le cercle polaire: Mackenzie. Paris: E. Dentu.

1891   Autour du Grand Lac des Esclaves. Paris: A. Savine.

1893   Exploration de la région du Grand Lac des Ours (fin de quinze ans sous le cercle polaire). Paris: Téqui.

1899   De Carlton-House au Fort Pitt, Saskatchewan. *Bulletin de la Société Neuchâteloise de Géographie* 11:176-195. Neuchâtel, Switzerland.

Pettipas, Leo
1970   Early Man in Manitoba. Pp. 5-28 in Ten Thousand Years: Archaeology in Manitoba. Walter M. Hlady, ed. Altona: Manitoba Archaeological Society.

Pettipas, Leo, and John Bissett
1976   A Review of the Archaeology of Northern Manitoba. (Unpublished manuscript in Manitoba Department of Tourism, Recreation and Cultural Affairs, Historic Resources Branch, Winnipeg.)

Petroff, Ivan
1884   Report on the Population, Industries, and Resources of Alaska. 10th Census, 1880. Washington: U.S. Government Printing Office.

1900   The Population and Resources of Alaska, 1880. Pp. 55-284 in Compilation of Narratives of Explorations in Alaska. Washington: U.S. Government Printing Office.

Péwé, Troy L.
1966   Permafrost and Its Effect on Life in the North. Corvallis: Oregon State University Press.

Phillips, R.A.J.
1967   Canada's North. New York: St. Martin's Press.

Piché, Victor
1977   Migration chez la population indienne de la Baie James: Une étude de cas. *Anthropologica* n.s. 19(2):153-167. Ottawa.

Piddington, Ralph
1950-1957   An Introduction to Social Anthropology. 2 vols. Edinburgh: Oliver and Boyd.

Pierronet, Thomas
1800   Specimen of the Mountaineer, or Sheshatapooshshoish, Scoffie, and Micmac Languages. *Collections of the Massachusetts Historical Society*, ser. 1, Vol. 6:16-33. Boston.

Piggott, Glyne L.
1978   Algonquin and Other Ojibwa Dialects: A Preliminary Report. Pp. 160-187 in *Papers of the Ninth Algonquian Conference*. William Cowan, ed. Ottawa: Carleton University.

Piggott, Glyne L., and Jonathan Kaye
1973   Odawa Language Project: Second Report. Toronto: University of Toronto.

Pike, Warburton M.
1892   The Barren Ground of Northern Canada. London and New York: Macmillan.

Pilling, James C.
1891   Bibliography of the Algonquian Languages. *Bureau of American Ethnology Bulletin* 13. Washington.

1892   Bibliography of the Athapascan Languages. *Bureau of American Ethnology Bulletin* 14. Washington.

Pinnow, Heinz-Jürgen
1976   Geschichte der Na-Dene Forschung. *Indiana* suppl. 5. Berlin.

Pitts, Roger S.
1972   The Changing Settlement Patterns and Housing Types of the Upper Tanana Indians. (Unpublished M.A. Thesis in Anthropology, University of Alaska, College.)

Plaskett, David C.
1977   The Nenana River Gorge Site: A Late Prehistoric Athapaskan Campsite in Central Alaska. (Unpublished M.A. Thesis in Anthropology, University of Alaska, Fairbanks.)

Pohorecky, Zenon S., and T.E.H. Jones
1967   Aboriginal Pictographs on Kipahigan Lake in the Precambrian Shield of Saskatchewan and Manitoba. *The Musk-Ox* 2:3-36. Saskatoon, Sask.

Pollock, John W.
1975   Algonquian Culture Development and Archaeological Sequences In Northeastern Ontario. *Bulletin of the Canadian Archaeological Association* 7:1-53. Ottawa.

Pond, Peter
1931   Peter Pond, Fur Trader and Adventurer. H.A. Innis, ed. Toronto: Macmillan.

Pope, Frank L.
1865   Report of the Exploration from Quesnel to Lake Tatla via Natla and Nakosla. (Manuscript No. 1682(2) in National Anthropological Archives, Smithsonian Institution, Washington.)

1866   Report of the British Columbia and Stekine Exploring Expedition. (Manuscript No. 1682 (3) in National Anthropological Archives, Smithsonian Institution, Washington.)

Porsild, Alf E.
1945   The Alpine Flora of the East Slope of Mackenzie Mountains, Northwest Territories. *Biological Series 27, National Museum of Canada Bulletin* 101. Ottawa.

Porter, James
1800-1801   [Slave Lake Journal, 1800-1801.] (Manuscript Series MG 19/C (1)/6, in Public Archives of Canada, Ottawa; Copy in Beryl C. Gillespie's possession.)

Portlock, Nathaniel
1789   A Voyage Round the World; But More Particularly to the North-west Coast of America: Performed in 1785, 1786, 1787, 1788 in the King George and Queen Charlotte. London: J. Stockdale and G. Goulding.

Pothier, Roger
1965   Relations inter-ethniques et acculturation à Mistassini. *Université Laval, Centre d'Etudes Nordiques, Travaux Divers* 9. Quebec.

1968   Community Complexity and Indian Isolation. Pp. 33-45 in Conflict in Culture: Problems of Developmental Change Among the Cree; Working Papers of the Cree Developmental Change Project. Norman A. Chance, ed. Ottawa: Saint Paul University, Canadian Research Centre for Anthropology.

Powell, Addison M.
1909   Trailing and Camping in Alaska. New York: A. Wessels.

Powell, John Wesley
1891   Indian Linguistic Families of America North of Mexico. Pp. 1-142 in *7th Annual Report of the Bureau of American Ethnology for the Years 1885-1886*. Washington.

Powers, William R.
1978   Dry Creek 1977. (Paper presented at the 5th Annual Alaska Anthropological Association Conference, Anchorage.)

Preble, Edward A.
1908   A Biological Investigation of the Athabasca-Mackenzie Region. (*North American Fauna 27*) Washington: U.S. Government Printing Office.

Preston, Richard J., III
[1963-1979]   [Ethnographic Notes, from Approximately 16 Months' Fieldwork Among the Eastern Cree, Quebec.] (Manuscripts in Preston's possession.)

1964   Ritual Hangings: An Aboriginal 'Survival' in a Northern North American Trapping Community. *Man* 64(180):142-144.

1966   The Conjuring House of the Eastern Cree. (Unpublished research report in National Museum of Man, Ottawa.)

1969   Eastern Cree Songs: The Expression of Personal Symbolism in the Use of Culture Patterns. (Unpublished paper prepared for the Northeastern Anthropological Association Meeting, Providence, R.I.)

1969a   Eastern Cree Attitudes Towards Hardship: Emotional Responses to the Contingencies of Bush Life. (Unpublished paper read at the Second Conference on Algonquian Studies, St. John's, Newf.)

1969-1972   Functional Politics in a Northern Indian Community. Pp. 169-178 in Vol. 3 of *Proceedings of the 38th International Congress of Americanists*, Stuttgart-München, 1968. 4 vols. München, Germany: Klaus Renner.

1970   The Relationships Between Human Persons and Food-animal Persons. (Unpublished paper prepared for the Third Conference on Algonquian Studies, Peterborough, Ont.)

1971   Eastern Cree Symbolism: The Use of Metaphor in the Expression of Beliefs. (Unpublished paper read at the 11th Meeting of the Northeastern Anthropological Association, Albany, N.Y.)

1971a   Cree Narration: An Expression of the Personal Meanings of Events. (Unpublished Ph.D. Dissertation in Anthropology, University of North Carolina, Chapel Hill.)

1971b   Problèmes humains reliés au développement de la Baie James. *Recherches Amérindiennes au Québec, Bulletin d'Information* 1(4-5):58-68. Montreal.

1974   The Means to Academic Success for Eastern Cree Students. Pp. 87-96 in Proceedings of the First Congress, Canadian Ethnology Society. Jerome H. Barkow, ed. *Canada. National Museum of Man, Mercury Series, Ethnology Service Paper* 17. Ottawa.

1975   Eastern Cree Community in Relation to Fur Trade Post in the 1830s: The Background of the Posting Process. Pp. 324-335 in Papers of the 6th Algonquian Conference, 1974. William Cowan, ed. *Canada. National Museum of Man, Mercury Series, Ethnology Service Paper* 23. Ottawa.

1975a   Belief in the Context of Rapid Change: An Eastern Cree Example. Pp. 117-129 in Symbols and Society: Essays on Belief Systems in Action. Carole E. Hill, ed. (*Southern Anthropological Proceedings* 9) Athens: University of Georgia Press.

1975b   Cree Narrative: Expressing the Personal Meanings of Events. *Canada. National Museum of Man, Mercury Series, Ethnology Service Paper* 30. Ottawa.

1975c   Symbolic Aspects of Eastern Cree Goose Hunting. Pp. 479-489 in Vol. 2 of Proceedings of the Second Congress, Canadian Ethnological Society. Jim Freedman and Jerome H. Barkow, eds. 2 vols *Canada. National Museum of Man, Mercury Series, Ethnology Service Paper* 28. Ottawa.

1976   Reticence and Self-expression: A Study of Style in Social Relationships. Pp. 450-494 in *Papers of the Seventh Algonquian Conference, 1975*. William Cowan, ed. Ottawa: Carleton University.

1977   Wiitiko: Algonquian Knowledge and Whiteman Interest. Pp. 101-106 in *Papers of the Eighth Algonquian Conference*. William Cowan, ed. Ottawa: Carleton University.

1978   La Relation sacrée entre les Cris et les oies. Françoy Raynauld, trans. *Recherches Amérindiennes au Québec* 8(2):147-152. Montreal.

1978a   Ethnographic Reconstruction of Witigo. Pp. 61-67 in *Papers of the Ninth Algonquian Conference*. William Cowan, ed. Ottawa: Carleton University.

1979   The Development of Self-control in the Eastern Cree Life Cycle. Pp. 83-96 in Childhood and Adolescence in Canada. K. Ishwaran, ed. Toronto: McGraw-Hill Ryerson.

1979a   The Cree Way Project: An Experiment in Grass-roots Curriculum Development. Pp. 92-101 in *Papers of the Tenth Algonquian Conference, 1978*. William Cowan, ed. Ottawa: Carleton University.

1980   Eastern Cree Notions of Social Grouping. Pp. 40-48 in *Papers of the Eleventh Algonquian Conference*. William Cowan, ed. Ottawa: Carleton University.

1980a   The Witigo: Algonkian Knowledge and Whiteman Knowledge. Pp. 111-131 in Manlike Monsters on Trial: Early Records and Modern Evidence. M. Halpin and M. Ames, eds. Vancouver: University of British Columbia Press.

Prevost, Jules L.
[1892] [Papers.] (Domestic and Foreign Missionary Society Papers, in Alaska Papers, 1884-1939, Box 48, The Church Historical Society, Austin, Tex.)

Pruitt, William O., Jr.
1967   Animals of the North. New York: Harper and Row.

1970   Some Ecological Aspects of Snow. Pp. 83-99 in Ecology of Subarctic Regions: Proceedings of the Helsinki Symposium, 1966. Paris: UNESCO.

Pullen, Hugh F.
1979   The Pullen Expedition in Search of Sir John Franklin: The Original Diaries, Log and Letters of Commander W.J.S. Pullen, Selected and Introduced by H.F. Pullen. Toronto: The Arctic History Press.

Quebec (Province)
1976   The James Bay and Northern Quebec Agreement... [Quebec]: Editeur Officiel du Quebec.

Quill, Norman
1965   The Moons of Winter and Other Stories. Charles Fiero, ed. and trans. Red Lake, Ont.: Northern Light Gospel Mission.

Quimby, George I.
1960   Indian Life in the Upper Great Lakes, 11,000 B.C. to A.D. 1800. Chicago: University of Chicago Press.

1960a   Habitat, Culture and Archaeology. Pp. 380-389 in Essays in the Science of Culture, in Honor of Leslie A. White in Celebration of His Sixtieth Birthday and His Thirtieth Year of Teaching at the University of Michigan. Gertrude E. Dole and Robert L. Carneiro, eds. New York: Thomas Y. Crowell.

1962   The Old Copper Culture and the Copper Eskimos, an Hypothesis. Pp. 76-79 in Prehistoric Cultural Relations Between the Arctic and Temperate Zones of North America. John M. Campbell, ed. *Arctic Institute of North America Technical Paper* 11. Montreal.

Radisson, Pierre E.
1961   The Explorations of Pierre Esprit Radisson, from the Original Manuscript in the Bodleian Library and the British Museum. Arthur T. Adams, ed. Minneapolis: Ross and Haines.

Radloff, Leopold
1858   Über die Sprache der Ugalachmut. *Bulletin de la Classe Historico-Philologique de l'Académie Impériale des Sciences* 15:25-37, 49-63, 125-139; *Mélanges Russes* 3:468-524. St. Petersburg.

1874   Leopold Radloffs Wörterbuch der Kinai-Sprache. A. Schiefner, ed. *Mémoires de l'Academie Impériale des Sciences de St. Pétersbourg*, 7th ser. Vol. 21(8). St. Petersburg.

Radojicic, D.
1969   Great Slave Lake-South Shore: An Area Economic Survey, 1967. G. Anders, ed. *Canada. Department of Indian Affairs and Northern Development, Industrial Division, Area Economic Surveys Report* 67/3. Ottawa.

Rae, George R.
1963   The Settlement of the Great Slave Lake Frontier, Northwest Territories, Canada: From the Eighteenth to the Twentieth Century. (Unpublished Ph.D. Dissertation in Anthropology, University of Michigan, Ann Arbor.)

Rae, John
1882   On the Conditions and Characteristics of Some of the Native Tribes of the Hudson's Bay Company Territories. *Journal of the Society of Arts* 30(1):483-499. London.

————
1953   Correspondence with the Hudson's Bay Company on Arctic Exploration, 1844-1855. (Publications of the Hudson's Bay Record Society 16) London: The Hudson's Bay Record Society.

Rainey, Froelich G.
1939   Archaeology in Central Alaska. *Anthropological Papers of the American Museum of Natural History* 36(4):351-405. New York.

————
1940   Archaeological Investigation in Central Alaska. *American Antiquity* 5(4):299-308.

————
1947   The Whale Hunters of Tigara. *Anthropological Papers of the American Museum of Natural History* 41(2). New York.

Ralph, Julian
1892   On Canada's Frontier: Sketches of History, Sport, and Adventure and of the Indians, Missionaries, Fur-traders, and Newer Settlers of Western Canada. New York: Harper.

Rand, Austin L.
1945   Mammals of the Yukon. *Biological Series 29, National Museum of Canada Bulletin* 100. Ottawa.

————
1945a   Mammal Investigations on the Canol Road, Yukon and Northwest Territories, 1944. *Biological Series 28, National Museum of Canada Bulletin* 99. Ottawa.

[Raudot, Antoine D.]
1904   Relation par lettres de l'Amérique septentrionale (années 1709 et 1710). Camille de Rochemonteix, ed. Paris: Letouzey et Ané.

Raup, Hugh M.
1946   Phytogeographic Studies in the Athabaska-Great Slave Lake Region, II. *Journal of the Arnold Arboretum, Harvard University* 27(1):1-85.

Ray, Arthur J.
1971   Indian Exploitation of the Forest-grassland Transition Zone in Western Canada, 1650-1860: A Geographical View of Two Centuries of Change. (Unpublished Ph.D. Dissertation in Geography, University of Wisconsin, Madison.)

————
1972   Indian Adaptations to the Forest-Grassland Boundary of Manitoba and Saskatchewan, 1650-1821: Some Implications for Inter-regional Migrations. *Canadian Geographer* 16(2):103-118.

————
1974   Indians in the Fur Trade: Their Role as Trappers, Hunters, and Middlemen in the Lands Southwest of Hudson Bay, 1660-1870. Toronto: University of Toronto Press.

————
1975   The Factor and the Trading Captain in the Hudson's Bay Company Fur Trade Before 1763. Pp. 586-602 in Vol. 2 of Proceedings of the Second Congress, Canadian Ethnological Society. Jim Freedman and Jerome H. Barkow, eds. 2 vols. *Canada. National Museum of Man, Mercury Series, Ethnology Service Paper* 28. Ottawa.

————
1975a   Some Conservation Schemes of the Hudson's Bay Company, 1821-50: An Examination of the Problems of Resource Management in the Fur Trade. *Journal of Historical Geography* 1(1):49-68.

Ray, Arthur J., and Donald B. Freeman
1978   "Give Us Good Measure:" An Economic Analysis of Relations Between the Indians and the Hudson's Bay Company Before 1763. Toronto: University of Toronto Press.

Ray, Charles K.
1959   A Program of Education for Alaskan Natives: A Research Report. Rev. ed. College: University of Alaska, Native Education Project.

Ray, Dorothy Jean
1964   [Review of] Napaskiak and Mission of Change in Alaska, by Wendell H. Oswalt. *The Beaver* 295 (Autumn):55.

————
1975   The Eskimos of Bering Strait, 1650-1898. Seattle: University of Washington Press.

Ray, Verne F.
1939   Cultural Relations in the Plateau of North-western America. (*Publications of the Frederick Webb Hodge Anniversary Publication Fund* 3) Los Angeles: The Southwest Museum.

————
1942   Culture Element Distributions, XXII: Plateau. *University of California Anthropological Records* 8(2). Berkeley.

Raymond, Charles [P.]
1900   Reconnoissance of the Yukon River, 1869. Pp. 19-41 in Compilation of Narratives of Explorations in Alaska. Washington: U.S. Government Printing Office.

Raymond, Charles W.
1870   Letter from Capt. C.W. Raymond, U.S.A. on the Youkon River and Tribes. Pp. 591-594 in *Annual Report of the U.S. Commissioner of Indian Affairs for the Year 1869*. Washington.

————
1871   Report of a Reconnaissance of the Yukon River, Alaska Territory July to September, 1869. *42d Congress, 1st sess., Senate Executive Doc. No.* 12. Washington: U.S. Government Printing Office.

————
1873   The Yukon River Region, Alaska. *Journal of the American Geographical Society* 3:158-192. New York.

Raymond, Marcel
1945   Notes ethnobotaniques sur les Tête-de-Boule de Manouan. *Contributions de l'Institut Botanique de l'Université de Montréal* 55:113-134. Montreal.

Rea, Kenneth J.
1968   The Political Economy of the Canadian North: An Interpretation of the Course of Development in the Northern Territories of Canada to the Early 1960s. Toronto: University of Toronto Press.

Reeves, Brian
1973   The Concept of an Altithermal Cultural Hiatus in Northern Plains Prehistory. *American Anthropologist* 75(5):1221-1253.

Reger, Douglas R.
1977   An Eskimo Site Near Kenai, Alaska. *Anthropological Papers of the University of Alaska* 18(2):37-52. Fairbanks.

————
1977a   Prehistory in the Upper Cook Inlet, Alaska. Pp. 16-21 in Prehistory of the North American Subarctic: The Athapaskan Question. J.W. Helmer, S. VanDyke, and F.J. Kense, eds. Calgary: no publisher.

Remington, Charles H. [Copper River Joe]
1939   Golden Cross (?) on Trails from the Valdez Glacier. Los Angeles: White-Thompson.

Renner, Louis L.
1975   Julius Jetté: Distinguished Scholar in Alaska; a Jesuit Priest and Accomplished Linguist on the Yukon. *The Alaska Journal* 5(4):239-247.

787

Rezanov, Nikolai Petrovich
1805   [Tanaina Vocabulary.] (Manuscript No. 118, in Fond Ade-
            lunga, Academy of Sciences, Leningrad.)

Rhodes, Richard A.
1976   A Preliminary Report on the Dialects of Eastern Ojibwa-
            Ottawa. Pp. 129-156 in *Papers of the Seventh Algonquian
            Conference, 1975.* William Cowan, ed. Ottawa: Carleton
            University.

———
1977   French Cree—A Case of Borrowing. Pp. 6-25 in *Papers of
            the Eighth Algonquian Conference.* William Cowan, ed. Ot-
            tawa: Carleton University.

Rhodes, William R., Lorraine Ruffing, Paul Alexander, and Michael Cox
1976   Special Joint Task Force Report on Alaskan Native Issues
            to the American Indian Policy Review Commission. Wash-
            ington: U.S. Government Printing Office.

Rice, Keren Dichter
1977   A Preliminary Grammar of Fort Good Hope Slave (Hare).
            Ottawa: Department of Indian Affairs and Northern Devel-
            opment.

———
1977a   The Continuants in Hare. *International Journal of American
            Linguistics* 43(4):315-326.

———
1978   Hare Dictionary. Ottawa: Department of Indian and North-
            ern Affairs, Northern Social Research Division.

Rich, Edwin E., ed.
1938   Posts and Districts. Pp. 413-427 (App. A.) in Journal of
            Occurrences in the Athabasca Department, by George Simp-
            son, 1820 and 21, and Report. Toronto: The Champlain So-
            ciety.

———, ed.
1945   Minutes of the Hudson's Bay Company 1679-1684: First Part,
            1679-82. (Publications of the Hudson's Bay Record Society
            8) London: The Hudson's Bay Record Society.

———, ed.
1957   Hudson's Bay Copy Booke of Letters, Commissions, Instruc-
            tions Outward, 1688-1696. (Publications of the Hudson's Bay
            Record Society 20) London: The Hudson's Bay Record So-
            ciety.

———
1967   The Fur Trade and the Northwest to 1857. Toronto: Mc-
            Clelland and Stewart.

Rich, Edwin E., and Alice M. Johnson, eds.
1951   Cumberland House Journals and Inland Journal, 1775-82:
            First Series, 1775-79. (Publications of the Hudson's Bay Rec-
            ord Society 14) London: The Hudson's Bay Record Society.

Richardson, Boyce
1972   James Bay: The Plot to Drown the North Woods. Toronto:
            Clarke, Irwin.

———
1975   Strangers Devour the Land: A Chronicle of the Assault upon
            the Last Coherent Hunting Culture in North America, the
            Cree Indians of Northern Quebec, and Their Vast Primeval
            Homelands. New York: Knopf, Distributed by Random
            House.

Richardson, Boyce, and Tony Lanzelo
1974   Cree Hunters and the Mistassini. Film, 16mm Color, Sound,
            58 Minutes. Toronto: National Film Board of Canada.

Richardson, Sir John
1851   Arctic Searching Expedition: A Journal of a Boat-voyage
            Through Rupert's Land and the Arctic Sea, in Search of the
            Discovery of Ships Under Command of Sir John Franklin
            with an Appendix on the Physical Geography of North
            America. 2 vols. London: Longman, Brown, Green, and
            Longmans.

———
1852   Arctic Searching Expedition: A Journal of a Boat-voyage
            Through Rupert's Land and the Arctic Sea. New York: Har-
            per.

Richardson, Murray
1968   Chipewyan Grammar. Cold Lake, Alta.: Northern Canada
            Evangelical Mission.

Ridge, Marian F., and Geraldine A. Cooke
1977   Yukon Bibliography Update to 1975. Edmonton: University
            of Alberta, Boreal Institute of Northern Studies.

Ridington, Robin
[1965-1972] [Fieldnotes and Texts on the Beaver.] (Manuscripts in Special
            Collections Library, University of British Columbia, Van-
            couver.)

———
1968   The Medicine Fight: An Instrument of Political Process
            Among the Beaver Indians. *American Anthropologist*
            70(6):1152-1160.

———
1968a   The Environmental Context of Beaver Indian Behavior.
            (Unpublished Ph.D. Dissertation in Anthropology, Harvard
            University, Cambridge, Mass.)

———
1969   Kin Categories versus Kin Groups: A Two-section System
            without Sections. *Ethnology* 8(4):460-467.

———
1969a   Culture and Creation. (Unpublished manuscript on Beaver
            Ecology in Special Collections Library, University of British
            Columbia, Vancouver.)

———
1971   Beaver Dreaming and Singing. Pp. 115-128 in Pilot Not Com-
            mander: Essays in Memory of Diamond Jenness. Pat Lotz
            and Jim Lotz, eds. *Anthropologica* n.s. 13(1-2):115-128. Ot-
            tawa.

———
1972   The Last Generation: A Book Length Ethnography of Bea-
            ver Indians Focusing on Meaning and Symbolism of Oral
            Tradition. (Unpublished manuscript in Ridington's posses-
            sion.)

———
1976   Wechuge and Windigo: A Comparison of Cannibal Belief
            Among Boreal Forest Athapaskans and Algonkians. *An-
            thropologica* n.s. 18(2):107-129. Ottawa.

———
1978   Swan People: A Study of the Dunne-za Prophet Dance. *Can-
            ada. National Museum of Man, Mercury Series, Ethnology
            Service Paper* 38. Ottawa.

———
1978a   Metaphor and Meaning: Healing in Dunne-za Music and
            Dance. *Western Canadian Journal of Anthropology* 8(2-4):9-
            17.

———
1979   Changes of Mind: Dunne-za Resistance to Empire. *British
            Columbia Studies* 43:65-80.

Ridington, Robin, and Tonia Ridington
1970   The Inner Eye of Shamanism and Totemism. *History of Re-
            ligions* 10(1):49-61.

Ridington, Tonia, and Robin Ridington
[1967]   [Beaver Tales, as Told or Translated by Johnny Chipesia and
            Others at Mile 232, Alaska Highway, British Columbia.]
            Mimeo.

Ridley, Frank
1954   The Frank Bay Site, Lake Nipissing, Ontario. *American An-
            tiquity* 20(1):40-50.

———
1956   An Archaeological Reconnaissance of Lake Abitibi, Prov-
            ince of Ontario. *Pennsylvania Archaeologist* 26(1):32-36.

———
1958   Sites on Ghost River, Lake Abitibi. *Pennsylvania Archae-
            ologist* 28(1):39-56.

———
1962   The Ancient Sites of Lake Abitibi. *Canadian Geographical
            Journal* 64(3):86-93.

———
1964   The Red Pine Point Site. *Anthropological Journal of Canada*
            2(3):7-10.

1966   Archaeology of Lake Abitibi, Ontario-Quebec. *Anthropological Journal of Canada* 4(2):2-50.

Rink, Henry
1887   The Eskimo Tribes: Their Distribution and Characteristics, Especially in Regard to Language, with a Comparative Vocabulary and a Sketch-map. *Meddelelser om Grønland* 11. Copenhagen.

Ritchie, James C., and F.K. Hare
1971   Late-Quaternary Vegetation and Climate Near the Arctic Tree Line of Northwestern North America. *Quaternary Research* 1(3):331-342.

Ritchie, William A.
1965   The Archaeology of New York State. Garden City, N.Y.: Natural History Press.

Ritter, John T.
1976   Mayo Indian Language: Dictionary. Whitehorse: Government of the Yukon Territory, Department of Education.

1976a   Gwich'in (Loucheux) Athapaskan Noun Dictionary: Fort McPherson Dialects. Whitehorse: The Queen's Printer for the Yukon.

1976b   Tutchone Historical Phonology. Mimeo.

1979   Han. (Unpublished paper presented to the 43d International Congress of Americanists, Vancouver, B.C., August 1979.)

[1980]   Han Gwich'in: Athabaskan Noun Dictionary. Fairbanks: University of Alaska, Native Language Center. (In Press.)

Ritter, John T., Tommy McGinty, and Johnson Edwards
1977   The Selkirk Indian Language Noun Dictionary (Northern Tutchone Athapaskan). Whitehorse: Council for Yukon Indians, Yukon Native Languages Project.

Ritzenthaler, Robert E., and Pat Ritzenthaler
1970   The Woodland Indians of the Western Great Lakes. Garden City, N.Y.: Natural History Press.

Rivers, William H.R.
1914   Kinship and Social Organization. London: Constable.

1915   Marriage (Introductory and Primitive). Pp. 423-432 in Vol. 8 of Encyclopedia of Religion and Ethics. James Hastings, ed. 13 vols. Edinburgh: T. and T. Clark. (Reprinted: Charles Scribner's Sons, New York, 1928.)

Robbins, Richard H.
1967   The Two Chiefs: Changing Leadership Patterns Among the Great Whale River Cree. (Paper read at the 7th Annual Meeting of the Northeastern Anthropological Association, Dartmouth College, Hanover, N.H.)

1973   Alcohol and the Identity Struggle: Some Effects of Economic Change on Interpersonal Relations. *American Anthropologist* 75(1):99-122.

Roberts, Frank H.H., Jr.
1940   Developments in the Problem of the North American Paleo-Indian. Pp. 51-116 in Essays in Historical Anthropology of North America, Published in Honor of John R. Swanton in Celebration of His Fortieth Year With the Smithsonian Institution. *Smithsonian Miscellaneous Collections* 100. Washington.

Roberts, John M., and Brian Sutton-Smith
1966   Cross-cultural Correlates of Games of Chance. *Behavior Science Notes* 1(3):131-144. New Haven, Conn.

Robertson, Colin
1939   Colin Robertson's Correspondence Book, September 1817 to September 1822. E.E. Rich, ed. Toronto: The Champlain Society.

Robertson, R. Gordon
1967   The Coming Crisis in the North. *North* 14(2):44-52.

Robinson, J. Lewis
1968   Geography of Hudson Bay. Pp. 201-235 in Vol. 1 of Science, History and Hudson Bay. C.S. Beals, ed. 2 vols. Ottawa: Department of Energy, Mines and Resources.

Robinson, M.J., and J.L. Robinson
1946   Exploration and Settlement of the Mackenzie District, N.W.T. 2 Pts. *Canadian Geographical Journal* 32(6):246-255; 33(1):43-49

1947   Fur Production in the North-West. Pp. 133-153 in The New Northwest. C.A. Dawson, ed. Toronto: University of Toronto Press.

Rogers, Edward S.
1958-1959   [Ethnographic Fieldnotes from Weagamow Lake, Weagamow, Ontario.] (Manuscript in Rogers's possession.)

1962   The Round Lake Ojibwa. *Royal Ontario Museum, Art and Archaeology Division Occasional Paper* 5. Toronto.

1963   Changing Settlement Patterns of the Cree-Ojibwa of Northern Ontario. *Southwestern Journal of Anthropology* 19(1):64-88.

1963a   The Hunting Group–Hunting Territory Complex Among the Mistassini Indians. *Anthropological Series 63, National Museum of Canada Bulletin* 195. Ottawa.

1963b   Notes on Lodge Plans in the Lake Indicator Area of South-central Quebec. *Arctic* 16(4):219-227.

1963c   The Canoe-sled Among the Montagnais-Naskapi. Pp. 74-76, 125 in *Royal Ontario Museum, Art and Archaeology Division Report for 1962*. Toronto.

1964   The Eskimo and Indian in the Quebec-Labrador Peninsula. Pp. 211-249 in Le Nouveau-Québec: Contribution à l'étude de l'occupation humaine. Jean Malaurie and Jacques Rousseau, eds. Paris: Mouton.

1965   Leadership Among the Indians of Eastern Subarctic Canada. *Anthropologica* n.s. 7(2):263-284. Ottawa.

1965-1972   [Ethnographic Fieldnotes of Northern Ontario Ojibwa.] (Manuscript in Rogers's possession.)

1966   A Cursory Examination of the Fur Returns from Three Indian Bands of Northern Ontario 1950-1964. *Ontario. Department of Lands and Forests Research Report* 75. Toronto.

1967   Subsistence Areas of the Cree-Ojibwa of the Eastern Subarctic: A Preliminary Study. *Anthropological Series 70, National Museum of Canada Bulletin* 204:59-99. Ottawa.

1967a   The Material Culture of the Mistassini. *Anthropological Series 80, National Museum of Canada Bulletin* 218. Ottawa.

1969   Band Organization Among the Indians of Eastern Subarctic Canada. Pp. 21-50 in Contributions to Anthropology: Band Societies. David Damas, ed. *Anthropological Series 84, National Museum of Canada Bulletin* 228. Ottawa.

1969a   Natural Environment—Social Organization—Witchcraft: Cree versus Ojibwa—a Test Case. Pp. 24-39 in Contributions to Anthropology: Ecological Essays. *Anthropological Series 86, National Museum of Canada Bulletin* 230. Ottawa.

1972   Ojibwa Fisheries in Northwestern Ontario. Toronto: Department of Lands and Forests, Resource Products Division. Mimeo.

1972a   The Mistassini Cree. Pp. 90-137 in Hunters and Gatherers Today. M.G. Bicchieri, ed. New York: Holt Rinehart and Winston.

1973   The Quest for Food and Furs: The Mistassini Cree, 1953-1954. *Canada. National Museum of Man, Publications in Ethnology* 5. Ottawa.

Rogers, Edward S., and Mary B. Black
1976   Subsistence Strategy in the Fish and Hare Period, Northern Ontario: The Weagamow Ojibwa, 1880-1920. *Journal of Anthropological Research* 32(1):1-43.

Rogers, Edward S., and Roger A. Bradley
1953   An Archaeological Reconnaissance in South-central Quebec, 1950. *American Antiquity* 19(2):138-144.

Rogers, Edward S., and Jean H. Rogers
1959   The Yearly Cycle of the Mistassini Indians. *Arctic* 12(3):131-138.

Rogers, Edward S., and Mary B. Rogers
1980   The Puzzle of the Crane Indians: A Name-game Through Two Centuries in Northern Ontario. *Rotunda: Bulletin of the Royal Ontario Museum* 12(4):11-19. Toronto.

Rogers, Edward S., and Murray H. Rogers
1948   Archaeological Reconnaissance of Lakes Mistassini and Albanel, Province of Quebec, 1947. *American Antiquity* 14(2):81-90.

1950   Archaeological Investigations in the Region about Lakes Mistassini and Albanel, Province of Quebec, 1948. *American Antiquity* 15(4):322-337.

Rogers, Edward S., and John Trudeau
1969-1972   The Indians of the Central Subarctic of Canada. Pp. 133-149 in Vol. 3 of *Proceedings of the 38th International Congress of Americanists*, Stuttgart-München, 1968. 4 vols. München, Germany: Klaus Renner.

Rogers, George W.
1971   Goodbye, Great White Father-figure. *Anthropologica* n.s. 13(1-2):279-306. Ottawa.

Rogers, Jean H.
1958   Notes on Mistassini Phonemics and Morphology. *National Museum of Canada Bulletin* 167. Ottawa.

1975   Prediction of Transitive Animate Verbs in an Ojibwa Dialect. *International Journal of American Linguistics* 41(2):114-139.

Rogers, Mary B., and Edward S. Rogers
1980   Adoption of Patrilineal Surname System by Bilateral Northern Ojibwa: Mapping the Learning of an Alien System. Pp. 198-230 in *Papers of the Eleventh Algonquian Conference.* William Cowan, ed. Ottawa: Carleton University.

Rogers, Patricia A.
1965   Aspirations and Acculturation of Cree Women at Great Whale River. (Unpublished M.A. Thesis in Anthropology, University of North Carolina, Chapel Hill.)

Rohn, Oscar
1900   Trails and Routes. Pp. 780-784 in Compilation of Narratives of Explorations in Alaska. Washington: U.S. Government Printing Office.

1900a   An Expedition into the Mount Wrangell Region. Pp. 790-803 in Compilation of Narratives of Explorations in Alaska. Washington: U.S. Government Printing Office.

Rohrl, Vivian J.
1970   A Nutritional Factor in Windigo Psychosis. *American Anthropologist* 72(1):97-101.

Roppel, Patricia
1975   Porcupine. *The Alaska Journal* 5(1):2-10.

Rosenstiel, Annette
1971   The Changing Focus of Native Education in Alaska. *Arctic and Alpine Research* 3:187-197.

Ross, Alexander
1855   The Fur Hunters of the Far West: A Narrative of Adventures in the Oregon and Rocky Mountains. 2 vols. London: Smith, Elder.

1856   The Red River Settlement: Its Rise, Progress, and Present State: With Some Account of the Native Races and Its General History, to the Present Day. London: Smith, Elder.

Ross, Bernard R.
1861   An Account of the Animals Useful in an Economic Point of View to the Various Chipewyan Tribes. *Canadian Naturalist and Geologist* 6(6):433-444.

1862   An Account of the Botanical and Mineral Products, Useful to the Chipewyan Tribes of Indians, Inhabiting the McKenzie River District. *Canadian Naturalist and Geologist* 7(2):133-137.

1872   The Eastern Tinneh. Pp. 303-311 in Notes on the Tinneh or Chepewyan Indians of British and Russian America, by George Gibbs. *Annual Report of the Smithsonian Institution for 1866.* Washington.

Rossignol, M.
1938   Cross-cousin Marriage Among the Saskatchewan Cree. *Primitive Man* 11(1-2):26-28.

1938a   Religion of the Saskatchewan and Western Manitoba Cree. *Primitive Man* 11(3-4):67-71.

1939   Property Concepts Among the Cree of the Rocks. *Primitive Man* 12(3):61-70.

Rousseau, Jacques
1945   Chez les Mistassini, indiens chasseurs de la forêt canadienne. *Revue de l'Institut Français de l'Amérique Latine* 2:64-91. Mexico.

1946   Notes sur l'ethnozoologie mistassini (résumé). *Annales de l'Association Canadienne-Française pour l'Avancement des Sciences* 12:95. Quebec.

1946a   Le "Couteau croche" des Indiens de la fôret boréale. *Technique* 21(6):447.

1947   Ethnobotanique des Mistassini. *Annales de l'Association Canadienne-Française pour l'Avancement des Sciences* 13:118. Quebec.

1952   Persistances païennes chez les indiens de la forêt boréale. *Cahiers des Dix* 17:183-208.

Rousseau, Madeleine, and Jacques Rousseau
1948   La Cérémonie de la tente agitée chez les Mistassini. Pp. 307-315 in *Proceedings of the 28th International Congress of Americanists.* Paris, 1947.

1948a   La Crainte des Iroquois chez les Mistassins. *Revue d'Histoire de l'Amérique Française* 2: 13-26. Montreal.

1952   Le Dualisme religieux des peuplades de la forêt boréale. Pp. 118-126 in Vol. 2 of Acculturation in the Americas. Sol Tax, ed. *Proceedings of the 29th International Congress of Americanists.* 3 vols. New York, 1949.

Rostlund, Erhard
1952   Freshwater Fish and Fishing in Native North America. *University of California Publications in Geography* 9. Berkeley.

Rowand, John
1842   Letter to the Governor, Chief Factor and Chief Trader, Northern Department. (Manuscript in Charles Bell Collection, 1828-1859, Public Archives of Canada, Manuscript Series MG 19/A 30: North West Papers, Ottawa.)

Rowe, John
1972   Forest Regions of Canada. Rev. ed. *Canadian Forestry Service Publication* 1300. Ottawa.

Rowe, Peter T.
[1910-1940] [Papers.] (Domestic and Foreign Missionary Society Papers, in Alaska Papers, 1884-1939, Boxes 51-65, The Church Historical Society, Austin, Tex.)

1920   Historical Data of Alaskan Missions. *The Alaskan Churchman* 14:80-91.

Rue, Leonard L., III
1961   Barrière Indians. *The Beaver* 292(Autumn):27-32.

Ruggles, Richard I.
1971   The West of Canada in 1763: Imagination and Reality. *Canadian Geographer* 15(4):235-260.

Rushforth, Scott
1976   The Dene and Their Land. Pp. 1-65 in Vol. 3, Pt. 2 of Recent Land-use by the Great Bear Lake Indians. (Study Done for Indian Brotherhood of the Northwest Territories for Submission to the Mackenzie Valley Pipeline Inquiry [Berger Inquiry].) Mimeo.

1977   Country Food. Pp. 32-46 in Dene Nation: The Colony Within. Mel Watkins, ed. Toronto: University of Toronto Press.

Russell, Dale
1975   The Effects of the Spring Goose Hunt on the Crees in the Vicinity of York Factory and Churchill River in the 1700s. Pp. 420-432 in Vol. 2 of Proceedings of the Second Congress, Canadian Ethnology Society. Jim Freedman and Jerome H. Barkow, eds. 2 vols. *Canada. National Museum of Man, Mercury Series, Ethnology Service Paper* 28. Ottawa.

Russell, Frank
1898   Explorations in the Far North: Being the Report of an Expedition Under the Auspices of the University of Iowa During the Years 1892, '93, and '94. Iowa City: University of Iowa Press.

Russian-American Company
1841   [Records, Communications Sent October 15, 1841 in vol. 20, no. 486, fol. 403-404.] (Manuscripts in National Archives, Washington.)

Rutherford, A.A., J. Wittenberg, and K.J. McCallum
1973   University of Saskatchewan Radiocarbon Dates, VI. *Radiocarbon* 15(1):193-211.

1975   University of Saskatchewan Radiocarbon Dates, [VI]. *Radiocarbon* 17(3):328-353.

Ryerson, John
1855   Hudson's Bay; or, a Missionary Tour in the Territory of the Hon. Hudson's Bay Company. Toronto: G.R. Sanderson.

Sadler, Patricia
1976   The Human Windigo in Northern Algonquian Oral Tradition. (Unpublished M.A. Thesis in Anthropology, University of Iowa, Iowa City.)

Saindon, Emile
1928   En Missionnant: Essai sur les missions des Pères Oblats de Marie Immaculée à la Baie James. Ottawa: Imprimerie du Droit.

St. Joseph's Mission
1852-1972   [Miscellaneous Mission Records.] (Manuscripts, on file at Fort Resolution, N.W.T.)

Salisbury, Richard F., Fernand G. Filion, Farida Rawji, and Donald Stewart
1972   Development and James Bay: Socio-economic Implications of the Hydro-electric Project. (Report Prepared for the James Bay Development Corporation) Montreal: McGill University.

Sametz, Zenon W.
1964   Big Trout Lake. (Report IG-3) Ottawa: Department of Citizenship and Immigration, Economic and Social Research Division.

Samson, Gilles
1977   Le Projet Mushuau Nipi (1973-1977): Historique, objectifs et méthodologique. *Ministère des Affaires Culturelles, Direction Générale du Patrimoine, Dossier* 31:21-39. Quebec.

Sanders, Douglas
1974   [Letter to June Helm, Dated Department of Law, Carleton University, Ottawa, February 19, 1974.] (Letter in Helm's possession.)

Sapir, Edward
1915   The Na-Dene Languages: A Preliminary Report. *American Anthropologist* 17(3):534-558.

1925   Pitch Accent in Sarcee, an Athabaskan Language. *Journal de la Société des Américanistes de Paris* 17:185-205.

1958   Selected Writings in Language, Culture and Personality. David G. Mandelbaum, ed. Berkeley: University of California Press.

Savage, Howard
1971   Faunal Analyses of the Frank Channel Site (KeP1-1) and the Acasta Lake Site (LiPk-1), Northwest Territories. (Unpublished manuscript in Savage's possession.)

Savard, Rémi
1969   L'Hôte maladroit, essai d'analyse d'un conte montagnais. *Interprétation* 3(4):5-52.

1971   Les Tentes et les maisons à Saint-Augustin. *Interprétation* 5(1):99-103.

1972   Note sur le mythe indien de ayãsẽw à partir d'une version montagnaise. *Recherches Amérindiennes au Québec, Bulletin d'Information* 2(1):3-16. Montreal.

1973   Structure du récit: L'Enfant couvert de poux. *Recherches Amérindiennes au Québec* 3(1-2):13-37. Montreal.

Savishinsky, Joel S.
1967-1971   [Fieldwork in the Hare Communities of Colville Lake and Fort Good Hope, August 1967 to August 1968, and at Colville Lake During June and July, 1971.] (Manuscripts in Savishinsky's possession.)

1970   Kinship and the Expression of Values in an Athabascan Bush Community. Pp. 31-59 in Athabascan Studies. Regna Darnell, ed. *Western Canadian Journal of Anthropology* 2(1).

1970a   Stress and Mobility in an Arctic Community: The Hare Indians of Colville Lake, Northwest Territories. (Unpublished Ph.D. Dissertation in Anthropology, Cornell University, Ithaca, N.Y.)

1971   Mobility as an Aspect of Stress in an Arctic Community. *American Anthropologist* 73(3):604-618.

1972   Coping with Feuding: The Missionary, the Fur Trader, and the Ethnographer. *Human Organization* 31(3):281-290.

1974   The Trail of the Hare: Life and Stress in an Arctic Community. New York: Gordon and Breach.

1975   The Dog and the Hare: Canine Culture in an Athapaskan Band. Pp. 462-515 in Vol. 2 of Proceedings: Northern Athapaskan Conference, 1971. A. McFadyen, Clark, ed. 2 vols. *Canada. National Museum of Man, Mercury Series, Ethnology Service Paper* 27. Ottawa.

Savishinsky, Joel S., and Susan B. Frimmer
1973   The Middle Ground: Social Change in an Arctic Community, 1967-1971. *Canada. National Museum of Man, Mercury Series, Ethnology Service Paper* 7. Ottawa.

Savoie, Donat, ed.
1971   The Amerindians of the Canadian North-West in the 19th Century, as Seen by Emile Petitot. Vol. 2: The Loucheux Indians. (MDRP 10) Ottawa: Department of Indian Affairs and Northern Development, Northern Science Research Group.

1971a   Bibliographie d'Emile Petitot, missionnaire dans le Nord-ouest canadien. *Anthropologica* n.s. 13(2):159-168. Ottawa.

Schanz, Alfred B.
1890   Our Alaska Expedition. *Frank Leslie's Illustrated Newspaper* 70:262, 440, 466-467.

Schanz, Alfred B., and E.H. Wells
1974   From Kluckwan to the Yukon, by A.B. Schanz and E.H. Wells of the Frank Leslie's Illustrated Newspaper Expedition to Alaska. Ro Sherman, ed. *The Alaska Journal* 4(3):169-180.

Schledermann, Peter, and Wallace Olson
1969   Archaeological Survey of C.O.D. Lake Area, Minto Flats. *Anthropological Papers of the University of Alaska* 14(2):67-76. College.

Schmidt, Richard C.
1971   The Integration of Subsistence Life in a Broader Socio-economic System: A Subarctic Community. (Unpublished Ph.D. Dissertation in Anthropology, Tulane University, New Orleans.)

Schmitter, Ferdinand
1910   Upper Yukon Native Customs and Folk-Lore. *Smithsonian Miscellaneous Collections* 56(4). Washington.

Scholefield, Ethelbert O.S.
1914   British Columbia from the Earliest Times to the Present. 4 vols. Vancouver: S.J. Clarke.

Schrader, Frank C.
1900   Preliminary Report on a Reconnaissance Along the Chandlar and Koyukuk Rivers, Alaska, in 1899. Pp. 441-486 in Vol. 2 of *21st Annual Report of the U.S. Geological Survey for the Years 1899-1900*. 2 vols. Washington.

Schrader, Frank C., and Arthur C. Spencer
1901   The Geology and Mineral Resources of a Portion of the Copper River District, Alaska. Washington: U.S. Government Printing Office.

Schwatka, Frederick
1885   Report of a Military Reconnoissance Made in Alaska in 1883. Washington: U.S. Government Printing Office.

1885a   Along Alaska's Great River: A Popular Account of the Travels of the Alaska Exploring Expedition of 1883; Along the Great Yukon River, from Its Source to Its Mouth, in the British North-West Territory, and in the Territory of Alaska. New York: Cassell.

1893   A Summer in Alaska. St. Louis: J.W. Henry. (Reprinted in 1894.)

1900   A Military Reconnoissance Made in Alaska in 1883. Pp. 285-362 in Compilation of Narratives of Explorations in Alaska. Washington: U.S. Government Printing Office.

Scollon, Ronald
1979   236 Years of Variability in Chipewyan Consonants. *International Journal of American Linguistics* 45(4):332-342.

Scollon, Ronald, and Suzanne B.K. Scollon
1979   Linguistic Convergence: An Ethnography of Speaking at Fort Chipewyan, Alberta. New York: Academic Press.

Scott, Duncan C.
1906   The Last of the Indian Treaties. *Scribner's Magazine* 40(5):573-583.

Scott, Lloyd, and Douglas Leechman
1952   The Swampy Cree. *The Beaver* 283(Winter):26-27.

Scott, Robert N.
1870   Indians Living on and Near the Boundary Between British Columbia and the Russian-American Territory Recently Ceded to the United States. Pp. 563-564 in *Annual Report of the United States Commissioner of Indian Affairs for the Year 1869*. Washington.

Scouler, John
1841   Observations on the Indigenous Tribes of the Northwest Coast of America. *Journal of the Royal Geographical Society of London* 11:215-251.

1848   On the Indian Tribes Inhabiting the North-west Coast of America. *Journal of the Ethnological Society of London* 1:228-252.

Seguin, Jocelyne
1979   Reconnaissance archéologique du futur réservoir LG-3, Complexe La Grande, Baie de James. (Unpublished manuscript in Ministère des Affaires Culturelles, Service du Patrimoine Autochtone, Direction Générale du Patrimoine, Quebec.)

Selkregg, Lidia L., ed.
1974   Southcentral Region. (Alaska Regional Profiles 1) Juneau: State of Alaska, Division of Planning and Research.

Service, Elman R.
1962   Primitive Social Organization: An Evolutionary Perspective. New York: Random House.

Seton, Ernest T.
1909   Life-histories of Northern Animals: An Account of the Mammals of Manitoba. 2 vols. New York: C. Scribner's Sons.

1911   The Arctic Prairies: A Canoe-journey of 2,000 Miles in Search of the Caribou: Being the Account of a Voyage to the Region North of Aylmer Lake. New York: Scribner. (Reprinted: International Press, New York, 1943.)

Seton-Karr, Heywood W.
1887   Shores and Alps of Alaska. London: Low, Marston, Searle, and Rivington.

Sharp, Bob
1977   Changes in Ross River During the Anvil Mine Development; Yukon Case Studies: Alaska Highway and Ross River. Whitehorse, Yukon Terr.: University of Canada North, (Yukon) Research Division.

Sharp, Henry S.
1973   The Kinship System of the Black Lake Chipewyan. (Unpublished Ph.D. Dissertation in Anthropology, Duke University, Durham, N.C.)

1975   Introducing the Sororate to a Northern Saskatchewan Chipewyan Village. *Ethnology* 14(1):71-82.

1975a   Trapping and Welfare: The Economics of Trapping in a Northern Saskatchewan Chipewyan Village. *Anthropologica* n.s. 17(1):29-44. Ottawa.

1976   Man: Wolf: Woman: Dog. *Arctic Anthropology* 13(1):25-34.

1977   The Caribou-eater Chipewyan: Bilaterality, Strategies of Caribou Hunting, and the Fur Trade. *Arctic Anthropology* 14(2):35-40.

1977a   The Chipewyan Hunting Unit. *American Ethnologist* 4(2):377-393.

1978   Comparative Ethnology of the Wolf and the Chipewyan. Pp. 55-79 in Wolf and Man: Evolution in Parallel. Roberta L. Hall and Henry S. Sharp, eds. New York: Academic Press.

1979   Chippewyan Marriage. *Canada. National Museum of Man, Mercury Series, Ethnology Service Paper* 58. Ottawa.

Shearwood, Mary Howard
1943   By Water and the Word: A Transcription of the Diary of the Right Rev. J.A. Newnham... While Plying the Waters and Ice Fields of Northern Canada in the Diocese of Moosonee. Toronto: Macmillan of Canada.

Sheldon, Charles
1911   The Wilderness of the Upper Yukon: A Hunter's Explorations for Wild Sheep in Sub-arctic Mountains. New York: Charles Scribner's Sons.

Shelford, Victor E.
1972   The Ecology of North America. Urbana: University of Illinois Press.

Sherwood, Morgan B.
1965   Exploration of Alaska, 1865-1900. New Haven, Conn.: Yale University Press.

Shinkwin, Anne D.
1974   Dakah De'nin's Village: An Early Historic Atna Site. *Arctic Anthropology* 11 (suppl.): 54-64.

1975   The Dixthada Site: Results of 1971 Excavations. *Western Canadian Journal of Anthropology* 5(3-4): 148-158.

1977   The Archaeological Visibility of Northern Athapaskans in the Tanana River Area, Central Alaska: A Discussion. Pp. 40-45 in Prehistory of the North American Subarctic: The Athapaskan Question. J.W. Helmer, S.VanDyke, and F.J. Kense, eds. Calgary: no publisher.

1979   Dakah De'nin's Village and the Dixthada Site: A Contribution to Northern Athapaskan Prehistory. *Canada. National Museum of Man, Mercury Series, Archaeological Survey Paper* 91. Ottawa.

Siebert, Frank T., Jr.
1967   The Original Home of the Proto-Algonquian People. Pp. 13-47 in Contributions to Anthropology: Linguistics I (Algonquian). *Anthropological Series 78, National Museum of Canada Bulletin* 214. Ottawa.

Silvy, Antoine
1931   Journal of Father Silvy from Belle Isle to Port Nelson. Pp. 35-101 in Documents Relating to the Early History of Hudson Bay. Joseph B. Tyrrell, ed. (Publications of the Champlain Society 18) Toronto: The Champlain Society.

1974   Dictionnaire montagnais-français [1678-1684]. Lorenzo Angers, David E. Cooter, and Gérard E. McNulty, transcribers. Montreal: Les Presses de l'Université du Québec.

Simard, Robert
1970   Le Site de Métabetchouan, Lac Saint-Jean: Rapport préliminaire. Chicoutimi [Quebec: Société d'Archéologie du Saguenay.]

Simmons, Norman M.
1968   Big Game in the Mackenzie Mountains, Northwest Territories. *Transactions of the Federal Provincial Wildlife Conference* 32:35-40. Ottawa.

Simms, S.C.
1906   The Metawin Society of the Bungees or Swampy Indians of Lake Winnipeg. *Journal of American Folk-Lore* 19(75):330-333.

Simpson, Sir George
1847   Narrative of a Journey Round the World, During the Years 1841 and 1842. 2 vols. London: Henry Colburn.

1938   Journal of Occurrences in the Athabasca Department 1820 and 1821, and Report. E.E. Rich, ed. Toronto: The Champlain Society.

1947   Part of Dispatch from George Simpson, Esqr., Governor of Ruperts Land to the Governor and Committee of the Hudson's Bay Company, London, March 1, 1829. Continued and Completed March 24 and June 5, 1829. E.E. Rich, ed. (Publications of the Champlain Society, Hudson's Bay Company Series 10) Toronto: The Champlain Society.

1968   Fur Trade and Empire: George Simpson's Journal Entitled Remarks Connected with the Fur Trade in the Course of a Voyage from York Factory to Fort George and Back to York Factory, 1824-25, with Related Documents. Frederick Merk, ed. Rev. ed. Cambridge, Mass.: Belknap Press of Harvard University Press.

Simpson, Thomas
1843   Narrative of the Discoveries on the North Coast of America; Effected by the Officers of the Hudson's Bay Company During the Years 1836-1839. London: Richard Bentley.

Sindell, Peter S.
1968   Some Discontinuities in the Enculturation of Mistassini Cree Children. Pp. 83-92 in Conflict in Culture: Problems of Developmental Change Among the Cree: Working Papers of the Cree Developmental Change Project. Norman A. Chance, ed. Ottawa: Saint Paul University, Canadian Research Centre for Anthropology.

Sioui, Anne-Marie
1979   Qui est l'auteur du Codex canadiensis? *Recherches Amérindiennes au Québec* 8(4):271-279. Montreal.

Skarland, Ivar, and J.L. Giddings
1948   Flint Stations in Central Alaska. *American Antiquity* 14(2):116-120.

Skarland, Ivar, and Charles J. Keim
1958   Archaeological Discoveries on the Denali Highway, Alaska. *Anthropological Papers of the University of Alaska* 6(2):79-88. College.

Skinner, Alanson B.
1912   Notes on the Eastern Cree and Northern Saulteaux. *Anthropological Papers of the American Museum of Natural History* 9(1). New York.

1916   Plains Cree Tales. *Journal of American Folk-Lore* 29(113):341-367.

Skinner, Alanson B., and John V. Saterlee
1915   Folklore of the Menomini Indians. *Anthropological Papers of the American Museum of Natural History* 13(3):217-546. New York.

Skoog, Ronald O.
1968   Ecology of the Caribou (*Rangifer tarandus granti*) in Alaska. (Unpublished Ph.D. Dissertation in Zoology, University of California, Berkeley.)

Slobodin, Richard
1938-1968 [Kutchin Fieldnotes.] (Manuscript in Slobodin's possession.)

1960   Some Social Functions of Kutchin Anxiety. *American Anthropologist* 62(1):122-133.

1960a   Eastern Kutchin Warfare. *Anthropologica* n.s. 2(1):76-94. Ottawa.

1962   Band Organization of the Peel River Kutchin. *Anthropological Series 55, National Museum of Canada Bulletin* 179. Ottawa.

1963   The Dawson Boys. *Polar Notes* 5:24-36.

1964   The Subarctic Métis as Products and Agents of Culture Contact. *Arctic Anthropology* 2(2):50-55.

1966   Métis of the Mackenzie District. Ottawa: Saint Paul University, Canadian Research Centre for Anthropology.

1969   Leadership and Participation in a Kutchin Trapping Party. Pp. 56-89 in Contributions to Anthropology: Band Societies. David Damas, ed. *Anthropological Series 84, National Museum of Canada Bulletin* 228. Ottawa.

1969a   Criteria for Identification of Bands. Pp. 191-211 in Contributions to Anthropology: Band Societies. David Damas, ed. *Anthropological Series 84, National Museum of Canada Bulletin* 228. Ottawa.

1970   Kutchin Concepts of Reincarnation. Pp. 67-79 in Athabascan Studies. Regna Darnell, ed. *Western Canadian Journal of Anthropology* 2(1).

1975   Without Fire: A Kutchin Tale of Warfare, Survival, and Vengeance. Pp. 259-301 in Vol. 1 of Proceedings: Northern Athapaskan Conference, 1971. A. McFadyen Clark, ed. 2 vols. *Canada. National Museum of Man, Mercury Series, Ethnology Service Paper* 27. Ottawa.

1975a   Canadian Subarctic Athapaskans in the Literature to 1965. *Canadian Review of Sociology and Anthropology* 12(3):278-289.

Smith, Barbara S.
1974   Preliminary Survey of Documents in the Archives of the Russian Orthodox Church in Alaska. Boulder, Colo.: Resources Development Internship Program, Western Interstate Commission for Higher Education.

Smith, David M.
[1968-1972] [Ethnographic Notes from Approximately 14 Months' Fieldwork Among the Métis and Chipewyan of Fort Resolution, Northwest Territories, Canada.] (Manuscripts in Smith's possession.)

1973   I^{n}ko^{n}ze: Magico-religious Beliefs of Contact-traditional Chipewan Trading at Fort Resolution, NWT, Canada. *Canada. National Museum of Man, Mercury Series, Ethnology Service Paper* 6. Ottawa.

1973a   [Ethnographic Notes from Fieldwork Among the Chipewyan, Northwest Territories, 1968-1973.] (Manuscript in Smith's possession.)

1973b   Ecological Change and the Chipewyan of Fort Resolution. (Paper read at the Symposium on Variation in Cultural Ecology: The Chipewyan of Subarctic Canada, Annual Meeting of the American Anthropological Association, New Orleans.)

1975   Fort Resolution People: An Historical Study of Ecological Change. (Unpublished Ph.D. Dissertation in Anthropology, University of Minnesota, Minneapolis.)

1976   Differential Adaptations Among the Chipewyan of the Great Slave Lake Area in the Early Twentieth Century. (Paper read at the Athapaskan Conference, Calgary, 1976.)

Smith, Derek G.
1975   Natives and Outsiders: Pluralism in the Mackenzie River Delta, Northwest Territories. (MDRP 12) Ottawa: Department of Indian Affairs and Northern Development, Northern Research Division.

Smith, Edward
1823-1827   [Mackenzie River District Report, March 7, 1826.] (Manuscript B.200/e/6, fo. 8 and 9 in Hudson's Bay Company Archives, Provincial Archives of Manitoba, Winnipeg, Canada.)

1825   [Mackenzie River District Report for 1823-24.] (Manuscript B.200/e/4 in Hudson's Bay Company Archives, Provincial Archives of Manitoba, Winnipeg, Canada.)

1829-1830   [Fort Simpson Post Journal.] (Manuscript B.200/a/11 in Hudson's Bay Company Archives, Provincial Archives of Manitoba, Winnipeg, Canada.)

1831   [Public Letter, Dated November 1831 in Fort Simpson Correspondence, 1831-1832.] (Manuscript B.200/b/7 in Hudson's Bay Company Archives, Provincial Archives of Manitoba, Winnipeg, Canada.)

Smith, James G.E.
1967-1970   [Fieldnotes on Rocky Cree of Reindeer Lake.] (Manuscript in Smith's possession.)

1967-1973   [Fieldnotes on Barren Lands Band of Caribou-eater Chipewyan.] (Manuscript in Smith's possession.)

1967-1976   [Fieldnotes on the Chipewyans.] (Manuscript in Smith's possession.)

1970   The Chipewyan Hunting Group in a Village Context. *Western Canadian Journal of Anthropology* 2(1):60-66. (Reprinted: Pp. 315-322 in Cultural Ecology: Readings on the Canadian Indians and Eskimos. Bruce Cox, ed. McClelland and Stewart, Toronto, 1973.)

1973   The Local Band of the Caribou Eater Chipewyan. (Paper read at the Symposium on Variation in Cultural Ecology: The Chipewyan of Subarctic Canada, Annual Meeting of the American Anthropological Association, New Orleans.)

1975   The Ecological Basis of Chipewyan Socio-territorial Organization. Pp. 389-461 in Vol. 2 of Proceedings: Northern Athapaskan Conference, 1971. A. McFadyen Clark, ed. 2 vols. *Canada. National Museum of Man, Mercury Series, Ethnology Service Paper* 27. Ottawa.

1975a   Preliminary Notes on the Rocky Cree of Reindeer Lake. Pp. 171-189 in Contributions to Canadian Ethnology, 1975. David B. Carlisle, ed. *Canada. National Museum of Man, Mercury Series, Ethnology Service Paper* 31. Ottawa.

1976   Local Band Organization of the Caribou-eater Chipewyan in the 18th and Early 19th Centuries. *Western Canadian Journal of Anthropology* 6(1):72-90.

1976a   On the Territorial Distribution of the Western Woods Cree. Pp. 414-435 in *Papers of the Seventh Algonquian Conference, 1975.* William Cowan, ed. Ottawa: Carleton University.

1976b   Local Band Organization of the Caribou Eater Chipewyan. *Arctic Anthropology* 13(1):12-24.

1976c   Notes on the Wittiko. Pp. 18-38 in *Papers of the Seventh Algonquian Conference, 1975.* William Cowan, ed. Ottawa: Carleton University.

1976d   Chipewyan Adaptations. (Papers from a Symposium on the Chipewyan of Subarctic Canada, James G.E. Smith, ed.) *Arctic Anthropology* 13(1).

1978   The Emergence of the Micro-urban Village Among the Caribou-eater Chipewyan. *Human Organization* 37(1):38-49.

1978a   Economic Uncertainty in an "Original Affluent Society:" Caribou and Caribou Eater Chipewyan Adaptive Strategies. *Arctic Anthropology* 15(1):68-88.

_____, ed.
1979   Indian-Eskimo Relations: Studies in the Inter-ethnic Relations of Small Societies. *Arctic Anthropology* 16(2).

Smith, James G.E., and Ernest S. Burch, Jr.
1979   Chipewyan and Inuit in the Central Canadian Subarctic, 1613-1977. *Arctic Anthropology* 16(2):76-101.

Smith, Jason W.
1969   Archaeological Investigation at Ice Mountain Near Telegraph Creek, Northern British Columbia: Preliminary Report. Mimeo.

1970   Preliminary Report of Archaeological Investigation in Northern British Columbia. Pp. 87-97 in Early Man and Environments in Northwest North America. R.A. Smith and J.W. Smith, eds. (Proceedings of the 2d Annual Paleoenvironmental Workshop of the University of Calgary Archaeological Association) Calgary: The Students' Press.

1971   The Ice Mountain Microblade and Core Industry, Cassiar District, Northern British Columbia, Canada. *Arctic and Alpine Research* 3(3):199-213.

1974   The Northeast Asian-Northwest American Microblade Tradition (NANAMT). *Journal of Field Archaeology* 1(3-4):347-364.

Smith, Ralph, and William Barr
1971   Marble Island: A Search for the Knight Expedition, August 6-15, 1970. *The Musk-Ox* 8:40-46. Saskatoon, Sask.

Sniffen, Matthew K., and Thomas S. Carrington
1914   The Indians of the Yukon and Tanana Valleys, Alaska. Philadelphia: Indian Rights Association.

Snook, Delores et al.
1972   Ojibwe Lessons, 1-12. Minneapolis: University of Minnesota, Department of American Indian Studies.

Snow, Dean R.
1976   The Archaeological Implications of the Proto-Algonquian Urheimat. Pp. 339-346 in *Papers of the Seventh Algonquian Conference, 1975*. William Cowan, ed. Ottawa: Carleton University.

La Société du Parler Français au Canada
1968   Glossaire du parler français au Canada. Quebec: Les Presses de l'Université Laval.

Sokolov, Alexander Petrovich
1852   The Copper River, from the Report of [Pilot Ruff] Serebrennikov, 1847-8. *Glavnoe Gidrograficheskoe Upravlenie, Zapiski* 10:167-177. St. Petersburg. (Manuscript translation by Ivan Petroff in *Alaska Miscellany* P-K 28:3, Bancroft Library, University of California, Berkeley.)

Sorenson, C.J., and J.C. Knox
1974   Paleosols and Paleoclimates Related to Late Holocene Forest/Tundra Border Migrations: Mackenzie and Keewatin, N.W.T., Canada. Pp. 187-203 in *5th International Conference on the Prehistory and Paleoecology of Western North American Arctic and Subarctic*. Scott Raymond and Peter Schledermann, eds. Calgary, 1972.

Souther, J.G.
1970   Recent Volcanism and Its Influence on Early Native Cultures of Northwestern British Columbia. Pp. 53-64 in Early Man and Environments in Northwest North America. R.A. Smith and J.W. Smith, eds. (Proceedings of the 2d Annual Paleoenvironmental Workshop of the University of Calgary Archaeological Association) Calgary: The Students' Press.

Spaulding, Albert C.
1946   Northeastern Archaeology and General Trends in the Northern Forest Zone. Pp. 143-167 in Man in Northeastern North America. Frederick Johnson, ed. *Papers of the Robert S. Peabody Foundation for Archaeology* 3. Andover, Mass.

Spaulding, Philip
1966   The Social Integration of a Northern Community: White Mythology and Métis Reality. Pp. 90-111 in A Northern Dilemma: Reference Papers. Arthur K. Davis, ed. 2 vols. Bellingham: Western Washington State College.

Speck, Frank G.
1914   The Double-curve Motive in Northeastern Algonkian Art. *Anthropological Series 1, Memoirs of the Canadian Geological Survey* 42. Ottawa.

————
1915   Family Hunting Territories and Social Life of Various Algonkian Bands of the Ottawa Valley. *Anthropological Series 8, Memoirs of the Canadian Geological Survey* 70:1-10. Ottawa.

————
1915a   The Family Hunting Band as the Basis of Algonkian Social Organization. *American Anthropologist* 17(2):289-305.

————
1916   An Ancient Archeological Site on the Lower St. Lawrence. Pp. 427-433 in Holmes Anniversary Volume: Anthropological Essays Presented to William Henry Holmes in Honor of His Seventieth Birthday, December 1, 1916, by His Friends and Colaborers. F.W. Hodge, ed. Washington: J.W. Bryan Press.

————
1918   Kinship Terms and the Family Band Among the Northeastern Algonkian. *American Anthropologist* 20(2):143-161.

————
1923   Mistassini Hunting Territories in the Labrador Peninsula. *American Anthropologist* 25(4):452-471.

————
1925   Central Eskimo and Indian Dot Ornamentation. *Museum of the American Indian, Heye Foundation, Indian Notes* 2(3):151-172. New York.

————
1925a   Dogs of the Labrador Indians. *Natural History* 25(1):58-64.

————
1926   Culture Problems in Northeastern North America. *Proceedings of the American Philosophical Society* 65(4):272-311. Philadelphia.

————
1927   Family Hunting Territories of the Lake St. John Montagnais and Neighbouring Bands. *Anthropos* 22:387-403.

————
1928   Land Ownership Among Hunting Peoples in Primitive America and the World's Marginal Areas. Pp. 323-332 in Vol. 2 of *Proceedings of the 22d International Congress of Americanists*. 2 vols. Rome, 1926.

————
1930   Mistassini Notes. *Museum of the American Indian, Heye Foundation, Indian Notes* 7(4):410-457. New York.

————
1931   Montagnais-Naskapi Bands and Early Eskimo Distribution in the Labrador Peninsula. *American Anthropologist* 33(4):557-600.

————
1935   Naskapi: The Savage Hunters of the Labrador Peninsula. Norman: University of Oklahoma Press. (Reprinted in 1977.)

————
1935-1936   Eskimo and Indian Backgrounds in Southern Labrador. *General Magazine and Historical Chronicle* 38(1):1-17, (2):143-163. Philadelphia.

————
1937   Analysis of Eskimo and Indian Skin-dressing Methods in Labrador. *Ethnos* 2(6):345-353.

————
1937a   Montagnais Art in Birch-bark: A Circumpolar Trait. *Museum of the American Indian, Heye Foundation, Indian Notes and Monographs* 11(2):45-125. New York.

————
1937b   Swimming Paddles Among the Northern Indians. *American Anthropologist* 39(4):726-727.

Speck, Frank G., and Loren C. Eiseley
1939   The Significance of Hunting Territory Systems of the Algonkian in Social Theory. *American Anthropologist* 41(2):269-280.

————
1942   Montagnais-Naskapi Bands and Family Hunting Districts of the Central and Southeastern Labrador Peninsula. *Proceedings of the American Philosophical Society* 85(2):215-242. Philadelphia.

Speck, Frank G., and George G. Heye
1921   Hunting Charms of the Montagnais and the Mistassini. *Museum of the American Indian, Heye Foundation, Indian Notes and Monographs, Misc. Series* 13(1). New York.

Spence, J.A., ed.
1972   Not by Bread Alone. (Report prepared for the James Bay Task Force of the Indians of Quebec Association. Mimeo.)

Spencer, Robert F., and Jesse D. Jennings, eds.
1965   The Native Americans: Prehistory and Ethnology of the North American Indians. New York: Harper and Row. (2d ed. published in 1977.)

Spier, Leslie
1935   The Prophet Dance of the Northwest and Its Derivatives: The Source of the Ghost Dance. *General Series in Anthropology* 1. Menasha, Wis.

Spindler, George D., and Louise S. Spindler
1957   American Indian Personality Types and Their Sociocultural Roots. *Annals of the American Academy of Political and Social Science* 311:147-157. Philadelphia.

Spurr, Josiah E.
1900   A Reconnaissance in Southwestern Alaska in 1898. Pp. 31-

264 in *20th Annual Report of the U.S. Geological Survey for the Years 1898-1899*. Washington.

Staffeief, Vladimir, and Ivan Petroff
1885-1886 ["KanKünä or Kankünats Kŏgtana" Vocabulary; Shores of Cook Inlet, Alaska, South of North Foreland.] (Manuscript No. 77 in National Anthropological Archives, Smithsonian Institution, Washington.)

Stager, John K.
1962 Fur Trading Posts in the Mackenzie Region up to 1850. *Canadian Association of Geographers, B.C. Division, Occasional Papers in Geography* 3:37-46. Vancouver.

——— 1974 Old Crow, Y.T. and the Proposed Northern Gas Pipeline. *Report of the Environmental-Social Committee, Task Force on Northern Oil Development* 74-21. Ottawa.

Starbuck, A.
1878 History of the American Whale Fishery from its Earliest Inception to the Year 1876. Waltham, Mass.: Published by the Author.

Steensby, H.P.
1917 An Anthropogeographical Study of the Origin of Eskimo Culture. *Meddelelser om Grønland* 53:39-228. Copenhagen.

Steinbring, Jack H.
1964 Recent Studies Among the Northern Ojibwa. *Manitoba Archaeological Newsletter* 1(4):9-12. Winnipeg.

——— 1965 The Sturgeon Skin "Jar." *Manitoba Archaeological Newsletter* 2(3):3-6. Winnipeg.

——— 1965a Environmental Knowledge Among the Northern Ojibwa Indians. Winnipeg: Natural History Society of Manitoba.

——— 1966 The Manufacture and Use of Bone Defleshing Tools. *American Antiquity* 31(4):575-581.

——— 1967 Ojibwa Culture: The Modern Situation and Problems. Pp. 46-71 in Kenora 1967: Resolving Conflicts—a Cross-cultural Approach. Winnipeg: University of Manitoba Press.

——— 1969-1972 Acculturational Phenomena Among the Lake Winnipeg Ojibwa of Canada. Pp. 179-188 in Vol. 3 of *Proceedings of the 38th International Congress of Americanists*. 4 vols. Stuttgart-München, 1968. München, Germany: Klaus Renner.

——— 1978 Ethnological Identification in Rock Pictography of the Canadian Shield. Pp. 3-35 in Manitoba Rock Art, II: Rock Paintings. *Papers in Manitoba Archaeology, Miscellaneous Paper* 8. Winnipeg.

——— 1980 Television on the Jackhead Indian Reserve, 1969-1980. Pp. 182-261 in Television and the Canadian Indian: Impact and Meaning Among Algonkians of Central Canada. G. Greenberg and S. Steinbring, eds. Winnipeg: Department of Communication.

——— 1980a Alcoholics Anonymous: Cultural Reform Among the Saulteaux. Pp. 89-107 in Alcohol and Native Peoples of the North. John Hammer and Jack Steinbring, eds. Washington: University Press of America.

Steinbring, Jack H., and Douglas Elias
1968 A Key Pictograph from the Bloodvein River, Manitoba. *American Antiquity* 33(4):499-501.

Steinbring, Jack H., J.P. Whelan, P.D. Elias, and T.E.H. Jones
1969 Preliminary Report: Rock Painting Investigations of the Churchill River Diversion Project, 1969. Winnipeg: University of Manitoba, Department of Anthropology.

Stevens, F.G.
1919 The Crane and Sucker Indians in Far North-Western Ontario. *Missionary Bulletin* [United Church Archives] 15(1). Toronto.

Steward, Julian H.
1941 Recording Culture Changes Among the Carrier Indians of British Columbia. Pp. 83-90 in *Explorations and Field Work of the Smithsonian Institution in 1940*. Washington.

——— 1942 The Direct Historical Approach to Archaeology. *American Antiquity* 7(4):337-343.

——— 1955 Theory of Culture Change: The Methodology of Multilinear Evolution. Urbana: University of Illinois Press.

——— 1960 Carrier Acculturation: The Direct Historical Approach. Pp. 732-744 in Culture in History: Essays in Honor of Paul Radin. Stanley Diamond, ed. New York: Columbia University Press.

Stewart, Elihu
1913 Down the Mackenzie and Up the Yukon in 1906. London and New York: John Lane.

Stoney, George M.
1899 Explorations in Alaska. *Proceedings of the United States Naval Institute* 25(3)533-584, (4):800-864. Annapolis, Md.

Story, Gillian L., and Constance M. Naish
1973 Tlingit Verb Dictionary. College: University of Alaska, Native Language Center.

Strahler, Arthur N.
1969 Physical Geography. 3d ed. New York: Wiley.

Strong, B. Stephen
1972 A History of Mentasta. (Unpublished M.A. Thesis in Anthropology, McGill University, Montreal.)

Strong, W. Duncan
1928 [Photos and Fieldnotes of 1928. In Papers of William Duncan Strong, 1923-1946.] (Unnumbered manuscript in National Anthropological Archives, Smithsonian Institution, Washington.)

——— 1929 Cross-cousin Marriage and the Culture of the Northeastern Algonkian. *American Anthropologist* 31(2):277-288.

——— 1930 A Stone Culture from Northern Labrador and Its Relation to the Eskimo-like Cultures of the Northeast. *American Anthropologist* 32(1):126-144.

Stuck, Hudson
[1906] [Account of the Founding of Mission at Allakaket.] (Manuscript in St. John's-in-the-Wilderness Mission Record Book, Allakaket, Alaska.)

——— [1906a] [Papers.] (Domestic and Foreign Missionary Society Papers, in Alaska Papers, 1884-1939. The Church Historical Society, Austin, Tex.)

——— 1914 Ten Thousand Miles with a Dog Sled: A Narrative of Winter Travel in Interior Alaska. New York: Charles Scribner's Sons.

——— 1917 Voyages on the Yukon and Its Tributaries: A Narrative of Summer Travel in the Interior of Alaska. New York: Charles Scribner's Sons.

——— 1920 A Winter Circuit of Our Arctic Coast: A Narrative of a Journey with Dog-sleds Around the Entire Arctic Coast of Alaska. New York: C. Scribner's Sons.

Sue, Hiroko
1961-1963 [Fieldwork at Fort Good Hope, June-September 1961, and at Colville Lake and Fort Good Hope, June 1962-January 1963.] (Manuscripts in Sue's possession.)

——— 1964 Hare Indians and Their World. (Unpublished Ph.D. Dissertation in Anthropology, Bryn Mawr College, Bryn Mawr, Pa.)

——— 1965 Pre-school Children of the Hare Indians. (NCRC 65-2) Ottawa: Department of Northern Affairs and National Resources, Northern Co-ordination and Research Centre.

Sue, Hiroko *see also* Hara, Hiroko Sue

Sullivan, Robert J.
1942   The Ten'a Food Quest. *Catholic University of America Anthropological Series* 11. Washington.

1942a   Temporal Concepts of the Ten'a. *Primitive Man* 15(3-4):57-65.

Sulte, Benjamin
1911   Les Attikamègues et les Têtes-de-Boule. *Bulletin de la Société de Géographie de Québec* 5(2):121-130. Quebec.

Sutherland, James
1815   [Norway House District Report by James Sutherland.] (Manuscript B.154/e/1, fo. 5d in Hudson's Bay Company Archives, Provincial Archives of Manitoba, Winnipeg, Canada.)

Swanton, John R.
1908   Social Condition, Beliefs, and Linguistic Relationship of the Tlingit Indians. Pp. 391-485 in *26th Annual Report of the Bureau of American Ethnology for the Years 1904-1905.* Washington.

1910   Nahane. P. 10 in Vol. 2 of Handbook of American Indians North of Mexico. Frederick W. Hodge, ed. 2 vols. *Bureau of American Ethnology Bulletin* 30. Washington.

1910a   Tagish. P. 669 in Vol. 2 of Handbook of American Indians North of Mexico. Frederick W. Hodge, ed. 2 vols. *Bureau of American Ethnology Bulletin* 30. Washington.

1910b   Taku. P. 675 in Vol. 2 of Handbook of American Indians North of Mexico. Frederick W. Hodge, ed. 2 vols. *Bureau of American Ethnology Bulletin* 30. Washington.

1952   The Indian Tribes of North America. *Bureau of American Ethnology Bulletin* 145. Washington. (Reprinted in 1968.)

Syncrude Canada
1974   The Beaver Creek Site: A Prehistoric Stone Quarry on Syncrude Lease No. 22. Edmonton: Syncrude Canada Limited.

Taggart, Harold F., ed.
1956   Journal of George Russell Adams, Member, Exploring Expedition in Russian America, 1865-67. *California Historical Society Quarterly* 35(4):291-307. San Francisco.

Tamplin, Morgan
1967   The Glacial Lake Agassiz Survey, 1966. *Plains Anthropologist* 12(36):220-221.

Tanner, Adrian
1966   Trappers, Hunters and Fishermen. (Yukon Research Project 5) Ottawa: Department of Northern Affairs and National Resources, Northern Co-ordination and Research Centre.

1968   Occupation and Life Style in Two Minority Communities. Pp. 47-67 in Conflict in Culture: Problems of Developmental Change Among the Cree. (Working Papers of the Cree Developmental Change Project) Norman A. Chance, ed. Ottawa: Saint Paul University, Canadian Research Centre for Anthropology.

1971   Existe-t-il des territoires de chasse? *Recherches Amérindiennes au Québec, Bulletin d'Information* 1(4-5):69-83. Montreal.

1973   The Significance of Hunting Territories Today. Pp. 101-114 in Cultural Ecology: Readings on the Canadian Indians and Eskimos. Bruce Cox, ed. Toronto: McClelland and Stewart.

1975   The Hidden Feast: Eating and Ideology Among the Mistassini Cree. Pp. 291-313 in Papers of the Sixth Algonquian Conference, 1974. William Cowan, ed. *Canada. National Museum of Man, Mercury Series, Ethnology Service Paper* 23. Ottawa.

1978   Game Shortage and the Inland Fur Trade in Northern Quebec, 1915-1940. Pp. 146-159 in *Papers of the Ninth Algonquian Conference.* William Cowan, ed. Ottawa: Carleton University.

1979   Bringing Home Animals: Religious Ideology and Mode of Production of the Mistassini Cree Hunters. New York: St. Martin's Press.

Tanner, Helen H.
1974   The Chippewa of Eastern Lower Michigan [1965]. Pp. 347-377 in Chippewa Indians, V. D.A. Horr, ed. New York: Garland.

Tanner, John
1956   A Narrative of the Captivity and Adventures of John Tanner During Thirty Years' Residence Among the Indians in the Interior of North America [1830]. Minneapolis: Ross and Haines.

Tanner, V.
1944   Outlines of the Geography, Life and Customs of Newfoundland-Labrador (the Eastern Part of the Labrador Peninsula). *Acta Geographica* 8(1): 1-907. Helsinki.

Taylor, Griffith
1947   A Yukon Domesday: 1944. Pp. 39-88 in The New North-West. Carl A. Dawson, ed. Toronto: University of Toronto Press.

Taylor, J. Garth
1969   [Ethnographic Fieldnotes from Lansdowne House, May 14-September 8, 1969.] (Manuscript in Taylor's possession.)

1970   [Ethnographic Fieldnotes from Webiquie, July 8-August 22, 1970.] (Manuscript in Taylor's possession.)

1971   [Ethnographic Fieldnotes from Wunnummin Lake, July 20-August 27, 1971.] (Manuscript in Taylor's possession.)

1972   Northern Ojibwa Communities of the Contact-traditional Period. *Anthropologica* n.s. 14(1):19-30. Ottawa.

1974   Labrador Eskimo Settlements of the Early Contact Period. *Canada. National Museum of Man, Publications in Ethnology* 9. Ottawa.

1978   Did the First Eskimos Speak Algonquian? Pp. 96-103 in *Papers of the Ninth Algonquian Conference.* William Cowan, ed. Ottawa: Carleton University.

1980   Canoe Construction in a Cree Cultural Tradition. *Canada. National Museum of Man, Mercury Series, Ethnology Service Paper* 64. Ottawa.

Taylor, William E., Jr.
1964   The Prehistory of the Quebec-Labrador Peninsula. Pp. 181-210 in Le Nouveau Québec: Contribution à l'étude de l'occupation humaine. Jean Malaurie and Jacques Rousseau, eds. Paris: Mouton.

1964a   Interim Account of an Archaeological Survey in the Central Arctic, 1963. *Anthropological Papers of the University of Alaska* 12(1):46-55. College.

1967   Summary of Archaeological Field Work on Banks and Victoria Islands, Arctic Canada, 1965. *Arctic Antropology* 4(1):221-243.

1968   The Arnapik and Tyara Sites: An Archaeological Study of Dorset Culture Origins. *Memoirs of the Society for American Archaeology* 22. Salt Lake City.

1972   An Archaeological Survey Between Cape Parry and Cambridge Bay, N.W.T., Canada in 1963. *Canada. National Museum of Man, Mercury Series, Archaeological Survey Paper* 1. Ottawa.

Teicher, M.I.
1960   Windigo Psychosis: A Study of a Relationship Between Belief and Behavior Among the Indians of Northeastern Canada.

(*Proceedings of the 1960 Annual Spring Meeting of the American Ethnological Society*) Seattle: University of Washington Press.

Teit, James
1906   Notes on the Tahltan Indians of British Columbia. Pp. 337-349 in Boas Anniversary Volume: Anthropological Papers Written in Honor of Franz Boas, Presented to Him on the Twenty-fifth Anniversary of His Doctorate, Ninth of August, Nineteen Hundred and Six. Berthold Laufer, ed. New York: G.E. Stechert.

1907   Notes on the Chilcotin Indians. *Memoirs of the American Museum of Natural History* 4(7):759-789. New York.

1909   Two Tahltan Traditions. *Journal of American Folk-Lore* 22 (85):314-318.

1909a   The Shuswap. *Memoirs of the American Museum of Natural History* 4(7):443-813. New York. (Reprinted as Vol. 2, Pt. 7 of the Jesup Expedition, AMS, New York, 1975.)

1909b   Notes on the Chilcotin Indians, in Pp. 759-789. The Shuswap. *Memoirs of the American Museum of Natural History* 4(7). New York.

[1912-1915]   [Manuscript Map Showing Location of Tahltan and Kaska Indians.] (Map in National Museum of Man, Ottawa.)

1914   On Tahltan (Athabaskan) Work, 1912. Pp. 484-487 in *Summary Report of the Canadian Geological Survey for the Year 1912.* Ottawa.

[1915]   [Notes on the Tahltan and Kaska Indians.] (Manuscript in National Museum of Canada, Ottawa.)

1917   Kaska Tales. *Journal of American Folk-Lore* 30(118):427-473.

1919-1921   Tahltan Tales. *Journal of American Folk-Lore* 32(124):198-250; 34(133):223-253, (134):335-356.

1921   Two Plains Cree Tales. *Journal of American Folk-Lore* 34(133):320-321.

1956   Field Notes on the Tahltan and Kaska Indians: 1912-15. June Helm MacNeish, ed. *Anthropologica* 3:40-171. Ottawa.

Tenenbaum, Joan M.
1975   Nondalton Tanaina Noun Dictionary: Preliminary Version. Fairbanks: University of Alaska, Native Language Center.

1976   Dena'ina Sukdu'a I-IV: Tanaina Stories I-IV. 4 vols. Fairbanks: University of Alaska, Native Language Center.

1977   Morphology and Semantics of the Tanaina Verb. (Unpublished Ph.D. Dissertation in Linguistics, Columbia University, New York City.)

Tener, J.S.
1965   Muskoxen in Canada: A Biological and Taxonomic Review. (*Wildlife Service Monograph 2*) Ottawa: Queen's Printer.

Tero, Richard O.
1973   E.J. Glave and the Alsek River. *The Alaska Journal* 3(3):180-188.

Teslin Women's Institute
1972   A History of the Settlement of Teslin. Teslin, Yukon Terr.: no publisher.

Tetso, John
1970   Trapping Is My Life. Toronto: Martin Associates.

Tharp, George W.
1971   Preliminary Report on the 'Nahanni' and Other Bands in the Southern Yukon and Northern British Columbia. (Manuscript in Gillespie's possession.)

1972   The Position of the Tsetsaut Among Northern Athapaskans. *International Journal of American Linguistics* 38(1):14-25.

Thériault, Yves
1972   N'Tsuk: A Novel. Gwendolyn Moore, trans. Montreal: Harvest House.

1972a   Ashini. Gwendolyn Moore, trans. Montreal: Harvest House.

Thomas, Heather L., Geraldine A. Cooke, and Geraldine D. Perry, comps.
1978   Yukon Bibliography: Update to 1977. (Boreal Institute for Northern Studies Occasional Publication 8-4) Edmonton: University of Alberta, Boreal Institute of Northern Studies.

Thomas, Tay
1967   Cry in the Wilderness: "Hear Ye the Voice of the Lord." Anchorage: Color Art Printing Company.

Thompson, Albert E.
1973   Chief Peguis and His Descendants. Winnipeg: Peguis Publishers.

Thompson, Chad L.
[1980]   Koyukon Verb Prefixes. *Alaska Native Language Center Research Series.* In Press.

Thompson, David
1916   David Thompson's Narrative of His Explorations in Western America, 1784-1812. J.B. Tyrrell, ed. (Publications of the Champlain Society 12) Toronto: The Champlain Society.

1962   David Thompson's Narrative, 1784-1812. Richard Glover, ed. 2d. ed. (Publications of the Champlain Society 40) Toronto: The Champlain Society.

Thompson, H. Paul
1966   A Technique Using Anthropological and Biological Data. *Current Anthropology* 7(4):417-424.

Thompson, Judy
1972   Preliminary Study of Traditional Kutchin Clothing in Museums. *Canada. National Museum of Man, Mercury Series, Ethnology Service Paper* 1. Ottawa.

Thompson, R.
1972   Peace River Drainage. (Paper delivered at the International Conference on the Prehistory and Paleoecology of the Western Arctic and Subarctic, University of Calgary, November 23-26, 1972, Calgary, Alta.)

Thompson, Stith
1953   The Star Husband Tale. *Studia Septentrionalia* 4:93-163. Oslo. (Reprinted: Pp. 414-474 in The Study of Folklore, A. Dundes, ed., Prentice-Hall, Englewood Cliffs, N.J., 1965.)

Thorman, W.P.
[1915]   [Tahltan Notes.] (Manuscript in British Columbia Provincial Archives, Victoria.)

Thorson, Robert M., and Thomas D. Hamilton
1977   Geology of the Dry Creek Site: A Stratified Early Man Site in Interior Alaska. *Quaternary Research* 7(2):149-176.

Thwaites, Reuben G., ed.
1904   Voyages and Travels of an Indian Interpreter and Trader. Cleveland: Arthur H. Clark.

Tikhmenev, Petr Aleksandrovich
1861-1863   Istoricheskoe obozrēnie obrazovanīa Rossisko-amerikanskoĭ kompanii dvistvii eīa do nastoīashchago vremeni. St. Petersburg: E. Veĭmara.

1978   A History of the Russian-American Company. Richard A. Pierce and Alton S. Donnelly, eds. and trans. Seattle and London: University of Washington Press.

Titus, Dorothy, and Matthew Titus
1979   Dats'en' lo K'eytth'ok Tr'eghonh: This is the Way We Make Our Baskets. Deborah Niedermeyer, ed. Fairbanks: Village Art Program and Alaska Native Language Center.

Todd, Evelyn M.
1970   A Grammar of the Ojibwa Language: The Severn Dialect.
           (Unpublished Ph.D. Dissertation in Anthropology, Univer-
           sity of North Carolina, Chapel Hill.)

1972   Ojibwa Syllabic Writing and Its Implications for a Standard
           Ojibwa Alphabet. *Anthropological Linguistics* 14(9):357-360.

Tolmie, William F., and George M. Dawson
1884   Comparative Vocabularies of the Indian Tribes of British
           Columbia, with a Map Illustrating Distribution. Montreal:
           Dawson Brothers.

Tompkins, Stuart R.
1952   Alaska: Promyshlennik and Sourdough. 2d ed. Norman:
           University of Oklahoma Press.

Tough, D.G.
1972   Mining in the Canadian North. Pp. 71-90 in The North.
           William C. Wonders, ed. Toronto: University of Toronto
           Press.

Tout, D.C.
1964   The Climate of Knob Lake. *McGill University, Subarctic
           Research Laboratory Paper* 17. Montreal.

Townsend, Charles W.
1910   A Labrador Spring. Boston: D. Estes.

1913   A Short Trip into the Labrador Peninsula by Way of the
           Natashquan River. *Bulletin of the Geographical Society of
           Philadelphia* 11(3):39-50. Philadelphia.

Townsend, Joan B.
[1960-1973] [Ethnographic Fieldnotes, from Approximately 21 Months'
           Archeological and Ethnographic Fieldwork Among the Il-
           iamna Area Tanaina, Alaska.] (Manuscript in Townsend's
           possession.)

1965   Ethnohistory and Culture Change of the Iliamna Tanaina.
           (Unpublished Ph.D. Dissertation in Anthropology, Univer-
           sity of California, Los Angeles.)

1969   Introduction. Pp. xix-xxxvi in Tanaina Tales from Alaska,
           by Bill Vaudrin. Norman: University of Oklahoma Press.

1970   The Tanaina of Southwestern Alaska: An Historical Syn-
           opsis. Pp. 2-16 in Athapaskan Studies. Regna Darnell, ed.
           Western Canadian Journal of Anthropology 2(1).

1970a   Tanaina Ethnohistory: An Example of a Method for the
           Study of Culture Change. Pp. 71-102 in Ethnohistory in
           Southwestern Alaska and the Southern Yukon: Method and
           Content. Margaret Lantis, ed. (*Studies in Anthropology* 7)
           Lexington: University of Kentucky Press.

1970b   Tanaina Archaeology in the Iliamna Lake Region, Alaska.
           Bulletin of the Canadian Archaeological Association 2:36-43.
           Ottawa.

1970c   Tanaina Athapaskan Ethnohistory and Socioeconomic Change.
           Pp. 186-188 in Vol. 2 of *Proceedings of the 8th International
           Congress of Anthropological and Ethnological Sciences.* 3
           vols. Tokyo, 1968.

1970d   The Archaeology of Pedro Bay, Alaska. (Paper prepared for
           the Annual Meeting of the Society for American Archaeol-
           ogy, Mexico City, April 30, 1970.)

1973   Ethnoarchaeology in Nineteenth Century Southern and
           Western Alaska: An Interpretive Model. *Ethnohistory*
           20(4):393-412.

1974   Journals of Nineteenth Century Russian Priests to the Tan-
           aina: Cook Inlet, Alaska. *Arctic Anthropology* 11(1):1-30.

1975   Alaskan Natives and the Russian-American Company: Var-
           iations in Relationships. Pp. 555-570 in Vol. 2 of Proceedings

of the 2d Congress, Canadian Ethnology Society. Jim Freedman and Jerome H. Barkow, eds. 2 vols. *Canada. National
Museum of Man, Mercury Series, Ethnology Service Paper*
28. Ottawa.

1975a   Mercantilism and Societal Change: An Ethnohistoric Ex-
           amination of Some Essential Variables. *Ethnohistory* 22(1):21-
           32.

1979   Indian or Eskimo? Interaction and Identity in Southern
           Alaska. *Arctic Anthropology* 16(2):160-182.

[1980]   The Ranked Societies of Southern Alaska. In Alaska Native
           History and Culture. (Senri Ethnological Studies) *Occasional
           Papers of the National Museum of Ethnology.* Osaka, Japan.
           In Press.

Townsend, Joan B., and Sam-Joe Townsend
1961   Archaeological Investigations at Pedro Bay, Alaska. *An-
           thropological Papers of the University of Alaska* 10(1):25-58.
           College.

1964   Additional Artifacts from Iliamna Lake, Alaska. *Anthro-
           pological Papers of the University of Alaska* 12(1):14-16. Col-
           lege.

Troufanoff, I.P.
1967   Kenaĭskie tomagavki iz ėtnograficheskoĭ kollekt͡sii I.G. Voz-
           nesenskogo. *Sbornik Muzeĭ Antropologii i Etnografii* 24:85-
           92. Leningrad.

1970   The Ahtena Tomahawks in the Museum of Anthropology
           and Ethnography of the Academy of Sciences of the U.S.S.R.
           Current Anthropology 11(2):155-159.

Trudeau, Jean
1963   [Review of] Foodways in a Muskeg Community, by John J.
           Honigmann. *Anthropologica* n.s. 5(1):86-90. Ottawa.

1966   Culture Change Among the Swampy Cree Indians of Winisk,
           Ontario. (Unpublished Ph.D. Dissertation in Anthropology,
           The Catholic University of America, Washington.)

Tucker, L. Norman
[1908]   Western Canada. London: A.R. Mowbray; New York: T.
           Whitaker.

Turner, David H.
1977   Windigo Mythology and the Analysis of Cree Social Struc-
           ture. *Anthropologica* n.s. 19(1):63-73. Ottawa.

1979   Hunting and Gathering: Cree and Australian. Pp. 195-213
           in Challenging Anthropology. David H. Turner and Gavin
           A. Smith, eds. Toronto: McGraw-Hill Ryerson.

Turner, Geoffrey J.
1955   Hair Embroidery in Siberia and North America. *Oxford
           University, Pitt Rivers Museum Occasional Papers on Tech-
           nology* 7. Oxford, England.

Turner, Lucien M.
1888   On the Indians and Eskimos of the Ungava District, Labra-
           dor. *Proceedings and Transactions of the Royal Society of
           Canada for the Year 1887,* ser. 1, sect. 2, Vol. 5:99-119.
           Montreal.

1894   Ethnology of the Ungava District, Hudson Bay Territory.
           Pp. 159-350 in *11th Annual Report of the Bureau of American
           Ethnology for the Years 1889-1890.* Washington.

Turner, William W.
1856   Vocabularies of North American Languages. Collected by
           A.W. Whipple, Classified by W.W. Turner. Pp. 54-103 in
           Pt. 3 of Reports of Explorations and Surveys to Ascertain
           the Most Practicable and Economical Route for a Railroad
           from the Mississippi to the Pacific Ocean, in 1853-4. *33d
           Cong., 2d sess., House of Representatives Executive Doc.* No.
           91. Washington.

Turnor, Philip
1934   Journal of a Journey from Cumberland House, North America in Latitude 53° 56¾' North and Longitude 102° 13' West of Greenwich Towards the Athapiscow Country and Back to York Factory, [September 13, 1790 to July 17, 1792]. Pp. 325-491 in Journals of Samuel Hearne and Philip Turnor Between the Years 1774 and 1792. J.B. Tyrrell, ed. (Publications of the Champlain Society 21) Toronto: The Champlain Society.

1934a   A Journal of the Most Remarkable Transactions and Occurrences from York Fort to Cumberland House, and from Said House to York Fort from 9th Septr 1778 to 15th Septr 1779. Pp. 195-258 in Journals of Samuel Hearne and Philip Turnor Between the Years 1774 and 1792. J.B. Tyrrell, ed. (Publications of the Champlain Society 21) Toronto: The Champlain Society.

Tyrrell, Joseph B.
1893   Northwestern Manitoba with Portions of the Adjacent Districts of Assiniboia and Saskatchewan. *Geological and Natural History Survey of Canada, Report of Progress for 1890-91*, Vol. 5, Pt. E. Ottawa.

————, ed.
1931   Documents Relating to the Early History of Hudson Bay. (Publications of the Champlain Society 18) Toronto: The Champlain Society.

Umfreville, Edward
1954   The Present State of Hudson's Bay, Containing a Full Description of That Settlement and the Adjacent Country and Likewise of the Fur Trade, with Hints for Its Improvement, etc. [1790]. W. Stewart Wallace, ed. Toronto: Ryerson Press.

U.S. Bureau of Education
1893   Education in Alaska: 1889-1890. Pp. 1245-1300 in Report of the Commissioner of Education for 1889-90 (Whole No. 191). Washington: U.S. Government Printing Office.

1896   Education in Alaska: 1894-95. Pp. 1424-1455 in Report of the Commissioner of Education for 1894-95 (Whole No. 231). Washington: U.S. Government Printing Office.

1906   Fifteenth Annual Report on Introduction of Domestic Reindeer into Alaska, 1905. Sheldon Jackson, comp. Washington: U.S. Government Printing Office.

1911   Report on Education in Alaska. Pp. 1343-1370 in Vol. 2 of Annual Report of the Commissioner of Education for the Year 1910 (Whole No. 443). Washington: U.S. Government Printing Office.

U.S. Bureau of the Census
1915   Indian Population in the United States and Alaska, 1910. Washington: U.S. Government Printing Office.

1973   1970 Census of Population. Vol. 1: Characteristics of Population, Pt. 3: Alaska. Washington: U.S. Government Printing Office.

U.S. Census Office. 11th Census
1893   Report on Population and Resources of Alaska at the 11th Census: 1890. Washington: U.S. Government Printing Office.

U.S. Geological Survey
1970   National Atlas of the United States of America. Arch C. Gerlach, ed. Washington: U.S. Government Printing Office.

Usher, Peter J.
1970   The Bankslanders: Economy and Ecology of a Frontier Trapping Community (NSRG 71-1). 3 vols. Ottawa: Department of Indian Affairs and Northern Development, Northern Science Research Group.

1971   Fur Trade Posts of the Northwest Territories, 1870-1970. (NSRG 71-4) Ottawa: Department of Indian Affairs and Northern Development, Northern Science Research Group.

Valentine, V.F.
1954   Some Problems of the Métis of Northern Saskatchewan. *Canadian Journal of Economics and Political Science* 20(1):89-95.

Vancouver, George
1798   A Voyage of Discovery to the North Pacific Ocean, and Round the World: In Which the Coast of North-west America has been Carefully Examined and Accurately Surveyed . . . Performed in the Years 1790-1795 in the Discovery Sloop of War and Armed Tender Chatham, Under the Command of Captain George Vancouver. 3 vols. London: G.G. and J. Robinson.

Van Kirk, Sylvia
1974   Thanadelthur. *The Beaver* 304 (Winter):40-45.

VanStone, James W.
1955   Exploring the Copper River Country. *Pacific Northwest Quarterly* 46(4):115-123.

1959   Russian Exploration in Interior Alaska: An Extract from the Journal of Andrei Glazunov. *Pacific Northwest Quarterly* 50(2):37-47.

1963   Changing Patterns of Indian Trapping in the Canadian Subarctic. *Arctic* 16(3):159-174.

1963a   The Snowdrift Chipewyan. (NCRC 63-64) Ottawa: Department of Northern Affairs and National Resources, Northern Co-ordination and Research Centre.

1965   The Changing Culture of the Snowdrift Chipewyan. *Anthropological Series 74, National Museum of Canada Bulletin* 209. Ottawa.

1967   Eskimos of the Nushagak River: An Ethnographic History. Seattle: University of Washington Press.

1974   Athapaskan Adaptations: Hunters and Fishermen of the Subarctic Forests. Chicago: Aldine.

1978   E.W. Nelson's Notes on Indians of the Yukon and Innoko Rivers, Alaska. *Fieldiana: Anthropology* 70. Chicago.

1979   Ingalik Contact Ecology: An Ethnohistory of the Lower-Middle Yukon, 1790-1935. *Fieldiana: Anthropology* 71. Chicago.

1979a   Historic Ingalik Settlements Along the Yukon, Innoko, and Anvik Rivers, Alaska. *Fieldiana: Anthropology* 72. Chicago.

[1979b]   The Yukon River Ingalik: Subsistence, the Fur Trade, and a Changing Resource Base. (Paper read at American Society for Ethnohistory Annual Meeting, October 1977.)

VanStone, James W., and Joan B. Townsend
1970   Kijik: An Historic Tanaina Indian Settlement. *Fieldiana: Anthropology* 59. Chicago.

Vaudrin, Bill
1963   The Amigook, the Eiukna, and the Joncha. *Alaska Review* 1(1):20-35.

1969   Tanaina Tales from Alaska. Norman: University of Oklahoma Press.

Veillette, John, and Gary White
1977   Early Indian Village Churches: Wooden Frontier Architecture in British Columbia. Vancouver: University of British Columbia Press.

Verwyst, Chrysostom
1901   Chippewa Exercises: Being a Practical Introduction into the Study of the Chippewa Language. Harbor Springs, Mich.: Holy Childhood School. (Reprinted: Ross and Haines, Minneapolis, 1971.)

Villiers, D.
1967   The Central Mackenzie: An Area Economic Survey. Ottawa: Department of Indian Affairs and Northern Development, Industrial Division.

Vincent, Sylvie
1973   Structure du rituel: La tente tremblante et le concept de mista-pe-w. *Recherches Amérindiennes au Québec* 3(1-2):69-83. Montreal.

_____
1978   Tradition orale et action politique montagnaises: Le cas de la rivière Natashquan. Pp. 138-145 in *Papers of the Ninth Algonquian Conference.* William Cowan, ed. Ottawa: Carleton University.

Vivian, R.P.
1948   The Nutrition and Health of the James Bay Indians. *Canadian Medical Association Journal* 59(6):505-518.

Voorhis, Ernest
1930   Historic Forts and Trading Posts of the French Regime and of the English Fur Trading Companies. Ottawa: Department of the Interior, Natural Resources Intelligence Service. Mimeo.

WHC = Draper, Lyman C., and Reuben G. Thwaites
1855-1911   Collections of the State Historical Society of Wisconsin. 21 vols. Madison: The Society.

Waddell, James M.
1970   Dominion City Facts: Fiction and Hyperbole. Steinbach, Man.: Derksen.

Wahrhaftig, Clyde
1965   Physiographic Divisions of Alaska. *U.S. Geological Survey Professional Paper* 482. Washington.

Waisberg, Leo G.
1975   Boreal Forest Subsistence and the Windigo: Fluctuation of Animal Populations. *Anthropologica* n.s. 17(2):169-185. Ottawa.

Walker, Richard
1979   Central Carrier Phonemics. *Canada. National Museum of Man, Mercury Series, Ethnology Service Paper* 50:93-107. Ottawa.

Walker, T.A.
1976   Spatsizi. Surrey, B.C.: Antonson Publishing.

Walker, Willard B.
1953   Acculturation of the Great Whale River Cree. (Unpublished M.A. Thesis in Anthropology, University of Arizona, Tucson.)

Wallace, Anthony F.C.
1952   The Modal Personality Structure of the Tuscarora Indians, as Revealed by the Rorschach Test. *Bureau of American Ethnology Bulletin* 150. Washington.

Wallace, Dillon
1907   The Long Labrador Trail. New York: Outing Publishing Company.

Wallace, J.N.
1929   The Wintering Partners on Peace River, from the Earliest Records to the Union in 1821, with a Summary of the Dunvegan Journal, 1806. Ottawa: Thorburn and Abbott.

Wallace, Williams S., ed.
1934   Documents Relating to the North West Company. (Publications of the Champlain Society 22) Toronto: The Champlain Society.

Wallis, Wilson D., and Ruth Sawtell Wallis
1955   The Micmac Indians of Eastern Canada. Minneapolis: University of Minnesota Press.

Warkentin, John, and Richard I. Ruggles, eds.
1970   Manitoba Historical Atlas: A Selection of Facsimile Maps, Plans and Sketches from 1612 to 1969. Winnipeg: Historical and Scientific Society of Manitoba.

Wassillie, Albert, and James M. Kari, comps. and eds.
1979   Dena'ina Qenaga Duch'duldih: Denaina Athabaskan Junior Dictionary. Anchorage: National Bilingual Materials Development Center.

Watts, F.B.
1968   Climate, Vegetation, Soil. Pp. 78-111 in Canada: A Geographical Interpretation. J. Warkentin, ed. Toronto, London: Methuen.

Watts, J., ed.
1971   The Round Lake Ojibwa—the People, the Land, the Resources, 1968-70. (Indian Development Study in Northwestern Ontario, A.R.D.A. Project 25075) Toronto: Ontario Department of Lands and Forests.

Waugh, F.
1925   The Naskapi Indians of Labrador and Their Neighbors. *Transactions of the Women's Canadian Historical Society of Ottawa* 9:126-136. Ottawa.

Webber, Alika Podolinsky
1973   Birchbark Baskets. *Imperial Oil Review* 57(4). Toronto.

Weekes, Mary
1949   Trader King. Regina and Toronto: School Aids and Textbook Publishing Company.

Weinstein, Martin S.
1977   Hares, Lynx, and Trappers. *American Naturalist* 111(980):806-808.

Wells, E. Hazard
1890   Our Alaska Expedition. *Frank Leslie's Illustrated Newspaper* 70:419.

_____
1891   Leslie's Alaska Expedition. *Frank Leslie's Illustrated Newspaper* 72:354-355, 378, 412, 431, 448; 73:10, 59, 75, 106.

_____
1974   Down the Yukon and up the Forty Mile, by E.H. Wells of the Frank Leslie's Illustrated Newspaper Expedition to Alaska. R. Sherman, ed. *Alaska Journal* 4(4):205-213.

Welsh, Ann N.
1970   Community Pattern and Settlement Pattern in the Development of the Old Crow Village, Yukon Territory. Pp. 17-30 in Athabascan Studies. Regna Darnell, ed. *Western Canadian Journal of Anthropology* 2(1).

_____
1970a   Changing Settlement Patterns at Old Crow. (Paper presented at the 10th Annual Meeting of the Northeastern Anthropological Association, Ottawa.)

Wentzel, Willard-Ferdinand
1821   [Account of Mackenzie River, 1821.] (Manuscript MG19/A20 in Public Archives of Canada, Ottawa; copy in the Royal Commonwealth Society, London.)

_____
1889-1890   Letters to the Hon. Roderic McKenzie, 1807-1824. Pp. 67-153 in Vol. 1 of Les Bourgeois de la Compagnie du Nord-Ouest. L.R. Masson, ed. 2 vols. Quebec: A. Coté.

West, Charles E.
1978   Archeology of the Birches Site, Lake Minchumina, Alaska. (Unpublished M.A. Thesis in Anthropology, University of Alaska, Fairbanks.)

West, Frederick Hadley *see* Hadleigh-West, Frederick

West, George A.
1934   Tobacco, Pipes and Smoking Customs of the American Indians. *Bulletin of the Public Museum of the City of Milwaukee* 17(1). Milwaukee.

West, John
1967   The Substance of a Journal During a Residence at the Red River Colony, British North America, in the Years 1820-1823. Vancouver: Alcuin Society.

Westbrook, Mary E.
1969   A Venture into Ethnohistory: The Journal of Rev. V.C. Sims, Pioneer Missionary on the Yukon. *Polar Notes* 9:34-45.

Wettlaufer, Boyd, and William J. Mayer-Oakes, eds.
1960   The Long Creek Site. *Saskatchewan Department of Natural Resources, Anthropological Series* 2. Regina.

Wheeler, Clinton J.
1977   The Historic Assiniboine: A Territorial Dispute in the Ethnohistoric Literature. Pp. 115-123 in *Papers of the Eighth Algonquian Conference.* William Cowan, ed. Ottawa: Carleton University.

Wheeler, David E.
1914   The Dog-Rib Indian and His Home. *Bulletin of the Geographical Society of Philadelphia* 12(2):47-69. Philadelphia.

Wherrett, G.J.
1947   Health Conditions and Services in the North-West. Pp. 229-244 in The New North-West. C.A. Dawson, ed. Toronto: University of Toronto Press.

White, George M.
1972   Craft Manual of Yukon Tlingit. Ronan, Mont.: no publisher.

White, Lena
[1978]   [A Survey of Language Use on Walpole Island.] (Manuscript in Walpole Island Language Centre Files, Walpole Island, Ont.)

White, Lena, Eliza John, Joanne Day, Beulah Johnson, and Teresa A. Altman
[1977]   "Table Talk": A Primer. Wallaceburg, Ont.: no publisher.

Whitney, Casper
1896   On Snow-shoes to the Barren Grounds: Twenty-eight Hundred Miles After Musk-oxen and Wood-bison. New York: Harper and Brothers.

Whymper, Frederick
1868   A Journey from Norton Sound, Bering Sea, to Fort Youkon (Junction of Porcupine and Youkon Rivers). *Journal of the Royal Geographical Society* 38:219-237. London.

_____
1869   Travel and Adventure in the Territory of Alaska, Formerly Russian America—Now Ceded to the United States—and in Various Other Parts of the North Pacific. New York: Harper and Bros.

_____
1869a   Russian America, or "Alaska:" The Natives of the Youkon River and Adjacent Country. *Transactions of the Ethnological Society of London* n.s. 7:167-185. London.

Wickersham, James
1938   Old Yukon: Tales—Trails—and Trials. Washington: Washington Law Book Company.

Wilford, Lloyd A.
1955   A Revised Classification of the Prehistoric Cultures of Minnesota. *American Antiquity* 21(2):130-142.

Wilkinson, David B., and Mildred Martin
1976   Nak'azdli Bughuni, 2: Workbook. Fort Saint James B.C.: Carrier Linguistic Committee.

Wilkinson, David B. and Kay Wilkinson
1969   Sekani Reading Book. Fort Saint James, B.C.: Wilkinson and Wilkinson.

_____
1969a   Sekani Bible Story Book. Fort Saint James, B.C.: Wilkinson and Wilkinson.

Williams, Frank, and Emma Williams
1978   Tongass Texts. Jeff Leer, ed. Fairbanks: University of Alaska, Native Language Center.

Williams, Glyndwr
1963   Introduction. Pp. xv-lxxix in Northern Quebec and Labrador Journals and Correspondence, 1819-35. Kenneth G. Davies, ed. London: The Hudson's Bay Record Society.

_____
1970   Highlights in the History of the First Two Hundred Years of the Hudson's Bay Company. *The Beaver* 301(Autumn):4-55.

_____, ed.
1975   Hudson's Bay Miscellany, 1670-1970. (Publications of the Hudson's Bay Record Society 30) Winnipeg: The Hudson's Bay Record Society.

Williams, Sophia, and Saul Williams
1978a   Weagamow Notebook. Toronto: Amethyst Publications.

Williamson, Robert G.
1955-1956   Slave Indian Legends. *Anthropologica* 1:119-143, 2:61-92. Ottawa.

Willis, Jane
1973   Geniesh: An Indian Girlhood. Toronto: New Press.

Wills, Richard H., Jr.
1965   Perceptions and Attitudes of the Montagnais-Naskapi of the Great Whale River Concerning the Western World. (Unpublished M.A. Thesis in Anthropology, University of North Carolina, Chapel Hill.)

Wilmeth, Roscoe, comp.
1969   Canadian Archaeological Radiocarbon Dates. *Anthropological Series 87, National Museum of Canada Bulletin* 232:68-127. Ottawa.

_____
[1970]   Excavations at Anahim Lake, B.C., Second Season. (Unpublished manuscript in National Museum of Man, Ottawa.)

_____
1970a   Chilcotin Archaeology. *Bulletin of the Canadian Archaeological Association* 2:42-43. Ottawa.

_____
1971   Historic Chilcotin Archaeology at Anahim Lake, British Columbia. Pp. 56-59 in Aboriginal Man and Environments on the Plateau of Northwest America. Arnoud H. Stryde and R.A. Smith, eds. Calgary: Calgary Archaeological Association.

_____
1973   Distribution of Several Types of Obsidian from Archaeological Sites in British Columbia. *Bulletin of the Canadian Archaeological Association* 5:27-60. Ottawa.

_____
1975   The Proto-historic and Historic Athapaskan Occupation of British Columbia: The Archaeological Evidence. Pp. 4-20 in Athapaskan Archaeology. *Western Canadian Journal of Anthropology* 5(3-4).

_____
1977   Chilcotin Archaeology: The Direct Historic Approach. Pp. 97-101 in Prehistory of the North American Subarctic: The Athapaskan Question. J.W. Helmer, S. VanDyke, and F.J. Kense, eds. Calgary: no publisher.

_____
1978   Anahim Lake Archaeology and the Early Historic Chilcotin Indians. *Canada. National Museum of Man, Mercury Series, Archaeological Survey Paper* 82. Ottawa.

_____
1978a   Canadian Archaeological Radiocarbon Dates (Revised Version). *Canada. National Museum of Man, Mercury Series, Archaeological Survey Paper* 77. Ottawa.

Wilson, Clifford
1947   Founding Fort Yukon. *The Beaver* 278 (Summer): 38-43.

_____
1970   Campbell of the Yukon. Toronto: Macmillan of Canada.

Wilson, Edward F.
1874   The Ojebway Language: A Manual for Missionaries and Others Employed Among the Ojebway Indians. Toronto: Printed by Roswell and Hutchinson for the Society for Promoting Christian Knowledge, London. (Reprinted: Department of Indian and Northern Affairs, Ottawa, 1968.)

Wilson, Godfrey, and Monica Wilson
1945   The Analysis of Social Change Based on Observations in Central Africa. Cambridge, England: University Press.

Wilson, Ian R.
1978   Archaeological Investigations at the Atigun Site, Central Brooks Range, Alaska. *Canada. National Museum of Man, Mercury Series, Archaeological Survey Paper* 78. Ottawa.

Wilson, J. Tuzo
1952   Some Considerations Regarding Geochronology with Special

Reference to Precambrian Time. *Transactions of the American Geophysical Union* 33(2):195-203. Washington.

Winsor, Justin, ed.
1884-1889   Narrative and Critical History of America. 8 vols. Boston and New York: Houghton, Mifflin.

Wintemberg, William J.
1929   Preliminary Report on Field Work in 1927. *Annual Report for 1927, National Museum of Canada Bulletin* 56:40-41. Ottawa.

1943   Artifacts from Ancient Workshop Sites Near Tadoussac, Saguenay County, Quebec. *American Antiquity* 8(4):313-340.

Wintrob, Ronald M., and Peter S. Sindell
1969   Education and Identity Conflict Among Cree Youth. Annex C in Developmental Change Among the Cree Indians of Quebec. Norman A. Chance, ed. Ottawa: Department of Regional Economic Expansion. Mimeo.

Wissler, Clark
1915   Culture of the North American Indians Occupying the Caribou Area and Its Relation to Other Types of Culture. *Proceedings of the National Academy of Sciences* 1(1):51-54. Washington.

1922   The American Indian: An Introduction to the Anthropology of the New World. 2d ed. New York: Oxford University Press.

Wolfart, H. Christoph
1973   Boundary Maintenance in Algonquian: A Linguistic Study of Island Lake, Manitoba. *American Anthropologist* 75(5):1305-1323.

1973a   Plains Cree: A Grammatical Study. *Transactions of the American Philosophical Society* n.s. 63(5). Philadelphia.

1977   Les Paradigmes verbaux ojibwa et la position du dialecte de Severn. Pp. 188-207 in *Papers of the Eighth Algonquian Conference*. William Cowan, ed. Ottawa: Carleton University.

Wolforth, John R.
1971   The Evolution and Economy of the MacKenzie Delta Community. *Canada. Department of Indian Affairs and Northern Development, Northern Science Research Group, Mackenzie Delta Research Project Report* 11. Ottawa.

Wonders, William C.
1968   The Forest Frontier and the Subarctic. Pp. 473-507 in Canada: A Geographical Interpretation. J. Warkentin, ed. Toronto: Methuen.

_____, ed.
1972   The North. Le Nord. (Studies in Canadian Geography) Toronto: University of Toronto Press.

Workman, Karen Wood, comp.
1972   Alaskan Archaeology: A Bibliography. (*Miscellaneous Publications, History and Archaeology Series 1*) Anchorage: Alaska Division of Parks.

Workman, William B.
1969   Archaeological Investigations in the Upper Aishihik Valley, Preliminary Report. Mimeo.

1971   Preliminary Report on 1971 Archeological Survey in the Middle Copper River Country, Alaska. (Department of Interior Permit 71-AK-20) (Unpublished manuscript at Alaska Methodist University, Anchorage.)

1974   First Dated Traces of Early Holocene Man in the Southwest Yukon Territory, Canada. *Arctic Anthropology* 11(suppl.):94-103.

1974a   The Cultural Significance of a Volcanic Ash Which Fell in the Upper Yukon Basin About 1400 Years Ago. Pp. 239-259 in International Conference on the Prehistory and Paleoecology of Western North American Arctic and Sub-Arctic,

University of Calgary, 1972. Scott Raymond and Peter Schledermann, eds. Calgary: University of Calgary, Department of Archaeology.

1974b   Continuity and Change in the Prehistoric Record from the Aishihik-Kluane Region, Southwest Yukon, Canada. (Paper read at the 7th Annual Meeting of the Canadian Archaeological Association, Whitehorse, Yukon Terr., March 1974.)

1977   Ahtna Archaeology: A Preliminary Report. Pp. 22-39 in Prehistory of the North American Subarctic: The Athapaskan Question. J.W. Helmer, S. VanDyke, and F.J. Kense, eds. Calgary: no publisher.

1977a   The Prehistory of the Southern Tutchone Area. Pp. 46-54 in Prehistory of the North American Subarctic: The Athapaskan Question. J.W. Helmer, S. VanDyke, and F.J. Kense, eds. Calgary: no publisher.

1978   Prehistory of the Aishihik-Kluane Area, Southwest Yukon Territory. *Canada. National Museum of Man, Mercury Series, Archaeological Survey Paper* 74. Ottawa.

Wormington, H. Marie
1957   Ancient Man in North America. 4th rev. ed. *Denver Museum of Natural History Popular Series* 4. Denver.

Wormington, H. Marie, and Richard G. Forbis
1965   An Introduction to the Archaeology of Alberta, Canada. *Proceedings of the Denver Museum of Natural History* n.s. 11. Denver.

Worsley, P.M., H. Buckley, and H.K. Davis
1961   Economic and Social Survey of Northern Saskatchewan. *University of Saskatchewan, Research Division, Centre for Community Studies Interim Report* 1. Saskatoon.

Wrangell, Ferdinand Petrovich von
1839   Obitateli severo—zapadnikh beregov Ameriki (Northwest Inhabitants of the Coast of America). *Syn Otechestva* 7:51-82. St. Petersburg.

1839a   Statistische und ethnographische Nachrichten über die russischen Besitzungen an der Nordwestküste von Amerika. K.E. von Baer, ed. St. Petersburg: Buchdruckerei der Kaiserlichen Akademie der Wissenschaften.

1970   The Inhabitants of the Northwest Coast of America [1839]. James VanStone, trans. *Arctic Anthropology* 6(2):5-20.

Wright, Allen A.
1976   Prelude to Bonanza: The Discovery and Exploration of the Yukon. Sidney, B.C.: Gray's Publishing.

Wright, James V.
1963   An Archaeological Survey Along the North Shore of Lake Superior. *National Museum of Canada, Anthropology Paper* 3. Ottawa.

1964   [Notebook "1964-Ont/Man/Sask/Alta."] (Unpublished manuscript in Archaeological Survey of Canada, National Museum of Man, Ottawa.)

1965   A Regional Examination of Ojibwa Culture History. *Anthropologica* n.s. 7(2):189-227. Ottawa.

1967   The Laurel Tradition and the Middle Woodland Period. *Anthropological Series 79, National Museum of Canada Bulletin* 217. Ottawa.

1967a   The Pic River Site: A Stratified Late Woodland Site on the North Shore of Lake Superior. *Anthropological Series 72, National Museum of Canada Bulletin* 206:54-99. Ottawa.

1968   The Application of the Direct Historical Approach to the Iroquois and the Ojibwa. *Ethnohistory* 15(1):96-111.

1968a   The Boreal Forest. Pp. 55-68 in Vol. 1 of Science, History and Hudson Bay. C.S. Beals, ed. 2 vols. Ottawa: Department of Energy, Mines and Resources.

1969   The Michipicoten Site. Contributions to Anthropology, IV: Archaeology and Physical Anthropology. *Anthropological Series 82, National Museum of Canada Bulletin* 224:1-85. Ottawa.

1970   The Shield Archaic in Manitoba: A Preliminary Statement. Pp. 29-45 in Ten Thousand Years: Archaeology in Manitoba. Walter M. Hlady, ed. Altona: Manitoba Archaeological Society.

1971   Cree Culture History in the Southern Indian Lake Region. *Anthropological Series 87, National Museum of Canada Bulletin* 232:1-31. Ottawa.

1972   The Aberdeen Site, Keewatin District, N.W.T. *Canada. National Museum of Man, Mercury Series, Archaeological Survey Paper* 2. Ottawa.

1972a   Ontario Prehistory: An Eleven-thousand Year Archaeological Outline. Ottawa: National Museum of Man, Archaeological Survey of Canada.

1972b   The Shield Archaic. *Canada. National Museum of Man, Publications in Archaeology* 3. Ottawa.

1975   The Prehistory of Lake Athabasca: An Initial Statement. *Canada. National Museum of Man, Mercury Series, Archaeological Survey Paper* 29. Ottawa.

1975a   [History of Research—Shield Region.] (Manuscript in Wright's possession.)

Yukon Native Brotherhood
1973   Together Today for Our Children Tomorrow, a Statement of Grievances and an Approach to Settlement by the Yukon Indian People: A Report Prepared by the Yukon Native Brotherhood for the Commissioner on Indian Claims and the Government of Canada. Whitehorse, Yukon Terr.: no publisher. (Reprinted in 1977.)

Zagoskin, Lavrentiĭ Alekseevich
1847   Peshekhodnaĭa opis'chasti russkikh vladēniĭ v Amerikīe. 2 vols. St. Petersburg: K. Kraĭĭa.

1956   Puteshestiviia i issledovaniia leitenanta Lavrentiia Zagoskina v Russkoi Amerike v 1842-1844 gg (The Travels and Explorations of Lt. Lavrentii Zagoskin in Russian America in 1842-1844). M.B. Chernenko, G.A. Agranat, and Y.E. Blomkist, eds. Moscow: Gos. izd-vo geogr. lit-ry.

1967   Lieutenant Zagoskin's Travels in Russian America, 1842-1844. Henry N. Michael, ed. (*Anthropology of the North: Translations from Russian Sources 7*) Toronto: Published for the Arctic Institute of North America by University of Toronto Press.

Zaslow, Morris
1971   The Opening of the Canadian North, 1870-1914. Toronto: McClelland and Stewart.

Zibert, Erna V.
1967   Kollektsii pervoĭ poloviny XIX v. po severnym atapaskam. *Sbornik Muzeĭ Antropologii i Etnografii* 24:55-72. Leningrad. [Translation: Erna V. Siebert. "Sammlungen von den nördlichen Athapasken aus der ersten Hälfte des 19. Jahrhunderts" in *Jahrbuch des Museums für Völkerkunde zu Leipzig* 31:113-131. Berlin, 1977; and "Northern Athapaskan Collections of the First Half of the Nineteenth Century" in *Arctic Anthropology* 17(1):49-76, 1980.]

Zimmerly, David W.
1975   Cain's Land Revisited: Culture Change in Central Labrador, 1775-1972. *Memorial University of Newfoundland, Institute of Social and Economic Research Studies* 16. St. John's.

Index

Italic numbers indicate material in a figure; roman numbers, material in the text and tables.

All variant names of groups are indexed, with the occurrences under synonymy *discussing the equivalences Variants of group names that differ from those cited only in their capitalization, hyphenation, italicization, or accentuation have generally been omitted; variants that differ only in the presence or absence of one (noninitial) letter or compound element have been collapsed into a single entry with that letter or element in parentheses.*

Specific reserves and reservations are at reserves and reservations.

The entry Indian and Eskimo words *indexes, by language, all words appearing in the standard orthographies and some others.*

The letter 8 is alphabetized as ou, and θ as th.

A

Abbãto-tenã´; synonymy: 505
Abbatotine; synonymy: 337
Abbitibbes; synonymy: 228
Abel, Elise: *306*
Abel, Kaarina: *554*
Abenaki; external relations: 170, 190. trade: 170
Aberdeen site: 89, *89*
Abitibi; synonymy: 228. *See also* Algonquin; Cree, West Main
Abít·ibi· anicənàbi; synonymy: 228
Abitibi bands. *See* Algonquin
abortion. *See* birth
Abri, Gens de l'; synonymy: *37*
Acasta Lake complex: 97–98, *98, 99,* 100
ʔa·čin; synonymy: 348
Adams, George R.: 49
Adams, Joseph: 160
ʔa·dna·ʔyaʔdəlahğəyu·; synonymy: 662
Adney, Edwin Tappan: 39
adoption: 277, 301, 320, 344, 633
adornment: 438, 503. Assomption sashes: *358, 365, 368, 438.* body and face painting: 221, *250, 262, 263,* 403, 408, 445, 474, 498–499, 509, 517, *522,* 629, 649, 652. body greasing: 403. ear piercing: 221, 445, 498, *522, 571, 572,* 629, 649, *650.* facial hair: 221, 340. hairstyles: *180,* 221, 261, 341, 403, 445, 448, 498, 502, 517, *522,* 571, 629, 652. lip piercing: 420, 424, 430, 629. nose piercing: 221, *250,* 341, 445, 498, 517, *520, 522,* 571, *572,* 577, 629, 649, *650.* ornaments: *48, 224, 246, 250, 340, 343, 359,* 403, 420, 424–425, 430, 445, *464,* 498, *512,* 517, *520, 522, 530,* 570–571, *571, 572,* 575, 629, 649, *650, 656, 710, 728.* tattooing: 221, 263, *294,* 318, 340–341, 403, 420, 425, 445, 499, 517, 571, 609, 629. *See also* beads; clothing; technology

Adsit, George: 468
adzes: 101, *102,* 113, 118, *119,* 122, 124, 126, 127, 219, 570, 612
Aesquimaux; synonymy: 187
afterlife: 195, 408, 448, 465, 519, 527, 620. *See also* supernatural beings
Agate Basin culture: 87–88, *88,* 98
agriculture: 95, 170, 171–172, 246, 356
ʔaɣełne; synonymy: 430
Ahbahaetais: 328. synonymy: 330
Ah-hah-to-din-ne; synonymy: 330, 505
ahδapaska·w; synonymy: 269
ahpiht si·piy; synonymy: 269
Ahtena; synonymy: 662
Ahtna: 43, 47, 50, 622, 633, 638, 641–663. adornment: *48,* 649, *650,* 652, *656,* 661. birth: 657. Cantwell-Denali band: *642.* ceremonies: 577–580, 647–649, 652, 659–600, *660.* childrearing: 649, 657. Chitina-Taral band: *642.* clothing: 649, *649, 650, 651,* 658, 660, *660,* 661. cosmology: 646. curing: 661. death: 658–659, 661. division of labor: 648, 649. education: 643. environment: *9, 12,* 373, *533.* external relations: 494, 502, 565, 641–643, 651, 653. Gulkana band: *642.* history: 643–644, 651, 652, *656.* kinship: 653, 655, 656. Klutina-Copper Center band: *642.* language: 48, 68, *70,* 71–73, 75, 77, 563, 623, 641, 643, *643,* 644. life cycle: 657–659. Lower: 45, 641, *642,* 643–646, *645–647,* 648–652, *650, 651,* 654, *656,* 662. Lower Tonsina band: *642.* marriage: 658, 659. menstrual practices: 658. Mentasta band: 641, 642, *642.* Middle and Western: 624, 641, *642,* 644, 646–648, 654, 662. migrations: 624, 643, 646. music: 649, 660, 661. mythology: 647, 653, 657. orthography: 641. political organization: 641, 656–657, *656.* population: 643, 644. prehistory: 45, 120, 124. puberty: 657–658. religion: 643. Sanford River–Chistochina band: *642.* settlement pattern: 644. settlements: 120, 639, 641, *642, 643,* 644–645. shamanism: 660–661. Slana-Batzulnetas band: *642.* social organization: 631, 653–656. structures: 120, 645–646, *645, 646,* 658. subsistence: 643, 646–649, *647.* synonymy: 661–662. Tonsina-Klutina band: *642.* technology: 645, 647. territory: 641, *642.* trade: 388, 643, 650–652. transport: 649–650, *651.* Tyone-Mendeltna band: *642.* Upper: 641, *642,* 643–646, *650,* 652, 654, 657, *660,* 661, 662. warfare: 642–643, 652, *652*

Ahtnah; synonymy: 662
Ahtna Natives Regional Corporation: 48, 641, 643
Ahtna Tannah Ninnan Association: 641
Ahyunais; synonymy: *37*
Airport site: *113*
air transport: 237, 282, 399, 475, 485, 498, 549, 550, *551,* 553, 567, 587, 597, 621, 630, 671, *674,* 696, 707, 709, 712, 715
Aishihik phase: 115, 124–125
Ai-ya´-na; synonymy: 512, 513
Ai-yan (Indians); synonymy: 505, 512
Akaitcho: 286–288, *286,* 294, 296, 298, 302, 685

Akmak complex: 111
Akat: *669*
akwa·niči·winnu; synonymy: 187
Akwilgét; synonymy: 430
Alaska Central Missions: 643
Alaska Commercial Company: 49, 509, *510,* 548, 612, 636, 643
Alaska Federation of Natives: 554, *554,* 627
Alaska Highway: 399, *400,* 443, 444, 460, 470, 475, 485, 503–504, 553, 567
Alaska Native Brotherhood: 401, 643, 660
Alaska Native Claims Settlement Act of 1971: 3, 48, 81, 401, 554–555, 562, 613, 622, 708, 715
Alaska Native Cooperative movement: 529
Alaska Native Language Center: 47, 562
Alaska native organizations: 401, *554,* 562, 598, 627, 643, 660. *See also* Alaska regional corporations
Alaska Railroad: 549, 568, 587, 705, 706
Alaska regional corporations: 46 48, 401, 555, 587, 598, 613, 641, 643, 708
Alaska Road Commission: 549
Alaska Statehood Act of 1958: 554, 708
Alaska State Housing Authority: 553, 709
Alaxia, Nikolai: *619*
Albany band; synonymy: 228–230. *See also* Cree, West Main
alcohol: 148, 173, 194, 212, 224, 226, 251, 254, 296, 323, 391, 394, 400, 443, 445, 716, 732. abuse: 568, 643, 671, 701, 705–706, 733, 737
Alcoholics Anonymous: 254, 733
Alememipigon; synonymy: 229
Aleut: *631,* 635, 636. synonymy: 642
Alexander (Tanana): *552, 574*
Alexander, Titus: *536*
Alexandria band; synonymy: 431. *See also* Carrier; Chilcotin
Alexis Creek band. *See* Chilcotin
Alex, Mike: 632
Algatcho; synonymy: 431
Algonquian language grouping; Central: 52, 53. Cree branch: 52–56, *53,* 58–64, *61–64.* Eastern: 52, 53. Ojibwa branch: 52–54: *54,* 56–65, *59, 61, 63, 64*
Algonquians: 1, 205, 209–210, 215. ceremonies: 132. external relations: 386. history: 147, 391. marriage: 27, 144. prehistory: 60, 86–87, *93,* 94, 95. religion: 27–28, 719. social organization: 25–26, 28, 86, 151–152, 720. structures: 138. subsistence: 28. synonymy: 64–66. technology: 134, 141, 248. territory: 158–160, *159.* trade: 134, 147. warfare: 164
Algonquin: 208, 209, 215, 241, 243. Abitibi bands: *54, 58,* 243. Argonaut band: 243. Barrière Lake band: *54, 58,* 243. Brennan Lake band: 243. external relations: 170, 190, 212. Grand Lac Victoria band: *54, 58, 59,* 243. history: 147, 148. Kipawa band: 243. Lac Simon band: *54, 58, 59,* 243. language: 52, 56–60, *59, 61,* 227, 228, 243. Long Point band: *54, 58,* 243. migration: 160. population: 160, 243. prehistory: 94, 95. synonymy: 58, 64, 243. Timiskaming band: *54, 58,* 228, 243. territory: 158, 160. trade: 147, 170, 208. Wolf Lake band: 243

Algonquins à têtes-de-Boule; synonymy: 211
Alimibegouek; synonymy: 158. territory: *159*
alimipi·k; synonymy: 229
Alim8spigoiak; synonymy: 306
Alimouspigui; synonymy: 306
Alimouspigut; synonymy: 306
Alkatcho; synonymy: 431
Allard, E.: 443, 450
Allen, Henry T.: 560–561, 566, 569, 586, 705
Al-ta´-tin; synonymy: 441
ʔaẋsmx; synonymy: 430
Áma: 356
Amba-ta-ut-'tinne; synonymy: 330
Ambawtawhoot-din-neh; synonymy: 330
Amiska-Sepee; synonymy: 269
amiskiwiyiniw; synonymy: 359
amisko-si·piy; synonymy: 269
Anaham band. *See* Chilcotin
Anahim: 126, 407
Anaktuvuk Pass site: 122
Anderson, James: 36, 312
ʔangi-daẋnuxʼana; synonymy: 638
Angling Lake band. *See* Ojibwa, Northern
Angoon: 485
animal respect: 132, 177, *177*, 184, *185*, 192,
    194, 201, 202, *202*, 203, 223, 409, 593, 607,
    608, 647–648, 670, *698*, 702, 724, *724, 725*
aniššina·pe·; synonymy: 241, 244
aniššinini; synonymy: 241
An Kutchins; synonymy: 512
Antigun site: 122
antlerwork. *See* technology
Anus-de-l'Eau, gens de l'; synonymy: 295
Apache; Chiricahua: 67. Jicarilla: 67.
    language: 67, 68, 84–85. Lipan: 67, 68.
    Mescalero: 67. migration: 68. Western: 67
Apachean language grouping: 67, 68, 84–85
Apacheans; prehistory: 68
Apet-Sepee; synonymy: 269
a·pihtawikosisa·n; synonymy: 371
apittipi· aniššina·pe·; synonymy: 228
appliqué: *266, 369, 391, 422,* 474, *542, 650,*
    729
Arabuthcow; synonymy: 269
Arathapescow Indians; synonymy: 166, 269
Archaic tradition: 33, *87,* 88–89, *89,* 98
archeology: 257–258, 415, 416, 546. contact
    period sites: 120–121, 124–125. direct
    historical approach: 30–31, 91. fieldwork:
    31–34, 44–46, *46,* 107. historic period sites:
    92, 118–121, 123, 125–126. protohistoric
    sites: 124–126. radiocarbon dating: 88–92,
    94, 95, 98, 99, 101, 103–104, 106, 111, 114–
    117, 123–127. salvage: 34, 45, 46. sites: 31,
    33, 44–46, 87–90, *87–91,* 92, 95, 97–99,
    98, 101, *101,* 102, *103, 108,* 110, 114–117,
    120–127, 575. *See also* prehistory
Arctic Red River band; synonymy: 531. *See
    also* Kutchin
Arctic Slope Native Association: *554*
Arctic Small Tool tradition: 32, 89, 100, 101,
    102, 109, 113, 116–117
Arctic Village band. *See* Kutchin
Argonaut band. *See* Algonquin
armor. *See* clothing
Arrowmaker, Alexis: *304*
arrows. *See* bows and arrows; projectile points
art: 263, 502–503, 509, *611.* circle and dot

design: *503.* chevron designs: 570, *571.*
circle designs: 570, *571.* curvilinear designs:
    523, 722. double curved design: 138, *179.*
floral designs: 248, *249,* 262, *266, 316, 344,*
    392, 392, 422, 429, 474, *486, 500,* 518, *699,*
    722. geometric design: *139, 210,* 262, *288,*
    294, 295, 316, 386, *386, 392,* 410, *410,* 464,
    486, 509, 518, *523,* 652, *721.* human motif:
    410. linear designs: 539. zoomorphic design:
    125, *210,* 246, 378, 410, *410, 464,* 474, *474,*
    475, 476, 478, 485, *486,* 592, 616, *630, 722,*
    728, 729. See also adornment; appliqué;
    basketry; clothing; embroidery; masks;
    pictographs; technology
Artillery Lake complex: 99, 100
Asch, Michael I.: 22
As-ick-an-a; synonymy: *441*
asini·ska·wiδiniwak; synonymy: 270
assemblies: 190, 198, 212, 213, 236, 252, 260,
    298–299, *300,* 303, 315, 320, 343, 346, 352,
    357, 376, 392, 406, 410, 445, 462, 482, 494,
    588, 589, 690. subsistence-related: 133, 137,
    235, 245, 247, 259, 260, 376, 406, 425, 443,
    462, 472, 483, 646, 684. trade-related: 158–
    159, 173, 182, 190, 232, 266, 294–295, 297–
    299, *299, 300,* 303, 322, 346, 389, 392, 462,
    690, 695. war-related: 159. *See also*
    ceremonies; potlatches
Assiniboëls; synonymy: 306
Assiniboin (Saulteaux chief): *249*
Assiniboin; external relations: 84, 264.
    migration: 165. prehistory: 94. synonymy:
    306. territory: 158, *159,* 165–166, 245.
    trade: 160. warfare: 159, 260
Assiniboin, Charlie: *249*
Ataouabouscatouek; synonymy: 158, 229
Ata8ab8skat8cia; synonymy: 229
Ateem Uspeki; synonymy: 283, 309
Athabasca band; synonymy: 168, 269. *See also*
    Cree, Western Woods
Athabasca division. *See* Chipewyan
Athabascan; synonymy: 168
Athabaskan; synonymy: 168
Athabaskaw; synonymy: 269
Athapascan; synonymy: 168
Athapascas; synonymy: 163, 168
Athapaskan; synonymy: 168, 305, 306, 348,
    622
Athapaskan-Eyak: 67–68
Athapaskan language grouping; Northern: 22,
    36, 48, *63,* 67–85, *70, 71,* 315, 326. Pacific
    Coast: 67, 68, 82, 83
Athapaskans, Northern: 1, *2,* 53, 41, 42.
    animal respect: 132. classification: 41–42,
    47, 451–453. clothing: 141. history: 43, 67–
    85, *70, 71.* languages: 67–85. marriage: 27,
    144. prehistory: 30, 33, 44–46, 67–68, 117–
    129. religion: 28. social organization: 26, 27.
    subsistence: 132, *132.* technology: 134, 141.
    territory: 40, 47, 161–168, *162, 165, 166.*
    transport: 138. warfare: 148, 164
Athapaskan tradition in archeology: 113, 114,
    124
athapaskisch; synonymy: 168
Athapeeska Indians; synonymy: 166, 269
Athapescow; synonymy: 166, 168
Athăpeškow; synonymy: 269
Atha-pis-co; synonymy: 269

Athapuscow; synonymy: 168, 228, 269
Atha,pus,kow; synonymy: 269
Atheneuwuck; synonymy: 268
At(h)naer; synonymy: 662
A,tho,pus,cow; synonymy: 269
A'Thopuskow; synonymy: 269
Athupescow; synonymy: 269
Athup pe scau; synonymy: 269
A,thup'pes'cau; synonymy: 269
Aticamegues; synonymy: 214
atihkame·kʷ(ak); synonymy: 208, 213, 214
Atikamègues; synonymy: 214
atikkame·k(ok); synonymy: 214
atima·pi·simwiyiyu·č; synonymy: 196
atimospikay; synonymy: 283, 303
Atim-us-peki; synonymy: 309
Atim-uspiki; synonymy: 283
Atlāshimih; synonymy: 430
atlatls: 443, 612, 626
Atlin band; synonymy: 480. *See also* Tlingit,
    Inland
Atna; synonymy: 661, 662
ʔatnaʔ; synonymy: 662
a·tna·ẏmiut; synonymy: 662
Atnah; synonymy: 662
ʔatnahie·ne; synonymy: 662
Atnakhtāne; synonymy: 662
Atnatána; synonymy: 662
atna't'ene; synonymy: 662
ʔatnaWie·ne; synonymy: 662
Attawapiskat; synonymy: 229, 230. *See also*
    Cree, West Main
Aticameges; synonymy: 214
Atticmospiscayes; synonymy: 306
Attikameg(ouek); synonymy: 213
Attikameg8ek; synonymy: 213
Attikamegouekhi; synonymy: 213
Attikamègues; 3, 208–211. synonymy: 214
Attikamek (Tête de Boule): 186, 205, 208–
    216. ceremonies: *724.* Coocoocash band:
    215. Cuscudidah band: 215. clothing: *722.*
    disease: 208, 211. employment: 213.
    environment: 208, 212, 213. external
    relations: 208, 212, 215. history: 208–213.
    Kikendatch band: 213, 215. language: *53,*
    55, 63, 196, 212, 213, 215, 243. Manouane:
    212, 213, 215. marriage: 208. migration:
    209–211. Obedjiwan: 209, *210,* 212, 215,
    243. orthography: 208. political
    organization: 208, 213. population: 208,
    209, 211–213. reserves: 212. settlement
    pattern: 212. settlements: 213. social
    organization: 212. structures: 213.
    subsistence: 208, *211,* 212, 213. synonymy:
    186, 213–216, 243. technology: *210, 211,*
    215, 722. territory: *159,* 208–211, *209.*
    trade: 208–212. transport: *214–215.*
    warfare: 160, 208, 211. Weymontachingue:
    210, 212, 213, 215
Attimospiquai(e)s; synonymy: 306
Attimospiquay; synonymy: 306
Au Kotchins; synonymy: 512
Aumoussonnites; synonymy: 229
Aurora River complex: 100–102, *102*
avoidance relationships. *See* social
    organization
awahka·n(ak); synonymy: 348
awls: *90,* 92, *93,* 95, 104, *105, 119,* 120, 124,

125, 219, 570, 612

axes: 219, 280, *319*

Ayabaskawiyiniwok; synonymy: 269

aya·hciyiniw; synonymy: 348

A-yan; synonymy: 505, 512

aya·pittawisit; synonymy: 371

ayasčime·w; synonymy: 187

Aylmer Lake site: *103*

Ayonais; synonymy: 512

Aysenatah: *650*

ʔazehne hʷəien; synonymy: 431

B

babiche: 280, *301,* 318, *393,* 424, 462, 511, 518, 570, *570, 613, 633.* bow strings: *132,* 220, 378. containers: *145,* 381, *508,* 734. defined: 280. nets: 134, 175, 201, 340, 424, 436, 443, 516, 596, 604. snareline: 307, 340, 377, *377,* 506, 516, 612. snowshoe lacing: 138, *176,* 221, 233, 262, 341, 381, *382,* 443, 517, 630

Babine Indians; synonymy: 430

Babine Lake band; synonymy: 430. *See also* Carrier

Babines; synonymy: 430

Back site: *103*

bags. *See* containers

Baillargeon, Alfred: *735*

Balikci, Asen: 22

bannock. *See* food

Baouichtigouian; synonymy: 254

Barbue tribe; synonymy: 242

Barger, W. Kenneth: 22

Barnston, George: 241

Barren Ground band. *See* Montagnais-Naskapi

Barren Lands band. *See* Chipewyan; Ojibwa, Northern

Barrière Lake band. *See* Algonquin

Barrières; synonymy: 215

basketry: 406. bark: 118, 120, 125, 340, *383,* 403, 511, 535, *538,* 610, 612, 648. coiled: 141, *145, 410.* decoration: *145, 383, 410,* 509. items: 120, 125, *145, 383,* 403, 405, 425, 516, 518, 535, 626. prehistoric: 118, 125. splint: 235. twined: 612. wicker: 235. woven: 403, 506, 518

Bas,que,ah; synonymy: 270

Bas,qui,a; synonymy: 270

Basquio Indians; synonymy: 270

Bastard Beaver Indians; synonymy: 348

Bastard Loucheux: 323

Bastien, Marie: *135*

Bâtards Loucheux; synonymy: 315

Bates,—: 566

Batza téna site: *113,* 114

Baucannes; synonymy: 440

beads: 221, *222, 554,* 652. berry: 498, 517, *522.* brass: *145.* bone: 92, *93.* clothing decoration: *143, 154,* 177, *180,* 224, *249,* 262, 263, *266, 336, 391, 392, 392, 439, 467,* 474, *474, 483,* 485, 498, 517, *520–523, 542, 570, 571,* 596, 629, *629,* 549, 632, *650, 711, 722, 733.* copper: *90, 95,* 125. dentalium: 120, 125. glass: 106, 120, 123–125, 391, 392, *508,* 518, *520, 609,* 629, *630,* 632, 649, *722.* ornamentation with: *185, 202, 343, 344, 386, 393,* 485, *491, 500, 507,* 610, *630,* 650, *652, 699, 722, 725.* ornaments of: *224, 250,*

512, 609, 628. seed: *143, 145, 154, 180, 202, 249, 391,* 392, 474, 498, 508, 517, *521,* 596, *629, 722.* shell: 120, 125, 517. steel: 518

Beale, Anthony: 159

beamers. *See* fleshers and beamers

Bearlake, Harry: 132

Bearlake Indians: 22, 310–313, 371. education: 311. environment: 310. external relations: 291, 310, 731. health care: 311, 312. history: 310–311, *311,* 401. language: *69, 70,* 72, 77, 79, 80, 310, 315, 326, 339. marriage: 316. migration: 311. population: 312, 313. religion: 311. settlements: 311, *312,* 313. subsistence: *311.* synonymy: 297, 312–313, 315–316, 348. technology: *311.* territory: 161, *162,* 310, *310,* 311

Bear Lakers: *462*

Bear Lake Nomads: 82

Bear Lake tribe; synonymy: 455

Beartooth Island site: *103*

bear tribe; synonymy: 242

Beaulieu, Alexis: *691*

Beaulieu, Elizabeth: *365*

Beaulieu Fort: 364

Beaulieu, François: 363–364, 367

Beaulieu, François, II: 685

Beaulieu, Isadore: *365*

Beaulieu, Jacques: 364

Beaulieu, Jean-Marie: 690, 691

Beaulieu, Joseph: 364

Beaulieu, Joseph King: 364

Beaulieu, Pierre: 689, *690*

Beaver: 20, 22, 268, 345, 350–360, *368,* 373, 433, 440, 452. adornment: *359.* ceremonies: 357. clothing: 352, *358.* cosmology: 353–354, *354.* education: 359. employment: 359. environment: 351–352, 357. external relations: 92, 388, 391, 435. history: 148, 357–359, 391. kinship: 350, 352–353. language: *70,* 72, 77, 81, 82, 84, 167, 350, 359. marriage: 353. migration: 163–167, 357, 435. music: 353, *354, 356,* 357, 358. mythology: 353–355. orthography: 350. population: 351. Prophet River band: 338, 351. puberty: *359.* religion: 353–358, *354, 356.* reserves: *351,* 359. shamanism: *356.* social organization: 350, 352–353. structures: 352, *352,* 357, *359.* subsistence: 167, 350–353, 357–359. synonymy: 163–167, 348, 359. territory: 161–165, *162,* 167–168, 350–351, *351.* trade: 357, 358, *358.* transport: 358. warfare: 148, 162–164, 167, 357, 391, 435

"Beaver" Indians: 163–167

Beaverlodge Portage component: 99

Beaver River band; synonymy: 269. *See also* Cree, Western Woods

Beaver River Indians; synonymy: 166

Beaverskin Lake band. *See* Ojibwa, Northern

bedding: 141, 175, 539, 619

Bella Coola: 413, 422, 430. ceremonies: 425. external relations: 384, 406, 415, 423, 425. history: 388, 394. marriage: 417. prehistory: 416. social organization: 388, 418. subsistence: 375, 376. territory: 402. trade: 388, 404, 406, 411, 416–418, 424

Bell, John: 36

Bell, Robert: 31

Bennett Lake phase: 115, 124–125

bentaWie·ne; synonymy: 576

bəNtə hóianə; synonymy: 576

bəntaxʷiænæ; synonymy: 576

berdaches: 27, *611*

Berens River band. *See* Saulteaux of Lake Winnipeg

Berens, William: *23*

Beringian culture: 128

Bering, Vitus: 635

Bersiamitæ; synonymy: 186

Bersiamites; synonymy: 186

Bersimis; synonymy: 186

Bertiamistes; synonymy: 186

bèpa rédhkkpan; synonymy: 371

Besant phase: 127

Betsiamites band; synonymy: 186. *See also* Montagnais-Naskapi

Beverly Lake-8 site: *103*

Bez Yaz House: 117

Big Bay site: 127

Big Grassy band. *See* Saulteaux of Lake Winnipeg

Big Island band. *See* Saulteaux of Lake Winnipeg

Big Lake Charlie: *486*

Big Men; synonymy: 434, 435, 440

Big Quartz site: *98*

Big Salmon Harry: *486*

Big Salmon Jim: *486*

Big Seymour: *729*

Bigstone band. *See* Cree, Western Woods

bilingualism. *See* language

Billum, Doctor: *646*

Billum, Douglas: *650*

Billum, Mary Ann. *See* Tsacotina

birchbark. *See* basketry; containers; technology

Birch Creek band; synonymy: 532. *See also* Kutchin

Birches site: 46, *108,* 122–123

Birch Indians; synonymy: 532

Birch-rind Indians; synonymy: 289

Birch-rind people; synonymy: 289

Birket-Smith, Kaj: 22, 24, 30

Birote, Albert: 215

birth: 385, 448, 487. abortion: 437. afterbirth: 427, 437, *437,* 508, 590, 610. assistance: 260, 277, 301, 335, 344, 404, 427, 437, 447, 477, 508, 571, 590, 610, 632. ceremonies: 260, 344, 385, 404, 437, 445, 447, 508, 527. fertility rate: 362, 572. illegitimacy: 721. infanticide: 260, 277, 301, 322, 331, 335, 437, 500, 591. location: 260, 301, 335, 344, 380, 404, 427, 437, 447, 487, 498, 508, 571, 590, 632–633, 645, 657. position at: 301, 344, 404, 437, 508, 590. ritual observances: 344, 385, 404, 437, 447, 487, 500, 590, 657, 726. taboos: 404, 427, 487, 526, 571–572, 590–591, 610, 657. umbilical cord: 508, 590

Bishop, Charles A.: 22

Blackduck complex: 92, *93,* 94

Blackfoot: 164, 347, 348. external relations: 84. history: *149.* language: 53

Black Lake band. *See* Chipewyan

Black Lake site: *103*

Black, Mary: 22

Blackned, John: 197, 198

Black River Indians; synonymy: *37*
Black River band; synonymy: 532. *See also* Kutchin
Black, Samuel: 35–36, 433, 434, 439, 441
blackwater "tribe"; synonymy: 431
blankets. *See* clothing
Blood: 164
Bloodvein band. *See* Cree, Western Woods; Saulteaux of Lake Winnipeg
Bloody Falls site: 101, *101*
Boas, Franz: 39
boats. *See* transport
Bod Indians; synonymy: 200
body painting: *See* adornment
bois-brûlé; synonymy: 371
Bois Forts, Gens des; synonymy: 348
Bois, Gens de(s); synonymy: 504, 512
bolas: 201, 626
Bompas, William C.: 396, 511
Bonanza Creek site: 114
Bone, Billy: *486*
bonework. *See* technology
Boniface, Roger: *322*
Boreal Archaic tradition: 32
Bortnovsky, John: 44
Bourget, Clermont: 688–689
Bouscouttons; synonymy: 229
bow drill: 517, 535, 619, 652, *670*
bows and arrows: 106, *172*, 262, 303, 318, 378, 408, 436, 497, 518, 652. arrows: 92, 95, 103, 118, *118*, 120, 124, *132*, 220, 234, *261*, 280, 307, 378, 424, 473, 496, 506, 516, 517, *535*, 566, 569, 612, 626. bows: *132*, *246*, *261*, 280, 307, 378, 424, 436, 456, 473, *507*, 517, *522*, *535*, 612, 626. crossbow: 175, *197*, 201, 234. fishing: 343. holding and release: *132*, *197*, 307, 378, *507*, 517, *535*, 612, *670*. hunting: 132, *132*, 133, 174, 175, 201, 220, 260, 276, 317, 340, 376, *377*, 390, 403, 425, 436, 443, 456, 462, 473, 484, 496, 506, 516, 517, 535, 566, 569, 604, 612, 619, 626, 647, 648, *670*. manufacture: 132, *132*, 220, 234, 280, 378, 436, 473, 496, 517, *535*, 569, *670*. prehistoric: 103. quivers: *172*, *246*, 307, 378, 403, *507*, *522*, 612, *630*. toy: 197, 221
boxes. *See* containers
Brador site: 95, *96*
breed; synonymy: 371
Brennan Lake band. *See* Algonquin
Breynat, Gabriel: *690*
bridges. *See* structures
Brie, Gens de; synonymy: *37*
Bristol Bay Native Corporation: 48
British Columbia Native Brotherhood: 401
British North America Act of 1867: 398
Brokenhead band. *See* Saulteaux of Lake Winnipeg
Broken Slavey: 347, 392, 529
Brown Corporation: 213
Brown, Johnny: *486*
Bruneau, Jimmy: 298, *304, 305*
Bruneau, Joseph (Susie): 298
Bruno. *See names at* Bruneau
Brunswick House band. *See* Cree, Western Woods
Buchanan site: 101, 102
Bulkley Carrier; synonymy: 430
Bulkley River; synonymy: 430

Bulkley River band. *See* Carrier
Bungee(s); synonymy: 241, 244
Bungi; synonymy: 241
Bureau of Indian Affairs (U.S.); education: 567, 597, 643. health care: 401. housing: 553, 707–709
burial: 405, 439, 465. abandonment: 279, 548. caches: 223, 448, 519, 591. cemeteries: *611*. coffins: 420, 425, 438, 448, 610, *611*, 659. cremated remains: 634, 659. dog: 95. grave construction: 262, 659. grave houses: 405, *405*, 428, 465, 478, 501, *501*, 502, 572, 591, *592, 611*, 616, *634*, 659. grave markers: 223, 262, 301, 405, 425, 428, *428*, 448, 465, *487*, 501, *611*, 634, *634*, 727. grave offerings: 223, 262, 301, 320, 344, 519, 591, 616, 634. inhumation: 323, 344, 405, 438, 448, 478, 488, 548, 572, 591, 610, 634. mounds: 90, 94. prehistoric: 90, 94, 101. scaffold: 301, 320, 323, 344, 438. tombs: 106. *See also* death practices; mourning
Burns, Charlie: *486*
Burns Lake band; synonymy: 430. *See also* Carrier
Burwash Landing band. *See* Tutchone
Bute, Gens de; synonymy: *37*
Buteux, Jacques: 209
buttes, gens des; synonymy: 575

C

Cache River people; synonymy: 515
caches: 318, 332, 340, 341, 376, 380, 443, 473, 483, 484, 496, 498, 508, 549, *549*, 588, 646. corpse: 223, 448, 519, 591. pits: 120, 124, 125, 220, 472, 566, 588, 645, 648. platforms: 406, 444, *497, 573*, 628, 645, *646*, 668, *698*. racks: 135, 176–177, 220. watercraft: 177, 182, 474, 484
Cadzow Lake site: *108*, 120
cahkatina·w si·piy; synonymy: 269
Cahto; language: 67
calendars. *See* cosmology
Calison site: 116
Calista Corporation: 48
Callbreath, J.C.: 38, 468
Cameron, Duncan: 242
Campbell, Johnny: 706
Campbell, Robert: 35, 36, 452, 503, 509, 512
camps: 126, *140*, 182, 236, 243, *247, 263, 279, 318, 319*, 327, 333, *335*, 405, 484, 496, 566, 604, 618, *669*. fishing: 46, 122, 133, 137, 298, *312*, 341, 375, 379, 462, 471, 483, *497*, 498, 507, 508, 545, 551, 558, 560–561, 565, 566, *568*, 569, 571, 588, 597, 598, 612, 627, 628, 646, 668, 694, 695, *707*. gathering: *247*. hunting: 120, 121, 137, 177, *177, 224, 281, 378*, 558, 565, 566, *573*, 588, 604, 646, 668, *669*. prehistoric: 46, 87, 121, 122
Campus site: 44, 45, 46, 107, *108*, 110, 111, 113
Camsell, Julian S.: 364
Canada, government of: 328, 345, 423, 469, 664, 674, *674*. adoption: 301. administration: 268, 311, 323, 399, 400, 529, 716. economic development: 268, 323, 346, 426, 678, *678*, 692, 713. education: 218, 237, 238–239, 282, 296, 311, 322, 347, 399, 400, 504, 529, 680, 691, 696. employment: 401,

682. health care: 218, 238, 254, *265*, 282, 291, 296, 311, 322, 323, 328, 347, 400–401, 691, 696. housing: 149, 267, 282, 281, *292*, 296, 311, 323, 498, 682, 696. land rights policy: 148–149, 203, 398, 401, 425–426, 482, 504, 702–703, 715. relocation: 282. welfare: 218, 226, 237, 239, 254, 282, 291, 296, 323, 347, 401, 504, 691, 692, 696, 712, 713. wildlife preserves: 218, 690. *See also* Department of Indian Affairs and Northern Development; legislation, Canadian; litigation, Canadian; treaties, Canadian
Canadian National Railway: 237, 397
Canadian Pacific Railway: 237, 397
Canadian Tundra tradition: 100–102, *101, 102*
Canham, Thomas: 38
cannibalism: 173, 249, 253, *263*, 322, 443. mythological: 184, 200, 223, 233, 253, 263, 319, 356–357, 365, 595. ritual: 194, 377, 443, 652
Canoe Lake band. *See* Cree, Western Woods
canoes: *21*, 137, 177, 198, 199, 259, 260, 299, 328, 390, 417, *568*, 604, *678*. bark: 390, 444, 456, 462. birchbark: 86, 138, 155, 199, *200*, *215*, 221, 223, 234, 235, *236*, 237, 248, *248*, 262, *263*, 280, *295*, 303, *305*, 307, 318, 341, 377, 380, 425, 498, 506, 518, *538, 539*, 569, 612, 618, 630, 650, *689*. canvas: 223, 234, *236*, 237, 307, *530*. construction: 138, 158, 177, *181, 215*, 234, 235, *236*, 262, 280, *343*, 380, *538*, 596. dugout: 380, *381*, 390, 403, 425, *427*, 437, *437*, 444, 474, 485, 498. fishing from: 174, 379, 403, 405, 566, 569, 604, 605. freight: 155, *156*, 197, 199, 202, 237, 318, 365, 462, 612, 618, *689*. hunting from: 132, 175, *215*, 221, 276, 280, 378, 380, *538*, 612, 626, 648, 650. paddles: *172*. prehistoric: 86. races: 198, 199. sails: 462, 474. sleds: 138, 177, 233, 234, 604. spruce bark: 307, 333, *341, 343*, 380, 425, 485, 498, 650. storage of: 177, 182, 474
Canteen site: *101*
Cantwell-Denali band. *See* Ahtna
Cantwell, George G.: 39
Canyon site: *108*, 115
Captain Slim. *See* Slim Jim
Carcross band. *See* Tagish
Caribou Eaters. *See* Chipewyan
Caribou Eskimo; territory: 271
Caribou Indians; synonymy: 505
Caribou Island complex: 99–100, *99*
Caribou Island site: 98
Caribou Lake Band. *See* Ojibwa, Northern
Caribou site: *103*
Carmack, George: 482, 491
Carmacks band. *See* Tutchone
Carribeau Eaters; synonymy: 683, 684
Carrier: 1, 3, 40, 41, 373, 387, 408, 413–433, 440, *441*, 451. adornment: 420, *420*, 424–425, 430. Alexandria band: 414–416, *414*, 431. Babine Lake band: 41, 69, *70*, 72, 77, 83, *414*, 415, 416, 418, 419–421, 424–426, 429–431, 455, 530. birth: 427. Bulkley River band: 83, *414*, 415, 416, 418–421, 424–426, 428–432, 435. Burns Lake band: 416, 430. ceremonies: 418–424, 428, 429. Cheslatta band: *414*, 415, 416, 431. childrearing: 427. clothing: 420, *421, 422*, 424, 425, 428, *429*.

curing: 425, 429. death: 420, 421, 423, 425, 428, *428*, 429. disease: 418. division of labor: 427. employment: 418, 426–427. environment: 374, 375, 420, 425, 426. external relations: 384, 415, 435, 438, 439, 455. Fort Fraser band: 423, 432. Fort George band: *414*, 416, 431. Fraser Lake band: *414*, 416, 429, 431, 435. Hagwilget band: 414, 415, *422, 428*. history: 35, 38, 39, 388, 389, 391, 394, 397, 410, 416, 425, 431, 441. kinship: 419. Kluskus band: 415, 416, 422, 431. language: 38, 69, *70*, 72, 77, 83, 84, *84*, 372, 402, 413, 415, 420, 430. life cycle: 425, 427–428. Lower: 394, 415. marriage: 417–420, 422–424, 428, 435, 438. menstruation: 425, 428. migration: 117, 126, 413, 415. Moricetown band: 416. music: 423, 425, 429. mythology: 420. Nazko band: *414*, 415, 416, 422, 431. Necoslie band: 416, 430. Northern: 415, 416, 418–423, 427, 428, 430, 432. Nulki band: *414*. Omineca band: 416, 430. orthography: 413. political organization: 418, 421. population: 413, 415–416, 418, 425. prehistory: 117, 125–126, 415–416. puberty: 425, 427–428. Quesnel band: 416, 431. religion: 428–430. reserves: 413, 425–426. settlement pattern: 413. settlements: 125–126, *394*, 413. shamanism: 425, 429. social organization: 384, 413–415, 417–424, *421*. Southern: 415, 416, 418, 419, 422–423, 425. Stellaquo band: *414*, 416, 431. Stony Creek band: 413, 416, 419, 429, 431. structures: 126, 379, 417, 420, 421, 425, 427, 428. Stuart Lake band: 38, 384, 414, 415, 416, 429, 432, 435. Stuart-Trembleur Lake band: *414*, 415, 416, 430. subsistence: 375, 379, 381, *383*, 415, 417, 420, 424–426, *426, 427*. synonymy: 430–431. Tachick band: *414*. Takla Lake band: 413, 415, 416, 431. Takulli band: 41, 430. technology: 378, *383*, 388, 397, *417, 419*, 424–425. territory: 413, *414*, 421–422. trade: 126, 375, 388, 410, 415, 419, 435. transport: 378, 380–381, 390, *393*, 417, 425, *427, 437, 434*. Ulkatcho band: 126, 413, *414*, 415, 416, 419, 422, 424, 425, 430–432. Upper: 397, 415. warfare: 162, 388, 410, 435.
Cartier, Jacques: 147, 171
Casca; synonymy: 449
Caspit: *428*
Cassiar; synonymy: 449
Castor, Gens de; synonymy: 359
Castors; synonymy: 359
Cat Lake band. *See* Ojibwa, Northern
Catlin, George: 248
caxĭana; synonymy: 638, 662
caynən xĭan; synonymy: 638
ca·y Wĭe·ne; synonymy: 662
če·ma·nipistikwinnu; synonymy: 187
čəntezni²ai; synonymy: 431
Central Ojibwa-Odawa; synonymy: 65
ceramics. *See* pottery
ceremonies: *503*, 522, 567, 721, 724. bear: 257, 320, 409, 577. birth: 260, 344, 385, 404, 437, 445, 447, 508, 527. Bladder: 607, *728*. Circle Dance: 519. curing: 251–253, *252*, 262, 266, 319, 409, 465, 634. dancing at: 149, 198, 221, 224, 263, 279, 298, 299, 303,

315, 320, 336, 343, 352, 357, 376, 385, 386, 391, 392, 396, 406, 408–410, 423, 429, 445, 465, *476*, 478, 488, 490, 503, 509, *510*, 527, 528, 571, 579, 580, 591, 593, *594*, 595, 608, 649, 660, *660*, 702, *710, 711*, 730, 732, 733, *735*. death: 344, 385, 421, 423, 438, 445, 465, 478, *486*, 488, 501–502, 508, 509, 519, 527, 541, 544, 574, 578–580, 591–593, *594*, 607, 608, 610, 616, 620, 632, 634, 659–660, 697, 698, 702, 705, 709, 727, 728–730, *729, 732*. disposition of goods at: 385, *422, 423*, 463, 488, 501–502, 527, 580–581, 591, *594*, 607, 608, 610, 620, 634, 659, 660, 705. Doll's: 607. Drum Dance: 303, 343, 732, *735*. eclipse: 527, 577. fasting: 409, 439, 657. Feast of Animals' Souls: 607, 608, *609*. feasts at: 149, 182, 184, *185*, 192, 198, 260, 263, 320, 344, 385, 391, 404, 405, 408, 410, 438, 445, 462, 463, 465, 478, 484, 501, 527, 541, 579, 588, 591, 593, *594*, 607, 608, 620, 634, 647, 659, 697, *698*, 702, 730–731. first kill: 260, 320, 385, 445, 527, 577, 608, 633, 657. first salmon: 527, 593, 608, 647. fishing: 202, 484, 647. games at: 149, 198–199, 263, 527, 593, 608, 709. gathering: 484, 648. geese: 28, 202. gunho dance: 580. Hot Dance: 607, 608, 728. hunting: *177, 179, 185*, 192, 202, 220–223, 260, 319, *337*, 484, 518, 577, 593, 607, 608, 620, 635, 647–648. *makusa·n:* 670. *manito·hke·wak:* 231. marriage: 261, 279, 301, 303, 319, 405, 445, 465, 591, 593, 608, 632, 633. Mask Dance: 607, *729, 730*. mimetic: 303. music at: 184, 198, 221, 251, 263, 343, 408, 409, 423, 478, *486*, 488, 490, 501, 571, 579–580, 593, *594*, 608, 649, 652. naming: 260, 423, 427. Partner's Potlatch: 607, *608*, 610. peace: 445, 478–479. postcontact: 202, 252, *253*, 265, 303, 488, 502, 527, 577, 593, 607, 621, 634, 658, 659, 660, *660*, 702, 709, *710, 711*, 731–732. Prophet Dance: 429, 439. puberty: 277, 301, 335, 336, 344, 405, 465, 508, 527, 608, 633. Round Dance: 343. sacrifices: 263. shaking-tent: 28, 177, 184, 223, 238, 251, *251*, 262, 266, 719, 733, 735. shamanistic: 429, 595, 607, 637, 661, 719. smoking at: 478. spring: 320, 527, 730. Stick Dance: *594*. structures for: 126, 177, 184, 198, 220, *251*, 252–253, *252*, 357, 380, 421, 444, 591, 608, 610, 613, 616. Tea Dance: 303, 339, 343, 732, *735*. war: 319, 408, 519, 652. weather related: 192. *See also* clothing, ceremonial; potlatches
Chalkyitsik people; synonymy: 515
Champagne-Aishihik band. *See* Tutchone
Champagne band. *See* Tutchone
Champagne complex: 115
Champlain, Samuel de: 173, 191, *192*
Chandalar band; synonymy: 515, 532. *See also* Kutchin
Chandelar; synonymy: 515
Chapleau Cree band. *See* Cree, Western Woods
Chapman, Henry H.: 50
Chapman, John W.: 44, 50, 51
Charley, Frank: *48*
Charley's Indians; synonymy: 513
Charley, Tenas: *647*

Charlie (Tanana): *552, 574,* 705
Charlie, Bessie: *710*
Charlie Creek Indians; synonymy: 513
Charlie, Mabel: 538
Charlie, Moses: *571, 710*
Charlie, Neal: *710*
Charlo, Angus: *735*
Charlo, Charles: *306*
Charlo, Joe: *735*
Charlo, Narcisse: *735*
Charlot River site: *91, 103,* 104
Chasta Costa; language: 67
Chawchinahaw: 276
Cheechov, Clayton: *224*
Cheepawyans; synonymy: 161, 283
Chekamekiriniwak; synonymy: 211
Chek8timiens; synonymy: 186
Chemahawin band. *See* Cree, Western Woods
Chena band. *See* Tanana
Chepawyans; synonymy: 92, 283
Chepewyan; synonymy: 283
Cheslatta; synonymy: 431. *See also* Carrier
Cheslatta Lake Indians; synonymy: 431
Cheta-ut-tdinnè; synonymy: 336, 337
Chetco; language: 67
Chettyna; synonymy: 662
Cheyenne; migration: 229
Chicanee; synonymy: 440
Chic(h)edec; synonymy: 187
Chichesedecum; synonymy: 187
Chickalusion, Simeon: 632
Chicoutimi band; synonymy: 186. *See also* Montagnais-Naskapi
Chicoutimiens; synonymy: 186
chieftainship. *See* political organization
Chilcotin: 1, 35, 41, 373, 387, 402–413, 416, 431. adornment: 403. Alexandria band: 407, 411, 414, 430. Alexis Creek band: 407, 411, 412. Anaham band: 407, 411. art: 410. birth: 404. ceremonies: 126, 408, 409. childrearing: 404. clothing: 403. curing: 409. death: 405, *405*. disease: 411, 418. division of labor: 403–404, 406. education: 412. employment: 412. environment: 374, 375, 402, 405, 412. external relations: 406–407, 423. games: 403, 410. history: 38, 39, 394, 410–412. kinship: 407. language: 38, 68, *70*, 72, 77, 83–84, 372, 402, 408, 415. life cycle: 404–405. marriage: 405. migration: 117, 388, 402, 406, 412. music: 403, 408–410. mythology: 402, 410. Nemaiah Valley band: 407, 411, 412. orthography: 402. political organization: 406, 407, 411–412. population: 411, 418. prehistory: 117, 125. puberty: 404–405, 409. religion: 408–409. reserves: *402*, 407, 412. Riske Creek band: 407, 411. settlement pattern: 406. settlements: 126, *402*, 407, 411. shamanism: 409. social organization: 384, 388, 404, 407, 408. Stone band: 407, 411. structures: 126, 379, 403, *403*, 405, *405*, 406. subsistence: 375, 376, 379, 403, 405–406, 412. synonymy: 412, 415. technology: 378, 402–403, *403, 404*, 406, 408, *410*. territory: 402, *402*. Toosey band: 407, 411. trade: 388, 404, 406, 410–411, 418. transport: 381, 403, 406, 412. warfare: 388, 394, 403, 406–408, 411
children: 607, 611, 657. adoption: 277, 301,

320, 344, 633. adornment: *512, 520.*
clothing: *139,* 141, 177, *178–179,* 262, *286,*
334, 344, *364,* 383, 508, *520, 542, 650.*
custody: 261, 591. discipline: 193, 260, 447,
448. duties: 180, 192, 193, 260, 277, 404,
487, 588, 627. games: 221, *221,* 487.
hunting: *197.* infants: 177, 192–193, 222,
235, *236,* 260, 277, *277, 299,* 301, 331, 335,
341, 344, *344,* 403, 404, *404,* 425, 427, 437,
438, 448, 477, 487, *499, 500,* 508, *520,* 572,
572, 573, 590, 610, 613, 633, 648–650, 651,
699. marriage: 261, 277, 319, 336, 508, 591.
mixed blood: 392. naming: 260, 301, 423,
427, 437, 590, 633. number of: 277. nursing:
260, 344, 404, 437, 438, 610. orphans: 192.
prayers: 194. toys: *197,* 221. training: 182,
355, 376, 391–392, 427, 428, 447, 477, 490,
572, 595, 610, 633, 635, 649, 657. twins:
260, 404. *See also* puberty
Chilkat. *See* Tlingit
Chilkhodins; synonymy: 412
Chimi site: 115
Chimo band. *See* Montagnais-Naskapi
Chinashagun, Sam: *274*
Chindadn complex: 114, 128
Chinlac site: 125–126
Chinook Jargon: 466, 504
Chip; synonymy: 283
Chi-pa-why-ans; synonymy: 283
Chipewyan: 2, 20, 22, *165, 166,* 166–168, 219,
228, 267, 271–286, 288, 289, 293, 306, 309,
325, 338, 348, 350, 359, 371, 392, 683–693.
Athabasca division: 271, 273. Barren Lands
band: *268, 274,* 275, 280–282, 284. birth:
277. Black Lake band: 275, 280, 282, 283.
Caribou Eaters division: 271, 273–275, 280–
283, 683, 684. ceremonies: 277. Churchill
band: 271, 275, 280, 282. Churchill River
division: 273. clothing: *277,* 279, 280, *280,*
281, 283. Cold Lake band: 81, 275, 284.
curing: 279. death: 279. disease: 273, 274.
division of labor: 279, *279,* 282. Duck Lake
band: 275, 280, 282. education: 274, 282.
employment: 282. English River band: 275.
environment: 271–273, 275, 282. external
relations: 92, 282, 285–287, 291, 315, 316,
391. Fitz-Smith band: 275. Fond Du Lac
band: 275, 280, 283. Fort Chipewyan band:
275. Fort McKay band: 275. Fort McMurray
band: 275. games: 279. Hatchet Lake band:
275, 280. health care: 274, 282. history: 80,
148, 273–274, *274,* 280–283, 285, 287, 288,
368, 391, 401, 682–693, *690.* Janvier band:
275. kinship: 277. language: 69, *70,* 72, 77,
80–81, *81,* 271, 275, 291, 339, 685. life
cycle: 277, 279. marriage: 276, 277, 279,
286, 297, 361, 364, 685. migration: 92, 163,
164, 167, 168, 258, 276–277, 282. music:
279. mythology: 279, 302. Northland band:
275. orthography: 271. Peter Pond band:
275. population: 273–275, 282, 691. political
organization: 684–685, 688. Portage La
Loche band: 275. prehistory: 92, 100, 102,
103, 106, 258. puberty: 277. religion: 273,
279. reserves: 359. Resolution band: 275,
683–693. settlements: 281, *281,* 282.
Snowdrift band: 275, 284. social
organization: 28, 141, 275–277, 280–282,

684. Stony Rapids band: 275, 280.
structures: 131–132, *140,* 279, 280, 281, *281,*
282. subsistence: 131–133, 273–277, 279–
281, *281,* 684. synonymy: 185, 283, 305,
306, 325, 337. technology: 134, *139, 145,*
275, *279,* 280. territory: 92, 162–164, *162,*
166, 167, 168, 258, 271, *272, 279,* 280, 285.
trade: 148, *153,* 273, 276, 283, 288, 296,
321, 345. transport: *139,* 276, 279, 281, 282,
689. warfare: 106, 148, 161–164, 260, 273.
See also Yellowknife
Chippewa: language: 52, 65–66. synonymy:
66, 244, 255
Chippewa, Southwestern; synonymy: 243. *See
also* Ojibwa
Chippew(e)yans; synonymy: 283
Chip-pe-wi-yan; synonymy: 283
Chisana Joe: *537*
Chisdec; synonymy: 187
Chisedech; synonymy: 187
Chisedeck; synonymy: 187
chithos: *91, 93,* 103, 104, *105,* 106, 118, 123–
125, 570
Chitina band. *See* Ahtna
Chi-tra-gottinék(h)é; synonymy: 336
Choris culture: 113
Chouart des Groseilliers, Médard: 147, 201
Chrétien, Jean: *678*
Christean; synonymy: 227
Christeens; synonymy: 227
Christian(aux); synonymy: 227
Christian Indians; synonymy: 199
Christianity: 75, 148, 150, 183–185, 191, 194,
202, 203, 218, 238, 240, 253, 259, 264, 273,
294, 299, 303, 311, 322, 357–358, 362, *394,*
395–396, *397, 422,* 429–430, 439, 448, 449,
479, 488, 490, 509, 511, 515, 548, 551, 567,
586, 599, 611, 620, 621, 634, 643, 673, 675–
677, *702,* 710, 724, 731. *See also*
missionaries; missions
Christianux; synonymy: 227
Christinaux: 160. synonymy: 158, 227, 257.
territory: *159*
Christinos; synonymy: 227
Chucketanaw; synonymy: 269
Chuckitanau; synonymy: 269
Chugach Eskimo: 635, 662. marriage: 636.
synonymy: 642. territory: 641. trade: 651.
warfare: 642–643, 651
Chukchi: 546, 561, 650
Chuki-tanu sipi; synonymy: 269
Churchill band. *See* Chipewyan
Churchill River band; synonymy: 269. *See also*
Cree, Western Woods
Churchill River division. *See* Chipewyan
chutes and pounds. *See* structures, hunting
enclosures
cicisbeism. *See* marriage
ci·gèhⁿẑik gʷičin; synonymy: 531
Cigne; synonymy: 440
či gotine; synonymy: 295
ciłkoⁱtin; synonymy: 412
činⁱquⁱin; synonymy: 412
či·pwaya·n; synonymy: 283
Circumpolar complex: 24
čiše·-ša·či·winnu; synonymy: 187
čiše·-ši·pi·winnu; synonymy: 205
čiše·-si·pi·wiyiyu; synonymy: 205

čí· žak gʷičin gí·; synonymy: 371
Clairmont, D.H.T.: 22
clans. *See* social organization
Clark, Isaiah: *267*
Clatchotin; synonymy: 576
Clearwater Lake phase. *See* Selkirk complex
climate. *See* environment
Clisteens; synonymy: 160
clothing: 260, 283, 298, *304,* 314, 315, 335,
358, 420, *421,* 425, 632. armor: 408, 424,
652. blankets: 138, 141, *143, 144,* 155, 175,
177, 219, *224,* 235, *236, 250,* 262, 294, 294,
296, 308, 318, 333, 334, *364, 391,* 403, 420,
424, 437, 462, 474, *474,* 572, 578, 613, *669,*
729. ceremonial: 202, *202,* 261, 335–336,
385, 390, 420, *422,* 425, 427, 448, *464,* 465,
467, 474, 475, 476, 477, 485, *486,* 488, *489,*
500, 524–525, *544,* 572, 580, *590,* 591, *594,*
596, *608,* 610, 633, 658, *660, 710, 711, 729,*
730, 733. children: 141, 177, *178–179,* 262,
286, 334, 344, *364,* 383, *520, 542, 650, 669.*
Cordillera area: 383, *383.* decoration: 138,
143, 153, 154, *154,* 177, *178–179,* 221, 224,
224, 246, 248–249, *249,* 262, 263, *266, 267,*
294, *316,* 318, *336,* 340, *340,* 342, 343, 369,
383, 386, *391,* 392, *392,* 420, *421, 422, 429,*
439, 445, *465, 467, 474, 474, 475, 476, 483,*
485, *486, 498,* 503, 509, 517, 518, *520–523,*
539, 542, 570, *571,* 596, 615, 619, *629, 629,*
632, 649, *649, 650, 710, 711, 720, 721, 733.*
dog: 155, *391, 392.* footwear: *20,* 138, 141,
142–143, 154, *176,* 177, 179, 179, 220, *223,*
224, *224,* 233, 235, 237, *239,* 246, *250,* 262,
266, 286, 308, 318, 333–334, 340, 383, 392,
392, 403, 424, 437, *438,* 443, 445, 456, 462,
465, 474, 485, 506–507, 517, 518, *521,* 539,
570, *570,* 588, 596, 597, 613, 619, 629, 668,
722. garments: *144,* 177, 220, *223, 224,* 233,
235, *238,* 246, 247, *249, 250,* 261, 262, *266,*
267, 280, *281, 286,* 288, 308, 318, 333–334,
340, 383, *392,* 403, *421, 422,* 424, *429,* 437,
438, 439, 443, 445, 456, 462, *464, 465,* 474,
474, 475, 483, 485, *486, 489,* 498, *499,* 506,
517, 518, *520–523, 530,* 539, *542,* 566, 570,
570, 571, 574, 588, *594,* 596, 613, 619, 628–
629, *629,* 649, *649–651, 660, 669, 721.*
handwear: 141, 154, 220, *223,* 224, 233, 235,
237, 248–249, *249,* 262, *266,* 267, *286,* 308,
318, 340, *369,* 383, 424, 437, 443, 445, 456,
498, 517, *521,* 539, *570,* 588, 596, 613, 619,
649, *669.* headgear: 138, *176, 180,* 220, *220,*
224, 261, 262, *316,* 335, *336,* 340, *364,* 365,
367, 383, 403, 420, *422,* 424, 425, 427, 437,
464, 467, 474, 474, 475, 477, *486,* 488, *489,*
500, 517, *521,* 524–525, *530,* 539, *544,* 570,
570, 572, 588, *590,* 591, *594,* 596, 610, 613,
619, 633, 649, 658, *710,* 722, *726, 726, 727.*
manufacture: 137, 138, *142–143,* 177, *178–*
179, 219, 220, 224, 262, 294, 318, 334, 340,
351, 377, 383, 392, 437, 443, 445, 473, *476,*
485, 498, 506–508, 516–518, *521,* 539, 566,
570, 596, 597, 613, 615–616, 629, 632, 649.
postcontact: 153, 154, *154, 178–179,* 185,
220–221, 224, *224,* 232, 233, *238, 247,* 262,
288, 308, 445, 474, *530, 574,* 597, 629, *660.*
Shield Subarctic area: 138, 141, *142–143,*
144, 153–154, *154. See also* adornment
clubs: 133, *152, 172,* 484, 570, 612

Clut, Isidore: 78
Coast culture: 24, 30
Coaster(s); synonymy: 205, 229. *See also* Cree, East Main
Coaster, Willie: *239*
coast Indians; synonymy: 230
Codzi, Charlie: *317*
ċo· godn ni·gn ii·n; synonymy: 576
Cohen, Ronald: 22
Colcharnies; synonymy: 652
Cold Lake band. *See* Chipewyan
Collins, Raymond L.: 75, 622
Collison, W.H.: 456
Common Indian; synonymy: 228
Conaquanta: *656*
ċoⁿdik hwəiin; synonymy: 513
Connenagh (tribe); synonymy: 466, 467
Conseil Attikamek-Montagnais: 213
Constance Lake band. *See* Cree, Western Woods; Cree, West Main
containers: 224, 232, *249*, 377, 393, *421*, 462, 477, 485, *486*, *537*, *649*; bark: 141, 340, 381, 403, 436, 437, 443. birchbark: 135, 141, *145*, 175, 201, *210*, 219, 235, 237, *237*, 248, 262, *383*, 424, 535, 542, 569, 619. birdskin: *145*. bone: *379*. cedar root: 424. fishskin: 141, 249. hide: 135, 141, *145*, 175, 232, 381, 403, 437, 443, *466*, *485*, 506, *508*, *522*, 612, 722. metal: 175, 232, 263. moss bags: 177, *236*, *277*, 341, 344, *344*, *364*, 383, 573, 633, *651*, *669*, 722. octopus bags: *486*, *491*, *722*. pine bark: 141. spruce bark: 141, 424, 648. spruceroot: 141, *145*, 220, 333, 340, 381, *383*, 436, 506, 596. stomach: 201, 220, 318, *335*, 381, 443, 612. stone: 220, 232. wood: 141, 175, *379*, 424, 437, 459, 612, *633*. *See also* basketry; pottery
Coocoocash band; synonymy: 215. *See also* Attikamek (Tête de Boule)
Cook Inlet Historic Sites Project: 46
Cook Inlet Native Association: *554*
Cook Inlet Region, Inc.: 46, 48
Cook, James: 43, 635
Cooper, John M.: 20–22, *21*, 24–26
COPE (Committee for Original Peoples' Entitlement): 715
Copper Chief: 494, 500
Copper Eskimo; Kiluhikturmiut band: 106. prehistory: 30, 106. technology: 30, 106
Copper Indians: 285, *286*, 287, 293, 294. synonymy: 289
Coppermine (river) Indians; synonymy: 289
Copper River Native Association: 641
cosmology: 376. calendar: 320, 646. directions: 341. world view: 353–357, *354*, 479, 490, 502, 526–527, 595, 718. *See also* mythology
Cosna-Manley subdivision. *See* Koyukon
Cote, J.A.: *368*
Côtes-de-Chien; synonymy: 309
còtiè goiine; synonymy: 295
còti hoii; synonymy: 297. *See also* Dogrib
Council for Yukon Indians: 41, 79
Couteaux Jaunes; synonymy: 289
Couteaux rouge; synonymy: 289
Cox, Bruce: 22
Cox, Ross: 410
Co-Y(o)ukon; synonymy: 599
ċoʒu· wəčin; synonymy: 513

cradles: 403, *404*, 427, 487, *520*, 572, *573*, 633, 649–650, *651*. cradleboards: *222*, *224*, 234, 235, *236*, 260, *261*, 425, 518
Cramer, G.F.: 552
Cranes band. *See* Ojibwa, Northern
crasse de l'eau, ĝens de la; synonymy: 289
Crazy, Thomas: *274*
creation. *See* mythology
Cree: 2–3, 20, 22, 23, 26, *157*, 161, *165*, *166*, 198, 201, 208, 215, 238, 241, 246, 247, 255, 271, 279, 283, 289, 292, 294, 303, *305*, 309, 338, 348, 350, 371, *433*. ceremonies: 251, *725*, 735. clothing: *155*. employment: 245, 391. external relations: 92, 199–200, 231, 282, 296, 316, 388, 391, 435. games: 732. history: 148, 151, 203, 245, 273, 282, *368*, 391. language: *24*, 27, 52–56, *53*, 58–66, 80, *153*, 169, 185, 208, 217, 227, 240–242, 243, 245, 733–734. marriage: *24*, 27, 94, 200, 245, 361, 364. migration: 60, 92, 160, 163, 164, 166–168, 245. population: 160. 247, 273, 275, 282. prehistory: 60, 92, 94–96, 127, 164. religion: 718, 719, 724. reserves: 56, 61, 245, 359. settlements: *53*, 245, 282, 683. social organization: 26, 156, 158, 250, 736. subsistence: *133*, 135, 137, *152*, 167, 282. Swampy: 66, 148, *154*, 159, 160, 217, 241, 256, 257, 258, 348. synonymy: 3, 64, 66, 214, 227, 228, 241, 254, 268, 283. technology: 92, 248, 249, *722*. territory: *53*, 92, 158–160, *159*, 161–163, 164, 166–168, 242, 244–245. trade: 148, 151, 156, 160, 245, 282, 283, 345. transport: 158, 245. warfare: 148, 160, 162–164, 167, 199, 200, 273, 321, 345, 391, 435
Cree band. *See* Cree, Western Woods
Cree, East Main: 3, 196–207, 217, 673–682. ceremonies: 198, 201, 202, *202*. Coasters: 196–203, 205, 229. education: 203, 673, 680. employment: 197–199, 201–203, 676–677, 679, 682, *682*. environment: 197–198. external relations: 197–200. Fort George band: *53*, 172, 203, 205. games: 198–199, *204*. Great Whale River band: *53*, 203, 205, 673–682. history: 200–203, 205, 673–674. Home Guard Indians: 196–197, 200, 201. Inlanders: 196–203, 205. Kanaaupscow band: 197, 203. Kaniapiscow band: 205. language: 196, 673, 680, 681. marriage: 197, 198, 199, 200, 203, 676, 679, 681. menstrual practices: 201. migration: 203, 205. music: 198, 201, 202. mythology: 200. Nemaska band: 205. Nichikun band: 205–206. orthography: 196. Painted Hills band: 197, 203. political organization: 202, 203. population: 202, 203, 673, 676. religion: 201, 202, 203. Rupert House band: *53*, 133, 197, 203, 206, 733. settlement pattern: 197, 201–202. settlements: 197, 202, 665, *665*, 673, *674*, 676–678. social organization: 199, 203. structures: 198, *199*, *200*, *201*, *204*, *206*. subsistence: 133, 197, *197*, 198, *198*, 199, 201–203, 673, 676–677, *677*. synonymy: 169, 205–206, 228. technology: *197*, *198*, 201. territory: *159*, 196–198, *196*. trade: *156*, 196, 197, 199, 201. transport: *156*, 197–198, *199*, *200*. Uplanders: 196, 200. warfare: 199–200

Cree, Plains: 1, 84, 227, 228, 255, 268, 348, 359, 430. language: *24*, 52, *53*, 55, 56, 59, 60, 61, 61, 63, 256, 264
Cree Regional Committee: 203
Cree School Board: 203
Cree Villages Act: 203
Cree, Western Woods: 2–3, *25*, 228, 256–270. adornment: 261, 263. art: 263. Athabasca band: 168, 256, 269. Beaver River band: 166, 168, 269. Bigstone band: 269. birth: 260. Bloodvein band: 269. Brunswick House band: 269. Canoe Lake band: 269. ceremonies: 260–263, 266. Chapleau Cree band: 269. Chemahawin band: 269. child rearing: 260. Churchill River Band: 269. clothing: 260, 261, *261*, 262, 263, *266*, 267. Constance Lake band: *53*, 243, 269. Cross Lake band: *53*, 249, 269. Cumberland House band: *53*, 269. Cree band: 269. curing: 261–263, 266. death: 262. diseases: 267. division of labor: 261. Driftpile band: 269. Duncan's band: 269. education: 267. employment: 258, 259, 266, 267, *268*. environment: 130, 256–258, 264. external relations: 264. Firesteel River band: 269. Fisher River band: 269. Flying Post band: 269. Fort McMurray band: 269. games: 263. God's Lake band: 269. Grand Rapids band: 269. Grass River band: 269. Grouard band: 269. Hayes River band: 269. health care: 266, 267. Hill River band: 269. history: 257–259, 266–267. Île-à-la-Crosse band: 269. kinship: 259–260. Lac la Ronge band: *53*, 269. language: *53*, 55, 59–61, 256, 263, 266. life cycle: 260–261. Little Red River band: 269. Lubicon Lake band: 269. marriage: 259–261, 266. Matachewan band: 269. Mathias Colomb band: *53*, 269. migration: 257, 258, 264. Missanabie band: 269. Montreal Lake band: *53*, 269. Moose Lake band: 269–270. music: 263. mythology: 262, 263. Nelson House band: *53*, 258, 269. Nelson River band: 270. New Post band: 269. Norway House band: *53*, 245, 269. orthography: 256. Oxford House band: 245, 269. Peguis band: 269. Peter Ballantyne band: *53*, 269. political organization: 259, 260, 264. Poplar River band: *53*, 269. population: 258, 267. prehistory: 257–258. puberty: 260–261. Red Deer River band: 270. Red Earth band: *53*, 269. religion: 259, 263, 264. reserves: *257*, 259, 267. Rocky Cree: 256–258, 267, 269, 282. Sawridge band: 269. settlement pattern: 258, 259. settlements: 259, 264, 266. shamanism: 261–262. Shoal Lake band: *53*, 269. social organization: 259–260, 264, 282. Split Lake band: *53*, 269. Strongwoods Cree: 130, 256, 257, 264, 267. structures: 259, 260, 261, 262, *263*, 267. Sturgeon Lake band: *53*, 269. subsistence: 257, 258, 260, 261, 262, 264, *264*, 266, *266*. Sucker Lake band: 269. Swampy Cree (Western): *53*, 55, 59, 60, *159*, 256–258, 263, 264, 267. Swan River band: 269. synonymy: 186, 267–270. technology: 258, 260, *260*, *261*, 262–264, *264*, *267*, *268*. territory: *159*, 256, 257, *257*. The Pas: *53*,

268, 270. Timagami band: 269. trade: 147–
148, 258. transport: 259, 260, 262, *263*, 264,
267. Wabasca band: 53, 269. warfare: 260.
Waterhen Lake band: 269. Whitefish Lake
band: 269. *For some bands, see also* Cree,
West Main
Cree, West Main: 2, *25*, 217–230, 241.
Abitibi: *159*, 160, 228, 229. adornment: 221.
Albany: *53*, 137, 219, 221, 228–229.
Attawapiskat band: *53*, 137, 158, 217, 219,
220–222, 224–225, 229, 719, 720, 724, 726,
735. ceremonies: 220, 221–223. Churchill
band: *53*, 219. clothing: *154*, 219–221, *220,
223*, 224, *224*. Constance Lake band: 243.
curing: 23. death practices: 223. education:
217, 218, 224, 225. employment: 218, 225–
226. environment: 217, 218. external
relations: 199. Fox Lake band: *53*, 219.
games: 221, *221*, 224. health care: 218, 225.
history: 148, 217–218, 224–227. kinship:
221. language: *53*, 54, 55, 217, 224, 225,
228, 243. marriage: 221, 224. menstrual
practices: 220. migration: 218, 219, 225.
Monsoni band: 229. Moose: *27, 53*, 55, 61,
196, 227, 242, 256. Moose Factory band:
230. music: 221, 224, 225. mythology: 221,
223. New Post band: 230. Nipigon band:
228, 229. orthography: 217. Piscotagami
band: 228, 229. political organization: 221–
222. population: 160, 218–219, 225.
puberty: 220–223. religion: 218, 223–225,
719, 720, 724. reserves: 228. settlements:
219, 225. Severn band: 219, 229, 230, 242.
shamanism: 223. Shamattawa band: *53*, 219.
social organization: 159, 221, 224–227, 735.
structures: 220, *220*, 223, *224*. subsistence:
135, 217, 219–221, 223–225, *225, 226*.
Swampy Cree (Eastern): *53*, 54, 55, *159*,
229. synonymy: 227–230. technology: 219,
222, 223, *225*. territory: 159, *159*, 160, 217,
218, 228. trade: 148, *151*, 217–218, 221,
227, 229. transport: 221, 223. warfare: 160.
Winisk band: *53*, 219, 229. Winnipeg band:
229–230. York Factory band: *53*, 219, 230.
For some bands, see also Cree, Western
Woods
cremation. *See* death practices
Creoles: 624, 636, 639
Cri; synonymy: 227
Crics; synonymy: 227
Criqs; synonymy: 227
Cris; synonymy: 227
Cris des Bois; synonymy: 268
Cristeens; synonymy: 227
Cristians; synonymy: 227
Cristinau(x); synonymy: 227
Cristinaux du Bois fort; synonymy: 268
Cristineaux; synonymy: 227
Cristinos; synonymy: 227
Crists; synonymy: 227
Croockedhand, Noel: *735*
crossbows: 175, *197*, 201, 234
Cross Lake band; synonymy: 269. *See also*
Cree, Western Woods
Crow Flats band; synonymy: 531–532. *See
also* Kutchin
Crow River Kutchin; synonymy: 532
Crows; synonymy: 479, 505

Cruikshank, Robert: *400*
Cuivre, Gens du; synonymy: 289
culture heroes. *See* mythology
Cumberland House band. *See* Cree, Western
Woods
Cuneskapi; synonymy: 185
Cunningham, J.F.: *686*
curing: 184, 279, 302–303, 595, 607, 620, 661.
bloodletting method: 249. blowing water
method: 449, 574. body manipulation: 409.
bone setting: 261. cannibalism: 249, 253.
ceremonies: 251–253, *252*, 262, 266, 319,
409, 465, 634. confession method: 223, 303,
720. enemas: 223. foreign object intrusion:
409, 439, 449, 465. medicinal: 135, 223, 249,
252, 261, 317, 319, 344, 409. music for: 319,
439. possession: 409, 429, 465, 574, 634.
postcontact practice: 246, 266, 319, 323.
soul loss: 409, 429, 439, 634. spirit helpers:
251, 261–263, 319, 344, 409. sucking
method: 223, 244, 319, 439, 574. sweating
method: 223, 262, 344. *See also* health care;
shamans
Curtis, Asahel: 39
Curve Lake band. *See* Ojibwa, Northern
Cuscudidah; synonymy: 215. *See also*
Attikamek (Tête de Boule)
Cyr, Pierre: *368*

D

dačan tat gʷičin; synonymy: 504
dagaδ gʷičin; synonymy: 531
dago· gʷičin; synonymy: 531
Dahadinnè; synonymy: 337
Daha-'dtinne; synonymy: 330, 337
Dahautinnes: 329. synonymy: 327
Dahodinne(s); synonymy: 327, 330
Dahoteena: 329; synonymy: 327, 330
Dahotine: 328
Dahotinnais; synonymy: 329, 330
Dahotinnes; synonymy: 327, 329
Daudinnes: 329
dakeⱡne; synonymy: 430
Dakkadehè; synonymy: 531
Dakkadhœ; synonymy: 531
Dakota (Sioux): *554*. history: 148. prehistory:
94. technology: 248. territory: 244. trade:
148. warfare: 148, 159, 160, 260
Dalles band. *See* Ojibwa, Northern
Dall, William H.: 38, 43, 51, 561, 584
Dalton, Jack: 503
dances. *See* ceremonies
dandé·y ín; synonymy: 575
Dandjalee. *See* Levi
Dandy Jim: *464*
Daniel (Carrier): *429*
Daniktco site: 117
dasǫ́əxiana; synonymy: 639
dastne·y; synonymy: 638
daqⱡawe·dí; synonymy: 461
Daudinnes: 329
Dauhaudinnes: 328, 330
David, Johnny: *711*
David, Jonathan: *711*
David's camp; synonymy: 513
David's people; synonymy: 513
Davie's band; synonymy: 434, 440
Davis Inlet band. *See* Montagnais-Naskapi

Davis, Twelve Foot: 358
Dawes Severalty Act of 1877: 399
Dawson Charlie: 482, *483, 486, 487*
Dawson, George M.: 38, 452, 503
Dawson, Johnny: *486*
daxⱡawe·dí; synonymy: 461
Dease Lake band. *See* Tahltan
Dease River Kaska; synonymy: 450
death: 262, 320, 344, 408, 409, 429, 448, 465,
487, 501, 511, 527, 620, 658
death practices: 252, 262, 342, 428, 465, 658.
avoidance relationships: 320. camp
abandonment: 279, 405, 438. cremation:
438. ceremonies: 344, 385, 421, 423, 438,
445, 446, 465, 478, *486*, 488, 501–502, 508,
509, 519, 527, 541, 544, 578–580, 591, 593,
594, 607, 608, 610, 616, 634, 659–660, 697,
698, 702, 709, 727, 729. corpse treatment:
223, 320, 447, 448, 488, 501, 509, 541, 591,
634, 659, 727. cremation: 114, 124, 385,
405, 425, 428, 438, 448, 478, 488, 501, 509,
548, 572, 620, 634, 659. disposal of
property: 279, 320, 344, 448, 572, 593, 610,
632, 634, 659, 727. haunting prevention:
262, 320, 591. house abandonment: 405,
498, 659. prehistoric: 114, 124. *See also*
burial; death; mourning
dečan to hoiyan; synonymy: 504
Deception Point site: *101*, 102
déchiné; synonymy: 269
dečįla hoįį; synonymy: 297. *See also* Dogrib
de·cinʔ; synonymy: 505
Decutla: 356
Deer Lake band. *See* Ojibwa, Northern
dəgë·; synonymy: 531
degeδe; synonymy: 531
degewi goįine; synonymy: 531
Deguthee Dinees; synonymy: 531
deh neδe goįine; synonymy: 348
deities. *See* supernatural beings
dəkənaniǫə hōįanə; synonymy: 622
Dek'on. *See* Tecon
dela goįine; synonymy: 322. *See also* Hare
De Laguna, Frederica: 44, 47, *48*, 72
delzən-tue dene; synonymy: 280
Demers, Modeste: 429
dəna; synonymy: 168, 599
Dena'ina; synonymy: 638
dənaʔina; synonymy: 622, 638
Denali complex: 46, 111, 113–115, 128
Denbigh phase: 113
de·ⁿdyu· gʷičin; synonymy: 532
Dene: 26, 364. synonymy: 168, 325
Déné; synonymy: 168
dene; synonymy: 168, 283, 338, 348
Dènè-Dindjié; synonymy: 168
deneδa; synonymy: 348
Dené Thá; synonymy: 348
Deneyou, Michel: *81*
dəneza; synonymy: 350
Department of Indian Affairs and Northern
Development (Canada): 203, 267, 328, 399,
426, 477, 529, *678*. economic development:
282, 682. treaties: 311
descent groups. *See* social organization
designs. *See* art
desná(ho)įįne; synonymy: 348
Des-nèdhè-kkè-nadé; synonymy: 271

Des-nèdhè-yapè-l'Ottinè; synonymy: 348
desneδe-ke-náde; synonymy: 271
desneθéhotine; synonymy: 348
dẏela·y taWie·ne; synonymy: 639
dẏəlaytəxiana; synonymy: 639
dẏili ʔuĉen xian; synonymy: 638
D'Herbomez, L.J.: 429
dialects. *See* language
Diamond, Widow George: *153*
Dick, Louise: *467*
Dick, William: *61, 238*
dieho gá gotine; synonymy: 316
Diguthe Dinees; synonymy: 531
di ʔhai· gⁿicin; synonymy: 532
Dihai band; synonymy: 532. *See also* Kutchin
dindjié; synonymy: 531
dineh šu·; synonymy: 575
Dinneh; synonymy: 168
Dinnie; synonymy: 161, 168
diⁿʒi·; synonymy: 168
diⁿʒi· žu·; synonymy: 531
diⁿʒi· žuh; synonymy: 531
directions. *See* cosmology
disease: 148, 201, 331, 351, 360, 510, 529, 530, 611, 636, 637, 647, 695. cholera: 323. diphtheria: 511, 621, 637. influenza: 274, 288, *292,* 296, 323, 511, 529, 569, 621, 627, 637, 643, 691, 692, 706. measles: 274, 322, 328, 393, 418, 511, 529, 558, 569, 587, 637. mumps: 511. scarlet fever: 322, 529, 560, 569. smallpox: 172, 173, 208, 211, 212, 246, 258, 273, 274, 328, 393, 394, 411, 418, *421,* 496, 511, 559, 569, 586, 615, 636, 643, 695. tuberculosis: 172, 258, 267, 274, 296, 322, 323, 328, 553, 569, 597, 636, 637, 643, 692. venereal: 568, 636. *See also* curing; health care
Dismal Lake site: *98,* 101
distant Rat Indians; synonymy: 532
divination: 301, 409, 449, 574, 620, 647. scapulimancy: 184, *184,* 194, 223, 518
division of labor: 138, 144, 192, 261, 279, *279,* 282, 340, 376, 377, 403–404, 406, 443–445, 462, 484, 508, 566, 569, 588, 611, 620, 627, 645, 647–649
divorce. *See* marriage
Dixthada phase: 107, *119,* 120, 122, 123, *123,* 124, 575
Doctor, Gabriel: *735*
Doggside Indians; synonymy: 306
Dog Rib: 287, 288, 321. synonymy: 327
Dogrib: *19, 22, 153,* 271, 283, 286, 288–290, 291–309, 312–314, 337, 338, 364, 373, 684. adornment: *294.* birth: 301. ceremonies: 301–303, *735.* clothing: 141, *142–143,* 154, *294,* 298, *304,* 308. *coti hoti:* 292, 297. curing: 302–303. death: 301. *decila hoti:* 292, 297. Edge of the Woods: 154, *292,* 297. education: 291–292, 296. employment: 288, 292. environment: *7, 11,* 291, 298–299, *299.* *ʔeiati (ʔeia hoti):* 292, 297. external relations: 291, 293, 296, 310, 315, 316, 327, 329. games: 27, 279, 298, 301, 303, *304, 305,* 528. health care: 291, 296. history: 148, *150,* 286–288, 291–296, 298, *300, 306,* 401, 688, 733. kinship: 301–302, *302.* language: *70,* 71, 72, 77, 79–80, 83, 291, 292, 310, 315, 339. life cycle: 299, 301. marriage: 286,

297, 299, 303, 331. menstrual practices: 301. migration: 106, 161, 291. music: 303, *304, 735.* mythology: 302, 305. orthography: 291. political organization: 296–298. population: 291, 293, 296, 312. prehistory: 106. puberty: 301. Rae band: 298, 303, *306,* 687, 733. religion: *150,* 299, 302–303, *312,* 733. *sati hóti:* 292, 297. settlements: 291, 292, *292,* 295, 297, 299, 683. social organization: 297, 301–302, 433, 737–738. structures: *140, 291, 292, 294, 299, 300, 301,* 308, 686. subsistence: *132, 136,* 291, 292, 297–299, *299,* 307. synonymy: 293, 303, 305–306, 309, 312–313, 347, 348. *ta ga hoti:* 292, 295. technology: *132, 292,* 303, *306,* 307–308. territory: 161–162, *162,* 286, 291, *292,* 294, 295, 297, 310, 311. trade: 148, 273, 276, 288, 291, 293, 294, *294,* 296–299, 303, 310, 311, 321, 684, *689.* transport: *21, 157,* 295, 298, 299, *301, 305,* 307–308. Yellowknife band: 298. warfare: 106, 161–162, 164, 273, 286–288, 294, 296, 310. *Wulede hoti: 292,* 297
Dog-ribbed Indians: 287
Dog rib(bed) tribe; synonymy: 306, 309
DogRib(b) Indians: 296. synonymy: 306, 309, 327
Dog-rib nation; synonymy: 294
dogs: *301, 379,* 598. burials: 95, 578. clothing for: 155, *391, 392.* eating of: 220, 320. food for: 16, 17, 154, 217, 281, 390, 484, 544, 549, 566. hunting with: 132, 133, 175, 318, 333, 381, 405, 485, 518, 626, 630, 648. packing: 133, 221, *333,* 390, 403, 437, 444, *446,* 462, 474, 485, 498, *570,* 618, 630, 649. sacrifice of: 263. sleds: *19, 177, 179,* 235, *301, 319,* 444, 462, *487, 540,* 544, 549, *551,* 596, 630. teams: 152, 154, 234, 262, *263,* 281, 299, *301,* 308, 333, 381, 444, 473, 484, 553, 567, 596–597, 621, 630, 699, 709. traction: 154, *155,* 181, 221, 235, 259, 262, 281, 318, 344, 374, 381, 390, 485, 498, 518, *540,* 544, 549, *551,* 553, 621, 630, *669, 696*
dogside Nation; synonymy: 305, 306
doẏ həian; synonymy: 616
done; synonymy: 306
Dǫnękǫ. *See* Tecon
Donnelly Ridge site: 46, *108,* 111, 114
Dorset culture: 30
Dorset Eskimo; prehistory: 30
Dorsh, John B.: 107
Douglas, James: 398
Dounè; synonymy: 309
Doyon Ltd.: 48, 401, 555, 587, 598, 613
dreams: 182, 195, 221, 223, 233, 251, 260, 263, 279, 319, 320, 335, 344, 353, 355–357, *356,* 385, 409, 427, 437, 439, 448, 478, 490, 502, 509, 518, 527, 574, 595, 607, 620, 634, 647, 661, 719
dress. *See* adornment; clothing
Driftpile band. *See* Cree, Western Woods
drums. *See* musical instruments
Drunken Point site: 89
Drybones site: *103*
Dry Creek site: *101, 108, 113,* 114, 128
Drygeese: 296, 297
'Dtinnè; synonymy: 168
Duck Lake band. *See* Chipewyan

Duff, Wilson: 40
Duke, Jimmy: 705
Duncan complex. *See* Caribou Island complex
Duncan Indians: 100
Duncan's band. *See* Cree, Western Woods
Duncan, William: 456
Duné, synonymy: 309
Dunning, Robert W.: 22
duta gotine; synonymy: 316
dutna; synonymy: 557
δahcài· gⁿicin; synonymy: 505

E

Eagle City; synonymy: 513
Eagle Eyed Indians; synonymy: 160. territory: *159*
Eagle Lake band. *See* Ojibwa, Northern
Eagle people; synonymy: 513
eagle tribe; synonymy: 242
Eaka site: 89
Early Prehistoric period: 117, 126
Early Woodland. *See* Initial Woodland
ear piercing. *See* adornment
East Cree; synonymy: 66. *See also* Montagnais-Naskapi
Eastern Archaic tradition: 31
Eastern Cree; synonymy: 205
East Foreland Tanainas: *625.* synonymy: 638
East Fork band. *See* Kolchan
East Main Indians; synonymy: 205
ʔeĉa gotine; synonymy: 348
Echel-la-o-tuna; synonymy: 348
ʔeĉide deh gotine; synonymy: 348
ʔeda; synonymy: 268
Edaot'ine; synonymy: 330
Edge of the Woods band. *See* Dogrib
education: 149, 185, 203, 213, 218, 237, 238, 291, 311, *340,* 359, 392, 482, 484, 529, 553, 587, 621, 637, 667, 676, 680, 691. boarding schools: 203, 213, 217, 224, 225, 239, 267, 274, 292, 322, 396–397, *397,* 399, 400, 401, 477, 529, 597, 612, 637, 695, 696, 707, 715. church-affiliated schools: 217, 224, 225, 292, 322, 396, *397,* 399, 400, 412, 477, 482, 504, 529, 567, 586–587, 597, 599, 612, *614, 673, 688,* 695, 706, *706.* college: 267, 400, 401, 412, 554, 710. community: 203, 213, 239, 274, 296, 323, 328, 347, 396, 399, 400, 529, 587, 691, 696, 707, 712, 715. language: 64, 74, 75, 77, 79, 217, *397.* secondary schools: 401, 412, 477, 554, 637, 696, 707, 710, 715. vocational: 400, 696, 715
Edwardson, Charlie, Jr.: *554*
Edzagwo: 298
Edze. *See* Edzo
Edzo: 294, 296, 298, 302
Egon, Samuel: *81*
Ehba got'ine; synonymy: 329, 330, 337
ʔehda gotine; synonymy: 337
Ehta-Gottinè; synonymy: 330, 336–337
eiyô·na; synonymy: 505
Ekawi Jimi (Jimmy): 298
elderly: 254, 262, 279, 405, 477–478, 483, 488, *524,* 525, 553, 588, 589, 610, 649, 650, 658, 660
elections. *See* political organization
Él'é-idlin-Gottinè; synonymy: 348
ʔəłkaĉo; synonymy: 431

Elk Island site: *89*

embroidery: *142–143, 145*, 223, 369, 392, *422, 429*, 445, *467*, 629, *629*, 632, *649*, 652, *721, 722*

Emmons, George T.: 39

employment: 213, 218, 225–226, 237, 239, 254, 267, 322, 323, 365, 368–370, 395, 397–400, 412, 418, 426, 460, 484, 504, 511, 549, 553, 554, 568, 587, 621, 627, 637, 643, 668, 675, 679, 682, 690, *692*, 700, 705, 710, 712, 716. fur trade: 155–156, 197–199, 201–202, 245, 258, 266, 282, 288, 365, 367, 390–391, 685. government: 511, 553, 667, 668, *682*, 690, *692*, 696, 713. wage work: 150, 172, 202–203, 394, 551, 553, 554, 587, 598, 668, *682*, 691, 692, 696, 699, 713

ʔená; synonymy: 268, 271

ʔenayčel: 402. synonymy: 402

enda; synonymy: 269

Endako River subtribe; synonymy: 431

ʔeneʒhǝʔan; synonymy: 600, 622

English River band. *See* Chipewyan

ʔenüq hǝʔan; synonymy: 616

environment: 5–14, *6*. Alaska Plateau area: 533–534, *533*. animal resources: 15–18, *16*, 86–88, 90, 95, 97, 98, 101, 102, 104, 130–133, 135, 137, 151, 169, 172–175, 190, 197, 208, 213, 217, 218, 233, 235–237, 248, 257, 258, 264, 272, 273, 275, 282, 291, 298–299, 317, 326, 374–376, 388, 390, 405, 406, 412, 420, 425, 433, 436, 444, 454, 458, 462, 470–472, 481, 482, 493, 506, 534, 543, 540–551, 584, 603, 605–606, 618, 627, 668. climate: *6*, 9–10, 86–89, 91, 130, 271, 310, 326, 373–374, 390, 406, 425, 433, 458, 470, 481, 493, 514, 533–534, 564, 584, 641, 667–668. Cordillera area: 372–375, *372*. forest fires: 18, 86, 97, 98, 100, 130, 173, 213, 390, 458, 481. geology: 5–9, *7*, 97, *299*, 514. hydrology: 10–12, *10, 11*, 86–88, 97, 130, 217, 326, 433, 470–471, 493, 514, 563–564, 602, 618, 641. Indian impact on: 257, 258, 264, 388, 482, 549–551. mineral resources: 13–14, 373. prehistoric: 86–90, 95, 97, 98, 100–102. Shield Subarctic area: 130–131, *131*. soils: 9, 13. terrain: 5–9, *7–9*, 12, 130, *131*, 197, 257, 310, 317, 326, 372, *372*, 373, 433, 470, 481, 514, 533, *533*, 563, 584, 602–603, 618, 641, 668. vegetation: 5, *6–9, 11*, 12–13, 18, 89, 97, 101, 130, 131, 217, 231, 256–257, 271–272, 291, 310, 317, 326, 374, *374*, 402, 433, 443, 458, 481, 493, 506, 514, 534, 564–565, 584, 618. White impact on: 13–14, 212–213, 418, 426

Epinette Nation; synonymy: 241

Esai, Dora: *622*

Esai, Phillip: *622*

ʔesbata gotine; synonymy: 337

Esbataottinè; synonymy: 330, 336–337, 505

Esclave; synonymy: 347, 348

Escoumains; synonymy: 186. *See also* Montagnais-Naskapi

e·šiši·pi·wi(ši·puwi)lnuč; synonymy: 186

Eskeimoes: 205

Esker End site: *101*

eskimeaux; synonymy: 187

Eskimo: 1, 39, 47, 51, 186–188, 271, 325, 361,

364, 365, 370, 378, 381, 401, 517, 531, *537, 539*, 543, 546, 549, 557, 559, 580, 596, 599, 600, 604, 607, 613–615, 618, 631, 632, 639, 643, 662, 673–682, 709, 713–714, 734. clothing: 177. disease: 611. education: 676, 680. employment: 668, 675, 679, 682, *682*, 705. external relations: 25, 171, 197, 199–200, 291, 315, 316, 322, 362, 389, 395, 525, 559, 582, 588, 603, 606, 618, 678–681, *681*. history: 44, 48, 171, 673–682. language: *63*, 68, 602, 680, 681. marriage: 199, 559, 582, 590, 602, 603, 612, 623, 679, 681, 714. migration: 89, 91, 92, 106, 121–123, 170, 514, 546–547. political organization: 150, 203, 675, *678*. population: 664, 673, 675, 676, 697. prehistory: 30, 44–46, 89, 106, 110, 113–114, 117, 118, 121–123, 129, 546. religion: 673, 675. settlements: 44, 46, 566, 602, *605*, 613, 639, 665, *665*, 667, 673, *674*, 675–676, 705. social organization: 524, 675, 736. structures: 675, 677, *677*. subsistence: 68, 606, 673, 676, *676*. synonymy: 557, 615. technology: 110, 122, *123*, 722. territory: 92, 165, 170, *516*, 557, 559, 602. trade: 120, 171, 321, 322, 388, 389, 528, 544, 546, 547, 559, 561, 582, 589, 595–596, 603, 616, 631, 635, 650–651. transport: 177, 630, *631*. warfare: 164, 173, 199, 260, 273, 515, 529, 547, 559, 582, 596, 623, 642–643

Eskimo language grouping: 53

Eskimo words. *See* Indian and Eskimo words

Esmailka, Marylene: *589*

Espatodena; synonymy: 329

Espato-ten(a); synonymy: 330

Es-pā-to-tī-na; synonymy: 505

Espa-tpa-Ottinè; synonymy: 330

Esquimau(x): 529. synonymy: 171, 187

Esquimawes; synonymy: 187

Estaloda: *650*

estikhe·n; synonymy: 466

Eta-gottiné; synonymy: 330, 337

ʔeta hoṭį; synonymy: 297. *See also* Dogrib

ʔetaṭį; synonymy: 297. *See also* Dogrib

Etcha-Ottinè; synonymy: 348

Etchareottine; synonymy: 349

Etchapè-ottiné; synonymy: 348

Etetnot-otna: *650*

Ethen-eldèli. *See* Chipewyan

ʔeθǝn heldéṭi; synonymy: 271

etiquette: 192, 220, 649, 726

Etolin, A.K.: 50

Ettchéri-dié-Gottinè; synonymy: 348

Euchinico band; synonymy: 431

euthanasia: 262, 658

Evans, James: 62, *63*, 217

éwié-étti; synonymy: 371

Exch-na: *650*

Excomminqui; synonymy: 187

Excomminquois; synonymy: 187

Exmouth Lake site: *98*

exogamy. *See* marriage

exploration. *See* history

Eyak: 67–68, 623, 662. external relations: 642. social organization: 631. territory: 641. trade: 645, 650, 651

ʔeža·n; synonymy: 512

ežan kučin; synonymy: 513

F

face painting. *See* adornment

Fairchild Bay complex: 100, *103*, 104–105

Fairford band. *See* Ojibwa, Northern

Faries, Richard: 238

farming. *See* agriculture

Farrand, Livingston: 39

Fathzei-Kootchin; synonymy: 505

Fct(o)utlin; synonymy: 513

Fidler, Peter: 289

Fidler, Robert: *238*

figurines and effigies: 221, 425

Filthy Lake Indians; synonymy: 309

fine, Gens-de-; synonymy: 512

Finlay, John: 439

Finlay River band. *See* Ojibwa, Northern

firearms: 106, 218, 234, 235, *246, 261*, 262, *262*, 280, 281, 307, 315, 327, 485, *486*, 509, 519, 548. hunting with: 133, 154, 201, 223, 333, 345, 357, 484, 497, 550, 619, 626, 648. trade of: 218, 548, 586, 652. warring with: 164

firemaking: 219, 341, 444, 456, 517, 535, *537*, 569, 619, *649*

Firesteel River band; synonymy: 268. *See also* Cree, Western Woods

Firth, John: 364

fish. *See* fishing; food

Fisherman Lake site: *98, 99, 113*

Fisher River band. *See* Cree, Western Woods

fishing: 25, 150, 169, 197, 201, 208, 212, 232, 233, 258, 261, 291, 299, 332, 362, 365, 376, 417, 425, 456, 544–545, 549, 553, 554, 569, 725. camps: 46, 122, 133, 137, 298, *312*, 341, 375, 379, 462, 471, 483, *497*, 507, 508, 545, 551, 565, 566, *568*, 569, 571, 588, 597, 598, 612, 627, 628, 646, 694, 695, *707*. commercial: 259, 266, 267, 274, 282, 368–369, 426, 485, 627, 636, 637, 668. communal: 247, 315, 407, 418, 425, 566, 647. eels: 174, *192*. fish wheels: *545*, 550, 567, 587, 588, 606, 621, 647, 705. ice: *136*, 220, 234, 236, 262, 303, 369, 376, *378, 379*, 405, 406, 425, 472–473, *473*, 484, 416, *536*, 553, 589, *589*, 604, *606*, 626, 647. implements: 16, *89, 90, 90, 93, 136*, 154, 174, 175, *192, 198, 211*, 219–220, 223, 232, 234–236, 247, 262, 281, 303, 307, *311*, 317, 340, 377, 379, *379, 381*, 390, 402–403, 405, 406, 424, 425, 436, 462, 484, 497, *497*, 506, 507, 518, 535, *536*, 569, 604, *606*, 612, *619*, 620, *626, 647*. resources: 15–18, 86, 137, 169, 174, 175, 208, 217, 233, 236, 248, 257, 272, 317, 326, 339, 351, 374–376, 405, 420, 425, 436, 454, 458, 459, 462, 470–472, 483, 493, 496, 506, 507, 516, 534, 565, 566, 584, 588, 589, 602–604, *606*, 618, 626, 646. ritual observances: 202, 484, 647, 652. Shield Subarctic area: 133–134. sites: 418, 421–422, 459–461, 585, 632, 644, 647. species: 134–135, 175, 379, 405, 425, 436, 456, 484, 497, 507–508, 516, 566, 567, 569, 588, 589, 604–606, 615, 619, 626, 646–647, 668. taboos: 320, 428, 610, 647. techniques: *11*, 133–134, *136*, 137, 174, 219–220, 235, 236, 247, 279, 298, 340, 368–369, 376, 377, *378*, 379, 403, 405, 407, 425, *426*, 443, 472–473,

484, *497,* 516, 535, *536,* 566, 569, 588, 589, 604, 605, *619,* 626, *626,* 647, *647.* weirs: 133, 134, 174, 219, 497, *497,* 506, 516, 518, 535, 566, 569, 570, 588, 604, 612, 619, *619,* 620, 644

fishhooks: *198,* 219, 516, 518, 604, 612, 626

Fish Lake complex: 116

Fish Lake Cultural Centre: 84

Fitz-Smith band. *See* Chipewyan

Flancs-de-Chien; synonymy: 293, 309

Flannery, Regina: 20, 22

fleshers and beamers: 92, *110,* 118, *119,* 125, 175, 219, 570

Florendo, Nora: 480

flutes. *See* musical instruments

Flying Post band. *See* Cree, Western Woods

Folger, John: *552*

Fond Du Lac band. *See* Chipewyan

food: 239, 244. annual cycle: 201, 232, 260, 276–277, 298–299, *299,* 332, 375–376, 425, 436, 443–444, 483–484, 496, 507–508, 543, 544, 546, 553, 554, 565–566, 588–589, 604–606, *606,* 615, 618–619, 626–627, 646. avoidances: 648. bannock: *226,* 444. birds: 16, 18, 133, 137, 151, 174–175, 198, 201, 223, 257, 375, 593. fish: 15–18, 104, 133, 135, 137, 151, 174, 201, 219, 220, 233, 247, 248, 264, 281, 298, 299, *318,* 332, 340, 351, *363,* 374–376, 381, 390, 400, 406, 417, 424, 425, 436, 443, 444, 456, 458, 459, 462, 471–472, 484, 496, 507, 508, 511, 516, *535, 537,* 565, 566, 588, 593, *598,* 604, *612,* 615, 618, 626, 627, 646, 649, 670. game: 15–18, *16,* 131–133, 135, 137, 151, 174, 198, 201, 202, *202,* 220, 233, 237, 257, 263, *267,* 276–277, 315, 317, 332, 351, 376, 381, 400, 405, 424, 425, 436, 443, 444, 456, 462, 472, 484, 496, 516, 534, 565, 566, 593, 604, 606, 618, 627, 648, 670. grease, fat, and oil: 198, 201, 220, 249, 318, 340, 425, 443, 569, 648, 649. intake: 135, 352. pemmican: 135, 318, 340. prehistoric: 86, 90. preparation: 97, 124, 135, 137, *145,* 174, 175, 201, 220, *225, 238,* 247, 263, 277, 317–318, 332, 340, 353, *363, 376,* 381, 436, 443, 506, 535, *537,* 569, 605, *612,* 619, *626,* 648. preservation: 135, *137,* 174, 198, 201, 220, 233, *267, 292,* 298, 299, 318, *318,* 327, 332, *335,* 340, *340,* 375, 376, *376,* 379, 406, 425, *427,* 436, 443, 444, 456, 458, 459, 462, 484, 496, 508, 511, *537,* 566, 588, *598,* 615, 619, 620. ritual observances: 201–203, *202,* 251, *337,* 344, 427–428, 447, 593, 647, 648, 670. sap: *363, 403.* sea mammals: 15, 133, 137, 174, 220. Shield Subarctic area: 134–135, 137. storage: 120, 124–126, 135, 174, 175, 201, 220, 249, 262, 318, 332, 340, 376, 381, 383, 406, 424, 425, 436, 443, 444, 471, 472, 483, 484, 496, 506, 508, 566, 588, 604, 605, 628, 645, 646, *646,* 648, 649, 668, 670. store bought: 173, 208, 218, 223, 233, 237, 346, 358, 375, 393, 400, 444, 548, 668. taboos: 220, 250, 277, 320, 336, 355, 404, 405, 420, 427, 438, 465. utensils: 175, 220, *238,* 262–263, *294, 300,* 333, 340, 386, *386,* 403, 424, 436–437, 443, 465, *503,* 506, 535, *537,* 569, *571, 612,* 619, *626, 633,* 648, 649. vegetal: 134–135, 174,

201, 220, 245, 247, 257, 258, 317, 318, 340, 374–376, 381, 405–406, 425, 443, 444, 458, 472, 484, 496, 565, 588, 605, 606, *612,* 648. wild rice: 135, 244, 245, 247, 258. *See also* gathering; hunting

footwear. *See* clothing; snowshoes

forest fires. *See* environment

Fort Albany: 159, 218, 219, 228, 231

Fort Alexander band. *See* Ojibwa, Northern

Fort Alexandria: *389,* 410, 411

Fort Anderson: 316, 322

Fort Babine: *389,* 390, *394*

Fort Bourbon: 258

Fort Castor: 345

Fort Chilcotin: 410

Fort Chimo: 20, *20,* 171, 173, 197

Fort Chipewyan: 273

Fort Chipewyan band. *See* Chipewyan

Fort Churchill: 218, 228, 273, *274,* 285, 287, 288

Fort Confidence: 296

Fort Connelly: *389,* 391, 413, 418, 435, 439, 440, 461

Fort D'Epinette: *108,* 125, 440

Fort Egbert: 568

Fort Enterprise: *103,* 106

Fort Frances: 389

Fort Franklin: 79, 291, 294, 296, 297, 311, 312, *312,* 313, 315, 328, 332, 348

Fort Fraser: *389,* 418, 439, 440

Fort Fraser band. *See* Carrier

Fort George (B.C.): *389,* 418, 439, 440

Fort George (Que.): *53,* 172, 200, *200,* 202, 203

Fort George band (Carrier). *See* Carrier

Fort George band (Cree): synonymy: 205. *See also* Cree, East Main

Fort Gibbon: 568

Fort Good Hope: 36, 311, 315, 316, *316,* 321, *321,* 322–324, 327–331, 348, *389*

Fort Grahame: *434, 438,* 440

Fort Grahame Nomads; synonymy: 450

Fort Halkett: 328, 331, 345, 389, *389,* 391, 439, 440, 442, 452

Fort Hope: *232*

Fort Hope band. *See* Ojibwa, Northern

Fort Indians; synonymy: 532

Fort Kilmars: 418, 440

Fort Liard: 79, 326, 328–331, 345, 347, *389,* 452, 713

Fort Liard complex: 125

Fort McLeod: 389, *389,* 417, 439, 440

Fort McMurray: *368*

Fort McMurray band. *See* Chipewyan; Cree, Western Woods

Fort McPherson: *108, 389,* 529, *529,* 531

Fort McPherson people; synonymy: 531

Fort Nelson: 221, 345, 347, 359, 442

Fort Nelson band. *See* Slavey

Fort Norman: 79, 296, 297, 310–312, 313, 315–316, 326, 327–332, 335, 345, 347, 348

Fort Norman Indians; synonymy: 311

Fort Prince of Wales: *152,* 161, *165,* 218, 273, 293

Fort Providence: 345, 347

Fort Rae: *21,* 153, 294, 296, 297, 299, *300,* 303, 311

Fort Reliance: *103,* 106, *389,* 494, 503, 567

Fort Resolution: 80, *140,* 280, 286, 288, *289,* 295–297, *295,* 345–346, 362, 370, 683–693

Fort Saint James: 389, 418, 427, 439, 440

Fort Saint John: 359, 439–440

Fort Selkirk: 36, 389, *389,* 494, 503, 509, 652

Fort Severn: 218, 231, 241

Fort Severn band; synonymy: 230. *See also* Cree, West Main

Fort Simpson: 36, 294, 296, 327–331, 345, 347, *389,* 452, 456

Fort Snelling: 248

Fort Timiscamingue: 212

Fort Vermilion: 346, *358,* 359

Fort Ware: 440

Fort Ware band. *See* Ojibwa, Northern

Fort Wrigley: 79, 326, 329

Fort Yukon: 36, 38, 389, *389,* 390, 391, 395, 396, 494, 509, 511, 515, 529, *547,* 548, 567, 569, 584, 586, 652, 695, 701, 704

Fort Yukon Indians; synonymy: 515, 532

Fou, Gens de; synonymy: *37,* 512

Fou, Gens des: 328

Fou, Gens du; synonymy: 505, 512

Foux, Gens de(s); synonymy: 504, 512

Fox; territory: 244

Fox Lake band. *See* Cree, West Main

Frances Lake Kaska; synonymy: 450. *See also* Kaska

Frances Lake Indians: 328

François Lake "tribe"; synonymy: 430

Frank (Ahtna): *650*

Frank Channel complex: 100, 104, *105*

Frank Channel site: *101, 103*

Franklin, John: 36, 286, *286,* 287, 294, 364

Franklin Tanks complex: 108, *113,* 116, 127

Fraser Lake subtribe; synonymy: 431. *See also* Carrier

Fraser, Simon: 35, 417, 431, 439, 441

Frawtsee-Kootchin; synonymy: 505, 513

Frazer, Johnny: *486*

Fredson, John: 78

French Cree dialect: 56, 61

French Indians; synonymy: 160

Frost, Steven: *540*

fur trade: *153,* 169, 196, 242, 686–687, 689. competitive period: 218, 232, 258, 273. credit: 212, 225, 264, 394, 549. decline: 224–225, 239, 394, 418, 484, 504, 529, 549–551, *551,* 553, 584, 612, 621. dependence on: 212, 213, 223, 231, 258, 264, 393–394, 529, 548, 549. exchange value: *153,* 154, *155.* French: 146, 147, 160, 208–210, 231, 258. impact: 26, 87, 92, 126, 148, 149, 151–160, 162–164, 170–172, 180, 212, 223–224, 232, 258, 280, 282, 383, 389–393, 417, 423, 443, 472, 482, 498, 500, 509, 544, 547, 548, 549, 620–621. Indian employment in: 197–199, 201–202, 245, 282, 288, 390–393, 511. intertribal conflict: 164, 388, 389, 411, 458, 478, 651. middlemen: 199, 208, 232, 258, 273, 276, 293, 375, 384, 388, 389, 410–411, 417, 418, 436, 452, 455–456, 460, 478, 481–483, 489, 494–496, 547, 548, 567, *588,* 620, 627, 650, 651. provisioning of: 237, 258, 294, 417, 511. routes: 156, 651–652. Sheild Subarctic area: 146–157. trading posts: 147,

147, 148, 151, 155, 156, 159–160, 171–173, 197, 199–201, 210, 212, 218, 231, 232, *232*, 239, 260, 266, 273, 280, 288, 294, 375, 388, 389–390, *389, 390*, 410, 417–418, 482, 503, 509, 515, 528–529, *529*, 547–548, *547, 548*, 566–567, 584, 586, 589, 611, 620, 621, 651, 652, 673, 683, *684*, 686, *687, 689*, 691, 695, 704–706. trade items: 462, 509, 547–549, 651, 652, 689, 705

fur trapping: 181, 212, 218, 239, 260, 264, 266, *267*, 281–282, 291, 299, 346, 362, 365, 376, *377, 379, 381*, 400, 403, 405, 406, 412, 418, 423, 424, 425, 436, 458, *471*, 484, 496, 509, 511, 544, 549–551, 553, 554, 589, 597, 598, 615, 620, 627, 647, 668, 676–677, 690, 692, 696, 699, 700, 713

futvūd'iê´; synonymy: 455

G

gahwiế gotine; synonymy: 325
Gakona Indians; synonymy: 662
Galice-Applegate; language: 67
Gallatin, Albert: 163
Galtsan: 631. synonymy: 559
Gal'ʦane; synonymy: 622
Galtzanes; synonymy: 622
Galzanen; synonymy: 622
gambling: 149, 301, 303, 315, 320, 323, *386*, 396, 406, 410, *466*, 489, 528, 690
game. *See* environment; food; hunting
games: 182, 221, *221*, 263, 303, *466*, 487, 509, 519, 528, 593, 732. ball: 509, 519, 528, 716. board: *204*, 224, 303, 678. card: 224, 303. competitions: 198, 199, 303, 343, *670*, 718. dice: 403. hand: 27, 263, 279, 298, 299, 303, *304, 305*, 320, 343, 396, 445, 509, 519, 528. hide and seek: 221, 445. music at: 303, *304*. postcontact: *204*, 224, 303. ring and pin: 279, 303, *305*, 403. stick: 279, 303, *386*, 509, 519, 528. tug-of-war: 198, 221, 445, 509, 732. wrestling: 279, 301, 403, 528, 732
gane-kúȩ́ dene; synonymy: 280
Garden Hill band. *See* Ojibwa, Northern
Garden site: 114
Gargan, Celine: *341*
gathering: 169, 175, 197, 403, 444. bark: 425, 472, 496, 538, 648. berries: 174, 232, 257, 279, 340, 374, 383, 405–406, 425, 443, 444, 458, 472, 484, 496, 565, 566, 588, 605, 648. bulbs: 174, 425, 443. camps: *247*. eggs: 605. fruit: 174. greens: 425. implements: 340, 383, *403*, 424, 643. nuts: 174. resources: 339, 374, 425, 443, 458, 472, 496, 565, 584, 605, 648. ritual observances: 484, 648. roots: 340, 405–406, 425, 443, 472, 484, 496, *538*, 565, 566, 648. sap: 135, 174, *363*, 443. sites: 585, 644. wild rice: 135, 244, 245, 247, 258
Gaudet, Charles Philip: 364
Geddes, Annie: *475*
Georgekish, Geordie: 198
Germain: 154
ghosts. *See* supernatural beings
GhPh-102: 127
GhPh-103: 127
GhPh-107: 127
Giant Mines sites: *103*
Gibbs, George: 36

gift exchange: 364, 376, 391, 405, 417, 446, 593, 608
gifts: 261, 344, 392, 404, 428, 488, 501, 502, 527, 580–581, 591, 608, 619, 633, 634, 648, 649, 657, 659
Gillam, Zachariah: 201
Gillespie, Beryl C.: 22
Gilstrap, Roger: 58
Gitksan: 413–415, 429, 430, 460. adornment: 420. ceremonies: 425. external relations: 425, 434, 435, 438–439, 454, 455. language: 456. Kitwancool: 455. marriage: 417, 434, 435, 438. migration: 455. prehistory: 416. religion: 420. social organization: 419–420. subsistence: 375, 376. territory: 455. trade: 388, 416, 418, 424, 462. transport: 437, *437*, 462. warfare: 455
Gitkun: 455
Gitlakwiyip; synonymy: 455
Gitxadin; synonymy: 455. *See also* Niska
Gladstone phase: 115
Gladstone site: 115
Gladu, Harriette: 336
Glave, E.J.: 38–39, 503, 505
Glazunov, Andrey: 43, 49, 548, 556, 557, 559, 586
Goat Indians: 328–331. synonymy: 329, 505
Goat People; synonymy: 330
Goat tribe; synonymy: 330
Godbout band. *See* Montagnais-Naskapi
Goddard, Pliny E.: 20, 22
God's Lake band. *See* Cree, Western Woods
Golden Lake band. *See* Ojibwa
Goldman, Irving: 40
gold rushes: 485, 503, 510, 549, 567–568, 584–587, 621, 705. Atlin: 469. Cariboo: 39, 394, 411, 418, 425. Cassiar: 394, 395, 397, 442, 460. Dawson: 322. Fairbanks: 567. Klondike: 39, 328, 329, 394, 395, 397, 442, 460, 469, 482, *483*, 510–511, 529, 549, 567. Omineca: 394, 440. Yellowknife Bay: 295, 296. Yukon: 38, 567
Goltsan; synonymy: 559, 622
Goltsan-Inkalikhlyuat; synonymy: 622
Goonennar; synonymy: 505
Goose Point site: 117, *119, 125*, 126
government, provincial: 203, 346, 398, 667, 668, 674, *674*, 677, 679, 712. education: 64, 267, 504. employment: 666, 668. housing: 692. land rights policy: 203, 398, 425–426, 504. trapline registration: 281, 418, 423. reserves: 148–149. welfare: 504, 666, 668. *See also* legislation, provincial; legislation, Canadian; Canada, government of
government, state: 401, 707. education: 567, 587, 597. housing: 553, 709. land claims: 554–555, 708. welfare: 401, 621. *See also* legislation, state; legislation, U.S.; U.S. government
Graham, A.: 532
Grand Council of the Crees (of Quebec): 150, 196, 203, 205
Grand Lac Victoria band. *See* Algonquin
Grand Lakers: 720. synonymy: 442, 450
Grand Rapids band. *See* Cree, Western Woods
Grand Rapids Reservoir Project: 33
Grand River Indians; synonymy: 309, 348

Grand Sault, Peuples du; synonymy: 254
grands Eskimaux, synonymy: 187
Grands Mistassins; synonymy: 186
Grand Trunk Pacific Railway: 418
Grant, Arthur, Sr.: 551
Grant, Cuthbert: 683
Grant Lake complex: 98, *98*
Grant, Peter: 242
Grass River band; synonymy: 260. *See also* Cree, Western Woods
Grass River phase. *See* Selkirk complex
Grassy Narrows band. *See* Ojibwa, Northern
Great Bear River complex: 116
Great Bear River site: 99, *113*
Great Cariboo Wagon Road: 394
Great Northern Airways: 696
Great Tabitabies; synonymy: 228
Great Water Indians; synonymy: 269
Great Whale River band; synonymy: 205. *See also* Cree, East Main
Great Winipeggons; synonymy: 230
Greenfield, William C.: 556
Green Stockings: *286*
Greenstockings Lake site: *101*
Greenwood, Tom: *702*
Gregory, McLeod, and Company: 683
Greysolon Dulhut, Daniel: 209
Gristeen, synonymy: 227
grooming: 403
Grouard band. *See* Cree, Western Woods
Groundhog people; synonymy: 461
guardian spirit. *See* supernatural beings
Guilistinous; synonymy: 228
GUL 077: *108*, 124
Gulkana band. *See* Ahtna
gunana·; synonymy: *466*, 490, 505
Gunena; synonymy: 505
guns. *See* firearms
gʷičà· gʷičin; synonymy: 532
Gwich'in; synonymy: 530
gʷičin; synonymy: 530
gʷičyà· gʷičin; synonymy: 532
gʷičyàh gʷičin; synonymy: 531
ɣalca·ne; synonymy: 622, 662
ɣəlcana; synonymy: 622
ɣəlcuna; synonymy: 622
ɣəlχonə; synonymy: 622

H

Habitans du Sault; synonymy: 254
Hadleigh-West, Frederick: 40
Hagwilget band; synonymy: 430. *See also* Carrier
Hagwilget tribe; synonymy: 430
Hahanudan complex: 123
hą hwəx̌in; synonymy: 512
Hai-ān´ -kŭt-chin´; synonymy: 512
Haida; history: 38. language: 67
Haig site: *103*, 104
hairstyles. *See* adornment
Haisla: 413
Hale, E.S.: 40, 515
Hale, Kenneth: 82
half-breed; synonymy: 371
Half-Breed Scrip Commission: *368*
Hallowell, A. Irving: 20–22, *23, 24*, 25–26
Hallowell, Maude F.: *23*
Hamilton, George: *702*

Hammond, David: *486*

Han: 40, *41*, 373, 387, 498, 500, 503, 505–513. adornment: *512*. art: 509. birth: 508. ceremonies: 486, 508, 509, *510*. clothing: 506–508. curing: 509. death: 508, 509. diseases: 510, 511. education: 401. employment: 511. environment: 374, 375, 506. external relations: 389, 482, 490, 494, 523, 565. games: 509. health care: 401, 511. history: 36, 38, 39, 390, 391, 394, 395, 397, 399–401, 494, 509–511. kinship: 508. Klondike band: *507*, 513. language: *70*, 72, 76–78, 83, 372, 506, 563. marriage: 508–509. menstrual practices: 508, 511. music: 509. mythology: 509. orthography: 506. political organization: 508. population: 511. puberty: 508. religion: 509–511. settlements: 511. shamanism: 509. social organization: 374, 499, 508, 509. structures: 379, 380, 507–509. subsistence: 374, 376, *378*, 506–509, 511. synonymy: *37*, 505, 511–513. technology: 377–379, *384*, *386*, 506, *507*, *508*, 511. territory: *37*, 506, *506*. trade: 388–389, 494. transport: 377, 380, 381, 390, 506, 511. warfare: 377, 379

handwear. *See* clothing

Han Gwich'in; synonymy: 512

han-gwičin; synonymy: 512

Han-Kootchin; synonymy: 512

Hankutchin; synonymy: 511, 512

Happy Valley band. *See* Montagnais-Naskapi

Hara, Hiroko Sue: 22

Hardisty, William L.: 36, *37*

Hare: 22, 268, 283, 312–313, 314–325, 336, 338, 371, 373. adornment: 318. birth: 320. ceremonies: 315, 319, 320. clothing: 141, 314, 315, *316*, 318. cosmology: 319. curing: 319, 323. death: 320, 322. *dela gotine*: 322. education: 322, 323. employment: 322, 323. environment: 317. external relations: 310, 315, 327, 329, 332. games: 320, 323. *Gens du Large* band: 316. health care: 322, 323. history: 148, 314–317, 320–324, 401. kinship: 319. language: 69, *70*, 72, 77, 79–80, 310, 313, 315, 322, 326, 339. life cycle: 320. marriage: 27, 315, 316, 319, 322, *322*, 324, 331. menstrual practices: 320. migration: 324. music: 319, 320. mythology: 315, 319, 320, 323. *ne la gotine*: 315. orthography: 314. political organization: 319, 321, 323. population: 312, 315, 317, 323, 324. puberty: 320. settlements: 315–316, *318*, *321*, 324. shamanism: 319. *sihta gotine*: 322. *sinta gotine*: 322. social organization: 314–316, 319, 320, 322, 323. structures: 319, *319*, 320, 322, 323. subsistence: 314–315, 317–318, *317*, *318*, 320, 323, 324, 725. synonymy: 312–313, 324–325, 336, 348. technology: *145*, 318–319, *318*, *319*, *322*. territory: 161, *162*, 310, 311, 314, *314*. trade: 310, 311, 315, 316, 320–323. transport: 318, *319*. warfare: 286, 287, 319, 321

Harmon, Daniel William: 35, 441

Harper, Arthur C.: *389*, 503, 566, 567

Harrington, John Peabody: 81, 82

Hatchet Lake band. *See* Chipewyan

hats. *See* clothing, headgear

Hattchénœ; synonymy: 600

Hayes River band; synonymy: 269. *See also* Cree, Western Woods

headwear. *See* clothing

health care: 149, 172, 254, 266, 291, 312, 322, 347, 399, 553, 569, 597, 599, 621, 690, 692, 712, 716. church-affiliated: 225, 553, 643, 671, 691, 695. hospitals: 218, 238, 267, 296, 328, 553, 569, 597, 633, 643, 667, 691, 696. nursing stations: 218, 238, 267, 274, 282, 311, 323, 328, 400–401, 691, 696. visiting nurses: 282

Healy: *571*, 579

Healy River–Joseph band. *See* Tanana

Hearne, Samuel: 92, 106, 167, 273, 287, 293, 296

Hegg, Eric A.: 39

Helm, June: 22, 26

Henderson, Patsy: *483*, *486*, 491

Hendriksen, Georg: 22

Hennessey complex: 100, 103, *103*, *105*

Hennessey site: *103*, 104

Henry, Alexander, the Elder: 215, 245

Henry, Alexander, the Younger: 241

Henry, David: 74

Henry, Joseph: 36

Heron Bay site: 90, *90*

highways and roads: 399, 400, 443, 444, 460, 470, 475, 485, 496, 498, 503–504, 511, 549, 553, 567, 568, 630, 643, 691, 709, 711, 712

Hill River band; synonymy: 269. *See also* Cree, Western Woods

Hislop and Nagle: *155*, 296, 687, *687*

Historic period: 126

history; American period: 38, 43, 44, 49, 51, 120, 121, 482, 548–551, 553–556, 567, 586–587, 636, 643. British period: 43, 146, 148, 160, 548, 586. Canadian period: 35–39, 120, 146, 148–149, *155*, 387. contact: 35, 36, 46, 92, 120, 146–148, 199, 201, 208, 212, 231, 388–389, 395, 410, 417, 431, 439, 441, 442, 460, 482, 493, 503, 509, 528, 556, *557*, 584, 586, 611. contact-traditional period: 211–213, 218, 233, 235–238, 240, 245, 258–259, 264, 267, *274*, 280–282, 286–288, 294–296, 298, 312, 322–323, 328, 345–346, 357–359, 361–364, 387, 393–399, 411–412, 417–418, 439–440, 442–443, 452, 460–461, 469, 482, 503, 509–511, 529, 548–551, 553, 567, 584–585, 586–587, 611–612, 620–621. early contact period: 201, 208–211, 218, 231–233, 244–245, 258, 273, 285–287, 293–294, 296, 310–311, 320–322, 327–329, 345, 357, 387–393, 410–411, 416–417, 439, 442, 452, 460, 482, 494–496, 503, 509, 528–529, 547–548, 566–567, 584, 586, 611, 620. 18th century: 171, 200, 218, 231–233, 244–245, 258–259, 273, 285, 287, 294, 296, 310, 321, 329, 345, 357, 417, 482, 586, 635–636, 643, 673, 683. exploration: 35–37, 43, 49, 147, 166, 171, 201, 208, 258, 270, 286, 293, 314–315, 410, 417, 439, 503, 509, 528–529, 548, 549, 556–561, 566, 584, 586, 611, 621. French period: 146, 147, *147*, 158, 160, 170–171, 208. modern period (since 1940): 213, 218, 224–227, 238, 245–246, 253–254, 259, 266–267, 282–283, 288, 291–292, 296, *306*, 311, 328, 331–332, 346–347, 359, 369–370, 387, 399–

401, 412, 418, 439, 443, 460, 461, 475, 482–483, 503–504, 511, 529–530, 553–555, 568, 587. 19th century: 171–172, 200–202, 212, 218, 232–233, 236, 286–288, 296, 310–311, 321–322, 327–329, 345–346, 357–358, 387–398, 410–412, 417–418, 435, 439–440, 442–443, 460, 482, 503, 509–511, 528–529, 546–549, 566–567, 584–587, 595, 599, 615, 620–621, 636, 643, 651, 673, 683–687, 695, 704–705. Russian period: 43–44, 49–50, 120, 387, 388–389, 547–548, *547–548*, 556, 567, 584, 586, 595, 611, 620, 631, 635, 643, 651. 17th century: 171, 200–201, 208–209, 217–218, 231, 258, 273, 293–294, 586. 20th century: 172, 185, 200, 202, 213, 218, 224–227, 236–240, 245–246, 253–254, 266–267, 273–274, 282–283, 288, 291–292, 295, 296, 311, 322–324, 328, 331–332, 346–347, 358–359, 370, 394, 396, 398–401, 412, 418, 440, 460, 503–504, 511, 529–530, 549–555, 567, 585, 587, 597–599, 621–622, 636–637, 643, 666, 674, 678, 688–692, 695–696, 705–711, 712–717. White settlement: 150, 202, 393, 394, 397–399, 440, 460, 503–504, 510–511, 548–549, 567, 664, 665, 674–675, 690. *See also* Canada, government of; fur trade; gold rushes; legislation; missionaries; treaties; U.S. government

Hoffman, Hans: 22

Hole River band. *See* Ojibwa, Northern

Holiaktzagmute; synonymy: 616

Holikachuk: 556, 559, 600, 602, 615–616, 622. ceremonies: 616. clothing: 615–616. death: 616. disease: 615. external relations: 74. history: 615. language: *70*, 72–74, 77, 534, 558, 616. orthography: 602. population: 615. settlements: 558, 615, 616. structures: 616. subsistence: 558, 615. synonymy: 599, 613–616. territory: *557*, 558, 615, *615*. trade: 615–616

Holikitsak; synonymy: 616

Holmes, William H.: 36

Hologochaket; synonymy: 616

Home Guard Indians: 156, 159, 196–197, 200, 201, 228, 282. synonymy: 228, 230, 259

Home Indians; synonymy: 228

Hong-Kutchin; synonymy: 512

Honigmann, Irma: 40

Honigmann, John J.: 22, 24–25, *25*, 40, *40*, 450

Hood, Robert: *286*

Hopson, Eben: *554*

Hoquel-got; synonymy: 430

Horn Mountain Indians; synonymy: 294, 309

horses: 485, 498

Hosley, Edward H.: 47

hotél'ená; synonymy: 271

hotél-náde dene; synonymy: 280

Houle, Joseph: *686*

houses. *See* structures

Howren, Robert: 80

Hrdlička, Aleš: 44, *46*

Hudson, Henry: 201

Hudson's Bay Company: 196, 198, 199, 205, 213, 232, 233, 264, 266, 270, 276, 294, 298, *300*, *686*, 712. economic role: 225, 280, 394. history: 35–38, 120, 146, 148, 151, *152*, 155, *155*, *156*, 172, 196–200, 212, 273, 288, 296,

310–311, 321, 322, 328, 329, 389, 391, 394, 395, 452. Indian employment: 197–199, 201–202, 225, 226, 266, 282, *316*, 361, 364, 367, 390–392. provisions: 201, 218. trade items: *64*, *151*, *154*, 172, 218, 652. trading posts: *147*, 197, 200, 218, 258, 273, 311, 345, *358*, *389*, 390–391, *390*, *398*, 417–418, 442, 452, 470, 494, 503, 509, *529*, 586, 652, 666, *667*, 673, *673*, 683, 687, 691

Hungwitchin; synonymy: 512

Hun-koo-chin; synonymy: 512

Hun-Kutchin; synonymy: 512

hunting: *25*, 31, 87, 97, 150, 169, 170, 182, 190, 197, 201, 208, 212, *224*, 247, 258, 261, 374, 375, 406, 444, 456, *543*. bear: 132, *134*, 174, 175, 220, 484, 496, 506, 535, *536*, 604, 612, 619, *620*, 648, 676. beaver: 133, 134, 152, 174, 175, 208, 220, 233, 340, 484, 497, 553, 604, 612, 615, 648. birds: 175, 201, 220, *225*, 233, 506, 516, *535*, 566, 589, 604, 612, 626, 648, 668, *670*, *677*. camps: 120, 121, 137, 177, *177*, *224*, *281*, *378*, 565, 566, *573*, 588, 604, 646, 688, *689*. caribou: 103, 120, 131–132, 137, 175, 201, 220, 232, 260, 276, *281*, 282, 297, 299, 307, 332, 362, 484, 496, 506, 508, 516–518, 534–535, *535*, 549, 554, 565–566, 569, 574, 588–589, 604, 612, 615, 618–619, 626, 627, 648, 650, 668, *671*, 699, 725. communal: 260, 264, 376, 406, 407, 418, 462, 534–535, 549, 550, 565, 566, 588–589, 604, 619, 648. distribution of kill: 26, 405, 517, 518, 657. dogs for: 132, 175, 381, 405, 572, 669, 670, 697, 709, 725. first kill: 260, 385, 445, 527, 608, 633, 657. furbearers: 15, 17, 213, 218, 233, 257, 258, 272, 375, 378, 388, 416, 436, 458, 473, 482, 484, 496, 497, 516, *543*, 549–550, 565, 589, 604, 612, 615, 648, 668. ground squirrels: 604, 632. hare: *135*, 174, 220, 484, 496, *535*, 604, 612, 699. implements: 97, 103, 108, 132, *132*, 133, *152*, 154, 169, 174, 175, *197*, 201, 220, 223, 234, 260, 262, 376–378, 389–390, 403, 424, 425, 436, 443, 462, 484, 496–497, 506, 508, 516–518, 535, *536*, 549, 566, 569, 604, 612, 619, *620*, 626, 647, 648. moose: 132, *133*, 137, 174, 175, 220, 332, 484, 496, 508, 517, 518, 535, *536*, 549, 554, 566, 569, 604, 626, 648, 699, 725. mountain goats: 484, 496, 526, 648. mountain sheep: 484, 496, 566, 569, 604, 619, 626, 627, 648. muskrat: 589, 604. prehistoric: 31, 87, 89, 97, 101, 103, 108, 122. resources: 15–18, *16*, 131–132, 136–137, 151, 169, 174, 208, 217, 223, 232–233, 375, 376, 405, 425, 436, 443, 458, 459, 462, 470–473, 481, 483, 493, 496, 506, 508, 515, 516, 534, 543, 549, 565–566, 569, 584, 588–589, 603–606, *606*, 627, 646, 648. ritual observance: *177*, *179*, *185*, 192, 201, 202, *202*, 220–223, 252, 260, 409, 427, 428, *471*, 473, 484, 517, 518, 574, 593, 607, 608, 620, 635, 647–648, 652. sea mammals: 68, 133, 197, 198, 220, 626, 668, *676*, *677*. sites: 458, 585, 632, 644. songs: 184, 201, 647. taboos: 201, 220, 428, 438, 447, 647–648. techniques: 131–133, *133–135*, 152, 174, 175, 201, 208, 220, *225*, 234, 376–378, *377*, *379*, 380, *380*, 405, 406, 425, 436, 443, 462, 474, 484, 496–497, 516, 517,

518, 534–535, *535*, 553, 565–566, 569, 604, 619, 620, 647, 648, 650. territories: 25–26, 28, 106, 141, 152, 172, 180, 181, 190–191, 197–198, 199, 233, 236, 259, 264, 280–281, 320, 418, 421–422, 669. wolves: 648, 668

Huntlatin; synonymy: 576

Hupa; language: 67

Hurlburt, Janice: 22

Huron; external relations: 190. technology: *93*. trade: 175, 208, 209

Huslia-Dalbi (Dulbi)-Hogatza subdivision. *See* Koyukon

Hutchins, Thomas: 229

Hutshi band. *See* Tutchone

Hwitsowitenne; synonymy: 430

hʷocoʔenne; synonymy: 430

Hwotsuʔtinni; synonymy: 430

hydrology. *See* environment

I

Ice-Hunting culture: 24, 30

Ice Mountain Microblade phase: 117

Ickes, L. Harold: 399

iδiniwak; synonymy: 268

IgOg-4: *103*

ihko-iriniwak; synonymy: 283

IhNh-2: *103*

IhOk-1: *103*, 104

IiOd-1: 99

Ikovirinioucks; synonymy: 283

Île-a-la-Crosse band; synonymy: 269. *See also* Cree, Western Woods

Iliamna Lake Tanainas; synonymy: 638. *See also* Tanaina

ililiw; synonymy: 227

Illarion, Hieromonk: 44, 558

illness. *See* curing; disease; health care

ilnu; synonymy: 186

Ina. *See* Setin-setna

Indian Act of 1876: 398

Indian Brotherhoods: 266, 283, 296

Indian Bureau. *See* Bureau of Indian Affairs

Indian organizations: 41, 79, 150, 203, 266–268, 283, 296, 401, *554*, 641, 675, 677, 680, 715

Indian Reorganization Act of 1934: 551

Indian Reserve Commission: 425–426

Indian rights movement: 267, 283, 292, 347, 369, 370, *370*, 479, 482, 675, 677, 703, 708, *708*, 715. cultural rights: 213. land rights: 3–4, 203, 213, 401, 426, 554–555, *554*, 587

Indian and Eskimo words; Ahtna: 575, 576, 622, 638, 639, 644, 646, *650*, 652–658, *660*, 661, 662. Beaver: 81, 350, 352–357. Bella Coola: 430. Carrier: *84*, 412, 414, 419, *422*, 430, 431, 441. Chilcotin: 84, 402, 407, 409, 412. Chinook Jargon: 504. Chipewyan: 69, 168, 268, 271, 276, 279–281, *281*, 283, 289, 348, 371, 531, 684, 685, 688, 691. Chugach Eskimo: 662. Cree: 27, 52, 55, 56, 59, 60, *153*, 168, *180*, 183–187, 193, 195, 196, 198, 200, 202, 205, 206, 208, 213–215, 217, 221, 223, 227–229, 240–242, 255, 259, 263, 264, 267–270, 283, 288, 303, 348, 359, 371, 430, 669, 670, 718, 737. Dogrib: 283, 289, 291, *292*, 295, 297, 298, 301–303, *302*, 306. Eyak: 662. Gitksan: 419–420. Han: 77, 512, 513, 531. Holikachuk: 600, 615, 616.

Ingalik: 69, 73, 168, 600, 604, 607, 608, 614, 616, 622. Inupiat: 599, 600. Kolchan: *618*, 619, 620, 622. Koyukon: 74, *75*, 168, 575, 576, 589, 593, *594*, 595, 599, 600, 614, 616, 622, 662. Kutchin: 69, 74, 78, 168, 348, 371, 451, 504, 505, 520, 523, *525*, 526, 528, 531, 532, 575, 696–698, *698*. Lower Tanana: 76, 576. Mackenzie Delta Eskimo: 531. Northern Tutchone: 79, 499, 512, 576. Ojibwa: 52, 57–60, *64*, 214, 215, 227–229, 231, 233, 240–242, 244, 246, 249, 250, *252*, 253–255, 268, 371. Pacific Eskimo: 638. Sekani: 430. Slavey-Hare: 268, 283, 312, 313, 315, 316, 319, 320, 322–325, 329, 336, 337, 338, 343, 345, 348, 371, 451, 531. Tahltan-Kaska-Tagish: 448, 449, 451, 466, 490. Tanacross: 76, 575. Tanaina: 557, 622, *625*, 627, 631, 632, 635, 638, 639, 662. Tlingit: 461, 465, 466, *474–476*, 475–476, 479, 485, 486, 489, 490, 495–496, 501, 505, 651, 662. Tsetsaut: 455, 456. Tsimshian: 455, 456. Upper Tanana: 76, 575–577, 580, 581, 654, 662. Yupik: 599, 600, 602, 613, 614, 616, 622

Indiūth; synonymy: *37*

infanticide. *See* birth

infants. *See* children

Ingalik: 3, 47, 50, 51, 168, 563, 596, 600–617, 623, 726. adornment: 613. Anvik-Shageluk group: 557–558, 602, 604–606. birth: 610. Bonsila group: 558. ceremonies: 607–608, *608*, *609*, 610, 728–730, *729*, *730*, 734. childrearing: 610. clothing: 610, 613, *726*. death: 610, *611*. disease: 558, 611. division of labor: 604, 611. education: 612, *614*. environment: *533*, 602–603, 605–606. external relations: 74, 603–604, *606*. history: 44, 552, 611–612, *614*. kinship: 542, 610. Kuskokwim: 558, 559, 600 602, 603, 605, 606, 610, 612, 613, 622. language: 68, 69, *70*, 72–75, 77, 602, 618. life cycle: 609–610. marriage: 590, 602, 603, 606–607, 609, 610, 612. menstrual practices: 610. migration: 557, 559. music: 607, 610. orthography: 602. political organization: 606. population: 534, 612–614. prehistory: *46*, 122. puberty: 610, *726*. religion: 607, 611, 612. settlement pattern: 604. settlements: 43, 557–558, *560*, 613, 615, 638. shamanism: 607, 719. social organization: 590, 606–610, 720. structures: 539, 604, *605*, *606*, 613. subsistence: *536*, *537*, *543*, 546, 603, 604–606, *606*, 611, 612, *612*. synonymy: 512, 599, 600, 613–616. technology: *536*, *606*, *611*, 612–613, *612*, *613*. territory: 556–558, *557*, *560*, 602, *603*. trade: 596, 603, 611–612. transport: 537, *538*, 604, 606, 612–613. warfare: 559, 582, 603, 618. Yukon: 602–605, *606*, 607, 608, 610, 612–614, 616, 617

Ingelete; synonymy: 599

Ingles, Frederick: 468

iŋqiliq; synonymy: 599

iŋqiliχɬuat; synonymy: 616

inheritance. *See* property

ininiw; synonymy: 227

Initial Woodland period: 87, 89–91, *90*

Inkalichlüaten; synonymy: 616

Inkalichmüten; synonymy: 616
inkalikhlūaty; synonymy: 616
Inkalikhlyuat; synonymy: 616, 622
Inkilik proper; synonymy: 599. territory: *557*
Inland culture: 24, 30
Inlander(s); synonymy: 196, 205. *See also*
    Cree, East Main
Inland Indians; synonymy: 348
Innocent. *See* Marsh, Gordon
Innoka-khotana; synonymy: 616
innu; synonymy: 186
International Paper Company: 213
Intsi-Dindjitch; synonymy: 600
Inuit; synonymy: 187. *See also* Eskimo
Inupiat Eskimo: 599, 600. language: 596.
    marriage: 582. trade: 582
Iotchininy; synonymy: 348
Ipiutak Eskimo; prehistory: 123
ʔiqk(ah)a· qʷa·n; synonymy: 662
Iroquoian language grouping: 53
Iroquois: 362. external relations: 170, 209,
    215, 361, 386, 435, 439. history: 148, 391,
    435. migration: 29, 165, 215. prehistory: 94,
    95, 170. subsistence: 170. technology: 94,
    95. territory: 165–166. trade: 148, 155, 170,
    171, 391. population: 155. warfare: 148,
    160, 173, 194, 200, 208, 211
ipkpélit; synonymy: 531
Isaac (Han): *378, 507*
iše·ⁿžik gʷičin; synonymy: 532
Isham, James: 152, 153, 268
Iskuamiskutsh; synonymy: 186
Iskut band. *See* Sekani
Island Lake band. *See* Ojibwa, Northern
Islington band. *See* Saulteaux of Lake
    Winnipeg
Itkillik complex: 122, 123
itkpéléit; synonymy: 531
Ivan: *552, 574*
Ivanov, Vasiliy: 556
ixe·ⁿžik gʷičin; synonymy: 532
I-yan; synonymy: 505

J

Jackhead band. *See* Saulteaux of Lake
    Winnipeg
Jackie, Jo: *486*
Jackson, Jake: *475, 476*
Jackson, Mary: *475*
Jacobsen, J. Adrian: 51, 556
James, Albert: *487*
James Bay Cree; synonymy: 66, 150, 169, 205
James Bay Hydroelectric project: 3, 150, 203,
    715
Janvier band. *See* Chipewyan
Jean site: *103*
Jenkins, W.H.: 22
Jenness, Diamond: 21, 39–40, 41
Jetté, Jules: 44, *45,* 50, 74, *75,* 601
Jim, Frankie: *486*
Joe (Kaska): *40*
Joe (Tanana): *552*
Joe, Bill: *660*
Joe, Johnny: *486*
Joe, Maggie: *660*
John (Chief, of Chena): *552, 574*
John, French: *274*
John, Joe: *536*

John, Peter: 708: *708*
John, Suslota: *650*
Johns, Johnny: *486*
Johnson, Andrew: *589*
Johnson, Billy: *486*
Johnson, W.D.: 22
Johnston, George: *396*
Johnston, William: *476*
Jolliet, Louis: 171
Jones, Charlotte: *363*
Jones, Eliza: 75
Jones, Volney: 65
Josie, Edith: 41, 694, *694*
Julian complex: *110,* 116
Jumbie, Augustine: *356*
Junction site: *101*
Juvenal, Hieromonk: 43–44

K

Kachadi group. *See* Tahltan
Kachemak Bay band. *See* Tanaina
Kā-cho-'dtinne; synonymy: 324
ǩá čo goǐine; synonymy: 324
Kah-cho tinneh; synonymy: 324
Kainhkhotana; synonymy: 600
Káiyuhk(h)atána; synonymy: 600
Kaiyuhkhotana; synonymy: 600. *See also*
    Koyukon
Kak8azakhi; synonymy: 186
Kакоuchac; synonymy: 186
kak8chak; synonymy: 186
Kакоuchakhi; synonymy: 186
Kak8echak; synonymy: 186
Kakovchaqvi; synonymy: 186
ka·kuš; synonymy: 186
ǩálat hotyánʔ; synonymy: 505
kalchan; synonymy: 622
Kalifornsky, Peter: 73, 640
Ka-lis-te-no; synonymy: 227
Kamut Lake site: *98, 103,* 106
Kanaaupscow band. *See* Cree, East Main
Kancho; synonymy: 325
Kane, Joe: *486*
Kane, Paul: 440
ka··ne·ya·piska·winnut; synonymy: 205
Kani·ápəckau wi·´nutᶜ; synonymy: 205
Kaniapiscow band; synonymy: 205. *See also*
    Cree, East Main
Kaniapiskau band. *See* Montagnais-Naskapi
Kankünā; synonymy: 638
Kankünats Kōqtana; synonymy: 638
Kari, James: 72–74
Kar-karwan; synonymy: 461
Karpinsky site: 127
kaša; synonymy: 449
Kasabonika Lake band. *See* Ojibwa, Northern
ǩáselehtine; synonymy: 283
Kasна; synonymy: 449
Kasini; synonymy: 82, 505
Kaska: 40, *40,* 41, 336, 373, 387, 433, 440,
    442–450, 466, 500, 505, 726. adornment:
    445, 448. birth: 445, 447, 448. ceremonies:
    445–446, 732. childrearing: 447, 448.
    clothing: 443, 445, 448–449. curing: 449.
    Dease River: 82, 442, *442,* 443, 446, 447,
    450. death: 445, 446, 448, 727, 732.
    division of labor: 443, 444, 445. education:
    448. environment: 374, 375, 444. external

relations: 162, 436, 454, 458, 470, 494, 502.
    Frances Lake band: 82, 442, *442,* 446, 450,
    494. games: 445. history: 36, 38, 39, 162,
    328, 389, 394, 395, 399, 442–443. kinship:
    446. language: 69, *70,* 72, 77, 79, 81, 82,
    372, 442–443, 451, 452, 458, 481, 482, 494.
    life cycle: 447–448. marriage: 447, 448,
    458, 470, 494. menstrual practices: 447.
    migration: 162, 443, 444. music: 445, 734.
    mythology: 449. Nelson Indians: 82, 329,
    442, *442,* 443, 447, 450. orthography: 442.
    political organization: 446, 447. population:
    331, 442. puberty: 447, 448. religion: 448,
    449, 719. Ross River band: 450.
    shamanism: 448–449, 720. social
    organization: 384, 446–447, 449, 720.
    structures: 444, 447, 473. subsistence: 376,
    443–444. synonymy: 327–328, 336, 449–
    450, 452, 453, 479, 480, 505. technology:
    379, 443, *445,* 446. territory: 161, 162, 442,
    442, 458. Titshotina band: 466. trade: 36,
    442, 470, 494. transport: 380, 381, 399,
    444, *445.* Tselona band: 82, 329, 442, *442,*
    446, 450. Upper Liard band: 82, 442, *442,*
    443, 446, 447, 450. warfare: 377, 388, 443,
    447, 470, 494
ǩá šo goǐine; synonymy: 324
Kastechewan; synonymy: 228
Kà-stichewan(uk); synonymy: 228
K'a-t'a-gottinè; synonymy: 324
Katchinak, William: *671*
K'a-tchó-gottinè; synonymy: 324
Kate (Tagish): 482
Kateel village site: 120
Ka-tshik-o-tin; synonymy: 513
Kavik complex: 122
Kavik site: 118
Kawchodinneh; synonymy: 324
kaxtnuxíana; synonymy: 638
Kayan: *354*
ǩàyⁿdik; synonymy: 513
KdPl-1 site: 106
Kechechewan; synonymy: 228
Keelshies: 276
Keewatin: 252
ǩeh ôi·gn; synonymy: 576
Keith, George: 451
Kenaeǐs; synonymy: 638
Kenai band. *See* Tanaina
Kenaier; synonymy: 638
Kenai Indians; synonymy: 638
Kenai Mountain Tanainas; synonymy: 638
Kenai Peninsula Tanainas; synonymy: 638. *See
    also* Tanaina
Kenai River Tanainas; synonymy: 638
Kenaískīi; synonymy: 638
Kenai-tená; synonymy: 638
Kenaïǐsy; synonymy: 638
Kenaitze; synonymy: 638
kənaiyuq; synonymy: 638
kənaiyut; synonymy: 638
Kenay, synonymy: 122
Kenayer; synonymy: 638
Kennicott, Robert: *27,* 36, 38
KeNo-2: *103,* 104
KePl-1: 104
Kerr, A.J.: 717

Kesichewan; synonymy: 228
Keskarrah: *286*
ke·yeho·ti·ne; synonymy: 466
KfNm-5: 99
KfNm-13: 102
KfNt-1: 104
Kha Sha, John: *498*
Kha-tchô-Gottinè; synonymy: 324
Kha-tpa-gottinè; synonymy: 324
Khuligichaɣat; synonymy: 616
Khŭn-ŭn-āh´; synonymy: 466, 505
Kichesipiiriniouek; synonymy: 229
Kijik site: 45, *108, 119*, 120. *121*, *121*
Kikendash; synonymy: 215
Kikendatch band; synonymy: 215. *See also*
  Attikamek (Tête de Boule)
ki·ke·nita·č; synonymy: 215
Kilistheno; synonymy: 228
Kilistinaux; synonymy: 228
kilištino·; synonymy: 227
Kilistinon(s); synonymy: 158, 159, 227.
  territory: *159*
Kilistinons Alimibegoueк; synonymy: 229
Kilistinons des Nipisiriniens; synonymy: 229.
  territory: *159*
Kilistinons Nisibourounik; synonymy: 205
Kilistinos; synonymy: 228
Kil-istinouc; synonymy: 227
Kilistones; synonymy: 228
Kilistones Nisibouк8nici; synonymy: 205
Killistinoes; synonymy: 228
Kinai; synonymy: 638
Kina-ïūt; synonymy: 638
kinajut; synonymy: 638
Kingfisher band. *See* Ojibwa, Northern
kingfisher tribe; synonymy: 242
King, James: 43
Kinishtineau; synonymy: 228
Kinistinaux; synonymy: 228
kiništino·; synonymy: 228
Kinistinons; synonymy: 228
KiNl-3: 99
kinship: 203, 221, 237, 301–302, 334, 341–
  342, 350, 352–353, 362, 384, 407, 419, 446,
  460, 475, 486–487, 508, 517, 519–520, 542,
  567, 589–590, 610, 631, 653–656, 669, 675,
  677, 696–697, 714, 735. bilateral: 144, 259–
  260, 276, 301, 319, 352, 384, 433, 590
kinship terminology: 24, 27, *27*, 183, 184, 250,
  277, *302*, 319, 341–342, 352–353, 384, 407,
  423–424, 572, 574, 620, 631, 654–656, 735.
  Crow system: 446, 476, 631. Eskimo system:
  486–487, 500, 501, 508, 517, 520, 542, 610.
  Hawaiian system: 342, 519, 631. Iroquois
  system: 221, 236, 319, 342, 446, 542, 574,
  589, 590, 620, 631
Kiowa-Apache; language: 67, 68. migration:
  68
Kipawa band. *See* Algonquin
Kippewa; synonymy: 243
Kiristin(n)ons; synonymy: 227
kirištino·; synonymy: 227
Kiristinous; synonymy: 227
Kirkby, W.W.: 701
Kischeripirini; synonymy: 229
kiše·-ma·ta·wa·w; synonymy: 242
Kitchen, Angus Willie: *153*
Kitchen, Mrs. Willie: *153*

Kitchichiouan; synonymy: 228
Kitwancool. *See* Gitksan
KkLn-2: *88*
Kkɒay-tsele-'ttiné; synonymy: 283
Kkɒayttchare Ottiné; synonymy: 325
Kkɒest'aylékkè ottiné. *See* Chipewyan
kkwi dyik; synonymy: 513
Klabbahnotin group. *See* Tahltan
Klat-ol-klin Indians; synonymy: 513
Klin-tchanɒè; synonymy: 295
Klimovskiy, Andrei Il'ich: 643
Klis-teno; synonymy: 228
Klo-a-tsul-tshik´; synonymy: 505
Klo-kut site: *108, 118, 119*, 120, *123*, 124
Klondike. *See* Han
Kloo Lake band. *See* Tutchone
Kluane band. *See* Tutchone
Kluksho-Champagne band. *See* Tutchone
Kluskoten; synonymy: 431
Kluskus band. *See* Carrier
Kluskus "tribe"; synonymy: 431
Klutena; synonymy: 662
Klutina–Copper Center band. *See* Ahtna
K'naí-ā-kho-tana; synonymy: 638
Knife Indians; synonymy: 494, 503, 505
Knight, James: *165*, 273, 276
Knight, Rolf: 22
Knik Arm Tanaina. *See* Tanaina
Knisteneaux; synonymy: 163, 228
Knistinaux; synonymy: 163
knives: 92, 95, *96*, 99, 101, 102, *102*, *105*, 110,
  113, 114, 118, 120, *121*, 125, *125*, 128, *152*,
  219, 518, *522, 536*, 570, *572*, 649. crooked:
  141, 175, *176*, 570, *571*, *613*. semilunar: 175,
  219, *626*, 649
Kobuk Eskimo: 596. external relations: 559.
  migration: 515. trade: 596. warfare: 596
Kodhell-vén-Kouttchin; synonymy: 531
kodilqaq̇ə x̌ŏianə; synonymy: 600
Koe, Andrew: *378*
K'Oghotaaineek. *See* Stickman, Anna
ko·hko·ka·šš; synonymy: 215
Kokrines Indians; synonymy: 600
Kolchan: 3, 47, 50, 556, 600, 618–622.
  ceremonies: 618, 620, 621. death: 620.
  clothing: 619. disease: 621. East Fork band:
  619. education: 621. employment: 621–622.
  environment: *533*, 618, 621. external
  relations: 75, 618. health care: 621, 622.
  history: *552*, 620–621. kinship: 620.
  language: 48, *70*, 72, 73, 74, 75–77, 618.
  marriage: 618–620. migration: 618–619,
  622. mythology: 620. Nikolai band: *619*.
  orthography: 618. political organization:
  618, 620, 621. population: 534, 615, 621,
  622. prehistory: 46. puberty: 619. religion:
  620, 621. settlement pattern: 618.
  settlements: *552*, 621, *621*. shamanism: 620.
  social organization: 618–621. structures:
  618, 619, *621*. subsistence: 535, *543, 545*,
  546, 618–619, *619*, 621. synonymy: 558–
  559, 600, 613, 614, 616, 622. Takotna band:
  619. Tatlawiksuk band: *619*. technology:
  619. Telida-Minchumina band: *619*.
  territory: *557, 588*–559, 618, *619*, 621.
  trade: 548, 559, 618, 620. transport: 537,
  618, 621, *621*, *622*. Vinasale band: *619*.
  warfare: 559, 603, 618

Kolchane: 657. synonymy: 662
Kolmakov, Fëdor: 554, 620
Kolmakov, Pëtr: 556, 558, 559, 615
Koltschanen; synonymy: 622
Koltschanes; synonymy: 622
Konē´·na; synonymy: 466
Koniag Eskimo; history: 547. marriage; 624,
  636
Koo cha Koo chin; synonymy: *37*, 532
Koolage, W.W.: 22
Kootcha-Kootchin; synonymy: 532
Kootchin; synonymy: 530
Korsakovskiy, Pëtr: 556
Koshon: *467*
kɔswa; synonymy: 449
Kotch-á-kutchins; synonymy: 532
Kotchile: *319*
k̇otene; synonymy: 430
Kotenich-etl: *650*
Kotzebue Sound Eskimo; trade: 596
Kouschâ-Kouttchin; synonymy: 532
Koyúkokhotáná; synonymy: 599
Koyukon: 45, 46, 47, 50, 168, *548*, 554, 556,
  575, 582–601, 602, 615, 616, 622, 623, 662.
  birth: 590–591. Central: 74. ceremonies:
  544, 590, 591, 593, *594*, 595. clothing: *542*,
  588, 590, 591, *594*, 596, 597. cosmology:
  595. Cosna-Manley subdivision: 582. death:
  591, *592*, 593, *594*, 728. disease: 559, 586,
  587, 597. division of labor: 588, 589.
  education: 586, 587, 597. employment: 586,
  597–598. environment: *533*, 584. external
  relations: 75, 523, 582, 603. games: 593.
  health care: 587, 597. history: 43, 44, *548*,
  584–587, *588*, 598–599. Huslia-Dalbi
  (Dulbi)-Hogatza subdivision: 582.
  Kaiyuhkhotana proper: 582, 600. kinship:
  542, 589–590. Koyukuk division: 47, *122*,
  388, 539, 559, 560, 582–587, *588*, 589–591,
  595, 596, 599–601. language: 48, *70*, 72–77,
  75, 84, 582–583, 585, 597, 599. Lower: 73,
  74. Lower Yukon division: 582–586, 589,
  590, 593, 595, 596, 599–601, 614. marriage:
  582, 585, 589, 591. menstrual practices: 590,
  591. migration: 559, 560, 562, 565, 582, 586,
  588–589. Minchumina-Bearpaw: 74, 75,
  582. music: 593, *594*, 595. mythology: 593,
  595, 600. Nowitna-Koyukuk subdivision:
  582. orthography: 582. political
  organization: *552*, 585, *588*, 598–599.
  population: 534, 584, 585, 597. prehistory:
  122, 124. puberty: 591. religion: 586, 593,
  594, 599. settlement pattern: 597.
  settlements: *548, 550, 551, 554*, 560, 584,
  597, *598*. shamanism: *589*, 593, 595. social
  organization: 585, 589–590, 653. South Fork
  subdivision: 582, 583, 599, 600. Stevens
  Village–Tanana subdivision: 582, 583.
  structures: *122*, 539, 591, *592*, *592*, 596, 597,
  598, *728*. subsistence: 535, *536*, *543*, 546,
  588–589, *589*, 597, *598*. synonymy: 575,
  599–600, 613, 614, 616. Takayaksa
  subdivision: 582, 600. Tanana-Nowitna
  subdivision: 582, 600. technology: *554*, 596.
  territory: *557*, 560, *560*, 582, *583*, 584.
  Todatonten-Kanuti subdivision: 582, 583,
  600. trade: 388, 582, 584–586, 588, *588*,
  589, 595–596, 603. transport: 537, *539, 551*,

589, 596–597. Ulukagmyut subdivision: 582, 600. Upper: 74, 75, 372, 563. Upper Yukon division: 582–585, 589, 590, 595, 596, 599–601. warfare: 559, 582, 585, 586, 596, 603, 618. Yukon-Kateel subdivision: 582, 584, 600

Koyukuk River division. *See* Koyukon
Koyukukhotana; synonymy: 599
Kóyukuks; synonymy: 599
Koyúkun; synonymy: 599
Rqızaɣətnu xĺan; synonymy: 638
Krause, Arthur: 503
Krauss, Michael: 47, 77, 616, 622
Krees; synonymy: 227
Krieger, Herbert W.: 44
Kriqs; synonymy: 227
Kris; synonymy: 227
Kristinos; synonymy: 227
Kroeber, A.L.: 41
Kroto Creek Tanainas; synonymy: 639. *See also* Tanaina
Ɽudəne; synonymy: 430
Kuilchana; synonymy: 616
kuīukanskiī; synonymy: 599
kuīukantsy; synonymy: 599
Kulchana; synonymy: 622
Kunana; synonymy: 466
Kŭn-ūn-ah´; synonymy: 466, 505
Kupfer-Galzanen; synonymy: 662
Kus-chē-o-tin; synonymy: 430
Kuskowagamiut Eskimo; disease: 611. external relations: 603. marriage: 602, 612. settlements: 602, 613. subsistence: 606. territory: 602. trade: 603. warfare: 603.
Kustatan Tanainas; synonymy: 638. *See also* Tanaina
Kutchakutchin; synonymy: 531, 532
Kutchiá-Kuttchin; synonymy: 532
Kutchin: 22, 40, 41, 161, 168, 269, 314, 330, 348, 361, 371, 373, 505, 514–532, 548, 575, 596, 623, 694–703. adornment: 517, *520, 522, 530.* Arctic Red River band: 514, 515, *516,* 528, 531. Arctic Village band: *397, 523.* Birch Creek band: *37,* 515, *516,* 532. birth: 526, 527. Black River band: *37,* 515, *516,* 532. ceremonies: 517, 519, 522, 524, 527, 528. Chandalar band: *37,* 40, 374, 375, *397, 399,* 515, *516,* 528, 532, 601, 697, *698,* 702, 727, 731, *733.* childrearing: 524. clothing: *392,* 516, 517, 518, *520–523,* 524, *733.* cosmology: 526–527. Crow Flats band: *37,* 120, 124, 515, *516,* 523, 531–532, 694–695. death: 519, 527, 697, *698,* 702. Dihai band: 515, *516,* 532. disease: 529, 560, 695. education: 401, 529, 695, 696. employment: 530, 696, 699, 700. environment: *9, 372,* 374, 375, 514, 515. external relations: 315, 316, 322, 389, 494, 506. games: 519, 528. health care: 401, 695, 696. history: 35–39, 148, 388–390, *389, 390,* 394, 395, 397, 399–401, 528–530, *529,* 547, 733. kinship: 517, 519–520. knowledge: 528. language: 36, 38, 69, *70,* 71–74, 76, 77–78, *78,* 83, 372, 396, 506, 514, 515, 529–530, 696. life cycle: 519. Loucheux: 78, 161, 315, 323, 512, 515, 529–531. Mackenzie Flats band: 125, 514, 515, *516,* 531. marriage: 316, 494, 524–526, 695, 697, 702. menstrual practices: 526.

migration: 122, 514, 515. music: *400,* 528. mythology: 526–528, 737. Old Crow band: *40,* 374, 399, *526, 530,* 531, 694–703. orthography: 514. Peel River band: 40, *378,* 451, 494, 504, 506, 514, 515, *516,* 520, 523, 528, 529, 530, 531, 695. political organization: 519, 522–523, *524,* 700–701, 720. population: 323, 530, 531, 696, 697. prehistory: 120, 122, 125. puberty: 524–525, 527, 727. religion: 395, *397,* 519, 526–527. reserves: 399. settlement pattern: 517, *524,* 699–700, *701.* settlements: 120, 515, *524,* 530, 531, 560, 694–703. shamanism: *397,* 527. social organization: 384, 514, 517, 519–520, 522–525, *524,* 653, 696–698, 721. structures: 379, 380, *390,* 518, *525, 526,* 695, 697, *698,* 700. subsistence: 374–376, *376, 377, 378,* 379, 515–518, 522, *530,* 694–695, 699. synonymy: *37,* 505, 512, 513, 530–532, *530–532.* technology: 377, *377,* 378–379, *382, 383, 391,* 517–519, *522, 722.* territory: *37,* 161, 514–515, *516,* 560. trade: 321, 322, 388, 389, *389–390,* 494, 515, 516, 522–523, 528–529, 652, 695. transport: 377, 380–381, *382,* 387, 390, 399, *400,* 517, 518, *525, 530, 540,* 696, 699, *699.* Tukudh: 38, 78, *78,* 515, 529, 531. Upper Porcupine River band: *37,* 515, *516,* 531. warfare: 377, 379, 494, 519, 522, 523, 528–529. Yukon Flats band: *37,* 515, *516,* 529, 532
Kutchin tribes; synonymy: 505, 512
Kutenai: 41, 373
Kuyukuk; synonymy: 599
Kuyukunski; synonymy: 599
Kwakiutl; social organization: 388. trade: 388
Kwalhioqua; language: 67, 68
kwa·niči·winnu; synonymy: 187
Kwitcha-Kouttchin; synonymy: 531
Kwitcha-Kut(t)chin; synonymy: 531
Kyltschanen; synonymy: 622
Kyltschanes; synonymy: 622
Kyristin8ns; synonymy: 227

L

Lac d'Ours, Gens du; synonymy: 311, 313
Lackweip; synonymy: 455
Lac la Ronge band. *See* Cree, Western Woods
Lacombe, Albert: *149*
Lac Seul band. *See* Saulteaux of Lake Winnipeg
Lac Simon band. *See* Algonquin
Ladue, Joe: 567, 569
Lafferty, Catherine: *364*
Lafferty, Edward: *364*
Lafferty, James: *364*
La France, Joseph: 306
Lagimodiere, J.B.: *368*
Lake Babine; synonymy: 430
Lake Clark Tanainas; synonymy: 638. *See also* Tanaina
Lake Iliamna band. *See* Tanaina
Lake Nipigon Cree; synonymy: 158
Lake Saint John band. *See* Montagnais-Naskapi
Lake Saint John–Saguenay River; synonymy: 186
Lake Saint John site: 95

Lake Saint Martin band. *See* Saulteaux of Lake Winnipeg
Lake Winnipeg Indians; synonymy: 230
Lakuyip; synonymy: 461
Lakweip; synonymy: 461
Lakwiyip; synonymy: 455
Lamöelle, Vital: *690*
land: 489. claims: 48, 150, 246, *306,* 398–400, 482, 496, 504, *552,* 703, 708, *708,* 715. disputes: 421–422. ownership: 26, 189, 191, 263, 418, 422, 426. rights: 26, 181, 236, 281, 418, 422. trespass: 181, 233, 421. use: 25, 141, 190–191, 281–282, 418. White encroachment: 13–14, 212–213, 259, 418, 426. *See also* environment; territory; treaties
language: 41, 47–48, 167, 212, 225, 273, 372, 387, 392, 396, 430, 442–443, 445, 458, 466, 529, 569, 599, 616, 667, 671, 733–734. bilingualism: 54, 61, 62, 80, 82, 150, 156, 196, 266, 529, 680, 681, 685, 696. borrowing: 56, 68, 72–76, *153,* 529–530. classification: 32, 52–53, 55–58, 67–69, 240, 245, 402, 442, 452, 454, 469, 481, 493, 506, 514, 562–563, 618. 641. dialects: 52, *53, 54,* 55–58, 60–61, *61,* 72–84, 169, 185, 196, 215, 217, 227, 228, 231, 241, 244, 256, 264, 271, 275, 288, 348, 408, 415, 442, 458, 469, 482, 514, 515, 563, 582–584, 602, 623, 624, *625,* 641, *643,* 644. distribution: 53–54, *53, 54,* 67–68. extinct: 67, 71, 73, 76, 83. kinship terminology: *24, 27, 27,* 302. literacy: 62, 78, 79, 81–84, 217, 224, 266, 397, 506, 529, 554, 643, 673. morphology: 52, 56–57, *59,* 69, *71,* 74. multilingualism: 54, 61, 73, 80. prehistory: 60–61, 67–68. sound system: 52, 55–60, *59,* 69, *70,* 71–85, 185, 227, 228, 623. teaching: 64, 74, 75, 77, 79. tone systems: 69, 71–85, 563. use: 54, 56, 62–64, 71–85, 213, 228, 241, 254, 451, 456, 469, 481, 494, 506, 530, 554, 584, 597, 602, 623, *643,* 696, 707, 710. writing systems: 38, *61,* 62–63, *62–64,* 65, 72–80, *81,* 82, 83, 217, 397, 515, 529
Laperrière, Nicolas: *150*
Lapiene's House Indians; synonymy: 531
La Pierre's House Indians; synonymy: 531
Lapointe site: *103,* 104
Laq·uyĭ´p; synonymy: 461
Large, Gens de; synonymy: *37,* 532
large, (Les) Gens du; synonymy: 434, 532
La Rusic, I.E.: 22
Late Prehistoric period: 126
Lake Woodland period. *See* Terminal Woodland period
Laurel culture: 90, *90,* 91, 94
Laurentian Archaic tradition: 32, 89
Laure, Pierre: 61
Lawrence, Harry: *46*
Laydliwotin; synonymy: 431
Leacock, Eleanor: 22
Leapers; synonymy: 255
leatherwork. *See* technology
Lebedev-Lastochkin Company: 547, 556, 636
Le Clercq, Chrétien: 724
Le Corre, A.: 78
Leechman, Douglas: 40
legislation, Canadian; antiquities: 34. drinking rights: 400. land: 3, 150, 203

legislation, provincial: 34. land: 203, 398
legislation, state; voting rights: 399
legislation, U.S.: 398. citizenship: 399. land:
3, 48, 81, 401, 554–555, 562, 587, 613, 622,
708, *708*, 715. land allotment: 399. political
organization: 551, 562. statehood: 554.
treaties: 399
Legoff, Laurent: *81*
Le Grand Jeune Homme: 685
teɣetnoʔ haʔan; synonymy: 616
teiλi hʷaʔienne; synonymy: 431
LeJac, Jean: 429
Le Jeune, Paul: 61, 190–195
Leroux, Laurent: 296, 683
Leslie's Illustrated Newspaper Expedition: 38–
39, 503
Levi: 455–457
life cycle; Ahtna: 657–659. Carrier: 425, 427–
28. Chilcotin: 404–405. Chipewyan: 277,
279. Dogrib: 299, 301. Han: 508–509. Hare:
320. Ingalik: 609–610. Kaska: 447–448.
Kolchan: 619–620. Koyukon: 590–591, 593.
Kutchin: 519. Mountain Indians: 335–336.
Sekani: 437–438. Slavey: 344. Tagish: 487–
488. Tanaina: 632–634. Tanana: 571–572.
Tlingit, Inland: 477–478. Tutchone: 500–
501. Western Woods Cree: 260–261
Lillooet; language: 84
łi·λi̧kó̧ȩ́ gotine; synonymy: 348
łingít λe·n: 501
LiNj-1: 106
Lintchanre; synonymy: 309
Lin-tchanpe; synonymy: 293, 309
LiPk-1: 98, 99
lip piercing. *See* adornment
Lips, Julius E.: 22
Lisīanskiĭ, ĪU. F.: 50
literacy: 62, 78, 79, 81–84, 217, 224, 266, 397,
506, 529, 554, 643, 673, 716
litigation, Canadian; land claims: 398, 401, 715
Little Arm phase: 115
Little Arm site: *113,* 115, *123*
Little Black River band. *See* Saulteaux of
Lake Winnipeg
Little Grand Rapids band. *See* Saulteaux of
Lake Winnipeg
Little John. *See* White River Johnny
Little Red River band. *See* Cree, Western
Woods
Little Salmon River Indians; synonymy: 505
Little Tabitabies; synonymy: 228
Little Winnipeggons; synonymy: 230
Livingston's Fort: 345
LjPh-1: 101
Lkátcoten; synonymy: 431
Lockhart River complex: 100, 104
Lockhart River site: *103*
to·ɣŭnʔ haʔan; synonymy: 616
Long Grass Indians; synonymy: 434, 460
Long Legs: 286, 287
Long Point band. *See* Algonquin
loon tribe; synonymy: 242
Loucheux; synonymy: 78, 512, 531. *See also*
Kutchin
Louchioux; synonymy: 531
Louzy Indians; synonymy: 283
Lower Ahtnas; synonymy: 662
Lower Dahotinne; synonymy: 327, 330

Lower Koyukuk; synonymy: 600
Lower Loucheux; synonymy: 323
Lower Nabesna band. *See* Tanana
Lower Post: *389*
Lower Rat Hunters: 323
Lower Susitna River Tanainas; synonymy: 639
Lower Tonsina band. *See* Ahtna
Lower Yukon division. *See* Koyukon
Lowie, Robert H.: 20, 22
Lowland dogs; synonymy: 306
łtaʔən; synonymy: 441
łtautenne; synonymy: 431
Lubicon Lake band. *See* Cree, Western
Woods
Lukin, Ivan Semënovich: 548, 584
Lukin, Semën: 547, 548
Lurie, Nancy Oestreich: 22
łuskez hʷaʔienne; synonymy: 431
λamas xötanə; synonymy: 600
λazienne; synonymy: 430
λi̧čaɣe; synonymy: 295
λi̧čo̧; synonymy: 306
λuɣotnoʔ xötanə; synonymy: 616

M

McClellan, Catharine: 40, 72
MacDonald, John A.: *81*
McDonald, Robert: 37–38, 77, 78, *78*, 396,
397, 506, 510, 515, 529, 531, 701
McDonnell, R.F.: 505
McDougall, James: 35, 439
MacFarlane, Roderick: 36
McGee, John T.: 22
McGinigle, Alan: 450
McGrath group: 588, 602. synonymy: 622. *See
also* Kolchan
Macha(n)dibi; synonymy: 214
Machantiby; synonymy: 214
Machatantibis; synonymy: 212, 214
Machkégons; synonymy: 227
Machkégous; synonymy: 227
McKenna-McBride Commission: 426
McKennan, Robert A.: 40, 46–47, 601
Mackenzie, Alexander: 35, 80, 163, 166, 296,
314, 345, 364, 388, 417, 431, 441, *441,* 528
Mackenzie complex: 116, *118,* 125
Mackenzie Eskimo; external relations: 315.
trade: 528
Mackenzie Flats band; synonymy: 531. *See
also* Kutchin
Mackenzie Indians: 329
Mackenzie River Indians: 323
MacKinlay River site: *101, 103*
MacLachlan, Bruce: 40
McLean, John: 35, 431
McLeod Lake band. *See* Sekani
McLeod, Mary: *512*
MacNeish, Richard S.: 32
McPherson, Murdoch: 36
McQuesten, Leroy N. (Jack): *389,* 503, 567,
569
McQuillan, Sister: *688*
McRoy, Nancy: 76, 77
McVicar, Robert: 683
Madara, Guy H.: *552, 574*
Mailhot, José: 22

Mair, Charles: *368*
Malakhov, Pëtr Vasil'evich: 547–548, *548,*
556, 584, 586, 643
Malimute, Alick: *45*
manawa·n; synonymy: 215
Mandeville, François: 289
manite·w si·piy; synonymy: 269
manitou. *See* supernatural beings
manitu·w-ši·pi·winnu; synonymy: 187
Maniwaki band. *See* Ojibwa
Manouane band; synonymy: 215. *See also*
Attikamek (Tête de Boule)
Manowan; synonymy: 215
Mansfield-Kechumstuk band. *See* Tanana
Mantotin; synonymy: 576
Mantua-Sepee; synonymy: 269
Many Hearths site: *103*
marriage: 183, 301, 385, 405, 428, 438, 500–
501, 591, 609, 619, 633, 634, 697. adultery:
261. age at: 183, 277, 319, 323, 447, 477,
488, 509, 524, 542, 606, 658. arranged: 144,
250, 261, 277, 320, 362, 385, 405, 464, 477,
488, 508–509, 525, 542, 619, 633, 658, 697.
betrothal: 261, 277, 319, 591. bride price:
448, 633, 634. bride service: 221, 250, 261,
299, 301, 319, 344, 428, 438, 447, 464, 477,
488, 525, 526, 542, 609, 620, 633, 634, 658.
ceremonies: 261, 279, 301, 319, 405, 445,
465, 591, 593, 633. cicisbeism: 526.
Christian: 447, 448. courtship: 170, 301,
428, 610, 619. cross-cousin: 24, 27, 144, 183,
221, 224, 236, 250, 259, 266, 277, 319, 424,
428, 447, 448, 464, 501, 508, 541, 572, 577,
590, 619, 633, 634, 653, 658. divorce: 192,
221, 261, 319, 438, 464, 488, 591, 609, 633,
658, 697. elopement: 405. endogamy: 524,
540, 585, 590, 607, 609, 623, 633, 634, 697.
Eskimo-Indian: 199, 559, 582, 590, 602, 603,
623, 681. Eskimo-White: 679. exogamy:
486, 499, 508, 540, 542, 565, 572, 577, 595,
618, 619, 633, 653. gifts: 261, 385, 405, 428,
488, 571, 619. incest: 363, 447. intergroup:
94, 194, 197, 198, 199, 200, 203, 208, 231,
237, 245, 249, 286, 297, 311, 316, 324, 331,
343–344, 363, 364, 387, 395, 397, 417, 419,
420, 422, 434, 435, 438, 439, 447, 456, 458,
461, 464, 469, 470, 475, 481, 482, 489, *489,*
494–496, 499, 565, 582, 590, 618, 619, 623,
624, 666, 685, 690, 695. levirate: 144, 183,
221, 266, 277, 319, 344, 447, 464, 590, 609,
620, 656. polyandry: 319, 447, 477, 488,
509, 525, 526, 590, 620, 658. polygyny: 144,
183, 192, 221, 236, 244, 259, 261, 266, 279,
301, 319, 344, 364, 396, 405, 428, 438, 447,
464, 477, 488, 500, 509, 525, 526, 571, 585,
590, 591, 609, 620, 632–634, 658. postcontact: 183, 203, 224, 250, 323, 509, 634.
remarriage: 144, 428, 438, 448, 488, 509,
577, 609, 697. residence: 144, 183, 191, 221,
250, 261, 319, 336, 344, 363, 384, 405, 428,
433, 447, 501, 508, 509, 525, 542, 571, 590,
609, 619–620, 633, 634, 658. sister
exchange: 319, 447, 619. sororate: 144, 183,
221, 224, 277, 319, 344, 438, 447, 464, 590,
609, 620, 634, 656. with Whites: 28, 35, 322,
361, 391, 398, 434, 488, 511, 636, 637, 679,
690, 692, 695, 702. wife exchange: 221, 224,
261, 619, 698

Marsh, Gordon: 77
Marsh, People of the; synonymy: 159
Marten Lake Indians: 294
Martin Falls band. *See* Ojibwa, Northern
Martin, Mrs.: *464*
Martin, Harry: *735*
Martin, Richard: *41*
Mashkegonhyrinis; synonymy: 159, 227
Mas-ke-gau; synonymy: 227
Maskego; synonymy: 227
Maskegon; synonymy: 159, 227
Maskegonehirinis; synonymy: 227, 258
Maskègowuk; synonymy: 227
maske·ko·wiyiniw; synonymy: 227
maski·ko·w; synonymy: 227
maskosi·ska·w si·piy; synonymy: 269
masks: *486*, 608, *609, 729, 730*
maskwa·nuwinnu; synonymy: 187
Mason, J. Alden: 20, *21*, 22, 290
Mason, Leonard: 21, 22, 25
Mason, M.H.: 532
Masquigon; synonymy: 227
Masquikoukioeks; synonymy: 227
Matachewan band. *See* Cree, Western Woods
Matanuskas; synonymy: 662
Mathew (Naskapi): *25*
Mathias Colomb band. *See* Cree, Western
  Woods
Matonabbee: 273, 276, 279
Mattole; language: 67
mauls: *570, 612*
Mayapoo, Charlie: *206*
Mayo, Alfred: 503, 567, 586
Mayo Indians; synonymy: 504. *See also*
  Tutchone
Mɑtacèwilnuts; synonymy: 215
Meadow Indians; synonymy: 440. *See also*
  Sekani
medicine bundles: 263, 353, 355–356, 490,
  502, 590, *719*
Medler, Andrew: 65–66
Meek, R.J.: 468
Menez, Louis: 693
Menez site: 101, 102
Menihek Lakes band. *See* Montagnais-Naskapi
Menominee; language: 54
menstrual practices: 201, 220, 223, 277, 299,
  301, 335–336, 344, 380, 385, 425, 427, 438,
  447, 488, 498, 502, 508, 511, 518, 526, 539,
  572, 591, 610, 628, 633, 645, 648, 657–658,
  725. *See also* puberty
Mentasta band. *See* Ahtna
Merasty, Angelique: *268*
Mercier, Moses: 509
Mer du Nord, Gens de la; synonymy: 209, 215
mer, gens de la; synonymy: 205
Mesa Lake site: *98*
Meshinnepee; synonymy: 269
Meso-Indian period: 100
Mestokosho, Marie: *176*
Metaketchouan site: 95
metalwork. *See* technology
Metawosenes: 160
Métif; synonymy: 370, 371
Métis: 3, 22, 28, 155, 165, 218, 230, 267, 289,
  293, *344*, 361–371, 686, *686*, 695, 701, 702,
  712–717. adornment: 365, *368*. clothing:
  154, *364*, 365, 366, *369*. defined: 150, 361.

education: 715. employment: 155–156, *156,
  316*, 361, 365–370, *366, 368*, 685, 690, 712–
  713, 716. external relations: 714. health
  care: 690, 712. history: 155–156, *156*, 361–
  364, *368*, 369–370, 391, 685, 688–692.
  kinship: 362. language: 150, 156, 361, 362,
  367, 685. marriage: 361–364, 370, 391, 685,
  690. music: 365. Northern: 150, 362–364,
  367. political organization: 370, *370*, 691,
  714–715. population: 370, 664, 689, 691,
  697, *713*. Red River: 150, 361–365, *367*,
  368, *368*. religion: 150, 362. social
  organization: 362–365, 697, 714–717.
  settlement pattern: 699–700. settlements:
  365, 665, *665*, 683, 688. structures: 369.
  subsistence: 153, 362, *363*, 365. synonymy:
  370–371. technology: *368, 369, 722–723*.
  territory: 361. trade: *153*, 155–156, *156*,
  364, 391. transport: 154, 365, *366*, 367, *367*,
  368
Métis Association of the Northwest
  Territories: 370, *370*, 371, 715
Michaud, A.: 22
Michel, Philip: *176*
Michikamau band. *See* Montagnais-Naskapi
Michipicoten site: *87, 93*
Micmac; ceremonies: 731. social organization:
  737. synonymy: 187
microblade cultures: 110–111, *112–113*, 113–
  117, 119, 123, 124, 127, 128, 575
microblades: 99, 101, 102, 110, *113*, 114–117,
  126, 128, 575
Middle Indians; synonymy: 532
Middle Prehistoric period: 117, 126
Middleton, Christopher: *165*
Middle Woodland period: 31. *See also* Initial
  Woodland period
Midewiwin: 28, 231, 244, 248, 249, 251–253,
  720. curing: 252–253. pictographs: 245,
  252–253. priests: 252, *252–253*. structures:
  252, 252–253
Midnoósky; synonymy: 662
Midnóvsti; synonymy: 662
Mĩednovskīe (Gal'tsane); synonymy: 662
Mĩednovtšy; synonymy: 662
Migod site: *101, 103*
migrations; prehistoric: 30, 31, 60, 67–68, 87–
  89, 91, 92, 95–96, 98, 103, 107–108, 110,
  115–118, 121–122, 124, 128, 245. seasonal:
  87, 106, 135, 137, 149, 170–172, 197–199,
  213, 232–233, 235–236, 245, 247, 254, 276–
  277, 291, 332, 350, 352, 375–376, 389, 406,
  425, 436, 443, 444, 456, 458, 462, 483–484,
  493, 496, 507–508, 566, 588–589, 604–605,
  627, 646. territorial: 29, 60, 67–68, 106,
  126, 160–164, 166–168, 170–173, 203, 205,
  209–211, 215, 218, 219, 225, 229, 244–245,
  249, 257, 258, 264, 282, 311, 324, 330, 357,
  388, 402, 413, *415*, 434, 440, 454–455, 458,
  460–461, 469, 493, 514, 515, 546–547, 557,
  559–562, 565, 566, 568, 615, 618, 624, 637.
  urban: 238, 254, 400, 567, 622, 692, 693
Mikenak, Maria: *236*
Milanowski, Paul: 77
minaikwinnu; synonymy: 187
Minchumina site: 114
Minchumina-Bearpaw subdivision. *See*
  Koyukon

Mingan band. *See* Montagnais-Naskapi
Mingan site: *87, 95*
Mining site: *103*
Minto band. *See* Tanana
MiPr-2: 101
Miscosinks; synonymy: 227
Mishenepe; synonymy: 269
mišikama·winnu; synonymy: 187
Misi-nipi; synonymy: 269
misi-nipiy; synonymy: 269
miskome·pin; synonymy: 242
Missabay: *731*
Missanabie band. *See* Cree, Western Woods
Mis se ne pe; synonymy: 269
Missin(n)epee; synonymy: 269
missionaries: 171, 172, 223, 250, 253, 264–266,
  411–412, 554, 585, 634–635, 671, 677.
  Anglican: 259, 328, 345, 395, 396, *397*, 477,
  504, 510–511, 529, 567, 673, 686, 695, 701.
  as anthropologists: 73, 74, 316. Assembly of
  God: 707. Baptist: 477, 504. Church of
  Canada: 504. Episcopalian: 37–38, 44, 50,
  61, 74, 78, 148, 202, 218, 224, 238, 240, 395,
  396, 567, 599, 706, 707. Evangelical: 202.
  Methodist: 395. Moravian: 44. native: 156.
  Pentecostal: 202, 253. Presbyterian: 395.
  Protestant: 396, 443, 686. Roman Catholic:
  19, *19*, 38, 44, 50, 74, 80, *81*, 148, *149*, 158,
  180, 184, 190–195, 202, 212, 218, 224–226,
  238, 259, 273, 282, 294, 296, 322, 345, 357–
  358, 395, 396, 411, 429, 439, 443, 477, 504,
  529, 586, 599, 666, 671, 685–686, *688*, 701.
  Russian Orthodox: 43–44, 49–50, 547, 548,
  558, 586, 629, 634, *637*. Wesleyan: 218
missions: 50, 156, 171, 193, 202, 213, 225, 277,
  296, 322, 328, 454, 456, 477, *550, 552*, 558,
  567, 584, 586, 587, 612, *614*, 685–686, *685*,
  688, 705, 706, *706*
Mississippian culture: 94
Mistapew. *See* supernatural beings
Mistasiniouek; synonymy: 186
mistasini·w; synonymy: 186
mistasini·wiyiyu; synonymy: 186
mista-ši·pi·winnu; synonymy: 187
Mistasirini(en)s; synonymy: 186
Mistassini band; synonymy: 169, 186. *See also*
  Montagnais-Naskapi
Mistassini complex: 96
Mistassin(irinin)s; synonymy: 186
Mistissinnys; synonymy: 186
Mistehay Sakahegan band. *See* Ojibwa,
  Northern
Mitchif: *54*, 56, 61. synonymy: 371
Mithcocoman; synonymy: 288
miθkohkoma·n; synonymy: 288
mittens. *See* clothing, handwear
mixed-blood; synonymy: 371
mocassins. *See* clothing, footwear
Mohawk: 228, 361
Móïseo; synonymy: 229
Moisie band; synonymy: 187. *See also*
  Montagnais-Naskapi
Molchatna; synonymy: 638
Monphwi: 296–298
Monsaunis; synonymy: 229
mo·nsoni·k; synonymy: 229
Monsoni(s): 159, *159*, 160. synonymy: 229.
  See also Cree, West Main

Monsonnis; synonymy: 229

Monsony; synonymy: 229

Monsounik; synonymy: 159, 229

Montagnairs; synonymy: 185

Montagnais: 3, 80, 684. synonymy: 185, 283, 337

Montagnais-Naskapi: 3, 20, *20*, 24, 169–189, *172*, 205, 206, 208, 209, 213, 215, 337, 666– 672. adornment: *180*. Barren Ground band: *170*, 171, *179*, 197, 666. Betsiamites band: *53*, 56, *170*, 171, 172, 173, 186. ceremonies: 177, *177*, 182, 184, *185*, 192, 670, 724, *725*. Chicoutimi band: *170*. Chimo band: *170*. childrearing: 192–193. clothing: 138, 141, *144*, *176*, 177, *179*, *180*, 185, 668, *669*, *721*. Davis Inlet band: *25*, 27, 53, 55, *170*, 171– 173, *174*, 175, 180, *181*, 666–672, *734*. division of labor: 192. East Cree: 55, 56, 59, 60, 169, 170, 181, 183, 184, 185, 196, 197, 205. education: 185, 667. employment: 172, 185, 668. environment: *12*, 130, *131*, 169, 190, 667–668. Escoumains band: *170*. external relations: 170, 190, 212, 667. Fort George band: 53, 172, 173. games: *670*. Godbout band: *170*. Happy Valley band: 172. health care: 667, 671. history: 147, 148, 170–171, 180–181, 666. Kaniapiskau band: 172. kinship: 181, 183–184. Lake Saint John band: 130, *144*, *170*, *174*, 186, 211. language: *24*, 52, *53*, 55, 56, 61, 63, 169, 185, 196, 667, 671, 673, 680, 681. marriage: *24*, 27, 170, 183, 191–192, 194, 197. Menihek Lakes band: *170*, 172. Michikamau band: *170*, 172. migration: 95–96, 170–171. Mingan band: *53*, *170*, 173. Mistassini band: *24*, *53*, 55, 56, 59, 60, 133, 137, *141*, 148, *170*, 172, 174–175, 177, *177*, 179, 181–184, *183*, *184*, 186, 196, 203, 212. Moisie band: *170*, 172, 187. music: 184, 192, *734*. mythology: 184. Natashquan band: *53*, *170*, 173, *176*, *181*, 183. North West River band: *53*, *170*, 171, 173, *176*. orthography: 169. Ouchestigoueki band: *170*. Oumamiouek band: *170*. Papinachois band: *170*. Petitsikapau: *170*, 172. Pointe-Bleue band: *24*, 53, 56, 173. political organization: 179, 181, 191, 213, 669–671. population: 172– 173, 181, 666–667. Porcs-épics: 141, 186. prehistory: 95, 170. religion: 28, 184, *184*, 185, *185*, 191, 194–195, 670, 719. reserves: 148. Romaine band: *53*, *170*, 173. Saint-Augustin band: *53*, *170*. Sainte-Marguerite band: 170, 172. Schefferville band: *53*, 172, 173. Sept-Îles band: *53*, *170*, 172, 173. settlement pattern: 170, 182, 190. settlements: 172, 666–672. shamanism: 181, 184, 191. Shelter Bay band: *170*, 172. social organization: 26, 28, 141, 170–172, 179– 183, *183*, 190, 668–672. structures: *140*, 169, 175–177, *177*, 184, 185, *192*, 667, *669*. subsistence: 15, 132, 133, *135*, 137, 169– 171, 174–175, 182, 190, 192, *192*, 666, 668, *670*, *671*. synonymy: 185–187, 283. Tadoussac band: *170*. technology: *153*, *174*, 175, *176*, *179*, *185*, 670. territory: 169–171, *170*, 196. trade: 20, 147, 148, 170, 171, 175, 177, *179*, 180, 197. transport: *139*, 177, 179, 181, *181*, 185, 668, *669*, 671. Ungava band:

178–179, 205. warfare: 148, 173, 194. Waswanipi band: *53*, 137, *153*, *170*, 186, 196, 203, 212

Montagnaits; synonymy: 185

Montagnar(d)s; synonymy: 185, 337, 452

Montagne(r)s; synonymy: 185

Montagnes, Gens des; synonymy: 337

Montagnets; synonymy: 185

Montaigna(i)rs; synonymy: 185

Montaigne(t)s; synonymy: 185

Monta(i)gnez; synonymy: 185

Montreal Lake band. *See* Cree, Western Woods

Monzoni; synonymy: 229

Moore, Patrick: 81

Moore, William: *237*

Moose; synonymy: 242. *See also* Ojibwa, Northern

Moose Cree; synonymy: 229. *See also* Cree, West Main

Moose Factory: *159*, 215, 217, 218, *218*, 227, 229

Moose Factory band; synonymy: 230. *See also* Cree, West Main

Moosehide Indians; synonymy: 513

Moose Lake band; synonymy: 269–270. *See also* Cree, Western Woods

Moose River Indians; synonymy: 229

moose tribe; synonymy: 242

Moose waw sepe; synonymy: 229

Moosonee; synonymy: 229

Moosu-Sepee; synonymy: 229

More, Mrs. *See* O-na-hä-ap-o-kwa

Morgan, Lewis Henry: 27, *27*, 36, 532

Morice, Adrien G.: 38, 429, 431, 452

Moricetown band; synonymy: 430. *See also* Carrier

Morning Star: *252*

Morphy. *See* Monphwi

Moses (Koyukon): 585, *588*

Moses, Myra: *530*

Moses, Peter: *530*, 698

mo·soni·hk; synonymy: 229

Mosonique; synonymy: 229

mo·so·si·piy; synonymy: 229

Mosquito Creek site: *98*

moss bags: 177, *236*, *277*, 341, 344, *344*, *364*, 383, 573, 633, 651, *669*, *722*

Mótacéwilnuts'; synonymy: 215

Mōtaignars; synonymy: 185

Mōtaignets; synonymy: 185

motifs. *See* art

Mountain. *See* Sagawan

Mountaineer(s); synonymy: 185, 283

Mountainees: 683. synonymy: 283

Mountain Indians; synonymy: 185, 505

Mountain Indians: 314, 326–337, 372. birth: 331, 335. ceremonies: 336, *337*. clothing: 333–335, *336*. environment: *8*, *131*, 326, 329, 332–333. external relations: 315, 316, 329, 332, 494. health care: 328. history: 148, 327–332, 401. language: 69, *70*, 72, 77, 79, 310, 315, 326, 339, 452. life cycle: 335–336. marriage: 331, 336, 494. menstrual practices: 336. migration: 330, 332. music: 336. orthography: 326. political organization: 335. population: 312, 327, 329–332. puberty: 335–336. religion: 336.

settlements: 332. social organization: 334– 335. structures: 333, 335, *335*. subsistence: 326–327, 330–333. synonymy: 327–328, 330, 336–337, 348, 451–453, 505. technology: 333. territory: 161, *162*, 326– 327, 329. trade: 148, 311, 321, 327–330, 332, 494. transport: 328, 332, 333, *333–335*. warfare: 328, 329, 494

mountain men; synonymy: 575

Mountain People: 624

mourning: 223, 262, 428, 438, 448, 488, 502, 509, 591, 610, 634, 659, 660, 727

Mouse River Indians; synonymy: 229

MS 23–0: 124

Muchiskewuck Athinuwick; synonymy: 269

Mulchatna Tanainas; synonymy: 638. *See also* Tanaina

Murdoch, Gertie: 198

Murphy. *See* Monphwi

Murphy site: *98*, 99

Murray, Alexander Hunter: *525*, *733*

Murray, John: 36, 38

mu·šawa·winnu; synonymy: 187

Muscagoes; synonymy: 227

Muscasiscow; synonymy: 269

Musce ko uck; synonymy: 227

Mus cus is cau; synonymy: 269

music: 198, 201, 202, 221, 225, 244, 251, 263, 279, 303, 353, 356, *356*, 357, 365, 376, 385, 386, 392, 396, 408–410, *411*, 429, 439, 478, 486, 488, 490, 501, 502, 509, 528, 571, 579, 581, 593, *594*, 595, 607, 608, 610, 647, 649, 652, 659–661, 732, 734, *734*

musical instruments; beating sticks: 386. clappers: 386. drums: 184, 192, 198, 251, 262, 279, 303, *304*, 320, 343, *354*, 386, 403, 410, *411*, 425, *478*, *486*, 490, 502, 509, 528, 571, 732, *734*. fiddles: 250–251, 445. flutes: 403, 410. gongs: 528. guitar: *400*, 445. postcontact: 224. rattles: 410, 425, *486*. whistles: 386, 410, 528

Muskagoes; synonymy: 227

Muska-siskow; synonymy: 269

Muskeegoo; synonymy: 227

Muskeggouck; synonymy: 227

Muskegoag; synonymy: 227

Muskegoe; synonymy: 227

Muskekowuck; synonymy: 227

Muskigos; synonymy: 227

Muskrat Dam Lake band. *See* Ojibwa, Northern

Musquaro; synonymy: 187

Muswà-sipi; synonymy: 229

mu·taše·wilnuč; synonymy: 215

mythology: 223, 251, 253, 279, 302, 315, 354– 356, 449, 456, 465, 479, 486, 490, 502, 509, 519, 581, 587, 593, 595, 600, 635, 647, 657. bushmen: 345, 519, 526, 527, 574, 595, 620, 635, 657, 661, 737. cannibals: 184, 200, 223, 233, 253, 319, 357, 449, 465, 595. creation: 195, 344, 354, *354*. creator-trickster: 479, 509, 653. culture heroes: 221, 354, 356, 385, 410, 449, 526–528, 574–575, 595, 620. Djokabish: 195, 221. dwarfs: 223, 385, 449. giants: 385, 449, 519, 595. monsters: 344, 354–356, 502, 519, 527, 574, 657. origin myths: 250, 279, 301, 305, 320, 420, 479, 485–486, 653, 654. Raven (Crow): 410, 465,

479, 490, 502, 527–528, 575, 595, *620*, 635, 653, 654. trickster-transformer: 184, 195, 263, 385, 410, 479, 527–528, 575, 635, 653. Windigo: 184, 200, 223, 233, 253. Wisakedjak: 221, 263, 528. *See also* cosmology; supernatural beings

N

Na-ai´; synonymy: 451, 505
na·ani; synonymy: 451, 466
Na´´anné; synonymy: 452
Nabesna; synonymy: 76, 575
Nabesna John: *535*
Nabesnatána; synonymy: 575
na·biah łi·n; synonymy: 576
Na-chon´-des; synonymy: 505
Nackowewuck; synonymy: 241
Na-Dene; synonymy: 46, 67
nadoienne; synonymy: 430
Nagailas; synonymy: 430
Nagailer; synonymy: 430
Nagle, Edward: *155*, 296, 687, *687*
na·gʷačo·ⁿǯik gʷičin; synonymy: 531
nahʔqa; synonymy: 451
nahʔa͌i·; synonymy: 451
Nahane; synonymy: 41, 82, 162, 336, 337, 450–453, 466, 480
nahʔá·neh; synonymy: 451
Nahani: 327, 373, 620. synonymy: 3, 82, 336, 436, 450, 451–453, 466
Nahanies: 312, 329. synonymy: 327
Nahanies of the Upper Stikine; synonymy: 467
Nahannies; synonymy: 452
Nahanny: 328. synonymy: 327, 330
Nahany; synonymy: 460, 467
Nahathaway(s); synonymy: 92, 268
Nahcowweeethinnuuck; synonymy: 241
Naheiy; synonymy: 451
Nahetheway; synonymy: 268
Nahhahwuk; synonymy: 268
nahkawe·-anišśinini; synonymy: 241
nahkawe·w(iδiniw)ak; synonymy: 241
nahkawe·wiyiniw; synonymy: 241
nahkawi·wiδiniwak; synonymy: 241
nahkawiyiniw; synonymy: 241
Nahlotin group. *See* Tahltan
Naka-we-wuk; synonymy: 241
Naidzo: 303, *312*
Naiyuk component: 111
Nakané(s); synonymy: 436, 450
Na-kas-le-tīn; synonymy: 430
Nakawawuck; synonymy: 231, 241, 242
Nakawewuck; synonymy: 240–242
nakͯazλiienne; synonymy: 430
Naketheway; synonymy: 268
nakkawe·; synonymy: 255
Nakotchokutchin; synonymy: 531
Nak-otchpô-ondjig K(o)uttchin; synonymy: 531
Na,kow,wa,vouck; synonymy: 241
Nä´kūtchū´ūnjūk kū´tchī´n; synonymy: 531
Nâle-ale-tain; synonymy: 430
naλoienne; synonymy: 431
Nama kou sepe; synonymy: 242
name·; synonymy: 242
name·ko-si·piy; synonymy: 242
name·pin; synonymy: 242
names; animal: 593, 649. ceremonies: 260,

423, 427. clan and moiety: 485, 501. personal: 260, 262, 280, 301, 320, 344, 363–364, 423, 427, 437, 487, 488, 501, 508, 519, 590, 610, 633, 658
Nameuilini; synonymy: 160
Nameu-Sepee band; synonymy: 242. *See also* Ojibwa, Northern
name·w si·piy; synonymy: 242
Naneai group. *See* Tahltan
na·nya·ʔa·yí; synonymy: 461
Napiou: *669*
Naqkyina; synonymy: 455, 461
Narrows complex: 100, 104, *105*
Narrows site: *103*
Nascapee(s); synonymy: 185, 186
Nascaupee; synonymy: 186
Nascobi; synonymy: 185
Nascopi(es); synonymy: 185, 186
Nascud Denee; synonymy: 431
Nascupi; synonymy: 186
Naskapi; synonymy: 3, 66, 185. *See also* Montagnais-Naskapi
Naskotenne; synonymy: 431
Naskotins; synonymy: 431
Naskupis; synonymy: 185
Nasquapee; synonymy: 185
Nasquapicks; synonymy: 185
Nasquitins; synonymy: 431
Nassgotin group; synonymy: 461. *See also* Tahltan
Nataotin; synonymy: 430
Natashquan band. *See* Montagnais-Naskapi
Na-taw-tīn; synonymy: 430
Natché Kutchin; synonymy: 532
Nate'a, Timoleon. *See* Ekawi Jimi
Nâte-ote-tains; synonymy: 430
Nathana; synonymy: 451
Nathèwy-withinyu; synonymy: 268
natikamiwiyiniwak; synonymy: 268
Native Language Teacher Training program: 63, 64
Natliáutin; synonymy: 431
Natliwoten; synonymy: 431
natq̇eʒi Wie·n; synonymy: 576
Na-tsik-koo-chin; synonymy: 532
Nãtsit´-kŭt-chin´; synonymy: 532
Natsitkutchin; synonymy: 532
Nattlewitenne; synonymy: 431
Nau-tle-a-tīn; synonymy: 431
Navajo; language: 67, 68, 84–85. prehistory: 117
naxkyina; synonymy: 455
Nayhaythaways; synonymy: 268
Nazko band; synonymy: 431. *See also* Carrier
nazko hʷəien; synonymy: 431
Nazkoten; synonymy: 431
nazkuienne; synonymy: 431
NbVk-1: 120
nearer Kolchanes; synonymy: 662
Né-a-ya-óg; synonymy: 268
ne·c̣q̇į gʷičin; synonymy: 532
nečauťen; synonymy: 431
ne·čit gʷičin; synonymy: 532
Necoslie band; synonymy: 430. *See also* Carrier
Necosliwoten; synonymy: 430
Ne-e-no-il-no; synonymy: 186
Neguia Dinais; synonymy: 431

neγá dék̇ǫ; synonymy: 371
Nehaunees; synonymy: 452, 479, 490, 505
Ne-hea-tha-way; synonymy: 268
Neheaway; synonymy: 228, 268
Ne-he-tha-wa(y); synonymy: 268
Nehethè-wuk; synonymy: 268
Něhethówuck; synonymy: 268
ne·hiδaw(e·w); synonymy: 227, 268
ne-hiδawiδiniw; synonymy: 268
ne·hinawe·wak; synonymy: 241
ne·hirawɪrɪnɪw; synonymy: 186
nehiro-iriniui; synonymy: 186
ne·hiyaw(ak); synonymy: 267
ne·hiyaw(e·w); synonymy: 267, 268
ne·hiyawiyiniw; synonymy: 268
Nehiyawok; synonymy: 268
nêhrane; synonymy: 466
Nekaslay(ans); synonymy: 429, 430
Nekasly; synonymy: 430
ne la gotine; synonymy: 315. *See also* Hare
Nel-cotly: *650*
Nelson, Edward William: 49, 556, 558
Nelson House band. *See* Cree, Western Woods
Nelson Indians; synonymy: 450. *See also* Kaska
Nelson River band; synonymy: 270. *See also* Cree, Western Woods
Nemaiah Valley band. *See* Chilcotin
Nemaska band. *See* Cree, East Main
Nanana-Toklat band. *See* Tanana
Nenawewack; synonymy: 241
Nena Wewhck; synonymy: 241
Nenawewhok; synonymy: 241
Neskaupe; synonymy: 186
Nətca´-hwoten; synonymy: 431
Nētcä´uťin; synonymy: 431
Netch-on´-dees; synonymy: 505
Netro, Linda: *699*
Netro, Mrs. Joe: *699*
nets; fishing: 133–134, 136, 137, 175, *192*, 201, 219–220, 223, 232, 484, 497, 506, 516, 518, 535, *536*, 553, 566, 569, 588, 589, 604, 605, 612, 619, 626, *626*, 647, *647*. hunting: 133, *152*, 174, 175, 220, 484, 612. manufacture: 134, 175, *211*, 596. twine: 16, 154, *211*, 223
Nétu'tinni; synonymy: 430
Newicargut; synonymy: 600
New Post band; synonymy: 230. *See also* Cree, Western Woods; Cree, West Main
New Severn Indian; synonymy: 229
Newton, W.H.: 567
nExa·ne; synonymy: 466
nexõni, synonymy: 466
Ney-et-se-Kootchin; synonymy: 532
Nichikun band; synonymy: 205–206. *See also* Cree, East Main
Nichols, John D.: 63
ničikuni·winnu; synonymy: 206
ničikwani·wiyiyu; synonymy: 205
Nicolai of Taral: 645, 652
ni·hiδaw; synonymy: 267
ni·hiyaw; synonymy: 267
ni·ʔina; synonymy: 241
ni·ʔinawe·(wak); synonymy: 241, 268
nikhto hot'ana; synonymy: 600
Nikita, Hieromonk: 44, 624

Nikolai band. *See* Kolchan
Nikolai, Hieromonk: 44, 636
Nikozliáutin; synonymy: 430
nilamna x̣iana; synonymy: 638
nilavəna x̣iana; synonymy: 638
NiNg-1: 101
NiNg-7: 101
NiNg-10: 101
Nipegons; synonymy: 229
Nipigon; synonymy: 229. *See also* Cree, West Main
Nipisirin(i)ens; synonymy: 158
Nipissing: 229. language: *59.* territory: *159.* trade: 158. warfare: 160
Nishga; synonymy: 455
Nisibourounik; synonymy: 158. territory: *159*
Niska: 456, 458. external relations: 454, 455. Gitxadin: 455. history: 455–456. language: 456. social organization: 455. trade: 455–456. warfare: 455
Nitchaotenne; synonymy: 431
Nitchequon; synonymy: 206
Nithè-wuk; synonymy: 268
Nitu'tinni; synonymy: 430
Njidh; synonymy: 531
*nkoxtna*ʔ *Wie·ne;* synonymy: 638
Nobili, John: 429
Noggoykhotana; synonymy: 600
noɣi x̣ŏiana; synonymy: 600
no·hpimink tašininiwak; synonymy: 215
Nokʼ: *174*
Nombahoteenais: 329. synonymy: 327, 330
Nool-kē-otīn; synonymy: 431
Noo-klak-ó; synonymy: 513
no·ppimink; synonymy: 240
no·ppimink taše· inini; synonymy: 215
no·ppimink taširiniwak; synonymy: 215
Nord, Gens du; synonymy: 215
nord, Nations du; synonymy: 215
Northeast culture area: 1. prehistory: 31, 86. technology: *197*
Northern Archaic tradition: 111, 113, 115, 116, 128
Northern Indian(s): 166, 273, 275, 285. synonymy: 161, 205, 228, 283
Northern Métis. *See* Métis
Northern Quebec Inuit Association: 150, 203
Northern Saulteaux; synonymy: 241
Northern Traders Limited: 691
Northern Trading Company: 322
Northern Transportation Company: 328
North Henik Lake site: *101*
Northland band. *See* Chipewyan
North River Indians; synonymy: 270
North Tacla Lake; synonymy: 431
North Takla Lake; synonymy: 431
Northward Indian(s); synonymy: 205, 228, 283
Northway band. *See* Tanana
Northwest Angle No. 33 band. *See* Saulteaux of Lake Winnipeg
Northwest Angle No. 37 band. *See* Saulteaux of Lake Winnipeg
Northwest Coast culture area: 1, 384, *405,* 410, 442, 498, *722.* history: 398, 401. mythology: 465. prehistory: 31, 416. structures: 425. technology: 417. trade: 387, 416, 424, 546
North West Company: 35, 36, 146, 147, 151,

200, 212, 232, 258, 273, 287, 294, 296, 310, 321, 327, 329, 345, 357, 361, 364, 388, 389, *389,* 391, 417, 439, 528
Northwest Microblade tradition: 46, 67, 98, 107, 111, 113, 115, 116
Northwest Mounted Police: 394, 482, 529
North West River band. *See* Montagnais-Naskapi
Norton, Moses: 166, *166*
Norton Sound Eskimo: external relations: 590, 603. trade: 559, 596, 603
Norway House band. *See* Cree, Western Woods
Norwegian, Louis: *343*
nose piercing. *See* adornment
Notti, Emil: *554*
Nouga; synonymy: 325
Noupiming-dach-iriniouek; synonymy: 215
Nowikákat; synonymy: 600
Nowitna-Koyukuk subdivision. *See* Koyukon
Noyakakat; synonymy: 600
Noyokakat; synonymy: 600
N.T. Docks complex: 111, 116
Ntshaáutin; synonymy: 431
nučaienne; synonymy: 431
nu·čimi·winnu; synonymy: 205, 215
Nuclaco; synonymy: 513
Nuctaco; synonymy: 513
nu·hcimi·w(ilnu); synonymy: 205
nu·hčimi·wiyiyu(·č); synonymy: 196, 205
Nu-kla-ko; synonymy: 513
Nukluktána; synonymy: 575
Nulaáutin; synonymy: 431
Nulato Massacre: 558, 586, 596
Nulki band. *See* Carrier
Nulkiwoten; synonymy: 431
Nunamiut Eskimo; migration: 515. trade: 596. warfare: 596
Nunarna'dene; synonymy: 280
Nus-koo-tain; synonymy: 431
nu·taskwa·ni·winnu; synonymy: 187
Nu'tseni; synonymy: 431
Nutzotin; synonymy: 576

O

Obedjiwan band; synonymy: 215. *See also* Attikamek (Tête de Boule)
Observation site: *103,* 106
Ochipawayons; synonymy: 283
oči·pwaya·ni·w; synonymy: 283
ocipwe·(w); synonymy: 240, 255
Odawa; synonymy: 65
Ogden, Peter Skene: 35
Ogicàʿkɑmiiu; synonymy: 215
Ogilvie, William: 480, 503
Ogishakamiiu; synonymy: 211
Ojibwa: 28, 244, 248, 249, 251–252, 255. Golden Lake band: *54, 58, 59,* 64, 243. Maniwaki band: *54, 58, 59,* 61, 243
Ojibwa/Chippewa; synonymy: 240, 255
Ojibwa, Northern: 20–22, 35, 211, 214, 215, 217, 229, 231–243, 244, 268, 269, 371. Angling Lake band: 241. Bearskin Lake band: *54,* 241. Caribou Lake band: *232,* 237, 240, 241. Cat Lake band: *54,* 241. ceremonies: 231, 238, *731,* 735. clothing: 141, 232, 233, 235, *236,* 237, *238, 239.* cosmology: 718. Cranes band: 233, 242.

Curve Lake band: *54, 58.* Deer Lake band: *54,* 64, *232,* 237, *238,* 240, 241. education: 237–239. employment: 237, 239, 713. environment: *131,* 231, 233, 235–237. external relations: 212, 221, 231. Fort Hope band: *54, 232,* 237, 240, 241, 243. Garden Hill band: 241. Gens de la Sapinière: 240, 241. health care: 238. history: 147, 148, 231–233, 236–240. Island Lake band: *54,* 237, 243, 244. Kasabonika Lake band: *54,* 241. Kingfisher band: *54,* 241. kinship: 236. language: 52–54, *54,* 56–66, *59,* 227, 228, 231, 240, 241, 243, 245. marriage: 94, 231, 236, 237–238, 361. Martin Falls band: *54,* 237, 240, 241, 243. migration: 60, 160, 165, 232–233, 235–236, 238, 239, 244–245. Mistehay Sakahegan band: 233. Moose: 240, 242. Muskrat Dam Lake band: *54,* 241. Nameu-Sepee band: 233. orthography: 231. Osnaburgh House band: *54,* 237, 241, 713. Ouassi: 240, 242. Outoulibis: 240, 242. political organization: 233, 236, 238, 240. population: 160, 237, 240, 241. prehistory: 60, 94, 95, 244. Red Sucker Lake band: 241. religion: 231, 233, 238, 240. reserves: 245. Sachigo Lake band: *54,* 241. St. Theresa Point band: 241. Sandy Lake band: 238, 242. settlement pattern: 235–237, 240. settlements: *54, 232,* 237–240. shamanism: 233, 719. Shumataway band: 233, 242. social organization: 27, 28, 231, 233, 236, 240, 249, 735. structures: 234–235, 237, 240. Sturgeons: *159,* 240, 242. subsistence: 133, 135, 137, 231–237, *238,* 239. Suckers: 233, 241, 242. synonymy: 64–66, 240–243, 244, 254. technology: 232–235, *236,* 237, *237, 238,* 239, *239.* territory: 158, *159,* 160, 165–166, 228, 229, 231, *232,* 242, 244. trade: 147, 148, *151,* 160, 231–233, 239, 242. transport: *139,* 233–235, *236,* 237, 239, *239.* Trout Lake band: *54,* 64, 237, 241. Uinescaw-Sepee: 233, 242. Wapus: 233, 240, 242. warfare: 160. Wasagamack band: 241. Weagamow Lake band: 233, 242. Winisk River band: 229, 233. Wunnumin band: *54,* 241. *See also* Saulteaux of Lake Winnipeg
Ojibwa, Plains; synonymy: 241. territory: 244
Ojibway; synonymy: 65, 66, 243
Old Chief Creek site: 124
Old Crow band. *See* Kutchin
Old Crow Indians; synonymy: 532
Old Crow people; synonymy: 513
Old Factory: 197, 199, 200, 203
Old Fort: 418
Old Fort Halkett: *389*
Old Fort Providence: 293–294, 296
Old Fort Rae: 106, 288, 296
Old Fort Selkirk: *389*
Old Fox: *476*
Old Lady Matoit: 724
Old Margaret: *178–179*
Old Matoit: *719*
Old Rocky Mountain Fort: 345
Old Sam: *573*
Old Stone culture: 30
Old Sulin: *411*
Omashkekok; synonymy: 227

(o)maške·ko·w; synonymy: 227
omaški·ko·; synonymy: 227
Omineca band; synonymy: 430. *See also*
Carrier
Omisk a sepe; synonymy: 269
Omiska-sipi; synonymy: 269
omo·soni·w; synonymy: 229
Omush-ke-goag; synonymy: 227
Omushke-goes; synonymy: 227
O-na-hä-ap-o-kwa: 27
onayahciki·w; synonymy: 430
one·hiδaw; synonymy: 268
one·hiyaw; synonymy: 268
One Man Lake group. *See* Saulteaux of Lake
Winnipeg
Onion Portage site: 46, 111, 122, 123
o·ⁿǯít gí·; synonymy: 371
opa·skwe·ya·w; synonymy: 270
Opemens d'Acheliny; synonymy: 209, 215
opi·čiwan; synonymy: 215
O'pimittish Ininiwac; synonymy: 211, 215
oratory: 294, 303, 385, 392, 488, 509, 528,
574, 580, 593, 634, 660, 702
Orchipoins; synonymy: 283
Organic Act of 1884: 399
ornaments. *See* adornment
Orturbi; synonymy: 242
Osgood, Cornelius: 22, 39, 40, 41, 47, 51
Oskemanettigons; synonymy: 160
Osnaburgh House band. *See* Ojibwa,
Northern
otapihtipi·w; synonymy: 228
Otcàkamiilnuts; synonymy: 215
Otchipiweons; synonymy: 283
oto·lipi·; synonymy: 241
oto·ripi·; synonymy: 241
Ottawa: 160, 241. history: 147. language: 52,
54, 56–62, 64, 227. synonymy: 64–66.
trade: 147, 160
Otter Falls site: 115
Otzane band. *See* Sekani
Otzosia. *See* Stickman, Joseph
Ouace: 159, 160
Ouasheo; synonymy: 229
Ouassi; synonymy: 242. *See also* Ojibwa,
Northern
Oubestamiouek; synonymy: 186
Ouchestigoüek; synonymy: 187
Ouchestigouetch; synonymy: 187
Ouchestigouets; synonymy: 187
Ouchestiguetch; synonymy: 187
Ouchestigueti; synonymy: 187
Oüenebigonchelinis; synonymy: 229
Oüenebigonhelinis; synonymy: 159, 229.
territory: 159
Oueperigoueiaouek; synonymy: 186
8iperig8e8a8ak; synonymy: 186
Oukesestigouck; synonymy: 187
Oumamiois; synonymy: 187
8mami8ec; synonymy: 186
Oumamiouek band; synonymy: 186–187. *See
also* Montagnais-Naskapi
8mami8eк(hi); synonymy: 186
8mami8etch; synonymy: 186
Ounachkapiouek; synonymy: 185
Ounadcapis; synonymy: 186
Ounascapis; synonymy: 185
Ounescapi; synonymy: 185

Ouneskapi; synonymy: 185
Ounhann-Koutànœ; synonymy: 600
Oupapinachiouek; synonymy: 187
8papinachi8eк(hi); synonymy: 187
8papinachi8j; synonymy: 187
Oupeeshepow; synonymy: 205
ouperigoue ouaouakhi; synonymy: 186
Oupeshepou; synonymy: 205
Oupeshepow; synonymy: 205
Outabitibecs; synonymy: 228
8tabitibecus; synonymy: 228
Outabitibek; synonymy: 228
8tabitibeux; synonymy: 228
Outabitikek; synonymy: 228
8tchisestig8 natione; synonymy: 187
Outer Hare Indians: 323
Outer Indians; synonymy: 287
Outer Inlet band. *See* Tanaina
Outoulibis; synonymy: 242. *See also* Ojibwa,
Northern
Outouloubys; synonymy: 242
Outurbi; synonymy: 241
Ovasovarin; synonymy: 242
Ovenigibonc; synonymy: 229
Ovpapinachoveti; synonymy: 187
Owashoes; synonymy: 229, 242
Oxbow complex: 99, 99, 100
Oxford House band. *See* Cree, Western
Woods

P

Pacific Eskimo: 638. synonymy: 632
Pacific Great Eastern Railroad: 418
paddles: dance: 580. swimming: 174.
watercraft: 172, 631, 650
Pagouitik; synonymy: 254
Pahoüiting dach Irini; synonymy: 254
Painted Hills band. *See* Cree, East Main
pakut-ši·pi·winnu; synonymy: 187
Palgrave, C.F.: 468
Paleo-Arctic tradition: 110, 111, 113, 114
Paleo-Eskimos: 32, 33, 89, 91, 100, 101, 103,
113–114
Paleo-Indian period: 87–88, 87–88, 107–108,
110, 114–116, 128
pan-Indian movement: 504, 563
Pa8itig8ecii; synonymy: 254
Papanashes: 159, 160
Papinacheois; synonymy: 187
Papinachioec; synonymy: 187
Papinachiois; synonymy: 187
Papinachioueki; synonymy: 187
Papinachiouek band; synonymy: 187. *See also*
Montagnais-Naskapi
Paouestigonce; synonymy: 254
Parsnip River band. *See* Sekani
Pauingassi band. *See* Saulteaux of Lake
Winnipeg
Paüoitigoüeieuhaк; synonymy: 254
Paouitikoungraentaouak; synonymy: 254
Paoutig8ejenhac; synonymy: 254
Peau(x) de Lièvre; synonymy: 324
Pechepoethinue; synonymy: 270
Peck, Edmund J.: 673
Pedro Bay site: 108, 121
Peel River Kutchin; synonymy: 531. *See also*
Kutchin

Peels River Indians; synonymy: 531
Pegogamow; synonymy: 269
Pegog eme ou; synonymy: 269
Pegogĕ-mè-u nipi; synonymy: 269
Peguis: 246, 246
Peguis band. *See* Cree, Western Woods;
Saulteaux of Lake Winnipeg
Peigan: 164
pe·kwa·kamiriniwak; synonymy: 186
Pelican Lake complex: 100
Pelican tribe; synonymy: 242
Pelly River Indians: 39, 328, 329, 451, 466,
478, 479
Peme chic emeou; synonymy: 269
pemmican. *See* food
Pemmichi-ke-mè-u; synonymy: 269
Pena say witchewan; synonymy: 269
Penashaway: 669
Penesay-wichewan sipi; synonymy: 269
Penesewichewan; synonymy: 269
Penesiwichewan Sepee; synonymy: 269
Pennesewagewan; synonymy: 269
Pentland, David: 55
Perrot, Nicolas: 158
pe·ssia·mi·winnut; synonymy: 186
pestles: 119, 124, 570, 612
Peter Ballantyne band. *See* Cree, Western
Woods
Peter Pond band. *See* Chipewyan
Peter, Tommy: 480
Petəs·əkupáuwi·nút·; synonymy: 187
Petitot, Émile: x, 19, 38, 78, 316, 322, 452,
586, 693
petits Eskimaux; synonymy: 187
Petits Mistassins; synonymy: 186
petsiámiwilnúts·; synonymy: 186
Pic River site: 93
pictographs: 149, 245–246, 252, 253, 479.
distribution: 87, 94
Piek8agamie(n)s; synonymy: 186
Piəkwágami·wilnúts·; synonymy: 186
Pigogomew; synonymy: 270
pi·ka·kama·w; synonymy: 269
Pikangikum band. *See* Saulteaux of Lake
Winnipeg
Pike's Portage site: 98, 99, 101, 103
Pike tribe; synonymy: 242
Pike, Warburton: 39
pi·kwa·kami·winnut; synonymy: 186
Pilot, Julius: 552, 574
pimicikama·w; synonymy: 269
Pimmechikemow; synonymy: 269
pinasiwe·ciwan si·piy; synonymy: 269
pipes: 93, 106, 120, 121, 185, 248, 248, 261,
261, 288, 393, 459, 466. *See also* tobacco
Piscotagame; synonymy: 229. *See also* Cree,
West Main
Piscotagemies; synonymy: 229
Piscoutagamis; synonymy: 229
Pishhapocanoes; synonymy: 205
pi·simuta·wiyiyu·č; synonymy: 196
Pisouotagamis; synonymy: 229
Pitchiboucouni; synonymy: 205
Pitchiboueoni; synonymy: 205
Pitchib8renik; synonymy: 205
Pitchibourouni; synonymy: 205
Pitchiboutounibueк; synonymy: 205
Plains Archaic tradition: 89

Plains Cree; synonymy: 66. *See also* Cree, Plains

Plains culture area: 1, *149*, 722. prehistory: *98*, 99–100, 108, 117, 127. structures: *352*

Plains Ojibwa; synonymy: 241. *See also* Ojibwa, Plains

Plano culture: 32, 87–88, 97–98, *98*, *99*, 100, 108, 115, 116, 127

Plascôtez de Chiens; synonymy: 306

Plat-coté-de-Chien; synonymy: 309

Plateau culture area: 1, 402, 410. prehistory: 116, 117

Plateau Microblade tradition: 116

Plats cotee de Chiens; synonymy: 306

Plats-Côtés de Chien; synonymy: 283, 305, 306

Plats côtez de Chiens; synonymy: 306

Poethinecaw; synonymy: 270

Poethinicau; synonymy: 270

Pointe-Bleue band. *See* Montagnais-Naskapi

Pointed Mountain complex: 116

Pointed Mountain site: 110–111, *113*

Point Peninsula culture: 89, 90

Poisson-blanc; synonymy: 214

Po-i-thinnè-kaw-sipi, synonymy: 270

Poker, John: *671*

political organization; bands: 208, 221–222, 233, 236, 259, 319, 408, 567, 582, 585, 644, 708, 715. elections: 202, 203, 240, 264, *274*, 296, 298, 306, 335, 447, 477, 482, 508, 551, 585, 598–599, 621, 632, 675, 677, *678*, 688, 700, 707, 714. leadership: 144, 179, 182, 183, 191, 202, 203, 208, 221–222, 233, 236, 238, 240, 259, 260, 275–276, 279, 297–298, 319, 321, 384, 406, 408, 411–412, 421, 446, 460, 463, 476, 489, 500, 508, 519, 522–523, *524*, 551, 574, 585, 588, 589, 606, 620, 631, 644–645, 656–657, 669–670, 684–685. local bands: 26, 143, 259, 260, 281–282, 297, 315, 320, 562, 641. postcontact: 150, 156, 196, 202, 203, 205, 213, 236, 238, 240, 323, 412, 489, 551, 567, 632, 669–671, 673, 675, 677, *678*, 714. regional bands: 26, 86, 141, 143, 161, 180, 259, 260, 275–276, 280–281, *292*, 295, 297, 298, 315, 514–515, 543–544, 562. social control: 181, 264, 343, 408, 421, 476–477, 489, 577, 606, 632, 652, 657, 671, 701, 721. trading chiefs: 154–156, 221–222, 233, 276, 298, *300*, 321, 346, 384, 392, 631, 684. village: 644. war leaders: 477, 478, 522, 523, 652, 657, 685

Pond, Peter: 148, 348, 364

Poplar Grove site: 117

Poplar River band. *See* Cree, Western Woods; Saulteaux of Lake Winnipeg

population: 218, 612. aboriginal: 1, 141, 267, 274, 317, 330, 339, 351, 411, 415–416, 442, 504, 511, 530, 534, 614, 621. band: 241, 243, 247, 269, 416, 434–435, 495. decline: 92, 172–173, 208, 219, 258, 273, 274, 286, 288, 296, 317, 322, 329–330, 351, 411, 418, 425, 456, 460, 530, 621. density: 141, 173, 275, 317, 351, 372, 416, 534, 621. 18th century: 160, 212, 219, 258, 273, 434–435, 530. increase: 173, 181, 238, 275, 291, 296, 312, 440, 530, 553, 621. 1960s: 219, 313, 370, 416, 460, 470, 495, 511, 531. 1970s: 173, 203, 218, 219, 240, 247, 269, 275, 313, 324,

331, 347, 351, 370, 399, 411, 416, 440, 460, 470, 483, 495, 504, 585, 689. 19th century: 43, 173, 212, 219, 288, 293, 312, 323, 324, 331, 347, 351, 411, 416, 434, 435, 440, 456, 460, 483, 495, 568, 585, 614, 691. settlements: 237, 240, 282, 312, 313, 332, 347, 369, 370, 398, 495, 511. 17th century: 173, 208. 20th century: 172, 173, 181, 203, 213, 218, 219, 240, 241, 243, 247, 254, 267, 269, 274, 275, 291, 293, 312, 313, 324, 327, 331, 332, 351, 369, 370, 398, 399, 411, 416, 440, 442, 470, 495, 568–569, 585, 614, 621, 667, 691, 697

Porc-épic, nation du; synonymy: 186

Porcs-épics, nation des; synonymy: 186

Porcupine, Nation of the: 141

Portage band. *See* Saulteaux of Lake Winnipeg

Portage La Loche band. *See* Chipewyan

Porteur; synonymy: 430

Portland Canal People; synonymy: 456

Potawatomi; language: 52, 54, 61, 63

Pothier, Roger: 22

potlatches: 376, 384, 396, 420–423, *421*, 425, 438, 439, 442, 445, 446, 465, 485, 487, 499, 524, 547, 567, 577–581, 607, 632, 634, 702, *710*, 727–729. activities: 385, 423, 478, 485, *486*, 488, 501, 527, 579–581, 591, 593, *594*, 607, 608, 634, 660, *660*, 728–730. death: 421, 423, 445–446, 478, *486*, 488, 501–502, 508, 527, 541, 544, *544*, 574, 578–580, 591, 593, *594*, 607, 608, 616, 620, 632, 634, 659–660, 697, *698*, 702, 709, 727–730, 732. distribution of property: 422, 423, 488, 501–502, 508, 527, 580–581, 591, 593, 607, 608, 620, 632, 634, 659, 660, 705, 729. hosting: 478, *486*, 578, 581, 607, 608, 659. intergroup: 482, *486*, 488, 494, 565, 579, 618, 659, 705, 709. invitations: 478, 579, 607, 608, 659–660. occasions for: 501, 577–578, 593, 632, 633, 659. postcontact: 488, 562, 577, 593, 607, 620, 621, 634, 659, 660, *660*, 702, 705, 709, 732. preparations for: 488, 578–579, 608, 634, 660. regalia: *486*, *489*, *544*, 580, *660*, 729. ritual observances: 501, 581, 660. structures: 126, 380, 421

Potlatch site: 117, *119*, 126

pottery: 619. historic: 120. prehistoric: 31, 32, 89–91, *90*, 92, *93*, 94–95, 122. styles: 122, 596. trade: 90. temper: *612*. types and uses: 535, 612, *612*

Potts, John: *222*

Pouoestingonce; synonymy: 254

Poux, Nation des; synonymy: 283

Pre-Dorset phase: 113

prehistory: 86–129. adornment: 575. Asian influence: 107–108, 110, 128, 381, 546. burial customs: 90, 94, 95, 101, 106, 114. environment: 86–90, 95, 97, 98, 100–102. language: 60–61, 67–68. marriage: 94. migration: 30, 31, 60, 67–68, 87–89, 91, 92, 95–96, 98, 103, 107–108, 110, 115–118, 121–122, 124, 128, 245. pottery: 31, 32, 89–91, *90*, 92, *93*, 94–95, 122. settlement patterns: 104. settlements: 46, 98, 126, 575. social organization: 86. structures: 89, 115, 117, 119, 122–126, *122*, 125, 126. subsistence: 86, 87, 90, 95, 97, 101, 102,

103, 104, 106, 170. technology: 30, 31, 33, 87–91, *88–91*, *93*, 94–106, *96*, *99*, *101*, *102*, *105*, 108, 110, 111, *112–113*, 113–129, *118*, *119*, *121*, *123*, *125*, 575. trade: 90, 546, 561. travel: 86. *See also* archeology

Preston, Richard J.: 22

Prevost, Jules: 74

Prince, Henry: 246

projectile points; prehistoric: 87, 88, *88–91*, 92, *93*, 95, *96*, 97–106, *99*, *102*, *105*, 108, 110, *110*, 111, *113*, 114–118, *118*, 120–122, *121*, 124–128, *124*, 575

property: 25–26, 28, 236, 279, 281–282, 320, 407, 420, 421, 423, 445, 460, 463. clan: 632. inheritance: 26, 191, 244, 249–250, 320, 408, 418, 420, 422, 423, 439, 446–447, 460, 463, 488, 574, 595, 607, 608, 609, *609*, 620, 632, 661. ownership: 528, 574, 585, 620–621, 632. trespass: 181, 233

Prophet River band. *See* Beaver

prophets. *See* religion

Proto-Algonquians: 30

Proto-Athapaskans: 575

Proto-Eskimos: 30, 110, 113–114

Prudhomme, J.F.: *368*

Punchaw Lake site: 126

puberty; boys': 277, 301, 320, 335, 344, 404–405, 427, 438, 447, 477, 485, 488, 500, 508, 524, 610, 633, 657–658, 719, 727. girls': 220, 260–261, 277, 301, 320, 335, 344, *359*, 385, 396, 405, 427–428, 438, 448, 456, 477, 488, 500, 508, 524, 572, 591, 610, 619, 633, 657–658, 726–727, *726*, *727*, *728*

(pwa·t-)čišaimu-innu; synonymy: 187

Q

qa·č’ádi; synonymy: 461

qayax xŏtanǝ; synonymy: 600

q̓esci·ge Wie·n; synonymy: 576

q̓etnaWie·n; synonymy: 662

qǝ́ynǝnxiana; synonymy: 638

qǝydǝýtna; synonymy: 638

qǝzdǝýtna; synonymy: 638

qižǯǝx xian; synonymy: 638

q̓ŏyǝƛ̓oč̓ǝnǝ xoianǝ; synonymy: 599

Quarrellers: 529. synonymy: 531

Quashe'o; synonymy: 229

Quebec Indian Association: 675, 677, 680

Quesnel band; synonymy: 431. *See also* Carrier

Quesnel "tribe"; synonymy: 431

quivers. *See* bows and arrows

q̓unutnǝ xŏianǝ; synonymy: 600

R

Rabaskaw; synonymy: 269

Rabbit Indians: *159*, 160

Rabbitskins; synonymy: 324

Rabesca, Martha: *318*

Rae band. *See* Dogrib

Rae phase: 106

railroads: 213, 218, 237, 397, 418, 481, 482, 484, 485, 549, 568, 582, 643, 687, 689, 705, 706

Rainier, Dorothy: 40

Ralph (Ingalik): *611*

Rampart Indians; synonymy: 505

Rapid Indians: 323

Rat Indian Creek site: 124

Rat Indians: 515. synonymy: *37, 532*
Rat Portage band. *See* Saulteaux of Lake Winnipeg
Rats, Gens des; synonymy: 532
rattles. *See* musical instruments
rattlesnake tribe; synonymy: 242
Raymond, Charles W.: 38, 556
Red Deer River band; synonymy: 269. *See also* Cree, Western Woods
Red Earth band. *See* Cree, Western Woods
rédhkkppan: 371
Red-knife Indians; synonymy: 289
Red Knives; synonymy: 289
Red River Métis. *See* Métis
Red Sucker Lake band. *See* Ojibwa, Northern
Red Suckers; synonymy: 242
reincarnation. *See* religion
reindeer tribe; synonymy: 242
Reliance complex: 100, 106
religion: 27–28, 203, 233, 263, 301, 336, 353–358, *354,* 385, 408–409, 428–430, 471, 479, 490, 502, 509, 511, 519, 718–720. Christian influence on: 148, 184, 195, 202, 203, 224, 238, 253, 259, 302, 357, 358, 395–396, 429, 449, 479, 490, 511, 527, 676, 701, 720, 731. prophets: 302, *312,* 357, 358, 396, *397,* 429, 439, 731. reincarnation: 279, 320, 385, 396, 448, 465, 477, 487, 501, 519, 527, 591, 595, 620, 659. shaking tent: 28, 177, 184, 223, 233, 238, 251, *251,* 262, 266, 719, 733, 735. *See also* afterlife; ceremonies; cosmology; mythology; shamans; supernatural beings
Remington, Frederic: 371
reserves and reservations: 267, 393, 407, 412, *462.* Anahim Lake: 413. Blueberry River: 359. Boyer: 359. Child Lake: 359. Clear Hills: 359. Doig River: 359. establishment of: 148–149, 212, 246, 259, 267, 359, 398, 399, 407, 411, 425–426. Fairford: 253. Fisher River: 245, 246. Halfway River: 359. Hole River: 245, 252. Horse Lakes: 359. Kasichuan: 228. Little Black River: 246. Jackhead: 252, *253.* Moquawkie: 637. Pequis: 246. maps: *257, 351, 402, 414, 471.* Prophet River: 359. Saint Peter's: 246. Turtle Mountain: 56, 61. Venetie: 399, 401. Weymontachingue: 212. White Dog: 246. Whiteshell Forest: 247
Resolution band. *See* Chipewyan
Revillon Frères: 218
Richardson Highway: 549, 568, *570,* 643
Richardson, John: 36, 316, 317
Rich, Joe. *See* Shushebish
Richmond, S.: 22
Ridington, Robin: 22
Ridley, Ruth: 77
Riggs, Thomas, Jr.: *552*
Riske Creek band. *See* Chilcotin
Ritchie, C.W.: *552*
Ritter, John: 79, 697
ritual. *See* ceremonies
River Desert band; synonymy: 243
roads. *See* highways and roads
Robinson-Superior Treaty: 148
Roche, Gens du: 328
rock art: 32, 33, 245–246
Rocknest Lake complex: 100–102, *101, 102*
Rocky Cree. *See* Cree, Western Woods

Rocky Mountain Indians; synonymy: 337, 347, 359, 440
Rodionov, Eremey: 556
Rogers, Edward S.: 22, 26, 32
Rolukekakat; synonymy: 616
Romaine band. *See* Montagnais-Naskapi
Ross, Bernard R.: 36, 317
Ross River band. *See* Kaska; Tutchone
Round Lake Tommy: *422*
Royal Canadian Mounted Police: 264, 296, 322, 328, 667, 688, 690, 695, 696, 701, 731
Roy, Louis: *686*
Rupert House band; synonymy: 206. *See also* Cree, East Main
Russell, Frank: 20, *20,* 22
Russian-American Company: 49, 50, 120, 436, 547, 548, 556, 561, 584, 627, 636, 704

S
Sabaskong band. *See* Saulteaux of Lake Winnipeg
Sabourin, Margarite: *342*
Sachigo Lake band. *See* Ojibwa, Northern
Sackaweé-thinyoowuc; synonymy: 268
sacred places: 251, 517
Sadilege; synonymy: 186
Sadiseg8; synonymy: 186
Sagami Indians; synonymy: 211, 215
Sagawan: 455–456
Sagseggons; synonymy: 186
sahtú gotine; synonymy: 312, 313
Sailor, Sam: 62
Saint-Augustin band. *See* Montagnais-Naskapi
Sainte-Marguerite band. *See* Montagnais-Naskapi
Saint Lawrence Iroquoians: 95
Saint Peter's band. *See* Saulteaux of Lake Winnipeg
Saint Theresa Point band. *See* Ojibwa, Northern
Sa-i-sa-'dtinnè; synonymy: 271
saka·wiδiniwak; synonymy: 268, 270
sak·wiyiniw(ak); synonymy: 268
Sakawiyiniwok; synonymy: 268
sa·kihtawa·w; synonymy: 269
Sakitawaweyinewuk; synonymy: 269
Sakitowawuk; synonymy: 269
Sakittawawiyiniwok; synonymy: 269
salca Wie·ne; synonymy: 576
Salcha-Goodpaster band. *See* Tanana
Salcomy Indians; synonymy: 215
Salish: 372, 373. prehistory: 415. religion: 429. structures: 379. territory: 402
Salish, Interior, language grouping: 41, 84
Salkemy(s): 159. synonymy: 215. territory: *159*
Salmon Indians; synonymy: 515
Samandré Lake site: *101*
Sandbluff site: *103*
Sandwillow site: 103, *103*
Sandy Lake Ojibwa; synonymy: 242. *See also* Ojibwa, Northern
Sanford, Charlie. *See* Aysenatah
Sanford River–Chistochina band. *See* Ahtna
Sangris, Isadore: *301*
Sangris, Rose: *301*
San-to-tin'; synonymy: 576
Sapinère, peuples de La; synonymy: 241

Sapinerie, gens de la; synonymy: 241
Sapinière, Gens de la; synonymy: 241. *See also* Ojibwa, Northern
Sapir, Edward: 20, 21, 78
Sarcee: 1, 52, 168. external relations: 84. language: 67, 68, *70,* 72, 77, 81, 84–85. migration: 68
Sasuchan band. *See* Sekani
sasutna? Wie·ne; synonymy: 639
Sa-tchó t'u gottiné; synonymy: 313
satl hoįł; synonymy: 297. *See also* Dogrib
Sa-tshi-o-tin'; synonymy: 576
Satudene; synonymy: 312
Saugeen culture: 89, 90
Sault; synonymy: 254
Saulteaux; synonymy: 240, 241
Saulteaux of Lake Winnipeg: 20, 22, *23,* 244–255, 733. adornment: *246, 250.* Berens River band: 28, 244, 247, *252,* 719. Big Grassy band: 247. Big Island band: 247. Bloodvein band: 247, *252.* Brokenhead band: 247, 252. ceremonies: 244, 251–253, *251–253.* clothing: *246, 247,* 248–249, *249, 250.* curing: 244, 246, 249, 252–253. Dalles band: 247. Eagle Lake band: *54,* 247. employment: 254. environment: 130, *131,* 248. external relations: 245, 246, 264. Fairford band: 247. Fort Alexander band: 247. Grassy Narrows band: *54,* 247. health care: 254. history: 148, 245–246, *249,* 253–254. Hole River band: 245, 247, 252. Islington band: *54,* 247. Jackhead band: *54,* 247. kinship: 250. Lac Seul band: *54,* 237, 247. Lake Saint Martin band: 247. language: 52, *54,* 56–58, 60, 61, 228, 244, 245, 254. Little Black River band: 246, 247. Little Grand Rapids band: *54,* 244, 245, 247, *249.* marriage: 27, 245, 249–250. migration: 245–247, 249, 254. music: 250–251. mythology: 246, 250, 251, 253. Northwest Angle No. 33 band: *54,* 247. Northwest Angle No. 37 band: *54,* 247. One Man Lake group: 246. orthography: 231. Pauingassi band: 244, 245, 247, *248.* Peguis band: 245–247. Pikangikum band: 27, 243, 244, 247, 253. Poplar River band: *54,* 247. population: 247, 254. Portage band: *249.* prehistory: 244, 245–246. Rat Portage band: *54,* 247. religion: 250–253. reserves: 245–247, 252, 253, *253.* Sabaskong band: 247. Saint Peter's band: 246. settlement patterns: 254. settlements: *140,* 245, *247.* shamanism: 250–252, *252, 253,* 719. Shoal Lake No. 39 band: *54,* 247. Shoal Lake No. 40 band: *54,* 247. social organization: 27, 28, 244, 248–250, 254. structures: *140, 247, 248, 250,* 251, *251,* 252, *252,* 253. subsistence: 244, 245–248, *247,* 249. synonymy: 243, 254–255. technology: 247–249, *248.* territory: 244–246, *245.* trade: 148, 248. transport: 246, 248, *248,* 253–254. Wabauskang band: 247. Wabigoon band: *54,* 247. Whitefish Bay band: *54,* 247. *See also* Ojibwa, Northern
Saulteurs; synonymy: 254
Saulteux; synonymy: 254
Sault, Nation des Gen du; synonymy: 254
Sault, Nation of the; synonymy: 254

Sautaux; synonymy: 254
Sauteur(s); synonymy: 241, 254, 255
Sauteux; synonymy: 254
Saut, Nation du; synonymy: 254
Sautors; synonymy: 254
Sauvages Bersiamiste; synonymy: 186
Savannahs: 159
Savishinsky, Joel S.: 22
Sawridge band. *See* Cree, Western Woods
Sawyer, Pierre. *See* Cyr, Pierre
sayisedene; synonymy: 280
Saykuswotin; synonymy: 431
Says-thau Dennehs; synonymy: 434, 440
Sa-zē-oo-ti-na; synonymy: 450
scalping. *See* warfare
scapulimancy. *See* divination
Schefferville band. *See* Montagnais-Naskapi
Schwatka, Frederick: 38, 482, 503, 556
Scoffis; synonymy: 185
Scollon, Ronald: 684
Scott, Mrs. *See* Keewatin
Scott, A.W.: *64*
Scottie Creek band. *See* Tanana
Scottie Creek Titus: *540*
scrapers: 88, *88–91*, 92, *93*, 95, *96*, 98, 99, *99*,
    101, *102*, 103, 104, 106, 110, *110*, *113*, 118,
    118, 120, 121, 124, *125*, *153*, 219, 518, 519,
    570, 612
Sea Horse Gully site: *101*, 102
Sea-Side Indians; synonymy: 159
Seauteaux; synonymy: 254
Seccanies; synonymy: 440
Secunnie; synonymy: 440
Séguin, Jean: 78
Sékanais; synonymy: 440
Sekani: 40, 41, 338, 350, 351, 364, 373, 387,
    430, 431, 433–441, *441*, 452, 456.
    adornment: 438. Baucanne band: 434, 435,
    440. Bear Lake: 450, 451, 458, 460. birth:
    437. ceremonies: 438, 439. clothing: 437,
    438, *439*. curing: 439. death: 438, 439.
    environment: *372*, 374, 375, 433, 435, 436.
    external relations: 162, 357, 388, 391, 413,
    435, 455, 458. Finlay River band: 439. Fort
    Ware band: 440. history: 35, 36, 38, 388,
    389, 391, 394, 395, 399, 434, 435, 439–440.
    Iskut band: 458. kinship: 433. language: *70*,
    72, 77, 81–82, *372*, 433. life cycle: 437, 438.
    McLeod Lake band: 436, *437*, 438.
    marriage: 433–435, 438, 439, 458. Meadow
    Indians: 434, 436, 440. menstrual practices:
    438. migration: 162, 434, 436, 440, 458,
    460–461. music: 439. orthography: 433.
    Otzane band: 434, 440. Parsnip River band:
    436. population: 434, 435, 440. puberty:
    438, 439. religion: 439. Sasuchan band: 434,
    435, 438, 461. settlements: 434, 435, 440,
    458. shamanism: 439. social organization:
    384, 433–434, 438–439. structures: 380,
    437, 438, *438*. subsistence: 375, 376, 437.
    synonymy: 440–441. technology: 378, 379,
    417, 436–437, *437–439*. territory: 161, 162,
    388, 433–435, *434*. T'lotona band: 434, 435,
    439, 461. trade: 36, 417, 418, 435, 436.
    transport: 380, 381, 399, 437, *437*. Tsekani
    band: 433–435, 438. Tseloni band: 434–435,
    450. warfare: 162, 417, 434–436.
    Yutuwichan band: 434, 435, 438

še·kutimi·wilnuč; synonymy: 186
Seldovia Tanainas; synonymy: 638. *See also*
    Tanaina
Selkirk band. *See* Tutchone
Selkirk complex: 92, *93*, 94
Selkirk people; synonymy: 505
Sept-Îles band. *See* Montagnais-Naskapi
Serebrennikov, Ruff: 643
Setin-setna: *650*
settlement pattern: 53–55, 101, 104, 149, 182–
    183, 190, 197, 201–202, 240, 257–258, 262,
    345, 376, 393, 406, 413, 456, 476, 497–498,
    517, *524*, 551, 553, 561, 604, 618, 627, 628,
    644, 699–700, *701*
settlements: 71, 73–75, 77–84, 197, 202, 239–
    240, 243, 281, 291, 292, *292*, 295, 297, 311,
    312, 315, 338, 347, 376, *394*, 413, 434, 455,
    460, 461, 494–496, 503, 511, 515, *550*, 557,
    558, 565, 566–568, 584, 602, *605*, 616, 621,
    623, 624, 637–639, 641, *642*, 664–711, *674*,
    695, 704. abandonment: 126, 173, 461, 504,
    559, 560, 566, 568, 621, 637, 643, 691. all-
    native: 237–239, 259, 264, 688. maps: *53*,
    54, *232*, *245*, *560*, *625*, *643*, *665*. population:
    213, 219, 238, 240, 282, 312, 313, 332, 347,
    369, 370, 398, 435, 440, 495, 511, 531.
    prehistoric: 98, 101, 124. winter: 120, *122*,
    123, 124
Severn band; synonymy: 229, 242. *See also*
    Cree, West Main
sexual behavior: 261, 385, 405, 443, 487, 501,
    526, 610, 647, 721
Sêzotêna; synonymy: 450
Shaggamies; synonymy: 215
shaking-tent rite. *See* religion
Shakoon: *486*
shamans: 233, 342, *357*, *540*, 591, 593, 607,
    616, 632, 661. contests: 250–251, 502.
    curing: 251, 261–262, 319, 344, 409, 429,
    439, 447–449, 456, 465, 490, 502, 553, 574,
    661. divination: 223, 553, 574. dreamers:
    357, 439. fees: 251, 409, 439, 490, 595, 661.
    functions: 181, 220, 319, 408, *408*, 479, 490,
    502, 508, 509, 519, 595, 607, 620, 634, 647,
    661, 685. influence: 191, 319, 479, 527, 620,
    656. music: 303, 490, 502, 607, 661.
    paraphernalia: 410, 425, 448, 490, 502, 595,
    634, 661, 719, *719*. performances: 490, 502,
    595, 607, 634, 661, 719. postcontact: 251,
    319, 509, 551, 553, 593, 634, 637, 661, 720.
    power acquisition: 184, 191, 223, 233, 310,
    355, 429, 439, 448, 490, 509, 574, 595, 607,
    620, 634, 660–661. ritual observances: 343,
    344. shaking-tent rite: 184, 233, 251.
    spiritual helpers: 251, 385, 409, 429, 479,
    487, 490, 502, 634, 661. sucking: 252, 319,
    574
Shantz, A.B.: 38
Sharp Eyes; synonymy: 531
Shatshegutsh; synonymy: 186
Sheep Indians; synonymy: 330
Sheldon, Daisy: *473*
Shelikov-Golikov Company: 547, 635–636
shellwork. *See* technology
Shelter Bay band. *See* Montagnais-Naskapi
Sheshatapoosh(shoish); synonymy: 187
Shiagamies; synonymy: 215
Shield Archaic tradition: 32, 33, 88–90, *89*, 95

shields: *172*
Shinabest: *734*
Shiogamys; synonymy: 215
Shi-ta-dene; synonymy: 336
Shoal Lake band. *See* Cree, Western Woods
Shoal Lake No. 39 band. *See* Saulteaux of
    Lake Winnipeg
Shoal Lake No. 40 band. *See* Saulteaux of
    Lake Winnipeg
Shoshoogamies: 159–160
Shukturalit; synonymy: 662
Shumat(t)away band; synonymy: 242. *See also*
    Ojibwa, Northern
Shushebish: *25*, *181*, *669*, *670*
Shuswap: 413, 433. external relations: 384,
    405. religion: 439. subsistence: 375.
    technology: 388, 405. trade: 388. warfare:
    162, 388, 434, 436
Shutin group. *See* Tahltan
Siberian Late Paleolithic period: 114
Sicannies; synonymy: 435, 440
Sicaunies; synonymy: 440
Siccan(n)ies; synonymy: 440
Siccany; synonymy: 440
Sidney, Angela: *489*
Sidney, George: *489*
Siffleur, Gens de; synonymy: 532
šíh gotine; synonymy: 336
Si-him-E-na; synonymy· 490
šíhta gotine; synonymy: 322, 336. *See also*
    Hare
Sikani; synonymy: 440
Sim, V.C.: 567
Simpson, George: *37*, 92, 273, 289, 529, *722*
Sindell, P.S.: 22
Sinkyone; language: 67
sinta gotine; synonymy: 322. *See also* Hare
Siouan language grouping: 53
Sioux. *See* Dakota
Sioux Company: 364
Sipary, Jessie: *594*
šitagottine; synonymy: 336
Skinner, Alanson B.: 20, 22
Skoffie; synonymy: 185
Skookum, Emma. *See* Áma
Skookum Jim: 482, *483*, 485, *486*, 490–492
Slana-Batzulnetas band. *See* Ahtna
Slave Indians; synonymy: 309
slavery: 463, 519, 623, 632, 657
Slave(s): 287, 293, 294, 312. synonymy: 79,
    163–164, 167, 309, 325, 338, 347–348
Slave Woman. *See* Thanadelther
Slavey: *21*, 22, 28, 269, 271, 293, 306, 309,
    314, 316, 325, 337, 338–339, 350, 364, 373,
    726. adornment: 340–341, *343*. birth: 344.
    ceremonies: 343, 724. childrearing: 344.
    clothing: *142–143*, 340, 344. cosmology:
    341. curing: 344. death: 342, 344. division of
    labor: 340, 341. education: *340*, 347.
    environment: *7*, *11*, *131*, 339, 346. external
    relations: 291, 293, 310, 315, 316, 329. Fort
    Nelson band: 338, 451, 720, 725, 731.
    games: 343. health care: 347. history: 148,
    345–346, 688. kinship: *302*, 341–342.
    language: *27*, 69, *70*, 72, 77, 79–82, 167,
    315, 338, 339. life cycle: 344. marriage: 331,
    343–344. menstrual practices: 344.
    migration: 162–167. music: 343, 344.

mythology: 302, 344–345. orthography: 339.
political organization: 342–343, 346, 347.
population: 339, 347. prehistory: 116, 125.
puberty: 344. religion: 303, 344, 345, 718,
731. settlements: 338, 347, 683. shamanism:
343, 344, 719. social organization: 339, 341–
344, 346, 347, 737. structures: 138, 140,
341, 344. subsistence: 145, 339–340, 340,
346, 347. synonymy: 306, 309, 347–348.
technology: 145, 340, 341–344, 344, 346.
territory: 161–164, 162, 167, 294, 310, 338,
338. trade: 288, 310, 311, 345, 346, 684.
transport: 341, 343. warfare: 163–164, 286,
345, 346, 451–452
Slavi; synonymy: 347
sleds: 381, 390, 403, 444, 474, 487, 506, 518,
525, 569, 589, 606, 613, 621, 630, 649, 668,
669. canoe: 138, 177, 604. dog-pulled: 177,
179, 498, 540, 544, 549, 551, 596, 630.
komatik: 177
Slim Jim: 486
Slobodin, Richard: 22, 40, 41, 41, 511
Sloua-cuss-Dinais; synonymy: 431
Slowercuss, Dinais; synonymy: 431
Smarch, Watson: 391
Smith, David M.: 22
Smith, Elsie: 500
Smith, Frankie: 500
Smith, Fred M.: 49
Smith, James G.E.: 22
Smith, Paddy: 486
Smith, Sam: 486
Smokey Lake site: 98
Snare River complex: 100, 105–106
Snare River site: 103, 106
Snowdrift band. See Chipewyan
Snowgoose site: 101
Snowshoe culture: 24, 30
snowshoes: 86, 223, 237, 286, 303, 308, 382,
403, 405, 437, 443, 485, 506, 511, 517, 525,
569, 596, 649, 669. introduction of: 30, 390,
498. manufacture: 138, 176, 221, 223, 239,
248, 262, 280, 318, 341, 381, 382, 406, 443,
444, 456, 508, 517, 540, 630. styles: 138,
139, 179, 233, 234, 235, 248, 262, 341, 381,
382, 443, 444, 498, 517, 518. use: 138, 197,
221
sobstvenno inkiliki; synonymy: 599
sobstvenno Ttynaïtsy; synonymy: 638
social organization; age-grading: 523, 524–525.
avoidance relationships: 221, 250, 320, 477,
487–488, 501, 610, 653, 656. bands: 26–27,
190, 208, 233, 259, 315–317, 319, 334, 339,
342, 346, 350, 384, 407, 433, 434, 446, 461,
522, 546, 585, 588–590, 618, 669, 684.
clans: 27, 191, 221, 231, 236, 244, 248, 249,
254, 301, 342, 384, 385, 388, 419–422, 421,
423, 427, 428, 439, 455, 456, 459–461, 463,
474–478, 474–476, 485–489, 495, 499, 508,
509, 519, 523–524, 526–527, 541, 542, 565,
572, 577, 578, 589–591, 619, 623, 629, 631–
634, 644–645, 651–654, 657, 659, 660, 696–
697, 698. 709. Cordillera area: 383–385,
388. descent groups: 26, 40, 221, 301, 342,
384, 407, 447, 459, 523, 541, 572, 577, 610,
619, 696–697. descent rules: 419, 589.
family groups: 143–144, 152, 182, 183, 191,
221, 233, 236, 240, 259, 262, 346, 352, 353,

362, 384, 400, 407, 418, 422, 446, 472, 489,
500, 508, 520, 529, 540, 567, 585, 588, 677,
697. joking relationships: 183, 250, 477, 519,
610, 653, 656, 734–735. lineage: 384, 385,
419, 474–479, 485–489, 500, 501, 631. local
bands: 500, 520, 540, 542, 545, 562, 565,
566. lodge-groups: 179–180, 190. moieties:
384, 385, 442, 445, 447, 448, 461, 463–465,
475–478, 475, 485–489, 486, 489, 499–502,
508, 509, 524, 572, 577, 578, 631, 633, 634,
651–654, 659, 660. phratries: 384, 385, 419–
422, 421, 423, 428, 438–439. partners: 519–
520, 542, 572, 698. postcontact: 151–152,
154–156, 179–183, 199, 203, 224–227, 240,
250, 254, 315, 391–392, 400, 509, 567, 590,
624, 630–632, 653, 668–672, 675, 677, 696–
698, 714–717. prehistoric: 86. ranking: 501,
524–526, 608–609, 623, 631–632, 714.
regional bands: 540–541, 562. reserve
relationship: 501, 656. trading post bands:
152, 171, 172, 180–182. See also assemblies;
division of labor; kinship; kinship
terminology
Sockemy Indians; synonymy: 215
songs. See music
sorcery: 202, 223, 250, 251, 253, 262, 279, 312,
320, 344, 357, 449, 478, 488, 490, 502, 574,
607, 719–720
Sotees; synonymy: 254
Sotoos; synonymy: 254
so·to·wiyiniwak; synonymy: 255
Sotto; synonymy: 255
Sourdough Rendezvous: 540
Sourdough Roadhouse: 550
Southern Indian(s): 273. synonymy: 228, 257,
283
Southern Tutchone. See Tutchone
South Fork people; synonymy: 600. See also
Koyukon
Southward Indian(s); synonymy: 205, 228
spears: 201. fishing: 133, 134, 174, 175, 484,
497, 506, 516, 518, 535, 569, 605, 612, 619,
620, 647. hunting: 131, 174, 175, 220, 484,
496, 496, 506, 517, 535, 536, 566, 612, 619,
620, 626, 647, 648. manufacture: 132.
warfare: 164, 484, 496, 652
Speck, Frank G.: 20–22, 24–26, 24, 211
Spencer River complex: 125
Split Lake band. See Cree, Western Woods
Spo-to-ti-na; synonymy: 505
Sqwam, Annie: 474
Sqwam, Joe: 474, 475
Sqwam, Mary: 474
Star, Jacob: 552, 574
starvation: 135, 137, 148, 173, 190, 199, 201,
208, 218, 232, 288, 317, 322, 328, 329, 376–
377
Steamboat, Robert: 530
steamboats: 485, 504, 511, 548–549, 550, 568,
584, 587, 611, 687, 687
Steese Highway: 568
Steinbring, Jack H.: 22
stela hʷəienne; synonymy: 431
Stel-a-tīn; synonymy: 431
Stellaquo band; synonymy: 431. See also
Carrier
Stella village; synonymy: 431
Stellawoten; synonymy: 431

Stellawotin; synonymy: 431
Stephen. See Stickwan
Stevens, Annie: 395
Stevens Village–Tanana subdivision. See
Koyukon
Steward, Julian H.: 40
Stewart River Indians; synonymy: 505
Stewart, William: 273, 283
Stick Indians; synonymy: 466, 490, 504
Stickman, Anna: 589
Stickman, Joseph: 589
Sticks; synonymy: 466
stick siwash; synonymy: 466
Stickwan: 651, 656
Stikine; synonymy: 466. See also Tlingit
Stikine Indians; synonymy: 466
Stone band. See Chilcotin
stonework. See technology
Stoney's expedition: 586
Stony Creek band; synonymy: 431. See also
Carrier
Stony Rapids band. See Chipewyan
Stony River Tanainas; synonymy: 638
storage. See structures
storytelling: 221, 260, 263, 279, 312, 320, 376,
385–386, 410, 420, 427, 465, 489, 502, 519,
649
Stringer, Isaac O.: 397
Strong Bow Indians; synonymy: 167, 348
Strong, William Duncan: 22, 25, 30, 174
Strong Wood Crees; synonymy: 268
Strongwoods Cree. See Cree, Western Woods
structures: 126, 369, 486, 596, 598, 604, 613,
620, 628, 628. abandonment: 498, 659. bark
houses: 169, 234, 569, 571, 613. bridges:
403, 415, 497. canvas-covered: 201, 223,
224, 289, 299, 335, 352. ceremonial: 126,
177, 184, 198, 220, 251, 252–253, 252, 357,
380, 421, 444, 579, 591, 604, 610, 613, 616.
childbirth: 301, 335, 380, 427, 447, 473, 487,
498, 571, 632, 645, 657. conical: 138, 140,
175, 192, 199, 200, 220, 220, 234, 248, 250,
281, 308, 333, 341, 379, 380, 437, 444, 473,
485, 498. construction: 131–132, 138, 140,
175, 220, 319, 333, 341, 379, 403, 457, 498,
525, 538, 570, 573, 596, 627, 645. decoration
of: 486, 503, 645. dome-shaped: 138, 140,
175, 192, 201, 220, 380, 390, 498, 526, 539,
541, 571, 571, 573, 604, 645. frame houses:
282, 291, 292, 308, 437, 443, 470, 473, 498,
518, 675, 677, 700, 709. gabled: 192, 462,
613. grave houses: 405, 405, 428, 465, 478,
572, 591, 592, 611, 616, 634, 634, 659, 728.
hide: 140, 169, 200, 281, 289, 299, 308, 319,
333, 380, 447, 498. hunting enclosures: 131–
132, 220, 377, 535, 462. internal
arrangement: 183, 206, 294, 605, 627–628,
645. lineage houses: 482, 483, 486, 628. log
cabins: 124, 199, 282, 308, 322, 333, 352,
437, 438, 444, 460, 463, 473, 497, 509, 518,
539, 549, 569, 597, 605, 613, 646, 688, 695,
695, 697, 700. menstrual: 220, 301, 320, 335,
344, 359, 380, 405, 425, 427, 438, 465, 473,
477, 488, 498, 500, 518, 539, 572, 628, 645,
657, 658. Northwest Coast style: 126, 498.
occupancy: 138, 140, 175, 183, 498, 540,
571, 585, 604, 628, 631, 645, 697. pit
houses: 115, 117, 119, 122–123, 122, 125,   *831*

126. postcontact: 185, *204, 206,* 213, 223, *224,* 597, 628. prehistoric: 89, 115, 117, 119–126, *122.* racks: 177, *177, 379,* 484, 498, 604, 628, *645, 669.* rectangular: 126, 175, 498, *498,* 518, 538, 613. ridgepole: 138, *140,* 175, *281,* 403, *403.* semisubterranean: 220, 507, 518, 539, 569, 575, 588, 596, 605, 613, 616, 618, 627. size: 125, 126, *140,* 206, 627–628. snow house: 613. sod: *206.* storage: 120, 124, 125, 126, 134, 176–177, 220, *497,* 498, 549, *550, 573,* 604, *605,* 628, 645, *646,* 668, *698.* summer: 175, 613. sweathouses: 120, 124, 138, 175, 220, 380, *390,* 403, 425, 443, 498, 518, 539, 571, 628, 645–646. temporary: 138, 176, 379, 403, 425, 437, 444, 456, 462, 473, 484–485, *497,* 498, 507, 509, 518, 538–539, 571, 604, 616, 627, 645, 646, *669,* 677, *677, 685, 686,* 695, *698.* tents: *299, 319, 335,* 473, *646.* tepees: *281, 299,* 308, 319, 352, *352,* 357, 380, 539, 613, 619. wigwams: 198, *199,* 200, *220.* winter: *140, 525, 541,* 596, 613, 628, *628*
Stuart, John: 35
Stuart Lake band. *See* Carrier
Stuart Lake tribe; synonymy: 430
Stuart-Trembleur Lake band; synonymy: 430. *See also* Carrier
Stuck, Hudson: 44, 50, 601
Stum, Julia: *404*
Sturgeon Indians; synonymy: 160, 242. territory: *159*
Sturgeon Lake band. *See* Cree, Western Woods
Sturgeons; synonymy: 242. *See also* Ojibwa, Northern
sturgeon tribe; synonymy: 242
Sturgoon Indians; synonymy: 242
Subarctic culture area: ix. defined: 1–4. environment: 5–18, *6.* history of research: 19–51. languages: 52–85. population: 1. prehistory: 86–106. subsistence: 15–18, *16*
subsistence. *See* fishing; food; gathering; hunting
Sucker Lake band. *See* Cree, Western Woods
Suckers; synonymy: 241, 242. *See also* Ojibwa, Northern
sucker tribe; synonymy: 242
suicide: 658, 701
Sullivan, Robert J.: 47
Summer Institute of Linguistics: 63, 74, 75, 77, 80, 83
supernatural beings: 194, 202, 527. animal spirits: 279, 301, 377, 385, 428, 439, 448, 449, 465, 477, 490, 502, 509, 635, 647, 648, 670. creator: 479, 509, 653. deities: 223, 408. ghosts: 262, 320, 409, 429, 448, 465, 478, 511, 591, 593, 620, 658–659, 727. guardian spirit: 251, 319, 409, 425, 439, 448, 479, 487, 490, 500, 502, 634, 661, 719, *728.* manitou: 202, 223, 253, 260, 263. Mistapew: 718, 720. spirits: 488, 490, 502, 519, 593, 634, 635. supreme being: 28, 202, 223, 253, 408, 449, 528. *See also* mythology
Susie. *See* Etetnot-otna
susitnu x̣iana; synonymy: 639
Sussex Lake site: *101*
Suss to'deen; synonymy: 455
Swamp Indian; synonymy: 227

Swamps, People of the; synonymy: 159
Swampy Cree; synonymy: 66, 217, 227. *See also* Cree, Western Woods; Cree, West Main
Swampy Indians; synonymy: 227, 241
Swan River band. *See* Cree, Western Woods
sweatbathing: 223, 262, 344, 519, 658, 659. introduction of: 646. *See also* structures, sweathouses
swimming: *174*

T

Tabitibis; synonymy: 228
Tabittee; synonymy: 228
taboos: 581, 660, 721, 724. bear: 648. childbirth: 500, 526, 571–572, 590–591, 610, 657, 660. death: *500,* 509, 610, 658. fishing: 320, 428, 610, 647. food: 192, 220, 250, 277, 320, 336, 385, 404, 405, 420, 427, 438, 465, 488, 508, 509, 571–572, 610, 657, 658, 721, 724. hunting: 201, 220, 277, 301, 320, 428, 438, 447, 647. incest: 447, 590, 609. menstrual: 201, 261, 277, 301, 320, 336, *359,* 438, 447, 488, 500, 524, 572, 591, 610, 619, 633, 647, 726. war-related: 652
tacán-hoṭine; synonymy: 271
tačotena; synonymy: 466
Tachick band. *See* Carrier
Tachickwoten; synonymy: 431
Tachiwoten; synonymy: 430
tačik hʷəien; synonymy: 431
Tâcullies; synonymy: 430
tadi móla; synonymy: 371
Tadoosh; synonymy: 513
Tadoussac band; synonymy: 186. *See also* Montagnais-Naskapi
Tadoussac site: 31
Tadush; synonymy: 513
ta ga ḣoṭį; synonymy: 295. *See also* Dogrib
tagisch; synonymy: 490
Tagish: 40, 41, 373, 387, 481–492. birth: 487. Carcross band: 482, 483. ceremonies: 482, 485, *486–487,* 487, 488, *489.* childrearing: 487, 490. clothing: *483,* 485, *486,* 488, *489.* cosmology: 490. death: *487,* 488. division of labor: 484, 485. education: 482, 484. employment: 484, 485. environment: *372, 374,* 375, 481. external relations: 470, 481–482, 485, 496, 506. games: 487, 489. history: 38, 394, 395, 399, 482, *483,* 485. language: 69, *70,* 72, 77, 79, 82, 372, 442, 470, 481, 482, 486, 506. life cycle: 487–488. marriage: 470, 481, 482, 485–489, 496. music: 486, 488, 490. mythology: 479, 486, 490. orthography: 481. political organization: 482, 489. population: 483. puberty: 487–488. religion: 487, 488, 490. settlements: 482, 483. shamanism: 490. social organization: 384, 481, 485–489, *489, 491.* structures: 482–488, *486.* subsistence: 375, 376, 378, 483–484. synonymy: 451–453, 480, 490–491. technology: 378, 379, 484, *485, 491.* territory: 481, *482.* trade: 378, 470, 481–484, 489–490. transport: 380, 381, *395, 396,* 484, 485, 487, *487.* warfare: 482, 484, 489
Tagish Jim: *486*
Tagishoten; synonymy: 461, 491
ta·giš qʷá·n; synonymy: 490

ta·gizi dene; synonymy: 490
taγγaviγmiut; synonymy: 600
taẏti·l Wie·ne; synonymy: 576
Tahgish; synonymy: 490
Tahkali; synonymy: 430
Tahk(h)eesh; synonymy: 490
Tahk-ong; synonymy: 512
Tāh́ko-tin´ neh; synonymy: 479, 490
Tahlagotin group; synonymy: 461. *See also* Tahltan
Tahltan: 39, 40, 41, 373, 387, 394, *398,* 440, 444, 450, 456, 458–468, 491. adornment: *464,* 728. art: 464–465. ceremonies: 445, *464,* 465, 467. childrearing: 464. clothing: 462, *464,* 465, *465,* 467. curing: 465. Dease Lake band: 391. death: 465. division of labor: 462. education: 460. employment: 460. environment: *372, 374,* 375, 458, 459, 462. external relations: 388, 435–436, 438–439, 445, 447, 454, 456, 458, 469, 486. games: *386,* 465. history: 36, 38, 391, 395, 397, 434, 459–461. Kachadi group: 461, 463. kinship: 487. Klabbahnotin group: 461. language: 69, *70,* 72, 77, 79, 82, 83, 372, 442, 452, 455, 458, 466, 469, 481, 482. marriage: 447, 458, 461, 463–465, 469. migration: 455, 458–462. music: 465. mythology: 465, 467, 479. Nahlotin group: 461, *464.* Naneai group: 461. Nassgotin group: 454–455, 458, 461. orthography: 458. political organization: 463. population: 460. prehistory: 462. puberty: 465, 726, *728.* religion: 465. reserve: *462.* settlements: 455, 460–462, *462, 467.* shamanism: 449, 465. Shutin group: 461. social organization: 384, 459–461, 463–464. structures: 379, 459, 460, 463, 465, *467.* subsistence: 379, 454, 458, 460–462. synonymy: 82, 451–454, 465–468, 480. Tahlagotin group: 461. Taxtlowedi group: 461. technology: 378, *379, 380, 386, 393,* 459, *463, 466, 722, 728.* Telegraph Creek: 82, *462.* territory: 458, *459.* Thlegtotin group: 458, 460. Thloadenni group: 434–436, 461. Tichanotin group: 461. trade: 378, 436, 458–463. transport: 380, 381, 390, 462, *463.* warfare: 377, 454, 455, 469, 472, 478, 479
Tahltan band; synonymy: 458
Tahltan subdivision; synonymy: 461
Tahowtin; synonymy: 431
Tait sa Koo chin; synonymy: *37*
Takaiak; synonymy: 600
takaīaksanskiī; synonymy: 600
takaīaksant̄sy; synonymy: 600
Takayaksa; synonymy: 600. *See also* Koyukon
Takellies; synonymy: 430
Takelly; synonymy: 430
Takio Tribe; synonymy: 470
Takla Lake band; synonymy: 431. *See also* Carrier
Takon Indians; synonymy: 512, 513
Ta-koŏs-oo-ti-na; synonymy: 479, 505
Takotna band. *See* Kolchan
Taku (Athapaskan); history: 451, 469. language: 82. synonymy: 451, 479, 480
Taku (Tlingit). *See* Tlingit
Takudh: 529, 531. synonymy: 531
Takulli band; synonymy: 430. *See also* Carrier

Tākŭ´ 'rdh; synonymy: 531
Takutine; synonymy: 479
Tā-küth-Kutchin; synonymy: 531
tak^ele gotine; synonymy: 295
talʒá-hotine; synonymy: 271, 289
Talkeetna River Ahtna-Tanainas; synonymy: 639. *See also* Tanaina
Talkotin; synonymy: 431
ta·tta·n; synonymy: 465
ta·ttanq^á·n; synonymy: 465
Taltheilei complex: 100, 103–104, *105*
Taltheilei Shale tradition: 33, 100, 102–106, *103, 105,* 108, 118, 127, 128
Taltheilei site: *103*
Talyan; synonymy: 465
ta·χa· ti·n; synonymy: 662
taχaWte·na; synonymy: 662
taχo· ti·n; synonymy: 662
Tanacross band. *See* Tanana
Tanaina: 47, 50, 51, 556–558, 622–640, 662, 727. adornment: 629. birth: 632–633. ceremonies: 632–634. childrearing: 633. clothing: 628–629, *629,* 632, 633. curing: 634. death: 634, *634.* disease: 624, 627, 636, 637. division of labor: 627. education: 637. employment: 627, 636, 637. environment: 9, 10, *533,* 626. external relations: 565, 603, 623, 624, 641, 653. health care: 633. history: 43–44, 547, 548, 624, 627, 635–637, 654. Iliamna Lake: 73, 623, 624, *625,* 626, 635, 638. Inland dialect: 73, 638. Interior society: 624, *625,* 633. Kenai Peninsula: 637–639. Kenai society: 73, 168, 624, *625,* 627. kinship: 631. Knik Arm: 623, *625.* Kroto Creek: *625,* 639. Kustatan: 624, *625,* 638. Lake Clark: 623, *625,* 638. language: 48, 68, *70,* 72–73, 75, 77, 623–624, *625,* 641. life cycle: 632–634. Lower Susitna River: *625,* 639. marriage: 623, 624, 631–634, 636, 637. menstrual practices: 626, 633. migrations: 121–122, 627, 637. Mulchatna: *625,* 638. mythology: 635. orthography: 623. Outer Inlet dialect: 73, 623. political organization: 631, 632. population: 624, 637–638. prehistory: 45–46, 107, 120, 121–122. puberty: 628, 633. religion: 634–637. reserves: 637. settlement pattern: 628, 663. settlements: 623, 624, *625,* 627, 637, 638. social organization: 623, 624, 630–632, 653. Stony River: 559, 603, *625,* 636, 638. structures: 627–628, *628,* 631, 632–633, 634, *634.* subsistence: 122, 624, 626–627, *626,* 632, 636, 713. Susitna society: 624, *625,* 627, 633. synonymy: 638–639. Talkeetna River Ahtna-Tanainas: 624, *625,* 639. technology: *626, 630,* 633. Telaquana Lake: *625,* 638. territory: 68, 559, *625.* trade: 388, 547, 548, 559, 603, 618, 623, 627, 631–632, 635–637, 654. transport: 624, 630, *631.* Tyonek: *625,* 627, 637. Upper Inlet dialect: 72, 73, 623, 639. warfare: 618, 623, 631, 643
Tanana: 50, 546, 556, 562–576. adornment: 570–571, *571, 572,* 575, *710.* birth: 571–572. ceremonies: 565, 567, 571, 574, 577–581, 618, 659, 660, 705, 709, *709–711.* Chena band: 76, 563, 566–569. childrearing: 472. clothing: *535, 542,* 570, *570–572, 574,* 710, 711. curing: 574. death: 572, 574, 577–580.

disease: 569, 706. division of labor: 569, *570.* education: 567, 706, 707, 710. employment: 568, 710. environment: 373, *533, 563–565.* external relations: 75, 76, 494, 495, 502, 506, 565, 618, 642, 651, 653. health care: 569. Healy River–Joseph band: *541,* 583, 565, 569, 573. history: 566–568, *574,* 704–711. kinship: 567, 572, 574. language: 48, 69, *70,* 72, 74–78, 506, 560–563, 567, 569, 618, 707, 710. Lower: 69, *70,* 72, 74–78, *538,* 562, 574, 600, 641, 654, 704–711. Lower Nabesna band: 563, 566. Mansfield-Kechumstuk band: 563, 576. marriage: 565, 571, 572, 577, 618, 619. menstrual practices: 572. migration: 561, 562, 566, 567. Minto band: 563, 566, 576, 704–711. music: 571, 579–580. mythology: 572, 574–575, 581. Nenana-Toklat band: 563, 566, 576. Northway band: 76, 77, 563, 576. orthography: 562. political organization: *552,* 562, 567, 574, 707, 708. population: 534, 568–569. prehistory: 46, 123, 575. religion: 567, 574–575, 710. Salcha-Goodpaster band: 75, 76, 563, 566, 569, *570,* 576. Scottie Creek band: 563, 566, *572,* 576. settlements: 560, 565–569, *568, 573,* 575, 576, 704–711, *704, 707.* shamanism: 574. social organization: 499, 562, 565–567, 572, 574, 577, 653, 709. structures: *541,* 569, *570,* 571, 572, *573,* 579, 709. subsistence: *535, 536, 543,* 546, 565–567, 569, *573,* 705. synonymy: *37,* 572, 575–576, 599, 575–576, 600. Tanacross band: 69, *70,* 72, 75–78, *541,* 562, 565, 572, 575–577, 662. technology: *535, 536, 538, 541, 542,* 569–570, *570, 571,* 573, 575. territory: *37,* 557, *557,* 560–561, *564,* 565, 566, 641. Tetlin band: 76, 77. Tetlin-Last Tetlin band: 563, 566, 576. Tolovana band: 566. trade: 388, 494, 565–567, 575, 582, 645, 651, 652, 704–705. transport: 537, *538–540, 551,* 566, 567, 568, *568,* 569, *570, 572, 573.* Upper: 46–48, *70,* 72, 76–78, 123, 373, 388, 494, 495, 499, 502, 506, *535–541,* 562, 565, 566, 569, *570,* 572, 575–581, 631, 642, 645, 652, 653, 654, 659–662. Upper Nabesna-Upper Chisana band: *540,* 566, 576. warfare: 565, 569, 570, 582, 642. Wood River band: 563, 566
Tanana Chiefs Conference: 562, 587, 598
Tanana Commercial Company: *551*
Tanana-Nowitna; synonymy: 600. *See also* Koyukon
Tananatána; synonymy: 575
tanan g^ačín; synonymy: 575
Tanan Kuttchin; synonymy: 575
Ta-nä´-tin-ne; synonymy: 325
Tandzán-hot!ínnè; synonymy: 289
Tangles Lakes sequence: 115
tani móla; synonymy: 371
Tanna-Kutchi; synonymy: 575
Tannatenne; synonymy: 431
Tanner, Adrien: 22
Tannin-Kootchin; synonymy: 575
Tā-non Kutchin; synonymy: 575
Tanoten; synonymy: 431
tanoienne; 431
Tantsa-ut-'dtinnè; synonymy: 289

Tantsawhot-dinneh; synonymy: 289
Taodennis Doadennis; synonymy: 436
Taral site: 120
Tatanchaks; synonymy: 505
Tatanchok Kutchins; synonymy: 504
Tatchatotenne; synonymy: 431
Tatchetenne; synonymy: 430
Tatche "tribe"; synonymy: 430
Tathzey-kutchi; synonymy: 505
Tatlatán; synonymy: 662
Tatlawiksuk band. *See* Kolchan
Tā-tlit-Kutchin; synonymy: 531
Tatlmain Lake band. *See* Tutchone
Tātltan; synonymy: 465
Tātsāh´-Kūtchin´; synonymy: *37*
T'atsan ottiné; synonymy: 271, 289
Tatshiáutin; synonymy: 430
Ta-tshik-o-tīn; synonymy: 431
tatsot'ine; synonymy: 289
tattín; synonymy: 371
tattinœ; synonymy: 269
tattooing. *See* adornment
Tauten; synonymy: 431
Taūtin; synonymy: 431
Taxlena; synonymy: 662
Taxtlowedi group; synonymy: 461. *See also* Tahltan
Taye Lake phase: 115, *118,* 124
Taylor, J. Garth: 22, 187
Tazlina; synonymy: 662
Tchi-cargut-kotan; synonymy: 512
Tēähĭ´ⁿ kūtchĭn; synonymy: 532
təbuγna; synonymy: 639
technology: 175, *222,* 645. antlerwork: 110, *113,* 121, 131, 132, 134, *153,* 175, *185,* 496, 569, 570, 575, 626, 645, *652.* bark work: 104, 106, 118, 120, 125, 131, 132, *133,* 135, *140,* 141, *145,* 175, *210,* 219, 484, 487, 506, 511, 518, *520,* 535, 538, *542,* 569, 572, *573,* 596, 610, 612, 619, 633, 648. bonework: 90, 92, *93,* 94–97, 101, 104, *105,* 110, 118, *119,* 120, 121, *123, 123,* 124, 125, 131, 132, 138, 141, 175, 496, 497, 516, 518, 569, 570, 575, 596, 604, 612, 629, 645, *652.* cordage: 219, 223, 518, 569, 570. fishskin: 141, 233, 249, 596, 619, 649. hornwork: *503, 535, 571,* 612, 645. leatherwork: *119,* 120, 124, 125, 131, 135, 137, 138, *140,* 141, *142–143, 145, 153,* 169, 175, 177, 219, *341, 342, 485, 498,* 506, *507, 508,* 517, 518, *522, 541,* 596, 619, 630, 645, *652.* metalwork: 30, *89, 90, 90, 93,* 95, 102, 104, *105,* 106, 114, 118, *121,* 123, *123,* 124, 125, *125,* 128, 496, 517, 518, *535,* 569, 570, 575, 626, 645, 649, 652. postcontact adaptations: 106, 118, 120–121, *121,* 123, 125, 132, 134, 141, 153, 175, *197,* 219, 223, 232, 484, 497, 519, *535, 536,* 548, 553, *613,* 626, 626, 652. quillwork: *142–143, 145,* 221, 340, *342, 343,* 485, 498, 509, 517, 518, *521, 522,* 539, 570, 596, 619, 629, *649, 649.* root: 516, 518, *538,* 570, *573,* 596, 632, 645, *647, 721, 733.* shellwork: 48, 120, 177, 499, *512,* 517, *522,* 539, *542,* 570–571, *571, 572,* 596, 629, 632, *649, 650, 656, 710.* sinew: 484, 497, 506, 517, 518, 535, 570, 575, 596, 604, 626, 645. stonework: 30, 33, 88–90, *88–91,* 92, *93,* 94–96, *96,* 97–99, *99,* 101–103, *102, 105,* 106, 108, 110–111,

110, 112–113, 113–118, *118*, *119*, 120–126, *123*, *125*, 132, 135, 175, *185*, 219, 220, 517, 518, 570, *570*, 575, 596, 612, 626, 645. textiles: 518. tooth: 570, *613*. woodwork: 97, 98, 101, 110, 131, 132, 134, 138, 141, 175, *222*, *225*, *507*, 517, 569, 570, *571*, 596, 612, *612*, 613, *633*, 645. *See also* art; basketry; beads; canoes; containers; pottery; projectile points; tools

Tecon: 298

Tecon-ne-betah. *See* Edzo

Teenjiraatsyaa; synonymy: 532

Tehanin-Kutchin; synonymy: 638

tehʒǫ́į̀; synonymy: 283, 289, 306

Teit, James: 39

Tekallies; synonymy: 430

Telaquana Lake; synonymy: 638. *See also* Tanaina

Telegraph Creek band. *See* Tahltan

telegraph system: 568, *568*, 584, 587, 643, 705, 707

Telida-Minchumina band. *See* Kolchan

Teltah: *464*

Telzoa River site: *101*

te·x̌it gʷič̣in; synonymy: 531

Temiskaming band. *See* Algonquin, Timiskaming band

Ten'a; synonymy: 43, 600

tēnaina; synonymy: 638

Tenanichna: *650*

Tenán-Kutchín: 568. synonymy: 575

Tenenbaum, Joan: 73

tənən hŏíanə; synonymy: 575

Tennŭth'-kŭt-chin'; synonymy: 532

Tênᵘth; synonymy: 532

tepees. *See* structures

Terminal Woodland period: 87, 90–91, *91*, *93*, 95, *96*

Terre(s), Gens de(s); synonymy: 209–211, 214, 215, 240–241. territory: *159*

territory; Ahtna: 641, *642*. Algonquin: 158, 160. Assiniboin: 158, 165–166, 245. Attikamek (Tête de Boule): 208–211, *209*. Bearlake Indians: 161, *162*, 310, *310*, 311. Beaver: 161–165, *162*, 167–168, 350–351, *351*. Bella Coola: 402. Carrier: 413, *414*, 421–422. Chilcotin: 402, *402*. Chipewyan: 92, 162–163, *162*, *165*, 166–168, 258, 271, *272*, *279*, 280, 285. Chugach Eskimo: 641. Copper Eskimo: 106. Cree: *53*, 92, 158–160, *159*, *166*, 161–163, 166–168, 242, 244–245. Dakota: 244. Dogrib: 161–162, *162*, 286, 291, *292*, 294, 295, 297, 310, 311. East Main Cree: 196–198, *196*. Eskimo: 92, 165, 170, *516*, 557, 559, 602. Eyak: 641. Han: *37*, 506, *506*. Hare: 161, *162*, 310, 311, 314, *314*. Holikachuk: *557*, 558, 615, *615*. Ingalik: 556–558, *557*, 602, *603*. Iroquois: 165–166. Kaska: 161, 162, 442, *442*, 458. Kolchan: *557*, 558–559, 618, *619*, 621. Koyukon: 582, *583*, 584. Kutchin: *37*, 161, 514–515, *516*. Métis: 165–166, 361. Montagnais-Naskapi: 169–171, *170*, 196. Mountain Indians: 161, *162*, 326–327, *327*, 329. Northern Ojibwa: 158, *159*, 160, 165–166, 229, 231, *232*, 242, 244, 288. Plains Ojibwa: 244. Saulteaux of Lake Winnipeg: 244–246, *245*. Sekani: 161, 162, 388, 433–435, *434*. Slavey: 161–164, *162*, 167, 294, 310, 338, *338*. Tagish: 481, *482*. Tahltan: 458, *459*. Tanaina: 68, 559, *625*. Tanana: *37*, *564*, 565. Tlingit: 458. Tlingit, Inland: 458, 469, *471*. Tsetsaut: 454, *454*, 455, 458. Tutchone: *37*, 493–495, *494*. Western Woods Cree: *166*, 256, 257, *257*. West Main Cree: 159, 160, 217, *218*, 228. Yellowknife: 106, 161–162, *162*, 285, *285*, 286, 310, 684

Teslin band; synonymy: 480. *See also* Tlingit, Inland

Tess-cho-tinneh; synonymy: 348

Testes de boeuf; synonymy: 214

Tete Plat (Nation); synonymy: 306

Tête(s)-de-Boule; synonymy: 211, 214, 215. *See also* Attikamek (Tête de Boule)

Tetlin band. *See* Tanana

Tetlin-Last Tetlin band. *See* Tanana

T'ètllet-Kuttchin; synonymy: 531

t'etsǫt'ine; synonymy: 289

T'éttchié-Dhidié; synonymy: 600

taxe·ldəlahgəyu·; synonymy: 662

Teytseh-Kootchin; synonymy: *37*

Tezli site: *108*, *113*, *118*, *125*, 126, 415

tyačik; synonymy: 513

tyatcık; synonymy: 513

Thanadelther: 273, 276, 279

Thatsan-o'tinne; synonymy: 289

θe· cǫ· x̌a· íi·n; synonymy: 576

Thecannies; synonymy: 440

Thè-kka-nè; synonymy: 440

Thelon complex: 99

θȩł-tue dene; synonymy: 280

The Pas band; synonymy: 269. *See also* Cree, Western Woods

θetahʊklį̀; synonymy: 513

Thetlíotin; synonymy: 431

θîlq-hołine; synonymy: 271

Thè-yé-Ottinè; synonymy: 271

Thick Wood Crees; synonymy: 268

Thikanies; synonymy: 440

θîlq-hołine; synonymy: 271

Thi-laṇ-ottiné; synonymy: 271

Thlakwair khit; synonymy: 455

Thlee-chaug-a; synonymy: 309

Thlegtotin group; synonymy: 461. *See also* Tahltan

Thlingcha-dinne(h); synonymy: 294, 309

Thling-è-ha-'dtinnè; synonymy: 309

Thloadenni group; synonymy: 461. *See also* Tahltan

Thlogosquin: *467*

Thnaina; synonymy: 638

Thomas (Tanana): *542*, *552*, *574*, 705

Thompson, Albert E.: 246

Thompson, David: 35, 92, 161

Thopiskow; synonymy: 269

Thorman, William P.: 468

Those Kuz Lake; synonymy: 431

θtahuklíⁿ; synonymy: 513

Thwaites, R.G.: 209

Tibithebe; synonymy: 228

Tibitiby: 160

Tič̣axhanoté·n; synonymy: 461, 465

Tichanotin group; synonymy: 461. *See also* Tahltan

Tichotina; synonymy: 450

Tikaihoten; synonymy: 461

Timagami band. *See* Cree, Western Woods

Timber Point complex: 100, *101*, 102, *102*

Timiskaming band. *See* Algonquin

Tinite: *21*

Tinnats-khotana; synonymy: 638

'Tinnè; synonymy: 168, 325

Tinneh; synonymy: 168

Tǐ·ⁿzǐt kutchin; synonymy: 505

Titcoténa; synonymy: 450

Titshotína; band. *See* Kaska

Ti-tsho-ti-na; synonymy: 450, 512

Titus, Alexander: *552*, *574*

Titus, Dorothy: *710*

Titus, Matthew: *710*

Tizya, John; 695

Tlatskanai; language: 67, 68

Tlegon-khotana; synonymy: 616

Tlepanoten; synonymy: 461

Tlingit: 39, 456, 465, 482, 490, 491, 500, 501, 503, 505, 580, 623, 645, 654, 662. ceremonies: 488. Chilkat: 375, 479, 495–496, 499, 503, 546, 569, 652. Chilkoot: 481, 482, 491. clothing: 485, *722*. disease: 496. external relations: 454, 455, 458, 460, 469, 481, 485, 488, 489, 490, 496, 499, 502, 642. history: 36, 389, 395, 452, 643, 660. language: 67–68, 82, 372, 469, 470, 479, 481, 486, 487, 501. migration: 67–68, 460. music: 660. prehistory: 67–68. settlement pattern: 470. settlements: 496. shamanism: 449, 502, 719. social organization: 461, 475, 476, 485, 651. Stikine: 458, 460. subsistence: 68, 375, 471. synonymy: 479. Taku: 375, 458, 469, 479, 480. technology: *380*. territory: 458, 481. trade: 388, 389, 395, 436, 452, 459, 471, 478, 481, 482, 483, 489, 490, 494, 495, 496, 503, 546, 645, 650, 652. transport: *395*, *396*. warfare: 447, 643. Yakutat: 375, 495

Tlingit, Inland: 1, 40, 373, 387, 469–480. adornment: 474. Atlin band: 469–471, 480. birth: 473, 477. ceremonies: 471, *471*, 473, 474, *474*, 475, 476, 477, 478, *478*, 482, *486*, 488. childrearing: 477. clothing: 474, *474*, 475, 476, 477, *486*, *489*, *722*. death: 477, 478. division of labor: 474. education: 477. employment: 470. environment: *372*, 374, 375, 470–471. external relations: 458, 469–470, 482, 485, 488. history: 394, 395, 397, 399, 469, 475. kinship: 375–376. language: 67–68, 82, 372, 452, 458, 469, 470, 479. life cycle: 477–478. marriage: 458, 469, 470, 475, 477, 478, 482. menstrual practices: 473. migration: 388, 469, 471–472. music: 478, *478*. mythology: 479. orthography: 469. political organization: 476–477. population: 470. puberty: 477. religion: 471, 477, 479. reserves: *471*. settlement pattern: 471, 476. settlements: 469, 470, *470*. shamanism: 479. social organization: 384, 472, *474*, 475–477, *475*, *476*, 485, *489*. structures: 379, *470*, 473, 476–478. subsistence: 374–376, 379, *383*, 470–473, *473*. synonymy: 451–453, 479–480. technology: 378, *471*, 472–473, *472*. territory: 458, 469, *471*. Teslin band: 469–471, 480. trade: 378, 389, 470, 472, 478. transport: 380, 381, *383*, *391*, *396*, 473–475. warfare: 469, 470, 472, 478–479

T'lokotan; synonymy: 460

T'lotona band. *See* Sekani

T'lukotene; synonymy: 460

Tnaïna; synonymy: 638

tobacco: 170, 208, 224, 251, 288, 391, 399, 488. carrot: *151*. pouches: 175. *See also* pipes

toboggans: 138, 179, 282, 303, *379, 391*, 403, 444, 506, 569, 618. dog traction: 133, 154, *155*, 221, 234, 235, 262, 308, 381, 390, 444, 474, 485, 498. hand-pulled: 180, 221, 262, 279, 318, 649. introduction of: *381*, 39, 437, 474, 485. manufacture: 138, 262, 280, 318, 444, *445*, 649. motor-drawn: *157*

Todatonten-Kanuti; synonymy: 600. *See also* Koyukon

Tolovana band. *See* Tanana

Tolowa; language; 67

Toltan; synonymy: 465

Tolwatin; synonymy: 576

Tomlinson, Robert: 456

Tonsina-Klutina band. *See* Ahtna

tools: 88–90, *88–91*, 92, *93*, 94, 95, *96*, 97–99, 101–105, 110, *110, 112–113*, 113, 116, 118, *119*, 120, 122, 127, *125*, 175, *179, 211*, 219, 223, 232, 235, 247, 263, 264, 275, 279, 280, 340, *342*, 381, *382*, 383, 388, 403, 424, 436, 443, 484, 517, 548, 553, 570, *570*, 575, 612, *613*

Toosey band. *See* Chilcotin

To-tshik-o-tin; synonymy: 505

Touchon-ta-Kutchin; synonymy: 504

Touetchoetinne: 328

totem poles: *486*

toys: *197*, 221

trade: 20, 126, 175, 498, 522–523, 546, 575, 615, 618. Asian: 544, 546, 561, 586, 595, 650. Eskimo-Indian: 120, 388, 528, 544, 546, 559, 561, 582, 589, 595–596, 603, 616, 631, 650. European goods: 94, 95, 96, 106. fairs: 208, 375, 388, 391, 489, 544, 546, 558, 586, 593, 595–596, 627. intergroup: 158, 190, 208, 315, 375, 387–388, 391, 404, 415, 416, 419, 424, 459, 469, 470, 472, 481–483, 489–490, 494–496, 528, 546, 548, 558, 565, 582, 586, 589, 595, 596, 603, 623, 627, 631, 645, 650, 652. items: *64*, 118, 120, 121, *121*, 125, 134, 151, *151*, 153, *154*, 170, 172, 175, 177, *179*, 197, 208, 218, 223, 232, 233, 237, 239, 288, 296, 303, 317, 375, 378, 387–388, 391, 416, 417, 424, 459, 462, 489, 499, 516, 517, 539, 544, 546, 586, 595, 603, 615, 627, 632, 649, 652. middlemen: 528, 645, 650. networks: 90, 544, 546, 561, 650. partners: 404, 424, 478, 489, 494, 523, 595, 596, 627, 631. prehistoric: 90, 546, 561. *See also* fur trade

trading posts: *147, 159, 389. See also* fur trade

Trading Nahannies; synonymy: 436

trail and road house system: 503, 549, 550, *550*, 621, 643

Tran-jik-koo-chin; synonymy: 532

Transitional cultures: 89

transport; boats: *11, 25*, 138, 155, 157, 177, 245, 377, 380, 390, 399, 405, 444, 462, 474, 484, 485, 498, 518, *539*, 551, 553, 569, 596, 612, 621, 627, 630, *631*, 650, *696*. carrying:

138, 202, *202*, 234, 279, *299, 395, 396*, 403, 405, 425, 437, 444, *446*, 462, *463*, 477, 485, 487, 498, *499, 500*, 518, *520, 570, 572, 573*, 618, 630, 649–650, *651, 666, 699*. dog-traction: *19*, 152, 154, *155*, 177, 179, 181, 235, 281, 282, 390, 400, 473, 484, 485, 498, 518, *540*, 544, 549, *551*, 553, 596–597, 621, 699. drags: 485, 498. kayak: 630. portages: 155, *156*. postcontact: 152, 154–156, *155–157*, 177, 179, 185, 223, 234, 400, *400*, 473, 484, 485, 498, 506, *540, 550, 551, 551*, 553, 568, *589*, 621, *622*, 630, 699, 709. rafts: *11*, 138, 177, 485, 498, 613, 650. sleds: *19*, 138, 177, 179, 381, 390, 403, 444, 474, *487*, 498, 506, 518, *525, 540*, 544, 549, *551*, 569, *586*, 596, 604, *606*, 613, *621*, 630, 649, 668, *669*. water: 155–156, *156, 157*, 177, *181*, 198, 221, 246, 566, 569, 668, *687. See also* canoes; dogs; snowshoes; toboggans

trapping. *See* fishing; fur trading; hunting

Trātzè-kutchi; synonymy: 505, 513

travel: 171, 172, 234, 251, 253, 262, 264, 277, 280, 292, 332, 334, 335, 341, 345, 376, 391, 395, 412, 500. dogsled: *19*. foot: 130, 138, 179, 197, 221, 390, 403, 437, 456, 474, 484, 485, 498, 630, 649. limitations: 130–131, 135, 137, 138, 260, 341, 374, 376, 391, 395, 406, 470, 534, 563, 624, 650. prehistoric: 86. signals and guides: 485. subsistence related: 197, 198, 201, 245, 376, 406, 442, 508, 509, 615, 627, 668, 669. trade for: 197, 199, 208, 232, 235, 248, 258, 260, 276, 277, 375, 388, 417, 443, 444, 483, 484, 509, 544, 486, 589, 615, 631. water: 130, 137, 138, 158, 177, 198, 217, 377, 380, 403, 437, *437*, 443, 474, 506, 650. *See also* dogs; snowshoes; transport

Traverse, George: 252, *253*

Traverse, Peter: 252

treaties, Canadian: 148–149, 237, 245, 259, 315, 322, 398–399, 469, 482, 702. commission: *368*. Fort Resolution: 297. No. 1: 246. No. 5: *274*. No. 8: 273, 288, 295, 296, 345, 346, 359, 399, 688–689. No. 9: *731*. No. 10: 273, *274*. No. 11: 295, 298, *306, 311*, 335, 345. payments: 237, 264, *264*, 266, 299, *300, 311*, 322, 346, 688, 731. Rae: 297. reserves: 259. restrictions on: 399. Selkirk: *249*

treaties, U.S.: 148

Tritt, Albert Edward: *397*

Tro-chu-tin; synonymy: 513

Troⁿčik; synonymy: 513

tronǯiuk; synonymy: 513

Tr′ōtsīk kū′tchīn; synonymy: 505, 532

Trout Lake band. *See* Ojibwa, Northern

Trudeau, Jean: 22

Tⲣa-kfwèlè-ⲣottinè; synonymy: 295

Tⲣa(l)tsan Ottinè; synonymy: 289

Tⲣa-nànœ-Kouttchin; synonymy: 575

Tⲣanata Kuttchin; synonymy: 575

Tⲣè-tliet-Kouttchin; synonymy: 531

Tⲣè-ttchié-dhidié-Kouttchin; synonymy: 532

Tⲣi-kka-Gottinè; synonymy: 348

Tsacotina: *650*

ts'ak'ê′; synonymy: 455

Tsan-tⲣottinè; synonymy: 295

Tsatsnótin; synonymy: 431

Tsa-ttiné; synonymy: 359

Tseco to tinneh; synonymy: 456

Tse etseta; synonymy: 455. *See also* Tsetsaut

Tsekani band. *See* Sekani

Tsekanies; synonymy: 440

Tsé-'kéh-ne; synonymy: 440

Tsekenné; synonymy: 440

Tselona; synonymy: 82, 450. *See also* Kaska

Tseloni band. *See* Sekani

tsǝtet'aič'in; synonymy: 532

Tsetsaut: 39, 41 373, 387, 451, 454–457, 460. clothing: 455, 456. curing: 456. environment: *372*, 454. external relations: 388, 454. history: 455–456. language: *70*, 71, 72, 77, 83, 372, 452, 454–456. mythology: 456. orthography: 454. population: 456. puberty: 456. settlement pattern: 456. social organization: 456. structures: 456, *457*. subsistence: 375, 456. Suss to'deen: 455. synonymy: 452, 454–456. technology: 378, 456. territory: 454, *454*, 455, 458. transport: 381, 456. Tse etseta: 455. warfare: 454, 455

T'setta, Isadore: *735*

Tshatsha, Marie Louise: *211*

Tshe-tsi-uetin-euerno; synonymy: 185

Tsilkotin; synonymy: 412

Tsilla-ta-ut-'tinnè; synonymy: 348

Tsillawdawhoot-dinneh; synonymy: 348

Tsimshian: 384, 401, 455, 460, 461, 466. external relations: 458. language: 420. prehistory: 416. trade: 388, 416–418, 435

Tsitka-ni; synonymy: 440

Tsit-o-klin-otin; synonymy: 513

Tsitsk band; synonymy: 430

Tsits Zaons; synonymy: 456

tθhéek'ehneh; synonymy: 440

T'trānjī′k kutchin; synonymy: 532

Ttsè-ⲣottinè; synonymy: 295

ttynaĭ(ɫ̄y); synonymy: 168, 638

tuba·ỵ́ne; synonymy: 639

tučotena; synonymy: 466

Tuk-kuth; synonymy: 531

Tŭkkŭth′-kŭtchin′; synonymy: 531

Tuktu complex: 46, 111, 113, 114

Tukudh; synonymy: 531. *See also* Kutchin

tuloγǝ xóťanǝ; synonymy: 600

tuɫuxťana; synonymy: 662

Turner, Lucien M.: 19–20, *20*, 22

Tuskey Moginicks: 166

Tŭt-chohn′-kŭt-chin; synonymy: 504

Tutchone: 40, 387, 493–505, 563. adornment: 498–499. art: 502–503. birth: 498. Burwash Landing band: 495. Carmacks band: 494. ceremonies: 482, *486*, 488, 494, 500–502, *503*. Champagne-Aishihik band: 495. Champagne band: 494. clothing: *392, 486*, 498, *499*, 500, *727*. cosmology: 502. curing: 502. death: 501–502, *501*. diseases: 569. education: 79, 504. employment: 504. environment: *8, 372*, 373–375, *374*, 493. external relations: 388–389, 482, 486, 488, 494–496, 506. history: 36, 38, 39, 389, 391, 394, 395, 397, 399, 494, 496, 503–504. Hutshi band: 495. kinship: 500. Kloo Lake band: 495. Kluane band: 494. Klukshu-Champagne band: 495. language: 38, *70*, 72, 76–79, 82, 83, 372, 451, 493, 494, 506, 563.

life cycle: 500–501. marriage: 482, 486, 494–496, 499–501. Mayo Indians: 504. menstrual practices: 498. music: 502, 503. mythology: 502. Northern: *37, 38, 70, 72,* 76, 77, 79, 451, 494, 496, 498–500, 503–504, 506, 512, 513, 532, 576. orthography: 493. political organization: 500. population: 495, 504. prehistory: 124, 495. puberty: 500, *727.* religion: 501, 502. Ross River band: 494, 495. Selkirk band: 494, 503. settlement pattern: 497–498. settlements: 494. shamanism: 449, 502. social organization: 384, 499–500. Southern: *70, 72, 76, 79,* 124, *380, 382, 392,* 450, 494–496, 499, 501, 563, 565, 569. structures: 380, *497, 498, 498, 500–502, 501.* subsistence: 375, 376, 379, 380, 496–497, *497.* synonymy: *37,* 337, 451–453, 479, 504–505, 512, 513, 532. Tatlmain Lake band: 503. technology: 378–380, *379,* 496–497, *503.* territory: *37,* 493–495, *494.* trade: 388–389, 482, 494–496, 498, 546, 652. transport: *379, 381, 382, 395,* 494, 498, *500,* 504. warfare: 378, 389, 482, 494, 496, 565. Whitehorse band: 450, 494

Tutchóne Kutchín; synonymy: 387, 504
Tutchon Kutchin; synonymy: 504
Tŭtchŭn tã´h kŭtchĭn; synonymy: 504
Tutna; synonymy: 556–557
Tututni; language: 67
tuvuýna; synonymy: 639
Twin Lakes site: *101,* 102
Tyonek Tanainas; synonymy: 639
Tyone-Mendeltna band. *See* Ahtna
Tyrrell, Joseph B.: 31, 306

U

U'anwitenne; synonymy: 430
U'Bas,que,a; synonymy: 270
U'Bas,qui,a; synonymy: 270
U'Basquio; synonymy: 270
U-che-pi-wy-an; synonymy: 283
učima·ssi·winnu; synonymy: 187
učiše·stiku·wakʸ; synonymy: 187
Ughaih: 78, *78*
Uinescaw-Sepee; synonymy: 242. *See also* Ojibwa, Northern
Uinnipiskowuck; synonymy: 205
ʔulčəna; synonymy: 632
Ulkatcho band; synonymy: 431. *See also* Carrier
Ulkatcho site: *108, 118, 121,* 126
Ulukagmyut; synonymy: 600. *See also* Koyukon
uma·mi·wakʸ; synonymy: 186
Umbahotin(n)e; synonymy: 327, 329, 330, 337
Umpqua, Upper; language: 67
Unakhotána; territory: 599
Unalakleet Eskimo; territory: 559
unaman-ši·pi·winnu; synonymy: 187
unaska·hpi·wakʸ; synonymy: 185
Unescapis; synonymy: 185
Ungava band. *See* Montagnais-Naskapi
United States government: *552.* Alaska purchase: 509, 544, 547, 548, 586, 611, 636, 643. Corps of Engineers: 556. Department of Defense: 587, 598. education: 401, 597. employment: 553. Office of Economic Opportunity: 707. Public Health Service:

401, 553, 569, 597, 707. welfare: 598. *See also* Bureau of Indian Affairs; legislation, U.S.; treaties, U.S.
Unnahathewunnutitto; synonymy: 268
upapinašiw; synonymy: 187
Upe-shipow; synonymy: 205
Uplander(s); synonymy: 196, 215. *See also* Cree, East Main
upland Indians: 159, 160. synonymy: 215, 257
Upper Ahtna; synonymy: 662
Upper Dahotinne; synonymy: 327
Upper Gens de Fou; synonymy: 505, 512
Upper Inlet band. *See* Tanaina
Upper Innoko people: 600
Upper Koyukuk; synonymy: 600
Upper Koyukon; synonymy: 600
Upper Kuskokwim Athapaskan; synonymy: 622
Upper Liard Kaska; synonymy: 450. *See also* Kaska
Upper Loucheux: 323
Upper Nabesna–Upper Chisana band. *See* Tanana
Upper Porcupine River band; synonymy: 531, 532. *See also* Kutchin
Upper Tanana(tánas); synonymy: 575
Upper Yukon division. *See* Koyukon
usa·čise·ku·w; synonymy: 186
Usquemays; synonymy: *165*
ʔutnuxtana; synonymy: 662

V

Vachon, Andrew: *551*
valčatnaxian; synonymy: 638
Valdez-Fairbanks Road: *550*
Valentine, Victor F.: 22, 717
value system: 144, 182, 190, 193, 194, 203, 276, 282, 320, 323, 353, 355, 363, 404, 406–407, 449, 608–609, 669–671, 677, 720–721, 725, 737–738
Vancouver, George: 388
Vànœ-ta-Kouttchin; synonymy: 532
VanStone, James W.: 22
Van-tah-koo-chin; synonymy: 532
Vanta Kootchin; synonymy: 531
Vanta-Kutchin; synonymy: 532
van tat gʷičin; synonymy: 532
van te· gʷičin; synonymy: 513, 532
Vasil'ev, Ivan Ya.: 554
Village site: 114, 575
Vinasale band. *See* Kolchan
vision quest: 233, 251, 353, *354,* 355, 719
visiting: 170, 208, 246, 324, 329, 364, 399, 406, 415, 425, 435, 436, 462, 481, 483, 544, 589
Vœn Kuttchin; synonymy: 532
Voyageurs; synonymy: 205
Voznesenskiĭ, I.G.: 50
Vunta Koo chin; synonymy: *37*
Vuntá Kutchin; synonymy: 513, 531, 532
vun tte kwi chin; synonymy: 513

W

Wabasca band. *See* Cree, Western Woods
Wabauskang band. *See* Saulteaux of Lake Winnipeg
Wabigoon band. *See* Saulteaux of Lake Winnipeg
Wailaki; language: 67

Waldron River complex: 100, 104, *105*
Waldron River site: *103*
Walker, Major: *368*
Walker, Richard: *84*
Walton, W.G.: 202, 673
wa·pame·kustiku·winnu; synonymy: 205
wa·panank. See Morning Star
wa·pos(o-si·piy); synonymy: 242
Wappuss; synonymy: 242
Wapus; synonymy: 242. *See also* Ojibwa, Northern
Wà-pusi-sipi; synonymy: 242
warfare: 106, 541. adornment: 517, 652. alliances: 159. casualties: 199, 286, 287, 294. causes: 148, 164, 167, 408, 494, 559, 596, 618, 642. ceremonies: 319, 408, 478–479, 519. equipment: 652. Eskimo-Indian: 164, 173, 529, 559, 596, 603, 623, 642–643, 651. Eskimo-White: 547. implements: 164, 378–379, 388, 403, 417, 435, 436, 484, 496, 570, 652, *652.* intergroup: 148, 159, 161–164, 173, 194, 199, 208, 211, 260, 285–287, 294, 296, 310, 328, 329, 357, 388, 389, 408, 411, 454–455, 469, 470, 472, 478, 482, 494, 528, 559, 565, 582, 596, 603, 618, 623, 642. leadership: 522, 523, 652, 657. music: 652. prisoners: 199, 273, 519, 657. results: 173. ritual observances: 408, 522, 652. scalping: 408. settlement: 199, 260, 273, 294, 296, 478–479, 530, 631, 652. tactics: 164, 570. torture: 194. weapons: 164, 484, 652, *652.* with Whites: 173, 346, 411, 503, 559, 643
Wasagamack band. *See* Ojibwa, Northern
wa·ša·winnu, synonymy: 187
Washahoe; synonymy: 229
Washe ho Sepe; synonymy: 229
Washeo-Sepee; synonymy: 229, 242
Washè-u-sipi; synonymy: 229
wa·ske·siw si·piy; synonymy: 270
Waske su sepe; synonymy: 270
Wasses; synonymy: 242
wa·ssi̧ irini; synonymy: 242
Wassilia, Devian: *620*
Waswanipi band; synonymy: 186. *See also* Montagnais-Naskapi
wa·šwa·nipi·wilnu; synonymy: 186
Waterhen Lake band. *See* Cree, Western Woods
Water, People of the; synonymy: 512
Watkins, E.A.: 202
Watson, Matthew: 39
Watt, Sophie: *499*
Waugh, F.W.: 20, 22
Waupus; synonymy: 242
wa·wiya·pe·ku·wilnu; synonymy: 187
Wca·y Wie·ne; synonymy: 662
WdisaWie·n; synonymy: 576
Weagamow Lake Ojibwa; synonymy: 242. *See also* Ojibwa, Northern
Wealth Woman: *483,* 490
Wəca·t' cékwilnuts'; synonymy: 186
Wechepawuck; synonymy: 283
Wechepowuck; synonymy: 283
Wechippianewuck; synonymy: 283
Weechepowack; synonymy: 283
Wee-chip-y-an-i-wuck; synonymy: 283
Weenusk; synonymy: 229
Weenusk band; synonymy: 230

Wekemouskunk: *248*
Wellington Bay site: 101, 102
Wells, E.H.: 38
Wenopsk complex: 95–96
Wentzel, W.F.: 294, 452
Wəsakwopətá·nwilnut'; synonymy: 187
Western Ahtnas; synonymy: 662
Western Dog-ribbed Indians; synonymy: 306
Western Montagnais; synonymy: 66
Western Nah·ane; synonymy: 466
Western Nascaupee, synonymy: 205
Western Union Telegraph Company: 49, 51,
    556, 561, 584, 586
West, Jennie: *404*
Wetalth; synonymy: 456
Weymontachie; synonymy: 215
Weymontachingue; synonymy: 215. *See also*
    Attikamek (Tête de Boule)
Whatten: 159
Whirl Lake site: 116, 125
whistles. *See* musical instruments
Whitefish: 685
Whitefish Bay band. *See* Saulteaux of Lake
    Winnipeg
Whitefish Lake band. *See* Cree, Western
    Woods
Whitefish Lake site: *98*, 100
Whitehorse band. *See* Tutchone
Whitehorse Billy: *486*
White Pass and Yukon Railway: 397, 481
White River Johnny: *572*
White Whale River band; synonymy: 205. *See
    also* Cree, East Main
Whymper, Frederick: 38, 584
Wickersham, James: *552*
wigwams. See structures
Wii´niskiiwiisakahikaniiwi´niiwak; synonymy:
    229
wi·łit; synonymy: 662
Wilkinson, David B.: 82, *84*
William (Tanana): *552, 574*
William, Alexander: *552, 574*
Williams, Billy: 47
Williams, Paul: *552, 574*
Willowherb site: *103*, 104
Wilson, Daniel: 36
Wilson, Francis D.: *358*
wi·nasko-sa·kahikan-ininiwak; synonymy: 229
Windigo. *See* mythology
Windigo psychosis: 28, 249, 737
Windy Point complex: 100, 104
Windy Point site: *103*
Winepeg; synonymy: 230
Wine pesk ko wuck; synonymy: 205
wi·nipe·ko·w(ak); synonymy: 205, 229
wi·nipe·ku·wa·skahikanis iyiyu; synonymy: 206

wi·nipe·ku·winnu; synonymy: 205
wi·nipe·ku·wiyiyu(·č); synonymy: 196, 205,
    206
wi·nipe·kwilnu; synonymy: 205
Winisk band; synonymy: 230
Winisk Cree; synonymy: 229. *See also* Cree,
    West Main
Winisk River band. *See* Ojibwa, Northern
Winnebago: 229, 230
Winnepeg: 230
Winne-peskowuk; synonymy: 205
Winne-peskowuk; synonymy: 205
Win nes cau sepe; synonymy: 242
Wisconsin Native American Languages
    Project: 63
wi·ssa·kkote·wikkwe·; synonymy: 371
wi·ssa·kkote·winini; synonymy: 371
Witsiwoten; synonymy: 430
wiz, Gens-de; synonymy: 505
Wolfe Lake band; synonymy: 243
Wolf Lake band. *See* Algonquin
Wolf, Mary: *359*
Wood Indians: 503. synonymy: 215, 504, 512
Woodland period: 32
Wood River band. *See* Tanana
Woods Cree; synonymy: 66, 270. *See also*
    Cree, Western Woods
world view. *See* cosmology
Wright, Arthur: 706
Wright, James V.: 258
Wright, Mary Rose: *340*
Wright, Paul: *340*
Wright, Tatsi: 332
writing systems. *See* language
Wulede hoįį; synonymy: 297. *See also* Dogrib
Wunnumin band. *See* Ojibwa, Northern
Wuskèsew-Sepee; synonymy: 270
Wuskesew-sipi; synonymy: 270

X

xcaxtana; synonymy: 638
xcayextana; synonymy: 662
xədəğdəlahğəyu·; synonymy: 662
XY Company: 35

Y

Yahey, Bella: *356*
Yahey, Charlie: *354*
Yakut: 631
Yakutat. *See* Tlingit
ya·nahğəyu·; synonymy: 662
Yanktonai Dakota; prehistory: 94
Yatchee-thin-yoowuc; synonymy: 164
Yaucen Indians; synonymy: *37*
yaxtana; synonymy: 638
Yellowknife: *19,* 273, 285–290, 293, 306, 309,
    373, 684, 693. clothing: *286, 288.* external

relations: 285, 286. history: 80, 285–288,
    293, 364, 688. language: 80, 273, 285.
    marriage: 286. migration: 106, 161.
    mythology: 302. orthography: 285. political
    organization: 684. population: 274, 275,
    286, 288, 691. prehistory: 102, 103.
    settlements: 691. social organization: 275.
    structures: 140, *289.* subsistence: 275, 285.
    synonymy: 288–289, 297, 306. technology:
    288. territory: 106, 161–162, *162,* 285, *285,*
    286, 310, 684. trade: 273, 276, 285–288,
    288, 293, 294, 296, 310. warfare: 106, 161–
    162, 164, 273, 285–288, 294, 310
Yellowknife band. *See* Dogrib
Yellow Knive(s): 683. synonymy: 289
yoday dene; synonymy: 280
yona^ʔ həʔan; synonymy: 600
yonəq həʔan; synonymy: 616
York Factory: *152,* 153, 158, 159, *159,* 215,
    217, *218,* 219, 228, 229, 231, 241, 242, 273,
    283
York Factory band; synonymy: 230. *See also*
    Cree, West Main
Youcan Indians; synonymy: 532
Youcon; synonymy: 532
Young, Robert W.: 81, 82
yudo^ʔ xôtanə; synonymy: 599
yudo yunğôt; synonymy: 600
Yukon Flats band; synonymy: 532. *See also*
    Kutchin
yukonikhotana; synonymy: 599
Yukon Indians: 328, 329. synonymy: 638
Yukon-Kateel; synonymy: 600. *See also*
    Koyukon
yullit; synonymy: 662
yunakhotana; synonymy: 599. territory: 557
yuna^ʔ xôtanə; synonymy: 599
yuqənə xôtanə; synonymy: 559
yun^ʔəhian; synonymy: 622
Yunnaka-khotana; synonymy: 599. territory:
    557
Yupik Eskimo: 599, 600, 613, 614, 616.
    language: 68, 73. settlements: 638.
    synonymy: 557, 615. trade: 582
yuqənə xôtanə; synonymy: 559
Yutawoteene; synonymy: 431
Yutuwichan band. *See* Sekani

Z

Zagoskin, Lavrentii A.: 43, 50, 548, 556, 558–
    561, *560,* 586
ʒà(h)ⁿʒik g^wičin; synonymy: 532
ʒan to hoʔyán^ʔ; synonymy: 576
ʒełtnaWie·n; synonymy: 576
Zjen Kuttchin; synonymy: 532
Zjén-ta-Kouttchin; synonymy: 532

837